AN INDEX TO

THE JEWISH COMMUNITY

OF THE BRITISH ISLES IN 1851

PETRA LAIDLAW

2010

Published 2010

ISBN 978-1-4457-5020-0

AN INDEX TO

THE JEWISH COMMUNITY OF THE BRITISH ISLES IN 1851

This volume is designed as a companion piece to the much larger database of the Anglo-Jewish community in 1851 which can be viewed freely at www.jgsgb.org.uk/1851. The two sources contain entries on just short of 29,000 people. This represents over 90 per cent of the estimated total Jewish population in England, Wales, Scotland, Ireland, the Channel Islands and the Isle of Man at that date, which was of the order of 31,000.

Each entry has a unique ID number, shown in the first column of the table printed here. The online database can be searched using this number. The online database lists, wherever available, details of each person's family, where they lived decade by decade throughout their lives, their occupations, their faith affiliations, and their death and burial. Some of these people lived long lives, and their entries may stretch well back into the 18th century or forward into the 2oth. Others lived only very short lives, and their entries are correspondingly brief. Other entries await fuller research.

The database has been a collaborative project, built up over ten years, and involving more than 250 contributors around the world. Their names are listed on the website above, as are the chief sources used.

The website also offers brief notes on the definitions and conventions used in the database. These should be consulted on any definitional queries arising from this index.

All entries have been subject to rigorous editorial control, but in a project of this size some errors will inevitably remain. Neither this volume nor the fuller database on the website could pretend to be definitive. Rather, they are intended as aids and spurs to further research.

Petra Laidlaw
London, April 2010

ID	surname	given names	born	birthplace	father	mother	spouse 1	1851 residence	1851 occupation
18215	Aaris	Isabella	1838	Middlesex, London	(?) Aaris			Mile End, London	scholar
6411	Aaron	Aaron	1828	?Barnstaple, Devon	Solomon Aarons	Caroline (?)	Julia Lazarus	Exeter, Devon	
25678	Aaron	Aaron	1839	St Giles, London	Noah Aaron	Catherine Phillips		Spitalfields, London	scholar
12865	Aaron	Abigail	1824	Birmingham	John Aaron	Matilda Solomon	Maurice (Morris) Aaron	Birmingham	pawnbroker
20918	Aaron	Abraham	1850	Whitechapel, London	Charles Aaron	Rachel Belais		Aldgate, London	
25679	Aaron	Adelaide	1843	Aldgate, London	Noah Aaron	Catherine Phillips		Spitalfields, London	
8173	Aaron	Alfred G	1850	Bloomsbury, London	Benjamin Wolf Aaron	Julia Jacobs		Soho, London	
4228	Aaron	Ann	1774	Birmingham	(?)			Birmingham	assistant
14316	Aaron	Ann M	1801	Manchester	(?)		John Aaron	Manchester	
20731	Aaron	Barnett	1828	Aldgate, London	Aaron Aaron	Catherine Crawcour		Whitechapel, London	shoe maker
8170	Aaron	Benjamin Wolf	1812	Painswick, Gloucestershire	Jacob Aaron		Julia Jacobs	Soho, London	watchmaker + jeweller
972	Aaron	Caroline	1806	Middlesex, London	(?)		Solomon Aaron	Exeter, Devon	wife of jeweller
25677	Aaron	Catherine	1818	Aldgate, London	Moses Phillips		Noah Aaron	Spitalfields, London	
30098	Aaron	Charles	1825	?, Germany	Levin Aron		Rachel Belais (Belize)	Aldgate, London	cigar maker
19741	Aaron	Charles B	1848	Aldgate, London	Benjamin Wolf Aaron	Julia Jacobs		Soho, London	
12866	Aaron	David	1846	Birmingham	Maurice (Morris) Aaron	Abigail Aaron		Birmingham	scholar
8169	Aaron	Deborah	1843	Aldgate, London	Benjamin Wolf Aaron	Julia Jacobs	Joseph Woolf Hobinstock	Soho, London	
22362	Aaron	Dina	1842	Finsbury, London	John Aaron	Hannah Jessel		Whitechapel, London	
22364	Aaron	Edward	1846	Stepney, London	John Aaron	Hannah Jessel		Whitechapel, London	
22363	Aaron	Elizabeth	1843	Stepney, London	John Aaron	Hannah Jessel		Whitechapel, London	
9731	Aaron	Elizabeth (Betsy)	1784	Whitechapel, London	Yehuda Leib Phillips		Phineas Aaron	Whitechapel, London	
26493	Aaron	Elizabeth (Betty)	1816	Rochester, Kent	Lewis Lion Aaron	Mary (?)		Dover, Kent	
4232	Aaron	Emma	1824	Birmingham	David Aaron	Maria Myers	Isaac Lotheim	Birmingham	
4229	Aaron	Esther	1772	Middlesex, London	(?)			Birmingham	retired pawnbroker
26494	Aaron	Fanny	1830	Liverpool	Lewis Lion Aaron	Mary (?)		Dover, Kent	
975	Aaron	Fanny	1833	Exeter, Devon	Solomon Aaron	Caroline (?)		Exeter, Devon	
22366	Aaron	Fanny	1849	Stepney, London	John Aaron	Hannah Jessel	Benjamin Lynes	Whitechapel, London	
4230	Aaron	Frances	1808	Birmingham	(?) Aaron	Esther (?)		Birmingham	
12588	Aaron	Hannah	1790	Ipswich, Suffolk	(?)		Simon Aaron	Torquay, Devon	
22361	Aaron	Hannah	1818	Whitechapel, London	Nathaniel Aaron Jessel	Frances (Fanny (?)	John Aaron	Whitechapel, London	dress maker
974	Aaron	Harriet	1831	Barnstaple, Devon	Solomon Aaron	Caroline (?)		Exeter, Devon	
4234	Aaron	Henry	1817	Birmingham	John Aaron	Matilda Solomon		Birmingham	shopman (pawnbroker)
12939	Aaron	Henry	1829	Birmingham	David Aaron	Maria Myers		Birmingham	
19742	Aaron	Henry Lewis	1849	Aldgate, London	Benjamin Wolf Aaron	Julia Jacobs		Soho, London	
25680	Aaron	Hyam	1847	Aldgate, London	Noah Aaron	Catherine Phillips		Spitalfields, London	
4830	Aaron	Isaac	1819	Birmingham	David Aaron	Maria Myers	Matilda Levin	Birmingham	clothier
8174	Aaron	Jane	1845	Aldgate, London	Benjamin Woolf Aaron	Julia Jacobs	Justus Bronkhorst	Soho, London	
4233	Aaron	John	1779	?, London			Matilda Solomon	Birmingham	pawnbroker
22360	Aaron	John	1813	Southwark, London	Phineas Aaron	Elizabeth (Betsy) Phillips	Hannah Jessel	Whitechapel, London	fruiterer
4231	Aaron	John	1814	Birmingham	David Aaron	Maria Myers	Harriet Nerwich	Birmingham	pawnbroker
14315	Aaron	John	1814	?, London			Ann (?)	Manchester	druggist
8171	Aaron	Julia	1812	Wapping, London	Cookey (Yechutiel) Jacobs	Jane Woolf	Benjamin Wolf Aaron	Soho, London	
8172	Aaron	Kate	1847	Aldgate, London	Benjamin Wolf Aaron	Julia Jacobs	Philip Charles Jacobs	Soho, London	
22365	Aaron	Lewis	1847	Stepney, London	John Aaron	Hannah Jessel		Whitechapel, London	
26489	Aaron	Lewis Lion	1782	Chatham, Kent			Mary (?)	Dover, Kent	pawnbroker

ID	surname	given names	born	birthplace	father	mother	spouse 1	1851 residence	1851 occupation
28677	Aaron	Louis	1828	?, London				Spitalfields, London	cigar maker
25681	Aaron	Louis (Lewis)	1849	Spitalfields, London	Noah Aaron	Catherine Phillips		Spitalfields, London	
4239	Aaron	Maria	1781	Birmingham	(?) Myers		David Aaron	Birmingham	pawnbroker
26490	Aaron	Mary	1791	Dover, Kent			Lewis Lion Aaron	Dover, Kent	
27020	Aaron	Matilda	1851	Birmingham	Maurice (Morris) Aaron	Abigail (?)		Birmingham	
12589	Aaron	Maurice	1815	Ipswich, Suffolk	(?Simon) Aaron	Hannah (?)		Torquay, Devon	silversmith + jeweller
12864	Aaron	Maurice (Morris)	1812	Birmingham	David Aaron	Maria Myers	Abigail Aaron	Birmingham	pawnbroker
11754	Aaron	Meyer	1821	?, Russia				Shoreditch, London	traveller
12867	Aaron	Moseley	1848	Birmingham	Maurice (Morris) Aaron	Abigail Aaron	Diana Miriam Solomon	Birmingham	scholar
16832	Aaron	Moses	1794	Kaliningrad, Russia [Konigsberg, Poland]				Bedminster, Somerset	teacher of Hebrew
16831	Aaron	Moses	1801	?, Poland				Witton, Cheshire	hawker
8818	Aaron	Moses	1815	?, Poland				Aldgate, London	tailor
9719	Aaron	Nathan	1775	Middlesex, London			?	Birmingham	
25676	Aaron	Noah	1812	Covent Garden, London	Aaron Aaron		Catherine Phillips	Spitalfields, London	clothier
9730	Aaron	Phineas	1773	Tower Hill, London	Yehuda Leib		Elizabeth (Betsy) Phillips	Whitechapel, London	general dealer
4237	Aaron	Phineas	1824	?, Poland			Rosie (?)	Birmingham	boot + shoe maker
26491	Aaron	Phoebe	1821	Chatham, Kent	Lewis Lion Aaron	Mary (?)		Dover, Kent	
20917	Aaron	Rachel	1823	Nice, France [Nice, Sardinia]	Abraham Belais (Belize)	Naomi (?)	Charles Aaron	Aldgate, London	
27571	Aaron	Rebecca	1777	City, London	(?)		(?) Aaron	Spitalfields, London	
12591	Aaron	Reuben	1826	Norwich, Norfolk	(?Simon) Aaron	Hannah (?)		Torquay, Devon	silversmith + jeweller
5614	Aaron	Rose	1827	Shoreditch, London	Phineas Aaron	Elizabeth (Betsy) Phillips	Samuel Lazarus	Whitechapel, London	dress maker
4238	Aaron	Rosie	1832	Birmingham			Phineas Aaron	Birmingham	
9732	Aaron	Samuel	1815	Southwark, London	Phineas Aaron	Elizabeth (Betsy) Phillips		Whitechapel, London	general dealer
12590	Aaron	Samuel	1820	Norwich, Norfolk	(?Simon) Aaron	Hannah (?)	Kate Reuben	Torquay, Devon	wholesale jeweller
4242	Aaron	Sarah	1795	Birmingham	Solomon Aaron	Abigail (?)		Birmingham	pawnbroker assistant
18343	Aaron	Sarah	1830	?, Russia	(?) Cohen		Simon Aaron	Wolverhampton, Staffordshire	
18342	Aaron	Simon	1821	?, Poland [?, Prussia]			Sarah Cohen	Wolverhampton, Staffordshire	pawnbroker + clothes dealer
30097	Aaron	Simon	1851	Whitechapel, London	Charles Aaron	Rachel Belais		Aldgate, London	
12493	Aaron	Soloman	1769	?, Poland				Exeter, Devon	
4235	Aaron	Solomon	1828	Birmingham	John Aaron	Matilda Solomon		Birmingham	pawnbroker shopman
12868	Aaron	Solomon	1850	Birmingham	Maurice (Morris) Aaron	Abigail Aaron		Birmingham	
4132	Aaron	Sophia	1831	Birmingham	John Aaron	Matilda Solomon	George Alexander	Birmingham	pawnbroker assistant
9604	Aaron (Aarons)	Abraham	1833	Aldgate, London	Barnet (Barnett) Aaron (Aarons)	Phoebe Lee		Spitalfields, London	dealer
9599	Aaron (Aarons)	Barnet (Barnett)	1799	Aldgate, London			Phoebe Lee	Spitalfields, London	clothier
9601	Aaron (Aarons)	John	1826	Aldgate, London	Barnet (Barnett) Aaron (Aarons)	Phoebe Lee		Spitalfields, London	cigar maker
9607	Aaron (Aarons)	Joseph	1841	Spitalfields, London	Barnet (Barnett) Aaron (Aarons)	Phoebe Lee		Spitalfields, London	scholar
9602	Aaron (Aarons)	Lewis	1828	Aldgate, London	Barnet (Barnett) Aaron (Aarons)	Phoebe Lee		Spitalfields, London	cigar maker
9608	Aaron (Aarons)	Martha	1846	Spitalfields, London	Barnet (Barnett) Aaron (Aarons)	Phoebe Lee		Spitalfields, London	scholar
9605	Aaron (Aarons)	Moss	1835	Aldgate, London	Barnet (Barnett) Aaron (Aarons)	Phoebe Lee	Moses Hart	Spitalfields, London	cigar makers apprentice
9600	Aaron (Aarons)	Phoebe	1803	Aldgate, London	(?) Lee		Barnet (Barnett) Aaron (Aarons)	Spitalfields, London	
9606	Aaron (Aarons)	Rachel	1839	Aldgate, London	Barnet (Barnett) Aaron (Aarons)	Phoebe Lee		Spitalfields, London	

ID	surname	given names	born	birthplace	father	mother	spouse 1	1851 residence	1851 occupation
9603	Aaron (Aarons)	Solomon	1830	Aldgate, London	Barnet (Barnett) Aaron (Aarons)	Phoebe Lee		Spitalfields, London	cigar maker
27240	Aarons	Aaron	1823	Amsterdam, Holland				Aldgate, London	general dealer
10764	Aarons	Aaron	1826	Spitalfields, London			Hannah (?)	Spitalfields, London	general dealer
28491	Aarons	Aaron	1829	Whitechapel, London				Spitalfields, London	quill merchant
10487	Aarons	Aaron	1835	Mile End, London	Solomon Aarons	Sarah (?)		Mile End, London	apprentice boot + shoe maker
27574	Aarons	Aaron	1841	Whitechapel, London	Solomon Aarons	Rosa Isaacs		Spitalfields, London	
29705	Aarons	Abraham	1831	Strand, London	Benjamin Aarons	Esther (?)		Aldgate, London	traveller
27075	Aarons	Amelia	1849	?, London	Daniel Aarons	Sarah Davis		Aldgate, London	
11723	Aarons	Angel	1825	Spitalfields, London	Samuel Aaron		Sarah Mendoza	Aldgate, London	tailor
29703	Aarons	Benjamin	1803	Aldgate, London			Esther (?)	Aldgate, London	baker + dealer
19271	Aarons	Caroline	1848	Liverpool	Henry Aarons	Kate (Katherine) Woolf		Liverpool	
27575	Aarons	Catherine	1843	Aldgate, London	Solomon Aarons	Rosa Isaacs		Spitalfields, London	
10782	Aarons	Catherine	1846	Spitalfields, London	Noah Aarons	Mary Selig		Spitalfields, London	scholar
27073	Aarons	Celia	1843	?, London	Daniel Aarons	Sarah Davis		Aldgate, London	scholar
13674	Aarons	Charles	1826	?, London				Manchester	manager in clothier's shop
28904	Aarons	Charlotte	1846	Spitalfields, London	John (Jacob) Aarons	Rosa (?)		Spitalfields, London	scholar
27069	Aarons	Daniel	1815	?, London	Michael Aarons	Rachel Joseph	Sarah Davis	Aldgate, London	general dealer
29706	Aarons	David	1833	?Bermondsey, London	Benjamin Aarons	Esther (?)		Aldgate, London	cabinet maker
10485	Aarons	Deborah	1827	Mile End, London	Solomon Aarons	Sarah (?)		Aldgate, London	tailoress
29108	Aarons	Esther	1783	Aldgate, London	(?) Aarons			Whitechapel, London	independent
29704	Aarons	Esther	1811	Aldgate, London	(?)		Benjamin Aarons	Aldgate, London	
27706	Aarons	Esther	1823	Whitechapel, London	Isaac Solomons		Joseph Aarons	Spitalfields, London	
29109	Aarons	Eve	1790	Aldgate, London	(?) Aarons			Whitechapel, London	monthly nurse
28906	Aarons	Gabriel	1850	Spitalfields, London	John (Jacob) Aarons	Rosa (?)		Spitalfields, London	
29707	Aarons	George	1835	?Bermondsey, London	Benjamin Aarons	Esther (?)		Aldgate, London	baker assistant
29710	Aarons	Grace	1841	?Bermondsey, London	Benjamin Aarons	Esther (?)		Aldgate, London	scholar
9704	Aarons	Hannah	1772	Aldgate, London	(?) Aarons			Aldgate, London	
10765	Aarons	Hannah	1822	Aldgate, London	(?)		Aaron Aarons	Spitalfields, London	
12788	Aarons	Hannah	1830	Manchester	Emmanuel Levy		Joseph Aarons	Manchester	
2739	Aarons	Henry	1801	?, London	Solomon Aaron		Katherine (Kate) Woolf	Liverpool	door keeper to Synagogue
29713	Aarons	Henry	1850	Aldgate, London	Benjamin Aarons	Esther (?)		Aldgate, London	
26391	Aarons	Jacob	1815	?, London				Aldgate, London	clothes dealer
20451	Aarons	Jacob Lyon (Lionel)	1851	Liverpool	Henry Aarons	Kate (Katherine) Woolf	?	Liverpool	
29708	Aarons	John	1837	?Bermondsey, London	Benjamin Aarons	Esther (?)		Aldgate, London	cabinet maker
28898	Aarons	John (Jacob)	1808	Spitalfields, London	Yosef		Rosa (?)	Spitalfields, London	general dealer
27705	Aarons	Joseph	1819	?London	Michael Aarons	(Rachel Joseph?)	Esther Solomons	Spitalfields, London	general dealer
12787	Aarons	Joseph	1830	Middlesex, London			Hannah Levy	Manchester	dealer in oil paintings
28900	Aarons	Joseph	1835	Spitalfields, London	John (Jacob) Aarons	Rosa (?)		Spitalfields, London	sofa maker
10784	Aarons	Joseph	1850	Spitalfields, London	Noah Aarons	Mary Selig		Spitalfields, London	
27074	Aarons	Julia	1845	?, London	Daniel Aarons	Sarah Davis		Aldgate, London	scholar
2740	Aarons	Kate (Katherine)	1823	?, Holland	Woolf Woolf		Henry Aarons	Liverpool	
10486	Aarons	Leah	1830	Mile End, London	Solomon Aarons	Sarah (?)		Mile End, London	waistcoat maker

ID	surname	given names	born	birthplace	father	mother	spouse 1	1851 residence	1851 occupation
28902	Aarons	Lewis	1842	Spitalfields, London	John (Jacob) Aarons	Rosa (?)		Spitalfields, London	scholar
29712	Aarons	Louis	1845	Aldgate, London	Benjamin Aarons	Esther (?)		Aldgate, London	scholar
28905	Aarons	Louisa	1847	Spitalfields, London	John (Jacob) Aarons	Rosa (?)		Spitalfields, London	scholar
10484	Aarons	Marion (Maria)	1824	Mile End, London	Solomon Aarons	Sarah (?)		Mile End, London	tailoress
10779	Aarons	Mary	1815	Whitechapel, London	Nachum Selig		Noah Aarons	Spitalfields, London	
28901	Aarons	Mary	1836	Aldgate, London	John (Jacob) Aarons	Rosa (?)		Spitalfields, London	dress maker
2734	Aarons	Mary	1845	Liverpool	Henry Aarons	Kate (Katherine) Woolf	Henry Solomon (Solomon Henry) Myers	Liverpool	
27577	Aarons	Mary	1848	Aldgate, London	Solomon Aarons	Rosa Isaacs		Spitalfields, London	
27708	Aarons	Michael	1847	Whitechapel, London	Joseph Aarons	Esther Solomons		Spitalfields, London	scholar
10767	Aarons	Michael	1850	Spitalfields, London	Aaron Aarons	Hannah (?)		Spitalfields, London	
1095	Aarons	Morris	1817	?, London				Falmouth, Cornwall	traveller
10780	Aarons	Nathaniel	1836	Spitalfields, London	Noah Aarons	Mary Selig		Spitalfields, London	apprentice to hat maker
10778	Aarons	Noah	1811	Whitechapel, London	Michael Aarons	Rachel Joseph	Mary Selig	Spitalfields, London	cigar maker
27072	Aarons	Noah	1840	?, London	Daniel Aarons	Sarah Davis		Aldgate, London	scholar
11724	Aarons	Phillip	1823	Covent Garden, London				Aldgate, London	tailor
27709	Aarons	Phineas	1849	Whitechapel, London	Joseph Aarons	Esther Solomons		Spitalfields, London	
27576	Aarons	Phoebe	1846	Aldgate, London	Solomon Aarons	Rosa Isaacs		Spitalfields, London	
21877	Aarons	Rachael	1835	Whitechapel, London	(?) Aarons			Clerkenwell, London	servant domestic
11352	Aarons	Racheal	1831	?, Poland	(?) Aarons			Aldgate, London	cap maker
9682	Aarons	Rachel	1811	Spitalfields, London	David Moses	Hannah (?)	Aaron Aaron	Aldgate, London	clothes dealer
27071	Aarons	Rachel	1836	?, London	Daniel Aarons	Sarah Davis		Aldgate, London	cap maker
10781	Aarons	Rachel	1837	Spitalfields, London	Noah Aarons	Mary Selig	George Hart	Spitalfields, London	domestic assistant
27707	Aarons	Rachel	1845	Whitechapel, London	Joseph Aarons	Esther Solomons		Spitalfields, London	scholar
3500	Aarons	Rachel	1847	Spitalfields, London	Aaron Aarons	Hannah (?)	Judah Wilks	Spitalfields, London	
24365	Aarons	Ralph	1821	?, Poland [?, Prussian Poland]				Covent Garden, London	tailor
17917	Aarons	Rayner	1817	Whitechapel, London	(?) Aarons			Lambeth, London	servant
29711	Aarons	Rebecca	1843	?Bermondsey, London	Benjamin Aarons	Esther (?)		Aldgate, London	scholar
28899	Aarons	Rosa	1817	Birmingham	(?)		John (Jacob) Aarons	Spitalfields, London	
27573	Aarons	Rosa	1821	Aldgate, London	(?) Isaacs		Solomon Aarons	Spitalfields, London	
10483	Aarons	Sarah	1793	Limehouse, London	(?)		Solomon Aarons	Mile End, London	
27070	Aarons	Sarah	1824	?, London	Isaac Davis		Daniel Aarons	Aldgate, London	
29709	Aarons	Silvester	1839	?Bermondsey, London	Benjamin Aarons	Esther (?)		Aldgate, London	scholar
10482	Aarons	Solomon	1781	?, Poland [?, Prussia]			Sarah (?)	Mile End, London	formerly general dealer
27572	Aarons	Solomon	1818	Aldgate, London			Rosa Isaacs	Spitalfields, London	butcher
28903	Aarons	Solomon	1844	Spitalfields, London	John (Jacob) Aarons	Rosa (?)		Spitalfields, London	scholar
10783	Aarons	Solomon	1848	Spitalfields, London	Noah Aarons	Mary Selig		Spitalfields, London	scholar
2741	Aarons	Solomon H	1850	Liverpool	Henry Aarons	Kate (Katherine) Woolf		Liverpool	
19270	Aarons	Sophia	1847	Liverpool	Henry Aarons	Kate (Katherine) Woolf		Liverpool	
12738	Aaronson	Abraham Mayer	1822	Cracow, Poland	Judah Aaronson		Rosetta Crabb	Ipswich, Suffolk	traveller in Sheffield goods
20815	Aaronson	Hannah	1833	?, Poland [?, Prussia]	Wolfe Abraham		Joseph Aaronson	Sunderland, Co Durham	
12790	Aaronson	Jacob Lyon (Yakov Yehuda)	1851	Sunderland, Co Durham	Joseph Aronson	Hannah Abraham		Sunderland, Co Durham	
12791	Aaronson	Joseph	1828	?, Poland [?, Prussia]	Levy Aronson		Hannah Abraham	Sunderland, Co Durham	clothes dealer

ID	surname	given names	born	birthplace	father	mother	spouse 1	1851 residence	1851 occupation
26488	Aaronson	Louisa	1826	Covent Garden, London	Mark Jacob Norden	Jane Arrobus	Maurice Aaronson	Bloomsbury, London	
26487	Aaronson	Maurice	1824	?, Holland			Louisa Norden	Bloomsbury, London	general upholsterer
31032	Aaronson	Thomas	1831	abroad				Sunderland, Co Durham	servant
18472	Aaronson (Aronson)	Andrew	1791	Amersfort, Holland	Abraham Aarons Samson Aronson	Matje Van Minden	Fanny Sanders	Bloomsbury, London	dealer
18474	Aaronson (Aronson)	Fanny	1819	?, Holland	(?) Sanders		Andrew Aaronson (Aronson)	Bloomsbury, London	
18473	Aaronson (Aronson)	Henry (Hyman)	1816	Amersfort, Holland	Abraham Aarons Samson Aronson	Matje Van Minden	Hannah Kesner	Bloomsbury, London	dealer
18475	Aaronson (Aronson)	Solomon	1842	?, Holland	Andrew Aaronson (Aronson)	Fanny (?)		Bloomsbury, London	
20015	Abady (Abadee, Abadaa)	Henry	1833	Mile End, London	Jonah de Moses Abady (Abadee, Abadaa)	Leah de Solomon		Spitalfields, London	tailor
20019	Abady (Abadee, Abadaa)	Jonah	1789	Aldgate, London	Moses Abady		Leah de Solomon	Spitalfields, London	pedlar
20020	Abady (Abadee, Abadaa)	Leah	1800	Aldgate, London	Solomon		Jonah de Moses Abady (Abadee, Abadaa)	Spitalfields, London	
20014	Abady (Abadee, Abadaa)	Moses	1830	Mile End, London	Jonah de Moses Abady (Abadee, Abadaa)	Leah de Solomon		Spitalfields, London	general dealer
20012	Abady (Abadee, Abadaa)	Simah (Simmy)	1831	Mile End, London	Jonah de Moses Abady (Abadee)	Leah de Solomon	Solomon Joel	Spitalfields, London	tailoress
20016	Abady (Abadee, Abadaa)	Solomon	1835	Mile End, London	Jonah de Moses Abady (Abadee, Abadaa)	Leah de Solomon	Rebecca Davis	Spitalfields, London	tailor
20018	Abady (Abadee, Abadaa, Aberdeen)	Hannah	1842	Mile End, London	Jonah de Moses Abady (Abadee, Abadaa)	Leah de Solomon	Joseph Rosenthal	Spitalfields, London	
20017	Abady (Abadee, Abadaa, Aberdeen)	Julia	1836	Mile End, London	Jonah de Moses Abady (Abadee, Abadaa)	Leah de Solomon	Joseph Rosenthal	Spitalfields, London	tailoress
20013	Abady (Abadee, Abadaa, Aberdeen)	Mark (Mordecai)	1828	Mile End, London	Jonah de Moses Abady (Abadee, Abadaa)	Leah de Solomon	Julia (Judith) Benjamin	Spitalfields, London	general dealer
13400	Abady (Aberdean)	David	1807	Spitalfields, London	Solomon Abady	Nelly (?)	Rebecca (Ribca) de Judah Leib	Spitalfields, London	hawker of clothes
13410	Abady (Aberdean)	Hannah	1833	Spitalfields, London	David Abady (Aberdean)	Rebecca (Ribca) de Judah Leib		Spitalfields, London	dressmaker
13409	Abady (Aberdean)	Rachel	1832	Spitalfields, London	David Abady (Aberdean)	Rebecca (Ribca) de Judah Leib	Joseph Barnett	Spitalfields, London	dressmaker
13408	Abady (Aberdean)	Rebecca (Ribca)	1810	Spitalfields, London	Judah Leib		David Abady (Aberdean)	Spitalfields, London	hawker of clothes
13411	Abady (Aberdean)	Sarrah	1837	Spitalfields, London	David Abady (Aberdean)	Rebecca (Ribca) de Judah Leib		Spitalfields, London	dressmaker
13412	Abady (Aberdean)	Solomon	1840	Spitalfields, London	David Abady (Aberdean)	Rebecca (Ribca) de Judah Leib		Spitalfields, London	scholar
23227	Abdullah	Abraham	1802	Baghdad, Iraq				Hammersmith, London	East India merchant
9040	Abecasis	Aaron	1822	City, London	Solomon Abecasis	Esther Daninos	Esther Brandon	Aldgate, London	merchant's clerk
7855	Abecasis	Ada (Meshoda)	1837	Finsbury, London	Solomon Abecassis	Esther Daninos	Philip Lucas	Aldgate, London	scholar
4176	Abecasis	Deborah (Dabby)	1836	Dublin, Ireland	Jacob Abecasis	Elizabeth (?)	Solomon Slupski	Aldgate, London	tailoress
4175	Abecasis	Diana	1831	Dublin, Ireland	Jacob Abecasis	Elizabeth (?)	Morris Brook	Aldgate, London	domestic servant
4173	Abecasis	Elizabeth	1800	Hamburg, Germany			Jacob Abecasis	Aldgate, London	

ID	surname	given names	born	birthplace	father	mother	spouse 1	1851 residence	1851 occupation
9044	Abecasis	Emily (Luna)	1839	Middlesex, London	Solomon Abecasis	Esther Daninos	Daniel de Pass	Aldgate, London	scholar
9039	Abecasis	Esther	1800	Algiers, Algeria	(?) Daninos		Solomon Abecasis	Aldgate, London	
4172	Abecasis	Jacob	1784	Essaouira, Morocco [Mogador, Morocco]	Shalem ?(Solomon) Abecasis		Elizabeth (?)	Aldgate, London	
4174	Abecasis	Jacob	1827	?, Morocco	Jacob Abecasis	Elizabeth (?)		Aldgate, London	traveller
4179	Abecasis	Joseph	1842	Dublin, Ireland	Jacob Abecasis	Elizabeth (?)		Aldgate, London	
9041	Abecasis	Judah Samuel	1829	Middlesex, London	Solomon Abecasis	Esther Daninos		Aldgate, London	gentleman
9042	Abecasis	Moses	1830	Middlesex, London	Solomon Abecasis	Esther Daninos		Aldgate, London	gentleman
4178	Abecasis	Rebecca	1841	Dublin, Ireland	Jacob Abecasis	Elizabeth (?)	Isidore (Israel) Glance	Aldgate, London	
232	Abecasis	Solomon	1792	Gibraltar	Aaron Abecasis		Esther Daninos	Aldgate, London	gentleman
4177	Abecasis	Solomon	1838	Dublin, Ireland	Jacob Abecasis	Elizabeth (?)		Aldgate, London	
18377	Abel	Elias	1848	Birmingham	Joseph Abel	Esther (?)		Birmingham	
9434	Abel	Elizabeth	1830	?, London	(?) Abel			Wapping, London	servant
18379	Abel	Esther	1821	Birmingham	(?)		Joseph Abel	Birmingham	
16975	Abel	Frances	1842	Birmingham	Joseph Abel	Esther (?)	Elias Abrahams	Birmingham	boarding school pupil
18376	Abel	Henry	1845	Birmingham	Joseph Abel	Esther (?)		Birmingham	
18378	Abel	Joseph	1811	abroad			Esther (?)	Birmingham	pawnbroker
28305	Abendana	Abigail	1811	Middlesex, London	Hananel Gomes Da Costa		Joseph de Raphael Abendana	Aldgate, London	
3318	Abendana	Abraham	1820	Middlesex, London	Solomon Abendana	Pindler (Prindla) de Judah Isaacs	Maria (Miriam) Levy	Aldgate, London	tailor
26423	Abendana	Amelia	1837	?, London	Elias Abendana	Ann (Hannah, Nancy, Yantla) de Jacob		Aldgate, London	
20646	Abendana	Celia	1832	?Whitechapel, London	Raphael de Joseph Abendana	Yahat (Jesse) de Isaac Israel		Spitalfields, London	dressmaker
5569	Abendana	Deborah	1794	Spitalfields, London	Hart [Naftali Hirts] Phillips		Moses Moses	Spitalfields, London	
26418	Abendana	Elias	1802	?, London	Isaac Abendana	Rachel Isaacs	Nancy (Hannah, Ann, Yantla) de Jacob	Aldgate, London	confectioner
20647	Abendana	Esther	1837	Whitechapel, London	Raphael de Joseph Abendana	Rachel de David Nunes Martinez		Spitalfields, London	dressmaker
5651	Abendana	Hananel	1834	City, London	Joseph de Raphael Abendana	Abigail de Hananel Gomes Da Costa	Rachael Lazarus	Aldgate, London	
15711	Abendana	Hannah	1832	Stepney, London	Solomon Abendana	Betsy (Batseba) (?)	Abraham Lyons	Spitalfields, London	
26422	Abendana	Hannah	1835	?, London	Elias Abendana	Ann (Hannah, Nancy, Yantla) de Jacob	Moses Harris	Aldgate, London	
18144	Abendana	Isaac	1810	?Barbados, West Indies	Raphael de Joseph Abendana	Yahat (Jesse) de Isaac Israel	Leah de Simon ben Nathan	Mile End, London	steward of Portuguese Jews' Hospital
5567	Abendana	Jacob	1846	Whitechapel, London	Solomon Abendana	Deborah Phillips	Sarah Nathan	Spitalfields, London	
28306	Abendana	Jesse	1832	Middlesex, London	Joseph de Raphael Abendana	Abigail de Hananel Gomes Da Costa		Aldgate, London	
18146	Abendana	Jesse (Simha)	1835	Spitalfields, London	Isaac Raphael Abendana	Leah de Simon ben Nathan	Abraham Moses	Mile End, London	
28304	Abendana	Joseph	1811	Barbados, West Indies	Raphael de Joseph Abendana	Yahat (Jesse) de Isaac Israel	Abigail de Hananel Gomes Da Costa	Aldgate, London	general dealer
26420	Abendana	Joseph	1828	?, London	Elias Abendana	Ann (Hannah, Nancy, Yantla) de Jacob		Aldgate, London	
26897	Abendana	Judah	1830	?, London	Solomon Abendana	Betsy (Batseba) (?)	Phoebe Hart	Aldgate, London	cigar maker

ID	surname	given names	born	birthplace	father	mother	spouse 1	1851 residence	1851 occupation
18145	Abendana	Leah	1815	Whitechapel, London	Simon ben Nathan		Isaac de Raphael Abendana	Mile End, London	matron of Portuguese Jews' Hospital
3317	Abendana	Maria (Miriam)	1826	?, London	Aaron Levy	Rachel Hart	Abraham Abendana	Aldgate, London	
26424	Abendana	Mary	1839	?, London	Elias Abendana	Ann (Hannah, Nancy, Yantla) de Jacob	Jacobs Jacobs	Aldgate, London	
26421	Abendana	Moses	1833	?, London	Elias Abendana	Ann (Hannah, Nancy, Yantla) de Jacob		Aldgate, London	
15712	Abendana	Moses	1834	Whitechapel, London	Solomon Abendana	Betsy (Batseba) (?)		Spitalfields, London	
26419	Abendana	Nancy (Hannah, Ann, Yantla)	1805	?, London	Jacob		Elias Abendana	Aldgate, London	
20645	Abendana	Rachel	1799	Whitechapel, London	David Nunes Martinez		Raphael de Joseph Abendana	Spitalfields, London	
20644	Abendana	Raphael	1789	Whitechapel, London	Joseph Abendana		Jesse (Yahat) de Isaac Israel	Spitalfields, London	
15710	Abendana	Solomon	1792	Spitalfields, London	Joseph Abendana	Esther (?)	Pindler de Judah Isaacs	Spitalfields, London	egg dealer
25184	Abendana	Solomon	1826	Whitechapel, London	Raphael de Joseph Abendana	Yahat (Jesse) de Isaac Israel		Finsbury, London	cigar dealer
3319	Abendana	Solomon	1850	Aldgate, London	Abraham Abendana	Maria (Miriam) Levy	Maria (?)	Aldgate, London	
5570	Abendana (Bendon)	Jacob (John)	1829	Whitechapel, London	Elias Abendana	Ann (Hannah, Nancy, Yantla) de Jacob	Catherine (Kate) Hyams	Aldgate, London	general dealer
9303	Abochbot	Debora	1795	Mile End, London	Isaac Vaz Martines		Jacob Abochbot	Aldgate, London	charwoman
17858	Abohbot	Abraham Prosper	1819	City, London	Prosper (Mesod) Abohbot (Bochbod)	Sarah (?)		Aldgate, London	spice dealer
17860	Abohbot	Julia	1831	City, London	Prosper (Mesod) Abohbot (Bochbod)	Sarah (?)	Michael Nathan	Aldgate, London	
5664	Abohbot	Miriam	1829	City, London	Prosper (Mesod) Abohbot (Bochbod)	Sarah (?)	Samuel de Moses Hassan	Aldgate, London	
17857	Abohbot	Sarah	1788	King's Lynn, Norfolk	(?)		Prosper (Mesod) Abohbot (Bochbod)	Aldgate, London	
17856	Abohbot (Bochbod)	Prosper (Mesod)	1788	Essaouira, Morocco [Mogador, Africa]			Sarah (?)	Aldgate, London	
13617	Abraham	A---	1811	Poznan, Poland [Posen, Germany]			Johanna (?)	Manchester	glazier
15146	Abraham	Aaron	1845	Whitechapel, London	Israel Abraham	Chashe (?)		Hoxton, London	scholar
5217	Abraham	Abraham	1799	Exeter, Devon	Jacob Abraham	Hannah (?)	Sarah Simons	Liverpool	fundholdr
18076	Abraham	Abraham	1800	Southwark, London			Sarah (?)	Southwark, London	mat weaver
3763	Abraham	Abraham	1840	Spitalfields, London	(?) Abraham	(?) Lyon		Spitalfields, London	scholar
895	Abraham	Abraham Woolf	1843	North Shields, Tyne & Wear	Wolf Abraham	Rachael (?)	Theresa W Sternberg	Sunderland, Co Durham	
31156	Abraham	Ada S	1850	Bristol	Joseph Abraham	Jane (?)		Bristol	
19008	Abraham	Adelaide	1830	Whitechapel, London	Godfrey Abraham	Sarah (?)		Whitechapel, London	
24262	Abraham	Adelaide	1845	Middlesex, London	Lewis Henry Abraham	Sophia (?)		Bloomsbury, London	
19006	Abraham	Alfred	1824	Whitechapel, London	Godfrey Abraham	Sarah (?)		Whitechapel, London	watchmaker
31081	Abraham	Alice	1839	Whitechapel, London	Michael Abraham	Frances (Brinah) Levy		Whitechapel, London	scholar
24219	Abraham	Amelia	1798	Portsmouth, Hampshire	(?)		(?) Abraham	Haggerston, London	wife of auctioneer
31083	Abraham	Amelia	1842	Whitechapel, London	Michael Abraham	Frances (Brinah) Levy		Whitechapel, London	assistant governess
21892	Abraham	Ann (Hannah)	1799	City, London	Gedalia Marks		Hyam Abraham	Clerkenwell, London	
19183	Abraham	Annie Bessie	1851	Bristol	Joseph Abraham	Jane (?)		Bristol	
13625	Abraham	Annranul	1850	Middlesex, London	A--- Abraham	Johanna (?)		Manchester	

ID	surname	given names	born	birthplace	father	mother	spouse 1	1851 residence	1851 occupation
18321	Abraham	Barnard	1819	?, Russia			Rachel (?)	Sunderland, Co Durham	traveller jeweller
19007	Abraham	Barnett	1827	Whitechapel, London	Godfrey Abraham	Sarah (?)		Whitechapel, London	watchmaker
27195	Abraham	Benjamin	1811	Gloucester, Gloucestershire	Solomon Abraham	Sarah Harris	Rachael Phillips	Aldgate, London	dressing glass maker
8556	Abraham	Benjamin	1814	Whitechapel, London			Julia Myers	Spitalfields, London	general dealer
21893	Abraham	Benjamin	1832	Clerkenwell, London	Hyam Abraham	Ann (Hannah) Marks		Clerkenwell, London	cabman
24264	Abraham	Benjamin	1847	Middlesex, London	Lewis Henry Abraham	Sophia (?)		Bloomsbury, London	
18384	Abraham	Bessie	1820	Frome, Somerset	Moses Abraham	Esther Emden	George (Gershon) Delgado	Bristol	
16689	Abraham	Betsey	1849	Middlesex, London	Joseph Abraham	Maria (?)		Spitalfields, London	
19288	Abraham	Caroline	1803	Bristol	(?)		John Abraham	Bristol	
8558	Abraham	Caroline	1839	Whitechapel, London	Benjamin Abraham	Julia Myers		Spitalfields, London	
26963	Abraham	Catherine	1841	Spitalfields, London	Ezekiel Abraham	Elizabeth (?)		Aldgate, London	scholar
15761	Abraham	Charlotte	1825	Covent Garden, London	Victor Abraham	Rebecca Levy		Soho, London	
15141	Abraham	Chashe	1811	?, Poland	(?)		Israel Abraham	Hoxton, London	
26960	Abraham	Dinah	1834	Aldgate, London	Ezekiel Abraham	Elizabeth (?)		Aldgate, London	tailoress
12968	Abraham	Dinah	1850	?, London	Isaac Abraham	Mary (?)		Aldgate, London	
13623	Abraham	Dorothy	1844	?, Poland [?, Prussia]	A--- Abraham	Johanna (?)		Manchester	scholar at home
15075	Abraham	Edward	1840	Whitechapel, London				Bethnal Green, London	
12185	Abraham	Elias	1806	Southwark, London			Sarah (?)	Whitechapel, London	umbrella maker
28345	Abraham	Elizabeth	1785	Whitechapel, London	(?)		Lazarus Abraham	Spitalfields, London	
26958	Abraham	Elizabeth	1803	?, Holland	(?)		Ezekiel Abraham	Aldgate, London	
24258	Abraham	Elizabeth	1837	Surrey, London	Lewis Henry Abraham	Sophia (?)		Bloomsbury, London	
21897	Abraham	Elizabeth	1840	Clerkenwell, London	Hyam Abraham	Ann (Hannah) Marks		Clerkenwell, London	
4078	Abraham	Elizabeth (Betsey)	1808	Portsmouth, Hampshire	Michael Emanuel	Hannah Isaacs	Benjamin Abraham	Norwich, Norfolk	
18334	Abraham	Ellen	1833	Corfu, Greece	(?) Abraham	Mary (?)		Chester, Cheshire	servant
17164	Abraham	Esther	1811	Margonin, Poland	(?) Israel		Jacob Abraham	Newcastle Upon Tyne	
13620	Abraham	Esther	1835	?, Poland [?, Prussia]	A--- Abraham	Johanna (?)		Manchester	cap maker
16687	Abraham	Esther	1845	Middlesex, London	Joseph Abraham	Maria (?)		Spitalfields, London	
26957	Abraham	Ezekiel	1806	Clerkenwell, London			Elizabeth (?)	Aldgate, London	coat dealer
22068	Abraham	Ezekiel	1807	?, London	Benjamin Abraham		Sarah Hart nee (?)	Spitalfields, London	refiner
15760	Abraham	Fanny	1824	Covent Garden, London	Victor Abraham	Rebecca Levy		Soho, London	dressmaker
15142	Abraham	Fanny	1831	?, Poland	Israel Abraham	Chashe (?)		Hoxton, London	shoemaker
8560	Abraham	Frances	1844	Whitechapel, London	Benjamin Abraham	Julia Myers		Spitalfields, London	school
31078	Abraham	Frances (Brinah)	1806	Aldgate, London	Solomon Levy		Michael Abraham	Whitechapel, London	
18078	Abraham	Frederick	1829	Southwark, London	Abraham Abraham	Sarah (?)		Southwark, London	mat weaver
31154	Abraham	Frederick	1844	Bristol	Joseph Abraham	Jane (?)		Bristol	
17071	Abraham	Godfrey	1793	Middlesex, London	Hayim Ze'ev		Sarah (?)	Glasgow, Scotland	watch maker
8561	Abraham	Godfrey	1847	Whitechapel, London	Benjamin Abraham	Julia Myers	Sarah Phillips	Spitalfields, London	school
31029	Abraham	Grace	1836	?, Poland [?, Poland]	Wolf Abraham	Rachael (?)		Sunderland, Co Durham	
4079	Abraham	Hannah	1841	Norwich, Norfolk	Benjamin Abraham	Elizabeth (Betsey) Emanuel		Norwich, Norfolk	
4246	Abraham	Hariette	1829	?, Poland [?, Prussia]			Julian Abraham	Birmingham	
13619	Abraham	Harriet	1833	?, Poland [?, Prussia]	A--- Abraham	Johanna (?)		Manchester	cap maker
7279	Abraham	Harriett	1826	Middlesex, London	Abraham Boss		Philip Abraham	Birmingham	
13621	Abraham	Harris	1837	?, Poland [?, Prussia]	A--- Abraham	Johanna (?)		Manchester	cap maker
8397	Abraham	Henry	1824	Frome, Somerset	Abraham Abraham	Esther Barnard	Mary Ann Docwra	Southampton, Hampshire	jeweller
24263	Abraham	Henry	1846	Middlesex, London	Lewis Henry Abraham	Sophia (?)		Bloomsbury, London	

ID	surname	given names	born	birthplace	father	mother	spouse 1	1851 residence	1851 occupation
31155	Abraham	Hester	1848	Bristol	Joseph Abraham	Jane (?)		Bristol	
19289	Abraham	Hester Evelina	1844	Bristol	John (Jacob) Abraham	Caroline (?)	Samuel Nunes Carvalho	Bristol	
2350	Abraham	Himan	1830	?, Poland				Hull, Yorkshire	glazier assistant
21891	Abraham	Hyam	1795	Holborn, London	Isaac Cow Cross		Ann (Hannah) Marks	Clerkenwell, London	furrier
28446	Abraham	Isaac	1744	Metz, France				Spitalfields, London	gentleman funded by [?]
12964	Abraham	Isaac	1822	?, Poland			Mary (?)	Aldgate, London	tailor
12462	Abraham	Isaac	1830	?, London				Spitalfields, London	cigar maker
27312	Abraham	Isaac	1836	Whitechapel, London	Lewis Abraham	(?)		Aldgate, London	
15759	Abraham	Isabella	1822	Covent Garden, London	Victor Abraham	Rebecca Levy		Soho, London	embroideress
24261	Abraham	Isabella	1843	Middlesex, London	Lewis Henry Abraham	Sophia (?)		Bloomsbury, London	
27197	Abraham	Isiah	1837	?, London	Benjamin Abraham	Rachael Phillips		Aldgate, London	
15140	Abraham	Israel	1806	?, Poland			Chashe (?)	Hoxton, London	shoemaker
31028	Abraham	Israel	1833	?, Poland [?, Poland]	Wolf Abraham	Rachael (?)		Sunderland, Co Durham	
15144	Abraham	Israel	1841	Whitechapel, London	Israel Abraham	Chashe (?)		Hoxton, London	scholar
27201	Abraham	Israel	1850	?Aldgate, London	Benjamin Abraham	Rachael Phillips		Aldgate, London	
17163	Abraham	Jacob	1813	Margonin, Poland			Esther Israel	Newcastle Upon Tyne	general dealer
26962	Abraham	Jacob	1839	Whitechapel, London	Ezekiel Abraham	Elizabeth (?)		Aldgate, London	boot maker
21894	Abraham	James	1834	Clerkenwell, London	Hyam Abraham	Ann (Hannah) Marks		Clerkenwell, London	furrier
19182	Abraham	Jane	1817	Middlesex, London	(?)		Joseph Abraham	Bristol	
24259	Abraham	Janette	1840	Surrey, London	Lewis Henry Abraham	Sophia (?)		Bloomsbury, London	
17166	Abraham	Jette	1850	Newcastle Upon Tyne	Jacob Abraham	Esther Israel		Newcastle Upon Tyne	
13618	Abraham	Johanna	1814	?, Poland [?, Prussia]	(?)		(?) Abraham	Manchester	
19287	Abraham	John	1805	Frome, Somerset	Moses Abraham	Esther Emden	Caroline (?)	Bristol	wine merchant
27200	Abraham	John	1848	?, London	Benjamin Abraham	Rachael Phillips		Aldgate, London	
27178	Abraham	Jonas	1793	?, London				Aldgate, London	tailor
31152	Abraham	Joseph	1815	Frome, Somerset	Moses Abraham	Esther Emden	Jane (?)	Bristol	wine + spirit merchant
438	Abraham	Joseph	1821	?, Poland			Maria (?)	Spitalfields, London	tailor
1418	Abraham	Joseph	1822	Amsterdam, Holland				Plymouth, Devon	
18079	Abraham	Joseph	1831	Southwark, London	Abraham Abraham	Sarah (?)		Southwark, London	mat weaver
16688	Abraham	Joseph	1847	Middlesex, London	Joseph Abraham	Maria (?)		Spitalfields, London	
16690	Abraham	Juley	1851	Spitalfields, London	Joseph Abraham	Maria (?)		Spitalfields, London	
8557	Abraham	Julia	1815	Aldgate, London	(?) Myers		Benjamin Abraham	Spitalfields, London	
19010	Abraham	Julia	1835	Whitechapel, London	Godfrey Abraham	Sarah (?)		Whitechapel, London	
21895	Abraham	Julia	1836	Clerkenwell, London	Hyam Abraham	Ann (Hannah) Marks		Clerkenwell, London	
12966	Abraham	Julia	1848	?, London	Isaac Abraham	Mary (?)		Aldgate, London	
4245	Abraham	Julian	1817	?, Poland [?, Prussia]			Hariette (?)	Birmingham	master tailor
15764	Abraham	Kate	1831	Covent Garden, London	Victor Abraham	Rebecca Levy		Soho, London	dressmaker
28344	Abraham	Lazarus	1785	Whitechapel, London			Elizabeth (?)	Spitalfields, London	tailor
27198	Abraham	Leah	1840	?, London	Benjamin Abraham	Rachael Phillips		Aldgate, London	scholar
31030	Abraham	Levi	1844	Sunderland, Co Durham	Wolf Abraham	Rachael (?)		Sunderland, Co Durham	
27311	Abraham	Lewis	1798	Warsaw, Poland			(?)	Aldgate, London	tailor formerly
22165	Abraham	Lewis	1829	Whitechapel, London				Whitechapel, London	cigar maker
17624	Abraham	Lewis	1832	?, Poland				Aldgate, London	tailor
24266	Abraham	Lewis	1850	Middlesex, London	Lewis Henry Abraham	Sophia (?)		Bloomsbury, London	
24255	Abraham	Lewis Henry	1808	Middlesex, London			Sophia (?)	Bloomsbury, London	attorney at law

ID	surname	given names	born	birthplace	father	mother	spouse 1	1851 residence	1851 occupation
15145	Abraham	Lezer	1843	Whitechapel, London	Israel Abraham	Chashe (?)		Hoxton, London	scholar
30792	Abraham	Louis	1799	?, Germany				Preston, Lancashire	hawker
2221	Abraham	Louis	1826	?, Poland				Leeds, Yorkshire	general dealer
3934	Abraham	Lydia	1787	Portsmouth, Hampshire	Simon Abrahams	Elizabeth (?)		Portsmouth, Hampshire	
23507	Abraham	Lyon	1839	Middlesex, London				Liverpool	
21375	Abraham	Marcus	1832	?, Germany [Treisapan, Germany]				Lincoln, Lincolnshire	billiard maker
16686	Abraham	Maria	1823	?, Poland	(?)		Joseph Abraham	Spitalfields, London	
4080	Abraham	Maria (Mariah) (Marie)	1843	Norwich, Norfolk	Benjamin Abraham	Elizabeth (Betsey) Emanuel		Norwich, Norfolk	
21896	Abraham	Mariah	1839	Clerkenwell, London	Hyam Abraham	Ann (Hannah) Marks		Clerkenwell, London	
18333	Abraham	Mary	1791	Portsmouth, Hampshire	(?)		(?) Abraham	Chester, Cheshire	laundress
12965	Abraham	Mary	1822	?, London	(?)		Isaac Abraham	Aldgate, London	
18323	Abraham	Mary	1848	Sunderland, Co Durham	Barnard Abraham	Rachel (?)		Sunderland, Co Durham	
15762	Abraham	Matilda	1827	Covent Garden, London	Victor Abraham	Rebecca Levy		Soho, London	embroideress
31153	Abraham	Matilda	1846	Bristol	Joseph Abraham	Jane (?)		Bristol	
18641	Abraham	Maurice	1809	Bath	Jacob Abraham	Hannah (?)		Cheltenham, Gloucestershire	optician
17165	Abraham	Meyer	1846	Plymouth, Devon	Jacob Abraham	Esther Israel		Newcastle Upon Tyne	
31077	Abraham	Michael	1799	Whitechapel, London	Moshe (?)		Frances (Brinah) Levy	Whitechapel, London	slopman clothiers
4081	Abraham	Michael	1845	Norwich, Norfolk	Benjamin Abraham	Elizabeth (Betsey) Emanuel		Norwich, Norfolk	
7272	Abraham	Moses	1772	?, London			Esther Emden	Bristol	optician
31082	Abraham	N---	1843	Whitechapel, London	Michael Abraham	Frances (Brinah) Levy		Whitechapel, London	scholar
22302	Abraham	Nathan	1812	?, Bavaria, Germany				Whitechapel, London	glass dealer
15147	Abraham	Nathan	1846	Whitechapel, London	Israel Abraham	Chashe (?)		Hoxton, London	scholar
7278	Abraham	Philip	1805	Middlesex, London	Avigdor Abraham		Harriett Boss	Birmingham	professor of languages
23551	Abraham	Philip	1830	Berlin, Germany [Berlin, Prussia]				Liverpool	furrier
12967	Abraham	Philip	1849	?, London	Isaac Abraham	Mary (?)		Aldgate, London	
15765	Abraham	Phoebe	1833	Covent Garden, London	Victor Abraham	Rebecca Levy		Soho, London	embroideress
12463	Abraham	Phoebe	1837	?, London				Spitalfields, London	servant
27828	Abraham	Polly	1848	Whitechapel, London	Michael Abrahams	Ann Davis		Spitalfields, London	
31079	Abraham	R---	1827	Whitechapel, London	Michael Abraham	Frances (Brinah) Levy		Whitechapel, London	
27196	Abraham	Rachael	1811	?, London	(?) Phillips		Benjamin Abraham	Aldgate, London	
31027	Abraham	Rachael	1806	?, Poland [?, Poland]	(?)		Wolf Abraham	Sunderland, Co Durham	
18322	Abraham	Rachel	1820	?, Russia	(?)		Barnard Abraham	Sunderland, Co Durham	
14768	Abraham	Rachel	1826	Poole, Dorset	Abraham Braham (Abraham)	Hannah Moses		Finsbury, London	
18324	Abraham	Rebeca	1850	Sunderland, Co Durham	Barnard Abraham	Rachel (?)		Sunderland, Co Durham	
15758	Abraham	Rebecca	1787	?, London	Shlomeh Zalman Michael Levy		Victor Abraham	Soho, London	embroideress
26959	Abraham	Rebecca	1830	Aldgate, London	Ezekiel Abraham	Elizabeth (?)		Aldgate, London	tailoress
11177	Abraham	Rebecca	1839	Middlesex, London	(?) Abraham	(?) Myers		Aldgate, London	scholar
31031	Abraham	Rebecca	1848	Sunderland, Co Durham	Wolf Abraham	Rachael (?)		Sunderland, Co Durham	
24260	Abraham	Rosetta	1841	Middlesex, London	Lewis Henry Abraham	Sophia (?)		Bloomsbury, London	
31080	Abraham	S---	1834	Whitechapel, London	Michael Abraham	Frances (Brinah) Levy		Whitechapel, London	cabinet maker
15763	Abraham	Samuel	1830	Covent Garden, London	Victor Abraham	Rebecca Levy		Soho, London	embroiderer

ID	surname	given names	born	birthplace	father	mother	spouse 1	1851 residence	1851 occupation
4082	Abraham	Samuel	1847	Norwich, Norfolk	Benjamin Abraham	Elizabeth (Betsey) Abraham		Norwich, Norfolk	
24265	Abraham	Samuel	1848	Middlesex, London	Lewis Henry Abraham	Sophia (?)		Bloomsbury, London	
27204	Abraham	Sarah	1774	?, London	Benjamin Schneider Harris		Solomon Abraham	Aldgate, London	
19005	Abraham	Sarah	1781	Aldgate, London	(?)		Godfrey Abraham	Whitechapel, London	watchmaker's wife
22069	Abraham	Sarah	1797	Amsterdam, Holland	Yehuda Leib		(?) Hart	Spitalfields, London	
5190	Abraham	Sarah	1800	Plymouth, Devon	(?) Simons		Abraham Abraham	Liverpool	
18077	Abraham	Sarah	1801	Holborn, London	(?)		Abraham Abraham	Southwark, London	
1032	Abraham	Sarah	1802	Exeter, Devon				Exeter, Devon	annuitant
18380	Abraham	Sarah	1803	Frome, Somerset	Moses Abraham	Esther Emden		Bristol	
12186	Abraham	Sarah	1818	Aldgate, London	(?)		Elias Abraham	Whitechapel, London	
15143	Abraham	Sarah	1833	?, Poland	Israel Abraham	Chashe (?)		Hoxton, London	shoemaker
24257	Abraham	Sarah	1836	Surrey, London	Lewis Henry Abraham	Sophia (?)		Bloomsbury, London	
26961	Abraham	Sarah	1838	Whitechapel, London	Ezekiel Abraham	Elizabeth (?)		Aldgate, London	tailoress
18080	Abraham	Sarah	1839	Southwark, London	Abraham Abraham	Sarah (?)		Southwark, London	
4083	Abraham	Sarah	1847	Norwich, Norfolk	Benjamin Abraham	Elizabeth (Betsey) Emanuel		Norwich, Norfolk	
19009	Abraham	Sidney	1831	Whitechapel, London	Godfrey Abraham	Sarah (?)		Whitechapel, London	
2351	Abraham	Simon	1831	?, Poland				Hull, Yorkshire	glazier assistant
13622	Abraham	Simon	1839	?, Poland [?, Prussia]	A--- Abraham	Johanna (?)		Manchester	scholar at home
27203	Abraham	Solomon	1767	?, London	Joshua Solomon from Gloucester		Sarah Harris	Aldgate, London	general dealer
29191	Abraham	Solomon	1769	Poole, Dorset				Whitechapel, London	member of the Stock Exchange
16897	Abraham	Solomon	1807	?, Poland [?, Prussia]				Sheffield, Yorkshire	hatter
5723	Abraham	Solomon	1829	Soho, London	Victor Abraham	Rebecca Levy	Sarah Bloom Phillips	Soho, London	embroiderer
26438	Abraham	Solomon	1830	?, Poland				Aldgate, London	cabinet maker
21065	Abraham	Solomon	1839	?, London				Dover, Kent	boarding school pupil
27199	Abraham	Solomon	1842	?, London	Benjamin Abraham	Rachael Phillips		Aldgate, London	
8562	Abraham	Solomon	1850	Spitalfields, London	Benjamin Abraham	Julia Myers		Spitalfields, London	
14769	Abraham	Sophia	1816	Portsmouth, Hampshire	Abraham Braham (Abraham)	Hannah Moses		Finsbury, London	
24256	Abraham	Sophia	1818	Middlesex, London	(?)		Lewis Henry Abraham	Bloomsbury, London	
5191	Abraham	Sophia	1821	Bath	Jacob Abraham	Hannah (?)		Cheltenham, Gloucestershire	optician's sister
8559	Abraham	Sophia	1841	Whitechapel, London	Benjamin Abraham	Julia Myers		Spitalfields, London	school
18690	Abraham	Victor Abraham	1851	Birmingham	Philip Abraham	Harriet Boss		Birmingham	
31026	Abraham	Wolf	1801	?, Poland [?, Poland]			Rachael (?)	Sunderland, Co Durham	clothes dealer
13624	Abraham	Yeaty	1847	Middlesex, London	A--- Abraham	Johanna (?)		Manchester	
10217	Abraham (Abrahams)	Abigail	1804	?, Holland	(?)		David Abraham (Abrahams)	Spitalfields, London	
10220	Abraham (Abrahams)	Abraham	1839	?, London	David Abraham (Abrahams)	Abigail (?)		Spitalfields, London	
26484	Abraham (Abrahams)	Benjamin	1827	Spitalfields, London			Rosina Leo	Boston, Lincolnshire	
10221	Abraham (Abrahams)	Daniel	1842	?, London	David Abraham (Abrahams)	Abigail (?)		Spitalfields, London	
10216	Abraham (Abrahams)	David	1806	?, Holland			Abigail (?)	Spitalfields, London	general dealer

ID	surname	given names	born	birthplace	father	mother	spouse 1	1851 residence	1851 occupation
10222	Abraham (Abrahams)	Emanuel	1848	?, London	David Abraham (Abrahams)	Abigail (?)		Spitalfields, London	
10219	Abraham (Abrahams)	George	1834	?, London	David Abraham (Abrahams)	Abigail (?)		Spitalfields, London	shoe maker
10218	Abraham (Abrahams)	Simmey (Simma)	1832	Mile End, London	David Abraham (Abrahams)	Abigail (?)	Solomon Silver	Spitalfields, London	
19846	Abraham (Abrahams, Abrams)	Elizabeth	1815	Strand, London	Samuel Abraham (Abrahams, Abrams)	Harriett (?)		St Giles, London	tailoress
19849	Abraham (Abrahams, Abrams)	Hannah	1826	Strand, London	Samuel Abraham (Abrahams, Abrams)	Harriett (?)		St Giles, London	dressmaker
19845	Abraham (Abrahams, Abrams)	Harriett	1787	Norwich, Norfolk			Samuel Abraham (Abrahams, Abrams)	St Giles, London	
19847	Abraham (Abrahams, Abrams)	Leah	1817	Strand, London	Samuel Abraham (Abrahams, Abrams)	Harriett (?)		St Giles, London	housemaid
19848	Abraham (Abrahams, Abrams)	Rachel	1824	Strand, London	Samuel Abraham (Abrahams, Abrams)	Harriett (?)		St Giles, London	tailoress
19844	Abraham (Abrahams, Abrams)	Samuel	1784	Middlesex, London			Harriett (?)	St Giles, London	tailor
8494	Abraham (Abrahams, Stockman)	Leah (Amelia)	1828	Portsmouth, Hampshire	John Stockman		Lewis Pinner	Southwark, London	
10897	Abrahams	?	1815	?			Sarah (?)	Spitalfields, London	dealer in musical instruments
2895	Abrahams	Aaron	1779	?, Poland			Julia Levi	Birmingham	steel pen mfr
19219	Abrahams	Aaron	1800	Plymouth, Devon			Hannah (?)	Liverpool	watch maker (repairer)
6662	Abrahams	Aaron	1833	Westminster, London	Barnett Abrahams	Leah (?)	Catherine (Kitty, Kate) Raphael	Spitalfields, London	slipper maker
20925	Abrahams	Aaron	1838	Warminster, Wiltshire	Morris Abrahams	Louisa (?)		Devizes, Wiltshire	
25990	Abrahams	Aaron	1846	Whitechapel, London	Woolf Abrahams	Deborah Joseph		Aldgate, London	scholar
19493	Abrahams	Abby	1824	Southwark, London			Flora (?)	Covent Garden, London	tobacconist
20688	Abrahams	Abigail	1802	Aldgate, London	(?)		(?) Abrahams	Spitalfields, London	annuitant
17228	Abrahams	Abigail	1836	Aldgate, London	Ellis (Elias) Abrahams	Rachael (?)	Joseph Cohen	Aldgate, London	
2115	Abrahams	Abigail	1842	Aldgate, London	Colman (Coleman) Abrahams	Leah Myers	Samuel Hassan	Aldgate, London	scholar
26214	Abrahams	Abraham	1771	Amsterdam, Holland			(?)	Aldgate, London	supported by family
22749	Abrahams	Abraham	1781	City, London			Hannah (?)	Whitechapel, London	watchmaker
31106	Abrahams	Abraham	1790	?, London			(?)	Gloucester, Gloucestershire	baker + fishmonger
205	Abrahams	Abraham	1794	?, London [St James, London]	Yehudah (?Abrahams)		Elizabeth Solomons ?nee Isaacs	Strand, London	master tailor
1382	Abrahams	Abraham	1794	Plymouth, Devon			Betsey (Betty) (?)	Plymouth, Devon	pensioner

ID	surname	given names	born	birthplace	father	mother	spouse 1	1851 residence	1851 occupation
24454	Abrahams	Abraham	1797	Hitchin, Hertfordshire			Deborah (?)	Strand, London	broker + furniture dealer
26126	Abrahams	Abraham	1802	Amsterdam, Holland			Rachael (?)	Aldgate, London	jeweller
8349	Abrahams	Abraham	1806	Canterbury, Kent			Elizabeth (Betsy) Levi	Canterbury, Kent	watchmaker + clothier
439	Abrahams	Abraham	1814	St Giles, London			Rachel Fileman (Freeman)	Spitalfields, London	general dealer
10578	Abrahams	Abraham	1814	Whitechapel, London	Baruch Abrahams		Sarah Gomes da Costa	Spitalfields, London	pencil maker
17070	Abrahams	Abraham	1814	Sheerness, Kent				Aberdeen, Scotland	commercial traveller
10854	Abrahams	Abraham	1818	?, London	George Abrahams		Polly (Mary) Abrahams	Spitalfields, London	wholesale stationer
5989	Abrahams	Abraham	1819	Bath	Joshua Abrahams	Hannah (?)	Elizabeth Jacobs	Whitechapel, London	general dealer
5990	Abrahams	Abraham	1823	Middlesex, London	Michael Abrahams		Sarah Levy	Liverpool	dealer in clothes
3321	Abrahams	Abraham	1826	Aldgate, London	Solomon Abrahams	Maria Solomons	Sarah Levy	Aldgate, London	matzo manufacturer
16821	Abrahams	Abraham	1826	Colchester, Essex	Isaac Abrahams	Hanial (?)		Wolverhampton, Staffordshire	musician
10844	Abrahams	Abraham	1830	?, Holland			Rosa (?)	Spitalfields, London	general dealer
16694	Abrahams	Abraham	1831	Finsbury, London			Sarah (?)	Spitalfields, London	cigar maker
8100	Abrahams	Abraham	1832	Birmingham	(?) Abrahams	Rebekah (?)	Adelaide Blaine	Whitechapel, London	tailor
21769	Abrahams	Abraham	1833	Whitechapel, London	(?) Abrahams	Sarah (?)		Aldgate, London	grocer
29820	Abrahams	Abraham	1835	Whitechapel, London	(?) Abrahams	Alice (?)		Whitechapel, London	cigar maker
30743	Abrahams	Abraham	1838	Spitalfields, London	Jacob Abrahams	Isabella (?)		Aldgate, London	scholar
27561	Abrahams	Abraham	1839	Aldgate, London	Barnett Abrahams	Leah (?)		Spitalfields, London	scholar
30721	Abrahams	Abraham	1842	Covent Garden, London	John Abrahams	Rosetta (?)		Covent Garden, London	scholar
20963	Abrahams	Abraham	1847	Whitechapel, London	Barnett Abrahams	Priscilla Cohen	Maria Barnett	Spitalfields, London	scholar
25991	Abrahams	Abraham	1848	Whitechapel, London	Woolf Abrahams	Deborah Joseph		Aldgate, London	scholar
17233	Abrahams	Abraham	1849	Aldgate, London	Ellis (Elias) Abrahams	Rachael (?)		Aldgate, London	scholar
9371	Abrahams	Abraham	1850	Whitechapel, London	Tobias Abrahams	Rebecca (?)	Rebecca (?)	Spitalfields, London	
6573	Abrahams	Abraham	1851	Liverpool	Isaac Abrahams	Hannah (?)	Harriette Hinda Lyon	Liverpool	
2890	Abrahams	Abraham (Abram)	1789	Clerkenwell, London	Phineas Halevi		Juliet Cohen	Clerkenwell, London	fancy cabinet maker
19691	Abrahams	Abraham (Alfred)	1850	Spitalfields, London	Nathan Abrahams	Clara Harris		Spitalfields, London	
17865	Abrahams	Abraham Emanuel	1839	Bodmin, Cornwall	Alexander Abrahams	Harriett Solomons		Whitechapel, London	scholar
5033	Abrahams	Abram	1830	Liverpool	David Abrahams			Portsmouth, Hampshire	fishmonger
2352	Abrahams	Aby	1842	?, Poland [?, Prussia]	Victor Abrahams	Tobe (Thresa) (?)		Hull, Yorkshire	scholar
7432	Abrahams	Adelaide	1831	?Elephant & Castle, London	Samson Abrahams		Abraham Levy	Aldgate, London	waistcoat maker
24459	Abrahams	Adelaide	1840	Clerkenwell, London	Abraham Abrahams	Deborah (?)		Strand, London	scholar
25049	Abrahams	Adelaide	1848	Middlesex, London	Solomon Abrahams	Susannah (?)		Clerkenwell, London	
18327	Abrahams	Albert	1850	Hull, Yorkshire	Isaac Abrahams	M--- A--- (Mary Ann?) (?)		York, Yorkshire	
29526	Abrahams	Alexander	1781	?, London				Spitalfields, London	
17863	Abrahams	Alexander	1803	?, Germany			Harriett Solomons	Whitechapel, London	slipper maker
5249	Abrahams	Alexander	1808	Whitechapel, London	Abraham Abrahams		Rosetta Kisch	Wapping, London	shoemaker
20629	Abrahams	Alexander	1822	Spitalfields, London	Michael Abrahams	Nancy Hart	Amelia Harris	Spitalfields, London	general dealer
31116	Abrahams	Alexander	1830	Amsterdam, Holland			Deborah (?)	Spitalfields, London	travelling hawker
20896	Abrahams	Alfred	1831	Chersey, Surrey			Selina (Semanya) Moryoseph	Twickenham, London	assistant auctioneer + upholsterer
12067	Abrahams	Alfred	1843	Whitechapel, London	Solomon Abrahams	Maria Simmons		Whitechapel, London	
16829	Abrahams	Alfred	1843	Hull, Yorkshire	Isaac Abrahams	Hanial (?)		Wolverhampton, Staffordshire	scholar
18617	Abrahams	Alfred	1845	Whitechapel, London	Joseph Abrahams	Eliza (?)		Tower Hill, London	

ID	surname	given names	born	birthplace	father	mother	spouse 1	1851 residence	1851 occupation
5717	Abrahams	Alfred	1850	Brighton, Sussex	Lawrence Abrahams	Matilda (?)		Brighton, Sussex	
15234	Abrahams	Alice	1781	Spitalfields, London	(?) Jacobs		(?) Abrahams	Shoreditch, London	housekeeper
29817	Abrahams	Alice	1791	Whitechapel, London	(?)		(?) Abrahams	Whitechapel, London	cook
9923	Abrahams	Alice	1815	Deal, Kent	(?) Abrahams			Canterbury, Kent	dressmaker
20957	Abrahams	Alice	1849	Whitechapel, London	Barnett Abrahams	Priscilla Cohen	Moss Benjamin	Spitalfields, London	
18640	Abrahams	Amelia	1791	Gloucester, Gloucestershire	Isaiah Abrahams	Sarah (?)		Gloucester, Gloucestershire	
13383	Abrahams	Amelia	1817	Deal, Kent	Abraham Abrahams	Sarah (?)		Spitalfields, London	tailoress
20594	Abrahams	Amelia (Emily)	1833	Whitechapel, London	Hyam Abrahams	Phoebe Solomons	Simon Garbar	Spitalfields, London	capmaker
16112	Abrahams	Angel	1850	?, London	Isaac Abrahams	Martha (?)	Hannah Franklin	Aldgate, London	
18999	Abrahams	Ann	1817	Whitechapel, London	(?) Levy	Rosetta (?)	(?) Abrahams	Whitechapel, London	watchmaker
28487	Abrahams	Ann	1817	Aldgate, London	Yitzhak HaLevi		Lewis Abrahams	Spitalfields, London	dressmaker
27829	Abrahams	Ann	1827	Whitechapel, London	Isaac Davis	Sarah (?)	Michael Abrahams	Spitalfields, London	
5170	Abrahams	Ann	1832	?Elephant & Castle, London	Samson Abrahams	Matilda (?)	Elias Levy	Aldgate, London	furrier
26028	Abrahams	Ann (Nancy)	1808	Whitechapel, London	Mordecai Barnett		Henry Abrahams	Aldgate, London	embroideress
23649	Abrahams	Ann Elizabeth	1844	Liverpool	Isaac Abrahams	Hannah (?)		Liverpool	
26129	Abrahams	Anna	1827	Amsterdam, Holland	Abraham Abrahams	Rachael (?)		Aldgate, London	
8341	Abrahams	Barnet	1837	Canterbury, Kent	Joel Abrahams	Frances Nathan		Canterbury, Kent	scholar
10581	Abrahams	Barnet	1839	Whitechapel, London	Abraham Abrahams	Elizabeth Gomes Da Costa		Spitalfields, London	scholar
2685	Abrahams	Barnett	1790	?, Poland	Abraham		?	Manchester	rabbi + print dealer
13523	Abrahams	Barnett	1805	?			Rosa (Rosetta) (?)	Manchester	fent + rag dealer
20958	Abrahams	Barnett	1812	Amsterdam, Holland	Emanuel Abrahams		Priscilla Cohen	Spitalfields, London	traveller
7005	Abrahams	Barnett	1831	Warsaw, Poland	Abraham Susman (Abrahams)	Esther Reisel	Jane Rodrigues Brandon	Aldgate, London	Minister
20631	Abrahams	Barnett	1835	Spitalfields, London	Michael Abrahams	Nancy Hart		Spitalfields, London	cigar maker apprentice
27560	Abrahams	Barnett	1837	Euston, London	Barnett Abrahams	Leah (?)		Spitalfields, London	
26033	Abrahams	Barnett	1840	Aldgate, London	Henry Abrahams	Ann (Nancy) Barnett		Aldgate, London	scholar
15309	Abrahams	Barrett	1844	Shoreditch, London	Woolf Abrahams	Leah de Samuel Shannon		Shoreditch, London	scholar
25823	Abrahams	Benjamin	1798	Aldgate, London	Isaac Bacharach		Sarah Cohen	Aldgate, London	clothes dealer
7654	Abrahams	Benjamin	1811	Gloucester, Gloucestershire			Rachael (?)	Aldgate, London	looking glass maker
441	Abrahams	Benjamin	1840	Spitalfields, London	John (Jacob) Abrahams	Jane Harris		Spitalfields, London	scholar
6681	Abrahams	Benjamin	1843	Bermondsey, London	Benjamin Abraham	Sarah Cohen	Dinah Solomons	Aldgate, London	
19664	Abrahams	Benjamin	1844	Aldgate, London	Lewis Abrahams	(?)		Spitalfields, London	scholar
3741	Abrahams	Benjamin	1849	Whitechapel, London	Abraham Abrahams	Rachel Fileman		Spitalfields, London	
8348	Abrahams	Benjamin	1849	Canterbury, Kent	Joel Abrahams	Frances Nathan		Canterbury, Kent	
2114	Abrahams	Betsey	1837	Aldgate, London	Colman (Coleman) Abrahams	Leah Myers		Aldgate, London	tailoress
16699	Abrahams	Betsey	1846	?, Holland	N J Abrahams	Elizabeth Fry		Spitalfields, London	
30331	Abrahams	Betsey	1851	Aldgate, London	David Abrahams	Fanny (?)		Aldgate, London	
1381	Abrahams	Betsey (Betty)	1799	Callington, Cornwall			Abraham Abrahams	Plymouth, Devon	seamstress + pensioner's wife
27717	Abrahams	Betsy	1764	?, Holland	(?)		(?) Abrahams	Spitalfields, London	washer to the dead for the Jews
4265	Abrahams	Bloom	1782	Dover, Kent			Michael Abrahams	Birmingham	
22841	Abrahams	Bloom	1785	?, Poland [?, Prussia]	(?)		Samuel Abrahams	Whitechapel, London	slopper?, Poland [?, Prussia]
24460	Abrahams	Bolina	1842	Clerkenwell, London	Abraham Abrahams	Deborah (?)	Joseph Mathews	Strand, London	scholar

ID	surname	given names	born	birthplace	father	mother	spouse 1	1851 residence	1851 occupation
17226	Abrahams	Caroline	1832	Aldgate, London	Ellis (Elias) Abrahams	Rachael (?)		Aldgate, London	
16132	Abrahams	Caroline	1834	Amsterdam, Holland	Isaac D Abrahams	Henriette (?)		Whitechapel, London	
14944	Abrahams	Caroline	1835	Bolton, Lancashire	(?) Abrahams			Bethnal Green, London	boarding school pupil
11876	Abrahams	Caroline	1839	Middlesex, London	(?) Abrahams	(?)		Whitechapel, London	inmate of orphan school
28104	Abrahams	Catharine	1781	City, London	(?)		(?) Abrahams	Spitalfields, London	nurse
11588	Abrahams	Catharine	1837	Whitechapel, London	Simon Abrahams	Rebecca (?)	Joseph Harris	Aldgate, London	
6833	Abrahams	Catharine	1839	Spitalfields, London	Michael Abrahams	Hannah (?)		Spitalfields, London	
19391	Abrahams	Catherine	1810	Southwark, London	Elias Abrahams	(?)		Southwark, London	cap maker
4256	Abrahams	Catherine	1829	?, Germany			Joseph Abrahams	Birmingham	tailoress
26852	Abrahams	Catherine	1849	?Aldgate, London	Abraham Abrahams	Sarah Levy		Aldgate, London	
23516	Abrahams	Cathrine	1849	Liverpool	Abraham Abrahams	Sarah Levy		Liverpool	
17227	Abrahams	Cecilia (Celia)	1833	Aldgate, London	Ellis (Elias) Abrahams	Rachael (?)	Henry Benjamin	Aldgate, London	dressmaker
24456	Abrahams	Charles	1833	St Pancras, London	Abraham Abrahams	Deborah (?)		Strand, London	cigar maker
13005	Abrahams	Charlotte	1772	Birmingham	Lipman Levy		Jacob Abrahams	Bethnal Green, London	
14955	Abrahams	Charlotte	1837	Bolton, Lancashire	(?) Abrahams			Bethnal Green, London	boarding school pupil
19686	Abrahams	Clara	1818	Whitechapel, London	Solomon Harris	Susan Solomon	Nathan Abrahams	Spitalfields, London	
16698	Abrahams	Clara	1841	?, Holland	N J Abrahams	Elizabeth Fry		Spitalfields, London	
2849	Abrahams	Coleman	1785	Bristol	Abraham Abrahams		Frances Moses	Chatham, Kent	outfitter
2112	Abrahams	Colman (Coleman)	1808	Middlesex, London	Baruch Abrahams		Leah Myers	Aldgate, London	cabman
4261	Abrahams	Dan Elias	1838	Birmingham	(?) Abrahams	Mary (?)		Birmingham	scholar
11745	Abrahams	Daniel	1821	Exeter, Devon	(?) Abrahams	Sarah (?)		Shoreditch, London	shopman
16133	Abrahams	Daniel	1837	Amsterdam, Holland	Isaac D Abrahams	Henriette (?)		Whitechapel, London	cigar maker apprentice
16058	Abrahams	Daniel	1849	Aldgate, London	Lewis Abrahams	Esther Genese		Aldgate, London	
5032	Abrahams	David	1797	Portsmouth, Hampshire			Elizabeth (?)	Portsmouth, Hampshire	fishmonger (poor relief)
22842	Abrahams	David	1808	Hull, Yorkshire	Samuel Abrahams	Bloom (?)		Whitechapel, London	
21982	Abrahams	David	1815	Tiverton, Devon				Whitechapel, London	warehouseman
27483	Abrahams	David	1819	Spitalfields, London				Aldgate, London	general dealer
27111	Abrahams	David	1821	?, Gloucestershire	Pinhas		Fanny (?)	Aldgate, London	cigar maker
29819	Abrahams	David	1832	Whitechapel, London	(?) Abrahams	Alice (?)		Whitechapel, London	shoe maker
20632	Abrahams	David	1837	Spitalfields, London	Michael Abrahams	Nancy Hart	Phoebe Solomns	Spitalfields, London	cigar maker apprentice
4263	Abrahams	David	1842	Birmingham	(?) Abrahams	Mary (?)		Birmingham	scholar
21044	Abrahams	David	1842	?, London				Dover, Kent	boarding school pupil
25047	Abrahams	David	1843	?, France	Solomon Abrahams	Susannah (?)		Clerkenwell, London	scholar
26036	Abrahams	David	1846	Aldgate, London	Henry Abrahams	Ann (Nancy) Barnett		Aldgate, London	scholar
15010	Abrahams	David	1849	Spitalfields, London	Simon (Simeon) Abrahams	Sarah Moses	Esther Van Praag	Spitalfields, London	
443	Abrahams	Davis	1810	?, Holland			Hannah (?)	Spitalfields, London	silk mercer
24455	Abrahams	Deborah	1808	Aldgate, London	(?)		Abraham Abrahams	Strand, London	
25989	Abrahams	Deborah	1817	Whitechapel, London	(?) Joseph		Woolf Abrahams	Aldgate, London	
6677	Abrahams	Deborah	1819	Amsterdam, Holland	Menachem Mendel Raphael		Morris Abrahams	Spitalfields, London	
31117	Abrahams	Deborah	1824	Amsterdam, Holland			Alexander Abrahams	Spitalfields, London	travelling hawker
26136	Abrahams	Deborah	1845	Amsterdam, Holland	Abraham Abrahams	Rachael (?)		Aldgate, London	scholar
28529	Abrahams	Dinah	1785	Spitalfields, London			(?) Abrahams	Spitalfields, London	fruiterer
28389	Abrahams	Dinah	1793	Spitalfields, London	(?)		(?) Abrahams	Spitalfields, London	housekeeper
25048	Abrahams	Edmond	1846	?, France	Solomon Abrahams	Susannah (?)		Clerkenwell, London	scholar
13820	Abrahams	Edward	1821	Farnham, Surrey	Natan		Julia Myers	Twickenham, London	auctioneer + upholsterer

15

ID	surname	given names	born	birthplace	father	mother	spouse 1	1851 residence	1851 occupation
18616	Abrahams	Edward	1843	Whitechapel, London	Joseph Abrahams	Eliza (?)		Tower Hill, London	
24743	Abrahams	Elias	1761	?, Poland [?, Prussia]			(?)	Southwark, London	general dealer
17314	Abrahams	Elias	1845	Whitechapel, London	Hyman Abrahams	Priscilla Jacobs	Rosetta Cohen	Whitechapel, London	scholar
28874	Abrahams	Elias	1850	Spitalfields, London	Henry Abrahams	Sarah Levy		Spitalfields, London	
19387	Abrahams	Elisha	1809	Southwark, London	Elias Abrahams		Maria Joseph	Waterloo, London	military cap maker
18614	Abrahams	Eliza	1819	Sheerness, Kent	(?)		Joseph Abrahams	Tower Hill, London	
10901	Abrahams	Eliza	1845	Spitalfields, London	(?) Abrahams	Sarah (?)		Spitalfields, London	scholar
18618	Abrahams	Eliza	1849	Whitechapel, London	Joseph Abrahams	Eliza (?)		Tower Hill, London	
13432	Abrahams	Elizabeth	1785	?, London	(?)		(?) Abrahams	Shoreditch, London	
206	Abrahams	Elizabeth	1791	Aldgate, London	Samuel (Shmuel) (?Isaacs)		(?) Solomons	Strand, London	
24375	Abrahams	Elizabeth	1801	Poole, Dorset [Poole, Surrey]	(?)		(?) Abrahams	Soho, London	monthly nurse
447	Abrahams	Elizabeth	1805	?, Holland	Moses Fry		N J Abrahams	Spitalfields, London	independent
7945	Abrahams	Elizabeth	1805	Portsmouth, Hampshire	(?) Emanuel	Hannah (?)	Benjamin Abrahams	Norwich, Norfolk	
8492	Abrahams	Elizabeth	1808	Portsmouth, Hampshire				Portsmouth, Hampshire	dressmaker
26557	Abrahams	Elizabeth	1817	Whitechapel, London	Solomon Jacobs		Abraham Abrahams	Whitechapel, London	
17975	Abrahams	Elizabeth	1821	Whitechapel, London	Isaac Samuel		Joseph Abrahams	Aldgate, London	
16692	Abrahams	Elizabeth	1823	Amsterdam, Holland	Emanuel Abrahams	Esther (?)		Spitalfields, London	cap maker
26169	Abrahams	Elizabeth	1826	?, London	Solomon Abrahams	Maria Solomons		Aldgate, London	tailoress
30711	Abrahams	Elizabeth	1826	Covent Garden, London	(?) Isaacs	Hannah (?)	(?) Abrahams	Covent Garden, London	servant
2854	Abrahams	Elizabeth	1828	Chatham, Kent	Coleman Abrahams	Frances Moses	Philip Hyman	Chatham, Kent	tobacconist
11746	Abrahams	Elizabeth	1828	Exeter, Devon	(?) Abrahams	Sarah (?)		Shoreditch, London	necklace maker
6828	Abrahams	Elizabeth	1830	Spitalfields, London	(?)		Jacob Abrahams	Spitalfields, London	tailoress
30126	Abrahams	Elizabeth	1831	Aldgate, London	Lewis Abrahams	Julia Phillips	Isaac Hart	Aldgate, London	
10839	Abrahams	Elizabeth	1833	?, Holland	Davis Abrahams	Hannah (?)		Spitalfields, London	domestic
10580	Abrahams	Elizabeth	1836	Whitechapel, London	Abraham Abrahams	Elizabeth Gomes Da Costa		Spitalfields, London	
24458	Abrahams	Elizabeth	1838	Clerkenwell, London	Abraham Abrahams	Deborah (?)		Strand, London	scholar
18220	Abrahams	Elizabeth	1839	Middlesex, London	(?) Abrahams			Mile End, London	scholar
22755	Abrahams	Elizabeth	1839	Whitechapel, London	Abraham Abrahams	Hannah (?)		Whitechapel, London	scholar
4257	Abrahams	Elizabeth	1847	Birmingham	Joseph Abrahams	Catherine (?)		Birmingham	
17315	Abrahams	Elizabeth	1847	Whitechapel, London	Hyman Abrahams	Priscilla Jacobs	Samuel Levene	Whitechapel, London	
16696	Abrahams	Elizabeth	1849	Spitalfields, London	Abraham Abrahams	Sarah (?)		Spitalfields, London	
8350	Abrahams	Elizabeth (Betsy)	1806	Canterbury, Kent	(?) Levi		Abraham Abrahams	Canterbury, Kent	
12700	Abrahams	Elizabeth (Betsy)	1835	Birmingham	Jacob (Joseph) Abrahams	Elizabeth (?)	William Sandiland	Birmingham	polisher
30168	Abrahams	Elizabeth (Eliza)	1831	Middlesex, London	Lewis Abrahams		Isaac Hart	Lambeth, London	lady
16733	Abrahams	Ellen	1811	Covent Garden, London	Joseph Abrahams	Rachel (?)		Spitalfields, London	fur sewer
19390	Abrahams	Ellen	1813	Southwark, London	Elias Abrahams	(?)		Southwark, London	assistant at home
17867	Abrahams	Ellen	1842	?, Cornwall	Alexander Abrahams	Harriett Solomons	Henry Hymans	Whitechapel, London	scholar
17224	Abrahams	Ellis (Elias)	1797	Aldgate, London			Rachael (?)	Aldgate, London	fishmonger
16691	Abrahams	Emanuel	1785	Amsterdam, Holland			Esther (?)	Spitalfields, London	general dealer
22705	Abrahams	Emanuel	1808	Amsterdam, Holland	Abraham		Phoebe (Simha) Saltiel	Whitechapel, London	wholesale dealer in British and foreign merchandise
13010	Abrahams	Emanuel	1833	Middlesex, London	Joel Abrahams	(?)		Spitalfields, London	skin dyer
6678	Abrahams	Emanuel	1849	Limehouse, London	Morris Abrahams	Deborah Raphael		Spitalfields, London	
10662	Abrahams	Ephraim	1824	?			Rachel (?)	Spitalfields, London	dealer
17816	Abrahams	Esther	1768	Aldgate, London	(?)		Henry Abrahams	Aldgate, London	

ID	surname	given names	born	birthplace	father	mother	spouse 1	1851 residence	1851 occupation
446	Abrahams	Esther	1791	Aldgate, London	(?) Abrahams			Spitalfields, London	general dealer
445	Abrahams	Esther	1800	Amsterdam, Holland	(?)		Emanuel Abrahams	Spitalfields, London	
16055	Abrahams	Esther	1814	Aldgate, London	Samuel de Isaac Genese	Rebecca de Emanuel Capua	Lewis Abrahams	Aldgate, London	
24611	Abrahams	Esther	1814	Whitechapel, London	(?) Abrahams			Lambeth, London	independent
15125	Abrahams	Esther	1822	Dorking, Surrey	(?)		(?) Abrahams	Haggerston, London	dressmaker
1383	Abrahams	Esther	1833	Plymouth, Devon	Abraham Abrahams	Betsey (Betty) (?)		Plymouth, Devon	
10898	Abrahams	Esther	1833	Spitalfields, London	(?) Abrahams	Sarah (?)		Spitalfields, London	tailoress
6040	Abrahams	Esther	1835	Spitalfields, London	Joel Abrahams	Rose (?)	Moss (Moses) Cantor	Aldgate, London	
2353	Abrahams	Esther	1837	?, Poland [?, Prussia]	Victor Abrahams	Tobe (Thresa) (?)	(Israel Abrahams?)	Hull, Yorkshire	
5566	Abrahams	Esther	1837	Plymouth, Devon	Alexander Abrahams	Harriet Solomons	Samuel Morris Samuel	Whitechapel, London	scholar
11589	Abrahams	Esther	1839	Whitechapel, London	Simon Abrahams	Rebecca (?)	Emanuel Joseph Solomon	Aldgate, London	
26133	Abrahams	Esther	1839	Amsterdam, Holland	Abraham Abrahams	Rachael (?)		Aldgate, London	scholar
5716	Abrahams	Esther	1843	Brighton, Sussex	Lawrence Abrahams	Matilda (?)		Brighton, Sussex	
20961	Abrahams	Esther	1844	Spitalfields, London	Barnett Abrahams	Priscilla Cohen		Spitalfields, London	scholar
10583	Abrahams	Esther	1845	Whitechapel, London	Abraham Abrahams	Elizabeth Gomes Da Costa	Moses (Moss) Joel	Spitalfields, London	scholar
8103	Abrahams	Esther	1847	Whitechapel, London	(?) Abrahams	Rebekah (?)		Whitechapel, London	scholar
23361	Abrahams	Evelina	1832	?, London	Lewis Abrahams	Julia Phillips		Strand, London	silversmith's assistant
27112	Abrahams	Fanny	1823	Southwark, London	(?)		David Abrahams	Aldgate, London	
4260	Abrahams	Fanny	1836	Birmingham	(?) Abrahams	Mary (?)		Birmingham	scholar
13011	Abrahams	Fanny	1837	Middlesex, London	Joel Abrahams	(?)	Abraham Isaac Ereira	Spitalfields, London	skin dyer
2896	Abrahams	Fanny	1838	Birmingham	Aaron Abrahams	Julia Levi	Benjamin Rubenstein	Birmingham	pawnbroker's assistant
5713	Abrahams	Fanny	1839	Brighton, Sussex	Lawrence Abrahams	Matilda (?)	Joseph Phillips Joseph	Brighton, Sussex	
10903	Abrahams	Fanny	1844	Spitalfields, London	(?) Abrahams	Sarah (?)		Spitalfields, London	
13527	Abrahams	Fanny	1844	Liverpool	Barnett Abrahams	Rosa (Rosetta) (?)		Manchester	scholar
30333	Abrahams	Fanny	1851	Aldgate, London	Lewis Abrahams	Sarah Cohen		Aldgate, London	
23650	Abrahams	Fanny R	1848	Liverpool	Isaac Abrahams	Hannah (?)		Liverpool	
19494	Abrahams	Flora	1822	?, London	(?)		Abby Abrahams	Covent Garden, London	
13433	Abrahams	Flora	1826	Bristol	(?) Abrahams	Elizabeth (?)		Shoreditch, London	
29311	Abrahams	Florreta	1813	?, London	(?)		Joseph Abrahams	Wapping, London	
2848	Abrahams	Frances	1787	Chatham, Kent	Ephraim Moses	Elizabeth (Bella) (?)	Coleman Abrahams	Chatham, Kent	tobacconist
2892	Abrahams	Frances	1831	Clerkenwell, London	Abraham (Abram) Abrahams	Juliet Cohen	Barnett Barnett	Clerkenwell, London	
10582	Abrahams	Frances	1841	Whitechapel, London	Abraham Abrahams	Elizabeth Gomes Da Costa		Spitalfields, London	scholar
417	Abrahams	Frances	1845	Whitechapel, London		Julia (?)		Spitalfields, London	
15395	Abrahams	Frances	1845	Waterloo, London	Lewis Abrahams	Julia Moses		Waterloo, London	
4258	Abrahams	Frances	1850	Birmingham	Joseph Abrahams	Catherine (?)		Birmingham	
8340	Abrahams	Frances (Fanny)	1808	Dover, Kent	Barnett Nathan	Julia (?)	Joel Abrahams	Canterbury, Kent	
13525	Abrahams	Frederick	1834	Nottingham, Nottinghamshire	Barnett Abrahams	Rosa (Rosetta) (?)		Manchester	clothier's assistant
20630	Abrahams	George	1830	Spitalfields, London	Michael Abrahams	Nancy Hart		Spitalfields, London	cigar maker apprentice
16846	Abrahams	George	1836	Brighton, Sussex	Lawrence Abrahams	Matilda (?)		Brighton, Sussex	
10856	Abrahams	George	1839	?, London	Abraham Abrahams	Polly (Mary) Abrahams		Spitalfields, London	scholar
26558	Abrahams	George	1839	Whitechapel, London				Whitechapel, London	scholar
23648	Abrahams	George? H	1842	Liverpool	Isaac Abrahams	Hannah (?)		Liverpool	
17866	Abrahams	Gertrude	1841	?, Cornwall	Alexander Abrahams	Harriett Solomons	Charles Hymans	Whitechapel, London	scholar
17870	Abrahams	Geta	1850	?, Cornwall	Alexander Abrahams	Harriett Solomons	Lewis Canter	Whitechapel, London	
15492	Abrahams	Haah	1822	Hamburg, Germany	(?)		Solomon Abrahams	Covent Garden, London	

17

ID	surname	given names	born	birthplace	father	mother	spouse 1	1851 residence	1851 occupation
10584	Abrahams	Hananel	1847	Whitechapel, London	Abraham Abrahams	Elizabeth Gomes Da Costa		Spitalfields, London	
16820	Abrahams	Hanial	1805	Middlesex, London	(?)		Isaac Abrahams	Wolverhampton, Staffordshire	
22750	Abrahams	Hannah	1789	City, London	(?)		Abraham Abrahams	Whitechapel, London	general dealer
6831	Abrahams	Hannah	1794	Spitalfields, London	(?)		Michael Abrahams	Spitalfields, London	
19220	Abrahams	Hannah	1794	Plymouth, Devon	(?)		Aaron Abrahams	Liverpool	
20274	Abrahams	Hannah	1795	Bath	(?)		Joshua Abrahams	Spitalfields, London	
6572	Abrahams	Hannah	1806	?, Yorkshire	(?)		Isaac Abrahams	Liverpool	
2684	Abrahams	Hannah	1810	Leszno, Poland [Lissa, Prussia], Poland [Lissa, Prussia]	Levy Levy (Yehuda Leib)	Fanny (?)	Barnet Abrahams	Manchester	
10838	Abrahams	Hannah	1812	?, Holland	(?)		Davis Abrahams	Spitalfields, London	domestic
11454	Abrahams	Hannah	1819	Aldgate, London	Lambeth (Lambert) Ellis	Sarah (?)	Mark Abrahams	Aldgate, London	tailoress
22708	Abrahams	Hannah	1830	Spitalfields, London	Emanuel Abrahams	Phoebe Saltiel		Whitechapel, London	dressmaker
8099	Abrahams	Hannah	1831	Birmingham	(?) Abrahams	Rebekah (?)		Whitechapel, London	tailoress
16127	Abrahams	Hannah	1838	Aldgate, London	Henry Abrahams	Matilda (?)		Stepney, London	scholar
8266	Abrahams	Hannah	1840	Aldgate, London	Benjamin Abrahams	Elizabeth Emanuel		Norwich, Norfolk	scholar
8343	Abrahams	Hannah	1841	Canterbury, Kent	Joel Abrahams	Frances Nathan	Joseph Hart	Canterbury, Kent	scholar
30081	Abrahams	Hannah	1841	Middlesex, London	(?) Abrahams	Phoebe (?)		Aldgate, London	
16719	Abrahams	Hannah	1848	Spitalfields, London	Louis (Lewis) Abrahams	Julia (Judith) (?)	Cohen Joseph Proops	Spitalfields, London	
30225	Abrahams	Hannah (Annie)	1851	Aldgate, London	Ellis Abrahams	Rachael (?)		Aldgate, London	
11747	Abrahams	Harriet	1830	Aldgate, London	(?) Abrahams	Sarah (?)		Shoreditch, London	fancy cap maker
17864	Abrahams	Harriett	1813	?, Poland	(?) Solomons		Alexander Abrahams	Whitechapel, London	
16130	Abrahams	Henriette	1805	Amsterdam, Holland	(?)		Isaac D Abrahams	Whitechapel, London	
15322	Abrahams	Henry	1787	Westminster, London			Sarah (?)	Shoreditch, London	general dealer
26027	Abrahams	Henry	1796	?, London	Michael Abrahams		Ann (Nancy) Barnett	Aldgate, London	printer
16125	Abrahams	Henry	1808	Whitechapel, London			Matilda (?)	Stepney, London	dock labourer
30024	Abrahams	Henry	1809	Hull, Yorkshire	Samuel Abrahams		Rebecca Defries	Aldgate, London	
16061	Abrahams	Henry	1825	Manchester				Aldgate, London	clothier
28872	Abrahams	Henry	1826	Spitalfields, London	Henry Abrahams		Sarah Levy	Spitalfields, London	pencil maker
370	Abrahams	Henry	1828	Spitalfields, London			Theresa Abrahams	Spitalfields, London	hawker
11748	Abrahams	Henry	1831	Aldgate, London	(?) Abrahams	Sarah (?)		Shoreditch, London	shoe maker
28493	Abrahams	Henry	1835	Aldgate, London				Spitalfields, London	jeweller
18615	Abrahams	Henry	1840	Whitechapel, London	Joseph Abrahams	Eliza (?)		Tower Hill, London	
8352	Abrahams	Henry	1844	Canterbury, Kent	Abraham Abrahams	Elizabeth (Betsy) Levi		Canterbury, Kent	scholar
8345	Abrahams	Henry	1845	Canterbury, Kent	Joel Abrahams	Frances Nathan		Canterbury, Kent	scholar
15396	Abrahams	Henry	1847	Waterloo, London	Lewis Abrahams	Julia Moses		Waterloo, London	
23517	Abrahams	Henry	1851	Liverpool	Abraham Abrahams	Sarah Levy		Liverpool	
6683	Abrahams	Henry (Harry)	1841	Southwark, London	Benjamin Abrahams	Sarah Cohen	Elizabeth (?)	Aldgate, London	
6669	Abrahams	Henry P	1847	Whitechapel, London	Henry Abrahams	Matilda (?)	Jane Dan	Stepney, London	scholar
20592	Abrahams	Hyam	1811	Aldgate, London	Benjamin Abrahams		Phoebe Solomons	Spitalfields, London	general dealer
17736	Abrahams	Hyam	1829	?, Poland [?, Prussia]				Aldgate, London	tailor
26032	Abrahams	Hyam	1836	Wapping, London	Henry Abrahams	Ann (Nancy) Barnett		Aldgate, London	printer
17229	Abrahams	Hyam	1838	Aldgate, London	Ellis (Elias) Abrahams	Rachael (?)		Aldgate, London	scholar
19687	Abrahams	Hyam	1842	Spitalfields, London	Nathan Abrahams	Clara Harris		Spitalfields, London	

ID	surname	given names	born	birthplace	father	mother	spouse 1	1851 residence	1851 occupation
19000	Abrahams	Hyman	1834	Whitechapel, London	(?) Abrahams	Ann (?)		Whitechapel, London	apprentice (?watchmaker?
31107	Abrahams	Hyman	1838	?, London	Abraham Abrahams	(?)		Gloucester, Gloucestershire	
16819	Abrahams	Isaac	1805	?, London			Hanial (?)	Wolverhampton, Staffordshire	inn keeper
16113	Abrahams	Isaac	1810	?, London	Avraham Avinu		Elizabeth Levy	Aldgate, London	logwood cutter
18325	Abrahams	Isaac	1813	?, Shropshire			M--- A--- (Mary Ann?) (?)	York, Yorkshire	hawker
6571	Abrahams	Isaac	1818	Sheerness, Kent			Hannah (?)	Liverpool	outfitter + clothier empl 2
25808	Abrahams	Isaac	1827	Amsterdam, Holland				Aldgate, London	cigar maker journeyman
209	Abrahams	Isaac	1828	Strand, London	Abraham Abrahams	Elizabeth Solomons (?nee Isaacs)		Strand, London	journeyman painter
11108	Abrahams	Isaac	1833	Deal, Kent				Aldgate, London	coal boy
8102	Abrahams	Isaac	1835	Whitechapel, London	(?) Abrahams	Rebekah (?)		Whitechapel, London	
25825	Abrahams	Isaac	1835	Aldgate, London	Benjamin Abrahams	Sarah Cohen		Aldgate, London	hawker
5718	Abrahams	Isaac	1841	Godstone, Surrey	Abraham Abrahams		Jane Levy	?London	
5035	Abrahams	Isaac	1842	Portsmouth, Hampshire	David Abrahams			Portsmouth, Hampshire	
26034	Abrahams	Isaac	1842	Aldgate, London	Henry Abrahams	Ann (Nancy) Barnett		Aldgate, London	scholar
19665	Abrahams	Isaac	1846	Aldgate, London	Lewis Abrahams	(?)	Esther Jonas	Spitalfields, London	
11592	Abrahams	Isaac	1848	Aldgate, London	Simon Abrahams	Rebecca (?)		Aldgate, London	
24464	Abrahams	Isaac	1848	Covent Garden, London	(?) Abrahams			Strand, London	scholar
15398	Abrahams	Isaac	1850	Waterloo, London	Lewis Abrahams	Julia Moses	Priscilla Lazarus	Waterloo, London	
17976	Abrahams	Isaac	1850	Aldgate, London	Joseph Abrahams	Elizabeth Samuels		Aldgate, London	
16129	Abrahams	Isaac D	1801	Amsterdam, Holland			Henriette (?)	Whitechapel, London	diamond broker
30740	Abrahams	Isabella	1812	Covent Garden, London	(?)		Jacob Abrahams	Aldgate, London	
22843	Abrahams	Isabella	1821	Manchester	Samuel Abrahams	Bloom (?)		Whitechapel, London	tambour worker
8850	Abrahams	Isabella	1833	Aldgate, London				Aldgate, London	
22752	Abrahams	Isace	1823	Whitechapel, London	Abraham Abrahams	Hannah (?)		Whitechapel, London	general dealer
31130	Abrahams	Isaiah	1837	?, London	Benjamin Abrahams	Rachael (?)		Aldgate, London	
6735	Abrahams	Isidore (Israel)	1821	Amsterdam, Holland	Isaac D Abrahams	Henriette (?)	Sophia Marks	Whitechapel, London	shipping agent commission
26128	Abrahams	Israel	1822	Amsterdam, Holland	Abraham Abrahams	Rachael (?)		Aldgate, London	jeweller
6664	Abrahams	Israel	1843	Whitechapel, London	Isaac Abrahams	Martha (?)	Julia Levy	Aldgate, London	scholar
31134	Abrahams	Israel	1850	?Aldgate, London	Benjamin Abrahams	Rachael (?)		Aldgate, London	
16134	Abrahams	Jacob	1838	Amsterdam, Holland	Isaac D Abrahams	Henriette (?)		Whitechapel, London	cigar maker apprentice
27150	Abrahams	Jacob	1776	?, Poland				Aldgate, London	cook merchant
30739	Abrahams	Jacob	1808	Spitalfields, London			Isabella (?)	Aldgate, London	?sausage maker
6827	Abrahams	Jacob	1831	Spitalfields, London	(?) Abrahams	(?) Levy	Elizabeth (?)	Spitalfields, London	cigar maker
27738	Abrahams	Jacob	1835	?, Russia				Spitalfields, London	tailor
8351	Abrahams	Jacob	1840	Canterbury, Kent	Abraham Abrahams	Elizabeth (Betsy) Levi		Canterbury, Kent	scholar
8344	Abrahams	Jacob	1843	Canterbury, Kent	Joel Abrahams	Frances Nathan		Canterbury, Kent	scholar
21770	Abrahams	Jacob	1843	Whitechapel, London	(?) Abrahams	Sarah (?)		Aldgate, London	
5036	Abrahams	Jacob	1847	Portsmouth, Hampshire	David Abrahams			Portsmouth, Hampshire	
12696	Abrahams	Jacob (Joseph)	1785	?Westphalia, Germany [West Falland]			Elizabeth (?)	Birmingham	tailor

ID	surname	given names	born	birthplace	father	mother	spouse 1	1851 residence	1851 occupation
19389	Abrahams	Jane	1775	Hamburg, Germany	Yehuda		(?) Solomons	Southwark, London	
440	Abrahams	Jane	1811	Whitechapel, London	Jacob Harris		John (Jacob) Abrahams	Spitalfields, London	
26131	Abrahams	Jane	1835	Amsterdam, Holland	Abraham Abrahams	Rachael (?)		Aldgate, London	
15397	Abrahams	Jane	1849	Waterloo, London	Lewis Abrahams	Julia Moses		Waterloo, London	
30332	Abrahams	Jane	1851	Spitalfields, London	Louis (Lewis) Abrahams	Julia (Judith) (?)		Spitalfields, London	
16131	Abrahams	Jeanette	1828	Amsterdam, Holland	Isaac D Abrahams	Henriette (?)		Whitechapel, London	
26132	Abrahams	Jeanette	1836	Amsterdam, Holland	Abraham Abrahams	Rachael (?)		Aldgate, London	
13529	Abrahams	Jennette	1849	Manchester	Barnett Abrahams	Rosa (Rosetta) (?)		Manchester	
5251	Abrahams	Jessie	1837	Wapping, London	Alexander Abrahams	Rosetta Kisch	Michael Harris	Wapping, London	scholar
20423	Abrahams	Joel	1791	Amsterdam, Holland			Rose (?)	Aldgate, London	general dealer
13009	Abrahams	Joel	1804	?, Holland			(?)	Spitalfields, London	skin dyer
8339	Abrahams	Joel	1811	Canterbury, Kent	Jacob Abrahams		Frances Nathan	Canterbury, Kent	china + glass dealer
17231	Abrahams	Joel	1844	Aldgate, London	Ellis (Elias) Abrahams	Rachael (?)		Aldgate, London	scholar
29717	Abrahams	John	1836	Aldgate, London	Lewis Abrahams	Julia Phillips		Aldgate, London	
17817	Abrahams	John	1807	Aldgate, London	Henry Abrahams	Esther (?)		Aldgate, London	cabinet manufacturer
30718	Abrahams	John	1814	Shoreditch, London			Rosetta (?)	Covent Garden, London	dealer in wearing apparel
19424	Abrahams	John	1831	Finsbury, London	Abraham Abrahams		Marianne (Marion) Hyman	Peckham, London	journeyman
27557	Abrahams	John	1831	Westminster, London	Barnett Abrahams	Leah (?)		Spitalfields, London	chair maker
16128	Abrahams	John	1842	Aldgate, London	Henry Abrahams	Matilda (?)		Stepney, London	scholar
19689	Abrahams	John	1847	Spitalfields, London	Nathan Abrahams	Clara Harris		Spitalfields, London	
31133	Abrahams	John	1848	?, London	Benjamin Abrahams	Rachael (?)		Aldgate, London	
11593	Abrahams	John	1850	Aldgate, London	Simon Abrahams	Rebecca (?)		Aldgate, London	
25992	Abrahams	John	1850	Whitechapel, London	Woolf Abrahams	Deborah Joseph		Aldgate, London	
442	Abrahams	John (Jacob)	1814	Spitalfields, London	Joseph Rodrigues Abrahams	Sarah (?)	Jane Harris	Spitalfields, London	general dealer
12306	Abrahams	Joseph	1793	Taunton, Somerset			Esther (?)	Romsey, Hampshire	wool sorter
1419	Abrahams	Joseph	1794	?, Holland				Plymouth, Devon	general dealer
17974	Abrahams	Joseph	1811	?, Kent	Michael (Meir) Abrahams		Elizabeth Samuels	Aldgate, London	hardwareman empl 2
29310	Abrahams	Joseph	1813	?, London			Florreta (?)	Wapping, London	tailor
4254	Abrahams	Joseph	1817	Strand, London			Eliza (?)	Tower Hill, London	gasfitter + whitesmith
4255	Abrahams	Joseph	1824	?, Germany			Catherine (?)	Birmingham	tailor
26170	Abrahams	Joseph	1833	?, London	Solomon Abrahams	Maria Solomons		Aldgate, London	dealer
23362	Abrahams	Joseph	1835	?, London	Lewis Abrahams	Julia Phillips		Strand, London	porter
29801	Abrahams	Joseph	1836	Birmingham	Jacob (Joseph) Abrahams	Elizabeth (?)	Mary Ann Guest	Birmingham	iron founder
16827	Abrahams	Joseph	1838	Manchester	Isaac Abrahams	Hanial (?)		Wolverhampton, Staffordshire	scholar
19001	Abrahams	Joseph	1839	Whitechapel, London	(?) Abrahams	Ann (?)		Whitechapel, London	scholar at home
16056	Abrahams	Joseph	1843	Aldgate, London	Lewis Abrahams	Esther Genese		Aldgate, London	
20960	Abrahams	Joseph	1843	Whitechapel, London	Barnett Abrahams	Priscilla Cohen		Spitalfields, London	scholar
16111	Abrahams	Joseph	1844	?, London	Isaac Abrahams	Martha (?)		Aldgate, London	
17313	Abrahams	Joseph	1844	Whitechapel, London	Hyman Abrahams	Priscilla Jacobs	Maria Harris	Whitechapel, London	scholar
3740	Abrahams	Joseph	1845	Whitechapel, London	Abraham Abrahams	Rachel Fileman		Spitalfields, London	
15009	Abrahams	Joseph	1848	Spitalfields, London	Simon (Simeon) Abrahams	Sarah Moses		Spitalfields, London	
6829	Abrahams	Joseph	1850	Spitalfields, London	Jacob Abrahams	Elizabeth (?)		Spitalfields, London	
12068	Abrahams	Joshua	1851	Whitechapel, London	Solomon Abrahams	Maria Simmons		Whitechapel, London	
19662	Abrahams	Judah	1838	Aldgate, London	Lewis Abrahams	(?)	Frances Priscilla Hands	Spitalfields, London	general dealer

ID	surname	given names	born	birthplace	father	mother	spouse 1	1851 residence	1851 occupation
17752	Abrahams	Julia	1777	?, Germany	(?)			Aldgate, London	nurse
29715	Abrahams	Julia	1795	Aldgate, London	(?) Phillips		Lewis Abrahams	Aldgate, London	
3295	Abrahams	Julia	1797	Birmingham	(?) Levi		Aaron Abrahams	Birmingham	
418	Abrahams	Julia	1815	Whitechapel, London				Spitalfields, London	
15394	Abrahams	Julia	1822	?, London	Isaac Moses	Jane (?)	Lewis Abrahams	Waterloo, London	
13821	Abrahams	Julia	1828	Birmingham	Isaac Myers	Rachael (?)	Edward Abrahams	Twickenham, London	
26029	Abrahams	Julia	1831	Spitalfields, London	Henry Abrahams	Ann (Nancy) Barnett		Aldgate, London	embroideress
26134	Abrahams	Julia	1840	Amsterdam, Holland	Abraham Abrahams	Rachael (?)		Aldgate, London	scholar
30744	Abrahams	Julia	1841	Spitalfields, London	Jacob Abrahams	Isabella (?)		Aldgate, London	scholar
7872	Abrahams	Julia	1842	Canterbury, Kent	Abraham Abrahams	Elizabeth (?)	Henry Harris	Canterbury, Kent	scholar
13012	Abrahams	Julia	1844	Middlesex, London	Joel Abrahams	(?)		Spitalfields, London	
15126	Abrahams	Julia	1847	?Cambridge	(?) Abrahams	Esther (?)		Haggerston, London	
16718	Abrahams	Julia (Judith)	1817	Amsterdam, Holland	(?)		Louis (Lewis) Abrahams	Spitalfields, London	
10000	Abrahams	Julia (Judith)	1838	Canterbury, Kent	Joel Abrahams	Frances Nathan	Maurice (Morris) Jacobs	Canterbury, Kent	
2891	Abrahams	Juliet (Gittel)	1796	Whitechapel, London	Isaac Hacohen		Abraham (Abram) Abrahams	Clerkenwell, London	
16505	Abrahams	Kate	1827	Kidderminster, Worcestershire	(?) Davis		Samuel Abrahams	Birmingham	
4262	Abrahams	Kate	1840	Birmingham	(?) Abrahams	Mary (?)		Birmingham	scholar
13528	Abrahams	Kate	1846	Liverpool	Barnett Abrahams	Rosa (Rosetta) (?)		Manchester	scholar
27831	Abrahams	Katherine	1849	Whitechapel, London	Michael Abrahams	Ann Davis		Spitalfields, London	
10904	Abrahams	Kitty	1850	Spitalfields, London	(?) Abrahams	Sarah (?)		Spitalfields, London	
5711	Abrahams	Lawrence	1810	Sheerness, Kent			Matilda (?)	Brighton, Sussex	tailor + outfitter
20950	Abrahams	Lazarus	1818	Spitalfields, London				Aldgate, London	sponge dealer
16828	Abrahams	Lazea	1841	Manchester	Isaac Abrahams	Hanial (?)		Wolverhampton, Staffordshire	scholar
27556	Abrahams	Leah	1800	Westminster, London	(?)		Barnett Abrahams	Spitalfields, London	shoe binder
2113	Abrahams	Leah	1811	Middlesex, London	Yehuda Leib Myers		Colman (Coleman) Abrahams	Aldgate, London	
15307	Abrahams	Leah	1819	Shoreditch, London	Samuel de Masaod Shannon	Miriam de Uri Sheraga Pais	Woolf Abrahams	Shoreditch, London	
1385	Abrahams	Leah	1837	Plymouth, Devon	Abraham Abrahams	Betsey (Betty) (?)		Plymouth, Devon	
31131	Abrahams	Leah	1840	?, London	Benjamin Abrahams	Rachael (?)		Aldgate, London	scholar
20427	Abrahams	Leah	1842	Spitalfields, London	Joel Abrahams	Rose (?)		Aldgate, London	
30722	Abrahams	Leah	1846	Covent Garden, London	John Abrahams	Rosetta (?)		Covent Garden, London	scholar
26605	Abrahams	Leah (Selina, Lena)	1824	Hanover, Germany	(?) Abrams (Abrahams)		Simon Abrahams	Chester, Cheshire	
21771	Abrahams	Leon	1845	Whitechapel, London	(?) Abrahams	Sarah (?)	Jane Catherine Twitchett	Aldgate, London	
29714	Abrahams	Lewis	1794	Aldgate, London			Julia Phillips	Aldgate, London	licensed victualler
15393	Abrahams	Lewis	1806	?, London			Julia Moses	Waterloo, London	furniture broker
409	Abrahams	Lewis	1807	Aldgate, London	Abraham Abrahams		Sarah Cohen	Aldgate, London	fruiterer
19661	Abrahams	Lewis	1809	Spitalfields, London	Lewis Abrahams		(?)	Spitalfields, London	general dealer
28486	Abrahams	Lewis	1817	Birmingham	Yehuda Leib HaLevi		Ann Levy	Spitalfields, London	general dealer
16054	Abrahams	Lewis	1821	Exeter, Devon	Joseph Abrahams		Esther Genese	Aldgate, London	cigar traveller
22753	Abrahams	Lewis	1825	Whitechapel, London	Abraham Abrahams	Hannah (?)		Whitechapel, London	general dealer
29818	Abrahams	Lewis	1830	Whitechapel, London	(?) Abrahams	Alice (?)		Whitechapel, London	cigar maker
17230	Abrahams	Lewis	1842	Aldgate, London	Ellis (Elias) Abrahams	Rachael (?)		Aldgate, London	scholar

ID	surname	given names	born	birthplace	father	mother	spouse 1	1851 residence	1851 occupation
25828	Abrahams	Lewis	1845	Southwark, London	Benjamin Abrahams	Sarah Cohen		Aldgate, London	
26238	Abrahams	Lewis	1845	Surrey, London	Samson Abrahams	Matilda (?)		Aldgate, London	scholar
16830	Abrahams	Lewis	1846	Birmingham	Isaac Abrahams	Hanial (?)		Wolverhampton, Staffordshire	scholar
27832	Abrahams	Lewis	1850	Whitechapel, London	Michael Abrahams	Ann Davis		Spitalfields, London	
19690	Abrahams	Lewis (Louis)	1849	Spitalfields, London	Nathan Abrahams	Clara Harris	Millie (?)	Spitalfields, London	
10900	Abrahams	Louis	1843	Spitalfields, London	(?) Abrahams	Sarah (?)		Spitalfields, London	scholar
450	Abrahams	Louis (Lewis)	1818	Amsterdam, Holland	Avraham Levi		Julia (Judith) (?)	Spitalfields, London	general dealer
2686	Abrahams	Louis Barnett	1839	Swansea, Wales	Barnett Abrahams	Hannah Levy	Fanny Rosetta Moseley	Manchester	pupil-teacher
20924	Abrahams	Louisa	1811	Scowbridge, Wiltshire	(?)		Morris Abrahams	Devizes, Wiltshire	
29716	Abrahams	Louisa	1833	Aldgate, London	Lewis Abrahams	Julia Phillips		Aldgate, London	
26237	Abrahams	Louisa	1841	Surrey, London	Samson Abrahams	Matilda (?)		Aldgate, London	scholar
28530	Abrahams	Lydia	1813	Spitalfields, London	(?) Abrahams	Dinah (?)		Spitalfields, London	fruiterer
18326	Abrahams	M--- A--- (Mary Ann?)	1827	Hull, Yorkshire	(?)		Isaac Abrahams	York, Yorkshire	
15011	Abrahams	Manassah	1850	Spitalfields, London	Simon (Simeon) Abrahams	Sarah Moses		Spitalfields, London	
26168	Abrahams	Maria	1792	?, London	Joseph Solomons		Solomon Abrahams	Aldgate, London	
25771	Abrahams	Maria	1806	Aldgate, London	Moses Isaacs		(?) Phillips	Aldgate, London	
22751	Abrahams	Maria	1819	City, London	Abraham Abrahams	Hannah (?)		Whitechapel, London	umbrella maker
19388	Abrahams	Maria	1820	Southwark, London	Lewis (Yehuda) Joseph	Dinah Benjamin	Maria Joseph	Waterloo, London	
12066	Abrahams	Maria	1821	Middlesex, London	Azreal Simmons		Solomon Abrahams	Whitechapel, London	
6832	Abrahams	Maria	1829	Spitalfields, London	Michael Abrahams	Hannah (?)		Spitalfields, London	
20216	Abrahams	Maria	1831	Bristol				Wandsworth, London	house servant
20276	Abrahams	Maria	1831	Plymouth, Devon	Joshua Abrahams	Hannah (?)	Benjamin (Barnet) Davis	Spitalfields, London	dress maker
16109	Abrahams	Maria	1838	?, London	Isaac Abrahams	Martha (?)		Aldgate, London	
22845	Abrahams	Mariah	1827	Manchester	Samuel Abrahams	Bloom (?)		Whitechapel, London	slopper
7948	Abrahams	Marie Elizabeth	1843	Whitechapel, London	Benjamin Abrahams	Elizabeth Emanuel	Harry Hyman	Norwich, Norfolk	
11453	Abrahams	Mark	1818	Strand, London	Samuel Abraham (Abrahams, Abrams)	Harriett (?)	Hannah Ellis	Aldgate, London	tailor
26030	Abrahams	Mark	1832	Spitalfields, London	Henry Abrahams	Ann (Nancy) Barnett		Aldgate, London	printer
16108	Abrahams	Mark	1849	Whitechapel, London	Isaac Abrahams	Martha (?)	Sarah Lyons	Aldgate, London	
1387	Abrahams	Mark (Markes)	1841	Plymouth, Devon	Abraham Abrahams	Betsey (Betty) (?)		Plymouth, Devon	
6819	Abrahams	Martha	1839	Whitechapel, London				Spitalfields, London	servant
30252	Abrahams	Mary	1780	Greenwich, London	(?) Abrahams			Greenwich, London	
4259	Abrahams	Mary	1807	Houghton, Staffordshire			(?) Abrahams	Birmingham	stay-maker employer
16826	Abrahams	Mary	1836	Manchester	Isaac Abrahams	Hanial (?)		Wolverhampton, Staffordshire	
11590	Abrahams	Mary	1843	Whitechapel, London	Simon Abrahams	Rebecca (?)		Aldgate, London	
30723	Abrahams	Mary	1848	Covent Garden, London	John Abrahams	Rosetta (?)		Covent Garden, London	
15311	Abrahams	Mary	1850	Shoreditch, London	Woolf Abrahams	Leah de Samuel Shannon		Shoreditch, London	
4925	Abrahams	Mathilda	1836	Birmingham				Birmingham	servant
5715	Abrahams	Matilda	1806	Maldon, Essex			Lawrence Abrahams	Brighton, Sussex	
16126	Abrahams	Matilda	1806	Spitalfields, London	(?)		Henry Abrahams	Stepney, London	bonnet maker
26233	Abrahams	Matilda	1808	Surrey, London	(?)		Samson Abrahams	Aldgate, London	
20089	Abrahams	Matilda	1835	?Birmingham	Aaron Abrahams	Julia Levi	Moses Levenberg	Birmingham	

ID	surname	given names	born	birthplace	father	mother	spouse 1	1851 residence	1851 occupation
20962	Abrahams	Matilda	1845	Spitalfields, London	Barnett Abrahams	Priscilla Cohen		Spitalfields, London	scholar
4264	Abrahams	Michael	1782	Chatham, Kent			Bloom (?)	Birmingham	provision dealer
6830	Abrahams	Michael	1795	Spitalfields, London			Hannah (?)	Spitalfields, London	mackintosh dealer
19272	Abrahams	Michael	1796	Middlesex, London				Liverpool	dealer in watches
20627	Abrahams	Michael	1797	Spitalfields, London	Pinchas Zelig		Nancy Hart	Spitalfields, London	general dealer
2223	Abrahams	Michael	1806	?, Poland				Leeds, Yorkshire	dealer, watch materials
27830	Abrahams	Michael	1824	Whitechapel, London			Ann Davis	Spitalfields, London	clothes dealer
16822	Abrahams	Michael	1827	Middlesex, London	Isaac Abrahams	Hanial (?)		Wolverhampton, Staffordshire	gilder
11712	Abrahams	Michael	1831	?, Germany				Aldgate, London	tailor
26031	Abrahams	Michael	1834	Spitalfields, London	Henry Abrahams	Ann (Nancy) Barnett		Aldgate, London	cigar maker
8265	Abrahams	Michael	1845	Whitechapel, London	Benjamin Abrahams	Elizabeth Emanuel		Norwich, Norfolk	scholar
11591	Abrahams	Michael	1847	Whitechapel, London	Simon Abrahams	Rebecca (?)		Aldgate, London	
5235	Abrahams	Michael B	1841	Swansea, Wales	Barnet Abrahams	Hannah Levy	Leah Cohen	Manchester	
16847	Abrahams	Miller	1841	Brighton, Sussex	Lawrence Abrahams	Matilda (?)		Brighton, Sussex	
20895	Abrahams	Miriam	1850	Twickenham, London	Edward Abrahams	Julia Myers		Twickenham, London	
30334	Abrahams	Montague	1851	Twickenham, London	Edward Abrahams	Julia Myers		Twickenham, London	
20923	Abrahams	Morris	1801	?, Poland [?, Prussia]			Louisa (?)	Devizes, Wiltshire	pedlar
17753	Abrahams	Morris	1807	City, London	(?) Abrahams	Julia (?)		Aldgate, London	boot maker
6676	Abrahams	Morris	1820	Amsterdam, Holland	Aharon HaLevi Abrahams		Deborah Raphael	Spitalfields, London	
13757	Abrahams	Morris	1829	?, Poland [?, Prussia]				Manchester	glazier
30018	Abrahams	Morris	1832	Middlesex, London	Isaac Abrahams	Hanial (?)	Clara Hyams	Wolverhampton, Staffordshire	vocalist
19688	Abrahams	Morris	1844	Spitalfields, London	Nathan Abrahams	Clara Harris	Anna Leah Solomons	Spitalfields, London	
6390	Abrahams	Morton (Mordecai)	1847	Aldgate, London	Lewis Abrahams	Esther Genese	Sylvia (Bathsheba) Green	Aldgate, London	
12695	Abrahams	Moses	1820	Birmingham	Jacob (Joseph) Abrahams	Elizabeth (?)	Harriet Hickens	Birmingham	polisher
27658	Abrahams	Moses	1829	Whitechapel, London				Aldgate, London	pencil maker
29312	Abrahams	Moss	1828	?, London	Joseph Abrahams	Florreta (?)		Wapping, London	shipman
10317	Abrahams	Moss	1848	Spitalfields, London	John (Jacob) Abrahams	Jane Harris		Spitalfields, London	
16697	Abrahams	N--- J---	1806	Hamburg, Germany			Elizabeth Fry	Spitalfields, London	general dealer
20628	Abrahams	Nancy	1799	Spitalfields, London	Gershon Hart		Nancy Hart	Spitalfields, London	
5692	Abrahams	Nancy	1828	Plymouth, Devon	Aaron Abrahams	Hannah (?)		Liverpool	
10314	Abrahams	Nancy	1842	Spitalfields, London	John (Jacob) Abrahams	Jane Harris		Spitalfields, London	scholar
16720	Abrahams	Nancy?	1849	Spitalfields, London	Louis (Lewis) Abrahams	Julia (Judith) (?)		Spitalfields, London	
19685	Abrahams	Nathan	1814	Bristol	H--- Abraham		Clara Harris	Spitalfields, London	general dealer
24457	Abrahams	Nathan	1835	Clerkenwell, London	Abraham Abrahams	Deborah (?)		Strand, London	broker + furniture dealer's assistant
13384	Abrahams	Nathaniel	1824	Deal, Kent	Abraham Abrahams	Sarah (?)		Spitalfields, London	fruiterer
8347	Abrahams	Nathaniel	1849	Canterbury, Kent	Joel Abrahams	Frances Nathan		Canterbury, Kent	
10307	Abrahams	Opshire	1806	?, Poland				Spitalfields, London	traveller
10857	Abrahams	Phebe	1844	?, London	Abraham Abrahams	Polly (Mary) Abrahams		Spitalfields, London	scholar
16825	Abrahams	Pheby	1833	Middlesex, London	Isaac Abrahams	Hanial (?)		Wolverhampton, Staffordshire	
4266	Abrahams	Pheeley	1826	Sheerness, Kent	Michael Abrahams	Bloom (?)		Birmingham	
4253	Abrahams	Philip	1775	?, Poland [?, Prussia]				Birmingham	clothier

ID	surname	given names	born	birthplace	father	mother	spouse 1	1851 residence	1851 occupation
29800	Abrahams	Philip	1827	Birmingham	Jacob (Joseph) Abrahams	Elizabeth (?)	Louisa Wigley	Birmingham	iron caster
26035	Abrahams	Philip	1843	Aldgate, London	Henry Abrahams	Ann (Nancy) Barnett		Aldgate, London	scholar
2893	Abrahams	Phineas	1833	Clerkenwell, London	Abraham Abrahams	Juliet Cohen	Rebecca Samuel	Clerkenwell, London	cabinet maker
13997	Abrahams	Phobe	1811	Whitechapel, London				Whitechapel, London	servant
30742	Abrahams	Phobe	1835	Spitalfields, London	Jacob Abrahams	Isabella (?)		Aldgate, London	
25568	Abrahams	Phoebe	1790	?, London	(?)		(?) Abrahams	Aldgate, London	
20593	Abrahams	Phoebe	1811	Holborn, London	Raphael Solomons		Hyam Abrahams	Spitalfields, London	
8101	Abrahams	Phoebe	1833	Birmingham	(?) Abrahams	Rebekah (?)		Whitechapel, London	tailoress
22706	Abrahams	Phoebe (Simha)	1804	Whitechapel, London	Isaac de Yomtob Saltiel	Hanah de Abraham Moses	Emanuel Abrahams	Whitechapel, London	
10855	Abrahams	Polly (Mary)	1819	?, London	Henry Abrahams		Abraham Abrahams	Spitalfields, London	
748	Abrahams	Priscilla	1811	Whitechapel, London	Elias Jacobs		Samuel Marks	Whitechapel, London	
20959	Abrahams	Priscilla	1817	Whitechapel, London	Joseph Cohen	Clara Cohen	Barnett Abrahams	Spitalfields, London	
2688	Abrahams	Priscilla	1848	Manchester	Barnett Abrahams	Hannah Levy	Emanuel Jacobs	Manchester	
26127	Abrahams	Rachael	1802	Amsterdam, Holland	(?)		Abraham Abrahams	Aldgate, London	
31129	Abrahams	Rachael	1811	?, London	(?)		Benjamin Abrahams	Aldgate, London	
17225	Abrahams	Rachael	1812	Aldgate, London	(?)		Ellis (Elias) Abrahams	Aldgate, London	
29313	Abrahams	Rachael	1844	?, London	Joseph Abrahams	Florreta (?)		Wapping, London	
4267	Abrahams	Rachel	1789	Rochford, Essex	Moses Rochford Lazarus		Abraham Abrahams	Birmingham	proprietor of houses
16732	Abrahams	Rachel	1790	Norwich, Norfolk	(?)		Joseph Abrahams	Spitalfields, London	nurse
5904	Abrahams	Rachel	1815	Spitalfields, London	Benjamin Fileman	Elizabeth (?)	Abraham Abrahams	Spitalfields, London	
207	Abrahams	Rachel	1824	Strand, London	Abraham Abrahams	Elizabeth Solomons (?nee Isaacs)	Ezekiel Lowenstark (Loewenstark)	Strand, London	
10663	Abrahams	Rachel	1825	?	(?)		Ephraim Abrahams	Spitalfields, London	dealer
6408	Abrahams	Rachel	1827	Bath	Joshua Abrahams	Hannah (?)	Joseph Lazarus	Spitalfields, London	dress maker
22754	Abrahams	Rachel	1827	City, London	Abraham Abrahams	Hannah (?)		Whitechapel, London	umbrella maker
30720	Abrahams	Rachel	1840	Covent Garden, London	John Abrahams	Rosetta (?)		Covent Garden, London	scholar
19663	Abrahams	Rachel	1842	Aldgate, London	Lewis Abrahams	(?)	Isaac Price	Spitalfields, London	scholar
1386	Abrahams	Rachel	1846	Plymouth, Devon	Abraham Abrahams	Betsey (Betty) (?)		Plymouth, Devon	
20894	Abrahams	Rachel	1848	Twickenham, London	Edward Abrahams	Julia Myers		Twickenham, London	
6107	Abrahams	Rachel	1849	Twickenham, Middlesex	Edward Abrahams	Julia Myers		Twickenham, London	
2354	Abrahams	Rachel	1850	Hull, Yorkshire	Victor Abrahams	Tobe (Thresa) (?)		Hull, Yorkshire	
10846	Abrahams	Rachel	1851	Spitalfields, London	Abraham Abrahams	Rosa		Spitalfields, London	
26606	Abrahams	Rachel	1851	Liverpool	Simon Abrahams	Leah (Selina, Lena) Abrams (Abrahams)	Isaac Israel	Chester, Cheshire	
10315	Abrahams	Rachel Ada	1849	Spitalfields, London	John (Jacob) Abrahams	Jane Harris	Harry S Parker	Spitalfields, London	scholar
27559	Abrahams	Rebbeca	1835	Westminster, London	Barnett Abrahams	Leah (?)		Spitalfields, London	tailoress
28083	Abrahams	Rebecca	1789	?, Holland	(?)		(?) Abrahams	Spitalfields, London	
30023	Abrahams	Rebecca	1810	?, London	Daniel (Gedalia) Defries	Charlotte Nathan	Henry Abrahams	Aldgate, London	
11587	Abrahams	Rebecca	1818	Aldgate, London	(?)		Simon Abrahams	Aldgate, London	dealer in old clothes
9370	Abrahams	Rebecca	1828	Middlesex, London	(?)		Tobias Abrahams	Spitalfields, London	
1388	Abrahams	Rebecca	1844	Plymouth, Devon	Abraham Abrahams	Betsey (Betty) (?)		Plymouth, Devon	
7439	Abrahams	Rebecca	1845	Spitalfields, London	John (Jacob) Abrahams	Jane Harris		Spitalfields, London	
8353	Abrahams	Rebecca	1845	Canterbury, Kent	Abraham Abrahams	Elizabeth (Betsy) Levi		Canterbury, Kent	scholar
10902	Abrahams	Rebecca	1847	Spitalfields, London	(?) Abrahams	Sarah (?)		Spitalfields, London	
20964	Abrahams	Rebecca	1850	Whitechapel, London	Barnett Abrahams	Priscilla Cohen		Spitalfields, London	

ID	surname	given names	born	birthplace	father	mother	spouse 1	1851 residence	1851 occupation
30335	Abrahams	Rebecca	1851	Aldgate, London	Henry Abrahams	Ann (Nancy) Barnett		Aldgate, London	
8097	Abrahams	Rebekah	1810	Whitechapel, London	(?)		(?) Abrahams	Whitechapel, London	tailoress
1296	Abrahams	Reuben	1791	Exeter, Devon				Plymouth, Devon	general dealer
10845	Abrahams	Rosa	1831	Whitechapel, London	(?)		Abraham Abrahams	Spitalfields, London	
26302	Abrahams	Rosa	1849	?, London	(?) Abrahams	(?) Isaacs		Aldgate, London	
13524	Abrahams	Rosa (Rosetta)	1811	Boston, Lincolnshire	(?)		Barnett Abrahams	Manchester	
20424	Abrahams	Rose	1795	Amsterdam, Holland	(?)		Joel Abrahams	Aldgate, London	
19913	Abrahams	Rose	1812	Amsterdam, Holland	(?) Abrahams		Philip Cohen	Spitalfields, London	servant
5250	Abrahams	Rosetta	1807	Furth by Nuremberg, Germany	Aryeh Leib Kisch		Alexander Abrahams	Wapping, London	
30719	Abrahams	Rosetta	1817	Aldgate, London	(?)		John Abrahams	Covent Garden, London	
26621	Abrahams	Rosetta	1829	?, Germany	(?) Abrahams			Aldgate, London	servant
20633	Abrahams	Rosetta	1840	Spitalfields, London	Michael Abrahams	Nancy Hart		Spitalfields, London	
24461	Abrahams	Rosetta	1844	Clerkenwell, London	Abraham Abrahams	Deborah (?)		Strand, London	scholar
2118	Abrahams	Rosetta	1850	Aldgate, London	Colman (Coleman) Abrahams	Leah Myers	John Lazarus	Aldgate, London	
26232	Abrahams	Samson	1801	?, London			Matilda (?)	Aldgate, London	clothes + general dealer
22840	Abrahams	Samuel	1778	?, Poland [?, Prussia]			Bloom (?)	Whitechapel, London	hawker hardware
30251	Abrahams	Samuel	1783	Greenwich, London			Rachel (?)	Greenwich, London	proprietor of houses
25770	Abrahams	Samuel	1815	Deal, Kent	Abraham Abrahams		Maria Phillips nee Isaacs	Aldgate, London	clothes dealer
4249	Abrahams	Samuel	1817	?, Poland [?, Prussia]	Avraham		Kate Davis	Birmingham	jeweller
208	Abrahams	Samuel	1826	Strand, London	Abraham Abrahams	Elizabeth Solomons (?nee Isaacs)	Eliza Emanuel	Strand, London	journeyman cigar maker
10899	Abrahams	Samuel	1835	Spitalfields, London	(?) Abrahams	Sarah (?)		Spitalfields, London	cigar maker
10847	Abrahams	Samuel	1836	?, Holland				Spitalfields, London	general dealer
16057	Abrahams	Samuel	1845	Aldgate, London	Lewis Abrahams	Esther Genese		Aldgate, London	
15310	Abrahams	Samuel	1846	Shoreditch, London	Woolf Abrahams	Leah de Samuel Shannon		Shoreditch, London	
17232	Abrahams	Samuel	1848	Aldgate, London	Ellis (Elias) Abrahams	Rachael (?)		Aldgate, London	scholar
25391	Abrahams	Samuel Benjamin	1823	St Pancras, London			Marianne Goldshede	Holborn, London	solicitor in practice
16693	Abrahams	Sara	1832	Spitalfields, London	Emanuel Abrahams	Esther (?)		Spitalfields, London	tailoress
29430	Abrahams	Sarah	1779	Aldgate, London	(?)		(?) Abrahams	Spitalfields, London	general dealer
13382	Abrahams	Sarah	1785	?, Kent	(?)		Abraham Abrahams	Spitalfields, London	
15323	Abrahams	Sarah	1790	Whitechapel, London	(?)		Henry Abrahams	Shoreditch, London	
25824	Abrahams	Sarah	1795	Aldgate, London	Joseph Yosefa Cohen		Benjamin Abrahams	Aldgate, London	
10319	Abrahams	Sarah	1796	Spitalfields, London	(?)		Joseph Rodrigues Abrahams	Spitalfields, London	
11744	Abrahams	Sarah	1796	Westminster, London	(?)		(?) Abrahams	Shoreditch, London	
21768	Abrahams	Sarah	1806	Whitechapel, London	(?)		(?) Abrahams	Aldgate, London	general dealer
4268	Abrahams	Sarah	1808	?, Kent	(?) Abrahams	Rachel (?)		Birmingham	annuitant
17674	Abrahams	Sarah	1811	Aldgate, London	Naftali (Hart) Cohen	Leah (?)	Lewis Abrahams	Aldgate, London	
10579	Abrahams	Sarah	1815	Whitechapel, London	Hananel Gomes Da Costa		Abraham Abrahams	Spitalfields, London	
28531	Abrahams	Sarah	1817	Spitalfields, London	(?) Abrahams	Dinah (?)		Spitalfields, London	fruiterer
10896	Abrahams	Sarah	1818	Amsterdam, Holland	(?)		(?) Abrahams	Spitalfields, London	wife of dealer in musical instruments
15008	Abrahams	Sarah	1818	Aldgate, London	David Moses	Hannah (?)	Simon (Simeon) Abrahams	Spitalfields, London	
5991	Abrahams	Sarah	1824	Middlesex, London	Henry Levy	Simmy (Sarah) Levy	Abraham Abrahams	Liverpool	

ID	surname	given names	born	birthplace	father	mother	spouse 1	1851 residence	1851 occupation
22844	Abrahams	Sarah	1825	Manchester	Samuel Abrahams	Bloom (?)		Whitechapel, London	slopper
22707	Abrahams	Sarah	1827	Spitalfields, London	Emanuel Abrahams	Phoebe Saltiel		Whitechapel, London	dressmaker
3320	Abrahams	Sarah	1828	Whitechapel, London	Aaron Levy	Rachel Hart	Abraham Abrahams	Aldgate, London	
28873	Abrahams	Sarah	1828	Spitalfields, London	Isaac Levy		Henry Abrahams	Spitalfields, London	pencil maker
26130	Abrahams	Sarah	1829	Amsterdam, Holland	Abraham Abrahams	Rachael (?)		Aldgate, London	
16695	Abrahams	Sarah	1831	Shoreditch, London	(?)		Abraham Abrahams	Spitalfields, London	
25569	Abrahams	Sarah	1832	?, London	(?) Abrahams	Phoebe (?)		Aldgate, London	cape maker
26236	Abrahams	Sarah	1834	?Elephant & Castle, London	Samson Abrahams	Matilda (?)		Aldgate, London	vest maker
30741	Abrahams	Sarah	1834	Spitalfields, London	Jacob Abrahams	Isabella (?)		Aldgate, London	
1384	Abrahams	Sarah	1835	Plymouth, Devon	Abraham Abrahams	Betsey (Betty) (?)		Plymouth, Devon	
8985	Abrahams	Sarah	1835	Portsmouth, Hampshire				Portsmouth, Hampshire	servant
29702	Abrahams	Sarah	1837	Middlesex, London	(?) Abrahams			Aldgate, London	
13526	Abrahams	Sarah	1840	Newcastle-under-Lyme, Staffordshire	Barnett Abrahams	Rosa (Rosetta) (?)		Manchester	scholar
3296	Abrahams	Sarah	1841	Birmingham	Aaron Abrahams	Julia Levi	Louis Marcusson	Birmingham	
11877	Abrahams	Sarah	1841	Middlesex, London	(?) Abrahams	(?)		Whitechapel, London	inmate of orphan school
14988	Abrahams	Sarah	1842	Middlesex, London	(?) Abrahams			Bethnal Green, London	boarding school pupil
17868	Abrahams	Sarah	1844	Bodmin, Cornwall	Alexander Abrahams	Harriett Solomons		Whitechapel, London	scholar
2116	Abrahams	Sarah	1845	Aldgate, London	Colman (Coleman) Abrahams	Leah Myers		Aldgate, London	scholar
5712	Abrahams	Sarah	1845	Brighton, Sussex	Lawrence Abrahams	Matilda (?)	Jacob Mosley Joseph	Brighton, Sussex	
8104	Abrahams	Sarah	1845	Whitechapel, London	(?) Abrahams	Rebekah (?)		Whitechapel, London	scholar
24462	Abrahams	Sarah	1845	Clerkenwell, London	Abraham Abrahams	Deborah (?)		Strand, London	scholar
5798	Abrahams	Sarah	1846	Aldgate, London	Ellis Abrahams	Rachel (?)	John (Jacob, Jack) Jacobs	Aldgate, London	scholar
5257	Abrahams	Sarah	1847	Whitechapel, London	Abraham Abrahams	Rachel Fileman	John (Jack) Jacobs	Spitalfields, London	scholar
27113	Abrahams	Sarah	1847	?, London	David Abrahams	Fanny (?)		Aldgate, London	
7438	Abrahams	Sarah	1849	Spitalfields, London	John (Jacob) Abrahams	Jane Harris		Spitalfields, London	
25050	Abrahams	Sarah	1850	Middlesex, London	Solomon Abrahams	Susannah (?)		Clerkenwell, London	
30724	Abrahams	Sarah	1850	Covent Garden, London	John Abrahams	Rosetta (?)		Covent Garden, London	
7946	Abrahams	Sarah E	1847	Norwich, Norfolk	Benjamin Abrahams	Elizabeth Emanuel	Samuel Edward Marks	Norwich, Norfolk	
16823	Abrahams	Sarrah	1831	Middlesex, London	Isaac Abrahams	Hanial (?)		Wolverhampton, Staffordshire	
5225	Abrahams	Saul	1811	?, Germany				Leeds, Yorkshire	general dealer, jewellery
2222	Abrahams	Saul	1835	Birmingham	Michael Abrahams	Bloom (?)	Henrietta Blanckensee	Leeds, Yorkshire	dealer in watch materials
26135	Abrahams	Selina	1842	Amsterdam, Holland	Abraham Abrahams	Rachael (?)		Aldgate, London	scholar
21772	Abrahams	Simmy	1831	Liverpool	David Abrahams		Solomon Silver	Aldgate, London	servant
26604	Abrahams	Simon	1813	?, Poland [?, Prussia]			Leah (Selina, Lena) Abrahams	Chester, Cheshire	
272	Abrahams	Simon	1816	Whitechapel, London	Avraham		Rebecca (?)	Aldgate, London	general dealer
15007	Abrahams	Simon (Simeon)	1820	St Giles, London	Samuel Abraham (Abrahams, Abrams)	Harriett (?)	Sarah Moses	Spitalfields, London	clothier
26167	Abrahams	Solomon	1788	?, London	Abraham		Maria Solomons	Aldgate, London	baker
25045	Abrahams	Solomon	1821	?, France			Susannah (?)	Clerkenwell, London	clothier
15491	Abrahams	Solomon	1822	?, Holland			Haah (?)	Covent Garden, London	master tailor empl 2
11797	Abrahams	Solomon	1823	?, Holland			Martha Lewis	Shoreditch, London	cigar manufacturer
12065	Abrahams	Solomon	1823	Bath	Joshua Abrahams	Hannah (?)	Maria Simmons	Whitechapel, London	general dealer

ID	surname	given names	born	birthplace	father	mother	spouse 1	1851 residence	1851 occupation
29802	Abrahams	Solomon	1824	Birmingham	Jacob (Joseph) Abrahams	Elizabeth (?)	Ann Forester	Northampton, Northamptonshire	iron caster
31132	Abrahams	Solomon	1842	?, London	Benjamin Abrahams	Rachael (?)		Aldgate, London	
17869	Abrahams	Solomon	1847	?, Cornwall	Alexander Abrahams	Harriett Solomons		Whitechapel, London	
27114	Abrahams	Solomon	1849	?, London	David Abrahams	Fanny (?)		Aldgate, London	
30336	Abrahams	Solomon	1851	Spitalfields, London	Simon (Simeon) Abrahams	Sarah Moses		Spitalfields, London	
8346	Abrahams	Solomon Lyon	1847	Canterbury, Kent	Joel Abrahams	Frances Nathan		Canterbury, Kent	
20426	Abrahams	Sophia	1837	Spitalfields, London	Joel Abrahams	Rose (?)	Samuel Abrahams	Aldgate, London	
2117	Abrahams	Sophia	1848	Aldgate, London	Colman (Coleman) Abrahams	Leah Myers	Harry David Sampson	Aldgate, London	
26853	Abrahams	Sophia	1851	Aldgate, London	Abraham Abrahams	Sarah Levy		Aldgate, London	
25046	Abrahams	Susannah	1822	?, France	(?)		Solomon Abrahams	Clerkenwell, London	
24463	Abrahams	Sylvia	1845	Covent Garden, London	(?) Abrahams			Strand, London	scholar
28082	Abrahams	Theresa	1825	?, Holland	(?) Abrahams	Rebecca (?)	Henry Abrahams	Spitalfields, London	
2355	Abrahams	Tobe (Thresa)	1811	Czarnkow, Poland [Czarnakow, Prussia]			Victor Abrahams	Hull, Yorkshire	
9369	Abrahams	Tobias	1829	?, Czech Republic [?, Bohemia]	Avraham		Rebecca (?)	Spitalfields, London	cap maker
2119	Abrahams	Victor	1811	Czarnkow, Poland [Czarnakow, Prussia]			Tobe (Thresa) (?)	Hull, Yorkshire	master tea dealer empl 2
5223	Abrahams	Wolfe	1793	Amsterdam, Holland				Leeds, Yorkshire	hawker
5714	Abrahams	Wolfe (Walter)	1840	Brighton, Sussex	Lawrence Abrahams	Matilda (?)	Addie Salomons	Brighton, Sussex	
25988	Abrahams	Woolf	1818	Whitechapel, London			Deborah Joseph	Aldgate, London	general dealer
15308	Abrahams	Woolf	1821	Shoreditch, London	Baruch Abrahams		Leah Shannon	Shoreditch, London	
8098	Abrahams	Woolf	1830	Birmingham	(?) Abrahams	Rebekah (?)		Whitechapel, London	cab driver
5034	Abrahams	Zachariah	1797	Amsterdam, Holland				Portsmouth, Hampshire	traveller
7871	Abrahams (Abraham)	Benjamin	1809	Portsmouth, Hampshire	Simon Abrahams	Elizabeth Emanuel	Elizabeth (Betsey) Emanuel	Norwich, Norfolk	watchmaker
24710	Abrahams (Abraham)	David	1834	Aldgate, London	Soesman (Simon, Eliezer) Abrahams (Abraham)	Elizabeth Hart		Walworth, London	
24711	Abrahams (Abraham)	Esther	1846	Whitechapel, London	Soesman (Simon, Eliezer) Abrahams (Abraham)	Elizabeth Hart		Walworth, London	scholar
7831	Abrahams (Abraham)	George Leon	1836	Brighton, Sussex			Rebecca Oppenheim	Brighton, Sussex	scholar
24708	Abrahams (Abraham)	Kate (Catherine)	1829	Aldgate, London	Soesman (Simon, Eliezer) Abrahams (Abraham)	Elizabeth Hart	Jacob Abraham Cantor	Walworth, London	
24709	Abrahams (Abraham)	Mary Ann (Miriam)	1833	Aldgate, London	Soesman (Simon, Eliezer) Abrahams (Abraham)	Elizabeth Hart		Walworth, London	
8267	Abrahams (Abraham)	Samuel Simon	1799	Portsmouth, Hampshire	Simon Abrahams	Elizabeth Emanuel		Norwich, Norfolk	watchmaker
24707	Abrahams (Abraham)	Soesman (Simon, Eliezer)	1803	Middlesex, London	Jacob		Elizabeth Hart	Walworth, London	wholesale grocer?
10849	Abrahams (Vos)	Esther	1832	Amsterdam, Holland			Woolf Van Praagh	Spitalfields, London	
24739	Abrahms	Dinah	1827	St Pancras, London	(?) Abrahms		Sarah (?)	Southwark, London	cloth cap maker
10602	Abrams	Abram	1830	Aldgate, London	Lewis Abrams (Abrahams)	(?)		Spitalfields, London	baker at home
13804	Abrams	Amelia	1838	Manchester	(?) Abrams	Sarah (?)		Manchester	
10604	Abrams	Edward	1844	?Spitalfields, London	(?) Abrams	(?)		Spitalfields, London	

ID	surname	given names	born	birthplace	father	mother	spouse 1	1851 residence	1851 occupation
15054	Abrams	Henry	1844	Aldgate, London				Bethnal Green, London	
10603	Abrams	Ralph	1837	Spitalfields, London	Lewis Abrams (Abrahams)	(?)		Spitalfields, London	baker at home
13803	Abrams	Sarah	1797	?, Germany				Manchester	lodging house keeper
10601	Abrams (Abrahams)	Lewis	1791	City, London			(?)	Spitalfields, London	master baker
29955	Adarney	?Dolores	1841	?, London	(?) Adarney			Whitechapel, London	
29949	Adarny	Jacob	1791	?, Germany			Margarett (?)	Whitechapel, London	skin dresser
29950	Adarny	Margarett	1817	?, Germany	(?)		Jacob Adarny	Whitechapel, London	
8401	Adelsdorf	Joseph	1811	?, Germany				Southampton, Hampshire	travelling jeweller
12141	Adler	Aaron	1812	?, Poland [?, Prussia]			Terasia (?)	Spitalfields, London	tailor's assistant
7002	Adler	Henrietta	1801	?, Germany	(?) Worms		Nathan Marcus Adler	Aldgate, London	
7003	Adler	Hermann	1839	Hanover, Germany	Nathan Marcus Adler	Henrietta Worms	Rachel Joseph	Aldgate, London	
26189	Adler	Isaac	1803	?, Germany			Rosa (?)	Aldgate, London	slipper maker
12144	Adler	Isaac	1850	?, Poland [?, Prussia]	Aaron Adler	Terasia (?)		Spitalfields, London	
30003	Adler	Jeanette	1833	Hanover, Germany	Nathan Marcus Adler	Henrietta Worms		Aldgate, London	
26193	Adler	Julia	1840	?, Germany	Isaac Adler	Rosa (?)		Aldgate, London	
26192	Adler	Levy	1837	?, Germany	Isaac Adler	Rosa (?)		Aldgate, London	slipper maker
30005	Adler	Marcus	1838	Hanover, Germany	Nathan Marcus Adler	Henrietta Worms	Fanny Myers	Aldgate, London	scholar at home
12143	Adler	Marcus	1845	?, Poland [?, Prussia]	Aaron Adler	Terasia (?)		Spitalfields, London	scholar
30004	Adler	Minna	1834	Hanover, Germany	Nathan Marcus Adler	Henrietta Worms	Jacob Nathan Israel	Aldgate, London	
7001	Adler	Nathan Marcus	1803	Hanover, Germany	Mordecai Baer Adler		Henrietta Worms	Aldgate, London	Chief Rabbi of the Synagogue
19672	Adler	Philippina	1831	Cassel, Germany				Aldgate, London	cook
19091	Adler	Rebecca	1837	?, Holland				Spitalfields, London	nurse
26191	Adler	Reuben	1834	?, Germany	Isaac Adler	Rosa (?)		Aldgate, London	slipper maker
26190	Adler	Rosa	1802	?, Germany	(?)		Isaac Adler	Aldgate, London	
12142	Adler	Terasia	1819	?, Poland [?, Prussia]	(?)		Aaron Adler	Spitalfields, London	
14813	Adolphus	Abraham	1792	City, London			(?)	Finsbury, London	dealer
15259	Adolphus	Amelia	1821	?, London	Ephraim Adolphus	Esther de Raphael Mendes Alvares	Morris Lenzberg	Shoreditch, London	dress maker
15261	Adolphus	Elias (Edward)	1823	?, London	Ephraim Adolphus	Esther de Raphael Mendes Alvares	Emma Moses	Shoreditch, London	annuitant
15263	Adolphus	Elizabeth	1828	?, London	Ephraim Adolphus	Esther de Raphael Mendes Alvares		Shoreditch, London	dress maker
15258	Adolphus	Esther	1782	?, London	Raphael Mendes Alvares	Miriam de Ishac Arby	Ephraim Adolphus	Shoreditch, London	
15262	Adolphus	Fanny	1826	?, London	Ephraim Adolphus	Esther de Raphael Mendes Alvares		Shoreditch, London	dress maker
29477	Adolphus	Jack	1825	?, Holland				Spitalfields, London	cigar maker
24838	Adolphus	Joseph	1827	Middlesex, London			Isabella Leggett	Elephant & Castle, London	surgeon MRS--- ?Apothecaries Hall
15260	Adolphus	Louis	1822	?, London	Ephraim Adolphus	Esther de Raphael Mendes Alvares		Shoreditch, London	annuitant
15149	Adolphus	Mary A	1821	Finsbury, London	(?)		William H J Adolphus	Hoxton, London	
19212	Adolphus	Rosa	1828	Spitalfields, London	(?) Adolphus			Belgravia, London	cook
14669	Adolphus	Sarah	1828	Islington, London	(?)		William Adolphus	Hoxton, London	book binder

ID	surname	given names	born	birthplace	father	mother	spouse 1	1851 residence	1851 occupation
14668	Adolphus	William	1829	Clerkenwell, London			Sarah (?)	Hoxton, London	?pensioner
14814	Adolphus	William	1841	Finsbury, London	(?) Adolphus			Finsbury, London	scholar
15148	Adolphus	William H J	1813	Chelmsford, Essex			Mary A (?)	Hoxton, London	clerk
24915	Adrechi	Solomon	1816	Hamburg, Germany			Ann (?)	Bethnal Green, London	cigar maker
9633	Aflalo	Alice	1842	Middlesex, London	Isaac Aflalo	Hannah Daninos	Abraham (Edward) Jacobs	Whitechapel, London	scholar at home
9635	Aflalo	Hannah (Nina)	1812	?, Italy	Jacob de Abraham Daninos		Isaac de Moses Aflalo	Whitechapel, London	
9634	Aflalo	Isaac	1801	?, Africa	Moses de Joseph Aflalo		Hannah (Nina) de Jacob Daninos	Whitechapel, London	merchant colonial
9636	Aflalo	Judah	1844	Middlesex, London	Isaac Aflalo	Hannah (Nina) Daninos		Aldgate, London	scholar at home
7631	Aflalo	Louisa (Luna L)	1840	Middlesex, London	Isaac Aflalo	Hannah (Nina) Daninos	Henry (Hillel) Benham	Aldgate, London	scholar at home
7635	Aflalo	Moses	1836	Middlesex, London	Isaac Aflalo		Annie Guedalla	Aldgate, London	scholar
7633	Aflalo	Selina (Simha)	1838	Middlesex, London	Isaac Aflalo	Hannah (Nina) Daninos	Ludovic (Mordecai) Loria	Aldgate, London	scholar
21287	Aflalo	Solomon	1839	Spitalfields, London				Edmonton, London	boarding school pupil
15874	Aguilar	David	1792	Kingston, Jamaica, West Indies	Joseph de Emanuel Aguilar	Gracia de Abraham Aguilar	Maria (Miriam) Belisario	Hackney, London	fundholder
6999	Aguilar	Emanuel Abraham	1824	Clapham, London	Emanuel de Joseph Aguilar	Sarah Dias Fernandes	Sarah (?)	Fitzrovia, London	professor of music
15877	Aguilar	Esther	1828	Middlesex, London	David de Joseph Aguilar	Maria (Miriam) Belisario		Hackney, London	boarding school inmate
15876	Aguilar	Grace	1826	Middlesex, London	David de Joseph Aguilar	Maria (Miriam) Belisario		Hackney, London	boarding school inmate
17937	Aguilar	Grace	1849	Marylebone, London	Emanuel Abraham Aguliar	Sarah Dias Fernandes		Fitzrovia, London	
24591	Aguilar	Joseph	1804	Lambeth, London			Caroline (?)	Lambeth, London	accountant
15881	Aguilar	Lydia (Leah)	1836	Hackney, London	David de Joseph Aguilar	Maria (Miriam) Belisario		Hackney, London	boarding school scholar
15875	Aguilar	Maria (Miriam)	1797	Kingston, Jamaica, West Indies	Abraham Mendes Belisario	Esther (?)	David de Joseph Aguilar	Hackney, London	
15879	Aguilar	Miriam (Marianne)	1831	Middlesex, London	David de Joseph Aguilar	Maria (Miriam) Belisario	Leopold Loewenthal	Hackney, London	boarding school inmate
15882	Aguilar	Octavius (Haim)	1839	Hackney, London	David de Joseph Aguilar	Maria (Miriam) Belisario		Hackney, London	boarding school scholar
15880	Aguilar	Rebecca	1834	Hackney, London	David de Joseph Aguilar	Maria (Miriam) Belisario		Hackney, London	boarding school scholar
6998	Aguilar	Sarah	1786	Jamaica, West Indies	Jacob Dias Fernandes	Esther (?)	Emanuel de Joseph Aguilar	Fitzrovia, London	fundholder
18972	Aguilar	Sarah	1787	Middlesex, London	(?) Dias	Esther (?)	(?) Aguilar	Whitechapel, London	gentlewoman
7000	Aguilar	Sarah	1827	Middlesex, London	Emanuel Abraham Aguilar	Sarah Dias Fernandes		Fitzrovia, London	
15878	Aguilar	Sarah	1830	Middlesex, London	David de Joseph Aguilar	Maria (Miriam) Belisario		Hackney, London	boarding school inmate
7697	Ahlborn	Abraham	1844	Liverpool	Louis Ahlborn	Fanny Keller	Rosetta Samuel	Liverpool	
7696	Ahlborn	Fanny	1818	Hamburg, Germany	(?)		Julius Ahlborn	Liverpool	
23693	Ahlborn	Fanny	1818	Liverpool	(?) Keller		Lewis Ahlborn	Liverpool	
23696	Ahlborn	Gershon	1849	Liverpool	Lewis Ahlborn	Fanny Keller		Liverpool	
20899	Ahlborn	Henrietta	1849	Liverpool	Julius Ahlborn	Fanny (?)		Liverpool	
20897	Ahlborn	Jane	1847	Liverpool	Julius Ahlborn	Fanny (?)	Moses Friedenwald	Liverpool	
20898	Ahlborn	Julia	1848	Liverpool	Julius Ahlborn	Fanny (?)		Liverpool	
7683	Ahlborn	Julius	1818	Hanover, Germany			Fanny (?)	Liverpool	haberdasher
23692	Ahlborn	Lewis	1817	?, Germany			Fanny Keller	Liverpool	toy merchant
23694	Ahlborn	Lewis	1839	Liverpool	Lewis Ahlborn	Fanny Keller		Liverpool	
23695	Ahlborn	Sarah	1845	Liverpool	Lewis Ahlborn	Fanny Keller		Liverpool	
24470	Ahrenfeld	Alfred	1837	Liverpool	Jacob (Jacques) Ahrenfeld	Eliza (?)	Dinah Davis	Peckham, London	at cigar manufactory
24468	Ahrenfeld	Edward	1835	Liverpool	Jacob (Jacques) Ahrenfeld	Eliza (?)		Peckham, London	apprentice to a commission agent
24467	Ahrenfeld	Eliza	1810	Liverpool			Jacob (Jacques) Ahrenfeld	Peckham, London	

ID	surname	given names	born	birthplace	father	mother	spouse 1	1851 residence	1851 occupation
24466	Ahrenfeld	Jacob (Jacques)	1801	?, Germany			Eliza (?)	Peckham, London	commission agent
24472	Ahrenfeld	Jenett	1840	Manchester	Jacob (Jacques) Ahrenfeld	Eliza (?)		Peckham, London	scholar
24469	Ahrenfeld	John	1836	Liverpool	Jacob (Jacques) Ahrenfeld	Eliza (?)		Peckham, London	
24471	Ahrenfeld	Lucy	1838	Manchester	Jacob (Jacques) Ahrenfeld	Eliza (?)	Isaac Lazarus	Peckham, London	scholar
24473	Ahrenfeld	Miriam	1841	Hoxton, London	Jacob (Jacques) Ahrenfeld	Eliza (?)		Peckham, London	scholar
24474	Ahrenfeld	Moss	1847	Clapham, London	Jacob (Jacques) Ahrenfeld	Eliza (?)		Peckham, London	
18336	Ahronsberg	Isidor	1830	?, Latvia [Jalsingen, Courland]				Brighton, Sussex	shopman
25792	Ahronson	Joseph	1833	?, Poland [?, Prussia]				Aldgate, London	scholar
2356	Akerman	John	1818	?, Germany				Hull, Yorkshire	clockmaker
4147	Albert	Adolphus Ephraim	1851	City, London	Meyer Ephraim Albert	Rebecca Catherine Davis		City, London	
4146	Albert	Alfred Samuel	1849	City, London	Meyer Ephraim Albert	Rebecca Catherine Davis		City, London	
4148	Albert	Edward Meyer	1842	City, London	Meyer Ephraim Albert	Rebecca Catherine Davis	Amy Hannah Lowe	City, London	
4149	Albert	James Valek	1848	City, London	Meyer Ephraim Albert	Rebecca Catherine Davis	Fanny Davis	City, London	scholar
4152	Albert	John Gabriel	1846	Covent garden, London	Meyer Ephraim Albert	Rebecca Catherine Davis	Hannah (Annie) Rabinowitz	City, London	
4153	Albert	Louisa Amelia	1841	Finsbury, London	Meyer Ephraim Albert	Rebecca Catherine Davis	George Prescott Mallan	City, London	
4150	Albert	Meyer Ephraim	1812	Surrey, London	Michael Meyers		Rebecca Catherine Davis	City, London	surgeon dentist
4151	Albert	Rebecca Catherine	1812	Middlesex, London	John Gabriel Davis	Catherine Davis	Meyer Ephraim Albert	City, London	
26102	Albrecht	Davis	1806	?, Poland			(?)	Aldgate, London	teacher
6413	Albu	Berthold	1825	Berlin, Germany	Israel Albu	(?)	Bella Silverstone	Exeter, Devon	synagogue minister
6414	Albu	Israel	1806	?, Germany [?, Prussia]			(?)	Aldgate, London	general merchant
6415	Albu	Solomon	1836	?, Germany	Israel Albu	(?)	Bluma Blumenthal	Aldgate, London	
4600	Alder	Henry	1824	Bridgenorth, Staffordshire				Birmingham	tailor
5198	Alex	Belinda	1819	Great Yarmouth, Norfolk	David Jones	Leah Micholls	Montague Alex	Cheltenham, Gloucestershire	
6991	Alex	Catherine	1801	King's Lynn, Norfolk	Aaron Jones		Barron Jones	Strand, London	
5196	Alex	Ephraim (Edward)	1800	Shoreditch, London	Solomon Alex	Rachel Jones	Catherine Jones nee Jones	Strand, London	surgeon dentist
5199	Alex	Leah Rachael	1840	Cheltenham, Gloucestershire	Montague Alex	Belinda Jones	Henry Joseph Phillips	Cheltenham, Gloucestershire	
5197	Alex	Montague	1817	?, London	Solomon Alex	Rachel Jones	Belinda Jones	Cheltenham, Gloucestershire	dentist
18236	Alex	Montague	1850	Cheltenham, Gloucestershire	Montague Alex	Belinda Jones		Cheltenham, Gloucestershire	
5195	Alex	Sophia Rose	1845	Cheltenham, Gloucestershire	Montague Alex	Belinda (?)	Sidney Myer	Cheltenham, Gloucestershire	
5816	Alexander	Aaron	1828	Clerkenwell, London	Israel Alexander	Eva (?)	Sarah Israel	Clerkenwell, London	
27872	Alexander	Aaron	1849	Whitechapel, London	John (Jacob) Alexander	Golda (Goulder) Levy		Spitalfields, London	
30029	Alexander	Abraham	1828	Finsbury, London	Israel Alexander	Eve (?)		Clerkenwell, London	
23123	Alexander	Abraham (Braham)	1811	City, London			Louisa Lazarus	City, London	auctioneer's assistant
18704	Alexander	Adelaide	1829	Middlesex, London	Lewis Alexander	Hannah (?)		Whitechapel, London	vocalist
26598	Alexander	Adolphus (Abraham)	1819	Wurtemberg, Germany			Violet Abrahams	Liverpool	boarding house keeper
18700	Alexander	Albert Lewis (Louis)	1835	Whitechapel, London	Lewis Alexander	Hannah (?)	Esther Somers	Whitechapel, London	

ID	surname	given names	born	birthplace	father	mother	spouse 1	1851 residence	1851 occupation
18466	Alexander	Alex	1814	Whitechapel, London	Barnet (Issachar Berman) Alexander		Elizabeth Pesman	Whitechapel, London	cigar dealer
17206	Alexander	Alexander	1800	Spitalfields, London	Meir Alexander		Frances Lazarus	Spitalfields, London	fruiterer
1075	Alexander	Alexander	1806	Sheerness, Kent			Tryphenia (Fanny) Johnson	Exeter, Devon	optician
7752	Alexander	Alexander	1807	Portsmouth, Hampshire	Solomon Alexander	Amelia Hart	Rose Constance Coleman	Holborn, London	jeweller
30133	Alexander	Alexander	1818	?, Poland [?, Prussia]	Wolff Alexander	Gitel Friedlander	Louise Friedlander	Liverpool	professor of languages
5027	Alexander	Alexander	1834	Whitechapel, London	Isaac Alexander	Susan Levy	Charlotte E Alloway	Whitechapel, London	ledger maker
4142	Alexander	Alfred	1826	Fitzrovia, London	Simon Alexander	Elizabeth Aarons	Sarah Myers	St Pancras, London	
959	Alexander	Alfred	1846	Exeter, Devon	Alexander Alexander	Tryphenia (Fanny) Johnson		Exeter, Devon	scholar
16508	Alexander	Alice Flora	1850	Holborn, London	Alexander Alexander	Rose Constance Coleman	Alfred Pyke	Holborn, London	
17935	Alexander	Amelia	1778	Aldgate, London	Moses Hart	Eleanor Adolphus	Solomon Alexander	Aldgate, London	supported by son
30799	Alexander	Amelia	1791	Wapping, London	(?) Alexander			Whitechapel, London	milliner
7679	Alexander	Amelia	1805	Southampton, Hampshire	Solomon Alexander	Amelia Hart		Aldgate, London	supported by [brother]
4139	Alexander	Amelia	1826	Fitzrovia, London	Simon Alexander	Elizabeth Aarons	Woolf Samuel	Whitechapel, London	
30800	Alexander	Ann	1796	Wapping, London	(?) Alexander			Whitechapel, London	servant's assistant
22559	Alexander	Ann	1810	Norwich, Norfolk	Barnett Crawcour	Fanny Alexander Crawcour	Reuben Alexander	Chatham, Kent	
30803	Alexander	Anna	1807	Southampton, Hampshire	Solomon Alexander	Amelia Hart		Aldgate, London	dressmaker + milliner
23608	Alexander	Benjamin	1843	?, Austria	John Alexander	Rose (?)		Liverpool	
27871	Alexander	Betsey	1846	Whitechapel, London	John (Jacob) Alexander	Golda (Goulder) Levy		Spitalfields, London	
1174	Alexander	Betsey (Elizabeth)	1806	Plymouth, Devon	Sander Alexander	Rose (?)		Plymouth, Devon	independent means
1173	Alexander	Blooming (Bloomey)	1816	Plymouth, Devon	Sander Alexander	Rose (?)		Plymouth, Devon	independent means
4141	Alexander	Caroline	1827	Fitzrovia, London	Simon Alexander	Elizabeth Aarons	Meyer Cohen	Whitechapel, London	
3665	Alexander	Catherine	1835	Whitechapel, London	Isaac Alexander	Susan Levy	Woolf Lazarus	Whitechapel, London	
9754	Alexander	Charles	1836	Bristol				Kew, London	boarding school pupil
20649	Alexander	Clara	1803	Bedford, Bedfordshire	(?) Pyke		John Alexander	Spitalfields, London	
9237	Alexander	David	1821	Whitechapel, London			Mary (?)	Spitalfields, London	sealing wax maker journeyman
5938	Alexander	David Lindo	1842	Finsbury, London	Joshua Alexander	Jemima Lindo	Hester Joseph	Finsbury, London	scholar at home
14566	Alexander	Edward B	1843	Middlesex, London	Lewis Alexander	Julia Asher	Esther Beck	Holborn, London	
23539	Alexander	Elias	1827	?, Poland			Hannah Goldbach	Liverpool	fringe manufacturer
30028	Alexander	Eliza	1824	Finsbury, London	Israel Alexander	Eve (?)		Clerkenwell, London	
18707	Alexander	Eliza	1834	Middlesex, London	Lewis Alexander	Hannah (?)		Whitechapel, London	
29739	Alexander	Eliza	1835	Aldgate, London	Moses Alexander	Elizabeth (?)		Aldgate, London	dressmaker apprentice
954	Alexander	Eliza	1836	Exeter, Devon	Alexander Alexander	Tryphenia (Fanny) Johnson		Exeter, Devon	
18111	Alexander	Elizabeth	1782	Aldgate, London	(?)		(?) Alexander	Mile End, London	
29734	Alexander	Elizabeth	1793	Aldgate, London	(?)		Moses Alexander	Aldgate, London	
4133	Alexander	Elizabeth	1799	City, London	Aaron Aarons		Simon Alexander	Whitechapel, London	annuitant
18467	Alexander	Elizabeth	1821	Whitechapel, London	Jacob Pesman	Esther Capua	Alex Alexander	Whitechapel, London	
14569	Alexander	Elizabeth	1847	Middlesex, London	Lewis Alexander	Julia Asher	Abraham Silverston	Holborn, London	
23126	Alexander	Elizabeth	1850	Wapping, London	Abraham (Braham) Alexander	Louisa Lazarus		City, London	
7751	Alexander	Ellen	1815	Southampton, Hampshire	Solomon Alexander	Amelia Hart		Aldgate, London	dressmaker + milliner
22561	Alexander	Emma	1847	Chatham, Kent	Reuben Alexander	Ann Crawcour		Chatham, Kent	
4144	Alexander	Esther	1783	?, Norfolk	(?) Goldsmith		Moses Alexander	Aldgate, London	
16215	Alexander	Esther	1797	Colchester, Essex	(?) Alexander			Finsbury, London	cook

ID	surname	given names	born	birthplace	father	mother	spouse 1	1851 residence	1851 occupation
7750	Alexander	Esther	1825	Southampton, Hampshire	Solomon Alexander	Amelia Hart			
30032	Alexander	Eve	1786	City, London	(?)			Aldgate, London	dress maker + milliner
29738	Alexander	Eve	1829	Aldgate, London	Moses Alexander	Elizabeth (?)	Israel Alexander	Clerkenwell, London	horse dealer
1057	Alexander	Fanny	1762	?, Germany				Aldgate, London	milliner
25292	Alexander	Fanny	1821	?, London	(?) Samuel	Lydia (?)	Levy Alexander	Exeter, Devon	
953	Alexander	Fanny	1832	Exeter, Devon	Alexander Alexander	Tryphenia (Fanny) Johnson	Morris (Maurice) Alexander	Holborn, London	
958	Alexander	Fanny (Frances) T	1844	Exeter, Devon	Alexander Alexander	Tryphenia (Fanny) Johnson		Exeter, Devon	
17207	Alexander	Frances	1793	Canterbury, Kent	Joseph HaLevi Lazarus		Alexander Alexander	Spitalfields, London	scholar
9753	Alexander	Frankel Isaac	1836	Bristol	Abraham HaLevi Alexander			Kew, London	boarding school pupil
2120	Alexander	George	1791	Hull, Yorkshire				Hull, Yorkshire	silversmith + general dealer
4131	Alexander	George	1829	Fitzrovia, London	Simon Alexander	Elizabeth Aarons	Sophia Aaron	Whitechapel, London	picture frame maker empl 5
27870	Alexander	Golda (Goulder)	1826	Spitalfields, London	Jacob Levy		John (Jacob) Alexander	Spitalfields, London	
18703	Alexander	Hannah	1803	Middlesex, London	Moses called Abraham		Lewis Alexander	Whitechapel, London	
30802	Alexander	Hannah	1815	Aldgate, London	Moses Alexander	Elizabeth (?)	Joseph Gaskell b Ezekiel	Whitechapel, London	milliner
23540	Alexander	Hannah	1827	?, Poland	(?) Goldbach		Elias Alexander	Whitechapel, London	
23541	Alexander	Hannah	1850	Liverpool	Elias Alexander	Hannah Goldbach		Liverpool	
7781	Alexander	Hannah (Ann)	1816	Middlesex, London	Isaac Alexander	Esther Barnard		Covent Garden, London	boarding house keeper
18705	Alexander	Harriette	1831	Middlesex, London	Lewis Alexander	Hannah (?)		Whitechapel, London	vocalist
30027	Alexander	Henrietta	1818	Finsbury, London	Israel Alexander	Eve (?)		Clerkenwell, London	
29106	Alexander	Henry	1829	Clerkenwell, London	Moss (Moses) Alexander	Jane (?)	Frances Phillips	Clerkenwell, London	cigar maker
29740	Alexander	Henry	1837	Aldgate, London	Moses Alexander	Elizabeth (?)		Aldgate, London	cigar maker apprentice
962	Alexander	Henry	1842	Plymouth, Devon	John Alexander	Isabella (?)		Exeter, Devon	scholar
14568	Alexander	Henry	1846	Middlesex, London	Lewis Alexander	Julia Asher		Holborn, London	
30807	Alexander	Henry	1848	Covent Garden, London	Henry Alexander	Sophia Leman		Covent Garden, London	
17635	Alexander	Herman	1829	?, Germany			Catherine (Zussie) (?)	Aldgate, London	traveller
30806	Alexander	Hester	1847	Covent Garden, London	Henry Alexander	Sophia Leman		Covent Garden, London	
8833	Alexander	Isaac	1828	Aldgate, London				Aldgate, London	cigar maker
23125	Alexander	Isaac	1848	Fitzrovia, London	Abraham (Braham) Alexander	Louisa Lazarus		City, London	
961	Alexander	Isabella	1809	Plymouth, Devon	(?) Johnson		John Alexander	Exeter, Devon	
15844	Alexander	Isabella Lindo	1841	Finsbury, London	Joshua Alexander	Jemima Lindo	Alfred Henry Moses	Finsbury, London	scholar at home
30031	Alexander	Israel	1787	Wapping, London			Eve (?)	Clerkenwell, London	horse dealer
15724	Alexander	Jacob	1803	Chatham, Kent				Euston, London	general merchant
956	Alexander	Jacob A	1840	Exeter, Devon	Alexander Alexander	Tryphenia (Fanny) Johnson	Elizabeth (Lizzie) Jessel	Exeter, Devon	scholar
22562	Alexander	James (Moses)	1849	Chatham, Kent	Reuben Alexander	Ann Crawcour	Florence Helen Healy	Chatham, Kent	
29104	Alexander	Jane	1789	Aldgate, London	(?)		Moss (Moses) Alexander	Clerkenwell, London	dealer in glass
15525	Alexander	Jane	1831	?London	(?) Alexander			Aldgate, London	housemaid
15843	Alexander	Jemima	1820	Whitechapel, London	David Abarbanel Lindo		Joshua Alexander	Shoreditch, London	
5934	Alexander	Jemima Lindo	1845	Shoreditch, London	Joshua Alexander	Jemima Lindo	John Henry Moses (Beddington)	Shoreditch, London	
1076	Alexander	John	1797	Sheerness, Kent			Isabella Johnson	Exeter, Devon	
20648	Alexander	John	1802	?, Russia [?, Rushland]			Clara Pyke	Spitalfields, London	labourer
23604	Alexander	John	1815	?, Austria			Rose (?)	Liverpool	jeweller hawker
965	Alexander	John	1848	Exeter, Devon	John Alexander	Isabella (?)	Bertha Lyons	Exeter, Devon	

ID	surname	given names	born	birthplace	father	mother	spouse 1	1851 residence	1851 occupation
27869	Alexander	John (Jacob)	1823	Aldgate, London	Alexander Alexander		Golda (Goulder) Levy	Spitalfields, London	general dealer
5936	Alexander	Joseph Lindo	1840	Finsbury, London	Joshua Alexander	Jemima Lindo	Ada Rachel Montefiore	Shoreditch, London	schola at home
9240	Alexander	Josh	1844	?, Northumberland	David Alexander	Mary (?)		Spitalfields, London	
5935	Alexander	Joshua	1804	Whitechapel, London	Joseph Alexander		Jemima Lindo	Shoreditch, London	solicitor in all the Superior Courts
6748	Alexander	Julia	1800	Colchester, Essex	(?) Alexander			Whitechapel, London	dressmaker
29735	Alexander	Julia	1816	Aldgate, London	Moses Alexander	Elizabeth (?)		Aldgate, London	domestic
17936	Alexander	Julia	1825	Southampton, Hampshire	Solomon Alexander	Amelia Hart		Aldgate, London	dressmaker + milliner
18706	Alexander	Julia	1832	Middlesex, London	Lewis Alexander	Hannah (?)		Whitechapel, London	vocalist
27886	Alexander	Julia	1844	City, London	(?) Alexander			Spitalfields, London	
14565	Alexander	Julia	1814	Middlesex, London	Meir Asher		Lewis Alexander	Holborn, London	
9747	Alexander	Kate	1840	Plymouth, Devon	(?) Alexander			Truro, Cornwall	shop assistant
30804	Alexander	Kate (Catherine)	1808	Middlesex, London	Isaac Alexander	Esther Barnard		Covent Garden, London	boarding house keeper
955	Alexander	Lawrence (Lauren A)	1838	Exeter, Devon	Alexander Alexander	Tryphenia (Fanny) Johnson		Exeter, Devon	scholar
17208	Alexander	Lazarus	1831	Whitechapel, London	Alexander Alexander	Frances Lazarus	Dinah Martin	Spitalfields, London	fruiterer
20523	Alexander	Leah	1821	?, Poland [?, Prussia]	Woolf Harris		Samuel Alexander	Aldgate, London	
7874	Alexander	Levi	1816	Turin, Italy			Emma (?)	?London	
23606	Alexander	Levi	1839	?, Austria	John Alexander	Rose (?)		Liverpool	
1056	Alexander	Levy	1753	?, Germany			Fanny (?)	Exeter, Devon	
18702	Alexander	Lewis	1800	Chatham, Kent	Isaiah		Hannah (?Abraham)	Whitechapel, London	cattle salesman
14564	Alexander	Lewis	1817	Middlesex, London	Issachar		Julia Asher	Holborn, London	tobacconist
29737	Alexander	Lewis	1826	Aldgate, London	Moses Alexander	Elizabeth (?)		Aldgate, London	furniture broker
1343	Alexander	Lewis	1836	Exeter, Devon	John Alexander	Isabella (?)	Rebecca Lyons	Plymouth, Devon	shop assistant
23124	Alexander	Louisa	1814	Aldgate, London	(?) Lazarus		Abraham (Braham) Alexander	City, London	
14234	Alexander	Luman	1835	?, Poland				Manchester	tinplate worker
30801	Alexander	Maria	1807	Whitechapel, London	(?) Alexander			Whitechapel, London	milliner
30749	Alexander	Maria	1824	Middlesex, London	Isaac Alexander	Esther Barnard	Benjamin Eliazer Emrik	Covent Garden, London	
9238	Alexander	Mary	1817	?, America			David Alexander	Spitalfields, London	
29105	Alexander	Mary	1827	?, London	Moss (Moses) Alexander	Jane (?)		Clerkenwell, London	pattern maker
26600	Alexander	Matilda	1844	Liverpool	Adolphus (Abraham) Alexander	Violet Abrahams	Morris Samuel	Liverpool	
27647	Alexander	Michael	1761	?, Germany			(?)	Aldgate, London	hairdresser
3666	Alexander	Michael	1837	Whitechapel, London	Isaac Alexander	Susan Levy		Whitechapel, London	
957	Alexander	Miriam	1842	Exeter, Devon	Alexander Alexander	Tryphenia (Fanny) Johnson	Isaac Marks	Exeter, Devon	scholar
30337	Alexander	Miriam	1851	Spitalfields, London	Israel Alexander	Phoebe Mendoza		Spitalfields, London	
25290	Alexander	Morris (Maurice)	1816	Portsmouth, Hampshire	Solomon Alexander	Amelia Hart	Fanny Samuel	Holborn, London	watch maker
14567	Alexander	Morris (Maurice) Lewis	1844	Middlesex, London	Lewis Alexander	Julia Asher	Sarah Beck	Holborn, London	
4145	Alexander	Moses	1783	?, Yorkshire			Esther Goldsmith	Aldgate, London	landed proprietor
29733	Alexander	Moses	1791	Wapping, London			Elizabeth (?)	Aldgate, London	furniture broker
17030	Alexander	Moses	1826	?, Poland				Edinburgh, Scotland	costermonger
10513	Alexander	Moses	1828	?, Poland [?, Prussia]			Rebecca (?)	Aldgate, London	traveller - jewelry
987	Alexander	Moses	1834	Exeter, Devon	Alexander Alexander	Tryphenia (Fanny) Johnson	Eliza Davidson	Exeter, Devon	assistant jeweller
30338	Alexander	Moses	1851	Spitalfields, London	John (Jacob) Alexander	Golda (Goulder) Levy		Spitalfields, London	

ID	surname	given names	born	birthplace	father	mother	spouse 1	1851 residence	1851 occupation
29103	Alexander	Moss (Moses)	1792	Aldgate, London			Jane (?)	Clerkenwell, London	dealer in glass
7754	Alexander	Naphtali Hart	1811	Southampton, Hampshire	Solomon Alexander	Amelia Hart		Aldgate, London	manufacturing jeweller
28766	Alexander	Nathan	1825	?, Germany	Israel Alexander		Phoebe Mendoza	Spitalfields, London	tailor
28767	Alexander	Phoebe	1824	Middlesex, London	Moses de Mordecai Mendoza	Maria (Miriam) Sarah Mathews	Israel Alexander	Spitalfields, London	
30529	Alexander	Rachel	1809	?Southampton, Hampshire	Isaac Alexander	Esther Barnard		Covent Garden, London	boarding house keeper
29736	Alexander	Rachel	1821	Aldgate, London	Moses Alexander	Elizabeth (?)		Aldgate, London	milliner
1303	Alexander	Rachel	1829	?, Poland			Samuel Alexander	Plymouth, Devon	
22430	Alexander	Rachel	1840	Chatham, Kent	Reuben Alexander	(?) Crawcour	Samuel Lazarus	Gravesend, Kent	boarding school pupil
964	Alexander	Rachel	1846	Exeter, Devon	John Alexander	Isabella (?)	Daniel Levy	Exeter, Devon	scholar
10514	Alexander	Rebecca	1830	?, Poland [?, Prussia]	(?)		Moses Alexander	Aldgate, London	
963	Alexander	Rebecca	1844	Exeter, Devon	John Alexander	Isabella (?)	Sussman Ragowsky	Exeter, Devon	scholar
22558	Alexander	Reuben	1804	Chatham, Kent	(?Joshua) Alexander		Ann Crawcour	Chatham, Kent	clothier
9241	Alexander	Richard	1846	?, Northumberland	David Alexander	Mary (?)		Spitalfields, London	
23605	Alexander	Rose	1817	?, Austria	(?)		John Alexander	Liverpool	
7753	Alexander	Rose Constance	1828	Liverpool	Sylvester Coleman	Flora Yates	Alexander Alexander	Holborn, London	
18199	Alexander	Rosetta	1777	Middlesex, London	(?) Alexander			Mile End, London	
20522	Alexander	Samuel	1813	?, Poland	Alexander Phillips		Leah Harris	Aldgate, London	fur dealer
8834	Alexander	Samuel	1826	Aldgate, London				Aldgate, London	cigar maker
1302	Alexander	Samuel	1830	?, Poland			Rachel (?)	Plymouth, Devon	licensed hawker
23607	Alexander	Samuel	1841	?, Austria	John Alexander	Rose (?)		Liverpool	
20651	Alexander	Samuel	1845	Aldgate, London	John Alexander	Clara Pyke		Spitalfields, London	scholar
966	Alexander	Samuel	1850	Exeter, Devon	John Alexander	Isabella (?)		Exeter, Devon	
29107	Alexander	Sarah	1832	?, London	Moss (Moses) Alexander	Jane (?)	Ettie Tickton	Clerkenwell, London	[---] maker
9239	Alexander	Sarah	1841	?, Northumberland	David Alexander	Mary (?)		Spitalfields, London	
960	Alexander	Sarah (Tryphenia)	1848	Exeter, Devon	Alexander Alexander	Tryphenia (Fanny) Johnson		Exeter, Devon	scholar
15845	Alexander	Sarah Lindo	1844	Finsbury, London	Joshua Alexander	Jemima Lindo		Finsbury, London	scholar at home
26601	Alexander	Selina	1849	Liverpool	Adolphus (Abraham) Alexander	Violet Abrahams		Liverpool	
3664	Alexander	Solomon	1834	Whitechapel, London	Isaac Alexander	Susan Levy	Aaron Marks	Whitechapel, London	ledger maker
20650	Alexander	Solomon	1844	Chatham, Kent	John Alexander	Clara Pyke	Rosetta Nathan	Spitalfields, London	scholar
30805	Alexander	Sophia	1822	Middlesex, London	(?) Leman		Henry Alexander	Covent Garden, London	grocer
25291	Alexander	Stephen Lewis	1851	Holborn, London	Morris (Maurice) Alexander	Fanny Samuel		Holborn, London	
27646	Alexander	Susan	1799	Elephant & Castle, London	Michael Alexander		(?) Alexander	Aldgate, London	fruiterer
30026	Alexander	Sylvester Solomon	1851	Holborn, London	Alexander Alexander	Rose Constance Coleman		Holborn, London	
952	Alexander	Tryphenia (Fanny)	1810	Plymouth, Devon	(?) Johnson		Alexander Alexander	Exeter, Devon	optician's assistant
26599	Alexander	Violet	1826	Hanover, Germany	(?) Abrahams		Adolphus (Abraham) Alexander	Liverpool	
21639	Alexander	William Wolfe	1798	Bristol	Joseph Alexander	Dinah (?)	Angelina Brandon	Bristol	commission merchant + ship agent + City Alderman
28589	Alisia	Eliza	1840	?, London	Henry Alisia	Hannah (?)		Spitalfields, London	scholar
28588	Alisia	Hannah	1814	?, London	(?)		Henry Alisia	Spitalfields, London	
28587	Alisia	Henry	1816	?, London			Hannah (?)	Spitalfields, London	general dealer
28590	Alisia	Joseph	1842	?, London	Henry Alisia	Hannah (?)		Spitalfields, London	scholar
28592	Alisia	Judah	1850	?, London	Henry Alisia	Hannah (?)		Spitalfields, London	

ID	surname	given names	born	birthplace	father	mother	spouse 1	1851 residence	1851 occupation
28591	Alisia	Michael	1846	?, London	Henry Alisia	Hannah (?)	-	Spitalfields, London	scholar
28593	Alisia	Sophia	1831	?, London	(?) Alisia			Spitalfields, London	servant
25267	Allen	Abraham	1804	?, Suffolk	Pinchas Zelig		Judith Miranda	Holborn, London	shoemaker
11043	Allen	Ann	1813	Aldgate, London	Yehuda Leib Myers		John (Jacob) Allen	Aldgate, London	
25640	Allen	Benjamin	1849	Aldgate, London	Lewis Allen	Isabella Simmonds	Julia Lydia Goldsmid	Aldgate, London	
25272	Allen	Betsy	1837	Holborn, London	Abraham Allen	Rebecca (?)		Holborn, London	
25275	Allen	Charles	1843	Holborn, London	Abraham Allen	Rebecca (?)		Holborn, London	
25271	Allen	Eliza	1835	Holborn, London	Abraham Allen	Rebecca (?)		Holborn, London	
25273	Allen	Fanny	1839	Holborn, London	Abraham Allen	Rebecca (?)		Holborn, London	
25276	Allen	George	1849	Holborn, London	Abraham Allen	Rebecca (?)		Holborn, London	
25639	Allen	Hannah	1846	Aldgate, London	Lewis Allen	Isabella Simmonds		Aldgate, London	
25638	Allen	Henry	1845	Aldgate, London	Lewis Allen	Isabella Simmonds	Louisa Solomon	Aldgate, London	
11044	Allen	Isaac	1837	Aldgate, London	John (Jacob) Allen	Ann Myers	Clara Hart	Aldgate, London	cigar maker
25637	Allen	Isaac	1844	Aldgate, London	Lewis Allen	Isabella Simmonds		Aldgate, London	
25636	Allen	Isabella	1827	Aldgate, London	Aaron Simmonds		Lewis Allen	Holborn, London	
25274	Allen	Isabella	1841	Holborn, London	Abraham Allen	Rebecca (?)		Edmonton, London	assistant teacher
21306	Allen	James	1830	Westminster, London				Aldgate, London	scholar
11046	Allen	John	1847	Aldgate, London	John (Jacob) Allen	Ann Myers		Aldgate, London	scholar
11042	Allen	John (Jacob)	1811	Aldgate, London	Jacob		Ann Myers	Aldgate, London	cigar maker
25641	Allen	Julia	1850	Aldgate, London	Lewis Allen	Isabella Simmonds		Aldgate, London	
25635	Allen	Lewis	1824	Aldgate, London	Isaac Allen		Isabella Simmonds	Aldgate, London	cigar maker
7441	Allen	Lewis	1842	Aldgate, London	John (Jacob) Allen	Ann Myers	Rosa Nelson	Aldgate, London	
11047	Allen	Michael	1849	Aldgate, London	John (Jacob) Allen	Ann Myers	Rose Nathan	Aldgate, London	
25268	Allen	Rebecca	1806	Holborn, London	Jacob		(?)	Holborn, London	
25270	Allen	Thomas	1833	Holborn, London	Abraham Allen	Rebecca (?)		Holborn, London	shoemaker
25269	Allen	William	1831	Holborn, London	Abraham Allen	Rebecca (?)		Holborn, London	shoemaker
20520	Allport	Abraham	1835	St Helier, Jersey, Channel Islands			Diana Asher	St Helier, Jersey, Channel Islands	
16755	Alman	Abraham	1849	Bristol	Lazarus Alman	Hannah (?)		Bristol	
16766	Alman	Deborah	1836	?, London	(?) Alman			Bristol	
16758	Alman	Emma	1809	Bristol	(?)		Joseph Alman	Bristol	
16764	Alman	Esther	1828	Bristol	Mosely Moses Alman	Hannah (?)	Moses Haim Botibol	Bristol	
16752	Alman	Frederick	1843	Bristol	Lazarus Alman	Hannah (?)		Bristol	
16762	Alman	Hannah	1791	Plymouth, Devon	Eliezer (?)		Mosely Moses Alman	Bristol	
16749	Alman	Hannah	1815	Gloucester, Gloucestershire	(?)		Lazarus Alman	Bristol	
16753	Alman	Isabella	1845	Bristol	Lazarus Alman	Hannah (?)		Bristol	
16756	Alman	Israel	1850	Bristol	Lazarus Alman	Hannah (?)		Bristol	
16757	Alman	Joseph	1807	Bristol	(?Mosely) Alman	(?Henel) (?)	Emma (?)	Bristol	--- coaf wharf
16751	Alman	Joseph	1841	Bristol	Lazarus Alman	Hannah (?)		Bristol	
16750	Alman	Julia	1839	Bristol	Lazarus Alman	Hannah (?)		Bristol	
16748	Alman	Lazarus	1814	Bristol	(?Mosely) Alman	(?Henel) (?)	Hannah (?)	Bristol	accountant + general dealer
16763	Alman	Leah	1826	Bristol	Mosely Moses Alman	Hannah (?)	Abraham Barnett Simmons	Bristol	
16761	Alman	Mosely Moses	1786	Bristol	Benjamin Joseph Alman		Hannah (?)	Bristol	silversmith + auctioneer
16760	Alman	Myrsha	1843	Bristol	Joseph Alman	Emma (?)		Bristol	

ID	surname	given names	born	birthplace	father	mother	spouse 1	1851 residence	1851 occupation
16754	Alman	Phoebe Jane	1848	Bristol	Lazarus Alman	Hannah (?)		Bristol	
16765	Alman	Rebecca	1833	Bristol	Mosely Moses Alman	Hannah (?)	Jacob Levy	Bristol	
16759	Alman	William	1836	Bristol	Joseph Alman	Emma (?)		Bristol	
21039	Almande	Judah	1838	Essaouira, Morocco [Mogadour, Africa]				Dover, Kent	boarding school pupil
19131	Almond	Abraham	1816	Bristol			Elesha (?)	Aldgate, London	feather merchant's clerk
19136	Almond	Dinah	1847	Bristol	Abraham Almond	Elesha (?)		Aldgate, London	
19132	Almond	Elesha	1821	?, West Indies	(?)		Abraham Almond	Aldgate, London	schoolmistress
19134	Almond	Fleurette	1843	Bristol	Abraham Almond	Elesha (?)		Aldgate, London	scholar
19133	Almond	Justinia	1841	Cincinnati, USA	Abraham Almond	Elesha (?)		Aldgate, London	pupil
19135	Almond	Samuel	1844	Swansea, Wales	Abraham Almond	Elesha (?)		Aldgate, London	scholar
29640	Almosnino	Donna	1798	Middlesex, London	Haim Hazday Almosnino	Orabuena (?)		Aldgate, London	
16380	Almosnino	Sarah	1809	Southwark, London	Elias Haim Lindo		Solomon Almosnino	Aldgate, London	
16379	Almosnino	Solomon	1792	City, London	Haim Hasday Almosnino	Orabuena (?)	Esther de Benjamin Mendes Pereira	Aldgate, London	secretary of Synagogue
7624	Aloof	Abraham	1837	?, London	Judah Aloof	Grace Lindo	Mesoda Sequerra	Whitechapel, London	
7622	Aloof	Esther	1825	?, London	Judah Aloof	Grace Lindo	Daniel Picciotto	Whitechapel, London	
7758	Aloof	Grace	1799	St Kitts, West Indies	David Abarbanel Lindo	Sarah (?)	Judah Aloof	Whitechapel, London	
7621	Aloof	Judah	1796	Gibraltar	Solomon Aloof		Grace Lindo	Whitechapel, London	fund holder
11954	Aloof	Menachem	1833	?, London	Judah Aloof	Grace Lindo	Ellen Burke	Whitechapel, London	
7759	Aloof	Mesodah	1828	?, London	Judah Aloof	Grace Lindo	Asher Solomon	Whitechapel, London	
7627	Aloof	Sarah	1837	?, London	Judah Aloof	Grace Lindo	Daniel Nunes Castello	Whitechapel, London	
23026	Altman	Abraham Joseph	1808	Plymouth, Devon	Natan HaCohen Altman		(?)	Shoreditch, London	importer of fancy goods
23029	Altman	Albert Joseph	1840	City, London	Abraham Joseph Altman	(?)		Shoreditch, London	scholar
23027	Altman	Esther	1832	City, London	Abraham Joseph Altman	(?)		Shoreditch, London	
23028	Altman	Fanny	1838	City, London	Abraham Joseph Altman	(?)		Shoreditch, London	scholar
23031	Altman	Henry	1829	Plymouth, Devon	(?) Cohen			Shoreditch, London	medical student
23030	Altman	Josephine	1842	City, London	Abraham Joseph Altman	(?)		Shoreditch, London	
21110	Alton	Israel	1806	?, Poland [?, Prussia]				Aldgate, London	general merchant
11515	Alvares	Aaron	1838	Middlesex, London	Abraham Alvares	Abigail Hart	Sarah Toledano	Aldgate, London	scholar
11514	Alvares	Abigail	1819	Middlesex, London	Isaac Hart		Abraham Alvares	Aldgate, London	
11513	Alvares	Abraham	1816	Middlesex, London	Aaron Alvares	Hanah Jesurun	Abigail Hart	Aldgate, London	pen cutter
11517	Alvares	Alice (Ellis, Jael)	1846	Middlesex, London	Abraham Alvares	Abigail Hart	Abraham Martin (Nunes Martines)	Aldgate, London	scholar
11518	Alvares	Barnett	1848	Spitalfields, London	Abraham Alvares	Abigail Hart	Rachel Mitchell	Aldgate, London	scholar
30483	Alvares	Benjamin Thomas	1812	Shoreditch, London	Aaron de David Alvarez	Hannah de David de Jacob Jessurun	Maria Dowling	Hoxton, London	painter &c
15727	Alvares	David	1800	Amsterdam, Holland	Aaron de David Alvarez	Hannah de David de Jacob Jessurun	Rachel de David Rodrigues	Hackney, London	retired missionary
11519	Alvares	David	1849	Middlesex, London	Abraham Alvares	Abigail Hart	Hannah Martin (Nunes Martines)	Aldgate, London	
15728	Alvares	Hannah	1823	Mile End, London	David de Aaron Alvares	Rachel de David Rodrigues		Hackney, London	needlewoman
11516	Alvares	Isaac	1841	Middlesex, London	Abraham Alvares	Abigail Hart	Elizabeth (Bathsheba) Henriques Valentine	Aldgate, London	scholar

ID	surname	given names	born	birthplace	father	mother	spouse 1	1851 residence	1851 occupation
15729	Alvares	John Solomon	1827	Mile End, London	David de Aaron Alvares	Rachel de David Rodrigues	Sophia (Siporah, Zipporah) Bensabat	Hackney, London	lithographer
11521	Alvares	Miriam	1851	Aldgate, London	Abraham Alvares	Abigail Hart		Aldgate, London	
15730	Alvares	Rebecca	1831	Finsbury, London	David de Aaron Alvares	Rachel de David Rodrigues		Hackney, London	general servant
15731	Alvares	Sarah	1838	Betrhnal Green, London	David de Aaron Alvares	Rachel de David Rodrigues	Michael Phillips	Hackney, London	scholar at home
11520	Alvares	Woolf	1849	Middlesex, London	Abraham Alvares	Abigail Hart		Aldgate, London	
17275	Alvarez	Morry	1799	?, Hungary				Aldgate, London	glazier
5658	Alvarez	Rachel	1785	Whitechapel, London	David de Mordecai Rodrigues	Esther Rodrigues	David de Aaron Alvares	Hackney, London	
14395	Amschel	Leopold	1821	?, Germany				Manchester	merchant
11817	Amsell	Benjamin	1823	Amerack (?Amerang), Germany	Philip Amsel		Sarah Ornstein	Whitechapel, London	tailor (journeyman)
28470	Ancona (D'Ancona)	Abraham	1841	Spitalfields, London	Isaac Ancona (D'Ancona)	Sarah Nunes Cardoza		Spitalfields, London	
28473	Ancona (D'Ancona)	Esther	1847	Spitalfields, London	Isaac Ancona (D'Ancona)	Sarah Nunes Cardoza		Spitalfields, London	
28468	Ancona (D'Ancona)	Isaac	1822	Spitalfields, London	Abraham de Jacob Haim Ancona	Rebecca (Ribca) de David	Sarah Nunes Cardoza	Spitalfields, London	furrier
28471	Ancona (D'Ancona)	Jacob	1843	Spitalfields, London	Isaac Ancona (D'Ancona)	Sarah Nunes Cardoza		Spitalfields, London	
28474	Ancona (D'Ancona)	Mary Ann (Miriam)	1850	Spitalfields, London	Isaac Ancona (D'Ancona)	Sarah Nunes Cardoza		Spitalfields, London	
28472	Ancona (D'Ancona)	Rebecca	1846	Spitalfields, London	Isaac Ancona (D'Ancona)	Sarah Nunes Cardoza		Spitalfields, London	
28469	Ancona (D'Ancona)	Sarah	1823	Spitalfields, London	Jacob de Isaac Nunes Cardoza	Esther de Isaac Mendoza	Isaac Ancona (D'Ancona)	Spitalfields, London	
9336	Andrade	Abigail	1797	City, London	(?) Andrade			Aldgate, London	feather dresser
24496	Andrade	Alexander Benjamin	1850	Camberwell, London	Benjamin Andrade	Eliza Levy		Walworth, London	
24492	Andrade	Benjamin	1813	Shoreditch, London			Eliza Levy	Walworth, London	master butcher empl 32
24493	Andrade	Eliza	1815	Whitechapel, London	(?) Levy		Benjamin Andrade	Walworth, London	
24494	Andrade	Emily Louisa	1848	Camberwell, London	Benjamin Andrade	Eliza Levy		Walworth, London	
24495	Andrade	Rosina? Eliza	1849	Camberwell, London	Benjamin Andrade	Eliza Levy		Walworth, London	
9328	Andrade	Sarah	1794	Aldgate, London	(?) Andrade			Aldgate, London	poor
29978	Andrade (Andrade Da Costa	Ann	1848	?, London	Benjamin Andrade (Andrade Da Costa)	Elizabeth (?)		Whitechapel, London	
29970	Andrade (Andrade Da Costa	Benjamin	1813	?, London	David Andrade Da Costa	Leah de Benjamin Alvarenga	Elizabeth (?)	Whitechapel, London	brush maker
29973	Andrade (Andrade Da Costa	Benjamin	1837	?, London	Benjamin Andrade (Andrade Da Costa)	Elizabeth (?)		Whitechapel, London	brush maker
29972	Andrade (Andrade Da Costa	David	1834	?, London	Benjamin Andrade (Andrade Da Costa)	Elizabeth (?)		Whitechapel, London	brush maker
29971	Andrade (Andrade Da Costa	Elizabeth	1814	?, London	(?)		Benjamin Andrade (Andrade Da Costa)	Whitechapel, London	
29975	Andrade (Andrade Da Costa	Elizabeth	1841	?, London	Benjamin Andrade (Andrade Da Costa)	Elizabeth (?)		Whitechapel, London	

ID	surname	given names	born	birthplace	father	mother	spouse 1	1851 residence	1851 occupation
29974	Andrade (Andrade Da Costa	Esther	1839	?, London	Benjamin Andrade (Andrade Da Costa)	Elizabeth (?)		Whitechapel, London	
29980	Andrade (Andrade Da Costa	Henry	1851	?Whitechapel, London	Benjamin Andrade (Andrade Da Costa)	Elizabeth (?)		Whitechapel, London	
29979	Andrade (Andrade Da Costa	Jane	1850	?, London	Benjamin Andrade (Andrade Da Costa)	Elizabeth (?)		Whitechapel, London	
29976	Andrade (Andrade Da Costa	Louisa	1844	?, London	Benjamin Andrade (Andrade Da Costa)	Elizabeth (?)		Whitechapel, London	
29977	Andrade (Andrade Da Costa	Lucy	1846	?, London	Benjamin Andrade (Andrade Da Costa)	Elizabeth (?)		Whitechapel, London	
24620	Andrade (Andrade Da Costa)	David	1817	Whitechapel, London	Saul de Benjamin Da Costa Andrade	Leah de Abraham Haim Benjamin	Eliza (Elisheba) Da Costa Andrade	Kennington, London	meat salesman
29554	Andrade (Andrade Da Costa)	David	1845	Whitechapel, London	Solomon Andrade (Andrade Da Costa)	Hannah Isaacs		Whitechapel, London	scholar
24622	Andrade (Andrade Da Costa)	Emma	1830	Whitechapel, London	Saul de Benjamin Da Costa Andrade	Leah de Abraham Haim Benjamin		Kennington, London	
29552	Andrade (Andrade Da Costa)	Hannah	1819	Portsmouth, Hampshire	Lewis Isaacs		Solomon Andrade (Andrade Da Costa)	Whitechapel, London	
29555	Andrade (Andrade Da Costa)	Julia	1848	Whitechapel, London	Solomon Andrade (Andrade Da Costa)	Hannah Isaacs		Whitechapel, London	
29553	Andrade (Andrade Da Costa)	L--- (Leah?)	1844	Whitechapel, London	Solomon Andrade (Andrade Da Costa)	Hannah Isaacs		Whitechapel, London	scholar
29556	Andrade (Andrade Da Costa)	Lucy	1850	Whitechapel, London	Solomon Andrade (Andrade Da Costa)	Hannah Isaacs		Whitechapel, London	
24619	Andrade (Andrade Da Costa)	Saul	1788	Whitechapel, London	Benjamin de David Da Costa Andrade	Judith de Saul Rodrigues	Leah de Abraham Haim Benjamin	Kennington, London	butcher
29551	Andrade (Andrade Da Costa)	Solomon	1817	Whitechapel, London	David Andrade Da Costa	Leah de Benjamin Alvarenga	Hannah Isaacs	Whitechapel, London	cigar maker
24621	Andrade (Andrade Da Costa)	Sophia	1820	Whitechapel, London	Saul de Benjamin Da Costa Andrade	Leah de Abraham Haim Benjamin		Kennington, London	
16033	Andrade Da Costa	Abigail Amelia	1847	?City, London	Solomon Haim de Moses Andrade Da Costa	Esther de Joseph Zamira	Phineas Hands	Stratford, London	
21369	Andrade Da Costa	Alfred	1822	Limehouse, London	Saul Andrade Da Costa	Leah de Haim Bendahan	Mary A Thompson nee (?)	Walworth, London	butcher (journeyman)
16029	Andrade Da Costa	David	1830	City, London	Solomon Haim de Moses Andrade Da Costa	Esther de Joseph Zamira	Sarah Nunes Carvalho	Aldgate, London	dealer in feathers
16032	Andrade Da Costa	Esther	1805	?, London	Joseph Zamira	Sarah (?)	Solomon Haim de Moses Andrade Da Costa	Stratford, London	
21610	Andrade Da Costa	Esther	1851	Finsbury, London	Moses Andrade Da Costa	Rachel Nunes Carvalho	Albert (Eliezer) Levin Lee	Finsbury, London	
16030	Andrade Da Costa	Joseph H	1836	City, London	Solomon Haim de Moses Andrade Da Costa	Esther de Joseph Zamira	Rebecca Suhami (Samuel)	Aldgate, London	ostrich feather manufacturer
20906	Andrade Da Costa	Joshua	1843	City, London	Solomon Haim de Moses Andrade Da Costa	Esther de Joseph Zamira		Stratford, London	
20907	Andrade Da Costa	Louisa (Leah)	1841	City, London	Solomon Haim de Moses Andrade Da Costa	Esther de Joseph Zamira	Levy Benatar	Stratford, London	
20905	Andrade Da Costa	Lucy	1834	City, London	Solomon Haim de Moses Andrade Da Costa	Esther de Joseph Zamira	Mark (Mordecai) Daniel Suhami	Stratford, London	

ID	surname	given names	born	birthplace	father	mother	spouse 1	1851 residence	1851 occupation
16034	Andrade Da Costa	Moses	1827	Whitechapel, London	Solomon Haim de Moses Andrade Da Costa	Esther de Joseph Zamira	Rachel Nunes Carvalho	Finsbury, London	warehouseman + artificial flower importer
16035	Andrade Da Costa	Rachel	1827	Finsbury, London	David de Samuel Nunes Carvalho	Hanah de Abraham Solomons	Moses Andrade Da Costa	Finsbury, London	
16028	Andrade Da Costa	Rebecca	1845	City, London	Solomon Haim de Moses Andrade Da Costa	Esther de Joseph Zamira	Phillip Samuel	Stratford, London	
9755	Andrade Da Costa	Samuel	1838	Middlesex, London	Solomon Haim de Moses Andrade Da Costa	Esther de Joseph Zamira	Maria (Miriam) Nunes Carvalho	Aldgate, London	boarding school pupil
20904	Andrade Da Costa	Sarah	1832	City, London	Solomon Haim de Moses Andrade Da Costa	Esther de Joseph Zamira	John Pesman Capua	Stratford, London	
6064	Andrade Da Costa	Sarah (Louisa)	1849	Southwark, London	Alfred Andrade Da Costa	Mary A Thompson nee (?)		Walworth, London	
16031	Andrade Da Costa	Solomon Haim	1802	?, London	Moses Andrade Da Costa	Lucia (?)	Esther de Joseph Zamira	Stratford, London	feather maker
13176	Andrews	Sarah	1849	?London	(?) Andrews			Aldgate, London	
14006	Andries	Sophia	1826	?, Holland				Manchester	annuitant
21898	Angel	Abraham	1791	Clerkenwell, London			Charlotte (?)	Clerkenwell, London	silversmith
4243	Angel	Abraham	1829	Islington, London			Mary-Ann (?)	Birmingham	silversmith
18171	Angel	Amelia	1841	Stepney, London	John Angel	(?)		Mile End, London	
21900	Angel	Caroline	1832	Clerkenwell, London	Abraham Angel	Charlotte (?)		Clerkenwell, London	
18169	Angel	Charles	1833	Stepney, London	John Angel	(?)		Mile End, London	
21901	Angel	Charles	1840	Clerkenwell, London	Abraham Angel	Charlotte (?)		Clerkenwell, London	
21899	Angel	Charlotte	1798	Clerkenwell, London	(?)		Abraham Angel	Clerkenwell, London	
12940	Angel	Daniel	1785	?, Germany			Rachel (?)	Dalston, London	tailor
20470	Angel	Daniel	1847	Middlesex, London	Morris (Maurice) Angel	Sarah Hyman	Blumer Isaacs	Covent Garden, London	
20480	Angel	Edward	1823	Middlesex, London	Daniel Angel	Rachel (?)	Julia Isaacs	Covent Garden, London	clothier
18168	Angel	Eliza	1826	Stepney, London	John Angel	(?)		Mile End, London	
20472	Angel	Ellen (Helen, Nellie)	1849	Middlesex, London	Morris (Maurice) Angel	Sarah Hyman	Alexander Jonas	Covent Garden, London	
18170	Angel	Emma	1839	Stepney, London	John Angel	(?)		Mile End, London	
30175	Angel	George	1821	?, Poland				Dudley, Worcestershire	
18167	Angel	John	1800	Stepney, London			(?)	Mile End, London	private coachman
12942	Angel	Josephine	1827	Strand, London	Daniel Angel	Rachel (?)		Dalston, London	
20481	Angel	Julia	1827	Middlesex, London	(?) Isaacs		Edward Angel	Covent Garden, London	
20469	Angel	Julia	1845	Middlesex, London	Morris (Maurice) Angel	Sarah Hyman		Covent Garden, London	
4244	Angel	Mary-Ann	1832	Birmingham			Abraham Angel	Birmingham	
20467	Angel	Morris (Maurice)	1824	Strand, London	Daniel Angel	Rachel (?)	Sarah Hyman	Covent Garden, London	clothier
12941	Angel	Rachel	1787	Holborn, London	(?)		Daniel Angel	Dalston, London	
20471	Angel	Rachel	1848	Middlesex, London	Morris (Maurice) Angel	Sarah Hyman	Alexander Cohen	Covent Garden, London	
20468	Angel	Sarah	1815	?, Somerset	Jacob Hyman		Morris (Maurice) Angel	Covent Garden, London	
18172	Angel	Walter	1843	Stepney, London	John Angel	(?)		Mile End, London	
3836	Angel [Moses]	Emanuel M	1843	Spitalfields, London	Moses (Angel) Angel (Moses)	Rebecca Godfrey		Spitalfields, London	scholar
3839	Angel [Moses]	Godfrey L	1850	Spitalfields, London	Moses (Angel) Angel (Moses)	Rebecca Godfrey		Spitalfields, London	
3837	Angel [Moses]	Maria Hannah	1847	Spitalfields, London	Moses (Angel) Angel (Moses)	Rebecca Godfrey	John Hart	Spitalfields, London	scholar
3834	Angel [Moses]	Moses [Angel]	1818	City, London	Emmanuel Moses	Sarah (?)	Rebecca Godfrey	Spitalfields, London	teacher of languages
3838	Angel [Moses]	Moses C	1849	Spitalfields, London	Moses (Angel) Angel (Moses)	Rebecca Godfrey		Spitalfields, London	scholar

ID	surname	given names	born	birthplace	father	mother	spouse 1	1851 residence	1851 occupation
3835	Angel [Moses]	Rebecca	1818	Westminster, London	Godfrey Godfrey (Levy)	Sarah Crawcour	Moses (Angel) Angel (Moses)	Spitalfields, London	
17442	Angell	Esther	1845	Warsaw, Poland	John Angell	Sarah (?)		Aldgate, London	scholar
17443	Angell	Jacob	1847	Warsaw, Poland	John Angell	Sarah (?)		Aldgate, London	
17440	Angell	John	1811	Warsaw, Poland			Sarah (?)	Aldgate, London	tailor
17444	Angell	Moses	1848	Warsaw, Poland	John Angell	Sarah (?)		Aldgate, London	
17441	Angell	Sarah	1816	Warsaw, Poland	(?)		John Angell	Aldgate, London	tailoress
29959	Anhooner	Elly	1824	Dublin, Ireland	(?) Anhooner			Whitechapel, London	dressmaker
22529	Ansell	?	1848	Whitechapel, London	Joseph Ansell	Abigail Cohen		Whitechapel, London	
19645	Ansell	Aaron	1835	?, London	Jacob Ansell	Rachel Isaacs	Angela Nunes	Whitechapel, London	
22522	Ansell	Abigail	1814	Chatham, Kent	Dan HaCohen		Joseph Ansell	Whitechapel, London	
29965	Ansell	Abigail	1820	Southwark, London	(?) Ansell			Whitechapel, London	dressmaker
22213	Ansell	Abraham	1813	?, Poland	Joseph		Dina (?)	Whitechapel, London	tailor
19110	Ansell	Amelia	1826	?, London	Hyam (Hyman) Ansell	Fanny (?)	John Lorrimer	Haggerston, London	fancy knitting?
19643	Ansell	Amelia	1830	Chelsea, London	Jacob Ansell	Rachel Isaacs		Whitechapel, London	hat binder
30080	Ansell	Amelia	1841	Kensington, London	Moses Ansell	Rebecca (?)		Whitechapel, London	
22217	Ansell	Angel	1845	Whitechapel, London	Abraham Ansell	Dina (?)		Whitechapel, London	scholar
22527	Ansell	Anna	1844	Whitechapel, London	Joseph Ansell	Abigail Cohen	Joseph Flatau	Whitechapel, London	scholar
22526	Ansell	Ansell	1842	Whitechapel, London	Joseph Ansell	Abigail Cohen		Whitechapel, London	scholar
19647	Ansell	Arthur Davidson	1840	Dublin, Ireland	Jacob Ansell	Rachel Isaacs	Hannah Davis	Whitechapel, London	
19646	Ansell	Asher	1838	Whitechapel, London	Jacob Ansell	Rachel Isaacs	Evelyn Charlotte Samuels	Whitechapel, London	shoe maker
7762	Ansell	Caroline	1830	?, London	Hyam (Hyman) Ansell	Fanny (?)		Haggerston, London	
18719	Ansell	Catherine	1849	Whitechapel, London	Moss Ansell	Mary Cantor		Haggerston, London	
2227	Ansell	David	1840	Middlesex, London	Myer Ansell	Jessie (?)	Amelia Booth	Leeds, Yorkshire	
22214	Ansell	Dina	1813	Finsbury, London	(?)		Abraham Ansell	Whitechapel, London	
2349	Ansell	Elizabeth	1851	Leeds, Yorkshire	Myer Ansell	Jessie (?)	Solomon Bodlander (Budlender)	Leeds, Yorkshire	
19650	Ansell	Elizabeth (Eliza)	1844	Whitechapel, London	Jacob Ansell	Rachel Isaacs	Adolphus Gluckstein	Whitechapel, London	
22524	Ansell	Emily	1838	Whitechapel, London	Joseph Ansell	Abigail Cohen	Edward Altman	Whitechapel, London	knitter?
18385	Ansell	Fanny	1798	Margate, Kent	(?)		Hyam (Hyman) Ansell	Haggerston, London	
29897	Ansell	Grace	1789	Spitalfields, London	Anshel Casper		Moses Ansell	Wapping, London	
19111	Ansell	Hannah	1832	?, London	Hyam (Hyman) Ansell	Fanny (?)		Haggerston, London	fancy knitting?
19648	Ansell	Henry	1841	Whitechapel, London	Jacob Ansell	Rachel Isaacs		Whitechapel, London	scholar
22219	Ansell	Henry	1848	Whitechapel, London	Abraham Ansell	Dina (?)		Whitechapel, London	scholar
7760	Ansell	Hyam (Hyman)	1793	?, London	Solomon (Zalman) Ansell	Rosetta (?)	Fanny (?)	Haggerston, London	commission agent + bookmaker
22528	Ansell	Isaac	1846	Whitechapel, London	Joseph Ansell	Abigail Cohen		Whitechapel, London	scholar
19641	Ansell	Jacob	1800	Ipswich, Suffolk	Ansell (Asher) Ansell		Rachel Isaacs	Whitechapel, London	merchant jeweller
22220	Ansell	Jacob	1850	Whitechapel, London	Abraham Ansell	Dina (?)		Whitechapel, London	
2225	Ansell	Jessie	1813	?, London			Myer Ansell	Leeds, Yorkshire	
7491	Ansell	Jonas	1820	?London				Haggerston, London	
22521	Ansell	Joseph	1803	Ipswich, Suffolk	Asher Ansell		Abigail Cohen	Whitechapel, London	optician
21613	Ansell	Joseph	1806	Harwich, Essex				Brighton, Sussex	
19653	Ansell	Julia	1850	Whitechapel, London	Jacob Ansell	Rachel Isaacs	Joseph Myers	Whitechapel, London	scholar
22218	Ansell	Lazarus	1846	Whitechapel, London	Abraham Ansell	Dina (?)		Whitechapel, London	scholar

ID	surname	given names	born	birthplace	father	mother	spouse 1	1851 residence	1851 occupation
22576	Ansell	Lewis	1824	Ipswich, Suffolk	Moses Ansell	Rebecca (?)		Whitechapel, London	travelling stationer
2228	Ansell	Lewis	1844	?, London	Myer Ansell	Jessie (?)		Leeds, Yorkshire	
22525	Ansell	Martha	1840	Whitechapel, London	Joseph Ansell	Abigail Cohen		Whitechapel, London	scholar
19649	Ansell	Martha	1842	Whitechapel, London	Jacob Ansell	Rachel Isaacs	George Lewis Levy	Whitechapel, London	scholar
7845	Ansell	Mary	1825	City, London	Joseph Cantor	Rachael (?)	Moss Ansell	Haggerston, London	
19651	Ansell	Michael	1846	Whitechapel, London	Jacob Ansell	Rachel Isaacs	Rachel (Martha) Solomon	Whitechapel, London	
22523	Ansell	Moses	1836	Whitechapel, London	Joseph Ansell	Abigail Cohen	Sarah Lazarus	Whitechapel, London	cigar maker apprentice
19652	Ansell	Moses (Morris)	1848	Whitechapel, London	Jacob Ansell	Rachel Isaacs	Phoebe Solomons	Whitechapel, London	
7482	Ansell	Moss	1823	City, London	Hyam (Hyman) Ansell	Fanny (?)	Mary Cantor	Haggerston, London	clerk to accountant
2224	Ansell	Myer	1810	?, London	Asher Ansell		Jessie (?)	Leeds, Yorkshire	chiropodist
22215	Ansell	Priscilla	1840	Whitechapel, London	Abraham Ansell	Dina (?)	Abraham Jacobs	Whitechapel, London	scholar
30339	Ansell	Rachael	1851	Haggerston, London	Moss Ansell	Mary Cantor		Haggerston, London	
19642	Ansell	Rachel	1805	Deptford, London	Michael Isaacs	Elizabeth Levy	Jacob Ansell	Whitechapel, London	
2229	Ansell	Rachel	1838	?, London	Myer Ansell	Jessie (?)	Leon Gross	Leeds, Yorkshire	
22575	Ansell	Rebecca	1799	Aldgate, London	(?)		Moses Ansell	Whitechapel, London	general dealer
22216	Ansell	Rebecca	1843	Whitechapel, London	Abraham Ansell	Dina (?)	Isaac Jacobs	Whitechapel, London	scholar
19020	Ansell	Rose	1834	?, Ireland	Jacob Ansell	Rachel Isaacs	Barnard Levy	Whitechapel, London	dressmaker
22577	Ansell	Sarah	1828	Middlesex, London	Moses Ansell	Rebecca (?)		Whitechapel, London	
19644	Ansell	Sarah	1832	Dublin, Ireland	Jacob Ansell	Rachel Isaacs	Samuel (Arthur) Wolff	Whitechapel, London	dressmaker
22578	Ansell	Simon	1832	Middlesex, London	Moses Ansell	Rebecca (?)	Rose Samuels	Whitechapel, London	journeyman chair maker
22579	Ansell	Solomon	1836	Dublin, Ireland	Moses Ansell	Rebecca (?)		Whitechapel, London	apprentice to tailor
18718	Ansell	Solomon	1847	Haggerston, London	Moss Ansell	Mary Cantor		Haggerston, London	
13702	Ansorge	Barnett	1850	Manchester	Solomon Ansorge	Sophia (?)		Manchester	
13701	Ansorge	Janette	1849	Manchester	Solomon Ansorge	Sophia (?)		Manchester	
13703	Ansorge	Janette	1849	Manchester	Solomon Ansorge	Sophia (?)		Manchester	
13699	Ansorge	Solomon	1825	?, Poland [?, Prussia]			Sophia (?)	Manchester	cap manufacturer
13700	Ansorge	Sophia	1826	?, Poland [?, Prussia]			Sophia (?)	Manchester	
2357	Aosen	Blehanderine	1811	Geneva, Switzerland			Herman Aosen	Hull, Yorkshire	teacher of French
30938	Aosen	Herman	1810	Warsaw, Poland			Blehanderine (?)	Hull, Yorkshire	teacher of German
21105	Appelman	Abraham	1801	?, Poland			Esther (?)	Aldgate, London	butcher
21107	Appelman	Barnet	1832	?, Poland	Abraham Appelman	Esther (?)		Aldgate, London	teacher of mathematics
21106	Appelman	Esther	1811	?, Poland	(?)		Abraham Appelman	Aldgate, London	
21109	Appelman	Mordecai	1844	?, London	Abraham Appelman	Esther (?)		Aldgate, London	scholar
21108	Appelman	Solomon	1842	?, London	Abraham Appelman	Esther (?)		Aldgate, London	scholar
20909	Apple	Charlotte	1837	?, Germany	(?) Apple			Hull, Yorkshire	
7656	Apple	Harris	1812	?, Germany			Rosalia (Rosetta) Nathan	Hull, Yorkshire	furrier
20908	Apple	Julia	1850	?Hull, Yorkshire	Harris Apple	Rosalia (Rosetta) Nathan		Hull, Yorkshire	
7704	Apple	Rosalia (Rosetta)	1818	?, Germany	Solomon Nathan		Harris Apple	Hull, Yorkshire	
27210	Appleby	John	1838	Mile End, London	(?) Appleby	Rebecca Myers		Limehouse, London	scholar
27209	Appleby	Rebecca	1821	Spitalfields, London	George Myers	Abigail (?)	(?) Appleby	Limehouse, London	tambour worker
27722	Applemoss	Anne	1850	Whitechapel, London	Bares Applemoss	Phoebe (Fridey) Horn		Spitalfields, London	
27719	Applemoss	Bares	1810	?	Judah Applemoss		(?)	Spitalfields, London	
27721	Applemoss	Henry	1849	Whitechapel, London	Bares Applemoss	Phoebe (Fridey) Horn		Spitalfields, London	
27720	Applemoss	Lyons	1848	Whitechapel, London	Bares Applemoss	Phoebe (Fridey) Horn		Spitalfields, London	
27718	Applemoss	Phoebe (Fridey)	1815	?, Poland	Judah Horn		(?)	Spitalfields, London	dealer in clothes

ID	surname	given names	born	birthplace	father	mother	spouse 1	1851 residence	1851 occupation
14353	Appleton	Abraham	1823	?, Poland [?, Prussia]			Lenia (?)	Manchester	cap maker
14354	Appleton	Lenia	1827	?, Poland [?, Prussia]	(?)		Abraham Appleton	Manchester	cap maker
14355	Appleton	Mary	1850	Manchester	Abraham Appleton	Lenia (?)		Manchester	
23577	Arends	Charles	1819	Hanover, Germany			Margaret (?)	Liverpool	commission merchant
23578	Arends	Margaret	1824	Hanover, Germany	(?)		Charles Arends	Liverpool	
13657	Arensberg	Henry	1846	Manchester	Julius Arensberg	Rika (?)		Manchester	
13655	Arensberg	Julius	1809	?, Germany			Rika (?)	Manchester	cigar merchant
13656	Arensberg	Rika	1817	?, Germany	(?)		Julius Arensberg	Manchester	
17293	Arnsberg	John	1832	?, Russia				Spitalfields, London	glazier
15171	Arons	?Elizabeth	1767	?	(?)		(?) Arons	Shoreditch, London	
15173	Arons	Debrah	1847	Shoreditch, London	Simon Arons	Rachel (?)		Shoreditch, London	
15174	Arons	George	1849	Shoreditch, London	Simon Arons	Rachel (?)		Shoreditch, London	
15172	Arons	Isaac	1844	Shoreditch, London	Simon Arons	Rachel (?)		Shoreditch, London	
15170	Arons	Rachel	1829	Elephant & Castle, London	(?)		Simon Arons	Shoreditch, London	scholar at home
15169	Arons	Simon	1818	Whitechapel, London		?Elizabeth (?)	Rachel (?)	Shoreditch, London	general dealer
18477	Aronson	Betsy	1850	St Giles, London	(?) Aronson			Bloomsbury, London	
26467	Aronson	Charles Henry	1845	Bangor, Wales	John Aronson	Maria Lazarus		Bangor, Wales	
26470	Aronson	David	1850	Bangor, Wales	John Aronson	Maria Lazarus		Bangor, Wales	
7437	Aronson	Eliza (Elizabeth) Mary Anne	1840	Bangor, Wales	John Aronson	Maria Lazarus	Abraham Berens	Bangor, Wales	
26465	Aronson	Emilia Louisa	1842	Bangor, Wales	John Aronson	Maria Lazarus		Bangor, Wales	
26471	Aronson	Frederick	1851	Bangor, Wales	John Aronson	Maria Lazarus		Bangor, Wales	
26468	Aronson	George	1847	Bangor, Wales	John Aronson	Maria Lazarus		Bangor, Wales	
7436	Aronson	John	1807	Wągrowiec, Poland [Wongrovitz, Prussia]	Aharon		Maria Lazarus	Bangor, Wales	jeweller + draper
26463	Aronson	Julia	1838	Bangor, Wales	John Aronson	Maria Lazarus		Bangor, Wales	
26464	Aronson	Lewis Henry	1841	Bangor, Wales	John Aronson	Maria Lazarus	Leah Barnard	Bangor, Wales	
3464	Aronson	Maria	1812	Aldgate, London	Lewis Henry Lazarus	Elizabeth (Eliza) Aaron	John Aronson	Bangor, Wales	
18476	Aronson	Samson	1843	?, Holland				Bloomsbury, London	
26466	Aronson	Saul	1844	Bangor, Wales	John Aronson	Maria Lazarus		Bangor, Wales	
20283	Aronstein	Salmon	1831	?, Russia	Salomon Moses	Jetta Todorno		Spitalfields, London	artist
24941	Arrobus	Abraham	1791	Altona, Germany	Moses Arrobas		Rachel de Samuel Suhami	Bethnal Green, London	general dealer
24945	Arrobus	Harriett	1835	Bethnal Green, London	Abraham de Moses Arrobus	Rachel de Samuel Suhami		Bethnal Green, London	
24943	Arrobus	Morris (Moses)	1830	Bethnal Green, London	Abraham de Moses Arrobus	Rachel de Samuel Suhami	Fanny Mendoza	Bethnal Green, London	cabinet maker
24942	Arrobus	Rachel	1792	Whitechapel, London	Samuel Suhami	Ribca de Jacob Da Silva Porto	Abraham Arrobus	Bethnal Green, London	
24944	Arrobus	Samuel	1834	Bethnal Green, London	Abraham de Moses Arrobus	Rachel de Samuel Suhami	Sarah Hyman	Bethnal Green, London	
14067	Arstall	Mary	1847	Manchester	(?) Arstall			Manchester	
19094	Ascher	Abraham	1831	City, London	Simon A Ascher	Eva (?)		Manchester	
19096	Ascher	Bella (Isabella)	1836	City, London	Simon A Ascher	Eva (?)	Abraham Bensabat	Aldgate, London	
7765	Ascher	Benjamin Henry (Hyam)	1812	Poznan, Poland [Pizern, Posen]	Moses Ascher		Hannah Messeena	Aldgate, London	reader to Synagogue
19093	Ascher	Eva	1809	?, Germany	(?)	Louisa (?)	Simon A Ascher	Aldgate, London	
19097	Ascher	Flora	1837	City, London	Simon A Ascher	Eva (?)		Aldgate, London	

ID	surname	given names	born	birthplace	father	mother	spouse 1	1851 residence	1851 occupation
7766	Ascher	Hannah	1825	City, London	John Nathaniel Messeena	Rachel Gomes	Benjamin Henry (Hyam) Ascher	Aldgate, London	
7764	Ascher	Joseph	1829	Groningen, Holland	Simon Ascher	Eva (?)		Aldgate, London	music composer + pianist
7767	Ascher	Moses Morris)	1850	Aldgate, London	Benjamin Hyam Ascher	Hannah Messeena		Aldgate, London	
18715	Ascher	Rachael	1848	Aldgate, London	Benjamin Hyam Ascher	Hannah Messeena		Aldgate, London	
19095	Ascher	Selkel	1834	City, London	Simon A Ascher	Eva (?)		Aldgate, London	
19092	Ascher	Simon A	1796	?, Poland [?, Prussia]	Moses Ascher		Eva (?)	Aldgate, London	Reader to Synagogue
1417	Aschfield	Aaron	1811	?, Germany			Sarai	Plymouth, Devon	teacher of languages
22280	Ascoli	Augustus	1848	?Whitechapel, London	Augustus (Abraham) Ascoli	Clara Nunez		Whitechapel, London	
22277	Ascoli	Augustus (Abraham)	1823	?, France	Joseph Ascoli		Clara Nunez	Whitechapel, London	cigar maker
22278	Ascoli	Clara	1819	Mile End, London	Moses Nunez	Sarah (?)	Augustus (Abraham) Ascoli	Whitechapel, London	
14991	Ascoli	Esther	1843	Whitechapel, London	Moses Ascoli	Elizabeth Lee (Levy)	Jonas Vaz Martines	Bethnal Green, London	boarding school pupil
14987	Ascoli	Jane (Jeanette)	1841	Aldgate, London	Moses Ascoli	Elizabeth Lee (Levy)	James MacCarthy	Bethnal Green, London	boarding school pupil
22279	Ascoli	Joseph	1845	?Whitechapel, London	Augustus (Abraham) Ascoli	Clara Nunez		Whitechapel, London	
4273	Ash	Bernard	1850	Birmingham	Joseph Ash	Rosiwia (?)		Birmingham	
4271	Ash	Elizabeth	1846	Birmingham	Joseph Ash	Rosiwia (?)	David Tobias	Birmingham	
4272	Ash	Emily	1847	Birmingham	Joseph Ash	Rosiwia (?)		Birmingham	
4269	Ash	Joseph	1812	?, Poland [?, Prussia]			Rosiwia (?)	Birmingham	clothier
4270	Ash	Rosiwia	1821	?, Poland [?, Prussia]			Joseph Ash	Birmingham	
7499	Ashenheim	Charles	1828	Edinburgh, Scotland	Jacob Ashenheim	Matilda Aaron		Edinburgh, Scotland	surgeon
7705	Ashenheim	Jacob	1787	Poznan, Poland [Posen, Prussia]	Joseph Ashenheim	Jane (?)	Matilda (?)	Edinburgh, Scotland	jeweller master empl 1
7500	Ashenheim	Lewis	1816	Edinburgh, Scotland	Jacob Ashenheim	Matilda Aaron		Edinburgh, Scotland	physician
17022	Ashenheim	Matilda	1791	?, Poland [Shilank, Prussia]	(?) Aaron		Jacob Ashenheim	Edinburgh, Scotland	jeweller master empl 1
7498	Ashenheim	Michael	1824	?Edinburgh, Scotland	Jacob Ashenheim	Matilda Aaron		Edinburgh, Scotland	
12955	Asher	Alice (Ailsey, Elsey)	1801	Spitalfields, London	Abraham Jacobs		Henry Asher	Spitalfields, London	general dealer
22511	Asher	Andrew	1793	Middlesex, London	Benjamin Asher		Rosetta Joseph	Whitechapel, London	perfumer
7029	Asher	Asher	1814	Wapping, London	Isaac Benjamin Asher	Mary Moses	Jane (?)	Holborn, London	clerk
7007	Asher	Asher	1836	Glasgow, Scotland	Philip Asher	Hannah (?)	Lucy Garcia	Glasgow, Scotland	student
4274	Asher	Benjamin	1779	?, London			Lydia (?)	Birmingham	
12956	Asher	Benjamin	1830	Finsbury, London	Henry Asher	Alice (Ailsey) Jacobs		Spitalfields, London	cigar maker
19276	Asher	Benjamin	1843	Holborn, London	Asher Asher	Jane (?)		Holborn, London	
6736	Asher	Benjamin Henry	1799	Amsterdam, Holland			Rayner Jacobs	Wapping, London	glass importer
28858	Asher	David	1817	Wapping, London			Sarah Cohen	Spitalfields, London	hatter
28861	Asher	Deborah	1850	Spitalfields, London	David Asher	Sarah Cohen		Spitalfields, London	
20518	Asher	Diana	1836	?, London	Isaac Benjamin Asher	Mary Moses	Abraham Allport	St Helier, Jersey, Channel Islands	
12957	Asher	Elizabeth (Eliza)	1831	Spitalfields, London	Henry Asher	Alice (Ailsey) Jacobs	David Jacobs	Spitalfields, London	tailoress
20517	Asher	Esther	1833	?, London	Isaac Benjamin Asher	Mary Moses	George Goldstein	St Helier, Jersey, Channel Islands	
12962	Asher	Esther	1840	Spitalfields, London	Henry Asher	Alice (Ailsey) Jacobs	Joseph Fernandes	Spitalfields, London	cap maker
7008	Asher	Hannah	1814	Amsterdam, Holland	Naftali		Philip Asher	Glasgow, Scotland	

ID	surname	given names	born	birthplace	father	mother	spouse 1	1851 residence	1851 occupation
21429	Asher	Hannah	1827	Nottingham, Nottinghamshire	Joseph Asher	Margaret (?)		Nottingham, Nottinghamshire	mender of lace
12959	Asher	Henry	1834	Shoreditch, London	Henry Asher	Alice (Ailsey) Jacobs		Spitalfields, London	cigar maker
20913	Asher	Herty	1850	Glasgow, Scotland	Asher Asher	Hannah (?)		Glasgow, Scotland	
19744	Asher	Isaac Benjamin	1782	?, London			Mary Moses	St Helier, Jersey, Channel Islands	salesman, clothier + pawnbroker
7030	Asher	Jane	1820	Marylebone, London			Asher Asher	Holborn, London	
12961	Asher	Jane	1839	Spitalfields, London	Henry Asher	Alice (Ailsey) Jacobs		Spitalfields, London	tailoress
21430	Asher	John	1828	Nottingham, Nottinghamshire	Joseph Asher	Margaret (?)		Nottingham, Nottinghamshire	white smith
21427	Asher	Joseph	1797	Ashby de la Zouche, Leicestershire			Margaret (?)	Nottingham, Nottinghamshire	journeyman tailor
15124	Asher	Joseph	1818	Stepney, London			Annis Soppitt	Haggerston, London	general dealer
21431	Asher	Joseph	1831	Nottingham, Nottinghamshire	Joseph Asher	Margaret (?)		Nottingham, Nottinghamshire	turner of wood
24392	Asher	Joseph	1831	?, Poland				Soho, London	cap maker
12963	Asher	Julia	1841	Spitalfields, London	Henry Asher	Alice (Ailsey) Jacobs		Spitalfields, London	scholar
28584	Asher	Julia	1841	?Spitalfields, London	Abraham Asher	Jeanette (Jenetta) Solomon		Spitalfields, London	
4275	Asher	Lydia	1781	?, London			Benjamin Asher	Birmingham	
22513	Asher	M---	1820	Middlesex, London	Andrew Asher	Rosetta (Rosa) Joseph		Whitechapel, London	
21428	Asher	Margaret	1792	Loughborough, Leicestershire	(?)		Joseph Asher	Nottingham, Nottinghamshire	
22514	Asher	Maria	1824	Stepney, London	Andrew Asher	Rosetta (Rosa) Joseph		Whitechapel, London	
20516	Asher	Mary	1792	?, London	Emanuel Moses	Dinah (?)	Isaac Benjamin Asher	St Helier, Jersey, Channel Islands	
21432	Asher	Mary	1836	Nottingham, Nottinghamshire	Joseph Asher	Margaret (?)		Nottingham, Nottinghamshire	lace mender
7031	Asher	Mary	1845	Holborn, London	Asher Asher	Jane (?)		Holborn, London	
28860	Asher	Moses	1846	Spitalfields, London	David Asher	Sarah Cohen		Spitalfields, London	
7009	Asher	Philip	1801	Lublin, Poland	Zev Wolf		Hannah (?)	Glasgow, Scotland	furrier
14164	Asher	Rachel	1772	Liverpool	(?) Stiebel		Joseph Asher	Manchester	
6737	Asher	Rayner	1800	Mile End, London	(?) Jacobs	(?Hannah Hart)	Benjamin Henry Asher	Wapping, London	
6741	Asher	Rebecca	1830	Whitechapel, London	Benjamin Henry Asher	Rayner Jacobs	Emanuel Davis	Wapping, London	
12958	Asher	Rebecca	1833	Spitalfields, London	Henry Asher	Alice (Ailsey) Jacobs	Isaac Garcia	Spitalfields, London	tailoress
6500	Asher	Rebecca	1837	Bristol	(?) Asher	(?) Aaron	Solomon Levy Green	Birmingham	
20911	Asher	Rebecca Amelia	1840	Glasgow, Scotland	Asher Asher	Hannah (?)		Glasgow, Scotland	
20912	Asher	Rosetta	1842	Glasgow, Scotland	Asher Asher	Hannah (?)		Glasgow, Scotland	
22512	Asher	Rosetta (Rosa)	1796	Shoreditch, London	Joseph Schneider		Andrew Asher	Whitechapel, London	
28859	Asher	Sarah	1820	Mile End, London	(?) Cohen		David Asher	Spitalfields, London	
12960	Asher	Sarah	1837	?Shoreditch, London	Henry Asher	Alice (Ailsey) JacobsAlice (Ailsey) Jacobs		Spitalfields, London	tailoress
28121	Asher	Sarah (Sally)	1780	?, London	Wolf Opich Abrahams		Solomon Asher	Spitalfields, London	
28120	Asher	Solomon	1762	?, Holland	Asher Schneider		Sarah (Sally) Abrahams	Spitalfields, London	tailor
20519	Asher	Solomon	1830	?, London	Isaac Benjamin Asher	Mary Moses		St Helier, Jersey, Channel Islands	broker + outfitter

ID	surname	given names	born	birthplace	father	mother	spouse 1	1851 residence	1851 occupation
28583	Asher	Solomon	1837	?, London	Abraham Asher	Jeanette (Jenetta) Solomon		Spitalfields, London	apprentice to bootmaker
20910	Asher	Wiliam	1838	Glasgow, Scotland	Asher Asher	Hannah (?)		Glasgow, Scotland	
21433	Asher	William	1838	Nottingham, Nottinghamshire	Joseph Asher	Margaret (?)		Nottingham, Nottinghamshire	turner of wood
20350	Aspenheimer	Esther	1825	?, London	(?) Aspenheimer			Wapping, London	cook
27082	Assenheim	Aaron	1844	Whitechapel, London	Isadore (Isaac) Assenheim	Hannah (?)		Aldgate, London	scholar
27079	Assenheim	Charlotte	1836	Plymouth, Devon	Isadore (Isaac) Assenheim	Hannah (?)		Aldgate, London	parasol maker
27081	Assenheim	Esther	1840	Plymouth, Devon	Isadore (Isaac) Assenheim	Hannah (?)	Louis Levy	Aldgate, London	scholar
27083	Assenheim	Frances	1851	Aldgate, London	Isadore (Isaac) Assenheim	Hannah (?)		Aldgate, London	
27077	Assenheim	Hannah	1803	Dartmouth, Devon			Isadore (Isaac) Assenheim	Aldgate, London	hawker
27076	Assenheim	Isadore (Isaac)	1798	?, Holland			Hannah (?)	Aldgate, London	hawker
27078	Assenheim	Rachel	1834	Plymouth, Devon	Isadore (Isaac) Assenheim	Hannah (?)		Aldgate, London	shoe binder
27080	Assenheim	Sarah	1838	Plymouth, Devon	Isadore (Isaac) Assenheim	Hannah (?)	Nathan Benjamin	Aldgate, London	servant
23209	Asser	Adelaide	1791	Whitechapel, London	(?) Asser			Paddington, London	fundholder
23207	Asser	Ann	1836	Piccadilly, London	Solomon Asser	Eliza (?)		Paddington, London	
14907	Asser	Charles	1839	Croydon, Surrey				Bethnal Green, London	boarding school pupil
23876	Asser	Daniel Gotheil	1832	Soho, London	Louis Asser	Harriet (?)		Soho, London	clerk
23205	Asser	Edward	1831	Piccadilly, London	Solomon Asser	Eliza (?)		Paddington, London	assistant to artificial florist
23204	Asser	Eliza	1813	Holborn, London	(?)		Solomon Asser	Paddington, London	
23206	Asser	Ellen	1831	Piccadilly, London	Solomon Asser	Eliza (?)		Paddington, London	
23873	Asser	Harriet	1801	South Mimms, Hertfordhire	(?)		Louis Asser	Soho, London	
23211	Asser	Henry	1788	Whitechapel, London	(?) Asser			Paddington, London	annuitant
23874	Asser	Juliet	1828	Soho, London	Louis Asser	Harriet (?)		Soho, London	outfitter's shopwoman
23872	Asser	Louis	1797	Whitechapel, London			Harriet (?)	Soho, London	outfitter
23208	Asser	Louisa	1836	Piccadilly, London	Solomon Asser	Eliza (?)		Paddington, London	
23875	Asser	Louisa Elizabeth	1830	Soho, London	Louis Asser	Harriet (?)		Soho, London	governess
23877	Asser	Maria Sarah	1836	Soho, London	Louis Asser	Harriet (?)		Soho, London	
23210	Asser	Rachel	1797	Whitechapel, London	(?) Asser			Paddington, London	fundholder
23203	Asser	Solomon	1805	?, London			Eliza (?)	Paddington, London	rtificial florist
23878	Asser	William Walter	1838	Soho, London	Louis Asser	Harriet (?)		Soho, London	
30939	Assman	Mark	1828	?, Poland [?, Prussia]				Hull, Yorkshire	licensed hawker
4276	Assman	Polim	1829	?, Poland [?, Prussia]				Birmingham	hawker
26021	Assur	Leah	1787	Stockholm, Sweden	(?)		Moses Assur	Aldgate, London	
26020	Assur	Moses	1785	Stockholm, Sweden			Leah (?)	Aldgate, London	inspector of cattle
26022	Assur	Sarah	1826	Whitechapel, London	Moses Assur	Leah (?)	Alexander Friedlander	Aldgate, London	
4277	Aston	George	1819	?, Poland [?, Prussia]				Birmingham	traveller in watches
16934	Auerbach	Elijah	1831	?, Poland				Sheffield, Yorkshire	hawker
16302	Auerbach	Ezekiel Caspar	1800	?, Germany				?Inverness, Scotland	
9944	Ayling	Rebecca (Jane)	1821	?, England	Samuel Ayling		Henry Barnard	Brighton, Sussex	
21055	Azuelos	Abraham	1838	?Middlesex, London	Judah Azuelos	Hannah (?)		Aldgate, London	boarding school pupil
29638	Azuelos	Clara	1836	Middlesex, London	Judah Azuelos	Hannah (?)	Joseph Haliva	Aldgate, London	
21036	Azuelos	Hasday A	1842	?Middlesex, London	Judah Azuelos	Hannah (?)		Aldgate, London	boarding school pupil
29637	Azuelos	Judah	1805	Gibraltar	Judah de Salom Azuelos	Clara de Hazday Almosnino	Hanah (?)	Aldgate, London	merchant
29639	Azuelos	Rachel (Dona)	1840	Middlesex, London	Judah Azuelos	Hannah (?)	Elias Haim Lindo	Aldgate, London	

ID	surname	given names	born	birthplace	father	mother	spouse 1	1851 residence	1851 occupation
25487	Azulay	Bella	1791	?, Germany	(?)		Isaac Azulay	Tower Hill, London	stall keeper
24502	Azulay	Bella Elizabeth	1851	Rotherhithe, London	Bondy (Yomtob) Azulay	Catherine Moses		Rotherhithe, London	
24497	Azulay	Bondy (Yomtob)	1813	Hamburg, Germany	Isaac Azulay		Catherine Moses	Rotherhithe, London	publisher + patentee
24498	Azulay	Catherine	1813	Middlesex, London	Emanuel Moses	Dinah (?)	Bondy (Yomtob) Azulay	Rotherhithe, London	
24501	Azulay	Doris T	1848	Rotherhithe, London	Bondy (Yomtob) Azulay	Catherine Moses		Rotherhithe, London	
30776	Azulay	Isaac	1845	Aldgate, London	Maurice (Moses) Azulay	Rachel Matilda Nunes Lara	Clara Isaac Susskind	Whitechapel, London	
24500	Azulay	Isaac Leon	1845	Rotherhithe, London	Bondy (Yomtob) Azulay	Catherine Moses	Sarah (?)	Rotherhithe, London	scholar
30774	Azulay	Maurice (Moses)	1814	?, Germany	Isaac Leon Azulay		Rachel Matilda Nunes Lara	Whitechapel, London	umbrella maker
24499	Azulay	Rachel	1843	Bermondsey, London	Bondy (Yomtob) Azulay	Catherine Moses		Rotherhithe, London	scholar
30775	Azulay	Rachel Matilda	1805	Whitechapel	Aaron Nunes Lara	Leah (?)	Maurice (Moses) Azulay	Whitechapel, London	umbrella maker
25488	Azulay	Yetta	1821	?, Germany	Isaac Azulay	Bella (?)		Tower Hill, London	stall keeper
18191	Babel	Nathan	1787	?, Poland			(?)	Mile End, London	teacher
16849	Bach	Fanny Laura	1851	Sheffield, Yorkshire	Henry Bach	Zillah (?)		Sheffield, Yorkshire	
5122	Bach	Helen Ada	1847	Sheffield, Yorkshire	Henry Bach	Zillah (?)	(?) Wild	Sheffield, Yorkshire	
5120	Bach	Henry	1821	Birmingham			Zillah (?)	Sheffield, Yorkshire	gentleman's mercer
5121	Bach	Zilla	1821	Middlesex, London			Henry Bach	Sheffield, Yorkshire	
16214	Bachrach	Rosa	1818	Holstein, Germany	Baruch Bachrach		Nehemias Joseph Alexander	Finsbury, London	governess
1742	Bademir	Ernst	1829	Saxony, Germany				Swansea, Wales	gentleman
27905	Baek	Betsey	1849	City, London	Lewis Baek	Miriam (?)		Spitalfields, London	
27903	Baek	Caroline	1843	?, Poland	Lewis Baek	Miriam (?)		Spitalfields, London	scholar
27904	Baek	Hannah	1847	?, Poland	Lewis Baek	Miriam (?)		Spitalfields, London	
27902	Baek	Jonathan	1842	?, Poland	Lewis Baek	Miriam (?)		Spitalfields, London	scholar
27900	Baek	Lewis	1820	?, Poland			Miriam (?)	Spitalfields, London	glazier
27901	Baek	Miriam	1818	?, Poland	(?)		Lewis Baek	Spitalfields, London	glazier
27906	Baek	Moses	1850	City, London	Lewis Baek	Miriam (?)		Spitalfields, London	
14996	Baer	Moses	1829	?, Poland [?, Prussian Poland]				Bethnal Green, London	printer
4278	Balden	Gershon	1833	?, Belgium				Birmingham	traveller in jewellery
8980	Ballin	Emma	1841	Bristol	Isaac Ballin	Frances Sarah (?)		Bristol	scholar at home
8982	Ballin	Frances (Fanny)	1835	Bristol	Isaac Ballin	Frances Sarah (?)	Emanuel Samuel	Bristol	scholar at home
8978	Ballin	Isaac	1812	Wells, Somerset	(Jacob?) Ballin		Frances Sarah (?)	Bristol	furrier, straw hat + bonnet manufacturer
8981	Ballin	Jacob S	1848	Bristol	Isaac Ballin	Frances Sarah (?)		Bristol	scholar at home
8979	Ballin	Marian	1838	Bristol	Isaac Ballin	Frances Sarah (?)		Bristol	scholar at home
28599	Balson	Abraham	1846	Spitalfields, London	Moses Balson	Zephiah (?)		Spitalfields, London	scholar
28596	Balson	Israel	1838	Spitalfields, London	Moses Balson	Zephiah (?)		Spitalfields, London	scholar
28597	Balson	Leah	1840	Whitechapel, London	Moses Balson	Zephiah (?)		Spitalfields, London	scholar
28601	Balson	Mark	1850	Spitalfields, London	Moses Balson	Zephiah (?)		Spitalfields, London	
28600	Balson	Michael	1848	Whitechapel, London	Moses Balson	Zephiah (?)		Spitalfields, London	
28594	Balson	Moses	1815	Whitechapel, London			Zephiah (?)	Spitalfields, London	general dealer
28598	Balson	Robina	1844	Whitechapel, London	Moses Balson	Zephiah (?)		Spitalfields, London	scholar
28595	Balson	Zephiah	1814	Aldgate, London	(?)		Moses Balson	Spitalfields, London	
30340	Bamberg	Lewis	1851	Whitechapel, London	Samuel (Simon) Bamberg	Rachel Barnett		Whitechapel, London	
29815	Bamberg	Rachel	1825	Manchester	Godfrey Barnett		Samuel (Simon) Bamberg	Whitechapel, London	
29814	Bamberg	Samuel (Simon)	1813	?, Germany	Lemel Bamberg		Rachel Barnett	Whitechapel, London	furrier

ID	surname	given names	born	birthplace	father	mother	spouse 1	1851 residence	1851 occupation
25033	Bamberger	Abraham	1831	?, Germany	Simon Bamberger	Malche (?)		Clerkenwell, London	assistant in leather trade
25038	Bamberger	Amelia	1825	?, London	(?)		Elias Bamberger	Clerkenwell, London	
23971	Bamberger	Caroline	1841	Marylebone, London	Samuel Bamberger	Rachel Marks		Marylebone, London	
25414	Bamberger	David	1819	?, Germany	Simon Bamberger	Malche (?)	Rosa Mollerich	Holborn, London	leather merchant
25037	Bamberger	Elias	1823	?, Germany	Simon Bamberger	Malche (?)	Amelia (?)	Clerkenwell, London	leather merchant
25416	Bamberger	Gerson	1848	Holborn, London	David Bamberger	Rosa Mollerich		Holborn, London	
23972	Bamberger	John	1843	?Westminster, London	Samuel Bamberger	Rachel Marks		Marylebone, London	
25034	Bamberger	Joseph	1838	?, Germany	Simon Bamberger	Malche (?)		Clerkenwell, London	scholar
25040	Bamberger	Julia	1850	Clerkenwell, London	Elias Bamberger	Amelia (?)		Clerkenwell, London	
30341	Bamberger	Julius Lyon	1851	Haggerston, London	Elias Bamberger	Amelia (?)		Haggerston, London	
140	Bamberger	Katherine	1776	Paris, France			Simon Bamberger	Soho, London	
25036	Bamberger	Leon (Lyon)	1846	Clekenwell, London	Simon Bamberger	Malche (?)	Elizabeth Cohen	Clerkenwell, London	
25030	Bamberger	Malche	1807	?, Germany	(?)		Simon Bamberger	Clerkenwell, London	leather merchant
23970	Bamberger	Rachel	1819	Aldgate, London	(?) Marks	Sarah (?)	Samuel Bamberger	Marylebone, London	teacher
25032	Bamberger	Rachel	1827	?, Germany	Simon Bamberger	Malche (?)		Clerkenwell, London	
25039	Bamberger	Rachel	1848	Clerkenwell, London	Elias Bamberger	Amelia (?)		Clerkenwell, London	
25417	Bamberger	Rachel	1851	Holborn, London	David Bamberger	Rosa Mollerich		Holborn, London	
25031	Bamberger	Rochel	1825	?, Germany	Simon Bamberger	Malche (?)		Clerkenwell, London	
25415	Bamberger	Rosa	1821	?, Germany	(?) Mollerich		David Bamberger	Holborn, London	
25035	Bamberger	Rosine	1841	?, Germany	Simon Bamberger	Malche (?)		Clerkenwell, London	scholar
23973	Bamberger	Sarah	1847	Marylebone, London	Samuel Bamberger	Rachel Marks		Marylebone, London	
25029	Bamberger	Simon	1793	?, Germany			Malche (?)	Clerkenwell, London	leather merchant
27362	Bann	Angel	1811	?, London				Aldgate, London	gun maker
2358	Banofke	David	1826	Klaipeda, Lithuania [Memel, Prussia]				Hull, Yorkshire	
14989	Barchinski	Harriet	1843	Middlesex, London	(?) Barchinski			Bethnal Green, London	boarding school pupil
21625	Barclay	Esther	1850	Portsmouth, Hampshire	Wolf (William) Barclay	Phoebe Cohen		Brighton, Sussex	
21624	Barclay	Morris (Maurice)	1848	Aldgate, London	Wolf (William) Barclay	Phoebe Cohen	Miriam Shottlander	Brighton, Sussex	scholar
21621	Barclay	Phoebe	1824	?, Holland	Jacob Cohen		Wolf (William) Barclay	Brighton, Sussex	
21622	Barclay	Priscilla	1842	Sunderland, Co Durham	Wolf (William) Barclay	Phoebe Cohen		Brighton, Sussex	scholar
21623	Barclay	Samuel	1846	Liverpool	Wolf (William) Barclay	Phoebe Cohen	Hannah (?)	Brighton, Sussex	scholar
21620	Barclay	Wolf (William)	1815	?, Belgium	Abraham Barclay		Phoebe Cohen	Brighton, Sussex	hawker
12025	Barend	Elizabeth	1832	?, Germany	Simon Barend	Frances (?)		Haggerston, London	crochet worker
12023	Barend	Frances	1793	Aldgate, London	(?)		Simon Barend	Haggerston, London	haberdasher
12024	Barend	George	1825	Southwark, London	Simon Barend	Frances (?)		Haggerston, London	cigar maker
12026	Barend	Marian (Miriam)	1837	Southwark, London	Simon Barend	Frances (?)	Eleazer (Elhazar) Meldola	Haggerston, London	
13781	Barenstine	Louis	1829	?, London			Mary (?)	Manchester	dealer or hawker of jewellery
13782	Barenstine	Mary	1829	Manchester	(?)		Louis Barenstine	Manchester	housewife
13783	Barenstine	Sarah	1849	?, London			Mary (?)	Manchester	
4377	Baritz	Isaac	1830	?, Poland			Ruth (?)	Birmingham	cap-maker
4378	Baritz	Ruth	1831	?, Poland			Isaac Baritz	Birmingham	tailoress
10059	Barnard	Adelaide	1849	Elephant & Castle, London	Henry Barnard	Helena (Helen) Franks		Walworth, London	
10075	Barnard	Alfred Francis	1821	Norwich, Norfolk	Francis Barnard		Ann (Mary) Marks	Canonbury, London	general clerk to solicitor
8470	Barnard	Alice	1839	Portsmouth, Hampshire	George Barnard	Esther Isaac	Julius Michael Amsberg	Portsmouth, Hampshire	

ID	surname	given names	born	birthplace	father	mother	spouse 1	1851 residence	1851 occupation
9931	Barnard	Amelia	1823	Strand, London	Joseph Levy		Daniel Barnard	Chatham, Kent	
26790	Barnard	Ann	1850	?London	Morris Barnard	Henrietta (?)		Aldgate, London	cigar maker
10017	Barnard	Arthur	1850	Middlesex, London	Benedict Barnard	Bertha Solomons		Brixton, London	
10021	Barnard	Asher	1810	Canterbury, Kent	Daniel Barnard	Zipporah (Sippy) Levy	Hannah Salomons	Wapping, London	commercial traveller
9948	Barnard	Asher	1825	Rochester, Kent	Berman Issachar Barnard	Hannah Tobias	Rebecca Nathan	Ipswich, Suffolk	hardwareman
10050	Barnard	Asher (Alfred)	1835	Middlesex, London	Israel (Francis) Barnard	Elizabeth Cohen	Mary Ann (Sarah) Onions	Whitechapel, London	general dealer's assistant
10012	Barnard	Benedict	1821	Portsmouth, Hampshire	David Barnard	Rebecca Davids	Bertha Solomons	Brixton, London	silk manufacturer
8298	Barnard	Benjamin	1789	Canterbury, Kent	Daniel Barnard	Zipporah (Sippy) Levy	Caroline Abrahams	Canterbury, Kent	annuitant
10026	Barnard	Benjamin	1841	Aldgate, London	Asher Barnard	Hannah Salomons		Wapping, London	scholar
9951	Barnard	Benjamin	1849	Ipswich, Suffolk	Asher Barnard	Rebecca Nathan	Harriette Madson	Ipswich, Suffolk	
10047	Barnard	Berman Isacher	1842	Dover, Kent	David Barnard	Kate (Kitty) Nathan	Abigail Samuel	Gravesend, Kent	boarding school pupil
10013	Barnard	Bertha	1824	Middlesex, London	(?) Solomons		Benedict Barnard	Brixton, London	
8299	Barnard	Caroline	1787	Canterbury, Kent	(?) Abrahams		Benjamin Barnard	Canterbury, Kent	
10058	Barnard	Caroline	1846	Middlesex, London	Henry Barnard	Helena (Helen) Franks		Walworth, London	
3884	Barnard	Catharine (Kate)	1826	Norwich, Norfolk	Mordecai Barnard	Elizabeth (?)	Coleman Joel	Spitalfields, London	fur sewing
10080	Barnard	Catherine	1794	Southwark, London	(?)		Joseph Benjamin Barnard	Brighton, Sussex	
18312	Barnard	Cecilia	1819	?, Russia	(?) Barnard	Syephia (?)		Cambridge	
9936	Barnard	Charles Daniel	1851	Chatham, Kent	Daniel Barnard	Amelia Levy	Deborah Levy	Chatham, Kent	
24072	Barnard	Clara F	1819	Portsmouth, Hampshire	(?David) Barnard			Regent's Park, London	
9953	Barnard	Daniel	1816	Rochester, Kent	Berman Issachar Barnard	Hannah Tobias	Rosetta Solomon	Rochester, Kent	
4279	Barnard	Daniel	1822	Whitechapel, London	Israel Barnard	Elizabeth Cohen	Hannah Cohen	Birmingham	cigar dealer
9930	Barnard	Daniel	1824	Chatham, Kent	Samuel Barnard	Louisa Benjamin	Amelia Levy	Chatham, Kent	victualler
9958	Barnard	Daniel	1847	Dover, Kent	David Barnard	Kitty (Kate) Nathan	Rebecca Rose	Dover, Kent	
9952	Barnard	Daniel	1850	Ipswich, Suffolk	Asher Barnard	Rebecca Nathan	Fanny Michaelson	Ipswich, Suffolk	
10025	Barnard	Daniel (Don)	1839	Aldgate, London	Asher Barnard	Hannah Salomons	Flora Salomons	Wapping, London	scholar
9955	Barnard	David	1818	Rochester, Kent	Berman Issachar Barnard	Hannah Tobias	Kitty (Kate) Nathan	Dover, Kent	fancy repository
10015	Barnard	David	1846	Middlesex, London	Benedict Barnard	Bertha Solomons		Brixton, London	
26507	Barnard	David	1847	Dover, Kent				Dover, Kent	
8466	Barnard	Eliza	1833	Portsmouth, Hampshire	George Barnard	Esther Isaac	Bezaliel Gollin	Portsmouth, Hampshire	
9962	Barnard	Elizabeth	1798	Middlesex, London	Baruch HaCohen		Israel (Francis) Barnard	Whitechapel, London	
3883	Barnard	Elizabeth	1803	?, Poland			Mordecai Barnard	Spitalfields, London	
9963	Barnard	Ella (Elizabeth, Ellen)	1818	?, Warwickshire	Israel (Francis) Barnard	Elizabeth Cohen		Whitechapel, London	dressmaker
9967	Barnard	Emanuel (Edward)	1823	Whitechapel, London	Israel (Francis) Barnard	Elizabeth Cohen	Frances Myers	Wapping, London	dealer
8464	Barnard	Esther	1807	Portsmouth, Hampshire	(?) Isaac		George Barnard	Portsmouth, Hampshire	
9946	Barnard	Esther	1822	Rochester, Kent	Berman Issachar Barnard	Hannah Tobias	Edward Nathan	Brighton, Sussex	
8485	Barnard	Esther	1851	Portsmouth, Hampshire	Alexander Bernard Barnard	Phoebe Moses		Portsmouth, Hampshire	
9959	Barnard	Fanny (Jeanette)	1849	Dover, Kent	David Barnard	Kitty (Kate) Nathan		Dover, Kent	
10076	Barnard	Frances	1819	Norwich, Norfolk	Francis Barnard			Canonbury, London	governess
10073	Barnard	Frances	1827	Whitechapel, London	Michael Abrahams		Joel Morris Barnard	Spitalfields, London	
9968	Barnard	Frances	1828	Southwark, London	Michael Myers		Emanuel Barnard	Wapping, London	
10077	Barnard	Francis	1797	Norwich, Norfolk			?	Canonbury, London	fundholder
10056	Barnard	Frederick	1843	?Middlesex, London	Henry Barnard	Helena (Helen) Franks	Hannah Davis	Walworth, London	
8463	Barnard	George	1803	Portsmouth, Hampshire	David Barnard	Rebecca (?)	Esther Isaac	Portsmouth, Hampshire	ship breaker + timber merchant

ID	surname	given names	born	birthplace	father	mother	spouse 1	1851 residence	1851 occupation
8473	Barnard	George	1848	Portsmouth, Hampshire	George Barnard	Esther Isaac		Portsmouth, Hampshire	
18314	Barnard	H---	1825	?, Russia	(?) Barnard	Syephia (?)		Cambridge	
9942	Barnard	Hannah	1798	Middlesex, London	Yehuda Leib Tobias		Berman Isaachar Barnard	Brighton, Sussex	china + general dealer
10022	Barnard	Hannah	1817	Aldgate, London	Lyon Salomons	Ann (Nancy) Hart	Asher Barnard	Wapping, London	
4280	Barnard	Hannah	1825	?, London	Emanuel (Menachem) Cohen		Daniel Barnard	Birmingham	
10054	Barnard	Hannah	1838	Middlesex, London	Henry Barnard	Helena (Helen) Franks	David Davis	Walworth, London	
10061	Barnard	Hannah	1851	Dover, Kent	David Barnard	Kate Nathan		Dover, Kent	
10053	Barnard	Helena (Helen)	1815	Gothenburg, Sweden	David Franks	Caroline (?)	Henry Barnard	Walworth, London	
26789	Barnard	Henrietta	1829	?, Germany	(?)		Morris Barnard	Aldgate, London	
10052	Barnard	Henry	1810	Middlesex, London	Moses Barnard	Betsy Isaacs	Helena (Helen) Franks	Walworth, London	umbrella maker
9943	Barnard	Henry	1818	?Hastings, Sussex	Berman Issachar Barnard	Hannah Tobias	Rebecca (Jane) Ayling	Brighton, Sussex	china + general dealer
9971	Barnard	Henry	1830	Middlesex, London	Israel Barnard	Elizabeth Cohen	Jeanette (Janet) Jacob	Manchester	
10066	Barnard	Henry	1834	Whitechapel, London				Wapping, London	fruiterer
10033	Barnard	Henry Benjamin	1834	Chatham, Kent	Samuel Barnard	Louisa Benjamin	Julia (Leah) Harris	Aldgate, London	
18313	Barnard	Isaac	1821	?, Russia	(?) Barnard	Syephia (?)		Cambridge	mariner
9961	Barnard	Israel (Francis)	1796	?, Kent	Daniel Barnard	Sippy (Zipporah) Levy	Elizabeth Cohen	Whitechapel, London	general dealer
9950	Barnard	Issachar	1848	Ipswich, Suffolk	Asher Barnard	Rebecca Nathan		Ipswich, Suffolk	
4311	Barnard	Jacob	1802	Canterbury, Kent	Daniel Barnard	Zipporah (Sippy) Levy	Kitty (Jetta) Jacobs	Birmingham	clothes dealer
18237	Barnard	Jacob	1823	?, Poland				Cheltenham, Gloucestershire	traveller
10028	Barnard	Jacob (John)	1847	Wapping, London	Asher Barnard	Hannah Salomons	Gertrude Deborah Levy	Wapping, London	
10072	Barnard	Joel Morris	1822	Norwich, Norfolk	Mordecai Barnard		Frances Abrahams	Spitalfields, London	attorney's clerk
9933	Barnard	Joseph	1848	Chatham, Kent	Daniel Barnard	Amelia Levy		Chatham, Kent	
10079	Barnard	Joseph Benjamin	1799	Brighton, Sussex			Catherine (?)	Brighton, Sussex	journeyman cordwainer
10019	Barnard	Julia	1818	Portsmouth, Hampshire	David Barnard	Rebecca Davids	Zander Alexander	Brixton, London	gentlewoman
10016	Barnard	Julia	1848	Middlesex, London	Benedict Barnard	Bertha Solomons	(?) Hill	Brixton, London	
9947	Barnard	Kate (Katharine)	1826	Rochester, Kent	Berman Issachar Barnard	Hannah Tobias	Louis Defries	Brighton, Sussex	
8422	Barnard	Kate (Kitty)	1830	?, London	Lyon Barnard	Kitty (?)		Portsmouth, Hampshire	straw bonnet
8421	Barnard	Kitty	1804	Falmouth, Cornwall	(?)		Lyon Barnard	Portsmouth, Hampshire	lodgehousekeeper
9964	Barnard	Kitty	1821	?, Kent	Israel (Francis) Barnard	Elizabeth Cohen		Whitechapel, London	domestic
4312	Barnard	Kitty (Jetta, Catharine)	1800	?, Poland	(?) ?Jacobs		(?) ?Jacobs	Birmingham	
9956	Barnard	Kitty (Kate)	1816	Dover, Kent	Barnet Nathan	Julia (?)	David Barnard	Dover, Kent	
10063	Barnard	Leah	1828	?, London	Israel Barnard	Elizabeth Cohen	Samuel Barnett	Whitechapel, London	
8423	Barnard	Leah	1830	Portsmouth, Hampshire	Lyon Barnard	Kitty (?)		Portsmouth, Hampshire	dressmaker
3938	Barnard	Leah	1849	Portsmouth, Hampshire	Alexander Bernard Barnard	Phoebe Moses	Lewis Henry Aronson	Portsmouth, Hampshire	
8469	Barnard	Louis	1838	Portsmouth, Hampshire	George Barnard	Esther Isaac		Portsmouth, Hampshire	
8974	Barnard	Louisa	1798	Aldgate, London	(?) Benjamin		Samuel Barnard	Aldgate, London	general dealer + dealer in china, glass + hardware
8468	Barnard	Louisa (Leah)	1836	Portsmouth, Hampshire	George Barnard	Esther Isaac	Moritz Alexander	Portsmouth, Hampshire	
9934	Barnard	Lyon (Lewis) Benjamin	1850	Chatham, Kent	Daniel Barnard	Amelia Levy	Susanna (?)	Chatham, Kent	
10023	Barnard	Lyon (Lewis, Louis)	1837	Aldgate, London	Asher Barnard	Hannah Salomons	Ellen Melody	Wapping, London	cigar maker

ID	surname	given names	born	birthplace	father	mother	spouse 1	1851 residence	1851 occupation
9938	Barnard	Lyon (Lionel)	1829	Chatham, Kent	Samuel Barnard	Louisa Benjamin	Julia Emanuel	Waterloo, London	rag merchant + dealer in marine stores
28996	Barnard	M---	1827	?, Poland [?, Prussia]				Whitechapel, London	
5038	Barnard	Mary	1775	Frankfurt, Germany	(?)		Philip Barnard	Portsmouth, Hampshire	
10029	Barnard	Michael (Myer)	1849	Whitechapel, London	Asher Barnard	Hannah Salomons		Wapping, London	
3882	Barnard	Mordecai	1795	?, Poland			Elizabeth (?)	Spitalfields, London	general dealer
26788	Barnard	Morris	1828	?, Poland			Henrietta (?)	Aldgate, London	cigar maker
9945	Barnard	Moss (Henry)	1851	Brighton, Sussex	Henry Barnard	Rebecca (Jane) Ayling		Brighton, Sussex	
5037	Barnard	Philip	1766	Rochford, Essex			Mary (?)	Portsmouth, Hampshire	annuitant, formerly Sheriff's Officer
8471	Barnard	Philip	1843	Portsmouth, Hampshire	George Barnard	Esther Isaac		Portsmouth, Hampshire	
10055	Barnard	Rachel	1840	Middlesex, London	Henry Barnard	Helena (Helen) Franks		Walworth, London	
10018	Barnard	Rebecca	1782	Portsmouth, Hampshire	(?) Davids		David Barnard	Brixton, London	retired
9949	Barnard	Rebecca	1828	Dover, Kent	Barnet Nathan	Julia (?)	Asher Barnard	Ipswich, Suffolk	
8467	Barnard	Rebecca	1835	Portsmouth, Hampshire	George Barnard	Esther Isaac		Portsmouth, Hampshire	
3885	Barnard	Rebecca	1836	Spitalfields, London	Mordecai Barnard	Elizabeth (?)	Joshua Tournoff	Spitalfields, London	fur sewing
10027	Barnard	Reuben	1843	Canterbury, Kent	Asher Barnard	Hannah Salomons	Frances Beatrice Levy	Wapping, London	scholar
22431	Barnard	Richard	1847	?				Gravesend, Kent	boarding school pupil
9932	Barnard	Samuel	1846	Chatham, Kent	Daniel Barnard	Amelia Levy	Elizabeth Levy	Chatham, Kent	
10074	Barnard	Samuel G	1851	Whitechapel, London	Joel Morris Barnard	Frances Abrahams	Rebecca Samuel	Spitalfields, London	
9965	Barnard	Sarah	1829	Middlesex, London	Israel (Francis) Barnard	Elizabeth Cohen		Whitechapel, London	
3886	Barnard	Sarah	1839	Spitalfields, London	Mordecai Barnard	Elizabeth (?)		Spitalfields, London	
10057	Barnard	Sarah	1844	Middlesex, London	Henry Barnard	Helena (Helen) Franks	John Davis	Walworth, London	
10014	Barnard	Sarah	1845	Middlesex, London	Benedict Barnard	Bertha Solomons		Brixton, London	
8472	Barnard	Simeon	1845	Portsmouth, Hampshire	George Barnard	Esther Isaac	Janetta Lee	Portsmouth, Hampshire	
25629	Barnard	Solomon	1811	?			(?) Joseph	Dublin, Ireland	manufacturer of brushes, fancy sticks, umbrellas + japanned cloth
9957	Barnard	Solomon Lyon (Lionel) (Saul)	1844	Dover, Kent	David Barnard	Kitty (Kate) Nathan		Dover, Kent	
18311	Barnard	Syephia	1791	?, Russia	(?)		(?) Barnard	Cambridge	annuitant
8465	Barnard	William	1831	Portsmouth, Hampshire	George Barnard	Esther Isaac		Portsmouth, Hampshire	
10024	Barnard	Zipporah (Sophia)	1839	Whitechapel, London	Asher Barnard	Hannah Salomons	Carl Hillebrandt	Wapping, London	
3936	Barnard (Barnad)	Alexander Bernard	1821	Hull, Yorkshire	Barnard (Barnett) Barnard		Phoebe Moses	Portsmouth, Hampshire	jeweller
3935	Barnard (Barnad)	Bernard Alexander	1850	Portsmouth, Hampshire	Alexander Bernard Barnard (Barnad)	Phoebe Moses		Portsmouth, Hampshire	tobacco + toy (dealer)
3937	Barnard (Barnad)	Phoebe	1816	Portsmouth, Hampshire	Isaac Moses	Esther (?)	Alexander Bernard Barnard (Barnad)	Portsmouth, Hampshire	
16577	Barned	Amelia	1791	Portsmouth, Hampshire	(?)		Israel Barned	Liverpool	
16576	Barned	Israel	1779	Portsmouth, Hampshire			Amelia (?)	Liverpool	banker
25905	Barnet	Amelia	1819	?, Poland [?, Prussia]	(?)		Henry Barnet	Aldgate, London	
17483	Barnet	Barnet	1806	Whitechapel, London			(?) Lyons	Spitalfields, London	general dealer
19858	Barnet	Barnet	1823	?, Holland	Judah Barnett		Hannah Fernandez	Spitalfields, London	clothes dealer
6818	Barnet	Benjamin	1796	Spitalfields, London				Spitalfields, London	general dealer
29748	Barnet	Elijah	1815	Whitechapel, London				Aldgate, London	cabman

ID	surname	given names	born	birthplace	father	mother	spouse 1	1851 residence	1851 occupation
19862	Barnet	Esther	1848	Whitechapel, London	Barnet Barnet	Hannah Fernandez		Spitalfields, London	
19859	Barnet	Hannah	1813	Stepney, London	Jacob Fernandez	Rebecca de Joseph Abendana	Barnet Barnet	Spitalfields, London	
25904	Barnet	Henry	1811	?, Poland [?, Prussia]			Amelia (?)	Aldgate, London	jobbing glazier
29385	Barnet	Isaac	1832	Whitechapel, London				Wapping, London	shopman to clothier
25909	Barnet	Isaac	1849	?, Yorkshire	Henry Barnet	Amelia (?)		Aldgate, London	
18320	Barnet	Jacob	1832	?, Poland [?, Prussia]				Sheffield, Yorkshire	hawker
17485	Barnet	John	1840	Whitechapel, London	Barnet Barnet	(?) Lyons		Spitalfields, London	scholar
25906	Barnet	Joseph	1842	?, Poland [?, Prussia]	Henry Barnet	Amelia (?)		Aldgate, London	scholar
19863	Barnet	Judah Judah	1849	Whitechapel, London	Barnet Barnet	Hannah Fernandez		Spitalfields, London	
19860	Barnet	Julia	1842	Spitalfields, London	Barnet Barnet	Hannah Fernandez		Spitalfields, London	
9158	Barnet	Leopold	1833	Kalisz, Poland				Whitechapel, London	journeyman cap maker
8032	Barnet	Mary	1844	Sunderland, Co Durham	Behr Barnet		Isaac Joseph	?Sunderland, Co Durham	
17484	Barnet	Moss	1839	Whitechapel, London	Barnet Barnet	(?) Lyons		Spitalfields, London	scholar
19861	Barnet	Rebecca	1846	Whitechapel, London	Barnet Barnet	Hannah Fernandez		Spitalfields, London	scholar
25907	Barnet	Sarah	1844	?, Poland [?, Prussia]	Henry Barnett	Amelia (?)		Aldgate, London	scholar
1743	Barnet	Simon	1821	?, Poland [?, Prussia]				Swansea, Wales	hawker
25908	Barnet	William	1847	?, Poland [?, Prussia]	Henry Barnet	Amelia (?)		Aldgate, London	
30456	Barnet (Baruch)	Reuben	1791	?, Poland				Hanley, Staffordshire	pedlar
26568	Barnett	?	1851	Middlesex, London	Samuel Barnett	Frances (?)		Whitechapel, London	
11455	Barnett	Aaron	1785	Warsaw?, Poland			Sarah (?)	Aldgate, London	cap maker
25871	Barnett	Aaron	1843	Spitalfields, London	Samuel Barnett	Sarah (?)		Aldgate, London	scholar
19579	Barnett	Aaron	1850	?Whitechapel, London	Barnett Barnett	Esther Michaels		Whitechapel, London	
27147	Barnett	Aaron	1850	?Aldgate, London	Barnett Barnett	Catherine (Kitty) Jacobs		Aldgate, London	
22106	Barnett	Abigail	1785	Hull, Yorkshire	(?)		(?) Barnett	Whitechapel, London	parasol maker
28460	Barnett	Abigail	1791	Aldgate, London	(?)		Henry Barnett	Spitalfields, London	general dealer
28046	Barnett	Abigail	1846	Whitechapel, London	Samuel Barnett	Sarah (?)		Spitalfields, London	scholar
13837	Barnett	Abraham	1795	?, Poland [?, Prussia]			Hannah Abrahams	Manchester	print dealer
6370	Barnett	Abraham	1809	Middlesex, London	David Barnett		Caroline Lazarus	City, London	independent minister
2122	Barnett	Abraham	1810	?, Poland [Breschen, Prussia]			Hannah Canter	Hull, Yorkshire	dealer in clocks, fancy goods + antiques
17142	Barnett	Abraham	1818	Anderton?, Cheshire			Hannah Cantor	Stoke-on-Trent, Staffordshire	hawker
29546	Barnett	Abraham	1830	Spitalfields, London	Eleazer Barnett		Rebecca Coleman	Spitalfields, London	cigar manufacturer
3878	Barnett	Abraham	1832	Spitalfields, London	Judah Barnett	Julia Cohen	Eve Cohen	Spitalfields, London	general dealer
25918	Barnett	Abraham	1844	Aldgate, London	Asher Barnett	Kitty (Catharine) Barnett		Aldgate, London	scholar
28181	Barnett	Abraham	1848	Whitechapel, London	Barnet Barnett	Maria (Brynah) Franks		Spitalfields, London	
933	Barnett	Abraham	1849	Aldgate, London	Joshua Barnett	Nancy (Mary) Benjamin		Aldgate, London	
25873	Barnett	Abraham	1849	Spitalfields, London	Samuel Barnett	Sarah (?)		Aldgate, London	
21380	Barnett	Abraham	1850	Spitalfields, London	Barnett Barnett	Elizabeth (?)		Spitalfields, London	
17144	Barnett	Abraham	1851	Stoke-on-Trent, Staffordshire	Abraham Barnett	Hannah (?)		Stoke-on-Trent, Staffordshire	
6378	Barnett	Abraham (John)	1809	?, America	Mordecai Barnett	Judith (Julia) Abrahams nee Zinger	Mary (Polly, Miriam) Franks	Marylebone, London	dealer in clothes

ID	surname	given names	born	birthplace	father	mother	spouse 1	1851 residence	1851 occupation
8682	Barnett	Abraham Alfred	1832	?, Poland [?, Prussia]	Arie Leib (Ari Lev) Barnett	Charlotte (Sheindel) (?)	Julia Joshua	Aldgate, London	clerk to a clothier
18025	Barnett	Abram	1839	Chatham, Kent	Barnett Barnett	(?)		Chatham, Kent	scholar
8684	Barnett	Adelaide	1837	?, London	Arie Leib (Ari Lev) Barnett	Charlotte (Sheindel) (?)		Aldgate, London	scholar
19164	Barnett	Adelaide	1851	Haggerston, London	Henry Barnett	Dinah Phillips		Haggerston, London	
30285	Barnett	Albert	1842	Bristol				Soho, London	
33	Barnett	Albert	1846	?, Poland	Moses Barnett	Esther (?)		Aldgate, London	
11807	Barnett	Alexander	1838	Aldgate, London	Hyam (Hyman) Barnett	Sarah Hart	Isabella Jacobs	Whitechapel, London	scholar
28182	Barnett	Alexander	1850	Whitechapel, London	Barnet Barnett	Maria (Brynah) Franks		Spitalfields, London	
24193	Barnett	Alfred	1817	Stepney, London			Rebecca (?)	De Beauvoir, London	umbrella manufacturer
20490	Barnett	Alice	1849	Westminster, London	Bennet Barnett	Julia Davis		Soho, London	
3698	Barnett	Amelia	1809	Spitalfields, London			Henry Barnett	Spitalfields, London	waistcoat maker
20705	Barnett	Amelia	1843	Wapping, London	David Barnett	Harriet (Hannah) Myers		Whitechapel, London	scholar
28335	Barnett	Amelia	1847	Aldgate, London	Isaac Barnett	Maria (?)		Aldgate, London	
13827	Barnett	Amelia	1848	Manchester	Lewis Barnett	Sarah Mayers	Abraham Abadi	Manchester	
20704	Barnett	Andrew	1842	Wapping, London	David Barnett	Harriet (Hannah) Myers		Whitechapel, London	scholar
143	Barnett	Ann Nancy)	1822	Spitalfields, London	Morris Myers		Barnett Barnett	Whitechapel, London	
3715	Barnett	Anna	1849	Spitalfields, London	David Barnett	Maria (?)		Spitalfields, London	
4292	Barnett	Anne	1809	?, Poland			Joseph Barnett	Birmingham	
25265	Barnett	Annette (Jeannnette)	1850	Holborn, London	Gabriel Barnett	Phoebe Jacobs		Holborn, London	
8679	Barnett	Arie Leib (Ari Lev)	1798	Poznan, Poland [Krotoschin, Prussia]			Charlotte (Sheindel) (?)	Aldgate, London	Rabbi
11808	Barnett	Ariel	1845	Aldgate, London	Hyam (Hyman) Barnett	Elizabeth Samuel		Whitechapel, London	scholar
25913	Barnett	Asher	1817	Aldgate, London	Isaac Eizak		Kitty (Catharine) Barnett	Aldgate, London	pastry cook empl 2
2359	Barnett	Barnard (Barney, Barnet)	1840	Hull, Yorkshire	Abraham Barnett	Hannah Canter	Esther Moses	Hull, Yorkshire	scholar
19872	Barnett	Barnet	1812	Aldgate, London	(?) Barnett	Nancy (?)		Spitalfields, London	clothes dealer
28173	Barnett	Barnet	1815	Whitechapel, London	Mordecai Barnett	Judith (Julia) Abrahams nee Zinger	Maria (Brynah) Franks	Spitalfields, London	clothes dealer
30342	Barnett	Barnet	1851	Aldgate, London	Barnett Barnett	Ann (Nancy) Myers		Aldgate, London	
9337	Barnett	Barnett	1784	?, London				Aldgate, London	
18023	Barnett	Barnett	1795	Chatham, Kent			(?)	Chatham, Kent	watch maker
25755	Barnett	Barnett	1810	Aldgate, London	Michael Barnett		Phoebe Isaacs	Aldgate, London	clothes dealer
7960	Barnett	Barnett	1816	Whitechapel, London			Elizabeth (?)	Spitalfields, London	clothier
142	Barnett	Barnett	1817	Aldgate, London	Isaac Barnett		Ann (Nancy) Myers	Aldgate, London	furrier empl 6
7968	Barnett	Barnett	1821	Whitechapel, London	Henry (Aharon) Barnett		Esther Michaels	Whitechapel, London	grocer (empl 1 lad)
23050	Barnett	Barnett	1821	Manchester	Lazarus Barnett	Esther Aaron		Aldgate, London	general dealer
27146	Barnett	Barnett	1821	?, London	Aaron Barnett		Catherine (Kitty) Jacobs	Aldgate, London	
2894	Barnett	Barnett	1824	?, Poland	Isaac Barnett	Sifra (?)	Selina Stadthagen	Birmingham	general dealer
2	Barnett	Barnett	1826	Whitechapel, London	Moses Barnett	Dinah (?)	Henrietta Defries	Euston, London	commercial traveller + clothes dealer
30	Barnett	Barnett	1829	?, Poland	Moses Barnett	Esther (?)		Aldgate, London	furrier
3703	Barnett	Barnett	1839	Spitalfields, London	Henry Barnett	Amelia (?)		Spitalfields, London	
7959	Barnett	Barnett	1842	Aldgate, London	Reuben Barnett	Julia Aarons		Aldgate, London	scholar
27177	Barnett	Barnett	1844	?, London	(?) Barnett	Judy (?)		Aldgate, London	scholar

ID	surname	given names	born	birthplace	father	mother	spouse 1	1851 residence	1851 occupation
11191	Barnett	Barney	1822	Aldgate, London	Henry Barnett	Rachael (?)	Betsy (Elizabeth) Moses	Aldgate, London	general dealer
927	Barnett	Baron	1848	Aldgate, London	Joshua Barnett	Nancy (Mary) Benjamin	Agnes Nunes Martines (Martin)	Aldgate, London	
20706	Barnett	Baron (Barnard) David	1845	Wapping, London	David Barnett	Harriet (Hannah) Myers	Kate Myers	Whitechapel, London	scholar
8686	Barnett	Baron (Behrend)	1842	Middlesex, London	Arie Leib (Ari Lev) Barnett	Charlotte (Sheindel) (?)	Adelaide Cowen	Aldgate, London	scholar
8363	Barnett	Bearman	1838	Ramsgate, Kent	Israel Barnett	Elizabeth (?)	Kate Jacobs	Ramsgate, Kent	scholar
13825	Barnett	Bearon	1844	Middlesex, London	Lewis Barnett	Sarah Mayers		Manchester	
25752	Barnett	Bearon	1847	Spitalfields, London	Michael Barnett	Leah Simmons		Spitalfields, London	
24107	Barnett	Benjamin	1810	Bristol			Charlotte (?)	Bloomsbury, London	tobacconist empl 6
3881	Barnett	Benjamin	1838	Spitalfields, London	Judah Barnett	Julia Cohen	Julia Phillips	Spitalfields, London	
28175	Barnett	Benjamin	1839	Whitechapel, London	Barnet Barnett	Maria (Brynah) Franks		Spitalfields, London	scholar
23951	Barnett	Benjamin	1844	Middlesex, London	John Barnett	Mary (?)		Marylebone, London	scholar
15740	Barnett	Benjamin	1846	Marylebone, London	Abraham (John) Barnett	Mary (Polly, Miriam) Franks		Marylebone, London	scholar
20487	Barnett	Bennett	1812	Strand, London			Julia	Soho, London	picture restorer
2907	Barnett	Berrin	1834	Birmingham	David Barnett	Fanny Lyon		Birmingham	
920	Barnett	Bloomah	1829	Middlesex, London	Lazarus (Eliezer, Lewis) Barnett	Ann (Miriam) (?)	Morris Solomons	Aldgate, London	tailoress
6371	Barnett	Caroline	1815	Exeter, Devon	Eleazer Lazarus	Julia Solomon	Abraham Barnett	City, London	
125	Barnett	Caroline	1818	?, Poland [?, Prussia]	Yehuda Leib Joseph		Moses (Morris) Barnett	Woolwich, London	
16787	Barnett	Caroline	1834	Bristol	(?) Barnett			Bristol	pawnbroker's assistant
5233	Barnett	Caroline	1842	Aldgate, London	Harris Barnett	Leah Levy	Harris Franks	Spitalfields, London	scholar
23449	Barnett	Caroline	1850	Liverpool	Henry Barnett	Julia (?)		Liverpool	
13824	Barnett	Catharine	1843	Birmingham	Lewis Barnett	Sarah Mayers	Saul Bigio	Manchester	
14686	Barnett	Catherine	1828	Amsterdam, Holland	Yehuda Barnett			Spitalfields, London	house servant
21383	Barnett	Catherine	1844	Exeter, Devon	Lewis Barnett	Charlotte (?)		Newton Abbot, Devon	
3	Barnett	Catherine (Kate)	1834	Whitechapel, London	Moses Barnett	Dinah (?)		Wapping, London	embroiderer
27145	Barnett	Catherine (Kitty)	1826	Lambeth, London	David Jacobs	Hannah Solomons	Barnett Barnett	Aldgate, London	waistcoat maker
30377	Barnett	Chapman (Yekutiel)	1801	Aldgate, London	Yehuda Leib		Hannah Gershon	Wapping, London	clothier
24108	Barnett	Charlotte	1813	Aldgate, London	(?)		Benjamin Barnett	Bloomsbury, London	
21382	Barnett	Charlotte	1818	Dawlish, Devon	(?)		Lewis Barnett	Newton Abbot, Devon	
10544	Barnett	Charlotte	1827	?, Wales	(?)		Samuel Barnett	Elephant & Castle, London	
8680	Barnett	Charlotte (Sheindel)	1800	?, Poland [?, Prussia]	(?)		Arie Leib (Ari Lev) Barnett	Aldgate, London	
5231	Barnett	Clara	1843	Aldgate, London	Harris Barnett	Leah Levy	Solomon Solomon	Spitalfields, London	scholar
8362	Barnett	Coleman	1836	Ramsgate, Kent	Israel Barnett	Elizabeth (?)		Ramsgate, Kent	jeweller's assistant
25868	Barnett	Daniel	1838	Stepney, London	Samuel Barnett	Sarah (?)		Aldgate, London	assistant to greengrocer
28461	Barnett	David	1785	Aldgate, London			Leah (?)	Spitalfields, London	general dealer
158	Barnett	David	1796	?, Lithuania			Fanny Lyon	Birmingham	merchant, factor + communal worker
20701	Barnett	David	1815	Aldgate, London	Barnet Barnett		Harriet (Hannah) Myers	Whitechapel, London	clothier, dealer in furniture + misc goods, + broker of household goods

ID	surname	given names	born	birthplace	father	mother	spouse 1	1851 residence	1851 occupation
8689	Barnett	David	1819	Poznan, Poland [Posen, Prussia]			Deborah Barnett	Wapping, London	general outfitter
3713	Barnett	David	1825	Spitalfields, London			Maria (?)	Spitalfields, London	watch finisher
27974	Barnett	David	1828	Whitechapel, London	John Barnett	Rachel Fernandes		Spitalfields, London	general dealer
6651	Barnett	David	1839	Liverpool	Samuel Barnett	Esther Marks	Esther Marks	Liverpool	
25869	Barnett	David	1839	Spitalfields, London	Samuel Barnett	Sarah (?)		Aldgate, London	scholar
95	Barnett	David	1843	Woolwich, London	Isaac Barnett	Rebecca (?)		Woolwich, London	
21379	Barnett	David	1849	Spitalfields, London	Barnett Barnett	Elizabeth (?)		Spitalfields, London	
30343	Barnett	David	1851	Spitalfields, London	Henry (Hyam) Barnett	Sarah Davis		Spitalfields, London	
21524	Barnett	David P	1832	Whitechapel, London				Wapping, London	clothier's shopman
24196	Barnett	Dawson Alexander	1848	Whitechapel, London	Alfred Barnett	Rebecca (?)	Sarah Levy (Levi)	De Beauvoir, London	
24774	Barnett	Deborah	1817	Southwark, London	(?)		(?) Barnett	Elephant & Castle, London	milliner + dressmaker
8688	Barnett	Deborah	1819	Poznan, Poland [Posen, Prussia]	Arie Leib (Ari Lev) Barnett	Charlotte (Sheindel) (?)	David Barnett	Wapping, London	
22122	Barnett	Deborah	1824	?, Germany	(?)		Jacob Barnett	Whitechapel, London	
4	Barnett	Dinah	1795	?, London			Moses Barnett	Wapping, London	general dealer
9742	Barnett	Dinah	1816	City, London	(?) Phillips		Henry Barnett	Haggerston, London	
5	Barnett	Edward	1839	Whitechapel, London	Moses Barnett	Dinah (?)		Wapping, London	scholar
14603	Barnett	Edward	1842	Whitechapel, London	Morris Barnett	Frances (?)		Hoxton, London	scholar
4294	Barnett	Eli Louis	1841	Exeter, Devon	Joseph Barnett	Anne (?)	Julia Jessel	Birmingham	scholar
24109	Barnett	Elias	1833	Covent Garden, London	Benjamin Barnett	Charlotte (?)		Bloomsbury, London	tobacconist
6653	Barnett	Elisabeth (Bessie)	1835	Liverpool	Samuel Barnett	Esther Marks	Hyam Marks	Liverpool	
24351	Barnett	Eliza Esther	1822	Strand, London	(?)		Frederick Barnett	Bloomsbury, London	
11614	Barnett	Elizabeth	1791	Middlesex, London	(?)		(?) Barnett	Aldgate, London	general dealer
28576	Barnett	Elizabeth	1799	Whitechapel, London	(?)		Nathaniel Barnett	Spitalfields, London	waistcoat maker
8359	Barnett	Elizabeth	1804	Deal, Kent	(?)		Israel Barnett	Ramsgate, Kent	
11804	Barnett	Elizabeth	1815	Aldgate, London	Ariel Samuel		Hyam (Hyman) Barnett	Whitechapel, London	
29859	Barnett	Elizabeth	1816	Spitalfields, London	Wolf Josephson Gollin	Marlah (Martha) (?)	Emanuel Barnett	Wapping, London	
7961	Barnett	Elizabeth	1819	Aldgate, London	(?)		Barnet Barnet	Spitalfields, London	
2910	Barnett	Elizabeth	1839	Birmingham	David Barnett	Fanny Lyon		Birmingham	
14602	Barnett	Elizabeth	1839	Whitechapel, London	Morris Barnett	Frances (?)		Hoxton, London	scholar
16519	Barnett	Elizabeth	1847	Bristol	Isaac Barnett	Rachel (?)		Marylebone, London	
17707	Barnett	Elizabeth	1848	Aldgate, London	Phineas (Philip) Barnett	Sarah Jones		Spitalfields, London	
20709	Barnett	Elizabeth	1851	Wapping, London	David Barnett	Harriet (Hannah) Myers		Whitechapel, London	
23953	Barnett	Elizabeth	1851	?Marylebone, London	John Barnett	Mary (?)		Marylebone, London	scholar
6383	Barnett	Elizabeth (Betsey)	1851	Marylebone, London	Abraham (John) Barnett	Mary (Polly, Miriam) Franks		Marylebone, London	
9745	Barnett	Ellen	1850	City, London	Henry Barnett	Dinah (?)	Charles Haarburger	Hackney, London	
29858	Barnett	Emanuel	1804	?, Poland			Elizabeth Gollin	Wapping, London	clothier
23443	Barnett	Emanuel	1836	Liverpool	Henry Barnett	Julia (?)		Liverpool	
11693	Barnett	Emanuel	1844	City, London	Isaac Barnett	Phoebe (?)		Aldgate, London	
6372	Barnett	Ernest (Eleazer)	1849	Middlesex, London	Abraham Barnett	Caroline Lazarus	Rose Leah Davis	City, London	
23049	Barnett	Esther	1793	City, London	Hollender Aharon		Lazarus Barnett	Aldgate, London	
29	Barnett	Esther	1813	?, Poland	(?)		Moses Barnett	Aldgate, London	
2843	Barnett	Esther	1821	Middlesex, London	Lyon (Judah) Marks	Frances Levey (Levy)	Samuel Barnett	Liverpool	

ID	surname	given names	born	birthplace	father	mother	spouse 1	1851 residence	1851 occupation
8681	Barnett	Esther	1825	?, Poland [?, Prussia]	Arie Leib (Ari Lev) Barnett	Charlotte (Sheindel) (?)	Philip Grizmish	Aldgate, London	
27973	Barnett	Esther	1827	Whitechapel, London	John Barnett	Rachel Fernandes	Nathan Block	Spitalfields, London	cap maker
7969	Barnett	Esther	1828	Whitechapel, London	Samuel Michaels	Rebecca Isaacs	Barnett Barnett	Whitechapel, London	
1748	Barnett	Esther	1835	Swansea, Wales	Joseph Barnett	Hannah Leah (?)	Isaac Samuel	Merthyr Tydfil, Wales	
11805	Barnett	Esther	1838	Aldgate, London	Hyam (Hyman) Barnett	Sarah Hart		Whitechapel, London	scholar
25917	Barnett	Esther	1843	Aldgate, London	Asher Barnett	Kitty (Catharine) Barnett	Jacob Symons	Aldgate, London	scholar
28580	Barnett	Esther	1850	Spitalfields, London	(?) Barnett			Spitalfields, London	
23788	Barnett	Esther	1851	Liverpool	Joseph Barnett	Mary Ann (?)		Liverpool	
6373	Barnett	Eve	1841	Aldgate, London	Abraham Barnett	Caroline Lazarus	William Harris	City, London	
29962	Barnett	Fanny	1803	Whitechapel, London	(?) Barnett	Rosa (?)		Whitechapel, London	furrier
2906	Barnett	Fanny	1811	Liverpool	Nathan Lyon	Phoebe Zipporah Aaron	David Barnett	Birmingham	merchant
8865	Barnett	Fanny	1813	Whitechapel, London				Aldgate, London	cook
23444	Barnett	Fanny	1838	Liverpool	Henry Barnett	Julia (?)		Liverpool	
24776	Barnett	Fanny	1845	Walworth, London	(?) Barnett	Deborah (?)		Elephant & Castle, London	scholar
5230	Barnett	Fanny	1847	Aldgate, London	Harris Barnett	Leah Levy	Maurice Cohen	Spitalfields, London	
11809	Barnett	Fanny	1847	Aldgate, London	Hyam (Hyman) Barnett	Elizabeth Samuel		Whitechapel, London	scholar at home
14600	Barnett	Frances	1815	Spitalfields, London	(?)		Morris Barnett	Hoxton, London	
22108	Barnett	Frances	1823	Wapping, London	(?) Barnett	Abigail (?)		Whitechapel, London	parasol maker
26567	Barnett	Frances	1825	Aldgate, London	(?)		Samuel Barnett	Whitechapel, London	marine store dealer
25262	Barnett	Frances	1841	Finsbury, London	Gabriel Barnett	Phoebe Jacobs		Holborn, London	scholar
8364	Barnett	Frances (Zipporah)	1840	Ramsgate, Kent	Israel Barnett	Elizabeth (?)	Henry Mayer Solomon	Ramsgate, Kent	scholar
6652	Barnett	Frances Deborah	1841	Liverpool	Samuel Barnett	Esther Marks		Liverpool	
19703	Barnett	Francis Lyon	1822	Lambeth, London				Elephant & Castle, London	pawnbroker
24350	Barnett	Frederick	1818	Finsbury, London			Eliza Esther (?)	Bloomsbury, London	general agent
14424	Barnett	Frederick	1839	Salford, Lancashire	Philip Barnett			Salford, Lancashire	
25259	Barnett	Gabriel	1810	Whitechapel, London	Joseph Shma'he		Phoebe Jacobs	Holborn, London	clothes dealer
13913	Barnett	George	1826	Whitechapel, London				Manchester	salesman to tailor + draper
28059	Barnett	George	1847	Spitalfields, London	Henry (Hyam) Barnett	(Sarah Davis?)		Spitalfields, London	
9211	Barnett	Godfrey	1788	?, London				Spitalfields, London	watch maker
3691	Barnett	Hannah	1795	Aldgate, London			Henry Barnett	Spitalfields, London	
22027	Barnett	Hannah	1801	?, London	Moshe Israel Barnett			Piccadilly, London	
13838	Barnett	Hannah	1812	?, Poland [?, Prussia]	(?) Abrahams		Abraham Barnett	Manchester	
2360	Barnett	Hannah	1813	Middlesex, London	(?) Canter		Abraham Barnett	Hull, Yorkshire	
29963	Barnett	Hannah	1815	Whitechapel, London	(?) Barnett	Rosa (?)		Whitechapel, London	furrier
25312	Barnett	Hannah	1821	Whitechapel, London	(?)		Joseph Barnett	Holborn, London	assistant clothier
17143	Barnett	Hannah	1824	?, Shropshire	(?) Cantor		Abraham Barnett	Stoke-on-Trent, Staffordshire	
18024	Barnett	Hannah	1836	Chatham, Kent	Barnett Barnett	(?)		Chatham, Kent	scholar
28045	Barnett	Hannah	1840	Amsterdam, Holland	Samuel Barnett	Sarah (?)		Spitalfields, London	scholar
14604	Barnett	Hannah	1844	Whitechapel, London	Morris Barnett	Frances (?)		Hoxton, London	scholar
28336	Barnett	Hannah	1849	Whitechapel, London	Isaac Barnett	Maria (?)		Aldgate, London	

ID	surname	given names	born	birthplace	father	mother	spouse 1	1851 residence	1851 occupation
23448	Barnett	Hannah	1850	Liverpool	Henry Barnett	Julia (?)		Liverpool	
1745	Barnett	Hannah Leah	1799	?, Poland			Joseph Barnett	Merthyr Tydfil, Wales	
22046	Barnett	Harriet	1848	Spitalfields, London	Isaac Barnett	Phoebe Hart		Spitalfields, London	
20702	Barnett	Harriet (Hannah)	1820	Wapping, London	Andrew Myers	Elizabeth Hains	David Barnett	Whitechapel, London	
5232	Barnett	Harris	1812	?, Poland	Saul Barnett		Leah Levy	Spitalfields, London	shoe maker
22109	Barnett	Henrietta	1821	Whitechapel, London	(?) Barnett	Abigail (?)		Whitechapel, London	parasol maker
8365	Barnett	Henrietta	1841	Ramsgate, Kent	Israel Barnett	Elizabeth (?)		Ramsgate, Kent	scholar
24353	Barnett	Henrietta Nora	1843	Marylebone, London	Frederick Barnett	Eliza Esther (?)		Bloomsbury, London	scholar at home
3690	Barnett	Henry	1788	Spitalfields, London			Hannah (?)	Spitalfields, London	general dealer
28459	Barnett	Henry	1790	Whitechapel, London			Abigail (?)	Spitalfields, London	general dealer
18238	Barnett	Henry	1791	?, Germany				Cheltenham, Gloucestershire	Hebrew teacher
3697	Barnett	Henry	1807	Spitalfields, London			Amelia (?)	Spitalfields, London	general dealer
23441	Barnett	Henry	1809	Middlesex, London			Julia (?)	Liverpool	stationer
17138	Barnett	Henry	1813	Holborn, London				Bradford, Yorkshire	clothier shopman
9741	Barnett	Henry	1818	City, London	Mordecai HaCohen Barnett		Dinah Phillips	Haggerston, London	warehouseman
21252	Barnett	Henry	1826	Whitechapel, London	(Joseph Myers?) Barnett	Sarah (?)		Spitalfields, London	general dealer
6	Barnett	Henry	1832	Whitechapel, London	Moses Barnett	Dinah (?)		Wapping, London	cigar-maker journeyman
21962	Barnett	Henry	1832	Swansea, Wales	Joseph Barnett	Hannah Leah (?)	Louisa Victoria Moses	Swansea, Wales	pawnbroker's assistant
7962	Barnett	Henry	1836	City, London	Henry Barnett	Amelia (?)	(?)	Spitalfields, London	
4296	Barnett	Henry	1845	Exeter, Devon	Joseph Barnett	Anne (?)	Jane (Jeannie) Moore	Birmingham	
25313	Barnett	Henry	1848	St Giles, London	Joseph Barnett	Hannah (?)		Holborn, London	
28054	Barnett	Henry (Hyam)	1821	Norwich, Norfolk	Mordecai Barnett		Sarah Harris nee Davis	Spitalfields, London	general dealer
24355	Barnett	Henry A	1848	St Giles, London	Frederick Barnett	Eliza Esther (?)		Bloomsbury, London	
1746	Barnett	Hinda (Hinder, Heinda)	1830	Swansea, Wales	Joseph Barnett	Hannah Leah (?)	Simon Goldberg	Merthyr Tydfil, Wales	
23786	Barnett	Hyam	1848	Liverpool	Joseph Barnett	Mary Ann (?)		Liverpool	
3707	Barnett	Hyam	1851	Spitalfields, London	Henry Barnett	Amelia (?)		Spitalfields, London	
11803	Barnett	Hyam (Hyman)	1811	Aldgate, London	Joseph Shma'ye (?Samuel) Barnett	(?Frances Phillips)	Sarah Hart	Whitechapel, London	draper + dealer
16274	Barnett	Isaac	1782	Whitechapel, London				Whitechapel, London	broker
4288	Barnett	Isaac	1792	?, Poland			Sifra (?)	Birmingham	general dealer
11690	Barnett	Isaac	1801	City, London	Abraham our Father		Sarah Joseph	Aldgate, London	coffee house keeper
28333	Barnett	Isaac	1801	Aldgate, London			Maria (?)	Aldgate, London	general dealer
16517	Barnett	Isaac	1804	Middlesex, London			Rachel (?)	Marylebone, London	broker
26815	Barnett	Isaac	1819	Whitechapel, London				Whitechapel, London	general dealer
92	Barnett	Isaac	1821	Bialystok, Poland [Bialystok, Russia]			Rebecca (?)	Woolwich, London	upholsterer
22042	Barnett	Isaac	1822	?, Holland	Jacob Barnett		Phoebe Hart	Spitalfields, London	fruiterer
7	Barnett	Isaac	1835	Whitechapel, London	Moses Barnett	Dinah (?)		Wapping, London	cigar maker apprentice
19876	Barnett	Isaac	1838	Aldgate, London				Spitalfields, London	scholar
23446	Barnett	Isaac	1842	Liverpool	Henry Barnett	Julia (?)		Liverpool	scholar
14607	Barnett	Isaac	1848	Whitechapel, London	Morris Barnett	Frances (?)		Hoxton, London	scholar
8358	Barnett	Israel	1803	?, Poland			Elizabeth (?)	Ramsgate, Kent	jeweller + hardwareman
22121	Barnett	Jacob	1821	Hanover, Germany			Deborah (?)	Whitechapel, London	jeweller
25872	Barnett	Jacob	1845	Spitalfields, London	Samuel Barnett	Sarah (?)		Aldgate, London	scholar

ID	surname	given names	born	birthplace	father	mother	spouse 1	1851 residence	1851 occupation
11810	Barnett	Jacob	1849	Aldgate, London	Hyam (Hyman) Barnett	Elizabeth Samuel		Whitechapel, London	scholar at home
25921	Barnett	Jacob	1849	Aldgate, London	Asher Barnett	Kitty (Catharine) Barnett		Aldgate, London	
2361	Barnett	Jacob	1850	Hull, Yorkshire	Abraham Barnett	Hannah Canter		Hull, Yorkshire	
8687	Barnett	Jane	1845	?, London	Arie Leib (Ari Lev) Barnett	Charlotte (Sheindel) (?)	Sampson Goldstone	Aldgate, London	scholar
24197	Barnett	Janetta	1850	De Beauvoir, London	Alfred Barnett	Rebecca (?)		De Beauvoir, London	
9743	Barnett	Jeanette	1846	Whitechapel, London	Henry Barnett	Dinah Phillips	Benjamin Benjamin	Haggerston, London	
25264	Barnett	Joel	1848	Holborn, London	Gabriel Barnett	Phoebe Jacobs		Holborn, London	scholar
3706	Barnett	Joel	1849	Spitalfields, London	Henry Barnett	Amelia (?)		Spitalfields, London	
24356	Barnett	Joel	1850	St Giles, London	Frederick Barnett	Eliza Esther (?)		Bloomsbury, London	
27970	Barnett	John	1789	Whitechapel, London	Joseph Barnett		Rachel Fernandes	Spitalfields, London	glass cutter
7032	Barnett	John	1802	Bedford, Bedfordshire	Bernhard Beer (Barnett)		Eliza Lindley	Cheltenham, Gloucestershire	composer + teacher
23946	Barnett	John	1804	Marylebone, London			Mary (?)	Marylebone, London	dealer in clothes
11615	Barnett	John	1823	Middlesex, London	(?) Barnett	Elizabeth (?)		Aldgate, London	general dealer
11032	Barnett	John	1835	Middlesex, London	Lazarus (Eliezer, Lewis) Barnett	Ann (Miriam) (?)		Aldgate, London	cigar maker
28579	Barnett	John	1837	Spitalfields, London	Nathaniel Barnett	Elizabeth (?)		Spitalfields, London	cigar maker
3695	Barnett	John	1838	Aldgate, London	Henry Barnett	Hannah (?)		Spitalfields, London	scholar
8179	Barnett	John	1845	Holborn, London	Gabriel Barnett	Phoebe Jacobs	Priscilla Jacobs	Holborn, London	scholar
1744	Barnett	Joseph	1801	?, Russia			Hannah Leah (?)	Merthyr Tydfil, Wales	pawnbroker
4291	Barnett	Joseph	1809	?, Poland			Anne (?)	Birmingham	travelling jeweller
25311	Barnett	Joseph	1816	Whitechapel, London			Hannah (?)	Holborn, London	clothier
27972	Barnett	Joseph	1823	Whitechapel, London	John Barnett	Rachel Fernandes		Spitalfields, London	glass cutter
23784	Barnett	Joseph	1828	Middlesex, London			Mary Ann (?)	Liverpool	tailor's assistant
19750	Barnett	Joseph	1831	Whitechapel, London	Chapman (Yekutiel) Barnett	Hannah Gershon	Rachael Abady (Aberdean)	Wapping, London	clothier
3694	Barnett	Joseph	1834	Spitalfields, London	Henry Barnett	Hannah (?)		Spitalfields, London	fruit seller
8361	Barnett	Joseph	1835	Ramsgate, Kent	Israel Barnett	Elizabeth (?)		Ramsgate, Kent	jeweller's assistant
94	Barnett	Joseph	1841	Woolwich, London	Isaac Barnett	Rebecca (?)		Woolwich, London	
20703	Barnett	Joseph	1841	Wapping, London	David Barnett	Harriet (Hannah) Myers		Whitechapel, London	scholar
25870	Barnett	Joseph	1841	Spitalfields, London	Samuel Barnett	Sarah (?)		Aldgate, London	scholar
23447	Barnett	Joseph	1849	Liverpool	Henry Barnett	Julia (?)		Liverpool	
22123	Barnett	Joseph	1850	?, Scotland	Jacob Barnett	Deborah (?)		Whitechapel, London	
24354	Barnett	Josephine J	1845	St Giles, London	Frederick Barnett	Eliza Esther (?)		Bloomsbury, London	scholar at home
923	Barnett	Joshua	1815	?, London	Lazarus (Eliezer, Lewis) Barnett	Ann (Miriam) (?)	Nancy (Mary) Benjamin	Aldgate, London	traveller + clothier
5228	Barnett	Joshua	1849	Whitechapel, London	Harris Barnett	Leah Levy	Miriam Phillips	Spitalfields, London	
3876	Barnett	Judah	1796	Amsterdam, Holland			Julia Cohen	Spitalfields, London	general dealer + clothes dealer
31	Barnett	Judah	1832	?, Poland	Moses Barnett	Esther (?)		Aldgate, London	
22044	Barnett	Judah	1843	Spitalfields, London	Isaac Barnett	Phoebe Hart		Spitalfields, London	
21377	Barnett	Judith	1847	Spitalfields, London	Barnett Barnett	Elizabeth (?)		Spitalfields, London	
27176	Barnett	Judy	1811	?, London	(?)		(?) Barnett	Aldgate, London	
7958	Barnett	Julia	1810	Middlesex, London	Michael Aarons	Rachel Joseph	Reuben Barnett	Aldgate, London	
23442	Barnett	Julia	1817	Newcastle-under-Lyme, Staffordshire	(?)		Henry Barnett	Liverpool	
20488	Barnett	Julia	1823	Soho, London	(?Henry) Davis		Bennett Barnett	Soho, London	
8571	Barnett	Julia	1826	Aldgate, London	(?) Barnett			Spitalfields, London	furrier finisher

ID	surname	given names	born	birthplace	father	mother	spouse 1	1851 residence	1851 occupation
28176	Barnett	Julia	1841	Spitalfields, London	Barnet Barnett	Maria (Brynah) Franks		Spitalfields, London	scholar
23950	Barnett	Julia	1842	Middlesex, London	John Barnett	Mary (?)		Marylebone, London	scholar
2362	Barnett	Julia	1843	Hull, Yorkshire	Abraham Barnett	Hannah Canter	(?Jacob Cohen)	Hull, Yorkshire	scholar
6381	Barnett	Julia	1843	Marylebone, London	Abraham (John) Barnett	Mary (Polly, Miriam) Franks		Marylebone, London	scholar
22045	Barnett	Julia	1845	Spitalfields, London	Isaac Barnett	Phoebe Hart		Spitalfields, London	
3877	Barnett	Julia	1801	Spitalfields, London	(?) Cohen		Judah Barnett	Spitalfields, London	clothes dealer
24778	Barnett	Kate	1850	Walworth, London	(?) Barnett	Deborah (?)		Elephant & Castle, London	
25914	Barnett	Kitty (Cathcrine)	1819	Aldgate, London	Abraham Barnett		Asher Barnett	Aldgate, London	
22110	Barnett	Lawrence	1829	Stepney, London	(?) Barnett	Abigail (?)		Whitechapel, London	umbrella maker
14601	Barnett	Lawrence	1837	Whitechapel, London	Morris Barnett	Frances (?)		Hoxton, London	scholar
23048	Barnett	Lazarus	1784	Poznan, Poland [Posen, Prussia]	Yissachar Baer		Esther Aaron	Aldgate, London	independent
21384	Barnett	Lazarus	1847	Exeter, Devon	Lewis Barnett	Charlotte (?)		Newton Abbot, Devon	
917	Barnett	Lazarus (Eliezer, Lewis)	1788	?, London	Barnet Barnett	Elizabeth (?)	Ann (Miriam) (?)	Aldgate, London	general dealer
28462	Barnett	Leah	1796	Stepney, London	(?)		David Barnett	Spitalfields, London	milliner
25748	Barnett	Leah	1803	Spitalfields, London	Aaron Simmons		Samuel Isaacs	Spitalfields, London	
2676	Barnett	Leah	1820	Leszno, Poland [Lissa, Prussia], Poland [Lissa, Prussia]	Yehuda Leib		Harris Barnett	Aldgate, London	
28042	Barnett	Leah	1834	Amsterdam, Holland	Samuel Barnett	Sarah (?)		Spitalfields, London	cap maker
23952	Barnett	Leah	1845	Middlesex, London	John Barnett	Mary (?)		Marylebone, London	
28467	Barnett	Leah	1847	Whitechapel, London	David Barnett	Leah (?)		Spitalfields, London	
6382	Barnett	Leah	1848	Marylebone, London	Abraham (John) Barnett	Mary (Polly, Miriam) Franks		Marylebone, London	
3716	Barnett	Leah	1850	Spitalfields, London	David Barnett	Maria (?)		Spitalfields, London	
18026	Barnett	Lear	1844	Chatham, Kent	Barnett Barnett	(?)		Chatham, Kent	scholar
13506	Barnett	Lewis	1814	Manchester				Manchester	porter dealer
21381	Barnett	Lewis	1816	Vilnius, Lithuania [Vilneaux, Poland]			Charlotte (?)	Newton Abbot, Devon	clothier + hatter
13822	Barnett	Lewis	1819	Middlesex, London	Issachar Barnett		Sarah Mayers	Manchester	carver + gilder, empl 2
3699	Barnett	Lewis	1830	Spitalfields, London	Henry Barnett	Amelia (?)		Spitalfields, London	
13839	Barnett	Lewis	1840	?, Wales	Abraham Barnett	Hannah Abrahams		Manchester	scholar
925	Barnett	Lewis	1845	Aldgate, London	Joshua Barnett	Nancy (Mary) Benjamin	Nancy Ellis	Aldgate, London	
24777	Barnett	Lewis	1847	Walworth, London	(?) Barnett	Deborah (?)		Elephant & Castle, London	scholar
97	Barnett	Lewis	1851	Woolwich, London	Isaac Barnett	Rebecca (?)		Woolwich, London	
1747	Barnett	Lewis (Louis)	1834	Swansea, Wales	Joseph Barnett	Hannah Leah (?)	Amelia Kisch	Merthyr Tydfil, Wales	pawnbroker
7862	Barnett	Lewis (Ludovik)	1801	?, Poland	Elkan Edelstein		(?)	?Aldgate, London	
27898	Barnett	Lipman	1803	Frankfurt-am-Main, Germany			Yette (?)	Spitalfields, London	journeyman tailor
7956	Barnett	Louis A	1839	Bristol	Isaac Barnett	Rachel (?)	Hannah Levy	Marylebone, London	
23987	Barnett	Louisa	1811	?, Jamaica, West Indies	(?)		Samuel B Barnett	St John's Wood, London	physician
8683	Barnett	Louisa	1837	?, London	Arie Leib (Ari Lev) Barnett	Charlotte (Sheindel) (?)	Solomon Temple	Aldgate, London	scholar
28578	Barnett	Lucy	1835	Spitalfields, London	Nathaniel Barnett	Elizabeth (?)		Spitalfields, London	waistcoat maker
12863	Barnett	Lyon	1843	Liverpool	Samuel Barnett	Esther Marks		Liverpool	

ID	surname	given names	born	birthplace	father	mother	spouse 1	1851 residence	1851 occupation
28334	Barnett	Maria	1823	Aldgate, London	(?)		Isaac Barnett	Aldgate, London	
3714	Barnett	Maria	1829	?, Holland			David Barnett	Spitalfields, London	dressmaker
24352	Barnett	Maria	1842	Marylebone, London	Frederick Barnett	Eliza Esther (?)		Bloomsbury, London	scholar at home
3705	Barnett	Maria	1843	Spitalfields, London	Henry Barnett	Amelia (?)		Spitalfields, London	
28172	Barnett	Maria (Brynah)	1817	Aldgate, London	Benjamin Franks	Priscilla Abrahams	Barnet Barnett	Spitalfields, London	
20708	Barnett	Marian	1850	Wapping, London	David Barnett	Harriet (Hannah) Myers	Alick Warschawsky	Whitechapel, London	
934	Barnett	Marian (Mary)	1851	Aldgate, London	Joshua Barnett	Nancy (Mary) Benjamin	(?) White	Aldgate, London	
9870	Barnett	Marione	1843	?, London				Fulham, London	boarding school pupil
28464	Barnett	Mark	1827	Aldgate, London	David Barnett	Leah (?)		Spitalfields, London	tailor
3702	Barnett	Mark	1837	Spitalfields, London	Henry Barnett	Amelia (?)		Spitalfields, London	
28180	Barnett	Mark	1846	Whitechapel, London	Barnet Barnett	Maria (Brynah) Franks		Spitalfields, London	scholar
17949	Barnett	Mark?	1821	Harrow, Middlesex				Whitechapel, London	sponge traveller
16937	Barnett	Martha	1819	Liverpool	(?)		Samuel Barnett	Sheffield, Yorkshire	
19116	Barnett	Mary	1791	?, London	(?)		(?) Barnett	Aldgate, London	annuitant
23947	Barnett	Mary	1811	?, America	(?)		John Barnett	Marylebone, London	
28577	Barnett	Mary	1825	Whitechapel, London	Nathaniel Barnett	Elizabeth (?)		Spitalfields, London	waistcoat maker
16725	Barnett	Mary	1831	Middlesex, London	Jacob Barnett		Michael Morris	Spitalfields, London	general dealer
28174	Barnett	Mary	1836	Whitechapel, London	Barnet Barnett	Maria (Brynah) Franks		Spitalfields, London	dressmaker
3696	Barnett	Mary	1839	Aldgate, London	Henry Barnett	Hannah (?)		Spitalfields, London	scholar
17708	Barnett	Mary	1850	Aldgate, London	Phineas (Philip) Barnett	Sarah Jones		Spitalfields, London	
11026	Barnett	Mary	1851	Aldgate, London	Joshua Barnett	Nancy Benjamin		Aldgate, London	
6379	Barnett	Mary (Polly, Miriam)	1811	Whitechapel, London	Benjamin Franks	Priscilla Abrahams	Abraham (John) Barnett	Marylebone, London	
23785	Barnett	Mary Ann	1829	Liverpool	(?)		Joseph Barnett	Liverpool	
3701	Barnett	Matilda	1835	Spitalfields, London	Henry Barnett	Amelia (?)		Spitalfields, London	
2909	Barnett	Matilda	1837	Birmingham	David Barnett	Fanny Lyon	Joseph Maurice Marks	Birmingham	
8685	Barnett	Matilda	1839	?, London	Arie Leib (Ari Lev) Barnett	Charlotte (Sheindel) (?)	Hyam S Besso	Aldgate, London	scholar
13828	Barnett	Matilda	1850	Manchester	Lewis Barnett	Sarah Mayers		Manchester	
22112	Barnett	Maurice	1845	?, London				Whitechapel, London	
24195	Barnett	Maurice	1846	Whitechapel, London	Alfred Barnett	Rebecca (?)	Julia Levy (Levi)	De Beauvoir, London	
26911	Barnett	Michael	1795	?, Germany			(?)	Aldgate, London	cap maker
25747	Barnett	Michael	1815	Spitalfields, London	Joseph Barnett		Leah Isaacs nee Simmons	Spitalfields, London	clothier
25758	Barnett	Michael	1850	Aldgate, London	Barnett Barnett	Phoebe Isaacs		Aldgate, London	
5710	Barnett	Montague	1844	Middlesex, London	Abraham Barnett	Caroline Lazarus	Phoebe Lewin	City, London	
3720	Barnett	Mordecai	1833	Spitalfields, London	Henry Barnett	Hannah (?)	Rosa Benjamin	Spitalfields, London	general dealer
126	Barnett	Mordicai	1843	Woolwich, London	Moses (Morris) Barnett	Caroline Joseph		Woolwich, London	scholar
20421	Barnett	Moris	1837	Bristol				Marylebone, London	
14599	Barnett	Morris	1813	Poplar, London			Frances (?)	Hoxton, London	umbrella + parasol maker
9744	Barnett	Morris (Maurice) Henry	1849	City, London	Henry Barnett	Dinah Phillips	Marie Sternberg	Hackney, London	
8	Barnett	Moses	1793	Aldgate, London	Barnett Barnett		Dinah (?)	Westminster, London	convict (general dealer)
28	Barnett	Moses	1801	?, Poland			Esther (?)	Aldgate, London	furrier
8691	Barnett	Moses	1850	Aldgate, London	David Barnett	Deborah Barnett		Wapping, London	scholar at home
22047	Barnett	Moses	1850	Spitalfields, London	Isaac Barnett	Phoebe Hart		Spitalfields, London	
124	Barnett	Moses (Morris)	1817	?, Russia	Mordecai Barnett		Caroline Joseph	Woolwich, London	general dealer

ID	surname	given names	born	birthplace	father	mother	spouse 1	1851 residence	1851 occupation
3721	Barnett	Moses (Morris)	1831	Spitalfields, London	Henry Barnett	Hannah (?)	Fanny Joseph	Spitalfields, London	general dealer
32	Barnett	Myer	1841	?, Poland	Moses Barnett	Esther (?)		Aldgate, London	scholar
19871	Barnett	Nancy	1788	Aldgate, London	(?)		(?) Barnett	Spitalfields, London	
28043	Barnett	Nancy	1835	Amsterdam, Holland	Samuel Barnett	Sarah (?)		Spitalfields, London	
25919	Barnett	Nancy	1845	Aldgate, London	Asher Barnett	Kitty (Catharine) Barnett		Aldgate, London	scholar
25757	Barnett	Nancy	1847	Aldgate, London	Barnett Barnett	Phoebe Isaacs	(?) Franks	Aldgate, London	
924	Barnett	Nancy (Mary)	1824	Middlesex, London	Abraham Benjamin		Joshua Barnett	Aldgate, London	
3704	Barnett	Nathan	1843	Spitalfields, London	Henry Barnett	Amelia (?)		Spitalfields, London	
24775	Barnett	Nathan	1844	Walworth, London	(?) Barnett	Deborah (?)		Elephant & Castle, London	scholar
28575	Barnett	Nathaniel	1798	Whitechapel, London			Elizabeth (?)	Spitalfields, London	general dealer
24110	Barnett	Nathaniel	1835	Covent Garden, London	Benjamin Barnett	Charlotte (?)		Bloomsbury, London	tobacconist
30873	Barnett	Nathaniel	1836	Bristol				Bristol	?harbour dealer's apprentice
19874	Barnett	Pheobe	1827	Spitalfields, London	(?) Barnett	Nancy (?)		Spitalfields, London	waistcoat maker
26910	Barnett	Philip	1781	?, Germany			(?)	Aldgate, London	general dealer
14423	Barnett	Philip	1806	?, Russia				Salford, Lancashire	tailor
8695	Barnett	Philip	1818	?, Poland [?, Prussia]	Arie Leib (Ari Lev) Barnett	Charlotte (Sheindel) (?)	Harriet Rebecca Goldstone	?London	
19873	Barnett	Phillip	1817	Aldgate, London	(?) Barnett	Nancy (?)		Spitalfields, London	clothes dealer
17705	Barnett	Phineas (Philip)	1819	?, Poland [?, Prussia]	Elikom Getz		Sarah Jones	Spitalfields, London	slipper maker
8690	Barnett	Phinias P	1848	Aldgate, London	David Barnett	Deborah Barnett		Wapping, London	scholar at home
25756	Barnett	Phoebe	1810	Aldgate, London	Samuel Isaacs		Barnett Barnett	Aldgate, London	clothier
25260	Barnett	Phoebe	1818	?, Derbyshire	Woolf Jacobs		Gabriel Barnett	Holborn, London	clothes dealer
22043	Barnett	Phoebe	1819	Middlesex, London	Mordecai Hart		Isaac Barnett	Spitalfields, London	
11691	Barnett	Phoebe	1824	City, London	(?)		Isaac Barnett	Aldgate, London	
28044	Barnett	Phoebe	1838	Amsterdam, Holland	Samuel Barnett	Sarah (?)		Spitalfields, London	scholar
25920	Barnett	Phoebe	1847	Aldgate, London	Asher Barnett	Kitty (Catharine) Barnett	Abraham Sampson	Aldgate, London	scholar
23949	Barnett	Priscilla	1840	Middlesex, London	John Barnett	Mary (?)		Marylebone, London	scholar
6380	Barnett	Priscilla	1841	Marylebone, London	Abraham (John) Barnett	Mary (Polly, Miriam) Franks		Marylebone, London	scholar
28179	Barnett	Priscilla	1843	Spitalfields, London	Barnet Barnett	Maria (Brynah) Franks		Spitalfields, London	scholar
13841	Barnett	Priscilla	1848	Manchester	Abraham Barnett	Hannah Abrahams		Manchester	
11190	Barnett	Rachael	1789	Aldgate, London	Yehuda Leib		Henry Barnett	Aldgate, London	tailoress
25915	Barnett	Rachael	1839	Aldgate, London	Asher Barnett	Kitty (Catharine) Barnett		Aldgate, London	
13840	Barnett	Rachael	1842	?, Wales	Abraham Barnett	Hannah Abrahams		Manchester	scholar
22902	Barnett	Rachel	1778	?, London	(?)		(?) Barnett	Wapping, London	
27971	Barnett	Rachel	1795	Spitalfields, London	Elias Jacobs		Moses de Aaron Mendoza	Spitalfields, London	dealer in fish
16518	Barnett	Rachel	1812	Middlesex, London	(?)		Isaac Barnett	Marylebone, London	
3693	Barnett	Rachel	1826	Aldgate, London	Henry Barnett	Hannah (?)		Spitalfields, London	tailoress
28466	Barnett	Rachel	1834	Aldgate, London	David Barnett	Leah (?)		Spitalfields, London	seamstress
129	Barnett	Rachel	1848	Woolwich, London	Moses (Morris) Barnett	Caroline Joseph		Woolwich, London	
28465	Barnett	Ralph	1830	Aldgate, London	David Barnett	Leah (?)		Spitalfields, London	general dealer
18027	Barnett	Rebeca	1847	Chatham, Kent	Barnett Barnett	(?)		Chatham, Kent	scholar
25309	Barnett	Rebecca	1781	?, Poland	(?)		(?) Barnett	Aldgate, London	annuitant
24194	Barnett	Rebecca	1817	Stepney, London	(?)		Alfred Barnett	De Beauvoir, London	
93	Barnett	Rebecca	1818	Woolwich, London			Isaac Barnett	Woolwich, London	

ID	surname	given names	born	birthplace	father	mother	spouse 1	1851 residence	1851 occupation
26816	Barnett	Rebecca	1823	Whitechapel, London	(?) Barnett			Whitechapel, London	garter maker
21251	Barnett	Rebecca	1824	Aldgate, London	(Joseph Myers?) Barnett	Sarah (?)		Spitalfields, London	general dealer
26841	Barnett	Rebecca	1824	?, Poland	(?) Barnett			Aldgate, London	slipper maker
23052	Barnett	Rebecca	1830	City, London	Lazarus Barnett	Esther Aaron		Aldgate, London	
29547	Barnett	Rebecca	1830	?, London	Coleman Coleman		Abraham Barnett	Spitalfields, London	dressmaker
15739	Barnett	Rebecca	1838	Middlesex, London	Abraham (John) Barnett	Mary (Polly, Miriam) Franks		Marylebone, London	scholar
23948	Barnett	Rebecca	1838	Middlesex, London	John Barnett	Mary (?)		Marylebone, London	scholar
24111	Barnett	Rebecca	1841	Covent Garden, London	Benjamin Barnett	Charlotte (?)		Bloomsbury, London	scholar
4295	Barnett	Rebecca	1843	?, Devon	Joseph Barnett	Anne (?)		Birmingham	scholar
16726	Barnett	Rebecca	1844	Middlesex, London	(?) Barnett			Spitalfields, London	scholar
14605	Barnett	Rebecca	1846	Whitechapel, London	Morris Barnett	Frances (?)		Hoxton, London	scholar
25314	Barnett	Reuben	1850	Holborn, London	Joseph Barnett	Hannah (?)		Holborn, London	
29961	Barnett	Rosa	1777	City, London	(?)		(?) Barnett	Whitechapel, London	furrier
23053	Barnett	Rose	1833	City, London	Lazarus Barnett	Esther Aaron		Aldgate, London	scholar
13826	Barnett	Rose	1846	Manchester	Lewis Barnett	Sarah Mayers	Abraham S Israel	Manchester	
20707	Barnett	Rose (Rosina)	1848	Wapping, London	David Barnett	Harriet (Hannah) Myers	Hyam Aarons	Whitechapel, London	scholar
3692	Barnett	Rosetta	1816	Aldgate, London	Henry Barnett	Hannah (?)		Spitalfields, London	domestic
3880	Barnett	Rosetta	1836	Spitalfields, London	Judah Barnett	Julia Cohen	Moss Cohen	Spitalfields, London	umbrella maker
25916	Barnett	Rosetta	1841	Aldgate, London	Asher Barnett	Kitty (Catharine) Barnett		Aldgate, London	scholar
2363	Barnett	Rosetta	1847	Hull, Yorkshire	Abraham Barnett	Hannah Canter	Joel Joseph Duveen	Hull, Yorkshire	
28047	Barnett	Rosetta	1847	Spitalfields, London	Samuel Barnett	Sarah (?)		Spitalfields, London	scholar
21378	Barnett	Rosetta	1848	Spitalfields, London	Barnett Barnett	Elizabeth (?)		Spitalfields, London	
20489	Barnett	Rowland Gideon Israel	1846	Westminster, London	Bennet Barnett	Julia Davis	Ellen Maria Lingham	Soho, London	
25465	Barnett	Samuel	1782	Aldgate, London			(?)	Aldgate, London	pensioner
27135	Barnett	Samuel	1801	?, London	Aaron Barnett			Aldgate, London	general dealer
25865	Barnett	Samuel	1803	?, Poland [?, Prussia]			Sarah (?)	Aldgate, London	greengrocer
28040	Barnett	Samuel	1807	Amsterdam, Holland			Sarah (?)	Spitalfields, London	jeweller
26571	Barnett	Samuel	1811	Aldgate, London			Frances (?)	Whitechapel, London	marine store dealer
6753	Barnett	Samuel	1813	Middlesex, London	David Levy (Barnett)		Esther Marks	Liverpool	tailor, draper + outfitter
10543	Barnett	Samuel	1821	Lambeth, London			Charlotte (?)	Elephant & Castle, London	pawnbroker
10062	Barnett	Samuel	1826	?, Poland [?, Prussia]	Isaac Barnett		Leah Barnard	Wolverhampton, Staffordshire	furniture dealer
11692	Barnett	Samuel	1826	City, London	Isaac Barnett	Sarah Joseph		Aldgate, London	cigar maker
23051	Barnett	Samuel	1827	City, London	Lazarus Barnett	Esther Aaron		Aldgate, London	warehouseman
12464	Barnett	Samuel	1829	Whitechapel, London	Abraham Barnett	Nancy (?)	Amelia (?)	Spitalfields, London	pastry cook
8360	Barnett	Samuel	1833	Ramsgate, Kent	Israel Barnett	Elizabeth (?)		Ramsgate, Kent	jeweller's assistant
25867	Barnett	Samuel	1835	Aldgate, London	Samuel Barnett	Sarah (?)		Aldgate, London	box maker apprentice
27464	Barnett	Samuel	1835	Aldgate, London				Whitechapel, London	apprentice to trunk + packing case maker
23445	Barnett	Samuel	1841	Liverpool	Henry Barnett	Julia (?)		Liverpool	scholar
128	Barnett	Samuel	1846	Woolwich, London	Moses (Morris) Barnett	Caroline Joseph	Jane Jacobs	Woolwich, London	scholar
96	Barnett	Samuel	1849	Woolwich, London	Isaac Barnett	Rebecca (?)		Woolwich, London	
23787	Barnett	Samuel	1849	Liverpool	Joseph Barnett	Mary Ann (?)		Liverpool	

ID	surname	given names	born	birthplace	father	mother	spouse 1	1851 residence	1851 occupation
25922	Barnett	Samuel	1850	Aldgate, London	Asher Barnett	Kitty (Catharine) Barnett		Aldgate, London	
23986	Barnett	Samuel B	1803	?, Suffolk			Louisa (?)	St John's Wood, London	physician
4293	Barnett	Samuel Woolf	1837	Exeter, Devon	Joseph Barnett	Anne (?)	Sarah Price	Birmingham	scholar
9111	Barnett	Sarah	1774	Aldgate, London	(?)		(?) Barnett	Covent Garden, London	independent
21250	Barnett	Sarah	1777	Aldgate, London	(?)		(Joseph Myers?) Barnett	Spitalfields, London	general dealer
9733	Barnett	Sarah	1785	Hamburg, Germany	(?)		(?) Barnett	Whitechapel, London	
11456	Barnett	Sarah	1791	Warsaw?, Poland	(?)		Aaron Barnett	Aldgate, London	
25866	Barnett	Sarah	1803	?, Poland [?, Prussia]	(?)		Samuel Barnett	Aldgate, London	greengrocer's wife
28041	Barnett	Sarah	1810	Amsterdam, Holland	(?)		Samuel Barnett	Spitalfields, London	
28055	Barnett	Sarah	1812	Whitechapel, London	Moses Davis		Joel Harris	Spitalfields, London	
13823	Barnett	Sarah	1820	Middlesex, London	(?Henry) Mayers	Catherine (?)	Lewis Barnett	Manchester	
22107	Barnett	Sarah	1821	Aldgate, London	(?) Barnett	Abigail (?)		Whitechapel, London	parasol maker
17706	Barnett	Sarah	1825	Aldgate, London	Abraham Jones		Phineas (Philip) Barnett	Spitalfields, London	slipper maker
28463	Barnett	Sarah	1826	Aldgate, London	David Barnett	Leah (?)		Spitalfields, London	dressmaker
11806	Barnett	Sarah	1840	Aldgate, London	Hyam (Hyman) Barnett	Sarah Hart	Mark Joel (Jewell)	Whitechapel, London	scholar
25261	Barnett	Sarah	1840	Finsbury, London	Gabriel Barnett	Phoebe Jacobs		Holborn, London	scholar
14606	Barnett	Sarah	1847	Whitechapel, London	Morris Barnett	Frances (?)		Hoxton, London	scholar
24113	Barnett	Sarah	1847	Aldgate, London	Benjamin Barnett	Charlotte (?)		Bloomsbury, London	scholar
144	Barnett	Sarah	1849	Aldgate, London	Barnett Barnett	Ann (Nancy) Myers		Whitechapel, London	
13877	Barnett	Sarah	1821	Middlesex, London	(?) Lazarus		(?) Barnett	Manchester	
20422	Barnett	Selim	1845	Bristol				Marylebone, London	
34	Barnett	Selina	1845	Aldgate, London	Moses Barnett	Dinah (?)		Wapping, London	scholar
4289	Barnett	Sifra	1795	?, Poland			Isaac Barnett	Birmingham	
2364	Barnett	Simon	1821	Pruszcz, Poland [Pruser, Prussia]			Henrietta (Jetty) Cohen	Hull, Yorkshire	jeweller
24112	Barnett	Simon	1844	Covent Garden, London	Benjamin Barnett	Charlotte (?)		Bloomsbury, London	scholar
3700	Barnett	Solomon	1833	Spitalfields, London	Henry Barnett	Amelia (?)		Spitalfields, London	
22781	Barnett	Sophia	1781	Whitechapel, London	(?)		Abraham Barnett	Whitechapel, London	
3879	Barnett	Sophia	1834	Spitalfields, London	Judah Barnett	Julia Cohen	Morris Phillips	Spitalfields, London	tailoress
127	Barnett	Sophia	1843	Woolwich, London	Moses (Morris) Barnett	Caroline Joseph	Isaac Harris	Woolwich, London	scholar
2908	Barnett	Sophie	1840	Birmingham	David Barnett	Fanny Lyon	Julius Wolff	Birmingham	scholar
27899	Barnett	Yette	1809	Frankfurt-am-Main, Germany	(?)		Lipman Barnett	Spitalfields, London	
16433	Barnett?	Coleman	1846	?, London	(?) Barnett?	Susan (?)		Aldgate, London	
16434	Barnett?	Joseph	1850	?, London	(?) Barnett?	Susan (?)		Aldgate, London	
16432	Barnett?	Susan	1816	Poznan, Poland [Posen, Prussia]	(?)		(?) Barnett?	Aldgate, London	general dealer
25507	Baron	Adolphus	1819	Poznan, Poland [Kozninoin, Posen]			Franchi (?)	Tower Hill, London	bootmaker
25508	Baron	Franchi	1822	Poznan, Poland [Kozninoin, Posen]	(?)		Adolphus Baron	Tower Hill, London	
25510	Baron	Herman	1850	City, London	Adolphus Baron	Franchi (?)		Tower Hill, London	
28985	Baron	Himan	1828	Kozmin, Poland [Kozmin, Posen, Prussia]				Whitechapel, London	tailor
28981	Baron	Jacob	1821	Rogajny, Poland [Roganin, Posen, Prussia]	Shmuel		Poline (Fagel) (?)	Whitechapel, London	tailor

ID	surname	given names	born	birthplace	father	mother	spouse 1	1851 residence	1851 occupation
25509	Baron	Natan	1845	?, Silesia, Poland [?, Philesia]	Adolphus Baron	Franchi (?)		Tower Hill, London	
28982	Baron	Poline (Fagel)	1823	Krotoszyn, Poland [Kratoshin, Posen, Prussia]	(?)		Jacob Baron	Whitechapel, London	tailor
28984	Baron	Rachel	1850	Whitechapel, London	Jacob Baron	Poline (Fagel) (?)		Whitechapel, London	
28983	Baron	Simon	1849	?, London	Jacob Baron	Poline (Fagel) (?)		Whitechapel, London	
8715	Barrada	Ally (?Eli)	1778	?, Morocco				Aldgate, London	merchant
13972	Barsam	Lasar	1818	Odessa, Ukraine [Odess, Russia]				Manchester	merchant
20436	Barschall	Catherine (Kate, Kitty)	1826	Spitalfields, London	Pincus Barschall		Aaron Levy	Aldgate, London	
20435	Barschall	Joseph	1822	?, Poland [?, Prussia]	Joel Abrahams	Rose (?)	Catherine (Kate, Kitty) Levy nee Barschall	Aldgate, London	tailor
20438	Barschall	Rachel	1849	Aldgate, London	Joseph Barschall	Catherine Abrahams		Aldgate, London	
2365	Bartles	John	1804	Mecklenburg Schwerin, Germany [Prussia]			Ann (?)	Hull, Yorkshire	beer shop keeper
22432	Bartlett	Sarah	1839	?	(?) Bartlett			Gravesend, Kent	boarding school pupil
11729	Baruch	Caroline	1824	?, Germany	(?)		Julius Baruch	Soho, London	
12169	Baruch	Esther	1826	?, Holland	Israel Keesing	Adelaide (?)	Isaac Zacharias Baruch	Whitechapel, London	dressmaker
24348	Baruch	Henrietta	1828	?, France	(?) Baruch			Bloomsbury, London	assistant to importer of fancy goods
12170	Baruch	Isaac Zacharias	1825	?, Holland	Zacharias Baruch		Esther Keesing	Whitechapel, London	cigar manufacturer
11728	Baruch	Julius	1822	?, Germany			Caroline (?)	Soho, London	watchmaker
19567	Baruch	Sarah	1851	Spitalfields, London	Isaac Zacharias Baruch	Esther Keesing	Hyman Rodrigues de Miranda	Whitechapel, London	
24188	Basan	Deborah	1801	Barbados, West Indies	Abraham de Isaac Nunes Israel	Sarah de Abraham Del Valle	David Basan	Hackney, London	
24189	Basan	Wallace	1828	?, Jamaica, West Indies	David Basan	Deborah Nunes (Nunes Israel)		Hackney, London	stock jobber
24057	Basch	Alfred	1838	Middlesex, London	John Basch	(?)		Euston, London	scholar
1390	Basch	Edward	1820	Leszno, Poland [Lissa, Prussia], Poland [Lissa, Prussia]			Julia Levi	Plymouth, Devon	master silversmith
24056	Basch	Fanny	1834	Middlesex, London	John Basch	(?)		Euston, London	dressmaker
24059	Basch	Frederick	1844	Middlesex, London	John Basch	(?)		Euston, London	scholar
1426	Basch	Jacob	1823	?, Russia			Sarah Marks	Plymouth, Devon	general hawker
24054	Basch	John	1801	Middlesex, London			(?)	Euston, London	tailor
1391	Basch	Julia	1828	Plymouth, Devon	John Levi	Elizabeth (?)	Edward Basch	Plymouth, Devon	
24058	Basch	Louisa	1841	Middlesex, London	John Basch	(?)		Euston, London	scholar
24055	Basch	Marian	1832	Middlesex, London	John Basch	(?)		Euston, London	father's housekeeper
9	Bash	Aaron	1817	Poznan, Poland [Posen, Prussia]	Samuel Bash		Leah Rosenthal Glück	Brighton, Sussex	tobacconist
1356	Bash	Elizabeth	1832	?, Cornwall				Plymouth, Devon	servant
2367	Battle	Azreal?	1850	Hull, Yorkshire	Robert Battle	Hannah (?)		Hull, Yorkshire	
2368	Battle	Hannah	1824	?, Poland			Robert Battle	Hull, Yorkshire	
2369	Battle	Pole (Powell, Robert)	1849	Berlin, Germany	Robert Battle	Hannah (?)	Alice (?)	Hull, Yorkshire	

ID	surname	given names	born	birthplace	father	mother	spouse 1	1851 residence	1851 occupation
2366	Battle	Robert	1826	?, Poland [?, Prussia]			Hannah (?)	Hull, Yorkshire	tailor
9810	Bauer	Alice	1837	Manchester	Abraham Bauer	Fanny (?)		Aldgate, London	scholar at home
9808	Bauer	Fanny	1803	Hamburg, Germany	(?)		Abraham Bauer	Aldgate, London	baker's wife
24409	Bauer	Harriet	1815	Whitechapel, London	(?)		Henry Bauer	Soho, London	
14030	Bauer	Henriette	1825	Hamburg, Germany	(?)		Phillip Bauer	Manchester	
24408	Bauer	Henry	1811	?, Germany	(?)		Harriet (?)	Soho, London	bootmaker
9809	Bauer	Juliette	1828	Hamburg, Germany	Abraham Bauer	Fanny (?)	Philip Gowa	Aldgate, London	teacher of languages
24410	Bauer	Louisa	1850	Soho, London	Henry Bauer	Harriet (?)		Soho, London	
14029	Bauer	Phillip	1813	Hamburg, Germany			Henriette (?)	Manchester	print merchant
9536	Baum	Abraham	1837	Poznan, Poland [Posen, Prussia]	Jacob Baum	Amelia Hiller		Spitalfields, London	scholar
147	Baum	Adolphus Saly	1826	Hamburg, Germany	Peter Frederick Baum	Hannah (Johanna) Behrens	Patti (?)	City, London	bullion dealer
9534	Baum	Amelia	1806	Poznan, Poland [Posen, Prussia]	Moses Hiller		Jacob Baum	Spitalfields, London	
5167	Baum	Cecilia (Celia)	1850	Portsmouth, Hampshire	David Baum	Jochabed (Caby) Barnett	Samuel Gomes da Costa	Portsmouth, Hampshire	
10	Baum	David	1811	Kornik, Poland [Kornick, Prussia]	Selig (Pinchas) Baum	Ottilie Ploczk	Jochabed (Caby) Barnett	Portsmouth, Hampshire	general dealer
149	Baum	Fanny	1836	Hamburg, Germany	Peter Frederick Baum	Hannah (Johanna) Behrens	Solomon Defries	City, London	scholar
150	Baum	Godfried (Godfrey)	1836	Hamburg, Germany	Peter Frederick Baum	Hannah (Johanna) Behrens	Julie Cohen	City, London	scholar
146	Baum	Hannah (Johanna)	1804	Altona, Germany	(?) Behrens		Peter Frederick Baum	City, London	
9533	Baum	Jacob	1797	Kornik, Poland [Kornick, Prussia]	Selig (Pinchas) Baum	Ottilie Ploczk	Amelia Hiller	Spitalfields, London	glazier
11	Baum	Jochabed (Caby)	1825	Aldgate, London	Moses Barnett	Dinah (?)	David Baum	Portsmouth, Hampshire	
17025	Baum	Joseph	1824	?, Poland [?, Prussia]				Greenock, Scotland	photographic artist
148	Baum	Joseph	1834	Hamburg, Germany	Peter Frederick Baum	Hannah (Johanna) Behrens		City, London	scholar
9538	Baum	Matilda	1843	Poznan, Poland [Posen, Prussia]	Jacob Baum	Amelia Hiller		Spitalfields, London	scholar
12	Baum	Maurice	1848	Portsmouth, Hampshire	David Baum	Jochabed (Caby) Barnett	Rachel Rosenthal Glück	Portsmouth, Hampshire	scholar
9537	Baum	Morris	1840	Poznan, Poland [Posen, Prussia]	Jacob Baum	Amelia Hiller		Spitalfields, London	scholar
151	Baum	Noe Meyer	1839	Hamburg, Germany	Peter Frederick Baum	Hannah (Johanna) Behrens	Caroline (?)	City, London	scholar
145	Baum	Peter Frederick	1795	Kornik, Poland [Kornick, Prussia]	Fischel Baum	Nuche (?)	Louise Pinner	City, London	bullion dealer
9535	Baum	Sarah	1835	Poznan, Poland [Posen, Prussia]	Jacob Baum	Amelia Hiller	Morris Fisher	Spitalfields, London	
9539	Baum	Solomon	1845	Poznan, Poland [Posen, Prussia]	Jacob Baum	Amelia Hiller	Mashe (?)	Spitalfields, London	scholar
13	Baum	Theresa	1846	Whitechapel, London	David Baum	Jochabed (Caby) Barnett	Joseph Pinkus (Pinkins)	Portsmouth, Hampshire	
14	Baum	Zallick (Zaleck) Louis	1843	Whitechapel, London	David Baum	Jochabed (Caby) Barnett	Miriam Gomes da Costa	Portsmouth, Hampshire	scholar
26948	Bauman	Aaron Moses	1828	?, Germany [?, Prussia]			Julia Nathan	Aldgate, London	cap maker empl 3
23147	Bauman	Alfred (Asher)	1816	?, Poland [?, Prussia]	Benjamin Bauman		Priscilla Isaacs	City, London	cap manufacturer
23150	Bauman	Benjamin	1845	City, London	Alfred (Asher) Bauman	Priscilla Isaacs		City, London	scholar
23154	Bauman	David	1831	?, Poland [?, Prussia]	Benjamin Bauman			City, London	
29235	Bauman	Eve	1823	?, Germany	(?)		Louis Bauman	Whitechapel, London	tailoress

ID	surname	given names	born	birthplace	father	mother	spouse 1	1851 residence	1851 occupation
23152	Bauman	James	1850	City, London	Alfred (Asher) Bauman	Priscilla Isaacs		City, London	
23151	Bauman	John	1848	City, London	Alfred (Asher) Bauman	Priscilla Isaacs		City, London	
26949	Bauman	Julia	1828	Spitalfields, London	Michael Nathan		Aaron Moses Bauman	Aldgate, London	
29234	Bauman	Louis	1812	?, Germany			Eve (?)	Whitechapel, London	tailor
29239	Bauman	Maria	1825	?, Germany	(?) Bauman			Whitechapel, London	servant
29236	Bauman	Maria	1844	?, Germany	Louis Bauman	Eve (?)		Whitechapel, London	
29238	Bauman	Michael	1850	?, Germany	Louis Bauman	Eve (?)		Whitechapel, London	
29237	Bauman	Philip	1848	?, Germany	Louis Bauman	Eve (?)		Whitechapel, London	
23148	Bauman	Priscilla	1826	?, London	(?) Isaacs		Alfred (Asher) Bauman	City, London	
23149	Bauman	Rebecca	1843	City, London	Alfred (Asher) Bauman	Priscilla Isaacs		City, London	scholar
25847	Bauman	Samuel	1834	?, Poland				Aldgate, London	slipper maker
26950	Bauman	Sarah	1851	Aldgate, London	Aaron Moses Baumann	Julia Nathan	Aron Joseph Selig	Aldgate, London	
21626	Baumgarten	Carl	1822	Vienna, Austria			Frederika (?)	Barnsbury, London	watchmaker
21629	Baumgarten	Catherine	1849	?, London	Carl Baumgarten	Frederika (?)		Barnsbury, London	
21628	Baumgarten	Frederika	1848	?, London	Carl Baumgarten	Frederika (?)		Barnsbury, London	
21627	Baumgarten	Frederika	1828	Vienna, Austria	(?)		Carl Baumgarten	Barnsbury, London	
24401	Baumgartner	Charles Henry	1807	?, Germany			Sophia Jeans	Soho, London	watch maker master
29336	Baxman	Aaron	1834	?, Poland				Whitechapel, London	capmaker
28051	Bear	Solomon	1831	Bydgoszcz, Poland [Bromberg, Prussia]				Spitalfields, London	shoemaker
4298	Bears	George	1829	?, Germany				Birmingham	musician
4297	Bears	Lewis	1833	?, Germany				Birmingham	musician
13481	Beaver	Albert	1850	Manchester	Louis Beaver	Rachael (?)		Manchester	
13480	Beaver	Evelyn	1847	Manchester	Louis Beaver	Rachael (?)	Julius Salenger	Manchester	
30810	Beaver	Laura	1851	Manchester	Louis Beaver	Rachael (?)		Manchester	
13478	Beaver	Louis	1820	?, Poland [?, Prussia]			Rachael (?)	Manchester	watch maker + jeweller
13479	Beaver	Rachael	1825	Hanley, Staffordshire	George Mayer	Amelia (Malka) (?)	Louis Beaver	Manchester	
42	Bebarfield (Bebarfald)	Abraham	1850	Aldgate, London	Solomon Bebarfield (Bebarfald)	Miriam Barnett		Aldgate, London	
40	Bebarfield (Bebarfald)	Barnett	1847	Aldgate, London	Solomon Bebarfield (Bebarfald)	Miriam Barnett		Aldgate, London	scholar
9736	Bebarfield (Bebarfald)	Barnett (Burnet)	1831	Wriezen, Germany [Wreshin, Prussia]	Myer Bebarfield (Bebarfald)	Shifra (Jane) (?)	Fanny Davis	Aldgate, London	cigar maker
41	Bebarfield (Bebarfald)	Esther	1848	Aldgate, London	Solomon Bebarfield (Bebarfald)	Miriam Barnett	John Lyon	Aldgate, London	scholar
9740	Bebarfield (Bebarfald)	Henry	1850	Aldgate, London	Solomon Bebarfield (Bebarfald)	Miriam Barnett		Aldgate, London	
9739	Bebarfield (Bebarfald)	Leah	1837	Wriezen, Germany [Wreshin, Prussia]	Myer Bebarfield (Bebarfald)	Shifra (Jane) (?)		Aldgate, London	tailoress
15	Bebarfield (Bebarfald)	Miriam	1825	Aldgate, London	Moses Barnett	Dinah (?)	Solomon M Bebarfield (Bebarfald)	Aldgate, London	
9734	Bebarfield (Bebarfald)	Myer	1801	Wriezen, Germany [Wreshin, Prussia]			Shifra (Jane) (?)	Aldgate, London	cap manufacturer
9738	Bebarfield (Bebarfald)	Priscilla	1835	Wriezen, Germany [Wreshin, Prussia]	Myer Bebarfield (Bebarfald)	Shifra (Jane) (?)	Philip Levy	Aldgate, London	cap maker

ID	surname	given names	born	birthplace	father	mother	spouse 1	1851 residence	1851 occupation
9737	Bebarfield (Bebarfald)	Rachel	1833	Wriezen, Germany [Wreshin, Prussia]	Myer Bebarfield (Bebarfald)	Shifra (Jane) (?)	Harris Jacobs	Aldgate, London	cap maker
9735	Bebarfield (Bebarfald)	Shifra (Jane)	1803	Wriezen, Germany [Wreshin, Prussia]	(?)		Myer Bebarfield (Bebarfald)	Aldgate, London	
39	Bebarfield (Bebarfald)	Solomon M	1822	Wriezen, Germany [Wreshin, Prussia]	Myer Bebarfield	Shifra (Jane) (?)	Miriam Barnett	Aldgate, London	
10385	Bebber	Aaron Isaacs	1847	Spitalfields, London	Isaac Isaacs Bebber	Amelia Simons		Spitalfields, London	scholar
10382	Bebber	Abraham Isaacs	1839	Spitalfields, London	Isaac Isaacs Bebber	Amelia Simons		Spitalfields, London	scholar
10381	Bebber	Amelia	1812	Amsterdam, Holland	Aaron Simons		Isaac Isaacs Bebber	Spitalfields, London	
10383	Bebber	Betsey Isaacs	1842	Spitalfields, London	Isaac Isaacs Bebber	Amelia Simons		Spitalfields, London	scholar
10380	Bebber	Isaac Isaacs	1801	Spitalfields, London	Abraham Isaacs Bebber		Amelia Simons	Spitalfields, London	general dealer
10384	Bebber	John Isaacs	1843	Spitalfields, London	Isaac Isaacs Bebber	Amelia Simons		Spitalfields, London	scholar
30934	Bebgebub	John	1835	Oldenburg, Germany [Holdenburg, Prussia]	(?) Liense			Hull, Yorkshire	mariner
13692	Bebro	Amelia	1817	Portsmouth, Hampshire	(?)		(?) Bebro	Manchester	
13695	Bebro	Ann	1839	Birmingham	(?) Bebro	Amelia (?)		Manchester	tailoress
13693	Bebro	Benjamin	1835	Manchester	(?) Bebro	Amelia (?)	Rosa (?)	Manchester	scholar
13698	Bebro	Henry	1845	Manchester	(?) Bebro	Amelia (?)		Manchester	commercial clerk
13697	Bebro	Joseph	1845	Manchester	(?) Bebro	Amelia (?)		Manchester	scholar
13696	Bebro	Marcus	1841	Birmingham	(?) Bebro	Amelia (?)	Clara Samuelson	Manchester	scholar
13694	Bebro	Sophia	1840	Birmingham	(?) Bebro	Amelia (?)		Manchester	scholar
14348	Bechtel	Abraham	1803	Hesse, Germany			Matilda (?)	Manchester	foreign export merchant
26696	Bechtel	Charles	1845	Manchester	Abraham Bechtel	Matilda (?)		Manchester	scholar
26698	Bechtel	Edmund	1850	Manchester	Abraham Bechtel	Matilda (?)		Manchester	
26697	Bechtel	Louisa Theresia Jeanette Colin	1846	Manchester	Abraham Bechtel	Matilda (?)		Manchester	
26694	Bechtel	Matilda	1825	Hesse, Germany	(?)		Abraham Hesse	Manchester	
26695	Bechtel	Philip Eberhard	1840	Manchester	Abraham Bechtel	Matilda (?)		Manchester	scholar
14562	Beck	Ann	1830	Spitalfields, London	Henry Beck	Sarah (?)	Joseph Bernal	Spitalfields, London	dress maker
14556	Beck	Dinah	1848	Spitalfields, London	Lewis Henry Beck	Maria (?)	Alexander Peartree	Spitalfields, London	
14563	Beck	Elizabeth	1832	Spitalfields, London	Henry Beck	Sarah (?)		Spitalfields, London	
14554	Beck	Esther	1845	Shoreditch, London	Lewis Henry Beck	Maria (?)	Edward B Alexander	Spitalfields, London	day scholar
14561	Beck	Laurence	1828	Spitalfields, London	Henry Beck	Sarah (?)		Spitalfields, London	cigar maker
14552	Beck	Lewis Henry	1818	Spitalfields, London	Henry Beck	Sarah (?)	Maria (?)	Spitalfields, London	glass + china dealer
14553	Beck	Maria	1823	?, London	(?)		Lewis Henry Beck	Spitalfields, London	
14559	Beck	Michael	1818	Spitalfields, London	Henry Beck	Sarah (?)		Spitalfields, London	china + glass dealer
14557	Beck	Rosetta	1845	Spitalfields, London	Lewis Henry Beck	Maria (?)	Samuel Heilbuth	Spitalfields, London	
14560	Beck	Samuel	1825	Spitalfields, London	Henry Beck	Sarah (?)	Elizabeth (Lizzie) Levy (Levi)	Spitalfields, London	servant
14558	Beck	Sarah	1796	Spitalfields, London	(?)		Henry Beck	Spitalfields, London	
14555	Beck	Sarah	1845	Spitalfields, London	Lewis Henry Beck	Maria (?)	Morris (Maurice) Lewis Alexander	Spitalfields, London	day scholar
16529	Behrend	David	1794	Hanover, Germany			Maria (?)	Liverpool	ship broker
7661	Behrend	George	1826	Liverpool	David Behrend	Maria (?)	Elkah Mendes Da Costa	Liverpool	ship broker
3632	Behrend	Henry	1828	Liverpool	David Behrend	Maria (?)	Priscilla Moses	Liverpool	scholar

ID	surname	given names	born	birthplace	father	mother	spouse 1	1851 residence	1851 occupation
2370	Behrend	Ludwig	1829	Pomerania, Germany				Hull, Yorkshire	tailor
16530	Behrend	Maria	1797	Liverpool			David Behrend	Liverpool	
16528	Behrend	Samuel	1841	Liverpool	David Behrend	Maria (?)		Liverpool	student
7028	Behrens	Adela Louise	1850	Manchester	Louis Behrens	Emilie (?)	Charles Moncriefe Simon	Manchester	
6718	Behrens	Alexander	1849	Holborn, London	Joseph Behrens	Frances (Fanny) Gollin	Agnes Carew Williams	Holborn, London	scholar
13983	Behrens	Alfred Emil M	1847	Manchester	Louis Behrens	Emilie (?)		Manchester	
23700	Behrens	August	1830	?, Germany				Liverpool	toy merchant's assistant
7794	Behrens	Bennet	1850	Nottingham, Nottinghamshire	Maurice Behrens	Rebecca (?)	Alice Kisch	Nottingham, Nottinghamshire	
7024	Behrens	Charles	1849	Bradford, Yorkshire	Jacob Behrens	Dorothea (Doris) Hohenemser		Bradford, Yorkshire	
31014	Behrens	Clara	1848	Bradford, Yorkshire	Jacob Behrens	Dorothea (Doris) Hohenemser		Bradford, Yorkshire	scholar
7020	Behrens	Dorothea (Doris)	1819	?, Germany	(?) Hohenemser		Jacob Behrens	Bradford, Yorkshire	
6704	Behrens	Edward	1836	Manchester	Salomon Behrens	Anne (?)	Abigail Lucas	?Manchester	
15110	Behrens	Elizabeth S	1818	Bloomsbury, London	(?) Palmer	Ann (?)		Bethnal Green, London	
20926	Behrens	Emilia	1849	Middlesex, London	Rudolph Behrens	Sophia (?)		Manchester	
7026	Behrens	Emilie	1823	Leipzig, Germany	(?)		Louis Behrens	Manchester	
21329	Behrens	Emma	1822	Manchester	(?) Behrens			Tonbridge, Kent	
2091	Behrens	Frances (Fanny)	1810	?, London	Wolf Josephson Gollin	Marlah (Martha) (?)	Joseph Behrens	Holborn, London	
7022	Behrens	Frederick	1850	Bradford, Yorkshire	Jacob Behrens	Dorothea (Doris) Hohenemser		Bradford, Yorkshire	
7023	Behrens	Gustav	1846	Bradford, Yorkshire	Jacob Behrens	Dorothea (Doris) Hohenemser	Fanny (?)	Bradford, Yorkshire	
7027	Behrens	Isaac (Oscar) Henry	1849	Manchester	Louis Behrens	Emilie (?)	Florence Louisa Salaman	Manchester	
20915	Behrens	Isabella	1849	Nottingham, Nottinghamshire	Maurice Behrens	Rebecca (?)		Nottingham, Nottinghamshire	
7019	Behrens	Jacob	1806	Pyrmont, Waldeck, Germany	Nathan Behrens	Clara Hahn	Dorothea (Doris) Hohenemser	Bradford, Yorkshire	stuff merchant
6654	Behrens	Joseph	1803	?, Germany	Dov Behr HaCohen		Frances (Fanny) Gollin	Holborn, London	jeweller + picture dealer
6712	Behrens	Joseph Barnett	1830	Holborn, London	Joseph Behrens	Frances (Fanny) Gollin	Sarah Lesser	Holborn, London	
6713	Behrens	Lewis Herbert	1845	Holborn, London	Joseph Behrens	Frances (Fanny) Gollin		Holborn, London	scholar
7025	Behrens	Louis	1813	Pyrmont, Waldeck, Germany	Nathan Behrens	Clara Hahn	Emilie (?)	Manchester	merchant
7793	Behrens	Maurice	1816	?, Germany			Rebecca (?)	Nottingham, Nottinghamshire	jeweller
6714	Behrens	Morris	1848	Holborn, London	Joseph Behrens	Frances (Fanny) Gollin		Holborn, London	scholar
6715	Behrens	Pauline Eve	1841	Holborn, London	Joseph Behrens	Frances (Fanny) Gollin	Morris Lawrence Levy	Holborn, London	scholar
20914	Behrens	Rebecca	1825	?, London	(?)		Maurice Behrens	Nottingham, Nottinghamshire	
13984	Behrens	Rudolph	1814	Pyrmont, Waldeck, Germany	Nathan Behrens	Clara Hahn	Sophia (?)	Manchester	merchant in cotton goods
15109	Behrens	Samuel Jacob	1816	?, Germany			Elizabeth S Palmer	Bethnal Green, London	teacher of German + Hebrew
6716	Behrens	Sarah	1838	Holborn, London	Joseph Behrens	Frances (Fanny) Gollin		Holborn, London	scholar
6717	Behrens	Solomon	1846	Holborn, London	Joseph Behrens	Frances (Fanny) Gollin		Holborn, London	scholar
13985	Behrens	Sophia	1831	Hamburg, Germany	(?)		Rudolph Behrens	Manchester	

ID	surname	given names	born	birthplace	father	mother	spouse 1	1851 residence	1851 occupation
7021	Behrens	Wilhelmina (Mina)	1841	Bradford, Yorkshire	Jacob Behrens	Dorothea (Doris) Hohenemser		Bradford, Yorkshire	
23109	Belais (Belize)	Abraham	1764	?, Africa			Naomi (?)	Aldgate, London	Rabbi of Portuguese Synagogue
23110	Belais (Belize)	Naomi	1801	?, Italy	(?)		Abraham Belais (Belize)	Aldgate, London	
16401	Belasco	Abraham	1803	?, London	Isaac Belasco	Rebecca (?)	Rachel Joseph	Aldgate, London	general dealer + butcher
11718	Belasco	Abraham	1844	Aldgate, London	Joseph Belasco	Rachel Tolano		Aldgate, London	
21818	Belasco	Abraham	1845	Spitalfields, London	Moses de Isaac Belasco	Sophia (Zipporah) Levy	Tanny (?)	Spitalfields, London	
7509	Belasco	Abraham (Aby) Henry	1796	Aldgate, London	Joseph de Abraham Belasco	Sarah de Joseph Nunes Martines	Leah (Eliza) Whaite	Aldgate, London	licensed victualler + rum dealer
15512	Belasco	Abraham (George)	1836	Covent Garden, London	Isaac de Joseph Belasco	Rosa (Raischa) de Alexander Isaac	Maria (Miriam) Davis	Covent Garden, London	apprentice
15500	Belasco	Abraham Julian	1811	Gibraltar	David de Abraham Belasco	Sarah de Moses Julian	Hagar de Joseph Belasco	Covent Garden, London	tobacconist
16406	Belasco	Adelaide (Addie)	1842	?, London	Abraham de Isaac Belasco	Rachel Joseph	Emanuel Lee	Aldgate, London	scholar
20919	Belasco	Agnes	1834	Covent Garden, London	Israel de Joseph Belasco	Sarah de Mordecai Samuel		Covent Garden, London	
21815	Belasco	Agnes (Agar	1803	Middlesex, London	Israel de Joseph Nunes Martines	Sarah de David Fernandes	John (Jacob) de Joseph Belasco	Aldgate, London	general dealer
16403	Belasco	Bella (Hanah, ?Anabella)	1850	?, London	Abraham de Isaac Belasco	Rachel Joseph		Aldgate, London	
7304	Belasco	Buena	1844	Spitalfields, London	David de Isaac de Joseph Belasco	Merla (Paloma, Polly, Mary) de Simha	Eleazar Ventura	Aldgate, London	
25944	Belasco	Daniel	1819	Stepney, London	Isaac Belasco	Rebecca (?)	Rachael Israel	Aldgate, London	clothes dealer
7299	Belasco	David	1808	Aldgate, London	Isaac de Joseph Belasco	Rebecca (?)	Merla (Paloma, Polly, Mary) de Simha	Aldgate, London	Beadle of Synagogue + general dealer
20511	Belasco	David	1825	Aldgate, London, London	Isaac de Joseph Belasco	Rosa (Raischa) de Alexander Isaac	Mary (Miriam, Pauline) Davis	Waterloo, London	tailor + coffee house + brothel keeper
20922	Belasco	Deborah	1843	Covent Garden, London	Israel de Joseph Belasco	Sarah de Mordecai Samuel		Covent Garden, London	
21822	Belasco	Ellen (Elsie)	1828	Covent Garden, London	Israel de Joseph Belasco	Sarah de Mordecai Samuel	John (Giovanni, Isaac) Levy Ximenes	Covent Garden, London	
9309	Belasco	Esther	1812	Aldgate, London	(?Isaac) Belasco			Aldgate, London	nurse
15508	Belasco	Esther	1824	City, London	Emanual Simmons		Joseph de Isaac de Abraham Belasco	Covent Garden, London	
16405	Belasco	Esther	1839	?, London	Abraham de Isaac Belasco	Rachel Joseph		Aldgate, London	umbrella maker maker
7312	Belasco	Esther	1843	Aldgate, London	David de Isaac de Joseph Belasco	Merla (Paloma, Polly, Mary) de Simha		Aldgate, London	
25948	Belasco	Esther	1850	Aldgate, London	Daniel Belasco	Rachael Israel		Aldgate, London	
15501	Belasco	Hagar	1794	Whitechapel, London	Joseph de Abraham Belasco	Sarah de Joseph Nunes Martines	Abraham Julian de David Belasco	Covent Garden, London	
8529	Belasco	Hannah	1798	Mile End, London	Aaron Gomes da Costa	Fanny (?)	Abraham (Aby) de Joseph Belasco	Aldgate, London	
7302	Belasco	Hannah	1841	Aldgate, London	David de Isaac de Joseph Belasco	Merla (Paloma, Polly, Mary) de Simha	Abraham Haim Nieto	Aldgate, London	
16408	Belasco	Hannah	1844	?, London	Abraham de Isaac Belasco	Rachel Joseph		Aldgate, London	scholar
18651	Belasco	Humphrey (Abraham)	1831	Covent Garden, London	Israel de Joseph Belasco	Sarah de Mordecai Samuel	Reyna Martin (Nunes Martines)	Covent Garden, London	general dealer

ID	surname	given names	born	birthplace	father	mother	spouse 1	1851 residence	1851 occupation
15505	Belasco	Isaac	1795	City, London	Joseph de Abraham Belasco	Sarah de Joseph Nunes Martines	Rosa (Raischa) de Alexander Isaac	Covent Garden, London	publican
16404	Belasco	Isaac	1836	?, London	Abraham de Isaac Belasco	Rachel Joseph		Aldgate, London	cigar maker
21820	Belasco	Isaac	1837	Middlesex, London	Moses de Isaac Belasco	Sophia (Zipporah) Levy		Spitalfields, London	
25946	Belasco	Isaac	1847	Stepney, London	Daniel Belasco	Rachael Israel		Aldgate, London	scholar
15509	Belasco	Isaac Doloro	1843	Covent Garden, London	Joseph de Isaac de Abraham Belasco	Esther Simmons	Selina Simmonds	Covent Garden, London	
18649	Belasco	Israel	1798	?Aldgate, London	Joseph de Abraham Belasco	Sarah de Joseph Nunes Martines	Sarah de Mordecai Samuel	Covent Garden, London	fruit dealer
21814	Belasco	John (Jacob)	1804	Middlesex, London	Joseph de Abraham Belasco	Sarah de Joseph Nunes Martines	Agnes (Agar) Nunes Martines	Aldgate, London	general dealer
15510	Belasco	John (Jacob)	1834	Covent Garden, London	Isaac de Joseph Belasco	Rosa (Raischa) de Alexander Isaac	Esther Toledano	Covent Garden, London	apprentice
14909	Belasco	John George	1836	Middlesex, London				Bethnal Green, London	boarding school pupil
16366	Belasco	Joseph	1806	Aldgate, London	Isaac Belasco	Rebecca (?)	Phoebe de Michael Isaacs	Aldgate, London	orphan school steward
7310	Belasco	Joseph	1823	Covent Garden, London	Abraham (Aby) Belasco	Leah (Eliza) Whaite	Rachel Tolano	Aldgate, London	general dealer
15507	Belasco	Joseph	1824	City, London	Isaac de Joseph Belasco	Rosa (Raischa) de Alexander Isaac	Esther Simmons	Covent Garden, London	coffee shop + brothel keeper
21816	Belasco	Joseph	1828	Middlesex, London	John (Jacob) de Joseph Belasco	Angnes (Agar) Nunes Martines	Julia (Judith) Levy	Aldgate, London	waterproofer
11726	Belasco	Joseph	1847	Aldgate, London	Joseph Belasco	Rachel Tolano		Aldgate, London	
20928	Belasco	Joseph S	1849	Strand, London	Joseph Simmons Belasco			Strand, London	
20927	Belasco	Joseph Simmons	1824	Strand, London	Emanuel Simmons	Rachael Belasco	Sarah Genese nee Tolano	Strand, London	
18653	Belasco	Julia	1837	Covent Garden, London	Israel de Joseph Belasco	Sarah de Mordecai Samuel		Covent Garden, London	
11720	Belasco	Kate (Kith, Keturah)	1849	Aldgate, London	Joseph Belasco	Rachel Tolano	Barnett Buckner	Aldgate, London	
11719	Belasco	Leah	1846	Aldgate, London	Joseph Belasco	Rachel Tolano		Aldgate, London	
20514	Belasco	Leah	1847	Covent Garden, London	David de Isaac Belasco	Mary (Miriam, Pauline) Davis		Waterloo, London	
21817	Belasco	Levy	1839	Middlesex, London	Moses de Isaac Belasco	Sophia (Zipporah) Levy	Abigail Nunes Martines	Spitalfields, London	
20512	Belasco	Mary (Miriam, Pauline)	1825	Whitechapel, London	Isaac Davis		David de Isaac Belasco	Waterloo, London	
7313	Belasco	Merla (Paloma, Polly, Mary)	1810	Aldgate, London	Simhah		David de Isaac de Joseph Belasco	Aldgate, London	
21819	Belasco	Mordecai	1850	Spitalfields, London	Moses de Isaac Belasco	Sophia (Zipporah) Levy	Rose Shannon	Spitalfields, London	
7309	Belasco	Moses	1815	Middlesex, London	Isaac Belasco	Rebecca (?)	Sophia (Zipporah) Levy	Spitalfields, London	
16367	Belasco	Phoebe	1812	Whitechapel, London	Michael Isaacs		Joseph de Isaac Belasco	Aldgate, London	
16407	Belasco	Phoebe	1842	?, London	Abraham de Isaac Belasco	Rachel Joseph	Isaac Rodrigues	Aldgate, London	scholar
25945	Belasco	Rachael	1823	Stepney, London	John William Kemp		Daniel Belasco	Aldgate, London	dressmaker
7316	Belasco	Rachel	1811	Portsmouth, Hampshire	Joseph Joseph		Abraham de Isaac Belasco	Aldgate, London	general dealer
7311	Belasco	Rachel	1820	Bethnal Green, London	Joseph Tolano	?Rebecca (?)	Joseph Belasco	Aldgate, London	
7314	Belasco	Rachel	1836	Aldgate, London	David de Isaac de Joseph Belasco	Merla (Paloma, Polly, Mary) de Simha		Aldgate, London	
18951	Belasco	Rachel	1836	Aldgate, London	David Belasco	Polly (Paloma, Merla) Simha		Aldgate, London	
20921	Belasco	Rachel	1840	Covent Garden, London	Israel de Joseph Belasco	Sarah de Mordecai Samuel	W H Sharpe	Covent Garden, London	

ID	surname	given names	born	birthplace	father	mother	spouse 1	1851 residence	1851 occupation
30101	Belasco	Rachel	1851	Covent Garden, London	David de Isaac Belasco	Mary (Miriam, Pauline) Davis		Covent Garden, London	
7307	Belasco	Rebecca	1829	Whitechapel, London	David de Isaac de JosephBelasco	Merla (Paloma, Polly, Mary) de Simha		Aldgate, London	
16402	Belasco	Rebecca	1833	?, London	Abraham de Isaac Belasco	Rachel Joseph	Jacob Jalfon	Aldgate, London	furrier
21821	Belasco	Rebecca	1843	Spitalfields, London	Moses Belasco	Sophia (Zipporah) Levy	Aaron Frisco	Spitalfields, London	
25947	Belasco	Rebecca	1848	Stepney, London	Daniel Belasco	Rachael Israel		Aldgate, London	scholar
15506	Belasco	Rosa	1801	City, London	Alexander Isaac		Isaac de Joseph Belasco	Covent Garden, London	
7298	Belasco	Rosetta	1833	Aldgate, London	David de Isaac de JosephBelasco	Merla (Paloma, Polly, Mary) Simha	Isaac Benoliel	Aldgate, London	
20513	Belasco	Rosey	1844	City, London	David de Isaac Belasco	Mary (Miriam, Pauline) Davis		Waterloo, London	
20920	Belasco	Sally	1836	Covent Garden, London	Israel de Joseph Belasco	Sarah de Mordecai Samuel		Covent Garden, London	
18950	Belasco	Samson	1833	Aldgate, London	David de Isaac de Joseph Belasco	Merla (Paloma, Polly, Mary) de Simha		Aldgate, London	
21827	Belasco	Samuel	1827	?London	Isaac de Joseph Belasco	Rosa (Raischa) de Alexander Isaac	Mary Ann Pooles	Covent Garden, London	
7300	Belasco	Samuel	1833	Aldgate, London	David de Isaac de Joseph Belasco	Merla (Paloma, Polly, Mary) de Simha	Hannah Isaacs	Aldgate, London	watchmaker
18650	Belasco	Sarah	1804	?	Mordecai Samuel		Israel Belasco	Covent Garden, London	
22048	Belasco	Sarah	1836	Middlesex, London	John (Jacob) de Joseph Belasco	Agnes (Agar) Nunes Martines		Aldgate, London	general dealer
15503	Belasco	Sarah	1837	Covent Garden, London	Abraham Julian de David Belasco	Agar de Joseph Belasco		Covent Garden, London	
7308	Belasco	Sarah	1838	Aldgate, London	David de Isaac de Joseph Belasco	Merla (Paloma, Polly, Mary) de Simha		Aldgate, London	
18654	Belasco	Solomon	1836	Covent Garden, London	Israel de Joseph Belasco	Sarah de Mordecai Samuel	Clara (?)	Covent Garden, London	waiter
8528	Belasco	Sophia (Zipporah)	1821	Middlesex, London	Levy Levy		Moses Belasco	Spitalfields, London	
18652	Belasco [Bland]	Joseph	1825	Covent Garden, London	Israel de Joseph Belasco	Sarah de Mordecai Samuel	Elizabeth Hart Whiteman	St Giles, London	dancer
15502	Belasco [James]	David	1835	Covent Garden, London	Abraham Julian de David Belasco	Hagar de Joseph Belasco	Mary Ann O'Hara	Covent Garden, London	
23162	Belilo	Abraham	1848	City, London	Israel Belilo	Sarah (?)		City, London	
23161	Belilo	Esther (Hester)	1844	City, London	Israel Belilo	Sarah (?)		City, London	
23155	Belilo	Israel	1803	Islington, London	Machluf Belilo	Judith de Moseh Rodrigues Moreira	Sarah (Jane) (?)	City, London	teacher of dancing
23158	Belilo	Julia	1836	Whitechapel, London	Israel Belilo	Sarah (?)	abraham Dupree	City, London	
23160	Belilo	Machluff	1838	Whitechapel, London	Israel Belilo	Sarah (?)	Elizabeth Moore	City, London	
23163	Belilo	Prosper (Masaod)	1850	City, London	Israel Belilo	Sarah (?)		City, London	
23159	Belilo	Rosetta (Rosa)	1841	Whitechapel, London	Israel Belilo	Sarah (?)	Elias Nunes Martines	City, London	
23157	Belilo	Sarah	1832	Whitechapel, London	Israel Belilo	Sarah (?)		City, London	
23156	Belilo	Sarah (Jane)	1813	Whitechapel, London	(?)		Israel Belilo	City, London	
24073	Belinfante	Abigail	1805	?, Jamaica, West Indies	Abraham Quixano Henriques		Daniel de Sadiq Cohen Belinfante	Regent's Park, London	fundholder
24074	Belinfante	Ellen	1835	Clapton, London	Daniel de Sadiq Cohen Belinfante	Abigail Quixano Henriques	Simeon Jacobs	Regent's Park, London	scholar at home
18138	Belinfante	Janetta (Jeanette, Tonati)	1794	Middlesex, London	Sadik de Isaac Cohen Belinfante	Abigail de Isaac Garcia		Mile End, London	formerly seamstress
24075	Belinfante	Julia	1837	Clapton, London	Daniel de Sadiq Cohen Belinfante	Abigail Quixano Henriques		Regent's Park, London	scholar at home
18137	Belinfante	Louisa	1795	Middlesex, London	Sadik de Isaac Cohen Belinfante	Abigail de Isaac Garcia		Mile End, London	seamstress

ID	surname	given names	born	birthplace	father	mother	spouse 1	1851 residence	1851 occupation
18139	Belinfante	Matilda	1798	Middlesex, London	Sadik de Isaac Cohen Belinfante	Abigail de Isaac Garcia		Mile End, London	seamstress
15873	Belisario	Caroline	1804	Middlesex, London	Abraham Mendes Belisario	Esther (?)		Hackney, London	partner in educational establishment
15903	Belisario	Clara Mendes	1784	Middlesex, London	Isaac Mendes Belisario	Leah (?)		Hackney, London	partner in educational establishment
24199	Belisario	David A	1792	Kingston, Jamaica, West Indies	Abraham Mendes Belisario			Hackney, London	fundholder
24201	Belisario	Esther A	1828	Middlesex, London	David A Belisario	(?)		Hackney, London	
24200	Belisario	Grace A	1826	Middlesex, London	David A Belisario	(?)		Hackney, London	
25482	Belisario	Hannah	1803	Whitechapel, London	(?)		Aaron (Haim) Mendes Belisario	Tower Hill, London	alms house recipient
15267	Belisario	Julia (Judith) Mendes	1791	?, London	Jacob de Isaac Mendes Da Costa	Rebecca de Elias Lindo	Jacob de Isaac Mendes Belisario	Shoreditch, London	fundholder
15871	Belisario	Lydia	1793	Kingston, Jamaica, West Indies	Abraham Mendes Belisario	Esther (?)		Hackney, London	Principal of educational establishment
25483	Belisario	Lydia (Leah)	1836	City, London	Aaron (Haim) Mendes Belisario	Hannah (?)		Tower Hill, London	
24205	Belisario	Lydia A	1836	Middlesex, London	David A Belisario	(?)		Hackney, London	scholar
24198	Belisario	Maria A	1797	Kingston, Jamaica, West Indies	Abraham Mendes Belisario	Esther (?)		Hackney, London	
15268	Belisario	Marian (Miriam) Mendes	1816	?, London	Jacob de Isaac Mendes Belisario	Julia (Judith) de Jacob Mendes Da Costa		Shoreditch, London	Hebrew teacher
24203	Belisario	Mir A	1832	Middlesex, London	David A Belisario	(?)		Hackney, London	
24206	Belisario	Octavius A	1840	Hackney, London	David A Belisario	(?)		Hackney, London	scholar
24204	Belisario	Rebecca A	1835	Middlesex, London	David A Belisario	(?)		Hackney, London	scholar
15872	Belisario	Rose	1796	Kingston, Jamaica, West Indies	Abraham Mendes Belisario	Esther (?)		Hackney, London	partner in educational establishment
24202	Belisario	Sarah A	1829	Middlesex, London	David A Belisario	(?)		Hackney, London	
18394	Belisha	Clara	1805	?, Africa	(?)		David Belisha	Aldgate, London	
18391	Belisha	Clara	1846	Aldgate, London	Isaac David Belisha	Julia (Judith) Senior Coronel	Felix Sahal	Aldgate, London	
18393	Belisha	David	1796	?, Africa			Clara (?)	Aldgate, London	traveller (various articles)
18389	Belisha	Isaac David	1815	Westminster, London	David Belisha	Clara (?)	Julia (Judith) Senior Coronel	Whitechapel, London	cigar maker empl 8
18392	Belisha	Sarah	1848	?Aldgate, London	Isaac David Belisha	Julia (Judith) Senior Coronel		Aldgate, London	
1245	Bellam	Jacob	1811	Dartmouth, Devon		Rachel (?)		Plymouth, Devon	general dealer
1247	Bellam (Bellem)	Abraham	1823	Dartmouth, Devon		Rachel (?)		Plymouth, Devon	dyer
1246	Bellam (Bellem)	Harriet	1811	Dartmouth, Devon		Rachel (?)		Plymouth, Devon	seamstress
1244	Bellam (Bellem)	Rachel	1783	Plymouth, Devon				Plymouth, Devon	housekeeper
1180	Bellem	Aaron	1850	Plymouth, Devon		Betsy Bellem		Plymouth, Devon	
1177	Bellem	Betsy	1808	Plymouth, Devon				Plymouth, Devon	clothes cleaner + dyer
1178	Bellem	George	1849	Plymouth, Devon		Betsy Bellem		Plymouth, Devon	
31121	Belman	Natan	1826	?Kalisz, Poland [Shalee, Poland]				Ipswich, Suffolk	dealer in jewellery
2897	Benabo	Abraham	1837	Middlesex, London	Masahod Benabo	Judith Mendel	Amelia Paris	Tower Hill, London	
15022	Benabo	Agnes	1846	Bethnal Green, London	Robert C Benabo	Edith (?)		Bethnal Green, London	
15024	Benabo	Benjamin G	1850	Bethnal Green, London	Robert C Benabo	Edith (?)		Bethnal Green, London	
15021	Benabo	Clifford	1846	Liverpool	Robert C Benabo	Edith (?)		Bethnal Green, London	scholar

ID	surname	given names	born	birthplace	father	mother	spouse 1	1851 residence	1851 occupation
15023	Benabo	Daniel M	1849	Bethnal Green, London	Robert C Benabo	Edith (?)		Bethnal Green, London	
15020	Benabo	Edith	1826	Bristol	(?)		Robert C Benabo	Bethnal Green, London	
15016	Benabo	Judith	1792	Bristol	Menahem Cohen Mendel		Masahod de Solomon Benabo	Tower Hill, London	
2898	Benabo	Masahod	1790	Essaouira, Morocco [Mogador, Morocco]	Solomon Benabu		Judith (Gitla) de Menahem Cohen Mendel	Tower Hill, London	interpreter of Arabic
15019	Benabo	Robert C	1824	Stepney, London			Edith (?)	Bethnal Green, London	scripture reader
15017	Benabo	Zara	1834	Middlesex, London	Masahod Benabo	Judith Mendel	Morris Lenzberg	Tower Hill, LondonCity, London	milliner
30382	Benas	Abraham	1847	Aldgate, London	Louis (Lewis) Benas	Rose (?)		Whitechapel, London	
30380	Benas	Baron	1844	Aldgate, London	Louis (Lewis) Benas	Rose (?)		Whitechapel, London	scholar
30383	Benas	Deborah	1848	Whitechapel, London	Louis (Lewis) Benas	Rose (?)		Whitechapel, London	
30381	Benas	Ester	1846	Aldgate, London	Louis (Lewis) Benas	Rose (?)		Whitechapel, London	scholar
30378	Benas	Louis (Lewis)	1820	Poznan, Poland [Posen, Prussia]	Binyamin		Rose (?)	Whitechapel, London	boot + shoe maker master empl 2 men
30384	Benas	Louisa	1850	Whitechapel, London	Louis (Lewis) Benas	Rose (?)		Whitechapel, London	
30379	Benas	Rose	1822	Poznan, Poland [Posen, Prussia]	(?)		Louis (Lewis) Benas	Whitechapel, London	
29868	Bendahan	Rebecca	1811	Whitechapel, London	Moses Bendahan	Simha (Jessie) de Abraham Benavente		Wapping, London	dressmaker
29869	Bendahan	Sarah	1812	Whitechapel, London	Moses Bendahan	Simha (Jessie) de Abraham Benavente		Wapping, London	upholsterer
28035	Bendin	Abraham	1823	Middlesex, London	(?) Bendin	Mary (?)		Spitalfields, London	shoemaker
28034	Bendin	Mary	1787	?, London	(?)		(?) Bendin	Spitalfields, London	glove maker
28036	Bendin	Solomon	1831	Middlesex, London	(?) Bendin	Mary (?)		Spitalfields, London	chair maker
12225	Bending	Hannah	1819	?, Poland [?, Prussia]	(?)		Solomon Bending	Whitechapel, London	
12226	Bending	Sarah	1851	Whitechapel, London	Solomon Bending	Hannah (?)		Whitechapel, London	
12224	Bending	Solomon	1819	?, Poland [?, Prussia]			Hannah (?)	Whitechapel, London	jeweller
24612	Bendix	Sarah	1823	Kettering, Norhamptonshire	(?) Bendix			Kennington, London	cook
17547	Bendof	Aaron	1834	City, London	Henry Bendof	Rosa (?)		Spitalfields, London	tailor
17545	Bendof	Hannah	1830	City, London	Henry Bendof	Rosa (?)	Samuel Lazarus	Spitalfields, London	furrier
17544	Bendof	Henry	1800	?			Rosa (?)	Spitalfields, London	
17546	Bendof	Rachael	1835	City, London	Henry Bendof	Rosa (?)		Spitalfields, London	tailoress
17543	Bendof	Rosa	1802	abroad [Colander, ?]	(?)		Henry Bendof	Spitalfields, London	furrier
12567	Bendon (Bandan)	Alice (Alcy)	1803	Cambridge, Cambridgeshire	Isaac Kyezor	Hannah Levy (Levi)	Moses (Mosiac, Macluf) Bendon (Bandan)	Norwich, Norfolk	
5559	Bendon (Bandan)	George	1835	Ely, Cambridgeshire	Moses (Mosiac, Macluf) Bendon	Alice (Alcy) Kyezor (Keyzor)	Julia Hart	Norwich, Norfolk	
12568	Bendon (Bandan)	Hannah	1829	Norwich, Norfolk	Moses (Mosiac, Macluf) Bendon (Bandan)	Alice (Alcy) Kyezor (Keyzor)	Joseph Levine	Norwich, Norfolk	
16876	Bendon (Bandan)	Moses	1821	Norwich, Norfolk	Moses (Mosiac, Macluf) Bendon (Bandan)	Moses (Mosiac, Macluf) Bendon (Bandan)		Cambridge	traveller
12566	Bendon (Bandan)	Moses (Mosiac, Macluf)	1778	Essaouira, Morocco [Mogador, Morocco]	Dahan		Alice (Alcy) Kyezor (Keyzor)	Norwich, Norfolk	retired merchant
19224	Bendon (Bandan)	Sarah	1842	Cambridge	Moses (Mosiac, Macluf) Bendon	Alice (Alcy) Kyezor (Keyzor)	Samuel Raphael Samuel	Norwich, Norfolk	

ID	surname	given names	born	birthplace	father	mother	spouse 1	1851 residence	1851 occupation
14967	Bendu	Hannah	1838	Middlesex, London	(?) Bendu			Bethnal Green, London	boarding school pupil
1999	Bene (Benny)	Jacob	1820	Szatmar, Hungary	Ferencz Benes	Maria (?)	Julia Seeman	Whitechapel, London	tailor
2001	Bene (Benny)	Philip	1851	Whitechapel, London	Jacob Bene (Benny)	Julia Zaman (Seeman)	Rosetta Woolf	Whitechapel, London	
19203	Benedict	Adele	1815	?, Italy	(?) Jean	Maria (?)	Julius Benedict	Marylebone, London	
19204	Benedict	Adeline	1837	Naples, Italy	Julius Benedict	Adele Jean	(?) Barrouss de Hingle	Marylebone, London	
19208	Benedict	Alice	1846	Marylebone, London	Julius Benedict	Adele Jean		Marylebone, London	
19206	Benedict	Edward	1841	Whitechapel, London	Julius Benedict	Adele Jean		Marylebone, London	
5694	Benedict	Frances	1803	Liverpool	(?)		Henry Benedict	Liverpool	dressmaker
19207	Benedict	Georgina	1843	Whitechapel, London	Julius Benedict	Adele Jean		Marylebone, London	
20870	Benedict	Henry	1803	Manchester			Frances (?)	Liverpool	mariner
7018	Benedict	Julius	1804	Stuttgart, Germany			Adele Jean	Marylebone, London	conductor, composer + musicologist
19205	Benedict	Julius	1839	Whitechapel, London	Julius Benedict	Adele Jean		Marylebone, London	
16472	Benhamu	Abraham	1795	Gibraltar			Rachel (?)	Mile End, London	general dealer
16470	Benhamu	Esther	1825	Gibraltar	Abraham Benhamu	Rachel (?)		Mile End, London	
16471	Benhamu	Isaac	1827	Gibraltar	Abraham Benhamu	Rachel (?)		Mile End, London	
21644	Benhamu	Leon (Judah)	1829	Gibraltar	Abraham Benhamu	Rachel (?)	Rachel Garcia	Mile End, London	ship broker
16473	Benhamu	Rachel	1803	Gibraltar	(?)		Abraham Benhamu	Mile End, London	general dealer
7632	Benhamu (Benham)	Henry (Hillel)	1839	Gibraltar	Abraham Benhamu	Rachel (?)	Louisa (Luna) Aflalo	Mile End, London	scholar
29488	Benhayon	David	1775	?, Morocco			Mary Ann (?)	Spitalfields, London	hawker in spices
29490	Benhayon	George Edward	1836	City, London	David Benhayon	Mary Ann (?)		Spitalfields, London	French polisher
29489	Benhayon	Mary Anne	1815	City, London			David Benhayon	Spitalfields, London	
29491	Benhayon	Solomon	1848	City, London	David Benhayon	Mary Ann (?)		Spitalfields, London	
21038	Benhile	Solomon	1843	Gibraltar				Dover, Kent	boarding school pupil
7013	Benisch	Abraham	1814	?Czech Republic [Drossau, Bohemia]			Harriet Levy	Bloomsbury, London	teacher of languages
29575	Benjamin	A---	1791	Spitalfields, London	(?)		Asher Benjamin	Whitechapel, London	
19370	Benjamin	Aaron	1808	Aldgate, London	Michael Benjamin (Menahem Menke)	Benlah bat Naftali Hirsh	(?)	Whitechapel, London	general dealer
10039	Benjamin	Abigail	1789	Aldgate, London	Jacob Benjamin			Waterloo, London	
27313	Benjamin	Abraham	1788	Middlesex, London			Amelia (?)	Aldgate, London	general dealer
29282	Benjamin	Abraham	1794	Whitechapel, London	Elias Benjamin		(?)	Whitechapel, London	general dealer
24366	Benjamin	Abraham	1798	Whitechapel, London			Phoebe (?)	St Giles, London	clothier
29291	Benjamin	Abraham	1800	Whitechapel, London	Joseph Benjamin		Julia (Juliet) Levy	Whitechapel, London	pencil maker
19361	Benjamin	Abraham	1809	Aldgate, London	Michael Benjamin (Menahem Menke)	Beulah bat Naftali Hirsh	Sarah Abrahams	Whitechapel, London	dairyman
14429	Benjamin	Abraham	1811	?, Poland [?, Prussian Poland]				Salford, Lancashire	rag sorter
9684	Benjamin	Abraham	1814	Leigh, Essex	Nathan Benjamin	Catherine Moses	Rebecca Simmonds	Strand, London	tailor + draper
17811	Benjamin	Abraham	1822	Whitechapel, London	Michael Benjamin	(?)		Aldgate, London	watch maker
4154	Benjamin	Abraham	1843	Whitechapel, London	Samuel Benjamin	Lydia Hart	Anne Joseph	Aldgate, London	
21392	Benjamin	Ada (Adele)	1844	Aldgate, London	Benjamin Benjamin	Hannah (?)	Abraham Isaac	Marylebone, London	
6620	Benjamin	Adelaide	1839	Euston, London	Elias Benjamin	Eve Barnet	Moses Mendoza	Euston, London	
9668	Benjamin	Adelaide	1849	Whitechapel, London	Abraham Benjamin	Louisa (?)		Whitechapel, London	scholar
30970	Benjamin	Alexander	1841	?, London	Lewis Benjamin	Rachael Jacobs		Hull, Yorkshire	

ID	surname	given names	born	birthplace	father	mother	spouse 1	1851 residence	1851 occupation
22129	Benjamin	Alfred	1828	Shoreditch, London			Rachel (?)	Whitechapel, London	cigar maker
20235	Benjamin	Alfred	1850	?, Canada	Goodman Benjamin	Julia Ballin		St John's Wood, London	
19407	Benjamin	Alice	1846	Southwark, London	Moses (Maurice) Benjamin	Emma (?)		Southwark, London	
12947	Benjamin	Alice	1851	Southwark, London	Joseph Benjamin	Dinah Davis		Southwark, London	scholar
25138	Benjamin	Alice (Eliza, Ailsie)	1830	Finsbury, London	Emanuel Benjamin	Jane Cohen	Ralph (Raphael) Lazarus	Finsbury, London	
25126	Benjamin	Amelia	1786	Finsbury, London	(?)		Lewis Benjamin	Finsbury, London	
27314	Benjamin	Amelia	1788	Middlesex, London	(?)		Abraham Benjamin	Aldgate, London	bonnet maker
6872	Benjamin	Amelia	1800	Spitalfields, London	(?)		(?) Benjamin	Edmonton, London	licensed victualler
14366	Benjamin	Amelia	1810	Liverpool	(?)		Joel Benjamin	Manchester	
6870	Benjamin	Amelia	1825	Spitalfields, London			Lewis Samuel	Aldgate, London	cap maker
20201	Benjamin	Amelia	1834	Spitalfields, London	Simon Benjamin	Hannah Elias		Spitalfields, London	general dealer
9591	Benjamin	Angel	1814	Shoreditch, London	Isaac Benjamin		Elizabeth Mosely	Spitalfields, London	general dealer
21390	Benjamin	Angelina	1839	Aldgate, London	Benjamin Benjamin	Hannah (?)		Marylebone, London	
13733	Benjamin	Ann	1788	?, London	Abraham Harris		Joel Benjamin	Bloomsbury, London	
25088	Benjamin	Ann	1825	Whitechapel, London	David Benjamin	Esther (?)	Abraham Aaron Harris	Finsbury, London	haberdasher
24168	Benjamin	Ann	1837	Euston, London	Elias Benjamin	Eve Barnet		Euston, London	
19366	Benjamin	Ann (Genandel)	1828	Aldgate, London	Lyon (Lionel) Benjamin	Mary Ann (Perle) Levi		Whitechapel, London	annuitant
29885	Benjamin	Ann (Hannah)	1842	Whitechapel, London	Moses Benjamin	Susan Solomon	Moss Judah Solomon	Wapping, London	scholar
830	Benjamin	Anne	1848	Marylebone, London	Henry Benjamin	Hannah Isaacs		Marylebone, London	
20956	Benjamin	Annie	1846	Soho, London	Lewis Benjamin	Rosetta Meyer		Soho, London	
29574	Benjamin	Asher	1781	Spitalfields, London			A--- (?)	Whitechapel, London	
29286	Benjamin	Asher	1838	Whitechapel, London	Abraham Benjamin	(?)		Whitechapel, London	[tailor's] shop boy
11787	Benjamin	Barnet	1848	Shoreditch, London	Samuel Benjamin	Elisa (?)		Shoreditch, London	scholar
30967	Benjamin	Ben	1833	?, London	Lewis Benjamin	Rachael Jacobs		Hull, Yorkshire	traveller in caps
21385	Benjamin	Benjamin	1790	?, London	Moshe		Hannah (?)	Marylebone, London	importer of antiquities
2207	Benjamin	Benjamin	1796	Aldgate, London	Michael Benjamin (Menahem Menke)	Benlah bat Naftali Hirsh	Rebecca (?)	Bristol	travelling hawker
14572	Benjamin	Benjamin	1815	Finsbury, London	Solomon Benjamin	Elizabeth (?)		Finsbury, London	cabman
6871	Benjamin	Benjamin	1823	Spitalfields, London	(?) Benjamin	Amelia (?)		Edmonton, London	
30787	Benjamin	Benjamin	1823	Finsbury, London			Esther Davis	Preston, Lancashire	clothier
25132	Benjamin	Benjamin	1824	Finsbury, London	Emanuel Benjamin	Jane Cohen	Jane Phillips	Finsbury, London	clothier
29006	Benjamin	Benjamin	1826	Finsbury, London	Asher Benjamin		Julia Marks	Whitechapel, London	clock [---]
20540	Benjamin	Benjamin	1829	?, Holland	Moses Benjamin	(?)		Aldgate, London	fishmonger
20543	Benjamin	Benjamin	1831	?London				Aldgate, London	tailor
27316	Benjamin	Benjamin	1832	Middlesex, London	Abraham Benjamin	Amelia (?)		Aldgate, London	cigar maker
10087	Benjamin	Benjamin	1833	Holborn, London	Henry Benjamin	Deborah Barnett		Holborn, London	apprentice to cigar maker
24856	Benjamin	Benjamin	1833	?Finsbury, London	Moss (Moses) Benjamin	Esther (?)	Frances (Fanny) Levy	Bermondsey, London	clothier
15655	Benjamin	Benjamin	1838	?, London	Samuel Benjamin	Lydia Hart	Hannah Benjamin	Aldgate, London	scholar
9666	Benjamin	Benjamin	1840	Whitechapel, London	Abraham Benjamin	Louisa (?)		Whitechapel, London	scholar
9026	Benjamin	Benjamin	1845	Soho, London	Lewis Benjamin	Rosetta Meyer	Jeannette Barnett	Soho, London	scholar at home
9903	Benjamin	Benjamin	1849	St Pancras, London	David Benjamin	Frances (?)		Marylebone, London	
18308	Benjamin	Benjamin	1851	Ramsgate, Kent	Jacob Benjamin	Paulina (?)		Ramsgate, Kent	
30385	Benjamin	Benjamin	1851	Spitalfields, London	Angel Benjamin	Elizabeth Mosely		Spitalfields, London	
30386	Benjamin	Benjamin	1851	Marylebone, London	Benjamin Benjamin	Hannah (?)		Marylebone, London	
816	Benjamin	Betsy (Elizabeth)	1822	Kensington, London	Saunders Solomon	Rachel Davis	Solomon Benjamin	Piccadilly, London	

ID	surname	given names	born	birthplace	father	mother	spouse 1	1851 residence	1851 occupation
25985	Benjamin	Blumer	1831	Whitechapel, London	(?) Weiller		Lazarus Benjamin	Aldgate, London	
25090	Benjamin	Caroline	1835	?Whitechapel, London	David Benjamin	Esther (?)		Finsbury, London	
25144	Benjamin	Catharine (Kate)	1845	Finsbury, London	Emanuel Benjamin	Jane Cohen	Phillip Jacob Solomon	Finsbury, London	scholar
9683	Benjamin	Catherine	1794	Westminster, London	Yehuda Moses		Nathan Benjamin	Strand, London	tailor + draper
15586	Benjamin	Catherine	1811	Aldgate, London	(?Tsevi Hirsh) Benjamin			Covent Garden, London	general servant
20544	Benjamin	Charles	1835	?London				Aldgate, London	clerk
24307	Benjamin	Charles	1848	Middlesex, London	Joseph David Benjamin	Martha Benjamin		St Giles, London	
19406	Benjamin	Charlotte	1844	Southwark, London	Moses (Maurice) Benjamin	Emma (?)		Southwark, London	scholar
30971	Benjamin	Charlotte	1844	Whitechapel, London	Lewis Benjamin	Rachael Jacobs		Hull, Yorkshire	
25419	Benjamin	Charlotte Mary	1825	Whitechapel, London			David Benjamin	Holborn, London	
3157	Benjamin	Cilia (Celia)	1847	Whitchurch, Shropshire	Emanuel Benjamin	Rebecca (Rebekah) Levy (Lewy)		Whitchurch, Shropshire	
19362	Benjamin	Clara	1832	Bristol	Benjamin Benjamin	Rebecca (?)		Whitechapel, London	[lady's] companion
9024	Benjamin	Daniel	1837	Marylebone, London	Lewis Benjamin	Rosetta Meyer		Soho, London	day scholar
25091	Benjamin	David	1787	?, London			Esther (?)	Finsbury, London	general dealer
9900	Benjamin	David	1814	Strand, London	Benjamin Benjamin		Frances South	Marylebone, London	working jeweller
25418	Benjamin	David	1825	Holborn, London			Charlotte Mary (?)	Holborn, London	greengrocer
30193	Benjamin	David	1827	?, Poland	(?)	Leane Benjamin		Dudley, Worcestershire	glazier
25310	Benjamin	David	1829	Whitechapel, London				Aldgate, London	cabinet maker
20203	Benjamin	David	1839	Spitalfields, London	Simon Benjamin	Hannah Elias		Spitalfields, London	scholar
827	Benjamin	David	1841	Marylebone, London	Mark Benjamin	Elizabeth Solomon	Elizabeth Solomon	Marylebone, London	
10091	Benjamin	David	1844	Holborn, London	Henry Benjamin	Deborah Barnett		Holborn, London	scholar
11562	Benjamin	David Joseph	1844	?Aldgate, London	Joseph Benjamin	Harriet (Hannah) Hart	Henry Benjamin	Aldgate, London	
10084	Benjamin	Deborah	1804	Aldgate, London	Hyam Barnett	Rachel Lazarus	John Aaron	Holborn, London	
16951	Benjamin	Diana (Dinah)	1822	Aldgate, London	Joel Benjamin	Frances Cohen	Joseph Benjamin	Hammersmith, London	school mistress
12944	Benjamin	Dinah	1829	Southwark, London	David Davis			Southwark, London	
2372	Benjamin	Edward	1813	?, Poland [?, Prussia]				Hull, Yorkshire	journeyman cigar maker
17809	Benjamin	Edward	1815	Middlesex, London	Michael Benjamin	(?)	Fanny Levy	Aldgate, London	watch maker
20233	Benjamin	Edward	1848	?, Canada	Goodman Benjamin	Julia Ballin		St John's Wood, London	scholar at home
21397	Benjamin	Edwin	1843	Soho, London	(?) Benjamin	Amelia (?)		Edmonton, London	scholar
24165	Benjamin	Elias	1805	Aldgate, London	Asher		Eve Barnet	Euston, London	engraver + stationer
22951	Benjamin	Elias	1820	City, London	Abraham Benjamin		Mary Lazarus	Wapping, London	general dealer
14594	Benjamin	Elias	1825	Whitechapel, London	Moshe Benjamin		Esther Jessurun	Hoxton, London	cigar maker
27085	Benjamin	Elias	1838	?, London	(?) Benjamin	Maria (?)		Aldgate, London	general dealer
11784	Benjamin	Elisa	1823	Shoreditch, London	(?)		Samuel Benjamin	Shoreditch, London	
14571	Benjamin	Elizabeth	1795	Finsbury, London			Solomon Benhamin	Finsbury, London	
821	Benjamin	Elizabeth	1799	Kensington, London	(?) Solomon		Mark Benjamin	Marylebone, London	
15527	Benjamin	Elizabeth	1803	Covent Garden, London	(?)		Philip Benjamin	Covent Garden, London	
9592	Benjamin	Elizabeth	1814	Spitalfields, London	Moshe Mosely		Angel Benjamin	Spitalfields, London	
22945	Benjamin	Elizabeth	1827	Wapping, London	Phillip Harris		Isaiah Benjamin	Wapping, London	
16772	Benjamin	Elizabeth	1829	Bristol	Benjamin Benjamin	Rebecca (?)		Bristol	dressmaker
29881	Benjamin	Elizabeth	1829	Whitechapel, London	Moses Benjamin	Susan Solomon	Isaac Asher Spiewkowsky (Isaac Asher)	Wapping, London	
833	Benjamin	Elizabeth	1846	Westminster, London	Henry Benjamin	Hannah Isaacs	Isaac Hart	Marylebone, London	
10092	Benjamin	Elizabeth	1847	Holborn, London	Henry Benjamin	Deborah Barnett	Lewis Henry Lyons	Holborn, London	at home

ID	surname	given names	born	birthplace	father	mother	spouse 1	1851 residence	1851 occupation
25135	Benjamin	Emanuel	1801	Finsbury, London	Henry Samuel Benjamin		Jane Cohen	Finsbury, London	clothier
3154	Benjamin	Emanuel	1805	?, Poland [?, Russian Poland]	Henry Benjamin		Rebecca (Rebekah) Levy (Lewy)	Whitchurch, Shropshire	cheese inspector for Jews
24306	Benjamin	Emily Eve	1846	Marylebone, London	Joseph David Benjamin	Martha Benjamin		St Giles, London	
20232	Benjamin	Emily?	1846	?, Canada	Goodman Benjamin	Julia Ballin		St John's Wood, London	scholar at home
14573	Benjamin	Emma	1820	Finsbury, London	Solomon Benjamin	Elizabeth (?)		Finsbury, London	
19405	Benjamin	Emma	1823	Southwark, London	(?)		Moses (Maurice) Benjamin	Southwark, London	milliner
25141	Benjamin	Emma	1837	Finsbury, London	Emanuel Benjamin	Jane Cohen		Finsbury, London	scholar
25421	Benjamin	Emma	1848	Holborn, London	David Benjamin	Charlotte Mary (?)		Holborn, London	
30789	Benjamin	Ephraim	1849	Strand, London	Benjamin Benjamin	Esther Davis		Preston, Lancashire	
20234	Benjamin	Ernest	1849	?, Canada	Goodman Benjamin	Julia Ballin		St John's Wood, London	
20431	Benjamin	Ester	1774	Amsterdam, Holland	(?)		(?) Benjamin	Aldgate, London	
24853	Benjamin	Esther	1795	Middlesex, London	(?)		Moss (Moses) Benjamin	Bermondsey, London	
25092	Benjamin	Esther	1795	?, London	(?)		David Benjamin	Finsbury, London	
28267	Benjamin	Esther	1810	?Aldgate, London	Yehuda Myers		Joseph Benjamin	Aldgate, London	
14595	Benjamin	Esther	1819	Finsbury, London	Eli Jessurun		Elias Benjamin	Hoxton, London	
30788	Benjamin	Esther	1821	Deptford, London	(?) Davis		Benjamin Benjamin	Preston, Lancashire	
321	Benjamin	Esther	1828	Whitechapel, London	Moses Benjamin			Aldgate, London	umbrella maker
10728	Benjamin	Esther	1835	Middlesex, London	Isaac Benjamin	Jane (?)	Julius Green	Spitalfields, London	tailoress
24167	Benjamin	Esther	1835	Euston, London	Elias Benjamin	Eve Barnet		Euston, London	
20202	Benjamin	Esther	1837	Spitalfields, London	Simon Benjamin	Hannah Elias		Spitalfields, London	tailoress
9902	Benjamin	Esther	1846	?Aldgate, London	David Benjamin	Frances (?)		Marylebone, London	
3159	Benjamin	Esther	1850	Whitchurch, Shropshire	Emanuel Benjamin	Rebecca (Rebekah) Levy (Lewy)	(?) Smith	Whitchurch, Shropshire	
22553	Benjamin	Esther	1850	Aldgate, London	(?) Benjamin			Aldgate, London	
9028	Benjamin	Esther	1851	Soho, London	Lewis Benjamin	Rosetta Meyer		Soho, London	
6431	Benjamin	Eugene	1834	Aldgate, London	Benjamin Benjamin	Hannah (?)	Ellen Davis	Marylebone, London	
24166	Benjamin	Eve	1803	Aldgate, London	(?) Barnet		Elias Benjamin	Euston, London	
4095	Benjamin	Fanny	1801	Surrey, London			(?) Benjamin	Soho, London	
29157	Benjamin	Fanny	1825	Aldgate, London	(?) Benjamin			Whitechapel, London	
29284	Benjamin	Fanny	1831	Whitechapel, London	Abraham Benjamin	(?)	Isaac Cohen	Whitechapel, London	tailoress
9020	Benjamin	Fanny	1840	Soho, London	Lewis Benjamin	Rosetta Meyer	Samson Genese	Soho, London	
14596	Benjamin	Fanny	1845	Hoxton, London	Elias Benjamin	Esther Jessurun		Hoxton, London	scholar
16950	Benjamin	Frances	1804	Middlesex, London	Jacob Moses Cohen		(?)	Hammersmith, London	retired
9901	Benjamin	Frances	1825	Marylebone, London	(?)		David Benjamin	Marylebone, London	
6621	Benjamin	Frances	1834	Euston, London	Elias Benjamin	Eve Barnet	Mordecai (Mark) Mendoza	Marylebone, London	leather dealer
28340	Benjamin	Francess	1769	Aldgate, London			(?Isaac) Benjamin	Aldgate, London	dealer in general
24308	Benjamin	Frederick Ephraim	1849	St Giles, London	Joseph David Benjamin	Martha Benjamin		St Giles, London	
20231	Benjamin	Frederick?	1844	?, Canada	Goodman Benjamin	Julia Ballin		St John's Wood, London	scholar at home
28950	Benjamin	George	1823	Whitechapel, London				Whitechapel, London	commercial traveller (cigars)
21396	Benjamin	George	1840	Strand, London	(?) Benjamin	Amelia (?)		Edmonton, London	scholar
21389	Benjamin	Georgina	1830	?, London	Benjamin Benjamin	Hannah (?)		Marylebone, London	
20229	Benjamin	Goodman	1815	Middlesex, London	Michael Benjamin	Sarah Goodman	Julia Ballin	St John's Wood, London	merchant
4157	Benjamin	Grace	1809	Spitalfields, London	Abraham Abrahams		Samuel Benjamin	Aldgate, London	

ID	surname	given names	born	birthplace	father	mother	spouse 1	1851 residence	1851 occupation
10886	Benjamin	Hannah	1765	Spitalfields, London	(?)		(?) Benjamin	Spitalfields, London	
28162	Benjamin	Hannah	1780	City, London	(?)		Abraham Benjamin	Shoreditch, London	
21386	Benjamin	Hannah	1796	New York, USA	(?)		Benjamin Benjamin	Marylebone, London	
18040	Benjamin	Hannah	1806	Elsford, Somerset	(?)		Isaac Benjamin	Dudley, Worcestershire	
30195	Benjamin	Hannah	1806	Olsford, Somerset	(?)		Isaac Benjamin	Dudley, Worcestershire	
29298	Benjamin	Hannah	1811	Whitechapel, London	Joseph Benjamin			Whitechapel, London	umbrella maker assistant
20200	Benjamin	Hannah	1813	Middlesex, London	Philip Elias		Simon Benjamin	Spitalfields, London	
829	Benjamin	Hannah	1821	Whitechapel, London	Samuel Isaacs	Elizabeth (?)	Henry Benjamin	Marylebone, London	
27047	Benjamin	Hannah	1823	Knightsbridge, London	Saunders Solomon	Rachel Davis	Jonas (Joseph) Benjamin	Marylebone, London	
823	Benjamin	Hannah	1831	Paddington, London	Mark Benjamin	Elizabeth Solomon	Henry Emanuel	Marylebone, London	
15529	Benjamin	Hannah	1831	Covent Garden, London	Philip Benjamin	Elizabeth (?)	(?) ?Hertz	Covent Garden, London	
25143	Benjamin	Hannah	1842	Finsbury, London	Emanuel Benjamin	Jane Cohen	Benjamin Benjamin	Finsbury, London	scholar
24371	Benjamin	Hannah	1844	?, London	Abraham Benjamin	Phoebe (?)		St Giles, London	scholar
25420	Benjamin	Hannah	1846	Holborn, London	David Benjamin	Charlotte Mary (?)		Holborn, London	scholar
19408	Benjamin	Hannah	1849	Southwark, London	Moses (Maurice) Benjamin	Emma (?)		Southwark, London	
20944	Benjamin	Henrietta Alexandra	1847	Worthing, Sussex	John Benjamin	Leah (?)	Moss (Moses) Benjamin	Birmingham	
14577	Benjamin	Henry	1791	Aldgate, London			Sophia (?)	Covent Garden, London	general dealer
10083	Benjamin	Henry	1801	Aldgate, London	Michael Benjamin (Menahem Menke)	Beulah bat Naftali Hirsh (Hirsch)	Deborah Barnett	Holborn, London	clothes salesman
17998	Benjamin	Henry	1805	Whitechapel, London	Solomon Benjamin	Judith Jonas	Martha Simmons	Aldgate, London	clothes dealer
828	Benjamin	Henry	1821	Knightsbridge, London	Mark Benjamin	Elizabeth Solomon	Hannah Isaacs	Marylebone, London	cab proprietor
20539	Benjamin	Henry	1821	?, Holland	Moses Benjamin	(?)	Cecilia (Celia) Abrahams	Aldgate, London	fishmonger
20542	Benjamin	Henry	1827	?London				Aldgate, London	jeweller
12481	Benjamin	Henry	1836	Spitalfields, London	Samuel Benjamin	Mary Simmons		Aldgate, London	fruit dealer
19369	Benjamin	Henry	1838	Cape, South Africa	Lyon (Lionel) Benjamin	Mary Ann (Perle) Levi	Kate Fink	Whitechapel, London	scholar
11560	Benjamin	Henry	1840	?Aldgate, London	Joseph Benjamin	Harriet (Hannah) Hart		Aldgate, London	
818	Benjamin	Henry	1849	Westminster, London	Solomon Benjamin	Betsy (Elizabeth) Solomon	Sarah Lipman	Piccadilly, London	
26220	Benjamin	Henry	1849	?, London	John Benjamin	Maria (Miriam) Baruk		Aldgate, London	
29008	Benjamin	Henry	1849	Whitechapel, London	Benjamin Benjamin	Julia Marks		Whitechapel, London	
14526	Benjamin	Hyam	1841	Holborn, London	Henry Benjamin	Deborah Barnett		Holborn, London	scholar
26221	Benjamin	Hyam	1850	Spitalfields, London	John Benjamin	Maria (Miriam) Baruk		Aldgate, London	
21940	Benjamin	Hyam (Hyman)	1824	Aldgate, London	Victor Benjamin		Adelaide (Betsey, Edella) Myers	Spitalfields, London	
18039	Benjamin	Isaac	1796	?, London			Hannah (?)	Dudley, Worcestershire	tailor
30194	Benjamin	Isaac	1796	?, London			Hannah (?)	Dudley, Worcestershire	tailor
19743	Benjamin	Isaac	1832	Hackney, London				Soho, London	shopman (jeweller + watchmaker's)
8678	Benjamin	Isaac	1835	Aldgate, London	(?) Benjamin	Rachel Jacobs		Aldgate, London	cigar maker
826	Benjamin	Isaac	1837	Paddington, London	Mark Benjamin	Elizabeth Solomon		Marylebone, London	
18001	Benjamin	Isaac	1839	Aldgate, London	Henry Benjamin	Martha Simmons		Aldgate, London	scholar
9594	Benjamin	Isaac	1842	Shoreditch, London	Angel Benjamin	Elizabeth Mosely	Rachel Ellis	Spitalfields, London	scholar
12479	Benjamin	Isaac	1843	Aldgate, London	Samuel Benjamin	Mary Simmons		Aldgate, London	scholar
20955	Benjamin	Isaac	1850	Whitechapel, London	Abraham Benjamin	Louisa (?)		Whitechapel, London	
12480	Benjamin	Isabella (Bella)	1840	Spitalfields, London	Samuel Benjamin	Mary Simmons		Aldgate, London	fruit dealer

ID	surname	given names	born	birthplace	father	mother	spouse 1	1851 residence	1851 occupation
22944	Benjamin	Isaiah	1822	Middlesex, London	Abraham Benjamin	(?)	Elizabeth Harris	Wapping, London	
22953	Benjamin	Isaiah	1844	Wapping, London	Elias Benjamin	Mary Lazarus		Wapping, London	outfitter + oilman
18003	Benjamin	Israel	1843	Aldgate, London	Henry Benjamin	Martha Simmons		Aldgate, London	
12476	Benjamin	Israel	1847	Aldgate, London	Samuel Benjamin	Mary Simmons	Rachel Sampson	Aldgate, London	scholar
26363	Benjamin	Jacob	1801	?, Germany				Aldgate, London	scholar
18306	Benjamin	Jacob	1807	?, Russia			Paulina (?)	Ramsgate, Kent	traveller
9542	Benjamin	Jacob	1830	Kornik, Poland [Kurnik, Prussia]				Spitalfields, London	glazier master
25136	Benjamin	Jane	1803	Finsbury, London	Shmuel HaCohen		Emanuel Benjamin	Finsbury, London	tailor
10727	Benjamin	Jane	1805	?, Holland	(?)		Isaac Benjamin	Spitalfields, London	licensed hawker
25142	Benjamin	Jane	1840	Finsbury, London	Emanuel Benjamin	Jane Cohen	Samuel Marks	Finsbury, London	scholar
6111	Benjamin	Jane	1846	Whitechapel, London	Abraham Benjamin	Louisa (?)	Woolf Emanuel	Whitechapel, London	scholar
3158	Benjamin	Jenette	1848	Whitchurch, Shropshire	Emanuel Benjamin	Rebecca (Rebekah) Levy (Lewy)		Whitchurch, Shropshire	
13732	Benjamin	Joel	1784	Brighton, Sussex	Abraham		Ann Harris	Bloomsbury, London	merchant
14365	Benjamin	Joel	1810	?, Poland [?, Prussia]			Amelia (?)	Manchester	rag dealer
4299	Benjamin	John	1794	Middlesex, London			Leah (?)	Birmingham	fishmonger
24357	Benjamin	John	1805	Spitalfields, London			Mary (?)	Covent Garden, London	clothes salesman
26217	Benjamin	John	1818	?, London	Moses Benjamin		Maria (Miriam) Baruk	Aldgate, London	cigar maker
11725	Benjamin	John	1830	Aldgate, London				Aldgate, London	general dealer
14525	Benjamin	John	1840	Holborn, London	Henry Benjamin	Deborah Barnett		Holborn, London	scholar
15657	Benjamin	John	1845	?, London	Samuel Benjamin	Lydia Hart		Aldgate, London	scholar
12946	Benjamin	Jonas	1850	Finsbury, London	Joseph Benjamin	Dinah Davis		Southwark, London	
27046	Benjamin	Jonas (Joseph)	1821	Marylebone, London	Mark Benjamin	Elizabeth Solomon	Hannah Solomon	Marylebone, London	orange merchant
11559	Benjamin	Joseph	1801	Middlesex, London			Harriet (Hannah) Hart	Aldgate, London	quill manufacturer
16795	Benjamin	Joseph	1808	?, Poland [?, Prussia]	Benjamin Theomin		(?) Braham	Bristol	deputy Minister of Synagogue
28266	Benjamin	Joseph	1811	Stepney, London	Moshe Benjamin		Esther Myers	Aldgate, London	cigar manufacturer
9685	Benjamin	Joseph	1818	Leigh, Essex	Nathan Benjamin	Catherine Moses	Phoebe Abrahams	Strand, London	
12943	Benjamin	Joseph	1824	Paddington, London	Jonah Benjamin		Dinah Davis	Southwark, London	general dealer
10090	Benjamin	Joseph	1839	Holborn, London	Henry Benjamin	Deborah Barnett	Rachel Harris	Holborn, London	scholar
21391	Benjamin	Joseph	1840	?, London	Benjamin Benjamin	Hannah (?)	Lizzie Bennett	Marylebone, London	
29294	Benjamin	Joseph	1840	Whitechapel, London	Abraham Benjamin	Julia (Juliet) Levy		Whitechapel, London	cigar maker assistant
15656	Benjamin	Joseph	1842	?, London	Samuel Benjamin	Lydia Hart		Aldgate, London	scholar
9597	Benjamin	Joseph	1850	Spitalfields, London	Angel Benjamin	Elizabeth Mosely		Spitalfields, London	
24304	Benjamin	Joseph David	1816	Whitechapel, London	David Benjamin		Martha Harris nee Lewis	St Giles, London	tobacconist
30387	Benjamin	Joshua	1851	Aldgate, London	Samuel Benjamin	Mary Simmons		Aldgate, London	
20949	Benjamin	Julia	1812	Whitechapel, London	Moses Cohen	Sophia (?)	Benjamin Benjamin	Aldgate, London	general dealer
20230	Benjamin	Julia	1817	Middlesex, London	(?) Ballin		Goodman Benjamin	St John's Wood, London	
29007	Benjamin	Julia	1827	Exeter, Devon	Moses Marks		Benjamin Benjamin	Whitechapel, London	
15528	Benjamin	Julia	1829	Covent Garden, London	Philip Benjamin	Elizabeth (?)		Covent Garden, London	
14574	Benjamin	Julia	1830	Finsbury, London	Solomon Benjamin	Elizabeth (?)		Finsbury, London	umbrella maker
29285	Benjamin	Julia	1834	Whitechapel, London	Abraham Benjamin	(?)		Whitechapel, London	tailoress
29883	Benjamin	Julia	1836	Whitechapel, London	Moses Benjamin	Susan Solomon	Philip Solomon	Wapping, London	apprentice to dressmaker
16954	Benjamin	Julia	1838	Camberwell, London	Joel Benjamin	Frances Cohen	A F Ornstein	Hammersmith, London	scholar

ID	surname	given names	born	birthplace	father	mother	spouse 1	1851 residence	1851 occupation
18002	Benjamin	Julia	1840	Aldgate, London	Henry Benjamin	Martha Simmons		Aldgate, London	scholar
819	Benjamin	Julia	1847	Westminster, London	Solomon Benjamin	Betsy (Elizabeth) Solomon	Nathan Harris	Piccadilly, London	
831	Benjamin	Julia	1850	Marylebone, London	Henry Benjamin	Hannah Isaacs	Charles Davis	Marylebone, London	
27048	Benjamin	Julia	1850	Marylebone, London	Jonas (Joseph) Benjamin	Hannah Solomon	Abraham Smith	Marylebone, London	orange merchant
29292	Benjamin	Julia (Juliet)	1808	Whitechapel, London	Solomon Levy		Abraham Benjamin	Whitechapel, London	umbrella maker
19365	Benjamin	Julia (Shana)	1825	Aldgate, London	Lyon (Lionel) Benjamin	Mary Ann (Perle) Levi		Whitechapel, London	annuitant
14581	Benjamin	Kate	1825	Strand, London	Henry Benjamin	Sophia (?)		Covent Garden, London	artificial florist
21394	Benjamin	Kate	1849	Marylebone, London	Benjamin Benjamin	Hannah (?)	Henry Levy	Marylebone, London	
19368	Benjamin	Kate (Yeska)	1831	Aldgate, London	Lyon (Lionel) Benjamin	Mary Ann (Perle) Levi	Alfred Abraham Marcus	Whitechapel, London	
20254	Benjamin	L--- M---	1829	Whitechapel, London			Leah (?)	Covent Garden, London	stationer
825	Benjamin	Lawrence	1835	Paddington, London	Mark Benjamin	Elizabeth Solomon	Elizabeth Solomon	Marylebone, London	
25984	Benjamin	Lazarus	1824	Whitechapel, London			Blumer Weiller	Aldgate, London	fishmonger empl 1
20948	Benjamin	Lazarus	1835	Middlesex, London	Benjamin Benjamin	Julia Cohen		Aldgate, London	cigar maker assistant
4300	Benjamin	Leah	1799	Birmingham	(?)		John Benjamin	Birmingham	
29283	Benjamin	Leah	1804	Whitechapel, London	Samuel Joseph		Abraham Benjamin	Whitechapel, London	tailoress
21387	Benjamin	Leah	1816	New York, USA	Benjamin Benjamin	Hannah (?)	Isaac Ramus	Marylebone, London	
20255	Benjamin	Leah	1831	Strand, London	(?)		L--- M--- Benjamin	Covent Garden, London	theatrical
14971	Benjamin	Leah	1839	Quebec, Canada	(?) Benjamin			Bethnal Green, London	boarding school pupil
25134	Benjamin	Leah	1839	Finsbury, London	Emanuel Benjamin	Jane Cohen		Finsbury, London	
30192	Benjamin	Leane	1791	?, Poland	(?)		(?) Benjamin	Dudley, Worcestershire	furniture dealer
14580	Benjamin	Leon	1823	Strand, London	Henry Benjamin	Sophia (?)	Kate Savren	Covent Garden, London	porter + packer
30968	Benjamin	Leon	1834	?, London	Lewis Benjamin	Rachael Jacobs		Hull, Yorkshire	traveller in caps
25125	Benjamin	Lewis	1784	Finsbury, London			Amelia (?)	Finsbury, London	clothes dealer
8990	Benjamin	Lewis	1792	?, Poland			Sarah (?)	Portsmouth, Hampshire	none (refugee)
8653	Benjamin	Lewis	1796	Aldgate, London			Sarah (?)	Aldgate, London	wine merchant
3118	Benjamin	Lewis	1807	Rotterdam, Holland			(?)	Hull, Yorkshire	cap maker
30966	Benjamin	Lewis	1807	Rotterdam, Holland	Benjamin		Rachael Jacobs	Hull, Yorkshire	cap maker
9021	Benjamin	Lewis	1810	Middlesex, London	Benjamin		Rosetta Meyer	Soho, London	jeweller
20946	Benjamin	Lewis	1831	Whitechapel, London	Benjamin Benjamin	Julia Cohen	Phoebe (?)	Aldgate, London	cigar maker
16796	Benjamin	Lewis	1835	?, Poland [?, Prussia]	Joseph Benjamin	(?) Braham		Bristol	furrier
6873	Benjamin	Lewis (Louis)	1830	Spitalfields, London	(?) Benjamin	Amelia (?)		Edmonton, London	barman
9667	Benjamin	Lewis (Louis)	1845	Whitechapel, London	Abraham Benjamin	Louisa (?)		Whitechapel, London	scholar
9665	Benjamin	Louisa	1819	Whitechapel, London	(?)		Abraham Benjamin	Whitechapel, London	artificial flower maker
9023	Benjamin	Louisa	1836	Marylebone, London	Lewis Benjamin	Rosetta Meyer		Soho, London	
7768	Benjamin	Louisa	1837	Plymouth, Devon	Henry Benjamin	Fanny (?)	Philip Beyfus	?Plymouth, Devon	
9689	Benjamin	Louisa (Leah)	1834	Leigh, Essex	Nathan Benjamin	Catherine Moses	Henry Naphtali Simmonds	Strand, London	
22956	Benjamin	Lydia	1850	Wapping, London	Elias Benjamin	Mary Lazarus		Wapping, London	
9897	Benjamin	Lyon	1779	Aldgate, London	Abraham Lyon		Miriam Moses	Whitechapel, London	retired slopseller
10089	Benjamin	Lyon (Louis)	1837	Holborn, London	Henry Benjamin	Deborah Barnett	Rebecca Davis	Holborn, London	scholar
16704	Benjamin	M---	1792	?Holland				Spitalfields, London	general dealer
3155	Benjamin	Maidishe (Madish, Maud)	1843	Whitchurch, Shropshire	Emanuel Benjamin	Rebecca (Rebekah) Levy (Lewy)	David H Davis	Whitchurch, Shropshire	
27084	Benjamin	Maria	1802	?, London	(?)		(?) Benjamin	Aldgate, London	general dealer
17810	Benjamin	Maria	1821	Middlesex, London	Michael Benjamin	(?)		Aldgate, London	
29293	Benjamin	Maria	1830	Whitechapel, London	Abraham Benjamin	Julia (Juliet) Levy		Whitechapel, London	umbrella maker

ID	surname	given names	born	birthplace	father	mother	spouse 1	1851 residence	1851 occupation
9904	Benjamin	Maria	1850	St Pancras, London	David Benjamin	Frances (?)		Marylebone, London	
26218	Benjamin	Maria (Miriam)	1821	?, London	Mordecai Baruk		John Benjamin	Aldgate, London	dressmaker
29287	Benjamin	Mariam	1840	Whitechapel, London	Abraham Benjamin	Leah Joseph		Whitechapel, London	scholar
24370	Benjamin	Marian	1833	?, London	Abraham Benjamin	Phoebe (?)		St Giles, London	
820	Benjamin	Mark	1795	Whitechapel, London	Samuel Benjamin		Elizabeth Solomon	Marylebone, London	corn merchant
17999	Benjamin	Martha	1808	Spitalfields, London	Isaac Simmons		Henry Benjamin	Aldgate, London	
24305	Benjamin	Martha	1810	City, London	Lewis Benjamin		Aaron Harris	St Giles, London	tobacconist
24358	Benjamin	Mary	1803	Aldgate, London	(?)		John Benjamin	Covent Garden, London	
12483	Benjamin	Mary	1812	Spitalfields, London	Isaac Simmons	Sarah (?)	Samuel Benjamin	Aldgate, London	
22952	Benjamin	Mary	1824	City, London	Moses Lazarus		Elias Benjamin	Wapping, London	
10088	Benjamin	Mary	1835	Holborn, London	Henry Benjamin	Deborah Barnett		Holborn, London	cap maker
9025	Benjamin	Mary	1842	Soho, London	Lewis Benjamin	Rosetta Meyer	Reuben Hyams	Soho, London	day scholar
24855	Benjamin	Mary (Marion)	1828	Finsbury, London	Moss (Moses) Benjamin	Esther (?)		Bermondsey, London	dressmaker
19364	Benjamin	Mary Ann (Perle)	1802	Deptford, Kent	(?Abraham) Levi	Jane (?)	Lyon (Lionel) Benjamin	Whitechapel, London	annuitant
25089	Benjamin	Matilda	1831	Whitechapel, London	David Benjamin	Esther (?)		Finsbury, London	
9687	Benjamin	Matilda (Ethyl)	1829	Leigh, Essex	Nathan Benjamin	Catherine Moses	Henry Nathan	Strand, London	tailor + draper
18062	Benjamin	Michael	1784	Middlesex, London	Hirsh Mulhausen		Sarah Goodman	Southwark, London	retired merchant
17808	Benjamin	Michael	1785	abroad	Benjamin Benjamin		(?)	Aldgate, London	watch maker
14576	Benjamin	Michael	1834	Finsbury, London	Solomon Benjamin	Elizabeth (?)	Rose (?)	Finsbury, London	fish dealer
9688	Benjamin	Miriam	1832	Leigh, Essex	Nathan Benjamin	Catherine Moses	Jacob Jacobs	Strand, London	
12477	Benjamin	Mordecai Mark)	1849	Aldgate, London	Samuel Benjamin	Mary Simmons	Fanny (?)	Aldgate, London	
14598	Benjamin	Morris (Moses)	1849	Hoxton, London	Elias Benjamin	Esther Jessurun		Hoxton, London	scholar
20538	Benjamin	Moses	1786	?, Holland		Sarah Jonas	(?)	Aldgate, London	fishmonger
29879	Benjamin	Moses	1797	Spitalfields, London	Elijah		Susan Solomon	Wapping, London	general dealer
18019	Benjamin	Moses	1821	Aldgate, London			Sarah Joel	Aldgate, London	clothes dealer
27315	Benjamin	Moses	1830	Middlesex, London	Abraham Benjamin	Amelia (?)		Aldgate, London	cigar maker
19404	Benjamin	Moses (Maurice)	1819	Soho, London	Victor Benjamin (Cohen)		Emma (?)	Southwark, London	tailor
25139	Benjamin	Moss	1833	Finsbury, London	Emanuel Benjamin	Jane Cohen		Finsbury, London	clothier
9596	Benjamin	Moss	1847	Spitalfields, London	Angel Benjamin	Elizabeth Mosely	Alice Abrahams	Spitalfields, London	
10085	Benjamin	Moss (Maurice)	1827	Holborn, London	Henry Benjamin	Deborah Barnett	Louisa Harris	Holborn, London	cigar maker
24852	Benjamin	Moss (Moses)	1791	Middlesex, London			Esther (?)	Bermondsey, London	clothier
20945	Benjamin	Moss (Moses)	1842	Middlesex, London	Benjamin Benjamin	Julia Cohen	Henrietta Alexandra Benjamin	Aldgate, London	scholar
9027	Benjamin	Naphtali	1849	Soho, London	Lewis Benjamin	Rosetta Meyer		Soho, London	
18000	Benjamin	Nathan	1836	Whitechapel, London	Henry Benjamin	Martha Simmons	Sarah Assenheim	Aldgate, London	fruit dealer
20204	Benjamin	Nathan	1842	Spitalfields, London	Simon Benjamin	Hannah Elias	Catherine Moses	Spitalfields, London	scholar
19402	Benjamin	Nathan (Nathaniel)	1840	Shoreditch, London	Moses Benjamin	Emma (?)	Hannah (Annie) Hyams	Southwark, London	scholar
18307	Benjamin	Paulina	1823	Ragoesen, Germany [Rogashin, Prussia]	(?)		Jacob Benjamin	Ramsgate, Kent	
15526	Benjamin	Philip	1803	Covent Garden, London			Elizabeth (?)	Covent Garden, London	general dealer
29886	Benjamin	Philip	1848	Whitechapel, London	Moses Benjamin	Susan Solomon	Minnie Cohen	Wapping, London	
29297	Benjamin	Philip	1849	Whitechapel, London	Abraham Benjamin	Julia (Juliet) Levy		Whitechapel, London	
24854	Benjamin	Philip (Lipman)	1821	Finsbury, London	Moss (Moses) Benjamin	Esther (?)		Bermondsey, London	clothier
20947	Benjamin	Phillip	1833	Middlesex, London	Benjamin Benjamin	Julia Cohen	Maria Isaacs	Aldgate, London	cigar maker assistant

ID	surname	given names	born	birthplace	father	mother	spouse 1	1851 residence	1851 occupation
11786	Benjamin	Phillip	1847	Shoreditch, London	Samuel Benjamin	Elisa (?)		Shoreditch, London	scholar
22946	Benjamin	Phillip Harris	1850	Wapping, London	Isaiah Benjamin	Elizabeth Harris		Wapping, London	
21346	Benjamin	Phoebe	1842	Middlesex, London	(?) Benjamin			Southwark, London	
29295	Benjamin	Phoebe	1842	Whitechapel, London	Abraham Benjamin	Julia (Juliet) Levy		Whitechapel, London	scholar
24367	Benjamin	Phoebe	1800	?, London	(?)		Abraham Benjamin	St Giles, London	
9686	Benjamin	Phoebe (Phila)	1823	Leigh, Essex	Nathan Benjamin	Catherine Moses		Strand, London	
19410	Benjamin	Priscilla	1822	Soho, London	Victor Benjamin (Cohen)		David Russell	Southwark, London	
17812	Benjamin	Priscilla	1827	Whitechapel, London	Michael Benjamin	(?)		Aldgate, London	
14579	Benjamin	Rachael	1821	Strand, London	Henry Benjamin	Sophia (?)		Covent Garden, London	?plumaner
18004	Benjamin	Rachael	1846	Aldgate, London	Henry Benjamin	Martha Simmons	Angel Cohen	Aldgate, London	scholar
29009	Benjamin	Rachael	1850	Whitechapel, London	Benjamin Benjamin	Julia Marks		Whitechapel, London	
9898	Benjamin	Rachel	1790	Aldgate, London	(?)		Lyon Benjamin	Whitechapel, London	
28488	Benjamin	Rachel	1800	?, London	(?) Benjamin			Spitalfields, London	charwoman
8677	Benjamin	Rachel	1809	Whitechapel, London	(?) Jacobs	Rebecca (?)		Aldgate, London	cloth cap maker
28343	Benjamin	Rachel	1824	Whitechapel, London	(?) Benjamin			Aldgate, London	dealer in general
22130	Benjamin	Rachel	1826	Whitechapel, London	(?)		Alfred Benjamin	Whitechapel, London	dressmaker
21388	Benjamin	Rachel	1828	?, London	Benjamin Benjamin	Hannah (?)		Marylebone, London	
19367	Benjamin	Rachel	1829	Aldgate, London	Lyon (Lionel) Benjamin	Mary Ann (Perle) Levi		Whitechapel, London	
16943	Benjamin	Rachel	1835	Aldgate, London	Joel Benjamin	Frances Cohen	Saul (Solomon) Cohen Spiers	Hammersmith, London	
24966	Benjamin	Rachel	1835	?, Canada		Elisa (?)		Haggerston, London	house servant
11788	Benjamin	Ralph	1849	Shoreditch, London	Samuel Benjamin			Shoreditch, London	scholar
22954	Benjamin	Raphael	1847	Wapping, London	Elias Benjamin	Mary Lazarus		Wapping, London	
16771	Benjamin	Rebecca	1801	Exeter, Devon	(?)		Benjamin Benjamin	Bristol	
25087	Benjamin	Rebecca	1819	?, London	David Benjamin	Esther (?)		Finsbury, London	haberdasher
28358	Benjamin	Rebecca	1827	Aldgate, London	Barnet Benjamin	Abigail de Leon (Lyon)	Abraham Joseph	Whitechapel, London	cap maker
10086	Benjamin	Rebecca	1832	Holborn, London	Henry Benjamin	Deborah Barnett	Emanuel Joseph	Holborn, London	
14575	Benjamin	Rebecca	1832	Finsbury, London	Solomon Benjamin	Elizabeth (?)		Finsbury, London	umbrella maker
9595	Benjamin	Rebecca	1844	Shoreditch, London	Angel Benjamin	Elizabeth Mosely		Spitalfields, London	scholar
16797	Benjamin	Rebecca	1846	Bristol	Joseph Benjamin	(?) Braham	Jesse Phillips	Bristol	scholar
3153	Benjamin	Rebecca (Rebekah)	1824	Poznan, Poland [Posen, Prussia]	Michael Levy (Lewy)	Adelaide (Adalanah) (?)	Emanuel Benjamin	Whitchurch, Shropshire	stall keeper
21395	Benjamin	Rosa	1829	Middlesex, London	(?) Benjamin	Amelia (?)		Edmonton, London	
13174	Benjamin	Rosa	1833	Spitalfields, London	(?) Benjamin			Aldgate, London	tailoress
18005	Benjamin	Rosa	1849	Aldgate, London	Henry Benjamin	Martha Simmons		Aldgate, London	scholar
16953	Benjamin	Rose	1833	Aldgate, London	Joel Benjamin	Frances Cohen		Hammersmith, London	school mistress
822	Benjamin	Rose (Rosetta)	1829	Middlesex, London	Mark Benjamin	Elizabeth Solomon		Marylebone, London	
9022	Benjamin	Rosetta	1810	Wapping, London	Jacob Meyer	Hannah (?)	Lewis Benjamin	Soho, London	
17813	Benjamin	Rosetta	1830	Whitechapel, London	Michael Benjamin	(?)		Aldgate, London	
11561	Benjamin	Rosetta	1842	?Aldgate, London	Joseph Benjamin	Harriet (Hannah) Hart		Aldgate, London	
25422	Benjamin	Rosetta	1849	Holborn, London	David Benjamin	Charlotte Mary (?)		Holborn, London	
9669	Benjamin	Rosetta	1850	Whitechapel, London	Abraham Benjamin	Louisa (?)		Whitechapel, London	
29576	Benjamin	S---	1815	Aldgate, London	Asher Benjamin	A--- (?)		Whitechapel, London	
11783	Benjamin	Samuel	1805	Shoreditch, London	Issachar Benjamin		Elisa (?)	Shoreditch, London	cane dealer
12482	Benjamin	Samuel	1806	Spitalfields, London	Tsevi Hirsh Benjamin		Mary Simmons	Aldgate, London	clothes dealer

ID	surname	given names	born	birthplace	father	mother	spouse 1	1851 residence	1851 occupation
4156	Benjamin	Samuel	1812	Clerkenwell, London	Moses Benjamin	Kitty Solomon	Lydia Hart	Aldgate, London	cigar maker + licensed victualler
25137	Benjamin	Samuel	1826	Finsbury, London	Emanuel Benjamin	Jane Cohen		Finsbury, London	clothier
31120	Benjamin	Samuel	1828	?Lublin, Poland [Labsens, Poland]				Ipswich, Suffolk	dealer in jewellery
824	Benjamin	Samuel	1833	Paddington, London	Mark Benjamin	Elizabeth Solomon	Deborah Fanny Marks	Marylebone, London	
27723	Benjamin	Samuel	1833	?, Poland				Spitalfields, London	travelling jeweller
29882	Benjamin	Samuel	1833	Whitechapel, London	Moses Benjamin	Susan Solomon		Wapping, London	apprentice cigar maker
9593	Benjamin	Sarnuel	1840	Spitalfields, London	Angel Benjamin	Elizabeth Mosely	Sophia (?)	Spitalfields, London	scholar
29288	Benjamin	Samuel	1843	Whitechapel, London	Abraham Benjamin	Leah Joseph		Whitechapel, London	scholar
11785	Benjamin	Samuel	1845	Shoreditch, London	Samuel Benjamin	Elisa (?)		Shoreditch, London	scholar
30790	Benjamin	Samuel	1850	Preston, Lancashire	Benjamin Benjamin	Esther Davis		Preston, Lancashire	
30030	Benjamin	Samuel Eugene	1846	Aldgate, London	Henry Benjamin	Marian Alexander		Clerkenwell, London	
817	Benjamin	Sanders (Saunders)	1844	Westminster, London	Solomon Benjamin	Betsy (Elizabeth) Solomon	Elizabeth Harris	Piccadilly, London	scholar
18063	Benjamin	Sarah	1779	Middlesex, London	Alexander Goodman		Michael Benjamin	Southwark, London	
30129	Benjamin	Sarah	1791	?			(?) Benjamin	Sunderland, Co Durham	
8654	Benjamin	Sarah	1794	Whitechapel, London	(?)		Lewis Benjamin	Aldgate, London	
8991	Benjamin	Sarah	1803	?, Isle of Wight	(?)		Lewis Benjamin	Portsmouth, Hampshire	stay stitcher
19360	Benjamin	Sarah	1812	Sheerness, Kent	(?) Abrahams		Abraham Benjamin	Whitechapel, London	
18020	Benjamin	Sarah	1823	Spitalfields, London	Daniel Joel	Elizabeth (Betsey) Cohen	Moses Benjamin	Aldgate, London	
16952	Benjamin	Sarah	1828	Aldgate, London	Joel Benjamin	Frances Cohen	Phineas Ezekiel Van Noorden	Hammersmith, London	school mistress
28359	Benjamin	Sarah	1829	Aldgate, London	Barnet Benjamin	Abigail de Leon (Lyon)		Whitechapel, London	housemaid
9899	Benjamin	Sarah	1830	Tower Hill, London	Lyon Benjamin	Rachel (?)		Whitechapel, London	
24369	Benjamin	Sarah	1832	?, London	Abraham Benjamin	Phoebe (?)		St Giles, London	
25140	Benjamin	Sarah	1834	Finsbury, London	Emanuel Benjamin	Jane Cohen		Finsbury, London	
29884	Benjamin	Sarah	1839	Whitechapel, London	Moses Benjamin	Susan Solomon	Emanuel Cohen	Wapping, London	scholar
24170	Benjamin	Sarah	1841	Euston, London	Elias Benjamin	Eve Barnet		Euston, London	scholar
3156	Benjamin	Sarah	1845	Whitchurch, Shropshire	Emanuel Benjamin	Rebecca (Rebekah) Levy (Lewy)		Whitchurch, Shropshire	
26219	Benjamin	Sarah	1847	?, London	John Benjamin	Maria (Miriam) Baruk		Aldgate, London	
22955	Benjamin	Sarah	1848	Wapping, London	Elias Benjamin	Mary Lazarus	John Isaacs	Wapping, London	
12945	Benjamin	Sarah	1849	Finsbury, London	Joseph Benjamin	Dinah Davis		Southwark, London	
20199	Benjamin	Simon	1812	Middlesex, London	Zadok Benjamin		Hannah Elias	Spitalfields, London	general dealer
27086	Benjamin	Simon	1840	?, London	(?) Benjamin	Maria (?)		Aldgate, London	cigar maker
14570	Benjamin	Solomon	1785	Middlesex, London			Elizabeth (?)	Finsbury, London	clothes salesman
815	Benjamin	Solomon	1820	Mayfair, London	Mark Benjamin	Elizabeth Solomon	Betsy (Elizabeth) Solomon	Piccadilly, London	master tailor
25133	Benjamin	Solomon	1834	Finsbury, London	Emanuel Benjamin	Jane Cohen	Hannah Barnett	Finsbury, London	clothier's shopman
30969	Benjamin	Solomon	1839	?, London	Lewis Benjamin	Rachael Jacobs		Hull, Yorkshire	
29296	Benjamin	Solomon	1844	Whitechapel, London	Abraham Benjamin	Julia (Juliet) Levy		Whitechapel, London	scholar
12478	Benjamin	Solomon	1845	Aldgate, London	Samuel Benjamin	Mary Simmons	Betsy (Elizabeth) Philips	Aldgate, London	scholar
14597	Benjamin	Solomon	1846	Shoreditch, London	Elias Benjamin	Esther Jessurun		Aldgate, London	
14578	Benjamin	Sophia	1787	?, Germany				Hoxton, London	
							Henry Benjamin	Covent Garden, London	
29880	Benjamin	Susan	1801	Spitalfields, London	Shemaya Solomon				
							Moses Benjamin	Wapping, London	
19409	Benjamin	Vigdor	1851	Southwark, London	Moses Benjamin	Emma (?)		Southwark, London	

ID	surname	given names	born	birthplace	father	mother	spouse 1	1851 residence	1851 occupation
21393	Benjamin	Zillah	1848	Aldgate, London	Benjamin Benjamin	Hannah (?)		Marylebone, London	
1175	Benjamin (Bengaman)	Leah	1800	Plymouth, Devon				Plymouth, Devon	annuitant
1176	Benjamin (Bengaman)	Rachel (Rachael)	1790	Plymouth, Devon				Plymouth, Devon	independent means
25622	Benmohel	Nathan Lazarus	1803	Hamburg, Germany	Eliezer Lazi	(?) Munk		Dublin, Ireland	
25623	Benmohel	Rosa	1800	Louth, Lincolnshire	(?) Hyams		Alexander Lazarus Benmohel	Dublin, Ireland	
30267	Bennett	Angelo	1820	Covent Garden, London	Solomon Bennett	Elizabeth (?)	Gertrude Emanuel	Camberwell, London	shorthand writer
30260	Bennett	Charles	1822	Middlesex, London	Solomon Bennett	Elizabeth (?)	Mary Ann Dyte	Strand, London	shorthand writer
30271	Bennett	Charles S	1850	Camberwell, London	Angelo Bennett	Gertrude Emanuel		Camberwell, London	
30259	Bennett	Elizabeth	1801	Middlesex, London	(?)		Solomon Bennett	Strand, London	
30269	Bennett	Elizabeth Miriam	1847	Covent Garden, London	Angelo Bennett	Gertrude Emanuel	Joseph Benjamin	Camberwell, London	
30266	Bennett	Eve	1838	Middlesex, London	Solomon Bennett	Elizabeth (?)		Strand, London	scholar at home
30268	Bennett	Gertrude	1824	Mayfair, London	(?) Emanuel		Angelo Bennett	Camberwell, London	
30261	Bennett	Isaac	1823	Middlesex, London	Solomon Bennett	Elizabeth (?)		Strand, London	shorthand writer
30264	Bennett	Israel	1828	Middlesex, London	Solomon Bennett	Elizabeth (?)		Strand, London	shorthand writer
30262	Bennett	Moses	1825	Middlesex, London	Solomon Bennett	Elizabeth (?)		Strand, London	shorthand writer
30265	Bennett	Nathaniel	1822	Middlesex, London	Solomon Bennett	Elizabeth (?)		Strand, London	general clerk in solicitor's office
30263	Bennett	Sarah	1827	Middlesex, London	Solomon Bennett	Elizabeth (?)		Strand, London	
30270	Bennett	Sophia	1849	Covent Garden, London	Angelo Bennett	Gertrude Emanuel		Camberwell, London	
12284	Benoliel	Abraham	1835	Gibraltar	(?) Benoliel			Finsbury, London	
7617	Benoliel	Esther	1831	Gibraltar	Joshua Benoliel	Hannah (?)	Moses Pariente	Shoreditch, London	
19036	Benoliel	Esther	1842	Gibraltar	Isaac Benoliel	Hannah (?)	Joseph Norsa Lindo	Shoreditch, London	scholar at home
12277	Benoliel	Hannah	1810	Gibraltar	(?)		Joshua Benoliel	Finsbury, London	
19034	Benoliel	Hannah	1818	Gibraltar	(?)		Isaac Benoliel	Shoreditch, London	
7297	Benoliel	Isaac	1811	?London	Abraham Benoliel		Rosetta Belasco	Finsbury, London	jeweller
7618	Benoliel	Isaac	1811	Gibraltar			Hannah (?)	Shoreditch, London	commission agent
7616	Benoliel	Joshua	1809	Gibraltar			Hannah (?)	Shoreditch, London	general merchant
19041	Benoliel	Judah	1850	Shoreditch, London	Isaac Benoliel	Hannah (?)		Shoreditch, London	
12279	Benoliel	Judith	1839	Gibraltar	Joshua Benoliel	Hannah (?)		Finsbury, London	
19035	Benoliel	Judith	1845	Gibraltar	Isaac Benoliel	Hannah (?)		Shoreditch, London	scholar at home
12278	Benoliel	Lerey	1834	Gibraltar	Joshua Benoliel	Hannah (?)		Finsbury, London	
12280	Benoliel	Miriam	1843	Gibraltar	Joshua Benoliel	Hannah (?)		Finsbury, London	
19040	Benoliel	Miriam	1846	Gibraltar	Isaac Benoliel	Hannah (?)		Shoreditch, London	scholar at home
12283	Benoliel	Moses	1820	Gibraltar	(?) Benoliel			Finsbury, London	general merchant
12282	Benoliel	Moses	1846	Gibraltar	Joshua Benoliel	Hannah (?)		Finsbury, London	
12281	Benoliel	Rachel	1844	Gibraltar	Joshua Benoliel	Hannah (?)		Finsbury, London	
16841	Benolier	Judah	1837	Gibraltar				Brighton, Sussex	scholar
16382	Benrimo	Buena (Orabuena)	1832	Finsbury, London	Daniel de Meir Benrimo	Rachel de Haim Hasdai Almosnino		Aldgate, London	
16381	Benrimo	Julia (Judith)	1831	Finsbury, London	Daniel de Meir Benrimo	Rachel de Haim Hasdai Almosnino		Aldgate, London	

ID	surname	given names	born	birthplace	father	mother	spouse 1	1851 residence	1851 occupation
16383	Benrimo	Meyer (Meir)	1835	Finsbury, London	Daniel de Meir Benrimo	Rachel de Haim Hasdai Almosnino		Aldgate, London	
20851	Bensabat	Abraham	1842	Spitalfields, London	David de Jacob Bensabat	Sarah de Jacob Mendes		Spitalfields, London	
19640	Bensabat	Charlotte	1837	?London	David de Joseph Bensabat	Hannah Casper	Joseph Kiet	Aldgate, London	
20849	Bensabat	Charlotte	1838	Spitalfields, London	David de Jacob Bensabat	Sarah de Jacob Mendes		Spitalfields, London	
15732	Bensabat	David	1811	Spitalfields, London	Jacob Bensabat	Rachel de David Rodrigues	Sarah de Jacob Mendes	Spitalfields, London	traveller + general dealer
19638	Bensabat	David	1811	Essaouira, Morocco [Mogador, Morocco]	Joseph Bensabat		Hannah Casper	Aldgate, London	merchant
20850	Bensabat	David	1840	Spitalfields, London	David de Jacob Bensabat	Sarah de Jacob Mendes		Spitalfields, London	
19639	Bensabat	Emma (Mesoda)	1833	?, London	David de Joseph Bensabat	Hannah Casper	Abraham Benares	Aldgate, London	
7315	Bensabat	Hannah	1819	City, London	Nathan Casper	Amelia Ansell	David de Joseph Bensabat	Aldgate, London	
20848	Bensabat	Jacob	1835	Spitalfields, London	David de Jacob Bensabat	Sarah de Jacob Mendes		Spitalfields, London	traveller
20852	Bensabat	Joseph	1843	Spitalfields, London	David de Jacob Bensabat	Sarah de Jacob Mendes		Spitalfields, London	
20853	Bensabat	Mordica	1849	Spitalfields, London	David de Jacob Bensabat	Sarah de Jacob Mendes		Spitalfields, London	
20854	Bensabat	Rachel	1784	Whitechapel, London	David de Hezekiah Daniel Rodrigues	Rachel de Benjamin Nunes Garcia	Jacob Bensabat	Spitalfields, London	fish dealer
5661	Bensabat	Sarah	1812	Southwark, London	Jacob Mendes	Charlotte (?)	David de Jacob Bensabat	Spitalfields, London	traveller
20855	Bensabat	Sophia (Siporah, Zipporah)	1825	Aldgate, London	Jacob Bensabat	Rachel Rodrigues	Solomon Alvarez	Spitalfields, London	dress maker
21043	Benshal	David	1839	Gibraltar				Dover, Kent	boarding school pupil
9017	Bensilum	Annette (Hannah)	1840	City, London	Haim Jacob Bensilum		Isaac Genese	Aldgate, London	
9018	Bensilum	Haim Jacob	1810	?	Isaac Bensilum			Aldgate, London	general dealer
9019	Bensilum	John Abraham	1842	?	Haim Jacob Bensilum		Rebecca Abulafia (Bolaffey)	Aldgate, London	
25239	Bensimon Levy	Edward	1800	Strand, London	(?) Bensimon Levy	Mary (?)		Clerkenwell, London	clerk in East India house
25240	Bensimon Levy	Mary	1766	Middlesex, London	(?)		(?) Bensimon Levy	Clerkenwell, London	
2952	Benson	Benjamin William	1809	Aldgate, London	(?) ?Lazarus	Ann Israel		?Chelsea, London	
4303	Benson	Michael	1821	?, Poland				Birmingham	hawker
24756	Bensusan	Aaron Levy	1827	Whitechapel, London	Samuel de Menahem Levy Bensusan	Stella (?)		Southwark, London	commercial traveller in perfumery + inks
18935	Bensusan	Abraham	1826	Istanbul, Turkey [Constantinople]	David Bensusan	Flora (Blooma) de Benjamin de Abraham	Rebecca Silver (Silva)	Aldgate, London	clothes dealer
25398	Bensusan	Abraham	1850	Bloomsbury, London	Moses Levy Bensusan	Emily (Esther) Levy Bensusan		Bloomsbury, London	
21706	Bensusan	Abraham Levi	1832	Middlesex, London	Jacob de Menahem Levi Bensusan	Sarah (?)		Holloway, London	
25392	Bensusan	Abraham Levy	1797	City, London	Menahem de Samuel Levy Bensusan	Simha de Jacob Levy Bensusan	Miriam (?)	Bloomsbury, London	merchant
27164	Bensusan	Benjamin	1822	?, London	David Bensusan	Flora (Blooma) de Benjamin de Abraham	Phoebe Solomons	Aldgate, London	licensed hawker
26863	Bensusan	Bloom (Flora)	1850	?Aldgate, London	Nathan (Nissim) Bensusan	Elizabeth (Betsy) Solomons		Aldgate, London	
25394	Bensusan	Celestine	1826	City, London	Abraham de Menahem Levy Bensusan	Miriam (?)	Hilel Beriro	Bloomsbury, London	
25164	Bensusan	Clara Levy	1829	Whitechapel, London	Jacob de Menahem Levi Bensusan	Sarah (?)		Finsbury, London	dressmaker
21710	Bensusan	Cressida	1842	Middlesex, London	Jacob de Menahem Levi Bensusan	Sarah (?)		Holloway, London	
18933	Bensusan	David	1775	Istanbul, Turkey [Constantinople]	Nissim Bensusan		Flora (Blooma) de Benjamin de Abraham	Aldgate, London	pauper (hawker)

ID	surname	given names	born	birthplace	father	mother	spouse 1	1851 residence	1851 occupation
26860	Bensusan	David	1844	?Aldgate, London	Nathan (Nissim) Bensusan	Elizabeth (Betsy) Solomons	Rosetta (Rahma) Solomons	Aldgate, London	
25162	Bensusan	David Levy	1826	Whitechapel, London	Jacob de Menahem Levy Bensusan	Sarah (?)		Finsbury, London	clerk in ship broker's office
24491	Bensusan	Elias Levy	1834	?, London	Joshua Levy Bensusan	Sarah de Elias Abenatar	Rebecca Rosina Louis	Walworth, London	
26859	Bensusan	Elizabeth (Betsy)	1821	?, London	Zachariah Solomons		Nathan (Nissim) Bensusan	Aldgate, London	
25395	Bensusan	Emily (Esther)	1827	St Pancras, London	Abraham de Menahem Levy Bensusan	Miriam (?)	Moses Levy Bensusan	Bloomsbury, London	
25393	Bensusan	Esther Levy	1812	City, London	Joseph Guttieres Bravo	Rebecca de Joseph Aguilar	Abraham de Menahem Levy Bensusan	Bloomsbury, London	
24484	Bensusan	Esther Levy	1831	?, London	Joshua Levy Bensusan	Sarah de Elias Abenatar		Walworth, London	
18934	Bensusan	Flora (Blooma)	1798	Aldgate, London	Benjamin de Abraham		David de Nissim Bensusan	Aldgate, London	mangling
25163	Bensusan	Fortune Levy	1828	Whitechapel, London	Jacob de Menahem Levy Bensusan	Sarah (?)		Finsbury, London	milliner
9333	Bensusan	Hannah	1777	Finsbury, London	(?) Bensusan			Aldgate, London	poor
26862	Bensusan	Isaac	1848	?Aldgate, London	Nathan (Nissim) Bensusan	Elizabeth (Betsy) Solomons	Ester Benjamin	Aldgate, London	
21704	Bensusan	Jacob Levi	1790	Middlesex, London	Menahem de Samuel Levy Bensusan	Simha de Jacob Levy Bensusan	Sarah (?)	Holloway, London	gentleman
24489	Bensusan	Jacob Levy	1842	Whitechapel, London	Joshua Levy Bensusan	Sarah de Elias Abenatar		Walworth, London	scholar
24488	Bensusan	Jemima Levy	1841	?, London	Joshua Levy Bensusan	Sarah de Elias Abenatar		Walworth, London	scholar
9335	Bensusan	Joseph	1796	Aldgate, London				Aldgate, London	poor
24481	Bensusan	Joshua Levy	1800	?, London	Menahem de Samuel Levy Bensusan	Simha de Jacob Levy Bensusan	Sarah de Elias Abenatar	Walworth, London	late general merchant
21709	Bensusan	Judith Josephine	1840	Middlesex, London	Jacob de Menahem Levi Bensusan	Sarah (?)	Samuel Davis	Holloway, London	
24486	Bensusan	Julia Levy	1836	?, London	Joshua Levy Bensusan	Sarah de Elias Abenatar		Walworth, London	
9334	Bensusan	Louisa	1791	Aldgate, London	(?) Bensusan			Aldgate, London	poor
25397	Bensusan	Marian (Miriam)	1847	Gibraltar	Moses Levy Bensusan	Emily (Esther) Levy Bensusan	Jacob S Levy Bensusan	Bloomsbury, London	
25161	Bensusan	Menahem Levy	1825	Whitechapel, London	Jacob de Menahem Levy Bensusan	Sarah (?)	Caroline Hart	Finsbury, London	clerk in merchant's office
21708	Bensusan	Miriam Levi	1838	Middlesex, London	Jacob de Menahem Levi Bensusan	Sarah (?)		Holloway, London	
25396	Bensusan	Moses	1815	?, London	Joshua Levy Bensusan	Sarah de Elias Abenatar	Emily (Esther) Levy Bensusan	Bloomsbury, London	
26858	Bensusan	Nathan (Nissim)	1821	?, London	David de Nissim Bensusan	Flora (Blooma) de Benjamin de Abraham	Elizabeth (Betsy) Solomons	Aldgate, London	dealer
24490	Bensusan	Rachael Levy	1845	?, London	Joshua Levy Bensusan	Sarah de Elias Abenatar		Walworth, London	
25165	Bensusan	Rachel Levy	1833	Whitechapel, London	Jacob de Menahem Levy Bensusan	Sarah (?)		Finsbury, London	dressmaker
21711	Bensusan	Raphael Levi	1843	Middlesex, London	Jacob de Menahem Levi Bensusan	Sarah (?)		Holloway, London	
18937	Bensusan	Rebecca	1836	Aldgate, London	David Bensusan	Flora (Blooma) de Benjamin de Abraham	William Harris	Aldgate, London	mangling
21707	Bensusan	Rebecca Levi	1837	Middlesex, London	Jacob de Menahem Levi Bensusan	Sarah (?)		Holloway, London	
24485	Bensusan	Rebecca Levy	1832	?, London	Joshua Levy Bensusan	Sarah de Elias Abenatar		Walworth, London	
25166	Bensusan	Richeteria Levy	1837	Peckham, London	Jacob de Menahem Levy Bensusan	Sarah (?)		Finsbury, London	dressmaker
24487	Bensusan	Samuel Levy	1837	Whitechapel, London	Joshua Levy Bensusan	Sarah de Elias Abenatar		Walworth, London	scholar
21705	Bensusan	Sarah Levi	1804	Gibraltar	(?)		Jacob de Menahem Levi Bensusan	Holloway, London	fundholder
24482	Bensusan	Sarah Levy	1807	?, London	Elias Abenatar		Joshua Levy Bensusan	Walworth, London	
24483	Bensusan	Simha Levy	1825	?, London	Joshua Levy Bensusan	Sarah de Elias Abenatar		Walworth, London	

ID	surname	given names	born	birthplace	father	mother	spouse 1	1851 residence	1851 occupation
18936	Bensusan	Vida	1833	Aldgate, London	David Bensusan	Flora (Blooma) de Benjamin de Abraham		Aldgate, London	mangling
26861	Bensusan	Zachariah (Alic, Zalic)	1846	?Aldgate, London	Nathan (Nissim) Bensusan	Elizabeth (Betsy) Solomons	Rebecca Myers	Aldgate, London	
19334	Bentolelar	Aaron	1840	Windsor, Berkshire	Samuel Bentolelar	Hannah Philip		Ramsgate, Kent	
7319	Bentolelar	Hannah	1818	Chatham, Kent	Jacob Philip		Samuel Bentolelar	Ramsgate, Kent	
19471	Bentolelar	Hannah	1851	Ramsgate, Kent	Samuel Bentolelar	Hannah Philip	Samuel Richard Smyth	Ramsgate, Kent	
19338	Bentolelar	Jacob	1836	?Whitechapel, London	Samuel Bentolelar	Hannah Philip		Ramsgate, Kent	
19333	Bentolelar	Juda	1838	Southampton, Hampshire	Samuel Bentolelar	Hannah Philip		Ramsgate, Kent	
19326	Bentolelar	Julia	1836	Whitechapel,, London	Samuel Bentolelar	Hannah (?)		Ramsgate, Kent	
7321	Bentolelar	Leah	1839	?Southampton, Hampshire	Samuel Bentolelar	Hannah Philip	Woolf Phillips	Ramsgate, Kent	
19337	Bentolelar	Mesoda (Esther)	1849	Ramsgate, Kent	Samuel Bentolelar	Hannah Philip	Solomon Elboz	Ramsgate, Kent	
19336	Bentolelar	Rachel	1846	Ramsgate, Kent	Samuel Bentolelar	Hannah Philip		Ramsgate, Kent	
7323	Bentolelar	Rebecca	1842	Winchester, Hampshire	Samuel Bentolelar	Hannah Philip	Solomon Amiel	Ramsgate, Kent	
7320	Bentolelar	Samuel	1796	?	Semah Bentulela		Philip Avigdor Garcia	Ramsgate, Kent	
							Hannah Philip	Ramsgate, Kent	
16485	Benzaquen	Clara	1822	Hackney, London	Jacob de Vidal de Judah Benzaquen	Simha (Simy) de Solomon Benamor		Mile End, London	needlewoman
18390	Benzaquen	Elizabeth (Betsey, Bathsheba)	1825	Hackney, London	Jacob de Vidal de Judah Benzaquen	Simha (Simy) de Solomon Benamor	Isaac David Belisha	Mile End, London	embroideress
18331	Benzaquen	Estella	1822	Aldgate, London	Jacob Benzaquen		Judah Atrutel	Cheltenham, Gloucestershire	governess
16488	Benzaquen	Esther	1832	Hackney, London	Jacob de Vidal de Judah Benzaquen	Simha (Simy) de Solomon Benamor	Isaac Bensaude	Mile End, London	
16489	Benzaquen	Hannah	1835	Mile End, London	Jacob de Vidal de Judah Benzaquen	Simha (Simy) de Solomon Benamor	Hyam Solomon Levy Yuly	Mile End, London	
22585	Benzaquen	Josiah	1831	Hackney, London	Jacob de Vidal de Judah Benzaquen	Simha (Simy) de Solomon Benamor		Stepney, London	cigar maker
22584	Benzaquen	Judah M	1829	Hackney, London	Jacob de Vidal de Judah Benzaquen	Simha (Simy) de Solomon Benamor		Stepney, London	cigar maker
16486	Benzaquen	Louisa	1823	Hackney, London	Jacob de Vidal de Judah Benzaquen	Simha (Simy) de Solomon Benamor	Abraham Tolano	Mile End, London	milliner
16484	Benzaquen	Rachel	1817	Aldgate, London	Jacob de Vidal de Judah Benzaquen	Simha (Simy) de Solomon Benamor		Mile End, London	needlewoman
16483	Benzaquen	Simha (Simy)	1799	Gibraltar	Solomon de Isaiah Benamor		Jacob de Vidal de Judah Benzaquen	Mile End, London	
13654	Benzieri	Moses	1826	Gibraltar				Manchester	interpreter
27185	Bercus	Bertha	1841	?, Germany	Simon Bercus	Hannah (?)		Aldgate, London	
27186	Bercus	Hanchen	1842	?, Germany	Simon Bercus	Hannah (?)		Aldgate, London	
27183	Bercus	Hannah	1811	?, Germany	(?)		Simon Bercus	Aldgate, London	
27184	Bercus	Israel	1835	?, Germany	Simon Bercus	Hannah (?)		Aldgate, London	tailor
27187	Bercus	Mandel	1843	?, London	Simon Bercus	Hannah (?)		Aldgate, London	
27188	Bercus	Moses	1849	?, London	Simon Bercus	Hannah (?)		Aldgate, London	
27182	Bercus	Simon	1791	?, Germany			Hannah (?)	Aldgate, London	tailor
12223	Berenberg	Julius	1831	Hamburg, Germany				Whitechapel, London	commission agent
21690	Berend	Adolph	1825	?, Germany			Emily (?)	Islington, London	importer of foreign cigars
14399	Berend	Dina	1807	?	(?)		Louis Berend	Manchester	

ID	surname	given names	born	birthplace	father	mother	spouse 1	1851 residence	1851 occupation
21691	Berend	Emily	1825	St Pancras, London	(?)		Adolph Berend	Islington, London	
30949	Berend	Jacob	1801	Hamburg, Germany				Bradford, Yorkshire	stuff merchant (worsted)
14401	Berend	Lana	1827	Manchester	Louis Berend	Dina (?)		Manchester	
14398	Berend	Louis	1804	Hanover, Germany			Dina (?)	Manchester	dentist
14402	Berend	Matilda	1829	Manchester	Louis Berend	Dina (?)		Manchester	
14400	Berend	Pamela	1825	Manchester	Louis Berend	Dina (?)		Manchester	
4310	Berens	Abraham	1834	?, Poland [?, Prussia]			Eliza Aronson	Birmingham	assistant jeweller
24559	Berens	Alexander	1802	?, Poland [?, Prussia]			Charlotte Dempster	Brixton, London	foreign merchant
3475	Berens	Henry	1822	?, Poland [?, Prussia]	(?) Berens		Julia Lazarus	Birmingham	
8020	Berg	Benedictus Salomon	1796	?, Holland			(?)	Whitechapel, London	bitters manufacturer
30900	Berg	Dinah	1838	Dover, Kent	(?) Berg	(?) Solomon		Deal, Kent	
19101	Berg	Eva	1849	Whitechapel, London	Benedictus Salomon Berg	Sarah Moss		Whitechapel, London	
17277	Berg	Jacob	1834	?, Poland [?, Prussia]				Aldgate, London	tailor
16882	Berg	Moses	1816	?, Ireland				Cambridge	traveller
19100	Berg	Sarah	1815	Portsmouth, Hampshire	Joseph Moss	Amelia (?)	Benedictus Salomon Moss	Whitechapel, London	
23916	Bergenstein	Julius?	1801	?, Poland			Emma (?)	Fitzrovia, London	watch maker
24515	Berger	Abraham	1821	?, Bavaria, Germany				Greenwich, London	journeyman glazier
14248	Berger	Elias	1828	?, Poland [?, Prussia]				Manchester	traveller
22311	Berger	Joseph Charles	1807	Trieste, Italy [Trieste, Austria]	Moise Maurizio Berger	Estelle Diamante	Sophia Wilcock nee Waterfield	Liverpool	
24386	Berger	Julius	1822	?, Poland [?, Prussia]				Soho, London	chaser in brass journeyman
21283	Berger	Samuel	1841	Gibraltar				Edmonton, London	boarding school pupil
13790	Bergheim	Moses	1832	?, Poland [?, Prussia]				Manchester	cap maker
30443	Bergman	Abraham	1787	?Frankfurt am Main, Germany			Sarah Crawford (Crowfoot)	Bethnal Green, London	marine store dealer
2381	Bergman	Abram	1835	Wejherowo, Poland [New Town, Prussia]	Ansell (Hansell) Bergman	Rebecca (?)		Hull, Yorkshire	cap maker
30440	Bergman	Agatha	1842	?Bethnal Green, London	Abraham Bergman	Sarah Crawford (Crowfoot)		Bethnal Green, London	
2123	Bergman	Ansell (Hansell)	1811	Wejherowo, Poland [New Town, Prussia]			Rebecca (?)	Hull, Yorkshire	cap maker
2382	Bergman	Bella	1841	Wejherowo, Poland [New Town, Prussia]	Ansell (Hansell) Bergman	Rebecca (?)		Hull, Yorkshire	
14908	Bergman	David	1837	Norwich, Norfolk	Abraham Bergman	Sarah Crawford (Crowfoot)	Elizabeth (?)	Bethnal Green, London	boarding school pupil
14978	Bergman	Hannah	1840	Norwich, Norfolk	Abraham Bergman	Sarah Crawford (Crowfoot)		Bethnal Green, London	boarding school pupil
2383	Bergman	Harris	1851	Hull, Yorkshire	Ansell (Hansell) Bergman	Rebecca (?)		Hull, Yorkshire	
18286	Bergman	Hunsell	1817	?, Poland [?, Polish Russia]				Salisbury, Wiltshire	traveller in jewellery
2384	Bergman	Levin (Lewis) Hansell	1849	Hull, Yorkshire	Ansell (Hansell) Bergman	Rachel (?)	Mathilde Strelitzer	Hull, Yorkshire	
30439	Bergman	Morris	1833	Norwich, Norfolk	Abraham Bergman	Sarah Crawford (Crowfoot)		Bethnal Green, London	clock case maker
2385	Bergman	Rachel	1844	Wejherowo, Poland [Newchtat, Poland]	Ansell (Hansell) Bergman	Rebecca (?)	Davis Horwitz	Hull, Yorkshire	
2386	Bergman	Rebecca	1814	Wejherowo, Poland [Newchtat, Poland]			Ansell (Hansell) Bergman	Hull, Yorkshire	
30441	Bergman	Rebecca	1845	?Bethnal Green, London	Abraham Bergman	Sarah Crawford (Crowfoot)		Bethnal Green, London	scholar

ID	surname	given names	born	birthplace	father	mother	spouse 1	1851 residence	1851 occupation
30444	Bergman	Sarah	1806	Norwich, Norfolk	(?) Crawford (Crowfoot)		Abraham Bergman	Bethnal Green, London	
30442	Bergman	Sarah	1848	?Bethnal Green, London	Abraham Bergman	Sarah Crawford (Crowfoot)	Esther (?)	Bethnal Green, London	[coat?] manufacturer
20966	Bergman	Simson	1849	Hull, Yorkshire	Ansell (Hansell) Bergman	Rebecca (?)		Hull, Yorkshire	
14016	Bergmann	Emma	1834	?, Poland [?, Prussia]	(?) Bergmann			Manchester	
14089	Bergson	Bertha	1844	Glasgow, Scotland	Wolff Bergson	Frances (?)	Solomon Solomon	Manchester	scholar
14088	Bergson	Eader	1839	?, Scotland	Wolff Bergson	Frances (?)		Manchester	scholar
14090	Bergson	Elias	1849	Glasgow, Scotland	Wolff Bergson	Frances (?)		Manchester	
14092	Bergson	Frances	1813	?, Poland	(?)		Wolff Bergson	Manchester	
14087	Bergson	Wolff	1810	?, Poland			Frances (?)	Manchester	traveller - fancy goods
16313	Bergtheil	John (Jonas)	1820	Bavaria, Germany	Myer Bergtheil		Louisa Salomons	Bloomsbury, London	export merchant
16314	Bergtheil	Louisa	1827	?, London	(?)		John (Jonas) Bergtheil	Bloomsbury, London	
27934	Berkein	Caroline	1846	Berwick-upon-Tweed, Northumberland	Jacob Berkein	Paulina (?)		Spitalfields, London	
27932	Berkein	Estella	1841	Berwick-upon-Tweed, Northumberland	Jacob Berkein	Paulina (?)		Spitalfields, London	
27929	Berkein	Jacob	1821	?			Paulina (?)	Spitalfields, London	
27930	Berkein	Paulina	1821	Berwick-upon-Tweed, Northumberland	(?)		Jacob Berkein	Spitalfields, London	
27933	Berkein	Rose	1843	Berwick-upon-Tweed, Northumberland	Jacob Berkein	Paulina (?)		Spitalfields, London	
27931	Berkein	Theodore	1839	Berwick-upon-Tweed, Northumberland	Jacob Berkein	Paulina (?)		Spitalfields, London	
21446	Berkowitz	Henry	1822	?, Poland	Isaac Beer Berkowitz		Rosetta Poland	Gravesend, Kent	teacher of Hebrew + German
14113	Berlack	John	1850	?, London	William Berlack	Martha Cohen		Manchester	
14111	Berlack	Martha	1821	Hanover, Germany	(?) Cohen		William Berlack	Manchester	
14112	Berlack	Meyer	1849	?, London	William Berlack	Martha Cohen		Manchester	
14114	Berlack	Rose	1851	Manchester	William Berlack	Martha Cohen		Manchester	
14110	Berlack	William	1803	?, Poland [?, Prussia]			Martha Cohen	Manchester	merchant's clerk
21675	Berlandina	Amelia	1817	?, Monmouthshire, Wales	Nathan Isaacs	Sarah (?)	David Berlandina	Islington, London	annuitant
21674	Berlandina	David	1814	Gibraltar	Solomon Berlandina		Amelia Isaacs	Islington, London	foreign commission merchant
21678	Berlandina	Edward Emanuel	1851	Islington, London	David Berlandina	Amelia Isaacs		Islington, London	
21677	Berlandina	Sarah Julia	1847	Islington, London	David Berlandina	Amelia Isaacs	Adolphus Croft	Islington, London	
21676	Berlandina	William (Hillel)	1846	Islington, London	David Berlandina	Amelia Isaacs	Hilda Arabella Cohen	Islington, London	
16851	Berlin	Barnett	1817	?, Poland [?, Prussia]				Egham, Berkshire	licensed hawker
9813	Berlin	Mandalina	1831	?, Germany	(?) Berlin			Finsbury, London	chamber attendant
5119	Berlin	Marcus	1825	?, Germany				Sheffield, Yorkshire	tailor + woollen draper master empl 6
9802	Berliner	Benjamin	1797	?, Germany			(?)	Aldgate, London	baker empl 2
7580	Berliner	Bero	1834	?, Germany	Benjamin Berliner	Phoebe (?)		Aldgate, London	baker
29875	Berliner	Caroline	1821	?, Germany	Abraham Rosenbaum		Herman (Henry) Berliner	Wapping, London	
9805	Berliner	Fanny	1834	?, Germany	Benjamin Berliner	Phoebe (?)		Aldgate, London	
29874	Berliner	Herman (Henry)	1824	?, Germany	Jacob Berliner		Caroline Rosenbaum	Wapping, London	boot + shoe maker empl 10

ID	surname	given names	born	birthplace	father	mother	spouse 1	1851 residence	1851 occupation
30388	Berliner	Jacob	1851	Wapping, London	Herman (Henry) Berliner	Caroline Rosenbaum	Rudolphine Berliner	Wapping, London	
9807	Berliner	Jeanette	1837	?, Germany	Benjamin Berliner	Phoebe (?)	Philip London	Aldgate, London	
29876	Berliner	Matilda	1848	Whitechapel, London	Herman (Henry) Berliner	Caroline Rosenbaum	Bendiz Stern	Wapping, London	scholar
9803	Berliner	Phoebe	1807	?, Germany	(?)		Benjamin Berliner	Aldgate, London	
9806	Berliner	Rachel	1835	?, Germany	Benjamin Berliner	Phoebe (?)		Aldgate, London	
9804	Berliner	Theresa	1830	?, Germany	Benjamin Berliner	Phoebe (?)		Aldgate, London	
29877	Berliner	Theresa	1850	Whitechapel, London	Herman (Henry) Berliner	Caroline Rosenbaum	Moritz Oppenheimer	Wapping, London	
10164	Berlyn	Abraham Moses	1811	Amsterdam, Holland	Moses Abraham Berlyn	Mariane (?)	Rachael Shyre	Spitalfields, London	clicker
4305	Berlyn	Catherine	1823	?, London	Mark (Mordecai) Davis		Charles Berlyn	Birmingham	
4304	Berlyn	Charles	1815	Amsterdam, Holland			Catherine Davis	Birmingham	general dealer
10167	Berlyn	Isaac	1846	Aldgate, London	Abraham Moses Berlyn	Rachael Shyre		Spitalfields, London	scholar
3335	Berlyn	John (Jonah)	1850	Birmingham	Charles Berlyn	Catherine (?)	Sophia Cohen	Birmingham	
20967	Berlyn	Joseph	1851	Aldgate, London	Abraham Moses Berlyn	Rachael Shyre		Spitalfields, London	
10168	Berlyn	Marian (Marie, Mary A)	1850	Whitechapel, London	Abraham Moses Berlyn	Rachael Shyre	Julius Jacobs	Spitalfields, London	
10575	Berlyn	Mariane	1788	Amsterdam, Holland			Moses Abraham Berlyn	Spitalfields, London	
4306	Berlyn	Mary Ann	1846	Birmingham	Charles Berlyn	Catherine Davis		Birmingham	
10166	Berlyn	Moses	1844	Aldgate, London	Abraham Moses Berlyn	Rachael Shyre	Leah Lewis	Spitalfields, London	scholar
10574	Berlyn	Moses Abraham	1789	?Amsterdam, Holland			Mariane (?)	Spitalfields, London	dealer in old clothes
4307	Berlyn	Phoebe	1848	Birmingham	Charles Berlyn	Catherine Davis		Birmingham	
10165	Berlyn	Rachael	1816	Amsterdam, Holland	Isaac Shyre		Abraham Moses Berlyn	Spitalfields, London	
18581	Bernal	Abraham	1801	Bethnal Green, London	Benjamin Bernal		Catherine (Keturah) de Elisha Wolf	Whitechapel, London	china + glass dealer
18583	Bernal	Benjamin	1833	Whitechapel, London	Abraham Bernal	Catherine (Keturah) Wolf		Whitechapel, London	
18582	Bernal	Catherine (Keturah)	1805	Whitechapel, London	Elisha Wolf		Abraham Bernal	Whitechapel, London	
24892	Bernal	Elizabeth	1783	Bermondsey, London	(?)		(?) Bernal	Lewisham, London	gentlewoman: annuitant
18580	Bernal	Elizabeth	1838	Whitechapel, London	Abraham Bernal	Catherine (?)	Lewis A White	Whitechapel, London	butcher at home
24894	Bernal	Esther A	1822	Lewisham, London	(?) Bernal	Elizabeth (?)		Lewisham, London	
24893	Bernal	Isaac	1806	Bermondsey, London	(?) Bernal	Elizabeth (?)		Lewisham, London	house decorator's manager's clerk
18584	Bernal	Joseph	1836	Whitechapel, London	Abraham Bernal	Catherine (Keturah) Wolf	Annie (Hannah) Beck	Whitechapel, London	
18585	Bernal	Lewis	1849	Whitechapel, London	Abraham Bernal	Catherine (Keturah) Wolf		Whitechapel, London	
7017	Bernal	Ralph (Raphael)	1783	Colchester, Essex	Jacob de Jacob Israel Bernal	Leah de Refael Vas Da Silva	Anne Elizabeth White	Belgravia, London	MP (Rochester) + Chairman of House of Commons + art collector
21074	Bernard	Edmond	1839	Paris, France				Dover, Kent	boarding school pupil
16734	Bernays	Adolphus (Aaron Beer)	1794	Mainz, Germany	Jacob Bernays	Martha Walsch	Martha Arrowsmith	Paddington, London	Professor of German, King's College
14403	Bernheim	Leopold	1820	?Germany				Manchester	pattern designer
14388	Bernstein	Adolphus	1826	?, Germany	Ludwig Bernstein	(?)		Manchester	
27683	Bernstein	Aharon?	1810	?, Poland [?, Prussia]			Sarah (?)	Aldgate, London	furrier + warehouse keeper
27687	Bernstein	Hannah	1840	Middlesex, London	Aharon? Bernstein	Sarah (?)		Aldgate, London	scholar
27691	Bernstein	Isaac	1846	Middlesex, London	Aharon? Bernstein	Sarah (?)		Aldgate, London	scholar

ID	surname	given names	born	birthplace	father	mother	spouse 1	1851 residence	1851 occupation
13779	Bernstein	Isidore (Isaac)	1815	?	Ezra Bernstein		Jane Isaacs	Strand, London	tailor
13778	Bernstein	Israel	1851	Strand, London	Isidore (Isaac) Bernstein	Jane Isaacs		Covent Garden, London	
6032	Bernstein	Jane	1816	Covent Garden, London	David Isaacs	Elizabeth (?)	Isidore (Isaac) Bernstein	Covent Garden, London	
22143	Bernstein	Julius	1828	?, Germany			Rebecca Joseph	Whitechapel, London	tailor
14387	Bernstein	Ludwig	1801	?, Germany			(?)	Manchester	professor of languages
27688	Bernstein	Presilla	1842	Middlesex, London	Aharon? Bernstein	Sarah (?)		Aldgate, London	scholar
27685	Bernstein	Rachel	1835	Middlesex, London	Aharon? Bernstein	Sarah (?)		Aldgate, London	scholar
27689	Bernstein	Raphael	1844	Middlesex, London	Aharon? Bernstein	Sarah (?)		Aldgate, London	scholar
22142	Bernstein	Rebecca	1825	?, Germany	Simon Joseph		Julius Bernstein	Whitechapel, London	tailoress
27692	Bernstein	Rebecca	1829	?, Poland [?, Prussia]	(?) Bernstein			Aldgate, London	assistant in publican's business
20616	Bernstein	Samuel	1781	?, Poland				Spitalfields, London	tailor
27014	Bernstein	Samuel	1827	?, Poland [Ruzwill, Prussia]				Aldgate, London	tailor
27690	Bernstein	Samuel	1845	Middlesex, London	Aharon? Bernstein	Sarah (?)		Aldgate, London	scholar
27684	Bernstein	Sarah	1814	Middlesex, London	(?)		Aharon? Bernstein	Aldgate, London	
27686	Bernstein	Solomon	1838	Middlesex, London	Aharon? Bernstein	Sarah (?)		Aldgate, London	scholar
20860	Berrick	Amelia Sarah	1838	Liverpool	Barned Berrick	Paulina (?)	Elias Coppel	Liverpool	
20856	Berrick	Barned	1802	?, Poland			Paulina (?)	Liverpool	watchmaker
20862	Berrick	Fanny	1845	Liverpool	Barned Berrick	Paulina (?)	Henry Gedaliah Franckel	Liverpool	scholar
20859	Berrick	George	1835	Liverpool	Barned Berrick	Paulina (?)		Liverpool	chemist + druggist
18838	Berrick	Hannah Rebecca	1847	Liverpool	Barned Berrick	Paulina (?)	Emanuel Nelson	Liverpool	
20863	Berrick	Joseph	1850	Liverpool	Barned Berrick	Paulina (?)		Liverpool	
20861	Berrick	Lesser	1840	Liverpool	Barned Berrick	Paulina (?)		Liverpool	scholar
20858	Berrick	Lewin	1833	Liverpool	Barned Berrick	Paulina (?)	Theresa Nathan	Liverpool	watch finisher
20857	Berrick	Paulina	1806	?, Poland			Barned Berrick	Liverpool	
11758	Berrin	Lewis	1825	?, Poland [?, Prussia]				Shoreditch, London	hawker
11840	Berthonie	Abigail	1787	?, London	(?) Berthonie			Whitechapel, London	annuitant
137	Bertram	Miriam	1825	Middlesex, London				Woolwich, London	governess
24896	Bertram	Miriam Sophia A	1825	Middlesex, London	(?) Bertram			Plumstead, London	governess
29005	Berwin	Julius	1832	?, Poland				Whitechapel, London	shoe maker
21372	Bessunger	Bernhard	1849	Lincoln, Lincolnshire	Morrice Bessunger	Louisa Simon		Lincoln, Lincolnshire	
21373	Bessunger	Jacob	1850	Lincoln, Lincolnshire	Morrice Bessunger	Louisa Simon		Lincoln, Lincolnshire	
21371	Bessunger	Louisa	1825	Mainz, Germany	(?) Simon		Morrice Bessunger	Lincoln, Lincolnshire	
21370	Bessunger	Morrice	1820	Damstadt, Germany			Louisa Simon	Lincoln, Lincolnshire	picture dealer + billiard table keeper
30374	Betsman	Jacob	1821	?, Poland				Cheadle, Staffordshire	traveller vagrant
30487	Betsman	Jacob	1821	?, Poland				Cheadle, Cheshire	traveller vagrant
24297	Beusten	Fredericka	1833	?, Poland [?, Prussia]	(?) Beusten			Bloomsbury, London	nurse
13141	Beyfus	Alfred	1850	City, London	Solomon Gotze Beyfus	Charlotte Abrahams	Emma Plumstead	Aldgate, London	
13137	Beyfus	Charlotte	1819	Aldgate, London	Henry Abrahams	Esther (?)	Solomon Gotze Beyfus	Aldgate, London	
13147	Beyfus	Cippy	1784	Plymouth, Devon	(?)		Gotze Philip Beyfus	Aldgate, London	Berlin woolworker
13139	Beyfus	Gertrude	1846	Aldgate, London	Solomon Gotze Beyfus	Charlotte Abrahams	Michael John Garcia	Aldgate, London	
13138	Beyfus	Henry	1844	Aldgate, London	Solomon Gotze Beyfus	Charlotte Abrahams	Jane (Jeannie) Moss	Aldgate, London	
13142	Beyfus	Julia	1842	Aldgate, London	Solomon Gotze Beyfus	Charlotte Abrahams	Albert Isaac Boss	Aldgate, London	boarding school pupil
22599	Beyfus	Louis	1850	Stepney, London	Marcus Levin Beyfus	Mary (?)		Stepney, London	

ID	surname	given names	born	birthplace	father	mother	spouse 1	1851 residence	1851 occupation
22598	Beyfus	Marcus	1843	Glasgow, Scotland	Marcus Levin Beyfus	Mary (?)		Stepney, London	scholar
22596	Beyfus	Marcus Levin	1804	Hamburg, Germany			Mary (?)	Stepney, London	clerk
22597	Beyfus	Mary	1824	Glasgow, Scotland	(?)		Marcus Levin Beyfus	Stepney, London	
7457	Beyfus	Philip	1819	Aldgate, London	Gotz Philip Beyfus	Cippy (?)	Louisa Benjamin	Aldgate, London	gentleman
10045	Beyfus	Phillip	1848	Aldgate, London	Solomon Gotze Beyfus	Charlotte Abrahams	Ella Ansell Jacobs	Aldgate, London	
22600	Beyfus	Rose	1851	Stepney, London	Marcus Levin Beyfus	Mary (?)		Stepney, London	
13136	Beyfus	Solomon Gotze	1820	Plymouth, Devon	Gotz Philip Beyfus	Cippy (?)	Charlotte Abrahams	Aldgate, London	traveller (mahogany trade)
29113	Bialy (Baily)	Mendel Elias	1822	?, Poland [?, Russia Poland]			Lucretia Margaret Blundell	Whitechapel, London	tailor
2373	Biberew	Abraham	1849	Hull, Yorkshire	Levy Biberew	Mary (?)		Hull, Yorkshire	scholar
2374	Biberew	Hannah	1850	Hull, Yorkshire	Levy Biberew	Mary (?)		Hull, Yorkshire	
2375	Biberew	Levy	1815	?, Germany			Mary (?)	Hull, Yorkshire	licensed hawker
2376	Biberew	Marcus	1838	?, Germany	Levy Biberew	Mary (?)		Hull, Yorkshire	scholar
2377	Biberew	Mary	1822	?, Germany	Levy Biberew			Hull, Yorkshire	
2378	Biberew	Mary ary	1840	Hull, Yorkshire	Levy Biberew	Mary (?)		Hull, Yorkshire	scholar
2379	Biberew	Nancy	1842	Hull, Yorkshire	Levy Biberew	Mary (?)		Hull, Yorkshire	scholar
2380	Biberew	Sarah	1846	Hull, Yorkshire	Levy Biberew	Mary (?)		Hull, Yorkshire	scholar
2387	Bick	Benjamin	1814	Poznan, Poland [Posen, Prussia]			Eliza (?)	Hull, Yorkshire	
2388	Bick	Eliza	1813	Shoreditch, London			Benjamin Bick	Hull, Yorkshire	
2389	Bick	Hannah	1850	Hull, Yorkshire	Bejamin Bick	Eliza (?)		Hull, Yorkshire	
22139	Biglizan	Colman	1831	Poznan, Poland [Posen, Prussia]				Whitechapel, London	tailor
25504	Bing	Jacob	1834	Copenhagen, Denmark				Tower Hill, London	
4315	Birks	Michael	1825	?, Poland				Birmingham	hawker
11373	Birne	Cecilia (Selia)	1850	Aldgate, London	Joseph Barnet Birne	Sarah Levy	Jacob Solomon	Aldgate, London	
11369	Birne	Elizabeth	1836	Middlesex, London	Joseph Barnet Birne	Sarah Levy	Joseph Reichfeld	Aldgate, London	tailoress
11372	Birne	Jane	1843	Aldgate, London	Joseph Barnet Birne	Sarah Levy	Michael Rees	Aldgate, London	
11370	Birne	Joseph	1840	?Aldgate, London	Joseph Barnet Birne	Sarah Levy	Rebecca Lupinski nee Hyams	Aldgate, London	
11367	Birne	Joseph Barnet	1803	?, Poland [?, Prussia]	Yosef		Sarah Levy	Aldgate, London	tailor
11371	Birne	Rachael	1841	Middlesex, London	Joseph Barnet Birne	Sarah Levy	Abraham Charles Jacobs	Aldgate, London	
11368	Birne	Sarah	1813	Middlesex, London	Michael Levy		Joseph Barnet Birne	Aldgate, London	tailor
30752	Birnstingl	Helen	1831	Chelsea, London			Louis Birnstingl	Bloomsbury, London	
30751	Birnstingl	Louis	1821	Budapest, Hungary [Pesth, Hungary]			Helen (?)	Bloomsbury, London	coral merchant
22994	Birwin	Isaac	1827	?, Poland [?, Prussia]				Whitechapel, London	tailor
22392	Bittan	Alexander (Abraham)	1837	Middlesex, London	Joshua Bittan	Phoebe de Jacob Nunes Martinez	Mary (Miriam) Solomons	Aldgate, London	general dealer
22391	Bittan	Benjamin	1835	Middlesex, London	Joshua Bittan	Phoebe de Jacob Nunes Martinez	Esther Levy	Aldgate, London	traveller
22394	Bittan	Dinah	1842	Stepney, London	Joshua Bittan	Phoebe de Jacob Nunes Martinez	Abraham Nathan	Aldgate, London	

ID	surname	given names	born	birthplace	father	mother	spouse 1	1851 residence	1851 occupation
22397	Bittan	Esther	1850	City, London	Joshua Bittan	Phoebe de Jacob Nunes Martinez		Aldgate, London	
22389	Bittan	Joshua	1811	?, Morocco	Yamin Betan		Phoebe de Jacob Nunes Martinez	Aldgate, London	traveller + general dealer
22395	Bittan	Julia	1844	Stepney, London	Joshua Bittan	Phoebe de Jacob Nunes Martinez	Joseph Valantine	Aldgate, London	
22390	Bittan	Phoebe	1815	Middlesex, London	Jacod de Isaac Nunes Martinez		Joshua Bittan	Aldgate, London	
22393	Bittan	Rebecca	1839	Spitalfields, London	Joshua Bittan	Phoebe de Jacob Nunes Martinez	Benjamin Rees	Aldgate, London	
22396	Bittan	Samuel	1848	City, London	Joshua Bittan	Phoebe de Jacob Nunes Martinez		Aldgate, London	
18061	Bitton	Leah	1840	Spitalfields, London	Jacob Bitton		Lion Blits	Southwark, London	boarding school pupil
17359	Bitton (Bitto)	Abigail	1834	Spitalfields, London	Isaac Bitton	Elizabeth (Eve, Hava) de Getschlik Elyakim	Joseph Rodrigues Mendez	Spitalfields, London	cap maker
17358	Bitton (Bitto)	David	1832	Spitalfields, London	Isaac Bitton	Elizabeth (Eve, Hava) de Getschlik Elyakim		Spitalfields, London	
17357	Bitton (Bitto)	Elizabeth (Eve, Hava)	1801	Amsterdam, Holland	Getschlik Eliakim		Isaac Bitton	Spitalfields, London	general dealer
17360	Bitton (Bitto)	Joel	1843	Spitalfields, London	Isaac Bitton	Elizabeth (Eve, Hava) de Getschlik Elyakim		Spitalfields, London	
17361	Bitton (Bitto)	Phoebe	1847	Aldgate, London	Isaac Bitton	Elizabeth (Eve, Hava) de Getschlik Elyakim		Spitalfields, London	
4331	Blanckensee	Aaron	1842	Bristol	Solomon (Salaman) Blanckensee	Julia Joseph	Elizabeth (Eliza, Lizzie) Hart	Birmingham	scholar
4341	Blanckensee	Abraham	1846	Bristol	Meyer Blanckensee	Julia Levy	Celine Warradyn	Birmingham	scholar at home
4326	Blanckensee	Abraham Solomon	1830	Bristol	Solomon (Salaman) Blanckensee	Julia Joseph	Hannah Joseph	Birmingham	wholesale jeweller
4321	Blanckensee	Charles	1844	Birmingham	Isaac Blanckensee	Eliza (?)		Birmingham	scholar
4317	Blanckensee	Eliza	1814	Birmingham	John Aaron		Isaac Blanckensee	Birmingham	
4339	Blanckensee	Eliza	1842	Bristol	Meyer Blanckensee	Julia Levy		Birmingham	scholar at home
4343	Blanckensee	Florence Rosetta	1851	Birmingham	Meyer Blanckensee	Julia Levy	Solomon Warschauer	Birmingham	
4333	Blanckensee	Georgina	1847	Bristol	Solomon (Salaman) Blanckensee	Julia Joseph	Nathan Jacob Hyman	Birmingham	scholar
4319	Blanckensee	Hannah (Marinda)	1841	Birmingham	Isaac Blanckensee	Eliza (?)		Birmingham	scholar
4329	Blanckensee	Helen	1837	Bristol	Solomon (Salaman) Blanckensee	Julia Joseph	Morris (Maurice) Moses	Birmingham	scholar
4327	Blanckensee	Henrietta	1833	Bristol	Solomon (Salaman) Blanckensee	Julia Joseph	Joel Solomon	Birmingham	
897	Blanckensee	Henrietta	1841	Bristol	Meyer Blanckensee	Julia Levy	Saul Abrahams	Birmingham	scholar at home
7442	Blanckensee	Henrietta	1844	?, London	Moses Blanckensee	Mary Ann Lazarus	Isaac Silverstone	Bristol	
4316	Blanckensee	Isaac	1807	?, Poland [?, Prussia]	Simon Blanckensee		Eliza Aaron	Birmingham	gold chain maker
4330	Blanckensee	Isabella	1840	Bristol	Solomon (Salaman) Blanckensee	Julia Joseph	Barnet Henry Joseph	Birmingham	scholar
4342	Blanckensee	Joel	1848	Bristol	Meyer Blanckensee	Julia Levy		Birmingham	scholar at home
4325	Blanckensee	Julia	1809	Falmouth Cornwall			Solomon (Salaman) Blanckensee	Birmingham	
4337	Blanckensee	Julia	1810	Plymouth, Devon	(?) Levy	?	Meyer Blanckensee	Birmingham	tailor's wife
4318	Blanckensee	Julius	1839	Birmingham	Isaac Blanckensee	Eliza (?)		Birmingham	scholar
4334	Blanckensee	Julius	1850	Birmingham	Solomon (Salaman) Blanckensee	Julia Joseph		Birmingham	
3469	Blanckensee	Mary Ann	1819	Aldgate, London	Lewis Henry Lazarus	Elizabeth (Eliza) Aaron	Moses Blankensee	Bristol	
4324	Blanckensee	Matilda	1850	Birmingham	Isaac Blanckensee	Eliza (?)		Birmingham	

ID	surname	given names	born	birthplace	father	mother	spouse 1	1851 residence	1851 occupation
178	Blanckensee	Meyer	1805	?, Germany	Levin Blanckensee		Julia Levy	Birmingham	jeweller
4323	Blanckensee	Meyer	1847	Birmingham	Isaac Blanckensee	Eliza (?)		Birmingham	
4332	Blanckensee	Miriam	1845	Bristol	Solomon (Salaman) Blanckensee	Julia Joseph		Birmingham	scholar
3470	Blanckensee	Moses	1813	?, Germany [Felshorn, Prussia, Germany]	Moses Judah Levy		Mary Ann Lazarus	Bristol	?harbour dealer
4322	Blanckensee	Moses	1845	Birmingham	Isaac Blanckensee	Eliza (?)		Birmingham	scholar
4340	Blanckensee	Rachel	1845	Bristol	Meyer Blanckensee	Julia Levy		Birmingham	scholar at home
7443	Blanckensee	Rose	1850	Bristol	Moses Blanckensee	Mary Ann Lazarus	Charles Marcus	Bristol	
4328	Blanckensee	Rosetta	1834	Bristol	Solomon (Salaman) Blanckensee	Julia Joseph	Simeon Joseph	Birmingham	scholar
4320	Blanckensee	Solomon	1842	Birmingham	Isaac Blanckensee	Eliza (?)		Birmingham	scholar
4335	Blanckensee	Solomon (Salaman)	1801	?, Germany	Levin Blanckensee		Julia Joseph	Birmingham	jeweller
24105	Blandes	Natje	1816	?< Holland	(?) Blandes			Bloomsbury, London	general servant
16633	Blankensy	Isaac	1806	?, Poland				Liverpool	commercial traveller lace
18056	Blankidney	Abraham	1792	?, Poland				Dudley, Worcestershire	tailor master empl 3
23004	Blaun	David	1811	Poznan, Poland [Posen, Prussia]				Finsbury, London	wholesale hat + cap manufacturer
14027	Bles	Abraham	1839	The Hague, Holland	Samuel D Bles	Sophia (?)		Manchester	
14025	Bles	David Samuel	1834	The Hague, Holland	Samuel D Bles	Sophia (?)		Manchester	
14024	Bles	Esther	1833	The Hague, Holland	Samuel D Bles	Sophia (?)		Manchester	
14028	Bles	Marcus	1846	Manchester	Samuel D Bles	Sophia (?)	Josephine Bles	Manchester	
14026	Bles	Rebecca	1836	The Hague, Holland	Samuel D Bles	Sophia (?)		Manchester	
14022	Bles	Samuel D	1798	The Hague, Holland			Sophia (?)	Manchester	merchant manufactory goods
14023	Bles	Sophia	1810	Rotterdam, Holland	(?)		Samuel D Bles	Manchester	
24143	Blitz	Esther	1814	?, Holland	Laurence Levy		Charlotte Levy	Bloomsbury, London	cook
12994	Blitz	Solomon	1785	Amsterdam, Holland	Simon Solomon Blits		Leah Levy nee Dagon	Aldgate, London	optician
12573	Bloch	Israel	1815	Moisling, Germany			Annie Kisch	Norwich, Norfolk	silversmith + jeweller
4344	Bloch	Samuel	1820	Copenhagen, Denmark				Birmingham	merchant
7876	Block	Albert	1792	?, Lower Saxony, Germany				Maidstone, Kent	Professor of languages
12681	Block	Edward	1849	King's Lynn, Norfolk	Marcus Block	Frances (?)		King's Lynn, Norfolk	
12678	Block	Elizabeth	1840	King's Lynn, Norfolk	Marcus Block	Frances (?)		King's Lynn, Norfolk	scholar
12677	Block	Frances	1819	King's Lynn, Norfolk	(?)		Marcus Block	King's Lynn, Norfolk	
12679	Block	George	1842	King's Lynn, Norfolk	Marcus Block	Frances (?)		King's Lynn, Norfolk	scholar
12680	Block	Harriett	1845	King's Lynn, Norfolk	Marcus Block	Frances (?)		King's Lynn, Norfolk	scholar
28093	Block	Isaac	1799	?, Hessen, Germany			(?)	Spitalfields, London	clothes dealer
12676	Block	Marcus	1813	Hamburg, Germany			Frances (?)	King's Lynn, Norfolk	general dealer
26748	Block	Mary	1806	Metz, France	(?)		(?) Block	Aldgate, London	annuitant
28094	Block	Nathan	1828	?, Germany	Isaac Block		Esther Barnett	Spitalfields, London	
20595	Blomberg (Bloomberg)	Annette	1808	Liepaja, Lilthuania [Libau, Russia]	(?)		Moses Blomberg (Bloomberg)	Spitalfields, London	seamstress
20597	Blomberg (Bloomberg)	Emily	1839	Liepaja, Lilthuania [Libau, Russia]	(?) Blomberg	Annette (?)		Spitalfields, London	capmaker
20596	Blomberg (Bloomberg)	Rebecca	1838	Liepaja, Lilthuania [Libau, Russia]	Moses Blomberg (Bloomberg)	Annette (?)	Henry Meyer Chapkowski	Spitalfields, London	capmaker

ID	surname	given names	born	birthplace	father	mother	spouse 1	1851 residence	1851 occupation
12495	Blondskai	Lewis	1820	?, Poland				Barnstaple, Devon	linguist
1755	Bloom	Abraham	1828	Merthyr Tydfil, Wales	Solomon Bloom	Leah (?)	Marian (Miriam) King	Merthyr Tydfil, Wales	painter, glazier
2230	Bloom	Gershon	1826	?, Poland				Leeds, Yorkshire	general dealer
1757	Bloom	Hynda (Hinda)	1850	Merthyr Tydfil, Wales	Abraham Bloom	Marian (Miriam) King	Wolfe Phillips	Merthyr Tydfil, Wales	
1750	Bloom	Isaac David	1830	Merthyr Tydfil, Wales	Solomon Bloom	Leah (?)	Hannah Harris	Merthyr Tydfil, Wales	glazier
14476	Bloom	Jacob	1821	?, Hungary			Rachel (?)	Manchester	hawks pencils
1751	Bloom	Jacob	1832	Merthyr Tydfil, Wales	Solomon Bloom	Leah (?)	Leah Himes	Merthyr Tydfil, Wales	glazier
1752	Bloom	Leah	1794	?, Poland	(?)		Solomon Bloom	Merthyr Tydfil, Wales	pawnbroker's wife
1754	Bloom	Maria	1839	Merthyr Tydfil, Wales	Solomon Bloom	Leah (?)	Simon Harris	Merthyr Tydfil, Wales	scholar
1756	Bloom	Marian (Miriam)	1832	Bristol	Moses King	Ann (?)	Abraham Bloom	Merthyr Tydfil, Wales	milliner
14477	Bloom	Mary	1831	?, Hungary	(?)		Jacob Bloom	Manchester	hawks pencils
4345	Bloom	Nathan	1841	?, Gloucestershire				Birmingham	
14478	Bloom	Rachel	1849	Manchester	Jacob Bloom	Mary (?)	Rachel (?)	Manchester	
1749	Bloom	Solomon	1786	Włodawa, Poland [Bladwa, Poland]	Kalonymous Bloom		Leah (?)	Merthyr Tydfil, Wales	pawnbroker
1753	Bloom	Sophia	1836	Merthyr Tydfil, Wales	Solomon Bloom	Leah (?)	Jacob Isaacs	Merthyr Tydfil, Wales	
27947	Bloomfield	David	1804	?, Poland [?, Prussia]	Tsadok		Matilda (?)	Spitalfields, London	waistcoat maker
27949	Bloomfield	Elizabeth	1831	Spitalfields, London	David Bloomfield	Matilda (?)		Spitalfields, London	waistcoat maker
27953	Bloomfield	Esther	1841	Aldgate, London	David Bloomfield	Matilda (?)		Spitalfields, London	scholar
14446	Bloomfield	Henry	1816	Middlesex, London				Salford, Lancashire	ticket writer
27954	Bloomfield	Isaac	1843	Aldgate, London	David Bloomfield	Matilda (?)		Spitalfields, London	scholar
27951	Bloomfield	Laurence	1836	Spitalfields, London	David Bloomfield	Matilda (?)		Spitalfields, London	butcher
27948	Bloomfield	Matilda	1804	Whitechapel, London	(?)		David Bloomfield	Spitalfields, London	waistcoat maker
27952	Bloomfield	Samuel	1839	Spitalfields, London	David Bloomfield	Matilda (?)	Clara Hart	Spitalfields, London	scholar
27950	Bloomfield	Zadoc (Zachariah)	1834	Whitechapel, London	David Bloomfield	Matilda (?)	Elizabeth (Betsy) Eisendrath	Spitalfields, London	cap maker
28084	Blouth	Jacob	1813	?, Germany			Sarah (?)	Spitalfields, London	
28085	Blouth	Sarah	1821	?, Germany	(?)		Jacob Blouth	Spitalfields, London	
28086	Blouth	Selina	1845	?, London	Jacob Blouth	Sarah (?)		Spitalfields, London	
23185	Blucher	Maria	1827	?, Germany	(?) Blucher			City, London	box maker
14443	Bluemenfeld	Abraham	1801	Cracow, Poland				Salford, Lancashire	merchant
14325	Bluhm	Arabella	1842	Manchester	Theodore Bluhm	Martha (?)		Manchester	
14323	Bluhm	Martha	1820	Stockport, Cheshire	(?)		Theodore Bluhm	Manchester	
14322	Bluhm	Theodore	1814	?, Germany			Martha (?)	Manchester	export merchant
14324	Bluhm	Theodore	1845	Manchester	Theodore Bluhm	Martha (?)		Manchester	
25540	Blum	?	1825	?	(?)		Joseph Blum	Dublin, Ireland	
25541	Blum	Bilah?	1851	Dublin, Ireland	Joseph Blum	?		Dublin, Ireland	
25535	Blum	Ephraim (Robert)	1815	?Hanover, Germany	Morris Blum		Minna (?)	Dublin, Ireland	toy warehouse
14911	Blum	Gustav	1838	?, Poland [Velbiret, Prussia]				Bethnal Green, London	boarding school pupil
25537	Blum	Henriette	1845	Dublin, Ireland	Ephraim (Robert) Blum	Minna (?)	Leopold Drechsfeld	Dublin, Ireland	
14910	Blum	Israel James	1839	Warsaw, Poland				Bethnal Green, London	boarding school pupil
2231	Blum	Jacob	1817	?, Germany			Miriam (?)	Leeds, Yorkshire	hawker
19755	Blum	Joseph	1820	Hanover, Germany	Morris Blum		(?)	Dublin, Ireland	fancy warehouseman
25536	Blum	Minna	1820	?	(?)		Ephraim (Robert) Blum	Dublin, Ireland	
2232	Blum	Miriam	1822	?, Germany			Jacob Blum	Leeds, Yorkshire	

ID	surname	given names	born	birthplace	father	mother	spouse 1	1851 residence	1851 occupation
25542	Blum	Morris	1846	Dublin, Ireland	Joseph Blum	?		Dublin, Ireland	
25538	Blum	Myer	1849	Dublin, Ireland	Ephraim (Robert) Blum	Minna (?)		Dublin, Ireland	
25539	Blum	Rachel	1851	Dublin, Ireland	Ephraim (Robert) Blum	Minna (?)		Dublin, Ireland	
6416	Blumenthal	Bluma	1843	?, London	Elias Blumenthal		Solomon Albu	?Spitalfields, London	
17223	Blumenthal	Bluma	1844	Whitechapel, London	Morris Blumenthal	Marian (?)		Spitalfields, London	
16500	Blumenthal	Fanny	1816	Aldgate, London	(?)		William Blumenthal	Lambeth, London	
16501	Blumenthal	Goodman	1845	Whitechapel, London	William Blumenthal	Fanny (?)		Lambeth, London	
13469	Blumenthal	Gustavus	1803	?, Germany				Manchester	agent
9814	Blumenthal	Hannah	1830	?Mecklenburg, Germany	(?) Blumenthal			Finsbury, London	cook
17221	Blumenthal	Marian	1816	?, Germany [?, Saxony]	(?)		Morris Blumenthal	Spitalfields, London	
16502	Blumenthal	Montague	1846	Aldgate, London	William Blumenthal	Fanny (?)		Lambeth, London	
17220	Blumenthal	Morris	1813	?, Germany			Marian (?)	Spitalfields, London	horse hair merchant empl 12
16504	Blumenthal	Samuel	1850	Aldgate, London	William Blumenthal	Fanny (?)		Lambeth, London	
16503	Blumenthal	Sarah	1848	Lambeth, London	William Blumenthal	Fanny (?)		Lambeth, London	
17222	Blumenthal	Solomon	1843	Whitechapel, London	Morris Blumenthal	Marian (?)		Spitalfields, London	
16499	Blumenthal	William	1819	Frankfurt, Germany			Fanny (?)	Lambeth, London	tailor + draper
16498	Blumenthal (Bloomenthal)	Barnett	1851	Whitechapel, London	Isaac (Jonas) Blumenthal (Bloomenthal)	Sarah Shard		Stepney, London	
24695	Blumenthal (Bloomenthal)	Caroline	1803	Mecklenburg, Germany	(?)		Isidore Blumenthal (Bloomenthal)	Walworth, London	
16497	Blumenthal (Bloomenthal)	Clara	1845	Whitechapel, London	Isaac (Jonas) Blumenthal (Bloomenthal)	Sarah Shard		Stepney, London	scholar
24699	Blumenthal (Bloomenthal)	Herman	1834	Greenwich, London	John Samson Blumenthal (Bloomenthal)	Johanna (?)		Walworth, London	
5909	Blumenthal (Bloomenthal)	Isaac (Jonas)	1813	?, Poland [?, Prussia]	Barnett Blumenthal (Bloomenthal)		Sarah Shard [Moses]	Whitechapel, London	hair brush dresser
24694	Blumenthal (Bloomenthal)	Isidore	1800	Hanover, Germany			Caroline (?)	Walworth, London	cigar merchant
24698	Blumenthal (Bloomenthal)	Johanna	1821	Brunswick, Germany			John Samson Blumenthal (Bloomenthal)	Walworth, London	
24697	Blumenthal (Bloomenthal)	John Samson	1811	Hanover, Germany			Johanna (?)	Walworth, London	cigar manufacturer
16496	Blumenthal (Bloomenthal)	Moses	1843	Whitechapel, London	Isaac (Jonas) Blumenthal (Bloomenthal)	Sarah Shard		Stepney, London	scholar
7448	Blumenthal (Bloomenthal)	Sarah	1819	?, Suffolk	Richard Shard		Isaac (Jonas) Blumenthal (Bloomenthal)	Whitechapel, London	
24700	Blumenthal (Bloomenthal)	Theodore	1838	Southwark, London	John Samson Blumenthal (Bloomenthal)	Johanna (?)	(?Henrietta Josephine Schott)	Walworth, London	scholar
11998	Boam	Adelaide	1842	Whitechapel, London	Barnett Boam	Fanny Phillips	Henry Isaac Lyon	Whitechapel, London	scholar
12004	Boam	Amelia	1805	Amsterdam, Holland	Zanvil Shmuel		Moses (Morris) Jacob Boam	Spitalfields, London	
16634	Boam	Barnett	1803	?, Holland				Liverpool	commercial traveller lace
11992	Boam	Barnett	1809	Amsterdam, Holland	Jacob Boam		Fanny Phillips	Whitechapel, London	diamond merchant
17677	Boam	Elizabeth	1837	Whitechapel, London	Moses (Morris) Jacob Boam	Amelia Samuel	John Jacobs	Spitalfields, London	furrier
11999	Boam	Elizabeth	1843	Whitechapel, London	Barnett Boam	Fanny Phillips	Mordecai Morris Cohen	Whitechapel, London	scholar

ID	surname	given names	born	birthplace	father	mother	spouse 1	1851 residence	1851 occupation
11993	Boam	Fanny	1807	Amsterdam, Holland	Aryeh Paivel Phillips		Barnett Boam	Whitechapel, London	
17676	Boam	Hannah	1836	Whitechapel, London	Moses (Morris) Jacob Boam	Amelia Samuel	Samuel Stretetsky	Spitalfields, London	dress maker
11994	Boam	Hannah (Henrietta)	1833	Whitechapel, London	Barnett Boam	Fanny Phillips	Isaac Jonas	Whitechapel, London	
17680	Boam	Jacob	1768	?, Holland			(?)	Spitalfields, London	
18060	Boam	Joseph	1839	Whitechapel, London				Southwark, London	boarding school pupil
12001	Boam	Joseph	1850	Whitechapel, London	Barnett Boam	Fanny Phillips	Priscilla Lyons	Whitechapel, London	
11995	Boam	Maria	1834	Whitechapel, London	Barnett Boam	Fanny Phillips		Whitechapel, London	
11997	Boam	Mitchel	1840	Whitechapel, London	Barnett Boam	Fanny Phillips		Whitechapel, London	
9756	Boam	Mitchell	1847	Middlesex, London				Kew, London	boarding school pupil
12000	Boam	Morris	1847	Whitechapel, London	Barnett Boam	Fanny Phillips		Whitechapel, London	
250	Boam	Moses (Morris) Jacob	1803	Amsterdam, Holland	Jacob Boam		Amelia Samuel	Spitalfields, London	attendant on the Sick to the Jews
17678	Boam	Rosa	1841	Whitechapel, London	Moses (Morris) Jacob Boam	Hannah Samuel	Barnet Rosenthall	Spitalfields, London	scholar
11996	Boam	Sarah	1837	Whitechapel, London	Barnett Boam	Fanny Phillips	Moses Jonas	Whitechapel, London	scholar
17679	Boam	Sarah	1842	Whitechapel, London	Moses (Morris) Jacob Boam	Hannah Samuel	Elias Silkman (Harrar)	Spitalfields, London	scholar
11919	Boas	Eliza (Elizabeth)	1849	Middlesex, London	Morris (Moses) H Boas	Theresa (Teibchen) Leepman	Marcus Leuw	Whitechapel, London	
11917	Boas	Morris (Moses) H	1825	Rotterdam, Holland	Samson Boas	Elizabeth (?)	Theresa (Teibchen) Leepman	Whitechapel, London	cattle agent
12168	Boas	Samuel	1828	?, Holland				Whitechapel, London	general dealer
11920	Boas	Samuel (Samson)	1850	Whitechapel, London	Morris (Moses) H Boas	Theresa (Teibchen) Leepman		Whitechapel, London	
11918	Boas	Theresa (Teibchen)	1822	Hanover, Germany	Abraham Leepman		Morris (Moses) H Boas	Whitechapel, London	
9162	Bock	Jenet	1818	Kornik, Poland [Prussia]	(?)		Michaelis Bock	Whitechapel, London	
9164	Bock	Lewis	1828	Poznan, Poland [Posen, Prussia]				Whitechapel, London	tailor
9163	Bock	Markus	1836	?, London	Michaelis Bock	Jenet (?)		Whitechapel, London	
9161	Bock	Michaelis	1822	Poznan, Poland [Posen, Prussia]			Jenet (?)	Whitechapel, London	journeyman tinman
2390	Bogovitz	Matteo	1822	?, Austria				Hull, Yorkshire	prisoner (mariner)
2391	Bogwitz	William	1823	Hamburg, Germany				Hull, Yorkshire	shoemaker
28856	Boman	Abraham	1820	Spitalfields, London			Debrah (?)	Spitalfields, London	general dealer
28857	Boman	Debrah	1821	Spitalfields, London	(?)		Abraham Boman	Spitalfields, London	
13008	Bomberg	Moses	1827	?, Holland				Spitalfields, London	dealer
23639	Bomm	Amelia	1828	?, Germany	(?)		Barnet Barnet Bomm	Liverpool	
23638	Bomm	Barnet Barnet	1830	?, Poland			Amelia (?)	Liverpool	glazier
22119	Bone	Jacobs	1822	?, Hungary				Whitechapel, London	tailor
18626	Booth	Amelia	1846	Selby, Yorkshire	John (Jonathan) Booth	Ann Hawcroft	David Ansell	Selby, Yorkshire	
2392	Born	Jacob	1842	?, Poland [?, Prussia]	Julius Born	Rosetta (?)		Hull, Yorkshire	
2124	Born	Julius	1813	?, Poland [?, Prussia]			Rosetta (?)	Hull, Yorkshire	licensed hawker jewellery
2393	Born	Rosetta	1812	?, Poland [?, Prussia]			Julius Born	Hull, Yorkshire	
9088	Bosman	Aaron	1796	?, Holland				Spitalfields, London	
27293	Bosman	Elizabeth	1827	Whitechapel, London	Zelig (Solomon) Phillips	Ann (Nancy) Woolf	Levy Bosman	Aldgate, London	

ID	surname	given names	born	birthplace	father	mother	spouse 1	1851 residence	1851 occupation
27292	Bosman	Levy	1824	Rotterdam, Holland	Simon Bosman		Elizabeth Phillips	Aldgate, London	tailor
27294	Bosman	Matilda	1844	Middlesex, London	Levy Bosman	Elizabeth Phillips	Abraham Myers	Aldgate, London	
27296	Bosman	Simon	1850	Aldgate, London	Levy Bosman	Elizabeth Phillips		Aldgate, London	
27295	Bosman	Zadok (Zalig)	1848	Aldgate, London	Levy Bosman	Elizabeth Phillips	Kate Polak	Aldgate, London	
21302	Boss	Albert Isaac	1837	Aldgate, London	Isaac Abraham Boss	Rose Alexander	Julia Beyfus	Aldgate, London	boarding school pupil
23099	Boss	Isaac Abraham	1809	Middlesex, London	Abraham Boss	Juliet (?)	Rose Alexander	Aldgate, London	parasol merchant
20660	Boss	Marcus	1822	?, Poland [?, Prussia]				Spitalfields, London	shoemaker
23100	Boss	Rose	1805	Middlesex, London	Moshe Alexander		Isaac Abraham Boss	Aldgate, London	
23101	Boss	Sarah	1838	Aldgate, London	Isaac Abraham Boss	Rose Alexander	Leopold Morris	Aldgate, London	
18720	Botibol	Abraham	1848	Marylebone, London	Moss (Moses) Botibol	Jessie Myers	Rachel Cohen nee Angel	Marylebone, London	
20971	Botibol	Asher	1850	Marylebone, London	Moss (Moses) Botibol	Jessie Myers		Marylebone, London	
16949	Botibol	Catherine	1846	Marylebone, London	Moss (Moses) Botibol	Jessie Myers		Marylebone, London	
20970	Botibol	Cecilia	1849	Marylebone, London	Moss (Moses) Botibol	Jessie Myers		Marylebone, London	
5663	Botibol	Elizabeth	1819	Bloomsbury, London	Moses Haim Botibol	Hanah Solomons		Shoreditch, London	
16946	Botibol	Esther	1836	Clerkenwell, London	Moss (Moses) Botibol	Jessie Myers		Marylebone, London	feather maker
21646	Botibol	Hannah	1793	?London	Aaron Solomons		Moses Haim Botibol	Shoreditch, London	
16948	Botibol	Isaac	1845	St Pancras, London	Moss (Moses) Botibol	Jessie Myers	Annie Benjamin	Marylebone, London	
16945	Botibol	Jessie	1816	Middlesex, London	Abraham Myers		Moses Botibol	Marylebone, London	
20969	Botibol	Maria	1840	Marylebone, London	Moss (Moses) Botibol	Jessie Myers		Marylebone, London	
21645	Botibol	Moses Haim	1790	?, London	Masaod (Prospero) Botibol	Abigail de Solomon Benamor	Hanah Solomons	Shoreditch, London	feather manufacturer
16944	Botibol	Moss (Moses)	1809	?, Ireland	Isaac Botibol	Hannah Abigail de Moses Rodrigues Moreira	Jessie Myers	Marylebone, London	feather manufacturer
16947	Botibol	Phoebe	1839	St Pancras, London	Moss (Moses) Botibol	Jessie Myers		Marylebone, London	
18165	Botibol	Solomon	1788	Middlesex, London				Mile End, London	patient in the Portuguese Jews Hospital
20972	Botibol	Solomon	1851	Marylebone, London	Moss (Moses) Botibol	Jessie Myers		Marylebone, London	
14442	Bottibos	Isaac	1798	Middlesex, London				Salford, Lancashire	merchant
30995	Braham	Abraham	1848	Newcastle Upon Tyne	Samuel A Braham	Ester (?)		Newcastle Upon Tyne	
20103	Braham	Adelaide	1833	Strand, London	Israel Joseph	Rosetta (?)	Louis Braham	Marylebone, London	
19760	Braham	Adelaide	1845	Middlesex, London	Lewis Henry Braham	Sophia (?)		Bloomsbury, London	
19761	Braham	Benjamin	1847	Middlesex, London	Lewis Henry Braham	Sophia (?)		Bloomsbury, London	
21279	Braham	David	1839	Holborn, London				Edmonton, London	boarding school pupil
19756	Braham	Elizabeth	1837	Surrey, London	Lewis Henry Braham	Sophia (?)		Bloomsbury, London	
1141	Braham	Ellen	1805	Plymouth, Devon				Torquay, Devon	independent means
14280	Braham	Emily	1814	Salford, Lancashire	(?)		Isaac Braham	Manchester	
30993	Braham	Ester	1824	?, Poland [?, Prussia]	(?)		Samuel A Braham	Newcastle Upon Tyne	
5777	Braham	Frederick Joseph	1832	Bristol	John Braham	Henrietta (?)	Phoebe Levy	Bristol	
18399	Braham	Frederick R	1850	Middlesex, London	Lewis Henry Braham	Sophia (?)		Bloomsbury, London	
29012	Braham	Hannah	1836	Stepney, London	(?) Braham			Whitechapel, London	servant
7192	Braham	Henrietta	1801	Bristol	Jacob (?)		John Braham	Bristol	
7193	Braham	Henry	1829	?, Gloucestershire	John Braham	Henrietta (?)		Bristol	
18398	Braham	Henry Arthur	1846	Middlesex, London	Lewis Henry Braham	Sophia (?)		Bloomsbury, London	
14279	Braham	Isaac	1807	Manchester			Emily (?)	Manchester	landed proprietor
19759	Braham	Isabella	1843	Middlesex, London	Lewis Henry Braham	Sophia (?)		Bloomsbury, London	

ID	surname	given names	born	birthplace	father	mother	spouse 1	1851 residence	1851 occupation
1140	Braham	James	1806	Plymouth, Devon			(?)	Torquay, Devon	retired watchmaker
31142	Braham	James	1841	Bristol	John Braham	Henrietta (?)		Bristol	
19757	Braham	Janette	1840	Surrey, London	Lewis Henry Braham	Sophia (?)		Bloomsbury, London	
7016	Braham	John	1774	?, London	(?John Abraham)	Esther (?Abrams)	Nancy Storace	Mayfair, London	retired opera singer
7191	Braham	John	1800	Plymouth, Devon	David Braham		Henrietta (?)	Bristol	
14278	Braham	Joseph	1775	Middlesex, London			(?)	Manchester	landed proprietor
7190	Braham	Joseph I---	1836	Bristol	John Braham	Henrietta (?)	Catherine Jessel	Bristol	
19763	Braham	Lewis	1850	Middlesex, London	Lewis Henry Braham	Sophia (?)		Bloomsbury, London	
7512	Braham	Lewis Henry	1808	Middlesex, London			Sophia (?)	Bloomsbury, London	attorney at law
5039	Braham	M---	1818	Portsmouth, Hampshire				Portsmouth, Hampshire	
31143	Braham	Octavius	1846	Bristol	John Braham	Henrietta (?)		Bristol	
19758	Braham	Rosetta	1841	Middlesex, London	Lewis Henry Braham	Sophia (?)		Bloomsbury, London	
19762	Braham	Samuel	1848	Middlesex, London	Lewis Henry Braham	Sophia (?)		Bloomsbury, London	
30992	Braham	Samuel A	1822	?, Poland [?, Prussia]			Ester (?)	Newcastle Upon Tyne	southwester maker
18397	Braham	Sara L	1836	Surrey, London	Lewis Henry Braham	Sophia (?)		Bloomsbury, London	
30994	Braham	Sarah A	1848	North Shields, Tyne & Wear	Samuel A Braham	Ester (?)		Newcastle Upon Tyne	
18396	Braham	Sophia	1818	Middlesex, London	(?)		Lewis Henry Braham	Bloomsbury, London	
6686	Braham (Abraham)	Abraham	1788	Arundel, Sussex	Nathan Papea	Lidia Barnett	Hannah Moses	Finsbury, London	annuitant + daguerrotypist
18395	Braham (Abraham)	Hannah	1795	Whitechapel, London	Yaacov Bromidsham Moses		Abraham Braham (Abraham)	Finsbury, London	
18549	Braham (Abrahams)	Asher	1849	Whitechapel, London	Mark Braham (Abrahams)	Sophia Isaacs		Whitechapel, London	
18548	Braham (Abrahams)	Elias	1844	Spitalfields, London	Mark Braham (Abrahams)	Sophia Isaacs		Whitechapel, London	
18547	Braham (Abrahams)	Lewis	1842	Whitechapel, London	Mark Braham (Abrahams)	Sophia Isaacs		Whitechapel, London	
18545	Braham (Abrahams)	Mark	1819	Spitalfields, London	Michael Abrahams		Sophia Isaacs	Whitechapel, London	commercial traveller (clothing)
18546	Braham (Abrahams)	Sophia	1817	Whitechapel, London	Asher Isaacs	Judith Cohen	Mark Braham (Abrahams)	Whitechapel, London	
16362	Brandon	Abraham	1839	City, London				Aldgate, London	boarding school pupil
9048	Brandon	Esther Rodrigues	1825	Barbados, West Indies	Abraham Rodrigues Brandon		Aaron Abecasis	Finsbury, London	fundholder
7015	Brandon	John Raphael Rodrigues	1817	?, London	Joshua de Isaac Moses Rodrigues Brandon	Sarah (?)	(?)	Strand, London	architect + writer
9049	Brandon	Joseph Rodrigues	1828	Barbados, West Indies	Abraham Rodrigues Brandon			Finsbury, London	merchant
9050	Brandon	Julia Rodrigues	1823	Barbados, West Indies	Abraham Rodrigues Brandon			Finsbury, London	fundholder
9486	Brandon (Brandon Rodrigues)	Abigail (Adelaide)	1840	Aldgate, London	Abraham Brandon (Brandon Rodrigues)	Sophia Nunes Martinez	Hyman Frankenburg	Aldgate, London	
9481	Brandon (Brandon Rodrigues)	Abraham	1806	Mile End, London	Moses Rodrigues Brandon	(Luna) (?)	Sophia (Simha) de David Nunes Martinez	Aldgate, London	shoe maker empl 5
28620	Brandon (Brandon Rodrigues)	Ellen (Luna)	1835	Spitalfields, London	Joseph de Moses Brandon (Brandon Rodrigues)	Sophia de Jacob Noah (Da Costa Noah)	Jacob Mendoza	Spitalfields, London	cap maker
9485	Brandon (Brandon Rodrigues)	Esther	1838	Aldgate, London	Abraham Brandon (Brandon Rodrigues)	Sophia Nunes Martinez	Hyman Enoch	Aldgate, London	

ID	surname	given names	born	birthplace	father	mother	spouse 1	1851 residence	1851 occupation
7006	Brandon (Brandon Rodrigues)	Jane (Jael)	1834	City, London	Abraham Brandon (Brandon Rodrigues)	Sophia Nunes Martinez	Barnett Abrahams	Aldgate, London	
28621	Brandon (Brandon Rodrigues)	Jane (Jael)	1841	Spitalfields, London	Joseph de Moses Brandon (Brandon Rodrigues)	Sophia de Jacob Noah (Da Costa Noah)		Spitalfields, London	tailoress
9484	Brandon (Brandon Rodrigues)	John (Jacob)	1836	Aldgate, London	Abraham Brandon (Brandon Rodrigues)	Sophia Nunes Martinez	Mary Lazarus	Aldgate, London	
9487	Brandon (Brandon Rodrigues)	Julia (Judith)	1842	Aldgate, London	Abraham Brandon (Brandon Rodrigues)	Sophia Nunes Martinez	Moses Corcos	Aldgate, London	
9118	Brandon (Brandon Rodrigues)	Moses	1828	Acton, London	Abraham Brandon (Brandon Rodrigues)	Sophia Nunes Martinez	Elizabeth Davis	Aldgate, London	
28619	Brandon (Brandon Rodrigues)	Moses	1832	Spitalfields, London	Joseph de Moses Brandon (Brandon Rodrigues)	Sophia de Jacob Noah (Da Costa Noah)		Spitalfields, London	cap maker
9483	Brandon (Brandon Rodrigues)	Sarah	1832	Mile End, London	Abraham Brandon (Brandon Rodrigues)	Sophia Nunes Martinez	Salomon Saunders	Aldgate, London	
9482	Brandon (Brandon Rodrigues)	Sophia	1799	Whitechapel, London	David Nunes Martinez	Sarah de Elisah Arobas	Abraham Brandon (Brandon Rodrigues)	Aldgate, London	
28618	Brandon (Brandon Rodrigues)	Sophia	1806	Spitalfields, London	Jacob de Isaac Noah (Da Costa Noah)	Esther de Joseph Cohen	Joseph de Moses Brandon (Brandon Rodrigues)	Spitalfields, London	tailoress
10333	Brandon (Rodrigues Brandon)	Amelia	1848	Middlesex, London	Elias Brandon (Rodrigues Brandon)	Sarah Davis		Holborn, London	at home
5653	Brandon (Rodrigues Brandon)	David	1815	City, London	Moses Rodrigues Brandon	Luna (?)	Jane Magnus	Bethnal Green, London	boot + shoe maker
10332	Brandon (Rodrigues Brandon)	David	1844	Middlesex, London	Elias Brandon (Rodrigues Brandon)	Sarah Davis		Holborn, London	at home
10329	Brandon (Rodrigues Brandon)	Elias	1817	Middlesex, London	Moses Rodrigues Brandon	Luna (?)	Sarah Davis	Holborn, London	clothes salesman
10331	Brandon (Rodrigues Brandon)	Ellen (Luna)	1840	Middlesex, London	Elias Brandon (Rodrigues Brandon)	Sarah Davis		Holborn, London	at home
21640	Brandon (Rodrigues Brandon)	Jane	1816	Middlesex, London	Nathan Magnus	Simony Solomon (Solomons)	David Brandon (Rodrigues Brandon)	Bethnal Green, London	
10334	Brandon (Rodrigues Brandon)	Joseph	1850	Middlesex, London	Elias Brandon (Rodrigues Brandon)	Sarah Davis		Holborn, London	at home
10330	Brandon (Rodrigues Brandon)	Sarah	1818	Middlesex, London	David Davis		Elias Brandon (Rodrigues Brandon)	Holborn, London	
10335	Brandon (Rodrigues Brandon)	Susan	1851	Middlesex, London	Elias Brandon (Rodrigues Brandon)	Sarah Davis		Holborn, London	
14426	Brandt	Ellen Sarah	1832	Wigan, Lancashire	(?) Lever	Abigail (?)	Marcus Brandt	Salford, Lancashire	
14428	Brandt	Louisa	1851	Salford, Lancashire	Marcus Brandt	Ellen Sarah Lever		Salford, Lancashire	

ID	surname	given names	born	birthplace	father	mother	spouse 1	1851 residence	1851 occupation
14427	Brandt	Marcus	1822	?, Poland [?, Prussia]			Ellen Sarah Lever	Salford, Lancashire	hatter
18932	Branner	Solomon	1803	Aldgate, London				Aldgate, London	baker journeyman
12172	Brasch	Solomon	1813	?, Poland [?, Prussia]	Tsevi Hirsh		Yatte (Jetty) Brody	Whitechapel, London	goldsmith
16817	Brasch	Wolf	1826	?, Poland [?, Prussia]				Colchester, Essex	jeweller
12173	Brasch	Yatte (Jetty)	1827	?, Poland [?, Prussia]	Chaim HaLevi Brody		Solomon Brasch	Whitechapel, London	
7950	Braunstein	Annie	1848	Leeds, Yorkshire	Newman Braunstein	Esther (?)	Edward Leman	Euston, London	
2233	Braunstein	Catherine	1821	?, Germany				Leeds, Yorkshire	
7949	Braunstein	Esther	1824	Whitechapel, London	(?)		Newman Braunstein	Euston, London	
7877	Braunstein	Newman	1813	Cracow, Poland			Esther (?)	Euston, London	tea merchant
15295	Bravo	Joseph	1808	Whitechapel, London	Jacob de Isaac Bravo	Rachel de Joseph Sagre		Shoreditch, London	traveller
9327	Bravo	Rachel	1778	Aldgate, London	(?)		(?) Bravo	Aldgate, London	poor
2394	Brebin	Edward	1832	Riga, Latvia [Russia]				Hull, Yorkshire	engineer
28003	Bremer	Aaron	1839	Amsterdam, Holland	Isaac Bremer	(?)		Spitalfields, London	scholar
2125	Bremer	Albert	1826	?, Germany				Hull, Yorkshire	jeweller's assistant
28001	Bremer	Anne	1835	Amsterdam, Holland	Isaac Bremer	(?)		Spitalfields, London	
28002	Bremer	Barnett	1837	Amsterdam, Holland	Isaac Bremer	(?)		Spitalfields, London	cigar maker
27999	Bremer	Esther	1829	Amsterdam, Holland	Isaac Bremer	(?)		Spitalfields, London	dressmaker
28004	Bremer	Henry (Hyman)	1841	Amsterdam, Holland	Isaac Bremer	(?)	Aaltje Moses Yzer	Spitalfields, London	scholar
27998	Bremer	Isaac	1803	Amsterdam, Holland			(?)	Spitalfields, London	general dealer
28000	Bremer	Philip	1830	Amsterdam, Holland	Isaac Bremer	(?)		Spitalfields, London	diamond polisher
7011	Breslau	Marcus Hyman	1808	Hamburg, Germany				Whitechapel, London	professor of languages + journalist + editor, Jewish Chronicle
26286	Breslaw	Harris	1831	?, Poland				Aldgate, London	slipper maker
14163	Brieger	Adolph	1822	?, Poland [?, Prussia]				Manchester	shipping merchant
23731	Bright	?	1832	Doncaster, Yorkshire	Philip Bright	Sarah Jacobs		Liverpool	merchant's apprentice
16890	Bright	Annette Esther	1836	Buxton, Derbyshire	Selim Bright	Estella de Lara		Buxton, Derbyshire	
23910	Bright	C---	1795	Sheffield, Yorkshire	(?) Bright			Marylebone, London	lady
23729	Bright	Caroline	1826	Doncaster, Yorkshire	Philip Bright	Sarah Jacobs		Liverpool	railway proprietor
23730	Bright	Charles	1830	Doncaster, Yorkshire	Philip Bright	Sarah Jacobs		Liverpool	mortgagee
16893	Bright	Edith Estella	1850	Buxton, Derbyshire	Selim Bright	Estella de Lara		Buxton, Derbyshire	
6509	Bright	Eleanor	1829	Doncaster, Yorkshire	Philip Bright	Sarah Jacobs	Adam Casper	Manchester	
16888	Bright	Estella	1806	Gibraltar	(?) De Lara		Selim Bright	Buxton, Derbyshire	
20099	Bright	Frances	1831	Sheffield, Yorkshire	Maurice Bright	Henrietta de Metz	Solomon Spyer	Sheffield, Yorkshire	
16892	Bright	Georgiana	1844	Buxton, Derbyshire	Selim Bright	Estella de Lara		Buxton, Derbyshire	
5146	Bright	Horatio	1828	Sheffield, Yorkshire	Selim Bright	Estella de Lara	Mary Alice Turton	Sheffield, Yorkshire	wire merchant
16891	Bright	Justina	1838	Buxton, Derbyshire	Selim Bright	Estella de Lara		Buxton, Derbyshire	
20119	Bright	Maurice Delara	1826	Buxton, Derbyshire	Selim Bright	Estella de Lara	Harriet Ann Turton	?Buxton, Derbyshire	
16889	Bright	Michael Octavius	1833	Buxton, Derbyshire	Selim Bright	Estella de Lara		Buxton, Derbyshire	
23728	Bright	Sarah	1788	?, Devon	(?) Jacobs		Philip Bright	Liverpool	railway proprietor
16887	Bright	Selim	1799	Sheffield, Yorkshire	Isaac (John) Bright	Ann Micholls	Estella de Lara	Buxton, Derbyshire	merchant goldsmith (master)
19061	Brillman	Reuben	1822	?, Poland	Simcha Brillman		Harriet Casper	Aldgate, London	watchmaker
5781	Britton	Daniel Abraham	1849	City, London	Lewis Abraham Britton		Annie (Annie) Raphael	Middlesex, London	
4346	Brock	Abraham	1791	?, Poland				Birmingham	hawker

ID	surname	given names	born	birthplace	father	mother	spouse 1	1851 residence	1851 occupation
1164	Brock	Betsey	1850	?, Cornwall	John Brock	Sohie (?)		Plymouth, Devon	
6490	Brock	Emma	1843	Plymouth, Devon	William Brock	Sophia (?)		Plymouth, Devon	
6517	Brock	George	1819	?, Poland [?, Prussia]			Sarah Levi	Plymouth, Devon	general dealer
1162	Brock	Irfuss	1840	?, Cornwall	John Brock	Sophie (?)		Plymouth, Devon	scholar abroad
1159	Brock	John	1805	?, Cornwall			Sophie (?)	Plymouth, Devon	horse poster
6477	Brock	Lewis	1839	Plymouth, Devon	George Brock	Sarah Levi	Henrietta Nathan	Plymouth, Devon	scholar
1161	Brock	Mary	1838	?, Cornwall	John Brock	Sophie (?)		Plymouth, Devon	scholar abroad
122	Brock	Morris	1823	Poznan, Poland [Posen, Prussia]				Woolwich, London	glass cutter
6518	Brock	Sarah	1814	Plymouth, Devon	(?) Levi	Leah (?)	George Brock	Plymouth, Devon	school teacher
1163	Brock	Shmuel	1843	?, Cornwall	John Brock	Sophie (?)		Plymouth, Devon	scholar abroad
6489	Brock	Sophia	1817	Plymouth, Devon	(?)		William Brock	Plymouth, Devon	
1160	Brock	Sophie	1809	?, Cornwall			John Brock	Plymouth, Devon	
6488	Brock	William	1812	Plymouth, Devon			Sophia (?)	Plymouth, Devon	
22084	Brode	Solomon	1831	?, Russia [Widshan, Russia]	(?) Eskelbach			Whitechapel, London	dealer in trinkets
30473	Brodick	Rica	1830	?, Poland				Mayfair, London	servant
26289	Brody	Sarah	1811	?, Russia	(?) Brody			Aldgate, London	tailoress
12777	Brokselig	Sarah	1824	?, Cornwall				Aldgate, London	general servant
4314	Brotek	Morris	1833	?, Poland				Birmingham	glazier
13747	Brower	Caroline	1824	Middlesex, London	Aharon Samuel Isaacs	(?Sarah Jacobs)	Henry Brower	Manchester	fancy box maker
13746	Brower	Henry	1817	?, Russia			Caroline Isaacs	Manchester	fancy box maker
4349	Brown	Barnett	1841	Bilston, Staffordshire	Joseph Brown	Hannah Levy		Birmingham	
30942	Brown	Hannah	1801	Great Yarmouth, Norfolk	(?)		(?) Brown	Hull, Yorkshire	lodging house keeper
4348	Brown	Hannah	1810	?, London	Issachar Parla HaLevi		Joseph Brown	Birmingham	
2237	Brown	Jacob	1839	Leeds, Yorkshire	John (Morris) Brown	Matilda (?)	Rosetta (?)	Leeds, Yorkshire	
2234	Brown	John (Morris)	1804	?, Poland [?, Prussia]	Lazarus Brown		Matilda (?)	Leeds, Yorkshire	general dealer
4347	Brown	Joseph	1810	?, Austria	Asher HaLevi		Hannah Levy	Birmingham	clothier + pawnbroker
2236	Brown	Lazarus	1771	?, Poland				Leeds, Yorkshire	
2235	Brown	Matilda	1810	?, Poland [?, Prussia]			John (Morris) Brown	Leeds, Yorkshire	
21980	Brown	Matilda	1821	Piccadilly, London	(?)		Solomon Brown	Swansea, Wales	
2241	Brown	Nathan	1851	Leeds, Yorkshire	John (Morris) Brown	Matilda (?)		Leeds, Yorkshire	
2431	Brown	Pheab	1828	Great Yarmouth, Norfolk	(?) Brown	Hannah (?)		Hull, Yorkshire	dressmaker
2238	Brown	Rebecca	1847	Leeds, Yorkshire	John (Morris) Brown	Matilda (?)	Alfred Asher Soman	Leeds, Yorkshire	
2239	Brown	Rosetta	1848	Leeds, Yorkshire	John (Morris) Brown	Matilda (?)	Michael Lazarus Marks	Leeds, Yorkshire	
8599	Brown	Simon	1831	?, Poland				Spitalfields, London	cap maker
21979	Brown	Solomon	1815	Poznan, Poland			Matilda (?)	Swansea, Wales	jeweller
11735	Bruck	Constance	1841	Amsterdam, Holland	(?) Bruck	Henrietta (?)		Shoreditch, London	scholar
11736	Bruck	Elizabeth	1844	Amsterdam, Holland	(?) Bruck	Henrietta (?)		Shoreditch, London	scholar
11733	Bruck	Fanny	1836	Rotterdam, Holland	(?) Bruck	Henrietta (?)		Shoreditch, London	teacher of music
11734	Bruck	George	1839	Amsterdam, Holland	(?) Bruck	Henrietta (?)	Ellen (?)	Shoreditch, London	scholar
11731	Bruck	Henrietta	1806	?, Holland	(?)		(?) Bruck	Shoreditch, London	annuitant
11737	Bruck	Louis	1847	Islington, London	(?) Bruck	Henrietta (?)		Shoreditch, London	scholar
11732	Bruck	Maurice	1833	Rotterdam, Holland	(?) Bruck	Henrietta (?)		Shoreditch, London	ship broker's clerk
11738	Bruck	William	1849	Islington, London	(?) Bruck	Henrietta (?)		Shoreditch, London	

ID	surname	given names	born	birthplace	father	mother	spouse 1	1851 residence	1851 occupation
20973	Brunswick	Annette (Jeannette)	1822	Paris, France	Myrthil Brunswick	Fanny (?)		Finsbury, London	lady's companion
18254	Brunswick	Clara	1832	?, Belgium	Myrthil Brunswick	Fanny (?)		Hull, Yorkshire	governess
31122	Bruth	Abraham	1816	Swarzędz, Poland [Schwersenz, Prussia]				Ipswich, Suffolk	dealer in jewellery
2395	Bryce	Augustus	1825	Kaliningrad, Russia [Konigsberg, Russia]				Hull, Yorkshire	
4350	Buckston	Julia	1827	?, Poland [?, Prussia]				Birmingham	
30932	Budwig	Michael	1832	Jezioro?, Poland [Jericho, Prussia]				Hull, Yorkshire	tailor
15883	Buensurate	Julie	1826	Paris, France	(?) Buensurate			Hackney, London	French teacher
28068	Bullock	Henry	1846	Spitalfields, London	(?) Bullock	(?) Gabriel		Spitalfields, London	scholar
14480	Buranstine	Kalman	1826	?, Belgium				Manchester	hawks pencils
13495	Burchwald	Samuel	1829	?, Poland				Manchester	cap maker
18442	Burdis	Esther	1830	Poplar, London	John Nathaniel Messeena	Rachel Gomes	Joseph Garnett Burdis	Poplar, London	
26791	Burke	Elias	1828	?, Poland				Aldgate, London	tailor
17628	Burnett	Abraham	1831	?, London	Lewis Burnett	Leah (?)		Aldgate, London	cigar maker
17627	Burnett	Leah	1805	?, London	(?)		Lewis Burnett	Aldgate, London	
17626	Burnett	Lewis	1800	?, London			Leah (?)	Aldgate, London	general dealer
17630	Burnett	Lewis	1841	?, London	Lewis Burnett	Leah (?)		Aldgate, London	scholar
17629	Burnett	Phoebe	1835	?, London	Lewis Burnett	Leah (?)		Aldgate, London	parasol maker
14073	Burnett	Sarah	1848	Liverpool				Manchester	scholar
14072	Burnett	Simeon	1845	Liverpool				Manchester	scholar
6542	Burstein	Abraham	1821	?, Poland			Rose Solomon	Exeter, Devon	
6533	Burstin	Marks	1825	Bristol			Esther Solomon	Bristol	
28563	Burtins	Susanah	1822	Amsterdam, Holland	(?)		(?) Burtins	Spitalfields, London	seamstress
11076	Buski	Elizabeth	1834	Aldgate, London	Moses Buski	Dora (?)		Aldgate, London	tailoress
11077	Buski	Judah	1839	Aldgate, London	Moses Buski	Dora (?)		Aldgate, London	scholar
11075	Buski	Moses	1795	abroad			Dora (?)	Aldgate, London	general dealer + jeweller
11642	Busnach	Rachael	1791	Aldgate, London	Moses de Juda		Solomon de Michael Busnach	Aldgate, London	dealer
27500	Butler?	John	1831	Middlesex, London				Aldgate, London	dealer in clothes
16149	Butnany	Abraham	1829	?, Poland [?, Prussia]				Whitechapel, London	tailor
18147	Buzaglo	Isaac	1785	Amsterdam, Holland				Mile End, London	inmate of Portuguese Jews Hospital
14155	Cababe	Paul	1816	Aleppo, Syria			Mariam (?)	Manchester	commission agent
21048	Caham	Mortimer	1842	?, London				Dover, Kent	boarding school pupil
14204	Caher	Telisch	1829	?, Poland				Manchester	hawker
23068	Cahn	Meyer	1819	?, France			Pauline (?)	Aldgate, London	slipper dealer
23069	Cahn	Pauline	1819	?, Poland [?, Prussia]	(?)		Meyer Cahn	Aldgate, London	
9722	Calisher	Adelaide (Adela)	1830	Whitechapel, London	Nathan Jacob Calisher	Phoebe (?)	(?) Curtis	Strand, London	
9723	Calisher	Bertram James	1834	Middlesex, London	Nathan Jacob Calisher	Phoebe (?)	Jane (?)	Strand, London	shorthand writer
9727	Calisher	Edward (Edmund)	1850	?, London	Nathan Jacob Calisher	Phoebe (?)		Strand, London	
9724	Calisher	Esther (Hester) Edith	1839	?Aldgate, London	Nathan Jacob Calisher	Phoebe (?)	Joseph Morris	Strand, London	

ID	surname	given names	born	birthplace	father	mother	spouse 1	1851 residence	1851 occupation
9725	Calisher	Helen	1845	?, London	Nathan Jacob Calisher	Phoebe (?)		Strand, London	
4351	Calisher	Henry C M	1831	Whitechapel, London	Nathan Jacob Calisher	Phoebe (?)	Marian (?)	Birmingham	diamond merchant
9726	Calisher	Joseph	1847	?, London	Nathan Jacob Calisher	Phoebe (?)	(?)	Strand, London	
7458	Calisher	Julius	1828	Birmingham	Nathan Jacob Calisher	Phoebe (?)	Julia Lazarus	Strand, London	dealer in jewellery
30391	Calisher	Lewis	1851	Aldgate, London	Solomon Calisher	Theresa (?)		Aldgate, London	
9728	Calisher	Lewis Llewellyn	1837	Greenwich, London	Nathan Jacob Calisher	Phoebe (?)	Rachel Morris	Strand, London	
9720	Calisher	Nathan Jacob	1800	?Kalisz, Poland	Yehuda		Phoebe (?)	Strand, London	dealer in jewellery
9721	Calisher	Phoebe	1808	Birmingham	(?)		Nathan Jacob Calisher	Strand, London	
7391	Calisher	Rose (Rosetta) A	1839	Aldgate, London	Nathan Jacob Calisher	Phoebe (?)	Alexander Pyke	Strand, London	
30389	Calisher	Solomon	1820	?	Yehuda		Theresa (?)	Aldgate, London	
30390	Calisher	Theresa	1825	?	(?)		Solomon Calisher	Aldgate, London	
29390	Calman	Albert	1844	Whitechapel, London	Lyon Woolf Calman	Julia Solomon		Wapping, London	scholar
29393	Calman	Anne M	1851	Whitechapel, London	Lyon Woolf Calman	Julia Solomon		Wapping, London	
29389	Calman	David	1843	Whitechapel, London	Lyon Woolf Calman	Julia Solomon		Wapping, London	scholar
29388	Calman	Julia	1821	Aldgate, London	David Solomon		Lyon Woolf Calman	Wapping, London	
29387	Calman	Lyon Woolf	1816	?, Poland	Moses Calman		Julia Solomon	Wapping, London	furrier master empl 1
29392	Calman	Morris B	1849	Whitechapel, London	Lyon Woolf Calman	Julia Solomon		Wapping, London	
29391	Calman	Rosetta	1847	Whitechapel, London	Lyon Woolf Calman	Julia Solomon		Wapping, London	scholar
22062	Calo	David	1841	Middlesex, London	Moses Calo	Rebecca Coronel		Spitalfields, London	
22061	Calo	Ester	1839	Amsterdam, Holland	Moses Calo	Rebecca Coronel		Spitalfields, London	
22064	Calo	Fanny	1845	Middlesex, London	Moses Calo	Rebecca Coronel		Spitalfields, London	
22065	Calo	Leah	1850	Middlesex, London	Moses Calo	Rebecca Coronel		Spitalfields, London	
22058	Calo	Moses	1813	Amsterdam, Holland			Rebecca Coronel	Spitalfields, London	Hebrew school teacher
22063	Calo	Moses	1843	Middlesex, London	Moses Calo	Rebecca Coronel		Spitalfields, London	
22059	Calo	Rebecca	1815	Amsterdam, Holland	David Coronel	Leah (?)	Moses Calo	Spitalfields, London	
22060	Calo	Sarah	1837	Amsterdam, Holland	Moses Calo	Rebecca Coronel	Philip Silverbergh	Spitalfields, London	
9415	Canstatt	Amelia	1800	?Middlesex, London	Jacob Canstatt	Elizabeth Hyams		Aldgate, London	
17795	Canstatt	Amelia	1845	Aldgate, London	Nathan Jacob Canstatt	Hannah Isaacs		Aldgate, London	
17794	Canstatt	Hannah	1808	City, London	Elias Isaacs		Nathan Jacob Canstatt	Aldgate, London	
17793	Canstatt	Nathan Jacob	1794	Whitechapel, London	Jacob Canstatt	Elizabeth Hyams	Yentla Bendelman	Aldgate, London	member of College of Surgeons
17796	Canstatt	Sarah	1848	Aldgate, London	Nathan Jacob Canstatt	Hannah Isaacs	David Cuby	Aldgate, London	
18721	Canter	Alexander	1851	Whitechapel, London	Henry Canter	Hannah (?)	Jeannette Harris	Whitechapel, London	
26327	Canter	Alexander David	1848	Whitechapel, London	David Canter	Sophia Moses	Henrietta Goldsmith	Spitalfields, London	
26328	Canter	Barnet	1850	Whitechapel, London	David Canter	Sophia Moses		Spitalfields, London	
12872	Canter	Charles	1828	?London				Spitalfields, London	slipper maker
26324	Canter	David	1817	Leeuwarden, Holland	Levy Canter		Sophia Moses	Spitalfields, London	pastry cook
26326	Canter	Esther	1846	Spitalfields, London	David Canter	Sophia Moses		Spitalfields, London	
11832	Canter	Hannah	1821	Haarlem, Holland	(?)		Henry Canter	Whitechapel, London	
11831	Canter	Henry	1816	Harlingen, Holland	Yehuda		Hannah (?)	Whitechapel, London	master tailor empl 3
11834	Canter	Joseph	1850	Whitechapel, London	Henry Canter	Hanna (?)	Deborah Joseph	Whitechapel, London	
11833	Canter	Lewis	1848	Whitechapel, London	Henry Canter	Hannah (?)	Geta Abrahams	Whitechapel, London	
26325	Canter	Sophia	1817	Amsterdam, Holland	Hyam Moses	Gertrude (?)	David Canter	Spitalfields, London	
18478	Cantine	Samson	1835	?, Holland				Bloomsbury, London	cigar maker
15477	Cantor	Abraham	1849	Whitechapel, London	Moss Cantor	Charlotte Newton		Covent Garden, London	

ID	surname	given names	born	birthplace	father	mother	spouse 1	1851 residence	1851 occupation
3452	Cantor	Abraham Jacob	1799	Aldgate, London	Aaron Jacob Cantor	Kitty (?)	Phoebe Jacobs	City, London	pen cutter
3443	Cantor	Agnes	1789	City, London	Aaron (Ahron Rahts) Woolf	?	Lewis Cantor	Stepney, London	
23065	Cantor	Alice	1821	Middlesex, London	Samuel Cantor		Herman Goldring	Aldgate, London	dressmaker
6022	Cantor	Alice	1829	Aldgate, London	Joseph Jacob Cantor	Rachel (?)	Simeon Moses Cantor	Aldgate, London	sponge merchant
6098	Cantor	Alice	1830	City, London	Jacob (Abraham) Cantor	Phoebe Jacobs	Samuel Hess	Aldgate, London	cap peak maker
27167	Cantor	Caroline	1802	?, London	Isaac Solomons		Moses Cantor	Aldgate, London	pen cutter
27168	Cantor	Catherine	1832	?, London	Moses Cantor	Caroline Solomons	Daniel Joseph	Aldgate, London	cap maker
15475	Cantor	Charlotte	1817	Westminster, London	Isaac Newton		Moss Cantor	Covent Garden, London	
27169	Cantor	Coleman	1833	?, London	Moses Cantor	Caroline Solomons		Aldgate, London	cabinet maker
2042	Cantor	Elizabeth (Lizzie, Lucy)	1837	City, London	Jacob (Abraham) Cantor	Phoebe Jacobs	Joseph Davis	City, London	cap maker
3449	Cantor	Emanuel	1828	City, London	Lewis Cantor	Agnes Woolf		Whitechapel, London	cigar maker
30768	Cantor	Emma	1795	?, Holland	(?)		Joseph Cantor	Whitechapel, London	capmaker
27173	Cantor	Hannah	1851	?Aldgate, London	Jacob Cantor	Leah Emanuel		Aldgate, London	
30772	Cantor	Heyman	1836	?, London	Joseph Cantor	Emma (?)		Whitechapel, London	chairmaker
3462	Cantor	Hyam	1840	City, London	Abraham Jacob Cantor	Phoebe Jacobs		City, London	scholar
27172	Cantor	Hyman	1839	?, London	Moses Cantor	Caroline Solomons	Leah Hart	Aldgate, London	scholar
14592	Cantor	Isidore	1846	Finsbury, London	Samuel Cantor	Louisa Davis		Hoxton, London	scholar
6020	Cantor	Israel	1817	Aldgate, London	Joseph Jacob Cantor	Rachel (?)		Aldgate, London	sponge merchant
30769	Cantor	Jacob	1826	?, Holland	Joseph Cantor	Emma (?)		Whitechapel, London	dealer
15476	Cantor	Jacob (John)	1846	Whitechapel, London	Moss Cantor	Charlotte Newton		Covent Garden, London	scholar
3456	Cantor	Jacob Abraham	1826	Whitechapel, London	Abraham Jacob Cantor	Phoebe Jacobs	Kate (Catherine) Abrahams	City, London	draper
30767	Cantor	Joseph	1789	?, Holland			Emma (?)	Whitechapel, London	seller on commission
3431	Cantor	Joseph Jacob	1785	Aldgate, London	Aaron Jacob Cantor	Kitty (?)	Rachel (?)	Aldgate, London	sponge merchant
3450	Cantor	Joseph Jacob	1829	City, London	Lewis Cantor	Agnes Woolf		Whitechapel, London	cloth cap manufacturer
2037	Cantor	Julia	1842	City, London	Jacob (Abraham) Cantor	Phoebe Jacobs	Sydney Davis	City, London	scholar
6096	Cantor	Kate	1824	Whitechapel, London	Jacob (Abraham) Cantor	Phoebe Jacobs	Morris Hess	City, London	cap peak maker
23066	Cantor	Kate	1829	Middlesex, London	Samuel Cantor			Aldgate, London	milliner
30770	Cantor	Louis	1828	?, Holland	Joseph Cantor	Emma (?)		Whitechapel, London	light porter
3435	Cantor	Louisa	1814	City, London	Alexander Davis	?	Samuel Cantor	Hoxton, London	
17973	Cantor	Louisa	1831	Aldgate, London	Joseph Jacob Cantor	Rachel (?)		Aldgate, London	sponge merchant
3461	Cantor	Mary	1839	City, London	Jacob (Abraham) Cantor	Phoebe Jacobs	Alexander Hart	City, London	scholar
27170	Cantor	Mary (Miriam)	1834	?, London	Moses Cantor	Caroline Solomons	Abraham Myers	Aldgate, London	dress maker
14591	Cantor	Morris	1845	Finsbury, London	Samuel Cantor	Louisa Davis		Hoxton, London	scholar
27166	Cantor	Moses	1798	?, London	Aaron Jacob Cantor	Kitty (?)	Caroline Solomons	Aldgate, London	pen cutter
3445	Cantor	Moss	1815	Portsmouth, Hampshire	Lewis Cantor	Agnes Woolf	Charlotte Newton	Covent Garden, London	masquerade tailor
6039	Cantor	Moss (Moses)	1831	City, London	Jacob (Abraham) Cantor	Phoebe Jacobs	Esther Abrahams	Aldgate, London	tailor
14593	Cantor	Phillip	1849	Finsbury, London	Samuel Cantor	Louisa Davis	Eva (?)	Hoxton, London	
3453	Cantor	Phoebe	1800	Aldgate, London	Henry (Zvi Hirsh) Jacobs	Rosetta (?)	Abraham Jacob Cantor	City, London	housekeeper
9650	Cantor	Rebecca	1831	City, London	Meshullam Cantor		Henry Bruck	Shoreditch, London	
3455	Cantor	Rosetta	1825	Whitechapel, London	Abraham Jacob Cantor	Phoebe Jacobs	Solomon Rains	City, London	cap peak maker
3434	Cantor	Samuel	1812	City, London	Joseph Jacob Cantor	Rachel (?)	Louisa Davis	Hoxton, London	dealer in fancy wool + sponge
3451	Cantor	Samuel	1831	City, London	Lewis Cantor	Agnes Woolf		Whitechapel, London	cigar maker's apprentice
30771	Cantor	Samuel	1831	?, London	Joseph Cantor	Emma (?)		Whitechapel, London	butcher

ID	surname	given names	born	birthplace	father	mother	spouse 1	1851 residence	1851 occupation
27171	Cantor	Samuel	1837	?, London	Moses Cantor	Caroline Solomons		Aldgate, London	scholar
30773	Cantor	Sarah	1838	?, London	Joseph Cantor	Emma (?)		Whitechapel, London	capmaker
6936	Cantor	Sophia	1833	Bristol	(?) Cantor			Aldgate, London	servant
15066	Cantorfitz	Fanny	1844	Whitechapel, London	(?) Cantorfitz			Bethnal Green, London	scholar
18117	Capoa	Ann	1805	Devizes, Wiltshire	(?)		Joseph Capoa	Mile End, London	monthly nurse
18123	Capoa	Edmund	1848	Stepney, London	Joseph Capoa	Ann (?)		Mile End, London	scholar
18120	Capoa	Elisa	1842	Stepney, London	Joseph Capoa	Ann (?)		Mile End, London	scholar
18121	Capoa	Jane	1844	Stepney, London	Joseph Capoa	Ann (?)		Mile End, London	scholar
18116	Capoa	Joseph	1806	?, Bedfordshire			Ann (?)	Mile End, London	coke dealer
18118	Capoa	Joseph	1831	Bow, London	Joseph Capoa	Ann (?)		Mile End, London	labourer
18122	Capoa	Louisa	1846	Stepney, London	Joseph Capoa	Ann (?)		Mile End, London	scholar
18119	Capoa	Sopa	1840	Stepney, London	Joseph Capoa	Ann (?)		Mile End, London	scholar
19027	Capua	Amelia	1832	Aldgate, London	Lewis Pesman Capua	Jane Jacobs		Aldgate, London	schoolmistress
19028	Capua	Esther	1835	Aldgate, London	Lewis Pesman Capua	Jane Jacobs	Isaiah (Josiah) Lazarus	Aldgate, London	schoolmistress
5916	Capua	Hannah	1812	Middlesex, London	Isaac Costa		Nehemiah de Raphael Capua Barzilay	?Stepney, London	dress maker
26709	Capua	Jane	1816	?, London	Jacob (John) Jacobs	Phillis Jacobs	Lewis Pesman Capua	Aldgate, London	
17958	Capua	John	1836	City, London				Aldgate, London	general shopman
20975	Capua	Lewis Pesman	1810	Wapping, London	John Pesman	Esther Capua	Jane Jacobs	Finsbury, London	prisoner + fruit merchant
19026	Capua	Mark	1830	Aldgate, London	Lewis Pesman Capua	Jane Jacobs		Aldgate, London	clerk in a mercantile house
15018	Capua	Nehemiah Barzilay	1810	?	Raphael Barzilay Capua	Esther (?)	Hannah de Isaac Costa	?Stepney, London	
28721	Capua	Rosetta	1837	Middlesex, London	(?) Capua			Spitalfields, London	waistcoat maker
9286	Carcas	Hannah	1790	Whitechapel, London	Isaac de Abraham Dias	Abigail de Isaac Gomes Da Costa	Joseph de Aaron Carcas	Aldgate, London	general dealer
9287	Carcas	Hannah	1831	Whitechapel, London	Joseph Carcas	Hannah Dias		Aldgate, London	dress maker
9291	Carcas	Rachel	1821	Whitechapel, London	Joseph Carcas	Hannah Dias	Aaron Gomes Da Costa	Bethnal Green, London	
8613	Cardoza	Abigal	1817	City, London				Wapping, London	house servant
13312	Cardoza	Samuel	1829	?				Spitalfields, London	shoe maker
29193	Cardozo	?Harriet	1825	Stepney, London	(?)		Solomon Cardozo	Whitechapel, London	
29195	Cardozo	?Mary Ann	1847	Spitalfields, London	Solomon Cardozo	?Harriet (?)		Whitechapel, London	scholar
29197	Cardozo	?Sarah	1850	Whitechapel, London	Solomon Cardozo	?Harriet (?)		Whitechapel, London	
29667	Cardozo	Abigail	1808	Spitalfields, London	Sadok Levy		Isaac de Abraham Nunes Cardozo	Spitalfields, London	shoe maker
29668	Cardozo	Abraham Nunes	1829	?, London	Isaac de Abraham Nunes Cardozo	Abigail de Sadok Levy		Spitalfields, London	shoe maker
28528	Cardozo	Amelia	1819	Aldgate, London	(?) Cardozo		Henry Phillips	Spitalfields, London	
26574	Cardozo	Deborah Nunes	1851	Spitalfields, London	Isaac Nunes Cardozo	Elizabeth Benjamin		Spitalfields, London	
25668	Cardozo	Elizabeth	1825	Finsbury, London	Emanuel Benjamin	Jane Cohen	Isaac Nunes Cardozo	Spitalfields, London	clothes dealer
23879	Cardozo	Emanuel Nunes	1807	Hackney, London	Samuel de Isaac Nunes Cardozo	Rachel (?)		Westminster, London	merchant of Madras East Indies
29666	Cardozo	Isaac Nunes	1806	Spitalfields, London	Abraham Nunes Cardozo		Abigail de Sadok Levy	Spitalfields, London	shoe maker
25667	Cardozo	Isaac Nunes	1824	Lambeth, London	Phineas de Isaac Nunes Cardozo	Sophia (Siporah) de Isaac	Elizabeth Benjamin	Spitalfields, London	cigar maker
29500	Cardozo	Isaac Nunes	1851	Spitalfields, London	Zechariah de Isaac Nunes Cardozo	Rachel Jonas		Spitalfields, London	
29669	Cardozo	Joseph Nunes	1833	Middlesex, London	Isaac de Abraham Nunes Cardozo	Abigail de Sadok Levy		Spitalfields, London	errand boy
25670	Cardozo	Julia Nunes	1849	Aldgate, London	Isaac Nunes Cardozo	Elizabeth Benjamin		Spitalfields, London	

ID	surname	given names	born	birthplace	father	mother	spouse 1	1851 residence	1851 occupation
9323	Cardozo	Leah	1824	Mile End, London	David de Uziel Cardozo	Rachel (?)		Aldgate, London	dress maker
29499	Cardozo	Mordecai Nunes	1850	Spitalfields, London	Zechariah de Isaac Nunes Cardozo	Rachel Jonas		Spitalfields, London	
20579	Cardozo	Moses Henriques	1816	Mile End, London	Abraham Henriques Cardozo	Rebecca (?)	Rosetta Simmons	Spitalfields, London	pen cutter
9322	Cardozo	Rachel	1800	Amsterdam, Holland	(?)		David de Uziel Cardozo	Aldgate, London	poor
29498	Cardozo	Rachel	1831	Southwark, London	David Jonas		Rachel Jonas	Spitalfields, London	dressmaker
29670	Cardozo	Raphael Nunes	1836	Whitechapel, London	Isaac de Abraham Nunes Cardozo	Abigail de Sadok Levy		Spitalfields, London	errand boy
29196	Cardozo	Rebecca	1849	Spitalfields, London	Solomon Cardozo	?Harriet (?)		Whitechapel, London	scholar
20580	Cardozo	Rosetta	1816	Spitalfields, London	Eliezer Simmons		Moses Henriques Cardozo	Spitalfields, London	
29194	Cardozo	Samuel	1842	Spitalfields, London	Solomon Cardozo	?Harriet (?)		Whitechapel, London	scholar
29192	Cardozo	Solomon	1823	Mile End, London			?Harriet (?)	Whitechapel, London	carver and gilder
25669	Cardozo	Sophia Nunes	1847	Aldgate, London	Isaac Nunes Cardozo	Elizabeth Benjamin		Spitalfields, London	
29497	Cardozo	Zachariah Nunes	1830	Mile End, London	Isaac de Abraham Nunes Cardozo	Abigail de Sadok Levy	Rachel Jonas	Spitalfields, London	sofa + couch maker
28863	Cardozo Paz	Betsy (Elizabeth, Bilha, Bella)	1812	Portsmouth, Hampshire	Moses Emanuel		Samson (Saunders) Cardozo Paz	Spitalfields, London	general dealer
9312	Cardozo Paz	Catherine (Keturah)	1777	Portsmouth, Hampshire	(?) Simson		David de Semuel Paz Cardozo	Aldgate, London	poor
28864	Cardozo Paz	David	1840	Elephant & Castle, London	Samson (Saunders) Cardozo Paz	Betsy (Elizabeth, Bilha, Bella) Emanuel		Spitalfields, London	scholar
9314	Cardozo Paz	Elizabeth (Bathsheba)	1819	Aldgate, London	David Cardozo Paz	Catherine (Keturah) Simson		Aldgate, London	dress maker
28866	Cardozo Paz	Henry (Zebi)	1843	Elephant & Castle, London	Samson (Saunders) Cardozo Paz	Betsy (Elizabeth, Bilha, Bella) Emanuel		Spitalfields, London	scholar
9313	Cardozo Paz	Judith (Julia)	1807	Aldgate, London	David Cardozo Paz	Catherine (Keturah) Simson		Aldgate, London	bonnet maker
28862	Cardozo Paz	Samson (Saunders)	1814	Aldgate, London	David Paz Cardozo	Catherine (Keturah) Simson	Betsy (Elizabeth, Bilha, Bella) Emanuel	Spitalfields, London	general dealer
28865	Cardozo Paz	Samuel	1841	Elephant & Castle, London	Samson (Saunders) Cardozo Paz	Betsy (Elizabeth, Bilha, Bella) Emanuel		Spitalfields, London	scholar
28867	Cardozo Paz	Solomon	1846	Elephant & Castle, London	Samson (Saunders) Cardozo Paz	Betsy (Elizabeth, Bilha, Bella) Emanuel		Spitalfields, London	scholar
12562	Caro	David	1844	Norwich, Norfolk	Simon Caro	Maria (?)		Norwich, Norfolk	scholar
12563	Caro	Esther	1844	Norwich, Norfolk	Simon Caro	Maria (?)		Norwich, Norfolk	
31021	Caro	Henrietta	1811	?, Poland [?, Poland]	(?)		Joseph Caro	Newcastle Upon Tyne	Reader of the Synagogue
31022	Caro	Jacob	1832	?, Poland [?, Poland]	Joseph Caro	Henrietta (?)		Newcastle Upon Tyne	coal exporter's clerk
12564	Caro	Jacob	1845	Norwich, Norfolk	Simon Caro	Maria (?)	Alice Haldinstein	Norwich, Norfolk	scholar
31020	Caro	Joseph	1804	?, Poland [?, Poland]			Henrietta (?)	Newcastle Upon Tyne	Reader of the Synagogue
12561	Caro	Maria	1812	?, Poland [?, Prussia]	Jacob Levy		Simon Caro	Norwich, Norfolk	
12565	Caro	Mority Levi	1847	Norwich, Norfolk	Simon Caro	Maria (?)		Norwich, Norfolk	at home
31023	Caro	Raphael	1816	?, Poland [?, Poland]				Newcastle Upon Tyne	brass founder
12560	Caro	Simon	1811	Poznan, Poland [Posen, Prussia]	David Caro		(?)	Norwich, Norfolk	reader in the Hebrew Synagogue
30179	Carol	Lazarus	1824	?, Germany			Roealler (?)	Dudley, Worcestershire	glazier
30180	Carol	Roealler	1826	?, Germany	(?)		Lazarus Carol	Dudley, Worcestershire	
12330	Carter	Catherine	1810	City, London	Lewis Lyons		William Carter	Marylebone, London	
12449	Carter	William	1809	Bloomsbury, London			Catherine Lyons	Marylebone, London	lodging house keeper
5659	Carvalho	Abraham Nunes	1791	Whitechapel, London	Solomon Nunes Carvalho	Judith Henriques Pimentel	Sarah Abraham	Aldgate, London	stationer

ID	surname	given names	born	birthplace	father	mother	spouse 1	1851 residence	1851 occupation
21718	Carvalho	Clara Nunes	1838	Finsbury, London	Raphael Nunes Carvalho	Rachel Delgado		Highbury, London	
25007	Carvalho	David Nunes	1800	?, London	Samuel Nunes Carvalho	Rachel (?)	Hannah de Abraham Solomons	Strand, London	bookseller
25008	Carvalho	Elizabeth (Bathsheba) Nunes	1828	?, London	David de Samuel Nunes Carvalho	Hannah de Abraham Solomons	Robert Levy	Strand, London	
21720	Carvalho	Isaac Nunes	1845	?, Jamaica, West Indies	Raphael Nunes Carvalho	Rachel Delgado	Hester Isaacs	Highbury, London	
25011	Carvalho	Isabella (Welcome) Nunes	1838	?, London	David de Samuel Nunes Carvalho	Hannah de Abraham Solomons	Sidney Woolf	Strand, London	
21717	Carvalho	Louisa Nunes	1836	?, Jamaica, West Indies	Raphael Nunes Carvalho	Rachel Delgado		Highbury, London	
25012	Carvalho	Maria (Miriam) Nunes	1843	?, London	David de Samuel Nunes Carvalho	Hannah de Abraham Solomons	Samuel Andrade Da Costa	Strand, London	
21716	Carvalho	Rachel Nunes	1814	?, Jamaica, West Indies	(?) Delgado		Raphael Nunes Carvalho	Highbury, London	
21715	Carvalho	Raphael Nunes	1809	Kingston, Jamaica, West Indies			Rachel Delgado	Highbury, London	West India merchant
25010	Carvalho	Rebecca (Welcome) Nunes	1836	?, London	David de Samuel Nunes Carvalho	Hannah de Abraham Solomons		Strand, London	
21719	Carvalho	Samuel Nunes	1840	Finsbury, London	Raphael Nunes Carvalho	Rachel Delgado	Hester Evelina Abraham	Highbury, London	
25009	Carvalho	Sarah Nunes	1830	?, London	David de Samuel Nunes Carvalho	Hannah de Abraham Solomons	David Andrade Da Costa	Strand, London	
7459	Cashmore	John	1820	Aldgate, London	Moses Joseph Cashmore (Moshe Kashman)	Rachel (Rela) bat Joshua	Hannah Van de Praagh	Aldgate, London	watch maker
8091	Cashmore	Moses Joseph	1781	Whitechapel, London	(?Joseph) Kashman		Rachel Cashmore	Aldgate, London	retired merchant
15709	Cashmore	Rebecca	1821	City, London	Moses Joseph Cashmore (Moshe Kashman)	Rachel (Rela) bat Joshua	Samuel Adolphus Jonas	Aldgate, London	
12635	Cashpole	Earn	1816	?, Poland				Plymouth, Devon	glazier
14232	Caspary	Jacob	1826	?, Poland [?, Prussia]				Manchester	traveller
13836	Casper	Abraham	1849	Manchester	Louis Casper	Minnie (Minah) (?)		Manchester	
6508	Casper	Adam	1819	?, Poland [?, Prussia]			Eleanor Bright	Manchester	tailor + draper
19055	Casper	Amelia	1784	Aldgate, London	Solomon (Zalman) Ansell	Rosetta (?)	Nathan Casper	Aldgate, London	
17930	Casper	Catherine	1823	City, London	(?)		Henry Casper	Aldgate, London	
14226	Casper	Elizabeth	1820	?, Germany	(?)		Lenz Casper	Manchester	lodging house keeper
17932	Casper	Frank	1849	City, London	Henry Casper	Catherine (?)		Aldgate, London	
17929	Casper	Henry	1824	City, London			Catherine (?)	Aldgate, London	late leather seller
14227	Casper	Henry	1841	Manchester	Lenz Casper	Elizabeth (?)		Manchester	scholar
17931	Casper	Henry	1848	City, London	Henry Casper	Catherine (?)		Aldgate, London	
6513	Casper	Hesokia (Ezekiel)	1851	Manchester	Louis Casper	Minnie (Minah) (?)	Gertrude Mirlo	Manchester	
6506	Casper	Jacob	1813	?, Poland [?, Prussia]			Mathilda Hyman	Manchester	tailor + draper
6507	Casper	Joel	1797	?, Germany [?, Prussia]			Rebecca (?)	Manchester	tailor + draper
11781	Casper	Judah	1793	?, Poland [?, Prussia]	Ezekiel Casper		Rachael Michaels	Shoreditch, London	general dealer + jeweller
14225	Casper	Lenz	1801	?, Germany			Elizabeth (?)	Manchester	tailor
6511	Casper	Louis	1821	Poznan, Poland [Posen, Prussia]			Minnie (Minah) (?)	Manchester	cap maker empl 7
6505	Casper	Mathilda	1811	Plymouth, Devon	Nathan Hyman		Jacob Casper	Manchester	
6512	Casper	Minnie (Minah)	1826	Poznan, Poland [Posen, Prussia]	(?)		Louis Casper	Manchester	
7644	Casper	Nathan	1783	Aldgate, London	Anschil Votch Macher		Amelia Ansell	Aldgate, London	watchmaker

ID	surname	given names	born	birthplace	father	mother	spouse 1	1851 residence	1851 occupation
19056	Casper	Philip Nathan (Uri)	1824	Aldgate, London	Nathan Casper	Amelia Ansell	Julia Joseph	Aldgate, London	watchmaker
26840	Casper	Phoebe	1795	?, Poland	(?)		(?) Casper	Aldgate, London	slipper maker
11782	Casper	Rachel	1805	Chesham, Buckinghamshire	Abraham Asher Anshel Michaels		Judah Casper	Shoreditch, London	
6510	Casper	Rebecca	1799	Liverpool			Joel Casper	Manchester	
17062	Casper	Samuel	1829	?, Poland [?, Prussia]				Edinburgh, Scotland	hawker of jewellery
27732	Castelberg	Betta	1799	?, Russia	(?)		Motel Castelberg	Spitalfields, London	
27734	Castelberg	Isaac	1830	?, Russia				Spitalfields, London	traveller
27733	Castelberg	Jacob	1830	?, Russia	Motel Castelberg	Betta (?)		Spitalfields, London	watchmaker
27731	Castelberg	Motel	1805	?, Russia	Joseph Castelberg		Betta (?)	Spitalfields, London	jeweller + watchmaker
19052	Castello	Baruch Nunes	1829	Mile End, London	Jacob de Emanuel Nunes Castello	Sarah de Beher Alevy	Sophia Woolf	Whitechapel, London	
20976	Castello	Daniel Nunes	1831	Mile End, London	Jacob de Emanuel Nunes Castello	Sarah de Beher Alevy	Sarah Aloof	Whitechapel, London	stock + general agent
19051	Castello	Esther Nunes	1828	Hoxton, London	Jacob de Emanuel Nunes Castello	Sarah de Beher Alevy		Whitechapel, London	
19053	Castello	Hannah Nunes	1833	Mile End, London	Jacob de Emanuel Nunes Castello	Sarah de Beher Alevy		Whitechapel, London	
19049	Castello	Jacob Nunes	1797	Whitechapel, London	Emanuel Nunes Castello		Sarah de Beher Alevy	Whitechapel, London	stock + general agent
7460	Castello	Manuel Nunes	1827	Middlesex, London	Jacob de Emanuel Nunes Castello	Sarah de Beher Alevy	Elizabeth (Lizzie) Magnus	Whitechapel, London	member of Stock Exchange
19054	Castello	Manuel Nunes	1846	Middlesex, London				Whitechapel, London	
19050	Castello	Sarah Nunes	1795	Deal, Kent	Beher de Issachar Alevy		Jacob de Emanuel Nunes Castello	Whitechapel, London	
16881	Caster	Moses	1801	?, Ireland			(?)	Cambridge	traveller
26505	Cavaleh?	Abraham	1841	Middlesex, London				Dover, Kent	
14870	Cazitsewitz	Hannah	1833	?, Poland [?, Prussia]	Samuel C Wolf	Sarah (?)	Robert Cazitsewitz	Bethnal Green, London	
14869	Cazitsewitz	Robert	1826	?, Poland [?, Prussia]			Hannah (?)	Bethnal Green, London	printer
5042	Ceref	Charlotte	1837	Manchester	Edwin Ceref	Sarah (?)		Portsmouth, Hampshire	
5040	Ceref	Edwin	1797	Brussels, Belgium			Sarah (?)	Portsmouth, Hampshire	clothes cleaner
5041	Ceref	Sarah	1817	Dublin, Ireland			Edwin Ceref	Portsmouth, Hampshire	
31017	Chamanski	David	1821	?, Poland				Halifax, Yorkshire	bazaar keeper
31018	Chamanski	Joseph	1824	?, Poland				Halifax, Yorkshire	bazaar keeper
31015	Chamanski	Lazarus	1816	?, Poland				Halifax, Yorkshire	dealer in jewellery
18724	Chapman	Abigail	1796	?, London	Avidor Cohen		Lewis (Louis) Chapman	Birmingham	
4353	Chapman	Abigail (Adelaide)	1810	Holborn, London	Moss (Moses) Abraham Colliss	Hannah (?)	Lewis Chapman	Holborn, London	
29981	Chapman	Barnett	1815	Finsbury, London	Joseph Chapman	Jane (?)	Esther De Souza	Whitechapel, London	hatter
16666	Chapman	Edwin	1827	Liverpool	Moses Chapman	Hannah (?)		Liverpool	book keeper
10094	Chapman	Elizabeth (Ella)	1816	Lambeth, London	Jacob Harris		Maurice Chapman	Holborn, London	
29982	Chapman	Esther	1815	Portsmouth, Hampshire	Daniel Henriques De Souza	Sarah de Eliau Henriques	Barnett Chapman	Whitechapel, London	
16664	Chapman	Hannah	1796	Liverpool	(?)		Moses Chapman	Liverpool	
24858	Chapman	Hannah	1842	Liverpool	(?) Chapman	Amelia Benjamin	John (Jacob) Myers	Bermondsey, London	
10096	Chapman	Henry M	1848	Holborn, London	Maurice Chapman	Elizabeth (Ella) Harris	Dinah Gershon	Holborn, London	at home
29985	Chapman	Jacob	1848	?, London	Barnett Chapman	Esther De Souza		Whitechapel, London	
5720	Chapman	John	1845	Holborn, London	Lewis Chapman	Abigail Colliss	Annie Rosenbaum	Holborn, London	scholar
10095	Chapman	John	1846	Spitalfields, London	Maurice Chapman	Elizabeth (Ella) Harris		Holborn, London	at home
5722	Chapman	Joseph	1847	Holborn, London	Lewis Chapman	Abigail Colliss	Fanny Jacobs	Holborn, London	scholar
29983	Chapman	Judina	1842	?, London	Barnett Chapman	Esther De Souza	Louis Pyzer	Whitechapel, London	

ID	surname	given names	born	birthplace	father	mother	spouse 1	1851 residence	1851 occupation
4352	Chapman	Lewis	1811	Whitechapel, London	Chapman (Meshullam) Chapman	Rebecca Samuel	Abigail (Adelaide) Colliss	Holborn, London	potato salesman + dealer in ladies wardrobes
18723	Chapman	Lewis (Louis)	1805	?, London	Jacob Chapman		Abigail Cohen	Birmingham	clothes salesman
10093	Chapman	Maurice	1808	Whitechapel, London	Chapman (Meshullam) Chapman	Rebecca Samuel	Elizabeth (Ella) Harris	Holborn, London	quill dresser
16663	Chapman	Moses	1780	Middlesex, London			Hannah (?)	Liverpool	retired silversmith
24859	Chapman	Moss	1843	Middlesex, London	(?) Chapman	Amelia Benjamin		Bermondsey, London	scholar
24857	Chapman	Rebecca	1840	Liverpool	(?) Chapman	Amelia Benjamin	Morris Menser	Bermondsey, London	apprentice
29986	Chapman	Rosetta	1850	?Whitechapel, London	Barnett Chapman	Esther De Souza		Whitechapel, London	
16665	Chapman	Sarah	1825	Liverpool	Moses Chapman	Hannah (?)		Liverpool	
29984	Chapman	Sarah	1843	?, London	Barnett Chapman	Esther De Souza		Whitechapel, London	
10098	Chapman	Selina	1850	Holborn, London	Maurice Chapman	Elizabeth (Ella) Harris		Holborn, London	
25644	Charig	Fanny	1843	Leszno, Poland [Lissa, Prussia]	Marcus (Mark) C Charig	Louisa Bellafield		Whitechapel, London	scholar
29467	Charig	Fanny	1847	Whitechapel, London	Samuel Charig	Louisa Fox		Spitalfields, London	scholar
25645	Charig	Henry Marks	1845	Leszno, Poland [Lissa, Prussia]	Marcus (Mark) C Charig	Louisa Bellafield	Amelia Shuter	Whitechapel, London	scholar
25646	Charig	Hyman Marks	1849	Spitalfields, London	Marcus (Mark) C Charig	Louisa Bellafield	Julia Lyons	Whitechapel, London	
25643	Charig	Louisa	1820	Leszno, Poland [Lissa, Prussia]	(?) Bellafield [Bieberfeld?]		Marcus (Mark) C Charig	Whitechapel, London	tailoress
25642	Charig	Marcus (Mark) C	1810	Leszno, Poland [Lissa, Prussia]			Louisa Bellafield	Whitechapel, London	tailor
28074	Charik	Meyer	1831	?, Poland [?, Prussia]	Israel Charik		Matilde (Rebecca) Borchardt	Spitalfields, London	saddler
17622	Chiesbergh	Moses	1822	?, Poland				Aldgate, London	tailor
16286	Chose	Victor	1820	?, Germany				Dundee, Scotland	
21751	Clarke	Adeline	1824	Chelsea, London	Joseph de Masahod Delevante	Judith (Julia) de Abraham Abendelack	James Clarke	Chelsea, London	
2611	Cochen	Isaac	1831	?, Germany				Glasgow, Scotland	assistant clothier
16646	Cohan	Asher	1780	Chatham, Kent			Esther (?)	Liverpool	pawnbroker + silversmith?/salesman?
3682	Cohan	Elias	1830	Aldgate, London				Spitalfields, London	general dealer
16647	Cohan	Esther	1769	Middlesex, London	(?)		Asher Cohan	Liverpool	
16531	Cohan	Henry	1811	Barking, Essex				Liverpool	tailor + draper
16648	Cohan	Mark	1818	Chatham, Kent	Asher Cohen	Esther (?)		Liverpool	merchant
4380	Cohen	(?)	1803	Birmingham			Jacob Cohen	Birmingham	
16222	Cohen	?	1851	Middlesex, London	Henry Cohen	Caroline S (?)		Paddington, London	
4388	Cohen	?Katie	1807	?, London			Joseph Colman Cohen	Birmingham	
16490	Cohen	A---	1765	Gibraltar				Mile End, London	
29577	Cohen	Aaron	1797	Amsterdam, Holland			Mary (?)	Stepney, London	optician
24835	Cohen	Aaron	1795	Middlesex, London			Rachel Davis	Elephant & Castle, London	merchant
25383	Cohen	Aaron	1803	Holborn, London			Rachel (?)	Clerkenwell, London	tool dealer
28012	Cohen	Aaron	1803	Aldgate, London	Abraham Cohen		Rachael Harris	Spitalfields, London	general dealer
22224	Cohen	Aaron	1811	Middlesex, London				Whitechapel, London	pawnbroker
1497	Cohen	Aaron	1818	Spitalfields, London	Michael Cohen		Julia Solomon Wilks	Spitalfields, London	furniture broker

ID	surname	given names	born	birthplace	father	mother	spouse 1	1851 residence	1851 occupation
3373	Cohen	Aaron	1821	Wapping, London	Benjamin Wolf Cohen	Frances Phillips	Phoebe Solomon (Sailman)	Holborn, London	wholesale fruiterer
11542	Cohen	Aaron	1822	Spitalfields, London			Sarah (?)	Spitalfields, London	furniture broker
11836	Cohen	Aaron	1822	?, Germany	Chaim Cohen		Ann Moss	Whitechapel, London	foreman to a tailor
1521	Cohen	Aaron	1831	Southwark, London	Samuel Cohen	Rebecca Joseph		Aldgate, London	furniture dealer
19912	Cohen	Aaron	1835	Amsterdam, Holland	Philip Cohen	Rose Abrahams		Spitalfields, London	errand boy
3899	Cohen	Aaron	1838	Amsterdam, Holland	Emanuel Cohen	Sally (?)	Kate Isaacs	Spitalfields, London	confectioner
5222	Cohen	Aaron	1838	Dobrzyn, Poland	Isaac Aaron	Jeanette (?)	Sophia Newhouse	Liverpool	
10404	Cohen	Aaron	1847	Spitalfields, London	Michael Cohen	Sarah Jacobs		Spitalfields, London	
17341	Cohen	Aaron	1847	Spitalfields, London	Samuel Cohen	Sarah (?)		Spitalfields, London	
5152	Cohen	Aaron (Alfred) Judah	1844	Spitalfields, London	Judah Cohen	Caroline Davis	Lydia Bardo nee Cohen	Wapping, London	
1519	Cohen	Abigail	1769	Aldgate, London	(?) Aarons		Moses Cohen	Aldgate, London	
17382	Cohen	Abigail	1803	Aldgate, London	Reuben		Lewis Cohen	Wapping, London	
15188	Cohen	Abigail	1809	?, London	Abraham Torres	Esther de Isaac Dias	Raphael (Ralph) Cohen	Shoreditch, London	
15313	Cohen	Abraham	1773	Whitechapel, London			Sarah (?)	Shoreditch, London	carpet dealer
11702	Cohen	Abraham	1789	Whitechapel, London	Jesse Cohen		Deborah Genese	Aldgate, London	tailor
21745	Cohen	Abraham	1808	Aldgate, London	Solomon Cohen	Hannah Moses Samuel		Canonbury, London	dealer in the Funds
4356	Cohen	Abraham	1809	?, London			Hannah (?)	Birmingham	confectioner
19459	Cohen	Abraham	1812	Spitalfields, London	Isaac Cohen		Esther Moses	Aldgate, London	pastry cook
17158	Cohen	Abraham	1815	Bristol			Mary A (?)	Newcastle Upon Tyne	?sidewaiter
11637	Cohen	Abraham	1816	Wapping, London	Moses de Samuel Cohen	Nancy (Yenta) de Isaiah	Elizabeth Busnach	Aldgate, London	cigar maker
25703	Cohen	Abraham	1816	Whitechapel, London	Joseph Cohen	Clara Cohen	Maria Samuel	Spitalfields, London	clothes dealer
23067	Cohen	Abraham	1821	Middlesex, London				Aldgate, London	clerk to general merchant
24740	Cohen	Abraham	1822	Whitechapel, London			Amelia Jacobs	Southwark, London	professor of music
6271	Cohen	Abraham	1825	Whitechapel, London	Joshua Cohen		Rosetta Levy	Spitalfields, London	clothier
14759	Cohen	Abraham	1827	Southwark, London	Moses Cohen	Henrietta (?)		Finsbury, London	watch finisher
29998	Cohen	Abraham	1829	Brighton, Sussex	Solomon Cohen	Susan (?)		Brighton, Sussex	
1590	Cohen	Abraham	1833	?, Holland				Spitalfields, London	
1610	Cohen	Abraham	1833	Spitalfields, London	Lewis (Lyon) Cohen	Harriet Lear		Spitalfields, London	cigar maker apprentice
13333	Cohen	Abraham	1833	Spitalfields, London	David Cohen	Harriet Woolf		Spitalfields, London	labourer
18301	Cohen	Abraham	1835	?, Russia	Moses Cohen	Jane (?)		Sheffield, Yorkshire	hawker
18589	Cohen	Abraham	1835	Aldgate, London	(?Abraham) Cohen	Elizabeth (?)		Stepney, London	
28015	Cohen	Abraham	1835	Whitechapel, London	Aaron Cohen	Rachael Harris		Spitalfields, London	
15192	Cohen	Abraham	1837	?, London	Raphael (Ralph) Cohen	Abigail Torres		Shoreditch, London	scholar
28965	Cohen	Abraham	1837	Aldgate, London	Solomon Isaac Cohen	Hannah Levie		Whitechapel, London	scholar
11858	Cohen	Abraham	1840	Middlesex, London	(?) Cohen	(?)		Whitechapel, London	inmate of orphan school
26975	Cohen	Abraham	1842	Whitechapel, London	Joseph Cohen	Esther (?)		Aldgate, London	scholar
21759	Cohen	Abraham	1843	New York, USA	Ezekiel Cohen	Elizabeth Myers	Emma Ansell	Aldgate, London	
11965	Cohen	Abraham	1844	Whitechapel, London	Moses Cohen	Flora (?)		Whitechapel, London	scholar
1498	Cohen	Abraham	1845	Spitalfields, London	Aaron Cohen	Julia Solomon Wilks		Spitalfields, London	scholar
1566	Cohen	Abraham	1846	Spitalfields, London	Henry Cohen	Esther Levy	Elizabeth Levy	Aldgate, London	
15089	Cohen	Abraham	1846	Stepney, London	Joseph Cohen	Catharine (?)		Mile End, London	scholar
29232	Cohen	Abraham	1846	?, Germany	Louis Cohen	Sophia (?)		Whitechapel, London	
19658	Cohen	Abraham	1847	Aldgate, London	Joseph Cohen	Rebecca Lazarus		Spitalfields, London	
5166	Cohen	Abraham	1850	Spitalfields, London	Barnet Cohen	Sarah Hyman		Spitalfields, London	

ID	surname	given names	born	birthplace	father	mother	spouse 1	1851 residence	1851 occupation
2187	Cohen	Abraham David	1843	Oxford, Oxfordshire	Isaac Jacob Cohen	Sarah Levi		Oxford, Oxfordshire	
18357	Cohen	Abraham Joseph	1824	St Pancras, London	Joseph Cohen	Elizabeth Benjamin	Adelaide Harris	Elephant & Castle, London	furniture broker
6288	Cohen	Abraham Mark	1814	Totnes, Devon	Mark Cohen		Fanny Millingen	Bloomsbury, London	paper hanger
2831	Cohen	Abraham Robert	1851	Spitalfields, London	Victor Cohen	Henrietta Magnus	Eliza Mary Driscoll	Spitalfields, London	
2242	Cohen	Abram (Abraham)	1824	?, Poland			Rosetta Fox	Leeds, Yorkshire	hawker
3908	Cohen	Adaline (Ada, Idyl)	1787	?, Poland [?, Prussia]			Michael Cohen	Sunderland, Co Durham	
1482	Cohen	Adelaide	1843	Spitalfields, London	Phineas Cohen	Rebecca Hyams	Simeon Moss	Spitalfields, London	scholar
10567	Cohen	Adelaide	1846	Whitechapel, London	Joseph Cohen	Maria (?)		Whitechapel, London	
7842	Cohen	Adelaide (Ada)	1830	Finsbury, London	Louis Cohen	Rebecca Floretta Keyser	Joseph Montefiore Sebag	Finsbury, London	
8498	Cohen	Adolph	1815	?, Poland [?, Prussia]				?Glasgow, Scotland	
15816	Cohen	Adolph	1824	?, Poland [?, Prussia]				Aldgate, London	furrier
80	Cohen	Adolphus	1815	Hamburg, Germany				Woolwich, London	glazier
18340	Cohen	Adolphus	1828	Mitau, Latvia [Milan, Curland]				Brighton, Sussex	musician
15755	Cohen	Albert A	1849	Middlesex, London	Selim Cohen	Sarah Kahn		Aldgate, London	
8911	Cohen	Alexander	1770	?, Italy				Aldgate, London	annuitant
23904	Cohen	Alexander	1806	Spitalfields, London	(?) Cohen	Ann (?)		Marylebone, London	Beadle of the West London Synagogue
11250	Cohen	Alexander	1839	Aldgate, London	Phillip Cohen	Catharine (?)	?	Aldgate, London	
8242	Cohen	Alexander	1850	Whitechapel, London	Isaac Cohen	Louisa Cowan	Marie Myers	Aldgate, London	
18257	Cohen	Alexander E	1814	?, Russia			Ann (?)	Cambridge	teacher of Hebrew
29849	Cohen	Alfred	1825	Spitalfields, London			Elizabeth Oswald	Whitechapel, London	musician
4384	Cohen	Alfred	1843	Birmingham	Jacob Cohen	(?) (?)		Birmingham	scholar
31187	Cohen	Alfred	1844	Southwark, London	Hyman Cohen	Maria (?)		Gravesend, Kent	scholar
21194	Cohen	Alfred (Aaron)	1843	Middlesex, London	Barnet Cohen	Sarah Hyman	Catherine Moss	Spitalfields, London	
7047	Cohen	Alfred Louis	1836	Finsbury, London	Louis Cohen	Rebecca Floretta Keyser	Marie Javal	Finsbury, London	scholar at home
13391	Cohen	Aliande	1850	?, London	Julius Cohen	Esther Jacobs		Spitalfields, London	
23058	Cohen	Amelia	1813	Hamburg, Germany	(?)		Saunder Cohen	Aldgate, London	
24736	Cohen	Amelia	1821	Southwark, London	Philip Cohen	Jane (?)	Solomon Henry Jaffa	Southwark, London	milliner + dress maker
1615	Cohen	Amelia	1827	Aldgate, London	Barnet Henry Cohen	Esther (?)		Spitalfields, London	
1517	Cohen	Amelia	1828	Middlesex, London	Isaac Cohen	Esther Davis	Samuel Isaacs Parks	Spitalfields, London	milliner
28538	Cohen	Amelia	1828	Middlesex, London	(?) Cohen			Aldgate, London	
24741	Cohen	Amelia	1829	Whitechapel, London	(?) Jacobs		Abraham Cohen	Southwark, London	
1513	Cohen	Amelia	1832	Aldgate, London	Woolf Cohen	Hannah (Ann) Prince (Prins))	Mordecai Symmons	Spitalfields, London	tailoress
19152	Cohen	Amelia	1834	Aldgate, London	Leman Cohen	Clara Lyon		Aldgate, London	furrier
21757	Cohen	Amelia	1839	Aldgate, London	Ezekiel Cohen	Elizabeth Myers		Aldgate, London	waistcoat maker
29789	Cohen	Amelia	1840	City, London	David Abraham Cohen	Hannah Solomon		Whitechapel, London	scholar
1597	Cohen	Amelia	1843	?, London	(?) Cohen			Spitalfields, London	scholar
10402	Cohen	Amelia	1843	Spitalfields, London	Michael Cohen	Sarah Jacobs	Abraham Collins	Spitalfields, London	
17339	Cohen	Amelia	1844	Spitalfields, London	Samuel Cohen	Sarah (?)		Spitalfields, London	
25709	Cohen	Amelia	1847	Spitalfields, London	Abraham Cohen	Maria Samuel		Spitalfields, London	
5677	Cohen	Amelia (Meije)	1796	?, Holland	(?) van der Reis		Benjamin Cohen	Sunderland, Co Durham	
24284	Cohen	Andrew	1791	?, Jamaica, West Indies	Hyam HaCohen		Hannah Oppenheim	Bloomsbury, London	retired West Indies merchant

ID	surname	given names	born	birthplace	father	mother	spouse 1	1851 residence	1851 occupation
9490	Cohen	Andrew	1798	Guernsey, Channel Islands			Catherine (?)	Aldgate, London	
21066	Cohen	Angel	1840	?, London				Dover, Kent	silk merchant
1632	Cohen	Angel	1846	Spitalfields, London	Ralph (Raphael) Cohen	Julia Lazarus	Rachel Benjamin	Spitalfields, London	boarding school pupil
23905	Cohen	Ann	1767	Aldgate, London			(?) Cohen	Marylebone, London	
136	Cohen	Ann	1791	Middlesex, London				Woolwich, London	servant
18258	Cohen	Ann	1812	Shrewsbury, Shropshire	(?)		Alexander E Cohen	Cambridge	
23881	Cohen	Ann	1815	Holborn, London	(?) Davis		Solomon Hyman Cohen	Westminster, London	
4363	Cohen	Ann	1816	Longford, Warwickshire			Daniel Cohen	Birmingham	
23330	Cohen	Ann	1821	Westminster, London				Westminster, London	
13646	Cohen	Ann	1826	?, London	Emanuel (Menachem Mendele) Solomons	Phoebe (?)	Franklin Cohen	Manchester	shoe mfr's wife
11837	Cohen	Ann	1828	Aldgate, London	Aryeh Pais Moss	Rosa (Rosy) (?)	Aaron Cohen	Whitechapel, London	
16541	Cohen	Ann	1829	Liverpool	(?) Moss	Rachael (?)	Henry Cohen	Liverpool	
1505	Cohen	Ann	1831	Spitalfields, London	Solomon Cohen	Rachel (?)		Spitalfields, London	
3366	Cohen	Ann (Isabella)	1818	Portsmouth, Hampshire	Moshe Solomon (Sailman)	Elizabeth (?)	Daniel Cohen	Holborn, London	
24817	Cohen	Ann (Nancy)	1813	?, London	Henry Harris		Samuel Cohen	Waterloo, London	
19153	Cohen	Ann (Nancy)	1836	Aldgate, London	Leman Cohen	Clara Lyon	Philip Cohen	Aldgate, London	general servant
11142	Cohen	Anna	1818	Aldgate, London	(?) Cohen	Frances (?)		Aldgate, London	tailoress
23309	Cohen	Anna Louisa	1835	Mayfair, London	Isaac Cohen	Sarah Samuel		Mayfair, London	scholar at home
18423	Cohen	Annetta	1829	Elephant & Castle, London	Michael Castle Levy	Ann Benjamin	Henry Cohen	Elephant & Castle, London	
5463	Cohen	Annette	1844	Southwark, London	Moses Cohen	Kate Joseph		Elephant & Castle, London	
24661	Cohen	Annette	1846	Elephant & Castle, London	Zachariah Cohen	Flora (?)		Kennington, London	
8497	Cohen	Annie Frances	1847	Glasgow, Scotland	Adolph Cohen		Abraham (Albert) N Magnus	?Glasgow, Scotland	
1762	Cohen	Antonia	1848	Cardiff, Wales	Marinus Thomas Cohen (CHECK)	Frederica Hanna (?)		Cardiff, Wales	
16294	Cohen	Arnold	1820	?, Germany				Dundee, Scotland	
4355	Cohen	Aron	1822	?, Poland				Birmingham	slipper maker
7034	Cohen	Arthur Joseph	1829	Marylebone, London	Benjamin Cohen	Justina Montefiore	Emmeline Micholls	Cambridge	student
22617	Cohen	Asher	1804	Whitechapel, London			Rachel (?)	Stepney, London	inspector, Bill department, Moses & Son, Aldgate
30689	Cohen	Asher John	1803	Southwark, London			H--- (?)	Whitechapel, London	house agent + appraiser
29065	Cohen	B---	1810	Whitechapel, London	Ezekiel Cohen	R--- (?)		Whitechapel, London	shopman
5161	Cohen	Barnet	1817	Middlesex, London	Isaac Cohen	Esther Davis	Sarah Hyman	Spitalfields, London	furniture broker
18344	Cohen	Barnet	1830	?, Russia				Wolverhampton, Staffordshire	pawnbroker + old clothes merchant
1613	Cohen	Barnet Henry	1791	Canterbury, Kent	Tsevi Hirsh Cohen		Esther Mathews	Spitalfields, London	journeyman glass cutter
6257	Cohen	Barnet Solomon	1816	Aldgate, London	Solomon Cohen	Mary (?)	Eliza Myers	St John's Wood, London	general merchant
11323	Cohen	Barnett	1802	Aldgate, London			(?)	Aldgate, London	butcher
16233	Cohen	Barnett	1843	Clerkenwell, London	Samuel Cohen	Rosetta (?)	Sarah Edwards	Clerkenwell, London	scholar
5169	Cohen	Barnett (Baruch)	1780	Bavaria, Germany	Judah Cohen		Sarah (Sierlah, Tserele) Levy	Lambeth, London	'out of business'

ID	surname	given names	born	birthplace	father	mother	spouse 1	1851 residence	1851 occupation
26801	Cohen	Bella	1811	Middlesex, London	Daniel Cohen	Leah (?)		Aldgate, London	fruiterer
7036	Cohen	Benjamin	1789	?, London	Levy Barent Cohen		Justina Moses Montefiore	Marylebone, London	exchange broker + magistrate
27640	Cohen	Benjamin	1789	City, London			(?)	Aldgate, London	clothier
29182	Cohen	Benjamin	1795	Sunderland, Co Durham				Whitechapel, London	merchant
5676	Cohen	Benjamin	1796	Leeuwarden, Holland	Wolf Benjamin Cohen	Hester Jacob Berand Linneweil	Reinje de Groot	Sunderland, Co Durham	general dealer
21119	Cohen	Benjamin	1803	?, Germany			Bluma (?)	Aldgate, London	cap maker
1476	Cohen	Benjamin	1804	Whitechapel, London	Moses (Yeshaya) Cohen		Rebecca Cohen	Spitalfields, London	general dealer
5123	Cohen	Benjamin	1808	Poznan, Poland [Wronke, Duchy Posen, Prussia]			Dinah (?)	Sheffield, Yorkshire	general dealer
17061	Cohen	Benjamin	1814	Norwich, Norfolk				Edinburgh, Scotland	pinches dealer
11705	Cohen	Benjamin	1831	Aldgate, London	Abraham Cohen	Deborah Genese		Aldgate, London	weaver
25785	Cohen	Benjamin	1837	Aldgate, London	Solomon Cohen	Catherine Myers		Aldgate, London	confectioner
29127	Cohen	Benjamin	1837	Whitechapel, London	Moses Cohen	Rebecca (?)		Whitechapel, London	tailor
4359	Cohen	Benjamin	1838	?, London	Abraham Cohen	Hannah (?)		Birmingham	scholar
11962	Cohen	Benjamin	1838	Whitechapel, London	Moses Cohen	Flora (?)	Rachel Montefiore	Whitechapel, London	scholar
23260	Cohen	Benjamin	1841	Hammersmith, London	Isaac Cohen	Louisa (?)		Notting Hill, London	
2612	Cohen	Benjamin	1848	Glasgow, Scotland	Simon M Cohen	Harriet (?)		Glasgow, Scotland	
1628	Cohen	Benjamin	1849	Spitalfields, London	Emanuel Cohen	Esther (?)		Spitalfields, London	
15070	Cohen	Benjamin	1849	Whitechapel, London	John Cohen	Louisa (?)		Bethnal Green, London	scholar
8910	Cohen	Benjamin Haim	1801	?, London	Alexander Cohen		Amelia (Miriam) Costa	Aldgate, London	translator of languages
29929	Cohen	Benjamin Israel	1833	Brighton, Sussex	Solomon Cohen	Susan (?)		Brighton, Sussex	shoemaker
7038	Cohen	Benjamin Louis	1844	Finsbury, London	Louis Cohen	Rebecca Floretta Keyser	Louisa Emily Merton	Finsbury, London	scholar at home
17886	Cohen	Benjamin Wolfe	1845	Holborn, London	Nathan Cohen	Deborah Cohen		Holborn, London	
15756	Cohen	Bernard	1850	Spitalfields, London	Selim Cohen	Sarah Kahn		Aldgate, London	
7140	Cohen	Bertha	1830	Hamburg, Germany	Raphael Isaac Cohen	Hannah (?)	David Levy (Lewis)	Dover, Kent	
24662	Cohen	Betsey	1847	Elephant & Castle, London	Zachariah Cohen	Flora (?)		Kennington, London	
14115	Cohen	Betsy	1831	Hanover, Germany	(?) Cohen			Manchester	tailor
1611	Cohen	Betsy	1836	Spitalfields, London	Lewis (Lyon) Cohen	Harriet Lear		Spitalfields, London	scholar
1542	Cohen	Betsy	1848	Spitalfields, London	James Cohen	Sarah (?)		Spitalfields, London	
21083	Cohen	Bloom	1799	Dover, Kent	(?)		Raphael Isaac Cohen	Dover, Kent	
6281	Cohen	Bloomah	1828	Finsbury, London	(?) Solomons		Michael Cohen	Aldgate, London	
21120	Cohen	Bluma	1806	Berlin, Germany	(?)		Benjamin Cohen	Aldgate, London	cap maker
29068	Cohen	C---	1819	Whitechapel, London	Ezekiel Cohen	R--- (?)		Whitechapel, London	tailoress
1588	Cohen	Caroline	1772	Spitalfields, London	(?)		(?) Cohen	Spitalfields, London	general dealer
24615	Cohen	Caroline	1814	Elephant & Castle, London	Philip Cohen	Sarah (?)		Kennington, London	
5150	Cohen	Caroline	1816	Aldgate, London	Joshua Davis	Sarah Zusman	Judah Cohen	Wapping, London	
23331	Cohen	Caroline	1819	Westminster, London	(?) Cohen			Westminster, London	ironmonger
2616	Cohen	Caroline	1822	?Liverpool	(?) Sewill		Henry Cohen	Glasgow, Scotland	traveller's wife
15996	Cohen	Caroline	1829	Aldgate, London	(?)		Hyman Cohen	Mile End, London	
1574	Cohen	Caroline	1835	Spitalfields, London	Michael Cohen	Elizabeth (?)		Spitalfields, London	dress maker
1551	Cohen	Caroline	1836	Spitalfields, London	Isaiah Cohen			Spitalfields, London	tailoress
5681	Cohen	Caroline	1837	?, London	Benjamin Cohen	Amelia (Mieje) van der Reis	David Sussman	Sunderland, Co Durham	
14965	Cohen	Caroline	1838	Middlesex, London	(?) Cohen			Bethnal Green, London	boarding school pupil

ID	surname	given names	born	birthplace	father	mother	spouse 1	1851 residence	1851 occupation
15440	Cohen	Caroline	1839	Aldgate, London	Moses Cohen			Covent Garden, London	
25659	Cohen	Caroline	1843	Lambeth, London	Zachariah Cohen	Flora (?)		Kennington, London	
16916	Cohen	Caroline	1850	Sheffield, Yorkshire	Benjamin Cohen	Dinah (?)		Sheffield, Yorkshire	
16218	Cohen	Caroline S	1826	?, Shropshire	(?)		Henry Cohen	Paddington, London	
11248	Cohen	Catharine	1812	Aldgate, London	(?)		Phillip Cohen	Aldgate, London	
25365	Cohen	Catharine	1815	Holborn, London	(?) Cohen	Maria (?)		Clerkenwell, London	
15088	Cohen	Catharine	1823	Whitechapel, London	(?)		Joseph Cohen	Mile End, London	
1506	Cohen	Catharine	1836	Spitalfields, London	Mark Cohen	Rachel (?)		Spitalfields, London	cap maker
21951	Cohen	Catherine	1771	Middlesex, London	(?)		Jacob Cohen	Swansea, Wales	proprietor of houses
18198	Cohen	Catherine	1779	Middlesex, London	(?) Cohen			Mile End, London	
29098	Cohen	Catherine	1794	Aldgate, London	(?)		Michael Cohen	Whitechapel, London	
9491	Cohen	Catherine	1796	Millbrook, Kent	(?)		Andrew Cohen	Aldgate, London	
25783	Cohen	Catherine	1803	Aldgate, London	Moshe Myers		Solomon Cohen	Aldgate, London	confectioner's wife
30373	Cohen	Catherine	1811	Middlesex, London	(?)		Myer Cohen	Tutbury, Staffordshire	dressmaker
29308	Cohen	Catherine	1815	Whitechapel, London	(?) Cohen	Rebecca (?)		Whitechapel, London	shoe binder
1486	Cohen	Catherine	1832	Spitalfields, London	Sampson Cohen	Rebecca (?)		Spitalfields, London	lint maker
13134	Cohen	Catherine	1832	King's Lynn, Norfolk	(?) Cohen	Eve (?)		Hoxton, London	boot binder
29060	Cohen	Catherine	1836	Whitechapel, London	Simon Cohen	Isabella (?)		Whitechapel, London	
27643	Cohen	Catherine	1838	City, London	Benjamin Cohen	(?)		Aldgate, London	
25706	Cohen	Catherine	1839	Whitechapel, London	Abraham Cohen	Maria Samuel		Spitalfields, London	
9269	Cohen	Catherine	1841	?, Holland	Myers S Cohen	Jane (?)		Aldgate, London	
11878	Cohen	Catherine	1841	?, Holland	(?) Cohen	(?)		Whitechapel, London	inmate of orphan school
10390	Cohen	Catherine (Kitty)	1836	Spitalfields, London	Philip Cohen	Rachael Jacobs	Abraham Garcia	Spitalfields, London	cap maker
1565	Cohen	Catherine (Kitty)	1842	Aldgate, London	Henry Cohen	Esther Levy		Aldgate, London	
1475	Cohen	Catherine (Kitty)	1850	Spitalfields, London	Benjamin Cohen	Rebecca (?)		Spitalfields, London	
21123	Cohen	Cecilia	1833	?, Germany	Benjamin Cohen	Bluma (?)		Aldgate, London	cap maker journeyman
30393	Cohen	Celia (Cecilia)	1851	?, London	Julius Cohen	Esther Jacobs		Spitalfields, London	
11951	Cohen	Charles	1821	?, Germany	Lazarus Cohen		Frances (Fanny) Solomons	Whitechapel, London	jeweller
8037	Cohen	Charles	1834	?London	Barnett (Baruch) Cohen	Sarah (Sierlah, Tserele) Levy		Lambeth, London	
4383	Cohen	Charles	1841	Birmingham	Jacob Cohen	(?) (?)		Birmingham	scholar
25789	Cohen	Charles	1846	Aldgate, London	Solomon Cohen	Catherine Myers		Aldgate, London	scholar
99	Cohen	Charlotte	1813	Woolwich, London			Joseph Cohen	Woolwich, London	schoolmistress
21953	Cohen	Charlotte	1815	Swansea, Wales	Jacob Cohen	Catherine (?)		Swansea, Wales	
12604	Cohen	Charlotte	1821	Briston, Norfolk	(?)		Joseph L Cohen	Norwich, Norfolk	
100	Cohen	Charlotte	1850	?Woolwich, London	Joseph Cohen	Charlotte (?)		Woolwich, London	
22899	Cohen	Ciper	1794	Aldgate, London	(?) Cohen			Wapping, London	
27567	Cohen	Clara	1788	Aldgate, London	Abraham Cohen		Joseph Cohen	Spitalfields, London	tailoress
19150	Cohen	Clara	1810	Aldgate, London	Isaac (Yitzhak Zelkel) Lyon	Rosa Levy	Leman Judah Cohen	Aldgate, London	furrier
1544	Cohen	Clara	1822	Aldgate, London	Simon HaLevi Michael		Moses Cohen	Spitalfields, London	
26803	Cohen	Clara	1825	Sheerness, Kent	Daniel Cohen	Leah (?)		Aldgate, London	shopwoman
25707	Cohen	Clara	1841	Aldgate, London	Abraham Cohen	Maria Samuel		Spitalfields, London	scholar
18587	Cohen	Clara	1843	Aldgate, London	Abraham Cohen		Isaac Woolf	Stepney, London	
22196	Cohen	Cosman	1806	Middlesex, London			Sarah Hyams nee (?)	Whitechapel, London	sponge dealer
21052	Cohen	D---	1842	?, London				Dover, Kent	boarding school pupil
26799	Cohen	Daniel	1784	Middlesex, London			Leah (?)	Aldgate, London	grocer

ID	surname	given names	born	birthplace	father	mother	spouse 1	1851 residence	1851 occupation
18261	Cohen	Daniel	1799	?, Poland [?, Prussia]			Sarah (?)	Boston, Lincolnshire	smallware dealer
4362	Cohen	Daniel	1806	Whitechapel, London			Ann (?)	Birmingham	general dealer
3365	Cohen	Daniel	1818	Middlesex, London	Benjamin Wolf Cohen	Frances Phillips	Ann (Isabella) Solomon (Sailman)	Holborn, London	general dealer
17535	Cohen	Daniel	1827	Whitechapel, London	Moshe Levi Cohen		Frances Hyams	Spitalfields, London	looking glass dealer
30394	Cohen	Daniel	1851	Holborn, London	Simon Cohen	Dinah Solomon		Holborn, London	
11981	Cohen	David	1792	?, Poland [?, Prussia]				Whitechapel, London	fancy store dealer
22916	Cohen	David	1796	Amsterdam, Holland	Benjamin Benedet HaCohen		Julia Cantor	Wapping, London	jeweller
23820	Cohen	David	1797	?, Germany			(?)	Liverpool	optician
13329	Cohen	David	1799	Spitalfields, London			Harriet Woolf	Spitalfields, London	labourer
12494	Cohen	David	1806	?, Poland				Exeter, Devon	traveller
28997	Cohen	David	1812	?, Poland [?, Prussia]				Whitechapel, London	fancy store dealer
8038	Cohen	David	1823	Lambeth, London	Barnett (Baruch) Cohen	Sarah (Sierlah, Tserele) Levy	Julia Nathan	Finsbury, London	colonial merchant
11144	Cohen	David	1825	Spitalfields, London	(?) Cohen	Frances (?)		Aldgate, London	musician
18296	Cohen	David	1828	?, Poland [?, Prussia]				Sunderland, Co Durham	general dealer, jewellery
1518	Cohen	David	1829	Middlesex, London	Isaac Cohen	Esther Davis	Rachel Marks	Spitalfields, London	cigar maker
1616	Cohen	David	1829	Aldgate, London	Barnet Henry Cohen	Esther (?)		Spitalfields, London	journeyman cigar maker
21876	Cohen	David	1829	Holborn, London	Jacob de Enoch (Hanoj) Cohen	Welcome (Benvenida) de David Nunes Carvalho		Clerkenwell, London	confectioner
22105	Cohen	David	1829	?, Germany				Whitechapel, London	tailor
19657	Cohen	David	1846	Aldgate, London	Joseph Cohen	Rebecca Lazarus		Spitalfields, London	
31188	Cohen	David	1846	Southwark, London	Hyman Cohen	Maria (?)		Gravesend, Kent	scholar
9200	Cohen	David	1849	Whitechapel, London	George Cohen	Hannah (?)		Whitechapel, London	
29786	Cohen	David Abraham	1801	City, London	Emanuel Cohen		Hannah Solomon	Whitechapel, London	master pencil maker
23329	Cohen	David Joseph	1819	Strand, London				Westminster, London	plumber, painter + glazier
12597	Cohen	David Leyser	1793	?, London			?	Great Yarmouth, Norfolk	fruiterer
22619	Cohen	David?	1826	Whitechapel, London	Asher Cohen	Rachel (?)		Stepney, London	inspector, Bill department, Moses & Son, Aldgate
26366	Cohen	Davis	1828	?, Germany				Aldgate, London	glazier
18152	Cohen	Deborah	1764	abroad	(?)		(?) Cohen	Mile End, London	inmate of Portuguese Jews Hospital
28228	Cohen	Deborah	1791	Bethnal Green, London	Gershon Jeweller Michael		Lewis Cohen	Spitalfields, London	
11703	Cohen	Deborah	1792	Aldgate, London	Samuel Genese	Rebecca Capua	Abraham Cohen	Aldgate, London	tailor
3359	Cohen	Deborah	1818	Holborn, London	Wolf (Benjamin) Cohen	Hannah (?)	Nathan Cohen	Holborn, London	
15437	Cohen	Deborah	1825	Whitechapel, London	Moses Cohen			Covent Garden, London	dress maker
16961	Cohen	Deborah	1836	Birmingham	(?) Cohen			Hammersmith, London	boarding school pupil
26097	Cohen	Deborah	1836	?, Poland	(?) Cohen	Rebecca (?)		Aldgate, London	dressmaker
18303	Cohen	Deborah	1843	?, Russia	Moses Cohen	Jane (?)		Sheffield, Yorkshire	scholar at home
8248	Cohen	Deborah (Dora)	1823	Holborn, London	Samuel Levy		Philip Cohen	Shoreditch, London	
20433	Cohen	Debrah	1783	Amsterdam, Holland	(?)		(?) Joseph	Aldgate, London	
16913	Cohen	Dinah	1817	?, London	(?)		Benjamin Cohen	Sheffield, Yorkshire	
9450	Cohen	Dinah	1823	?, London	Henry (Naftali) Solomon		Simon Cohen	Aldgate, London	
16098	Cohen	Dinah	1827	?, London	(?) Cohen			Whitechapel, London	servant
24818	Cohen	Dinah	1839	?, London	Samuel Cohen	Ann (Nancy) Harris		Waterloo, London	scholar

ID	surname	given names	born	birthplace	father	mother	spouse 1	1851 residence	1851 occupation
21954	Cohen	Douglas	1807	Swansea, Wales	Jacob Cohen	Catherine (?)		?Liverpool	
16915	Cohen	Edward	1845	Sheffield, Yorkshire	Benjamin Cohen	Dinah (?)		Sheffield, Yorkshire	
23733	Cohen	Edward	1846	Liverpool	Aaron Judah Cohen	Flora Lyon		Liverpool	scholar
8451	Cohen	Edward	1847	Bristol	Simon Cohen	Mary Ann (?)		Portsmouth, Hampshire	
23647	Cohen	Edward	1850	Liverpool	Henry Cohen	Ann Moss		Liverpool	
969	Cohen	Edward Aaron	1835	Walworth, London	Abraham Aaron Cohen		Ellen Joseph	Exeter, Devon	boarding school pupil
17161	Cohen	Eleanor	1843	North Shields, Tyne & Wear	Abraham Cohen	Mary A (?)		Newcastle Upon Tyne	scholar
1617	Cohen	Eleazer	1801	Amsterdam, Holland			Elizabeth (?)	Spitalfields, London	general dealer
16914	Cohen	Elena	1844	Sheffield, Yorkshire	Benjamin Cohen	Dinah (?)		Sheffield, Yorkshire	
24238	Cohen	Elenor	1842	Whitechapel, London	Mark Cohen	Reyna (?)		Hackney, London	scholar at home
6300	Cohen	Elias	1824	Sheerness, Kent	D Cohen		Jane Phillips	Brighton, Sussex	cigar manufacturer
10518	Cohen	Elias	1837	?, London	Levy Jacob Cohen	Esther Isaacs	Catherine (Kate) Levy	Aldgate, London	scholar
21035	Cohen	Elias	1844	?, London				Dover, Kent	boarding school pupil
1489	Cohen	Elias	1846	Spitalfields, London	Sampson Cohen	Rebecca (?)		Spitalfields, London	scholar
1523	Cohen	Elias	1846	Spitalfields, London	Samuel Cohen	Rebecca Joseph		Aldgate, London	scholar
6258	Cohen	Eliza	1829	Chelmsford, Essex	Woolf Myers	Hannah Samuel	Barnet Solomon Cohen	St John's Wood, London	
23257	Cohen	Eliza	1836	Whitechapel, London	Isaac Cohen	Louisa (?)	Isidor Oelsner	Notting Hill, London	
27452	Cohen	Elizabeth	1771	Aldgate, London	(?)		(?) Cohen	Whitechapel, London	
10479	Cohen	Elizabeth	1779	?, Germany	(?)		(?) Cohen	Mile End, London	formerly broker
16525	Cohen	Elizabeth	1779	?abroad	(?)		Moses Cohen	Whitechapel, London	
28409	Cohen	Elizabeth	1791	Whitechapel, London	(?)		(?) Cohen	Spitalfields, London	general dealer
18356	Cohen	Elizabeth	1798	Marylebone, London	(?) Benjamin		Joseph Cohen	Elephant & Castle, London	furniture broker
1471	Cohen	Elizabeth	1799	Whitechapel, London	(?) Cohen			Spitalfields, London	cook
28227	Cohen	Elizabeth	1801	Spitalfields, London	(?)		(?) Cohen	Spitalfields, London	
1571	Cohen	Elizabeth	1802	Spitalfields, London	(?)		Michael Cohen	Spitalfields, London	
1581	Cohen	Elizabeth	1802	?, Holland	(?)		Henry Cohen	Spitalfields, London	general dealer
6283	Cohen	Elizabeth	1802	Finsbury, London	Samuel Cohen		Isaac Cohen	Finsbury, London	
1618	Cohen	Elizabeth	1807	Amsterdam, Holland			Eleazer Cohen	Spitalfields, London	
18588	Cohen	Elizabeth	1811	Aldgate, London	(?)		(?Abraham) Cohen	Stepney, London	
27279	Cohen	Elizabeth	1811	Walthamstow, London	(?)		Joseph Cohen	Aldgate, London	
6287	Cohen	Elizabeth	1812	Whitechapel, London	Jacob Myers		Ezekiel Cohen	Aldgate, London	
27551	Cohen	Elizabeth	1814	Aldgate, London	(?)		Hyam Cohen	Spitalfields, London	
11638	Cohen	Elizabeth	1819	Amsterdam, Holland	Solomon de Michael Busnach	Rachael de Moses de Juda	Abraham Cohen	Aldgate, London	dressmaker
1527	Cohen	Elizabeth	1823	Spitalfields, London	Hart Cohen			Spitalfields, London	general dealer
23042	Cohen	Elizabeth	1823	?, London	(?) Cohen			Aldgate, London	dressmaker
24640	Cohen	Elizabeth	1825	Whitechapel, London	(?)		(?) Cohen	Waterloo, London	clothes dealer
3377	Cohen	Elizabeth	1826	Middlesex, London	Benjamin Wolf Cohen	Frances Phillips		Holborn, London	
6586	Cohen	Elizabeth	1830	Middlesex, London	Lewis Harris	Leah Marks	Henry Cohen (Cohan)	Liverpool	
1573	Cohen	Elizabeth	1831	Aldgate, London	Michael Cohen	Elizabeth (?)		Spitalfields, London	dress maker
10517	Cohen	Elizabeth	1834	Aldgate, London	Levy Jacob Cohen	Esther Isaacs		Aldgate, London	waistcoat maker
17947	Cohen	Elizabeth	1834	?, London	Emanuel Cohen	Theresa (?)		Whitechapel, London	
15092	Cohen	Elizabeth	1839	Whitechapel, London	(?) Cohen			Mile End, London	scholar
16231	Cohen	Elizabeth	1839	Clerkenwell, London	Samuel Cohen	Rosetta (?)	Benjamin Lyons	Clerkenwell, London	scholar
22433	Cohen	Elizabeth	1842	?	(?) Cohen			Gravesend, Kent	boarding school pupil

ID	surname	given names	born	birthplace	father	mother	spouse 1	1851 residence	1851 occupation
1488	Cohen	Elizabeth	1843	Spitalfields, London	Sampson Cohen	Rebecca (?)		Spitalfields, London	scholar
4368	Cohen	Elizabeth	1849	Birmingham	Francis Cohen	Mary (?)		Birmingham	
3368	Cohen	Elizabeth (Betsey)	1842	Holborn, London	Daniel Cohen	Ann (Isabella) Solomon (Sailman)	William Thompson	Holborn, London	scholar
23252	Cohen	Elizabeth J	1825	Whitechapel, London	Isaac Cohen	Louisa (?)		Notting Hill, London	
11325	Cohen	Elizebeth	1841	Aldgate, London	Barnett Cohen	Hannah (?)		Aldgate, London	butcher
14093	Cohen	Ellen	1796	Hanover, Germany	(?)		(?) Cohen	Manchester	
1474	Cohen	Ellen	1799	Shoreditch, London	(?) Cohen			Spitalfields, London	servant
14422	Cohen	Ellen	1827	Lancaster, Lancashire	Yaacov			Salford, Lancashire	
7050	Cohen	Ellen	1828	Middlesex, London	Lazarus (Eleazer) Goodman	Catherine (?)	Moss (Moses) Cohen	Whitechapel, London	
3607	Cohen	Ellen	1843	Finsbury, London	Louis Cohen	Rebecca Floretta Keyser	Montagu (Samuel) Samuel [Montagu]	Finsbury, London	scholar at home
4390	Cohen	Ellen	1848	Birmingham	Joseph Colman Cohen	?Katie (?)		Birmingham	
12610	Cohen	Ellen Charlotte	1851	Norwich, Norfolk	Joseph L Cohen	Charlotte (?)		Norwich, Norfolk	
12818	Cohen	Elsy	1802	Aldgate, London	(?)		Henry Cohen	Southwark, London	clicker
10223	Cohen	Emanuel	1790	Whitechapel, London			Hannah (?)	Aldgate, London	general dealer
17943	Cohen	Emanuel	1793	Amsterdam, Holland			Theresa (?)	Whitechapel, London	sponge + cigar dealer
3897	Cohen	Emanuel	1804	Amsterdam, Holland			Sally (?)	Spitalfields, London	confectioner
4365	Cohen	Emanuel	1804	?, Holland				Birmingham	cigar mfr
5757	Cohen	Emanuel	1806	Finsbury, London				Spitalfields, London	porter
2703	Cohen	Emanuel	1817	?, England	Henry Cohen	Sarah Barrow?	Phoebe Cohen	Glasgow, Scotland	stationer
1624	Cohen	Emanuel	1823	Southwark, London			Esther (?)	Spitalfields, London	scourer
12606	Cohen	Emanuel	1841	Norwich, Norfolk	Joseph L Cohen	Charlotte (?)		Norwich, Norfolk	
21128	Cohen	Emanuel	1843	Aldgate, London	Benjamin Cohen	Bluma (?)		Aldgate, London	scholar
15754	Cohen	Emanuel	1848	Middlesex, London	Selim Cohen	Sarah Kahn		Aldgate, London	
28971	Cohen	Emanuel	1848	Aldgate, London	Solomon Isaac Cohen	Hannah Levie		Whitechapel, London	scholar
29793	Cohen	Emanuel	1850	Whitechapel, London	David Abraham Cohen	Hannah Solomon		Whitechapel, London	
26804	Cohen	Emily	1829	Sheerness, Kent	Daniel Cohen	Leah (?)		Aldgate, London	milliner
4385	Cohen	Emily	1845	Birmingham	Jacob Cohen	(?) (?)		Birmingham	scholar
2794	Cohen	Emma	1832	Finsbury, London	Joseph Cohen		Asher (Isaac) Jonas	Bermondsey, London	
27642	Cohen	Emma	1836	City, London	Benjamin Cohen	(?)		Aldgate, London	
9199	Cohen	Emma	1847	Finsbury, London	George Cohen	Hannah (?)	Aaron Solomon	Whitechapel, London	to school [---]
11864	Cohen	Emmanuel	1846	Amsterdam, Holland	(?) Cohen	(?)		Whitechapel, London	inmate of orphan school
15190	Cohen	Enoch	1834	?, London	Raphael (Ralph) Cohen	Abigail Torres		Shoreditch, London	cigar maker
4358	Cohen	Enoch Baruch	1833	?, London	Abraham Cohen	Hannah (?)	Deborah Barnett	Birmingham	confectioner
5227	Cohen	Ephraim	1830	Peizer, Poland	Lazarus Cohen	?Esther (?)	Fanny Levy	Leeds, Yorkshire	rabbi
17386	Cohen	Ephriam A	1847	Whitechapel, London	Lewis Cohen	Abigail Reuben		Wapping, London	scholar at home
27553	Cohen	Ester	1850	Aldgate, London	Hyam Cohen	Elizabeth (?)		Spitalfields, London	
779	Cohen	Esther	1788	Middlesex, London	Daniel Rees		Benjamin Benjamin	Soho, London	assistant (to husband)
1614	Cohen	Esther	1801	Amsterdam, Holland	Abraham Mathews	Phebhe (?)	Barnet Henry Cohen	Spitalfields, London	
8240	Cohen	Esther	1804	Aldgate, London	Moses Cohen	Elizabeth (?)		Whitechapel, London	
10516	Cohen	Esther	1809	?, London	Isaac Isaacs		Levy Jacob Cohen	Aldgate, London	waistcoat maker
21170	Cohen	Esther	1813	Aldgate, London	(?)		John Cohen	Aldgate, London	
26972	Cohen	Esther	1813	Aldgate, London	(?)		Joseph Cohen	Aldgate, London	
1562	Cohen	Esther	1816	?, Holland	Joseph HaLevi		Henry Cohen	Aldgate, London	

ID	surname	given names	born	birthplace	father	mother	spouse 1	1851 residence	1851 occupation
19460	Cohen	Esther	1818	Spitalfields, London	Hyam Moses		Abraham Cohen	Aldgate, London	
13390	Cohen	Esther	1822	?, London	Moshe Jacobs		Julius Cohen	Spitalfields, London	
4397	Cohen	Esther	1823	?, Poland [?, Prussia]			Morris Cohen	Birmingham	
11984	Cohen	Esther	1823	Aldgate, London	Jacob Cohen	Katherine (?)		Whitechapel, London	
25377	Cohen	Esther	1823	Middlesex, London	Moses Isaacs		Joseph Cohen	Clerkenwell, London	
1625	Cohen	Esther	1826	?, Holland	(?)		Emanuel Cohen	Spitalfields, London	washerwoman
2724	Cohen	Esther	1826	Aldgate, London	Moses Cohen	Fanny (?)		Aldgate, London	waistcoat maker
1548	Cohen	Esther	1827	Amsterdam, Holland	Isaiah Cohen			Spitalfields, London	cap maker
23819	Cohen	Esther	1831	?, Ireland	(?) Irwin	Margaret (?)	George Cohen	Liverpool	
28232	Cohen	Esther	1832	Spitalfields, London	Lewis Cohen	Deborah Michael		Spitalfields, London	cap maker
19711	Cohen	Esther	1834	Whitechapel, London	Herman Jacob Cohen	Rebecca Samuel		Whitechapel, London	
1480	Cohen	Esther	1835	Wapping, London	Phineas Cohen	Rebecca Hyams		Spitalfields, London	shopkeeper
29072	Cohen	Esther	1835	?, London	(?) Cohen			Covent Garden, London	servant
15191	Cohen	Esther	1836	?, London	Raphael (Ralph) Cohen	Abigail Torres		Shoreditch, London	scholar
23258	Cohen	Esther	1836	Hammersmith, London	Isaac Cohen	Louisa (?)		Notting Hill, London	
5680	Cohen	Esther	1837	?, London	Benjamin Cohen	Amelia (Mieje) van der Reis	Holfman Wolfe	Sunderland, Co Durham	
1515	Cohen	Esther	1839	Dublin, Ireland	Woolf Cohen	Hannah (Ann) Prince (Prins))		Spitalfields, London	day servant
19609	Cohen	Esther	1839	Spitalfields, London	David Cohen	Harriet Woolf		Spitalfields, London	
1487	Cohen	Esther	1841	Spitalfields, London	Sampson Cohen	Rebecca (?)		Spitalfields, London	scholar
30678	Cohen	Esther	1841	Spitalfields, London	David Cohen			Finsbury, London	
1541	Cohen	Esther	1843	Whitechapel, London	James Cohen	Sarah (?)		Spitalfields, London	scholar
11063	Cohen	Esther	1844	Aldgate, London	Samuel Cohen	Hannah Phillips		Aldgate, London	
2188	Cohen	Esther	1846	Oxford, Oxfordshire	Isaac Jacob Cohen	Sarah Levi	Simon Henschel	Oxford, Oxfordshire	
5154	Cohen	Esther	1846	Spitalfields, London	Judah Cohen	Caroline Davis		Wapping, London	
1508	Cohen	Esther	1847	Spitalfields, London	Mark Cohen	Rachel (?)		Spitalfields, London	scholar
27630	Cohen	Esther	1847	?Aldgate, London	Judah Cohen	Rachel Solomon		Aldgate, London	scholar
6282	Cohen	Esther	1848	Aldgate, London	Michael Cohen	Bloomah (?)		Aldgate, London	
4391	Cohen	Esther	1849	Birmingham	Joseph Colman Cohen	?Katie (?)		Birmingham	
19660	Cohen	Esther	1849	Spitalfields, London	Joseph Cohen	Rebecca Lazarus		Spitalfields, London	
4376	Cohen	Esther	1850	Birmingham	Israel Cohen	Jane (?)		Birmingham	
8250	Cohen	Esther	1850	Islington, London	Philip Cohen	Deborah (Dora) Levy		Shoreditch, London	
23888	Cohen	Esther	1850	Westminster, London	Solomon Hyman Cohen	Ann Davis		Westminster, London	
22620	Cohen	Esther?	1828	Whitechapel, London	Asher Cohen	Rachel (?)		Stepney, London	boot binder
13132	Cohen	Eve	1798	King's Lynn, Norfolk	(?) Dorris		(?) Cohen	Hoxton, London	
8241	Cohen	Evelina	1848	Whitechapel, London	Isaac Cohen	Louisa Cowan		Aldgate, London	
25600	Cohen	Eveline	1833	Dublin, Ireland	Joseph Wolfe Cohen	Rebecca Lazarus	Joseph Isaacs	Dublin, Ireland	
1605	Cohen	Evy	1841	Spitalfields, London	Isaiah Cohen	Rosa Solomon		Spitalfields, London	tailoress
6286	Cohen	Ezekiel	1809	Spitalfields, London	Isaac HaCohen		Elizabeth Myers	Aldgate, London	pastry cook
25787	Cohen	Ezekiel	1841	Aldgate, London	Solomon Cohen	Catherine Myers		Aldgate, London	scholar
4381	Cohen	F---	1834	Birmingham	Jacob Cohen	(?) (?)		Birmingham	scholar
4382	Cohen	F---	1835	Birmingham	Jacob Cohen	(?) (?)		Birmingham	scholar
2719	Cohen	Fanny	1786	Aldgate, London			Moses Cohen	Aldgate, London	
6289	Cohen	Fanny	1821	Middlesex, London	(?) Millingen		Abraham Mark Cohen	Bloomsbury, London	
18263	Cohen	Fanny	1826	?, Poland [?, Prussia]	Daniel Cohen	Sarah (?)		Boston, Lincolnshire	

ID	surname	given names	born	birthplace	father	mother	spouse 1	1851 residence	1851 occupation
30909	Cohen	Fanny	1831	Norwich, Norfolk	Solomon Cohen	Rachel (?)		Lincoln, Lincolnshire	silversmith &c
6127	Cohen	Fanny	1833	Spitalfields, London	Lewis (Lyon) Cohen	Harriet Lear	Moss (Moses) Emanuel	Spitalfields, London	tailoress
26100	Cohen	Fanny	1843	?, London	(?) Cohen	Rebecca (?)		Aldgate, London	scholar
30403	Cohen	Fanny	1851	Aldgate, London	Abraham Cohen	Esther Moses		Aldgate, London	
11968	Cohen	Flora	1814	?, Holland	(?)		Moses Cohen	Whitechapel, London	general dealer
23732	Cohen	Flora	1822	Liverpool	(?) Lyon		Aaron Judah Cohen	Liverpool	dressmaker
24659	Cohen	Flora	1822	Paddington, London	(?)		Zachariah Cohen	Kennington, London	
23253	Cohen	Flora	1827	Whitechapel, London	Isaac Cohen	Louisa (?)		Notting Hill, London	
19710	Cohen	Flora	1833	?Whitechapel, London	Herman Jacob Cohen	Rebecca Samuel	Philipp Meyer	Whitechapel, London	
11140	Cohen	Frances	1782	Aldgate, London	(?)		(?) Cohen	Aldgate, London	governess
3357	Cohen	Frances	1792	Middlesex, London	(Alexander?) (Pais Lemon-man)Phillips		Benjamin Wolf Cohen	Holborn, London	
23054	Cohen	Frances	1801	City, London	(?) Cohen			Aldgate, London	
16526	Cohen	Frances	1812	Aldgate, London	Moses Cohen	Elizabeth (?)		Whitechapel, London	
1510	Cohen	Frances	1814	Spitalfields, London	(?) Cohen			Spitalfields, London	fruit seller
27310	Cohen	Frances	1819	Aldgate, London	(?) Cohen			Aldgate, London	cap maker
12612	Cohen	Frances	1825	?, London	(?)		Lazarus Cohen	Wymondham, Norfolk	
17536	Cohen	Frances	1829	Aldgate, London	Joseph Hyams		Daniel Cohen	Spitalfields, London	
21755	Cohen	Frances	1831	Aldgate, London	Ezekiel Cohen	Elizabeth Myers	Joseph Samuels	Aldgate, London	
16229	Cohen	Frances	1833	Clerkenwell, London	Samuel Cohen	Rosetta (?)		Clerkenwell, London	
22198	Cohen	Frances	1837	Bristol	Cosman Cohen	Sarah (?)		Whitechapel, London	dressmaker
25389	Cohen	Frances	1840	Holborn, London	Aaron Cohen	Rachel (?)		Clerkenwell, London	scholar
19715	Cohen	Frances	1843	Whitechapel, London	Herman Jacob Cohen	Rebecca Samuel		Whitechapel, London	
3370	Cohen	Frances (Fanny)	1848	Holborn, London	Daniel Cohen	Ann (Isabella) Solomon (Sailman)	Isaac Solomon	Holborn, London	
4366	Cohen	Francis	1820	?, London			Mary (?)	Birmingham	cigar mfr
1763	Cohen	Francois Antoine	1848	Cardiff, Wales	Marinus Thomas Cohen (CHECK)	Frederica Hanna (?)		Cardiff, Wales	
13645	Cohen	Franklin	1825	?, Poland			Ann (?)	Manchester	shoe mfr
1760	Cohen	Frederica Hanna	1814	?, Holland			Marinus Thomas Cohen (CHECK)	Cardiff, Wales	
16221	Cohen	Frederick J	1850	Middlesex, London	Henry Cohen	Caroline S (?)	Constance (?)	Paddington, London	
29380	Cohen	George	1818	Whitechapel, London	Lazarus Cohen		Rachel (?)	Wapping, London	clothier master
9195	Cohen	George	1821	Whitechapel, London	Henry Davis		Hannah Mordecai	Whitechapel, London	stay maker
5986	Cohen	George	1823	Whitechapel, London			Esther Irwin	Liverpool	draper + outfitter
1619	Cohen	George	1824	Amsterdam, Holland				Spitalfields, London	tailor empl 1
3332	Cohen	George	1828	Whitechapel, London	Moss Cohen	Sarah Hart	Sarah Isaacs	Spitalfields, London	dealer in iron
25786	Cohen	George	1840	Aldgate, London	Solomon Cohen	Catherine Myers		Aldgate, London	scholar
17330	Cohen	George	1848	Spitalfields, London	Benjamin Cohen	Rebecca (?)		Spitalfields, London	
5155	Cohen	George Solomon	1847	Wapping, London	Judah Cohen	Caroline Davis	Catherine Franks	Wapping, London	
19461	Cohen	Golda	1838	Aldgate, London	Abraham Cohen	Esther Moses		Aldgate, London	
16491	Cohen	H---	1781	Gibraltar	(?) Cohen			Mile End, London	
30690	Cohen	H---	1803	Whitechapel, London	(?)		Asher John Cohen	Whitechapel, London	house agent + appraiser
12602	Cohen	H---	1813	?, Poland				Norwich, Norfolk	dealer
21744	Cohen	Hannah	1778	Aldgate, London	Moses Samuel		Solomon Cohen	Canonbury, London	retired merchant

ID	surname	given names	born	birthplace	father	mother	spouse 1	1851 residence	1851 occupation
1478	Cohen	Hannah	1789	Aldgate, London	(?)		(?) Cohen	Spitalfields, London	fruit seller
22828	Cohen	Hannah	1799	Middlesex, London	(?)		Joseph Cohen	Whitechapel, London	
11324	Cohen	Hannah	1801	Aldgate, London			Barnett Cohen	Aldgate, London	
10224	Cohen	Hannah	1803	Aldgate, London	(?)		Emanuel Cohen	Aldgate, London	
4357	Cohen	Hannah	1807	?, London			Abraham Cohen	Birmingham	
20690	Cohen	Hannah	1807	Spitalfields, London			Moses Cohen	Spitalfields, London	general dealer
29787	Cohen	Hannah	1812	Spitalfields, London	Samuel Solomon		David Abraham Cohen	Whitechapel, London	
6354	Cohen	Hannah	1814	Aldgate, London	Yehuda Leib Phillips		Samuel Cohen	Aldgate, London	
17652	Cohen	Hannah	1815	?, Poland	(?)		Solomon Cohen	Aldgate, London	
28964	Cohen	Hannah	1819	Leyden, Holland	Menachem Levie		Solomon Isaac Cohen	Whitechapel, London	wholesale clothes dealer
1580	Cohen	Hannah	1821	Strood, Kent				Spitalfields, London	
1598	Cohen	Hannah	1821	Aldgate, London	(?)		(?) Cohen	Spitalfields, London	cloth cap maker
9196	Cohen	Hannah	1822	Strand, London	Benjamin Mordecai		George Cohen	Whitechapel, London	stay maker
1596	Cohen	Hannah	1823	Birmingham				Spitalfields, London	dress maker
27915	Cohen	Hannah	1825	Aldgate, London	(?)		Myer Cohen	Spitalfields, London	
25448	Cohen	Hannah	1826	Amsterdam, Holland	(?) Cohen			Spitalfields, London	servant
4370	Cohen	Hannah	1827	Paris, France				Birmingham	general dealer
1572	Cohen	Hannah	1830	Aldgate, London	Michael Cohen	Elizabeth (?)		Spitalfields, London	tailoress
3336	Cohen	Hannah	1830	Whitechapel, London	Moss Cohen	Sarah Hart	Samuel Harris	Spitalfields, London	waistcoat maker
27554	Cohen	Hannah	1835	Aldgate, London	(?) Cohen			Spitalfields, London	servant
1105	Cohen	Hannah	1837	Penzance, Cornwall	(?) Cohen	Rose (?)	E S Hart	Falmouth, Cornwall	milliner's apprentice
21756	Cohen	Hannah	1837	Whitechapel, London	Ezekiel Cohen	Elizabeth Myers	Abraham Levy	Aldgate, London	
29062	Cohen	Hannah	1840	Whitechapel, London	Simon Cohen	Isabella (?)		Whitechapel, London	scholar
15194	Cohen	Hannah	1841	?, London	Raphael (Ralph) Cohen	Abigail Torres		Shoreditch, London	scholar
23882	Cohen	Hannah	1841	Holborn, London	Solomon Hyman Cohen	Ann Davis		Westminster, London	
25370	Cohen	Hannah	1842	Holborn, London	Henry Cohen	Rosetta (?)		Clerkenwell, London	scholar
1606	Cohen	Hannah	1843	Spitalfields, London	Isaiah Cohen	Rosa Solomon		Spitalfields, London	scholar
19463	Cohen	Hannah	1845	Aldgate, London	Abraham Cohen	Esther Moses		Aldgate, London	
3360	Cohen	Hannah	1847	Holborn, London	Nathan Cohen	Deborah Cohen	Morris L Jacobs	Holborn, London	
1567	Cohen	Hannah	1848	Spitalfields, London	Henry Cohen	Esther Levy		Spitalfields, London	
1545	Cohen	Hannah	1849	Spitalfields, London	Moses Cohen	Clara Michael		Spitalfields, London	
10397	Cohen	Hannah	1850	Spitalfields, London	Philip Cohen	Rachael Jacobs		Spitalfields, London	
1585	Cohen	Hannah	1851	Spitalfields, London	Henry Cohen	Sarah (?)		Spitalfields, London	
3314	Cohen	Hannah	1851	Whitechapel, London	George Cohen	Sarah Isaacs	Lewis Levy	Aldgate, London	
24285	Cohen	Hannah	1802	Middlesex, London	Yechiel HaCohen Oppenheim		Andrew Cohen	Bloomsbury, London	
1511	Cohen	Hannah (Ann)	1800	?, Holland [Lutkind, Gilderland]	Asher Prince	Amelia (?)	Woolf Cohen	Spitalfields, London	
13330	Cohen	Harriet	1804	Soho, London	(?) Woolf		David Cohen	Spitalfields, London	
2617	Cohen	Harriet	1806	Plymouth, Devon	(?)		Simon M Cohen	Glasgow, Scotland	
1607	Cohen	Harriet	1809	Spitalfields, London	Isaac Lear		Lewis (Lyon) Cohen	Spitalfields, London	nurse
26802	Cohen	Harriet	1816	Chatham, Kent	Daniel Cohen	Leah (?)		Aldgate, London	shopwoman
23984	Cohen	Harriet	1817	Marylebone, London	(?)		(?) Cohen	Marylebone, London	laundress
1525	Cohen	Harriet	1850	Spitalfields, London	Samuel Cohen	Rebecca Joseph	Henry Haim Gomes Da Costa	Aldgate, London	
2396	Cohen	Harriet	1850	Hull, Yorkshire	(?) Cohen	Rosalie (?)		Hull, Yorkshire	

ID	surname	given names	born	birthplace	father	mother	spouse 1	1851 residence	1851 occupation
11755	Cohen	Harris	1826	?, Poland [?, Prussia]				Shoreditch, London	hawker
4371	Cohen	Harris	1827	?, Poland				Birmingham	hawker
18299	Cohen	Harris	1829	?, Russia	Moses Cohen	Jane (?)	Phoebe Herman	Sheffield, Yorkshire	hawker
13568	Cohen	Harris	1831	Poznan, Poland [Posen, Prussia]				Manchester	glazier
2189	Cohen	Harris	1848	Oxford, Oxfordshire	Isaac Jacob Cohen	Sarah Levi		Oxford, Oxfordshire	
22434	Cohen	Harry	1847	?				Gravesend, Kent	boarding school pupil
1526	Cohen	Hart	1776	?, Holland				Spitalfields, London	general dealer
2618	Cohen	Hart	1802	Sunderland, Co Durham				Glasgow, Scotland	traveller
2622	Cohen	Helen	1841	?, England	Joseph Cohen	Rachel Goodman		Glasgow, Scotland	scholar
14757	Cohen	Henrietta	1794	Whitechapel, London	(?)		Moses Cohen	Finsbury, London	
2826	Cohen	Henrietta	1814	Chatham, Kent	Lazarus Magnus	Sarah Moses	Victor Cohen	Spitalfields, London	
19712	Cohen	Henrietta	1836	Whitechapel, London	Herman Jacob Cohen	Rebecca Samuel		Whitechapel, London	
3634	Cohen	Henrietta	1838	Finsbury, London	Louis Cohen	Rebecca Floretta Keyser	Assur Henry Moses	Finsbury, London	scholar at home
21367	Cohen	Henrietta Rachael	1828	?, England	Joseph Salamons		Lionel Benjamin Cohen	Marylebone, London	
1582	Cohen	Henry	1802	?, Holland			Elizabeth (?)	Spitalfields, London	general dealer
12817	Cohen	Henry	1802	Southwark, London			Elsy (?)	Southwark, London	master shoemaker
25366	Cohen	Henry	1813	Holborn, London			Rosetta Levy	Clerkenwell, London	iron founder
1561	Cohen	Henry	1815	Aldgate, London	Aryeh Leib Cohen		Esther Levy	Aldgate, London	fruit dealer
17058	Cohen	Henry	1815	?, London				Edinburgh, Scotland	fustie maker
4372	Cohen	Henry	1817	?, Germany				Birmingham	dealer in watch materials
7048	Cohen	Henry	1819	Herne Hill, London			Caroline S (?)	Paddington, London	stockbroker
5124	Cohen	Henry	1820	?			Elizabeth (?)	Sheffield, Yorkshire	tobacconist
6742	Cohen	Henry	1820	Middlesex, London	Henry Cohen	Sarah (?)	Elizabeth Harris	Liverpool	draper + outfitter
1473	Cohen	Henry	1825	?, Denmark				Spitalfields, London	furrier journeyman
29309	Cohen	Henry	1825	Whitechapel, London			Margaret (?)	Wapping, London	dealer in marine stores
12682	Cohen	Henry	1826	?, Germany			Mary A (?)	Norwich, Norfolk	printer (journeyman)
3378	Cohen	Henry	1828	Middlesex, London	Benjamin Wolf Cohen	Frances Phillips		Holborn, London	
28410	Cohen	Henry	1828	Whitechapel, London	(?) Cohen	Elizabeth (?)		Spitalfields, London	general dealer
1586	Cohen	Henry	1829	?, Holland			Sarah (?)	Spitalfields, London	cigar maker
22829	Cohen	Henry	1830	Middlesex, London	Joseph Cohen	Hannah (?)		Whitechapel, London	cabinet maker
22927	Cohen	Henry	1830	Wapping, London				Wapping, London	errand boy
29999	Cohen	Henry	1832	Brighton, Sussex	Solomon Cohen	Susan (?)		Brighton, Sussex	
1522	Cohen	Henry	1835	Strand, London	Samuel Cohen	Rebecca Joseph		Aldgate, London	cigar maker
1469	Cohen	Henry	1836	Spitalfields, London				Spitalfields, London	general dealer
1621	Cohen	Henry	1837	Amsterdam, Holland	Eleazer Cohen	Elizabeth (?)		Spitalfields, London	cigar maker
25388	Cohen	Henry	1837	Holborn, London	Aaron Cohen	Rachel (?)		Clerkenwell, London	scholar
21288	Cohen	Henry	1838	Essaouira, Morocco [Mogaore, Africa]				Edmonton, London	boarding school pupil
18360	Cohen	Henry	1841	Southwark, London	Joseph Cohen	Elizabeth Benjamin	Esther Cashmore	Elephant & Castle, London	scholar
25982	Cohen	Henry	1841	Aldgate, London	Lipman Cohen	Jane Isaacs		Aldgate, London	scholar
12331	Cohen	Henry	1843	Marylebone, London	(?) Cohen	(?) ?Lyons		Marylebone, London	scholar
24820	Cohen	Henry	1843	?, London	Samuel Cohen	Ann (Nancy) Harris	Julia Solomons	Waterloo, London	scholar
25371	Cohen	Henry	1844	Holborn, London	Henry Cohen	Rosetta (?)		Clerkenwell, London	scholar

ID	surname	given names	born	birthplace	father	mother	spouse 1	1851 residence	1851 occupation
9198	Cohen	Henry	1845	Finsbury, London	George Cohen	Hannah (?)		Whitechapel, London	to school [---]
1626	Cohen	Henry	1846	Aldgate, London	Emanuel Cohen	Esther (?)		Spitalfields, London	
3903	Cohen	Henry	1846	Amsterdam, Holland	Emanuel Cohen	Sally (?)		Spitalfields, London	
26645	Cohen	Henry	1846	Whitechapel, London	Samuel Cohen	Mary (?)		Aldgate, London	scholar
2829	Cohen	Henry	1847	Whitechapel, London	Victor Cohen	Henrietta Magnus		Spitalfields, London	
17162	Cohen	Henry	1847	North Shields, Tyne & Wear	Abraham Cohen	Mary A (?)		Newcastle Upon Tyne	
12608	Cohen	Henry	1848	Norwich, Norfolk	Joseph L Cohen	Charlotte (?)		Norwich, Norfolk	
27917	Cohen	Henry	1849	Whitechapel, London	Myer Cohen	Hannah (?)		Spitalfields, London	
18422	Cohen	Henry Aron	1822	Southwark, London			Annetta Castle Levy	Elephant & Castle, London	general merchant
23821	Cohen	Henry David	1834	?, Germany	David Cohen			Liverpool	optician
19702	Cohen	Henry Lewis	1835	?, London	Moses Cohen	Elizabeth Nathan	Priscilla Joseph	Elephant & Castle, London	
7045	Cohen	Henry Louis	1827	Finsbury, London	Louis Cohen	Rebecca Floretta Keyser	Ellen de Castro	Finsbury, London	clerk
16219	Cohen	Herbert	1847	Middlesex, London	Henry Cohen	Caroline S (?)		Paddington, London	
16288	Cohen	Herman	1820	?, Germany				Dundee, Scotland	
19708	Cohen	Herman Jacob	1795	?, Holland	Yaacov Hacohen		Rebecca Samuel	Whitechapel, London	merchant
8581	Cohen	Humphrey	1782	City, London			Louisa (?)	Soho, London	master tailor
27550	Cohen	Hyam	1810	Westminster, London			Elizabeth (?)	Spitalfields, London	metal merchant
1470	Cohen	Hyam	1838	Spitalfields, London				Spitalfields, London	
19462	Cohen	Hyam	1842	Spitalfields, London	Abraham Cohen	Esther Moses		Aldgate, London	
1543	Cohen	Hyam	1850	Spitalfields, London	James Cohen	Sarah (?)		Spitalfields, London	
31182	Cohen	Hyman	1807	Southwark, London			Maria (?)	Gravesend, Kent	bottle merchant
6290	Cohen	Hyman	1820	Plymouth, Devon			Caroline (?)	Mile End, London	paper hanging manufacturer empl 11
21078	Cohen	Hyman	1839	Westminster, London				Dover, Kent	boarding school pupil
24641	Cohen	Hyman	1849	Strand, London	(?) Cohen	Elizabeth (?)		Waterloo, London	
7603	Cohen	I---	1825	?				Dover, Kent	
29063	Cohen	I---	1843	Whitechapel, London	Simon Cohen	Isabella (?)		Whitechapel, London	
28167	Cohen	Isaac	1775	City, London				Spitalfields, London	general dealer
31024	Cohen	Isaac	1789	?, Holland				Newcastle Upon Tyne	Beadle of the Synagogue
30457	Cohen	Isaac	1791	?, Poland				Newcastle-under-Lyme, Staffordshire	hawker
4373	Cohen	Isaac	1811	?, Germany				Birmingham	hawker
18535	Cohen	Isaac	1813	Finsbury, London	Benjamin Zeev Wolf Cohen		Elizabeth Cohen	Finsbury, London	fishmonger
6656	Cohen	Isaac	1818	Middlesex, London	Joshua Cohen		Louisa Cowan	Aldgate, London	clothes dealer
11704	Cohen	Isaac	1829	Southwark, London	Abraham Cohen	Deborah Genese	Fanny Benjamin	Aldgate, London	scourer
13133	Cohen	Isaac	1829	King's Lynn, Norfolk	(?) Cohen	Eve (?)		Hoxton, London	leather cutter
27570	Cohen	Isaac	1829	Whitechapel, London	Joseph Cohen	Clara Cohen		Spitalfields, London	tailor
7145	Cohen	Isaac	1832	Lambeth, London	Henry Cohen	Elsy (?)		Spitalfields, London	butcher
1583	Cohen	Isaac	1833	Middlesex, London	Henry Cohen	Elizabeth (?)		Spitalfields, London	general dealer
25784	Cohen	Isaac	1834	Aldgate, London	Solomon Cohen	Catherine Myers		Aldgate, London	confectioner
25387	Cohen	Isaac	1835	Holborn, London	Aaron Cohen	Rachel (?)		Clerkenwell, London	engineer's apprentice
11249	Cohen	Isaac	1836	Liverpool	Phillip Cohen	Catharine (?)		Aldgate, London	
22832	Cohen	Isaac	1837	Middlesex, London	Joseph Cohen	Hannah (?)		Whitechapel, London	baker

ID	surname	given names	born	birthplace	father	mother	spouse 1	1851 residence	1851 occupation
19911	Cohen	Isaac	1839	Amsterdam, Holland	Philip Cohen	Rose Abrahams	Elizabeth Phillips	Spitalfields, London	scholar
19154	Cohen	Isaac	1843	Aldgate, London	Leman Cohen	Clara Lyon		Aldgate, London	scholar
28968	Cohen	Isaac	1843	Aldgate, London	Solomon Isaac Cohen	Hannah Levie		Whitechapel, London	scholar
11860	Cohen	Isaac	1844	Middlesex, London	(?) Cohen	(?)		Whitechapel, London	inmate of orphan school
15196	Cohen	Isaac	1844	?, London	Raphael (Ralph) Cohen	Abigail Torres	Hannah Cohen	Shoreditch, London	scholar
5165	Cohen	Isaac	1846	Spitalfields, London	Barnet Cohen	Sarah Hyman		Spitalfields, London	
10521	Cohen	Isaac	1848	?, London	Levy Jacob Cohen	Esther Isaacs	Sophia Solomons	Aldgate, London	scholar
1490	Cohen	Isaac	1849	Spitalfields, London	Sampson Cohen	Rebecca (?)		Spitalfields, London	scholar
8249	Cohen	Isaac	1849	Islington, London	Philip Cohen	Deborah (Dora) Levy		Shoreditch, London	
19465	Cohen	Isaac	1850	Aldgate, London	Abraham Cohen	Esther Moses		Aldgate, London	
13086	Cohen	Isaac Henry	1819	Whitechapel, London				Southwark, London	convict + cheese factor
2186	Cohen	Isaac Jacob	1818	?, Poland			Sarah Levi	Oxford, Oxfordshire	jeweller
7044	Cohen	Isaac Louis	1844	Finsbury, London	Louis Cohen	Rebecca Floretta Keyser		Finsbury, London	scholar at home
29057	Cohen	Isabella	1806	Aldgate, London	Yehuda Leib		Simon Cohen	Whitechapel, London	
22225	Cohen	Isabella	1833	Middlesex, London	Aaron Cohen	(?)		Whitechapel, London	pawnbroker
2397	Cohen	Isabella	1848	Hull, Yorkshire	(?) Cohen	Rosalie Bremer		Hull, Yorkshire	
1547	Cohen	Isaiah	1791	Amsterdam, Holland				Spitalfields, London	general dealer
5878	Cohen	Isaiah Henry	1828	?England	Henry Cohen	Sarah Barrow?	Elizabeth Phillips	?London	
21046	Cohen	Isidor	1840	Canterbury, Kent				Dover, Kent	boarding school pupil
22903	Cohen	Israel	1781	?, Germany				Wapping, London	clothes dealer
5409	Cohen	Israel	1823	Middlesex, London	Emanuel Cohen	Trevena? (?)	Rachel Isaacs	Whitechapel, London	sponge dealer
4374	Cohen	Israel	1826	?, Russia			Jane (?)	Birmingham	waterproofer
11863	Cohen	Israel	1840	Amsterdam, Holland	(?) Cohen	(?)		Whitechapel, London	inmate of orphan school
29128	Cohen	Israel	1840	Whitechapel, London	Moses Cohen	Rebecca (?)		Whitechapel, London	tailor
22935	Cohen	Jacob	1789	Whitechapel, London	Jacob Cohen	(?)		Wapping, London	dealer
20652	Cohen	Jacob	1795	?, Russia [?, Rushland]				Spitalfields, London	
13600	Cohen	Jacob	1801	?, Poland [?, Prussia]				Manchester	hawker of jewellery
4379	Cohen	Jacob	1803	?, Poland [?, Prussia]			(?)	Birmingham	merchant
11982	Cohen	Jacob	1805	?, Poland			Katherine (?)	Whitechapel, London	butcher
23825	Cohen	Jacob	1809	?, Russia				Liverpool	hawker
20692	Cohen	Jacob	1810	Amsterdam, Holland	Solomon Cohen		Rosetta Lyon	Spitalfields, London	butcher
24734	Cohen	Jacob	1811	Southwark, London	Philip Cohen	Jane (?)		Southwark, London	bottle merchant
27003	Cohen	Jacob	1815	Amsterdam, Holland			Rachael (?)	Aldgate, London	agent
14083	Cohen	Jacob	1828	?, Poland [?, Prussia]				Manchester	watch maker
23056	Cohen	Jacob	1829	Gdansk, Poland [Dantsic, Prussia]				Aldgate, London	lithographer
21787	Cohen	Jacob	1831	?, Germany				Aldgate, London	shoe maker
13586	Cohen	Jacob	1832	Inowroclaw, Poland [Inauroclau, Prussia]				Manchester	hawker of jewellery
1620	Cohen	Jacob	1835	Amsterdam, Holland	Eleazer Cohen	Elizabeth (?)		Spitalfields, London	cigar maker
12776	Cohen	Jacob	1839	Whitechapel, London				Aldgate, London	scholar
9268	Cohen	Jacob	1840	?, Holland	Myers S Cohen	Jane (?)		Aldgate, London	apprentice cigar maker
11866	Cohen	Jacob	1841	Middlesex, London	(?) Cohen	(?)		Whitechapel, London	inmate of orphan school
11966	Cohen	Jacob	1846	Whitechapel, London	Moses Cohen	Flora (?)		Whitechapel, London	
15197	Cohen	Jacob	1846	?, London	Raphael (Ralph) Cohen	Abigail Torres		Shoreditch, London	

ID	surname	given names	born	birthplace	father	mother	spouse 1	1851 residence	1851 occupation
12613	Cohen	Jacob	1850	Norwich, Norfolk	Lazarus Cohen	Frances (?)		Wymondham, Norfolk	
21761	Cohen	Jacob (James)	1846	Aldgate, London	Ezekiel Cohen	Elizabeth Myers		Aldgate, London	
2721	Cohen	Jacob (John)	1819	Aldgate, London	Moses Cohen	Fanny (?)	Alice Moses	Aldgate, London	general dealer
19721	Cohen	Jacob Herman	1838	Middlesex, London	Herman Jacob Cohen	Rebecca Samuel	Sarah Weiller	Whitechapel, London	
16955	Cohen	Jacob Moses	1781	?, Isle of Wight			(?)	Hammersmith, London	annuitant
13392	Cohen	Jahab	1833	?	(?Ezekiel) HaCohen			Spitalfields, London	tailor
1601	Cohen	James	1778	Aldgate, London				Spitalfields, London	
4386	Cohen	James	1806	?, Ireland				Birmingham	pawnbroker
1539	Cohen	James	1819	Aldgate, London	Moshe Cohen		Sarah (?Moses)	Spitalfields, London	general dealer
12816	Cohen	James	1830	Southwark, London	Henry Cohen	Elsy (?)		Southwark, London	butcher
24733	Cohen	Jane	1778	?, England	(?)		Philip Cohen	Southwark, London	
18298	Cohen	Jane	1807	?, Russia	(?)		Moses Cohen	Sheffield, Yorkshire	
9266	Cohen	Jane	1811	?, Holland	(?)		Myers S Cohen	Aldgate, London	
25981	Cohen	Jane	1817	Spitalfields, London	(?) Isaacs		Lipman Cohen	Aldgate, London	
25544	Cohen	Jane	1824	?	(?)		Lewis (Louis) Cohen	Dublin, Ireland	snuff + tobacco dealer
12600	Cohen	Jane	1825	Whitechapel, London	Moses Cohen	Sophia (?)		Norwich, Norfolk	
4375	Cohen	Jane	1828	?, Russia			Israel Cohen	Birmingham	
28966	Cohen	Jane	1839	Aldgate, London	Solomon Isaac Cohen	Hannah Levie		Whitechapel, London	scholar
23883	Cohen	Jane	1843	Holborn, London	Solomon Hyman Cohen	Ann Davis		Westminster, London	
21763	Cohen	Jane	1850	Aldgate, London	Ezekiel Cohen	Elizabeth Myers		Aldgate, London	
19718	Cohen	Jane (Jeanette)	1846	Whitechapel, London	Herman Jacob Cohen	Rebecca Samuel	Judah Henriques Valentine	Whitechapel, London	
29233	Cohen	Jeanette	1791	?, Germany	(?)		(?) Cohen	Whitechapel, London	tailoress
1604	Cohen	Jenett	1838	Spitalfields, London	Isaiah Cohen	Rosa Solomon		Spitalfields, London	tailoress
11059	Cohen	Jesey	1837	Bloomsbury, London	Samuel Cohen	Hannah (?Phillips)		Aldgate, London	
11707	Cohen	Jesse (Simha)	1837	Aldgate, London	Abraham Cohen	Deborah Genese		Aldgate, London	
1592	Cohen	John	1796	Aldgate, London			Phoebe (?)	Spitalfields, London	clothes salesman
21169	Cohen	John	1809	Aldgate, London			Esther (?)	Aldgate, London	clothes dealer
15067	Cohen	John	1822	Bristol			Louisa (?)	Bethnal Green, London	sealing wax maker + preacher
22830	Cohen	John	1832	Middlesex, London	Joseph Cohen	Hannah (?)		Whitechapel, London	cigar maker
13917	Cohen	John	1834	Aldgate, London				Manchester	salesman to tailor + draper
21127	Cohen	John	1841	Aldgate, London	Benjamin Cohen	Bluma (?)		Aldgate, London	scholar
15069	Cohen	John	1844	Stepney, London	John Cohen	Louisa (?)		Bethnal Green, London	scholar
25390	Cohen	John	1844	Holborn, London	Aaron Cohen	Rachel (?)		Clerkenwell, London	scholar
15575	Cohen	John	1848	City, London	(?) Cohen	Rosa (?)		Covent Garden, London	
970	Cohen	John Aaron	1837	Walworth, London	Abraham Aaron Cohen		Amelia Joseph	Exeter, Devon	boarding school pupil
14408	Cohen	John William	1820	abroad				Manchester	salesman
1528	Cohen	Jonas	1829	Spitalfields, London	Hart Cohen			Spitalfields, London	general dealer
20697	Cohen	Joseph	1844	Aldgate, London	Jacob Cohen	Rosetta Lyon		Spitalfields, London	scholar
22827	Cohen	Joseph	1797	Middlesex, London			Hannah (?)	Whitechapel, London	furniture broker
98	Cohen	Joseph	1800	Woolwich, London	? Eleazer Cohen		Charlotte (?)	Woolwich, London	schoolmaster
27278	Cohen	Joseph	1801	Aldgate, London			Elizabeth (?)	Aldgate, London	tobacconist
2619	Cohen	Joseph	1805	?, Germany	Moshe Cohen		Rachel Goodman	Glasgow, Scotland	leech merchant

ID	surname	given names	born	birthplace	father	mother	spouse 1	1851 residence	1851 occupation
10565	Cohen	Joseph	1819	Poznan, Poland [Posen, Prussia]			Maria (?)	Whitechapel, London	tailor
25376	Cohen	Joseph	1819	Middlesex, London	Joshua Cohen		Esther Isaacs	Clerkenwell, London	rag merchant
14522	Cohen	Joseph	1820	Paris, France				Bideford, Devon	commercial traveller
19655	Cohen	Joseph	1821	Whitechapel, London	David Cohen	Harriet (?)	Rebecca Lazarus	Spitalfields, London	cab driver
15087	Cohen	Joseph	1822	Whitechapel, London			Catharine (?)	Mile End, London	rag merchant
26971	Cohen	Joseph	1822	Warsaw, Poland [Warschau, Prussia]			Esther (?)	Aldgate, London	clothier
11722	Cohen	Joseph	1828	Spitalfields, London				Aldgate, London	general dealer
1514	Cohen	Joseph	1835	Whitechapel, London	Woolf Cohen	Hannah (Ann) Prince (Prins))		Spitalfields, London	general dealer
24237	Cohen	Joseph	1839	Stepney, London	Mark Cohen	Reyna (?)		Hackney, London	scholar at home
4360	Cohen	Joseph	1840	Birmingham	Abraham Cohen	Hannah (?)	Abigail Abrahams	Birmingham	scholar
26099	Cohen	Joseph	1840	?, London	(?) Cohen	Rebecca (?)		Aldgate, London	scholar
23884	Cohen	Joseph	1844	Holborn, London	Solomon Hyman Cohen	Ann Davis		Westminster, London	
28969	Cohen	Joseph	1845	Aldgate, London	Solomon Isaac Cohen	Hannah Levie		Whitechapel, London	scholar
10395	Cohen	Joseph	1846	Spitalfields, London	Philip Cohen	Rachael Jacobs		Spitalfields, London	
17336	Cohen	Joseph	1846	Spitalfields, London	Mark Cohen	Rachel (?)		Spitalfields, London	scholar
22131	Cohen	Joseph	1846	Spitalfields, London				Whitechapel, London	scholar
29792	Cohen	Joseph	1846	Whitechapel, London	David Abraham Cohen	Hannah Solomon		Whitechapel, London	scholar
25717	Cohen	Joseph	1851	Spitalfields, London	Solomon (Selig) Cohen	Simela (Simlah) Moses		Spitalfields, London	
30401	Cohen	Joseph Barnet	1851	Whitechapel, London	Barnet Solomon Cohen	Eliza Myers		Whitechapel, London	
4387	Cohen	Joseph Colman	1806	Norwich, Norfolk			?Katie (?)	Birmingham	merchant
23254	Cohen	Joseph J	1829	Whitechapel, London	Isaac Cohen	Louisa (?)		Notting Hill, London	clerk to the Stock Exchange
12603	Cohen	Joseph L	1816	Lambeth, London			Charlotte (?)	Norwich, Norfolk	type founder
19595	Cohen	Joshua	1829	Spitalfields, London	David Cohen	Harriet (?)	Nancy (Ann) Jacobs	Spitalfields, London	
25379	Cohen	Joshua	1840	Middlesex, London	Joseph Cohen	Esther Isaacs		Clerkenwell, London	scholar
5151	Cohen	Joshua	1843	Spitalfields, London	Judah Cohen	Caroline Davis		Wapping, London	
6273	Cohen	Joshua	1850	Whitechapel, London	Abraham Cohen	Rosetta (?)		Spitalfields, London	
1108	Cohen	Josiah	1841	Plymouth, Devon	(?) Cohen	Rose (?)		Falmouth, Cornwall	scholar
17331	Cohen	Josiah	1848	Spitalfields, London	Benjamin Cohen	Rebecca (?)		Spitalfields, London	
5160	Cohen	Judah	1820	Spitalfields, London	Isaac Cohen	Esther Davis	Caroline Davis	Wapping, London	furniture broker
27628	Cohen	Judah	1825	Aldgate, London	Pinchas HaCohen		Rachel Solomon	Aldgate, London	furniture broker
11545	Cohen	Judah	1849	Spitalfields, London	Aaron Cohen	Sarah (?)	Rachel Cohen	Spitalfields, London	
18987	Cohen	Judith	1819	Aldgate, London	(?) Cohen			Aldgate, London	
10256	Cohen	Judith	1845	Aldgate, London	Moses Cohen	Clara Michael		Spitalfields, London	
5465	Cohen	Judith	1848	Elephant & Castle, London	Moses Cohen	Kate Joseph	Lawrence B Phillips	Elephant & Castle, London	
21232	Cohen	Julia	1791	Spitalfields, London	(?)		Michael Cohen	Spitalfields, London	
22917	Cohen	Julia	1792	Aldgate, London	Jacob Cantor		David Cohen	Wapping, London	pencutter
12809	Cohen	Julia	1803	Spitalfields, London	(?) Cohen	Caroline (?)		Spitalfields, London	general dealer
17353	Cohen	Julia	1819	Spitalfields, London	Levy Lazarus		Ralph (Raphael) Cohen	Spitalfields, London	domestic
18942	Cohen	Julia	1820	Bristol	(?) Cohen			Aldgate, London	general servant
14758	Cohen	Julia	1822	Southwark, London	Moses Cohen	Henrietta (?)		Finsbury, London	

ID	surname	given names	born	birthplace	father	mother	spouse 1	1851 residence	1851 occupation
28013	Cohen	Julia	1823	Middlesex, London	Samuel Samuel		Aaron Cohen	Spitalfields, London	
8039	Cohen	Julia	1828	Whitechapel, London	N--- Nathan		David Cohen	Finsbury, London	
10480	Cohen	Julia	1828	Southwark, London				Mile End, London	shoe binder
11985	Cohen	Julia	1829	Portsmouth, Hampshire	Jacob Cohen	Katherine (?)		Whitechapel, London	
16227	Cohen	Julia	1829	Clerkenwell, London	Samuel Cohen	Rosetta (?)		Clerkenwell, London	
17946	Cohen	Julia	1833	?, London	Emanuel Cohen	Theresa (?)		Whitechapel, London	
25386	Cohen	Julia	1833	Holborn, London	Aaron Cohen	Rachel (?)		Clerkenwell, London	dressmaker
7216	Cohen	Julia	1834	Finsbury, London	Louis Cohen	Rebecca Floretta Keyser	Henry Jessel	Finsbury, London	
14951	Cohen	Julia	1836	Middlesex, London	(?) Cohen			Bethnal Green, London	boarding school pupil
18590	Cohen	Julia	1837	Aldgate, London	(?Abraham) Cohen	Elizabeth (?)		Stepney, London	
27552	Cohen	Julia	1837	Aldgate, London	Hyam Cohen	Elizabeth (?)		Spitalfields, London	
10391	Cohen	Julia	1838	Spitalfields, London	Philip Cohen	Rachael Jacobs	John Jacobs	Spitalfields, London	scholar
20695	Cohen	Julia	1840	Aldgate, London	Jacob Cohen	Rosetta Lyon		Spitalfields, London	scholar
10403	Cohen	Julia	1844	Spitalfields, London	Michael Cohen	Sarah Jacobs	(?) Phillips	Spitalfields, London	
11478	Cohen	Julia	1844	Aldgate, London	Nathan Cohen	Maria (?Rintel)		Aldgate, London	
17340	Cohen	Julia	1845	Spitalfields, London	Samuel Cohen	Sarah (?)		Spitalfields, London	
3369	Cohen	Julia	1846	Holborn, London	Daniel Cohen	Ann (Isabella) Solomon (Sailman)	?	Holborn, London	scolar
24822	Cohen	Julia	1848	?, London	Samuel Cohen	Ann (Nancy) Harris	Henry Barnett	Waterloo, London	scholar
23887	Cohen	Julia	1849	Westminster, London	Solomon Hyman Cohen	Ann Davis		Westminster, London	
15189	Cohen	Julia (Judith)	1833	?, London	Raphael (Ralph) Cohen	Abigail Torres	David Cohen	Shoreditch, London	dress maker
10576	Cohen	Julia (Judy)	1825	Whitechapel, London	Moses Abraham Berlyn	Mariane (?)	Solomon Cohen	Spitalfields, London	
3482	Cohen	Julia Solomon	1814	Spitalfields, London	Abraham Solomon Wilks	Rosetta Abrahams	Aaron Cohen	Spitalfields, London	
15091	Cohen	Juliet	1790	Aldgate, London	(?)		(?) Cohen	Mile End, London	dealer in wardrobes
2625	Cohen	Julius	1817	?, Russia				Glasgow, Scotland	wholesale traveller
13389	Cohen	Julius	1821	?, Germany	Ezekiel HaCohen		Esther Jacobs	Spitalfields, London	tailor
8563	Cohen	Julius	1828	?, Denmark				Spitalfields, London	furrier
19146	Cohen	Julius	1830	?, Poland [?, Prussia]				Aldgate, London	tailor
14084	Cohen	Julius	1833	?, Poland [?, Prussia]				Manchester	cloth cap maker
13647	Cohen	Justatius	1837	Ironbridge, Shropshire				Manchester	shop boy
7037	Cohen	Justina	1800	?, London	Joseph Eliahu Montefiore	Raquel (?)	Benjamin Cohen	Marylebone, London	
24286	Cohen	Justina	1832	Whitechapel, London	Andrew Cohen	Hannah Oppenheim		Bloomsbury, London	
16220	Cohen	Justinian Charles	1848	Middlesex, London	Henry Cohen	Caroline S (?)		Paddington, London	
5460	Cohen	Kate	1807	Falmouth, Cornwall	Lyon Joseph	Judith Levy	Moses Cohen	Elephant & Castle, London	
24664	Cohen	Kate	1851	Elephant & Castle, London	Zachariah Cohen	Flora (?)		Kennington, London	
9702	Cohen	Kate (Catherine)	1844	Spitalfields, London	Samuel Cohen	Rebecca Joseph	Mordecai (Morris) Rodrigues (Rogers)	Spitalfields, London	scholar
9705	Cohen	Kate (Kitty)	1804	Southwark, London	Moses Cohen	Abigail (?)	Solomon Barnett	Aldgate, London	
11983	Cohen	Katherine	1803	Aldgate, London	(?)		Jacob Cohen	Whitechapel, London	
2615	Cohen	Katherine	1846	Glasgow, Scotland	Simon M Cohen	Harriet (?)		Glasgow, Scotland	
2006	Cohen	Katherine (Kate)	1836	Mile End, London	Simon Cohen		Myer Woolf	Chatham, Kent	
9452	Cohen	Kaufman	1850	Holborn, London	Simon Cohen	Dinah Solomon		Aldgate, London	
28230	Cohen	Kitty	1820	Aldgate, London	Lewis Cohen	Deborah Michael		Spitalfields, London	house servant
11964	Cohen	Laurence	1842	Whitechapel, London	Moses Cohen	Flora (?)		Whitechapel, London	scholar

ID	surname	given names	born	birthplace	father	mother	spouse 1	1851 residence	1851 occupation
31186	Cohen	Laurence	1842	Southwark, London	Hyman Cohen	Maria (?)		Gravesend, Kent	scholar
24692	Cohen	Lawrence	1830	Lambeth, London	Joseph Cohen			Elephant & Castle, London	cabinet maker
29383	Cohen	Lazarus	1775	?, Hungary			(?)	Wapping, London	general dealer
1764	Cohen	Lazarus	1791	?, Poland				Cardiff, Wales	leader, Jews' congregation
12611	Cohen	Lazarus	1819	Malavar, Poland			Frances (?)	Wymondham, Norfolk	traveller with jewellery
27422	Cohen	Lazarus	1826	?, Germany			Rosetta (?)	Whitechapel, London	tailor
25382	Cohen	Lazarus	1850	Middlesex, London	Joseph Cohen	Esther Isaacs		Clerkenwell, London	
30400	Cohen	Lazarus	1850	Spitalfields, London	Ralph (Raphael) Cohen	Julia Lazarus		Spitalfields, London	
8243	Cohen	Lazarus	1851	Aldgate, London	Isaac Cohen	Louisa Cowan		Aldgate, London	
28229	Cohen	Lazarus (Lawrence)	1822	Aldgate, London	Lewis Cohen	Deborah Michael		Spitalfields, London	labourer
2827	Cohen	Lazarus (Lawrence)	1842	Canterbury, Kent	Victor Cohen	Henrietta Magnus	Catherine Cohen	Spitalfields, London	
2399	Cohen	Lea	1826	?, Germany				Hull, Yorkshire	cap maker
12080	Cohen	Leah	1760	Whitechapel, London	(?)		(?) Cohen	Spitalfields, London	
17675	Cohen	Leah	1782	Aldgate, London	(?)		Naftali (Hart) Cohen	Aldgate, London	
26800	Cohen	Leah	1789	Middlesex, London	(?)		Daniel Cohen	Aldgate, London	grocer
1399	Cohen	Leah	1791	Newton Abbot, Devon [Newton, Devon]	(?) Levi		(?) Cohen	Plymouth, Devon	
8650	Cohen	Leah	1801	Whitechapel, London	(?)		(?) Levy	Aldgate, London	orange dealer
28231	Cohen	Leah	1830	Spitalfields, London	Lewis Cohen	Deborah Michael		Spitalfields, London	house servant
14070	Cohen	Leah	1831	Sheffield, Yorkshire	(?) Cohen	Priscilla (?)		Manchester	governess
2727	Cohen	Leah	1834	Aldgate, London	Moses Cohen	Fanny (?)		Aldgate, London	tailoress
27641	Cohen	Leah	1834	City, London	Benjamin Cohen	(?)		Aldgate, London	
10519	Cohen	Leah	1839	Aldgate, London	Levy Jacob Cohen	Esther Isaacs	Michael Isaacs	Aldgate, London	scholar
18536	Cohen	Leah	1840	Finsbury, London	Isaac Cohen	Elizabeth Cohen		Finsbury, London	
2193	Cohen	Leah	1845	Oxford, Oxfordshire	Isaac Jacob Cohen	Sarah Levi	Gustav Frankel	Oxford, Oxfordshire	scholar
20698	Cohen	Leah	1847	Aldgate, London	Jacob Cohen	Rosetta Lyon		Spitalfields, London	scholar
5678	Cohen	Leah (Lidia)	1830	Leeuwarden, Holland	Benjamin Cohen	Amelia (Mieje) van der Reis	David Cohen	Sunderland, Co Durham	
19156	Cohen	Lemon (Leman, Judah)	1851	Aldgate, London	Leman Cohen	Clara Lyon	Hannah Hurne (Hearne)	Aldgate, London	
21670	Cohen	Leon	1806	?, Holland				Finsbury, London	gentleman
12607	Cohen	Leon	1846	Norwich, Norfolk	Joseph L Cohen	Charlotte (?)		Norwich, Norfolk	
4394	Cohen	Leopold	1817	?, Germany			Henrietta Myers	Birmingham	watch materials dealer
13090	Cohen	Levi	1808	Amsterdam, Holland				Clerkenwell, London	convict + Jew clothes salesman
17537	Cohen	Levi	1851	Whitechapel, London	Daniel Cohen	Frances Hyams	Rebecca Pollock	Spitalfields, London	
27005	Cohen	Levy	1837	Amsterdam, Holland	Jacob Cohen	Rachael (?)		Aldgate, London	cigar maker
10515	Cohen	Levy Jacob	1801	Leicester, Leicestershire	Elias		Esther Isaacs	Aldgate, London	waistcoat maker
2614	Cohen	Lewin H	1843	Glasgow, Scotland	Simon M Cohen	Harriet (?)		Glasgow, Scotland	
17381	Cohen	Lewis	1807	Whitechapel, London	Yacov HaCohen		Abigail Reuben	Wapping, London	dealer
2720	Cohen	Lewis	1815	Aldgate, London	Moses Cohen	Fanny (?)		Aldgate, London	dealer
27308	Cohen	Lewis	1819	Aldgate, London			(?)	Aldgate, London	traveller in plated articles
10871	Cohen	Lewis	1821	Whitechapel, London	Shmuel HaCohen		Sarah Solomon	Spitalfields, London	general dealer

ID	surname	given names	born	birthplace	father	mother	spouse 1	1851 residence	1851 occupation
15438	Cohen	Lewis	1832	Spitalfields, London	Moses Cohen			Covent Garden, London	cigar maker
21124	Cohen	Lewis	1835	Spitalfields, London	Benjamin Cohen	Bluma (?)		Aldgate, London	apprentice cigar maker
29061	Cohen	Lewis	1838	Whitechapel, London	Simon Cohen	Isabella (?)		Whitechapel, London	scholar
10392	Cohen	Lewis	1840	Spitalfields, London	Philip Cohen	Rachael Jacobs	Julia Cohen	Spitalfields, London	scholar
11251	Cohen	Lewis	1843	Aldgate, London	Phillip Cohen	Catharine (?)		Aldgate, London	
26644	Cohen	Lewis	1844	Whitechapel, London	Samuel Cohen	Mary (?)		Aldgate, London	scholar
21037	Cohen	Lewis	1845	?, London				Dover, Kent	boarding school pupil
10605	Cohen	Lewis	1848	Spitalfields, London	(?)	Hannah (?)		Spitalfields, London	scholar
11065	Cohen	Lewis	1848	?Aldgate, London	Samuel Cohen	Hannah (?Phillips)		Aldgate, London	
13336	Cohen	Lewis	1848	Spitalfields, London	David Cohen	Harriet Woolf		Spitalfields, London	
13723	Cohen	Lewis	1848	Finsbury, London	Isaac Cohen	Elizabeth Cohen		Finsbury, London	
6743	Cohen	Lewis	1849	Liverpool	Henry Cohen	Elizabeth Harris	Selina Marks	Liverpool	
25543	Cohen	Lewis (Louis)	1802	?	Isaac Cohen		Jane (?)	Dublin, Ireland	snuff + tobacco dealer
968	Cohen	Lewis (Louis)	1831	Walworth, London	Abraham Aaron Cohen			Exeter, Devon	apprentice
7053	Cohen	Lewis (Louis)	1841	Middlesex, London	Levy Cohen	Esther (?)	Esther Isaacs	Aldgate, London	scholar
7060	Cohen	Lewis (Louis)	1845	Clerkenwell, London	Samuel Cohen	Rosetta (?)	Annie Woolf	Clerkenwell, London	scholar
13006	Cohen	Lewis Reuben	1832	Middlesex, London	Henry Cohen	Elizabeth (?)		Spitalfields, London	general dealer
24575	Cohen	Lionel	1838	Whitechapel, London				Clapham, London	boarding school pupil
31185	Cohen	Lionel	1840	Southwark, London	Hyman Cohen	Maria (?)		Gravesend, Kent	scholar
5464	Cohen	Lionel	1845	Southwark, London	Moses Cohen	Kate Joseph		Elephant & Castle, London	
6179	Cohen	Lionel Benjamin	1826	Marylebone, London	Benjamin Cohen	Justina Montefiore	Henrietta Rachael Salomons	Marylebone, London	exchange broker
3636	Cohen	Lionel Louis	1832	Finsbury, London	Louis Cohen	Rebecca Floretta Keyser	Esther Moses	Finsbury, London	clerk
22895	Cohen	Lipman	1794	Aldgate, London				Wapping, London	dealer in wearing apparel
25980	Cohen	Lipman	1821	Aldgate, London			Jane Isaacs	Aldgate, London	cap maker empl 2
7042	Cohen	Louis	1799	City, London	Joseph Cohen		Rebecca Floretta Keyser	Shoreditch, London	merchant
15681	Cohen	Louis	1808	?, London				Aldgate, London	general dealer
13791	Cohen	Louis	1811	?, Poland [?, Prussia]				Manchester	dealer + hawker
2956	Cohen	Louis	1817	Poznan, Poland [Schokerley, Posen, Prussia]	Joel Cohen		Esther Moses	Wolverhampton, Staffordshire	clothier
29229	Cohen	Louis	1819	?, Germany	(?) Cohen	Jeanette (?)	Sophia (?)	Whitechapel, London	tailor
11143	Cohen	Louis	1821	Spitalfields, London	(?) Cohen	Frances (?)		Aldgate, London	tailor
14081	Cohen	Louis	1823	?, Poland [?, Prussia]			Sarah (?)	Manchester	watch maker + repairer
23823	Cohen	Louis	1833	?, Russia				Liverpool	commercial traveller (pedlar)
10568	Cohen	Louis	1848	Whitechapel, London	Joseph Cohen	Maria (?)		Whitechapel, London	
3380	Cohen	Louis (Lewis)	1835	Middlesex, London	Benjamin Wolf Cohen	Frances Phillips		Holborn, London	
8582	Cohen	Louisa	1792	Strand, London	(?)		Humphrey Cohen	Soho, London	
23251	Cohen	Louisa	1798	Aldgate, London	(?)		Isaac Cohen	Notting Hill, London	schoolmistress
15068	Cohen	Louisa	1815	Islington, London	(?)		John Cohen	Bethnal Green, London	
6657	Cohen	Louisa	1819	Southwark, London	Joseph Cowan		Isaac Cohen	Aldgate, London	
29126	Cohen	Louisa	1834	Whitechapel, London	Moses Cohen	Rebecca (?)		Whitechapel, London	tailor
16230	Cohen	Louisa	1836	Clerkenwell, London	Samuel Cohen	Rosetta (?)		Clerkenwell, London	
26974	Cohen	Louisa	1838	Whitechapel, London	Joseph Cohen	Esther (?)		Aldgate, London	

ID	surname	given names	born	birthplace	father	mother	spouse 1	1851 residence	1851 occupation
17384	Cohen	Louisa	1841	Whitechapel, London	Lewis Cohen	Abigail Reuben		Wapping, London	scholar
29911	Cohen	Louisa (Leah)	1823	Whitechapel, London	Lazarus Jacobs		Ralph Cohen	Whitechapel, London	
24236	Cohen	Lucy	1838	Stepney, London	Mark Cohen	Reyna (?)		Hackney, London	
23310	Cohen	Lucy	1839	Mayfair, London	Isaac Cohen	Sarah Samuel		Mayfair, London	scholar at home
25378	Cohen	Lydia	1839	Middlesex, London	Joseph Cohen	Esther Isaacs		Clerkenwell, London	scholar
5153	Cohen	Lydia	1846	Whitechapel, London	Isaac Cohen	Louisa Cowan	Samuel Bardo	Aldgate, London	
24240	Cohen	Lydia	1847	Stepney, London	Mark Cohen	Reyna (?)		Hackney, London	
21870	Cohen	Lyon	1835	Spitalfields, London				Clerkenwell, London	assistant to fancy cabinet maker
1765	Cohen	Manasseh	1828	Peizer, Poland	Lazarus Cohen	?Esther (?)	Harriet (Harriette) Moses	Cardiff, Wales	leader
2702	Cohen	Marcus	1806	?, Poland [?, Prussia]				Glasgow, Scotland	general broker
2244	Cohen	Marcus	1823	?, Poland			Sarah (?)	Leeds, Yorkshire	jewellery hawker
5679	Cohen	Margaret (Grietje)	1832	Leeuwarden, Holland	Benjamin Cohen	Amelia (Meije) van der Reis	Henry Marks	Sunderland, Co Durham	
25364	Cohen	Maria	1786	Whitechapel, London	(?)		(?) Cohen	Clerkenwell, London	tool dealer
25123	Cohen	Maria	1806	?, America	(?)		(?) Cohen	Finsbury, London	rag merchant
21233	Cohen	Maria	1812	Spitalfields, London	Michael Cohen	Julia (?)		Spitalfields, London	
31183	Cohen	Maria	1813	Clerkenwell, London	(?)		Hyman Cohen	Gravesend, Kent	
25704	Cohen	Maria	1818	Spitalfields, London	Shlomeh Samuel		Abraham Cohen	Spitalfields, London	
2248	Cohen	Maria	1820	Leeds, Yorkshire			Sim Cohen	Leeds, Yorkshire	
7058	Cohen	Maria	1820	Spitalfields, London			Nathan Cohen	Aldgate, London	
10566	Cohen	Maria	1822	?, Scotland	(?)			Whitechapel, London	
24693	Cohen	Maria	1834	Lambeth, London	Joseph Cohen			Elephant & Castle, London	
18302	Cohen	Maria	1839	?, Russia	Moses Cohen	Jane (?)		Sheffield, Yorkshire	scholar at home
17335	Cohen	Maria	1842	Spitalfields, London	Mark Cohen	Rachel (?)		Spitalfields, London	scholar
26977	Cohen	Maria	1849	Aldgate, London	Joseph Cohen	Esther (?)		Aldgate, London	
24742	Cohen	Maria	1850	Southwark, London	Abraham Cohen	Amelia Jacobs		Southwark, London	
1761	Cohen	Marinus Thomas	1810	?, Holland			Frederica Hanna (?)	Cardiff, Wales	ship broker
24232	Cohen	Mark	1787	Bristol			Reyna (?)	Hackney, London	income from houses
13055	Cohen	Mark	1807	?				Spitalfields, London	shoemaker
17333	Cohen	Mark	1811	Southwark, London			Rachel (?)	Spitalfields, London	furniture broker
15997	Cohen	Mark	1850	Stepney, London	Hyman Cohen	Caroline (?)		Mile End, London	
10229	Cohen	Mark (Mordecai)	1831	Aldgate, London	Emanuel Cohen	Hannah (?)		Aldgate, London	cigar maker
17126	Cohen	Marks	1826	?, Poland [?, Prussia]				Darlington, Co Durham	jeweller
27508	Cohen	Martha	1816	Middlesex, London	Moshe Cohen			Aldgate, London	
2726	Cohen	Martha	1831	Aldgate, London	Moses Cohen	Fanny (?)	Alexander Abrahams	Aldgate, London	waistcoat maker
14864	Cohen	Mary	1777	?, Norfolk				Bethnal Green, London	laundress
15993	Cohen	Mary	1788	?, London	(?)		Solomon Cohen	St John's Wood, London	
27451	Cohen	Mary	1809	Aldgate, London	(?)		Moss Cohen	Whitechapel, London	
4367	Cohen	Mary	1815	Wolverhampton, Staffordshire			Francis Cohen	Birmingham	
26643	Cohen	Mary	1825	Aldgate, London	(?)		Samuel Cohen	Aldgate, London	clothes dealer
2725	Cohen	Mary	1826	Aldgate, London	Moses Cohen	Fanny (?)		Aldgate, London	
10289	Cohen	Mary	1831	?, Ireland	(?) Cohen			Spitalfields, London	general servant
20691	Cohen	Mary	1831	Spitalfields, London	Moses Cohen	Hannah (?)	Lemon (Lemel) Lemon	Spitalfields, London	
2626	Cohen	Mary	1840	Jamaica, West Indies				Glasgow, Scotland	scholar

129

ID	surname	given names	born	birthplace	father	mother	spouse 1	1851 residence	1851 occupation
4364	Cohen	Mary	1841	Birmingham	Daniel Cohen	Ann (?)		Birmingham	
13602	Cohen	Mary	1841	?, Poland	(?) Cohen	Rachael (?)		Manchester	
9197	Cohen	Mary	1842	Canterbury, Kent	George Cohen	Hannah (?)		Whitechapel, London	to school [---]
9270	Cohen	Mary	1850	Aldgate, London	Myers S Cohen	Jane (?)		Aldgate, London	
18305	Cohen	Mary	1850	Sheffield, Yorkshire	Moses Cohen	Jane (?)		Sheffield, Yorkshire	
17159	Cohen	Mary A	1808	York, Yorkshire	(?)		Abraham Cohen	Newcastle Upon Tyne	
12683	Cohen	Mary A	1832	Norwich, Norfolk	(?)		Henry Cohen	Norwich, Norfolk	
17160	Cohen	Mary A	1833	North Shields, Tyne & Wear	Abraham Cohen	Mary A (?)		Newcastle Upon Tyne	scholar
12596	Cohen	Mary A	1838	Lowestoft, Suffolk	Samuel Cohen	Mary Ann (?)		Great Yarmouth, Norfolk	scholar
12595	Cohen	Mary Ann	1807	Great Yarmouth, Norfolk	(?)		Samuel Cohen	Great Yarmouth, Norfolk	
8450	Cohen	Mary Ann	1826	Louth, Lincolnshire	(?)		Simon Cohen	Portsmouth, Hampshire	
25051	Cohen	Mary Ann	1833	?, France	(?) Cohen			Clerkenwell, London	general servant
23985	Cohen	Mary Ann	1851	Marylebone, London	(?) Cohen	Harriet (?)		Marylebone, London	
6259	Cohen	Mary Frances	1848	Whitechapel, London	Barnet Solomon Cohen	Eliza Myers	Bernhard (Bernard) Blume	St John's Wood, London	
24660	Cohen	Maryann (Marion)	1843	Elephant & Castle, London	Zachariah Cohen	Flora (?)	Abraham Levy	Kennington, London	
21952	Cohen	Matilda	1805	Swansea, Wales	Jacob Cohen	Catherine (?)		Swansea, Wales	
20965	Cohen	Matilda	1819	Whitechapel, London	Joseph Cohen	Clara Cohen		Spitalfields, London	tailoress
15998	Cohen	Matilda	1823	Whitechapel, London	(?) Cohen			Mile End, London	
5461	Cohen	Matilda	1841	Elephant & Castle, London	Moses Cohen	Kate Joseph	Nathanael Levy	Elephant & Castle, London	
29791	Cohen	Matilda	1842	Whitechapel, London	David Abraham Cohen	Hannah Solomon		Whitechapel, London	scholar
5156	Cohen	Matilda	1849	?, London	Judah Cohen	Caroline Davis		Wapping, London	
13878	Cohen	May Priscilla	1819	Middlesex, London	(?) Lazarus		(?) Cohen	Manchester	
13596	Cohen	Meyer	1826	?, Poland			Sarah (?)	Manchester	cap maker
3123	Cohen	Michael	1767	Margonin, Poland [Prussia]	Eliezer(?) Cohen		Adaline (?)	Sunderland, Co Durham	Jewish priest
21231	Cohen	Michael	1781	Aldgate, London			Julia (?)	Spitalfields, London	furniture broker
29097	Cohen	Michael	1791	Aldgate, London			Catherine (?)	Whitechapel, London	
12810	Cohen	Michael	1807	Spitalfields, London			Elizabeth (?)	Spitalfields, London	gas fitter + brass finisher
14523	Cohen	Michael	1816	Paris, France				Bideford, Devon	commercial traveller
10400	Cohen	Michael	1818	Aldgate, London	Aaron Cohen		Sarah Isaacs	Spitalfields, London	clothier
17327	Cohen	Michael	1820	Middlesex, London				Mile End, London	paper stainer journeyman
6280	Cohen	Michael	1828	Spitalfields, London	Isaac Cohen	Esther Davis	Bloomah Solomons	Aldgate, London	furniture broker
13332	Cohen	Michael	1828	Spitalfields, London	David Cohen	Harriet Woolf		Spitalfields, London	labourer
13918	Cohen	Michael	1828	Whitechapel, London				Manchester	salesman to tailor + draper
17338	Cohen	Michael	1829	Euston, London	Woolf Cohen	Hannah (Ann) Prince (Prins))	Abigail Jacobs	Spitalfields, London	general dealer
21122	Cohen	Michael	1831	?, Germany	Benjamin Cohen	Bluma (?)		Aldgate, London	cap maker journeyman
17334	Cohen	Michael	1837	Spitalfields, London	Mark Cohen	Rachel (?)		Spitalfields, London	furniture broker
10393	Cohen	Michael	1842	Spitalfields, London	Philip Cohen	Rachael Jacobs		Spitalfields, London	scholar
13722	Cohen	Michael	1846	Finsbury, London	Isaac Cohen	Elizabeth Cohen	Leah Hart	Finsbury, London	
25373	Cohen	Michael	1848	Holborn, London	Henry Cohen	Rosetta (?)		Clerkenwell, London	scholar
21235	Cohen	Michael	1849	Spitalfields, London				Spitalfields, London	
2627	Cohen	Michael	1850	Manchester	Henry Cohen	Caroline Sewill		Glasgow, Scotland	
30402	Cohen	Michael	1851	Aldgate, London	Joseph Cohen	Rebecca Lazarus		Spitalfields, London	

ID	surname	given names	born	birthplace	father	mother	spouse 1	1851 residence	1851 occupation
26787	Cohen	Mier	1823	Middlesex, London				Aldgate, London	servant
23886	Cohen	Miriam	1846	Holborn, London	Solomon Hyman Cohen	Ann Davis		Westminster, London	
15198	Cohen	Miriam (Minnie)	1847	?, London	Raphael (Ralph) Cohen	Abigail Torres	Hermann Harris	Shoreditch, London	
5163	Cohen	Mordecai (Morris)	1841	Middlesex, London	Barnet Cohen	Sarah Hyman	Elizabeth Boam	Spitalfields, London	
4396	Cohen	Morris	1821	?, Poland [?, Prussia]			Esther (?)	Birmingham	jeweller
9451	Cohen	Morris	1821	Kepno, Poland [Kempen, Prussia]	Tsevi HaCohen			Aldgate, London	
13007	Cohen	Morris	1829	?, Holland	Henry Cohen	Elizabeth (?)	Sarah Levy	Spitalfields, London	general dealer
2243	Cohen	Morris	1839	?, Poland	Morris Cohen		Fanny Hickman	Leeds, Yorkshire	hawker, jewellery dealer
11061	Cohen	Morris	1841	Finsbury, London	Samuel Cohen	Hannah Phillips		Aldgate, London	
9757	Cohen	Morris	1842	Middlesex, London				Kew, London	boarding school pupil
9586	Cohen	Morris	1847	Spitalfields, London	James Cohen	Sarah (?)		Spitalfields, London	
10957	Cohen	Morris	1848	Amsterdam, Holland	Eleazer Cohen	Elizabeth (?)		Spitalfields, London	
19884	Cohen	Morris (Moses)	1821	?, Russia			(?)	Dover, Kent	watch + clockmaker, optician, silversmith + jeweller
17697	Cohen	Morris T	1836	Nottingham, Nottinghamshire	Joseph Cohen	Rachel Goodman	Ada Moss	Glasgow, Scotland	leecher traveller
11641	Cohen	Morriss	1851	Aldgate, London	Abraham Cohen	Elizabeth Busnach (?Barnett)		Aldgate, London	
16524	Cohen	Moses	1777	?abroad			Elizabeth (?)	Whitechapel, London	traveller (jewellery)
2718	Cohen	Moses	1781	?, Poland			Fanny (?)	Aldgate, London	general dealer
778	Cohen	Moses	1785	High Wycombe, Buckinghamshire	Hart Cohen		Esther Benjamin	Soho, London	warehouseman for antique goods keeper
29124	Cohen	Moses	1786	Whitechapel, London			Rebecca (?)	Whitechapel, London	tailor
14756	Cohen	Moses	1795	Whitechapel, London			Henrietta (?)	Finsbury, London	annuitant
175	Cohen	Moses	1799	Cambridge	Henry Cohen	(Silah Moses?)	Elizabeth Nathan	Elephant & Castle, London	general merchant
18297	Cohen	Moses	1803	?, Russia			Jane (?)	Sheffield, Yorkshire	hawker
15436	Cohen	Moses	1804	Cambridge			(?)	Covent Garden, London	looking glass dealer
11967	Cohen	Moses	1809	?, Poland [?, Prussia]			Flora (?)	Whitechapel, London	general dealer
20689	Cohen	Moses	1809	Spitalfields, London			Hannah (?)	Spitalfields, London	general dealer
16252	Cohen	Moses	1813	?, London				Spitalfields, London	
10255	Cohen	Moses	1821	Wapping, London	Joseph Cohen		Clara Michael	Spitalfields, London	general dealer
4395	Cohen	Moses	1829	?, Poland				Birmingham	slipper-maker
22938	Cohen	Moses	1830	Whitechapel, London	Jacob Cohen	(?)		Wapping, London	salesman
15574	Cohen	Moses	1836	Whitechapel, London	(?) Cohen	Rosa (?)		Covent Garden, London	apprentice fancy brush maker
9701	Cohen	Moses	1839	Strand, London	Samuel Cohen	Rebecca Joseph	Emma (?)	Spitalfields, London	
8652	Cohen	Moses	1841	Aldgate, London	(?) Cohen	Leah (?)		Aldgate, London	scholar
10956	Cohen	Moses	1841	Amsterdam, Holland	Eleazer Cohen	Elizabeth (?)		Spitalfields, London	scholar
25380	Cohen	Moses	1843	Middlesex, London	Joseph Cohen	Esther Isaacs		Clerkenwell, London	scholar
3904	Cohen	Moses	1849	Amsterdam, Holland	Emanuel Cohen	Sally (?)		Spitalfields, London	
10577	Cohen	Moses	1850	Whitechapel, London	Solomon Cohen	Julia (Judy) Berlyn		Spitalfields, London	
18359	Cohen	Moses (Morris) Joseph	1829	St Pancras, London	Joseph Cohen	Elizabeth Benjamin	Isabella Jones	Elephant & Castle, London	furniture broker

ID	surname	given names	born	birthplace	father	mother	spouse 1	1851 residence	1851 occupation
27450	Cohen	Moss	1806	Aldgate, London	(?) Cohen	Elizabeth (?)	Mary (?)	Whitechapel, London	cigar maker
11706	Cohen	Moss	1833	Aldgate, London	Abraham Cohen	Deborah Genese		Aldgate, London	general dealer
28967	Cohen	Moss	1842	Aldgate, London	Solomon Isaac Cohen	Hannah Levie		Whitechapel, London	scholar
23885	Cohen	Moss	1845	Holborn, London	Solomon Hyman Cohen	Ann Davis		Westminster, London	
17329	Cohen	Moss	1846	City, London	Benjamin Cohen	Rebecca (?)		Spitalfields, London	scholar
26508	Cohen	Moss	1847	Middlesex, London				Dover, Kent	
3372	Cohen	Moss (Morris) Daniel	1850	Holborn, London	Daniel Cohen	Ann (Isabella) Solomon (Sailman)	Frances Abrahams	Holborn, London	
7049	Cohen	Moss (Moses)	1827	Middlesex, London	Emanuel Cohen	Trevena? (?)	Ellen Goodman	Whitechapel, London	sponge dealer
10522	Cohen	Moss (Moses)	1850	Aldgate, London	Levy Jacob Cohen	Esther Isaacs		Aldgate, London	
3364	Cohen	Moss (Moses)	1851	Holborn, London	Nathan Cohen	Deborah Cohen	Phoebe Isaacs	Holborn, London	
16228	Cohen	Moss [Tsadok]	1831	Clerkenwell, London	Samuel Cohen	Rosetta (?)	Sarah Myers	Clerkenwell, London	engineer
11481	Cohen	Mosses	1850	Aldgate, London	Nathan Cohen	Maria (?Rintel)		Aldgate, London	
27914	Cohen	Myer	1818	Amsterdam, Holland	Naphtali haCohen		Hannah (?)	Spitalfields, London	working jeweller
30372	Cohen	Myer	1818	Middlesex, London			Catherine (?)	Tutbury, Staffordshire	French polisher
27569	Cohen	Myer	1824	Whitechapel, London	Joseph Cohen	Clara Cohen	Sarah Phillips	Spitalfields, London	tailor
9265	Cohen	Myers S	1805	?, Holland			Jane (?)	Aldgate, London	Jewish Reader
30910	Cohen	Nahan	1833	Norwich, Norfolk	Solomon Cohen	Rachel (?)		Lincoln, Lincolnshire	silversmith &c
5767	Cohen	Nancy	1841	Strand, London	Samuel Cohen	Rebecca Joseph	Aaron Gomes da Costa	Aldgate, London	scholar
11640	Cohen	Nancy	1849	Aldgate, London	Abraham Cohen	Elizabeth Busnach (?Barnett)		Aldgate, London	
3358	Cohen	Nathan	1811	Wapping, London	Benjamin Wolf Cohen	Frances Phillips	Deborah Cohen	Holborn, London	clothes salesman
7057	Cohen	Nathan	1819	Chatham, Kent			Maria (?Rintel)	Aldgate, London	general dealer
27568	Cohen	Nathan	1823	Whitechapel, London	Joseph Cohen	Clara Cohen		Spitalfields, London	hatter
25124	Cohen	Nathan	1825	Whitechapel, London	(?) Cohen	Maria (?)		Finsbury, London	rag merchant
11835	Cohen	Nathan	1829	?, Germany				Whitechapel, London	master boot + shoe maker
22226	Cohen	Nathan	1841	Middlesex, London	Aaron Cohen	(?)		Whitechapel, London	pawnbroker
19717	Cohen	Nathan	1846	Whitechapel, London	Herman Jacob Cohen	Rebecca Samuel		Whitechapel, London	
26647	Cohen	Nathan	1850	Aldgate, London	Samuel Cohen	Mary (?)		Aldgate, London	
16213	Cohen	Nathan (Nathaniel) Louis	1846	Finsbury, London	Louis Cohen	Rebecca Floretta Keyser	Julia M Waley	Finsbury, London	scholar at home
30634	Cohen	Nathaniel	1851	Spitalfields, London	Aaron Cohen	Julia Solomon Wilks		Spitalfields, London	
6705	Cohen	Nathaniel Benjamin	1827	Marylebone, London	Benjamin Cohen	Justina Montefiore	Rebecca Lucas	Marylebone, London	
9969	Cohen	Paris	1805	?, Germany			Rebecca (?)	Manchester	stationery agent
24613	Cohen	Philip	1780	Oxford, Oxfordshire			Sarah (?)	Kennington, London	bottle merchant
24732	Cohen	Philip	1782	?, Germany			Jane (?)	Southwark, London	bottle merchant
14420	Cohen	Philip	1811	Liverpool	Yaacov			Salford, Lancashire	clothes dealer
10387	Cohen	Philip	1813	Spitalfields, London	Aryeh Leib HaCohen		Rachael Jacobs	Spitalfields, London	general dealer
12599	Cohen	Philip	1819	Whitechapel, London	Moses Cohen	Sophia (?)		Norwich, Norfolk	orange merchant
8247	Cohen	Philip	1821	Spitalfields, London	Isaac Cohen	Esther Davis	Deborah (Dora) Levy	Shoreditch, London	dealer in china + glass
22346	Cohen	Philip	1822	City, London			(?) Green	Aldgate, London	dock porter
29058	Cohen	Philip	1832	Chelsea, London	Simon Cohen	Isabella (?)		Whitechapel, London	
2828	Cohen	Philip	1844	Gravesend, Kent	Victor Cohen	Henrietta Magnus		Spitalfields, London	

ID	surname	given names	born	birthplace	father	mother	spouse 1	1851 residence	1851 occupation
10406	Cohen	Philip	1850	Spitalfields, London	Michael Cohen	Sarah Jacobs		Spitalfields, London	
17343	Cohen	Philip	1850	Spitalfields, London	Samuel Cohen	Sarah (?)		Spitalfields, London	
11247	Cohen	Phillip	1781	Warsaw, Poland			Catharine (?)	Aldgate, London	hawker
22894	Cohen	Phillip	1789	Aldgate, London				Wapping, London	dealer in wearing apparel
8708	Cohen	Phillip	1814	Aldgate, London				Aldgate, London	general dealer
30829	Cohen	Phillip	1827	?, Poland [?, Prussia]				Coventry, Warwickshire	watch manufacturer empl 13
27015	Cohen	Phillip	1830	Wriezen, Germany [Wreshin, Prussia]				Aldgate, London	tailor
21125	Cohen	Phillip	1837	Whitechapel, London	Benjamin Cohen	Bluma (?)	Elizabeth Marks	Aldgate, London	apprentice cigar maker
26646	Cohen	Phillip	1848	Aldgate, London	Samuel Cohen	Mary (?)		Aldgate, London	
17332	Cohen	Phineas	1813	Whitechapel, London	Naftali Cohen		Rebecca Hyams	Spitalfields, London	ironmonger
19826	Cohen	Phoebe	1780	Aldgate, London	(?)		Isaac Cohen	Gravesend, Kent	
17344	Cohen	Phoebe	1806	Aldgate, London	(?)		John Cohen	Spitalfields, London	
3374	Cohen	Phoebe	1821	Middlesex, London	Moses Solomon (Sailman)	Elizabeth (?)	Aaron Cohen	Holborn, London	
5877	Cohen	Phoebe	1826	Liverpool	Yaacov		Emanuel Cohen	Salford, Lancashire	
15573	Cohen	Phoebe	1834	Whitechapel, London	(?) Cohen	Rosa (?)		Covent Garden, London	scholar
22831	Cohen	Phoebe	1834	Middlesex, London	Joseph Cohen	Hannah (?)		Whitechapel, London	umbrella maker
1107	Cohen	Phoebe	1839	Falmouth, Cornwall	(?) Cohen	Rose (?)		Falmouth, Cornwall	scholar
21758	Cohen	Phoebe	1841	Aldgate, London	Ezekiel Cohen	Elizabeth Myers		Aldgate, London	
13334	Cohen	Phoebe	1844	Spitalfields, London	David Cohen	Harriet Woolf		Spitalfields, London	
18499	Cohen	Phoebe	1850	Whitechapel, London	Israel Cohen	Rachel Isaacs	Benjamin Woolf Hyman	Whitechapel, London	
14068	Cohen	Priscilla	1793	Middlesex, London	(?)		(?) Cohen	Manchester	teacher
17945	Cohen	Priscilla	1830	?, London	Emanuel Cohen	Theresa (?)		Whitechapel, London	
3379	Cohen	Priscilla	1833	Middlesex, London	Benjamin Wolf Cohen	Frances Phillips	Francis Slade Coaker	Holborn, London	flower maker
18591	Cohen	Priscilla	1838	Aldgate, London	(?Abraham) Cohen	Elizabeth (?)		Stepney, London	
3367	Cohen	Priscilla	1839	?, London	Daniel Cohen	Ann (Isabella) Solomon (Sailman)		Holborn, London	
16232	Cohen	Priscilla	1841	Clerkenwell, London	Samuel Cohen	Rosetta (?)	John Phillips	Clerkenwell, London	scholar
25708	Cohen	Priscilla	1844	Aldgate, London	Abraham Cohen	Maria Samuel		Spitalfields, London	scholar
6314	Cohen	Priscilla	1849	Holborn, London	Nathan Cohen	Deborah Cohen	Lewis Solomon	Holborn, London	
4369	Cohen	Priscilla	1850	Birmingham	Francis Cohen	Mary (?)		Birmingham	
3375	Cohen	Priscilla	1851	Holborn, London	Aaron Cohen	Phoebe Solomon (Sailman)		Holborn, London	
29066	Cohen	R---	1772	Whitechapel, London	(?)		Ezekiel Cohen	Whitechapel, London	feather maker
29064	Cohen	R---	1846	Whitechapel, London	Simon Cohen	Isabella (?)		Whitechapel, London	
10388	Cohen	Rachael	1814	Spitalfields, London	Michael Jacobs		Philip Cohen	Spitalfields, London	
27004	Cohen	Rachael	1814	Amsterdam, Holland	(?)		Jacob Cohen	Aldgate, London	
13601	Cohen	Rachael	1821	?, Poland	(?)		(?) Cohen	Manchester	
29788	Cohen	Rachael	1835	Whitechapel, London	David Abraham Cohen	Hannah Solomon		Whitechapel, London	scholar
9700	Cohen	Rachael	1837	Covent Garden, London	Samuel Cohen	Rebecca Joseph		Spitalfields, London	
26098	Cohen	Rachael	1839	?, London	(?) Cohen	Rebecca (?)		Aldgate, London	
23259	Cohen	Rachael	1840	Hammersmith, London	Isaac Cohen	Louisa (?)	Solomon Elsner	Notting Hill, London	
17716	Cohen	Rachael	1850	Aldgate, London	Michael Cohen	Bloomah Solomons		Spitalfields, London	
10227	Cohen	Racheal	1825	Aldgate, London	Emanuel Cohen	Hannah (?)		Aldgate, London	tailoress
1501	Cohen	Rachel	1789	Aldgate, London	(?)		Solomon Cohen	Spitalfields, London	

ID	surname	given names	born	birthplace	father	mother	spouse 1	1851 residence	1851 occupation
24836	Cohen	Rachel	1800	Exeter, Devon	Samuel Davis	Harriet (?)	Aaron Cohen	Elephant & Castle, London	
12081	Cohen	Rachel	1802	Aldgate, London	(?) Cohen	Leah (?)		Spitalfields, London	monthly nurse
25384	Cohen	Rachel	1803	Clerkenwell, London	(?)		Aaron Cohen	Clerkenwell, London	tool dealer
22618	Cohen	Rachel	1809	Colchester, Essex	(?)		Asher Cohen	Stepney, London	
30908	Cohen	Rachel	1809	Ipswich, Suffolk	(?)		Solomon Cohen	Lincoln, Lincolnshire	
1502	Cohen	Rachel	1810	?, London	(?)		Mark Cohen	Spitalfields, London	
2628	Cohen	Rachel	1813	?, England	Tobias (Tevli Shmuel) Goodman		Joseph Cohen	Glasgow, Scotland	
1589	Cohen	Rachel	1815	Spitalfields, London	(?) Cohen	Caroline (?)		Spitalfields, London	general dealer
27629	Cohen	Rachel	1825	City, London	(?) Solomon		Judah Cohen	Aldgate, London	
29381	Cohen	Rachel	1825	?, Ireland	(?)		George Cohen	Wapping, London	
24616	Cohen	Rachel	1826	Elephant & Castle, London	Philip Cohen	Sarah (?)		Kennington, London	
5410	Cohen	Rachel	1827	Middlesex, London	Joseph Isaacs		Israel Cohen	Whitechapel, London	
24234	Cohen	Rachel	1836	Stepney, London	Mark Cohen	Reyna (?)		Hackney, London	
14095	Cohen	Rachel	1837	Hanover, Germany	(?) Cohen	Ellen (?)		Manchester	scholar
31184	Cohen	Rachel	1838	Southwark, London	Hyman Cohen	Maria (?)		Gravesend, Kent	scholar
5908	Cohen	Rachel	1839	Bloomsbury, London	Samuel Cohen	Hannah (?Phillips)	Isaac Hart	Aldgate, London	
11963	Cohen	Rachel	1840	Whitechapel, London	Moses Cohen	Flora (?)		Whitechapel, London	scholar
1630	Cohen	Rachel	1841	Spitalfields, London	Ralph (Raphael) Cohen	Julia Lazarus		Spitalfields, London	apprentice tailor
1516	Cohen	Rachel	1843	Aldgate, London	Woolf Cohen	Hannah (Ann) Prince (Prins))		Spitalfields, London	scholar
19716	Cohen	Rachel	1844	Whitechapel, London	Herman Jacob Cohen	Rebecca Samuel	Judah Samuel	Whitechapel, London	
21760	Cohen	Rachel	1845	Birmingham	Ezekiel Cohen	Elizabeth Myers		Aldgate, London	
7941	Cohen	Rachel	1848	Aldgate, London	Nathan Cohen	Maria (?Rintel)	Solomon Moss (Moses)	Aldgate, London	
29382	Cohen	Rachel	1849	Whitechapel, London	George Cohen	Rachel (?)		Wapping, London	
24663	Cohen	Rachel (Ray)	1849	Elephant & Castle, London	Zachariah Cohen	Flora (?)		Kennington, London	
26978	Cohen	Rachell	1849	Aldgate, London	Joseph Cohen	Esther (?)		Aldgate, London	
29910	Cohen	Ralph	1816	Whitechapel, London	Joseph Cohen		Louisa (Leah) Jacobs	Whitechapel, London	?draper
15439	Cohen	Ralph	1834	Aldgate, London	Moses Cohen			Covent Garden, London	cigar maker
1629	Cohen	Ralph (Raphael)	1817	Spitalfields, London	Moses Cohen		Julia Lazarus	Spitalfields, London	general dealer
15187	Cohen	Raphael (Ralph)	1806	?, London	Enoch (Hanoj) Cohen	Judith de Joseph Bendan	Abigail de Abraham Torres	Shoreditch, London	confectioner
18633	Cohen	Raphael Isaac	1805	?, Germany			Hannah (?)	Dover, Kent	Synagogue Minister + secretary + schoolmaster
29307	Cohen	Rebecca	1778	Aldgate, London	(?)		(?) Cohen	Whitechapel, London	cook
29125	Cohen	Rebecca	1798	Whitechapel, London	(?)		Moses Cohen	Whitechapel, London	tailor
9970	Cohen	Rebecca	1806	?, Germany	(?)		Paris Cohen	Manchester	
1484	Cohen	Rebecca	1808	Spitalfields, London	(?)		Sampson Cohen	Spitalfields, London	
9699	Cohen	Rebecca	1811	City, London	John (Jacob) Joseph		Samuel Cohen	Aldgate, London	
19709	Cohen	Rebecca	1812	?, Holland	Natan Halevi Samuel	Hannah (?)	Herman Jacob Cohen	Whitechapel, London	
1479	Cohen	Rebecca	1813	Aldgate, London	(?) Hyams		Phineas Cohen	Spitalfields, London	
26095	Cohen	Rebecca	1813	?, Poland	(?)		(?) Cohen	Aldgate, London	dealer
1477	Cohen	Rebecca	1817	Southwark, London	Abraham Cohen		Benjamin Cohen	Spitalfields, London	
23032	Cohen	Rebecca	1822	City, London	Natan HaCohen Altman			Shoreditch, London	
19656	Cohen	Rebecca	1825	Whitechapel, London	Jacob (John) Lazarus	Sarah (?)	Joseph Cohen	Spitalfields, London	
10228	Cohen	Rebecca	1828	Aldgate, London	Emanuel Cohen	Hannah (?)		Aldgate, London	parasol maker

ID	surname	given names	born	birthplace	father	mother	spouse 1	1851 residence	1851 occupation
1472	Cohen	Rebecca	1831	Middlesex, London	(?) Cohen			Spitalfields, London	tailoress
14094	Cohen	Rebecca	1831	Hanover, Germany	(?) Cohen	Ellen (?)		Manchester	tailor
23255	Cohen	Rebecca	1831	Whitechapel, London	Isaac Cohen	Louisa (?)	Joseph Isaac Solomon	Notting Hill, London	
1584	Cohen	Rebecca	1833	Middlesex, London	Henry Cohen	Elizabeth (?)		Spitalfields, London	general dealer
28014	Cohen	Rebecca	1835	Whitechapel, London	Aaron Cohen	Rachael Harris		Spitalfields, London	
24819	Cohen	Rebecca	1841	?, London	Samuel Cohen	Ann (Nancy) Harris		Waterloo, London	scholar
1623	Cohen	Rebecca	1845	Amsterdam, Holland	Eleazer Cohen	Elizabeth (?)		Spitalfields, London	scholar
10396	Cohen	Rebecca	1847	Spitalfields, London	Philip Cohen	Rachael Jacobs		Spitalfields, London	
11544	Cohen	Rebecca	1847	Spitalfields, London	Aaron Cohen	Sarah (?)		Spitalfields, London	
10569	Cohen	Rebecca	1849	Whitechapel, London	Joseph Cohen	Maria (?)		Whitechapel, London	
1568	Cohen	Rebecca	1850	Spitalfields, London	Henry Cohen	Esther Levy		Aldgate, London	
18592	Cohen	Rebecca	1850	Aldgate, London	(?Abraham) Cohen	Elizabeth (?)		Stepney, London	
3900	Cohen	Rebecca (Elizabeth)	1840	Amsterdam, Holland	Emanuel Cohen	Sally (?)	Levy (Lewis) Lazarus	Spitalfields, London	
15195	Cohen	Rebecca (Rachel)	1842	?, London	Raphael (Ralph) Cohen	Abigail Torres	Emanuel Sperling	Shoreditch, London	scholar
7043	Cohen	Rebecca Floretta	1807	Finsbury, London	Asher Ansel Keyser		Louis Cohen	Finsbury, London	
3902	Cohen	Rena	1844	Amsterdam, Holland	Emanuel Cohen	Sally (?)		Spitalfields, London	
21121	Cohen	Reuben	1829	?, Germany	Benjamin Cohen	Bluma (?)		Aldgate, London	cap maker journeyman
17383	Cohen	Reuben	1835	Whitechapel, London	Lewis Cohen	Abigail Reuben		Wapping, London	cigar maker
24233	Cohen	Reyna	1791	Stepney, London	(?)		Mark Cohen	Hackney, London	
24239	Cohen	Reyna	1844	Stepney, London	Mark Cohen	Reyna (?)		Hackney, London	scholar at home
15572	Cohen	Rosa	1804	City, London	(?)		(?) Cohen	Covent Garden, London	general line
1602	Cohen	Rosa	1811	?, Holland	Jonah Solomon		Isaiah Cohen	Spitalfields, London	hawker
1608	Cohen	Rosa	1830	Spitalfields, London	Lewis (Lyon) Cohen	Harriet Lear		Spitalfields, London	tailoress
18300	Cohen	Rosa	1833	?, Russia	Moses Cohen	Jane (?)	Harris Davies	Sheffield, Yorkshire	hawker
26973	Cohen	Rosa	1835	Aldgate, London	Joseph Cohen	Esther (?)		Aldgate, London	house servant
1603	Cohen	Rosa	1836	Spitalfields, London	Isaiah Cohen	Rosa Solomon		Spitalfields, London	tailoress
19714	Cohen	Rosa	1841	Whitechapel, London	Herman Jacob Cohen	Rebecca Samuel		Whitechapel, London	
1631	Cohen	Rosa	1843	Spitalfields, London	Ralph (Raphael) Cohen	Julia Lazarus	Lewis Benjamin	Spitalfields, London	scholar
11064	Cohen	Rosa	1847	Aldgate, London	Samuel Cohen	Hannah Phillips		Aldgate, London	
15090	Cohen	Rosa	1849	Stepney, London	Joseph Cohen	Catharine (?)		Mile End, London	
29231	Cohen	Rosalia	1843	?, Germany	Louis Cohen	Sophia (?)		Whitechapel, London	
2398	Cohen	Rosalie	1827	?, Germany	(?) Bremer		(?Marks, ?Moses, ?Solomon) Cohen	Hull, Yorkshire	jeweller's wife
1104	Cohen	Rose	1804	Falmouth, Cornwall			(?) Cohen	Falmouth, Cornwall	pedlar's wife
21996	Cohen	Rose	1831	Middlesex, London				Whitechapel, London	
1499	Cohen	Rose	1850	Spitalfields, London	Aaron Cohen	Julia Solomon Wilks		Spitalfields, London	
19155	Cohen	Rose (Rosetta)	1846	Aldgate, London	Leman Cohen	Clara Lyon	Abraham Polack	Aldgate, London	scholar
9201	Cohen	Rosena	1850	Whitechapel, London	George Cohen	Hannah (?)		Whitechapel, London	
14760	Cohen	Rosetta	1799	Whitechapel, London	(?) Cohen			Finsbury, London	
16226	Cohen	Rosetta	1807	Whitechapel, London	(?)		Samuel Cohen	Clerkenwell, London	
25367	Cohen	Rosetta	1813	Wapping, London	Goodman Levy	Sarah (?)	Henry Cohen	Clerkenwell, London	
24735	Cohen	Rosetta	1815	Southwark, London	Philip Cohen	Jane (?)		Southwark, London	milliner + dress maker
11141	Cohen	Rosetta	1816	Aldgate, London	(?) Cohen	Frances (?)		Aldgate, London	governess
20693	Cohen	Rosetta	1819	Amsterdam, Holland	Israel Lyon		Jacob Cohen	Spitalfields, London	

ID	surname	given names	born	birthplace	father	mother	spouse 1	1851 residence	1851 occupation
10226	Cohen	Rosetta	1822	Aldgate, London	Emanuel Cohen	Hannah (?)		Aldgate, London	parasol maker
6272	Cohen	Rosetta	1825	Whitechapel, London	Moshe Levy		Abraham Cohen	Spitalfields, London	
18358	Cohen	Rosetta	1827	St Pancras, London	Joseph Cohen	Elizabeth Benjamin		Elephant & Castle, London	
27423	Cohen	Rosetta	1829	?, Germany	(?)		Lazarus Cohen	Whitechapel, London	tailoress
1564	Cohen	Rosetta	1840	Whitechapel, London	Henry Cohen	Esther Levy		Aldgate, London	
5164	Cohen	Rosetta	1845	Spitalfields, London	Barnet Cohen	Sarah Hyman	Henry Magnus	Spitalfields, London	
12609	Cohen	Rosetta	1849	Norwich, Norfolk	Joseph L Cohen	Charlotte (?)		Norwich, Norfolk	
27424	Cohen	Rosetta	1850	Aldgate, London	Lazarus Cohen	Rosetta (?)		Whitechapel, London	
18264	Cohen	Rosey	1828	Boston, Lincolnshire	Daniel Cohen	Sarah (?)		Boston, Lincolnshire	
4389	Cohen	Ruth	1841	Birmingham	Jacob Colman Cohen	?Katie (?)	?Lewis Lewis?)	Birmingham	scholar
3898	Cohen	Sally	1806	Amsterdam, Holland			Emanuel Cohen	Spitalfields, London	
5158	Cohen	Sampson	1808	Southwark, London	Isaac Cohen	Esther Davis	Rebecca (?)	Spitalfields, London	furniture broker
1622	Cohen	Samson	1839	Amsterdam, Holland	Eleazer Cohen	Elizabeth (?)		Spitalfields, London	cigar maker
16225	Cohen	Samuel	1796	Whitechapel, London	Baruch HaCohen		Rosetta (?)	Clerkenwell, London	tool dealer
6357	Cohen	Samuel	1807	Southwark, London	Moses Cohen	Abigail (?)	Rebecca Joseph	Aldgate, London	furniture dealer
1759	Cohen	Samuel	1811	?, Poland [?, Prussia]				Merthyr Tydfil, Wales	hawker
6353	Cohen	Samuel	1811	Aldgate, London	Moshe HaCohen		Hannah Phillips	Aldgate, London	clothes man
15315	Cohen	Samuel	1815	Southwark, London	Abraham Cohen	Sarah (?)		Shoreditch, London	carpet dealer
24816	Cohen	Samuel	1815	?, London	Abraham Cohen		Ann (Nancy) Harris	Waterloo, London	tailor
1529	Cohen	Samuel	1818	Aldgate, London			Sarah (?)	Spitalfields, London	clothier
26642	Cohen	Samuel	1819	Aldgate, London			Mary (?)	Aldgate, London	clothes dealer
12594	Cohen	Samuel	1822	Lowestoft, Suffolk			Mary Ann (?)	Great Yarmouth, Norfolk	twine spinner
4282	Cohen	Samuel	1823	?, Poland [?, Prussia]				Birmingham	jeweller
1758	Cohen	Samuel	1825	Aldgate, London				Merthyr Tydfil, Wales	outfitter, tailor
13331	Cohen	Samuel	1825	Spitalfields, London	David Cohen	Harriet Woolf	Rachel Solomon	Spitalfields, London	labourer
24837	Cohen	Samuel	1825	Southwark, London	Aaron Cohen	Rachel Davis		Elephant & Castle, London	assistant to merchant
13713	Cohen	Samuel	1829	?Budapest, Hungary [Pesth]				Bloomsbury, London	journeyman tailor
15662	Cohen	Samuel	1829	?, Poland [?, Prussia]				Aldgate, London	tailor
11347	Cohen	Samuel	1831	?, Poland				Aldgate, London	tailor
25385	Cohen	Samuel	1831	Holborn, London	Aaron Cohen	Rachel (?)		Clerkenwell, London	cigar maker
1550	Cohen	Samuel	1834	Spitalfields, London	Isaiah Cohen			Spitalfields, London	cigar maker
24235	Cohen	Samuel	1837	Stepney, London	Mark Cohen	Reyna (?)		Hackney, London	
1481	Cohen	Samuel	1841	Spitalfields, London	Phineas Cohen	Rebecca Hyams		Spitalfields, London	scholar
18537	Cohen	Samuel	1841	Finsbury, London	Isaac Cohen	Elizabeth Cohen		Finsbury, London	
29790	Cohen	Samuel	1841	Whitechapel, London	David Abraham Cohen	Hannah Solomon		Whitechapel, London	scholar
2629	Cohen	Samuel	1844	Liverpool	Henry Cohen	Caroline (?)		Glasgow, Scotland	
25372	Cohen	Samuel	1846	Holborn, London	Henry Cohen	Rosetta (?)		Clerkenwell, London	scholar
1627	Cohen	Samuel	1847	Aldgate, London	Emanuel Cohen	Esther (?)		Spitalfields, London	scholar
28970	Cohen	Samuel	1847	Aldgate, London	Solomon Isaac Cohen	Hannah Levie		Whitechapel, London	scholar
19659	Cohen	Samuel	1848	Spitalfields, London	Joseph Cohen	Rebecca Lazarus		Spitalfields, London	
18304	Cohen	Samuel	1849	Sheffield, Yorkshire	Moses Cohen	Jane (?)	Fanny Lewis	Sheffield, Yorkshire	
25347	Cohen	Sanders	1798	?, Northamptonshire				Finsbury, London	commission salesman
15314	Cohen	Sarah	1776	City, London	(?)		Abraham Cohen	Shoreditch, London	

ID	surname	given names	born	birthplace	father	mother	spouse 1	1851 residence	1851 occupation
24614	Cohen	Sarah	1782	Aldgate, London	(?)		Philip Cohen	Kennington, London	
29026	Cohen	Sarah	1785	Whitechapel, London	(?)			Whitechapel, London	needlewoman
3331	Cohen	Sarah	1792	Whitechapel, London	Barnett Hart		Moss Cohen	Spitalfields, London	
26616	Cohen	Sarah	1792	Whitechapel, London	(?)		(?) Cohen	City, London	house servant
22197	Cohen	Sarah	1793	Middlesex, London	(?)			Whitechapel, London	
18262	Cohen	Sarah	1801	?, Poland [?, Prussia]	(?)		Daniel Cohen	Boston, Lincolnshire	
29067	Cohen	Sarah	1804	Whitechapel, London	Ezekiel Cohen	R--- (?)		Whitechapel, London	feather maker
18187	Cohen	Sarah	1806	Middlesex, London	(?) Cohen			Mile End, London	cook to house
23308	Cohen	Sarah	1811	Middlesex, London	Pinchas Samuel		Isaac Cohen	Mayfair, London	fundholder
27509	Cohen	Sarah	1811	Middlesex, London	Moshe Cohen			Aldgate, London	
1538	Cohen	Sarah	1814	Spitalfields, London	(?Abraham Moses)		James Cohen	Spitalfields, London	
5162	Cohen	Sarah	1815	Middlesex, London	Mordecai Hyman		Barnet Cohen	Spitalfields, London	
1531	Cohen	Sarah	1819	Spitalfields, London	(?)		Samuel Cohen	Spitalfields, London	
10225	Cohen	Sarah	1819	Aldgate, London	Emanuel Cohen	Hannah (?)		Aldgate, London	furrier
10401	Cohen	Sarah	1819	Spitalfields, London	Samson Isaacs		Michael Cohen	Spitalfields, London	
15753	Cohen	Sarah	1821	Middlesex, London	Menachem Mendel Kahn (Cohen)		Selim Cohen	Aldgate, London	
11543	Cohen	Sarah	1823	Whitechapel, London	(?)		Aaron Cohen	Spitalfields, London	
10872	Cohen	Sarah	1825	Whitechapel, London	Jacob Solomon	Ann (?Hart)	Lewis Cohen	Spitalfields, London	shoe binder
3333	Cohen	Sarah	1826	Whitechapel, London	Michael Isaacs		George Cohen	Spitalfields, London	
14069	Cohen	Sarah	1826	Sheffield, Yorkshire	(?) Cohen	Priscilla (?)		Manchester	governess
14082	Cohen	Sarah	1826	?, Poland [?, Prussia]	(?)		Louis Cohen	Manchester	
22936	Cohen	Sarah	1826	Whitechapel, London			(?)	Wapping, London	dressmaker
26222	Cohen	Sarah	1826	?, London	(?) Cohen			Aldgate, London	servant
1587	Cohen	Sarah	1828	?, Holland	(?)		Henry Cohen	Spitalfields, London	
8583	Cohen	Sarah	1828	Soho, London	Humphrey Cohen	Louisa (?)	James Phillips	Soho, London	
2245	Cohen	Sarah	1830	Leeds, Yorkshire			Marcus Cohen	Leeds, Yorkshire	
1549	Cohen	Sarah	1831	Spitalfields, London	Isaiah Cohen			Spitalfields, London	dress maker
10389	Cohen	Sarah	1833	Whitechapel, London	Philip Cohen	Rachael Jacobs		Spitalfields, London	
6202	Cohen	Sarah	1834	Spitalfields, London	Lewis Cohen	Deborah Michael	Joseph Nathan	Spitalfields, London	waistcoat maker
9267	Cohen	Sarah	1834	?, Holland	Myers S Cohen	Jane (?)		Aldgate, London	
29059	Cohen	Sarah	1834	Whitechapel, London	Simon Cohen	Isabella (?)		Whitechapel, London	
14761	Cohen	Sarah	1837	Whitechapel, London	(?) Cohen			Finsbury, London	
19713	Cohen	Sarah	1837	?, Holland	Herman Jacob Cohen	Rebecca Samuel		Whitechapel, London	
1106	Cohen	Sarah	1838	Penzance, Cornwall	(?) Cohen	Rose (?)		Falmouth, Cornwall	scholar
20694	Cohen	Sarah	1838	Whitechapel, London	Jacob Cohen	Rosetta Lyon		Spitalfields, London	scholar
15193	Cohen	Sarah	1839	?, London	Raphael (Ralph) Cohen	Abigail Torres		Shoreditch, London	scholar
21126	Cohen	Sarah	1839	Aldgate, London	Benjamin Cohen	Bluma (?)	Aaron Levy	Aldgate, London	apprentice tailoress
27309	Cohen	Sarah	1840	Shoreditch, London	Lewis Cohen	(?)		Aldgate, London	
6356	Cohen	Sarah	1842	Aldgate, London	Samuel Cohen	Hannah Phillips	Solomon Jacobs	Aldgate, London	
25788	Cohen	Sarah	1843	Aldgate, London	Solomon Cohen	Catherine Myers		Aldgate, London	scholar
1507	Cohen	Sarah	1844	Spitalfields, London	Mark Cohen	Rachel (?)		Spitalfields, London	scholar
17385	Cohen	Sarah	1844	Whitechapel, London	Lewis Cohen	Abigail Reuben		Wapping, London	scholar
26976	Cohen	Sarah	1844	Aldgate, London	Joseph Cohen	Esther (?)		Aldgate, London	scholar
10405	Cohen	Sarah	1848	Spitalfields, London	Michael Cohen	Sarah Jacobs		Spitalfields, London	
21762	Cohen	Sarah	1848	Aldgate, London	Ezekiel Cohen	Elizabeth Myers	Noah Woolf	Aldgate, London	

ID	surname	given names	born	birthplace	father	mother	spouse 1	1851 residence	1851 occupation
2624	Cohen	Sarah	1849	Glasgow, Scotland	Joseph Cohen	Rachel Goodman		Glasgow, Scotland	
17342	Cohen	Sarah	1849	Spitalfields, London	Samuel Cohen	Sarah (?)		Spitalfields, London	
25374	Cohen	Sarah	1849	Holborn, London	Henry Cohen	Rosetta (?)		Clerkenwell, London	scholar
25381	Cohen	Sarah	1849	Middlesex, London	Joseph Cohen	Esther Isaacs		Clerkenwell, London	scholar
18500	Cohen	Sarah	1850	Middlesex, London	Moss Cohen	Ellen Goodman		Whitechapel, London	
24823	Cohen	Sarah	1850	?, London	Samuel Cohen	Ann (Nancy) Harris		Waterloo, London	
28972	Cohen	Sarah	1850	Aldgate, London	Solomon Isaac Cohen	Hannah Levie		Whitechapel, London	
5157	Cohen	Sarah	1851	Wapping, London	Judah Cohen	Caroline Davis		Wapping, London	
8040	Cohen	Sarah (Sierlah, Tserele)	1788	Aldgate, London	Eliezer Zessel Levy		Barnett (Baruch) Cohen	Lambeth, London	
12605	Cohen	Sarah A	1840	Norwich, Norfolk	Joseph L Cohen	Charlotte (?)		Norwich, Norfolk	
15199	Cohen	Saul	1849	?, London	Raphael (Ralph) Cohen	Abigail Torres		Shoreditch, London	
20573	Cohen	Saul (Sell)	1791	Whitechapel, London			Welcome (?)	Spitalfields, London	general dealer
23057	Cohen	Saunder	1803	Hamburg, Germany			Amelia (?)	Aldgate, London	cigar maker
15752	Cohen	Selim	1817	Piccadilly, London	Humphrey Cohen	Louisa (?)	Sarah Kahn	Aldgate, London	hardwareman
2247	Cohen	Sim	1812	Spitalfields, London			Maria (?)	Leeds, Yorkshire	French polisher
25716	Cohen	Simela (Simlah)	1827	?, Poland	Solomon Moses		Solomon (Selig) Cohen	Spitalfields, London	
13951	Cohen	Simeon	1766	Middlesex, London			(?)	Manchester	retired trunk dealer
5145	Cohen	Simeon	1803	?, Poland [?, Prussia-Poland]				Sheffield, Yorkshire	rabbi
1524	Cohen	Simeon	1848	Spitalfields, London	Samuel Cohen	Rebecca Joseph	Mary Ann Levi	Aldgate, London	
15682	Cohen	Simon	1796	?, Poland [?, Prussia]				Aldgate, London	teacher
29056	Cohen	Simon	1799	Whitechapel, London	Ezekiel Cohen	R--- (?)	Isabella (?)	Whitechapel, London	pencil maker
2630	Cohen	Simon	1803	?, Poland [?, Prussia]				Glasgow, Scotland	Hebrew teacher
9449	Cohen	Simon	1819	Kepno, Poland [Kempen, Prussia]	Tsevi HaCohen		Dinah Solomon	Aldgate, London	wholesale jeweller
8449	Cohen	Simon	1821	?, Poland			Mary Ann (?)	Portsmouth, Hampshire	travelling labourer
123	Cohen	Simon	1823	Poznan, Poland [Posen, Prussia]				Woolwich, London	
3125	Cohen	Simon	1825	?	Michael Cohen	Adaline (?)	Hortense Vallet	South Shields, Tyne & Wear	artificial flower maker + traveller
16923	Cohen	Simon	1825	?, Poland [?, Prussia]				Sheffield, Yorkshire	traveller
17734	Cohen	Simon	1829	?, Poland [?, Prussia]				Aldgate, London	tailor
2613	Cohen	Simon M	1806	Exeter, Devon			Harriet (?)	Glasgow, Scotland	optician
1599	Cohen	Soloman	1846	Spitalfields, London	(?)	Hannah (?)		Spitalfields, London	scholar
21743	Cohen	Solomon	1778	Aldgate, London	Levi Cohen		Hannah Moses Samuel	Canonbury, London	retired merchant
15992	Cohen	Solomon	1780	?, London			Mary (?)	St John's Wood, London	retired merchant
1500	Cohen	Solomon	1784	Whitechapel, London			Rachel (?)	Spitalfields, London	furniture broker
18275	Cohen	Solomon	1785	Aldgate, London			(?)	Salisbury, Wiltshire	manufacturer of flowers
25782	Cohen	Solomon	1799	Spitalfields, London	Isaac Cohen		Catherine Myers	Aldgate, London	confectioner
29928	Cohen	Solomon	1799	?, London			Susan (?)	Brighton, Sussex	confectioner
30907	Cohen	Solomon	1801	?, Poland [?, Prussia]			Rachel (?)	Lincoln, Lincolnshire	silversmith &c
17651	Cohen	Solomon	1805	?, Poland			Hannah (?)	Aldgate, London	hawker
17042	Cohen	Solomon	1806	?, Poland [?, Prussia]				Edinburgh, Scotland	travelling dealer
3376	Cohen	Solomon	1823	Middlesex, London	Benjamin Wolf Cohen	Frances Phillips		Holborn, London	fishmonger
2692	Cohen	Solomon	1824	Peizer, Poland	Lazarus Cohen		Sarah (?)	Coventry, Warwickshire	rabbi

ID	surname	given names	born	birthplace	father	mother	spouse 1	1851 residence	1851 occupation
22566	Cohen	Solomon	1826	Bethnal Green, London				Whitechapel, London	cigar maker
2127	Cohen	Solomon	1828	Sheffield, Yorkshire			Miriam Hart	Hull, Yorkshire	clothier
27498	Cohen	Solomon	1833	Middlesex, London				Aldgate, London	dealer in clothes
1591	Cohen	Solomon	1837	Spitalfields, London	(?) Cohen			Spitalfields, London	apprentice
25705	Cohen	Solomon	1837	Whitechapel, London	Abraham Cohen	Maria Samuel		Spitalfields, London	apprentice to clothes dealer
3901	Cohen	Solomon	1842	Amsterdam, Holland	Emanuel Cohen	Sally (?)		Spitalfields, London	
20696	Cohen	Solomon	1842	Aldgate, London	Jacob Cohen	Rosetta Lyon		Spitalfields, London	scholar
25983	Cohen	Solomon	1844	Aldgate, London	Lipman Cohen	Jane Isaacs		Aldgate, London	scholar
2623	Cohen	Solomon	1845	Glasgow, Scotland	Joseph Cohen	Rachel Goodman		Glasgow, Scotland	scholar
2795	Cohen	Solomon	1845	Aldgate, London	Nathan Cohen	Mary (Maria) Moses	Martha Mendoza	Bermondsey, London	
11479	Cohen	Solomon	1845	Aldgate, London	Nathan Cohen	Maria (?Rintel)		Aldgate, London	
11639	Cohen	Solomon	1848	Aldgate, London	Abraham Cohen	Elizabeth Busnach (?Barnett)		Aldgate, London	
25715	Cohen	Solomon (Selig)	1829	?, Poland	Eleazer Zimmerman		Simela (Simlah) Moses	Spitalfields, London	tailor
30911	Cohen	Solomon G	1840	Halifax, Yorkshire				Halifax, Yorkshire	scholar
27918	Cohen	Solomon Henry	1850	Whitechapel, London	Myer Cohen	Hannah (?)		Spitalfields, London	
23880	Cohen	Solomon Hyman	1811	Holborn, London	Hyman Benjamin Cohen		Ann Davis	Westminster, London	china dealer
28963	Cohen	Solomon Isaac	1806	Aldgate, London	Isaac Cohen		Hannah Levie	Whitechapel, London	wholesale clothes dealer
12601	Cohen	Sophia	1778	?, London	(?)		Moses Cohen	Norwich, Norfolk	
29230	Cohen	Sophia	1824	?, Germany	(?)		Louis Cohen	Whitechapel, London	tailoress
15995	Cohen	Sophia	1825	Middlesex, London	(?) Cohen			Bloomsbury, London	
22937	Cohen	Sophia	1828	Whitechapel, London	Jacob Cohen	(?)		Wapping, London	dressmaker
23256	Cohen	Sophia	1833	Whitechapel, London	Isaac Cohen	Louisa (?)	I--- N--- Schnurmann	Notting Hill, London	
10394	Cohen	Sophia	1844	Aldgate, London	Philip Cohen	Rachael Jacobs		Spitalfields, London	scholar
24821	Cohen	Sophia	1846	Wapping, London	Samuel Cohen	Ann (Nancy) Harris	John Joel	Waterloo, London	scholar
19464	Cohen	Sophia	1847	Aldgate, London	Abraham Cohen	Esther Moses		Aldgate, London	
27916	Cohen	Sophia	1847	Portsmouth, Hampshire	Myer Cohen	Hannah (?)		Spitalfields, London	
2830	Cohen	Sophia	1849	?, America	Victor Cohen	Henrietta Magnus	Henry Cohen	Spitalfields, London	
1546	Cohen	Sophia	1850	Spitalfields, London	Moses Cohen	Clara Michael		Spitalfields, London	
3334	Cohen	Sophia	1850	Spitalfields, London	George Cohen	Sarah Isaacs	John (Jonah) Berlyn	Spitalfields, London	
23043	Cohen	Susan	1840	?, London	(?) Cohen			Aldgate, London	scholar
17944	Cohen	Theresa	1798	?, London	(?)		Emanuel Cohen	Whitechapel, London	
13981	Cohen	Theresa	1828	Hamburg, Germany	(?) Cohen			Manchester	governess
20548	Cohen	Tobias	1812	Aldgate, London				Aldgate, London	jeweller
26096	Cohen	Tobias	1833	?, Poland	(?) Cohen	Rebecca (?)		Aldgate, London	tailor
2825	Cohen	Victor	1815	?, Poland [?, Prussia]	Isaac		Henrietta Magnus	Spitalfields, London	general dealer
25368	Cohen	Victoria	1838	Holborn, London	Henry Cohen	Rosetta (?)		Clerkenwell, London	scholar
20572	Cohen	Welcome	1788	Aldgate, London	(?)		Saul (Sell) Cohen	Spitalfields, London	general dealer
5408	Cohen	Welcome	1849	Aldgate, London	Israel Cohen	Rachel Isaacs	Alfred Joseph (Jay)	Whitechapel, London	
21872	Cohen	Welcome (Benvenida)	1801	Aldgate, London	David Nunes Carvalho		Jacob de Enoch (Hanoj) Cohen	Clerkenwell, London	confectioner
25369	Cohen	William	1840	Holborn, London	Henry Cohen	Rosetta (?)		Clerkenwell, London	scholar
5125	Cohen	Wolf	1816	?, Russia				Sheffield, Yorkshire	watchmaker + jeweller
30947	Cohen	Wolf	1830	?, Poland				Hull, Yorkshire	hawker - jewellery

ID	surname	given names	born	birthplace	father	mother	spouse 1	1851 residence	1851 occupation
5219	Cohen	Wolf	1831	?, Poland	Isaac Cohen	Jeanette (?)	Yetta Levin	Liverpool	jeweller
4393	Cohen	Wolf	1838	Birmingham	Joseph Colman Cohen	?Katie (?)	Hannah (?)	Birmingham	
6260	Cohen	Wolf Henry	1850	Whitechapel, London	Barnet Solomon Cohen	Eliza Myers		St John's Wood, London	
1512	Cohen	Woolf	1804	Rotterdam, Holland	Yechiel HaCohen		Hannah (Ann) Prince (Prins))	Spitalfields, London	tailor
6306	Cohen	Woolf	1838	Whitechapel, London	Henry Cohen	Esther (?)	Mary (Pollie) Jacobs	Spitalfields, London	
13721	Cohen	Woolf	1843	Finsbury, London	Isaac Cohen	Elizabeth Cohen	Rebecca Cortissos	Finsbury, London	
13335	Cohen	Woolf	1846	Spitalfields, London	David Cohen	Harriet Woolf		Spitalfields, London	
30392	Cohen	Woolf	1851	Spitalfields, London	Michael Cohen	Sarah Jacobs		Spitalfields, London	
6261	Cohen	Woolf H	1838	?, Russia	Moses Cohen	Yetta (?)	Harriet Phillips	?	
30830	Cohen	Yetta	1817	?, Poland [?, Prussia]	(?) Cohen			Coventry, Warwickshire	housekeeper
2621	Cohen	Ynassy	1839	?, England	Joseph Cohen	Rachel Goodman		Glasgow, Scotland	scholar
24658	Cohen	Zachariah	1815	Elephant & Castle, London	Philip Cohen	Sarah (?)	Flora (?)	Kennington, London	commercial traveller
2400	Colbourne	Frederick	1819	?, Poland [?, Prussia]				Hull, Yorkshire	waiter
18239	Cole	Eliza	1770	?, London	(?)		(?) Cole	Cheltenham, Gloucestershire	
16277	Coleman	Abigail	1842	Spitalfields, London	Jacob Coleman	Esther (?)	Abraham Polack	Spitalfields, London	scholar
28741	Coleman	Ally (Eli?)	1849	Middlesex, London				Spitalfields, London	
27043	Coleman	Angel	1842	?, Poland	Lewis Coleman	Hannah (?)		Aldgate, London	scholar
19476	Coleman	Barnett	1801	?, Poland	Kalonymus Kalman		Maria Isaacs	Stepney, London	labourer
21205	Coleman	Barnett	1847	Spitalfields, London	Coleman Coleman	Frances Henry		Spitalfields, London	scholar
17405	Coleman	Benjamin	1787	Aldgate, London			Jane (?)	Wapping, London	general dealer + clothier
28742	Coleman	Benjamin	1824	Middlesex, London				Spitalfields, London	glass dealer
17407	Coleman	Catherine	1810	Aldgate, London	(?) Coleman			Wapping, London	general dealer + clothier
23756	Coleman	Charlotte	1821	Liverpool	Sylvester Coleman	Flora Yates		Liverpool	
21198	Coleman	Coleman	1808	Middlesex, London	Eliezer Coleman		Frances Henry	Spitalfields, London	clothier
15013	Coleman	Eleazer	1846	Spitalfields, London	Jacob Coleman	Esther (?)		Spitalfields, London	scholar
16279	Coleman	Esther	1814	?, Holland	(?)		Jacob Coleman	Spitalfields, London	cap maker
13439	Coleman	Esther	1816	Aldgate, London	(?) Coleman	Sarah (?)		Aldgate, London	
378	Coleman	Esther	1822	?, Holland	Soloman Coleman	Sarah (?)		Spitalfields, London	cap maker
26296	Coleman	Esther	1828	?, London	(?) Coleman			Aldgate, London	tailoress
6392	Coleman	Flora	1785	?, London	(?) Yates		Sylvester Coleman	Holborn, London	annuitant
21199	Coleman	Frances	1809	Middlesex, London	Isaac Henry	Tamar (?)	Frances Henry	Spitalfields, London	
27041	Coleman	Hannah	1820	?, Poland	(?)		Lewis Coleman	Aldgate, London	
21206	Coleman	Hannah	1849	Spitalfields, London	Coleman Coleman	Frances Henry		Spitalfields, London	
19472	Coleman	Hannah (Anna)	1841	Stepney, London	Barnett Coleman	Maria Isaacs	Judah Lewis	Stepney, London	
21204	Coleman	Henry	1841	Spitalfields, London	Coleman Coleman	Frances Henry		Spitalfields, London	scholar
21200	Coleman	Isaac	1832	Middlesex, London	Coleman Coleman	Frances Henry	(?)	Spitalfields, London	cigar maker
19474	Coleman	Isaac	1835	Stepney, London	Barnett Coleman	Maria Isaacs	Betsy Levy	Stepney, London	cigar maker
8236	Coleman	Isabella (Elizabella)	1849	Whitechapel, London	Israel Coleman	Julia Cohen	Moses Hyman	Whitechapel, London	
8237	Coleman	Israel	1819	?, Poland	Kalonymus (Woolf) Kalman		Julia Cohen	Whitechapel, London	master tailor
16278	Coleman	Jacob	1807	?, Holland	Kalonymus		Esther (?)	Spitalfields, London	cap maker
27044	Coleman	Jacob	1843	?, Poland	Lewis Coleman	Hannah (?)		Aldgate, London	scholar
17406	Coleman	Jane	1791	Aldgate, London	(?)		Benjamin Coleman	Wapping, London	general dealer + clothier

ID	surname	given names	born	birthplace	father	mother	spouse 1	1851 residence	1851 occupation
27042	Coleman	Jane	1837	?, Poland	Lewis Coleman	Hannah (?)		Aldgate, London	scholar
19475	Coleman	John	1845	Whitechapel, London	Barnett Coleman	Maria Isaacs		Stepney, London	
8238	Coleman	Julia	1819	Stepney, London	Moses Cohen	Elizabeth (?)	Israel Coleman	Whitechapel, London	
27040	Coleman	Lewis	1820	?, Poland			Hannah (?)	Aldgate, London	tailor
19473	Coleman	Lewis	1832	Spitalfields, London	Barnett Coleman	Maria Isaacs		Stepney, London	cigar maker
28052	Coleman	Lewis	1832	Bydgoszcz, Poland [Bromberg, Prussia]				Spitalfields, London	tailor
19477	Coleman	Maria	1811	Whitechapel, London	Yaacov Isaacs		Barnett Coleman	Stepney, London	tailoress
21201	Coleman	Mark	1834	Middlesex, London	Coleman Coleman	Frances Henry		Spitalfields, London	cigar maker
15014	Coleman	Phillip	1848	Spitalfields, London	Jacob Coleman	Esther (?)		Spitalfields, London	scholar
16275	Coleman	Phoeby	1836	Spitalfields, London	Jacob Coleman	Esther (?)		Spitalfields, London	cap maker
13440	Coleman	Rosetta	1822	Aldgate, London	(?) Coleman	Sarah (?)		Aldgate, London	
6577	Coleman	Samuel Yates	1825	Liverpool	Sylvester Coleman	Flora Yates	Elizabeth Fairhurst	Liverpool	clerk to print seller
13438	Coleman	Sarah	1773	Aldgate, London	(?)			Aldgate, London	
377	Coleman	Sarah	1779	?, Holland			Soloman Coleman	Spitalfields, London	cap maker
23757	Coleman	Sarah	1803	Liverpool	(?) Coleman			Liverpool	
21203	Coleman	Sarah	1839	Spitalfields, London	Coleman Coleman	Frances Henry	(?) Raphael	Spitalfields, London	scholar
15012	Coleman	Sarah	1844	Spitalfields, London	Jacob Coleman	Esther (?)	Lewis Harris	Spitalfields, London	scholar
8239	Coleman	Sarah	1848	Whitechapel, London	Israel Coleman	Julia Cohen	Henry Cohen	Whitechapel, London	
376	Coleman	Soloman	1784	?, Holland			Sarah (?)	Spitalfields, London	cap maker
15015	Coleman	Sophier	1842	Spitalfields, London	Jacob Coleman	Esther (?)		Spitalfields, London	scholar
21202	Coleman	Tamar	1836	Spitalfields, London	Coleman Coleman	Frances Henry		Spitalfields, London	
16276	Coleman	Woolf	1838	Spitalfields, London	Jacob Coleman	Esther (?)		Spitalfields, London	cigar maker
3130	Collins	Abraham	1841	Sunderland, Co Durham	John Collins	Mary (Meriel) Cohen	Amelia Cohen	Sunderland, Co Durham	scholar
20479	Collins	Abraham	1849	?, London	Mark Collins	Lydia (?)		Covent Garden, London	
18683	Collins	Adelaide	1830	Bristol	Solomon George Coliins	Kate Isaacs	John Collins	Euston, London	
20477	Collins	Amelia	1846	?, London	Mark Collins	Lydia (?)		Covent Garden, London	
3134	Collins	Anne	1850	Sunderland, Co Durham	John Collins	Mary (Meriel) Cohen		Sunderland, Co Durham	
16309	Collins	Augustus	1846	Covent Garden, London	Henry Hirsch Collins	Floretta (?)		Covent Garden, London	
25447	Collins	Catherine	1810	Amsterdam, Holland	(?)		Eleazer Collins	Aldgate, London	licensed hawker
16086	Collins	Charles	1843	Spitalfields, London	Lewis Collins	Julia Isaacs	Jane Moses	Euston, London	scholar
16311	Collins	Edward	1848	Covent Garden, London	Henry Hirsch Collins	Floretta (?)		Covent Garden, London	
25446	Collins	Eleazer	1806	Rotterdam, Holland			Catherine (?)	Aldgate, London	licensed hawker
16308	Collins	Eliza	1844	Covent Garden, London	Henry Hirsch Collins	Floretta (?)		Covent Garden, London	
6143	Collins	Elizabeth	1839	Middlesex, London	Simeon (Simon) Collins	Rosetta Solomon	Joseph Nathan	Marylebone, London	
3131	Collins	Elizabeth	1844	Sunderland, Co Durham	John Collins	Mary (Meriel) Cohen	George Pyser	Sunderland, Co Durham	scholar
30363	Collins	Ellen	1839	Middlesex, London	Hyman Collins	Mary (Maria) Davis		Marylebone, London	charwoman
3133	Collins	Esther	1848	Sunderland, Co Durham	John Collins	Mary (Meriel) Cohen		Sunderland, Co Durham	
16306	Collins	Floretta	1811	Westminster, London	(?)		Henry Hirsch Collins	Covent Garden, London	
16307	Collins	Frances	1837	Covent Garden, London	Henry Hirsch Collins	Floretta (?)		Covent Garden, London	
16305	Collins	Henry Hirsch	1807	Westminster, London			Floretta (?)	Covent Garden, London	auctioneer
7063	Collins	Hyman Henry	1833	Westminster, London	Henry Hirsch Collins	Floretta (?)	Matilda Marcus	Soho, London	
3129	Collins	Jane	1840	Sunderland, Co Durham	John Collins	Mary (Meriel) Cohen		Sunderland, Co Durham	scholar
16087	Collins	Jane	1845	?, Gloucestershire	Lewis Collins	Julia Isaacs		Euston, London	scholar
3132	Collins	Janet Cissie	1848	Sunderland, Co Durham	John Collins	Mary (Meriel) Cohen		Sunderland, Co Durham	scholar

ID	surname	given names	born	birthplace	father	mother	spouse 1	1851 residence	1851 occupation
3127	Collins	John	1810	?, Poland [?, Prussia]	Abraham Collins		Mary Cohen	Sunderland, Co Durham	jeweller
18682	Collins	John	1828	Soho, London	Woolf Collins		Adelaide Collins	Euston, London	hatter
16088	Collins	Joseph	1850	St Pancras, London	Lewis Collins	Julia Isaacs	Esther Harris	Euston, London	
16084	Collins	Julia	1815	Westminster, London	Solomon Isaacs	Julia Isaacs	Lewis Collins	Euston, London	hat maker's wife
30258	Collins	Julius	1815	Covent Garden, London	Hyman Collins	Mary (Maria) Davis	Rosa Emma Salaman	Euston, London	general practice medicine
6537	Collins	Kate	1807	Marylebone, London	(?) Isaacs		Solomon George Collins	Euston, London	
16083	Collins	Lewis	1817	Soho, London	Isaac Collins		Julia Isaacs	Euston, London	hat maker
16312	Collins	Lionel	1850	Covent Garden, London	Henry Hirsch Collins	Floretta (?)		Covent Garden, London	
20475	Collins	Lydia	1811	?, London	(?)		Mark Collins	Covent Garden, London	
10746	Collins	Maria	1769	?, Holland	(?)		(?) Collins	Spitalfields, London	supported by her children
20474	Collins	Mark	1818	?, London	William (Wolf) Collins	Priscilla Marks	Lydia (?)	Covent Garden, London	hatmaker
30361	Collins	Mary (Maria)	1787	Middlesex, London	Simon ben Sam Irishman		Hyman Collins	Marylebone, London	greengrocer
30362	Collins	Mary (Marianne)	1826	Middlesex, London	Hyman Collins	Mary (Maria) Davis		Marylebone, London	charwoman
3128	Collins	Mary (Meriel)	1814	Margonin, Poland [Prussia]	Michael Cohen	Adaline (?)	John Collins	Sunderland, Co Durham	
21286	Collins	Phineas	1842	Spitalfields, London				Edmonton, London	boarding school pupil
20478	Collins	Priscilla	1847	?, London	Mark Collins	Lydia (?)		Covent Garden, London	
6140	Collins	Rosetta	1815	Middlesex, London	Jacob Solomon	Priscilla (?)	Simeon (Simon) Collins	Marylebone, London	
30398	Collins	Sarah	1814	Middlesex, London	Hyman Collins	Mary (Maria) Davis		Marylebone, London	
16310	Collins	Simeon	1847	Covent Garden, London	Henry Hirsch Collins	Floretta (?)		Covent Garden, London	
6139	Collins	Simeon (Simon)	1809	Middlesex, London	Hayim HaLevi		Rosetta Solomon	Marylebone, London	picture restorer
20482	Collins	Solomon	1832	Middlesex, London	(?Mark) Collins	(?Lydia) (?)		Covent Garden, London	hatter
16085	Collins	Solomon	1839	St Pancras, London	Lewis Collins	Julia Isaacs		Euston, London	
6538	Collins	Solomon George	1804	Soho, London			Kate Isaacs	Euston, London	hatter
31002	Collins	William	1828	Westminster, London	Solomon George Collins	Kate Isaacs		Euston, London	
20476	Collins	William	1844	?, London	Mark Collins	Lydia (?)		Covent Garden, London	
25330	Colliss	Catherine	1811	Southwark, London	Moses Colliss		Joseph Colliss	Holborn, London	
25335	Colliss	David	1845	Holborn, London	Joseph Colliss	Catherine Colliss		Holborn, London	scholar
25337	Colliss	Dinah	1828	Holborn, London	Mosses Colliss?			Holborn, London	artificial flower maker
25334	Colliss	Elizabeth	1842	Holborn, London	Joseph Colliss	Catherine Colliss		Holborn, London	scholar
25332	Colliss	Esther	1834	Holborn, London	Joseph Colliss	Catherine Colliss	Judah Jacobs	Holborn, London	
25285	Colliss	Hannah	1786	Holborn, London	(?)		Moss (Moses) Abraham Colliss	Holborn, London	
25331	Colliss	Hannah	1832	Holborn, London	Joseph Colliss	Catherine Colliss		Holborn, London	
25286	Colliss	Harriet	1821	Clerkenwell, London	Moss (Moses) Abraham Colliss	Hannah (?)		Holborn, London	
25287	Colliss	Jemima	1827	Holborn, London	Moss (Moses) Abraham Colliss	Hannah (?)		Holborn, London	dressmaker
25329	Colliss	Joseph	1810	Clerkenwell, London	Moss (Moses) Abraham Colliss	Hannah (?)	Catherine Colliss	Holborn, London	glass maker
25333	Colliss	Lydia	1840	Holborn, London	Joseph Colliss	Catherine Colliss		Holborn, London	scholar
25336	Colliss	Moses	1781	?, Germany			(?)	Holborn, London	clothes salesman
25284	Colliss	Moss (Moses) Abraham	1783	City, London			Hannah (?)	Holborn, London	glass cutter
17373	Colman	David	1849	Aldgate, London	(?) Colman	(?) Jacobs		Whitechapel, London	
12496	Coln	Louis	1830	?, Poland [?, Prussia]				Plymouth, Devon	traveller (with jewellery box)
23722	Columbia	John	1826	?, Germany				Liverpool	pedlar
27987	Cone	Isaac	1851	?Spitalfields, London	Solomon Cohen	Marie (?)		Spitalfields, London	

ID	surname	given names	born	birthplace	father	mother	spouse 1	1851 residence	1851 occupation
27986	Cone	Izzy	1848	?	Solomon Cohen	Marie (?)		Spitalfields, London	
27984	Cone	Marie	1827	?	(?)		Solomon Cone	Spitalfields, London	
27985	Cone	Owen	1847	?	Solomon Cohen	Marie (?)		Spitalfields, London	
27983	Cone	Solomon	1819	?			Marie (?)	Spitalfields, London	tailor
29348	Conick	Esther	1850	?, Germany	Jules Conick	Rebecca (?)		Whitechapel, London	
29346	Conick	Jules	1821	?, Poland			Rebecca (?)	Whitechapel, London	glazier
29347	Conick	Rebecca	1826	?, Germany	(?)		Jules Conick	Whitechapel, London	
30011	Constadt	Hannah	1815	Bethnal Green, London			(?) Constadt	Aldgate, London	
4398	Cook	Alexander	1815	Jerusalem, Israel	Samuel Cook		Frances (Fanny) Hart	Birmingham	pedlar
4399	Cook	Frances (Fanny)	1816	Jerusalem, Israel	Yehuda Leib Hart		Alexander Cook	Birmingham	hawker
4401	Cook	Hannah	1849	Birmingham	Alexander, Hannah	Frances (Fanny) Hart		Birmingham	
4402	Cook	Katharine	1851	Birmingham	Alexander Cook	Frances (Fanny) Hart		Birmingham	
4400	Cook	Samuel	1848	Birmingham	Alexander Cook	Frances (Fanny) Hart		Birmingham	
6240	Coomer	Leah (Ann)	1831	Fulham, London	William Coomer		Judah Solomon	St Giles, London	
28525	Cooper	Sarah	1781	Amsterdam, Holland	(?)		Simeon Cooper	Spitalfields, London	
28524	Cooper	Simeon	1769	Amsterdam, Holland			Sarah (?)	Spitalfields, London	general dealer
30777	Coppel	Charles	1809	Hanover, Germany			Kate Hess	Preston, Lancashire	dentist
30782	Coppel	David Behrend	1849	Preston, Lancashire	Charles Coppel	Kate Hess		Preston, Lancashire	
30779	Coppel	Israel	1844	Preston, Lancashire	Charles Coppel	Kate Hess		Preston, Lancashire	
30783	Coppel	Joseph	1851	Preston, Lancashire	Charles Coppel	Kate Hess		Preston, Lancashire	
30781	Coppel	Julia	1847	Preston, Lancashire	Charles Coppel	Kate Hess		Preston, Lancashire	
30778	Coppel	Kate	1807	Liverpool	Israel Hess	Rosetta (?)	Charles Coppel	Preston, Lancashire	
30780	Coppel	Raphael (Ralph)	1845	Preston, Lancashire	Charles Coppel	Kate Hess		Preston, Lancashire	
4491	Coppel	Zallel	1811	Cracow, Poland	Jacob Coppel		(?)	Liverpool	silversmith + watch manufacturer
2401	Cora	August	1820	?, Poland [?, Prussia]				Hull, Yorkshire	journeymanshoemaker
25061	Corbey	Elizabeth	1808	Whitechapel, London	(?)		Joseph Moses	Spitalfields, London	tailoress
25060	Corbey	Marcus	1803	?, Poland [?, Prussia]			Elizabeth Moses nee (?)	Spitalfields, London	journeyman tailor
12389	Core	Fanny	1818	?, Poland	Abraham Joel	Sarah (?)	Morris Core	North Shields, Tyne & Wear	
12391	Core	Hannah	1850	North Shields, Tyne & Wear	Morris Core	Fanny Joel		North Shields, Tyne & Wear	
12390	Core	Morris	1822	?, Poland			Fanny Joel	North Shields, Tyne & Wear	glazier
28308	Corlesh	Esther	1828	?, Poland [?, Prussia]	(?)		Solomon Corlesh	Aldgate, London	cap maker
28307	Corlesh	Solomon	1826	?, Poland [?, Prussia]			Esther (?)	Aldgate, London	cap maker
3476	Corlyn	Leah	1795	Mile End, London	Simon Solomon Wilks	Elizabeth (?)	Solomon Tobias Zack Corlyn	Marylebone, London	
3477	Corlyn	Solomon Tobias Zack	1794	Amsterdam, Holland	Tobias (Benjamin Kornalijnslijper?)		Leah Solomon (Wilks)	Marylebone, London	dealer in furniture + metals
5590	Cornbloom	Amelia	1811	Plymouth, Devon			Nahum Cornbloom	Plymouth, Devon	
1266	Cornbloom	Caroline	1839	Plymouth, Devon	Nahum Cornbloom	Amelia (?)		Plymouth, Devon	scholar
1267	Cornbloom	Charles	1841	Plymouth, Devon	Nahum Cornbloom	Amelia (?)		Plymouth, Devon	scholar
27067	Cornbloom	Fanny	1825	?, Germany	(?)		Michael Cornbloom	Aldgate, London	
5592	Cornbloom	Frances	1846	Plymouth, Devon	Nahum Cornbloom	Amelia (?)	Solomon Bornstein	Plymouth, Devon	scholar

ID	surname	given names	born	birthplace	father	mother	spouse 1	1851 residence	1851 occupation
27068	Cornbloom	Hannah	1850	?Aldgate, London	Michael Cornbloom	Fanny (?)		Aldgate, London	
1270	Cornbloom	Henry	1848	Plymouth, Devon	Nahum Cornbloom	Amelia (?)		Plymouth, Devon	scholar
27066	Cornbloom	Michael	1823	?, Germany			Fanny (?)	Aldgate, London	cap maker
5591	Cornbloom	Nahum	1801	?, Poland	(?) Cornbloom		Amelia (?)	Plymouth, Devon	merchant + money broker
5594	Cornbloom	Rosetta	1844	Plymouth, Devon	Nahum Cornbloom	Amelia (?)		Plymouth, Devon	scholar
5593	Cornbloom (Cohen)	Simeon	1836	Plymouth, Devon	Nahum Cornbloom	Amelia (?)		Plymouth, Devon	
19886	Cornely (Cohen)	Max Leonard	1822	?, Germany				Islington, London	commission merchant
19887	Cornely (Cohen)	Sigismond	1820	?, Germany				Islington, London	commission merchant
11955	Coronel	Abraham Senior	1813	Aldgate, London	Jacob Senior Coronel	Judith de Moseh Rodrigues Moreira	Rosetta (Reise) de Jacob Cohen	Whitechapel, London	cigar manufacturer
11957	Coronel	Catherine (Judith)	1840	Whitechapel, London	Abraham Senior Coronel	Rosetta (Reise) de Jacob Cohen		Whitechapel, London	
22066	Coronel	David	1791	?, Holland			Leah (?)	Spitalfields, London	general dealer
11960	Coronel	Emanuel (Edward)	1847	Whitechapel, London	Abraham Senior Coronel	Rosetta (Reise) de Jacob Cohen	Eugenie Jacob	Whitechapel, London	
27006	Coronel	Emanuel Senior	1819	Holborn, London	Jacob Senior Coronel	Judith de Moseh Rodrigues Moreira	Esther Delevante	Aldgate, London	cigar maker
27007	Coronel	Esther	1820	Whitechapel, London	Prosper (Haim) Delevante	Miryam (Polly, Perla) (?)	Emanuel Senior Coronel	Aldgate, London	school mistress
11961	Coronel	Frances (Fanny)	1849	Whitechapel, London	Abraham Senior Coronel	Rosetta (Reise) de Jacob Cohen	Max Mendlesohn	Whitechapel, London	
11959	Coronel	Hannah (Annie)	1844	Whitechapel, London	Abraham Senior Coronel	Rosetta (Reise) de Jacob Cohen	Adolph Mendelssohn	Whitechapel, London	
11958	Coronel	John (Jacob) S	1842	Whitechapel, London	Abraham Senior Coronel	Rosetta (Reise) de Jacob Cohen	Kate Emanuel	Whitechapel, London	
23273	Coronel	Julia (Judith)	1838	Aldgate, London	Abraham Senior Coronel	Rosetta (Reise) de Jacob Cohen	Benjamin Cohen	Whitechapel, London	
22067	Coronel	Leah	1795	?, Holland	(?)		David Coronel	Spitalfields, London	
11956	Coronel	Rosetta	1817	Aldgate, London	Jacob de Moses Cohen		Abraham de Jacob Senior Coronel	Whitechapel, London	
13028	Corper	Adelaid	1849	Spitalfields, London	Isaac Corper	Hannah (?)		Spitalfields, London	
13027	Corper	Esther	1845	?, Holland	Isaac Corper	Hannah (?)	Charles Stodell	Spitalfields, London	
13023	Corper	Hannah	1814	?, Holland	(?)		Isaac Corper	Spitalfields, London	
13022	Corper	Isaac	1807	?, Holland	Shimon HaLevi		Hannah (?)	Spitalfields, London	
13026	Corper	Jacob	1843	?, Holland	Isaac Corper	Hannah (?)		Spitalfields, London	cigar maker
13024	Corper	Julia	1837	?, Holland	Isaac Corper	Hannah (?)	Leon Kesner	Spitalfields, London	
13025	Corper	Samuel	1841	?, Holland	Isaac Corper	Hannah (?)		Spitalfields, London	
22037	Cortissos	Abigail	1830	?, London	Elias de Emanuel Cortissos	Rachel de Raphael Barzilay Capua		Spitalfields, London	
22041	Cortissos	Benjamin	1847	Middlesex, London	Elias de Emanuel Cortissos	Rachel de Raphael Barzilay Capua		Spitalfields, London	
19048	Cortissos	Cynthia	1826	Middlesex, London	Josiah de Joseph Cortissos	Esther de Jacob Sarfaty de Penna		Aldgate, London	daily governess
19047	Cortissos	David	1823	Middlesex, London	Josiah de Joseph Cortissos	Esther de Jacob Sarfaty de Penna		Aldgate, London	lithographic printer

ID	surname	given names	born	birthplace	father	mother	spouse 1	1851 residence	1851 occupation
22034	Cortissos	Elias	1802	?, London	Emanuel de Elias Cortissos	Sarah de David Rodrigues	Rachel de Raphael Barzilay Capua	Spitalfields, London	coal dealer
19046	Cortissos	Esther	1792	Middlesex, London	Jacob Sarfaty de Penna		Josiah de Joseph Cortissos	Aldgate, London	school mistress
22036	Cortissos	Esther	1828	?, London	Elias de Emanuel Cortissos	Rachel de Raphael Barzilay Capua	Isaac Jonas	Spitalfields, London	
22039	Cortissos	Hannah	1842	Middlesex, London	Elias de Emanuel Cortissos	Rachel de Raphael Barzilay Capua	Lipman Phillips	Spitalfields, London	
22035	Cortissos	Rachel	1805	?, Kent	Raphael Barzilay Capua	Esther de Jacob Carcas	Elias de Emanuel Cortissos	Spitalfields, London	
22040	Cortissos	Rachel	1845	Middlesex, London	Elias de Emanuel Cortissos	Rachel de Raphael Barzilay Capua		Spitalfields, London	
22038	Cortissos	Rebecca	1838	Middlesex, London	Elias de Emanuel Cortissos	Rachel de Raphael Barzilay Capua		Spitalfields, London	
26166	Costa	Abigail	1849	?, London	Gabriel Costa	Ann Levy		Aldgate, London	
25793	Costa	Abraham	1791	Aldgate, London				Aldgate, London	clothes dealer
8909	Costa	Amelia (Miriam)	1820	?Aldgate, London	Raphael (Ralph) Costa	Rachael Zundel Jacobs	Benjamin Haim Cohen	Aldgate, London	
26158	Costa	Ann	1832	?Spitalfields, London	Nathan Levy	Abigail Noah (Noah Da Costa)	Gabriel Costa	Aldgate, London	cap maker
10160	Costa	Barnet (Baruh)	1834	?Aldgate, London	Moses de Isaac Costa	Matilda de Zeheb Arye	Louisa (Leah) Myers	Spitalfields, London	general dealer
8915	Costa	Betsey	1831	Spitalfields, London	Raphael (Ralph) Costa	Rachael Zundel Jacobs		Aldgate, London	
22385	Costa	Elizabeth	1831	Stepney, London	Jacob de Isaac Costa	Esther de Zeheb Arye		Whitechapel, London	
21654	Costa	Ellen Sarah	1850	Aldgate, London	Samuel de Raphael Costa	Sarah Levy	Benjamin Costa	Aldgate, London	
22383	Costa	Esther	1795	Whitechapel, London	Zeheb Arye	Sarah	Jacob de Isaac Costa	Whitechapel, London	
9308	Costa	Esther	1805	Aldgate, London	(?) Costa			Aldgate, London	cape maker
8916	Costa	Esther	1825	Aldgate, London	Raphael (Ralph) Costa	Rachael Zundel Jacobs		Aldgate, London	general dealer
6918	Costa	Fanny	1836	Aldgate, London	Moses Costa	Matilda de Zeheb Arye		Spitalfields, London	
6988	Costa	Gabriel	1828	Middlesex, London	Samuel de Gabriel Costa	Hannah Levy	Ann Levy	Aldgate, London	general dealer
6919	Costa	Henry	1843	Aldgate, London	Moses Costa	Matilda de Zeheb Arye		Spitalfields, London	
8907	Costa	Isaac	1816	Middlesex, London	Raphael (Ralph) Costa	Rachel Zundel Jacobs	Rebecca Donati	Aldgate, London	butcher
15836	Costa	Isaac	1824	Whitechapel, London	Benjamin Costa		Phoebe Cohen	Spitalfields, London	watch maker
2744	Costa	Isaac (Eleazar)	1848	Spitalfields, London	Jacob (John) Costa	Julia Gitele Barnett		Spitalfields, London	scholar
22382	Costa	Jacob	1796	City, London	Isaac de Gabriel Costa	Sarah (?)	Esther de Zeheb Arye	Whitechapel, London	dealer in clothes
919	Costa	Jacob (John)	1821	Aldgate, London	Raphael (Ralph) Costa	Rachel Zundel Jacobs	Julia (Judith Gitele) Barnett	Spitalfields, London	tailor
22386	Costa	Jane	1832	Stepney, London	Jacob de Isaac Costa	Esther de Zeheb Arye		Whitechapel, London	
5922	Costa	Jane	1849	Spitalfields, London	Isaac Costa	Phoebe Cohen		Spitalfields, London	
22387	Costa	Judah	1835	Stepney, London	Jacob de Isaac Costa	Esther de Zeheb Arye	Esther Hart	Whitechapel, London	
918	Costa	Julia (Judith Gitele)	1824	Aldgate, London	Lazarus (Eliezer, Lewis) Barnett	Ann (Miriam) (?)	Jacob (John) Costa	Spitalfields, London	
15837	Costa	Lydia	1850	Spitalfields, London	Isaac Costa	Phoebe Cohen		Spitalfields, London	
2746	Costa	Mary (Miriam)	1850	Spitalfields, London	Jacob Costa	Julia Gitele Barnett		Spitalfields, London	
6917	Costa	Matilda	1799	Whitechapel, London	Zeheb Arye		Moses de Isaac Costa	Spitalfields, London	
6916	Costa	Moses	1798	Mile End, London	Isaac Costa	Sarah (?)	Matilda (Malca de Zeheb Arye)	Spitalfields, London	renovator
10843	Costa	Moss	1832	Spitalfields, London				Spitalfields, London	couch maker
5923	Costa	Phoebe	1823	Whitechapel, London	Joshua Cohen		Isaac Costa	Spitalfields, London	
8904	Costa	Rachael	1790	Aldgate, London	Nethanel (Judah) Zundel Jacobs		Raphael (Ralph) Costa	Aldgate, London	

ID	surname	given names	born	birthplace	father	mother	spouse 1	1851 residence	1851 occupation
2747	Costa	Rachael	1851	Spitalfields, London	Jacob (John) Costa	Julia Gitele Barnett		Spitalfields, London	
22388	Costa	Ralph (Raphael)	1837	Stepney, London	Jacob de Isaac Costa	Esther de Zeheb Arye		Whitechapel, London	scholar
16527	Costa	Raphael	1847	Aldgate, London	Samuel de Raphael Costa	Sarah Levy	Rachel Barnett	Aldgate, London	scholar
8903	Costa	Raphael (Ralph)	1793	Whitechapel, London	Isaac Costa		Rachel de Nethanel (Judah) Zundel Jacobs	Aldgate, London	tailor
8905	Costa	Samuel	1818	Aldgate, London	Raphael (Ralph) Costa	Rachael Zundel Jacobs	Sarah Levy	Aldgate, London	tailor master
8906	Costa	Sarah	1808	Aldgate, London	Jacob Levy		Samuel de Raphael Costa	Aldgate, London	
22384	Costa	Sarah	1829	Whitechapel, London	Jacob de Isaac Costa	Esther de Zeheb Arye		Whitechapel, London	
15955	Coster	Mary	1823	Limerick, Ireland	(?) Coster			Whitechapel, London	servant
28845	Costima	Abraham	1824	Amsterdam, Holland			Jeannet (?)	Spitalfields, London	cigar maker
28851	Costima	Barnett Abraham	1850	Whitechapel, London	Abraham Costima	Jeannet (?)		Spitalfields, London	
28850	Costima	Elizabeth	1849	Whitechapel, London	Abraham Costima	Jeannet (?)		Spitalfields, London	
28847	Costima	Esther	1843	Amsterdam, Holland	Abraham Costima	Jeannet (?)		Spitalfields, London	scholar
28849	Costima	Feby	1847	Amsterdam, Holland	Abraham Costima	Jeannet (?)		Spitalfields, London	scholar
28848	Costima	Henerota	1845	Amsterdam, Holland	Abraham Costima	Jeannet (?)		Spitalfields, London	scholar
28846	Costima	Jeannet	1821	Amsterdam, Holland	(?)		Abraham Costima	Spitalfields, London	
3213	Cotton	Edward	1801	?, Kent			Hannah Levy	Rochester, Kent	
3214	Cotton	Hannah	1810	?, Kent	Isaac Levy	Sarah Levy	Edward Cotton	Rochester, Kent	
22257	Cowan	Abigal	1845	Whitechapel, London	Israel Cowan	Rachel (?)		Whitechapel, London	scholar
22254	Cowan	Catherine	1840	Whitechapel, London	Israel Cowan	Rachel (?)		Whitechapel, London	scholar
3543	Cowan	Hannah	1797	Camberwell, London	(?) Solomon		Lewis Cowan	Whitechapel, London	
3544	Cowan	Henry	1817	Chatham, Kent	Lewis Cohan	Hannah Solomon	Charlotte Sophia Levy	Whitechapel, London	assistant to soapmaker
13222	Cowan	Isaac	1828	Whitechapel, London				Spitalfields, London	traveller hardware
22249	Cowan	Israel	1804	Aldgate, London			Rachel (?)	Whitechapel, London	commercial traveller, clothing
3547	Cowan	John	1830	Chatham, Kent	Lewis Cowan	Hannah Solomon		Whitechapel, London	
25150	Cowan	Julia	1824	Middlesex, London	(?Yechutiel HaCohen)			Finsbury, London	shopwoman
22252	Cowan	Julia	1836	Whitechapel, London	Israel Cowan	Rachel (?)	Daniel Benjamin Herts	Whitechapel, London	scholar
3542	Cowan	Lewis	1788	Rochester, Kent	Solomon Cohan	Lydia (?)	Hannah Solomon	Whitechapel, London	soapmaker
22251	Cowan	Lewis	1831	Aldgate, London	Israel Cowan	Rachel (?)	Fanny (?)	Whitechapel, London	jeweller
25149	Cowan	Lewis	1844	Middlesex, London	Solomon Cowan	Lydia Harris		Finsbury, London	
25146	Cowan	Lydia	1812	Middlesex, London	Jacob Harris		Solomon Cowan	Finsbury, London	
22256	Cowan	Maria	1842	Whitechapel, London	Israel Cowan	Rachel (?)		Whitechapel, London	scholar
10308	Cowan	Maria	1844	Whitechapel, London	(?) Cowan			Spitalfields, London	scholar
22255	Cowan	Mark	1841	Whitechapel, London	Israel Cowan	Rachel (?)		Whitechapel, London	scholar
23453	Cowan	Nathan	1809	?, Poland			(?)	Liverpool	cabinet maker
3550	Cowan	Phineas (Ben)	1832	Chatham, Kent	Lewis Cowan	Hannah Solomon	Rose (Rosetta) Moses	Wapping, London	?
22258	Cowan	Pricella	1850	Whitechapel, London	Israel Cowan	Rachel (?)		Whitechapel, London	
22250	Cowan	Rachel	1810	Southwark, London	(?)		Israel Cowan	Whitechapel, London	
25147	Cowan	Rebecca	1837	Middlesex, London	Solomon Cowan	Lydia Harris		Finsbury, London	flower maker
3548	Cowan	Samuel	1825	?, Kent	Lewis Cowan	Hannah Solomon	Marion Levy	Whitechapel, London	assistant to soapmaker
25148	Cowan	Sarah	1841	Middlesex, London	Solomon Cowan	Lydia Harris		Finsbury, London	
25145	Cowan	Solomon	1810	Middlesex, London	Yechutiel HaCohen		Lydia Harris	Finsbury, London	general dealer
22253	Cowan	Sophia	1838	Whitechapel, London	Israel Cowan	Rachel (?)		Whitechapel, London	scholar
15940	Cowen	Abigal	1831	Whitechapel, London	Lewis Cowen	Elizabeth (?)		Marylebone, London	

ID	surname	given names	born	birthplace	father	mother	spouse 1	1851 residence	1851 occupation
8693	Cowen	Adelaide	1850	Manchester	David Cowen	Martha Lyons	Baron Barnett	Manchester	
15034	Cowen	Caroline	1814	Spitalfields, London	(?)		Henry Cowen	Bethnal Green, London	lint maker
14972	Cowen	Caroline	1839	Gravesend, Kent	(?) Cowen			Bethnal Green, London	boarding school pupil
7530	Cowen	David	1817	?, Poland [?, Prussia]			Martha Lyons	Manchester	watchmaker
15939	Cowen	Elizabeth	1811	Whitechapel, London	(?)		Lewis Cohen	Marylebone, London	
15036	Cowen	Emanuel	1839	Bethnal Green, London	Henry Cowen	Caroline (?)		Bethnal Green, London	scholar
15945	Cowen	Folk	1846	Marylebone, London	Lewis Cowen	Elizabeth (?)		Marylebone, London	
15033	Cowen	Henry	1808	Spitalfields, London			Caroline (?)	Bethnal Green, London	journeyman pencil maker
14479	Cowen	Isaac	1831	?, Poland [?, Prussia]				Manchester	hawks jewellery
15037	Cowen	Isaac	1841	Whitechapel, London	Henry Cowen	Caroline (?)		Bethnal Green, London	scholar
13687	Cowen	Jacob	1850	Manchester	Marks Cohen	Mena (?)		Manchester	
15946	Cowen	John	1848	Marylebone, London	Lewis Cowen	Elizabeth (?)		Marylebone, London	
15943	Cowen	Joseph	1839	Marylebone, London	Lewis Cowen	Elizabeth (?)		Marylebone, London	scholar
15941	Cowen	Julia	1832	Whitechapel, London	Lewis Cowen	Elizabeth (?)		Marylebone, London	
15938	Cowen	Lewis	1809	City, London			Elizabeth (?)	Marylebone, London	clothier
15947	Cowen	Lewis	1850	Marylebone, London	Lewis Cowen	Elizabeth (?)		Marylebone, London	
14956	Cowen	Louisa	1837	?, London	(?) Cowen			Bethnal Green, London	boarding school pupil
15038	Cowen	Mark	1843	Bethnal Green, London	Henry Cowen	Caroline (?)		Bethnal Green, London	scholar
13685	Cowen	Marks	1828	?, Germany			Mena (?)	Manchester	hawker of jewellery
8694	Cowen	Martha	1824	?, Poland [?, Prussia]	Goldstone Lyons	Louisa (Theresa) (?)	David Cowen	Manchester	
13686	Cowen	Mena	1831	?, Germany	(?)		Marks Cowen	Manchester	
15035	Cowen	Nathan	1838	Bethnal Green, London	Henry Cowen	Caroline (?)		Bethnal Green, London	errand boy
15942	Cowen	Ralph	1836	Marylebone, London	Lewis Cowen	Elizabeth (?)		Marylebone, London	
15039	Cowen	Rossetta	1847	Bethnal Green, London	Henry Cowen	Caroline (?)		Bethnal Green, London	scholar
15944	Cowen	Sophia	1841	Marylebone, London	Lewis Cowen	Elizabeth (?)		Marylebone, London	scholar
2402	Cowhen	Harris	1811	Schapen, Germany			Sarah (?)	Hull, Yorkshire	glazier
2403	Cowhen	Moses	1840	Schapen, Germany	Harris Cowhen	Sarah (?)		Hull, Yorkshire	
2404	Cowhen	Sarah	1825	Volkovysk, Russia			Harris Cowhen	Hull, Yorkshire	
26288	Cowron	Simon	1801	?, Poland				Aldgate, London	hawker
7564	Cowvan	Bernard (Bernhard, Barnard)	1795	?, Poland [?, Prussia]	Bernard Corvan (Dov Behr HaCohen)		Henrietta Poole	Tower Hill, London	manufacturer of razors, bags, ink + cork
8124	Cowvan	Henrietta	1793	Poole, Dorset	Abraham HaLevi Poole		Bernard (Bernhard, Barnard) Cowvan	Tower Hill, London	
8089	Cowvan	Isabella	1808	Middlesex, London	Isaiah Israel	Jane (?)	Samuel Cowvan	Elephant & Castle, London	
5270	Cowvan	Theresa	1841	Tower Hill, London	Samuel Cowvan (Corvan, Cowan, Coward, Cowvam)	Isabella Israel	Jacques Lang	Elephant & Castle, London	
5271	Cowvan (Corvan, Cowan, Coward, Cowvam)	Samuel	1803	?, Poland [?, Prussia]	Bernard Corvan (Dov Behr HaCohen)		Isabella Israel	Elephant & Castle, London	razor strop maker + carper bag + fur cap merchant
18736	Cox	Marian	1850	Clerkenwell, London	(?) Cox		David Solomon Davis	Clerkenwell, London	
24349	Coyvich	Amelia	1830	?, France	(?) Coyvich			Bloomsbury, London	servant
6863	Crabb	Abraham	1798	Spitalfields, London			Catherine (?)	Whitechapel, London	dealer in clothes
6859	Crabb	Abraham Emanuel	1850	Aldgate, London	Michael Crabb	Elizabeth Harris	Elizabeth (Betsy) Levy	Spitalfields, London	

ID	surname	given names	born	birthplace	father	mother	spouse 1	1851 residence	1851 occupation
25630	Crabb	Benjamin	1785	?	Uri Shraga			Kilkee, County Clare, Ireland	
25196	Crabb	Catharine	1803	Middlesex, London				Clerkenwell, London	
16141	Crabb	Catherine	1803	Middlesex, London	(?)		Abraham Crabb	Whitechapel, London	dealer in clothes
6858	Crabb	Deborah	1848	Spitalfields, London	Michael Crabb	Elizabeth Harris		Spitalfields, London	scholar
16143	Crabb	Dinah	1840	Middlesex, London	Abraham Crabb	Catherine (?)		Whitechapel, London	
6852	Crabb	Elizabeth	1812	Whitechapel, London	Eliakim Getschlik Harris		Michael Crabb	Spitalfields, London	
6867	Crabb	Elizabeth	1825	City, London	Abraham Crabb	Catherine (?)		Whitechapel, London	parasol maker
6854	Crabb	Emanuel	1834	Whitechapel, London	Michael Crabb	Elizabeth Harris	Hannah Isaacs	Spitalfields, London	general dealer
6869	Crabb	Frances (Fannie)	1833	Whitechapel, London	Abraham Crabb			Whitechapel, London	dressmaker
6853	Crabb	Godfrey	1832	Whitechapel, London	Michael Crabb	Elizabeth Harris	Sarah Jacobs	Spitalfields, London	general dealer
6864	Crabb	Isaac	1827	Wapping, London	Abraham Crabb	Catherine (?)		Whitechapel, London	cigar maker
6857	Crabb	Israel	1840	Aldgate, London	Michael Crabb	Elizabeth Harris	Rachel Jacobs	Spitalfields, London	scholar
6866	Crabb	John	1831	Whitechapel, London	Abraham Crabb	Catherine (?)		Whitechapel, London	cigar maker
6856	Crabb	John	1836	Whitechapel, London	Michael Crabb	Elizabeth Harris		Spitalfields, London	baker
6865	Crabb	Joseph	1829	Wapping, London	Abraham Crabb	Catherine (?)		Whitechapel, London	cigar maker
6868	Crabb	Mary	1837	Whitechapel, London	Abraham Crabb	Catherine (?)		Whitechapel, London	
6851	Crabb	Michael	1810	Aldgate, London	Menachem Mendele		Elizabeth Harris	Spitalfields, London	fruiterer
18203	Crabb	Morris	1839	Middlesex, London				Mile End, London	scholar
18194	Crabb	Phillip	1759	Middlesex, London			(?)	Mile End, London	pencil maker
6861	Crabb	Samuel	1833	Aldgate, London	Michael Crabb	Elizabeth Harris	Michel (?)	Spitalfields, London	
16142	Crabb	Susan	1823	Middlesex, London	Abraham Crabb	Catherine (?)		Whitechapel, London	parasol maker
11871	Crabbe	Philip	1846	Middlesex, London	(?) Crabbe	(?)		Whitechapel, London	inmate of orphan school
11879	Crabbe	Rachel	1841	Middlesex, London	(?) Crabbe	(?)		Whitechapel, London	inmate of orphan school
27354	Crafus	John	1830	Muschen, Germany [Musheen, Germany]				Aldgate, London	wholesale jeweller
11978	Crane	Ellis	1823	?, Poland				Whitechapel, London	tailor
11979	Crane	Hyman	1819	?, Poland				Whitechapel, London	tailor
15471	Crawcar	Sophia	1823	Covent Garden, London	Moses Solomon	Betsy (?)	(?) Crawcar	Covent Garden, London	
14792	Crawcour	Amelia	1797	?, London	(?) Barnes		David Crawcour	Finsbury, London	
14662	Crawcour	Amelia	1836	Birmingham	Morris Crawcour	(?)		Hoxton, London	
14794	Crawcour	Amelia	1850	Finsbury, London	Henry Crawcour	Rosa Isaacs	Benjamin Bernstein	Finsbury, London	
14663	Crawcour	Ann Louisa	1849	Southwark, London	Morris Crawcour	(?)	George Croft Bayley (Bailey)	Hoxton, London	
14791	Crawcour	David	1796	?, London	Samuel (Zanvil) Crawcour	Rebecca (?)	Miriam (?)	Finsbury, London	dentist
14793	Crawcour	David	1848	Finsbury, London	Henry Crawcour	Rosa Isaacs	Mary Ann Samuels	Finsbury, London	
22425	Crawcour	Elizabeth (Eliza)	1830	Norwich, Norfolk	Barnett Crawcour	Fanny (?)	Samuel Barczinsky	Gravesend, Kent	housekeeper
22422	Crawcour	Emma Esther	1817	Norwich, Norfolk	Barnett Crawcour	Fanny (?)	(?) Simons	Gravesend, Kent	governess
22423	Crawcour	Fanny	1819	Norwich, Norfolk	Barnett Crawcour	Fanny (?)		Gravesend, Kent	governess
22421	Crawcour	Fanny Alexander	1794	?, London	(?)		Barnett Crawcour	Gravesend, Kent	head governess
20507	Crawcour	Hanna	1796	Middlesex, London	(?)		Moses Crawcour	Hyde Park, London	
22427	Crawcour	Hannah	1827	Norwich, Norfolk	Barnett Crawcour	Fanny (?)	Benjamin Simons	Gravesend, Kent	monitor
7205	Crawcour	Henry	1822	Middlesex, London	David Crawcour	Miriam (?)	Rosa Isaacs	Finsbury, London	dentist
30842	Crawcour	Henry J	1811	Norwich, Norfolk				Wapping, London	dentist

148

ID	surname	given names	born	birthplace	father	mother	spouse 1	1851 residence	1851 occupation
22564	Crawcour	Isaac Henry	1813	Norwich, Norfolk	(?Barnett) Crawcour		Jane Mann	Walworth, London	tobacconist + bill discounter
22163	Crawcour	Jemima	1781	Whitechapel, London	(?)		Isaac Crawcour	Whitechapel, London	
22426	Crawcour	Martha	1831	Norwich, Norfolk	Barnett Crawcour	Fanny (?)		Gravesend, Kent	housekeeper
7206	Crawcour	Morris	1813	Finsbury, London	David Crawcour	Miriam (?)	(?)	Finsbury, London	commercial traveller in bone, wood + glass goods
20506	Crawcour	Moses	1781	Hull, Yorkshire	Samuel Crawcour	Rebecca (?)	Hannah (?)	Hyde Park, London	fund holder + landed proprietor
22424	Crawcour	Rebecca	1827	Norwich, Norfolk	Barnett Crawcour	Fanny (?)		Gravesend, Kent	housekeeper
7204	Crawcour	Rosa	1823	Chatham, Kent	John Isaacs	Deborah (?)	Henry Crawcour	Finsbury, London	
22563	Crawcour	Samuel Walter	1829	Norwich, Norfolk	Barnett Crawcour	Fanny (?)	Emily Barnes	Chatham, Kent	assistant
22428	Crawcour	Sarah	1830	Norwich, Norfolk	Barnett Crawcour	Fanny (?)	Bernhard Barczinsky	Gravesend, Kent	pupil
4406	Creamer	Joseph	1849	Birmingham	William Creamer	Sophie (?)		Birmingham	
4405	Creamer	Selina (Lilian)	1847	Birmingham	William Creamer	Sophie (?)	Arthur Lynes	Birmingham	
4404	Creamer	Sophie	1816	Liverpool			William Creamer	Birmingham	
4403	Creamer	William	1818	Leszno, Poland [Lissa, Prussia]			Sophie (?)	Birmingham	furniture mfr
26285	Cress	Joseph	1801	?, Poland				Aldgate, London	hawker
23828	Cronenberg	Lazarus	1829	?, Poland				Liverpool	hawker
23846	Crow	Julius	1824	?, Russia				Soho, London	tailor
17026	Crown	Raphael	1788	?, Poland [?, Prussia]				Falkirk, Scotland	shopman
18156	Cusster	Rachel	1791	Spitalfields, London	(?) Cusster			Mile End, London	inmate of Portuguese Jews Hospital
1096	Da Costa	A G	1818	?, London				Falmouth, Cornwall	traveller
9292	Da Costa	Aaron Gomes	1825	Bethnal Green, London	Isaac Gomes Da Costa	Ann (?)	Rachel Carcas	Bethnal Green, London	commercial traveller
9363	Da Costa	Aaron Gomes	1825	Whitechapel, London	Moses de Isaac Gomes Da Costa	Rachel (?)	Caroline Siegenberg	Spitalfields, London	cigar maker
8620	Da Costa	Aaron Gomes	1834	Spitalfields, London	Benjamin Gomes da Costa	Sarah de Aaron Gomes Da Costa	Catherine Lyons	Spitalfields, London	traveller gas fittings
8772	Da Costa	Aaron Gomes	1836	Aldgate, London	Abraham Gomes Da Costa	Hannah Joseph	Rachel Gomes da Costa	Aldgate, London	
72	Da Costa	Aaron Haim Gomes	1832	?, London	Isaac de Aaron Gomes da Costa	Esther de Hananel Gomes da Costa	Maria Pinkus	Mile End, London	traveller
5660	Da Costa	Abigail Gomes	1803	Whitechapel, London	Moses de Isaac Gomes Da Costa	Rachel Beraha		?Margate, Kent	
12321	Da Costa	Abraham (Alfred) Gomes	1847	Spitalfields, London	Benjamin de Moses Gomes Da Costa	Sarah de Aaron Gomes Da Costa	Mary Elizabeth Henshaw	Spitalfields, London	scholar
8781	Da Costa	Abraham Gomes	1812	Spitalfields, London	Aaron Gomes Da Costa	Fanny (?)	Hannah de Benjamin Joseph	Aldgate, London	dealer in stationery + traveller
5826	Da Costa	Abraham Gomes	1820	Middlesex, London	Moses de Isaac Gomes Da Costa	Rachel Beraha	Jane (Jael) Barnett	Spitalfields, London	lemon dealer
8766	Da Costa	Angelo (Mordecai)	1837	Whitechapel, London	Hyam de Moses Gomes Da Costa	Rosa de Mordecai Baruh	Rachel Gomes Da Costa	Whitechapel, London	
24951	Da Costa	Ann Gomes	1796	Finsbury, London	(?)		Isaac Gomes Da Costa	Bethnal Green, London	
15954	Da Costa	Anne (Hannah) Gomes	1849	Spitalfields, London	Philip Avigdor Gomes Da Costa	Rebecca Suhamy (Samuel)		Whitechapel, London	
5761	Da Costa	Barnett (Baruch) Gomes	1851	Aldgate, London	Abraham Gomes Da Costa	Bilha (?)	Miriam (Marian) Myers	Aldgate, London	
8765	Da Costa	Belah	1835	Whitechapel, London	Hyam Gomes Da Costa	Rosa de Mordecai Baruh		Whitechapel, London	
8777	Da Costa	Benjamin	1839	Aldgate, London	Abraham Gomes Da Costa	Hannah Joseph	Agnes Lazarus	Aldgate, London	

149

ID	surname	given names	born	birthplace	father	mother	spouse 1	1851 residence	1851 occupation
8769	Da Costa	Benjamin	1844	Whitechapel, London	Hyam Gomes Da Costa	Rosa de Mordecai Baruh		Whitechapel, London	
12316	Da Costa	Benjamin Gomes	1808	Whitechapel, London	Moses de Isaac Gomes Da Costa	Rachel Beraha	Sarah de Aaron Gomes Da Costa	Spitalfields, London	dealer in gas burners + glasses
9367	Da Costa	Benjamin Gomes	1850	Whitechapel, London	Aaron de Moses Gomes Da Costa	Caroline Siegenberg		Spitalfields, London	
8593	Da Costa	Betsy Gomes	1838	Aldgate, London	Isaac de Hananel Gomes da Costa	Esther Barnett		Spitalfields, London	
9364	Da Costa	Caroline	1824	Whitechapel, London	Jonas Siegenberg		Aaron Gomes Da Costa	Spitalfields, London	
8779	Da Costa	Daniel	1849	Aldgate, London	Abraham Gomes Da Costa	Hannah Joseph	Sarah Levy	Aldgate, London	
25	Da Costa	Dinah Gomes	1850	Aldgate, London	Isaac de Hananel Gomes da Costa	Esther Barnett		Spitalfields, London	
8621	Da Costa	Elizabeth (Bella) Gomes	1834	Whitechapel, London	Isaac de Aaron Gomes da Costa	Esther de Hananel Gomes Da Costa		Mile End, London	
14678	Da Costa	Elizabeth Gomes	1851	Spitalfields, London	Moses Gomes Da Costa	Phoebe Solomons	Henry (Haim) Israel	Spitalfields, London	
31101	Da Costa	Ellen	1829	Stoke Newington, London	(?) Da Costa	Rachel (?)		Camberwell, London	
8771	Da Costa	Emanuel Gomes	1841	Aldgate, London	Abraham Gomes Da Costa	Hannah Joseph	Maria (Miriam) Gomes da Costa	Aldgate, London	
19114	Da Costa	Esther	1822	Southwark, London	(?) Da Costa	Lydia (?)		Aldgate, London	
8783	Da Costa	Esther	1851	Aldgate, London	Abraham Gomes Da Costa	Hannah Joseph	Barnett Isaacs	Aldgate, London	
8767	Da Costa	Esther (Aster)	1839	Whitechapel, London	Hyam Gomes Da Costa	Rosa de Mordecai Baruh		Whitechapel, London	
8618	Da Costa	Esther Gomes	1800	City, London	Hananel Gomes Da Costa	Elizabeth (Betsey) (?)	Isaac de Aaron Gomes Da Costa	Mile End, London	
26	Da Costa	Esther Gomes	1818	Whitechapel, London	Moses Barnett	Dinah (?)	Isaac de Hananel Gomes da Costa	Spitalfields, London	
15953	Da Costa	Esther Gomes	1847	Spitalfields, London	Philip Avigdor Gomes Da Costa	Rebecca Suhamy (Samuel)	Judah Fox	Whitechapel, London	
8641	Da Costa	Fanny	1843	Aldgate, London	(?) Da Costa			Aldgate, London	scholar
23233	Da Costa	Fanny Nunes	1805	Portsmouth, Hampshire	Elias Levi		Maurice (Moses) Nunes Da Costa	Kensington, London	
24953	Da Costa	Frances	1839	Bethnal Green, London	Isaac Gomes Da Costa	Ann (?)		Bethnal Green, London	
12322	Da Costa	Frances (Fanny) Gomes	1832	Whitechapel, London	Benjamin de Moses Gomes Da Costa	Sarah de Aaron Gomes Da Costa	David Nunes Martin (Martines)	Spitalfields, London	
30102	Da Costa	Frances Gomes	1851	Whitechapel, London	Philip Avigdor Gomes Da Costa	Rebecca Suhamy (Samuel)		Whitechapel, London	
15885	Da Costa	Grace Mendes	1835	St Thomas, Virgin Islands, West Indies	Elias Charles Mendes Da Costa	Leah (?)	Abraham Mocatta	Hackney, London	boarding school pupil
9288	Da Costa	Haim Gomes	1831	Bethnal Green, London	Isaac de Moses Gomes da Costa	Leah (?)	Judith Carcas	Bethnal Green, London	hawker
8619	Da Costa	Hananel Gomes	1832	Whitechapel, London	Isaac de Aaron Gomes Da Costa	Esther de Hananel Gomes Da Costa		Mile End, London	apprentice cigar maker
37	Da Costa	Hananel Gomes	1841	Whitechapel, London	Isaac de Hananel Gomes da Costa	Esther Barnett		Spitalfields, London	
8782	Da Costa	Hannah	1812	Aldgate, London	Benjamin Joseph		Abraham de Aaron Gomes Da Costa	Aldgate, London	
10713	Da Costa	Hannah	1820	Middlesex, London	(?)		Solomon Da Costa	Spitalfields, London	general dealer
8760	Da Costa	Hyam Gomes	1806	Whitechapel, London	Moses Gomes da Costa		Rosa de Mordecai Baruh	Whitechapel, London	commercial traveller
30033	Da Costa	Hyam Gomes	1850	Spitalfields, London	Benjamin de Moses Gomes Da Costa	Sarah de Isaac Gomes Da Costa		Spitalfields, London	
8778	Da Costa	Isaac	1847	Aldgate, London	Abraham Gomes Da Costa	Hannah Joseph		Aldgate, London	
24950	Da Costa	Isaac Gomes	1796	Whitechapel, London			Ann (?)	Bethnal Green, London	traveller
12318	Da Costa	Isaac Gomes	1800	?, London	Aaron Gomes Da Costa	Fanny (?)	Esther de Hananel Gomes Da Costa	Mile End, London	traveller
27	Da Costa	Isaac Gomes	1813	Whitechapel, London	Hananel de Isaac Gomes da Costa	Elizabeth (?)	Esther Barnett	Spitalfields, London	general dealer

ID	surname	given names	born	birthplace	father	mother	spouse 1	1851 residence	1851 occupation
12319	Da Costa	Isaac Gomes	1842	Spitalfields, London	Benjamin de Moses Gomes Da Costa	Sarah de Aaron Gomes Da Costa	Alice (Jael) Joseph	Spitalfields, London	scholar
10879	Da Costa	Isaac Gomes	1845	Spitalfields, London	Jacob de Moses Gomes Da Costa	Sarah Martin (Nunes Martinez)	Rachel Solomons	Spitalfields, London	scholar
9290	Da Costa	Isaac Gomes	1851	Bethnal Green, London	Haim Gomes da Costa	Judith Carcas		Bethnal Green, London	
8775	Da Costa	Jacob	1837	Aldgate, London	Abraham Gomes Da Costa	Hannah Joseph	Rosetta Israel	Aldgate, London	
8622	Da Costa	Jacob (John) Gomes	1841	Whitechapel, London	Isaac de Aaron Gomes Da Costa	Esther de Hananel Gomes Da Costa	Hannah Symons	Mile End, London	educated at home
10876	Da Costa	Jacob Gomes	1818	Spitalfields, London	Moses de Isaac Gomes Da Costa	Rachel Beraha	Sarah Martin (Nunes Martinez)	Spitalfields, London	general dealer
9366	Da Costa	Jacob Gomes	1846	Whitechapel, London	Aaron de Moses Gomes Da Costa	Caroline Siegenberg		Spitalfields, London	scholar
5827	Da Costa	Jane (Jael)	1819	Mile End, London	Jacob Barnett		Abraham Gomes Da Costa	Spitalfields, London	lemon dealer
16721	Da Costa	John (Jacob) Gomes	1847	Middlesex, London	Abraham de Isaac Gomes Da Costa	Jane (Jael) Barnett	Miriam Jacobs	Spitalfields, London	scholar
10878	Da Costa	Joseph Gomes	1843	Glasgow, Scotland	Jacob de Moses Gomes Da Costa	Sarah Martin (Nunes Martinez)	Hannah Symonds	Spitalfields, London	scholar
16723	Da Costa	Josua Gomes	1851	Spitalfields, London	Abraham de Isaac Gomes Da Costa	Jane (Jael) Barnett		Spitalfields, London	
9289	Da Costa	Judith	1823	Whitechapel, London	Joseph Carcas	Hannah Dias	Haim Gomes Da Costa	Bethnal Green, London	dress maker
30007	Da Costa	Lucy (Mazaltob)	1789	Bethnal Green, London	Moses Zachariah Foligno	Rachel de Isaac Sabitay Salom	Benjamin de Benjamin de Isaac Gomes Da Costa	Aldgate, London	
19113	Da Costa	Lydia	1792	City, London	(?)		(?) Da Costa	Aldgate, London	annuitant
15778	Da Costa	Margaret	1811	Whitechapel, London	(?) Da Costa			Aldgate, London	sponge dealer's assistant
8768	Da Costa	Maria (Miriam)	1842	Birmingham	Hyam Gomes Da Costa	Rosa de Mordecai Baruh	Emanuel Gomes Da Costa	Whitechapel, London	
15887	Da Costa	Marian (Miriam) Mendes	1839	St Thomas, Virgin Islands, West Indies	Elias Charles Mendes Da Costa	Leah (?)	Gabriel Lindo	Hackney, London	boarding school pupil
23232	Da Costa	Maurice (Moses) Nunes	1769	?, Switzerland	Gabriel Nunes Da Costa		(?)	Kensington, London	annuitant
31100	Da Costa	Miriam	1807	Hackney, London	(?) Da Costa	(?)		Camberwell, London	
35	Da Costa	Miriam (Marian) Gomes	1844	Aldgate, London	Isaac de Hananel Gomes da Costa	Esther Barnett	Zaleck Baum	Spitalfields, London	
10881	Da Costa	Mordecai Gomes	1850	Spitalfields, London	Jacob de Moses Gomes Da Costa	Sarah Martin (Nunes Martinez)	Rebecca Barker	Spitalfields, London	
16253	Da Costa	Moses	1775	?, London				Spitalfields, London	
8763	Da Costa	Moses	1831	Whitechapel, London	Hyam Gomes Da Costa	Rosa de Mordecai Baruh		Whitechapel, London	cap peak maker
30010	Da Costa	Moses Gomes	1816	Whitechapel, London				Aldgate, London	silversmith
14676	Da Costa	Moses Gomes	1830	Spitalfields, London	Benjamin Gomes da Costa	Sarah de Aaron Gomes Da Costa	Phoebe Solomons	Spitalfields, London	traveller
9365	Da Costa	Moses Gomes	1843	Whitechapel, London	Aaron de Moses Gomes Da Costa	Caroline Siegenberg	Rosey Joseph	Spitalfields, London	scholar
36	Da Costa	Moses Gomes	1848	Aldgate, London	Isaac de Hananel Gomes da Costa	Esther Barnett	Jane (?)	Spitalfields, London	
15888	Da Costa	Olivia	1843	St Thomas, Virgin Islands, West Indies	(?) Da Costa			Hackney, London	boarding school pupil
6169	Da Costa	Philip Avigdor Gomes	1820	Whitechapel, London	Isaac Gomes Da Costa		Rebecca Suhamy (Samuel)	Whitechapel, London	commercial traveller
14677	Da Costa	Phoebe Gomes	1833	Whitechapel, London	David Solomons		Moses Gomes Da Costa	Spitalfields, London	
8764	Da Costa	Rachael	1833	Whitechapel, London	Hyam Gomes Da Costa	Rosa de Mordecai Baruh		Whitechapel, London	

151

ID	surname	given names	born	birthplace	father	mother	spouse 1	1851 residence	1851 occupation
31099	Da Costa	Rachel	1803	Middlesex, London	(?)		(?) Da Costa	Camberwell, London	fundholder
24952	Da Costa	Rachel Gomes	1835	Bethnal Green, London	Isaac Gomes Da Costa	Ann (?)	Lewis Abrahams	Bethnal Green, London	
8773	Da Costa	Rachel Gomes	1836	Spitalfields, London	Benjamin de Moses Gomes Da Costa	Sarah de Isaac Gomes Da Costa	Aaron de Abraham Gomes da Costa	Spitalfields, London	scholar
8770	Da Costa	Rachel Gomes	1844	Aldgate, London	Abraham de Aaron Gomes Da Costa	Hannah Joseph	Angelo (Mordecai) Gomes Da Costa	Aldgate, London	
16722	Da Costa	Rachel Gomes	1849	Middlesex, London	Abraham de Isaac Gomes Da Costa	Jane (Jael) Barnett		Spitalfields, London	scholar
10880	Da Costa	Rachel Gomes	1847	Spitalfields, London	Jacob de Moses Gomes Da Costa	Sarah Martin (Nunes Martinez)		Spitalfields, London	scholar
15886	Da Costa	Ramah Mendes	1837	St Thomas, Virgin Islands, West Indies	Elias Charles Mendes Da Costa	Leah (?)		Hackney, London	boarding school pupil
6170	Da Costa	Rebecca Gomes	1823	Mile End, London	Jacob Suhamy (Samuel)		Philip Avigdor Gomes Da Costa	Whitechapel, London	dressmaker
21671	Da Costa	Rebecca Mendes	1785	City, London	Jacob de Abraham Samuda	Abigail de Isaac de Pina	Moseh de Hananel Mendes Da Costa	Islington, London	fundholder
8761	Da Costa	Rosa	1809	Whitechapel, London	Mordecai Baruh		Hyam Gomes da Costa	Whitechapel, London	
24949	Da Costa	Samuel	1821	Shoreditch, London			Martha Bengough	Bethnal Green, London	hawker
12317	Da Costa	Sarah Gomes	1810	Spitalfields, London	Aaron Gomes Da Costa	Fanny (?)	Benjamin de Moses Gomes Da Costa	Spitalfields, London	
10877	Da Costa	Sarah Gomes	1818	Spitalfields, London	Joseph Nunes Martinez	Lucky (Mazaltob) de Abraham Levy	Jacob de Moses Gomes Da Costa	Spitalfields, London	house keeper
9311	Da Costa	Sarah L	1767	?	(?)		(?) Da Costa	Aldgate, London	poor
8623	Da Costa	Simmy (Simcha)	1845	Whitechapel, London	Isaac de Aaron Gomes Da Costa	Esther de Hananel Gomes Da Costa		Mile End, London	
10712	Da Costa	Solomon	1810	Middlesex, London			Hannah (?)	Spitalfields, London	general dealer
8762	Da Costa	Susannah Gomes	1829	Whitechapel, London	Hyam Gomes Da Costa	Rosa de Mordecai Baruh		Whitechapel, London	
15951	Da Silva	Abraham	1848	Finsbury, London	Jacob Da Silva	Maria (Miriam) Jones		Finsbury, London	
6163	Da Silva	Abraham	1849	Aldgate, London	Samuel Da Silva	Sophia Cardozo Paz	Hannah Levy	Aldgate, London	
21714	Da Silva	Alice Esther S J	1847	Islington, London	Johnson Da Silva	(?)	Julius Adler	Highbury, London	
9319	Da Silva	David	1850	?Aldgate, London	Samuel Silva	Sophia Cardozo Paz		Aldgate, London	
9318	Da Silva	Esther	1850	?Aldgate, London	Samuel Silva	Sophia Cardozo Paz		Aldgate, London	
24066	Da Silva	Francesca	1838	Liverpool	(?) Gomes Da Silva			Euston, London	scholar at home
6167	Da Silva	Jacob	1824	Mile End, London	Abraham de Abraham Da Silva	Esther de David Nunes Martines	Maria (Miriam) Jones	Finsbury, London	
21712	Da Silva	Johnson	1811	Finsbury, London			(?)	Highbury, London	patent medicine vendor + fund holder
6165	Da Silva	Jonah	1849	Finsbury, London	Jacob Da Silva	Maria (Miriam) Jones	Esther Osborn	Finsbury, London	
15952	Da Silva	Joseph	1850	Finsbury, London	Jacob Da Silva	Maria (Miriam) Jones	Rachel (Ray) Joseph	Finsbury, London	
21713	Da Silva	Leo C	1835	Bermondsey, London	Johnson Da Silva	(?)		Highbury, London	scholar
6166	Da Silva	Maria (Miriam)	1823	Aldgate, London	Jonas Jones	Rebecca (?)	Jacob da Silva	Finsbury, London	
24065	Da Silva	Mary A Gomes	1807	Fulham, London	(?)		(?) Gomes Da Silva	Euston, London	independent
9316	Da Silva	Samuel	1821	Mile End, London	Abraham de Abraham Da Silva	Esther de David Nunes Martines	Sophia Cardozo Paz	Aldgate, London	boot maker
9315	Da Silva	Sophia	1823	Aldgate, London	David Cardozo Paz	Catherine (Keturah) Simson	Samuel Da Silva	Aldgate, London	

ID	surname	given names	born	birthplace	father	mother	spouse 1	1851 residence	1851 occupation
5667	Da Silva	Sophia (Siporah, Zipporah)	1828	Mile End, London	Abraham de Abraham Da Silva	Esther de David Nunes Martines		?Spitalfields, London	
11977	Danell	Mary	1769	?, Holland	(?)		(?) Danell (?Daniel)	Whitechapel, London	annuitant
2405	Daniel	Catherine	1787	?, Poland [?, Prussia]			Isaac Daniel	Hull, Yorkshire	
2128	Daniel	Isaac	1785	?, Poland [?, Prussia]			Catherine (?)	Hull, Yorkshire	jeweller
17171	Daniel	Marcus	1834	Margonin, Poland				Newcastle Upon Tyne	dealer in sponges
15835	Danieli	Rebecca	1801	Portsmouth, Hampshire	(?) Levi		(?) Danieli	Aldgate, London	
18149	Daniels	Abraham	1760	Middlesex, London			Leah (?)	Mile End, London	inmate of Portuguese Jews Hospital
24917	Daniels	Ann	1804	Hammersmith, London	(?)		Solomon Daniels	Bethnal Green, London	
24918	Daniels	Ann	1838	Spitalfields, London	Solomon Daniels	Ann (?)		Bethnal Green, London	
24921	Daniels	Benjamin	1843	Bethnal Green, London	Solomon Daniels	Ann (?)		Bethnal Green, London	scholar
28706	Daniels	Daniel	1810	Spitalfields, London	Moses Daniels		Elizabeth (?)	Spitalfields, London	confectioner
2406	Daniels	Diana	1816	?, Germany				Hull, Yorkshire	tobacconist
28707	Daniels	Elizabeth	1821	Middlesex, London	(?)		Daniel Daniels	Spitalfields, London	
25564	Daniels	Emanuel	1838	Walworth, London	Daniel (Gedalia, Joseph) Daniels	Esther Crabb	Julia Levy	Aldgate, London	cigar maker
28712	Daniels	Emanuel	1850	Middlesex, London	Daniel Daniels	Elizabeth (?)		Spitalfields, London	
28708	Daniels	Ester	1841	Middlesex, London	Daniel Daniels	Elizabeth (?)		Spitalfields, London	
25565	Daniels	Esther	1809	?, London	Menachem Mendel Crabb		Daniel (Gedalia, Joseph) Daniels	Aldgate, London	tailoress
24920	Daniels	George	1840	Bethnal Green, London	Solomon Daniels	Ann (?)		Bethnal Green, London	scholar
28710	Daniels	Henry	1846	Middlesex, London	Daniel Daniels	Elizabeth (?)		Spitalfields, London	scholar
2407	Daniels	Isabel	1835	Hull, Yorkshire		Diana (?)		Hull, Yorkshire	milliner
24919	Daniels	John	1839	Bethnal Green, London	Solomon Daniels	Ann (?)		Bethnal Green, London	scholar
28711	Daniels	Julia	1848	Middlesex, London	Daniel Daniels	Elizabeth (?)		Spitalfields, London	
18150	Daniels	Leah	1769	Middlesex, London	(?)		Abraham Daniels	Mile End, London	inmate of Portuguese Jews Hospital
28709	Daniels	Moses	1844	Middlesex, London	Daniel Daniels	Elizabeth (?)		Spitalfields, London	
24916	Daniels	Solomon	1804	Chelmsford, Essex			Ann (?)	Bethnal Green, London	cabinet maker
24398	Dantziger	Elizabeth	1789	?, Devon	(?)		Jacob M Dantziger	Soho, London	
24400	Dantziger	Henry Charles	1830	Soho, London	Jacob M Dantziger	Elizabeth (?)		Soho, London	asssistant to jeweller
24397	Dantziger	Jacob M	1780	?, Poland [?, Silesia]			Elizabeth (?)	Soho, London	jeweller
24399	Dantziger	James W	1827	Soho, London	Jacob M Dantziger	Elizabeth (?)		Soho, London	
4407	Danziger	Abraham	1820	?, Poland [?, Prussia]	Joseph Danziger		Esther Emanuel	Birmingham	wholesale jeweller
4409	Danziger	Elizabeth (Lizzie)	1848	Birmingham	Abraham Danziger	Esther Emanuel	Henry E Isaacs	Birmingham	
4408	Danziger	Esther	1812	Northampton, Northamptonshire	Barnett Emanuel		Abraham Danziger	Birmingham	
18725	Danziger	Isidor	1836	Gdansk, Poland [Danzig]				Manchester	importer
14233	Danziger	William	1821	Gdansk, Poland [Danzig]			Amelia (?)	Manchester	jeweller
9306	David	Hannah	1795	Whitechapel, London	(?)		(?) David	Aldgate, London	working confectioner
17131	David	Judah	1834	?, Poland [?, Prussia]				Darlington, Co Durham	jeweller
17129	David	Phillip	1825	?, Poland [?, Prussia]				Darlington, Co Durham	jeweller
17132	David	Samuel	1830	?, Poland [?, Prussia]				Darlington, Co Durham	jeweller
20193	Davids	Abraham	1806	Spitalfields, London			Elizabeth (?)	Spitalfields, London	hawker
8398	Davids	Elhanan	1792	Portsmouth, Hampshire	Lemla Davids	Hannah (?)		Southampton, Hampshire	jeweller

ID	surname	given names	born	birthplace	father	mother	spouse 1	1851 residence	1851 occupation
20194	Davids	Elizabeth	1815	Aldgate, London	(?)		Abraham Davids	Spitalfields, London	
20195	Davids	Mary Ann	1847	Whitechapel, London	Abraham Davids	Elizabeth (?)		Spitalfields, London	
9175	Davidsohn	David	1836	?, Poland [?, Prussia]				Whitechapel, London	
9176	Davidsohn	Solomon	1839	?, Poland [?, Prussia]				Whitechapel, London	
8313	Davidson	Abraham	1801	?, Sweden			Rosetta Joseph	Wapping, London	clothier
24968	Davidson	Anne	1816	Portsmouth, Hampshire	(?) (Solomon?)		Sigismund Davidson	Holborn, London	
18425	Davidson	Arrabella	1837	Falmouth, Cornwall	Abraham Davidson	Rosetta Joseph	Julius Neustadt	Wapping, London	
15376	Davidson	Benjamin	1807	?, Poland [?, Prussia]			Ann Fitzpatrick	Waterloo, London	teacher of languages
25545	Davidson	Catherine	1797	Ipswich, Suffolk	Asher Ansell		Isaac Davidson	Dublin, Ireland	annuitant
7461	Davidson	David Meyer	1817	Finsbury, London	Meyer Davidson	Jesse Cohen	Henrietta Cohen	Belgravia, London	stockbroker
8312	Davidson	Eliza	1832	Falmouth, Cornwall	Abraham Davidson	Rosetta Joseph	Moses Alexander	Wapping, London	assistant jeweller
7639	Davidson	Ellis A	1828	Hull, Yorkshire			Catherine Levy	Holborn, London	drawing master
1085	Davidson	Grace	1795	Sheerness, Kent				Falmouth, Cornwall	milliner
18968	Davidson	Henrietta	1830	Brixton, London	Samuel Cohen		David Meyer Davidson	Belgravia, London	
18462	Davidson	Isaac	1803	?, Sweden	Moshe		Sarah (?)	Whitechapel, London	dealer in jewellery
18424	Davidson	Isaac	1830	Falmouth, Cornwall	Abraham Davidson	Rosetta Joseph	Amelia Simmons	Wapping, London	
24971	Davidson	James	1845	Middlesex, London				Holborn, London	scholar
25546	Davidson	Joseph	1836	Dublin, Ireland	Isaac Davidson	Catherine Ansell		Dublin, Ireland	
30460	Davidson	Julian	1833	Warsaw, Poland				Burslem, Staffordshire	jeweller
6706	Davidson	Louis	1841	Bloomsbury, London	Meyer Davidson	Jesse Cohen	Amelia R Lucas	Belgravia, London	scholar at home
18464	Davidson	Morris	1841	Aldgate, London	Isaac Davidson	Sarah (?)		Whitechapel, London	
18465	Davidson	Rebecca	1842	Whitechapel, London	Isaac Davidson	Sarah (?)		Whitechapel, London	
2249	Davidson	Rika	1826	?, Poland [?, Prussia]				Leeds, Yorkshire	hawker
8314	Davidson	Rosetta	1804	Redruth, Cornwall			Abraham Davidson	Wapping, London	
18463	Davidson	Sarah	1814	Whitechapel, London	(?)		Isaac Davidson	Whitechapel, London	
24967	Davidson	Sigismund	1818	?, Sweden			Anne (Solomon?)	Holborn, London	embroiderer
21063	Davidson	Thomas	1840	Falmouth, Cornwall				Dover, Kent	boarding school pupil
25547	Davidson	Wolfe	1833	Dublin, Ireland	Isaac Davidson	Catherine Ansell	Fanny Nathan	Dublin, Ireland	
10947	Davies	?	1800	?Holland			Jane (?)	Spitalfields, London	traveller
26839	Davies	Caroline	1850	?, London	Solomon Davies	Rose (?)		Aldgate, London	
28661	Davies	Darby	1837	?, Poland	Samuel Davies	Maria (?)		Spitalfields, London	tailor
15817	Davies	David F	1821	?, London				Aldgate, London	salesman
28662	Davies	Debrah	1841	?, Poland	Samuel Davies	Maria (?)		Spitalfields, London	
8254	Davies	Harris	1825	?, Poland [?, Rusia Poland]	David Orchinski		Rosa Cohen	Hull, Yorkshire	hawker
10946	Davies	Jane	1806	?, Holland	(?)		(?) Davies	Spitalfields, London	wife of traveller
10949	Davies	Julia	1842	Paris, France	(?) Davies	Jane (?)		Spitalfields, London	
22113	Davies	Magnus	1820	Poznan, Poland [Posen, Prussia]				Whitechapel, London	tailor
28660	Davies	Maria	1811	?, Poland	(?)		Samuel Davies	Spitalfields, London	
27280	Davies	Newman	1815	?, Poland [?, Prussia]				Aldgate, London	wholesale jeweller
28664	Davies	Rayheh	1850	Middlesex, London	Samuel Davies	Maria (?)		Spitalfields, London	
10948	Davies	Rheuben	1840	Paris, France	(?) Davies	Jane (?)		Spitalfields, London	
26837	Davies	Rose	1821	?,London	(?)		Solomon Davies	Aldgate, London	
28659	Davies	Samuel	1787	?, Poland			Maria (?)	Spitalfields, London	glazier
28663	Davies	Samuel	1844	?, Poland	Samuel Davies	Maria (?)		Spitalfields, London	

ID	surname	given names	born	birthplace	father	mother	spouse 1	1851 residence	1851 occupation
26838	Davies	Sarah	1848	?, London	Solomon Davies	Rose (?)		Aldgate, London	
26836	Davies	Solomon	1824	?, Germany			Rose (?)	Aldgate, London	shoemaker
982	Davies (Davis)	Elizabeth	1849	Exeter, Devon	Hyman Davis	Rebecca Jacobs		Exeter, Devon	
25558	Davis	?	1851	Dublin, Ireland	John Isaac Davis	Selina Davis		Dublin, Ireland	
9254	Davis	Abagail	1847	Birmingham	Solomon Davis	Hannah Hart	Herman Heilbluth	Spitalfields, London	
28289	Davis	Abraham	1799	?, Poland			Rosa (?)	Aldgate, London	cap maker
3753	Davis	Abraham	1801	Mile End, London	Isaac Eizak Davis		Catharine (Kate) Harris	Spitalfields, London	furniture broker
17657	Davis	Abraham	1803	?, London	(Jacob?) Davis	(Nancy Jonas?)	Hannah (?)	Aldgate, London	clothes salesman
18480	Davis	Abraham	1804	Holborn, London	Moshe Davis		Rosetta (?)	Bloomsbury, London	glass dealer
6590	Davis	Abraham	1809	Aldgate, London				Aldgate, London	shoe maker
13327	Davis	Abraham	1831	Spitalfields, London	Judah Davis	Leah Mendoza	Sophia Levy	Spitalfields, London	clothes dealer
9584	Davis	Abraham	1835	Spitalfields, London	(?) Davis	Sarah (?)		Spitalfields, London	general dealer
111	Davis	Abraham	1849	Woolwich, London	David Davis	Rosetta Davis		Woolwich, London	
52	Davis	Abraham Richard	1848	Woolwich, London	Lewis Davis	Anne Jacobs		Plumstead, London	
15403	Davis	Abraham Rufus	1836	Whitechapel, London	Daniel Davis	Frances (?)		Waterloo, London	assistant in china, glass + earthenware dealer's business
2172	Davis	Abram (Abraham)	1816	?, Poland			Maria Harris	Oxford, Oxfordshire	wholesale dealer in jewellery &c
25522	Davis	Ada	1844	Liverpool	David Marcus Davis	Sarah (?)	Samuel Lewis	Dublin, Ireland	
2408	Davis	Adelaide	1829	Middlesex, London	John J Davis	Sarah (?)	Benjamin Jacobs	Hull, Yorkshire	
25554	Davis	Adolph	1841	Dublin, Ireland	John Isaac Davis	Selina Davis	Henrietta Friedlander	Dublin, Ireland	
20095	Davis	Agnes	1851	Whitechapel, London	Henry Davis	Hannah Woolf nee Ascher		Mayfair, London	
25553	Davis	Albert John	1838	?London	John Isaac Davis	Selina Davis		Dublin, Ireland	
30356	Davis	Alex	1834	Stepney, London				St Giles, London	tailor's assistant
30228	Davis	Alexander	1807	Chodzież, Poland [Chodziessen, Prussia]			Polina (?)	Sunderland, Co Durham	clothes dealer
9115	Davis	Alexander	1811	?, London			Anne (?)	Strand, London	sadler empl 5
9125	Davis	Alexander	1848	Strand, London	Alexander Davis	Anne (?)		Strand, London	
7558	Davis	Alfred	1811	?, London	Moses Davis	Catherine (?)		Aldgate, London	Birmingham + Sheffield merchants in British + foreign fancy goods
31192	Davis	Alfred	1836	Glasgow, Scotland	David Davis	Elizabeth (?)		Glasgow, Scotland	watchmaker's clerk
19890	Davis	Alfred	1844	Derby, Derbyshire	John Davis	Amelia (?)		Derby, Derbyshire	
23934	Davis	Alfred	1845	Marylebone, London	David Davis	Louisa (?)		Marylebone, London	
6230	Davis	Alice	1806	?, London	(?)		(?) Samuel	Covent Garden, London	
20096	Davis	Alice	1832	Whitechapel, London	Henry Davis	(?)		Mayfair, London	
3778	Davis	Alice	1833	Whitechapel, London	David Davis	Hannah (?)		Spitalfields, London	dressmaker
19888	Davis	Amelia	1820	?, London	(?)		John Davis	Derby, Derbyshire	
29871	Davis	Amelia	1820	Stratford, London	Mordecai Davis	Esther Bendahan		Wapping, London	dressmaker
3777	Davis	Amelia	1831	Whitechapel, London	David Davis	Hannah (?)	Henry Nathan Levy	Spitalfields, London	tailoress
30706	Davis	Amelia	1845	Strand, London	Solomon Davis	Solomon Davis		Covent Garden, London	scholar
11084	Davis	Angel	1808	Middlesex, London			Catherine (?)	Aldgate, London	general dealer
2251	Davis	Ann	1791	Birmingham	(?) Aaron		Gabriel Davis	Leeds, Yorkshire	

ID	surname	given names	born	birthplace	father	mother	spouse 1	1851 residence	1851 occupation
985	Davis	Ann	1832	Exeter, Devon	Morris Davis	Elizabeth (?)		Exeter, Devon	assistant to haberdasher + jeweller
26754	Davis	Ann	1832	Aldgate, London	Isaac Davis	Louisa (?)		Aldgate, London	oilman
10700	Davis	Ann	1835	Spitalfields, London	Elias Davis	Esther Harris		Spitalfields, London	at home
50	Davis	Ann	1845	Woolwich, London	Lewis Davis	Anne Jacobs	Augustus Davis	Plumstead, London	scholar
3609	Davis	Anne	1790	?, London	Isaac (John Zekel Neubrenner) Solomon	Maria (Merle) Israel	Jacob Davis	Cheltenham, Gloucestershire	
9116	Davis	Anne	1819	Strand, London	(?)		Alexander Davis	Strand, London	
12268	Davis	Anne	1836	Finsbury, London	Jacob Davis			Finsbury, London	
30231	Davis	Anne	1841	Chodzież, Poland [Chodziessen, Prussia]	Alexander Davis	Polina (?)		Sunderland, Co Durham	
9124	Davis	Anne	1846	Strand, London	Alexander Davis	Anne (?)	Hyam Abrahams	Strand, London	
30212	Davis	Annette	1840	Liverpool	David Marcus Davis	Sarah Mordecai	Joseph J Davis	Dublin, Ireland	
8482	Davis	Annie	1848	Gosport, Hampshire	Joseph Davis	Emma (?)		Gosport, Hampshire	
30234	Davis	Aron	1847	Sunderland, Co Durham	Alexander Davis	Polina (?)		Sunderland, Co Durham	
19891	Davis	Arthur	1846	Derby, Derbyshire	John Davis	Amelia (?)	Louise Jonas	Derby, Derbyshire	
18482	Davis	Asher	1835	Holborn, London	Abraham Davis	Rosetta (?)		Bloomsbury, London	glass dealer's assistant
10142	Davis	Asher	1837	Spitalfields, London	Coleman Davis	Rebecca Jacobs		Spitalfields, London	brush maker
20094	Davis	Asher	1849	Whitechapel, London	Henry Davis	Hannah Woolf nee Ascher		Mayfair, London	
28628	Davis	Barny	1841	Whitechapel, London	Isaac Davis	Harriet Henry		Spitalfields, London	scholar
44	Davis	Benjamin	1834	Woolwich, London	Lewis Davis	Anne Jacobs		Plumstead, London	scholar
27826	Davis	Benjamin	1844	Spitalfields, London	Isaac Davis	Sarah (?)		Spitalfields, London	scholar
22805	Davis	Benjamin (Barnet)	1828	Spitalfields, London	David Davis	Elizabeth (?)	Maria Abrahams	Whitechapel, London	furrier
8591	Davis	Benn (Barnet)	1847	Kensington, London	James Phineas Davis	Eliza Davis	Belle Elizabeth Davis	Notting Hill, London	scholar (at home)
30155	Davis	Berinder (Merinda, Brenda)	1843	Piccadilly, London	Joseph Davis	Jeannette Mallan		Hendon, London	scholar at home
2631	Davis	Bernard	1827	Marylebone, London			Adelaide (?)	Glasgow, Scotland	clothier traveller
22402	Davis	Bertha	1851	Whitechapel, London	Jacob Davis	Rosa Schwaba		Whitechapel, London	
30076	Davis	Betsy	1827	?, London	Henry Davis	Ellen Lewis		Bloomsbury, London	
7860	Davis	Caroline	1850	Aldgate, London	Saul (Solomon) Davis	Rosetta (Rosa) Costa		Aldgate, London	
3754	Davis	Catharine (Kate)	1800	Spitalfields, London	Pinchas Zelig Harris		Abraham Davies	Spitalfields, London	
30150	Davis	Catherine	1800	Aldgate, London	Shimon Simmons		Gabriel Davis	Victoria, London	formerly in business
2410	Davis	Catherine	1813	abroad			John Davis	Hull, Yorkshire	
11085	Davis	Catherine	1813	Middlesex, London	(?)		Angel Davis	Aldgate, London	general dealer
25257	Davis	Catherine	1844	Middlesex, London	Joseph Davis	Esther (?)		Holborn, London	attends school
5149	Davis	Catherine (Kitty)	1828	Aldgate, London	Joshua Davis	Sarah Zusman		Aldgate, London	
11974	Davis	Charles	1827	Whitechapel, London	Angel Davis	Maria Davis	(?)	Whitechapel, London	compositor
22019	Davis	Charles	1847	Whitechapel, London	Myer Davis	Hannah Moses		Covent Garden, London	
15406	Davis	Charles	1849	Waterloo, London	Daniel Davis	Frances (?)		Waterloo, London	
3198	Davis	Charles Elias	1834	Greenwich, London	Elias Davis	Elizabeth Moses	Clara Rosetta Moses	Bloomsbury, London	
781	Davis	Charles Isaac	1843	?, London	Charles Davis	Sarah Benjamin	Kate Sprague Hamilton	Soho, London	scholar
22804	Davis	Charles Mordecai	1831	Spitalfields, London	David Davis	Elizabeth (?)	Nancy Cohen	Whitechapel, London	lamp cotton manufacturer
30236	Davis	Charlotte	1820	Finsbury, London	(?) Myers		Henry Asher Davis	Mile End, London	

ID	surname	given names	born	birthplace	father	mother	spouse 1	1851 residence	1851 occupation
108	Davis	Charlotte	1822	Middlesex, London	(?) Jacobs	Leah (?)	David Davis	Woolwich, London	
29969	Davis	Clara	1773	Gdansk, Poland [Danzig, Prizen]	Klonymus Zadok		Marks Davis	Whitechapel, London	
12265	Davis	Clara	1829	City, London	Jacob Davis			Finsbury, London	
10143	Davis	Clara	1840	Spitalfields, London	Coleman Davis	Rebecca Jacobs	(?Joseph) Hart	Spitalfields, London	scholar
10046	Davis	Clara	1842	Liverpool	Saul Davis	Evelyn (Evelene) (?)		Liverpool	
18733	Davis	Clara Emma	1842	Liverpool	David Marcus Davis	Sarah Mordecai	Augustus (Asher) Jacobs	Dublin, Ireland	
2159	Davis	Coleman	1800	Southwark, London	John Jacob Davis	Maria Joel	Mary Jacob	Southwark, London	musician, teacher of music
10697	Davis	Coleman	1827	Spitalfields, London	Elias Davis	Esther Harris	Esther Solomon	Spitalfields, London	cigar maker
980	Davis	Coleman	1840	Birmingham	Hyman Davis	Rebecca Jacobs	Amelia Samuel	Exeter, Devon	
15400	Davis	Daniel	1811	Holborn, London	Moses Davis from Kassel		Frances (?)	Waterloo, London	china, glass + earthenware dealer
11976	Davis	Daniel	1831	Whitechapel, London	Angel Davis	Maria Davis		Whitechapel, London	pianoforte tuner
9122	Davis	Daniel Reginald	1844	Strand, London	Alexander Davis	Anne (?)		Strand, London	scholar at home
19987	Davis	David	1780	Birmingham	Meir Davis		Feigele Katz	Birmingham	
27180	Davis	David	1781	?, London			Julia (?)	Aldgate, London	tailor
23854	Davis	David	1791	?, Poland	Shmuel		Hannah Cohen	Piccadilly, London	dealer in regimentals
23929	Davis	David	1799	Spitalfields, London			Louisa (?)	Marylebone, London	general dealer
2030	Davis	David	1801	Aldgate, London	Jacob Davis		Jane Myers	Aldgate, London	tailor master
18430	Davis	David	1801	?, London	Samuel Davis	Ann Aaron	Elizabeth (?)	Glasgow, Scotland	watch manufacturer
9928	Davis	David	1804	Great Yarmouth, Norfolk	(?Simon) Davis			?Great Yarmouth, Norfolk	
6228	Davis	David	1809	?, London	Mark (Mordecai) Davis		Alice Samuel nee (?)	Covent Garden, London	lodging house keeper
8393	Davis	David	1813	Portsmouth, Hampshire	Moses Davis	Rosey Nathan	Sophia (?)	Southampton, Hampshire	clothier
15168	Davis	David	1813	?, London				Shoreditch, London	dealer in jewellery
107	Davis	David	1817	Woolwich, London	Israel Davis	Rosetta Levy	Charlotte Jacobs	Woolwich, London	clothier, pawnbroker + outfitter
30151	Davis	David	1824	Covent Garden, London	Gabriel Davis	Catherine Simmons		Victoria, London	dentist
12264	Davis	David	1830	City, London	Jacob Davis			Finsbury, London	agent + traveller
16985	Davis	David	1834	Bethnal Green, London				Wapping, London	shoemaker apprentice
30109	Davis	David	1834	Middlesex, London	Moses Davis	Julia Hart	Rachel Nathan	Hackney, London	draper
6321	Davis	David	1835	?, London	Moses Davis	Julia (Judith) Myers		Aldgate, London	
29200	Davis	David	1838	Aldgate, London	Henry Asher Davis	Frances Wolff		Whitechapel, London	scholar
26756	Davis	David	1839	Aldgate, London	Isaac Davis	Louisa (?)		Aldgate, London	
9252	Davis	David	1844	Whitechapel, London	Solomon Davis	Hannah Hart		Whitechapel, London	
26433	Davis	David	1844	?, London	(?)	Matilda Davis		Aldgate, London	
19855	Davis	David	1845	Spitalfields, London	Isaac Davis	Rosa Solomon		Spitalfields, London	scholar
24585	Davis	David	1845	Lambeth, London	Isaac Davis	Mary Levy		Lambeth, London	
30233	Davis	David	1845	Chodzież, Poland [Chodziessen, Prussia]	Alexander Davis	Polina (?)		Sunderland, Co Durham	
11089	Davis	David	1846	Middlesex, London	Angel Davis	Catherine (?)	Sophia Louisson	Aldgate, London	scholar
22401	Davis	David	1848	Whitechapel, London	Jacob Davis	Rosa Schwaba		Whitechapel, London	
30636	Davis	David	1851	Whitechapel, London	John Davis	Dinah Abrahams		Whitechapel, London	

ID	surname	given names	born	birthplace	father	mother	spouse 1	1851 residence	1851 occupation
3201	Davis	David (Frederick) Elias	1838	Walworth, London	Elias Davis	Elizabeth Moses	Gertrude Moses	Bloomsbury, London	scholar
6342	Davis	David Barnett	1820	Whitechapel, London			Elizabeth Cohen	Aldgate, London	broker
6309	Davis	David John	1839	Middlesex, London	Jacob David Davis	Dinah Alexander	Lina Meyer	Aldgate, London	scholar
2679	Davis	David Levi	1833	Nottingham, Nottinghamshire	Joel Davis	Rosa Levy		Nottingham, Nottinghamshire	assistant pawnbroker
18734	Davis	David Marcus	1808	Cambridge			Sarah Mordecai	Dublin, Ireland	dentist
15279	Davis	David Solomon	1831	?, London	(?) Davis	Sarah (?)	Marian Cox	Shoreditch, London	commercial traveller
10837	Davis	Davis	1835	Whitechapel, London				Spitalfields, London	apprentice
17885	Davis	Davis	1836	Middlesex, London	Moss Davis	Sarah Jonas		Elephant & Castle, London	
10144	Davis	Dinah	1803	Southwark, London	Asher Jacobs	Esther Israel	Joseph Davis	Whitechapel, London	
6310	Davis	Dinah	1811	?, London	Moshe Alexander		Jacob David Davis	Aldgate, London	
20278	Davis	Dinah	1832	Wapping, London	Alexander Abrahams	Rosetta Kisch	John Davis	Wapping, London	tailor
2164	Davis	Dinah	1839	Southwark, London	Coleman Davis	Mary Jacob	Alfred Ahrenfeld	Southwark, London	
19892	Davis	Edith	1848	Derby, Derbyshire	John Davis	Amelia (?)	Leopold Zossenheim	Derby, Derbyshire	
8590	Davis	Edmund Francis	1846	Chiswick, London	James Phineas Davis	Eliza Davis	Florence Aria	Notting Hill, London	scholar (at home)
19936	Davis	Edward	1813	Aldgate, London	David Davis	Elizabeth Lazarus		Whitechapel, London	merchant
25361	Davis	Edward	1827	Holborn, London	John (Jacob) Davis	Maria (Mary) Pyke	Louisa Joseph	Clerkenwell, London	--- maker
12267	Davis	Edward	1834	Finsbury, London	Jacob Davis			Finsbury, London	furrier
26757	Davis	Edward	1842	Aldgate, London	Isaac Davis	Louisa (?)		Aldgate, London	
14548	Davis	Edward	1843	Paddington, London	Henry Davis	Mary (?)		Walworth, London	scholar
15524	Davis	Edward	1846	?, London	Jacob David Davis	Dinah Alexander	?	Aldgate, London	
2672	Davis	Edward (Elijah)	1837	Nottingham, Nottinghamshire	Joel Davis	Rosa Levy	Ella Joseph	Nottingham, Nottinghamshire	cigar maker
22435	Davis	Edwin	1846	?				Gravesend, Kent	boarding school pupil
15744	Davis	Eleazer	1830	Exeter, Devon				Aldgate, London	assistant to wholesale clothier
10695	Davis	Elias	1801	Bethnal Green, London	Isaac Davis		Esther Harris	Spitalfields, London	general dealer
16	Davis	Elias	1809	Woolwich, London	Israel Davis	Rosetta Levy	Elizabeth Moses	Bloomsbury, London	merchant
22661	Davis	Elias	1812	Spitalfields, London	David HaLevi		Rachel Moses	Whitechapel, London	general dealer
3762	Davis	Elias	1842	Spitalfields, London	Abraham Davis	Catharine (Kate) Harris		Spitalfields, London	
29695	Davis	Elijah	1837	Nottingham, Nottinghamshire				Aldgate, London	
8587	Davis	Eliza	1816	Montego Bay, Jamaica, West Indies	David I Davis	Rebecca (?)	James Phineas Davis	Notting Hill, London	
30535	Davis	Eliza	1828	St Pancras, London	Lewis Lazarus		Moss Davis	Soho, London	milliner
14546	Davis	Eliza	1835	Walworth, London	Henry Davis	Mary (?)		Walworth, London	
19939	Davis	Elizabeth	1788	?, London	Jacob from Worms Lazarus		David Davis	Whitechapel, London	
23474	Davis	Elizabeth	1792	?, London	(?)		(?) Davis	Liverpool	housekeeper
18431	Davis	Elizabeth	1803	Birmingham	(?)		David Davis	Glasgow, Scotland	
3207	Davis	Elizabeth	1806	Westminster, London	Asher Anshel HaCohen		Solomon Davis	Walworth, London	
17	Davis	Elizabeth	1815	Whitechapel, London	David Moses	Abigail Solomons	Elias Davis	Bloomsbury, London	
25360	Davis	Elizabeth	1822	Aldgate, London	John (Jacob) Davis	Maria (Mary) Pyke		Clerkenwell, London	seamstress
6343	Davis	Elizabeth	1825	Spitalfields, London	Isaac Cohen	Esther Davis	David Barnett Davis	Aldgate, London	
3756	Davis	Elizabeth	1828	Aldgate, London	Abraham Davis	Catharine (Kate) Harris		Spitalfields, London	

ID	surname	given names	born	birthplace	father	mother	spouse 1	1851 residence	1851 occupation
19992	Davis	Elizabeth	1830	Birmingham	David Davis	Feigele Katz	Alexis Alexander	Birmingham	companion
2161	Davis	Elizabeth	1831	Southwark, London	Coleman Davis	Mary Jacob	Samuel Weingott	Southwark, London	dancing mistress
10145	Davis	Elizabeth	1834	Spitalfields, London	Joseph Davis	Dinah Jacobs		Whitechapel, London	dressmaker
26755	Davis	Elizabeth	1838	Aldgate, London	Isaac Davis	Louisa (?)		Aldgate, London	scholar
9117	Davis	Elizabeth	1839	Strand, London	Alexander Davis	Anne (?)	Moses Brandon (Brandon Rodrigues)	Strand, London	scholar
10777	Davis	Elizabeth	1840	Spitalfields, London	(?) Davis	Rebecca (?)		Spitalfields, London	parasol maker
28629	Davis	Elizabeth	1843	Spitalfields, London	Isaac Davis	Harriet Henry		Spitalfields, London	scholar
30705	Davis	Elizabeth	1844	Strand, London	Solomon Davis	Solomon Davis		Covent Garden, London	scholar
15405	Davis	Elizabeth	1846	Waterloo, London	Daniel Davis	Frances (?)		Waterloo, London	
16591	Davis	Elizabeth	1846	Liverpool	Saul Davis	Evelyn (Evelene) (?)		Liverpool	
28809	Davis	Elizabeth	1850	Whitechapel, London	Joseph Davis	Esther (?)		Spitalfields, London	
10835	Davis	Elizabeth (Betsey)	1825	Whitechapel, London	Emanuel Emanuel		Woolf (Benjamin) Davis	Spitalfields, London	domestic
30235	Davis	Elizabeth Victoria	1843	Mile End, London	Henry Asher Davis	Charlotte Myers		Mile End, London	
23473	Davis	Ellen	1824	?, London	(?) Davis	Elizabeth (?)		Liverpool	
27817	Davis	Ellen	1831	Whitechapel, London	Isaac Davis	Sarah (?)		Spitalfields, London	artificial flower maker
25550	Davis	Ellen (Elkela)	1851	?, London	Hyman Davis	Isabella Davis	Eugene Benjamin	Dublin, Ireland	
8592	Davis	Ellis James	1850	Kensington, London	James Phineas Davis	Eliza Davis	Florence Louisa Rosenthal	Notting Hill, London	
17661	Davis	Emanuel	1828	?, London	Abraham Davis	Hannah (?)	Rebecca Asher	Aldgate, London	
9585	Davis	Emanuel	1836	Spitalfields, London	(?) Davis	Sarah (?)		Spitalfields, London	general dealer
24583	Davis	Emanuel	1841	Lambeth, London	Isaac Davis	Mary Levy		Lambeth, London	
8588	Davis	Emily Sarah	1837	Marylebone, London	James Phineas Davis	Eliza Davis	Lewis Abraham Franklin	St Pancras, London	
31075	Davis	Emma	1808	Portsmoth, Hampshire	(?) Moses		Abraham Davis	Maida Vale, London	annuitant
8478	Davis	Emma	1814	Gosport, Hampshire	(?)		Joseph Davis	Gosport, Hampshire	
11970	Davis	Emma	1816	Whitechapel, London	Angel Davis	Maria Davis	George Benjamin	Whitechapel, London	
17662	Davis	Emma	1830	?, London	Abraham Davis	Hannah (?)		Aldgate, London	dressmaker
47	Davis	Emma	1838	Woolwich, London	Lewis Davis	Anne Jacobs		Plumstead, London	scholar
19893	Davis	Emma	1850	Derby, Derbyshire	John Davis	Amelia (?)	Lucien Marcan (March)	Derby, Derbyshire	
19619	Davis	Ester	1829	Whitechapel, London	Joseph Davis	Julia (?)		Spitalfields, London	teacher in a school
21493	Davis	Ester	1832	?, Holland	Solomon Davis	Rebecca (?)		Spitalfields, London	
30232	Davis	Ester	1842	Chodzież, Poland [Chodziessen, Prussia]	Alexander Davis	Polina (?)		Sunderland, Co Durham	
29870	Davis	Esther	1792	Whitechapel, London	Benjamin de Samuel Bendahan	Ribca de Moseh Jesurun Alveres	Mordecai Davis	Wapping, London	shopkeeper
10696	Davis	Esther	1803	Spitalfields, London	Pinchas Zelig Harris		Elias Davis	Spitalfields, London	
25254	Davis	Esther	1803	Middlesex, London	Mordecai		Joseph Davis	Holborn, London	general dealer
27493	Davis	Esther	1815	Middlesex, London	Tsevi Hirsh Solomon		George Davis	Aldgate, London	
23856	Davis	Esther	1816	Piccadilly, London	David Davis	Hannah Cohen		Piccadilly, London	
13325	Davis	Esther	1825	Spitalfields, London	Judah Davis	Leah Mendoza	Angelo Myers	Spitalfields, London	shoe binder
28805	Davis	Esther	1828	Whitechapel, London	(?)		Joseph Davis	Spitalfields, London	
11975	Davis	Esther	1830	Whitechapel, London	Angel Davis	Maria Davis		Whitechapel, London	
10141	Davis	Esther	1833	Spitalfields, London	Coleman Davis	Rebecca Jacobs		Spitalfields, London	umbrella maker
27824	Davis	Esther	1838	St Giles, London	Isaac Davis	Sarah (?)		Spitalfields, London	tailoress
22438	Davis	Esther	1839	Whitechapel, London	Daniel Davis	Frances (?)	William L Miller	Waterloo, London	boarding school pupil
30112	Davis	Esther	1843	Whitechapel, London	Moses Davis	Julia Hart		Hackney, London	scholar

ID	surname	given names	born	birthplace	father	mother	spouse 1	1851 residence	1851 occupation
5649	Davis	Esther	1848	Liverpool	Saul Davis	Evelyn (Evelene) (?)	(?) Tibe	Liverpool	
30159	Davis	Esther	1849	Marylebone, London	Joseph Davis	Jeannette Mallan		Hendon, London	scholar
6344	Davis	Esther (Ellen)	1851	Spitalfields, London	David Barnett Davis	Elizabeth Cohen	Joshua Cohen	Aldgate, London	
28291	Davis	Eve	1828	?, Poland	Abraham Davis	Rosa (?)		Aldgate, London	cap maker
27820	Davis	Eve	1833	St Giles, London	Isaac Davis	Sarah (?)		Spitalfields, London	servant
5646	Davis	Evelyn (Evelene)	1820	Liverpool	(?)		Saul (D M) Davis	Liverpool	
6587	Davis	Fanny	1827	Aldgate, London	David Davis	Jane Myers		Aldgate, London	tailoress
18691	Davis	Fanny	1834	Exeter, Devon	Morris Davis	Elizabeth (?)	Barnett (Burnet) Bebarfield (Bebarfald)	Whitechapel, London	
46	Davis	Fanny	1837	Woolwich, London	Lewis Davis	Anne Jacobs	David Joseph	Plumstead, London	
15404	Davis	Fanny	1837	Clerkenwell, London	Daniel Davis	Frances (?)		Waterloo, London	scholar
27665	Davis	Fanny	1838	Middlesex, London	Moses Davis	Julia Hart		Aldgate, London	
17663	Davis	Fanny	1839	?, London	Abraham Davis	Hannah (?)		Aldgate, London	book worker
11088	Davis	Fanny	1841	Middlesex, London	Angel Davis	Catherine (?)		Aldgate, London	scholar
15523	Davis	Fanny	1844	Aldgate, London	Jacob David Davis	Dinah Alexander	Judah (Joseph) Isaacson	Aldgate, London	scholar
26758	Davis	Fanny	1844	Aldgate, London	Isaac Davis	Louisa (?)		Aldgate, London	
29202	Davis	Fanny	1845	Whitechapel, London	Henry Asher Davis	Isabella Hart	Jonas Weiskopf [White]	Whitechapel, London	scholar
18740	Davis	Fanny	1847	Middlesex, London	Noah Davis	Henrietta (?)	Nathaniel Harris	Elephant & Castle, London	
28807	Davis	Fanny	1848	Whitechapel, London	Joseph Davis	Esther (?)		Spitalfields, London	
9123	Davis	Flora	1845	Strand, London	Alexander Davis	Anne (?)		Strand, London	
15401	Davis	Frances	1814	Aldgate, London	(?)		Daniel Davis	Waterloo, London	
17592	Davis	Frances	1823	Spitalfields, London	Isaac Davis	Rachael (?)		Spitalfields, London	general dealer
26564	Davis	Frances	1833	Whitechapel, London	Simon Davis	Sarah Nunes Martin (Martines)		Whitechapel, London	
16589	Davis	Frances	1840	Liverpool	Saul Davis	Evelyn (Evelene) (?)		Liverpool	
19994	Davis	Frances Rose (Fanny)	1849	Sunderland, Co Durham	Michael Davis	Sarah Jacobs	John Davis	Dublin, Ireland	
30154	Davis	Frederick	1840	City, London	Joseph Davis	Jeannette Mallan		Hendon, London	scholar
19889	Davis	Frederick	1843	Cheltenham, Gloucestershire	John Davis	Amelia (?)		Derby, Derbyshire	mechanical engineer & iron merchant
3200	Davis	Frederick Elias	1835	Greenwich, London	Elias Davis	Elizabeth Moses	Gertrude Moses [Nathan]	Bloomsbury, London	
2250	Davis	Gabriel	1790	?, Germany			Ann Aaron	Leeds, Yorkshire	optician
27492	Davis	George	1811	Middlesex, London	Yehuda		Esther Solomon	Aldgate, London	general dealer
19995	Davis	George	1827	Birmingham	David Davis	Feigele Katz	Susanna Amelia Brown	Barnsbury, London	
19854	Davis	George	1839	Spitalfields, London	Isaac Davis	Rosa Solomon		Spitalfields, London	scholar
26759	Davis	George	1849	Aldgate, London	Isaac Davis	Louisa (?)		Aldgate, London	
112	Davis	George	1850	Woolwich, London	David Davis	Charlotte Davis		Woolwich, London	
11090	Davis	George	1850	Middlesex, London	Angel Davis	Catherine (?)		Aldgate, London	
51	Davis	George Robert David	1846	Woolwich, London	Lewis Davis	Anne Jacobs		Plumstead, London	
8479	Davis	Georgiana	1843	Gosport, Hampshire	Joseph Davis	Emma (?)		Gosport, Hampshire	
19624	Davis	Godfrey	1843	Whitechapel, London	Joseph Davis	Julia (?)		Spitalfields, London	scholar
4845	Davis	Hannah	1785	?, Poland			(?) Davis	Birmingham	family tailoress
15030	Davis	Hannah	1787	?, Wales [Gwent, Wales]	(?)		(?) Davis	Bethnal Green, London	

ID	surname	given names	born	birthplace	father	mother	spouse 1	1851 residence	1851 occupation
23855	Davis	Hannah	1791	Aldgate, London	Isaac Isaac Cohen		David Davis	Piccadilly, London	
22913	Davis	Hannah	1793	Whitechapel, London	(?)		(?) Samuel	Wapping, London	waistcoat maker
3775	Davis	Hannah	1801	Deal, Kent	(?)		David Davis	Spitalfields, London	fruiteress
17658	Davis	Hannah	1805	?, London	(?)		Abraham Davis	Aldgate, London	
27224	Davis	Hannah	1809	?, Poland	Baruch Benedet Moses		(?)	Aldgate, London	
22017	Davis	Hannah	1820	Boston, Lincolnshire	Emanuel Moses	Ann (?)	Myer Davis	Covent Garden, London	
9251	Davis	Hannah	1823	Whitechapel, London	Solomon Hart		Solomon Davis	Spitalfields, London	town traveller
6738	Davis	Hannah	1825	Aldgate, London	Benjamin Henry Asher	Rayner Jacobs	Goodman Woolf	Mayfair, London	
11000	Davis	Hannah	1825	Aldgate, London	(?)		Lewis Davis	Aldgate, London	
6588	Davis	Hannah	1828	Aldgate, London	David Davis	Jane Myers	Isaac Lyon (Lyons)	Aldgate, London	tailoress
28955	Davis	Hannah	1828	?, London	(?) Benjamin		Solomon Davis	Whitechapel, London	
3760	Davis	Hannah	1839	Aldgate, London	Abraham Davis	Catharine (Kate) Harris		Spitalfields, London	
11087	Davis	Hannah	1839	Middlesex, London	Angel Davis	Catherine (?)		Aldgate, London	scholar
14544	Davis	Hannah	1845	Elephant & Castle, London	Henry Davis	Mary (?)	Frederick Barnard	Walworth, London	scholar
28806	Davis	Hannah	1845	Whitechapel, London	Joseph Davis	Esther (?)		Spitalfields, London	
18645	Davis	Hannah	1851	Northampton, Northamptonshire	Joseph Davis	Paulina Gonski	David Lewis Isaacs	Northampton, Northamptonshire	
30708	Davis	Hannah	1851	Covent Garden, London	Solomon Davis	Solomon Davis		Covent Garden, London	
13326	Davis	Hannah (Ann)	1829	Spitalfields, London	Judah Davis	Leah Mendoza	Daniel Joseph	Spitalfields, London	seamstress
859	Davis	Hannah (Anne)	1838	Liverpool	Saul Davis	Evelyn (Evelene) (?)	Montague (Moses) Moses (Montague)	Liverpool	
28627	Davis	Harriet	1820	Whitechapel, London	Solomon Henry		Isaac Davis	Spitalfields, London	general dealer
18737	Davis	Harriet	1829	Whitechapel, London	Angel Davis	Maria Davis		Whitechapel, London	
27225	Davis	Harriet	1842	?, London	Joseph Israel Davis	(?)		Aldgate, London	
24846	Davis	Harriett	1766	Hanover, Germany	(?)		Samuel Davis	Elephant & Castle, London	
30921	Davis	Harris	1817	?, Poland				Hull, Yorkshire	hawker
10573	Davis	Helen	1845	Glasgow, Scotland	David Davis	Elizabeth (?)	Montague Jacobs	Glasgow, Scotland	scholar
18417	Davis	Henrietta	1825	Brighton, Sussex	(?)		Noah Davis	Elephant & Castle, London	
3195	Davis	Henry	1790	?, London	Hyman Mossbach [Davis]	Esther (?)	Ellen Lewis	Bloomsbury, London	
14549	Davis	Henry	1806	Plymouth, Devon			Mary (?)	Walworth, London	carpenter joiner
20093	Davis	Henry	1809	Whitechapel, London			(?Alice) (?)	Mayfair, London	lodging house keeper
12263	Davis	Henry	1826	Middlesex, London	Jacob Davis			Finsbury, London	clerk, East India Agency
2039	Davis	Henry	1835	Aldgate, London	David Davis	Jane Myers	Esther Phillips	Aldgate, London	clothier warehouseman
18418	Davis	Henry	1848	Middlesex, London	Noah Davis	Henrietta (?)		Elephant & Castle, London	
28631	Davis	Henry	1851	Spitalfields, London	Isaac Davis	Harriet Henry		Spitalfields, London	
30022	Davis	Henry	1851	Shoreditch, London	Moses (Moss) Davis	Jane Davis		Shoreditch, London	
29198	Davis	Henry Asher	1818	Whitechapel, London	David Davis		Frances Wolff	Whitechapel, London	glass ?dealer
30162	Davis	Henry Asher	1840	Mile End, London	Henry Asher Davis	Charlotte Myers	Ann Mann	Mile End, London	
7254	Davis	Henry David	1839	Holborn, London	Abraham Davis	Emma Moses	Sarah Lindo Baber Isaacs	Maida Vale, London	
30111	Davis	Henry E	1842	?, London	Moses Davis	Julia Hart	Elizabeth (Betsy, Lizzie) Lialter	Hackney, London	scholar
3205	Davis	Henry Elias	1844	Aldgate, London	Elias Davis	Elizabeth Moses		Bloomsbury, London	scholar

ID	surname	given names	born	birthplace	father	mother	spouse 1	1851 residence	1851 occupation
29759	Davis	Hyam	1831	?, London				Aldgate, London	
6589	Davis	Hyam	1834	Aldgate, London	David Davis	Jane Myers		Aldgate, London	poulterer
978	Davis	Hyman	1800	Middlesex, London				Aldgate, London	butcher's lad
25548	Davis	Hyman	1824	Middlesex, London			Rebecca Jacobs	Exeter, Devon	general merchant
43	Davis	Hyman	1831	Woolwich, London	Henry Davis	Ellen Lewis	Isabella Davis	Dublin, Ireland	dentist
19620	Davis	Hyman	1833	Whitechapel, London	Lewis Davis	Anne Jacobs		Plumstead, London	articled clerk, solicitor
21040	Davis	Hyman	1846	?, London	Joseph Davis	Julia (?)	Amelia Rees	Spitalfields, London	fishmonger
								Dover, Kent	boarding school pupil
2675	Davis	Hyman (Henry)	1845	Nottingham, Nottinghamshire	Joel Davis	Rosa Levy	Emily Isaacs	Nottingham, Nottinghamshire	
27815	Davis	Isaac	1781	?, Poland [?, Prussia]			Sarah (?)	Spitalfields, London	general dealer
26751	Davis	Isaac	1803	City, London			Louisa (?)	Aldgate, London	oilman
28626	Davis	Isaac	1810	Spitalfields, London	David Davis		Harriet Henry	Spitalfields, London	general dealer
19850	Davis	Isaac	1815	Whitechapel, London	Judah Davis	Leah Mendosa	Rosa Solomon	Spitalfields, London	clothes dealer
24580	Davis	Isaac	1817	Deal, Kent	David Davis		Mary Levy	Lambeth, London	furniture dealer
6231	Davis	Isaac	1830	Middlesex, London	Mark (Mordecai) Davis		Rachel (?)	Soho, London	dealer in curiosities + works of art
6292	Davis	Isaac	1830	Aldgate, London	Abraham Davis	Catharine (Kate) Harris	Hannah Nathan	Spitalfields, London	
21492	Davis	Isaac	1830	?, Holland	Solomon Davis	Rebecca (?)		Spitalfields, London	butcher
31091	Davis	Isaac	1830	?, London	Michael Davis	Rebecca (?)		Northampton, Northamptonshire	cigar maker
4412	Davis	Isaac	1834	Birmingham			Esther Emanuel	Birmingham	commercial traveller in watches
2163	Davis	Isaac	1837	Southwark, London	Coleman Davis	Mary Jacob	Catherine Everitt	Southwark, London	
8245	Davis	Isaac	1847	Middlesex, London	David Barnett Davis	Elizabeth Cohen	Julia Isaacs	Aldgate, London	
30114	Davis	Isaac	1847	?, London	Moses Davis	Julia Hart		Hackney, London	
30707	Davis	Isaac	1847	Covent Garden, London	Solomon Davis	Solomon Davis		Covent Garden, London	scholar
30021	Davis	Isaac	1850	Bermondsey, London	Moses (Moss) Davis	Jane Davis	Rebecca Susan Branston	Covent Garden, London	
29199	Davis	Isabella	1823	Whitechapel, London	Joel Hart	Mary Hyams	Henry Asher Davis	Shoreditch, London	
25549	Davis	Isabella	1825	St Giles, London	Phineas Davis	(Jane Isaacs?)	Hyman Davis	Whitechapel, London	
22441	Davis	Isabella	1840	?	(?) Davis			Dublin, Ireland	
30115	Davis	Isabella	1846	Aldgate, London	Moses Davis	Julia Hart		Gravesend, Kent	boarding school pupil
19622	Davis	Israel	1839	Whitechapel, London	Joseph Davis	Julia (?)		Hackney, London	
21061	Davis	Israel	1841	Woolwich, London	(Israel?) Davis	(Anne Jacobs?)		Spitalfields, London	scholar
110	Davis	Israel	1847	Woolwich, London	David Davis	Charlotte Davis	Jane Jaffe	Dover, Kent	boarding school pupil
2680	Davis	Israel (Charles)	1840	Nottingham, Nottinghamshire	Joel Davis	Rosa Levy		Woolwich, London	scholar
3610	Davis	Jacob	1778	?, Germany	David Mulhausen		Anne Solomon	Cheltenham, Gloucestershire	pawnbroker
22398	Davis	Jacob	1809	?, Poland [?, Prussia]	David Schultz		Rosa Schwaba	Whitechapel, London	travelling jeweller
2674	Davis	Jacob	1843	Nottingham, Nottinghamshire	Joel Davis	Rosa Levy	Sophia Shoeps	Nottingham, Nottinghamshire	scholar
3940	Davis	Jacob David	1823	?, London	David Davis		Sarah Lazarus	Portsmouth, Hampshire	general dealer + Hebrew teacher + mohel
15519	Davis	Jacob Davis	1810	?, London	David Davis	(?Sarah Moses)	Dinah Alexander	Aldgate, London	wine merchant
8586	Davis	James Phineas	1811	Whitechapel, London	Phineas Davis	(?Jane Isaacs)	Eliza Davis	Notting Hill, London	attorney at law

ID	surname	given names	born	birthplace	father	mother	spouse 1	1851 residence	1851 occupation
2031	Davis	Jane	1797	Aldgate, London	Jacob Myers	Fanny Simons	David Davis	Aldgate, London	
30075	Davis	Jane	1821	?, London	Henry Davis	Ellen Lewis		Bloomsbury, London	
11973	Davis	Jane	1824	Whitechapel, London	Angel Davis	Maria Davis		Whitechapel, London	
23858	Davis	Jane	1826	Piccadilly, London	David Davis	Hannah Cohen		Piccadilly, London	milliner
18428	Davis	Jane	1827	Middlesex, London	(?) Davis			Bloomsbury, London	annuitant
6437	Davis	Jane	1830	City, London	Henry Davis		Moses (Moss) Davis	Shoreditch, London	
25359	Davis	Jane	1830	Holborn, London	John (Jacob) Davis	Maria (Mary) Pyke	Joseph Gashion	Clerkenwell, London	dressmaker
22440	Davis	Jane (Jeannette)	1844	?, London	Daniel Davis	Frances (?)		Waterloo, London	boarding school pupil
30153	Davis	Jeannette	1819	Bloomsbury, London	Vallek (Falk) Mallan (Milleman)	Bracha Lippschutz	Joseph Davis	Hendon, London	
27818	Davis	Jessie	1831	Whitechapel, London	Isaac Davis	Sarah (?)		Spitalfields, London	
2671	Davis	Joel	1784	Pinsk, Belarus [Gorodnow, nr Pinsk, Poland]	David Davidovitz		Rosa Levy	Nottingham, Nottinghamshire	jewellery dealer
29201	Davis	Joel	1845	Whitechapel, London	Henry Asher Davis	Isabella Hart	Sophia Michaelis	Whitechapel, London	scholar
30113	Davis	Joel	1845	Whitechapel, London	Moses Davis	Julia Hart		Hackney, London	scholar
2411	Davis	John	1809	abroad			Catherine (?)	Hull, Yorkshire	cabinet maker
19881	Davis	John	1811	Thame, Oxfordshire			Amelia (?)	Derby, Derbyshire	optician master empl 4
7707	Davis	John	1816	?, London	Moses Davis	Catherine (?)	Rachel Adelaide Moses	Aldgate, London	
20277	Davis	John	1820	Whitechapel, London	David HaLevi		Dinah Abrahams	Wapping, London	tailor
17660	Davis	John	1827	?, London	Abraham Davis	Hannah (?)		Aldgate, London	clothes salesman
31189	Davis	John	1828	Glasgow, Scotland	David Davis	Elizabeth (?)		Glasgow, Scotland	silk manufactuerer's clerk
20036	Davis	John	1829	Spitalfields, London	(?) Davis	Rachael (?)		Aldgate, London	tailor
10699	Davis	John	1834	Spitalfields, London	Elias Davis	Esther Harris		Spitalfields, London	at home
19853	Davis	John	1837	Finsbury, London	Isaac Davis	Rosa Solomon		Spitalfields, London	errand boy
23933	Davis	John	1838	Marylebone, London	David Davis	Louisa (?)		Marylebone, London	
14547	Davis	John	1841	Paddington, London	Henry Davis	Mary (?)	Sarah Barnard	Walworth, London	scholar
981	Davis	John	1842	Exeter, Devon	Hyman Davis	Rebecca Jacobs		Exeter, Devon	
22436	Davis	John	1845	?				Gravesend, Kent	boarding school pupil
25362	Davis	John (Jacob)	1796	Aldgate, London	David		Maria (Mary) Pyke	Clerkenwell, London	tailor
24588	Davis	John (Jacob)	1851	Lambeth, London	Isaac Davis	Mary Levy	Rachel Hyman	Lambeth, London	
25551	Davis	John Isaac	1803	?Leeds, Yorkshire	Samuel Davis	Ann Aaron	Selina Davis	Dublin, Ireland	surgeon dentist
2130	Davis	John J	1786	Middlesex, London			Sarah (?)	Hull, Yorkshire	medicine vendor
9583	Davis	Jonas	1833	Spitalfields, London	(?) Davis	Sarah (?)		Spitalfields, London	general dealer
19618	Davis	Joseph	1801	Aldgate, London			Julia (?)	Spitalfields, London	dealer in clothes
8477	Davis	Joseph	1807	Portsmouth, Hampshire	Moses Davis	Rosey Nathan	Emma (?)	Gosport, Hampshire	clothier
30152	Davis	Joseph	1812	Woolwich, London	Israel Davis	Rosetta Levy	(?)	Hendon, London	surgeon dentist
28804	Davis	Joseph	1815	Stratford, London	Mordecai		Esther (?)	Spitalfields, London	general dealer
18644	Davis	Joseph	1819	Middlesex, London	Mordecai Davis		Paulina Gonski	Northampton, Northamptonshire	hardwareman + dealer in china, glass, toys + fancy goods
7857	Davis	Joseph	1832	?, Poland	David Davis	Rosa Barnett	Jane Marks	Aldgate, London	
27822	Davis	Joseph	1835	St Giles, London	Isaac Davis	Sarah (?)		Spitalfields, London	general dealer
2041	Davis	Joseph	1837	Aldgate, London	David Davis	Jane Myers	Lizzie Cantor	Aldgate, London	clothier warehouseman
8481	Davis	Joseph	1845	Gosport, Hampshire	Joseph Davis	Emma (?)		Gosport, Hampshire	
11002	Davis	Joseph	1849	Spitalfields, London	Lewis Davis	Hannah (?)		Aldgate, London	scholar
27223	Davis	Joseph Israel	1805	Amsterdam, Holland	David Davis		(?)	Aldgate, London	general dealer

ID	surname	given names	born	birthplace	father	mother	spouse 1	1851 residence	1851 occupation
27819	Davis	Joshua	1832	St Giles, London	Isaac Davis	Sarah (?)		Spitalfields, London	general dealer
8244	Davis	Joshua	1845	Middlesex, London	David Barnett Davis	Elizabeth Cohen		Aldgate, London	
11001	Davis	Joshua	1847	Whitechapel, London	Lewis Davis	Hannah (?)		Aldgate, London	scholar
13323	Davis	Judah	1791	Aldgate, London	Isaac Lemplek		Leah de Isaac Mendoza	Spitalfields, London	clothes dealer
15472	Davis	Judah	1823	Spitalfields, London			Julia Jewell	Covent Garden, London	fruiterer
19852	Davis	Judah	1835	Spitalfields, London	Isaac Davis	Rosa Solomon		Spitalfields, London	butcher
26432	Davis	Judah	1841	?, London	(?)	Matilda Davis		Aldgate, London	
2673	Davis	Judah (John)	1839	Nottingham, Nottinghamshire	Joel Davis	Rosa Levy		Nottingham, Nottinghamshire	scholar
27181	Davis	Julia	1791	?, Poland	(?)		David Davis	Aldgate, London	
19617	Davis	Julia	1807	Whitechapel, London	(?)		Joseph Davis	Spitalfields, London	
27664	Davis	Julia	1815	Middlesex, London	Yoel Hart	Mary (?)	Moses Davis	Aldgate, London	
4414	Davis	Julia	1823	Glasgow, Scotland	(?) Myers	Rebecca (?)	Louis [James] Myers	Birmingham	
15473	Davis	Julia	1830	Strand, London	(?) Jewell		Judah Davis	Covent Garden, London	
31190	Davis	Julia	1830	Glasgow, Scotland	David Davis	Elizabeth (?)		Glasgow, Scotland	
3758	Davis	Julia	1834	Aldgate, London	Abraham Davis	Catharine (Kate) Harris		Spitalfields, London	
45	Davis	Julia	1835	Woolwich, London	Lewis Davis	Anne Jacobs	Henry Meyers	Plumstead, London	
986	Davis	Julia	1836	Exeter, Devon	Morris Davis	Elizabeth (?)		Exeter, Devon	scholar
29204	Davis	Julia	1849	Whitechapel, London	Henry Asher Davis	Isabella Hart		Whitechapel, London	
13219	Davis	Julia	1824	Spitalfields, London	Eli Hyams		Lewis Davis	Spitalfields, London	
27258	Davis	Julia (Judith)	1798	?, London	Hyam Myers		Moses Davis	Aldgate, London	
22437	Davis	Kate	1845	?	(?) Davis			Gravesend, Kent	boarding school pupil
27827	Davis	Kitty	1848	Whitechapel, London	Isaac Davis	Sarah (?)		Spitalfields, London	
19937	Davis	Lawrence	1821	Aldgate, London	David Davis	Elizabeth Lazarus		Whitechapel, London	merchant
18738	Davis	Lawrence	1833	Whitechapel, London	Angel Davis	Maria Davis		Whitechapel, London	
17460	Davis	Leah	1802	Surrey, London	(?)			Spitalfields, London	lemon stripper
6346	Davis	Leah	1846	Woolwich, London	David Davis	Charlotte Jacobs	Joseph Solomon	Kensington, London	scholar at home
19857	Davis	Leah	1850	Spitalfields, London	Isaac Davis	Rosa Solomon		Spitalfields, London	
3759	Davis	Lealia	1836	Aldgate, London	Abraham Davis	Catharine (Kate) Harris		Spitalfields, London	
12266	Davis	Leon	1832	City, London	Jacob Davis			Finsbury, London	furrier
15304	Davis	Lewis	1798	?, Poland [?, Prussia]				Shoreditch, London	cap maker
19	Davis	Lewis	1807	Woolwich, London	Israel Davis	Rosetta Levy	Anne Jacobs	Plumstead, London	auctioneer, builder + surveyor
13218	Davis	Lewis	1821	Spitalfields, London	Benjamin Davis		Julia Hyams	Spitalfields, London	clothes dealer
10999	Davis	Lewis	1824	Whitechapel, London	Joshua Davis		Hannah (?)	Aldgate, London	cigar maker
49	Davis	Lewis	1844	Woolwich, London	Lewis Davis	Anne Jacobs		Plumstead, London	scholar
24586	Davis	Lewis	1846	Lambeth, London	Isaac Davis	Mary Levy		Lambeth, London	
30156	Davis	Lionel Cartwright	1844	Piccadilly, London	Joseph Davis	Jeannette Mallan		Hendon, London	scholar at home
4413	Davis	Louis	1813	?, Poland [?, Prussia]			Julia Myers	Birmingham	pawnbroker
23472	Davis	Louis	1826	?, London	(?) Davis	Elizabeth (?)		Liverpool	tailor &c empl 4
23932	Davis	Louis	1834	Marylebone, London	David Davis	Louisa (?)		Marylebone, London	
23930	Davis	Louisa	1800	Spitalfields, London	(?)		David Davis	Marylebone, London	
26752	Davis	Louisa	1806	Aldgate, London	(?)		Isaac Davis	Aldgate, London	
11972	Davis	Louisa	1822	Whitechapel, London	Angel Davis	Maria Davis		Whitechapel, London	
23860	Davis	Louisa	1830	Piccadilly, London	David Davis	Hannah Cohen		Piccadilly, London	

ID	surname	given names	born	birthplace	father	mother	spouse 1	1851 residence	1851 occupation
15214	Davis	Louisa	1835	?, London	(?) Davis			Shoreditch, London	nurse maid
18433	Davis	Louise	1849	Glasgow, Scotland	David Davis	Elizabeth (?)	David Woolf	Glasgow, Scotland	scholar
6591	Davis	Lydia	1800	Aldgate, London	(?) Davis			Aldgate, London	
23426	Davis	Lydia	1824	?, London	(?) Davis			Aldgate, London	tailoress
11969	Davis	Maria	1793	Whitechapel, London	Joseph Davis		Angel Davis	Whitechapel, London	coal merchant
2173	Davis	Maria	1816	Walworth, London	Abraham Harris	Rose (Rosa) Jessel	Abram (Abraham) Davis	Oxford, Oxfordshire	
25555	Davis	Maria	1840	?, Scotland	John Isaac Davis	Selina Davis	Joseph S Levy	Dublin, Ireland	
29203	Davis	Maria	1848	Whitechapel, London	Henry Asher Davis	Isabella Hart		Whitechapel, London	
19625	Davis	Maria	1849	Spitalfields, London	Joseph Davis	Julia (?)		Spitalfields, London	
15513	Davis	Maria (Miriam)	1848	Covent Garden, London	Solomon Davis	Mary Franks	Abraham (George) Belasco	Covent Garden, London	
30158	Davis	Marian (Miriam)	1848	Marylebone, London	Joseph Davis	Jeannette Mallan		Hendon, London	
18204	Davis	Mark	1838	Middlesex, London				Mile End, London	scholar
15531	Davis	Mark	1845	?, London				Covent Garden, London	
28808	Davis	Mark	1849	Whitechapel, London	Joseph Davis	Esther (?)		Spitalfields, London	
11336	Davis	Mary	1761	Aldgate, London	(?)		Levy Davis	Aldgate, London	
24425	Davis	Mary	1792	Strand, London	(?)		Moss Davis	Strand, London	
25363	Davis	Mary	1794	Aldgate, London	Yehuda Leib Pyke		John (Jacob) Davis	Clerkenwell, London	
2160	Davis	Mary	1807	Stepney, London	Yehoshua Hessel Jacob		Coleman Davis	Southwark, London	dancing mistress
14550	Davis	Mary	1808	?Romsey, Hampshire [Rumsey]	(?)		Henry Davis	Walworth, London	
30704	Davis	Mary	1811	Aldgate, London	Isaac Franks		Solomon Davis	Covent Garden, London	
24581	Davis	Mary	1819	Elephant & Castle, London	Emanuel Levy		Isaac Davis	Lambeth, London	
10698	Davis	Mary	1832	Spitalfields, London	Elias Davis	Esther Harris	Judah Levy	Spitalfields, London	dealer
18479	Davis	Mary A (Miriam, Marian)	1839	St Giles, London	Abraham Davis	Rosetta (?)	Julius Jacobson	Bloomsbury, London	scholar
25256	Davis	Mary Ann	1841	Middlesex, London	Joseph Davis	Esther (?)	Henry Phillips	Holborn, London	attends school
26431	Davis	Matilda	1813	?, London	(?) Davis			Aldgate, London	
15522	Davis	Matilda	1839	?, London	Jacob David Davis	Dinah Alexander	Maurice Meyer	Aldgate, London	scholar
12262	Davis	Maurice Lionel	1824	City, London	Jacob Davis		Esther Lewis	Finsbury, London	surgeon dentist
12269	Davis	Michael	1779	?, Yorkshire				Finsbury, London	annuitant
31089	Davis	Michael	1785	?, London			Rebecca (?)	Northampton, Northamptonshire	clothes + glass dealer
19988	Davis	Michael	1826	Birmingham	David Davis	Feigele Katz	Sarah Adele Jacobs	Sunderland, Co Durham	
23931	Davis	Michael	1833	Marylebone, London	David Davis	Louisa (?)		Marylebone, London	
2681	Davis	Michael	1848	Nottingham, Nottinghamshire	Joel Davis	Rosa Levy	Hilda (?)	Nottingham, Nottinghamshire	
25556	Davis	Minna	1836	?Scotland	John Isaac Davis	Selina Davis	Julius Frankel	Dublin, Ireland	
30116	Davis	Minnie (Mary)	1850	Aldgate, London	Moses Davis	Julia Hart		Aldgate, London	
22020	Davis	Miranda	1849	Covent Garden, London	Myer Davis	Hannah Moses		Covent Garden, London	
27667	Davis	Miriam	1841	Middlesex, London	Moses Davis	Julia Hart		Aldgate, London	
5648	Davis	Miriam	1849	Liverpool	Saul Davis	Evelyn (Evelene) (?)	Henry B Hart	Liverpool	
4924	Davis	Montagu	1843	Liverpool	David Marcus Davis	Sarah (?)	Elizabeth (Lizzie) Samuel	Dublin, Ireland	
5650	Davis	Montague	1850	Liverpool	Saul Davis	Evelyn (Evelene) (?)	(Angelina?) (?)	Liverpool	
9119	Davis	Montague Alexander	1840	Strand, London	Alexander Davis	Anne (?)	Grace Parker	Strand, London	scholar at home

ID	surname	given names	born	birthplace	father	mother	spouse 1	1851 residence	1851 occupation
20097	Davis	Moris	1836	Whitechapel, London	Henry Davis	(?)		Mayfair, London	cigar maker
983	Davis	Morris	1793	?, London				Exeter, Devon	haberdasher + jeweller
24516	Davis	Morris	1820	?, Poland [?, Prussia]			Elizabeth (?)	Greenwich, London	tailor
25255	Davis	Morris	1830	Middlesex, London	Joseph Davis	Esther (?)		Holborn, London	cigar maker
9253	Davis	Morris	1846	Whitechapel, London	Solomon Davis	Hannah Hart	Minnie I Davis	Spitalfields, London	
9126	Davis	Morris	1850	Strand, London	Alexander Davis	Anne (?)		Strand, London	
27257	Davis	Moses	1803	?, London	Joseph Davis		Julia (Judith) Myers	Aldgate, London	clothes salesman
11756	Davis	Moses	1811	?, Russia				Shoreditch, London	hawker
27663	Davis	Moses	1815	Middlesex, London	David Davis	Elizabeth (?)	Julia Hart	Aldgate, London	draper &c
19938	Davis	Moses	1823	Aldgate, London	David Davis	Elizabeth Lazarus		Whitechapel, London	watch manufacturer
9582	Davis	Moses	1832	Spitalfields, London	(?) Davis	Sarah (?)		Spitalfields, London	general dealer
27823	Davis	Moses	1836	St Giles, London	Isaac Davis	Sarah (?)		Spitalfields, London	general dealer
2033	Davis	Moses	1838	Aldgate, London	David Davis	Jane Myers	Catherine Samuels	Aldgate, London	scholar
29205	Davis	Moses	1850	Whitechapel, London	Henry Asher Davis	Isabella Hart	Fanny Davis	Whitechapel, London	
6436	Davis	Moses (Moss)	1826	Shoreditch, London	Isaac Davis		Jane Davis	Shoreditch, London	general dealer
24424	Davis	Moss	1789	Strand, London			Mary (?)	Strand, London	wine merchant
17883	Davis	Moss	1811	Canterbury, Kent	David Davis		Sarah Jonas	Elephant & Castle, London	broker
26753	Davis	Moss	1831	Aldgate, London	Isaac Davis	Louisa (?)		Aldgate, London	oilman
23861	Davis	Moss	1834	Piccadilly, London	David Davis	Hannah Cohen	Ada Zox	Piccadilly, London	dealer in regimentals
30534	Davis	Moss (Morris)	1823	Clerkenwell, London	John (Jacob) Davis	Mary (?)	Eliza Lazarus	Soho, London	tailor's warehouseman
21299	Davis	Murray	1841	Strand, London				Edmonton, London	boarding school pupil
22018	Davis	Myer	1826	Middlesex, London			Hannah Moses	Covent Garden, London	tailor merchant empl 1
2034	Davis	Myer David	1830	Aldgate, London	David Davis	Jane Myers	Frances Wolfson	Aldgate, London	schoolmaster, JFS
30230	Davis	Myers	1838	Chodzież, Poland [Chodziessen, Prussia]	Alexander Davis	Polina (?)		Sunderland, Co Durham	
27666	Davis	Nancy	1838	Middlesex, London	Moses Davis	Julia (Judith) Myers		Aldgate, London	
30108	Davis	Nancy	1840	Middlesex, London	Moses Davis	Julia Hart	Samuel Solomon	Aldgate, London	scholar
24757	Davis	Nathan	1812	?, Poland [?, Prussia]			Catherine Brown	Waterloo, London	Minister, Church of Scotland
18416	Davis	Noah	1825	Middlesex, London			Henrietta (?)	Elephant & Castle, London	cigar manufacturer
18643	Davis	Paulina	1828	Poznan, Poland [Posen, Prussia]	(?) Gonski		Joseph Davis	Northampton, Northamptonshire	
28630	Davis	Pheeby	1845	Spitalfields, London	Isaac Davis	Harriet Henry		Spitalfields, London	scholar
17659	Davis	Philip	1825	?, London	Abraham Davis	Hannah (?)		Aldgate, London	bookbinder
9255	Davis	Philip	1848	Whitechapel, London	Solomon Davis	Hannah Hart		Spitalfields, London	
15407	Davis	Philip	1850	Waterloo, London	Daniel Davis	Frances (?)		Waterloo, London	
9581	Davis	Phillip	1831	Spitalfields, London	(?) Davis	Sarah (?)		Spitalfields, London	general dealer
14946	Davis	Phoebe	1836	Middlesex, London	(?) Davis			Bethnal Green, London	boarding school pupil
22439	Davis	Phoebe	1840	Whitechapel, London	Daniel Davis	Frances (?)	Henry L Miller	Waterloo, London	boarding school pupil
19856	Davis	Phoebe	1847	Spitalfields, London	Isaac Davis	Rosa Solomon		Spitalfields, London	scholar
9121	Davis	Phoebe Ann	1844	Strand, London	Alexander Davis	Anne (?)	Julius Frankenburg	Strand, London	scholar at home
30229	Davis	Polina	1818	Chodzież, Poland [Chodziessen, Prussia]	(?)		Alexander Davis	Sunderland, Co Durham	

ID	surname	given names	born	birthplace	father	mother	spouse 1	1851 residence	1851 occupation
984	Davis	Priscilla	1826	Exeter, Devon	Morris Davis	Elizabeth (?)	Benjamin Lazarus	Exeter, Devon	assistant to haberdasher + jeweller
2162	Davis	Priscilla	1836	Southwark, London	Coleman Davis	Mary Jacob	Jacob Frederick (Frederick Jacob) Turner	Southwark, London	
17591	Davis	Rachael	1791	Aldgate, London	(?)		Isaac Davis	Spitalfields, London	servant
20035	Davis	Rachael	1801	Aldgate, London	(?)		(?) Davis	Aldgate, London	monthly nurse
30149	Davis	Rachael	1832	Covent Garden, London	John Gabriel Davis	Catherine Simmons	James Michael Mallan	Victoria, London	
22164	Davis	Racheal	1839	Whitechapel, London	David Davis	Ann Crawcour		Whitechapel, London	
22662	Davis	Rachel	1813	Spitalfields, London	Zeev Aryeh Wolf Leib Moses		Elias Davis	Whitechapel, London	blouse maker
20098	Davis	Rachel	1837	Whitechapel, London	Henry Davis	(?)		Mayfair, London	
11971	Davis	Ralph	1821	Whitechapel, London	Angel Davis	Maria Davis		Whitechapel, London	cigar maker
31090	Davis	Rebecca	1787	Banbury, Oxfordshire	(?)		Michael Davis	Northampton, Northamptonshire	
21491	Davis	Rebecca	1799	?, Holland	(?)		Solomon Davis	Spitalfields, London	
10140	Davis	Rebecca	1804	Wapping, London	Asher Jacobs	Esther Israel	Coleman Davis	Spitalfields, London	umbrella maker
9172	Davis	Rebecca	1813	?, London	Abraham Davis	Sarah (?)	Joseph Lipschutz	Whitechapel, London	keeper of seminary
18468	Davis	Rebecca	1813	Wapping, London	Jacob Pesman	Esther Capua	Lewis Davis	Whitechapel, London	
979	Davis	Rebecca	1814	Exeter, Devon	Jacob Jacobs	Esther (?)	Hyman Davis	Exeter, Devon	
23857	Davis	Rebecca	1818	Piccadilly, London	David Davis	Hannah Cohen		Piccadilly, London	
23425	Davis	Rebecca	1822	?, London	(?) Davis			Aldgate, London	tailoress
29872	Davis	Rebecca	1822	Stratford, London	Mordecai Davis	Esther Bendahan		Wapping, London	dressmaker
10776	Davis	Rebecca	1824	Spitalfields, London	(?)		(?) Davis	Spitalfields, London	clothes dealer
3776	Davis	Rebecca	1829	Whitechapel, London	David Davis	Hannah (?)		Spitalfields, London	dressmaker
14533	Davis	Rebecca	1840	?Exeter, Devon	Morris Davis	Elizabeth (?)	Lyon (Louis) Benjamin	Exeter, Devon	
27825	Davis	Rebecca	1840	St Giles, London	Isaac Davis	Sarah (?)		Spitalfields, London	scholar
22442	Davis	Rebecca	1842	?	(?) Davis			Gravesend, Kent	boarding school pupil
24584	Davis	Rebecca	1842	Lambeth, London	Isaac Davis	Mary Levy	Reuben Hyams	Lambeth, London	
10702	Davis	Rebecca	1843	Spitalfields, London	Elias Davis	Esther Harris	Isaac Levy	Spitalfields, London	scholar
5043	Davis	Rosa	1771	Whitechapel, London	Joseph Nathan		Moses Davis	Portsmouth, Hampshire	
28290	Davis	Rosa	1800	?, Poland	(?)		Abraham Davis	Aldgate, London	cap maker
2670	Davis	Rosa	1807	Leszno, Poland [Lissa, Prussia], Poland [Lissa, Prussia]	Levy Levy (Yehuda Leib)	Fanny (Frumit) (?)	Joel Davis	Nottingham, Nottinghamshire	
22399	Davis	Rosa	1817	?, Poland [?, Prussia]	Levy Schwaba		Jacob Davis	Whitechapel, London	
19851	Davis	Rosa	1819	Aldgate, London	Moshe Isaac Solomon		Isaac Davis	Spitalfields, London	
30110	Davis	Rosa	1836	?, London	Moses Davis	Julia Hart		Hackney, London	annuitant
16970	Davis	Rose	1839	Middlesex, London	(?) Davis			Hammersmith, London	boarding school pupil
8483	Davis	Rose	1850	Gosport, Hampshire	Joseph Davis	Emma (?)		Gosport, Hampshire	
3203	Davis	Rose Elizabeth	1841	?London	Elias Davis	Elizabeth Moses	Julius Zossenheim	Bloomsbury, London	
19990	Davis	Rose Leah	1851	Dublin, Ireland	Michael Davis	Sarah Adele Jacobs	Ernest (Eleazer) Barnett	Sunderland, Co Durham	
8589	Davis	Roseline (Rosalia)	1842	Bloomsbury, London	James Phineas Davis	Eliza Davis		Notting Hill, London	scholar (at home)
18481	Davis	Rosetta	1815	City, London	(?)		Abraham Davis	Bloomsbury, London	glass dealer
27821	Davis	Rosetta	1834	St Giles, London	Isaac Davis	Sarah (?)		Spitalfields, London	general dealer
48	Davis	Rosetta	1843	Woolwich, London	Lewis Davis	Anne Jacobs	Benoit Levy	Plumstead, London	
109	Davis	Rosetta	1844	Woolwich, London	David Davis	Charlotte Davis	Maurice A De Groot	Woolwich, London	scholar

ID	surname	given names	born	birthplace	father	mother	spouse 1	1851 residence	1851 occupation
30157	Davis	Rosetta	1846	Piccadilly, London	Joseph Davis	Jeannette Mallan		Hendon, London	scholar at home
24587	Davis	Rosetta	1850	Lambeth, London	Isaac Davis	Mary Levy		Lambeth, London	
7861	Davis	Rosetta (Rosa)	1817	Aldgate, London	Isaac Costa	Sarah (?)	Solomon Davis	Aldgate, London	
24845	Davis	Samuel	1767	Hanover, Germany			Harriett (?)	Elephant & Castle, London	general dealer
26542	Davis	Samuel	1832	Leeds, Yorkshire				Birmingham	assistant woollen draper
31191	Davis	Samuel	1834	Glasgow, Scotland	David Davis	Elizabeth (?)		Glasgow, Scotland	scholar
19621	Davis	Samuel	1837	Whitechapel, London	Joseph Davis	Julia (?)		Spitalfields, London	baker's boy
20037	Davis	Samuel	1839	Spitalfields, London	(?) Davis	Rachael (?)		Aldgate, London	apprentice to cigar maker
3761	Davis	Samuel	1840	Aldgate, London	Abraham Davis	Catharine (Kate) Harris		Spitalfields, London	
22400	Davis	Samuel	1845	Whitechapel, London	Jacob Davis	Rosa Schwaba		Whitechapel, London	
15521	Davis	Samuel A	1837	?, London	Jacob David Davis	Dinah Alexander	Jennie (?)	Aldgate, London	scholar
30160	Davis	Samuel Edmund	1851	Hendon, London	Joseph Davis	Jeannette Mallan		Hendon, London	
9120	Davis	Samuel Solomon	1842	Strand, London	Alexander Davis	Anne (?)	Frances Samuel	Strand, London	scholar at home
9171	Davis	Sarah	1779	Aldgate, London	(?)		Abraham Davis	Whitechapel, London	none
22111	Davis	Sarah	1783	Hull, Yorkshire	(?)		(?) Davis	Whitechapel, London	
2409	Davis	Sarah	1792	Middlesex, London	(?)		John J Davis	Hull, Yorkshire	
26563	Davis	Sarah	1794	Middlesex, London	David de Joseph de Moses Nunes Martines	Sarah de Mordecai Vitta	Simon Davis	Whitechapel, London	
9580	Davis	Sarah	1796	Spitalfields, London	(?)		(?) Davis	Spitalfields, London	greengrocer
15278	Davis	Sarah	1796	Maldon, Essex	(?)		(?) Davis	Shoreditch, London	annuitant
27816	Davis	Sarah	1801	St Giles, London	(?)		Isaac Davis	Spitalfields, London	
18954	Davis	Sarah	1803	?, London				Whitechapel, London	
780	Davis	Sarah	1812	Middlesex, London	Benjamin Benjamin	Esther (?)	Charles Davis	Soho, London	assistant to warehouseman for antique goods
3941	Davis	Sarah	1815	Portsmouth, Hampshire	David Lazarus	Hannah Phillips	Lazarus Rapheles	Portsmouth, Hampshire	
17884	Davis	Sarah	1816	Middlesex, London	Solomon (Samuel, Pinchas Zelig) Jonas	Rosetta Joseph	Moss Davis	Elephant & Castle, London	
18735	Davis	Sarah	1821	Great Yarmouth, Norfolk	Isaac Mordecai	Ann Mayers	David Marcus Davis	Dublin, Ireland	
29873	Davis	Sarah	1822	Stratford, London	Mordecai Davis	Esther Bendahan		Wapping, London	tailoress
3755	Davis	Sarah	1825	Aldgate, London	Abraham Davis	Catharine (Kate) Harris		Spitalfields, London	
23859	Davis	Sarah	1829	Piccadilly, London	David Davis	Hannah Cohen		Piccadilly, London	
15402	Davis	Sarah	1834	Whitechapel, London	Daniel Davis	Frances (?)	Joseph Michael Isaacs	Waterloo, London	assistant in china, glass + earthenware dealer's business
23202	Davis	Sarah	1834	Whitechapel, London	(?) Davis			City, London	
15520	Davis	Sarah	1835	?, London	Jacob David Davis	Dinah Alexander		Aldgate, London	
18483	Davis	Sarah	1837	Bloomsbury, London	Abraham Davis	Rosetta (?)		Bloomsbury, London	glass dealer's assistant
10701	Davis	Sarah	1839	Spitalfields, London	Elias Davis	Esther Harris		Spitalfields, London	at home
24582	Davis	Sarah	1839	Lambeth, London	Isaac Davis	Mary Levy		Lambeth, London	
19623	Davis	Sarah	1841	Whitechapel, London	Joseph Davis	Julia (?)		Spitalfields, London	scholar
18432	Davis	Sarah	1842	Glasgow, Scotland	David Davis	Elizabeth (?)	Samuel Woolf	Glasgow, Scotland	scholar
5647	Davis	Sarah	1844	Liverpool	Saul Davis	Evelyn (Evelene) (?)		Liverpool	
7859	Davis	Sarah	1847	Aldgate, London	Saul (Solomon) Davis	Rosetta (Rosa) Costa	Jacob Rocen	Aldgate, London	

ID	surname	given names	born	birthplace	father	mother	spouse 1	1851 residence	1851 occupation
11091	Davis	Sarah	1850	Middlesex, London	Angel Davis	Catherine (?)		Aldgate, London	
18419	Davis	Sarah	1850	Middlesex, London	Noah Davis	Henrietta (?)		Elephant & Castle, London	
30635	Davis	Sarah	1851	Whitechapel, London	Solomon Davis	Hannah Benjamin		Whitechapel, London	
19989	Davis	Sarah Adele	1824	Middlesex, London	Samuel Jacobs	Rose Alexander	Michael Davis	Sunderland, Co Durham	
8480	Davis	Sarah J	1844	Gosport, Hampshire	Joseph Davis	Emma (?)		Gosport, Hampshire	
5644	Davis	Saul	1810	Middlesex, London			Evelyn (Evelene) (?)	Liverpool	dealer in medicine
7858	Davis	Saul (Solomon)	1826	?, Poland	David Davis	Rosa (Rosetta) Barnett	Rosetta (Rosa) Costa	Aldgate, London	shoemaker
25552	Davis	Selina	1810	?, London	Jacob Davis	(?Nancy Jonas)	John Isaac Davis	Dublin, Ireland	
25557	Davis	Selina	1843	Piccadilly, London	John Isaac Davis	Selina Davis		Dublin, Ireland	
17664	Davis	Selina	1844	?, London	Abraham Davis	Hannah (?)		Aldgate, London	scholar
2035	Davis	Sidney	1832	Aldgate, London	David Davis	Jane Myers	Sarah Mordecai	Aldgate, London	tailor
26562	Davis	Simon	1796	Whitechapel, London	Moshe Datshya		Sarah Nunes Martin (Martines)	Whitechapel, London	tailor, draper + confectioner
9758	Davis	Simon	1840	Middlesex, London				Kew, London	boarding school pupil
3206	Davis	Solomon	1798	Southwark, London	John Jacob Davis	Maria Joel	Elizabeth Cohen	Walworth, London	money lender
21490	Davis	Solomon	1798	?, Holland			Rebecca (?)	Spitalfields, London	general dealer
30703	Davis	Solomon	1809	Aldgate, London	Daniel Davis	(?Betsy Abrahams)	Mary Franks	Covent Garden, London	general dealer
23618	Davis	Solomon	1821	?, Poland				Liverpool	hardware traveller
9250	Davis	Solomon	1822	Shoreditch, London			Hannah Hart	Spitalfields, London	town traveller
28954	Davis	Solomon	1822	?, London	David HaLevi		Hannah Benjamin	Whitechapel, London	outfitter master
11086	Davis	Solomon	1834	Middlesex, London	Angel Davis	Catherine (?)		Aldgate, London	general dealer
22663	Davis	Solomon	1837	Spitalfields, London	Elias Davis	Rachel Moses		Whitechapel, London	cigar maker
8394	Davis	Sophia	1812	?, London	(?)		David Davis	Southampton, Hampshire	
9108	Davis	Sophia	1838	Strand, London	Alexander Davis	Anne (?)	Simeon John Simmons	Strand, London	
31193	Davis	Sophia	1838	Glasgow, Scotland	David Davis	Elizabeth (?)		Glasgow, Scotland	scholar
26565	Davis	Sophia	1839	Whitechapel, London	Simon Davis	Sarah Nunes Martin (Martines)		Whitechapel, London	scholar
5445	Davis	Sophia	1845	Exeter, Devon	Hyman Davis	Rebecca Jacobs	Solomon Lyon	Exeter, Devon	scholar
27262	Davis	Sophia	1845	?, London	Moses Davis	Julia (Judith) Myers		Aldgate, London	
15895	Davis	Sophie	1837	Middlesex, London	(?) Davis			Hackney, London	boarding school pupil
27261	Davis	Susan	1839	?, London	Moses Davis	Julia (Judith) Myers		Aldgate, London	
13324	Davis	Tilcy (Telsey, Telcey)	1823	Spitalfields, London	Judah Davis	Leah Mendoza	Philip Davis	Spitalfields, London	seamstress
22996	Davis	William	1826	?, Wales				Whitechapel, London	tailor
28292	Davis	Wolf	1837	?, Poland	Abraham Davis	Rosa (?)		Aldgate, London	cap maker
10834	Davis	Woolf (Benjamin)	1827	City, London	Joseph Davis		Elizabeth (Betsey) Emanuel	Spitalfields, London	general dealer
23427	Davis	Zippy	1827	?, London	(?) Davis			Aldgate, London	tailoress
9419	Davis (Davies)	Ann	1832	Aldgate, London	Isaac Davis (Davies)	Louisa (?)		Aldgate, London	oilman
9421	Davis (Davies)	David	1839	Aldgate, London	Isaac Davis (Davies)	Louisa (?)		Aldgate, London	
9422	Davis (Davies)	Edward	1842	Aldgate, London	Isaac Davis (Davies)	Louisa (?)		Aldgate, London	
9420	Davis (Davies)	Elizabeth	1838	Aldgate, London	Isaac Davis (Davies)	Louisa (?)		Aldgate, London	scholar
9423	Davis (Davies)	Fanny	1844	Aldgate, London	Isaac Davis (Davies)	Louisa (?)		Aldgate, London	
9424	Davis (Davies)	George	1849	Aldgate, London	Isaac Davis (Davies)	Louisa (?)	Abigail Pass	Aldgate, London	

ID	surname	given names	born	birthplace	father	mother	spouse 1	1851 residence	1851 occupation
9416	Davis (Davies)	Isaac	1803	Finsbury, London			Louisa (?)	Aldgate, London	oil + colourman + pickle merchant
9417	Davis (Davies)	Louisa	1806	Aldgate, London	(?)		Isaac Davis (Davies)	Aldgate, London	
9418	Davis (Davies)	Moss	1831	Aldgate, London	Isaac Davis (Davies)	Louisa (?)		Aldgate, London	oilman
21494	Davis [Solomons]	Solomon (Saul)	1830	?, Holland	Solomon Davis	Rebecca (?)	Kitty (Catherine) Phillips	Aldgate, London	oilman
21111	Davison	E---	1817	?, Poland				Spitalfields, London	shoe maker
2412	Davison	Susannah	1791	abroad				Aldgate, London	ornamental writer
2413	Dawes	Elizabeth	1832	Hamburg, Germany	(?) Dawes			Hull, Yorkshire	
14954	Dayalim	Fatye	1837	?, Poland [?, Prussia]	(?) Dayalim			Hull, Yorkshire	
23365	Dayan	Fortuna	1827	Strasbourg, France [Strasburgh, Germany]	(?) Dayan			Bethnal Green, London	boarding school pupil
23363	Dayan	Prosper	1835	?, Holland				Strand, London	fancy goods stall keeper (arcade)
23364	Dayan	Rosine	1825	?, Italy	(?) Dayan			Strand, London	fancy goods stall keeper (arcade)
19745	De Azavedo	Aaron Cohen	1775	Middlesex, London	Moses Cohen De Azavedo	Sarah (?)	Judith (?)	City, London	ostrich feather manufacturer
10625	De Azevedo	Daniel Cohen	1839	Whitechapel, London	Joseph Cohen De Azevedo	Hannah Henriques		Spitalfields, London	cabinet maker
10623	De Azevedo	Hannah Cohen	1807	Whitechapel, London	Jacob Henriques	Constance Henriques Se Souza	Joseph de Aron Cohen De Azevedo	Spitalfields, London	cabinet maker's wife
10626	De Azevedo	Henry (Aaron) Cohen	1836	Whitechapel, London	Joseph Cohen De Azevedo	Hannah Henriques		Spitalfields, London	cabinet maker
17940	De Azevedo	Isaac Cohen	1820	Middlesex, London	Aaron Cohen De Azevedo	Judith (?)		City, London	foreman at cigar manufactory
10624	De Azevedo	Joseph Cohen	1813	?, London	Aaron Cohen De Azevedo	Judith (?)	Hannah de Jacob Henriques	Spitalfields, London	cabinet maker
10627	De Azevedo	Julia (Judith) Cohen	1837	Mile End, London	Joseph Cohen De Azevedo	Hannah Henriques		Spitalfields, London	domestic assistant
10628	De Azevedo	Louisa Cohen	1844	Spitalfields, London	Joseph Cohen De Azevedo	Hannah Henriques	Abraham Isaacs	Spitalfields, London	scholar
7330	De Azevedo	Miriam	1804	Bethnal Green, London	Aaron Cohen De Azevedo	Judith (?)		City, London	ostrich feather manufacturer
10629	De Azevedo	Moses	1847	Spitalfields, London	Joseph Cohen De Azevedo	Hannah Henriques		Spitalfields, London	scholar
16216	De Castro	Deborah	1790	Aldgate, London	Jacob de Hananel Mendes Da Costa	Sarah de Jacob Machoro	Hananel de Moses De Castro	Shoreditch, London	lady
7046	De Castro	Ellen	1832	Aldgate, London	Hananel de Moses De Castro	Deborah de Jacob Mendes Da Costa	Henry Louis Cohen	Shoreditch, London	
25167	De Castro	Esther	1786	Aldgate, London	Moses de David De Castro	Judith de Hananel Mendes Da Costa		Finsbury, London	independent
7462	De Castro	Joseph	1834	Aldgate, London	Hananel de Moses De Castro	Deborah de Jacob Mendes Da Costa	Sarah Oppenheim	Shoreditch, London	apprentice
25168	De Castro	Maria (Miriam)	1786	Aldgate, London	Moses de David De Castro	Judith de Hananel Mendes Da Costa		Finsbury, London	independent
21559	De Frece	Abraham	1802	?, Holland	Baruch Bendit		Mary Isaacs	Aldgate, London	print seller + stationer
21561	De Frece	Blumah	1825	Spitalfields, London	Abraham De Frece	Mary Isaacs	Louis De Jongh	Aldgate, London	
3415	De Frece	Elizabeth	1828	Spitalfields, London	Abraham De Frece	Mary (?)	Jacob (Jack) Lazarus	Aldgate, London	
21563	De Frece	Esther	1835	Aldgate, London	Abraham De Frece	Mary Isaacs		Aldgate, London	cap maker

ID	surname	given names	born	birthplace	father	mother	spouse 1	1851 residence	1851 occupation
21562	De Frece	Eva	1833	Spitalfields, London	Abraham De Frece	Mary Isaacs		Aldgate, London	cap maker
6019	De Frece	Henry	1837	Spitalfields, London	Abraham De Frece	Mary Isaacs		Aldgate, London	fancy stationer
21560	De Frece	Mary	1806	Whitechapel, London	Abraham Isaacs		Abraham De Frece	Aldgate, London	
21564	De Frece	Moss	1842	Spitalfields, London	Abraham De Frece	Mary Isaacs		Aldgate, London	scholar
21565	De Frece	Sarah	1844	Spitalfields, London	Abraham De Frece	Mary Isaacs		Aldgate, London	scholar
14445	De Freece	John	1830	Middlesex, London				Salford, Lancashire	merchant
27783	De Groot	Abraham	1825	Amsterdam, Holland				Spitalfields, London	cigar maker
29967	De Groot	Elizabeth	1821	Middlesex, London	Marks Davis	Clara Zadok	Louis De Groot	Whitechapel, London	
29968	De Groot	Jacob	1845	?, Holland	Louis De Groot	(?)		Whitechapel, London	
29966	De Groot	Louis	1815	?, Holland	Samuel De Groot		(?)	Whitechapel, London	traveller
28951	De Groot	Marcus	1829	?, Holland	Moses De Groot		Mietje (Marianne) Bosman	Whitechapel, London	master bootmaker
28952	De Groot	Mietje (Marianne)	1827	?, Holland	Moses Bosman		Marcus De Groot	Whitechapel, London	
29264	De Groot	Solomon	1823	Rotterdam, Holland				Whitechapel, London	commercial traveller
25477	De Jongh	Abraham Louis	1796	?, Holland			Sarah Leo	Tower Hill, London	dealer in precious stones
25479	De Jongh	Adelaide L	1843	?, London	Abraham Louis De Jongh	Sarah Leo	Solomon Jewell	Tower Hill, London	scholar
25480	De Jongh	Fanny L	1838	?, London	Abraham Louis De Jongh	Sarah Leo	Ignitz Levy	Tower Hill, London	scholar
25481	De Jongh	Moss L	1841	?, London	Abraham Louis De Jongh	Sarah Leo		Tower Hill, London	scholar
25478	De Jongh	Sarah	1799	?, London	Leisman Leo	Elizabeth (?)	Abraham Louis de Jongh	Tower Hill, London	
13085	De Joudea	A---	1830	?, France				Southwark, London	prisoner + gentleman
30493	De Lara (De Lara Cohen)	Alfred (Isaac)	1833	Middlesex, London	David Laurent de David De Lara	Sarah Abigail Cracour	?	Bloomsbury, London	
30495	De Lara (De Lara Cohen)	Anne	1839	Middlesex, London	David Laurent de David De Lara	Sarah Abigail Cracour	Joseph Laurence	Bloomsbury, London	--- + singeer
23070	De Lara (De Lara Cohen)	David Emanuel	1800	?	Isaac De Lara Cohen		Sarah de David de Jehiel	Aldgate, London	
30496	De Lara (De Lara Cohen)	David Laurent	1810	Middlesex, London	David Laurant De Lara		Sarah Abigail Cracour	Bloomsbury, London	illuminating artist + lithographic printer
23072	De Lara (De Lara Cohen)	Emma	1827	Middlesex, London	David Emanuel de Isaac De Lara Cohen	Sarah de David de Jehiel		Aldgate, London	dressmaker
23073	De Lara (De Lara Cohen)	Flora	1835	Liverpool	David Emanuel de Isaac De Lara Cohen	Sarah de David de Jehiel		Aldgate, London	dressmaker
7348	De Lara (De Lara Cohen)	Hannah (Emma)	1844	Stepney, London	David Laurent de David De Lara	Sarah Abigail Cracour	Henry Russell	Bloomsbury, London	
30494	De Lara (De Lara Cohen)	Rachel	1836	Middlesex, London	David Laurent de David De Lara	Sarah Abigail Cracour		Bloomsbury, London	
23071	De Lara (De Lara Cohen)	Sarah	1802	Middlesex, London	David de Jehiel		David Emanuel de Isaac De Lara Cohen	Aldgate, London	
30497	De Lara (De Lara Cohen)	Sarah	1806	Amsterdam, Holland	Isaac Cracour	Simha Cohen De Lara	David Laurent de David De Lara	Bloomsbury, London	
30492	De Lara (De Lara Cohen)	Semira (Zemira)	1830	Middlesex, London	David Laurent de David De Lara	Sarah Abigail Cracour	?	Bloomsbury, London	
23074	De Lara (De Lara Cohen)	Victoria	1837	Liverpool	David Emanuel de Isaac De Lara Cohen	Sarah de David de Jehiel		Aldgate, London	dressmaker
13420	De Leon	Cornelia	1827	Kingston, Jamaica, West Indies	Hananel de Solomon De Leon	Maria (?)		Bloomsbury, London	

ID	surname	given names	born	birthplace	father	mother	spouse 1	1851 residence	1851 occupation
13423	De Leon	Eustace	1832	Kingston, Jamaica, West Indies	Hananel de Solomon De Leon	Maria (?)		Bloomsbury, London	student, University College
13422	De Leon	Felicia	1831	Kingston, Jamaica, West Indies	Hananel de Solomon De Leon	Maria (?)		Bloomsbury, London	
13418	De Leon	Hananel	1797	Middlesex, London	Solomon De Leon	Rachel de Hananel Mendes Da Costa	Maria (?)	Bloomsbury, London	physician LCP
13419	De Leon	Maria	1808	Kingston, Jamaica, West Indies	(?)		Hananel de Solomon De Leon	Bloomsbury, London	
13421	De Leon	Miranda	1828	Kingston, Jamaica, West Indies	Hananel de Solomon De Leon	Maria (?)		Bloomsbury, London	
19720	De Maza	Sarah	1813	?, Holland	(?)		(?) De Maza	Whitechapel, London	nurse
22055	De Meza	Adelade	1824	?, Holland	(?) De Meza	Sarah (?)		Spitalfields, London	
20804	De Meza	Adelaide (Alida)	1827	Amsterdam, Holland	(?)		Jacob De Meza	Spitalfields, London	
22056	De Meza	David	1827	?, Holland	(?) De Meza	Sarah (?)		Spitalfields, London	cigar maker
20805	De Meza	David	1845	Amsterdam, Holland	Jacob De Meza	Adelaide (Alida) (?)		Spitalfields, London	
20803	De Meza	Jacob	1821	Amsterdam, Holland			Adelaide (Alida) (?)	Spitalfields, London	cigar maker
22057	De Meza	Moses	1830	?, Holland	(?) De Meza	Sarah (?)		Spitalfields, London	cigar maker
20808	De Meza	Rebecca	1851	Spitalfields, London	Jacob De Meza	Adelaide (Alida) (?)	Emanuel Baruch	Spitalfields, London	
22054	De Meza	Sarah	1792	?, Holland			(?) De Meza	Spitalfields, London	nurse
20807	De Meza	Sarah	1849	Aldgate, London	Jacob De Meza	Adelaide (Alida) (?)		Spitalfields, London	
20806	De Meza	Simeon	1847	Amsterdam, Holland	Jacob De Meza	Adelaide (Alida) (?)	Rachel Live Isaacson	Spitalfields, London	
9046	De Pass	Aaron	1814	?, London	Daniel de Aaron De Pass	Rachel de Meir Davis	Esther de Benjamin Gomes Da Costa	City, London	merchant
9338	De Pass	Abraham Daniel	1824	King's Lynn, Norfolk	Daniel de Aaron De Pass	Rachel de Meir Davis	Judith Lazarus	Holloway, London	merchant
24271	De Pass	Alfred Hyam	1850	Middlesex, London	David De Pass	Alice (Esther) Hyam	Florence Levy	Bloomsbury, London	
24269	De Pass	Alice (Esther)	1825	Colchester, Essex	Hyam Hyam	Hannah Lazarus	David de Pass	Bloomsbury, London	
9045	De Pass	Daniel	1839	?	Aaron de Pass	Esther Gomes da Costa	Emily (Luna) Abecasis	City, London	
9340	De Pass	Daniel	1847	Kingston, Jamaica, West Indies	Abraham Daniel de Pass	Judith Lazarus		Holloway, London	
24270	De Pass	Daniel	1849	Middlesex, London	David De Pass	Alice (Esther) Hyam		Bloomsbury, London	
24268	De Pass	David	1818	King's Lynn, Norfolk	Daniel de Aaron De Pass	Rachel de Meir Davis	Alice (Esther) Hyam	Bloomsbury, London	merchant
3638	De Pass	Elias	1830	King's Lynn, Norfolk	Daniel de Aaron De Pass	Rachel de Meir Davis	Floretta Moses	Finsbury, London	merchant
9342	De Pass	Elias Abram	1851	?Holloway, London	Abraham Daniel de Pass	Judith Lazarus		Holloway, London	
9047	De Pass	Esther	1819	Middlesex, London	Benjamin Gomes Da Costa		Aaron de Daniel De Pass	City, London	
9339	De Pass	Judith	1822	Kingston, Jamaica, West Indies	(?Eleazer) Lazarus		Abraham Daniel De Pass	Holloway, London	merchant's wife
21725	De Pass	Michael	1821	King's Lynn, Norfolk	Daniel de Aaron De Pass	Rachel de Meir Davis	Simmy (Simcha) Levi Bensusan	Highbury, London	general merchant
9341	De Pass	Rachel	1849	Kingston, Jamaica, West Indies	Abraham Daniel de Pass	Judith Lazarus		Holloway, London	
21726	De Pass	Simmy (Simcha)	1823	Middlesex, London	Jacob de Menahem Levi Bensusan	Sarah (?)	Michael de Daniel De Pass	Highbury, London	
22050	De Saxe	Abigail	1826	Aldgate, London	Asher Isaacs	Judith Cohen	Morris De Saxe	Spitalfields, London	
15614	De Saxe	Ann	1826	Gibraltar	John Isaac De Saxe	Fanny Lyons		Spitalfields, London	assistant to fancy whalebone manufacturer
15619	De Saxe	Ann	1843	?, London	Charles De Saxe	Isabella (?)	Samuel Simmons	Soho, London	scholar
22051	De Saxe	Anne	1847	Spitalfields, London	Morris De Saxe	Abigail Isaacs		Spitalfields, London	

ID	surname	given names	born	birthplace	father	mother	spouse 1	1851 residence	1851 occupation
15617	De Saxe	Charles	1817	Gibraltar	John Isaac De Saxe	Fanny Lyons	Isabella (?)	Soho, London	umbrella manufacturer
5730	De Saxe	Fanny	1801	Edinburgh, Scotland	Herman Lyons		John Isaac De Saxe	Spitalfields, London	
15620	De Saxe	Henry	1845	Sheffield, Yorkshire	Charles De Saxe	Isabella (?)		Soho, London	scholar
15618	De Saxe	Isabella	1815	Liverpool	(?)		Charles De Saxe	Soho, London	
15616	De Saxe	Isabella	1837	Whitechapel, London	John Isaac De Saxe	Fanny Lyons	Alfred Davis	Spitalfields, London	
5728	De Saxe	John Isaac	1792	Bath			Fanny Lyons	Spitalfields, London	fancy whalebone manufacturer
22052	De Saxe	Joseph Alexander	1850	Spitalfields, London	Morris De Saxe	Abigail Isaacs		Spitalfields, London	
5731	De Saxe	Louis (Lewis)	1833	Gibraltar	John Isaac De Saxe	Fanny Lyons		Spitalfields, London	
15615	De Saxe	Maria	1831	Liverpool	John Isaac De Saxe	Fanny Lyons		Spitalfields, London	assistant to fancy whalebone manufacturer
22049	De Saxe	Morris	1820	Edinburgh, Scotland	John Isaac de Saxe	Fanny Lyons	Abigail Isaacs	Spitalfields, London	umbrella + parasol maker
22053	De Saxe	Selian	1832	Edinburgh, Scotland	Solomon Isaacs			Spitalfields, London	
15700	De Sola	Aaron	1826	City, London	David Aaron De Sola	Rebecca (Rica) Meldola		Aldgate, London	goldsmith
5382	De Sola	Annette	1839	Middlesex, London	David Aaron De Sola	Rebecca (Rica) Meldola	Maurice (Moses) Cohen Rogers	Whitechapel, London	scholar
15698	De Sola	David Aaron	1796	Amsterdam, Holland	Isaac De Sola		Rebecca (Rica) de Raphael Meldola	Aldgate, London	Minister to Synagogue
5383	De Sola	Esther	1835	City, London	David Aaron De Sola	Rebecca (Rica) Meldola	Simeon Langner	Aldgate, London	
5388	De Sola	Isaac	1827	City, London	David Aaron De Sola	Rebecca (Rica) Meldola		Aldgate, London	tobacco manufacturer
15702	De Sola	Julia	1843	?, London	David Aaron De Sola	Rebecca (Rica) Meldola		Aldgate, London	
15701	De Sola	Margo	1834	City, London	David Aaron De Sola	Rebecca (Rica) Meldola		Aldgate, London	
5381	De Sola	Rebecca (Rica)	1799	Livorno, Italy [Leghorn, Italy]	Raphael Meldola		David Aaron De Sola	Aldgate, London	
5380	De Sola	Samuel	1839	City, London	David Aaron de Sola	Rebecca (Rica) Meldola	Jemima Lindo Henry	Aldgate, London	scholar
15699	De Sola	Stella	1823	City, London	David Aaron De Sola	Rebecca (Rica) Meldola	Julius David Langner	Aldgate, London	
15229	De Souza	Daniel Henriques	1781	City, London	Jacob Henriques De Souza	Hannah (?)	Sarah de Eliau Henriques	Shoreditch, London	retired army agent
15230	De Souza	Hannah Henriques	1807	Aldgate, London	Daniel Henriques De Souza	Sarah de Eliau Henriques		Shoreditch, London	
7336	De Souza	Leah	1826	?	Gabriel De Souza		Israel de Israel Ottolengui	Spitalfields, London	
18722	De Souza	Louisa	1811	Portsmouth, Hampshire	Daniel Henriques De Souza	Sarah de Eliau Henriques	Lewis Chapman	Finsbury, London	
14009	De Symons	Aaron	1794	Whitechapel, London	Lyon De Symons	Polly (Michla) bat Aaron	Matilda Israel	Kensington, London	merchant in British + foreign funds + securities
14011	De Symons	Emily Eliza	1829	Brighton, Sussex	Aaron De Symons	Matilda Israel		Kensington, London	
14010	De Symons	Matilda	1799	Holborn, London	Azreal Israel		Aaron De Symons	Kensington, London	
3643	De Symons	Matilda Maria	1826	Walthamstow, London	Aaron De Symons	Matilda Israel	Eliezer Moses [Merton]	Kensington, London	
7556	De Symons	Samuel Lyon	1824	Wanstead, London	Aaron De Symons	Matilda Israel		Kensington, London	
6837	De Wilde (Gervilder)	Abraham	1851	Spitalfields, London	Nathan De Wilde (Gevilder)	Esther (?)	Rebecca Harris	Spitalfields, London	
6836	De Wilde (Gervilder)	Esther	1827	Amsterdam, Holland	(?)		Nathan de Wilde (Gervilder)	Spitalfields, London	
6835	De Wilde (Gervilder)	Nathan	1821	Amsterdam, Holland			Esther (?)	Spitalfields, London	cigar maker
10267	De Young (Deyong)	Elizabeth	1851	Spitalfields, London	Simon de Young	Priscilla (Paissy) Moss	Leon Michaels	Spitalfields, London	
10266	De Young (Deyong)	Priscilla (Paissy)	1825	Spitalfields, London	(?) Moss		Simon De Young (Deyong)	Spitalfields, London	

ID	surname	given names	born	birthplace	father	mother	spouse 1	1851 residence	1851 occupation
10265	De Young (Deyong)	Simon	1821	?Holland			Priscilla (Paissy) Moss	Spitalfields, London	tailor
25486	Defreiza	Cynthia	1778	Aldgate, London	(?) Defreiza			Tower Hill, London	bead stringer
28886	Defries	Catherine	1791	Amsterdam, Holland	(?)		(?) Defries	Spitalfields, London	
6333	Defries	Charlotte	1766	Middlesex, London	Leib Makach Nathan		Daniel (Gedalia) Defries	Aldgate, London	supported by family
5861	Defries	Coleman	1828	Aldgate, London	Jonas Defries	Esther Coleman	Cordelia Magnus	Aldgate, London	commercial traveller
21295	Defries	Daniel	1839	King's Lynn, Norfolk				Edmonton, London	boarding school pupil
21006	Defries	Daniel	1845	Shoreditch, London	Henry Defries	Maria (Miriam) Davis		Finsbury, London	scholar
16166	Defries	Daniel N	1845	St Pancras, London	Nathan Defries	Isabella Lazarus		Fitzrovia, London	
8233	Defries	Dinah	1817	Hull, Yorkshire	Lyon Samson	Sarah (?)	Henry Hyman Defries	Whitechapel, London	
16163	Defries	Eleazor	1838	Marylebone, London	Nathan Defries	Isabella Lazarus	Julia La Mert	Fitzrovia, London	
21005	Defries	Ester	1843	Aldgate, London	Henry Defries	Maria (Miriam) Davis		Finsbury, London	scholar
6327	Defries	Esther	1807	Aldgate, London	(?) Coleman	Sarah (?)	Jonas Defries	Aldgate, London	
18742	Defries	Ethel	1839	St Pancras, London	Nathan Defries	Isabella Lazarus		Fitzrovia, London	
6304	Defries	Hannah	1829	Middlesex, London	Jacob (John) Harris		Henry Defries	Aldgate, London	
6623	Defries	Henry	1798	Aldgate, London	Daniel (Gedalia) Defries	Charlotte Nathan	Elizabeth Barnett	Finsbury, London	gas fitter
6303	Defries	Henry	1826	Middlesex, London	Henry Defries	Elizabeth Barnett	Hannah Harris	Aldgate, London	brass founder
13436	Defries	Henry	1830	Aldgate, London	Jonas Defries	Esther Coleman	Susan Myers	Aldgate, London	
30419	Defries	Henry	1851	Aldgate, London	Henry Defries	Hannah (?)		Aldgate, London	
8232	Defries	Henry Hyam (Hyman)	1818	Middlesex, London			Dinah Samson	Whitechapel, London	warehouseman
6331	Defries	Isaac	1838	Shoreditch, London	Henry Defries	Maria (Miriam) Davis	Amelia Moses	Finsbury, London	scholar
16159	Defries	Isabella	1809	Finsbury, London	Eliezer Lezer	(?Eliza Aaron)	Nathan Defries	Fitzrovia, London	
28887	Defries	Jacob	1831	Amsterdam, Holland	(?) Defries	Catherine (?)		Spitalfields, London	cigar maker
21003	Defries	John	1841	Shoreditch, London	Henry Defries	Maria (Miriam) Davis		Finsbury, London	scholar
6305	Defries	John	1849	?Aldgate, London	Henry Defries	Hannah (?)		Aldgate, London	
6326	Defries	Jonas	1805	Aldgate, London	Daniel (Gedalia) Defries	Charlotte Nathan	Esther Coleman	Aldgate, London	gas glass + lamp glass warehouseman
16160	Defries	Julia	1833	Middlesex, London	Nathan Defries	Isabella Lazarus		Fitzrovia, London	
8231	Defries	Julia	1849	Mile End, London	Henry Hyam (Hyman) Defries	Dinah Samson	Moses Hyman Phillips	Whitechapel, London	
16165	Defries	Leonora	1842	St Pancras, London	Nathan Defries	Isabella Lazarus	Simeon Klean	Fitzrovia, London	
9960	Defries	Louis (Lewis) H	1826	Whitechapel, London	(?) Defries	Rosetta (?)	Kate Barnard	Brighton, Sussex	tailor's assistant
6622	Defries	Maria	1839	Shoreditch, London	Henry Defries	Maria (Miriam) Davis	Abraham Mendoza	Finsbury, London	scholar
6624	Defries	Maria (Miriam)	1809	Bethnal Green, London	Isaac Davis		Henry Defries	Finsbury, London	
6329	Defries	Morris	1830	Shoreditch, London	Henry Defries	Elizabeth Barnett	Esther Saunders	Finsbury, London	
6325	Defries	Moss	1832	Aldgate, London	Jonas Defries	Esther Coleman	Flora Lyons	Aldgate, London	
16158	Defries	Nathan	1803	Aldgate, London	Daniel (Gedalia) Defries	Charlotte Nathan	Isabella Lazarus	Fitzrovia, London	gas engineer/gas meter maker empl 50
21289	Defries	Nathan	1833	Birmingham				Edmonton, London	boarding school pupil
18434	Defries	Nathan	1839	Aldgate, London	Jonas Defries	Esther Coleman	Sara Lazarus	Aldgate, London	
16161	Defries	Rachael	1834	Marylebone, London	Nathan Defries	Isabella Lazarus	Alfred Colman Cohen	Fitzrovia, London	
21000	Defries	Rachel	1827	Shoreditch, London	Henry Defries	Elizabeth Barnett		Finsbury, London	
16162	Defries	Rebecca	1836	Marylebone, London	Nathan Defries	Isabella Lazarus		Fitzrovia, London	
16164	Defries	Rosetta	1840	St Pancras, London	Nathan Defries	Isabella Lazarus	Edward Jessel	Fitzrovia, London	
13437	Defries	Samuel	1837	Aldgate, London	Jonas Defries	Esther Coleman		Aldgate, London	

ID	surname	given names	born	birthplace	father	mother	spouse 1	1851 residence	1851 occupation
21004	Defries	Sarah	1842	Southwark, London	Henry Defries	Maria (Miriam) Davis		Finsbury, London	scholar
16167	Defries	Sarah	1847	St Pancras, London	Nathan Defries	Isabella Lazarus	John Marcus	Fitzrovia, London	
13424	Defriez	David	1823	Whitechapel, London			Esther Moses	Spitalfields, London	clothes dealer
16481	Delare	Rachel	1775	?, London	(?) Delare			Mile End, London	
16482	Delare	Sarah	1777	?, London	(?) Delare			Mile End, London	
19739	Delevante	Abraham	1841	Essaouira, Morocco [Mogadore, Africa]	Moses de David Delevante	Esther de Jacob Nunes Martinez		Spitalfields, London	scholar
14890	Delevante	Absalom	1796	?Algiers, Algeria			Ellen Wyer	Lambeth, London	interpreter of Arabic languages
14945	Delevante	Dinah	1836	Middlesex, London	(?) Delevante			Bethnal Green, London	boarding school pupil
14861	Delevante	Edward Riches	1828	Middlesex, London	Prospero Delevante	Sarah Riches	Elizabeth Whittle	Bethnal Green, London	teacher of Latin, Greek &c
19736	Delevante	Esther	1818	Spitalfields, London	Jacob Nunes Martinez		Moses de David Delevante	Spitalfields, London	nurse
14862	Delevante	Frederick David	1834	Middlesex, London	Prospero Delevante	Sarah Riches	Sophia L (?)	Bethnal Green, London	teacher of organ + pianoforte
19735	Delevante	George Riches	1822	Norwich, Norfolk	Prospero Delevante	Sarah Riches	Rachel Becket	Plaistow, London	clerk to feather merchant
19737	Delevante	Julia (Simha)	1832	Spitalfields, London	Moses de David Delevante	Esther de Jacob Nunes Martinez	Joseph Hains	Spitalfields, London	tailoress
14858	Delevante	Prospero	1787	Algiers, Algeria			Sarah Riches	Bethnal Green, London	interpreter of Arabic, Spanish &c
24146	Delevante	Prospero	1821	Norwich, Norfolk	Prospero Delevante	Sarah Riches	Mary Hutchings	Euston, London	professor of music
14860	Delevante	Rachael	1825	Norwich, Norfolk	Prospero Delevante	Sarah Riches		Bethnal Green, London	
19738	Delevante	Rebecca	1835	Spitalfields, London	Moses de David Delevante	Esther de Jacob Nunes Martinez	Samuel Jacobs	Spitalfields, London	tailoress
14859	Delevante	Sarah	1791	?, Norfolk	(?) Riches		Prospero Delevante	Bethnal Green, London	
21752	Delevante (Dalevant)	Charlotte	1827	Chelsea, London	Joseph de Masahod Delevante	Judith (Julia) de Abraham Abendelack	William Mann Crosland	Chelsea, London	
21753	Delevante (Dalevant)	Emma Matilda	1833	Chelsea, London	Joseph de Masahod Delevante	Judith (Julia) de Abraham Abendelack	Edward Montague Burrell	Chelsea, London	
19733	Delevante (Dalevant)	Joseph	1784	Mile End, London	Masahod Sarique Delevante	Miryam de Joseph Bendelak	Judith (Julia) de Abraham Abendelack	Chelsea, London	West India merchant
19734	Delevante (Dalevant)	Judith (Julia)	1802	Finsbury, London	Abraham Abendelack	Rachel de Mordecai Cohen del Medico	Joseph de Masahod Delevante (Dalevant)	Chelsea, London	
7276	Delgado	George (Gershon)	1801	Port Royal, Jamaica, West Indies	Menasse Delgado	Rachel De Moses Cohen D'Azevedo	Louisa (?)	Highbury, London	merchant
21721	Delgado	Manasseh	1831	?, Jamaica, West Indies	George Delgado	Louisa (?)		Highbury, London	scholar
24190	Delvalle	Isaac	1804	Islington, London			Sarah (?)	Stoke Newington, London	fire insurance clerk
14339	Dessau	Adolph	1846	?, Germany	Philip Dessau	Minna (?)		Manchester	
14337	Dessau	Caroline	1842	?, Germany	Philip Dessau	Minna (?)		Manchester	
20901	Dessau	David	1836	Hamburg, Germany				Liverpool	servant
14338	Dessau	Isaac	1844	?, Germany	Philip Dessau	Minna (?)		Manchester	
14340	Dessau	Lipman	1848	?, Germany	Philip Dessau	Minna (?)		Manchester	
14336	Dessau	Minna	1819	?, Germany	(?)		Philip Dessau	Manchester	
14341	Dessau	Morris	1850	Manchester	Philip Dessau	Minna (?)		Manchester	
14335	Dessau	Philip	1820	?, Germany			Minna (?)	Manchester	reader at Synagogue
4417	Devley	Isaac	1820	?, Holland				Birmingham	cigar mfr

175

ID	surname	given names	born	birthplace	father	mother	spouse 1	1851 residence	1851 occupation
13513	Devonsky	David	1830	?, Scotland	Lewis Devonsky	(?)		Manchester	traveller in stationery
13517	Devonsky	Leah	1844	?, Scotland	Lewis Devonsky	(?)		Manchester	scholar
13512	Devonsky	Lewis	1795	?, Poland [?, Prussia Poland]			(?)	Manchester	traveller in stationery
13514	Devonsky	Paulina	1832	Liverpool	Lewis Devonsky	(?)		Manchester	
13515	Devonsky	Rebecca	1838	?, Scotland	Lewis Devonsky	(?)		Manchester	scholar
13516	Devonsky	Sarah	1841	?, Scotland	Lewis Devonsky	(?)		Manchester	scholar
16137	Devries	Fanny	1843	Amsterdam, Holland	Meyer Benedictus Devries	Hannah (?)		Whitechapel, London	scholar
16136	Devries	Hannah	1802	Amsterdam, Holland	(?)		Meyer Benedictus Devries	Whitechapel, London	
16703	Devries	L---	1824	?, Holland				Spitalfields, London	general dealer
260	Devries	Meyer Benedictus	1816	Amsterdam, Holland			Hannah (?)	Spitalfields, London	cigar maker journeyman
14469	Di Moro	David	1826	?Italy				Manchester	merchant
14468	Di Moro	Giuseppe Rabino	1816	?Italy				Manchester	merchant
23617	Diamond	Henry	1851	Liverpool	Tobias Diamond	Sarah Harper		Liverpool	
23615	Diamond	Sarah	1831	Liverpool	(?) Harper		Tobias Diamond	Liverpool	
23616	Diamond	Sarah A	1849	Liverpool	Tobias Diamond	Sarah Harper		Liverpool	
23614	Diamond	Tobias	1821	?, Poland			Sarah Harper	Liverpool	glazier
15852	Dias	Abigail	1793	Middlesex, London				Bloomsbury, London	cook
9302	Dias	Abigail	1795	Mile End, London	Isaac de Abraham Dias	Abigail de Isaac Gomes Da Costa		Aldgate, London	charwoman
20555	Dias	Abigail	1832	Aldgate, London	John (Johannan) de Daniel Dias	Rachel de Naphtali Pass (Paz De Leon)		Aldgate, London	
20552	Dias	Buena (Orabuena)	1825	Aldgate, London	John (Johannan) de Daniel Dias	Rachel de Naphtali Pass (Paz De Leon)		Aldgate, London	dress maker
7463	Dias	David	1785	Jamaica, West Indies	(?) Dias	Esther (?)		Whitechapel, London	merchant
15293	Dias	David	1843	City, London	Elisha de Jacob Dias	Rachel de Priscilla Arrobas		Shoreditch, London	
15290	Dias	Elisha	1797	Bethnal Green, London	Jacob Dias	Sarah (?)	Rachel de Priscilla Arrobas	Shoreditch, London	furniture broker
18974	Dias	Esther	1763	Jamaica, West Indies	(?)		(?) Dias	Whitechapel, London	gentlewoman
20553	Dias	Esther	1828	Aldgate, London	John (Johannan) de Daniel Dias	Rachel de Naphtali Pass (Paz De Leon)		Aldgate, London	
19115	Dias	Hannah	1824	?, London	(?) Dias			Aldgate, London	general servant
21736	Dias	Isaac	1786	?, London			Sarah (?)	Islington, London	assistant surgeon, Royal Navy
20550	Dias	John (Johannan)	1796	Aldgate, London	Daniel de Isaac Dias	Rachel de Isaac Delgado	Rachel de Naphtali Pass (Paz De Leon)	Aldgate, London	butcher
18162	Dias	Michael Santillana	1778	Middlesex, London	Samuel Dias Santeliano		Abigail de Moseh Rochelt	Mile End, London	patient in the Portuguese Jews Hospital
24511	Dias	Nathaniel	1799	Whitechapel, London	Isaac Haim de Abraham Dias	Abigail de Moses Cohen D'Azevedo	Keturah (Gell) de Jacob Levi	Deptford, London	glass dealer
15292	Dias	Precilla (Priscella)	1828	Paddington, London	Elisha de Jacob Dias	Rachel de Priscilla Arrobas		Shoreditch, London	
18973	Dias	Rachel	1792	Middlesex, London	(?) Dias	Esther (?)		Whitechapel, London	gentlewoman
20551	Dias	Rachel	1793	Aldgate, London	Naphtali Pass (Paz De Leon)	Buena de David Azogui	John (Johannan) de Daniel Dias	Aldgate, London	
15291	Dias	Rachel	1807	Cork, Ireland	(?) Arrobas	Priscilla (?)	Elisha de Jacob Dias	Shoreditch, London	
18971	Dias	Rebecca	1781	Jamaica, West Indies	(?) Dias	Esther (?)		Whitechapel, London	
15294	Dias	Rebecca	1850	Shoreditch, London	Elisha Dias	Rachel de Priscilla Arrobas		Shoreditch, London	

ID	surname	given names	born	birthplace	father	mother	spouse 1	1851 residence	1851 occupation
20554	Dias	Samuel Cardozo	1829	Aldgate, London	John (Johannan) de Daniel Dias	Rachel de Naphtali Pass (Paz De Leon)	Hannah Levi	Aldgate, London	butcher
21737	Dias	Sarah	1795	Donhead, Wiltshire	(?)		Isaac Dias	Islington, London	
25511	Diney	Luis	1831	?Hungary [Arrad Ungarn]				Tower Hill, London	artist
5669	Disraeli	Benjamin	1804	Chelsea, London	Isaac D'Israeli	Maria Basevi	Mary Anne Lewis	Mayfair, London	landed proprietor + Cabinet Minister
30562	Disraeli	James (Jacob)	1813	Marylebone, London	Isaac D'Israeli	Maria Basevi	Isabella Anne Cave	Bradenham, Buckinghamshire	fundholder + farmer empl 12
30561	Disraeli	Ralph (Raphael)	1809	Brighton, Sussex	Isaac D'Israeli	Maria Basevi	Katharine Trevor	Mayfair, London	
30560	Disraeli	Sarah (Sa)	1802	Middlesex, London	Isaac D'Israeli	Maria Basevi		Twickenham, London	fundholder
5724	Dix	Josephine	1846	Bristol	Frederick Dix	Charlotte (?)	Nelson Marks	Bristol	
23090	D'Monty	Chevalier	1826	?, France				Aldgate, London	professor of French language
28073	Doblienski	Hannah	1847	?, Poland [?, Prussia]	Morris Doblienski	Rosa (?)		Spitalfields, London	
28070	Doblienski	Morris	1821	?, Poland [?, Prussia]			Rosa (?)	Spitalfields, London	tinplate worker
28071	Doblienski	Rosa	1820	?, Poland [?, Prussia]	(?)		Morris Doblienski	Spitalfields, London	
28072	Doblienski	Theodore	1846	?, Poland [?, Prussia]	Morris Doblienski	Rosa (?)		Spitalfields, London	
28081	Doblilin	Isaac	1830	Poznan, Poland [Posan, Prussia]				Spitalfields, London	tailor
8913	Donatty (Donati)	Hannah	1784	Whitechapel, London	Abraham Belasco		David de David Donati	Aldgate, London	poor
8912	Donatty (Donati)	Rachel	1809	Mile End, London	David Donati	Hannah de Abraham Belasco		Aldgate, London	furrier
8908	Donatty (Donati)	Rebecca	1825	Mile End, London	David Donati	Hannah de Abraham Belasco	Isaac Costa	Aldgate, London	furrier
11909	Doodeward	Abraham	1839	Rotterdam, Holland	Jeremiah Doodeward	Harriet (?)		Whitechapel, London	
11906	Doodeward	Harriet	1814	Rotterdam, Holland	(?)		Jeremiah Doodeward	Whitechapel, London	
11911	Doodeward	Isaac	1849	Whitechapel, London	Jeremiah Doodeward	Harriet (?)		Whitechapel, London	
11905	Doodeward	Jeremiah	1811	Rotterdam, Holland			Harriet (?)	Whitechapel, London	general merchant
11907	Doodeward	Rebecca	1835	Rotterdam, Holland	Jeremiah Doodeward	Harriet (?)	Joseph Jacobs	Whitechapel, London	
11910	Doodeward	Rosetta	1846	Rotterdam, Holland	Jeremiah Doodeward	Harriet (?)	Moses Koopman Speelman	Whitechapel, London	
11908	Doodeward	Samuel	1837	Rotterdam, Holland	Jeremiah Doodeward	Harriet (?)		Whitechapel, London	
13744	Dornkar	Behrens	1801	?, Poland [?, Prussia]				Manchester	cap maker
13135	Dorris	Alexander	1790	King's Lynn, Norfolk				Hoxton, London	warehouseman
28885	Dounkirk	Abram	1847	Amsterdam, Holland	Isaac Dounkirk	Deborah Defries		Spitalfields, London	scholar
28884	Dounkirk	Deborah	1817	Amsterdam, Holland	(?) Defries	Catherine (?)	Isaac Dounkirk	Spitalfields, London	
28883	Dounkirk	Isaac	1819	Amsterdam, Holland			Deborah Defries	Spitalfields, London	dealer in confectionery
28888	Dounkirk	Moss	1827	Amsterdam, Holland				Spitalfields, London	cigar maker
9301	Drago	Abigail	1788	Whitechapel, London	Aaron Drago	Esther Fernandes		Aldgate, London	embroideress
9300	Drago	Cynthia	1777	Whitechapel, London	(?Aaron Drago)	(?Esther Fernandes)		Aldgate, London	embroideress
24547	Drefries	Julia	1771	Aldgate, London	(?)		(?) Defries	Brixton, London	
9090	Driazeldor	Joel	1829	?, Holland				Spitalfields, London	hawker
22977	Drielsma	Anne	1851	Liverpool	Mozes Jonas (Maurice, Morris) Drielsma	Sarah Jones	Adolph (Abraham) Gottschalk	Liverpool	
23010	Drielsma	Caroline	1848	Liverpool	Mozes Jonas (Maurice, Morris) Drielsma	Sarah Jones	Ruben Rubens	Liverpool	

ID	surname	given names	born	birthplace	father	mother	spouse 1	1851 residence	1851 occupation
23811	Drielsma	David	1849	Liverpool	Mozes Jonas (Maurice, Morris) Drielsma	Sarah Jones		Liverpool	
363	Drielsma	Isaac Jonas	1793	Groningen, Holland	Simon Jonas Drielsma		Theresa (Mietje) Meyer (Moses) Loewenstein	Liverpool	watch, chronometer + clockmaker
22973	Drielsma	Mozes Jonas (Maurice, Morris)	1817	Groningen, Holland	Isaac Jonas Drielsma	Theresa (Mietje) Meyer (Moses) Loewenstein	Sarah Jones	Liverpool	watchmaker
364	Drielsma	Rose (Roosje) Isaac	1822	Groningen, Holland	Isaac Jonas Drielsma	Theresa (Mietje) Meyer (Moses) Loewenstein	Samuel Kisch	Liverpool	grocer, provision dealer + outfitter
22974	Drielsma	Sarah	1817	Great Yarmouth, Norfolk	David Jones	Leah Micholls	Mozes Jonas (Maurice, Morris) Drielsma	Liverpool	
365	Drielsma	Simon	1835	Nijmegen, Holland	Isaac Jonas Drielsma	Theresa (Mietje) Meyer (Moses)	Jane Crellin	Liverpool	
19895	Drielsma	Theresa (Mietje)	1787	Hessen, Germany	Meijer Mozes Levie Loewnstein	Roosje Levie Furth	Isaac Jonas Drielsma	Liverpool	watch + chronometer maker
26005	Drukker	Alexander	1842	Whitechapel, London	Simon Samuel Drukker	Mary Emanuel		Aldgate, London	
26004	Drukker	Bertha	1842	Whitechapel, London	George Moss	Mary Emanuel		Aldgate, London	
26006	Drukker	Blumer	1844	Whitechapel, London	Simon Samuel Drukker	Mary Emanuel		Aldgate, London	
25883	Drukker	Elizabeth	1846	Rotterdam, Holland	Nathan (Naphthali) Drukker	Sarah (?)		Aldgate, London	
29476	Drukker	Emanuel	1827	?, Holland	Marks Drukker	Julia (?)	Catherine Schornesham	Spitalfields, London	general dealer
25881	Drukker	Hannah	1835	Rotterdam, Holland	Nathan (Naphthali) Drukker	Sarah (?)		Aldgate, London	
26008	Drukker	Isaac	1845	Whitechapel, London	Simon Samuel Drukker	Mary Emanuel		Aldgate, London	
26007	Drukker	Israel	1844	Whitechapel, London	George Moss	Mary Emanuel		Aldgate, London	
26010	Drukker	Joseph	1850	?Aldgate, London	Simon Samuel Drukker	Lucy Lippschutz		Aldgate, London	
29475	Drukker	Julia	1799	?, Holland	(?)		Marks Drukker	Spitalfields, London	
26002	Drukker	Julia	1838	Middlesex, London	Simon Samuel Drukker	Mary Emanuel		Aldgate, London	
26001	Drukker	Kate	1831	Middlesex, London	Simon Samuel Drukker	Mary Emanuel		Aldgate, London	
25999	Drukker	Lucy	1816	Middlesex, London	Israel Lippschutz		George Moss	Aldgate, London	pickle merchant
26000	Drukker	Lydia (Leah)	1827	Aldgate, London	Simon Samuel Drukker	Mary Emanuel		Aldgate, London	
29474	Drukker	Marks	1792	?, Holland			Julia (?)	Spitalfields, London	cloth traveller
25879	Drukker	Nathan (Naphthali)	1800	Amsterdam, Holland			Sarah (?)	Aldgate, London	clothes dealer
26003	Drukker	Phoebe	1840	Middlesex, London	Simon Samuel Drukker	Mary Emanuel		Aldgate, London	
25884	Drukker	Phoebe	1848	?, London	Nathan (Naphthali) Drukker	Sarah (?)		Aldgate, London	
25882	Drukker	Samuel	1840	Rotterdam, Holland	Nathan (Naphthali) Drukker	Sarah (?)		Aldgate, London	
25880	Drukker	Sarah	1807	Amsterdam, Holland	(?)		Nathan (Naphthali) Drukker	Aldgate, London	clothes dealer
26009	Drukker	Sarah	1847	Whitechapel, London	Simon Samuel Drukker	Mary Emanuel		Aldgate, London	
25885	Drukker	Simon	1851	Aldgate, London	Nathan (Naphthali) Drukker	Sarah (?)		Aldgate, London	
25998	Drukker	Simon Samuel	1802	Amsterdam, Holland	Samuel Marcus Drukker		Blumer Angel	Aldgate, London	pickle merchant
14986	Dubois	Elizabeth	1842	Middlesex, London	(?) Dubois		Mary Emanuel	Bethnal Green, London	boarding school pupil
14912	Dubois	Thomas	1838	Middlesex, London				Bethnal Green, London	boarding school pupil
23642	Duckett	Isaac	1830	?, Poland				Liverpool	tailor
23643	Duckett	Ralph	1832	?, Poland				Liverpool	glazier
10670	Duica	Abraham	1826	Amsterdam, Holland			Sarah (?)	Spitalfields, London	cigar maker
10673	Duica	Elizabeth	1847	Amsterdam, Holland	Abraham Duica	Sarah (?)		Spitalfields, London	
10674	Duica	Nancy	1848	Amsterdam, Holland	Abraham Duica	Sarah (?)		Spitalfields, London	

ID	surname	given names	born	birthplace	father	mother	spouse 1	1851 residence	1851 occupation
10675	Duica	Rebecca	1850	Spitalfields, London	Abraham Duica	Sarah (?)		Spitalfields, London	
10671	Duica	Sarah	1829	Amsterdam, Holland	(?)		Abraham Duica	Spitalfields, London	
10672	Duica	Solomon	1845	Amsterdam, Holland	Abraham Duica	Sarah (?)		Spitalfields, London	scholar
9662	Duran	Abraham	1829	Whitechapel, London	Baruch (Baron) Duran	Sophia (Simha) Racah	Rebecca Montefiore	Aldgate, London	cigar maker
9653	Duran	Baruch (Baron)	1795	Algiers, Algeria	Isaac Duran		Sophia (Simha) de Abraham Israel Racah	Aldgate, London	general dealer
8074	Duran	Esther	1842	Aldgate, London	Baruch (Baron) Duran	Sophia (Simha) Racah	Woolf Myers	?Aldgate, London	scholar
9656	Duran	Guarella	1833	?, London	Baruch (Baron) Duran	Sophia (Simha) Racah		Aldgate, London	?dress maker
9657	Duran	Hannah	1835	?, London	Baruch (Baron) Duran	Sophia (Simha) Racah		Aldgate, London	tailoress
9655	Duran	Isaac	1832	?, London	Baruch (Baron) Duran	Sophia (Simha) Racah		Aldgate, London	cigar maker
9659	Duran	Jacob	1844	?, London	Baruch (Baron) Duran	Sophia (Simha) Racah		Aldgate, London	scholar
14830	Duran	Joseph	1827	Soho, London			Rebecca (?)	Bethnal Green, London	mariner
9658	Duran	Miriam	1838	?, London	Baruch (Baron) Duran	Sophia (Simha) Racah		Aldgate, London	scholar
9663	Duran	Moses	1840	?, London	Baruch (Baron) Duran	Sophia (Simha) Racah		Aldgate, London	scholar
9661	Duran	Rachel	1851	?Aldgate, London	Baruch (Baron) Duran	Sophia (Simha) Racah	Phil Phillips	Aldgate, London	
14831	Duran	Rebecca	1830	Poplar, London	(?)		Joseph Duran	Bethnal Green, London	shape maker
9664	Duran	Rebecca	1831	Mile End, London	Abraham de Samuel Montefiore	Stella (Estrella) de Isaac Hatchwell	Rebecca Montefiore	Aldgate, London	
9660	Duran	Rebecca	1847	?, London	Baruch (Baron) Duran	Sophia (Simha) Racah		Aldgate, London	scholar
9654	Duran	Sophia (Simha)	1807	?, London	Abraham Israel Racah	Hanah (?)	Baruch (Baron) de Isaac Duran	Aldgate, London	
14511	Durlacher	Adelaide	1831	Mayfair, London	Godfrey Zimmerman	Martha (?)	Henry Durlacher	Mayfair, London	
4117	Durlacher	Alexander	1823	Piccadilly, London	Lewis Durlacher	Susanna Levi		Piccadilly, London	bookseller
4094	Durlacher	Deborah	1825	Westminster, London	(?) Benjamin	Fanny (?)	Montague Durlacher	Soho, London	
4118	Durlacher	Elizabeth	1829	Piccadilly, London	Lewis Durlacher	Susanna Levi		Piccadilly, London	bookseller
4119	Durlacher	George	1829	Piccadilly, London	Lewis Durlacher	Susanna Levi		Piccadilly, London	bookseller
14510	Durlacher	Henry	1827	Mayfair, London			Adelaide Zimmerman	Mayfair, London	china + picture dealer
4115	Durlacher	Lewis	1792	?, Warwickshire	Solomon Abraham Durlacher	Elizabeth Harris	Susanna Levi	Piccadilly, London	surgeon chiropodist to the Royal Household
4093	Durlacher	Montague	1825	Westminster, London			Deborah Benjamin	Soho, London	surgeon chiropodist
4116	Durlacher	Susanna	1798	Piccadilly, London	David Levi		Lewis Durlacher	Piccadilly, London	
29247	Dusseldorf	E--- M---	1814	?, Holland				Whitechapel, London	diamond merchant
25563	Dutch	?	1805	?	(?) (?Nelson)		Lewis Lesser Dutch	Dublin, Ireland	
25560	Dutch	?	1825	?	(?)		Samuel Lewis Dutch	Dublin, Ireland	
25562	Dutch	Lewis Lesser	1807	?	Avraham		(?) (?Nelson)	Dublin, Ireland	
25561	Dutch	Louis Lesser	1850	Dublin, Ireland	Samuel Lewis Dutch	(?)		Dublin, Ireland	
25559	Dutch	Samuel Lewis	1822	?	Lewis Lesser Dutch	(?) (?Nelson)	(?)	Dublin, Ireland	tobacconist + cigar manufacturer
12056	Dyea	Victoa	1776	Paris, France				Whitechapel, London	
13935	Dyte	Charles	1819	Aldgate, London	David Moses Dyte	Hannah Lazarus	Eliza (Evelina) Nathan	Manchester	tailor
9413	Dyte	David Hyman	1839	Aldgate, London	Maurice Dyte	Louisa Canstatt	Sarah Solomon	Aldgate, London	scholar
13936	Dyte	Eliza (Evelina)	1821	Liverpool	(?) Nathan		Charles Dyte	Manchester	
19213	Dyte	Fanny	1818	?Middlesex, London	David Moses Dyte	Hannah Lazarus	William Smith	Strand, London	tradesman's daughter
7708	Dyte	Hannah	1777	Middlesex, London	Henry (Hirsh) Lazarus	Perla (?)	David Moses Dyte	Strand, London	quill merchant
13937	Dyte	Hannah	1849	Whitechapel, London	Charles Dyte	Eliza (Evelina) Nathan		Manchester	

ID	surname	given names	born	birthplace	father	mother	spouse 1	1851 residence	1851 occupation
7709	Dyte	Henry	1807	?Middlesex, London	David Moses Dyte	Hannah Lazarus		Strand, London	solicitor
7518	Dyte	John	1811	Middlesex, London	David Moses Dyte	Hannah Lazarus	Marianne Beazley	Strand, London	stationer
9412	Dyte	Louisa	1809	Middlesex, London	Jacob Canstatt	Elizabeth Hyams	Maurice Dyte	Aldgate, London	chemist
9425	Dyte	Maria Louisa	1841	Aldgate, London	Maurice Dyte	Louisa Canstatt	Richard Moss	Aldgate, London	
19214	Dyte	Mary Ann	1823	?Middlesex, London	David Moses Dyte	Hannah Lazarus	Charles Bennett	Strand, London	tradesman's daughter
13938	Dyte	Rosina	1851	Manchester	Charles Dyte	Eliza (Evelina) Nathan		Manchester	
9414	Dyte	Sarah Hannah	1844	Aldgate, London	Maurice Dyte	Louisa Canstatt		Aldgate, London	scholar
18232	Dyte (Dight)	Catharine Sophia	1845	Cheltenham, Gloucestershire	Lewis Asher Dyte (Dight)	Eliza H Dyte		Cheltenham, Gloucestershire	scholar
18234	Dyte (Dight)	Charles	1842	Cheltenham, Gloucestershire	Lewis Asher Dyte (Dight)	Eliza H Dyte		Cheltenham, Gloucestershire	scholar
18229	Dyte (Dight)	David	1836	Cheltenham, Gloucestershire	Lewis Asher Dyte (Dight)	Eliza H Dyte		Cheltenham, Gloucestershire	scholar
30475	Dyte (Dight)	Edward	1850	Cheltenham, Gloucestershire	Lewis Asher Dyte (Dight)	Eliza H Dyte		Cheltenham, Gloucestershire	
18228	Dyte (Dight)	Eliza H	1812	City, London	David Moses Dyte	Hannah Lazarus	Lewis Asher Dyte (Dight)	Cheltenham, Gloucestershire	
18235	Dyte (Dight)	Fanny Eliza	1848	Cheltenham, Gloucestershire	Lewis Asher Dyte (Dight)	Eliza H Dyte	Lewis Lyons	Cheltenham, Gloucestershire	scholar
18233	Dyte (Dight)	Hannah	1846	Cheltenham, Gloucestershire	Lewis Asher Dyte (Dight)	Eliza H Dyte	Sidney Jackson	Cheltenham, Gloucestershire	scholar
18230	Dyte (Dight)	Henry	1838	Cheltenham, Gloucestershire	Lewis Asher Dyte (Dight)	Eliza H Dyte		Cheltenham, Gloucestershire	scholar
18231	Dyte (Dight)	John	1840	Cheltenham, Gloucestershire	Lewis Asher Dyte (Dight)	Eliza H Dyte		Cheltenham, Gloucestershire	scholar
5213	Dyte (Dight)	Lewis Asher	1806	Bristol	D--- M--- Dyte		Eliza H Dyte	Cheltenham, Gloucestershire	quill manufacturer + stationer
6532	Dyte (Dight)	Maurice Lewis	1834	?Cheltenham, Gloucestershire	Lewis Asher Dyte (Dight)	Eliza H Dyte	Esther Lazarus	Cheltenham, Gloucestershire	
16990	Eardensohn	Isaac	1808	?, Russia			Jeanetta (?)	Wapping, London	wholesale shoemaker empl 8 apps
16991	Eardensohn	Jeanetta	1811	?, Russia	(?)		Isaac Eardensohn	Wapping, London	
16992	Eardensohn	Joseph	1837	?, Russia	Isaac Eardensohn	Jeanetta (?)		Wapping, London	scholar
14913	Ebeinstein	Nathan	1840	Douglas, Isle of Man				Bethnal Green, London	boarding school pupil
25712	Eckstein	David	1827	Teplice, Czech Republic [Teplila in Bohemia]	Jacob Eckstein		Simeh (Simah) Paris	Spitalfields, London	tailor
2171	Edelman	Hirsch	1811	Moldova, Rumania				Oxford, Oxfordshire	Hebrew teacher
27782	Edelsheim	Philip	1832	Amsterdam, Holland				Spitalfields, London	cigar maker
7065	Edersheim	Alfred	1825	Vienna, Austria	Marcus Edersheim	Stephanie Beifuss	Mary Broomfield	Aberdeen, Scotland	Free Church minister
18460	Edersheim	Joel	1783	Amsterdam, Holland			(?)	Whitechapel, London	merchant
18461	Edersheim	Morris	1823	Amsterdam, Holland	Joel Edersheim	(?)		Whitechapel, London	potato salesman
3945	Edwards	Esther	1844	Portsmouth, Hampshire	John Edwards	Jane Hart	Isaac Phillips	Portsmouth, Hampshire	
3944	Edwards	Hannah	1850	Portsmouth, Hampshire	John Edwards	Jane Hart	Samuel Joseph Epstein	Portsmouth, Hampshire	
3948	Edwards	Jane	1819	Wapping, London	Michael Henry Hart	Esther Davis	John Edwards	Portsmouth, Hampshire	
3947	Edwards	John	1805	?, London	Samuel Edward (?Moses)		Hannah Sophia (?)	Portsmouth, Hampshire	navy agent councillor + navy agent

ID	surname	given names	born	birthplace	father	mother	spouse 1	1851 residence	1851 occupation
3946	Edwards	John	1848	Portsmouth, Hampshire	John Edwards	Jane Hart		Portsmouth, Hampshire	
3943	Edwards	Michael Henry	1846	Portsmouth, Hampshire	John Edwards	Jane Hart		Portsmouth, Hampshire	
3942	Edwards	Samuel	1843	Portsmouth, Hampshire	John Edwards	Jane Hart		Portsmouth, Hampshire	
2414	Efrom	Kalman	1829	?, Poland [?, Prussia]				Hull, Yorkshire	hawker
29607	Ehrenberg	Hannah	1827	?, Russia	Marcus Manuel		Hyman Ehrenberg	Aldgate, London	
29606	Ehrenberg	Hyman	1823	?, Poland	Levin Ehrenberg		Hannah Manuel	Aldgate, London	tailor
30420	Ehrenberg	Solomon	1851	Aldgate, London	Hyman Ehrenberg	Hannah Manuel		Aldgate, London	
29263	Ehrensperger	Carel	1824	Amsterdam, Holland				Whitechapel, London	ship agent's clerk
18415	Eifel	Solomon	1829	?, Poland [?, Prussia]				Aldgate, London	tailor
9447	Eiger	Charles	1850	Aldgate, London	Henry Solomon Eiger	Jane Woolf		Aldgate, London	
9446	Eiger	David	1845	Aldgate, London	Henry Solomon Eiger	Jane Woolf		Aldgate, London	scholar at home
9445	Eiger	Henry Solomon	1812	?, Poland [?, Prussia]	Shlomeh		Jane Woolf	Aldgate, London	stock and share agent
9444	Eiger	Jane	1814	Brighton, Sussex	David Woolf	Rosetta (?)	Henry Solomon Eiger	Aldgate, London	wife to share agent
9448	Eiger	Saul L	1833	Warsaw, Poland	(?Shlomeh)	Mary (?)		Aldgate, London	apprentice to lithographer
18674	Eisenberg	Betsy	1811	?Zemplén, Hungary [Semplin, Hungary]	(?)		Henry Eisenberg	Spitalfields, London	
18673	Eisenberg	Henry	1809	Zemplén, Hungary [Semplin, Hungary]			Betsy (?)	Spitalfields, London	licensed hawker
22728	Eisendrath	Elizabeth (Betsy)	1828	Whitechapel, London	Levy Eisendrath	Esther (?)	Zadoc (Zachariah) Bloomfield	Whitechapel, London	dress maker
22727	Eisendrath	Esther	1808	Whitechapel, London	(?)		Levy Eisendrath	Whitechapel, London	cap maker
22731	Eisendrath	Eve	1838	Spitalfields, London	Levy Eisendrath	Esther (?)		Whitechapel, London	scholar
22730	Eisendrath	Isaac	1834	Finsbury, London	Levy Eisendrath	Esther (?)		Whitechapel, London	cigar maker apprentice
22726	Eisendrath	Levy	1798	?, Germany	Nathan Eisendrath		Esther (?)	Whitechapel, London	cap maker
22733	Eisendrath	Rosetta	1843	Whitechapel, London	Levy Eisendrath	Esther (?)		Whitechapel, London	scholar
22734	Eisendrath	Samuel	1849	Whitechapel, London	Levy Eisendrath	Esther (?)		Whitechapel, London	
22729	Eisendrath	Sarah	1830	Whitechapel, London	Levy Eisendrath	Esther (?)		Whitechapel, London	tailoress
22732	Eisendrath	Sophia	1840	Whitechapel, London	Levy Eisendrath	Esther (?)		Whitechapel, London	scholar
2415	Eizenberg	Fishel	1831	?, Poland				Hull, Yorkshire	travelling jeweller
7322	Elboz	Solomon	1829	?	Judah Elboz		Wellcome (?)	?Spitalfields, London	
30025	Elboz	Welcome	1830	?	(?)		Solomon Elboz	?Spitalfields, London	
13962	Eli	Maria	1831	Hamburg, Germany				Manchester	dressmaker
28321	Elias	Angelo	1832	Watford, Hertfordshire	Samuel Elias	Sarah Myers		Aldgate, London	
28320	Elias	Ann	1830	Watford, Hertfordshire	Samuel Elias	Sarah Myers		Aldgate, London	
22897	Elias	Catherine	1778	Whitechapel, London	(?)		(?) Elias	Wapping, London	nurse
28322	Elias	Charlotte	1831	Watford, Hertfordshire	Samuel Elias	Sarah Myers		Aldgate, London	
17371	Elias	Clara	1847	Spitalfields, London	Nathan Elias	Sarah (Elizabeth) Moses	Michael Hart	Spitalfields, London	
28183	Elias	Elias (Iley, Eli)	1817	Spitalfields, London	Philip Elias	Esther Nathan	Sarah Hyams	Spitalfields, London	master cattle drover
28323	Elias	Elizabeth	1834	Watford, Hertfordshire	Samuel Elias	Sarah Myers		Aldgate, London	
17370	Elias	Esther	1846	Spitalfields, London	Nathan Elias	Sarah (Elizabeth) Moses		Spitalfields, London	
28187	Elias	Esther	1851	Whitechapel, London	Elias (Iley, Eli) Elias	Sarah Hyams		Spitalfields, London	
28318	Elias	Evelina	1827	Watford, Hertfordshire	Samuel Elias	Sarah Myers	Jacob Ehrenberg	Aldgate, London	
28186	Elias	Hyam	1849	Whitechapel, London	Elias (Iley, Eli) Elias	Sarah Hyams		Spitalfields, London	
17369	Elias	Jonas	1844	Spitalfields, London	Nathan Elias	Sarah (Elizabeth) Moses		Spitalfields, London	
28319	Elias	Julia	1829	Watford, Hertfordshire	Samuel Elias	Sarah Myers		Aldgate, London	

ID	surname	given names	born	birthplace	father	mother	spouse 1	1851 residence	1851 occupation
17367	Elias	Nathan	1813	Spitalfields, London	Philip Elias	Esther Nathan	Sarah (Elizabeth) Moses	Spitalfields, London	general dealer
20198	Elias	Philip	1780	Amsterdam, Holland	Eliyahu Klavier-Meister		Esther Nathan	Spitalfields, London	general dealer
17372	Elias	Phillip	1848	Spitalfields, London	Nathan Elias	Sarah (Elizabeth) Moses		Spitalfields, London	
28185	Elias	Phillip	1848	Whitechapel, London	Elias (Iley, Eli) Elias	Sarah Hyams		Spitalfields, London	
22474	Elias	Rebecca I	1786	?, Poland	(?)		(?) Elias	St Helier, Jersey, Channel Islands	
28316	Elias	Samuel	1795	Aldgate, London	Aharon		Sarah Myers	Aldgate, London	greengrocer
27038	Elias	Sarah	1781	?, London	(?) Elias			Aldgate, London	
28317	Elias	Sarah	1793	Aldgate, London	Yeshayahu (Isaiah) Myers		Samuel Elias	Aldgate, London	
28184	Elias	Sarah	1818	Aldgate, London	Henry Hyams		Elias (Iley, Eli) Elias	Spitalfields, London	
17368	Elias	Sarah (Elizabeth)	1819	Southwark, London	Jonas Moses		Nathan Elias	Spitalfields, London	
26834	Elias (Ellis)	Simon	1849	Aldgate, London	Lipman Ellis	Theresa (?)		Aldgate, London	
7380	Elkin	Catherine	1831	Finsbury, London	Benjamin Elkin		Sigismund Schloss	Hastings, Sussex	
19082	Elkin	Emily Dinah Rachel	1830	Bristol	William Wolfe Alexander		Jacob Levy Elkin	Marylebone, London	
7693	Elkin	Jacob Levy	1823	Barbados, West Indies	Benjamin Elkin		Emily Dinah Rachel Alexander	Marylebone, London	merchant
11291	Ellice	Rosa	1821	Aldgate, London	(?)		(?) Ellice	Aldgate, London	general dealer
2860	Ellinger	Alexander Adolphus	1820	Mainz, Germany	Isaak (Issac) Ellinger	Sophia Cahn	Mathilda Van Oven	?Manchester	
3728	Ellis	Abraham	1814	Aldgate, London	Lambert (Lambeth) Ellis	Sarah (?)	Ailsey Harris	Spitalfields, London	general dealer
27250	Ellis	Abraham	1832	?, London	David Ellis	Hannah (?)		Aldgate, London	commission agent
3729	Ellis	Ailsey	1815	Whitechapel, London	(?) Harris		Abraham Ellis	Spitalfields, London	
18943	Ellis	Alexander	1788	Westminster, London	Aharon		Frances (?)	Whitechapel, London	slopseller
12686	Ellis	Alice	1818	Rudham, Norfolk	(?)		William Ellis	Norwich, Norfolk	
11429	Ellis	Asher	1844	Aldgate, London	Jonas Ellis	Sarah Jacobs		Aldgate, London	
3733	Ellis	Asher	1845	Spitalfields, London	Abraham Ellis	Ailsey Harris	Isabella Israel	Spitalfields, London	scholar
27256	Ellis	Asher	1849	?, London	David Ellis	Hannah (?)	Catherine (Kate) Hyams	Aldgate, London	scholar
16904	Ellis	Aurther	1841	Sheffield, Yorkshire	Benjamin Ellis	Mary (?)		Sheffield, Yorkshire	
5126	Ellis	Benjamin	1810	?, Yorkshire			Mary (?)	Sheffield, Yorkshire	hairdresser + smallwear + toy dealer
12690	Ellis	Benjamin	1850	Norwich, Norfolk	William Ellis	Alice (?)		Norwich, Norfolk	
18205	Ellis	Bennett	1838	Middlesex, London				Mile End, London	scholar
12433	Ellis	Catherine	1816	?, Holland	Issachar HaLevi Kessner		Nathan Ellis	Spitalfields, London	
15446	Ellis	Charles (Carig)	1811	?, Germany	Dov Baer		Louisa Myers	Covent Garden, London	cap maker
27248	Ellis	David	1794	?, Poland			Hannah (?)	Aldgate, London	furrier
21075	Ellis	David	1839	?, London				Dover, Kent	boarding school pupil
15451	Ellis	Dinah	1847	?, London	Charles (Carig) Ellis	Louisa Myers		Covent Garden, London	
17802	Ellis	Elias	1848	Aldgate, London	Michael Ellis	Lavinia Hart		Aldgate, London	
16903	Ellis	Eliza	1838	Sheffield, Yorkshire	Benjamin Ellis	Mary (?)		Sheffield, Yorkshire	
15452	Ellis	Emma	1849	Aldgate, London	Charles (Carig) Ellis	Louisa Myers		Covent Garden, London	
27253	Ellis	Esther	1841	?, London	David Ellis	Hannah (?)		Aldgate, London	scholar
12693	Ellis	Esther	1844	Norwich, Norfolk	Samuel Ellis	Hannah (?)		Norwich, Norfolk	
12688	Ellis	Esther	1846	Norwich, Norfolk	William Ellis	Alice (?)		Norwich, Norfolk	scholar
11430	Ellis	Esther	1848	Aldgate, London	Jonas Ellis	Sarah Jacobs		Aldgate, London	

ID	surname	given names	born	birthplace	father	mother	spouse 1	1851 residence	1851 occupation
17806	Ellis	Eve	1828	City, London	(?) Ellis			Aldgate, London	watch maker
18944	Ellis	Frances	1789	Middlesex, London	(?)		Alexander Ellis	Whitechapel, London	
17805	Ellis	Frances	1826	City, London	(?) Ellis			Aldgate, London	dressmaker
16906	Ellis	Frederick	1846	Sheffield, Yorkshire	Benjamin Ellis	Mary (?)		Sheffield, Yorkshire	
27249	Ellis	Hannah	1804	?, Germany	(?)		David Ellis	Aldgate, London	general dealer
6802	Ellis	Hannah	1817	Cambridge	Abraham Jacobs		Asher Ellis	Spitalfields, London	
12692	Ellis	Hannah	1818	?, Norfolk [---dsley, Norfolk]			Samuel Ellis	Norwich, Norfolk	
3730	Ellis	Henry	1839	Whitechapel, London	Abraham Ellis	Ailsey Harris		Spitalfields, London	
25762	Ellis	Henry	1842	Aldgate, London	Isaac Ellis	Julia (?)		Aldgate, London	
25759	Ellis	Isaac	1813	Southwark, London			Julia (?)	Aldgate, London	clothier
11428	Ellis	Jacob	1842	Aldgate, London	Jonas Ellis	Sarah Jacobs		Aldgate, London	
27255	Ellis	Jacob	1847	?, London	David Ellis	Hannah (?)		Aldgate, London	scholar
17804	Ellis	John	1824	City, London				Aldgate, London	watch maker
27254	Ellis	John	1843	?, London	David Ellis	Hannah (?)		Aldgate, London	scholar
3736	Ellis	John	1850	Spitalfields, London	Abraham Ellis	Ailsey Harris	Dinah Alexander	Spitalfields, London	
5577	Ellis	Jonas	1818	Aldgate, London	Lambert (Lambeth) Ellis		Sarah Jacobs	Aldgate, London	general dealer
8399	Ellis	Joseph	1812	Aldgate, London			Sarah (?)	Southampton, Hampshire	watchmaker + jeweller
15448	Ellis	Joseph	1839	?, London	Charles (Carig) Ellis	Louisa Myers		Covent Garden, London	scholar
16908	Ellis	Joseph	1849	Sheffield, Yorkshire	Benjamin Ellis	Mary (?)		Sheffield, Yorkshire	
25760	Ellis	Julia	1819	Lambeth, London	(?)		Isaac Ellis	Aldgate, London	
26966	Ellis	Julia	1834	Whitechapel, London	(?) Ellis			Aldgate, London	
17800	Ellis	Julia	1842	Aldgate, London	Michael Ellis	Lavinia Hart		Aldgate, London	
15450	Ellis	Julia	1843	?, London	Charles (Carig) Ellis	Louisa Myers		Covent Garden, London	scholar
19732	Ellis	Lambert	1851	Aldgate, London	Moses Ellis	Hannah Jacobs	Hannah Levy	Aldgate, London	
3735	Ellis	Lambeth (Samuel)	1848	Spitalfields, London	Abraham Ellis	Ailsey Harris		Spitalfields, London	
17798	Ellis	Lavinia	1815	City, London	(?) Hart	Judith (?)	Michael Ellis	Aldgate, London	
18945	Ellis	Lewis	1826	Whitechapel, London	Alexander Ellis	Frances (?)		Whitechapel, London	merchant + shipper
26832	Ellis	Lipman (Goodman)	1820	?, Germany	Elia		Theresa (?)	Aldgate, London	glazier
15447	Ellis	Louisa	1817	?, London	Hanoch Myers		Charles (Carig) Ellis	Covent Garden, London	
27252	Ellis	Louisa	1838	?, London	David Ellis	Hannah (?)		Aldgate, London	fur sewer
16902	Ellis	Mary	1810	Sheffield, Yorkshire	(?)		Benjamin Ellia	Sheffield, Yorkshire	
16905	Ellis	Mary	1843	Sheffield, Yorkshire	Benjamin Ellis	Mary (?)		Sheffield, Yorkshire	
17797	Ellis	Michael	1817	City, London			Lavinia Hart	Aldgate, London	watch maker
6801	Ellis	Moses	1822	Aldgate, London	Lambert Ellis	Sarah (?)	Hannah Jacobs	Spitalfields, London	clothes + general dealer
6804	Ellis	Nancy	1843	Aldgate, London	Asher Ellis	Hannah Jacobs	Lewis Cohen	Spitalfields, London	scholar
926	Ellis	Nancy	1845	Aldgate, London	Jonas Ellis	Sarah (?)	Lewis Barnett	Aldgate, London	
3732	Ellis	Nancy (Ann)	1843	Spitalfields, London	Abraham Ellis	Ailsey Harris		Spitalfields, London	scholar
12432	Ellis	Nathan	1808	Whitechapel, London	Abraham Ellis		Catherine Kesner	Spitalfields, London	general dealer
27251	Ellis	Rachael	1835	?, London	David Ellis	Hannah (?)	Aaron Jacobs	Aldgate, London	general dealer
11431	Ellis	Rachael	1850	Aldgate, London	Jonas Ellis	Sarah Jacobs	Isaac Benjamin	Aldgate, London	
15449	Ellis	Rebecca	1841	?, London	Charles (Carig) Ellis	Louisa Myers		Covent Garden, London	scholar
3734	Ellis	Rebecca	1847	Spitalfields, London	Abraham Ellis	Ailsey Harris		Spitalfields, London	scholar
17803	Ellis	Reuben	1850	Aldgate, London	Michael Ellis	Lavinia Hart		Aldgate, London	
17801	Ellis	Rosa (Rosetta)	1844	Aldgate, London	Michael Ellis	Lavinia Hart		Aldgate, London	

ID	surname	given names	born	birthplace	father	mother	spouse 1	1851 residence	1851 occupation
12691	Ellis	Samuel	1821	Norwich, Norfolk			Hannah (?)	Norwich, Norfolk	general dealer
12689	Ellis	Samuel	1848	Norwich, Norfolk	William Ellis	Alice (?)		Norwich, Norfolk	scholar
8400	Ellis	Sarah	1809	Aldgate, London	(?)		(?)	Southampton, Hampshire	
11426	Ellis	Sarah	1823	Aldgate, London	Abraham Jacobs	Rachel Raphael	Jonas Ellis	Aldgate, London	
2935	Ellis	Sarah (Sally)	1837	Spitalfields, London	Abraham Ellis	Ailsey Harris	Israel Levy	Spitalfields, London	
6803	Ellis	Solomon	1838	Aldgate, London	Asher Ellis	Hannah Jacobs		Spitalfields, London	scholar
11427	Ellis	Solomon	1841	Aldgate, London	Jonas Ellis	Sarah Jacobs		Aldgate, London	
25761	Ellis	Sophia	1835	Southwark, London	Isaac Ellis	Julia (?)		Aldgate, London	
17799	Ellis	Sophia	1841	Aldgate, London	Michael Ellis	Lavinia Hart		Aldgate, London	scholar
26833	Ellis	Theresa	1824	?, Germany	(?)		Lipman (Goodman) Ellis	Aldgate, London	
16907	Ellis	Walter	1847	Sheffield, Yorkshire	Benjamin Ellis	Mary (?)		Sheffield, Yorkshire	
12685	Ellis	William	1818	Norwich, Norfolk			Alice (?)	Norwich, Norfolk	greengrocer
12687	Ellis	William	1840	Norwich, Norfolk	William Ellis	Alice (?)		Norwich, Norfolk	scholar
24106	Ellison	Isaac M	1791	?, Poland [?, Prussia]				Bloomsbury, London	grocery agent
13585	Ellison	Jacob	1828	?, Poland				Manchester	cabinet maker
14472	Ellissen	Philip David	1820	?				Salford, Lancashire	shipping merchant
6524	Elsner (Elzner)	Solomon	1831	?, Poland [?, Prussia]	Abraham Elzner		Rosina Silverstone	Exeter, Devon	optician
16702	Elsor	Catherine	1833	?, Holland	(?) Elsor			Spitalfields, London	needlewoman
30274	Ely	Jacques	1801	?, Poland [?, Prussia]			Julia Davis	Westminster, London	
30273	Ely	Julia	1822	Exeter, Devon	(?) Davis		Jacques Ely	Westminster, London	jeweller
8629	Emanuel	Abigail	1820	Middlesex, London	Yehuda Simmons		Philip Emanuel	Aldgate, London	general dealer
4418	Emanuel	Abraham	1795	?, Germany			Adele (?)	Birmingham	independent
6108	Emanuel	Abraham	1817	Southwark, London	Uzziel (Azreal) Emanuel	Jane Solomonson	Clara Joseph	Marylebone, London	rag + metal dealer
12731	Emanuel	Abraham	1820	Peterborough, Cambridgeshire				Coventry, Warwickshire	watch manufacturer
6123	Emanuel	Abraham	1844	Aldgate, London	Barnet Emanuel	Amelia Isaacs	Sarah Samuel	Aldgate, London	
4429	Emanuel	Abraham Alfred	1843	Birmingham	Michael Emanuel	Frances (?)		Birmingham	
3969	Emanuel	Abraham Leon (Levi)	1848	Portsmouth, Hampshire	Henry Michael Emanuel	Anne Moses	Julia Lazarus	Portsmouth, Hampshire	
21573	Emanuel	Adelaide	1837	Whitechapel, London	Emanuel Emanuel	Mary (?)		Spitalfields, London	umbrella maker
28023	Emanuel	Adelaide	1850	Spitalfields, London	(?) Emanuel			Spitalfields, London	
4419	Emanuel	Adele	1791	?, Germany			Abraham Emanuel	Birmingham	
15167	Emanuel	Alfred	1850	Shoreditch, London	David Emanuel	Amelia Davis		Shoreditch, London	
8636	Emanuel	Amelia	1811	Aldgate, London	Abraham Isaacs		Barnet Emanuel	Aldgate, London	orange dealer
15165	Emanuel	Amelia	1821	Birmingham	Morris (Menachem) Davis		David Emanuel	Shoreditch, London	
352	Emanuel	Amelia	1841	Spitalfields, London	John (Jacob) Emanuel	Frances Levy		Spitalfields, London	scholar
8634	Emanuel	Amelia	1850	Aldgate, London	Philip Emanuel	Abigail Simmonds	Samuel Hyams	Aldgate, London	
24101	Emanuel	Amin	1809	City, London	Emanuel Emanuel	Julia (?)	(?)	Bloomsbury, London	
19558	Emanuel	Ann	1821	Whitechapel, London	Abraham Emanuel	Elizabeth (?)		Covent Garden, London	
3965	Emanuel	Anne	1813	Gosport, Hampshire	Joseph Moses	Catherine Symonds	Henry Michael Emanuel	Portsmouth, Hampshire	
4066	Emanuel	Annie	1848	Southampton, Hampshire	Samuel Michael Emanuel	Sarah Jacobs		Southampton, Hampshire	
23229	Emanuel	Appy	1791	Plymouth, Devon	(?)		Ezekiel (Uzziel) Emanuel	Hammersmith, London	
3959	Emanuel	Arthur	1843	Portsmouth, Hampshire	Ezekiel Emanuel	Rebecca Lewis		Portsmouth, Hampshire	
8635	Emanuel	Barnet	1804	?, London	Moshe Emanuel		Amelia Isaacs	Aldgate, London	orange dealer
8638	Emanuel	Barnet (Baruch)	1805	Poznan, Poland [Posen, Prussia]	Menachem Manly		Catherine Moses	Aldgate, London	cap manufacturer

ID	surname	given names	born	birthplace	father	mother	spouse 1	1851 residence	1851 occupation
4100	Emanuel	Barrow	1842	Portsmouth, Hampshire	Emanuel Emanuel	Julia Moss		Portsmouth, Hampshire	
3967	Emanuel	Benjamin Elkin	1842	Portsmouth, Hampshire	Henry Michael Emanuel	Anne Moses	Annie Stanley	Portsmouth, Hampshire	
21571	Emanuel	Betsey	1832	Whitechapel, London	Emanuel Emanuel	Mary (?)		Spitalfields, London	
16073	Emanuel	Braham	1841	Covent Garden, London	Moses (Moss) Emanuel	Elizabeth (?)		St Giles, London	
3658	Emanuel	Caroline	1812	?, London	Michael Benjamin		Morris Emanuel	Aldgate, London	
13393	Emanuel	Caroline	1830	Canterbury, Kent	(?) Emanuel			Spitalfields, London	plain cook
19898	Emanuel	Catherine	1781	Aldgate, London	(?)		Joseph Emanuel	Aldgate, London	
8639	Emanuel	Catherine	1801	Aldgate, London	Raphael Moses		Baruch (Barnet) Emanuel]	Aldgate, London	
12927	Emanuel	Catherine	1806	?, Germany	(?)		Simon Emanuel	Spitalfields, London	
10748	Emanuel	Catherine	1848	Spitalfields, London	John (Jacob) Emanuel	Frances Levy		Spitalfields, London	scholar
4423	Emanuel	Charles Alfred	1834	Birmingham	Michael Emanuel	Frances (?)		Birmingham	
6109	Emanuel	Clara	1818	Southwark, London	Abraham Joseph		Abraham Emanuel	Marylebone, London	
4422	Emanuel	Clara	1831	Birmingham	Michael Emanuel	Frances (?)		Birmingham	
15164	Emanuel	David	1820	Whitechapel, London	Lewis (Yehuda) Emanuel	(?Rachel Hendriks?)	Amelia Davis	Shoreditch, London	dealer in millinery
24102	Emanuel	Edward	1834	St Giles, London	Amin Emanuel	(?)		Bloomsbury, London	
4426	Emanuel	Elias	1839	Birmingham	Michael Emanuel	Frances (?)	Annie Flora Lazarus	Birmingham	
19557	Emanuel	Eliza	1820	Whitechapel, London	Abraham Emanuel	Elizabeth (?)		Covent Garden, London	
220	Emanuel	Eliza	1832	Whitechapel, London	Joseph Emanuel	Jane Lazarus	Samuel Abrahams	Spitalfields, London	
4098	Emanuel	Eliza	1837	Portsmouth, Hampshire	Emanuel Emanuel	Julia Moss		Portsmouth, Hampshire	
18328	Emanuel	Eliza H	1800	Aldgate, London	Abraham Lyon Moses	Abigail Lazarus	Morris Joel Emanuel	Cheltenham, Gloucestershire	landed + stock proprietor
28564	Emanuel	Elizabeth	1781	Spitalfields, London	(?)		(?) Emanuel	Spitalfields, London	clothes dealer
8630	Emanuel	Elizabeth	1786	Middlesex, London	(?)		(?) Emanuel	Aldgate, London	
19555	Emanuel	Elizabeth	1787	?, London	(?)		Abraham Emanuel	Covent Garden, London	annuitant
16071	Emanuel	Elizabeth	1810	Tottenham, London	Menahem Mendel		Moses (Moss) Emanuel	St Giles, London	
30243	Emanuel	Elizabeth	1815	Covent Garden, London	(?) Emanuel			Holborn, London	artificial florist
8637	Emanuel	Elizabeth	1846	?, London	Barnet Emanuel	Amelia Isaacs	Isaac Lewis	Aldgate, London	scholar
19896	Emanuel	Elizabeth	1849	Aldgate, London	Morris Emanuel	Caroline Benjamin		Aldgate, London	
8633	Emanuel	Elizabeth (Sarah)	1849	Aldgate, London	Philip Emanuel	Abigail Simmonds		Aldgate, London	scholar
6105	Emanuel	Elliot	1848	Marylebone, London	Abraham Emanuel	Clara (?)	Jane Isaacs	Marylebone, London	
30242	Emanuel	Ellis	1796	Covent Garden, London				Holborn, London	artificial florist
24005	Emanuel	Emanuel	1782	City, London			Julia (?)	Bloomsbury, London	diamond merchant
3987	Emanuel	Emanuel	1808	Fitzrovia, London	Moses Emanuel	Kitty (?)	Julia Moss	Portsmouth, Hampshire	silversmith, magistrate + City Councillor
269	Emanuel	Emanuel	1819	Spitalfields, London	(?) ?Jacobs			Aldgate, London	waiter
3950	Emanuel	Emanuel	1830	Portsmouth, Hampshire	Ezekiel Emanuel	Rebecca Lewis	Eliza (Lizzie) Lewis	Portsmouth, Hampshire	goldsmith's assistant
221	Emanuel	Emanuel	1834	?, London	Joseph Emanuel	Jane Lazarus		Whitechapel, London	teacher (Jewish Free School)
4099	Emanuel	Emanuel	1839	Portsmouth, Hampshire	Emanuel Emanuel	Julia Moss	Kate Levin	Portsmouth, Hampshire	
4428	Emanuel	Emanuel	1843	Birmingham	Michael Emanuel	Frances (?)		Birmingham	
16075	Emanuel	Emanuel	1848	Covent Garden, London	Moses (Moss) Emanuel	Elizabeth (?)		St Giles, London	
10469	Emanuel	Esther	1815	Deal, Kent	(?) Emanuel	Priscilla (?)		Mile End, London	
15660	Emanuel	Esther	1835	?, Poland	Mark Emanuel	Rose (?)		Aldgate, London	tailoress
20084	Emanuel	Eve	1819	Strand, London	Michael Braham		Lawrence Emanuel	Marylebone, London	
3954	Emanuel	Ezekiel	1801	?, London	Moses Emanuel	Kitty (?)	Rebecca Lewis	Portsmouth, Hampshire	goldsmith

185

ID	surname	given names	born	birthplace	father	mother	spouse 1	1851 residence	1851 occupation
23228	Emanuel	Ezekiel (Uzziel)	1786	Plymouth, Devon			Appy (?)	Hammersmith, London	commission agent
4421	Emanuel	Frances	1809	Birmingham	Avraham HaCohen		Michael Emanuel	Birmingham	
3957	Emanuel	Frances	1838	Portsmouth, Hampshire	Ezekiel Emanuel	Rebecca Lewis		Portsmouth, Hampshire	
21011	Emanuel	Frances	1850	Marylebone, London	Abraham Emanuel	Clara Joseph		Marylebone, London	
421	Emanuel	Frances	1815	Whitechapel, London	Henry Levy	Simmy Levy	John (Jacob) Emanuel	Spitalfields, London	
222	Emanuel	George Joseph	1837	Whitechapel, London	Joseph Emanuel	Jane Lazarus	Elizabeth (Lizzie) Hyman	Whitechapel, London	teacher (Jewish Free School)
354	Emanuel	Guldah (Golda)	1843	Aldgate, London	Barnet Emanuel	Amelia Isaacs		Aldgate, London	scholar
5044	Emanuel	Hannah	1767	Portsmouth, Hampshire	Levy Isaac	Boonley Lazarus	Michael Emanuel	Portsmouth, Hampshire	gentlewoman
26671	Emanuel	Hannah	1798	Spitalfields, London	(?)		(?) Emanuel	Spitalfields, London	hawker
30470	Emanuel	Hannah	1809	?, London	Abraham Levy		Michael Emanuel	Mayfair, London	
10474	Emanuel	Hannah	1810	?, London	Mosely Solomon		Lipman Emanuel	Mile End, London	
8631	Emanuel	Hannah	1842	Aldgate, London	Philip Emanuel	Abigail Simmonds	Morris Myers	Aldgate, London	scholar
10749	Emanuel	Hannah	1850	Spitalfields, London	John (Jacob) Emanuel	Frances Levy		Spitalfields, London	
17757	Emanuel	Henry	1808	Aldgate, London	Joel Emanuel	Julia (Juliet) Lazarus	Rosalie Josephs	Aldgate, London	formerly goldsmith
18955	Emanuel	Henry	1822	Deal, Kent				Whitechapel, London	general agent
20088	Emanuel	Henry	1830	Soho, London	Uzziel (Azreal) Emanuel	Jane Solomonson	Hannah Benjamin	Hammersmith, London	
3952	Emanuel	Henry	1844	Portsmouth, Hampshire	Ezekiel Emanuel	Rebecca Lewis		Portsmouth, Hampshire	
16074	Emanuel	Henry	1844	Covent Garden, London	Moses (Moss) Emanuel	Elizabeth (?)		St Giles, London	
10747	Emanuel	Henry	1846	Spitalfields, London	John (Jacob) Emanuel	Frances Levy		Spitalfields, London	scholar
30471	Emanuel	Henry (Harry)	1830	Aldgate, London	Michael Emanuel	Hannah Levy	Rosalie Coster	Mayfair, London	
4060	Emanuel	Henry Herschel	1836	Southampton, Hampshire	Samuel Michael Emanuel	Sarah Jacobs	Julia Spier	Southampton, Hampshire	assistant silversmith + pawnbroker
18329	Emanuel	Henry Joel	1846	Acton, London	Morris Joel Emanuel	Eliza H Moses	Emma Sarah Langdon	Cheltenham, Gloucestershire	
3964	Emanuel	Henry Michael	1807	Portsmouth, Hampshire	Michael Emanuel	Hannah Isaac	Anne Moses	Portsmouth, Hampshire	silversmith
8447	Emanuel	Henry Osborne	1849	Portsmouth, Hampshire	Judah Emanuel	Phoebe (?)		Portsmouth, Hampshire	
3966	Emanuel	Isaac Henry	1840	Portsmouth, Hampshire	Henry Michael Emanuel	Anne Moses		Portsmouth, Hampshire	
4065	Emanuel	Isaac Samuel	1842	Southampton, Hampshire	Samuel Michael Emanuel	Sarah Jacobs		Southampton, Hampshire	
423	Emanuel	Jacob	1841	?, London	Simon Emanuel	Catherine (?)		Spitalfields, London	
218	Emanuel	Jane	1801	Gainsborough, Lincolnshire	Asher (Lewis) Halevi Lazarus		Joseph Emanuel	Spitalfields, London	umbrella maker
4069	Emanuel	Jane	1811	?, London	Henry Jacobs	Kitty Samuel	Isaac Michael Emanuel	Southampton, Hampshire	
21008	Emanuel	Jane	1844	Marylebone, London	Abraham Emanuel	Clara Joseph		Marylebone, London	
6114	Emanuel	Jane	1846	Aldgate, London	Philip Emanuel	Abigail Simmonds		Aldgate, London	scholar
24103	Emanuel	Janette	1837	St Pancras, London	Amin Emanuel	(?)		Bloomsbury, London	
18533	Emanuel	Jeannette	1850	?, London	Solomon Emanuel	Phoebe Benjamin		Soho, London	
17754	Emanuel	Joel	1767	Bavaria, Germany	Menahem		Julia (Juliet) Lazarus	Aldgate, London	retired merchant
4067	Emanuel	Joel	1845	Southampton, Hampshire	Samuel Michael Emanuel	Sarah Jacobs	Georgiana Rousseau	Southampton, Hampshire	
4103	Emanuel	Joel Edward	1850	Portsmouth, Hampshire	Emanuel Emanuel	Julia Moss		Portsmouth, Hampshire	
5045	Emanuel	John	1779	Portsmouth, Hampshire				Portsmouth, Hampshire	
425	Emanuel	John (Jacob)	1815	Spitalfields, London	Jonah Emanuel		Frances Levy	Spitalfields, London	general dealer
9939	Emanuel	John Herbert	1832	City, London	Uzziel (Azreal) Emanuel	Jane Solomonson	Harriet Gabriel	Lambeth, London	rag merchant's assistant
8448	Emanuel	John Osborne	1851	Portsmouth, Hampshire	Judah Emanuel	Phoebe (?)		Portsmouth, Hampshire	
217	Emanuel	Joseph	1801	Portsmouth, Hampshire	Solomon (?Emanuel)		Jane Lazarus	Spitalfields, London	umbrella maker

ID	surname	given names	born	birthplace	father	mother	spouse 1	1851 residence	1851 occupation
20086	Emanuel	Joseph	1848	Marylebone, London	Lawrence Emanuel	Eve Braham	Elizabeth Angel	Marylebone, London	scholar
19897	Emanuel	Joseph	1850	Aldgate, London	Morris Emanuel	Caroline Benjamin		Aldgate, London	
3968	Emanuel	Joseph Moses	1845	Portsmouth, Hampshire	Henry Michael Emanuel	Anne Moses		Portsmouth, Hampshire	
8445	Emanuel	Judah	1803	Aldgate, London			Phoebe (?)	Portsmouth, Hampshire	general dealer
24100	Emanuel	Julia	1779	City, London	(?)		Emanuel Emanuel	Bloomsbury, London	
4097	Emanuel	Julia	1813	Plymouth, Devon	Barrow Moss	Sarah (Sally) Isaac	Emanuel Emanuel	Portsmouth, Hampshire	
19556	Emanuel	Julia	1816	Whitechapel, London	Abraham Emanuel	Elizabeth (?)		Covent Garden, London	
2416	Emanuel	Julia	1821	Middlesex, London	(?)		Lewis Emanuel	Hull, Yorkshire	clothier
23230	Emanuel	Julia	1823	?, London	Ezekiel (Uzziel) Emanuel	Appy (?)	Barnard Lyon	Hammersmith, London	
9941	Emanuel	Julia	1827	Southwark, London	Uzziel Emanuel	Jane Solomonson	Lyon (Lionel) Barnard	Hammersmith, London	
17760	Emanuel	Julia	1836	Aldgate, London	Henry Emanuel	Rosalie Josephs	Guillaume Frederic Isidore Costa	Aldgate, London	scholar
359	Emanuel	Julia	1839	Aldgate, London	Barnet Emanuel	Amelia Isaacs		Aldgate, London	
3962	Emanuel	Kate	1826	Middlesex, London	Israel Emanuel		Emanuel Hyams	Portsmouth, Hampshire	
22756	Emanuel	Kate	1831	Spitalfields, London	(?) Emanuel			Whitechapel, London	general servant
6972	Emanuel	Kate	1833	Aldgate, London	Barnet Emanuel	Amelia Isaacs		Aldgate, London	
3956	Emanuel	Kate	1835	Portsmouth, Hampshire	Ezekiel Emanuel	Rebecca Lewis		Portsmouth, Hampshire	
2760	Emanuel	Kate	1840	Southampton, Hampshire	Samuel Michael Emanuel	Sarah Jacobs	Henry Jacobs	Southampton, Hampshire	
4101	Emanuel	Kate	1845	Portsmouth, Hampshire	Emanuel Emanuel	Julia Moss	Philip Magnus	Portsmouth, Hampshire	
20083	Emanuel	Lawrence	1821	Southwark, London	Uzziel (Azreal) Emanuel	Jane Solomonson	Eve Braham	Marylebone, London	general dealer
3960	Emanuel	Lawrence (Lawrie)	1850	Portsmouth, Hampshire	Ezekiel Emanuel	Rebecca Lewis		Portsmouth, Hampshire	
12929	Emanuel	Lazarus	1843	?, London	Simon Emanuel	Catherine (?)		Spitalfields, London	
30244	Emanuel	Leah	1817	Covent Garden, London	(?) Emanuel			Holborn, London	artificial florist
4425	Emanuel	Leah	1837	Birmingham	Michael Emanuel	Frances (?)	Elkan Davies	Birmingham	
4062	Emanuel	Leon	1838	Southampton, Hampshire	Samuel Michael Emanuel	Sarah Jacobs	Mary Ollendorf	Southampton, Hampshire	
17759	Emanuel	Leonard	1835	Aldgate, London	Henry Emanuel	Rosalie Josephs		Aldgate, London	scholar
2417	Emanuel	Lewis	1819	Portsmouth, Hampshire			Julia (?)	Hull, Yorkshire	tailor + shopman
219	Emanuel	Lewis	1829	?, London	Joseph Emanuel	Jane Lazarus	Amelia Hart	Spitalfields, London	
7742	Emanuel	Lewis	1832	Portsmouth, Hampshire	Ezekiel Emanuel	Rebecca Lewis	Julia Salomons	Portsmouth, Hampshire	
6125	Emanuel	Lewis	1837	Aldgate, London	Barnet Emanuel	Amelia Isaacs	Kate Benjamin	Aldgate, London	fruit merchant
8632	Emanuel	Lewis	1844	Aldgate, London	Philip Emanuel	Abigail Simmonds		Aldgate, London	scholar
15166	Emanuel	Lewis	1845	Whitechapel, London	David Emanuel	Amelia Davis		Shoreditch, London	
30472	Emanuel	Lionel	1833	Aldgate, London	Michael Emanuel	Hannah Levy		Mayfair, London	
6946	Emanuel	Lipman	1804	Deal, Kent	Emanuel (Menachem Mendel) Emanuel	(?Amelia Levy?)	Hannah Mosely	Mile End, London	dealer in sponges
3958	Emanuel	Lizzy	1841	Portsmouth, Hampshire	Ezekiel Emanuel	Rebecca Lewis	Philip Cohen	Portsmouth, Hampshire	
24104	Emanuel	Louis	1838	City, London	Amin Emanuel	(?)		Bloomsbury, London	
427	Emanuel	Lydia	1826	?, London	(?) Emanuel	Rachel (?)		Spitalfields, London	umbrella maker
16223	Emanuel	Manuel (Menahem Menky)	1802	Shoreditch, London	Judah Emanuel	Hatty (Esther)	Matilda Pass	Clerkenwell, London	rag merchant
28565	Emanuel	Maria	1821	Spitalfields, London	(?) Emanuel	Elizabeth		Spitalfields, London	tailoress
4073	Emanuel	Maria	1837	Portsmouth, Hampshire	Henry Michael Emanuel	Anne Moses	Henry Lewis	Portsmouth, Hampshire	boarding school pupil
15661	Emanuel	Marian	1842	?, Poland	Mark Emanuel	Rose (?)		Aldgate, London	scholar
15658	Emanuel	Mark	1797	?, Poland			Rose (?)	Aldgate, London	tailor

ID	surname	given names	born	birthplace	father	mother	spouse 1	1851 residence	1851 occupation
21569	Emanuel	Mary	1793	Whitechapel, London	(?)		Emanuel Emanuel	Spitalfields, London	clothes dealer
4424	Emanuel	Mary	1835	Birmingham	Michael Emanuel	Frances (?)	Maurice Michaels	Birmingham	
358	Emanuel	Mary	1836	Aldgate, London	Barnet Emanuel	Amelia Isaacs		Aldgate, London	tailoress
17755	Emanuel	Mary Ann	1805	City, London	Joel Emanuel	Julia (Juliet) Lazarus		Aldgate, London	
4427	Emanuel	Mathilda	1841	Birmingham	Michael Emmanuel	Frances (?)	Abraham Harris	Birmingham	
16224	Emanuel	Matilda	1813	Aldgate, London	David Pass (Paz de Leon)	Rebecca de Jacob Selomoh Solomons	Manuel (Menahem Menky) Emanuel	Clerkenwell, London	
4420	Emanuel	Michael	1799	Gdansk, Poland [Danzig, Prussia]			Frances (?)	Birmingham	pawnbroker
30469	Emanuel	Michael	1804	Aldgate, London	Joel Emanuel	Julia (Juliet) Lazarus	Hannah Levy	Mayfair, London	silversmith + jeweller master
4058	Emanuel	Michael	1835	Southampton, Hampshire	Samuel Michael Emanuel	Sarah Jacobs	Eleanor Spier	Southampton, Hampshire	assistant silversmith + pawnbroker
20087	Emanuel	Michael	1849	?Marylebone, London	Lawrence Emanuel	Eve Braham		Marylebone, London	scholar
3949	Emanuel	Michael Henry	1851	Portsmouth, Hampshire	Henry Michael Emanuel	Ann Moses	Julia Jacobs	Portsmouth, Hampshire	
4070	Emanuel	Michael Isaac	1841	Southampton, Hampshire	Michael Emanuel	Martha Jacob	Isabel (Isobel) Jacobs	Southampton, Hampshire	
3659	Emanuel	Morris	1812	Portsmouth, Hampshire	Joseph Emanuel	Catherine (?)	Caroline Benjamin	Aldgate, London	coffee house keeper
3961	Emanuel	Moses	1761	Steinhardt, Bavaria, Germany			Kitty Aaron	Portsmouth, Hampshire	retired silversmith
28021	Emanuel	Moses	1794	Canterbury, Kent			(?)	Spitalfields, London	general dealer
3951	Emanuel	Moses	1846	Portsmouth, Hampshire				Portsmouth, Hampshire	
16070	Emanuel	Moses (Moss)	1802	Tottenham, London	Abraham Emanuel		Elizabeth b. Menahem Mendel	St Giles, London	clothes salesman + timber merchant
4102	Emanuel	Moses Maurice	1847	Portsmouth, Hampshire	Emanuel Emanuel	Julia Moss	Jeanne Marguerite Cremnitz	Portsmouth, Hampshire	
21572	Emanuel	Moss	1834	Whitechapel, London	Emanuel Emanuel	Mary (?)		Spitalfields, London	cigar maker
343	Emanuel	Moss (Moses)	1830	?, London	Barnet Emanuel	Amelia Isaacs	Fanny Cohen	Aldgate, London	fruit dealer
22898	Emanuel	Phaba	1781	Plymouth, Devon			(?) Emanuel	Wapping, London	dealer in clothes
340	Emanuel	Philip	1818	Middlesex, London	Menachem Emanuel	Elizabeth (?)	Abigail Simmons	Aldgate, London	general dealer + clothier
8446	Emanuel	Phoebe	1811	Chatham, Kent			Judah Emanuel	Portsmouth, Hampshire	
10470	Emanuel	Phoebe	1817	Deal, Kent	(?) Emanuel	Priscilla (?)		Mile End, London	
19559	Emanuel	Phoebe	1823	Whitechapel, London	Abraham Emanuel	Elizabeth (?)		Covent Garden, London	
832	Emanuel	Phoebe	1826	Shoreditch, London	Mark Benjamin	Elizabeth Solomon	Solomon Emanuel	Soho, London	
23231	Emanuel	Phoebe	1829	?, London	Ezekiel (Uzziel) Emanuel	Appy (?)		Hammersmith, London	
10468	Emanuel	Priscilla	1780	Margate, Kent	(?)		(?) Emanuel	Mile End, London	annuitant
428	Emanuel	Rachel	1801	?, London	(?)		(?) Emanuel	Spitalfields, London	monthly nurse
21009	Emanuel	Ralph	1845	Marylebone, London	Abraham Emanuel	Clara Joseph		Marylebone, London	
3955	Emanuel	Rebecca	1807	Brighton, Sussex	Hyam Lewis	Susan (Sally) Harris	Ezekiel Emanuel	Portsmouth, Hampshire	
12930	Emanuel	Rebecca	1845	?, London	Simon Emanuel	Catherine (?)		Spitalfields, London	
4068	Emanuel	Rebecca	1849	Southampton, Hampshire	Samuel Michael Emanuel	Sarah Jacobs	Jacob Flatau	Southampton, Hampshire	
20085	Emanuel	Rosa (Rose)	1845	?Marylebone, London	Lawrence Emanuel	Eve Braham		Marylebone, London	scholar
17758	Emanuel	Rosalie	1814	Whitechapel, London	Shlomeh Aryeh Zalman Leib Josephs	Deborah (?)	Henry Emanuel	Aldgate, London	
15659	Emanuel	Rose	1799	?, Poland	(?)		Mark Emanuel	Aldgate, London	

ID	surname	given names	born	birthplace	father	mother	spouse 1	1851 residence	1851 occupation
12928	Emanuel	Samuel	1835	?, London	Simon Emanuel	Catherine (?)		Spitalfields, London	
3963	Emanuel	Samuel	1849	Portsmouth, Hampshire	Henry Michael Emanuel	Anne Moses		Portsmouth, Hampshire	
28567	Emanuel	Samuel	1850	Spitalfields, London				Spitalfields, London	
4056	Emanuel	Samuel Michael	1803	Portsmouth, Hampshire	Michael Emanuel		Sarah Jacobs	Southampton, Hampshire	silversmith + pawnbroker
4057	Emanuel	Sarah	1818	?, London	Henry Jacobs	Kitty Samuel	Samuel Michael Emanuel	Southampton, Hampshire	
21570	Emanuel	Sarah	1827	Whitechapel, London	Emanuel Emanuel	Mary (?)		Spitalfields, London	
28022	Emanuel	Sarah	1827	Canterbury, Kent	Moses Emanuel	(?)		Spitalfields, London	milliner
8309	Emanuel	Sarah	1833	?, Poland	(?)		Hyman Isaacs	North Shields, Tyne & Wear	
6973	Emanuel	Sarah	1834	Aldgate, London	Barnet Emanuel	Amelia Isaacs	(?) Levy	Aldgate, London	tailoress
21010	Emanuel	Sarah	1846	Marylebone, London	Abraham Emanuel	Clara Joseph		Marylebone, London	
28566	Emanuel	Sarah	1849	Spitalfields, London	(?) Emanuel			Spitalfields, London	
426	Emanuel	Sarah (Simha)	1842	Spitalfields, London	John (Jacob) Emanuel	Frances Levy		Spitalfields, London	scholar
429	Emanuel	Sarah Mary	1817	?, London	(?) Emanuel	Rachel (?)		Spitalfields, London	umbrella maker
5914	Emanuel	Simeon	1833	Covent Garden, London	Moses (Moss) Emanuel	Elizabeth (?)	Caroline Magnus	St Giles, London	apprentice cabinet maker
422	Emanuel	Simon	1782	?, Poland			Catherine (?)	Spitalfields, London	shoe maker
7446	Emanuel	Solomon	1826	?Southwark, London	Uzziel (Azreal) Emanuel	Jane Solomonson	Phoebe Benjamin	Soho, London	rag merchant + dealer in marine stores
223	Emanuel	Sylvester	1840	Wapping, London	Joseph Emanuel	Jane Lazarus		Spitalfields, London	
9940	Emanuel	Uzziel (Azreal)	1797	City, London	Yehuda Edel		Jane Solomonson	Hammersmith, London	rag merchant
6110	Emanuel	Woolf	1829	Whitechapel, London	Emanuel Emanuel	Mary (?)	Jane Benjamin	Spitalfields, London	dealer in fruit
24639	Emanuels	Samuel	1823	Middlesex, London			Eleanor Apthorp	Waterloo, London	professor of dancing
28095	Embden	Ram	1826	?, Holland				Spitalfields, London	cigar maker
18197	Embden (Emdin)	Rosetta	1781	?, Holland	(?) Embden			Mile End, London	
1400	Emden	Abraham	1799	Plymouth, Devon	(? Eleazar) Emden	Kitty (?)	Lydia (?)	Plymouth, Devon	pawnbroker
17614	Emden	Amelia	1816	Whitechapel, London	(?) Levy	Catherine (?)	Elias Emden	Spitalfields, London	
1405	Emden	Caroline	1848	Plymouth, Devon	Abraham Emden	Lydia (?)		Plymouth, Devon	
353	Emden	Catherine (Kate)	1851	Spitalfields, London	Elias Emden	Amelia Levy	Lewis Marks	Spitalfields, London	
1403	Emden	Clare (Clara)	1843	Plymouth, Devon	Abraham Emden	Lydia (?)	H--- Sampson	Plymouth, Devon	
17613	Emden	Elias	1810	?, Holland			Rosetta Lazarus	Spitalfields, London	shoemaker
1402	Emden	Eliezer (Eleazar)	1840	Plymouth, Devon	Abraham Emden	Lydia (?)	Eliza Joseph	Plymouth, Devon	scholar
30426	Emden	Elizabeth (Betsy)	1842	?, London	Joseph Emden	Rachael Marks	Morris Krukziener	Aldgate, London	
17612	Emden	Hannah	1848	Aldgate, London	Elias Emden	Amelia Levy	Louis Granger	Spitalfields, London	
30428	Emden	Isaac	1848	?, London	Joseph Emden	Rachael Marks		Aldgate, London	
15777	Emden	Jane	1838	Aldgate, London	Joseph Emden	Rachael Marks		Aldgate, London	scholar
30430	Emden	Jane	1839	?London	Joseph Emden	Rachael Marks	Henry Isaacs	Aldgate, London	
17610	Emden	Jane	1840	Whitechapel, London	Elias Emden	Rosetta Lazarus		Spitalfields, London	
30424	Emden	Joseph	1811	?, London	Woolf Emden		Rachael Marks	Aldgate, London	general dealer
17611	Emden	Leah	1842	Aldgate, London	Elias Emden	Rosetta Lazarus	Lewis Samuel	Spitalfields, London	
1401	Emden	Lydia	1811	Plymouth, Devon				Plymouth, Devon	
1406	Emden	Mark	1849	Plymouth, Devon	Abraham Emden	Lydia (?)	Rachel Michael	Plymouth, Devon	
17609	Emden	Phoebe	1838	Whitechapel, London	Elias Emden	Rosetta Lazarus	Harris Rosenbloom	Spitalfields, London	
6554	Emden	Rachael	1814	?Aldgate, London	Simon Marks	Kitty Jacobs	Joseph Emden	Aldgate, London	
22921	Emden	Ralph	1792	Hackney, London				Wapping, London	stay maker
1325	Emden	Rebecca	1814	Plymouth, Devon	(?) (Franco?)		Wolf Emden	Plymouth, Devon	

ID	surname	given names	born	birthplace	father	mother	spouse 1	1851 residence	1851 occupation
30427	Emden	Simon	1846	?, London	Joseph Emden	Rachael Marks	Sarah Abrahams	Aldgate, London	
1404	Emden	Solomon	1845	Plymouth, Devon	Abraham Emden	Lydia (?)	Isadora Amelia Labatt	Plymouth, Devon	scholar
1324	Emden	Wolf	1811	Plymouth, Devon	(Solomon Emden?)	(Phoeby?) (?)	Rebecca (Franco?)	Plymouth, Devon	draper
30425	Emden	Woolf	1841	?, London	Joseph Emden	Rachael Marks		Aldgate, London	
18675	Endlick	Joseph	1818	?, Poland				Spitalfields, London	teacher of Hebrew
15610	Engel	Amelia	1832	Whitechapel, London	Jonas (Joseph) Engel	Sarah (Louisa) Barnett	A--- Mayer	Shoreditch, London	
5599	Engel	Bernard	1836	Whitechapel, London	Jonas (Joseph) Engel	Sarah (Louisa) Barnett	Kate Benjamin	Shoreditch, London	scholar
13635	Engel	Charles	1814	?, Poland [?, Prussia]			Dorothea (?)	Manchester	watchmaker
13636	Engel	Dorothea	1815	?, Poland [?, Prussia]	(?)		Charles Engel	Manchester	
15613	Engel	Elizabeth	1849	Shoreditch, London	Jonas (Joseph) Engel	Sarah (Louisa) Barnett		Shoreditch, London	
15611	Engel	Hannah	1834	Whitechapel, London	Jonas (Joseph) Engel	Sarah (Louisa) Barnett		Shoreditch, London	
5598	Engel	Jonas (Joseph)	1797	?, London	Issachar Berl (Behr?) Engel		Sarah (Louisa) Barnett	Shoreditch, London	umbrella + parasol mfr
15612	Engel	Julia	1847	Whitechapel, London	Jonas (Joseph) Engel	Sarah (Louisa) Barnett		Shoreditch, London	
5595	Engel	Lawrence	1838	Whitechapel, London	Jonas (Joseph) Engel	Sarah (Louisa) Barnett	Elizabeth Garcia	Shoreditch, London	
5601	Engel	Leon	1844	Whitechapel, London	Jonas Engel	Louisa Barnett		Shoreditch, London	scholar
5597	Engel	Samuel	1846	Whitechapel, London	Jonas (Joseph) Engel	Sarah (Louisa) Barnett		Shoreditch, London	
5600	Engel	Sarah (Louisa)	1810	?, London	Issachar HaCohen Barnett		Jonas Engel	Shoreditch, London	
21281	Engle	Albert	1839	Spitalfields, London				Edmonton, London	boarding school pupil
21282	Engle	Lawrence	1838	Spitalfields, London				Edmonton, London	boarding school pupil
17312	Enlick	Isaac	1820	?, Poland				Whitechapel, London	band? Maker
26476	Enoch	Elizabeth	1842	Bedford, Bedfordshire	Joseph Enoch	Mary Levy	Morris Sions	Bedford, Bedfordshire	
26475	Enoch	Hyman	1839	Bedford, Bedfordshire	Joseph Enoch	Mary Levy	Esther Brandon (Brandon Rodrigues)	Bedford, Bedfordshire	
26473	Enoch	Joseph	1809	?, Poland			Mary Levy	Bedford, Bedfordshire	jeweller + watchmaker
26474	Enoch	Mary	1809	Bedford, Bedfordshire	(?) Levy		Joseph Enoch	Bedford, Bedfordshire	
26477	Enoch	Moses	1844	Bedford, Bedfordshire	Joseph Enoch	Mary Levy		Bedford, Bedfordshire	
26478	Enoch	Rosa	1846	Bedford, Bedfordshire	Joseph Enoch	Mary Levy		Bedford, Bedfordshire	
18819	Enthoven	Amelia (Amy)	1839	Tower Hill, London	Henry Israel Enthoven	Ann (?)		Euston, London	scholar at home
18813	Enthoven	Ann	1797	Amsterdam, Holland	(?)		Henry Israel Enthoven	Euston, London	
18817	Enthoven	Catherine	1833	Tower Hill, London	Henry Israel Enthoven	Ann (?)		Euston, London	
18815	Enthoven	Frances	1824	Tower Hill, London	Henry Israel Enthoven	Ann (?)		Euston, London	
18818	Enthoven	Frederick	1835	Tower Hill, London	Henry Israel Enthoven	Ann (?)		Euston, London	scholar
18812	Enthoven	Henry Israel	1799	?, Holland	Israel Enthoven		Ann (?)	Euston, London	metal merchant + tin ---
18814	Enthoven	James Henry	1823	Tower Hill, London	Henry Israel Enthoven	Ann (?)	Matilda Lucas	Euston, London	metal merchant + tin ---
18816	Enthoven	John	1827	Tower Hill, London	Henry Israel Enthoven	Ann (?)	Sophia A (?)	Euston, London	metal merchant + tin ---
18820	Enthoven	Julia	1843	City, London	Henry Israel Enthoven	Ann (?)		Euston, London	scholar at home
2254	Ephraim	Adolphus	1849	Leeds, Yorkshire	Morris Ephraim	Selina A C (?)	Jane (?)	Leeds, Yorkshire	
25179	Ephraim	Henry	1790	Whitechapel, London				Finsbury, London	journeyman trimming maker + East India Company pensioner
20428	Ephraim	Joseph	1826	Amsterdam, Holland				Aldgate, London	tailor
2252	Ephraim	Morris	1822	?, Poland [?, Prussia]			Selina A. C. (?)	Leeds, Yorkshire	jewellery traveller
4430	Ephraim	Moses	1831	?, Poland				Birmingham	glazier
2253	Ephraim	Selina A C	1825	Leeds, Yorkshire				Leeds, Yorkshire	
18259	Epstein	Israel Hayman	1819	?, Russia			Euphemia (?)	Liverpool	student of St Aidan's

ID	surname	given names	born	birthplace	father	mother	spouse 1	1851 residence	1851 occupation
29473	Erdlick	Joseph	1818	?, Poland				Spitalfields, London	teacher of Hebrew
11892	Erlick	Abraham	1823	?, Poland [?, Prussia]				Whitechapel, London	tailor
2418	Ermorom	Jacob	1828	?, Germany				Hull, Yorkshire	cap maker
2419	Esberger	Charlotte	1821	Middlesex, London	(?) Esberger			Hull, Yorkshire	house servant
16935	Eschenschied	Henry	1823	?, Germany				Sheffield, Yorkshire	wine merchant
17655	Eschwege	Charles	1847	?, Germany	Morris Eschwege	Hanahen (?)	Louisa Isaacs	Aldgate, London	
17653	Eschwege	Hanahen	1818	?, Germany			Morris Eschwege	Aldgate, London	needlewoman
17654	Eschwege	Simon	1842	?, Germany	Morris Eschwege	Hanahen (?)	Leah Mendoza	Aldgate, London	
22081	Eskelbach	Amelia	1831	?, Russia [Betenheim, Russia]	(?) Eskelbach			Whitechapel, London	tailoress
14257	Eskell	?	1849	?, Lancashire	Albert (Abraham) Eskell	Sarah Eskell		Manchester	
4431	Eskell	Abraham Clifford	1824	Edinburgh, Scotland	Ezekiel Moses Eskell	Katherine (?)	Frances Eskell	Birmingham	surgeon dentist
5142	Eskell	Albert (Abraham)	1810	?, London	(?) Eskell		Sarah Eskell	Manchester	surgeon-dentist
14259	Eskell	Ann	1851	Manchester	Albert (Abraham) Eskell	Sarah Eskell		Manchester	
4432	Eskell	Frances	1827	Hull, Yorkshire	Phillip Eskell	Sophia Lyons		Birmingham	
7884	Eskell	Frederick Abraham	1818	?, Scotland	Philip Eskell	Sophia Lyons	Sarah Jordan	Manchester	dentist
14258	Eskell	Julia	1848	?Lancashire	Albert (Abraham) Eskell	Sarah Eskell	Isidor Saunders	Manchester	
31059	Eskell	Katherine	1797	Arundel, Sussex	(?Israel Abrahams)	(?Elizabeth Davids)	Ezekiel Moses Eskell	Newcastle Upon Tyne	jeweller's shop
7885	Eskell	Louis Ezekiel	1832	Edinburgh, Scotland	Ezekiel Moses Eskell	Katherine (?)	Emily Woolf	Newcastle Upon Tyne	assistant in jeweller's shop
31058	Eskell	Louisa	1838	Newcastle Upon Tyne	Ezekiel Moses Eskell	Katherine (?)		Newcastle Upon Tyne	scholar
31057	Eskell	Marian	1829	Edinburgh, Scotland	Ezekiel Moses Eskell	Katherine (?)		Newcastle Upon Tyne	assistant in jeweller's shop
4433	Eskell	Morris (Maurice)	1845	Birmingham	Abraham Eskell	Frances Eskell	Sarah Samuel	Birmingham	
4435	Eskell	Phillip	1786	?, Holland	Abraham Ezechiel Moses	(?) Saloman/Van Noorden	Sophia Lyons	Sheffield, Yorkshire	surgeon dentist
14256	Eskell	Sarah	1815	Sheffield, Yorkshire	Philip Eskell	Sophia Lyons	Albert (Abraham) Eskell	Manchester	
7951	Eskell	Sarah	1833	Middlesex, London	(?) Jordan		Frederick Abraham Eskell	Manchester	
4434	Eskell	Sophia	1799	?, Scotland	Herman Lyons		Philip Eskell	Sheffield, Yorkshire	
19899	Essinger	Louisa	1850	Bristol	Max Essinger	Rachel Solomon	Charles Julius Kino	Bloomsbury, London	
5822	Essinger	Max	1822	?, Germany	Solomon (Shlomeh Zalman) Essinger		Rachel Solomon	Bloomsbury, London	straw hat manufacturer master
5821	Essinger	Rachel	1827	Middlesex, London	Maurice Solomon	Louisa Raphael	Max Essinger	Bloomsbury, London	
12079	Estenber	Isaac	1826	Hamburg, Germany				Spitalfields, London	upholsterer
9203	Ezakyhah	Selim	1827	?, Germany				Whitechapel, London	tailor
23465	Ezekiel	Alfred	1840	Tiverton, Devon	Elias Ezekiel	Ellenor (?)		Liverpool	
14074	Ezekiel	Alfred A	1818	Newton Abbot, Devon [Newton, Devon]	(?Benjamin) Ezekiel	(?Florence) (?)	Angelica M (?)	Manchester	tailor + draper
14076	Ezekiel	Angelica M	1819	Liverpool	(?)		Alfred A Ezekiel	Manchester	
1451	Ezekiel	Benjamin	1815	Falmouth, Cornwall			Priscilla Holmes	Plymouth, Devon	confectioner
14078	Ezekiel	Benjamin	1848	Liverpool	Alfred A Ezekiel	Angelica M (?)		Manchester	
1456	Ezekiel	Benjamin	1849	Plymouth, Devon	Benjamin Ezekiel	Priscilla Holmes		Plymouth, Devon	
7600	Ezekiel	Elias	1798	Newton Abbot, Devon			Ellenor (?)	Liverpool	watchmaker
1454	Ezekiel	Elizabeth	1843	Plymouth, Devon	Benjamin Ezekiel	Priscilla Holmes		Plymouth, Devon	
16631	Ezekiel	Ellenor	1803	Birmingham	(?)		Elias Ezekiel	Liverpool	
14079	Ezekiel	Florence	1850	Manchester	Alfred A Ezekiel	Angelica M (?)		Manchester	
1119	Ezekiel	Hannah	1776	Redruth, Cornwall	Moses Jacob	Sarah Moses	Solomon Ezekiel	Penzance, Cornwall	
1453	Ezekiel	John	1840	Redruth, Cornwall	Benjamin Ezekiel	Priscilla Holmes		Plymouth, Devon	

ID	surname	given names	born	birthplace	father	mother	spouse 1	1851 residence	1851 occupation
14077	Ezekiel	Miriam	1846	Liverpool	Alfred A Ezekiel	Angelica M (?)		Manchester	
1455	Ezekiel	Moses	1845	Plymouth, Devon	Benjamin Ezekiel	Priscilla Holmes		Plymouth, Devon	
13905	Ezekiel	Phillip	1823	Tiverton, Devon				Manchester	tailor + draper
1452	Ezekiel	Priscilla	1817	Bath	(?) Holmes	Ann (?)		Plymouth, Devon	
1118	Ezekiel	Solomon	1781	Newton Abbot, Devon			Hannah Jacob	Penzance, Cornwall	tin plate worker
2420	Fajen	Louise	1830	Altona, Germany			Wilhelm Fajen	Hull, Yorkshire	
2421	Fajen	Wilhelm	1829	Hamburg, Germany			Louise (?)	Hull, Yorkshire	shipbroker's clerk
14071	Falck	James	1842	Middlesex, London				Manchester	scholar
7072	Falcke	Adelaide	1837	?Mayfair, London	Jacob Falcke	Hannah (?)	Aaron Wolfe	Marylebone, London	
7075	Falcke	Anna	1830	Westminster, London	(?)		Edward Falcke	Soho, London	
19906	Falcke	Antoinette	1850	Mayfair, London	David Falcke	Emily (?)		Mayfair, London	
7076	Falcke	Beare	1819	?, Germany [?, Prussia]	Falcke Behr		Eliza Levine	Norwich, Norfolk	pawnbroker
19905	Falcke	Blanche	1848	Mayfair, London	David Falcke	Emily (?)		Mayfair, London	
7067	Falcke	David	1818	Great Yarmouth, Norfolk	Jacob Falcke	Hannah (?)	Emily Isaacs	Mayfair, London	picture importer, antique furniture, bronze, curiosity + china dealer empl 2
7071	Falcke	Edward	1825	Great Yarmouth, Norfolk	(?Jacob) Falcke	(Hannah?) (?)	Anna (?)	Soho, London	dealer in articles of vertu
7077	Falcke	Eliza	1824	?, London	Myer Levine	Charlotte (?)	Beare Falcke	Norwich, Norfolk	
16315	Falcke	Elizabeth	1850	Soho, London	Edward Falcke	Anna (?)		Soho, London	
7070	Falcke	Elizah (Bella)	1832	Great Yarmouth, Norfolk	(?) Falcke			Bloomsbury, London	jeweller
7074	Falcke	Emily	1829	?Westminster, London	Samuel Isaacs		David Falcke	Mayfair, London	
24123	Falcke	Hannah	1798	Middlesex, London	(?)		Jacob Falcke	Bloomsbury, London	
7066	Falcke	Isaac	1819	Great Yarmouth, Norfolk	Jacob Falcke	Hannah (?)	Mary Ann Reid	Mayfair, London	picture importer, antique furniture, bronze, curiosity + china dealer
7068	Falcke	James	1815	Great Yarmouth, Norfolk	Jacob Falcke	Hannah (?)	Henrietta Edersheim	Great Yarmouth, Norfolk	picture dealer
7078	Falcke	Meyerbeer Philip	1850	Norwich, Norfolk	Beare Falcke	Eliza Levine		Norwich, Norfolk	
18436	Falcke	Uriah Philip	1848	Norwich, Norfolk	Beare Falcke	Eliza Levine		Norwich, Norfolk	
30929	Faldman	Aaron	1829	?, Poland				Hull, Yorkshire	hawker
14370	Falk	?	1850	Manchester	David Falk	Amelia Mayer		Manchester	
14369	Falk	Alfred	1848	Manchester	David Falk	Amelia Mayer		Manchester	
18438	Falk	Amelia	1843	?Manchester	David Falk	Amelia Mayer	Marcus Brasch	Manchester	
13856	Falk	Bertha	1831	Hamburg, Germany	(?) Falk			Manchester	
14367	Falk	David	1815	?, Poland [?, Prussia]			Fanny Mayer	Manchester	hardware dealer (warehouse)
14368	Falk	Fanny	1816	?, Poland [?, Prussia]	George Mayer	Amelia (Malka) (?)	David Falk	Manchester	
16877	Falk	Morris	1816	Gdansk, Poland [Danzig, Prussia]				Cambridge	traveller
30376	Falk	Moses	1825	?				Burton-on-Trent, Staffordshire	surgeon
11074	Fanry	Lemon	1831	?, Poland [?, Prussian Poland]				Aldgate, London	cap maker
11073	Fanry	Leon	1831	?, Poland [?, Prussian Poland]				Aldgate, London	shopman
7559	Faudel	Henry	1808	City, London	(?Samuel?) Faudel			Finsbury, London	wholesale furrier

ID	surname	given names	born	birthplace	father	mother	spouse 1	1851 residence	1851 occupation
5454	Feinberg	Catherine (Kate)	1819	Penzance, Cornwall	Barnet Asher Simmons	Flora Jacob	Hyman Feinberg	Newport, Glamorgan, Wales	broker
12772	Feinberg	Hyman	1811	?, Cornwall	Moses Feinberg		Catherine (Kate) Simmons	Newport, Glamorgan, Wales	broker
26316	Feiner?	Julia	1831	?, Hungary	(?) Feiner?			Aldgate, London	cap maker
26315	Feiner?	Rosetta	1833	?, Hungary	(?) Feiner?			Aldgate, London	cap maker
18337	Felarek	Bernhard	1821	Brandenburg, Germany				Brighton, Sussex	jeweller
18338	Felarek	Salheza	1823	Brandenburg, Germany				Brighton, Sussex	jeweller
8263	Feldman	Moses	1833	Shackey, Poland			Hannah Myers	Hull, Yorkshire	
20993	Ferdsburg	Naamy	1781	?, Poland	(?)		(?) Ferdsberg	Aldgate, London	
19033	Fernandes	Abraham	1831	?, Italy				Aldgate, London	general merchant
19031	Fernandes	Anna	1815	?, Poland [?, Prussia]	(?)		Marco Fernandes	Aldgate, London	manufacturer of embroidery
18970	Fernandes	Caroline	1807	Fareham, Hampshire	(?)		Francis Fernandes	Belgravia, London	cook
19032	Fernandes	Cecile	1850	Middlesex, London	Marco Fernandes	Anna (?)		Aldgate, London	
13185	Fernandes	David	1813	?London	Jacob Fernandez	Rebecca de Joseph Abendana	Rebecca Kincey	Whitechapel, London	shoemaker
11618	Fernandes	Elizabeth (Betsy)	1830	Middlesex, London	Isaac Fernandes	Sarah (?)	Moses Mendoza	Aldgate, London	bakeress
18969	Fernandes	Francis	1806	Madeira, Portugal			Caroline (?)	Belgravia, London	butler
13177	Fernandes	Jacob	1774	Whitechapel, London	David Fernandez	Miriam de Natan Espinosa	Rebecca de Joseph Abendana	Aldgate, London	china dealer
13179	Fernandes	Jacob	1819	?Whitechapel, London	Jacob Fernandez	Rebecca de Joseph Abendana	Simla (Simey, Simha) Gompertz	Whitechapel, London	clothes dealer
11617	Fernandes	Jacob	1827	Middlesex, London	Isaac Fernandes	Sarah (?)	Sarah Abrahams	Aldgate, London	traveller
13183	Fernandes	James	1849	Whitechapel, London	Jacob Fernandez	Simey (Simha) Gompertz		Whitechapel, London	
11619	Fernandes	Joseph	1833	City, London	Isaac Fernandes	Sarah (?)	Esther Asher	Aldgate, London	carver + gilder
7604	Fernandes	Marco	1815	?, Italy			Anna (?)	Aldgate, London	importer of foreign goods + babylinen + outfitting
13182	Fernandes	Michael	1846	Whitechapel, London	Jacob Fernandez	Simey (Simha) Gompertz		Whitechapel, London	
13186	Fernandes	Nathan	1835	Whitechapel, London	Jacob Fernandes		Rosa (?)	Aldgate, London	jeweller
13178	Fernandes	Rebecca	1779	Whitechapel, London	Joseph Abendana	(?Esther) (?)	Jacob de Abraham Leon	Aldgate, London	
13184	Fernandes	Samuel	1850	Whitechapel, London	Jacob Fernandez	Simey (Simha) Gompertz		Whitechapel, London	
11616	Fernandes	Sarah	1796	Middlesex, London	(?)		Isaac Fernandes	Aldgate, London	general dealer
13181	Fernandes	Sarah	1845	?, London	Jacob Fernandez	Simey (Simha) Gompertz		Whitechapel, London	
13180	Fernandes	Simla (Simey, Simha)	1819	?Holland	Michael Gompertz		Jacob Fernandes	Whitechapel, London	
11620	Fernandes	Solomon	1834	Middlesex, London	Isaac Fernandes	Sarah (?)		Aldgate, London	clicker
14458	Fichel	Sepinal C	1823	?, Germany			Rebecca (?)	Manchester	clerk
5900	Fileman	Benjamin	1841	Whitechapel, London	John Fileman	Mary (Miriam, Maria) Levy		Spitalfields, London	scholar
5902	Fileman	Elizabeth (Lizzie)	1848	Spitalfields, London	John Fileman	Mary (Miriam, Maria) Levy	Henry Levi	Spitalfields, London	scholar
18670	Fileman	Hannah (Annie)	1847	Spitalfields, London	John Fileman	Mary (Miriam, Maria) Levy		Spitalfields, London	scholar
5901	Fileman	Henry	1842	Whitechapel, London	John Fileman	Mary (Miriam, Maria) Levy	Theresa Clara Leopold	Spitalfields, London	scholar
5898	Fileman	John	1822	Spitalfields, London	Benjamin Fileman	Elizabeth (?)	Mary (Miriam, Maria) Levy	Spitalfields, London	general dealer
2818	Fileman	Maria	1820	Shoreditch, London	Benjamin Fileman	Elizabeth (?)		Shoreditch, London	

ID	surname	given names	born	birthplace	father	mother	spouse 1	1851 residence	1851 occupation
5899	Fileman	Mary (Miriam, Maria)	1823	Spitalfields, London	Jacob Levy	Hannah (?)	John Fileman	Spitalfields, London	
18671	Fileman	Myer	1851	Spitalfields, London	John Fileman	Mary (Miriam, Maria) Levy	Hannah Wolff	Spitalfields, London	
5897	Fileman (Freeman)	Elizabeth	1790	Spitalfields, London	Israel (?)		Benjamin Fileman	Spitalfields, London	general dealer
25112	Filipowski	Abrahajm	1850	Finsbury, London	Herschell Filipowski	Esther (?)		Finsbury, London	
25111	Filipowski	Concordia	1849	Finsbury, London	Herschell Filipowski	Esther (?)		Finsbury, London	scholar at home
25110	Filipowski	Denison	1847	Finsbury, London	Herschell Filipowski	Esther (?)		Finsbury, London	scholar at home
25108	Filipowski	Esther	1817	?, Poland	(?)		Herschell Filipowski	Finsbury, London	
25107	Filipowski	Herschell	1818	?, Poland			Esther (?)	Finsbury, London	printer
25109	Filipowski	Matilda	1836	?, Poland	Herschell Filipowski	Esther (?)		Finsbury, London	scholar at home
2632	Fine	Michael	1814	?, Ireland				Glasgow, Scotland	
27194	Finglestein	Isaac	1786	?, Poland			(?)	Aldgate, London	traveller
21028	Fink	Benjamin Josman	1847	Guernsey, Channel Islands	Moses Fink	Gertrude Ascher	Catherine Fink	St Peter Port, Guernsey, Channel Islands	
21027	Fink	Cornelia	1846	Guernsey, Channel Islands	Moses Fink	Gertrude Ascher		St Peter Port, Guernsey, Channel Islands	scholar
21026	Fink	Gertrude	1822	?, Poland [?, Prussia]	(?) Ascher		Moses Fink	St Peter Port, Guernsey, Channel Islands	tradesman's wife
29997	Fink	Henry	1801	Hanover, Germany				Whitechapel, London	tailor
2422	Fink	Hermann	1833	Plastau, Germany	Zvi Fink		Rebecca Volberg	Hull, Yorkshire	tailor
19637	Fink	Hirsch Henry	1821	?, Poland [?, Prussia]	Benjamin Josman Fink	Johannah Manassa	Amelia Oppenheim	St Peter Port, Guernsey, Channel Islands	dealer in jewellery, draper + pawnbroker
21030	Fink	Magnus	1850	Guernsey, Channel Islands	Moses Fink	Gertrude Ascher		St Peter Port, Guernsey, Channel Islands	
21029	Fink	Mark	1849	Guernsey, Channel Islands	Moses Fink	Gertrude Ascher	Amy Wilmot Levey	St Peter Port, Guernsey, Channel Islands	
26519	Fink	Moses	1810	?, Poland	Benjamin Josman Fink	Johannah Manassa	Gertrude Ascher	St Peter Port, Guernsey, Channel Islands	tradesman
21012	Fink	Rebecca	1828	?, Poland [?, Prussia]	(?) Fink			St Peter Port, Guernsey, Channel Islands	housekeeper
26520	Fink	Theodora	1851	Guernsey, Channel Islands	Moses Fink	Gertrude Ascher	Samuel Leon	St Peter Port, Guernsey, Channel Islands	
26521	Finsterer	Babette (Barbet)	1816	Furth, Bavaria, Germany	Isaac Leibman Leopold	Ruth (?)	Jacob Finsterer	Spitalfields, London	
26525	Finsterer	Isaac	1839	Whitechapel, London	Jacob Finsterer	Babette (Barbet) Leopold		Spitalfields, London	scholar
26522	Finsterer	Jacob	1802	?, Germany	Yehuda Leib		Babette (Barbet) Leopold	Spitalfields, London	dealer in jewellery
26524	Finsterer	Louisa Isabella	1837	Whitechapel, London	Jacob Finsterer	Babette (Barbet) Leopold	Joseph Henry Magnus	Spitalfields, London	dealer in jewellery
26523	Finsterer	Matilda	1835	Whitechapel, London	Jacob Finsterer	Babette (Barbet) Leopold	Samuel Simpson	Spitalfields, London	dealer in jewellery
7273	Finzi	Harriette	1813	Frome, Somerset	Moses Abraham	Esther Emden	Samuel Leon Finzi	Finsbury, London	
7277	Finzi	Leon (Judah) Moses	1851	Islington, London	Samuel Leon Finzi	Harriette Abraham	Henrietta Lawrence	Islington, London	
7274	Finzi	Samuel Leon	1813	Finsbury, London	Leon Finzi		Harriette Abraham	Finsbury, London	surgeon dentist
2261	Firestine	Isaac	1813	?, Poland				Leeds, Yorkshire	hawker
4436	Firestone	Abraham	1828	?, Germany				Birmingham	slipper maker
12497	Fischel	Louis	1826	?, Poland			Reschew (?)	Birmingham	tailor
12498	Fischel	Reschew	1827	?, Poland [?, Prussia]	(?)		Louis Fischel	Birmingham	tailor's wife
27544	Fishel	Morris	1831	Bath				Spitalfields, London	jeweller

ID	surname	given names	born	birthplace	father	mother	spouse 1	1851 residence	1851 occupation
81	Fisher	Jacob	1819	?, Russia			Julia (?)	Woolwich, London	clothier + general dealer
82	Fisher	Julia	1808	?, Poland	(?)		Jacob Fisher	Woolwich, London	domestick
28038	Fishfield	Moses	1817	?, Russia			Sarah (?)	Spitalfields, London	cap maker
4049	Flatau	Abram (Abraham)	1808	Braunschweig, Germany [Prussia]	Solomon Flatau	Tobie (?)	Sarah (?)	Whitechapel, London	boot + shoe mfr
10103	Flatau	Barnett	1847	Spitalfields, London	Morris (Maurice) Flatau	Nancy Woolf	Priscilla Cohen	Spitalfields, London	
25437	Flatau	Emily	1848	?Berlin, Germany [?, Prussia]	Samuel Flatau	Jane Woolf	Ascher Cruley	Mile End, London	
4053	Flatau	Emily	1850	Whitechapel, London	Abram (Abraham) Flatau	Sarah (?)	Alfred Jacobs	Whitechapel, London	
25435	Flatau	Frances	1838	Whitechapel, London	Samuel Flatau	Jane Woolf	Joseph Ferdinand Wertheimstein	Mile End, London	
4051	Flatau	Jacob	1843	?, Poland [?, Prussia]	Abram (Abraham) Flatau	Sarah (?)	Rebecca Emanuel	Whitechapel, London	
25433	Flatau	Jane	1816	Dublin, Ireland	Benjamin Woolf	Phoebe (?)	Leon Meyer	Mile End, London	
10104	Flatau	Joseph Maurice	1848	Spitalfields, London	Morris (Maurice) Flatau	Nancy Woolf	Esther Hyams	Spitalfields, London	
18439	Flatau	Julia	1834	Poplar, London	John Nathaniel Messeena	Rachel Gomes	William (Woolf) Flatau	Poplar, London	
6764	Flatau	Morris (Maurice)	1818	?, Poland [?, Prussia]	Shlomeh		Nancy Woolf	Spitalfields, London	dealer in plate
10102	Flatau	Nancy	1818	Spitalfields, London	(?) Woolf	Frances (?)	Morris (Maurice) Flatau	Spitalfields, London	dealer in plate
6763	Flatau	Rosetta (Rose)	1845	Spitalfields, London	Morris (Maurice) Flatau		Tobias Goodman	Spitalfields, London	
25432	Flatau	Samuel	1816	Berlin, Germany	Solomon Flatau	Tobie (?)	Jane Woolf	Mile End, London	oil man + grocer
4050	Flatau	Sarah	1813	?, Poland [?, Prussia]			Abram (Abraham) Flatau	Whitechapel, London	
25436	Flatau	Saul Albert	1844	Whitechapel, London	Samuel Flatau	Jane Woolf	Ann Lydia Townley	Mile End, London	
4052	Flatau	Solomon	1848	Whitechapel, London	Abram (Abraham) Flatau	Sarah (?)	Rebecca Emanuel	Whitechapel, London	
25438	Flatau	Solomon	1850	Mile End, London	Samuel Flatau	Jane Woolf		Mile End, London	
4055	Flatau	William (Woolf)	1811	?, Germany	Solomon Flatau	Tobie (?)	Julia Messeena	Whitechapel, London	boot + shoe mfr
29784	Flatow	Harris	1829	?, Poland				Whitechapel, London	baker
2258	Flatow	Henry	1832	Nottingham, Nottinghamshire	Solomon Flatow	Maria (?)		Leeds, Yorkshire	
2257	Flatow	Manasseh	1819	?, Poland [?, Prussia]	Solomon Flatow	Maria (?)		Leeds, Yorkshire	
2256	Flatow	Maria	1800	?, Poland [?, Prussia]			Solomon Flatow	Leeds, Yorkshire	
2255	Flatow	Solomon	1793	?, Poland [?, Prussia]			Maria (?)	Leeds, Yorkshire	dealer, watch materials
13576	Fleirsheim	Feibel	1811	?, Poland				Manchester	slipper maker
2423	Flister	Levine	1811	?, Germany				Hull, Yorkshire	
4441	Flohm	Isaac D	1850	Birmingham	Solomon Flohm	Jane R (?)		Birmingham	
4438	Flohm	Jane R	1823	?, Poland			Solomon (?)	Birmingham	
4442	Flohm	Levi	1829	?, Poland				Birmingham	glazier
4440	Flohm	Sarah	1846	?, Poland	Solomon Flohm	Jane R (?)		Birmingham	scholar
4437	Flohm	Solomon	1817	?, Poland			Jane R (?)	Birmingham	furniture dealer
4439	Flohm	William	1842	?, Poland	Solomon Flohm	Jane R (?)		Birmingham	scholar
15641	Floriday	Frances	1810	Warwick, Warwickshire	(?)		(?) Joseph	Birmingham	
7620	Foligno	Edward	1801	Bethnal Green, London	Moses Zachariah Foligno	Rachel de Isaac Baquis		Aldgate, London	silversmith
30009	Foligno	Rachel	1772	Aldgate, London	Isaac Baquis	Simha (?)	Moses Zachariah Foligno	Aldgate, London	fundholder
30008	Foligno	Rosa	1809	Bethnal Green, London	Moses Zachariah Foligno	Rachel de Isaac Baquis		Aldgate, London	
22070	Fonseca	Daniel H H	1786	Livorno, Italy [Leghorn]				Whitechapel, London	agent for drugs
13542	Fonseca	Joseph	1829	?, London				Manchester	cutler
9329	Fonseca	Rebecca	1797	Aldgate, London	(?) Fonseca			Aldgate, London	poor
26544	Fonseca	Samuel	1834	City, London				Birmingham	hatter assistant

ID	surname	given names	born	birthplace	father	mother	spouse 1	1851 residence	1851 occupation
11275	Fonseca (Pimentel Fonseca)	Aaron	1831	Aldgate, London	Phineas Fonseca (Pimentel Fonseca)	Keturah de Moses Silveira De Mattos		Aldgate, London	watch maker
11274	Fonseca (Pimentel Fonseca)	Betsy (Bilha)	1850	Aldgate, London	Isaac Fonseca (Pimentel Fonseca	Hannah de Hananel Gomez Da Costa		Aldgate, London	
11273	Fonseca (Pimentel Fonseca)	Caroline (Keturah)	1848	Aldgate, London	Isaac Fonseca (Pimentel Fonseca	Hannah de Hananel Gomez Da Costa		Aldgate, London	
26337	Fonseca (Pimentel Fonseca)	Catherine (Keturah)	1830	?, London	Joseph de Jacob Fonseca (Pimentel Fonseca)	Rachel de Moses Silveira de Mattos	Mark Levy	Aldgate, London	cap maker
5733	Fonseca (Pimentel Fonseca)	Catherine (Keturah, Golda)	1822	Aldgate, London	Jacob Marks		Samuel Fonseca (Pimentel)	Aldgate, London	
26335	Fonseca (Pimentel Fonseca)	David	1830	?, London	Joseph de Jacob Fonseca (Pimentel Fonseca)	Rachel de Moses Silveira de Mattos		Aldgate, London	cigar maker
28016	Fonseca (Pimentel Fonseca)	Emanuel	1823	Aldgate, London	Phineas de Phineas Fonseca (Pimentel Fonseca)	Rebecca de Abraham Roxas	Julia Hart	Spitalfields, London	cigar maker
18402	Fonseca (Pimentel Fonseca)	Fanny	1848	?, London	Samuel Fonseca (Pimentel Fonseca)	Catherine (Keturah, Golda) Marks	Henry Harris	Aldgate, London	scholar
26336	Fonseca (Pimentel Fonseca)	Goulding (Ora)	1832	?, London	Joseph de Jacob Fonseca (Pimentel Fonseca)	Rachel de Moses Silveira de Mattos	Jacob Pacifico	Aldgate, London	furrier
11272	Fonseca (Pimentel Fonseca)	Hannah	1825	Aldgate, London	Hananel Gomez Da Costa	Ketura (?)	Isaac Fonseca (Pimentel Fonseca)	Aldgate, London	
5735	Fonseca (Pimentel Fonseca)	Henry (Haim)	1843	?Aldgate, London	Samuel Fonseca (Pimentel Fonseca)	Catherine (Keturah, Golda) Marks	(?)	Aldgate, London	scholar
11271	Fonseca (Pimentel Fonseca)	Isaac	1825	Aldgate, London	Phineas Fonseca (Pimentel Fonseca)	Keturah de Moses Silveira De Mattos	Hannah de Hananel Gomez Da Costa	Aldgate, London	gas meter repairer
18404	Fonseca (Pimentel Fonseca)	Jacob	1849	?, London	Samuel Fonseca (Pimentel Fonseca)	Catherine (Keturah, Golda) Marks	Julia (Judith) Symons	Aldgate, London	
27861	Fonseca (Pimentel Fonseca)	Jane	1800	Whitechapel, London	Jacob Marks		Louis Gideon	Spitalfields, London	
5736	Fonseca (Pimentel Fonseca)	Jane (Jael)	1846	Aldgate, London	Samuel Fonseca (Pimentel Fonseca)	Catherine (Keturah, Golda) Marks	Henry Barnett	Aldgate, London	
26333	Fonseca (Pimentel Fonseca)	Joseph	1794	?, London	Jacob de Phineas Da Fonseca (Pimentel Fonseca)	Blanca de Jacob Mendoza	Rachel de Moses Silveira de Mattos	Aldgate, London	butcher
28017	Fonseca (Pimentel Fonseca)	Julia	1824	Whitechapel, London	Isaac Hart		Emanuel Fonseca (Pimentel Fonseca)	Spitalfields, London	
27862	Fonseca (Pimentel Fonseca)	Leah	1827	Whitechapel, London	Phineas de Phineas Fonseca (Pimentel Fonseca)	Rebecca de Abraham Roxas	Solomon Cohen	Spitalfields, London	furrier
18401	Fonseca (Pimentel Fonseca)	Leah	1841	?, London	Samuel Fonseca (Pimentel Fonseca)	Catherine (Keturah, Golda) Marks		Aldgate, London	scholar
18403	Fonseca (Pimentel Fonseca)	Louisa	1845	?, London	Samuel Fonseca (Pimentel Fonseca)	Catherine (Keturah, Golda) Marks		Aldgate, London	scholar
27860	Fonseca (Pimentel Fonseca)	Phineas	1800	Bethnal Green, London	Phineas Fonseca (Pimentel Fonseca)	Fanny (?)	Rebecca de Abraham Roxas	Spitalfields, London	general dealer
26338	Fonseca (Pimentel Fonseca)	Phineas	1836	?, London	Joseph de Jacob Fonseca (Pimentel Fonseca)	Rachel de Moses Silveira de Mattos		Aldgate, London	cigar maker
21653	Fonseca (Pimentel Fonseca)	Phineas	1851	Aldgate, London	Samuel Fonseca (Pimentel Fonseca)	Catherine (Keturah, Golda) Marks		Aldgate, London	

ID	surname	given names	born	birthplace	father	mother	spouse 1	1851 residence	1851 occupation
26334	Fonseca (Pimentel Fonseca)	Rachel	1800	?, London	Moses de Abraham Silveira de Mattos	Oro (Golding) de Abraham Benhamu	Joseph Fonseca (Pimentel Fonseca)	Aldgate, London	
18400	Fonseca (Pimentel Fonseca)	Samuel	1812	?, London	Phineas de Phineas Fonseca (Pimentel Fonseca)	Leah Jacobs	Catherine (Keturah, Golda) Marks (Moses)	Aldgate, London	cigar maker
25848	Foulkes	Michael	1831	?, Poland				Aldgate, London	hawker
17155	Fox	Abraham	1822	Ragoesen, Germany [Ragusar, Prussia]			Bertha (?)	Newcastle Upon Tyne	hawker
29466	Fox	Abraham	1833	Leszno, Poland [Lissa, Prussia]	Wolf Fox	Flora (?)	Elizabeth Phillips	Spitalfields, London	cigar maker apprentice
12517	Fox	Alexander	1830	?, London	Joel Fox	Eliza Emanuel	Rosetta Phillips	Norwich, Norfolk	furrier
4076	Fox	Anna (Anne, Annie)	1833	Norwich, Norfolk	Joel Fox	Eliza Emanuel	Maurice Fryer	Norwich, Norfolk	
29465	Fox	Anna (Hannah)	1826	Leszno, Poland [Lissa, Prussia]	Wolf Fox	Flora (?)	Solomon Levy	Spitalfields, London	working tailor
4853	Fox	Annie	1817	?, Poland [?, Prussia]	(?)		Ralph Fox	Pontypool, Wales	
2346	Fox	Barnett	1793	Leszno, Poland [Lissa, Prussia]	Alexander Fox	Rechil (?)	Rosella (?)	Aldgate, London	furrier
17156	Fox	Bertha	1824	Ragoesen, Germany [Ragusar, Prussia]	(?)		Abraham Fox	Newcastle Upon Tyne	
20559	Fox	Charles	1845	?Poland	Simon Fox	Sarah (Fanny) (?)		Aldgate, London	
20558	Fox	Dora	1844	?Poland	Simon Fox	Sarah (Fanny) (?)	Mendel Kime	Aldgate, London	
29464	Fox	Flora	1795	Leszno, Poland [Lissa, Prussia]	(?)		Wolf Fox	Spitalfields, London	
21015	Fox	George	1850	Pontypool, Wales	Ralph Fox	Annie (?)		Pontypool, Wales	
4855	Fox	Harriet	1844	Pontypool, Wales	Ralph Fox	Annie (?)	Louis Robert	Pontypool, Wales	
21014	Fox	Isaac	1847	Pontypool, Wales	Ralph Fox	Annie (?)		Pontypool, Wales	
4074	Fox	Joel	1805	Leszno, Poland [Lissa, Prussia]	Alexander Fox	Rechil (?)	Eliza Emanuel	Norwich, Norfolk	furrier + town councillor
21013	Fox	Joseph	1843	Pontypool, Wales	Ralph Fox	Annie (?)		Pontypool, Wales	
20560	Fox	Julius (Judah)	1849	Aldgate, London	Simon Fox	Sarah (Fanny) (?)	Esther Da Costa	Aldgate, London	
30431	Fox	Lewis	1851	Aldgate, London	Simon Fox	Sarah (Fanny) (?)		Aldgate, London	
4854	Fox	Morris	1841	Pontypool, Wales	Ralph Fox	Annie (?)		Pontypool, Wales	
17157	Fox	Pola	1847	Ragoesen, Germany [Ragusar, Prussia]	Abraham Fox	Bertha (?)		Newcastle Upon Tyne	
2348	Fox	Rachel	1826	Aldgate, London	Barnett Fox	Rosella (?)	Simon Tannenberg	Aldgate, London	furrier
4852	Fox	Ralph	1803	?, Poland [?, Prussia]			Annie (?)	Pontypool, Wales	jeweller + furniture broker
18898	Fox	Rosella	1793	?, Poland [?, Prussia]	(?)		Barnett Fox	Aldgate, London	furrier
2347	Fox	Rosetta	1832	Leeds, Yorkshire	Barnett Fox	Rosella (?)	Abram (Abraham) Cohen	Aldgate, London	furrier
20557	Fox	Sarah (Fanny)	1818	?Poland	(?)		Simon Fox	Aldgate, London	
20556	Fox	Simon	1818	?, Poland [?, Prussia]	Uri Shraga		Sarah (Fanny) (?)	Aldgate, London	journeyman tailor
29463	Fox	Wolf	1786	?, Poland [?, Prussia]			Flora (?)	Spitalfields, London	furrier
25469	Franckel	Eliza	1822	Hanover, Germany	(?)		Martin Levin	Aldgate, London	house servant
30450	Francks	Elias Holliday	1823	Newcastle-under-Lyme, Staffordshire	Abraham Francks	Mary (?)		Newcastle-under-Lyme, Staffordshire	

197

ID	surname	given names	born	birthplace	father	mother	spouse 1	1851 residence	1851 occupation
30366	Francks	Henry H	1815	Newcastle-under-Lyme, Staffordshire	Abraham Francks	Mary (?)		Newcastle-under-Lyme, Staffordshire	optician + jeweller
30364	Francks	Naomi	1811	Newcastle-under-Lyme, Staffordshire	Abraham Francks	Mary (?)		Newcastle-under-Lyme, Staffordshire	
30365	Francks	Rosina	1819	Newcastle-under-Lyme, Staffordshire	Abraham Francks	Mary (?)		Newcastle-under-Lyme, Staffordshire	
1433	Franco	Daniel	1819	Tavistock, Devon			Isabella (?)	Plymouth, Devon	last maker
21738	Franco	Francis	1800	?, Jamaica, West Indies				Islington, London	gentleman
1434	Franco	Isabella	1822	Plymouth, Devon			Daniel Franco	Plymouth, Devon	
21739	Franco	Maria	1806	Middlesex, London	(?) Franco			Islington, London	lady
27472	Frank	Mina	1828	?, Germany [Prussia, Germany]	(?) Frank			Whitechapel, London	cook
4449	Frankel	Benjamin	1844	Birmingham	Morris Frankel	Maria (?)		Birmingham	scholar
4450	Frankel	Edward	1846	Birmingham	Morris Frankel	Maria (?)		Birmingham	scholar
4448	Frankel	Henry	1842	Birmingham	Morris Frankel	Maria (?)		Birmingham	scholar
30371	Frankel	Hyman	1822	?, Poland [?, Prussia]			Rose (?)	Uttoxeter, Staffordshire	traveller, jewels, pedlar
4446	Frankel	Isaiah	1836	Birmingham	Morris Frankel	Maria (?)		Birmingham	cigar maker
4445	Frankel	Maria	1807	Birmingham			Morris Frankel	Birmingham	
4447	Frankel	Mathilda (Matilda)	1840	Birmingham	Morris Frankel	Maria (?)		Birmingham	scholar
4444	Frankel	Morris	1802	?, Poland [?, Prussia]			Maria (?)	Birmingham	general dealer
27420	Frankel	Samuel	1806	Berlin, Germany				Whitechapel, London	shoe maker
14997	Frankel	Selig	1828	?, Poland [?, Prussian Poland]				Bethnal Green, London	printer
1766	Frankell	David	1811	?, Poland [?, Prussia]	Isaac Frankel		Esther Phillips	Swansea, Wales	pawnbroker
1767	Frankell	Esther	1823	Whitechapel, London	Meir Phillips		David Frankell	Swansea, Wales	
1769	Frankell	Frederick Phineas	1844	Swansea, Wales	David Frankell	Esther Phillips		Swansea, Wales	scholar
1774	Frankell	Hanna	1781	?, Poland [?, Prussia]			Isaac Frankell	Swansea, Wales	
1776	Frankell	Henry	1816	?, Poland [?, Prussia]				Swansea, Wales	pawnbroker
1775	Frankell	Isaac	1776	?, Poland [?, Prussia]			Hanne (?)	Swansea, Wales	hawker
1770	Frankell	James	1846	Swansea, Wales	David Frankell	Esther Phillips		Swansea, Wales	scholar
1771	Frankell	Michael	1849	Swansea, Wales	David Frankell	Esther Phillips	Sophia Jacobs	Swansea, Wales	
1768	Frankell	Miriam	1843	Swansea, Wales	David Frankell	Esther Phillips		Swansea, Wales	scholar
1773	Frankell	Morris (Moses)	1808	?, Poland [?, Prussia]				Swansea, Wales	pawnbroker
13569	Frankenstein	Adolphus	1830	Wroclaw, Poland [Breslau]				Manchester	tailor
8424	Frankenstein	Isaac	1825	?, Poland				Portsmouth, Hampshire	licensed hawker (jeweller)
12849	Frankford	Alfred	1846	Whitechapel, London	Isaac Frankford	Hannah Henricks		Spitalfields, London	scholar
28375	Frankford	Anne	1850	Whitechapel, London	Moss Frankford	Rebecca Nathan	Felix Beale	Whitechapel, London	
17351	Frankford	Caroline	1847	Spitalfields, London	Israel Frankford	Rosetta Cohen		Spitalfields, London	scholar
12850	Frankford	Celia	1849	Spitalfields, London	Isaac Frankford	Hannah Henricks	Ellis Harris	Spitalfields, London	scholar
30432	Frankford	Emma	1851	Spitalfields, London	Isaac Frankford	Hannah Henricks	Ernest R Harris	Spitalfields, London	
12845	Frankford	Hannah	1786	?, Bedfordshire	(?)		Isaiah (Josiah) Simon Frankford	Whitechapel, London	
12847	Frankford	Hannah	1816	Whitechapel, London	Aaron Hendriks	Ann Mosely	Isaac Frankford	Spitalfields, London	sugar + sponge dealer
28374	Frankford	Henry	1847	Whitechapel, London	Moss Frankford	Rebecca Nathan		Whitechapel, London	scholar
12846	Frankford	Isaac	1818	?Whitechapel, London	Isaiah (Josiah) Simon Frankford	Hannah (?)	Hannah Hendricks	Spitalfields, London	sugar + sponge dealer
17349	Frankford	Isaac	1840	Spitalfields, London	Israel Frankford	Rosetta Cohen		Spitalfields, London	scholar

ID	surname	given names	born	birthplace	father	mother	spouse 1	1851 residence	1851 occupation
17347	Frankford	Isaiah	1836	Aldgate, London	Israel Frankford	Rosetta Cohen		Spitalfields, London	cigar maker
12848	Frankford	Isaiah	1843	Whitechapel, London	Isaac Frankford	Hannah Henricks		Spitalfields, London	scholar
12844	Frankford	Isaiah (Josiah) Simon	1778	Amsterdam, Holland			Hannah (?)	Whitechapel, London	supported by his family
17345	Frankford	Israel	1814	Whitechapel, London	Joshua Frankford		Rosetta Cohen	Spitalfields, London	cigar maker
17352	Frankford	Julia	1850	Spitalfields, London	Israel Frankford	Rosetta Cohen		Spitalfields, London	
28373	Frankford	Katherine	1846	Whitechapel, London	Moss Frankford	Rebecca Nathan		Whitechapel, London	scholar
17348	Frankford	Morris	1833	Spitalfields, London	Israel Frankford	Rosetta Cohen		Spitalfields, London	cigar maker
28371	Frankford	Moss	1822	Whitechapel, London			Rebecca Nathan	Whitechapel, London	cigar manufacturer
17350	Frankford	Rachael	1842	Spitalfields, London	Israel Frankford	Rosetta Cohen		Spitalfields, London	scholar
28372	Frankford	Rebecca	1821	Spitalfields, London	(?) Nathan		Moss Frankford	Whitechapel, London	
17346	Frankford	Rosetta	1813	Spitalfields, London	James Cohen		Israel Frankford	Spitalfields, London	
12852	Frankford	Rosetta	1830	Whitechapel, London	Isaiah (Josiah) Simon Frankford	Hannah (?)		Spitalfields, London	furrier
12851	Frankford	Sarah	1825	Whitechapel, London	Isaiah (Josiah) Simon Frankford	Hannah (?)		Spitalfields, London	furrier
25965	Frankfort	Elizabeth	1850	Spitalfields, London	Leon Frankfort	Hannah (?)		Aldgate, London	
25961	Frankfort	Hannah	1819	Aldgate, London	(?) Hyams		Leon Frankfort	Aldgate, London	
25963	Frankfort	Julia (Emily)	1841	Amsterdam, Holland	Leon Frankfort	(?)	Lewis Proops	Aldgate, London	scholar
25960	Frankfort	Leon	1815	Amsterdam, Holland			(?)	Aldgate, London	hawker
25962	Frankfort	Rebecca	1838	Amsterdam, Holland	Leon Frankfort	(?)		Aldgate, London	tailoress
25964	Frankfort	Solomon	1849	Aldgate, London	Leon Frankfort	Hannah (?)		Aldgate, London	
30486	Frankill	Hyman	1832	?, Poland [?, Prussia]				Uttoxeter, Staffordshire	traveller jewels pedlar
2259	Frankinstein	Jacob	1830	?, Poland				Leeds, Yorkshire	hawker
17779	Frankle	Kalman	1829	?, Poland				Spitalfields, London	tailor
17778	Frankle	Mark	1827	?, Poland				Spitalfields, London	tailor
7082	Franklin	Abraham	1784	?, England			Miriam (Polly, Ann) Aaron	Manchester	
11854	Franklin	Abraham	1843	Jersey, Channel Islands	Gershon Franklin	Jessy (?)		Whitechapel, London	
1427	Franklin	Abraham Gabay	1821	Liverpool	Abraham Franklin	Miriam (Polly, Ann) Aaron	Phebe Harris	Plymouth, Devon	traveller in drapery + fancy hardware
28844	Franklin	Amelia	1829	Whitechapel, London	Abraham Abrahams		Mark Franklin	Spitalfields, London	parasol maker
15736	Franklin	Ann	1811	Ipswich, Suffolk	(?) Graumann		Samuel Franklin	Spitalfields, London	
21016	Franklin	Annie	1819	City, London	Lewis Israel		Jonas Franklin	St Helier, Jersey, Channel Islands	
5701	Franklin	Berryman	1839	Spitalfields, London	Samuel Franklin	Ann Graumann	Esther Jacob (Jacobs)	Spitalfields, London	boarding school pupil
4821	Franklin	Bloomah	1838	Birmingham				Birmingham	scholar at home
4451	Franklin	David	1828	?, Poland			Jane (?)	Birmingham	glazier + plumber
21017	Franklin	Dorah	1851	St Helier, Jersey, Channel Islands	Jonas Franklin	Annie Israel		St Helier, Jersey, Channel Islands	
13866	Franklin	Elias	1849	Manchester	Morris Levy Franklin	Kate (?)		Manchester	
7085	Franklin	Ellis Abraham	1822	Liverpool	Abraham Franklin	Miriam (Polly, Ann) Aaron	Adelaide Samuel	Aldgate, London	manager BR + grocer
11853	Franklin	Frances Dinah	1841	?, Hampshire	Gershon Franklin	Jessy (?)	Maurice Coopman	Whitechapel, London	
11851	Franklin	Gershon	1817	Kalisz, Poland [Kalish, Poland]			Jessy (?)	Whitechapel, London	superintendent of orphan asylum
10478	Franklin	Hannah	1786	?, Poland	(?)		(?) Franklin	Mile End, London	annuitant
13865	Franklin	Harriet	1848	Manchester	Morris Levy Franklin	Kate (?)	Alexander Harris	Manchester	
7088	Franklin	Henry Abraham	1827	?, Lancashire	Abraham Franklin	Miriam (Polly, Ann) Aaron	Victoria Segre	Manchester	

ID	surname	given names	born	birthplace	father	mother	spouse 1	1851 residence	1851 occupation
5703	Franklin	Isaac	1840	Spitalfields, London	Samuel Franklin	Ann Graumann	Kate Isaacs	Spitalfields, London	scholar
11880	Franklin	Isaac	1848	Whitechapel, London	Gershon Franklin	Jessy (?)		Whitechapel, London	
7084	Franklin	Isaac Abraham	1812	Portsmouth, Hampshire	Abraham Franklin	Miriam (Polly, Ann) Aaron	Theresa Segre	Manchester	surgeon, MRCS
7081	Franklin	Jacob Abraham	1809	Portsmouth, Hampshire	Abraham Franklin	Miriam (Polly, Ann) Aaron		Aldgate, London	professional auditor
11852	Franklin	Jessy	1819	Plymouth, Devon	(?)		Gershon Franklin	Whitechapel, London	mistress of orphan asylum
19914	Franklin	Jonas	1815	?, Germany	Burman Franklin		Annie Israel	St Helier, Jersey, Channel Islands	dealer in jewellery, perfumery, watches, tobacco, haberdashery + fancy goods
27394	Franklin	Julius	1832	Scheiden, Germany				Aldgate, London	cap maker
13864	Franklin	Kate	1816	Sheerness, Kent	(?)		Morris Levy Franklin	Manchester	trimming mfr master empl 1
17324	Franklin	Lewis	1802	?, Germany			Rachel (?)	Wapping, London	outfitter
28843	Franklin	Mark	1825	Spitalfields, London	Myer Franklin		Amelia Abrahams	Spitalfields, London	tailor
15737	Franklin	Matilda	1837	Spitalfields, London	Samuel Franklin	Ann Graumann		Spitalfields, London	
17326	Franklin	Meyers	1850	?Wapping, London	Lewis Franklin	Rachel (?)		Wapping, London	
7083	Franklin	Miriam (Polly, Ann)	1789	Portsmouth, Hampshire	Jacob Aaron	Alice (?)	Abraham Franklin	Manchester	
13863	Franklin	Morris Levy	1812	Leszno, Poland [Lissa, Prussia], Poland [Lisser, Germany]			Kate (?)	Manchester	trimming mfr master empl 1
8405	Franklin	Myers	1791	?, Poland [Polish Russia]				Southampton, Hampshire	jeweller
11855	Franklin	Phebe	1846	Portsmouth, Hampshire	Gershon Franklin	Jessy (?)		Whitechapel, London	
15738	Franklin	Rachael	1845	Spitalfields, London	Samuel Franklin	Ann Graumann		Spitalfields, London	
17325	Franklin	Rachel	1810	Aldgate, London	(?)		Lewis Franklin	Wapping, London	
5702	Franklin	Samuel	1807	?, Germany			Ann Graumann	Spitalfields, London	shoe manufacturer
5705	Franklin	Simon Hyam	1841	Spitalfields, London	Samuel Franklin	Ann Graumann	Adelaide Lewin	Spitalfields, London	
1326	Franko (Franco)	Blum (Bluma)	1813	Plymouth, Devon				Plymouth, Devon	
7489	Franks	Abraham	1806	Manchester	(?) Franks	Amelia Cohen	(?)	Manchester	optician
30733	Franks	Abraham	1811	Aldgate, London	Benjamin Franks		Sophia Levy	Aldgate, London	coffee house keeper
13053	Franks	Abraham	1831	Spitalfields, London	Henry Franks	Sarah (?)	Rosetta Jacobs	Spitalfields, London	general dealer
13950	Franks	Amelia	1790	Manchester	Simeon Cohen		(?) Franks	Manchester	
1428	Franks	Anne	1786	Crediton, Devon			(?) Franks	Plymouth, Devon	slop seller
14615	Franks	Arthur	1850	Middlesex, London	John W Franks	Eliza (?)		Hoxton, London	
30736	Franks	Barnett	1844	Spitalfields, London	Abraham Franks	Sophia Levy		Aldgate, London	scholar
30735	Franks	Benjamin	1840	Spitalfields, London	Abraham Franks	Sophia Levy		Aldgate, London	scholar
24701	Franks	Caroline	1773	Gothenburg, Sweden			David Franks	Walworth, London	kept by children
15583	Franks	Caroline	1847	Spitalfields, London	Samuel Franks	Rebecca Benjamin		Covent Garden, London	
14611	Franks	Clara	1842	Middlesex, London	John W Franks	Eliza (?)		Hoxton, London	scholar
2260	Franks	Edward	1832	?, Poland				Leeds, Yorkshire	hawker
13948	Franks	Edwin	1838	Manchester	(?) Franks	Amelia Cohen		Manchester	
14609	Franks	Eliza	1824	Middlesex, London	(?)		John W Franks	Hoxton, London	
13946	Franks	Eliza	1832	Manchester	(?) Franks	Amelia Cohen		Manchester	
14610	Franks	Elizabeth	1840	Middlesex, London	John W Franks	Eliza (?)		Hoxton, London	scholar

ID	surname	given names	born	birthplace	father	mother	spouse 1	1851 residence	1851 occupation
30738	Franks	Elizabeth	1850	Aldgate, London	Abraham Franks	Sophia Levy		Aldgate, London	
15578	Franks	Elizabeth (Betsy)	1840	Spitalfields, London	Samuel Franks	Rebecca Benjamin	Eleazer (Ezekar) Proops	Covent Garden, London	scholar
28170	Franks	Esther	1823	Whitechapel, London	Benjamin Franks	Priscilla Abrahams		Spitalfields, London	tailoress
30737	Franks	Esther	1847	Aldgate, London	Abraham Franks	Sophia Levy		Aldgate, London	scholar
17091	Franks	Fanny Amelia	1838	Leeds, Yorkshire	Martin W Franks	Sarah (?)		Bedford, Bedfordshire	scholar
14613	Franks	Frances	1847	Middlesex, London	John W Franks	Eliza (?)		Hoxton, London	scholar
17095	Franks	Frederick Antone	1848	Bedford, Bedfordshire	Martin W Franks	Sarah (?)		Bedford, Bedfordshire	scholar at home
14616	Franks	George	1826	Middlesex, London				Hoxton, London	messenger
14614	Franks	Hanah	1849	Middlesex, London	John W Franks	Eliza (?)		Hoxton, London	
15585	Franks	Hannah	1851	Covent Garden, London	Samuel Franks	Rebecca Benjamin		Covent Garden, London	
13049	Franks	Henry	1793	?London			Sarah (?)	Spitalfields, London	general dealer
13944	Franks	Henry	1824	Manchester	(?) Franks	Amelia Cohen		Manchester	optician
15580	Franks	Henry	1842	Spitalfields, London	Samuel Franks	Rebecca Benjamin		Covent Garden, London	scholar
17094	Franks	Henry	1843	Middlesex, London	Martin W Franks	Sarah (?)		Bedford, Bedfordshire	scholar
13947	Franks	Jane	1834	Manchester	(?) Franks	Amelia Cohen		Manchester	
14608	Franks	John W	1819	Middlesex, London			Eliza (?)	Hoxton, London	clerk in newspaper office
14085	Franks	Joseph	1831	Manchester			Rose (?)	Manchester	optician
15584	Franks	Joseph	1849	Westminster, London	Samuel Franks	Rebecca Benjamin		Covent Garden, London	
14612	Franks	Joseph H	1843	Middlesex, London	John W Franks	Eliza (?)		Hoxton, London	scholar
13051	Franks	Julia	1829	Spitalfields, London	Henry Franks	Sarah (?)	Moses Isaacs	Spitalfields, London	general dealer
15582	Franks	Julia	1846	Spitalfields, London	Samuel Franks	Rebecca Benjamin		Covent Garden, London	
17093	Franks	Julius Solomon	1842	Leeds, Yorkshire	Martin W Franks	Sarah (?)		Bedford, Bedfordshire	scholar
17096	Franks	Kate Ida	1850	Bedford, Bedfordshire	Martin W Franks	Sarah (?)		Bedford, Bedfordshire	
15581	Franks	Mark	1844	Spitalfields, London	Samuel Franks	Rebecca Benjamin		Covent Garden, London	scholar
17090	Franks	Martin W	1806	?, Germany			Sarah (?)	Bedford, Bedfordshire	commercial traveller
13945	Franks	Matilda	1828	Manchester	(?) Franks	Amelia Cohen		Manchester	
28489	Franks	Nathan	1830	?, Poland [Neufcover, Prussia]				Spitalfields, London	tailor
28168	Franks	Priscilla	1781	Aldgate, London	Avraham Canterbury		Benjamin Franks	Spitalfields, London	clothes dealer
6594	Franks	Rebecca	1819	Spitalfields, London	Tsevi Hirsh Benjamin		Samuel Franks	Covent Garden, London	
14086	Franks	Rose	1831	Middlesex, London	(?)		Joseph Franks	Manchester	
6593	Franks	Samuel	1819	Spitalfields, London	Shlomeh Zalman Franks		Rebecca Benjamin	Covent Garden, London	tailor
13052	Franks	Samuel	1830	Spitalfields, London	Henry Franks	Sarah (?)	Emma Moss	Spitalfields, London	general dealer
13399	Franks	Sarah	1779	?, Germany	(?)		(?) Franks	Spitalfields, London	
13050	Franks	Sarah	1798	?London	(?)		Henry Franks	Spitalfields, London	general dealer
17089	Franks	Sarah	1811	Hanley, Staffordshire	(?)		Martin W Franks	Bedford, Bedfordshire	commercial traveller's wife
28490	Franks	Sarah	1828	?, Poland [Neufcover, Prussia]	(?) Franks			Spitalfields, London	tailoress
17092	Franks	Sarah	1840	Leeds, Yorkshire	Martin W Franks	Sarah (?)		Bedford, Bedfordshire	scholar
30734	Franks	Sophia	1813	Spitalfields, London	Jacob Levy		Abraham Franks	Aldgate, London	coffee house keeper
13054	Franks	Tilley	1832	Spitalfields, London	Henry Franks	Sarah (?)		Spitalfields, London	general dealer
13949	Franks	Victoria	1839	Manchester	(?) Franks	Amelia Cohen	Joseph Saltiel	Manchester	
28169	Franks	Woolf	1821	Whitechapel, London	Benjamin Franks	Priscilla Abrahams		Spitalfields, London	quill dresser
15579	Franks	Zilpah (Elizabeth)	1841	Spitalfields, London	Samuel Franks	Rebecca Benjamin		Covent Garden, London	scholar
3974	Freedbergh	Elizabeth	1782	Portsmouth, Hampshire				Portsmouth, Hampshire	pauper + almswoman
3970	Freedbergh	Rachel	1793	?, London	Abraham Levy		Morris Freedbergh	Portsmouth, Hampshire	

ID	surname	given names	born	birthplace	father	mother	spouse 1	1851 residence	1851 occupation
17271	Freedburgh	Dora	1831	Poznan, Poland [Posen, Prussia]	(?) Freedburgh			Aldgate, London	tailoress
1781	Freedman	Adelaide (Adilid)	1846	Merthyr Tydfil, Wales	Solomon Freedman	Sarah Rachael (?)		Merthyr Tydfil, Wales	
1779	Freedman	Ann	1836	?, Poland	Solomon Freedman	Sarah Rachael (?)		Merthyr Tydfil, Wales	
1784	Freedman	Aron	1831	?, Poland	Samson Freedman			Merthyr Tydfil, Wales	glazier
1782	Freedman	Barnet	1848	Merthyr Tydfil, Wales	Solomon Freedman	Sarah Rachael (?)		Merthyr Tydfil, Wales	
1783	Freedman	Lewis (Louis)	1850	Merthyr Tydfil, Wales	Solomon Freedman	Sarah Rachael (?)	Elizabeth (Lizzie) Phillips	Merthyr Tydfil, Wales	
1780	Freedman	Mary Ann	1841	?, Poland	Solomon Freedman	Sarah Rachael (?)		Merthyr Tydfil, Wales	
30544	Freedman	Phineas	1851	Merthyr Tydfil, Wales	Solomon Freedman	Sarah Rachael (?)	Augusta Horwitz	Merthyr Tydfil, Wales	
1785	Freedman	Samson	1795	?, Poland				Merthyr Tydfil, Wales	glazier
1778	Freedman	Sarah Rachael	1817	Kalvarija, Lithuania [Kalwaria, Poland]			Solomon Freedman	Merthyr Tydfil, Wales	
1777	Freedman	Solomon	1815	Kalvarija, Lithuania [Kalwaria, Poland]	Samson Freedman		Sarah Rachael (?)	Merthyr Tydfil, Wales	pawnbroker
1786	Freedman	Solomon	1818	?, Poland				Merthyr Tydfil, Wales	glazier
4452	Freelander	David	1825	?, Germany				Birmingham	glazier
7989	Freeman	Benjamin	1850	?London				Spitalfields, London	
2424	Freeman	Fanny	1840	?, Poland	Jacob Freeman	Selina (?)	George Tickton	Hull, Yorkshire	scholar
2429	Freeman	Isaac	1817	?, Poland			Mary A Brown	Hull, Yorkshire	professor
30941	Freeman	Jacob	1817	?, Poland			Selina (?)	Hull, Yorkshire	watchmaker finisher
2432	Freeman	James	1848	Great Yarmouth, Norfolk	Isaac Freeman	Mary A Brown		Hull, Yorkshire	
2433	Freeman	Marcus	1822	?, Poland			Mary (?)	Hull, Yorkshire	
2427	Freeman	Marcus	1848	?, Poland	Jacob Freeman	Selina (?)		Hull, Yorkshire	
2434	Freeman	Mary	1822	Hamburg, Germany			Marcus Freeman	Hull, Yorkshire	
2430	Freeman	Mary A	1825	Great Yarmouth, Norfolk	(?) Brown	Hannah (?)	Isaac Freeman	Hull, Yorkshire	dressmaker
5869	Freeman	Mary A	1841	Great Yarmouth, Norfolk	Isaac Freeman	Mary A (?)	(?) Nuttel (Nuttle)	Hull, Yorkshire	
2426	Freeman	Rachael	1836	?, Poland	Jacob Freeman	Selina (?)	Charles Stern	Hull, Yorkshire	scholar
2428	Freeman	Sarah	1851	Hull, Yorkshire	(?) Freeman	Selina (?)	Isaac Mechilisky	Hull, Yorkshire	
2425	Freeman	Selina	1821	?, Poland	(?)		Jacob Freeman	Hull, Yorkshire	
12671	Freestone	Abraham	1828	?, Germany				Birmingham	slipper maker
23826	Freitag	Mark	1831	?, Poland [?, Prussia]				Liverpool	glazier
4455	Fridlander	Alfred	1841	Birmingham	David Fridlander	Esther (?)	Flora J Solomon	Birmingham	scholar
4458	Fridlander	Augustus(Abraham)	1849	Birmingham	David Fridlander	Esther (?)		Birmingham	
4453	Fridlander	David	1807	Bavaria, Germany			Esther (?)	Birmingham	pawnbroker
4454	Fridlander	Esther	1808	Cambridge			David Fridlander	Birmingham	
4456	Fridlander	Mary	1844	Birmingham	David Fridlander	Esther (?)	M Klean	Birmingham	scholar
4457	Fridlander	Moses (Moss)	1848	Birmingham	David Fridlander	Esther (?)	Minnie Abrahams	Birmingham	
16815	Friedberg	Henry	1820	?, Poland [?, Prussia]				Cheltenham, Gloucestershire	general dealer
20330	Friedeberg	Abraham	1809	?, Poland [?, Prussia]	Eliezer Lezer		Rebecca Phillips	Aldgate, London	furrier
20333	Friedeberg	Annie	1835	Whitechapel, London	Abraham Friedeberg	Rebecca Phillips	Israel Charles Marshall	Aldgate, London	
25653	Friedeberg	Buena	1804	Aldgate, London	David Pass (Paz de Leon)	Rebecca de Jacob Selomoh Solomons	Mark Friedeberg	Aldgate, London	
20338	Friedeberg	Edward	1845	Whitechapel, London	Abraham Friedeberg	Rebecca Phillips		Aldgate, London	

ID	surname	given names	born	birthplace	father	mother	spouse 1	1851 residence	1851 occupation
20337	Friedeberg	Godfrey	1844	Whitechapel, London	Abraham Friedeberg	Rebecca Phillips		Aldgate, London	
22091	Friedeberg	Henry	1816	Portsmouth, Hampshire				Aldgate, London	dealer in beads
20340	Friedeberg	Henry	1849	Whitechapel, London	Abraham Friedeberg	Rebecca Phillips	Katie Elkan	Aldgate, London	
8442	Friedeberg	Jacob	1828	Portsmouth, Hampshire	Morris Friedeberg	Rachel (?)	Isabella Harris	Portsmouth, Hampshire	tailor
20334	Friedeberg	Julia	1838	Whitechapel, London	Abraham Friedeberg	Rebecca Phillips	Adolphus Reich	Aldgate, London	
20332	Friedeberg	Louisa	1834	Whitechapel, London	Abraham Friedeberg	Rebecca Phillips	Isaac Samuel	Aldgate, London	
20335	Friedeberg	Matilda	1840	Whitechapel, London	Abraham Friedeberg	Rebecca Phillips		Aldgate, London	
20339	Friedeberg	Morris	1847	Whitechapel, London	Abraham Friedeberg	Rebecca Phillips		Aldgate, London	
16816	Friedeberg	Moses	1816	?, Poland [?, Prussia]				Warrington, Cheshire	watchmaker + jeweller
20331	Friedeberg	Rebecca	1813	?, Poland	Eliakim Getshlik Phillips		Abraham Friedeberg	Aldgate, London	
20336	Friedeberg	Semira (Simisa)	1843	Whitechapel, London	Abraham Friedeberg	Rebecca Phillips	Edward Siegismund Slomowski	Aldgate, London	
3972	Friedeberg (Freedbergh)	Lewis	1830	Portsmouth, Hampshire	Morris Freedbergh	Rachel Levy		Portsmouth, Hampshire	clothes dealer
3971	Friedeberg (Freedbergh)	Mark	1830	Portsmouth, Hampshire	Morris Freedbergh	Rachel Levy	Amelia Jacobs	Portsmouth, Hampshire	clothes dealer
3973	Friedeberg (Freedbergh)	Morris	1787	?, London	Jacob Friedeberg		Rachel Levy	Portsmouth, Hampshire	clothes dealer
29956	Friedengamer	Ann	1821	?, Germany			(?) Friedengamer	Whitechapel, London	shoe binder
29957	Friedengamer	Ann Maria	1850	?, London	(?) Friedengamer	Ann (?)		Whitechapel, London	
29958	Friedengamer	John	1842	?, London	(?) Friedengamer	Ann (?)		Whitechapel, London	
16292	Friedheim	Otto	1820	?, Germany				Dundee, Scotland	
14187	Friedlander	Charles	1850	Oxford, Oxfordshire	Morris (Moses) Friedlander	Ellen (?)		Manchester	
24224	Friedlander	Charles Jacob	1850	Bethnal Green, London	Morris (Moses) Friedlander	Eliza Harris		Hackney, London	
24221	Friedlander	Eliza	1823	?, Essex	(?) (Harris)		Morris (Moses) Friedlander	Hackney, London	dressmaker
26012	Friedlander	Elizabeth	1820	Whitechapel, London	Moses Assur	Leah (?)	Lesser Friedlander	Aldgate, London	
14186	Friedlander	Ellen	1829	?, London	(?)		Morris (Moses) Friedlander	Manchester	
26014	Friedlander	Esther	1841	Whitechapel, London	Lesser Friedlander	Elizabeth Assur	Meyer Friedlander	Aldgate, London	scholar
24223	Friedlander	F---	1848	Bethnal Green, London	Morris (Moses) Friedlander	Eliza Harris		Hackney, London	
26015	Friedlander	Fanny	1842	Whitechapel, London	Lesser Friedlander	Elizabeth Assur		Aldgate, London	scholar
26017	Friedlander	Henrietta	1847	Whitechapel, London	Lesser Friedlander	Elizabeth Assur	Adolph Davis	Aldgate, London	scholar
26023	Friedlander	Henry	1835	Hamburg, Germany				Aldgate, London	
26018	Friedlander	Henry Lesser	1849	Aldgate, London	Lesser Friedlander	Elizabeth Assur	Rose Lenzberg	Aldgate, London	
20284	Friedlander	Isaac	1822	?, Russia				Spitalfields, London	traveller
24222	Friedlander	Joseph George	1846	Bethnal Green, London	Morris (Moses) Friedlander	Eliza Harris		Hackney, London	
26019	Friedlander	Julius	1851	Aldgate, London	Lesser Friedlander	Elizabeth Assur		Aldgate, London	
30445	Friedlander	Leon (Lennard)	1851	Whitechapel, London	Morris (Moses) Friedlander	Ellen (?)		Whitechapel, London	
26011	Friedlander	Lesser	1811	Hamburg, Germany	Hirsch Friedlander		Elizabeth Assur	Aldgate, London	foreign goods merchant
15210	Friedlander	Louisa	1824	?, London	Chaim Ventura	Paulina (?)	Robert (Raphael) Joseph Friedlander	Shoreditch, London	domestic duties
24220	Friedlander	Morris (Moses)	1818	?, Poland [Golup, Poland]			Eliza Harris	Hackney, London	bookbinder
14185	Friedlander	Morris (Moses)	1824	?, Poland [Russia Poland]	Abraham Friedlander		Ellen (?)	Manchester	India rubber waterproofer
15209	Friedlander	Robert (Raphael) Joseph	1819	?, Germany	David Friedlander		Louisa Ventura	Shoreditch, London	turner in general

ID	surname	given names	born	birthplace	father	mother	spouse 1	1851 residence	1851 occupation
26016	Friedlander	Rose (Rosetta)	1844	Whitechapel, London	Lesser Friedlander	Elizabeth Assur		Aldgate, London	scholar
26013	Friedlander	Selina	1840	Whitechapel, London	Lesser Friedlander	Elizabeth Assur	H Michaelsohn	Aldgate, London	scholar
27891	Friedman	Abraham	1849	Plock, Poland	Joseph Friedman	Terese (?)		Spitalfields, London	
27889	Friedman	Joseph	1815	Plock, Poland			Terese (?)	Spitalfields, London	tailor
13794	Friedman	Nathan	1828	Guernsey, Channel Islands				Manchester	cloth cap maker
27890	Friedman	Terese	1830	Plock, Poland	(?)		Joseph Friedman	Spitalfields, London	tailoress
27355	Frilanda	Abraham	1833	?, Germany [Landermester, Germany]				Aldgate, London	wholesale jeweller
28974	Frind	Jacob	1830	?, Poland				Whitechapel, London	tailor
28975	Frind	Lewis	1832	?, Poland				Whitechapel, London	tailor
14964	Fristel	Esther J	1838	Middlesex, London	(?) Fristel			Bethnal Green, London	boarding school pupil
14914	Fristil	Robert Alexander	1840	Middlesex, London				Bethnal Green, London	boarding school pupil
27784	From	Edward	1826	Hamburg, Germany				Spitalfields, London	cigar maker
25842	Fromberg	Abraham	1837	?, Poland	Barnet Fromberg	Hannah (?)		Aldgate, London	scholar
25837	Fromberg	Barnet	1781	?, Poland			Hannah (?)	Aldgate, London	lodging house keeper
25838	Fromberg	Hannah	1797	?, Poland	(?)		Barnet Fromberg	Aldgate, London	wife of lodging house keeper
25841	Fromberg	Henry	1833	?, Poland	Barnet Fromberg	Hannah (?)	Jane Hart	Aldgate, London	furrier journeyman
25840	Fromberg	Isaac	1830	?, Poland	Barnet Fromberg	Hannah (?)	Sarah Moses	Aldgate, London	furrier journeyman
25839	Fromberg	Samuel	1827	?, Poland	Barnet Fromberg	Hannah (?)	Rosetta Jacobs	Aldgate, London	furrier journeyman
26322	Frost	Saul	1831	?, Poland [?, Prussia]				Aldgate, London	butcher
26287	Frusia	Isaac	1829	?, Poland				Aldgate, London	slipper maker
16700	Fry	Betsey	1827	?, Holland	Moses Fry		Edward Porten	Spitalfields, London	independent
18036	Fry	Catherine	1824	Spitalfields, London	Eliezer Lezer Park	Blume (?)	Philip (Flip) Fry	Whitechapel, London	
26932	Fry	Herman	1846	?, Poland [?, Prussia]	Simpson Fry	Jane (?)		Aldgate, London	
26931	Fry	Jane	1819	?, Poland [?, Prussia]	(?)		Simpson Fry	Aldgate, London	
26933	Fry	Louis	1848	?, London	Simpson Fry	Jane (?)		Aldgate, London	
26935	Fry	Michael	1851	Aldgate, London	Simpson Fry	Jane (?)		Aldgate, London	
30446	Fry	Moses	1851	Spitalfields, London	Philip (Flip) Fry	Catherine Park		Spitalfields, London	
18035	Fry	Philip (Flip)	1827	?, Holland	Moshe Chaim		Catherine Park	Whitechapel, London	general dealer
16701	Fry	Rose (Rosa)	1835	?, Holland	Moses Fry		Simon Winkel	Spitalfields, London	
26934	Fry	Rosetta	1849	?, London	Simpson Fry	Jane (?)		Aldgate, London	
26930	Fry	Simpson	1820	?, Poland [?, Prussia]			Jane (?)	Aldgate, London	cap maker
12656	Fuld	Frances M	1795	Middlesex, London			Israel M Fuld	Plymouth, Devon	
12655	Fuld	Israel M	1791	Amsterdam, Holland			Frances M (?)	Plymouth, Devon	annuitant
18260	Furdenthal	Joseph	1816	?, Poland [?, Poland Russia]				Northampton, Northamptonshire	traveller
14992	Furst	Simon	1818	?, Poland [?, Prussian Poland]				Bethnal Green, London	bookbinder
18054	Futter	Rafel	1829	?, Poland				Dudley, Worcestershire	glazier
6566	Fyerman	Louisa J	1851	Plymouth, Devon	(?) Fyerman	Mary Ann (?)		Plymouth, Devon	
6565	Fyerman	Mary Ann	1820	Bloomsbury, London	(?)		(?) Fyerman	Plymouth, Devon	
26277	Fzik	Herman	1825	?Poland [Lessle, ?]			Rosa (?)	Aldgate, London	tailor
26279	Fzik	Herz	1848	?Poland [Lessle, ?]	Herman Fzik	Rosa (?)		Aldgate, London	
26278	Fzik	Rosa	1823	Szubin, Poland [Schubin, Prussia]	(?)		Herman Fzik	Aldgate, London	

ID	surname	given names	born	birthplace	father	mother	spouse 1	1851 residence	1851 occupation
29281	Gabay	Isaac	1821	Whitechapel, London			Mary (?)	Wapping, London	cigar maker
27290	Gabay	Isabella (Bella)	1821	Whitechapel, London	David Valentine		Raphael Gabay	Aldgate, London	
27289	Gabay	Raphael	1827	?, Holland	Samuel Gabay		Isabella (Bella) Valentine	Aldgate, London	cigar maker
27291	Gabay	Samuel	1848	Whitechapel, London	Raphael Gabay	Isabella (Bella) Valentine		Aldgate, London	
19549	Gabriel	Abraham	1849	Strand, London	Henry Montague	Fanny (?)	Hannah Levy	Strand, London	
21659	Gabriel	Adelaide	1805	Brussels, Belgium	(?)		Lyon Gabriel	City, London	
21665	Gabriel	Adolphe	1839	Hull, Yorkshire	Lyon Gabriel	Adelaide (?)	Martha Cohen	City, London	
16585	Gabriel	Arnold	1833	?, London	Lyon Gabriel	Adelaide (?)	Jane Sewill	Liverpool	surgeon dentist
28067	Gabriel	Benjamin	1838	Aldgate, London	Gabriel Gabriel	Sarah (?Levy)		Spitalfields, London	cigar maker
21666	Gabriel	Caroline	1841	Hull, Yorkshire	Lyon Gabriel	Adelaide (?)	Willem Van Straaten	City, London	scholar
21668	Gabriel	Celine	1844	Liverpool	Lyon Gabriel	Adelaide (?)	Samuel Neumann (Newman)	City, London	
19498	Gabriel	Charlotte	1827	Westminster, London	(?) Gabriel	Martha (?)		Strand, London	
19548	Gabriel	Esther	1848	Strand, London	Henry Montague	Fanny (?)		Strand, London	scholar
19546	Gabriel	Fanny	1818	Finsbury, London			Henry Gabriel	Strand, London	
21177	Gabriel	Fanny	1826	Strand, London, London	(?) Gabriel			Aldgate, London	furrier
14624	Gabriel	Frances	1796	Whitechapel, London	(?)		Michael Gabriel	Hoxton, London	
28060	Gabriel	Gabriel	1794	City, London	Yaacov		Rebecca Marks	Spitalfields, London	tailor
21661	Gabriel	Gustave	1835	?London	Lyon Gabriel	Adelaide (?)	Louisa Rheuben	City, London	
21662	Gabriel	Harriett	1836	Hull, Yorkshire	Lyon Gabriel	Adelaide (?)	John Emanuel	City, London	dressmaker
19545	Gabriel	Henry	1819	Strand, London			Fanny (?)	Strand, London	tailor
21663	Gabriel	Henry	1837	Hull, Yorkshire	Lyon Gabriel	Adelaide (?)	Kate Levy	City, London	
21660	Gabriel	Jeannette (Joanna)	1829	abroad	Lyon Gabriel	Adelaide (?)	Michael Levy Romberg	City, London	
21664	Gabriel	John	1839	Hull, Yorkshire	Lyon Gabriel	Adelaide (?)	Maud Hyman	City, London	
19550	Gabriel	John	1850	Strand, London	Henry Montague	Fanny (?)		Strand, London	
19499	Gabriel	Levy	1828	Westminster, London	(?) Gabriel	Martha (?)		Strand, London	tailor
28066	Gabriel	Levy	1834	Aldgate, London	Gabriel Gabriel	Sarah (?Levy)		Spitalfields, London	pastrycook
14625	Gabriel	Lewis	1822	Aldgate, London	Michael Gabriel	Frances (?)		Hoxton, London	miller
19496	Gabriel	Louis	1823	Westminster, London	(?) Gabriel	Martha (?)		Strand, London	tailor
21658	Gabriel	Lyon	1786	Amsterdam, Holland			Adelaide (?)	City, London	surgeon dentist
19495	Gabriel	Martha	1790	?, London	(?)		(?) Gabrial	Strand, London	
14623	Gabriel	Michael	1791	Whitechapel, London			Frances (?)	Hoxton, London	china agent
19497	Gabriel	Michael	1825	Westminster, London	(?) Gabriel	Martha (?)		Strand, London	tailor
19547	Gabriel	Montague	1847	Strand, London	Henry Montague	Fanny (?)		Strand, London	scholar
16586	Gabriel	Morris (Maurice)	1831	?, London	Lyon Gabriel	Adelaide (?)	Esther Myers	Liverpool	surgeon dentist
21667	Gabriel	Rose	1842	Liverpool	Lyon Gabriel	Adelaide (?)	Hermann Green	City, London	scholar
28061	Gabriel	Sarah	1792	Whitechapel, London	Avraham HaLevi		(?Benjamin) Lyons	Spitalfields, London	
21669	Gabriel	Solomon	1846	Liverpool	Lyon Gabriel	Adelaide (?)		City, London	
8899	Garcia	Abigail	1819	?Aldgate, London	Abraham de Abraham Garcia	Sarah de Moses Perez	David Henriques Valentine	Aldgate, London	furrier
15221	Garcia	Abigail Rebecca	1788	Aldgate, London	Abraham Gomes Soares	Rebecca de Eliau Lopes Pereira	Daniel de Moses Garcia	Shoreditch, London	annuitant
8879	Garcia	Abraham	1788	?, London	Abraham Garcia	Abigail (?)	Sarah de Moseh Perez	Aldgate, London	fishmonger
9143	Garcia	Abraham	1809	Aldgate, London	Abigador Garcia	Lucy de Samuel Lion	Emma (?)	Mayfair, London	picture dealer
8881	Garcia	Abraham	1813	?Aldgate, London	Abraham de Abraham Garcia	Sarah de Moses Perez		Aldgate, London	cab driver
8885	Garcia	Abraham	1840	Spitalfields, London	Moses Garcia	Hannah Samuel	Catherine (Kitty) Cohen	Spitalfields, London	scholar

ID	surname	given names	born	birthplace	father	mother	spouse 1	1851 residence	1851 occupation
8891	Garcia	Abraham	1843	?Aldgate, London	Isaac Garcia	Isabella (Betsey, Bilha) Simmons		Aldgate, London	
9151	Garcia	Charles	1847	Mayfair, London	Abraham Garcia	Emma (?)		Mayfair, London	
9146	Garcia	Clara	1838	Islington, London	Abraham Garcia	Emma (?)		Mayfair, London	
8851	Garcia	Daniel	1827	Aldgate, London	Abraham Garcia	Sarah Perez	Martha Henry	Aldgate, London	cigar maker
8901	Garcia	David	1833	?Aldgate, London	Abraham de Abraham Garcia	Sarah de Moses Perez	Julia (Judith) Jones	Aldgate, London	
8893	Garcia	David	1846	?Aldgate, London	Isaac Garcia	Isabella (Betsey, Bilha) Simmons	Rosa Isaacs	Aldgate, London	
9150	Garcia	Edward	1845	Marylebone, London	Abraham Garcia	Emma (?)		Mayfair, London	
5596	Garcia	Elizabeth	1844	Covent Garden, London	Samuel de Abigador Garcia	Sarah de Ari Bar Meir	Lawrence Engel	Covent Garden, London	
9149	Garcia	Emily	1843	Mayfair, London	Abraham Garcia	Emma (?)		Mayfair, London	
9144	Garcia	Emma	1815	Aldgate, London	(?)		Abraham Garcia	Mayfair, London	
9152	Garcia	Frederick	1848	Mayfair, London	Abraham Garcia	Emma (?)		Mayfair, London	
9147	Garcia	George	1839	St James, London	Abraham Garcia	Emma (?)		Mayfair, London	
8884	Garcia	Hannah	1822	Aldgate, London	Hyam Samuel	Katharine (?)	Moses Garcia	Spitalfields, London	general dealer
26184	Garcia	Hannah	1827	?, London	(?)		(?) Garcia	Aldgate, London	supported by family
15223	Garcia	Hannah	1830	Aldgate, London	Daniel de Moses Garcia	Abigail Rebecca de Abraham Gomes Soares	Daniel Lindo	Shoreditch, London	
9148	Garcia	Henry	1841	Camberwell, London	Abraham Garcia	Emma (?)		Mayfair, London	
8886	Garcia	Hyam	1843	Spitalfields, London	Moses Garcia	Hannah Samuel		Spitalfields, London	scholar
8889	Garcia	Isaac	1819	?, London	Abraham de Abraham Garcia	Sarah de Moses Perez	Isabella (Betsey, Bilha) Simmons	Aldgate, London	cigar maker
15629	Garcia	Isaac Alfred	1845	Covent Garden, London	Samuel de Abigador Garcia	Sarah de Ari Bar Meir		Covent Garden, London	
9153	Garcia	Isabella	1850	Mayfair, London	Abraham Garcia	Emma (?)		Mayfair, London	
8890	Garcia	Isabella (Betsey, Bilha)	1819	?, London	Joseph Simmons		Isaac Garcia	Aldgate, London	
8892	Garcia	Joseph	1844	?Aldgate, London	Isaac Garcia	Isabella (Betsey, Bilha) Simmons		Aldgate, London	
8882	Garcia	Julia	1815	?Aldgate, London	Abraham de Abraham Garcia	Sarah de Moses Perez		Aldgate, London	
9145	Garcia	Lucy	1834	Covent Garden, London	Abraham Garcia	Emma (?)		Mayfair, London	
7010	Garcia	Lucy	1841	Covent Garden, London	Samuel de Abigador Garcia	Sarah de Ari Bar Meir	Asher Asher	Covent Garden, London	scholar
8852	Garcia	Martha	1832	Aldgate, London	Joseph Henry		Daniel Garcia	Aldgate, London	
15631	Garcia	Martha	1850	Covent Garden, London	Samuel de Abigador Garcia	Sarah de Ari Bar Meir	Solomon J Phillips	Covent Garden, London	
15627	Garcia	Michael John	1839	Strand, London	Samuel de Abigador Garcia	Sarah de Ari Bar Meir	Gertrude Beyfus	Covent Garden, London	scholar
8883	Garcia	Moses	1817	Aldgate, London	Abraham de Abraham Garcia	Sarah de Moses Perez	Hannah Samuel	Spitalfields, London	cigar maker
8888	Garcia	Moss (Moses)	1850	Whitechapel, London	Moses Garcia	Hannah Samuel	Elizabeth Hart	Spitalfields, London	
15626	Garcia	Philip Henry (Avigdor)	1838	Covent Garden, London	Samuel de Abigador Garcia	Sarah de Ari Bar Meir	Rebecca Jessica Barnett Lawrie	Covent Garden, London	scholar
14749	Garcia	Rachael	1781	?, London	(?) Barrios		David Garcia	Spitalfields, London	general dealer
15222	Garcia	Rachael	1831	Aldgate, London	Daniel de Moses Garcia	Abigail Rebecca de Abraham Gomes Soares	Leon (Judah) Benhamu	Shoreditch, London	
14751	Garcia	Raphael	1822	?, London	David Garcia	Rachael Barrios		Spitalfields, London	general dealer
14752	Garcia	Rebecca	1850	?, London	(?) Garcia			Spitalfields, London	
15624	Garcia	Samuel	1810	Aldgate, London	Philip (Abigador) de Abraham Garcia	Lucy de Samuel Lion	Sarah de Ari Bar Meir	Covent Garden, London	fruiterer

ID	surname	given names	born	birthplace	father	mother	spouse 1	1851 residence	1851 occupation
8880	Garcia	Sarah	1792	?, London	Moses Perez	Judith de Moses Torres	Abraham de Abraham Garcia	Aldgate, London	
15625	Garcia	Sarah	1812	Covent Garden, London	Ari Bar Meir		Samuel de Abigador Garcia	Covent Garden, London	
8900	Garcia	Sarah	1831	?Aldgate, London	Abraham de Abraham Garcia	Sarah de Moses Perez		Aldgate, London	cap maker
8887	Garcia	Sarah	1845	Aldgate, London	Moses Garcia	Hannah Samuel		Spitalfields, London	scholar
14750	Garcia	Sophia (Siporah)	1811	?, London	David Garcia	Rachael Barrios		Spitalfields, London	
26185	Garcia	Susan	1849	?, London	(?) Garcia	Hannah (?)		Aldgate, London	
15630	Garcia	Walter (Benjamin)	1847	Covent Garden, London	Samuel de Abigador Garcia	Sarah de Ari Bar Meir		Covent Garden, London	
28928	Garrets	Esther	1845	Amsterdam, Holland	Levy (Louis) Garrets	Rebecca (?)	Asher Green	Spitalfields, London	scholar
28930	Garrets	Gerson	1850	Spitalfields, London	Levy (Louis) Garrets	Rebecca (?)	Deborah Levy	Spitalfields, London	
28927	Garrets	Hannah	1839	Amsterdam, Holland	Levy (Louis) Garrets	Rebecca (?)	Salomon Abraham Haringman	Spitalfields, London	scholar
28929	Garrets	Leah	1847	Amsterdam, Holland	Levy (Louis) Garrets	Rebecca (?)		Spitalfields, London	
28925	Garrets	Levy (Louis)	1816	Amsterdam, Holland			Rebecca (?)	Spitalfields, London	dealer in jewellery
28926	Garrets	Rebecca	1816	Amsterdam, Holland	(?)		Levy (Louis) Garrets	Spitalfields, London	
13413	Garrit	Harrod	1811	?, Holland			Silvar (?)	Spitalfields, London	hawker of tapes
13417	Garrit	Henery	1848	?, London	Harrod Garrit	Silvar (?)		Spitalfields, London	
13416	Garrit	Jacob	1846	?, Holland	Harrod Garrit	Silvar (?)		Spitalfields, London	scholar
13415	Garrit	Sarrah	1844	Paris, France	Harrod Garrit	Silvar (?)		Spitalfields, London	school
13414	Garrit	Silvar	1808	?, Holland			Silvar (?)	Spitalfields, London	
27780	Gasen	Hartog	1831	Amsterdam, Holland				Spitalfields, London	cigar maker
2262	Gashan	Abraham	1813	?, London				Leeds, Yorkshire	hawker
25358	Gashion	Catherine	1830	?London	Joseph Isaacs		Isaac Gashion	Aldgate, London	
25355	Gashion	Fanny	1837	Walworth, London	Michael Gashion		Hyaman Abraham Cohen	Clerkenwell, London	
25354	Gashion	Isaac	1828	?London	Michael Gashion		Catherine Isaacs	Aldgate, London	?
30447	Gashion	Jane	1850	Aldgate, London	Isaac Gashion	Catherine Isaacs	Coleman Joel	Aldgate, London	
30448	Gashion	Joseph	1851	Aldgate, London	Isaac Gashion	Catherine Isaacs		Aldgate, London	
25353	Gashion	Joseph	1828	?London	Michael Gashion		Jane Davis	Clerkenwell, London	?
25356	Gashion	Louis	1844	St Giles, London	Michael Gashion			Clerkenwell, London	scholar
25350	Gashion	Maria [Leah]	1811	?, Isle of Wight	John Beacham		Michael Gashion	Clerkenwell, London	
25349	Gashion	Michael	1796	Whitechapel, London	Gershon Gashion		(?)	Clerkenwell, London	iron dealer
25357	Gashion	Rachael	1846	St Giles, London	Michael Gashion			Clerkenwell, London	scholar
25352	Gashion	Samuel	1831	St Giles, London	Michael Gashion		Julia Kauffman	Clerkenwell, London	assistant to iron broker
25351	Gashion	Sarah	1831	Walworth, London	Michael Gashion			Clerkenwell, London	dress maker
16386	Genese	Abigail	1796	City, London	Haim Daniel Dias		Samson de Samuel Genese	Aldgate, London	
9016	Genese	Abraham	1798	City, London	Samson de Isaac Genese	Esther de Abraham Bernal		Aldgate, London	
9003	Genese	Abraham	1841	Strand, London	David Genese	Sarah (?)		Strand, London	scholar
8519	Genese	Abraham	1846	Finsbury, London	Samuel Genese	Rachel Levy		Piccadilly, London	scholar
19122	Genese	Catherine (Keturah)	1846	Aldgate, London	Emanuel Genese	Sarah Tolano		Aldgate, London	
8998	Genese	David	1807	Islington, London	Samson de Isaac Genese	Esther de Abraham Bernal	Sarah (?)	Strand, London	glass cutter
8994	Genese	David	1837	Middlesex, London	(?) Genese			Piccadilly, London	errand boy
9001	Genese	David	1837	City, London	David Genese	Sarah (?)		Strand, London	scholar
9014	Genese	David	1847	Aldgate, London	Samson Genese	Hannah Simons		Aldgate, London	
9000	Genese	Emily	1834	Strand, London	David Genese	Sarah (?)		Strand, London	bookfolder

ID	surname	given names	born	birthplace	father	mother	spouse 1	1851 residence	1851 occupation
9320	Genese	Esther	1771	Aldgate, London	Abraham de Isaac Bernal	Sarah de Isaac Soares	Samson de Isaac Genese	Aldgate, London	poor
9010	Genese	Esther	1838	City, London	Samson Genese	Hannah Simons	Leon (Judah) Zabban	Aldgate, London	scholar
8996	Genese	Hannah	1804	Middlesex, London	Samson Genese			Piccadilly, London	
9009	Genese	Hannah	1808	Aldgate, London	Isaac Simons		Sampson Genese	Aldgate, London	
9005	Genese	Hannah	1846	Strand, London	David Genese	Sarah (?)		Strand, London	
8513	Genese	Hannah (Anna)	1840	Strand, London	Samuel Genese	Rachel (?)	Elias Jacobs	Piccadilly, London	scholar
9011	Genese	Isaac	1838	City, London	Samson Genese	Hannah Simons	Annette Bensilum	Aldgate, London	scholar
8995	Genese	John	1838	Middlesex, London	(?) Genese			Piccadilly, London	errand boy
9002	Genese	John	1839	Strand, London	David Genese	Sarah (?)		Strand, London	scholar
8518	Genese	Joseph	1842	?Strand, London	Samuel Genese	Rachel Levy		Piccadilly, London	boarding school pupil
9015	Genese	Julia (Judith)	1849	Aldgate, London	Samson Genese	Hannah Simons		Aldgate, London	
16623	Genese	Margaret	1827	?, Ireland	(?) Kelly		Samuel Genese	Liverpool	
8520	Genese	Philip Avigdor	1848	Finsbury, London	Samuel Genese	Rachel Levy	Sarah Jane Isaacs	Piccadilly, London	
9013	Genese	Rachael	1844	Aldgate, London	Samson Genese	Hannah Simons		Aldgate, London	
9006	Genese	Rachael	1849	Strand, London	David Genese	Sarah (?)		Strand, London	
8515	Genese	Rachel	1820	Whitechapel, London	Levy Levy		Samuel Genese	Piccadilly, London	
19123	Genese	Rachel	1848	Aldgate, London	Emanuel Genese	Sarah Tolano	Isaac de Aaron Gomes Da Costa	Aldgate, London	
19120	Genese	Rebecca	1843	Aldgate, London	Emanuel Genese	Sarah Tolano	Abraham Zagury	Aldgate, London	
16624	Genese	Robert	1848	?, Ireland	Samuel Genese	Margaret Kelly		Liverpool	
9008	Genese	Samson	1800	City, London	Samson de Isaac Genese	Esther de Abraham Bernal	Hannah de Isaac Simons	Aldgate, London	general dealer + porter
16385	Genese	Samson	1804	City, London	Samuel Genese	Rebecca de Emanuel Capua	Abigail de Haim Daniel Dias	Aldgate, London	sexton to Synagogue
9012	Genese	Samson	1841	Dublin, Ireland	Samson Genese	Hannah Simons	Fanny Benjamin	Aldgate, London	scholar
8517	Genese	Samson (Samuel)	1842	Strand, London	Samuel Genese	Rachel Levy	Eliza	Piccadilly, London	boarding school pupil
8514	Genese	Samuel	1805	Aldgate, London	Samson de Isaac Genese	Esther de Abraham Bernal	Rachel Levy	Piccadilly, London	coffee house keeper + dealer in plate, watches, jewels + pictures
5394	Genese	Samuel	1820	Middlesex, London	Isaac Haim de Hezekiah Genese	Esther de Isaac Isaac	Margaret Kelly	Liverpool	auctioneer
9004	Genese	Samuel	1843	Strand, London	David Genese	Sarah (?)		Strand, London	scholar
9034	Genese	Samuel	1845	City, London	Emanuel Genese	Sarah Tolano	Dinah Jacobs	Aldgate, London	
8521	Genese	Samuel	1850	Westminster, London	Samuel Genese	Rachel Levy		Piccadilly, London	
9321	Genese	Sarah	1795	Aldgate, London	Samson de Isaac Genese	Esther de Abraham Bernal		Aldgate, London	feather dresser
8999	Genese	Sarah	1813	Middlesex, London	(?)		David Genese	Strand, London	
19119	Genese	Sarah	1825	Bethnal Green, London	Joseph Tolano		Emanuel de Samuel Genese	Aldgate, London	mangling woman
8516	Genese	Sarah	1838	Whitechapel, London	Samuel Genese	Rachel Levy		Piccadilly, London	scholar
25534	Genese	Solomon	1820	?			(?)	Dublin, Ireland	tobacconist?
10125	Gershon	Aaron	1813	Whitechapel, London	Samuel Gershon	Elizabeth Kahn (Cohen)	Rose (Rosetta) Sims	Stepney, London	commission agent
26050	Gershon	Aaron	1835	Birmingham	Isaac Gershon	Harriet? (?)		Whitechapel, London	cigar maker
26051	Gershon	Catharine	1839	?, London	Isaac Gershon	Harriet? (?)		Whitechapel, London	scholar
10097	Gershon	Dinah	1851	Mile End, London	Aaron Gershon	Rose (Rosetta) Sims	Henry M Chapman	Stepney, London	
22610	Gershon	Elizabeth	1781	?, London	(?) Kahn (Cohen)		Samuel Gershon	Stepney, London	furniture dealer
22189	Gershon	Emanuel	1844	Whitechapel, London	George Gershon	Rachael Jane (?)	Rose Solomons (Solomon)	Whitechapel, London	scholar
22184	Gershon	George	1804	Whitechapel, London	Samuel Gershon	Elizabeth Kahn (Cohen)	Rachael Jane (?)	Whitechapel, London	furniture broker

ID	surname	given names	born	birthplace	father	mother	spouse 1	1851 residence	1851 occupation
27504	Gershon	Hannah	1795	Middlesex, London			(?) Gershon	Aldgate, London	furniture broker
22613	Gershon	Hannah	1819	Whitechapel, London	Samuel Gershon	Elizabeth Kahn (Cohen)		Stepney, London	furniture dealer
26048	Gershon	Harriet?	1807	Birmingham	(?)		Isaac Gershon	Whitechapel, London	quill pen maker
12971	Gershon	Hyam (Hyman)	1847	?, London	Michael Gershon	Martha (?)	Hannah Hart	Aldgate, London	
26047	Gershon	Isaac	1805	Whitechapel, London	Samuel Gershon	Elizabeth Kahn (Cohen)	Harriet?	Whitechapel, London	quill pen maker
22188	Gershon	Joseph	1836	Colchester, Essex	George Gershon	Rachael Jane (?)		Whitechapel, London	cigar maker
10131	Gershon	Joseph	1850	Elephant & Castle, London	Aaron Gershon	Rose (Rosetta) Sims	Rachael Simons	Stepney, London	
10130	Gershon	Julia	1847	Bermondsey, London	Aaron Gershon	Rose (Rosetta) Sims	John Jones	Stepney, London	scholar
22614	Gershon	Maria	1831	?, London	(?) Gershon			Stepney, London	furniture dealer
26049	Gershon	Maria	1833	Birmingham	Isaac Gershon	Harriet? (?)		Whitechapel, London	dressmaker
12970	Gershon	Martha	1826	?, Poland	(?)		Michael Gershon	Aldgate, London	
12969	Gershon	Michael	1824	?, Poland			Martha (?)	Aldgate, London	clothes dealer + rag merchant
12973	Gershon	Myer	1850	?, London	Michael Gershon	Martha (?)		Aldgate, London	
22186	Gershon	Phoebe	1830	Whitechapel, London	George Gershon	Rachael Jane (?)		Whitechapel, London	seamstress
22185	Gershon	Rachael Jane	1804	Chelmsford, Essex	(?)		George Gershon	Whitechapel, London	
10129	Gershon	Rachel	1845	Spitalfields, London	Aaron Gershon	Rose (Rosetta) Sims	Mordecai Haas	Stepney, London	scholar
22611	Gershon	Raphael	1811	Whitechapel, London	Samuel Gershon	Elizabeth Kahn (Cohen)		Stepney, London	furniture dealer
22612	Gershon	Rebecca	1812	Whitechapel, London	(Samuel Gershon	Elizabeth Kahn (Cohen)		Stepney, London	furniture dealer
22187	Gershon	Rose	1833	Colchester, Essex	George Gershon	Rachael Jane (?)		Whitechapel, London	seamstress
10126	Gershon	Rose (Rosetta)	1814	Spitalfields, London	G--- Sims	Judith (?)	Aaron Gershon	Stepney, London	
10127	Gershon	Samuel	1841	Spitalfields, London	Aaron Gershon	Rose (Rosetta) Sims		Stepney, London	scholar
12972	Gershon	Samuel	1848	?, London	Michael Gershon	Martha (?)		Aldgate, London	
10128	Gershon	Selim	1843	Spitalfields, London	Aaron Gershon	Rose (Rosetta) Sims	Elizabeth J Bryan	Stepney, London	scholar
18034	Gersonn	Heiman	1827	?, Poland				Grimsby, Lincolnshire	jeweller
21689	Gerstenberg	Isidor	1822	?, Poland [?, Prussia]				Islington, London	merchant + exchange broker
14209	Geyer	Maurice	1811	?, Germany				Manchester	clerk
4459	Gheckman	Solomon	1825	?, Poland [?, Prussia]				Birmingham	glazier
810	Gideon	David	1801	City, London	Jonas Gideon		Caroline Lawrence	Uxbridge, Middlesex	clothier servant
31141	Gideon	Esther	1791	?, London	(?)		(?) Gideon	Croydon, Surrey	
31138	Gideon	Jonah	1824	?, London	(?) Gideon	Esther (?)	Sarah Myers	Croydon, Surrey	clothier
31140	Gideon	Louisa	1850	Croydon, Surrey	Jonah Gideon	Sarah Myers		Croydon, Surrey	
31139	Gideon	Sarah	1828	?, London	(?) Myers		Jonah Gideon	Croydon, Surrey	
27863	Gideon	Sarah	1832	Whitechapel, London	Louis Gideon	Jane Marks	Herman Pizer	Spitalfields, London	waistcoat maker
12227	Gilbert	Morris	1828	?, Poland				Whitechapel, London	tailor
27387	Gilbert	Moses	1817	?, Poland [Plosick, Poland]				Aldgate, London	tailor
8283	Giller	Laura	1837	Bristol	(?) Giller			North Shields, Tyne & Wear	scholar
15383	Ginsburg	Christian Daniel	1831	Warsaw, Poland			Emily (?)	Waterloo, London	student
15382	Ginsburg	James	1826	?, Russia				Waterloo, London	student
2264	Girson	Abel	1823	?, Poland				Leeds, Yorkshire	hawker
2132	Glassman	Victor	1829	?, Poland [?, Prussia]			Minna Haberland	Hull, Yorkshire	tea dealer's assistant
14405	Glatz	Joseph	1801	abroad				Manchester	watch + clock maker
4461	Glistone	Ann	1829	?, Poland [?, Prussia]			Samuel Glistone	Birmingham	

ID	surname	given names	born	birthplace	father	mother	spouse 1	1851 residence	1851 occupation
4460	Glistone	Samuel	1829	?, Poland			Ann (?)	Birmingham	shoemaker
20	Glück	Jacob Rosenthal	1834	Poznan, Poland [Posen, Prussia]	Louis Rosenthal Glück	Amalia (Male) (?)	Maria Levy	Charlton, London	printer's apprentice
21	Glück	Leah Rosenthal	1832	Poznan, Poland [Posen, Prussia]	Louis Rosenthal Glück	Amalia (Male) (?)	Aaron Bash	Charlton, London	
1	Glück	Louis Rosenthal	1804	Poznan, Poland [Posen, Prussia]	Pielte Elimelech Glück	(?)	Amalie (Male) (?)	Charlton, London	professor of languages
23	Glück	Pielte (Philip) Rosenthal	1848	Charlton, London	Louis Rosenthal Glück	Rebecca Levy	Dinah Baum	Charlton, London	scholar
24	Glück	Rebecca Rosenthal	1818	Woolwich, London	Nathan Levy	Sarah (Mary) Palmer	Louis Rosenthal Glück	Charlton, London	dressmaker
22	Glück [Rosebery]	Morris Rosenthal	1850	Charlton, London	Louis Rosenthal Glück	Rebecca Levy	Rebecca Hyam	Charlton, London	
30918	Gluckman	Isaac	1832	?, Poland [?, Prussia]				Sheffield, Yorkshire	engraver
12628	Glucksman	Solomon	1825	?, Poland [?, Prussia]				Birmingham	glazier
17732	Gluckstein	Adolphus	1843	?, Belgium	Lehmann (Asher) Meyer Gluckstein	Helena Horn	Elizabeth (Eliza) Ansell	Whitechapel, London	scholar
17731	Gluckstein	Bertha	1835	?, Holland	Lehmann (Asher) Meyer Gluckstein	Helena Horn	Lawrence Abrahams	Whitechapel, London	governess of a school
10862	Gluckstein	Bertha (Betsey)	1848	Spitalfields, London	Samuel Gluckstein	Hannah (Ann) Josephs	Julius Koppenhagen	Spitalfields, London	scholar
10863	Gluckstein	Catherine (Kate, Kitty)	1850	Spitalfields, London	Samuel Gluckstein	Hannah (Ann) Josephs	Samuel Joseph	Spitalfields, London	
10859	Gluckstein	Hannah (Ann)	1821	?, Holland	Yekutiel HaCohen Josephs		Samuel Gluckstein	Spitalfields, London	
17728	Gluckstein	Helena	1798	?, Poland [?, Prussia]	(?) Horn		Lehmann (Asher) Meyer Gluckstein	Whitechapel, London	
17730	Gluckstein	Henry (Harry)	1833	Arnhem, Holland	Lehmann (Asher) Meyer Gluckstein	Helena Horn	Rose Levien	Whitechapel, London	cigar maker
10861	Gluckstein	Julia	1847	Spitalfields, London	Samuel Gluckstein	Hannah (Ann) Josephs	Abraham Abrahams	Spitalfields, London	scholar
17727	Gluckstein	Lehmann (Asher) Meyer	1791	Oldenburg, Germany			Helena Horn	Whitechapel, London	professor of languages
10860	Gluckstein	Lena	1846	Spitalfields, London	Samuel Gluckstein	Hannah (Ann) Josephs	Barnett Solomons (Salmon)	Spitalfields, London	scholar
10858	Gluckstein	Samuel	1821	?, Germany	Asher Gluckstein		Hannah (Ann) Josephs	Spitalfields, London	cigar dealer
17729	Gluckstein	Solly	1831	?, Holland	Lehmann (Asher) Meyer Gluckstein	Helena Horn		Whitechapel, London	cigar maker
13018	Gobertz	Abraham	1794	?, Holland			(?)	Spitalfields, London	jeweller
30449	Gobertz	Abraham	1851	Aldgate, London	Isaac Abraham Gobertz	Julia A Levy		Aldgate, London	
17433	Gobertz	Amelia A	1850	?Spitalfields, London	Isaac Abraham Gobertz	Julia A Levy		Spitalfields, London	
17430	Gobertz	Isaac Abraham	1822	?, Holland	Abraham Gobertz	(?)	Julia A Levy	Spitalfields, London	jeweller
13019	Gobertz	Julia	1830	?, Holland	Abraham Gobertz	(?)	David Levy	Spitalfields, London	
17431	Gobertz	Julia A	1823	?, Holland	Asher Anshel Levy		Isaac Abraham Gobertz	Spitalfields, London	
17435	Gobertz	Mary	1825	?, Holland	Solomon Mossel	(?)	Moses Abraham Gobertz	Spitalfields, London	
17434	Gobertz	Moses Abraham	1827	?, Holland	Abraham Gobertz	(?)	Mary Solomon Mossel	Spitalfields, London	cigar maker
13020	Gobertz	Rebecca	1832	?, Holland	Abraham Gobertz	(?)		Spitalfields, London	
17432	Gobertz	Rebecca A	1849	?Spitalfields, London	Isaac Abraham Gobertz	Julia A Levy	Barnett Miller	Spitalfields, London	
13584	Gobinsky	Juda	1828	?, Poland				Manchester	cap maker
7177	Godfrey	Samuel	1817	Middlesex, London	Solomon Godfrey		Rachel Catherine Isaac	Hull, Yorkshire	clerk
24396	Goetze	Esther	1829	Soho, London	Noah Goetze	(?)		Soho, London	
24395	Goetze	Noah	1781	Covent Garden, London			(?)	Soho, London	stationer

ID	surname	given names	born	birthplace	father	mother	spouse 1	1851 residence	1851 occupation
13681	Goldberg	Aaron	1850	Manchester	Solomon Goldberg	Margaret (?)		Manchester	scholar
19295	Goldberg	Anne	1838	?, Poland [?, Prussia]	Lewis Goldberg	Hannah Brasch	Jacob Hollander	Nottingham, Nottinghamshire	
23544	Goldberg	Ashley	1835	Liverpool	(?) Goldberg	Sarah (?)		Liverpool	glazier + silverer
17646	Goldberg	Barnet	1850	?, London	George (Juda) Goldberg	Louisa (Leah) Isaacs		Aldgate, London	
30369	Goldberg	Casimir Joseph Adam	1823	Warsaw, Poland			Emily Farn	Great Heywood, Staffordshire	brewer, empl 3
23545	Goldberg	Clara	1836	Liverpool	(?) Goldberg	Sarah (?)		Liverpool	scholar
14333	Goldberg	David	1823	?, Austria				Manchester	bookbinder
26944	Goldberg	Davis	1834	?, Poland				Aldgate, London	tailor
19296	Goldberg	Elizabeth	1840	?, Poland [?, Prussia]	Lewis Goldberg	Hannah Brasch	Lewis Karmel	Nottingham, Nottinghamshire	
17644	Goldberg	Elizabeth	1847	Aldgate, London	George (Juda) Goldberg	Louisa (Leah) Isaacs	Simon Henri Wheirman	Aldgate, London	
17642	Goldberg	George (Judah)	1823	?, Poland	Baruch Goldberg		Louisa (Leah) Isaacs	Aldgate, London	slipper maker
19292	Goldberg	Hannah	1814	Hamburg, Germant	Simon Brasch	Hannah (?)	Lewis Goldberg	Nottingham, Nottinghamshire	
17645	Goldberg	Isaac	1850	?, London	George (Juda) Goldberg	Louisa (Leah) Isaacs		Aldgate, London	
4462	Goldberg	Israel	1821	?, Poland			Sophia (?)	Birmingham	shoemaker
30785	Goldberg	Joseph	1827	Warsaw, Poland				Preston, Lancashire	traveller
19294	Goldberg	Joseph	1836	?, Poland [?, Prussia]	Lewis Goldberg	Hannah Brasch		Nottingham, Nottinghamshire	
2695	Goldberg	Lewis	1797	?, Poland [?, Prussia]			Hannah Brasch	Nottingham, Nottinghamshire	rabbi
23543	Goldberg	Louis	1821	?, Poland	(?) Goldberg	Sarah (?)		Liverpool	steel pen dealer
17643	Goldberg	Louisa (Leah)	1819	?, London	Isaac Isaacs		George (Juda) Goldberg	Aldgate, London	
13678	Goldberg	Margaret	1822	?, Poland [?, Prussia]	(?)		Solomon Goldberg	Manchester	attends house + shop
25864	Goldberg	Michael	1831	?Latvia [?Kurland]				Aldgate, London	cigar maker journeyman
19298	Goldberg	Philip	1844	?, Poland [?, Prussia]	Lewis Goldberg	Hannah Brasch		Nottingham, Nottinghamshire	
19297	Goldberg	Phoebe	1842	?, Poland [?, Prussia]	Lewis Goldberg	Hannah Brasch	Wolf Flegeltaub	Nottingham, Nottinghamshire	
19299	Goldberg	Rebecca	1849	Swansea, Wales	Lewis Goldberg	Hannah Brasch	Simon Harris	Nottingham, Nottinghamshire	
23542	Goldberg	Sarah	1791	?, Poland	(?)		(?) Goldberg	Liverpool	
13679	Goldberg	Selina	1846	?, Poland [?, Prussia]	Solomon Goldberg	Margaret (?)		Manchester	scholar
13680	Goldberg	Simeon	1848	Manchester	Solomon Goldberg	Margaret (?)		Manchester	scholar
1787	Goldberg	Simon	1821	Schneidermahl, Germany	Joseph Goldberg		Hinda (Hinder, Heinda) Barnett	Swansea, Wales	pawnbroker
19293	Goldberg	Simon	1835	?, Poland [?, Prussia]	Lewis Goldberg	Hannah Brasch		Nottingham, Nottinghamshire	
13677	Goldberg	Solomon	1822	?, Poland [?, Prussia]			Margaret (?)	Manchester	cabinet maker
4463	Goldberg	Sophia	1821	?, Austria			Israel Goldberg	Birmingham	
1788	Goldblink	Nathaniel	1833	?				Swansea, Wales	traveller
4464	Goldburg	Nathan	1825	?, Poland				Birmingham	hawker
13567	Goldenkranz	David	1832	Silesia, Poland				Manchester	glazier
26444	Goldhill	Albert Morris	1842	Finsbury, London	Samuel Goldhill	Matilda Moss	Elizabeth Harris	Aldgate, London	

211

ID	surname	given names	born	birthplace	father	mother	spouse 1	1851 residence	1851 occupation
26603	Goldhill	Benjamin Moss	1838	Whitechapel, London	Samuel Goldhill	Matilda Moss	Sarah Nunes Martin (Martines)	Aldgate, London	
26447	Goldhill	Jeanette	1850	Aldgate, London	Samuel Goldhill	Matilda Moss		Aldgate, London	
26443	Goldhill	John Isaac	1840	?, London	Samuel Goldhill	Matilda Moss	Sarah Hyman	Aldgate, London	
26446	Goldhill	Lewis (Louis)	1850	Aldgate, London	Samuel Goldhill	Matilda Moss	Julia Joseph	Aldgate, London	
26442	Goldhill	Matilda	1819	Whitechapel, London	Benjamin Moss		Samuel Goldhill	Aldgate, London	
26441	Goldhill	Samuel	1813	?, Poland	Isaac Nachum HaCohen		Matilda Moss	Aldgate, London	sponge dealer
26445	Goldhill	Sophia Deborah	1847	Whitechapel, London	Samuel Goldhill	Matilda Moss	Simon Saks	Aldgate, London	
13801	Goldman	Cecilia	1851	Hamburg, Germany	David Goldman	Emma (?)		Manchester	
13795	Goldman	David	1817	?, Poland [?, Prussia]			Emma (?)	Manchester	cap mfr
13798	Goldman	Dorothy	1845	Hamburg, Germany	David Goldman	Emma (?)		Manchester	scholar
13796	Goldman	Emma	1807	Hamburg, Germany	(?)		David Goldman	Manchester	house
14647	Goldman	Emma	1821	Southwark, London	(?)		Leopold Goldman	Hoxton, London	
14650	Goldman	Emma	1850	Shoreditch, London	Leopold Goldman	Emma (?)		Hoxton, London	
14649	Goldman	Frederick	1846	Shoreditch, London	Leopold Goldman	Emma (?)		Hoxton, London	
13799	Goldman	Hannah (Annie)	1847	Hamburg, Germany	David Goldman	Emma (?)	Joseph Schwersenz	Manchester	scholar
14648	Goldman	Henrietta	1846	Finsbury, London	Leopold Goldman	Emma (?)		Hoxton, London	scholar
8377	Goldman	Jacob A	1805	abroad	Ezriel Goldman		(?)	Southampton, Hampshire	Jewish clergyman
27847	Goldman	Judah	1829	?, Poland				Spitalfields, London	slipper maker
14646	Goldman	Leopold	1816	?, Poland [?, Prussia]			Emma (?)	Hoxton, London	warehouseman at furriers
13797	Goldman	Priscilla	1843	Hamburg, Germany	David Goldman	Emma (?)		Manchester	scholar
13800	Goldman	Theodore	1850	Hamburg, Germany	David Goldman	Emma (?)		Manchester	
23064	Goldring	Herman	1816	?, Germany	Raphael Abraham Goldring		Alice Cantor	Aldgate, London	tailor
2698	Goldschmidt	Edward	1827	Cassel, Germany				Nottingham, Nottinghamshire	silk trader + manufacturer
14151	Goldschmidt	Nathan	1809	?, Germany				Manchester	merchant
14382	Goldschmidt	Philip	1815	?, Germany				Manchester	cotton merchant
19581	Goldschmidt	Rose	1811	?, London	Moses Solomon		Solomon Lyon	?Plymouth, Devon	
2435	Goldskin	Abraham	1829	?, Poland				Hull, Yorkshire	pedlar
7105	Goldsmid	Aaron	1785	Whitechapel, London	Abraham Goldsmid			Bloomsbury, London	general merchant
7421	Goldsmid	Aaron Asher	1786	?, London	Asher Goldsmid		Sophia Solomons	Marylebone, London	funded proprietor
29832	Goldsmid	Abraham	1838	Middlesex, London	(?) Goldsmid	Frances (?)		Wapping, London	apprentice biscuit baker
27678	Goldsmid	Abraham	1847	Middlesex, London	Joseph Goldsmid	Celia Jacobs		Aldgate, London	scholar
30087	Goldsmid	Abraham	1851	Spitalfields, London	Jacob Goldsmid	Rachel Isaacs	Elizabeth Moses	Spitalfields, London	
24868	Goldsmid	Adelaide	1831	Bath	George Goldsmid	Hester (Esther) Solomon	John Davis	Bermondsey, London	cap maker
23906	Goldsmid	Albert	1793	Stamford Hill, London	Benjamin Goldsmid	Jessy	Caroline Goldsmid	Marylebone, London	Lieut. Col. Army
27677	Goldsmid	Albert	1846	Middlesex, London	Joseph Goldsmid	Celia Jacobs		Aldgate, London	scholar
15958	Goldsmid	Albert A	1841	Marylebone, London	Frederick David Goldsmid	Caroline Samuel		Marylebone, London	scholar at home
27674	Goldsmid	Alfred	1841	Middlesex, London	Joseph Goldsmid	Celia Jacobs		Aldgate, London	scholar
7092	Goldsmid	Anna Maria	1805	Spitalfields, London	Isaac Lyon Goldsmid	Isabel Goldsmid		Regent's Park, London	benefactor + translator
19626	Goldsmid	Aron	1833	Spitalfields, London				Spitalfields, London	tailor
7098	Goldsmid	Caroline	1815	Finsbury, London	Shmuel Zenvil Samuel		Frederick Henry Goldsmid	Marylebone, London	
23907	Goldsmid	Caroline	1815	Finsbury, London	(?) Goldsmid		Albert Goldsmid	Marylebone, London	
7106	Goldsmid	Caroline	1817	Spitalfields, London	Isaac Lyon Goldsmid	Isabel Goldsmid		Regent's Park, London	

212

ID	surname	given names	born	birthplace	father	mother	spouse 1	1851 residence	1851 occupation
24829	Goldsmid	Caroline	1821	Lambeth, London	Lamert Goldsmid	Esther (?)		Elephant & Castle, London	
16344	Goldsmid	Cecelia	1829	Middlesex, London	Sampson Goldsmid	Jane (?)		Bloomsbury, London	
27669	Goldsmid	Celia	1811	Middlesex, London	Aaron Jacobs		Joseph Goldsmid	Aldgate, London	
27675	Goldsmid	Celina	1843	Middlesex, London	Joseph Goldsmid	Celia Jacobs		Aldgate, London	scholar
24866	Goldsmid	Charlotte	1826	Bath	George Goldsmid	Hester (Esther) Solomon	Lewis Marcusson	Bermondsey, London	straw bonnet maker
24865	Goldsmid	Clara	1823	Waltham Abbey, Essex	George Goldsmid	Hester (Esther) Solomon		Bermondsey, London	cap maker
18206	Goldsmid	Daniel	1837	Middlesex, London				Mile End, London	scholar
29833	Goldsmid	David	1840	Middlesex, London	(?) Goldsmid	Frances (?)		Wapping, London	scholar
24869	Goldsmid	Deborah	1833	Bath	George Goldsmid	Hester (Esther) Solomon		Bermondsey, London	cap maker
20823	Goldsmid	Edward (Moses)	1764	Dover, Kent	Hirsch Goldsmid		Rose Joachim	Marylebone, London	Chairman of the Globe Insurance
24830	Goldsmid	Edwin	1834	Elephant & Castle, London	Lamert Goldsmid	Esther (?)		Elephant & Castle, London	
16343	Goldsmid	Elizabeth	1827	Middlesex, London	Sampson Goldsmid	Jane (?)		Bloomsbury, London	
30084	Goldsmid	Elizabeth	1847	Aldgate, London	Jacob Goldsmid	Rachel Isaacs		Spitalfields, London	
24828	Goldsmid	Esther	1796	Elephant & Castle, London	(?)		Lamert Goldsmid	Elephant & Castle, London	
20825	Goldsmid	Esther	1809	Shoreditch, London	Edward (Moses) Goldsmid	Rose Joachim		Marylebone, London	
29831	Goldsmid	Esther	1836	Middlesex, London	(?) Goldsmid	Frances (?)		Wapping, London	apprentice umbrella maker
15950	Goldsmid	Esther	1850	Aldgate, London	Isaac Goldsmid	Rosetta Isaacs	Isaac Solomon	Aldgate, London	
15959	Goldsmid	Flora	1845	Hastings, Sussex	Frederick David Goldsmid	Caroline Samuel		Marylebone, London	scholar at home
7095	Goldsmid	Francis Henry	1807	Spitalfields, London	Isaac Lyon Goldsmid	Isabel Goldsmid	Louisa Sophia Goldsmid	Marylebone, London	barrister in actual practice
7097	Goldsmid	Frederick David	1812	Spitalfields, London	Isaac Lyon Goldsmid	Isabel Goldsmid	Caroline Samuel	Marylebone, London	bullion broker
24863	Goldsmid	George	1784	abroad			Hester (Esther) Solomon	Bermondsey, London	
16342	Goldsmid	George	1816	Middlesex, London	Sampson Goldsmid	Jane (?)		Bloomsbury, London	
15956	Goldsmid	Helen	1836	Marylebone, London	Frederick David Goldsmid	Caroline Samuel	Lionel Lucas	Marylebone, London	scholar at home
7115	Goldsmid	Henry	1845	Aldgate, London	Jacob Goldsmid	Rachel Isaacs		Spitalfields, London	
27679	Goldsmid	Henry	1849	Middlesex, London	Joseph Goldsmid	Celia Jacobs		Aldgate, London	
23908	Goldsmid	Hertz? Henry	1816	Marylebone, London				Marylebone, London	merchant (foreign)
24864	Goldsmid	Hester (Esther)	1796	Hanover, Germany	(?) Solomon		George Goldsmid	Bermondsey, London	cap maker
15949	Goldsmid	Isaac	1822	Elephant & Castle, London			Rosetta Isaacs	Aldgate, London	fruiterer
7093	Goldsmid	Isaac Lyon	1778	City, London	Asher N Goldsmid	Rachel Keyser	Isabel Goldsmid	Regent's Park, London	financier + community leader
7094	Goldsmid	Isabel	1788	Middlesex, London	Abraham Goldsmid		Isaac Lyon Goldsmid	Regent's Park, London	
20826	Goldsmid	Isabel	1811	Shoreditch, London	Edward (Moses) Goldsmid	Rose Joachim		Marylebone, London	
7107	Goldsmid	Isabel	1842	Marylebone, London	Frederick David Goldsmid	Caroline Samuel		Marylebone, London	scholar at home
30082	Goldsmid	Jacob	1810	Middlesex, London	Eli HaLevi Goldsmid		Rachel Isaacs	Spitalfields, London	
29830	Goldsmid	Jacob	1834	Middlesex, London	(?) Goldsmid	Frances (?)		Wapping, London	cigar maker
16341	Goldsmid	Jane	1797	?, Shropshire	(?)		Sampson Goldsmid	Bloomsbury, London	
27408	Goldsmid	Joel	1850	Aldgate, London	Solomon Goldsmid	Rosina Hart		Whitechapel, London	
24831	Goldsmid	Johnny	1844	Elephant & Castle, London	Lamert Goldsmid	Esther (?)		Elephant & Castle, London	scholar
27668	Goldsmid	Joseph	1811	Middlesex, London	Michael Goldsmid		Fanny Mordecai	Aldgate, London	Birmingham warehouse

ID	surname	given names	born	birthplace	father	mother	spouse 1	1851 residence	1851 occupation
24870	Goldsmid	Joseph	1836	Bath	George Goldsmid	Hester (Esther) Solomon		Bermondsey, London	cigar maker
7104	Goldsmid	Julia	1823	Middlesex, London	Isaac Lyon Goldsmid	Isabel Goldsmid		Regent's Park, London	
27673	Goldsmid	Julia	1840	Middlesex, London	Joseph Goldsmid	Celia Jacobs	Abraham Abrahams	Aldgate, London	scholar
7099	Goldsmid	Julian	1838	Marylebone, London	Frederick David Goldsmid	Caroline Samuel	Virginia Philipson	Marylebone, London	scholar at home
7114	Goldsmid	Kate	1841	Aldgate, London	Jacob Goldsmid	Rachel Isaacs		Spitalfields, London	
24827	Goldsmid	Lamert	1796	Whitechapel, London			Esther (?)	Elephant & Castle, London	fruiterer
8409	Goldsmid	Lewis	1832	Southwark, London				Newport, Isle of Wight	fruiterer
27680	Goldsmid	Lionel	1850	?Aldgate, London	Joseph Goldsmid	Celia Jacobs		Aldgate, London	
7096	Goldsmid	Louisa Sophia	1819	Shoreditch, London	Moses Asher Goldsmid	Eliza Salomons	Francis Henry Goldsmid	Marylebone, London	feminist + promoter of women's education
30085	Goldsmid	Martha	1849	Aldgate, London	Jacob Goldsmid	Rachel Isaacs	Joseph Cohen	Spitalfields, London	
6189	Goldsmid	Mary Ada	1836	Marylebone, London	Frederick David Goldsmid	Caroline Samuel	Frederick David Mocatta	Marylebone, London	
27672	Goldsmid	Michael	1838	Middlesex, London	Joseph Goldsmid	Celia Jacobs		Aldgate, London	scholar
24867	Goldsmid	Miriam	1828	Bath	George Goldsmid	Hester (Esther) Solomon		Bermondsey, London	cap maker
7113	Goldsmid	Rachel	1815	Aldgate, London	Tsevi Hirsh Isaacs		Jacob Goldsmid	Spitalfields, London	
27671	Goldsmid	Rebecca	1835	Middlesex, London	Joseph Goldsmid	Fanny Mordecai		Aldgate, London	
10706	Goldsmid	Rebecca	1843	Amsterdam, Holland	Shmuel Goldsmid			Spitalfields, London	scholar
30083	Goldsmid	Rebecca	1843	Aldgate, London	Jacob Goldsmid	Rachel Isaacs	Abraham Fingelstein	Spitalfields, London	
20824	Goldsmid	Rose	1775	?, Holland	Eli Hanover Joachim	Esther (?)	Edward (Moses) Goldsmid	Marylebone, London	
6146	Goldsmid	Rosetta	1820	Aldgate, London	Shmuel Isaacs		Isaac Goldsmid	Aldgate, London	
27406	Goldsmid	Rosina	1831	Whitechapel, London	Joel Hart	Mary Hyams	Solomon Goldsmid	Whitechapel, London	
27676	Goldsmid	Rosina	1845	Middlesex, London	Joseph Goldsmid	Celia Jacobs		Aldgate, London	scholar
16340	Goldsmid	Sampson	1795	Whitechapel, London	Abraham Goldsmid	Patty (?)	Jane (?)	Bloomsbury, London	dealer in funds + foreign stocks
30086	Goldsmid	Samuel	1850	Aldgate, London	Jacob Goldsmid	Rachel Isaacs		Spitalfields, London	
27670	Goldsmid	Sarah	1834	Middlesex, London	Joseph Goldsmid	Fanny Mordecai		Aldgate, London	dressmaker
7109	Goldsmid	Septimus Corbet	1830	Middlesex, London	Sampson Goldsmid	Jane (?)	Gertrude Elizabeth Huffam	Bloomsbury, London	dealer in foreign stocks
27407	Goldsmid	Solomon	1825	Cheltenham, Gloucestershire	George Goldsmid		Rosina Hart	Whitechapel, London	clothier's assistant
15957	Goldsmid	Walter H	1840	Marylebone, London	Frederick David Goldsmid	Caroline Samuel		Marylebone, London	scholar at home
19614	Goldsmid (Goldsmith)	Aaron	1844	Spitalfields, London	Raphael (Ralph) Goldsmid (Goldsmith)	Elizabeth (Betsy) Davis	Hannah Woolf	Spitalfields, London	
19616	Goldsmid (Goldsmith)	Catherine (Caroline)	1851	Spitalfields, London	Raphael (Ralph) Goldsmid (Goldsmith)	Elizabeth (Betsy) Davis		Spitalfields, London	
19611	Goldsmid (Goldsmith)	Elizabeth (Betsy)	1823	Spitalfields, London	Joseph Davis	Julia (?)	Raphael (Ralph) Goldsmid (Goldsmith)	Spitalfields, London	
19612	Goldsmid (Goldsmith)	Esther	1843	Spitalfields, London	Raphael (Ralph) Goldsmid (Goldsmith)	Elizabeth (Betsy) Davis	Isaac Abraham Levy	Spitalfields, London	scholar
19613	Goldsmid (Goldsmith)	Rachel (Rosetta)	1844	Spitalfields, London	Raphael (Ralph) Goldsmid (Goldsmith)	Elizabeth (Betsy) Davis	Hyam Hyams	Spitalfields, London	scholar
19610	Goldsmid (Goldsmith)	Raphael (Ralph)	1820	Spitalfields, London	Samuel Goldsmid	Calo Esperance Sprintze	Elizabeth (Betsy) Davis	Spitalfields, London	general dealer
19615	Goldsmid (Goldsmith)	Sarah	1850	Spitalfields, London	Raphael (Ralph) Goldsmid (Goldsmith)	Elizabeth (Betsy) Davis	Samuel Woolf	Spitalfields, London	
24274	Goldsmith	Aboulafel	1837	?, Jamaica, West Indies	Phineas Goldsmith	Cecilia (?)		Bloomsbury, London	

ID	surname	given names	born	birthplace	father	mother	spouse 1	1851 residence	1851 occupation
19798	Goldsmith	Abraham Davy	1849	Sheffield, Yorkshire	Samuel Goldsmith	Elizabeth Rachel Greaves		Sheffield, Yorkshire	
4466	Goldsmith	Ann	1825	Sheffield, Yorkshire			Lewis Goldsmith	Birmingham	
27926	Goldsmith	Benjamin	1848	Whitechapel, London	Henry Goldsmith	Sarah Landeshut		Whitechapel, London	
19785	Goldsmith	Catherine	1791	Whitechapel, London	(?)		(?) Goldsmith	Spitalfields, London	clothes dealer
3978	Goldsmith	Catherine	1807	Portsmouth, Hampshire	Lazarus Hart		David Goldsmith	Portsmouth, Hampshire	
24273	Goldsmith	Cecilia	1811	?, London	(?)		Phineas Goldsmith	Bloomsbury, London	
3977	Goldsmith	David	1806	?, Poland [?, Prussia]			Catherine Hart	Portsmouth, Hampshire	clothes dealer
22071	Goldsmith	Elizabeth	1797	?, Germany	(?)		(?) Goldsmith	Whitechapel, London	
11644	Goldsmith	Elizabeth	1802	?, Holland	(?)		(?) Goldsmith	Aldgate, London	nurse
24277	Goldsmith	Elizabeth	1841	?, Jamaica, West Indies	Phineas Goldsmith	Cecilia (?)		Bloomsbury, London	
19794	Goldsmith	Elizabeth Rachel	1812	Sheffield, Yorkshire	John Greaves	(?) Davy	Samuel Goldsmith	Sheffield, Yorkshire	
27927	Goldsmith	Emanuel	1850	Whitechapel, London	Henry Goldsmith	Sarah Landeshut		Whitechapel, London	
24278	Goldsmith	Esther	1843	?, Jamaica, West Indies	Phineas Goldsmith	Cecilia (?)		Bloomsbury, London	
3976	Goldsmith	Esther	1845	Portsmouth, Hampshire	David Goldsmith	Catherine Hart	Judah Joel	Portsmouth, Hampshire	
3147	Goldsmith	Frances	1792	?, Germany			Morris Goldsmith	Chatham, Kent	
27923	Goldsmith	Henry	1823	?, Poland [?, Prussia]			Sarah Landeshut	Whitechapel, London	cigar maker
24275	Goldsmith	Henry	1838	?, Jamaica, West Indies	Phineas Goldsmith	Cecilia (?)		Bloomsbury, London	
9089	Goldsmith	Isaac	1834	?, Holland				Spitalfields, London	general dealer
4471	Goldsmith	Isaac	1849	Manchester	Lewis Goldsmith	Ann (?)		Birmingham	
19797	Goldsmith	Isaac John	1846	Sheffield, Yorkshire	Samuel Goldsmith	Elizabeth Rachel Greaves		Sheffield, Yorkshire	
18941	Goldsmith	Jacob	1785	?, Norfolk				Aldgate, London	
14207	Goldsmith	Jacob	1821	?, Poland [?, Prussia]				Manchester	clerk
24281	Goldsmith	Julia	1846	?Knightsbridge, London	Phineas Goldsmith	Cecilia (?)		Bloomsbury, London	
23628	Goldsmith	Leah	1822	?, Holland	Levi Themans		Lyon Goldsmith	Liverpool	
4465	Goldsmith	Lewis	1812	?, Poland			Ann (?)	Birmingham	glazier
29781	Goldsmith	Lewis	1826	?, Poland				Whitechapel, London	jeweller
22073	Goldsmith	Lionel	1825	Whitechapel, London	(?) Goldsmith	Elizabeth (?)		Whitechapel, London	agent for French merinos
2214	Goldsmith	Lipman	1817	Poznan, Poland [Posen, Prussia]			Augusta (Gertrude) Phillips	Oxford, Oxfordshire	jeweller
24276	Goldsmith	Louis	1839	?, Jamaica, West Indies	Phineas Goldsmith	Cecilia (?)		Bloomsbury, London	
3975	Goldsmith	Louis	1845	Portsmouth, Hampshire	David Goldsmith	Catherine Hart		Portsmouth, Hampshire	
27925	Goldsmith	Louis (Lewis)	1846	Whitechapel, London	Henry Goldsmith	Sarah Landeshut		Whitechapel, London	
23627	Goldsmith	Lyon	1821	?, Holland			Leah Themans	Liverpool	cigar dealer
19795	Goldsmith	Maria	1840	Manchester	Samuel Goldsmith	Elizabeth Rachel Greaves	Hyman Cohen	Sheffield, Yorkshire	
24280	Goldsmith	Michael	1844	?, Jamaica, West Indies	Phineas Goldsmith	Cecilia (?)		Bloomsbury, London	
24282	Goldsmith	Miriam	1848	Bloomsbury, London	Phineas Goldsmith	Cecilia (?)		Bloomsbury, London	
27928	Goldsmith	Montague	1851	Whitechapel, London	Henry Goldsmith	Sarah Landeshut		Whitechapel, London	
3146	Goldsmith	Morris	1793	?, London			Frances (?)	Chatham, Kent	clothier + chiropodist
10836	Goldsmith	Moses	1820	Whitechapel, London				Spitalfields, London	general dealer
24272	Goldsmith	Phineas	1810	?, Germany			Cecilia (?)	Bloomsbury, London	general merchant
3979	Goldsmith	Priscilla	1843	Portsmouth, Hampshire	David Goldsmith	Catherine Hart	Barnett Joel	Portsmouth, Hampshire	
20023	Goldsmith	Rachael	1799	Aldgate, London	(?)		(?) Goldsmith	Aldgate, London	jeweller
3148	Goldsmith	Rachel	1828	Chatham, Kent	Morris Goldsmith	Frances (?)	Solomon Joseph	Chatham, Kent	
4470	Goldsmith	Rachel	1848	Birmingham	Lewis Goldsmith	Ann (?)		Birmingham	
24279	Goldsmith	Rebecca	1843	?, Jamaica, West Indies	Phineas Goldsmith	Cecilia (?)		Bloomsbury, London	

ID	surname	given names	born	birthplace	father	mother	spouse 1	1851 residence	1851 occupation
19793	Goldsmith	Samuel	1814	Liverpool	Simon Goldsmith		Elizabeth Rachel Greaves	Sheffield, Yorkshire	
22072	Goldsmith	Samuel	1825	Whitechapel, London	(?) Goldsmith	Elizabeth (?)		Whitechapel, London	agent for French merinos
19799	Goldsmith	Samuel	1850	Sheffield, Yorkshire	Samuel Goldsmith	Elizabeth Rachel Greaves		Sheffield, Yorkshire	
27924	Goldsmith	Sarah	1821	?, Poland [?, Prussia]	Meyer Landeshut	Charlotte Myer	Henry Goldsmith	Whitechapel, London	
19796	Goldsmith	Simon Jon	1843	Sheffield, Yorkshire	Samuel Goldsmith	Elizabeth Rachel Greaves		Sheffield, Yorkshire	
23629	Goldsmith	Solomon	1850	Liverpool	Lyon Goldsmith	Leah Themans		Liverpool	
7200	Goldstein	Abraham	1810	?, Poland	Lyon Goldstein		Kate Isaacs	Rochester, Kent	traveller, jewellery
30204	Goldstein	Ann	1794	Cheltenham, Gloucestershire	(?)		(?) Goldstein	Dudley, Worcestershire	grocer
4475	Goldstein	Ann	1845	Birmingham	John D Goldstein	Eliza (?)		Birmingham	
4476	Goldstein	Caroline	1847	Birmingham	John D Goldstein	Eliza (?)		Birmingham	
7201	Goldstein	Deborah	1849	Chatham, Kent	Abraham Goldstein	Kate Isaacs	Reuben Barnett Lyons	Rochester, Kent	
4473	Goldstein	Eliza	1817	Charlton, London			John D Goldstein	Birmingham	
27421	Goldstein	Haroud	1815	?, Poland [?, Prussia]				Whitechapel, London	gilder
18265	Goldstein	Harris	1801	Poznan, Poland [Posen, Prussia]				Newport Pagnell, Buckinghamshire	Prussian Jew jeweller
30943	Goldstein	Isaac	1811	?, Poland				Wolverhampton, Staffordshire	traveller
4472	Goldstein	John D	1810	?, Poland [?, Prussia]			Eliza (?)	Birmingham	plater
7199	Goldstein	Kate	1815	Sheerness, Kent	John Isaacs	Deborah (?)	Abraham Goldstein	Rochester, Kent	
30880	Goldstein	Louis	1815	?, Poland [?, Prussia]				Bradford, Yorkshire	manager of a stuff business
2438	Goldstein	Louis	1842	?, Poland	Morris Goldstein	Rebecca (?)		Hull, Yorkshire	
19225	Goldstein	Louis	1850	Rochester, Kent	Abraham Goldstein	Kate Isaacs		Rochester, Kent	
30881	Goldstein	Martin	1814	?, Poland [?, Prussia]				Bradford, Yorkshire	worsted stuff merchant
21269	Goldstein	Martin	1816	?, Poland			Mary Maria Childs nee (?)	Barnsbury, London	silversmith
4478	Goldstein	Mordechai	1801	?, Poland				Birmingham	traveller
4477	Goldstein	Moretly	1849	Birmingham	John D Goldstein	Eliza (?)		Birmingham	
2436	Goldstein	Morris	1819	?, Poland			Rebecca (?)	Hull, Yorkshire	tailor
7203	Goldstein	Morris	1827	Warsaw, Poland	Lyon Goldstein		Elizabeth Isaacs	Chatham, Kent	jeweller
2437	Goldstein	Rebecca	1825	?, Poland			Morris Goldstein	Hull, Yorkshire	
4474	Goldstein	Susannah	1842	Dudley, Worcestershire	John D Goldstein	Eliza (?)		Birmingham	
3117	Goldston	Abraham	1812	?, Poland				Canterbury, Kent	jeweller
14364	Goldstone	Charles	1848	Salford, Lancashire	Michael Goldstone	Hannah (?)		Salford, Lancashire	
14361	Goldstone	Elizabeth	1838	Manchester	Michael Goldstone	Hannah (?)		Salford, Lancashire	
14358	Goldstone	Esther	1833	Liverpool	Michael Goldstone	Hannah (?)		Salford, Lancashire	
4480	Goldstone	Hannah	1812	?, Poland			Maurice Goldstone	Birmingham	
14357	Goldstone	Hannah	1817	Liverpool	(?)		Michael Goldstone	Salford, Lancashire	
14363	Goldstone	Joseph	1844	Salford, Lancashire	Michael Goldstone	Hannah (?)		Salford, Lancashire	
14359	Goldstone	Louisa	1835	Liverpool	Michael Goldstone	Hannah (?)		Salford, Lancashire	
4479	Goldstone	Maurice	1812	?, Poland			Hannah (?)	Birmingham	glazier
14356	Goldstone	Michael	1790	Warsaw, Poland			Hannah (?)	Salford, Lancashire	jeweller + watchmaker
4481	Goldstone	Rebecca (Harriet)	1838	?, Poland	Maurice Goldstone	Hannah (?)	Philip Barnett	Birmingham	tailoress
8692	Goldstone	Sampson	1839	Birmingham	Maurice Goldstone	Hannah (?)	Jane Barnett	Birmingham	
14362	Goldstone	Sophia	1841	Manchester	Michael Goldstone	Hannah (?)		Salford, Lancashire	
29002	Goldwater	Abra	1829	?, Poland				Whitechapel, London	tailor

ID	surname	given names	born	birthplace	father	mother	spouse 1	1851 residence	1851 occupation
4484	Goldwater	Ann	1807	?, Poland	(?)		Maks Goldwater	Birmingham	
26762	Goldwater	Caroline	1851	Aldgate, London	Michael Goldwater (Goldwasser)	Sarah Nathan		Aldgate, London	
26900	Goldwater	Fanny	1845	?, Poland	Sawl Goldwater	Maria (?)		Aldgate, London	scholar
4485	Goldwater	Hannah (Ann)	1851	Birmingham	Maks Goldwater	Ann (?)	Harris Goodman	Birmingham	
21139	Goldwater	Joseph	1833	?, Poland	Hirsh Goldwasser			Aldgate, London	tailor
4483	Goldwater	Maks	1812	?, Poland			Ann (?)	Birmingham	hawker
26899	Goldwater	Maria	1821	?, Poland	(?)		Sawl Goldwater	Aldgate, London	tailor
12704	Goldwater	Mark	1825	?, Germany				Coventry, Warwickshire	travelling hawker
26901	Goldwater	Samuel	1829	?, Poland				Aldgate, London	tailor
26761	Goldwater	Sarah	1826	Aldgate, London	Moses Nathan		Michael Goldwater (Goldwasser)	Aldgate, London	dressmaker
26898	Goldwater	Sawl	1816	?, Poland			Maria (?)	Aldgate, London	tailor
26760	Goldwater (Goldwasser)	Michael	1821	Konin, Poland	Hirsh Goldwasser		Sarah Nathan	Aldgate, London	master tailor empl 3
2834	Gollin	Bearman	1819	Spitalfields, London	Wolf Josephson Gollin	Marlah (Martha) (?)	Mary (Maria) Marks	Liverpool	warehouseman
2835	Gollin	Mary (Maria)	1830	Wapping, London	Lyon (Judah) Marks	Fanny Levey (Levy)	Bearman Gollin	Liverpool	domestic duties
2832	Gollin	Mary Ann (Miriam)	1851	Liverpool	Bearman Gollin	Mary Marks	Baron Joseph Levi de Menasce	Liverpool	
2837	Gollin	Walter Wolf (Woolf)	1849	Liverpool	Bearman Gollin	Mary Marks	Julia Bell	Liverpool	
2440	Golstein	Betty	1816	Hamburg, Germany			Isaac Golstein	Hull, Yorkshire	
24993	Golstein	George	1835	Gdansk, Poland [Dantzig, Prussia]				Strand, London	tobacconist's assistant
2439	Golstein	Isaac	1811	?, Poland			Betty	Hull, Yorkshire	plumber + glazier
2441	Golstein	Solomon	1849	Hull, Yorkshire	Isaac Golstein	Betty (?)		Hull, Yorkshire	
18716	Gomes	Esther	1805	City, London	Abraham Gomes			Aldgate, London	annuitant
15220	Gomes	Judith Suares	1783	Aldgate, London	Isaac Suares Gomes	Rebecca (?)		Shoreditch, London	
15219	Gomes	Mordecai Suares	1782	Aldgate, London	Isaac Suares Gomes	Rebecca (?)	Leah Bernal	Shoreditch, London	clerk to an outfitter
9081	Gompers	Catherine (Harriet)	1807	?, Holland	Salomon Haring	Mietje Koekverkoper	Salomon (Samuel) Mozes Gompers	Spitalfields, London	general dealer
9085	Gompers	Catherine (Kate, Grietje)	1841	Amsterdam, Holland	Salomon (Samuel) Mozes Gompers	Catherine (Jette, Harriet) Salomon Haring	Samuel Pennamacoor	Spitalfields, London	cabinet maker
5173	Gompers	Clara	1842	Spitalfields, London	Emanuel Gompers	Leah Levy	Nathan Cohen van Vlijmen	Plymouth, Devon	
1420	Gompers	Emanuel (Emanuel)	1819	Amsterdam, Holland	Solomon Gompers	Jansje Abraham Horloos	Leah Levy	Plymouth, Devon	general hawker
9083	Gompers	Fanny (Femmetje)	1836	Amsterdam, Holland	Salomon (Samuel) Mozes Gompers	Catherine (Jette, Harriet) Salomon Haring	Jacob Cohen	Spitalfields, London	cabinet maker
6700	Gompers	Jane	1843	Whitechapel, London	Emanuel Gompers	Leah Levy	Samuel Lasker	Plymouth, Devon	
1421	Gompers	Leah	1819	Middlesex, London	Naphtali Levy		Emanuel Gompers	Plymouth, Devon	drapery
9084	Gompers	Mary (Clara, Mietje)	1838	Amsterdam, Holland	Salomon (Samuel) Mozes Gompers	Catherine (Jette, Harriet) Salomon Haring	Francois Jacques Le Bosse	Spitalfields, London	cabinet maker
9080	Gompers	Moses	1851	Spitalfields, London	Solomon (Salomon) Phineas Gompers (Gompert)	Sarah Root		Spitalfields, London	
9114	Gompers	Moses Solomon	1851	Spitalfields, London	Salomon (Samuel) Mozes Gompers	Catherine (Jette, Harriet) Salomon Haring		Spitalfields, London	

ID	surname	given names	born	birthplace	father	mother	spouse 1	1851 residence	1851 occupation
9082	Gompers	Salomon (Samuel) Mozes	1807	Amsterdam, Holland			Catherine (Jette, Harriet) Salomon Haring	Spitalfields, London	
9086	Gompers	Sarah	1843	Amsterdam, Holland	Salomon (Samuel) Mozes Gompers	Catherine (Jette, Harriet) Salomon Haring	Marcus (Mark) Levy	Spitalfields, London	
9087	Gompers	Simeon (Simon)	1849	Spitalfields, London	Salomon (Samuel) Mozes Gompers	Catherine (Jette, Harriet) Salomon Haring	Elizabeth (Lizzie, Leah) Fagg	Spitalfields, London	cabinet maker
1422	Gompers	Solomon	1845	Spitalfields, London	Emanuel Gompers	Leah Levy	Sophie Anne Lazarus	Plymouth, Devon	scholar
9079	Gompers (Gompert)	Samuel	1850	Spitalfields, London	Solomon (Salomon) Phineas Gompers (Gompert)	Sarah Root	Sophia Julian	Spitalfields, London	
9078	Gompers (Gompert)	Sarah	1827	Amsterdam, Holland	Moshe Root	Betje Bellefleur	Solomon (Salomon) Phineas Gompers (Gompert)	Spitalfields, London	
9077	Gompers (Gompert)	Solomon (Salomon Salomon) Phineas	1827	Amsterdam, Holland	Salomon (Samuel) Mozes Gompers	Catherine (Jette, Harriet) Salomon Haring	Sarah Root	Spitalfields, London	cigar maker
5177	Gomperts	Barnett	1847	Spitalfields, London	Salomon Barend Gomperts	Elizabeth Daniels		Spitalfields, London	
6695	Gomperts	Betsy-Barend	1826	Amsterdam, Holland	Barend Moses Gomperts	Betje Salomon Knipschaar	Moses Aaron Witmond	Spitalfields, London	
5176	Gomperts	Elizabeth	1829	Amsterdam, Holland	Isaac Daniels		Salomon Barend Gomperts	Spitalfields, London	
5179	Gomperts	Mark (Mordecai)	1850	Spitalfields, London	Salomon Barend Gomperts	Elizabeth Daniels		Spitalfields, London	
30510	Gomperts	Moses	1851	Spitalfields, London	Salomon Barend Gomperts	Elizabeth Daniels		Spitalfields, London	
5175	Gomperts (Gompertz)	Solomon (Salomon) Barend	1824	Amsterdam, Holland	Barend Moses Gomperts	Betje Salomon Knipschaar	Elizabeth Daniels	Spitalfields, London	
14959	Gomperty	Julia	1837	?, London	(?) Gomperty			Bethnal Green, London	boarding school pupil
874	Gompertz	Abigail Joseph	1790	Middlesex, London	Joseph Elias Montefiore		Benjamin Gompertz	Kennington, London	
26213	Gompertz	Abraham	1847	?, London	Moses Gompertz	Rachael Abrahams		Aldgate, London	scholar
5183	Gompertz	Abraham	1850	Whitechapel, London	Barnet (Barend) Machiel Gompertz	Jane Hart	Ann Israel	Aldgate, London	
5172	Gompertz	Alexander	1839	Lambeth, London	Alexander Gompertz	Hannah Louise Cater	Lavinia Charlotte Wane	Bethnal Green, London	boarding school pupil
915	Gompertz	Amelia	1782	Middlesex, London	Solomon Barent Gompertz	Leah Gompertz		Brixton, London	
23981	Gompertz	Amelia	1848	Elephant & Castle, London	Herbert Gompertz	Susan (?)		Marylebone, London	
26212	Gompertz	Barnett	1845	?, London	Moses Gompertz	Rachael Abrahams		Aldgate, London	scholar
5180	Gompertz	Barnett (Barend) Machiel	1826	Amsterdam, Holland	Michael Gompertz	Sarah (Abrahams?)	Jane Hart	Aldgate, London	licensed hawker
873	Gompertz	Benjamin	1779	Aldgate, London	Solomon Barent Gompertz	Leah Cohen	Abigail Joseph Montefiore	Kennington, London	retired actuary
14915	Gompertz	Charles Felix	1835	Lambeth, London				Bethnal Green, London	boarding school pupil
30827	Gompertz	Charlotte Florence (Flora)	1795	?, France	(?) Wattier		Isaac Gompertz	Belgravia, London	independent fundholder
15722	Gompertz	Clara	1832	Amsterdam, Holland	Solomon Gompertz	Jane Horloon (?)		Spitalfields, London	tailoress
15721	Gompertz	Elizabeth	1830	Amsterdam, Holland	Solomon Gompertz	Jane Horloon (?)		Spitalfields, London	
15153	Gompertz	Emily	1833	Southwark, London	Alexander Gompertz	Hannah Louise Cater		Lambeth, London	servant
913	Gompertz	Ephraim	1776	Middlesex, London	Solomon Barent Gompertz	Leah Cohen	Adelaide Smith	Twickenham, London	annuitant + fund holder
26215	Gompertz	Esther	1834	?, London	Michael Gompertz	Sarah (Abrahams?)		Aldgate, London	tailoress
15723	Gompertz	Fanny	1838	Whitechapel, London	Solomon Gompertz	Jane Horloon (?)		Spitalfields, London	scholar
6699	Gompertz	Francis Trimmer	1830	Pimlico, London	Isaac Gompertz	Charlotte Florence (Flora) Wattier	Therese Perkin	Belgravia, London	architect's student
6697	Gompertz	Frederick Octavius	1831	Southwark, London	Alexander Gompertz	Hannah Louise Cater	Emily Jane Trewin	Lambeth, London	cabinet carver

ID	surname	given names	born	birthplace	father	mother	spouse 1	1851 residence	1851 occupation
15154	Gompertz	Hannah Louise	1801	Spitalfields, London	(?) Cater		Alexander Gompertz	Lambeth, London	dress maker + embroideress
908	Gompertz	Henry Louis Aaron	1796	Kennington, London	Barent Gompertz	Miriam Keyser	Elizabeth Wilks	Kensington, London	2nd lieutenant in the Army on half pay
5184	Gompertz	Henry William	1850	Shoreditch, London	Walter Edmund Gompertz	Matilda Green	Caroline Buskin	Liverpool	
23979	Gompertz	Herbert	1823	Southwark, London			Susan (?)	Marylebone, London	printer compositor
23983	Gompertz	Herbert Edmund	1850	Marylebone, London	Herbert Gompertz	Susan (?)		Marylebone, London	
912	Gompertz	Isaac	1774	Middlesex, London	Solomon Barent Gompertz	Leah Cohen	Florence Charlotte Wattier	Belgravia, London	independent fundholder
30826	Gompertz	Isaac	1775	Middlesex, London			Charlotte Florence (Flora) Wattier	Belgravia, London	independent fundholder
5182	Gompertz	Isaac	1848	Whitechapel, London	Barnet (Barend) Machiel Gompertz	Jane Hart	Sarah Jacobs	Aldgate, London	scholar
5181	Gompertz	Jane	1830	Whitechapel, London	Isaac Hart		Barnet (Barend) Machiel Gompertz	Aldgate, London	
27649	Gompertz	Jane	1844	Middlesex, London	(?) Gompertz			Aldgate, London	
15719	Gompertz	Jane Horloon	1799	Amsterdam, Holland	(?)		Solomon Gompertz	Spitalfields, London	
887	Gompertz	Lewis	1784	Aldgate, London	Solomon Barent Gompertz	Leah (Lydia) Cohen	Ann (?)	Kennington, London	fundholder + proprietor + inventor
23982	Gompertz	Louisa	1849	Southwark, London	Herbert Gompertz	Susan (?)		Marylebone, London	
6698	Gompertz	Lydia Anna	1828	Lambeth, London	Alexander Gompertz	Hannah Louise Cater	Thomas Wilbey Rawlinson	Lambeth, London	
5187	Gompertz	Matilda	1824	Bethnal Green, London	(?) Green		Walter Edmund Gompertz	Liverpool	
26206	Gompertz	Michael	1794	Amsterdam, Holland			Sarah (Abrahams?)	Aldgate, London	general dealer
26210	Gompertz	Michael	1838	?, London	Moses Gompertz	Rachael Abrahams		Aldgate, London	cigar maker
26208	Gompertz	Moses	1814	Amsterdam, Holland	Michael Gompertz	Sarah (Abrahams?)	Rachael Abrahams	Aldgate, London	licensed hawker
15720	Gompertz	Moses	1826	Amsterdam, Holland	Solomon Gompertz	Jane Horloon (?)		Spitalfields, London	cap maker
26209	Gompertz	Rachael	1817	?, London	Joel HaLevi Abrahams		Moses Gompertz	Aldgate, London	
914	Gompertz	Rachel	1778	Middlesex, London	Solomon Barent Gompertz	Leah Cohen		Brixton, London	
30825	Gompertz	Richard	1821	?, France	Isaac Gompertz	Charlotte Florence (Flora) Wattier		Belgravia, London	official employment
26211	Gompertz	Rosetta	1839	?, London	Moses Gompertz	Rachael Abrahams		Aldgate, London	scholar
26207	Gompertz	Sarah	1792	Amsterdam, Holland	(Abraham Abrahams?)		Michael Gompertx	Aldgate, London	
15718	Gompertz	Solomon	1792	Amsterdam, Holland			Jane Horloon (?)	Spitalfields, London	
909	Gompertz	Solomon	1806	?Kennington, London	Barent Gompertz	Miriam Keyser	Catherine Amelia Chamberlain	Chalford, Gloucestershire	Anglican vicar
23980	Gompertz	Susan	1825	Middlesex, London	(?)		Herbert Gompertz	Marylebone, London	
5186	Gompertz	Walter Edmund	1825	Clapton, London	Alexander Gompertz Gompertz	Hannah Louise Cater	Matilda Green	Liverpool	clockmaker
18642	Gonski	Adolph	1810	Poznan, Poland [Posen, Prussia]				Northampton, Northamptonshire	merchant/dealer
18285	Goodday	Immanuel	1830	Wroclaw, Poland [Preslieu, Prussia]				Salisbury, Wiltshire	traveller in spices
30454	Goodheim	Hannah (?Mary Ann)	1821	Hanley, Staffordshire	(?) (?Turner)		Samson Goodheim	Hanley, Staffordshire	
13457	Goodheim	Myer	1843	Hanley, Staffordshire	Samson Goodheim	Hannah (?Mary Ann Turner)		Manchester	scholar
30455	Goodheim	Rebecca	1845	Stoke-on-Trent, Staffordshire	Samson Goodheim	Hannah (?Mary Ann Turner)		Hanley, Staffordshire	

ID	surname	given names	born	birthplace	father	mother	spouse 1	1851 residence	1851 occupation
30367	Goodheim	Samson	1809	?Obensdorf, Germany [Louper Opensdorf]			Hannah (?Mary Ann Turner)	Hanley, Staffordshire	cap manufacturer
13456	Goodheim	Samuel	1839	Hanley, Staffordshire	Samson Goodheim	Hannah (?Mary Ann Turner)		Manchester	scholar
23644	Goodman	Abraham	1824	Hamburg, Germany				Liverpool	traveller
903	Goodman	Abraham (Alfred)	1806	Frankfurt-am-Main, Germany			Sarah (?)	Taunton, Somerset	traveller in various articles
18523	Goodman	Alice	1848	St Pancras, London	Louis Goodman	Julia Salaman		Bloomsbury, London	
5359	Goodman	Amelia	1822	Penzance, Cornwall	Samuel Jacob	Sarah (Sally) Levy	Charles Goodman	Pontypridd, Wales	
3300	Goodman	Annie (Hannah)	1840	Leeds, Yorkshire	Abraham Goodman	Sarah (?)	Morriss (Maurice) Montagu Jacobs	Cheltenham, Gloucestershire	
4190	Goodman	Arthur	1842	St Giles, London	Louis Goodman	Julia Salaman		Bloomsbury, London	scholar
1793	Goodman	Barnett	1850	Merthyr Tydfil, Wales	Joseph Goodman	Mary (?)		Merthyr Tydfil, Wales	
21591	Goodman	Bernard (Barnett)	1833	Aldgate, London	Lazarus (Eleazer) Goodman	Catherine (?)	Elizabeth Cohen	Whitechapel, London	boot maker
3150	Goodman	Caroline	1827	Chatham, Kent			Morris Goodman	Chatham, Kent	
21590	Goodman	Catherine	1790	Aldgate, London	(?)		Lazarus (Eleazer) Goodman	Whitechapel, London	
12769	Goodman	Charles	1827	?, Poland	George Goodman		Amelia Jacob	Pontypridd, Wales	glazier + clothier
4191	Goodman	Constance	1840	Islington, London	Louis Goodman	Julia Salaman		Bloomsbury, London	scholar
21592	Goodman	Deborah	1835	Aldgate, London	Lazarus (Eleazer) Goodman	Catherine (?)		Whitechapel, London	
18521	Goodman	Edward J	1837	Paddington, London	Louis Goodman	Julia Salaman		Bloomsbury, London	colonial broker's clerk
7374	Goodman	Eliza	1827	Islington, London	John Goodman	Maria Ballin	(?) Scott	Piccadilly, London	
1796	Goodman	George	1773	?, Poland				Merthyr Tydfil, Wales	
1794	Goodman	George	1825	Poland [Poland/Russia]	Harris Goodman	Pauly (?)	Rose Joseph	Merthyr Tydfil, Wales	
27897	Goodman	Hannah	1841	Elephant & Castle, London, London	Israel Goodman	Phoebe Moses	Joseph Lubinski	Spitalfields, London	scholar
1789	Goodman	Harris	1801	?, Poland	George Goodman		Pauly (?)	Merthyr Tydfil, Wales	pawnbroker
27895	Goodman	Israel	1799	Whitechapel, London	Tobias Shmuel		Hannah Cohen	Spitalfields, London	teacher of languages
1797	Goodman	Israel	1830	?, Russia				Merthyr Tydfil, Wales	assistant pawnbroker
7372	Goodman	John	1804	Aldgate, London	Perets Goodman		Maria Ballin	Piccadilly, London	proprietor of houses + annuitant
14485	Goodman	Joseph	1821	?, Poland [?, Silesia]			Zepherina (?)	Manchester	cigar merchant
1791	Goodman	Joseph	1822	?, Russia	Harris Goodman	Pauly (?)	Mary (?)	Merthyr Tydfil, Wales	
4187	Goodman	Julia	1812	Strand, London	Simeon Kensington Salaman	Alice Cowen	Louis Goodman	Bloomsbury, London	portrait painter
21589	Goodman	Lazarus (Eleazer)	1793	Middlesex, London			Catherine (?)	Whitechapel, London	general clothes dealer
4188	Goodman	Louis	1810	Islington, London			Julia Salaman	Bloomsbury, London	linen draper master empl 5
7373	Goodman	Maria	1806	Holloway, London	Samuel Ballin		John Goodman	Piccadilly, London	
1792	Goodman	Mary (Miriam)	1832	?, Russia			Joseph Goodman	Merthyr Tydfil, Wales	
905	Goodman	Matilda	1843	Birmingham	Abraham Goodman	Sarah (?)	Abraham Cassell	Cheltenham, Gloucestershire	
18524	Goodman	Miriam	1850	St Pancras, London	Louis Goodman	Julia Salaman		Bloomsbury, London	
18310	Goodman	Morishire	1786	?, Germany				Hereford, Herefordshire	traveller in various articles
16637	Goodman	Morris	1820	?, Germany			Rose (?)	Liverpool	clothier
3149	Goodman	Morris	1823	?, Germany			Caroline (?)	Chatham, Kent	clothier
1795	Goodman	Moses	1833	Wlodawa, Russia	Harris Goodman	Pauly (?)	Phoebe (?)	Merthyr Tydfil, Wales	

ID	surname	given names	born	birthplace	father	mother	spouse 1	1851 residence	1851 occupation
1790	Goodman	Pauly	1803	?, Russia			Harris Goodman	Merthyr Tydfil, Wales	
27896	Goodman	Phoebe	1803	City, London	Shlomo Dov Moses		Israel Goodman	Spitalfields, London	
16639	Goodman	Rebecca	1850	Liverpool	Morris Goodman	Rose (?)		Liverpool	
18522	Goodman	Robert	1845	St Giles, London	Louis Goodman	Julia Salaman		Bloomsbury, London	scholar
16638	Goodman	Rose	1824	Middlesex, London	(?)		Morris Goodman	Liverpool	
904	Goodman	Sarah	1815	Amsterdam, Holland			Abraham Goodman	Cheltenham, Gloucestershire	traveller
6762	Goodman	Tobias	1838	Aldgate, London	Lazarus (Eleazer) Goodman	Catherine (?)	Rosetta (Rose) Flatau	Whitechapel, London	tailor apprentice
4189	Goodman	Walter	1838	Islington, London	Louis Goodman	Julia Salaman		Bloomsbury, London	scholar
14231	Goodman	William	1816	?, Poland [?, Prussia]			(?)	Manchester	jeweller
14486	Goodman	Zepherina	1823	?, Ireland	(?)		Joseph Goodman	Manchester	
5466	Gordon	Betsy (Elizabeth)	1827	Lincoln, Lincolnshire	Jonas Lazarus	Rosceia Nathan	Marcus Gordon	Wolverhampton, Staffordshire	
16956	Gordon	Esther	1806	Middlesex, London	Joel Benjamin	Rachael Levy	Michael Abraham Gordon	Hammersmith, London	dress maker
168	Gordon	Marcus	1826	Wejherowo, Poland [Neustadt, Germany]	Maurice Gordon	Sarah Cohen	Betsy Lazarus	Wolverhampton, Staffordshire	pawnbroker
16957	Gordon	Michael Abraham	1800	?	Abraham Gordon		Esther Benjamin	?Soho, London	
5468	Gordon	Rachel	1850	Wolverhampton, Staffordshire	Marcus Gordon	Betsy Lazarus	Meyer Mindelsohn	Wolverhampton, Staffordshire	
5467	Gordon	Samuel	1848	Wolverhampton, Staffordshire	Marcus Gordon	Betsy Lazarus	Esther Caro	Wolverhampton, Staffordshire	
13952	Gore	Ann	1812	?, London	(?)		Joseph Gore	Manchester	fancy cap maker
7606	Gore	Louisa	1832	?, London	Joseph Gore	Ann (?)	Isaac Frederick Keesing	Manchester	fancy cap dealer
22594	Gottheil	Ann	1825	Whitechapel, London	Moses Levy		Elias (Elisha) Gottheil	Stepney, London	
22593	Gottheil	Elias (Elisha)	1821	?, Germany	Bernherd (Yissachar) Gottheil		Ann Levy	Stepney, London	shoemaker
22595	Gottheil	Rosa	1850	Stepney, London	Elias (Elisha) Gottheil	Ann Levy	Edward Harris	Stepney, London	
25412	Gottheimer	Berton	1799	?, Poland [?, Prussia]	Moshe		Julia Zachariah	Bloomsbury, London	commission agent
25413	Gottheimer	Julia	1811	Portsmouth, Hampshire	Yehuda Leib Zachariah		Berton Gottheimer	Bloomsbury, London	
25411	Gottheimer	Lavinia	1832	Strand, London	Berton Gottheimer	Julia Zachariah		Bloomsbury, London	
11819	Gottheimer	Lesser	1797	?, Poland [?, Prussia]	Abraham Gottheimer		Eliza Zachariah	Whitechapel, London	annuitant
25410	Gottheimer	Morris	1836	Middlesex, London	Berton Gottheimer	Julia Zachariah		Bloomsbury, London	solicitor's clerk
18207	Gottheimer	Morris	1838	City, London	Lesser Gottheimer	Eliza Zachariah		Mile End, London	scholar
7116	Gottheimer (Grant)	Albert (Abraham) Zachariah	1831	Dublin, Ireland	Berton Gottheimer	Julia Zachariah	Emily Isabella Robinson	Holborn, London	architect's clerk
14160	Gottschalk	Godfrey	1821	?, Germany				Manchester	merchant
27769	Goudsmid	Gerson?	1832	Amsterdam, Holland				Spitalfields, London	cigar maker
27761	Goudsmid	Hartog	1806	Amsterdam, Holland			Sarah (?)	Spitalfields, London	cap maker
27764	Goudsmid	Henry?	1833	Amsterdam, Holland	Hartog Goudsmid	Sarah (?)		Spitalfields, London	cigar maker
27767	Goudsmid	Isaac	1844	Amsterdam, Holland	Hartog Goudsmid	Sarah (?)		Spitalfields, London	scholar
27765	Goudsmid	Jonas	1839	Amsterdam, Holland	Hartog Goudsmid	Sarah (?)		Spitalfields, London	cigar maker
27768	Goudsmid	Mary	1845	Amsterdam, Holland	Hartog Goudsmid	Sarah (?)		Spitalfields, London	scholar
27763	Goudsmid	Moses	1832	Amsterdam, Holland	Hartog Goudsmid	Sarah (?)		Spitalfields, London	cigar maker
27766	Goudsmid	Myers	1841	Amsterdam, Holland	Hartog Goudsmid	Sarah (?)		Spitalfields, London	scholar
27762	Goudsmid	Sarah	1803	Amsterdam, Holland	(?)		Hartog Goudsmid	Spitalfields, London	cap maker
13544	Goulding	Augusta	1837	Manchester	(?) Goulding			Manchester	scholar

ID	surname	given names	born	birthplace	father	mother	spouse 1	1851 residence	1851 occupation
13545	Goulding	Phoebe	1840	Manchester	(?) Goulding			Manchester	scholar
13546	Goulding	Rosetta	1843	Manchester	(?) Goulding			Manchester	scholar
28103	Gouldsmith	Harris	1833	?, Germany				Spitalfields, London	tailor
28102	Goulstein	Harris	1833	?, Poland [?, Russia Poland]				Spitalfields, London	tailor
28101	Goulstein	Isabella	1829	?, Germany	(?)		Israel Goulstein	Spitalfields, London	
28100	Goulstein	Israel	1827	?, Poland [?, Russia Poland]			Isabella (?)	Spitalfields, London	tailor empl 4
22246	Goulston	Edward Morris	1814	Middlesex, London			Frances (?)	Whitechapel, London	watch? Maker
22247	Goulston	Frances	1813	Middlesex, London	(?)		Edward Morris Goulston	Whitechapel, London	
28234	Goulston	Henry	1818	Whitechapel, London			Sarah Levy	Spitalfields, London	?quill manufacturer
4486	Goulston	Joseph	1821	?, Poland [?, Prussia]				Birmingham	tailor
22248	Goulston	Manasah	1842	Middlesex, London	Edward Morris Goulston	Frances (?)		Whitechapel, London	scholar
28235	Goulston	Sarah	1814	Whitechapel, London	(?) Levy		Henry Goulston	Spitalfields, London	
13562	Grabouski	Aaron	1848	Poznan, Poland [Posen, Prussia]	Meyer Grabouski	Pauline (?)		Manchester	
13563	Grabouski	Emily	1850	Manchester	Meyer Grabouski	Pauline (?)		Manchester	
13561	Grabouski	Leopold	1846	Poznan, Poland [Posen, Prussia]	Meyer Grabouski	Pauline (?)		Manchester	
13559	Grabouski	Meyer	1809	Ostrow, Poland			Pauline (?)	Manchester	watch materials dealer
13560	Grabouski	Pauline	1819	Poznan, Poland [Posen, Prussia]	(?)		Meyer Grabouski	Manchester	
30489	Grabowsky	Henry	1820	?, Poland				Cheadle, Cheshire	
23108	Graff	Abraham	1841	?, Poland	(?) Graff	Hanna (?)		Aldgate, London	scholar
23102	Graff	Hanna	1806	?, Poland	(?)		(?) Graff	Aldgate, London	independent
23106	Graff	Hoodsa	1831	?, Poland	(?) Graff	Hanna (?)		Aldgate, London	furrier
23107	Graff	Jacob	1839	?, Poland	(?) Graff	Hanna (?)		Aldgate, London	cap maker
23104	Graff	Louiza	1827	?, Poland	(?) Graff	Hanna (?)		Aldgate, London	furrier
23105	Graff	Samuel	1829	?, Poland	(?) Graff	Hanna (?)		Aldgate, London	furrier
23103	Graff	Woolf	1826	?, Poland	(?) Graff	Hanna (?)		Aldgate, London	slipper maker
4794	Grant	Henry	1815	?, Germany [?, Prussia]			Sophia (?)	Liverpool	outfitter
4793	Grant	Jacob Reuben	1849	Liverpool	Henry Grant	Sophia (?)	Mala (Matilda) Myers	Liverpool	
16645	Grant	Solomon	1850	Liverpool	Henry Grant	Sophia (?)	Amelia Frances Leon	Liverpool	
16644	Grant	Sophia	1825	Newcastle Upon Tyne	(?)		Henry Grant	Liverpool	
27781	Graunbour	Moris	1822	Amsterdam, Holland				Spitalfields, London	general dealer
8540	Green	Aaron	1791	?, Holland	Ephraim HaLevi Green	Jane Nathan	Rose Myers	Spitalfields, London	provision dealer
25890	Green	Aaron	1837	Aldgate, London	Abraham Green	Rachael (?)		Aldgate, London	scholar
6495	Green	Aaron Levy	1821	Middlesex, London	Levy Ephraim Green	Amelia Hyams	Phoebe Levy	Aldgate, London	Minister of Great Synagogue Duke's Place
25886	Green	Abraham	1794	Whitechapel, London	Ephraim Levy Green	Piepa Eva (?)	Rachael (?)	Aldgate, London	provision dealer
7434	Green	Amelia	1779	Aldgate, London	(?)		Levy Ephraim Green	Aldgate, London	
16369	Green	Amelia	1814	Middlesex, London	Aaron Hart	(?) Levy	Edward (Ephraim) Levy Green	Aldgate, London	
6388	Green	Amelia	1842	Exeter, Devon	Michael Levy Green	Rosetta Davis	Isidor Gallewski	Aldgate, London	
16372	Green	Amelia	1846	Spitalfields, London	Edward (Ephraim) Levy Green	Amelia Hart		Aldgate, London	scholar
14882	Green	Ann	1794	Morden, London	(?)		(?) Green	Finsbury, London	
12532	Green	Ann C	1848	Norwich, Norfolk	Jacob Green	Mary (?)		Norwich, Norfolk	

ID	surname	given names	born	birthplace	father	mother	spouse 1	1851 residence	1851 occupation
12592	Green	Asher	1827	Middlesex, London	Aaron Green	Rose Myers	Leah Green	Norwich, Norfolk	commercial traveller
22345	Green	Catherine	1802	abroad	Isaachar Perle HaLevi Casner		Isaac Green	Aldgate, London	
22352	Green	Catherine	1840	Spitalfields, London	Isaac Green	Catherine Casner		Aldgate, London	scholar
14844	Green	Charles	1841	Hackney, London	James Green	Rebecca (?Cooke)		Bethnal Green, London	
11353	Green	David	1816	?, Holland			Elizabeth (?)	Aldgate, London	pencil maker
28715	Green	David	1847	?, London	Solomon Green	Sophia (?)		Spitalfields, London	
14847	Green	Davis	1849	Bethnal Green, London	James Green	Rebecca (?Cooke)		Bethnal Green, London	
11925	Green	Deborah	1851	Whitechapel, London	Philip Green	Gestje (Gitcha, Goodie) (?)		Whitechapel, London	scholar
16368	Green	Edward (Ephraim) Levy	1809	?Spitalfields, London	Levy Ephraim Green	Amelia Hyams	Amelia Hart	Aldgate, London	clothier
11355	Green	Elizabeth	1803	Aldgate, London	(?)		David Green	Aldgate, London	feather maker
11924	Green	Elizabeth	1850	Whitechapel, London	Philip Green	Gestje (Gitcha, Goodie) (?)	Jacob Van Gelder	Whitechapel, London	
6395	Green	Elizabeth (Lizzie)	1849	Aldgate, London	Michael Levy Green	Rosetta Davis	Samuel L Harris	Aldgate, London	
12527	Green	Elizabeth A	1836	Norwich, Norfolk	Jacob Green	Mary (?)		Norwich, Norfolk	braces maker
16373	Green	Ellen	1848	Spitalfields, London	Edward (Ephraim) Levy Green	Amelia Hart	Angel Levy	Aldgate, London	
25888	Green	Ephraim	1822	Whitechapel, London	Abraham Green	Rachael (?)		Aldgate, London	assistant to provision dealer
6497	Green	Ephraim A	1849	Bristol	Aaron Levy Green	Phoebe Levy		Aldgate, London	
16371	Green	Esther	1841	Aldgate, London	Edward (Ephraim) Levy Green	Amelia Hart	Godfrey Levy	Aldgate, London	scholar
14883	Green	Frederick	1827	Islington, London	(?) Green	Ann (?)		Finsbury, London	telescope maker
17559	Green	Gershon	1828	?, Poland	Hyam Green			Spitalfields, London	tailor
11922	Green	Gestje (Gitcha, Goodie)	1821	?, Holland	(?)		Philip Green	Whitechapel, London	
8541	Green	Godfrey	1829	Middlesex, London	Aaron Green	Rose Myers	Matilda Jacobs	Spitalfields, London	baker
15663	Green	Harris	1829	?, Poland [?, Prussia]				Aldgate, London	tailor
12531	Green	Harry M	1848	Norwich, Norfolk	Jacob Green	Mary (?)		Norwich, Norfolk	
26382	Green	Henry	1830	?, Germany				Aldgate, London	tailor
22344	Green	Isaac	1804	abroad	Mordecai HaLevi		Catherine Casner	Aldgate, London	printer
11816	Green	Isaac	1830	New Diep, Holland				Whitechapel, London	cigar maker/journeyman
12528	Green	Isaac Y	1838	Norwich, Norfolk	Jacob Green	Mary (?)		Norwich, Norfolk	match maker
16769	Green	Isabella	1851	Bristol	Aaron Levy Green	Phoebe Levy		Aldgate, London	
6394	Green	Isabella Levy	1847	Aldgate, London	Michael Levy Green	Rosetta Davis	Louis Phillips	Aldgate, London	scholar
12525	Green	Jacob	1812	Norwich, Norfolk			Mary (?)	Norwich, Norfolk	silk weaver
12529	Green	Jacob	1841	Norwich, Norfolk	Jacob Green	Mary (?)		Norwich, Norfolk	scholar
15741	Green	Jacob	1845	Aldgate, London	Michael Levy Green	Rosetta Davis		Aldgate, London	scholar
14842	Green	James	1815	Islington, London			Rebecca (?Cooke)	Bethnal Green, London	painter glazier
22351	Green	John	1838	City, London	Isaac Green	Catherine Casner		Aldgate, London	scholar
9547	Green	Judah	1827	Aldgate, London	Abraham Green		Betsey (Elizabeth) Jacobs	Aldgate, London	general dealer + victualler
25943	Green	Julia	1801	?, Holland	(?)		Henry Green	Aldgate, London	
27124	Green	Julia	1820	?, London	(?) Green	Sarah (?)		Aldgate, London	needlewoman
16374	Green	Julia	1850	Middlesex, London	Edward (Ephraim) Levy Green	Amelia Hart		Aldgate, London	
17556	Green	Julius	1825	?, Poland	Hyam Green		Mary Solomons	Spitalfields, London	tailor
16081	Green	Leah	1817	Spitalfields, London	Levy Ephraim Green	Amelia Hyams	Asher Green	Aldgate, London	passover cake baker
15743	Green	Leah	1850	Aldgate, London	Michael Levy Green	Rosetta Davis	Lewis Judah Anidjar	Aldgate, London	
22353	Green	Levy	1842	Spitalfields, London	Isaac Green	Catherine Casner		Aldgate, London	scholar

ID	surname	given names	born	birthplace	father	mother	spouse 1	1851 residence	1851 occupation
7433	Green	Levy Ephraim	1784	Amsterdam, Holland	Ephraim Green		Amelia Hyams	Aldgate, London	Passover cake baker + confectionery journeyman
16370	Green	Lewis	1840	?Aldgate, London	Edward (Ephraim) Levy Green	Amelia Hart		Aldgate, London	scholar
16767	Green	Lewis (Louis) A	1846	Bristol	Aaron Levy Green	Phoebe Levy	Fannie Unger	Aldgate, London	
11923	Green	Louis	1849	Whitechapel, London	Philip Green	Gestje (Gitcha, Goodie) (?)		Whitechapel, London	scholar
11354	Green	Lydia	1801	?, Holland	(?)		(?) Green	Aldgate, London	nurse
22350	Green	Mark	1834	City, London	Isaac Green	Catherine Casner		Aldgate, London	printer
6242	Green	Martha	1835	Spitalfields, London	Aaron Green	Rose Myers	Moses (Moss) Solomon	Spitalfields, London	
12526	Green	Mary	1812	Norwich, Norfolk	(?)		Jacob Green	Norwich, Norfolk	
17557	Green	Mary	1826	Aldgate, London	Woolf Solomons		Julius Green	Spitalfields, London	tailoress
28387	Green	Mary	1829	?, Poland [?, Russia Poland]	(?)		Michael A Green	Spitalfields, London	tailoress
16768	Green	Mary	1848	Bristol	Aaron Levy Green	Phoebe Levy	Isidore Harris	Aldgate, London	
28386	Green	Michael A	1828	?, Poland [?, Russia Poland]			Mary (?)	Spitalfields, London	tailor
6386	Green	Michael Levy	1812	Aldgate, London	Levy Ephraim Green	Amelia Hyams	Rosetta Davis	Aldgate, London	wholesale clothier
14845	Green	Nathaniel	1845	Bethnal Green, London	James Green	Rebecca (?Cooke)		Bethnal Green, London	
11921	Green	Philip	1813	?, Holland	Eleazer		Gestje (Gitcha, Goodie) (?)	Whitechapel, London	dealer in slops
28717	Green	Phillip	1850	?Spitalfields, London	Solomon Green	Sophia (?)		Spitalfields, London	
6496	Green	Phoebe	1825	Bristol	Joseph Levy		Aaron Levy Green	Aldgate, London	
25887	Green	Rachael	1798	Whitechapel, London	(?)		Abraham Green	Aldgate, London	
14843	Green	Rebecca	1815	Hackney, London	(?) ?Cooke		James Green	Bethnal Green, London	
16770	Green	Rebecca	1821	Middlesex, London	(?)			Aldgate, London	
17558	Green	Rebecca	1850	Spitalfields, London	Julius Green	Mary Solomons	Louis Seroka	Spitalfields, London	
28716	Green	Reuben	1848	?, London	Solomon Green	Sophia (?)		Spitalfields, London	
6387	Green	Rosetta	1823	Exeter, Devon	(?) Davis		Michael Levy Green	Aldgate, London	
22349	Green	Rosetta	1832	City, London	Isaac Green	Catherine Casner		Aldgate, London	furrier
14846	Green	Samuel	1847	Bethnal Green, London	James Green	Rebecca (?Cooke)		Bethnal Green, London	
12530	Green	Samuel W	1844	Norwich, Norfolk	Jacob Green	Mary (?)		Norwich, Norfolk	scholar
27123	Green	Sarah	1778	?, London	(?)		(?) Green	Aldgate, London	general dealer
28713	Green	Solomon	1821	?, London			Sophia (?)	Spitalfields, London	tailor
25986	Green	Solomon	1822	?, Poland [?, Prussia]				Aldgate, London	tailor journeyman
6501	Green	Solomon Abraham	1834	Aldgate, London	Abraham Green	Rachael (?)	Jane Moses	Aldgate, London	assistant to provision dealer
6499	Green	Solomon Levy	1815	?Spitalfields, London	Levy Ephraim Green	Amelia Hyams	Rebecca Asher	Birmingham	
28714	Green	Sophia	1826	?, London	(?)		Solomon Green	Spitalfields, London	
6389	Green	Sylvia (Bathsheba)	1846	Aldgate, London	Michael Levy Green	Rosetta Davis	Morton (Mordecai) Abrahams	Aldgate, London	
29332	Greenbaum	Ellis	1831	?, Poland [?, Prussia]				Whitechapel, London	capmaker
20620	Greenbaum	Hannah	1851	Spitalfields, London	Simon (Simeon) Greenbaum	Mary (Miriam) Crownson		Spitalfields, London	
20618	Greenbaum	Mary (Miriam)	1826	?, Poland	(?) Crownson		Simon (Simeon) Greenbaum	Spitalfields, London	
20619	Greenbaum	Rachael	1850	Aldgate, London	Simon (Simeon) Greenbaum	Mary (Miriam) Crownson		Spitalfields, London	
20617	Greenbaum	Simon (Simeon)	1825	Vilnius, Lithuania [Vilna, Russia]			Mary (Miriam) Crownson	Spitalfields, London	tailor
25903	Greenberg	Jacob	1829	?, Poland				Aldgate, London	barber journeyman

ID	surname	given names	born	birthplace	father	mother	spouse 1	1851 residence	1851 occupation
4487	Greenberg	Morris	1824	?, Germany			Sarah Lees	Birmingham	master tailor
8404	Greenberg	Simeon	1828	?, Russia [Sawgand/Morgon/Smorgan, Russia]	Solomon Greenberg		Matilda Sampson	Southampton, Hampshire	Jew traveller
29641	Greenboam	Isaac	1829	?, Poland	Elias Greenboam		Sophia (Siporah) Mendoza	Aldgate, London	tailor
29642	Greenboam	Sophia (Siporah)	1827	Bow, London	Moses de Mordecai Mendoza	Maria (Miriam) Sarah Mathews	Isaac Greenboam	Aldgate, London	tailoress
17308	Greenburg	Harris	1825	?, Poland [?, Prussia Poland]			Jane (?)	Whitechapel, London	tailor
17623	Greenburg	Isaac	1826	?, Poland				Aldgate, London	shopman
17309	Greenburg	Jane	1825	?, Poland [?, Prussia Poland]	(?)		Harris Greenburg	Whitechapel, London	
17310	Greenburg	Marks	1844	?, Poland [?, Prussia Poland]	Harris Greenburg	Jane (?)		Whitechapel, London	scholar
17311	Greenburg	Sarah	1850	Whitechapel, London	Harris Greenburg	Jane (?)		Whitechapel, London	
17127	Greenwold	Casper	1828	?, Poland [?, Prussia]				Darlington, Co Durham	jeweller
17128	Greenwold	Philip	1831	?, Poland [?, Prussia]				Darlington, Co Durham	jeweller
12627	Greiffenberg	Joseph	1799	?, Poland [?, Prussia]				Aylsham, Norfolk	hawker jeweller
20612	Greistein (Gunstein)	Caroline	1844	?, Poland	Lewis Greistein (Gunstein)	Eve (?)	Barnett Silverstone	Spitalfields, London	
20611	Greistein (Gunstein)	Eve	1819	?, Poland	(?)		Lewis Greistein (Gunstein)	Spitalfields, London	
20610	Greistein (Gunstein)	Lewis	1819	?, Poland			Eve (?)	Spitalfields, London	glazier
20613	Greistein (Gunstein)	Rebecca	1848	Aldgate, London	Lewis Greistein (Gunstein)	Eve (?)		Spitalfields, London	
20614	Greistein (Gunstein)	Simlia	1850	Aldgate, London	Lewis Greistein (Gunstein)	Eve (?)		Spitalfields, London	
4488	Grims	Moses	1832	?, Poland				Birmingham	traveller
21786	Grin	Mark	1829	?, Poland				Aldgate, London	shoe maker
2134	Grodditer	Harris	1810	?, Poland	Moses Grodditer		Sarah Fox	Hull, Yorkshire	
9178	Grodzinski	Davis	1828	?, Poland	(?) Grodzinski	Hannah (?)		Whitechapel, London	[---] purse maker
9182	Grodzinski	Esther	1842	?, Poland	(?) Grodzinski	Hannah (?)		Whitechapel, London	school [---]
9177	Grodzinski	Hannah	1801	?, Poland	(?)		(?) Grodzinski	Whitechapel, London	lodging house keeper
9180	Grodzinski	Morris	1835	?, Poland	(?) Grodzinski	Hannah (?)		Whitechapel, London	cigar maker
9181	Grodzinski	Moses	1839	?, Poland	(?) Grodzinski	Hannah (?)		Whitechapel, London	cigar maker
9179	Grodzinski	Samuel	1833	?, Poland	(?) Grodzinski	Hannah (?)		Whitechapel, London	cigar maker
2263	Gross	Leon	1827	?Poland [?, Galicia]	Hyman Gross		Rachel Ansell	Leeds, Yorkshire	general dealer
4489	Gross	Simon	1824	Poznan, Poland [Posen, Prussia]				Birmingham	traveller
8601	Grossman	Abraham	1827	?, Poland				Spitalfields, London	
8602	Grossman	Michal	1827	?, Poland				Spitalfields, London	cap maker
24389	Grouse	Catharine	1831	Aldgate, London	Hart Davis		Michael Grouse	Soho, London	
24388	Grouse	Michael	1821	Kolo, Poland	Eliezer Grouse		Catharine Davis	Soho, London	master tailor empl 6
24390	Grouse	Rebecca	1849	Soho, London	Michael Grouse	Catherine Davis		Soho, London	
27736	Grunbarg	Isaih	1829	?, Russia				Spitalfields, London	glazier
16942	Grunbaum	Maximilian	1819	?, Germany				Brighton, Sussex	teacher
26365	Gruner	Davis	1814	?, Poland				Aldgate, London	goldsmith

ID	surname	given names	born	birthplace	father	mother	spouse 1	1851 residence	1851 occupation
26512	Grunwald	Julius	1829	?, Poland [?, Prussia]				Dover, Kent	
26511	Grunwald	Pauline	1851	Dover, Kent	William Grunwald	Rachel Millengen		Dover, Kent	
26510	Grunwald	Rachel	1825	Whitechapel, London	(?) Millengen		William Grunwald	Dover, Kent	
26509	Grunwald	William	1818	?, Poland [?, Prussia]			Rachel Millengen	Dover, Kent	silversmith
2442	Grunwald (Greenwald)	Harris	1851	Hull, Yorkshire	Saul Grunwald (Greenwald)	Tina (Ernestine, Esther) Heymann		Hull, Yorkshire	
2443	Grunwald (Greenwald)	Hyman	1846	Poznan, Poland [Fordon, Posen, Prussia]	Saul Grunwald (Greenwald)	Tina (Ernestine, Esther) Heymann		Hull, Yorkshire	
2444	Grunwald (Greenwald)	Jacob	1849	Hull, Yorkshire	Saul Grunwald (Greenwald)	Tina (Ernestine, Esther) Heymann		Hull, Yorkshire	
2445	Grunwald (Greenwald)	Jeanetta	1845	Poznan, Poland [Fordon, Posen, Prussia]	Saul Grunwald (Greenwald)	Tina (Ernestine, Esther) Heymann	Simon (Zeaman, Joshua) Cohen	Hull, Yorkshire	
2446	Grunwald (Greenwald)	Michael	1831	?, Poland [?, Prussia]				Hull, Yorkshire	dealer in jewellery
2135	Grunwald (Greenwald)	Saul	1823	Poznan, Poland [Fordon, Posen, Prussia]			Tina (Ernestine, Esther) Heymann	Hull, Yorkshire	dealer in jewellery
2447	Grunwald (Greenwald)	Tina (Ernestine, Esther)	1824	?, Poland [?, Prussia]	(?) Heymann		Saul Grunwald (Greenwald)	Hull, Yorkshire	
7636	Guedalla	Anna	1851	Islington, London	Moses Guedalla	Phoebe Samuel Phillips	Moses Aflalo	Islington, London	
15898	Guedalla	Ester	1841	Middlesex, London	(?) Guedalla			Hackney, London	boarding school pupil
21301	Guedalla	George	1842	Bloomsbury, London				Edmonton, London	boarding school pupil
8054	Guedalla	Grace	1817	?, London	Judah Guedalla		Gershom Kursheedt	Finsbury, London	
7494	Guedalla	Haim	1815	Finsbury, London	Judah Guedalla		Jemima Sebag	Belgravia, London	merchant trading to Barbary (North + South American coffee house)
21300	Guedalla	Jacob	1841	Bloomsbury, London				Edmonton, London	boarding school pupil
8053	Guedalla	Jemima	1820	Kennington, London	Solomon Sebag		Haim Guedalla	Belgravia, London	
21019	Guedalla	Joseph	1847	Islington, London	Moses Guedalla	Phoebe Samuel Phillips	Rowena Florance	Finsbury, London	
8051	Guedalla	Judah	1773	Essaouira, Morocco [Mogador]	Haim Guedalla		Esther de Samuel Montefiore	Finsbury, London	gentleman annuitant
7615	Guedalla	Moses	1816	Finsbury, London	Judah Guedalla		Phoebe Samuel Phillips	Islington, London	fundholder
8052	Guedalla	Phoebe Samuel	1819	Jamaica, West Indies	Samuel Phillips		Moses Guedalla	Islington, London	fundholder
13789	Guisii	Prarnard (?Bernard)	1801	?, Poland				Manchester	hawker
2862	Gumpelson	Amelia	1851	Birmingham	Joseph Gumpelson	Matilda Samuel	Marcus (Michael) Myers	Birmingham	
2861	Gumpelson	Joseph	1800	Berlin, Germany	Cohen Gumpelson		Matilda Samuel	Birmingham	pawnbroker + jeweller
2866	Gumpelson	Marcus (Marquis) Abraham	1850	Manchester	Joseph Gumpelson	Matilda Samuel	Frances Maria Aaron	Birmingham	
2867	Gumpelson	Matilda	1819	Birmingham	Abraham Samuel	Lydia (?)	Joseph Gumpelson	Birmingham	
4490	Gumpet	Abraham	1833	?, Russia				Birmingham	assistant jeweller + silversmith
23847	Gustave	Adolph	1824	?, Russia				Soho, London	tailor
13760	Gutkind	Charlotte	1816	?, Poland [?, Prussia]	(?)		Wolf Gutkind	Manchester	tailor
13761	Gutkind	Maria	1848	?, Poland [?, Prussia]	Wolf Gutkind	Charlotte (?)		Manchester	
13759	Gutkind	Wolf	1814	?, Poland [?, Prussia]			Charlotte (?)	Manchester	traveller
23602	Guttle	Joel	1830	?, Poland				Liverpool	glazier's jobbing

ID	surname	given names	born	birthplace	father	mother	spouse 1	1851 residence	1851 occupation
30395	Guttmann	Isaac	1827	Kalisz, Poland	Jozef Gutman	Bluma Schefl	Charlotte Redlich	Sheffield, Yorkshire	general dealer
30399	Guttmann	Tobias	1829	Kalisz, Poland	Jozef Gutman	Bluma Schefl	Louisa (?)	Sheffield, Yorkshire	hawker of jewellery
14162	Haarbleiche	Henry	1828	Hamburg, Germany				Manchester	book keeper
5769	Haberland	Minna	1828	?Poland [?Labashin, Prussia]		Yette Goldstein	Victor Glassman	Hull, Yorkshire	
2136	Haberland (Haborland)	Morris	1829	?, Poland [Labashin, Prussia]		Yette Goldstein		Hull, Yorkshire	tea dealer's assistant
19591	Hadida	Abraham	1842	Aldgate, London	Jacob de Solomon Hadida	Esther de Abraham Da Silva		Whitechapel, London	
14059	Hadida	Charlotte	1825	Manchester	(?)		Samuel Hadida	Manchester	
19587	Hadida	Esther	1815	?Aldgate, London	Abraham Da Silva	Esther de David Nunes Martines	Jacob de Solomon Hadida	Whitechapel, London	interpreter's wife
9189	Hadida	Esther	1830	Whitechapel, London	Jacob de Joseph Hadida	Sarah Silva	Isaac De Frece	Whitechapel, London	dress maker
19586	Hadida	Jacob	1796	?, Morocco	Solomon Hadida		Esther de Abraham Da Silva	Whitechapel, London	interpreter
9185	Hadida	Jacob	1800	Tangier, Morocco	Joseph Hadida		Sarah de Abraham Silva	Whitechapel, London	general dealer
9190	Hadida	Jessie	1832	Whitechapel, London	Jacob de Joseph Hadida	Sarah Silva		Whitechapel, London	dress maker
9187	Hadida	Joseph	1824	Whitechapel, London	Jacob de Joseph Hadida	Sarah Silva		Whitechapel, London	cigar maker
19594	Hadida	Joseph	1849	Aldgate, London	Jacob de Solomon Hadida	Esther de Abraham Da Silva	Rachel Hyman	Whitechapel, London	
9188	Hadida	Lucy	1828	Whitechapel, London	Jacob de Joseph Hadida	Sarah Silva	Benjamin Hyam	Whitechapel, London	dress maker
19592	Hadida	Lucy (Meshoda)	1844	Aldgate, London	Jacob de Solomon Hadida	Esther de Abraham Da Silva	Louis Henry Moore	Whitechapel, London	
19593	Hadida	Moses	1847	Aldgate, London	Jacob de Solomon Hadida	Esther de Abraham Da Silva	Amelia Baum	Whitechapel, London	
19589	Hadida	Rachel	1837	Whitechapel, London	Jacob de Solomon Hadida	Esther de Abraham Da Silva		Whitechapel, London	
14058	Hadida	Samuel	1810	Gibraltar			Charlotte (?)	Manchester	merchant
9186	Hadida	Sarah	1798	Whitechapel, London	Abraham Silva		Jacob de Joseph Hadida	Whitechapel, London	
19590	Hadida	Simcha (Simmy)	1838	Whitechapel, London	Jacob de Solomon Hadida	Esther de Abraham Da Silva		Whitechapel, London	scholar
19588	Hadida	Solomon	1835	Aldgate, London	Jacob de Solomon Hadida	Esther de Abraham Da Silva		Whitechapel, London	
14494	Hadkins	Clara	1814	Birmingham	John Hadkins	Maria (?)	Jacob Coppel	Birmingham	
17814	Hagman	Judah	1820	abroad				Aldgate, London	tailor
14404	Hahn	Bernard	1820	?, Germany				Manchester	merchant
27175	Hains	Charles	1821	Southwark, London	Henry (Hiam) Hains (Haines)	Catherine (?)	Hannah Myers	Limehouse, London	ship's steward
27207	Hains	Hannah	1822	Whitechapel, London	George Myers	Abigail (?)	Charles Hains	Limehouse, London	tambour worker
18195	Hains	Henry	1779	Middlesex, London			Catherine (?)	Mile End, London	tailor
27211	Hains	Joseph	1828	Whitechapel, London	Henry (Hiam) Hains (Haines)	Catherine (?)	Julia (Simha) Delevante	Limehouse, London	ship's steward
27208	Hains	Joseph	1846	Mile End, London	Charles Hains	Hannah Myers	Hannah Barnett	Limehouse, London	scholar
20288	Hakel	Moses	1791	?, Russia				Spitalfields, London	cap maker
13690	Halbram	Esther	1849	Ramsgate, Kent	Samuel Halbram	Sarah (?)		Manchester	
13688	Halbram	Samuel	1824	Brussels, Belgium			Sarah (?)	Manchester	jeweller
13689	Halbram	Sarah	1830	Caernavon, Wales	(?)		Samuel Halbram	Manchester	furrier
12577	Haldinstein	Alfred Isaac	1850	Norwich, Norfolk	Philip Haldinstein	Rachel Solomon	Emma Samuel	Norwich, Norfolk	

ID	surname	given names	born	birthplace	father	mother	spouse 1	1851 residence	1851 occupation
12574	Haldinstein	Philip Victor	1820	?, Poland [?, Prussia]	W Haldinstein	Rachel (?)	Rachel Soman	Norwich, Norfolk	cap maker empl 6
12575	Haldinstein	Rachel	1827	Norwich, Norfolk	David Soman	Rosetta Solomon	Philip Victor Haldinstein	Norwich, Norfolk	
12576	Haldinstein	Woolf	1849	Norwich, Norfolk	Philip Haldinstein	Rachel Solomon	Ada Jonas	Norwich, Norfolk	
20987	Haliva	Abraham	1791	?Meknes, Morocco [Mequrnez, Barbaria]			Mesoda (?)	Aldgate, London	rabbi Jews
20990	Haliva	Esther	1835	City, London	Abraham Haliva	Mesoda (?)		Aldgate, London	
20991	Haliva	Joseph N	1839	City, London	Abraham Haliva	Mesoda (?)	Clara Azuelos	Aldgate, London	
20988	Haliva	Mesoda	1806	?Meknes, Morocco [Mequrnez, Barbaria]	(?)		Abraham Haliva	Aldgate, London	
20989	Haliva	Miriam	1834	City, London	Abraham Haliva	Mesoda (?)	Solomon Hurwitz	Aldgate, London	
20992	Haliva	Rachel	1842	City, London	Abraham Haliva	Mesoda (?)		Aldgate, London	
14299	Halle	Arthur	1841	Manchester	Emmanuel Halle	Sarah Anne Shuttleworth		Manchester	
14294	Halle	Emmanuel	1797	Hamburg, Germany			Sarah Anne Shuttleworth	Manchester	export merchant
14297	Halle	Francis Emmanuel	1836	Manchester	Emmanuel Halle	Sarah Anne Shuttleworth		Manchester	
14298	Halle	George Albert	1840	Manchester	Emmanuel Halle	Sarah Anne Shuttleworth		Manchester	
14300	Halle	Henry	1844	Manchester	Emmanuel Halle	Sarah Anne Shuttleworth		Manchester	
14301	Halle	Lucy Jane	1846	Manchester	Emmanuel Halle	Sarah Anne Shuttleworth		Manchester	
14296	Halle	Mary Alice	1834	Manchester	Emmanuel Halle	Sarah Anne Shuttleworth		Manchester	
14295	Halle	Sarah Anne	1808	Manchester	(?) Shuttleworth		Emmanuel Halle	Manchester	
4492	Hamam	Charles	1825	?, Germany				Birmingham	jeweller
9093	Hambice	Alice	1816	?, Holland			Moses Hambice	Spitalfields, London	
9097	Hambice	Henry	1845	?, Holland	Moses Hambice	Alice (?)		Spitalfields, London	scholar
9094	Hambice	Jacob	1837	?, Holland	Moses Hambice	Alice (?)		Spitalfields, London	tailor
9099	Hambice	Jane	1849	?, London	Moses Hambice	Alice (?)		Spitalfields, London	
9095	Hambice	Louis	1839	?, Holland	Moses Hambice	Alice (?)		Spitalfields, London	scholar
9092	Hambice	Moses	1816	?, Holland			Alice (?)	Spitalfields, London	tailor
9098	Hambice	Rosa	1847	?, London	Moses Hambice	Alice (?)		Spitalfields, London	
9100	Hambice	Samuel	1850	?, London	Moses Hambice	Alice (?)		Spitalfields, London	
9096	Hambice	Solomon	1842	?, Holland	Moses Hambice	Alice (?)		Spitalfields, London	scholar
24465	Hambro	Carl (Charles) Joachim	1807	Copenhagen, Denmark			Caroline Maria Gostenhofer	Putney, London	foreign banker business
21582	Hamburger	Amelia	1806	Mile End, London	Mordecai Mendoza		Myer Hamburger	Spitalfields, London	
21585	Hamburger	Julia	1837	Whitechapel, London	Myer Hamburger	Sophia Cohen		Spitalfields, London	dress maker
21586	Hamburger	Millie	1839	Whitechapel, London	Myer Hamburger	Sophia Cohen		Spitalfields, London	cap maker
21581	Hamburger	Myer	1793	Amsterdam, Holland	Samuel Cohen		Sophia Cohen	Spitalfields, London	pedlar
21584	Hamburger	Sarah	1827	Spitalfields, London	Myer Hamburger	Sophia Cohen		Spitalfields, London	
22128	Hamburger	Simon	1817	?, Germany [Inprush, Germany]				Whitechapel, London	merchant
21882	Hamburgh	Ann	1824	?, London	(?)		John Hamburgh	Clerkenwell, London	
21883	Hamburgh	Henry	1844	?, London	John Hamburgh	Ann (?)		Clerkenwell, London	
21881	Hamburgh	John	1822	?, London			Ann (?)	Clerkenwell, London	furrier
21884	Hamburgh	John	1847	Clerkenwell, London	John Hamburgh	Ann (?)		Clerkenwell, London	
21885	Hamburgh	William	1850	Clerkenwell, London	John Hamburgh	Ann (?)		Clerkenwell, London	
16297	Hamel	?	1820	?, Germany				Dundee, Scotland	

ID	surname	given names	born	birthplace	father	mother	spouse 1	1851 residence	1851 occupation
22643	Hamer	Calmen	1823	Cracow, Poland [Krakuz, Poland]				Whitechapel, London	slipper manufacturer
22644	Hamer	Schlag	1821	Cracow, Poland [Krakuz, Poland]				Whitechapel, London	journeyman slipper maker
11891	Hammerstein	Morris	1826	?, Poland			Caroline Campen	Whitechapel, London	tailor
18189	Hanbury	Harriot	1806	Plymouth, Devon	(?) Hanbury			Mile End, London	Governess
16044	Hands	Alfred	1844	Marylebone, London	Solomon Hands	Frances (?)		St John's Wood, London	scholar
16039	Hands	Amelia	1846	Paddington, London	Joshua Hands	Hannah Mitchell		Maida Vale, London	
16046	Hands	Anna	1848	Paddington, London	Solomon Hands	Frances (?)		St John's Wood, London	
16045	Hands	Benjamin	1846	Paddington, London	Solomon Hands	Frances (?)		St John's Wood, London	scholar
16043	Hands	Elizabeth	1841	Marylebone, London	Solomon Hands	Frances (?)	Joseph Benjamin	St John's Wood, London	scholar
22443	Hands	Elizabeth (Lizzie)	1846	?	(?) Hands		Coleman Defries	Gravesend, Kent	boarding school pupil
16049	Hands	Frances	1818	Whitechapel, London	(?)		Solomon John Hands	St John's Wood, London	
16042	Hands	Hannah	1760	Aldgate, London	(?)		(?) Hands	Maida Vale, London	
16037	Hands	Hannah	1816	?Aldgate, London	M--- Mitchell		Joshua Hands	Maida Vale, London	
16040	Hands	Henry	1849	Paddington, London	Joshua Hands	Hannah Mitchell		Maida Vale, London	
16047	Hands	Jeannette	1850	Paddington, London	Solomon Hands	Frances (?)		St John's Wood, London	
16036	Hands	Joshua	1800	?Aldgate, London	Joseph? Hands	Hannah (?)	Hannah Mitchell	Maida Vale, London	
16041	Hands	Joshua	1850	Paddington, London	Joshua Hands	Hannah Mitchell	Ruth Meyers	Maida Vale, London	
16038	Hands	Phineas	1842	Middlesex, London	Joshua Hands	Hannah Mitchell	Abigail Amelia Andrade Da Costa	Maida Vale, London	boarding school pupil
6148	Hands	Rebecca	1842	Marylebone, London	Solomon Hands	Frances (?)		St John's Wood, London	
16048	Hands	Solomon John	1815	Aldgate, London			Frances (?)	St John's Wood, London	coachman
18267	Hanigbaum	Morris	1822	?, Russia				Whitby, Yorkshire	hawker
18266	Hanigbaum	Solomon	1817	?, Russia				Whitby, Yorkshire	hawker
27996	Happman	Julius	1829	Wroclaw, Poland [Breslau, Germany]				Spitalfields, London	tailor jouneyman
6522	Harding	John	1837	Exeter, Devon			Amelia (?)	Exeter, Devon	
14126	Harebleachar	John	1801	?, Germany				Manchester	yarn agent
9638	Harfeld	Ellis	1830	?, Poland [?, Prussia]	Levy Harfeld		Catherine Marks	Dalston, London	glazier
28092	Haris	Nanse	1803	Warsaw, Poland				Spitalfields, London	clothes dealer
11824	Harkman	Isaac	1824	Rotterdam, Holland				Whitechapel, London	gun maker/journeyman
25580	Harris	?	1820	?Poznan, Poland [Posen, Prussia]	(?)		Joseph Harris	Dublin, Ireland	
10368	Harris	Aaron	1836	Aldgate, London	Henry Harris	Eve Woolf	Leah Isaacs	Spitalfields, London	general dealer
6469	Harris	Aaron	1838	Aldgate, London	Abraham Harris	Catherine (?)	Esther Raphael	Aldgate, London	slipper maker
6461	Harris	Aaron Ellis	1835	Whitechapel, London	Abraham Ellis Harris	Zipporah (?)		Whitechapel, London	
20605	Harris	Abey	1844	Aldgate, London	Lewis (Louis) Harris	Esther Cohen		Spitalfields, London	
11940	Harris	Abigail	1826	Spitalfields, London	Abraham Ellis Harris	Zipporah (?)		Whitechapel, London	
29379	Harris	Abigail	1848	Wapping, London	Woolf Harris	Hannah Solomon		Wapping, London	
11107	Harris	Abraham	1775	?, Holland				Aldgate, London	general dealer
24713	Harris	Abraham	1779	Whitechapel, London			Rose (Rosa) Jessel	Walworth, London	clothes dealer
30292	Harris	Abraham	1790	Coventry, Warwickshire				Chelsea, London	retired pawnbroker
27153	Harris	Abraham	1801	?, Germany			Fanny (?)	Aldgate, London	traveller
24006	Harris	Abraham	1807	Middlesex, London			Alice (?)	Marylebone, London	clothier

ID	surname	given names	born	birthplace	father	mother	spouse 1	1851 residence	1851 occupation
4493	Harris	Abraham	1816	Aldgate, London			Leah (?)	Birmingham	glass dealer
22782	Harris	Abraham	1816	?, Poland [?, Prussia]	Tsvi		Fanny (?)	Whitechapel, London	furrier
28979	Harris	Abraham	1825	Marylebone, London	Woolf Harris	Hannah Solomon	Sarah Joseph	Whitechapel, London	clothes salesman
11939	Harris	Abraham	1828	Spitalfields, London	Abraham Ellis Harris	Zipporah (?)	Leah Brandon	Whitechapel, London	cigar maker
13579	Harris	Abraham	1832	?, Poland				Manchester	slipper maker
23636	Harris	Abraham	1836	Liverpool	Lazarus Harris	Polina (?)		Liverpool	watchmaker's apprentice
3346	Harris	Abraham	1843	Spitalfields, London	Joseph Alexander Harris	Elizabeth Levy		Spitalfields, London	
11687	Harris	Abraham	1844	Spitalfields, London	Phillip Harris	Priscilla (Powell) Marks		Aldgate, London	
5049	Harris	Abraham	1848	Portsmouth, Hampshire	Newman (Shearesa) Harris	Fanny (Sarah) Cracouer		Portsmouth, Hampshire	
10716	Harris	Abraham	1849	Middlesex, London	John Harris	Sarah (?)		Spitalfields, London	
8669	Harris	Abraham	1850	?, London	Barnett (Baruch) Harris	Rose Myers		Holborn, London	
24309	Harris	Abraham Aaron	1830	Middlesex, London	Aaron Harris	Martha Benjamin	Ann Benjamin	St Giles, London	
2633	Harris	Abraham E	1812	?, Poland [?, Prussia]			Hannah (Hana) (?)	Glasgow, Scotland	wholesale traveller
18335	Harris	Abram	1791	?, Poland [?, Russia Poland]				Bristol	pauper, late a hawker
5540	Harris	Adelaide	1840	Waterloo, London	Morris Harris	Amelia Benjamin		Waterloo, London	scholar
5474	Harris	Adelaide	1850	Wolverhampton, Staffordshire	Levi Harris	Sarah Lazarus		Wolverhampton, Staffordshire	
790	Harris	Adelaide	1851	Lambeth, London	Myer Harris	Rebecca Braham	Edward Foligno Lee	Lambeth, London	
12437	Harris	Agnes	1824	City, London	(?) Abrahams		Joseph (Myer) Harris	Spitalfields, London	
19331	Harris	Alexander	1818	Whitechapel, London	Samuel Harris	Deborah (?)		King's Cross, London	engraver
24364	Harris	Alexander	1844	St Giles, London	Mark Harris	(?)		Covent Garden, London	scholar
31148	Harris	Alexander	1849	?, Kent	Lewis (Judah Lion) Harris	Sarah Solomon		Bath	
9233	Harris	Alfred	1847	Spitalfields, London	Lawrence (Lazarus) Harris	Hannah (?)		Spitalfields, London	
4500	Harris	Alfred	1849	Birmingham	Benjamin Harris	Sarah (?)		Birmingham	
7450	Harris	Alfred (Abraham) Ellis	1836	Middlesex, London	Abraham Ellis Harris	Zipporah (?)	Ellen Hendriks	Whitechapel, London	apprentice student
21806	Harris	Alfred Abraham	1845	Whitechapel, London	Samuel Harris	Hannah (Sarah) Simpson		Wapping, London	
25586	Harris	Alfred Wormser	1837	Dublin, Ireland	Louis (Lewis) Harris	Caroline (Ellen) Picard	Miriam Lazarus	Dublin, Ireland	
24007	Harris	Alice	1809	Whitechapel, London	(?)		Abraham Harris	Marylebone, London	clothier
30096	Harris	Alice	1850	Bath	Lewis (Judah Lion) Harris	Sarah Solomon		Bath	
10036	Harris	Amelia	1805	Aldgate, London	Jacob Benjamin		Morris Harris	Waterloo, London	
17756	Harris	Amelia	1817	City, London	(?) Harris			Aldgate, London	cook
11682	Harris	Amelia	1830	Whitechapel, London	Phillip Harris	Priscilla (Powell) Marks		Aldgate, London	furrier
23526	Harris	Amelia	1830	Bedford, Bedfordshire	(?) Rosenberg		Julius Harris	Liverpool	
28057	Harris	Amelia	1832	Spitalfields, London	Joel Harris	Sarah Davis	Michael Abrahams	Spitalfields, London	
9234	Harris	Amelia	1848	Spitalfields, London	Lawrence (Lazarus) Harris	Hannah (?)		Spitalfields, London	
28315	Harris	Angel	1781	Aldgate, London				Aldgate, London	
8664	Harris	Angel	1835	?, London	Barnett (Baruch) Harris	Rose Myers		Holborn, London	apprentice tailor
29374	Harris	Angel	1837	Wapping, London	Woolf Harris	Hannah Solomon		Wapping, London	scholar
18058	Harris	Ann	1811	Ledbury, Herefordshire	(?)		Jacob Harris	Dudley, Worcestershire	
27879	Harris	Ann	1826	Aldgate, London	(?) Harris			Spitalfields, London	carpet bag maker
18668	Harris	Ann	1839	?, London	Isaac Harris	Dinah (?)		Whitechapel, London	
8668	Harris	Ann (Annie)	1842	Cincinnati, USA	Barnett (Baruch) Harris	Rose Myers	Henry Liebler (Leibler)	Holborn, London	
30503	Harris	Ann (Hannah) Deborah	1820	?, Poland	Solomon Bloom	Leah (?)	Ephraim Harris	Merthyr Tydfil, Wales	

ID	surname	given names	born	birthplace	father	mother	spouse 1	1851 residence	1851 occupation
13729	Harris	Anne	1823	?, London	Ralph Harris	Rachel Shannon		Bloomsbury, London	
27374	Harris	Anne	1823	Aldgate, London			Isaac Harris	Aldgate, London	
5541	Harris	Annie	1846	Waterloo, London	Morris Harris	Amelia Benjamin	Maurice Abraham Hyman	Waterloo, London	scholar
24008	Harris	Asher	1838	Marylebone, London	Abraham Harris	Alice (?)		Marylebone, London	
6578	Harris	Asher Selig	1824	Liverpool	Raphael Harris		Leah Nathan	Aldgate, London	watch maker
18510	Harris	Barnett	1806	Westminster, London	Meir HaLevi		Rosetta (?)	Chatham, Kent	
8662	Harris	Barnett	1810	Middlesex, London	Michael (Meyer) Harris	Simmie (Sima, Simha) b. Dov Ber	Rose Myers	Holborn, London	tailor + secretary of loan office
8600	Harris	Barnett	1811	?, Poland				Spitalfields, London	
18272	Harris	Barnett	1825	?, Russia			(?)	Whitby, Yorkshire	dealer
17052	Harris	Barnett	1840	Glasgow, Scotland	Abraham Harris	Anna (?)		Glasgow, Scotland	
14451	Harris	Benjamin	1808	Manchester			Sarah (?)	Manchester	boot maker
11102	Harris	Benjamin	1809	?, Holland	Abraham Harris		Eleanor (?)	Aldgate, London	general dealer
4495	Harris	Benjamin	1812	Birmingham		Mary (?)	Sarah (?)	Birmingham	jewellery mfr
13313	Harris	Benjamin	1828	Whitechapel, London	John (Jacob) Harris	Rebecca Moses	Hannah Abrahams	Spitalfields, London	clothes dealer
11167	Harris	Benjamin	1833	Aldgate, London	Abraham Harris	Catharine (?)		Aldgate, London	cigar maker
24311	Harris	Benjamin	1840	Middlesex, London	Aaron Harris	Martha Benjamin		St Giles, London	scholar
20607	Harris	Benjamin	1847	Aldgate, London	Lewis (Louis) Harris	Esther Cohen		Spitalfields, London	
18196	Harris	Betsey	1761	Middlesex, London	(?) Harris			Mile End, London	
18512	Harris	Betsey	1831	?, London	Barnett Harris	Rosetta (?)		Chatham, Kent	
10983	Harris	Betsy	1823	Aldgate, London	Woolf Harris	Rachel Pounser		Aldgate, London	greengrocer
25455	Harris	Betsy (Elizabeth)	1850	Spitalfields, London	Henry Harris	Hannah Joseph	(?) Hyams	Aldgate, London	
27382	Harris	Blumah	1811	Pruszkow, Poland [Pritzkow, Poland]	(?)		Jarman Harris	Aldgate, London	
13666	Harris	Caroline	1811	Portsmouth, Hampshire	(?) Levy		Lewis Henry Harris	Manchester	attends to house &c
25585	Harris	Caroline (Ellen)	1817	?, France	Raphael Picard		Louis (Lewis) Harris	Dublin, Ireland	
11164	Harris	Catharine	1799	Aldgate, London	(?)		Abraham Harris	Aldgate, London	general dealer
20603	Harris	Catharine	1838	Whitechapel, London	Lewis (Louis) Harris	Esther Cohen		Spitalfields, London	
4517	Harris	Catherine	1813	Lambeth, London	Moshe Harris		Isaac Harris	Birmingham	
26527	Harris	Catherine	1832	Holborn, London	George Harris	Louisa (?)	Jacob Levy Miers	Marylebone, London	warehouseman
5275	Harris	Catherine	1844	Bethnal Green, London	Hyam (Hyman) Harris	Mary Samson	Woolf Turner	Stepney, London	scholar
27159	Harris	Catherine	1846	?, London	Abraham Harris	Fanny (?)		Aldgate, London	
16101	Harris	Catherine (Kitty)	1775	King's Lynn, Norfolk	(?) Levy		Godfrey Harris	Wapping, London	
30505	Harris	Cecile Hindah	1846	Merthyr Tydfil, Wales	Ephraim Harris	Ann (Hannah) Deborah Bloom		North Shields, Tyne & Wear	
11148	Harris	Cecilia	1831	Whitechapel, London	Solomon Harris	Frances Myers		Aldgate, London	umbrella maker
25588	Harris	Charles	1802	?			Mary Samuel	Dublin, Ireland	watch + clock maker
25202	Harris	Charlotte	1834	Marylebone, London	Lewis Harris	Sarah (?)		Clerkenwell, London	shirt front maker
28284	Harris	Clara	1770	Aldgate, London	(?)		(?) Harris	Aldgate, London	invalid
13728	Harris	Clara	1819	Spitalfields, London	Ralph Harris	Rachel Shannon	Ernest Oppenheim	Bloomsbury, London	
27274	Harris	Daniel	1809	City, London	Lazarus (Eliezer) Harris	Rachel Abrahams	Elizabeth Pavano	Aldgate, London	general dealer
11685	Harris	Daniel	1837	Whitechapel, London	Phillip Harris	Priscilla (Powell) Marks		Aldgate, London	cigar maker
20606	Harris	Daniel	1846	Aldgate, London	Lewis (Louis) Harris	Esther Cohen		Spitalfields, London	
10257	Harris	David	1822	Whitechapel, London	John (Jacob) Harris	Rebecca Moses	Isabella Barnett	Spitalfields, London	general dealer
6789	Harris	David	1824	Aldgate, London	Mordecai Harris	Sarah Lyon (Lyons)		Spitalfields, London	

ID	surname	given names	born	birthplace	father	mother	spouse 1	1851 residence	1851 occupation
30930	Harris	David	1831	?, Poland [?, Prussia]				Hull, Yorkshire	tailor
11168	Harris	David	1835	Aldgate, London	Abraham Harris	Catharine (?)		Aldgate, London	general dealer
29376	Harris	David	1843	Wapping, London	Woolf Harris	Hannah Solomon		Wapping, London	scholar
25582	Harris	David	1845	?	Joseph Harris			Dublin, Ireland	
10374	Harris	David	1849	Spitalfields, London	Henry Harris	Julia Jacobs		Spitalfields, London	
2639	Harris	David	1850	Glasgow, Scotland	Abraham Harris	Hannah (Hana) (?)		Glasgow, Scotland	
26312	Harris	David	1851	Aldgate, London	Henry Harris	Esther Mordecai		Aldgate, London	
14208	Harris	Davis	1830	?				Manchester	tailor
26992	Harris	Davis	1849	Aldgate, London	Nathan Harris	Hannah (?)		Aldgate, London	
19330	Harris	Deborah	1791	City, London	(?)		Samuel Harris	King's Cross, London	
11683	Harris	Deborah	1833	Whitechapel, London	Phillip Harris	Priscilla (Powell) Marks		Aldgate, London	furrier
29866	Harris	Deborah	1833	Whitechapel, London	Joseph Harris	Rachel (?)		Whitechapel, London	assistant to broker
4520	Harris	Deborah	1841	Birmingham	Isaac Harris	Catherine Harris		Birmingham	scholar
29372	Harris	Diana (Dinah)	1833	Wapping, London	Woolf Harris	Hannah Solomon		Wapping, London	waistcoat maker
18664	Harris	Dinah	1807	?, London	(?)		Isaac Harris	Whitechapel, London	
27148	Harris	Dinah	1824	Lambeth, London	David Jacobs	Hannah Solomons	George Harris	Aldgate, London	general dealer
24310	Harris	Dinah	1836	Middlesex, London	Aaron Harris	Martha Benjamin		St Giles, London	
29118	Harris	Dinah	1845	Bermondsey, London	Lewis Harris	Hannah Nathan		Whitechapel, London	
29378	Harris	Edward	1846	Wapping, London	Woolf Harris	Hannah Solomon		Wapping, London	scholar
25207	Harris	Edward E	1844	Islington, London	Lewis Harris	Sarah (?)		Clerkenwell, London	
11103	Harris	Eleanor	1813	Great Yarmouth, Norfolk	(?)		Benjamin Harris	Aldgate, London	
27276	Harris	Eleazer	1841	City, London	Daniel Harris	Hannah Solomon		Aldgate, London	
4502	Harris	Elias	1804	?, Poland [?, Prussia]			Fanny (?)	Birmingham	cap maker
10768	Harris	Elisha (Elias)	1826	Aldgate, London			Rebecca (?)	Spitalfields, London	cabman
11934	Harris	Eliza	1813	Whitechapel, London	Henry Harris	(?)		Whitechapel, London	
25201	Harris	Eliza	1831	Marylebone, London	Lewis Harris	Sarah (?)		Clerkenwell, London	shirt front maker
29377	Harris	Eliza (Ailsey)	1843	Wapping, London	Woolf Harris	Hannah Solomon		Wapping, London	scholar
21971	Harris	Eliza (Elvira)	1833	Swansea, Wales	Mordecai Harris	Leah (?)		Swansea, Wales	
20460	Harris	Elizabeth	1767	?, France				Soho, London	
11138	Harris	Elizabeth	1781	Lublin, Poland	(?)		Isaac Harris	Aldgate, London	carpet bag maker
25086	Harris	Elizabeth	1795	Middlesex, London	(?) Harris			City, London	
12270	Harris	Elizabeth	1797	Clerkenwell, London	(?)		(?) Harris	Finsbury, London	proprietor of houses
30766	Harris	Elizabeth	1798	?, London	(?) Harris			Finsbury, London	
21588	Harris	Elizabeth	1799	Holborn, London	(?)		Nathaniel Harris	Holborn, London	
4507	Harris	Elizabeth	1802	?, Belgium [Flanders]	Shmuel (?Samuels)		Henry Harris	Birmingham	
19930	Harris	Elizabeth	1804	?Warwick, Warwickshire	(?)		Samuel Harris	Whitechapel, London	
3339	Harris	Elizabeth	1805	Plymouth, Devon	Chaim Levy		Joseph Alexander Harris	Spitalfields, London	
30287	Harris	Elizabeth	1811	City, London	Isaac Harris	Esther (?)		Holborn, London	
11028	Harris	Elizabeth	1818	Middlesex, London	Lazarus (Eliezer, Lewis) Barnett	Ann (Miriam) (?)	Isaac Harris	Aldgate, London	
794	Harris	Elizabeth	1827	Middlesex, London	Nathan Harris	Rebecca (?)	(?) Young	Lambeth, London	
6791	Harris	Elizabeth	1830	Aldgate, London	Mordecai Harris	Sarah Lyon (Lyons)		Spitalfields, London	furrier
2934	Harris	Elizabeth	1831	Whitechapel, London	John (Jacob) Harris	Rebecca Moses	Israel Levy	Spitalfields, London	
27384	Harris	Elizabeth	1833	Pruszkow, Poland [Pritzkow, Poland]	Jarman Harris	Blumah (?)		Aldgate, London	tailoress
19931	Harris	Elizabeth	1839	Whitechapel, London	Samuel Harris	Elizabeth (?)		Whitechapel, London	

ID	surname	given names	born	birthplace	father	mother	spouse 1	1851 residence	1851 occupation
2197	Harris	Elizabeth	1842	Oxford, Oxfordshire	Wolf Harris	Esther Barnett	George Leopold Michel	Oxford, Oxfordshire	scholar
24009	Harris	Elizabeth	1845	Marylebone, London	Abraham Harris	Alice (?)	Lewis (Louis) Michael Myers	Marylebone, London	scholar
789	Harris	Elizabeth	1848	Lambeth, London	Myer Harris	Rebecca Braham	Saunders Benjamin	Lambeth, London	
20509	Harris	Elizabeth (Bluma)	1813	Strand, London	Jacob		Morris (Moses) James Harris	Waterloo, London	
13670	Harris	Ellen	1844	Manchester	Lewis Henry Harris	Caroline Levy		Manchester	scholar
9231	Harris	Ellenor (Ellen)	1842	Spitalfields, London	Lawrence (Lazarus) Harris	Hannah (?)		Spitalfields, London	
9762	Harris	Ellis	1838	Middlesex, London	Alfred Harris		Celia Frankford	Kew, London	boarding school pupil
20615	Harris	Emanuel	1791	?, Poland				Spitalfields, London	tailor
11937	Harris	Emanuel	1824	Spitalfields, London	Abraham Ellis Harris	Zipporah (?)		Whitechapel, London	printer
13669	Harris	Emanuel	1840	Manchester	Lewis Henry Harris	Caroline Levy		Manchester	scholar
31147	Harris	Emanuel	1847	Bath	Lewis (Judah Lion) Harris	Sarah Solomon		Bath	
7895	Harris	Emanuel	1849	?, London	Henry Harris	Hannah Joseph	Sarah Harris	Aldgate, London	
27645	Harris	Emilia	1816	Aldgate, London	Isaac Harris	(?)		Aldgate, London	
19980	Harris	Ephraim	1819	?, Austria			Ann (Hannah) Deborah Bloom	Merthyr Tydfil, Wales	
9651	Harris	Ephraim	1844	Bethnal Green, London	Hyam (Hyman) Harris	Mary Samson	Rebecca Joel	Stepney, London	scholar
2638	Harris	Ephraim	1848	Glasgow, Scotland	Abraham Harris	Hannah (Hana) (?)		Glasgow, Scotland	
28666	Harris	Ester	1766	?, London	(?) Harris			Spitalfields, London	tobacco stripper
28667	Harris	Ester	1830	?, London	Rubin Harris	(?)		Spitalfields, London	tobacco stripper
5304	Harris	Esther	1784	Redruth, Cornwall	Moses Jacob	Sarah Moses	Henry Harris	Truro, Cornwall	
20600	Harris	Esther	1811	Aldgate, London	Joseph Benjamin Zeev Wolf HaCohen		Lewis (Louis) Harris	Spitalfields, London	
16100	Harris	Esther	1814	King's Lynn, Norfolk	Godfrey Harris	Catherine (Kitty) Levy		Wapping, London	tobacconist
13727	Harris	Esther	1815	Spitalfields, London	Ralph Harris	Rachel Shannon		Bloomsbury, London	
26310	Harris	Esther	1817	?, Poland	Barnett Mordecai	Deborah (?)	Henry Harris	Aldgate, London	dressmaker
17261	Harris	Esther	1820	?, London	(?)		Joseph Harris	Aldgate, London	
8123	Harris	Esther	1830	Chatham, Kent	Isaac Samuel	Rebecca (?)	Moses (Joseph) Solomon Harris	Whitechapel, London	
18665	Harris	Esther	1830	?, London	Isaac Harris	Dinah (?)	Samuel Levy	Whitechapel, London	
13884	Harris	Esther	1837	Wigan, Lancashire	Moses Harris	Rachel (?)		Manchester	
3752	Harris	Esther	1838	Spitalfields, London	Morris Harris	Nancy (?)	Laurence Jacobs	Spitalfields, London	scholar
21973	Harris	Esther	1838	Swansea, Wales	Mordecai Harris	Leah (?)		Swansea, Wales	
19932	Harris	Esther	1840	Whitechapel, London	Samuel Harris	Elizabeth (?)		Whitechapel, London	
10991	Harris	Esther	1846	Aldgate, London	Woolf Harris	Phoebe Solomons	Lewis Samuel Silver	Aldgate, London	scholar
12438	Harris	Esther	1851	Whitechapel, London	Joseph (Myer) Harris	Agnes (?)	Emanuel Gompertz	Spitalfields, London	
2194	Harris	Esther (Hester)	1811	Lambeth, London	Daniel Barnett		Wolf Harris	Oxford, Oxfordshire	clothier's wife
22790	Harris	Eve	1850	Whitechapel, London	Abraham Harris	Fanny (?)		Whitechapel, London	
6457	Harris	Ezra	1823	Whitechapel, London	Abraham Ellis Harris	Zipporah (?)	Sarah Hannah Harris	Whitechapel, London	printer
2749	Harris	Fanny	1801	City, London	(Abraham) Henry Hirsch Jacobs	Kitty Samuel	Lewis Harris	Whitechapel, London	
24643	Harris	Fanny	1801	Aldgate, London	Philip (Avigdor) Marks	Phoebe Cohen	Hyam Phillips	Waterloo, London	job buyer
27154	Harris	Fanny	1808	?, Germany	(?)		Abraham Harris	Aldgate, London	
22783	Harris	Fanny	1816	?, Poland	(?)		Abraham Harris	Whitechapel, London	furrier
4503	Harris	Fanny	1824	?, Poland [?, Prussia]			Elias Harris	Birmingham	

ID	surname	given names	born	birthplace	father	mother	spouse 1	1851 residence	1851 occupation
27385	Harris	Fanny	1835	Pruszkow, Poland [Pritzkow, Poland]	Jarman Harris	Blumah (?)		Aldgate, London	cloth cap maker
9229	Harris	Fanny	1837	Liverpool	Lawrence (Lazarus) Harris	Hannah (?)		Spitalfields, London	cap maker
17916	Harris	Fanny	1839	Lambeth, London	(?) Harris	(?) Marks		Lambeth, London	scholar
10990	Harris	Fanny	1841	Aldgate, London	Woolf Harris	Phoebe Solomons	Michael Silver	Aldgate, London	scholar
5473	Harris	Fanny	1845	Wolverhampton, Staffordshire	Levi Harris	Sarah Lazarus	Joseph Harris	Wolverhampton, Staffordshire	
21975	Harris	Fanny	1845	Swansea, Wales	Mordecai Harris	Leah (?)		Swansea, Wales	scholar
17265	Harris	Fanny	1850	?, London	Joseph Harris	Esther (?)		Aldgate, London	
5047	Harris	Fanny (Sarah)	1811	Berlin, Germany	(?) Cracouer		Newman (Shearesa) Harris	Portsmouth, Hampshire	
11145	Harris	Frances	1789	Tower Hill, London	Meir Myers		Solomon Harris	Aldgate, London	umbrella maker
27149	Harris	George	1823	Lambeth, London	Woolf Harris	Rachel Pounser	Dinah Jacobs	Aldgate, London	general dealer
26529	Harris	George	1829	Finsbury, London	George Harris	Louisa (?)		Marylebone, London	
4524	Harris	George	1833	?, Poland				Birmingham	glazier
11689	Harris	Georgina	1850	Aldgate, London	Phillip Harris	Priscilla (Powell) Marks		Aldgate, London	
20685	Harris	Godfrey	1837	Whitechapel, London	Zalig Harris	Lucy (?)		Spitalfields, London	scholar
10372	Harris	Hanah	1847	Spitalfields, London	Henry Harris	Julia Jacobs		Spitalfields, London	scholar
27396	Harris	Hannah	1782	Brussels, Belgium [Brussels in Flanders]	Mordecai Marks		Isaac Harris	Whitechapel, London	
29370	Harris	Hannah	1807	Whitechapel, London	David Solomon		Woolf Harris	Wapping, London	
29115	Harris	Hannah	1809	Aldgate, London	Yehuda Leib Nathan		Lewis Harris	Whitechapel, London	
9226	Harris	Hannah	1810	Birmingham	(?)		Lawrence (Lazarus) Harris	Spitalfields, London	wife to wholesale flock dealer
27275	Harris	Hannah	1815	City, London	Eliezer Lipman Solomon		Daniel Harris	Aldgate, London	dressmaker
26991	Harris	Hannah	1816	?, Germany	(?)		Nathan Harris	Aldgate, London	
24714	Harris	Hannah	1820	Walworth, London	Abraham Harris	Rose (Rosa) Jessel		Walworth, London	
25453	Harris	Hannah	1824	Aldgate, London	Emanuel Joseph		Henry Harris	Aldgate, London	
29469	Harris	Hannah	1825	Rotterdam, Holland	(?) Lavy		Joel Harris	Spitalfields, London	
13314	Harris	Hannah	1826	Spitalfields, London	Yechutiel Abrahams		Benjamin Harris	Spitalfields, London	
29861	Harris	Hannah	1827	Spitalfields, London	Abraham White	Elizabeth Levy	Morris (Moses) Harris	Whitechapel, London	
3750	Harris	Hannah	1831	Wapping, London	Morris Harris	Nancy (?)	Charles White	Spitalfields, London	tailoress
10985	Harris	Hannah	1831	Aldgate, London	Woolf Harris	Phoebe Solomons		Aldgate, London	tailoress
27156	Harris	Hannah	1832	?, London	Abraham Harris	Fanny (?)		Aldgate, London	seamstress
23272	Harris	Hannah	1841	Leicester, Leicestershire	(?) Harris			Notting Hill, London	boarding school pupil
18515	Harris	Hannah	1846	Chatham, Kent	Barnett Harris	Rosetta (?)		Chatham, Kent	
13673	Harris	Hannah	1850	Manchester	Lewis Henry Harris	Caroline Levy		Manchester	
25587	Harris	Hannah (Annie)	1838	Dublin, Ireland	Louis (Lewis) Harris	Caroline (Ellen) Picard	Henry Simmons	Dublin, Ireland	
8121	Harris	Hannah (Annie)	1850	Whitechapel, London	Moses (Joseph) Solomon Harris	Esther Samuel	Isaac Asher Isaacs	Whitechapel, London	
2641	Harris	Hannah (Hana)	1818	?, London			Abraham Harris	Glasgow, Scotland	
22785	Harris	Harriet	1839	Spitalfields, London	Abraham Harris	Fanny (?)		Whitechapel, London	
21977	Harris	Harris Lyons	1783	?, Poland			(?)	Swansea, Wales	general dealer
25205	Harris	Hellen	1840	Birmingham	Lewis Harris	Sarah (?)		Clerkenwell, London	
18192	Harris	Henry	1772	Middlesex, London	Shmuel Buch Binder		Keila Cohen	Mile End, London	bookbinder
11932	Harris	Henry	1783	Whitechapel, London			(?)	Whitechapel, London	stationer
188	Harris	Henry	1784	Penzance, Cornwall	Samuel Harris	Judith Solomon	Esther Jacob	Truro, Cornwall	silversmith

ID	surname	given names	born	birthplace	father	mother	spouse 1	1851 residence	1851 occupation
19332	Harris	Henry	1796	City, London				King's Cross, London	
4506	Harris	Henry	1802	?, London	Simcha Isaac HeLevi Harris		Elizabeth Samuels	Birmingham	frame maker
10363	Harris	Henry	1808	Middlesex, London	John (Jacob) Harris	Rebecca Moses	Eve Woolf	Spitalfields, London	fishmonger
4511	Harris	Henry	1812	Aldgate, London	Shmuel Harris		Phoebe Joseph	Birmingham	clothier
26309	Harris	Henry	1818	?, Poland [?, Prussia]	Raphael Harris		Esther Mordecai	Aldgate, London	furrier
26528	Harris	Henry	1820	Aldgate, London	George Harris	Louisa (?)		Marylebone, London	solicitor + attorney
25452	Harris	Henry	1824	Aldgate, London	Solomon Harris	Susan Solomons	Hannah Joseph	Aldgate, London	clothier
13911	Harris	Henry	1826	Whitechapel, London				Manchester	manager to tailor + draper
11166	Harris	Henry	1828	Aldgate, London	Abraham Harris	Catharine (?)		Aldgate, London	cigar maker
29373	Harris	Henry	1834	Wapping, London	Woolf Harris	Hannah Solomon		Wapping, London	clothier's shopman
10987	Harris	Henry	1835	Aldgate, London	Woolf Harris	Phoebe Solomons		Aldgate, London	cigar maker
2195	Harris	Henry	1839	Oxford, Oxfordshire	Wolf Harris	Esther Barnett	Julia Abrahams	Oxford, Oxfordshire	scholar
4519	Harris	Henry	1839	Oxford, Oxfordshire	Isaac Harris	Catherine Harris		Birmingham	scholar
13668	Harris	Henry	1839	Manchester	Lewis Henry Harris	Caroline Levy		Manchester	scholar
9761	Harris	Henry	1841	Middlesex, London				Kew, London	boarding school pupil
24363	Harris	Henry	1842	St Giles, London	Mark Harris	(?)		Covent Garden, London	scholar
25206	Harris	Henry	1842	Clerkenwell, London	Lewis Harris	Sarah (?)		Clerkenwell, London	
25583	Harris	Henry	1847	?	Joseph Harris			Dublin, Ireland	
20608	Harris	Henry	1848	Aldgate, London	Lewis (Louis) Harris	Esther Cohen		Spitalfields, London	
19675	Harris	Henry	1850	Spitalfields, London	Woolf Harris	Phoebe (?)	Fanny Fonseca	Spitalfields, London	
29862	Harris	Henry	1850	Whitechapel, London	Morris (Moses) Harris	Hannah White		Whitechapel, London	
5545	Harris	Henry (Harry) M	1843	Waterloo, London	Morris Harris	Amelia Benjamin	Sophia Hyman	Waterloo, London	
2634	Harris	Henry (Hendry)	1838	Edinburgh, Scotland	Abraham Harris	Hannah (Hana) (?)	Rosie (?)	Glasgow, Scotland	
24646	Harris	Henry A	1844	Lambeth, London	Moses Harris	Fanny Marks		Waterloo, London	scholar
2750	Harris	Henry Lewis	1831	Aldgate, London	Lewis Harris	Fanny Jacobs	Amelia Magnus	Whitechapel, London	cigar apprentice
8547	Harris	Henry Samuel	1841	Middlesex, London	Samuel Harris	Jane (?)	Kate Isaacs	Spitalfields, London	
29352	Harris	Herman	1829	?, Poland [?, Prussia]				Whitechapel, London	tailor
27878	Harris	Hyam	1821	Aldgate, London				Spitalfields, London	clothes dealer
3343	Harris	Hyam	1829	Spitalfields, London	Joseph Alexander Harris	Elizabeth Levy		Spitalfields, London	traveller
10719	Harris	Hyam	1850	Spitalfields, London	Sime Harris	Rozetta (?)		Spitalfields, London	
5273	Harris	Hyam (Hyman)	1806	Spitalfields, London	Benjamin (Hyam) Harris		Mary Samson	Stepney, London	pen cutter + dealer
6453	Harris	Hyman Ellis	1821	Spitalfields, London	Abraham Ellis Harris	Zipporah (?)	Rachel Dias	Whitechapel, London	merchant
30286	Harris	Isaac	1771	Whitechapel, London			Esther (?)	Holborn, London	annuitant
27644	Harris	Isaac	1773	Aldgate, London			(?)	Aldgate, London	Hebrew teacher
27395	Harris	Isaac	1778	Aldgate, London	Shmuel Bekbender		Hannah Marks	Whitechapel, London	general dealer
27636	Harris	Isaac	1801	Aldgate, London			Isabella (?)	Aldgate, London	general dealer of fruit
18663	Harris	Isaac	1805	?, London			Dinah (?)	Whitechapel, London	broker
4516	Harris	Isaac	1815	?, London	Jacob Bas		Catherine Harris	Birmingham	glass dealer
11027	Harris	Isaac	1816	Middlesex, London	Woolf Harris		Elizabeth Barnett	Aldgate, London	furniture dealer
27373	Harris	Isaac	1825	Aldgate, London			Anne (?)	Aldgate, London	gentleman
27383	Harris	Isaac	1831	Pruszkow, Poland [Pritzkow, Poland]	Jarman Harris	Blumah (?)		Aldgate, London	tailor
4518	Harris	Isaac	1836	Spitalfields, London	Isaac Harris	Catherine Harris		Birmingham	slipper maker
29116	Harris	Isaac	1841	Aldgate, London	Lewis Harris	Hannah Nathan		Whitechapel, London	

ID	surname	given names	born	birthplace	father	mother	spouse 1	1851 residence	1851 occupation
27158	Harris	Isaac	1843	?, London	Abraham Harris	Fanny (?)		Aldgate, London	
19979	Harris	Isaac	1851	Merthyr Tydfil, Wales	Ephraim Harris	Ann (Hannah) Deborah Bloom	Flora Norma Woolf	Merthyr Tydfil, Wales	
27637	Harris	Isabella	1811	Whitechapel, London	(?)		Isaac Harris	Aldgate, London	laundress
10258	Harris	Isabella	1823	Whitechapel, London	Lazarus (Eliezer, Lewis) Barnett	Ann (Miriam) (?)	David Harris	Spitalfields, London	
19341	Harris	Isabella	1832	Bloomsbury, London	(?) Harris	(?) (?Isaacs)		Bloomsbury, London	
21802	Harris	Isabella	1836	Whitechapel, London	Samuel Harris	Hannah (Sarah) Simpson		Wapping, London	waistcoat maker
19977	Harris	Isabella (Bella)	1838	Spitalfields, London	Henry Harris	Eve Woolf	Jacob King	Spitalfields, London	
18513	Harris	Isabella (Bella)	1840	Chatham, Kent	Barnett Harris	Rosetta (?)		Chatham, Kent	
5313	Harris	Israel	1823	Truro, Cornwall	Henry Harris	Esther Jacob		Truro, Cornwall	watchmaker
12439	Harris	Izzy	1831	?London				Spitalfields, London	
10292	Harris	Jacob	1768	?, Poland [?, Prussia]			(?)	Spitalfields, London	rag + general dealer
18057	Harris	Jacob	1811	?, Poland			Ann (?)	Dudley, Worcestershire	hardware dealer
28668	Harris	Jacob	1836	?, London	Rubin Harris	(?)		Spitalfields, London	tobacco stripper
22788	Harris	Jacob	1847	Stepney, London	Abraham Harris	Fanny (?)		Whitechapel, London	
9235	Harris	Jacob	1850	Spitalfields, London	Lawrence (Lazarus) Harris	Hannah (?)		Spitalfields, London	
10099	Harris	Jacob (Morris)	1831	Elephant & Castle, London	Morris Harris	Amelia Benjamin	Mary (Miriam) Joel	Waterloo, London	rag merchant
30107	Harris	Jane	1778	Whitechapel, London	(?)		Samuel Harris	Wapping, London	
17216	Harris	Jane	1801	?, London	(?)		Samuel Harris	Spitalfields, London	
8546	Harris	Jane	1819	Middlesex, London	Lyon Benjamin		Samuel Harris	Spitalfields, London	
11139	Harris	Jane	1826	Aldgate, London	Isaac Harris	Elizabeth (?)		Aldgate, London	carpet bag maker
18059	Harris	Jane	1830	Ledbury, Herefordshire	Jacob Harris	Ann (?)		Dudley, Worcestershire	straw bonnet maker
10365	Harris	Jane	1831	Spitalfields, London	Henry Harris	Eve Woolf	Lamert Isaacs	Spitalfields, London	servant
29867	Harris	Jane	1836	Whitechapel, London	Joseph Harris	Rachel (?)		Whitechapel, London	
30511	Harris	Jane	1851	Spitalfields, London	David Harris	Isabella Barnett		Spitalfields, London	
31224	Harris	Jane	1851	Spitalfields, London	Elisha (Elias) Harris	Rebecca (?)		Spitalfields, London	
27381	Harris	Jarman	1795	Pruszkow, Poland [Pritzkow, Poland]			Blumah (?)	Aldgate, London	painter + glazier
29468	Harris	Joel	1817	Aldgate, London			Hannah Levy	Spitalfields, London	broker
28058	Harris	Joel	1835	Spitalfields, London	Joel Harris	Sarah Davis		Spitalfields, London	cigar maker apprentice
3340	Harris	Joel	1836	?Spitalfields, London	Joseph Alexander Harris	Elizabeth Levy	Julia Mendoza	Spitalfields, London	furniture dealer
11106	Harris	Joel	1848	Middlesex, London	Benjamin Harris	Eleanor (?)	Nancy Isaacs	Aldgate, London	
9208	Harris	John	1827	?, Poland				Whitechapel, London	tailor
10714	Harris	John	1827	?, Holland			Sarah (?)	Spitalfields, London	tailor
3344	Harris	John	1831	Spitalfields, London	Joseph Alexander Harris	Elizabeth Levy		Spitalfields, London	traveller
10369	Harris	John	1838	Spitalfields, London	Henry Harris	Eve Woolf		Spitalfields, London	scholar
10989	Harris	John	1839	Aldgate, London	Woolf Harris	Phoebe Solomons	Clara Silver	Aldgate, London	scholar
13671	Harris	John	1846	Manchester	Lewis Henry Harris	Caroline Levy		Manchester	scholar
13315	Harris	John	1849	Spitalfields, London	Benjamin Harris	Hannah Abrahams		Spitalfields, London	
3708	Harris	John (Jacob)	1781	Aldgate, London	Hirsch Van Berg [Weinberg]		Rebecca Moses	Spitalfields, London	general dealer
30215	Harris	John Solomon	1802	Covent Garden, London	Joseph Harris		Rose (Rosetta) Phillips	Piccadilly, London	shellfish monger
11933	Harris	Jonathan	1815	Whitechapel, London	Henry Harris	(?)		Whitechapel, London	commercial traveller
29864	Harris	Joseph	1793	?, Poland	Tsvi		Rachel (?)	Whitechapel, London	broker
17260	Harris	Joseph	1817	?, London			Esther (?)	Aldgate, London	furniture broker
791	Harris	Joseph	1823	Middlesex, London	Nathan Harris	Rebecca (?)		Lambeth, London	jeweller

ID	surname	given names	born	birthplace	father	mother	spouse 1	1851 residence	1851 occupation
6790	Harris	Joseph	1828	Aldgate, London	Mordecai Harris	Sarah Lyon (Lyons)	Eve Jacobs	Spitalfields, London	cigar maker
17428	Harris	Joseph	1830	?, Poland				Spitalfields, London	
11581	Harris	Joseph	1834	Whitechapel, London			Maria Saunders	Aldgate, London	apprentice cigar maker
23635	Harris	Joseph	1834	Liverpool	Lazarus Harris	Polina (?)		Liverpool	general dealer + [---]
16989	Harris	Joseph	1836	Marylebone, London				Wapping, London	shoemaker apprentice
11105	Harris	Joseph	1842	Middlesex, London	Benjamin Harris	Eleanor (?)		Aldgate, London	scholar
21974	Harris	Joseph	1842	Swansea, Wales	Mordecai Harris	Leah (?)		Swansea, Wales	scholar
23527	Harris	Joseph	1848	Liverpool	Julius Harris	Amelia Rosenberg		Liverpool	
29119	Harris	Joseph	1849	Whitechapel, London	Lewis Harris	Hannah Nathan		Whitechapel, London	
12436	Harris	Joseph (Myer)	1825	City, London	Tsvi		Agnes Abrahams	Spitalfields, London	bookseller
3338	Harris	Joseph Alexander	1806	Spitalfields, London	Pinchas Zelig Harris		Elizabeth Levy	Spitalfields, London	furniture broker
25579	Harris	Joseph Levi	1817	Poznan, Poland [Exin, Posen, Prussia]	Tsvi		(?)	Dublin, Ireland	jeweller
14481	Harris	Josiah	1814	Middlesex, London				Manchester	clerk: general Manchester warehouse
10367	Harris	Judah	1835	Spitalfields, London	Henry Harris	Eve Woolf		Spitalfields, London	general dealer
25456	Harris	Julia	1800	?, London	(?)		(?) Harris	Aldgate, London	nurse
24824	Harris	Julia	1801	?, London	Samuel Cohen	Ann (Nancy) Harris		Waterloo, London	
10364	Harris	Julia	1815	Spitalfields, London	Michael Jacobs		(?) Israel	Spitalfields, London	general dealer
13203	Harris	Julia	1821	Middlesex, London	(?) Samuels		Simcha Harris	Whitechapel, London	
3342	Harris	Julia	1825	Spitalfields, London	Joseph Alexander Harris	Elizabeth Levy	Lewis Price	Spitalfields, London	furrier
21801	Harris	Julia	1835	Shoreditch, London	Samuel Harris	Hannah (Sarah) Simpson		Wapping, London	waistcoat maker
25203	Harris	Julia	1835	Marylebone, London	Lewis Harris	Sarah (?)		Clerkenwell, London	shirt front maker
20602	Harris	Julia	1836	Whitechapel, London	Lewis (Louis) Harris	Esther Cohen		Spitalfields, London	dressmaker
11170	Harris	Julia	1838	Aldgate, London	Abraham Harris	Catharine (?)	Edward Angell	Aldgate, London	cap maker
4508	Harris	Julia	1839	?, London	Henry Harris	Elizabeth Samuels		Birmingham	
9230	Harris	Julia	1839	Liverpool	Lawrence (Lazarus) Harris	Hannah (?)		Spitalfields, London	furrier
29375	Harris	Julia	1840	Wapping, London	Woolf Harris	Hannah Solomon		Wapping, London	scholar
10260	Harris	Julia	1844	Spitalfields, London	David Harris	Isabella Barnett		Spitalfields, London	scholar
22787	Harris	Julia	1845	Stepney, London	Abraham Harris	Fanny (?)		Whitechapel, London	
10034	Harris	Julia (Leah)	1839	Southwark, London	Morris Harris	Amelia Bejamin	Henry Benjamin Barnard	Waterloo, London	
23525	Harris	Julius	1817	?, Poland			Amelia Rosenberg	Liverpool	watch manufacturer
10984	Harris	Kate (Catherine)	1829	Aldgate, London	Woolf Harris	Phoebe Solomons	Michael Silver	Aldgate, London	tailoress
5470	Harris	Kitty (Catherine)	1841	Wolverhampton, Staffordshire	Levi Harris	Sarah Lazarus	Myers Mandy	Wolverhampton, Staffordshire	
11686	Harris	Lawrence	1841	Whitechapel, London	Phillip Harris	Priscilla (Powell) Marks		Aldgate, London	cigar maker
13672	Harris	Lawrence	1848	Manchester	Lewis Henry Harris	Caroline Levy	Matilda Maillet	Manchester	
9225	Harris	Lawrence (Lazarus)	1808	Holborn, London	Tsvi HaCohen		Hannah (?)	Spitalfields, London	wholesale flock dealer
23633	Harris	Lazarus	1802	?, Poland			Polina (?)	Liverpool	watch manufacturer
20601	Harris	Lazarus	1833	Aldgate, London	Lewis (Louis) Harris	Esther Cohen		Spitalfields, London	cigar maker
3751	Harris	Lazarus	1836	Spitalfields, London	Morris Harris	Nancy (?)		Spitalfields, London	errand boy
4494	Harris	Leah	1811	Lambeth, London			Abraham Harris	Birmingham	
21970	Harris	Leah	1813	?, Poland			Mordecai Harris	Swansea, Wales	
16102	Harris	Leah	1823	Hackney, London	(?) Harris	Catherine (?)		Wapping, London	

ID	surname	given names	born	birthplace	father	mother	spouse 1	1851 residence	1851 occupation
18514	Harris	Leah	1843	Chatham, Kent	Barnett Harris	Rosetta (?)		Chatham, Kent	
4505	Harris	Leah	1845	Birmingham	Elias Harris	Fanny (?)		Birmingham	
4523	Harris	Leah	1849	Birmingham	Isaac Harris	Catherine Harris		Birmingham	
2196	Harris	Leah (Leza)	1840	Oxford, Oxfordshire	Wolf Harris	Esther Barnett	Samuel Kronson	Oxford, Oxfordshire	scholar
170	Harris	Levi	1800	?, Poland			Sarah Lazarus	Wolverhampton, Staffordshire	pawnbroker + clothier
24010	Harris	Levi	1847	Marylebone, London	Abraham Harris	Alice (?)		Marylebone, London	scholar
11684	Harris	Levy	1835	Whitechapel, London	Phillip Harris	Priscilla (Powell) Marks		Aldgate, London	cigar maker
30293	Harris	Lewis	1787	Coventry, Warwickshire				Chelsea, London	retired pawnbroker
25197	Harris	Lewis	1802	Marylebone, London			Sarah (?)	Clerkenwell, London	coal merchant
2748	Harris	Lewis	1803	Aldgate, London	Henry Harris	Frances Levy	Fanny Jacobs	Whitechapel, London	commission agent
29114	Harris	Lewis	1808	Whitechapel, London	Eliakim Getshlik		Hannah Nathan	Whitechapel, London	turner
12670	Harris	Lewis	1827	?, Germany				Birmingham	slipper maker
27386	Harris	Lewis	1837	Pruszkow, Poland [Pritzkow, Poland]	Jarman Harris	Blumah (?)		Aldgate, London	cloth cap maker
21804	Harris	Lewis	1841	Whitechapel, London	Samuel Harris	Hannah (Sarah) Simpson	Elizabeth Gibbs	Wapping, London	
27398	Harris	Lewis	1842	Spitalfields, London				Whitechapel, London	scholar
30093	Harris	Lewis (Judah Lion)	1818	Middlesex, London	Emanuel Harris		Sarah Solomon	Bath	glass dealer
20599	Harris	Lewis (Louis)	1812	Spitalfields, London	Lazarus (Eliezer Lezer) Harris	(?Rachel Abrahams)	Esther Cohen	Spitalfields, London	watchmaker
13665	Harris	Lewis Henry	1806	?, London	(Henry?) Harris		Caroline Levy	Manchester	ink manufacturer
25204	Harris	Lionel	1838	Birmingham	Lewis Harris	Sarah (?)		Clerkenwell, London	
20686	Harris	Louis	1839	Whitechapel, London	Zalig Harris	Lucy (?)		Spitalfields, London	scholar
22786	Harris	Louis	1843	Stepney, London	Abraham Harris	Fanny (?)		Whitechapel, London	scholar
25584	Harris	Louis (Lewis)	1812	Stuttgart, Germany	Isaac Wormser		Caroline (Ellen) Picard	Dublin, Ireland	Army and Navy agent
26530	Harris	Louisa	1801	Strand, London	(?)		George Harris	Marylebone, London	annuitant
10037	Harris	Louisa	1828	Elephant & Castle, London	Morris Harris	Amelia Benjamin	Moss (Maurice) Benjamin	Waterloo, London	assistant, rag merchant's business
20683	Harris	Lucy	1804	Spitalfields, London	(?)		Zalig Harris	Spitalfields, London	greengrocer
4499	Harris	Lydia	1847	Birmingham	Benjamin Harris	Sarah (?)		Birmingham	
5472	Harris	Lyon	1846	Wolverhampton, Staffordshire	Levi Harris	Sarah Lazarus		Wolverhampton, Staffordshire	
4521	Harris	M---- (Moses?)	1843	Birmingham	Isaac Harris	Catherine (Harris)		Birmingham	scholar
6459	Harris	Malvina	1835	Holborn, London	Bartholomew Harris		William Oppenheim	Holborn, London	boarding school pupil
25200	Harris	Maria	1829	Marylebone, London	Lewis Harris	Sarah (?)		Clerkenwell, London	shirt front maker
21799	Harris	Maria	1830	Soho, London	Samuel Harris	Hannah (Sarah) Simpson		Wapping, London	waistcoat maker
5539	Harris	Maria	1835	Waterloo, London	Morris Harris	Amelia Benjamin		Waterloo, London	
11580	Harris	Maria	1836	Whitechapel, London	Goodman Saunders	Phoebe (?)	Joseph Harris	Aldgate, London	
10988	Harris	Maria	1837	Aldgate, London	Woolf Harris	Phoebe Solomons		Aldgate, London	dress maker
3347	Harris	Maria	1843	Whitechapel, London	Zalig Harris	Lucy (?)	Joseph Abrahams	Spitalfields, London	scholar
4514	Harris	Maria	1845	Cheltenham, Gloucestershire	Henry Harris	Phoebe (?)		Birmingham	
24360	Harris	Mark	1808	St Giles, London			(?)	Covent Garden, London	tailor
793	Harris	Mark (Montague)	1825	Middlesex, London	Nathan Harris	Rebecca (?)	Frances Cohen	Lambeth, London	traveller
4501	Harris	Mary	1784	Birmingham			(?) Harris	Birmingham	
23926	Harris	Mary	1803	?, Poland	(?)		(?) Harris	Marylebone, London	housekeeper
5272	Harris	Mary	1816	Whitechapel, London	Ephraim Samson	Hannah Myers	Hyam (Hyman) Harris	Stepney, London	

238

ID	surname	given names	born	birthplace	father	mother	spouse 1	1851 residence	1851 occupation
20684	Harris	Mary	1835	Whitechapel, London	Zalig Harris	Lucy (?)		Spitalfields, London	
17263	Harris	Mary	1844	?, London	Joseph Harris	Esther (?)		Aldgate, London	scholar
4498	Harris	Mary	1845	Birmingham	Benjamin Harris	Sarah (?)		Birmingham	
10261	Harris	Mary	1848	Spitalfields, London	David Harris	Isabella Barnett		Spitalfields, London	
18517	Harris	Mary	1849	Chatham, Kent	Barnett Harris	Rosetta (?)		Chatham, Kent	
30513	Harris	Mary	1851	Aldgate, London	Isaac Harris	Elizabeth Barnett		Aldgate, London	
22354	Harris	Mary Ann	1824	Chelsea, London	(?) Harris			Aldgate, London	dressmaker
20609	Harris	Mary Ann	1850	Aldgate, London	Lewis (Louis) Harris	Esther Cohen		Spitalfields, London	
30294	Harris	Matilda	1796	Coventry, Warwickshire	(?) Harris			Chelsea, London	
19825	Harris	Matilda	1845	Portsmouth, Hampshire	Samuel Harris	Rebecca Cohen		Gravesend, Kent	
18519	Harris	Michael	1836	Chatham, Kent	Barnett Harris	Rosetta (?)	Jessie Abrahams	Chatham, Kent	
20604	Harris	Michael	1842	Aldgate, London	Lewis (Louis) Harris	Esther Cohen		Spitalfields, London	
23528	Harris	Montague	1849	Liverpool	Julius Harris	Amelia Rosenberg		Liverpool	
6076	Harris	Mordecai	1806	?, Holland	Eliakim Getshlik		Sarah Lyon (Lyons)	Spitalfields, London	general dealer
21969	Harris	Mordecai	1807	?, Poland	Harris Lyons Harris		Leah (?)	Swansea, Wales	jeweller
3748	Harris	Morris	1800	Spitalfields, London	Eliezer Lezer Harris		Nancy Mendoza	Spitalfields, London	watchmaker
7527	Harris	Morris	1800	?				Manchester	
10035	Harris	Morris	1805	Vauxhall, London	Jacob Harris		Amelia Benjamin	Waterloo, London	rag merchant
795	Harris	Morris	1829	Middlesex, London	Nathan Harris	Rebecca (?)	Catherine Myers	Lambeth, London	engineer
2754	Harris	Morris	1836	City, London	Lewis Harris	Fanny Jacobs	Teresa Cowvan (Lang)	Whitechapel, London	scholar
24362	Harris	Morris	1838	Strand, London	Mark Harris	(?)		Covent Garden, London	scholar
4504	Harris	Morris	1843	Wolverhampton, Staffordshire	Elias Harris	Fanny (?)		Birmingham	
8666	Harris	Morris (Mark)	1838	?, London	Barnett (Baruch) Harris	Rose Myers		Holborn, London	
29860	Harris	Morris (Moses)	1825	Spitalfields, London	Joseph Harris		Hannah White	Whitechapel, London	fixture dealer
20508	Harris	Morris (Moses) James	1799	Covent Garden, London	Joseph Harris		Elizabeth (Bluma b. Jacob)	Waterloo, London	shellfish monger
5315	Harris	Morris Hart	1821	Truro, Cornwall	Henry Harris	Esther Jacob	Rebecca Jacob	Bristol	
13882	Harris	Moses	1798	Poznan, Poland [Posen, Prussia]			Rachel (?)	Manchester	tailor + draper
24642	Harris	Moses	1804	Aldgate, London			Fanny Phillips nee Marks	Waterloo, London	general dealer + clothier
2266	Harris	Moses	1821	?, London				Leeds, Yorkshire	general dealer
25064	Harris	Moses	1822	Aldgate, London	(?Abraham) Harris			Spitalfields, London	general dealer
28056	Harris	Moses	1829	Spitalfields, London	Joel Harris	Sarah Davis		Spitalfields, London	furniture broker
21972	Harris	Moses	1835	Swansea, Wales	Mordecai Harris	Leah (?)		Swansea, Wales	watchmaker
11104	Harris	Moses	1837	Middlesex, London	Benjamin Harris	Eleanor (?)	Hannah Abendana	Aldgate, London	
23927	Harris	Moses	1844	Marylebone, London	(?) Harris	Mary (?)		Marylebone, London	scholar
8122	Harris	Moses (Joseph) Solomon	1828	Warsaw, Poland			Esther Samuel	Whitechapel, London	slipper maker
17262	Harris	Moses (Moss)	1842	?, London	Joseph Harris	Esther (?)		Aldgate, London	scholar
7896	Harris	Moss	1824	Elephant & Castle, London	Abraham Harris	Rose (Rosa) Jessel		Peckham, London	master tailor
785	Harris	Myer	1821	Covent Garden, London	Nathan Harris	Rebecca (?)	Rebecca Braham	Lambeth, London	jeweller
8665	Harris	Myer	1836	?, London	Barnett (Baruch) Harris	Rose Myers		Holborn, London	apprentice engraver
18662	Harris	Myer	1841	Middlesex, London	Isaac Harris	Dinah (?)	Rosetta Stibbe	Whitechapel, London	
3749	Harris	Nancy	1807	Aldgate, London	David Mendoza		Morris Harris	Spitalfields, London	Leghorn bonnet maker
11688	Harris	Nancy	1847	Aldgate, London	Phillip Harris	Priscilla (Powell) Marks		Aldgate, London	

ID	surname	given names	born	birthplace	father	mother	spouse 1	1851 residence	1851 occupation
19328	Harris	Naphtali	1823	Spitalfields, London	Samuel Harris	Deborah (?)	Rebecca Kyezor (Keyzor, Keysor)	King's Cross, London	engraver
784	Harris	Nathan	1796	St Giles, London			Rebecca (?)	Lambeth, London	
2137	Harris	Nathan	1800	?, Poland			Sarah(?)	Hull, Yorkshire	appraiser + engraver
26990	Harris	Nathan	1816	?, Germany			Hannah (?)	Aldgate, London	hawker
21060	Harris	Nathan	1840	?, London				Dover, Kent	glazier
788	Harris	Nathan	1843	Lambeth, London	Myer Harris	Rebecca Braham	Julia Benjamin	Lambeth, London	boarding school pupil
21587	Harris	Nathaniel	1799	Clerkenwell, London			Elizabeth (?)	Holborn, London	scholar
24716	Harris	Nathaniel	1823	Walworth, London	Abraham Harris	Rose (Rosa) Jessel		Walworth, London	shopman
18741	Harris	Nathaniel	1833	Holborn, London	Nathaniel Harris	Elizabeth (?)	Fanny Davis	Holborn, London	clothes dealer
18518	Harris	Nathaniel	1850	Chatham, Kent	Barnett Harris	Rosetta (?)		Chatham, Kent	apprentice to a compellator
5046	Harris	Newman (Shearesa)	1795	Berlin, Germany			Fanny (Sarah) Cracouer	Portsmouth, Hampshire	glazier
5048	Harris	Nieman	1840	Portsmouth, Hampshire	Newman (Shearesa) Harris	Fanny (Sarah) Cracouer		Portsmouth, Hampshire	
18443	Harris	Phebe	1828	Truro, Cornwall	Henry Harris	Esther Jacob	Abraham Gabay Franklin	Truro, Cornwall	shop assistant
11680	Harris	Phillip	1801	Aldgate, London	Tsevi Hirsh		Priscilla (Powell) Marks	Aldgate, London	tailor
27638	Harris	Phillip	1831	Middlesex, London	Issac Harris	Isabella (?)		Aldgate, London	general dealer of fruit
24647	Harris	Phillip	1850	Lambeth, London	Moses Harris	Fanny Marks		Waterloo, London	
30512	Harris	Phineas	1851	Whitechapel, London	Lewis Harris	Hannah Nathan		Whitechapel, London	
9227	Harris	Phobe	1834	Liverpool	Lawrence (Lazarus) Harris	Hannah (?)		Spitalfields, London	milliner
10982	Harris	Phoebe	1803	Aldgate, London	Eliezer Lipman Solomons		Woolf Harris	Aldgate, London	greengrocer
4512	Harris	Phoebe	1815	Aldgate, London	Naphtali Hirts Joseph		Henry Harris	Birmingham	
25199	Harris	Phoebe	1826	Marylebone, London	Lewis Harris	Sarah (?)		Clerkenwell, London	milliner
27155	Harris	Phoebe	1829	?, London	Abraham Harris	Fanny (?)		Aldgate, London	seamstress
19674	Harris	Phoebe	1830	Aldgate, London	Jacob Romaine		Woolf Harris	Spitalfields, London	
13667	Harris	Phoebe	1837	Manchester	Lewis Henry Harris	Caroline Levy		Manchester	scholar
23634	Harris	Polina	1806	?, Poland	(?)		Lazarus Harris	Liverpool	
11681	Harris	Priscilla (Powell)	1803	Aldgate, London	Eliezer Lazer Marks		Phillip Harris	Aldgate, London	
27277	Harris	Rachael	1842	City, London	Daniel Harris	Hannah Solomon		Aldgate, London	
10373	Harris	Rachael	1848	Spitalfields, London	Henry Harris	Julia Jacobs		Spitalfields, London	scholar
22789	Harris	Rachael	1848	Whitechapel, London	Abraham Harris	Fanny (?)		Whitechapel, London	
11029	Harris	Rachael	1849	Aldgate, London	Isaac Harris	Elizabeth Barnett		Aldgate, London	
26993	Harris	Rachael	1850	Aldgate, London	Nathan Harris	Hannah (?)		Aldgate, London	
13726	Harris	Rachel	1789	?, London	Masaod Shannon	Esther (?)	Ralph Harris	Bloomsbury, London	
13883	Harris	Rachel	1797	Poznan, Poland [Posen, Prussia]	(?)		Moses Harris	Manchester	
29865	Harris	Rachel	1807	?, Poland	(?)		Joseph Harris	Whitechapel, London	
6454	Harris	Rachel	1822	Aldgate, London	John (Johannan) Dias	Rachel de Naphtali Pass (Paz De Leon)	Hyman Ellis Harris	Whitechapel, London	professor of music
17217	Harris	Rachel	1826	?, London	Samuel Harris	Jane (?)		Spitalfields, London	
3710	Harris	Rachel	1831	Aldgate, London	John (Jacob) Harris	Rebecca Moses	Henry Polack	Spitalfields, London	
2449	Harris	Rachel	1836	?, Poland	Nathan Harris	Sarah (?)	Aaron Feldman	Hull, Yorkshire	scholar
10038	Harris	Rachel	1837	Waterloo, London	Morris Harris	Amelia Benjamin	Joseph Benjamin	Waterloo, London	scholar

ID	surname	given names	born	birthplace	father	mother	spouse 1	1851 residence	1851 occupation
5469	Harris	Rachel	1838	Wolverhampton, Staffordshire	Levi Harris	Sarah Lazarus		Wolverhampton, Staffordshire	
2637	Harris	Rachel	1848	Glasgow, Scotland	Abraham Harris	Hannah (Hana) (?)	Joseph Rogers	Glasgow, Scotland	
5277	Harris	Rachel	1850	Stepney, London	Hyam (Hyman) Harris	Mary Samson	Moss Woolf	Stepney, London	
13725	Harris	Ralph	1786	?, London	Abraham Emzer		Rachel Shannon	Bloomsbury, London	dealer in china
11938	Harris	Ralph	1826	Spitalfields, London	Abraham Ellis Harris	Zipporah (?)		Whitechapel, London	cigar maker
2752	Harris	Raphael	1835	Aldgate, London	Lewis Harris	Fanny Jacobs	Julia Solomon	Whitechapel, London	teacher
26311	Harris	Raphael	1849	Aldgate, London	Henry Harris	Esther Mordecai		Aldgate, London	
23637	Harris	Rebbecca	1838	Liverpool	Lazarus Harris	Polina (?)		Liverpool	
786	Harris	Rebecca	1816	St Pancras, London	Abraham Braham (Abraham)	Hannah Moss (Moses)	Myer Harris	Lambeth, London	
27880	Harris	Rebecca	1816	Whitechapel, London	(?) Harris			Spitalfields, London	domestic servant
19824	Harris	Rebecca	1823	Portsmouth, Hampshire	Isaac Cohen	Phoebe Myer	Samuel Harris	Gravesend, Kent	
5316	Harris	Rebecca	1824	Falmouth, Cornwall	Jacob Jacob	Sarah Simons	Morris Hart Harris	Bristol	
10769	Harris	Rebecca	1826	Whitechapel, London	(?)		Elisha (Elias) Harris	Spitalfields, London	slipper binder out doors
21800	Harris	Rebecca	1832	Soho, London	Samuel Harris	Hannah (Sarah) Simpson		Wapping, London	waistcoat maker
18666	Harris	Rebecca	1833	?, London	Isaac Harris	Dinah (?)		Whitechapel, London	
9228	Harris	Rebecca	1835	Liverpool	Lawrence (Lazarus) Harris	Hannah (?)		Spitalfields, London	cap maker
2755	Harris	Rebecca	1839	Aldgate, London	Lewis Harris	Fanny Jacobs		Whitechapel, London	
787	Harris	Rebecca	1842	Lambeth, London	Myer Harris	Rebecca Braham	David Isaacs	Lambeth, London	
5471	Harris	Rebecca	1842	Wolverhampton, Staffordshire	Levi Harris	Sarah Lazarus	Heyman Heymanson	Wolverhampton, Staffordshire	
10259	Harris	Rebecca	1843	City, London	David Harris	Isabella Barnett		Spitalfields, London	scholar
10370	Harris	Rebecca	1844	Spitalfields, London	Henry Harris	Julia Jacobs	Barnet Levy	Spitalfields, London	scholar
19934	Harris	Rebecca	1845	Whitechapel, London	Samuel Harris	Elizabeth (?)		Whitechapel, London	
6838	Harris	Rebecca	1847	Bethnal Green, London	Hyam (Hyman) Harris	Mary Samson	Abraham De Wilde (Gervilder)	Stepney, London	scholar
6816	Harris	Rebecca	1848	Aldgate, London	Joseph Harris	Esther (?)	Ezekiel Moss	Aldgate, London	
10770	Harris	Rebecca	1848	Spitalfields, London	Elisha (Elias) Harris	Rebecca (?)		Spitalfields, London	
2265	Harris	Rosa	1801	?, Poland [?, Prussia]				Leeds, Yorkshire	
25923	Harris	Rosa	1824	City, London	Solomon Harris	Susan Solomons	Godfrey C Phillips	Spitalfields, London	
27157	Harris	Rosa	1841	?, London	Abraham Harris	Fanny (?)		Aldgate, London	
29371	Harris	Rosa (Rosetta)	1831	Wapping, London	Woolf Harris	Hannah Solomon	Jacob Myers	Wapping, London	housekeeper
30095	Harris	Rosalie	1846	Bath	Lewis (Judah Lion) Harris	Sarah Solomon		Bath	
8663	Harris	Rose	1811	Aldgate, London	Angel (Abraham Asher Anshel) Myers	Hannah (Anna) (?)	Barnett Harris	Holborn, London	
25581	Harris	Rose	1850	Dublin, Ireland	Joseph Harris			Dublin, Ireland	
30216	Harris	Rose (Rosetta)	1808	Strand, London	Joseph Phillips	Elizabeth (Pessa) Sarah bat Abraham	John Solomon Harris	Piccadilly, London	
18511	Harris	Rosetta	1806	?, London	Meir HaLevi		Barnett Harris	Chatham, Kent	
21803	Harris	Rosetta (Rosa)	1839	Whitechapel, London	Samuel Harris	Hannah (Sarah) Simpson	Morris Goldstein	Wapping, London	waistcoat maker
2636	Harris	Rosetta (Roselly)	1844	Glasgow, Scotland	Abraham Harris	Hannah (Hana)	Barnett (Baruck) Lazarus [Lawrence]	Glasgow, Scotland	
5323	Harris	Rosina	1836	Wolverhampton, Staffordshire	Levi Harris	Sarah Lazarus	Joseph Wolfe	Wolverhampton, Staffordshire	
10718	Harris	Rozetta	1828	Middlesex, London	(?)		Sime Harris	Spitalfields, London	tailoress

ID	surname	given names	born	birthplace	father	mother	spouse 1	1851 residence	1851 occupation
28665	Harris	Rubin	1793	?, London			(?)	Spitalfields, London	general dealer
19329	Harris	Samuel	1781	City, London			Deborah (?)	King's Cross, London	dealer in glass
17215	Harris	Samuel	1787	?, London			Jane (?)	Spitalfields, London	general dealer
25794	Harris	Samuel	1797	?, Poland [?, Prussia]				Aldgate, London	formerly a broker? --- Great Synagogue
19929	Harris	Samuel	1805	City, London	(Henry?) Harris		Elizabeth (?)	Whitechapel, London	blacking + ink manufacturer + drysalter
21797	Harris	Samuel	1805	Whitechapel, London	Samuel Harris	Jane (?)	Hannah (Sarah) Simpson	Wapping, London	fishmonger
19823	Harris	Samuel	1818	?, Poland [?, Prussia]			Rebecca Cohen	Gravesend, Kent	glazier
27397	Harris	Samuel	1818	Whitechapel, London	Isaac Harris	Hannah Marks		Whitechapel, London	general dealer
8545	Harris	Samuel	1819	Middlesex, London	Henry Harris	Keila Cohen	Jane Benjamin	Spitalfields, London	shoe maker + jeweller
5318	Harris	Samuel	1825	Truro, Cornwall	Henry Harris	Esther Jacob	Sophia Levi	Truro, Cornwall	
3337	Harris	Samuel	1827	Spitalfields, London	Joseph Alexander Harris	Elizabeth Levy	Hannah Cohen	Spitalfields, London	dealer
26623	Harris	Samuel	1831	?, Germany				Aldgate, London	tailor
10366	Harris	Samuel	1834	Aldgate, London	Henry Harris	Eve Woolf		Spitalfields, London	general dealer
27639	Harris	Samuel	1835	Middlesex, London	Issac Harris	Isabella (?)		Aldgate, London	general dealer of fruit
4513	Harris	Samuel	1839	Cheltenham, Gloucestershire	Henry Harris	Phoebe (?)		Birmingham	scholar
4130	Harris	Samuel	1842	Lambeth, London	Moses Harris	Frances Marks	Mary Anne (Polly) George	Waterloo, London	scholar
19933	Harris	Samuel	1842	Whitechapel, London	Samuel Harris	Elizabeth (?)		Whitechapel, London	
5321	Harris	Samuel	1845	Penzance, Cornwall	Morris Hart Harris	Rebecca Jacob		Bristol	
17264	Harris	Samuel	1846	?, London	Joseph Harris	Esther (?)		Aldgate, London	scholar
24011	Harris	Samuel	1850	Marylebone, London	Abraham Harris	Alice (?)		Marylebone, London	
4509	Harris	Samuel H	1841	?, France	Henry Harris	Elizabeth Samuels	Catherine (?)	Birmingham	
9194	Harris	Sarah	1795	Birmingham	(?) Harris			Whitechapel, London	label cutter
6788	Harris	Sarah	1801	Spitalfields, London	Israel Lyon (Lyons)	Lear (?)	Mordecai Harris	Spitalfields, London	laundress
2448	Harris	Sarah	1803	?, Poland			Nathan Harris	Hull, Yorkshire	dressmaker
25198	Harris	Sarah	1805	Warwick, Warwickshire	(?)		Lewis Harris	Clerkenwell, London	
14452	Harris	Sarah	1806	Ipswich, Suffolk	(?)		Benjamin Harris	Manchester	
5324	Harris	Sarah	1813	Lincoln, Lincolnshire	Jonas Lazarus	Rosceia Nathan	Levi Harris	Wolverhampton, Staffordshire	
11165	Harris	Sarah	1815	Aldgate, London	Abraham Harris	Catharine (?)		Aldgate, London	cap maker
24715	Harris	Sarah	1822	Walworth, London	Abraham Harris	Rose (Rosa) Jessel	Israel Morris Levi (Levy)	Walworth, London	
4496	Harris	Sarah	1823	Birmingham			Benjamin Harris	Birmingham	
792	Harris	Sarah	1824	Middlesex, London	Nathan Harris	Rebecca (?)	George Rhind	Lambeth, London	dressmaker
30094	Harris	Sarah	1826	Middlesex, London	(?) Solomon		Lewis (Judah Lion) Harris	Bath	
10715	Harris	Sarah	1827	?, Holland	(?)		John Harris	Spitalfields, London	tailoress
17218	Harris	Sarah	1828	?, London	Samuel Harris	Jane (?)	Barnett Rains	Spitalfields, London	tailoress
28980	Harris	Sarah	1830	Aldgate, London	Israel Joseph		Abraham Harris	Whitechapel, London	womans apparel
10986	Harris	Sarah	1833	Aldgate, London	Woolf Harris	Phoebe Solomons		Aldgate, London	fancy cap maker
18667	Harris	Sarah	1835	?, London	Isaac Harris	Dinah (?)	Jacob Simmonds	Whitechapel, London	
24644	Harris	Sarah	1836	City, London	Moses Harris	Fanny Marks	Joseph Van Diepenheim	Waterloo, London	nurse
30056	Harris	Sarah	1838	Marylebone, London	Abraham Harris	Alice (?)	Solomon Benjamin	Marylebone, London	
2198	Harris	Sarah	1843	Oxford, Oxfordshire	Wolf Harris	Esther Barnett	Emanuel Harris	Oxford, Oxfordshire	scholar
4497	Harris	Sarah	1844	Birmingham	Benjamin Harris	Sarah (?)		Birmingham	
4522	Harris	Sarah	1846	Birmingham	Isaac Harris	Catherine (Harris		Birmingham	scholar

ID	surname	given names	born	birthplace	father	mother	spouse 1	1851 residence	1851 occupation
21976	Harris	Sarah	1847	Swansea, Wales	Mordecai Harris	Leah (?)		Swansea, Wales	
30504	Harris	Sarah	1848	Merthyr Tydfil, Wales	Ephraim Harris	Ann (Hannah) Deborah Bloom	Moses Noach Lotinga	North Shields, Tyne & Wear	scholar
23529	Harris	Sarah	1850	Liverpool	Julius Harris	Amelia Rosenberg		Liverpool	
30514	Harris	Sarah	1851	Spitalfields, London	Benjamin Harris	Hannah Abrahams		Spitalfields, London	
21798	Harris	Sarah (Hannah)	1807	Clerkenwell, London	Abraham Simpson		Samuel Harris	Wapping, London	
6458	Harris	Sarah Hannah	1827	Holborn, London	Bartholomew Harris		Ezra Harris	Holborn, London	
13730	Harris	Sarah Hannah	1833	?, London	Ralph Harris	Rachel Shannon		Bloomsbury, London	
5317	Harris	Sarah Kate	1849	Penzance, Cornwall	Morris Hart Harris	Rebecca Jacob		Bristol	
18516	Harris	Saul Solomon	1847	Chatham, Kent	Barnett Harris	Rosetta (?)		Chatham, Kent	
8667	Harris	Selina (Sarah)	1840	Holborn, London	Barnett (Baruch) Harris	Rose Myers	Isaac Daniel Soares	Holborn, London	
13202	Harris	Simcha	1829	Middlesex, London			Julia Samuels	Whitechapel, London	lapidary master
10717	Harris	Sime	1826	?, Poland			Rozetta (?)	Spitalfields, London	tailor
9232	Harris	Simeon	1846	Spitalfields, London	Lawrence (Lazarus) Harris	Hannah (?)		Spitalfields, London	
5536	Harris	Simeon (Simon) (Morris)	1833	Waterloo, London	Morris Harris	Amelia Benjamin	Kate Isaacs	Waterloo, London	assistant, rag merchant's business
11867	Harris	Simon	1840	Middlesex, London	(?) Harris	(?)		Whitechapel, London	inmate of orphan school
18758	Harris	Simon	1843	Aldgate, London	Woolf Harris	Phoebe Solomons	Mary (Polly) Harris	Aldgate, London	scholar
10375	Harris	Simon	1851	Spitalfields, London	Henry Harris	Julia Jacobs		Spitalfields, London	
14698	Harris	Solomon	1784	Aldgate, London	(?Abraham) Harris	(?Leah Davis)	Susan Solomons	Spitalfields, London	general dealer
12447	Harris	Solomon	1809	Whitechapel, London			Sarah (?)	Spitalfields, London	furniture broker
10291	Harris	Solomon	1831	?, Poland [?, Prussia]				Spitalfields, London	tailor
11149	Harris	Solomon	1833	Whitechapel, London	Solomon Harris	Frances Myers		Aldgate, London	cigar maker
10371	Harris	Solomon	1846	Spitalfields, London	Henry Harris	Julia Jacobs	Jessie Phillips	Spitalfields, London	scholar
13204	Harris	Solomon	1850	Middlesex, London	Simcha Harris	Julia Samuels		Whitechapel, London	
5322	Harris	Sophia	1831	?Truro, Cornwall	Henry Harris	Esther Jacob		Truro, Cornwall	
29117	Harris	Sophia	1843	Aldgate, London	Lewis Harris	Hannah Nathan		Whitechapel, London	
14699	Harris	Susan	1791	Aldgate, London	(?) Solomon	Leah (?)	Solomon Harris	Spitalfields, London	
21805	Harris	Virginia	1844	Whitechapel, London	Samuel Harris	Hannah (Sarah) Simpson	Samuel Romain	Wapping, London	
24361	Harris	Welcome	1834	St Giles, London	Mark Harris	(?)		Covent Garden, London	milliner
2199	Harris	Wolf (Woolf)	1803	Lambeth, London	Moses Harris		Esther Barnett	Oxford, Oxfordshire	clothier
29369	Harris	Woolf	1809	Whitechapel, London	Tsvi Hirsch		Hannah Solomon	Wapping, London	clothier
19673	Harris	Woolf	1828	Aldgate, London	Solomon Harris	Susan Solomons	Phoebe Romaine	Spitalfields, London	general dealer
22784	Harris	Woolf	1838	Spitalfields, London	Abraham Harris	Fanny (?)		Whitechapel, London	
9563	Harris	Woolfe	1838	Spitalfields, London				Spitalfields, London	fruit dealer
5050	Harris	Zachariah	1850	Portsmouth, Hampshire	Newman (Shearesa) Harris	Fanny (Sarah) Cracouer		Portsmouth, Hampshire	
3345	Harris	Zelig	1840	Aldgate, London	Joseph Alexander Harris	Elizabeth Levy		Spitalfields, London	
11935	Harris	Zipporah	1800	Brighton, Sussex	(?)		Abraham Ellis Harris	Whitechapel, London	
6455	Harris	Zipporah	1850	Whitechapel, London	Hyman Ellis Harris	Rachel (?)		Whitechapel, London	
16438	Harris (Hamis de Fonseca)	Hagar	1805	Strand, London	(?)	Betsy Yom Tob	Jacob de Abraham Harris (Hamis Fonseca)	Aldgate, London	
7335	Harris (Hamis de Fonseca)	Jacob	1803	Aldgate, London	Abraham Hamis Fonseca	Eve de Samuel	Hagar de Betsy Yom Tob	Aldgate, London	ginger beer maker
21415	Harrison	Wolf	1822	Cracow, Poland				Dewsbury, Yorkshire	traveller
11451	Harriss	Dinah	1779	Rotterdam, Holland	(?)		(?) Harriss	Aldgate, London	general dealer

ID	surname	given names	born	birthplace	father	mother	spouse 1	1851 residence	1851 occupation
12625	Harriss	Esther	1805	Bialystok, Poland	(?)		(?) Harriss	Birmingham	
11452	Harriss	Jacob	1807	Spitalfields, London	(?) Harriss	Dinah (?)		Aldgate, London	fishmonger
11711	Harriss	Morriss	1832	?, Germany				Aldgate, London	tailor
12626	Harriss	Rachel	1825	Bialystok, Poland	(?) Harriss	Esther (?)		Birmingham	
12434	Hart	Aaron	1788	Middlesex, London			(?) Levy	Spitalfields, London	glass cutter
22328	Hart	Aaron	1811	Whitechapel, London	Henry Hart	Phoebe Myers	Rebecca (Anne) Crawcour	Stepney, London	shoe manufacturer empl 13
10664	Hart	Aaron	1822	Aldgate, London	Tsebi Hart		Sarah (?)	Spitalfields, London	pedlar
27760	Hart	Aaron	1841	?, Holland	(?) Hart	Julia (?)		Spitalfields, London	
18132	Hart	Abigail	1840	Middlesex, London	Naphtali Hart	Elizabeth Solomon		Mile End, London	
8145	Hart	Abigail	1847	Spitalfields, London	Joseph Hart	Rachel Martin (Nunes Martines)		Aldgate, London	
22836	Hart	Abraham	1799	Middlesex, London			Julia (?)	Whitechapel, London	general dealer
26889	Hart	Abraham	1808	?, London			Esther (?)	Aldgate, London	orange merchant + general dealer
17540	Hart	Abraham	1812	Aldgate, London	Isaac Hart	Kitty (?)	Mary (?)	Spitalfields, London	quill dresser
9589	Hart	Abraham	1827	Whitechapel, London	Henry Hart	Elizabeth (?)		Spitalfields, London	cigar maker
3144	Hart	Abraham	1831	Aldgate, London				Newcastle Upon Tyne	shoemaker
8798	Hart	Abraham	1833	Aldgate, London	Benjamin Hart	Caroline (?)	Elizabeth (?)	Aldgate, London	fruiterer's assistant
27583	Hart	Abraham	1833	Middlesex, London				Spitalfields, London	
8146	Hart	Abraham	1850	Aldgate, London	Joseph Hart	Rachel Martin (Nunes Martines)	Jane Levy	Aldgate, London	
10921	Hart	Abraham	1850	Spitalfields, London	Henry Hart	Phoebe Solomon		Spitalfields, London	
28558	Hart	Abraham	1850	Spitalfields, London	Henry Hart	Matilda Abrahams		Aldgate, London	
9498	Hart	Abraham Henry Hart	1850	Spitalfields, London	Henry (Hart) Hart	Caroline Matilda Cohen	Rachel Isaacs	Aldgate, London	
16463	Hart	Abraham Septimus	1801	Bristol	Naphtali Hart		Julia (?)	Knightsbridge, London	dentist
25775	Hart	Abraham?	1833	Aldgate, London	(?) Hart	Hannah (?)		Aldgate, London	fishmonger
4529	Hart	Abram	1842	Birmingham	Lewis Hart	Sarah (?)		Birmingham	
16467	Hart	Adolphus Daniel	1833	Westminster, London	Abraham Septimus Hart	Julia (?)		Knightsbridge, London	dentist
23462	Hart	Albert	1841	Liverpool	Naphtali Hart	Mary Sewill		Liverpool	scholar
25776	Hart	Alexander	1834	Aldgate, London	(?) Hart	Hannah (?)		Aldgate, London	fishmonger
10916	Hart	Alexander	1836	Spitalfields, London	Henry Hart	Phoebe Solomon	Mary Cantor	Spitalfields, London	at home
28028	Hart	Alexander	1849	Whitechapel, London	John Hart	Esther (?)		Spitalfields, London	
14660	Hart	Alfred	1850	Hoxton, London	Joseph Hart	Maria (?)		Hoxton, London	
22990	Hart	Alfred	1850	Whitechapel, London	Reuben Hart	Amelia Cohen	Josephine Flora Wilson	Whitechapel, London	
14100	Hart	Alice	1821	Aldgate, London	Abraham Hart			Marylebone, London	annuitant
4530	Hart	Alice	1844	Birmingham	Lewis Hart	Sarah (?)		Birmingham	
8144	Hart	Alice	1846	Spitalfields, London	Joseph Hart	Rachel Martin (Nunes Martines)	Abraham Israel	Aldgate, London	
6100	Hart	Alice	1848	Portsmouth, Hampshire	Henry Hart	Fanny Barnett	Lazarus Mordecai	Spitalfields, London	
6807	Hart	Amelia	1811	Aldgate, London	Jonah Lipman		Emanuel Hart	Spitalfields, London	
28117	Hart	Amelia	1822	Middlesex, London	(?)		(?) Hart	Spitalfields, London	furrier
22988	Hart	Amelia	1827	Whitechapel, London	Solomon Cohen	Jane (?)	Reuben Hart	Whitechapel, London	
8605	Hart	Amelia	1832	City, London	Henry Hart	Rosa (?)		Wapping, London	waistcoat maker

ID	surname	given names	born	birthplace	father	mother	spouse 1	1851 residence	1851 occupation
25774	Hart	Amelia	1832	Aldgate, London	(?) Hart	Hannah (?)		Aldgate, London	
9632	Hart	Amelia	1837	Spitalfields, London	Henry Hart	Elizabeth (?)	Lewis Emanuel	Mile End, London	
9890	Hart	Amelia	1838	Whitechapel, London	Henry Hart	Ann Mordecai	Morris Harris	Whitechapel, London	hatter trimmer
5459	Hart	Amelia	1839	?, Staffordshire	Emanuel Hart	Sheba Lazarus	Joseph Wolfe	Wolverhampton, Staffordshire	
4528	Hart	Amelia	1840	Birmingham	Lewis Hart	Sarah (?)		Birmingham	
22330	Hart	Amelia	1841	Whitechapel, London	Aaron Hart	Rebecca (Anne) Crawcour	Henry Chapman Hart	Stepney, London	scholar
9398	Hart	Amelia	1844	Aldgate, London	Henry Hart	Jane (?)		Aldgate, London	
26714	Hart	Amelia	1844	?Marylebone, London	John Hart	Elizabeth Jacobs	Maurice Davies	Piccadilly, London	
15049	Hart	Amelia	1845	Bethnal Green, London	Joseph Hart	Ann (?)		Bethnal Green, London	
15932	Hart	Amelia	1846	Portsmouth, Hampshire	Henry Hart	Fanny Barnett		Spitalfields, London	
20939	Hart	Ann	1826	Spitalfields, London	(?)		Judah Hart	Aldgate, London	fishmonger's wife
27403	Hart	Ann	1829	Whitechapel, London	Joel Hart	Mary Hyams		Whitechapel, London	
9400	Hart	Ann	1848	City, London	Henry Hart	Jane (?)	Alfred Seroka	Aldgate, London	
11570	Hart	Ann	1848	Spitalfields, London	Joseph Hart	Rosetta (?)		Aldgate, London	
29421	Hart	Ann	1850	Spitalfields, London	Henry Hart	Elizabeth (Batseba) Mendoza		Spitalfields, London	
9887	Hart	Ann	1811	Aldgate, London	(?) Mordecai		Henry Hart	Whitechapel, London	
15041	Hart	Ann	1811	Finsbury, London	(?)		Joseph Hart	Bethnal Green, London	
22331	Hart	Anne	1842	Whitechapel, London	Aaron Hart	Rebecca (Anne) Crawcour		Stepney, London	scholar
16867	Hart	Arthur Robert	1845	Cambridge	Benjamin Hart	Margaret Hopkins		Cambridge	
19966	Hart	Asher	1826	Canterbury, Kent	Joseph Hart	Miriam (Marian, Mary) Abrahams	Esther Solomons	Aldgate, London	tailor
9896	Hart	Asher	1848	Whitechapel, London	Henry Hart	Ann Mordecai		Whitechapel, London	school
23463	Hart	Augustus	1843	Liverpool	Naphtali Hart	Mary Sewill		Liverpool	scholar
22007	Hart	Barnet	1786	Whitechapel, London			Elizabeth (?)	Whitechapel, London	annuitant
27436	Hart	Barnett	1795	Whitechapel, London	Isaac Ari		Catherine (?)	Whitechapel, London	clothier
3351	Hart	Barnett (Barney, Bennett)	1839	Whitechapel, London	Joseph Hart	Deborah Franks	Annie Levy	Whitechapel, London	
8795	Hart	Benjamin	1802	Aldgate, London			Caroline (?)	Aldgate, London	fruiterer
16864	Hart	Benjamin	1811	Cambridge			Margaret Hopkins	Cambridge	solicitor general clerk
20267	Hart	Benjamin	1826	?, London	Moses Hart	Leah Benjamin		Spitalfields, London	general dealer
9895	Hart	Benjamin	1830	Whitechapel, London	Henry Hart	Ann Mordecai		Whitechapel, London	school
26893	Hart	Benjamin	1834	?, London	Abraham Hart	Esther (?)		Aldgate, London	carver + gilder
26715	Hart	Benjamin	1835	Strand, London	John Hart	Elizabeth Jacobs		Piccadilly, London	
10619	Hart	Benjamin	1837	Middlesex, London	Mordecai Hart	Kitty Moses		Spitalfields, London	
105	Hart	Benjamin	1843	Woolwich, London	Henry Hart			Woolwich, London	scholar
12826	Hart	Benjamin	1845	Whitechapel, London	Ezekiel Hart	Sylvia Green		Covent Garden, London	
26545	Hart	Benjamin	1845	Whitechapel, London	Lipman Hart	Emma (Abigail) Franks	Ann Harris	Spitalfields, London	
25223	Hart	Benjamin	1851	Aldgate, London	Solomon (Zalig) Hart	Mary Joel	Matilda Solomon	Aldgate, London	
16866	Hart	Benjamin Barnett	1843	Cambridge	Benjamin Hart	Margaret Hopkins		Cambridge	
18136	Hart	Benjamin John	1850	Middlesex, London	Naphtali Hart	Elizabeth Solomon		Mile End, London	
2138	Hart	Bethel	1828	Hull, Yorkshire	(?) Hart	Hannah Alexander		Hull, Yorkshire	assistant to silversmith + general dealer
11568	Hart	Betsey	1837	Spitalfields, London	Joseph Hart	Rosetta (?)		Aldgate, London	tailoress

ID	surname	given names	born	birthplace	father	mother	spouse 1	1851 residence	1851 occupation
12442	Hart	Betsey (Elizabeth)	1825	Spitalfields, London	Aaron Hart	(?) Levy		Spitalfields, London	tailoress
21207	Hart	Betsy	1846	Spitalfields, London	(?) Hart			Spitalfields, London	scholar
3350	Hart	Caroline	1807	Portsmouth, Hampshire	(?) Cohen		Joseph Hart	Whitechapel, London	
8796	Hart	Caroline	1807	Portsmouth, Hampshire			Benjamin Hart	Aldgate, London	
7231	Hart	Caroline	1820	Aldgate, London	Stephen (Solomon) Hart	Esther Solomon	Manuel (Menahem) Levi Bensusan	Whitechapel, London	
22342	Hart	Caroline	1830	Whitechapel, London	Henry Hart	Phoebe Myers		Aldgate, London	
9883	Hart	Caroline	1844	Stepney, London	Henry Hart	Elizabeth (?)		Mile End, London	scholar
30515	Hart	Caroline	1851	Spitalfields, London	Joseph Hart	Eve (Elizabeth, Sarah) Berlyn		Aldgate, London	
9496	Hart	Caroline Matilda	1826	Soho, London	Humphrey Cohen		Henry (Hart) Hart	Aldgate, London	
28027	Hart	Catharine	1836	Whitechapel, London	John Hart	Esther (?)		Spitalfields, London	
27437	Hart	Catherine	1795	Aldgate, London	(?)		Barnett Hart	Whitechapel, London	
14829	Hart	Catherine	1810	Deptford, London	Moshe Jones		Michael Hart	Bethnal Green, London	clothes salesman
12435	Hart	Catherine	1816	Middlesex, London	Aaron Hart	(?) Levy		Spitalfields, London	servant
26254	Hart	Catherine	1827	?, London	(?) Hart	Mary (?)		Aldgate, London	dressmaker
11563	Hart	Catherine	1831	?abroad	(?) Hart			Aldgate, London	
29932	Hart	Catherine	1835	Whitechapel, London	(?) Hart	Hannah (?)		Whitechapel, London	waistcoat maker
17274	Hart	Catherine	1842	?, Poland	(?) Hart			Aldgate, London	scholar
27598	Hart	Catherine	1850	City, London	Lewis (Louis) Hart	Maria (Miryam) Rodriguez		Spitalfields, London	
5475	Hart	Catherine (Kate)	1840	Darlaston, Staffordshire	Emanuel Hart	Sheba Lazarus	Abraham Finger	Wolverhampton, Staffordshire	
26713	Hart	Catherine (Kate) Rebecca	1831	?, London	John Hart	Elizabeth Jacobs	Abraham Crawcour	Piccadilly, London	
16465	Hart	Charlotte	1829	Knightsbridge, London	Abraham Septimus Hart	Julia (?)		Knightsbridge, London	
15047	Hart	Charlotte	1841	Bethnal Green, London	Joseph Hart	Ann (?)		Bethnal Green, London	
12804	Hart	Clara	1839	Whitechapel, London	Isaac Hart	Sarah Phillips		Spitalfields, London	scholar
28118	Hart	Clara	1843	Whitechapel, London	(?) Hart	Amelia (?)	Samuel Bloomfield	Spitalfields, London	
5507	Hart	Cordelia	1834	Margate, Kent	Michael Hart	Pamela Magnus	Joseph Levy	Ramsgate, Kent	
3143	Hart	Daniel	1828	Aldgate, London				Newcastle Upon Tyne	hawker
20941	Hart	Daniel	1848	Aldgate, London	Judah Hart	Ann (?)		Aldgate, London	scholar
17963	Hart	Daniel	1850	Whitechapel, London	Solomon (Zalig) Hart	Mary Joel	Elizabeth Lazarus	Aldgate, London	
27908	Hart	David	1800	Spitalfields, London			(?)	Spitalfields, London	shoemaker
29685	Hart	David	1827	Aldgate, London			Sarah Lipman	Shoreditch, London	cigar maker
20363	Hart	David	1837	Stepney, London	(?Moses) Hart			Aldgate, London	
22719	Hart	David	1843	Whitechapel, London	Moses (Moss) Hart	Sarah Moses		Whitechapel, London	scholar
24139	Hart	Edward	1808	City, London	Samuel Hart	Fanny (Frances) Solomon		Bloomsbury, London	professor of singing
8495	Hart	Eleazer	1787	Portsmouth, Hampshire	Yehuda Cohen		Sarah Levy	Tottenham, London	house properties
27757	Hart	Eleazer	1832	?, Holland	(?) Hart	Julia (?)		Spitalfields, London	cigar maker
20940	Hart	Eleazer	1843	Whitechapel, London	Judah Hart	Ann (?)		Aldgate, London	scholar
27909	Hart	Elijah	1832	Spitalfields, London	David Hart	(?)		Spitalfields, London	cigar maker
30326	Hart	Eliza	1830	?, London	John Naphtali Hart			Edinburgh, Scotland	
9588	Hart	Elizabeth	1791	Aldgate, London	(?)		Henry Hart	Spitalfields, London	
22008	Hart	Elizabeth	1792	Whitechapel, London	(?)		Barnet Hart	Whitechapel, London	
22023	Hart	Elizabeth	1794	Sandwich, Kent	(?) Lamert		Michael Hart	Ramsgate, Kent	

ID	surname	given names	born	birthplace	father	mother	spouse 1	1851 residence	1851 occupation
22803	Hart	Elizabeth	1794	Spitalfields, London	(?)		David Davis	Whitechapel, London	lamp cotton manufacturer
3330	Hart	Elizabeth	1798	Whitechapel, London	Barnett Hart			Spitalfields, London	
26711	Hart	Elizabeth	1800	Aldgate, London	Henry Jacobs	Kitty Moses	John Hart	Piccadilly, London	
18131	Hart	Elizabeth	1810	Middlesex, London	B--- Solomon		Naphtali Hart	Mile End, London	
9879	Hart	Elizabeth	1813	Holborn, London	(?)		Henry Hart	Mile End, London	
15250	Hart	Elizabeth	1817	?, London	(?)		John W Hart	Shoreditch, London	
25299	Hart	Elizabeth	1818	Aldgate, London	Henry Hart	Frances Isaacs		Aldgate, London	tailoress
11179	Hart	Elizabeth	1821	Aldgate, London	Tsevi Hart		Israel Hart	Aldgate, London	umbrella maker
22623	Hart	Elizabeth	1823	Whitechapel, London	Lewis Levy	Mary (?)	(?) Hart	Stepney, London	
22094	Hart	Elizabeth	1825	Aldgate, London	(?) Hart	Rebecca (?)		Aldgate, London	furrier
12314	Hart	Elizabeth	1833	?, Berkshire	Eleazer Hart	Sarah Levy		Tottenham, London	
24359	Hart	Elizabeth	1838	Aldgate, London	(?) Hart			Covent Garden, London	scholar
19503	Hart	Elizabeth	1844	Westminster, London	Louis (Lewis) Hart	Julia (?)		Strand, London	
27913	Hart	Elizabeth	1845	Spitalfields, London	David Hart	(?)		Spitalfields, London	
13032	Hart	Elizabeth	1848	Spitalfields, London	Robert Hart	Leah (?)		Spitalfields, London	
30064	Hart	Elizabeth	1851	Marylebone, London	Lewis Hart	Rosetta Jonas	Benjamin Phillips	Marylebone, London	
29419	Hart	Elizabeth (Batseba)	1825	Whitechapel, London	Moses de David Mendoza	Hannah Jonas	Henry Hart	Spitalfields, London	domestic
27439	Hart	Elizabeth (Betsey)	1838	Spitalfields, London	Barnett Hart	Catherine (?)	Abraham Lee	Whitechapel, London	scholar
5946	Hart	Elizabeth (Betsy)	1847	Whitechapel, London	Solomon (Zalig) Hart	Mary Joel	Michael Joseph	Aldgate, London	
871	Hart	Elizabeth (Eliza, Lizzie)	1841	Canterbury, Kent	Mordecai (Maurice) Hart	Frances Moses	Aaron Blanckensee	Canterbury, Kent	
7401	Hart	Ella	1838	Knightsbridge, London	Abraham Septimus Hart	Julia (?)	Abraham Solomon	Knightsbridge, London	scholar
8802	Hart	Ellis	1845	Aldgate, London	Benjamin Hart	Caroline (?)	Ellen (Eleanor) Phillips	Aldgate, London	scholar
9893	Hart	Elvina	1843	Whitechapel, London	Henry Hart	Ann Mordecai	Mitchell Tartakover	Whitechapel, London	school
169	Hart	Emanuel	1800	?, Germany			Sheba Lazarus	Wolverhampton, Staffordshire	clothier
6806	Hart	Emanuel	1810	Aldgate, London	Chaim Hart		Amelia Lipman	Spitalfields, London	general dealer
6778	Hart	Emanuel	1826	Tottenham, London			Esther Alexander	Edmonton, London	fruiterer + confectioner
8612	Hart	Emanuel	1845	City, London	Henry Hart	Rosa (?)		Wapping, London	scholar
18227	Hart	Emanuel	1846	Wolverhampton, Staffordshire	Emanuel Hart	Sheba Lazarus		Wolverhampton, Staffordshire	
13640	Hart	Emma	1847	Manchester	Philip Hart	Sarah Southwick nee (?)		Manchester	scholar
14659	Hart	Emma	1847	Hoxton, London	Joseph Hart	Maria (?)		Hoxton, London	
25065	Hart	Emma (Abigail)	1819	Whitechapel, London	Benjamin Franks		Lipman Hart	Spitalfields, London	
7122	Hart	Ernest Abraham	1835	Knightsbridge, London	Abraham Septimus Hart	Julia (?)	Rosetta Levy	Knightsbridge, London	scholar + medical student
15251	Hart	Ernest L	1838	?, London	John W Hart	Elizabeth (?)	Leah Hertz	Shoreditch, London	scholar
27599	Hart	Ester	1830	Middlesex, London	(?) Hart			Spitalfields, London	
7225	Hart	Esther	1782	Aldgate, London	(?) Solomon		Stephen (Solomon) Hart	Whitechapel, London	
16641	Hart	Esther	1793	Amsterdam, Holland	(?)		Moses Hart	Liverpool	
3981	Hart	Esther	1799	Finsbury, London	David Davis		Michael Henry Hart	Portsmouth, Hampshire	
28025	Hart	Esther	1806	Aldgate, London	(?)		John Hart	Spitalfields, London	
7226	Hart	Esther	1809	Whitechapel, London	Stephen (Solomon) Hart	Esther Solomon		Whitechapel, London	
26890	Hart	Esther	1810	?, London	(?)		Abraham Hart	Aldgate, London	

247

ID	surname	given names	born	birthplace	father	mother	spouse 1	1851 residence	1851 occupation
26253	Hart	Esther	1822	?, London	(?) Hart	Mary (?)		Aldgate, London	dressmaker
19972	Hart	Esther	1824	Canterbury, Kent	Joseph Hart	Miriam (Marian, Mary) Abrahams	(?Samuel Cohen) (?Morris Plymouth)	Aldgate, London	tailor
21615	Hart	Esther	1827	Whitechapel, London	Joseph Hart	Deborah Franks		Whitechapel, London	tailoress
5024	Hart	Esther	1832	Whitechapel, London	Isaac Alexander	Susan Levy	Emanuel Hart	Edmonton, London	
28026	Hart	Esther	1832	Spitalfields, London	John Hart	Esther (?)		Spitalfields, London	tailoress
24957	Hart	Esther	1836	Finsbury, London	Hayman Hart	Rebekah (?)		Haggerston, London	dressmaker
27440	Hart	Esther	1840	Finsbury, London	Barnett Hart	Catherine (?)		Whitechapel, London	scholar
10918	Hart	Esther	1841	Spitalfields, London	Henry Hart	Phoebe Solomon		Spitalfields, London	scholar
11180	Hart	Esther	1842	Aldgate, London	Israel Hart	Elizabeth (?)	Nathan Hart	Aldgate, London	
22721	Hart	Esther	1847	Whitechapel, London	Moses (Moss) Hart	Sarah Moses		Whitechapel, London	
10668	Hart	Esther	1848	Spitalfields, London	Aaron Hart	Sarah (?)		Spitalfields, London	
22334	Hart	Eve	1848	Stepney, London	Aaron Hart	Rebecca (Anne) Crawcour		Stepney, London	
6797	Hart	Eve (Elizabeth, Sarah)	1819	Amsterdam, Holland	Moses Abraham Berlyn	Mariane (?)	Joseph Hart	Spitalfields, London	
12823	Hart	Ezekiel	1803	Whitechapel, London	Chaim HaLevi		Sylvia Green	Covent Garden, London	fish salesman
21949	Hart	Ezekiel	1836	Margate, Kent	Michael Hart	Pamela Magnus	Amelia (?)	Ramsgate, Kent	
10669	Hart	Ezekiel	1850	Spitalfields, London	Aaron Hart	Sarah (?)		Spitalfields, London	
15937	Hart	Fanny	1814	Strand, London	Abraham Barnett		Henry Hart	Spitalfields, London	tailoress
24956	Hart	Fanny	1833	Finsbury, London	Hayman Hart	Rebekah (?)		Haggerston, London	dressmaker
9105	Hart	Fanny	1842	?, London	Louis (Lewis) Hart	Julia Levy	Henry John Simmons	South Kensington, London	
26895	Hart	Fanny	1842	?, London	Abraham Hart	Esther (?)		Aldgate, London	scholar
24140	Hart	Fanny	1845	Fitzrovia, London	(?) Hart			Bloomsbury, London	
24138	Hart	Fanny (Frances)	1774	City, London	Zelig Solomon		Samuel Hart	Bloomsbury, London	dependent of son
7227	Hart	Fanny (Frances)	1810	Whitechapel, London	Stephen (Solomon) Hart	Esther Solomon		Whitechapel, London	
25302	Hart	Frances	1794	Aldgate, London	Baruch Moshe Bek Betser Isaacs		Frances Isaacs	Aldgate, London	
29803	Hart	Frances	1807	Lambeth, London	Naftali Hertz Phillips		Samuel Michael Hart	Whitechapel, London	umbrella maker
849	Hart	Frances	1812	Gloucester, Gloucestershire	Moses Moses	Jane (?)	Mordecai (Maurice) Hart	Canterbury, Kent	
22127	Hart	Frances	1838	?, London	(?) Hart			Whitechapel, London	servant
29935	Hart	Frances	1841	Whitechapel, London	(?) Hart	Hannah (?)		Whitechapel, London	scholar
9590	Hart	George	1830	Whitechapel, London	Henry Hart	Elizabeth (?)		Spitalfields, London	cigar maker
30121	Hart	George	1837	Whitechapel, London	Henry Hart	Rose Cohen		Wapping, London	scholar
9396	Hart	George	1840	Whitechapel, London	Henry Hart	Jane (?)		Aldgate, London	
23464	Hart	George	1846	Liverpool	Naphtali Hart	Mary Sewill		Liverpool	
9708	Hart	George	1847	Spitalfields, London	Michael Hart	Sarah Cohen		Whitechapel, London	
22335	Hart	Gertrude	1850	Stepney, London	Aaron Hart	Rebecca (Anne) Crawcour	Louis Courlander	Stepney, London	
16643	Hart	Grace	1824	Plymouth, Devon	Moses Hart	Esther (?)		Liverpool	
16138	Hart	Hanah	1783	Whitechapel, London	(?)		(?) Jacobs/Hart	Wapping, London	
2450	Hart	Hannah	1794	Hull, Yorkshire	(?) Alexander		(?) Hart	Hull, Yorkshire	
9357	Hart	Hannah	1800	Aldgate, London	(?) Israel		Henry Hart	Holborn, London	
3984	Hart	Hannah	1803	?, London			Solomon Hart	Portsmouth, Hampshire	
29930	Hart	Hannah	1806	Portsmouth, Hampshire	(?)		(?) Hart	Whitechapel, London	
25773	Hart	Hannah	1809	Whitechapel, London	(?)		(?) Hart	Aldgate, London	fishmonger
104	Hart	Hannah	1821	?, Germany			Nathan Hart	Woolwich, London	

ID	surname	given names	born	birthplace	father	mother	spouse 1	1851 residence	1851 occupation
22095	Hart	Hannah	1826	Whitechapel, London	(?) Hart	Rebecca (?)		Aldgate, London	
11450	Hart	Hannah	1827	Middlesex, London				Aldgate, London	cap maker
20574	Hart	Hannah	1828	Whitechapel, London	(?) Hart			Spitalfields, London	parasol maker
27438	Hart	Hannah	1837	Spitalfields, London	Barnett Hart	Catherine (?)		Whitechapel, London	scholar
30123	Hart	Hannah	1842	Finsbury, London	Henry Hart	Rose Cohen		Wapping, London	scholar
29936	Hart	Hannah	1843	Mile End, London	(?) Hart	Hannah (?)		Whitechapel, London	scholar
15933	Hart	Hannah	1846	Portsmouth, Hampshire	Henry Hart	Fanny Barnett		Spitalfields, London	
10618	Hart	Hanne	1843	Middlesex, London	Mordecai Hart	Kitty Moses		Spitalfields, London	
26896	Hart	Harriet	1844	?, London	Abraham Hart	Esther (?)		Aldgate, London	scholar
28119	Hart	Harriet Betsey	1851	Whitechapel, London	(?) Hart	Amelia (?)		Spitalfields, London	
18274	Hart	Harris	1829	?, Poland [?, Russia Poland]				Ilminster, Somerset	travelling jeweller
26255	Hart	Hart	1829	?, London	(?) Hart	Mary (?)		Aldgate, London	cigar maker
5478	Hart	Hart E	1846	Wolverhampton, Staffordshire	Emanuel Hart	Sheba Lazarus		Wolverhampton, Staffordshire	
12533	Hart	Harty	1814	Whitechapel, London	Henry Hart		Rebecca Abrahams [Masters]	Great Yarmouth, Norfolk	dealer in glass
8609	Hart	Harty	1839	City, London	Henry Hart	Rosa (?)		Wapping, London	cigar maker
24954	Hart	Hayman	1783	Middlesex, London			Rebekah (?)	Haggerston, London	stationer
15046	Hart	Hellen	1839	Bethnal Green, London	Joseph Hart	Ann (?)		Bethnal Green, London	
101	Hart	Henry	1790	?, Poland			(?)	Woolwich, London	silversmith + general dealer
25301	Hart	Henry	1791	Great Yarmouth, Norfolk	Simon from Yarmouth		Frances Isaacs	Aldgate, London	tailor
8603	Hart	Henry	1800	Portsmouth, Hampshire			Rosa (?)	Wapping, London	general dealer
9356	Hart	Henry	1801	Westminster, London			(?)	Holborn, London	tailor
9587	Hart	Henry	1801	Whitechapel, London			Elizabeth (?)	Spitalfields, London	clothes man
9109	Hart	Henry	1802	?, London	Benjamin Hart		Rose Lyons	South Kensington, London	proprietor of houses
9886	Hart	Henry	1808	Aldgate, London			Ann Mordecai	Whitechapel, London	master hatter
10914	Hart	Henry	1808	Whitechapel, London	Shlomeh Hart		Phoebe Solomon	Spitalfields, London	master tailor
31195	Hart	Henry	1811	?, Germany			Rosa (?)	Bath	dealer in cigars
9878	Hart	Henry	1813	Spitalfields, London			Elizabeth (?)	Mile End, London	greengrocer + fruiterer
15936	Hart	Henry	1815	Shoreditch, London	Moshe Hart		Fanny Barnett	Spitalfields, London	tailor
28555	Hart	Henry	1816	Whitechapel, London			Matilda Abrahams	Aldgate, London	coal dealer
30117	Hart	Henry	1817	Whitechapel, London	Joel Hart	Mary Hyams	Rose Cohen	Wapping, London	iron dealer
9394	Hart	Henry	1822	?, London			Jane (?)	Aldgate, London	metal miller
29418	Hart	Henry	1826	Whitechapel, London	Mordecai Hart		Elizabeth (Batseba) Mendoza	Spitalfields, London	general dealer
29931	Hart	Henry	1829	Whitechapel, London	(?) Hart	Hannah (?)		Whitechapel, London	journeyman cigar maker
21944	Hart	Henry	1830	Margate, Kent	Michael Hart	Pamela Magnus	Clara Myers	Dover, Kent	
29804	Hart	Henry	1830	Whitechapel, London	Samuel Michael Hart	Frances Phillips		Whitechapel, London	cigar maker
13088	Hart	Henry	1831	Spitalfields, London				Clerkenwell, London	prisoner + general labourer
22096	Hart	Henry	1832	Whitechapel, London	(?) Hart	Rebecca (?)		Aldgate, London	apprentice cigar maker
27910	Hart	Henry	1834	Spitalfields, London	David Hart	(?)		Spitalfields, London	cigar maker
9880	Hart	Henry	1836	Spitalfields, London	Henry Hart	Elizabeth (?)		Mile End, London	stationer

ID	surname	given names	born	birthplace	father	mother	spouse 1	1851 residence	1851 occupation
26716	Hart	Henry	1838	?, London	John Hart	Elizabeth Jacobs	Amelia Hart	Piccadilly, London	
15048	Hart	Henry	1843	Bethnal Green, London	Joseph Hart	Ann (?)		Bethnal Green, London	
27596	Hart	Henry	1844	City, London	Lewis (Louis) Hart	Maria (Miryam) Rodriguez		Spitalfields, London	scholar
9399	Hart	Henry	1845	Aldgate, London	Henry Hart	Jane (?)		Aldgate, London	scholar
10667	Hart	Henry	1846	Spitalfields, London	Aaron Hart	Sarah (?)		Spitalfields, London	scholar
8803	Hart	Henry	1847	Aldgate, London	Benjamin Hart	Caroline (?)		Aldgate, London	scholar
15256	Hart	Henry	1847	Middlesex, London	John W Hart	Elizabeth (?)		Shoreditch, London	
22333	Hart	Henry	1847	Stepney, London	Aaron Hart	Rebecca (Anne) Crawcour		Stepney, London	
13033	Hart	Henry	1848	Spitalfields, London	Robert Hart	Leah (?)		Spitalfields, London	
14661	Hart	Henry	1850	Hoxton, London	Joseph Hart	Maria (?)		Hoxton, London	
6779	Hart	Henry (Harry)	1851	Edmonton, London	Emanuel Hart	Esther Alexander		Edmonton, London	
9495	Hart	Henry (Hart)	1816	Whitechapel, London	Hyam Hart		Caroline Matilda Cohen	Aldgate, London	coal dealer
863	Hart	Henry A	1833	Canterbury, Kent	Mordecai (Maurice) Hart	Frances Moses	Rosa Nathan	Folkestone, Kent	
15257	Hart	Herman	1850	?Shoreditch, London	John W Hart	Elizabeth (?)		Shoreditch, London	
9889	Hart	Hyam	1832	Paddington, London	Henry Hart	Ann Mordecai		Whitechapel, London	hatter
9359	Hart	Hyam	1835	St Giles, London	Henry Hart	(?)		Holborn, London	cutter
6808	Hart	Hyam	1840	Spitalfields, London	Emanuel Hart	Amelia Lipman		Spitalfields, London	
6798	Hart	Hyam	1841	Spitalfields, London	Joseph Halevi Hart	Eve (Elizabeth, Sarah) Berlyn	Elizabeth Levy	Spitalfields, London	scholar
12827	Hart	Hyam	1847	Strand, London	Ezekiel Hart	Sylvia Green		Covent Garden, London	
9497	Hart	Hyam	1849	Spitalfields, London	Henry (Hart) Hart	Caroline Matilda Cohen		Aldgate, London	
28557	Hart	Hyam	1849	Spitalfields, London	Henry Hart	Matilda Abrahams		Aldgate, London	
20265	Hart	I---	1818	?, London	Moses Hart	Leah Benjamin	(?)	Spitalfields, London	general dealer
17538	Hart	Isaac	1787	Aldgate, London			Kitty (?)	Spitalfields, London	pencil maker
12801	Hart	Isaac	1801	Spitalfields, London	Yechiel Michael Hart		Sarah Phillips	Spitalfields, London	clothes dealer
2216	Hart	Isaac	1823	?, Poland				Oxford, Oxfordshire	jeweller
27402	Hart	Isaac	1826	Whitechapel, London	Joel Hart	Mary Hyams	Elizabeth (Eliza) Abrahams	Whitechapel, London	job draper
11566	Hart	Isaac	1833	Spitalfields, London	Joseph Hart	Rosetta (?)		Aldgate, London	butcher
27758	Hart	Isaac	1836	?, Holland	(?) Hart	Julia (?)		Spitalfields, London	apprentice slipper maker
8141	Hart	Isaac	1839	Spitalfields, London	Joseph Hart	Rachel Martin (Nunes Martines)	Rachel Cohen	Aldgate, London	
10917	Hart	Isaac	1839	Spitalfields, London	Henry Hart	Phoebe Solomon	Esther Ellis	Spitalfields, London	scholar
9397	Hart	Isaac	1842	Aldgate, London	Henry Hart	Jane (?)	Miriam Woolf	Aldgate, London	
30124	Hart	Isaac	1847	Whitechapel, London	Henry Hart	Rose Cohen		Wapping, London	
5670	Hart	Isaac Hermann	1828	Canterbury, Kent	Joseph Hart	Miriam Abrahams	Louisa Levy	Sunderland, Co Durham	
9894	Hart	Isabella	1845	Whitechapel, London	Henry Hart	Ann Mordecai	Joseph Simmons	Whitechapel, London	school
11178	Hart	Israel	1816	Aldgate, London	Meir HaCohen		Elizabeth Hart	Aldgate, London	fish porter
866	Hart	Israel	1835	Canterbury, Kent	Mordecai (Maurice) Hart	Frances Moses	Caroline Sewill	Folkestone, Kent	tailor
22097	Hart	Jacob	1832	Shoreditch, London				Aldgate, London	apprentice
20192	Hart	Jacob	1834	Whitechapel, London				Spitalfields, London	slipper maker
5052	Hart	Jane	1795	Portsmouth, Hampshire	Moses Hart	Rachael (?)		Portsmouth, Hampshire	needlework
9395	Hart	Jane	1822	Whitechapel, London	(?)		Henry Hart	Aldgate, London	
31115	Hart	Jane	1823	Tottenham, London	(?) Hart			Edmonton, London	
27405	Hart	Jane	1834	Aldgate, London	Joel Hart	Mary Hyams	Henry Fromberg	Whitechapel, London	
15044	Hart	Jane	1835	Spitalfields, London	Joseph Hart	Ann (?)		Bethnal Green, London	servant

ID	surname	given names	born	birthplace	father	mother	spouse 1	1851 residence	1851 occupation
21942	Hart	Jane	1838	Canterbury, Kent	Mordecai (Maurice) Hart	Frances Moses		Canterbury, Kent	
24958	Hart	Jane	1839	Finsbury, London	Hayman Hart	Rebekah (?)		Haggerston, London	dressmaker
18134	Hart	Jane	1842	Middlesex, London	Naphtali Hart	Elizabeth Solomon		Mile End, London	
22989	Hart	Jane	1848	Islington, London	Reuben Hart	Amelia Cohen	David Lowe	Whitechapel, London	
7229	Hart	Jeanette	1817	Whitechapel, London	Stephen (Solomon) Hart	Esther Solomon		Whitechapel, London	
30120	Hart	Joel	1835	Whitechapel, London	Henry Hart	Rose Cohen		Wapping, London	scholar
16377	Hart	Joel	1849	City, London	Moss (Moses) Hart	Sophia Abrahams		Aldgate, London	
26710	Hart	John	1798	Strand, London	Benjamin Hart		Elizabeth Jacobs	Piccadilly, London	tailor
28024	Hart	John	1805	Aldgate, London			Esther (?)	Spitalfields, London	pencil maker
22337	Hart	John	1816	Whitechapel, London	Henry Hart	Phoebe Myers		Aldgate, London	shoe manufacturer empl 130
21614	Hart	John	1824	Whitechapel, London	Joseph Hart	Deborah Franks		Whitechapel, London	cigar maker
20269	Hart	John	1830	?, London	Moses Hart	Leah Benjamin		Spitalfields, London	general dealer
15042	Hart	John	1831	Spitalfields, London	Joseph Hart	Ann (?)		Bethnal Green, London	cigar maker
17356	Hart	John	1831	Whitechapel, London				Spitalfields, London	general dealer
18444	Hart	John	1836	Middlesex, London	Isaac Hart		Maria Hannah Moses	?, London	
29933	Hart	John	1836	Whitechapel, London	(?) Hart	Hannah (?)		Whitechapel, London	[?slip] cutter apprentice
21080	Hart	John	1840	?, London	Moses Hart	Rachael Solomons		Aldgate, London	boarding school pupil
15255	Hart	John	1845	?, London	John W Hart	Elizabeth (?)		Shoreditch, London	scholar
15249	Hart	John W	1806	?, London	Napthali		Elizabeth (?)	Shoreditch, London	annuitant
5330	Hart	Jonas	1851	Wolverhampton, Staffordshire	Emanuel Hart	Sheba Lazarus	Amelia Cohen	Wolverhampton, Staffordshire	
29687	Hart	Joseph	1781	Southampton, Hampshire			(?)	Shoreditch, London	parish relief
3349	Hart	Joseph	1791	Cambridge	Barnett Hart		Deborah Franks	Whitechapel, London	
14654	Hart	Joseph	1802	Hungerford, Berkshire			Maria (?)	Hoxton, London	printer pressman
11564	Hart	Joseph	1806	Whitechapel, London			Rosetta (?)	Aldgate, London	general dealer
15040	Hart	Joseph	1809	Spitalfields, London			Ann (?)	Bethnal Green, London	wine porter
8139	Hart	Joseph	1812	Aldgate, London	Isaac Hart		Rachel Martin (Nunes Martines)	Aldgate, London	fishmonger
6796	Hart	Joseph	1819	Spitalfields, London	Hyam Hart		Eve (Elizabeth, Sarah) Berlyn	Spitalfields, London	cab proprietor
19921	Hart	Joseph	1820	?				Belfast, Ireland	music + musical instrument merchant
30499	Hart	Joseph	1827	Spitalfields, London	Moses Hart	Leah Benjamin	Phoebe Jonas	Spitalfields, London	general dealer
14656	Hart	Joseph	1834	Banbury, Oxfordshire	Joseph Hart	Maria (?)		Hoxton, London	printer
21058	Hart	Joseph	1836	Middlesex, London	Eleazer Hart	Sarah Levy	Hannah Abrahams	Tottenham, London	boarding school pupil
15045	Hart	Joseph	1837	Bethnal Green, London	Joseph Hart	Ann (?)		Bethnal Green, London	errand boy
29937	Hart	Joseph	1846	Mile End, London	(?) Hart	Hannah (?)		Whitechapel, London	scholar
10920	Hart	Joseph	1848	Spitalfields, London	Henry Hart	Phoebe Solomon		Spitalfields, London	
21617	Hart	Joseph	1850	Whitechapel, London	Joseph Hart	Caroline Cohen		Whitechapel, London	
23460	Hart	Joseph M	1837	Liverpool	Naphtali Hart	Mary Sewill		Liverpool	apprentice
11314	Hart	Joshua	1839	Spitalfields, London	(?)			Aldgate, London	scholar
17855	Hart	Judah	1801	Portsmouth, Hampshire				Aldgate, London	merchant + jeweller
7465	Hart	Judah	1821	Tottenham, London	Eleazer Hart	Sarah Levy	Hannah Nathan	Aldgate, London	rag merchant
20938	Hart	Judah	1822	Tottenham, London	Tsvi		Ann (?)	Aldgate, London	fishmonger

ID	surname	given names	born	birthplace	father	mother	spouse 1	1851 residence	1851 occupation
17807	Hart	Judith	1777	City, London	(?)		(?) Hart	Aldgate, London	
16464	Hart	Julia	1801	Bethnal Green, London	(?)		Abraham Septimus Hart	Knightsbridge, London	
22837	Hart	Julia	1801	Middlesex, London	(?)		Abraham Hart	Whitechapel, London	
27754	Hart	Julia	1806	?, Holland	(?)		(?) Hart	Spitalfields, London	cap maker
19501	Hart	Julia	1814	Westminster, London	Joseph Levy		Louis (Lewis) Hart	Strand, London	
22338	Hart	Julia	1824	Whitechapel, London	Henry Hart	Phoebe Myers		Aldgate, London	
12774	Hart	Julia	1826	Aldgate, London	Moses Hart	Rachael Solomons		Aldgate, London	
26712	Hart	Julia	1826	?, London	John Hart	Elizabeth Jacobs		Piccadilly, London	
12443	Hart	Julia	1829	Spitalfields, London	Aaron Hart	(?) Levy		Spitalfields, London	tailoress
8606	Hart	Julia	1834	City, London	Henry Hart	Rosa (?)		Wapping, London	waistcoat maker
3985	Hart	Julia	1836	Portsmouth, Hampshire	Solomon Hart	Hannah Crabb		Portsmouth, Hampshire	
852	Hart	Julia	1839	Canterbury, Kent	Mordecai (Maurice) Hart	Frances Moses	George Bendon	Canterbury, Kent	
29934	Hart	Julia	1839	Lambeth, London	(?) Hart	Hannah (?)		Whitechapel, London	scholar
10919	Hart	Julia	1844	Spitalfields, London	Henry Hart	Phoebe Solomon		Spitalfields, London	scholar
22722	Hart	Julia	1849	Whitechapel, London	Moses (Moss) Hart	Sarah Moses		Whitechapel, London	
14657	Hart	Julius	1840	Shoreditch, London	Joseph Hart	Maria (?)		Hoxton, London	printer
7232	Hart	Justina (Hannah)	1822	Aldgate, London	Stephen (Solomon) Hart	Esther Solomon	Hilel de Moses Beriro	Whitechapel, London	
27939	Hart	Kate	1826	Whitechapel, London	Moses Hart			Spitalfields, London	dressmaker
17539	Hart	Kitty	1796	Aldgate, London	(?)		Isaac Hart	Spitalfields, London	
10622	Hart	Kitty	1798	?, Holland	Moshe Mannheim		Mordeca Hart	Spitalfields, London	
9892	Hart	Lawrence	1840	Whitechapel, London	Henry Hart	Ann Mordecai		Whitechapel, London	school
21950	Hart	Lazarus	1832	Margate, Kent	Philip Hart	Pamela Magnus		Ramsgate, Kent	
30516	Hart	Lazarus	1851	Whitechapel, London	Moses (Moss) Hart	Sarah Moses		Whitechapel, London	
20264	Hart	Leah	1795	?, London	Binyamin Halevi		Moses Hart	Spitalfields, London	
25296	Hart	Leah	1809	Aldgate, London	John Solomons (Solomon)		Simon Hart	Holborn, London	
13030	Hart	Leah	1821	Shoreditch, London	(?)		Robert Hart	Spitalfields, London	
8797	Hart	Leah	1828	Aldgate, London	Benjamin Hart	Caroline (?)	Michal Lyons	Aldgate, London	fruiterer's assistant
27582	Hart	Leah	1835	City, London	(?) Hart			Spitalfields, London	servant
4527	Hart	Leah	1838	Mile End, London	Lewis Hart	Sarah (?)		Birmingham	
18594	Hart	Leah	1838	City, London	Henry Hart	Phoebe Myers	Herman Wulfson	Aldgate, London	
27593	Hart	Leah	1838	City, London	Lewis (Louis) Hart	Maria (Miryam) Rodriguez		Spitalfields, London	scholar
25891	Hart	Leah	1842	Spitalfields, London	Ezekiel Hart	Sylvia Green		Covent Garden, London	
8022	Hart	Leah	1847	Spitalfields, London	Emanuel Hart	Amelia Lipman	Saul Lyons	Spitalfields, London	
6800	Hart	Leah	1850	Spitalfields, London	Joseph Hart	Eve (Elizabeth, Sarah) Berlyn		Spitalfields, London	
4525	Hart	Lewis	1809	Finsbury, London	Moshe Hart		Sarah Roxas (Rochas)	Birmingham	tailor
30065	Hart	Lewis	1811	Portsmouth, Hampshire	Michael Hart		Rosetta Jonas	Marylebone, London	clothier
25300	Hart	Lewis	1831	Whitechapel, London	Henry Hart	Frances Isaacs	Elizabeth Solomons	Aldgate, London	cigar maker
27404	Hart	Lewis	1832	Aldgate, London	Joel Hart	Mary Hyams	Ann Levy	Whitechapel, London	cigar maker
11567	Hart	Lewis	1835	Spitalfields, London	Joseph Hart	Rosetta (?)	Adelaide Levy	Aldgate, London	butcher
9360	Hart	Lewis	1837	St Giles, London	Henry Hart	(?)		Holborn, London	book seller
23461	Hart	Lewis	1839	Liverpool	Naphtali Hart	Mary Sewill		Liverpool	scholar
27591	Hart	Lewis (Louis)	1808	City, London	Raphael Hart		Maria (Miryam) Rodriguez	Spitalfields, London	general dealer
16868	Hart	Lewis Edward	1849	Cambridge	Benjamin Hart	Margaret Hopkins		Cambridge	
16466	Hart	Lewis Joseph	1831	Westminster, London	Abraham Septimus Hart	Julia (?)		Knightsbridge, London	dentist

ID	surname	given names	born	birthplace	father	mother	spouse 1	1851 residence	1851 occupation
27982	Hart	Lion	1779	Aldgate, London				Spitalfields, London	shoemaker
15254	Hart	Lionel	1843	?, London	John W Hart	Elizabeth (?)		Shoreditch, London	scholar
20266	Hart	Lipman	1821	Whitechapel, London	Moses Hart	Leah Benjamin	Sarah Asher	Spitalfields, London	fishmonger
30125	Hart	Louis	1850	Whitechapel, London	Henry Hart	Rose Cohen		Wapping, London	
19500	Hart	Louis (Lewis)	1804	Middlesex, London	Benjamin Hart		Julia Levy	Strand, London	clothes salesman
15252	Hart	Louisa	1840	?Shoreditch, London	John W Hart	Elizabeth (?)		Shoreditch, London	scholar
18133	Hart	Louisa	1841	Middlesex, London	Naphtali Hart	Elizabeth Solomon		Mile End, London	
17272	Hart	Lyon	1797	?, Poland			Rachael (?)	Aldgate, London	tailor
18341	Hart	Marcus	1827	Amsterdam, Holland				Brighton, Sussex	musician
16865	Hart	Margaret	1811	Cambridge	(?) Hopkins		Benjamin Hart	Cambridge	
14655	Hart	Maria	1812	Hackney, London	(?)		Joseph Hart	Hoxton, London	
3982	Hart	Maria	1830	Wapping, London	Michael Henry Hart	Esther Davis	Nathan Samuel Braun	Portsmouth, Hampshire	
8610	Hart	Maria	1840	City, London	Henry Hart	Rosa (?)		Wapping, London	scholar
14658	Hart	Maria	1844	Shoreditch, London	Joseph Hart	Maria (?)		Hoxton, London	
8801	Hart	Maria (Miriam)	1844	Aldgate, London	Benjamin Hart	Caroline (?)	Isaac Mendoza	Aldgate, London	scholar
27592	Hart	Maria (Miryam)	1809	City, London	Abraham de Mordecai Rodrigues	Leah de Isaac Nunes Martines	Lewis (Louis) Hart	Spitalfields, London	
14099	Hart	Marianne	1819	Strand, London	Abraham Hart		Aaron Levy	Marylebone, London	annuitant
27755	Hart	Mark	1826	?, Holland	(?) Hart	Julia (?)		Spitalfields, London	tailor
27937	Hart	Mark	1851	Whitechapel, London	Naphtali Hart	Deborah Levy		Spitalfields, London	
9358	Hart	Martha	1833	St Giles, London	Henry Hart	(?)		Holborn, London	dressmaker
30325	Hart	Mary	1777	?, London	Reuben Jacob Katz (Cohen)		Naphtali (Nathaniel) Hart	Edinburgh, Scotland	
27401	Hart	Mary	1791	Whitechapel, London	Tsevi Hirsh Hyams		Joel Hart	Whitechapel, London	retired draper
26251	Hart	Mary	1797	?, London			(?) Hart	Aldgate, London	dressmaker
18639	Hart	Mary	1811	?, London	(?) Sewill		Naphtali Hart	Liverpool	
17960	Hart	Mary	1819	Whitechapel, London	Daniel Joel	Elizabeth (Betsey) Cohen	Solomon (Zalig) Hart	Aldgate, London	
13192	Hart	Mary	1839	Aldgate, London	(?) Hart			Aldgate, London	
9882	Hart	Mary	1840	Stepney, London	Henry Hart	Elizabeth (?)		Mile End, London	scholar
30119	Hart	Mary	1844	Whitechapel, London	Henry Hart	Rose Cohen		Wapping, London	scholar
22720	Hart	Mary	1845	Whitechapel, London	Moses (Moss) Hart	Sarah Moses		Whitechapel, London	scholar
6799	Hart	Mary (Marianne)	1843	Spitalfields, London	Joseph Hart	Eve (Elizabeth, Sarah) Berlyn		Spitalfields, London	scholar
20984	Hart	Mary Ann	1832	City, London	(?) Hart			Aldgate, London	general servant
13639	Hart	Mary E	1845	Manchester	Philip Hart	Sarah Southwick nee (?)		Manchester	scholar
4092	Hart	Matilda	1813	Whitechapel, London	Stephen (Solomon) Hart	Esther Solomon	Joel Woolf Solomon	Aldgate, London	
28556	Hart	Matilda	1826	Soho, London	(?) Abrahams		Henry Hart	Aldgate, London	
106	Hart	Matilda	1847	Woolwich, London	Henry Hart			Woolwich, London	
7224	Hart	Maurice	1777	Portsmouth, Hampshire				Whitechapel, London	retired merchant
5053	Hart	Maurice	1830	Tottenham, London	Eleazer Hart	Sarah Levy		Portsmouth, Hampshire	
3390	Hart	Maurice	1835	Aldgate, London	Moses Hart	Rachael Solomons	Ailsie Miers	Aldgate, London	hardware dealer's assistant
15935	Hart	Maurice (Morris)	1842	Whitechapel, London	Henry Hart	Fanny Barnett		Spitalfields, London	scholar
14828	Hart	Michael	1799	Middlesex, London	Jacob Hart		Catherine Jones	Bethnal Green, London	clothes salesman
21943	Hart	Michael	1805	?, Poland			Pamela Magnus	Ramsgate, Kent	
1798	Hart	Michael	1808	?, Holland				Merthyr Tydfil, Wales	spice traveller

ID	surname	given names	born	birthplace	father	mother	spouse 1	1851 residence	1851 occupation
9706	Hart	Michael	1819	Whitechapel, London	Henry Hart		Sarah Cohen	Whitechapel, London	general dealer
12441	Hart	Michael	1826	Spitalfields, London	Aaron Hart	(?) Levy		Spitalfields, London	cigar maker
20263	Hart	Michael	1835	?, London	Moses Hart	Leah Benjamin	Elizabeth Isaacs	Spitalfields, London	general dealer
10666	Hart	Michael	1844	Spitalfields, London	Aaron Hart	Sarah (?)		Spitalfields, London	
12806	Hart	Michael	1845	Whitechapel, London	Isaac Hart	Sarah Phillips		Spitalfields, London	scholar
26546	Hart	Michael	1848	Whitechapel, London	Lipman Hart	Emma (Abigail) Franks		Spitalfields, London	
16378	Hart	Michael	1850	City, London	Moss (Moses) Hart	Sophia Abrahams		Aldgate, London	
20942	Hart	Michael	1850	Aldgate, London	Judah Hart	Ann (?)		Aldgate, London	
3980	Hart	Michael Henry	1796	Georgetown, USA	Nathan Hart		Esther Davis	Portsmouth, Hampshire	clothes salesman + slopseller, watchmaker + jeweller &c
11569	Hart	Micheal	1839	Spitalfields, London	Joseph Hart	Rosetta (?)		Aldgate, London	scholar
7230	Hart	Miriam	1819	Aldgate, London	Stephen (Solomon) Hart	Esther Solomon	Saul Isaac	Whitechapel, London	
2451	Hart	Miriam	1829	Hull, Yorkshire	(?) Hart	Hannah Alexander	Solomon Cohen	Hull, Yorkshire	
19965	Hart	Miriam (Marian, Mary)	1795	Canterbury, Kent	(?) Abrahams		Joseph Hart	Deal, Kent	retired clothier's widow
15253	Hart	Montague Phineas	1841	Shoreditch, London	John W Hart	Elizabeth (?)	Clara Solomon	Shoreditch, London	scholar
27597	Hart	Mordecai	1847	City, London	Lewis (Louis) Hart	Maria (Miryam) Rodriguez		Spitalfields, London	scholar
850	Hart	Mordecai (Maurice)	1798	Bielsk, Poland			Frances Moses	Canterbury, Kent	pawnbroker
10621	Hart	Mordecai (Mordica)	1800	?, Holland	Yehuda Leib		Kitty Moses	Spitalfields, London	general dealer
16642	Hart	Morris	1816	Plymouth, Devon	Moses Hart	Esther (?)		Liverpool	watchmaker + general dealer
19922	Hart	Morris	1831	Tottenham, London			Isabella Vanderlyn	Ipswich, Suffolk	glass + earthenware man + general dealer
31194	Hart	Morris	1832	?, Germany	Henry Hart	Rosa (?)		Bath	dealer in cigars
16640	Hart	Moses	1782	Plymouth, Devon			Esther (?)	Liverpool	watchmaker + general dealer
17853	Hart	Moses	1806	Whitechapel, London			Rebecca (?)	Aldgate, London	general dealer
22838	Hart	Moses	1837	Middlesex, London	Abraham Hart	Julia (?)		Whitechapel, London	cigar maker
27911	Hart	Moses	1837	Spitalfields, London	David Hart	(?)		Spitalfields, London	cigar maker
10620	Hart	Moses	1839	Middlesex, London	Mordecai Hart	Kitty Moses	Amelia Hyams	Spitalfields, London	
25778	Hart	Moses	1839	Aldgate, London	(?) Hart	Hannah (?)		Aldgate, London	scholar
29420	Hart	Moses	1848	Spitalfields, London	Henry Hart	Elizabeth (Batseba) Mendoza		Spitalfields, London	
11571	Hart	Moses	1850	Aldgate, London	Joseph Hart	Rosetta (?)		Aldgate, London	
17961	Hart	Moses (Morris)	1846	Whitechapel, London	Solomon (Zalig) Hart	Mary Joel	Martha Aarons	Aldgate, London	
22716	Hart	Moses (Moss)	1815	Aldgate, London	David Hart		Sarah Moses	Whitechapel, London	black lead pencil maker
22339	Hart	Moss	1826	Whitechapel, London	Henry Hart	Phoebe Myers		Aldgate, London	shoe manufacturer
12444	Hart	Moss	1831	Spitalfields, London	Aaron Hart	(?) Levy		Spitalfields, London	cigar maker
16375	Hart	Moss (Moses)	1820	City, London	Joel Hart	Mary Hyams	Sophia Abrahams	Aldgate, London	draper
8804	Hart	Moss (Moses)	1850	Aldgate, London	Benjamin Hart	Caroline (?)	Louisa (Lucy) Phillips	Aldgate, London	
21418	Hart	Myres	1830	Kutnow, Poland				Dewsbury, Yorkshire	traveller
18130	Hart	Naphtali	1809	Shoreditch, London	Tobe Hart		Elizabeth Solomon	Mile End, London	clerk in the Customs

ID	surname	given names	born	birthplace	father	mother	spouse 1	1851 residence	1851 occupation
18634	Hart	Naphtali	1811	Plymouth, Devon			Mary Sewill	Liverpool	watch manufacturer + goldsmith
22340	Hart	Naphtali	1828	Whitechapel, London	Henry Hart	Phoebe Myers		Aldgate, London	
26894	Hart	Naphtali	1840	?, London	Abraham Hart	Esther (?)		Aldgate, London	scholar
27935	Hart	Napthali	1820	Whitechapel, London			Deborah Levy	Spitalfields, London	trunk maker
103	Hart	Nathan	1819	?, Poland	Henry Hart		Hannah (?)	Woolwich, London	silversmith + general dealer
27938	Hart	Nathan	1822	Whitechapel, London	Moses Hart		Julia Nathan	Spitalfields, London	cigar maker
13031	Hart	Nathan	1842	Spitalfields, London	Robert Hart	Leah (?)		Spitalfields, London	
7681	Hart	Nathan (Nathaniel) Samuel	1828	Wapping, London	Michael Henry Hart	Esther (?)	Priscilla Borchardt	Liverpool	grocer + provision dealer
5054	Hart	Nathaniel	1832	Tottenham, London	Eleazer Hart	Sarah Levy	Dinah Nathan	Portsmouth, Hampshire	
13637	Hart	Philip	1789	?, Germany			Sarah Southwick nee (?)	Manchester	dealer in stationery
102	Hart	Philip	1813	?, Poland	Henry Hart			Woolwich, London	shipman
851	Hart	Philip	1836	Canterbury, Kent	Mordecai (Maurice) Hart	Frances Moses	Adelaide (?)	Canterbury, Kent	
25777	Hart	Philip	1836	Aldgate, London	(?) Hart	Hannah (?)		Aldgate, London	
21946	Hart	Philip	1841	Margate, Kent	Michael Hart	Pamela Magnus	Rosetta Frances Moses	Ramsgate, Kent	
12805	Hart	Phillip	1842	Spitalfields, London	Isaac Hart	Sarah Phillips		Spitalfields, London	scholar
22336	Hart	Phoebe	1791	Aldgate, London	Jacob Myers	Eve (?)	Henry Hart	Aldgate, London	
10915	Hart	Phoebe	1810	Aldgate, London	Shlomeh		Henry Hart	Spitalfields, London	
26892	Hart	Phoebe	1832	?, London	Abraham Hart	Esther (?)	Judah Abendana	Aldgate, London	slipper maker
22332	Hart	Phoebe	1841	Whitechapel, London	Aaron Hart	Rebecca (Anne) Crawcour	Albert Aaron Goldsmid	Stepney, London	scholar
6004	Hart	Phoebe	1849	Whitechapel, London	Michael Hart	Sarah Cohen	Hyam Hyams	Whitechapel, London	
27443	Hart	Prescilla	1845	Finsbury, London	Barnett Hart	Catherine (?)		Whitechapel, London	scholar
5051	Hart	Rachael	1758	?, Germany	(?)		Moses Hart	Portsmouth, Hampshire	
17273	Hart	Rachael	1791	?, Poland	(?)		Lyon Hart	Aldgate, London	
12773	Hart	Rachael	1795	?, London	Pinchas Zelig Solomons		Moses Hart	Aldgate, London	hardware dealer
17541	Hart	Rachael	1816	Whitechapel, London	Isaac Hart	Kitty (?)		Spitalfields, London	
26252	Hart	Rachael	1820	?, London	(?) Hart	Mary (?)		Aldgate, London	dressmaker
26891	Hart	Rachael	1831	?, London	Abraham Hart	Esther (?)		Aldgate, London	slipper maker
21616	Hart	Rachael	1840	Whitechapel, London	Joseph Hart	Deborah Franks		Whitechapel, London	
12825	Hart	Rachael	1843	Whitechapel, London	Ezekiel Hart	Sylvia Green		Covent Garden, London	
8140	Hart	Rachel	1812	?, London	Isaac Nunes Martines	Sarah (?)	Joseph Hart	Aldgate, London	
12440	Hart	Rachel	1819	Middlesex, London	Aaron Hart	(?) Levy		Spitalfields, London	tailoress
20268	Hart	Rachel	1828	?, London	Moses Hart	Leah Benjamin	Aaron Nathan	Spitalfields, London	
22718	Hart	Rachel	1842	Whitechapel, London	Moses (Moss) Hart	Sarah Moses		Whitechapel, London	scholar
27594	Hart	Raphael	1840	Aldgate, London	Lewis (Louis) Hart	Maria (Miryam) Rodriguez	Sarah Isaacs	Spitalfields, London	scholar
22093	Hart	Rebecca	1791	Aldgate, London	(?)		(?) Hart	Aldgate, London	sextoness
17854	Hart	Rebecca	1803	Whitechapel, London	(?)		Moses Hart	Aldgate, London	
12534	Hart	Rebecca	1819	Great Yarmouth, Norfolk	William Masters		Harty Hart	Great Yarmouth, Norfolk	
15588	Hart	Rebecca	1831	Ware, Hertfordshire	Mordecai Marks		Samuel Hart	Covent Garden, London	
27941	Hart	Rebecca	1831	Whitechapel, London	(?) Hart			Spitalfields, London	dressmaker
9891	Hart	Rebecca	1839	City, London	Henry Hart	Ann Mordecai		Whitechapel, London	hatter timmer
27441	Hart	Rebecca	1840	Finsbury, London	Barnett Hart	Catherine (?)		Whitechapel, London	scholar
27595	Hart	Rebecca	1842	City, London	Lewis (Louis) Hart	Maria (Miryam) Rodriguez		Spitalfields, London	scholar

ID	surname	given names	born	birthplace	father	mother	spouse 1	1851 residence	1851 occupation
18135	Hart	Rebecca	1846	Middlesex, London	Naphtali Hart	Elizabeth Solomon		Mile End, London	
22329	Hart	Rebecca (Anne)	1823	Finsbury, London	David Crawcour	Miriam (?)	Aaron Hart	Stepney, London	
24955	Hart	Rebekah	1805	Amsterdam, Holland	(?)		Hayman Hart	Haggerston, London	
22987	Hart	Reuben	1820	Szubin, Poland [Schubin, Prussia]	Arendt Zadok Hart	Mirjam Abraham	Amelia Cohen	Whitechapel, London	dealer in jewellery
13029	Hart	Robert	1824	Whitechapel, London			Leah (?)	Spitalfields, London	jeweller
8426	Hart	Rosa	1768	Portsmouth, Hampshire	(?)		(?) Hart	Portsmouth, Hampshire	annuitant
8604	Hart	Rosa	1801	City, London	(?)		Henry Hart	Wapping, London	
31196	Hart	Rosa	1811	?, Germany	(?)		Henry Hart	Bath	
29806	Hart	Rosa	1841	Whitechapel, London	Samuel Michael Hart	Frances Phillips		Whitechapel, London	umbrella maker
9110	Hart	Rose	1806	?, London	(?)		Henry Hart	South Kensington, London	
30118	Hart	Rose	1818	Strand, London	Benjamin Wolf Cohen		Henry Hart	Wapping, London	
5326	Hart	Rose	1833	Wolverhampton, Staffordshire	Emanuel Hart	Sheba Lazarus	Abraham Noah Richardson	Wolverhampton, Staffordshire	
30066	Hart	Rosetta	1811	Aldgate, London	Isaac Jonas		Lewis Hart	Marylebone, London	capmaker
11565	Hart	Rosetta	1812	Whitechapel, London	(?)		Joseph Hart	Aldgate, London	tailoress
27940	Hart	Rosetta	1829	Whitechapel, London	Moses Hart		Judah (Lewis) Henry	Spitalfields, London	tailoress
8143	Hart	Rosetta	1841	Spitalfields, London	Joseph Hart	Rachel Martin (Nunes Martines)		Aldgate, London	
9401	Hart	Rosetta	1850	City, London	Henry Hart	Jane (?)		Aldgate, London	
12803	Hart	Rosetta (Rosa)	1830	Aldgate, London	Isaac Hart	Sarah Phillips		Spitalfields, London	
30999	Hart	Rosina	1836	Manchester	(?) Hart			Wolverhampton, Staffordshire	assistant to a pawnbroker
10617	Hart	Sally	1833	Middlesex, London	Mordecai Hart	Kitty Moses		Spitalfields, London	
8607	Hart	Sampson	1836	City, London	Henry Hart	Rosa (?)		Wapping, London	cigar maker
24137	Hart	Samuel	1774	Whitechapel, London	Naphtali Fretter		Fanny (Frances) Solomon	Bloomsbury, London	dependent of son
11410	Hart	Samuel	1811	Aldgate, London				Aldgate, London	shopman
15587	Hart	Samuel	1825	City, London	Jacob HaLevi Hart		Rebecca Marks	Covent Garden, London	rag merchant
25298	Hart	Samuel	1827	Spitalfields, London	Henry Hart	Frances Isaacs	Elizabeth Solomons	Aldgate, London	cigar maker
8608	Hart	Samuel	1838	City, London	Henry Hart	Rosa (?)		Wapping, London	cigar maker
9885	Hart	Samuel	1849	Stepney, London	Henry Hart	Elizabeth (?)		Mile End, London	
12003	Hart	Sarah	1798	Coventry, Warwickshire	(?) Hart			Whitechapel, London	
12802	Hart	Sarah	1800	Aldgate, London	Aryeh Pais Phillips		Isaac Hart	Spitalfields, London	
4526	Hart	Sarah	1809	Mile End, London	Abraham Rochas		Lewis Hart	Birmingham	
13638	Hart	Sarah	1812	Sheffield, Yorkshire	(?)		(?William) Southwick	Manchester	
22717	Hart	Sarah	1816	Whitechapel, London	Eliezer Moses		Moses (Moss) Hart	Whitechapel, London	dress maker
30500	Hart	Sarah	1820	?, London	Moses Hart	Leah Benjamin		Spitalfields, London	
10665	Hart	Sarah	1823	Aldgate, London			Aaron Hart	Spitalfields, London	
9707	Hart	Sarah	1826	Spitalfields, London	Samson Cohen		Michael Hart	Whitechapel, London	
29686	Hart	Sarah	1827	Whitechapel, London	(?) Lipman		David Hart	Shoreditch, London	
9888	Hart	Sarah	1830	City, London	Henry Hart	Ann Mordecai		Whitechapel, London	hatter trimmer
22341	Hart	Sarah	1830	Whitechapel, London	Henry Hart	Phoebe Myers		Aldgate, London	
19974	Hart	Sarah	1832	Canterbury, Kent	Joseph Hart	Miriam (Marian, Mary) Abrahams	Harris King [Henry Harris]	Aldgate, London	tailor

ID	surname	given names	born	birthplace	father	mother	spouse 1	1851 residence	1851 occupation
15043	Hart	Sarah	1833	Spitalfields, London	Joseph Hart	Ann (?)		Bethnal Green, London	seamstress
2452	Hart	Sarah	1834	Hull, Yorkshire	(?) Hart	Hannah Alexander		Hull, Yorkshire	
8142	Hart	Sarah	1838	?Spitalfields, London	Joseph Hart	Rachel Martin (Nunes Martines)		Aldgate, London	
22839	Hart	Sarah	1838	Middlesex, London	Abraham Hart	Julia (?)		Whitechapel, London	fancy trimmer
19502	Hart	Sarah	1840	Westminster, London	Louis (Lewis) Hart	Julia Levy		Strand, London	
27912	Hart	Sarah	1841	Spitalfields, London	David Hart	(?)		Spitalfields, London	
5476	Hart	Sarah	1842	Darlaston, Staffordshire	Emanuel Hart	Sheba Lazarus	Solomon Auerbach	Wolverhampton, Staffordshire	
8800	Hart	Sarah	1842	Aldgate, London	Benjamin Hart	Caroline (?)		Aldgate, London	scholar
27442	Hart	Sarah	1842	Finsbury, London	Barnett Hart	Catherine (?)		Whitechapel, London	scholar
12828	Hart	Sarah	1848	Strand, London	Ezekiel Hart	Sylvia Green		Covent Garden, London	
13034	Hart	Sarah	1850	Spitalfields, London	Robert Hart	Leah (?)		Spitalfields, London	
15934	Hart	Sarah	1850	Whitechapel, London	Henry Hart	Fanny Barnett		Spitalfields, London	
29807	Hart	Selina	1842	Whitechapel, London	Samuel Michael Hart	Frances Phillips		Whitechapel, London	scholar
5325	Hart	Sheba	1813	Lincoln, Lincolnshire	Jonas Lazarus	Rosceia Nathan	Emanuel Hart	Wolverhampton, Staffordshire	
10615	Hart	Sheba (Phoebe, Sophia)	1829	Middlesex, London	Mordecai Hart	Kitty Moses	Moses Perez	Spitalfields, London	
29805	Hart	Simeon	1833	Aldgate, London	Samuel Michael Hart	Frances Phillips		Whitechapel, London	frame maker
25297	Hart	Simon	1816	Aldgate, London	Henry Hart	Frances Isaacs	Leah Solomons	Holborn, London	
27759	Hart	Simon	1839	?, Holland	(?) Hart	Julia (?)		Spitalfields, London	
5477	Hart	Simon	1844	Birmingham	Emanuel Hart	Sheba Lazarus		Wolverhampton, Staffordshire	
22802	Hart	Solomon	1779	Whitechapel, London			Elizabeth (?)	Whitechapel, London	pencutter
3983	Hart	Solomon	1809	Portsmouth, Hampshire	Lazarus Hart	Rosa Simpson	Hannah Crabb	Portsmouth, Hampshire	clothes
27756	Hart	Solomon	1830	?, Holland	(?) Hart	Julia (?)		Spitalfields, London	cigar maker
17959	Hart	Solomon (Zalig)	1818	Whitechapel, London	Moses Hart	Leah Benjamin	Mary Joel	Aldgate, London	fishmonger + pickle dealer
7547	Hart	Solomon Abraham	1822	Aldgate, London			Maria Isaacs	Aldgate, London	merchant + warehouseman
7124	Hart	Solomon Alexander	1806	Plymouth, Devon	Samuel Hart			Fitzrovia, London	professor of painting, Royal Academy + journalist
16376	Hart	Sophia	1821	Aldgate, London	Lewis Abrahams	Julia Phillips	Moss (Moses) Hart	Aldgate, London	
8799	Hart	Sophia	1836	Aldgate, London	Benjamin Hart	Caroline (?)		Aldgate, London	fruiterer's assistant
8611	Hart	Sophia	1842	City, London	Henry Hart	Rosa (?)		Wapping, London	scholar
5327	Hart	Sophia	1849	Wolverhampton, Staffordshire	Emanuel Hart	Sheba Lazarus	Bernard Jacoby	Wolverhampton, Staffordshire	
12824	Hart	Sylvia	1811	Whitechapel, London	Abraham Green	Rachael (?)	Ezekiel Hart	Covent Garden, London	
12829	Hart	Sylvia	1850	Strand, London	Ezekiel Hart	Sylvia Green	Henry Shuter	Covent Garden, London	
15050	Hart	Thomas Edward	1849	Bethnal Green, London	Joseph Hart	Ann (?)		Bethnal Green, London	
10616	Hart	Tommy	1828	Middlesex, London	Mordecai Hart	Kitty Moses		Spitalfields, London	
13641	Hart	Wiiliam J	1850	Manchester	Philip Hart	Sarah Southwick nee (?)		Manchester	
9884	Hart	William	1847	Stepney, London	Henry Hart	Elizabeth (?)		Mile End, London	

ID	surname	given names	born	birthplace	father	mother	spouse 1	1851 residence	1851 occupation
30122	Hart	Woolf	1838	Whitechapel, London	Henry Hart	Rose Cohen		Wapping, London	scholar
26547	Hart	Woolf	1850	Spitalfields, London	Lipman Hart	Emma (Abigail) Franks		Spitalfields, London	
13187	Hart (Hyams)	Michael	1795	Tottenham, London	Bezaliel Hyams		Rachel Hyams nee Davis	Aldgate, London	fishmonger
13188	Hart (Hyams)	Rachel	1806	Spitalfields, London	Joshua Davis	Sarah Zussman	Solomon Hyams	Aldgate, London	
1799	Hartman	Morris	1818	Leiban Carlan, Russia				Merthyr Tydfil, Wales	sponge hawker
25209	Hartmeyer	Adela	1808	Mons, Belgium	(?)		George Hartmeyer	Clerkenwell, London	
25210	Hartmeyer	Eugene	1833	Utrecht, Holland	George Hartmeyer	Adela (?)		Clerkenwell, London	errand boy
25208	Hartmeyer	George	1803	Amsterdam, Holland			Adela (?)	Clerkenwell, London	musician
25211	Hartmeyer	George J H	1837	Thiel, Holland	George Hartmeyer	Adela (?)		Clerkenwell, London	
25213	Hartmeyer	Johanna	1843	Limbourg, Belgium	George Hartmeyer	Adela (?)		Clerkenwell, London	
25212	Hartmeyer	Lazarus	1840	Limbourg, Belgium	George Hartmeyer	Adela (?)		Clerkenwell, London	
7126	Hartog	Alphonse	1815	?, France	Menachem Mendel Hartog		Marian Moss	Whitechapel, London	Professor of languages
8019	Hartog	Amelia	1850	Whitechapel, London	Alphonse Hartog	Marion Moss		Whitechapel, London	
19240	Hartog	Helena (Nellie)	1848	Whitechapel, London	Alphonse Hartog	Marion Moss		Whitechapel, London	
7128	Hartog	Marcus Manuel	1851	Paddington, London	Alphonse Hartog	Marion Moss	Blanche Levy-Brandes	Paddington, London	
7127	Hartog	Marion	1821	Portsmouth, Hampshire	Joseph Moss	Amelia Davids	Alphonse Hartog	Whitechapel, London	governess
7125	Hartog	Numa Edward	1846	Whitechapel, London	Alphonse Hartog	Marion Moss		Whitechapel, London	
29487	Harwitz	Adolph	1846	Poznan, Poland [Posen, Prussia]	Bernhard Harwitz	July (?)		Spitalfields, London	
29485	Harwitz	Albertina	1838	Poznan, Poland [Posen, Prussia]	Bernhard Harwitz	July (?)		Spitalfields, London	scholar
29482	Harwitz	Bernhard	1805	Poznan, Poland [Posen, Prussia]			July (?)	Spitalfields, London	cap peak manufacturer
29484	Harwitz	Julius	1836	Poznan, Poland [Posen, Prussia]	Bernhard Harwitz	July (?)		Spitalfields, London	[cap] peak maker
29483	Harwitz	July	1807	Poznan, Poland [Posen, Prussia]	(?)		Bernhard Harwitz	Spitalfields, London	
29486	Harwitz	Malvina	1844	Poznan, Poland [Posen, Prussia]	Bernhard Harwitz	July (?)		Spitalfields, London	scholar
14350	Hasche	Ave	1820	?				Manchester	
9554	Hass	Aaron	1846	Spitalfields, London	Angel Hass	Elizabeth Cohen		Aldgate, London	scholar
9548	Hass	Angel	1806	?, Germany	Isaac Hass		Elizabeth Mendoza	Aldgate, London	tinman
9553	Hass	Elias	1845	Spitalfields, London	Angel Hass	Elizabeth Cohen		Aldgate, London	scholar
9549	Hass	Elizabeth	1811	Spitalfields, London	Moshe Cohen		Angel Hass	Aldgate, London	
9550	Hass	Isaac	1834	Spitalfields, London	Angel Hass	Elizabeth Mendoza		Aldgate, London	cigar maker
9551	Hass	Mordecai	1836	Spitalfields, London	Angel Hass	Elizabeth Mendoza		Aldgate, London	tinman at home
9555	Hass	Moses	1848	Spitalfields, London	Angel Hass	Elizabeth Cohen		Aldgate, London	
9552	Hass	Myer	1837	Spitalfields, London	Angel Hass	Elizabeth Mendoza		Aldgate, London	tinman at home
9556	Hass	Phoebe	1850	Spitalfields, London	Angel Hass	Elizabeth Mendoza		Aldgate, London	
10199	Hassan	Abraham	1830	Gibraltar	Moses de M Hassan	Dinah (?)	Esther Pacifico	Aldgate, London	gentleman
28645	Hassan	Aron	1836	Mile End, London	Isaac Hassan	Sophia (Zipporah) de Salman		Spitalfields, London	scholar
28649	Hassan	Catherine	1850	Mile End, London	Isaac Hassan	Sophia (Zipporah) de Salman		Spitalfields, London	
10201	Hassan	Dinah	1804	Gibraltar	(?)		Moses Hassan	Aldgate, London	

ID	surname	given names	born	birthplace	father	mother	spouse 1	1851 residence	1851 occupation
28647	Hassan	Esther	1844	Mile End, London	Isaac Hassan	Sophia (Zipporah) de Salman	Morris Ellis Poolosky	Spitalfields, London	scholar
5655	Hassan	Isaac	1802	Mile End, London	Mordecai Hassan	Sipporah de Abraham Silva	Sophia (Zipporah) de Salman	Spitalfields, London	tailor
28263	Hassan	Isaac	1840	Whitechapel, London	Judah Hassan	Susanah (Sarah, Simha) de Jacob Netto		Aldgate, London	
15717	Hassan	Jacob	1833	Stepney, London				Spitalfields, London	egg seller
5654	Hassan	Judah	1802	Aldgate, London	Mordecai Hassan	Sipporah de Abraham Silva	Susanah (Sarah, Simha) de Jacob Netto	Aldgate, London	clothes dealer
28644	Hassan	Mark	1832	Bristol	Isaac Hassan	Sophia (Zipporah) de Salman		Spitalfields, London	shoe maker
28648	Hassan	Mary (Miriam)	1846	Mile End, London	Isaac Hassan	Sophia (Zipporah) de Salman		Spitalfields, London	scholar
28265	Hassan	Mordecai	1847	Whitechapel, London	Judah Hassan	Susanah (Sarah, Simha) de Jacob Netto		Aldgate, London	
10200	Hassan	Moses	1801	Gibraltar	Abraham Hassan		Dinah (?)	Aldgate, London	landed proprietor
17942	Hassan	Rayna	1795	Middlesex, London	(?) Hassan			City, London	ostrich feather manufacturer
10202	Hassan	Samuel	1833	Gibraltar	Moses Hassan	Dinah (?)	Miriam Abohbot	Aldgate, London	
28264	Hassan	Samuel	1845	Whitechapel, London	Judah Hassan	Susanah (Sarah, Simha) de Jacob Netto	Abigail Abrahams	Aldgate, London	
28262	Hassan	Sophia (Siporah)	1827	Spitalfields, London	Judah Hassan	Susanah (Sarah, Simha) de Jacob Netto		Aldgate, London	
28646	Hassan	Sophia (Ziporah)	1841	Mile End, London	Isaac Hassan	Sophia (Zipporah) de Salman	Abraham Jacobs	Spitalfields, London	scholar
28643	Hassan	Sophia (Zipporah)	1805	Walworth, London	Salman		Isaac Hassan	Spitalfields, London	tailor
28261	Hassan	Susanah (Sarah, Simha)	1812	Aldgate, London	Jacob Netto	Miriam (?)	Judah Hassan	Aldgate, London	
27238	Hassenham	Isaac	1846	Amsterdam, Holland	Judah Hassenham	Sarah (?)		Aldgate, London	
27239	Hassenham	Joseph	1849	?, London	Judah Hassenham	Sarah (?)		Aldgate, London	
27236	Hassenham	Judah	1819	?, London			Sarah (?)	Aldgate, London	pickle dealer
27237	Hassenham	Sarah	1817	Amsterdam, Holland	(?)		Judah Hassenham	Aldgate, London	
22029	Hatchwell	Ann	1806	Birmingham	(?)		Joshua Hatchwell	Spitalfields, London	hawker
22030	Hatchwell	Eliza	1838	?, Gloucestershire	Joshua Hatchwell	Ann (?)		Spitalfields, London	servant
22031	Hatchwell	Ellen	1843	Spitalfields, London	Joshua Hatchwell	Ann (?)		Spitalfields, London	scholar
22028	Hatchwell	Joshua	1805	Clerkenwell, London			Ann (?)	Spitalfields, London	hawker
22032	Hatchwell	Joshua	1844	Spitalfields, London	Joshua Hatchwell	Ann (?)		Spitalfields, London	scholar
22033	Hatchwell	Martha	1844	Spitalfields, London	Joshua Hatchwell	Ann (?)		Spitalfields, London	scholar
23013	Hauff	Esther	1843	Middlesex, London	Samuel Hauff	Thresa (?)		City, London	
23018	Hauff	Harriett	1849	Middlesex, London	Samuel Hauff	Thresa (?)		City, London	
23017	Hauff	Henrietta	1848	Middlesex, London	Samuel Hauff	Thresa (?)		City, London	
23020	Hauff	Julius	1823	?, Poland [?, Prussia]	Samuel Hauff	Thresa (?)		City, London	jeweller + watchmaker
23016	Hauff	Louis	1846	Middlesex, London	Samuel Hauff	Thresa (?)		City, London	
23014	Hauff	Matilda	1844	Middlesex, London	Samuel Hauff	Thresa (?)		City, London	
23015	Hauff	Moses	1845	Middlesex, London	Samuel Hauff	Thresa (?)		City, London	
23019	Hauff	Rebecca	1850	Middlesex, London	Samuel Hauff	Thresa (?)		City, London	

ID	surname	given names	born	birthplace	father	mother	spouse 1	1851 residence	1851 occupation
23011	Hauff	Samuel	1812	?, Poland [?, Prussia]			Thresa (?)	City, London	cap manufacturer
23012	Hauff	Thresa	1824	?, Poland [?, Prussia]	(?)		Samuel Hauff	City, London	
4532	Hayman	Doris	1827	?, Poland [?, Prussia]			Louis Hayman	Birmingham	
14974	Hayman	Henrietta	1839	Bristol	(?) Hayman			Bethnal Green, London	boarding school pupil
4533	Hayman	Henry	1850	Birmingham	Louis Hayman	Doris (?)	Annie Clara Myers	Birmingham	
4531	Hayman	Louis	1815	?, Poland [?, Prussia]			Doris (?)	Birmingham	tobacconist
14983	Hayman	Maria	1841	Bristol	(?) Hayman			Bethnal Green, London	boarding school pupil
13682	Hayman	Michael	1834	?, Poland [?, Prussia]				Manchester	apprentice to joiner
4812	Hayman	Philip	1820	?, Poland [?, Prussia]			Rebecca (?)	Birmingham	
22630	Heartstein	Abraham	1817	?, Germany	Moses Heartstein		Rebecca Swayne	Whitechapel, London	journeyman skin dresser
22634	Heartstein	Hannah	1846	Middlesex, London	Abraham Heartstein	Rebecca Swayne		Whitechapel, London	scholar
22632	Heartstein	Jacob	1840	Middlesex, London	Abraham Heartstein	Rebecca Swayne		Whitechapel, London	scholar
22631	Heartstein	Rebecca	1818	Middlesex, London	James Swayne		Abraham Heartstein	Whitechapel, London	
22633	Heartstein	Sarah	1844	Middlesex, London	Abraham Heartstein	Rebecca Swayne		Whitechapel, London	scholar
22635	Heartstein	Solomon	1851	?Whitechapel, London	Abraham Heartstein	Rebecca Swayne		Whitechapel, London	
27976	Heiams	Hannah	1810	?, Poland [?, Prussia]	(?)		Marcus Heiams	Spitalfields, London	
27979	Heiams	Hannah	1842	?, Poland [?, Prussia]	Marcus Heiams	Hannah (?)		Spitalfields, London	
27975	Heiams	Marcus	1805	?, Poland [?, Prussia]			Hannah (?)	Spitalfields, London	tailor
27980	Heiams	Rachel	1844	?, Poland [?, Prussia]	Marcus Heiams	Hannah (?)		Spitalfields, London	
27977	Heiams	Sarah	1834	?, Poland [?, Prussia]	Marcus Heiams	Hannah (?)		Spitalfields, London	
27978	Heiams	Woolf	1836	?, Poland [?, Prussia]	Marcus Heiams	Hannah (?)		Spitalfields, London	
9156	Heilbron	Abraham	1846	Poznan, Poland [Posen, Prussia]	Jacob Heilbron	Hannah (Hancher) Kempner		Whitechapel, London	scholar
4536	Heilbron	Alexander	1836	Birmingham	Lewis Heilbron	Frances Phillips		Birmingham	pawnbroker's assistant
7198	Heilbron	David	1844	Breda, Holland	Lewis (Levy) Heilbron		Fanny Jessel	?Glasgow, Scotland	
4535	Heilbron	Frances	1806	Birmingham	Shmuel HaLevi Phillips		Lewis Heilbron	Birmingham	
4537	Heilbron	Hannah	1838	Birmingham	Lewis Heilbron	Frances Phillips		Birmingham	scholar
9155	Heilbron	Hannah (Hancher)	1818	Ostrow, Poland [Ostrowo, Prussia]	(?) Kempner		Jacob Heilbron	Whitechapel, London	
27446	Heilbron	Hannale	1840	Aldgate, London	Raphael Heilbron	Hester (?)		Whitechapel, London	
27445	Heilbron	Hester	1811	?, Holland			Hester (?)	Whitechapel, London	
9154	Heilbron	Jacob	1818	Poznan, Poland [Posen, Prussia]	Eleazer Heilbron		Hannah (Hancher) Kempner	Whitechapel, London	journeyman tailor
27447	Heilbron	Jacob	1843	Aldgate, London	Raphael Heilbron	Hester (?)		Whitechapel, London	scholar
12771	Heilbron	Jonas (Joseph)	1804	?, Germany	Isaac Heilbron		Phoebe Simmons	Whitechapel, London	general dealer
3989	Heilbron	Levi	1831	Amsterdam, Holland	Samuel Heilbron	Sarah (?)		Portsmouth, Hampshire	hawker
27449	Heilbron	Levi	1847	Aldgate, London	Raphael Heilbron	Hester (?)		Whitechapel, London	
4534	Heilbron	Lewis	1798	?, Poland [?, Prussia]	Hanoch Zundel Moshe Heilbron		Frances Phillips	Birmingham	dealer in embroidery
9157	Heilbron	Marcus	1849	?, London	Jacob Heilbron	Hannah (Hancher) Kempner		Whitechapel, London	scholar at home
5055	Heilbron	Mary Hannah	1839	Manchester	Samuel Heilbron	Sarah (?)		Portsmouth, Hampshire	
4539	Heilbron	Miriam	1845	Birmingham	Lewis Heilbron	Frances Phillips		Birmingham	scholar
30518	Heilbron	Moses	1851	Whitechapel, London	Jacob Heilbron	Hannah (Hancher) Kempner		Whitechapel, London	
5452	Heilbron	Phoebe	1815	Penzance, Cornwall	Barnet Asher Simmons	Flora Jacob	Joseph Heilbron	Whitechapel, London	

ID	surname	given names	born	birthplace	father	mother	spouse 1	1851 residence	1851 occupation
27448	Heilbron	Rachel	1845	Aldgate, London	Raphael Heilbron	Hester (?)		Whitechapel, London	scholar
27444	Heilbron	Raphael	1814	?, Holland			Hester (?)	Whitechapel, London	furrier
31006	Heilbron	Rebecca	1834	Birmingham	Lewis Heilbron	Frances Phillips	Lewis Lask	Wolverhampton, Staffordshire	assistant to pawnbroker
4538	Heilbron	Roselia	1843	Birmingham	Lewis Heilbron	Frances Phillips		Birmingham	scholar
3990	Heilbron	Rosetta	1833	Amsterdam, Holland	Samuel Heilbron	Sarah (?)		Portsmouth, Hampshire	
3986	Heilbron	Samuel	1797	Amsterdam, Holland			Sarah (?)	Portsmouth, Hampshire	Reader of Synagogue
3988	Heilbron	Sarah	1801	Amsterdam, Holland			Samuel Heibron	Portsmouth, Hampshire	
29161	Heilbut	Adeline	1850	Whitechapel, London	Reuben Samuel Heilbut	Matilda Symons	Charles Lindo	Whitechapel, London	
29159	Heilbut	Matilda	1821	Whitechapel, London	Eleazer Jacob Symons	Hester (Esther) (?)	Reuben Samuel Heilbut	Whitechapel, London	
29158	Heilbut	Reuben Samuel	1809	Hamburg, Germany	Samuel Joseph Heilbut		Matilda Symons	Whitechapel, London	export merchant
29160	Heilbut	Samuel	1849	?, London	Reuben Samuel Heilbut	Matilda Symons	Emma Levy	Whitechapel, London	
29878	Heilbut	Solly J	1812	?, Germany			Mary Ann Wright	Wapping, London	importer of leeches
22980	Heilbuth	Jane Jenetta	1844	Stepney, London	Samuel Heilbuth	Matilda Furst	Charles David de Pinna	Limehouse, London	
22979	Heilbuth	Matilda	1812	Walworth, London	Samson Furst		Samuel Heilbuth	Limehouse, London	
22978	Heilbuth	Samuel	1812	Copenhagen, Denmark	Simon Heilbuth		Matilda Furst	Limehouse, London	ship chandler
22981	Heilbuth	Samuel Samson	1846	Limehouse, London	Samuel Heilbuth	Matilda Furst	Rosetta Beck	Limehouse, London	
23579	Heilmann	Emily	1835	Hamburg, Germany	(?) Heilmann			Liverpool	house servant
24067	Heimann	Adolph	1807	?, Poland [?, Prussia]	Hyman Heimann		Amelia Barnard	Regent's Park, London	doctor of philosophy + Professor of German in University College London
24068	Heimann	Amelia	1825	Portsmouth, Hampshire	David Barnard		Adolph Heimann	Regent's Park, London	
24069	Heimann	Charles Adolph	1844	Holborn, London	Adolph Heimann	Amelia Barnard	(?)	Regent's Park, London	
24070	Heimann	Golde Alexandrine	1849	St Pancras, London	Adolph Heimann	Amelia Barnard		Regent's Park, London	
24071	Heimann	Henriette Marianne	1851	Regent's Park, London	Adolph Heimann	Amelia Barnard		Regent's Park, London	
5056	Heineman	Rachel	1795	?, London	Abraham Moses	Rosy Nathan	Wolf Heineman	Portsmouth, Hampshire	pawnbroker
5057	Heineman	William	1823	?, London	Wolf Heineman	Rachel Moses		Portsmouth, Hampshire	tailor
24696	Heinemann	Amalie	1783	Altona, Germany	(?)		(?) Heinemann	Walworth, London	
29351	Heinemann	Jacob	1811	?, Bavaria, Germany			Babette Finsterer nee Leifmann	Whitechapel, London	teacher of languages
14152	Heinemann	Louis	1825	Hanover, Germany				Manchester	agent
13708	Heinenm	?	1830	?, Poland				Bloomsbury, London	journeyman tailor
4540	Heiris	Jacob	1836	?, Poland				Birmingham	glazier
25860	Heiser	Abraham	1826	?, Poland [?, Prussia]	Shmuel		Sarah Levy	Aldgate, London	bead maker journeyman
30531	Helbert [Israel]	Adeline	1801	?, London	Joshua Levy Katz Cohen		John Hilbert Helbert [Israel]	Marylebone, London	
30533	Helbert [Israel]	Frederick John Herbert	1829	Marylebone, London	John Hilbert Helbert [Israel]	Adeline Cohen	Sarah Magdalen Lane	Marylebone, London	Indian Army
30530	Helbert [Israel]	John Hilbert	1793	?, London	Azreal		Adeline Cohen	Marylebone, London	stockbroker
7495	Helbert [Israel]	Lionel Herbert	1817	?, London	John Hilbert Helbert [Israel]	Adeline Cohen	Amelia Mozley	Marylebone, London	stockbroker
30532	Helbert [Israel]	Lydia	1819	?, London	John Hilbert Helbert [Israel]	Adeline Cohen		Marylebone, London	
11845	Hendle	Joseph	1817	Trieste, Italy				Whitechapel, London	chief clerk to coffee + sugar importer

ID	surname	given names	born	birthplace	father	mother	spouse 1	1851 residence	1851 occupation
12854	Hendriks	Aaron	1783	Aldgate, London	Chaim Gakesh		Ann Mosely	Spitalfields, London	undertaker to the Great Synagogue
12855	Hendriks	Ann	1798	Aldgate, London	Moshe Gykerla Mosely		Aaron Hendriks	Spitalfields, London	
12856	Hendriks	Charles	1827	Whitechapel, London	Aaron Hendriks	Ann Mosely		Spitalfields, London	shopman
7451	Hendriks	Ellen	1835	Whitechapel, London	Aaron Hendriks	Ann Mosely	Alfred (Abraham) Ellis Harris	Spitalfields, London	dressmaker
12857	Hendriks	Jane	1830	Whitechapel, London	Aaron Hendriks	Ann Mosely		Spitalfields, London	
12860	Hendriks	Louisa	1839	Whitechapel, London	Aaron Hendriks	Ann Mosely	Alfred Jacobson	Spitalfields, London	scholar
12858	Hendriks	Priscilla	1833	Whitechapel, London	Aaron Hendriks	Ann Mosely	Benjamin Levy	Spitalfields, London	dressmaker
12634	Hennesky	Joseph R	1820	?, Poland				Plymouth, Devon	traveller (with jewellery box)
20818	Henriques	Arthur (Abraham) Quixano	1836	?, London	David Quixano Henriques	Rebecca de Menahem Naphtali	Isabel Strauss	Marylebone, London	scholar
21680	Henriques	David Nunes	1793	?, Jamaica, West Indies	Abraham Nunes Henriques	Mary Ann (Miriam) (?)		Islington, London	fundholder
20816	Henriques	David Quixano	1804	Jamaica, West Indies	Abraham Quixano Henriques		Rebecca de Menahem Naphtali	Marylebone, London	merchant
6710	Henriques	David Quixano	1851	Marylebone, London	Jacob Quixano Henriques	Elizabeth Waley	Agnes Charlotte Lucas	Marylebone, London	
20819	Henriques	Edward Micholls (Menahem) Quixano	1837	?, London	David Quixano Henriques	Rebecca de Menahem Naphtali	Rose Emily Straus	Marylebone, London	scholar
20821	Henriques	Elizabeth L	1822	Middlesex, London	Solomon Jacob Waley	Rachel Hort	Jacob Quixano Henriques	Marylebone, London	
5212	Henriques	Elizabeth Mary	1807	Bristol	(?)		Moses Quixano Henriques	Cheltenham, Gloucestershire	
31180	Henriques	Grace Rachel	1834	?, Jamaica, West Indies	Moses Quixano Henriques	Elizabeth Mary (?)		Cheltenham, Gloucestershire	
20820	Henriques	Jacob Quixano	1811	Spanish Town, Jamaica, West Indies	Abraham Quixano Henriques		Elizabeth Waley	Marylebone, London	merchant
20822	Henriques	Julian Quixano	1849	Marylebone, London	Jacob Quixano Henriques	Elizabeth Waley		Marylebone, London	
21681	Henriques	Mary Ann (Miriam) Nunes	1775	?, Jamaica, West Indies	(?)		Abraham Nunes Henriques	Islington, London	fundholder
21682	Henriques	Matilda Nunes	1802	Kingston, Jamaica, West Indies	Abraham Nunes Henriques	Mary Ann (Miriam) (?)		Islington, London	fundholder
24161	Henriques	Moritz Bernhard	1824	Copenhagen, Denmark			Kezia Hassell	Euston, London	upholsterer
5211	Henriques	Moses Quixano	1800	?, Jamaica, West Indies			Elizabeth Mary (?)	Cheltenham, Gloucestershire	librarian + bookseller
20817	Henriques	Rebecca	1815	?, London	Menahem Naphtali		David Quixano Henriques	Marylebone, London	
31181	Henriques	William Abraham Luddington	1850	Cheltenham, Gloucestershire	Moses Quixano Henriques	Elizabeth Mary (?)		Cheltenham, Gloucestershire	
8859	Henry	Abigail	1818	Aldgate, London	Joseph Henry	Esther Garcia	David Nunes Cardozo	Aldgate, London	fruiterer's assistant
8857	Henry	Abraham	1819	Aldgate, London	Joseph Henry	Esther Garcia		Aldgate, London	fruiterer's assistant
2919	Henry	Alexander	1825	Whitechapel, London	Abraham Henry	Emma Lyon		Bloomsbury, London	commercial traveller for importer + dealer in foreign and british fancy goods
2911	Henry	Alexander George	1834	City, London	George Henry	Kate Lyon		Bloomsbury, London	clerk in foreign warehouse

ID	surname	given names	born	birthplace	father	mother	spouse 1	1851 residence	1851 occupation
8856	Henry	Amelia?	1816	Aldgate, London	Joseph Henry	Esther Garcia		Aldgate, London	fruiterer's assistant
19985	Henry	Ann	1839	Clerkenwell, London	(?) Henry			Southwark, London	
8858	Henry	Barnet	1821	Aldgate, London	Joseph Henry	Esther Garcia		Aldgate, London	fruiterer's assistant
12499	Henry	Benjamin	1832	?, Poland				Kingsbridge, Devon	traveller in jewellery
15275	Henry	Bilha Lindo	1836	?, London	Edward (Elias) Lindo Henry	Sarah de David Abarbanel Lindo	Benjamin Lindo	Shoreditch, London	
2922	Henry	Charles	1823	City, London	Abraham Henry	Emma Lyon	Eliza Andrews	Manchester	
14746	Henry	Coleman	1846	Aldgate, London	Henry Henry	Rachael Isaacs		Spitalfields, London	scholar
15277	Henry	David Lindo	1851	?Shoreditch, London	Edward (Elias) Lindo Henry	Sarah de David Abarbanel Lindo	Rebecca Henry	Shoreditch, London	
19984	Henry	Deborah	1799	Finsbury, London	Nathan Henry	Mary (?)		Southwark, London	
14742	Henry	Deborah	1830	Spitalfields, London	Henry Henry	Rachael Isaacs	Jacob Myers	Spitalfields, London	cap maker
12378	Henry	Dora	1826	?, Germany	(?)		Isaac Henry	North Shields, Tyne & Wear	
15273	Henry	Edward (Elias) Lindo	1810	?Kent	Levi Abraham		Sarah de David Abarbanel Lindo	Shoreditch, London	merchant
2925	Henry	Elise	1836	City, London	George Henry	Kate Lyon		Bloomsbury, London	
21618	Henry	Emily	1850	Middlesex, London	Richard Loew Henry	Rebecca Lyon		Islington, London	
155	Henry	Emma	1788	Portsmouth, Hampshire	Solomon Lyon	Rachel Hart	Abraham Henry	Bloomsbury, London	annuitant
8855	Henry	Esther	1787	Aldgate, London	Abraham Garcia		Joseph Henry	Aldgate, London	
8864	Henry	Esther	1830	Aldgate, London	Joseph Henry	Esther Garcia		Aldgate, London	fruiterer's assistant
5963	Henry	Esther	1838	Shoreditch, London	Edward (Elias) Lindo Henry	Sarah de David Abarbanel Lindo	Isaac A Joseph	Shoreditch, London	boarding school pupil
10162	Henry	Eve	1791	Spitalfields, London	(?)		(?) Henry	Elephant & Castle, London	householder
19986	Henry	Eve	1840	Westminster, London	(?) Henry			Southwark, London	
8861	Henry	Fanny	1821	Aldgate, London	Joseph Henry	Esther Garcia		Aldgate, London	fruiterer's assistant
9759	Henry	Fiedler	1844	Bristol				Kew, London	boarding school pupil
162	Henry	George	1803	Ramsgate, Kent	Levi Abraham	Elizabeth Moses	Kate Lyon	Bloomsbury, London	clerk to insurance company
14739	Henry	Henry	1797	Aldgate, London	Isaac Henry		Rachael Isaacs	Spitalfields, London	general dealer
30491	Henry	Henry	1814	Mogilev Oblast, Belarus	Phineas Henry		Ann Alice Milman	Manchester	
12377	Henry	Isaac	1827	?, Germany			Dora (?)	North Shields, Tyne & Wear	glazier
8863	Henry	Isaac	1829	Aldgate, London	Joseph Henry	Esther Garcia		Aldgate, London	fruiterer's assistant
29892	Henry	Jane	1791	City, London	(?)		Solomon Henry	Wapping, London	
5379	Henry	Jemima Lindo	1845	Finsbury, London	Edward Henry	Sarah de David Abarbanel	Samuel de Sola	Shoreditch, London	
14743	Henry	John	1835	Aldgate, London	Henry Henry	Rachael Isaacs	Amelia Levy	Spitalfields, London	general dealer
8854	Henry	Joseph	1790	Aldgate, London	Moshe Cakbyt		Esther Garcia	Aldgate, London	fruiterer
14741	Henry	Judah (Lewis)	1828	Aldgate, London	Henry Henry	Rachael Isaacs	Rosetta Hart	Spitalfields, London	journeyman tailor
161	Henry	Kate	1807	Chelsea, London	Solomon Lyon	Rachel Hart	George Henry	Bloomsbury, London	
13971	Henry	Leah	1776	Cork, Ireland	(?)		(?) Henry	Manchester	draper's widow
19983	Henry	Mary	1766	Aldgate, London			Nathan Henry	Southwark, London	
29893	Henry	Michael	1821	Middlesex, London	Solomon Henry	Jane (?)		Wapping, London	cigar business
2921	Henry	Michael	1830	Kennington, London	Abraham Henry	Emma Lyon		Bloomsbury, London	clerk at Patent Office

ID	surname	given names	born	birthplace	father	mother	spouse 1	1851 residence	1851 occupation
15900	Henry	Miriam Eliza	1837	Liverpool	Michael Henry		David Lindo	Hackney, London	boarding school pupil
8860	Henry	Moses	1823	Aldgate, London	Joseph Henry	Esther Garcia	Martha Gracia	Aldgate, London	fruiterer's assistant
12380	Henry	Moses	1850	North Shields, Tyne & Wear	Isaac Henry	Dora (?)		North Shields, Tyne & Wear	
19982	Henry	Nathan	1767	Aldgate, London			Mary (?)	Southwark, London	iron dealer
14747	Henry	Philip	1848	Aldgate, London	Henry Henry	Rachael Isaacs		Spitalfields, London	
14317	Henry	Phineas	1788	Mogilev, Belarus [Podaloc, Russia]				Manchester	merchant
14740	Henry	Rachael	1806	Aldgate, London	Yehuda Isaacs		Henry Henry	Spitalfields, London	
2926	Henry	Rachel Isabel	1835	Finsbury, London	George Henry	Kate Lyon		Bloomsbury, London	
2916	Henry	Rebecca	1830	Bridgetown, Barbados, W Indies	Hart Lyon	Sarah Miriam Mendes da Costa	Richard Loew Henry	Islington, London	
2920	Henry	Richard Loew	1819	Whitechapel, London	Abraham Henry	Emma Lyon	Rebecca Lyon	Islington, London	
15276	Henry	Rosa	1839	?, London	Edward (Elias) Lindo Henry	Sarah de David Abarbanel Lindo		Shoreditch, London	
26225	Henry	Samuel	1831	?Poland [Friezgrod]				Aldgate, London	tailor
14744	Henry	Samuel	1837	Aldgate, London	Henry Henry	Rachael Isaacs		Spitalfields, London	
2924	Henry	Saphira (Zipporah)	1822	City, London	Abraham Henry	Emma Lyon	Solomon Lindo	Bloomsbury, London	
12379	Henry	Sarah	1848	North Shields, Tyne & Wear	Isaac Henry	Dora (?)		North Shields, Tyne & Wear	
14748	Henry	Sarah	1849	Spitalfields, London	Henry Henry	Rachael Isaacs		Spitalfields, London	
15274	Henry	Sarah Lindo	1814	?, London	David Abarbanel Lindo	Sarah de Abraham Mocatta	Edward (Elias) Lindo Henry	Shoreditch, London	
14745	Henry	Simon	1843	Aldgate, London	Henry Henry	Rachael Isaacs	Harriet Hannah Saunders	Spitalfields, London	scholar
29891	Henry	Solomon	1787	?, Germany			Jane (?)	Wapping, London	watchmaker
8862	Henry	Sophia	1827	Aldgate, London	Joseph Henry	Esther Garcia		Aldgate, London	fruiterer's assistant
21209	Henry	Tamar	1763	?, London	(?)		Isaac Henry	Spitalfields, London	
30937	Hepper	Emanuel	1831	?, Germany				Hull, Yorkshire	travelling jeweller
14961	Herbert	Esther S	1837	?, London	(?) Herbert			Bethnal Green, London	boarding school pupil
18602	Herbert	Georgiana Eleanor (Sarah)	1822	Middlesex, London	(?) Herbert		Solomon Marcus Schiller-Szinessy	Ross-on-Wye, Herefordshire	governess
14979	Herbert	Margaret	1841	Liverpool	(?) Herbert			Bethnal Green, London	boarding school pupil
15386	Herbertman	Bezaliel	1818	?, Poland [?, Russia Poland]				Waterloo, London	student
17169	Herch	Chum	1833	Margonin, Poland				Newcastle Upon Tyne	jeweller
1081	Herman	Abraham David	1828	Konin, Poland	Samuel Herman	Frances (?)	Esther Cohen	Falmouth, Cornwall	bookbinder
1080	Herman	Frances	1800	Wejherowo, Poland [Neustadt, Germany]			Samuel Herman	Falmouth, Cornwall	
14406	Herman	Jacob	1820	abroad				Salford, Lancashire	clock maker
26230	Herman	Jacob	1838	?Germany [Herzogthum]				Aldgate, London	bag maker
25625	Herman	Michael	1780	?, Germany				Dublin, Ireland	in receipt of allowance from congregation
1083	Herman	Phoebe	1841	Babiak, Poland	Samuel Herman	Frances (?)	Harris Cohen	Falmouth, Cornwall	
1082	Herman	Rose	1831	Konin, Poland	Samuel Herman	Frances (?)		Falmouth, Cornwall	
1079	Herman	Samuel	1802	Konin, Poland			Frances (?)	Falmouth, Cornwall	rabbi
16974	Heron	Debora	1842	Walworth, London	(?Henry) Heron			Hammersmith, London	boarding school pupil

ID	surname	given names	born	birthplace	father	mother	spouse 1	1851 residence	1851 occupation
12630	Herris	Jacob	1836	?, Poland				Birmingham	glazier
7136	Herschell	Ridley Haim	1807	Strzelno, Poland	Judah Herschell	Ghetal (?)	Helen Skirving Mowbray	Marylebone, London	independent minister of [---] chapel
23128	Herschorn	Kate	1829	Bethnal Green, London	John Jonas		Maurice Herschorn	City, London	
23130	Herschorn	Matilda	1850	City, London	Maurice Herschorn	Kate Jonas		City, London	
23127	Herschorn	Maurice	1813	?, Germany	Seiskind Herschorn		Kate Jonas	City, London	importer of French flowers
23129	Herschorn	Sidney	1848	City, London	Maurice Herschorn	Kate Jonas		City, London	
16959	Herson	Mary	1834	Camberwell, London	(?) Herson			Hammersmith, London	school assistant
23533	Hertsfeld	Caroline	1833	?, London	Solomon Hertsfeld	(?)		Liverpool	
23534	Hertsfeld	Mary Ann	1835	?, London	Solomon Hertsfeld	(?)		Liverpool	
23532	Hertsfeld	Solomon	1810	Schiedan, Holland			(?)	Liverpool	dentist
19924	Hertz	Amelia	1809	Frankfurt, Germany	(?)		Bram Hertz	Soho, London	
19923	Hertz	Bram	1794	Hanover, Germany			Amelia (?)	Soho, London	diamond merchant
19925	Hertz	Clara	1836	Soho, London	Bram Hertz	Amelia (?)		Soho, London	
7137	Hertz	Fanny	1830	Hanover, Germany	Bram Hertz	Amelia (?)	William David Hertz	Soho, London	feminist, educationist + positivist
26226	Hertz	Jacob	1826	Cracow, Poland				Aldgate, London	tailor
14462	Hertz	James	1818	?, Germany	Marcus Hertz		Tryphena Esther Da Costa	Manchester	calico printer
19926	Hertz	James P	1846	Soho, London	Bram Hertz	Amelia (?)		Soho, London	
21643	Hertz	Tryphena Esther	1828	?, London	Solomon Gomes Da Costa	Canandla (Mary) de Judah Samuel	James Hertz	Manchester	
7138	Hertz	William David	1825	Hamburg, Germany			Fanny Hertz	Bradford, Yorkshire	yarn merchany
14352	Hertzberger	Karl	1817	?, Germany				Manchester	tailor
17291	Herzberg	Joseph	1825	?, Russia				Spitalfields, London	tailor
22118	Herzfeld	Louis	1831	?, Hungary				Whitechapel, London	tailor
14397	Hess	Alexander James	1817	?, Germany				Manchester	
12258	Hess	Augustus	1818	Frankfurt-am-Main, Germany			Rebecca (?)	Finsbury, London	MD in general practice
23586	Hess	Esther	1815	Liverpool	Israel Hess	Rosetta (?)		Liverpool	
12261	Hess	Ferdinand	1849	Frankfurt-am-Main, Germany	Augustus Hess	Rebecca (?)		Finsbury, London	
23580	Hess	Joseph	1794	Liverpool			Sarah Yates	Liverpool	engraver
23585	Hess	Miriam	1811	Liverpool	Israel Hess	Rosetta (?)		Liverpool	
18090	Hess	Morris	1822	Merzig, Saarland, Germany	Solomon Hess		Kate Cantor	?Spitalfields, London	
14396	Hess	Nathan	1815	?, Germany				Manchester	merchant
12260	Hess	Pauline	1847	Frankfurt-am-Main, Germany	Augustus Hess	Rebecca (?)	Emil Meyerstein	Finsbury, London	
23588	Hess	Rachel	1818	Liverpool	Israel Hess	Rosetta (?)		Liverpool	
23587	Hess	Ralph	1813	Liverpool	Israel Hess	Rosetta (?)		Liverpool	merchant
12259	Hess	Rebecca	1820	Frankfurt-am-Main, Germany	(?)		Augustus Hess	Finsbury, London	
23583	Hess	Rosetta	1772	Liverpool	(?)		Israel Hess	Liverpool	proprietor of houses
18089	Hess	Samuel	1824	Merzig, Saarland, Germany	Solomon Hess		Alice Cantor	Spitalfields, London	cap peak manufacturer empl 5
7660	Hess	Samuel Yates	1822	Liverpool			Julia Samuel	Liverpool	engraver
23581	Hess	Sarah	1792	Lichfield, Staffordshire	(?) Yates		Joseph Hess	Liverpool	
23584	Hess	Sarah	1808	Liverpool	(?) Hess	Rosetta (?)		Liverpool	
23589	Hess	Sophia	1821	Liverpool	(?) Hess	Rosetta (?)		Liverpool	

ID	surname	given names	born	birthplace	father	mother	spouse 1	1851 residence	1851 occupation
14377	Hesse	Barbara	1786	?, Germany [?, Prussia]	(?)		Nathan Hesse	Salford, Lancashire	
14372	Hesse	Clare	1806	?, Germany	Nathan Hesse	Barbara (?)	Clare	Salford, Lancashire	
14371	Hesse	David	1810	Cologne, Germany	(?)		David Hesse	Salford, Lancashire	shirt manufacturer
14374	Hesse	Esther	1838	Manchester	David Hesse	Clare (?)	Isaac Heine	Salford, Lancashire	
14373	Hesse	Max	1836	?, Germany	David Hesse	Clare (?)	Emily Samuel	Salford, Lancashire	
14376	Hesse	Nathan	1780	?, Germany [?, Prussia]			Barbara (?)	Salford, Lancashire	retired rabbi
14375	Hesse	Rosetta	1841	Manchester	David Hesse	Clare (?)		Salford, Lancashire	
26403	Hesselburgh	Elkan	1820	Amsterdam, Holland			Julia (?)	Aldgate, London	cigar maker
26406	Hesselburgh	Henry	1847	Amsterdam, Holland	Elkan Hesselburgh	Julia (?)		Aldgate, London	
26404	Hesselburgh	Julia	1818	Amsterdam, Holland	(?)		Elkan Hesselburgh	Aldgate, London	
26407	Hesselburgh	Mary	1851	?Aldgate, London	Elkan Hesselburgh	Julia (?)		Aldgate, London	
26405	Hesselburgh	Michael	1845	Amsterdam, Holland	Elkan Hesselburgh	Julia (?)		Aldgate, London	
26689	Hestermann	Matilda	1827	Frankfurt-am-Main, Germany	(?) Hestermann			Manchester	governess
23674	Heyman	Caralloline	1850	Liverpool	Lewis Heyman	Sarah Elias		Liverpool	
23673	Heyman	Cicilla	1849	Liverpool	Lewis Heyman	Sarah Elias		Liverpool	
23670	Heyman	Ellis	1841	Liverpool	Lewis Heyman	Sarah Elias		Liverpool	
23671	Heyman	Hanny	1843	Liverpool	Lewis Heyman	Sarah Elias		Liverpool	
29324	Heyman	Henry	1842	?, Poland [?, Prussia]	Moses Heyman	Marian (?)		Whitechapel, London	scholar
23672	Heyman	Henry	1846	Liverpool	Lewis Heyman	Sarah Elias		Liverpool	
23668	Heyman	Lewis	1806	?, Poland [?, Prussia]	Heyman Heyman		Sarah Elias	Liverpool	pawnbroker empl 2
29323	Heyman	Marian	1816	?, Holland	(?)		Moses Heyman	Whitechapel, London	
29322	Heyman	Moses	1818	?, Poland [?, Prussia]			Marian (?)	Whitechapel, London	clothier
23669	Heyman	Sarah	1816	?, London	Elias Elias		Lewis Heyman	Liverpool	
7171	Heymann	Henrietta	1814	?Germany	A--- Hirsch		Lewis Heymann	Nottingham, Nottinghamshire	
2697	Heymann	Lewis	1802	Teterow, Mecklenburg, Germany	Gabriel Heymann	Nascha (?)	Henrietta Hirsch	Nottingham, Nottinghamshire	lace merchant + manufacturer + alderman
30438	Heymanson	Rebecca	1850	Holborn, London	William Heymanson	Sophia Woolfe		Stepney, London	
30437	Heymanson	Sophia	1824	Aldgate, London	Benjamin Woolfe		William Heymanson	Stepney, London	
30436	Heymanson	William	1826	?, Germany	Abraham Heymanson		Sophia Woolfe	Stepney, London	stationer
28342	Hiam	Catherine	1827	Whitechapel, London	(?Hyam Hyams)	Elizabeth Benjamin		Aldgate, London	fur worker
28341	Hiam	Elizabeth	1805	Whitechapel, London	(?Isaac) Benjamin	Francess (?)		Aldgate, London	dealer in general
13784	Hiam	Joseph	1791	?, Poland				Manchester	lace weaver
29671	Hiams	Abraham	1803	?, Germany			Sarah (?)	Spitalfields, London	hawker
29673	Hiams	Mary	1849	Aldgate, London	Abraham Hiams	Sarah (?)		Spitalfields, London	
29672	Hiams	Sarah	1832	?, Germany	(?)		Abraham Hiams	Spitalfields, London	
2270	Hickman	Fanny	1840	Leeds, Yorkshire	Marcus Hickman	Sarah (?)	Morris Cohen	Leeds, Yorkshire	
2269	Hickman	Hannah	1838	Leeds, Yorkshire	Marcus Hickman	Sarah (?)	Henry Levy	Leeds, Yorkshire	
2271	Hickman	Isaac	1841	Leeds, Yorkshire	Marcus Hickman	Sarah (?)		Leeds, Yorkshire	
2274	Hickman	Joseph	1847	Leeds, Yorkshire	Marcus Hickman	Sarah (?)	Harriet (?)	Leeds, Yorkshire	
2267	Hickman	Marcus	1811	?, Poland			Sarah (?)	Leeds, Yorkshire	fancy goods dealer, shopkeeper
2273	Hickman	Pauline	1845	Leeds, Yorkshire	Marcus Hickman	Sarah (?)	Samuel Jacob Jordain	Leeds, Yorkshire	
2275	Hickman	Samson	1851	Leeds, Yorkshire	Marcus Hickman	Sarah (?)	Rachael (?)	Leeds, Yorkshire	
2272	Hickman	Samuel	1843	Leeds, Yorkshire	Marcus Hickman	Sarah (?)	Rebecca Blashker	Leeds, Yorkshire	

ID	surname	given names	born	birthplace	father	mother	spouse 1	1851 residence	1851 occupation
2268	Hickman	Sarah	1818	?, Poland [?, Prussia]			Marcus Hickman	Leeds, Yorkshire	
14942	Hidderheimer	Rosetta	1835	?, Northumberland	(?) Hidderheimer			Bethnal Green, London	boarding school pupil
18075	Higham	Sarah J	1830	Paddington, London	(?) Higham			Southwark, London	cook
4541	Higleston	Joseph	1829	?, Poland				Birmingham	slipper maker
1800	Higletough	Abraham	1826	?, Poland				Merthyr Tydfil, Wales	glazier
18276	Hill	Abraham	1830	Cracow, Poland				Salisbury, Wiltshire	traveller in jewellery
14329	Hiller	Albert	1849	Manchester	Harry Hiller	Caroline (?)		Manchester	
14327	Hiller	Caroline	1826	Manchester	(?)		Harry Hiller	Manchester	
14326	Hiller	Harry	1810	?, Germany			Caroline (?)	Manchester	commission agent
14328	Hiller	Harry C	1847	Manchester	Harry Hiller	Caroline (?)		Manchester	
14330	Hiller	William	1850	Manchester	Harry Hiller	Caroline (?)		Manchester	
13663	Hilsbach	Edward	1850	?, London	Joseph Hilsbach	Rosa (?)		Manchester	
13664	Hilsbach	Henry	1851	Manchester	Joseph Hilsbach	Rosa (?)		Manchester	
13661	Hilsbach	Joseph	1821	Hamburg, Germany			Rosa (?)	Manchester	tobacconist
13662	Hilsbach	Rosa	1827	Rotterdam, Holland	(?)		Joseph Hillsbach	Manchester	
8375	Hime	Benjamin	1795	Liverpool	Humphrey Hime	Sarah Levy	Ann Cooper Coulthard	Manchester	music dealer + composer
8372	Hime	Benjamin	1828	Liverpool	Maurice Edward Hime	Jane Davis		?Liverpool	
8320	Hime	Charles Edward	1829	Liverpool	Edward Elias Hime	Priscilla Elkin		Liverpool	pianoforte teacher
8315	Hime	Edward Elias	1782	?, London	Humphrey Hime	Sarah Levy	Priscilla Elkin	Liverpool	music seller
8369	Hime	Edward Lawrence	1823	Liverpool	Maurice Edward Hime	Jane Davis	Susanna Sarah Sadler	?Liverpool	composer + actor + singer
8370	Hime	Esther	1825	Liverpool	Maurice Edward Hime	Jane Davis	John Evans	Liverpool	governess
8371	Hime	Harriett (Hatty) Louisa	1826	Liverpool	Maurice Edward Hime	Jane Davis		Liverpool	governess
8376	Hime	Henry	1807	Liverpool	Humphrey Hime	Sarah Levy	Jane Baldwin	Birkenhead, Cheshire	attorney
7665	Hime	Henry Edward	1820	Liverpool	Edward Elias Hime	Priscilla Elkin		Liverpool	music seller
8368	Hime	Henry Joseph	1822	Liverpool	Maurice Edward Hime	Jane Davis	Ann Wilkinson	Liverpool	watchmaker
8373	Hime	James Walwyn	1830	Liverpool	Maurice Edward Hime	Jane Davis	Rachel Rosenthal	?Liverpool	
8367	Hime	Jane	1799	Middlesex, London	(?) Davis		Maurice Edward Hime	Liverpool	annuitant
8317	Hime	Julia	1811	Liverpool	Edward Elias Hime	Priscilla Elkin		Liverpool	
8316	Hime	Priscilla	1793	Kingston, Jamaica, West Indies	Solomon Elkin		Edward Elias Hime	Liverpool	
8319	Hime	Rosa	1824	Liverpool	Edward Elias Hime	Priscilla Elkin		Liverpool	
8322	Hime	Sarah	1766	?, London	(?) Levy		Humphrey Hime	Liverpool	
8318	Hime	Sarah Ann	1818	Liverpool	Edward Elias Hime	Priscilla Elkin		Liverpool	
20871	Hime	Sarah Jane	1834	Liverpool	Maurice Edward Hime	Jane Davis		Liverpool	governess
8321	Hime	Sophia	1830	Liverpool	Edward Elias Hime	Priscilla Elkin		Liverpool	
8323	Hime	William Henry	1831	Liverpool	Edward Hime	Priscilla Elkin	Clara (?)	?Liverpool	
5058	Himes	Annie	1827	?, London				Portsmouth, Hampshire	
19243	Himes	Barnett	1850	Whitechapel, London	Edward S Himes	Emma Moss		Whitechapel, London	
19241	Himes	Edward S	1818	Portsmouth, Hampshire	Barnet Himes		Emma Moss	Whitechapel, London	tailor
19242	Himes	Emma	1824	Portsmouth, Hampshire	Joseph Moss		Edward S Himes	Whitechapel, London	
8793	Himes	Mary	1765	Aldgate, London	(?) Myers		(?) Himes	Aldgate, London	
21650	Hinton	Edmund Jubilee	1845	Marylebone, London	Edmund Hinton	Esther Emanuel	Isabella Louisa Lewis	Mayfair, London	
21619	Hinton	Esther	1821	Southwark, London	Uzziel Emanuel	Jane Solomonson	Edmund Hinton	Mayfair, London	

ID	surname	given names	born	birthplace	father	mother	spouse 1	1851 residence	1851 occupation
21648	Hinton	Louisa	1849	Marylebone, London	Edmund Hinton	Esther Emanuel	John Thomas Ferry	Mayfair, London	
21649	Hinton	Lyon (Lionel)	1850	Marylebone, London	Edmund Hinton	Esther Emanuel	Mary Ann Pope	Mayfair, London	
2454	Hirchfield (Hirschfield)	Hane	1828	?, Poland [?, Prussia]			Heiman Hirchfield (Hirschfield)	Hull, Yorkshire	
2139	Hirchfield (Hirschfield)	Heiman	1825	?, Poland			Hane (?)	Hull, Yorkshire	glazier
2455	Hirchfield (Hirschfield)	Louis	1850	Hull, Yorkshire	Heiman Hirchfield (Hirschfield)	Hane (?)		Hull, Yorkshire	
31218	Hirsch	Henrietta	1833	Teterow, Germany	(?) Hirsch			Matlock, Derbyshire	
16289	Hirsch	Hermann Anselm	1820	Mecklenburg Schwerin, Germany			Betsy (?)	Dundee, Scotland	linen merchant
14994	Hirsch	Mirels	1829	?, Poland [?, Prussian Poland]				Bethnal Green, London	bookbinder
4542	Hirsch	Solly	1830	?, Germany				Birmingham	cigar maker
13843	Hirsch	Susman	1823	?, Poland [?, Prussia]				Manchester	warehouseman
23040	Hirschel	David	1786	Wroclaw, Poland [Preslau, Prussia]	Hirsch		Sarah Ansell	Aldgate, London	general dealer
23041	Hirschel	Sarah	1788	City, London	Dayan Zalman		David Hirschel	Aldgate, London	
20800	Hirschfield	Elizabeth (Betsey)	1848	Whitechapel, London	Henry (Harris) Hirschfield	Rachel Raphael		Whitechapel, London	
20798	Hirschfield	Henry (Harris)	1815	?, Germany	Eliezer Hirschfield		Rachael Raphael	Whitechapel, London	traveller
20801	Hirschfield	Maria	1850	Whitechapel, London	Henry (Harris) Hirschfield	Rachel Raphael		Whitechapel, London	
20799	Hirschfield	Rachel	1820	Portsmouth, Hampshire	Ralph Raphael	Leah Hart	Henry (Harris) Hirschfield	Whitechapel, London	
29635	Hirsh	Jule	1827	?, Poland [?, Prussia]				Aldgate, London	
4543	Hischel	Louis	1826	?, Poland			Reschen (Gretchen?)	Birmingham	tailor
4544	Hischel	Reschen (?Gretchen)	1827	?, Poland [?, Prussia]			Louis Hischel	Birmingham	
8061	Hobinstock	Clara	1823	Poznan, Poland [Posen, Prussia]	(?) Cohen		Joseph Woolf Hobinstock	Guernsey, Channel Islands	
8062	Hobinstock	Gustavus	1847	Halle, Germany	Joseph Woolf Hobinstock	Clara Cohen	?	Guernsey, Channel Islands	
18388	Hobinstock	Hannah	1821	?, Poland	Hyam Hobinstock	Phoebe Cohen		Aldgate, London	
18386	Hobinstock	Hyam	1793	?, Poland			Phoebe Cohen	Aldgate, London	merchant
8060	Hobinstock	Joseph Woolf	1825	?, Poland	Hyam Hobinstock	Phoebe Cohen	Clara Cohen	Guernsey, Channel Islands	hatter
8063	Hobinstock	Julius	1851	Guernsey, Channel Islands	Joseph Woolf Hobinstock	Clara Cohen	Rachel Braham	Guernsey, Channel Islands	
8057	Hobinstock	Leah Catherine	1835	?, Poland	Hyam Hobinstock	Phoebe Cohen	Levi Woolf	Aldgate, London	
8058	Hobinstock	Louis	1848	Shoreditch, London	Joseph Woolf Hobinstock	Clara Cohen	Emilie Woolf	Guernsey, Channel Islands	
18387	Hobinstock	Phoebe	1793	?, Poland	(?) Cohen		Hyam Hobinstock	Aldgate, London	
6479	Hocking	Martha	1829	Bodmin, Cornwall	(?) Hocking		Henry Woolf	?Cornwall	
11801	Hoelzel	Herman	1812	?, Hungary			Mina (?)	Whitechapel, London	Minister of the Synagogue
11802	Hoelzel	Mina	1821	?, Poland [?, Prussia]	(?)		Herman Hoelzel	Whitechapel, London	
26271	Hoff	Dore	1817	?, Poland [?, Prussia]	(?)		Michael Hoff	Aldgate, London	
26275	Hoff	Fanny	1850	?, London	Michael Hoff	Dore (?)		Aldgate, London	
26274	Hoff	Hane	1848	?, Poland [?, Prussia]	Michael Hoff	Dore (?)		Aldgate, London	

ID	surname	given names	born	birthplace	father	mother	spouse 1	1851 residence	1851 occupation
26270	Hoff	Michael	1819	?, Poland [?, Prussia]			Dore (?)	Aldgate, London	tailor
26273	Hoff	Reuben	1843	?, Poland [?, Prussia]	Michael Hoff	Dore (?)		Aldgate, London	scholar
26272	Hoff	Riekie	1843	?, Poland [?, Prussia]	Michael Hoff	Dore (?)		Aldgate, London	scholar
15027	Hoffman	Anne	1823	City, London	(?) Davis	Hannah (?)	Edward Hoffman	Bethnal Green, London	
15029	Hoffman	Anne L	1845	Bethnal Green, London	Edward Hoffman	Anne Davis		Bethnal Green, London	
15026	Hoffman	Edward	1817	Bethnal Green, London			Ann Davis	Bethnal Green, London	oil + colourman and proprietor of houses
15028	Hoffman	Edward J	1847	Bethnal Green, London	Edward Hoffman	Anne Davis		Bethnal Green, London	
20732	Hoffman	Susan	1835	Southwark, London	(?) Hoffman			Whitechapel, London	house servant
4411	Hoffnung	Abraham	1833	Berlin, Germany				Birmingham	clerk
1038	Hoffnung	Bertha C	1841	Exeter, Devon	Samuel Hoffnung	Caroline (?)	George Garcia Wolf	Exeter, Devon	
1037	Hoffnung	Caroline	1813	?, Poland			Samuel Hoffnung	Exeter, Devon	
1036	Hoffnung	Samuel	1810	?, Poland			Caroline (?)	Exeter, Devon	synagogue reader
16298	Holdheim	?	1820	?, Germany				Dundee, Scotland	
916	Hollander	Lewis Adolphus	1775	Amsterdam, Holland	Abraham Yerovshulama of Amsterdam		Sarah Gompertz	De Beauvoir, London	annuitant
15225	Hollander	Samuel	1781	Berlin, Germany	Yechiel		Phebe Abrahams	Shoreditch, London	retired merchant
2696	Hollander	Solomon	1820	Liverpool				Nottingham, Nottinghamshire	watchmaker
28091	Holsman	Caspar	1827	?, Switzerland				Spitalfields, London	tailor
2140	Holt	Louis (Lewis)	1824	?, Poland [?, Prussia]			Janette (?)	Hull, Yorkshire	hawker of jewellery
27994	Holtman	Manuel	1798	Poznan, Poland [Posen, Germany]			(?)	Spitalfields, London	traveller
27995	Holtman	Tobias	1833	Poznan, Poland [Posen, Germany]	Manuel Holtman			Spitalfields, London	capmaker journeyman
28248	Holtz	Isadore	1839	?, Poland [?, Prussia]	Samuel Holtz	Jeanette (?)		Spitalfields, London	
28247	Holtz	Jeanette	1809	?, Poland [?, Prussia]	(?)		Samuel Holtz	Spitalfields, London	
28250	Holtz	Magnus	1845	?, Poland [?, Prussia]	Samuel Holtz	Jeanette (?)		Spitalfields, London	
28249	Holtz	Mary	1843	?, Poland [?, Prussia]	Samuel Holtz	Jeanette (?)		Spitalfields, London	
28246	Holtz	Samuel	1807	?, Poland [?, Prussia]			Jeanette (?)	Spitalfields, London	tailor
2456	Holtzman	Paul	1810	?, Russia				Hull, Yorkshire	Secretary for the Relief of Distressed Russians
14453	Holzhauer	Edward	1831	?, Russia				Manchester	merchant
29417	Horsa	Hyam	1824	Amsterdam, Holland				Spitalfields, London	cigar maker
5690	Hort	Florence	1830	Liverpool				Liverpool	
30822	Hort	Joel	1807	Liverpool				Liverpool	pencil maker
30823	Hort	Rachael	1826	Liverpool	(?) Hort			Liverpool	
22926	Horwitz	Amelia	1844	Wapping, London	Morris (Manuel) Horwitz	Hannah Hart	Joseph Wacks	Wapping, London	scholar
22924	Horwitz	Esther	1839	Wapping, London	Morris (Manuel) Horwitz	Hannah Hart		Wapping, London	scholar
22923	Horwitz	Hannah	1818	Wapping, London	Michael Hart		Morris (Manuel) Horwitz	Wapping, London	
22925	Horwitz	Michael	1842	Wapping, London	Morris (Manuel) Horwitz	Hannah Hart		Wapping, London	scholar
22922	Horwitz	Morris (Manuel)	1811	?, Poland [?, Prussia]	Abraham Hurwitz		Hannah Hart	Wapping, London	tailor
14251	Houseman	Charles	1830	?, Germany				Manchester	traveller - jewellery
22910	Houseman	Rebecca	1833	Liverpool	(?)		Woolf Houseman	Wapping, London	
22909	Houseman	Woolf	1827	Bavaria, Germany			Rebecca (?)	Wapping, London	butcher

ID	surname	given names	born	birthplace	father	mother	spouse 1	1851 residence	1851 occupation
18271	Housman	Emanuel	1790	?, Russia				Brighton, Sussex	professor of the German language and philosophy
4547	Hovins	Lewis	1827	?, Germany				Birmingham	slipper maker
18182	How	Samuel	1800	Tiverton, Devon			(?)	Mile End, London	head of House + superintendent + tutor in school
14130	Howitz	Isaac	1817	?, Hungary				Manchester	commission agent
29179	Huagman	Mark	1825	Rotterdam, Holland				Whitechapel, London	servant
2276	Hunsman	David	1830	?, Poland				Leeds, Yorkshire	hawker
2277	Hunty	Solomon	1819	?, Poland				Leeds, Yorkshire	glazier
24423	Hurwitz	Esther	1835	Whitechapel, London	Judah Hurwitz			Strand, London	
20290	Husel	Lebe	1839	?, Russia				Spitalfields, London	
13793	Hyam	Abraham	1824	Bristol				Manchester	clothier's salesman
19248	Hyam	Abraham	1850	Birmingham	Samuel Hyam	Phoebe Levy		Paddington, London	
13975	Hyam	Adeline	1841	Manchester	Benjamin Hyam	Kate (?)	Benjamin Ephraim Mosely	Manchester	scholar at home
13978	Hyam	Adolph	1849	Manchester	Benjamin Hyam	Kate (?)		Manchester	
4550	Hyam	Alfred	1850	Southampton, Hampshire	Samuel Hyam	Amelia (?)		Birmingham	
18760	Hyam	Alice Dove	1848	Euston, London	Lawrence Hyam	Catherine Levy		Euston, London	
4549	Hyam	Amelia	1827	Portsmouth, Hampshire			Samuel Hyam	Birmingham	
19246	Hyam	Arthur	1842	Birmingham	Samuel Hyam	Phoebe Levy	Orovida Bensusan	Paddington, London	
12740	Hyam	Benjamin	1810	Ipswich, Suffolk	Hyam Hyam	Hannah Lazarus	Kate (?)	Manchester	tailor + clothier
22199	Hyam	Benjamin	1817	Middlesex, London	(?) Hyam	Sarah (?)		Whitechapel, London	clothes dealer
29053	Hyam	C---	1841	Soho, London	(?) Hyam			Whitechapel, London	scholar
18759	Hyam	Catherine	1818	Bury St Edmunds, Suffolk	Nathaniel Levy		Lawrence Hyam	Euston, London	
19249	Hyam	Charles	1851	Paddington, London	Samuel Hyam	Phoebe Levy		Paddington, London	
7467	Hyam	David	1810	Ipswich, Suffolk			Hannah (?)	Bristol	clothier
7504	Hyam	David	1819	Bristol				Bristol	stationer
22098	Hyam	David	1824	City, London	Isaac Hyam	Frances Lazarus	Alice Moses	Aldgate, London	
27681	Hyam	David	1824	Aldgate, London				Aldgate, London	merchant hardware
16394	Hyam	Edward	1835	City, London	Isaac Hyam	Frances Lazarus		Aldgate, London	brush maker
13976	Hyam	Edward	1845	Manchester	Benjamin Hyam	Kate (?)		Manchester	scholar at home
13979	Hyam	Eliza	1850	Manchester	Benjamin Hyam	Kate (?)		Manchester	
7468	Hyam	Ellis	1832	Bury St Edmunds, Suffolk	Lawrence Hyam	Caroline Elias	Adelaide Emily (?)	Euston, London	outfitter
13980	Hyam	Emma	1834	Bury St Edmunds, Suffolk	(?) Hyam			Manchester	
16388	Hyam	Frances	1798	Whitechapel, London	Jacob Lazarus		Isaac Hyam	Aldgate, London	
3552	Hyam	Hannah	1773	Rochford, Essex	Moses Lazarus	Esther Davis	Hyam Hyam	Bloomsbury, London	
16810	Hyam	Hannah	1815	?, London	(?)		David Hyam	Bristol	
24393	Hyam	Henry Lewis	1825	City, London			Mary (?)	Soho, London	general dealer
3553	Hyam	Hyam	1775	Ipswich, Suffolk	Simcha of Ipswich (Simon Hyam?)		Hannah Lazarus	Bloomsbury, London	holder of railway stock
7535	Hyam	Isaac	1795	Aldgate, London	David Hyam	Sarah Shannon	Frances Lazarus	Aldgate, London	pawnbroker
24929	Hyam	Isaac	1831	?, Somerset				Bethnal Green, London	silk weaver
19247	Hyam	Isabel	1843	Birmingham	Samuel Hyam	Phoebe Levy		Paddington, London	
29052	Hyam	J---	1839	Soho, London				Whitechapel, London	scholar
13977	Hyam	Jeanette	1847	Manchester	Benjamin Hyam	Kate (?)		Manchester	scholar at home
16389	Hyam	Jeannette (Jemima)	1827	City, London	Isaac Hyam	Frances Lazarus		Aldgate, London	

ID	surname	given names	born	birthplace	father	mother	spouse 1	1851 residence	1851 occupation
20832	Hyam	Jessie	1829	City, London	Isaac Hyam	Frances Lazarus	Mark (Mordecai) Marcus	Aldgate, London	
16391	Hyam	John	1830	City, London	Isaac Hyam	Frances Lazarus		Aldgate, London	hardwareman's clerk
13802	Hyam	Joseph	1811	?Yorkshire [York Clowit]				Manchester	carter
3817	Hyam	Joseph	1848	Spitalfields, London	Solomon Hyams	Maria Levy		Spitalfields, London	scholar
13974	Hyam	Kate	1814	Middlesex, London			Benjamin Hyam	Manchester	
18764	Hyam	Lawrence	1807	Ipswich, Suffolk	Hyam Hyam	Hannah Lazarus	Caroline Elias	Euston, London	outfitter
18762	Hyam	Lewis	1850	Euston, London	Lawrence Hyam	Catherine Levy		Euston, London	
22444	Hyam	Lionel	1845	Middlesex, London				Gravesend, Kent	boarding school pupil
18761	Hyam	Louise Frances	1849	Euston, London	Lawrence Hyam	Catherine Levy	Algernon Moses [Marsden]	Euston, London	
24394	Hyam	Mary	1825	Westminster, London	(?)		Henry Lewis Hyam	Soho, London	
16813	Hyam	Montague	1843	Bristol	David Hyam	Hannah (?)		Bristol	scholar at home
16393	Hyam	Phineas	1832	City, London	Isaac Hyam	Frances Lazarus	Rebecca Abrahams [Amelia Marshall]	Aldgate, London	brush maker
19245	Hyam	Phoebe	1820	?, London	Abraham Levy		Samuel Hyam	Paddington, London	
18786	Hyam	Rachel	1831	City, London	Isaac Hyam	Frances Lazarus	Nathan Joseph	Aldgate, London	
16811	Hyam	Rachel	1837	Coventry, Warwickshire	David Hyam	Hannah (?)		Bristol	scholar at home
16812	Hyam	Ruth	1840	Bristol	David Hyam	Hannah (?)		Bristol	scholar at home
19244	Hyam	Samuel	1813	Ipswich, Suffolk	Hyam Hyam	Hannah Lazarus	Phoebe Levy	Paddington, London	tailor clothier
4548	Hyam	Samuel	1818	Liverpool			Amelia (?)	Birmingham	dyer
29051	Hyam	Solomon	1836	Clerkenewell, London				Whitechapel, London	apprentice to cigar maker
19080	Hyam [Halford]	Augustus Lawrence	1847	Bloomsbury, London	Montagu (Moses) Hyam [Halford]	Rachel Levy	Ada Levinsohn	Bloomsbury, London	
7117	Hyam [Halford]	Frederic Michael	1844	Birmingham	Samuel Hyam	Phoebe Levy	Florence St Losky	Paddington, London	
19081	Hyam [Halford]	Lewis Albert	1850	Bloomsbury, London	Montagu (Moses) Hyam [Halford]	Rachel Levy		Bloomsbury, London	
19078	Hyam [Halford]	Montagu (Moses)	1814	Ipswich, Suffolk	Hyam Hyam	Hannah Lazarus	Rachel Levy	Bloomsbury, London	merchant
19079	Hyam [Halford]	Rachel	1822	Kensington, London	(?) Levy		Montagu (Moses) Hyam [Halford]	Bloomsbury, London	
18766	Hyam [Halford]	Rebecca	1825	King's Lynn, Norfolk	(?)		Simon Hyam [Haldord]	Hornsey, London	
12742	Hyam [Halford]	Simon	1818	Colchester, Essex	Hyam Hyam	Hannah Lazarus	Rebecca (?)	Hornsey, London	merchant
8408	Hyams	?	1796	?				Newport, Isle of Wight	traveller
3811	Hyams	Abigail	1836	Whitechapel, London	Solomon Hyams	Maria Levy		Spitalfields, London	scholar
3800	Hyams	Abigail	1839	Spitalfields, London	Samuel Hyams	Sarah Phillips		Spitalfields, London	see Notes
24176	Hyams	Abraham	1846	Covent Garden, London	Hyam J Hyams	Betsy (?)		Euston, London	
11113	Hyams	Abraham	1821	Cambridge	Simon Hyams	(Judy Moses?)	Elizabeth Joseph	Aldgate, London	general dealer
16190	Hyams	Abraham	1837	Wapping, London	Henry Hyams	Julia Levy		Wapping, London	scholar
10238	Hyams	Abraham	1843	Aldgate, London	David Hyams	Hannah Barnett		Aldgate, London	scholar
17787	Hyams	Abraham	1845	Spitalfields, London	Mark (Mordecai) Hyams	Hannah Cohen	Hannah Myers	Aldgate, London	
24175	Hyams	Adelaide	1844	Covent Garden, London	Hyam J Hyams	Betsy (?)		Euston, London	
9670	Hyams	Adelaide (Adel, Addie)	1849	Spitalfields, London	Hyam Hyams	Jane Levy		Spitalfields, London	
6595	Hyams	Alexander (Sander)	1810	Aldgate, London			Esther Lazarus	Aldgate, London	general dealer
28286	Hyams	Amelia	1825	Whitechapel, London	Michael Abrahams		Hyam Hyams	Aldgate, London	
3812	Hyams	Amelia	1838	Whitechapel, London	Solomon Hyams	Maria Levy		Spitalfields, London	scholar
3993	Hyams	Amelia (Julia)	1815	Portsmouth, Hampshire	David Lazarus	Hannah Phillips	Wolf Hyams	Portsmouth, Hampshire	
8419	Hyams	Barnard	1776	?, Poland			Tobia (?)	Chichester, Sussex	jeweller

ID	surname	given names	born	birthplace	father	mother	spouse 1	1851 residence	1851 occupation
26121	Hyams	Barnett	1851	Aldgate, London	Michael Hyams	Elizabeth (Betsey) Lewis		Aldgate, London	
19392	Hyams	Barnett (Barnet, Dov Behr)	1818	Walworth, London	David Hyams		Elizabeth (Betsey) Davis	Elephant & Castle, London	rag merchant
22795	Hyams	Benjamin	1823	Finsbury, London			Rosetta (?)	Whitechapel, London	cigar maker
31003	Hyams	Benjamin	1825	?, Poland			Sophia (?)	Wolverhampton, Staffordshire	pawnbroker
24172	Hyams	Betsy	1815	?, Poland	(?)		Hyam J Hyams	Euston, London	
3819	Hyams	Betsy	1850	Spitalfields, London	Solomon Hyams	Maria Levy		Spitalfields, London	
10551	Hyams	Bloom (Flora)	1828	Westminster, London	Hyam Hyams	Catharine (?)	Marcus Levy	Elephant & Castle, London	tailor's assistant
4551	Hyams	Blume	1788	Birmingham				Birmingham	
20239	Hyams	Camelia	1840	Spitalfields, London	Joseph Hyams	Jane Benjamin		Spitalfields, London	
18213	Hyams	Caroline	1838	Spitalfields, London	Michael Hyams	Isabella (?)		Spitalfields, London	scholar
17526	Hyams	Catharine	1781	Aldgate, London	(?)		(?) Hyams	Spitalfields, London	formerly a nurse
10430	Hyams	Catharine	1850	Spitalfields, London	Joseph Hyams	Sarah Jacobs nee (?)		Spitalfields, London	
10546	Hyams	Catherine	1796	Whitechapel, London			Hyam Hyams	Elephant & Castle, London	
28294	Hyams	Catherine	1800	?, Poland [?, Prussia]	Joseph Levy		Jacob Hyams	Aldgate, London	
10233	Hyams	Catherine	1834	Aldgate, London	David Hyams	Hannah Barnett		Aldgate, London	slipper binder
8087	Hyams	Catherine	1846	Spitalfields, London	Alexander (Sander) Hyams	Esther Lazarus	Joseph Israel	Aldgate, London	
8200	Hyams	Catherine (Kate)	1821	Whitechapel, London			Jacob Hyams	Aldgate, London	
5571	Hyams	Catherine (Kate)	1829	Aldgate, London	Emanuel (Manuel) Hyams	Rachael Lyon	Jacob (John) Abendana (Bendon)	Spitalfields, London	laundress
13189	Hyams	Catherine (Kate)	1832	Aldgate, London	Solomon Hyams	Rachel Davis		Aldgate, London	
6961	Hyams	Catherine (Kate)	1847	Aldgate, London	Hyam Hyams	Jane Levy	Barnett Levy	Spitalfields, London	
26120	Hyams	Catherine (Kate)	1849	Aldgate, London	Michael Hyams	Elizabeth (Betsey) Lewis	Asher Ellis	Aldgate, London	
27853	Hyams	Charles	1816	Whitechapel, London				Spitalfields, London	traveller of caps
6675	Hyams	Clara	1834	Lambeth, London	Hyam Hyams	Catherine (?)	Morris Abrahams	Elephant & Castle, London	tailor's assistant
19456	Hyams	Daniel	1841	Whitechapel, London	Joseph Mitchell Hyams	Julia Joel		Aldgate, London	scholar
11115	Hyams	Daniel	1846	Aldgate, London	Abraham Hyams	Elizabeth Joseph		Aldgate, London	
13242	Hyams	David	1781	?, Poland			Franny (?)	Spitalfields, London	clothes dealer
24730	Hyams	David	1781	Aldgate, London				Southwark, London	general dealer
10232	Hyams	David	1795	Aldgate, London	Abraham Hyam		Hannah Barnett	Aldgate, London	slipper maker
19927	Hyams	David	1827	Aldgate, London	Solomon Hyams	Rachel Davis	Rebecca Arrobas	Covent Garden, London	fishmonger
3995	Hyams	David	1843	Portsmouth, Hampshire	Wolf Hyams	Julia (?)		Portsmouth, Hampshire	
10429	Hyams	David	1843	Spitalfields, London	Joseph Hyams			Spitalfields, London	
19397	Hyams	David	1846	Lambeth, London	Barnett (Barnet, Dov Behr) Hyams	Elizabeth (Betsey) Davis	Rebecca Hyams	Elephant & Castle, London	scholar
20243	Hyams	David	1848	Spitalfields, London	Joseph Hyams	Jane Benjamin		Spitalfields, London	
3873	Hyams	Dinah	1826	Spitalfields, London	Joseph Moses		Isaac Hyams	Spitalfields, London	
10548	Hyams	Edward	1829	Lambeth, London	Hyam Hyams	Catharine (?)		Elephant & Castle, London	cigar maker
28216	Hyams	Elizabeth	1806	Whitechapel, London	Joseph Hyams			Spitalfields, London	waistcoat maker
11114	Hyams	Elizabeth	1819	Aldgate, London	Benjamin Joseph		Abraham Hyams	Aldgate, London	

ID	surname	given names	born	birthplace	father	mother	spouse 1	1851 residence	1851 occupation
15905	Hyams	Elizabeth	1824	Middlesex, London	Shmuel Levy		Mark Hyams	Finsbury, London	
25194	Hyams	Elizabeth	1831	Aldgate, London	Joshua Hyams	Mary Crabb	James Ochse	Clerkenwell, London	dressmaker
10552	Hyams	Elizabeth	1832	Lambeth, London	Hyam Hyams	Catharine (?)		Elephant & Castle, London	
13190	Hyams	Elizabeth	1835	Aldgate, London	Solomon Hyams	Rachel Davis		Aldgate, London	
13221	Hyams	Elizabeth	1836	Whitechapel, London	(?) Hyams			Spitalfields, London	
17519	Hyams	Elizabeth	1836	Whitechapel, London	Michael Hyams	Isabella (?)	Hermann Tasch	Spitalfields, London	
20678	Hyams	Elizabeth	1837	Whitechapel, London	Emanuel (Manuel) Hyams	Rachael Lyon		Spitalfields, London	scholar
19514	Hyams	Elizabeth	1838	Strand, London	George Hyams	Esther Jacobs		Strand, London	scholar
13240	Hyams	Elizabeth	1839	Spitalfields, London	(?) Hyams			Spitalfields, London	
10428	Hyams	Elizabeth	1840	Whitechapel, London	Joseph Hyams			Spitalfields, London	
8193	Hyams	Elizabeth	1841	Middlesex, London	Jacob Hyams	Catherine (Kate) (?)	Abraham Henriques Valentine	Aldgate, London	scholar
26111	Hyams	Elizabeth (Betsey)	1811	?, London	Samuel Lewis	Isabella (?)	Michael Hyams	Aldgate, London	
19393	Hyams	Elizabeth (Betsey)	1822	Whitechapel, London	David Davis		Barnett (Barnet, Dov Behr) Hyams	Elephant & Castle, London	
25015	Hyams	Ellen	1827	Clerkenwell, London	(?) Solomon		Michael Hyams	Finsbury, London	
3991	Hyams	Emanuel	1829	Stepney, London			Kate Emanuel	Portsmouth, Hampshire	
20671	Hyams	Emanuel (Manuel)	1802	Aldgate, London	Joseph Hyams		Rachael Lyon	Spitalfields, London	pencil maker
13220	Hyams	Esther	1778	Whitechapel, London	(?)		(?) Hyams	Spitalfields, London	
19510	Hyams	Esther	1806	Surrey, London	Moshe Halevi		George Hyams	Strand, London	
6596	Hyams	Esther	1812	Spitalfields, London	Michael Lazarus		Alexander (Sander) Hyams	Aldgate, London	
13248	Hyams	Esther	1833	Soho, London	David Hyams	Franny (?)		Spitalfields, London	
8945	Hyams	Fanny	1824	Aldgate, London	(?) Levy	Ann (?)	Solomon Hyams	Aldgate, London	
17789	Hyams	Fanny	1849	Aldgate, London	Mark (Mordecai) Hyams	Hannah Cohen		Aldgate, London	
28288	Hyams	Fanny	1851	Whitechapel, London	Hyam Hyams	Amelia Abrahams		Aldgate, London	
3801	Hyams	Frances	1841	Spitalfields, London	Samuel Hyams	Sarah Phillips		Spitalfields, London	scholar
13243	Hyams	Franny	1791	Aldgate, London	(?)		David Hyams	Spitalfields, London	
19509	Hyams	George	1802	?, London	Zev Wolff		Esther Jacobs	Strand, London	master tailor
16855	Hyams	George	1846	Bath	Henry Hyams	Harriet (?)		Bath	
28287	Hyams	George	1849	Whitechapel, London	Hyam Hyams	Amelia Abrahams		Aldgate, London	
16983	Hyams	Godfrey	1833	Aldgate, London	Michael Hyams	Isabella (?)		Wapping, London	shoemaker apprentice
3804	Hyams	Godfry	1849	Spitalfields, London	Samuel Hyams	Sarah Phillips		Spitalfields, London	
19448	Hyams	H---	1837	Whitechapel, London	Joseph Hyams	Rose Isaacs		Whitechapel, London	
17463	Hyams	Hannah	1789	Middlesex, London	Hirsh Davis		Lazarus Hyams	Spitalfields, London	
10163	Hyams	Hannah	1806	Spitalfields, London	(?)		Philip Hyams	Elephant & Castle, London	annuitant
17786	Hyams	Hannah	1816	Spitalfields, London	Henry Hart (Naphtali) Cohen		Mark (Mordecai) Hyams	Aldgate, London	
25192	Hyams	Hannah	1827	Aldgate, London	Joshua Hyams	Mary Crabb		Clerkenwell, London	
3813	Hyams	Hannah	1840	Whitechapel, London	Solomon Hyams	Maria Levy		Spitalfields, London	scholar
19516	Hyams	Hannah	1843	Strand, London	George Hyams	Esther Jacobs		Strand, London	scholar
3997	Hyams	Hannah	1848	?, Isle of Wight	Wolf Hyams	Julia (?)		Portsmouth, Hampshire	
19396	Hyams	Hannah (Annie)	1844	Lambeth, London	Barnett (Barnet, Dov Behr) Hyams	Elizabeth (Betsey) Davis	Nathan Benjamin	Elephant & Castle, London	scholar
16854	Hyams	Harriet	1827	Bath			Henry Hyams	Bath	

ID	surname	given names	born	birthplace	father	mother	spouse 1	1851 residence	1851 occupation
16188	Hyams	Henry	1802	?, Poland	Chaim		Julia Levy	Wapping, London	furrier + hair cap maker
16853	Hyams	Henry	1822	?, Poland			Harriet (?)	Bath	stationer
9908	Hyams	Henry	1823	Whitechapel, London	Eliezer Hyams		Rachael Phillips	Southwark, London	fishmonger
19780	Hyams	Henry	1823	Soho, London	David Hyams		Mary (Polly) Davis	Spitalfields, London	clothes dealer
10549	Hyams	Henry	1837	Lambeth, London	Hyam Hyams	Catharine (?)		Elephant & Castle, London	assistant to cigar maker
9763	Hyams	Henry	1838	Middlesex, London				Kew, London	boarding school pupil
17523	Hyams	Henry	1845	Spitalfields, London	Michael Hyams	Isabella (?)		Spitalfields, London	scholar
3803	Hyams	Henry	1847	Spitalfields, London	Samuel Hyams	Sarah Phillips		Spitalfields, London	scholar
3816	Hyams	Henry	1848	Spitalfields, London	Solomon Hyams	Maria Levy		Spitalfields, London	scholar
22797	Hyams	Henry	1849	Finsbury, London	Benjamin Hyams	Rosetta (?)		Whitechapel, London	
9459	Hyams	Hyam	1796	Hull, Yorkshire	Shlomeh Zalman Hyams			Aldgate, London	shopkeeper
10545	Hyams	Hyam	1798	Westminster, London			Catharine (?)	Elephant & Castle, London	tailor
6016	Hyams	Hyam	1816	Aldgate, London	Joseph Hyams		Jane Levy	Spitalfields, London	fishmonger
28285	Hyams	Hyam	1816	Aldgate, London	Simon Hyams	(?Judy Moses)	Amelia Abrahams	Aldgate, London	general dealer
14219	Hyams	Hyam	1818	Chichester, Sussex			Jane (?)	Manchester	commercial traveller
10235	Hyams	Hyam	1838	Aldgate, London	David Hyams	Hannah Barnett		Aldgate, London	slipper server
21297	Hyams	Hyam	1839	Bury St Edmunds, Suffolk	(Lawrence Hyam?)	(Caroline Elias?)		Edmonton, London	boarding school pupil
26115	Hyams	Hyam	1840	Aldgate, London	Michael Hyams	Elizabeth (Betsey) Lewis		Aldgate, London	scholar
5977	Hyams	Hyam	1843	Whitechapel, London	Mark Hyams	Elizabeth Levy	Clara Jacobs	Finsbury, London	scholar
6003	Hyams	Hyam	1844	Whitechapel, London	Sander Hyams	Esther Lazarus	Phoebe (?)	Aldgate, London	
20242	Hyams	Hyam	1846	Spitalfields, London	Joseph Hyams	Jane Benjamin	Rosetta Goldsmith	Spitalfields, London	
3874	Hyams	Hyam	1848	Spitalfields, London	Isaac Hyams	Dinah Moses		Spitalfields, London	
19784	Hyams	Hyam	1850	Spitalfields, London	Henry Hyams	Mary (Polly) Davis		Spitalfields, London	
9909	Hyams	Hyam (Henry)	1850	Southwark, London	Henry Hyams	Rachael Phillips		Southwark, London	
3316	Hyams	Hyam (Hyman)	1850	Aldgate, London	Joseph Mitchell Hyams	Julia Joel	Catherine (Kate) Levy	Aldgate, London	
24171	Hyams	Hyam J	1810	?, Poland			Betsy (?)	Euston, London	tinplate worker
29758	Hyams	Hyman	1788	?, London				Aldgate, London	dealer
3994	Hyams	Hyman	1842	Portsmouth, Hampshire	Wolf Hyams	Julia (?)		Portsmouth, Hampshire	
8086	Hyams	Hyman	1843	Spitalfields, London	Alexander (Sander) Hyams	Esther Lazarus		Aldgate, London	
3818	Hyams	Hyman	1849	Spitalfields, London	Solomon Hyams	Maria Levy		Spitalfields, London	
3872	Hyams	Isaac	1824	Whitechapel, London	Chaim		Dinah Moses	Spitalfields, London	clothes dealer
10547	Hyams	Isaac	1826	Westminster, London	Hyam Hyams	Catharine (?)		Elephant & Castle, London	hatter
17466	Hyams	Isaac	1827	?, London	Lazarus Hyams	Hannah Davis		Spitalfields, London	fishmonger
13239	Hyams	Isaac	1828	Spitalfields, London	(?) Hyams	Pricila (?)		Spitalfields, London	clothes dealer
10234	Hyams	Isaac	1836	Aldgate, London	David Hyams	Hannah Barnett		Aldgate, London	slipper server
24173	Hyams	Isaac	1837	?, Poland	Hyam J Hyams	Betsy (?)		Euston, London	
17518	Hyams	Isabella	1807	Whitechapel, London	(?)		Michael Hyams	Spitalfields, London	
28217	Hyams	Isabella	1819	Whitechapel, London	Joseph Hyams			Spitalfields, London	servant
26119	Hyams	Isabella	1848	Aldgate, London	Michael Hyams	Elizabeth (Betsey) Lewis		Aldgate, London	
28293	Hyams	Jacob	1809	?, Poland [?, Prussia]	Joseph Hyams		Catherine Levy	Aldgate, London	trimming seller
8194	Hyams	Jacob	1819	Aldgate, London			Catherine (Kate) (?)	Aldgate, London	fishmonger
13247	Hyams	Jacob	1830	Soho, London	David Hyams	Franny (?)		Spitalfields, London	clothes dealer

ID	surname	given names	born	birthplace	father	mother	spouse 1	1851 residence	1851 occupation
20677	Hyams	Jacob	1836	Whitechapel, London	Emanuel (Manuel) Hyams	Rachael Lyon	Amelia Levy	Spitalfields, London	general dealer
24174	Hyams	Jacob	1842	Aldgate, London	Hyam J Hyams	Betsy (?)		Euston, London	
26116	Hyams	Jacob	1842	Aldgate, London	Michael Hyams	Elizabeth (Betsey) Lewis		Aldgate, London	scholar
20237	Hyams	Jane	1811	Whitechapel, London	Zadock Benjamin		Joseph Hyams	Spitalfields, London	
6017	Hyams	Jane	1814	Aldgate, London	Isaac Levy		Hyam Hyams	Spitalfields, London	
25966	Hyams	Jane	1817	Aldgate, London	(?) Hyams			Aldgate, London	servant
14220	Hyams	Jane	1823	Truro, Cornwall	(?)		Hyam Hyams	Manchester	commercial traveller
29545	Hyams	John	1846	Finsbury, London	(?) Hyams	So[phia (?)		Spitalfields, London	
19398	Hyams	John	1850	Southwark, London	Barnett (Barnet, Dov Behr) Hyams	Elizabeth (Betsey) Davis	Sophia Rees	Elephant & Castle, London	
11278	Hyams	Joseph	1776	Aldgate, London			Sarah (?)	Aldgate, London	clothes man
10421	Hyams	Joseph	1806	Aldgate, London			(?)	Spitalfields, London	shoe manufacturer
20236	Hyams	Joseph	1812	Middlesex, London	Hyam Hyams		Jane Benjamin	Spitalfields, London	general dealer
19446	Hyams	Joseph	1819	Middlesex, London	Menahem Mendel		Rose Isaacs	Whitechapel, London	general dealer
19976	Hyams	Joseph	1833	Whitechapel, London	Emanuel (Manuel) Hyams	Rachael Lyon	Julia Joel	Spitalfields, London	general dealer
21869	Hyams	Joseph	1835	Whitechapel, London				Clerkenwell, London	assistant to fancy cabinet maker
26113	Hyams	Joseph	1835	Aldgate, London	Michael Hyams	Elizabeth (Betsey) Lewis		Aldgate, London	cigar maker
10236	Hyams	Joseph	1840	Aldgate, London	David Hyams	Hannah Barnett		Aldgate, London	scholar
15908	Hyams	Joseph	1849	Middlesex, London	Mark Hyams	Elizabeth Levy		Finsbury, London	
3875	Hyams	Joseph	1850	Spitalfields, London	Isaac Hyams	Dinah Moses		Spitalfields, London	
3805	Hyams	Joseph	1851	Spitalfields, London	Samuel Hyams	Sarah Phillips		Spitalfields, London	
19451	Hyams	Joseph Mitchell	1810	Shoreditch, London	Nachum Hyams		Julia Joel	Aldgate, London	fishmonger + fish curer empl 3
25189	Hyams	Joshua	1795	Aldgate, London	Menahem Mendel		Mary Crabb	Clerkenwell, London	watch maker
6959	Hyams	Julia	1806	Whitechapel, London	Yehuda Leib		Henry Hyams	Wapping, London	domestic
19452	Hyams	Julia	1819	Spitalfields, London	Jacob Joel		Joseph Mitchell Hyams	Aldgate, London	fishmonger empl 3
13244	Hyams	Julia	1824	Soho, London	David Hyams	Franny (?)		Spitalfields, London	tailoress
3814	Hyams	Julia	1842	Whitechapel, London	Solomon Hyams	Maria Levy		Spitalfields, London	scholar
19449	Hyams	Julia	1843	Whitechapel, London	Joseph Hyams	Rose Isaacs		Whitechapel, London	
11116	Hyams	Julia	1848	Aldgate, London	Abraham Hyams	Elizabeth Joseph		Aldgate, London	
19783	Hyams	Julia	1848	Spitalfields, London	Henry Hyams	Mary (Polly) Davis	Henry Goldstein	Spitalfields, London	scholar
17735	Hyams	Julius	1831	?, Poland [?, Prussia]				Aldgate, London	tailor
17462	Hyams	Lazarus	1787	?, London	Chaim the Shammes		Hannah Davis	Spitalfields, London	clothes dealer
20673	Hyams	Leah	1824	Aldgate, London	Emanuel (Manuel) Hyams	Rachael Lyon		Spitalfields, London	laundress
19453	Hyams	Leah	1833	Whitechapel, London	Joseph Mitchell Hyams	Julia Joel		Aldgate, London	
6597	Hyams	Leah	1840	?Aldgate, London	Alexander (Sander) Hyams	Esther Lazarus		Aldgate, London	
13241	Hyams	Leah	1841	Spitalfields, London	(?) Hyams			Spitalfields, London	
26118	Hyams	Leah	1846	Aldgate, London	Michael Hyams	Elizabeth (Betsey) Lewis		Aldgate, London	scholar
15907	Hyams	Leah	1847	Aldgate, London	Mark Hyams	Elizabeth Levy		Finsbury, London	
17788	Hyams	Leah	1847	Spitalfields, London	Mark (Mordecai) Hyams	Hannah Cohen		Aldgate, London	
30519	Hyams	Leah	1851	Spitalfields, London	Hyam Hyams	Jane Levy		Spitalfields, London	
16189	Hyams	Lewis	1833	Wapping, London	Henry Hyams	Julia Levy		Wapping, London	cigar maker
25016	Hyams	Lewis	1845	?, London	Michael Hyams	Ellen Solomon		Finsbury, London	

ID	surname	given names	born	birthplace	father	mother	spouse 1	1851 residence	1851 occupation
5732	Hyams	Louis	1845	Wolverhampton, Staffordshire	Benjamin Hyams	Sophia (?)	Emily Amelia Moses	Wolverhampton, Staffordshire	scholar
8728	Hyams	Louisa	1839	Aldgate, London	(?) Hyams	(?) (?Metz)		Aldgate, London	
22798	Hyams	Louisa	1850	Shoreditch, London	Benjamin Hyams	Rosetta (?)		Whitechapel, London	
3809	Hyams	Maria	1809	Mile End, London	Hyam Levy		Solomon Hyams	Spitalfields, London	
13246	Hyams	Maria	1829	Soho, London	David Hyams	Franny (?)		Spitalfields, London	
29163	Hyams	Maria	1829	?, London	(?) Hyams			Whitechapel, London	cook
20240	Hyams	Maria	1842	Spitalfields, London	Joseph Hyams	Jane Benjamin		Spitalfields, London	
17524	Hyams	Maria	1847	Spitalfields, London	Michael Hyams	Isabella (?)		Spitalfields, London	scholar
17464	Hyams	Mariah	1821	?, London	Lazarus Hyams	Hannah Davis		Spitalfields, London	
3996	Hyams	Mariam	1847	?, Isle of Wight	Wolf Hyams	Julia (?)	David Bartoles	Portsmouth, Hampshire	
15904	Hyams	Mark	1820	Middlesex, London	Chaim Hyams		Elizabeth Levy	Finsbury, London	general dealer
20238	Hyams	Mark	1839	Whitechapel, London	Joseph Hyams	Jane Benjamin	Elizabeth Abrahams	Spitalfields, London	
17785	Hyams	Mark (Mordecai)	1815	Bermondsey, London	Abraham Hyams	(Lidia Hart?)	Hannah Cohen	Aldgate, London	fruiterer
26114	Hyams	Martha	1839	Aldgate, London	Michael Hyams	Elizabeth (Betsey) Lewis		Aldgate, London	
21368	Hyams	Mary	1795	?, London				Mayfair, London	cook
25190	Hyams	Mary	1799	Whitechapel, London	Aryeh Shirga Pais Crabb		Joshua Hyams	Clerkenwell, London	
20679	Hyams	Mary (Miriam)	1841	Spitalfields, London	Emanuel (Manuel) Hyams	Rachael Lyon		Spitalfields, London	scholar
19781	Hyams	Mary (Polly)	1826	Whitechapel, London	David Davis		Henry Hyams	Spitalfields, London	clothes dealer
19395	Hyams	Matilda	1842	Southwark, London	Barnett (Barnet, Dov Behr) Hyams	Elizabeth (Betsey) Davis	Lawrence Rees	Elephant & Castle, London	
11117	Hyams	Matilda	1849	Aldgate, London	Abraham Hyams	Elizabeth Joseph		Aldgate, London	
26110	Hyams	Michael	1801	?, London	Joseph Hyams		Elizabeth (Betsey) Lewis	Aldgate, London	general dealer
17517	Hyams	Michael	1805	Aldgate, London	(?) Hyams	Catharine (?)	Isabella (?)	Spitalfields, London	shoemaker
25014	Hyams	Michael	1817	Covent Garden, London			Ellen Solomon	Finsbury, London	shoemaker
10427	Hyams	Michael	1838	Aldgate, London	Joseph Hyams			Spitalfields, London	
6599	Hyams	Michael	1848	?Aldgate, London	Alexander (Sander) Hyams	Esther Lazarus		Aldgate, London	
25017	Hyams	Michael	1850	?, London	Michael Hyams	Ellen Solomon		Finsbury, London	
5758	Hyams	Morris	1816	Middlesex, London			(?)	Spitalfields, London	gentleman
17522	Hyams	Morris	1843	Spitalfields, London	Michael Hyams	Isabella (?)		Spitalfields, London	scholar
3807	Hyams	Moses	1777	Spitalfields, London			(?)	Spitalfields, London	tailor
3810	Hyams	Moses	1835	Spitalfields, London	Solomon Hyams	Maria Levy		Spitalfields, London	scholar
16191	Hyams	Moses	1844	Wapping, London	Henry Hyams	Julia Levy		Wapping, London	scholar
30521	Hyams	Moses	1851	Spitalfields, London	Isaac Hyams	Dinah Moses		Spitalfields, London	
17465	Hyams	Moses (Morris)	1825	?, London	Lazarus Hyams	Hannah Davis	Rebecca (Betsey) Israel	Spitalfields, London	butcher
31212	Hyams	Moss	1824	Lambeth, London				Winchester, Hampshire	stationer
8088	Hyams	Nancy	1850	Aldgate, London	Alexander (Sander) Hyams	Esther Lazarus	Simon Hyams	Aldgate, London	
30520	Hyams	Nancy	1851	Spitalfields, London	Henry Hyams	Mary (Polly) Davis		Spitalfields, London	
19454	Hyams	Nathan	1835	Whitechapel, London	Joseph Mitchell Hyams	Julia Joel	Rebecca Solomons	Aldgate, London	
19399	Hyams	Philip	1851	Southwark, London	Barnett (Barnet, Dov Behr) Hyams	Elizabeth (Betsey) Davis	Betsey Harris	Elephant & Castle, London	
25193	Hyams	Philip J	1828	Aldgate, London	Joshua Hyams	Mary Crabb		Clerkenwell, London	watch maker
10237	Hyams	Phillip	1841	Aldgate, London	David Hyams	Hannah Barnett		Aldgate, London	scholar
13237	Hyams	Pricila	1795	Bamberg, Germany	(?)		(?) Hyams	Spitalfields, London	clothes dealer
6598	Hyams	Priscilla	1843	?Aldgate, London	Alexander (Sander) Hyams	Esther Lazarus		Aldgate, London	

ID	surname	given names	born	birthplace	father	mother	spouse 1	1851 residence	1851 occupation
25754	Hyams	Rachael	1793	Bialystok, Poland [Bialystok, Russia]	(?)		Samuel Hyams	Aldgate, London	
20672	Hyams	Rachael	1802	St Giles, London	Azreal Lyon		Emanuel (Manuel) Hyams	Spitalfields, London	laundress
9907	Hyams	Rachael	1825	Elephant & Castle, London	Henry Phillips	Abigail Solomons	Henry Hyams	Southwark, London	
25195	Hyams	Rachael	1832	Aldgate, London	Joshua Hyams	Mary Crabb		Clerkenwell, London	milliner's apprentice
19512	Hyams	Rachael	1834	Westminster	George Hyams	Esther Jacobs	Henry Harris	Strand, London	
30522	Hyams	Rachael	1851	Covent Garden, London	David Hyams	Rebecca Arrobas		Covent Garden, London	
19928	Hyams	Rebecca	1833	Bethnal Green, London	Abraham de Moses Arrobus	Rachel de Samuel Suhami	David Hyams	Covent Garden, London	
9475	Hyams	Rebecca	1837	?, London	(?) Hyams			Aldgate, London	
17521	Hyams	Rebecca	1840	Spitalfields, London	Michael Hyams	Isabella (?)	Louis Blashker	Spitalfields, London	scholar
19515	Hyams	Rebecca	1841	Strand, London	George Hyams	Esther Jacobs		Strand, London	scholar
19403	Hyams	Rebecca	1844	Aldgate, London	Joseph Mitchell Hyams	Julia Joel	David Hyams	Aldgate, London	scholar
24759	Hyams	Reuben	1824	Hackney, London				Southwark, London	professional
13245	Hyams	Rosa	1828	Soho, London	David Hyams	Franny (?)		Spitalfields, London	
2669	Hyams	Rosa	1836	Southwark, London	Philip Hyams	Hannah (?)	Israel Aaron Levy	Elephant & Castle, London	
19457	Hyams	Rosa	1843	Whitechapel, London	Joseph Mitchell Hyams	Julia Joel		Aldgate, London	
19782	Hyams	Rosa	1846	Spitalfields, London	Henry Hyams	Mary (Polly) Davis		Spitalfields, London	scholar
19447	Hyams	Rose	1815	Portsmouth, Hampshire	Asher Isaacs		Joseph Hyams	Whitechapel, London	
8729	Hyams	Rose	1841	Marylebone, London	(?) Hyams	(?) (?Metz)		Aldgate, London	
20681	Hyams	Rose	1845	Spitalfields, London	Emanuel (Manuel) Hyams	Rachael Lyon		Spitalfields, London	scholar
19450	Hyams	Rose (Rosetta)	1845	Whitechapel, London	Joseph Hyams	Rose Isaacs		Whitechapel, London	
22796	Hyams	Rosetta	1824	Aldgate, London	(?)		Benjamin Hyams	Whitechapel, London	
25191	Hyams	Rosetta (Rosa)	1834	Whitechapel, London	Joshua Hyams	Mary Crabb	Alexander Moses	Clerkenwell, London	scholar
8079	Hyams	Rosetta (Rosea)	1841	?, London	Alexander (Sander) Hyams	Esther Lazarus	Lyon Jacobs	Aldgate, London	
25753	Hyams	Samuel	1781	Cracow, Poland			Rachael (?)	Aldgate, London	general dealer
3798	Hyams	Samuel	1819	Spitalfields, London	Moses Hyams		Sarah Phillips	Spitalfields, London	general dealer
20674	Hyams	Samuel	1826	Aldgate, London	Emanuel (Manuel) Hyams	Rachael Lyon	Leah Saunders	Spitalfields, London	general dealer
16982	Hyams	Samuel	1833	Whitechapel, London				Wapping, London	shoemaker apprentice
26112	Hyams	Samuel	1833	Aldgate, London	Michael Hyams	Elizabeth (Betsey) Lewis		Aldgate, London	shoe maker
16988	Hyams	Samuel	1835	Whitechapel, London				Wapping, London	shoemaker apprentice
3815	Hyams	Samuel	1843	Spitalfields, London	Solomon Hyams	Maria Levy		Spitalfields, London	scholar
15906	Hyams	Samuel	1846	Middlesex, London	Mark Hyams	Elizabeth Levy		Finsbury, London	scholar
20244	Hyams	Samuel	1850	Spitalfields, London	Joseph Hyams	Jane Benjamin	Amelia Emanuel	Spitalfields, London	
11279	Hyams	Sarah	1795	Aldgate, London	(?)		Joseph Hyams	Aldgate, London	
3799	Hyams	Sarah	1820	Spitalfields, London	(?) Phillips	Sarah (?)		Spitalfields, London	
10240	Hyams	Sarah	1823	Finsbury, London	(?)		Solomon Hyams	Spitalfields, London	
10550	Hyams	Sarah	1824	Westminster, London	Hyam Hyams	Catharine (?)		Elephant & Castle, London	cap maker
13238	Hyams	Sarah	1826	Spitalfields, London	(?) Hyams	Pricila (?)		Spitalfields, London	dress maker
19198	Hyams	Sarah	1833	Clerkenwell, London	(?) Hyams	(?) Samuel		City, London	wig maker
19513	Hyams	Sarah	1836	Strand, London	George Hyams	Esther Jacobs		Strand, London	scholar
19394	Hyams	Sarah	1841	Lambeth, London	Barnett (Barnet, Dov Behr) Hyams	Elizabeth (Betsey) Davis	Isaac Hyman	Elephant & Castle, London	capmaker
26117	Hyams	Sarah	1844	Aldgate, London	Michael Hyams	Elizabeth (Betsey) Lewis		Aldgate, London	scholar

277

ID	surname	given names	born	birthplace	father	mother	spouse 1	1851 residence	1851 occupation
17525	Hyams	Sarah	1850	Spitalfields, London	Michael Hyams	Isabella (?)		Spitalfields, London	
17790	Hyams	Sarah	1850	Aldgate, London	Mark (Mordecai) Hyams	Hannah Cohen		Aldgate, London	
3820	Hyams	Sarah	1851	Spitalfields, London	Solomon Hyams	Maria Levy		Spitalfields, London	
15909	Hyams	Sarah	1851	Finsbury, London	Mark Hyams	Elizabeth Levy		Finsbury, London	
10422	Hyams	Sarah	1816	Chelmsford, Essex	Shlomo Zalman Levy		Lewis Jacobs	Spitalfields, London	
20241	Hyams	Simon	1844	Spitalfields, London	Joseph Hyams	Jane Benjamin		Spitalfields, London	
3808	Hyams	Solomon	1811	Whitechapel, London	Moses Hyams		Maria Levy	Spitalfields, London	tailor
10239	Hyams	Solomon	1813	Aldgate, London			Sarah (?)	Spitalfields, London	general dealer
8946	Hyams	Solomon	1822	Aldgate, London			Fanny Lyons	Aldgate, London	cigar maker
17520	Hyams	Solomon	1832	Whitechapel, London	Michael Hyams	Isabella (?)		Spitalfields, London	cigar maker
3802	Hyams	Solomon	1843	Spitalfields, London	Samuel Solomon	Sarah Phillips		Spitalfields, London	scholar
20680	Hyams	Solomon	1843	Spitalfields, London	Emanuel (Manuel) Hyams	Rachael Lyon	Dinah Harris	Spitalfields, London	scholar
24177	Hyams	Solomon	1848	St Pancras, London	Hyam J Hyams	Betsy (?)		Euston, London	
31004	Hyams	Sophia	1821	?, Poland	(?)		Benjamin Hyams	Wolverhampton, Staffordshire	
29544	Hyams	Sophia	1826	Bethnal Green, London	(?)		(?) Hyams	Spitalfields, London	silk winder
19511	Hyams	Susan	1830	Holborn, London	George Hyams	Esther Jacobs		Strand, London	
8420	Hyams	Tobia	1779	?, Poland	(?)		Barnard Hyams	Chichester, Sussex	
3992	Hyams	Wolf	1816	?, Poland	Hyam Hyams		Julia (Amelia) Lazarus	Portsmouth, Hampshire	hardware foreman
19455	Hyams (Mitchell)	John (Jack)	1837	Whitechapel, London	Joseph Mitchell Hyams	Julia Joel		Aldgate, London	scholar
1301	Hyman	Abraham	1788	?, Poland				Plymouth, Devon	hawker
5543	Hyman	Abraham	1816	Aldgate, London	Mordecai Hyams	Rose Elkan	Amelia Barnett	Spitalfields, London	furrier + skinner master empl 7 + parasol + umbrella maker
11195	Hyman	Abraham	1819	Whitechapel, London	Judah Hyman	Jane (?)	Hannah Barnett	Aldgate, London	tailor
2729	Hyman	Abraham	1823	Falmouth, Cornwall	Moses Hyman (Moshe Chaim)	Sarah (Sally) Levy (Levi)	Kate (Catherine) Myers	Whitechapel, London	furrier
22608	Hyman	Alexander	1849	Stepney, London	Solomon Hyman	Bluma Lyon		Stepney, London	
8565	Hyman	Amelia	1822	Aldgate, London	(?) Barnett		Abraham Hyman	Spitalfields, London	
8572	Hyman	Ann	1850	Spitalfields, London	Abraham Hyman	Amelia Barnett		Spitalfields, London	
22609	Hyman	Ann	1850	Stepney, London	Solomon Hyman	Bluma Lyon		Stepney, London	
19421	Hyman	Ann (Nancy)	1830	Vauxhall, London	Solomon Hyman (Hyams)	Sarah Davis	Hyam Joseph	Bloomsbury, London	
8206	Hyman	Barnett	1849	Camberwell, London	Hyam Hyman	Jane Cohen	Julia Goldman	Camberwell, London	
12374	Hyman	Benjamin	1847	?, Germany	Selig Hyman	Yetta (?)		North Shields, Tyne & Wear	
8569	Hyman	Benjamin Woolf	1847	Spitalfields, London	Abraham Hyman	Amelia Barnett	Phoebe Cohen	Spitalfields, London	
2855	Hyman	Bertha	1841	Liverpool	Solomon Hyman	Esther Ernestine (?)	Philip Frenkel (Frenklin)	Liverpool	
13109	Hyman	Betsey (Lizzie)	1850	Southwark, London	David Hyman	Frances (Fanny) Israel	L--- H--- Phillips	Camden Town, London	
27747	Hyman	Betsy	1805	?, Holland	(?)		(?) Hyman	Spitalfields, London	
6504	Hyman	Betsy	1817	Birmingham	(?) Nathan		Joseph Hyman	Manchester	
27750	Hyman	Betsy	1836	?, Holland	(?) Hyman	Betsy (?)		Spitalfields, London	cap maker
22607	Hyman	Bluma	1826	Aldgate, London	Alexander Lyon		Solomon Hyman	Stepney, London	tailoress
27753	Hyman	Brenir	1843	?, Holland	(?) Hyman	Betsy (?)		Spitalfields, London	
30523	Hyman	Catherine	1851	Spitalfields, London	Abraham Hyman	Amelia Barnett		Spitalfields, London	
19428	Hyman	Catherine (Kate, Kitty)	1823	Vauxhall, London	Solomon Hyman (Hyams)	Sarah Davis	Moses (Moss) Samuel	Peckham, London	

ID	surname	given names	born	birthplace	father	mother	spouse 1	1851 residence	1851 occupation
13104	Hyman	David	1818	Vauxhall, London	Solomon (Shlomeh) Hyman (Hyams)	Sarah Davis	Frances (Fanny) Israel	Camden Town, London	marine store keeper
8207	Hyman	David	1850	Camberwell, London	Hyam Hyman	Jane Cohen		Camberwell, London	
19561	Hyman	Eliza C	1827	Epsom, Surrey	(?)		Joseph H Hyman	Covent Garden, London	
13874	Hyman	Elizabeth	1847	Bolton, Lancashire	Joseph Hyman	Bestsy Nathan		Manchester	
3914	Hyman	Elizabeth (Lizzie)	1842	Plymouth, Devon	Hyman Hyman	Zipporah Jacob	George Joseph Emanuel	Plymouth, Devon	scholar
19562	Hyman	Elizabeth J	1850	Middlesex, London	Joseph H Hyman	Eliza C (?)		Covent Garden, London	
19426	Hyman	Emanuel	1825	Vauxhall, London	Solomon Hyman (Hyams)	Sarah Davis	Sarah Abrahams	Peckham, London	rag merchant
8221	Hyman	Esther	1844	Spitalfields, London	Jacob Hyman	Frances Phillips		Spitalfields, London	scholar
2851	Hyman	Esther (Ernestine) Rose	1810	?Poland			Solomon Hyman	Liverpool	
8649	Hyman	Esther (Hester)	1837	Whitechapel, London	Jacob Hyman	Jane (?)		Whitechapel, London	scholar
8646	Hyman	Fanny	1826	Whitechapel, London	Jacob Hyman	Jane (?)		Whitechapel, London	tailoress
8220	Hyman	Frances	1813	Amsterdam, Holland	Phillip Phillips		Jacob Hyman	Spitalfields, London	
13105	Hyman	Frances (Fanny)	1819	Southwark, London	Israel Israel		David Hyman	Camden Town, London	
8235	Hyman	Frederick Moses	1850	Stepney, London	Abraham Hyman	Catherine (Kate) Myers	Isabella Coleman	Whitechapel, London	
28765	Hyman	Hannah	1831	?, Poland	(?) Hyman			Spitalfields, London	
8204	Hyman	Hannah	1843	Lambeth, London	Hyam Hyman	Jane Cohen	Abraham Brodziak	Camberwell, London	
2857	Hyman	Harris	1848	Liverpool	Solomon Hyman	Esther Ernestine (?)	Angela Cohen	Liverpool	
8208	Hyman	Hyam	1815	?, Oxfordshire	Solomon (Shlomeh) Hyman (Hyams)	Sarah Davis	Jane Cohen	Camberwell, London	general dealer
184	Hyman	Hyman	1815	Plymouth, Devon	Nathan Hyman		Zipporah Jacob	Plymouth, Devon	goldsmith + silversmith
27487	Hyman	Hyman	1827	Middlesex, London				Aldgate, London	clothes dealer
12373	Hyman	Hyman	1845	?, Germany	Selig Hyman	Yetta (?)		North Shields, Tyne & Wear	scholar
19400	Hyman	Isaac	1836	Lambeth, London	Solomon Hyman	Sarah Davis	Sarah Hyams	Lambeth, London	assistant to father [marine store dealer]
13107	Hyman	Isaac	1846	Southwark, London	David Hyman	Frances (Fanny) Israel		Camden Town, London	scholar
8570	Hyman	Isaac	1849	Spitalfields, London	Abraham Hyman	Amelia Barnett		Spitalfields, London	
13106	Hyman	Israel	1843	Southwark, London	David Hyman	Frances (Fanny) Israel	Esther Coleman	Camden Town, London	scholar
8644	Hyman	Jacob	1767	?, Poland			Jane (?)	Whitechapel, London	tailor
19422	Hyman	Jacob	1832	Vauxhall, London	Solomon Hyman (Hyams)	Sarah Davis	Jane Hillyer	Peckham, London	rag merchant
27752	Hyman	Jacob	1840	?, Holland	(?) Hyman	Betsy (?)		Spitalfields, London	cigar maker
8219	Hyman	Jacob (John)	1815	Falmouth, Cornwall	Moses Hyman	Sarah (Sally) Levy (Levi)	Frances Phillips	Spitalfields, London	constable, London Docks
13103	Hyman	Jacob (John)	1845	Southwark, London	David Hyman	Frances (Fanny) Israel	Priscilla Isaacs	Bloomsbury, London	scholar
19427	Hyman	Jacob (John)	1851	Peckham, London	Emanuel Hyman	Sarah Abrahams	Catherine Cohen	Peckham, London	
8645	Hyman	Jane	1795	Saffron Walden, Essex			Jacob Hyman	Whitechapel, London	
8209	Hyman	Jane	1817	Lambeth, London	Barnett Cohen	Sarah (Sierlah, Tserele) Levy	Hyam Hyman	Camberwell, London	
6503	Hyman	Joseph	1821	Plymouth, Devon	Samuel Hyman	Betsy Moses	Betsy Nathan	Manchester	tailor + draper empl 6
19560	Hyman	Joseph H	1829	Middlesex, London			Eliza C (?)	Covent Garden, London	potato salesman
2930	Hyman	Judah	1822	Whitechapel, London	Jacob Hyman	Jane (?)	Julia Levy	Whitechapel, London	
2728	Hyman	Kate (Catherine)	1826	Spitalfields, London	Moses Myers	Sarah Cohen	Abraham Hyman	Whitechapel, London	
27751	Hyman	Leah	1838	?, Holland	(?) Hyman	Betsy (?)		Spitalfields, London	tailoress
6563	Hyman	Lewis	1809	?, Germany			Rosetta Davis	Plymouth, Devon	general dealer, hardware + toys

ID	surname	given names	born	birthplace	father	mother	spouse 1	1851 residence	1851 occupation
27748	Hyman	Lewis	1832	?, Holland	(?) Hyman	Betsy (?)		Spitalfields, London	cigar maker
8205	Hyman	Lewis Hyam	1846	Lambeth, London	Hyam Hyman	Jane Cohen	Sarah Levey	Camberwell, London	
8648	Hyman	Maria	1834	Whitechapel, London	Jacob Hyman	Jane (?)		Whitechapel, London	tailoress
19423	Hyman	Marianne (Marion)	1834	Vauxhall, London	Solomon Hyman (Hyams)	Sarah Davis	John Abrahams	Marylebone, London	assistant
19420	Hyman	Mark	1851	Lambeth, London	Solomon Hyman (Hyams)	Maria (Mary, Sarah) Friedeburg		Lambeth, London	
1276	Hyman	Maud	1846	Plymouth, Devon	Hyman Hyman	Zipporah Jacob	John Gabriel	Plymouth, Devon	scholar
13108	Hyman	Maurice	1848	Southwark, London	David Hyman	Frances (Fanny) Israel	Millie Joseph	Camden Town, London	
5542	Hyman	Maurice (Mordecai) Abraham	1844	Aldgate, London	Abraham Hyman	Amelia Barnett	Annie Harris	Spitalfields, London	scholar
12375	Hyman	Michael	1850	North Shields, Tyne & Wear	Selig Hyman	Yetta (?)		North Shields, Tyne & Wear	
1340	Hyman	Mosely	1826	Plymouth, Devon	Samuel Hyman	Betsy Moses	Sarah Johnson	Plymouth, Devon	tailor + outfitter
2852	Hyman	Myer	1837	?, Poland	Solomon Hyman	Esther Ernestine (?)	Esther Davis	Liverpool	tailor + clothier
1274	Hyman	Nathan Jacob	1843	Plymouth, Devon	Hyman Hyman	Zipporah Jacob	Georgina Blanckensee	Plymouth, Devon	scholar
2853	Hyman	Philip	1840	?Poznan, Poland [Posen, Prussia]	Solomon Hyman	Esther Ernestine (?)	Elizabeth Abrahams	Liverpool	scholar
13875	Hyman	Philip	1849	Manchester	Joseph Hyman	Bestsy Nathan	(?)	Manchester	
2730	Hyman	Phoebe	1850	Whitechapel, London	Abraham Hyman	Kate (Catherine) Myers		Whitechapel, London	
8647	Hyman	Rebecca	1825	Whitechapel, London	Jacob Hyman	Jane (?)		Whitechapel, London	housekeeper
8234	Hyman	Rose (Rosetta, Rosan)	1822	Falmouth, Cornwall	Moses Hyman	Sarah (Sally) Levy (Levi)		Spitalfields, London	furrier
6564	Hyman	Rosetta	1825	Cheltenham, Gloucestershire	(?) Davis		Lewis Hyman	Plymouth, Devon	
8566	Hyman	Rosetta	1840	Spitalfields, London	Abraham Hyman	Amelia Barnett		Spitalfields, London	scholar
27749	Hyman	Samuel	1834	?, Holland	(?) Hyman	Betsy (?)		Spitalfields, London	cigar maker
1275	Hyman	Samuel	1845	Plymouth, Devon	Hyman Hyman	Zipporah Jacob	Lydia (Lillie) Mosely	Plymouth, Devon	scholar
1341	Hyman	Sarah	1823	Exeter, Devon	(?) Johnson	Eliza (?)	Mosely Hyman	Plymouth, Devon	
13921	Hyman	Sarah	1823	Whitechapel, London	(?) Hyman			Manchester	house servant to tailor + draper
19425	Hyman	Sarah	1826	Finsbury, London	Abraham Abrahams		Emanuel Hyman	Peckham, London	
8222	Hyman	Sarah	1849	Spitalfields, London	Jacob Hyman	Frances Phillips	Humphrey James Phillips	Spitalfields, London	
8215	Hyman	Sarah (Sally)	1776	Helston, Cornwall	Abraham Levy (Levi)		Moses Hyman	Spitalfields, London	supported by daughter
12371	Hyman	Selig	1818	?, Germany			Yetta (?)	North Shields, Tyne & Wear	jeweller
14228	Hyman	Selig	1827	Poznan, Poland [Posen, Prussia]				Manchester	hawker
2850	Hyman	Solomon	1807	Poznan, Poland [Posen, Prussia]			Esther (Ernestine) Rose (?)	Liverpool	outfitter
22606	Hyman	Solomon	1824	Whitechapel, London	Jacob Hyman		Bluma Lyon	Stepney, London	tailor
5544	Hyman	Sophia	1845	Aldgate, London	Abraham Hyman	Amelia Barnett	Henry (Harry) M Harris	Spitalfields, London	scholar
30524	Hyman	Sophia	1851	Spitalfields, London	Jacob Hyman	Frances Phillips		Spitalfields, London	
12372	Hyman	Yetta	1823	?, Germany	(?)		Selig Hyman	North Shields, Tyne & Wear	
5331	Hyman	Zipporah	1813	Dartmouth, Devon	(?) Jacob		Hyman Hyman	Plymouth, Devon	
2856	Hyman	Zipporah (Sarah)	1847	Liverpool	Solomon Hyman	Esther Ernestine (?)	Michael Rittenberg	Liverpool	

ID	surname	given names	born	birthplace	father	mother	spouse 1	1851 residence	1851 occupation
19413	Hyman (Hyams)	Maria (Mary, Sarah)	1809	Portsmouth, Hampshire	Mark Friedeburg		Solomon Hyman (Hyams)	Lambeth, London	
19412	Hyman (Hyams)	Solomon (Shlomeh)	1790	Watford, Hertfordshire	Jacob Hyman		Sarah Davis	Lambeth, London	marine store dealer
13021	Hymans	David	1834	?, Holland				Spitalfields, London	cigar maker
22763	Hymas	Jane	1833	City, London	Samuel Hymas	Sarah (?)		Whitechapel, London	parasol maker
22760	Hymas	Samuel	1803	City, London			Sarah (?)	Whitechapel, London	pedlar
22761	Hymas	Sarah	1815	Wapping, London	(?)		Samuel Hymas	Whitechapel, London	general dealer
22762	Hymas	Sarah	1831	City, London	Samuel Hymas	Sarah (?)		Whitechapel, London	parasol maker
16428	Hymer	Joseph	1806	Poznan, Poland [Posen, Prussia]			Rebecca (?)	Aldgate, London	tailor
16429	Hymer	Rebecca	1808	Poznan, Poland [Posen, Prussia]	(?)		Joseph Hymer	Aldgate, London	
967	Hynes	Kitty	1806	Exeter, Devon				Exeter, Devon	
22138	Indig	Louis	1830	?, Poland [Indewitz, Prussia]				Whitechapel, London	tailor
12500	Inkerladen	Hyman	1806	Warsaw, Poland				Hindolveston, Norfolk	hawker
25067	Isaac	Abigail	1821	Dublin, Ireland	Joseph Wolfe Cohen	Rebecca Lazarus	Benjamin Ralph Isaac	Liverpool	
4552	Isaac	Abraham	1822	?, Russia				Birmingham	glazier
1804	Isaac	Abraham B	1822	?, Poland	Jacob Isaac	Lydia (?)	Lydia (?)	Merthyr Tydfil, Wales	glazier
21365	Isaac	Adelaide	1832	Finsbury, London	Alexander Isaac	Sophia Levy		New Cross, London	
21360	Isaac	Alexander	1778	Portsmouth, Hampshire	Shlomeh from Portsmouth		Sophia Levy	New Cross, London	general merchant
21366	Isaac	Alexander	1835	Finsbury, London	Alexander Isaac	Sophia Levy		New Cross, London	solicitor articled
1801	Isaac	Alfred	1813	Llanelli, Wales				Swansea, Wales	jeweller
14432	Isaac	Alice	1825	Liverpool	Frank Isaac	Sophia Aaron		Salford, Lancashire	
17720	Isaac	Amelia	1837	Aldgate, London	Jacob Isaac	Nancy (?)		Whitechapel, London	cap maker
21363	Isaac	Annie	1820	Whitechapel, London	Alexander Isaac	Sophia Levy		New Cross, London	
29011	Isaac	Barnet	1825	?				Whitechapel, London	annuitant
17719	Isaac	Barnet	1835	Aldgate, London	Jacob Isaac	Nancy (?)		Whitechapel, London	cigar maker
25066	Isaac	Benjamin Ralph	1817	Liverpool	Ralph Isaac	Sophia Aaron (Arayne)	Abigail Cohen	Liverpool	teacher of music
23753	Isaac	Blanche E	1846	Liverpool	John Raphael Isaac	Sarah Amelia Coleman		Liverpool	
7175	Isaac	Catherine	1789	Margate, Kent	Nathaniel Solomon	Phoebe de Metz	Lewis Isaac	Chelsea, London	
5060	Isaac	Dinah	1796	?, London	Moses Davis	Rosey Nathan	Reuben Isaac	Portsmouth, Hampshire	
23754	Isaac	Edith Rose	1849	Liverpool	John Raphael Isaac	Sarah Amelia Coleman	Leopold Farmer	Liverpool	
25069	Isaac	Elizabeth Sophia	1816	Liverpool	Ralph Isaac	Sophia Aaron (Arayne)		Liverpool	
11020	Isaac	Ellen	1821	Aldgate, London	(?Jacob Solomons)		Phillip Isaac	Aldgate, London	general dealer
7173	Isaac	Emma	1814	Aldgate, London	Stephen (Solomon) Hart	Esther Solomon	Samuel Isaac	Kensington, London	
30882	Isaac	Esther	1831	Chatham, Kent	Lewis Isaac	Catherine Solomon		Chelsea, London	
23750	Isaac	Esther F	1842	Liverpool	John Raphael Isaac	Sarah Amelia Coleman		Liverpool	
28562	Isaac	Ezekiel	1825	Spitalfields, London	Samuel Isaac	Rachael (?)		Spitalfields, London	clothes dealer
5064	Isaac	Frances	1825	Manchester	Reuben Isaac	Dinah Davis	Alexander Nelson	Portsmouth, Hampshire	straw hat maker
8505	Isaac	Frederick S	1830	Finsbury, London	Alexander Isaac	Sophia Levy	Sara Levin	New Cross, London	
23755	Isaac	Georgina Eugenie	1851	Liverpool	John Raphael Isaac	Sarah Amelia Coleman	Maurice (Morris) John Alexander	Liverpool	
17726	Isaac	Harry	1848	Whitechapel, London	Jacob Isaac	Nancy (?)		Whitechapel, London	

ID	surname	given names	born	birthplace	father	mother	spouse 1	1851 residence	1851 occupation
7710	Isaac	Henrietta Rose	1837	Salford, Lancashire	John Michael Isaacs	Sarah Frances Aaron (Arayne)	Samuel Jacob	Salford, Lancashire	
17722	Isaac	Henry	1839	Whitechapel, London	Jacob Isaac	Nancy (?)		Whitechapel, London	cap maker
30883	Isaac	Henry E S	1837	Chatham, Kent				Chelsea, London	
1802	Isaac	Jacob	1803	?, Poland			Lydia (?)	Merthyr Tydfil, Wales	traveller, hawker
17717	Isaac	Jacob	1808	Frankfurt, Germany			Nancy (?)	Whitechapel, London	cap maker
13614	Isaac	Jettie	1831	?, Poland				Manchester	
30275	Isaac	John Colman	1811	Covent Garden, London	Joseph Isaac	Mary (?)	Sarah (?)	Soho, London	dealer in curiosities
7453	Isaac	John Michael	1801	Middlesex, London			Esther Sophia Isaac	Salford, Lancashire	silversmith + pawnbroker
23747	Isaac	John Raphael	1809	Liverpool	Frank Isaac	Sophia Aaron	Sarah Amelia Coleman	Liverpool	craftsman engraver + lithographer empl 9
5062	Isaac	Joseph	1839	Portsmouth, Hampshire	Reuben Isaac	Dinah Davis		Portsmouth, Hampshire	
7174	Isaac	Lewis	1788	Poole, Dorset	Samuel Isaacs		Catherine Solomon	Chelsea, London	independent
1806	Isaac	Lewis	1825	?, Poland	Jacob Isaac	Lydia (?)		Merthyr Tydfil, Wales	glazier
21364	Isaac	Louisa	1830	Finsbury, London	Alexander Isaac	Sophia Levy		New Cross, London	
1803	Isaac	Lydia	1802	?, Poland			Jacob Isaac	Merthyr Tydfil, Wales	
1805	Isaac	Lydia	1827	?, Poland			Abraham B Isaac	Merthyr Tydfil, Wales	
5067	Isaac	Maria	1833	Portsmouth, Hampshire	Reuben Isaac	Dinah Davis		Portsmouth, Hampshire	
30277	Isaac	Mary	1772	Aldgate, London	(?)		Joseph Isaac	Soho, London	
21362	Isaac	Matilda	1819	Whitechapel, London	Alexander Isaac	Sophia Levy		New Cross, London	
17723	Isaac	Michael	1841	Whitechapel, London	Jacob Isaac	Nancy (?)		Whitechapel, London	cap maker
7239	Isaac	Michael	1846	Chatham, Kent	Samuel Isaac	Isabella Simons		Kensington, London	
17725	Isaac	Moses	1848	Whitechapel, London	Jacob Isaac	Nancy (?)		Whitechapel, London	
17718	Isaac	Nancy	1809	Nordhausen, Germany	(?)		Jacob Isaac	Whitechapel, London	cap maker
23752	Isaac	Percy Lewis	1845	Liverpool	John Raphael Isaac	Sarah Amelia Coleman		Liverpool	
11019	Isaac	Phillip	1823	Aldgate, London			Ellen (?Solomons)	Aldgate, London	general dealer
7238	Isaac	Phoebe Grace	1843	Chatham, Kent	Samuel Isaac	Isabella Simons	Julius Bernard Levy	Kensington, London	
28561	Isaac	Rachael	1791	Spitalfields, London	(?)		Samuel Isaac	Spitalfields, London	
3864	Isaac	Rachael	1803	Spitalfields, London			Isaac Isaacs	Spitalfields, London	
17721	Isaac	Rachel	1838	Whitechapel, London	Jacob Isaac	Nancy (?)		Whitechapel, London	cap maker
7176	Isaac	Rachel Catherine	1829	Chatham, Kent	Lewis Isaac	Catherine Solomon	Samuel Godfrey	Chelsea, London	
25068	Isaac	Ralph H	1849	Liverpool	Benjamin Ralph Isaac	Abigail Cohen		Liverpool	
23749	Isaac	Raphael Coleman	1840	Liverpool	John Raphael Isaac	Sarah Amelia Coleman		Liverpool	
5065	Isaac	Rebecca	1827	Manchester	Reuben Isaac	Dinah Davis		Portsmouth, Hampshire	
25070	Isaac	Rebecca	1851	Liverpool	Benjamin Ralph Isaac	Abigail Cohen	Alfred M Jackson	Liverpool	
5059	Isaac	Reuben	1791	?, London			Dinah Davis	Portsmouth, Hampshire	clothier
14142	Isaac	Rose	1786	Middlesex, London	(?)		(?) Isaac	Manchester	
17724	Isaac	Sally	1844	Whitechapel, London	Jacob Isaac	Nancy (?)		Whitechapel, London	scholar
28560	Isaac	Samuel	1781	Whitechapel, London			Rachael (?)	Spitalfields, London	clothes dealer
7172	Isaac	Samuel	1812	Chatham, Kent	Lewis Isaac	Catherine Solomon	Isabella Simons	Kensington, London	army contractor, accoutrement maker + general East India agent
7237	Isaac	Samuel Edward Henry	1836	Chatham, Kent	Samuel Isaac	Isabella Simons		Kensington, London	
30276	Isaac	Sarah	1791	?, Germany	(?)		John Colman Isaac	Soho, London	

ID	surname	given names	born	birthplace	father	mother	spouse 1	1851 residence	1851 occupation
5066	Isaac	Sarah	1831	Portsmouth, Hampshire	Reuben Isaac	Dinah Davis		Portsmouth, Hampshire	
23748	Isaac	Sarah Amelia	1813	Charleston, USA	Sylvester Coleman	Flora Yates	John Raphael Isaac	Liverpool	
14430	Isaac	Sarah Frances	1800	Portsmouth, Hampshire	Jacob Aaron (Arayne)	Alice (?)	John Michael Isaac	Salford, Lancashire	
7178	Isaac	Saul	1823	Chatham, Kent	Lewis Isaac	Catherine Solomon	Miriam Hart	Chatham, Kent	
5061	Isaac	Simon	1834	Portsmouth, Hampshire	Reuben Isaac	Dinah Davis		Portsmouth, Hampshire	jeweller
4546	Isaac	Solomon	1826	?, Poland				Birmingham	glazier
14431	Isaac	Sophia	1780	Portsmouth, Hampshire	Jacob Aaron (Arayne)	Alice (?)	Frank Isaac	Salford, Lancashire	
21361	Isaac	Sophia	1791	Dover, Kent	Benjamin Levy from Canterbury		Alexander Isaac	New Cross, London	
7240	Isaac	Stephen H	1850	Kensington, London	Samuel Isaac	Emma Hart		Kensington, London	
23751	Isaac	Theresa Sophia	1844	Liverpool	John Raphael Isaac	Sarah Amelia Coleman	Joseph Frederick Ehrenbacher	Liverpool	
22697	Isaacs	Aaron	1781	City, London	Baruch Benedet Moshe		Pheby Abrahams	Whitechapel, London	journeyman butcher
18939	Isaacs	Aaron	1807	Aldgate, London	(?) Isaacs	Esther (?)		Aldgate, London	master tailor empl 9
20077	Isaacs	Aaron	1831	Southwark, London	John Isaacs	Eve Joshua	Esther Moses	Spitalfields, London	butcher
11498	Isaacs	Aaron	1844	Aldgate, London	David Isaacs			Aldgate, London	scholar
6932	Isaacs	Abby	1845	Amsterdam, Holland	Solomon Isaacs	Deborah (?)	Juda Jakobs	Aldgate, London	scholar
27519	Isaacs	Abigail	1826	Middlesex, London	(?) Benjamin		Simeon Isaacs	Aldgate, London	tailoress
12187	Isaacs	Abigal	1811	Finsbury, London	(?)		(?) Isaacs	Whitechapel, London	needlewoman
19022	Isaacs	Abraham	1775	Aldgate, London	Leib Deshuler		Judith Barnett	Aldgate, London	general dealer
29524	Isaacs	Abraham	1801	?, London				Spitalfields, London	fruit salesman
22961	Isaacs	Abraham	1812	Aldgate, London			Martha (?)	Aldgate, London	fishmonger
9557	Isaacs	Abraham	1822	Marylebone, London	John Isaacs	Eve Joshua	Elizabeth Jacobs	Aldgate, London	butcher empl 1
1425	Isaacs	Abraham	1826	?, Russia				Plymouth, Devon	general hawker
19836	Isaacs	Abraham	1827	Spitalfields, London	(?) Isaacs	Martha (?)		Spitalfields, London	clothes dealer
22699	Isaacs	Abraham	1828	Aldgate, London	Aaron Isaacs	Pheby Abrahams		Whitechapel, London	cigar maker
18908	Isaacs	Abraham	1831	Aldgate, London	(?) Isaacs	Ellen (?)		Aldgate, London	cigar maker journeyman
13226	Isaacs	Abraham	1832	Whitechapel, London	Mordecai Isaacs	Rebecca (?)		Spitalfields, London	cigar maker
15456	Isaacs	Abraham	1832	Strand, London	Michael Isaacs	Elizabeth (Bloomer) (?)		Covent Garden, London	assistant to orange merchant
20455	Isaacs	Abraham	1832	Middlesex, London	Israel Levy Isaacs	Hannah (?)		Soho, London	
7211	Isaacs	Abraham	1833	Chatham, Kent	John Isaacs	Deborah (?)		Chatham, Kent	assistant general dealer
3858	Isaacs	Abraham	1836	Spitalfields, London	Lewis Isaacs	Hannah (?)		Spitalfields, London	
26180	Isaacs	Abraham	1842	?, London	Zadoc Isaacs	Julia (?)		Aldgate, London	scholar
11163	Isaacs	Abraham	1843	Aldgate, London	Isaac Isaacs	Sarah Lyon		Aldgate, London	scholar
3745	Isaacs	Abraham	1844	Aldgate, London	Isaac Isaacs	Phoebe Jacobs		Spitalfields, London	scholar
17209	Isaacs	Abraham	1844	Paddington, London				Spitalfields, London	
26092	Isaacs	Abraham	1844	?, London	Samuel Isaacs	Jane (?)		Aldgate, London	
2108	Isaacs	Abraham	1845	Canterbury, Kent	Judah Isaacs	Leah Moses	Flora Joel	Canterbury, Kent	
27611	Isaacs	Abraham	1845	Aldgate, London	Mark Isaacs	Esther Abrahams		Aldgate, London	scholar
29534	Isaacs	Abraham	1845	Spitalfields, London	Joseph Isaacs	Ann (?)		Spitalfields, London	scholar
22571	Isaacs	Abraham	1846	Shoreditch, London	Elias Isaacs	Rebecca De Souza		Whitechapel, London	
25665	Isaacs	Abraham	1848	Aldgate, London	Elias Isaacs	Amelia Mendoza		Spitalfields, London	
28198	Isaacs	Abraham	1848	Spitalfields, London	Samuel Isaacs	Frances Nathan		Spitalfields, London	scholar
17475	Isaacs	Abraham	1849	Spitalfields, London	Coleman Isaacs	Rosetta Davis		Spitalfields, London	
19143	Isaacs	Abraham	1849	Aldgate, London	Joseph Isaacs	Esther Lyons		Aldgate, London	

ID	surname	given names	born	birthplace	father	mother	spouse 1	1851 residence	1851 occupation
25724	Isaacs	Abraham	1849	Aldgate, London	Alexander Isaacs	Amelia (?)		Spitalfields, London	
5063	Isaacs	Abraham Pinchas	1792	Bury St Edmunds, Suffolk	Israel Isaacs	(?Dinah) (?)	Sophia (?Isaacs)	Portsmouth, Hampshire	general dealer
28755	Isaacs	Adelade	1843	Middlesex, London	Moses Isaacs	Jane Isaacs		Spitalfields, London	
24302	Isaacs	Adelaide	1833	Norwich, Norfolk	Naphtali Isaacs	Louisa (?)		St Giles, London	bonnet maker
26658	Isaacs	Adelaide	1837	Poznan, Poland [Pozen, Prussia]	Henry Isaacs	Rosetta (?)		Aldgate, London	tailoress
10645	Isaacs	Adelaide	1842	Spitalfields, London	Lazarus (Eliezer) Zusman Isaacs	Rachael (?)		Spitalfields, London	
22569	Isaacs	Adelaide	1842	Poplar, London	Elias Isaacs	Rebecca De Souza		Whitechapel, London	
25732	Isaacs	Adelaide	1846	Spitalfields, London	Lewis Isaacs	Eve Myers		Spitalfields, London	
24036	Isaacs	Agnes	1836	?, Jamaica, West Indies	Jacob Isaacs	Eliza (?)		Marylebone, London	
9544	Isaacs	Ailsa (Alsey, Alice)	1826	Whitechapel, London	Isaac Hart		Barnet Isaacs	Aldgate, London	
26046	Isaacs	Albert Abraham	1846	Whitechapel, London	Isaac Isaacs	Catherine Pyke		Whitechapel, London	
15931	Isaacs	Alex	1847	Spitalfields, London	Israel Isaacs	Rachael Simmons		Whitechapel, London	scholar
25718	Isaacs	Alexander	1815	?, Poland			Amelia (?)	Spitalfields, London	general dealer
7393	Isaacs	Alexander	1817	?, Poland	Isaac Moses/Slubowski		Frances Meyer	Aldgate, London	trimming manufacturer
12034	Isaacs	Alexander	1823	Portsmouth, Hampshire	Lewis (Aryeh, Uriel) Isaacs	Judith Barnett	Sophia Cohen	Whitechapel, London	cigar maker
14832	Isaacs	Alexander	1828	Finsbury, London	Abraham		Rose (Rayner) (?)	Haggerston, London	fruiterer
12038	Isaacs	Alexander	1850	Whitechapel, London	Henry Isaacs	Maria Isaacs		Whitechapel, London	
20325	Isaacs	Alfred	1835	Aldgate, London	Lewis Isaacs	Sarah Elizabeth Abrahams		Aldgate, London	cigar maker
20998	Isaacs	Alfred John	1830	Strand, London	John Isaacs	Esther (?)	(?)	Aldgate, London	teacher of dancing
19253	Isaacs	Alice	1806	Whitechapel, London	(?)		Lewis Isaacs	Aldgate, London	
6106	Isaacs	Alice	1851	Strand, London	John Isaacs	Amelia Isaacs		Strand, London	
19478	Isaacs	Amelia	1814	Marylebone, London	Isaac Isaacs	Deborah (?)	John Isaacs	Strand, London	
25660	Isaacs	Amelia	1815	Aldgate, London	Eliezer Mendoza	Esther de Micael Jonas	Elias Isaacs	Spitalfields, London	
25719	Isaacs	Amelia	1817	?, Poland	(?)		Alexander Isaacs	Spitalfields, London	
21596	Isaacs	Amelia	1835	Cambridge, Cambridgeshire	Ralph Isaacs	Fanny (?)		Strand, London	milliner
9264	Isaacs	Amelia	1839	Aldgate, London	Samuel Isaacs	Catherine (?)	John Keesing	Aldgate, London	
1214	Isaacs	Amelia	1840	Plymouth, Devon	Isaac Isaacs	Fanny (?)		Plymouth, Devon	
21229	Isaacs	Amelia	1849	Spitalfields, London	Isaac Isaacs	Kitty (Catherine) (?)		Spitalfields, London	
10111	Isaacs	Amelia	1850	Euston, London	Lewis (Lazarus) Isaacs	Caroline Jones	Emanuel Moses [Albert M Moss]	Euston, London	
27332	Isaacs	Ami	1807	?, Poland [?, Prussia]	(?)		(?) Isaacs	Aldgate, London	general dealer
10653	Isaacs	Angel	1830	Aldgate, London	Mark (Mordecai) Isaacs	Elizabeth (?)	Sarah Moses	Spitalfields, London	glass dealer
6052	Isaacs	Angel Abraham	1814	?, London	Abraham Isaacs		Sarah Benjamin	Aldgate, London	general dealer
19963	Isaacs	Angelina	1791	?, London	(?)			Whitechapel, London	annuitant
10998	Isaacs	Angell	1826	Middlesex, London				Aldgate, London	general dealer
29529	Isaacs	Ann	1808	Spitalfields, London	(?)		Joseph Isaacs	Spitalfields, London	
8444	Isaacs	Ann	1815	Plymouth, Devon	(?)		Samuel Isaacs	Portsmouth, Hampshire	
799	Isaacs	Ann	1826	Whitechapel, London	Samuel Isaacs	Elizabeth (?)		Spitalfields, London	cap maker
24938	Isaacs	Ann	1848	Spitalfields, London	Lewis Isaacs	Sarah (?)		Bethnal Green, London	
1328	Isaacs	Ann (Hannah)	1820	?, London			John Isaacs	Plymouth, Devon	
7326	Isaacs	Ann (Hannah, Nancy)	1831	Spitalfields, London	Isaac Isaacs	Sarah (?)	Phineas Nunez	Spitalfields, London	
15388	Isaacs	Anna	1805	Jamaica, West Indies	Solomon Marks	Phoebe (?)	Barnett Isaacs	Waterloo, London	

ID	surname	given names	born	birthplace	father	mother	spouse 1	1851 residence	1851 occupation
19998	Isaacs	Anna	1805	Frome, Somerset	(?) Lyons	Bella (?)	Samuel Isaacs	Bristol	silversmith + dealer in plate + jewellery
6051	Isaacs	Anne	1820	Hackney, London	(?) Strutton		Elias Isaacs	Aldgate, London	
20458	Isaacs	Anne	1840	Middlesex, London	Israel Levy Isaacs	Hannah (?)		Soho, London	day scholar
26554	Isaacs	Anne	1779	Middlesex, London	(?)		Wolfe Isaacs	Abergavenny, Wales	
24303	Isaacs	Anne R	1843	Finsbury, London	Naphtali Isaacs	Louisa (?)		St Giles, London	scholar
17979	Isaacs	Annie	1836	Spitalfields, London	Isaac Isaacs	Mary (Miriam, Polly) Solomons	Simeon S Josephs	Aldgate, London	furniture broker
5336	Isaacs	Annie	1841	Whitechapel, London	Lewis Isaacs	Jane (?)	Joseph Levi	Whitechapel, London	
20080	Isaacs	Annie (Hannah)	1847	Lambeth, London	Lamert Isaacs	(?Ann) (?)	Thomas Coley Bills	Waterloo, London	
21812	Isaacs	Annie (Hannah)	1847	Aldgate, London	Isaac Isaacs	Rachel Lazarus	Frederick Lewis Lewisson (Louisson)	Aldgate, London	
5346	Isaacs	Arabella	1850	Liverpool	David Myer Isaacs	Esther Levy		Liverpool	
22701	Isaacs	Aron	1830	City, London	Aaron Isaacs	Pheby Abrahams		Whitechapel, London	cigar maker
17951	Isaacs	Asher	1789	Aldgate, London	Eli Isaacs		Judith Cohen	Aldgate, London	victualler
5768	Isaacs	Asher	1826	?, Russia	Isaac (?)		Esther Davis	Whitechapel, London	tailor + trimming seller
14917	Isaacs	Asher	1836	Middlesex, London				Bethnal Green, London	boarding school pupil
21222	Isaacs	Asher	1838	Spitalfields, London	Isaac Isaacs	Kitty (Catherine) (?)	Catherine Marks	Spitalfields, London	
27609	Isaacs	Asher	1841	?Aldgate, London	Mark Isaacs	Esther Abrahams		Aldgate, London	scholar
30539	Isaacs	Asher	1851	Whitechapel, London	Mark Isaacs	Julia Solomon		Whitechapel, London	
30540	Isaacs	Asher	1851	Aldgate, London	Elias Isaacs	Jane Simmons		Aldgate, London	
24039	Isaacs	Augusta Mary	1843	Middlesex, London	Jacob Isaacs	Eliza (?)		Marylebone, London	
10203	Isaacs	Barnard	1829	Poznan, Poland [Posen, Prussia]	Benjamin or Yitzhak		Maria Jacobs	Aldgate, London	wholesale jeweller
11359	Isaacs	Barnard	1847	Middlesex, London	(?) Isaacs			Aldgate, London	scholar
18986	Isaacs	Barnard (Barnet)	1826	Aldgate, London	Israel Isaacs	Rachel Andrade Da Costa		Aldgate, London	tailor
10249	Isaacs	Barnet	1794	Spitalfields, London	Benjamin Ze'ev Wolf		Catherine (Kitty) Magnus	Spitalfields, London	clothes dealer
9543	Isaacs	Barnet	1824	Aldgate, London	Chaim Isaacs		Ailsa (Alsey, Alice) Hart	Aldgate, London	licensed victualler
9570	Isaacs	Barnet	1849	Spitalfields, London	John Isaacs	Mary Solomons		Spitalfields, London	
8811	Isaacs	Barnet (Baron)	1846	Aldgate, London	Israel Loly Isaacs	Rachel Cohen	Betsy Lipman	Aldgate, London	
15387	Isaacs	Barnett	1797	Whitechapel, London	Michael Isaacs	Elizabeth (?)	Anna Marks	Waterloo, London	retired West India merchant
13232	Isaacs	Barnett	1850	Spitalfields, London	Lewis Isaacs	Phoebe (?)		Spitalfields, London	
25713	Isaacs	Baruh	1781	?, Poland			Mary (?)	Spitalfields, London	clothes dealer
15917	Isaacs	Benjamin	1814	?, Shropshire	Chaim Isaacs		Esther Allen	Aldgate, London	retailer of beer
10205	Isaacs	Benjamin	1820	Miloslav, Poland [Melaslaw, Prussia]	Benjamin or Yitzhak		Rebecca (?)	Aldgate, London	wholesale jeweller
26765	Isaacs	Benjamin	1839	Liverpool	Solomon Isaacs	(?)		Aldgate, London	scholar
10252	Isaacs	Benjamin	1841	Spitalfields, London	Barnet Isaacs	Catherine (Kitty) Magnus		Spitalfields, London	scholar
21034	Isaacs	Benjamin	1843	?, London				Dover, Kent	boarding school pupil
17782	Isaacs	Benjamin	1844	Aldgate, London	Isaac Isaacs	Esther (?)		Aldgate, London	
19348	Isaacs	Benjamin	1845	Middlesex, London	Solomon Isaacs	Phoebe (?)		Fitzrovia, London	
29210	Isaacs	Benjamin	1847	Aldgate, London	Mark Isaacs	Julia Solomon		Whitechapel, London	
28211	Isaacs	Betsey	1836	Whitechapel, London	Morris Isaacs	Harriet (Hannah) Hyams		Spitalfields, London	tailoress

ID	surname	given names	born	birthplace	father	mother	spouse 1	1851 residence	1851 occupation
13776	Isaacs	Blumer	1846	Strand, London	Philip Isaacs	Fanny Solomons	Daniel Angel	Covent Garden, London	assistant to dealer in iron + marine stores
10107	Isaacs	Caroline	1819	City, London	(?) Jones		Lewis (Lazarus) Isaacs	Euston, London	
10207	Isaacs	Caroline	1820	Miloslav, Poland [Melaslaw, Prussia]	(?) Alexander		Louis (Lewis) Isaacs	Aldgate, London	
22234	Isaacs	Caroline	1836	Aldgate, London	(?) Isaacs	Rachael (?)		Whitechapel, London	parasol maker
10643	Isaacs	Caroline	1839	Spitalfields, London	Lazarus (Eliezer) Zusman Isaacs	Rachael (?)		Spitalfields, London	umbrella maker
6834	Isaacs	Catharine	1830	Aldgate, London				Spitalfields, London	furrier
11186	Isaacs	Catharine	1843	Aldgate, London	Michael Isaacs	Leah (?)		Aldgate, London	
11162	Isaacs	Catharine (Kate)	1838	Aldgate, London	Isaac Isaacs	Sarah Lyon		Aldgate, London	scholar
10440	Isaacs	Catherine	1792	Spitalfields, London	(?)		Emanuel Isaacs	Spitalfields, London	general dealer
19014	Isaacs	Catherine	1799	Middlesex, London	Michael Isaacs	Elizabeth (?)		Whitechapel, London	
10745	Isaacs	Catherine	1811	?, Holland	(?)			Spitalfields, London	domestic assistant
26044	Isaacs	Catherine	1814	City, London	Lewis Eleazer Pyke	Charlotte Woolf	Isaac Isaacs	Whitechapel, London	jeweller
22834	Isaacs	Catherine	1822	Middlesex, London	(?)		Samuel Isaacs	Whitechapel, London	dealer
26885	Isaacs	Catherine	1842	Middlesex, London	Simon Isaacs	Rose Michaels		Aldgate, London	scholar
27610	Isaacs	Catherine	1843	Aldgate, London	Mark Isaacs	Esther Abrahams		Aldgate, London	scholar
10658	Isaacs	Catherine	1844	Spitalfields, London	Mark (Mordecai) Isaacs	Elizabeth (?)		Spitalfields, London	scholar
25439	Isaacs	Catherine (Kate)	1838	?, London	Isaac Isaacs	Leah Harris	Joel Joel	Spitalfields, London	
8968	Isaacs	Catherine (Kate)	1840	Aldgate, London	Henry Isaacs	Sarah (?)	Michael Victor (Haim) Cavaliero	Aldgate, London	
5535	Isaacs	Catherine (Kate)	1842	St Pancras, London	Lewis (Lazarus) Isaacs	Caroline Jones	Simeon (Simon) (Morris) Harris	Euston, London	
20309	Isaacs	Catherine (Kate)	1842	Aldgate, London	Elias Isaacs	Jane Simmons	Aaron Cohen	Aldgate, London	scholar
6130	Isaacs	Catherine (Kate) (Kate)	1825	Finsbury, London	Shlomeh Zalman Benjamin?)		Elias Isaacs	Covent Garden, London	
800	Isaacs	Catherine (Kate, Yetta)	1828	Whitechapel, London	Samuel Isaacs	Elizabeth (?)	Joseph Follick [Pontiel Wallach]	Spitalfields, London	cap maker
7179	Isaacs	Charles	1823	Chatham, Kent	Isaac Isaacs	Katherine (?)	Julia Samuel	Chatham, Kent	
13775	Isaacs	Charles	1838	Strand, London	Phillip Isaacs	Blumer (?)	Deborah Isaacs	Covent Garden, London	assistant to dealer in iron + marine stores
19705	Isaacs	Charles Samuel	1835	?Portsmouth, Hampshire	Samuel Isaacs	Ann (?)		Portsmouth, Hampshire	
15337	Isaacs	Clara	1819	Westminster, London	Henry Abrahams		Emanuel Isaacs	Southwark, London	
17472	Isaacs	Coleman	1821	Spitalfields, London	Abraham Isaacs		Rosetta Davis	Spitalfields, London	cabman
28514	Isaacs	Daniel	1819	Aldgate, London			Harriet (?)	Spitalfields, London	general dealer
22570	Isaacs	Daniel	1844	Poplar, London	Elias Isaacs	Rebecca De Souza		Whitechapel, London	
29718	Isaacs	David	1776	Aldgate, London			Leah (?)	Aldgate, London	watch finisher
29721	Isaacs	David	1777	Aldgate, London				Aldgate, London	infirm + receiving parish relief
11492	Isaacs	David	1809	Whitechapel, London			(?)	Aldgate, London	sponge dealer
26556	Isaacs	David	1813	Abergavenny, Wales	Wolfe Isaacs	Anne (?)		Abergavenny, Wales	occasional assistant (to pawnbroker + clothier?)
3865	Isaacs	David	1828	Spitalfields, London	Isaac Isaacs	Rachael (?)		Spitalfields, London	cigar maker
6101	Isaacs	David	1828	St Giles, London	Philip Isaacs	Blumer (?)	Rebecca Harris	Covent Garden, London	dealer in iron + marine stores

ID	surname	given names	born	birthplace	father	mother	spouse 1	1851 residence	1851 occupation
13195	Isaacs	David	1835	Aldgate, London				Aldgate, London	furrier
26883	Isaacs	David	1835	Middlesex, London	Simon Isaacs	Rose Michaels	Esther (?)	Aldgate, London	furrier
19139	Isaacs	David	1838	Aldgate, London	Joseph Isaacs	Esther Lyons		Aldgate, London	cigar maker
14919	Isaacs	David	1839	Middlesex, London				Bethnal Green, London	boarding school pupil
10108	Isaacs	David	1840	Euston, London	Lewis (Lazarus) Isaacs	Caroline Jones		Euston, London	scholar
22380	Isaacs	David	1840	Spitalfields, London	Samuel Isaacs	Sarah Jacobs		Whitechapel, London	scholar
30715	Isaacs	David	1840	Covent Garden, London	(?) Isaacs	Hannah (?)		Covent Garden, London	scholar
19479	Isaacs	David	1845	Strand, London	John Isaacs	Amelia Isaacs		Strand, London	
2109	Isaacs	David	1846	Canterbury, Kent	Judah Isaacs	Leah Moses		Canterbury, Kent	
6080	Isaacs	David	1846	Clerkenwell, London	Judah Isaacs	Maria (Mary, Miriam) Isaacs		Clerkenwell, London	
22572	Isaacs	David	1848	Poplar, London	Elias Isaacs	Rebecca De Souza		Whitechapel, London	
12820	Isaacs	David	1850	Strand, London	Elias Isaacs	Catharine (Kate) Benjamin		Covent Garden, London	
26183	Isaacs	David	1850	?Aldgate, London	Zadoc Isaacs	Julia (?)		Aldgate, London	
8119	Isaacs	David Asher	1849	Spitalfields, London	Asher Isaacs	Esther Davis	Rosetta Marks	Whitechapel, London	
6131	Isaacs	David James	1845	Strand, London	James David Isaacs	Rachael Belasco	Annie Phoebe Tuckwell	Covent Garden, London	
19466	Isaacs	David Lewis	1842	Covent Garden, London	Lewis Isaacs	Phoebe Davis		Covent Garden, London	
167	Isaacs	David Myer	1810	Leuwarden, Holland	Myer Isaacs		Esther Levy	Liverpool	Minister (Jews)
25013	Isaacs	David Samuel	1819	Finsbury, London	Samuel Isaacs		Ann Stone	Finsbury, London	orange merchant
7186	Isaacs	Deborah	1795	Middlesex, London	(?)		John Isaacs	Chatham, Kent	
6931	Isaacs	Deborah	1825	Amsterdam, Holland	(?)		Solomon Isaacs	Aldgate, London	
6102	Isaacs	Deborah	1845	Strand, London	John Isaacs	Amelia Isaacs	Charles Isaacs	Strand, London	
19349	Isaacs	Deborah	1849	Middlesex, London	Solomon Isaacs	Phoebe (?)		Fitzrovia, London	
24041	Isaacs	Edith Annie	1847	Middlesex, London	Jacob Isaacs	Eliza (?)		Marylebone, London	
9566	Isaacs	Edward	1838	Spitalfields, London	John Isaacs	Mary Solomons		Spitalfields, London	apprentice
19347	Isaacs	Edward	1843	Middlesex, London	Solomon Isaacs	Phoebe (?)		Fitzrovia, London	
22626	Isaacs	Edward A	1829	Manchester	(?) Isaacs	Sarah (?)		Stepney, London	general factor
9411	Isaacs	Edward Abraham	1833	?, London	Isaac Isaacs	Mary (Miriam, Polly) Solomons	Eliza Isaacs	Aldgate, London	assistant
25128	Isaacs	Eleanor (Ellen)	1808	Aldgate, London	Isaac Benjamin		Ellen Benjamin	Finsbury, London	
26045	Isaacs	Eleazer	1844	Whitechapel, London	Isaac Isaacs	Catherine Pyke		Whitechapel, London	
192	Isaacs	Elias	1776	Middlesex, London			Julia (?)	Aldgate, London	solicitor
6047	Isaacs	Elias	1813	Aldgate, London	Abraham Isaacs		Amelia Mendoza	Spitalfields, London	dealer
20305	Isaacs	Elias	1814	?, London	Asher Isaacs		Jane Simmons	Aldgate, London	waterproof clothing maker
6050	Isaacs	Elias	1816	Aldgate, London			Anne Strutton	Aldgate, London	tailor
6026	Isaacs	Elias	1820	Strand, London	David Isaacs	Elizabeth (?)	Catherine (Kate) Benjamin	Covent Garden, London	fishmonger empl 3
22567	Isaacs	Elias	1820	Bethnal Green, London	Israel Isaacs		Rebecca De Souza	Whitechapel, London	cigar maker
11496	Isaacs	Elias	1838	Aldgate, London	David Isaacs			Aldgate, London	scholar
29208	Isaacs	Elias	1844	Aldgate, London	Mark Isaacs	Julia Solomon		Whitechapel, London	
5481	Isaacs	Elias	1845	?Liverpool	David Myer Isaacs	Esther Levy		Liverpool	
4557	Isaacs	Elija	1848	?, London	John Isaacs	Hannah (?)		Birmingham	
24034	Isaacs	Eliza	1810	?, Jamaica, West Indies	(?)		Jacob Isaacs	Marylebone, London	
21092	Isaacs	Eliza	1826	Middlesex, London	(?)		Moses Isaacs	Islington, London	
12039	Isaacs	Eliza	1827	Portsmouth, Hampshire	Lewis (Aryeh, Uriel) Isaacs	Judith Barnett	Abraham Goldsmith	Whitechapel, London	
19251	Isaacs	Eliza	1836	Liverpool	(?) Isaacs			Aldgate, London	

ID	surname	given names	born	birthplace	father	mother	spouse 1	1851 residence	1851 occupation
24038	Isaacs	Eliza	1841	?, Jamaica, West Indies	Jacob Isaacs	Eliza (?)		Marylebone, London	
11404	Isaacs	Eliza	1848	Aldgate, London	(?) Isaacs			Aldgate, London	
29299	Isaacs	Elizabeth	1773	Aldgate, London	(?)		(?) Isaacs	Whitechapel, London	traveller
19013	Isaacs	Elizabeth	1776	Middlesex, London	(?) Levy		Michael Isaacs	Whitechapel, London	
19488	Isaacs	Elizabeth	1780	Aldgate, London	(?)		David Isaacs	Covent Garden, London	
797	Isaacs	Elizabeth	1781	Whitechapel, London			Samuel Isaacs	Spitalfields, London	
8751	Isaacs	Elizabeth	1788	?, London	(?) Levy		Lazarus Isaacs	Aldgate, London	
26150	Isaacs	Elizabeth	1801	Middlesex, London	(?)		(?) Isaacs	Aldgate, London	pen maker
6025	Isaacs	Elizabeth	1802	?London	David Isaacs	Elizabeth (?)		Covent Garden, London	
10652	Isaacs	Elizabeth	1805	Spitalfields, London	Menahem called Nahum		Mark (Mordecai) Isaacs	Spitalfields, London	dress maker
12509	Isaacs	Elizabeth	1810	Aldgate, London	(?)		Philip Isaacs	Great Yarmouth, Norfolk	
7202	Isaacs	Elizabeth	1821	Chatham, Kent	John Isaacs	Deborah (?)	Morris Goldstein	Chatham, Kent	
22230	Isaacs	Elizabeth	1822	Whitechapel, London	(?) Isaacs	Rachael (?)		Whitechapel, London	parasol maker
25749	Isaacs	Elizabeth	1822	Marylebone, London	Samuel Isaacs	Leah Simmons		Spitalfields, London	
29720	Isaacs	Elizabeth	1823	Aldgate, London	David Isaacs			Aldgate, London	furrier
20584	Isaacs	Elizabeth	1824	Whitechapel, London	Nathan Isaacs	Mary (?)		Spitalfields, London	dressmaker
7181	Isaacs	Elizabeth	1825	Chatham, Kent	Isaac Isaacs	Katherine (?)		Chatham, Kent	
20405	Isaacs	Elizabeth	1825	Westminster, London	(?) Nathan		Michael Isaacs	Southwark, London	general salesman
21020	Isaacs	Elizabeth	1830	Bristol	Samuel Isaacs	Anna Lyons		Bristol	
9558	Isaacs	Elizabeth	1831	Spitalfields, London	Reuben Jacobs		Abraham Isaacs	Aldgate, London	
10641	Isaacs	Elizabeth	1835	Spitalfields, London	Lazarus (Eliezer) Zusman Isaacs	Rachael (?)		Spitalfields, London	
25720	Isaacs	Elizabeth	1835	?, Poland	Alexander Isaacs	Amelia (?)		Spitalfields, London	
20079	Isaacs	Elizabeth	1836	Southwark, London	John Isaacs	Eve Joshua	Michael Hart	Waterloo, London	
15920	Isaacs	Elizabeth	1841	Aldgate, London	Benjamin Isaacs	Esther Allen		Aldgate, London	scholar
19467	Isaacs	Elizabeth	1844	Covent Garden, London	Lewis Isaacs	Phoebe Davis		Covent Garden, London	
26660	Isaacs	Elizabeth	1845	Poznan, Poland [Pozen, Prussia]	Henry Isaacs	Rosetta (?)		Aldgate, London	scholar
25733	Isaacs	Elizabeth	1848	Spitalfields, London	Lewis Isaacs	Eve Myers		Spitalfields, London	
15454	Isaacs	Elizabeth (Bloomer)	1805	Aldgate, London			Michael Isaacs	Covent Garden, London	
12515	Isaacs	Elizabeth M	1847	Great Yarmouth, Norfolk	Philip Isaacs	Elizabeth (?)		Great Yarmouth, Norfolk	scholar
13881	Isaacs	Ellen	1796	Liverpool	(?)		Samuel Isaacs	Manchester	
18905	Isaacs	Ellen	1800	Aldgate, London	(?)		(?) Isaacs	Aldgate, London	greengrocer
14779	Isaacs	Ellen	1829	Bath	(?)		Henry Isaacs	Finsbury, London	
5345	Isaacs	Ellen	1839	Liverpool	David Myer Isaacs	Esther Levy		Liverpool	scholar
19692	Isaacs	Ellen	1840	Portsmouth, Hampshire	Samuel Isaacs	Ann (?)		Portsmouth, Hampshire	
18346	Isaacs	Ellen Jane	1825	Weston, Staffordshire	(?)		Julius Isaacs	Wolverhampton, Staffordshire	
24042	Isaacs	Ellen Octavia	1849	Middlesex, London	Jacob Isaacs	Eliza (?)		Marylebone, London	
1330	Isaacs	Elvina (Evelina)	1846	Plymouth, Devon	John Isaacs	Ann (Hannah) (?)		Plymouth, Devon	scholar
11402	Isaacs	Emanuel	1782	Aldgate, London	Simon Isaacs		Harriet Myers	Aldgate, London	coal dealer
10439	Isaacs	Emanuel	1787	Spitalfields, London			Catherine (?)	Spitalfields, London	general dealer
15336	Isaacs	Emanuel	1817	Spitalfields, London	Isaac Isaacs	Mary (Miriam, Polly) Solomons	Clara Abrahams	Southwark, London	furniture dealer + warehouseman
22963	Isaacs	Emanuel	1839	Spitalfields, London	Abraham Isaacs	Martha (?)		Aldgate, London	scholar

ID	surname	given names	born	birthplace	father	mother	spouse 1	1851 residence	1851 occupation
26887	Isaacs	Emanuel	1846	Middlesex, London	Simon Isaacs	Julia Israel		Aldgate, London	scholar
29338	Isaacs	Emma	1821	Whitechapel, London	(?) Hart		Samuel Isaacs	Whitechapel, London	
15389	Isaacs	Emma	1829	Jamaica, West Indies	Barnett Isaacs	Anna Marks	Alfred Rosenthall	Waterloo, London	
21597	Isaacs	Emma	1834	Cambridge, Cambridgeshire	Ralph Isaacs	Fanny (?)		Strand, London	milliner
27494	Isaacs	Ester	1801	Middlesex, London	(?)		(?) Isaacs	Aldgate, London	furniture dealer
7210	Isaacs	Ester	1830	Chatham, Kent	John Isaacs	Deborah (?)	(?) Bernstein	Chatham, Kent	
27521	Isaacs	Ester	1850	Middlesex, London	Simeon Isaacs	Abigail Benjamin		Aldgate, London	
18938	Isaacs	Esther	1766	Aldgate, London	(?)		(?) Isaacs	Aldgate, London	supported by her son
20996	Isaacs	Esther	1799	Bath	(?)		John Isaacs	Aldgate, London	
25506	Isaacs	Esther	1810	?, London	(?)		Henry Isaacs	Tower Hill, London	glass cutter's wife
5342	Isaacs	Esther	1816	Plymouth, Devon	(?) Levy		David Myer Isaacs	Liverpool	
27608	Isaacs	Esther	1816	Middlesex, London	Abraham Abrahams		Mark isaacs	Aldgate, London	
19138	Isaacs	Esther	1817	Aldgate, London	Lyon (Lewis) Lyons		Joseph Isaacs	Aldgate, London	
17781	Isaacs	Esther	1819	Aldgate, London	(?)		Isaac Isaacs	Aldgate, London	
2606	Isaacs	Esther	1821	Southwark, London	Humphrey Isaacs	Rosetta (?)		Spitalfields, London	
15918	Isaacs	Esther	1822	Aldgate, London	Isaac Allen		Benjamin Isaacs	Aldgate, London	
19130	Isaacs	Esther	1824	City, London	(?) Isaacs	Rebecca (?)		Aldgate, London	needlewoman
2032	Isaacs	Esther	1825	Aldgate, London	David Davis	Jane Myers	Asher Isaacs	Whitechapel, London	
18907	Isaacs	Esther	1826	Aldgate, London	(?) Isaacs	Ellen (?)		Aldgate, London	seamstress
16469	Isaacs	Esther	1830	Slough, Berkshire	(?) Isaacs			Knightsbridge, London	domestic servant
21018	Isaacs	Esther	1831	Chatham, Kent	(?) Isaacs			Rochester, Kent	
26882	Isaacs	Esther	1833	Middlesex, London	Simon Isaacs	Rose Michaels		Aldgate, London	
11495	Isaacs	Esther	1834	Aldgate, London	David Isaacs			Aldgate, London	general servant
9262	Isaacs	Esther	1835	Aldgate, London	Samuel Isaacs	Catherine (?)	Abraham Keesing	Aldgate, London	
3859	Isaacs	Esther	1838	Spitalfields, London	Lewis Isaacs	Hannah (?)		Spitalfields, London	
25661	Isaacs	Esther	1840	Aldgate, London	Elias Isaacs	Amelia Mendoza	Naphtali Levy	Spitalfields, London	
22381	Isaacs	Esther	1843	Whitechapel, London	Samuel Isaacs	Sarah Jacobs		Whitechapel, London	scholar
7054	Isaacs	Esther	1844	Spitalfields, London	Isaac Isaacs	Kitty (?)	Lewis (Louis) Cohen	Spitalfields, London	
12132	Isaacs	Esther	1845	Whitechapel, London	Lewis Isaacs	Frances (?)		Spitalfields, London	scholar
19830	Isaacs	Esther	1845	Whitechapel, London	Isaac Isaacs	Hanah (?)	Solomon Henry Lazarus	Spitalfields, London	scholar
1331	Isaacs	Esther	1849	Plymouth, Devon	John Isaacs	Ann (Hannah) (?)	John (Selig) Nelson	Plymouth, Devon	
24578	Isaacs	Esther	1849	Lambeth, London	Isaac Isaacs	Julia Lyons		Lambeth, London	
19707	Isaacs	Esther Ann	1849	Portsmouth, Hampshire	Samuel Isaacs	Ann (?)		Portsmouth, Hampshire	
14973	Isaacs	Esther Elizabeth	1839	Middlesex, London	(?) Isaacs			Bethnal Green, London	boarding school pupil
20074	Isaacs	Eve	1797	Aldgate, London	Ephraim Cohen Joshua		John Isaacs	Waterloo, London	
25728	Isaacs	Eve	1806	Aldgate, London	Michael Myers	Hannah Israel	Lewis Isaacs	Spitalfields, London	
11159	Isaacs	Eve	1825	Aldgate, London	Isaac Isaacs	Sarah Lyon		Aldgate, London	dress maker
29110	Isaacs	Fanny	1777	?, Germany	(?)		(?) Isaacs	Whitechapel, London	furrier
13777	Isaacs	Fanny	1805	Whitechapel, London	(?)		Phillip Isaacs	Covent Garden, London	
1213	Isaacs	Fanny	1812	Exeter, Devon			Isaac Isaacs	Plymouth, Devon	
29111	Isaacs	Fanny	1818	?, Germany	(?) Isaacs	Fanny (?)		Whitechapel, London	furrier
5697	Isaacs	Fanny	1830	Chatham, Kent	John Isaacs	Deborah (?)	Simon Jacob (Jacobs)	Chatham, Kent	
26154	Isaacs	Fanny	1836	Middlesex, London	Isaac Isaacs	Elizabeth (?)	Morris Perkins	Aldgate, London	tailoress
14963	Isaacs	Fanny	1838	Middlesex, London	(?) Isaacs			Bethnal Green, London	boarding school pupil
30714	Isaacs	Fanny	1838	Whitechapel, London	(?) Isaacs	Hannah (?)		Covent Garden, London	scholar

ID	surname	given names	born	birthplace	father	mother	spouse 1	1851 residence	1851 occupation
15921	Isaacs	Fanny	1845	Aldgate, London	Benjamin Isaacs	Esther Allen		Aldgate, London	
21221	Isaacs	Fanny (Frances)	1836	Spitalfields, London	Isaac Isaacs	Kitty (Catherine) (?)		Spitalfields, London	
27613	Isaacs	Fanny (Frances)	1847	Aldgate, London	Mark Isaacs	Esther Abrahams		Aldgate, London	scholar
10647	Isaacs	Flora	1846	Spitalfields, London	Lazarus (Eliezer) Zusman Isaacs	Rachael (?)		Spitalfields, London	
12131	Isaacs	Frances	1809	Whitechapel, London	(?)		Lewis Isaacs	Spitalfields, London	general dealer
18508	Isaacs	Frances	1824	Whitechapel, London	Jacob Meyer		Alexander Isaacs	Aldgate, London	
28197	Isaacs	Frances	1830	Whitechapel, London	Philip Nathan		Samuel Isaacs	Spitalfields, London	
21595	Isaacs	Frances	1831	Middlesex, London	Ralph Isaacs	Fanny (?)		Strand, London	milliner
16246	Isaacs	Frances	1839	?, London	Moses Isaacs	Jessie Polack		Spitalfields, London	scholar
29515	Isaacs	Frances	1846	Spitalfields, London	Moses Isaacs	Mary (?)		Spitalfields, London	
3747	Isaacs	Frances	1850	Aldgate, London	Isaac Isaacs	Phoebe Jacobs		Spitalfields, London	
20081	Isaacs	Francis	1848	Lambeth, London	Lamert Isaacs	(?Ann) (?)		Waterloo, London	
19018	Isaacs	Frederick	1839	Jamaica, West Indies	Barnett Isaacs	Anna Marks		Whitechapel, London	scholar
27476	Isaacs	George	1791	?, Germany	Yitzhak		Martha Davis	Aldgate, London	general dealer
2608	Isaacs	George	1828	Southwark, London	Humphrey Isaacs	Rosetta (?)		Spitalfields, London	
7182	Isaacs	George	1828	Chatham, Kent	Isaac Isaacs	Katherine (?)		Chatham, Kent	
24452	Isaacs	George	1829	Norwich, Norfolk				Strand, London	general dealer
20456	Isaacs	George	1833	Middlesex, London	Israel Levy Isaacs	Hannah (?)		Soho, London	
9263	Isaacs	George	1838	Aldgate, London	Samuel Isaacs	Catherine (?)	Esther Jacobs	Aldgate, London	
24037	Isaacs	Georgina	1838	?, Jamaica, West Indies	Jacob Isaacs	Eliza (?)		Marylebone, London	
21023	Isaacs	Gertrude	1837	Bristol	Samuel Isaacs	Anna Lyons		Bristol	
19706	Isaacs	Gregory Henry David	1846	Portsmouth, Hampshire	Samuel Isaacs	Ann (?)	Rosina Cowen	Portsmouth, Hampshire	
19828	Isaacs	Hanah	1813	Whitechapel, London	(?)		Isaac Isaacs	Spitalfields, London	
19837	Isaacs	Hanah	1829	Spitalfields, London	(?) Isaacs	Martha (?)		Spitalfields, London	tailoress
11648	Isaacs	Hannah	1771	?, Holland	(?)		Levy Isaacs	Aldgate, London	
20953	Isaacs	Hannah	1786	Spitalfields, London	(?)		(?) Isaacs	Aldgate, London	tobacco shipper
28670	Isaacs	Hannah	1793	Amsterdam, Holland	(?)		Lewis Isaacs	Spitalfields, London	
20453	Isaacs	Hannah	1805	Middlesex, London	(?)		Israel Levy Isaacs	Soho, London	
4554	Isaacs	Hannah	1810	?, London	(?Mordecai Davis?)		John Isaacs	Birmingham	
30710	Isaacs	Hannah	1811	Whitechapel, London	(?)		(?) Isaacs	Covent Garden, London	lodging house keeper
3857	Isaacs	Hannah	1815	Spitalfields, London			Lewis Isaacs	Spitalfields, London	
9574	Isaacs	Hannah	1819	Spitalfields, London	(?) Jacobs	Sarah (?)	Joseph Isaacs	Spitalfields, London	
21909	Isaacs	Hannah	1824	Middlesex, London	(?)		(?) Isaacs	Clerkenwell, London	
10441	Isaacs	Hannah	1825	Whitechapel, London	Emanuel Isaacs	Catherine (?)	Joseph Barnett	Spitalfields, London	
25729	Isaacs	Hannah	1829	Aldgate, London	Lewis Isaacs	Eve Myers	Samuel Hyam Isaacs	Spitalfields, London	
2610	Isaacs	Hannah	1833	Southwark, London	Humphrey Isaacs	Rosetta (?)		Spitalfields, London	
7301	Isaacs	Hannah	1835	Whitechapel, London	Isaac Isaacs		Samuel Belasco	Aldgate, London	
25751	Isaacs	Hannah	1835	Spitalfields, London	Samuel Isaacs	Leah Simmons		Spitalfields, London	tailoress
10250	Isaacs	Hannah	1836	Spitalfields, London	Barnet Isaacs	Catherine (Kitty) Magnus		Spitalfields, London	tailoress
22550	Isaacs	Hannah	1837	Aldgate, London	Isaac Isaacs	Sarah Barnett		Aldgate, London	servant
5344	Isaacs	Hannah	1841	?Liverpool	David Myer Isaacs	Esther Levy	(?) Cassell	Liverpool	
6855	Isaacs	Hannah	1842	Aldgate, London	Michael Isaacs	Leah (?)	Emanuel Crabb	Aldgate, London	
17014	Isaacs	Hannah	1843	Strand, London	Michael Isaacs	Elizabeth (?)		Covent Garden, London	scholar
19469	Isaacs	Hannah	1848	Covent Garden, London	Lewis Isaacs	Phoebe Davis		Covent Garden, London	

ID	surname	given names	born	birthplace	father	mother	spouse 1	1851 residence	1851 occupation
19487	Isaacs	Hannah	1849	Strand, London	Mark Isaacs	Sarah (?)		Covent Garden, London	
15930	Isaacs	Hannah	1845	Aldgate, London	Israel Isaacs	Rachael Simmons		Whitechapel, London	scholar
11403	Isaacs	Harriet	1817	Aldgate, London	Raphael Myers		Emanuel Isaacs	Aldgate, London	
28515	Isaacs	Harriet	1824	Aldgate, London	(?)		Daniel Isaacs	Spitalfields, London	
9261	Isaacs	Harriet	1831	Aldgate, London	Samuel Isaacs	Catherine (?)	Ephraim Israel	Aldgate, London	
2094	Isaacs	Harriet	1832	?, Poland	Judah Isaacs	Leah Moses	Myer Joseph Isaacs	Canterbury, Kent	
28209	Isaacs	Harriet (Hannah)	1809	Whitechapel, London	Joseph Hyams		Morris Isaacs	Spitalfields, London	
13227	Isaacs	Hebe	1849	Spitalfields, London	Mordecai Isaacs	Rebecca (?)		Spitalfields, London	
20311	Isaacs	Henrietta (Ann)	1848	Aldgate, London	Elias Isaacs	Jane Simmons		Aldgate, London	
29525	Isaacs	Henry	1807	?, London				Spitalfields, London	fruit salesman?
26999	Isaacs	Henry	1810	?, Holland	Judah Isaacs		Mary Benjamin	Aldgate, London	wholesale boot + shoe dealer
26656	Isaacs	Henry	1811	Poznan, Poland [Pozen, Prussia]	Shlomo		Rosetta (?)	Aldgate, London	jobbing glazier
25505	Isaacs	Henry	1812	?, London			Esther (?)	Tower Hill, London	glass cutter
29537	Isaacs	Henry	1813	Whitechapel, London				Spitalfields, London	greengrocer
8966	Isaacs	Henry	1814	Aldgate, London			Sarah (?)	Aldgate, London	cigar maker
6024	Isaacs	Henry	1818	Covent Garden, London	David Isaacs	Elizabeth (?)	Isabella Isaacs	Strand, London	tailor
29794	Isaacs	Henry	1819	Aldgate, London			Mary (?)	Whitechapel, London	dyer + general dealer
22546	Isaacs	Henry	1824	Spitalfields, London	Isaac Isaacs	Sarah Barnett		Aldgate, London	shoe maker
20324	Isaacs	Henry	1831	Aldgate, London	Lewis Isaacs	Sarah Elizabeth Abrahams		Aldgate, London	cigar maker
8311	Isaacs	Henry	1832	?, Poland	Isaac Jacobs	Blume (?)		South Shields, Tyne & Wear	hawker
19016	Isaacs	Henry	1833	Jamaica, West Indies	Barnett Isaacs	Anna Marks		Whitechapel, London	jeweller
7184	Isaacs	Henry	1835	Chatham, Kent	Isaac Isaacs	Katherine (?)		Chatham, Kent	
26299	Isaacs	Henry	1836	?, London	Isaac Isaacs	Rebecca Marks		Aldgate, London	carver + gilder
22703	Isaacs	Henry	1838	City, London	Aaron Isaacs	Pheby Abrahams		Whitechapel, London	
29532	Isaacs	Henry	1839	Spitalfields, London	Joseph Isaacs	Ann (?)		Spitalfields, London	scholar
15928	Isaacs	Henry	1840	Spitalfields, London	Israel Isaacs	Rachael Simmons	Julia Samuels	Whitechapel, London	scholar
29513	Isaacs	Henry	1841	Spitalfields, London	Moses Isaacs	Mary (?)		Spitalfields, London	
10254	Isaacs	Henry	1845	Spitalfields, London	Barnet Isaacs	Catherine (Kitty) Magnus		Spitalfields, London	scholar
27615	Isaacs	Henry	1850	Aldgate, London	Mark Isaacs	Esther Abrahams		Aldgate, London	
10656	Isaacs	Henry (Harry)	1840	Spitalfields, London	Mark (Mordecai) Isaacs	Elizabeth (?)	Rachel Cohen	Spitalfields, London	cigar maker
14778	Isaacs	Henry Aaron	1830	Aldgate, London	Michael Isaacs	Sarah (?)	Ellen (?)	Finsbury, London	fruit merchant
15339	Isaacs	Henry E	1845	Southwark, London	Emanuel Isaacs	Clara Abrahams	Lizzie Danziger	Southwark, London	
12036	Isaacs	Henry Israel	1826	Portsmouth, Hampshire	Lewis (Aryeh, Uriel) Isaacs	Judith Barnett	Maria Isaacs	Whitechapel, London	cigar maker
18509	Isaacs	Hinda	1850	Aldgate, London	Alexander Isaacs	Frances Meyer	David Politi	Aldgate, London	
9567	Isaacs	Holloday	1840	Spitalfields, London	John Isaacs	Mary Solomons		Spitalfields, London	errand boy
2090	Isaacs	Humphrey	1777	Aldgate, London			Rosetta (?)	Spitalfields, London	dealer in glass
19340	Isaacs	Hyam	1801	St Giles, London	Isaac Isaacs	Deborah (?)		Bloomsbury, London	bottle dealer
25723	Isaacs	Hyam	1847	Aldgate, London	Alexander Isaacs	Amelia (?)		Spitalfields, London	
10649	Isaacs	Hyam (Hyman)	1850	Spitalfields, London	Lazarus (Eliezer) Zusman Isaacs	Rachael (?)		Spitalfields, London	
8308	Isaacs	Hyman	1828	?, Poland	Isaac Jacobs	Blume (?)	Sarah (?)	South Shields, Tyne & Wear	hawker
2106	Isaacs	Hyman	1841	Canterbury, Kent	Judah Isaacs	Leah Moses	Maria Hart	Canterbury, Kent	

ID	surname	given names	born	birthplace	father	mother	spouse 1	1851 residence	1851 occupation
11189	Isaacs	Hyman	1849	Aldgate, London	Michael Isaacs	Leah (?)		Aldgate, London	
17977	Isaacs	Isaac	1788	Aldgate, London	Aaron Isaacs		Mary (Miriam, Polly) Solomons	Aldgate, London	furniture broker
11156	Isaacs	Isaac	1796	Whitechapel, London	Yehuda Leib		Sarah Lyon	Aldgate, London	tailor
3791	Isaacs	Isaac	1800	Aldgate, London			Sarah (?)	Spitalfields, London	fishmonger
3863	Isaacs	Isaac	1800	Rotterdam, Holland	(?Simon Isaacs)		Rachael (?Mordecai)	Spitalfields, London	general dealer
1212	Isaacs	Isaac	1803	Bavaria, Germany			Fanny (?)	Plymouth, Devon	master jeweller
11390	Isaacs	Isaac	1804	Middlesex, London			(?)	Aldgate, London	pickle merchant
17780	Isaacs	Isaac	1810	Aldgate, London			Esther (?)	Aldgate, London	fruiterer
26043	Isaacs	Isaac	1811	?, London	Yitzhak		Catherine Pyke	Whitechapel, London	jeweller
26555	Isaacs	Isaac	1811	Abergavenny, Wales	Wolfe Isaacs	Anne (?)		Abergavenny, Wales	pawnbroker + clothier
25440	Isaacs	Isaac	1813	Newcastle-under-Lyme, Staffordshire	Chaim		Leah Harris	Aldgate, London	clothier
21025	Isaacs	Isaac	1815	?, Poland [?, Prussia Poland]				Bristol	jeweller
19827	Isaacs	Isaac	1816	Whitechapel, London			Hanah (?)	Spitalfields, London	clothes dealer
21219	Isaacs	Isaac	1817	Spitalfields, London	Abraham		Kitty (Catherine) (?)	Spitalfields, London	furniture broker
21809	Isaacs	Isaac	1817	Spitalfields, London	Samuel Isaacs	Sarah Jacobs	Rachel Lazarus	Aldgate, London	general dealer
3742	Isaacs	Isaac	1821	Marylebone, London	John Isaacs	Eve Joshua	Phoebe Jacobs	Spitalfields, London	dealer
24576	Isaacs	Isaac	1825	Spitalfields, London			Julia Lyons	Lambeth, London	tailor
22233	Isaacs	Isaac	1831	Aldgate, London	(?) Isaacs	Rachael (?)		Whitechapel, London	cigar maker
24453	Isaacs	Isaac	1833	Norwich, Norfolk				Strand, London	
21557	Isaacs	Isaac	1836	Finsbury, London	Elias Isaacs	Anne Strutton		Aldgate, London	scholar
21059	Isaacs	Isaac	1838	?, London				Dover, Kent	boarding school pupil
1329	Isaacs	Isaac	1842	Plymouth, Devon	John Isaacs	Ann (Hannah) (?)		Plymouth, Devon	scholar
10657	Isaacs	Isaac	1842	Spitalfields, London	Mark (Mordecai) Isaacs	Elizabeth (?)		Spitalfields, London	scholar
2107	Isaacs	Isaac	1843	Canterbury, Kent	Judah Isaacs	Leah Moses	Deborah ?Solovachevick	Canterbury, Kent	
12513	Isaacs	Isaac	1843	Great Yarmouth, Norfolk	Philip Isaacs	Elizabeth (?)		Great Yarmouth, Norfolk	scholar
10109	Isaacs	Isaac	1844	Euston, London	Lewis (Lazarus) Isaacs	Caroline Jones	Sarah Jacobs	Euston, London	scholar
19468	Isaacs	Isaac	1846	Covent Garden, London	Lewis Isaacs	Phoebe Davis		Covent Garden, London	
15340	Isaacs	Isaac	1850	Southwark, London	Emanuel Isaacs	Clara Abrahams		Southwark, London	
30548	Isaacs	Isaac	1851	Aldgate, London	Alexander Isaacs	Frances Meyer		Aldgate, London	
6103	Isaacs	Isaac (John James Irving)	1849	Strand, London	John Isaacs	Amelia Isaacs		Strand, London	
8120	Isaacs	Isaac Asher	1851	Whitechapel, London	Asher Isaacs	Esther Davis	Hannah (Annie) Harris	Whitechapel, London	
19344	Isaacs	Isaacs	1838	Middlesex, London	Solomon Isaacs	Phoebe (?)		Fitzrovia, London	bottle merchant
19339	Isaacs	Isabella	1810	Marylebone, London	Isaac Isaacs	Deborah (?)	Henry Isaacs	Bloomsbury, London	
21594	Isaacs	Isabella	1824	Middlesex, London	Ralph Isaacs	Fanny (?)		Strand, London	milliner
20322	Isaacs	Isabella	1827	Aldgate, London	Lewis Isaacs	Sarah Elizabeth Abrahams		Aldgate, London	
1215	Isaacs	Isabella	1844	Plymouth, Devon	Isaac Isaacs	Fanny (?)	David Abrahams	Plymouth, Devon	
29211	Isaacs	Isabella	1850	Aldgate, London	Mark Isaacs	Julia Solomon		Whitechapel, London	
26089	Isaacs	Isaiah	1791	?, Poland [?, Prussia]			(?)	Aldgate, London	clothes dealer
7554	Isaacs	Israel	1787	Aldgate, London	Naphtali Hirts		Rachel Andrade Da Costa	Aldgate, London	butcher
15923	Isaacs	Israel	1806	Whitechapel, London	Reuben Zelig Isaacs		Rachael Simmons	Whitechapel, London	commercial traveller in stationery
22378	Isaacs	Israel	1832	Spitalfields, London	Samuel Isaacs	Sarah Jacobs		Whitechapel, London	tailor

ID	surname	given names	born	birthplace	father	mother	spouse 1	1851 residence	1851 occupation
26153	Isaacs	Israel	1833	Middlesex, London	Isaac Isaacs	Elizabeth (?)		Aldgate, London	cigar maker
22573	Isaacs	Israel	1849	Bethnal Green, London	Elias Isaacs	Rebecca De Souza		Whitechapel, London	
20452	Isaacs	Israel Levy	1807	Middlesex, London			Hannah (?)	Soho, London	bird + animal dealer
8807	Isaacs	Israel Loly	1802	Aldgate, London	Abraham Isaacs	Judith Barnett	Rachel Cohen	Aldgate, London	general dealer, fruit merchant + clothier
27735	Isaacs	Jacob	1791	?, Russia				Spitalfields, London	traveller
24033	Isaacs	Jacob	1800	?, Jamaica, West Indies			Eliza (?)	Marylebone, London	merchant
11150	Isaacs	Jacob	1821	Spitalfields, London				Aldgate, London	poulterer
13743	Isaacs	Jacob	1822	?, Poland [?, Prussia]				Manchester	smallware dealer
27361	Isaacs	Jacob	1822	?, Poland				Aldgate, London	slipper maker
20888	Isaacs	Jacob	1830	?, Poland [?, Prussia]				Bedford, Bedfordshire	watchmaker
22377	Isaacs	Jacob	1830	Spitalfields, London	Samuel Isaacs	Sarah Jacobs		Whitechapel, London	clothes dealer
13093	Isaacs	Jacob	1833	Frankfurt, Germany				Clerkenwell, London	convict + cigar maker
25115	Isaacs	Jacob	1835	?, London				Finsbury, London	shoemaker
25721	Isaacs	Jacob	1842	Aldgate, London	Alexander Isaacs	Amelia (?)		Spitalfields, London	
20591	Isaacs	Jacob	1844	Whitechapel, London	Nathan Isaacs	Mary (?)		Spitalfields, London	scholar
29535	Isaacs	James	1849	Spitalfields, London	Joseph Isaacs	Ann (?)		Spitalfields, London	
5333	Isaacs	Jane	1803	Middlesex, London	(?)		Lewis Isaacs	Whitechapel, London	
20306	Isaacs	Jane	1812	?, London	Isaac Simmons	(?Sarah Israel)	Elias Isaacs	Aldgate, London	
28753	Isaacs	Jane	1815	Surrey, London	(?) Isaacs		Moses Isaacs	Spitalfields, London	
2605	Isaacs	Jane	1816	Kennington, London	Humphrey Isaacs	Rosetta (?)		Spitalfields, London	
26091	Isaacs	Jane	1823	?, Poland [?, Prussia]	(?)		Samuel Isaacs	Aldgate, London	
26151	Isaacs	Jane	1827	Middlesex, London	Isaac Isaacs	Elizabeth (?)		Aldgate, London	tailoress
31092	Isaacs	Jane	1837	?, London	(?) Isaacs	(?) Davis		Northampton, Northamptonshire	scholar
15919	Isaacs	Jane	1839	Aldgate, London	Benjamin Isaacs	Esther Allen		Aldgate, London	dressmaker
22965	Isaacs	Jane	1843	Spitalfields, London	Abraham Isaacs	Martha (?)		Aldgate, London	scholar
12819	Isaacs	Jane	1849	Strand, London	Elias Isaacs	Catharine (Kate) Benjamin		Covent Garden, London	
6104	Isaacs	Jane	1850	Strand, London	John Isaacs	Amelia Isaacs	Elliot Emanuel	Strand, London	
26888	Isaacs	Jane	1851	?Aldgate, London	Simon Isaacs	Julia Israel		Aldgate, London	
1218	Isaacs	Jeanette	1850	Plymouth, Devon	Isaac Isaacs	Fanny (?)		Plymouth, Devon	
16245	Isaacs	Jessie	1819	?, London	Michael Polack		Moses Isaacs	Spitalfields, London	
19346	Isaacs	Jessie	1841	Middlesex, London	Solomon Isaacs	Phoebe (?)	Maurice Makower	Fitzrovia, London	scholar
6054	Isaacs	Jessie	1842	Whitechapel, London	Angel Abraham Isaacs	Sarah Benjamin	Abraham Phillips	Aldgate, London	scholar
11151	Isaacs	Jessy	1817	Aldgate, London	(?) Isaacs			Aldgate, London	
5479	Isaacs	Joel	1845	Liverpool	David Myer Isaacs	Esther Levy		Liverpool	scholar
12516	Isaacs	Joel	1848	Great Yarmouth, Norfolk	Philip Isaacs	Elizabeth (?)		Great Yarmouth, Norfolk	
7185	Isaacs	John	1787	Middlesex, London	Samuel Isaacs		Deborah (?)	Chatham, Kent	silversmith + navy agent
8378	Isaacs	John	1794	Southampton, Hampshire			Frances Blake	Southampton, Hampshire	spectacles maker
20073	Isaacs	John	1798	Elephant & Castle, London	Jacob Isaac Printsman (Frenchman?)		Eve Joshua	Waterloo, London	harness maker
1327	Isaacs	John	1803	?, Poland			Ann (Hannah) (?)	Plymouth, Devon	oilcoat mfr
4553	Isaacs	John	1812	?, London			Hannah (?)	Birmingham	tailor
6031	Isaacs	John	1815	Piccadilly, London	David Isaacs	Elizabeth (?)	Amelia Isaacs	Strand, London	tailor
9564	Isaacs	John	1819	Limehouse, London	Hayim Yehiel HaLevi		Mary Solomons	Spitalfields, London	general dealer

ID	surname	given names	born	birthplace	father	mother	spouse 1	1851 residence	1851 occupation
22702	Isaacs	John	1832	City, London	Aaron Isaacs	Pheby Abrahams		Whitechapel, London	cigar maker
28673	Isaacs	John	1834	Middlesex, London	Lewis Isaacs	Hannah (?)		Spitalfields, London	
29511	Isaacs	John	1835	Spitalfields, London	Moses Isaacs	Mary (?)		Spitalfields, London	
22545	Isaacs	John	1839	Aldgate, London	Isaac Isaacs	Sarah Barnett	Sarah Lazarus	Aldgate, London	scholar
10644	Isaacs	John	1841	Spitalfields, London	Lazarus (Eliezer) Zusman Isaacs	Rachael (?)		Spitalfields, London	
3744	Isaacs	John	1842	Aldgate, London	Isaac Isaacs	Phoebe Jacobs	Sarah Benjamin	Spitalfields, London	scholar
30717	Isaacs	John	1844	Covent Garden, London	(?) Isaacs	Hannah (?)		Covent Garden, London	scholar
11187	Isaacs	John	1845	Aldgate, London	Michael Isaacs	Leah (?)		Aldgate, London	
19470	Isaacs	John	1848	Covent Garden, London	Lewis Isaacs	Phoebe Davis		Covent Garden, London	
29797	Isaacs	Jonas	1847	Spitalfields, London	Henry Isaacs	Mary (?)		Whitechapel, London	
4559	Isaacs	Jos	1810	?, London				Birmingham	tailor
11281	Isaacs	Joseph	1779	Whitechapel, London			Leah (?)	Aldgate, London	general dealer
2092	Isaacs	Joseph	1795	?, Poland				Plymouth, Devon	oil cloth mfr
29528	Isaacs	Joseph	1806	Spitalfields, London			Ann (?)	Spitalfields, London	fruiterer
19137	Isaacs	Joseph	1813	Aldgate, London	David Isaacs		Esther Lyons	Aldgate, London	cigar maker
9573	Isaacs	Joseph	1816	Spitalfields, London	Solomon Abendana		Hannah Jacobs	Spitalfields, London	pencil maker
22835	Isaacs	Joseph	1818	Middlesex, London				Whitechapel, London	dealer
20028	Isaacs	Joseph	1824	Aldgate, London				Aldgate, London	butcher
2278	Isaacs	Joseph	1827	?, Poland				Leeds, Yorkshire	hawker
26323	Isaacs	Joseph	1831	?, Poland				Aldgate, London	tailor
28210	Isaacs	Joseph	1832	Whitechapel, London	Morris Isaacs	Harriet (Hannah) Hyams		Spitalfields, London	cigar maker
28672	Isaacs	Joseph	1833	Middlesex, London	Lewis Isaacs	Hannah (?)		Spitalfields, London	
26884	Isaacs	Joseph	1841	Middlesex, London	Simon Isaacs	Rose Michaels		Aldgate, London	furrier
3746	Isaacs	Joseph	1846	Aldgate, London	Isaac Isaacs	Phoebe Jacobs	Charlotte (?)	Spitalfields, London	scholar
26182	Isaacs	Joseph	1849	?, London	Zadoc Isaacs	Julia (?)		Aldgate, London	
17784	Isaacs	Joseph	1850	Aldgate, London	Isaac Isaacs	Esther (?)		Aldgate, London	
30543	Isaacs	Joseph	1851	Whitechapel, London	Asher Isaacs	Esther Davis		Whitechapel, London	
8826	Isaacs	Joseph Michael	1832	Aldgate, London	Michael Isaacs	Sarah (?)	Sarah Davis	Aldgate, London	fruiterer
6077	Isaacs	Judah	1803	Holborn, London	David		Maria (Mary, Miriam) Isaacs	Clerkenwell, London	coal dealer
2095	Isaacs	Judah	1808	?, Poland	Isaac Isaacs	Elizabeth Solomons	Leah Moses	Canterbury, Kent	rabbi
20585	Isaacs	Judah	1830	Bethnal Green, London	Nathan Isaacs	Mary (?)		Spitalfields, London	general dealer
27267	Isaacs	Judah	1831	?, London	(?) Isaacs	Sarah (?)		Aldgate, London	cigar maker
22549	Isaacs	Judah	1835	Aldgate, London	Isaac Isaacs	Sarah Barnett	Rachel Barnett	Aldgate, London	errand boy
27001	Isaacs	Judah	1848	?Aldgate, London	Henry Isaacs	Mary Benjamin		Aldgate, London	
22551	Isaacs	Judas	1841	Aldgate, London	Isaac Isaacs	Sarah Barnett		Aldgate, London	scholar
19023	Isaacs	Judith	1778	Aldgate, London	Baruch Katsov Barnett		Abraham Isaacs	Aldgate, London	
17952	Isaacs	Judith	1793	Aldgate, London	Joseph Benjamin Zeev Wolf Cohen		Asher Isaacs	Aldgate, London	victualler
24043	Isaacs	Judith	1803	?, Jamaica, West Indies	(?) Isaacs			Marylebone, London	
25663	Isaacs	Judith	1844	Aldgate, London	Elias Isaacs	Amelia Mendoza		Spitalfields, London	
30542	Isaacs	Judith	1851	Aldgate, London	Israel Loly Isaacs	Rachel Cohen		Aldgate, London	
26178	Isaacs	Julia	1815	?, London	(?)		Zadoc Isaacs	Aldgate, London	
21593	Isaacs	Julia	1822	King's Lynn, Norfolk	Ralph Isaacs	Fanny (?)		Strand, London	milliner
29207	Isaacs	Julia	1822	Aldgate, London	Lewis Solomon	(?)	Mark Isaacs	Whitechapel, London	

ID	surname	given names	born	birthplace	father	mother	spouse 1	1851 residence	1851 occupation
21135	Isaacs	Julia	1824	Marylebone, London	Samuel Isaacs	Leah Simmons		Aldgate, London	dress maker
26881	Isaacs	Julia	1826	Middlesex, London	(?) Israel		Simon Isaacs	Aldgate, London	
4562	Isaacs	Julia	1827	Birmingham	(?) Isaacs	Sarah (?)		Birmingham	
24577	Isaacs	Julia	1828	Lambeth, London	(?) Lyons		Isaac Isaacs	Lambeth, London	
27495	Isaacs	Julia	1830	Middlesex, London	(?) Isaacs	Ester (?)		Aldgate, London	needlewoman
15925	Isaacs	Julia	1833	Spitalfields, London	Israel Isaacs	Rachael Simmons	Solomon Jacobs	Whitechapel, London	
10444	Isaacs	Julia	1834	Spitalfields, London	Emanuel Isaacs	Catherine (?)	Abraham Isaacs	Spitalfields, London	tailoress
14948	Isaacs	Julia	1836	Middlesex, London	(?) Isaacs			Bethnal Green, London	boarding school pupil
19017	Isaacs	Julia	1836	Jamaica, West Indies	Barnett Isaacs	Anna Marks		Whitechapel, London	
23006	Isaacs	Julia	1836	Covent Garden, London	Abraham Isaacs	Rachael Belasco		Covent Garden, London	
3796	Isaacs	Julia	1837	Spitalfields, London	Isaac Isaacs	Sarah (?)		Spitalfields, London	
10415	Isaacs	Julia	1837	Spitalfields, London	(?) Isaacs			Spitalfields, London	
19704	Isaacs	Julia	1837	?Portsmouth, Hampshire	Samuel Isaacs	Ann (?)		Portsmouth, Hampshire	
10251	Isaacs	Julia	1838	Spitalfields, London	Barnet Isaacs	Catherine (Kitty) Magnus		Spitalfields, London	apprentice tailoress
22552	Isaacs	Julia	1844	Aldgate, London	Isaac Isaacs	Sarah Barnett		Aldgate, London	scholar
4556	Isaacs	Julia	1846	Birmingham	John Isaacs	Hannah (?)		Birmingham	
1217	Isaacs	Julia	1848	Plymouth, Devon	Isaac Isaacs	Fanny (?)		Plymouth, Devon	
5484	Isaacs	Julia	1848	Liverpool	David Myer Isaacs	Esther Levy		Liverpool	scholar
30541	Isaacs	Julia	1851	Aldgate, London	Elias Isaacs	Jane Simmons		Aldgate, London	
15499	Isaacs	Julien	1835	Covent Garden, London	(?) Isaacs			Covent Garden, London	servant
18345	Isaacs	Julius	1815	Cracow, Poland			Ellen Jane (?)	Wolverhampton, Staffordshire	painter + glazier
21813	Isaacs	Kate	1851	Aldgate, London	Isaac Isaacs	Rachel Lazarus	Henry Samuel Harris	Aldgate, London	
15338	Isaacs	Kate (Catherine)	1843	Finsbury, London	Emanuel Isaacs	Clara Abrahams	Isaac Franklin	Southwark, London	
15457	Isaacs	Katherine	1836	Strand, London	Michael Isaacs	Elizabeth (Bloomer) (?)		Covent Garden, London	
21220	Isaacs	Kitty (Catherine)	1816	Spitalfields, London	(?)		Isaac Isaacs	Spitalfields, London	
20076	Isaacs	Lamert	1829	Lambeth, London	John Isaacs	Eve Joshua	Ann (?)	Waterloo, London	harness maker
20589	Isaacs	Lawrence	1839	Whitechapel, London	Nathan Isaacs	Mary (?)		Spitalfields, London	scholar
12571	Isaacs	Lazarus	1760	Amsterdam, Holland			(?)	Norwich, Norfolk	tailor
8750	Isaacs	Lazarus	1791	?, London			Elizabeth Levy	Aldgate, London	fruiterer
28213	Isaacs	Lazarus	1842	Whitechapel, London	Morris Isaacs	Harriet (Hannah) Hyams		Spitalfields, London	scholar
25664	Isaacs	Lazarus	1846	Aldgate, London	Elias Isaacs	Amelia Mendoza		Spitalfields, London	
30538	Isaacs	Lazarus	1851	Haggerston, London	Alexander Isaacs	Rose (Rayner) (?)		Haggerston, London	
10639	Isaacs	Lazarus (Eliezer) Zusman	1815	Whitechapel, London	Hayim		Rachael (?)	Spitalfields, London	general dealer
29719	Isaacs	Leah	1783	Aldgate, London	(?)		David Isaacs	Aldgate, London	
11282	Isaacs	Leah	1787	Whitechapel, London	(?)		Joseph Isaacs	Aldgate, London	general dealer
13211	Isaacs	Leah	1800	Middlesex, London	(?)		Mordecai (Morris) Isaacs	Bloomsbury, London	furniture dealer's wife
2096	Isaacs	Leah	1810	?, Poland	(?) Moses		Judah Isaacs	Canterbury, Kent	
11182	Isaacs	Leah	1818	Whitechapel, London	Jacob Myers		Michael Isaacs	Aldgate, London	
25441	Isaacs	Leah	1818	?, London	Shlomeh Harris		Isaac Isaacs	Aldgate, London	clothier
18770	Isaacs	Leah	1826	Whitechapel, London	Joshua Davis		Lewis (Louis) Isaacs	Aldgate, London	
13225	Isaacs	Leah	1834	Whitechapel, London	Mordecai Isaacs	Rebecca (?)		Spitalfields, London	tailoress
6462	Isaacs	Leah	1836	Southwark, London	John Isaacs	Eve Joshua	Aaron Harris	Waterloo, London	
12510	Isaacs	Leah	1838	Great Yarmouth, Norfolk	Philip Isaacs	Elizabeth (?)		Great Yarmouth, Norfolk	scholar

ID	surname	given names	born	birthplace	father	mother	spouse 1	1851 residence	1851 occupation
28212	Isaacs	Leah	1838	Whitechapel, London	Morris Isaacs	Harriet (Hannah) Hyams	Hyman Levy	Spitalfields, London	
22964	Isaacs	Leah	1841	Spitalfields, London	Abraham Isaacs	Martha (?)		Aldgate, London	scholar
14834	Isaacs	Leah	1850	Haggerston, London	Alexander Isaacs	Rose (Rayner) (?)	Samuel Green	Haggerston, London	
26661	Isaacs	Leah	1851	Aldgate, London	Henry Isaacs	Rosetta (?)		Aldgate, London	
7481	Isaacs	Leon	1833	Liverpool	Lewis Isaacs	Alice (?)		Aldgate, London	articled to a solicitor
11647	Isaacs	Levy	1763	?, Holland			Hannah (?)	Aldgate, London	tailor
12572	Isaacs	Levy	1776	?, Holland				Norwich, Norfolk	teacher of Hebrew
19141	Isaacs	Levy	1842	Aldgate, London	Joseph Isaacs	Esther Lyons		Aldgate, London	
28669	Isaacs	Lewis	1794	?, London			Hannah (?)	Spitalfields, London	tailor
29300	Isaacs	Lewis	1800	Aldgate, London	(?) Isaacs	Elizabeth (?)		Whitechapel, London	traveller
12130	Isaacs	Lewis	1805	Whitechapel, London			Frances (?)	Spitalfields, London	general dealer
25727	Isaacs	Lewis	1805	Whitechapel, London	Shlomo Zalman		Eve Myers	Spitalfields, London	clothier
5332	Isaacs	Lewis	1807	?, Holland			Jane (?)	Whitechapel, London	general dealer in the [jewellery trade?]
19252	Isaacs	Lewis	1807	Liverpool			Alice (?)	Aldgate, London	landed proprietor
6027	Isaacs	Lewis	1810	Spitalfields, London	David Isaacs	Elizabeth (?)	Phoebe Davis	Covent Garden, London	
19834	Isaacs	Lewis	1813	Spitalfields, London	(?) Isaacs	Martha (?)		Spitalfields, London	clothes dealer
3856	Isaacs	Lewis	1814	Spitalfields, London	Mordecai		Hannah (?)	Spitalfields, London	lint dealer
19024	Isaacs	Lewis	1815	Aldgate, London	Abraham Isaacs	Judith Barnett	Sarah Lazarus	Aldgate, London	fruiterer
361	Isaacs	Lewis	1819	Aldgate, London	Shmuel Isaacs			Aldgate, London	cigar maker
4560	Isaacs	Lewis	1819	Whitechapel, London				Birmingham	wax doll maker foreman
13230	Isaacs	Lewis	1821	Spitalfields, London	Mordecai		Phoebe (?)	Spitalfields, London	clothes dealer
21007	Isaacs	Lewis	1826	?, Poland				Liverpool	prisoner + hawker
13773	Isaacs	Lewis	1828	St Giles, London	Philip Isaacs	Blumer (?)		Covent Garden, London	dealer in iron + marine stores
24936	Isaacs	Lewis	1828	Aldgate, London			Sarah (?)	Bethnal Green, London	bootmaker
20587	Isaacs	Lewis	1833	Shoreditch, London	Nathan Isaacs	Mary (?)		Spitalfields, London	general dealer
10655	Isaacs	Lewis	1838	Spitalfields, London	Mark (Mordecai) Isaacs	Elizabeth (?)		Spitalfields, London	cigar maker
11358	Isaacs	Lewis	1838	Middlesex, London	(?) Isaacs			Aldgate, London	scholar
4555	Isaacs	Lewis	1841	Birmingham	John Isaacs	Hannah (?)		Birmingham	
30549	Isaacs	Lewis	1841	Whitechapel, London	Angel Abraham Isaacs	Sarah Benjamin	Julia Angel	Aldgate, London	
6062	Isaacs	Lewis	1842	Middlesex, London	Benjamin Isaacs	Esther Allen	Selina (Simelia, Serina) Phillips	Aldgate, London	scholar
8809	Isaacs	Lewis	1842	Wapping, London	Israel Loly Isaacs	Rachel Cohen		Aldgate, London	
9577	Isaacs	Lewis	1842	Spitalfields, London	Joseph Isaacs	Hannah Jacobs		Spitalfields, London	scholar
29533	Isaacs	Lewis	1842	Spitalfields, London	Joseph Isaacs	Ann (?)		Spitalfields, London	scholar
10646	Isaacs	Lewis	1845	Spitalfields, London	Lazarus (Eliezer) Zusman Isaacs	Rachael (?)		Spitalfields, London	
21230	Isaacs	Lewis	1850	Spitalfields, London	Isaac Isaacs	Kitty (Catherine) (?)		Spitalfields, London	
29798	Isaacs	Lewis	1850	Spitalfields, London	Henry Isaacs	Mary (?)		Whitechapel, London	
3413	Isaacs	Lewis (Lazarus)	1818	Euston, London	Mordecai (Morris) Isaacs	Leah (?)	Caroline Jones	Euston, London	furniture dealer + broker
18769	Isaacs	Lewis (Louis)	1830	Southwark, London	Isaac Isaacs	Sarah (?)	Leah Davis	Aldgate, London	
20310	Isaacs	Lewis (Louis)	1845	Aldgate, London	Elias Isaacs	Jane Simmons	Helena Levy	Aldgate, London	
22627	Isaacs	Lewis H	1829	Manchester	(?) Isaacs	Sarah (?)		Stepney, London	general factor
20586	Isaacs	Lion	1832	Shoreditch, London	Nathan Isaacs	Mary (?)		Spitalfields, London	general dealer
5480	Isaacs	Lionel (Lyon)	1843	Liverpool	David Myer Isaacs	Esther Levy		Liverpool	scholar

ID	surname	given names	born	birthplace	father	mother	spouse 1	1851 residence	1851 occupation
4558	Isaacs	Livia	1850	Birmingham	John Isaacs	Hannah (?)		Birmingham	
22232	Isaacs	Louis	1826	Aldgate, London	(?) Isaacs	Rachael (?)		Whitechapel, London	cigar maker
10208	Isaacs	Louis (Lewis)	1819	Miloslav, Poland [Melaslaw, Prussia]	Benjamin or Yitzhak		Caroline Alexander	Aldgate, London	wholesale jeweller
24301	Isaacs	Louisa	1802	Norwich, Norfolk	(?)		Naphtali Isaacs	St Giles, London	bonnet maker
22379	Isaacs	Louisa	1836	Spitalfields, London	Samuel Isaacs	Sarah Jacobs	Samuel Genese	Whitechapel, London	
20406	Isaacs	Louisa	1850	Southwark, London	Michael Isaacs	Elizabeth Nathan		Southwark, London	
20457	Isaacs	Lucy	1838	Middlesex, London	Israel Levy Isaacs	Hannah (?)		Soho, London	
17593	Isaacs	Lydia	1842	Whitechapel, London	(?Joseph) Isaacs			Spitalfields, London	scholar
24040	Isaacs	Lydia	1846	Middlesex, London	Jacob Isaacs	Eliza (?)	Robert Boyd	Marylebone, London	
2824	Isaacs	Maria	1786	?, Holland				Aldgate, London	
8675	Isaacs	Maria	1821	Aldgate, London	(?) Jacobs	Rebecca (?)	(?) Isaacs	Aldgate, London	cloth cap maker
18985	Isaacs	Maria	1823	Aldgate, London	Israel Isaacs	Rachel Andrade Da Costa		Aldgate, London	
7548	Isaacs	Maria	1827	Strand, London	John Isaacs	Esther (?)	Solomon Abraham Hart	Aldgate, London	stationer
12037	Isaacs	Maria	1829	Middlesex, London	Aharon Shmuel Isaacs	(?Sarah Jacobs)	Henry Isaacs	Whitechapel, London	
10443	Isaacs	Maria	1831	Spitalfields, London	Emanuel Isaacs	Catherine (?)		Spitalfields, London	tailoress
12040	Isaacs	Maria	1831	Portsmouth, Hampshire	Lewis (Aryeh, Uriel) Isaacs	Judith Barnett		Whitechapel, London	
13212	Isaacs	Maria	1834	Aldgate, London	Mordecai (Morris) Isaacs	Leah (?)		Bloomsbury, London	
25730	Isaacs	Maria	1834	Aldgate, London	Lewis Isaacs	Eve Myers		Spitalfields, London	
15927	Isaacs	Maria	1836	Spitalfields, London	Israel Isaacs	Rachael Simmons		Whitechapel, London	apprentice dressmaker
26300	Isaacs	Maria	1839	?, London	Isaac Isaacs	Rebecca Marks		Aldgate, London	
19740	Isaacs	Maria	1851	Portsmouth, Hampshire	Samuel Isaacs	Ann (?)		Portsmouth, Hampshire	
6078	Isaacs	Maria (Mary, Miriam)	1813	Spitalfields, London	(?) Isaacs		Judah Isaacs	Clerkenwell, London	
27607	Isaacs	Mark	1818	Middlesex, London	Abraham Isaacs		Esther Abrahams	Aldgate, London	furniture broker
29206	Isaacs	Mark	1820	Spitalfields, London	Asher Isaacs		Julia Solomon	Whitechapel, London	outfitter
19484	Isaacs	Mark	1821	Covent Garden, London			Sarah (?)	Covent Garden, London	picture frame maker
19486	Isaacs	Mark	1842	Strand, London	Mark Isaacs	Sarah (?)		Covent Garden, London	scholar
25722	Isaacs	Mark	1844	Aldgate, London	Alexander Isaacs	Amelia (?)		Spitalfields, London	
3861	Isaacs	Mark	1850	Spitalfields, London	Lewis Isaacs	Hannah (?)		Spitalfields, London	
10651	Isaacs	Mark (Mordecai)	1790	Spitalfields, London	Asher Anshel Isaacs		Elizabeth bat Menahem called Nahum	Spitalfields, London	glass dealer
19832	Isaacs	Martha	1784	Aldgate, London	(?)		(?) Isaacs	Spitalfields, London	
27477	Isaacs	Martha	1798	Aldgate, London	Enslie Asher Davis		George Isaacs	Aldgate, London	
22962	Isaacs	Martha	1816	Spitalfields, London	(?)		Abraham Isaacs	Aldgate, London	general dealer
27496	Isaacs	Martha	1831	Middlesex, London	(?) Isaacs	Ester (?)		Aldgate, London	needlewoman
2105	Isaacs	Martha	1839	Canterbury, Kent	Judah Isaacs	Leah Moses	Isaac Lewis	Canterbury, Kent	
29514	Isaacs	Martha	1845	Spitalfields, London	Moses Isaacs	Mary (?)		Spitalfields, London	
20583	Isaacs	Mary	1803	Shoreditch, London	(?)		Nathan Isaacs	Spitalfields, London	
25714	Isaacs	Mary	1809	?, Poland	(?)		Baruh Isaacs	Spitalfields, London	
29510	Isaacs	Mary	1813	Spitalfields, London	(?)		Moses Isaacs	Spitalfields, London	
27000	Isaacs	Mary	1816	?, London	Michael Benjamin		Henry Isaacs	Aldgate, London	
9565	Isaacs	Mary	1820	Spitalfields, London	(?) Solomons	Hannah Solomons	John Isaacs	Spitalfields, London	
29795	Isaacs	Mary	1829	Aldgate, London			Henry Isaacs	Whitechapel, London	general dealer
7183	Isaacs	Mary	1831	Chatham, Kent	Isaac Isaacs	Katherine (?)		Chatham, Kent	

ID	surname	given names	born	birthplace	father	mother	spouse 1	1851 residence	1851 occupation
22276	Isaacs	Mary	1833	Middlesex, London	(?) Isaacs			Whitechapel, London	
20307	Isaacs	Mary	1835	Aldgate, London	Elias Isaacs	Jane Simmons	Ferdinand Nauheim	Aldgate, London	scholar
15458	Isaacs	Mary	1838	Strand, London	Michael Isaacs	Elizabeth (Bloomer) (?)	Phillip Kaufman	Covent Garden, London	scholar
3797	Isaacs	Mary	1839	Spitalfields, London	Isaac Isaacs	Sarah (?)		Spitalfields, London	
28754	Isaacs	Mary	1840	Middlesex, London	Moses Isaacs	Jane Isaacs		Spitalfields, London	
21910	Isaacs	Mary	1842	Middlesex, London	(?) Isaacs	Hannah (?)		Clerkenwell, London	
15518	Isaacs	Mary	1848	Covent Garden, London	Isaac Isaacs	Sarah Rachael Belasco		Covent Garden, London	
17978	Isaacs	Mary (Miriam. Polly)	1790	Whitechapel, London	David Solomons		Isaac Isaacs	Aldgate, London	furniture broker
13160	Isaacs	Mary Ann	1839	Covent Garden, London	(?) Isaacs			Aldgate, London	scholar
19140	Isaacs	Matilda	1841	Aldgate, London	Joseph Isaacs	Esther Lyons		Aldgate, London	
29722	Isaacs	Matilda	1841	Aldgate, London	(?) Isaacs			Aldgate, London	
20308	Isaacs	Matilda	1842	Aldgate, London	Elias Isaacs	Jane Simmons	Lewis Morris Hurst	Aldgate, London	scholar
16250	Isaacs	Matilda	1847	?, London	Moses Isaacs	Jessie Polack		Spitalfields, London	scholar
27612	Isaacs	Maurice	1846	Aldgate, London	Mark Isaacs	Esther Abrahams		Aldgate, London	scholar
9405	Isaacs	Meyer	1786	Whitechapel, London				Aldgate, London	glass dealer
19012	Isaacs	Michael	1771	Oxford, Oxfordshire			Elizabeth Levy	Whitechapel, London	housekeeper
8824	Isaacs	Michael	1802	Aldgate, London	Samuel Isaacs		Sarah (?)	Aldgate, London	fruiterer
11181	Isaacs	Michael	1802	Wapping, London	Hayim Isaacs		Leah Myers	Aldgate, London	fishmonger
15453	Isaacs	Michael	1803	Aldgate, London			Elizabeth (Bloomer) (?)	Covent Garden, London	orange merchant
20404	Isaacs	Michael	1818	Spitalfields, London	Shmuel		Elizabeth Nathan	Southwark, London	dealer in ironmongery, tinware, boots + shoes
11161	Isaacs	Michael	1836	Aldgate, London	Isaac Isaacs	Sarah Lyon		Aldgate, London	scholar
9575	Isaacs	Michael	1838	Spitalfields, London	Joseph Isaacs	Hannah Jacobs		Spitalfields, London	cigar maker
21223	Isaacs	Michael	1839	Spitalfields, London	Isaac Isaacs	Kitty (Catherine) (?)	Leah Cohen	Spitalfields, London	
9568	Isaacs	Michael	1842	Spitalfields, London	John Isaacs	Mary Solomons		Spitalfields, London	scholar
19019	Isaacs	Michael	1843	Jamaica, West Indies	Barnett Isaacs	Anna Marks		Whitechapel, London	scholar
29796	Isaacs	Michael	1844	Aldgate, London	Henry Isaacs	Mary (?)		Whitechapel, London	
22967	Isaacs	Michael	1849	Spitalfields, London	Abraham Isaacs	Martha (?)		Aldgate, London	
14780	Isaacs	Michael	1850	Finsbury, London	Henry Isaacs	Ellen (?)		Finsbury, London	
25666	Isaacs	Michael	1850	Aldgate, London	Elias Isaacs	Amelia Mendoza		Spitalfields, London	
27002	Isaacs	Michael (Meyer)	1850	Aldgate, London	Henry Isaacs	Mary Benjamin		Aldgate, London	
19025	Isaacs	Miriam	1822	Aldgate, London	Abraham Isaacs	Judith Barnett		Aldgate, London	
13223	Isaacs	Mordecai	1791	Middlesex, London	Isaac		Rebecca (?)	Spitalfields, London	
13210	Isaacs	Mordecai (Morris)	1794	Middlesex, London	Eliezer Valz		Leah (?)	Bloomsbury, London	furniture dealer
28208	Isaacs	Morris	1809	Middlesex, London	Mordecai Isaacs		Harriet (Hannah) Hyams	Spitalfields, London	clothes dealer
19831	Isaacs	Morris	1847	Whitechapel, London	Isaac Isaacs	Hanah (?)		Spitalfields, London	scholar
29509	Isaacs	Moses	1808	Spitalfields, London			Mary (?)	Spitalfields, London	general dealer
28752	Isaacs	Moses	1809	Surrey, London			Jane Isaacs	Spitalfields, London	hatter
16244	Isaacs	Moses	1811	?, London	Simon Isaacs		Jessie Polack	Spitalfields, London	dealer in fish
19996	Isaacs	Moses	1811	Middlesex, London			Eliza (?)	Islington, London	livery stable keeper
14918	Isaacs	Moses	1838	Middlesex, London				Bethnal Green, London	boarding school pupil
21226	Isaacs	Moses	1843	Spitalfields, London	Isaac Isaacs	Kitty (Catherine) (?)		Spitalfields, London	
25662	Isaacs	Moses	1843	Aldgate, London	Elias Isaacs	Amelia Mendoza		Spitalfields, London	
21911	Isaacs	Moses	1846	Middlesex, London	(?) Isaacs	Hannah (?)		Clerkenwell, London	

ID	surname	given names	born	birthplace	father	mother	spouse 1	1851 residence	1851 occupation
10206	Isaacs	Moses (Marcus, Marks)	1850	Aldgate, London	Louis (Lewis) Isaacs	Caroline Alexander		Aldgate, London	
8395	Isaacs	Moses (Moss)	1836	Portsmouth, Hampshire	Reuben Isaacs	Dinah Davis		Southampton, Hampshire	clothier's assistant
1807	Isaacs	Moses Lewis	1809	Tower Hill, London				Merthyr Tydfil, Wales	clothier
22966	Isaacs	Mosey	1845	Spitalfields, London	Abraham Isaacs	Martha (?)		Aldgate, London	scholar
6030	Isaacs	Moss	1823	St Giles, London	David Isaacs	Elizabeth (?)	Mary A (?)	Covent Garden, London	dealer in old iron
11160	Isaacs	Moss	1833	Aldgate, London	Isaac Isaacs	Sarah Lyon		Aldgate, London	cigar maker
25457	Isaacs	Moss	1835	Swansea, Wales				City, London	apprentice
5483	Isaacs	Myer	1837	Liverpool	David Myer Isaacs	Esther Levy		Liverpool	student
11184	Isaacs	Myer	1839	Whitechapel, London	Michael Isaacs	Leah (?)		Aldgate, London	
5334	Isaacs	Myer Lewis	1839	Whitechapel, London	Lewis Isaacs	Jane (?)	Julia Levy	Whitechapel, London	
10648	Isaacs	Nancy	1847	Spitalfields, London	Lazarus (Eliezer) Zusman Isaacs	Rachael (?)		Spitalfields, London	
1216	Isaacs	Nancy	1848	Plymouth, Devon	Isaac Isaacs	Fanny (?)	Z--- Rudelsheim	Plymouth, Devon	
8812	Isaacs	Nancy	1848	Aldgate, London	Israel Loly Isaacs	Rachel Cohen	Benjamin Harris	Aldgate, London	
10209	Isaacs	Nancy	1851	Aldgate, London	Louis (Lewis) Isaacs	Caroline Alexander		Aldgate, London	
24300	Isaacs	Naphtali	1801	Chatham, Kent			Louisa (?)	St Giles, London	straw bonnet maker
20582	Isaacs	Nathan	1801	Shoreditch, London			Mary (?)	Spitalfields, London	general dealer
11494	Isaacs	Nathan	1832	Aldgate, London	David Isaacs			Aldgate, London	general dealer
10642	Isaacs	Nathan	1837	Spitalfields, London	Lazarus (Eliezer) Zusman Isaacs	Rachael (?)		Spitalfields, London	
11183	Isaacs	Nathan	1837	Whitechapel, London	Michael Isaacs	Leah (?)	(?)	Aldgate, London	
6075	Isaacs	Nathan	1849	Spitalfields, London	Israel Isaacs	Rachael Simmons		Whitechapel, London	
21810	Isaacs	Nathan	1849	Aldgate, London	Isaac Isaacs	Rachel Lazarus	Sarah Myers	Aldgate, London	
801	Isaacs	Nathan (Nathaniel) Samuel	1832	Whitechapel, London	Samuel Isaacs	Elizabeth (?)	Rebecca Lazarus	Spitalfields, London	cigar maker
22700	Isaacs	Nathaniel	1830	Aldgate, London	Aaron Isaacs	Pheby Abrahams		Whitechapel, London	journeyman butcher
12188	Isaacs	Phebe	1825	Finsbury, London	(?) Isaacs	Abigal (?)		Whitechapel, London	needlewoman
22704	Isaacs	Pheby	1850	Mile End, London	(?) Isaacs			Whitechapel, London	
27333	Isaacs	Pheobe	1840	Wapping, London	(?) Isaacs	Ami (?)		Aldgate, London	scholar
16249	Isaacs	Pheoby	1845	?, London	Moses Isaacs	Jessie Polack		Spitalfields, London	scholar
12508	Isaacs	Philip	1811	Whitechapel, London			Elizabeth (?)	Great Yarmouth, Norfolk	clothier + furrier
30716	Isaacs	Philip	1841	Covent Garden, London	(?) Isaacs	Hannah (?)		Covent Garden, London	scholar
21228	Isaacs	Philip	1847	Spitalfields, London	Isaac Isaacs	Kitty (Catherine) (?)		Spitalfields, London	
28199	Isaacs	Phillip	1849	Spitalfields, London	Samuel Isaacs	Frances Nathan	Sarah Aylesburg (Nuremberg)	Spitalfields, London	
2609	Isaacs	Phineas	1830	Southwark, London				Spitalfields, London	butcher
6028	Isaacs	Phoebe	1812	Aldgate, London	Mordecai Davis		Lewis Isaacs	Covent Garden, London	
3743	Isaacs	Phoebe	1821	Spitalfields, London	Reuben Jacobs	Frances (?)	Isaac Isaacs	Spitalfields, London	
19343	Isaacs	Phoebe	1821	Middlesex, London	Jacob		Solomon Isaacs	Fitzrovia, London	
13231	Isaacs	Phoebe	1830	Aldgate, London	(?)		Lewis Isaacs	Spitalfields, London	
10253	Isaacs	Phoebe	1842	Spitalfields, London	Barnet Isaacs	Catherine (Kitty) Magnus		Spitalfields, London	scholar
15455	Isaacs	Priscilla	1828	Strand, London	Michael Isaacs	Elizabeth (Bloomer) (?)		Covent Garden, London	
13214	Isaacs	Priscilla	1840	Aldgate, London	Mordecai (Morris) Isaacs	Leah (?)		Bloomsbury, London	scholar
12512	Isaacs	Priscilla	1841	Soho, London	Philip Isaacs	Elizabeth (?)		Great Yarmouth, Norfolk	scholar
10110	Isaacs	Priscilla	1845	Euston, London	Lewis (Lazarus) Isaacs	Caroline Jones	Jacob (John) Hyman	Euston, London	scholar
6079	Isaacs	Priscilla	1849	Clerkenwell, London	Judah Isaacs	Maria (Mary, Miriam) Isaacs		Clerkenwell, London	

ID	surname	given names	born	birthplace	father	mother	spouse 1	1851 residence	1851 occupation
22229	Isaacs	Rachael	1787	Aldgate, London	(?)		(?) Isaacs	Whitechapel, London	parasol maker
11333	Isaacs	Rachael	1791	Aldgate, London	Levy Davis	Mary (?)	(?) Isaacs	Aldgate, London	laundress
18459	Isaacs	Rachael	1800	Montego Bay, Jamaica, West Indies	Solomon Marks	Phoebe (?)	(?) Isaacs	Whitechapel, London	annuitant
12822	Isaacs	Rachael	1811	Gibraltar	David de Abraham Belasco	Sarah de Moses Julian	Abraham Isaacs	Covent Garden, London	
15924	Isaacs	Rachael	1815	Spitalfields, London	Aaron Simmons	Judith Harris	Israel Isaacs	Whitechapel, London	
10640	Isaacs	Rachael	1817	Spitalfields, London	(?)		Lazarus (Eliezer) Zusman Isaacs	Spitalfields, London	general dealer
27265	Isaacs	Rachael	1819	?Amsterdam, Holland	(?) Isaacs	Sarah (?)		Aldgate, London	(?) maker
10442	Isaacs	Rachael	1827	Spitalfields, London	Emanuel Isaacs	Catherine (?)		Spitalfields, London	tailoress
13224	Isaacs	Rachael	1827	Whitechapel, London	Mordecai Isaacs	Rebecca (?)		Spitalfields, London	
20590	Isaacs	Rachael	1842	Whitechapel, London	Nathan Isaacs	Mary (?)		Spitalfields, London	scholar
27614	Isaacs	Rachael	1849	Aldgate, London	Mark Isaacs	Esther Abrahams		Aldgate, London	scholar
23975	Isaacs	Rachel	1811	Aldgate, London	(?) Isaacs			Marylebone, London	assistant to lodging house keeper
8808	Isaacs	Rachel	1815	Aldgate, London	Moshe Cohen		Israel Loly Isaacs	Aldgate, London	
21811	Isaacs	Rachel	1822	?London	Nathan Lazarus		Isaac Isaacs	Aldgate, London	
5699	Isaacs	Rachel	1826	Chatham, Kent	John Isaacs	Deborah (?)	Chapman Jacobs	Manchester	
29055	Isaacs	Rachel	1828	Poznan, Poland [Duchy of Posen, Prussia]	(?) Isaacs			Whitechapel, London	seamstress
22547	Isaacs	Rachel	1830	Aldgate, London	Isaac Isaacs	Sarah Barnett		Aldgate, London	tailoress
5343	Isaacs	Rachel	1835	Bristol	David Myer Isaacs	Esther Levy	Henry Josephi	Liverpool	scholar
21224	Isaacs	Rachel	1840	Spitalfields, London	Isaac Isaacs	Kitty (Catherine) (?)		Spitalfields, London	
17474	Isaacs	Rachel	1841	Spitalfields, London	Coleman Isaacs	Rosetta Davis		Spitalfields, London	
16248	Isaacs	Rachel	1842	?, London	Moses Isaacs	Jessie Polack		Spitalfields, London	scholar
5338	Isaacs	Rachel	1843	Whitechapel, London	Lewis Isaacs	Jane (?)	Marcus Pool	Whitechapel, London	
12514	Isaacs	Rachel	1845	Great Yarmouth, Norfolk	Philip Isaacs	Elizabeth (?)		Great Yarmouth, Norfolk	scholar
6935	Isaacs	Rachel	1849	Aldgate, London	Solomon Isaacs	Deborah (?)		Aldgate, London	
2111	Isaacs	Rachel (Rachael)	1851	Canterbury, Kent	Judah Isaacs	Leah Moses	Marks Joseph Samuel Lyons	Canterbury, Kent	
25130	Isaacs	Rachell	1845	Southwark, London	Woolf Isaacs	Eleanor (Ellen) Benjamin		Finsbury, London	
6570	Isaacs	Ralph	1797	Middlesex, London	Samuel Isaacs		Fanny b. Isaac	Strand, London	traveller
21598	Isaacs	Ralph	1837	Middlesex, London	Ralph Isaacs	Fanny (?)		Strand, London	no calling
11405	Isaacs	Ralph	1838	Aldgate, London	(?) Isaacs			Aldgate, London	
9579	Isaacs	Raphael	1848	Spitalfields, London	Joseph Isaacs	Hannah Jacobs		Spitalfields, London	
16251	Isaacs	Rebeca	1849	?, London	Moses Isaacs	Jessie Polack		Spitalfields, London	scholar
19129	Isaacs	Rebecca	1796	City, London	(?)		(?) Isaacs	Aldgate, London	
19580	Isaacs	Rebecca	1801	Whitechapel, London	(?) (?Isaacs)		(?Samuel Michaels)	Whitechapel, London	tailoress
22568	Isaacs	Rebecca	1818	Portsmouth, Hampshire	Daniel De Souza		Elias Isaacs	Whitechapel, London	cigar maker
27266	Isaacs	Rebecca	1821	?Amsterdam, Holland	(?) Isaacs	Sarah (?)		Aldgate, London	
10204	Isaacs	Rebecca	1823	Miloslav, Poland [Melaslaw, Prussia]	(?)		Benjamin Isaacs	Aldgate, London	
22698	Isaacs	Rebecca	1824	Aldgate, London	Aaron Isaacs	Pheby Abrahams		Whitechapel, London	dress maker
16027	Isaacs	Rebecca	1827	?, London	(?) Isaacs			Whitechapel, London	
862	Isaacs	Rebecca	1830	St Pancras, London	Woolf Lyon	Dinah Isaacs	Simeon Isaacs	Manchester	

ID	surname	given names	born	birthplace	father	mother	spouse 1	1851 residence	1851 occupation
11334	Isaacs	Rebecca	1832	Aldgate, London	(?) Isaacs	Rachael Davis		Aldgate, London	parasol maker
26764	Isaacs	Rebecca	1832	Liverpool	Solomon Isaacs	(?)		Aldgate, London	
21928	Isaacs	Rebecca	1837	?, London	(?) Isaacs	(?) Myers		Aldgate, London	
27247	Isaacs	Rebecca	1837	?Aldgate, London	Lewis Isaacs	Eve Myers		Aldgate, London	
30307	Isaacs	Rebecca	1837	Whitechapel, London	Lewis Isaacs	Jane (?)	Abraham Solomons	Whitechapel, London	
26181	Isaacs	Rebecca	1844	Aldgate, London	Zadoc Isaacs	Julia (?)		Aldgate, London	scholar
26093	Isaacs	Rebecca	1846	Aldgate, London	Samuel Isaacs	Jane (?)		Aldgate, London	
28215	Isaacs	Rebecca	1846	Whitechapel, London	Morris Isaacs	Harriet (Hannah) Hyams		Spitalfields, London	scholar
17783	Isaacs	Rebecca	1848	Aldgate, London	Isaac Isaacs	Esther (?)		Aldgate, London	
27520	Isaacs	Rebecca	1848	Middlesex, London	Simeon Isaacs	Abigail Benjamin		Aldgate, London	
22628	Isaacs	Rebecca A	1832	Manchester	(?) Isaacs	Sarah (?)		Stepney, London	
2110	Isaacs	Reuben	1849	Canterbury, Kent	Judah Isaacs	Leah Moses		Canterbury, Kent	
6933	Isaacs	Rosa	1846	Amsterdam, Holland	Solomon Isaacs	Deborah (?)		Aldgate, London	scholar
28757	Isaacs	Rosa	1849	Middlesex, London	Moses Isaacs	Jane Isaacs		Spitalfields, London	
22231	Isaacs	Rose	1823	Aldgate, London	(?) Isaacs	Rachael (?)		Whitechapel, London	parasol maker
11356	Isaacs	Rose	1831	Middlesex, London	(?) Isaacs			Aldgate, London	servant
14833	Isaacs	Rose (Rayner)	1830	Manchester	(?)		Alexander Isaacs	Haggerston, London	fruiterer
2604	Isaacs	Rosetta	1788	Aldgate, London			Humphrey Isaacs	Spitalfields, London	
20954	Isaacs	Rosetta	1791	Spitalfields, London	(?) Isaacs			Aldgate, London	
26657	Isaacs	Rosetta	1813	Poznan, Poland [Pozen, Prussia]	(?)		Henry Isaacs	Aldgate, London	
17473	Isaacs	Rosetta	1821	Spitalfields, London	Henry Davis		Coleman Isaacs	Spitalfields, London	
3860	Isaacs	Rosetta	1840	Spitalfields, London	Lewis Isaacs	Hannah (?)		Spitalfields, London	
11158	Isaacs	Rosetta (Rose)	1822	Aldgate, London	Isaac Isaacs	Sarah Lyon		Aldgate, London	tailoress
29531	Isaacs	Rossetta	1837	Spitalfields, London	Joseph Isaacs	Ann (?)		Spitalfields, London	scholar
29112	Isaacs	Rosy	1819	?, Germany	(?) Isaacs	Fanny (?)		Whitechapel, London	furrier
29033	Isaacs	S---	1835	Whitechapel, London	Lewis Isaacs	Jane (?)		Whitechapel, London	
30525	Isaacs	Samson	1851	Spitalfields, London	Isaac Isaacs	Kitty (Catherine) (?)		Spitalfields, London	
796	Isaacs	Samuel	1764	Frankfurt-am-Main, Germany			Elizabeth (?)	Spitalfields, London	general dealer
8827	Isaacs	Samuel	1766	Aldgate, London	Wolf Isaacs		Sarah (?)	Aldgate, London	retired fruiterer
8443	Isaacs	Samuel	1793	Ipswich, Suffolk	Israel Isaacs	(?Dinah) (?)	Ann (?)	Portsmouth, Hampshire	clothier
22375	Isaacs	Samuel	1797	Spitalfields, London	Isaac Aharon Isaacs		Sarah Jacobs	Whitechapel, London	clothes salesman
9260	Isaacs	Samuel	1798	Aldgate, London			Catherine (?)	Aldgate, London	fruiterer
19997	Isaacs	Samuel	1804	?, Poland [?, Prussia Poland]			Anna Lyons	Bristol	silversmith + dealer in plate + jewellery
26090	Isaacs	Samuel	1811	?, Poland [?, Prussia]	Yitzhak		Jane (?)	Aldgate, London	traveller
29337	Isaacs	Samuel	1817	Gloucester, Gloucestershire			Emma Hart	Whitechapel, London	merchant
25750	Isaacs	Samuel	1820	Marylebone, London	Samuel Isaacs	Leah Simmons	Hannah Isaacs	Spitalfields, London	clothier
22833	Isaacs	Samuel	1821	Stepney, London			Catherine (?)	Whitechapel, London	dealer
2089	Isaacs	Samuel	1822	Southwark, London	Humphrey Isaacs	Rosetta (?)	Jane Samuels	Spitalfields, London	glass dealer
28196	Isaacs	Samuel	1826	Whitechapel, London	Mordecai Isaacs		Frances Nathan	Spitalfields, London	clothes dealer
7212	Isaacs	Samuel	1827	Chatham, Kent	John Isaacs	Deborah (?)	Esther Leon	Manchester	dealer: china, glass &c
20323	Isaacs	Samuel	1828	Aldgate, London	Lewis Isaacs	Sarah Elizabeth Abrahams		Aldgate, London	cigar maker
24451	Isaacs	Samuel	1828	Norwich, Norfolk				Strand, London	presser + dyer
11493	Isaacs	Samuel	1831	Aldgate, London	David Isaacs		Mary (?)	Aldgate, London	general dealer

ID	surname	given names	born	birthplace	father	mother	spouse 1	1851 residence	1851 occupation
20454	Isaacs	Samuel	1831	Middlesex, London	Israel Levy Isaacs	Hannah (?)		Soho, London	carver + gilder journeyman
13774	Isaacs	Samuel	1833	St Giles, London	Philip Isaacs	Blumer (?)	Sarah Sophia Marks	Covent Garden, London	assistant to dealer in iron + marine stores
29530	Isaacs	Samuel	1833	Spitalfields, London	Joseph Isaacs	Ann (?)		Spitalfields, London	fruiterer
30712	Isaacs	Samuel	1833	Whitechapel, London	(?) Isaacs	Hannah (?)		Covent Garden, London	cigar maker
20588	Isaacs	Samuel	1836	Whitechapel, London	Nathan Isaacs	Mary (?)		Spitalfields, London	general dealer
25129	Isaacs	Samuel	1836	Spitalfields, London	Woolf Isaacs	Eleanor (Ellen) Benjamin		Finsbury, London	assistant to rag merchant
17972	Isaacs	Samuel	1837	Clerkenwell, London	Judah Isaacs	Maria (Mary, Miriam) Isaacs		Clerkenwell, London	
19829	Isaacs	Samuel	1840	Whitechapel, London	Isaac Isaacs	Hanah (?)		Spitalfields, London	scholar
15459	Isaacs	Samuel	1841	Strand, London	Michael Isaacs	Elizabeth (Bloomer) (?)	Catherine Jacobs	Covent Garden, London	scholar
8810	Isaacs	Samuel	1843	Aldgate, London	Israel Loly Isaacs	Rachel Cohen		Aldgate, London	
15929	Isaacs	Samuel	1843	Spitalfields, London	Israel Isaacs	Rachael Simmons		Whitechapel, London	scholar
18347	Isaacs	Samuel	1843	Wolverhampton, Staffordshire	Julius Isaacs	Ellen Jane (?)		Wolverhampton, Staffordshire	
19142	Isaacs	Samuel	1846	Aldgate, London	Joseph Isaacs	Esther Lyons		Aldgate, London	
8828	Isaacs	Sarah	1773	Aldgate, London	(?)		Samuel Isaacs	Aldgate, London	
27264	Isaacs	Sarah	1791	?Amsterdam, Holland	(?)		(?) Isaacs	Aldgate, London	boot + shoe dealer
8825	Isaacs	Sarah	1794	Aldgate, London	(?)		Michael Isaacs	Aldgate, London	
3792	Isaacs	Sarah	1796	Aldgate, London			Isaac Isaacs	Spitalfields, London	
22376	Isaacs	Sarah	1797	Hanover, Germany	Akriel Jacobs		Samuel Isaacs	Whitechapel, London	
22625	Isaacs	Sarah	1800	Liverpool	(?)		(?) Isaacs	Stepney, London	wife of lawyer's clerk
11157	Isaacs	Sarah	1801	Aldgate, London	Moshe Lyon		Isaac Isaacs	Aldgate, London	
22554	Isaacs	Sarah	1805	Spitalfields, London	Yosef HaLevi Barnett		Isaac Isaacs	Aldgate, London	
23974	Isaacs	Sarah	1809	Aldgate, London	(?) Isaacs			Marylebone, London	lodging house keeper
4561	Isaacs	Sarah	1810	?, London			(?) Isaacs	Birmingham	shopkeeper
19833	Isaacs	Sarah	1811	Aldgate, London	(?) Isaacs	Martha (?)		Spitalfields, London	cap maker
8967	Isaacs	Sarah	1814	Whitechapel, London	(?)		Henry Isaacs	Aldgate, London	
6053	Isaacs	Sarah	1815	?, London	Moses Benjamin		Angel Abraham Isaacs	Aldgate, London	
19015	Isaacs	Sarah	1815	Middlesex, London	Michael Isaacs	Elizabeth (?)		Whitechapel, London	
19485	Isaacs	Sarah	1819	?Whitechapel, London	(?)		Mark Isaacs	Covent Garden, London	
798	Isaacs	Sarah	1824	Whitechapel, London	Samuel Isaacs	Elizabeth (?)		Spitalfields, London	cap maker
20075	Isaacs	Sarah	1827	Lambeth, London	John Isaacs	Eve Joshua	Michael Moses	Waterloo, London	furrier
24937	Isaacs	Sarah	1827	Aldgate, London	(?)		Lewis Isaacs	Bethnal Green, London	
22676	Isaacs	Sarah	1830	Aldgate, London	(?)		Selim Isaacs	Whitechapel, London	
23153	Isaacs	Sarah	1830	?, London	(?) Isaacs			City, London	
28671	Isaacs	Sarah	1830	Middlesex, London	Lewis Isaacs	Hannah (?)		Spitalfields, London	
11357	Isaacs	Sarah	1831	Middlesex, London	(?) Isaacs			Aldgate, London	servant
12821	Isaacs	Sarah	1832	Strand, London	Abraham Isaacs	Rachael Belasco	John Edwards	Covent Garden, London	
10654	Isaacs	Sarah	1834	Whitechapel, London	Mark (Mordecai) Isaacs	Elizabeth (?)		Spitalfields, London	dress maker
21022	Isaacs	Sarah	1835	Bristol	Samuel Isaacs	Anna Lyons		Bristol	
30713	Isaacs	Sarah	1836	Whitechapel, London	(?) Isaacs	Hannah (?)		Covent Garden, London	scholar
13213	Isaacs	Sarah	1837	Aldgate, London	Mordecai (Morris) Isaacs	Leah (?)		Bloomsbury, London	scholar
26155	Isaacs	Sarah	1837	Middlesex, London	Isaac Isaacs	Elizabeth (?)	Lewis Moses	Aldgate, London	tailoress
29512	Isaacs	Sarah	1837	Spitalfields, London	Moses Isaacs	Mary (?)		Spitalfields, London	

ID	surname	given names	born	birthplace	father	mother	spouse 1	1851 residence	1851 occupation
12511	Isaacs	Sarah	1839	Great Yarmouth, Norfolk	Philip Isaacs	Elizabeth (?)		Great Yarmouth, Norfolk	scholar
19345	Isaacs	Sarah	1839	Middlesex, London	Solomon Isaacs	Phoebe (?)		Fitzrovia, London	
16247	Isaacs	Sarah	1840	?, London	Moses Isaacs	Jessie Polack	Nathan Romaine (Romano)	Spitalfields, London	scholar
6071	Isaacs	Sarah	1841	Aldgate, London	David Isaacs		Nathan Nathan	Aldgate, London	scholar
21225	Isaacs	Sarah	1841	Spitalfields, London	Isaac Isaacs	Kitty (Catherine) (?)	(?) Hyams	Spitalfields, London	
8676	Isaacs	Sarah	1843	Whitechapel, London	(?) Isaacs	Maria Jacobs		Aldgate, London	scholar
25443	Isaacs	Sarah	1843	Aldgate, London	Isaac Isaacs	Leah Harris	Abraham (Alfred) Rantzen	Aldgate, London	
26659	Isaacs	Sarah	1843	Poznan, Poland [Pozen, Prussia]	Henry Isaacs	Rosetta (?)		Aldgate, London	scholar
20459	Isaacs	Sarah	1844	Middlesex, London	Israel Levy Isaacs	Hannah (?)		Soho, London	day scholar
25731	Isaacs	Sarah	1844	Spitalfields, London	Lewis Isaacs	Eve Myers		Spitalfields, London	
9578	Isaacs	Sarah	1845	Spitalfields, London	Joseph Isaacs	Hannah Jacobs		Spitalfields, London	scholar
26886	Isaacs	Sarah	1845	Middlesex, London	Simon Isaacs	Julia Israel		Aldgate, London	scholar
29209	Isaacs	Sarah	1846	Aldgate, London	Mark Isaacs	Julia Solomon		Whitechapel, London	
19480	Isaacs	Sarah	1848	Strand, London	John Isaacs	Amelia Isaacs		Strand, London	
5482	Isaacs	Sarah	1850	Liverpool	David Myer Isaacs	Esther Levy		Liverpool	
21679	Isaacs	Sarah	1775	Middlesex, London	(?)		Nathan Isaacs	Islington, London	annuitant
20082	Isaacs	Sarah (Leah?)	1850	Lambeth, London	Lamert Isaacs	(?Ann) (?)		Waterloo, London	
24035	Isaacs	Sarah C	1835	?, Jamaica, West Indies	Jacob Isaacs	Eliza (?)		Marylebone, London	
20321	Isaacs	Sarah Elizabeth	1792	Aldgate, London	Henry Abrahams	Esther (?)	Lewis Isaacs	Aldgate, London	watchmaker + cigar manufacturer
22675	Isaacs	Selim	1831	Aldgate, London			Sarah (?)	Whitechapel, London	musician
27518	Isaacs	Simeon	1825	Witney, Oxfordshire			Abigail Benjamin	Aldgate, London	tailor
861	Isaacs	Simeon	1830	Manchester	Moshe Abraham Isaacs		Rebecca Lyon	Manchester	tailor's manager
26880	Isaacs	Simon	1808	Middlesex, London	Joseph Isaacs		Rose Michaels	Aldgate, London	furrier
11335	Isaacs	Simon	1841	Aldgate, London	(?) Isaacs			Aldgate, London	scholar
9569	Isaacs	Simon	1848	Spitalfields, London	John Isaacs	Mary Solomons		Spitalfields, London	
30019	Isaacs	Simon	1851	Spitalfields, London	Joseph Isaacs	Hannah Jacobs		Spitalfields, London	
15926	Isaacs	Simon (Simeon)	1834	Spitalfields, London	Israel Isaacs	Rachael Simmons		Whitechapel, London	apprentice cigar maker
6081	Isaacs	Soloman	1846	Clerkenwell, London	Judah Isaacs	Maria (Mary, Miriam) Isaacs		Clerkenwell, London	
26763	Isaacs	Solomon	1797	Liverpool			(?)	Aldgate, London	watchmaker
19342	Isaacs	Solomon	1809	Middlesex, London	Isaac Isaacs	Deborah (?)	Phoebe (Fredcha b. Jacob)	Fitzrovia, London	bottle merchant
6930	Isaacs	Solomon	1813	Amsterdam, Holland	Yitzhak		Deborah (?)	Aldgate, London	tailor
19835	Isaacs	Solomon	1818	Spitalfields, London	(?) Isaacs	Martha (?)		Spitalfields, London	clothes dealer
21434	Isaacs	Solomon	1819	?, London				Nottingham, Nottinghamshire	hawker of jewellery
18906	Isaacs	Solomon	1823	Aldgate, London	(?) Isaacs	Ellen (?)		Aldgate, London	boot maker journeyman
3793	Isaacs	Solomon	1827	Spitalfields, London	Isaac Isaacs	Sarah (?)		Spitalfields, London	general dealer
26152	Isaacs	Solomon	1830	Middlesex, London	Isaac Isaacs	Elizabeth (?)	Jane Abrahams	Aldgate, London	cigar maker
28214	Isaacs	Solomon	1844	Whitechapel, London	Morris Isaacs	Harriet (Hannah) Hyams		Spitalfields, London	scholar
28756	Isaacs	Solomon	1846	Middlesex, London	Moses Isaacs	Jane Isaacs		Spitalfields, London	
24579	Isaacs	Solomon	1850	Lambeth, London	Isaac Isaacs	Julia Lyons		Lambeth, London	
6580	Isaacs	Solomon (Judah)	1841	Spitalfields, London	Joseph Isaacs	Hannah Jacobs	Sarah Saunders	Spitalfields, London	scholar
8435	Isaacs	Sophia	1796	Portsmouth, Hampshire	(?) Isaacs			Portsmouth, Hampshire	Jewess (lodger)

ID	surname	given names	born	birthplace	father	mother	spouse 1	1851 residence	1851 occupation
12035	Isaacs	Sophia	1829	Whitechapel, London	Menachem Mendel HaCohen		Alexander Isaacs	Whitechapel, London	
21021	Isaacs	Sophia	1832	Bristol	Samuel Isaacs	Anna Lyons		Bristol	
6934	Isaacs	Sophia	1848	Amsterdam, Holland	Solomon Isaacs	Deborah (?)		Aldgate, London	
25131	Isaacs	Sophia	1848	Southwark, London	Woolf Isaacs	Eleanor (Ellen) Benjamin		Finsbury, London	
22548	Isaacs	Sophy	1833	Aldgate, London	Isaac Isaacs	Sarah Barnett		Aldgate, London	tailoress
11188	Isaacs	Susan	1847	Aldgate, London	Michael Isaacs	Leah (?)		Aldgate, London	
14138	Isaacs	William	1837	Manchester				Manchester	house servant
26094	Isaacs	William	1848	?, London	Samuel Isaacs	Jane (?)		Aldgate, London	
26553	Isaacs	Wolfe	1784	Vishsa, Poland			Anne (?)	Abergavenny, Wales	railway proprietor
27648	Isaacs	Wolfe	1833	Finsbury, London				Aldgate, London	fruiterer
25127	Isaacs	Woolf	1805	?, Holland	Moshe		Eleanor (Ellen) Benjamin	Finsbury, London	rag merchant
3794	Isaacs	Woolf	1829	Spitalfields, London	Isaac Isaacs	Sarah (?)		Spitalfields, London	general dealer
26179	Isaacs	Woolf	1840	?, London	Zadoc Isaacs	Julia (?)	Sarah Lederman	Aldgate, London	scholar
25442	Isaacs	Woolf	1841	?Finsbury, London	Isaac Isaacs	Leah Harris		Aldgate, London	
15922	Isaacs	Woolf	1847	Aldgate, London	Benjamin Isaacs	Esther Allen		Aldgate, London	
9545	Isaacs	Woolfe	1843	Spitalfields, London	Barnet Isaacs	Ailsa (Alsey) Hart		Aldgate, London	scholar
26177	Isaacs	Zadoc	1815	Mile End, London			Julia (?)	Aldgate, London	undertaker
10726	Isaacs (Izaaks)	Abigail	1778	Aldgate, London	Lezer Shweinfeld (Levy)		Chapman Isaacs (Izaaks)	Spitalfields, London	
10725	Isaacs (Izaaks)	Chapman	1783	Whitechapel, London	Asher Lemon-man		Abigail Levy	Spitalfields, London	watch maker
681	Isaacs (Jacobs)	Harriet	1811	Portsmouth, Hampshire	Joel Isaacs			Whitechapel, London	
2093	Isaacs (Joseph)	Myer Joseph (Josh Henry)	1829	?, Poland	Joseph Isaacs		Harriet Isaacs	Plymouth, Devon	oil cloth mfr
25445	Isaacs [Barnato]	Barnett	1851	?Spitalfields, London	Isaac Isaacs	Leah Harris	Fanny Bees	Aldgate, London	
25444	Isaacs [Barnato]	Henry	1849	?, London	Isaac Isaacs	Leah Harris	Charlotte (?)	Aldgate, London	
14784	Isaacson	Alexander	1837	Aldgate, London	Bernard (Barnet) Isaacson	Catherine Leo (Lee)	Annie Isaacs	Finsbury, London	clerk
24210	Isaacson	Anne	1848	Dalston, London	Walter Isaacson	Katherine Walter Nathan		Dalston, London	
14782	Isaacson	Bernard (Barnet)	1813	Spitalfields, London	Menachem Isaacson		Catherine Leo (Lee)	Finsbury, London	professor of music
14783	Isaacson	Catherine	1812	Whitechapel, London	Shmuel HaLevi Leo	Sarah (?)	Bernard (Barnet) Isaacson	Finsbury, London	
8166	Isaacson	Isaac	1804	Whitechapel, London	Aharon Isaacson		Maria (Miriam) Moseley	Whitechapel, London	furrier + cigar maker
8168	Isaacson	Judah (Joseph)	1834	Aldgate, London	Isaac Isaacson	Maria (Miriam) Moseley	Fanny Davis	Whitechapel, London	lithographic printer
14785	Isaacson	Julia	1838	Whitechapel, London	Bernard (Barnet) Isaacson	Catherine Leo (Lee)		Finsbury, London	scholar
24209	Isaacson	Katherine	1811	Whitechapel, London	Walter (Falk) Nathan	Sophia Friedberg	Walter Isaacson	Dalston, London	
24211	Isaacson	Lionel	1849	Dalston, London	Walter Isaacson	Katherine Walter Nathan		Dalston, London	
11765	Isaacson	Lydia	1847	Whitechapel, London	Isaac Isaacson	Maria (Miriam) Moseley	Jacob Van Den Bergh	Whitechapel, London	scholar
8167	Isaacson	Maria (Miriam, Polly)	1802	Aldgate, London	Moses Moseley	Rosetta Samuel	Isaac Isaacson	Whitechapel, London	
11764	Isaacson	Rachael Live	1839	Aldgate, London	Isaac Isaacson	Maria (Miriam) Moseley	Simeon De Meza	Whitechapel, London	scholar
8165	Isaacson	Sophia Catherine	1836	Aldgate, London	Isaac Isaacson	Maria (Miriam) Moseley	Joseph Hobinstock	Whitechapel, London	scholar
24208	Isaacson	Walter	1805	Haggerston, London	Isaac Isaacson		Katherine Walter Nathan	Dalston, London	commercial traveller + general dealer in watches + plate
1808	Isaak	Morgety (Mordecai?)	1791	?, Poland				Swansea, Wales	Jew hawker, sundries
1809	Isace	Harris	1810	?, Poland				Merthyr Tydfil, Wales	rabbi
22891	Isachar	Hyam	1779	?, Germany			Rosetta (?)	Wapping, London	retired clergyman

ID	surname	given names	born	birthplace	father	mother	spouse 1	1851 residence	1851 occupation
22892	Isachar	Rosetta	1786	Whitechapel, London	(?)		Hyam Isachar	Wapping, London	
2458	Isaiah	Elijah	1798	Altona, Germany				Hull, Yorkshire	teacher of languages
9204	Isbick	David	1824	Izbica, Poland [Isbick, Poland]			Sophia (?)	Whitechapel, London	tailor
9206	Isbick	Isaac	1850	City, London	David Isbick	Sophia (?)		City, London	
9205	Isbick	Sophia	1827	City, London	(?)		David Isbick	Whitechapel, London	tailor
5127	Isele	Bernard	1823	Baden, Germany			Marey (?)	Sheffield, Yorkshire	watchmaker
2457	Isenberg	Abraham	1830	?, Poland				Hull, Yorkshire	glazier
29542	Isenberg	Alfred Louis	1848	Gutersloh, Germany [Guterslock, Westphalen, Germany]	Louis Isenberg	Rebecca (?)		Spitalfields, London	
29543	Isenberg	Charles Louis	1850	Spitalfields, London	Louis Isenberg	Rebecca (?)		Spitalfields, London	
19230	Isenberg	Jacob	1823	?, Germany	Abraham Isenberg		Esther Isaacs	Aldgate, London	commercial agent
29540	Isenberg	Louis	1820	Gutersloh, Germany [Guterslock, Westphalen, Germany]	Abraham		Rebecca (?)	Spitalfields, London	leather merchant
29541	Isenberg	Rebecca	1821	Gutersloh, Germany [Guterslock, Westphalen, Germany]	(?)		Louis Isenberg	Spitalfields, London	
23701	Isenstein	Mordy	1825	?, Germany				Liverpool	toy merchant's apprentice
988	Israel	Aaron	1801	?, Poland			Ester (Esther) (?)	Exeter, Devon	jeweller
11663	Israel	Aaron	1842	Aldgate, London	Henry Israel	Hannah Abrahams		Aldgate, London	
13168	Israel	Aaron	1849	Whitechapel, London	Isaac (Israel) Israel	Elizabeth Jones		Aldgate, London	
6553	Israel	Aaron	1851	Exeter, Devon	Aaron Israel	Ester (Esther) (?)		Exeter, Devon	
11660	Israel	Abigail	1834	Aldgate, London	Henry Israel	Hannah Abrahams	Henry Laurence	Aldgate, London	furrier
10309	Israel	Abraham	1788	Spitalfields, London	(?) Israel	Abigail de Aaron Joel	Sarah de Phineas Mordecai Cohen	Spitalfields, London	general dealer
538	Israel	Abraham	1811	Aldgate, London	Menachem Mendele Israel		Sarah Lyons	Spitalfields, London	furniture broker
21156	Israel	Abraham	1822	?, Poland {?, Prussia]				Aldgate, London	tailor
521	Israel	Abraham	1823	Spitalfields, London	Israel (Ezekiel) Israel	Rebecca Jonas	Nancy (Ann, Jane) Harris	Spitalfields, London	greengrocer
993	Israel	Abraham	1845	Exeter, Devon	Aaron Israel	Ester (Esther) (?)		Exeter, Devon	
8927	Israel	Abraham	1848	Aldgate, London	Moses Israel	Elizabeth Solomon		Aldgate, London	
15804	Israel	Albert	1845	Aldgate, London	Henry Ash Israel	Hannah Cohen		Aldgate, London	
3596	Israel	Amelia	1787	Aldgate, London	Israel Israel	Rebecca Pearl Solomon		Whitechapel, London	dressmaker retired
8917	Israel	Amelia	1812	Whitechapel, London	Abraham HaCohen Woolf		Moses (Morris) Israel	Aldgate, London	marine store dealer
415	Israel	Amelia	1829	Spitalfields, London	Abraham Israel	Sarah de Phineas Mordecai Cohen		Spitalfields, London	cap maker
8925	Israel	Amelia	1844	?Aldgate, London	Moses Israel	Elizabeth Solomon		Aldgate, London	
3862	Israel	Andrew	1814	Middlesex, London	Israel (Ezekiel) Israel	Rebecca Jonas	Sarah Harris	Spitalfields, London	general dealer
28337	Israel	Ann	1791	Whitechapel, London	(?)		(?) Israel	Aldgate, London	dealer in old clothes
24027	Israel	Ann	1806	Covent Garden, London	(?)		Henry Israel	Marylebone, London	
31076	Israel	Ann (Nancy)	1791	Aldgate, London	Israel Israel	Rebecca Pearl Solomon		Whitechapel, London	dressmaker retired
19117	Israel	Anne	1828	?, London	(?) Israel			Aldgate, London	
5810	Israel	Annette	1846	Aldgate, London	Henry Ash Israel	Hannah Cohen	Charles Moss Lavey	Aldgate, London	
17167	Israel	Barnett	1820	Margonin, Poland			Lessina? (?)	Newcastle Upon Tyne	general dealer
8921	Israel	Benjamin	1841	Whitechapel, London	Moses (Morris) Israel	Amelia Woolf		Aldgate, London	scholar

ID	surname	given names	born	birthplace	father	mother	spouse 1	1851 residence	1851 occupation
11665	Israel	Benjamin	1844	Aldgate, London	Henry Israel	Hannah Abrahams		Aldgate, London	
15423	Israel	Betsy	1834	Covent Garden, London	(?) Israel			Covent Garden, London	scholar
524	Israel	Car	1850	Middlesex, London	David Israel	Harriet (Hannah) Joseph		Spitalfields, London	
11154	Israel	Caroline	1821	Portsmouth, Hampshire	Boaz Lyons		Elkin Israel	Aldgate, London	
523	Israel	Caroline	1850	Middlesex, London	Michael Israel	Rachel Solomons		Spitalfields, London	
525	Israel	Catherine	1849	Spitalfields, London	Abraham Israel	Nancy (Ann, Jane) Harris		Spitalfields, London	
13167	Israel	Charles	1847	Spitalfields, London	Isaac (Israel) Israel	Elizabeth Jones		Aldgate, London	scholar
469	Israel	Cobby	1783	?, London	(?)		Lewis Israel	Aldgate, London	
28338	Israel	David	1811	Whitechapel, London	(?) Israel	Ann (?)		Aldgate, London	dealer in old clothes
412	Israel	David	1815	?, Poland [?, Prussia]	Israel Israel		Harriet (Hannah) Joseph	Spitalfields, London	slipper maker
28269	Israel	David	1821	Whitechapel, London	Simon Israel	Bluma (?)	Rachel Jacobs	Aldgate, London	poulterer
4567	Israel	Deborah	1848	Birmingham	Wolf Israel	Sarah Jacobs		Birmingham	
13162	Israel	Elizabeth	1809	Whitechapel, London	(?) Jones		Isaac (Israel) Israel	Aldgate, London	
6091	Israel	Elizabeth	1819	Aldgate, London	David Solomons		Moses Israel	Aldgate, London	
6989	Israel	Elizabeth	1835	Spitalfields, London	Moses Israel		Gabriel Costa	Aldgate, London	parasol trimmer
11666	Israel	Elizabeth	1847	Aldgate, London	Henry Israel	Hannah Abrahams		Aldgate, London	
11153	Israel	Elkin	1824	Spitalfields, London	Israel (Ezekiel) Israel	Rebecca Jonas	Caroline Lyons	Aldgate, London	general dealer
30053	Israel	Ester	1826	Aldgate, London	(?) Israel			Soho, London	assistant to beef butcher
989	Israel	Ester (Esther)	1813	?, Poland [?, Prussia]			Aaron Israel	Exeter, Devon	
5813	Israel	Esther	1842	Aldgate, London	Henry Ash Israel	Hannah Cohen	Nathan Moss	Aldgate, London	
28436	Israel	Esther	1842	Spitalfields, London	Israel Israel	Leah Lyon		Spitalfields, London	scholar
2459	Israel	Fisher	1812	?				Hull, Yorkshire	lunatic
30550	Israel	Flora	1849	Aldgate, LondonAldgate, London	David Israel	Rachel Jacobs		Aldgate, London	
8919	Israel	Frances	1837	Whitechapel, London	Moses (Morris) Israel	Amelia Woolf	Bernhard Kauffmann	Aldgate, London	?soap grinder
8090	Israel	Hannah	1800	Aldgate, London	Isaiah Israel	Jane (?)		Belgravia, London	
5808	Israel	Hannah	1814	Chatham, Kent	Asher Cohen	Esther (?)	Henry Ash Israel	Aldgate, London	
12830	Israel	Hannah	1821	Spitalfields, London	(?) Israel			Strand, London	servant
539	Israel	Hannah	1848	Spitalfields, London	Abraham Israel	Sarah Lyons		Spitalfields, London	scholar
11659	Israel	Hannah	1817	Spitalfields, London	Yehuda Leib Abrahams		Henry Israel	Aldgate, London	waistcoat maker
411	Israel	Harriet (Hannah)	1813	Middlesex, London	Isaac Joseph	(?Bedice) (?)	David Israel	Spitalfields, London	
4565	Israel	Henrietta	1843	Birmingham	Wolf Israel	Sarah Jacobs	Abraham A Meyers	Birmingham	scholar
24026	Israel	Henry	1813	Middlesex, London			Ann (?)	Marylebone, London	solicitor's clerk
11658	Israel	Henry	1817	Aldgate, London	Benjamin Israel		Hannah Abrahams	Aldgate, London	general dealer
527	Israel	Henry	1830	Spitalfields, London	Abraham Israel	Sarah de Phineas Mordecai Cohen	Leah Michaels	Spitalfields, London	cigar maker
526	Israel	Henry	1847	Spitalfields, London	Abraham Israel	Nancy (Ann, Jane) Harris		Spitalfields, London	scholar
14679	Israel	Henry (Haim)	1851	Spitalfields, London	Solomon Israel	Rebecca Barnett	Elizabeth Gomes Da Costa	Spitalfields, London	
5807	Israel	Henry Ash	1805	Aldgate, London			Hannah Cohen	Aldgate, London	carcass butcher empl 2
5809	Israel	Henry Ash	1840	Aldgate, London	Henry Ash Israel	Hannah Cohen		Aldgate, London	
8920	Israel	Isaac	1839	Whitechapel, London	Moses (Morris) Israel	Amelia Woolf		Aldgate, London	scholar
13161	Israel	Isaac (Israel)	1810	Whitechapel, London			Elizabeth Jones	Aldgate, London	dairy man
6592	Israel	Isabella	1847	Aldgate, London	Moses Israel	Elizabeth (?)	Asher Ellis	Aldgate, London	
22811	Israel	Israel	1781	Whitechapel, London				Whitechapel, London	incapable of work: idiotic
2279	Israel	Israel	1827	?, London				Leeds, Yorkshire	hawker

ID	surname	given names	born	birthplace	father	mother	spouse 1	1851 residence	1851 occupation
24028	Israel	Israel	1837	Covent Garden, London	Henry Israel	Ann (?)		Marylebone, London	
13110	Israel	Israel	1839	Southwark, London				Camden Town, London	scholar
24719	Israel	Israel	1839	Elephant & Castle, London	(?) Israel	Marian (?)		Walworth, London	scholar
994	Israel	Israel	1849	Exeter, Devon	Aaron Israel	Ester (?)		Exeter, Devon	
28433	Israel	Israel (Ezekiel)	1786	Aldgate, London	Moses Israel		Rebecca Jonas	Spitalfields, London	greengrocer
528	Israel	Jacob	1836	Spitalfields, London				Spitalfields, London	scholar
2285	Israel	Jacob	1840	?, London	Solomon Israel	Mary Polack		Leeds, Yorkshire	
992	Israel	Jacob	1842	Exeter, Devon	Aaron Israel	Ester (Esther) (?)		Exeter, Devon	
24029	Israel	James	1839	Covent Garden, London	Henry Israel	Ann (?)		Marylebone, London	scholar
529	Israel	Jane	1848	Middlesex, London	Michael Israel	Rachel Solomons		Spitalfields, London	
2286	Israel	Jessie	1842	Spitalfields, London	Solomon Israel	Mary Polack		Leeds, Yorkshire	
2280	Israel	John	1819	?, Germany				Leeds, Yorkshire	wool merchant
30051	Israel	John Isaac	1803	Aldgate, London				Soho, London	beef butcher
28339	Israel	Jonah	1828	Whitechapel, London	(?) Israel	Ann (?)		Aldgate, London	idiot
15343	Israel	Joseph	1778	Hackney, London				Waterloo, London	plasterer
24032	Israel	Joseph	1846	Covent Garden, London	Henry Israel	Ann (?)		Marylebone, London	scholar
28438	Israel	Joseph	1847	Spitalfields, London	Israel Israel	Leah Lyon		Spitalfields, London	
11664	Israel	Joshua	1843	Aldgate, London	Henry Israel	Hannah Abrahams	Esther Martin	Aldgate, London	
14680	Israel	Judah	1843	Spitalfields, London	Solomon Israel	Rebecca Barnett	Leah Hyams	Spitalfields, London	
13165	Israel	Julia	1842	Spitalfields, London	Isaac (Israel) Israel	Elizabeth Jones	Isaac Israel	Aldgate, London	scholar
14683	Israel	Julia	1849	Whitechapel, London	Solomon Israel	Rebecca Barnett		Spitalfields, London	
8922	Israel	Lazarus	1846	Aldgate, London	Moses (Morris) Israel	Amelia Woolf	Ann Joseph	Aldgate, London	scholar
23371	Israel	Leah	1813	Spitalfields, London	(?) Israel			Strand, London	nurse
28434	Israel	Leah	1816	Portsmouth, Hampshire	Barnet Lyon		Israel Israel	Spitalfields, London	
530	Israel	Leah	1840	Middlesex, London	Michael Israel	Rachel Solomons		Spitalfields, London	
30551	Israel	Leah	1851	Aldgate, London	Henry Israel	Hannah Abrahams		Aldgate, London	
17168	Israel	Lessina?	1826	Margonin, Poland	(?)		Barnett Israel	Newcastle Upon Tyne	dressmaker
467	Israel	Lewis	1789	Aldgate, London			Cobby (?)	Aldgate, London	annuitant
11661	Israel	Lewis	1835	Aldgate, London	Henry Israel	Hannah Abrahams		Aldgate, London	
5806	Israel	Lewis (Louis) Ash	1838	Aldgate, London	Henry Ash Israel	Hannah (?)	Jessie Myers	Aldgate, London	scholar
13164	Israel	Louis	1840	Whitechapel, London	Isaac (Israel) Israel	Elizabeth Jones		Aldgate, London	scholar
10542	Israel	Louisa	1838	?, London	(?) Israel	(?) (?Lazarus)		Piccadilly, London	apprentice milliner
24717	Israel	Marian	1808	Bristol	(?)		(?) Israel	Walworth, London	needlewoman
5812	Israel	Mark	1815	Aldgate, London				Aldgate, London	carcass butcher
24720	Israel	Mark	1841	Elephant & Castle, London	(?) Israel	Marian (?)		Walworth, London	scholar
15805	Israel	Mark (Marcus)	1847	Aldgate, London	Henry Ash Israel	Hannah Cohen		Aldgate, London	
14682	Israel	Martha (Maria)	1846	Whitechapel, London	Solomon Israel	Rebecca Barnett	(?) Kalischer	Spitalfields, London	
2282	Israel	Mary	1802	?, London	David Polack		Solomon Israel	Leeds, Yorkshire	
27138	Israel	Mary	1832	?, London	(?) Israel			Aldgate, London	furrier
24030	Israel	Mary	1842	Covent Garden, London	Henry Israel	Ann (?)		Marylebone, London	scholar
13163	Israel	Mary Ann	1839	Whitechapel, London	Isaac (Israel) Israel	Elizabeth Jones		Aldgate, London	scholar
1226	Israel	Maurice	1766	?, Poland				Plymouth, Devon	travelling jeweller
8108	Israel	Meyer	1851	Birmingham	Wolf Israel	Sarah Jacobs		Birmingham	
532	Israel	Michael	1818	Middlesex, London	Nathan HaLevi Israel		Rachel Solomons	Spitalfields, London	general dealer
20777	Israel	Michael	1832	Covent Garden, London	Woolf Israel	Julia Moses		Covent Garden, London	cigar maker

ID	surname	given names	born	birthplace	father	mother	spouse 1	1851 residence	1851 occupation
531	Israel	Michael	1838	Whitechapel, London				Spitalfields, London	scholar
8928	Israel	Michael	1850	Aldgate, London	Moses Israel	Elizabeth Solomon		Aldgate, London	
10310	Israel	Mordecai	1832	Spitalfields, London	Abraham Israel	Sarah de Phineas Mordecai Cohen		Spitalfields, London	general dealer
24718	Israel	Morris	1836	Lambeth, London	(?) Israel	Marian (?)		Walworth, London	newsboy
28273	Israel	Morris	1850	Whitechapel, London	David Israel	Rachel Jacobs		Aldgate, London	
8924	Israel	Moses	1813	Middlesex, London	Abraham Israel		Elizabeth Solomon	Aldgate, London	fruit merchant
20778	Israel	Moses	1838	Covent Garden, London	Woolf Israel	Julia Moses		Covent Garden, London	scholar
28437	Israel	Moses	1843	Spitalfields, London	Israel Israel	Leah Lyon		Spitalfields, London	scholar
6990	Israel	Moses (Morris)	1802	Aldgate, London	Isaac HaCohen Israel		Amelia Woolf	Aldgate, London	marine store dealer
15807	Israel	Moss	1826	Aldgate, London				Aldgate, London	butcher's man
22715	Israel	Nancy	1844	Whitechapel, London	(?) Israel	(?) Myers		Whitechapel, London	
414	Israel	Nancy (Ann, Jane)	1821	Spitalfields, London	John Harris		Abraham Israel	Spitalfields, London	
540	Israel	Nathan	1844	Spitalfields, London	Abraham Israel	Sarah Lyons		Spitalfields, London	scholar
20768	Israel	Phillip	1814	?, Poland				Whitechapel, London	
24031	Israel	Priscilla	1844	Covent Garden, London	Henry Israel	Ann (?)		Marylebone, London	scholar
11662	Israel	Rachael	1841	Aldgate, London	Henry Israel	Hannah Abrahams		Aldgate, London	
413	Israel	Rachel	1815	Middlesex, London	Pinchas Zelig HaLevi Solomons		Michael Israel	Spitalfields, London	
30052	Israel	Rachel	1821	Aldgate, London	(?) Israel			Soho, London	assistant to beef butcher
28271	Israel	Rachel	1823	Whitechapel, London	Moss Jacobs		David Israel	Aldgate, London	
2283	Israel	Rachel	1836	?, London	Solomon Israel	Mary Polack	Louis Harris	Leeds, Yorkshire	
541	Israel	Rachel	1850	Spitalfields, London	Abraham Israel	Sarah Lyons		Spitalfields, London	
18159	Israel	Rebecca	1791	Middlesex, London	(?)		(?) Israel	Mile End, London	inmate of Portuguese Jews Hospital
14685	Israel	Rebecca	1819	Amsterdam, Holland	Judah Barnett		Solomon Israel	Spitalfields, London	wife to general dealer
991	Israel	Rebecca	1839	Exeter, Devon	Aaron Israel	Ester (Esther) (?)		Exeter, Devon	
6090	Israel	Rebecca	1842	Aldgate, London	Moses Israel	Elizabeth (?)	Philip Myers	Aldgate, London	
533	Israel	Rebecca	1844	Spitalfields, London	Abraham Israel	Nancy (Ann, Jane) Harris		Spitalfields, London	scholar
28439	Israel	Rebecca	1849	Spitalfields, London	Israel Israel	Leah Lyon		Spitalfields, London	
11155	Israel	Rebecca	1850	Aldgate, London	Elkin Israel	Caroline Lyons	Abraham Isaacs	Aldgate, London	
13194	Israel	Rebecca (Betsey)	1823	Spitalfields, London	Simon Israel	Sarah Emanuel	Moses (Morris) Hyams	Aldgate, London	tailoress
4568	Israel	Rosa (Rosetta)	1850	Birmingham	Wolf Israel	Sarah Jacobs	A--- Abrahams	Birmingham	
8776	Israel	Rosetta	1841	Middlesex, London	Moses Israel	Elizabeth (?)	Jacob Gomes da Costa	Aldgate, London	
8918	Israel	Samuel	1833	Whitechapel, London	Moses (Morris) Israel	Amelia Woolf		Aldgate, London	assists marine store dealer
15806	Israel	Samuel	1850	Aldgate, London	Henry Ash Israel	Hannah Cohen		Aldgate, London	
13193	Israel	Sarah	1785	Spitalfields, London	David Emanuel		Simon Israel	Aldgate, London	general dealer + poulterer
28270	Israel	Sarah	1791	Spitalfields, London	Phineas Mordecai Cohen		Abraham Israel	Spitalfields, London	general dealer
535	Israel	Sarah	1815	Middlesex, London	Eliakim Getshlik Harris		Andrew Israel	Spitalfields, London	
12792	Israel	Sarah	1817	Whitechapel, London	Yehuda Leib Lyon		Abraham Israel	Spitalfields, London	
4564	Israel	Sarah	1820	Sheffield, Yorkshire	Samuel Jacobs	Eva (Eve) (?)	Wolf Israel	Birmingham	
2917	Israel	Sarah	1828	Tottenham, London	Lewis Israel	(?Ann) (?)	Solomon Mendes Lyon	Aldgate, London	
5815	Israel	Sarah	1836	Aldgate, London	Henry Ash Israel	Hannah Cohen	Aaron Alexander	Aldgate, London	
990	Israel	Sarah	1837	Exeter, Devon	Aaron Israel	Ester (Esther) (?)		Exeter, Devon	
2284	Israel	Sarah	1838	?, London	Solomon Israel	Mary Polack		Leeds, Yorkshire	
28435	Israel	Sarah	1841	Spitalfields, London	Israel Israel	Leah Lyon		Spitalfields, London	scholar

ID	surname	given names	born	birthplace	father	mother	spouse 1	1851 residence	1851 occupation
536	Israel	Sarah	1842	Middlesex, London	David Israel	Harriet (Hannah) Joseph		Spitalfields, London	
534	Israel	Sarah	1848	Spitalfields, London	Abraham Israel	Nancy (Ann, Jane) Harris		Spitalfields, London	scholar
8923	Israel	Sarah	1850	Aldgate, London	Moses (Morris) Israel	Amelia Woolf		Aldgate, London	
4566	Israel	Selim (Selig)	1846	Birmingham	Wolf Israel	Sarah Jacobs		Birmingham	scholar
242	Israel	Simon	1765	Amsterdam, Holland			(?)	Spitalfields, London	pensioner
14681	Israel	Simon	1845	Spitalfields, London	Solomon Israel	Rebecca Barnett		Spitalfields, London	
28272	Israel	Simon	1848	Whitechapel, London	David Israel	Rachel Jacobs		Aldgate, London	
2281	Israel	Solomon	1799	?, London	Jacob Solomon		Mary Polack	Leeds, Yorkshire	chiropodist
14684	Israel	Solomon	1813	Whitechapel, London	Israel (Ezekiel) Israel	Rebecca Jonas	Rebecca Barnett	Spitalfields, London	general dealer
13166	Israel	Solomon	1845	Spitalfields, London	Isaac (Israel) Israel	Elizabeth Jones		Aldgate, London	scholar
4563	Israel	Wolf	1801	?, Poland			Sarah Jacobs	Birmingham	shopkeeper
20776	Israel	Woolf	1809	Aldgate, London	Isaac HaCohen Israel		Julia Moses	Covent Garden, London	orange merchant
11667	Israel	Woolf	1849	Aldgate, London	Henry Israel	Hannah Abrahams		Aldgate, London	
537	Israel	Zachariah	1838	Middlesex, London	Michael Israel	Rachel Solomons		Spitalfields, London	
21874	Israel (Cohen)	Abraham	1827	Brighton, Sussex	Salomon Cohen		Judith Cohen	Clerkenwell, London	confectioner
21875	Israel (Cohen)	Jacob	1850	Clerkenwell, London	Abraham Israel (Cohen)	Judith Cohen		Clerkenwell, London	
21873	Israel (Cohen)	Judith	1823	Clerkenwell, London	Jacob de Enoch (Hanoj) Cohen	Welcome (Benvenida) de David Nunes Carvalho	Abraham Israel	Clerkenwell, London	confectioner
11360	Isreal	David	1771	Middlesex, London				Aldgate, London	butcher
15224	Isreels	Amelia	1806	Aldgate, London	(?) Isreels			Shoreditch, London	annuitant
10721	Izaaks	Esther	1801	Plymouth, Devon	(?)		Izaak Izaaks	Spitalfields, London	
10724	Izaaks	Frances	1845	Spitalfields, London	Izaak Izaaks	Esther (?)		Spitalfields, London	
10720	Izaaks	Izaak	1807	Middlesex, London	Chapman Isaacs (Izaaks)	Abigail Levy	Esther (?)	Spitalfields, London	shopman
10722	Izaaks	Julia	1838	Spitalfields, London	Izaak Izaaks	Esther (?)		Spitalfields, London	scholar
10723	Izaaks	Sophia	1840	Spitalfields, London	Izaak Izaaks	Esther (?)		Spitalfields, London	scholar
8273	Jackson	Abraham	1817	Margonin, Poland [Prussia]	Jacob ben Myer		Rosanna (?)	North Shields, Tyne & Wear	painter + glazier
25073	Jackson	Alfred Moss	1849	Liverpool	George Isaac	Caroline Moss	Rebecca Isaac	Liverpool	
18777	Jackson	Annie	1847	Whitechapel, London	John (Isaac) Jackson	Isabella (?)	Samuel Edward Benjamin	Stepney, London	scholar
23727	Jackson	Arthur	1817	Bristol				Liverpool	commission agent
25072	Jackson	Caroline	1817	Plymouth, Devon	(?) Moss		George Isaac Jackson	Liverpool	
16557	Jackson	David I	1781	Liverpool			Kitty (?)	Liverpool	retired draper
21056	Jackson	Edwin	1839	Dover, Kent				Dover, Kent	boarding school pupil
16560	Jackson	Eliza	1812	Liverpool	David I Jackson	Kitty (?)		Liverpool	
3138	Jackson	Eva	1841	Sunderland, Co Durham	Myers Jackson	Sarah Cohen		Sunderland, Co Durham	
25071	Jackson	George Isaac	1812	Liverpool			Caroline Moss	Liverpool	tailor + draper
23726	Jackson	Hannah	1785	?, Devon				Liverpool	annuitant
8270	Jackson	Hannah (Ann)	1823	Sunderland, Co Durham			Henry Jackson	North Shields, Tyne & Wear	
16561	Jackson	Henrietta	1816	Liverpool	David I Jackson	Kitty (?)		Liverpool	
3142	Jackson	Henry	1819	Margonin, Poland [Prussia]			Hannah (Ann) Jacobs	North Shields, Tyne & Wear	plumber + glazier + general dealer + clothier
21087	Jackson	Henry	1820	Hoxton, London				Dover, Kent	teacher
8275	Jackson	Henry	1838	North Shields, Tyne & Wear	Abraham Jackson	Rosanna (?)	Jane Jackson	North Shields, Tyne & Wear	apprentice painter + glazier

ID	surname	given names	born	birthplace	father	mother	spouse 1	1851 residence	1851 occupation
16559	Jackson	Henry I	1812	Liverpool	David I Jackson	Kitty (?)		Liverpool	retired draper
18772	Jackson	Isabella	1813	Whitechapel, London	(?)		John (Isaac) Jackson	Stepney, London	
8278	Jackson	Jacob	1845	North Shields, Tyne & Wear	Henry Jackson	Hannah (Ann) Jacobs	Annie Frend	North Shields, Tyne & Wear	scholar
8030	Jackson	Jacob	1846	North Shields, Tyne & Wear	Abraham Jackson	Rosanna (?)	Hannah Frend	North Shields, Tyne & Wear	scholar
3137	Jackson	Jane	1840	Sunderland, Co Durham	Myers Jackson	Sarah Cohen		Sunderland, Co Durham	
18771	Jackson	John (Isaac)	1803	Whitechapel, London			Isabella (?)	Stepney, London	commercial traveller
8277	Jackson	Joseph	1849	North Shields, Tyne & Wear	Abraham Jackson	Rosanna (?)		North Shields, Tyne & Wear	scholar
8271	Jackson	Julius (Judah)	1847	North Shields, Tyne & Wear	Henry Jackson	Hannah (Ann) Jacobs	Esther Sagar	North Shields, Tyne & Wear	scholar
16558	Jackson	Kitty	1781	Liverpool	(?)		David I Jackson	Liverpool	
7939	Jackson	Margaret Ellen	1850	Shrewsbury, Shropshire			Michael Levy	Shrewsbury, Shropshire	
8276	Jackson	Mary	1844	North Shields, Tyne & Wear	Abraham Jackson	Rosanna (?)		North Shields, Tyne & Wear	scholar
18773	Jackson	Michael	1834	Whitechapel, London	John (Isaac) Jackson	Isabella (?)	Louisa Van Goor	Stepney, London	cigar maker
25182	Jackson	Montague	1843	?, London				Finsbury, London	
18774	Jackson	Moss	1837	Whitechapel, London	John (Isaac) Jackson	Isabella (?)		Stepney, London	scholar
3135	Jackson	Myers	1801	Margonin, Poland [Prussia]	Ya'acov (Jacob)		Sarah Cohen	Sunderland, Co Durham	painter + glazier
18775	Jackson	Rebecca	1842	Whitechapel, London	John (Isaac) Jackson	Isabella (?)		Stepney, London	scholar
8274	Jackson	Rosanna	1819	?, Holland			Abraham Jackson	North Shields, Tyne & Wear	
3139	Jackson	Rose	1843	Sunderland, Co Durham	Myers Jackson	Sarah Cohen		Sunderland, Co Durham	
25074	Jackson	Sara	1850	Liverpool	George Isaac	Caroline Moss		Liverpool	
3136	Jackson	Sarah	1807	Margonin, Poland [Prussia]	Michael Cohen	Adaline (?)	Myers Jackson	Sunderland, Co Durham	
18776	Jackson	Sarah	1844	Whitechapel, London	John (Isaac) Jackson	Isabella (?)	Lewis Moses	Stepney, London	scholar
8272	Jackson	Simon	1850	North Shields, Tyne & Wear	Henry Jackson	Hannah (Ann) Jacobs		North Shields, Tyne & Wear	
17083	Jacob	Aaron	1825	?, Poland			Frederika (?)	Ardrossan, Scotland	travelling jeweller
20053	Jacob	Aaron	1832	Manchester	Henry Jacobs	Esther Lyons		Liverpool	stationer
2704	Jacob	Abraham	1840	Edinburgh, Scotland	Jenkin Jacob	Hannah (?)		Glasgow, Scotland	
8112	Jacob	Abraham	1850	Bradford, Yorkshire	Bernard Jacob	Maria Moss		Bradford, Yorkshire	
13121	Jacob	Alexander	1800	Manchester	Aaron Jacob	Leah Solomons	Julia (?)	Salford, Lancashire	
4569	Jacob	Alexander	1821	?, Poland				Birmingham	slippermaker
1091	Jacob	Alexander	1841	Falmouth, Cornwall	Moss J Jacob	Frances (?)	Leah Myer	Falmouth, Cornwall	scholar
20011	Jacob	Alfred Alexander	1840	Salford, Lancashire	Alexander Jacob	Julia Asher	Ann Marks	Salford, Lancashire	
30171	Jacob	Barnet	1832	?, Poland				Dudley, Worcestershire	glazier
13847	Jacob	Baruch	1846	Chatham, Kent	Nathan Jacob	Rachael (?)		Manchester	scholar
8109	Jacob	Bernard	1822	Sheffield, Yorkshire	Samuel Jacobs	Eve (Eva) (?)	Maria Moss	Bradford, Yorkshire	
1111	Jacob	Bettesy	1825	Penzance, Cornwall	Samuel Jacob	Sarah (Sally) Levy		Penzance, Cornwall	dressmaker
13786	Jacob	Catharine	1821	Manchester	(?)		Joseph Jacob	Manchester	lodging house keeper's wife
2706	Jacob	Charles	1849	Edinburgh, Scotland	Jenkin Jacob	Hannah (?)		Glasgow, Scotland	
16079	Jacob	Charles Jabez	1851	Plymouth, Devon	Jacob Jacob	Mary (?)		Plymouth, Devon	

ID	surname	given names	born	birthplace	father	mother	spouse 1	1851 residence	1851 occupation
8117	Jacob	Daniel	1851	Wellington, Shropshire	Maurice Jacob	Fanny Myers		Wellington, Shropshire	
8111	Jacob	Deborah	1847	Liverpool	Bernard Jacob	Maria Moss		Bradford, Yorkshire	
1156	Jacob	Ebenezer	1844	Plymouth, Devon	Mark Jacob	Eliza (?)		Plymouth, Devon	
1157	Jacob	Edwin	1847	Plymouth, Devon	Mark Jacob	Eliza (?)		Plymouth, Devon	
4574	Jacob	Eleanor	1850	Birmingham	Moses Levi Jacob	Sarah Lyons	M--- D--- Marks	Birmingham	
1152	Jacob	Eliza	1803	Plymouth, Devon			Mark Jacob	Plymouth, Devon	
1153	Jacob	Eliza	1827	Plymouth, Devon	Mark Jacob	Eliza (?)		Plymouth, Devon	shoebinder
1158	Jacob	Eliza	1835	Plymouth, Devon	Mark Jacob	Eliza (?)		Plymouth, Devon	
12524	Jacob	Ephraim	1827	Norwich, Norfolk				Norwich, Norfolk	journeyman tailor
20052	Jacob	Esther	1810	Portsmouth, Hampshire	Charles Lyons	Phoebe Levy	Henry Jacobs	Liverpool	
23716	Jacob	Esther	1811	?, Germany	(?)		Wolf Jacob	Liverpool	
13574	Jacob	Esther	1850	Manchester	Levy Jacob	Hannah (?)		Manchester	
8116	Jacob	Fanny	1828	Birmingham	Daniel Myers		Maurice Jacob	Wellington, Shropshire	
1155	Jacob	Feargus	1842	Plymouth, Devon	Mark Jacob	Eliza (?)		Plymouth, Devon	
1088	Jacob	Frances	1812	Portsmouth, Hampshire			Moss J Jacob	Falmouth, Cornwall	
14302	Jacob	Frances Matilda	1825	Calcutta, India [Calcutta, East Indies]	(?) Jacob			Manchester	
2643	Jacob	Hannah	1810	Ragoesen, Germany [Rogassen, Prussia]			Jenkin Jacob	Glasgow, Scotland	
18007	Jacob	Hannah	1813	?, Germany	(?)		Jacob Israel	Aldgate, London	tailor
13572	Jacob	Hannah	1826	?, Poland	(?)		Levy Jacob	Manchester	
1089	Jacob	Hannah	1840	Falmouth, Cornwall	Moss J Jacob	Frances (?)		Falmouth, Cornwall	scholar
20051	Jacob	Henry	1805	Manchester			Esther Lyons	Liverpool	general dealer
23719	Jacob	Hyam	1847	Liverpool	Wolf Jacob	Esther (?)		Liverpool	
1820	Jacob	Isaac	1821	Falmouth, Cornwall			Sophia Lazarus	Swansea, Wales	jeweller, silversmith
18006	Jacob	Israel	1815	?, Germany			Hannah (?)	Aldgate, London	tailor
182	Jacob	Jacob	1774	Falmouth, Cornwall	Moses Jacob	Sarah Moses	Sarah Kate Simons	Falmouth, Cornwall	dealer
6472	Jacob	Jacob	1793	Ilminster, Dorset [Yelminster, Dorset]			Mary (?)	Plymouth, Devon	master baker empl 1
2705	Jacob	Jacob	1849	Edinburgh, Scotland	Jenkin Jacob	Hannah (?)		Glasgow, Scotland	
13787	Jacob	James Lyons	1842	Manchester	Joseph Jacob	Catharine (?)		Manchester	
8106	Jacob	Jane	1827	Poplar, London	Abraham Moss		Meyer Jacob	Poplar, London	
13848	Jacob	Jane	1848	Chatham, Kent	Nathan Jacob	Rachael (?)		Manchester	
10040	Jacob	Jeanette (Janet)	1838	Salford, Lancashire	Alexander Jacob	Julia Asher	Henry Barnard	Salford, Lancashire	
2642	Jacob	Jenkin	1809	Ragoesen, Germany [Rogassen, Prussia]			Hannah (?)	Glasgow, Scotland	jeweller traveller
13788	Jacob	John	1850	Manchester	Joseph Jacob	Catharine (?)		Manchester	
1154	Jacob	Jonas	1840	Plymouth, Devon	Mark Jacob	Eliza (?)		Plymouth, Devon	
23603	Jacob	Jos	1829	?, Poland				Liverpool	glazier's jobbing
2460	Jacob	Joseph	1799	?, Poland				Hull, Yorkshire	jeweller
13785	Jacob	Joseph	1811	?, Poland			Catharine (?)	Manchester	lodging house keeper
8107	Jacob	Joseph	1850	Portsmouth, Hampshire	Meyer Jacob	Jane Moss		Poplar, London	
10041	Jacob	Josephine	1840	Salford, Lancashire	Alexander Jacob	Julia Asher		Salford, Lancashire	
2461	Jacob	Julia	1849	Hull, Yorkshire	Lazarus Jacob	Zilla (Celia) (?)		Hull, Yorkshire	
5378	Jacob	Lawrence	1844	Falmouth, Cornwall	Moss Jacob	Frances Emanuel	Julia Joseph	Falmouth, Cornwall	scholar

ID	surname	given names	born	birthplace	father	mother	spouse 1	1851 residence	1851 occupation
2462	Jacob	Lazarus	1811	Riga, Latvia [Riga, Russia]			Zilla (Celia) (?)	Hull, Yorkshire	cap maker
13571	Jacob	Levy	1827	?, Poland			Hannah (?)	Manchester	slipper maker
16936	Jacob	Lusia	1837	Sheffield, Yorkshire				Sheffield, Yorkshire	
8110	Jacob	Maria	1828	Dartford, Kent	Abraham Moss		Bernard Jacob	Bradford, Yorkshire	
1151	Jacob	Mark	1804	Plymouth, Devon			Eliza (?)	Plymouth, Devon	shoemaker
23720	Jacob	Marks	1849	Liverpool	Wolf Jacob	Esther (?)		Liverpool	
16078	Jacob	Mary	1809	Plymouth, Devon	(?)		Jacob Jacob	Plymouth, Devon	
8115	Jacob	Maurice	1825	Sheffield, Yorkshire	Samuel Jacobs	Eva (Eve) (?)	Fanny Myers	Wellington, Shropshire	
8105	Jacob	Meyer	1818	Sheffield, Yorkshire	Samuel Jacobs	Eva (Eve) (?)	Jane Moss	Poplar, London	draper
1090	Jacob	Michael	1841	Falmouth, Cornwall	Moss J Jacob	Frances (?)		Falmouth, Cornwall	scholar
19999	Jacob	Moses	1803	?				Edinburgh, Scotland	broker + dealer in old books
2463	Jacob	Moses	1847	Middlesex, London	Lazarus Jacob	Zilla (Celia) (?)		Hull, Yorkshire	scholar
4572	Jacob	Moses Levi	1819	Falmouth, Cornwall	Levi Jacob	Sophia Mordecai	Sarah Lyons	Birmingham	factor
5358	Jacob	Moses Samuel	1815	?Falmouth, Cornwall	Samuel Jacob	Sarah (Sally) Levy		Falmouth, Cornwall	?
1087	Jacob	Moss Jacob	1813	Cambourne, Cornwall	Jacob Jacob	Sarah Kate Simons	Frances (?)	Penzance, Cornwall	pawnbroker + tailor
13844	Jacob	Nathan	1816	?, Poland			Rachael (?)	Manchester	labourer
2464	Jacob	Philip	1851	Hull, Yorkshire	Lazarus Jacob	Zilla (Celia) (?)		Hull, Yorkshire	
13845	Jacob	Rachael	1823	?, Poland	(?)		Nathan Jacob	Manchester	attends home
10042	Jacob	Rebecca	1841	Salford, Lancashire	Alexander Jacob	Julia Asher	Charles Pyke	Salford, Lancashire	
13573	Jacob	Reuben	1848	Manchester	Levy Jacob	Hannah (?)		Manchester	
18009	Jacob	Rosa	1839	?, Germany	Israel Jacob	Hannah (?)		Aldgate, London	
183	Jacob	Samuel	1777	Falmouth, Cornwall	Moses Jacob	Sarah Moses	Sarah (Sally) Levy	Penzance, Cornwall	Jew jeweller
7711	Jacob	Samuel	1836	Falmouth, Cornwall			Henrietta Rose Isaacs	Dover, Kent	boarding school pupil
2644	Jacob	Samuel	1838	Edinburgh, Scotland	Jenkin Jacob	Hannah (?)		Glasgow, Scotland	
13846	Jacob	Samuel	1844	Chatham, Kent	Nathan Jacob	Rachael (?)		Manchester	scholar
4573	Jacob	Sarah	1825	Portsmouth, Hampshire	Charles Lyons	Phoebe Levy	Moses Levi Jacob	Birmingham	
23717	Jacob	Sarah	1841	?, Germany	Wolf Jacob	Esther (?)		Liverpool	
18010	Jacob	Sarah	1843	?, Germany	Israel Jacob	Hannah (?)		Aldgate, London	
5357	Jacob	Sarah (Sally)	1780	Truro, Cornwall	Israel Levy	Hannah Moses	Samuel Jacob	Penzance, Cornwall	
1093	Jacob	Sarah K	1850	Falmouth, Cornwall	Moss J Jacob	Frances (?)		Falmouth, Cornwall	
5643	Jacob	Sarah M	1835	Manchester	Henry Jacob	Esther Lyons	Jacob Mordecai Levi	Liverpool	
17063	Jacob	Sawkin	1811	?, Poland [?, Prussia-Poland]				Edinburgh, Scotland	broker
18008	Jacob	Sela	1837	?, Germany	Israel Jacob	Hannah (?)		Aldgate, London	tailor
31045	Jacob	Sophia	1779	Portsmouth, Hampshire	(?)		(?) Jacob	Liverpool	
1821	Jacob	Sophia	1827	Leigh, Essex	Laurence Lazarus	Catharine Phillips	Isaac Jacob	Swansea, Wales	jeweller's wife
23718	Jacob	Susannah	1843	?, Germany	Wolf Jacob	Esther (?)		Liverpool	
20055	Jacob	Theresa	1838	Manchester	Henry Jacobs	Esther Lyons		Liverpool	
23715	Jacob	Wolf	1811	?, Germany			Esther (?)	Liverpool	pedlar
2465	Jacob	Zilla (Celia)	1824	?, Germany [Gloustine, Germany]			Lazarus Jacob	Hull, Yorkshire	
30405	Jacob (Bing-Jacob)	Bing (Joseph)	1780	?, France			Collette Brunswick	Brighton, Sussex	
30423	Jacob (Bing-Jacob)	Celestine	1833	Metz, France	Bing (Joseph) Jacob (Bing-Jacob)	Collette Brunswick	Nathan Norman	Brighton, Sussex	
30421	Jacob (Bing-Jacob)	Collette	1795	?, France	Nathan Brunswick	Rosine Levy	Bing (Joseph) Jacob (Bing-Jacob)	Brighton, Sussex	

ID	surname	given names	born	birthplace	father	mother	spouse 1	1851 residence	1851 occupation
30422	Jacob (Bing-Jacob)	Elisa Alice	1831	Metz, France	Bing (Joseph) Jacob (Bing-Jacob)	Collette Brunswick	Ferdinand Jonas	Brighton, Sussex	
5698	Jacob (Jacobs)	Chapman	1829	Swansea, Wales	Greenbone (Granbone) Jacob (Jacobs)	Rosetta (Rozeta) (?)	Rachel Isaacs	Swansea, Wales	jeweller + pawnbroker
1813	Jacob (Jacobs)	Esther	1838	Swansea, Wales	Greenbone (Granbone) Jacob (Jacobs)	Rosetta (Rozeta) (?)	Berryman Franklin	Swansea, Wales	
1810	Jacob (Jacobs)	Greenbone (Granbone)	1798	Gdansk, Poland [Danzig, Prussia]			Rosetta (Rozeta) (?)	Swansea, Wales	tailor + general outfitter
1816	Jacob (Jacobs)	Harriet	1843	Swansea, Wales	Greenbone (Granbone) Jacob (Jacobs)	Rosetta (Rozeta) (?)		Swansea, Wales	
21956	Jacob (Jacobs)	Hyam (Imon)	1830	Swansea, Wales	Greenbone (Granbone) Jacob (Jacobs)	Erosetta (Rozeta) (?)	Sarah Best	Exeter, Devon	traveller in pens
1819	Jacob (Jacobs)	Isaac (Franc)	1850	Swansea, Wales	Greenbone (Granbone) Jacob (Jacobs)	Rosetta (Rozeta) (?)	Lizzie (?)	Swansea, Wales	
1815	Jacob (Jacobs)	Joel	1841	Swansea, Wales	Greenbone (Granbone) Jacob (Jacobs)	Rosetta (Rozeta) (?)	Julia Langner	Swansea, Wales	
1812	Jacob (Jacobs)	Lazarus	1833	Swansea, Wales	Greenbone (Granbone) Jacob (Jacobs)	Rosetta (Rozeta) (?)	Elizabeth Levy	Swansea, Wales	
1833	Jacob (Jacobs)	Lewin (Louis)	1835	Swansea, Wales	Greenbone (Granbone) Jacob (Jacobs)	Rosetta (Rozeta) (?)	Nancy Davis	Swansea, Wales	hawker
1814	Jacob (Jacobs)	Michael	1839	Swansea, Wales	Greenbone (Granbone) Jacob (Jacobs)	Rosetta (Rozeta) (?)		Swansea, Wales	
1817	Jacob (Jacobs)	Miriam (Minnie)	1845	Swansea, Wales	Greenbone (Granbone) Jacob (Jacobs)	Rosetta (Rozeta) (?)	Joseph Berg	Swansea, Wales	
1811	Jacob (Jacobs)	Rosetta (Rozeta)	1804	Szczecin, Poland [Stettin, Prussia]	(?)		Greenbone (Granbone) Jacob	Swansea, Wales	
5696	Jacob (Jacobs)	Simon	1834	Swansea, Wales	Greenbone (Granbone)) Jacob (Jacobs)	Rosetta (?)	Fanny Isaacs	Swansea, Wales	jeweller + pawnbroker
1818	Jacob (Jacobs)Swansea, Wales	Frederick	1848	Swansea, Wales	Greenbone (Granbone) Jacob (Jacobs)	Rosetta (Rozeta) (?)	Kate Elkan	Swansea, Wales	
8118	Jacob (Spiers)	Ellen	1830	Sheffield, Yorkshire	Samuel Jacobs	Eva (Eve) (?)		Birmingham	shop assistant
1431	Jacobowitch	Frederick	1841	?, Poland	Signor Jacobowitch	Madame (?)		Plymouth, Devon	musician
1430	Jacobowitch	Madame	1811	?, Poland			Signor Jacobowitch	Plymouth, Devon	musician - harpist
1429	Jacobowitch	Signor	1806	?, Poland			Madame (?)	Plymouth, Devon	musician - vocalist
27888	Jacobowitz	Betsey	1829	?, Poland [Magestin, Prussia]	(?)		Henry Jacobowitz	Spitalfields, London	tailoress
27887	Jacobowitz	Henry	1824	Bydgoszcz, Poland [Bromberg, Prussia]			Betsey (?)	Spitalfields, London	tailor
17605	Jacobs	?	1829	Aldgate, London	Joseph Jacobs	Rachael Mendoza		Aldgate, London	waistcoat maker
17606	Jacobs	?	1831	Aldgate, London	Joseph Jacobs	Rachael Mendoza		Aldgate, London	
25972	Jacobs	?	1849	Aldgate, London	Isaac Henry Jacobs	Matilda Levy		Aldgate, London	
17082	Jacobs	Aaron	1771	?, Poland [?, Prussia]				Glasgow, Scotland	retired broker
777	Jacobs	Aaron	1809	Finsbury, London	Jacob Jacobs		Rosetta Aaron Jessel	Whitechapel, London	cane dealer
13435	Jacobs	Aaron	1817	?, London				Shoreditch, London	warehouseman
8598	Jacobs	Aaron	1829	?, Poland				Spitalfields, London	cap maker
28148	Jacobs	Aaron	1841	Aldgate, London	Ezra Jacobs	Nancy Cohen		Aldgate, London	scholar
634	Jacobs	Aaron	1846	Spitalfields, London	Israel Jacobs	Elizabeth (Betsy) Phillips	Sarah Jacobs	Spitalfields, London	

ID	surname	given names	born	birthplace	father	mother	spouse 1	1851 residence	1851 occupation
26607	Jacobs	Aaron	1851	Aldgate, London	Benjamin Jacobs	Julia Lyons		Aldgate, London	
2167	Jacobs	Aaron Joseph	1845	Oxford, Oxfordshire	Nathan Jacobs	Hannah Woolf	Sarah Dora Samuel	Oxford, Oxfordshire	
21889	Jacobs	Abagail	1847	Clerkenwell, London	Abraham Jacobs	Marian (?)		Clerkenwell, London	
772	Jacobs	Abely	1833	City, London	John Jacobs	Elizabeth (?)		Whitechapel, London	general dealer
19228	Jacobs	Abigail	1822	Sheerness, Kent	(?) Jacobs			Aldgate, London	house servant
281	Jacobs	Abigail	1827	Whitechapel, London	(?) Jacobs			Spitalfields, London	clothes dealer
27321	Jacobs	Abigail	1832	Aldgate, London	Isaac Jacobs	Sophia Garcia		Aldgate, London	
12799	Jacobs	Abigail	1846	Whitechapel, London	Benjamin Jacobs	Julia Levy	Joseph Cohen	Spitalfields, London	scholar
11656	Jacobs	Abigail	1849	Aldgate, London	Joseph Jacobs	Catherine Moses		Aldgate, London	
16879	Jacobs	Abraham	1773	Aldgate, London			(?)	Cambridge	traveller
15231	Jacobs	Abraham	1791	Spitalfields, London			(?)	Shoreditch, London	dealer in boots, shoes, clothing, china + glass
12729	Jacobs	Abraham	1793	Coventry, Warwickshire			Maria (?)	Coventry, Warwickshire	trunk maker
1227	Jacobs	Abraham	1806	?, Poland [?, Prussia-Poland]			Julia (?)	Plymouth, Devon	master tailor
676	Jacobs	Abraham	1807	Amsterdam, Holland			Lea (?)	Spitalfields, London	cigar maker
15974	Jacobs	Abraham	1810	Aldgate, London			Rosetta (?)	Covent Garden, London	fruit salesman
739	Jacobs	Abraham	1820	Middlesex, London	Elias Jacobs		Frances Coleman	Aldgate, London	clothier
30370	Jacobs	Abraham	1820	?, London				Stafford, Staffordshire	traveller
30485	Jacobs	Abraham	1821	Chesterfield, Derbyshire				Stafford, Staffordshire	hawker
570	Jacobs	Abraham	1824	Spitalfields, London	Yaacov		Esther (?)	Spitalfields, London	general dealer
21886	Jacobs	Abraham	1824	Holborn, London	Zev		Marian (?)	Clerkenwell, London	furrier
708	Jacobs	Abraham	1826	?, Poland	Yitzhak		Fanny (?)	Whitechapel, London	tailor
22417	Jacobs	Abraham	1826	Middlesex, London	Joshua Jacobs	Dinah Cohen		Southwark, London	cab driver
11269	Jacobs	Abraham	1834	?, Holland	Barney Jacobs	Hanah (?)		Aldgate, London	tailor
28157	Jacobs	Abraham	1834	Shoreditch, London	Ralph Jacobs	Mary Benjamin		Shoreditch, London	cap maker
774	Jacobs	Abraham	1838	City, London	John Jacobs	Elizabeth (?)	Priscilla Ansell	Whitechapel, London	scholar
21784	Jacobs	Abraham	1838	Whitechapel, London	David Jacobs	Amelia (?)	Julia Isaacs	Aldgate, London	cigar maker apprentice
27221	Jacobs	Abraham	1839	?, London	Emanuel Jacobs	Sarah (?)		Aldgate, London	
21099	Jacobs	Abraham	1843	Liverpool	(?) Jacobs	Henrietta (?)		Liverpool	
624	Jacobs	Abraham	1844	City, London	Mark Jacobs	Fanny Solomons		Spitalfields, London	
1829	Jacobs	Abraham	1846	Swansea, Wales	Charles Jacobs	Augusta (?)		Swansea, Wales	
11597	Jacobs	Abraham	1848	Bethnal Green, London	Mosses Jacobs	Ester Daniel		Aldgate, London	
20598	Jacobs	Abraham	1849	Aldgate, London				Spitalfields, London	
14736	Jacobs	Abraham	1850	City, London	Lazarus Jacobs	Rosa (?)		Spitalfields, London	
28432	Jacobs	Abraham	1850	Spitalfields, London	John (Jacob) Jacobs	Maria Israel		Spitalfields, London	
25973	Jacobs	Abraham	1851	Aldgate, London	Isaac Henry Jacobs	Matilda Levy		Aldgate, London	
693	Jacobs	Abraham (Edward)	1837	Aldgate, London	Levy Jacobs	Caroline Davis	Alice Aflalo	Whitechapel, London	scholar
5259	Jacobs	Abraham Lewis	1848	Aldgate, London	Lewis Jacobs	Rachel Solomons	Abigail Nathan	Spitalfields, London	scholar
5355	Jacobs	Alexander	1813	Dartmouth, Devon	?Nathan Jacob	?Miriam Alexander	Harriet Lyons	Paignton, Devon	silversmith
706	Jacobs	Alexander	1849	Spitalfields, London	Levi (Levy) Jacobs	Janette (?)		Whitechapel, London	scholar
686	Jacobs	Alfred	1790	Hull, Yorkshire			Elizabeth? (Elos'h) (?)	Whitechapel, London	watch maker + jeweller
21070	Jacobs	Alfred	1839	?, London				Dover, Kent	boarding school pupil
21079	Jacobs	Alfred	1839	Manchester				Dover, Kent	boarding school pupil
697	Jacobs	Alfred	1849	Aldgate, London	Levy Jacobs	Caroline Davis	Emily Flatau	Whitechapel, London	scholar

ID	surname	given names	born	birthplace	father	mother	spouse 1	1851 residence	1851 occupation
21890	Jacobs	Alfred	1850	Clerkenwell, London	Abraham Jacobs	Marian (?)		Clerkenwell, London	
721	Jacobs	Alfred Moss	1839	Aldgate, London	Moss Jacobs	Martha Davis	Caroline Apperley	Aldgate, London	scholar
20378	Jacobs	Alice	1842	Aldgate, London	Joseph Jacobs	Maria Benjamin		Aldgate, London	
13931	Jacobs	Ambrosia	1840	Barnsley, Yorkshire	Isaac Jacobs	Catharine (?)		Manchester	scholar
21779	Jacobs	Amelia	1801	Whitechapel, London	(?)		David Jacobs	Aldgate, London	
653	Jacobs	Amelia	1809	City, London	David Mendoza		Jacob (John) Jacobs	Spitalfields, London	
639	Jacobs	Amelia	1819	Hanover, Germany	(?)		Wolf Solomon Jacobs	Spitalfields, London	
25341	Jacobs	Amelia	1821	Holborn, London	(?) Jacobs	Elizabeth (?)		Holborn, London	fur sewer
23324	Jacobs	Amelia	1830	Middlesex, London	Lewis Jacobs	Milcah (Malcha) Levi		Westminster, London	dress maker
9390	Jacobs	Amelia	1834	Whitechapel, London	Joseph Jacobs	Rebecca (?)	Louis Abrahams	Spitalfields, London	shoe binder
26856	Jacobs	Amelia	1834	?, Poland [?, Prussia]	(?) Jacobs			Aldgate, London	cap maker
26148	Jacobs	Amelia	1836	?, London	Levy Jacobs	Hannah (?)		Aldgate, London	furrier
12796	Jacobs	Amelia	1838	Whitechapel, London	Benjamin Jacobs	Julia Levy		Spitalfields, London	scholar
28145	Jacobs	Amelia	1839	Whitechapel, London	Ezra Jacobs	Nancy Cohen		Aldgate, London	scholar
632	Jacobs	Amelia	1841	Spitalfields, London	Israel Jacobs	Elizabeth (Betsy) Phillips		Spitalfields, London	
20379	Jacobs	Amelia (Annie)	1845	Aldgate, London	Joseph Jacobs	Maria Benjamin		Aldgate, London	
17670	Jacobs	Amelia (Emily)	1816	Kornik, Poland [Cornick, Prussia]	(?)		Morris (Moses) Jacobs	Aldgate, London	
5631	Jacobs	Angelo	1850	Piccadilly, London	David Jacobs	Matilda Jacobs	Leah Nathan	Piccadilly, London	
13094	Jacobs	Ann	1786	Whitechapel, London				Whitechapel, London	pauper + dealer
679	Jacobs	Ann	1799	Portsmouth, Hampshire	Joel Isaacs		Eleazer Elias Jacobs	Whitechapel, London	
19227	Jacobs	Ann	1799	Middlesex, London	Abraham Jacobs	Rebecca Catherine (?)		Aldgate, London	
25994	Jacobs	Ann	1827	Aldgate, London	(?) Jacobs	Sarah (?)		Aldgate, London	general dealer's assistant
545	Jacobs	Ann	1836	Amsterdam, Holland	Meyer Jacobs	Jacoba (?)		Spitalfields, London	
20009	Jacobs	Ann	1842	Plumstead, London	Joseph Jacobs	Ellen (?)		Plumstead, London	
23338	Jacobs	Ann	1849	Covent Garden, London	George Jacobs	Rose (?)		Piccadilly, London	
1040	Jacobs	Ann (Anna)	1818	?, Poland	(?) Harris		Henry Jacobs	Exeter, Devon	
25246	Jacobs	Ann (Hannah)	1851	Holborn, London	Solomon Jacobs	Hannah (Ann) Myers		Holborn, London	
13896	Jacobs	Ann M	1815	Cheltenham, Gloucestershire	(?) Jacobs	Hannah (?)		Manchester	dressmaker
543	Jacobs	Anna	1781	Coventry, Warwickshire	(?)		Jacob Jacobs	Spitalfields, London	
24428	Jacobs	Anne	1842	Strand, London	Henry Jacobs	Emma Davis		Strand, London	scholar at home
642	Jacobs	Anne (Hannah)	1793	Aldgate, London	Naphtali Hirts Bevrik Solomon		Moses Jacobs	Spitalfields, London	general dealer
17122	Jacobs	Asher	1811	Sheerness, Kent	(?) Jacobs	Catherine (?)		Sheerness, Kent	master pawnbroker
10138	Jacobs	Asher	1831	Whitechapel, London	Lazarus Jacobs	Catherine Marks		Whitechapel, London	looking glass manufacturer
1823	Jacobs	Augusta	1817	?, Poland			Charles Jacobs	Swansea, Wales	
14243	Jacobs	Augusta	1841	?, Poland	Elias Jacobs	Hetty (Henrietta) Seifersohn		Manchester	scholar
9977	Jacobs	Augustus (Asher)	1836	Canterbury, Kent	Jacob Jacobs	Ella Barnard	Clara Emma Davis	Great Yarmouth, Norfolk	general dealer's assistant
16050	Jacobs	Barnard	1801	Holborn, London				Marylebone, London	dealer (chiefly in glass)
8548	Jacobs	Barnard	1841	Middlesex, London				Spitalfields, London	
20570	Jacobs	Barnard	1847	Shoreditch, London	Moses Jacobs	Mary Lipman		Spitalfields, London	
263	Jacobs	Barnet	1806	Aldgate, London	Abraham		Catharine (Kitty) (?)	Aldgate, London	general dealer
18208	Jacobs	Barnett	1838	Middlesex, London				Mile End, London	scholar
11265	Jacobs	Barney	1806	?, Holland			Hanah (?)	Aldgate, London	bullock driver
11632	Jacobs	Barney (Barnett)	1825	Middlesex, London	Jacob Jacobs	(?)	Rachel Jacobs	Aldgate, London	general dealer

ID	surname	given names	born	birthplace	father	mother	spouse 1	1851 residence	1851 occupation
17596	Jacobs	Baron	1847	Wapping, London	Simon Jacobs	Dinah (Diana) Jewell		Wapping, London	scholar
268	Jacobs	Benjamin	1809	Sheerness, Kent	Isaac Jacobs		Julia Benjamin	Aldgate, London	boot maker
280	Jacobs	Benjamin	1819	Aldgate, London	Samuel Jacobs		Julia Levy	Spitalfields, London	clothes dealer
11503	Jacobs	Benjamin	1823	Whitechapel, London	Michael Jacobs		Julia Hyams nee Lyons	Aldgate, London	general dealer
2141	Jacobs	Benjamin	1828	Middlesex, London			Adelaide Davis	Hull, Yorkshire	Rabbi
616	Jacobs	Benjamin	1839	Amsterdam, Holland	Mark (Mordecai) Jacobs	Esta (?)		Spitalfields, London	cordwainer
264	Jacobs	Benjamin	1842	?, London	(?) Jacobs	Rosetta (?Lyons?)		Aldgate, London	scholar
11510	Jacobs	Benjamin	1842	?Whitechapel, London	Hyam Hyams	Julia Lyons		Aldgate, London	scholar
26353	Jacobs	Benjamin	1843	?, London	Simon Jacobs	Sarah (?)		Aldgate, London	scholar
19417	Jacobs	Benjamin	1846	Camden Town, London	Isaac Jacobs	Phoebe Hyman		Bloomsbury, London	
581	Jacobs	Benjamin	1847	Spitalfields, London	Henry Jacobs	Julia Jacobs		Aldgate, London	
2142	Jacobs	Bethel	1812	Hull, Yorkshire	Israel Jacobs	Sarah Barnett	Esther Lyon	Hull, Yorkshire	silversmith + jeweller
16060	Jacobs	Betsey	1806	Aldgate, London				Aldgate, London	
17302	Jacobs	Betsey	1827	Whitechapel, London	Moses Jacobs	Anne (Hannah) Solomon		Spitalfields, London	
14241	Jacobs	Betsey	1837	?, Poland	Elias Jacobs	Hetty (Henrietta) Seifersohn		Manchester	scholar
618	Jacobs	Betsey	1844	Amsterdam, Holland	Mark (Mordecai) Jacobs	Esta (?)		Spitalfields, London	scholar
11635	Jacobs	Betsey	1849	Middlesex, London	Barney (Barnett) Jacobs	Rachel Jacobs		Aldgate, London	
11599	Jacobs	Betsey (Elizabeth)	1829	Aldgate, London	Barnet Jacobs	Catharine (Kitty) (?)	Judah Green	Aldgate, London	
3308	Jacobs	Betsie (Bessie)	1847	Cheltenham, Gloucestershire	Isaac Jacobs	Hannah Foist	Barnett Davis Rigal	Birmingham	
11677	Jacobs	Betsy	1832	Spitalfields, London	(?) Jacobs			Aldgate, London	
25326	Jacobs	Betsy	1848	Middlesex, London	Louis Jacobs	Rebecca Barnett		Holborn, London	
631	Jacobs	Bloomer	1840	Middlesex, London	Israel Jacobs	Elizabeth (Betsy) Phillips		Spitalfields, London	
28243	Jacobs	Bluma	1796	Southwark, London	(?)		John (Jacob) Jacobs	Spitalfields, London	pencil maker
8307	Jacobs	Blume	1801	?, Poland	(?)		Isaac Jacobs	South Shields, Tyne & Wear	
16636	Jacobs	Caroline	1809	Totnes, Devon	(?) Jacobs			Liverpool	annuitant
692	Jacobs	Caroline	1817	Thame, Oxfordshire	Jacob Davis	Ann (Nancy) Solomon	Levy Jacobs	Whitechapel, London	
12087	Jacobs	Caroline	1826	Aldgate, London	Simon Simmons		Isaac Jacobs	Spitalfields, London	
547	Jacobs	Caroline	1844	Amsterdam, Holland	Meyer Jacobs	Jacoba (?)		Spitalfields, London	
554	Jacobs	Caroline	1849	Spitalfields, London	John Jacobs	Frances (?)		Spitalfields, London	
13926	Jacobs	Catharine	1818	Nottingham, Nottinghamshire			Isaac Jacobs	Manchester	
11268	Jacobs	Catharine	1839	?, Holland	Barney Jacobs	Hanah (?)		Aldgate, London	scholar
11598	Jacobs	Catharine (Kitty)	1808	Aldgate, London	(?)		Barnet Jacobs	Aldgate, London	
17123	Jacobs	Catherine	1776	Innsbruck, Austria	(?)		(?) Jacobs	Sheerness, Kent	retired grocer
18406	Jacobs	Catherine	1780	?, London	(?) Jacobs			Aldgate, London	
628	Jacobs	Catherine	1789	Aldgate, London	(?)		(?) Jacobs	Spitalfields, London	broker of household goods
10133	Jacobs	Catherine	1801	Whitechapel, London	Mordecai Marks		Lazarus Jacobs	Whitechapel, London	staymaker
563	Jacobs	Catherine	1815	St Giles, London				Spitalfields, London	rag dealer
15484	Jacobs	Catherine	1824	Strand, London	(?) Jacobs			Covent Garden, London	
26720	Jacobs	Catherine	1831	Spitalfields, London	Edward (Aaron) Jacobs	Jane (Shava, Sylvia) Green		Spitalfields, London	tailoress
27786	Jacobs	Catherine	1834	Aldgate, London	Lewis Jacobs	Sarah Levy		Spitalfields, London	waistcoat maker
649	Jacobs	Catherine	1836	Spitalfields, London	Henry Jacobs	Maria (?)		Spitalfields, London	tailoress apprentice
11306	Jacobs	Catherine	1836	Middlesex, London	Lewis Jacobs	(?)		Aldgate, London	cap maker
18219	Jacobs	Catherine	1838	Middlesex, London	(?) Jacobs			Mile End, London	scholar

ID	surname	given names	born	birthplace	father	mother	spouse 1	1851 residence	1851 occupation
25244	Jacobs	Catherine	1838	Clerkenwell, London	Solomon Jacobs	Hannah (Ann) Myers		Holborn, London	cigar maker
27152	Jacobs	Catherine	1839	?, London	(?) Jacobs			Aldgate, London	
26149	Jacobs	Catherine	1840	?, London	Levy Jacobs	Hannah (?)		Aldgate, London	scholar
27024	Jacobs	Catherine	1841	?Aldgate, London	Mordecai Jacobs	Rachael Nathan		Aldgate, London	scholar
13301	Jacobs	Catherine	1847	Whitechapel, London	Isaac Jacobs	Louisa (Leah) Nathan		Spitalfields, London	
15602	Jacobs	Catherine	1848	Soho, London	Joseph Jacobs	Sarah (?)		Covent Garden, London	
17597	Jacobs	Catherine	1850	Wapping, London	Simon Jacobs	Dinah (Diana) Jewell	Samuel Isaacs	Wapping, London	
5913	Jacobs	Catherine (Kate, Kitty)	1847	Aldgate, London	Isaac Jacobs	Caroline Simmons	Benjamin Magnus	Spitalfields, London	
11650	Jacobs	Catherine (Kitty)	1820	Aldgate, London	David Moses	Hannah (?)	Joseph Jacobs	Aldgate, London	
1824	Jacobs	Chapman	1835	Swansea, Wales	Charles Jacobs	Augusta (?)		Swansea, Wales	watchmaker
1822	Jacobs	Charles	1802	?, Poland			Augusta (?)	Swansea, Wales	hawker
21096	Jacobs	Charles	1836	Liverpool	(?) Jacobs	Henrietta (?)		Liverpool	
23725	Jacobs	Charles	1839	?, Devon				Liverpool	scholar
15606	Jacobs	Charles	1850	Covent Garden, London	Joseph Jacobs	Sarah Davis		Covent Garden, London	
2475	Jacobs	Charles M	1850	Hull, Yorkshire	Bethel Jacobs	Esther (?)		Hull, Yorkshire	
25942	Jacobs	Charlot	1851	Aldgate, London	Jacob Jacobs	Leah (Louisa) Green		Aldgate, London	
25523	Jacobs	Clara	1820	?	(?) Samuel	(?) Wolfe	Phineas Jacobs	Dublin, Ireland	
4570	Jacobs	Clara	1834	Sheffield, Yorkshire	Samuel (Emmanuel) Jacobs	Eve (Eva) (?)		Birmingham	
19520	Jacobs	Clara	1835	Lambeth, London	(?) Jacobs	Elizabeth (?)	Abraham Isaacs	Covent Garden, London	
15983	Jacobs	Clara	1849	Covent Garden, London	Abraham Jacobs	Rosetta (?)		Covent Garden, London	
8993	Jacobs	Clara (Clarissa)	1831	Spitalfields, London	Lewis Jacobs	Jane (?)	Lewis L Levy	Spitalfields, London	
773	Jacobs	Clary	1835	City, London	John Jacobs	Elizabeth (?)		Whitechapel, London	tailoress
12880	Jacobs	Coleman	1844	Spitalfields, London	(?) Jacobs	Maria Coleman		Spitalfields, London	scholar
22516	Jacobs	Constantia	1811	Canterbury, Kent	(?)		Joseph Jacobs	Whitechapel, London	
760	Jacobs	Daniel	1831	Bethnal Green, London	Edward Jacobs	Hannah (?)		Wapping, London	
15327	Jacobs	Daniel	1836	Strand, London	(?) Jacobs	Hannah (?)		Southwark, London	tailor
21778	Jacobs	David	1785	Whitechapel, London			Amelia (?)	Aldgate, London	fishmonger
27139	Jacobs	David	1795	?, London	Issachar		Hannah Solomons	Aldgate, London	general dealer
18529	Jacobs	David	1819	Piccadilly, London	Moses Jacobs		Matilda Rebecca Jacobs	Piccadilly, London	glass warehouseman master empl 2
575	Jacobs	David	1826	Whitechapel, London	(?) Jacobs	Esther (?)		Spitalfields, London	dealer in fruit
11208	Jacobs	David	1826	Aldgate, London	Jacob		Rebecca Harris	Aldgate, London	cigar maker
17303	Jacobs	David	1827	Whitechapel, London	Moses Jacobs	Anne (Hannah) Solomon	Martha Nathan	Spitalfields, London	dealer in fruit
27319	Jacobs	David	1828	Aldgate, London	Isaac Jacobs	Sophia Garcia		Aldgate, London	city marker
28154	Jacobs	David	1829	City, London	Ralph Jacobs	Mary Benjamin		Shoreditch, London	general dealer
28144	Jacobs	David	1831	Whitechapel, London	Ezra Jacobs	Nancy Simmons		Aldgate, London	master butcher
371	Jacobs	David	1833	Spitalfields, London	Henry Jacobs	Maria (?)		Spitalfields, London	cap peak cutter
25346	Jacobs	David	1837	Holborn, London	(?) Jacobs	Elizabeth (?)		Holborn, London	at home
15328	Jacobs	David	1838	Strand, London	(?) Jacobs	Hannah (?)		Southwark, London	scholar
15135	Jacobs	David	1840	Finsbury, London	John Jacobs	Sarah Phillips		Hoxton, London	
548	Jacobs	David	1846	Amsterdam, Holland	Meyer Jacobs	Jacoba (?)		Spitalfields, London	
657	Jacobs	David	1847	Spitalfields, London	Jacob (John) Jacobs	Amelia Mendoza	Phoebe White	Spitalfields, London	
25941	Jacobs	David	1849	Aldgate, London	Jacob Jacobs	Leah (Louisa) Green		Aldgate, London	
1831	Jacobs	David	1850	Swansea, Wales	Charles Jacobs	Augusta (?)		Swansea, Wales	

ID	surname	given names	born	birthplace	father	mother	spouse 1	1851 residence	1851 occupation
5261	Jacobs	David	1850	Spitalfields, London	Lewis Jacobs	Rachel Solomons		Spitalfields, London	
17280	Jacobs	David Henry	1823	Shoreditch, London	Henry Jacobs	Elizabeth Myers	Mary Ann Broadfoot	Shoreditch, London	glass dealer
718	Jacobs	David Moss	1834	Aldgate, London	Moss Jacobs	Martha Davis		Whitechapel, London	cigar maker
9829	Jacobs	Deborah	1820	Aldgate, London	Aaron Isaacs	Rebecca (?)	Moss Jacobs	Bethnal Green, London	clerk
27023	Jacobs	Deborah	1834	?, London	Mordecai Jacobs	Rachael Nathan		Aldgate, London	
8082	Jacobs	Deborah	1850	Whitechapel, London	John (Ellis, Jacob Eleazer, Isaac) Jacobs	Frances Samson		Whitechapel, London	
12083	Jacobs	Dinah	1795	Aldgate, London	Joseph Benjamin Zeev Wolf Cohen		Joshua Jacobs	Spitalfields, London	
27151	Jacobs	Dinah	1803	?, London	(Issachar?) Jacobs			Aldgate, London	waistcoat maker
8732	Jacobs	Dinah	1815	Aldgate, London	(?) Jacobs	Julia (?)		Aldgate, London	dress maker
258	Jacobs	Dinah	1827	Spitalfields, London	Moses Jacobs	Rosetta Solomon	Nathan Nelson	Spitalfields, London	umbrella maker
290	Jacobs	Dinah	1838	Whitechapel, London	Henry Jacobs	Maria (?)		Spitalfields, London	tailoress apprentice
25325	Jacobs	Dinah	1846	Middlesex, London	Louis Jacobs	Rebecca Barnett		Holborn, London	
562	Jacobs	Dinah	1850	Spitalfields, London	John Jacobs	Louisa Levi		Spitalfields, London	
17594	Jacobs	Dinah (Diana)	1821	Wapping, London	Baruch Jewell		Simon Jacobs	Wapping, London	
30991	Jacobs	Dorothy	1785	?, Poland [?, Prussia]	(?)		(?) Jacobs	Newcastle Upon Tyne	
758	Jacobs	Edward	1798	Bethnal Green, London			Hannah (?)	Whitechapel, London	licensed victualler
15981	Jacobs	Edward	1846	Covent Garden, London	Abraham Jacobs	Rosetta (?)		Covent Garden, London	scholar
26717	Jacobs	Edward (Aaron)	1802	Spitalfields, London	Solomon Jacobs		Jane (Shava, Sylvia) Green	Spitalfields, London	tailor
2468	Jacobs	Edward Lewis	1839	Hull, Yorkshire	Bethel Jacobs	Esther (?)		Hull, Yorkshire	
28244	Jacobs	Eleanor	1821	Whitechapel, London	John (Jacob) Jacobs	Bluma (?)		Spitalfields, London	
385	Jacobs	Eleazer	1832	Spitalfields, London	Jacob Jacobs	Hannah (?)	Dinah Kizar	Spitalfields, London	slipper maker
26352	Jacobs	Eleazer	1837	?, London	Simon Jacobs	(?)		Aldgate, London	
680	Jacobs	Eleazer Elias	1802	Wapping, London	Elias Jacobs		Sarah Maria Lazarus	Whitechapel, London	clothier
623	Jacobs	Eli	1843	City, London	Mark Jacobs	Fanny Solomons		Spitalfields, London	
747	Jacobs	Elias	1767	Whitechapel, London			(?)	Whitechapel, London	
14238	Jacobs	Elias	1810	Grudziadz, Poland [Graudenz, Prussia]		Hetty (Henrietta) Seifersohn		Manchester	glazier
11421	Jacobs	Elias	1829	Middlesex, London				Aldgate, London	dealer in clothes and unredeemed pledges
8512	Jacobs	Elias	1831	Spitalfields, London	Lewis Jacobs	Jane (?)	Anna Genese	Spitalfields, London	scholar
28257	Jacobs	Elias	1839	Spitalfields, London	Elias Jacobs	Jane Mendoza		Spitalfields, London	scholar
10425	Jacobs	Elias	1842	Spitalfields, London	Lewis Jacobs	Sarah Levy		Spitalfields, London	
13829	Jacobs	Elis	1813	?, Poland [?, Prussia]				Manchester	watch maker
8510	Jacobs	Eliza	1831	Spitalfields, London	Lewis Jacobs	Jane (?)		Aldgate, London	tailoress
28255	Jacobs	Eliza	1831	Spitalfields, London	Elias Jacobs	Jane Mendoza		Spitalfields, London	tailoress
8417	Jacobs	Eliza	1836	Manchester	Henry Jacobs	Esther Lyons		Liverpool	
28161	Jacobs	Eliza	1848	Shoreditch, London	Ralph Jacobs	Mary Benjamin		Shoreditch, London	scholar
13897	Jacobs	Eliza F	1823	Cheltenham, Gloucestershire	(?) Jacobs	Hannah (?)		Manchester	milliner
19517	Jacobs	Elizabeth	1787	Whitechapel, London	(?)		(?) Jacobs	Covent Garden, London	
25338	Jacobs	Elizabeth	1793	Holborn, London	(?)		(?) Jacobs	Holborn, London	clothes dealer
769	Jacobs	Elizabeth	1798	City, London	(?)		John Jacobs	Whitechapel, London	
17279	Jacobs	Elizabeth	1798	Aldgate, London	Angel (Asher Anshel) Myers	Hannah (Anna) Joseph	Henry Jacobs	Shoreditch, London	
663	Jacobs	Elizabeth	1802	Aldgate, London	(?)		Lewis (Levy) Jacobs	Spitalfields, London	

ID	surname	given names	born	birthplace	father	mother	spouse 1	1851 residence	1851 occupation
8355	Jacobs	Elizabeth	1806	Norwich, Norfolk	Asher Jacobs			Canterbury, Kent	draper
21172	Jacobs	Elizabeth	1811	Strand, London	Levy Gabriel		John (Jacob) Jacobs	Aldgate, London	
24338	Jacobs	Elizabeth	1817	Sheerness, Kent	Lazarus Jacobs	Catherine (?)		Holborn, London	
601	Jacobs	Elizabeth	1825	Aldgate, London	(?)		Lewis Jacobs	Spitalfields, London	
24672	Jacobs	Elizabeth	1827	Aldgate, London	(?)		Henry Isaac	Kennington, London	
26350	Jacobs	Elizabeth	1828	?, London	Simon Jacobs	(?)		Aldgate, London	
765	Jacobs	Elizabeth	1829	?	(?) Jacobs			Wapping, London	furrier
12794	Jacobs	Elizabeth	1829	Whitechapel, London	(?) Jacobs			Spitalfields, London	clothes dealer
27141	Jacobs	Elizabeth	1831	?Spitalfields, London	David Jacobs	Hannah Solomons		Aldgate, London	umbrella maker
11825	Jacobs	Elizabeth	1832	Aldgate, London				Whitechapel, London	house servant
757	Jacobs	Elizabeth	1836	Wapping, London	Michael Jacobs	Rachel (?)	Cecil Louisson	Wapping, London	scholar
10424	Jacobs	Elizabeth	1839	Spitalfields, London	Lewis Jacobs	Sarah Levy		Spitalfields, London	
393	Jacobs	Elizabeth	1842	Spitalfields, London	(?) Jacobs			Spitalfields, London	
736	Jacobs	Elizabeth	1842	Whitechapel, London	Nathaniel Jacobs	Sarah (?)		Whitechapel, London	
293	Jacobs	Elizabeth	1844	City, London	Jacob (John) Jacobs	Amelia Mendoza		Spitalfields, London	
12800	Jacobs	Elizabeth	1848	Whitechapel, London	Benjamin Jacobs	Julia Levy	Solomon Mendes Coutinho	Spitalfields, London	
507	Jacobs	Elizabeth	1849	Aldgate, London	Lewis Jacobs	Sarah (?)		Spitalfields, London	
28241	Jacobs	Elizabeth	1849	Spitalfields, London	Joseph Charles Jacobs	Sarah Myers		Spitalfields, London	
15603	Jacobs	Elizabeth	1850	Soho, London	Henry Jacobs	Rachel (?)		Covent Garden, London	
310	Jacobs	Elizabeth (Betsy)	1807	Whitechapel, London		Tsipora (?)	Israel Jacobs	Spitalfields, London	
5255	Jacobs	Elizabeth (Lizzie, Lesley)	1842	Aldgate, London	Lewis Jacobs	Rachel Solomons	Hyam Abrahams	Spitalfields, London	scholar
687	Jacobs	Elizabeth? (Elos'h)	1795	Whitechapel, London			Alfred Jacobs	Whitechapel, London	
9973	Jacobs	Ella	1800	Canterbury, Kent	Daniel Barnard	Zipporah (Sippy) Levy	Jacob Jacobs	Great Yarmouth, Norfolk	
9999	Jacobs	Ellah	1847	Canterbury, Kent	Nathan Jacobs	Hannah Barnard	Barnet Joseph Vanderlyn	Canterbury, Kent	
20005	Jacobs	Ellen	1806	?, Northumberland	(?)		Joseph Jacobs	Plumstead, London	
1828	Jacobs	Ellen	1842	Swansea, Wales	Charles Jacobs	Augusta (?)		Swansea, Wales	
27218	Jacobs	Emanuel	1801	?, Poland			Sarah (?)	Aldgate, London	tailor
16051	Jacobs	Emanuel	1802	Bath			Esther (?)	Marylebone, London	dealer (chiefly in glass)
26723	Jacobs	Emanuel	1804	Spitalfields, London	Solomon Jacobs			Spitalfields, London	clothes dealer
1022	Jacobs	Emanuel	1822	Exeter, Devon	Jacob Jacobs	Esther (?)	Sarah (?)	Exeter, Devon	stationer
25052	Jacobs	Emanuel	1836	Whitechapel, London				Clerkenwell, London	prisoner + hawker in (Hants?)
2168	Jacobs	Emanuel	1847	Oxford, Oxfordshire	Nathan Jacobs	Hannah Woolf	Priscilla Abrahams	Oxford, Oxfordshire	
550	Jacobs	Emanuel	1850	Middlesex, London	Meyer Jacobs	Jacoba (?)		Spitalfields, London	
30553	Jacobs	Emanuel	1851	Whitechapel, London	Joseph Jacobs	Rachel Jacobs		Whitechapel, London	
719	Jacobs	Emily	1836	Aldgate, London	Moss Jacobs	Martha Davis		Aldgate, London	
23339	Jacobs	Emily	1850	Covent Garden, London	George Jacobs	Rose (?)		Piccadilly, London	
24427	Jacobs	Emma	1812	Strand, London	Moss Davis	Mary (?)	Henry Jacobs	Strand, London	
584	Jacobs	Ephraim	1810	Spitalfields, London			(Fanny Michaels?)	Aldgate, London	Hackney carriage proprietor, victualler + dealer in paintings
5143	Jacobs	Ephraim	1811	?, Poland			Jane (?)	Newcastle Upon Tyne	jeweller + watchmaker
28429	Jacobs	Ephraim	1840	Whitechapel, London	John (Jacob) Jacobs	Maria Israel		Spitalfields, London	scholar
6915	Jacobs	Esta	1817	Amsterdam, Holland			Mark (Mordecai) Jacobs	Spitalfields, London	

ID	surname	given names	born	birthplace	father	mother	spouse 1	1851 residence	1851 occupation
20327	Jacobs	Ester	1779	?	(?)		(?) Jacobs	Aldgate, London	annuitant
11596	Jacobs	Ester	1828	Dalston, London	Abraham Daniel		Mosses Jacobs	Aldgate, London	
30990	Jacobs	Ester	1830	?, Poland [?, Prussia]	(?) Jacobs	Dorothy (?)		Newcastle Upon Tyne	dressmaker
569	Jacobs	Esther	1787	Spitalfields, London	(?)		(?) Jacobs	Spitalfields, London	dealer in fruit
1023	Jacobs	Esther	1795	Lyme Regis, Dorset	(?)		Jacob Jacobs	Exeter, Devon	lady
712	Jacobs	Esther	1800	Whitechapel, London				Whitechapel, London	
2466	Jacobs	Esther	1811	Hull, Yorkshire	Joseph Lyon	Rosa Ralph	Bethel Jacobs	Hull, Yorkshire	
11715	Jacobs	Esther	1811	Whitechapel, London	(?)		Joseph Jacobs	Aldgate, London	cook
25339	Jacobs	Esther	1813	Holborn, London	(?) Jacobs	Elizabeth (?)		Holborn, London	
16052	Jacobs	Esther	1815	?	(?)		Emanuel Jacobs	Marylebone, London	
18421	Jacobs	Esther	1822	Hull, Yorkshire	(?) Jacobs			Elephant & Castle, London	house servant
698	Jacobs	Esther	1825	?, Holland	(?) Spyer	Rosea (?)	Herman Jacobs	Whitechapel, London	
26985	Jacobs	Esther	1825	?, Germany	(?) Jacobs			Aldgate, London	house servant
571	Jacobs	Esther	1828	Spitalfields, London	(?)		Abraham Jacobs	Spitalfields, London	
591	Jacobs	Esther	1828	Aldgate, London			John Jacobs	Spitalfields, London	dress maker
771	Jacobs	Esther	1831	City, London	John Jacobs	Elizabeth (?)		Whitechapel, London	house servant
7645	Jacobs	Esther	1831	Finsbury, London	John Jacobs	Sarah (?)		Aldgate, London	
13151	Jacobs	Esther	1831	Finsbury, London	John Jacobs	Sarah (?)		Spitalfields, London	
10137	Jacobs	Esther	1836	Whitechapel, London	Lazarus Jacobs	Catherine Marks	George Isaacs	Whitechapel, London	staymaker
11547	Jacobs	Esther	1837	Shoreditch, London	Moses Jacobs	Mary Lipman		Spitalfields, London	cap maker
15977	Jacobs	Esther	1839	Covent Garden, London	Abraham Jacobs	Rosetta (?)		Covent Garden, London	scholar
5555	Jacobs	Esther	1841	Clerkenwell, London	Solomon Jacobs	Hannah (Ann) Myers		Holborn, London	scholar
25321	Jacobs	Esther	1841	Middlesex, London	Louis Jacobs	Rebecca Barnett		Holborn, London	scholar
1041	Jacobs	Esther	1843	Exeter, Devon	Henry Jacobs	Ann (Anna) Harris	Jacob Abel	Exeter, Devon	scholar
552	Jacobs	Esther	1846	Spitalfields, London	John Jacobs	Frances (?)		Spitalfields, London	
26354	Jacobs	Esther	1846	?, London	Simon Jacobs	Sarah (?)		Aldgate, London	scholar
22520	Jacobs	Esther	1849	Stepney, London	Joseph Jacobs	Constantia (?)		Whitechapel, London	
9929	Jacobs	Esther Ella	1833	Canterbury, Kent	Jacob Jacobs	Ella Barnard	George Mitchell	Great Yarmouth, Norfolk	general dealer's assistant
2936	Jacobs	Eve	1794	?, Russia			Samuel (Emmanuel) Jacobs	Birmingham	
609	Jacobs	Eve	1833	Spitalfields, London	Moses Jacobs		Joseph Harris	Spitalfields, London	dressmaker
15431	Jacobs	Ezekiel	1796	?, London	Simcha Lemon		Sarah Levy	Covent Garden, London	fruiterer
28142	Jacobs	Ezra	1807	Whitechapel, London	Jacob (John) Jacobs (Coppel)	Phillis (?)	Nancy Simmons	Aldgate, London	master butcher
26088	Jacobs	Fanny	1803	Warsaw, Poland	(?)		Moses Jacobs	Aldgate, London	
622	Jacobs	Fanny	1816	Whitechapel, London	Lipman (Eliezer) Solomons		Mark Jacobs	Spitalfields, London	
707	Jacobs	Fanny	1823	?, Poland			Abraham Jacobs	Whitechapel, London	
26147	Jacobs	Fanny	1833	?, London	Levy Jacobs	Hannah (?)		Aldgate, London	furrier
20376	Jacobs	Fanny	1838	Aldgate, London	Joseph Jacobs	Maria Benjamin		Aldgate, London	
28245	Jacobs	Fanny	1840	Whitechapel, London	John (Jacob) Jacobs	Bluma (?)		Spitalfields, London	
22175	Jacobs	Fanny	1843	Shoreditch, London	John Jacobs	Martha Lazarus		Whitechapel, London	
291	Jacobs	Fanny	1844	Spitalfields, London	Henry Jacobs	Maria (?)		Spitalfields, London	scholar
11676	Jacobs	Fanny	1845	Aldgate, London	Henry Jacobs	Sarah Jacobs		Aldgate, London	
388	Jacobs	Fanny	1848	Spitalfields, London	Raphael Jacobs	Rebecca Barnett		Spitalfields, London	scholar
637	Jacobs	Fanny	1850	?London	Wolf Solomon Jacobs	Amelia (?)		Spitalfields, London	

ID	surname	given names	born	birthplace	father	mother	spouse 1	1851 residence	1851 occupation
22207	Jacobs	Fanny (Frances)	1821	Aldgate, London	Henry Jacobs	Rosetta (?)		Whitechapel, London	parasol + umbrella maker
11774	Jacobs	Flora	1831	City, London	(?) Jacobs			Aldgate, London	house servant
26025	Jacobs	Frances	1814	Norwich, Norfolk	Aaron Jones		Judah Jacobs	Aldgate, London	
738	Jacobs	Frances	1818	Middlesex, London	Benjamin Coleman		Abraham Jacobs	Wapping, London	
2025	Jacobs	Frances	1821	Liverpool	Lyon Samson	Sarah (?)	John (Ellis, Jacob Eleazer, Isaac) Jacobs	Whitechapel, London	
551	Jacobs	Frances	1823	Whitechapel, London			John Jacobs	Spitalfields, London	cap maker
27144	Jacobs	Frances	1840	?, London	David Jacobs	Hannah Solomons		Aldgate, London	scholar
633	Jacobs	Frances	1844	Spitalfields, London	Israel Jacobs	Elizabeth (Betsy) Phillips		Spitalfields, London	
22519	Jacobs	Frances	1846	Stepney, London	Joseph Jacobs	Constantia (?)		Whitechapel, London	scholar
17608	Jacobs	Frances	1847	Aldgate, London	Joseph Jacobs	Rachael (?)		Aldgate, London	
2472	Jacobs	Frances Louise	1846	Hull, Yorkshire	Bethel Jacobs	Esther (?)	Daniel Hirsch Schloss	Hull, Yorkshire	
21054	Jacobs	Fred	1844	?, London				Dover, Kent	boarding school pupil
23724	Jacobs	Frederick	1837	?, Devon				Liverpool	merchant's apprentice
22286	Jacobs	G--- M---	1829	Birmingham	Joseph Jacobs	Mary (?)		Whitechapel, London	general dealer
20007	Jacobs	George	1833	Plumstead, London	Joseph Jacobs	Ellen (?)		Plumstead, London	labourer cow keeper
1827	Jacobs	George	1840	Swansea, Wales	Charles Jacobs	Augusta (?)	Rose Amy Moses	Swansea, Wales	
14733	Jacobs	George	1842	City, London	Lazarus Jacobs	Rosa (?)		Spitalfields, London	
24429	Jacobs	George	1845	Strand, London	Henry Jacobs	Emma Davis		Strand, London	scholar at home
11266	Jacobs	Hanah	1802	?, Holland	(?)		Barney Jacobs	Aldgate, London	
26486	Jacobs	Hannah	1773	Whitechapel, London	Ahraron from Frankfurt am Oder		Jacob Jacobs	Southwark, London	
13895	Jacobs	Hannah	1781	Thornbury, Gloucestershire	(?)		(?) Jacobs	Manchester	dressmaker
608	Jacobs	Hannah	1790	Spitalfields, London	Joseph Levy		Jacob Jacobs	Spitalfields, London	
15324	Jacobs	Hannah	1799	Spitalfields, London	(?)		(?) Jacobs	Southwark, London	
27140	Jacobs	Hannah	1799	?, London	(?) Solomons		David Jacobs	Aldgate, London	general dealer
759	Jacobs	Hannah	1801	Bethnal Green, London	(?)		Edward Jacobs	Wapping, London	
26146	Jacobs	Hannah	1801	?, Germany	(?)		Levy Jacobs	Aldgate, London	furrier
8354	Jacobs	Hannah	1804	Norwich, Norfolk	Asher Jacobs			Canterbury, Kent	draper
9994	Jacobs	Hannah	1804	Canterbury, Kent	Daniel Barnard	Zipporah (Sippy) Levy	Nathan Jacobs	Canterbury, Kent	
3298	Jacobs	Hannah	1806	Wiesbaden, Germany	(?) Foist		Isaac Jacobs	Birmingham	
19518	Jacobs	Hannah	1813	Finsbury, London	(?) Jacobs	Elizabeth (?)		Covent Garden, London	
11447	Jacobs	Hannah	1822	Middlesex, London	(?)		(?) Jacobs	Aldgate, London	needlewoman
2166	Jacobs	Hannah	1824	?, Poland	Isaiah Woolf	Catherine (?)	Nathan Jacobs	Oxford, Oxfordshire	
4313	Jacobs	Hannah	1825	Brighton, Sussex	(?) Jacobs	Kitty (Jetta, Catharine) (?)		Birmingham	shop woman
28155	Jacobs	Hannah	1831	Whitechapel, London	Ralph Jacobs	Mary Benjamin	Solomon Goldsmid	Shoreditch, London	cap maker
12085	Jacobs	Hannah	1832	Aldgate, London	Joshua Jacobs	Dinah Cohen	Isaac Hyman	Spitalfields, London	furrier
13152	Jacobs	Hannah	1833	Finsbury, London	John Jacobs	Sarah (?)		Spitalfields, London	
666	Jacobs	Hannah	1834	Aldgate, London	Lewis (Levy) Jacobs	Elizabeth (?)		Spitalfields, London	tailoress
11507	Jacobs	Hannah	1835	?Whitechapel, London	Hyam Hyams	Julia Lyons		Aldgate, London	general dealer
17607	Jacobs	Hannah	1835	Spitalfields, London	Joseph Jacobs	Rachael (?)		Aldgate, London	waistcoat maker
11602	Jacobs	Hannah	1836	Aldgate, London	Barnet Jacobs	Catharine (Kitty) (?)		Aldgate, London	
27220	Jacobs	Hannah	1836	?, London	Emanuel Jacobs	Sarah (?)		Aldgate, London	
6585	Jacobs	Hannah	1843	Covent Garden, London	Abraham Jacobs	Rosetta (?)	Solomon Joel	Covent Garden, London	scholar
11655	Jacobs	Hannah	1845	Aldgate, London	Joseph Jacobs	Catherine (Kitty) Moses		Aldgate, London	

ID	surname	given names	born	birthplace	father	mother	spouse 1	1851 residence	1851 occupation
604	Jacobs	Hannah	1847	Aldgate, London	Lewis Jacobs	Sarah (?)		Spitalfields, London	scholar
2773	Jacobs	Hannah	1850	Spitalfields, London	Abraham Jacobs	Hannah (?)	Joseph Marks	Spitalfields, London	
3719	Jacobs	Hannah	1850	Spitalfields, London	Raphael Jacobs	Rebecca Barnett		Spitalfields, London	
5554	Jacobs	Hannah (Ann)	1817	Aldgate, London	Yehuda Myers		Solomon Jacobs	Holborn, London	
6527	Jacobs	Harriet	1794	?, Poland				Exeter, Devon	pauper
20002	Jacobs	Harriet	1810	Portsmouth, Hampshire	Charles Lyons	Phoebe Levy	Alexander Jacobs	Paignton, Devon	
21095	Jacobs	Harriet	1833	?, London	(?) Jacobs	Henrietta (?)		Liverpool	
12501	Jacobs	Harris	1807	?, Poland				Exeter, Devon	traveller
20568	Jacobs	Hart	1841	Shoreditch, London	Moses Jacobs	Mary Lipman		Spitalfields, London	
22290	Jacobs	Harty	1837	Birmingham	Joseph Jacobs	Mary (?)		Whitechapel, London	
20003	Jacobs	Henrietta	1802	?, Germany	(?)		(?) Jacobs	Liverpool	dealer in groceries, fents, muslin, tobacco, snuff + cigars
13155	Jacobs	Henrietta	1838	City, London	John Jacobs	Sarah (?)		Spitalfields, London	
2470	Jacobs	Henrietta Matilda	1842	Hull, Yorkshire	Bethel Jacobs	Esther (?)	Elim Henry D'Avigdor	Hull, Yorkshire	
21549	Jacobs	Henry	1772	Aldgate, London	David Jacobs		Kitty Moses	Bloomsbury, London	no business
323	Jacobs	Henry	1796	Spitalfields, London	Philip Jacobs (Uri Shirga Pais)		Elizabeth Myers	Shoreditch, London	glass dealer
2476	Jacobs	Henry	1801	Arnhem, Holland			(?)	Hull, Yorkshire	cattle dealer
17461	Jacobs	Henry	1801	Coventry, Warwickshire				Spitalfields, London	general dealer
262	Jacobs	Henry	1805	City, London	Jacob Jacobs	Hannah Jacobs	Sarah Jacobs	Aldgate, London	general dealer
1039	Jacobs	Henry	1810	?, Poland	(?) Jacobs	Harriet (?)	Ann (Anna) Harris	Exeter, Devon	jeweller
15600	Jacobs	Henry	1812	Sheerness, Kent	Lazarus Jacobs	Catherine (?)	Rachel (?)	Covent Garden, London	general dealer
24426	Jacobs	Henry	1812	Strand, London			Emma Davis	Strand, London	wine merchant
576	Jacobs	Henry	1813	City, London	Phillip Jacobs	Rosa (Rosetta) Hyams	Julia Jacobs	Aldgate, London	glass cutter
12934	Jacobs	Henry	1826	Amsterdam, Holland				Spitalfields, London	cigar maker
6600	Jacobs	Henry	1828	Sheffield, Yorkshire	Samuel Jacobs	Eve (?)	Paulina Wulfson	Manchester	salesman
13928	Jacobs	Henry	1828	Manchester	Isaac Jacobs	(?)	Sarah (?)	Manchester	tailor + clothes dealer
15233	Jacobs	Henry	1828	Whitechapel, London	Abraham Jacobs	(?)	(?)	Shoreditch, London	dealer in boots, shoes, clothing, china + glass
15483	Jacobs	Henry	1828	Strand, London				Covent Garden, London	cigar maker
13916	Jacobs	Henry	1829	Sheffield, Yorkshire				Manchester	salesman to tailor + draper
17304	Jacobs	Henry	1831	Whitechapel, London	Moses Jacobs	Anne (Hannah) Solomon		Spitalfields, London	scholar
2759	Jacobs	Henry	1836	Whitechapel, London	Levy Jacobs	Caroline Davis	Kate Emanuel	Aldgate, London	scholar
20008	Jacobs	Henry	1836	Plumstead, London	Joseph Jacobs	Ellen (?)		Plumstead, London	apprentice to cow keeper
20377	Jacobs	Henry	1840	Aldgate, London	Joseph Jacobs	Maria Benjamin		Aldgate, London	
11604	Jacobs	Henry	1841	Aldgate, London	Barnet Jacobs	Catharine (Kitty) (?)		Aldgate, London	
13156	Jacobs	Henry	1841	City, London	John Jacobs	Sarah (?)		Spitalfields, London	
15978	Jacobs	Henry	1841	Covent Garden, London	Abraham Jacobs	Rosetta (?)		Covent Garden, London	scholar
28159	Jacobs	Henry	1841	?Shoreditch, London	Ralph Jacobs	Mary Benjamin		Shoreditch, London	scholar
24673	Jacobs	Henry	1844	Tasmania, Australia [Van Diemen's Land]	Henry Isaac Jacobs	Elizabeth (?)		Kennington, London	
24674	Jacobs	Henry	1844	Newcastle Upon Tyne	Henry Isaac Jacobs	Elizabeth (?)		Kennington, London	
17671	Jacobs	Henry	1846	Kornik, Poland [Cornick, Prussia]	Morris (Moses) Jacobs	Amelia (Emily) (?)		Aldgate, London	scholar

ID	surname	given names	born	birthplace	father	mother	spouse 1	1851 residence	1851 occupation
9982	Jacobs	Henry (Harry)	1828	Canterbury, Kent	Jacob Jacobs	Ella Barnard	Martha Mordecai	Canterbury, Kent	general dealer
9998	Jacobs	Henry (Naphtali)	1843	Canterbury, Kent	Nathan Jacobs	Hannah Barnard		Canterbury, Kent	
24671	Jacobs	Henry Isaac	1821	?, Norfolk			Elizabeth (?)	Kennington, London	artist
720	Jacobs	Henry Moss	1837	Aldgate, London	Moss Jacobs	Martha Davis	Sarah Levy	Aldgate, London	scholar
2474	Jacobs	Henry R	1849	Hull, Yorkshire	Bethel Jacobs	Esther	Charlotte (?)	Hull, Yorkshire	
700	Jacobs	Herman	1819	?, Holland			Rebecca (?)	Whitechapel, London	tailor
14239	Jacobs	Hetty (Henrietta)	1813	?, Poland	(?) Seifersohn		Elias Jacobs	Manchester	at home
13927	Jacobs	Horatia	1827	Manchester	Isaac Jacobs	(?)		Manchester	
298	Jacobs	Hyam	1788	?, Holland			Julie (?)	Spitalfields, London	general dealer
25322	Jacobs	Hyam	1842	Middlesex, London	Louis Jacobs	Rebecca Barnett		Holborn, London	scholar
14734	Jacobs	Hyam	1845	City, London	Lazarus Jacobs	Rosa (?)		Spitalfields, London	
27336	Jacobs	Hyam	1849	Aldgate, London	Lewis Jacobs	Rachael (?)		Aldgate, London	
17673	Jacobs	Hyam	1851	Aldgate, London	Morris (Moses) Jacobs	Amelia (Emily) (?)		Aldgate, London	
1826	Jacobs	Hyman (Hyam)	1838	Swansea, Wales	Charles Jacobs	Augusta (?)	Elizabeth Solomon nee Samuels	Swansea, Wales	
8306	Jacobs	Isaac	1796	?, Poland			Blume (?)	South Shields, Tyne & Wear	general dealer
13925	Jacobs	Isaac	1800	?, Poland			(?)	Manchester	tailor + clothes dealer
27317	Jacobs	Isaac	1801	Aldgate, London	Jacob b. Meir		Sophia Garcia	Aldgate, London	orange dealer
3297	Jacobs	Isaac	1805	?, Germany	Jacob ben (?)		Hannah Foist	Birmingham	commercial traveller in boots + shoes
19415	Jacobs	Isaac	1816	Bath	John Jacobs	Phoebe (?)	Phoebe Hyman	Bloomsbury, London	general dealer
12086	Jacobs	Isaac	1821	Whitechapel, London	Joshua HaLevi Jacobs	(?Dinah Cohen)	Caroline Simmons	Spitalfields, London	cigar maker
10134	Jacobs	Isaac	1822	Whitechapel, London	Lazarus Jacobs	Catherine Marks	Rachel Joshua	Whitechapel, London	picture frame maker
13299	Jacobs	Isaac	1826	Spitalfields, London	Jacob		Louisa (Leah) Nathan	Spitalfields, London	clothes dealer
15325	Jacobs	Isaac	1827	Strand, London	(?) Jacobs	Hannah (?)		Southwark, London	general dealer
21094	Jacobs	Isaac	1829	?, London	(?) Jacobs	Henrietta (?)		Liverpool	cigar maker
14240	Jacobs	Isaac	1835	?, Poland	Elias Jacobs	Hetty (Henrietta) Seifersohn		Manchester	shop boy
22174	Jacobs	Isaac	1841	Shoreditch, London	John Jacobs	Martha Lazarus		Whitechapel, London	
775	Jacobs	Isaac	1843	Newmarket, Suffolk	John Jacobs	Elizabeth (?)	Rebecca Ansell	Whitechapel, London	scholar
27790	Jacobs	Isaac	1845	Aldgate, London	Lewis Jacobs	Sarah Levy		Spitalfields, London	scholar
25940	Jacobs	Isaac	1849	Aldgate, London	Jacob Jacobs	Leah (Louisa) Green		Aldgate, London	
25967	Jacobs	Isaac Henry	1807	Whitechapel, London	Yaakov		Matilda Levy	Aldgate, London	pencil maker
9053	Jacobs	Isabella	1808	City, London	(?) Nathan	Elizabeth (?)	Joseph Jacobs	Aldgate, London	
683	Jacobs	Isabella	1838	Wapping, London	Eleazer Elias Jacobs	Sarah Maria Lazarus	Abraham Samuel	Whitechapel, London	scholar
740	Jacobs	Isabella	1848	Whitechapel, London	Abraham Jacobs	Frances Coleman	Alexander Barnett	Aldgate, London	
4072	Jacobs	Isobel (Isabel)	1843	Whitechapel, London	Levy Jacobs	Caroline Davis	Michael Isaac Emanuel	Aldgate, London	scholar
2143	Jacobs	Israel	1775	?, Poland [?, Prussia]	B'zalel		Sarah Barnett	Hull, Yorkshire	goldsmith
309	Jacobs	Israel	1807	Whitechapel, London	Issachar Behr Jacobs		Elizabeth (Betsy) Phillips	Spitalfields, London	general dealer
27502	Jacobs	Israel	1811	Middlesex, London				Aldgate, London	hawker
18270	Jacobs	Israel	1822	?, Poland [?, Prussia]				Whitby, Yorkshire	confectioner
9974	Jacobs	Israel	1824	Canterbury, Kent	Jacob Jacobs	Ella Barnard	Kate Mitchell	Great Yarmouth, Norfolk	general dealer's assistant
30989	Jacobs	Israel	1828	?, Poland [?, Prussia]	(?) Jacobs	Dorothy (?)		Newcastle Upon Tyne	cloth cap maker
28427	Jacobs	Israel	1833	Whitechapel, London	John (Jacob) Jacobs	Maria Israel		Spitalfields, London	general dealer
12798	Jacobs	Israel	1842	Whitechapel, London	Benjamin Jacobs	Julia Levy		Spitalfields, London	scholar

ID	surname	given names	born	birthplace	father	mother	spouse 1	1851 residence	1851 occupation
15984	Jacobs	Israel	1851	Covent Garden, London	Abraham Jacobs	Rosetta (?)		Covent Garden, London	
17288	Jacobs	Jacob	1779	?			Anna (?)	Spitalfields, London	
386	Jacobs	Jacob	1783	Aldgate, London		Hannah (?)		Spitalfields, London	general dealer
245	Jacobs	Jacob	1791	?, Holland			(?)	Spitalfields, London	general dealer
9972	Jacobs	Jacob	1798	Norwich, Norfolk	Asher Jacobs		Ella Barnard	Great Yarmouth, Norfolk	general dealer
25936	Jacobs	Jacob	1821	?, Holland	Moses Jacobs		Leah (Louisa) Green	Aldgate, London	general dealer
567	Jacobs	Jacob	1826	?, Poland				Spitalfields, London	cap maker
26855	Jacobs	Jacob	1830	?, Poland [?, Prussia]				Aldgate, London	cap maker
380	Jacobs	Jacob	1834	Spitalfields, London	(?) Jacobs	Maria Coleman		Spitalfields, London	general dealer
11603	Jacobs	Jacob	1839	Aldgate, London	Barnet Jacobs	Catharine (Kitty) (?)		Aldgate, London	
16886	Jacobs	Jacob	1839	Sheffield, Yorkshire	Ephraim Jacobs	Jane (?)		Newcastle Upon Tyne	
20569	Jacobs	Jacob	1843	Shoreditch, London	Moses Jacobs	Mary Lipman		Spitalfields, London	
28160	Jacobs	Jacob	1844	City, London	Ralph Jacobs	Mary Benjamin		Shoreditch, London	scholar
25971	Jacobs	Jacob	1845	Aldgate, London	Isaac Henry Jacobs	Matilda Levy		Aldgate, London	
292	Jacobs	Jacob (John)	1809	City, London	Aryeh Pais Jacobs		Amelia Mendoza	Spitalfields, London	glass cutter
19416	Jacobs	Jacob (John)	1844	Camden Town, London	Isaac Jacobs	Phoebe Hyman	Hannah J (?Davis)	Bloomsbury, London	
17595	Jacobs	Jacob (John)	1846	Wapping, London	Simon Jacobs	Dinah (Diana) Jewell	Jane Freedman	Wapping, London	scholar
17287	Jacobs	Jacoba	1818	Amsterdam, Holland	(?)		Meyer Jacobs	Spitalfields, London	
22890	Jacobs	Jane	1777	Whitechapel, London	(?)		(?) Jacobs	Wapping, London	dairy keeper
8509	Jacobs	Jane	1798	Aldgate, London	(?)		Lewis Jacobs	Spitalfields, London	clothes dealer
28254	Jacobs	Jane	1798	Aldgate, London	Aaron Mendoza		Lewis Jacobs	Spitalfields, London	clothes dealer
26172	Jacobs	Jane	1815	?, London	Solomon Abrahams	Maria Solomons	Mark Jacobs	Aldgate, London	
25342	Jacobs	Jane	1827	Holborn, London	(?) Jacobs	Elizabeth (?)		Holborn, London	fur business
28158	Jacobs	Jane	1837	Shoreditch, London	Ralph Jacobs	Mary Benjamin	David Heller	Shoreditch, London	scholar
21097	Jacobs	Jane	1838	Liverpool	(?) Jacobs	Henrietta (?)		Liverpool	
23707	Jacobs	Jane	1838	Liverpool	(?) Jacobs			Liverpool	scholar
14242	Jacobs	Jane	1839	?, Poland	Elias Jacobs	Hetty (Henrietta) Seifersohn		Manchester	scholar
16260	Jacobs	Jane	1840	Middlesex, London	(?) Jacobs			Spitalfields, London	
28146	Jacobs	Jane	1841	Spitalfields, London	Ezra Jacobs	Nancy Cohen		Aldgate, London	scholar
9830	Jacobs	Jane	1842	Aldgate, London	Moss Jacobs	Deborah Isaacs		Bethnal Green, London	scholar
26026	Jacobs	Jane	1848	Aldgate, London	Judah Jacobs	Frances Jones		Aldgate, London	
16884	Jacobs	Jane	1812	?, Yorkshire	(?)		Ephraim Jacobs	Newcastle Upon Tyne	
26718	Jacobs	Jane (Shava, Sylvia)	1807	Spitalfields, London	Judah Levy Green		Edward (Aaron) Jacobs	Spitalfields, London	
702	Jacobs	Janette	1813	Amsterdam, Holland	(?)		Levi (Levy) Jacobs	Whitechapel, London	licensed hawker
21174	Jacobs	Jeannette	1847	Aldgate, London	John (Jacob) Jacobs	Elizabeth Gabriel		Aldgate, London	
2477	Jacobs	Jennetta	1833	Middlesex, London	(?) Jacobs			Hull, Yorkshire	
776	Jacobs	Jesse	1825	Southwark, London				Mile End, London	railway guard
26722	Jacobs	Jessy	1841	Spitalfields, London	Edward (Aaron) Jacobs	Jane (Shava, Sylvia) Green		Spitalfields, London	scholar
5260	Jacobs	Jewell (Julia)	1846	Aldgate, London	Lewis Jacobs	Rachel Solomons		Spitalfields, London	
770	Jacobs	John	1800	Whitechapel, London			Elizabeth (?)	Whitechapel, London	general dealer
17829	Jacobs	John	1801	Walton-on-Thames, London			Rosa (?)	Aldgate, London	auctioneer + appraiser
26054	Jacobs	John	1801	Sheerness, Kent	Lazarus Jacobs	Catherine (?)		Mayfair, London	general dealer
22170	Jacobs	John	1803	Shoreditch, London	Elias Jacobs		Martha Lazarus	Whitechapel, London	clothier
410	Jacobs	John	1805	City, London			Sarah (?)	Spitalfields, London	clothier
560	Jacobs	John	1810	Whitechapel, London	Tsebi		Louisa Levi	Spitalfields, London	town traveller

ID	surname	given names	born	birthplace	father	mother	spouse 1	1851 residence	1851 occupation
15133	Jacobs	John	1816	Derby, Derbyshire	Woolf Jacobs		Sarah Phillips	Hoxton, London	furrier empl 2 + dealer in china, glass + earthenware
27854	Jacobs	John	1821	Whitechapel, London	Joseph Jacobs		Martha Lipman	Spitalfields, London	general tailor
590	Jacobs	John	1822	Spitalfields, London			Esther (?)	Spitalfields, London	general dealer
5558	Jacobs	John	1823	Spitalfields, London			Frances (?)	Spitalfields, London	cap maker
15232	Jacobs	John	1827	Whitechapel, London	Abraham Jacobs	(?)		Shoreditch, London	dealer in boots, shoes, clothing, glass + china
586	Jacobs	John	1829	Spitalfields, London	Abraham Jacobs	Sarah (?)	Julia Cohen	Spitalfields, London	dealer in fruit
289	Jacobs	John	1830	Whitechapel, London	Henry Jacobs	Maria (?)		Spitalfields, London	general dealer
27320	Jacobs	John	1830	Aldgate, London	Isaac Jacobs	Sophia Garcia		Aldgate, London	city marker
21780	Jacobs	John	1831	Whitechapel, London	David Jacobs	Amelia (?)		Aldgate, London	fishmonger
635	Jacobs	John	1832	Middlesex, London				Spitalfields, London	furrier
6555	Jacobs	John	1832	Middlesex, London	Samuel Jacobs	Rose Alexander	Maria (Marion) Jacobs	Sunderland, Co Durham	glass dealer
15486	Jacobs	John	1832	Strand, London				Covent Garden, London	fruit dealer
630	Jacobs	John	1834	Middlesex, London	Israel Jacobs	Elizabeth (Betsy) Phillips		Spitalfields, London	
735	Jacobs	John	1834	Whitechapel, London	Nathaniel Jacobs	Sarah (?)		Whitechapel, London	musician
10136	Jacobs	John	1835	Whitechapel, London	Lazarus Jacobs	Catherine Marks		Whitechapel, London	clerk or scholar
5556	Jacobs	John	1843	Holborn, London	Solomon Jacobs	Hannah (Ann) Myers		Holborn, London	scholar
25323	Jacobs	John	1843	Middlesex, London	Louis Jacobs	Rebecca Barnett		Holborn, London	scholar
15329	Jacobs	John	1844	Strand, London	(?) Jacobs	Hannah (?)		Southwark, London	scholar
1042	Jacobs	John	1846	Exeter, Devon	Henry Jacobs	Ann (Anna) Harris		Exeter, Devon	scholar
572	Jacobs	John	1847	Spitalfields, London	Abraham Jacobs	Esther (?)		Spitalfields, London	
11210	Jacobs	John	1849	Aldgate, London	David Jacobs	Rebecca (?Harris)		Aldgate, London	
566	Jacobs	John	1850	Whitechapel, London	(?) Jacobs	Catherine (?)		Spitalfields, London	
8177	Jacobs	John	1851	Hackney, London	John Jacobs	Sarah Phillips		Hackney, London	
2024	Jacobs	John (Ellis, Jacob Eleazer, Isaac)	1816	?, London	Samuel Jacobs	Eva (Eve) (?)	Frances Samson	Whitechapel, London	bazaar keeper
28242	Jacobs	John (Jacob)	1778	Gloucester, Gloucestershire			Bluma (?)	Spitalfields, London	pencil maker
21171	Jacobs	John (Jacob)	1808	Aldgate, London	Hyam Barnett Jacobs		(?)	Aldgate, London	tailor
28425	Jacobs	John (Jacob)	1811	Spitalfields, London	Zebulon		Maria Israel	Spitalfields, London	general dealer
11636	Jacobs	John (Jacob)	1850	Aldgate, London	Barney (Barnett) Jacobs	Rachel Jacobs		Aldgate, London	
9628	Jacobs	John (Jacob)	1851	Spitalfields, London	Simon Jacobs	Phoebe Nathan		Spitalfields, London	
20280	Jacobs	John (Jacob, Jack)	1843	City, London	Lewis Jacobs	Rachel Solomons	Matilda Marks	Spitalfields, London	scholar
21173	Jacobs	Jonah	1837	Bristol	John (Jacob) Jacobs	(?)		Aldgate, London	
12396	Jacobs	Jonas	1789	?, Holland			Sarah Juda (?)	North Shields, Tyne & Wear	glazier
2756	Jacobs	Jonas	1793	Aldgate, London	Henry Jacobs	Kitty Samuel		Aldgate, London	grocer
25345	Jacobs	Jonas	1834	Holborn, London	(?) Jacobs	Elizabeth (?)		Holborn, London	fur business
9385	Jacobs	Joseph	1782	?, Holland			Rebecca (?)	Spitalfields, London	optician
22284	Jacobs	Joseph	1783	Bedford, Bedfordshire			Mary (?)	Whitechapel, London	general dealer
15517	Jacobs	Joseph	1789	City, London			(?)	Covent Garden, London	dealer
23923	Jacobs	Joseph	1796	?, Poland			Kitty (?)	Marylebone, London	
750	Jacobs	Joseph	1800	Aldgate, London				Whitechapel, London	gunsmith
320	Jacobs	Joseph	1801	Aldgate, London	Moshe		Rachael Mendoza	Aldgate, London	fruiterer

325

ID	surname	given names	born	birthplace	father	mother	spouse 1	1851 residence	1851 occupation
9052	Jacobs	Joseph	1801	Amsterdam, Holland			Isabella Nathan	Aldgate, London	general merchant
20372	Jacobs	Joseph	1806	Whitechapel, London	Pinchas Jacobs		Maria Benjamin	Aldgate, London	tobacconist
11714	Jacobs	Joseph	1808	Sheerness, Kent			Ester (?)	Aldgate, London	general dealer
20004	Jacobs	Joseph	1808	Plumstead, London			Ellen (?)	Plumstead, London	cow keeper
22515	Jacobs	Joseph	1808	Canterbury, Kent			Constantia (?)	Whitechapel, London	optician
11649	Jacobs	Joseph	1816	Cambridge	Abraham Jacobs		Catherine (Kitty) Moses	Aldgate, London	commercial traveller
15604	Jacobs	Joseph	1817	Sheerness, Kent	Lazarus Jacobs	Catherine (?)	Sarah Davis	Covent Garden, London	
2645	Jacobs	Joseph	1826	?, England				Glasgow, Scotland	assistant clothier
30988	Jacobs	Joseph	1826	?, Poland [?, Prussia]	(?) Jacobs	Dorothy (?)		Newcastle Upon Tyne	cloth cap maker
577	Jacobs	Joseph	1827	City, London	Phillip Jacobs	Rosa (Rosetta) Hyams		Aldgate, London	servant
21525	Jacobs	Joseph	1827	Walton-on-Thames, Surrey				City, London	clothier's assistant
15485	Jacobs	Joseph	1831	Strand, London				Covent Garden, London	fruit dealer
20006	Jacobs	Joseph	1831	Plumstead, London	Joseph Jacobs	Ellen (?)		Plumstead, London	cow keeper
22172	Jacobs	Joseph	1832	Shoreditch, London	John Jacobs	Martha Lazarus		Whitechapel, London	rag warehouseman
22210	Jacobs	Joseph	1833	Aldgate, London	Henry Jacobs	Rosetta (?)		Whitechapel, London	cigar maker
30128	Jacobs	Joseph	1836	Coventry, Warwickshire	Samuel Jacobs	Rose Alexander		Sunderland, Co Durham	
13154	Jacobs	Joseph	1837	City, London	John Jacobs	Sarah (?)		Spitalfields, London	
662	Jacobs	Joseph	1839	Amsterdam, Holland	Abraham Jacobs	Lea (?)		Spitalfields, London	cigar maker
25938	Jacobs	Joseph	1841	Aldgate, London	Jacob Jacobs	Leah (Louisa) Green		Aldgate, London	
22518	Jacobs	Joseph	1844	Stepney, London	Joseph Jacobs	Constantia (?)		Whitechapel, London	scholar
28430	Jacobs	Joseph	1844	Spitalfields, London	John (Jacob) Jacobs	Maria Israel		Spitalfields, London	scholar
19418	Jacobs	Joseph	1847	St Pancras, London	Isaac Jacobs	Phoebe Hyman	Katherine Lynes	Bloomsbury, London	
8081	Jacobs	Joseph	1849	?, London	John (Ellis, Jacob Eleazer, Isaac) Jacobs	Frances Samson		Whitechapel, London	scholar
28239	Jacobs	Joseph Charles	1827	Whitechapel, London	John (Jacob) Jacobs	Bluma (?)	Sarah Myers	Spitalfields, London	pencil maker
1830	Jacobs	Joseph Charles	1848	Swansea, Wales	Charles Jacobs	Augusta (?)	Esther Migel	Swansea, Wales	
6546	Jacobs	Joseph I	1837	Exeter, Devon			Kate Morris	Strand, London	apprentice jeweller
2467	Jacobs	Joseph Lyon	1838	Hull, Yorkshire	Bethel Jacobs	Esther (?)	Emily Sarah Meyer	Hull, Yorkshire	
12082	Jacobs	Joshua	1794	Aldgate, London	Isaac Eizak		Dinah Cohen	Spitalfields, London	fishmonger
24337	Jacobs	Joshua	1819	Sheerness, Kent	Lazarus Jacobs	Catherine (?)		Holborn, London	dealer in furniture
21157	Jacobs	Joshua	1821	Sheerness, Kent				Aldgate, London	orange merchant
27025	Jacobs	Joshua	1838	?, London	Mordecai Jacobs	Rachael Nathan		Aldgate, London	scholar
26024	Jacobs	Judah	1808	Aldgate, London	Abraham		Frances Jones	Aldgate, London	clothier + warehouseman empl 3
23326	Jacobs	Judah	1834	Middlesex, London	Lewis Jacobs	Milcah (Malcha) Levi		Westminster, London	cigar maker
25243	Jacobs	Judah	1836	Finsbury, London	Solomon Jacobs	Hannah (Ann) Myers	Esther Colliss	Holborn, London	cigar maker
13157	Jacobs	Judah (Julius)	1844	City, London	John Jacobs	Sarah (?)		Spitalfields, London	
11270	Jacobs	Julia	1768	?, Holland	(?)		(?) Jacobs	Aldgate, London	formerly a general dealer
8730	Jacobs	Julia	1779	?, London	(?)		(?) Jacobs	Aldgate, London	bath house keeper
22949	Jacobs	Julia	1812	Spitalfields, London	(?)		(?) Jacobs	Wapping, London	monthly nurse
1228	Jacobs	Julia	1813	?, Poland			Abraham Jacobs	Plymouth, Devon	
11504	Jacobs	Julia	1813	Whitechapel, London	Simcha Benim Lyons		Hyam Hyams	Aldgate, London	general dealer
9387	Jacobs	Julia	1818	Whitechapel, London	Joseph Jacobs	Rebecca (?)		Spitalfields, London	shoe binder
273	Jacobs	Julia	1819	Whitechapel, London	Benjamin (?Benjamin)		Benjamin Jacobs	Aldgate, London	umbrella maker
12795	Jacobs	Julia	1820	Whitechapel, London	Asher Levy		Benjamin Jacobs	Spitalfields, London	

ID	surname	given names	born	birthplace	father	mother	spouse 1	1851 residence	1851 occupation
12084	Jacobs	Julia	1825	Aldgate, London	Joshua Jacobs	Dinah Cohen	Cohen Joseph Proops	Spitalfields, London	furrier
11267	Jacobs	Julia	1831	?, Holland	Barney Jacobs	Hanah (?)		Aldgate, London	tailoress
11051	Jacobs	Julia	1834	Whitechapel, London	(?) Jacobs	Leah (?)		Aldgate, London	
15433	Jacobs	Julia	1834	?, London	Ezekiel Jacobs	Sarah Levy		Covent Garden, London	
654	Jacobs	Julia	1836	City, London	Jacob (John) Jacobs	Amelia Mendoza	David Davis	Spitalfields, London	servant of all work
27788	Jacobs	Julia	1838	Aldgate, London	Lewis Jacobs	Sarah Levy		Spitalfields, London	dressmaker
579	Jacobs	Julia	1842	Spitalfields, London	Henry Jacobs	Julia Jacobs		Aldgate, London	
8077	Jacobs	Julia	1842	Liverpool	John (Ellis, Jacob Eleazer, Isaac) Jacobs	Frances Samson	Jonas (John) Seigenberg	Whitechapel, London	scholar
704	Jacobs	Julia	1843	Spitalfields, London	Levi (Levy) Jacobs	Janette (?)		Whitechapel, London	scholar
13861	Jacobs	Julia	1843	Ashton, Lancashire				Manchester	scholar
619	Jacobs	Julia	1847	Spitalfields, London	Mark (Mordecai) Jacobs	Esta (?)	Michael Tapper	Spitalfields, London	scholar
21176	Jacobs	Julia	1850	Aldgate, London	John (Jacob) Jacobs	Elizabeth Gabriel	(?) Edmonds	Aldgate, London	
24431	Jacobs	Julia	1850	Strand, London	Henry Jacobs	Emma Davis		Strand, London	
27858	Jacobs	Julia	1850	Whitechapel, London	John Jacobs	Martha Lipman		Spitalfields, London	
674	Jacobs	Julie	1787	?, Holland			Hyam Jacobs	Spitalfields, London	
17831	Jacobs	Julie	1832	Aldgate, London	John Jacobs	Rosa (?)		Aldgate, London	
549	Jacobs	Julius	1848	Middlesex, London	Meyer Jacobs	Jacoba (?)		Spitalfields, London	
29896	Jacobs	Julius	1851	Whitechapel, London	Louis Jacobs	Leah Henry		Wapping, London	
2169	Jacobs	Julius (Jehiel)	1849	Oxford, Oxfordshire	Nathan Jacobs	Hannah Woolf	Mary Ann (Marie, Mariane) Berlyn Berlyn	Oxford, Oxfordshire	
25181	Jacobs	Kate	1817	Spalding, Lincolnshire	(?) Jacobs	Rosina (?)	Asher Myers	Finsbury, London	dressmaker
9840	Jacobs	Kate	1835	Aldgate, London	Moss Jacobs	Martha Davis	Henry Isaacs	Aldgate, London	
9979	Jacobs	Kate	1835	Canterbury, Kent	Jacob Jacobs	Ella Barnard	Bearman Barnett	Canterbury, Kent	
11634	Jacobs	Katharine	1847	Middlesex, London	Barney (Barnett) Jacobs	Rachel Jacobs		Aldgate, London	
2757	Jacobs	Kitty	1771	Middlesex, London	Israel (Ensley Cohen) Samuel	Susie Phillips	Henry Jacobs	Aldgate, London	annuitant
23924	Jacobs	Kitty	1786	?, Poland	(?)		Joseph Jacobs	Marylebone, London	
21781	Jacobs	Kitty	1831	Whitechapel, London	David Jacobs	Amelia (?)		Aldgate, London	
2473	Jacobs	Laura	1847	Hull, Yorkshire	Bethel Jacobs	Esther (?)		Hull, Yorkshire	
25970	Jacobs	Lawrence	1843	Aldgate, London	Isaac Henry Jacobs	Matilda Levy		Aldgate, London	scholar
243	Jacobs	Lazarus	1792	Amsterdam, Holland			Rosa (?)	Spitalfields, London	general dealer
10132	Jacobs	Lazarus	1796	Wapping, London	Asher Jacobs	Esther Israel	Catherine Marks	Whitechapel, London	looking glass maker
606	Jacobs	Lazarus	1835	Spitalfields, London	Reuben Jacobs	Frances (?)		Spitalfields, London	hawker
1825	Jacobs	Lazarus	1838	Swansea, Wales	Charles Jacobs	Augusta (?)		Swansea, Wales	shoemaker
27789	Jacobs	Lazarus	1840	Aldgate, London	Lewis Jacobs	Sarah Levy		Spitalfields, London	scholar
659	Jacobs	Lea	1807	Amsterdam, Holland	(?)		Abraham Jacobs	Spitalfields, London	cigar maker
16017	Jacobs	Leah	1788	Ipswich, Suffolk	(?)		Abraham R Jacobs	Kensington, London	annuitant
749	Jacobs	Leah	1795	Whitechapel, London	Elias Jacobs			Whitechapel, London	shop woman
11050	Jacobs	Leah	1817	Aldgate, London	(?)		(?) Jacobs	Aldgate, London	nurse
26796	Jacobs	Leah	1818	Aldgate, London	(?) Jacobs			Aldgate, London	
18532	Jacobs	Leah	1827	Shoreditch, London	Henry Jacobs	Elizabeth Myers		Piccadilly, London	
29894	Jacobs	Leah	1827	Whitechapel, London	Solomon Henry	Jane (?)	Louis Jacobs	Wapping, London	cigar business
26786	Jacobs	Leah	1830	Middlesex, London	(?) Jacobs			Aldgate, London	servant
16018	Jacobs	Leah	1833	Middlesex, London	Abraham R Jacobs	Leah (?)		Kensington, London	proprietor of houses
23327	Jacobs	Leah	1836	Middlesex, London	Lewis Jacobs	Milcah (Malcha) Levi		Westminster, London	

ID	surname	given names	born	birthplace	father	mother	spouse 1	1851 residence	1851 occupation
26721	Jacobs	Leah	1836	Spitalfields, London	Edward (Aaron) Jacobs	Jane (Shava, Sylvia) Green		Spitalfields, London	tailoress
14245	Jacobs	Leah	1847	Liverpool	Elias Jacobs	Hetty (Henrietta) Seifersohn	Moss Davis	Manchester	scholar
625	Jacobs	Leah	1848	Spitalfields, London	Mark Jacobs	Fanny Solomons	Isaac Cohen	Spitalfields, London	
25245	Jacobs	Leah	1848	Holborn, London	Solomon Jacobs	Hannah (Ann) Myers		Holborn, London	
1044	Jacobs	Leah	1850	Exeter, Devon	Henry Jacobs	Ann (Anna) Harris		Exeter, Devon	
25934	Jacobs	Leah (Louisa)	1822	?, Holland	Henry Green	Julia (?)	Jacob Jacobs	Aldgate, London	
5068	Jacobs	Levi	1823	?, Poland				Portsmouth, Hampshire	assistant hawker
28156	Jacobs	Levi	1833	Shoreditch, London	Ralph Jacobs	Mary Benjamin		Shoreditch, London	cap maker
701	Jacobs	Levi (Levy)	1811	Rotterdam, Holland			Janette (?)	Whitechapel, London	tailor/journeyman
25466	Jacobs	Levy	1773	?, Poland				Aldgate, London	pensioner
691	Jacobs	Levy	1792	Aldgate, London	Henry Jacobs	Kitty Samuel	Caroline Davis	Whitechapel, London	grocer empl 1
26145	Jacobs	Levy	1801	?, Germany			Hannah (?)	Aldgate, London	furrier
21093	Jacobs	Levy	1827	?, London	(?) Jacobs	Henrietta (?)		Liverpool	cigar maker
9643	Jacobs	Lewis	1837	?, Poland [Russia Poland]	Solomon Jacobs	Rosa (?)		Spitalfields, London	
23322	Jacobs	Lewis	1792	Spitalfields, London	Philip Jacobs		Milcah (Malcha) Levi	Westminster, London	glass dealer
11302	Jacobs	Lewis	1801	Middlesex, London			(?)	Aldgate, London	general dealer
8508	Jacobs	Lewis	1803	Aldgate, London			Jane (?)	Spitalfields, London	clothes dealer
24517	Jacobs	Lewis	1806	City, London	Shmuel		Sophia Daniels	Stockwell, London	attorney + solicitor
28253	Jacobs	Lewis	1808	Spitalfields, London	Eliyahu		Jane Mendoza	Spitalfields, London	clothes dealer
5253	Jacobs	Lewis	1819	Cambridge	Abraham Jacobs	Rachel Raphael	Rachel Solomons	Spitalfields, London	butcher
113	Jacobs	Lewis	1820	Middlesex, London	(?) Jacobs			Woolwich, London	shop assistant
598	Jacobs	Lewis	1823	Spitalfields, London			Elizabeth (?)	Spitalfields, London	fish salesman
27334	Jacobs	Lewis	1824	?, Poland [?, Prussia]			Rachael (?)	Aldgate, London	tailor
390	Jacobs	Lewis	1825	Amsterdam, Holland	Yissachar		Sarah (?)	Spitalfields, London	tailor
22211	Jacobs	Lewis	1834	Aldgate, London	Henry Jacobs	Rosetta (?)		Whitechapel, London	shopman
20375	Jacobs	Lewis	1835	Aldgate, London	Joseph Jacobs	Maria Benjamin		Aldgate, London	
11679	Jacobs	Lewis	1836	Spitalfields, London	(?) Jacobs			Aldgate, London	general dealer
5557	Jacobs	Lewis	1846	Holborn, London	Solomon Jacobs	Hannah (Ann) Myers		Holborn, London	
21175	Jacobs	Lewis	1849	Aldgate, London	John (Jacob) Jacobs	Elizabeth Gabriel		Aldgate, London	
21462	Jacobs	Lewis	1849	Sheerness, Kent	(?) Jacobs	(?) Russell		Sheerness, Kent	
555	Jacobs	Lewis	1850	Spitalfields, London	John Jacobs	Frances (?)		Spitalfields, London	
709	Jacobs	Lewis	1850	Aldgate, London	Abraham Jacobs	Fanny (?)		Whitechapel, London	
664	Jacobs	Lewis (Levy)	1803	Aldgate, London	Yaacov		Elizabeth (?)	Spitalfields, London	clothes dealer
696	Jacobs	Lionel	1845	Aldgate, London	Levy Jacobs	Caroline Davis	Zillah Davis	Whitechapel, London	scholar
25319	Jacobs	Louis	1817	Southwark, London	Moses Jacobs		Rebecca Barnett	Holborn, London	clothes salesman
29895	Jacobs	Louis	1824	?, Poland	Henry Jacobs		Leah Henry	Wapping, London	slipper maker
25344	Jacobs	Louis	1831	Holborn, London	(?) Jacobs	Elizabeth (?)		Holborn, London	cigar maker
25939	Jacobs	Louis	1847	Aldgate, London	Jacob Jacobs	Leah (Louisa) Green		Aldgate, London	
16053	Jacobs	Louis	1850	Marylebone, London	Emanuel Jacobs	Esther (?)		Marylebone, London	
561	Jacobs	Louisa	1818	Elephant + Castle, London	(?) Levi		John Jacobs	Spitalfields, London	
11678	Jacobs	Louisa	1833	Spitalfields, London	(?) Jacobs			Aldgate, London	cap maker
10426	Jacobs	Louisa	1843	Spitalfields, London	Lewis Jacobs	Sarah Levy		Spitalfields, London	
15982	Jacobs	Louisa	1848	Covent Garden, London	Abraham Jacobs	Rosetta (?)		Covent Garden, London	
13300	Jacobs	Louisa (Leah)	1819	Spitalfields, London	Simon Nathan		Isaac Jacobs	Spitalfields, London	

ID	surname	given names	born	birthplace	father	mother	spouse 1	1851 residence	1851 occupation
8078	Jacobs	Lyon	1844	Liverpool	John (Ellis, Jacob Eleazer, Isaac) Jacobs	Frances Samson	Rosetta Hyams	Whitechapel, London	scholar
288	Jacobs	Maria	1803	Whitechapel, London			Henry Jacobs	Spitalfields, London	
12730	Jacobs	Maria	1807	Coventry, Warwickshire	(?)		Abraham Jacobs	Coventry, Warwickshire	filler of silk
20373	Jacobs	Maria	1808	Whitechapel, London	(?) Benjamin		Joseph Jacobs	Aldgate, London	
28426	Jacobs	Maria	1811	Spitalfields, London	Ezekiel Israel		John (Jacob) Jacobs	Spitalfields, London	
1416	Jacobs	Maria	1821	?, Poland			Simon Jacobs	Plymouth, Devon	
14731	Jacobs	Maria	1832	Amsterdam, Holland	Lazarus Jacobs	Rosa (?)		Spitalfields, London	
2758	Jacobs	Maria	1833	Aldgate, London	Moss Jacobs	Martha Davis	Barnard Isaacs	Aldgate, London	
12797	Jacobs	Maria	1841	Whitechapel, London	Benjamin Jacobs	Julia Levy		Spitalfields, London	scholar
27026	Jacobs	Maria	1847	Aldgate, LondonAldgate, London	Mordecai Jacobs	Rachael Nathan		Aldgate, London	scholar
2469	Jacobs	Maria A	1840	Hull, Yorkshire	Bethel Jacobs	Esther (?)	Frederick B Hyam	Hull, Yorkshire	
610	Jacobs	Mariah	1812	Spitalfields, London	(?)		(?) Jacobs	Spitalfields, London	general dealer
21887	Jacobs	Marian	1826	Whitechapel, London	(?)		Abraham Jacobs	Clerkenwell, London	furrier
15892	Jacobs	Marian	1837	Middlesex, London	(?) Jacobs			Hackney, London	boarding school pupil
379	Jacobs	Marie	1809	?, Holland	Soloman Coleman	Sarah (?)	(?) Jacobs	Spitalfields, London	?sponge maker
24430	Jacobs	Marion	1848	Strand, London	Henry Jacobs	Emma Davis		Strand, London	
621	Jacobs	Mark	1810	?, Holland	Eliezer Jacobs		Fanny Solomon	Spitalfields, London	cap maker
26171	Jacobs	Mark	1815	?, London	Moses Jacobs		Jane Abrahams	Aldgate, London	dealer
9642	Jacobs	Mark	1831	?, Poland [Russia Poland]	Solomon Jacobs	Rosa (?)	Sarah Marks	Spitalfields, London	
573	Jacobs	Mark	1849	Spitalfields, London	Abraham Jacobs	Esther (?)		Spitalfields, London	
6914	Jacobs	Mark (Mordecai)	1809	Amsterdam, Holland			Esta (?)	Spitalfields, London	jeweller
715	Jacobs	Martha	1806	City, London	David Davis	(?Phoebe Moses)	Moss Jacobs	Whitechapel, London	
22171	Jacobs	Martha	1807	Shoreditch, London	Eleazer Lazarus		John Jacobs	Whitechapel, London	shirt maker
767	Jacobs	Martha	1817	Middlesex, London				Wapping, London	shopwoman
27855	Jacobs	Martha	1819	Whitechapel, London	(?) Lipman		John Jacobs	Spitalfields, London	general tailor
668	Jacobs	Martha	1841	Southwark, London	Lewis (Levy) Jacobs	Elizabeth (?)	Leendesh Wins	Spitalfields, London	scholar
22285	Jacobs	Mary	1795	Bedford, Bedfordshire	(?)		Joseph Jacobs	Whitechapel, London	
247	Jacobs	Mary	1811	Shoreditch, London	(?) Lipman	Sarah (?)	Moses Jacobs	Spitalfields, London	
10955	Jacobs	Mary	1811	Amsterdam, Holland	(?) Jacobs			Spitalfields, London	house servant
17437	Jacobs	Mary	1811	Whitechapel, London	(?)		Moses Jacobs	Aldgate, London	
28153	Jacobs	Mary	1811	Whitechapel, London	Abraham Benjamin	Hannah (?)	Ralph Jacobs	Shoreditch, London	
660	Jacobs	Mary	1833	Amsterdam, Holland	Abraham Jacobs	Lea (?)		Spitalfields, London	dress maker
26351	Jacobs	Mary	1835	?, London	Simon Jacobs	(?)		Aldgate, London	
617	Jacobs	Mary	1840	Amsterdam, Holland	Mark (Mordecai) Jacobs	Esta (?)		Spitalfields, London	scholar
11653	Jacobs	Mary	1842	Aldgate, London	Joseph Jacobs	Catherine (Kitty) Moses		Aldgate, London	
11716	Jacobs	Mary	1843	Cheltenham, Gloucestershire	Joseph Jacobs	Ester (?)		Aldgate, London	scholar
6307	Jacobs	Mary (Pollie)	1840	Spitalfields, London	Hyam Hyams	Julia Lyons	Woolf Cohen	Aldgate, London	scholar
713	Jacobs	Mary Ann	1803	Whitechapel, London				Whitechapel, London	
10135	Jacobs	Mary Ann	1825	Whitechapel, London	Lazarus Jacobs	Catherine Marks	Baruch (Barnet) Emanuel	Whitechapel, London	staymaker
764	Jacobs	Mary Ann	1835	Stepney, London	(?) Jacobs			Aldgate, London	house servant
24099	Jacobs	Matilda	1801	Whitechapel, London	I--- E--- Jacobs (Jacob Syklese)		Solomon Levy (Louis) Jacobs	Bloomsbury, London	
15664	Jacobs	Matilda	1827	?, Poland [?, Prussia]	(?) Jacobs			Aldgate, London	tailoress

ID	surname	given names	born	birthplace	father	mother	spouse 1	1851 residence	1851 occupation
16082	Jacobs	Matilda	1834	Aldgate, London	Edward (Aaron) Jacobs	Jane (Shava, Sylvia) Green	Godfrey Green	Aldgate, London	seamstress
25968	Jacobs	Matilda	1815	Chelmsford, Essex	Shlomo Zalman Levy		Isaac Henry Jacobs	Aldgate, London	
18530	Jacobs	Matilda Rebecca	1822	Shoreditch, London	Henry Jacobs	Elizabeth Myers	David Jacobs	Piccadilly, London	
24521	Jacobs	Matthew Henry	1834	City, London	Lewis Jacobs	Sophia Daniels		Stockwell, London	articled clerk to a solicitor
9995	Jacobs	Maurice (Morris)	1838	Canterbury, Kent	Nathan Jacobs	Hannah Barnard	Julia Abrahams	Canterbury, Kent	scholar
669	Jacobs	May	1843	Southwark, London	Lewis (Levy) Jacobs	Elizabeth (?)		Spitalfields, London	scholar
544	Jacobs	Meyer	1813	Groningen, Holland	Jacob Jacobs	Anna (?)	Jacoba (?)	Spitalfields, London	manufacturers of lace
21783	Jacobs	Meyer	1835	Whitechapel, London	David Jacobs	Amelia (?)		Aldgate, London	fishmonger
753	Jacobs	Michael	1798	Whitechapel, London			Rachel (?)	Wapping, London	clothes dealer
19314	Jacobs	Michael	1804	Wapping, London	Jacob Jacobs	Hannah (?)	Rosetta Kyezor	Newcastle-under-Lyme, Staffordshire	clothier
24336	Jacobs	Michael	1809	Sheerness, Kent	Lazarus Jacobs	Catherine (?)		Holborn, London	dealer in furniture
11546	Jacobs	Michael	1835	Shoreditch, London	Moses Jacobs	Mary Lipman		Spitalfields, London	cigar maker
6308	Jacobs	Michael	1845	Spitalfields, London	Benjamin Jacobs	Julia Lyons		Aldgate, London	scholar
17672	Jacobs	Michael	1849	Whitechapel, London	Morris (Moses) Jacobs	Amelia (Emily) (?)		Aldgate, London	
30554	Jacobs	Michael	1851	Spitalfields, London	Jacob (John) Jacobs	Amelia Mendoza		Spitalfields, London	
11673	Jacobs	Micheal	1830	Aldgate, London	Henry Jacobs	Sarah Jacobs		Aldgate, London	
11305	Jacobs	Micheal	1838	Middlesex, London	Lewis Jacobs	(?)		Aldgate, London	general dealer
23323	Jacobs	Milcah (Malcha)	1796	Middlesex, London	Yaacov Levi		Lewis Jacobs	Westminster, London	
26173	Jacobs	Milly?	1833	?, London	(?) Jacobs			Aldgate, London	
24522	Jacobs	Miriam	1838	?City, London	Lewis Jacobs	Sophia Daniels	Jonah Nathan	Stockwell, London	
565	Jacobs	Miriam	1849	Aldgate, London	(?) Jacobs	Catherine (?)		Spitalfields, London	
694	Jacobs	Montague	1839	Aldgate, London	Levy Jacobs	Caroline Davis	Helena Davis	Whitechapel, London	scholar
558	Jacobs	Morca (Mordecai)	1842	Holborn, London				Spitalfields, London	
27021	Jacobs	Mordecai	1799	?, London	Jacob		Rachael Nathan	Aldgate, London	general dealer
8655	Jacobs	Mordecai	1814	Hackney, London				Aldgate, London	merchant
11651	Jacobs	Mordecai (Mark)	1839	Spitalfields, London	Joseph Jacobs	Catherine (Kitty) Moses	Henrietta Schram	Aldgate, London	
15137	Jacobs	Moris	1843	Finsbury, London	John Jacobs	Sarah Phillips		Hoxton, London	
682	Jacobs	Morris	1828	Shoreditch, London	Eleazer Elias Jacobs	Sarah Maria Lazarus		Whitechapel, London	warehouseman
762	Jacobs	Morris	1830	Whitechapel, London				Wapping, London	clothier
10139	Jacobs	Morris	1833	Whitechapel, London	Lazarus Jacobs	Catherine Marks		Whitechapel, London	looking glass manufacturer + carver + gilder
13932	Jacobs	Morris	1845	Blackburn, Lancashire	Isaac Jacobs	Catharine (?)		Manchester	scholar
670	Jacobs	Morris	1846	Spitalfields, London	Lewis (Levy) Jacobs	Elizabeth (?)		Spitalfields, London	scholar
599	Jacobs	Morris	1847	Whitechapel, London	Lewis Jacobs	Elizabeth (?)		Spitalfields, London	scholar
21888	Jacobs	Morris	1847	Middlesex, London	Abraham Jacobs	Marian (?)		Clerkenwell, London	
408	Jacobs	Morris (Moses)	1820	Kornik, Poland [Cornick, Prussia]	Yaakov		Amelia (Emily) (?)	Aldgate, London	glazier
3299	Jacobs	Morris (Moses, Maurice) Montague	1838	Middlesex, London	Isaac Jacobs	Hannah Foist	Annie (Hannah) Goodman	Birmingham	scholar
501	Jacobs	Moses	1771	Spitalfields, London				Spitalfields, London	broker
512	Jacobs	Moses	1793	Aldgate, London	(?Barnet) Jacobs (Issachar Behr Paris)		Rosetta Solomon	Spitalfields, London	general dealer

ID	surname	given names	born	birthplace	father	mother	spouse 1	1851 residence	1851 occupation
26087	Jacobs	Moses	1803	Warsaw, Poland			Fanny (?)	Aldgate, London	tailor
17436	Jacobs	Moses	1809	Whitechapel, London			Mary (?)	Aldgate, London	licensed victualler
246	Jacobs	Moses	1810	Shoreditch, London	Jacob Jacobs	Hannah Jacobs	Mary Lipman	Spitalfields, London	general dealer
26485	Jacobs	Moses	1811	Shoreditch, London	Jacob Jacobs	Hannah (?)		Southwark, London	cane merchant
761	Jacobs	Moses	1813	Whitechapel, London				Wapping, London	clothier
387	Jacobs	Moses	1826	Spitalfields, London	Jacob Jacobs	Hannah (?)		Spitalfields, London	general dealer
9388	Jacobs	Moses	1826	Whitechapel, London	Joseph Jacobs	Rebecca (?)		Spitalfields, London	general dealer
26857	Jacobs	Moses	1836	?, Poland [?, Prussia]				Aldgate, London	cap maker
8511	Jacobs	Moses	1837	Spitalfields, London	Lewis Jacobs	Jane (?)		Spitalfields, London	apprentice
28256	Jacobs	Moses	1837	Spitalfields, London	Elias Jacobs	Jane Mendoza		Spitalfields, London	apprentice [tailor?]
615	Jacobs	Moses	1838	Amsterdam, Holland	Mark (Mordecai) Jacobs	Esta (?)		Spitalfields, London	
656	Jacobs	Moses	1840	City, London	Jacob (John) Jacobs	Amelia Mendoza		Spitalfields, London	
11675	Jacobs	Moses	1840	Aldgate, London	Henry Jacobs	Sarah Jacobs		Aldgate, London	
25937	Jacobs	Moses	1847	Aldgate, London	Jacob Jacobs	Leah (Louisa) Green		Aldgate, London	
11657	Jacobs	Moses	1850	Aldgate, London	Joseph Jacobs	Catherine Moses		Aldgate, London	
717	Jacobs	Moss	1804	Whitechapel, London				Whitechapel, London	retired colonial merchant
716	Jacobs	Moss	1806	Aldgate, London	Henry Jacobs	Kitty Samuel	Martha Davis	Whitechapel, London	cigar manufacturer
9828	Jacobs	Moss	1817	Wapping, London	Charles (Coolie) Jacobs	Jane Solomons	Deborah Isaacs	Bethnal Green, London	clerk
25343	Jacobs	Moss	1829	Holborn, London	(?) Jacobs	Elizabeth (?)		Holborn, London	fur + skin dealer
22173	Jacobs	Moss	1834	Shoreditch, London	John Jacobs	Martha Lazarus		Whitechapel, London	rag warehouseman
25969	Jacobs	Moss	1839	Middlesex, London	Isaac Henry Jacobs	Matilda Levy	Louisa Jacobs	Aldgate, London	scholar
25324	Jacobs	Moss	1845	Middlesex, London	Louis Jacobs	Rebecca Barnett		Holborn, London	scholar
11595	Jacobs	Mosses	1829	Aldgate, London	Joseph Jacobs		Ester Daniel	Aldgate, London	general dealer
11601	Jacobs	Mosses	1833	Aldgate, London	Barnet Jacobs	Catharine (Kitty) (?)		Aldgate, London	
9976	Jacobs	Myer	1827	Canterbury, Kent	Jacob Jacobs	Ella Barnard	Matilda Nathan	Canterbury, Kent	printer compositor
18209	Jacobs	Myer	1835	Middlesex, London				Mile End, London	scholar
9996	Jacobs	Myer	1839	Canterbury, Kent	Nathan Jacobs	Hannah Barnard		Canterbury, Kent	scholar
20571	Jacobs	Myer	1841	Shoreditch, London	Moses Jacobs	Mary Lipman		Spitalfields, London	
28149	Jacobs	Myer (Morris, Moses)	1849	Whitechapel, London	Ezra Jacobs	Nancy Cohen	Sophia Lazarus	Aldgate, London	scholar
28143	Jacobs	Nancy	1809	Whitechapel, London	Moses Cohen		Ezra Jacobs	Aldgate, London	master butcher
11605	Jacobs	Nancy	1845	Aldgate, London	Barnet Jacobs	Catharine (Kitty) (?)		Aldgate, London	
11652	Jacobs	Nancy (Ann)	1840	Spitalfields, London	Joseph Jacobs	Catherine (Kitty) Moses	Joshua Cohen	Aldgate, London	
9993	Jacobs	Nathan	1810	Norwich, Norfolk	Asher Jacobs		Hannah Barnard	Canterbury, Kent	hardwareman, dealer in china + glass, master empl 8
2165	Jacobs	Nathan	1825	?, Poland	Aaron Jacobs		Hannah Woolf	Oxford, Oxfordshire	jeweller + tobacconist + Synagogue reader
11508	Jacobs	Nathan	1837	?Whitechapel, London	Hyam Hyams	Julia Lyons		Aldgate, London	scholar
580	Jacobs	Nathan	1843	Spitalfields, London	Henry Jacobs	Julia Jacobs		Aldgate, London	
711	Jacobs	Nathaniel	1795	Whitechapel, London			Sarah (?)	Whitechapel, London	musician
27856	Jacobs	Nathaniel	1845	Whitechapel, London	John Jacobs	Martha Lipman		Spitalfields, London	
24520	Jacobs	Nathaniel Henry	1832	Aldgate, London	Lewis Jacobs	Sophia Daniels		Stockwell, London	clerk to a ship broker
641	Jacobs	Phidias	1849	?, Holland	Wolf Solomon Jacobs	Amelia (?)		Spitalfields, London	
30358	Jacobs	Philip	1835	Strand, London				St Giles, London	cashier

ID	surname	given names	born	birthplace	father	mother	spouse 1	1851 residence	1851 occupation
9833	Jacobs	Philip Charles	1849	Old Ford, London	Moss Jacobs	Deborah Isaacs	Kate Aaron	Bethnal Green, London	
395	Jacobs	Phillip	1780	City, London	Simcha Lemon-man		Rose (Rosetta) Hyams	Aldgate, London	glass cutter
26622	Jacobs	Phillip	1816	?, Germany				Aldgate, London	furrier
23925	Jacobs	Phillip	1825	?, Poland	Joseph Jacobs	Kitty (?)	Rachael Solomon	Marylebone, London	
15139	Jacobs	Phillip	1845	Finsbury, London	John Jacobs	Sarah Phillips		Hoxton, London	
18531	Jacobs	Phillip D	1849	Piccadilly, London	David Jacobs	Matilda Jacobs	Harriette Matilda Nerwich	Piccadilly, London	
28147	Jacobs	Phillis	1844	Spitalfields, London	Ezra Jacobs	Nancy Cohen		Aldgate, London	scholar
20063	Jacobs	Phineas	1807	?			Clara Samuel	Dublin, Ireland	manager, clothing trade
585	Jacobs	Phoebe	1814	Whitechapel, London	Joseph Nathan		Simon Jacobs	Spitalfields, London	
19414	Jacobs	Phoebe	1816	Vauxhall, London	Solomon (Shlomeh) Hyman (Hyams)	Sarah Davis	Isaac Jacobs	Bloomsbury, London	
689	Jacobs	Phoebe	1827	Mile End, London	Alfred Jacobs	Elizabeth? (Elos'h) (?)		Whitechapel, London	
1139	Jacobs	Phoebe	1828	Penzance, Cornwall	(?) Jacobs			Penzance, Cornwall	assistant to pawnbroker
22208	Jacobs	Phoebe	1831	Aldgate, London	Henry Jacobs	Rosetta (?)	Benjamin (Phineas) Jonas	Whitechapel, London	parasol + umbrella maker
27142	Jacobs	Phoebe	1833	?, London	David Jacobs	Hannah Solomons		Aldgate, London	dressmaker
755	Jacobs	Phoebe	1834	Wapping, London	Michael Jacobs	Rachel (?)	Edward Jacob Jones	Wapping, London	dressmaker
26998	Jacobs	Priscilla	1776	?, Poland	(?)		(?) Jacobs	Aldgate, London	
2823	Jacobs	Priscilla	1835	St Giles, London				Aldgate, London	lady's maid
8178	Jacobs	Priscilla	1841	Finsbury, London	John Jacobs	Fanny Aaron	John Barnett	Hoxton, London	
685	Jacobs	Priscilla	1842	Whitechapel, London	Eliezer Jacobs	Sarah Maria Lazarus		Whitechapel, London	scholar
865	Jacobs	Priscilla	1845	Spitalfields, London	Levi (Levy) Jacobs	Janette (?)	Henry A Hart	Whitechapel, London	scholar
27027	Jacobs	Priscilla	1850	Spitalfields, London	Mordecai Jacobs	Rachael Nathan		Aldgate, London	
17604	Jacobs	Rachael	1809	Aldgate, London	Moses Mendoza		Joseph Jacobs	Aldgate, London	
27022	Jacobs	Rachael	1809	?, London	Yehuda Leib HaLevi Nathan		Mordecai Jacobs	Aldgate, London	
26672	Jacobs	Rachael	1824	Spitalfields, London	(?) Jacobs			Spitalfields, London	needlewoman
27335	Jacobs	Rachael	1825	?, Poland [?, Prussia]	(?)		Lewis Jacobs	Aldgate, London	
11512	Jacobs	Rachael	1847	Whitechapel, London	Benjamin Jacobs	Julia Lyons	Henry Levy	Aldgate, London	scholar
14735	Jacobs	Rachael	1847	City, London	Lazarus Jacobs	Rosa (?)		Spitalfields, London	
5254	Jacobs	Rachel	1818	Spitalfields, London	David HaLevi Solomons	Betsy (Elizabeth) Cohen	Lewis Jacobs	Spitalfields, London	
15601	Jacobs	Rachel	1822	Westminster, London	(?)		Henry Jacobs	Covent Garden, London	
665	Jacobs	Rachel	1828	Spitalfields, London	Lewis (Levy) Jacobs	Elizabeth (?)		Spitalfields, London	cap maker
26559	Jacobs	Rachel	1828	Whitechapel, London	Solomon Jacobs		Joseph Jacobs	Whitechapel, London	dressmaker
611	Jacobs	Rachel	1831	Whitechapel, London	(?) Jacobs			Spitalfields, London	cap maker
11633	Jacobs	Rachel	1831	Middlesex, London	Tsevi Hirsh Jacobs		Barney (Barnett) Jacobs	Aldgate, London	
22209	Jacobs	Rachel	1833	Aldgate, London	Henry Jacobs	Rosetta (?)	Israel Crabb	Whitechapel, London	parasol + umbrella maker
6560	Jacobs	Rachel	1841	Hull, Yorkshire	Samuel Jacobs	Rose Alexander	Emanuel Braham (Abrahams)	Sunderland, Co Durham	
607	Jacobs	Rachel	1843	Amsterdam, Holland	Mark Jacobs	Esta (?)		Spitalfields, London	scholar
27857	Jacobs	Rachel	1848	Whitechapel, London	John Jacobs	Martha Lipman		Spitalfields, London	
4571	Jacobs	Rachel	1850	Birmingham	Isaac Jacobs	Hanna Foist		Birmingham	
25328	Jacobs	Rachel	1850	Middlesex, London	Louis Jacobs	Rebecca Barnett		Holborn, London	
28152	Jacobs	Ralph	1803	Spitalfields, London	Philip Jacobs		Mary Benjamin	Shoreditch, London	glass dealer
13930	Jacobs	Ralph	1839	Blackburn, Lancashire	Isaac Jacobs	Catharine (?)		Manchester	scholar

ID	surname	given names	born	birthplace	father	mother	spouse 1	1851 residence	1851 occupation
17449	Jacobs	Raphael	1812	Aldgate, London	Simon Jacobs		Sarah Assenheim	Aldgate, London	poulterer + dealer in wearing apparel
3717	Jacobs	Raphael	1820	Spitalfields, London	Moses Jacobs	Rosetta Solomon	Rebecca Barnett	Spitalfields, London	general dealer
15498	Jacobs	Rebeca	1786	Aldgate, London	(?)		(?) Jacobs (?Jacob Davis)	Covent Garden, London	
244	Jacobs	Rebecca	1781	Rotterdam, Holland	(?)		(?) Jacobs	Spitalfields, London	
8674	Jacobs	Rebecca	1784	Aldgate, London	(?)		(?) Jacobs	Aldgate, London	cloth cap maker
9386	Jacobs	Rebecca	1793	Whitechapel, London	(?)		Joseph Jacobs	Spitalfields, London	optician
27222	Jacobs	Rebecca	1795	?, Poland	(?)		(?) Jacobs	Aldgate, London	general dealer
3718	Jacobs	Rebecca	1816	Spitalfields, London	Aaron Barnett		Raphael Jacobs	Spitalfields, London	
25320	Jacobs	Rebecca	1818	Middlesex, London	Hyam Barnett		Louis Jacobs	Holborn, London	
11209	Jacobs	Rebecca	1826	Aldgate, London	Abraham Harris		David Jacobs	Aldgate, London	
9641	Jacobs	Rebecca	1830	?, Poland [Russia Poland]	Solomon Jacobs	Rosa (?)		Spitalfields, London	
11506	Jacobs	Rebecca	1833	?Whitechapel, London	Hyam Hyams	Julia Lyons		Aldgate, London	general dealer
13153	Jacobs	Rebecca	1835	Clerkenwell, London	John Jacobs	Sarah (?)		Spitalfields, London	
3301	Jacobs	Rebecca	1841	?, London	Isaac Jacobs	Hannah Foist	Morris (Moris) Lintine	Birmingham	
9831	Jacobs	Rebecca	1844	Spitalfields, London	Moss Jacobs	Deborah Isaacs		Bethnal Green, London	scholar
14244	Jacobs	Rebecca	1844	?, Poland	Elias Jacobs	Hetty (Henrietta) Seifersohn		Manchester	scholar
11448	Jacobs	Rebecca	1846	Middlesex, London	(?) Jacobs	Hannah (?)		Aldgate, London	
22212	Jacobs	Rebecca	1848	Whitechapel, London	(?) Jacobs			Whitechapel, London	scholar
25327	Jacobs	Rebecca	1849	Middlesex, London	Louis Jacobs	Rebecca Barnett		Holborn, London	
28150	Jacobs	Rebecca	1850	Aldgate, London	Ezra Jacobs	Nancy Cohen		Aldgate, London	scholar
26561	Jacobs	Reuben	1850	Spitalfields, London	Joseph Jacobs	Rachel Jacobs		Whitechapel, London	
587	Jacobs	Rosa	1801	?, Poland [Prussia Poland]			Solomon Jacobs	Spitalfields, London	
17830	Jacobs	Rosa	1811	Aldgate, London	(?)		John Jacobs	Aldgate, London	
614	Jacobs	Rosa	1835	Amsterdam, Holland	Mark (Mordecai) Jacobs	Esta (?)		Spitalfields, London	
2023	Jacobs	Rosa	1846	Liverpool	John (Ellis, Jacob Eleazer, Isaac) Jacobs	Frances Samson	Michael Levy	Whitechapel, London	
2170	Jacobs	Rosa	1850	Oxford, Oxfordshire	Nathan Jacobs	Hannah Woolf	Michael Franks	Oxford, Oxfordshire	
13929	Jacobs	Rosabel	1838	Manchester	Isaac Jacobs	Catharine (?)		Manchester	scholar
8356	Jacobs	Rose	1806	Norwich, Norfolk	Asher Jacobs			Canterbury, Kent	draper
6559	Jacobs	Rose	1808	Pembroke, Wales	(?) Alexander		Samuel Jacobs	Sunderland, Co Durham	
14730	Jacobs	Rose	1808	Amsterdam, Holland	(?)		Lazarus Jacobs	Spitalfields, London	
11303	Jacobs	Rose	1823	Middlesex, London	Lewis Jacobs	(?)	Samuel Fromberg	Aldgate, London	tailoress
23337	Jacobs	Rose	1826	Ipswich, Suffolk	Michael Samuel		George Jacobs	Piccadilly, London	umbrella manufacturer
6095	Jacobs	Rose	1835	Spitalfields, London	(?) Jacobs	Maria Coleman	David Isaacs	Spitalfields, London	umbrella maker
27787	Jacobs	Rose	1835	Spitalfields, London	Lewis Jacobs	Sarah Levy		Spitalfields, London	waistcoat maker
347	Jacobs	Rose (Rosetta)	1788	City, London	Joseph Hyams		Phillip Jacobs	Aldgate, London	
2471	Jacobs	Rose Jane	1844	Hull, Yorkshire	Bethel Jacobs	Esther (?)	Maurice E Solomons	Hull, Yorkshire	
729	Jacobs	Rosea	1849	Aldgate, London	Herman Jacobs	Esther Spyer		Whitechapel, London	
513	Jacobs	Rosetta	1791	Aldgate, London	Raphael Solomon		Moses Jacobs	Spitalfields, London	
22206	Jacobs	Rosetta	1795	Aldgate, London	(?)		Henry Jacobs	Whitechapel, London	
319	Jacobs	Rosetta	1806	?, London	(?) (?Lyons?)		(?) Jacobs	Aldgate, London	fruiterer
19313	Jacobs	Rosetta	1809	Cambridge	Isaac Kyezor	Hannah Levy (Levi)	Michael Jacobs	Newcastle-under-Lyme, Staffordshire	
15975	Jacobs	Rosetta	1817	Aldgate, London	(?)		Abraham Jacobs	Covent Garden, London	

ID	surname	given names	born	birthplace	father	mother	spouse 1	1851 residence	1851 occupation
20374	Jacobs	Rosetta	1832	Aldgate, London	Joseph Jacobs	Maria Benjamin		Aldgate, London	
16885	Jacobs	Rosetta	1834	Sheffield, Yorkshire	Ephraim Jacobs	Jane (?)		Newcastle Upon Tyne	
11674	Jacobs	Rosetta	1836	Aldgate, London	Henry Jacobs	Sarah Jacobs		Aldgate, London	
684	Jacobs	Rosetta	1841	?Whitechapel, London	Eleazer Elias Jacobs	Sarah Maria Lazarus	Abraham Franks	Whitechapel, London	scholar
25180	Jacobs	Rosina	1796	Bedford, Bedfordshire			(?) Jacobs	Finsbury, London	wife of silversmith
688	Jacobs	Rossetta	1825	Mile End, London	Alfred Jacobs	Elizabeth? (Elos'h) (?)		Whitechapel, London	
13158	Jacobs	Samson	1847	City, London	John Jacobs	Sarah (?)		Spitalfields, London	
12502	Jacobs	Samuel	1803	?, Poland				Norwich, Norfolk	jeweller
26055	Jacobs	Samuel	1803	Sheerness, Kent	Lazarus Jacobs	Catherine (?)		Mayfair, London	general dealer
4575	Jacobs	Samuel	1804	Hull, Yorkshire				Birmingham	
6558	Jacobs	Samuel	1806	Middlesex, London	Zebulon b. Joseph		Rose Alexander	Sunderland, Co Durham	tailor, draper + general merchant, empl 5
19519	Jacobs	Samuel	1822	Finsbury, London	(?) Jacobs	Elizabeth (?)		Covent Garden, London	fruit salesman
18931	Jacobs	Samuel	1827	Aldgate, London				Aldgate, London	fish dealer
754	Jacobs	Samuel	1831	Wapping, London	Michael Jacobs	Rachel (?)	Theresa Lesser	Wapping, London	shopman
661	Jacobs	Samuel	1836	Amsterdam, Holland	Abraham Jacobs	Lea (?)		Spitalfields, London	cigar maker
15434	Jacobs	Samuel	1837	?, London	Ezekiel Jacobs	Sarah Levy		Covent Garden, London	
248	Jacobs	Samuel	1839	Shoreditch, London	Moses Jacobs	Mary Lipman		Spitalfields, London	cigar maker
9978	Jacobs	Samuel	1839	Canterbury, Kent	Jacob Jacobs	Ella Barnard	Julia Kisch	Great Yarmouth, Norfolk	general dealer's assistant
23328	Jacobs	Samuel	1839	Middlesex, London	Lewis Jacobs	Milcah (Malcha) Levi		Westminster, London	
752	Jacobs	Samuel	1842	?, London	Joseph Jacobs			Whitechapel, London	scholar
3303	Jacobs	Samuel	1842	Spitalfields, London	Isaac Jacobs	Hannah Foist	Bessie (?)	Birmingham	scholar
15980	Jacobs	Samuel	1845	Covent Garden, London	Abraham Jacobs	Rosetta (?)		Covent Garden, London	scholar
671	Jacobs	Samuel	1848	Spitalfields, London	Lewis (Levy) Jacobs	Elizabeth (?)		Spitalfields, London	scholar
9627	Jacobs	Samuel	1848	Spitalfields, London	Simon Jacobs	Phoebe Nathan		Spitalfields, London	
12089	Jacobs	Samuel	1849	Whitechapel, London	Isaac Jacobs	Caroline Simmons		Spitalfields, London	
658	Jacobs	Samuel	1850	Spitalfields, London	Jacob (John) Jacobs	Amelia Mendoza		Spitalfields, London	
710	Jacobs	Samuel	1851	Whitechapel, London	Abraham Jacobs	Fanny (?)		Whitechapel, London	
741	Jacobs	Samuel	1851	Middlesex, London	Abraham Jacobs	Frances Coleman		Aldgate, London	
2026	Jacobs	Samuel (Emmanuel)	1782	?, London	Joseph Jacobs		Eve (Eva) (?)	Birmingham	general agent
2478	Jacobs	Sarah	1771	?, Germany	Ephraim Barnett		Israel Jacobs	Hull, Yorkshire	
25993	Jacobs	Sarah	1777	Aldgate, London	(?)		(?) Jacobs	Aldgate, London	general dealer
583	Jacobs	Sarah	1784	Aldgate, London	(?)		Abraham Jacobs	Spitalfields, London	general dealer
732	Jacobs	Sarah	1797	Aldgate, London	(?)		Nathaniel Jacobs	Whitechapel, London	
15432	Jacobs	Sarah	1800	?, London	Eliezer HaLevi		Ezekiel Jacobs	Covent Garden, London	
13150	Jacobs	Sarah	1801	Whitechapel, London	(?)		John Jacobs	Spitalfields, London	
27219	Jacobs	Sarah	1801	?, Poland	(?)		Emanuel Jacobs	Aldgate, London	
26349	Jacobs	Sarah	1803	?, London	Samuel Benjamin		(?)	Aldgate, London	
11672	Jacobs	Sarah	1805	Whitechapel, London	(?) Jacobs		Henry Jacobs	Aldgate, London	
27785	Jacobs	Sarah	1810	Aldgate, London	Gershon Levy		Lewis Jacobs	Spitalfields, London	
15134	Jacobs	Sarah	1816	Holborn, London	Alexander Phillips		John Jacobs	Hoxton, London	
25340	Jacobs	Sarah	1816	Holborn, London	(?) Jacobs	Elizabeth (?)		Holborn, London	fur sewer
17450	Jacobs	Sarah	1817	Whitechapel, London	Joseph Assenheim		Raphael Jacobs	Aldgate, London	
627	Jacobs	Sarah	1818	Spitalfields, London	(?)		(?) Jacobs	Spitalfields, London	silk weaver

ID	surname	given names	born	birthplace	father	mother	spouse 1	1851 residence	1851 occupation
15605	Jacobs	Sarah	1818	Westminster, London	(?) Davis		Joseph Jacobs	Covent Garden, London	
9391	Jacobs	Sarah	1821	Aldgate, London				Aldgate, London	cap maker
578	Jacobs	Sarah	1822	City, London	Phillip Jacobs	Rosa (Rosetta) Hyams		Aldgate, London	tailoress
18484	Jacobs	Sarah	1822	Paddington, London	(?) Jacobs			Bloomsbury, London	domestic
603	Jacobs	Sarah	1824	Aldgate, London	(?)		Lewis Jacobs	Spitalfields, London	
675	Jacobs	Sarah	1827	?, Holland	Hyam Jacobs	Julie (?)		Spitalfields, London	cap maker
26854	Jacobs	Sarah	1827	?, Poland [?, Prussia]	(?) Jacobs			Aldgate, London	cap maker
28240	Jacobs	Sarah	1829	Whitechapel, London	Benjamin Woolf Myers		Joseph Charles Jacobs	Spitalfields, London	clothes dealer
8310	Jacobs	Sarah	1830	?, Poland	Isaac Jacobs	Blume (?)		South Shields, Tyne & Wear	
11505	Jacobs	Sarah	1831	?Whitechapel, London	Hyam Hyams	Julia Lyons		Aldgate, London	general dealer
647	Jacobs	Sarah	1832	Whitechapel, London	Henry Jacobs	Maria (?)		Spitalfields, London	tailoress
9389	Jacobs	Sarah	1832	Whitechapel, London	Joseph Jacobs	Rebecca (?)	Nathaniel Nathan	Spitalfields, London	needle woman
15767	Jacobs	Sarah	1833	Bloomsbury, London	(?) Jacobs			Soho, London	embroideress
15326	Jacobs	Sarah	1834	Southwark, London	(?) Jacobs	Hannah (?)		Southwark, London	servant
21782	Jacobs	Sarah	1834	Whitechapel, London	David Jacobs	Amelia (?)		Aldgate, London	
546	Jacobs	Sarah	1837	Amsterdam, Holland	Meyer Jacobs	Jacoba (?)		Spitalfields, London	
652	Jacobs	Sarah	1837	Spitalfields, London	(?) Jacobs	Maria Coleman		Spitalfields, London	umbrella maker
655	Jacobs	Sarah	1838	City, London	Jacob (John) Jacobs	Amelia Mendoza	Samuel Garcia	Spitalfields, London	tailoress
14732	Jacobs	Sarah	1838	City, London	Lazarus Jacobs	Rosa (?)		Spitalfields, London	
667	Jacobs	Sarah	1839	Southwark, London	Lewis (Levy) Jacobs	Elizabeth (?)		Spitalfields, London	scholar
22517	Jacobs	Sarah	1841	Stepney, London	Joseph Jacobs	Constantia (?)		Whitechapel, London	scholar
11654	Jacobs	Sarah	1844	Aldgate, London	Joseph Jacobs	Catherine (Kitty) Moses	Henry Simmons	Aldgate, London	
15138	Jacobs	Sarah	1844	Finsbury, London	John Jacobs	Sarah Phillips		Hoxton, London	
20010	Jacobs	Sarah	1846	Plumstead, London	Joseph Jacobs	Ellen (?)		Plumstead, London	
553	Jacobs	Sarah	1847	Spitalfields, London	John Jacobs	Frances (?)		Spitalfields, London	
564	Jacobs	Sarah	1847	Aldgate, London	(?) Jacobs	Catherine (?)		Spitalfields, London	
1043	Jacobs	Sarah	1847	Exeter, Devon	Henry Jacobs	Ann (Anna) Harris		Exeter, Devon	scholar
13933	Jacobs	Sarah	1847	Blackburn, Lancashire	Isaac Jacobs	Catharine (?)		Manchester	
28431	Jacobs	Sarah	1847	Spitalfields, London	John (Jacob) Jacobs	Maria Israel		Spitalfields, London	scholar
600	Jacobs	Sarah	1848	Spitalfields, London	Lewis Jacobs	Elizabeth (?)		Spitalfields, London	
22176	Jacobs	Sarah	1848	Shoreditch, London	John Jacobs	Martha Lazarus		Whitechapel, London	
620	Jacobs	Sarah	1849	Spitalfields, London	Mark (Mordecai) Jacobs	Esta (?)		Spitalfields, London	
9629	Jacobs	Sarah	1849	Aldgate, London	Simon Jacobs	Phoebe Nathan		Aldgate, London	
19419	Jacobs	Sarah	1850	St Pancras, London	Isaac Jacobs	Phoebe Hyman	Isaac Isaacs	Bloomsbury, London	
27337	Jacobs	Sarah	1850	?Aldgate, London	Lewis Jacobs	Rachael (?)		Aldgate, London	
30552	Jacobs	Sarah	1851	Spitalfields, London	Joseph Charles Jacobs	Sarah Myers		Spitalfields, London	
3304	Jacobs	Sarah (Bertha)	1844	Cheltenham, Gloucestershire	Isaac Jacobs	Hannah Foist		Birmingham	
13898	Jacobs	Sarah F	1824	Cheltenham, Gloucestershire	(?) Jacobs	Hannah (?)		Manchester	straw bonnet maker
12397	Jacobs	Sarah Juda	1793	?, Holland	(?)		Jonas Jacobs	North Shields, Tyne & Wear	
2761	Jacobs	Sidney	1842	?, London	Levy Jacobs	Caroline Davis	Frances Joseph	Aldgate, London	scholar
24519	Jacobs	Simeon	1831	Aldgate, London	Lewis Jacobs	Sophia Daniels	Ellen Belinfante	Stockwell, London	member of the Inner Temple
26348	Jacobs	Simon	1801	?, London	John Jacobs		(?)	Aldgate, London	greengrocer

ID	surname	given names	born	birthplace	father	mother	spouse 1	1851 residence	1851 occupation
582	Jacobs	Simon	1813	Aldgate, London	Aryeh (Uri) Jacobs		Phoebe Nathan	Spitalfields, London	clothier
302	Jacobs	Simon	1823	Wapping, London	Ezekiel Jacobs		Dinah (Diana) Jewell	Wapping, London	outfitter
1415	Jacobs	Simon	1828	?, Poland			Maria (?)	Plymouth, Devon	journeyman tailor
15976	Jacobs	Simon	1837	Covent Garden, London	Abraham Jacobs	Rosetta (?)	Sarah Mordecai	Covent Garden, London	scholar
13302	Jacobs	Simon	1850	Spitalfields, London	Isaac Jacobs	Louisa (Leah) Nathan		Spitalfields, London	
27737	Jacobs	Slyllia	1833	?, Russia				Spitalfields, London	tailor
714	Jacobs	Soloman	1808	Whitechapel, London				Whitechapel, London	commission agent
734	Jacobs	Soloman	1831	Whitechapel, London	Nathaniel Jacobs	Sarah (?)		Whitechapel, London	musician
419	Jacobs	Solomon	1801	?, Poland [Prussia Poland]			Rosa (?)	Spitalfields, London	general dealer
5553	Jacobs	Solomon	1813	Elephant & Castle, London	Moshe HaLevi		Hannah (Ann) Myers	Holborn, London	clothier
11304	Jacobs	Solomon	1831	Middlesex, London	Lewis Jacobs	(?)	Julia Isaacs	Aldgate, London	general dealer
11600	Jacobs	Solomon	1831	Aldgate, London	Barnet Jacobs	Catharine (Kitty) (?)	Mary Ann Jones	Aldgate, London	
26719	Jacobs	Solomon	1831	Spitalfields, London	Edward (Aaron) Jacobs	Jane (Shava, Sylvia) Green		Spitalfields, London	cigar maker apprentice
23325	Jacobs	Solomon	1832	Middlesex, London	Lewis Jacobs	Milcah (Malcha) Levi		Westminster, London	cigar maker
756	Jacobs	Solomon	1835	Wapping, London	Michael Jacobs	Rachel (?)		Wapping, London	apprentice
10423	Jacobs	Solomon	1837	Spitalfields, London	Lewis Jacobs	Sarah Levy		Spitalfields, London	
28428	Jacobs	Solomon	1837	Whitechapel, London	John (Jacob) Jacobs	Maria Israel		Spitalfields, London	scholar
21098	Jacobs	Solomon	1840	Liverpool	(?) Jacobs	Henrietta (?)		Liverpool	
26560	Jacobs	Solomon	1847	Spitalfields, London	Joseph Jacobs	Rachel Jacobs		Whitechapel, London	
11449	Jacobs	Solomon	1848	Middlesex, London	(?) Jacobs	Hannah (?)		Aldgate, London	
25974	Jacobs	Solomon	1851	Aldgate, London	Isaac Henry Jacobs	Matilda Levy		Aldgate, London	
24098	Jacobs	Solomon Levy (Louis)	1804	Amsterdam, Holland	Leib Syklese? Amsterdam		Matilda Jacobs	Bloomsbury, London	stock jobber
27318	Jacobs	Sophia	1798	Aldgate, London	Abraham Garcia	Abigail (?)	Isaac Jacobs	Aldgate, London	orange dealer
19226	Jacobs	Sophia	1801	Middlesex, London	Abraham Jacobs	Rebecca Catherine (?)		Aldgate, London	lodging hose keeper
26956	Jacobs	Sophia	1803	Aldgate, London	(?)		(?) Jacobs	Aldgate, London	nurse
24518	Jacobs	Sophia	1807	City, London	Moshe Daniels		Lewis Jacobs	Stockwell, London	
733	Jacobs	Sophia	1825	Whitechapel, London	Nathaniel Jacobs	Sarah (?)		Whitechapel, London	umbrella maker
9997	Jacobs	Sophia	1841	Canterbury, Kent	Nathan Jacobs	Hannah Barnard	Daniel Mitchell	Canterbury, Kent	
699	Jacobs	Sophia	1847	Aldgate, London	Herman Jacobs	Esther Spyer		Whitechapel, London	
9832	Jacobs	Sophia	1847	Whitechapel, London	Moss Jacobs	Deborah Isaacs		Bethnal Green, London	
14246	Jacobs	Sophia	1850	Manchester	Elias Jacobs	Hetty (Henrietta) Seifersohn		Manchester	
30555	Jacobs	Sophia	1851	Spitalfields, London	Israel Jacobs	Elizabeth (Betsy) Phillips		Spitalfields, London	
18437	Jacobs	Susan	1839	?, London	(?) Jacobs			Norwich, Norfolk	
17953	Jacobs	Sushannah	1778	Birmingham	(?) ?Isaacs		(?) Jacobs	Aldgate, London	
27143	Jacobs	Thomas	1838	?, London	David Jacobs	Hannah Solomons		Aldgate, London	scholar
15435	Jacobs	Tobias	1839	?, London	Ezekiel Jacobs	Sarah Levy		Covent Garden, London	
751	Jacobs	Walter	1838	Aldgate, London	Joseph Jacobs			Whitechapel, London	scholar
9975	Jacobs	William	1830	Canterbury, Kent	Jacob Jacobs	Ella Barnard		Great Yarmouth, Norfolk	general dealer's assistant
640	Jacobs	Wolf Solomon	1827	?, Holland	Nathaniel		Amelia (?)	Spitalfields, London	shoe maker
25266	Jacobs	Woolf	1786	?, Poland			(?)	Holborn, London	general dealer
26393	Jacobs	Yetta	1828	?, Holland	(?) Jacobs			Aldgate, London	needlewoman
22287	Jacobs	Zipporah	1832	Hull, Yorkshire	Joseph Jacobs	Mary (?)		Whitechapel, London	
22227	Jacobsen	Julius	1823	?, Denmark	Aaron Jacobsen		Maria Bolaffey	Whitechapel, London	foreign shipping + commission agent

ID	surname	given names	born	birthplace	father	mother	spouse 1	1851 residence	1851 occupation
22228	Jacobsen	Maria (Miriam)	1827	Middlesex, London	Hananiya Bolaffey (Bolaffia)	Grace (de Samuel Bendelack)	Julius Jacobsen	Whitechapel, London	
5207	Jacobsohn	Raphael	1807	Chodzież, Poland [Chodjiesten, Prussia]				Cheltenham, Gloucestershire	Jew priest
24085	Jacobson	Abigail	1849	St Pancras, London	Nathan Woolf Jacobson	Rosa Davis		Fitzrovia, London	
22488	Jacobson	Abraham (Alfred)	1850	Whitechapel, London	Henry Jacobson	Phoebe (?)		Whitechapel, London	
8738	Jacobson	Abraham (Braham)	1843	Aldgate, London	Nathan (Nathaniel) Jacobson	Hannah Jacobs	Josephine Emma Davis	Aldgate, London	scholar
21261	Jacobson	Ada M	1850	Islington, London	Nathaniel Jacobson	Sarah (?)		Barnsbury, London	
8736	Jacobson	Alfred	1841	Aldgate, London	Nathan (Nathaniel) Jacobson	Hanna) Jacobs	Louisa Hendriks	Aldgate, London	scholar
24086	Jacobson	Alice Woolf	1850	St Pancras, London	Nathan Woolf Jacobson	Rosa Davis		Fitzrovia, London	
25849	Jacobson	Behr?	1826	?, Poland				Aldgate, London	shoe maker
22485	Jacobson	Caroline	1845	Whitechapel, London	Henry Jacobson	Phoebe (?)		Whitechapel, London	
21259	Jacobson	Catherine	1845	Barnsbury, London	Nathaniel Jacobson	Sarah (?)	John W Bolton	Barnsbury, London	
30556	Jacobson	Catherine	1851	Aldgate, London	Nathan (Nathaniel) Jacobson	Hannah Jacobs		Aldgate, London	
19200	Jacobson	Daniel	1840	Middlesex, London	Samuel Jacobson	Katherine Barnard		Whitechapel, London	scholar
21263	Jacobson	Emily F	1851	Islington, London	Nathaniel Jacobson	Sarah (?)		Barnsbury, London	
15155	Jacobson	Esther	1771	City, London	(?) Jacobson			Haggerston, London	annuitant
18240	Jacobson	Eve	1800	St Giles, London	(?)		Isaac Jacobson	Mayfair, London	
21262	Jacobson	Frances	1774	Middlesex, London	(?)		(?) Jacobson	Barnsbury, London	
21258	Jacobson	Frances Ann	1843	Islington, London	Nathaniel Jacobson	Sarah (?)		Barnsbury, London	scholar
8731	Jacobson	Hannah	1814	Aldgate, London	(?) Jacobs	Julia (?)	Nathan (Nathaniel) Jacobson	Aldgate, London	stay maker
28129	Jacobson	Hannah	1820	?, Poland [?, Prussia]	Zev Woolf Prince		Mark Jacobson	Spitalfields, London	
19199	Jacobson	Hannah	1838	Middlesex, London	Samuel Jacobson	Katherine Barnard	William Gunn	Whitechapel, London	scholar
22486	Jacobson	Hannah	1846	Whitechapel, London	Henry Jacobson	Phoebe (?)		Whitechapel, London	
22481	Jacobson	Henry	1815	Leyden, Holland			Phoebe (?)	Whitechapel, London	cigar maker
18241	Jacobson	Henry	1839	Bloomsbury, London	Isaac Jacobson	Eve (?)		Mayfair, London	scholar
7552	Jacobson	Isaac	1799	?, Poland [?, Prussia]			Eve (?)	Mayfair, London	silversmith + dealer master
8734	Jacobson	Isabella	1837	Aldgate, London	Nathan (Nathaniel) Jacobson	Hannah Jacobs		Aldgate, London	stay maker
17709	Jacobson	Jacob	1826	?, Poland [?, Prussia]				Spitalfields, London	slipper maker
8735	Jacobson	Julia	1839	Aldgate, London	Nathan (Nathaniel) Jacobson	Hannah Jacobs		Aldgate, London	scholar
18242	Jacobson	Julius	1839	Bloomsbury, London	Isaac Jacobson	Eve (?)	Miriam Davis	Marylebone, London	scholar
10064	Jacobson	Katherine	1806	Canterbury, Kent	Daniel Barnard	Zipporah (Sippy) Levy	Samuel Jacobson	Whitechapel, London	dressmaker
19202	Jacobson	Leonora	1847	Finsbury, London	Samuel Jacobson	Katherine Barnard	Andrew Cochrane	Whitechapel, London	
28131	Jacobson	Louisa	1848	Spitalfields, London	Mark Jacobson	Hannah Prince	Joseph Bernstein	Spitalfields, London	
28128	Jacobson	Mark	1816	?, London	Yaakov		Hannah Prince	Spitalfields, London	furrier
21257	Jacobson	Mary W	1841	Islington, London	Nathaniel Jacobson	Sarah (?)		Barnsbury, London	scholar
9637	Jacobson	Michael	1780	Amsterdam, Holland				Whitechapel, London	retired merchant
8733	Jacobson	Nathan (Nathaniel)	1811	Aldgate, London	Alexander Jacobson		Hannah Jacobs	Aldgate, London	cap maker
24083	Jacobson	Nathan Woolf	1827	Middlesex, London	Moses Jacobson		Rosa Davis	Fitzrovia, London	watch maker empl 4
21253	Jacobson	Nathaniel	1804	Middlesex, London	(?) Jacobson	Frances (?)	Sarah (?)	Barnsbury, London	medical and estate agent
22482	Jacobson	Phoebe	1815	Shoreditch, London	(?)		Henry Jacobson	Whitechapel, London	

ID	surname	given names	born	birthplace	father	mother	spouse 1	1851 residence	1851 occupation
14098	Jacobson	Rebecca	1842	Newcastle Upon Tyne	(?) Jacobson			Marylebone, London	scholar at home
21260	Jacobson	Rebecca M	1847	Barnsbury, London	Nathaniel Jacobson	Sarah (?)	Albert E Dixey	Barnsbury, London	
24084	Jacobson	Rosa	1826	Whitechapel, London	(?) Davis		Nathan Woolf Jacobson	Fitzrovia, London	
22487	Jacobson	Rose	1848	Whitechapel, London	Henry Jacobson	Phoebe (?)		Whitechapel, London	
8739	Jacobson	Rosina	1848	Aldgate, London	Nathan (Nathaniel) Jacobson	Hannah Jacobs	Bernard Frank Davis	Aldgate, London	
10065	Jacobson	Samuel	1814	Leyden, Holland			Katherine Barnard	Whitechapel, London	musician
15127	Jacobson	Sarah	1780	?, Cambridgeshire	(?)		(?) Jacobson	Haggerston, London	annuitant
21254	Jacobson	Sarah	1808	Mile End, London	(?)		Nathaniel Jacobson	Barnsbury, London	
22483	Jacobson	Sarah	1841	Middlesex, London	Henry Jacobson	Phoebe (?)		Whitechapel, London	
21255	Jacobson	Sarah M	1835	Middlesex, London	Nathaniel Jacobson	Sarah (?)		Barnsbury, London	scholar
22484	Jacobson	Simeon	1843	Whitechapel, London	Henry Jacobson	Phoebe (?)		Whitechapel, London	
8737	Jacobson	Solomon	1843	Aldgate, London	Nathan (Nathaniel) Jacobson	Hannah Jacobs	Louisa Davis	Aldgate, London	scholar
19201	Jacobson	Sophia	1844	Finsbury, London	Samuel Jacobson	Katherine Barnard	Alfred Goldsmith Bright	Whitechapel, London	
21256	Jacobson	Susannah H	1839	Middlesex, London	Nathaniel Jacobson	Sarah (?)		Barnsbury, London	scholar
28130	Jacobson	William	1839	City, London	Mark Jacobson	Hannah Prince	Hannah Hyams	Spitalfields, London	
21723	Jacoby	Alexander	1830	?, Germany				Highbury, London	Madeira merchant
2701	Jacoby	John Henry	1849	Nottingham, Nottinghamshire	Moritz Jacoby	Violetta Hirsch		Matlock, Derbyshire	
2700	Jacoby	Moritz	1817	Teterow, Germany			Violetta Hirsch	Matlock, Derbyshire	merchant
31217	Jacoby	Violetta	1829	Teterow, Germany	(?) Hirsch		Moritz Jacoby	Matlock, Derbyshire	
20258	Jacques	Alfred A	1835	Liverpool	Isaac Abraham Jacques	Elizabeth A (?)		Newcastle Upon Tyne	optician's apprentice
20257	Jacques	Elizabeth A	1811	?, London	(?)		Isaac Abraham Jacques	Newcastle Upon Tyne	
20256	Jacques	Isaac Abraham	1807	?, London			Elizabeth A (?)	Newcastle Upon Tyne	medical practitioner
20261	Jacques	Lewis A	1847	Newcastle Upon Tyne	Isaac Abraham Jacques	Elizabeth A (?)		Newcastle Upon Tyne	
20262	Jacques	Sarah A	1848	Newcastle Upon Tyne	Isaac Abraham Jacques	Elizabeth A (?)		Newcastle Upon Tyne	
20260	Jacques	Solomon A	1843	?Newcastle Upon Tyne	Isaac Abraham Jacques	Elizabeth A (?)		Newcastle Upon Tyne	scholar
9852	Jacques [Parker]	Hyam (Henry)	1844	Newcastle Upon Tyne	Isaac A Jacques	Elizabeth A (?)	Rose (Ruth) J Raphael	Newcastle Upon Tyne	
20259	Jacques [Parker]	Joseph A	1839	Newcastle Upon Tyne	Isaac Abraham Jacques	Elizabeth A (?)	Matilda Abraham	Newcastle Upon Tyne	scholar
2288	Jael	Jane	1827	?, Scotland	Solomon Flatow		Louis (Levin) Jael	Leeds, Yorkshire	
2287	Jael	Louis (Levin)	1818	?, Poland [?, Prussia]	Levin Jael		Jane Flatow	Leeds, Yorkshire	jewellery traveller
19321	Jaffe	Caroline	1842	Hamburg, Germany	Daniel Joseph Jaffe	Friedrike (Rike) Josephy	Bernhard Cohn	Holywood, Co Down, Ireland	
16285	Jaffe	Daniel Joseph	1809	Schwerin, Germany	Joseph M Jaffe	Jette L Daniel	Friedrike (Rika) Josephy	Holywood, Co Down, Ireland	linen merchant/manufacturer
16304	Jaffe	Friedrike (Rike)	1819	Mecklenburg, Germany	Isaac Josephy	Sara Sophie Hirsch	Daniel Joseph Jaffe	Holywood, Co Down, Ireland	
19323	Jaffe	Ida	1845	Hamburg, Germany	Daniel Joseph Jaffe	Friedrike (Rike) Josephy	Edward Silz	Holywood, Co Down, Ireland	
2479	Jaffe	Isaac	1826	?, Germany				Hull, Yorkshire	tailor
11913	Jaffe	Jacob	1828	?, Poland [?, Prussia]				Whitechapel, London	cap maker
19322	Jaffe	Joseph John	1843	Hamburg, Germany	Daniel Joseph Jaffe	Friedrike (Rike) Josephy		Holywood, Co Down, Ireland	
19320	Jaffe	Malvina	1841	Hamburg, Germany	Daniel Joseph Jaffe	Friedrike (Rike) Josephy	Robert Marcus Mendelssohn	Holywood, Co Down, Ireland	
16303	Jaffe	Martin	1839	Hamburg, Germany	Daniel Joseph Jaffe	Friedrike (Rike) Josephy	Catherine (Kate) Samuel	Holywood, Co Down, Ireland	

ID	surname	given names	born	birthplace	father	mother	spouse 1	1851 residence	1851 occupation
19324	Jaffe	Otto Moses	1846	Hamburg, Germany	Daniel Joseph Jaffe	Friedrike (Rike) Josephy	Paula Hertz	Holywood, Co Down, Ireland	
19325	Jaffe	Pauline	1849	Belfast, Ireland	Daniel Joseph Jaffe	Friedrike (Rike) Josephy	Siegmund Oppse	Holywood, Co Down, Ireland	
7678	Jaffe	Samuel L---	1820	?				Liverpool	
26472	Jaffe	Solomon	1829	?, Poland [?, Prussia]				Bangor, Wales	clerk
17294	Jamatsky	Robert	1831	?, Poland [?, Prussia]				Spitalfields, London	cap maker
556	Jameson	Elizabeth	1819	Hamburg, Germany	David Phillips		Isaac Jameson	Spitalfields, London	
17289	Jameson	Isaac	1813	Hamburg, Germany	Jacob Jameson		Elizabeth Phillips	Spitalfields, London	tailor
17290	Jankelsohn	Isaac	1827	?, Russia				Spitalfields, London	cap maker
22120	Jarman	Julia	1828	?, Germany	(?) Jarman			Whitechapel, London	tailoress
26946	Jarmusch	Ephraim	1831	?, Poland				Aldgate, London	tailor
12629	Jaskulch	Maxe	1827	?, Poland [?, Prussia]				Birmingham	tailor
19210	Jean	Julietta	1834	?, Italy	(?) Jean	Maria (?)		Marylebone, London	
19209	Jean	Maria	1797	?, Italy	(?)		(?) Jean	Marylebone, London	
2205	Jeremiah	Simon	1811	Bialystok, Poland [Beyalla, Poland]				Oxford, Oxfordshire	jewellery dealer
27549	Jessel	?	1851	Maidstone, Kent	Michael Aaron Jessel	Mary Isaacs		Maidstone, Kent	
7222	Jessel	Amelia	1820	City, London	Zadok Aaron Jessel	Mary Harris	Ignace Cahn	Mayfair, London	
22238	Jessel	Amelia	1823	Whitechapel London, London	Nathaniel Aaron Jessel	Frances (Fanny) (?)		Whitechapel, London	dressmaker
7189	Jessel	Catherine	1837	Maidstone, Kent	Michael Aaron Jessel	Mary Isaacs	Joseph I Braham	Maidstone, Kent	
7196	Jessel	Deborah	1841	Maidstone, Kent	Michael Aaron Jessel	Mary Isaacs		Maidstone, Kent	
7221	Jessel	Edward	1822	City, London	Zadok Aaron Jessel	Mary Harris	Rebecca Julia Levy	Mayfair, London	attorney solicitor
27545	Jessel	Edward	1836	Maidstone, Kent	Michael Aaron Jessel	Mary Isaacs		Maidstone, Kent	
7195	Jessel	Elizabeth (Lizzie)	1838	Maidstone, Kent	Michael Aaron Jessel	Mary Isaacs	Jacob A Alexander	Maidstone, Kent	
7197	Jessel	Fanny	1845	Maidstone, Kent	Michael Aaron Jessel	Mary Isaacs	David Heilbron	Maidstone, Kent	
22236	Jessel	Frances (Fanny)	1783	City, London, London	(?)		Nathaniel Aaron Jessel	Whitechapel, London	
7217	Jessel	George	1824	City, London	Zadok Aaron Jessel	Mary Harris	Amelia Moses	Mayfair, London	barrister in actual practice
27548	Jessel	Godfrey	1849	Ramsgate, Kent	Michael Aaron Jessel	Mary Isaacs		Maidstone, Kent	
7215	Jessel	Henry	1821	City, London	Zadok Aaron Jessel	Mary Harris	Julia Cohen	Mayfair, London	barrister in actual practice
22237	Jessel	Isabella	1821	Whitechapel London, London	Nathaniel Aaron Jessel	Frances (Fanny) (?)		Whitechapel, London	dressmaker
27547	Jessel	John	1843	Maidstone, Kent	Michael Aaron Jessel	Mary Isaacs		Maidstone, Kent	
7187	Jessel	Mary	1813	Middlesex, London	John Isaacs	Deborah (?)	Michael Aaron Jessel	Maidstone, Kent	
7188	Jessel	Michael Aaron	1809	Whitechapel, London	Nathaniel Aaron Jessel	Frances (Fanny) (?)	Mary Isaacs	Maidstone, Kent	hardwareman
22235	Jessel	Nathaniel Aaron	1786	City, London, London	Aharon Frankfurt		Frances (Fanny) (?)	Whitechapel, London	jeweller
27546	Jessel	Rose	1841	Maidstone, Kent	Michael Aaron Jessel	Mary Isaacs		Maidstone, Kent	
19327	Jessel	Rosetta Aaron	1812	Lambeth, London	Joseph Aaron Jessel		Aaron Jacobs	Whitechapel, London	cane dealer
7214	Jessel	Zadok Aaron	1793	Middlesex, London	Aharon Frankfurt		Mary Harris	Mayfair, London	pearl + diamond merchant
14693	Jessurun	Agnes	1818	Whitechapel, London	(?)		Robert Jessurun	Stepney, London	
14695	Jessurun	Agnes	1847	Dalston, London	Robert Jessurun	Agnes (?)	Emanuel Menahem Norden	Stepney, London	
14694	Jessurun	Louisa Agnes	1846	Finsbury, London	Robert Jessurun	Agnes (?)		Stepney, London	
14692	Jessurun	Robert	1818	Finsbury, London			Agnes (?)	Stepney, London	solicitor's general clerk

ID	surname	given names	born	birthplace	father	mother	spouse 1	1851 residence	1851 occupation
17104	Jewel	Rachel	1830	?, England	(?)	Sarah (?)	(?) Jewel	St Helier, Jersey, Channel Islands	
30415	Jewell	Abraham	1846	Whitechapel, London	Joel Jewell	Mary Solomon		Holborn, London	
30435	Jewell	Adelaide	1831	Middlesex, London	Moss Jewell	Ellen (Eleanor, Hellen) Joseph	Michael Heymanson	Norwich, Norfolk	
30418	Jewell	Amelia	1850	Covent Garden, London	Joel Jewell	Mary Solomon		Holborn, London	
20700	Jewell	Ann (Nancy)	1835	Aldgate, London	Abraham Jewell (Joel)	Elizabeth de David Ventura	Aaron Phillips	Whitechapel, London	general dealer
30250	Jewell	Benjamin	1850	Marylebone, London	Morris Jewell	Sophia (?)	Katherine (Kate) Myers	Marylebone, London	
15474	Jewell	Catherine	1834	Covent Garden, London	(?) Jewell			Covent Garden, London	
30416	Jewell	David	1849	Whitechapel, London	Joel Jewell	Mary Solomon		Holborn, London	
30409	Jewell	David Solomon	1848	St Helier, Jersey, Channel Islands	Simeon Jewell	Rebecca (?)		St Helier, Jersey, Channel Islands	
30433	Jewell	Ellen (Eleanor, Hellen)	1795	?, London	Samson Sampea Joseph		Moss Jewell	Whitechapel, London	annuitant
30413	Jewell	Esther	1843	St Helier, Jersey, Channel Islands	Joel Jewell	Mary Solomon	Emanuel Sampson	Holborn, London	
30411	Jewell	Joel	1813	?, London	Moss Jewell	Ellen (Eleanor, Hellen) Joseph	Mary (?)	Holborn, London	furniture dealer
30247	Jewell	Joseph	1838	Liverpool	Morris Jewell	Sophia (?)		Marylebone, London	scholar
30249	Jewell	Marcus	1848	Middlesex, London	Morris Jewell	Sophia (?)		Marylebone, London	scholar
30412	Jewell	Mary	1814	?, London	Lyon (Yehuda) Solomon	Esther (?)	Joel Jewell	Holborn, London	
30434	Jewell	Matilda	1835	?, London	Moss Jewell	Ellen (Eleanor, Hellen) Joseph	Edward Godfrey	Whitechapel, London	annuitant
30245	Jewell	Morris	1808	Middlesex, London			Sophia (?)	Marylebone, London	rag merchant
30408	Jewell	Moses (Moss)	1845	St Helier, Jersey, Channel Islands	Simeon Jewell	Rebecca (?)		St Helier, Jersey, Channel Islands	
30414	Jewell	Moss	1845	St Helier, Jersey, Channel Islands	Joel Jewell	Mary Solomon		Holborn, London	
30410	Jewell	Raphael	1850	St Helier, Jersey, Channel Islands	Simeon Jewell	Rebecca (?)		St Helier, Jersey, Channel Islands	
30407	Jewell	Rebecca	1825	?, England	(?)		Simeon Jewell	St Helier, Jersey, Channel Islands	
30406	Jewell	Simeon	1820	?London	Moss Jewell	Ellen (Eleanor, Hellen) Joseph	Rebecca (?)	St Helier, Jersey, Channel Islands	general dealer
30248	Jewell	Solomon	1842	Middlesex, London	Morris Jewell	Sophia (?)		Marylebone, London	scholar
30417	Jewell	Solomon	1847	Whitechapel, London	Joel Jewell	Mary Solomon	Adelaide de Jongh	Holborn, London	
30246	Jewell	Sophia	1816	Middlesex, London	(?)		Morris Jewell	Marylebone, London	
4587	Jewski	Thomas	1806	?, Poland				Birmingham	shoemaker
12387	Joel	Abraham	1799	?, Poland			Sarah (?)	North Shields, Tyne & Wear	hawker jewellery
30865	Joel	Anne	1841	Chichester, Sussex	Jacob Joel	Rosetta (?)		Brighton, Sussex	scholar
18489	Joel	Annette	1839	?, London	Joel (Joseph) Coleman Joel	Sophia Samuel		Finsbury, London	scholar
1206	Joel	Asher (Arthur)	1811	?, Poland			Rosina (Rose) Hyman	Plymouth, Devon	jeweller
27055	Joel	Barnet	1850	Aldgate, London	Henry Joel	Sarah Simmons		Aldgate, London	
27063	Joel	Benjamin Jacob	1836	Edinburgh, Scotland	Moses (Mark) Joel	Susan Moses		Edinburgh, Scotland	stockbroker's clerk
27744	Joel	Bloomah	1820	Middlesex, London	Solomon Solomons		David Coleman Joel	Spitalfields, London	furrier

ID	surname	given names	born	birthplace	father	mother	spouse 1	1851 residence	1851 occupation
1211	Joel	Caroline (Carrie)	1850	Plymouth, Devon	Asher (Arthur) Joel	Rosina (Rose) (?)		Plymouth, Devon	
18021	Joel	Catherine	1820	Spitalfields, London				Aldgate, London	
27058	Joel	Catherine	1825	Edinburgh, Scotland	Moses (Mark) Joel	Susan Moses		Edinburgh, Scotland	furrier
20750	Joel	Coleman	1799	Spitalfields, London	Joel Joel	(Mary Benjamin?)	Esther Mitchel	Spitalfields, London	furniture broker
10100	Joel	Coleman	1832	Spitalfields, London	Isaac Joel	Rebecca Solomons	Catherine (Kate) Barnard	Spitalfields, London	
27745	Joel	Coleman	1848	Spitalfields, London	David Coleman Joel	Bloomah Solomons		Spitalfields, London	
19290	Joel	Daniel	1790	Spitalfields, London	Jacob Joel		Elizabeth (Betsey) Cohen	Romford, Essex	fishmonger
15280	Joel	David	1803	Middlesex, London	Joel Joel		Julia Simmons	Shoreditch, London	furniture broker
27555	Joel	David	1837	Hackney, London				Spitalfields, London	servant
27743	Joel	David Coleman	1824	Middlesex, London	Coleman Joel	Esther Mitchel	Bloomah Solomons	Spitalfields, London	furrier
15053	Joel	Dinah	1806	Whitechapel, London	David Joel			Bethnal Green, London	hat + bonnet maker (out of employ)
11875	Joel	Dinah	1839	Spitalfields, London	Isaac Joel	Rebecca Solomons		Whitechapel, London	inmate of orphan school
9648	Joel	Dinah	1843	Aldgate, London	Mark Joel	Mary (Marian) Cantor	Morris Fordonski	Shoreditch, London	
3354	Joel	Dinah	1850	Middlesex, London	David Joel	Julia Simmons	Joshua Levy	Shoreditch, London	
20757	Joel	Dinah (Dianna)	1850	Spitalfields, London	Coleman Joel	Esther Mitchel		Spitalfields, London	
10101	Joel	Elizabeth	1802	Spitalfields, London	Michael Davis		Isaac Joel	Spitalfields, London	shopkeeper
8805	Joel	Elizabeth	1834	Aldgate, London	(?) Joel	Louisa (?)		Aldgate, London	
13819	Joel	Elizabeth	1838	?, Poland [?, Prussia]	(?) Joel			Manchester	cloth cap maker
1207	Joel	Elizabeth	1843	Plymouth, Devon	Asher (Arthur) Joel	Rosina (Rose) (?)	Henry Golding	Plymouth, Devon	scholar
19291	Joel	Elizabeth (Betsey)	1790	Spitalfields, London	Shlomeh Cohen		Daniel Joel	Romford, Essex	fishmonger
10123	Joel	Emanuel	1848	Spitalfields, London	Solomon Joel	Phoebe Lazarus		Aldgate, London	
27062	Joel	Ephraim	1832	Edinburgh, Scotland	Moses (Mark) Joel	Susan Moses		Edinburgh, Scotland	tailor's cutter
20751	Joel	Esther	1799	Islington, London	David Mitchel	(?Mary Emanuel)	Coleman Joel	Spitalfields, London	
20756	Joel	Flora	1843	Spitalfields, London	Coleman Joel	Esther Mitchel		Spitalfields, London	
27061	Joel	Frederick	1831	Edinburgh, Scotland	Moses (Mark) Joel	Susan Moses		Edinburgh, Scotland	
433	Joel	George	1798	Whitechapel, London				Spitalfields, London	labourer
27060	Joel	Hannah	1827	Edinburgh, Scotland	Moses (Mark) Joel	Susan Moses	(?) McPherson	Edinburgh, Scotland	capmaker
11301	Joel	Hannah	1838	Middlesex, London	(?) Joel			Aldgate, London	cap maker
27049	Joel	Henry	1810	?, London	Solomon Joel		Amelia Alvers	Aldgate, London	general dealer
27065	Joel	Henry	1830	Edinburgh, Scotland	Moses (Mark) Joel	Susan Moses	(?) Hyams	Edinburgh, Scotland	
18486	Joel	Henry Edward	1834	Shoreditch, London	Joel (Joseph) Coleman Joel	Sophia Samuel		Finsbury, London	merchant clerk
15051	Joel	Isaac	1811	Whitechapel, London	David Joel		Leah Abrahams	Bethnal Green, London	sponge + general dealer
30860	Joel	Isaac	1849	Brighton, Sussex	Samuel Joel	Mary Levy		Brighton, Sussex	
27052	Joel	Isaac?	1843	?, London	Henry Joel	Sarah Simmons		Aldgate, London	
1210	Joel	Isabella	1848	Plymouth, Devon	Asher (Arthur) Joel	Rosina (Rose) (?)	Robert Jordan	Plymouth, Devon	scholar
23234	Joel	Isidore	1850	Kensington, London	Joseph Frederick Joel	Marguerite Nathan		Kensington, London	
15287	Joel	Issiac	1845	Shoreditch, London	David Joel	Julia Simmons		Shoreditch, London	scholar
14385	Joel	Jacob	1804	?, Russia			Leah (?)	Manchester	hardware dealer
30861	Joel	Jacob	1806	Biala, Poland			Rosetta (?)	Brighton, Sussex	silversmith + tobacconist
1835	Joel	Jacob	1823	?, Russia				Merthyr Tydfil, Wales	travelling jeweller
434	Joel	Jacob	1826	Spitalfields, London	Daniel Joel	Elizabeth (Betsey) Cohen	Bethsheba (Betsey) Costa	Spitalfields, London	general dealer
24231	Joel	Jane	1837	Hackney, London	Michael Joel	Harriet Solomons		Hackney, London	scholar
10122	Joel	Jane	1843	Spitalfields, London	Solomon Joel	Phoebe Lazarus		Aldgate, London	scholar
15283	Joel	Joel	1834	?Aldgate, London	David Joel	Julia Simmons		Shoreditch, London	cigar maker

ID	surname	given names	born	birthplace	father	mother	spouse 1	1851 residence	1851 occupation
430	Joel	Joel	1835	Spitalfields, London	Isaac Joel	Rebecca Solomons	Catherine (Kate) Isaacs	Spitalfields, London	
30864	Joel	Joel	1837	Portsmouth, Hampshire	Jacob Joel	Rosetta (?)		Brighton, Sussex	scholar
20755	Joel	Joel	1841	Spitalfields, London	Coleman Joel	Esther Mitchel		Spitalfields, London	
5551	Joel	Joel	1847	Finsbury, London	Mark Joel	Mary (Marian) Cantor	Esther Solomons	Shoreditch, London	
27054	Joel	John	1848	?, London	Henry Joel	Sarah Simmons	Sophia Cohen	Aldgate, London	
18488	Joel	John A	1835	?, London	Joel (Joseph) Coleman Joel	Sophia Samuel		Finsbury, London	stationer assistant
24136	Joel	John Daniel	1822	Aldgate, London			Caroline Hannah Wood	Bloomsbury, London	watchmaker + jeweller journeyman
24618	Joel	Joseph	1807	Lambeth, London			Elizabeth (?)	Kennington, London	gold beater
12381	Joel	Joseph	1822	?, Poland			Rebecca (?)	North Shields, Tyne & Wear	glazier
20754	Joel	Joseph	1835	Spitalfields, London	Coleman Joel	Esther Mitchel		Spitalfields, London	cigar maker
1208	Joel	Joseph	1845	Plymouth, Devon	Asher (Arthur) Joel	Rosina (Rose) (?)		Plymouth, Devon	scholar
23236	Joel	Joseph Frederick	1816	Bristol			Marguerite Nathan	Kensington, London	jeweller + diamond merchant
15281	Joel	Julia	1811	Surrey, London	Azreal Simmons		David Joel	Shoreditch, London	
10118	Joel	Julia	1837	Aldgate, London	Solomon Joel	Phoebe Lazarus		Aldgate, London	scholar
19975	Joel	Julia	1838	Spitalfields, London	Daniel Joel	Elizabeth (Betsey) Cohen	Joseph Hyams	Romford, Essex	
30868	Joel	Julia	1847	Brighton, Sussex	Jacob Joel	Rosetta (?)		Brighton, Sussex	scholar
8525	Joel	Kate	1842	Aldgate, London	Mark Joel	Mary (Marian) Cantor	Abraham Levy	Shoreditch, London	
30859	Joel	Kate	1848	Brighton, Sussex	Samuel Joel	Mary Levy		Brighton, Sussex	
30866	Joel	Kitty	1843	Brighton, Sussex	Jacob Joel	Rosetta (?)		Brighton, Sussex	scholar
15052	Joel	Leah	1801	Spitalfields, London	Judah Abrahams		Isaac Joel	Bethnal Green, London	
14386	Joel	Leah	1814	Manchester	(?)		Jacob Joel	Manchester	
11874	Joel	Leah	1837	?Spitalfields, London	Isaac Joel	Rebecca Solomons		Whitechapel, London	inmate of orphan school
12384	Joel	Levy	1791	?, Poland			Rachael (?)	North Shields, Tyne & Wear	hawker
13092	Joel	Lewis	1824	Preston, Lancashire	Isaac Joel	Hannah (?)	Sophia Levy	Clerkenwell, London	prisoner + jeweller
30856	Joel	Lewis	1842	Brighton, Sussex	Samuel Joel	Mary Levy		Brighton, Sussex	scholar
6584	Joel	Louisa	1808	Aldgate, London	(?)		Isaac Joel	Aldgate, London	fruiterer
30870	Joel	Lyon	1850	Brighton, Sussex	Jacob Joel	Rosetta (?)		Brighton, Sussex	
23235	Joel	Marguerite	1829	?, Brazil	(?) Nathan		Joseph Frederick Joel	Kensington, London	
9646	Joel	Mark	1812	City, London	Joel Joel		Mary (Marian) Cantor	Shoreditch, London	furniture broker
15285	Joel	Mark	1841	Shoreditch, London	David Joel	Julia Simmons		Shoreditch, London	scholar
15288	Joel	Marks	1847	Shoreditch, London	David Joel	Julia Simmons		Shoreditch, London	scholar
30853	Joel	Mary	1818	Aldgate, London	Moses Levy		Samuel Joel	Brighton, Sussex	
15282	Joel	Mary	1833	Aldgate, London	David Joel	Julia Simmons		Shoreditch, London	
431	Joel	Mary	1835	Spitalfields, London	Isaac Joel	Rebecca Solomons		Spitalfields, London	
8524	Joel	Mary (Marian)	1820	City, London	Meshullam Cantor		Mark Joel	Shoreditch, London	
10117	Joel	Mary (Miriam)	1836	Aldgate, London	Solomon Joel	Phoebe Lazarus	Jacob (Morris) Harris	Aldgate, London	scholar
16217	Joel	Mary A	1785	Aldgate, London	(?)		(?) Joel	Finsbury, London	cook
30854	Joel	Maurice	1837	Brighton, Sussex	Samuel Joel	Mary Levy		Brighton, Sussex	scholar
30857	Joel	Michael	1844	Brighton, Sussex	Samuel Joel	Mary Levy		Brighton, Sussex	scholar
5838	Joel	Miriam	1835	Newport, Glamorgan, Wales	Isaac Joel		Lewis Leapman	Bristol	
20753	Joel	Miriam (Mary)	1832	Spitalfields, London	Coleman Joel	Esther Mitchel		Spitalfields, London	

ID	surname	given names	born	birthplace	father	mother	spouse 1	1851 residence	1851 occupation
20521	Joel	Morris	1850	Shoreditch, London	Mark Joel	Mary (Marian) Cantor		Shoreditch, London	
27056	Joel	Moses (Mark)	1790	?, Bavaria, Germany	Joel Moses Joel	Fanny Ephraim	Susan Moses	Edinburgh, Scotland	Reader in Jewish Synagogue
27053	Joel	Moses (Moss)	1845	?, London	Henry Joel	Sarah Simmons	Esther Abrahams	Aldgate, London	
30869	Joel	Myer B	1849	Brighton, Sussex	Jacob Joel	Rosetta (?)		Brighton, Sussex	scholar
10116	Joel	Phoebe	1813	Middlesex, London	Emanuel (Manly) Lazarus	Sophia Simmons	Solomon Joel	Aldgate, London	
12385	Joel	Rachael	1791	?, Poland	(?)		Levy Joel	North Shields, Tyne & Wear	
30863	Joel	Rachael	1835	Portsmouth, Hampshire	Jacob Joel	Rosetta (?)		Brighton, Sussex	scholar
12382	Joel	Rebecca	1825	?, Poland	(?)		Joseph Joel	North Shields, Tyne & Wear	
30855	Joel	Rebecca	1838	Brighton, Sussex	Samuel Joel	Mary Levy		Brighton, Sussex	scholar
9647	Joel	Rebecca	1839	Shoreditch, London	Mark Joel	Mary (Marian) Cantor	Ephraim Harris	Shoreditch, London	
10119	Joel	Rebecca	1839	Aldgate, London	Solomon Joel	Phoebe Lazarus	Solomon Fernandez	Aldgate, London	scholar
30862	Joel	Rosetta	1816	Chichester, Sussex	(?)		Jacob Joel	Brighton, Sussex	
8806	Joel	Rosetta	1836	Aldgate, London	(?) Joel	Louisa (?)		Aldgate, London	
30867	Joel	Rosina	1845	Brighton, Sussex	Jacob Joel	Rosetta (?)		Brighton, Sussex	scholar
1205	Joel	Rosina (Rose)	1813	Plymouth, Devon	Nathan Hyman		Asher (Arthur) Joel	Plymouth, Devon	
324	Joel	Rosy	1841	Aldgate, London	(?) Joel			Spitalfields, London	scholar
15284	Joel	Ruben	1835	Middlesex, London	David Joel	Julia Simmons		Shoreditch, London	cigar maker
30852	Joel	Samuel	1816	Middlesex, London	Moshe Aryeh Leib		Mary Levy	Brighton, Sussex	orange merchant
18487	Joel	Samuel	1835	Shoreditch, London	Joel (Joseph) Coleman Joel	Sophia Samuel		Finsbury, London	lithographer apprentice
9649	Joel	Samuel	1845	Aldgate, London	Mark Joel	Mary (Marian) Cantor		Shoreditch, London	
1209	Joel	Samuel	1846	Plymouth, Devon	Asher (Arthur) Joel	Rosina (Rose) (?)		Plymouth, Devon	scholar
27050	Joel	Sarah	1814	?, London	Simon Simmons		Henry Joel	Aldgate, London	
9036	Joel	Sarah	1822	Preston, Lancashire	(?) Joel			Aldgate, London	
27059	Joel	Sarah	1829	Edinburgh, Scotland	Moses (Mark) Joel	Susan Moses	John Phelps	Edinburgh, Scotland	seamstress
432	Joel	Sarah	1833	Spitalfields, London	Isaac Joel	Rebecca Solomons		Spitalfields, London	
10121	Joel	Sarah	1842	Spitalfields, London	Solomon Joel	Phoebe Lazarus		Aldgate, London	scholar
15286	Joel	Sarah	1843	Shoreditch, London	David Joel	Julia Simmons	Solomon Jewell	Shoreditch, London	scholar
12388	Joel	Sarah	1798	?, Poland	(?)		Abraham Joel	North Shields, Tyne & Wear	
27051	Joel	Simeon	1841	?, London	Henry Joel	Sarah Simmons		Aldgate, London	
10124	Joel	Simeon Solomon	1851	Aldgate, London	Solomon Joel	Phoebe Lazarus	Julia Aarons	Aldgate, London	
10115	Joel	Solomon	1807	Spitalfields, London	Joel		Phoebe Lazarus	Aldgate, London	furniture dealer
18022	Joel	Solomon	1827	Spitalfields, London				Aldgate, London	fishmonger
17964	Joel	Solomon	1829	Whitechapel, London	Daniel Joel	Elizabeth (Betsey) Cohen	Elizabeth Lazarus	Aldgate, London	fishmonger's assistant
20752	Joel	Solomon	1830	Spitalfields, London	Coleman Joel	Esther Mitchel		Spitalfields, London	cigar maker
6583	Joel	Solomon	1832	Aldgate, London	Isaac Joel	Louisa (?)	Hannah Jacobs	Aldgate, London	fruiterer
435	Joel	Solomon	1833	Spitalfields, London	Henry Joel		Simah (Simmy) Abady (Abadee, Abadaa)	Spitalfields, London	
30858	Joel	Solomon	1846	Brighton, Sussex	Samuel Joel	Mary Levy		Brighton, Sussex	scholar
468	Joel	Sophia	1780	Gelderland, Holland				Aldgate, London	almswoman
18485	Joel	Sophia	1811	Chichester, Sussex	Shmuel HaLevi Samuel		Joel (Joseph) Coleman Joel	Finsbury, London	bookseller + stationer
9037	Joel	Sophia	1826	Exeter, Devon	(?)		(?) Joel	Aldgate, London	

ID	surname	given names	born	birthplace	father	mother	spouse 1	1851 residence	1851 occupation
27064	Joel	Sophia	1835	Edinburgh, Scotland	Moses (Mark) Joel	Susan Moses	(?) Abrams	Edinburgh, Scotland	vest maker
10120	Joel	Sophia	1840	Aldgate, London	Solomon Joel	Phoebe Lazarus		Aldgate, London	scholar
5833	Joel	Sophia (Priscilla)	1837	Portsmouth, Hampshire	Jacob Joel	Rosetta	Samuel Leapman	Brighton, Sussex	scholar
27057	Joel	Susan	1801	?, England	(?) Moses		Moses (Mark) Joel	Edinburgh, Scotland	
21655	Joel	Zuseman (Zuice, Solomon)	1830	Spitalfields, London	Daniel Joel	Elizabeth (Betsey) Cohen	Elizabeth Michael	Aldgate, London	fishmonger
4581	Joel (Jael)	Adelaide	1834	King's Lynn, Norfolk	Hyams Joel	Esther (?)		Birmingham	milliner + dressmaker
4582	Joel (Jael)	Elias	1840	King's Lynn, Norfolk	Hyams Joel	Esther (?)		Birmingham	scholar
4576	Joel (Jael)	Esther	1801	Thurston, Norfolk			Hyams Joel	Birmingham	boarding house keeper
4583	Joel (Jael)	George	1837	King's Lynn, Norfolk	Hyams Joel	Esther (?)		Birmingham	scholar
4577	Joel (Jael)	Hannah	1826	King's Lynn, Norfolk	Hyams Joel	Esther (?)		Birmingham	milliner + dressmaker
4580	Joel (Jael)	Hyman	1833	King's Lynn, Norfolk	Hyams Joel	Esther (?)		Birmingham	travelling optician
4579	Joel (Jael)	Joseph	1829	King's Lynn, Norfolk	Hyams Joel	Esther (?)	Betsy Myers	Birmingham	travelling optician
4578	Joel (Jael)	Rachel	1828	King's Lynn, Norfolk	Hyams Joel	Esther (?)		Birmingham	milliner + dressmaker
18490	Johnson	Adelaide	1837	Strand, London	John Morris Johnson	Rosa (?)		Holborn, London	scholar
6523	Johnson	Amelia (Louisa Amelia)	1836	Exeter, Devon	(?) Johnson		John Harding	Exeter, Devon	
7713	Johnson	Charles	1840	Holborn, London	John Morris Johnson	Rosa (?)	Annie Jones	Holborn, London	scholar
7712	Johnson	Edmund	1835	Strand, London	John Morris Johnson	Rosa (?)	Ada A A (?)	Holborn, London	scholar
1342	Johnson	Eliza	1781	Portsmouth, Hampshire			(?) Johnson	Plymouth, Devon	formerly pawnbroker
18492	Johnson	Emma	1842	Holborn, London	John Morris Johnson	Rosa (?)		Holborn, London	scholar
18491	Johnson	James	1839	Marylebone, London	John Morris Johnson	Rosa (?)		Holborn, London	scholar
7517	Johnson	John Morris	1804	Gothenburg, Sweden			Rosa (Reizecha b. Judah Leib)	Holborn, London	engraver + printer
6531	Johnson	Lavinia	1816	Plymouth, Devon	Moses Johnson		Abraham Samuel	?London	
7785	Johnson	Rosa	1814	Whitechapel, London	Judah Leib		John Morris Johnson	Holborn, London	
18493	Johnson	Rosa	1844	Holborn, London	John Morris Johnson	Rosa (?)		Holborn, London	scholar
2949	Jonas	Adele Juliet	1851	Manchester	Benjamin Julius Jonas	Isabella Salamon	Ferdinand Heilborn	Manchester	
20813	Jonas	Adolph Samuel	1849	Finsbury, London	Samuel Adolphus Jonas	Esther Cashmore		Finsbury, London	
30557	Jonas	Alexander	1851	Aldgate, London	John (Jacob) Jonas	Sarah Levi (Levy)		Aldgate, London	
26295	Jonas	Amelia	1849	?, London	Shmuel (Samuel) Jonas	Elizabeth (Passy, Betsy) Green		Aldgate, London	
12133	Jonas	Andrew	1788	Aldgate, London			Ann (?)	Spitalfields, London	general dealer
28792	Jonas	Andrew	1843	Spitalfields, London	John (Jonas) Jonas	Catherine Levy	Sophia Solomons	Spitalfields, London	scholar
26259	Jonas	Angel	1778	?, London	Michael Lemon Man		Nancy Michel	Aldgate, London	
12134	Jonas	Ann	1781	Whitechapel, London	(?)		Andrew Jonas	Spitalfields, London	general dealer
20064	Jonas	Ann	1791	Acton, London	(?)		Jacob Jonas	Southwark, London	
22908	Jonas	Ann	1815	Aldgate, London	B--- Harris		Joseph Jonas	Wapping, London	
4165	Jonas	Anna (Hannah)	1847	Exeter, Devon	Benjamin Jonas	Eliza Levi		Exeter, Devon	scholar
9792	Jonas	Asher (Isaac)	1825	Aldgate, London	Solomon (Samuel, Pinchas Zelig) Jonas	Rosetta Joseph	Emma Cohen	Waterloo, London	tailor
8549	Jonas	Benjamin	1805	Middlesex, London	Isaac Jonas		Jane Norden	Spitalfields, London	general dealer
4162	Jonas	Benjamin	1809	Topsham, Devon			Eliza Levi	Exeter, Devon	general dealer
27656	Jonas	Benjamin	1817	Middlesex, London				Aldgate, London	pencil maker

ID	surname	given names	born	birthplace	father	mother	spouse 1	1851 residence	1851 occupation
30545	Jonas	Benjamin (Phineas)	1829	Brighton, Sussex	Benjamin Jonas	Jane Norden	Phoebe Jacobs	Spitalfields, London	parasol + umbrella maker
2946	Jonas	Benjamin Julius	1824	Hamburg, Germany	Abraham Heymann Jonas	Adelheid Fraenkel	Isabella Salamon	Manchester	merchant
18496	Jonas	Bloom	1826	Aldgate, London	(?) Abrahams		Nathaniel Jonas	Maida Vale, London	warehouseman
22885	Jonas	Caroline	1843	Liverpool	Moss Jonas	Mary (?)		Stepney, London	
18544	Jonas	Catherine	1789	Amsterdam, Holland	Zekel Mahler		Henry Hart Jonas	Stoke Newington, London	annuitant
17767	Jonas	Catherine	1803	Middlesex, London	Yehuda Leib Lyon		Jonas Jonas	Spitalfields, London	
28791	Jonas	Catherine	1818	Whitechapel, London	Isaac Levy		John (Jonas) Jonas	Spitalfields, London	
12042	Jonas	Catherine (Kate)	1828	Whitechapel, London	(?) Barnett		David Jonas	Whitechapel, London	
12047	Jonas	Catherine (Kate)	1850	Whitechapel, London	John Jonas	Sarah Reuben	Lewis Barnett Lazarus	Whitechapel, London	
8551	Jonas	Clara	1834	?Brighton, Sussex	Benjamin Jonas	Jane Norden	Samuel Levy	Spitalfields, London	
29479	Jonas	David	1788	Southwark, London			(?)	Spitalfields, London	drug broker
12041	Jonas	David	1822	Aldgate, London	Jacob HaCohen Jonas		Catherine (Kate) Barnett	Whitechapel, London	cigar importer
22886	Jonas	David	1848	Liverpool	Moss Jonas	Mary (?)		Stepney, London	
10750	Jonas	Elias	1817	Aldgate, London	Yechiel Michael		Ellen Solomons	Spitalfields, London	general dealer
2899	Jonas	Eliza	1822	Southampton, Hampshire	John Levi	Elizabeth (?)	Benjamin Jonas	Exeter, Devon	
14966	Jonas	Eliza M	1838	Middlesex, London	(?) Jonas			Bethnal Green, London	boarding school pupil
20065	Jonas	Elizabeth	1815	Whitechapel, London	Jacob Jonas	Ann (?)		Southwark, London	dress maker
26291	Jonas	Elizabeth (Passy, Betsy)	1808	Aldgate, London	Levy Ephraim Green	Amelia Hyams	Shmuel (Samuel) Jonas	Aldgate, London	
10751	Jonas	Ellen	1818	Middlesex, London	Samson Solomons		Elias Jonas	Spitalfields, London	
30786	Jonas	Emmanuel	1810	?, London				Preston, Lancashire	tobacco manufacturer
20811	Jonas	Esther	1822	City, London	Moses Joseph Cashmore	Rachel (Rela) bat Joshua	George Hollander	Finsbury, London	
8555	Jonas	Esther	1847	Spitalfields, London	Benjamin Jonas	Jane Norden	Isaac Abrahams	Spitalfields, London	
4167	Jonas	Esther (Pet)	1850	Exeter, Devon	Benjamin Jonas	Eliza Levi	Henry Samson	Exeter, Devon	
4163	Jonas	Frances	1843	Exeter, Devon	Benjamin Jonas	Eliza Levi		Exeter, Devon	scholar
22883	Jonas	Frank	1837	Middlesex, London	Moss Jonas	Mary (?)		Stepney, London	
27160	Jonas	Godfrey	1772	Amsterdam, Holland				Aldgate, London	general dealer
27241	Jonas	Hannah (Ann)	1791	?, London	Michael Hart		Barnet Solomon	Aldgate, London	general dealer
14947	Jonas	Harriett	1836	Middlesex, London	(?) Jonas			Bethnal Green, London	boarding school pupil
4166	Jonas	Henry	1849	Exeter, Devon	Benjamin Jonas	Eliza Levi		Exeter, Devon	
26261	Jonas	Hyam	1821	?, London	Angel Jonas	Nancy Michel		Aldgate, London	general dealer
31220	Jonas	Isaac	1806	Strand, London				Nottingham, Nottinghamshire	general dealer
30546	Jonas	Isaac	1831	?Brighton, Sussex	Benjamin Jonas		Esther Cortissos	Spitalfields, London	
17768	Jonas	Isaac	1839	Middlesex, London	Jonas Jonas	Catherine Lyon		Spitalfields, London	
2947	Jonas	Isabella	1826	?, London	Moses Salamon	Ann Israel	Benjamin Julius Jonas	Manchester	
25458	Jonas	Israel	1811	Aldgate, London	Samuel Jonas		Louisa Levy	Aldgate, London	attendant at vestry, Jews' Synagogue
7537	Jonas	Jacob	1781	Aldgate, London			Ann (?)	Southwark, London	accountant
20812	Jonas	James Hollander	1843	Aldgate, London	George Hollander	Esther Cashmore		Finsbury, London	
8550	Jonas	Jane	1803	Middlesex, London	Jacob Moshe Norden		Benjamin Jonas	Spitalfields, London	
26292	Jonas	Jane	1837	Spitalfields, London	Shmuel (Samuel) Jonas	Elizabeth (Passy, Betsy) Green	Isaac Philip Cohen	Aldgate, London	
10755	Jonas	Jane	1847	Middlesex, London	Elias Jonas	Ellen Solomons	Lewis Lyons	Spitalfields, London	

ID	surname	given names	born	birthplace	father	mother	spouse 1	1851 residence	1851 occupation
12045	Jonas	John	1810	Aldgate, London	Jacob HaCohen Jonas		Sarah Reuben	Whitechapel, London	cigar importer
25655	Jonas	John (Jacob)	1823	Aldgate, London	Angel Jonas		Elizabeth Abrahams	Aldgate, London	vest maker
28790	Jonas	John (Jonas)	1817	Whitechapel, London	Andrew Jonas	Ann (?)	Catherine Levy	Spitalfields, London	labourer
31222	Jonas	Jonah	1838	Nottingham, Nottinghamshire				Nottingham, Nottinghamshire	scholar
24934	Jonas	Jonah	1839	Bethnal Green, London	(?) Jonas	Rachael (?)		Bethnal Green, London	scholar
17766	Jonas	Jonas	1803	?, London	Isaac Eizak		Catherine Lyon	Spitalfields, London	general dealer
20068	Jonas	Jonathan	1819	Whitechapel, London	Jacob Jonas	Ann (?)		Southwark, London	cigar maker
22907	Jonas	Joseph	1811	Tower Hill, London			Ann Harris	Wapping, London	pencil maker
20066	Jonas	Joseph	1817	Whitechapel, London	Jacob Jonas	Ann (?)		Southwark, London	attorney's clerk
27657	Jonas	Joseph	1831	Middlesex, London				Aldgate, London	pencil maker
15399	Jonas	Julia	1834	?, London	(?) Jonas			Waterloo, London	nurserymaid
20070	Jonas	Kate	1827	Whitechapel, London	Jacob Jonas	Ann (?)		Southwark, London	dress maker
19169	Jonas	Kate Bloom	1851	Maida Vale, London	Nathaniel Jonas	Bloom Abrahams	Samuel Ellis Harron	Maida Vale, London	
23429	Jonas	Lazarus (Lewis, Eliezer)	1813	Soho, London	Solomon (Samuel, Pinchas Zelig) Jonas	Rosetta Joseph	Sarah Levy	Chelmsford, Essex	pawnbroker + clothier
27716	Jonas	Leah	1779	Middlesex, London	(?)		(?) Jonas	Spitalfields, London	funded by her children
17633	Jonas	Lewis	1828	?, Germany	Yohanan		Pauline (?)	Aldgate, London	traveller
28793	Jonas	Lewis	1845	Spitalfields, London	John (Jonas) Jonas	Catherine Levy		Spitalfields, London	scholar
24932	Jonas	Louis	1830	Bethnal Green, London	(?) Jonas	Rachael (?)		Bethnal Green, London	ostrich feather dealer
12043	Jonas	Louis (Lewis) E	1850	Whitechapel, London	David Jonas	Catherine (Kate) Barnett	Nelly Hyam	Whitechapel, London	
25459	Jonas	Louisa	1811	Spitalfields, London	Joseph Levy		Israel Jonas	Aldgate, London	matron of the Hand in Hand Asylum
19168	Jonas	Louisa	1851	Whitechapel, London	John Jonas	Sarah Reuben	Arthur Davis	Whitechapel, London	
28794	Jonas	Maria	1847	Spitalfields, London	John (Jonas) Jonas	Catherine Levy		Spitalfields, London	scholar
23432	Jonas	Maria	1851	Chelmsford, Essex	Lazarus (Lewis, Eliezer) Jonas	Sarah Levy		Chelmsford, Essex	
24935	Jonas	Marian	1845	Bethnal Green, London	(?) Jonas	Rachael (?)		Bethnal Green, London	scholar
22882	Jonas	Mary	1811	Middlesex, London	(?)		Moss Jonas	Stepney, London	
28795	Jonas	Mary	1849	Spitalfields, London	John (Jonas) Jonas	Catherine Levy		Spitalfields, London	
9794	Jonas	Mary Ann	1823	Aldgate, London	Solomon (Samuel, Pinchas Zelig) Jonas	Rosetta Joseph	Barnett Hart	Waterloo, London	dressmaker
26260	Jonas	Michael	1813	?, London	Angel Jonas	Nancy Michel		Aldgate, London	shoe maker
10754	Jonas	Michel	1845	Middlesex, London	Elias Jonas	Ellen Solomons		Spitalfields, London	scholar
8553	Jonas	Moses (Moss)	1839	?Brighton, Sussex	Benjamin Jonas	Jane Norden	Dinah (?)	Spitalfields, London	
12044	Jonas	Moses Frederick	1851	Whitechapel, London	David Jonas	Catherine (Kate) Barnett		Whitechapel, London	
22881	Jonas	Moss	1806	Middlesex, London			Mary (?)	Stepney, London	tailor
12135	Jonas	Moss	1825	Whitechapel, London	Andrew Jonas	Ann (?)		Spitalfields, London	general dealer
7470	Jonas	Nathaniel	1819	Aldgate, London			Bloom Abrahams	Maida Vale, London	cigar manufacturer
20071	Jonas	Nathaniel	1832	Southwark, London	Jacob Jonas	Ann (?)		Southwark, London	cigar maker
17634	Jonas	Pauline	1830	?, Germany	(?)		Lewis Jonas	Aldgate, London	
8552	Jonas	Phoebe	1836	?Brighton, Sussex	Benjamin Jonas	Jane Norden	Joseph Hart	Spitalfields, London	
24930	Jonas	Rachael	1805	?, London			(?) Jonas	Bethnal Green, London	ostrich feather maker
31221	Jonas	Rachael	1830	Marylebone, London	(?) Jonas			Nottingham, Nottinghamshire	general dealer
17769	Jonas	Rachael	1842	Spitalfields, London	Jonas Jonas	Catherine Lyon		Spitalfields, London	

ID	surname	given names	born	birthplace	father	mother	spouse 1	1851 residence	1851 occupation
31219	Jonas	Rachel	1791	Aldgate, London	(?) Jonas			Nottingham, Nottinghamshire	housekeeper
20069	Jonas	Rachel	1819	Whitechapel, London	Jacob Jonas	Ann (?)		Southwark, London	dress maker
23431	Jonas	Rachel	1849	?Chelmsford, Essex	Lazarus (Lewis, Eliezer) Jonas	Sarah Levy		Chelmsford, Essex	
24933	Jonas	Rebecca	1833	Bethnal Green, London	(?) Jonas	Rachael (?)		Bethnal Green, London	ostrich feather maker
20067	Jonas	Reuben	1818	Whitechapel, London	Jacob Jonas	Ann (?)		Southwark, London	carver + gilder
30558	Jonas	Rosa	1851	Spitalfields, London	John (Jonas) Jonas	Catherine Levy		Spitalfields, London	
20814	Jonas	Rosalia	1850	Aldgate, London	Samuel Adolphus	Esther Cashmore	David Oppenheimer	Finsbury, London	
24931	Jonas	Rose	1824	?, London	(?) Jonas	Rachael (?)		Bethnal Green, London	ostrich feather maker
9793	Jonas	Rosetta	1788	Aldgate, London	Tsevi Hirtseva Joseph		Solomon (Samuel, Pinchas Zelig) Jonas	Waterloo, London	
29481	Jonas	Rosetta	1823	Middlesex, London	David Jonas	(?)		Spitalfields, London	housekeeper
8554	Jonas	Rubin	1842	?Brighton, Sussex	Benjamin Jonas	Jane Norden		Spitalfields, London	
16984	Jonas	Samuel	1834	Aldgate, London				Wapping, London	shoemaker apprentice
26293	Jonas	Samuel	1842	?, London	Shmuel (Samuel) Jonas	Elizabeth (Passy, Betsy) Green	Amelia Walters	Aldgate, London	scholar
28796	Jonas	Samuel	1850	Spitalfields, London	John (Jonas) Jonas	Catherine Levy		Spitalfields, London	
20810	Jonas	Samuel Adolphus	1815	Hamburg, Germany	Abraham Heyman Jonas	Adelheid Fraenkel	Esther Hollander nee Cashmore	Finsbury, London	
12046	Jonas	Sarah	1820	Dover, Kent	(?) Reuben		John Jonas	Whitechapel, London	
25656	Jonas	Sarah	1823	Aldgate, London	Alexander Levy		John (Jacob) Jonas	Aldgate, London	
23430	Jonas	Sarah	1826	Whitechapel, London	Henry Levy		Lazarus (Lewis, Eliezer) Jonas	Chelmsford, Essex	
25658	Jonas	Sarah	1837	Spitalfields, London	(?) Jonas			Aldgate, London	cap maker
26290	Jonas	Shmuel (Samuel)	1817	?, London			Elizabeth (Passy, Betsy) Green	Aldgate, London	general merchant
26294	Jonas	Silvia	1843	?, London	Shmuel (Samuel) Jonas	Elizabeth (Passy, Betsy) Green	Lewis Phillips	Aldgate, London	scholar
29480	Jonas	Simon	1822	Southwark, London	David Jonas	(?)		Spitalfields, London	drug dealer
10752	Jonas	Solomon	1841	Middlesex, London	Elias Jonas	Ellen Solomons		Spitalfields, London	scholar
25085	Jonas	Sophia	1783	Middlesex, London	Joseph (Jezfa Haarschneider) Solomons		Joshua Jonas	City, London	
22884	Jonas	Sophia	1839	Liverpool	Moss Jonas	Mary (?)		Stepney, London	
4164	Jonas	Sophia	1845	Exeter, Devon	Benjamin Jonas	Eliza Levi		Exeter, Devon	scholar
10753	Jonas	Susan	1843	Middlesex, London	Elias Jonas	Ellen Solomons		Spitalfields, London	scholar
14921	Jonas	William	1839	?, London				Bethnal Green, London	boarding school pupil
2699	Jonas	Woolf	1794	?, London				Nottingham, Nottinghamshire	general dealer
7668	Jonassohn	David	1797	?, Holland			Charlotte Bouer	Durham, Co Durham	proprietor of coal mines
30104	Jonassohn	Fanny	1830	Sunderland, Co Durham	David Jonassohn	Charlotte Bouer		Durham, Co Durham	
7714	Jonassohn	Julia	1831	Sunderland, Co Durham	David Jonassohn	Charlotte Bouer	Caesar Hartog Gerson	Durham, Co Durham	
30105	Jonassohn	Moses John	1833	Sunderland, Co Durham	David Jonassohn	Charlotte Bouer	Mathilda (?)	Durham, Co Durham	
22308	Jones	Aaron	1845	?Aldgate, London	Joseph Jones	Sarah Simmons		Aldgate, London	
7520	Jones	Abraham Jacob	1804	Whitechapel, London	Aaron Jones		Sophia Goldsmid	Whitechapel, London	quill dealer
2791	Jones	Adelaide	1847	Bermondsey, London	Alexander Jones	Sarah Simon Moses	Adolph Rapp	Bermondsey, London	scholar

ID	surname	given names	born	birthplace	father	mother	spouse 1	1851 residence	1851 occupation
18695	Jones	Albert	1840	Whitechapel, London	Abraham Jacob Jones	Sophia Goldsmid		Whitechapel, London	scholar
2782	Jones	Alexander	1809	Shoreditch, London	Jonas Jones		Sarah Simon Moses	Bermondsey, London	fishmonger
18993	Jones	Alexander	1816	Aldgate, London			Fanny (?)	Aldgate, London	cigar traveller
4791	Jones	Alexander	1845	Piccadilly, London	Henry Jones	Elizabeth Benjamin	Henrietta Myers	Piccadilly, London	scholar at home
15640	Jones	Alfred Barron	1827	Elephant & Castle, London	Barron Jones	Catherine Jones		Strand, London	surgeon dentist (MNCSE)
30218	Jones	Amelia	1796	Strand, London	Joseph Harris		Benjamin Joseph	Fitzrovia, London	
22310	Jones	Amelia	1850	Aldgate, London	Joseph Jones	Sarah Simmons		Aldgate, London	
2793	Jones	Ann (Annie)	1850	Bermondsey, London	Alexander Jones	Sarah Simon Moses	Michael Eliezer Goldstein	Bermondsey, London	
17966	Jones	Annie	1833	Knightsbridge, London	Henry Jones	Elizabeth Benjamin		Piccadilly, London	
30219	Jones	Blume	1838	Covent Garden, London	Benjamin Joseph	Amelia Harris	James Hastings	Fitzrovia, London	
14493	Jones	Brina	1805	Exeter, Devon	(?) Levy		Henry Micholls Jones	Shrewsbury, Shropshire	
18697	Jones	C---	1846	Whitechapel, London	Abraham Jacob Jones	Sophia Goldsmid		Whitechapel, London	scholar
6890	Jones	Catharine	1835	Spitalfields, London	Michael Jones (Jonas)	Hannah Simmons		Spitalfields, London	tailoress
7716	Jones	Celia Esther	1834	Whitechapel, London	Abraham Jacob Jones	Sophia Goldsmid	Moses Marks	Whitechapel, London	cap maker
18995	Jones	Charles	1847	Aldgate, London	Alexander Jones	Fanny (?)		Aldgate, London	
27227	Jones	Charlotte	1781	?, Poland	(?)		(?) Jones	Aldgate, London	supported by children
6894	Jones	David	1848	Spitalfields, London	Michael Jones (Jonas)	Hannah Simmons	Nancy Jacobs	Spitalfields, London	scholar
29396	Jones	Deborah (Dalby)	1824	Amsterdam, Holland	Emanuel Abrahams	Esther (?)	Lewis Jones	Spitalfields, London	
18696	Jones	E---	1842	Whitechapel, London	Abraham Jacob Jones	Sophia Goldsmid		Whitechapel, London	scholar
18693	Jones	Edward Jacob	1829	Whitechapel, London	Abraham Jacob Jones	Sophia Goldsmid	Phoebe Jacobs	Whitechapel, London	cigar maker
14491	Jones	Edward Newton	1851	Southampton, Hampshire	Samuel Aaron Jones	Maria Emanuel	Frances Durlacher	Southampton, Hampshire	
4725	Jones	Eliza	1831	?, London	Braham Madenburg	Hannah (?)		Birmingham	
24677	Jones	Elizabeth	1791	Cambridge	(?)		Samuel Jones	Elephant & Castle, London	
17965	Jones	Elizabeth	1803	Whitechapel, London	Joel Benjamin	Ann Harris	Henry Jones	Piccadilly, London	
4800	Jones	Elizabeth (Eliza)	1842	Middlesex, London	Henry Jones	Elizabeth Benjamin	David Joshua Myers	Piccadilly, London	
21959	Jones	Ellen N	1835	Chester, Cheshire	Henry Micholls Jones	Brina Levy		Shrewsbury, Shropshire	scholar at home
21960	Jones	Emanuel L	1837	Chester, Cheshire	Henry Micholls Jones	Brina Levy		Shrewsbury, Shropshire	scholar
21961	Jones	Emily Brina	1838	Chester, Cheshire	Henry Micholls Jones	Brina Levy		Shrewsbury, Shropshire	scholar at home
19877	Jones	Esther	1803	Aldgate, London	(?)		(?) Jones	Spitalfields, London	clothes dealer
6888	Jones	Esther	1829	Spitalfields, London	Michael Jones (Jonas)	Hannah Simmons	Moses Cohen	Spitalfields, London	
4087	Jones	Esther	1842	Norwich, Norfolk	Samuel Aaron Jones	Maria Emanuel	Leon (Judah) Coriat	Southampton, Hampshire	
29399	Jones	Esther	1845	Spitalfields, London	Lewis Jones	Deborah (Dalby) Abrahams		Spitalfields, London	scholar
18994	Jones	Fanny	1816	Aldgate, London	(?)		Alexander Jones	Aldgate, London	
21958	Jones	Frances E	1831	Chester, Cheshire	Henry Micholls Jones	Brina Levy		Shrewsbury, Shropshire	
6887	Jones	Hannah	1806	Aldgate, London	Yehuda Simmons		Michael Jones (Jonas)	Spitalfields, London	
24680	Jones	Hannah	1836	Elephant & Castle, London	Samuel Jones	Elizabeth (?)	Henry Hart	Elephant & Castle, London	scholar
4089	Jones	Hannah	1846	Portsmouth, Hampshire	Samuel Aaron Jones	Maria Emanuel	Charles Johnston	Southampton, Hampshire	
7901	Jones	Henry	1799	?, England	Aaron Jones	(?)	Elizabeth Benjamin	Piccadilly, London	dentist
28581	Jones	Henry	1812	?, London	John Jones		Jeanette (Jenetta) Asher nee Solomon	Spitalfields, London	master bootmaker empl 2
24679	Jones	Henry	1831	Elephant & Castle, London	Samuel Jones	Elizabeth (?)		Elephant & Castle, London	cigar manufacturer

ID	surname	given names	born	birthplace	father	mother	spouse 1	1851 residence	1851 occupation
17967	Jones	Henry	1834	Canterbury, Kent	Henry Jones	Elizabeth Benjamin		Piccadilly, London	apprentice dentist
22307	Jones	Henry	1840	Whitechapel, London	Joseph Jones	Sarah Simmons	Bella (Isabella) Myers	Aldgate, London	
14492	Jones	Henry Micholls	1802	East Dereham, Norfolk	David Jones	Leah Micholls	Brina Levy	Shrewsbury, Shropshire	surgeon dentist
27228	Jones	Hyam	1811	?, London	(?) Jones	Charlotte (?)	(?)	Aldgate, London	general dealer
4585	Jones	Isaac	1795	?, London				Birmingham	ribbon dealer
18694	Jones	Isabella	1830	Whitechapel, London	Abraham Jacob Jones	Sophia Goldsmid	Morris Cohen	Whitechapel, London	dressmaker
30559	Jones	Isaiah	1850	Spitalfields, London	Henry Jones	Jeanette (Jenetta) Solomon		Spitalfields, London	
18692	Jones	J---	1826	Whitechapel, London	Abraham Jacob Jones	Sophia Goldsmid		Whitechapel, London	dressmaker
22445	Jones	James	1845	?				Gravesend, Kent	boarding school pupil
19879	Jones	Jane	1839	Whitechapel, London	(?) Jones	Esther (?)		Spitalfields, London	scholar
28582	Jones	Jeanette (Jenetta)	1814	Naples, Italy	Jonas Solomon		Abraham Asher	Spitalfields, London	
17970	Jones	Joel B	1843	Piccadilly, London	Henry Jones	Elizabeth Benjamin		Piccadilly, London	scholar at home
4584	Jones	Johanna	1824	?, London	(?Isaac Jones?)			Birmingham	ribbon dealer
14920	Jones	John	1838	Wednesbury, Staffordshire				Bethnal Green, London	boarding school pupil
2789	Jones	John	1840	Aldgate, London	Alexander Jones	Sarah Simon Moses	Julia Marks	Bermondsey, London	scholar
28585	Jones	John	1844	?Spitalfields, London	Henry Jones	Jeanette (Jenetta) Solomon		Spitalfields, London	scholar
29400	Jones	John	1848	Spitalfields, London	Lewis Jones	Deborah (Dalby) Abrahams		Spitalfields, London	scholar
22304	Jones	Joseph	1817	Aldgate, London	Solomon (Samuel, Pinchas Zelig) Jonas	Rosetta Joseph	Sarah Simmons	Aldgate, London	general dealer
4090	Jones	Josiah (Isaiah)	1848	Southampton, Hampshire	Samuel Aaron Jones	Maria Emanuel		Southampton, Hampshire	
22306	Jones	Julia	1836	Whitechapel, London	Joseph Jones	Sarah Simmons		Aldgate, London	
6891	Jones	Julia	1839	Spitalfields, London	Michael Jones (Jonas)	Hannah Simmons		Spitalfields, London	tailoress
17969	Jones	Kate	1840	Piccadilly, London	Henry Jones	Elizabeth Benjamin	Joshua Moses [Moses Jones]	Piccadilly, London	scholar at home
22724	Jones	Lazarus	1787	?, Holland				Whitechapel, London	optician
21957	Jones	Leah N	1829	Exeter, Devon	Henry Micholls Jones	Brina Levy		Shrewsbury, Shropshire	
28586	Jones	Levy	1847	?Spitalfields, London	Henry Jones	Jeanette (Jenetta) Solomon		Spitalfields, London	scholar
29397	Jones	Lewis	1820	?	Moses Jonas		Deborah (Dalby) Abrahams	Spitalfields, London	
2790	Jones	Lewis	1845	Bermondsey, London	Alexander Jones	Sarah Simon Moses	Rose Hart	Bermondsey, London	scholar
26602	Jones	Lionel Jacob	1841	Whitechapel, London	Abraham Jacob Jones	Sophia Goldsmid		Whitechapel, London	
23706	Jones	Luis	1829	Holstein, Germany				Liverpool	cigar manufacturer
4086	Jones	Maria	1813	Portsmouth, Hampshire	Michael Emanuel	Hannah Isaacs	Samuel Aaron Jones	Southampton, Hampshire	
14976	Jones	Mary Ann	1839	Walsall, Staffordshire	(?) Jones			Bethnal Green, London	boarding school pupil
6889	Jones	Mary Ann (Maria)	1831	Spitalfields, London	Michael Jones (Jonas)	Hannah Simmons	Solomon Jacobs	Spitalfields, London	tailoress
4088	Jones	Michael	1843	Norwich, Norfolk	Samuel Aaron Jones	Maria Emanuel		Southampton, Hampshire	
19878	Jones	Morris	1837	Whitechapel, London	(?) Jones	Esther (?)		Spitalfields, London	scholar
29398	Jones	Morris	1844	Spitalfields, London	Lewis Jones	Deborah (Dalby) Abrahams		Spitalfields, London	scholar
18996	Jones	Moss	1850	Aldgate, London	Alexander Jones	Fanny (?)		Aldgate, London	
24678	Jones	Nathan	1826	Elephant & Castle, London	Samuel Jones	Elizabeth (?)	Catherine Aarons	Elephant & Castle, London	clothes salesman
6893	Jones	Priscilla	1844	Spitalfields, London	Michael Jones (Jonas)	Hannah Simmons	Israel Mendoza	Spitalfields, London	scholar
2788	Jones	Rachael	1837	Southwark, London	Alexander Jones	Sarah Simon Moses	John Levi	Bermondsey, London	at home
29401	Jones	Rebecca	1850	Spitalfields, London	Lewis Jones	Deborah (Dalby) Abrahams		Spitalfields, London	
17968	Jones	Rosa	1835	Canterbury, Kent	Henry Jones	Elizabeth Benjamin		Piccadilly, London	

ID	surname	given names	born	birthplace	father	mother	spouse 1	1851 residence	1851 occupation
2768	Jones	Rosa (Rosetta)	1843	Aldgate, London	Alexander Jones	Sarah Moses	Henry Marks	Bermondsey, London	scholar
7718	Jones	Rose (Rosina)	1839	Whitechapel, London	Abraham Jacob Jones	Sophia Goldsmid	Gabriel Freedman	Whitechapel, London	crochet work
22309	Jones	Rosetta	1848	Aldgate, London	Joseph Jones	Sarah Simmons		Aldgate, London	
24676	Jones	Samuel	1791	?, Germany	Yehonatan		Elizabeth (?)	Elephant & Castle, London	clothes salesman
2792	Jones	Samuel (Charlie)	1849	Bermondsey, London	Alexander Jones	Sarah Simon Moses	Alice (Ellis) Holt?	Bermondsey, London	
4085	Jones	Samuel Aaron	1816	Great Yarmouth, Norfolk	Isaiah Jones	Hannah (?)	Maria Emanuel	Southampton, Hampshire	dentist
22725	Jones	Sarah	1785	?, London	(?) Jones			Whitechapel, London	
2787	Jones	Sarah	1813	Whitechapel, London	Simon Moses		Alexander Jones	Bermondsey, London	fishmonger's wife
22305	Jones	Sarah	1821	Whitechapel, London	Aaron Simmons	Julia Harris	Joseph Jones	Aldgate, London	
6892	Jones	Simon	1841	Spitalfields, London	Michael Jones (Jonas)	Hannah Simmons	Esther (?)	Spitalfields, London	scholar
30765	Jones	Sophia	1783	Aldgate, London	(?)		Joshua Jones	Finsbury, London	
7715	Jones	Sophia	1804	Whitechapel, London	Yechiel Michael Goldsmid		Abraham Jacob Jones	Whitechapel, London	
15639	Jones	Walter B	1825	Westminster, London	Barron Jones	Catherine Jones		Strand, London	surgeon dentist
21081	Jones	William	1841	?, London				Dover, Kent	boarding school pupil
6886	Jones (Jonas)	Michael	1801	Spitalfields, London	Jacob Jonas		Hannah Simmons	Spitalfields, London	general dealer
4091	Jones [Durlacher]	Edward Newton	1851	Southampton, Hampshire	Samuel Aaron Jones	Maria Emanuel	Frances Susan Durlacher	Southampton, Hampshire	
30814	Jordan	Anne	1835	Middlesex, London	(?) Jordan	Maria (?)		Liverpool	
30812	Jordan	Louisa	1831	Middlesex, London	(?) Jordan	Maria (?)		Liverpool	
20289	Jordan	Mache	1834	?, Russia				Spitalfields, London	
30811	Jordan	Maria	1829	Middlesex, London	(?) Jordan	Maria (?)		Liverpool	
30816	Jordan	Maria	1831	Middlesex, London	(?)		(?) Jordan	Liverpool	dentist
30813	Jordan	Phoebe	1833	Middlesex, London	(?) Jordan	Maria (?)		Liverpool	
30815	Jordan	Rebecca	1843	Middlesex, London	(?) Jordan	Maria (?)		Liverpool	
5866	Jordan	Samuel Jacob	1836	Middlesex, London	(?) Jordan	Maria (?)	Pauline Hickman	Liverpool	dentist
13583	Joseph	Aaron	1776	Wejherowo, Poland [Newstad, Poland]				Manchester	hawker + jeweller
11760	Joseph	Aaron	1786	?, Germany			Esther (?)	Shoreditch, London	dealer
1468	Joseph	Aaron	1788	?, London	Samuel Joseph	Catherine (?)	(?)	Aldgate, London	navy agent
17179	Joseph	Aaron	1796	Middlesex, London	Nathan Joseph		Matilda Phillips	Fitzrovia, London	merchant
26589	Joseph	Aaron	1836	Sunderland, Co Durham	Hyam (Esau) Joseph	Hannah Davis		Sunderland, Co Durham	watch + clockmaker
15644	Joseph	Abraham	1789	Southwark, London	Abraham		Elizabeth (?)	Holborn, London	general dealer
1283	Joseph	Abraham	1799	Plymouth, Devon	Joseph Joseph	Edal (?)	Eliza Woolf	Plymouth, Devon	bill broker
15649	Joseph	Abraham	1818	Westminster, London			Sarah Falcke	Piccadilly, London	importer of works of art + dlr in cabinet + fancy goods, china, glass, articles of curiosity + vertu
939	Joseph	Abraham	1830	Whitechapel, London	Jacob (John) Joseph	Esther (?)		Whitechapel, London	cigar business
5392	Joseph	Abraham	1830	?Bristol	Joseph Joseph	Phoebe Alexander		Liverpool	
27532	Joseph	Abraham	1830	Middlesex, London	(?) Joseph	Elenor (?)		Aldgate, London	cab driver
20108	Joseph	Abraham	1846	?Whitechapel, London	Samuel Joseph	Sarah (?)		Spitalfields, London	
8579	Joseph	Abraham	1849	New York, USA	Moses Joseph	Leah Benjamin	Caroline Solomons	Spitalfields, London	
5398	Joseph	Alexander	1849	Liverpool	Joseph Joseph	Phoebe Alexander		Liverpool	
29729	Joseph	Alexander	1850	Aldgate, London	Solomon Joseph	Jane Moses		Aldgate, London	

ID	surname	given names	born	birthplace	father	mother	spouse 1	1851 residence	1851 occupation
5407	Joseph	Alfred	1846	Whitechapel, London	Henry Joseph	Rosetta (Rose) (?)	Welcome Cohen	Aldgate, London	
17404	Joseph	Alfred	1850	Aldgate, London	Samuel Joseph	Rosa (?)		Wapping, London	
5406	Joseph	Alfred Barnett	1836	Leeds, Yorkshire	Barnet Joseph	Fanny Moses	Hannah (?)	Newcastle Upon Tyne	
1840	Joseph	Alice	1837	Swansea, Wales	Benjamin Joseph	Matilda Moseley		Swansea, Wales	
17188	Joseph	Alice	1840	Middlesex, London	Aaron Joseph	Matilda Phillips		Fitzrovia, London	scholar
26708	Joseph	Alice (Ella)	1851	Middlesex, London	Moss Jacob Joseph	Frances Lialter		Whitechapel, London	
12320	Joseph	Alice (Jael)	1846	Whitechapel, London	Isaac Joseph	Ellen (?)	Isaac de Benjamin Gomes Da Costa	Spitalfields, London	
8033	Joseph	Amelia	1803	North Shields, Tyne & Wear	Phillips Samuel		Tobias Joseph	Sunderland, Co Durham	
1121	Joseph	Amelia	1811	Cambourne, Cornwall	Jacob Jacob	Sarah Simons	Henry Joseph	Penzance, Cornwall	pawnbroker's wife
11697	Joseph	Amelia	1818	Finsbury, London	Ephraim Benjamin		Barnett Joseph	Aldgate, London	
15557	Joseph	Amelia	1821	Covent Garden, London	(?)		Joseph Myer	Covent Garden, London	
24368	Joseph	Amelia	1821	?, London	Abraham Benjamin	Phoebe (?)	(?) Joseph	St Giles, London	
7243	Joseph	Amelia	1822	Bermondsey, London	(?) Levi		David Joseph	St Giles, London	
17695	Joseph	Amelia	1834	Covent Garden, London	Moses Joseph	Hannah Moss	Emanuel Berlin	Holborn, London	stay manufacturer
13489	Joseph	Amelia	1844	Manchester	Simon Joseph	Fanny Simmons	John Aaron Cohen	Manchester	
22993	Joseph	Amelia	1850	Spitalfields, London	Mark (Mordecai) Joseph	(Rosa) Rosetta Abrahams		Whitechapel, London	
28500	Joseph	Amelia (Emily)	1846	Spitalfields, London	Samuel Joseph	Sarah Jonas		Spitalfields, London	
29727	Joseph	Angel	1845	Aldgate, London	Solomon Joseph	Jane Moses		Aldgate, London	
24535	Joseph	Ann	1793	?, London	(?) Joseph			Kennington, London	
10595	Joseph	Ann	1823	Norwich, Norfolk	(?)		(?) Joseph	Aldgate, London	tailoress
16123	Joseph	Ann	1846	?, London	Samuel Joseph	Sarah (?)		Aldgate, London	scholar
28220	Joseph	Ann	1847	Spitalfields, London	(?) Joseph	Clara Phillips		Spitalfields, London	
10346	Joseph	Ann	1848	Spitalfields, London	Elias Joseph	Hannah (?)		Spitalfields, London	
937	Joseph	Ann (Nancy)	1828	Whitechapel, London	Jacob (John) Joseph	Esther (?)	Joseph Marks	Whitechapel, London	waistcoat maker
28499	Joseph	Ann (Nancy)	1844	Spitalfields, London	Samuel Joseph	Sarah Jonas	Henry Levy	Spitalfields, London	scholar
29728	Joseph	Anna	1847	Aldgate, London	Solomon Joseph	Jane Moses		Aldgate, London	
1843	Joseph	Anna	1848	Swansea, Wales				Swansea, Wales	
9871	Joseph	Anne	1844	?, London				Fulham, London	boarding school pupil
7244	Joseph	Anne	1845	Soho, London	David Joseph	Amelia Levi	Abraham Isaac Hassan	St Giles, London	
1339	Joseph	Annie	1823	Plymouth, Devon	Nathan Joseph	Briney (Briny) (?)		Plymouth, Devon	daily governess
23591	Joseph	Annie	1828	Liverpool	Moss Joseph	(?)		Liverpool	
5415	Joseph	Annie	1849	Middlesex, London	Henry Joseph	Rosetta (Rose) (?)	Jules Cohen	Aldgate, London	
5369	Joseph	Arabella	1836	Frome, Somerset	Joseph Joseph	Phoebe Alexander	Zallel Coppel	Liverpool	
20872	Joseph	Arabella	1838	Liverpool	Barnet Lyon Joseph	Betsy Jacob		Liverpool	school
3562	Joseph	Arabella	1845	Newcastle Upon Tyne	Barnet Joseph	Fanny Moses	Maurice Meyer	Newcastle Upon Tyne	
27393	Joseph	Asher	1832	?, Poland				Aldgate, London	cap maker
23761	Joseph	Barned	1801	?, London			Rose (?)	Liverpool	merchant
3559	Joseph	Barnet	1805	Falmouth, Cornwall	Abraham Joseph	Hannah Levy	Fanny Moses	Newcastle Upon Tyne	woollen draper
16207	Joseph	Barnet	1840	?London	Solomon Joseph	Jane Selig		Whitechapel, London	scholar at home
18497	Joseph	Barnet Henry	1837	Penzance, Cornwall	Henry Joseph	Amelia Jacob	Isabella Blanckensee	Penzance, Cornwall	assistant woollen draper
164	Joseph	Barnet Lyon	1801	Falmouth, Cornwall	Lyon Joseph	Judith Levy	Betsy Jacob	Liverpool	silversmith + merchant
11696	Joseph	Barnett	1812	Finsbury, London	Meir Joseph		Amelia Benjamin	Aldgate, London	metal dealer
28503	Joseph	Barnett	1823	Spitalfields, London			Rachel (?)	Spitalfields, London	general dealer

ID	surname	given names	born	birthplace	father	mother	spouse 1	1851 residence	1851 occupation
1836	Joseph	Benjamin	1790	?, Germany	Ephraim Joseph		Matilda Moseley	Swansea, Wales	clockmaker + watch dealer
27129	Joseph	Benjamin	1844	?, London	Joseph Joseph	Grace Jacobs		Aldgate, London	
23191	Joseph	Benjamin	1847	Spitalfields, London	Joseph Joseph	Rachel (?)		City, London	
15858	Joseph	Benjamin	1851	Holborn, London	Simeon Joseph	Rebecca (?)		Holborn, London	
1130	Joseph	Betsey (Elizabeth)	1848	Penzance, Cornwall	Henry Joseph	Amelia Jacob		Penzance, Cornwall	
1467	Joseph	Betsy	1791	Ipswich, Suffolk	Asher (Israel) Isaacs	Dinah bat Daniel	Barnett Solomons	Aldgate, London	
5361	Joseph	Betsy	1802	Dartmouth, Devon	Nathan Jacob	Miriam Alexander	Barnet Lyon Joseph	Liverpool	
28501	Joseph	Betsy	1848	Spitalfields, London	Samuel Joseph	Sarah Jonas		Spitalfields, London	
27515	Joseph	Bloomer	1844	Soho, London	Samuel Joseph	Rebecca (?)		Aldgate, London	
27130	Joseph	Bluma	1846	?, London	Joseph Joseph	Grace Jacobs		Aldgate, London	
1335	Joseph	Briney (Briny)	1783	Plymouth, Devon			Nathan Joseph	Plymouth, Devon	property owner + annuitant
5370	Joseph	Caroline	1841	Liverpool	Barnet Lyon Joseph	Betsy Jacob	Jonas Lang	Liverpool	school
17895	Joseph	Caroline	1841	Lambeth, London	Moss Joseph	Rachel Blitz		Waterloo, London	
12401	Joseph	Catharine	1846	Spitalfields, London	Mordecai Joseph	Julia Dacosta		Spitalfields, London	
22919	Joseph	Catherine	1781	Spitalfields, London	(?)		Joseph Joseph	Wapping, London	
17189	Joseph	Catherine	1799	Middlesex, London	Nathan Joseph			Fitzrovia, London	
17184	Joseph	Catherine	1833	Middlesex, London	Aaron Joseph	Matilda Phillips		Fitzrovia, London	
27534	Joseph	Catherine	1838	Middlesex, London	(?) Joseph	Elenor (?)		Aldgate, London	
28498	Joseph	Catherine	1843	Spitalfields, London	Samuel Joseph	Sarah Jonas		Spitalfields, London	
5071	Joseph	Catherine	1848	Portsmouth, Hampshire	Lewis Joseph	Frances Simon		Portsmouth, Hampshire	
11220	Joseph	Catherine (Kitty)	1801	Portsmouth, Hampshire	Asher Nathan		John Joseph	Aldgate, London	
24947	Joseph	Celia	1824	Spitalfields, London	Samuel Moss	(?Alice Benjamin)	Isaiah Joseph	Bethnal Green, London	dressmaker
16063	Joseph	Charles	1807	Middlesex, London			Charlotte (?)	St Giles, London	hatter
23765	Joseph	Charles	1831	Liverpool	Barned Joseph	Rose (?)		Liverpool	book keeper
16065	Joseph	Charles	1841	Middlesex, London	Charles Joseph	Charlotte (?)		St Giles, London	
13490	Joseph	Charles M	1847	Manchester	Simon Joseph	Fanny Simmons		Manchester	
16064	Joseph	Charlotte	1821	Middlesex, London	(?)		Charles Joseph	St Giles, London	
28219	Joseph	Clara	1801	Spitalfields, London	(?) Phillips	Elizabeth (?)	(?) Joseph	Spitalfields, London	
26590	Joseph	Clara	1828	Sunderland, Co Durham	(?) Joseph			Sunderland, Co Durham	
26581	Joseph	Clara	1838	Sunderland, Co Durham	David Joseph	Fanny Samuel	Jacob Cohen	Sunderland, Co Durham	
17403	Joseph	Clara	1844	Aldgate, London	Samuel Joseph	Rosa (?)		Wapping, London	scholar
29777	Joseph	Daniel	1822	Whitechapel, London	Emanuel Joseph	Frances Cohen	Hannah (Ann) Davis	Spitalfields, London	pastrycook
27131	Joseph	Daniel	1848	?, London	Joseph Joseph	Grace Jacobs		Aldgate, London	
26577	Joseph	David	1805	Amsterdam, Holland			Fanny Samuel	Sunderland, Co Durham	hardwareman
7242	Joseph	David	1816	Strand, London			Amelia Levi	St Giles, London	secretary of Jewish synagogue
7902	Joseph	David	1817	?, Germany [?, Prussia]			Rebecca (?)	Pontypool, Wales	glazier
31038	Joseph	David	1841	Sunderland, Co Durham	Lionel Joseph	Sarah (?)		Sunderland, Co Durham	scholar
31067	Joseph	David	1849	Sunderland, Co Durham	Tobias Joseph	Amelia Samuel		Sunderland, Co Durham	scholar
14532	Joseph	Dinah	1796	Aldgate, London	Jacob Benjamin		Lewis Joseph	Southwark, London	
26587	Joseph	Dinah	1829	Birmingham	David Davis	Feigele Katz	Joseph Joseph	Sunderland, Co Durham	
1143	Joseph	Edal	1775	Liskeard, Cornwall	(?)		Joseph Joseph	Plymouth, Devon	annuitant
23763	Joseph	Edward	1828	Liverpool	Barned Joseph	Rose (?)		Liverpool	book keeper

ID	surname	given names	born	birthplace	father	mother	spouse 1	1851 residence	1851 occupation
15653	Joseph	Edward	1845	Piccadilly, London	Abraham Joseph	Sarah Falcke	Lizzie Jonas	Piccadilly, London	scholar
5943	Joseph	Edward (Nathan)	1827	Portsmouth, Hampshire	Yosef		Mary (?)	Bermondsey, London	tailor
13491	Joseph	Edward J	1850	Manchester	Simon Joseph	Fanny Simmons		Manchester	
8580	Joseph	Eleanor	1850	Spitalfields, London	Moses Joseph	Leah Benjamin		Spitalfields, London	
27527	Joseph	Elenor	1798	Aldgate, London	(?)		(?) Joseph	Aldgate, London	general dealer
10343	Joseph	Elias	1818	Covent Garden, London			Hannah (?)	Spitalfields, London	tailor
31040	Joseph	Elijah	1847	Sunderland, Co Durham	Lionel Joseph	Sarah (?)		Sunderland, Co Durham	scholar
5958	Joseph	Eliza	1818	Middlesex, London	Joseph Joseph		Simon Joseph Joseph	Bloomsbury, London	
17185	Joseph	Eliza	1834	Middlesex, London	Aaron Joseph	Matilda Phillips		Fitzrovia, London	
20110	Joseph	Eliza	1849	?Whitechapel, London	Samuel Joseph	Sarah (?)		Spitalfields, London	
1288	Joseph	Eliza	1850	Plymouth, Devon	Abraham Joseph	Eliza Woolf		Plymouth, Devon	
15645	Joseph	Elizabeth	1786	Whitechapel, London	Eli Ari Laza		Abraham Joseph	Holborn, London	
12002	Joseph	Elizabeth	1797	Coventry, Warwickshire	(?)		(?) Joseph	Whitechapel, London	
26245	Joseph	Elizabeth	1830	?, London	Joseph Simmons		Lewis Joseph	Aldgate, London	
26597	Joseph	Elizabeth	1831	Sunderland, Co Durham	Hyam (Esau) Joseph	Hannah Davis		Sunderland, Co Durham	
17893	Joseph	Elizabeth	1837	Hoxton, London	Moss Joseph	Rachel Blitz	Lyon Abraham Hart	Waterloo, London	
15651	Joseph	Elizabeth	1839	Mayfair, London	Abraham Joseph	Sarah Falcke		Piccadilly, London	scholar
20109	Joseph	Elizabeth	1848	?Whitechapel, London	Samuel Joseph	Sarah (?)		Spitalfields, London	
5957	Joseph	Elizabeth E	1822	Aldgate, London	(?)		Hyman Joseph	Holborn, London	
2678	Joseph	Ella	1838	Portsmouth, Hampshire	Isaac Joseph	Sarah Jacobs	Elijah (Edward) Davis	Portsmouth, Hampshire	
12426	Joseph	Ellen	1813	Aldgate, London	Michael Lazarus		Isaac Joseph	Spitalfields, London	
5363	Joseph	Ellen	1824	Bristol	Barnet Lyon Joseph	Betsy Jacob	(?) Gordon	Liverpool	assistant to silversmith + merchant
5393	Joseph	Ellen	1832	Bristol	Joseph Joseph	Phoebe Alexander	Samuel Genese	Liverpool	
12357	Joseph	Ellen	1837	Soho, London	Moses Joseph	Hannah Moss	Nathan Solomon	Holborn, London	
13488	Joseph	Ellen	1842	Manchester	Simon Joseph	Fanny Simmons	Edward Aaron Cohen	Manchester	
14527	Joseph	Emanuel	1825	Southwark, London	Lewis Joseph	Dinah Benjamin	Rebecca Benjamin	Southwark, London	shoe maker
28502	Joseph	Emanuel (Morris)	1850	Spitalfields, London	Samuel Joseph	Sarah Jonas		Spitalfields, London	
18790	Joseph	Emma	1834	Whitechapel, London	Joshua Joseph	Esther (Hester) Jacobs		Holborn, London	
17187	Joseph	Emma	1838	Middlesex, London	Aaron Joseph	Matilda Phillips		Fitzrovia, London	
11699	Joseph	Ephraim	1844	Aldgate, London	Barnett Joseph	Amelia Benjamin		Aldgate, London	
5371	Joseph	Ephraim Samuel	1830	Swansea, Wales	Benjamin Joseph	Matilda Moseley	Sarah Marks	Swansea, Wales	assistant clockmaker
27529	Joseph	Ester	1829	Middlesex, London	(?) Joseph	Elenor (?)		Aldgate, London	
11761	Joseph	Esther	1803	Covent Garden, London			Aaron Joseph	Shoreditch, London	
936	Joseph	Esther	1804	?, London	(?)		(?) Joseph	Whitechapel, London	
15863	Joseph	Esther	1818	Spitalfields, London	Eliezer Lezer Samuel		Moses Joseph	Spitalfields, London	
24504	Joseph	Esther	1828	Bedford, Bedfordshire	(?) Joseph	Rosa (?)		Rotherhithe, London	seamstress
5364	Joseph	Esther	1830	Bristol	Barnet Lyon	Betsy Jacob		Liverpool	
27512	Joseph	Esther	1830	St Giles, London	Samuel Joseph	Rebecca (?)		Aldgate, London	
17400	Joseph	Esther	1838	Aldgate, London	Samuel Joseph	Rosa (?)		Wapping, London	scholar
1846	Joseph	Esther	1839	Merthyr Tydfil, Wales	Harris Joseph	Margaret (?)	Wolf Lyons	Swansea, Wales	scholar
5396	Joseph	Esther	1841	New York, USA	Joseph Joseph	Phoebe Alexander		Liverpool	
1309	Joseph	Esther	1843	Redruth, Cornwall	Joseph Joseph	Fanny (?)		Plymouth, Devon	
20116	Joseph	Esther	1843	St Giles, London	Solomon Joseph	Priscilla (?)		St Giles, London	scholar
1127	Joseph	Esther	1844	Penzance, Cornwall	Henry Joseph	Amelia Jacob	H Biernstein	Penzance, Cornwall	scholar

ID	surname	given names	born	birthplace	father	mother	spouse 1	1851 residence	1851 occupation
3563	Joseph	Esther	1849	Newcastle Upon Tyne	Barnet Joseph	Fanny Moses		Newcastle Upon Tyne	
15857	Joseph	Esther	1850	Holborn, London	Simeon Joseph	Rebecca (?)		Holborn, London	
19726	Joseph	Esther	1850	Middlesex, London	Moss Jacob Joseph	Frances Lialter		Whitechapel, London	
16069	Joseph	Esther	1851	Middlesex, London	Charles Joseph	Charlotte (?)		St Giles, London	
18784	Joseph	Esther (Hester)	1801	Middlesex, London	Nathan Jacobs		Joshua Joseph	Holborn, London	
27981	Joseph	Eva	1833	?, Poland [?, Prussia]	(?) Joseph			Spitalfields, London	
16067	Joseph	Ezekiel	1845	Middlesex, London	Charles Joseph	Charlotte (?)		St Giles, London	
18990	Joseph	Fanny	1755	?, Germany			(?) Joseph	Aldgate, London	
4515	Joseph	Fanny	1801	Aldgate, London	(?) Joseph			Birmingham	housekeeper
26578	Joseph	Fanny	1803	North Shields, Tyne & Wear	(?) Samuel		David Joseph	Sunderland, Co Durham	
3558	Joseph	Fanny	1814	Bristol	Elias Moses [Marsden]	Judith Jacobs	Barnett Joseph	Newcastle Upon Tyne	
1305	Joseph	Fanny	1815	?, Poland			Joseph Joseph	Plymouth, Devon	
13484	Joseph	Fanny	1815	Manchester	(?) Simmons	Rachal (?)	Simon Joseph	Manchester	deriving income from property
31039	Joseph	Fanny	1845	Sunderland, Co Durham	Lionel Joseph	Sarah (?)		Sunderland, Co Durham	scholar
27161	Joseph	Fanny	1786	?, Germany	(?)		(?) Joseph	Aldgate, London	
16964	Joseph	Fanny (Frances) Hester	1837	Whitechapel, London	Joshua Joseph	Esther (Hester) Jacobs	Goodman Levy	Holborn, London	boarding school pupil
15652	Joseph	Felix	1840	Mayfair, London	Abraham Joseph	Sarah Falcke		Piccadilly, London	scholar
5950	Joseph	Flora	1847	Middlesex, London	Abraham Joseph	Sarah Falcke	Asher Wertheimer	Piccadilly, London	scholar
31096	Joseph	Frances	1795	?, Jamaica	Chaim Cohen		Aaron Joseph	Bloomsbury, London	fundholder
29776	Joseph	Frances	1800	?, Holland	Eliyahu HaCohen		Emanuel Joseph	Spitalfields, London	slop shirt maker
19724	Joseph	Frances	1825	Middlesex, London	Isaac Lialter	Priscilla Joseph	Moss Jacob Joseph	Whitechapel, London	
5069	Joseph	Frances	1826	Portsmouth, Hampshire	Simon Joseph	Sarah (?)	Lewis Joseph	Portsmouth, Hampshire	shirt manufactor
27530	Joseph	Frances	1833	Middlesex, London	(?) Joseph	Elenor (?)		Aldgate, London	
22446	Joseph	Frederick	1843	?				Gravesend, Kent	boarding school pupil
23189	Joseph	Gabriel	1841	Spitalfields, London	Joseph Joseph	Rachel (?)		City, London	
5492	Joseph	George Philip	1835	Swansea, Wales	Benjamin Joseph	Matilda Moseley		Southampton, Hampshire	watchmaker + jeweller's assistant
16209	Joseph	George Solomon	1845	?London	Solomon Joseph	Jane Selig	Henrietta Marian Franklin	Whitechapel, London	scholar at home
1311	Joseph	Gertrude	1847	Redruth, Cornwall	Joseph Joseph	Fanny (?)	Mordecai (Mark) Nathan	Plymouth, Devon	
27128	Joseph	Grace	1816	?, London	Jacob Jacobs		Joseph Joseph	Aldgate, London	
30757	Joseph	Greville Demund	1851	Holborn, London	Hyman Joseph	Elizabeth E (?)		Holborn, London	
28924	Joseph	H---	1826	?, Holland	(?)		J--- Joseph	Spitalfields, London	
1122	Joseph	Hannah	1771	Falmouth, Cornwall	Barnet Levy	Esther Elias	Abraham Joseph	Penzance, Cornwall	pawnbroker's widow
24534	Joseph	Hannah	1788	?, London	(?) Joseph			Kennington, London	funded py [property?]
26585	Joseph	Hannah	1789	King's Lynn, Norfolk	(?) Davis		Hyam (Esau) Joseph	Sunderland, Co Durham	jeweller
17692	Joseph	Hannah	1802	Lambeth, London	Naftali Hertz Moss		Moses Joseph	Holborn, London	stay manufacturer
24840	Joseph	Hannah	1807	Shoreditch, London	Shmuel Cohen		Joseph Joseph	Elephant & Castle, London	furrier
10344	Joseph	Hannah	1816	Covent Garden, London	(?)		Elias Joseph	Spitalfields, London	
10399	Joseph	Hannah	1824	Aldgate, London	(?) Joseph			Spitalfields, London	servant
23764	Joseph	Hannah	1830	Liverpool	Barned Joseph	Rose (?)		Liverpool	
940	Joseph	Hannah	1832	Whitechapel, London	Jacob (John) Joseph	Esther (?)	Jacob Levy	Whitechapel, London	waistcoat maker
16206	Joseph	Hannah	1839	?Aldgate, London	Solomon Joseph	Jane Selig		Whitechapel, London	scholar at home

ID	surname	given names	born	birthplace	father	mother	spouse 1	1851 residence	1851 occupation
1286	Joseph	Hannah	1843	Plymouth, Devon	Abraham Joseph	Eliza Woolf	Henry Nathan	Plymouth, Devon	
11850	Joseph	Hannah	1843	Amsterdam, Holland	(?) Joseph			Whitechapel, London	
1848	Joseph	Hannah	1849	Swansea, Wales	Harris Joseph	Margaret (?)		Swansea, Wales	
11701	Joseph	Hannah	1849	Aldgate, London	Barnett Joseph	Amelia Benjamin		Aldgate, London	
11290	Joseph	Hannah (Ann)	1807	Aldgate, London	Michael Lazarus		Lewis Henry (Hyam) Joseph	Aldgate, London	watchmaker
4155	Joseph	Hannah (Anna, Annie)	1846	Whitechapel, London	Samuel Joseph	Sarah (?)	Abraham Benjamin	Spitalfields, London	
1844	Joseph	Harris	1803	Warsaw, Poland			Margaret (?)	Swansea, Wales	hawker
5404	Joseph	Harry	1841	Newcastle Upon Tyne	Barnet Joseph	Fanny Moses		Newcastle Upon Tyne	
31035	Joseph	Hart	1833	Sunderland, Co Durham	Lionel Joseph	Sarah (?)		Sunderland, Co Durham	
17650	Joseph	Hatel	1836	?, Poland	Michael Joseph	Louisa (?)		Aldgate, London	
3227	Joseph	Henrietta (Hannah)	1827	Aldgate, London	Aaron Joseph	Matilda Phillips	Solomon Weil	Fitzrovia, London	
17897	Joseph	Henriette	1841	Lambeth, London	Moss Joseph	Rachel Blitz		Waterloo, London	
10586	Joseph	Henry	1782	Whitechapel, London	(?) Joseph			Spitalfields, London	general dealer?
1120	Joseph	Henry	1806	Falmouth, Cornwall	Abraham Joseph	Hannah Levy	Amelia Jacob	Penzance, Cornwall	pawnbroker + outfitter
185	Joseph	Henry	1815	Falmouth, Cornwall	Lyon Joseph	Judith Levy	Maria Samuel	Whitechapel, London	jeweller
5411	Joseph	Henry	1815	Middlesex, London	Jacob Joseph		Rosetta (Rose, Rosina) Michaels	Aldgate, London	
18788	Joseph	Henry	1831	Whitechapel, London	Joshua Joseph	Esther (Hester) Jacobs		Holborn, London	clerk to boot manufacturer
5488	Joseph	Henry	1834	?Plymouth, Devon	Abraham Joseph	Eliza Woolf		Plymouth, Devon	
16205	Joseph	Henry	1837	?Aldgate, London	Solomon Joseph	Jane Selig		Whitechapel, London	scholar at home
12427	Joseph	Henry	1838	Aldgate, London	Isaac Joseph	Ellen (?)		Spitalfields, London	
20874	Joseph	Henry	1839	Bristol	Joseph Joseph	Phoebe Alexander		Liverpool	
31065	Joseph	Henry	1843	Sunderland, Co Durham	Tobias Joseph	Amelia Samuel		Sunderland, Co Durham	scholar
8296	Joseph	Henry	1849	Sunderland, Co Durham	Nesham (Nathan) Joseph	Matilda Cohen		Sunderland, Co Durham	
20118	Joseph	Henry	1849	St Giles, London	Solomon Joseph	Priscilla (?)		St Giles, London	
16124	Joseph	Henry	1850	?, London	Samuel Joseph	Sarah (?)		Aldgate, London	
17899	Joseph	Henry	1850	Lambeth, London	Moss Joseph	Rachel Blitz		Waterloo, London	
1308	Joseph	Henry I	1840	Redruth, Cornwall	Joseph Joseph	Fanny (?)	Sarah Suhami	Plymouth, Devon	
5939	Joseph	Hester	1845	Bloomsbury, London	Simon Joseph Joseph	Eliza (?)	David Lindo Alexander	Bloomsbury, London	
29726	Joseph	Hyam	1844	Aldgate, London	Solomon Joseph	Jane Moses		Aldgate, London	
26584	Joseph	Hyam (Esau)	1784	Amsterdam, Holland			Hannah (?)	Sunderland, Co Durham	jeweller
5956	Joseph	Hyman	1823	Aldgate, London			Elizabeth E (?)	Holborn, London	
17402	Joseph	Hyman	1842	Aldgate, London	Samuel Joseph	Rosa (?)		Wapping, London	scholar
5486	Joseph	Hyman (Henry)	1830	Plymouth, Devon	Abraham Joseph	Eliza Woolf		Soho, London	scientific chemist
2875	Joseph	Isaac	1799	Zollochiz, Poland	Joseph (?)		Sarah Jacobs	Portsmouth, Hampshire	
12425	Joseph	Isaac	1815	Aldgate, London	H--- Joseph		Ellen Lazarus	Spitalfields, London	pencil maker
16202	Joseph	Isaac	1832	Whitechapel, London	Solomon Joseph	Jane Selig		Whitechapel, London	
8584	Joseph	Isaac	1833	Windsor, Berkshire				Soho, London	engineer
17656	Joseph	Isaac	1837	?, Poland				Aldgate, London	tailor
29780	Joseph	Isaac	1837	Whitechapel, London	Emanuel Joseph	Frances Cohen		Spitalfields, London	butcher boy
8031	Joseph	Isaac	1839	Sunderland, Co Durham	Lyonel Joseph	Sarah (?)	Mary Barnet	Sunderland, Co Durham	scholar

ID	surname	given names	born	birthplace	father	mother	spouse 1	1851 residence	1851 occupation
29725	Joseph	Isaac	1840	Aldgate, London	Solomon Joseph	Jane Moses	Miriam Solomon	Aldgate, London	
20115	Joseph	Isaac	1842	St Giles, London	Solomon Joseph	Priscilla (?)		St Giles, London	scholar
16066	Joseph	Isaac	1843	Middlesex, London	Charles Joseph	Charlotte (?)		St Giles, London	
28332	Joseph	Isaac	1846	Whitechapel, London	(?) Joseph	Sarah (?)		Aldgate, London	
15856	Joseph	Isaac	1848	Holborn, London	Simeon Joseph	Rebecca (?)		Holborn, London	
12402	Joseph	Isaac	1849	Spitalfields, London	Mordecai Joseph	Julia Dacosta		Spitalfields, London	
12431	Joseph	Isaac	1850	Whitechapel, London	Isaac Joseph	Ellen (?)		Spitalfields, London	
5962	Joseph	Isaac Aaron	1837	Whitechapel, London	Aaron Joseph	Frances Cohen	Esther Henry	Bloomsbury, London	scholar at London University
12586	Joseph	Isabella	1820	Middlesex, London	(?)		Maurice Joseph	Norwich, Norfolk	
20510	Joseph	Isabella (Belle)	1835	Waterloo, London	Benjamin Joseph	Amelia Harris	Abraham Joseph Murray	Waterloo, London	
24946	Joseph	Isaiah	1823	Amsterdam, Holland	Coleman Joseph		Celia Moss	Bethnal Green, London	general dealer
13486	Joseph	Israel	1838	Manchester	Simon Joseph	Fanny Simmons	Sarah Cohen	Manchester	
28923	Joseph	J---	1825	?, Holland			H--- (?)	Spitalfields, London	cigar maker
20111	Joseph	Jack	1851	?Whitechapel, London	Samuel Joseph	Sarah (?)		Spitalfields, London	
29344	Joseph	Jacob	1770	?, Poland			(?)	Whitechapel, London	furrier
1850	Joseph	Jacob	1807	?, Poland			Phoebe (?)	Swansea, Wales	pawnbroker
29778	Joseph	Jacob	1832	Whitechapel, London	Emanuel Joseph	Frances Cohen	Rachael Lazarus	Spitalfields, London	pastrycook
14530	Joseph	Jacob	1838	Southwark, London	Lewis Joseph	Dinah Benjamin		Southwark, London	cigar maker
10596	Joseph	Jacob	1844	Surrey, London	(?) Joseph	Ann (?)		Aldgate, London	scholar
26771	Joseph	Jacob	1849	Spitalfields, London	Michael Joseph	Sarah (?)		Aldgate, London	
935	Joseph	Jacob (John)	1780	?, London	Samuel Jacob Joseph		Esther (?)	Whitechapel, London	former fruit merchant
1841	Joseph	Jacob Mosley	1839	Swansea, Wales	Benjamin Joseph	Matilda Moseley	Sarah Abrahams	Swansea, Wales	scholar at home
29395	Joseph	James	1825	?, Holland	(?) Joseph	Julia (?)		Spitalfields, London	silk merchant
16201	Joseph	Jane	1812	Finsbury, London	Avigdor Selig		Solomon Joseph	Whitechapel, London	
29724	Joseph	Jane	1820	Aldgate, London	Emanuel Moses		Solomon Joseph	Aldgate, London	
18787	Joseph	Jane	1829	Whitechapel, London	Joshua Joseph	Esther (Hester) Jacobs		Holborn, London	
30214	Joseph	Jane	1832	Fitzrovia, London	Benjamin Joseph	Amelia Harris	Abraham Keyzor [Bandan]	Piccadilly, London	
20106	Joseph	Joe	1841	?Whitechapel, London	Samuel Joseph	Sarah (?)		Spitalfields, London	
9703	Joseph	John	1769	Spitalfields, London				Aldgate, London	general dealer
11219	Joseph	John	1785	Aldgate, London			(?)	Aldgate, London	general dealer
25995	Joseph	John	1811	Aldgate, London				Aldgate, London	tailor
29345	Joseph	John	1811	Manchester	Joseph Jacob	(?)		Whitechapel, London	furrier
5954	Joseph	John	1837	Aldgate, London	John Joseph	Catherine (Kitty) Nathan	Elizabeth (Betsy, Bilha) Romain	Aldgate, London	
20117	Joseph	John	1846	St Giles, London	Solomon Joseph	Priscilla (?)		St Giles, London	scholar
25464	Joseph	Joseph	1773	Aldgate, London				Aldgate, London	pensioner
15848	Joseph	Joseph	1782	Middlesex, London			(?)	Bloomsbury, London	
22918	Joseph	Joseph	1785	Aldgate, London			Catherine (?)	Wapping, London	shopkeeper
174	Joseph	Joseph	1802	Falmouth, Cornwall	Abraham Joseph	Hannah Levy	Phoebe Alexander	Liverpool	jeweller
1304	Joseph	Joseph	1802	Redruth, Cornwall			Fanny (?)	Plymouth, Devon	silversmith + mineralogist
24839	Joseph	Joseph	1806	Spitalfields, London	Reuben Joseph		Hannah Cohen	Elephant & Castle, London	furrier
28029	Joseph	Joseph	1806	Whitechapel, London			(?)	Spitalfields, London	general dealer
27127	Joseph	Joseph	1814	?, London	Benjamin Joseph		Grace Jacobs	Aldgate, London	dealer in china + glass

ID	surname	given names	born	birthplace	father	mother	spouse 1	1851 residence	1851 occupation
23187	Joseph	Joseph	1816	Aldgate, London			Rachel (?)	City, London	clothes dealer
11789	Joseph	Joseph	1817	?, Holland	Yechutiel HaCohen Joseph		Sarah Miriam Park	Shoreditch, London	silk mercer
26586	Joseph	Joseph	1820	Sunderland, Co Durham	Hyam (Esau) Joseph	Hannah Davis	Dinah Davis	Sunderland, Co Durham	general dealer
15647	Joseph	Joseph	1827	Southwark, London	Abraham Joseph	Elizabeth (?)		Holborn, London	musician
938	Joseph	Joseph	1828	Whitechapel, London	Jacob (John) Joseph	Esther (?)		Whitechapel, London	cigar maker
2874	Joseph	Joseph	1830	Portsmouth, Hampshire	Isaac Joseph	Sarah Jacobs	Elizabeth Nerwich	Southampton, Hampshire	jeweller
16203	Joseph	Joseph	1833	Aldgate, London	Solomon Joseph	Jane Selig		Whitechapel, London	merchant's clerk
17398	Joseph	Joseph	1833	Aldgate, London	Samuel Joseph	Rosa (?)		Wapping, London	cigar maker
9764	Joseph	Joseph	1839	Middlesex, London				Kew, London	boarding school pupil
5413	Joseph	Joseph	1842	Middlesex, London	Henry Joseph	Rosetta (Rose) (?)		Aldgate, London	
9872	Joseph	Joseph	1843	?, London				Fulham, London	boarding school pupil
28331	Joseph	Joseph	1843	Whitechapel, London	(?) Joseph	Sarah (?)		Aldgate, London	
17896	Joseph	Joseph	1844	Lambeth, London	Moss Joseph	Rachel Blitz		Waterloo, London	
15869	Joseph	Joseph	1846	Spitalfields, London	(?) Joseph	Priscilla (?Levy)		Bethnal Green, London	scholar
15859	Joseph	Joseph	1847	Spitalfields, London	Edward (Nathan) Joseph	Mary (?)		Bermondsey, London	scholar
12430	Joseph	Joseph	1849	Whitechapel, London	Isaac Joseph	Ellen (?)		Spitalfields, London	
1128	Joseph	Joseph	1850	Penzance, Cornwall	Henry Joseph	Amelia Jacob	Emily Clara Jacob	Penzance, Cornwall	
13487	Joseph	Joseph Albert	1840	Manchester	Simon Joseph	Fanny Simmons		Manchester	
26591	Joseph	Joseph Nesham	1851	Sunderland, Co Durham	Nesham (Nathan) Joseph	Matilda Cohen		Sunderland, Co Durham	
1852	Joseph	Joseph Phillips	1832	Swansea, Wales	Benjamin Joseph	Matilda Moseley	Fanny Abrahams	Swansea, Wales	assistant jeweller
5362	Joseph	Josephus B	1828	Falmouth, Cornwall	Barnet Lyon Joseph	Betsy Jacob		Liverpool	watchmaker
7563	Joseph	Joshua	1790	Taunton, Somerset	Raphael Joseph		Jane Hyams	Holborn, London	ladies boots manufacturer empl 50
24842	Joseph	Judah	1819	Spitalfields, London	Reuben Joseph		Elizabeth Moses	Elephant & Castle, London	furrier
29394	Joseph	Julia	1789	Amsterdam, Holland	(?)		(?) Joseph	Spitalfields, London	
20101	Joseph	Julia	1796	Whitechapel, London	(?)		(?) Joseph	Mayfair, London	
1336	Joseph	Julia	1811	Plymouth, Devon	Nathan Joseph	Briney (Briny) (?)		Plymouth, Devon	general instructress + teacher of drawing
12399	Joseph	Julia	1821	Spitalfields, London	Isaac Dacosta		Mordecai Joseph	Spitalfields, London	
2873	Joseph	Julia	1827	Portsmouth, Hampshire	Isaac Joseph	Sarah Jacobs	Philip Nathan (Uri) Casper	Portsmouth, Hampshire	
27528	Joseph	Julia	1827	Middlesex, London	(?) Joseph	Elenor (?)		Aldgate, London	
17397	Joseph	Julia	1831	Aldgate, London	Samuel Joseph	Rosa (?)		Wapping, London	
5375	Joseph	Julia	1834	Liverpool	Barnet Lyon Joseph	Betsy Jacob	Israel Levy	Liverpool	school
3560	Joseph	Julia	1835	Bristol	Barnet Joseph	Fanny Moses		Newcastle Upon Tyne	
4000	Joseph	Julia	1838	Penzance, Cornwall	Henry Joseph	Amelia Jacob	Maurice Bischofweder	Penzance, Cornwall	
10553	Joseph	Julia	1841	Westminster, London	(?) Joseph			Elephant & Castle, London	
5399	Joseph	Julia	1845	Liverpool	Joseph Joseph	Phoebe Alexander		Liverpool	
5377	Joseph	Julia	1847	Bristol	Henry Joseph	Maria Samuel	Lawrence Jacob	Whitechapel, London	
15642	Joseph	Julia	1848	Bristol	(?) Joseph	Frances (?)		Birmingham	
24948	Joseph	Julia	1849	Shoreditch, London	Isaiah Joseph	Celia Moss		Bethnal Green, London	
1313	Joseph	Julia	1850	Redruth, Cornwall	Joseph Joseph	Fanny (?)		Plymouth, Devon	
29730	Joseph	Julia (Judith)	1771	Brighton, Sussex	Zelig Myers from Brighton		Isaac Joseph	Aldgate, London	
17181	Joseph	Julia (Juliet)	1822	Whitechapel, London	Aaron Joseph	Matilda Phillips	Louis (Lewis) Harris	Fitzrovia, London	

357

ID	surname	given names	born	birthplace	father	mother	spouse 1	1851 residence	1851 occupation
5405	Joseph	Kate	1843	Newcastle Upon Tyne	Barnet Joseph	Fanny Moses	Lionel Barnet Joseph	Newcastle Upon Tyne	
1129	Joseph	Kate	1846	Penzance, Cornwall	Henry Joseph	Amelia Jacob	Abraham Freedman	Penzance, Cornwall	scholar
27516	Joseph	Katherine	1847	Soho, London	Samuel Joseph	Rebecca (?)		Aldgate, London	
15866	Joseph	Lazarus	1845	Spitalfields, London	Moses Joseph	Esther Samuel		Spitalfields, London	
8578	Joseph	Leah	1829	Middlesex, London	Henry Benjamin	Martha Simmons	Moses Joseph	Spitalfields, London	
16068	Joseph	Leah	1849	St Giles, London	Charles Joseph	Charlotte (?)		St Giles, London	
15861	Joseph	Leah	1850	Bermondsey, London	Edward (Nathan) Joseph	Mary (?)		Bermondsey, London	
5403	Joseph	Levine	1836	?Leeds, Yorkshire	Barnet Joseph	Fanny Moses		Newcastle Upon Tyne	
14531	Joseph	Lewis	1798	Fulham, London			Dinah Benjamin	Southwark, London	glass cutter
26244	Joseph	Lewis	1822	?, London	Emanuel Joseph		Elizabeth Simmons	Aldgate, London	pastrycook
17399	Joseph	Lewis	1835	Aldgate, London	Samuel Joseph	Rosa (?)		Wapping, London	
30564	Joseph	Lewis	1851	Spitalfields, London	Moses Joseph	Esther Samuel		Spitalfields, London	
11289	Joseph	Lewis Henry (Hyams)	1787	Aldgate, London	Joseph Joseph		Hannah (Ann) Lazarus	Aldgate, London	watch + clockmaker + dealer in bullion
17894	Joseph	Lion	1839	Lambeth, London	Moss Joseph	Rachel Blitz		Waterloo, London	
31033	Joseph	Lionel	1805	Amsterdam, Holland			Sarah (?)	Sunderland, Co Durham	pawnbroker
1125	Joseph	Lionel	1841	Penzance, Cornwall	Henry Joseph	Amelia Jacob		Penzance, Cornwall	scholar
26583	Joseph	Lionel	1843	Sunderland, Co Durham	David Joseph	Fanny Samuel		Sunderland, Co Durham	scholar
165	Joseph	Lionel Barnet	1826	Bristol	Barnet Lyon Joseph	Betsy Jacob	Kate Joseph	Liverpool	
17648	Joseph	Louisa	1811	?, Poland	(?)		Michael Joseph	Aldgate, London	
31095	Joseph	Louisa A	1832	Aldgate, London	Aaron Joseph	Frances Cohen		Bloomsbury, London	
18093	Joseph	Luisa	1815	?, England	(?)		Moses Joseph	Holborn, London	
22906	Joseph	Lydia	1781	?, Germany	(?)		(?) Joseph	Wapping, London	milliner
5390	Joseph	Lyon J	1828	Falmouth, Cornwall	Joseph Joseph	Phoebe Alexander	Esther Levy	Birmingham	commercial traveller, jewellery
31066	Joseph	Lyonel	1845	Sunderland, Co Durham	Tobias Joseph	Amelia Samuel		Sunderland, Co Durham	scholar
1845	Joseph	Margaret	1819	Warsaw, Poland	(?)		Harris Joseph	Swansea, Wales	hawker's wife
5376	Joseph	Maria	1817	Middlesex, London	Abraham Samuel	Phoebe Levy	Henry Joseph	Whitechapel, London	
12429	Joseph	Maria	1844	Whitechapel, London	Isaac Joseph	Ellen (?)	Solomon Siegenberg	Spitalfields, London	
23190	Joseph	Maria	1845	Spitalfields, London	Joseph Joseph	Rachel (?)		City, London	
11700	Joseph	Maria	1846	Aldgate, London	Barnett Joseph	Amelia Benjamin		Aldgate, London	
1839	Joseph	Maria (Miriam) Fanny	1833	Swansea, Wales	Benjamin Joseph	Matilda Moseley		Swansea, Wales	
12167	Joseph	Mark	1809	?, Holland	(?) Joseph	Julia (?)	(?)	Whitechapel, London	silk merchant, provision merchant + fruiterer
5960	Joseph	Mark	1848	Spitalfields, London	(?) Joseph	Priscilla (?)	Rebecca (?)	Bethnal Green, London	scholar
22991	Joseph	Mark (Mordecai)	1827	?, Germany	Joseph Joseph		(Rosa) Rosetta Abrahams	Whitechapel, London	tailor empl 3
8389	Joseph	Martha L---	1832	?, London	(?) Joseph			Southampton, Hampshire	servant
5944	Joseph	Mary	1826	City, London	(?)		Edward (Nathan) Joseph	Bermondsey, London	tailoress
17694	Joseph	Mary	1833	Covent Garden, London	Moses Joseph	Hannah Moss		Holborn, London	stay manufacturer
10347	Joseph	Mary	1850	Spitalfields, London	Elias Joseph	Hannah (?)		Spitalfields, London	
15558	Joseph	Mary Ann	1840	Spitalfields, London	Joseph Myer	Amelia (?)		Covent Garden, London	
1837	Joseph	Matilda	1805	Swansea, Wales	Jacob Moseley		Benjamin Joseph	Swansea, Wales	
17180	Joseph	Matilda	1805	Middlesex, London	Yehuda Leib Phillips		Aaron Joseph	Fitzrovia, London	
20827	Joseph	Matilda	1825	King's Lynn, Norfolk	Henry Cohen		Nesham (Nathan) Joseph	Sunderland, Co Durham	

ID	surname	given names	born	birthplace	father	mother	spouse 1	1851 residence	1851 occupation
16969	Joseph	Matilda	1839	Middlesex, London	(?) Joseph			Hammersmith, London	boarding school pupil
5373	Joseph	Matilda	1843	Liverpool	Barnet Lyon Joseph	Betsy Jacob	Israel Oppenheim	Liverpool	school
12585	Joseph	Maurice	1804	Middlesex, London			Isabella (?)	Norwich, Norfolk	pawnbroker
18789	Joseph	Maurice	1832	Whitechapel, London	Joshua Joseph	Esther (Hester) Jacobs		Holborn, London	dentist
5414	Joseph	Maurice	1848	Whitechapel, London	Henry Joseph	Rosetta (Rose) (?)	(?)	Aldgate, London	
17647	Joseph	Michael	1800	?, Poland			Louisa (?)	Aldgate, London	
26766	Joseph	Michael	1817	Portsmouth, Hampshire			Sarah Simmons nee (?)	Aldgate, London	general dealer
26592	Joseph	Michael	1826	Sunderland, Co Durham	Hyam (Esau) Joseph	Hannah Davis	Rebecca Jacobs	Sunderland, Co Durham	watchmaker + jeweller
14528	Joseph	Michael	1832	Southwark, London	Lewis Joseph	Dinah Benjamin		Southwark, London	cigar maker
12428	Joseph	Michael	1841	Whitechapel, London	Isaac Joseph	Ellen (?)		Spitalfields, London	
1847	Joseph	Michael	1847	Swansea, Wales	Harris Joseph	Margaret (?)		Swansea, Wales	scholar
5945	Joseph	Michael	1848	Spitalfields, London	Moses Joseph	Esther Samuel	Elizabeth (Betsy) Hart	Spitalfields, London	
23192	Joseph	Michael	1850	City, London	Joseph Joseph	Rachel (?)		City, London	
26588	Joseph	Michael	1851	Sunderland, Co Durham	Joseph Joseph	Dinah Davis		Sunderland, Co Durham	
26579	Joseph	Milcah Perla	1835	Sunderland, Co Durham	David Joseph	Fanny Samuel	Joseph David Kaufman	Sunderland, Co Durham	
31093	Joseph	Miriam	1822	Aldgate, London	Aaron Joseph	Frances Cohen		Bloomsbury, London	
30845	Joseph	Montague	1848	Newcastle Upon Tyne	Barnet Joseph	Fanny Moses		Newcastle Upon Tyne	
12398	Joseph	Mordecai	1820	Spitalfields, London	Emanuel Joseph		Julia Dacosta	Spitalfields, London	general dealer
9765	Joseph	Morris	1842	Middlesex, London				Kew, London	boarding school pupil
30224	Joseph	Morris	1843	Middlesex, London				Bayswater, London	scholar at home
1126	Joseph	Morris (Maurice)	1843	Penzance, Cornwall	Henry Joseph	Amelia Jacob		Penzance, Cornwall	scholar
7241	Joseph	Morris David	1848	Covent Garden, London	David Joseph	Amelia Levi	Frances Amelia Henry	St Giles, London	
13485	Joseph	Morris S	1837	Manchester	Simon Joseph	Fanny Simmons	Rachel M Abrahams	Manchester	
18092	Joseph	Moses	1809	?, England			Luisa (?)	Holborn, London	general dealer
23508	Joseph	Moses	1821	?, Poland [?, Prussia]				Liverpool	traveller watchmaker
15862	Joseph	Moses	1822	Bath	Yehuda Leib		Esther Samuel	Spitalfields, London	general dealer
8577	Joseph	Moses	1825	Middlesex, London	Joseph Joseph	Eleanor Myers	Leah Benjamin	Spitalfields, London	cab driver
1094	Joseph	Moses	1826	Plymouth, Devon	Isaac Joseph	Hannah (?)		Falmouth, Cornwall	shop assistant, pawnbroker + tailor
27513	Joseph	Moses	1831	Windsor, Berkshire	Samuel Joseph	Rebecca (?)		Aldgate, London	
10345	Joseph	Moses	1846	Spitalfields, London	Elias Joseph	Hannah (?)		Spitalfields, London	
26594	Joseph	Moses J	1834	Sunderland, Co Durham	Hyam (Esau) Joseph	Hannah Davis		Sunderland, Co Durham	clock- and watchmaker
23590	Joseph	Moss	1798	?, London			(?)	Liverpool	merchant
17891	Joseph	Moss	1800	Groningen, Holland	Joseph		Rachel Blitz	Waterloo, London	jeweller
16122	Joseph	Moss	1842	?, London	Samuel Joseph	Sarah (?)		Aldgate, London	scholar
2872	Joseph	Moss (Maurice)	1832	Portsmouth, Hampshire	Isaac Joseph	Sarah Jacobs	Emma Davis	Birmingham	jeweller
19723	Joseph	Moss Jacob	1815	Middlesex, London			Frances Lialter	Whitechapel, London	attends sales
15556	Joseph	Myer	1823	Aldgate, London			Amelia (?)	Covent Garden, London	general dealer
31063	Joseph	Naomi	1839	Sunderland, Co Durham	Tobias Joseph	Amelia Samuel		Sunderland, Co Durham	
5368	Joseph	Nathan	1833	Bristol	Barnet Lyon Joseph	Betsy Jacob		Liverpool	school
17186	Joseph	Nathan	1836	Middlesex, London	Aaron Joseph	Matilda Phillips		Fitzrovia, London	
18785	Joseph	Nathan (Nathaniel)	1827	Whitechapel, London	Joshua Joseph	Esther (Hester) Jacobs	Rachel Hyam	Holborn, London	
7245	Joseph	Nathan Solomon	1834	Aldgate, London	Solomon Joseph	Jane Selig	Alice Samuel	Whitechapel, London	scholar at home
1855	Joseph	Nathaniel	1776	?, Poland				Cardiff, Wales	hawker

ID	surname	given names	born	birthplace	father	mother	spouse 1	1851 residence	1851 occupation
8297	Joseph	Nesham	1850	Sunderland, Co Durham	Nesham (Nathan) Joseph	Matilda Cohen		Sunderland, Co Durham	
8295	Joseph	Nesham (Nathan)	1816	North Shields, Tyne & Wear	Hyam (Esau) Joseph	Hannah Davis	Matilda Cohen	Sunderland, Co Durham	clock, watch and compass maker
26582	Joseph	Nissan	1841	Sunderland, Co Durham	David Joseph	Fanny Samuel		Sunderland, Co Durham	scholar
31036	Joseph	Perle	1837	Sunderland, Co Durham	Lionel Joseph	Sarah (?)		Sunderland, Co Durham	
26580	Joseph	Philip	1836	Sunderland, Co Durham	David Joseph	Fanny Samuel		Sunderland, Co Durham	tailor
31064	Joseph	Phillip	1841	Sunderland, Co Durham	Tobias Joseph	Amelia Samuel		Sunderland, Co Durham	scholar
9873	Joseph	Phineas	1848	?, London				Fulham, London	
5389	Joseph	Phoebe	1805	Plymouth, Devon	Sander Alexander	Rose Jacob	Joseph Joseph	Liverpool	
1851	Joseph	Phoebe	1808	?, Poland			Jacob Joseph	Swansea, Wales	
1307	Joseph	Phoebe	1838	Redruth, Cornwall	Joseph Joseph	Fanny (?)	A H Van Nierop	Plymouth, Devon	
1849	Joseph	Phoebe	1844	Swansea, Wales	Harris Joseph	Margaret (?)		Swansea, Wales	scholar
20114	Joseph	Priscilla	1812	Soho, London	(?)		Solomon Joseph	St Giles, London	
15868	Joseph	Priscilla	1824	Whitechapel, London	(?) (?Levy)	(?Hannah) (?)		Bethnal Green, London	clothes dealer
6128	Joseph	Priscilla	1839	Middlesex, London	Judah Joseph	Elizabeth Moses	Henry Lewis Cohen	Hammersmith, London	boarding school pupil
19725	Joseph	Priscilla	1849	Middlesex, London	Moss Jacob Joseph	Frances Lialter		Whitechapel, London	
2871	Joseph	Rachael	1834	Portsmouth, Hampshire	Isaac Joseph	Sarah Jacobs	Simon Barnett Simmons	Portsmouth, Hampshire	
3561	Joseph	Rachael	1840	Leeds, Yorkshire	Barnet Joseph	Fanny Moses		Newcastle Upon Tyne	
15855	Joseph	Rachael	1847	St Giles, London	Simeon Joseph	Rebecca (?)		Holborn, London	
27132	Joseph	Rachael	1850	?Aldgate, London	Joseph Joseph	Grace Jacobs		Aldgate, London	
14529	Joseph	Rachael	1835	Southwark, London	Lewis Joseph	Dinah Benjamin	Solomon Jacobs	Southwark, London	tailoress
10585	Joseph	Rachel	1772	Whitechapel, London	(?) Joseph			Spitalfields, London	general dealer?
17892	Joseph	Rachel	1811	Amsterdam, Holland	Yehuda Leib Blitz		Moss Joseph	Waterloo, London	
23188	Joseph	Rachel	1817	Aldgate, London	(?)		Joseph Joseph	City, London	clothes dealer
28504	Joseph	Rachel	1821	Spitalfields, London	(?)		Barnett Joseph	Spitalfields, London	
1250	Joseph	Rachel	1831	Plymouth, Devon	Isaac Joseph	Hannah (?)	Myer Jacobi	Plymouth, Devon	milliner
17182	Joseph	Rachel	1831	Middlesex, London	Aaron Joseph	Matilda Phillips	Simon Price	Fitzrovia, London	
28973	Joseph	Rachel	1831	Aldgate, London	(?) Joseph			Whitechapel, London	general servant
5365	Joseph	Rachel	1833	Bristol	Barnet Lyon Joseph	Betsy Jacob	Alexander Levin	Liverpool	assistant to silversmith + merchant
7004	Joseph	Rachel	1839	Aldgate, London	Solomon Joseph	Jane Selig	Hermann Adler	Whitechapel, London	
28330	Joseph	Rachel	1841	Aldgate, London	(?) Joseph	Sarah (?)		Aldgate, London	scholar
3401	Joseph	Rachel	1842	?, London	Abraham Joseph	Sarah Falcke	Frederick Samuel David Phillips	Marylebone, London	scholar
20875	Joseph	Rachel	1843	New York, USA	Joseph Joseph	Phoebe Alexander		Liverpool	
15646	Joseph	Raphael	1813	Southwark, London	Abraham Joseph	Elizabeth (?)		Holborn, London	rag merchant + metal dealer
24766	Joseph	Rebecca	1795	Aldgate, London				Southwark, London	employed in domestic duties
27511	Joseph	Rebecca	1807	Westminster, London	(?)		Samuel Joseph	Aldgate, London	
15854	Joseph	Rebecca	1820	?Aldgate, London	(?)		Simeon Joseph	Holborn, London	tailor's wife
8163	Joseph	Rebecca	1822	?, Poland [?, Prussia]	(?)		David Joseph	Cardiff, Wales	
26596	Joseph	Rebecca	1831	Sunderland, Co Durham	Hyam (Esau) Joseph	Hannah Davis		Sunderland, Co Durham	
26593	Joseph	Rebecca	1832	Middlesex, London	Samuel Jacobs	Rose Alexander	Michael Joseph	Sunderland, Co Durham	
5367	Joseph	Rebecca	1835	Bristol	Barnet Lyon Joseph	Betsy Jacob	Ephraim Samuel Joseph	Liverpool	school

ID	surname	given names	born	birthplace	father	mother	spouse 1	1851 residence	1851 occupation
15893	Joseph	Rebecca	1835	Middlesex, London	(?) Joseph			Hackney, London	boarding school pupil
17649	Joseph	Rebecca	1835	?, Poland	Michael Joseph	Louisa (?)		Aldgate, London	
24505	Joseph	Rebecca	1835	Amsterdam, Holland	(?) Joseph	Rosa (?)		Rotherhithe, London	shopwoman
27533	Joseph	Rebecca	1835	Middlesex, London	(?) Joseph	Elenor (?)		Aldgate, London	
15865	Joseph	Rebecca	1842	Spitalfields, London	Moses Joseph	Esther Samuel	Samuel Moses	Spitalfields, London	
18792	Joseph	Rebecca	1845	Holborn, London	Joshua Joseph	Esther (Hester) Jacobs		Holborn, London	scholar
5961	Joseph	Rebecca	1849	Bermondsey, London	Edward (Nathan) Joseph	Mary (?)	Mark Joseph	Bermondsey, London	scholar
1842	Joseph	Robert Ellis	1845	Swansea, Wales	Benjamin Joseph	Matilda Moseley	Clara Mier	Swansea, Wales	scholar at home
24503	Joseph	Rosa	1797	Finsbury, London	(?)		(?) Joseph	Rotherhithe, London	shopkeeper &c
17396	Joseph	Rosa	1809	Whitechapel, London	(?)		Samuel Joseph	Wapping, London	
1338	Joseph	Rosa	1819	Plymouth, Devon	Nathan Joseph	Briney (Briny) (?)		Plymouth, Devon	daily governess
27535	Joseph	Rosa	1843	Middlesex, London	(?) Joseph	Elenor (?)		Aldgate, London	
22992	Joseph	Rosa (Rosetta)	1829	Whitechapel, London	Abraham Abrahams		Mark (Mordecai) Joseph	Whitechapel, London	
23762	Joseph	Rose	1805	Liverpool	(?)		Barned Joseph	Liverpool	
1124	Joseph	Rose	1840	Penzance, Cornwall	Henry Joseph	Amelia Jacob	George Goodman	Penzance, Cornwall	scholar
1312	Joseph	Rose	1849	Redruth, Cornwall	Joseph Joseph	Fanny (?)		Plymouth, Devon	
5400	Joseph	Rose	1851	Liverpool	Joseph Joseph	Phoebe Alexander	Hyman Moses	Liverpool	
20102	Joseph	Rosetta	1805	?, London	(?)		Israel Joseph	Marylebone, London	
11698	Joseph	Rosetta	1842	Aldgate, London	Barnett Joseph	Amelia Benjamin		Aldgate, London	
5412	Joseph	Rosetta (Rose, Rosina)	1822	?, London	Joseph Michaels		Henry Joseph	Aldgate, London	seamstress
17898	Joseph	Salomon	1848	Lambeth, London	Moss Joseph	Rachel Blitz		Waterloo, London	
17395	Joseph	Samuel	1803	Guernsey, Channel Islands			Rosa (?)	Wapping, London	clothier
27510	Joseph	Samuel	1805	St Giles, London			Rebecca (?)	Aldgate, London	ironmonger
4158	Joseph	Samuel	1811	?, Holland			Sarah (?)	Spitalfields, London	general dealer
16120	Joseph	Samuel	1811	?, London	Yaakov		Sarah (?)	Aldgate, London	hawker
28496	Joseph	Samuel	1819	Spitalfields, London	Emanuel Joseph		Sarah Jonas	Spitalfields, London	general dealer
27531	Joseph	Samuel	1830	Middlesex, London	(?) Joseph	Elenor (?)		Aldgate, London	cab driver
16208	Joseph	Samuel	1843	?London	Solomon Joseph	Jane Selig		Whitechapel, London	scholar at home
27517	Joseph	Samuel	1849	?Aldgate, London	Samuel Joseph	Rebecca (?)		Aldgate, London	
15867	Joseph	Samuel	1850	Spitalfields, London	Moses Joseph	Esther Samuel		Spitalfields, London	
15847	Joseph	Samuel Joseph	1843	Bloomsbury, London	Simon Joseph Joseph	Eliza Joseph		Bloomsbury, London	
5070	Joseph	Samuel Solomon	1846	Portsmouth, Hampshire	Lewis Joseph	Frances Simon		Portsmouth, Hampshire	
27746	Joseph	Sarah	1765	Amsterdam, Holland	(?)		(?) Joseph	Spitalfields, London	supported by her family
20430	Joseph	Sarah	1781	Amsterdam, Holland	(?)		(?) Joseph	Aldgate, London	
16677	Joseph	Sarah	1801	Liverpool	(?) ?Joseph			Liverpool	gentlewoman
2877	Joseph	Sarah	1803	Poole, Dorset	Abraham Jacobs	Elizabeth (Belly, Beila) Moses	Isaac Joseph	Portsmouth, Hampshire	
31034	Joseph	Sarah	1808	North Shields, Tyne & Wear	(?)		Lionel Joseph	Sunderland, Co Durham	
1337	Joseph	Sarah	1813	Plymouth, Devon	Nathan Joseph	Briney (Briny) (?)		Plymouth, Devon	school mistress
16121	Joseph	Sarah	1813	?, London	(?)		Samuel Joseph	Aldgate, London	
15650	Joseph	Sarah	1815	Great Yarmouth, Norfolk	Jacob Falcke	Hannah (?)	Abraham Joseph	Piccadilly, London	
26767	Joseph	Sarah	1815	Spitalfields, London	(?)		(?) Simmons	Aldgate, London	
4159	Joseph	Sarah	1816	?, Holland	(?)		Samuel Joseph	Spitalfields, London	
28329	Joseph	Sarah	1821	Aldgate, London	(?)		(?) Joseph	Aldgate, London	fruit seller

ID	surname	given names	born	birthplace	father	mother	spouse 1	1851 residence	1851 occupation
28497	Joseph	Sarah	1821	Whitechapel, London	Henry Jonas		Samuel Joseph	Spitalfields, London	
26595	Joseph	Sarah	1826	Sunderland, Co Durham	Hyam (Esau) Joseph	Hannah Davis		Sunderland, Co Durham	
1249	Joseph	Sarah	1831	Plymouth, Devon	Isaac Joseph	Hannah (?)	Solomon Ullmann	Plymouth, Devon	
29779	Joseph	Sarah	1834	Whitechapel, London	Emanuel Joseph	Frances Cohen	Jacob Goodman	Spitalfields, London	slop shirt maker
5397	Joseph	Sarah	1835	Bristol	Joseph Joseph	Phoebe Alexander		Liverpool	
2753	Joseph	Sarah	1836	Plymouth, Devon	Abraham Joseph	Eliza Woolf	Raphael Harris	Mayfair, London	
27514	Joseph	Sarah	1838	Windsor, Berkshire	Samuel Joseph	Rebecca (?)		Aldgate, London	
1853	Joseph	Sarah	1839	Swansea, Wales				Swansea, Wales	scholar
15864	Joseph	Sarah	1841	Middlesex, London	Moses Joseph	Esther Samuel	Moses Henriques Valentine	Spitalfields, London	
1310	Joseph	Sarah	1845	Redruth, Cornwall	Joseph Joseph	Fanny (?)		Plymouth, Devon	
11762	Joseph	Sarah	1845	Aldgate, London	Aaron Joseph	Esther (?)		Shoreditch, London	
12400	Joseph	Sarah	1845	Spitalfields, London	Mordecai Joseph	Julia Dacosta		Spitalfields, London	
11790	Joseph	Sarah Miriam	1818	?, Holland	Eliezer Lezer Park	Blume (?)	Joseph Joseph	Shoreditch, London	
18783	Joseph	Selim	1829	Aldgate, London	Joseph Joseph	Mary Ann (?)	Louisa M (?)	Waterloo, London	tailor
1123	Joseph	Selina	1835	Penzance, Cornwall	Henry Joseph	Amelia Jacob		Penzance, Cornwall	scholar
15853	Joseph	Simeon	1812	St Giles, London			Rebecca (?)	Holborn, London	tailor
5395	Joseph	Simeon	1835	Bristol	Joseph Joseph	Phoebe Alexander	Rose Blanckensee	Birmingham	jeweller's clerk
8425	Joseph	Simon	1759	?, Germany				Portsmouth, Hampshire	clothes dealer
22141	Joseph	Simon	1791	?, Germany			(?)	Whitechapel, London	glazier
7486	Joseph	Simon	1807	Manchester			Fanny Simmons	Manchester	furrier empl 3
24841	Joseph	Simon	1809	Spitalfields, London	Reuben Joseph		(?)	Elephant & Castle, London	furrier
15559	Joseph	Simon	1842	Spitalfields, London	Joseph Myer	Amelia (?)		Covent Garden, London	
15846	Joseph	Simon Joseph	1806	Middlesex, London	Joseph Joseph		Eliza Joseph	Bloomsbury, London	stockbroker
16200	Joseph	Solomon	1801	Aldgate, London	Nathan Joseph		Jane Selig	Whitechapel, London	importer of foreign goods
20113	Joseph	Solomon	1807	St Giles, London			Priscilla (?)	St Giles, London	tailor
29723	Joseph	Solomon	1809	Aldgate, London	Isaac Joseph	Julia (Judith) Myers	Jane Moses	Aldgate, London	licensed victualler
1854	Joseph	Solomon	1823	Klaipeda, Lithuania [Memel, Prussia]	Joseph Solomon		Rachel Goldsmith	Merthyr Tydfil, Wales	travelling jeweller
1285	Joseph	Solomon	1834	Plymouth, Devon	Abraham Joseph	Eliza Woolf	Caroline Cohen	Plymouth, Devon	
26770	Joseph	Solomon	1847	Spitalfields, London	Michael Joseph	Sarah (?)		Aldgate, London	
1306	Joseph	Solomon L	1837	Redruth, Cornwall	Joseph Joseph	Fanny (?)		Plymouth, Devon	
7903	Joseph	Solomon William	1839	?, Germany	David Joseph	Rebecca (?)	Amelia Cohen	Pontypool, Wales	glazier
17183	Joseph	Sophia	1832	Middlesex, London	Aaron Joseph	Matilda Phillips		Fitzrovia, London	
17401	Joseph	Sophia	1840	Aldgate, London	Samuel Joseph	Rosa (?)		Wapping, London	scholar
5959	Joseph	Sophia	1847	Bloomsbury, London	(?) Joseph	Eliza (?)		Bloomsbury, London	
15643	Joseph	Susan	1849	Birmingham	(?) Joseph	Frances (?)		Birmingham	
8034	Joseph	Tobias	1807	Margonin, Poland [Margonin, Prussia]	Joseph Joseph		Amelia Samuel	Sunderland, Co Durham	jeweller
18791	Joseph	Walter	1844	Holborn, London	Joshua Joseph	Esther (Hester) Jacobs		Holborn, London	scholar
31094	Joseph	Zipporah A	1826	Aldgate, London	Aaron Joseph	Frances Cohen		Bloomsbury, London	
17693	Joseph (Josephs)	Alexander	1832	Covent Garden, London	Moses Joseph	Hannah Moss	Hannah Myers	Holborn, London	stay manufacturer
15392	Josephs	Amelia	1806	Brussels, Belgium	(?)		(?) Josephs	Waterloo, London	cook
4748	Josephs	Caroline	1837	Alsace, France	(?) Josephs			Birmingham	

ID	surname	given names	born	birthplace	father	mother	spouse 1	1851 residence	1851 occupation
17761	Josephs	Deborah	1778	Leiden, Holland	(?)		Shlomeh Aryeh Zalman Leib Josephs	Aldgate, London	
10477	Josephs	Elizabeth	1826	Shoreditch, London	Emanuel Josephs			Mile End, London	artificial florist
10476	Josephs	Emanuel	1774	Aldgate, London				Mile End, London	formerly furniture broker
18794	Josephs	Emily Sarah	1847	Bloomsbury, London	Walter Josephs	Sarah Henriques		Bloomsbury, London	
24825	Josephs	Esther	1792	Finsbury, London	(?)		(?) Josephs	Waterloo, London	bonnet maker
24826	Josephs	Esther	1831	Lambeth, London	(?) Josephs	Esther (?)		Waterloo, London	bonnet maker maker
24145	Josephs	Grace	1796	St Pancras, London	Issachar Behr		Joseph Josephs	Bloomsbury, London	
4747	Josephs	Jacob	1796	Birmingham	(?) Josephs		Caroline (?)	Birmingham	cabinet maker's assistant
9561	Josephs	Joseph	1773	Aldgate, London				Spitalfields, London	general dealer
24144	Josephs	Joseph	1801	Whitechapel, London	Meir		Grace Nathan	Bloomsbury, London	retired tobacco manufacturer
15441	Josephs	Louis	1820	Shoreditch, London	Joshua Josephs		Sarah Franks	Covent Garden, London	tailor
15443	Josephs	Maria	1843	Shoreditch, London	Louis Josephs	Sarah Franks		Covent Garden, London	scholar
18795	Josephs	Michael	1849	Bloomsbury, London	Walter Josephs	Sarah Henriques		Bloomsbury, London	
15444	Josephs	Minkey	1846	Shoreditch, London	Louis Josephs	Sarah Franks		Covent Garden, London	
15445	Josephs	Rachael	1848	Shoreditch, London	Louis Josephs	Sarah Franks		Covent Garden, London	
8462	Josephs	Samuel	1816	Portsmouth, Hampshire				Portsmouth, Hampshire	pauper
18793	Josephs	Sarah	1811	Jamaica, West Indies	Abraham L Henriques		Walter Josephs	Bloomsbury, London	
15442	Josephs	Sarah	1822	Shoreditch, London	Isaac Franks	Mary (?)	Louis Josephs	Covent Garden, London	
29915	Josephs	Sarah Betsy	1850	Middlesex, London	(?) Josephs	Ann Levy		Whitechapel, London	
7480	Josephs	Walter	1805	Middlesex, London	Michael Josephs		Sarah Henriques	Bloomsbury, London	merchant
18796	Josephs	Walter	1850	Bloomsbury, London	Walter Josephs	Sarah Henriques		Bloomsbury, London	
21922	Josephs (Joseph)	Emanuel	1846	Clerkenwell, London	Saul Josephs (Joseph)	Sarah Isaacs		Clerkenwell, London	scholar
21925	Josephs (Joseph)	Esther	1850	Clerkenwell, London	Saul Josephs (Joseph)	Sarah Isaacs		Clerkenwell, London	
21921	Josephs (Joseph)	Lewis (Louis)	1841	Clerkenwell, London	Saul Josephs (Joseph)	Sarah Isaacs	MariaTheresa Calderra	Clerkenwell, London	scholar
21920	Josephs (Joseph)	Sarah	1812	Spitalfields, London	Menachem Isaacs		Saul Josephs (Joseph)	Clerkenwell, London	
21924	Josephs (Joseph)	Sarah	1849	Clerkenwell, London	Saul Josephs (Joseph)	Sarah Isaacs		Clerkenwell, London	
21919	Josephs (Joseph)	Saul	1806	Whitechapel, London	Menachem Manos		Sarah Isaacs	Clerkenwell, London	furniture dealer
21923	Josephs (Joseph)	Simon (Simeon) S	1837	Clerkenwell, London	Saul Josephs (Joseph)	Sarah Isaacs	Annie Isaacs	Clerkenwell, London	
23450	Josephson	Bernard	1819	?, Poland			Jane (?)	Liverpool	cabinet maker
23452	Josephson	Eliza	1839	?, Poland	Bernard Josephson	Jane (?)		Liverpool	scholar
23451	Josephson	Jane	1820	?, Poland	(?)		Barnard Josephson	Liverpool	
10155	Joshua	Abraham	1769	Aldgate, London	Joshua Joshua		Sarah (?)	Whitechapel, London	fishmonger
10158	Joshua	Charlotte	1804	City, London	(?)		John Joshua	Whitechapel, London	
10157	Joshua	John	1803	City, London	Abraham Joshua	Sarah (?)	Charlotte (?)	Whitechapel, London	fishmonger
10156	Joshua	Joshua	1793	Middlesex, London	Abraham Joshua	Sarah (?)	Rebecca Levi	Brighton, Sussex	formerly butcher
10159	Joshua	Joshua Michael	1827	City, London	Michael Joshua	Sarah Solomon		Whitechapel, London	merchant
14524	Joshua	Rebecca	1801	Middlesex, London	Moshe Levi		Joshua Joshua	Brighton, Sussex	
26795	Judah	Fanny (Frances)	1801	Aldgate, London	Shlomeh Zalman		Moses Judah	Aldgate, London	
26794	Judah	Moses	1803	Aldgate, London	Joseph Judah		Fanny (Frances) Solomon	Aldgate, London	clothes dealer
4588	Judge	Abraham	1791	?, Germany				Birmingham	hawker
17640	Judman	Hannah	1844	?, Poland [?, Prussia]	Joachim Judman	Jette (?)		Aldgate, London	
17639	Judman	Jacob	1842	?, Poland [?, Prussia]	Joachim Judman	Jette (?)		Aldgate, London	
17641	Judman	Jane	1847	?, London	Joachim Judman	Jette (?)		Aldgate, London	

ID	surname	given names	born	birthplace	father	mother	spouse 1	1851 residence	1851 occupation
17637	Judman	Jette	1814	?, Poland [?, Prussia]	(?)		Joachim Judman	Aldgate, London	
17636	Judman	Joachim	1813	?, Poland [?, Prussia]			Jette (?)	Aldgate, London	tailor
17638	Judman	Leni	1841	?, Poland [?, Prussia]	Joachim Judman	Jette (?)		Aldgate, London	
9071	Julian	David Henriques	1819	City, London	Moses Henriques Julian	Esther de Aaron de Pass	Rosetta Aaron	Hoxton, London	shoe manufacturer emp 12
9073	Julian	Esther Sophia	1846	Hackney, London	David Henriques Julian	Rosetta Aaron		Hoxton, London	
9075	Julian	Henry	1849	Shoreditch, London	David Henriques Julian	Rosetta Aaron		Hoxton, London	
9074	Julian	Moses Henriques	1847	Stepney, London	David Henriques Julian	Rosetta Aaron		Hoxton, London	
9072	Julian	Rosetta	1820	Whitechapel, London	Harry Aaron		David Henriques Julian	Hoxton, London	
9076	Julian	Sophia	1850	Shoreditch, London	David Henriques Julian	Rosetta Aaron	Samuel Gompers	Hoxton, London	
10437	Julius	Julia	1827	?, Germany	(?)		Moses Julius	Spitalfields, London	
10438	Julius	Leah	1849	Aldgate, London	Moses Julius	Julia (?)		Spitalfields, London	
10436	Julius	Moses	1826	?, Germany			Julia (?)	Spitalfields, London	carpenter + glazier
2292	Kahn	Adelaide	1845	Leeds, Yorkshire	Adolphus Kahn	Lisette (Lisetta) (?)		Leeds, Yorkshire	
2290	Kahn	Adolphus	1805	?, Germany			Lisette	Leeds, Yorkshire	wool merchant
2293	Kahn	Albert	1846	Leeds, Yorkshire	Adolphus Kahn	Lisette (Lisetta) (?)	Helene	Leeds, Yorkshire	
2294	Kahn	Charles	1850	Leeds, Yorkshire	Adolphus Kahn	Lisette (Lisetta) (?)		Leeds, Yorkshire	
15757	Kahn	Isaac	1834	?, Germany	Menachem Mendel Kahn (Cohen)			Aldgate, London	shopman
2291	Kahn	Lisette (Lisetta)	1822	?, Germany			Adolphus Kahn	Leeds, Yorkshire	
7248	Kalisch	Marcus Moritz	1825	Treptow, Pomerania, Germany			Clara Stern	Whitechapel, London	doctor + secretary to the Chief Rabbi
26281	Kaliski	Moses	1834	Poznan, Poland [Posen, Prussia]				Aldgate, London	cap maker
27339	Kaller	Abraham	1829	?, Poland [?, Prussia]				Aldgate, London	traveller
11929	Kalman	Hannah (Henrietta)	1845	Aldgate, London	Henry Kalman	Theresa Seligman		Whitechapel, London	scholar
11927	Kalman	Henry	1804	?, Germany	Judah Kalman		Theresa Seligman	Whitechapel, London	boot + shoe maker
11931	Kalman	Juda	1803	?, Germany	Judah Kalman			Whitechapel, London	boot + shoe maker
11930	Kalman	Louisa	1848	Aldgate, London	Henry Kalman	Theresa Seligman	Sander Lazarus	Whitechapel, London	
11928	Kalman	Theresa	1815	?, Germany	Abraham Seligman		Henry Kalman	Whitechapel, London	
18246	Kanselbury	Jetty	1834	?, Poland [?, Prussia]	Louis Kanselbury	Leah (?)		Bristol	
18245	Kanselbury	Leah	1816	?, Poland	(?)		Louis Kanselbury	Bristol	
18244	Kanselbury	Louis	1815	?, Poland [?, Prussia]			Leah (?)	Bristol	jeweller
18248	Kanselbury	Mayer	1843	?, Poland	Louis Kanselbury	Leah (?)		Bristol	
18247	Kanselbury	Michael	1839	?, Poland	Louis Kanselbury	Leah (?)		Bristol	
18250	Kanselbury	Rebecca	1851	Bristol	Louis Kanselbury	Leah (?)		Bristol	
18249	Kanselbury	William	1847	?, Poland	Louis Kanselbury	Leah (?)		Bristol	
14128	Kantrovitz	Baer	1785	?, Poland			(?)	Manchester	retired Minister
14127	Kantrovitz	Jacob	1825	?, Poland	Baer Kantrovitz			Manchester	reader, Jewish Synagogue
14407	Kantrovitz	Nathan	1820	abroad				Salford, Lancashire	tobacco + cigar dealer
5673	Kariet (Karet)	Julius (Joseph)	1831	Plock, Poland	Benjamin Kariet		Rebecca Levy	Spitalfields, London	tin man
5675	Kariet (Karet)	Rosetta (Rose)	1851	Spitalfields, London	Julius (Joseph) Kariet (Karet)	Rebecca Levy		Spitalfields, London	
21439	Karninski	Simon	1824	?, Poland [?, Prussia]				Nottingham, Nottinghamshire	hawker of jewellery

ID	surname	given names	born	birthplace	father	mother	spouse 1	1851 residence	1851 occupation
5209	Karo	Hertz	1813	?, Poland [?, Prussia]			Kate (?)	Cheltenham, Gloucestershire	proprietor of fancy repository
7787	Karo	Kate	1813	Ipswich, Suffolk	(?)		Hertz Karo	Cheltenham, Gloucestershire	
26330	Kary	Caroline	1824	?, Poland [?, Prussia]	(?)		Solomon Kary	Spitalfields, London	
26332	Kary	Jacob	1849	?, Poland [?, Prussia]	Solomon Kary	Caroline (?)		Spitalfields, London	
26331	Kary	Jesse	1845	?, Poland [?, Prussia]	Solomon Kary	Caroline (?)		Spitalfields, London	scholar
26329	Kary	Solomon	1819	?, Poland [?, Prussia]			Caroline (?)	Spitalfields, London	tailor
24129	Katz	Jannette	1822	Wurtemberg, Germany	(?) Katz			Bloomsbury, London	cook
18886	Kaube	Isaac	1829	Berlin, Germany [Berlin, Prussia]	(?) Kaube	Sarah (?)		Spitalfields, London	tailor
18887	Kaube	Lia	1836	Berlin, Germany [Berlin, Prussia]	(?) Kaube	Sarah (?)		Spitalfields, London	tailor
18888	Kaube	Lora	1838	Berlin, Germany [Berlin, Prussia]	(?) Kaube	Sarah (?)		Spitalfields, London	tailoress
18885	Kaube	Sarah	1801	Berlin, Germany [Berlin, Prussia]	(?)		(?) Kaube	Spitalfields, London	needlewoman
18890	Kaube	Sarah	1828	Berlin, Germany [Berlin, Prussia]	(?) Levy			Spitalfields, London	needlewoman
23249	Kauffman	Betsey (Elizabeth)	1842	St Giles, London	Carl Kauffman	Sarah (?)		Chelsea, London	scholar
23244	Kauffman	Carl	1791	?, Germany			Sarah (?)	Chelsea, London	watchmaker
31118	Kauffman	David	1811	?, Poland	David Kauffman	(?)		Portsmouth, Hampshire	Rabbi of Hebrew Congregation
5023	Kauffman	Diana (Dinah)	1830	Whitechapel, London	Carl Kauffman		Lewis Solomon	Oxford, Oxfordshire	
23246	Kauffman	Henrietta (Harriette)	1834	Middlesex, London	Carl Kauffman	Sarah (?)		Chelsea, London	
6649	Kauffman	Jessie Sophia	1826	Doncaster, Yorkshire	Louis Kyezor	Sophia Flora Myers	David Kauffman	Piccadilly, London	
23055	Kauffman	Louis	1829	Kalisz, Poland [Kolish, Poland]				Aldgate, London	cap manufacturer
23247	Kauffman	Louisa	1837	Middlesex, London	Carl Kauffman	Sarah (?)	Joseph Bornstone	Chelsea, London	
31119	Kauffman	Marie	1842	?, Poland			(?)	Portsmouth, Hampshire	scholar
15123	Kauffman	Mary Ann	1828	Aldgate, London	(?) Kauffman			Haggerston, London	milliner
23248	Kauffman	Rosalind	1841	Middlesex, London	Carl Kauffman	Sarah (?)		Chelsea, London	scholar
23245	Kauffman	Sarah	1802	Middlesex, London	(?)		Carl Kauffman	Chelsea, London	watchmaker
23250	Kauffman	Theresa	1845	St Giles, London	Carl Kauffman	Sarah (?)		Chelsea, London	scholar
15266	Kauffmann	Diana	1827	?, London	(?) Kauffmann			Shoreditch, London	domestic servant
12624	Kauffmann	Moses	1812	?, Poland [?, Prussia]				Newton Abbot, Devon	cabinet maker
24295	Kaufinger	Jacob	1815	?, Czech Republic [?, Bohemia]				Bloomsbury, London	author
1423	Kaufman	Abraham	1809	?, Poland [?, Prussia]				Plymouth, Devon	general awker
5072	Kaufman	David	1811	Kalisz, Poland			?	Portsmouth, Hampshire	rabbi
1437	Kaufman	Herman	1840	?, Poland [?, Prussia]	Bernard (Bernet) Kaufman (Kaupman)	(?)	Yetta (Cohen?)	Plymouth, Devon	
1424	Kaufman	Israel	1830	?, Poland [?, Prussia]				Plymouth, Devon	master glazier
31124	Kaufman	Kaufman	1826	Marburg, Germany				Ipswich, Suffolk	dealer in shoes
2480	Kaufman	Ludwig	1830	?, Poland				Hull, Yorkshire	professor of languages

ID	surname	given names	born	birthplace	father	mother	spouse 1	1851 residence	1851 occupation
5073	Kaufman	Marie	1839	Kalisz, Poland	David Kaufman	(?)		Portsmouth, Hampshire	
14203	Kaufman	Wulf	1829	?, Germany				Manchester	hawker
1436	Kaufman (Kaupman)	Anna (Anne, Hannah)	1828	Berlin, Germany	Mathias Joske Perl	Hinda Jacobsohn	Bernard (Bernet) Kaufman	Plymouth, Devon	
1435	Kaufman (Kaupman)	Bernard (Bernet)	1816	Berlin, Germany			(?)	Plymouth, Devon	hawker
14205	Kayser	Wolf	1835	?, Poland				Manchester	hawker
18553	Keeling	Frederick	1845	Piccadilly, London	Henry Levy Keeling	Sophia (?)		Regent's Park, London	scholar at home
7569	Keeling	Henry Levy	1806	Piccadilly, London	David Levy	Hannah Solomons	Sophia (?)	Regent's Park, London	fruit broker
7788	Keeling	Sophia S	1806	Liverpool	(?)		Henry Levy Keeling	Regent's Park, London	
13451	Keesing	Elizabeth	1795	Amsterdam, Holland	(?)		Joseph Keesing	Manchester	
13452	Keesing	Frederick	1823	?, London	Joseph Keesing	Elizabeth (?)		Manchester	furrier
7605	Keesing	Isaac Frederick	1822	Middlesex, London	(?) Keesing	Julia (?)	Louisa Gore	Manchester	stationer
8456	Keesing	James	1818	Amsterdam, Holland			Sarah (?)	Portsmouth, Hampshire	general dealer
13450	Keesing	Joseph	1790	Amsterdam, Holland			Elizabeth (?)	Manchester	clothes dealer
8458	Keesing	Moris	1822	Amsterdam, Holland				Portsmouth, Hampshire	general dealer
8457	Keesing	Sarah	1825	Plymouth, Devon	(?)		James Keesing	Portsmouth, Hampshire	
25912	Keiser	Samuel	1833	?, Poland				Aldgate, London	cap maker journeyman
23697	Keller	Rebecca	1821	Liverpool	(?) Keller			Liverpool	
4591	Kerkopsky	Dinah	1847	?, Poland	Israel Kerkopsky	Rosanna (?)		Birmingham	
4592	Kerkopsky	Isaac	1848	Birmingham	Israel Kerkopsky	Rosanna (?)		Birmingham	
4589	Kerkopsky	Israel	1823	?, Poland			Rosanna (?)	Birmingham	clothier
4590	Kerkopsky	Rosanna	1822	?, Poland			Israel Kerkopsky	Birmingham	
4593	Kerkopsky	Solomon	1851	Birmingham	Israel Kerkopsky	Rosanna (?)		Birmingham	
1856	Kern	Joseph	1812	Baden Neukirch, Germany			Ann	Swansea, Wales	clockmaker
13853	Keron	Adilow (?Adele/Adelaide)	1822	Hamburg, Germany	(?) (?Falk)		Samuel Keron	Manchester	shopkeeper + jeweller
13854	Keron	Bertha	1847	Manchester	Samuel Keron	Adilow (?Adele/Adelaide) (?Falk)		Manchester	
13855	Keron	Emilly	1850	Manchester	Samuel Keron	Adilow (?Adele/Adelaide) (?Falk)		Manchester	
13852	Keron	Samuel	1821	?, Poland [?, Prussia]			Adilow (?Adele/Adelaide) (?Falk)	Manchester	shopkeeper + jeweller
21164	Kesner	Barnett	1813	Amsterdam, Holland	Lyon Kesner	Isabella [Matilda, Elizbeth] David	Hannah Lyon	Pimlico, London	clothier
21165	Kesner	Hannah	1811	Islington, London	Moses Lyon	Sara Minden	Barnett Kesner	Pimlico, London	
20461	Kesner	Hannah	1824	Chelsea, London	Lyon Kesner	Isabella [Matilda, Elizbeth] David	Henry (Hyman) Aaronson (Aronson)	Chelsea, London	
23891	Kesner	Isaac	1791	?, Holland			Rebecca (?Abrahams)	Westminster, London	general dealer
21166	Kesner	Isabella	1840	Pimlico, London	Barnett Kesner	Hannah Lyon	William Collins	Pimlico, London	
21163	Kesner	Isabella [Matilda, Elizbeth]	1783	Amsterdam, Holland	Abraham David		Lyon Kesner	Chelsea, London	
23893	Kesner	Julia	1831	Chelsea, London	Isaac Kesner	Rebecca (?Abrahams)		Westminster, London	
21168	Kesner	Kate	1840	Pimlico, London	Barnett Kesner	Hannah Lyon		Pimlico, London	

ID	surname	given names	born	birthplace	father	mother	spouse 1	1851 residence	1851 occupation
21162	Kesner	Lyon	1784	Amsterdam, Holland	Barend Kesnich	Hannah Raphael	Isabella [Matilda, Elizbeth] David	Chelsea, London	collector - poor rate
21167	Kesner	Moses Morris	1842	Pimlico, London	Barnett Kesner	Hannah Lyon	Louisa (Leah) Smetham	Pimlico, London	
23892	Kesner	Rebecca	1789	?, Holland	(?Abraham)		Isaac Kesner	Westminster, London	
27488	Kesner	Solomon	1831	?, Holland				Aldgate, London	cigar maker
23243	Kessenger	Albert	1829	Middlesex, London				Chelsea, London	stenographer
6424	Kestenberg	Abraham	1808	Cracow, Poland			Phoebe Jacob	Liverpool	bill broker + jeweller
31041	Kestenberg	Hinda	1848	Plymouth, Devon	Abraham Kestenberg	Phoebe Jacob		Liverpool	
1410	Kestenberg	Joseph	1823	?, Poland				Plymouth, Devon	teacher of German
31042	Kestenberg	Lionel	1851	Liverpool	Abraham Kestenberg	Phoebe Jacob		Liverpool	
6423	Kestenberg	Phoebe	1824	Penzance, Cornwall	(?) Jacob	Sophia (?)	Abraham Kestenberg	Liverpool	
6426	Kestenberg	Rachel	1849	Plymouth, Devon	Abraham Kestenberg	Phoebe Jacob	Thomas Haining Reid	Liverpool	
6425	Kestenberg	Sarah	1847	Plymouth, Devon	Abraham Kestenberg	Phoebe Jacob		Liverpool	
20249	Keys (Israel)	Abraham	1836	Spitalfields, London	Henry (Asher) Keys (Israel)	Sarah de Simon Cohen	Sarah Nunez	Spitalfields, London	
29221	Keys (Israel)	Abraham	1851	Whitechapel, London	Benjamin Keys (Israel)	Rosa Levy		Whitechapel, London	
29215	Keys (Israel)	Benjamin	1808	Whitechapel, London	Abraham de Moseh Israel (Keys)	Keturah de Benjamin de Crasto	Rosa Levy	Whitechapel, London	general dealer
29220	Keys (Israel)	Catherine	1848	Whitechapel, London	Benjamin Keys (Israel)	Rosa Levy		Whitechapel, London	
29217	Keys (Israel)	Elias	1839	Whitechapel, London	Benjamin Keys (Israel)	Rosa Levy		Whitechapel, London	scholar
20245	Keys (Israel)	Henry (Asher)	1804	Middlesex, London	Abraham de Moseh Israel	Keturah de Benjamin de Isaac de Crasto	Sarah de Simon Cohen	Spitalfields, London	traveller
29219	Keys (Israel)	Isaac	1844	Whitechapel, London	Benjamin Keys (Israel)	Rosa Levy		Whitechapel, London	
20247	Keys (Israel)	Julia	1826	Manchester	Henry (Asher) Keys (Israel)	Sarah de Simon Cohen		Spitalfields, London	cook
20251	Keys (Israel)	Kate	1839	Spitalfields, London	Henry (Asher) Keys (Israel)	Sarah de Simon Cohen		Spitalfields, London	traveller
20252	Keys (Israel)	Lawrence (Eliezer)	1841	Spitalfields, London	Henry (Asher) Keys (Israel)	Sarah de Simon Cohen	Rosetta (Rosa) Rodrigues	Spitalfields, London	
20248	Keys (Israel)	Moses	1834	Spitalfields, London	Henry (Asher) Keys (Israel)	Sarah de Simon Cohen		Spitalfields, London	traveller
29218	Keys (Israel)	Moses	1841	Whitechapel, London	Benjamin Keys (Israel)	Rosa Levy		Whitechapel, London	scholar
20253	Keys (Israel)	Rebecca	1844	Spitalfields, London	Henry (Asher) Keys (Israel)	Sarah de Simon Cohen	Lazarus Mendoza	Spitalfields, London	
29216	Keys (Israel)	Rosa	1816	Whitechapel, London	(?)	Rachel Levy	Benjamin Keys (Israel)	Whitechapel, London	
20246	Keys (Israel)	Sarah	1802	?, Warwickshire	Simon Cohen		Henry (Asher) Keys (Israel)	Spitalfields, London	
6214	Keyser	Assur	1844	Aldgate, London	Moses Solomon Asher Keyser	Esther (?)	Isabel Samuel	Shoreditch, London	scholar at home
21091	Keyser	Augusta	1824	Bristol	Jacob Keyser	Harriet Jacobs		Bristol	professor of dancing
6217	Keyser	Esther	1818	Middlesex, London	(?)		Moses Solomon Asher Keyser	Shoreditch, London	
18821	Keyser	H---	1791	?, Holland	(?) Enthoven		(?) Keyser	Euston, London	
6216	Keyser	Hannah	1840	Shoreditch, London	Moses Solomon Asher Keyser	Esther (?)	George Samuel Yates	Finsbury, London	scholar at home
21089	Keyser	Harriet	1791	Bristol	Isaac Jacobs		Jacob Keyser	Bristol	fundholder
9811	Keyser	Leah	1839	Shoreditch, London	Moses Solomon Asher Keyser	Esther (?)	Alexander Mosely	Shoreditch, London	scholar at home
21090	Keyser	Miriam	1812	Bristol	Jacob Keyser	Harriet Jacobs		Bristol	
6215	Keyser	Moses Solomon Asher	1809	Middlesex, London	Assur Keyser	Leah (?)	Esther (?)	Shoreditch, London	house proprietor + fund holder
14879	Keyzer	?	1820	?			Augusta Green	Finsbury, London	diamond dealer
14881	Keyzer	Annie	1849	Hackney, London	(?) Keyzer	Augusta Green		Finsbury, London	
14878	Keyzer	Augusta	1825	Marylebone, London	(?) Green	Ann (?)	(?) Keyzer	Finsbury, London	wife of diamond dealer
11926	Keyzer	Esther	1807	?, Holland	(?)		(?) Keyzer	Whitechapel, London	nurse

ID	surname	given names	born	birthplace	father	mother	spouse 1	1851 residence	1851 occupation
21535	Kisch	Joseph	1807	Middlesex, London	Benjamin Kisch		(?)	Shoreditch, London	surgeon + Society of Apothecaries practising generally
12584	Kisch	Joseph	1846	?Norwich, Norfolk	Moses Kisch		Hannah de Pass	Norwich, Norfolk	
19084	Kisch	Joel Seymour	1847	Westminster, London	Simon Abraham Kisch	Flora Davis	Sarah (Tobie) Levy	Marylebone, London	
21540	Kisch	Herman Michael	1850	Middlesex, London	Joseph Kisch	Louisa Selig	Alice Elkin	Shoreditch, London	
21538	Kisch	Henry J	1846	Middlesex, London	Joseph Kisch	Louisa Selig	Helen Schlesinger	Shoreditch, London	
10010	Kisch	Henry	1809	Middlesex, London	Simon Kisch			Norwich, Norfolk	commercial traveller (shoes)
5875	Kisch	Hannah	1818	King's Lynn, Norfolk	Daniel de Aaron De Pass	Rachel de Meir Davis	Moses Kisch	Shoreditch, London	
23269	Kisch	Flora	1839	Aldgate, London	Joseph Kisch		(?)	Shoreditch, London	boarding school pupil
7720	Kisch	Flora	1824	Middlesex, London	(?) Davis		Simon Abraham Kisch	Marylebone, London	
19255	Kisch	Fleur	1851	Marylebone, London	Simon Abraham Kisch	Flora Davis		Marylebone, London	
21539	Kisch	Emma	1849	Shoreditch, London	Joseph Kisch	Louisa Selig		Shoreditch, London	
23863	Kisch	Elizabeth	1837	Piccadilly, London	(?) Kisch			Piccadilly, London	apprentice to dealer in regimentals
23268	Kisch	Eliza	1833	City, London	Joseph Kisch		(?)	Shoreditch, London	boarding school pupil
10007	Kisch	David Hy.	1848	Norwich, Norfolk	Moses Kisch	Hannah de Pass		Norwich, Norfolk	scholar
10004	Kisch	Daniel	1841	Wisbech, Cambridgeshire	Moses Kisch	Hannah de Pass	Rebecca Spier	Norwich, Norfolk	scholar
21537	Kisch	Benjamin	1843	Middlesex, London	Joseph Kisch	Louisa Selig		Shoreditch, London	scholar
10005	Kisch	Benjamin	1843	Wisbech, Cambridgeshire	Moses Kisch	Hannah de Pass		Norwich, Norfolk	scholar
23840	Kisch	Benjamin	1804	?, London	Simon Kisch		Julia (Yetta b. Solomon)	Soho, London	tailor
10009	Kisch	Annie	1831	Middlesex, London	Joseph Kisch		Israel Bloch	Norwich, Norfolk	companion
23862	Kisch	Amelia	1834	Piccadilly, London	(?) Kisch			Piccadilly, London	apprentice to dealer in regimentals
10008	Kisch	Alfred	1849	Norwich, Norfolk	Moses Kisch	Hannah de Pass		Norwich, Norfolk	
7778	Kisch	Albert	1845	City, London	Joseph Kisch	Louisa (?)	Annie Davidson	Shoreditch, London	scholar
19254	Kisch	Abraham	1849	Middlesex, London	Simon Abraham Kisch	Flora Davis		Marylebone, London	
14168	Kirstaff	Julius	1820	Berlin, Germany				Manchester	merchant
23063	Kirschfeld	Zelina	1850	Aldgate, London	Adolph Kirschfeld		Hannah (?)	Aldgate, London	
23062	Kirschfeld	Rosetta	1849	Aldgate, London	Adolph Kirschfeld		Hannah (?)	Aldgate, London	
23061	Kirschfeld	Kate	1847	Aldgate, London	Adolph Kirschfeld		Hannah (?)	Aldgate, London	
23060	Kirschfeld	Hannah	1814	Aldgate, London			Adolph Kirschfeld	Aldgate, London	
23059	Kirschfeld	Adolph	1805	Portsmouth, Hampshire			Hannah (?)	Aldgate, London	watchmaker + jeweller
15705	Kirch	Rebecca	1801	Covent Garden, London	(?) Kirch			Southwark, London	embroideress
30547	King	Barrett	1834	Bristol	Moses King		Ann (?)	Merthyr Tydfil, Wales	
12583	Keyzor [Bandau]	Abraham	1825	Norwich, Norfolk	Moses (Mosiac, Machul) Bendon (Bandau)	Alice Kyezor (Keyzor)	Jane Joseph	Norwich, Norfolk	optician
12582	Keyzor	Theresa (Treaza)	1849	Norwich, Norfolk	Michael Kyezor (Keyzor)	Fanny Jacobs	Alfred Bronkhorst	Norwich, Norfolk	
19317	Keyzor	Isaac	1848	Norwich, Norfolk	Michael Kyezor (Keyzor)	Fanny Jacobs	Bessie Edwards nee Andrews	Norwich, Norfolk	
12581	Keyzor	Isaac	1848	Norwich, Norfolk	Michael Kyezor (Keyzor)	Fanny Jacobs	Bessie Edwards nee Andrews	Norwich, Norfolk	
12580	Keyzor	Fanny	1821	Middlesex, London	Jacob Jacobs		Michael Keyzor	Norwich, Norfolk	
14880	Keyzer	Henry	1847	Islington, London	(?) Keyzer		Augusta Green	Finsbury, London	

ID	surname	given names	born	birthplace	father	mother	spouse 1	1851 residence	1851 occupation
23841	Kisch	Julia	1803	?, Hampshire	Solomon		Benjamin Kisch	Soho, London	
10003	Kisch	Julia	1837	King's Lynn, Norfolk	Moses Kisch	Hannah de Pass	Samuel Jacobs	Norwich, Norfolk	scholar
21536	Kisch	Louisa	1816	Middlesex, London	I--- Selig		Joseph Kisch	Shoreditch, London	
5876	Kisch	Moses Judah	1810	Middlesex, London	Simon Kisch		Hannah de Pass	Norwich, Norfolk	wholesale shoe manufacturer
10006	Kisch	Rachall	1845	Wisbech, Cambridgeshire	Moses Kisch	Hannah de Pass		Norwich, Norfolk	scholar
5873	Kisch	Rebecca Louise	1851	Norwich, Norfolk	Moses Kisch	Hannah de Pass	Ludwig Grunbaum	Norwich, Norfolk	
17909	Kisch	Selim	1832	Middlesex, London				Mayfair, London	shopman
5874	Kisch	Simeon	1838	King's Lynn, Norfolk	Moses Kisch	Hannah de Pass		Norwich, Norfolk	scholar
7519	Kisch	Simon Abraham	1823	Westminster, London			Flora Davis	Marylebone, London	clerical tailor + robe maker
14269	Kisel	Isaac	1829	?, Germany			Rebecca (?)	Manchester	shoe maker
14270	Kisel	Rebecca	1829	?, Germany	(?)		Isaac Kisel	Manchester	
14342	Kissel	George	1809	?, Germany			Julia (?)	Manchester	calico + general print merchant
16852	Kitch	Elijah Abraham	1833	Bridgewater, Somerset				Bath	shopman (grocer's shop)
17911	Kitz (Kisch?)	Ellen	1822	?, Devon			Louis Kitz (Kisch?)	Mayfair, London	
17912	Kitz (Kisch?)	Jane	1847	?, London	Louis Kitz (Kisch?)	Ellen (?)		Mayfair, London	
17910	Kitz (Kisch?)	Louis	1821	?, Germany			Ellen (?)	Mayfair, London	watchmaker + jeweller
17913	Kitz (Kisch?)	Mathilda	1850	?, London	Louis Kitz (Kisch?)	Ellen (?)		Mayfair, London	
18294	Kiva	Alexander	1826	?, Poland [?, Prussia]				Hull, Yorkshire	dealer in jewellery
18295	Kiva	Solomon	1828	?, Poland [?, Prussia]				Hull, Yorkshire	dealer in jewellery
28879	Kizar	?	1808	?	(?)		Lewis Kizar	Spitalfields, London	nurse
28881	Kizar	Dinah (Diana)	1832	?	Lewis Kizar	(?)	Eleazer Jacobs	Spitalfields, London	tailoress
28880	Kizar	Hannah	1829	?	Lewis Kizar	(?)		Spitalfields, London	tailoress
28882	Kizar	Morris	1837	?	Lewis Kizar	(?)		Spitalfields, London	slipper maker
15368	Kizer	Charles	1815	Miskolc, Hungary			Eliza (?)	Waterloo, London	furrier
15370	Kizer	Charles	1846	Clerkenwell, London	Charles Kizer	Eliza (?)		Waterloo, London	
15369	Kizer	Eliza	1815	Clerkenwell, London	(?)		Charles Kizer	Waterloo, London	
15371	Kizer	Guylai	1850	Waterloo, London	Charles Kizer	Eliza (?)		Waterloo, London	
13494	Klattshosky	Aron	1834	?, Poland				Manchester	cap maker
13493	Klattshosky	Jacob	1830	?, Poland				Manchester	cap maker
24506	Klein	Frederick	1823	?, Prussia, Germany [Preussen (Germany)]			Louisa (?)	Rotherhithe, London	master japanner empl 5
24508	Klein	Jacob	1827	?, Prussia, Germany [Preussen (Germany)]				Rotherhithe, London	foreman to master japanner
24507	Klein	Louisa	1830	Bermondsey, London	(?)		Frederick Klein	Rotherhithe, London	
24509	Klein	Philip	1833	?, Prussia, Germany [Preussen (Germany)]				Rotherhithe, London	workman (with master japanner?)
23708	Kleine	Moyse	1802	?, France			(?)	Liverpool	smallware dealer
23709	Kleine	Teresa	1844	Liverpool	Moyse Kleine	(?)		Liverpool	
21856	Klimcke	Benjamin	1839	?, London	Charles Klimcke	May (?)		Clerkenwell, London	school
21852	Klimcke	Charles	1803	?, London			May (?)	Clerkenwell, London	furrier
21854	Klimcke	Charles	1835	?, London	Charles Klimoiki	May (?)		Clerkenwell, London	apprentice
21857	Klimcke	Charlotte	1845	?, London	Charles Klimcke	May (?)		Clerkenwell, London	school

ID	surname	given names	born	birthplace	father	mother	spouse 1	1851 residence	1851 occupation
21853	Klimcke	May	1803	?, London	(?)		Charles Klimcke	Clerkenwell, London	
21855	Klimcke	Moses	1838	?, London	Charles Klimcke	May (?)		Clerkenwell, London	school
21101	Kling	Constance	1827	?, Belgium	(?)		Julius Kling	Manchester	
21102	Kling	Constantine	1848	Manchester	Julius Kling	Constance (?)		Manchester	
21103	Kling	Gustava	1841	Manchester	Julius Kling	Constance (?)		Manchester	
14351	Kling	Julius	1804	?, Germany			Constance (?)	Manchester	merchant
12503	Klingleston	Joseph	1829	?, Poland				Birmingham	slipper maker
28770	Klock	Abraham	1829	?, Holland	Tsvi HaCohen		Jane Braham	Spitalfields, London	cigar maker
25102	Knacksberg	Caroline	1823	Strand, London	(?)		Julius Knacksberg	Finsbury, London	
25104	Knacksberg	Irie	1847	City, London	Julius Knacksberg	Caroline (?)		Finsbury, London	
25103	Knacksberg	Joschi	1845	City, London	Julius Knacksberg	Caroline (?)		Finsbury, London	
25101	Knacksberg	Julius	1809	?, Germany			Caroline (?)	Finsbury, London	leather dealer + dresser
25106	Knacksberg	Morris	1850	City, London	Julius Knacksberg	Caroline (?)		Finsbury, London	
25105	Knacksberg	Samuel	1847	City, London	Julius Knacksberg	Caroline (?)		Finsbury, London	
20403	Koblinsky	Julius	1821	?, Poland [Frustar, Prussia]				Spitalfields, London	furrier chambermaster
18151	Kocha	Anna	1765	Amsterdam, Holland	(?)		(?) Kocha	Mile End, London	inmate of Portuguese Jews Hospital
22015	Kofski	Moss	1829	?, Poland [?, Prussia]				Whitechapel, London	porter
2481	Kohn	Jacob	1828	Hamburg, Germany				Hull, Yorkshire	journeyman baker
13973	Kohn	Joel A	1812	Brody, Ukraine [Brody Galzie, Russia]				Manchester	merchant
30948	Kohn	Julius	1817	Wurtemberg, Germany			(?)	Nottingham, Nottinghamshire	lace + general merchant
28987	Kohn	Moses	1806	Bydgoszcz, Poland [Chorzysk, Bromberg]			(?)	Whitechapel, London	tailor
27358	Kohner	Herman	1819	Budapest, Hungary [Pesth, Hungary]				Aldgate, London	tailor
7690	Kohnstamm	Morris	1821	?, Germany				Bloomsbury, London	professor of languages + literature
7795	Kohnstamm (Konstamm)	Heiman	1817	?, Germany			Teresina Friedmann	City, London	foreign commission agent
26943	Kolski	Harris	1834	?, Poland				Aldgate, London	tailor
18273	Kolski	Louis	1823	?, Poland [?, Russia Poland]				Ilminster, Somerset	travelling jeweller
18525	Koppel	Joseph	1835	?, Russia				Bloomsbury, London	unemployed clerk
28986	Koritowski	Moses	1825	Borki, Poland [Borike, Posen, Prussia]				Whitechapel, London	tailor
24391	Korminski	Marcus	1830	?, Poland				Soho, London	journeyman tailor
25178	Korn	Esther	1805	?, Hampshire			Philip Jacob Korn	Finsbury, London	
25177	Korn	Philip Jacob	1806	?, Poland [?, Prussia]			Esther Korn	Finsbury, London	furrier
29132	Koster	Isaac	1829	?, Poland [?, Prussia]			Sophia Levy	Whitechapel, London	tailor
29133	Koster	Sophia Levy	1825	?, Poland [?, Prussia]	(?) Levy		Isaac Koster	Whitechapel, London	tailor
23005	Kotoski	Marcus	1832	?, Poland [Sandberg, Prussia]				Finsbury, London	cap maker
25931	Kotzk	Jacob	1822	?, Poland [?, Prussia]			Sarah Lazarus nee (?)	Aldgate, London	tailor
25932	Kotzk	Sarah	1813	Mile End, London	(?)		(?) Lazarus	Aldgate, London	
4594	Kowalsky	Michael	1801	?, Poland				Birmingham	shoemaker

ID	surname	given names	born	birthplace	father	mother	spouse 1	1851 residence	1851 occupation
26430	Krackauer	Solomon	1817	?, Poland [?, Prussia]				Aldgate, London	general dealer
14875	Krauss	Antonia	1829	?, Germany	(?)		Julius Krauss	Finsbury, London	
14874	Krauss	Julius	1824	?, Germany			Antonia (?)	Finsbury, London	jeweller empl 3
14876	Krauss	Julius	1850	Middlesex, London	Julius Krauss	Antonia (?)		Finsbury, London	
30134	Kristeller	Samuel B	1818	?, Poland [?, Prussia]				Liverpool	commission agent
24387	Kritzman	Samuel	1831	Kolo, Poland				Soho, London	journeyman tailor
8712	Kroene	Abraham	1830	?, Denmark	Adolphus Kroene	Catherine (?)		Aldgate, London	tobacconist
8709	Kroene	Adolphus	1791	?, Czech Republic [?, Bohemia]			Catherine (?)	Aldgate, London	perfumer
8710	Kroene	Catherine	1803	?, Poland	(?)		Adolphus Kroene	Aldgate, London	
8713	Kroene	Henry	1832	?, London	Adolphus Kroene	Catherine (?)		Aldgate, London	tobacconist
8714	Kroene	Maurice	1837	?, London	Adolphus Kroene	Catherine (?)		Aldgate, London	tobacconist
8711	Kroene	Phoebe	1823	?, Poland	Adolphus Kroene	Catherine (?)		Aldgate, London	tobacconist
14877	Kronberg	Julius	1824	?, Poland [?, Prussia]				Finsbury, London	jeweller
23001	Krotoski	Benjamin	1822	?, Poland [Sandberg, Prussia]			Juliette Calisher	Finsbury, London	wholesale hat + cap manufacturer
23002	Krotoski	Juliette	1829	Birmingham	Nathan Jacob Calisher	Phoebe (?)	Benjamin Krotoski	Finsbury, London	
23003	Krotoski	Lewis	1850	Finsbury, London	Benjamin Krotoski	Juliette Calisher		Finsbury, London	
21724	Krueger	John	1827	?, Germany				Highbury, London	Madeira merchant
2482	Kruger	Jacob	1828	?, Poland				Hull, Yorkshire	journeyman tailor
17065	Kusel	Fanny	1828	Bortzenburg, Germany				Glasgow, Scotland	
13715	Kutner	?	1829	?, Poland				Bloomsbury, London	journeyman tinman
12705	Kuttner	Henry	1809	?, Poland				Coventry, Warwickshire	travelling hawker
4595	Kuttner	Henry	1821	?, Poland [?, Prussia]				Birmingham	
13766	Kutura	Ellen	1850	?, France	Samuel Kutura	Rachael (?)		Manchester	
13764	Kutura	Esther	1846	?, France	Samuel Kutura	Rachael (?)		Manchester	
13765	Kutura	Matthew	1846	?, London	Samuel Kutura	Rachael (?)		Manchester	
13763	Kutura	Rachael	1824	?, London	(?)		Samuel Kutura	Manchester	
13762	Kutura	Samuel	1816	Corfu, Greece			Rachael (?)	Manchester	confectioner
8064	Kyezor	Elizabeth	1784	Southwark, London	Isaac Joseph		Charles Ellis	Paddington, London	watchmaker's wife
6648	Kyezor	Henry Myers	1830	Doncaster. Yorkshire	Louis Kyezor	Sophia Flora (?)	Anne Burchett	Holborn, London	watchmaker
6644	Kyezor	Julia	1833	Marylebone, London	Benjamin Joseph	Amelia Harris	Louis (Lewis) Kyezor	Marylebone, London	
6645	Kyezor	Louis	1797	Cambridge	Isaac Kyezor (Keyzor)	Hannah Levy (Levi)	Sophia Flora Myers	Marylebone, London	watchmaker
6643	Kyezor	Louis (Lewis)	1833	Doncaster, Yorkshire	Louis Kyezor	Sophia Flora Myers	Julia Joseph	Marylebone, London	watchmaker
6646	Kyezor	Matilda	1838	St Pancras, London	Louis Kyezor	Sophia Flora Myers	Henry Heilbron	Marylebone, London	
19316	Kyezor (Keyzor)	Fanny	1821	?London	Jacob Jacobs	Hannah (?)	Michael Kyezor (Keyzor)	Norwich, Norfolk	
12579	Kyezor (Keyzor)	Michael	1813	Cambridge	Isaac Kyezor (Keyzor)	Hannah Levy (Levi)	Fanny Jacobs	Norwich, Norfolk	optician
19306	Kyezor (Keyzor, Keysor)	Abraham	1842	Euston, London	Elias Kyezor (Keyzor, Keysor)	Caroline Lewis		King's Cross, London	
19301	Kyezor (Keyzor, Keysor)	Caroline	1809	St Pancras, London	(?) Lewis		Elias Kyezor (Keyzor, Keysor)	King's Cross, London	
19300	Kyezor (Keyzor, Keysor)	Elias	1795	Cambridge	Isaac Kyezor	Hannah Levy (Levi)	Caroline Lewis	King's Cross, London	engraver
19305	Kyezor (Keyzor, Keysor)	Jessie	1839	Euston, London	Elias Kyezor (Keyzor, Keysor)	Caroline Lewis	George Alfred Hunt	King's Cross, London	

ID	surname	given names	born	birthplace	father	mother	spouse 1	1851 residence	1851 occupation
19304	Kyezor (Keyzor, Keysor)	Joseph	1837	St Pancras, London	Elias Kyezor (Keyzor, Keysor)	Caroline Lewis	Julia Donovan	King's Cross, London	
19302	Kyezor (Keyzor, Keysor)	Rebecca	1831	King's Cross, London	Elias Kyezor (Keyzor, Keysor)	Caroline Lewis	Naphtali Harris	King's Cross, London	
19307	Kyezor (Keyzor, Keysor)	Rosina	1845	Clerkenwell, London	Elias Kyezor (Keyzor, Keysor)	Caroline Lewis	William Greenshields	King's Cross, London	
19303	Kyezor (Keyzor, Keysor)	Sophia	1833	St Pancras, London	Elias Kyezor (Keyzor, Keysor)	Caroline Lewis	Henry Salmon	Bloomsbury, London	
10787	Kymanska	?J---	1803	?, Poland			Ellen (?)	Spitalfields, London	general dealer
10790	Kymanska	Alexander	1845	Spitalfields, London	?J--- Kymanska	Ellen (?)		Spitalfields, London	scholar
10788	Kymanska	Ellen	1826	?, Ireland	(?)		?J--- Kymanska	Spitalfields, London	
10789	Kymanska	John	1843	Spitalfields, London	?J--- Kymanska	Ellen (?)		Spitalfields, London	scholar
10791	Kymanska	Joseph	1849	Spitalfields, London	?J--- Kymanska	Ellen (?)		Spitalfields, London	
14922	Labelsea	Solomon Phillips	1837	Wellington, Shropshire				Bethnal Green, London	boarding school pupil
27375	Labowitzky	Daniel	1813	Warsaw, Poland	Yehuda Aryeh Leib		Elizabeth Isaacs	Aldgate, London	cigar dealer
31123	Labzberg	Hiresh	1816	Cracow, Poland				Ipswich, Suffolk	dealer in jewellery
16836	Lacki	Cecilia	1823	?, Poland [?, Prussia]				Brighton, Sussex	housekeeper
19211	Laffert	Herman	1807	?, Germany				Marylebone, London	tutor
28048	Lahmann	Henry	1806	Berlin, Germany [Berlin, Prussia]			Katharine (?)	Spitalfields, London	cabinet maker
28049	Lahmann	Katharine	1820	Berlin, Germany [Berlin, Prussia]	(?)		Henry Lahmann	Spitalfields, London	
28050	Lahmann	Solomon	1842	Berlin, Germany [Berlin, Prussia]	Henry Lahmann	Katharine (?)		Spitalfields, London	
30272	Lalisha	Barham	1834	?				Strand, London	clerk to shorthand writer
22026	Lamert	Abraham	1843	Strand, London	Joseph Lamert	Eliza Barnett		Piccadilly, London	
7596	Lamert	Elisabeth	1790	?Sandwich, Kent	Shmuel Zanvil Abrahams		Abraham (Yehuda) Lima Lamert	Canterbury, Kent	
7847	Lamert	Eliza	1809	?, London	Moshe Israel Barnett		Joseph Lamert	Piccadilly, London	
22025	Lamert	John	1842	?, London	Joseph Lamert	Eliza Barnett		Piccadilly, London	
7597	Lamert	Joseph	1813	Canterbury, Kent	Abraham (Yehuda) Lima	Elisabeth Abrahams	Eliza Barnett	Piccadilly, London	medical man not practising
18368	Lamert	Julia	1840	Manchester	Samuel Lamert	Sarah (?)	Eleazer Defries	Bloomsbury, London	scholar at home
22024	Lamert	Julia (Judith)	1841	?, London	Joseph Lamert	Eliza Barnett	Morris Joseph	Piccadilly, London	
18366	Lamert	Lema	1837	Birmingham	Samuel Lamert	Sarah (?)		Bloomsbury, London	scholar
18367	Lamert	Lewis	1838	Birmingham	Samuel Lamert	Sarah (?)		Bloomsbury, London	scholar at home
7598	Lamert	Samuel	1811	Southwark, London	Abraham (Yehuda) Lima	Elisabeth Abrahams	Sarah (?)	Bloomsbury, London	physician + apothecary
7796	Lamert	Sarah	1811	Bristol	(?)		Samuel Lamert	Bloomsbury, London	
9007	Land	Elizabeth	1799	Strand, London				Strand, London	bookfolder
27379	Landau	Morris	1811	Cracow, Poland [Crakau, Austria]	Abraham Landau		Frances Marks nee Levy	Aldgate, London	cigar manufacturer empl 8
25845	Landeck	Lewis	1829	?, Poland				Aldgate, London	glazier journeyman
25846	Landeck	Samuel	1829	?, Poland				Aldgate, London	boot maker
22297	Landeshut	Charlotte	1801	?, Poland [?, Prussia]	(?) Myer		Meyer Landeshut	Whitechapel, London	
22300	Landeshut	Ester	1840	Middlesex, London	Meyer Landeshut	Charlotte Myer		Whitechapel, London	

ID	surname	given names	born	birthplace	father	mother	spouse 1	1851 residence	1851 occupation
22298	Landeshut	Marian (Miriam)	1829	?, Poland [?, Prussia]	Meyer Landeshut	Charlotte Myer	Abraham Adolphus Cohen	Whitechapel, London	
22296	Landeshut	Meyer	1798	?, Poland [?, Prussia]			Charlotte Myer	Whitechapel, London	teacher of Hebrew language
22301	Landeshut	Solomon	1843	Middlesex, London	Meyer Landeshut	Charlotte Myer		Whitechapel, London	
22299	Landeshut	Woolf	1835	Middlesex, London	Meyer Landeshut	Charlotte Myer		Whitechapel, London	solicitor's clerk
5700	Langner	Julia	1841	Leeds, Yorkshire	Julius (Judah) David Langner	Lydia Kirch	Joel Jacob (Jacobs)	Southwark, London	boarding school pupil
15703	Langner	Julius (Judah) David	1811	?, Poland [?, Prussia]			Lydia Kirch	Southwark, London	cap + hat manufacturer
15704	Langner	Lydia	1805	Covent Garden, London	(?) Kirch		Julius (Judah) David Langner	Southwark, London	
5384	Langner	Simeon	1839	Leeds, Yorkshire	Julius (Judah) David Langner	Lydia Kirch	Esther De Sola	Southwark, London	scolar
14146	Langsdorff	?Hannah	1820	?Germany	(?)		Frederick Langsdorff	Manchester	
14148	Langsdorff	Alice	1844	Hull, Yorkshire	Frederick Langsdorff	(?Hannah) (?)		Manchester	
14150	Langsdorff	Eliza	1806	Chesterfield, Derbyshire	(?)		(?) Langsdorff	Manchester	
14147	Langsdorff	Emma	1842	Hull, Yorkshire	Frederick Langsdorff	(?Hannah) (?)		Manchester	
14145	Langsdorff	Frederick	1816	Hamburg, Germany			(?Hannah) (?)	Manchester	clerk in general merchant's office
14149	Langsdorff	Frederick William	1851	Manchester	Frederick Langsdorff	(?Hannah) (?)		Manchester	
13587	Lanker	Hirsh	1801	?, Poland				Manchester	teacher of Hebrew
9169	Lansbury	Flora	1847	?, Poland	(?) Lansbury	Rosaline (?)		Whitechapel, London	
9170	Lansbury	Louis	1849	Aldgate, London	(?) Lansbury	Rosaline (?)		Whitechapel, London	
9168	Lansbury	Rosaline	1826	?, Poland	(?)		(?) Lansburg	Whitechapel, London	
4596	Lansrus	Myer	1806	?, Poland				Birmingham	licensed hawker
28912	Laon	Marcus	1839	Spitalfields, London	Phineas Laon	Margaret (?)		Spitalfields, London	scholar
28909	Laon	Margaret	1806	Amsterdam, Holland	(?)		Phineas Laon	Spitalfields, London	
28910	Laon	Maria	1835	Amsterdam, Holland	Phineas Laon	Margaret (?)	Jacob Lesser	Spitalfields, London	tailoress
28908	Laon	Phineas	1805	?Chorin, Germany [Corinah, Prussia]			Margaret (?)	Spitalfields, London	master tailor empl 3
28911	Laon	Rosa	1837	Amsterdam, Holland	Phineas Laon	Margaret (?)	Phineas Nunez	Spitalfields, London	tailoress
3164	Lapidus (Lapuds)	Elias	1815	?	Isaac Lapuds		Eleanor Brace	?Ledbury, Herefordshire	
8476	Lara	Bessie	1827	Portsmouth, Hampshire	Benjamin Lara	Rachel Walters		Portsmouth, Hampshire	
22583	Lara	Daniel	1827	Whitechapel, London	Phineas J Nunes Lara	Sarah de Jacob Mendes Furtado		Whitechapel, London	
22582	Lara	Emma	1824	Greenwich, London	Phineas J Nunes Lara	Sarah de Jacob Mendes Furtado		Whitechapel, London	
8475	Lara	Mary	1821	Portsmouth, Hampshire	Benjamin Lara	Rachel Walters		Portsmouth, Hampshire	
22580	Lara	Phineas Joseph Nunes	1797	Stepney, London	Aaron Nunes Lara	Leah (?)	Sarah de Jacob Mendes Furtado	Whitechapel, London	house agent + undertaker
8474	Lara	Rachel	1790	Wapping, London	Thomas Walters		Benjamin Lara	Portsmouth, Hampshire	
22581	Lara	Sarah Nunes	1785	Islington, London	Jacob Mendes Furtado	Clara de Aron Nunes Lara	Phineas J Nunes Lara	Whitechapel, London	
5074	Laray	Jacob	1800	Portsmouth, Hampshire				Portsmouth, Hampshire	labourer
13170	Lardinski	Betsey	1822	?, Poland [?, Prussia]	(?)		Jacob Lardinski	Aldgate, London	
13169	Lardinski	Jacob	1818	?, Poland [?, Prussia]			Betsey (?)	Aldgate, London	tailor
13171	Lardinski	Rosey	1850	Aldgate, London	Jacob Lardinski	Betsey (?)		Aldgate, London	
8493	Larry	Eve	1794	?, London				Portsmouth, Hampshire	needlewoman

ID	surname	given names	born	birthplace	father	mother	spouse 1	1851 residence	1851 occupation
18038	Larvinskey	Joseph	1813	?, Poland [?, Prussia]				Dudley, Worcestershire	musician
2295	Lascar	Samuel	1827	?, Poland [?, Prussia]				Leeds, Yorkshire	hawker
14249	Lasker	Henri	1831	?, Poland [?, Prussia]				Manchester	traveller
17267	Laskly	Davis	1828	?, Poland	Kracher Laskly	(?)		Aldgate, London	cap maker
17266	Laskly	Kracher	1811	?, Poland				Aldgate, London	cap maker
17268	Laskly	Pauline	1838	?, Poland	Kracher Laskly	(?)		Aldgate, London	cap maker
20285	Lasser	Jacob E	1827	?, Russia				Spitalfields, London	licensed hawker
15693	Laurence (Lawrence)	John Zachariah	1829	Bath	Samuel Lewis Laurence		Miriam Solomon	Hampstead, London	undergraduate, London University
4599	Lavenstein	Esther	1850	Birmingham	Samuel Lavenstein	Sarah (?)		Birmingham	
4597	Lavenstein	Samuel	1825	?, Germany			Sarah (?)	Birmingham	master tailor
4598	Lavenstein	Sarah	1825	Birmingham			Samuel Lavenstein	Birmingham	
12033	Laventoff	Zeman	1829	?, Poland [?, Prussia]				Whitechapel, London	tailor
5811	Lavey	Charles Moss	1840	Spitalfields, London	Solomon Charles Lavey	Theresa Levy	Annette Israel	Spitalfields, London	scholar
21541	Lavey	Solomon Charles	1813	Whitechapel, London	Moses Levy		Theresa Levy	Spitalfields, London	musician
21542	Lavey	Theresa	1811	Plymouth, Devon	Hyam Levy		Solomon Charles Lavey	Spitalfields, London	
17751	Lavinburg	Betsy	1844	?, Poland [?, Prussia]	Goetz Lavinburg	Julia (?)		Aldgate, London	scholar
17744	Lavinburg	Goetz	1805	?, Poland [?, Prussia]			Julia (?)	Aldgate, London	tailor
17749	Lavinburg	Goetz	1841	City, London	Goetz Lavinburg	Julia (?)		Aldgate, London	scholar
17745	Lavinburg	Julia	1807	?, Poland [?, Prussia]	(?)		Goetz Lavinburg	Aldgate, London	tailor
17746	Lavinburg	Lewis	1831	?, Poland [Whenica, Prussia]	Goetz Lavinburg	Julia (?)	Harriet Solomon	Aldgate, London	tailor
17747	Lavinburg	Rachael	1835	?, Poland [?, Prussia]	Goetz Lavinburg	Julia (?)		Aldgate, London	tailor
17750	Lavinburg	Rosa	1842	City, London	Goetz Lavinburg	Julia (?)		Aldgate, London	scholar
17748	Lavinburg	Samuel	1837	?, Poland [?, Prussia]	Goetz Lavinburg	Julia (?)		Aldgate, London	tailor
16837	Lavy	Lazare	1821	?, France				Brighton, Sussex	teacher of French language + literature
27700	Lawrence	Abraham	1786	Great Yarmouth, Norfolk	Yishay Vatchmaker		Sophia Cohen	Spitalfields, London	general dealer
27703	Lawrence	Allice	1826	Whitechapel, London	Abraham Lawrence	Sophia Cohen		Spitalfields, London	tailoress
17002	Lawrence	Amelia	1827	Covent Garden, London	(?) Lawrence			Strand, London	
27704	Lawrence	Caroline	1831	Whitechapel, London	Abraham Lawrence	Sophia Cohen		Spitalfields, London	umbrella maker
14666	Lawrence	Cornelius	1828	Southwark, London	(?Joseph) Lawrence	Hannah (?Myers)		Hoxton, London	warehouseman
19527	Lawrence	Fanny	1843	Covent Garden, London	(?) Lawrence	Julia (?)		Covent Garden, London	
14664	Lawrence	Hannah	1796	Spitalfields, London	Joseph Myers		(?Joseph) Lawrence	Hoxton, London	dressmaker
27702	Lawrence	Hannah	1824	Whitechapel, London	Abraham Lawrence	Sophia Cohen		Spitalfields, London	umbrella maker
29948	Lawrence	Jane	1820	Portsmouth, Hampshire	(?)		Moses Lawrence	Whitechapel, London	dressmaker
19522	Lawrence	Jessie	1831	Covent Garden, London	(?) Lawrence	Julia (?)		Covent Garden, London	
19523	Lawrence	Joel	1832	Covent Garden, London	(?) Lawrence	Julia (?)		Covent Garden, London	warehouseman
19521	Lawrence	Julia	1805	Covent Garden, London	(?)		(?) Lawrence	Covent Garden, London	
2948	Lawrence	Julia	1828	City, London	Moses (Moss) Lawrence Lawrence	Rayner Andrade Da Costa	Benjamin Julius Jonas	Maida Vale, London	
16967	Lawrence	Julia	1837	?, France	(?) Lawrence			Hammersmith, London	boarding school pupil
19524	Lawrence	Kate	1837	Covent Garden, London	(?) Lawrence	Julia (?)		Covent Garden, London	
18372	Lawrence	Lawrence	1833	City, London	Moses (Moss) Lawrence Lawrence	Rayner Andrade Da Costa		Maida Vale, London	
19526	Lawrence	Michael	1841	Covent Garden, London	(?) Lawrence	Julia (?)		Covent Garden, London	scholar
29947	Lawrence	Moses	1821	Whitechapel, London			Jane (?)	Whitechapel, London	clothes dealer

ID	surname	given names	born	birthplace	father	mother	spouse 1	1851 residence	1851 occupation
18369	Lawrence	Moses (Moss) Lawrence	1794	City, London	Yaacov		Rayner Andrade Da Costa	Maida Vale, London	merchant
7572	Lawrence	Philip	1799	City, London	?Yaacov			Aldgate, London	merchant
18373	Lawrence	Rachel	1834	City, London	Moses (Moss) Lawrence Lawrence	Rayner Andrade Da Costa		Maida Vale, London	
18370	Lawrence	Rayner	1801	City, London	Benjamin Andrade Da Costa	Judith de Saul Rodrigues	Moses (Moss) Lawrence Lawrence	Maida Vale, London	
14665	Lawrence	Rebecca	1819	Finsbury, London	(?Joseph) Lawrence	Hannah (?Myers)		Hoxton, London	dressmaker
25626	Lawrence	Samuel	1791	?London	Myer Lawrence			Dublin, Ireland	
18374	Lawrence	Sarah L	1841	Aldgate, London	Moses (Moss) Lawrence Lawrence	Rayner Andrade Da Costa		Maida Vale, London	scholar
19525	Lawrence	Solomon	1838	Covent Garden, London	(?) Lawrence	Julia (?)		Covent Garden, London	scholar
27701	Lawrence	Sophia	1789	Aldgate, London	Nathan Cohen		Abraham Lawrence	Spitalfields, London	
14275	Lazard	Helena	1847	Salford, Lancashire	Isidor Lazard	Henrietta (?)		Manchester	
14274	Lazard	Henrietta	1814	?, Germany	(?)		Isidor Lazard	Manchester	
14273	Lazard	Isidor	1805	?, France			Henrietta (?)	Manchester	agent, Shiffs & Co - calico
14276	Lazard	Sophia	1849	Salford, Lancashire	Isidor Lazard	Henrietta (?)		Manchester	
14277	Lazard	Victoria	1850	Manchester	Isidor Lazard	Henrietta (?)		Manchester	
13474	Lazarus	?	1804	?, Russia	(?)		Joseph George Lazarus	Manchester	
13476	Lazarus	?	1841	Liverpool	Joseph George Lazarus	?		Manchester	
13475	Lazarus	?	1837	Liverpool	Joseph George Lazarus	?		Manchester	
4604	Lazarus	?Anny	1845	Birmingham	Elias Lazarus	Sophie (?)		Birmingham	
26074	Lazarus	Aaron	1804	Middlesex, London	Nathan Lazarus		Rosetta Moses	Aldgate, London	carver + gilder
24313	Lazarus	Abraham	1791	?, London				Covent Garden, London	wood dealer
2201	Lazarus	Abraham	1815	?, London				Oxford, Oxfordshire	jewellery dealer
22115	Lazarus	Abraham	1817	?, Poland			(?)	Whitechapel, London	tailor
8542	Lazarus	Abraham	1819	Middlesex, London	Lazarus (Eliezer) Lazarus		Esther Silva Green	Spitalfields, London	clothier
21053	Lazarus	Abraham	1843	?, London				Dover, Kent	boarding school pupil
26785	Lazarus	Abraham	1844	Middlesex, London	Lewis Lazarus	Ellen (?)		Aldgate, London	
3425	Lazarus	Abraham	1847	Bethnal Green, London	Solomon Lazarus	Elizabeth Minden	Julia Alexander	Bethnal Green, London	
10806	Lazarus	Abraham	1848	Spitalfields, London	Mark Lazarus	Sarah Hyams		Spitalfields, London	scholar
3430	Lazarus	Abraham	1851	Euston, London	Henry Lazarus	Fanny Collins	Gladys (?)	Euston, London	
3397	Lazarus	Abraham Lewis	1841	Newcastle Upon Tyne	Lewis (Eliezer Jacob) Lazarus	Kate (Kila) Lazarus Miers	Caroline Levy	Aldgate, London	
22509	Lazarus	Adelaide	1830	Whitechapel, London	Isaac Lazarus	Sarah (?)		Whitechapel, London	
26141	Lazarus	Adolphus	1843	Manchester	Henry Lazarus	Ann (?)		Aldgate, London	scholar
5763	Lazarus	Agnes	1847	City, London	Eleazer Lazarus	Rachael (?)	Benjamin Da Costa	Aldgate, London	
3271	Lazarus	Ailsey (Ailsie)	1846	Spitalfields, London	Lewis (Eliezer Jacob) Lazarus	Kate (Kila) Lazarus Miers	Frederick Samuel David Phillips	Aldgate, London	scholar
9343	Lazarus	Alexander	1827	Kingston, Jamaica, West Indies				Holloway, London	merchant of New York
19357	Lazarus	Alexander	1840	Marylebone, London	David Lazarus	Amelia (?)		Fitzrovia, London	scholar
19257	Lazarus	Alfred Henry	1848	Aldgate, London	Henry George Lazarus	Emma Lazarus		Aldgate, London	
18875	Lazarus	Alfred L	1847	Dublin, Ireland	Henry Lazarus	Fanny (Frances) Barnett		Dublin, Ireland	
18869	Lazarus	Alice	1850	Dublin, Ireland	Henry Lazarus	Fanny (Frances) Barnett	Godfrey Zimmerman Samuel	Dublin, Ireland	
22920	Lazarus	Alicia	1777	Portsmouth, Hampshire	(?)		(?) Lazarus	Wapping, London	clothes dealer

ID	surname	given names	born	birthplace	father	mother	spouse 1	1851 residence	1851 occupation
19351	Lazarus	Amelia	1806	?, London	(?)		David Lazarus	Fitzrovia, London	dealer in furniture
14969	Lazarus	Amelia	1839	Middlesex, London	(?) Lazarus			Bethnal Green, London	boarding school pupil
19359	Lazarus	Amelia	1850	Marylebone, London	David Lazarus	Amelia (?)		Fitzrovia, London	
26144	Lazarus	Amelia	1850	?Aldgate, London	Henry Lazarus	Ann (?)		Aldgate, London	
22800	Lazarus	Ann	1788	Aldgate, London	Hirsh Fiorda		Samuel Lazarus	Whitechapel, London	
29769	Lazarus	Ann	1811	Aldgate, London	(?)		Israel Lazarus	Spitalfields, London	
26138	Lazarus	Ann	1817	Birmingham	(?)		Henry Lazarus	Aldgate, London	
1052	Lazarus	Ann	1825	Exeter, Devon	David Lazarus	Betsy (?)	Abraham Levy	Exeter, Devon	
9249	Lazarus	Ann	1851	Spitalfields, London	Isaac Lazarus	Martha (?)		Spitalfields, London	
30566	Lazarus	Ann	1851	Aldgate, London	Henry Lazarus	Ann (?)		Aldgate, London	
20892	Lazarus	Anny	1849	Southwark, London	Emanuel Lazarus	Emily (?)		Holborn, London	
11572	Lazarus	Barnett	1801	Aldgate, London			Elizabeth (?)	Aldgate, London	general dealer
27907	Lazarus	Barnett	1815	?, Poland			(?)	Spitalfields, London	glazier
3787	Lazarus	Barnett	1846	Aldgate, London	Benjamin Lazarus	Rebecca (?)	Julia Lyons	Spitalfields, London	scholar
10172	Lazarus	Benjamin	1802	Portsmouth, Hampshire	Mordecai		Maria Isaacs	Shoreditch, London	hawker
3783	Lazarus	Benjamin	1808	Wapping, London	Meir HaLevi Lazarus		Rebecca Moses	Spitalfields, London	boot maker
24749	Lazarus	Benjamin	1815	City, London	Eliezer Lazarus		Catherine Solomons	Southwark, London	clerk
2647	Lazarus	Benjamin	1820	?, England			Rebecca (?)	Glasgow, Scotland	clothier manager
30368	Lazarus	Benjamin	1829	Leigh, Essex	Laurence Lazarus	Laurence Lazarus		Burslem, Staffordshire	tailor empl [---]
29306	Lazarus	Benjamin	1850	Whitechapel, London	Samuel Lazarus	Sophia Cohen		Whitechapel, London	
8131	Lazarus	Benjamin C--- P---	1846	Wakefield, Yorkshire	James Philip Tait Lazarus	Lucy (?)	Marian Solomon	Wakefield, Yorkshire	scholar at home
23413	Lazarus	Betsey	1843	Aldgate, London	Eleazer Lazarus	Rachael (?)		Aldgate, London	
9489	Lazarus	Betsey (Fesco)	1830	Spitalfields, London	Abraham Lazarus	Mary Solomon Wilks	Lemuel Asher Levyno	Aldgate, London	
3511	Lazarus	Caroline	1823	Soho, London	Solomon Isaacs		Joseph Lazarus	Camden Town, London	
19029	Lazarus	Caroline	1824	Exeter, Devon	Morris Davis	Elizabeth (?)	Joseph Lazarus	Whitechapel, London	
19353	Lazarus	Caroline	1831	Marylebone, London	David Lazarus	Amelia (?)		Fitzrovia, London	dress maker
951	Lazarus	Caroline	1832	Exeter, Devon				Exeter, Devon	
24752	Lazarus	Caroline	1843	Whitechapel, London	Benjamin Lazarus	Catherine Solomons		Southwark, London	
10786	Lazarus	Catherine	1801	Aldgate, London	(?) Lazarus			Spitalfields, London	governess
19935	Lazarus	Catherine	1809	Aldgate, London	David Davis	Elizabeth Lazarus	Edward Lazarus	Whitechapel, London	merchant
24750	Lazarus	Catherine	1811	Spitalfields, London	Simon Solomons		Benjamin Lazarus	Southwark, London	
22156	Lazarus	Catherine	1826	Wapping, London	Isaac Lazarus	Hannah Zadocks		Whitechapel, London	parasol maker
13588	Lazarus	Catherine	1827	?, Poland [?, Prussia]				Manchester	jewellery traveller
29824	Lazarus	Catherine	1827	Whitechapel, London	Philip Lazarus	Amelia Barnes		Whitechapel, London	fur worker
5421	Lazarus	Catherine	1830	Lincoln, Lincolnshire	Jonas Lazarus	Rosceia Nathan	Isaac Levi	Wolverhampton, Staffordshire	pawnbroker's assistant
26811	Lazarus	Catherine	1848	Aldgate, London	Joshua Lazarus	Rachel (?)		Aldgate, London	
3427	Lazarus	Catherine	1851	Bethnal Green, London	Solomon Lazarus	Elizabeth Minden		Bethnal Green, London	
3395	Lazarus	Catherine (Kila)	1820	Spitalfields, London	Joseph Lazarus	Ailsie (Elze, Ailce) Cantor	Lewis (Eliezer Jacob) Lazarus	Aldgate, London	
2063	Lazarus	Catherine (Kitty)	1828	Aldgate, London	Lewis Lazarus	Jane Abraham		Aldgate, London	
29996	Lazarus	Cecilia	1831	Poznan, Poland [Posen, Germany]	(?) Lazarus			Whitechapel, London	tailoress
26809	Lazarus	Charles	1844	Aldgate, London	Joshua Lazarus	Rachel (?)		Aldgate, London	scholar
3468	Lazarus	Charles Henry	1847	Aldgate, London	Henry George Lazarus	Emma Lazarus		Aldgate, London	

ID	surname	given names	born	birthplace	father	mother	spouse 1	1851 residence	1851 occupation
10650	Lazarus	Charlotte	1766	?	(?)		(?) Lazarus	Spitalfields, London	china hawker
10540	Lazarus	Clara	1801	?, London	(?) Raphael		Lewis Lazarus	Piccadilly, London	
9711	Lazarus	Clara	1832	Aldgate, London	John Lazarus	Sarah Solomons		Covent Garden, London	domestic
21955	Lazarus	Coleman	1831	Leigh, Essex	Laurence Lazarus	Catharine Phillips		Swansea, Wales	jeweller + silversmith apprentice
1051	Lazarus	David	1793	Exeter, Devon			Betsy (?)	Exeter, Devon	quill mfr
19350	Lazarus	David	1796	?, Poland			Amelia (?)	Fitzrovia, London	dealer in furniture
4204	Lazarus	David	1813	Spitalfields, London	Tsevi Hirsh	(Elizabeth Israel?)	Rachel Solomon	Aldgate, London	clothes salesman
1058	Lazarus	David	1820	Exeter, Devon				Exeter, Devon	watch dealer
14584	Lazarus	David	1825	Shoreditch, London	Isaac Lazarus	Sarah (?)		Hoxton, London	
29384	Lazarus	David	1830	?, Sri Lanka [?, Ceylon]				Wapping, London	sailor
2296	Lazarus	David	1832	?, Poland				Leeds, Yorkshire	hawker
19942	Lazarus	David	1832	?, London	Edward Lazarus	Catherine Davis		Whitechapel, London	clerk
23411	Lazarus	David	1835	Aldgate, London	Eleazer Lazarus	Rachael (?)		Aldgate, London	
23571	Lazarus	David	1837	Hayle, Cornwall	Isaac Lazarus	Rachel (?)		Liverpool	scholar
18251	Lazarus	Deborah	1809	Hull, Yorkshire	Israel Jacobs	Sarah Barnett	I--- L--- Lazarus	Hull, Yorkshire	
10803	Lazarus	Deborah	1842	Spitalfields, London	Mark Lazarus	Sarah Hyams	Joseph Asher	Spitalfields, London	
15218	Lazarus	Diana	1832	?, London	Lewis Lazarus	Lydia (?)		Shoreditch, London	flower maker
20122	Lazarus	Dinah	1815	Middlesex, London	(?) Solomon		Nathaniel Lazarus	Canterbury, Kent	
22801	Lazarus	Dinah	1816	Stepney, London	Samuel Lazarus	Ann Joseph		Whitechapel, London	dressmaker + tobacconist
8138	Lazarus	Dinah	1833	Middlesex, London	(?) Lazarus			Wakefield, Yorkshire	
18802	Lazarus	Edward	1840	Middlesex, London	Samuel Mordecai Lazarus	Nancy (?)		Whitechapel, London	scholar
1068	Lazarus	Eleazar	1848	Exeter, Devon	Moses Lazarus	Rebecca Schultz	Lucy D (?)	Exeter, Devon	scholar
23408	Lazarus	Eleazer	1807	?, London	Michael Lazarus		Rachael (?)	Aldgate, London	clothes salesman
2056	Lazarus	Eleazer	1823	Aldgate, London	Lewis Lazarus	Jane Abraham	Sarah Jacobs	Aldgate, London	lead smelter
30567	Lazarus	Eleazer	1851	Whitechapel, London	Samuel Lazarus	Sophia Cohen		Whitechapel, London	
4601	Lazarus	Elias	1801	?, Poland			Sophie (?)	Birmingham	pawnbroker
948	Lazarus	Eliza	1815	Falmouth, Cornwall	Levy Jacobs		Isaac Eleazer Lazarus	Exeter, Devon	
19943	Lazarus	Eliza	1834	?, London	Edward Lazarus	Catherine Davis	Abraham Levy	Whitechapel, London	
22931	Lazarus	Eliza	1841	Wapping, London	Harris Lazarus	Mary Yozel		Wapping, London	
3411	Lazarus	Eliza (Elizabeth)	1826	Spitalfields, London	Emanuel Lazarus	Sophia Simmons	Simon Hamburger	Spitalfields, London	dress maker
25524	Lazarus	Eliza Matilda	1851	Dublin, Ireland	Henry Lazarus	Fanny (Frances) Barnett		Dublin, Ireland	
28134	Lazarus	Elizabeth	1781	Middlesex, London	(?)		(?) Lazarus	Spitalfields, London	general dealer
11573	Lazarus	Elizabeth	1806	Aldgate, London	(?)		Barnett Lazarus	Aldgate, London	general dealer
3422	Lazarus	Elizabeth	1823	Whitechapel, London	Emanuel (Menachem) Minden	Sarah Davis	Solomon Lazarus	Bethnal Green, London	
26779	Lazarus	Elizabeth	1829	Middlesex, London	Lewis Lazarus	Ellen (?)		Aldgate, London	
15217	Lazarus	Elizabeth	1830	?, London	Lewis Lazarus	Lydia (?)		Shoreditch, London	greengrocer's assistant
19319	Lazarus	Elizabeth	1831	Middlesex, London	Barnett Lazarus	Elizabeth (?)	Solomon Joel	Aldgate, London	
6135	Lazarus	Elizabeth	1834	Stepney, London			(?) Haytor	Mile End, London	
29771	Lazarus	Elizabeth	1839	Whitechapel, London	Israel Lazarus	Ann (?)		Spitalfields, London	scholar
18647	Lazarus	Elizabeth	1840	Middlesex, London	David Lazarus	Rachel Solomon		Aldgate, London	
19358	Lazarus	Elizabeth	1844	Marylebone, London	David Lazarus	Amelia (?)		Fitzrovia, London	scholar
2067	Lazarus	Elizabeth	1845	Middlesex, London	Henry Lazarus	Isabella Lyon		Spitalfields, London	
24015	Lazarus	Elizabeth	1849	Marylebone, London	Moses Lazarus	Louisa Samuel		Marylebone, London	
2062	Lazarus	Elizabeth (Betsy)	1816	Aldgate, London	Lewis Lazarus	Jane Abraham		Aldgate, London	

ID	surname	given names	born	birthplace	father	mother	spouse 1	1851 residence	1851 occupation
19748	Lazarus	Elizabeth (Betsy)	1834	Spitalfields, London	Jacob (John) Lazarus	Sarah (?)		Spitalfields, London	cap maker
3463	Lazarus	Elizabeth (Eliza)	1792	Birmingham	Moses Aaron	Friandla (?)	Lewis Henry Lazarus	Aldgate, London	former pencil maker
3467	Lazarus	Elizabeth (Lizzie) Julia	1845	Aldgate, London	Henry George Lazarus	Emma Lazarus	Ludolph Lowenstein	Aldgate, London	
30960	Lazarus	Ellen	1809	Sheffield, Yorkshire	(?)		Nathan Lazarus	Sheffield, Yorkshire	
26778	Lazarus	Ellen	1813	Middlesex, London	(?)		Lewis Lazarus	Aldgate, London	
6937	Lazarus	Emanuel	1804	Whitechapel, London			Sarah (?)	Spitalfields, London	watchmaker (finisher)
20890	Lazarus	Emanuel	1827	Hamburg, Germany			Emily (?)	Holborn, London	cap maker
3426	Lazarus	Emanuel	1849	Bethnal Green, London	Solomon Lazarus	Elizabeth Minden		Bethnal Green, London	
19283	Lazarus	Emanuel Lewis	1850	?, London	Lewis Emanuel (Eliezer) Lazarus	Sophia Isaacs	Rachel Barnett	Aldgate, London	
20891	Lazarus	Emily	1826	Aldgate, London	(?)		Emanuel Lazarus	Holborn, London	
18252	Lazarus	Emily	1839	Scarborough, Yorkshire	I--- L--- Lazarus	Deborah Jacobs		Hull, Yorkshire	scholar at home
3466	Lazarus	Emma	1820	Middlesex, London	Harris Lazarus	?	Henry George Lazarus	Aldgate, London	
225	Lazarus	Emma	1832	Whitechapel, London	Asher (Lewis) Halevy Lazarus			Whitechapel, London	parasol maker
14588	Lazarus	Emma	1834	Shoreditch, London	Isaac Lazarus	Sarah (?)		Hoxton, London	
26434	Lazarus	Ephraim	1810	?, Poland			Shine (?)	Aldgate, London	tailor
5418	Lazarus	Esther	1825	Hull, Yorkshire	Jonas Lazarus	Rosceia Nathan	Jacob Moses	Lincoln, Lincolnshire	
11136	Lazarus	Esther	1827	Aldgate, London	Isaac Harris	Elizabeth (?)	Simon Lazarus	Aldgate, London	carpet bag maker
1053	Lazarus	Esther	1831	Exeter, Devon	David Lazarus	Betsy (?)	Maures Dyte	Exeter, Devon	
22158	Lazarus	Esther	1836	Whitechapel, London	Isaac Lazarus	Hannah Zadocks		Whitechapel, London	parasol maker
26140	Lazarus	Esther	1841	Manchester	Henry Lazarus	Ann (?)		Aldgate, London	scholar
29774	Lazarus	Esther	1845	Whitechapel, London	Israel Lazarus	Ann (?)		Spitalfields, London	scholar
8543	Lazarus	Esther Silva	1823	Middlesex, London	Aaron Green	Rose Myers	Abraham Lazarus	Spitalfields, London	
24650	Lazarus	Fanny	1804	Bristol	(?)		Isaac Lazarus	Waterloo, London	
16168	Lazarus	Fanny	1823	St Pancras, London	Eliezer Lezer	(?Eliza Aaron)		Fitzrovia, London	
3429	Lazarus	Fanny	1826	Westminster, London	Wolf Collins	?	Henry Lazarus	Euston, London	
18988	Lazarus	Fanny	1831	?, London	Moses Lazarus	Clara Joseph		Aldgate, London	
14587	Lazarus	Fanny	1832	Shoreditch, London	Isaac Lazarus	Sarah (?)		Hoxton, London	
1221	Lazarus	Fanny	1834	Plymouth, Devon	Lippa (Lyon) Lazarus	Matilda (Lilli) Lyon	Nathan Lazarus	Plymouth, Devon	dressmaker
4168	Lazarus	Fanny	1834	Exeter, Devon				Exeter, Devon	
10170	Lazarus	Fanny	1845	Bath	Benjamin Lazarus	Maria Isaacs		Shoreditch, London	
10807	Lazarus	Fanny	1850	Spitalfields, London	Mark Lazarus	Sarah Hyams	Solomon Levy	Spitalfields, London	
18870	Lazarus	Fanny (Frances)	1820	?	(?Barnard) Barnett		Henry Lazarus	Dublin, Ireland	
16156	Lazarus	Fanny (Frances)	1849	Whitechapel, London	Lewis Lazarus	Fanny (Frances, Phoebe) Solomon		Whitechapel, London	
16155	Lazarus	Fanny (Frances, Phoebe)	1828	City, London	David Solomon		Lewis Lazarus	Whitechapel, London	shop assistant
28135	Lazarus	Frances	1819	Middlesex, London	(?) Lazarus	Elizabeth		Spitalfields, London	tailoress
24751	Lazarus	Frances	1837	Whitechapel, London	Benjamin Lazarus	Catherine Solomons		Southwark, London	
18803	Lazarus	Frances	1842	Middlesex, London	Samuel Mordecai Lazarus	Nancy (?)		Whitechapel, London	scholar
1222	Lazarus	Frank	1838	Plymouth, Devon	Lippa (Lyon) Lazarus	Matilda (Lilli) Lyon	Nettie Ballerstein	Plymouth, Devon	merchant apprentice
2483	Lazarus	Frederick	1826	?, Germany				Hull, Yorkshire	painter
6023	Lazarus	Frederick Henry (Walter)	1850	Middlesex, London	Henry George Lazarus	Emma Lazarus		Aldgate, London	
6133	Lazarus	Gabriel	1811	Whitechapel, London	Meir HaLevi Lazarus		Sophia Isaacs	Mile End, London	foreman at a quill factory

ID	surname	given names	born	birthplace	father	mother	spouse 1	1851 residence	1851 occupation
14884	Lazarus	Godfrey	1801	Bristol			Julia (?)	Islington, London	watch manufacturer
14887	Lazarus	Godfrey	1835	?abroad	Godfrey Lazarus	Julia (?)		Islington, London	law stationer
22154	Lazarus	Hannah	1795	Whitechapel, London	Nathaniel Zadocks		Isaac Lazarus	Whitechapel, London	
22075	Lazarus	Hannah	1821	Mile End, London	David Solomon Rodrigues	Sarah (?)	Lewis Lazarus	Whitechapel, London	
28106	Lazarus	Hannah	1823	?, Germany	(?) Lazarus			Spitalfields, London	needlewoman
19749	Lazarus	Hannah	1829	Whitechapel, London	Jacob (John) Lazarus	Sarah (?)		Spitalfields, London	
9523	Lazarus	Hannah	1832	Aldgate, London	Joseph Lazarus	Leah (?)	Joseph Mendoza	Spitalfields, London	tailoress
11331	Lazarus	Hannah	1832	Mile End, London	(?) Lazarus			Aldgate, London	laundress
18800	Lazarus	Hannah	1834	Middlesex, London	Samuel Mordecai Lazarus	Nancy (?)	(?) Lawrence	Whitechapel, London	
22793	Lazarus	Hannah	1848	Whitechapel, London	Lewis Lazarus	Rachael (?)		Whitechapel, London	
2069	Lazarus	Hannah	1849	Middlesex, London	Henry Lazarus	Isabella Lyon	Henry (Aaron) Barnett	Aldgate, London	
10169	Lazarus	Hannah (Annie)	1838	Bath	Benjamin Lazarus	Maria Isaacs	Goulden Oliver	Shoreditch, London	
23570	Lazarus	Harriet	1835	Hayle, Cornwall	Isaac Lazarus	Rachel (?)		Liverpool	
22928	Lazarus	Harris	1793	?, Germany	Eliezer Ezra		Mary Jacobs nee Yozel	Wapping, London	outfitter
14224	Lazarus	Harry M	1821	?, Germany				Manchester	merchant
14886	Lazarus	Henrietta	1832	?abroad	Godfrey Lazarus	Julia (?)		Islington, London	
18871	Lazarus	Henry	1808	Portsmouth, Hampshire	Lewis Lazarus	Elizabeth Bat Isaac of Portsmouth	Fanny (Frances) Barnett	Dublin, Ireland	goldsmith + silversmith
26137	Lazarus	Henry	1809	?, London	Meir HaLevi		Ann (?)	Aldgate, London	quill pen maker
3428	Lazarus	Henry	1825	Spitalfields, London	Abraham Lazarus	Mary Solomon Wilks	Fanny Collins	Euston, London	furniture broker
14585	Lazarus	Henry	1827	Shoreditch, London	Isaac Lazarus	Sarah (?)		Hoxton, London	
20578	Lazarus	Henry	1831	?				Spitalfields, London	general dealer
14926	Lazarus	Henry	1839	Whitechapel, London				Bethnal Green, London	boarding school pupil
1055	Lazarus	Henry	1846	Exeter, Devon	David Lazarus	Betsy (?)		Exeter, Devon	
29305	Lazarus	Henry	1847	Whitechapel, London	Samuel Lazarus	Sophia Cohen		Whitechapel, London	
2059	Lazarus	Henry (Aaron)	1818	?, London	Lewis Lazarus	Jane Abraham	Isabella Lyon	Spitalfields, London	metal refiner
3465	Lazarus	Henry George	1815	Aldgate, London	Lewis Henry Lazarus	Elizabeth (Eliza) Aaron	Emma Lazarus	Aldgate, London	watch manufacturer
25933	Lazarus	Henry S	1829	Clerkenwell, London	(?) Lazarus	Sarah (?)		Aldgate, London	plate worker
13714	Lazarus	Herman	1829	Hamburg, Germany				Bloomsbury, London	general dealer
806	Lazarus	Hester (Esther)	1849	Uxbridge, Middlesex	Lawrence (Lazarus, Eliezer) Lazarus	Sarah Levy	Edward Lawrence Levy	Uxbridge, Middlesex	scholar
11575	Lazarus	Hyman	1839	Middlesex, London	Barnett Lazarus	Elizabeth (?)		Aldgate, London	
14582	Lazarus	Isaac	1787	City, London			Sarah (?)	Hoxton, London	money broker
22504	Lazarus	Isaac	1793	Whitechapel, London			Sarah (?)	Whitechapel, London	watch finisher
24649	Lazarus	Isaac	1794	Bristol	Eleazer		Fanny (?)	Waterloo, London	watchmaker
5417	Lazarus	Isaac	1802	?, Poland			Rachel (?)	Liverpool	dealer in watches &c
24888	Lazarus	Isaac	1816	Whitechapel, London			Sarah (?)	Southwark, London	clerk to solicitor
9247	Lazarus	Isaac	1819	Middlesex, London			Martha (?)	Spitalfields, London	dealer
22508	Lazarus	Isaac	1828	Whitechapel, London	Isaac Lazarus	Sarah (?)		Whitechapel, London	
19356	Lazarus	Isaac	1838	Marylebone, London	David Lazarus	Amelia (?)		Fitzrovia, London	scholar
30961	Lazarus	Isaac	1841	Sheffield, Yorkshire	Nathan Lazarus	Ellen (?)		Sheffield, Yorkshire	?tack grinder
10804	Lazarus	Isaac	1844	Spitalfields, London	Mark Lazarus	Sarah Hyams		Spitalfields, London	scholar
29773	Lazarus	Isaac	1844	Whitechapel, London	Israel Lazarus	Ann (?)		Spitalfields, London	scholar
947	Lazarus	Isaac Eleazer	1817	Exeter, Devon	Eleazer Lazarus	Julia Solomon	Eliza Jacobs	Exeter, Devon	
2065	Lazarus	Isabella	1822	Bedford, Bedfordshire	Joseph Lyon		Henry Lazarus	Spitalfields, London	dress maker

ID	surname	given names	born	birthplace	father	mother	spouse 1	1851 residence	1851 occupation
11137	Lazarus	Isaiah (Isaac)	1851	Aldgate, London	Simon Lazarus	Esther Harris		Aldgate, London	
17956	Lazarus	Isaiah (Josiah)	1831	City, London	Moses Lazarus		Esther Capua	Aldgate, London	tea dealer
29768	Lazarus	Israel	1807	Whitechapel, London	Yitzhak		Ann (?)	Spitalfields, London	general dealer
19946	Lazarus	Israel	1827	?, London				Whitechapel, London	packing case maker
9529	Lazarus	Israel	1841	Spitalfields, London	Joseph Lazarus	Leah (?)		Spitalfields, London	
10729	Lazarus	Jacob	1819	?, Holland			Sarah (?Marks)	Spitalfields, London	general dealer
29993	Lazarus	Jacob	1828	Poznan, Poland [Posen, Germany]			Racca (?)	Whitechapel, London	tailor
19944	Lazarus	Jacob	1835	?, London	Edward Lazarus	Catherine Davis		Whitechapel, London	apprentice
26782	Lazarus	Jacob	1839	Middlesex, London	Lewis Lazarus	Ellen (?)		Aldgate, London	
3414	Lazarus	Jacob (Jack)	1828	Spitalfields, London	Emanuel Lazarus	Sophia Simmons	Elizabeth De Frece	Spitalfields, London	
19746	Lazarus	Jacob (John)	1796	Aldgate, London			Sarah (?)	Spitalfields, London	general dealer
22510	Lazarus	Jacob (John)	1835	Whitechapel, London	Isaac Lazarus	Sarah (?)		Whitechapel, London	
8129	Lazarus	James Philip Tait	1816	Friesland, Holland	Eleazar		Lucy (?)	Wakefield, Yorkshire	cloth merchant
3764	Lazarus	Jane	1786	Spitalfields, London			(?) Lazarus	Spitalfields, London	dealer
22930	Lazarus	Jane	1823	Wapping, London	Harris Lazarus	Mary Yozel		Wapping, London	
805	Lazarus	Jane	1841	Whitechapel, London	Lawrence (Lazarus, Eliezer) Lazarus	Sarah Levy		Uxbridge, Middlesex	
26077	Lazarus	Jane	1844	Whitechapel, London	Aaron Lazarus	Maria Israel		Aldgate, London	
2068	Lazarus	Jane	1847	Middlesex, London	Henry Lazarus	Isabella Lyon	Eleazer Staal	Spitalfields, London	
3788	Lazarus	Jane	1849	Aldgate, London	Benjamin Lazarus	Rebecca (?)	Abraham Litoun	Spitalfields, London	scholar
18806	Lazarus	Jane	1850	Middlesex, London	Samuel Mordecai Lazarus	Nancy (?)		Whitechapel, London	
2058	Lazarus	Jane (Yetla)	1786	Aldgate, London	(?) Abraham		Lewis Lazarus	Aldgate, London	
30088	Lazarus	Jessie	1828	Whitechapel, London	Isaac Lazarus	Sarah (?)		Whitechapel, London	
9709	Lazarus	John	1804	Aldgate, London			Sarah Solomons	Covent Garden, London	veal butcher
18989	Lazarus	John	1834	?, London	Moses Lazarus	Clara Joseph	Ellen Solomon	Aldgate, London	grocer
14927	Lazarus	John	1840	Whitechapel, London				Bethnal Green, London	boarding school pupil
163	Lazarus	Jonas	1770	?, Poland	Mendele		Rosceia Nathan	Lincoln, Lincolnshire	broker
9524	Lazarus	Joseph	1796	?, Holland	(?Eliezer) Moses	Maria (?)	?	Spitalfields, London	clothes dealer
10785	Lazarus	Joseph	1797	Aldgate, London				Spitalfields, London	general dealer
7573	Lazarus	Joseph	1813	Middlesex, London	Eleazer		Caroline Davis	Whitechapel, London	wholesale rag merchant
3510	Lazarus	Joseph	1822	Middlesex, London	Abraham Lazarus	Mary Solomon Wilks	Caroline Isaacs	Camden Town, London	dealer in horsehair, feathers + wool
6407	Lazarus	Joseph	1825	Spitalfields, London	Moses Lazarus		Rachel Abrahams	Spitalfields, London	butcher
22507	Lazarus	Joseph	1827	Whitechapel, London	Isaac Lazarus	Sarah (?)		Whitechapel, London	
19352	Lazarus	Joseph	1829	Marylebone, London	David Lazarus	Amelia (?)		Fitzrovia, London	
5787	Lazarus	Joseph	1830	Wapping, London	Isaac Lazarus	Hannah Zadocks		Whitechapel, London	cigar maker
26436	Lazarus	Joseph	1834	?, Poland	Ephraim Lazarus	Shine (?)		Aldgate, London	tailor
25116	Lazarus	Joseph	1835	Whitechapel, London				Finsbury, London	biscuit baker
26780	Lazarus	Joseph	1837	Middlesex, London	Lewis Lazarus	Ellen (?)		Aldgate, London	
1066	Lazarus	Joseph	1843	Exeter, Devon	Moses Lazarus	Rebecca Schultz		Exeter, Devon	scholar
14925	Lazarus	Joseph Eleazer	1842	Islington, London				Bethnal Green, London	boarding school pupil
13473	Lazarus	Joseph George	1800	?, Russia			(?)	Manchester	Minister to Jews
2070	Lazarus	Joseph Lyon	1851	Aldgate, London	Henry Lazarus	Isabella Lyon	Jane Levy	Aldgate, London	
26805	Lazarus	Joshua	1814	Finsbury, London	Raphael Lazarus		Rachel (?)	Aldgate, London	clothier

ID	surname	given names	born	birthplace	father	mother	spouse 1	1851 residence	1851 occupation
26783	Lazarus	Joshua	1840	Middlesex, London	Lewis Lazarus	Ellen (?)		Aldgate, London	
9714	Lazarus	Judah	1838	Aldgate, London	John Lazarus	Sarah Solomons		St Giles, London	out scholar
14885	Lazarus	Julia	1805	Bristol			Godfrey Lazarus	Islington, London	dress maker
25023	Lazarus	Julia	1817	?, London	(?) Lazarus			Finsbury, London	housekeeper
24651	Lazarus	Julia	1819	Southwark, London	Isaac Lazarus	Fanny (?)		Waterloo, London	
21544	Lazarus	Julia	1821	Hull, Yorkshire	(?) Barnard		Lewis Lazarus	Spitalfields, London	
14586	Lazarus	Julia	1829	Shoreditch, London	Isaac Lazarus	Sarah (?)		Hoxton, London	
3474	Lazarus	Julia	1833	?, London	Lewis Henry Lazarus	Elizabeth (Eliza) Aaron	Henry Berens	Bristol	
3481	Lazarus	Julia	1834	Mile End, London	Abraham Lazarus	Mary Solomon Wilks	Edward Simeon Wilks	Marylebone, London	
1054	Lazarus	Julia	1839	Exeter, Devon	David Lazarus	Betsy (?)	Aaron Aarons	Exeter, Devon	
1065	Lazarus	Julia	1841	Exeter, Devon	Moses Lazarus	Rebecca Schultz	Bernard Rubinstein	Exeter, Devon	scholar
7706	Lazarus	Julia	1842	Dublin, Ireland	Henry Lazarus	Fanny (Frances) Barnett	Julius Calisher	Dublin, Ireland	
14889	Lazarus	Julia	1842	?abroad	Godfrey Lazarus	Julia (?)		Islington, London	
949	Lazarus	Julia	1847	Exeter, Devon	Isaac Eleazer Lazarus	Eliza Jacobs	Louis Abelson	Exeter, Devon	scholar
6444	Lazarus	Julia	1847	Plymouth, Devon	Samuel Joyful Lazarus	Nancy Lazarus	Maximilian Stanislaus Hassfeld	Whitechapel, London	
3405	Lazarus	Julia	1850	Spitalfields, London	Lewis (Eliezer Jacob) Lazarus	Kate (Kila) Lazarus Miers	Abraham Leon Emanuel	Aldgate, London	
30637	Lazarus	Juliet	1851	Spitalfields, London	Lewis Lazarus	Julia Barnard		Spitalfields, London	
807	Lazarus	Kate (Kitty, Ruth)	1851	Uxbridge, Middlesex	Laurence (Lazarus) Lazarus	Sarah Levy	John Henry Strange	Uxbridge, Middlesex	scholar
3785	Lazarus	Katharine	1837	Aldgate, London	Benjamin Lazarus	Rebecca (?)		Spitalfields, London	
27039	Lazarus	Kitty	1777	?, London	(?) Lazarus			Aldgate, London	
22155	Lazarus	Lawrence	1822	Whitechapel, London	Isaac Lazarus	Hannah Zadocks		Whitechapel, London	fishmonger
802	Lazarus	Lawrence (Lazarus, Eliezer)	1810	Middlesex, London	Aharon		Sarah Levy	Uxbridge, Middlesex	clothier
23573	Lazarus	Lazarus	1840	Hayle, Cornwall	Isaac Lazarus	Rachel (?)		Liverpool	scholar
9525	Lazarus	Leah	1806	Spitalfields, London	(?)		Joseph Lazarus	Spitalfields, London	clothes dealer
3402	Lazarus	Leon (Lipman)	1847	Spitalfields, London	Lewis (Eliezer Jacob) Lazarus	Kate (Kila) Lazarus Miers	Grace Salmon	Aldgate, London	
25525	Lazarus	Lewis	1771	Portsmouth, Hampshire			Elizabeth bat Isaac of Portsmouth	Dublin, Ireland	silversmith + watch- and clockmaker
4606	Lazarus	Lewis	1777	Strasbourg, France				Birmingham	gentleman
10539	Lazarus	Lewis	1792	Bristol	Mordecai Lazarus		Clara Raphael	Piccadilly, London	special dealer + commercial agent
26777	Lazarus	Lewis	1800	Middlesex, London			Ellen (?)	Aldgate, London	
15215	Lazarus	Lewis	1809	?, London			Lydia (?)	Shoreditch, London	greengrocer
22791	Lazarus	Lewis	1817	?, Poland			Rachael (?)	Whitechapel, London	slipper maker master empl 4
21543	Lazarus	Lewis	1821	Exeter, Devon	Eliezer		Julia Barnard	Spitalfields, London	optician
22074	Lazarus	Lewis	1822	Mile End, London	Jacob Lazarus		Hannah Rodrigues	Whitechapel, London	hawker
16154	Lazarus	Lewis	1823	Aldgate, London	Woolf Lazarus		Fanny (Frances, Phoebe) Solomon	Whitechapel, London	general dealer
9712	Lazarus	Lewis	1834	Aldgate, London	John Lazarus	Sarah Solomons	Frances Isaacs	Covent Garden, London	veal butcher
19354	Lazarus	Lewis	1834	Marylebone, London	David Lazarus	Amelia (?)		Fitzrovia, London	polisher
26808	Lazarus	Lewis	1842	Aldgate, London	Joshua Lazarus	Rachel (?)		Aldgate, London	
950	Lazarus	Lewis	1844	Exeter, Devon	Isaac Eleazer Lazarus	Eliza Jacobs		Exeter, Devon	scholar
9530	Lazarus	Lewis	1847	Spitalfields, London	Joseph Lazarus	Leah (?)		Spitalfields, London	

ID	surname	given names	born	birthplace	father	mother	spouse 1	1851 residence	1851 occupation
18805	Lazarus	Lewis	1847	Middlesex, London	Samuel Mordecai Lazarus	Nancy (?)		Whitechapel, London	
29775	Lazarus	Lewis	1847	Whitechapel, London	Israel Lazarus	Ann (?)		Spitalfields, London	
22794	Lazarus	Lewis	1850	Shoreditch, London	Lewis Lazarus	Rachael (?)		Whitechapel, London	
3396	Lazarus	Lewis (Eliezer Jacob)	1814	Mile End, London	Abraham Lazarus	Mary Solomon Wilks	Catherine (Kila) Lazarus Miers	Aldgate, London	general agent + dealer in metals
2066	Lazarus	Lewis (Levy)	1843	Middlesex, London	Henry Lazarus	Isabella Lyon	Rebecca (Elizabeth) Cohen	Spitalfields, London	
3418	Lazarus	Lewis (Louis) Emanuel	1810	Spitalfields, London	Emanuel Lazarus	Sophia Simmons	Sophia Isaacs	Aldgate, London	ironmonger + tool dealer
2057	Lazarus	Lewis (Yehuda Leib)	1784	City, London	Aaron Lewis	Phoebe (?)	Jane Abraham	Aldgate, London	lead merchant
18872	Lazarus	Lewis Barnett	1843	Dublin, Ireland	Henry Lazarus	Fanny (Frances) Barnett	Catherine (Kate) Jonas	Dublin, Ireland	
19256	Lazarus	Lewis Henry	1846	Aldgate, London	Henry George Lazarus	Emma Lazarus		Aldgate, London	
24890	Lazarus	Lewis W	1845	Whitechapel, London	Isaac Lazarus	Sarah (?)		Southwark, London	scholar
24013	Lazarus	Louisa	1818	City, London	(?) Samuel	Nessel/Lissel (?)	Louisa Samuel	Marylebone, London	
8130	Lazarus	Lucy	1827	Leeds, Yorkshire	(?)		James Philip Tait Lazarus	Wakefield, Yorkshire	
15216	Lazarus	Lydia	1801	?, London	(?)		Lewis Lazarus	Shoreditch, London	
30958	Lazarus	Lyons	1796	?, Poland				York, Yorkshire	quill dresser
11886	Lazarus	Magnus	1781	Portsmouth, Hampshire				Whitechapel, London	
26075	Lazarus	Maria	1805	Middlesex, London	Jacob Israel		Benjamin Myers	Aldgate, London	
10173	Lazarus	Maria	1819	Shoreditch, London	(?) Isaacs		Benjamin Lazarus	Shoreditch, London	
10801	Lazarus	Mark	1819	Whitechapel, London	John (Jacob) Lazarus	Sarah (?)	Sarah Hyams	Spitalfields, London	general dealer
3828	Lazarus	Martha	1774	Aldgate, London			(?) Lazarus	Spitalfields, London	dealer in clothes
29821	Lazarus	Martha	1817	Wapping, London	Philip Lazarus	Amelia Barnes		Whitechapel, London	dressmaker
9248	Lazarus	Martha	1825	Birmingham	(?)		Isaac Lazarus	Spitalfields, London	
22929	Lazarus	Mary	1795	?, Somerset	Simcha Benem Mr Yozel		(?) Jacobs	Wapping, London	
3423	Lazarus	Mary (May)	1845	Bethnal Green, London	Solomon Lazarus	Elizabeth Minden	Lewis Levy (Levi)	Bethnal Green, London	
3266	Lazarus	Mary (May)	1848	Spitalfields, London	Lewis (Eliezer Jacob) Lazarus	Kate (Kila) Lazarus Miers	Henry Joseph Phillips	Aldgate, London	
30501	Lazarus	Matilda	1814	Aldgate, London	Lewis Henry Lazarus	Elizabeth (Eliza) Aaron		Bristol	annuitant
19941	Lazarus	Matilda	1831	?, London	Edward Lazarus	Catherine Davis		Whitechapel, London	
1219	Lazarus	Matilda (Lilli)	1801	Bideford, Devon	Francis Lyon	Sarah Woolfe	Lippa (Lyon) Lazarus	Plymouth, Devon	haberdasher
1251	Lazarus	Maurice (Morris)	1821	Leigh, Essex	Laurence Lazarus	Catharine Phillips	Selina Pearn	Plymouth, Devon	master tailor
18873	Lazarus	Miriam	1844	Dublin, Ireland	Henry Lazarus	Fanny (Frances) Barnett	Alfred Wormser Harris	Dublin, Ireland	
29248	Lazarus	Montague	1827	?, London				Whitechapel, London	commercial traveller
9713	Lazarus	Morris	1836	Aldgate, London	John Lazarus	Sarah Solomons		Covent Garden, London	veal butcher
26807	Lazarus	Morris (Moses)	1837	Aldgate, London	Joshua Lazarus	Rachel (?)		Aldgate, London	scholar
1220	Lazarus	Mosely (Moses)	1827	Plymouth, Devon	Lippa (Lyon) Lazarus	Matilda (Lilli) Lyon		Plymouth, Devon	general dealer
20270	Lazarus	Moses	1778	Aldgate, London			(?)	Spitalfields, London	butcher
7555	Lazarus	Moses	1800	?, London	Raphael Lazarus		Clara Joseph	Aldgate, London	tea dealer
1062	Lazarus	Moses	1812	Exeter, Devon	Eleazer Lazarus	Julia Solomon	Rebecca Schultz	Exeter, Devon	master watchmaker
24012	Lazarus	Moses	1812	Middlesex, London	Nathan Lazarus		Louisa Samuel	Marylebone, London	clothes salesman
1078	Lazarus	Moses	1814	Exeter, Devon	David Lazarus	Betsy (?)		Exeter, Devon	
29822	Lazarus	Moses	1818	Wapping, London	Philip Lazarus	Amelia Barnes		Whitechapel, London	printer
3765	Lazarus	Moses	1821	Spitalfields, London	(?) Lazarus	Jane (?)		Spitalfields, London	dealer
9526	Lazarus	Moses (Moss)	1823	?, Holland	Joseph Lazarus	(?)	Leah Cohen	Spitalfields, London	clothes dealer
10805	Lazarus	Moss	1846	Spitalfields, London	Mark Lazarus	Sarah Hyams		Spitalfields, London	scholar

ID	surname	given names	born	birthplace	father	mother	spouse 1	1851 residence	1851 occupation
20273	Lazarus	Myer	1826	Spitalfields, London	Moses Lazarus			Spitalfields, London	general dealer
26143	Lazarus	Myer	1849	?, London	Henry Lazarus	Ann (?)		Aldgate, London	scholar
28107	Lazarus	Myr?	1823	?, Germany				Spitalfields, London	journeyman baker
18798	Lazarus	Nancy	1809	Whitechapel, London	(?)		Samuel Mordecai Lazarus	Whitechapel, London	
16076	Lazarus	Nancy	1821	Plymouth, Devon	(?) Lazarus			Whitechapel, London	
6439	Lazarus	Nancy	1829	Plymouth, Devon	Lippa (Lyon) Lazarus	Matilda Lyon	Samuel Joyful Lazarus	Whitechapel, London	
24016	Lazarus	Nancy (Anne)	1851	Marylebone, London	Moses Lazarus	Louisa Samuel		Marylebone, London	
30959	Lazarus	Nathan	1817	Lincoln, Lincolnshire			Ellen (?)	Sheffield, Yorkshire	tailor
1069	Lazarus	Nathan	1849	Exeter, Devon	Moses Lazarus	Rebecca (Schultz	Sarah Braham	Exeter, Devon	
20121	Lazarus	Nathaniel	1803	Canterbury, Kent			Dinah Solomon	Canterbury, Kent	silversmith, jeweller, clothier + general salesman
10171	Lazarus	Nathaniel	1847	Bath	Benjamin Lazarus	Maria Isaacs		Shoreditch, London	
18874	Lazarus	Nellie (Helen)	1848	Dublin, Ireland	Henry Lazarus	Fanny (Frances) Barnett	Lesser Lesser	Dublin, Ireland	
18801	Lazarus	Newton	1837	Middlesex, London	Samuel Mordecai Lazarus	Nancy (?)	(?)	Whitechapel, London	cigar maker
24014	Lazarus	Phebe	1836	City, London	Moses Lazarus	Louisa Samuel		Marylebone, London	apprentice (?to clothes salesman)
13589	Lazarus	Phillip	1847	?, Poland [?, Prussia]	(?) Lazarus	Catherine (?)		Manchester	
6658	Lazarus	Phineas	1842	Bath	Benjamin Lazarus	Maria Isaacs	Sarah Smith	Shoreditch, London	
7905	Lazarus	Phineas S---	1797	Whitechapel, London				Sunderland, Co Durham	
26437	Lazarus	Phoebe	1834	?, Poland	Ephraim Lazarus	Shine (?)		Aldgate, London	tailoress
16077	Lazarus	Phoebe	1842	Plymouth, Devon	Lippa (Lyon) Lazarus	Matilda (Lilli) Lyon		Whitechapel, London	
26076	Lazarus	Phoebe	1842	Whitechapel, London	Aaron Lazarus	Maria Israel		Aldgate, London	
23574	Lazarus	Phoebe	1843	Hayle, Cornwall	Isaac Lazarus	Rachel (?)		Liverpool	scholar
29069	Lazarus	Priscilla	1781	Bethnal Green, London	(?) Lazarus			Whitechapel, London	late general dealer
29994	Lazarus	Racca	1826	Poznan, Poland [Posen, Germany]	(?)		Jacob Lazarus	Whitechapel, London	
23409	Lazarus	Rachael	1808	?, London	(?)		Eleazer Lazarus	Aldgate, London	
22792	Lazarus	Rachael	1829	Elephant & Castle, London	(?)		Lewis Lazarus	Whitechapel, London	
9527	Lazarus	Rachael	1833	Spitalfields, London	Joseph Lazarus	Leah (?)		Spitalfields, London	
5652	Lazarus	Rachael	1836	Aldgate, London	Moses Lazarus	Clara Joseph	Hananel Abendana	Aldgate, London	
29770	Lazarus	Rachael	1836	Whitechapel, London	Israel Lazarus	Ann (?)	Jacob Joseph	Spitalfields, London	furrier
29995	Lazarus	Rachael	1850	Whitechapel, London	Jacob Lazarus	Racca (?)		Whitechapel, London	
23569	Lazarus	Rachel	1805	?, Poland	(?)		Isaac Lazarus	Liverpool	
224	Lazarus	Rachel	1811	Whitechapel, London	Levy Lazarus		Benjamin Klepman	Spitalfields, London	parasol maker
4205	Lazarus	Rachel	1814	Spitalfields, London	Sampson Solomon		David Lazarus	Aldgate, London	
26806	Lazarus	Rachel	1816	Whitechapel, London	(?)		Joshua Lazarus	Aldgate, London	clothier
22900	Lazarus	Ralph	1776	?, London			Rosetta (?)	Wapping, London	general dealer
3409	Lazarus	Ralph (Raphael)	1823	Spitalfields, London	Emanuel Lazarus	Sophia Simmons	Alice (Ailsie) Benjamin	Spitalfields, London	general dealer
20434	Lazarus	Rebecca	1785	Middlesex, London	(?)		(?) Lazarus	Aldgate, London	
3784	Lazarus	Rebecca	1808	Whitechapel, London	Isaac Moses		Benjamin Lazarus	Spitalfields, London	
1063	Lazarus	Rebecca	1817	?, Poland	Lewis Schultz	Louisa (?)	Moses Lazarus	Exeter, Devon	
2648	Lazarus	Rebecca	1819	?, England			Benjamin Lazarus	Glasgow, Scotland	housekeeper
28136	Lazarus	Rebecca	1823	Middlesex, London	(?) Lazarus	Elizabeth		Spitalfields, London	tailoress
26781	Lazarus	Rebecca	1838	Middlesex, London	Lewis Lazarus	Ellen (?)		Aldgate, London	

ID	surname	given names	born	birthplace	father	mother	spouse 1	1851 residence	1851 occupation
804	Lazarus	Rebecca	1840	Whitechapel, London	Lawrence (Lazarus, Eliezer) Lazarus	Sarah Levy	Nathan Nathaniel Isaacs	Uxbridge, Middlesex	
4202	Lazarus	Rebecca	1850	Whitechapel, London	David Lazarus	Rachel Solomon	Henry Marks	Aldgate, London	
23576	Lazarus	Rebecca	1850	Liverpool	Isaac Lazarus	Rachel (?)		Liverpool	
20893	Lazarus	Rebecca	1851	Aldgate, London	Emanuel Lazarus	Emily (?)		Holborn, London	
4603	Lazarus	Rebecca Leah	1842	Birmingham	Elias Lazarus	Sophie (?)	Alfred Israel Moses	Birmingham	
20271	Lazarus	Rosa	1823	Spitalfields, London	Moses Lazarus			Spitalfields, London	cap maker
19355	Lazarus	Rosa	1836	Marylebone, London	David Lazarus	Amelia (?)		Fitzrovia, London	scholar
18253	Lazarus	Rosa	1839	Scarborough, Yorkshire	I--- L--- Lazarus	Deborah Jacobs		Hull, Yorkshire	scholar at home
22629	Lazarus	Rosa	1850	Canterbury, Kent	Nathaniel Lazarus	Dinah Solomon		Canterbury, Kent	
6939	Lazarus	Rose	1837	Spitalfields, London	Emanuel Lazarus	Sarah (?)		Spitalfields, London	parasol maker
11502	Lazarus	Rose	1840	Aldgate, London	(?) Lazarus	(?) ?Symons		Aldgate, London	tailoress
22901	Lazarus	Rosetta	1781	?, London	(?)		Ralph Lazarus	Wapping, London	
24667	Lazarus	Rosetta	1831	Aldgate, London	(?) Lazarus	(?) Levy		Kennington, London	milliner + dress maker
26142	Lazarus	Rosetta	1844	Clerkenwell, London	Henry Lazarus	Ann (?)		Aldgate, London	scholar
11576	Lazarus	Rosetta (Rosa)	1843	Aldgate, London	Barnett Lazarus	Elizabeth (?)	Israel Lyons	Aldgate, London	
8544	Lazarus	Rosetta (Rosa)	1850	Spitalfields, London	Abraham Lazarus	Esther Silva Green		Spitalfields, London	
23410	Lazarus	Rosetta (Rosy)	1835	Aldgate, London	Eleazer Lazarus	Rachael (?)		Aldgate, London	tailoress
26810	Lazarus	Rossetta	1846	Aldgate, London	Joshua Lazarus	Rachel (?)		Aldgate, London	
18648	Lazarus	Samson	1838	Middlesex, London	David Lazarus	Rachel Solomon		Aldgate, London	
22799	Lazarus	Samuel	1789	Spitalfields, London	Simon Heinspert		Ann Joseph	Whitechapel, London	furniture broker + dealer
29303	Lazarus	Samuel	1811	Whitechapel, London	Henry (Tsvi) Lazarus		Sophia Cohen	Whitechapel, London	cigar maker
5613	Lazarus	Samuel	1825	Whitechapel, London	Isaac Lazarus	Sarah (?)	Rose Aaron	Whitechapel, London	watch finisher
3416	Lazarus	Samuel	1831	Spitalfields, London	Emanuel Lazarus	Sophia Simmons	Ellen Marks	Spitalfields, London	cigar maker
17957	Lazarus	Samuel	1835	City, London	Moses Lazarus		Isabella Meyers	Aldgate, London	tea dealer
5608	Lazarus	Samuel	1839	Aldgate, London	John Lazarus	Sarah Solomons	Rachael Solomons	St Giles, London	
23572	Lazarus	Samuel	1839	Hayle, Cornwall	Isaac Lazarus	Rachel (?)		Liverpool	scholar
1067	Lazarus	Samuel	1844	Exeter, Devon	Moses Lazarus	Rebecca Schultz	Isabella Meyers (Myers)	Exeter, Devon	scholar
22560	Lazarus	Samuel	1847	Canterbury, Kent	Nathaniel Lazarus	Dinah Solomon	Rachel Alexander	Canterbury, Kent	scholar
6440	Lazarus	Samuel Joyful	1824	Exeter, Devon	Eleazer Lazarus	Julia Solomon	Nancy Lazarus	Whitechapel, London	optician empl 1
18797	Lazarus	Samuel Mordecai	1799	Winchester, Hampshire	Mordecai Lazarus		Nancy (?)	Whitechapel, London	bracelet manufacturer
2484	Lazarus	Sander	1827	?Wapping, London	Isaac Lazarus	Hannah Zadocks	Louisa Kalman	Hull, Yorkshire	dealer in hardware
27307	Lazarus	Sarah	1781	Aldgate, London	(?)			Aldgate, London	dealer in plated articles
22505	Lazarus	Sarah	1790	Mile End, London	(?)		Isaac Lazarus	Whitechapel, London	
19747	Lazarus	Sarah	1798	Spitalfields, London	(?)		Jacob (John) Lazarus	Spitalfields, London	
6938	Lazarus	Sarah	1800	Whitechapel, London	(?)		Emanuel Lazarus	Spitalfields, London	
9710	Lazarus	Sarah	1801	Aldgate, London	(?) Solomons	Catherine (?)	John Lazarus	Covent Garden, London	domestic
14583	Lazarus	Sarah	1801	City, London	(?)		Isaac Lazarus	Hoxton, London	
24889	Lazarus	Sarah	1811	Bermondsey, London	(?)		Isaac Lazarus	Southwark, London	clerk to solicitor
803	Lazarus	Sarah	1812	Middlesex, London	Moshe Levy	Jane (?)	Lawrence (Lazarus, Eliezer) Lazarus	Uxbridge, Middlesex	
2060	Lazarus	Sarah	1819	Aldgate, London	Lewis Lazarus	Jane Abraham	Jacob Boxen (Boxius)	Aldgate, London	
10730	Lazarus	Sarah	1821	Middlesex, London	(?Moshe Kashman Marks)		Jacob Lazarus	Spitalfields, London	general dealer
10802	Lazarus	Sarah	1821	Whitechapel, London	Hyam Hyams	Elizabeth Benjamin	Mark Lazarus	Spitalfields, London	
21808	Lazarus	Sarah	1821	Middlesex, London	(?) Lazarus		Judah Norden	Chelsea, London	bookbinder

ID	surname	given names	born	birthplace	father	mother	spouse 1	1851 residence	1851 occupation
19940	Lazarus	Sarah	1825	Whitechapel, London	Edward Lazarus	Catherine Davis		Whitechapel, London	
3412	Lazarus	Sarah	1828	Spitalfields, London	Emanuel Lazarus	Sophia Simmons	Lewis Isaacs	Spitalfields, London	cap maker
18799	Lazarus	Sarah	1832	Middlesex, London	Samuel Mordecai Lazarus	Nancy (?)	Moses Ansell	Whitechapel, London	dress maker
30565	Lazarus	Sarah	1832	Mile End, London	Abraham Lazarus	Mary Solomon (Wilks)		Bethnal Green, London	
11574	Lazarus	Sarah	1837	Aldgate, London	Barnett Lazarus	Elizabeth (?)	John Isaacs	Aldgate, London	tailoress
26139	Lazarus	Sarah	1840	Liverpool	Henry Lazarus	Ann (?)		Aldgate, London	scholar
3786	Lazarus	Sarah	1842	Aldgate, London	Benjamin Lazarus	Rebecca (?)		Spitalfields, London	scholar
23414	Lazarus	Sarah	1845	Aldgate, London	Eleazer Lazarus	Rachael (?)		Aldgate, London	
22076	Lazarus	Sarah	1850	Mile End, London	Lewis Lazarus	Hannah Rodrigues		Whitechapel, London	
26435	Lazarus	Shine	1810	?, Poland	(?)		Ephraim Lazarus	Aldgate, London	
13590	Lazarus	Silpby	1849	Hull, Yorkshire	(?) Lazarus	Catherine (?)		Manchester	
30962	Lazarus	Simeon	1843	Sheffield, Yorkshire	Nathan Lazarus	Ellen (?)		Sheffield, Yorkshire	
3398	Lazarus	Simeon	1844	Spitalfields, London	Lewis (Eliezer Jacob) Lazarus	Kate (Kila) Lazarus Miers	Florence Solomon)	Aldgate, London	scholar
3509	Lazarus	Simeon (Edward)	1816	Mile End, London	Abraham Lazarus	Mary Solomon Wilks		Marylebone, London	furniture + metal dealer
19282	Lazarus	Simeon Lewis	1845	?, London	Lewis Emanuel (Eliezer) Lazarus	Sophia Isaacs		Aldgate, London	
11135	Lazarus	Simon	1826	Vilnius, Lithuania [Vilna, Russia]	Eliezer		Esther Harris	Aldgate, London	cigar dealer
3408	Lazarus	Solomon	1814	Spitalfields, London	Emanuel Lazarus	Sophia Simmons	Rachel Benjamin	Spitalfields, London	tobacconist, broker of household goods + dealer in ironmongery
3421	Lazarus	Solomon	1818	Whitechapel, London	Abraham Lazarus	Mary Solomon (Wilks)	Elizabeth Minden	Bethnal Green, London	furniture broker
29823	Lazarus	Solomon	1821	Wapping, London	Philip Lazarus	Amelia Barnes		Whitechapel, London	general dealer
9528	Lazarus	Solomon	1835	Spitalfields, London	Joseph Lazarus	Leah (?)		Spitalfields, London	
29772	Lazarus	Solomon	1841	Whitechapel, London	Israel Lazarus	Ann (?)		Spitalfields, London	scholar
18804	Lazarus	Solomon	1844	Middlesex, London	Samuel Mordecai Lazarus	Nancy (?)		Whitechapel, London	
23575	Lazarus	Solomon	1844	Hayle, Cornwall	Isaac Lazarus	Rachel (?)		Liverpool	scholar
6134	Lazarus	Sophia	1815	Stepney, London	Eliezer Isaacs		Gabriel Lazarus	Mile End, London	
29304	Lazarus	Sophia	1817	Aldgate, London	(?) Cohen	Rebecca (?)	Samuel Lazarus	Whitechapel, London	
3419	Lazarus	Sophia	1820	Bethnal Green, London	Samuel Isaacs	?	Lewis (Louis) Emanuel Lazarus	Aldgate, London	
23412	Lazarus	Sophia	1840	Aldgate, London	Eleazer Lazarus	Rachael (?)		Aldgate, London	
26784	Lazarus	Sophia	1841	Middlesex, London	Lewis Lazarus	Ellen (?)		Aldgate, London	
4602	Lazarus	Sophie	1809	Birmingham			Elias Lazarus	Birmingham	
18646	Lazarus	Susan (Susannah)	1838	Spitalfields, London	David Lazarus	Rachel Solomon	Solomon Barnett	Aldgate, London	dress maker
10541	Lazarus	Tabitha	1801	Bristol	Mordecai Lazarus			Piccadilly, London	
16157	Lazarus	Woolf	1780	Aldgate, London			(?)	Whitechapel, London	general dealer
5786	Lazarus	Zadoc (Zadea)	1824	Wapping, London	Isaac Lazarus	Hannah Zadocks	Mary Ann (Marianne, Mary) Raphael	Whitechapel, London	hardware dealer
8132	Lazarus (Kingsley)	James Eleazar	1847	Wakefield, Yorkshire	James Philip Tait Lazarus	Lucy (?)	Emma Solomon	Wakefield, Yorkshire	scholar at home
14888	Lazarus [Godfrey]	Edward	1836	?abroad	Godfrey Lazarus	Julia (?)		Islington, London	
11577	Lazarus [Joel]	Julia	1849	Middlesex, London	Solomon Joel	Elizabeth Lazarus	Isaac Levy	Aldgate, London	
1223	Lazarus [Laurance, Lawtence]	Hezekiah (Henry)	1845	Plymouth, Devon	Lippa (Lyon) Lazarus)	Matilda (Lilli) Lyon	Isabel Druiff	Plymouth, Devon	scholar
1064	Lazarus [Lawrence]	Barnett (Baruck)	1838	Exmouth, Devon	Moses Lazarus	Rebecca Schultz	Rosetta (Roselly) Harris	Exeter, Devon	scholar

ID	surname	given names	born	birthplace	father	mother	spouse 1	1851 residence	1851 occupation
16421	Lazzadi	Abraham	1803	?, Germany			Sarah (?)	Aldgate, London	tailor's cutter
16425	Lazzadi	Isaac	1841	?, London	Abraham Lazzadi	Sarah (?)		Aldgate, London	scholar
16424	Lazzadi	Jacob	1839	?, London	Abraham Lazzadi	Sarah (?)		Aldgate, London	scholar
16423	Lazzadi	Lawrence	1837	?, London	Abraham Lazzadi	Sarah (?)		Aldgate, London	scholar
16427	Lazzadi	Michael	1849	?, London	Abraham Lazzadi	Sarah (?)		Aldgate, London	scholar
16422	Lazzadi	Sarah	1814	?, Suffolk	(?)		Abraham Lazzadi	Aldgate, London	
16426	Lazzadi	Simon	1843	?, London	Abraham Lazzadi	Sarah (?)		Aldgate, London	scholar
12183	Lea---	Sarah	1765	Amsterdam, Holland	(?)		(?)	Whitechapel, London	annuitant
204	Lealter	Judith	1791	Whitechapel, London	Benjamin De Samuel Bendahan	Ribca de Moseh Jesurun Alveres	Abraham Lealter	Wapping, London	annuitant
5836	Leapman	Fanny	1801	City, London			Isaac Leapman	Whitechapel, London	
22161	Leapman	Gordon	1841	Middlesex, London	Isaac Leapman	Fanny (?)		Whitechapel, London	
5835	Leapman	Isaac	1801	abroad			Fanny (?)	Whitechapel, London	black [---] manufacturer
5837	Leapman	Lewis	1835	Bristol	Isaac Leapman	Fanny (?)	Miriam Joel	Whitechapel, London	
22160	Leapman	Moss	1834	Bristol	Isaac Leapman	Fanny (?)	Charlotte (?)	Whitechapel, London	
5839	Leapman	Rachael	1837	Middlesex, London	Isaac Leapman	Fanny (?)	Jacob Szapira	Whitechapel, London	
22162	Leapman	Rebecca	1843	Middlesex, London	Isaac Leapman	Fanny (?)		Whitechapel, London	
5834	Leapman	Samuel	1830	?City, London	Isaac Leapman	Fanny (?)	Sophia Joel	Whitechapel, London	
22159	Leapman	Sarah	1827	City, London	Isaac Leapman	Fanny (?)		Whitechapel, London	
18551	Leavy	Henry	1833	Sheerness, Kent				Spitalfields, London	tailor apprentice
29694	Leavy	Philip? B	1787	?, Poland			(?)	Shoreditch, London	
11780	Leavy	Rachael	1781	Aldgate, London	(?) Leavy			Aldgate, London	fundholder
11792	Leck	Levy	1825	?, Holland				Shoreditch, London	cigar manufacturer
10851	Lee	Abraham	1784	?, London			Esther (?)	Spitalfields, London	general dealer
25575	Lee	Abraham	1832	?, London	Lewis Lee	Elizabeth (?)	Elizabeth (Betsey) Hart	Aldgate, London	general dealer
10853	Lee	Abraham	1835	?, London	Abraham Lee	Esther (?)		Spitalfields, London	general dealer
9766	Lee	Albert	1841	Middlesex, London				Kew, London	boarding school pupil
27810	Lee	Alexander	1842	Strand, London	Michael Montague Lee	Catherine Moses (Morse)	Annie Caird Cowen	Chelsea, London	
14518	Lee	Annie	1837	?Dublin, Ireland	Michael Lee	Mary (?)		Birmingham	
14977	Lee	Annie Elizabeth	1840	Middlesex, London	(?) Lee			Bethnal Green, London	boarding school pupil
27806	Lee	Barnard	1836	Strand, London	Michael Montague Lee	Catherine Moses (Morse)	Isabella Holmes	Chelsea, London	
6193	Lee	Barnard Isaac Foligno Godfrey Charles	1837	Westminster, London	Barnett Lee	Diamond Foligno	Miriam Mocatta	Notting Hill, London	
6194	Lee	Barnett	1804	Eton, Berkshire	Barnett Alexander Levy	Rosetta Isaacs	Diamond Foligno	Notting Hill, London	tailor
10562	Lee	Barnitt	1844	Lambeth, London	Solomon Isaac Lee	Caroline Solomon		Elephant & Castle, London	
6198	Lee	Benjamin Alexander	1848	Soho, London	Barnett Lee	Diamond Foligno		Notting Hill, London	
20123	Lee	Bernard	1796	Whitechapel, London			Hannah (?)	Soho, London	professor of music
14516	Lee	Betsy	1834	Middlesex, London	Michael Lee	Mary (?)		Birmingham	
10560	Lee	Caroline	1814	Portsmouth, Hampshire	Issachar Solomon		Solomon Isaac Lee	Elephant & Castle, London	
27803	Lee	Catherine	1807	Holborn, London	(?) Moses (Morse)	Sarah (?)	Michael Montague Lee	Chelsea, London	
24345	Lee	David	1842	St Giles, London	(?) Lee			Holborn, London	

ID	surname	given names	born	birthplace	father	mother	spouse 1	1851 residence	1851 occupation
6195	Lee	Diamond	1802	Bethnal Green, London	Moses Zachariah Foligno	Rachel de Isaac Baquis	Barnett Lee	Notting Hill, London	
25303	Lee	Dinah	1786	Windsor, Berkshire	(?)		(?) Lee	Aldgate, London	seamstress
24341	Lee	Edward	1834	Holborn, London				Holborn, London	lithographer
6196	Lee	Edward Foligno	1839	Piccadilly, London	Barnett Lee	Diamond Foligno	Adelaide Harris	Notting Hill, London	
14519	Lee	Elias (Ellis) Laurence	1839	Dublin, Ireland	Michael Lee	Mary (?)	Adelaide Mose Myers	Birmingham	
25571	Lee	Elizabeth	1800	?, London	(?)		Lewis Lee	Aldgate, London	tailor
27813	Lee	Elizabeth Amelia	1846	Kensington, London	Michael Montague Lee	Catherine Moses (Morse)	David Robert Hurt	Chelsea, London	
29495	Lee	Emanuel	1836	Spitalfields, London	Henry Lee	(?)		Spitalfields, London	general dealer
14517	Lee	Emma	1835	Middlesex, London	Michael Lee	Mary (?)	Lewin (Louis) Jacob (Jacobs)	Birmingham	
10852	Lee	Esther	1801	Aldgate, London	(?)		Abraham Lee	Spitalfields, London	
24340	Lee	Eve	1832	City, London	(?) Lee			Holborn, London	milliner
14923	Lee	George Edward	1835	Marylebone, London				Bethnal Green, London	boarding school pupil
20124	Lee	Hannah	1801	Bideford, Devon	(?)		Bernard Lee	Soho, London	
24342	Lee	Hannah	1837	Holborn, London	(?) Lee			Holborn, London	
15961	Lee	Hannah	1843	Westminster, London	Barnett Lee	Diamond Foligno		Notting Hill, London	
27812	Lee	Hannah	1847	Kensington, London	Michael Montague Lee	Catherine Moses (Morse)		Chelsea, London	
348	Lee	Harriet	1817	Whitechapel, London	Isaac Lee			Spitalfields, London	
29492	Lee	Henry	1801	Aldgate, London			(?)	Spitalfields, London	general dealer
27811	Lee	Henry	1844	Strand, London	Michael Montague Lee	Catherine Moses (Morse)	Emma Elizabeth Watson	Chelsea, London	
10564	Lee	Henry	1850	Lambeth, London	Solomon Isaac Lee	Caroline Solomon	Esther Jacobs	Elephant & Castle, London	
14924	Lee	Henry James	1838	Marylebone, London				Bethnal Green, London	boarding school pupil
253	Lee	Isaac	1789	Whitechapel, London				Spitalfields, London	dealer in glass
10561	Lee	Isaac	1843	Lambeth, London	Solomon Isaac Lee	Caroline Solomon		Elephant & Castle, London	
25576	Lee	Jacob (John)	1840	?, London	Lewis Lee	Elizabeth (?)	Kate (Kitty) Jacobs	Aldgate, London	scholar
13434	Lee	John	1830	?, London				Shoreditch, London	cigar maker
24343	Lee	John	1839	Holborn, London				Holborn, London	
27807	Lee	Joseph	1838	Covent Garden, London	Michael Montague Lee	Catherine Moses (Morse)	Phoebe Eliza Johnston	Chelsea, London	
29496	Lee	Joseph	1842	Spitalfields, London	Henry Lee	(?)		Spitalfields, London	scholar at home
25573	Lee	Julia	1830	?, London	Lewis Lee	Elizabeth (?)		Aldgate, London	
24346	Lee	Kate	1843	St Giles, London	(?) Lee			Holborn, London	
25577	Lee	Kitty	1842	?, London	Lewis Lee	Elizabeth (?)		Aldgate, London	scholar
24339	Lee	Lawrence	1829	Aldgate, London				Holborn, London	lithographer
24344	Lee	Leah	1841	Southampton, Hampshire	(?) Lee			Holborn, London	
25570	Lee	Lewis	1795	?, London			Elizabeth (?)	Aldgate, London	tailor
29494	Lee	Lewis	1834	Aldgate, London	Henry Lee	(?)		Spitalfields, London	general dealer
17286	Lee	Louis	1845	Bow, London	(?) Lee			Spitalfields, London	scholar
17285	Lee	Maria	1835	Bow, London	Isaac Lee			Spitalfields, London	cap maker
27809	Lee	Maria	1841	Strand, London	Michael Montague Lee	Catherine Moses (Morse)		Chelsea, London	
14515	Lee	Mary	1804	Middlesex, London	(?)		Michael Lee	Birmingham	
25572	Lee	Mary	1825	?, London	Lewis Lee	Elizabeth (?)		Aldgate, London	tailor
18225	Lee	Mary Ann	1839	Middlesex, London	(?) Lee			Mile End, London	scholar

ID	surname	given names	born	birthplace	father	mother	spouse 1	1851 residence	1851 occupation
14514	Lee	Michael	1804	Birmingham			Mary (?)	Birmingham	commercial traveller (tobacconist)
27802	Lee	Michael Montague	1801	Eton, Berkshire	Barnett Alexander Levy	Rosetta Isaacs	Catherine Moses (Morse)	Chelsea, London	tailor
27805	Lee	Montague Michael	1835	Covent Garden, London	Michael Montague Lee	Catherine Moses (Morse)	Mary Louisa Davis	Chelsea, London	
5075	Lee	Moses	1797	Middlesex, London			Sarah Davis	Portsmouth, Hampshire	clothier
10563	Lee	Rachael	1847	Lambeth, London	Solomon Isaac Lee	Caroline Solomon	Joseph Pearce	Elephant & Castle, London	
10558	Lee	Rachel	1762	Canterbury, Kent				Elephant & Castle, London	
15414	Lee	Rachel	1807	Aldgate, London	Zvi Hirsch Marks		John Levy	Covent Garden, London	
29493	Lee	Rachel	1833	Aldgate, London	Henry Lee	(?)		Spitalfields, London	general dealer
25574	Lee	Rebecca	1834	?, London	Lewis Lee	Elizabeth (?)		Aldgate, London	parasol maker
17283	Lee	Rose	1822	Spitalfields, London	Isaac Lee			Spitalfields, London	tailoress
22889	Lee	Rosetta	1778	Whitechapel, London	(?)		(?) Lee	Wapping, London	F-brokers
27804	Lee	Rosetta	1834	Covent Garden, London	Michael Montague Lee	Catherine Moses (Morse)		Chelsea, London	
6197	Lee	Rosetta	1841	Soho, London	Barnett Lee	Diamond Foligno	David Maurice Moses	Notting Hill, London	
25578	Lee	Rosetta	1843	?, London	Lewis Lee	Elizabeth (?)		Aldgate, London	scholar
17284	Lee	Samuel	1830	Whitechapel, London	Isaac Lee			Spitalfields, London	metal dealer
5076	Lee	Sarah	1803	Portsmouth, Hampshire	Moses Davis	Rosey Nathan	Moses Lee	Portsmouth, Hampshire	
27808	Lee	Sarah	1839	Covent Garden, London	Michael Montague Lee	Catherine Moses (Morse)		Chelsea, London	
24347	Lee	Solomon	1849	St Giles, London	(?) Lee			Holborn, London	
10559	Lee	Solomon Isaac	1801	Aldgate, London	Isaac HaLevi		Caroline Solomon	Elephant & Castle, London	general agent
11721	Lee	Toby	1830	Aldgate, London				Aldgate, London	general dealer
452	Leendert Park	Esther	1819	?, London				Spitalfields, London	
453	Leendert Park	Isaac	1825	Amsterdam, Holland				Spitalfields, London	
454	Leendert Park	Simon	1829	Amsterdam, Holland				Spitalfields, London	
17691	Lehman	Henrietta	1821	Holstein, Germany	(?) Lehman			Finsbury, London	governess
4607	Leichter	Samuel	1830	?, Poland [?, Prussia]				Birmingham	glazier
22006	Leigh	Henry	1828	Middlesex, London	Joseph Leigh	(?)		Whitechapel, London	dealer in plate
22004	Leigh	Joseph	1798	Middlesex, London			(?)	Whitechapel, London	dealer in plate
22005	Leigh	Rebecca	1826	Middlesex, London	Joseph Leigh	(?)		Whitechapel, London	
16838	Lein	Horatio S	1836	?, London				Brighton, Sussex	scholar
18222	Leiser	Adelaide	1838	?, Germany	(?) Leiser			Mile End, London	scholar
26684	Leisler	Agatha	1840	Manchester	John Leisler	Lydia (?)		Manchester	scholar
26686	Leisler	Agnes Caroline	1845	Manchester	John Leisler	Lydia (?)		Manchester	scholar
26687	Leisler	Fanny (Frances) Adelaide	1847	Manchester	John Leisler	Lydia (?)		Manchester	scholar
26685	Leisler	Frederick Alexander	1843	Manchester	John Leisler	Lydia (?)		Manchester	scholar
26688	Leisler	Helen	1848	Manchester	John Leisler	Lydia (?)	Pierce Adolphus Simpson	Manchester	scholar
14347	Leisler	John	1804	?, Germany			Lydia (?)	Manchester	merchant engaged in export trade
26682	Leisler	Lydia	1808	?, Germany			Lydia (?)	Manchester	
26683	Leisler	Margaret	1838	Manchester	John Leisler	Lydia (?)		Manchester	scholar

ID	surname	given names	born	birthplace	father	mother	spouse 1	1851 residence	1851 occupation
16933	Leizerynstey	J---	1831	?, Poland				Sheffield, Yorkshire	hawker
18961	Leman	A--- H---	1795	?, Holland			Elizabeth (?)	Whitechapel, London	watch maker
7728	Leman	Benedictus Lion	1814	?Whitechapel, London	Lyon Benedictus (Aryeh Leib) Leman	Leonora (?)	Eliza Levy	Whitechapel, London	jeweller, silversmith + dealer in precious stones
18962	Leman	Elizabeth	1805	Boston, Lincolnshire	(?)		A--- H--- Leman	Whitechapel, London	
18998	Leman	Jenny	1828	?Whitechapel, London	Lyon Benedictus (Aryeh Leib Leman)	Leonora (?)		Whitechapel, London	
20126	Leman	Leonora	1791	abroad	(?)		Lyon Benedictus (Aryeh Leib) Leman	Whitechapel, London	draper + outfitter
18963	Leman	Louisa	1833	Marylebone, London	A--- H--- Leman	Elizabeth (?)		Whitechapel, London	
18997	Leman	Lyon Benedictus (Aryeh Leib)	1782	abroad			Leonora (?)	Whitechapel, London	agent
18964	Leman	Selina	1833	Rochdale, Lancashire	A--- H--- Leman	Elizabeth (?)		Whitechapel, London	
14999	Lemon	Aaron	1824	?, Holland				Bethnal Green, London	printer
17106	Lemon	Abraham	1804	Liverpool			Amelia (?)	Douglas, Isle of Man	jeweller
19633	Lemon	Abraham	1849	Spitalfields, London	Abriam Lemon	Julia (?)		Spitalfields, London	scholar
19627	Lemon	Abriam	1813	Spitalfields, London			Julia (?)	Spitalfields, London	(hawker?) of china
17108	Lemon	Amelia	1822	Liverpool	(?)		Abraham Lemon	Douglas, Isle of Man	
19629	Lemon	Eliza	1835	Spitalfields, London	Abriam Lemon	Julia (?)		Spitalfields, London	
30000	Lemon	Ephraim	1800	Utrecht, Holland	Aron Lemon	Hester Samuel	Rebecca Wertheim	Finsbury, London	dealer
19631	Lemon	Ernest	1841	Spitalfields, London	Abriam Lemon	Julia (?)		Spitalfields, London	scholar
19628	Lemon	Julia	1809	Spitalfields, London	(?)		Abriam Lemon	Spitalfields, London	(hawker?) of china
17542	Lemon	Lemon (Lemel)	1829	Haarlem, Holland	Ephraim Lemon	Rebecca Wertheimer	Mary (Merle) Cohen	Spitalfields, London	dealer
19630	Lemon	Lidia	1837	Spitalfields, London	Abriam Lemon	Julia (?)		Spitalfields, London	dress maker
19632	Lemon	Louis	1846	Spitalfields, London	Abriam Lemon	Julia (?)		Spitalfields, London	scholar
17110	Lemon	Madeline	1847	Douglas, Isle of Man	Abraham Lemon	Amelia (?)		Douglas, Isle of Man	scholar
30001	Lemon	Mary	1806	Frome, Somerset	(?)		Ephraim Lemon	Finsbury, London	
17109	Lemon	Rachael	1845	Douglas, Isle of Man	Abraham Lemon	Amelia (?)		Douglas, Isle of Man	scholar
17111	Lemon	Sampson	1849	Douglas, Isle of Man	Abraham Lemon	Amelia (?)		Douglas, Isle of Man	
3145	Lemon	Samuel Ephraim	1826	Haarlem, Holland	Ephraim Lemon	Rebecca Wertheimer	Eleanor Austin	Newcastle Upon Tyne	shoemaker
30965	Lenkowski	Jeremiar	1826	Lask, Poland				Hull, Yorkshire	hawker, jewellery (licensed)
2489	Lensker	Alexander	1821	?, Italy			Mary (?)	Hull, Yorkshire	plaster figure dealer
2491	Lensker	John	1850	Hull, Yorkshire	Alexander Lensker	Mary (?)		Hull, Yorkshire	
2490	Lensker	Mary	1818	?, Germany			Alexander Lensker	Hull, Yorkshire	
14321	Lentz	Ernest	1820	?, Germany				Manchester	clerk to merchant in cotton manufactory
19902	Leo	Abigail	1825	Boston, Lincolnshire	Henry Lewis Leo	Mary Pamela Myers		Boston, Lincolnshire	
30798	Leo	Abraham	1824	?, London	Simeon Leo	Rosetta (?)		De Beauvoir, London	clerk in a distillery
25697	Leo	Abraham	1835	Spitalfields, London	David Leo	Esther (?)		Spitalfields, London	dealer in clothes
25698	Leo	Catherine (Kate)	1836	Spitalfields, London	David Leo	Esther (?)	David Samuel	Spitalfields, London	dealer in clothes
25702	Leo	Cecila	1844	Spitalfields, London	David Leo	Esther (?)		Spitalfields, London	
25695	Leo	David	1799	Aldgate, London			Esther (?)	Spitalfields, London	dealer in clothes
30288	Leo	Elizabeth	1760	?, London			Leisman Leo	Tower Hill, London	
19903	Leo	Elizabeth	1827	Boston, Lincolnshire	Henry Lewis Leo	Mary Pamela Myers		Boston, Lincolnshire	

ID	surname	given names	born	birthplace	father	mother	spouse 1	1851 residence	1851 occupation
30796	Leo	Ellen	1821	?, London	Simeon Leo	Rosetta (?)		De Beauvoir, London	professor of music
25696	Leo	Esther	1804	Deptford, London	(?)		David Leo	Spitalfields, London	dealer in clothes
19900	Leo	Henry Lewis	1802	Aldgate, London			Mary Pamela Myers	Boston, Lincolnshire	general shopkeeper
14343	Leo	Herman Edward	1798	?, Germany			Emily Maria (?)	Manchester	calico printer
25699	Leo	Isaac D	1837	Spitalfields, London	David Leo	Esther (?)		Spitalfields, London	dealer in clothes
25700	Leo	Jane	1839	Spitalfields, London	David Leo	Esther (?)		Spitalfields, London	dealer in clothes
25701	Leo	Leah	1842	Spitalfields, London	David Leo	Esther (?)		Spitalfields, London	
7130	Leo	Louis	1817	?, London	Simeon Leo	Rosetta (?)	Isabella Moss	De Beauvoir, London	professor of music
30795	Leo	Louisa	1815	?, London	Simeon Leo	Rosetta (?)		De Beauvoir, London	teacher of music
27484	Leo	Lydia	1790	Middlesex, London	(?)		(?) Samuel	Aldgate, London	dealer in hosiery
19901	Leo	Mary Pamela	1801	Boston, Lincolnshire	(?) Myers	Rosina (?)	Henry Lewis Leo	Boston, Lincolnshire	
30794	Leo	Rosetta	1796	?, London	(?)		Simeon Leo	De Beauvoir, London	housekeeper
19904	Leo	Rosina	1830	Boston, Lincolnshire	Henry Lewis Leo	Mary Pamela Myers	Benjamin Abraham (Abrahams)	Boston, Lincolnshire	
30797	Leo	Sarah	1823	?, London	Simeon Leo	Rosetta (?)		De Beauvoir, London	professor of music
12938	Leo	Sophia	1791	Rotterdam, Holland	(?)		(?) Leo	Liverpool	annuitant
14787	Leo (Lee)	Maria	1811	Whitechapel, London	Shmuel HaLevi Leo	Sarah (?)		Finsbury, London	dress maker
14786	Leo (Lee)	Sarah	1779	?, London			Shmuel HaLevi Leo	Finsbury, London	
16925	Leon	Abraham	1799	Hamburg, Germany			Eve (?)	Sheffield, Yorkshire	furrier?
5129	Leon	Abraham	1818	?, Germany	(?Abraham) Leon	(?Eve) (?)	Henrietta (?)	Sheffield, Yorkshire	hardware merchant
14441	Leon	Ada	1846	Salford, Lancashire	Samuel Leon	Fanny (?)		Salford, Lancashire	
16931	Leon	Alexander	1836	Hamburg, Germany	Abraham Leon	Eve (?)		Sheffield, Yorkshire	scholar
11742	Leon	Charles	1846	Spitalfields, London	Emanuel Leon	Rosetta (?)		Shoreditch, London	scholar
20829	Leon	Clara	1822	Sunderland, Co Durham	Hyam Joseph		Isaac Leon	Sunderland, Co Durham	
14440	Leon	Clara	1841	Salford, Lancashire	Samuel Leon	Fanny (?)		Salford, Lancashire	
4608	Leon	David	1838	?, Poland				Birmingham	glazier
20128	Leon	Eliza	1821	Marylebone, London	(?)		Levy Leon	Holborn, London	
14437	Leon	Elizabeth	1833	?, Lancashire	Samuel Leon	Fanny (?)		Salford, Lancashire	
19170	Leon	Elizabeth	1833	Bloomsbury, London	Joseph Jonas Leon	Sarah Lucas		Hyde Park, London	
17832	Leon	Ellen	1831	?, Essex	(?) Leon			Aldgate, London	servant
11739	Leon	Emanuel	1815	?, France			Rosetta (?)	Shoreditch, London	boot + shoe manufacturer
16745	Leon	Emanuel	1842	Bristol	Herentz Leon	Hannah Hart		Bath	
19171	Leon	Emily Rebecca	1840	Bloomsbury, London	Joseph Jonas Leon	Sarah Lucas		Hyde Park, London	
7213	Leon	Esther	1828	Manchester	Samuel Leon	Fanny (?)	Samuel Isaacs	Salford, Lancashire	
16926	Leon	Eve	1800	Hamburg, Germany	(?)		Abraham Leon	Sheffield, Yorkshire	
14435	Leon	Fanny	1804	?, Lancashire	(?)		Samuel Leon	Salford, Lancashire	
18528	Leon	Frank Philip	1848	Barnsbury, London	George Isaac Leon	Julianne Samuel		Bloomsbury, London	
18526	Leon	George Isaac	1821	Middlesex, London			Julianne Samuel	Bloomsbury, London	navy agent
16744	Leon	Hannah	1819	Plymouth, Devon	(?) Hart		Herentz (Hertz) Leon	Bath	
11743	Leon	Helene	1849	Spitalfields, London	Emanuel Leon	Rosetta (?)		Shoreditch, London	
3581	Leon	Herbert Samuel	1850	Barnsbury, London	George Isaac Leon	Julianne Samuel	Esther Julia Moses [Beddington]	Bloomsbury, London	
2691	Leon	Herentz (Hertz)	1810	Aiseldorp-on-the-Rhine, Germany			Hannah Hart	Bath	jeweller + general commission agent

ID	surname	given names	born	birthplace	father	mother	spouse 1	1851 residence	1851 occupation
20828	Leon	Isaac	1813	Bavaria, Germany	Leopold Leon		Clara Joseph	Sunderland, Co Durham	watch + jewellery factor
16927	Leon	Jane	1824	Hamburg, Germany	Abraham Leon	Eve (?)		Sheffield, Yorkshire	staymaker
19172	Leon	Joseph Jonas	1795	Portsmouth, Hampshire	Joseph Leon		Sarah Lucas	Hyde Park, London	merchant
18527	Leon	Julianne	1825	Chichester, Sussex	(?) Samuel		George Isaac Leon	Bloomsbury, London	
16932	Leon	Lais	1842	Hamburg, Germany	Abraham Leon	Eve (?)		Sheffield, Yorkshire	scholar
20127	Leon	Levy	1821	?, France			Eliza (?)	Holborn, London	chandler + cigar manufacturer
16746	Leon	Lewis (Louis) Henry	1847	Bath	Herentz (Hertz) Leon	Hannah Hart	Rosetta Davis	Bath	
19098	Leon	Louisa	1845	City, London	Szymanski Leon	Selina Ascher	Reuben Moss	Aldgate, London	
2690	Leon	Melina	1844	Bristol	Herentz (Hertz) Leon	Hannah Hart	Louis Symons	Bath	
16930	Leon	Morris	1834	Hamburg, Germany	Abraham Leon	Eve (?)		Sheffield, Yorkshire	hawker
9767	Leon	Philip (Eliczer)	1839	Fremantle, Australia	Lewis Leon		Alice Israel Montefiore	Kew, London	boarding school pupil
16842	Leon	Philip Lucas	1837	Bloomsbury, London	Joseph Jonas Leon	Sarah Lucas		Hyde Park, London	scholar
14438	Leon	Raphael	1835	?, Lancashire	Samuel Leon	Fanny (?)		Salford, Lancashire	
16928	Leon	Rica	1825	Hamburg, Germany	Abraham Leon	Eve (?)		Sheffield, Yorkshire	staymaker
11740	Leon	Rosetta	1815	?, France	(?)		Emanuel Leon	Shoreditch, London	
14439	Leon	Rosetta	1836	?, Lancashire	Samuel Leon	Fanny (?)		Salford, Lancashire	
14434	Leon	Samuel	1791	Zeevold, Holland			Fanny (?)	Salford, Lancashire	retired furrier
19173	Leon	Sarah	1803	Middlesex, London	(?) Lucas		Joseph Jonas Leon	Hyde Park, London	merchant
9768	Leon	Septimus	1838	Jamaica, West Indies				Kew, London	boarding school pupil
11741	Leon	Simon	1844	Spitalfields, London	Emanuel Leon	Rosetta (?)		Shoreditch, London	scholar
7655	Leon	Sophia	1810	?	(?)		Samuel Leon	Manchester	
16929	Leon	Sophia	1829	Hamburg, Germany	Abraham Leon	Eve (?)		Sheffield, Yorkshire	staymaker
16747	Leon	Zarylic	1850	Bath	Herentz Leon	Hannah Hart		Bath	
13388	Leopold	B---	1847	?London	Felix Leopold	Julia Abrahams		Spitalfields, London	scholar
20134	Leopold	Clement	1850	Jersey, Channel Islands	Lewis (Louis) Lipman Leopold	Marian Harriet Harvey		St Helier, Jersey, Channel Islands	
13386	Leopold	Felix	1817	Middlesex, London	Isaac Leibman Leopold	Ruth (?)	Julia Abrahams	Spitalfields, London	general dealer
13385	Leopold	Julia	1815	Deal, Kent	Abraham Abrahams	Sarah (?)	Felix Leopold	Spitalfields, London	tailoress
20130	Leopold	Lewis (Louis) Lipman	1818	Furth, Bavaria, Germany	Isaac Leibman Leopold	Ruth (?)	Marian Harriet Harvey	St Helier, Jersey, Channel Islands	tobacconist
20132	Leopold	Marian Harriet	1820	?, England	Andrew Harvey		Lewis (Louis) Lipman Leopold	St Helier, Jersey, Channel Islands	
20135	Leopold	Matilda	1851	Jersey, Channel Islands	Lewis (Louis) Lipman Leopold	Lewis (Louis) Lipman Leopold		St Helier, Jersey, Channel Islands	
13387	Leopold	Rachal	1846	?, London	Felix Leopold	Julia Abrahams		Spitalfields, London	
20131	Leopold	Sigmund Liebman	1829	Furth, Bavaria, Germany	Isaac Leibman Leopold	Ruth (?)	Emma (?)	St Helier, Jersey, Channel Islands	tobacconist
20133	Leopold	Theresa Clara	1848	Jersey, Channel Islands	Lewis (Louis) Lipman Leopold	Marian Harriet Harvey	Henry Fileman	St Helier, Jersey, Channel Islands	
14320	Leppoc	Henry J	1808	?, Germany			Jane Gibson	Manchester	merchant + commission agent
2302	Lesser	Abraham	1825	Skwierzyna, Poland [Schwerin, Prussia]	Ephraim Lesser	Hinda Pincus	Elizabeth May	Leeds, Yorkshire	general dealer

ID	surname	given names	born	birthplace	father	mother	spouse 1	1851 residence	1851 occupation
4609	Lesser	Boanna	1813	Spitalfields, London	Wolf Josephson Gollin	Marlah (Martha) (?)	Mathias Lesser	Birmingham	
7977	Lesser	Eliza	1841	Spitalfields, London	Isaac Lesser	Sophia Hart	Benjamin Mendoza	Spitalfields, London	scholar
10867	Lesser	Ellen	1831	Whitechapel, London	Isaac Lesser	Sophia Hart	Lazarus Bernstein	Spitalfields, London	fancy cap maker
7972	Lesser	Isaac	1801	?, Poland [?, Prussia]	Eliezer		Sophia Hart	Spitalfields, London	dealer in jewellery
7974	Lesser	Jacob	1832	Aldgate, London	Isaac Lesser	Sophia Hart	Maria Laon	Spitalfields, London	cigar maker
4612	Lesser	Lesser	1840	Birmingham	Mathias Lesser	Boanna Gollin	Helen Lazarus	Birmingham	scholar
11757	Lesser	Louis	1821	?, Poland [?, Prussia]				Shoreditch, London	hawker
2301	Lesser	Louis	1832	Skwierzyna, Poland [Skwierzyna, Poland, Prussia]	Ephraim Lesser	Hinda Pincus	Evelina May	Leeds, Yorkshire	general dealer
6722	Lesser	Mathias	1800	?Poland	Eliezer Lesser	Brital Elizabeth (?)	Boanna Gollin	Birmingham	
13943	Lesser	Maximillian	1804	?, Poland [?, Prussia]				Manchester	cigar dealer
10866	Lesser	Rosetta (Rose)	1829	Whitechapel, London	Isaac Lesser	Sophia Hart	Mordecai de Moses Mendoza	Spitalfields, London	milliner
7975	Lesser	Samuel	1836	Spitalfields, London	Isaac Lesser	Sophia Hart	Fanny Woolf	Spitalfields, London	cigar maker
4611	Lesser	Samuel	1838	Birmingham	Mathias Lesser	Boanna Gollin	Marion Rock	Birmingham	scholar
4610	Lesser	Sarah	1835	St Pancras, London	Mathias Lesser	Boanna Gollin	Joseph Barnett Behrens	Birmingham	
7973	Lesser	Sophia	1793	?Canterbury, Kent	Benjamin (Zeib Woolf) Hart	Beilah (Elizabeth, Betsy) Hart	Isaac Lesser	Spitalfields, London	
4613	Lesser	Wolf	1842	Birmingham	Mathias Lesser	Boanna Gollin		Birmingham	scholar
30177	Lesset	Emma	1825	?, Poland				Dudley, Worcestershire	traveller
30178	Lesset	Louisa	1829	?, Poland			Morris Side	Dudley, Worcestershire	traveller
13745	Lessey	Alpica	1822	?, Poland [?, Prussia]				Manchester	tailor
14840	Lessowski	Joseph	1799	?Poznan, Poland [?Posen, Prussia]			Susannah (?)	Bethnal Green, London	pensioner
14841	Lessowski	Susannah	1801	?, Essex	?)		Joseph Lessowski	Bethnal Green, London	laundress
14156	Leudesdorf	Henry	1821	Hamburg, Germany				Manchester	commission agent
5206	Levason	Catherine (Kate)	1801	?, Norfolk [East ?Thatcham, Norfolk]	David Jones	Leah Micholls	Lewis Levason	Clerkenwell, London	attends to family
14696	Levason	Henrietta	1834	Leamington, Warwickshire	Lewis Levason	Catherine (Kate) Jones		Clerkenwell, London	bead worker
5200	Levason	Joseph	1811	?Colchester, Essex	Samuel Levason	Kate (?)	Rebecca Jones	Hereford, Herefordshire	dentist
5203	Levason	Leah Jones	1839	Cheltenham, Gloucestershire	Joseph Levason	Rebecca Jones	Louis Mendelsohn	Cheltenham, Gloucestershire	
5205	Levason	Lewis	1800	Colchester, Essex	Samuel Levason	Kate (?)	Catherine (Kate) Jones	Clerkenwell, London	dentist (formerly dentist but without occupation)
5202	Levason	Lewis Edward	1837	Whitehaven, Cumbria	Joseph Levason	Rebecca Jones		Cheltenham, Gloucestershire	
5201	Levason	Rebecca	1812	Great Yarmouth, Norfolk	David Jones	Leah Micholls	Joseph Levason	Cheltenham, Gloucestershire	
14697	Levason	Rosetta	1839	Cheltenham, Gloucestershire	Lewis Levason	Catherine (Kate) Jones	Thomas Blamire	Clerkenwell, London	bead worker
18832	Levason	Victoria	1842	Cheltenham, Gloucestershire	Lewis Levason	Catherine (Kate) Jones	Edward I Myer	Clerkenwell, London	
5204	Levason	Walter Emanuel	1843	Cheltenham, Gloucestershire	Joseph Levason	Rebecca Jones		Cheltenham, Gloucestershire	
8094	Leveau	Abraham	1811	Gloucester, Gloucestershire			Maria Israel	Belgravia, London	
8093	Leveau	Maria	1811	Aldgate, London	Isaiah Israel	Jane (?)	Abraham Leveau	Belgravia, London	
14053	Leveaux	Adeline	1831	Bedford, Bedfordshire	Henry Leveaux	Catharine (?)		Manchester	

ID	surname	given names	born	birthplace	father	mother	spouse 1	1851 residence	1851 occupation
14056	Leveaux	Albert	1841	Bedford, Bedfordshire	Henry Leveaux	Catharine (?)	Maude Benjamin	Manchester	scholar
14051	Leveaux	Catharine	1802	Bedford, Bedfordshire	(?)		Henry Leveaux	Manchester	wine merchant
14052	Leveaux	Henry	1800	?			Catharine (?)	Manchester	wine merchant
14057	Leveaux	Joseph	1842	Bedford, Bedfordshire	Henry Leveaux	Catharine (?)		Manchester	scholar
14055	Leveaux	Montague	1834	Bedford, Bedfordshire	Henry Leveaux	Catharine (?)		Manchester	student
14054	Leveaux	Sarah	1839	Bedford, Bedfordshire	Henry Leveaux	Catharine (?)	Simon Katzenstein	Manchester	
4614	Levein	Wolf	1803	?, Poland			(?)	Birmingham	tailor
17146	Levenburg	Levin	1805	?, Poland			Rachel (?)	Newcastle Upon Tyne	glazier
20092	Levenburg	Nathan	1835	North Shields, Tyne & Wear	Levin Levenburg	Rachel (?)	Ellen Elizabeth Woomack	Newcastle Upon Tyne	
17147	Levenburg	Rachel	1794	?, Germany	(?)		Levin Levenburg	Newcastle Upon Tyne	
18052	Levene	Abraham	1825	?, Poland				Dudley, Worcestershire	traveller
18562	Levene	Alfred	1840	Shoreditch, London	Lewis Levene	Caroline (?)	Rosetta Barnett	Shoreditch, London	scholar
18559	Levene	Betsy	1834	Shoreditch, London	Lewis Levene	Caroline (?)	Moris Spyers	Shoreditch, London	
18558	Levene	Caroline	1803	Great Yarmouth, Norfolk	(?)		Lewis Levene	Shoreditch, London	
18561	Levene	Julia	1839	Shoreditch, London	Lewis Levene	Caroline (?)	Pierre John Nathan	Shoreditch, London	scholar
18557	Levene	Lewis	1807	Whitechapel, London			Caroline (?)	Shoreditch, London	master tailor
18563	Levene	Lipman E	1842	Shoreditch, London	Lewis Levene	Caroline (?)		Shoreditch, London	scholar
18560	Levene	Morris	1836	Shoreditch, London	Lewis Levene	Caroline (?)	Fanny (Frances) Nathan	Shoreditch, London	scholar
18564	Levene	Samuel	1844	Shoreditch, London	Lewis Levene	Caroline (?)	Elizabeth Abrahams	Shoreditch, London	scholar
18565	Levene	Sarah	1831	Norwich, Norfolk	Lewis Levene	Caroline (?)		Shoreditch, London	
30915	Levenson	Herman	1824	?, Russia				Sheffield, Yorkshire	
30912	Levenson	Joseph	1827	?, Russia			Rosalie (?)	Sheffield, Yorkshire	--- maker
30914	Levenson	Lewis	1850	Sheffield, Yorkshire	Joseph Levenson	Rosalie (?)		Sheffield, Yorkshire	
30913	Levenson	Rosalie	1827	Hanover, Germany	(?)		Joseph Levenson	Sheffield, Yorkshire	
14425	Lever	Abigail	1796	Wigan, Lancashire	(?)		(?) Lever	Salford, Lancashire	annuitant
20833	Leverson	George Bazett Colvin	1827	Piccadilly, London			Henriette Jonassohn	Kensington, London	diamond, pearl precious stone + coral merchant
30103	Leverson	Henrietta	1827	Sunderland, Co Durham	David Jonassohn	Charlotte Bouer	George Bazett Colvin Leverson	Durham, Co Durham	
2492	Leveson	Ester	1806	?, Poland			Joseph Leveson	Hull, Yorkshire	
16814	Leveson	Hinda	1825	Doncaster, Yorkshire	(?) Leveson			Bristol	governess
2493	Leveson	Joseph	1804	?, Poland			Ester (?)	Hull, Yorkshire	travelling hawker + jeweller
15808	Levett	Maria	1816	Aldgate, London	(?) Israel		(?) Levett	Aldgate, London	lodging house keeper
15810	Levett	Sarah	1837	Dublin, Ireland	(?) Levett	Maria Israel		Aldgate, London	
15809	Levett	Walter	1835	Dublin, Ireland	(?) Levett	Maria Israel		Aldgate, London	butcher
7131	Levetus	Celia	1823	Portsmouth, Hampshire	Joseph Moss	Amelia Davids	Lewis (Edward Hyman) Levetus	Birmingham	writer
7133	Levetus	Edward M	1850	Birmingham	Lewis (Edward Hyman) Levetus	Celia Moss	Sarah Isabelle Himes	Birmingham	
7134	Levetus	Hyman	1849	Birmingham	Lewis (Edward Hyman) Levetus	Celia Moss	Fanny Solomon	Birmingham	
7132	Levetus	Lewis (Edward Hyman)	1796	?, Moldova [Moldavia, Romania]			Celia Moss	Birmingham	shochet
10215	Levey	Aaron	1771	?, Germany			Rachel (?)	Spitalfields, London	general dealer
20141	Levey	Augusta M	1821	Margate, Kent	Emanuel Levey	Esther (?)		Marylebone, London	
15418	Levey	Catherine	1844	?	John Levey	Elizabeth (?)		Covent Garden, London	scholar

ID	surname	given names	born	birthplace	father	mother	spouse 1	1851 residence	1851 occupation
20140	Levey	Catherine R	1820	Margate, Kent	Emanuel Levey	Esther (?)		Marylebone, London	
20139	Levey	Clara	1811	Margate, Kent	Emanuel Levey	Esther (?)		Marylebone, London	
15420	Levey	David	1849	?	John Levey	Elizabeth (?)		Covent Garden, London	
15416	Levey	Elizabeth	1816	?	(?)		John Levey	Covent Garden, London	
20137	Levey	Esther	1789	Dover, Kent			Emanuel Levey	Marylebone, London	dealer in French fancy goods, clocks, toys &c
20142	Levey	Janet Louisa	1831	Margate, Kent	Emanuel Levey	Esther (?)		Marylebone, London	
15415	Levey	John	1815	?			Elizabeth (?)	Covent Garden, London	
15419	Levey	Louis	1847	Dublin, Ireland	John Levey	Elizabeth (?)		Covent Garden, London	
10214	Levey	Rachel	1744	Middlesex, London	(?)		Aaron Levey	Spitalfields, London	
15417	Levey	Rachel	1833	?	John Levey	Elizabeth (?)		Covent Garden, London	
18765	Levey	Sarah	1815	Amsterdam, Holland	(?) Levey			Bloomsbury, London	
29102	Levey	Sarah	1827	?London	(?) Levey			Southwark, London	
20138	Levey	Sarah Ann	1809	Margate, Kent	Emanuel Levey	Esther (?)		Marylebone, London	
13603	Levi	Abraham	1798	?, Poland [?, Prussia]			Minna (?)	Manchester	tailor
11842	Levi	Abraham	1801	Venice, Italy			(?)	Whitechapel, London	coffee + sugar importer
16622	Levi	Abraham	1803	?, Warwickshire				Liverpool	dealer in watch materials
4615	Levi	Abraham	1808	?, Poland			Maria (?Israel)	Birmingham	dealer in jewellery
29040	Levi	Abraham	1815	Whitechapel, London			R--- (?)	Whitechapel, London	tobacconist
2298	Levi	Abraham	1821	?, London				Leeds, Yorkshire	general dealer
7992	Levi	Abraham	1831	Spitalfields, London	Eleazer Levi	Catherine Moses		Spitalfields, London	clothier
4632	Levi	Abraham	1847	Sheffield, Yorkshire	David Levi	Tarisia (?Theresa) (?)		Birmingham	
15725	Levi	Alexander	1797	Canterbury, Kent			Louisa Leah (?)	Euston, London	watch maker
11843	Levi	Alexander	1823	Venice, Italy	Abraham Levi	(?)		Whitechapel, London	coffee + sugar importer
25657	Levi	Alexander	1831	Aldgate, London	Alexander Levy			Aldgate, London	watchmaker
9819	Levi	Alexander	1843	Whitechapel, London	Leman Levi	Elizabeth Myers (Koopman)		Whitechapel, London	scholar
23660	Levi	Alfred	1841	Liverpool	Joseph Levi	Sarah (?)		Liverpool	scholar
9816	Levi	Alfred Kaufman	1838	Whitechapel, London	Leman Levi	Elizabeth Myers (Koopman)	Kate Julia Rosenthal	Whitechapel, London	scholar
18807	Levi	Amelia	1795	Portsmouth, Hampshire	Elias Levi	Esther (?)		Portsmouth, Hampshire	
2494	Levi	Amelia	1830	Shantra, Russia	(?) Goldstein		Levi Levi	Hull, Yorkshire	
18212	Levi	Amelia	1837	Middlesex, London	(?) Levi			Mile End, London	scholar
23298	Levi	Ann	1805	?, London	David de Abraham Mendes	Sarah de Jacob Simhon	Elias Levi	Mayfair, London	dealer in apparel
23277	Levi	Ann	1815	Marylebone, London	(?)		Philip Levi	Kensal Green, London	shoe binder
23307	Levi	Ann	1846	Mayfair, London	Elias Levi	Ann Mendes		Mayfair, London	scholar
4004	Levi	Anna	1789	Portsmouth, Hampshire	Elias Levi	Sarah (?)		Portsmouth, Hampshire	
5305	Levi	Arabella (Isabella)	1821	Truro, Cornwall	Henry Harris	Esther Jacob	Joseph Levi	Aldgate, London	
29567	Levi	B---	1833	?, Scotland	Joseph Levi	Nancy Prince		Whitechapel, London	cabinet maker
23509	Levi	Barnet	1795	?, London			Sarah (?)	Liverpool	watch manufacurer
9818	Levi	Barnett	1841	Whitechapel, London	Leman Levi	Elizabeth Myers (Koopman)		Whitechapel, London	scholar
1396	Levi	Benjamin	1786	Newton Abbot, Devon				Plymouth, Devon	last maker
9821	Levi	Benjamin	1846	Whitechapel, London	Leman Levi	Elizabeth Myers (Koopman)		Whitechapel, London	scholar

ID	surname	given names	born	birthplace	father	mother	spouse 1	1851 residence	1851 occupation
4003	Levi	Benjamin Wolf	1792	Portsmouth, Hampshire	Elias Levi	Sarah (?)		Portsmouth, Hampshire	engraver + copper plate printer, stationer + furrier
5642	Levi	Blanche Selina	1849	St Pancras, London	John Levi	Georgiana (Georgina) Ezekiel		Kentish Town, London	
13172	Levi	Catherine	1795	Aldgate, London	(?)		(?) Levi	Aldgate, London	nurse
7991	Levi	Catherine	1802	Whitechapel, London	(?Abraham) Moses		Eleazer Levi	Whitechapel, London	
4646	Levi	Charles	1836	Birmingham	Nathan Levi	Matilda (?)		Birmingham	watchmaker's apprentice
4617	Levi	Charles Lyon	1794	Birmingham	Yehuda HaLevi		Ellis (?)	Birmingham	engraver
4642	Levi	Charlotte	1809	Birmingham	Lyon Levi			Birmingham	
4639	Levi	Clina	1825	?, Poland			Lazarus Levi	Birmingham	
4622	Levi	David	1800	Birmingham			Ris (?)	Birmingham	wine merchant
4005	Levi	David	1811	Portsmouth, Hampshire	Elias Levi	Sarah (?)		Portsmouth, Hampshire	assistant engraver
8532	Levi	David	1820	?Plymouth, Devon	Phineas Levi	Kitty Mordecai/Aschenberg	Eve Hyman	Plymouth, Devon	traveller, artificial flowers
2215	Levi	David	1821	?, Poland				Oxford, Oxfordshire	jeweller
4621	Levi	David	1821	Plymouth, Devon				Birmingham	artificial flowers
4630	Levi	David	1821	?, Poland			Tarisia (?Theresa) (?)	Birmingham	traveller
13597	Levi	David	1821	?, Poland				Manchester	cap maker
23299	Levi	David	1832	?, London	Elias Levi	Ann Mendes		Mayfair, London	dealer in apparel
2496	Levi	Davis	1821	Brod, Russia [Brott, Russia]			Hannah Levett	Hull, Yorkshire	jeweller
4127	Levi	Deborah	1826	Spitalfields, London	Eleazer Levi	Catherine Moses	Michael Solomon	Whitechapel, London	
12358	Levi	Deborah	1833	Bermondsey, London	John (Jacob) Levi	Ann Henry	Abraham Solomon	City, London	
12166	Levi	E--	1824	Whitechapel, London	(?) Levi	S--- (?)		Whitechapel, London	
29042	Levi	E---	1837	Whitechapel, London	Abraham Levi	R--- (?)		Whitechapel, London	
29043	Levi	E---	1839	Whitechapel, London	Abraham Levi	R--- (?)		Whitechapel, London	scholar
4586	Levi	Edward	1826	?, Poland [?, Prussia]				Birmingham	watch material dealer
4647	Levi	Edward	1839	Birmingham	Nathan Levi	Matilda (?)		Birmingham	
7990	Levi	Eleazer	1797	Aldgate, London			Catherine Moses	Whitechapel, London	pen maker
23297	Levi	Elias	1804	Strand, London	Jacob Levi		Ann Mendes	Mayfair, London	cut glass manufacturer
13605	Levi	Elias	1833	?, Poland [?, Prussia]	Abraham Levi	Minna (?)		Manchester	glazier
23282	Levi	Eliza	1848	Kensington, London	Philip Levi	Ann (?)		Kensal Green, London	
5307	Levi	Eliza H	1843	Exeter, Devon	Joseph Levi	Arabella Harris		Aldgate, London	scholar
2903	Levi	Elizabeth	1793	Portsmouth, Hampshire	Eliakim		John Levi	Plymouth, Devon	
23261	Levi	Elizabeth	1797	Aldgate, London	(?) Levi			Notting Hill, London	fundholder
4007	Levi	Elizabeth	1813	Portsmouth, Hampshire	Elias Levi	Esther (?)		Portsmouth, Hampshire	
5522	Levi	Elizabeth	1815	Whitechapel, London	Yechutiel Koopman HaCohen (Meyers)		Leman Levi	Whitechapel, London	
4619	Levi	Elizabeth	1829	?, London	Charles Lyon Levi	Ellis (?)		Birmingham	
23659	Levi	Elizabeth	1834	Liverpool	Joseph Levi	Sarah (?)		Liverpool	
4618	Levi	Ellis	1799	?, London			Charles Lyon Levi	Birmingham	
4625	Levi	Erne	1834	Birmingham	David Levi	Ris (?)		Birmingham	
22904	Levi	Esther	1782	Whitechapel, London	(?) Levi			Wapping, London	schoolmistress
4006	Levi	Esther	1794	Portsmouth, Hampshire	Elias Levi	Esther (?)		Portsmouth, Hampshire	
5523	Levi	Esther	1836	Whitechapel, London	Leman Levi	Elizabeth Meyers		Whitechapel, London	scholar
5309	Levi	Esther (Ethel) Harris	1850	Exeter, Devon	Joseph Levi	Arabella Harris		Aldgate, London	

ID	surname	given names	born	birthplace	father	mother	spouse 1	1851 residence	1851 occupation
8533	Levi	Eve	1821	?Plymouth, Devon	Samuel Hyman	Betsy Moses	David Levi	Plymouth, Devon	
1349	Levi	Evelina	1817	Plymouth, Devon	Phineas Levi	Kitty Mordecai/Aschenberg		Plymouth, Devon	
4648	Levi	Eveline	1841	Birmingham	Nathan Levi	Matilda (?)		Birmingham	
5524	Levi	Eveline	1848	Whitechapel, London	Leman Levi	Elizabeth Meyers	Saunders Solomon	Whitechapel, London	
23281	Levi	Fanny	1846	Kensington, London	Philip Levi	Ann (?)		Kensal Green, London	
1204	Levi	Frances	1835	Plymouth, Devon	Samuel Levi	Phoebe (?)		Plymouth, Devon	
23515	Levi	Frederick	1850	Liverpool	Barnet Levi	Sarah (?)		Liverpool	
11844	Levi	Gabriel	1827	Venice, Italy	Abraham Levi	(?)		Whitechapel, London	coffee + sugar importer
14993	Levi	Gabriel	1832	?, Turkey				Bethnal Green, London	bookbinder
23512	Levi	George	1837	Liverpool	Barnet Levi	Sarah (?)		Liverpool	scholar
5311	Levi	George Joseph	1846	Exeter, Devon	Joseph Levi	Arabella Harris	Kate Jacobs	Aldgate, London	scholar
5639	Levi	Georgiana (Georgina)	1824	?, Devon	Henry Ezekiel		John Levi	Kentish Town, London	
8535	Levi	Gerald Abraham	1843	Exeter, Devon	John Levi	Georgiana (Georgina) Ezekiel	Sarah Levy	Kentish Town, London	
5640	Levi	Gertrude Ezekiel	1842	Exeter, Devon	John Levi	Georgiana (Georgina) Ezekiel		Kentish Town, London	
7549	Levi	Godfrey	1822	Birmingham	Joseph Levi	Sarah (?)	Miriam Nathan	Liverpool	
29047	Levi	H---	1847	Whitechapel, London	Abraham Levi	R--- (?)		Whitechapel, London	scholar
4636	Levi	Hannah	1808	?, London	(?) Abrahams		Joel Levi	Birmingham	
1351	Levi	Hannah	1822	Plymouth, Devon	Phineas Levi	Kitty Mordecai/Aschenberg		Plymouth, Devon	
2497	Levi	Hannah	1824	Bristol	(?) Levett		Davis Levi	Hull, Yorkshire	
4652	Levi	Hannah	1830	Manchester	(?)		Hyam Levi	Birmingham	
23511	Levi	Hannah	1836	Liverpool	Barnet Levi	Sarah (?)		Liverpool	milliner (apprentice)
2192	Levi	Hannah (Anne)	1806	?, Poland			Harris Levi	Oxford, Oxfordshire	jeweller's widow
23280	Levi	Harriet	1844	Kensington, London	Philip Levi	Ann (?)		Kensal Green, London	
2144	Levi	Henry	1815	Hamburg, Germany				Hull, Yorkshire	licensed hawker
23278	Levi	Henry	1837	Whitechapel, London	Philip Levi	Ann (?)		Kensal Green, London	errand boy
24184	Levi	Henry	1840	Exeter, Devon	John Levi	Georgiana (Georgina) Ezekiel		Kentish Town, London	
5903	Levi	Henry	1844	Whitechapel, London	Leman Levi	Elizabeth Myers	Elizabeth (Lizzie) Fileman	Whitechapel, London	
1353	Levi	Henry (Harry) M	1830	Plymouth, Devon	Phineas Levi	Kitty Mordecai/Aschenberg		Plymouth, Devon	assistant to general dealer
23514	Levi	Henry B	1842	Liverpool	Barnet Levi	Sarah (?)		Liverpool	scholar
4640	Levi	Herman	1850	Aldgate, London	Lazarus Levi	Clina (?)		Birmingham	
23843	Levi	Horatia	1823	Poznan, Poland [Posen, Germany]	(?)		Samuel Levi	Soho, London	
4651	Levi	Hyam	1822	?, Germany ?, Prussia]			Hannah (?)	Birmingham	clothier
4482	Levi	Hyman	1828	?, Poland				Birmingham	glazier
2297	Levi	Inno	1811	?, Germany				Leeds, Yorkshire	shoemaker
30170	Levi	Isaac	1825	?, Poland				Dudley, Worcestershire	glass + paint seller
9817	Levi	Isaac	1840	Whitechapel, London	Leman Levi	Elizabeth Myers (Koopman)		Whitechapel, London	scholar
29099	Levi	Isabella	1828	Hanover, Germany	(?) Levi			Whitechapel, London	governess
6464	Levi	Isabelle	1829	Exeter, Devon	(?)		(?) Levi	Merthyr Tydfil, Wales	
29045	Levi	J---	1842	Whitechapel, London	Abraham Levi	R--- (?)		Whitechapel, London	scholar

ID	surname	given names	born	birthplace	father	mother	spouse 1	1851 residence	1851 occupation
29046	Levi	J---	1844	Whitechapel, London	Abraham Levi	R--- (?)		Whitechapel, London	scholar
1350	Levi	Jacob Mordecai	1819	Plymouth, Devon	Phineas Levi	Kitty Mordecai/Aschenberg	Sarah M Jacob	Plymouth, Devon	tobacconist + dealer
19363	Levi	Jane	1767	?, Germany	(?)		(?Abraham) Levi	Whitechapel, London	
808	Levi	Jane	1791	Whitechapel, London				Uxbridge, Middlesex	monthly nurse
22447	Levi	Jane	1844	?	(?) Levi			Gravesend, Kent	boarding school pupil
4635	Levi	Joel	1805	?, Germany			Hannah Abrahams	Birmingham	pawnbroker
1229	Levi	John	1793	Portsmouth, Hampshire	Judah		Elizabeth (?)	Plymouth, Devon	general dealer
16848	Levi	John	1803	Middlesex, London	Moshe Levi			Brighton, Sussex	orange merchant
5638	Levi	John	1815	Plymouth, Devon	Phineas Levi	Kitty Mordecai/Aschenberg	Georgiana (Georgina) Ezekiel	Kentish Town, London	
9815	Levi	John	1833	Whitechapel, London	Leman Levi	Elizabeth Myers (Koopman)	Rachel Jacobs	Whitechapel, London	apprentice jeweller
23302	Levi	John	1837	Mayfair, London	Elias Levi	Ann Mendes	Rachel Jones	Mayfair, London	
23513	Levi	John	1840	Liverpool	Barnet Levi	Sarah (?)		Liverpool	scholar
6465	Levi	John Henry	1851	Merthyr Tydfil, Wales	(?) Levi	Isabelle (?)		Merthyr Tydfil, Wales	
7996	Levi	Jonah	1840	Spitalfields, London	Eleazer Levi	Catherine Moses		Spitalfields, London	scholar
23655	Levi	Joseph	1793	?, London			Sarah (?)	Liverpool	quill + steel pen manufacturer + dealer
5306	Levi	Joseph	1811	Portsmouth, Hampshire	Phineas Levi	Kitty Mordecai/Aschenberg	Arabella Harris	Aldgate, London	hardwareman
5337	Levi	Joseph	1833	Plymouth, Devon	Samuel Levi	Phoebe (?)	Annie Isaacs	Plymouth, Devon	
23306	Levi	Joshua	1844	Mayfair, London	Elias Levi	Ann Mendes		Mayfair, London	scholar
4620	Levi	Julia	1837	Birmingham	Charles Lyon Levi	Ellis (?Alice) (?)		Birmingham	
4628	Levi	Julia	1844	Birmingham	David Levi	Ris (?)		Birmingham	scholar
4649	Levi	Juliana (Julia)	1843	Birmingham	Nathan Levi	Matilda (?)		Birmingham	
809	Levi	Kate	1818	Whitechapel, London				Uxbridge, Middlesex	servant
22448	Levi	Kate	1846	?	(?) Levi			Gravesend, Kent	boarding school pupil
1345	Levi	Kitty	1788	Portsmouth, Hampshire	(?) Mordecai/Aschenberg		Phineas Levi	Plymouth, Devon	
29566	Levi	L---	1828	?, Scotland	Joseph Levi	Nancy Prince		Whitechapel, London	dressmaker
29044	Levi	L---	1840	Whitechapel, London	Abraham Levi	R--- (?)		Whitechapel, London	scholar
9769	Levi	Lawrence	1837	Middlesex, London				Kew, London	boarding school pupil
4638	Levi	Lazarus	1831	?, Poland			Clina (?)	Birmingham	glazier
5521	Levi	Leman	1810	Portsmouth, Hampshire	(?) Levi		Elizabeth Myers (Koopman)	Whitechapel, London	dealer in jewellery + plate
6701	Levi	Leone	1821	Ancona, Italy	Isaac Levi		Margaret Ritchie	Edinburgh, Scotland	lecturer + writer on commercial law
2145	Levi	Levi	1825	Landrick, Russia			Amelia Goldstein	Hull, Yorkshire	plumber + glazier
8071	Levi	Levine (Leven, Levean)	1834	Spitalfields, London	Eleazer Levi	Catherine Moses		Whitechapel, London	pen cutter
4644	Levi	Lewis Lyon	1830	Birmingham	Nathan Levi	Matilda (?)		Birmingham	jeweller's journeyman
23844	Levi	Lily	1848	Soho, London			Horatia (?)	Soho, London	
13606	Levi	Lina	1835	?, Poland [?, Prussia]	Abraham Levi	Minna (?)		Manchester	cap maker
23303	Levi	Louisa	1838	Mayfair, London	Elias Levi	Ann Mendes		Mayfair, London	scholar
7995	Levi	Louisa	1839	Spitalfields, London	Eleazer Levi	Catherine Moses		Spitalfields, London	scholar
15726	Levi	Louisa Leah	1811	Arundel, Sussex	(?)		Alexander Levi	Euston, London	
23658	Levi	Lucy	1832	Liverpool	Joseph Levi	Sarah (?)		Liverpool	

ID	surname	given names	born	birthplace	father	mother	spouse 1	1851 residence	1851 occupation
4641	Levi	Lyon	1761	?, Germany				Birmingham	retired tradesman
4616	Levi	Maria	1804	Portsmouth, Hampshire	(Isaiah Israel?)			Birmingham	
23301	Levi	Maria	1835	Lambeth, London	Elias Levi	Ann Mendes		Mayfair, London	
29746	Levi	Marianne	1847	Aldgate, London	Wolf Levi	Phoebe (?)		Aldgate, London	scholar
30793	Levi	Mark	1809	Warsaw, Poland				Preston, Lancashire	traveller
4626	Levi	Martha	1837	Birmingham	David Levi	Ris (?)		Birmingham	scholar
2495	Levi	Mary	1850	Hull, Yorkshire	Levi Levi	Amelia (?)		Hull, Yorkshire	
7496	Levi	Mathilda	1767	?				Liverpool	
4643	Levi	Matilda	1801	Birmingham			Nathan Levi	Birmingham	factor's wife
5308	Levi	Maurice H	1844	Exeter, Devon	Joseph Levi	Arabella Harris		Aldgate, London	scholar
12737	Levi	Mier	1818	Ipswich, Suffolk				Ipswich, Suffolk	traveller in jewellery
13609	Levi	Minah	1849	?, Poland [?, Prussia]	Abraham Levi	Minna (?)		Manchester	
13604	Levi	Minna	1811	?, Poland [?, Prussia]	(?)		Abraham Levi	Manchester	
4653	Levi	Morris	1830	?, Germany				Birmingham	
29747	Levi	Moses	1850	Aldgate, London	Wolf Levi	Phoebe (?)		Aldgate, London	
4161	Levi	Mosley John	1837	Plymouth, Devon	John Levi	Elizabeth (?)	Frances (Fanny) Morris	Plymouth, Devon	
29565	Levi	Nancy	1799	?, Holland	Asher Prince	Amelia (?)	Joseph Levi	Whitechapel, London	
18808	Levi	Nathan	1797	Birmingham	Lyon Levi		Matilda (?)	Birmingham	factor
7590	Levi	Nathaniel	1830	Liverpool	Joseph Levi	Sarah (?)	Sarah (?)	Liverpool	tailor + draper
23304	Levi	Nathaniel	1840	Mayfair, London	Elias Levi	Ann Mendes		Mayfair, London	scholar
30169	Levi	Newman	1823	?, Poland				Dudley, Worcestershire	glass + paint seller
23276	Levi	Philip	1814	Whitechapel, London			Ann (?)	Kensal Green, London	shoe maker
4645	Levi	Philip	1835	Birmingham	Nathan Levi	Matilda (?)		Birmingham	lithographer
23279	Levi	Philip	1839	Whitechapel, London	Philip Levi	Ann (?)		Kensal Green, London	errand boy
1344	Levi	Phineas	1784	Portsmouth, Hampshire			Kitty Mordecai/Aschenberg	Plymouth, Devon	Navy agent
5310	Levi	Phineas Harris	1848	Exeter, Devon	Joseph Levi	Arabella Harris	Julia Wertheimer	Aldgate, London	scholar
5641	Levi	Phineas Samuel	1846	Whitechapel, London	John Levi	Georgiana (Georgina) Ezekiel		Kentish Town, London	
1203	Levi	Phoebe	1812	Exeter, Devon	(?)		Samuel Levi	Plymouth, Devon	dealer in toys
29744	Levi	Phoebe	1823	Aldgate, London	(?)		Wolf Levi	Aldgate, London	
1347	Levi	Phoebe	1832	Plymouth, Devon	Phineas Levi	Kitty Mordecai/Aschenberg	Levy (Levi) Barnett Simmons	Plymouth, Devon	
4637	Levi	Priscilla	1842	?, London	Joel Levi	Hannah Abrahams	Joseph Harris	Birmingham	
29041	Levi	R---	1817	?, Hampshire	(?)		Abraham Levi	Whitechapel, London	
13608	Levi	Rachael	1845	?, Poland [?, Prussia]	Abraham Levi	Minna (?)		Manchester	
13173	Levi	Rachel	1826	Aldgate, London	(?) Levi	Catherine (?)		Aldgate, London	general dealer
23305	Levi	Rebecca	1842	Mayfair, London	Elias Levi	Ann Mendes		Mayfair, London	scholar
1352	Levi	Rebecca (Rebbeca) M	1827	Plymouth, Devon	Phineas Levi	Kitty Mordecai/Aschenberg	Joseph Myers	Plymouth, Devon	housekeeper
4623	Levi	Ris	1803	Birmingham			David Levi	Birmingham	
4627	Levi	Ris	1841	Birmingham	David Levi	Ris (?)		Birmingham	scholar
4624	Levi	Ron	1832	Birmingham	David Levi	Ris (?)		Birmingham	
4634	Levi	Rosa	1851	Birmingham	David Levi	Tarisia (?Theresa) (?)		Birmingham	
1346	Levi	Rosa (Rose)	1824	Plymouth, Devon	Phineas Levi	Kitty Mordecai/Aschenberg	Simon Mordecai Levy	Plymouth, Devon	

ID	surname	given names	born	birthplace	father	mother	spouse 1	1851 residence	1851 occupation
13191	Levi	Ruban (?Judah)	1827	Whitechapel, London				Aldgate, London	general dealer
29048	Levi	S---	1850	Whitechapel, London	Abraham Levi	R--- (?)		Whitechapel, London	
1397	Levi	Sampson	1802	Newton Abbot, Devon				Plymouth, Devon	clog maker
30466	Levi	Samuel	1799	?, London				Newcastle-under-Lyme, Staffordshire	hardware dealer
4650	Levi	Samuel	1803	?, Germany				Birmingham	traveller
23842	Levi	Samuel	1823	Poznan, Poland [Posen, Germany]			Horatia (?)	Soho, London	tailor empl 3
120	Levi	Samuel	1846	Woolwich, London				Woolwich, London	
2498	Levi	Samuel	1851	Hull, Yorkshire	Davis Levi	Hannah Levett		Hull, Yorkshire	
30568	Levi	Samuel	1851	Walworth, London	David Levi	Eve Hyman		Walworth, London	
8534	Levi	Samuel Harris	1846	Exeter, Devon	Joseph Levi	Arabella Harris		Aldgate, London	scholar
1348	Levi	Samuel M	1815	Plymouth, Devon	Phineas Levi	Kitty Mordecai/Aschenberg		Plymouth, Devon	general dealer + agent
23656	Levi	Sarah	1797	Liverpool	(?)		Joseph Levi	Liverpool	
23510	Levi	Sarah	1811	Liverpool	(?)		Barnet Levi	Liverpool	
4160	Levi	Sarah	1833	Plymouth, Devon	John Levi	Elizabeth (?)	William Keiler	Plymouth, Devon	
23300	Levi	Sarah	1834	Lambeth, London	Elias Levi	Ann Mendes		Mayfair, London	
7997	Levi	Sarah	1843	Spitalfields, London	Eleazer Levi	Catherine Moses	Benjamin Levy	Spitalfields, London	scholar
23283	Levi	Sarah A	1850	Kensington, London	Philip Levi	Ann (?)		Kensal Green, London	
4169	Levi	Sarah Henrietta	1821	?, Devon	Phineas Levi	Kitty Mordecai/Aschenberg	Abraham Lemon Woolf	Plymouth, Devon	
4633	Levi	Simon	1849	Birmingham	David Levi	Tarisia (?Theresa) (?)		Birmingham	
7915	Levi	Simon (Simeon) Mordecai	1824	Plymouth, Devon	M--- M--- Levi		Rosa (Rose) Levi	Plymouth, Devon	clerk
29745	Levi	Solomon	1845	Aldgate, London	Wolf Levi	Phoebe (?)		Aldgate, London	scholar
1354	Levi	Sophia (Sophy)	1832	Plymouth, Devon	Phineas Levi	Kitty Mordecai/Aschenberg	Samuel Harris	Plymouth, Devon	
4631	Levi	Tarisia (?Theresa)	1826	?, Poland			David Levi	Birmingham	
29743	Levi	Wolf	1818	Aldgate, London			Phoebe (?)	Aldgate, London	cabman
13607	Levi	Woolf	1843	?, Poland [?, Prussia]	Abraham Levi	Minna (?)		Manchester	scholar
23087	Levi (Levy)	Abraham	1850	Aldgate, London	Isaac Levi (Levy)	Maria (Mary) Isaacs		Aldgate, London	
1183	Levi (Levy)	Abraham M	1842	Plymouth, Devon	Marks (Markes) Levi (Levy)	Betsy (Bella) (?)		Plymouth, Devon	scholar
21334	Levi (Levy)	Adelaide	1839	King's Lynn, Norfolk	Alkin Levi (Levy)	Sarah (?)		Lowestoft, Suffolk	scholar
17985	Levi (Levy)	Adelaide	1843	Aldgate, London	Alexander Levi (Levy)	Esther Asher		Aldgate, London	
5527	Levi (Levy)	Alexander	1806	Westminster, London	Isaac Levi		Esther Asher	Aldgate, London	jeweller
21331	Levi (Levy)	Alkin	1806	?, Holland			Sarah (?)	Lowestoft, Suffolk	fishmonger
21335	Levi (Levy)	Alkin	1841	King's Lynn, Norfolk	Alkin Levi (Levy)	Sarah (?)	Emma S (?)	Lowestoft, Suffolk	scholar
17980	Levi (Levy)	Benjamin	1834	City, London	Alexander Levi (Levy)	Esther Asher		Aldgate, London	
1182	Levi (Levy)	Betsy (Bella)	1817	Penzance, Cornwall			Marks (Markes) Levi (Levy)	Plymouth, Devon	
1187	Levi (Levy)	Caroline	1849	Plymouth, Devon	Marks (Markes) Levi (Levy)	Betsy (Bella) (?)		Plymouth, Devon	
17984	Levi (Levy)	Catherine	1840	City, London	Alexander Levi (Levy)	Esther Asher		Aldgate, London	
21333	Levi (Levy)	Clara	1837	King's Lynn, Norfolk	Alkin Levi (Levy)	Sarah (?)		Lowestoft, Suffolk	scholar
1188	Levi (Levy)	Eliza	1850	Plymouth, Devon	Marks (Markes) Levi (Levy)	Betsy (Bella) (?)		Plymouth, Devon	
5529	Levi (Levy)	Elizabeth	1832	Finsbury, London	Alexander Levi (Levy)	Esther Asher	Henry Levy	Aldgate, London	
1186	Levi (Levy)	Ellen (Esther) C	1848	Plymouth, Devon	Marks (Markes) Levi (Levy)	Betsy (Bella) (?)		Plymouth, Devon	
5528	Levi (Levy)	Esther	1811	Spitalfields, London	Benjamin Asher		Alexander Levi (Levy)	Aldgate, London	
23085	Levi (Levy)	Esther	1847	Aldgate, London	Isaac Levi (Levy)	Maria (Mary) Isaacs		Aldgate, London	

ID	surname	given names	born	birthplace	father	mother	spouse 1	1851 residence	1851 occupation
1398	Levi (Levy)	Galler (Gala, Gallah)	1789	Newton Abbot, Devon				Plymouth, Devon	
23082	Levi (Levy)	Isaac	1811	Whitechapel, London	Moses Levy		Maria (Mary) Isaacs	Aldgate, London	cocoa nut merchant
17982	Levi (Levy)	Julia	1837	City, London	Alexander Levi (Levy)	Esther Asher		Aldgate, London	
1185	Levi (Levy)	Julia	1844	Plymouth, Devon	Marks (Markes) Levi (Levy)	Betsy (Bella) (?)		Plymouth, Devon	
23083	Levi (Levy)	Maria (Mary)	1821	Spitalfields, London	Lazarus Isaacs		Isaac Levi (Levy)	Aldgate, London	
23084	Levi (Levy)	Mark	1846	Aldgate, London	Isaac Levi (Levy)	Maria (Mary) Isaacs		Aldgate, London	
1181	Levi (Levy)	Marks	1813	Plymouth, Devon			Betsy (?)	Plymouth, Devon	Navy agent + jeweller
23086	Levi (Levy)	Moss	1849	Aldgate, London	Isaac Levi (Levy)	Maria (Mary) Isaacs		Aldgate, London	
17983	Levi (Levy)	Rebecca	1838	City, London	Alexander Levi (Levy)	Esther Asher		Aldgate, London	
21332	Levi (Levy)	Sarah	1813	Downham Market, Norfolk	(?)		Alkin Levi (Levy)	Lowestoft, Suffolk	
17981	Levi (Levy)	Sarah	1835	City, London	Alexander Levi (Levy)	Esther Asher		Aldgate, London	
1184	Levi (Levy)	Sarah	1844	Plymouth, Devon	Marks (Markes) Levi (Levy)	Betsy (Bella) (?)		Plymouth, Devon	
21336	Levi (Levy)	Sarah	1844	King's Lynn, Norfolk	Alkin Levi (Levy)	Sarah (?)		Lowestoft, Suffolk	scholar
18055	Levia	Moses	1787	?, Poland				Dudley, Worcestershire	hawker
25772	Levie	Abraham	1821	?, Germany [Nerolph, Germany]				Aldgate, London	tailor
16713	Levie	Alexander	1845	Spitalfields, London	Henry Levie	Catherine (?)		Spitalfields, London	scholar
16706	Levie	Ann	1832	Spitalfields, London	Henry Levie	Catherine (?)		Spitalfields, London	
16705	Levie	Catherine	1807	Marylebone, London	(?)		Henry Levie	Spitalfields, London	wholesale clothier
16715	Levie	Ester	1848	Spitalfields, London	Henry Levie	Catherine (?)		Spitalfields, London	scholar
472	Levie	Henry	1807	Aldgate, London			Catherine (?)	Spitalfields, London	wholesale clothier
473	Levie	Henry	1844	Spitalfields, London	Henry Levie	Catherine (?)		Spitalfields, London	scholar
474	Levie	Isabella	1839	Spitalfields, London	Henry Levie	Catherine (?)		Spitalfields, London	scholar
2499	Levie	Jacob	1799	Hull, Yorkshire				Hull, Yorkshire	lunatic
16710	Levie	Jane	1838	Spitalfields, London	Henry Levie	Catherine (?)		Spitalfields, London	feather maker
16708	Levie	John	1835	Spitalfields, London	Henry Levie	Catherine (?)		Spitalfields, London	
16717	Levie	Leah	1851	Spitalfields, London	Henry Levie	Catherine (?)		Spitalfields, London	
16711	Levie	Lewis	1841	Spitalfields, London	Henry Levie	Catherine (?)		Spitalfields, London	scholar
16707	Levie	Mark	1834	Spitalfields, London	Henry Levie	Catherine (?)		Spitalfields, London	
16709	Levie	Morriss	1836	Spitalfields, London	Henry Levie	Catherine (?)		Spitalfields, London	
16716	Levie	Rachal	1851	Spitalfields, London	Henry Levie	Catherine (?)		Spitalfields, London	
16714	Levie	Rosetta	1846	Spitalfields, London	Henry Levie	Catherine (?)		Spitalfields, London	scholar
16712	Levie	Samuel	1850	Spitalfields, London	Henry Levie	Catherine (?)		Spitalfields, London	
22403	Levien	Barnett	1801	Hamburg, Germany			Hannah (?)	Whitechapel, London	general dealer
12933	Levien	Edward	1819	St Pancras, London				Bloomsbury, London	MA Oxford assistant in the ms department of the British Museum
22404	Levien	Hannah	1802	?, Holland	(?)		Barnett Levien	Whitechapel, London	
22406	Levien	Jacob	1837	Shoreditch, London	Barnett Levien	Hannah (?)		Whitechapel, London	cigar maker
24064	Levien	Louis	1795	Middlesex, London				Euston, London	annuitant
22407	Levien	Polly	1837	Whitechapel, London	Barnett Levien	Hannah (?)		Whitechapel, London	umbrella maker
22405	Levien	Rosa	1835	Whitechapel, London	Barnett Levien	Hannah (?)	Henry Gluckstein	Whitechapel, London	milliner
28388	Leviene	Israel	1826	?, Poland [?, Russia Poland]				Spitalfields, London	tailor
19004	Levin	Abigail	1805	Jamaica, West Indies	(?) Levin			Whitechapel, London	

ID	surname	given names	born	birthplace	father	mother	spouse 1	1851 residence	1851 occupation
8499	Levin	Alexander	1827	Penzance, Cornwall	Henry Levin	Julia (?)	Rachel Joseph	Bristol	
5429	Levin	Bernard (Barnard)	1842	Whitechapel, London	Moses Lewin Levin	Nanie (Sarah Nanette, Hannah) Joseph		Aldgate, London	
23121	Levin	Charles	1819	?, Germany				City, London	general merchant
8503	Levin	David	1833	Penzance, Cornwall	Henry (Zvi) Levin	Julia Levy		Penzance, Cornwall	
5428	Levin	Edwin	1842	City, London	Moses Lewin Levin	Nanie (Sarah Nanette, Hannah) Joseph		Aldgate, London	
17846	Levin	Elias	1830	?, Germany				Aldgate, London	tailor
16323	Levin	Ester	1824	?, London	(?) Levin			Regent's Park, London	scullery maid
5424	Levin	Esther	1835	City, London	Moses Lewin Levin	Nanie (Sarah Nanette, Hannah) Joseph		Aldgate, London	
8500	Levin	Henry	1799	?, Sweden			Julia Levy	Penzance, Cornwall	jeweller + dealer in fancy goods
6448	Levin	Isabel	1839	Whitechapel, London	Moses Lewin Levin	Nanie (Sarah Nanette, Hannah) Joseph	Lewis Levy	Aldgate, London	
8502	Levin	Israel	1829	Penzance, Cornwall	Henry (Zvi) Levin	Julia Levy		?Penzance, Cornwall	
14230	Levin	Jacob	1827	Vilnius, Lithuania [Willno, Russia]				Manchester	hawker
24207	Levin	James H	1781	Kaliningrad, Russia [Conningsburgh, East Prussia]			Mary A (?)	Clapton, London	wool merchant
5427	Levin	Jeanette	1849	Whitechapel, London	Moses Lewin Levin	Nanie (Sarah Nanette, Hannah) Joseph		Aldgate, London	
17845	Levin	Joseph	1828	?, Germany				Aldgate, London	tailor
8501	Levin	Julia	1793	Truro, Cornwall	Israel Levy		Henry (Zvi) Levin	Penzance, Cornwall	
24537	Levin	Kate	1821	Camberwell, London	(?) Levin			Kennington, London	
5430	Levin	Kate	1840	City, London	Moses Lewin Levin	Nanie (Sarah Nanette, Hannah) Joseph	Emanuel Emanuel	Aldgate, London	
25467	Levin	Martin	1818	Copenhagen, Denmark	Philip Levin		Racielle (?)	Aldgate, London	general merchant
8504	Levin	Matilda	1826	Penzance, Cornwall	Henry (Zvi) Levin	Julia Levy	Isaac Aaron	Penzance, Cornwall	
7649	Levin	Meyer	1783	?, Poland [?, Prussia]	Leib Levin		Esther Nathan	Whitechapel, London	merchant
24538	Levin	Miriam	1823	Camberwell, London	(?) Levin			Kennington, London	
176	Levin	Moses Lewin	1801	Middlesex, London	Yehuda Leib		Nanie (Sarah Nanette, Hannah) Joseph	Aldgate, London	importer of fancy French jewellery + beads &c from India and Africa
5422	Levin	Nanie (Sarah Nanette, Hannah)	1809	Falmouth, Cornwall	(?) Joseph	?	Moses Lewin Levin	Aldgate, London	
25461	Levin	Philip	1772	?, Denmark			(?)	Aldgate, London	pensioner
25468	Levin	Racielle	1823	Hamburg, Germany	(?)		Martin Levin	Aldgate, London	
8507	Levin	Rosa Rachel	1844	Whitechapel, London	Moses Lewin Levin	Nanie (Sarah Nanette, Hannah) Joseph	Charles David Levy	Aldgate, London	
24536	Levin	Rose	1819	Camberwell, London	(?) Levin			Kennington, London	
4654	Levin	Samuel	1831	?, Poland				Birmingham	traveller
5425	Levin	Sara	1837	?City, London	Moses Lewin Levin	Nanie (Sarah Nanette, Hannah) Joseph	Frederick Isaac	Aldgate, London	
19945	Levin	Sarah	1825	?, Germany				Whitechapel, London	house servant
24539	Levin	Sarah	1825	Camberwell, London	(?) Levin			Kennington, London	

ID	surname	given names	born	birthplace	father	mother	spouse 1	1851 residence	1851 occupation
16805	Levin	Sarah	1838	?, London	(?) Levin			Bristol	scholar at home
22117	Levin	Solomon	1830	?, Poland				Whitechapel, London	tailor
5221	Levin	Yetta (Kate)	1827	?, Germany			Wolf Cohen	Liverpool	
1861	Levine	Boaz	1844	Merthyr Tydfil, Wales	Isaac Levine	Sarah Ann Abrahams		Swansea, Wales	scholar
7080	Levine	Charlotte	1793	Ipswich, Suffolk	(?)		Myers Levine	Norwich, Norfolk	
12507	Levine	Henrietta	1849	Norwich, Norfolk	John M Levine	Rebecca (?)		Norwich, Norfolk	
1862	Levine	Henry	1849	Sheffield, Yorkshire	Isaac Levine	Sarah Ann Abrahams	Ellen (?)	Swansea, Wales	
1857	Levine	Isaac	1803	?, Poland [?, Prussia]			Sarah Ann Abrahams	Swansea, Wales	hardware dealer
12504	Levine	John Myers	1815	?, Poland [?, Russia Poland]			Rebecca (?)	Norwich, Norfolk	dealer in watches + jewellery
12506	Levine	Julia	1845	Norwich, Norfolk	John M Levine	Rebecca (?)		Norwich, Norfolk	
1860	Levine	Leah	1840	Merthyr Tydfil, Wales	Isaac Levine	Sarah Ann Abrahams		Swansea, Wales	scholar
7079	Levine	Myers	1787	?, Poland			Charlotte (?)	Norwich, Norfolk	pawnbroker
12505	Levine	Rebecca	1825	?, Holland	(?)		John M Levine	Norwich, Norfolk	
1859	Levine	Rodolph	1839	Merthyr Tydfil, Wales	Isaac Levine	Sarah Ann Abrahams		Swansea, Wales	scholar
1863	Levine	Samuel	1850	Swansea, Wales	Isaac Levine	Sarah Ann Abrahams		Swansea, Wales	
1858	Levine	Sarah Ann	1807	Liverpool	(?) Abrahams		Isaac Levine	Swansea, Wales	
5672	Levinsohn	Benjamin	1827	Aldgate, London	Yosef		Rachel Rubinstein	Aldgate, London	
20655	Levinsohn	Eve	1807	?, Poland [?, Prussia]	(?)		H--- Levinsohn	Spitalfields, London	
20654	Levinsohn	H---	1805	?, Poland [?, Prussia]			Eve (?)	Spitalfields, London	shoemaker
20658	Levinsohn	Jacob	1839	?, Poland [?, Prussia]	H--- Levinsohn	Eve (?)		Spitalfields, London	
20659	Levinsohn	Rachael	1847	Aldgate, London	H--- Levinsohn	Eve (?)		Spitalfields, London	
20656	Levinsohn	Rebecca	1833	?, Poland [?, Prussia]	H--- Levinsohn	Eve (?)		Spitalfields, London	
20657	Levinsohn	Zepora	1836	?, Poland [?, Prussia]	H--- Levinsohn	Eve (?)		Spitalfields, London	
23343	Levinson	Isidor	1801	?, Poland [?, Prussia]			Caroline Burkett	Strand, London	hosier
4301	Levinson	John	1822	Birmingham				Birmingham	printer
23344	Levinson	Joseph	1833	Hrzelno, Poland [Hrzelno, Prussia]				Strand, London	
16921	Levinson (Levison)	Benjamin	1850	Sheffield, Yorkshire	Michael Maurice Levinson (Levison)	Bertha Moses		Sheffield, Yorkshire	
16917	Levinson (Levison)	Bertha	1816	?, Poland [?, Prussia]	Lewin Moses	Rachel (?)	Michael Maurice Levinson (Levison)	Sheffield, Yorkshire	
16918	Levinson (Levison)	Hyam (Hyman)	1834	?, Poland [?, Prussia]	Michael Maurice Levinson (Levison)	Bertha Moses	Augusta Jacobs	Sheffield, Yorkshire	scholar
16920	Levinson (Levison)	Mark	1847	Sheffield, Yorkshire	Michael Maurice Levinson (Levison)	Bertha Moses		Sheffield, Yorkshire	
5130	Levinson (Levison)	Michael Maurice	1812	?, Poland [?, Prussia]			Bertha Moses	Sheffield, Yorkshire	watchmaker + jeweller
16919	Levinson (Levison)	Theresa	1841	?, Poland [?, Prussia]	Michael Maurice Levinson (Levison)	Bertha Moses		Sheffield, Yorkshire	scholar
14252	Levinthall	David	1829	?, Germany				Manchester	traveller - jewellery
4656	Levis (Louis)	Maria	1807	South Wales	(?) (?Mier)		Tobias Hyman Levis (Louis)	Birmingham	
4655	Levis (Louis)	Tobias Hyman	1807	?, Poland [?, Prussia]			Maria (?)	Birmingham	merchant
16850	Levison	Catherine	1830	Islington, London	Jacob Levi (Leslie) Levison	Catherine Isaacs	Michal Gabriel Bergson	Brighton, Sussex	governess

ID	surname	given names	born	birthplace	father	mother	spouse 1	1851 residence	1851 occupation
19286	Levison	Catherine (Kate)	1800	City, London	Naftali Hirsh Isaacs		Jacob Levi (Leslie) Levison	Brighton, Sussex	
26611	Levison	Hinda	1828	Hull, Yorkshire	Jacob Levi (Leslie) Levison	Catherine Isaacs	Zaleg Phillip Mosely	Brighton, Sussex	
12654	Levison	Isaac	1828	?, Holland				Norwich, Norfolk	professor of French + German
7490	Levison	Jacob Levi (Leslie)	1798	Colchester, Essex	Asher Levison		Catherine Isaacs	Brighton, Sussex	surgeon dentist
7725	Levison	Mary	1839	Doncaster, Yorkshire	Jacob Levi (Leslie) Levison	Catherine Isaacs	Adolph Arnholz	Brighton, Sussex	scholar at home
1142	Levison	Paul E	1812	Hanover, Germany				Torquay, Devon	professor of German
7724	Levison	Rachel	1837	Doncaster, Yorkshire	Jacob Levi (Leslie) Levison	Catherine Isaacs		Brighton, Sussex	scholar at home
8269	Levison	Samuel	1831	?, Poland				Birmingham	traveller
30972	Levistone	Jacob	1826	?, Germany				Sheffield, Yorkshire	traveller
20759	Levitt	Isaac	1817	Whitechapel, London	Lewis Levitt	Sarah Isaacs	Sophia Isaacs	Whitechapel, London	chronometer maker
20761	Levitt	Lewis	1789	Brighton, Sussex	Yitzhak miBrighton		Sarah Isaacs	Kennington, London	
30569	Levitt	Lewis	1851	Aldgate, London	Isaac Levitt	Sophia Isaacs		Aldgate, London	
29184	Levitt	Morris Tobias	1820	Kennington, London	Lewis Levitt	Sarah Isaacs	Maria Isaacs	Whitechapel, London	watchmaker
20762	Levitt	Sarah	1793	Mile End, London	Isaac		Lewis Levitt	Kennington, London	
20763	Levitt	Sophia	1815	Wapping, London	Lewis Levitt	Sarah Isaacs		Kennington, London	
20760	Levitt	Sophia	1818	Aldgate, London	Asher Isaacs		Isaac Levitt	Whitechapel, London	
27414	Levy	A---	1829	?, Poland [?, Prussia]				Whitechapel, London	tailor
20144	Levy	Aaron	1794	Middlesex, London			(?)	Soho, London	cabinet maker journeyman
2667	Levy	Aaron	1798	Leszno, Poland [Lissa, Prussia], Poland [Lissa, Prussia]	Levy Levy (Yehuda Leib)	Fanny (Frumit) (?)	Catherine (Kate) Moses	Aldgate, London	Jewish ecclesiastic
3309	Levy	Aaron	1800	Aldgate, London	Yehuda Leib (?Asher Leon Levy)		Rachel Hart	Aldgate, London	clothes dealer
2777	Levy	Aaron	1801	Whitechapel, London			(?)	Whitechapel, London	black lead pencil maker
21823	Levy	Aaron	1803	Covent Garden, London			Hannah (?)	Covent Garden, London	oil man at present
1189	Levy	Aaron	1811	Plymouth, Devon	Abraham Levy		Rosetta (Rozetta) Meyers	Plymouth, Devon	silversmith
10412	Levy	Aaron	1838	Whitechapel, London	(?) Levy	Catherine (?)		Spitalfields, London	
21218	Levy	Aaron	1838	Tower Hill, London				Spitalfields, London	
28684	Levy	Aaron	1839	Middlesex, London	Abraham Levy	Louisa Judah	Sarah Cohen	Spitalfields, London	
11319	Levy	Aaron	1841	Aldgate, London	Lewis Levy	Ann (Nancy) Israel		Aldgate, London	scholar
12116	Levy	Aaron	1845	Whitechapel, London	Abraham Levy	Mary Kapman	Miriam (Mary) Saunders	Spitalfields, London	scholar
398	Levy	Aaron	1850	Spitalfields, London	(?) Levy	Hannah (?)		Spitalfields, London	
26157	Levy	Abigail	1808	?, London	Benjamin Noah Da Costa	Agar de Joseph Abendanha	Nathan Levy	Aldgate, London	butcher
10068	Levy	Abigail	1829	Whitechapel, London	Chapman Barnett		Jacob Levy	Wapping, London	dressmaker
23871	Levy	Abigail	1832	City, London	(?) Levy			Soho, London	teacher
20179	Levy	Abigail	1841	Spitalfields, London	Michael Levy	Amelia Simmons		Spitalfields, London	scholar
3655	Levy	Abigail	1845	City, London	Moses Levy	Alice Moses		Shoreditch, London	
29249	Levy	Abraham	1791	?, London			Elizabeth (?)	Whitechapel, London	retired coal merchant
12111	Levy	Abraham	1792	Whitechapel, London	Yehuda Leib		Esther Silva	Spitalfields, London	pencil maker
28640	Levy	Abraham	1793	Aldgate, London			Sarah (?)	Spitalfields, London	greengrocer
20148	Levy	Abraham	1799	?, Berkshire	Jacob HaLevi		Julia Hart	Euston, London	watch + clockmaker + landed proprietor
28678	Levy	Abraham	1801	Middlesex, London	Moshe HaLevi		Louisa Judah	Spitalfields, London	dealer in miscellany
28750	Levy	Abraham	1809	Middlesex, London			(?)	Spitalfields, London	tailor

ID	surname	given names	born	birthplace	father	mother	spouse 1	1851 residence	1851 occupation
2708	Levy	Abraham	1811	Poznan, Poland [Posen, Prussia]	Yaacov Halevi		Rachel Wolfson	Manchester	glazier
15971	Levy	Abraham	1815	Finsbury, London			Adelaide (?)	Covent Garden, London	lodging house keeper
17387	Levy	Abraham	1818	City, London			Rebecca (?)	Whitechapel, London	clothes salesman
25763	Levy	Abraham	1819	Aldgate, London	Solomon Levy		Rosey (Rosa) Levy	Aldgate, London	clothier
14788	Levy	Abraham	1824	Whitechapel, London	Moses Levy	Catherine (?)	Julia Lawrence	Finsbury, London	journeyman furrier
26812	Levy	Abraham	1824	?Plonsko, Poland [Plotzky, Poland]			Sarah Barnett	Whitechapel, London	bookmaker empl 2
6525	Levy	Abraham	1825	?			Ann Lazarus	Exeter, Devon	
23034	Levy	Abraham	1825	Aldgate, London	Isaac Levy	Hannah Ansell		Aldgate, London	lithographer + stationer
29180	Levy	Abraham	1826	?, Holland				Whitechapel, London	general merchant
26223	Levy	Abraham	1827	?, London				Aldgate, London	cigar maker
21742	Levy	Abraham	1828	?, Jamaica, West Indies	(?) Levy	Hannah (?)		Canonbury, London	merchant
29289	Levy	Abraham	1828	City, London			Rebecca (?)	Whitechapel, London	clothes salesman
2778	Levy	Abraham	1830	Whitechapel, London	Aaron Levy	(?)	Amelia Joel Marks	Whitechapel, London	black lead pencil maker
12881	Levy	Abraham	1830	Aldgate, London	Aaron Levy	Rachel Hart	Rebecca (?)	Aldgate, London	cigar maker
16807	Levy	Abraham	1830	Bristol	Levy Levy	Elizabeth (?)		Bristol	glass + china maker
23368	Levy	Abraham	1830	Covent Garden, London	Samuel Levy	Julia (?)		Strand, London	military outfitter
9541	Levy	Abraham	1832	?Wriezen, Germany [Wreshen, Prussia]				Spitalfields, London	tailor
7431	Levy	Abraham	1834	?London	Samuel Levy		Adelaide Abrahams	Aldgate, London	warehouseman
16115	Levy	Abraham	1834	?, London				Aldgate, London	porter
20191	Levy	Abraham	1836	Whitechapel, London	Henry Levy	Jane Alexander		Spitalfields, London	cigar maker
8005	Levy	Abraham	1840	Aldgate, London	Benjamin Levy	Rosa Mandola		Spitalfields, London	
12237	Levy	Abraham	1840	Whitechapel, London	Moses Levy	Catherine Aarons	Deborah Aarons	Whitechapel, London	
26201	Levy	Abraham	1840	?, Germany	Simon Levy	Fanny (?)		Aldgate, London	
1198	Levy	Abraham	1841	Plymouth, Devon	Aaron Levy	Rosetta (Rozetta) Meyers		Plymouth, Devon	
5440	Levy	Abraham	1842	?Plymouth, Devon	Markes Levy	Bella Woolf		Plymouth, Devon	
16198	Levy	Abraham	1842	Covent Garden, London	(?) Levy	Sarah (?)		Whitechapel, London	scholar
25857	Levy	Abraham	1842	Spitalfields, London	Barnett Levy	Elizabeth (?)		Aldgate, London	scholar
8526	Levy	Abraham	1843	Mile End, London	Jacob Levy	Elizabeth (?)	Kate Joel	Mile End, London	scholar
17121	Levy	Abraham	1843	Sheerness, Kent	Isaac Levy	Frances (?)	Maryann (Marion) Cohen	Sheerness, Kent	scholar
11292	Levy	Abraham	1845	Aldgate, London				Aldgate, London	
10930	Levy	Abraham	1846	Aldgate, London	Lewis Levy	Sarah (?)		Spitalfields, London	scholar
13200	Levy	Abraham	1846	Whitechapel, London	Solomon Hyam (Hyman) Levy	Clara Joseph		Whitechapel, London	scholar
22876	Levy	Abraham	1846	Spitalfields, London	Samuel Levy	Regrena (?)		Whitechapel, London	scholar
6401	Levy	Abraham	1847	Whitechapel, London	Israel Levy	Frances (Fanny) (?)		Spitalfields, London	
24791	Levy	Abraham	1847	Southwark, London	Hyam Levy	Lydia (?)		Elephant & Castle, London	
15685	Levy	Abraham	1849	?, London	Solomon Levy	Elizabeth Hamburger		Aldgate, London	
10313	Levy	Abraham	1850	Spitalfields, London	Lewis Levy	Catharine Elias		Spitalfields, London	
23382	Levy	Abraham	1850	Aldgate, London	Mark Levy	Sarah Lazarus		Aldgate, London	
28961	Levy	Abraham	1850	?, London	Isaiah Levy	Brinette (?)		Whitechapel, London	
30304	Levy	Abraham	1850	Strand, London	Leon (Lewis) Levy	Caroline Saunders		Strand, London	
8010	Levy	Abraham (Moses)	1763	?, Holland				Spitalfields, London	hatter

ID	surname	given names	born	birthplace	father	mother	spouse 1	1851 residence	1851 occupation
53	Levy	Abraham Leopold	1823	Woolwich, London	Nathan Levy	Sarah (Mary) Palmer	Sarah Hart	?Woolwich, London	
63	Levy	Abraham Myers	1847	Woolwich, London	Jacob Levy	Sarah Levy		Woolwich, London	
17704	Levy	Adelade	1824	Whitechapel, London	(?)		Moses Levy	Spitalfields, London	
27540	Levy	Adelaid	1837	Aldgate, London	Mark (Mordecai) Levy	Phoebe Hyams		Spitalfields, London	cap maker
29444	Levy	Adelaide	1802	Amsterdam, Holland			Wolf Levy	Spitalfields, London	
29014	Levy	Adelaide	1803	Whitechapel, London	(?)		Samuel Levy	Whitechapel, London	
15972	Levy	Adelaide	1811	Aldgate, London	(?)		Abraham Levy	Covent Garden, London	lodging house keeper
4669	Levy	Adelaide	1833	Southwark, London	Lawrence Levy	Priscilla (?)		Birmingham	
23387	Levy	Adelaide	1841	?, London	Lipman (Eliezer) Levy	Hannah Jones		Aldgate, London	
29450	Levy	Adelaide	1845	Amsterdam, Holland	Joseph Levy	Amelia (?)		Spitalfields, London	scholar
8939	Levy	Adelaide	1847	Aldgate, London	Lewis Levy	Esther Noah (Da Costa Noah)		Aldgate, London	
11007	Levy	Adelaide (Adel)	1850	Aldgate, London	Philip Levy	Elizabeth Davis		Aldgate, London	
23961	Levy	Adolphus	1822	Clapham, London	Solomon Abraham Levy	Paulina (Pessy) (?)		Marylebone, London	barrister practising
24060	Levy	Adolphus	1826	?, Guernsey, Channel Islands			Louisa (?)	St John's Wood, London	gas fitter
11234	Levy	Agnes	1802	Whitechapel, London	(?) Wolf	Rachael (?)	Henry Levy	Aldgate, London	waistcoat maker
23960	Levy	Albert	1819	Clapham, London	Solomon Abraham Levy	Paulina (Pessy) (?)		Marylebone, London	Stock Exchange
8214	Levy	Albert	1839	St Pancras, London	Joseph Moses Levy	Esther Cohen		Bloomsbury, London	
24415	Levy	Albert	1847	Strand, London	Morrice (Morris) Levy	Hannah Alexander		Strand, London	
16195	Levy	Alex	1828	Shoreditch, London	Emanuel Levy	Sarah (?)		Whitechapel, London	butcher
5774	Levy	Alexander	1796	Eton, Berkshire	Barnett Alexander Levy	Rosetta Isaacs	Stella Foligno	Eton, Berkshire	watchmaker
14643	Levy	Alexander	1817	Finsbury, London	Jacob Levy	Polly (?)	Elizabeth (?)	Hoxton, London	clerk - insurance office
28165	Levy	Alexander	1819	City, London				Spitalfields, London	lemon dealer
7484	Levy	Alexander	1822	Middlesex, London			Julia Defries	Whitechapel, London	merchant shipper
16511	Levy	Alexander	1825	Covent Garden, London	Joseph Levy	Elizabeth (?)	Amelia Harris	Clerkenwell, London	publican
20189	Levy	Alexander	1825	Whitechapel, London	Henry Levy	Jane Alexander	Hannah Moses	Spitalfields, London	slipper maker
25217	Levy	Alexander	1840	Aldgate, London	Lewis Levy	Caroline Lee		Clerkenwell, London	scholar
29901	Levy	Alexandria	1847	Whitechapel, London	(?) Levy	Mary (?)		Wapping, London	
22986	Levy	Alfred	1824	?, Essex	Hymer Levy	Julia (?)	Phoebe Lyons	Poplar, London	tailor
21312	Levy	Alfred	1835	Sheerness, Kent				Chatham, Kent	
26506	Levy	Alfred	1842	Middlesex, London				Dover, Kent	
1199	Levy	Alfred	1843	Plymouth, Devon	Aaron Levy	Rosetta (Rozetta) meyers		Plymouth, Devon	
19192	Levy	Alfred	1848	Whitechapel, London	John Levy	Mary Lazarus		Whitechapel, London	
21407	Levy	Alfred	1850	Elephant & Castle, London	Solomon Levy	Maria Harris		Elephant & Castle, London	
31056	Levy	Alice	1789	Aldgate, London	(?)		Nathan Levy	Rochester, Kent	
3651	Levy	Alice	1819	Whitechapel, London	Abraham Lyon Moses	Abigail Lazarus	Moses Levy	Shoreditch, London	
13198	Levy	Alice	1840	Whitechapel, London	Solomon Hyam (Hyman) Levy	Clara Joseph		Whitechapel, London	scholar
29921	Levy	Alice	1847	York, Yorkshire	Louis J Levy	Rebecca (?)		Whitechapel, London	scholar
17843	Levy	Alice	1848	Aldgate, London	Henry Levy	Anna (?)		Aldgate, London	
57	Levy	Alice	1851	Stepney, London	Isaac Levy	Dinah Jacobs		Whitechapel, London	
3328	Levy	Alice (Abigail)	1851	Aldgate, London	Aaron Levy	Rachel Hart	Abraham Solomons	Aldgate, London	
29843	Levy	Alice Alexandrina	1847	Aldgate, London	(?) Levy	Mary (?)		Stepney, London	
24792	Levy	Allen (Ellen?)	1848	Southwark, London	Hyam Levy	Lydia (?)		Elephant & Castle, London	

ID	surname	given names	born	birthplace	father	mother	spouse 1	1851 residence	1851 occupation
3924	Levy	Amelia	1781	?, London	David Levy		Mordecai (Mark) Levy	Aldgate, London	
5849	Levy	Amelia	1803	Whitechapel, London	Henry Jacobs	Kitty Moses	Daniel Levy	Bloomsbury, London	
23963	Levy	Amelia	1809	Clapham, London	Jacob Abraham Levy	(?)		Marylebone, London	
8741	Levy	Amelia	1815	Aldgate, London	(?)		Nathan Levy	Aldgate, London	
29446	Levy	Amelia	1816	Amsterdam, Holland	(?)		Wolf Levy	Spitalfields, London	
15530	Levy	Amelia	1819	?, London	(?)		(?) Levy	Covent Garden, London	charwoman
20177	Levy	Amelia	1819	Whitechapel, London	Levy Simmons		Michael Levy	Spitalfields, London	
28482	Levy	Amelia	1821	Margonin, Poland [Prussia]	Moses Morris		Lewis Levy	Spitalfields, London	cloth cap maker
16898	Levy	Amelia	1826	Holborn, London	Reuben Levy	Polly Solomons		Sheffield, Yorkshire	
3312	Levy	Amelia	1827	Middlesex, London	Moss Cohen	Sarah Hart	Lawrence Levy	Aldgate, London	
16512	Levy	Amelia	1828	Whitechapel, London	(?) Harris		Alexander Levy	Clerkenwell, London	
23036	Levy	Amelia	1832	Southwark, London	(?) Levy	Hannah (?)		Aldgate, London	dressmaker
893	Levy	Amelia	1833	Manchester	Joseph Levy	Julia (?)	John Solomon	Manchester	
10533	Levy	Amelia	1834	Covent Garden, London	David Levy	Catherine Davids		Covent Garden, London	needlewoman
27539	Levy	Amelia	1836	Aldgate, London	Mark (Mordecai) Levy	Phoebe Hyams		Spitalfields, London	cap maker
20577	Levy	Amelia	1840	Whitechapel, London	(?) Levy	(?) Phillips		Spitalfields, London	
28224	Levy	Amelia	1843	Whitechapel, London	(?) Levy	Catherine (?)		Spitalfields, London	scholar
28423	Levy	Amelia	1843	Whitechapel, London	Moses Levy	(?)		Spitalfields, London	
13015	Levy	Amelia	1845	Middlesex, London	Emanuel Levy	Rebecca (?)		Spitalfields, London	
13872	Levy	Amelia	1849	Manchester	Lewis Levy	Mary Ann (?)		Manchester	at home
30570	Levy	Amelia	1851	Clerkenwell, London	Lewis Levy	Caroline Lee		Clerkenwell, London	
30571	Levy	Amelia	1851	Spitalfields, London	Lewis Levy	Catharine Elias		Spitalfields, London	
28458	Levy	Amelia (Emilia)	1850	Islington, London	Henry Levy	Rosetta Moses		Spitalfields, London	
28443	Levy	Angel	1841	Whitechapel, London	Simon Levy	Esther Abendana		Spitalfields, London	scholar
26266	Levy	Angel	1847	?, London	Samuel Levy	Louisa Jonas		Aldgate, London	
8210	Levy	Angelina	1831	Clerkenwell, London	Joseph Moses Levy	Esther Cohen	Edward Ludwig Goetz	Bloomsbury, London	
5848	Levy	Angelina	1840	Walworth, London	Daniel Levy	Amelia Jacobs	Joseph Lindow	Bloomsbury, London	
24633	Levy	Ann	1788	Whitechapel, London	(?)		Emanuel Levy	Waterloo, London	
8944	Levy	Ann	1791	Aldgate, London	(?)		(?) Levy	Aldgate, London	fruiterer
25492	Levy	Ann	1810	Whitechapel, London	(?) Levy			City, London	staymaker
17097	Levy	Ann	1811	?, England	(?) Marks		(?) Rosenthal	St Peter Port, Guernsey, Channel Islands	dealer in jewellery, cutlery, stationery, mathematical + optical instruments + wearing apparel
23320	Levy	Ann	1812	Canterbury, Kent	Moses Levy	Elizabeth (?)		Belgravia, London	
28729	Levy	Ann	1813	Middlesex, London	(?) Levy	Mary (?)	(?) Levy	Spitalfields, London	
6494	Levy	Ann	1817	?, Ireland	(?)		Lewis Levy	Birmingham	
13003	Levy	Ann	1819	Bethnal Green, London	Barnett Levy	Catherine Levy		Bethnal Green, London	
14313	Levy	Ann	1823	?Bow, London [Barmley, London]				Manchester	lodging house keeper
24638	Levy	Ann	1829	Aldgate, London	(?) Levy			Waterloo, London	
4743	Levy	Ann	1834	Oxford, Oxfordshire				Birmingham	servant
20180	Levy	Ann	1843	Spitalfields, London	Michael Levy	Amelia Simmons		Spitalfields, London	scholar
26174	Levy	Ann	1844	?, London	(?) Levy			Aldgate, London	

ID	surname	given names	born	birthplace	father	mother	spouse 1	1851 residence	1851 occupation
11316	Levy	Ann (Nancy)	1814	Aldgate, London	Binyamin Wolff Israel		Lewis Levy	Aldgate, London	
5287	Levy	Ann (Nancy)	1818	Finsbury, London	(?) Levy		Jacob Levy	Aldgate, London	general dealer
214	Levy	Ann (Nancy)	1834	Middlesex, London	Lyon (Lewis) Levy	Sarah Davis	Solomon Levy Abrahams	Spitalfields, London	
3352	Levy	Ann (Nancy)	1846	Aldgate, London	Philip Levy	Elizabeth Davis	Barnett Hart	Aldgate, London	scholar
29914	Levy	Ann J	1828	?, Holland	Louis J Levy	Rebecca (?)	(?) Josephs	Whitechapel, London	professor of languages
17834	Levy	Anna	1803	City, London	(?)		Henry Levy	Aldgate, London	
3925	Levy	Anna	1821	?, London	Mordecai (Mark) Levy	Amelia Levy		Aldgate, London	
1866	Levy	Anna	1835	Swansea, Wales	(?) Levy	Rebecca (?)		Swansea, Wales	teacher
28642	Levy	Anna	1841	Spitalfields, London	Abraham Levy	Sarah (?)		Spitalfields, London	scholar
22878	Levy	Anna	1850	Spitalfields, London	Samuel Levy	Regrena (?)		Whitechapel, London	scholar
12202	Levy	Anna	1851	?, London	Marks Levy	Rachel (?)		Whitechapel, London	
29506	Levy	Anna Hannah)	1846	Spitalfields, London	Henry Levy	Catherine (Kate, Kitty) Franks		Spitalfields, London	scholar
21866	Levy	Anna Louiza	1842	Clerkenwell, London	Charles Levy	Mary Ann (?)		Clerkenwell, London	
30163	Levy	Anne	1828	Middlesex, London	Abraham Levy	Hannah (Levi?)	Lewis Hart	Lambeth, London	annuitant
23783	Levy	Anne	1841	Liverpool	Henry Levy	Maria (?)		Liverpool	scholar
25218	Levy	Anne	1843	Finsbury, London	Lewis Levy	Caroline Lee		Clerkenwell, London	scholar
4675	Levy	Anne	1846	Birmingham	Lewis Levy	Sarah (?)		Birmingham	
8213	Levy	Annie	1844	St Pancras, London	Joseph Moses Levy	Esther Cohen		Bloomsbury, London	scholar at home
10463	Levy	Ansell	1829	Spitalfields, London	Jacob Levy	Elizabeth (?)		Mile End, London	cigar maker
16798	Levy	Arabella	1806	Falmouth, Cornwall	(?)		Solomon Levy	Bristol	jeweller + dealer in fancy articles
21868	Levy	Arthur	1850	Clerkenwell, London	Charles Levy	Mary Ann (?)		Clerkenwell, London	
17688	Levy	Arthur Abraham	1848	Shoreditch, London	Lawrence Levy	Eliza (Sarah) Emanuel		Shoreditch, London	
12974	Levy	Asher	1801	?, London	Yehuda		Julia Phillips	Aldgate, London	tailor
22637	Levy	Asher	1815	Ipswich, Suffolk	(?) Levy	Rachel (?)		Whitechapel, London	annuitant
20367	Levy	Asher	1839	Aldgate, London	Israel Levy	Sarah Harris		Aldgate, London	
26067	Levy	Asher Isaac	1787	Amsterdam, Holland			Rebecca (?)	Aldgate, London	jeweller
7641	Levy	Augustus Samuel	1816	Middlesex, London	David Levy		Miriam Tobias	Piccadilly, London	fruiterer
5775	Levy	Barnard	1830	?Eton, Berkshire	Alexander Levy	Stella Foligno	Rose Ansell	Eton, Berkshire	watchmaker
1202	Levy	Barnard	1848	Plymouth, Devon	Aaron Levy	Rosetta (Rozetta) Meyers		Plymouth, Devon	
17102	Levy	Barnet	1801	?, England			Sarah (?)	St Helier, Jersey, Channel Islands	pawnbroker
22875	Levy	Barnet	1844	Spitalfields, London	Samuel Levy	Regrena (?)		Whitechapel, London	scholar
23619	Levy	Barnet Isaac	1809	Hamburg, Germany	Isaac Levy		Elizabeth Levy	Liverpool	cigar manufacturer
13001	Levy	Barnett	1782	Birmingham	Lipman Levy		Catherine Levy	Bethnal Green, London	stonemason master empl 1
30037	Levy	Barnett	1788	Aldgate, London			Blumer (?)	Wapping, London	tailor
28166	Levy	Barnett	1797	City, London				Spitalfields, London	lemon dealer
25854	Levy	Barnett	1799	?, Germany			Elizabeth (?)	Aldgate, London	lodging house keeper
3919	Levy	Barnett	1823	Aldgate, London	Mordecai Levy	Jane (?)		Aldgate, London	tailor
8538	Levy	Barnett	1833	Bristol				Aldgate, London	apprentice carver + gilder
19815	Levy	Barnett	1844	Whitechapel, London	Elias Levy	Sarah Palachy		Spitalfields, London	scholar
27957	Levy	Barnett	1846	Spitalfields, London	John Levy	Julia Moses		Spitalfields, London	
12405	Levy	Barnett	1847	Spitalfields, London	Thomas Levy	Rose (?)		Spitalfields, London	

ID	surname	given names	born	birthplace	father	mother	spouse 1	1851 residence	1851 occupation
22348	Levy	Barnett (Bernhard)	1826	Poznan, Poland [Posen, Poland]	Myer Levy		Julia Green	Aldgate, London	furrier
6960	Levy	Barney (Barnett)	1846	Spitalfields, London	Samuel Levy		Kate (Catherine) Hyams	Spitalfields, London	
5439	Levy	Bella	1817	Penzance, Cornwall	Lemon Woolf	Rebecca (?)	Markes Levy	Plymouth, Devon	
29922	Levy	Bella	1849	York, Yorkshire	Louis J Levy	Rebecca (?)		Whitechapel, London	
4125	Levy	Benedict (Barnett) Henry	1849	Wapping, London	Hyam Levy	Sarah Moses		Wapping, London	
25463	Levy	Benjamin	1771	?, Germany				Aldgate, London	pensioner
7998	Levy	Benjamin	1820	Poznan, Poland [Posen, Prussia]	Abraham (Moses) Levy		Rosa Mandola	Spitalfields, London	furrier
22140	Levy	Benjamin	1823	?, Germany				Whitechapel, London	commercial traveller
26280	Levy	Benjamin	1825	?, Holland				Aldgate, London	tailor
5505	Levy	Benjamin	1826	Middlesex, London			Rachel Simon	Leicester, Leicestershire	tailor
10530	Levy	Benjamin	1826	Covent Garden, London	David Levy	Catherine Davids		Covent Garden, London	cigar manufacturer
10212	Levy	Benjamin	1830	Clerkenwell, London	John Levy	Sarah (?)		Aldgate, London	stationer
27126	Levy	Benjamin	1830	Elephant & Castle, London	(?) Levy	Catherine (?)		Aldgate, London	cigar maker
17470	Levy	Benjamin	1835	Lambeth, London	Emanuel Levy	Mary (?)		Aldgate, London	butcher journeyman
26160	Levy	Benjamin	1837	?Spitalfields, London	Nathan Levy	Abigail Noah (Noah Da Costa)		Aldgate, London	cigar maker
2715	Levy	Benjamin	1849	?, Poland [?, Prussia]	Abraham Levy	Rachel Wolfson	Florence (Florrie) (?)	Manchester	
11322	Levy	Benjamin	1850	Aldgate, London	Lewis Levy	Ann (Nancy) Israel		Aldgate, London	
2081	Levy	Benjamin Wolfe	1838	Carmarthen, Wales	Daniel Levy	Mary Anne Lazarus		Carmarthen, Wales	scholar
12201	Levy	Bernard	1849	?, London	Marks Levy	Rachel (?)		Whitechapel, London	
21867	Levy	Bertram	1846	Clerkenwell, London	Charles Levy	Mary Ann (?)		Clerkenwell, London	
28099	Levy	Bethseba (Beersheba)	1842	Aldgate, London	Emanuel Levy	Rosetta Asher		Spitalfields, London	scholar
20366	Levy	Betsey	1837	Aldgate, London	Israel Levy	Sarah Harris		Aldgate, London	
10928	Levy	Betsey	1842	City, London	Lewis Levy	Sarah (?)		Spitalfields, London	scholar
20166	Levy	Betsey	1850	Spitalfields, London	Isaac Levy	Catherine (?)		Spitalfields, London	
30060	Levy	Betsy	1843	Bedford, Bedfordshire	Lewis Levy	Jessy Selig	Frederick Stern	Bedford, Bedfordshire	
10661	Levy	Betsy	1850	Spitalfields, London	Morris (Moses) Levy	Esther Samuel	Isaac Leon Defries	Spitalfields, London	
2932	Levy	Blumah	1791	Spitalfields, London	(?) Jacobs		Joseph Levy	Spitalfields, London	
30038	Levy	Blumer	1800	Aldgate, London	(?)		Barnett Levy	Wapping, London	
28957	Levy	Brinette	1822	Metz, France [Metz, Germany]	(?)		Isaiah Levy	Whitechapel, London	
3907	Levy	Caroline	1793	Aldgate, London			(?) Levy	Spitalfields, London	general dealer
22723	Levy	Caroline	1817	Whitechapel, London	(?) Levy			Whitechapel, London	teacher at school
13338	Levy	Caroline	1819	Aldgate, London	(?)		Joseph Levy	Spitalfields, London	
25216	Levy	Caroline	1819	Aldgate, London	Joseph Lee		Lewis Levy	Clerkenwell, London	
1333	Levy	Caroline	1820	Plymouth, Devon	Abraham Levy	Zipporah Benjamin		Plymouth, Devon	
17918	Levy	Caroline	1822	Strand, London	(?) Saunders		Leon (Lewis) Levy	Strand, London	
24844	Levy	Caroline	1829	?Ongar, Essex	(?) Levy			Elephant & Castle, London	house servant
12235	Levy	Caroline	1836	Whitechapel, London	Moses Levy	Catherine Aarons		Whitechapel, London	
16237	Levy	Caroline	1837	Spitalfields, London	Nathan Levy	Rachael (?)		Spitalfields, London	seamstress

ID	surname	given names	born	birthplace	father	mother	spouse 1	1851 residence	1851 occupation
28958	Levy	Caroline	1845	Aldgate, London	Isaiah Levy	Brinette (?)		Whitechapel, London	scholar
4124	Levy	Caroline	1848	Wapping, London	Hyam Levy	Sarah Moses	Abraham Lewis Lazarus	Wapping, London	
30572	Levy	Caroline	1851	Aldgate, London	Abraham Levy	Rosey (Rosa) Levy		Aldgate, London	
5443	Levy	Caroline (Carrie)	1851	Plymouth, Devon	Markes Levy	Bella Woolf	Solomon Lyon	Plymouth, Devon	
3727	Levy	Catharine	1823	Spitalfields, London	Aryeh Elias		Lewis Levy	Spitalfields, London	
24419	Levy	Catharine	1832	?, London	Lawrence Levy	Rebecca Jacobs		Strand, London	
11436	Levy	Catharine	1843	Whitechapel, London	(?Hart) Levy	Julia (?)		Aldgate, London	
10279	Levy	Catharine (Kate)	1838	Whitechapel, London	Lewis Levy	Sarah (?)	Elias Cohen	Spitalfields, London	scholar
3916	Levy	Catherine	1791	Whitechapel, London	(?)		Lyon Levy	Waterloo, London	
13002	Levy	Catherine	1791	?, Holland	Zelig Lipman Levy		Barnet Levy	Bethnal Green, London	
6792	Levy	Catherine	1792	Whitechapel, London	(?)		Isaac Levy	Spitalfields, London	
23045	Levy	Catherine	1795	Whitechapel, London	(?)		Moses Levy	Aldgate, London	
15113	Levy	Catherine	1797	?, London	(?)		(?) Levy	Bethnal Green, London	annuitant
27125	Levy	Catherine	1800	?, Yorkshire	(?)		(?) Levy	Aldgate, London	general dealer
12232	Levy	Catherine	1801	Strand, London	(?) Aarons		Moses Levy	Whitechapel, London	annuitant + silversmith, jeweller + watchmaker
10407	Levy	Catherine	1803	Whitechapel, London	(?)		(?) Levy	Spitalfields, London	general dealer
10529	Levy	Catherine	1804	Covent Garden, London	(?) Davids		David Levy	Covent Garden, London	dealer in cigars
28222	Levy	Catherine	1811	Spitalfields, London	(?)		(?) Levy	Spitalfields, London	
20159	Levy	Catherine	1814	Spitalfields, London	(?)		Isaac Levy	Spitalfields, London	general dealer
15117	Levy	Catherine	1815	Boston, ?Lincolnshire	Joseph Levy	Elizabeth (?)		Hoxton, London	
18362	Levy	Catherine	1817	City, London	Isaac Samuel		Moses Levy	Elephant & Castle, London	
7779	Levy	Catherine	1821	Middlesex, London	David Levy	Hannah Solomons	Ellis A Davidson	Fitzrovia, London	
21268	Levy	Catherine	1821	Bedford, Bedfordshire	(?) Levy			Barnsbury, London	servant
13354	Levy	Catherine	1826	Whitechapel, London	Moses Levy	Sarah Lazarus	Nathan (Nathaniel) Levy	Spitalfields, London	
28421	Levy	Catherine	1838	Whitechapel, London	Moses Levy	(?)		Spitalfields, London	
28613	Levy	Catherine	1839	Spitalfields, London	Samuel Levy	Sarah (?)		Spitalfields, London	tailoress
29449	Levy	Catherine	1840	Amsterdam, Holland	Joseph Levy	Amelia (?)		Spitalfields, London	scholar
17120	Levy	Catherine	1841	Sheerness, Kent	Isaac Levy	Frances (?)		Sheerness, Kent	scholar
15490	Levy	Catherine	1842	Strand, London	(?) Levy			Covent Garden, London	
30061	Levy	Catherine	1845	Bedford, Bedfordshire	Lewis Levy	Jessy Selig		Bedford, Bedfordshire	
2666	Levy	Catherine (Kate)	1801	Leszno, Poland [Lissa, Prussia], Poland [Lissa, Prussia]	Yehuda Moses		Aaron Levy	Aldgate, London	
21216	Levy	Catherine (Kate)	1848	Spitalfields, London	David Levy	Jane Lazarus		Spitalfields, London	
29502	Levy	Catherine (Kate, Kitty)	1822	Spitalfields, London	Solomon Franks		Henry Levy	Spitalfields, London	general dealer
5863	Levy	Catherine Virginia	1842	Walworth, London	Daniel Levy	Amelia Jacobs	George Henry Russell (Russel)	Bloomsbury, London	
21864	Levy	Charles	1812	St Giles, London			Mary Ann (?)	Clerkenwell, London	chaser
28730	Levy	Charles	1828	Middlesex, London	(?) Levy	Mary (?)		Spitalfields, London	dealer in glass
7146	Levy	Charles	1830	Rochester, Kent	Nathan Levy	Alice (?)	Rebecca Wells	Rochester, Kent	general dealer
16901	Levy	Charles	1839	Sheffield, Yorkshire	Reuben Levy	Polly Solomons	Sarah Esther Samuel	Sheffield, Yorkshire	
20774	Levy	Charles	1841	Bethnal Green, London	Solomon Levy	Elizabeth (?)		Haggerston, London	

ID	surname	given names	born	birthplace	father	mother	spouse 1	1851 residence	1851 occupation
2084	Levy	Charles	1844	Carmarthen, Wales	Daniel Levy	Mary Anne Lazarus	Julia Michael	Carmarthen, Wales	scholar
21826	Levy	Charles	1845	St Pancras, London	Aaron Levy	Hannah (?)		Covent Garden, London	
13871	Levy	Charles	1847	Manchester	Lewis Levy	Mary Ann (?)		Manchester	at home
22242	Levy	Charles	1848	Whitechapel, London	Lewis Levy	Elizabeth (?)		Whitechapel, London	
28424	Levy	Charles	1849	Whitechapel, London	Moses Levy	(?)		Spitalfields, London	
23321	Levy	Charlotte	1812	Middlesex, London	Moses Levy	Elizabeth (?)		Belgravia, London	
20025	Levy	Charlotte	1823	Whitechapel, London	Abraham Hart (?Barnett)		Solomon Levy	Aldgate, London	
24142	Levy	Charlotte	1828	Walworth, London	Daniel Levy	Amelia Jacobs	Edward Laurence Levy	Bloomsbury, London	
16800	Levy	Charlotte	1831	Bristol	Solomon Levy	Arabella (?)		Bristol	assistant jeweller
10356	Levy	Charlotte	1845	Middlesex, London	Simon Levy	Moriah (?)		Spitalfields, London	scholar
28946	Levy	Charlotte	1845	Aldgate, London	Henry Levy	Phoebe Marks		Whitechapel, London	
13357	Levy	Charlotte	1849	Whitechapel, London	Nathan (Nathaniel) Levy	Catherine Levy		Spitalfields, London	
3545	Levy	Charlotte Sophia	1827	Kensington, London	Nathaniel Levy	Sophia (?)	Henry Cowan	Bloomsbury, London	
13197	Levy	Clara	1816	Whitechapel, London	(?) Joseph		Solomon Hyam (Hyman) Levy	Whitechapel, London	
25080	Levy	Clara	1824	?London	(?)		Raphael Levy	City, London	
12285	Levy	Clara	1832	Whitechapel, London	(?) Levy			Finsbury, London	servant
13520	Levy	Clara	1835	Birmingham	(?) Levy			Manchester	scholar
19816	Levy	Clara	1846	Whitechapel, London	Elias Levy	Sarah Palachy		Spitalfields, London	scholar
19864	Levy	Coleman	1817	Aldgate, London	Solomon Levy		Jael (?)	Spitalfields, London	boot maker
12882	Levy	Coleman	1832	Aldgate, London	Aaron Levy	Rachel Hart	Babette (Elizabeth) (?)	Aldgate, London	cigar maker
2078	Levy	Daniel	1790	Berlin, Germany			Mary Anne Lazarus	Carmarthen, Wales	traveller - spirits
21545	Levy	Daniel	1797	Mile End, London			Amelia Jacobs	Bloomsbury, London	glass + china dealer
20151	Levy	Daniel	1803	Bristol			Rachael (?)	Bristol	dealer in new + second hand clothes
1021	Levy	Daniel	1835	St Peter Port, Guernsey, Channel Islands	Mark Levy	Mary Lambert		Exeter, Devon	
16236	Levy	Daniel	1835	Spitalfields, London	Nathan Levy	Rachael (?)		Spitalfields, London	errand boy
29919	Levy	Daniel	1841	?, Holland	Louis J Levy	Rebecca (?)		Whitechapel, London	scholar
28445	Levy	Daniel	1850	Spitalfields, London	Simon Levy	Esther Abendana		Spitalfields, London	
30015	Levy	David	1771	?, Germany			Hannah Solomons	Fitzrovia, London	retired
29213	Levy	David	1795	?				Whitechapel, London	general dealer
4009	Levy	David	1799	Portsmouth, Hampshire	Solomon Levy	Sophia (?)	Rebecca Davids	Portsmouth, Hampshire	army agent
15424	Levy	David	1803	Middlesex, London			Maria (?)	Covent Garden, London	looking glass maker
11468	Levy	David	1808	Spitalfields, London			Julia (?)	Aldgate, London	dealer
21211	Levy	David	1810	Aldgate, London	Simcha		Jane Lazarus	Spitalfields, London	general dealer
11066	Levy	David	1811	?, Poland [?, Prussian Poland]	Moshe		Phoebe (?)	Aldgate, London	plumber + glazier
28413	Levy	David	1813	Whitechapel, London	Moses Levy		Sarah Phillips	Spitalfields, London	orange merchant
18420	Levy	David	1815	Poznan, Poland [Posen, Prussia]				Elephant & Castle, London	tailor
21828	Levy	David	1817	Whitechapel, London			(?)	Covent Garden, London	electro-gilder + brothel keeper
27884	Levy	David	1823	City, London	Jacob Levy	Julia (?)	Catherine (Kate) White	Spitalfields, London	general dealer
21741	Levy	David	1825	?, Jamaica, West Indies	(?) Levy	Hannah (?)		Canonbury, London	merchant
26069	Levy	David	1825	Amsterdam, Holland	Ansell Isaac Levy	Rebecca (?)	Julia Gobertz	Aldgate, London	general dealer

ID	surname	given names	born	birthplace	father	mother	spouse 1	1851 residence	1851 occupation
27997	Levy	David	1828	Poznan, Poland [Posen, Germany]				Spitalfields, London	tailor jouneyman
22642	Levy	David	1837	Bungay, Suffolk	(?) Levy	Rachel (?)		Whitechapel, London	apprentice to hatter
216	Levy	David	1840	Dublin, Ireland	Lyon (Lewis) Levy	Sarah Davis	Annie Theobalds	Spitalfields, London	
9280	Levy	David	1841	Aldgate, London	Nathan Levy	Rachel (?)		Aldgate, London	scholar
11005	Levy	David	1845	Aldgate, London	Philip Levy	Elizabeth Davis		Aldgate, London	scholar
20165	Levy	David	1846	Spitalfields, London	Isaac Levy	Catherine (?)		Spitalfields, London	scholar
11068	Levy	David	1848	Whitechapel, London	David Levy	Phoebe (?)		Aldgate, London	
25121	Levy	David	1848	Holborn, London	Philip Levy	Sarah (?)		Finsbury, London	
28803	Levy	David	1851	Spitalfields, London	Lewis Levy	Jeannette (Jane) Symons		Spitalfields, London	
8506	Levy	David (Charles)	1839	Elephant & Castle, London	Solomon Levy	Maria Harris	Rosa Rachel (Isobel) Levin	Elephant & Castle, London	
26224	Levy	Deborah	1761	Voronezh Oblast, Russia [Vron Plazt]	(?)		(?) Levy	Aldgate, London	
25780	Levy	Deborah	1781	?, Poland [?, Prussia]	(?)		(?) Levy	Aldgate, London	pauper clothes dealer
21244	Levy	Deborah	1807	?, London	Issachar Behr Barnett		Samuel Levy	Spitalfields, London	
17067	Levy	Deborah	1816	Amsterdam, Holland	(?) Defries	Rosetta (?)	Henry Levy	Edinburgh, Scotland	
13350	Levy	Deborah	1824	Spitalfields, London	Shlomeh Bendon		Isaac Levy	Spitalfields, London	
27936	Levy	Deborah	1827	Whitechapel, London	(?) Levy		Naphtali Hart	Spitalfields, London	
30039	Levy	Deborah	1836	Aldgate, London	Barnett Levy	Blumer (?)		Wapping, London	
18363	Levy	Deborah	1844	Bermondsey, London	Moses Levy	Catherine Samuel		Elephant & Castle, London	
24790	Levy	Deborah	1845	Southwark, London	Hyam Levy	Lydia (?)		Elephant & Castle, London	
9937	Levy	Deborah	1849	Covent Garden, London	David Levy	Catherine Davids	Charles Daniel Barnard	Covent Garden, London	
10523	Levy	Dinah	1816	?, London	(?) Levy			Aldgate, London	waistcoat maker
56	Levy	Dinah	1827	Birmingham	(?) Jacobs		Isaac Levy	Whitechapel, London	
12471	Levy	Dinah	1844	Whitechapel, London	Israel Levy	Frances (Fanny) (?)		Spitalfields, London	
28457	Levy	Dinah	1846	Hull, Yorkshire	Henry Levy	Rosetta Moses	Godfrey Levy Bamberg	Spitalfields, London	scholar
26203	Levy	Dorothea	1844	?, Germany	Simon Levy	Fanny (?)		Aldgate, London	
8830	Levy	Dorothy	1815	Portsmouth, Hampshire	(?)		Jonas Levy	Aldgate, London	
30688	Levy	E---	1835	Whitechapel, London	(?) Levy	Eve (?)		Whitechapel, London	
23919	Levy	Edmund	1846	Marylebone, London	Myer Levy	Hannah Levy		Fitzrovia, London	
30012	Levy	Edward	1809	?, London	David Levy	Hannah Solomons		Fitzrovia, London	
23958	Levy	Edward	1812	Hamburg, Germany	Solomon Abraham Levy	Paulina (Pessy) (?)		Marylebone, London	Stock Exchange
25741	Levy	Edward	1841	Spitalfields, London	Elias Levy	Matilda Harris		Spitalfields, London	scholar
8831	Levy	Edward	1845	Whitechapel, London	Jonas Levy	Dorothy (?)		Aldgate, London	scholar
17689	Levy	Edward	1849	Shoreditch, London	Lawrence Levy	Eliza (Sarah) Emanuel		Shoreditch, London	
28191	Levy	Edward	1849	Whitechapel, London	Samuel Levy	Ellen Abrahams		Spitalfields, London	
30575	Levy	Edward	1851	Aldgate, London	Abraham Levy	Julia Lawrence		Aldgate, London	
24141	Levy	Edward Laurence	1828	City, London	Laurence Levy		Charlotte Levy	Bloomsbury, London	solicitor
6685	Levy	Edward Lawrence	1851	Middlesex, London	Abraham Levy		Hester (Esther) Lazarus	Middlesex, London	
21825	Levy	Edwin	1843	St Pancras, London	Aaron Levy	Hannah (?)		Covent Garden, London	
8006	Levy	Eleazer	1843	Whitechapel, London	Benjamin Levy	Rosa Mandola	Rebecca Isaacs	Spitalfields, London	
19810	Levy	Elias	1813	Aldgate, London	Barnet Levy		Sarah Palachy	Spitalfields, London	clothes dealer

ID	surname	given names	born	birthplace	father	mother	spouse 1	1851 residence	1851 occupation
25738	Levy	Elias	1813	Whitechapel, London	Nathan Levy		Matilda Harris	Spitalfields, London	clothier
11381	Levy	Elias	1816	Aldgate, London	(?) Levy	Sarah (?)		Aldgate, London	pencil maker
213	Levy	Elias	1832	Middlesex, London	Lyon (Lewis) Levy	Sarah Davis	Anne Abrahams	Spitalfields, London	cigar maker
25898	Levy	Elias	1848	Aldgate, London	Hyam Levy	Frances Naphthali		Aldgate, London	scholar
19960	Levy	Eliza	1809	Middlesex, London	Jonas Levy	Sarah Israel Levy		Whitechapel, London	
27945	Levy	Eliza	1820	Chelmsford, Essex	Solomon Levy	Maria (?)		Spitalfields, London	waistcoat maker
17124	Levy	Eliza	1829	Shoreditch, London	(?) Levy			Sheerness, Kent	dressmaker
28612	Levy	Eliza	1834	Spitalfields, London	Samuel Levy	Sarah (?)		Spitalfields, London	cap maker
16900	Levy	Eliza	1837	Sheffield, Yorkshire	Reuben Levy	Polly Solomons		Sheffield, Yorkshire	
5441	Levy	Eliza	1846	?Plymouth, Devon	Markes Levy	Bella Woolf	Ernest A Lyons	Plymouth, Devon	
20164	Levy	Eliza	1846	Spitalfields, London	Isaac Levy	Catherine (?)		Spitalfields, London	scholar
17682	Levy	Eliza (Sarah)	1812	Aldgate, London	Joel Emanuel	Julia (Juliet) Lazarus	Lawrence Levy	Shoreditch, London	
1031	Levy	Elizabeth	1762	Exeter, Devon				Exeter, Devon	annuitant
18689	Levy	Elizabeth	1769	Whitechapel, London	(?)		Nathan Levy	Whitechapel, London	
15116	Levy	Elizabeth	1785	?, London	(?)		Joseph Levy	Hoxton, London	
3657	Levy	Elizabeth	1786	Rochford, Essex	Moses Lazarus		Abraham Levy	Finsbury, London	annuitant
25490	Levy	Elizabeth	1786	Whitechapel, London	(?) Levy			City, London	staymaker
15834	Levy	Elizabeth	1788	Portsmouth, Hampshire	(?) Levi		(?) Levy	Aldgate, London	
10413	Levy	Elizabeth	1789	Whitechapel, London	(?)		(?) Levy	Spitalfields, London	
3790	Levy	Elizabeth	1791	Aldgate, London				Spitalfields, London	servant
12445	Levy	Elizabeth	1791	Middlesex, London	(?) Levy			Spitalfields, London	retired servant
23319	Levy	Elizabeth	1792	Westminster, London	(?)		Moses Levy	Belgravia, London	
10453	Levy	Elizabeth	1793	Spitalfields, London	(?)		Woolf Levy	Aldgate, London	
7801	Levy	Elizabeth	1797	Plymouth, Devon	Abraham (?)		Levy Levy	Bristol	
29250	Levy	Elizabeth	1802	?, London	(?)		Abraham Levy	Whitechapel, London	
10462	Levy	Elizabeth	1803	?, Germany	(?)		Jacob Levy	Mile End, London	
9812	Levy	Elizabeth	1806	Rochford, Essex	(?)		(?) Levy	Finsbury, London	annuitant
29651	Levy	Elizabeth	1809	Middlesex, London	(?) Levy			Aldgate, London	needlewoman
23620	Levy	Elizabeth	1810	?, London	Israel Levy		Barnet Isaac Levy	Liverpool	
21831	Levy	Elizabeth	1811	Whitechapel, London	(?)		(?) Levy	Covent Garden, London	needlewoman
25855	Levy	Elizabeth	1811	Hessen, Germany	(?)		Barnett Levy	Aldgate, London	lodging house keeper's wife
3356	Levy	Elizabeth	1812	Spitalfields, London	Joshua (Jesse) Davis	Sarah Solomon	Philip Levy	Aldgate, London	
22240	Levy	Elizabeth	1814	Birmingham	(?)		Lewis Levy	Whitechapel, London	
20770	Levy	Elizabeth	1815	Bethnal Green, London	(?)		Solomon Levy	Haggerston, London	
14644	Levy	Elizabeth	1816	Whitechapel, London	(?)		Alexander Levy	Hoxton, London	
27944	Levy	Elizabeth	1816	Chelmsford, Essex	Solomon Levy	Maria (?)		Spitalfields, London	waistcoat maker
3906	Levy	Elizabeth	1820	Shoreditch, London			Lazarus Levy	Spitalfields, London	cap maker
6826	Levy	Elizabeth	1821	Spitalfields, London	Joseph Levy	Rosetta (?)		Spitalfields, London	servant
22100	Levy	Elizabeth	1821	Marylebone, London	(?)		Henry Levy	Whitechapel, London	
7727	Levy	Elizabeth	1824	Fulham, London	Nathaniel Levy	Sophia (?)	Benedictus L Leman	Bloomsbury, London	
20146	Levy	Elizabeth	1828	Middlesex, London	(?)		Isaac Levy	Soho, London	
15426	Levy	Elizabeth	1829	Whitechapel, London	David Levy	Maria (?)		Covent Garden, London	
15684	Levy	Elizabeth	1829	Aldgate, London	Meir HaLevi Hamburger		Solomon Levy	Aldgate, London	
20190	Levy	Elizabeth	1829	Whitechapel, London	Henry Levy	Jane Alexander		Spitalfields, London	tailoress

ID	surname	given names	born	birthplace	father	mother	spouse 1	1851 residence	1851 occupation
24422	Levy	Elizabeth	1829	Whitechapel, London	Judah Hurwitz		Henry Levy	Strand, London	
14043	Levy	Elizabeth	1830	?, London	(?)		Reuben Levy	Manchester	tailor + woollen draper
21400	Levy	Elizabeth	1830	Elephant & Castle, London	Solomon Levy	Maria Harris	Saul Reginald Solomon	Elephant & Castle, London	
8651	Levy	Elizabeth	1831	Aldgate, London	(?) Levy	Leah (?) [later Cohen]		Aldgate, London	
19841	Levy	Elizabeth	1833	Whitechapel, London	Jacob Levy	Sarah Samuel		Spitalfields, London	tailoress
24420	Levy	Elizabeth	1834	?, London	Lawrence Levy	Rebecca Jacobs		Strand, London	
27538	Levy	Elizabeth	1834	Aldgate, London	Mark (Mordecai) Levy	Phoebe Hyams		Spitalfields, London	
30353	Levy	Elizabeth	1834	Strand, London	Joseph Levy	Hannah (?)		Strand, London	
23370	Levy	Elizabeth	1835	Covent Garden, London	Samuel Levy	Julia (?)		Strand, London	
2781	Levy	Elizabeth	1840	Whitechapel, London	Aaron Levy	(?)		Whitechapel, London	scholar
28608	Levy	Elizabeth	1840	?, Holland	Samuel Levy	Sarah (?)		Spitalfields, London	scholar
28685	Levy	Elizabeth	1841	Middlesex, London	Abraham Levy	Louisa Judah	Hyam Hart	Spitalfields, London	
31178	Levy	Elizabeth	1841	Rochester, Kent	John Lewis Levy	Mary Ann (?)		Chatham, Kent	
10282	Levy	Elizabeth	1842	Aldgate, London	Lewis Levy	Sarah (?)	Abraham Cohen	Spitalfields, London	scholar
14984	Levy	Elizabeth	1842	Middlesex, London	(?) Levy			Bethnal Green, London	boarding school pupil
19814	Levy	Elizabeth	1842	Whitechapel, London	Elias Levy	Sarah Palachy	Israel Lazarus	Spitalfields, London	scholar
19866	Levy	Elizabeth	1846	Whitechapel, London	Coleman Levy	Jael (?)		Spitalfields, London	
20437	Levy	Elizabeth	1846	Spitalfields, London	Aaron Levy	Catherine Abrahams		Aldgate, London	
25859	Levy	Elizabeth	1846	Spitalfields, London	Barnett Levy	Elizabeth (?)		Aldgate, London	scholar
8742	Levy	Elizabeth	1847	Aldgate, London	Nathan Levy	Amelia (?)	Abraham Lazarus	Aldgate, London	
13341	Levy	Elizabeth	1847	Whitechapel, London	Joseph Levy	Caroline (?)		Spitalfields, London	
28802	Levy	Elizabeth	1848	Aldgate, London	Lewis Levy	Jeannette (Jane) Symons		Spitalfields, London	
30213	Levy	Elizabeth	1848	Finsbury, London	Henry Levy	Rosetta Moses		Spitalfields, London	
12117	Levy	Elizabeth	1849	Whitechapel, London	Abraham Levy	Mary Kapman		Spitalfields, London	
26265	Levy	Elizabeth	1850	?Aldgate, London	Samuel Levy	Louisa Jonas		Aldgate, London	
29946	Levy	Elizabeth	1850	Whitechapel, London	Morris Levy	Jane (?)		Whitechapel, London	
5291	Levy	Elizabeth	1851	Spitalfields, London	Jacob Levy	Ann Levy		Spitalfields, London	
16514	Levy	Elizabeth (Bessie)	1850	Aldgate, London	Alexander Levy	Amelia Harris	David Goldberg	Clerkenwell, London	
28412	Levy	Elizabeth (Betsey)	1824	Whitechapel, London	Aaron Phillips		Lewis Levy	Spitalfields, London	tailoress
8963	Levy	Elizabeth (Betsy)	1803	Aldgate, London	(?)		Samuel Levy	Aldgate, London	
6860	Levy	Elizabeth (Betsy)	1847	Whitechapel, London	Michael Levy	Sarah Harris	Abraham Emanuel Crabb	Whitechapel, London	
29837	Levy	Elizabeth (Betsy)	1849	Spitalfields, London	Moses Levy	Esther (?)		Wapping, London	
9935	Levy	Elizabeth (Lizzie)	1843	Covent Garden, London	David Levy	Catherine Davids	Samuel Barnard	Covent Garden, London	
23458	Levy	Elizabeth (Lizzie)	1845	?, London	Joseph Levy	Mary (?)	Henry John Nathan	Liverpool	scholar
2082	Levy	Elizabeth Maria	1840	Carmarthen, Wales	Daniel Levy	Mary Anne Lazarus		Carmarthen, Wales	scholar
13738	Levy	Elkin	1833	Wigan, Lancashire	(?) Levy	Sophia (?)		Manchester	tailor
28189	Levy	Ellen	1819	Aldgate, London	Solomon Abrahams		Samuel Levy	Spitalfields, London	clothes dealer
28705	Levy	Ellen	1844	Bristol	(?) Levy			Spitalfields, London	servant
17687	Levy	Ellen	1846	Shoreditch, London	Lawrence Levy	Eliza (Sarah) Emanuel		Shoreditch, London	scholar at home
2086	Levy	Ellen	1848	Carmarthen, Wales	Daniel Levy	Mary Anne Lazarus		Carmarthen, Wales	scholar
3278	Levy	Ellen (Helen) F	1841	St Pancras, London	Joseph Moses Levy	Esther Cohen	George Faudel Phillips [Faudel Phillips]	Bloomsbury, London	scholar at home
5442	Levy	Ellen E	1849	Plymouth, Devon	Markes Levy	Bella Woolf	Isaac S Frank Lyons	Plymouth, Devon	

ID	surname	given names	born	birthplace	father	mother	spouse 1	1851 residence	1851 occupation
5850	Levy	Ellen Maud (Nellie)	1845	Walworth, London	Daniel Levy	Amelia Jacobs	Henry Rossner	Bloomsbury, London	
17467	Levy	Emanuel	1790	Southwark, London			Mary (?)	Aldgate, London	clothes dealer
24632	Levy	Emanuel	1791	Whitechapel, London			Ann (?)	Waterloo, London	officer to the Sheriffs
28096	Levy	Emanuel	1792	Whitechapel, London	Lyon Levy		(?)	Spitalfields, London	tailor
13013	Levy	Emanuel	1815	Middlesex, London	Hayim Aryeh		Rebecca (?)	Spitalfields, London	general dealer
6964	Levy	Emanuel	1817	Whitechapel, London			Rachael Arnold	Finsbury, London	furrier
6957	Levy	Emanuel	1826	Aldgate, London	Mordecai Levy	Jane (?)	Esther Isaacs	Aldgate, London	cigar maker
23386	Levy	Emanuel	1839	?, London	Lipman (Eliezer) Levy	Hannah Jones	Sarah Levy	Aldgate, London	
4671	Levy	Emanuel	1840	Middlesex, London	Lawrence Levy	Priscilla (?)		Birmingham	scholar
29836	Levy	Emanuel	1846	Spitalfields, London	Moses Levy	Esther (?)		Wapping, London	scholar
18364	Levy	Emanuel	1848	Elephant & Castle, London	Moses Levy	Catherine Samuel		Elephant & Castle, London	
5290	Levy	Emanuel	1849	Middlesex, London	Jacob Levy	Ann Levy		Aldgate, London	scholar
9474	Levy	Emelia	1840	?, London	Samuel Levy	Henrietta (?)		Aldgate, London	
30709	Levy	Emilia	1836	Stepney, London	(?) Levy			Covent Garden, London	
8211	Levy	Emily	1832	Clerkenwell, London	Joseph Moses Levy	Esther Cohen		Bloomsbury, London	scholar at home
21132	Levy	Emily	1848	Aldgate, London	Joseph Levy	Ester (?)		Aldgate, London	
10924	Levy	Emily (Amelia)	1832	?, France			Jacob Levy	Spitalfields, London	
25473	Levy	Emma	1825	Middlesex, London	Solomon Levy			Tower Hill, London	
3656	Levy	Emma	1850	City, London	Moses Levy	Alice Moses		Shoreditch, London	
17690	Levy	Emma	1851	Shoreditch, London	Lawrence Levy	Eliza (Sarah) Emanuel	Samuel Heilbut	Shoreditch, London	
13521	Levy	Emmanuel	1776	Banbury, Oxfordshire			(?)	Manchester	traveller + clothes dealer
21548	Levy	Ernest Braham	1836	Walworth, London	Daniel Levy	Amelia Jacobs	(?)	Bloomsbury, London	scholar
21652	Levy	Estelle	1844	Whitechapel, London	Benjamin Levy	Rosa Mandola	Bernard (Behor) Carmona	Spitalfields, London	
21130	Levy	Ester	1817	Aldgate, London	(?)		Joseph Levy	Aldgate, London	
28719	Levy	Ester	1831	Middlesex, London	(?)		Joseph Levy	Spitalfields, London	cap maker
17069	Levy	Ester	1848	Edinburgh, Scotland	Henry Levy	Deborah Defries		Edinburgh, Scotland	scholar
23830	Levy	Esther	1783	?, London	(?)		Joseph Levy	Liverpool	tobacconist
10511	Levy	Esther	1807	?, Poland [?, Prussia]	(?)		Lewis Levy	Aldgate, London	furrier
17698	Levy	Esther	1811	Whitechapel, London	(?) Levy			Spitalfields, London	cloth cap maker
25471	Levy	Esther	1814	Middlesex, London	Solomon Levy			Tower Hill, London	
28441	Levy	Esther	1818	Whitechapel, London	Solomon Abendana	Pindler (Prindla) de Judah Isaacs	Angel Levy	Spitalfields, London	
8937	Levy	Esther	1820	Whitechapel, London	Samuel Noah (Da Costa Noah)	Dinah Levy	Lewis Levy	Aldgate, London	
10660	Levy	Esther	1821	Spitalfields, London	Shmuel		Morris (Moses) Levy	Spitalfields, London	
29835	Levy	Esther	1827	Amsterdam, Holland	(?)		Moses Levy	Wapping, London	
16799	Levy	Esther	1828	Exeter, Devon	Solomon Levy	Arabella (?)	Julius Cohen	Bristol	assistant jeweller
23263	Levy	Esther	1828	Whitechapel, London	(?) Levy			Notting Hill, London	fundholder
11471	Levy	Esther	1829	Aldgate, London	David Levy	Julia (?)		Aldgate, London	
25878	Levy	Esther	1830	Aldgate, London	(?)		James Jonas Levy	Aldgate, London	
17469	Levy	Esther	1831	Lambeth, London	Emanuel Levy	Mary (?)		Aldgate, London	
16153	Levy	Esther	1832	Whitechapel, London	Joseph Levy	Rebecca Johnson		Whitechapel, London	feather dealer
5391	Levy	Esther	1836	Eton, Berkshire	Alexander Levy	Stella Foligno	Lyon Joseph Joseph	Eton, Berkshire	
6846	Levy	Esther	1836	Spitalfields, London	Samuel Levy	Rebecca Pereira	Benjamin Bitton	Spitalfields, London	parasol maker

ID	surname	given names	born	birthplace	father	mother	spouse 1	1851 residence	1851 occupation
1197	Levy	Esther	1840	Plymouth, Devon	Aaron Levy	Rosetta (Rozetta) Meyers		Plymouth, Devon	
26164	Levy	Esther	1841	?Aldgate, London	Nathan Levy	Abigail Noah (Noah Da Costa)		Aldgate, London	scholar
23457	Levy	Esther	1843	?, London	Joseph Levy	Mary (?)		Liverpool	scholar
25766	Levy	Esther	1843	Whitechapel, London	Abraham Levy	Rosey (Rosa) Levy		Aldgate, London	
10311	Levy	Esther	1844	Spitalfields, London	Lewis Levy	Catharine Elias		Spitalfields, London	scholar
23624	Levy	Esther	1845	Liverpool	Barnet Isaac Levy	Elizabeth Levy		Liverpool	scholar
14790	Levy	Esther	1850	City, London	Abraham Levy	Julia Lawrence		Finsbury, London	
18977	Levy	Esther	1850	Whitechapel, London	Alexander Levy	Julia Defries		Whitechapel, London	
28139	Levy	Eve	1800	Hoxton, London	(?)		(?) Levy	Spitalfields, London	
30687	Levy	Eve	1818	Whitechapel, London	(?)		(?) Levy	Whitechapel, London	merchant's wife
17425	Levy	Eve	1832	Whitechapel, London	Solomon Levy	Fanny (?)		Spitalfields, London	
10931	Levy	Eve	1850	Spitalfields, London	Lewis Levy	Sarah (?)		Spitalfields, London	
1201	Levy	Eveline (Evelyn)	1846	Plymouth, Devon	Aaron Levy	Rosetta (Rozetta) Meyers		Plymouth, Devon	
17423	Levy	Fanny	1803	Whitechapel, London	(?)		Solomon Levy	Spitalfields, London	
26197	Levy	Fanny	1811	?, Germany	(?)		Simon Levy	Aldgate, London	
12862	Levy	Fanny	1821	Whitechapel, London	(?)		Mordecai Levy	Spitalfields, London	
14135	Levy	Fanny	1829	Manchester	Joseph Levy	Julia (?)		Manchester	
30351	Levy	Fanny	1829	Strand, London	Joseph Levy	Hannah (?)	Barnett Joshua Simmons	Strand, London	
5226	Levy	Fanny	1830	Leszno, Poland [Lissa, Prussia], Poland [Lissa, Prussia]	Yehuda Leib		Ephraim Cohen	Aldgate, London	dressmaker
23621	Levy	Fanny	1837	Liverpool	Barnet Isaac Levy	Elizabeth Levy		Liverpool	scholar
25767	Levy	Fanny	1845	Aldgate, London	Abraham Levy	Rosey (Rosa) Levy		Aldgate, London	
11477	Levy	Fanny	1847	Aldgate, London	David Levy	Julia (?)		Aldgate, London	
20371	Levy	Fanny	1848	Aldgate, London	Israel Levy	Sarah Harris		Aldgate, London	scholar
5135	Levy	Felix	1791	?, England			Elizabeth (?)	Sheffield, Yorkshire	tailor
17099	Levy	Flora	1846	St Peter Port, Guernsey, Channel Islands	Mark Levy	Ann Marks		St Peter Port, Guernsey, Channel Islands	scholar
17116	Levy	Frances	1800	Sheerness, Kent	(?)		Isaac Levy	Sheerness, Kent	
25893	Levy	Frances	1811	Aldgate, London	Joseph Naphthali	Leah (?)	Hyam Levy	Aldgate, London	
54	Levy	Frances	1821	Woolwich, London	Nathan Levy	Sarah (Mary) Palmer	Samuel Whiteman	Woolwich, London	seamstress
17699	Levy	Frances	1825	Whitechapel, London	(?) Levy			Spitalfields, London	cloth cap maker
11434	Levy	Frances	1838	Whitechapel, London	(?Hart) Levy	Julia (?)		Aldgate, London	
29941	Levy	Frances	1839	Whitechapel, London	Morris Levy	Jane (?)		Whitechapel, London	scholar
11320	Levy	Frances	1843	Aldgate, London	Lewis Levy	Ann (Nancy) Israel		Aldgate, London	scholar
28615	Levy	Frances	1843	Spitalfields, London	Samuel Levy	Sarah (?)		Spitalfields, London	scholar
30044	Levy	Frances	1843	Marylebone, London	(?) Levy	Hannah Moses		Aldgate, London	
13201	Levy	Frances	1845	Whitechapel, London	Solomon Hyam (Hyman) Levy	Clara Joseph	Lewis Phillips	Whitechapel, London	scholar
30574	Levy	Frances	1851	Wapping, London	Hyam Levy	Sarah Moses		Wapping, London	
6399	Levy	Frances (Fanny)	1812	Whitechapel, London	(?)		Israel Levy	Spitalfields, London	
28681	Levy	Frances (Fanny)	1831	Middlesex, London	Abraham Levy	Louisa Judah	Benjamin Benjamin	Spitalfields, London	
19778	Levy	Franny	1837	Spitalfields, London	Mark (Mordecai) Levy	Sarah Jacobs		Spitalfields, London	tailoress
16806	Levy	Frederick	1832	Bristol	Levy Levy	Elizabeth (?)		Bristol	glass + china maker
1200	Levy	Frederick	1844	Plymouth, Devon	Aaron Levy	Rosetta (Rozetta) Meyers		Plymouth, Devon	

ID	surname	given names	born	birthplace	father	mother	spouse 1	1851 residence	1851 occupation
26161	Levy	George	1838	?Spitalfields, London	Nathan Levy	Abigail Noah (Noah Da Costa)		Aldgate, London	cigar maker
29917	Levy	George	1838	?, Holland	Louis J Levy	Rebecca (?)		Whitechapel, London	errand boy
20174	Levy	George	1845	Spitalfields, London	Henry Levy	Hannah (?)		Spitalfields, London	
29945	Levy	George	1849	Whitechapel, London	Morris Levy	Jane (?)		Whitechapel, London	
30063	Levy	Godfrey	1773	Middlesex, London				Bedford, Bedfordshire	jeweller
8753	Levy	Godfrey	1825	Spitalfields, London	Barnett Judah Levy	Blumer Phillips	Hannah Isaacs	Aldgate, London	clothier
23381	Levy	Godfrey	1847	Aldgate, London	Mark Levy	Sarah Lazarus		Aldgate, London	
25375	Levy	Goodman	1788	Whitechapel, London	Moshe		Sarah (?)	Clerkenwell, London	
21401	Levy	Goodman	1832	Elephant & Castle, London	Solomon Levy	Maria Harris	Fanny (Frances) Hester Joseph	Elephant & Castle, London	scholar
22241	Levy	Goodman	1846	Whitechapel, London	Lewis Levy	Elizabeth (?)		Whitechapel, London	scholar
10534	Levy	Guldah	1838	Covent Garden, London	David Levy	Catherine Davids		Covent Garden, London	scholar
10408	Levy	Hanah	1828	Whitechapel, London	(?) Levy	Catherine (?)		Spitalfields, London	
19812	Levy	Hanah	1840	Whitechapel, London	Elias Levy	Sarah Palachy		Spitalfields, London	scholar
10355	Levy	Hanah	1844	Middlesex, London	Simon Levy	Moriah (?)		Spitalfields, London	scholar
13342	Levy	Hanah	1848	Whitechapel, London	Joseph Levy	Caroline (?)		Spitalfields, London	
9560	Levy	Hannah	1779	Whitechapel, London	(?)		(?) Levy	Spitalfields, London	
18672	Levy	Hannah	1781	Amsterdam, Holland	(?)		Jacob Levy	Spitalfields, London	
22893	Levy	Hannah	1783	?	(?)		(?) Levy	Wapping, London	
15870	Levy	Hannah	1786	?, Holland	(?)		(?) Levy	Bethnal Green, London	
23035	Levy	Hannah	1786	Aldgate, London	Shlomeh Zalman Ansell		Isaac Levy	Aldgate, London	
30349	Levy	Hannah	1794	Covent Garden, London	(?)		Joseph Levy	Strand, London	
21740	Levy	Hannah	1804	?, Jamaica, West Indies	(?)		(?) Levy	Canonbury, London	
21824	Levy	Hannah	1804	St Pancras, London	(?)		Aaron Levy	Covent Garden, London	
30164	Levy	Hannah	1805	Middlesex, London	(?Nathan Levi)		Abraham Levy	Lambeth, London	annuitant
20168	Levy	Hannah	1812	Aldgate, London	(?)		Henry Levy	Spitalfields, London	
24412	Levy	Hannah	1813	?, London	Naphtali Alexander		Morrice (Morris) Levy	Strand, London	
23384	Levy	Hannah	1816	?, London	Solomon (Samuel, Pinchas Zelig) Jonas	Rosetta Joseph	Lipman (Eliezer) Levy	Aldgate, London	dealer
10812	Levy	Hannah	1818	Spitalfields, London	(?) Levy			Spitalfields, London	
15689	Levy	Hannah	1819	Southwark, London				Aldgate, London	servant
3920	Levy	Hannah	1821	Aldgate, London	Mordecai Levy	Jane (?)		Aldgate, London	cap maker
23918	Levy	Hannah	1821	Elephant & Castle, London	(?) Levy		Myer Levy	Fitzrovia, London	
30059	Levy	Hannah	1822	Edinburgh, Scotland	Jacob Ashenheim	Jane (?)	Michael Abraham Levy	Edinburgh, Scotland	
28610	Levy	Hannah	1824	Spitalfields, London	Samuel Levy	Sarah (?)		Spitalfields, London	servant
2933	Levy	Hannah	1825	Spitalfields, London	Henry Benjamin		Henry (Savage) Levy	Spitalfields, London	
30043	Levy	Hannah	1825	Spitalfields, London	(?) Moses	Catherine (?)	(?) Levy	Aldgate, London	
397	Levy	Hannah	1826	Aldgate, London	(?)		(?) Levy	Spitalfields, London	picture dealer
8964	Levy	Hannah	1827	Aldgate, London	Samuel Levy	Elizabeth (Betsy) (?)		Aldgate, London	
11470	Levy	Hannah	1827	Aldgate, London	David Levy	Julia (?)		Aldgate, London	
19775	Levy	Hannah	1827	Spitalfields, London	Mark (Mordecai) Levy	Sarah Jacobs		Spitalfields, London	pen cutter
22638	Levy	Hannah	1827	Ipswich, Suffolk	(?) Levy	Rachel (?)		Whitechapel, London	dressmaker
8752	Levy	Hannah	1829	?, London	Lazarus Isaacs	Elizabeth Levy	Godfrey Levy	Aldgate, London	
9471	Levy	Hannah	1831	Aldgate, London	(?) Levy			Aldgate, London	

ID	surname	given names	born	birthplace	father	mother	spouse 1	1851 residence	1851 occupation
21246	Levy	Hannah	1833	Whitechapel, London	Samuel Levy	Deborah Barnett		Spitalfields, London	dressmaker
21314	Levy	Hannah	1834	Eton, Berkshire	Alexander Levy	Stella Foligno	Myer Erlich	Eton, Berkshire	
26159	Levy	Hannah	1834	Spitalfields, London	Nathan Levy	Abigail Noah (Noah Da Costa)		Aldgate, London	cap maker
26402	Levy	Hannah	1838	?, London	Mordecai Levy	Leah (?)		Aldgate, London	slipper maker
17427	Levy	Hannah	1839	Whitechapel, London	Solomon Levy	Fanny (?)		Spitalfields, London	
11435	Levy	Hannah	1840	Whitechapel, London	(?Hart) Levy	Julia (?)		Aldgate, London	
26202	Levy	Hannah	1842	?, Germany	Simon Levy	Fanny (?)		Aldgate, London	
25742	Levy	Hannah	1843	Spitalfields, London	Elias Levy	Matilda Harris		Spitalfields, London	scholar
6164	Levy	Hannah	1844	Mile End, London	Asher Levy	Julia (?)	Abraham Da Silva	Aldgate, London	
20154	Levy	Hannah	1845	Poplar, London	Henry Levy	Rachel (?)		Stepney, London	
8008	Levy	Hannah	1846	Whitechapel, London	Benjamin Levy	Rosa Mandola	Charles Carlish	Spitalfields, London	
7957	Levy	Hannah	1849	City, London	Alexander Levy	Amelia Harris	Louis A Barnett	Clerkenwell, London	
8744	Levy	Hannah	1850	Aldgate, London	Nathan Levy	Amelia (?)		Aldgate, London	
25122	Levy	Hannah	1850	Finsbury, London	Philip Levy	Sarah (?)		Finsbury, London	
29645	Levy	Hannah	1850	?Aldgate, London	Joseph Levy	Maria (?)		Aldgate, London	
21505	Levy	Hannah	1828	Middlesex, London	(?) Levy			Aldgate, London	furrier
26339	Levy	Hannah (Anna)	1849	?, London	Lawrence Levy	Amelia Cohen		Aldgate, London	
30576	Levy	Hannah Sophia	1851	Aldgate, London	Henry Levy	Jane Hart		Aldgate, London	
12615	Levy	Harman	1831	?, Poland				Norwich, Norfolk	general dealer
7014	Levy	Harriet	1814	?, London	David Levy	Hannah Solomons	Abraham Benisch	Fitzrovia, London	
15114	Levy	Harriet	1831	?, London	(?) Levy	Catherine (?)		Bethnal Green, London	
14839	Levy	Harriett	1828	Aldgate, London	Eliezer Lezer Samson		Joseph Levy	Bethnal Green, London	
25472	Levy	Harriette (Henriette, Judith)	1821	Middlesex, London	Solomon Levy		Morris (Moses) Shannon	Tower Hill, London	
17118	Levy	Harriott	1835	Sheerness, Kent	Isaac Levy	Frances (?)		Sheerness, Kent	
26228	Levy	Harris	1815	?Poland [Cursberg, Russian Poland]				Aldgate, London	cap maker
26042	Levy	Harris	1825	?, Poland [?, Russian Poland]				Whitechapel, London	tailor
26940	Levy	Harris	1836	?, Poland				Aldgate, London	tailor
11710	Levy	Harriss	1832	?, Germany				Aldgate, London	tailor
20155	Levy	Harry	1847	Poplar, London	Henry Levy	Rachel (?)		Stepney, London	
11437	Levy	Hart	1850	Whitechapel, London	(?Hart) Levy	Julia (?)		Aldgate, London	
9207	Levy	Hayman	1830	?, Poland				Whitechapel, London	tailor
2300	Levy	Heiman (Herman, Iman)	1826	?, Poland [?, Prussia]	Joshua Carenwood (?)		Paulina (Pauline) Wolfsohn	Leeds, Yorkshire	jeweller
16803	Levy	Helen	1840	Bristol	Solomon Levy	Arabella (?)	E--- Wolff	Bristol	scholar at home
21840	Levy	Helen (Ellen)	1824	Aldgate, London	Jonas (Jonathan) Levy	Matilda Moses		Clerkenwell, London	
9473	Levy	Henrietta	1822	?, London	(?)		Samuel Levy	Aldgate, London	
16199	Levy	Henry	1795	Aldgate, London				Whitechapel, London	general dealer
17833	Levy	Henry	1796	City, London			Anna (?)	Aldgate, London	tailor
11233	Levy	Henry	1797	Spitalfields, London			Agnes Wolf	Aldgate, London	general dealer
28453	Levy	Henry	1799	Southwark, London	Asher Levy		(?)	Spitalfields, London	piece broker
28236	Levy	Henry	1801	Whitechapel, London				Spitalfields, London	?quill manufacturer
20167	Levy	Henry	1808	Aldgate, London	Mordecai Levy	Abigail Levy	Hannah (?)	Spitalfields, London	general dealer

ID	surname	given names	born	birthplace	father	mother	spouse 1	1851 residence	1851 occupation
23779	Levy	Henry	1811	?, Poland [Lobertz, Prussia]			Maria (?)	Liverpool	grocer
17066	Levy	Henry	1815	?, London			Deborah Defries	Edinburgh, Scotland	tobacconist master
28944	Levy	Henry	1815	?			Phoebe Marks	Whitechapel, London	journeyman cigar maker
22099	Levy	Henry	1816	Aldgate, London			Elizabeth (?)	Whitechapel, London	salesman + tailor
29501	Levy	Henry	1816	Spitalfields, London	Jacob Levy		Catherine (Kate, Kitty) Franks	Spitalfields, London	general dealer
13099	Levy	Henry	1818	Whitechapel, London				Whitechapel, London	pauper + labourer
15118	Levy	Henry	1818	?, London	Joseph Levy	Elizabeth (?)		Hoxton, London	warehouseman
20152	Levy	Henry	1819	Stratford, London	Hyman Levy		Rachel (?)	Stepney, London	cabinet maker empl 2
17921	Levy	Henry	1821	Strand, London	Joseph Levy	Hannah (?)		Strand, London	clothier
20357	Levy	Henry	1823	Manchester	Samson Levy		Jane Hart	Aldgate, London	stationer, quill merchant + Birmingham warehouseman
24421	Levy	Henry	1823	Marylebone, London	William Levy		Elizabeth Hurwitz	Strand, London	solicitor
4660	Levy	Henry	1825	?, London			Katherine (?)	Birmingham	cordwinder (?cordwainer)
5133	Levy	Henry	1830	?Sheffield, Yorkshire	Reuben Levy	Polly (?)		Sheffield, Yorkshire	outfitter
19011	Levy	Henry	1830	Strand, London				Whitechapel, London	licensed hawker
10243	Levy	Henry	1832	Spitalfields, London	Lewis Levy	Rachel (?)		Spitalfields, London	cigar maker
16196	Levy	Henry	1832	Southwark, London	Emanuel Levy	Sarah (?)	Esther Myers	Whitechapel, London	waterproofer
13850	Levy	Henry	1835	Manchester	Joseph Levy	Julia (?)		Manchester	tailor + draper's assistant
11041	Levy	Henry	1837	?Aldgate, London	Samson Levy	Phoebe Simmons		Aldgate, London	cigar maker
16808	Levy	Henry	1837	Bristol	Levy Levy	Elizabeth (?)		Bristol	assistant glass + china maker
23385	Levy	Henry	1837	?, London	Lipman (Eliezer) Levy	Hannah Jones		Aldgate, London	
28521	Levy	Henry	1837	Whitechapel, London	(?) Levy	Rachael		Spitalfields, London	general dealer
29940	Levy	Henry	1837	Whitechapel, London	Morris Levy	Jane (?)		Whitechapel, London	butcher boy
19779	Levy	Henry	1839	Spitalfields, London	Mark (Mordecai) Levy	Sarah Jacobs	Ann (Nancy) Joseph	Spitalfields, London	cigar maker
2083	Levy	Henry	1842	Carmarthen, Wales	Daniel Levy	Mary Anne Lazarus	Elizabeth Levi	Carmarthen, Wales	scholar
3654	Levy	Henry	1843	City, London	Moses Levy	Alice Levy		Shoreditch, London	
27541	Levy	Henry	1843	Aldgate, London	Mark (Mordecai) Levy	Phoebe Hyams		Spitalfields, London	
20173	Levy	Henry	1844	Spitalfields, London	Henry Levy	Hannah (?)		Spitalfields, London	
29842	Levy	Henry	1844	Wapping, London	(?) Levy	Mary (?)		Stepney, London	scholar
29900	Levy	Henry	1844	Wapping, London	(?) Levy	Mary (?)		Wapping, London	
10283	Levy	Henry	1845	Whitechapel, London	Lewis Levy	Sarah (?)		Spitalfields, London	scholar
25744	Levy	Henry	1846	Spitalfields, London	Elias Levy	Matilda Harris		Spitalfields, London	scholar
28484	Levy	Henry	1846	Spitalfields, London	Lewis Levy	Amelia Morris		Spitalfields, London	scholar
17068	Levy	Henry	1847	Liverpool	Henry Levy	Deborah Defries	Kate Benjamin	Edinburgh, Scotland	scholar
13017	Levy	Henry	1848	Middlesex, London	Emanuel Levy	Rebecca (?)		Spitalfields, London	
17513	Levy	Henry	1850	Whitechapel, London	Ralph Levy	Phoebe Solomons		Spitalfields, London	
25899	Levy	Henry	1850	Aldgate, London	Hyam Levy	Frances Naphthali		Aldgate, London	
28949	Levy	Henry	1850	Whitechapel, London	Henry Levy	Phoebe Marks		Whitechapel, London	
2710	Levy	Henry (Harris)	1839	?, Poland [?, Prussia]	Abraham Levy	Rachel Wolfson		Manchester	
2020	Levy	Henry (Savage)	1825	Spitalfields, London	Joseph Levy	Blumah Jacobs	Hannah Benjamin	Spitalfields, London	fishmonger
21547	Levy	Henry Daniel	1833	Walworth, London	Daniel Levy	Amelia Jacobs		Bloomsbury, London	tailor's boy
17684	Levy	Herbert Michael	1840	Aldgate, London	Lawrence Levy	Eliza (Sarah) Emanuel		Shoreditch, London	scholar at home

ID	surname	given names	born	birthplace	father	mother	spouse 1	1851 residence	1851 occupation
28226	Levy	Hester	1849	Whitechapel, London	(?) Levy	Catherine (?)		Spitalfields, London	
25892	Levy	Hyam	1810	Aldgate, London	Isaac Levy	Sarah (?)	Frances Naphthali	Aldgate, London	butcher master
24787	Levy	Hyam	1819	Whitechapel, London			Lydia (?)	Elephant & Castle, London	clothes salesman
4120	Levy	Hyam	1821	Whitechapel, London			Sarah Moses	Wapping, London	general outfitter empl 6
12470	Levy	Hyam	1841	Whitechapel, London	Israel Levy	Frances (Fanny) (?)		Spitalfields, London	scholar
12233	Levy	Hyam Moses	1826	Aldgate, London	Moses Levy	Catherine Aarons		Whitechapel, London	silversmith, jeweller + watchmaker
3722	Levy	Hyman	1776	Spitalfields, London			Sarah (?)	Spitalfields, London	general dealer
11072	Levy	Hyman	1827	?, Poland [?, Prussian Poland]				Aldgate, London	plumber + glazier
11475	Levy	Hyman	1839	Aldgate, London	David Levy	Julia (?)	Leah Isaacs	Aldgate, London	
28947	Levy	Hyman	1847	Aldgate, London	Henry Levy	Phoebe Marks		Whitechapel, London	
22984	Levy	Hymer	1779	?, Holland			Julia (?)	Poplar, London	tailor
17115	Levy	Isaac	1790	Canterbury, Kent			Frances (?)	Sheerness, Kent	outfitter
24376	Levy	Isaac	1803	City, London	Matathias HaLevi		Elizabeth Russell	Soho, London	butcher
20197	Levy	Isaac	1805	Margate, Kent			Jane (?)	Chatham, Kent	slopseller + general dealer
20145	Levy	Isaac	1814	Oberhagenthal, France	Jacob Levy		Elizabeth (?)	Soho, London	haberdasher + cigar dealer
1027	Levy	Isaac	1815	Exeter, Devon	(?) Levy		Sarah (?)	Exeter, Devon	druggist
20158	Levy	Isaac	1815	Whitechapel, London			Catherine (?)	Spitalfields, London	general dealer
26065	Levy	Isaac	1818	Amsterdam, Holland	Ansell Isaac Levy	Rebecca (?)	Mary Kobas	Aldgate, London	jeweller
4662	Levy	Isaac	1821	?, Poland				Birmingham	glazier
12614	Levy	Isaac	1821	?, Poland				Norwich, Norfolk	general dealer
55	Levy	Isaac	1824	Woolwich, London	Nathan Levy	Sarah (Mary) Palmer	Dinah Jacobs	Whitechapel, London	
13349	Levy	Isaac	1825	Aldgate, London	Shlomeh		Deborah Bendon	Spitalfields, London	clothes dealer
27946	Levy	Isaac	1826	Aldgate, London	Solomon Levy	Maria (?)		Spitalfields, London	general dealer
11071	Levy	Isaac	1827	?, Poland [?, Prussian Poland]				Aldgate, London	plumber + glazier
14236	Levy	Isaac	1827	Abingdon, Oxfordshire [Abingdon, Berkshire]				Manchester	traveller (cedar)
11346	Levy	Isaac	1830	?, Poland				Aldgate, London	tailor
17354	Levy	Isaac	1831	Whitechapel, London				Spitalfields, London	pencil maker
26176	Levy	Isaac	1831	?, London				Aldgate, London	rag merchant
20210	Levy	Isaac	1832	Elephant & Castle, London	Moses Levy	Mary (?)		Wandsworth, London	
10244	Levy	Isaac	1834	Spitalfields, London	Lewis Levy	Rachel (?)		Spitalfields, London	cigar maker
17839	Levy	Isaac	1836	City, London	Henry Levy	Anna (?)		Aldgate, London	tailor
25894	Levy	Isaac	1836	Aldgate, London	Hyam Levy	Frances Naphthali		Aldgate, London	assistant to butcher
29916	Levy	Isaac	1836	?, Holland	Louis J Levy	Rebecca (?)		Whitechapel, London	errand boy
15430	Levy	Isaac	1839	Covent Garden, London	David Levy	Maria (?)		Covent Garden, London	
6400	Levy	Isaac	1840	Whitechapel, London	Israel Levy	Frances (Fanny) (?)		Spitalfields, London	scholar
19813	Levy	Isaac	1841	Whitechapel, London	Elias Levy	Sarah Palachy		Spitalfields, London	scholar
21833	Levy	Isaac	1841	Covent Garden, London	(?) Levy	Elizabeth (?)		Covent Garden, London	
28422	Levy	Isaac	1841	Whitechapel, London	Moses Levy	(?)		Spitalfields, London	
12200	Levy	Isaac	1843	?, Poland	Marks Levy	Rachel (?)		Whitechapel, London	
22102	Levy	Isaac	1845	Marylebone, London	Henry Levy	Elizabeth (?)		Whitechapel, London	scholar
28686	Levy	Isaac	1845	Spitalfields, London	Abraham Levy	Louisa Judah		Spitalfields, London	

ID	surname	given names	born	birthplace	father	mother	spouse 1	1851 residence	1851 occupation
10537	Levy	Isaac	1846	Covent Garden, London	David Levy	Catherine Davids		Covent Garden, London	scholar
11006	Levy	Isaac	1849	Aldgate, London	Philip Levy	Elizabeth Davis	Julia Lazarus [Joel]	Aldgate, London	
20026	Levy	Isaac	1849	Spitalfields, London	Solomon Levy	Charlotte Hart		Aldgate, London	
18365	Levy	Isaac	1850	Elephant & Castle, London	Moses Levy	Catherine Samuel		Elephant & Castle, London	
30579	Levy	Isaac	1851	Spitalfields, London	John (Jacob) Levy	Leah Myers		Spitalfields, London	
12115	Levy	Isaac A	1843	Whitechapel, London	Abraham Levy	Mary Kapman		Spitalfields, London	scholar
30013	Levy	Isabella	1811	?, London	David Levy	Hannah Solomons		Fitzrovia, London	
6446	Levy	Isabella	1832	Aldgate, London	Henry Levy	Anna (?)		Aldgate, London	milliner
20213	Levy	Isabella	1838	Aldgate, London	Moses Levy	Mary (?)		Wandsworth, London	
12886	Levy	Isabella	1843	Aldgate, London	Aaron Levy	Rachel Hart		Aldgate, London	scholar
12979	Levy	Isabella	1844	Whitechapel, London	Asher Levy	Julia Phillips		Aldgate, London	scholar
23622	Levy	Isac	1839	Liverpool	Barnet Isaac Levy	Elizabeth Levy		Liverpool	scholar
28956	Levy	Isaiah	1810	Luxembourg	Yitzhak		Brinette (?)	Whitechapel, London	teacher of the Hebrew language
22291	Levy	Isidore	1848	Manchester	(?) Levy	(?) Jacobs		Whitechapel, London	
20364	Levy	Israel	1803	Whitechapel, London	Moses Levy		Sarah Harris	Aldgate, London	dealer in fruit
6398	Levy	Israel	1811	Lambeth, London			Frances (Fanny) (?)	Spitalfields, London	general dealer
2021	Levy	Israel	1827	Spitalfields, London	Joseph Levy	Blumah Jacobs	Elizabeth Harris	Spitalfields, London	general dealer
10278	Levy	Israel	1836	Whitechapel, London	Lewis Levy	Sarah (?)		Spitalfields, London	scholar
13869	Levy	Israel	1845	Manchester	Lewis Levy	Mary Ann (?)		Manchester	scholar
2668	Levy	Israel Aaron	1824	Aldgate, London	Aaron Levy (Aaron ben Yehuda Leib)	Catherine Moses	Rosa Hyams	Piccadilly, London	rabbi
23623	Levy	Isreal	1843	Liverpool	Barnet Isaac Levy	Elizabeth Levy		Liverpool	scholar
14737	Levy	Jacob	1765	Amsterdam, Holland			Sarah (?)	Spitalfields, London	
19838	Levy	Jacob	1787	Aldgate, London			Sarah Samuel	Spitalfields, London	clothes dealer
10461	Levy	Jacob	1798	?, Germany			Elizabeth (?)	Mile End, London	general dealer
5286	Levy	Jacob	1818	Finsbury, London	Mordecai Levy		Ann (Nancy) Levy	Aldgate, London	general dealer
10067	Levy	Jacob	1819	Whitechapel, London	Solomon Levy		Abigail Barnett	Wapping, London	clothier
29548	Levy	Jacob	1819	Norwich, Norfolk	George Levy		Maria Levy	Spitalfields, London	furrier
23033	Levy	Jacob	1823	Amsterdam, Holland	Isaac Levy	Hannah Ansell		Aldgate, London	lithographer + stationer
10923	Levy	Jacob	1826	Amsterdam, Holland	Abraham Levy		Emily (Amelia) (?)	Spitalfields, London	cigar maker
11350	Levy	Jacob	1831	?, Poland	Mark Levy	Rebecca (?)		Aldgate, London	scholar
2500	Levy	Jacob	1833	Swansea, Wales	(?) Levy	Rebecca Levy	Sarah Levy	Swansea, Wales	watchmaker
21435	Levy	Jacob	1833	?, Poland [?, Prussia]				Nottingham, Nottinghamshire	hawker of jewellery
26200	Levy	Jacob	1838	?, Germany	Simon Levy	Fanny (?)		Aldgate, London	
29448	Levy	Jacob	1838	Amsterdam, Holland	Joseph Levy	Amelia (?)		Spitalfields, London	cigar maker
10248	Levy	Jacob	1844	Spitalfields, London	Lewis Levy	Rachel (?)		Spitalfields, London	scholar
23920	Levy	Jacob	1848	Marylebone, London	Myer Levy	Hannah Levy		Fitzrovia, London	
20175	Levy	Jacob	1849	Spitalfields, London	Henry Levy	Hannah (?)		Spitalfields, London	
29507	Levy	Jacob	1849	Spitalfields, London	Henry Levy	Catherine (Kate, Kitty) Franks		Spitalfields, London	
13642	Levy	Jacob	1850	Leeds, Yorkshire	Abraham Levy	Rachel Wolfson		Manchester	
19789	Levy	Jacob (John)	1833	Spitalfields, London	Moses Levy	Sarah Lazarus		Spitalfields, London	butcher

ID	surname	given names	born	birthplace	father	mother	spouse 1	1851 residence	1851 occupation
21981	Levy	Jacob (John)	1833	Woolwich, London	Nathan Levy	Sarah (Mary) Palmer		Whitechapel, London	clerk
23962	Levy	Jacob Abraham	1779	?, Holland	(?Abraham) Levy		(?)	Marylebone, London	fundholder
2080	Levy	Jacob Daniel	1836	North Shields, Tyne & Wear	Daniel Levy	Mary Anne Lazarus		Carmarthen, Wales	scholar
19865	Levy	Jael	1818	Aldgate, London	(?)		Coleman Levy	Spitalfields, London	dress maker
20150	Levy	James	1828	Aldgate, London	Abraham Levy	Julia Hart		Euston, London	
24416	Levy	James	1849	Strand, London	Morrice (Morris) Levy	Hannah Alexander		Strand, London	
25877	Levy	James Jonas	1823	Whitechapel, London			Esther (?)	Aldgate, London	clothes dealer
25222	Levy	Jane	1777	Finsbury, London	(?)		(?) Levy	Clerkenwell, London	
11343	Levy	Jane	1790	?, Holland	(?)		(?) Levy	Aldgate, London	butcher
5893	Levy	Jane	1794	Whitechapel, London	Meir Alexander		Henry Levy	Spitalfields, London	fruiterer
3918	Levy	Jane	1801	Whitechapel, London			Mordecai Levy	Aldgate, London	
21311	Levy	Jane	1811	Dover, Kent	(?)		Isaac Levy	Chatham, Kent	
29939	Levy	Jane	1813	Hackney, London	(?)		Morris Levy	Whitechapel, London	parasol coverer
21212	Levy	Jane	1814	Aldgate, London	Nathan Lazarus		David Levy	Spitalfields, London	
20358	Levy	Jane	1827	Middlesex, London	Moses Hart		Henry Levy	Aldgate, London	
23922	Levy	Jane	1831	Elephant & Castle, London	(?) Levy			Fitzrovia, London	
9279	Levy	Jane	1833	Aldgate, London	Nathan Levy	Rachel (?)		Aldgate, London	
10410	Levy	Jane	1833	Whitechapel, London	(?) Levy	Catherine (?)		Spitalfields, London	
10245	Levy	Jane	1836	Spitalfields, London	Lewis Levy	Rachel (?)		Spitalfields, London	tailoress
5719	Levy	Jane	1839	Aldgate, London	Philip Levy	Elizabeth Davis	Isaac Abrahams	Aldgate, London	scholar
13340	Levy	Jane	1841	Spitalfields, London	Joseph Levy	Caroline (?)		Spitalfields, London	
5981	Levy	Jane	1842	Aldgate, London	Lawrence Levy	Maria Hiam		Wapping, London	scholar
30573	Levy	Jane	1842	Wapping, London	Hyam Levy	Sarah Moses		Wapping, London	
8938	Levy	Jane	1843	Aldgate, London	Lewis Levy	Esther Noah (Da Costa Noah)		Aldgate, London	
10312	Levy	Jane	1846	Spitalfields, London	Lewis Levy	Catharine Elias		Spitalfields, London	scholar
29944	Levy	Jane	1846	Whitechapel, London	Morris Levy	Jane (?)		Whitechapel, London	scholar
23390	Levy	Jane	1847	?, London	Lipman (Eliezer) Levy	Hannah Jones	Abraham Hart	Aldgate, London	
12407	Levy	Jane	1849	Spitalfields, London	Thomas Levy	Rose (?)		Spitalfields, London	
19920	Levy	Jane	1850	Belfast, Ireland	Myer (Mier) Levy	Sarah Jacobs	Elliott Meyer	Belfast, Ireland	
24063	Levy	Jane?	1798	Middlesex, London	(?) Levy			St John's Wood, London	
5862	Levy	Jeanette	1830	Walworth, London	Daniel Levy	Amelia Jacobs		Bloomsbury, London	
28798	Levy	Jeannette (Jane)	1823	Whitechapel, London	Joseph Symons		Lewis Levy	Spitalfields, London	
13834	Levy	Jehuiakim	1803	Hamburg, Germany				Manchester	Professor of Hebrew
10925	Levy	Jenneat	1850	Spitalfields, London	Jacob Levy	Emily (Amelia)		Spitalfields, London	
1030	Levy	Jenny	1850	Exeter, Devon	Isaac Levy	Sarah (?)		Exeter, Devon	
4663	Levy	Jeremiah	1775	?, London			Lydia (?)	Birmingham	glass cutter
18688	Levy	Jesse	1850	Whitechapel, London	Michael Levy	Sarah Harris		Whitechapel, London	
19118	Levy	Jessy	1813	?, London	Nathan Selig		Lewis Levy	Bedford, Bedfordshire	
13368	Levy	Jette	1826	?, Germany	(?)		Joseph Levy	Holborn, London	
20196	Levy	Joel	1807	Sheerness, Kent				Chatham, Kent	slopseller + general dealer
22104	Levy	Joel	1828	Spitalfields, London				Whitechapel, London	cutter to a tailor
28682	Levy	Joel	1832	Middlesex, London	Abraham Levy	Louisa Judah	Sarah Marks	Spitalfields, London	cigar maker
10465	Levy	Joel	1840	Spitalfields, London	Jacob Levy	Elizabeth (?)	Lizzie Abrahams	Mile End, London	scholar
15665	Levy	Joesman	1833	?, London				Aldgate, London	general dealer

ID	surname	given names	born	birthplace	father	mother	spouse 1	1851 residence	1851 occupation
10210	Levy	John	1787	Spitalfields, London			Sarah (?)	Aldgate, London	wholesale stationer
7584	Levy	John	1804	Piccadilly, London	David Levy	Hannah Solomons		Southampton, Hampshire	Principal Officer, Southampton Docks
19194	Levy	John	1811	Bristol	Levi		Mary Lazarus	Whitechapel, London	grocer
27955	Levy	John	1818	Aldgate, London			Julia Moses	Spitalfields, London	cigar maker
8402	Levy	John	1821	?, Germany				Southampton, Hampshire	travelling jeweller
22245	Levy	John	1821	Whitechapel, London	(?) Levy	Rebecca (?)		Whitechapel, London	tailor
30350	Levy	John	1821	Strand, London	Joseph Levy	Hannah (?)		Strand, London	
17252	Levy	John	1822	Aldgate, London			Rebecca (?)	Aldgate, London	clothes dealer
26175	Levy	John	1825	?, London				Aldgate, London	rag merchant
28680	Levy	John	1829	Middlesex, London	Abraham Levy	Louisa Judah		Spitalfields, London	general dealer
10280	Levy	John	1840	Whitechapel, London	Lewis Levy	Sarah (?)		Spitalfields, London	scholar
26162	Levy	John	1840	?Aldgate, London	Nathan Levy	Abigail Noah (Noah Da Costa)		Aldgate, London	scholar
27885	Levy	John	1842	City, London				Spitalfields, London	scholar
11442	Levy	John	1843	Spitalfields, London	Mark (Mordecai) Levy	Maria Lyon		Aldgate, London	
31179	Levy	John	1843	Rochester, Kent	John Lewis Levy	Mary Ann (?)		Chatham, Kent	
18685	Levy	John	1846	Whitechapel, London	Michael Levy	Sarah Harris		Whitechapel, London	
28948	Levy	John	1848	Whitechapel, London	Henry Levy	Phoebe Marks		Whitechapel, London	
26662	Levy	John (Jacob)	1824	Whitechapel, London	Mark (Mordecai) Levy		Leah Myers	Spitalfields, London	cigar maker journeyman
3211	Levy	John Lewis	1807	Rochester, Kent	Isaac Levy	Sarah (?)	Mary Ann (?)	Chatham, Kent	victualling officer
5134	Levy	Jonah (Jonathon)	1830	?Holborn, London	Reuben Levy	Polly (?)		Sheffield, Yorkshire	draper + tailor
7143	Levy	Jonas	1813	Middlesex, London	Joseph Levy	Elizabeth (?)		Bloomsbury, London	toll contractor
8829	Levy	Jonas	1818	Whitechapel, London			Dorothy (?)	Aldgate, London	licensed victualler
18426	Levy	Jonas	1830	Kensington, London	Nathaniel Levy	Sophia (?)		Bloomsbury, London	clerk to a stockbroker
21837	Levy	Jonas (Jonathan)	1794	Newbury, Berkshire	Jacob Levy		Matilda Moses	Clerkenwell, London	merchant
22851	Levy	Joseph	1761	Strasbourg, France [Strasburg, Germany]				Whitechapel, London	retired jeweller
14133	Levy	Joseph	1763	?, Poland [?, Prussia]			Julia (?)	Manchester	retired tailor + draper
24665	Levy	Joseph	1772	Aldgate, London			Sophia (?)	Kennington, London	formerly jeweller
25910	Levy	Joseph	1773	?, Poland [?, Prussia]				Aldgate, London	clothes dealer
23829	Levy	Joseph	1775	?, Germany			Esther (?)	Liverpool	tobacconist
15115	Levy	Joseph	1778	Hanover, Germany			Elizabeth (?)	Hoxton, London	annuitant
30348	Levy	Joseph	1784	Middlesex, London			Hannah (?)	Strand, London	clothier
2019	Levy	Joseph	1789	Aldgate, London	Yechiel Michael Halevi		Blumah Jacobs	Spitalfields, London	cook + confectioner
16151	Levy	Joseph	1795	Coventry, Warwickshire	Jacob Levy		Rebecca Johnson	Whitechapel, London	feather dealer
23455	Levy	Joseph	1811	?, London			Mary (?)	Liverpool	
24634	Levy	Joseph	1811	Whitechapel, London	Emanuel Levy	Ann (?)		Waterloo, London	general dealer
29445	Levy	Joseph	1811	Amsterdam, Holland			Amelia (?)	Spitalfields, London	jeweller
4665	Levy	Joseph	1818	Norwich, Norfolk				Birmingham	glassblower
21129	Levy	Joseph	1819	Aldgate, London			Ester (?)	Aldgate, London	hatter
13337	Levy	Joseph	1821	Aldgate, London	Yitzhak		Caroline (?)	Spitalfields, London	butcher
13367	Levy	Joseph	1821	?, Germany			Jette (?)	Holborn, London	portmoney + cigar cases maker empl 5
10975	Levy	Joseph	1822	?, Dorset				Aldgate, London	journeyman baker

ID	surname	given names	born	birthplace	father	mother	spouse 1	1851 residence	1851 occupation
28718	Levy	Joseph	1826	Middlesex, London			Ester (?)	Spitalfields, London	cigar maker
13518	Levy	Joseph	1827	Manchester			Leah (?)	Manchester	cigar dealer
9202	Levy	Joseph	1828	?, Germany				Whitechapel, London	tailor
14838	Levy	Joseph	1828	Finsbury, London	Jacob Levy		Harriet Samson	Bethnal Green, London	wholesale stationer
29643	Levy	Joseph	1828	Whitechapel, London			Maria (?)	Aldgate, London	tailor
5506	Levy	Joseph	1829	Strand, London	(?) Levy		Cordelia Hart	Leicester, Leicestershire	tailor
10532	Levy	Joseph	1829	Covent Garden, London	David Levy	Catherine Davids		Covent Garden, London	warehouseman
4668	Levy	Joseph	1831	Southwark, London	Lawrence Levy	Priscilla (?)		Birmingham	apprentice watchmaker
30165	Levy	Joseph	1831	Middlesex, London	Abraham Levy	Hannah (Levi?)		Lambeth, London	warehouseman
12113	Levy	Joseph	1832	Whitechapel, London	Abraham Levy	(?Esther Silva)		Spitalfields, London	cigar maker
17355	Levy	Joseph	1833	Whitechapel, London				Spitalfields, London	pencil maker
28520	Levy	Joseph	1833	Whitechapel, London	(?) Levy	Rachael		Spitalfields, London	general dealer
16801	Levy	Joseph	1835	Bristol	Solomon Levy	Arabella (?)		Bristol	haberdasher apprentice
17119	Levy	Joseph	1837	Sheerness, Kent	Isaac Levy	Frances (?)		Sheerness, Kent	scholar
17426	Levy	Joseph	1837	Whitechapel, London	Solomon Levy	Fanny (?)		Spitalfields, London	
10246	Levy	Joseph	1838	Spitalfields, London	Lewis Levy	Rachel (?)		Spitalfields, London	cigar maker
29841	Levy	Joseph	1841	Wapping, London	(?) Levy	Mary (?)		Stepney, London	scholar
29899	Levy	Joseph	1841	Wapping, London	(?) Levy	Mary (?)		Wapping, London	
29920	Levy	Joseph	1844	?, Holland	Louis J Levy	Rebecca (?)		Whitechapel, London	scholar
2714	Levy	Joseph	1845	?, Poland [?, Prussia]	Abraham Levy	Rachel Wolfson	Lily Betts	Manchester	scholar
28225	Levy	Joseph	1845	Whitechapel, London	(?) Levy	Catherine (?)		Spitalfields, London	scholar
25220	Levy	Joseph	1846	Clerkenwell, London	Lewis Levy	Caroline Lee		Clerkenwell, London	
28190	Levy	Joseph	1846	Whitechapel, London	Samuel Levy	Ellen Abrahams		Spitalfields, London	
30303	Levy	Joseph	1846	Strand, London	Leon (Lewis) Levy	Caroline Saunders		Strand, London	
28801	Levy	Joseph	1847	Spitalfields, London	Lewis Levy	Jeannette (Jane) Symons		Spitalfields, London	scholar
16513	Levy	Joseph	1848	?, London	Alexander Levy	Amelia Harris		Clerkenwell, London	
28960	Levy	Joseph	1848	?, London	Isaiah Levy	Brinette (?)		Whitechapel, London	
13352	Levy	Joseph	1850	Aldgate, London	Isaac Lvy	Deborah Bendon		Spitalfields, London	
22243	Levy	Joseph	1851	Whitechapel, London	Lewis Levy	Elizabeth (?)		Whitechapel, London	
7253	Levy	Joseph Hiam	1838	Aldgate, London	Lawrence Levy	Maria Hiam	Emily Wheeler	Wapping, London	scholar
25897	Levy	Joseph Hyam	1841	Aldgate, London	Hyam Levy	Frances Naphthali	Amelia Lewis	Aldgate, London	scholar
30354	Levy	Joshua	1836	Strand, London	Joseph Levy	Hannah (?)		St Giles, London	
11321	Levy	Joshua	1846	Aldgate, London	Lewis Levy	Ann (Nancy) Israel		Aldgate, London	scholar
27959	Levy	Joshua	1850	Aldgate, London	John Levy	Julia Moses		Spitalfields, London	
3353	Levy	Joshua (John)	1841	Aldgate, London	Philip Levy	Elizabeth Davis	Dinah Joel	Aldgate, London	scholar
6794	Levy	Judah	1832	Spitalfields, London	Isaac Levy	Catherine (?)	Mary Davis	Spitalfields, London	general dealer
28522	Levy	Judah	1836	Whitechapel, London	(?) Levy	Rachael		Spitalfields, London	apprentice
13397	Levy	Judah	1840	Spitalfields, London	(?) Levy	(?) Mathews		Spitalfields, London	scholar
29503	Levy	Judah	1841	Spitalfields, London	Henry Levy	Catherine (Kate, Kitty) Franks		Spitalfields, London	scholar
25491	Levy	Judith	1791	Whitechapel, London	(?) Levy			City, London	staymaker
27881	Levy	Julia	1784	City, London	(?)		Jacob Levy	Spitalfields, London	
14134	Levy	Julia	1793	Liverpool	(?)		Joseph Levy	Manchester	
23367	Levy	Julia	1795	Finsbury, London	(?)		Samuel Levy	Strand, London	
22985	Levy	Julia	1799	?, London	(?)		Hymer Levy	Poplar, London	

ID	surname	given names	born	birthplace	father	mother	spouse 1	1851 residence	1851 occupation
19193	Levy	Julia	1801	Bristol	(?) Levy			Whitechapel, London	
20149	Levy	Julia	1802	?Portsmouth, Hampshire	Moses Hart	Rachel (?)	Abraham Levy	Euston, London	
11469	Levy	Julia	1808	Aldgate, London	(?)		David Levy	Aldgate, London	
12975	Levy	Julia	1815	Whitechapel, London	(?) Phillips		Asher Levy	Aldgate, London	
11433	Levy	Julia	1817	Aldgate, London	(?)		(?Hart) Levy	Aldgate, London	general dealer
20187	Levy	Julia	1819	Whitechapel, London	Henry Levy	Jane Alexander		Spitalfields, London	fruiterer
11277	Levy	Julia	1820	Aldgate, London	Joseph Isaacs		Samuel Levy	Aldgate, London	general dealer
13004	Levy	Julia	1821	Bethnal Green, London	Barnett Levy	Catherine Levy		Bethnal Green, London	
27956	Levy	Julia	1821	Aldgate, London	(?) Moses		John Levy	Spitalfields, London	
13522	Levy	Julia	1824	Manchester	Emmanuel Levy			Manchester	
3724	Levy	Julia	1826	Spitalfields, London	Hyman Levy	Sarah (?)		Spitalfields, London	carpet bag maker
18976	Levy	Julia	1826	Aldgate, London	Jonas Defries	Esther Coleman	Alexander Levy	Whitechapel, London	
21841	Levy	Julia	1826	Aldgate, London	Jonas (Jonathan) Levy	Matilda Moses		Clerkenwell, London	
22347	Levy	Julia	1826	Shoreditch, London	Isaac Green	Catherine Casner	Barnett (Bernhard) Levy	Aldgate, London	furrier
14789	Levy	Julia	1828	Soho, London	Benjamin Lawrence		Abraham Levy	Finsbury, London	
3922	Levy	Julia	1829	Aldgate, London	Mordecai Levy	Jane (?)		Aldgate, London	tailoress
10464	Levy	Julia	1832	Spitalfields, London	Jacob Levy	Elizabeth (?)		Mile End, London	shoebinder empl 1
22640	Levy	Julia	1833	Ipswich, Suffolk	(?) Levy	Rachel (?)		Whitechapel, London	milliner
11039	Levy	Julia	1834	?Aldgate, London	Samson Levy	Phoebe Simmons	Emanuel Daniels	Aldgate, London	home servant
58	Levy	Julia	1836	Woolwich, London	Nathan Levy	Sarah (Mary) Palmer		Woolwich, London	seamstress
30474	Levy	Julia	1837	Aldgate, London	Lawrence Levy	Eliza (Sarah) Emanuel		Shoreditch, London	scholar at home
215	Levy	Julia	1838	Whitechapel, London	Lyon (Lewis) Levy	Sarah Davis	Judah Hyman	Spitalfields, London	
28945	Levy	Julia	1839	Spitalfields, London	Henry Levy	Phoebe Marks		Whitechapel, London	scholar
28731	Levy	Julia	1840	Middlesex, London	(?) Levy	Ann Levy		Spitalfields, London	
6665	Levy	Julia	1841	Spitalfields, London	Samuel Levy	Rebecca Pereira	Israel Abrahams	Spitalfields, London	parasol maker
17841	Levy	Julia	1841	Aldgate, London	Henry Levy	Anna (?)		Aldgate, London	
26163	Levy	Julia	1841	?Aldgate, London	Nathan Levy	Abigail Noah (Noah Da Costa)		Aldgate, London	scholar
5335	Levy	Julia	1844	Plymouth, Devon	Markes Levy	Bella Woolf	Myer L Isaacs	Plymouth, Devon	
17686	Levy	Julius Laurence	1844	Shoreditch, London	Lawrence Levy	Eliza (Sarah) Emanuel		Shoreditch, London	scholar at home
11423	Levy	June	1839	Aldgate, London	Lazarus (Eleazer) Levy	Catherine Green		Aldgate, London	
27883	Levy	Kate	1818	City, London	Jacob Levy	Julia (?)		Spitalfields, London	tailoress
22639	Levy	Kate	1831	Ipswich, Suffolk	(?) Levy	Rachel (?)		Whitechapel, London	dressmaker
25221	Levy	Kate	1849	Clerkenwell, London	Lewis Levy	Caroline Lee		Clerkenwell, London	
22758	Levy	Kate (Catherine)	1815	Spitalfields, London	Shalom Levy		Michael Levy	Whitechapel, London	parasol maker
10351	Levy	Katharine	1834	Middlesex, London	Simon Levy	Moriah (?)	Simeon Raphael	Spitalfields, London	tailoress
65	Levy	Katherine	1775	Canterbury, Kent			Solomon Levy	Woolwich, London	hawker
4661	Levy	Katherine	1822	?, London			Henry Levy	Birmingham	tailoress
19917	Levy	Kathleen (Catherine) Matilda	1846	Belfast, Ireland	Myer (Mier) Levy	Sarah Jacobs	Charles Samuel	Belfast, Ireland	
4666	Levy	Lawrence	1790	?, London	Joseph Levy		Priscilla (?)	Birmingham	watchmaker
24417	Levy	Lawrence	1806	Middlesex, London	Yehuda		Rebecca Jacobs	Strand, London	wine merchant
17681	Levy	Lawrence	1811	Limehouse, London	Abraham Levy	Elizabeth Lazarus	Eliza (Sarah) Emanuel	Shoreditch, London	
15911	Levy	Lawrence	1812	Spitalfields, London	Shalom Levy		Maria Hiam	Wapping, London	outfitter

ID	surname	given names	born	birthplace	father	mother	spouse 1	1851 residence	1851 occupation
3311	Levy	Lawrence	1823	Middlesex, London	Aaron Levy	Rachel Hart	Amelia Cohen	Aldgate, London	cigar maker
6336	Levy	Lawrence J	1851	Spitalfields, London	Jacob Levy	Maria Levy	Jeannette Defries	Spitalfields, London	
28825	Levy	Lazarus	1781	?, Germany			Rebecca (?)	Spitalfields, London	general dealer
25489	Levy	Lazarus	1798	Whitechapel, London				City, London	sexton of Hambro Synagogue
3905	Levy	Lazarus	1812	Aldgate, London		Caroline (?)	Elizabeth (?)	Spitalfields, London	general dealer
15120	Levy	Lazarus	1823	Bristol	Joseph Levy	Elizabeth (?)		Hoxton, London	warehouseman
10816	Levy	Lazarus	1833	Spitalfields, London	(?) Levy			Spitalfields, London	boot maker's apprentice
10411	Levy	Lazarus	1835	Whitechapel, London	(?) Levy	Catherine (?)		Spitalfields, London	
2779	Levy	Lazarus	1837	Whitechapel, London	Aaron Levy	(?)		Whitechapel, London	scholar
21214	Levy	Lazarus	1842	Spitalfields, London	David Levy	Jane Lazarus		Spitalfields, London	
24793	Levy	Lazarus	1849	Southwark, London	Hyam Levy	Lydia (?)		Elephant & Castle, London	
11422	Levy	Lazarus (Eleazer)	1815	abroad	Simha		Catherine Green	Aldgate, London	grocer + pickle merchant
19919	Levy	Lazarus (Lawrence) Arthur	1849	Belfast, Ireland	Myer (Mier) Levy	Sarah Jacobs		Belfast, Ireland	
18889	Levy	Lea	1833	Berlin, Germany [Berlin, Prussia]	(?) Levy			Spitalfields, London	needlewoman
22500	Levy	Leah	1783	Margate, Kent			(?) Levy	Whitechapel, London	annuitant
10264	Levy	Leah	1795	?, Holland	(?)		(?) Levy	Spitalfields, London	
17112	Levy	Leah	1808	Whitechapel, London	Moshe Levy		Abraham Levy	Newport, Glamorgan, Wales	dealer in shoes
26400	Levy	Leah	1808	Amsterdam, Holland	(?)		Mordecai Levy	Aldgate, London	nurse
31054	Levy	Leah	1811	St Giles, London	(?)		(?) Levy	Rochester, Kent	
26663	Levy	Leah	1825	Aldgate, London	Isaac Myers		John (Jacob) Levy	Spitalfields, London	
59	Levy	Leah	1829	Woolwich, London	Nathan Levy	Sarah (Mary) Palmer		Woolwich, London	seamstress
10814	Levy	Leah	1829	Spitalfields, London	(?) Levy			Spitalfields, London	tailoress
13737	Levy	Leah	1830	Manchester	(?) Levy	Sophia (?)		Manchester	marine store dealer
13519	Levy	Leah	1833	Birmingham	(?)		Joseph Levy	Manchester	
30166	Levy	Leah	1834	Middlesex, London	Abraham Levy	Hannah (Levi?)		Lambeth, London	annuitant
24413	Levy	Leah	1842	Strand, London	Morrice (Morris) Levy	Hannah Alexander		Strand, London	
28799	Levy	Leah	1842	Spitalfields, London	Lewis Levy	Jeannette (Jane) Symons		Spitalfields, London	scholar
17100	Levy	Leah	1847	St Peter Port, Guernsey, Channel Islands	Mark Levy	Ann Marks		St Peter Port, Guernsey, Channel Islands	scholar
25120	Levy	Leah	1847	Covent Garden, London	Philip Levy	Sarah (?)		Finsbury, London	
22759	Levy	Leah	1848	Whitechapel, London	Michael Levy	Kate (Catherine) (?)		Whitechapel, London	
29838	Levy	Leah	1850	Spitalfields, London	Moses Levy	Esther (?)		Wapping, London	
23625	Levy	Leah?	1848	Liverpool	Barnet Isaac Levy	Elizabeth Levy		Liverpool	
28456	Levy	Lemuel	1844	Hull, Yorkshire	Henry Levy	Rosetta Moses		Spitalfields, London	scholar
19191	Levy	Leon	1845	Aldgate, London	John Levy	Mary Lazarus	Fannie Barkman	Whitechapel, London	
6445	Levy	Leon	1848	Aldgate, London	Henry Levy	Anna (?)		Aldgate, London	
8754	Levy	Leon	1850	?, London	Godfrey Levy	Hannah Isaacs		Aldgate, London	
22103	Levy	Leon	1850	Whitechapel, London	Henry Levy	Elizabeth (?)		Whitechapel, London	
5751	Levy	Leon (Lewis)	1811	Strand, London	Joseph Levy	Hannah (?)	Caroline Saunders	Strand, London	clothier (master)
2712	Levy	Leona (Poena)	1842	?, Poland [?, Prussia]	Abraham Levy	Rachel Wolfson	Louis Harrison	Manchester	

ID	surname	given names	born	birthplace	father	mother	spouse 1	1851 residence	1851 occupation
29918	Levy	Leonard	1839	?, Holland	Louis J Levy	Rebecca (?)		Whitechapel, London	scholar
7492	Levy	Levy	1788	Bristol	Moses Levy		Elizabeth (?)	Bristol	retired glass merchant
29447	Levy	Levy	1837	Amsterdam, Holland	Joseph Levy	Amelia (?)		Spitalfields, London	cigar maker
7142	Levy	Lewis	1786	Stratford, London			Elizabeth Levy nee (?)	Bloomsbury, London	toll contractor
22621	Levy	Lewis	1799	Whitechapel, London			Mary (?)	Stepney, London	general dealer
28164	Levy	Lewis	1799	City, London				Spitalfields, London	lemon dealer
28481	Levy	Lewis	1799	Poznan, Poland [Posen, Prussia]	Joseph Levy		(?)	Spitalfields, London	cloth cap maker
4672	Levy	Lewis	1806	Deal, Kent			Sarah (?)	Birmingham	licensed hawker
11315	Levy	Lewis	1810	Spitalfields, London	Yeruham HaLevi		Ann (Nancy) Israel	Aldgate, London	general dealer
28411	Levy	Lewis	1811	Whitechapel, London	Moses Levy		Elizabeth (Betsey) Phillips	Spitalfields, London	baker
13867	Levy	Lewis	1812	Manchester			Mary Ann (?)	Manchester	tailor + outfitter
10241	Levy	Lewis	1813	Spitalfields, London			Rachel (?)	Spitalfields, London	hatter
10275	Levy	Lewis	1813	Whitechapel, London	Yosef HaLevi		Sarah Martin	Spitalfields, London	general dealer
18628	Levy	Lewis	1813	Bedford, Bedfordshire	Godfey Levy		Jessy Selig	Bedford, Bedfordshire	Synagogue secretary
22239	Levy	Lewis	1813	City, London	(?) Levy	Rebecca (?)	Elizabeth (?)	Whitechapel, London	tailor
10510	Levy	Lewis	1815	?, Poland [?, Prussia]			Esther (?)	Aldgate, London	furrier
25215	Levy	Lewis	1816	Epsom, Surrey	Hyman Levy		Caroline Lee	Clerkenwell, London	cigar maker
6493	Levy	Lewis	1818	Middlesex, London			Ann (?)	Birmingham	
28797	Levy	Lewis	1819	Spitalfields, London	Samuel Levy		Jeannette (Jane) Symons	Spitalfields, London	labourer
3323	Levy	Lewis	1820	Whitechapel, London	Nathan Levy		Susan Solomons	Spitalfields, London	general dealer
3726	Levy	Lewis	1821	Spitalfields, London	Abraham Levy		Catharine Elias	Spitalfields, London	dealer
10926	Levy	Lewis	1821	City, London			Sarah (?)	Spitalfields, London	hawker of shoes
11264	Levy	Lewis	1823	Middlesex, London				Aldgate, London	hawker of ?shells
8936	Levy	Lewis	1824	Aldgate, London	Barnett Levy		Esther Noah (Da Costa Noah)	Aldgate, London	cigar maker
21313	Levy	Lewis	1824	Sheerness, Kent				Minster, Sheppey, Kent	cabinet maker
24731	Levy	Lewis	1825	Elephant & Castle, London			Elizabeth Burn	Southwark, London	greengrocer
19840	Levy	Lewis	1829	Whitechapel, London	Jacob Levy	Sarah Samuel		Spitalfields, London	clothes dealer
23870	Levy	Lewis	1829	City, London				Soho, London	assistant to glass factor
24635	Levy	Lewis	1829	Lambeth, London	Emanuel Levy	Ann (?)		Waterloo, London	clerk to a shoe maker
10815	Levy	Lewis	1832	Spitalfields, London	(?) Levy			Spitalfields, London	gasfitter
15428	Levy	Lewis	1833	Whitechapel, London	David Levy	Maria (?)		Covent Garden, London	cigar maker
21546	Levy	Lewis	1833	Walworth, London	Daniel Levy	Amelia Jacobs		Bloomsbury, London	clerk to a solicitor
6447	Levy	Lewis	1835	Elephant & Castle, London	Solomon Levy	Maria Harris	Isabel Levin	Elephant & Castle, London	
12883	Levy	Lewis	1836	Aldgate, London	Aaron Levy	Rachel Hart	Rachel Jacobs	Aldgate, London	butcher's boy
19790	Levy	Lewis	1836	Whitechapel, London	Moses Levy	Sarah Lazarus		Spitalfields, London	butcher
20212	Levy	Lewis	1836	Aldgate, London	Moses Levy	Mary (?)		Wandsworth, London	
23781	Levy	Lewis	1837	Liverpool	Henry Levy	Maria (?)		Liverpool	grocer apprentice
11440	Levy	Lewis	1838	Spitalfields, London	Mark (Mordecai) Levy	Maria Lyon		Aldgate, London	
12236	Levy	Lewis	1838	Whitechapel, London	Moses Levy	Catherine Aarons		Whitechapel, London	
20171	Levy	Lewis	1839	Whitechapel, London	Henry Levy	Hannah (?)		Spitalfields, London	cigar maker
20178	Levy	Lewis	1839	Spitalfields, London	Michael Levy	Amelia Simmons		Spitalfields, London	scholar
21832	Levy	Lewis	1839	Covent Garden, London	(?) Levy	Elizabeth (?)		Covent Garden, London	

ID	surname	given names	born	birthplace	father	mother	spouse 1	1851 residence	1851 occupation
5979	Levy	Lewis	1844	Wapping, London	Lawrence Levy	Maria Hiam		Wapping, London	scholar
7454	Levy	Lewis	1845	?Chatham, Kent	John Lewis Levy			Chatham, Kent	
26204	Levy	Lewis	1845	?, Germany	Simon Levy	Fanny (?)		Aldgate, London	
3313	Levy	Lewis	1847	Wapping, London	Lawrence Levy	Amelia Cohen	Hannah Cohen	Whitechapel, London	
8832	Levy	Lewis	1848	Whitechapel, London	Jonas Levy	Dorothy (?)		Aldgate, London	scholar
12469	Levy	Lewis	1850	Whitechapel, London	Israel Levy	Frances (Fanny) (?)		Spitalfields, London	
25745	Levy	Lewis	1850	Aldgate, London	Elias Levy	Matilda Harris		Spitalfields, London	
10070	Levy	Lewis	1851	Whitechapel, London	Jacob Levy	Abigail Barnett		Wapping, London	
7613	Levy	Lionel Solomon	1829	Bristol	Solomon Levy	Arabella (?)		Bristol	assistant jeweller
28607	Levy	Lions	1839	?, Holland	Samuel Levy	Sarah (?)		Spitalfields, London	
12446	Levy	Lipman	1801	Middlesex, London				Spitalfields, London	glass cutter
29015	Levy	Lipman	1822	Southwark, London	Samuel Levy	Adelaide (?)		Whitechapel, London	general dealer
23383	Levy	Lipman (Eliezer)	1813	Surrey, London	Menachem Levy		Hannah Jones	Aldgate, London	dealer
23959	Levy	Louis Henry?	1814	Clapham, London	Solomon Abraham Levy	Paulina (Pessy) (?)		Marylebone, London	professor of music
29912	Levy	Louis J	1800	?, France			Rebecca (?)	Whitechapel, London	professor of languages
28679	Levy	Louisa	1806	Middlesex, London	Joseph Judah		Abraham Levy	Spitalfields, London	dealer in miscellany
26258	Levy	Louisa	1815	?, London	Angel Jonas	Nancy Michel	Samuel Levy	Aldgate, London	
5671	Levy	Louisa	1827	Stratford, London	Hyman Levy		Isaac Hermann Hart	Stepney, London	
24061	Levy	Louisa	1828	?, Guernsey, Channel Islands	(?)		Adolphus Levy	St John's Wood, London	
17838	Levy	Louisa	1834	City, London	Henry Levy	Anna (?)		Aldgate, London	milliner
23782	Levy	Louisa	1839	Liverpool	Henry Levy	Maria (?)		Liverpool	scholar
13870	Levy	Louisa	1846	Manchester	Lewis Levy	Mary Ann (?)	M--- D--- Strelitz	Manchester	scholar
4664	Levy	Lydia	1775	?, London				Birmingham	
12673	Levy	Lydia	1803	Wallington, Norfolk	(?)		Samuel Levy	King's Lynn, Norfolk	
24788	Levy	Lydia	1824	Lambeth, London	(?)		Hyam Levy	Elephant & Castle, London	
27958	Levy	Lydia	1848	Aldgate, London	John Levy	Julia Moses		Spitalfields, London	
3915	Levy	Lyon	1790	Whitechapel, London			Catherine (?)	Waterloo, London	tailor + clothier
210	Levy	Lyon (Lewis)	1804	Spitalfields, London	Mordecai (?Levy)		Sarah Davis	Spitalfields, London	hat maker
20163	Levy	M---	1841	Whitechapel, London	Isaac Levy	Catherine (?)		Spitalfields, London	scholar
18956	Levy	M--- J---	1809	?, West Indies				Whitechapel, London	commission agent
11070	Levy	Marcus	1807	?, Poland [?, Prussian Poland]				Aldgate, London	plumber + glazier
17844	Levy	Marcus	1828	?, Germany				Aldgate, London	tailor
27943	Levy	Maria	1784	Soho, London	(?)		Solomon Levy	Spitalfields, London	
15425	Levy	Maria	1803	Spitalfields, London	(?)		David Levy	Covent Garden, London	
15912	Levy	Maria	1805	Aldgate, London	Joseph Hiam		Lawrence Levy	Wapping, London	
21399	Levy	Maria	1809	Aldgate, London	(?) Harris		Solomon Levy	Elephant & Castle, London	
23780	Levy	Maria	1816	?, Poland	(?)		Henry Levy	Liverpool	
11439	Levy	Maria	1820	Whitechapel, London	Yehuda HaLevi		Mark (Mordecai) Levy	Aldgate, London	
26479	Levy	Maria	1821	Bedford, Bedfordshire	(?) Levy			Bedford, Bedfordshire	
29549	Levy	Maria	1826	Strand, London	Samuel Levy		Jacob Levy	Spitalfields, London	
17835	Levy	Maria	1827	City, London	Henry Levy	Anna (?)		Aldgate, London	milliner
29644	Levy	Maria	1827	?, London	(?)		Joseph Levy	Aldgate, London	bookbinder
60	Levy	Maria	1831	Woolwich, London	Nathan Levy	Sarah (Mary) Palmer	Jacob Rosenthal Glück	Kensington, London	lady's companion

ID	surname	given names	born	birthplace	father	mother	spouse 1	1851 residence	1851 occupation
10281	Levy	Maria	1842	Whitechapel, London	Lewis Levy	Sarah (?)	John Harris	Spitalfields, London	scholar
23388	Levy	Maria	1843	?, London	Lipman (Eliezer) Levy	Hannah Jones		Aldgate, London	
12472	Levy	Maria	1846	Whitechapel, London	Israel Levy	Frances (Fanny) (?)		Spitalfields, London	
2087	Levy	Maria	1850	Carmarthen, Wales	Daniel Levy	Mary Anne Lazarus	John Mill Oborn	Carmarthen, Wales	
14645	Levy	Maria	1850	Bloomsbury, London	Alexander Levy	Elizabeth (?)		Hoxton, London	
3549	Levy	Maria (Marion)	1829	Kensington, London	Nathaniel Levy	Sophia (?)	Samuel Cowan	Bloomsbury, London	
28399	Levy	Maria (Miriam)	1782	Spitalfields, London	Yaakov Lam Potoy Isaacs		Angel Levy	Spitalfields, London	
20050	Levy	Mariah	1829	Cork, Ireland	(?) Levy			Covent Garden, London	cook
24624	Levy	Marian	1807	Lambeth, London	Shlomo Zalman HaLevi Solomonson		Rudolph Levy	Kennington, London	
22101	Levy	Marian	1843	Marylebone, London	Henry Levy	Elizabeth (?)		Whitechapel, London	scholar
30897	Levy	Marianne	1796	Whitechapel, London	(?) Levy			Chelmsford, Essex	governess
11348	Levy	Mark	1806	?, Poland			Rebecca (?)	Aldgate, London	cap maker
23379	Levy	Mark	1822	?, London	Daniel Levy	Hannah Davis	Sarah Lazarus	Aldgate, London	clothier
212	Levy	Mark	1829	Middlesex, London	Lyon (Lewis) Levy	Sarah Davis	Mary Collett	Spitalfields, London	hat maker
9540	Levy	Mark	1829	?Wriezen, Germany [Wreshen, Prussia]				Spitalfields, London	tailor
12675	Levy	Mark	1829	King's Lynn, Norfolk	Samuel Levy	Lydia (?)		King's Lynn, Norfolk	hairdresser
28614	Levy	Mark	1841	Spitalfields, London	Samuel Levy	Sarah (?)		Spitalfields, London	scholar
11004	Levy	Mark	1843	Aldgate, London	Philip Levy	Elizabeth Davis		Aldgate, London	scholar
10929	Levy	Mark	1844	Southwark, London	Lewis Levy	Sarah (?)		Spitalfields, London	scholar
5289	Levy	Mark	1845	Middlesex, London	Jacob Levy	Ann Levy		Aldgate, London	scholar
21131	Levy	Mark	1847	Aldgate, London	Joseph Levy	Ester (?)		Aldgate, London	
8743	Levy	Mark	1849	Aldgate, London	Nathan Levy	Amelia (?)		Aldgate, London	
27536	Levy	Mark (Mordecai)	1808	Middlesex, London	Yitzaak Izaak HaLevi		Phoebe Hyams	Spitalfields, London	general dealer
11438	Levy	Mark (Mordecai)	1815	Aldgate, London	Tsadok HaLevi		Maria Lyon	Aldgate, London	iron dealer
181	Levy	Markes	1812	Plymouth, Devon	Abraham Levy	Zipporah Benjamin	Bella Woolf	Plymouth, Devon	pawnbroker
12198	Levy	Marks	1824	?, Poland			Rachel (?)	Whitechapel, London	tailor empl 2
21437	Levy	Marks	1824	?, Poland [?, Prussia]				Nottingham, Nottinghamshire	hawker of jewellery
4227	Levy	Martha	1787	Aldgate, London	Eliezer Zissel Levy		Benjamin Wolfe Levy	Lambeth, London	
16005	Levy	Martha	1824	Covent Garden, London	Samuel Solomon	Ann (?)	Solomon Levy	Covent Garden, London	oil shop keeper
12406	Levy	Martha	1848	Spitalfields, London	Thomas Levy	Rose (?)		Spitalfields, London	
28728	Levy	Mary	1784	Middlesex, London	(?)		(?) Levy	Spitalfields, London	dealer in glass
10263	Levy	Mary	1791	?, Holland	(?)		Myer Levy	Spitalfields, London	
20208	Levy	Mary	1794	Whitechapel, London	(?)		Moses Levy	Wandsworth, London	
17468	Levy	Mary	1797	Aldgate, London	(?)		Emanuel Levy	Aldgate, London	
22622	Levy	Mary	1803	Whitechapel, London	(?)		Lewis Levy	Stepney, London	
12112	Levy	Mary	1809	Whitechapel, London	Isaac Kapman		Abraham Levy	Spitalfields, London	
23456	Levy	Mary	1810	?, London	(?)		Joseph Levy	Liverpool	
19195	Levy	Mary	1812	?, London	Samuel Lazarus	(Ann Joseph?)	John Levy	Whitechapel, London	
29898	Levy	Mary	1812	Whitechapel, London	(?)		(?) Levy	Wapping, London	dealer in milk
29840	Levy	Mary	1814	Wapping, London	(?)		(?) Levy	Stepney, London	cow keeper
26066	Levy	Mary	1820	Amsterdam, Holland	Abraham Kobas		Isaac Levy	Aldgate, London	
15119	Levy	Mary	1822	Bristol	Joseph Levy	Elizabeth (?)		Hoxton, London	

ID	surname	given names	born	birthplace	father	mother	spouse 1	1851 residence	1851 occupation
9278	Levy	Mary	1829	Aldgate, London	Nathan Levy	Rachel (?)	Pincous Lovisohn	Aldgate, London	
29016	Levy	Mary	1829	Elephant & Castle, London	Samuel Levy	Adelaide (?)		Whitechapel, London	tailor
17836	Levy	Mary	1830	City, London	Henry Levy	Anna (?)		Aldgate, London	milliner
8965	Levy	Mary	1831	Aldgate, London	Samuel Levy	Elizabeth (Betsy) (?)		Aldgate, London	
15427	Levy	Mary	1831	Whitechapel, London	David Levy	Maria (?)		Covent Garden, London	
20160	Levy	Mary	1833	Whitechapel, London	Isaac Levy	Catherine (?)		Spitalfields, London	tailoress
11040	Levy	Mary	1835	?Aldgate, London	Samson Levy	Phoebe Simmons		Aldgate, London	tailoress
28606	Levy	Mary	1837	?, Holland	Samuel Levy	Sarah (?)		Spitalfields, London	needleworker
19791	Levy	Mary	1838	Whitechapel, London	Moses Levy	Sarah Lazarus		Spitalfields, London	
24789	Levy	Mary	1841	Middlesex, London	Hyam Levy	Lydia (?)		Elephant & Castle, London	
13356	Levy	Mary	1845	Whitechapel, London	Nathan (Nathaniel) Levy	Catherine Levy	Abraham Abrahams	Spitalfields, London	
25076	Levy	Mary	1845	Hoxton, London	(?) Levy	Rose (?)		City, London	
13351	Levy	Mary	1846	Aldgate, London	Isaac Levy	Deborah Bendon		Spitalfields, London	
10357	Levy	Mary	1847	Middlesex, London	Simon Levy	Moriah (?)		Spitalfields, London	scholar
20181	Levy	Mary	1848	Spitalfields, London	Michael Levy	Amelia Simmons	Nathan Nathan	Spitalfields, London	
24062	Levy	Mary	1849	Middlesex, London	Adolphus Levy	Louisa (?)		St John's Wood, London	
30046	Levy	Mary	1849	Marylebone, London	(?) Levy	Hannah Moses		Aldgate, London	
19818	Levy	Mary	1850	Whitechapel, London	Elias Levy	Sarah Palachy		Spitalfields, London	
3212	Levy	Mary Ann	1810	Chatham, Kent			John Lewis Levy	Chatham, Kent	
14818	Levy	Mary Ann	1815	Edmonton, London	(?)		Moss Levy	Finsbury, London	
13868	Levy	Mary Ann	1816	?, London	(?)		Lewis Levy	Manchester	
21865	Levy	Mary Ann	1816	Newport, Essex	(?)		Charles Levy	Clerkenwell, London	
25078	Levy	Mary Ann	1833	Euston, London	(?) Levy			City, London	
13199	Levy	Mary Ann (Miriam)	1842	Whitechapel, London	Solomon Hyam (Hyman) Levy	Clara Joseph		Whitechapel, London	scholar
2079	Levy	Mary Anne	1813	Carmarthen, Wales	Jacob Lazarus	Elizabeth Lazarus	Daniel Levy	Carmarthen, Wales	spirit merchant traveller's wife
21838	Levy	Matilda	1805	Portsmouth, Hampshire	Abraham Moses		Jonas (Jonathan) Levy	Clerkenwell, London	merchant's wife
25739	Levy	Matilda	1816	Spitalfields, London	Nathan Harris		Elias Levy	Spitalfields, London	clothier
30352	Levy	Matilda	1832	Strand, London	Joseph Levy	Hannah (?)		Strand, London	
24832	Levy	Matilda	1833	?, Poland	(?) Levy			Elephant & Castle, London	servant
26198	Levy	Matilda	1833	?, Germany	Simon Levy	Fanny (?)		Aldgate, London	
7252	Levy	Matilda	1836	Clerkenwell, London	Joseph Moses Levy	Esther Cohen		Bloomsbury, London	
16802	Levy	Matilda	1838	Bristol	Solomon Levy	Arabella (?)	Michael Castle	Bristol	scholar at home
20215	Levy	Matilda	1844	Aldgate, London	Moses Levy	Mary (?)		Wandsworth, London	
30062	Levy	Matilda	1849	Bedford, Bedfordshire	Lewis Levy	Jessy Selig		Bedford, Bedfordshire	
19175	Levy	Matilda	1851	Edinburgh, Scotland	Michael Abraham Levy	Hannah Ashenheim		Edinburgh, Scotland	
21304	Levy	Matthias	1840	Soho, London	Isaac Levy	Elizabeth Russell	Louisa Solomon	Soho, London	boarding school pupil
17685	Levy	Maurice Emanuel	1841	Shoreditch, London	Lawrence Levy	Eliza (Sarah) Emanuel		Shoreditch, London	scholar at home
11865	Levy	Meyer	1840	Middlesex, London	(?) Levy	(?)		Whitechapel, London	inmate of orphan school
21248	Levy	Michael	1790	Spitalfields, London			Pia (?)	Spitalfields, London	fish dealer
3871	Levy	Michael	1795	Wapping, London			(?)	Spitalfields, London	sponge dealer
14811	Levy	Michael	1805	Covent Garden, London			Sarah (?)	Finsbury, London	furniture dealer

429

ID	surname	given names	born	birthplace	father	mother	spouse 1	1851 residence	1851 occupation
22757	Levy	Michael	1807	Spitalfields, London	Shmuel		Kate (Catherine) Levy	Whitechapel, London	general dealer
5224	Levy	Michael	1809	Middlesex, London				Leeds, Yorkshire	quill dresser
6442	Levy	Michael	1817	Whitechapel, London	Nathan Levy	Elizabeth (?)	Sarah Harris	Whitechapel, London	cab man
20176	Levy	Michael	1817	Whitechapel, London	Mordecai Levy	Abigail Levy	Amelia Simmons	Spitalfields, London	general dealer
9500	Levy	Michael	1831	Aldgate, London	(?) Levy	Rachel (?)		Aldgate, London	baker's shopman
20161	Levy	Michael	1834	Whitechapel, London	Isaac Levy	Catherine (?)		Spitalfields, London	tailor
10247	Levy	Michael	1842	Spitalfields, London	Lewis Levy	Rachel (?)		Spitalfields, London	scholar
26262	Levy	Michael	1844	?, London	Samuel Levy	Louisa Jonas		Aldgate, London	scholar
4122	Levy	Michael	1845	Wapping, London	Hyam Levy	Sarah Moses		Wapping, London	scholar
2022	Levy	Michael	1847	Spitalfields, London	Henry (Savage) Levy	Hannah Benjamin	Rosa Jacobs	Spitalfields, London	
4676	Levy	Michael	1849	Birmingham			Margaret Ellen Jackson	Birmingham	
19174	Levy	Michael Abraham	1821	Limehouse, London	Abraham Levy	Elizabeth Lazarus	Hannah Ashenheim	Edinburgh, Scotland	clothier + tailor
17429	Levy	Michal	1829	?, Holland				Spitalfields, London	
28959	Levy	Michel	1847	?, London	Isaiah Levy	Brinette (?)		Whitechapel, London	
18214	Levy	Miriam	1839	Middlesex, London	(?) Levy			Mile End, London	scholar
28098	Levy	Miriam	1840	Spitalfields, London	Emanuel Levy	Rosetta Asher		Spitalfields, London	
28523	Levy	Miriam	1840	Whitechapel, London	(?) Levy	Rachael		Spitalfields, London	
21404	Levy	Montague	1847	Elephant & Castle, London	Solomon Levy	Maria Harris		Elephant & Castle, London	
22896	Levy	Mordecai	1771	Colchester, Essex			(?)	Wapping, London	clothes shop
3917	Levy	Mordecai	1791	Whitechapel, London			Jane (?)	Aldgate, London	general dealer
12861	Levy	Mordecai	1826	Whitechapel, London			Fanny (?)	Spitalfields, London	cigar maker
3923	Levy	Mordecai (Mark)	1780	?, London	Moshe Levy		Amelia Levy	Aldgate, London	hatter
26814	Levy	Mordecai Joseph	1851	Whitechapel, London	Abraham Levy	Sarah Barnett		Whitechapel, London	
20369	Levy	Mordica	1842	Aldgate, London	Israel Levy	Sarah Harris		Aldgate, London	scholar
10350	Levy	Moriah	1809	Aldgate, London	(?)		Simon Levy	Spitalfields, London	
29302	Levy	Moris	1831	Aldgate, London				Whitechapel, London	cigar maker
24414	Levy	Morrice	1846	Strand, London	Morrice (Morris) Levy	Hannah Alexander		Strand, London	
24411	Levy	Morrice (Morris)	1810	?, London	Yehuda Leib		Hannah Alexander	Strand, London	wine merchant
29938	Levy	Morris	1802	Spitalfields, London			Jane (?)	Whitechapel, London	glass cutter
1252	Levy	Morris	1830	Jersey, Channel Islands	Mark Levy	Mary Lambert		Plymouth, Devon	assistant tailor
19776	Levy	Morris	1830	Spitalfields, London	Mark (Mordecai) Levy	Sarah Jacobs	Dinah Moseley	Spitalfields, London	cigar maker
26797	Levy	Morris	1830	Aldgate, London				Aldgate, London	
11713	Levy	Morris	1833	?, Germany				Aldgate, London	barber
23369	Levy	Morris	1833	Covent Garden, London	Samuel Levy	Julia (?)		Strand, London	military outfitter
4670	Levy	Morris	1836	Middlesex, London	Lawrence Levy	Priscilla (?)	Pauline Eve Behrens	Birmingham	apprentice watchmaker
12884	Levy	Morris	1839	Aldgate, London	Aaron Levy	Rachel Hart		Aldgate, London	cigar maker
17114	Levy	Morris	1841	Aldgate, London	Abraham Levy	Leah (?)		Newport, Glamorgan, Wales	scholar
25157	Levy	Morris	1845	Clerkenwell, London	Emanuel Levy	Rachael Arnold		Finsbury, London	
3114	Levy	Morris (Mordecai)	1832	Spitalfields, London	Henry Levy	Hannah (?)	Elizabeth Simons	Spitalfields, London	cigar maker
10659	Levy	Morris (Moses)	1823	?, Holland	Tsevi Hirsh		Esther Samuel	Spitalfields, London	general dealer
7850	Levy	Moses	1761	?, Germany			(?)	Aldgate, London	
28351	Levy	Moses	1784	Aldgate, London				Whitechapel, London	beadle, New Synagogue
19786	Levy	Moses	1788	Aldgate, London	Yehuda Leib Patriot		Sarah Lazarus	Spitalfields, London	black lead pencil maker

ID	surname	given names	born	birthplace	father	mother	spouse 1	1851 residence	1851 occupation
20207	Levy	Moses	1790	Aldgate, London			Mary (?)	Wandsworth, London	rag merchant + government contractor
23318	Levy	Moses	1790	?, Poland [?, Prussia]			Elizabeth (?)	Belgravia, London	fruiterer
23044	Levy	Moses	1795	Middlesex, London			Catherine (?)	Aldgate, London	furrier
27497	Levy	Moses	1811	Middlesex, London				Aldgate, London	tailor
28420	Levy	Moses	1814	Whitechapel, London			(?)	Spitalfields, London	general dealer
3652	Levy	Moses	1816	Limehouse, London	Abraham Levy	Elizabeth Lazarus	Alice Moses	Shoreditch, London	slopseller
18361	Levy	Moses	1818	Elephant & Castle, London	Emanuel Levy		Catherine Samuel	Elephant & Castle, London	clothes salesman + furniture dealer + dealer in children's chaises (perambulators)
28171	Levy	Moses	1821	Whitechapel, London			Esther Franks	Spitalfields, London	clothes dealer
14331	Levy	Moses	1823	?, Poland				Manchester	shoe maker
17703	Levy	Moses	1824	Whitechapel, London			Adelade (?)	Spitalfields, London	tailor
21785	Levy	Moses	1826	?, Poland				Aldgate, London	shoe maker
29834	Levy	Moses	1827	Spitalfields, London			Esther (?)	Wapping, London	dealer in marine stores
10352	Levy	Moses	1835	Middlesex, London	Simon Levy	Moriah (?)	Maria (?)	Spitalfields, London	scholar
13355	Levy	Moses	1840	Whitechapel, London	Nathan (Nathaniel) Levy	Catherine Levy		Spitalfields, London	
13016	Levy	Moses	1847	Middlesex, London	Emanuel Levy	Rebecca (?)		Spitalfields, London	
17512	Levy	Moses	1848	Aldgate, London	Ralph Levy	Phoebe Solomons		Spitalfields, London	
20361	Levy	Moses	1850	Aldgate, London	Henry Levy	Jane Hart		Aldgate, London	
30580	Levy	Moses	1851	Spitalfields, London	Lewis Levy	Elizabeth (Betsey) Phillips		Spitalfields, London	
7999	Levy	Moses (Moss) Benjamin	1850	Whitechapel, London	Benjamin Levy	Rosa Mandola	Julia Moss	Spitalfields, London	
11382	Levy	Moss	1818	Aldgate, London	(?) Levy	Sarah (?)		Aldgate, London	butcher
14817	Levy	Moss	1824	Aldgate, London			Mary Ann (?)	Finsbury, London	cigar maker
10414	Levy	Moss	1825	Whitechapel, London	(?) Levy	Elizabeth (?)		Spitalfields, London	general dealer
19842	Levy	Moss	1838	Whitechapel, London	Jacob Levy	Sarah Samuel		Spitalfields, London	scholar
11444	Levy	Moss	1847	Spitalfields, London	Mark (Mordecai) Levy	Maria Lyon		Aldgate, London	
6557	Levy	Moss	1849	Whitechapel, London	John Levy	Mary Lazarus	Abigail Newton	Whitechapel, London	
19918	Levy	Moss Myer	1848	Belfast, Ireland	Myer (Mier) Levy	Sarah Jacobs		Belfast, Ireland	
10262	Levy	Myer	1788	Hanover, Germany			Mary (?)	Spitalfields, London	locksmith
23917	Levy	Myer	1818	Middlesex, London	Yaacov		Hannah Levy	Fitzrovia, London	shopman
26367	Levy	Myer	1833	?, Germany				Aldgate, London	glazier
19915	Levy	Myer (Mier)	1814	?, London	Moses Levy		Sarah Jacobs	Belfast, Ireland	outfitter
16924	Levy	Myers	1830	?, Poland [?, Prussia]				Sheffield, Yorkshire	brass founder
29863	Levy	Nancey	1836	Spitalfields, London	(?) Levy			Whitechapel, London	house servant
12114	Levy	Nancy	1841	Whitechapel, London	Abraham Levy	Mary Kapman	Samuel Lyons	Spitalfields, London	scholar
25895	Levy	Naphthali	1838	Aldgate, London	Hyam Levy	Frances Naphthali	Esther Isaacs	Aldgate, London	assistant to butcher
31055	Levy	Nathan	1787	?, Germany			Alice (?)	Rochester, Kent	general dealer
9276	Levy	Nathan	1791	Aldgate, London			Rachel (?)	Aldgate, London	fruiterer
8947	Levy	Nathan	1796	Whitechapel, London				Aldgate, London	tailor
26156	Levy	Nathan	1802	?, London	Israel HaLevi		Abigail Noah (Noah Da Costa)	Aldgate, London	butcher
8740	Levy	Nathan	1809	Southwark, London			Amelia (?)	Aldgate, London	orange dealer

431

ID	surname	given names	born	birthplace	father	mother	spouse 1	1851 residence	1851 occupation
16234	Levy	Nathan	1817	?, Holland	Yehuda		Rachael (?)	Spitalfields, London	fruit vendor
10535	Levy	Nathan	1839	Covent Garden, London	David Levy	Catherine Davids	Rebecca Zox	Covent Garden, London	cigar maker
18684	Levy	Nathan	1843	Whitechapel, London	Michael Levy	Sarah Harris		Whitechapel, London	
21217	Levy	Nathan	1850	Spitalfields, London	David Levy	Jane Lazarus		Spitalfields, London	
13353	Levy	Nathan (Nathaniel)	1824	Whitechapel, London	David Levy	(Polly Nathan?)	Catherine Levy	Spitalfields, London	clothes dealer
7726	Levy	Nathaniel	1799	Middlesex, London	Yehuda Levy		Sophia (?)	Bloomsbury, London	toll contractor
5462	Levy	Nathaniel	1833	Elephant & Castle, London	Solomon Levy	Maria Harris	Matilda Cohen	Bermondsey, London	scholar
30581	Levy	Nathaniel	1851	Strand, London	Leon (Lewis) Levy	Caroline Saunders		Strand, London	
14060	Levy	Nissim	1797	Istanbul, Turkey [Constantinople]				Manchester	merchant
1029	Levy	Parnell	1848	Exeter, Devon	Isaac Levy	Sarah (?)		Exeter, Devon	
2299	Levy	Paulina (Pauline)	1828	?, Poland [?, Prussia]	Hirsh Wolfsohn		Heiman (Herman, Iman) Levy	Leeds, Yorkshire	
23957	Levy	Paulina (Pessy)	1790	Hamburg, Germany			Solomon Abraham Levy	Marylebone, London	
16089	Levy	Phebe	1786	Aldgate, London	(?)		(?) Levy	Covent Garden, London	
21208	Levy	Phebe	1837	Spitalfields, London	(?) Levy			Spitalfields, London	scholar
3355	Levy	Philip	1811	Aldgate, London	Isaac Levy		Elizabeth Davis	Aldgate, London	general dealer
25117	Levy	Philip	1814	?Spitalfields, London			Sarah (?)	Finsbury, London	traveller (sponges)
10213	Levy	Philip	1833	Clerkenwell, London	John Levy	Sarah (?)	Priscilla Bebarfield (Bebarfald)	Aldgate, London	stationer
29942	Levy	Philip	1841	Whitechapel, London	Morris Levy	Jane (?)		Whitechapel, London	scholar
21829	Levy	Philip	1843	Covent Garden, London	David Levy		Rose Benjamin Cohen	Covent Garden, London	
20773	Levy	Philip	1849	Bethnal Green, London	Solomon Levy	Elizabeth (?)		Haggerston, London	
15151	Levy	Phillip	1822	Hamburg, Germany				Hoxton, London	journeyman cigar manufacturer
25219	Levy	Phillip	1844	Clerkenwell, London	Lewis Levy	Caroline Lee		Clerkenwell, London	scholar
28011	Levy	Phoebe	1773	Aldgate, London	(?)		(?) Levy	Spitalfields, London	nurse
27537	Levy	Phoebe	1809	Middlesex, London	Hyam		Mark (Mordecai) Levy	Spitalfields, London	
11067	Levy	Phoebe	1816	?, Poland [?, Prussian Poland]	(?)		David Levy	Aldgate, London	
17511	Levy	Phoebe	1816	Shoreditch, London	Solomon (Pinchas Zelig) Solomons		Marks Abrahams	Spitalfields, London	cap maker
28140	Levy	Phoebe	1830	Hoxton, London	(?) Levy	Eve (?)		Spitalfields, London	tailoress
21210	Levy	Phoebe	1831	Whitechapel, London	(?) Levy			Spitalfields, London	shopwoman
15429	Levy	Phoebe	1835	Whitechapel, London	David Levy	Maria (?)	David Marks	Covent Garden, London	
28683	Levy	Phoebe	1836	Middlesex, London	Abraham Levy	Louisa Judah	Marks Rohstein	Spitalfields, London	
5776	Levy	Phoebe	1838	Eton, Berkshire	Alexander Levy	Stella Foligno	Frederick Joseph Braham	Eton, Berkshire	
20772	Levy	Phoebe	1847	Bethnal Green, London	Solomon Levy	Elizabeth (?)		Haggerston, London	
10069	Levy	Phoebe	1849	Tower Hill, London	Jacob Levy	Abigail Barnett		Wapping, London	
28943	Levy	Phoebe Marks	1817	Edmonton, London	(?) Marks		Henry Levy	Whitechapel, London	
21249	Levy	Pia	1796	Spitalfields, London	(?)		Michael Levy	Spitalfields, London	
5132	Levy	Polly	1799	Middlesex, London	Raphael Solomons		Reuben Levy	Sheffield, Yorkshire	
4667	Levy	Priscilla	1796	Middlesex, London	Emanuel Moses	Dinah (?)	Lawrence Levy	Birmingham	
22641	Levy	Priscilla	1835	Ipswich, Suffolk	(?) Levy	Rachel (?)		Whitechapel, London	cap maker
28442	Levy	Priscilla	1838	Whitechapel, London	Simon Levy	Esther Abendana		Spitalfields, London	scholar

ID	surname	given names	born	birthplace	father	mother	spouse 1	1851 residence	1851 occupation
3653	Levy	Priscilla	1840	Liverpool	Moses Levy	Alice Levy		Shoreditch, London	
28519	Levy	Rachael	1811	Chatham, Kent	(?)		(?) Levy	Spitalfields, London	general dealer
27465	Levy	Rachael	1822	Whitechapel, London	(?)		(?) Levy	Whitechapel, London	charwoman
61	Levy	Rachael	1828	Woolwich, London	Nathan Levy	Sarah (Mary) Palmer		Woolwich, London	seamstress
17117	Levy	Rachael	1832	Sheerness, Kent	Isaac Levy	Frances (?)		Sheerness, Kent	
25156	Levy	Rachael	1832	Clerkenwell, London	(?) Arnold		Emanuel Levy	Finsbury, London	
29470	Levy	Rachael	1835	Spitalfields, London	(?) Levy			Spitalfields, London	
12978	Levy	Rachael	1840	Whitechapel, London	Asher Levy	Julia Phillips		Aldgate, London	scholar
17840	Levy	Rachael	1840	Aldgate, London	Henry Levy	Anna (?)		Aldgate, London	
16804	Levy	Rachael	1842	Bristol	Solomon Levy	Arabella (?)		Bristol	scholar at home
25769	Levy	Rachael	1849	Spitalfields, London	Abraham Levy	Rosey (Rosa) Levy		Aldgate, London	
8009	Levy	Rachael (Ray)	1849	Whitechapel, London	Benjamin Levy	Rosa Mandola	Morris Friend	Spitalfields, London	
3789	Levy	Rachel	1781	Aldgate, London				Spitalfields, London	servant
22636	Levy	Rachel	1795	Colchester, Essex	(?)		(?) Levy	Whitechapel, London	annuitant
9277	Levy	Rachel	1797	Aldgate, London	(?)		Nathan Levy	Aldgate, London	
9499	Levy	Rachel	1798	?, Holland	(?)		(?) Levy	Aldgate, London	domestic
3310	Levy	Rachel	1805	Aldgate, London	Napthali Hart (Hirsh, Hirtz)		Aaron Levy	Aldgate, London	
25470	Levy	Rachel	1811	Middlesex, London	Solomon Levy			Tower Hill, London	publisher
10242	Levy	Rachel	1812	Spitalfields, London	(?)		Lewis Levy	Spitalfields, London	
16235	Levy	Rachel	1816	Whitechapel, London	(?)		Nathan Levy	Spitalfields, London	
2709	Levy	Rachel	1822	?, Poland [?, Prussia]	(?) Wolfson		Abraham Levy	Manchester	
12199	Levy	Rachel	1825	?, Poland	(?)		Marks Levy	Whitechapel, London	tailor's wife
28720	Levy	Rachel	1826	Middlesex, London	(?) Levy			Spitalfields, London	cap maker
10531	Levy	Rachel	1827	Covent Garden, London	David Levy	Catherine Davids		Covent Garden, London	needle woman
20153	Levy	Rachel	1829	City, London	(?)		Henry Levy	Stepney, London	
19788	Levy	Rachel	1830	Aldgate, London	Moses Levy	Sarah Lazarus		Spitalfields, London	clothes dealer
19777	Levy	Rachel	1832	Spitalfields, London	Mark (Mordecai) Levy	Sarah Jacobs		Spitalfields, London	pen cutter
6971	Levy	Rachel	1835	Southwark, London	Emanuel Levy	Sarah (?)	Benjamin Myers	Whitechapel, London	tailoress
9501	Levy	Rachel	1835	Aldgate, London	(?) Levy	Rachel (?)		Aldgate, London	mens cap maker
18550	Levy	Rachel	1836	abroad	(?) Levy			Whitechapel, London	servant
30311	Levy	Rachel	1837	City, London	Joseph Levy	Elizabeth (?)		City, London	flower maker
10353	Levy	Rachel	1839	Middlesex, London	Simon Levy	Moriah (?)		Spitalfields, London	scholar
25119	Levy	Rachel	1841	Covent Garden, London	Philip Levy	Sarah (?)		Finsbury, London	
28455	Levy	Rachel	1842	Bedford, Bedfordshire	Henry Levy	Rosetta Moses	David Solomon Amstell	Spitalfields, London	scholar
6849	Levy	Rachel	1844	Spitalfields, London	Samuel Levy	Rebecca Pereira		Spitalfields, London	scholar
20370	Levy	Rachel	1844	Aldgate, London	Israel Levy	Sarah Harris		Aldgate, London	scholar
29505	Levy	Rachel	1844	Spitalfields, London	Henry Levy	Catherine (Kate, Kitty) Franks		Spitalfields, London	scholar
28444	Levy	Rachel	1845	?Spitalfields, London	Simon Levy	Esther Abendana		Spitalfields, London	scholar
3325	Levy	Rachel	1850	Spitalfields, London	Lewis Levy	Susan Solomons		Spitalfields, London	
26340	Levy	Rachel	1850	?Aldgate, London	Lawrence Levy	Amelia Cohen		Aldgate, London	
29452	Levy	Rachel	1850	Spitalfields, London	Joseph Levy	Amelia (?)		Spitalfields, London	
17510	Levy	Ralph (Raphael)	1826	Whitechapel, London	Moses Levy	Sarah Lazarus	Phoebe Abrahams nee Solomons	Spitalfields, London	general dealer
6825	Levy	Raphael	1816	Spitalfields, London	Joseph Levy	Rosetta (?)	Hannah Jacobs	Spitalfields, London	general dealer

ID	surname	given names	born	birthplace	father	mother	spouse 1	1851 residence	1851 occupation
25079	Levy	Raphael	1819	Middlesex, London			Clara (?)	City, London	tailor
13756	Levy	Raphael	1829	?, Poland [?, Prussia]				Manchester	cap maker
8007	Levy	Raphael (Ralph)	1844	Whitechapel, London	Benjamin Levy	Rosa Mandola		Spitalfields, London	
23921	Levy	Rebbecca	1850	Marylebone, London	Myer Levy	Hannah Levy		Fitzrovia, London	
30612	Levy	Rebecca	1779	?, Jamaica, West Indies	(?)		(?) Levy	Bloomsbury, London	fundholder
22244	Levy	Rebecca	1782	City, London	(?)		(?) Levy	Whitechapel, London	
26068	Levy	Rebecca	1785	Amsterdam, Holland			Asher Isaac Levy	Aldgate, London	
28826	Levy	Rebecca	1792	?, Holland	(?)		Lazarus Levy	Spitalfields, London	
1864	Levy	Rebecca	1796	Swansea, Wales			(?) Levy	Swansea, Wales	librarian
16152	Levy	Rebecca	1802	Southwark, London	Joseph Johnson		Joseph Levy	Whitechapel, London	feather dealer
6824	Levy	Rebecca	1811	Amsterdam, Holland	Joseph Levy	Rosetta (?)	(?)	Spitalfields, London	general dealer
29913	Levy	Rebecca	1813	?, Holland	(?)		Louis J Levy	Whitechapel, London	professor of languages
10512	Levy	Rebecca	1816	?, Poland [?, Prussia]	(?) Levy			Aldgate, London	
8452	Levy	Rebecca	1817	Portsmouth, Hampshire	(?) Davids		David Levy	Portsmouth, Hampshire	
13014	Levy	Rebecca	1821	Middlesex, London	(?)		Emanuel Levy	Spitalfields, London	
17253	Levy	Rebecca	1824	Aldgate, London	(?)		John Levy	Aldgate, London	
17424	Levy	Rebecca	1825	Whitechapel, London	Solomon Levy	Fanny (?)	Alexander Marcuson	Spitalfields, London	
18427	Levy	Rebecca	1826	Middlesex, London	(?)		Lewis Levy	Bloomsbury, London	
5674	Levy	Rebecca	1827	Berlin, Germany	Abinulech Levy		Julius (Joseph) Kariet (Karet)	Spitalfields, London	
21317	Levy	Rebecca	1828	Bloomsbury, London	(?) Levy	(?) (?Solomon)		Eton, Berkshire	
17388	Levy	Rebecca	1829	City, London	(?)		Abraham Levy	Whitechapel, London	
29290	Levy	Rebecca	1829	City, London	(?)		Abraham Levy	Whitechapel, London	
11473	Levy	Rebecca	1834	Aldgate, London	David Levy	Julia (?)		Aldgate, London	
16899	Levy	Rebecca	1834	Sheffield, Yorkshire	Reuben Levy	Polly Solomons		Sheffield, Yorkshire	
17098	Levy	Rebecca	1834	St Peter Port, Guernsey, Channel Islands	Mark Levy	Mary Lambert		St Peter Port, Guernsey, Channel Islands	dressmaker
11197	Levy	Rebecca	1835	Aldgate, London	(?) Levy			Aldgate, London	
11317	Levy	Rebecca	1835	Aldgate, London	Lewis Levy	Ann (Nancy) Israel		Aldgate, London	
9795	Levy	Rebecca	1836	Aldgate, London	(?) Levy	(?) Jonas		Waterloo, London	
26199	Levy	Rebecca	1836	?, Germany	Simon Levy	Fanny (?)		Aldgate, London	
21402	Levy	Rebecca	1837	Elephant & Castle, London	Solomon Levy	Maria Harris	Alexander Saunders	Elephant & Castle, London	scholar
13339	Levy	Rebecca	1838	Aldgate, London	Joseph Levy	Caroline (?)		Spitalfields, London	
18221	Levy	Rebecca	1839	Middlesex, London	(?) Levy			Mile End, London	scholar
20214	Levy	Rebecca	1840	Aldgate, London	Moses Levy	Mary (?)	Jacques Van Praagh	Wandsworth, London	
30577	Levy	Rebecca	1843	Spitalfields, London	Simon Levy	Esther Abendana		Spitalfields, London	scholar
26165	Levy	Rebecca	1845	Aldgate, London	Nathan Levy	Abigail Noah (Noah Da Costa)		Aldgate, London	scholar
29451	Levy	Rebecca	1847	Amsterdam, Holland	Joseph Levy	Amelia (?)		Spitalfields, London	
26264	Levy	Rebecca	1848	Aldgate, London	Samuel Levy	Louisa Jonas	Mark (Markus) Solomon	Aldgate, London	
28192	Levy	Rebecca	1850	Whitechapel, London	Samuel Levy	Ellen Abrahams		Spitalfields, London	
11069	Levy	Rebecca	1851	Aldgate, London	David Levy	Phoebe (?)		Aldgate, London	
11446	Levy	Rebecca	1851	Aldgate, London	Mark (Mordecai) Levy	Maria Lyon		Aldgate, London	
11349	Levy	Rebecca	1815	?, Poland			Mark Levy	Aldgate, London	cap maker

ID	surname	given names	born	birthplace	father	mother	spouse 1	1851 residence	1851 occupation
8453	Levy	Rebecca (Rose)	1841	?Portsmouth, Hampshire	David Levy	Rebecca Davids	George Isaac Moss	Portsmouth, Hampshire	
19961	Levy	Rebecca Miriam	1816	Middlesex, London	Jonas Levy	Sarah Israel Levy	Eleazer (Albert) Pyke [Albert]	Whitechapel, London	
18687	Levy	Rebeka?	1848	Whitechapel, London	Michael Levy	Sarah Harris		Whitechapel, London	
22874	Levy	Regrena	1813	Frankfurt-am-Main, Germany	(?)		Samuel Levy	Whitechapel, London	
5131	Levy	Reuben	1788	Newbury, Berkshire	Jacob Levy		Polly Solomons	Sheffield, Yorkshire	tailor + draper empl 20
11008	Levy	Reuben	1803	Walworth, London				Aldgate, London	general dealer
14042	Levy	Reuben	1823	Manchester			Elizabeth (?)	Manchester	tailor + woollen draper
23047	Levy	Reuben	1830	Whitechapel, London	Moses Levy	Catherine (?)		Aldgate, London	furrier
11318	Levy	Reuben	1837	Aldgate, London	Lewis Levy	Ann (Nancy) Israel		Aldgate, London	
21839	Levy	Robert	1823	Aldgate, London	Jonas (Jonathan) Levy	Matilda Moses	Elizabeth Nunes Carvalho	Clerkenwell, London	watch maker
8004	Levy	Rosa	1821	?, Germany	(?) Mandola		Benjamin Levy	Spitalfields, London	
25858	Levy	Rosa	1845	Spitalfields, London	Barnett Levy	Elizabeth (?)		Aldgate, London	scholar
7782	Levy	Rose	1825	Hoxton, London	(?)		(?) Levy	City, London	
22499	Levy	Rose	1826	Canterbury, Kent	(?) Levy	Sophia (?)		Whitechapel, London	dressmaker
1355	Levy	Rose	1827	Hull, Yorkshire				Plymouth, Devon	watchmaker's wife
12404	Levy	Rose	1830	Whitechapel, London	(?)		Thomas Levy	Spitalfields, London	
12234	Levy	Rose	1835	Whitechapel, London	Moses Levy	Catherine Aarons		Whitechapel, London	
11445	Levy	Rose	1849	Aldgate, London	Mark (Mordecai) Levy	Maria Lyon		Aldgate, London	
21215	Levy	Rose (Rosetta)	1843	Spitalfields, London	David Levy	Jane Lazarus		Spitalfields, London	
19002	Levy	Rosetta	1772	Aldgate, London	(?)		(?) Levy	Whitechapel, London	
6823	Levy	Rosetta	1781	Amsterdam, Holland	(?)		Joseph Levy	Spitalfields, London	general dealer
17064	Levy	Rosetta	1796	Bortzenburg, Germany				Glasgow, Scotland	manufacturing furrier
28097	Levy	Rosetta	1799	Whitechapel, London	Solomon Asher		Emanuel Levy	Spitalfields, London	
28454	Levy	Rosetta	1809	Finsbury, London	Emanuel Moses	Dinah (?)	Henry Levy	Spitalfields, London	
20209	Levy	Rosetta	1829	Elephant & Castle, London	Moses Levy	Mary (?)		Wandsworth, London	
3725	Levy	Rosetta	1830	Spitalfields, London	Hyman Levy	Sarah (?)		Spitalfields, London	tailoress
11472	Levy	Rosetta	1831	Aldgate, London	David Levy	Julia (?)		Aldgate, London	
5773	Levy	Rosetta	1832	Eton, Berkshire	Alexander Levy	Stella Foligno	John Symons	Eton, Berkshire	
7123	Levy	Rosetta	1835	Kensington, London	Nathaniel Levy	Sophia (?)	Ernest Abraham Hart	Bloomsbury, London	
17683	Levy	Rosetta	1839	Aldgate, London	Lawrence Levy	Eliza (Sarah) Emanuel	Moses Henry Moses	Shoreditch, London	scholar at home
30045	Levy	Rosetta	1846	Marylebone, London	(?) Levy	Hannah Moses		Aldgate, London	
23459	Levy	Rosetta (Rosanne)	1847	Liverpool	Joseph Levy	Mary (?)	Pierre John Nathan	Liverpool	
1190	Levy	Rosetta (Rozetta)	1821	?, London	Kaufman (Yechutiel HaCohen) Meyers		Aaron Levy	Plymouth, Devon	
20368	Levy	Rosey	1840	Aldgate, London	Israel Levy	Sarah Harris		Aldgate, London	scholar
25764	Levy	Rosey (Rosa)	1819	Aldgate, London	Zacharia Levy		Abraham Levy	Aldgate, London	
20359	Levy	Rosina	1846	Aldgate, London	Henry Levy	Jane Hart		Aldgate, London	
11152	Levy	Rubben	1837	Aldgate, London				Aldgate, London	dealer
24623	Levy	Rudolph	1799	Kaliningrad, Russia [Koenigsberg, Prussia]	Haim HaLevi		Marian Solomonson	Kennington, London	merchant - Baltic
13873	Levy	Rueben	1850	Manchester	Lewis Levy	Mary Ann (?)		Manchester	at home
22877	Levy	Salomon	1848	Spitalfields, London	Samuel Levy	Regrena (?)		Whitechapel, London	
20360	Levy	Sampson Henry	1848	Aldgate, London	Henry Levy	Jane Hart		Aldgate, London	
29301	Levy	Samuel	1775	Aldgate, London			(?)	Whitechapel, London	traveller

ID	surname	given names	born	birthplace	father	mother	spouse 1	1851 residence	1851 occupation
23366	Levy	Samuel	1789	Aldgate, London			Julia (?)	Strand, London	military outfitter
12672	Levy	Samuel	1792	Great Yarmouth, Norfolk			Lydia (?)	King's Lynn, Norfolk	clothes dealer
28616	Levy	Samuel	1793	Aldgate, London			Sarah (?)	Spitalfields, London	general dealer
21245	Levy	Samuel	1796	?, London	Simcha		Deborah Barnett	Spitalfields, London	tailor
29013	Levy	Samuel	1796	Whitechapel, London			Adelaide (?)	Whitechapel, London	general dealer
8962	Levy	Samuel	1798	Aldgate, London			Elizabeth (Betsy) (?)	Aldgate, London	fruit merchant + box maker + van proprietor
28604	Levy	Samuel	1806	?, Holland			Sarah (?)	Spitalfields, London	hawker of china
6845	Levy	Samuel	1808	Aldgate, London	Yehuda Leib		Rebecca Pereira	Spitalfields, London	dealer in glass
11276	Levy	Samuel	1808	Aldgate, London	Isaac Levy		Julia Isaacs	Aldgate, London	general dealer
22873	Levy	Samuel	1813	Frankfurt-am-Main, Germany			Regrena (?)	Whitechapel, London	journeyman skin dresser
26257	Levy	Samuel	1813	?, London	Solomon Levy		Louisa Jonas	Aldgate, London	tailor
9472	Levy	Samuel	1815	?, Poland [?, Prussia]			Henrietta (?)	Aldgate, London	clothier
28188	Levy	Samuel	1818	Whitechapel, London	Nathan Levy		Ellen Abrahams	Spitalfields, London	clothes dealer
25863	Levy	Samuel	1821	?, Poland				Aldgate, London	slipper maker journeyman
28650	Levy	Samuel	1821	?, London				Spitalfields, London	hawker
28827	Levy	Samuel	1824	Spitalfields, London	Lazarus Levy	Rebecca (?)		Spitalfields, London	general dealer
13849	Levy	Samuel	1827	Manchester	Joseph Levy	Julia (?)		Manchester	tailor + draper
23046	Levy	Samuel	1827	Whitechapel, London	Moses Levy	Catherine (?)		Aldgate, London	commercial traveller
24636	Levy	Samuel	1830	Lambeth, London			Sarah (?)	Waterloo, London	French polisher
10348	Levy	Samuel	1831	Spitalfields, London				Spitalfields, London	fishmonger
17700	Levy	Samuel	1832	Whitechapel, London	(?) Levy			Spitalfields, London	cigar maker
20169	Levy	Samuel	1834	Whitechapel, London	Henry Levy	Hannah (?)	Clara Jonas	Spitalfields, London	general dealer
21247	Levy	Samuel	1836	Whitechapel, London	Samuel Levy	Deborah Barnett		Spitalfields, London	cigar maker apprentice
12977	Levy	Samuel	1837	Whitechapel, London	Asher Levy	Julia Phillips		Aldgate, London	apprentice (?tailor)
21213	Levy	Samuel	1839	Spitalfields, London	David Levy	Jane Lazarus		Spitalfields, London	
20172	Levy	Samuel	1841	Whitechapel, London	Henry Levy	Hannah (?)		Spitalfields, London	general dealer
28223	Levy	Samuel	1841	Whitechapel, London	(?) Levy	Catherine (?)		Spitalfields, London	scholar
5288	Levy	Samuel	1843	Middlesex, London	Jacob Levy	Ann Levy		Aldgate, London	scholar
29943	Levy	Samuel	1844	Whitechapel, London	Morris Levy	Jane (?)		Whitechapel, London	scholar
21406	Levy	Samuel	1845	Elephant & Castle, London	Solomon Levy	Maria Harris		Elephant & Castle, London	
25743	Levy	Samuel	1845	Spitalfields, London	Elias Levy	Matilda Harris		Spitalfields, London	scholar
28800	Levy	Samuel	1845	Spitalfields, London	Lewis Levy	Jeannette (Jane) Symons		Spitalfields, London	scholar
11424	Levy	Samuel	1847	Aldgate, London	Lazarus (Eleazer) Levy	Catherine Green		Aldgate, London	
19817	Levy	Samuel	1848	Whitechapel, London	Elias Levy	Sarah Palachy		Spitalfields, London	
20156	Levy	Samuel	1850	Stepney, London	Henry Levy	Rachel (?)		Stepney, London	
30582	Levy	Samuel	1851	Whitechapel, London	John Levy	Mary Lazarus		Whitechapel, London	
17448	Levy	Sarah	1764	Aldgate, London	(?)		(?) Levy	Aldgate, London	
14738	Levy	Sarah	1774	Amsterdam, Holland	(?)		Jacob Levy	Spitalfields, London	
11380	Levy	Sarah	1777	?, Holland	(?)		(?) Levy	Aldgate, London	butcher
3723	Levy	Sarah	1784	Spitalfields, London			Hyman Levy	Spitalfields, London	
3210	Levy	Sarah	1787	Spitalfields, London			Isaac Levy	Rochester, Kent	landowner + annuitant
10211	Levy	Sarah	1791	?, Germany	(?)		John Levy	Aldgate, London	
19839	Levy	Sarah	1791	Aldgate, London	(?) Samuel	Elizabeth (?)		Spitalfields, London	clothes dealer

ID	surname	given names	born	birthplace	father	mother	spouse 1	1851 residence	1851 occupation
19787	Levy	Sarah	1796	Aldgate, London	Raphael (Ralph) Lazarus		Moses Levy	Spitalfields, London	clothes dealer
28641	Levy	Sarah	1797	Shoreditch, London	(?)		Abraham Levy	Spitalfields, London	greengrocer
28617	Levy	Sarah	1798	Spitalfields, London	(?)		Samuel Levy	Spitalfields, London	
211	Levy	Sarah	1801	City, London	(?) Davis		Lyon (Lewis) Levy	Spitalfields, London	
16194	Levy	Sarah	1801	Spitalfields, London	(?)		Emanuel Levy	Whitechapel, London	tailoress
19774	Levy	Sarah	1801	Whitechapel, London	Yaacov Jacobs		Mark (Mordecai) Levy	Spitalfields, London	laundress
28163	Levy	Sarah	1801	City, London	(?) Levy			Spitalfields, London	household servant
17103	Levy	Sarah	1806	?, England	(?)		(?)	St Helier, Jersey, Channel Islands	
28605	Levy	Sarah	1807	?, Holland	(?)		Samuel Levy	Spitalfields, London	hawker of china
14812	Levy	Sarah	1808	Middlesex, London	(?)		Michael Levy	Finsbury, London	
23831	Levy	Sarah	1813	Southwark, London	Joseph Levy	Esther (?)		Liverpool	seamstress
10276	Levy	Sarah	1814	Whitechapel, London	Abraham Martin		Lewis Levy	Spitalfields, London	
19003	Levy	Sarah	1815	Whitechapel, London	(?) Levy	Rosetta (?)		Whitechapel, London	
24876	Levy	Sarah	1815	?, Devon	(?) Levy			Bermondsey, London	
25118	Levy	Sarah	1815	Covent Garden, London			Philip Levy	Finsbury, London	
28414	Levy	Sarah	1816	Whitechapel, London	Aaron Phillips		David Levy	Spitalfields, London	dressmaker
1028	Levy	Sarah	1817	Birmingham			Isaac Levy	Exeter, Devon	
6443	Levy	Sarah	1817	Whitechapel, London	Jacob Harris		Michael Levy	Whitechapel, London	
19811	Levy	Sarah	1819	?, Germany	Samuel Palachy		Elias Levy	Spitalfields, London	
10927	Levy	Sarah	1820	Bradford, Yorkshire	(?)		Lewis Levy	Spitalfields, London	hawker of shoes
4121	Levy	Sarah	1821	Deptford, London	(?) Moses		Hyam Levy	Wapping, London	
4673	Levy	Sarah	1823	?, Hampshire			Lewis Levy	Birmingham	
20188	Levy	Sarah	1823	Whitechapel, London	Henry Levy	Jane Alexander	Morris Cohen	Spitalfields, London	tailoress
23380	Levy	Sarah	1824	?, London	Isaac Lazarus		Mark Levy	Aldgate, London	
19916	Levy	Sarah	1825	?, London	Lazarus Jacobs	Catherine Marls	Myer (Mier) Levy	Belfast, Ireland	
6793	Levy	Sarah	1826	Whitechapel, London	Isaac Levy	Catherine (?)		Spitalfields, London	general dealer
26813	Levy	Sarah	1826	Middlesex, London	(?) Barnett		Abraham Levy	Whitechapel, London	
12674	Levy	Sarah	1828	King's Lynn, Norfolk	Samuel Levy	Lydia (?)		King's Lynn, Norfolk	dress maker
24637	Levy	Sarah	1829	Lambeth, London	(?)		Samuel Levy	Waterloo, London	
25781	Levy	Sarah	1831	?, Poland [?, Prussia]	(?) Levy			Aldgate, London	tailoress
28751	Levy	Sarah	1831	Middlesex, London	Abraham Levy	(?)		Spitalfields, London	
25856	Levy	Sarah	1832	?Darmstadt, Germany	Barnett Levy	Elizabeth (?)		Aldgate, London	slipper maker
26401	Levy	Sarah	1833	?, London	Mordecai Levy	Leah (?)	Isaac Solomons	Aldgate, London	tailoress
5872	Levy	Sarah	1835	Elephant & Castle, London	Moses Levy	Mary (?)	Jacob Levy	Wandsworth, London	
11432	Levy	Sarah	1835	Spitalfields, London	(?) Levy			Aldgate, London	general servant
12976	Levy	Sarah	1835	Whitechapel, London	Asher Levy	Julia Phillips	Isaac Rees	Aldgate, London	furrier
20170	Levy	Sarah	1836	Whitechapel, London	Henry Levy	Hannah (?)		Spitalfields, London	tailoress
17113	Levy	Sarah	1838	Whitechapel, London	Abraham Levy	Leah (?)		Newport, Glamorgan, Wales	
19190	Levy	Sarah	1839	Aldgate, London	John Levy	Mary Lazarus		Whitechapel, London	
20162	Levy	Sarah	1839	Whitechapel, London	Isaac Levy	Catherine (?)		Spitalfields, London	
6847	Levy	Sarah	1840	Spitalfields, London	Samuel Levy	Rebecca Pereira		Spitalfields, London	parasol maker
25740	Levy	Sarah	1840	Aldgate, London	Elias Levy	Matilda Harris	Emanuel Levy	Spitalfields, London	scholar
25896	Levy	Sarah	1840	Aldgate, London	Hyam Levy	Frances Naphthali		Aldgate, London	scholar

ID	surname	given names	born	birthplace	father	mother	spouse 1	1851 residence	1851 occupation
10536	Levy	Sarah	1841	Covent Garden, London	David Levy	Catherine Davids	Morris Harris	Covent Garden, London	scholar
25765	Levy	Sarah	1841	Aldgate, London	Abraham Levy	Rosey (Rosa) Levy		Aldgate, London	
27466	Levy	Sarah	1841	Whitechapel, London	(?) Levy	Rachael (?)		Whitechapel, London	hawker
10354	Levy	Sarah	1842	Middlesex, London	Simon Levy	Moriah (?)		Spitalfields, London	scholar
11351	Levy	Sarah	1842	?, Poland	Mark Levy	Rebecca (?)	Jacob Cohen	Aldgate, London	tailoress
13398	Levy	Sarah	1842	Spitalfields, London	(?) Levy	(?) Mathews		Spitalfields, London	scholar
28483	Levy	Sarah	1842	Spitalfields, London	Lewis Levy	Amelia Morris		Spitalfields, London	scholar
29017	Levy	Sarah	1842	Whitechapel, London	Samuel Levy	Adelaide (?)		Whitechapel, London	scholar
29504	Levy	Sarah	1842	Spitalfields, London	Henry Levy	Catherine (Kate, Kitty) Franks		Spitalfields, London	scholar
28609	Levy	Sarah	1843	?, Holland	Samuel Levy	Sarah (?)		Spitalfields, London	scholar
18809	Levy	Sarah	1844	Elephant & Castle, London	Solomon Levy	Maria Harris	Gerald Abraham Levi	Elephant & Castle, London	
11443	Levy	Sarah	1845	Spitalfields, London	Mark (Mordecai) Levy	Maria Lyon	Barnett Lyons	Aldgate, London	
23389	Levy	Sarah	1845	?, London	Lipman (Eliezer) Levy	Hannah Jones		Aldgate, London	
2085	Levy	Sarah	1846	Carmarthen, Wales	Daniel Levy	Mary Anne Lazarus	Jacob Barnett Smith	Carmarthen, Wales	scholar
27542	Levy	Sarah	1846	Aldgate, London	Mark (Mordecai) Levy	Phoebe Hyams		Spitalfields, London	
11425	Levy	Sarah	1847	Aldgate, London	Lazarus (Eleazer) Levy	Catherine Green		Aldgate, London	
8780	Levy	Sarah	1849	Whitechapel, London	Jonas Levy	Dorothy (?)	Daniel Gomes da Costa	Aldgate, London	
20147	Levy	Sarah	1849	Strand, London	Isaac Levy	Elizabeth (?)		Soho, London	
13358	Levy	Sarah	1850	Whitechapel, London	Nathan (Nathaniel) Levy	Catherine Levy	Hyman Lyons	Spitalfields, London	
19792	Levy	Sarah	1850	Aldgate, London	Moses Levy	Sarah Lazarus		Spitalfields, London	
20027	Levy	Sarah	1850	Spitalfields, London	Solomon Levy	Charlotte Hart		Aldgate, London	
21830	Levy	Sarah	1850	Covent Garden, London	David Levy			Covent Garden, London	
25077	Levy	Sarah	1850	Middlesex, London	(?) Levy	Rose (?)		City, London	
30583	Levy	Sarah	1851	Spitalfields, London	Joseph Levy	Caroline (?)		Spitalfields, London	
20365	Levy	Sarah	1806	Whitechapel, London	Asher Harris		Israel Levy	Aldgate, London	
62	Levy	Sarah (Mary)	1795	Walsall, Staffordshire	(?) Palmer		Nathan Levy	Woolwich, London	proprietress of houses
13369	Levy	Sarah Ann	1849	Holborn, London	Joseph Levy	Jette (?)		Holborn, London	
3388	Levy	Sarah Cecilia (Celia)	1846	Wapping, London	Hyam Levy	Sarah (?)	Joseph Lazarus Miers	Wapping, London	
19959	Levy	Sarah Israel	1776	?, London	Jacob Levy		Jonas Levy	Whitechapel, London	annuitant
23039	Levy	Selina	1828	Wapping, London	Isaac Levy	Hannah Ansell		Aldgate, London	lithographer + stationer's assistant
28962	Levy	Selinah	1851	?, London	Isaiah Levy	Brinette (?)		Whitechapel, London	
10409	Levy	Simeon	1831	Whitechapel, London	(?) Levy	Catherine (?)		Spitalfields, London	cigar manufacturer
15152	Levy	Simeon	1831	Hamburg, Germany				Hoxton, London	journeyman cigar manufacturer
23518	Levy	Simmy (Sarah)	1786	?, London	Segel Nahman		Henry Levy	Liverpool	
26196	Levy	Simon	1793	?, Germany			Fanny (?)	Aldgate, London	glazier
10349	Levy	Simon	1806	Aldgate, London			Moriah (?)	Spitalfields, London	general dealer
28440	Levy	Simon	1816	Aldgate, London	Angel Levy		Esther Abendana	Spitalfields, London	general dealer
27230	Levy	Simon	1829	?, Germany	Josef Tsvi HaLevi		Rebecca (?)	Aldgate, London	slipper maker
16238	Levy	Simon	1845	Spitalfields, London	Nathan Levy	Rachael (?)		Spitalfields, London	scholar
27942	Levy	Solomon	1775	?, Poland			Maria (?)	Spitalfields, London	general dealer

ID	surname	given names	born	birthplace	father	mother	spouse 1	1851 residence	1851 occupation
17422	Levy	Solomon	1776	?, Poland			Fanny (?)	Spitalfields, London	paste colourer
21398	Levy	Solomon	1805	Whitechapel, London			Maria Harris	Elephant & Castle, London	furniture broker
8997	Levy	Solomon	1806	Whitechapel, London				Piccadilly, London	
20769	Levy	Solomon	1817	Hamburg, Germany			Elizabeth (?)	Haggerston, London	cigar maker
20024	Levy	Solomon	1821	City, London	Isaac Levy		Charlotte Hart	Aldgate, London	general dealer
3926	Levy	Solomon	1823	?, London	Mordecai (Mark) Levy	Amelia Levy	Anna (Hannah) Fox	Aldgate, London	
15683	Levy	Solomon	1827	Spitalfields, London	Abraham Levy		Elizabeth Hamburger	Aldgate, London	teacher
10813	Levy	Solomon	1828	Spitalfields, London	(?) Levy			Spitalfields, London	artist
16004	Levy	Solomon	1830	St Pancras, London			Martha Solomon	Covent Garden, London	
9384	Levy	Solomon	1832	Middlesex, London				Spitalfields, London	waistcoat maker
10277	Levy	Solomon	1835	Whitechapel, London	Lewis Levy	Sarah (?)		Spitalfields, London	fruit dealer
17742	Levy	Solomon	1836	?, Poland [?, Prussia]				Aldgate, London	cap maker's apprentice
5980	Levy	Solomon	1840	Aldgate, London	Lawrence Levy	Maria Hiam		Wapping, London	scholar
2711	Levy	Solomon	1841	Skoki, Poland [Shocken, Prussia]	Abraham Levy	Rachel Wolfson		Manchester	scholar
11476	Levy	Solomon	1841	Aldgate, London	David Levy	Julia (?)		Aldgate, London	
4674	Levy	Solomon	1843	Birmingham	Lewis Levy	Sarah (?)		Birmingham	
20771	Levy	Solomon	1845	Bethnal Green, London	Solomon Levy	Elizabeth (?)		Haggerston, London	
26263	Levy	Solomon	1845	?, London	Samuel Levy	Louisa Jonas		Aldgate, London	scholar
12980	Levy	Solomon	1846	Aldgate, London	Asher Levy	Julia Phillips		Aldgate, London	at home
30578	Levy	Solomon	1847	Spitalfields, London	Simon Levy	Esther Abendana		Spitalfields, London	scholar
23391	Levy	Solomon	1849	?, London	Lipman (Eliezer) Levy	Hannah Jones		Aldgate, London	
19867	Levy	Solomon	1851	Whitechapel, London	Coleman Levy	Jael (?)		Spitalfields, London	
29508	Levy	Solomon	1851	Spitalfields, London	Henry Levy	Catherine (Kate, Kitty) Franks		Spitalfields, London	
23956	Levy	Solomon Abraham	1783	?, Holland	(?Abraham) Levy		Paulina (Pessy) (?)	Marylebone, London	Stock Exchange
13196	Levy	Solomon Hyam (Hyman)	1815	Whitechapel, London	(?Hyman) Levy		Clara Joseph	Whitechapel, London	watch manufacturer
24666	Levy	Sophia	1775	Aldgate, London	(?)		Joseph Levy	Kennington, London	
22497	Levy	Sophia	1776	Canterbury, Kent	(?)		(?) Levy	Whitechapel, London	annuitant
7676	Levy	Sophia	1802	Middlesex, London	(?)		Nathaniel Levy	Bloomsbury, London	
27882	Levy	Sophia	1816	Portsmouth, Hampshire	Jacob Levy	Julia (?)		Spitalfields, London	general dealer
2780	Levy	Sophia	1834	Whitechapel, London	Aaron Levy	(?)		Whitechapel, London	tailoress
16809	Levy	Sophia	1839	Bristol	Levy Levy	Elizabeth (?)		Bristol	scholar
3322	Levy	Sophia	1841	Aldgate, London	Aaron Levy	Rachel Hart	Lewis Levy	Aldgate, London	scholar
8976	Levy	Sophia	1842	Portsmouth, Hampshire	David Levy	Rebecca Davids	Jonathan Brandon	Portsmouth, Hampshire	
20038	Levy	Sophia	1850	Aldgate, London	(?) Levy			Aldgate, London	
19962	Levy	Sophia (Zipporah)	1818	Middlesex, London	Jonas Levy	Sarah Israel Levy		Whitechapel, London	
28611	Levy	Sophiah	1829	Spitalfields, London	Samuel Levy	Sarah (?)		Spitalfields, London	capmaker
19654	Levy	Stella	1797	Bethnal Green, London	Moses Zachariah Foligno	Rachel de Isaac Baquis	Alexander Levy	Eton, Berkshire	
22498	Levy	Susan	1810	Canterbury, Kent	(?) Levy	Sophia (?)		Whitechapel, London	dressmaker
3324	Levy	Susan	1829	Whitechapel, London	Phillip Solomons		Lewis Levy	Spitalfields, London	umbrella maker
11441	Levy	Susan	1840	Spitalfields, London	Mark (Mordecai) Levy	Maria Lyon		Aldgate, London	
13709	Levy	Theodore	1824	?, Poland [?, Prussia]				Bloomsbury, London	journeyman tailor

ID	surname	given names	born	birthplace	father	mother	spouse 1	1851 residence	1851 occupation
12403	Levy	Thomas	1826	Aldgate, London			Rose (?)	Spitalfields, London	pastry cook
29260	Levy	Victoria	1829	?, Italy	(?) Levy			Whitechapel, London	
24418	Levy	William	1830	?, London	Lawrence Levy	Rebecca Jacobs		Strand, London	auctioneer
29443	Levy	Wolf	1801	Amsterdam, Holland			Adelaide (?)	Spitalfields, London	jeweller
2713	Levy	Wolfe	1843	Ragoesen, Germany [Rogasen, Prussia]	Abraham Levy	Rachel Wolfson	Kate Joseph	Manchester	scholar
10452	Levy	Woolf	1795	?, Holland			Elizabeth (?)	Aldgate, London	furniture dealer
6795	Levy	Woolf	1850	Whitechapel, London	Moses Levy	Jane Isaacs		Spitalfields, London	
1867	Levy	Yentuv (Youtaff, Yomtaaf)	1795	?, Morocco				Merthyr Tydfil, Wales	clothier
11474	Levy	Zaccariah	1836	Aldgate, London	David Levy	Julia (?)		Aldgate, London	
25768	Levy	Zachariah	1848	Whitechapel, London	Abraham Levy	Rosey (Rosa) Levy		Aldgate, London	
1332	Levy	Zipporah	1787	Plymouth, Devon	(Aaron Moses?) Benjamin		Abraham Levy	Plymouth, Devon	pawnbroker
1865	Levy	Zipporah	1826	Barnstaple, Devon	(?) Levy	Rebecca (?)		Swansea, Wales	governess
10833	Levy (Lazarus)	Reyna	1833	Spitalfields, London	Eli Lazarus			Spitalfields, London	shoe binder
21310	Levy (Levey)	Anne	1841	Liverpool	Henry Levy (Levey)	Maria (?)		Liverpool	scholar
20143	Levy (Levey)	Henry	1811	?, Poland [Lobent, Prussia]			Maria (?)	Liverpool	grocer + smallware dealer, jeweller + clothier
21308	Levy (Levey)	Lewis	1837	Liverpool	Henry Levy (Levey)	Maria (?)		Liverpool	apprentice grocer
21309	Levy (Levey)	Louisa	1839	Liverpool	Henry Levy (Levey)	Maria (?)		Liverpool	scholar
21307	Levy (Levey)	Maria	1815	?, Poland [Lobent, Prussia]	(?)		Henry Levy (Levey)	Liverpool	
12156	Levy (Levi)	Abraham E	1814	Whitechapel, London	Enoch Levi	Sarah (Marjot) Smith	Rachel Isaacs	Whitechapel, London	tobacconist
21322	Levy (Levi)	Ann	1828	Ipswich, Suffolk	Moses Levy (Levi)	Zipporah (Sippy) Abrahams		Ipswich, Suffolk	
6486	Levy (Levi)	Bella (Isabella)	1821	Plymouth, Devon	(?) Levy (Levi)	Leah (?)		Plymouth, Devon	
12159	Levy (Levi)	Edward	1839	Whitechapel, London	Abraham E Levy (Levi)	Rachel Isaacs		Whitechapel, London	scholar
12158	Levy (Levi)	Elizabeth (Lizzie)	1837	Whitechapel, London	Abraham E Levy (Levi)	Rachel Isaacs	Samuel Beck	Whitechapel, London	scholar
6519	Levy (Levi)	Esther	1816	Plymouth, Devon	(?) Levy (Levi)	Leah (?)		Plymouth, Devon	
12163	Levy (Levi)	Henry	1847	Whitechapel, London	Abraham E Levy (Levi)	Rachel Isaacs		Whitechapel, London	scholar
7952	Levy (Levi)	Isaac (Israel)	1819	Ipswich, Suffolk	Moses Levy (Levi)	Zipporah (Sippy) Abrahams		Ipswich, Suffolk	journeyman watchmaker
2219	Levy (Levi)	Israel Morris	1814	?, Poland			Selina (?)	Oxford, Oxfordshire	watchmaker + jeweller
12162	Levy (Levi)	John	1844	Whitechapel, London	Abraham E Levy (Levi)	Rachel Isaacs		Whitechapel, London	scholar
18110	Levy (Levi)	Judith	1783	King's Lynn, Norfolk	Joseph Simon Magnus	Bela Eliezer Cohen	Moses Lazarus	Mile End, London	
6487	Levy (Levi)	Julia	1826	Plymouth, Devon	(?) Levy (Levi)	Leah (?)		Plymouth, Devon	
18604	Levy (Levi)	Julia	1830	Ipswich, Suffolk	Moses Levy (Levi)	Zipporah (Sippy) Abrahams		Ipswich, Suffolk	
12161	Levy (Levi)	Julia	1842	Whitechapel, London	Abraham E Levy (Levi)	Rachel Isaacs	Maurice Barnett	Whitechapel, London	scholar
31046	Levy (Levi)	Leah	1791	Portsmouth, Hampshire	(?)		(?) Levy (Levi)	Plymouth, Devon	
12160	Levy (Levi)	Lewis	1840	Whitechapel, London	Abraham E Levy (Levi)	Rachel Isaacs	Mary (May) Lazarus	Whitechapel, London	scholar
20217	Levy (Levi)	Moses	1791	Bury St Edmunds, Suffolk			Zipporah (Sippy) Abrahams	Ipswich, Suffolk	dealer in hardware + general dealer
12157	Levy (Levi)	Rachel	1816	Portsmouth, Hampshire	Ari Isaacs		Abraham E Levy (Levi)	Whitechapel, London	
18603	Levy (Levi)	Rose	1826	Ipswich, Suffolk	Moses Levy (Levi)	Zipporah (Sippy) Abrahams		Ipswich, Suffolk	
18109	Levy (Levi)	Samuel	1788	Whitechapel, London	Chaim Levy		Judith Lazarus nee Magnus	Mile End, London	clothier
12165	Levy (Levi)	Sarah	1788	Whitechapel, London	(?) Smith		Enoch Levy	Whitechapel, London	
12164	Levy (Levi)	Sarah	1850	Whitechapel, London	Abraham E Levy (Levi)	Rachel Isaacs	Dawson Alexander Barnett	Whitechapel, London	
2220	Levy (Levi)	Selina (Salina)	1819	Warsaw, Poland	Lewis Schultz	Louisa (?)	Israel Levy (Levi)	Oxford, Oxfordshire	

ID	surname	given names	born	birthplace	father	mother	spouse 1	1851 residence	1851 occupation
20218	Levy (Levi)	Zipporah (Sippy)	1796	Ipswich, Suffolk	Israel Abrahams		Moses Levy	Ipswich, Suffolk	
7139	Levy (Lewis)	David	1823	Lambeth, London	Benjamin Wolfe Levy	Martha Levy	Bertha Cohen	Liverpool	outfitter
3152	Levy (Lewy)	Adelaide (Adalanah)	1798	?, Poland [?, Prussia]			Michael Levy (Lewy)	Birmingham	
3160	Levy (Lewy)	Hannah	1829	Poznan, Poland [Posen, Prussia]	Michael Levy (Lewy)	Adelaide (Adalanah) (?)		Birmingham	
3161	Levy (Lewy)	Manassah	1840	Liverpool	Michael Levy (Lewy)	Adelaide (Adalanah)		Birmingham	
3151	Levy (Lewy)	Michael	1796	?, Poland [?, Prussia]			Adelaide (Adalanah) (?)	Birmingham	general dealer
7249	Levy [Lawson]	Edward	1833	Clerkenwell, London	Joseph Moses Levy	Esther Cohen	Harriette Georgiana Webster	Bloomsbury, London	journalist
7251	Levy [Lawson]	Esther	1812	Whitechapel, London	Godfrey Alexander Cohen		Joseph Moses Levy [Lawson]	Bloomsbury, London	
7250	Levy [Lawson]	Joseph Moses	1812	Whitechapel, London	Moses Lionel Levy	Helena Moses	Esther Cohen	Bloomsbury, London	printer, 'Sunday Times'
2485	Lewicky	Elizabeth	1818	abroad	(?)		(?) Lewicky	Hull, Yorkshire	shopkeeper
2487	Lewicky	Rosa	1845	abroad	(?) Lewicky	Elizabeth (?)		Hull, Yorkshire	scholar
2488	Lewicky	Sarah	1843	abroad	(?) Lewicky	Eliizabeth (?)		Hull, Yorkshire	scholar
2486	Lewicky	Simon S	1848	abroad	(?) Lewicky	Elizabeth (?)		Hull, Yorkshire	scholar
26939	Lewin	Abraham	1822	?, Poland				Aldgate, London	glazier
21342	Lewin	Adelaide	1851	Whitechapel, London	Isaac Lewin (Lewin Levy)	Rebecca Lyons	Simon Hyam Franklin	Whitechapel, London	
21343	Lewin	Anna	1849	Whitechapel, London	Isaac Lewin (Lewin Levy)	Rebecca Lyons		Whitechapel, London	
13370	Lewin	Benjamin	1832	?, Germany				Holborn, London	tailor
30964	Lewin	Dworaka	1804	Grudno, Poland	(?)		Solomon P Lewin	Hull, Yorkshire	hawker, jewellery wife
21178	Lewin	Lewis	1835	Waterloo, London				Aldgate, London	cigar maker
21189	Lewin	Lewis	1847	?, Germany	Wolf Lewin	Pauline (?)		Aldgate, London	
21188	Lewin	Pauline	1829	?, Germany	(?)		Wolf Lewin	Aldgate, London	
5709	Lewin	Phoebe	1847	Middlesex, London	Isaac Lewin (Lewin Levy)	Rebecca Lyons	Montague Barnett	City, London	
21190	Lewin	Rebecca	1850	Aldgate, London	Wolf Lewin	Pauline (?)		Aldgate, London	
30963	Lewin	Solomon P	1806	Grudno, Poland			Dworaka (?)	Hull, Yorkshire	hawker, jewellery (licensed)
21187	Lewin	Wolf	1819	?, Germany			Pauline (?)	Aldgate, London	tailor
5707	Lewin (Lewin Levy)	Isaac	1822	Bimingham	Lazarus Levy		Rebecca Lyons	Whitechapel, London	
5708	Lewin (Lewin Levy)	Rebecca	1820	Bristol	Joseph (Moshe) Lyons		Isaac Lewin (Lewin Levy)	Whitechapel, London	
4682	Lewinthal	Fanny	1850	Whitechapel, London	Jacob Lewinthal	Mary Abrahams		Birmingham	
4681	Lewinthal	Isabella	1848	Stepney, London	Jacob Lewinthal	Mary Abrahams		Birmingham	
4680	Lewinthal	Lavinia	1847	?, London	Jacob Lewinthal	Mary Abrahams		Birmingham	scholar
4679	Lewinthal	Lewis	1842	Birmingham	Jacob Lewinthal	Mary Abrahams		Birmingham	scholar
4678	Lewinthal	Mary	1815	?, London	Tsevi Hirsh Abrahams		Jacob Lewinthal	Birmingham	
4677	Lewinthal (Livingthall)	Jacob	1809	?, Poland	Yehuda Lewinthal		Mary Abrahams	Birmingham	general dealer
18044	Lewinthell	Levy	1825	?, Poland				Dudley, Worcestershire	glazier
24150	Lewis	Aaron	1812	?, Poland [?, Prussia]			Sarah (?)	Euston, London	tailor
17514	Lewis	Abraham	1773	Spitalfields, London	Moshe Lewis		Mary (Miriam) Saunders	Spitalfields, London	general dealer
28622	Lewis	Abraham	1811	?, Germany			(?)	Spitalfields, London	tailor

ID	surname	given names	born	birthplace	father	mother	spouse 1	1851 residence	1851 occupation
27008	Lewis	Abraham	1818	?, Germany	Lewis Lewis		Rachael Lutto nee Solomon	Aldgate, London	tailor
29134	Lewis	Abraham	1822	?, Poland			Rosalia (?)	Whitechapel, London	glazier
8015	Lewis	Albert S	1843	Brighton, Sussex	Benjamin Lewis	Henrietta Moss	Sarah Simmons	Brighton, Sussex	scholar
24153	Lewis	Alfred	1842	Bloomsbury, London	Aaron Lewis	Sarah (?)		Euston, London	scholar
25114	Lewis	Amelia	1811	Aldgate, London	(?) Hyams		Higham (Hyam) Lewis	Finsbury, London	
8957	Lewis	Amelia (Emilia)	1842	Aldgate, London	Phiilip Lewis	Ann Lyons		Aldgate, London	
8955	Lewis	Ann	1821	Aldgate, London	Aaron Lyons	Abigail Solomons	Phillip Lewis	Aldgate, London	
22416	Lewis	Ann	1847	Stepney, London	Solomon Lewis	Ann Levy		Whitechapel, London	
10288	Lewis	Anna	1850	Spitalfields, London	Isaac Lewis	Hannah (?)		Spitalfields, London	
8012	Lewis	Barrow	1834	Brighton, Sussex	Benjamin Lewis	Henrietta Moss		Brighton, Sussex	assistant gold- and silversmith
8011	Lewis	Benjamin	1804	Brighton, Sussex	Hyam Lewis	(?) (?Cohen)	Henrietta Moss	Brighton, Sussex	gold- and silversmith
16939	Lewis	Braham	1842	Brighton, Sussex	Benjamin Lewis	Henrietta (?)		Brighton, Sussex	scholar
11328	Lewis	Caroline	1821	Aldgate, London			Lewis Lewis	Aldgate, London	
19542	Lewis	Caroline	1838	Marylebone, London	Lewis Lewis	Louisa (?)		Strand, London	scholar at home
16283	Lewis	Daniel	1761	Aldgate, London				Spitalfields, London	
10287	Lewis	Deborah	1848	Spitalfields, London	Isaac Lewis	Hannah (?)		Spitalfields, London	scholar
28623	Lewis	Dinah	1844	?, London	Abraham Lewis	(?)		Spitalfields, London	scholar
22411	Lewis	Edward	1839	Stepney, London	Solomon Lewis	Ann Levy		Whitechapel, London	cigar maker
24156	Lewis	Edward	1847	Covent Garden, London	Aaron Lewis	Sarah (?)		Euston, London	
7164	Lewis	Edward John	1832	Holborn, London	James Graham Lewis	Harriet Davis		Euston, London	solicitor's articled clerk
2501	Lewis	Eliza	1818	Middlesex, London	Godfrey Solomon	(?Judith Davis)	Phineas (Pincus) Lewis	Hull, Yorkshire	
2504	Lewis	Eliza	1841	Sheffield, Yorkshire	Phineas Lewis	Deborah Jacobs		Hull, Yorkshire	
4011	Lewis	Eliza (Lizzie)	1836	Brighton, Sussex	Benjamin Lewis	Henrietta Moss	Emanuel Emanuel	Portsmouth, Hampshire	
4688	Lewis	Elizabeth	1811	?, Lincolnshire			Joseph Lewis	Birmingham	
20220	Lewis	Elizabeth	1819	?, London	Levy Levy		Moses Lewis	Aldgate, London	
4684	Lewis	Elizabeth	1822	Lambeth, London			Israel Lewis	Birmingham	
28624	Lewis	Ellen	1846	?, London	Abraham Lewis	(?)		Spitalfields, London	scholar
23038	Lewis	Emma	1848	Middlesex, London	John Lewis	(?)		Aldgate, London	
7167	Lewis	Emmeline	1841	Holborn, London	James Graham Lewis	Harriet Davis	Henry Gustavus Herz	Euston, London	scholar at home
16940	Lewis	Ernest	1844	Brighton, Sussex	Benjamin Lewis	Henrietta (?)		Brighton, Sussex	scholar
7168	Lewis	Esther	1830	Holborn, London	James Graham Lewis	Harriet Davis	Maurice Davis	Euston, London	
22414	Lewis	Esther	1841	Stepney, London	Solomon Lewis	Ann Levy		Whitechapel, London	scholar
19544	Lewis	Esther	1844	Soho, London	Lewis Lewis	Louisa (?)		Strand, London	scholar at home
7169	Lewis	Fanny	1835	Middlesex, London	James Graham Lewis	Harriet Davis	Sebastien Auguste Ettinghausen	Euston, London	scholar at home
2503	Lewis	Fanny	1838	Sheffield, Yorkshire	Phineas Lewis	Deborah Jacobs	Henry Godfrey	Hull, Yorkshire	
7160	Lewis	Frederick	1801	?			Sarah (?)	Birmingham	
19540	Lewis	Frederick	1825	Chatham, Kent	Lewis Lewis	Louisa (?)		Strand, London	clerk to a broker
7165	Lewis	Frederick Hyman	1835	Holborn, London	James Graham Lewis	Harriet Davis		Euston, London	scholar
22412	Lewis	Gabriel	1842	Stepney, London	Solomon Lewis	Ann Levy		Whitechapel, London	cigar maker
2928	Lewis	George	1823	Poznan, Poland [Posen, Prussia]	Solomon Levi	Zipporah (?)	Julia Lyon	Wapping, London	dealer
7161	Lewis	George Henry	1833	Holborn, London	James Graham Lewis	Harriet Davis	Victorine Kann	Euston, London	solicitor's articled clerk

ID	surname	given names	born	birthplace	father	mother	spouse 1	1851 residence	1851 occupation
10285	Lewis	Hannah	1821	Holstein, Germany [Holstein, Denmark]	(?)		Isaac Lewis	Spitalfields, London	
19541	Lewis	Hannah	1833	Chelsea, London	Lewis Lewis	Louisa (?)		Strand, London	book folder
29596	Lewis	Hannah	1849	Bath	Jude Lewis	Mary (?)		Whitechapel, London	
18414	Lewis	Hannah	1850	?, London	Joseph Lewis	Julia (?)		Aldgate, London	
24158	Lewis	Hannah	1850	St Pancras, London	Aaron Lewis	Sarah (?)		Euston, London	
7163	Lewis	Harriet	1805	Middlesex, London	Joseph Davis		James Graham Lewis	Holborn, London	
7170	Lewis	Harriet	1840	Middlesex, London	James Graham Lewis	Harriet Davis		Euston, London	scholar at home
16938	Lewis	Henrietta	1811	Plymouth, Devon	Barrow Moss	Sarah (Sally) Isaac	Benjamin Lewis	Brighton, Sussex	
22409	Lewis	Henry	1833	Whitechapel, London	Solomon Lewis	Ann Levy		Whitechapel, London	cigar maker
24154	Lewis	Henry	1844	Covent Garden, London	Aaron Lewis	Sarah (?)		Euston, London	scholar
19275	Lewis	Henry	1851	Aldgate, London	Philip Lewis	Ann Lyons	Esther (Hester) de Costa	Aldgate, London	
4104	Lewis	Henry (Harry) B	1840	Brighton, Sussex	Benjamin Lewis	Henrietta (?)	Maria Emanuel	Brighton, Sussex	
8013	Lewis	Herbert Hyam	1849	Brighton, Sussex	Benjamin Lewis	Henrietta Moss	Sophia (?)	Brighton, Sussex	
25113	Lewis	Higham (Hyam)	1802	?, Poland			Amelia Hyams	Finsbury, London	dealer in old clothes
8017	Lewis	Hyam (Hyman)	1768	Gdansk, Poland [Danziger, Germany]			(?) Cohen	Brighton, Sussex	
10284	Lewis	Isaac	1815	?, Poland [?Karaikar, Prussia]			Hannah (?)	Spitalfields, London	tailor
26122	Lewis	Isabella	1771	Amsterdam, Holland	(?)		Samuel Lewis	Aldgate, London	
29595	Lewis	Isabella	1846	Bath	Jude Lewis	Mary (?)		Whitechapel, London	
4683	Lewis	Israel	1820	?, Germany			Elizabeth (?)	Birmingham	tailor
18411	Lewis	Jacob	1839	?, Poland [?, Prussia]	Joseph Lewis	Julia (?)		Aldgate, London	scholar
7162	Lewis	James Graham	1804	Middlesex, London	Nachum Lewis		Harriet Davis	Euston, London	solicitor + clerk of indictments, Midland circuit
18811	Lewis	James Graham Louison	1843	Holborn, London	James Graham Lewis	Harriet Davis		Euston, London	scholar at home
14796	Lewis	Jane	1824	Middlesex, London	(?)		John Lewis	Finsbury, London	
19543	Lewis	Joel	1842	Marylebone, London	Lewis Lewis	Louisa (?)		Strand, London	scholar at home
22355	Lewis	John	1791	City, London			Rachal (?)	Aldgate, London	general dealer
14795	Lewis	John	1819	?, Poland [?, Prussia]			Jane (?)	Finsbury, London	foreign agent
23037	Lewis	John	1827	Norwich, Norfolk			(?)	Aldgate, London	commercial traveller
20221	Lewis	John	1844	?, London	Moses Lewis	Elizabeth Levy		Aldgate, London	
24157	Lewis	John	1849	Covent Garden, London	Aaron Lewis	Sarah (?)		Euston, London	
4687	Lewis	Joseph	1811	Amsterdam, Holland			Elizabeth (?)	Birmingham	hawker
18409	Lewis	Joseph	1811	?, Poland [?, Prussia]			Julia (?)	Aldgate, London	cabinet maker
2505	Lewis	Joseph	1843	Sheffield, Yorkshire	Phineas Lewis	Deborah Jacobs	Henrietta (Nettie) Mosely	Hull, Yorkshire	
16986	Lewis	Judah	1835	Aldgate, London	Barnett Lewis		Hannah (Anna) Coleman	Wapping, London	shoemaker apprentice
28625	Lewis	Jude	1848	?, London	Abraham Lewis	(?)		Spitalfields, London	scholar
29590	Lewis	Jude	1811	?, Poland			Mary (?)	Whitechapel, London	traveller
18410	Lewis	Julia	1816	?, Poland [?, Prussia]	(?)		Joseph Lewis	Aldgate, London	
154	Lewis	Julia	1830	Islington, London	Isaac Leo Lyon	Hannah (Anna) Levi	George Lewis	Spitalfields, London	dressmaker
14797	Lewis	Julius	1850	Finsbury, London	John Lewis	Jane (?)		Finsbury, London	
27350	Lewis	Lazarus	1823	Chelmno, Poland [Chelmns, Germany]			Rachael (?)	Aldgate, London	tailor

ID	surname	given names	born	birthplace	father	mother	spouse 1	1851 residence	1851 occupation
4689	Lewis	Lazarus	1829	?, Germany				Birmingham	traveller
4010	Lewis	Leah	1835	Brighton, Sussex	Benjamin Lewis	Henrietta Moss	Lewis Colman Cohen	Portsmouth, Hampshire	
2507	Lewis	Leon	1849	Hull, Yorkshire	Phineas Lewis	Eliza Godfrey Solomon	Rosetta (Rose) Rabinowitz	Hull, Yorkshire	
19538	Lewis	Lewis	1786	Whitechapel, London			Louisa (?)	Strand, London	broker
19894	Lewis	Lewis	1809	?, Kent				Whitechapel, London	assistant to soapmaker
11327	Lewis	Lewis	1823	?, Poland [?, Prussia]			Caroline (?)	Aldgate, London	painter + glazier
7166	Lewis	Louis	1838	Holborn, London	James Graham Lewis	Harriet Davis		Euston, London	scholar at home
8014	Lewis	Louis (Lewis)	1838	Brighton, Sussex	Benjamin Lewis	Henrietta Moss	Ruth (?Cohen)	Brighton, Sussex	scholar
19539	Lewis	Louisa	1804	Rochester, Kent	(?)		Lewis Lewis	Strand, London	
22624	Lewis	Louisa	1827	Walworth, London	Lewis Levy	Mary (?)		Stepney, London	
24155	Lewis	Louisa	1846	Covent Garden, London	Aaron Lewis	Sarah (?)		Euston, London	scholar
4685	Lewis	Louisa	1849	Birmingham	Israel Lewis	Elizabeth (?)		Birmingham	
18412	Lewis	Maria	1842	?, Poland [?, Prussia]	Joseph Lewis	Julia (?)		Aldgate, London	scholar
29591	Lewis	Mary	1813	?, Poland	(?)		Jude Lewis	Whitechapel, London	
17515	Lewis	Mary (Miriam)	1786	Spitalfields, London	Moshe Saunders		Abraham Lewis	Spitalfields, London	
22413	Lewis	Matilda	1839	Stepney, London	Solomon Lewis	Ann Levy		Whitechapel, London	
24152	Lewis	Matilda	1840	Bloomsbury, London	Aaron Lewis	Sarah (?)		Euston, London	scholar
22415	Lewis	Maurice	1843	Stepney, London	Solomon Lewis	Ann Levy		Whitechapel, London	scholar
22410	Lewis	Michael	1836	Whitechapel, London	Solomon Lewis	Ann Levy		Whitechapel, London	commission traveller
18884	Lewis	Moley (?Mosey)	1823	Spitalfields, London	(?) Lewis	Sarah (?)		Spitalfields, London	clothes dealer
20219	Lewis	Moses	1818	?, London	Abraham Lewis		Elizabeth Levy	Aldgate, London	general dealer
18413	Lewis	Moses	1846	?, London	Joseph Lewis	Julia (?)		Aldgate, London	scholar
4686	Lewis	Moses	1850	Birmingham	Israel Lewis	Elizabeth (?)		Birmingham	
4690	Lewis	Moss	1826	?, London				Birmingham	traveller in printing
8956	Lewis	Moss	1839	Aldgate, London	Phiilip Lewis	Ann Lyons	Rachel Joseph	Aldgate, London	
12386	Lewis	Nathan	1827	?, Poland				North Shields, Tyne & Wear	glazier
20224	Lewis	Philip	1850	Aldgate, London	Moses Lewis	Elizabeth Levy	Sophia Alexander	Aldgate, London	
8954	Lewis	Phillip	1818	Whitechapel, London	Abraham Lewis		Ann Lyons	Aldgate, London	general dealer
2502	Lewis	Phineas (Pincus)	1813	?, Poland [?, Prussia]			Deborah Jacobs	Hull, Yorkshire	wholesale jeweller + importer of foreign goods &c
16284	Lewis	Phoeby	1781	Spitalfields, London	(?) Lewis			Spitalfields, London	
29593	Lewis	Priscilla	1842	Bath	Jude Lewis	Mary (?)		Whitechapel, London	
27009	Lewis	Rachael	1816	Aldgate, London	Isaac Solomon		Joseph Lutto	Aldgate, London	
27351	Lewis	Rachael	1823	Leszno, Poland [Lissa, Germany]	(?)		Lazarus Lewis	Aldgate, London	
22356	Lewis	Rachal	1790	City, London	(?)		John Lewis	Aldgate, London	
17516	Lewis	Rebecca	1808	Spitalfields, London	Abraham Lewis	Mary (Miriam) Saunders		Spitalfields, London	domestic servant
29592	Lewis	Rebecca	1841	Markham, Wiltshire	Jude Lewis	Mary (?)		Whitechapel, London	
2506	Lewis	Rosa	1845	Sheffield, Yorkshire	Phineas Lewis	Deborah Jacobs		Hull, Yorkshire	
29135	Lewis	Rosalia	1824	?, Poland	(?)		Abraham Lewis	Whitechapel, London	
20223	Lewis	Rosetta	1849	?, London	Moses Lewis	Elizabeth Levy		Aldgate, London	
14268	Lewis	Samuel	1835	Blackford, Cheshire				Manchester	pawnbroker's apprentice
4692	Lewis	Samuel	1838	Birmingham	Frederick Lewis	Sarah (?)	Ada Davis	Birmingham	pedlar

ID	surname	given names	born	birthplace	father	mother	spouse 1	1851 residence	1851 occupation
10286	Lewis	Samuel	1845	Spitalfields, London	Isaac Lewis	Hannah (?)		Spitalfields, London	scholar
29136	Lewis	Samuel	1849	?, London	Abraham Lewis	Rosalia (?)		Whitechapel, London	
18882	Lewis	Sarah	1778	?, Germany [High Germany]	(?)		(?) Lewis	Spitalfields, London	clothes dealer
4691	Lewis	Sarah	1805	Bristol			Frederick Lewis	Birmingham	lodging house keeper
24151	Lewis	Sarah	1818	Bloomsbury, London	(?)		Aaron Lewis	Euston, London	
29594	Lewis	Sarah	1845	Bath	Jude Lewis	Mary (?)		Whitechapel, London	
20222	Lewis	Sarah	1846	Spitalfields, London	Moses Lewis	Elizabeth Levy		Aldgate, London	
29137	Lewis	Sarah	1850	?, London	Abraham Lewis	Rosalia (?)		Whitechapel, London	
18883	Lewis	Solomon	1800	Whitechapel, London	(?) Lewis	Sarah (?)		Spitalfields, London	clothes dealer
22408	Lewis	Solomon	1810	?, Poland [?, Prussia]	Shalom		Ann Levy	Whitechapel, London	jeweller + general dealer
8757	Lewisohn	Batdiol	1844	Berlin, Germany	Samuel Lewisohn	Helena (?)		Whitechapel, London	scholar
8756	Lewisohn	Helena	1823	Poznan, Poland [Posen, Prussia]	(?)		Samuel Lewisohn	Whitechapel, London	
8759	Lewisohn	Isaiah	1850	Aldgate, London	Samuel Lewisohn	Helena (?)		Whitechapel, London	
8755	Lewisohn	Samuel	1820	?, Germany [?, Prussia]			Helena (?)	Whitechapel, London	tailor
8758	Lewisohn (Levisohn)	Pincus	1848	Aldgate, London	Samuel Lewisohn	Helena (?)		Whitechapel, London	scholar
15157	Lewiston	George	1840	Brighton, Sussex	Henry Lewiston	(?)		Haggerston, London	
15156	Lewiston	Henry	1805	?, Germany			(?)	Haggerston, London	pipe manufacturer
15159	Lewiston	Isaac	1844	?Hoxton, London	Henry Lewiston	(?)		Haggerston, London	
15158	Lewiston	Rachel	1842	?Hoxton, London	Henry Lewiston	(?)		Haggerston, London	scholar
4354	Ley	Isaac	1839	New York, USA				Birmingham	
14184	Leypsiger	Elkan	1833	Poznan, Poland [Posen, Prussia]	Lewin Leypsiger	(?)		Manchester	cap maker
14180	Leypsiger	Lewin	1799	Poznan, Poland [Posen, Prussia]			Rosalia (?)	Manchester	tailor
14182	Leypsiger	Marcus	1829	Poznan, Poland [Posen, Prussia]	Lewin Leypsiger	(?)		Manchester	cap maker
14183	Leypsiger	Moritz	1831	Poznan, Poland [Posen, Prussia]	Lewin Leypsiger	(?)		Manchester	traveller
14181	Leypsiger	Rosalia	1827	Poznan, Poland [Posen, Prussia]	Lewin Leypsiger	(?)		Manchester	dressmaker
21552	Lezard	Charles	1839	Paris, France	Joseph Lezard	Zephirine (?)		Hoxton, London	
6018	Lezard	Edward Joseph	1847	Islington, London	Joseph Lezard	Zephirine (?)	Elizabeth (Lizzie) Lazarus	Hoxton, London	
5800	Lezard	Flavian Ernst	1844	Islington, London	Joseph Lezard	Zephirine (?)	Julia Myers	Hoxton, London	
5819	Lezard	Ida	1841	Whitechapel, London	Joseph Lezard	Zephirine (?)	Hector Inger	Hoxton, London	
5817	Lezard	Joseph	1812	?, Luxembourg			Zephirine (?)	Hoxton, London	dealer in watches
5820	Lezard	Lucy	1843	Islington, London	Joseph Lezard	Zephirine (?)		Hoxton, London	
5818	Lezard	Zephirine	1810	Paris, France	(?)		Joseph Lezard	Hoxton, London	
198	Lialter	Alice (Alcey)	1835	Middlesex, London	Isaac Lialter	Priscilla (Sprinza) Joseph	Moss Levy Jacobs	Aldgate, London	
199	Lialter	Elizabeth (Betsy, Lizzie)	1846	Aldgate, London	Isaac Lialter	Priscilla (Sprinza) Joseph	Henry E Davis	Aldgate, London	
189	Lialter	Elsey (Alcey/Alice)	1768	?	(?) Jacobs (Tedesco)		Uzziel (Josiah) Lialter	Aldgate, London	
190	Lialter	Isaac	1801	City, London	Uzziel (Josiah) Lialter	Elsey (Alcey/Alice) (?)	Priscilla (Sprinza) Joseph	Aldgate, London	master butcher empl 3

ID	surname	given names	born	birthplace	father	mother	spouse 1	1851 residence	1851 occupation
193	Lialter	Isaac	1829	Aldgate, London	Isaac Lialter	Priscilla (Sprinza) Joseph	Laura Isaacs	Aldgate, London	butcher
17792	Lialter	Isaac	1851	Aldgate, London	Isaac Lialter	Laura Isaacs		Aldgate, London	
200	Lialter	Joseph	1842	?Aldgate, London	Isaac Lialter	Priscilla (Sprinza) Joseph	Selina Sarah Solomon	Aldgate, London	scholar
194	Lialter	Laura	1827	City, London	Elias Isaacs	Julia (?)	Isaac Lialter	Aldgate, London	
195	Lialter	Moses Uzziel	1822	?, London	Isaac Lialter			Aldgate, London	butcher
196	Lialter	Priscilla	1831	Aldgate, London	Isaac Lialter	Priscilla (Sprinza) Joseph	John Jacob Moseley	Aldgate, London	
203	Lialter	Priscilla	1850	City, London	Isaac Lialter	Laura Isaacs	Julius Levin	Aldgate, London	
191	Lialter	Priscilla (Sprinza)	1802	Middlesex, London	Reuben Joseph		Isaac Lialter	Aldgate, London	
2654	Libberman	Abraham	1841	?, Poland	Samuel Libberman	Rachel (?)		Glasgow, Scotland	
2653	Libberman	Betsy	1837	?, Poland	Samuel Libberman	Rachel (?)		Glasgow, Scotland	
2651	Libberman	Jacob	1828	?, Poland	Samuel Libberman	Rachel (?)		Glasgow, Scotland	
2652	Libberman	Mary	1834	?, Poland	Samuel Libberman	Rachel (?)		Glasgow, Scotland	
2650	Libberman	Rachel	1803	?, Poland			Samuel Libberman	Glasgow, Scotland	
2649	Libberman	Samuel	1803	?, Poland			Rachel (?)	Glasgow, Scotland	cloth manufacturer
13566	Liberneich	Elizah	1833	?, Poland	Raphael Liberneich	Harriet (?)		Manchester	hawker of watches &c
13565	Liberneich	Harriet	1796	?, Poland	(?)		Raphael Liberneich	Manchester	
13564	Liberneich	Raphael	1793	?, Poland			Harriet (?)	Manchester	hawker of trinkets
22530	Lichtentien	Lipman	1831	Lubeck, Germany				Whitechapel, London	cigar maker
17669	Licoman	Meyer	1795	?, Germany			(?)	Aldgate, London	retired cook
13963	Liebert	Emil	1817	Berlin, Germany				Manchester	twist merchant
2951	Liebreich	Emil (Elias)	1804	Gadebusch Mecklenburg, Germany	Salomon Ephraim Liebreich	Malicha Wolff		Leeds, Yorkshire	wool merchant
2950	Liebreich	James	1797	Gadebusch Mecklenburg, Germany	Salomon Ephraim Liebreich	Malicha Wolff	Susannah Pratt	Leeds, Yorkshire	wool agent
23808	Liebschutz	A---	1826	Poznan, Poland [Posen, Prussia]				Liverpool	jeweller
30919	Liebus	Harris	1831	?, Poland				Sheffield, Yorkshire	shopman (formerly)
30933	Liense	Mary	1831	Ćmielów?, Poland [Culme, Prussia]	(?) Liense			Hull, Yorkshire	general servant
2508	Liepman	Jacob	1834	Hamburg, Germany				Hull, Yorkshire	house servant
13964	Liepman	Julius	1822	Berlin, Germany				Manchester	twist merchant
23806	Lieven	Alfred	1850	Liverpool	Jacob Lieven	Henrietta (?)		Liverpool	
23805	Lieven	Emmeline	1848	Liverpool	Jacob Lieven	Henrietta (?)		Liverpool	
23800	Lieven	Henrietta	1821	Hanover, Germany	(?)		Jacob Lieven	Liverpool	
23804	Lieven	Isidore	1844	Hanover, Germany	Jacob Lieven	Henrietta (?)		Liverpool	
23803	Lieven	Iweyn	1844	Hanover, Germany	Jacob Lieven	Henrietta (?)		Liverpool	
23799	Lieven	Jacob	1812	Kaliningrad, Russia [Konigsberg, Prussia]			Henrietta (?)	Liverpool	jeweller
23801	Lieven	Pauline	1840	Hanover, Germany	Jacob Lieven	Henrietta (?)		Liverpool	
23802	Lieven	Theodore	1842	Hanover, Germany	Jacob Lieven	Henrietta (?)		Liverpool	
4443	Ligt	U K	1806	?, Germany				Birmingham	traveller
2510	Limbach	Ann	1821	Hull, Yorkshire	(?) Bores		Louis Limbach	Hull, Yorkshire	
2511	Limbach	John Leonard	1850	Hull, Yorkshire			Louis Limbach	Hull, Yorkshire	
2509	Limbach	Louis	1824	?, Germany			Ann (?)	Hull, Yorkshire	
30940	Lind	Jenny	1832	Berlin, Germany	(?) Lind			Hull, Yorkshire	tailor

ID	surname	given names	born	birthplace	father	mother	spouse 1	1851 residence	1851 occupation
13919	Linde	David	1828	Hoxton, London				Manchester	manager to tailor + draper
18947	Lindenthal	Deborah	1804	Holborn, London	(?) Lyon		Israel Levy Lindenthal	City, London	Secretary to Synagogue
7155	Lindenthal	Gertrude	1825	Holstein, Germany	Israel Levy Lindenthal	Deborah Lyon	Albert (Abraham) Löwy	City, London	
18948	Lindenthal	Hannah	1839	City, London	Israel Levy Lindenthal	Deborah Lyon		City, London	
18946	Lindenthal	Israel Levy	1796	Brighton, Sussex			Deborah Lyon	City, London	Secretary to Synagogue
7511	Linder	Jacob	1826	?, Hungary				Bristol	officiating Minister of Synagogue
21684	Lindo	Alexander	1814	Kingston, Jamaica, West Indies	Abraham Alexander Lindo	Luna Nunes Henriques		Islington, London	merchant
25171	Lindo	Arthur (Aaron)	1839	?, London	Nathaneel de David Abarbanel Lindo	Sarah de Moses Da Costa Lindo	Sarah Selina Spyer	Finsbury, London	
15272	Lindo	Benjamin	1825	?, London	Benjamin de Moses de Elias Lindo	Rachel de Hananel Mendes Da Costa	Billah Lindo Henry	Shoreditch, London	clerk
21632	Lindo	Charles	1845	?, London	Zachariah (Zachel) Lindo	Isabel Levy	Adeline Heilbut	Holloway, London	
6994	Lindo	Daniel	1816	Whitechapel, London	David Abarbanel Lindo	Sarah de Abraham Mocatta	Hannah Garcia	Shoreditch, London	
6992	Lindo	David Abarbanel	1772	Clapton, London	Elias de Isaac Lindo	Grace de Moseh Lumbroso de Mattos	Sarah de Abraham Mocatta	Whitechapel, London	retired merchant
9453	Lindo	Elias Haim	1784	?, London			Hannah (?)	Aldgate, London	commission agent
15271	Lindo	Emma	1821	Finsbury, London	Benjamin de Moses de Elias Lindo	Rachel de Hananel Mendes Da Costa		Shoreditch, London	
13206	Lindo	Esther	1802	Surrey, London	David Abarbanel Lindo	Sarah de Abraham Mocatta		Whitechapel, London	
9455	Lindo	Grace	1810	St Thomas, Virgin Islands, West Indies	Elias Haim Lindo	Hannah (?)	Julius Isaac Valery	Aldgate, London	
9454	Lindo	Hannah	1785	Curaçao, West Indies	(?)		Elias Haim Lindo	Aldgate, London	
26413	Lindo	Herman	1826	Amsterdam, Holland			Rosa (?)	Aldgate, London	cigar maker
21631	Lindo	Isabel	1824	?, London	Abraham Levy		Zachariah (Zachel) Lindo	Holloway, London	
24187	Lindo	Jacintha	1800	Hackney, London	Isaac Lindo	Esther (Leah) de Abraham del Valle		Hackney, London	fundholder
13209	Lindo	Leah	1821	Middlesex, London	David Abarbanel Lindo	Sarah de Abraham Mocatta		Whitechapel, London	
15270	Lindo	Leonora	1820	Finsbury, London	Benjamin de Moses de Elias Lindo	Rachel de Hananel Mendes Da Costa		Shoreditch, London	
15355	Lindo	Maria	1822	Southwark, London	(?) (?Adolphus)		William Lindo	Waterloo, London	
15357	Lindo	Maria Elizabeth	1847	Strand, London	William Lindo	Maria (?Adolphus)		Waterloo, London	
26415	Lindo	Mariane	1845	Amsterdam, Holland	Herman Lindo	Rosa (?)		Aldgate, London	
13208	Lindo	Miriam	1818	Middlesex, London	David Abarbanel Lindo	Sarah de Abraham Mocatta		Whitechapel, London	
26417	Lindo	Mortzy	1849	Amsterdam, Holland	Herman Lindo	Rosa (?)		Aldgate, London	
25172	Lindo	Moses Da Costa	1784	?, London	Moses de Elias Lindo	Sarah de Moseh Da Costa	Leah de Moses Haim Norsa	Finsbury, London	retired broker
25169	Lindo	Nathaneel	1810	?, London	David Abarbanel Lindo	Sarah de Abraham Mocatta	Sarah de Moses Da Costa Lindo	Finsbury, London	solicitor
9456	Lindo	Rachael	1816	St Thomas, Virgin Islands, West Indies	Elias Haim Lindo	Hannah (?)		Aldgate, London	
15269	Lindo	Rachel	1796	Middlesex, London	Hananel de Isaac Mendes Da Costa	Rachel de Elias Lindo	Benjamin de Moses de Elias Lindo	Shoreditch, London	annuitant
13207	Lindo	Rebecca	1808	Middlesex, London	David Abarbanel Lindo	Sarah de Abraham Mocatta		Whitechapel, London	

ID	surname	given names	born	birthplace	father	mother	spouse 1	1851 residence	1851 occupation
26414	Lindo	Rosa	1822	Amsterdam, Holland	(?)		Herman Lindo	Aldgate, London	
18975	Lindo	Samuel	1805	Middlesex, London				Whitechapel, London	clerk at Atlas office
6996	Lindo	Samuel	1807	Islington, London	David Abarbanel Lindo	Sarah Mocatta	Clare Walter Nathan	Bloomsbury, London	insurance clerk
26416	Lindo	Samuel	1847	Amsterdam, Holland	Herman Lindo	Rosa (?)		Aldgate, London	
6993	Lindo	Sarah	1778	Whitechapel, London	Abraham Mocatta		Sarah de Abraham Mocatta	Whitechapel, London	
25170	Lindo	Sarah	1814	?, London	Moses Da Costa Lindo	Leah (?)	Nathaneel de David Abarbanel Lindo	Finsbury, London	
8065	Lindo	Solomon	1829	?, London	Elias Lindo	Sarah (?)	Saphira Henry	Bloomsbury, London	commercial traveller, foreign + British fancy goods (wine merchant)
15354	Lindo	William	1812	?, West Indies			Maria (?Adolphus)	Waterloo, London	wine cellarman
15356	Lindo	William Adolphus	1846	Strand, London	William Lindo	Maria (?Adolphus)		Waterloo, London	
21630	Lindo	Zachariah (Zachel)	1813	?, London	David de Elisah Abarbanel Lindo	Matilda de Jehiel Prager-Solomons	Isabel Levy	Holloway, London	medical profession not practisig
4695	Lindon	Catherine	1795	?, London			Solomon Lindon	Birmingham	
4694	Lindon	Solomon	1791	?, Poland [?, Russia Poland]			Catherine (?)	Birmingham	clothier
2178	Lindow	Joseph	1834	?, Poland			(?)	Oxford, Oxfordshire	jewellery traveller
3302	Lintine	Morris (Moris)	1836	Birmingham	Meir Lintine	?	Rebecca Jacobs	Birmingham	traveller
15248	Lion	Aaron Ernest	1850	Shoreditch, London	Mayer Alexander Lion	Fanny Salomon		Shoreditch, London	
15240	Lion	Abraham Jacob	1825	Metz, France	Alexander Lion	Fanny (Frances) Lambert	Rachel Myers	Shoreditch, London	shoe manufacturer
12951	Lion	Alexander	1816	Metz, France			Julia (?)	Whitechapel, London	shoe manufacturer
30404	Lion	Alice	1851	Shoreditch, London	Lion Lion	Rosine Jacob (Bing-Jacob)		Shoreditch, London	
15238	Lion	Celestine	1848	Shoreditch, London	Lion Lion	Rosine Jacob (Bing-Jacob)	Armand Levy	Shoreditch, London	
12948	Lion	Emanuel Lambert	1818	Metz, France	Alexander Lion	Fanny (Frances) Lambert	Rosette Medex	Whitechapel, London	shoe manufacturer
15245	Lion	Fanny	1822	?, France	Shmuel Salomon		Mayer Alexander Lion	Shoreditch, London	
30478	Lion	Fanny (Frances)	1783	Metz, France	Simon Lambert	Hannah Bing	Alexander Lion	Whitechapel, London	annuitant
12949	Lion	Hannah	1825	Walworth, London	(?) Jonas		Emanuel Lambert Lion	Whitechapel, London	
15239	Lion	Henriette	1849	Shoreditch, London	Lion Lion	Rosine Jacob (Bing-Jacob)	Hyppolite J Cahen	Shoreditch, London	
15247	Lion	Henry Simon	1849	Shoreditch, London	Mayer Alexander Lion	Fanny Salomon	Mathilda Marks	Shoreditch, London	
12952	Lion	Julia	1823	Dieur, France	(?)		Alexander Lion	Whitechapel, London	shoe manufacturer
15235	Lion	Lion	1817	Metz, France	Alexander Lion	Fanny (Frances) Lambert	Rosine Jacob (Bing-Jacob)	Shoreditch, London	shoe maker
12950	Lion	Maurice	1850	Whitechapel, London	Emanuel Lambert Lion	Hannah Jonas		Whitechapel, London	
15246	Lion	Maurice Michel	1847	Shoreditch, London	Mayer Alexander Lion	Fanny Salomon	Adelaide Lynes	Shoreditch, London	
15244	Lion	Mayer Alexander	1819	Metz, France	Alexander Lion	Fanny (Frances) Lambert	Fanny Salomon	Shoreditch, London	shoe manufacturer
15242	Lion	Michael (Mitchel) Abraham	1850	Shoreditch, London	Abraham Lion	Rachel Myers		Shoreditch, London	
15237	Lion	Michael L	1847	Shoreditch, London	Lion Lion	Rosine Jacob (Bing-Jacob)	Regine Levilion	Shoreditch, London	
15241	Lion	Rachel	1827	Whitechapel, London	Meir Myers	Ellen (?)	Abraham Lion	Shoreditch, London	
15236	Lion	Rosine	1824	Metz, France	Bing (Joseph) Jacob (Bing-Jacob)	Collette Brunswick	Lion Lion	Shoreditch, London	
19074	Lipman	?	1833	?, Scotland	(?) Lipman	Eve (?)		Aldgate, London	jeweller
19076	Lipman	?	1837	?, Scotland	(?) Lipman	Eve (?)		Aldgate, London	
13888	Lipman	Abraham	1807	?, Poland [?, Prussia]			Eliza (?)	Manchester	tailor + draper
9381	Lipman	Adelade	1838	Whitechapel, London	Mark Lipman	Louisa (?)		Spitalfields, London	
19072	Lipman	Amelia	1827	?, Scotland	(?) Lipman	Eve (?)		Aldgate, London	--- teacher
17438	Lipman	Amelia	1834	Aldgate, London	(?) Lipman			Aldgate, London	dress maker

ID	surname	given names	born	birthplace	father	mother	spouse 1	1851 residence	1851 occupation
9218	Lipman	Amelia	1850	Spitalfields, London	Elias Lipman	Hannah Raphael	Joseph Hart	Spitalfields, London	
9135	Lipman	Andrew (Asher) Philip	1769	Aldgate, London			(?)	Whitechapel, London	pencil manufacturer's assistant
9131	Lipman	Andrew Samuel Philips	1841	Whitechapel, London	Lewis Philip Lipman	Ann Moses		Whitechapel, London	scholar
9128	Lipman	Ann	1806	Portsmouth, Hampshire	Andrew (Moshe) Cohen		Lewis Philip Lipman	Whitechapel, London	
14381	Lipman	Annie	1847	Manchester	Michael Lipman	Mary Anne (?)	Julius Heynssen	Manchester	
17581	Lipman	Asher	1848	Whitechapel, London	Henry Lipman	Hannah (?)		Spitalfields, London	
29523	Lipman	Barnet	1831	Aldgate, London				Spitalfields, London	pastry cook
17528	Lipman	Benjamin	1845	Whitechapel, London	Morris Lipman	Rosetta (?)		Spitalfields, London	scholar
21320	Lipman	Bertha	1851	Dundee, Scotland	James Lipman	Ida Rothschild		Dundee, Scotland	
9214	Lipman	Caroline	1841	Spitalfields, London	Elias Lipman	Hannah Raphael	Lewis Lyons	Spitalfields, London	scholar
11549	Lipman	Catharine	1814	Shoreditch, London	(?) Lipman	Sarah (?)		Spitalfields, London	furrier
21319	Lipman	Cecelia	1849	Dundee, Scotland	James Lipman	Ida Rothschild		Dundee, Scotland	
13892	Lipman	Charles	1841	Manchester	Abraham Lipman	Eliza (?)		Manchester	scholar
9212	Lipman	Elias	1811	Aldgate, London	J--- (or I---) Lipman		Hannah Raphael	Spitalfields, London	glass cutter
11464	Lipman	Elias	1837	Aldgate, London	Michael Lipman	Rosy (?)		Aldgate, London	baker
13889	Lipman	Eliza	1815	Manchester	(?)		Abraham Lipman	Manchester	
9134	Lipman	Eliza	1848	Stepney, London	Lewis Philip Lipman	Ann Moses	Sylvester Solomon	Whitechapel, London	
11461	Lipman	Emily (Amelia)	1828	Aldgate, London	Michael Lipman	Rosy (?)		Aldgate, London	parasol maker
11548	Lipman	Esther	1804	Whitechapel, London	(?) Lipman	Sarah (?)		Spitalfields, London	servant
11463	Lipman	Esther	1836	Aldgate, London	Michael Lipman	Rosy (?)		Aldgate, London	servant
7646	Lipman	Eve	1803	?, London			(?) Lipman	Aldgate, London	sponge merchant
26775	Lipman	Fanny	1835	Aldgate, London	Lewis Lipman	Mary (?)		Aldgate, London	
22861	Lipman	Frances	1795	Amsterdam, Holland	Shmuel HaLevi		(?) Davis	Whitechapel, London	
9382	Lipman	Frances	1840	Whitechapel, London	Mark Lipman	Louisa (?)		Spitalfields, London	
9136	Lipman	Frances Phillips	1801	Aldgate, London	Andrew (Asher) Philip Lipman			Whitechapel, London	pencil manufacturer's assistant
13893	Lipman	Frederick	1844	Manchester	Abraham Lipman	Eliza (?)		Manchester	scholar
17579	Lipman	Hannah	1809	Aldgate, London	(?)		Henry Lipman	Spitalfields, London	
9213	Lipman	Hannah	1810	Spitalfields, London	R--- Raphael		Elias Lipman	Spitalfields, London	
14282	Lipman	Harriet	1847	Manchester	(?) Lipman	(?) Braham		Manchester	
267	Lipman	Henry	1808	?, Germany			Hannah (?)	Spitalfields, London	looking glass manufacturer
17439	Lipman	Henry	1838	Aldgate, London	(?) Lipman			Aldgate, London	cigar maker apprentice
9383	Lipman	Henry	1843	Whitechapel, London	Mark Lipman	Louisa (?)		Spitalfields, London	
9132	Lipman	Henry	1844	Stepney, London	Lewis Philip Lipman	Ann Moses		Whitechapel, London	scholar
21318	Lipman	Ida	1825	Hamburg, Germany	(?) Rothschild		James Lipman	Dundee, Scotland	
11467	Lipman	Isaac	1842	Aldgate, London	Michael Lipman	Rosy (?)		Aldgate, London	
16296	Lipman	James	1808	Hamburg, Germany			Ida Rothschild	Dundee, Scotland	linen merchant
9130	Lipman	Jane	1839	Stepney, London	Lewis Philip Lipman	Ann Moses		Whitechapel, London	scholar
13891	Lipman	Jeanette	1840	Manchester	Abraham Lipman	Eliza (?)		Manchester	scholar
11465	Lipman	John	1832	Aldgate, London	Michael Lipman	Rosy (?)		Aldgate, London	baker
11132	Lipman	Jonas	1827	Spitalfields, London			Rachael (?)	Aldgate, London	general dealer
10976	Lipman	Jonas	1831	?, Dorset			(?)	Aldgate, London	journeyman baker

ID	surname	given names	born	birthplace	father	mother	spouse 1	1851 residence	1851 occupation
11332	Lipman	Jonas	1832	Mile End, London				Aldgate, London	baker
22860	Lipman	Joseph	1784	Hanover, Germany	Eliezer HaLevi		Rachel Joseph	Whitechapel, London	umbrella maker
11407	Lipman	Joseph	1828	Aldgate, London	Lewis (Eliezer) Lipman		Julia Lipman	Aldgate, London	coffee house keeper
13890	Lipman	Joseph	1838	Manchester	Abraham Lipman	Eliza (?)	Louisa Solomon	Manchester	scholar
9216	Lipman	Joseph	1845	Spitalfields, London	Elias Lipman	Hannah Raphael		Spitalfields, London	scholar
19073	Lipman	Judah	1829	?, Scotland	(?) Lipman	Eve (?)		Aldgate, London	watch? Maker
24555	Lipman	Julia	1825	Edinburgh, Scotland	(?) Lipman			Brixton, London	resident governess
11408	Lipman	Julia	1829	Aldgate, London	Lewis Lipman	Mary (?)	Joseph Lipman	Aldgate, London	coffee house keeper
13894	Lipman	Kate	1846	Manchester	Abraham Lipman	Eliza (?)		Manchester	at home
252	Lipman	Leah	1840	Shoreditch, London				Spitalfields, London	scholar
26772	Lipman	Lewis	1799	Aldgate, London			Mary (?)	Aldgate, London	victualler + cookshop
9377	Lipman	Lewis	1805	Wapping, London	Phillip Lipman			Spitalfields, London	pencil maker
9127	Lipman	Lewis Philip	1806	Southwark, London	Andrew (Asher) Philip Lipman		Ann Moses	Whitechapel, London	pencil manufacturer empl 2
5602	Lipman	Lionel Philip	1842	Whitechapel, London	Lewis Philip Lipman	Ann Moses	Fanny Silverstone	Whitechapel, London	scholar
28393	Lipman	Lipman	1807	Whitechapel, London			Rachael (?)	Spitalfields, London	general dealer
9380	Lipman	Louisa	1814	Exeter, Devon	(?)		Mark Lipman	Spitalfields, London	furrier
9376	Lipman	Mark	1802	Middlesex, London	Phillip Lipman		Louisia (?)	Spitalfields, London	fur dyer
26773	Lipman	Mary	1791	Aldgate, London	(?)		Lewis Lipman	Aldgate, London	
9571	Lipman	Mary	1799	Spitalfields, London	(?) Solomons		(?) Lipman	Spitalfields, London	tavern keeper (out of business)
11462	Lipman	Mary (Polly)	1831	Aldgate, London	Michael Lipman	Rosy (?)		Aldgate, London	servant
14379	Lipman	Mary Anne	1822	Manchester	(?)		Michael Lipman	Manchester	
9133	Lipman	Maurice	1846	Stepney, London	Lewis Philip Lipman	Ann Moses		Whitechapel, London	scholar
11458	Lipman	Michael	1804	Aldgate, London	Jonah Lipman		Rosy (?)	Aldgate, London	cook
14378	Lipman	Michael	1811	?, Poland [?, Prussia]			Mary Anne (?)	Manchester	tailor + draper
11409	Lipman	Michael	1850	Aldgate, London	Joseph Lipman	Julia (?)		Aldgate, London	
20943	Lipman	Michael	1850	Aldgate, London	Michael Lipman	Rosy (?)		Aldgate, London	
19071	Lipman	Moris	1824	?, Scotland	(?) Lipman	Eve (?)		Aldgate, London	teacher of languages
301	Lipman	Morris	1826	Aldgate, London			Rosetta (?)	Spitalfields, London	general dealer
11293	Lipman	Moses	1821	Aldgate, London	Alexander Lipman		Hannah Hart	Aldgate, London	general dealer
11460	Lipman	Pheobe	1824	Aldgate, London	Michael Lipman	Rosy (?)		Aldgate, London	cap maker
9375	Lipman	Phillip	1769	Middlesex, London				Spitalfields, London	pencil maker
28394	Lipman	Rachael	1821	Whitechapel, London	(?)		Lipman Lipman	Spitalfields, London	
11133	Lipman	Rachael	1828	Aldgate, London	(?)		Jonas Lipman	Aldgate, London	general dealer
19075	Lipman	Rebecca	1835	?, Scotland	(?) Lipman	Eve (?)		Aldgate, London	
14281	Lipman	Rebecca	1845	Manchester	(?) Lipman	(?) Braham		Manchester	scholar
26774	Lipman	Rosa	1832	Aldgate, London	Lewis Lipman	Mary (?)		Aldgate, London	
9217	Lipman	Rose	1847	Spitalfields, London	Elias Lipman	Hannah Raphael		Spitalfields, London	scholar
17527	Lipman	Rosetta	1827	Whitechapel, London	(?)		Morris Lipman	Spitalfields, London	
14380	Lipman	Rosina	1845	Manchester	Michael Lipman	Mary Anne (?)		Manchester	
11459	Lipman	Rosy	1802	Aldgate, London	Samuel (?)		Michael Lipman	Aldgate, London	
17580	Lipman	Samuel	1843	Aldgate, London	Henry Lipman	Hannah (?)		Spitalfields, London	scholar
249	Lipman	Sarah	1771	Shoreditch, London	(?)		(?) Lipman	Spitalfields, London	
10303	Lipman	Sarah	1833	Spitalfields, London	(?) Lipman			Spitalfields, London	general servant

ID	surname	given names	born	birthplace	father	mother	spouse 1	1851 residence	1851 occupation
9129	Lipman	Sarah	1838	Stepney, London	Lewis Philip Lipman	Ann Moses	Aaron A Solomon	Whitechapel, London	scholar
19077	Lipman	Sarah	1839	?, Scotland	(?) Lipman	Eve (?)		Aldgate, London	
11466	Lipman	Sarah	1841	Aldgate, London	Michael Lipman	Rosy (?)		Aldgate, London	
9215	Lipman	Sarah	1843	Spitalfields, London	Elias Lipman	Hannah Raphael		Spitalfields, London	scholar
17529	Lipman	Sarah	1847	Whitechapel, London	Morris Lipman	Rosetta (?)	Moss Isaacs	Spitalfields, London	scholar
11134	Lipman	Sarah	1850	Aldgate, London	Jonas Lipman	Racheal (?)		Aldgate, London	
10290	Lipman	Solomon	1831	?, Poland [?, Prussia]				Spitalfields, London	tailor
4701	Lipmann	Hanna	1843	King's Lynn, Norfolk	Isaac Lipmann	Hannah (?)		Birmingham	
4697	Lipmann	Hannah	1811	?, Germany			Isaac Lipmann	Birmingham	
4696	Lipmann	Isaac	1809	?, Germany			Hannah (?)	Birmingham	tailor
4698	Lipmann	Isaac	1835	?, Germany	Isaac Lipmann	Hannah (?)		Birmingham	
4699	Lipmann	Myer	1842	Norwich, Norfolk	Isaac Lipmann	Hannah (?)		Birmingham	
4700	Lipmann	Rachel	1846	Birmingham	Isaac Lipmann	Hannah (?)		Birmingham	
4702	Lipmann	Sarah	1849	Birmingham	Isaac Lipmann	Hannah (?)		Birmingham	
4703	Lipmann	Simon	1850	Birmingham	Isaac Lipmann	Hannah (?)		Birmingham	
6358	Lippschutz	Amelia	1821	Spitalfields, London	Israel Lippscutz	Harriet (?)	Samuel Cohen	Bloomsbury, London	ccok
26256	Lippschutz	Harriet	1789	?, Holland			Israel Lippschutz	Aldgate, London	
18407	Lippschutz	Israel	1786	?, Germany			Harriet (?)	Aldgate, London	general dealer
12995	Lipschitz	Lazarus	1832	Warsaw, Poland	Yehoshe		Rebecca (?)	Aldgate, London	tailor
12996	Lipschitz	Rebecca	1830	Warsaw, Poland	(?)		Lazarus Lipschitz	Aldgate, London	
18408	Lipshitz	Angel	1791	?, Holland				Aldgate, London	
17087	Lissack	Deborah	1844	Bedford, Bedfordshire	Moses (Morris) Lissack	Hannah (?)	Wolf Cohen	Bedford, Bedfordshire	
17086	Lissack	Elizabeth	1842	Bedford, Bedfordshire	Moses (Morris) Lissack	Hannah (?)	Judah Hatchwell	Bedford, Bedfordshire	
17084	Lissack	Hannah	1814	Bedford, Bedfordshire	(?)		Moses (Morris) Lissack	Bedford, Bedfordshire	
17085	Lissack	Joel	1841	Bedford, Bedfordshire	Moses (Morris) Lissack	Hannah (?)		Bedford, Bedfordshire	
17088	Lissack	Miriam	1847	Bedford, Bedfordshire	Moses (Morris) Lissack	Hannah (?)		Bedford, Bedfordshire	
7452	Lissack	Moses (Morris)	1814	Poznan, Poland [Posen, Prussia]			Hannah (?)	Bedford, Bedfordshire	Professor of German
12728	Lissaman	Abraham	1850	Coventry, Warwickshire	David Lissaman	Mary Ann (?)		Coventry, Warwickshire	
12725	Lissaman	David	1818	Coventry, Warwickshire			Mary Ann (?)	Coventry, Warwickshire	ribbon weaver
12727	Lissaman	David	1848	Coventry, Warwickshire	David Lissaman	Mary Ann (?)		Coventry, Warwickshire	
12726	Lissaman	Mary Ann	1821	Coventry, Warwickshire	(?)		David Lissaman	Coventry, Warwickshire	ribbon weaver
26318	Livingstone	Esther	1801	?, Poland	(?)		Moses Livingstone	Aldgate, London	cap maker
26320	Livingstone	Hannah	1834	?, Poland	Moses Livingstone	Esther (?)		Aldgate, London	necklace maker
26317	Livingstone	Moses	1806	?, Poland			Esther (?)	Aldgate, London	dealer
26319	Livingstone	Rachael	1831	?, Poland	Moses Livingstone	Esther (?)		Aldgate, London	cap maker
15994	Livy	Elizabeth	1827	?, London	(?) Livy (?Levy)			St John's Wood, London	cook
18053	Lixton	David	1827	?, Poland				Dudley, Worcestershire	glazier
23601	Lizle	Sim	1833	?, Poland				Liverpool	glazier's jobbing
27419	Lodeman	Isaac	1791	?, Poland [?, Prussia]				Whitechapel, London	wool dealer
29143	Loewe	Benjamin Daniel	1807	?, Germany	Daniel Benjamin Loewe	Sipora (?)	Rose Simmons	Whitechapel, London	
29138	Loewe	Daniel Benjamin	1774	Emden, Hanover, Germany			Sipora (?)	Whitechapel, London	formerly a dealer
29142	Loewe	Daniel Benjamin	1848	Whitechapel, London	Benjamin Daniel Loewe	Rose Simmons		Whitechapel, London	
7159	Loewe	Emma	1824	?, Poland [?, Prussia]	(?)		Louis Loewe	Brighton, Sussex	
29140	Loewe	Jacob Daniel	1825	Aldgate, London	Daniel Benjamin Loewe	Sipora (?)		Whitechapel, London	journeyman cigar maker

ID	surname	given names	born	birthplace	father	mother	spouse 1	1851 residence	1851 occupation
16835	Loewe	Jessie	1850	Brighton, Sussex	Louis Loewe	Emma (?)	Adolf Kurrein	Brighton, Sussex	
29141	Loewe	Levy Benjamin	1845	Whitechapel, London	Benjamin Daniel Loewe	Rose Simmons		Whitechapel, London	
7158	Loewe	Louis	1809	?Poland [Zulz, Silesia]			Emma (?)	Brighton, Sussex	Doctor of Philiosophy and schoolmaster
16833	Loewe	Martin	1845	Whitechapel, London	Louis Loewe	Emma (?)		Brighton, Sussex	scholar
14672	Loewe	Oscar	1830	?, Germany [?, Prussia, Germany]				Hoxton, London	journeyman watchmaker
16834	Loewe	Philip	1847	Whitechapel, London	Louis Loewe	Emma (?)		Brighton, Sussex	
29144	Loewe	Rose	1814	Aldgate, London	Levi Simmons		Benjamin Daniel Loewe	Whitechapel, London	
29139	Loewe	Sipora	1784	Amsterdam, Holland	(?)		Daniel Benjamin Loewe	Whitechapel, London	
7157	Loewenthal	Johann (Janos) Jacob (Jakab)	1810	Budapest, Hungary				?, London	chess player
9331	Lombrozo	Luna	1793	Aldgate, London	Moses de Abraham Hassan	Esther de Joshua Alevy	Daniel Lumbrozo Nunes	Aldgate, London	charwoman
4044	Lopez	Isaac	1817	Paris, France	Samuel Lopez		Leah Leavy	Whitechapel, London	costermonger
4046	Lopez	Isaac	1840	Whitechapel, London	Isaac Lopez	Leah Leavy	Elizabeth Morris	Whitechapel, London	scholar
4045	Lopez	Leah	1819	Whitechapel, London	Isaac Leavy		Isaac Lopez	Whitechapel, London	furrier
4048	Lopez	Matilda (Miriam, Amelia)	1843	Whitechapel, London	Isaac Lopez	Leah Leavy	John Cuthbert	Whitechapel, London	scholar
29214	Lopez	Samuel John	1838	Whitechapel, London	Isaac Lopez	Leah Leavy	Sarah Anne Stanton	Whitechapel, London	scholar
5689	Lotinga	Aaron (Arend) Assur	1834	Groningen, Holland	Asser Moses Lotinga	Rachel Abrahams Hoffman	Leah Newman	Sunderland, Co Durham	
5684	Lotinga	Abraham	1828	Groningen, Holland	Asser Moses Lotinga	Rachel Abrahams Hoffman		Sunderland, Co Durham	
8292	Lotinga	Abraham	1846	?, Holland	Calmer Moses Lotinga	Caroline Susanna Hoffman	Fanny Cohen	North Shields, Tyne & Wear	
8285	Lotinga	Alida (Aaltje)	1791	Groningen, Holland	Meijer Joseph Cohen	Sara Izaaks Engers	Samuel Moses Lotinga	North Shields, Tyne & Wear	ship broker's wife
8282	Lotinga	Alida Martha	1849	North Shields, Tyne & Wear	Noah (Noack) Samuel Lotinga	Mary Giller		North Shields, Tyne & Wear	
5685	Lotinga	Anna	1834	Groningen, Holland	Asser Moses Lotinga	Rachel Abrahams Hoffman		Sunderland, Co Durham	
5682	Lotinga	Asser Moses	1805	Groningen, Holland	Mozes Noachs Levi	Sara Salomons	Rachel Abrahams Hoffman	Sunderland, Co Durham	general merchant
8287	Lotinga	Calmer Moses	1808	Groningen, Holland	Mozes Noachs Lotinga	Sara Kalmer	Caroline Susanna Hoffman	North Shields, Tyne & Wear	ship broker + agent
8288	Lotinga	Caroline Susanna	1814	Hanover, Germany	(?) Hoffman		Calmer Moses Lotinga	North Shields, Tyne & Wear	
5686	Lotinga	Isaac Asser	1837	Groningen, Holland	Asser Moses Lotinga	Rachel Abrahams Hoffman	Leah Newmann	Sunderland, Co Durham	
8280	Lotinga	Mary	1826	Bristol	(?) Giller		Noah (Noack) Samuel Lotinga	North Shields, Tyne & Wear	
8338	Lotinga	Meyer Frederick Noah	1851	North Shields, Tyne & Wear	Noah (Noack) Samuel Lotinga	Mary Giller		North Shields, Tyne & Wear	
8289	Lotinga	Moses Noach	1840	Groningen, Holland	Calmer Moses Lotinga	Caroline Susanna Hoffman	Sarah Harris	North Shields, Tyne & Wear	scholar
8279	Lotinga	Noah (Noack) Samuel	1819	Groningen, Holland	Samuel Moses Lotinga	Alida (Aaltje) Meijers Cohen	Mary Giller	North Shields, Tyne & Wear	ship + insurance broker
5683	Lotinga	Rachel	1802	Hanover, Germany	Abraham Hartog Hoffman	Röschen Aarons	Asser Moses Lotinga	Sunderland, Co Durham	
8293	Lotinga	Rachel	1849	South Shields, Tyne & Wear	Calmer Moses Lotinga	Caroline Susanna Hoffman		North Shields, Tyne & Wear	

ID	surname	given names	born	birthplace	father	mother	spouse 1	1851 residence	1851 occupation
8290	Lotinga	Rosetta	1842	?, Holland	Calmer Moses Lotinga	Caroline Susanna Hoffman		North Shields, Tyne & Wear	scholar
5687	Lotinga	Rosetta (Rose, Roosje))	1840	Groningen, Holland	Asser Moses Lotinga	Rachel Abrahams Hoffman	Adolph Cohen	Sunderland, Co Durham	
8294	Lotinga	Samuel	1851	North Shields, Tyne & Wear	Calmer Moses Lotinga	Caroline Susanna Hoffman		North Shields, Tyne & Wear	
8284	Lotinga	Samuel Moses	1790	Hanover, Germany	Mozes Noachs Levi	Sara Salomons	Alida (Aaltje) Meijers Cohen	North Shields, Tyne & Wear	ship broker
8281	Lotinga	Samuel Noah	1848	Cardiff, Wales	Noah (Noack) Samuel Lotinga	Mary Giller	Jane Hannah Workman	North Shields, Tyne & Wear	
8286	Lotinga	Sarah	1821	Groningen, Holland	Samuel Moses Lotinga	Alida (Aaltje) Meijers Cohen		North Shields, Tyne & Wear	
5688	Lotinga	Sarah	1843	Sunderland, Co Durham	Asser Moses Lotinga	Rachel Abrahams Hoffman	Jules Mason	Sunderland, Co Durham	
8291	Lotinga	Sarah	1844	?, Holland	Calmer Moses Lotinga	Caroline Susanna Hoffman		North Shields, Tyne & Wear	scholar
20903	Louis	Adolphus	1837	Hamburg, Germany			Annie Phillips	Liverpool	servant
27377	Louis	Alexander	1820	?, Poland [?, Prussia]				Aldgate, London	sponge dealer
14038	Louis	Alfred	1843	Salford, Lancashire	Levi Louis	Elizabeth (?)		Manchester	
7156	Louis	Alfred Hyman	1829	Birmingham	Hyman Tobias Louis		Emma Cunnington	?, London	barrister
14039	Louis	Celicia	1844	Manchester	Levi Louis	Elizabeth (?)		Manchester	
14041	Louis	Elain	1849	Manchester	Levi Louis	Elizabeth (?)		Manchester	
14032	Louis	Elizabeth	1807	Salford, Lancashire	(?)		Levi Louis	Manchester	
14037	Louis	Emily	1840	Salford, Lancashire	Levi Louis	Elizabeth (?)		Manchester	
14035	Louis	Frederick	1836	Salford, Lancashire	Levi Louis	Elizabeth (?)		Manchester	
14040	Louis	George	1847	Manchester	Levi Louis	Elizabeth (?)		Manchester	
14033	Louis	Gustavus	1829	Manchester	Levi Louis	Elizabeth (?)		Manchester	shipping merchant
17328	Louis	Joseph	1812	?, Poland				Mile End, London	lithography writer
14031	Louis	Levi	1802	Hanover, Germany			Elizabeth (?)	Manchester	shipping merchant
14036	Louis	Mary E	1838	Salford, Lancashire	Levi Louis	Elizabeth (?)		Manchester	
16395	Louis	Sarah	1811	City, London	(?)		(?) Louis	Aldgate, London	general servant
14034	Louis	Sarah	1831	Manchester	Levi Louis	Elizabeth (?)		Manchester	
18452	Louisson (Lewisson)	Alfred	1832	Whitechapel, London	George Melville Louisson (Lewisson)	Julia Pyke		Whitechapel, London	shipping agents clerk
18454	Louisson (Lewisson)	Caroline	1836	Whitechapel, London	George Melville Louisson (Lewisson)	Julia Pyke		Whitechapel, London	purse maker
18455	Louisson (Lewisson)	Cecil	1837	Whitechapel, London	George Melville Louisson (Lewisson)	Julia Pyke	Elizabeth Jacobs	Whitechapel, London	cigar maker apprentice
18456	Louisson (Lewisson)	Charles	1840	Whitechapel, London	George Melville Louisson (Lewisson)	Julia Pyke	H--- Harris	Whitechapel, London	scholar
18453	Louisson (Lewisson)	David	1834	Whitechapel, London	George Melville Louisson (Lewisson)	Julia Pyke		Whitechapel, London	painter
18451	Louisson (Lewisson)	Flora	1831	Whitechapel, London	George Melville Louisson (Lewisson)	Julia Pyke		Whitechapel, London	dressmaker
18446	Louisson (Lewisson)	Frederick Lewis	1838	Whitechapel, London	George Melville Louisson (Lewisson)	Julia Pyke	Annie (Hannah) Isaacs	Whitechapel, London	

ID	surname	given names	born	birthplace	father	mother	spouse 1	1851 residence	1851 occupation
18447	Louisson (Lewisson)	George Melville	1801	Portsmouth, Hampshire	Joel Isaac		Julia Pyke	Whitechapel, London	umbrella maker
18448	Louisson (Lewisson)	Julia	1802	Whitechapel, London	Eliezer Lezer Pyke		George Melville Louisson (Lewisson)	Whitechapel, London	
18458	Louisson (Lewisson)	Julia Georgina	1845	Whitechapel, London	George Melville Louisson (Lewisson)	Julia Pyke	Edward Ely Levy	Whitechapel, London	scholar
18450	Louisson (Lewisson)	Phoebe	1829	Whitechapel, London	George Melville Louisson (Lewisson)	Julia Pyke		Whitechapel, London	dressmaker
18449	Louisson (Lewisson)	Sarah	1828	Whitechapel, London	George Melville Louisson (Lewisson)	Julia Pyke	Abraham Symmons	Whitechapel, London	dressmaker
18457	Louisson (Lewisson)	Sophia	1843	Whitechapel, London	George Melville Louisson (Lewisson)	Julia Pyke	David Davis	Whitechapel, London	scholar
18613	Lousada	John B	1810	Shoreditch, London			Tryphena (?)	Winchester, Hampshire	
8414	Lousada	Mary J	1836	Bath	(?) Lousada			Ryde, Isle of Wight	scholar
24046	Lousada	Rebecca	1773	Twickenham, Middlesex	(?)		(?) Lousada	Marylebone, London	fundholder
23025	Lowe	Joseph	1830	?, Poland				City, London	stationer
23807	Lowenberg	J---	1823	Kaliningrad, Russia [Konigsberg, Prussia]				Liverpool	auctioneer
12335	Lowenstark (Loewenstark)	Abraham David	1818	Cracow, Poland	Simon (Sampson) Lowenstark (Loewenstark)	Esther (?)	Sarah (?)	Strand, London	working jeweller
12340	Lowenstark (Loewenstark)	Ezekiel	1824	Cracow, Poland	Simon (Sampson) Lowenstark (Loewenstark)	Esther (?)	Rachel Abrahams	Whitechapel, London	teacher of languages
12338	Lowenstark (Loewenstark)	Ezekiel	1846	?, London	Abraham David Lowenstark (Loewenstark)	Sarah (?)		Strand, London	
12339	Lowenstark (Loewenstark)	Marcus David	1850	Strand, London	Abraham David Lowenstark (Loewenstark)	Sarah (?)	Marian Samuel	Strand, London	
12337	Lowenstark (Loewenstark)	Meyer Abraham	1845	St Giles, London	Abraham David Lowenstark (Loewenstark)	Sarah (?)		Strand, London	
12336	Lowenstark (Loewenstark)	Sarah	1819	Middlesex, London	(?)		Abraham David Lowenstark (Loewenstark)	Strand, London	
12341	Lowenstark (Loewenstark)	Solomon	1821	Cracow, Poland	Simon (Sampson) Lowenstark (Loewenstark)	Esther (?)	Jane (?)	Whitechapel, London	watchmaker
5077	Lowenstein	Susan A	1830	Denham, ?Buckinghamshire				Portsmouth, Hampshire	
23092	Lowenthal	Abraham	1817	Aschaffenberg, Germany				Aldgate, London	tailor
31072	Lowenthal	Adele	1841	Hamburg, Germany	Louis Lowenthal	Ida (?)		Huddersfield, Yorkshire	
31070	Lowenthal	Ida	1814	Hamburg, Germany	(?)		Louis Lowenthal	Huddersfield, Yorkshire	
31074	Lowenthal	Joseph	1819	Mecklenburg, Germany				Huddersfield, Yorkshire	wool merchant
31069	Lowenthal	Louis	1806	Mecklenburg, Germany			Ida (?)	Huddersfield, Yorkshire	wool merchant
31073	Lowenthal	Maria	1848	Hamburg, Germany	Louis Lowenthal	Ida (?)		Huddersfield, Yorkshire	
31071	Lowenthal	Robert	1840	Hamburg, Germany	Louis Lowenthal	Ida (?)		Huddersfield, Yorkshire	scholar
2953	Lowenthall	Betty	1834	Hanover, Germany	Moses Moses		Hyman Lowenthall	Swansea, Wales	
2954	Lowenthall	Hyman	1827	?, Poland	Myer Lowenthall		Betty Moses	Swansea, Wales	Minister of the Hebrew Congregation
14293	Lowig	Fanny	1823	Hamburg, Germany	(?) Lowig			Manchester	professor of music
14292	Lowig	Mark	1824	Hamburg, Germany				Manchester	commission merchant - cotton goods

ID	surname	given names	born	birthplace	father	mother	spouse 1	1851 residence	1851 occupation
30174	Lowthrine	Isaac	1827	?, Germany				Dudley, Worcestershire	pawnbroker
7154	Löwy	Albert (Abraham)	1816	?, Czech Republic [Aussee, Moravia]	Leopold Löwy	Katty (?)	Gertrude Levy Lindenthal	Marylebone, London	Minister of the west London Synagogue
28701	Lubenston	Caroline	1850	?, France	Joseph Lubenston	Debera (?)		Spitalfields, London	
28698	Lubenston	Debera	1823	Poznan, Poland [Posen, Prussia]			Joseph Lubenston	Spitalfields, London	
28700	Lubenston	Elizabeth	1849	Whitechapel, London	Joseph Lubenston	Debera (?)		Spitalfields, London	
28697	Lubenston	Joseph	1821	Berlin, Germany			Debera (?)	Spitalfields, London	furrier
28699	Lubenston	Julious	1845	?, Germany	Joseph Lubenston	Debera (?)		Spitalfields, London	
8815	Luberliner	Hannah	1845	?, Poland [?, Prussia]	Loebel Luberliner	Rebecca (?)		Aldgate, London	
8816	Luberliner	Henry	1850	Aldgate, London	Loebel Luberliner	Rebecca (?)		Aldgate, London	
8813	Luberliner	Loebel	1820	?, Poland [?, Prussia]			Rebecca (?)	Aldgate, London	tailor
8817	Luberliner	Morris	1834	?, Poland [?, Prussia]	(?) Luberliner			Aldgate, London	tailor
8814	Luberliner	Rebecca	1821	?, Poland [?, Prussia]	(?)		Loebel Luberliner	Aldgate, London	
879	Lucas	Abigail	1843	Manchester	Philip Lucas	Juliana Gompertz	Edward Behrens	Manchester	
886	Lucas	Agnes Charlotte	1849	Manchester	Philip Lucas	Juliana Gompertz	David Quixano Henriques	Manchester	
880	Lucas	Alice Rose	1848	Manchester	Philip Lucas	Juliana Gompertz	Alfred Gutteres Henriques	Manchester	
881	Lucas	Amelia R	1846	Lincoln, Lincolnshire	Philip Lucas	Juliana Gompertz	Louis Davidson	Manchester	
16339	Lucas	Arthur	1846	?, London	Lewis (William Jeremiah Louis) Lucas	Frances Cohen		Hyde Park, London	
7153	Lucas	Edward	1841	Finsbury, London	Lewis (William Jeremiah Louis) Lucas	Frances Cohen	Laura M Salomons	Hyde Park, London	
7854	Lucas	Esther (Frances)	1802	?, London	(?) Louis		Lewis (William Jeremiah Louis) Lucas	Hyde Park, London	
7151	Lucas	Francis (Frank) Alfred	1850	Bayswater, London	Sampson Lucas	Lydia Davidson		Bayswater, London	
7103	Lucas	Henry	1843	Finsbury, London	Lewis (William Jeremiah Louis) Lucas	Frances Cohen	Alice Julia Montefiore	Hyde Park, London	
7148	Lucas	Horatio Joseph	1839	Shoreditch, London	Lewis (William Jeremiah Louis) Lucas	Frances Cohen	Isabel Olga D'Avigdor	Hyde Park, London	scholar
19176	Lucas	Jessie	1851	Bayswater, London	Sampson Lucas	Lydia Davidson		Bayswater, London	
877	Lucas	Juliana	1815	Kennington, London	Benjamin Gompertz	Abigail Montefiore	Philip Lucas	Manchester	
7152	Lucas	Lewis (William Jeremiah Louis)	1791	Kingston, Jamaica, West Indies	Samson Lucas		Esther Louis	Hyde Park, London	merchant general
7852	Lucas	Lionel	1822	Shoreditch, London	Lewis (William Jeremiah Louis) Lucas	Frances Cohen	Helen Goldsmid	Hyde Park, London	
883	Lucas	Louis Arthur	1851	Manchester	Philip Lucas	Juliana Gompertz		Manchester	
7150	Lucas	Lydia	1828	?, London	(?) Davidson		Sampson Lucas	Bayswater, London	
16338	Lucas	Matilda	1828	Shoreditch, London	Lewis (William Jeremiah Louis) Lucas	Frances Cohen		Hyde Park, London	
878	Lucas	Philip	1797	Kingston, Jamaica, West Indies	Sampson Lucas		Juliana Gompertz	Manchester	cotton merchant + city councillor
7853	Lucas	Philip	1824	Shoreditch, London	Lewis (William Jeremiah Louis) Lucas	Frances Cohen	Ada (Meshoda) Abecasis	Hyde Park, London	
16337	Lucas	Rebecca	1826	Shoreditch, London	Lewis (William Jeremiah Louis) Lucas	Frances Cohen		Hyde Park, London	

ID	surname	given names	born	birthplace	father	mother	spouse 1	1851 residence	1851 occupation
882	Lucas	Rebecca	1840	Manchester	Philip Lucas	Juliana Gompertz	Nathaniel Benjamin Cohen	Manchester	
7149	Lucas	Sampson	1821	Shoreditch, London	Lewis (William Jeremiah Louis) Lucas	Frances Cohen	Lydia Davidson	Bayswater, London	merchant general
13616	Luckman	Samuel	1818	?, Poland [?, Prussia]				Manchester	tailor
18163	Lupino	Raphael	1781	Livorno, Italy [Leghorn, Italy]			(?)	Mile End, London	patient in the Portuguese Jews Hospital
16478	Luria	Bella	1787	?, London	(?) Delare		Abraham Luria	Mile End, London	annuitant
16480	Luria	Esther	1815	Barbados, West Indies	Abraham Luria	Bella Delare		Mile End, London	
16479	Luria	Sarah Hannah	1812	Barbados, West Indies	Abraham Luria	Bella Delare		Mile End, London	
7917	Lutomirski	Isidor	1822	?, Poland [?, Prussia]				Marylebone, London	Professor of languages + author
27011	Lutto	Elizabeth	1845	Aldgate, London	Joseph Lutto	Rachael Solomons		Aldgate, London	
27012	Lutto	Hannah	1845	Aldgate, London	Joseph Lutto	Rachael Solomons		Aldgate, London	
27013	Lutto	Isaac	1847	Aldgate, London	Joseph Lutto	Rachael Solomons		Aldgate, London	
27010	Lutto	Sarah	1844	Aldgate, London	Joseph Lutto	Rachael Solomons	Phillip Brenner	Aldgate, London	
29608	Lynes	Abraham	1824	Whitechapel, London			Esther (?)	Aldgate, London	tailor
29609	Lynes	Esther	1817	Whitechapel, London	(?)		Abraham Lynes	Aldgate, London	
29610	Lynes	Solomon	1850	Aldgate, London	Abraham Lynes	Esther (?)		Aldgate, London	
13228	Lyon	Abigail	1823	?, Holland	(?)		(?) Lyon	Spitalfields, London	mangler
4710	Lyon	Abraham	1785	?, Sweden				Birmingham	calico printer
5078	Lyon	Abraham	1785	?, London			Martha (?)	Portsmouth, Hampshire	tailor
15549	Lyon	Abraham	1791	Aldgate, London	Michael Lyon	Sarah (?)	Esther Hart	Covent Garden, London	general dealer
4704	Lyon	Abraham	1819	Slurzewo(?), Poland			Ester (?)	Birmingham	tailor
2964	Lyon	Amelia	1848	City, London	David Lyon	Hannah (?)		Spitalfields, London	
18096	Lyon	Ann	1829	Clerkenwell, London	Lewis Lyon	Mary (?)		Holborn, London	artificial flower maker
4706	Lyon	Anne	1841	?, Poland	Abraham Lyon	Ester (?)		Birmingham	
2915	Lyon	Annie	1851	Islington, London	Hart Lyon	Sarah Miriam Mendes da Costa		Islington, London	
3096	Lyon	Barnett	1840	Whitechapel, London				Spitalfields, London	scholar
2960	Lyon	Benjaman	1842	City, London	David Lyon	Hannah (?)		Spitalfields, London	
11119	Lyon	Catherine	1804	Aldgate, London	Moss Lyon	Rachel (?)		Aldgate, London	
18098	Lyon	Catherine	1833	Finsbury, London	Lewis Lyon	Mary (?)		Holborn, London	
30319	Lyon	Charles James	1826	Whitechapel, London	James (Jacob) Walter Lyon	Louisa Hart		Edinburgh, Scotland	
2958	Lyon	David	1816	City, London			Hannah (?)	Spitalfields, London	tailor
14103	Lyon	Dinah	1843	Shoreditch, London	Isaac Lyon	Rosetta (?)		Manchester	scholar
4707	Lyon	Dora	1845	?, Poland	Abraham Lyon	Ester (?)		Birmingham	
1334	Lyon	Eliza	1832	Plymouth, Devon	Solomon Lyon	Rose Solomon	John Laziam	Plymouth, Devon	pawnbroker's assistant
30694	Lyon	Elizabeth	1806	Westminster, London	Joseph Lyon	Sarah (?)		Stoke Newington, London	
2961	Lyon	Elizabeth	1844	City, London	David Lyon	Hannah (?)		Spitalfields, London	
18101	Lyon	Elizabeth	1845	Holborn, London	Lewis Lyon	Mary (?)	Joseph Samuel	Holborn, London	scholar
3019	Lyon	Ellen	1830	?, Ireland				Spitalfields, London	general servant
15552	Lyon	Emanuel	1834	Covent Garden, London	Abraham Lyon	Esther Hart		Covent Garden, London	servant
5082	Lyon	Emma	1829	Portsmouth, Hampshire	Abraham Lyon	Martha		Portsmouth, Hampshire	dressmaker
18100	Lyon	Emma	1840	Holborn, London	Lewis Lyon	Mary (?)		Holborn, London	scholar
4705	Lyon	Ester	1821	?, Poland			Abraham Lyon	Birmingham	

ID	surname	given names	born	birthplace	father	mother	spouse 1	1851 residence	1851 occupation
15550	Lyon	Esther	1793	City, London	Tsevi Hirsh Hart		Abraham Lyon	Covent Garden, London	
20227	Lyon	Esther	1800	?				Liverpool	
3021	Lyon	Esther	1824	Spitalfields, London	(?) Lyon	Hannah (?)		Spitalfields, London	charwoman
2913	Lyon	Esther	1841	City, London	Hart Lyon	Sarah Miriam Mendes da Costa		Hackney, London	scholar
15902	Lyon	Esther	1842	Middlesex, London	(?) Lyon			Hackney, London	boarding school pupil
11118	Lyon	Eve	1797	Aldgate, London	(?) Lyon			Aldgate, London	dealer in wardrobes
1281	Lyon	Fanny	1797	Bideford, Devon	Francis Lyon	Sarah Woolfe		Plymouth, Devon	bonnet maker
1280	Lyon	Fanny	1803	Swansea, Wales			Judah Lyon	Plymouth, Devon	
14096	Lyon	Fanny	1813	Aldgate, London	Daniel Baruch		Isaac Lyon	Marylebone, London	
13229	Lyon	Gabriel	1846	Whitechapel, London	(?) Lyon	Abigail (?)		Spitalfields, London	
5081	Lyon	George L	1829	Portsmouth, Hampshire	Abraham Lyon	Martha (?)		Portsmouth, Hampshire	newspaper reporter
3020	Lyon	Hannah	1787	Whitechapel, London				Spitalfields, London	dealer in clothes
29612	Lyon	Hannah	1798	Aldgate, London	(?)		(?) Lyon	Aldgate, London	
2957	Lyon	Hannah	1815	City, London			David Lyon	Spitalfields, London	
23734	Lyon	Hannah	1826	Liverpool	(?) Lyon			Liverpool	
15555	Lyon	Hannah	1842	Covent Garden, London	Abraham Lyon	Esther Hart		Covent Garden, London	scholar
6574	Lyon	Harriette Hinda	1850	St Giles, London	Samuel Lyon		Abraham Abrahams	St Giles, London	
156	Lyon	Hart	1794	Cambridge	Solomon Lyon	Rachel Hart	Sarah Miriam Mendes da Costa	Islington, London	
12669	Lyon	Henry	1841	?, Germany				Birmingham	
2912	Lyon	Henry	1848	Aldgate, London	Hart Lyon	Sarah Miriam Mendes da Costa	Edith Jane Elizabeth (?)	Islington, London	
5083	Lyon	Henry	1850	Portsmouth, Hampshire	(?) Lyon			Portsmouth, Hampshire	
14097	Lyon	Henry Isaac	1836	Aldgate, London	Isaac Lyon	Fanny Baruch		Marylebone, London	shopman to grocer
14107	Lyon	Henry R	1850	Manchester	Isaac Lyon	Rosetta (?)		Manchester	
7506	Lyon	Isaac	1803	Aldgate, London	Yehuda Leib		Fanny Baruch	Marylebone, London	wine seller + oil + Italian warehouse + butterman
16515	Lyon	Isaac	1804	St Giles, London			Sarah (?)	Clerkenwell, London	artificial florist
14101	Lyon	Isaac	1809	Middlesex, London	Woolf Lyon	Dinah Isaacs	Rosetta Mordecai	Manchester	artificial flower maker (empl 20)
30322	Lyon	Isidor Bernadotte	1839	Edinburgh, Scotland	James (Jacob) Walter Lyon	Louisa Hart		Edinburgh, Scotland	
30316	Lyon	James (Jacob) Walter	1801	Cambridge, Cambridgeshire	Solomon Lyon	Rachel Hart	Louisa Hart	Edinburgh, Scotland	stock + bill broker
18949	Lyon	Jane	1821	City, London	(?) Lyon			City, London	
5080	Lyon	Jochabed	1827	?, London	Abraham Lyon	Martha (?)		Portsmouth, Hampshire	dressmaker
15553	Lyon	John	1838	Covent Garden, London	Abraham Lyon	Esther Hart		Covent Garden, London	cigar maker
2064	Lyon	Joseph	1767	Kunreuth, Germany				Aldgate, London	formerly a jeweller - supported by friends
20225	Lyon	Joseph	1771	City, London			Sarah (?)	Stoke Newington, London	retired [?coal dealer]
3022	Lyon	Joseph	1826	Spitalfields, London	Lyon	Hannah (?)		Spitalfields, London	general dealer
15554	Lyon	Joseph	1840	Covent Garden, London	Abraham Lyon	Esther Hart		Covent Garden, London	scholar
1279	Lyon	Judah (Jacob Pesach)	1794	Bideford, Devon	Francis Lyon	Sarah Woolfe	Fanny (?)	Plymouth, Devon	watchmaker + jeweller
1282	Lyon	Judah Solomon	1827	Plymouth, Devon	Solomon Lyon	Fanny Lazarus	Kate Levi	Plymouth, Devon	wholesale traveller

ID	surname	given names	born	birthplace	father	mother	spouse 1	1851 residence	1851 occupation
29614	Lyon	Julia	1831	Finsbury, London	(?) Lyon	Hannah (?)		Aldgate, London	dressmaker
2959	Lyon	Julia	1839	City, London	David Lyon	Hannah (?)		Spitalfields, London	
30323	Lyon	Julia Eleanor	1843	Edinburgh, Scotland	James (Jacob) Walter Lyon	Louisa Hart		Edinburgh, Scotland	
19585	Lyon	Juliet	1836	Plymouth, Devon	Solomon Lyon	Rose Solomon	Isaac Ahronsberg	?Plymouth, Devon	
21326	Lyon	Kitty	1787	Liverpool	(?)		Moses Lyon	Liverpool	
159	Lyon	Leah	1809	Liverpool	Nathan Lyon	Phoebe Zipporah Aaron		Birmingham	
21324	Lyon	Leah	1822	Aldgate, London	Moses Lyon	Phoebe Solomon		Liverpool	teacher of music
18094	Lyon	Lewis	1801	Marylebone, London			Mary (?)	Holborn, London	watch manufacturer
21327	Lyon	Lewis	1816	Liverpool	Moses Lyon	Kitty (?)		Liverpool	general broker
24077	Lyon	Louisa	1803	Cambridge	Solomon Lyon	Rachel Hart		Bloomsbury, London	
30318	Lyon	Louisa	1804	?, London	Naphtali (Nathaniel) Hart	Mary Katz	James (Jacob) Walter Lyon	Edinburgh, Scotland	
5079	Lyon	Martha	1791	?, London			Abraham Lyon	Portsmouth, Hampshire	
18095	Lyon	Mary	1807	Aldgate, London	(?)		Lewis Lyon	Holborn, London	
14104	Lyon	Mary	1844	Shoreditch, London	Isaac Lyon	Rosetta (?)		Manchester	scholar
30321	Lyon	Mary Miriam	1837	Edinburgh, Scotland	James (Jacob) Walter Lyon	Louisa Hart		Edinburgh, Scotland	
15551	Lyon	Morris	1832	Covent Garden, London	Abraham Lyon	Esther Hart	Sophia (Simha) Rogers (Rodrigues)	Covent Garden, London	cigar maker
6661	Lyon	Morris	1833	Aldgate, London				Aldgate, London	cheesemonger
4708	Lyon	Morris	1846	?, Poland	Abraham Lyon	Ester (?)		Birmingham	
18102	Lyon	Morris (Maurice)	1846	Holborn, London	Lewis Lyon	Mary (?)		Holborn, London	scholar
21325	Lyon	Moses	1776	?, London			Kitty (?)	Liverpool	retired broker
20228	Lyon	Moses	1794	?, London	Yehuda		Phoebe Solomon	Liverpool	licensed hawker + dealer in hats
2991	Lyon	Moses	1800	Whitechapel, London	Mordecai Lyon		Rachel Moses	Spitalfields, London	fruiterer + general dealer
30324	Lyon	Moses Wittering	1847	Edinburgh, Scotland	James (Jacob) Walter Lyon	Louisa Hart		Edinburgh, Scotland	
30320	Lyon	Nathaniel David	1830	Islington, London	James (Jacob) Walter Lyon	Louisa Hart		Edinburgh, Scotland	
12652	Lyon	Philip	1811	Warsaw, Poland				Birmingham	tobacconist
21323	Lyon	Phoebe	1797	?, London	Naftali Hertz Solomon		Moses Lyon	Liverpool	
2992	Lyon	Rachel	1790	Whitechapel, London	Moshe Moses		?	Spitalfields, London	
2994	Lyon	Rebecca	1830	Spitalfields, London	Moses Lyons	Rachel (?)		Spitalfields, London	
2963	Lyon	Rebecca	1847	City, London	David Lyon	Hannah (?)		Spitalfields, London	
18097	Lyon	Reuben	1832	Finsbury, London	Lewis Lyon	Mary (?)		Holborn, London	watch maker finisher
18099	Lyon	Rosa	1835	Holborn, London	Lewis Lyon	Mary (?)		Holborn, London	milliner
30317	Lyon	Rose (Rosetta, Rosina)	1796	Cambridge, Cambridgeshire	Solomon Lyon	Rachel Hart		Edinburgh, Scotland	fundholder
14102	Lyon	Rosetta	1817	Middlesex, London	Henry Mordecai		Isaac Lyon	Manchester	
14106	Lyon	Rosetta	1847	Shoreditch, London	Isaac Lyon	Rosetta (?)	George Robert Lyon	Manchester	scholar
21328	Lyon	Samuel	1823	Liverpool	Moses Lyon	Kitty (?)		Liverpool	tailor's shopman
18103	Lyon	Samuel	1848	Holborn, London	Lewis Lyon	Mary (?)		Holborn, London	scholar
9307	Lyon	Sarah	1783	?	(?)		(?) Lyon	Aldgate, London	poor
20226	Lyon	Sarah	1786	Bermondsey, London	(?)		Joseph Lyon	Stoke Newington, London	
16516	Lyon	Sarah	1806	?Aldgate, London	(?)		Isaac Lyon	Clerkenwell, London	
2993	Lyon	Sarah	1827	Whitechapel, London	Moses Lyons	Rachel (?)		Spitalfields, London	
2962	Lyon	Sarah	1846	City, London	David Lyon	Hannah (?)		Spitalfields, London	
2918	Lyon	Sarah Miriam	1811	?, London	Jacob Mendes da Costa		Hart Lyon	Islington, London	

ID	surname	given names	born	birthplace	father	mother	spouse 1	1851 residence	1851 occupation
29613	Lyon	Solomon	1823	Covent Garden, London	(?) Lyon	Hannah (?)		Aldgate, London	clerk
5444	Lyon	Solomon	1839	Plymouth, Devon	Solomon Lyon	Rose Solomon	Sophia Davis	?Plymouth, Devon	
2914	Lyon	Solomon Mendes	1831	Barbados, West Indies	Hart Lyon	Sarah Miriam Mendes da Costa	Sarah Israel	Islington, London	merchant
17021	Lyon	Sophia	1832	Glasgow, Scotland				Edinburgh, Scotland	house servant
18104	Lyon	Sophia	1850	Holborn, London	Lewis Lyon	Mary (?)	Philip Landstein	Holborn, London	
14105	Lyon	William W	1845	Shoreditch, London	Isaac Lyon	Rosetta (?)		Manchester	scholar
30584	Lyon (Lions)	Abigail	1851	Aldgate, London	Isaac Lyon (Lions)	Amelia Hart		Aldgate, London	
8930	Lyon (Lions)	Amelia	1810	Aldgate, London	(?)		Isaac Lyon (Lions)	Aldgate, London	
8932	Lyon (Lions)	Anna	1839	Aldgate, London	Isaac Lyon (Lions)	Amelia Hart		Aldgate, London	
8933	Lyon (Lions)	Esther	1840	Aldgate, London	Isaac Lyon (Lions)	Amelia Hart		Aldgate, London	
8929	Lyon (Lions)	Isaac	1801	Southwark, London	Yosef		Amelia Hart	Aldgate, London	hatter
8934	Lyon (Lions)	Joseph	1844	Aldgate, London	Isaac Lyon (Lions)	Amelia Hart		Aldgate, London	
8931	Lyon (Lions)	Mary	1835	Whitechapel, London	Isaac Lyon (Lions)	Amelia Hart		Aldgate, London	
5295	Lyon (Lyons)	Abigail	1793	Gloucester, Gloucestershire	Chaim (?Hyams)		Joseph (Reuben) Lyon (Lyons)	Aldgate, London	
13271	Lyon (Lyons)	Abigail	1846	Aldgate, London	Saul Lyon (Lyons)	Hannah Emanuel	Jacob Lyons	Spitalfields, London	
5298	Lyon (Lyons)	Catherine	1835	?Aldgate, London	Joseph (Reuben) Lyon (Lyons)	Abigail Hyams	Moses Woolf	Aldgate, London	umbrella maker
13272	Lyon (Lyons)	Emanuel	1849	Aldgate, London	Saul Lyon (Lyons)	Hannah Emanuel		Spitalfields, London	
8021	Lyon (Lyons)	Hannah	1820	Whitechapel, London	Menachem Emanuel		Saul Lyon (Lyons)	Spitalfields, London	
152	Lyon (Lyons)	Hannah (Anna)	1789	Aldgate, London	Moses Levi	Rachel (?)	Isaac Leo Lyon	Spitalfields, London	
4994	Lyon (Lyons)	Henry	1841	?, Germany	Levi Lyons		Rose Salmon	Birmingham	
5296	Lyon (Lyons)	Isaac	1827	Middlesex, London	Joseph (Reuben) Lyon (Lyons)	Abigail Hyams	Hannah Davis	Aldgate, London	fruit dealer
5294	Lyon (Lyons)	Joseph (Reuben)	1796	Whitechapel, London	Saul Peller Lyon	Katherine (?)	Abigail Hyams	Aldgate, London	clothes salesman
5299	Lyon (Lyons)	Lewis	1838	Aldgate, London	Joseph (Reuben) Lyon (Lyons)	Abigail Hyams	Caroline Lipman	Aldgate, London	scholar
5297	Lyon (Lyons)	Rosetta	1833	?Aldgate, London	Joseph (Reuben) Lyon (Lyons)	Abigail Hyams		Aldgate, London	
5300	Lyon (Lyons)	Saul	1821	Aldgate, London	Joseph (Reuben) Lyon (Lyons)	Abigail Hyams	Hannah Emanuel	Spitalfields, London	clothes dealer
8952	Lyons	Aaron	1777	Aldgate, London	Naftali Nathan		Abigail Solomon	Aldgate, London	glass cutter
3002	Lyons	Aaron	1801	Aldgate, London	Yehuda Leib		Rachel Nunes Martinez	Spitalfields, London	general dealer
25831	Lyons	Aaron	1831	Aldgate, London	Abraham Lyons	Leah Davis		Aldgate, London	fish dealer
28018	Lyons	Aaron	1831	Spitalfields, London	Aaron Lyons	(Rachel Martin?)	Frances (Fanny) Nathan	Spitalfields, London	general dealer
27367	Lyons	Aaron	1842	Whitechapel, London	Morris (Jacob) Lyons	Frederica Friederberg		Aldgate, London	scholar
15495	Lyons	Abay	1846	Covent Garden, London	Isaacs Lyons	R--- Jacobs		Covent Garden, London	
3055	Lyons	Abigail	1788	Aldgate, London	Asher ben Nathan Solomons		Aaron Lyons	Spitalfields, London	
24884	Lyons	Abigail	1790	Middlesex, London	(?)		Benjamin Lyons	Southwark, London	
3007	Lyons	Abigail	1838	Aldgate, London	Aaron Lyons	Rachel Nunes Martinez	(?) Mendoza	Spitalfields, London	apprentice to tailor
21574	Lyons	Abigail	1847	Whitechapel, London	(?) Lyons	(?) Emanuel		Spitalfields, London	
23355	Lyons	Abraham	1802	Aldgate, London			Rachel (?)	Strand, London	general dealer
26624	Lyons	Abraham	1803	Spitalfields, London			Rosetta (?)	Aldgate, London	clothes dealer
25829	Lyons	Abraham	1808	Aldgate, London	(?) Lyons	Chava (?)	Leah Davis	Aldgate, London	clothes dealer
28063	Lyons	Abraham	1826	Aldgate, London	(?Benjamin) Lyons	Sarah (?Levy)		Spitalfields, London	pastrycook
23357	Lyons	Abraham	1834	Covent Garden, London	Abraham Lyons	Rachel (?)		Strand, London	butcher's servant
11386	Lyons	Abraham	1838	Whitechapel, London	Samuel Lyons	Rachael Levy	Hannah Abendana	Aldgate, London	scholar
24688	Lyons	Abraham	1838	Elephant & Castle, London	Joseph Lyons	Catherine (?)	Sophia Hart	Elephant & Castle, London	scholar

459

ID	surname	given names	born	birthplace	father	mother	spouse 1	1851 residence	1851 occupation
3074	Lyons	Abraham	1848	City, London	Lewis Lyons	Sarah Hyam		Spitalfields, London	scholar
30452	Lyons	Abraham	1850	Southwark, London	Lewis (Lazarus) Lyons	Leonora (Eleanora) Francks		Newcastle-under-Lyme, Staffordshire	
3070	Lyons	Adelaid	1840	City, London	Lewis Lyons	Sarah Hyam		Spitalfields, London	scholar
16965	Lyons	Adelaide	1837	Middlesex, London	(?) Lyons			Hammersmith, London	boarding school pupil
3013	Lyons	Adelaide	1839	Spitalfields, London	Lewis Lyons	Sophia (?)		Spitalfields, London	
12325	Lyons	Alexander (Elisha)	1815	Middlesex, London	Lewis Lyons		Julia (?)	Spitalfields, London	
25097	Lyons	Alfred	1847	Whitechapel, London	Isaac Lyons	Rosetta Mordecai		Finsbury, London	
3031	Lyons	Amelia	1812	Spitalfields, London	Yehuda Leib Phillips		Saul Lyons	Spitalfields, London	
27287	Lyons	Amelia	1837	Aldgate, London	(?) Lyons	Rosetta (?)		Aldgate, London	tailoress
1363	Lyons	Amelia	1849	Plymouth, Devon	Jacob Lyons	Phoebe (Barina, Branah, Fanny) Solomon	Adolphe Posener	Plymouth, Devon	
3027	Lyons	Amelia	1849	Spitalfields, London	Philip Lyons	Catherine (Kitty) Levy		Spitalfields, London	
30078	Lyons	Ann	1807	?Middlesex, London	David Barnett		Morris Lyons	Aldgate, London	
7209	Lyons	Asher	1825	Canterbury, Kent			Sarah Isaacs	Chatham, Kent	silversmith
27094	Lyons	Asher	1836	?, London	(?) Lyons	Elizabeth		Aldgate, London	cigar maker
1880	Lyons	Barnett	1822	Warsaw, Poland			Jane (?)	Cardiff, Wales	pawnbroker
12453	Lyons	Barnett	1846	Aldgate, London	John Lyons	Martha Simonds	Sarah Levy	Aldgate, London	scholar
21024	Lyons	Bella	1765	Bristol	(?)		(?) Lyons	Bristol	
4719	Lyons	Ben	1843	East Retford, Nottinghamshire	Morris Lyons	Sarah (?)		Birmingham	
24883	Lyons	Benjamin	1788	City, London			Abigail (?)	Southwark, London	tailor
24685	Lyons	Benjamin	1830	Elephant & Castle, London	Joseph Lyons	Catherine (?)	Hannah Nathan	Elephant & Castle, London	cigar manufacturer
3072	Lyons	Benjamin	1844	City, London	Lewis Lyons	Sarah Hyam		Spitalfields, London	scholar
2974	Lyons	Benjamin (Benny)	1837	Spitalfields, London	Samuel Lyons	Catharine (Caroline) (?)	Elizabeth Cohen	Spitalfields, London	
11872	Lyons	Betsy	1835	Middlesex, London	(?) Lyons	(?)		Whitechapel, London	inmate of orphan school
3001	Lyons	Betsy	1848	Spitalfields, London	Samuel Lyons	Rebecca Symonds		Spitalfields, London	
3014	Lyons	Caroline	1840	Spitalfields, London	Lewis Lyons	Sophia (?)		Spitalfields, London	
24784	Lyons	Catharine	1848	Aldgate, London	Henry Lyons	Rachael (?)		Elephant & Castle, London	
2973	Lyons	Catharine (Caroline)	1806	Poznan, Poland [Posen, Prussia]			Samuel Lyons	Spitalfields, London	
3069	Lyons	Catherin	1838	City, London	Lewis Lyons	Sarah Hyam		Spitalfields, London	scholar
11491	Lyons	Catherine	1789	Aldgate, London	(?)		Humphrey Lyons	Aldgate, London	optician
24682	Lyons	Catherine	1793	Cambridge			Joseph Lyons	Elephant & Castle, London	
3028	Lyons	Catherine	1828	Portsmouth, Hampshire	(?)		(?) Lyons	Spitalfields, London	
10181	Lyons	Catherine	1838	Spitalfields, London	Alexander (Elisha) Lyons	Julia (?)	Aaron Gomes Da Costa	Spitalfields, London	tailoress
3083	Lyons	Catherine	1839	Middlesex, London	Isaac Lyons	Luisa (?)		Spitalfields, London	
25835	Lyons	Catherine	1845	Aldgate, London	Abraham Lyons	Leah Davis		Aldgate, London	scholar
27460	Lyons	Catherine	1848	Whitechapel, London	John Lyons	Esther Levy		Whitechapel, London	
26631	Lyons	Catherine	1850	Aldgate, London	Abraham Lyons	Rosetta (?)		Aldgate, London	
24722	Lyons	Catherine	1799	Middlesex, London	(?)		Moss Lyons	Walworth, London	
3024	Lyons	Catherine (Kitty)	1824	Aldgate, London	Lewis Levy		Philip Lyons	Spitalfields, London	slipper binder

ID	surname	given names	born	birthplace	father	mother	spouse 1	1851 residence	1851 occupation
8415	Lyons	Charles	1777	Abergavenny, Wales			Phoebe Levy	Ryde, Isle of Wight	fancy dealer
27035	Lyons	Charles	1843	?, London	Joseph Lyons	Mary (?)		Aldgate, London	scholar
16387	Lyons	Charles J	1827	Whitechapel, London				Aldgate, London	--- merchant clerk
27226	Lyons	Charlotte	1781	?, London	(?)		(?) Lyons	Aldgate, London	
23358	Lyons	Daniel	1836	Covent Garden, London	Abraham Lyons	Rachel (?)	Rosetta Myers	Strand, London	butcher's servant
25833	Lyons	David	1835	Aldgate, London	Abraham Lyons	Leah Davis		Aldgate, London	scholar
2976	Lyons	David	1841	Spitalfields, London	Samuel Lyons	Catharine (Caroline) (?)		Spitalfields, London	
27368	Lyons	David	1844	Whitechapel, London	Morris (Jacob) Lyons	Frederica Friederberg		Aldgate, London	scholar
22674	Lyons	David	1848	Mile End, London	(?) Lyons	Sarah (?)		Whitechapel, London	
24723	Lyons	David M	1830	Walworth, London	Moss Lyons	Catherine (?)		Walworth, London	floor cloth manufacturer
26835	Lyons	Dinah	1787	Plymouth, Devon	(?)		(?) Lyons	Aldgate, London	supported by family
3005	Lyons	Dinah	1834	Aldgate, London	Aaron Lyons	Rachel Nunes Martinez	Woolf Woolfson	Spitalfields, London	tailoress
6502	Lyons	Dinah	1841	Spitalfields, London	Joseph Lyons	Mary Barnett	Solomon Abraham Green	Spitalfields, London	
1876	Lyons	Dinah	1842	Swansea, Wales	(?) Lyons	Fanny (?)		Cardiff, Wales	scholar
3064	Lyons	Edward	1812	?, Germany			Hannah (?)	Spitalfields, London	boot maker
20292	Lyons	Edward Emanuel	1831	?Canterbury, Kent	Myer (Mayer) Lyons	Elizabeth Isaacs		Canterbury, Kent	pawnbroker + salesman
27365	Lyons	Eleazar	1836	Aldgate, London	Morris (Jacob) Lyons	Frederica Friederberg		Aldgate, London	apprentice to lithographic printer
12519	Lyons	Eliza	1821	Norwich, Norfolk	(?)		Philip Lyons	Norwich, Norfolk	
24725	Lyons	Eliza	1836	Walworth, London	Moss Lyons	Catherine (?)		Walworth, London	
12520	Lyons	Eliza	1843	Norwich, Norfolk	Philip Lyons	Eliza (?)		Norwich, Norfolk	
25096	Lyons	Eliza	1845	?, London	Isaac Lyons	Rosetta Mordecai		Finsbury, London	
28324	Lyons	Elizabeth	1802	Aldgate, London	(?)		(?) Lyons	Aldgate, London	tailoress
27093	Lyons	Elizabeth	1807	?, London	(?)		(?) Lyons	Aldgate, London	general dealer
2097	Lyons	Elizabeth	1813	Middlesex, London	Isaac Isaacs	Elizabeth Solomons	Myer (Mayer) Lyons	Canterbury, Kent	
1870	Lyons	Elizabeth	1814	?, Poland			Hyman Lyons	Merthyr Tydfil, Wales	
28064	Lyons	Elizabeth	1825	Aldgate, London	(?Benjamin) Lyons	Sarah (?Levy)		Spitalfields, London	
12327	Lyons	Elizabeth	1834	Middlesex, London	Alexander (Elisha) Lyons	Julia (?)	Joseph Jacobs	Spitalfields, London	
26626	Lyons	Elizabeth	1836	Whitechapel, London	Abraham Lyons	Rosetta (?)		Aldgate, London	
23479	Lyons	Elizabeth	1841	Manchester	Joseph Lyons	Esther (?)		Liverpool	scholar
27400	Lyons	Elizabeth	1831	Spitalfields, London	Levy Woolf		Woolf Lyons	Whitechapel, London	
11048	Lyons	Emanuel	1823	Portsmouth, Hampshire	Boaz Lyons		Sara Symons	Aldgate, London	cigar maker
12521	Lyons	Emily	1845	Norwich, Norfolk	Philip Lyons	Eliza (?)		Norwich, Norfolk	
3041	Lyons	Emma	1824	Spitalfields, London	(?) Lyons	Rebecca (?)		Spitalfields, London	furrier
23476	Lyons	Esther	1813	Middlesex, London	(?)		Joseph Lyons	Liverpool	oil + pickle dealer's wife
27459	Lyons	Esther	1827	Whitechapel, London	(?) Levy		John Lyons	Whitechapel, London	
477	Lyons	Esther	1832	Spitalfields, London	Joseph Lyons	Mary Barnett	Myer Myers	Spitalfields, London	
1874	Lyons	Esther	1836	Swansea, Wales	(?) Lyons	Fanny (?)		Cardiff, Wales	
28326	Lyons	Esther	1840	Aldgate, London	(?) Lyons	Elizabeth (?)		Aldgate, London	scholar
11388	Lyons	Esther	1843	Aldgate, London	Samuel Lyons	Rachael Levy		Aldgate, London	scholar
26629	Lyons	Esther	1846	Aldgate, London	Abraham Lyons	Rosetta (?)		Aldgate, London	scholar
12454	Lyons	Esther	1849	Aldgate, London	John Lyons	Martha Simonds	David Solomon	Aldgate, London	
1883	Lyons	Esther	1850	Cardiff, Wales	Barnett Lyons	Jane (?)		Cardiff, Wales	
27288	Lyons	Esther?	1840	Spitalfields, London	(?) Lyons	Rosetta (?)		Aldgate, London	scholar
12011	Lyons	Eve	1848	Middlesex, London	Henry Lyons	Rachel Hart		Waterloo, London	

461

ID	surname	given names	born	birthplace	father	mother	spouse 1	1851 residence	1851 occupation
1873	Lyons	Fanny	1811	?, Poland			(?) Lyons	Cardiff, Wales	
24683	Lyons	Fanny	1827	Elephant & Castle, London	Joseph Lyons	Catherine (?)	Lion Lyons	Elephant & Castle, London	household work
2975	Lyons	Fanny	1839	Spitalfields, London	Samuel Lyons	Catharine (Caroline) (?)		Spitalfields, London	
23480	Lyons	Fanny	1842	Manchester	Joseph Lyons	Esther (?)		Liverpool	scholar
24882	Lyons	Fanny	1850	Southwark, London	Simeon Lyons	Louisa Cowan		Southwark, London	
6328	Lyons	Flora	1832	Aldgate, London	Jacob Lyons (Lyon)	Elizabeth Abrahams	Moss Defries	Shoreditch, London	
28019	Lyons	Frances (Fanny)	1830	Spitalfields, London	Henry Nathan		Aaron Lyons	Spitalfields, London	dressmaker
27462	Lyons	Frances Rachel	1850	Whitechapel, London	John Lyons	Esther Levy		Whitechapel, London	
2967	Lyons	Francis	1833	Whitechapel, London	William Lyons	Mary (?)		Spitalfields, London	cigar maker
27364	Lyons	Frederica	1809	?, Poland [?, Prussia]	Eliezer Lezer Friedeberg		Morris (Jacob) Lyons	Aldgate, London	cap maker
3079	Lyons	George	1778	Middlesex, London	Yehuda Leib Lyons		Liddia (Lydia) Abrahams	Spitalfields, London	navy pensioner
7776	Lyons	Goldstone	1784	?, Poland [?, Prussia]			Louisa (Theresa) (?)	Manchester	retired tailor
10467	Lyons	Hannah	1778	Whitechapel, London	(?)		(?) Lyons	Mile End, London	receives poor relief
22651	Lyons	Hannah	1786	Whitechapel, London	(?)		(?) Lyons	Whitechapel, London	
3065	Lyons	Hannah	1811	?, Germany			Edward Lyons	Spitalfields, London	
24689	Lyons	Hannah	1819	St Pancras, London	Joseph Cohen		Nathaniel (Nathan) Lyons	Elephant & Castle, London	
1224	Lyons	Hannah	1830	Plymouth, Devon				Plymouth, Devon	dressmaker
24783	Lyons	Hannah	1844	Southwark, London	Henry Lyons	Rachael (?)		Elephant & Castle, London	
4720	Lyons	Hannah	1846	Birmingham	Morris Lyons	Sarah (?)		Birmingham	
1868	Lyons	Harris	1782	?, Poland				Swansea, Wales	general dealer
26851	Lyons	Henry	1813	?, London				Aldgate, London	general dealer
12014	Lyons	Henry	1815	?, Lincolnshire	Moshe		Rachel Hart	Waterloo, London	umbrella + parasol manufacturer
24781	Lyons	Henry	1819	Aldgate, London			Rachael (?)	Elephant & Castle, London	jeweller
3043	Lyons	Henry	1821	Aldgate, London	Lewis (Yehuda) Lyons		Mary (Mary Ann) Benjamin	Spitalfields, London	pedlar
8953	Lyons	Henry	1821	Aldgate, London	Aaron Lyons	Abigail Solomons		Aldgate, London	orange dealer
1875	Lyons	Henry	1838	Swansea, Wales	(?) Lyons	Fanny (?)		Cardiff, Wales	
3038	Lyons	Henry	1840	Spitalfields, London	(?) Lyons			Spitalfields, London	scholar
13653	Lyons	Henry	1841	Manchester	William Lyons	Isabella (?)		Manchester	scholar
3085	Lyons	Henry	1848	Middlesex, London	Isaac Lyons	Luisa (?)		Spitalfields, London	
5921	Lyons	Henry	1848	Aldgate, London	Nathan Lyons	Mary Barnett	Jane Costa	Aldgate, London	
3060	Lyons	Hester	1848	Spitalfields, London	Sampson Lyons	Lidy (?)		Spitalfields, London	
22085	Lyons	Hirschel	1833	?, Russia [Ryla, Russia]				Whitechapel, London	dealer in trinkets
11490	Lyons	Humphrey	1778	Spitalfields, London			Catherine (?)	Aldgate, London	optician
5292	Lyons	Hyam	1830	Aldgate, London	Joseph (Reuben) Lyons	Abigail Hyams	Esther Woolf	Aldgate, London	baker journeyman
3073	Lyons	Hyam	1846	City, London	Lewis Lyons	Sarah Hyam		Spitalfields, London	scholar
1869	Lyons	Hyman	1801	?, Poland			Elizabeth (?)	Merthyr Tydfil, Wales	general dealer
13651	Lyons	Hyman	1838	Manchester	William Lyons	Isabella (?)		Manchester	scholar
2979	Lyons	Hyman	1850	Spitalfields, London	Samuel Lyons	Catharine (Caroline) (?)	Rose Breeden	Spitalfields, London	
3081	Lyons	Isaac	1817	Middlesex, London	Gershon Lyons		Louisa Nelson	Spitalfields, London	shoemaker
25093	Lyons	Isaac	1822	Bristol			Rosetta Mordecai	Finsbury, London	umbrella maker

ID	surname	given names	born	birthplace	father	mother	spouse 1	1851 residence	1851 occupation
25834	Lyons	Isaac	1837	Aldgate, London	Abraham Lyons	Leah Davis		Aldgate, London	scholar
11383	Lyons	Isaac	1839	Aldgate, London	(?) Lyons	(?) Levy		Aldgate, London	scholar
12007	Lyons	Isaac	1839	Middlesex, London	Henry Lyons	Rachel Hart		Waterloo, London	scholar at home
16977	Lyons	Isaac	1843	Middlesex, London	(?) Lyons			Hammersmith, London	boarding school pupil
3009	Lyons	Isaac	1844	Aldgate, London	Aaron Lyons	Rachel Nunes Martinez	Leah Lyons	Spitalfields, London	scholar
12452	Lyons	Isaac	1845	Aldgate, London	John Lyons	Martha Simonds		Aldgate, London	scholar
24081	Lyons	Isaac	1848	Middlesex, London	Solomon Lyons	Julia (?)		Fitzrovia, London	
1362	Lyons	Isaac S Frank	1847	Plymouth, Devon	Jacob Lyons	Phoebe (Barina, Branah, Fanny) Solomon	Ellen (Ella) E Levy	Plymouth, Devon	
15493	Lyons	Isaacs	1828	Covent Garden, London			R--- Jacobs	Covent Garden, London	cabman
11330	Lyons	Isaacs	1833	Mile End, London	(?)	Julia Lyons		Aldgate, London	scholar
13650	Lyons	Isabella	1818	Blackburn, Lancashire	(?)		William Lyons	Manchester	
4721	Lyons	Isabella	1848	Birmingham	Morris Lyons	Sarah (?)		Birmingham	
27366	Lyons	Israel	1838	Aldgate, London	Morris (Jacob) Lyons	Frederica Friederberg		Aldgate, London	scholar
11387	Lyons	Israel	1841	Aldgate, London	Samuel Lyons	Rachael Levy	Rosetta (Rosa) Lazarus	Aldgate, London	scholar
26630	Lyons	Israel	1848	Aldgate, London	Abraham Lyons	Rosetta (?)		Aldgate, London	scholar
13758	Lyons	Jacob	1779	?, Poland [?, Prussia]				Manchester	
1357	Lyons	Jacob	1795	?, Poland			Phoebe (Barina, Branah, Fanny) Solomon	Plymouth, Devon	general dealer
24785	Lyons	Jacob	1850	Southwark, London	Henry Lyons	Rachael (?)		Elephant & Castle, London	
24082	Lyons	Jacob	1851	Fitzrovia, London	Solomon Lyons	Julia (?)		Fitzrovia, London	
1881	Lyons	Jane	1826	?, Poland			Barnett Lyons	Cardiff, Wales	
9874	Lyons	Jane	1827	?, London				Fulham, London	
4716	Lyons	Jane	1836	Plymouth, Devon	Morris Lyons	Sarah (?)		Birmingham	
26627	Lyons	Jesse	1838	Spitalfields, London	Abraham Lyons	Rosetta (?)		Aldgate, London	scholar
24686	Lyons	Jessie	1835	Elephant & Castle, London	Joseph Lyons	Catherine (?)		Elephant & Castle, London	dress maker
27378	Lyons	John	1815	Aldgate, London			(?)	Aldgate, London	fruit dealer
12450	Lyons	John	1817	Portsmouth, Hampshire	Boaz Lyons		Martha Simonds	Aldgate, London	fishmonger
27458	Lyons	John	1821	Finsbury, London	Nahum		Esther Levy	Whitechapel, London	trunk + packing case maker empl 6
27034	Lyons	John	1838	?, London	Joseph Lyons	Mary (?)		Aldgate, London	scholar
11859	Lyons	John	1841	Middlesex, London	(?) Lyons	(?)		Whitechapel, London	inmate of orphan school
2998	Lyons	John	1850	Spitalfields, London	Samuel Lyons	Rebecca Symonds		Spitalfields, London	
25832	Lyons	Jonah	1833	Aldgate, London	Abraham Lyons	Leah Davis		Aldgate, London	clothes dealer
3046	Lyons	Jonah	1847	Spitalfields, London	Henry Lyons	Mary (Mary Ann) Benjamin		Spitalfields, London	
24681	Lyons	Joseph	1790	?, Germany			Catherine (?)	Elephant & Castle, London	general dealer
27031	Lyons	Joseph	1793	?, Poland			Mary (?)	Aldgate, London	furrier
476	Lyons	Joseph	1795	Spitalfields, London	Moshe Lyon		Mary Barnett	Spitalfields, London	general dealer
23475	Lyons	Joseph	1801	Portsmouth, Hampshire			Esther (?)	Liverpool	oil + pickle dealer
26617	Lyons	Joseph	1828	Liverpool	(?)		(?) Cohen	City, London	tailor + draper shopman
3037	Lyons	Joseph	1829	Spitalfields, London	(?) Lyons	Rebeca (?)		Aldgate, London	slop seller
28065	Lyons	Joseph	1829	Aldgate, London	(?Benjamin) Lyons	Sarah (?Levy)		Spitalfields, London	warehouseman

ID	surname	given names	born	birthplace	father	mother	spouse 1	1851 residence	1851 occupation
13652	Lyons	Joseph	1840	Manchester	William Lyons	Isabella (?)		Manchester	scholar
30143	Lyons	Joseph	1843	New York, USA				Bloomsbury, London	
2970	Lyons	Joseph	1844	Whitechapel, London	William Lyons	Mary (?)		Spitalfields, London	
3026	Lyons	Joseph	1846	Spitalfields, London	Philip Lyons	Catherine (Kitty) Levy	Hannah Phillips	Spitalfields, London	scholar
24080	Lyons	Joseph	1847	Middlesex, London	Solomon Lyons	Julia (?)		Fitzrovia, London	
3075	Lyons	Joseph	1850	City, London	Lewis Lyons	Sarah Hyam		Spitalfields, London	
4722	Lyons	Joseph	1850	Birmingham	Morris Lyons	Sarah (?)		Birmingham	
30889	Lyons	Joseph	1850	Chatham, Kent	Asher Lyons	Sarah Isaacs		Chatham, Kent	
7144	Lyons	Joseph Nathaniel	1847	Kennington, London	Nathaniel (Nathan) Lyons	Hannah Cohen	Psyche Cohen	Lambeth, London	
22673	Lyons	Joshua	1839	Mile End, London	(?) Lyons	Sarah (?)		Whitechapel, London	
3062	Lyons	Juda	1806	Spitalfields, London				Spitalfields, London	ginger beer maker
8942	Lyons	Judah	1849	Aldgate, London	Nathan Lyons	Mary Barnett		Aldgate, London	
20835	Lyons	Julia	1806	Bristol	Jacob Lyons		Michael Abrahams	Bristol	
11329	Lyons	Julia	1811	Mile End, London	(?) Lyons			Aldgate, London	laundress
12326	Lyons	Julia	1811	Middlesex, London	(?)		Alexander (Elisha) Lyons	Spitalfields, London	
4968	Lyons	Julia	1815	Bristol				Birmingham	housekeeper
24079	Lyons	Julia	1821	Middlesex, London	(?)		Solomon Lyons	Fitzrovia, London	
24684	Lyons	Julia	1829	Elephant & Castle, London	Joseph Lyons	Catherine (?)		Elephant & Castle, London	cap maker
12522	Lyons	Julia	1847	Norwich, Norfolk	Philip Lyons	Eliza (?)		Norwich, Norfolk	
19284	Lyons	Julia	1851	Aldgate, London	Nathan Lyons	Mary Barnett	Barnett Lazarus	Aldgate, London	
2977	Lyons	Julia (Yetel)	1842	Spitalfields, London	Samuel Lyons	Catharine (Caroline) (?)		Spitalfields, London	
23478	Lyons	Julius	1838	Hull, Yorkshire	Joseph Lyons	Esther (?)		Liverpool	scholar
3040	Lyons	Kate	1822	Spitalfields, London	(?) Lyons	Rebecca (?)		Spitalfields, London	furrier
12009	Lyons	Katherine	1846	Spitalfields, London	Henry Lyons	Rachel Hart	Abraham Nathan	Waterloo, London	scholar at home
16973	Lyons	Larisia	1841	Middlesex, London	(?) Lyons			Hammersmith, London	boarding school pupil
23481	Lyons	Laura	1844	Liverpool	Joseph Lyons	Esther (?)		Liverpool	scholar
25830	Lyons	Leah	1811	Aldgate, London	Eliezer Lipman Davis		Abraham Lyons	Aldgate, London	clothes dealer
22652	Lyons	Leah	1823	Spitalfields, London	(?) Lyons	Hannah (?)		Whitechapel, London	cap maker
3089	Lyons	Leah	1834	Spitalfields, London	Joseph Lyons	Mary Barnett	Samuel Myers	Spitalfields, London	
12328	Lyons	Leah	1836	Middlesex, London	Alexander (Elisha) Lyons	Julia (?)	Moss Moses	Spitalfields, London	
3029	Lyons	Lear	1775	Spitalfields, London	(?)		Israel Lyons	Spitalfields, London	
30451	Lyons	Leonora (Eleanora)	1827	Newcastle-under-Lyme, Staffordshire	Abraham Francks	Mary (?)	Lewis (Lazarus) Lyons	Newcastle-under-Lyme, Staffordshire	
3010	Lyons	Levy	1836	Finsbury, London				Spitalfields, London	servant
4711	Lyons	Lewis	1777	Strasbourg, France				Birmingham	gentleman
11361	Lyons	Lewis	1779	Aldgate, London				Aldgate, London	broker + appraiser
28327	Lyons	Lewis	1801	Middlesex, London	Ezekiel Lyons		?	Reading, Berkshire	cigar maker apprentice
3011	Lyons	Lewis	1813	City, London	Yehuda Leib		Sophia (?)	Spitalfields, London	general dealer
3067	Lyons	Lewis	1817	City, London	Benjamin Lyons		Sarah Hyam	Spitalfields, London	shoemaker
15514	Lyons	Lewis	1823	City, London			Maria (?)	Covent Garden, London	cabman
22653	Lyons	Lewis	1826	Spitalfields, London	(?) Lyons	Hannah (?)		Whitechapel, London	glass dealer
3032	Lyons	Lewis	1831	Spitalfields, London	Saul Lyons	Amelia Phillips		Spitalfields, London	cigar maker
3095	Lyons	Lewis	1833	?, London	Abraham Lyons	Rachel (?)		Spitalfields, London	cigar maker
27033	Lyons	Lewis	1836	?, London	Joseph Lyons	Mary (?)		Aldgate, London	apprentice [to furrier?]

ID	surname	given names	born	birthplace	father	mother	spouse 1	1851 residence	1851 occupation
28325	Lyons	Lewis	1837	Aldgate, London	(?) Lyons	Elizabeth (?)		Aldgate, London	cigar maker apprentice
3045	Lyons	Lewis	1845	Spitalfields, London	Henry Lyons	Mary (Mary Ann) Benjamin		Spitalfields, London	
1878	Lyons	Lewis	1846	Swansea, Wales	(?) Lyons	Fanny (?)		Cardiff, Wales	
3092	Lyons	Lewis	1846	Spitalfields, London	Joseph Lyons	Mary Barnett		Spitalfields, London	
11389	Lyons	Lewis	1848	Aldgate, London	Samuel Lyons	Rachael Levy	Sarah Heilbron	Aldgate, London	scholar
15496	Lyons	Lewis	1849	Covent Garden, London	Isaacs Lyons	R--- Jacobs		Covent Garden, London	
3066	Lyons	Lewis	1850	?Spitalfields, London	Edward Lyons	Hannah (?)		Spitalfields, London	
3086	Lyons	Lewis	1850	Middlesex, London	Isaac Lyons	Luisa (?)		Spitalfields, London	
2999	Lyons	Lewis (Louis)	1844	Spitalfields, London	Samuel Lyons	Rebecca Symonds	Sarah Heilbron	Spitalfields, London	
14534	Lyons	Lewis Henry	1838	Middlesex, London	Henry Lyons	Rachel Hart	Elizabeth Benjamin	Waterloo, London	scholar at home
3080	Lyons	Liddia (Lydia)	1796	?, London	Isaac Abrahams		George Lyons	Spitalfields, London	
3058	Lyons	Lidy (Leah)	1829	Bethnal Green, London	(?)		Sampson Lyons	Spitalfields, London	
27370	Lyons	Louis	1850	Aldgate, London	Morris (Jacob) Lyons	Frederica Friederberg		Aldgate, London	
1872	Lyons	Louis (Lewis)	1839	?, Poland	Hyman Lyons	Elizabeth (?)		Merthyr Tydfil, Wales	scholar
3082	Lyons	Louisa	1816	Middlesex, London	Nathan Nelson		Isaac Lyons	Spitalfields, London	
24878	Lyons	Louisa	1821	Southwark, London	G--- Cowan		Simeon Lyons	Southwark, London	
3056	Lyons	Louisa	1829	Aldgate, London	Aaron Lyons	Abigail Solomon		Spitalfields, London	
5281	Lyons	Louisa	1846	Whitechapel, London	Morris (Jacob) Lyons	Frederica Friederberg	Samson Samson	Aldgate, London	scholar
13862	Lyons	Louisa (Theresa)	1787	?, Poland [?, Prussia]			Goldstone Lyons	Manchester	retired tailor
19145	Lyons	Lyon	1772	Spitalfields, London				Aldgate, London	formerly general dealer in receipt of parish relief
19144	Lyons	Lyon (Lewis)	1774	Spitalfields, London			(?)	Aldgate, London	
12793	Lyons	Maria	1808	Whitechapel, London	Yehuda Leib Lyon			Spitalfields, London	furniture broker
15515	Lyons	Maria	1830	Oldham, Lancashire	(?)		Lewis Lyons	Covent Garden, London	
1871	Lyons	Maria	1837	?, Poland	Hyman Lyons	Elizabeth (?)		Merthyr Tydfil, Wales	scholar
24886	Lyons	Maria (Marian)	1830	Middlesex, London	(?) Isaacs		Maurice Lyons	Southwark, London	
4718	Lyons	Maria (Marion)	1839	Norwich, Norfolk	Morris Lyons	Sarah (?)	John Jacobs	Birmingham	
28020	Lyons	Maria (Miriam)	1850	Spitalfields, London	Aaron Lyons	Frances (Fanny) Nathan		Spitalfields, London	
12013	Lyons	Marian	1850	Middlesex, London	Henry Lyons	Rachel Hart	Alexander Frankford	Waterloo, London	
3087	Lyons	Mark	1820	Middlesex, London	(?) Lyons	(?Esther Norden)		Spitalfields, London	general dealer
3047	Lyons	Mark	1850	Aldgate, London	Henry Lyons	Mary (Mary Ann) Benjamin		Spitalfields, London	
4712	Lyons	Mark Gumpel	1824	?, Poland	Moses Lyons		Matilda Robinzon	Birmingham	traveller in jewellery
12451	Lyons	Martha	1831	Aldgate, London	Isaac Simonds		John Lyons	Aldgate, London	
17210	Lyons	Mary	1801	Spitalfields, London	Yehuda Leib Barnett	Sarah (?)	Joseph Lyons	Spitalfields, London	
27032	Lyons	Mary	1801	?, London	(?)		Joseph Lyons	Aldgate, London	dealer
2966	Lyons	Mary	1815	Whitechapel, London			William Lyons	Spitalfields, London	
8941	Lyons	Mary	1827	Amsterdam, Holland	(?) Barnett	Julia (?)	Nathan Lyons	Aldgate, London	
3088	Lyons	Mary	1829	Middlesex, London				Spitalfields, London	
3017	Lyons	Mary	1847	Spitalfields, London	Lewis Lyons	Sophia (?)		Spitalfields, London	
1879	Lyons	Mary	1848	Swansea, Wales	(?) Lyons	Fanny (?)		Cardiff, Wales	
3044	Lyons	Mary (Mary Ann)	1827	Marylebone, London	Jonah Benjamin		Henry Lyons	Spitalfields, London	
24724	Lyons	Mary Ann	1834	Walworth, London	Moss Lyons	Catherine (?)		Walworth, London	
24880	Lyons	Mary Ann	1846	Westminster, London	Simeon Lyons	Louisa Cowan		Southwark, London	
24885	Lyons	Maurice	1831	Middlesex, London	Benjamin Lyons	Abigail (?)	Maria (Marian) Isaacs	Southwark, London	tailor
2995	Lyons	Michael	1841	Spitalfields, London	Samuel Lyons	Rebecca Symonds		Spitalfields, London	

ID	surname	given names	born	birthplace	father	mother	spouse 1	1851 residence	1851 occupation
30077	Lyons	Morris	1806	?, London			Ann Barnett	Aldgate, London	
4713	Lyons	Morris	1811	Coventry, Warwickshire	(?) Lyons	Mary (?)	Sarah (?)	Birmingham	dentist
3102	Lyons	Morris	1850	Aldgate, London	Abraham Lyons	Alice (?)	Sarah Lyons	Aldgate, London	
27363	Lyons	Morris (Jacob)	1802	?, Poland [?, Prussia]	Yehuda Leib		Frederica Friederberg	Aldgate, London	cap maker
21340	Lyons	Moses	1804	Philadelphia, USA				Liverpool	pauper
3090	Lyons	Moses	1836	Spitalfields, London	Joseph Lyons	Mary Barnett		Spitalfields, London	
3008	Lyons	Moses	1841	Aldgate, London	Aaron Moses	Rachel Nunes Martinez		Spitalfields, London	scholar
1877	Lyons	Moses	1844	Swansea, Wales	(?) Lyons	Fanny (?)		Cardiff, Wales	scholar
1361	Lyons	Moses	1845	Plymouth, Devon	Jacob Lyons	Phoebe (Barina, Branah, Fanny) Solomon	Esther Blanche Davis	Plymouth, Devon	
3061	Lyons	Moses	1850	Spitalfields, London	Sampson Lyons	Lidy (?)		Spitalfields, London	
24721	Lyons	Moss	1798	Middlesex, London			Catherine (?)	Walworth, London	floor cloth manufacturer
3042	Lyons	Moss	1829	Spitalfields, London	(?) Lyons	Rebecca (?)		Spitalfields, London	clothes salesman
2968	Lyons	Moss	1837	Wapping, London	William Lyons	Mary (?)		Spitalfields, London	
2978	Lyons	Myer	1844	Spitalfields, London	Samuel Lyons	Catharine (Caroline) (?)		Spitalfields, London	
2098	Lyons	Myer (Mayer)	1807	Kirchburg, Koblenz, Germany			Elizabeth Isaacs	Canterbury, Kent	tailor
8940	Lyons	Nathan	1820	Aldgate, London	Aaron Lyons	Abigail Solomons	Mary Barnett	Aldgate, London	orange dealer
13792	Lyons	Nathan B	1791	?, Turkey				Manchester	teacher
30079	Lyons	Nathaniel	1835	?, London	Morris Lyons	Ann Barnett		Aldgate, London	
24690	Lyons	Nathaniel (Nathan)	1820	?Elephant & Castle, London	Joseph Lyons	Catherine (?)	Hannah Cohen	Elephant & Castle, London	
2100	Lyons	Nathaniel (Nathan)	1836	?Canterbury, Kent	Myer (Mayer) Lyons	Elizabeth Isaacs		Canterbury, Kent	
3023	Lyons	Philip	1814	Aldgate, London	Joseph (Reuben) Lyon (Lyons)	Abigail Hyams	Catherine (Kitty) Levy	Spitalfields, London	slipper maker
12518	Lyons	Philip	1821	Norwich, Norfolk			Eliza (?)	Norwich, Norfolk	hand loom weaver mixed
12456	Lyons	Phillip	1827	Portsmouth, Hampshire	Boaz Lyons			Aldgate, London	fishmonger journeyman
8416	Lyons	Phoebe	1785	Portsmouth, Hampshire	Joseph Levy		Charles Lyons	Ryde, Isle of Wight	
2099	Lyons	Phoebe	1834	Canterbury, Kent	Myer (Mayer) Lyons	Elizabeth Isaacs	Alfred Levy	Canterbury, Kent	
1358	Lyons	Phoebe (Barina, Branah, Fanny)	1816	?, Poland	Woolf Solomon		Jacob Lyons	Plymouth, Devon	
12008	Lyons	Phoeby	1841	Middlesex, London	Henry Lyons	Rachel Hart		Waterloo, London	scholar at home
12005	Lyons	Priscilla	1844	Middlesex, London	Henry Lyons	Rachel Hart	Joseph Boam	Waterloo, London	scholar at home
15494	Lyons	R---	1826	Aldgate, London	(?) Jacobs	Rebecca (?)	Isaacs Lyons	Covent Garden, London	
11385	Lyons	Rachael	1806	Holborn, London	Yitzhak Levy		Samuel Lyons	Aldgate, London	greengrocer
12015	Lyons	Rachael	1817	Middlesex, London	Shlomeh Hart		Henry Lyons	Waterloo, London	
24782	Lyons	Rachael	1822	Southwark, London	(?)		Henry Lyons	Elephant & Castle, London	
3015	Lyons	Rachael	1843	Spitalfields, London	Lewis Lyons	Sophia (?)		Spitalfields, London	
24881	Lyons	Rachael	1848	Westminster, London	Simeon Lyons	Louisa Cowan		Southwark, London	
15497	Lyons	Rachael	1850	Covent Garden, London	Isaacs Lyons	R--- Jacobs		Covent Garden, London	
15516	Lyons	Rachael	1850	Covent Garden, London	Lewis Lyons	Maria (?)		Covent Garden, London	
23356	Lyons	Rachel	1804	Soho, London	(?)		Abraham Lyons	Strand, London	
3003	Lyons	Rachel	1807	Aldgate, London	Aaron Nunes Martinez		Aaron Lyons	Spitalfields, London	
3093	Lyons	Rachel	1811	?, London			Abraham Lyons	Spitalfields, London	slipper hawker

ID	surname	given names	born	birthplace	father	mother	spouse 1	1851 residence	1851 occupation
3036	Lyons	Rachel	1827	Spitalfields, London	(?) Lyons	Rebeca (?)		Aldgate, London	tailoress
3004	Lyons	Rachel	1832	Aldgate, London	Aaron Lyons	Rachel Nunes Martinez	Moses Nunes Martin (Martines)	Spitalfields, London	servant of all work
2990	Lyons	Rachel	1833	Whitechapel, London	(?) Lyons			Spitalfields, London	servant
23359	Lyons	Rachel	1840	Covent Garden, London	Abraham Lyons	Rachel (?)		Strand, London	scholar
3071	Lyons	Rachel	1842	City, London	Lewis Lyons	Sarah Hyam		Spitalfields, London	scholar
3034	Lyons	Rebeca	1777	Spitalfields, London	(?)		(?) Lyons	Aldgate, London	
3039	Lyons	Rebecca	1791	Bath				Spitalfields, London	
2997	Lyons	Rebecca	1820	Spitalfields, London	Yehuda Leib Symonds		Samuel Lyons	Spitalfields, London	
28062	Lyons	Rebecca	1821	Whitechapel, London	(?Benjamin) Lyons	Sarah (?Levy)		Spitalfields, London	capmaker
24687	Lyons	Rebecca	1836	Elephant & Castle, London	Joseph Lyons	Catherine (?)		Elephant & Castle, London	flower manufacturer
4717	Lyons	Rebecca	1838	Jersey, Channel Islands	Morris Lyons	Sarah (?)	Lewis Alexander	Birmingham	
1360	Lyons	Rebecca	1843	Plymouth, Devon	Jacob Lyons	Phoebe (Barina, Branah, Fanny) Solomon		Plymouth, Devon	
25095	Lyons	Rebecca	1844	?, London	Isaac Lyons	Rosetta Mordecai		Finsbury, London	
12010	Lyons	Rebecca	1847	Middlesex, London	Henry Lyons	Rachel Hart	Albert B Harris	Waterloo, London	
23483	Lyons	Rebecca	1849	Liverpool	Joseph Lyons	Esther (?)		Liverpool	scholar
24887	Lyons	Rebecca	1849	Southwark, London	Maurice Lyons	Maria (Marian) Isaacs		Southwark, London	
8943	Lyons	Rebecca	1851	Aldgate, London	Nathan Lyons	Mary Barnett		Aldgate, London	
1882	Lyons	Reuben Barnett	1848	Neath, Wales	Barnett Lyons	Jane (?)	Deborah Goldstein	Cardiff, Wales	
25098	Lyons	Robert	1850	Finsbury, London	Isaac Lyons	Rosetta Mordecai		Finsbury, London	
1359	Lyons	Rosa (Briny)	1840	Plymouth, Devon	Jacob Lyons	Phoebe (Barina, Branah, Fanny) Solomon	G--- Norman	Plymouth, Devon	
27286	Lyons	Rosetta	1807	Aldgate, London	(?)		(?) Lyons	Aldgate, London	dressmaker
26625	Lyons	Rosetta	1808	Aldgate, London	(?)		Abraham Lyons	Aldgate, London	clothes dealer's wife
25094	Lyons	Rosetta	1826	?, London	(?) Mordecai		Isaac Lyons	Finsbury, London	
3057	Lyons	Sampson	1820	Aldgate, London			Lidy (Leah) (?)	Spitalfields, London	pastry cook
2996	Lyons	Samuel	1807	City, London	Lewis Lyons		Rebecca Symonds	Spitalfields, London	general dealer
2972	Lyons	Samuel	1808	Poznan, Poland [Posen, Prussia]	Yehuda		Catharine (Caroline) (?)	Spitalfields, London	cap peak manufacturer
11384	Lyons	Samuel	1811	Spitalfields, London	Israel Lyon		Rachael Levy	Aldgate, London	greengrocer
22654	Lyons	Samuel	1829	Spitalfields, London	(?) Lyons	Hannah (?)		Whitechapel, London	glass dealer
3094	Lyons	Samuel	1830	?, London	Abraham Lyons	Rachel (?)	Anna Solomon	Spitalfields, London	slipper maker
22672	Lyons	Samuel	1830	Whitechapel, London	(?) Lyons	Sarah (?)		Whitechapel, London	general labourer
3006	Lyons	Samuel	1836	Aldgate, London	Aaron Lyons	Rachel Nunes Martinez	Nancy Levy	Spitalfields, London	general dealer
27095	Lyons	Samuel	1839	?, London	(?) Lyons	Elizabeth		Aldgate, London	cigar maker
26628	Lyons	Samuel	1840	Aldgate, London	Abraham Lyons	Rosetta (?)		Aldgate, London	scholar
23360	Lyons	Samuel	1842	Covent Garden, London	Abraham Lyons	Rachel (?)		Strand, London	scholar
3059	Lyons	Samuel	1845	Surrey, London	Sampson Lyons	Lidy (?)		Spitalfields, London	
2971	Lyons	Samuel	1846	Whitechapel, London	William Lyons	Mary (?)		Spitalfields, London	
25836	Lyons	Samuel	1848	Aldgate, London	Abraham Lyons	Leah Davis		Aldgate, London	scholar
11049	Lyons	Sara	1821	Aldgate, London	Isaac Symons		Emanuel Lyons	Aldgate, London	parasol maker
22670	Lyons	Sarah	1804	Whitechapel, London	(?)		(?) Lyons	Whitechapel, London	lodging house keeper
3063	Lyons	Sarah	1812	Spitalfields, London	(?) Lyons			Spitalfields, London	ginger beer maker

ID	surname	given names	born	birthplace	father	mother	spouse 1	1851 residence	1851 occupation
3068	Lyons	Sarah	1813	City, London	Hyam Hyams		Lewis Lyons	Spitalfields, London	
4714	Lyons	Sarah	1814	Portsmouth, Hampshire	(?)		Morris Lyons	Birmingham	
15331	Lyons	Sarah	1815	Southwark, London	(?)		(?) Lyons	Southwark, London	
7208	Lyons	Sarah	1822	Chatham, Kent	John Isaacs	Deborah (?)	Asher Lyons	Chatham, Kent	
21514	Lyons	Sarah	1840	Aldgate, London	Mordecai Lyon (Lyons)	Esther Levy		Soho, London	
2969	Lyons	Sarah	1842	Whitechapel, London	William Lyons	Mary (?)		Spitalfields, London	
3084	Lyons	Sarah	1843	Middlesex, London	Isaac Lyons	Luisa (?)		Spitalfields, London	
27461	Lyons	Sarah	1849	Whitechapel, London	John Lyons	Esther Levy		Whitechapel, London	
3018	Lyons	Sarah	1850	Spitalfields, London	Lewis Lyons	Sophia (?)	Mark Abrahams	Spitalfields, London	
12455	Lyons	Sarah	1850	Aldgate, London	John Lyons	Martha Simonds	Morris Lyons	Aldgate, London	
12523	Lyons	Sarah	1850	Norwich, Norfolk	Philip Lyons	Eliza (?)		Norwich, Norfolk	
3030	Lyons	Saul	1808	Spitalfields, London	Lewis (Lear, Yehuda Leib) Lyons		Amelia Phillips	Spitalfields, London	general dealer
3025	Lyons	Saul	1842	Spitalfields, London	Philip Lyons	Catherine (Kitty) Levy	Leah Hart	Spitalfields, London	scholar
3000	Lyons	Saul	1846	?Spitalfields, London	Samuel Lyons	Rebecca Symonds	Phoebe Myers	Spitalfields, London	
15897	Lyons	Selina	1840	Middlesex, London	(?) Lyons			Hackney, London	boarding school pupil
24877	Lyons	Simeon	1817	Whitechapel, London	Benjamin Lyons	Abigail (?)	Louisa Cowan	Southwark, London	tailor
24078	Lyons	Solomon	1812	Middlesex, London			Julia (?)	Fitzrovia, London	tailor
13934	Lyons	Solomon	1830	?, London				Manchester	tailor's shopman
11419	Lyons	Solomon	1834	Middlesex, London				Aldgate, London	butcher
24879	Lyons	Solomon	1841	Southwark, London	Simeon Lyons	Louisa Cowan		Southwark, London	
3016	Lyons	Solomon	1846	Spitalfields, London	Lewis Lyons	Sophia (?)		Spitalfields, London	
12012	Lyons	Solomon	1849	Waterloo, London	Henry Lyons	Rachel Hart		Waterloo, London	
3012	Lyons	Sophia	1816	Boston, Liincolnshire	(?)		Lewis Lyons	Spitalfields, London	
3035	Lyons	Sophie	1823	Spitalfields, London	(?) Lyons	Rebecca (?)		Aldgate, London	cap maker
19666	Lyons	Susan	1821	Whitechapel, London	(?) Lyons			Spitalfields, London	house servant
23477	Lyons	Theresa	1834	Liverpool	Joseph Lyons	Esther (?)		Liverpool	dress maker
23482	Lyons	Victoria	1846	Liverpool	Joseph Lyons	Esther (?)		Liverpool	scholar
2965	Lyons	William	1809	Aldgate, London			Mary (?)	Spitalfields, London	labourer
13649	Lyons	William	1815	?			Isabella (?)	Manchester	inkmaker empl 1
4715	Lyons	William	1834	Plymouth, Devon	Morris Lyons	Sarah (?)		Birmingham	electric gilder
27399	Lyons	Woolf	1826	Shoreditch, London	Lewes Lyon		Elizabeth Woolf	Whitechapel, London	general dealer
17493	Lyons (Lyon)	Abraham	1823	?, London	Myer Lyons		Alice Lyons	Aldgate, London	general dealer
13428	Lyons (Lyon)	Abraham	1834	Aldgate, London	Jacob Lyons (Lyon)	Elizabeth Abrahams		Shoreditch, London	clothier
17494	Lyons (Lyon)	Alice	1809	?, London	Lewis Lyons		Abraham Lyons (Lyon)	Aldgate, London	
12097	Lyons (Lyon)	Charles (Saul, Solomon)	1804	Aldgate, London	Yehuda Leib		Dinah Cohen	Spitalfields, London	general dealer
12098	Lyons (Lyon)	Dinah	1807	Aldgate, London	Eliyahu HaCohen		Charles (Saul, Solomon) Lyons (Lyon)	Spitalfields, London	
13429	Lyons (Lyon)	Edward	1835	?Shoreditch, London	Jacob Lyons (Lyon)	Elizabeth Abrahams		Shoreditch, London	clothier
12107	Lyons (Lyon)	Elias	1847	Spitalfields, London	Charles (Saul, Solomon) Lyons (Lyon)	Dinah Cohen		Spitalfields, London	
13426	Lyons (Lyon)	Elizabeth	1807	?, London	(?) Abrahams	Elizabeth (?)	Jacob Lyons (Lyon)	Shoreditch, London	
12099	Lyons (Lyon)	Emanuel	1830	Whitechapel, London	Charles (Saul, Solomon) Lyons (Lyon)	Dinah Cohen		Spitalfields, London	general dealer
13431	Lyons (Lyon)	Esther	1849	Shoreditch, London	Jacob Lyons (Lyon)	Elizabeth Abrahams	John Abrahams	Shoreditch, London	

ID	surname	given names	born	birthplace	father	mother	spouse 1	1851 residence	1851 occupation
17498	Lyons (Lyon)	Frances (Fanny)	1848	Aldgate, London	Abraham Lyons (Lyon)	Alice Lyons		Aldgate, London	scholar
13425	Lyons (Lyon)	Jacob	1807	?, London	Yehuda Lyon		Elizabeth Abrahams	Shoreditch, London	clothier
12105	Lyons (Lyon)	Jacob	1843	Whitechapel, London	Charles (Saul, Solomon) Lyons (Lyon)	Dinah Cohen		Spitalfields, London	scholar
11870	Lyons (Lyon)	Joel	1843	Shoreditch, London	Judah Lyon	Rose (Rosetta) Hart		Whitechapel, London	inmate of orphan school
24729	Lyons (Lyon)	John	1850	Elephant & Castle, London	Simon Lyons (Lyon)	Julia Levi		Walworth, London	
24727	Lyons (Lyon)	Julia	1819	Bermondsey, London	(?) Levi		Simon Lyons (Lyon)	Walworth, London	
12106	Lyons (Lyon)	Leah	1845	Spitalfields, London	Charles (Saul, Solomon) Lyons (Lyon)	Dinah Cohen		Spitalfields, London	scholar
12100	Lyons (Lyon)	Lewis	1832	Whitechapel, London	Charles (Saul, Solomon) Lyons (Lyon)	Dinah Cohen		Spitalfields, London	general dealer
17497	Lyons (Lyon)	Lewis	1846	Aldgate, London	Abraham Lyons (Lyon)	Alice Lyons	Jane Jonas	Aldgate, London	scholar
12101	Lyons (Lyon)	Lyon	1835	Whitechapel, London	Charles (Saul, Solomon) Lyons (Lyon)	Dinah Cohen		Spitalfields, London	butcher
17495	Lyons (Lyon)	Michael	1842	Aldgate, London	Abraham Lyons (Lyon)	Alice Lyons	Amelia Levy	Aldgate, London	scholar
12104	Lyons (Lyon)	Moses	1841	Aldgate, London	Charles (Saul, Solomon) Lyons (Lyon)	Dinah Cohen		Spitalfields, London	scholar
13430	Lyons (Lyon)	Moss	1845	Shoreditch, London	Jacob Lyons (Lyon)	Elizabeth Abrahams		Shoreditch, London	
12103	Lyons (Lyon)	Nancey	1839	Aldgate, London	Charles (Saul, Solomon) Lyons (Lyon)	Dinah Cohen		Spitalfields, London	waistcoat maker
12102	Lyons (Lyon)	Rachel	1830	Aldgate, London	Charles (Saul, Solomon) Lyons (Lyon)	Dinah Cohen		Spitalfields, London	cap maker
17496	Lyons (Lyon)	Rachel	1844	Aldgate, London	Abraham Lyons (Lyon)	Alice Lyons		Aldgate, London	scholar
30585	Lyons (Lyon)	Rebecca	1851	Spitalfields, London	Charles (Saul, Solomon) Lyons (Lyon)	Dinah Cohen		Spitalfields, London	
13427	Lyons (Lyon)	Samuel	1830	Aldgate, London	Jacob Lyons (Lyon)	Elizabeth Abrahams		Shoreditch, London	clothier
24726	Lyons (Lyon)	Simon	1825	Westminster, London			Julia Levi	Walworth, London	upholsterer
24728	Lyons (Lyon)	Wolf	1848	Bermondsey, London	Simon Lyons (Lyon)	Julia Levi		Walworth, London	
22959	Lyons [Pesman]	Emma Amelia	1842	Aldgate, London	Emanuel Pesman	Catherine (Kate) Lyons	Benjamin Noah Da Costa	Wapping, London	
21568	Lyons?	George	1850	Spitalfields, London	(?) Lyons?	(?) De Frece		Aldgate, London	
21566	Lyons?	Laurence	1846	Spitalfields, London	(?) Lyons?	(?) De Frece		Aldgate, London	
21567	Lyons?	Rebecca	1848	Spitalfields, London	(?) Lyons?	(?) De Frece		Aldgate, London	
13660	Lyrschitz	Solomon M	1817	?				Manchester	dealer in musical instruments
23945	Maccabi	Charles	1775	Surrey, London				Marylebone, London	surgeon
15129	Mackes	Elizabeth	1822	?, Essex	(?)		Reuben Mackes	Hoxton, London	
15132	Mackes	Ellen	1851	Shoreditch, London	Reuben Mackes	Elizabeth (?)		Hoxton, London	
15131	Mackes	Rebecca	1849	Shoreditch, London	Reuben Mackes	Elizabeth (?)		Hoxton, London	
15128	Mackes	Reuben	1818	Surrey, London			Elizabeth (?)	Hoxton, London	undertaker
15130	Mackes	Reuben	1843	Southwark, London	Reuben Mackes	Elizabeth (?)		Hoxton, London	
4723	Madenberg	Braham	1801	Warsaw, Poland			Hannah (?)	Birmingham	cabinet maker
4724	Madenberg	Hannah (Anna)	1795	Warsaw, Poland			Braham Madenberg	Birmingham	
24385	Maers	Angel	1845	Soho, London	Jacob Maers	Jane (?)		Soho, London	
24384	Maers	Betsy	1842	Soho, London	Jacob Maers	Jane (?)		Soho, London	
24379	Maers	Jacob	1799	?, Germany			Jane (?)	Soho, London	tailor

ID	surname	given names	born	birthplace	father	mother	spouse 1	1851 residence	1851 occupation
24380	Maers	Jane	1803	?, Belgium	(?)		Jacob Maers	Soho, London	
24381	Maers	Michael	1830	Covent Garden, London	Jacob Maers	Jane (?)		Soho, London	clerk
24383	Maers	Samuel	1836	Covent Garden, London	Jacob Maers	Jane (?)		Soho, London	tailor (apprentice)
24382	Maers	Sarah	1833	Covent Garden, London	Jacob Maers	Jane (?)		Soho, London	tailoress
2148	Magner	Morris	1822	?, Poland [Pruser, Prussia]	Levin Magner			Hull, Yorkshire	jeweller
17418	Magness	Catherine	1815	Aldgate, London	(?)		Philip Magness	Spitalfields, London	
17421	Magness	Catherine	1849	Spitalfields, London	Philip Magness	Catherine (?)		Spitalfields, London	
17419	Magness	Henry	1836	Spitalfields, London	Philip Magness	Catherine (?)		Spitalfields, London	cigar maker
17420	Magness	Julia	1847	Spitalfields, London	Philip Magness	Catherine (?)		Spitalfields, London	
17417	Magness	Philip	1816	Shoreditch, London			Catherine (?)	Spitalfields, London	general dealer
2808	Magnus	Abraham (Albert)	1837	Finsbury, London	Nathaniel Magnus	Hannah Moses	Annie Frances Cohen	Shoreditch, London	scholar
26449	Magnus	Amelia	1813	?, Poland	(?)		Elias Magnus	Aldgate, London	
2751	Magnus	Amelia	1842	Finsbury, London	Simon Magnus	Julia Moss	Henry Lewis Harris	Aldgate, London	
25790	Magnus	Barnett	1776	Hamburg, Germany			Sarah (?)	Aldgate, London	clothes dealer
22166	Magnus	Barnett	1788	Aldgate, London	Menachem Manes Cohen	Rachel (?)	Sarah Barnett	Whitechapel, London	general dealer
6902	Magnus	Barnett	1842	Aldgate, London	Philip Magnus	Rachel (?)		Spitalfields, London	scholar
10840	Magnus	Benjamin	1827	Aldgate, London	(?Barnett) Magnus	(?Sarah Barnett)	Esther Costa	Spitalfields, London	cigar maker
6910	Magnus	Benjamin	1846	Spitalfields, London	James (Simon) Magnus	Rosetta Nathan	Catherine (Kate) Jacobs	Spitalfields, London	
2817	Magnus	Benjamin	1848	Shoreditch, London	Joseph Magnus	Emma Fileman		Shoreditch, London	scholar
7262	Magnus	Caroline	1809	Rochester, Kent	Joel Barnett	Sarah (?)	Jacob (John) Magnus	Fitzrovia, London	
2820	Magnus	Caroline	1834	Aldgate, London	Henry Magnus	Rosetta Isaacs	Simeon Emanuel	Aldgate, London	
2803	Magnus	Caroline	1840	Aldgate, London	Simon Magnus	Julia Moss		Aldgate, London	scholar
6901	Magnus	Catharine	1836	Aldgate, London	Philip Magnus	Rachel (?)		Spitalfields, London	
6909	Magnus	Catharine	1842	Spitalfields, London	James (Simon) Magnus	Rosetta Nathan		Spitalfields, London	
22168	Magnus	Catherine	1831	Mile End, London	Barnett Magnus	Sarah Barnett		Whitechapel, London	
10842	Magnus	Catherine	1851	Spitalfields, London	Benjamin Magnus	Esther Costa		Spitalfields, London	
5860	Magnus	Cordelia	1831	Chatham, Kent	Simon Lazarus Magnus	Sarah Wolff	Coleman Defries	Soho, London	
6903	Magnus	David	1844	Spitalfields, London	Philip Magnus	Rachel (?)		Spitalfields, London	scholar
2807	Magnus	Dinah	1820	Stratford, London	Hyman Levy		Nathaniel Magnus	Shoreditch, London	
16350	Magnus	Edward	1848	Shoreditch, London	Jacob (John) Magnus	Caroline Barnett		Fitzrovia, London	
2812	Magnus	Edward (Nathan Henry)	1834	Aldgate, London	Henry Magnus	Rosetta Isaacs	Henrietta Magnus	Aldgate, London	
26448	Magnus	Elias	1803	?, Poland			Amelia (?)	Aldgate, London	cap maker
28350	Magnus	Elizabeth	1823	Whitechapel, London	(?) Magnus	Julia (?)		Whitechapel, London	
19430	Magnus	Elizabeth (Eliza)	1820	Vauxhall, London	Solomon Hyman	Sarah Davis	Lazarus (Lewis) Magnus	Camden Town, London	
30310	Magnus	Elizabeth (Lizzie)	1834	Chatham, Kent	Simon Magnus	Sarah Wolff	Manuel Nunes Castello	Chatham, Kent	
2810	Magnus	Emanuel	1847	Finsbury, London	Nathaniel Magnus	Esther Isaacs	Elizabeth Natali	Shoreditch, London	
2815	Magnus	Emma	1825	Whitechapel, London	Benjamin Fileman	Elizabeth (?)	Joseph Magnus	Shoreditch, London	
10841	Magnus	Esther	1822	Spitalfields, London	(?) Costa		Benjamin Magnus	Spitalfields, London	general dealer
2811	Magnus	Esther	1849	Finsbury, London	Nathaniel Magnus	Esther Isaacs		Shoreditch, London	
29079	Magnus	George	1836	Middlesex, London	James Magnus	Rebecca (?)		St Giles, London	hawker
29081	Magnus	Hannah	1842	Whitechapel, London	James Magnus	Rebecca (?)		St Giles, London	scholar
6906	Magnus	Hannah	1850	Spitalfields, London	Philip Magnus	Rachel (?)		Spitalfields, London	
26452	Magnus	Hannah	1838	?, Poland	Elias Magnus	Amelia (?)		Aldgate, London	

ID	surname	given names	born	birthplace	father	mother	spouse 1	1851 residence	1851 occupation
2813	Magnus	Henrietta	1838	Aldgate, London	Simon Nathan Magnus	Julia Moss	Edward (Nathan Henry) Magnus	Aldgate, London	scholar
2804	Magnus	Henry	1841	Aldgate, London	Simon Magnus	Julia Moss	Rosetta Cohen	Aldgate, London	scholar
21049	Magnus	Henry	1841	?, London				Dover, Kent	boarding school pupil
31168	Magnus	Henry	1847	Chatham, Kent	Samuel Magnus	Miriam (?)		Chatham, Kent	scholar
29082	Magnus	Henry	1849	Middlesex, London	James Magnus	Rebecca (?)		St Giles, London	
2822	Magnus	Henry H	1838	Aldgate, London	Henry Magnus	Rosetta Isaacs	Emily Barnett	Aldgate, London	
2801	Magnus	Isabella	1836	Aldgate, London	Simon Magnus	Julia Moss	Julius Lemel	Aldgate, London	childminder
19432	Magnus	Jacob	1848	St Pancras, London	Lazarus (Lewis) Magnus	Elizabeth (Eliza) Hyman		Camden Town, London	
7261	Magnus	Jacob (John)	1805	Chatham, Kent	Lazarus Magnus	Sarah Moses	Caroline Barnett	Fitzrovia, London	shipping agent
29077	Magnus	James	1811	Middlesex, London	Tsvi		Rebecca (?)	St Giles, London	general dealer
6907	Magnus	James (Simon)	1822	Aldgate, London	Barnett Magnus	(?Sarah Barnett)	Rosetta Nathan	Spitalfields, London	general dealer
14461	Magnus	Joseph	1806	?, Germany				Manchester	merchant
2814	Magnus	Joseph	1824	Aldgate, London	Nathan Joseph Magnus	Simony Solomon	Emma Fileman	Shoreditch, London	boot + shoe maker
2800	Magnus	Joseph	1835	Aldgate, London	Simon Magnus	Julia Moss	Sarah Natali	Aldgate, London	boot and shoe maker
6905	Magnus	Joseph	1846	Spitalfields, London	Philip Magnus	Rachel (?)		Spitalfields, London	scholar
2821	Magnus	Joseph Henry	1837	Aldgate, London	Henry Magnus	Rosetta Isaacs	Louisa Isabella Finsterer	Aldgate, London	
28349	Magnus	Julia	1781	Aldgate, London	(?)		(?) Magnus	Whitechapel, London	
2799	Magnus	Julia	1805	Deptford, London	Barnard (Baruch) Moss	Isabella (?)	Simon (Simeon) Magnus	Aldgate, London	
29080	Magnus	Julia	1838	Middlesex, London	James Magnus	Rebecca (?)		St Giles, London	servant
31167	Magnus	Kate	1843	Dover, Kent	Samuel Magnus	Miriam (?)		Chatham, Kent	scholar
19434	Magnus	Kate	1851	Camden Town, London	Lazarus (Lewis) Magnus	Elizabeth (Eliza) Hyman		Camden Town, London	
31165	Magnus	Laurence	1839	Dover, Kent	Samuel Magnus	Miriam (?)		Chatham, Kent	scholar
7260	Magnus	Laurie	1840	Ramsgate, Kent	Jacob (John) Magnus	Caroline Barnett		Fitzrovia, London	scholar
6904	Magnus	Lazarus	1846	Spitalfields, London	Philip Magnus	Rachel (?)		Spitalfields, London	scholar
19431	Magnus	Lazarus (Lewis)	1822	Middlesex, London			Elizabeth Hyman	Camden Town, London	general dealer
5856	Magnus	Lazarus Simon	1827	Chatham, Kent	Simon Magnus	Sarah Wolff		Chatham, Kent	coal factor + merchant
31170	Magnus	Lennie	1851	Chatham, Kent	Samuel Magnus	Miriam (?)		Chatham, Kent	
26450	Magnus	Levin	1832	?, Poland	Elias Magnus	Amelia (?)		Aldgate, London	cap maker
11344	Magnus	Michael	1834	Middlesex, London				Aldgate, London	shopman
31164	Magnus	Miriam	1813	Chatham, Kent	(?)		Samuel Magnus	Chatham, Kent	
2797	Magnus	Nathan	1780	Zwolle, Holland	Joseph Simon Magnus	Bela Eliezer Cohen	Simony Solomon (Solomons)	Aldgate, London	boot and shoe manufacturer
2809	Magnus	Nathan	1842	Finsbury, London	Nathaniel Magnus	Hannah Moses		Shoreditch, London	scholar
2806	Magnus	Nathaniel	1812	Aldgate, London	Nathan Magnus	Simony Solomon (Solomons)	Hannah Moses	Shoreditch, London	shoe manufacturer
31166	Magnus	Phebe	1841	Dover, Kent	Samuel Magnus	Miriam (?)		Chatham, Kent	scholar
6899	Magnus	Philip	1815	Aldgate, London	Issachar Behr Magnus		Rachel Levy	Spitalfields, London	general dealer
7257	Magnus	Philip	1842	Holborn, London	Jacob (John) Magnus	Caroline Barnett	Katie Emanuel	Fitzrovia, London	scholar
22169	Magnus	Rachel	1761	Southwark, London	(?)		Menachem Manes Cohen Magnus	Whitechapel, London	
6900	Magnus	Rachel	1819	Aldgate, London	Michael Levy		Philip Magnus	Spitalfields, London	
2717	Magnus	Rachel	1834	?, Poland	Elias Magnus	Amelia (?)	Woolf Davis	Aldgate, London	cap maker
29078	Magnus	Rebecca	1815	?, Holland	(?)		James Magnus	St Giles, London	music teacher
2819	Magnus	Rosetta	1811	?, London	Emanuel Isaacs	Maria (?)	Henry Magnus	Aldgate, London	shoe manufacturer

ID	surname	given names	born	birthplace	father	mother	spouse 1	1851 residence	1851 occupation
6908	Magnus	Rosetta	1827	Spitalfields, London	Joseph Nathan	Elizabeth (?)	James (Simon) Magnus	Spitalfields, London	dressmaker
31163	Magnus	Samuel	1795	Chatham, Kent			Miriam (?)	Chatham, Kent	plate glass dealer
7264	Magnus	Sarah	1774	?	Abraham Moses	Elizabeth (?)		Chatham, Kent	
25791	Magnus	Sarah	1778	?, Holland	(?)		Barnett Magnus	Aldgate, London	
22167	Magnus	Sarah	1798	Spitalfields, London	David [Straight Finger? Stratford?] Barnett		Barnett Magnus	Whitechapel, London	
7263	Magnus	Sarah	1846	Shoreditch, London	Jacob (John) Magnus	Caroline Barnett		Fitzrovia, London	
31169	Magnus	Sarah	1849	Chatham, Kent	Samuel Magnus	Miriam (?)		Chatham, Kent	scholar
19433	Magnus	Sarah	1850	St Pancras, London	Lazarus (Lewis) Magnus	Elizabeth (Eliza) Hyman		Camden Town, London	
26462	Magnus	Sarah	1851	Spitalfields, London	James (Simon) Magnus	Rosetta Nathan		Spitalfields, London	
2798	Magnus	Simon (Simeon)	1805	Aldgate, London	Nathan Magnus	Simony Solomon (Solomons)	Julia Moss	Aldgate, London	boot and shoe maker
5854	Magnus	Simon Lazarus	1800	Chatham, Kent	Lazarus Magnus	Sarah Moses	Sarah Wolff	Chatham, Kent	coal factor + merchant
2816	Magnus	Victoria (Simha)	1847	Finsbury, London	Joseph Magnus	Emma Fileman		Shoreditch, London	
26205	Mahler	Michael?	1822	?, Germany				Aldgate, London	furrier
4740	Maks	Isabella	1845	Birmingham	James Marks	Sarah (?)		Birmingham	scholar
30137	Mallan	Adelaide Eve	1831	Bloomsbury, London	Edward Mallan	Mary (Miriam) (?)	Solomon Meyers	Bloomsbury, London	
30145	Mallan	Diana (Dinah)	1811	City, London	Meir		James Michael Mallan	Bloomsbury, London	
30135	Mallan	Edward	1806	?, Holland	Vallek (Falk) Mallan (Milleman)	Bracha Lippschutz	Mary (Miriam) (?)	Bloomsbury, London	dentist
30138	Mallan	George Prescott	1834	?Bloomsbury, London	Edward Mallan	Mary (Miriam) (?)	Louisa Amelia Albert	Bloomsbury, London	
30142	Mallan	Hannah (Harriet) Prescott	1844	Lambeth, London	Edward Mallan	Mary (Miriam) (?)	Louis Meldola	Bloomsbury, London	
30144	Mallan	James Michael	1814	?, Holland	Vallek (Falk) Mallan (Milleman)	Bracha Lippschutz	Diana (Dinah) Myers	Bloomsbury, London	
30147	Mallan	John G A	1847	City, London				Bloomsbury, London	
30136	Mallan	Mary (Miriam)	1811	New York, USA	(?)		Edward Mallan	Bloomsbury, London	
30146	Mallan	Rebecca M	1842	City, London	(?) Mallan			Bloomsbury, London	scholar at home
30141	Mallan	Rosetta Eveline	1842	Bloomsbury, London	Edward Mallan	Mary (Miriam) (?)	Charles Henry Collick	Bloomsbury, London	
30140	Mallan	Victoria	1841	Bloomsbury, London	Edward Mallan	Mary (Miriam) (?)	Moses Samuel	Bloomsbury, London	
30139	Mallan	Zalinda (Yelena)	1833	Bloomsbury, London	Edward Mallan	Mary (Miriam) (?)		Bloomsbury, London	
15385	Mallis	Matthew L	1823	?, Austria				Waterloo, London	student
8018	Malone	John	1778	Belfast, Ireland			Eliza (?)	Portsmouth, Hampshire	
2512	Malonowski	Godel	1831	?, Poland				Hull, Yorkshire	glazier
14998	Mamroth	Alexander	1826	?, Poland [?, Prussian Poland]				Bethnal Green, London	printer
14200	Manasse	Adolf	1845	?, Poland [?, Prussia]	Baruch Manasse	Flora (?)		Manchester	
14199	Manasse	Augusta	1835	?, Poland [?, Prussia]	Baruch Manasse	Flora (?)		Manchester	
14197	Manasse	Baruch	1791	?, Poland [?, Prussia]			Flora (?)	Manchester	agent
14202	Manasse	Caroline	1850	?, London	Baruch Manasse	Flora (?)		Manchester	
14198	Manasse	Flora	1811	?, Poland [?, Prussia]	(?)		Baruch Manasse	Manchester	lodging house keeper
14201	Manasse	Samuel	1848	?, Russia	Baruch Manasse	Flora (?)		Manchester	
27467	Mandelbaum	David	1797	?, Bavaria, Germany			Fanny (?)	Whitechapel, London	importer of fancy goods empl 1
27468	Mandelbaum	Fanny	1811	?, Bavaria, Germany	(?)		David Mandelbaum	Whitechapel, London	
27470	Mandelbaum	Frances	1832	?, Bavaria, Germany	David Mandelbaum	Fanny (?)	Anton Benda	Whitechapel, London	
27469	Mandelbaum	Judith	1830	?, Bavaria, Germany	David Mandelbaum	Fanny (?)	David Philipp	Whitechapel, London	

ID	surname	given names	born	birthplace	father	mother	spouse 1	1851 residence	1851 occupation
1297	Mandovsky	Moses Jonas	1800	Mecklenburg Schwerin, Germany	Jonah Mandovsky		Sophia Simon	Plymouth, Devon	toy dealer
1278	Mandovsky	Sophia	1800	Plymouth, Devon	Abraham Simons		Moses Jonas Mandovsky	Plymouth, Devon	toy dealer's wife
22565	Mann	Jane	1825	Billericay, Essex	John Mann	Mary (?)	Isaac Henry Crawcour	Brentwood, Essex	
14982	Manns	Rose	1841	Middlesex, London	(?) Manns			Bethnal Green, London	boarding school pupil
19057	Manuel	Marian (Miriam)	1822	Aldgate, London	Nathan Casper	Amelia Ansell	Morris Manuel	Aldgate, London	
19058	Manuel	Morris	1821	?, Poland [?, Russia Poland]	Samuel Manuel		Marian (Miriam) Casper	Aldgate, London	watchmaker
19059	Manuel	Priscilla Harriet	1848	Aldgate, London	Morris Manuel	Marian Casper	Henry Coates	Aldgate, London	
19060	Manuel	Rosina Sarah	1850	Aldgate, London	Morris Manuel	Marian Casper		Aldgate, London	
2174	Marcks	Nathan	1815	?, Poland			Rose (?)	Oxford, Oxfordshire	itinerant jeweller
2176	Marcks	Philip	1850	Oxford, Oxfordshire	Nathan Marcks	Rose (?)		Oxford, Oxfordshire	
2175	Marcks	Rose	1815	?, Poland			Nathan Marcks	Oxford, Oxfordshire	
24513	Marcs	Augusta	1825	?, Poland [?, Prussia]	(?)		Phillip Marcs	Greenwich, London	
24512	Marcs	Phillip	1823	?, Poland [?, Prussia]			Augusta (?)	Greenwich, London	glazier empl 1
24514	Marcs	Samuel	1845	?, Poland [?, Prussia]	Phillip Marcs	Augusta (?)		Greenwich, London	scholar
23183	Marcus	Alex	1838	Hamburg, Germany	Louis Marcus	Eva (?)		City, London	
25530	Marcus	Benjamin	1810	?, Poland [?, Russian Poland]				Dublin, Ireland	
23184	Marcus	Bertha	1845	Hamburg, Germany	Louis Marcus	Eva (?)		City, London	
20830	Marcus	Charles	1849	Dublin, Ireland	Mark Marcus	Jessie (?)	Rose Blanckensee	Dublin, Ireland	
26654	Marcus	Elias	1827	?, Germany			Mina (?)	Aldgate, London	tailor journeyman
23180	Marcus	Eva	1815	?, Germany			Louis Marcus	City, London	
25526	Marcus	Isaac	1800	Gdansk, Poland [Danzig, Prussia]	Mordecai		Julia (?)	Dublin, Ireland	jeweller + silversmith
23181	Marcus	Isidor	1835	?, Germany	Louis Marcus	Eva (?)		City, London	box maker
25527	Marcus	Julia	1805	?			Isaac Marcus	Dublin, Ireland	
23179	Marcus	Louis	1809	?, Germany			Eva (?)	City, London	fancy box maker
4726	Marcus	Louis	1821	?, Germany				Birmingham	professor of the German language
20831	Marcus	Mark (Mordecai)	1824	Bristol	Isaac Marcus	Julia (?)	Sophia (?)	Dublin, Ireland	
25528	Marcus	Matilda	1837	Dublin, Ireland	Isaac Marcus	Julia (?)	Hyman Henry Collins	Dublin, Ireland	
26655	Marcus	Mina	1826	?, Germany	(?)		Elias Marcus	Aldgate, London	assisant to tailor journeyman
25529	Marcus	Priscilla (Bessie)	1848	Dublin, Ireland	Isaac Marcus	Julia (?)	Alphonse Mayer	Dublin, Ireland	
23182	Marcus	Rosalia	1836	Hamburg, Germany	Louis Marcus	Eva (?)		City, London	
21994	Marcuse	Alfred	1850	Middlesex, London	(?) Marcuse	Priscilla (?)		Whitechapel, London	
21995	Marcuse	Frederick	1826	Middlesex, London				Whitechapel, London	merchant
21993	Marcuse	Isabella	1848	Middlesex, London	(?) Marcuse	Priscilla (?)		Whitechapel, London	
21991	Marcuse	Maurice	1845	Middlesex, London	(?) Marcuse	Priscilla (?)		Whitechapel, London	scholar
21990	Marcuse	Priscilla	1823	Middlesex, London	(?)		(?) Marcuse	Whitechapel, London	merchant's wife
21992	Marcuse	Simon	1847	Middlesex, London	(?) Marcuse	Priscilla (?)		Whitechapel, London	scholar
24802	Marcusson	Lewis	1821	?, Poland [?, Prussia]			Charlotte Goldsmid	Elephant & Castle, London	cigar maker
2515	Margolinsky	Abram	1836	?, Poland [?, Prussia]	Joseph Margolinsky	Paulina (?)		Hull, Yorkshire	
2517	Margolinsky	Fredericka	1839	?, Poland [?, Prussia]	Joseph Margolinsky	Paulina (?)		Hull, Yorkshire	
2513	Margolinsky	Joseph	1804	?, Poland [?, Prussia]			Paulina (?)	Hull, Yorkshire	dealer in clothes

ID	surname	given names	born	birthplace	father	mother	spouse 1	1851 residence	1851 occupation
2514	Margolinsky	Paulina	1811	?, Poland [?, Prussia]			Joseph Margolinsky	Hull, Yorkshire	
2516	Margolinsky	Selick	1837	?, Poland [?, Prussia]	Joseph Margolinsky	Paulina (?)		Hull, Yorkshire	
2518	Margolinsky	Yetta	1844	?, Poland [?, Prussia]	Joseph Margolinsky	Paulina (?)		Hull, Yorkshire	
7266	Margoliouth	Ann (Chaja)	1818	?, Poland	Ber Goldberg	Rachel (?)	Moses Epstein Margoliouth	Liverpool	Protestant Minister's wife
7268	Margoliouth	Charles Lindsay	1844	Liverpool	Moses Margoliouth	Ann (Chaya) Goldberg		Liverpool	
25053	Margoliouth	Fanny	1846	Dublin, Ireland	Moses Margoliouth	Ann (Chaya) Goldberg		Liverpool	
7267	Margoliouth	Miriam	1835	?, Poland	Moses Margoliouth	Ann (Chaya) Goldberg	William Parker	Liverpool	
7265	Margoliouth	Moses Epstein	1815	Suwalki, Poland	Gershon Margoliouth (Epstein)		Ann (Chaja) Goldberg	Liverpool	Anglican minister
12649	Margorchis	Ezrel	1846	Cheltenham, Gloucestershire	Samuel Margorchis	Mary Ann (?)		Leamington, Warwickshire	
12646	Margorchis	John Thomas	1840	Cheltenham, Gloucestershire	Samuel Margorchis	Mary Ann (?)		Leamington, Warwickshire	
12650	Margorchis	Joshua E	1848	Leamington, Warwickshire	Samuel Margorchis	Mary Ann (?)		Leamington, Warwickshire	
12647	Margorchis	Martha L P	1841	Cheltenham, Gloucestershire	Samuel Margorchis	Mary Ann (?)		Leamington, Warwickshire	
12645	Margorchis	Mary Ann	1819	Newport, Glamorgan, Wales	(?)		Samuel Margorchis	Leamington, Warwickshire	
12648	Margorchis	Michael S A	1844	Cheltenham, Gloucestershire	Samuel Margorchis	Mary Ann (?)		Leamington, Warwickshire	
12651	Margorchis	Rebecca J	1849	Leamington, Warwickshire	Samuel Margorchis	Mary Ann (?)		Leamington, Warwickshire	
12644	Margorchis	Samuel	1807	?, Poland [Galicia in Poland]			Mary Ann (?)	Leamington, Warwickshire	jeweller + stationer
12300	Markes	Elizabeth	1804	?, London	(?)		Joseph Henry Markes	Finsbury, London	
12303	Markes	Elizabeth	1831	Southwark, London	Joseph Henry Markes	Elizabeth (?)		Finsbury, London	
12301	Markes	Henry	1828	Aldgate, London	Joseph Henry Markes	Elizabeth (?)		Finsbury, London	provision merchant
12702	Markes	Israel	1795	Exeter, Devon			Mary Ann (?)	Exeter, Devon	shoe maker
12302	Markes	Joseph	1832	Southwark, London	Joseph Henry Markes	Elizabeth (?)		Finsbury, London	provision merchant
12299	Markes	Joseph Henry	1801	Southwark, London			Elizabeth (?)	Finsbury, London	provision merchant
12304	Markes	Mary	1834	Southwark, London	Joseph Henry Markes	Elizabeth (?)		Finsbury, London	scholar
12703	Markes	Mary Ann	1791	Exeter, Devon	(?)		Israel Markes	Exeter, Devon	shoe maker wife
13613	Markland	Isacher	1833	?, Poland [?, Prussia]				Manchester	traveller, smware
13508	Marks	?	1815	Manchester	(?)		Uriah Marks	Manchester	
23139	Marks	?	1851	City, London	Aaron Marks	Louisa (?)		City, London	
23131	Marks	Aaron	1809	?, Poland	Michael Marks		Louisa (?)	City, London	trimming manufacturer
12778	Marks	Aaron	1823	Spitalfields, London				Aldgate, London	hat manufacturer empl 6
5141	Marks	Aaron	1825	?, Poland [?, Prussia]		Hannah (?)	Amelia (?)	Sheffield, Yorkshire	watchmaker + jeweller
28298	Marks	Aaron	1832	Aldgate, London	Joshua Marks	Rosetta (?)	Catherine Cohen	Aldgate, London	cigar maker
15798	Marks	Aaron	1844	Aldgate, London	Woolf Marks	Mary Simmons	Selina Alexander	Aldgate, London	scholar
29461	Marks	Aaron	1846	Spitalfields, London	Hyam Marks	Esther Coleman		Spitalfields, London	scholar
19178	Marks	Aaron	1851	Aldgate, London	David Marks	Rose Alexander		Aldgate, London	
1893	Marks	Abraham	1768	?, London				Cardiff, Wales	rabbi
15827	Marks	Abraham	1817	City, London	Jacob Coppel Marks		Phoebe Simmons	Spitalfields, London	tailor
22262	Marks	Abraham	1830	Stepney, Londob	(?) Marks	Hariett (?)		Whitechapel, London	foreman

ID	surname	given names	born	birthplace	father	mother	spouse 1	1851 residence	1851 occupation
8003	Marks	Abraham	1835	?St Giles, London	Mark Marks	Juliet Collins	Amelia Isaacs	St Giles, London	
23133	Marks	Abraham	1835	Plymouth, Devon	Aaron Marks	Louisa (?)		City, London	trimming manufacturer
29457	Marks	Abraham	1836	Spitalfields, London	Hyam Marks	Esther Coleman		Spitalfields, London	shirt maker
30974	Marks	Abram	1822	?				Sunderland, Co Durham	hawker, jewellery
2522	Marks	Abram	1842	Hull, Yorkshire	Benjamin Marks			Hull, Yorkshire	
6368	Marks	Ada	1850	Marylebone, London	David Woolf Marks	Cecilia S Woolf	Andrew Duncan	Marylebone, London	
17765	Marks	Adalade	1850	Middlesex, London	Jonas Marks	Sarah (?)		Spitalfields, London	
4750	Marks	Adelaide	1811	?, Poland				Birmingham	
4739	Marks	Adelaide	1844	Birmingham	James Marks	Sarah (?)		Birmingham	scholar
27799	Marks	Ailsey	1843	Liverpool	Mark Marks	Hannah Harris	William Frederick Isaacs	Liverpool	
1906	Marks	Albert P	1840	Cardiff, Wales	Mark Marks	Mary Marks		Cardiff, Wales	
1019	Marks	Alexander	1849	Exeter, Devon	Joseph Marks	Julia Solomon		Exeter, Devon	
13880	Marks	Alfred	1831	Manchester	John Marks	Kate (?)		Manchester	quill dresser
1072	Marks	Alfred	1844	Bristol	Samuel Marks	Susan (?)		Exeter, Devon	scholar
19801	Marks	Amelia	1786	Whitechapel, London	(?)		Isaac Marks	Spitalfields, London	
2762	Marks	Amelia	1804	Bethnal Green, London	George Joel	Mary (?)	Solomon Marks	Spitalfields, London	furniture broker
16894	Marks	Amelia	1827	Nottingham, Nottinghamshire	(?)		Aaron Marks	Sheffield, Yorkshire	
12936	Marks	Amelia	1845	Liverpool	Leon Marks	Esther Leo	(?) Berliner	Liverpool	scholar
2532	Marks	Amelia	1848	Hull, Yorkshire	Lewis Marks	Esther (?)		Hull, Yorkshire	
12204	Marks	Amelia (Millie)	1819	Deptford, London	Samuel Moss		Henry Marks	Whitechapel, London	
8261	Marks	Amelia D	1846	Aldgate, London	John Davis Marks	Rachel Cohen		Aldgate, London	scholar
23378	Marks	Ann	1779	Spitalfields, London	(?)		(?) Marks	Aldgate, London	
5320	Marks	Ann	1813	Plymouth, Devon			Samuel Marks	Plymouth, Devon	
3290	Marks	Ann	1827	Whitechapel, London	Henry Nathan	Sarah (?)	Barnard Marks	Mile End, London	
31128	Marks	Ann	1827	Whitechapel, London	Mark Marks	(?)		Paddington, London	
18281	Marks	Ann	1831	Darlington, Co Durham	(?) Lister		David Marks	Hartlepool, Co Durham	
20056	Marks	Ann	1851	Plymouth, Devon	Charles Marks	Louisa Lyons	Alfred Alexander Jacob	Plymouth, Devon	
4752	Marks	Ann (Hannah)	1833	?, Poland	Solomon Matks	Adelaide (?)	Samuel Isaac	Birmingham	
23665	Marks	Anne	1840	Liverpool	Edward Marks	Margaret (?)		Liverpool	
8253	Marks	Annie Davis	1839	Aldgate, London	John Davis Marks	Rachel Cohen	Harris Davies	Aldgate, London	
13808	Marks	Arthur	1849	Manchester	Edward Marks	Charlotte (?)		Manchester	
3289	Marks	Barnard (Bernard)	1813	Aldgate, London	Lyon (Judah) Marks	Frances (Fanny) Levy (Levey)	Ann Nathan	Mile End, London	merchant
1901	Marks	Barnett Samuel	1828	Cardiff, Wales	Mark Marks	Mary Marks	Zipporah Marks	Cardiff, Wales	artist
4736	Marks	Baron (Bearon) I---	1838	Birmingham	James Marks	Sarah (?)	(?)	Birmingham	scholar
25795	Marks	Benjamin	1787	Spitalfields, London				Aldgate, London	clothes dealer
2519	Marks	Benjamin	1810	Middlesex, London				Hull, Yorkshire	
26928	Marks	Benjamin	1822	?, Poland [?, Prussia]			Betsey (?)	Aldgate, London	tailor
2769	Marks	Benjamin	1839	Aldgate, London	Solomon Marks	Amelia Joel	Elizabeth Stubbings	Spitalfields, London	scholar
13319	Marks	Benjamin	1841	Westminster, London	Mark Marks	Sarah Levy		Spitalfields, London	
27801	Marks	Bernard	1851	Liverpool	Mark Marks	Hannah Harris	Jane Elizabeth Benjamin	Liverpool	
26929	Marks	Betsey	1823	?, Poland [?, Prussia]	(?)		Benjamin Marks	Aldgate, London	
28303	Marks	Betsy	1846	Aldgate, London	Joshua Marks	Rosetta (?)		Aldgate, London	
28302	Marks	Bluma	1844	Aldgate, London	Joshua Marks	Rosetta (?)		Aldgate, London	

ID	surname	given names	born	birthplace	father	mother	spouse 1	1851 residence	1851 occupation
15801	Marks	Caroline	1826	?, Kent	Montague Marks	Hannah Moses		Piccadilly, London	
23136	Marks	Caroline	1843	City, London	Aaron Marks	Louisa (?)		City, London	scholar
2528	Marks	Caroline	1849	Hull, Yorkshire	(?) Marks	Hannah (?)		Hull, Yorkshire	scholar
23376	Marks	Caroline	1849	Aldgate, London	Phillip Marks	Sarah (Sally) Jacobs		Aldgate, London	
2533	Marks	Caroline	1850	Hull, Yorkshire	Lewis Marks	Esther (?)		Hull, Yorkshire	
15696	Marks	Caroline	1850	City, London	David Marks	Rose Alexander	Abraham J W Samuel	Aldgate, London	
11082	Marks	Catharine	1841	Aldgate, London	Joseph Marks	Rose (?)		Aldgate, London	
30347	Marks	Catherine	1762	Middlesex, London	(?)		Gedalia Kesselflicker Marks	Clerkenwell, London	
2765	Marks	Catherine	1831	Aldgate, London	Solomon Marks	Amelia Joel	Ellis Harfeld	Spitalfields, London	looking glass silverer
17874	Marks	Catherine	1837	Whitechapel, London	Elias Henry Marks	Hannah Lyon	Asher Isaacs	Mayfair, London	
12208	Marks	Catherine (Kate)	1849	Whitechapel, London	Henry Marks	Amelia (Millie) Moss		Whitechapel, London	
6364	Marks	Cecilia S	1821	Middlesex, London	Moseley Woolf		David Woolf Marks	Marylebone, London	
8259	Marks	Celia D	1828	Middlesex, London	John Davis Marks	Rachel Cohen		Aldgate, London	
1258	Marks	Charles	1801	Portsmouth, Hampshire			Anne Phillips	Plymouth, Devon	Navy agent + silversmith
7586	Marks	Charles	1812	Aldgate, London	Samuel Marks	Sophia (Fyla, Fanny) Collins	Elizabeth Aaronson	Bloomsbury, London	upholsterer
4211	Marks	Charles	1835	St Giles, London	Mark Marks	Juliet (Julia) Collins	Rayner Woolf	St Giles, London	scholar
1013	Marks	Charles	1840	Exeter, Devon	Joseph Marks	Julia Solomon	Sophia Harris	Exeter, Devon	
16321	Marks	Charles	1848	Soho, London	Emanuel Marks	Jessey (?)		Soho, London	
14903	Marks	Charles Elijah	1835	?Marylebone, London				Bethnal Green, London	boarding school pupil
13807	Marks	Charlotte	1820	Manchester	(?)		Edward Marks	Manchester	
1890	Marks	Charlotte Cornelia	1835	Swansea, Wales	Michael Marks	Rosetta (?)		Swansea, Wales	
28396	Marks	Clara	1820	Emden, Hanover, Germany	(?)		Samuel Marks	Spitalfields, London	tailoress
19948	Marks	Clara	1822	Birmingham	(?)		Solomon Marks	Whitechapel, London	
16896	Marks	Claria	1850	Sheffield, Yorkshire	Aaron Marks	Amelia (?)		Sheffield, Yorkshire	
29460	Marks	Coleman	1844	Aldgate, London	Hyam Marks	Esther Coleman		Spitalfields, London	scholar
25307	Marks	Daniel	1849	Aldgate, London	Mark Marks	Elizabeth Benjamin		Aldgate, London	
4138	Marks	David	1816	Newton Abbot, Devon	Moshe Marks		Rose Alexander	Aldgate, London	print seller &c
20643	Marks	David	1823	?, Poland [?, Prussia]				Spitalfields, London	journeyman tailor
18280	Marks	David	1825	?, Poland [?, Prussia]			Eliza Lister	Hartlepool, Co Durham	glazier
20464	Marks	David	1832	Picadilly, London	Lewis Marks	Mary Solomons	Anna Levi	Holborn, London	artist
15410	Marks	David	1836	Whitechapel, London	Elias Henry Marks	Hannah Lyon		Covent Garden, London	cigar maker
16895	Marks	David	1850	Sheffield, Yorkshire	Aaron Marks	Amelia (?)		Sheffield, Yorkshire	
6363	Marks	David Woolf	1811	Middlesex, London	Woolf Marks	Mary (?)	Cecilia S Woolf	Marylebone, London	Chief Minister of the West London Synagogue of British Jews
27798	Marks	Deborah Fanny	1841	Liverpool	Mark Marks	Hannah Harris	Samuel Benjamin	Liverpool	
14808	Marks	Dinah	1839	Finsbury, London	Mark Marks	Jane Nathan		Finsbury, London	scholar
23661	Marks	Edward	1811	?, Poland [?, Prussia]			Margaret (?)	Liverpool	tailor
13806	Marks	Edward	1818	?, Poland [?, Prussia]			Charlotte (?)	Manchester	cap mfr
23902	Marks	Edward E	1849	Marylebone, London	David Woolf Marks	Cecilia S Woolf		Marylebone, London	
1889	Marks	Edward Lloyd	1833	Swansea, Wales	Michael Marks	Rosetta (?)	Emily Flatau	Swansea, Wales	druggist's assistant
17871	Marks	Elias Henry	1806	Whitechapel, London	Zvi Hirsch Marks		Hannah Lyon	Mayfair, London	lodging house keeper + general dealer
1074	Marks	Eliza	1830	Bristol				Exeter, Devon	dressmaker

ID	surname	given names	born	birthplace	father	mother	spouse 1	1851 residence	1851 occupation
22265	Marks	Eliza	1839	Stepney, London	(?) Marks	Hariett (?)		Whitechapel, London	feather maker
4746	Marks	Elizabeth	1800	Birmingham	(?) (?Josephs)		Simon King Marks	Birmingham	
10501	Marks	Elizabeth	1806	?London	(?)		(?) Marks	Mile End, London	
18471	Marks	Elizabeth	1811	Amersfort, Holland	Abraham Aarons Samson Aronson	Matje Van Minden	Charles Marks	Bloomsbury, London	milliner
15776	Marks	Elizabeth	1821	Aldgate, London	Simon Marks	Kitty Jacobs	David Abraham	Aldgate, London	sponge dealer's assistant
9055	Marks	Elizabeth	1823	City, London	Naphtali Isaacs		Joseph Marks	Aldgate, London	
17914	Marks	Elizabeth	1828	Whitechapel, London	(?) Marks	Phoebe (?)		Lambeth, London	glass + china dealer
18502	Marks	Elizabeth	1834	Aldgate, London	John Davis Marks	Rachel Cohen		Aldgate, London	
2018	Marks	Elizabeth	1839	Liverpool	Mark Marks	Hannah Harris	Samuel Cohen	Liverpool	
13318	Marks	Elizabeth	1840	Westminster, London	Mark Marks	Sarah Levy		Spitalfields, London	
13509	Marks	Elizabeth	1840	Manchester	Uriah Marks	(?)		Manchester	
25737	Marks	Elizabeth	1850	Aldgate, London	Philip Marks	Julia (?)		Spitalfields, London	
28855	Marks	Elizabeth	1850	Spitalfields, London	Joseph Marks	Julia White		Spitalfields, London	
25305	Marks	Elizabeth (Betsy)	1827	Whitechapel, London	Abraham Benjamin	(?)	Mark Marks	Aldgate, London	
75	Marks	Elizabeth E	1847	Greenwich, London	Israel Marks	Rebecca Meyers		Greenwich, London	scholar
22261	Marks	Ellen	1827	Tower Hill, London	(?) Marks	Hariett (?)		Whitechapel, London	feather maker
18216	Marks	Ellen	1837	Middlesex, London	(?) Marks			Mile End, London	scholar
23664	Marks	Ellen	1839	Liverpool	Edward Marks	Margaret (?)		Liverpool	
1015	Marks	Ellen	1843	Exeter, Devon	Joseph Marks	Julia Solomon	Samuel Lazarus	Exeter, Devon	
4741	Marks	Ellen	1848	Birmingham	James Marks	Sarah (?)		Birmingham	scholar
8260	Marks	Ellen D	1837	Aldgate, London	John Davis Marks	Rachel Cohen		Aldgate, London	
16316	Marks	Emanuel	1808	?, Holland			Jessey (?)	Soho, London	importer of antique china, furntiture &c
23418	Marks	Emanuel	1838	?, London				Aldgate, London	apprentice
29458	Marks	Emanuel	1838	Spitalfields, London	Hyam Marks	Esther Coleman		Spitalfields, London	cigar maker
23663	Marks	Emelia	1837	Liverpool	Edward Marks	Margaret (?)		Liverpool	
23641	Marks	Emma	1791	?, Germany	(?)		(?) Marks	Liverpool	
19910	Marks	Emma	1835	Chatham, Kent	Montague Marks	Hannah Moses		Chatham, Kent	
14985	Marks	Emma	1842	Middlesex, London	(?) Marks			Bethnal Green, London	boarding school pupil
1073	Marks	Emma	1846	Bristol	Samuel Marks	Susan (?)		Exeter, Devon	
2521	Marks	Ephraim	1840	Hull, Yorkshire	Benjamin Marks		Leah (?)	Hull, Yorkshire	
29454	Marks	Esther	1815	?, Holland	Kalonymous		Hyam Marks	Spitalfields, London	
2529	Marks	Esther	1821	Hull, Yorkshire			Lewis Marks	Hull, Yorkshire	
12935	Marks	Esther	1825	?, London	(?) Leo	Sophia (?)	Leon Marks	Liverpool	
23969	Marks	Esther	1832	Marylebone, London	(?) Marks	Sarah (?)		Marylebone, London	teacher
4210	Marks	Esther	1833	St Giles, London	Mark Marks	Juliet (Julia) Collins		St Giles, London	hat trimmer
18503	Marks	Esther	1841	Aldgate, London	John Davis Marks	Rachel Cohen		Aldgate, London	scholar
2525	Marks	Esther	1843	Hull, Yorkshire	(?) Marks	Hanah (?)		Hull, Yorkshire	scholar
78	Marks	Eveline R	1851	Greenwich, London	Israel Marks	Rebecca Meyers		Greenwich, London	
4732	Marks	Ezekiel	1850	?, Warwickshire	Henry Marks	Maria Coster	Annie Jaffe	Birmingham	
28133	Marks	Fanny	1811	Aldgate, London	Jacob Levy		Laurence (Lazarus) Marks	Spitalfields, London	
2836	Marks	Fanny (Frances)	1783	Whitechapel, London	Moses (Moshe Frenshman) Levy (Levey)	Deborah (?)	Lyon (Judah) Marks	Liverpool	annuitant
23137	Marks	Floretta	1846	City, London	Aaron Marks	Louisa (?)		City, London	scholar
10499	Marks	Frances	1769	Aldgate, London	(?) Marks	Frances (?)		Mile End, London	annuitant

ID	surname	given names	born	birthplace	father	mother	spouse 1	1851 residence	1851 occupation
15391	Marks	Frances	1813	Jamaica, West Indies	Solomon Marks	Phoebe (?)		Waterloo, London	
27380	Marks	Frances	1814	Ragoesen, Germany [Rogarson, Prussia]	Beil Levy		(?) Marks	Aldgate, London	eating house keeper
19635	Marks	Frances	1829	Spitalfields, London	Simon Israel		Isaac Marks	Spitalfields, London	
20466	Marks	Frances	1838	Picadilly, London	Lewis Marks	Mary Solomons		Holborn, London	
14810	Marks	Frances	1843	Finsbury, London	Mark Marks	Jane Nathan		Finsbury, London	scholar
19177	Marks	Frances Ann	1851	Mile End, London	Barnard Marks	Ann Nathan		Mile End, London	
6365	Marks	Francis Walter	1844	Middlesex, London	David Woolf Marks	Cecilia S Woolf		Marylebone, London	
1909	Marks	Frederick	1821	Cardiff, Wales				Cardiff, Wales	shoemaker
20465	Marks	George	1835	Picadilly, London	Lewis Marks	Mary Solomons		Holborn, London	
12206	Marks	George	1845	Whitechapel, London	Henry Marks	Amelia (Millie) Moss		Whitechapel, London	
28854	Marks	George	1845	Spitalfields, London	Joseph Marks	Julia White		Spitalfields, London	
2763	Marks	George Joel	1829	Bethnal Green, London	Solomon Marks	Amelia Joel	Elizabeth Samuels	Aldgate, London	looking glass maker
4737	Marks	Gertrude	1844	Birmingham	James Marks	Sarah (?)	Philip Brown	Birmingham	scholar
12619	Marks	Hadele	1816	Wejherowo, Poland [New Town, Prussia]	(?)		Isaac Marks	Great Yarmouth, Norfolk	
18405	Marks	Hannah	1769	?, London	(?)		(?) Marks	Aldgate, London	
19907	Marks	Hannah	1801	Middlesex, London	Jacob Moses		Montague Marks	Chatham, Kent	cigar impoorter
17872	Marks	Hannah	1807	Strand, London	Yehuda Leib Lyons		Elias Henry Marks	Mayfair, London	general dealer
2523	Marks	Hannah	1815	?, Wales	(?)		(?) Marks	Hull, Yorkshire	fruit merchant
2017	Marks	Hannah	1820	?, London	Henry Harris	Elizabeth Phillips	Mark Marks	Liverpool	
28297	Marks	Hannah	1829	Aldgate, London	Joshua Marks	Rosetta (?)		Aldgate, London	tailoress
12620	Marks	Hannah	1841	Wejherowo, Poland [New Town, Prussia]	Isaac Marks	Hadele (?)		Great Yarmouth, Norfolk	scholar
15833	Marks	Hannah	1850	Spitalfields, London	Abraham Marks	Phoebe Simmons		Spitalfields, London	
22259	Marks	Hariett	1791	Whitechapel, London	(?)		(?) Marks	Whitechapel, London	lodging housekeeper
7259	Marks	Harris	1797	?, Poland [?, Prussia]			Hannah Samuel	Wapping, London	outfitter
13887	Marks	Harris	1833	?, Germany				Manchester	tailor
13321	Marks	Helen	1844	Stepney, London	Mark Marks	Sarah Levy		Spitalfields, London	
4727	Marks	Henry	1815	?, Poland [?, Prussia]	Joshua Marks		Maria Coster	Birmingham	cap maker
12203	Marks	Henry	1818	Whitechapel, London	Simon Marks		Amelia (Millie) Moss	Whitechapel, London	dealer + traveller in sponge, brushes, turnery + cigars
26239	Marks	Henry	1823	?, Poland	Elkin Marks		Jesse Levy	Aldgate, London	tailor
26242	Marks	Henry	1823	?, Poland				Aldgate, London	tailor
30975	Marks	Henry	1828	?				Sunderland, Co Durham	hawker, window glass
15409	Marks	Henry	1831	Whitechapel, London	Elias Henry Marks	Hannah Lyon		Covent Garden, London	cigar maker
2767	Marks	Henry	1838	Aldgate, London	Solomon Marks	Amelia Joel	Rosetta Jones	Spitalfields, London	errand boy
5832	Marks	Henry	1838	Aldgate, London	Abraham Marks	Phoebe Simmons	Sarah Bowman	Spitalfields, London	tailor
1018	Marks	Henry	1847	Exeter, Devon	Joseph Marks	Julia Solomon	Elizabeth Levy	Exeter, Devon	
4203	Marks	Henry	1849	Whitechapel, London	Lewis Marks	Sarah Myers	Rebecca Lazarus	Whitechapel, London	
15800	Marks	Henry	1849	Aldgate, London	Woolf Marks	Mary Simmons		Aldgate, London	
19908	Marks	Henry (Harry)	1821	Chatham, Kent	Montague Marks	Hannah Moses		Chatham, Kent	furniture occupation
8255	Marks	Henry Davis	1843	Aldgate, London	John Davis Marks	Rachel Cohen	Miriam Myers	Aldgate, London	scholar

ID	surname	given names	born	birthplace	father	mother	spouse 1	1851 residence	1851 occupation
14901	Marks	Henry Edward Benjamin	1836	Marylebone, London				Bethnal Green, London	boarding school pupil
24610	Marks	Henry M	1841	Nottingham, Nottinghamshire	Lewis Marks	Priscilla Abrahams		Lambeth, London	scholar
29453	Marks	Hyam	1801	?, Holland	Mordecai Marks		Esther Coleman	Spitalfields, London	shoemaker
17733	Marks	Hyam	1825	?, Poland [?, Prussia]				Aldgate, London	tailor
14807	Marks	Hyam (Hyman)	1836	Finsbury, London	Mark Marks	Jane Nathan		Finsbury, London	apprentice to clothier
30346	Marks	Hyman	1835	Greenwich, London	Myer (Mark) Marks (Myers)	Rachel (?)		Hampstead, London	
10460	Marks	Isaac	1766	Aldgate, London				Aldgate, London	
19800	Marks	Isaac	1779	Whitechapel, London			Amelia (?)	Spitalfields, London	hatter
12653	Marks	Isaac	1793	?, Holland				Leamington, Warwickshire	optician
12618	Marks	Isaac	1813	Wejherowo, Poland [New Town, Prussia]			Hadele (?)	Great Yarmouth, Norfolk	Reader of the Hebrew Congregation
19909	Marks	Isaac	1823	Chatham, Kent	Montague Marks	Hannah Moses		Chatham, Kent	army clothier
19634	Marks	Isaac	1825	Spitalfields, London	Jacob Marks		Frances Israel	Spitalfields, London	gas fitter
11753	Marks	Isaac	1829	?, Russia				Shoreditch, London	traveller
1011	Marks	Isaac	1834	Exeter, Devon	Joseph Marks	Julia Solomon	Miriam Alexander	Exeter, Devon	
18505	Marks	Isaac	1844	Aldgate, London	John Davis Marks	Rachel Cohen		Aldgate, London	scholar
30130	Marks	Isaac	1845	Whitechapel, London	Abraham Marks	Phoebe Simmons	Maria Jacobs	Spitalfields, London	
23134	Marks	Isaachar	1836	Falmouth, Cornwall	Aaron Marks	Louisa (?)		City, London	trimming manufacturer
22014	Marks	Isabella	1791	?, Norfolk			(?) Marks	Whitechapel, London	servant
1017	Marks	Isabella	1846	Exeter, Devon	Joseph Marks	Julia Solomon	Samuel Hamburg	Exeter, Devon	
25306	Marks	Isaiah Mark	1847	Aldgate, London	Mark Marks	Elizabeth Benjamin	Rebecca Moses	Aldgate, London	scholar
27693	Marks	Israel	1795	?, France				Aldgate, London	general merchant
73	Marks	Israel	1819	Greenwich, London	Myer (Mark) Marks (Myers)	Elizabeth Davis	Rebecca Meyers	Greenwich, London	dealer in marine stores, brassfounder + engineer + metal merchant
28541	Marks	Israel	1833	Middlesex, London				Aldgate, London	broker
23640	Marks	Jacob	1830	?, Germany	(?) Marks	Emma (?)		Liverpool	traveller
15796	Marks	Jacob	1837	Aldgate, London	Woolf Marks	Mary Simmons		Aldgate, London	
23667	Marks	Jacob	1848	Liverpool	Edward Marks	Margaret (?)		Liverpool	
1888	Marks	Jacob Cohen	1829	Swansea, Wales	Michael Marks	Rosetta (?)		Swansea, Wales	assistant pawnbroker
4733	Marks	James	1811	?, Poland	Joshua Marks		Sarah (?)	Birmingham	cap mfr
2776	Marks	Jane	1806	Exeter, Devon	(?) Marks			Whitechapel, London	house servant
14806	Marks	Jane	1815	Finsbury, London	Chaim Nathan		Mark Marks	Finsbury, London	
8388	Marks	Jane	1826	?, London	(?) Marks			Southampton, Hampshire	nurse
22263	Marks	Jane	1833	Stepney, Londob	(?) Marks	Hariett (?)		Whitechapel, London	needlewoman
28300	Marks	Jane	1837	Aldgate, London	Joshua Marks	Rosetta (?)		Aldgate, London	
15797	Marks	Jane	1840	Aldgate, London	Woolf Marks	Mary Simmons	Daniel Levy	Aldgate, London	
2527	Marks	Jane	1845	Hull, Yorkshire	(?) Marks	Hannah (?)		Hull, Yorkshire	scholar
15831	Marks	Jane	1845	Spitalfields, London	Abraham Marks	Phoebe Simmons		Spitalfields, London	
26240	Marks	Jesse	1831	?, Germany	Levy Levy		Henry Marks	Aldgate, London	tailoress
26243	Marks	Jesse	1843	?, Poland [?, Prussia]				Aldgate, London	
16317	Marks	Jessey	1815	Soho, London	(?)		Emanuel Marks	Soho, London	
16320	Marks	Joel	1845	St Pancras, London	Emanuel Marks	Jessey (?)		Soho, London	scholar

ID	surname	given names	born	birthplace	father	mother	spouse 1	1851 residence	1851 occupation
7685	Marks	John	1818	Southwark, London	Mark Marks		Susan (?)	Paddington, London	coach broker
30278	Marks	John	1818	Arborfield, Berkshire	Thomas Marks		Adelaide Martin	Covent Garden, London	plumber + painter empl 3
13511	Marks	John	1840	Manchester	Uriah Marks	(?)		Manchester	
3293	Marks	John	1849	Mile End, London	Barnard Marks	Ann Nathan		Mile End, London	
10792	Marks	John (Jacob)	1794	Amsterdam, Holland	Mordecai		Sophia (?)	Spitalfields, London	general dealer
4212	Marks	John (Joshua) M	1838	St Giles, London	Mark Marks	Juliet (Julia) Collins	Adelaide Aarons	St Giles, London	scholar
8252	Marks	John Davis	1803	Aldgate, London			Rachel Cohen	Aldgate, London	furniture broker
17762	Marks	Jonas	1801	?, Poland			Sarah (?)	Spitalfields, London	tailor
1134	Marks	Joseph	1806	Portsmouth, Hampshire			Julia Solomon	Exeter, Devon	commercial traveller
6434	Marks	Joseph	1809	Mallaux, Poland			Nancy Lazarus	Oxford, Oxfordshire	jeweller
11078	Marks	Joseph	1811	?, Poland			Rose (?)	Aldgate, London	tailor
1077	Marks	Joseph	1814	?			Julia (?)	Exeter, Devon	clothier
9054	Marks	Joseph	1816	?, Poland [?, Prussia]	Yehuda		Elizabeth Isaacs	Aldgate, London	master tailor
28852	Marks	Joseph	1821	Whitechapel, London	George (Godfrey) Marks	Maria Joseph	Julia White	Spitalfields, London	metal dealer
13886	Marks	Joseph	1826	?, Germany				Manchester	tailor
14900	Marks	Joseph	1834	Whitechapel, London				Bethnal Green, London	boarding school pupil
22264	Marks	Joseph	1835	Stepney, London	(?) Marks	Hariett (?)		Whitechapel, London	junior foreman
4213	Marks	Joseph	1843	St Giles, London	Mark Marks	Juliet (Julia) Collins	Catherine Lindsay	St Giles, London	scholar
2772	Marks	Joseph	1847	Spitalfields, London	Solomon Marks	Amelia Joel		Spitalfields, London	scholar
18506	Marks	Joseph	1848	Aldgate, London	John Davis Marks	Rachel Cohen	Esther Amelia Cohen	Aldgate, London	scholar
28295	Marks	Joshua	1805	Aldgate, London	Yaakov		Rosetta (?)	Aldgate, London	tailor
19802	Marks	Joshua	1817	Whitechapel, London	Isaac Marks	Amelia (?)		Spitalfields, London	hatter
15799	Marks	Joshua	1847	Aldgate, London	Woolf Marks	Mary Simmons	Hannah Jacobs	Aldgate, London	
4751	Marks	Josiah	1828	?, Poland	Solomon Marks	Adelaide (?)	Fanny (?)	Birmingham	licensed hawker
4735	Marks	Josiah	1837	Birmingham	James Marks	Sarah (?)		Birmingham	scholar
1014	Marks	Josiah	1841	Exeter, Devon	Joseph Marks	Julia Solomon	Julia Solomon	Exeter, Devon	
4729	Marks	Josiah	1841	Birmingham	Henry Marks	Maria Coster		Birmingham	scholar
1900	Marks	Judith	1769	Portsmouth, Hampshire			?Levi Marks	Cardiff, Wales	
1010	Marks	Julia	1808	Exeter, Devon	Isaac Solomon	Rosetta Solomon	Joseph Marks	Exeter, Devon	
25735	Marks	Julia	1823	Aldgate, London	(?)		Philip Marks	Spitalfields, London	
28853	Marks	Julia	1823	?Spitalfields, London	Abraham White	Elizabeth Levy	Joseph Marks	Spitalfields, London	
1262	Marks	Julia	1839	Plymouth, Devon	Charles Marks	Ann Phillips		Plymouth, Devon	scholar
24609	Marks	Julia	1840	Nottingham, Nottinghamshire	Lewis Marks	Priscilla Abrahams		Lambeth, London	scholar
15412	Marks	Julia	1843	Mayfair, London	Elias Henry Marks	Hannah Lyon		Covent Garden, London	scholar
2771	Marks	Julia	1844	Aldgate, London	Solomon Marks	Amelia Joel	John Jones	Spitalfields, London	scholar
13809	Marks	Julia	1851	Manchester	Edward Marks	Charlotte (?)		Manchester	
1905	Marks	Julia H	1837	Cardiff, Wales	Mark Marks	Mary Marks		Cardiff, Wales	
1225	Marks	Juliana	1804	Portsmouth, Hampshire				Plymouth, Devon	dressmaker
4207	Marks	Juliet (Julia)	1799	?, Holland	Samuel (Zanvill) Collins (Hyman)		Mark Marks	St Giles, London	
28309	Marks	Julius	1816	?, Germany				Aldgate, London	tailor
15005	Marks	July	1781	Spitalfields, London	(?)		(?) Marks	Spitalfields, London	dealer
13879	Marks	Kate	1798	Liverpool	(?)		John Marks	Manchester	stationer
27618	Marks	Kate	1831	Aldgate, London	John Davis Marks	Rachel Cohen	Jonas Phillips	Aldgate, London	
1020	Marks	Kate	1850	Exeter, Devon	Joseph Marks	Julia Solomon		Exeter, Devon	

ID	surname	given names	born	birthplace	father	mother	spouse 1	1851 residence	1851 occupation
14229	Marks	Kaufman	1828	Poznan, Poland [Posen, Prussia]				Manchester	hawker
76	Marks	Kaufman I	1848	Greenwich, London	Israel Marks	Rebecca Meyers		Greenwich, London	scholar
15006	Marks	Kitty	1811	Spitalfields, London	(?) Marks	July (?)		Spitalfields, London	milliner
28299	Marks	Kitty	1834	Aldgate, London	Joshua Marks	Rosetta (?)		Aldgate, London	
28132	Marks	Laurence (Lazarus)	1801	Aldgate, London	Joshua Marks		Fanny Levy	Spitalfields, London	hatter
23374	Marks	Lazarus	1845	Aldgate, London	Phillip Marks	Sarah (Sally) Jacobs		Aldgate, London	
25308	Marks	Leah	1789	?, Poland	(?)		Michael Marks	Aldgate, London	almswoman
29459	Marks	Leah	1842	Spitalfields, London	Hyam Marks	Esther Coleman		Spitalfields, London	scholar
4742	Marks	Leah	1850	Birmingham	James Marks	Sarah (?)	Alfred Brooks	Birmingham	
8303	Marks	Lena	1825	Poznan, Poland [Posen, Prussia]	(?)		Moses Marks	North Shields, Tyne & Wear	
6728	Marks	Leon	1812	?, Poland [?, Prussia]	Meyer Marks	Cyrell (?)	Esther Leo	Liverpool	watch manufacturer
5084	Marks	Levi	1818	?, Poland	Mordecai Marks		Alice Theresa Moss	Portsmouth, Hampshire	travelling jeweller
1902	Marks	Levi M Johnson	1829	Cardiff, Wales	Mark Marks	Mary Marks	Frances Jane Carslake	Cardiff, Wales	watch maker
24606	Marks	Lewis	1795	Poznan, Poland [Posen, Prussia]	M--- Marks		Priscilla Abrahams	Lambeth, London	tailor
20462	Marks	Lewis	1797	Soho, London	Joel Marks		Mary Solomons	Holborn, London	paper stainer empl 2
2149	Marks	Lewis	1817	?, Poland [?, Prussia]			Esther (?)	Hull, Yorkshire	jeweller + silversmith
8001	Marks	Lewis	1827	Whitechapel, London	Elias Henry Marks	Hannah Lyon	Sarah Myers	Whitechapel, London	watch maker
24786	Marks	Lewis	1829	Elephant & Castle, London				Elephant & Castle, London	
16322	Marks	Lionel	1851	Soho, London	Emanuel Marks	Jessey (?)		Soho, London	
3294	Marks	Lionel (Lyon)	1844	Liverpool	Mark Marks	Hannah Harris	Eliza Rebecca Marks	Liverpool	
9057	Marks	Louis	1848	Aldgate, London	Joseph Marks	Elizabeth Isaacs		Aldgate, London	
23132	Marks	Louisa	1811	Plymouth, Devon	(?)		Aaron Marks	City, London	
1259	Marks	Louisa	1818	Portsmouth, Hampshire	Charles Lyons	Phoebe Levy	Charles Marks	Plymouth, Devon	
4738	Marks	Louisa	1842	Birmingham	James Marks	Sarah (?)		Birmingham	scholar
2531	Marks	Louisa	1847	Hull, Yorkshire	Lewis Marks	Esther (?)	Barnett Rubenstein	Hull, Yorkshire	
1907	Marks	Louisa R	1842	Cardiff, Wales	Mark Marks	Mary Marks		Cardiff, Wales	
2526	Marks	Lucy	1844	Hull, Yorkshire	(?) Marks	Hannah (?)		Hull, Yorkshire	
4226	Marks	Lyon (Lionel)	1850	Southwark, London	Moses (Moss) Marks	Rose (Rosetta) Levy		Lambeth, London	
3292	Marks	Lyon Henry	1846	Mile End, London	Barnard Marks	Ann Nathan		Mile End, London	
23662	Marks	Margaret	1814	Liverpool	(?)		Edward Marks	Liverpool	
4728	Marks	Maria	1822	?, London	Lyon Coster		Henry Marks	Birmingham	
15413	Marks	Maria	1848	Marylebone, London	Elias Henry Marks	Hannah Lyon		Covent Garden, London	scholar
19949	Marks	Marinella	1846	Whitechapel, London	Solomon Marks	Clara (?)		Whitechapel, London	
31127	Marks	Mark	1790	Aldgate, london			(?)	Paddington, London	coach broker
1898	Marks	Mark	1798	Cardiff, Wales	?Levi Marks	Judith (?)	Mary Marks	Cardiff, Wales	auctioneer
4206	Marks	Mark	1799	Spitalfields, London	Samuel Marks	Sophia (Fyla, Fanny) Collins	Juliet (Julia) Collins	St Giles, London	silk hat maker
14805	Marks	Mark	1804	Covent Garden, London	Joel Marks	Frances Solomon	Jane Nathan	Finsbury, London	master cabinet maker empl 3 + furniture broker
13316	Marks	Mark	1811	Aldgate, London	Woolf (Benjamin) Marks		Sarah Levy	Spitalfields, London	brush maker
2016	Marks	Mark	1815	?, London	Lyon Marks	Fanny Levey	Hannah Harris	Liverpool	banker, outfitter
25304	Marks	Mark	1817	?, Poland	Michael Marks	Leah (?)	Elizabeth Benjamin	Aldgate, London	Beadle of Synagogue

ID	surname	given names	born	birthplace	father	mother	spouse 1	1851 residence	1851 occupation
29455	Marks	Mark	1833	Spitalfields, London	Hyam Marks	Esther Coleman		Spitalfields, London	shoemaker
16352	Marks	Mark	1842	Swansea, Wales	(?) Marks	(?) Samuel		Wapping, London	
11083	Marks	Mark	1843	Aldgate, London	Joseph Marks	Rose (?)		Aldgate, London	
4225	Marks	Martha (Maud)	1848	Southwark, London	Moses (Moss) Marks	Rose (Rosetta) Levy		Lambeth, London	
9470	Marks	Mary	1786	?, London	(?)		(?) Marks	Aldgate, London	
1899	Marks	Mary	1803	Swansea, Wales	(?) Marks		Mark Marks	Cardiff, Wales	
20463	Marks	Mary	1806	Aldgate, London	Kalonymus Kalman Solomons		Lewis Marks	Holborn, London	
15795	Marks	Mary	1817	Aldgate, London	Jacob Simmons		Woolf Marks	Aldgate, London	
2774	Marks	Mary	1849	Aldgate, London	Solomon Marks	Amelia Joel	Simon Lancaster	Spitalfields, London	
12937	Marks	Mathilda	1850	Liverpool	Leon Marks	Esther Leo	Henry Simon Lion	Liverpool	
17875	Marks	Matilda	1845	Covent Garden, London	Elias Henry Marks	Hannah Lyon	Jacob (Jack) Jacobs	Mayfair, London	
18504	Marks	Michael	1838	Aldgate, London	John Davis Marks	Rachel Cohen		Aldgate, London	tailor
23375	Marks	Michael	1846	Aldgate, London	Phillip Marks	Sarah (Sally) Jacobs		Aldgate, London	
30976	Marks	Michael	1771	?, Poland				Ipswich, Suffolk	Rabbi
1908	Marks	Michael J	1848	Cardiff, Wales	Mark Marks	Mary Marks	Susan Jane Scholes	Cardiff, Wales	
23138	Marks	Michael J	1850	City, London	Aaron Marks	Louisa (?)		City, London	
1891	Marks	Michael Lazarus	1840	Swansea, Wales	Michael Marks	Rosetta (?)	Rosetta Brown	Swansea, Wales	scholar
4223	Marks	Montague	1844	Southwark, London	Moses (Moss) Marks	Rose (Rosetta) Levy	Deborah Harris	Lambeth, London	
6367	Marks	Montague Lawrence	1847	St Pancras, London	David Woolf Marks	Cecilia S Woolf	Agnes Lazarus	Marylebone, London	
1892	Marks	Morris	1801	?, Poland				Swansea, Wales	hawker
1414	Marks	Morris	1810	Spitalfields, London				Plymouth, Devon	artist
11893	Marks	Morris	1819	?, Poland [?, Prussia]				Whitechapel, London	tailor
8305	Marks	Moses	1786	?, Germany				North Shields, Tyne & Wear	
8302	Marks	Moses	1827	Margonin, Poland [Prussia]	Moses Marks		Lena (?)	North Shields, Tyne & Wear	glazier
15695	Marks	Moses	1847	City, London	David Marks	Rose Alexander		Aldgate, London	scholar
4221	Marks	Moses (Moss)	1816	Southwark, London	Mordecai Marks		Rose (Rosetta) Levy	Lambeth, London	furniture dealer
11080	Marks	Mosses	1837	Aldgate, London	Joseph Marks	Rose (?)		Aldgate, London	
16319	Marks	Murray	1841	St Pancras, London	Emanuel Marks	Jessey (?)		Soho, London	scholar
77	Marks	Myer Israel	1849	Greenwich, London	Israel Marks	Rebecca Meyers		Greenwich, London	
21450	Marks	Nathan	1838	Middlesex, London				Gravesend, Kent	boarding school pupil
130	Marks	Nathan (Mordecai)	1815	?, Poland	Nissan Marks		(?)	Woolwich, London	general dealer
1896	Marks	Nelson	1836	Cardiff, Wales	Samuel Marks	Rosetta (?)	Josephine Dix	Cardiff, Wales	
1903	Marks	Nelson D	1831	Cardiff, Wales	Mark Marks	Mary Marks		Cardiff, Wales	optician
1910	Marks	Nelson S	1836	Swansea, Wales				Cardiff, Wales	apprentice druggist
2177	Marks	Philip	1801	?, Poland				Oxford, Oxfordshire	jewellery traveller
25734	Marks	Philip	1814	Aldgate, London			Julia (?)	Spitalfields, London	hatter
16318	Marks	Philip	1834	St Pancras, London	Emanuel Marks	Jessey (?)		Soho, London	
2520	Marks	Philip	1836	Middlesex, London	Benjamin Marks			Hull, Yorkshire	
4731	Marks	Philip Alfred	1847	?, Warwickshire	Henry Marks	Maria Coster	Isabella Moore	Birmingham	
23372	Marks	Phillip	1811	Whitechapel, London	(?) Marks	Anne (?)	Sarah (Sally) Jacobs	Aldgate, London	hatter
15390	Marks	Phoebe	1777	Wapping, London	(?)		Solomon Marks	Waterloo, London	
17915	Marks	Phoebe	1796	Whitechapel, London	(?)		(?) Marks	Lambeth, London	

ID	surname	given names	born	birthplace	father	mother	spouse 1	1851 residence	1851 occupation
15828	Marks	Phoebe	1822	Spitalfields, London	Isaac Eizak Simmons		Abraham Marks	Spitalfields, London	dressmaker
23135	Marks	Phoebe	1840	City, London	Aaron Marks	Louisa (?)		City, London	scholar
9056	Marks	Phoebe	1846	Aldgate, London	Joseph Marks	Elizabeth Isaacs		Aldgate, London	
12209	Marks	Phoebe	1850	Whitechapel, London	Henry Marks	Amelia (Millie) Moss	Abraham (Alfred) Moore	Whitechapel, London	
24607	Marks	Priscilla	1815	Whitechapel, London	Henry Abrahams		Lewis Marks	Lambeth, London	
1897	Marks	Priscilla	1840	Cardiff, Wales	Samuel Marks	Rosetta (?)		Cardiff, Wales	
25736	Marks	Priscilla	1848	Spitalfields, London	Philip Marks	Julia (?)		Spitalfields, London	
13322	Marks	Rachael	1845	Stepney, London	Mark Marks	Sarah Levy		Spitalfields, London	
23666	Marks	Rachael	1845	Liverpool	Edward Marks	Margaret (?)		Liverpool	
23377	Marks	Rachael	1850	Aldgate, London	Phillip Marks	Sarah (Sally) Jacobs	Joseph Morris	Aldgate, London	
15832	Marks	Rachael (Ray)	1847	Spitalfields, London	Abraham Marks	Phoebe Simmons	Samuel Thomas Mossman	Spitalfields, London	
30344	Marks	Rachel	1801	?, Poland [?, Prussia]	(?)		Myer (Mark) Marks (Myers)	Hampstead, London	
8251	Marks	Rachel	1809	Southwark, London	Isaac Cohen	Esther Davis	John Davis Marks	Aldgate, London	
15408	Marks	Rachel	1833	Whitechapel, London	Elias Henry Marks	Hannah Lyon	David Cohen	Covent Garden, London	lodging house keeper
2770	Marks	Rachel	1841	Aldgate, London	Solomon Marks	Amelia Joel		Spitalfields, London	scholar
28301	Marks	Rachel	1842	Aldgate, London	Joshua Marks	Rosetta (?)		Aldgate, London	
74	Marks	Rebecca	1827	Aldgate, London	Kaufman Meyers	Eve Harris	Israel Marks	Greenwich, London	
30345	Marks	Rebecca	1831	Greenwich, London	Myer (Mark) Marks (Myers)	Rachel (?)		Hampstead, London	
24608	Marks	Rebecca	1839	Nottingham, Nottinghamshire	Lewis Marks	Priscilla Abrahams		Lambeth, London	gold + silver emroideress
21754	Marks	Rebecca	1846	Swansea, Wales	(?Harris? Marks			Swansea, Wales	
28633	Marks	Renan (Reyna?)	1831	Whitechapel, London	(?) Martin	Sarah	(?) Marks	Spitalfields, London	tailoress
17764	Marks	Rosa	1849	Middlesex, London	Jonas Marks	Sarah (?)		Spitalfields, London	
1887	Marks	Rosabella	1827	Swansea, Wales	Michael Marks	Rosetta (?)	(?) Joseph	Swansea, Wales	
11079	Marks	Rose	1809	Aldgate, London	(?)		Joseph Marks	Aldgate, London	
4137	Marks	Rose	1820	Deptford, London	Simon Alexander	Elizabeth Aarons	David Marks	Aldgate, London	
1260	Marks	Rose	1832	Plymouth, Devon	Charles Marks	Ann Phillips	Isaac Solomon Henry	Plymouth, Devon	
16169	Marks	Rose	1836	Aldgate, London	(?) Marks			Fitzrovia, London	servant
30498	Marks	Rose	1841	Aldgate, London	John Davis Marks	Rachel Cohen		Aldgate, London	
1016	Marks	Rose	1844	Exeter, Devon	Joseph Marks	Julia Solomon	Abraham Levy	Exeter, Devon	
4222	Marks	Rose (Rosetta)	1819	Lambeth, London	Benjamin Wolfe Levy	Martha Levy	Moses (Moss) Marks	Lambeth, London	
27800	Marks	Rose Rachel	1841	Liverpool	Mark Marks	Hannah Harris	Samuel Ackman	Liverpool	
1884	Marks	Rosetta	1801	Swansea, Wales			Michael Marks	Swansea, Wales	pawnbroker
1895	Marks	Rosetta	1804	Neath, Wales			Samuel Marks	Cardiff, Wales	
28296	Marks	Rosetta	1807	Aldgate, London	(?)		Joshua Marks	Aldgate, London	
2530	Marks	Rosetta	1846	Hull, Yorkshire	Lewis Marks	Esther (?)	Abraham Hiller	Hull, Yorkshire	
18507	Marks	Sampson	1849	Aldgate, London	John Davis Marks	Rachel Cohen		Aldgate, London	
15697	Marks	Samuel	1802	Plymouth, Devon			Ann (?)	Plymouth, Devon	broker
1894	Marks	Samuel	1805	?, London	Abraham Marks		Rosetta (?)	Cardiff, Wales	dyer
28395	Marks	Samuel	1815	Emden, Hanover, Germany			Clara (?)	Spitalfields, London	tailor
1911	Marks	Samuel	1820	Cardiff, Wales				Cardiff, Wales	watchmaker, repairer
1070	Marks	Samuel	1824	Bristol			Susan (?)	Exeter, Devon	railway clerk
4209	Marks	Samuel	1831	St Giles, London	Mark Marks	Juliet (Julia) Collins	Jane Louise Cheetham	St Giles, London	hatter
15411	Marks	Samuel	1840	Covent Garden, London	Elias Henry Marks	Hannah Lyon		Covent Garden, London	scholar
15830	Marks	Samuel	1842	Whitechapel, London	Abraham Marks	Phoebe Simmons	Elizabeth (Lucy) Samuel	Spitalfields, London	
12205	Marks	Samuel	1844	Whitechapel, London	Henry Marks	Amelia (Millie) Moss	Jane Benjamin	Whitechapel, London	

ID	surname	given names	born	birthplace	father	mother	spouse 1	1851 residence	1851 occupation
12622	Marks	Samuel	1848	Wejherowo, Poland [New Town, Prussia]	Isaac Marks	Hadele (?)		Great Yarmouth, Norfolk	scholar
29462	Marks	Samuel	1849	Spitalfields, London	Hyam Marks	Esther Coleman		Spitalfields, London	
19636	Marks	Samuel	1850	Spitalfields, London	Isaac Marks	Frances Israel		Spitalfields, London	
4730	Marks	Samuel Edward	1844	Birmingham	Henry Marks	Maria Coster	Sarah Elizabeth Abrahams	Birmingham	scholar
14902	Marks	Samuel Josiah	1840	Marylebone, London				Bethnal Green, London	boarding school pupil
2524	Marks	Sara	1839	Middlesex, London	(?) Marks	Hannah (?)		Hull, Yorkshire	scholar
9559	Marks	Sarah	1782	Whitechapel, London	(?)		(?) Marks	Spitalfields, London	general shopkeeper
23967	Marks	Sarah	1791	Aldgate, London	(?)		(?) Marks	Marylebone, London	fruiterer
13317	Marks	Sarah	1812	Whitechapel, London	Moses Levy		Mark Marks	Spitalfields, London	
4734	Marks	Sarah	1815	Lambeth, London			James Marks	Birmingham	
17763	Marks	Sarah	1815	Ramsgate, Kent	(?)		Jonas Marks	Spitalfields, London	
1885	Marks	Sarah	1824	Swansea, Wales	Michael Marks	Rosetta (?)	Ephraim Samuel Joseph	Swansea, Wales	
22260	Marks	Sarah	1824	Aldgate, London	(?) Marks	Hariett (?)		Whitechapel, London	needlewoman
12869	Marks	Sarah	1827	Spitalfields, London	Meir (Myers)		Lewis Marks	Whitechapel, London	
28540	Marks	Sarah	1829	Middlesex, London	(?) Marks			Aldgate, London	servant
17873	Marks	Sarah	1830	Strand, London	Elias Henry Marks	Hannah Lyon	(?) Levy	Mayfair, London	
10794	Marks	Sarah	1831	Whitechapel, London	John (Jacob) Marks	Sophia (?)	Isaac Jacob de Casseres	Spitalfields, London	umbrella maker
1904	Marks	Sarah	1833	Cardiff, Wales	Mark Marks	Mary Marks		Cardiff, Wales	
1261	Marks	Sarah	1834	Plymouth, Devon	Charles Marks	Ann Phillips		Plymouth, Devon	
29456	Marks	Sarah	1834	Spitalfields, London	Hyam Marks	Esther Coleman		Spitalfields, London	tailoress
1012	Marks	Sarah	1836	Exeter, Devon	Joseph Marks	Julia Solomon		Exeter, Devon	
2766	Marks	Sarah	1836	Aldgate, London	Solomon Marks	Amelia (?)	Mark Jacobs	Spitalfields, London	tailoress
15829	Marks	Sarah	1839	Aldgate, London	Abraham Marks	Phoebe Simmons	Lewis Harris	Spitalfields, London	tailoress
14809	Marks	Sarah	1841	Finsbury, London	Mark Marks	Jane Nathan		Finsbury, London	scholar
15694	Marks	Sarah	1844	Whitechapel, London	David Marks	Rose Alexander		Aldgate, London	scholar
12207	Marks	Sarah	1846	Whitechapel, London	Henry Marks	Amelia (Millie) Moss	Philip Moore	Whitechapel, London	
19950	Marks	Sarah	1849	Whitechapel, London	Solomon Marks	Clara (?)		Whitechapel, London	
12870	Marks	Sarah	1851	Whitechapel, London	Lewis Marks	Sarah Myers	Abraham Israel	Whitechapel, London	
30586	Marks	Sarah	1851	Aldgate, London	Mark Marks	Elizabeth Benjamin		Aldgate, London	
23373	Marks	Sarah (Sally)	1822	Aldgate, London	(?) Jacobs		Phiilip Marks	Aldgate, London	
13510	Marks	Sarah Ann	1840	Manchester	Uriah Marks	(?)		Manchester	
19564	Marks	Sarah Sophia	1837	Finsbury, London	Charles Marks	Elizabeth Aaronson	Samuel Isaacs	Bloomsbury, London	
28539	Marks	Selina	1828	Middlesex, London	(?) Marks			Aldgate, London	dressmaker
2838	Marks	Selina	1838	Wapping, London	Samuel Marks	Priscilla Jacobs	Wolf Michael Salomon	Liverpool	scholar
3291	Marks	Selina	1844	Mile End, London	Barnard Marks	Ann Nathan	Louis Simmons	Mile End, London	
4744	Marks	Simon	1789	?, Holland				Birmingham	hawker of jewellery
15775	Marks	Simon	1790	Aldgate, London	Tsvi Hirsch		Kitty Jacobs	Aldgate, London	dealer in brushes, sponge + second-hand harness
29010	Marks	Simon	1825	Aldgate, London	Moses Marks			Whitechapel, London	annuitant
22449	Marks	Simon	1844	?				Gravesend, Kent	boarding school pupil
4745	Marks	Simon King	1801	?, Poland			Elizabeth (?Josephs)	Birmingham	cabinet maker
4749	Marks	Solomon	1806	?, Poland	Joshua Marks		Adelaide (?)	Birmingham	licensed hawker
19947	Marks	Solomon	1812	?, London	Moshe		Clara (?)	Whitechapel, London	printseller
11081	Marks	Solomon	1839	Aldgate, London	Joseph Marks	Rose (?)		Aldgate, London	

ID	surname	given names	born	birthplace	father	mother	spouse 1	1851 residence	1851 occupation
10793	Marks	Sophia	1801	Whitechapel, London	(?)		John (Jacob) Marks	Spitalfields, London	general dealer
4208	Marks	Sophia	1827	St Giles, London	Mark Marks	Juliet (Julia) Collins	Israel Isidore Abrahams	St Giles, London	dress maker
22429	Marks	Sophia	1840	?	(?) Marks			Gravesend, Kent	boarding school pupil
13320	Marks	Sophia	1842	Stepney, London	Mark Marks	Sarah Levy		Spitalfields, London	
12623	Marks	Sophia	1850	?, London	Isaac Marks	Hadele (?)		Great Yarmouth, Norfolk	
6156	Marks	Sophia (Fyla, Fanny)	1766	?, Holland	Charles Collins (Yekutiel Kollum)		Samuel Marks	St Giles, London	
31126	Marks	Susan	1816	Aylesbury, Buckinghamshire	(?)		John Marks	Paddington, London	
1071	Marks	Susan	1824	Bristol			Samuel Marks	Exeter, Devon	
12779	Marks	Theresa	1828	Spitalfields, London	(?) Marks			Aldgate, London	
13507	Marks	Uriah	1811	?, Cornwall			(?)	Manchester	umbrella maker
30106	Marks	Wilhelmina	1808	?, Poland [?, Prussia]			Marks Myers	Sunderland, Co Durham	
29992	Marks	William	1831	Whitechapel, London				Whitechapel, London	tailor
12621	Marks	Wolf	1845	Wejherowo, Poland [New Town, Prussia]	Isaac Marks	Hadele (?)		Great Yarmouth, Norfolk	scholar
14314	Marks	Wolfe	1800	?, London				Manchester	hawker - hardware
5753	Marks	Woolf	1806	Aldgate, London	Jacob Coppel Marks		Mary Simmons	Aldgate, London	general dealer
4224	Marks	Woolf (Woolfred)	1846	Southwark, London	Moses (Moss) Marks	Rose (Rosetta) Levy	Esther (Essie) Solomon	Lambeth, London	
8304	Marks	Yetta	1851	North Shields, Tyne & Wear	Moses Marks	Lena (?)		North Shields, Tyne & Wear	
6366	Marks	Zillah	1845	St Pancras, London	David Woolf Marks	Cecilia S Woolf		Marylebone, London	
1886	Marks	Zipporah	1826	Swansea, Wales	Michael Marks	Rosetta (?)	Barnett Samuel Marks	Swansea, Wales	
3192	Marks (Myers)	Myer (Mark)	1786	Aldgate, London	Gedalia Kesselflicker Marks	Catherine (?)	Elizabeth Davis	Hampstead, London	retired brass founder
2534	Markwald (Markwell)	Marcus	1828	Samoczin, Poland	Benjamin Markwald		Tena Kasriel (Casriel, Casril)	Hull, Yorkshire	hawker of jewellery
11846	Marsiglio	Fanny	1817	Fellheim, Germany	(?)		(?) Marsiglio	Whitechapel, London	housekeeper
11847	Marsiglio	Josephine	1836	Venice, Italy	(?) Marsiglio	Fanny (?)		Whitechapel, London	assistant housekeeper
25929	Martin	Abigail	1823	Finsbury, London	Aron Martin	(?)		Aldgate, London	dressmaker
28542	Martin	Abigal	1801	Bethnal Green, London	(?)		(?) Martin	Aldgate, London	slipper maker
9091	Martin	Abraham	1826	?, Holland				Spitalfields, London	hawker
22691	Martin	Adam	1812	?, Germany			Mary Ann (?)	Whitechapel, London	greengrocer
8876	Martin	Adelaide	1837	Aldgate, London	Isaac de Abraham Martin	Emily (?)		Aldgate, London	
22693	Martin	Ann Catherine	1842	Bethnal Green, London	Adam Martin	Mary Ann (?)		Whitechapel, London	
25928	Martin	Aron	1795	Bethnal Green, London			(?)	Aldgate, London	general dealer
20402	Martin	Betsy	1832	Whitechapel, London	(?) Martin			Spitalfields, London	house servant
18030	Martin	Daniel	1830	Chatham, Kent	Jacob Martin	(?)		Chatham, Kent	general dealer
12953	Martin	David	1793	Spitalfields, London			Rosetta (?)	Spitalfields, London	confectioner
28544	Martin	David	1829	Bethnal Green, London				Aldgate, London	slipper maker
9295	Martin	David	1848	Bethnal Green, London	Judah Martin	Rebecca Carcas		Bethnal Green, London	
20296	Martin	Elizabeth	1833	Lambeth, London	(?) Martin			Brixton, London	assistant in cattle doctor + beer retailing business
8871	Martin	Emily	1803	Aldgate, London	(?)		Isaac de Abraham Martin	Aldgate, London	fruiterer
9310	Martin	Esther	1801	Aldgate, London	(?)		(?) Martin	Aldgate, London	dealer in fruit
18029	Martin	Hanah	1828	Mile End, London	Jacob Martin	(?)		Chatham, Kent	general dealer
25930	Martin	Hannah	1825	Finsbury, London	Aron Martin	(?)		Aldgate, London	cap maker

ID	surname	given names	born	birthplace	father	mother	spouse 1	1851 residence	1851 occupation
8874	Martin	Hannah Nunes	1835	Aldgate, London	Isaac de Abraham Martin	Emily (?)	Mordecai Henriques Valentine	Aldgate, London	
18031	Martin	Henry	1834	Chatham, Kent	Jacob Martin	(?)		Chatham, Kent	general dealer
22696	Martin	Herman	1850	Bethnal Green, London	Adam Martin	Mary Ann (?)		Whitechapel, London	
19808	Martin	Isaac	1776	Whitechapel, London				Spitalfields, London	confectioner
18033	Martin	Isaac	1840	Chatham, Kent	Jacob Martin	(?)		Chatham, Kent	scholar
19809	Martin	Isreal	1825	Whitechapel, London				Spitalfields, London	furrier
18028	Martin	Jacob	1795	Mile End, London			(?)	Chatham, Kent	general dealer
20297	Martin	James	1824	Erith, Kent			Rebecca (?)	Norwood, London	carman
8873	Martin	Jane	1833	Aldgate, London	Isaac de Abraham Martin	Emily (?)		Aldgate, London	
26566	Martin	Joseph	1836	Mile End, London				Whitechapel, London	
23312	Martin	Louisa	1827	Middlesex, London	(?) Martin			Mayfair, London	cook
8872	Martin	Mary	1831	Aldgate, London	Isaac de Abraham Martin	Emily (?)	Jacob Abraham	Aldgate, London	
20295	Martin	Mary A	1802	Bermondsey, London	(?)		Samuel Martin	Brixton, London	
22694	Martin	Mary A	1844	Bethnal Green, London	Adam Martin	Mary Ann (?)		Whitechapel, London	
22692	Martin	Mary Ann	1816	Whitechapel, London	(?)		Adam Martin	Whitechapel, London	
20293	Martin	Morris	1780	Whitechapel, London			Rebecca (?)	Brighton, Sussex	lodging house keeper
31135	Martin	Rebecca	1786	Whitechapel, London	(?)		Morris Martin	Brighton, Sussex	lodging house keeper
9293	Martin	Rebecca	1816	Bethnal Green, London	Joseph Carcas	Hannah Dias	Judah Martin	Bethnal Green, London	
20298	Martin	Rebecca	1824	Croydon, Surrey	(?)		James Martin	Norwood, London	carman
8877	Martin	Rebecca	1839	Aldgate, London	Isaac de Abraham Martin	Emily (?)	Emanuel Henriques Valentine	Aldgate, London	
20301	Martin	Rebecca	1850	Norwood, London	James Martin	Rebecca (?)		Norwood, London	
12954	Martin	Rosetta	1791	Spitalfields, London	(?)		David Martin	Spitalfields, London	
20300	Martin	Ruth	1848	Norwood, London	James Martin	Rebecca (?)		Norwood, London	scholar
20294	Martin	Samuel	1802	Lambeth, London			Mary A (?)	Brixton, London	cattle doctor + retailer of beer
20299	Martin	Samuel	1846	Norwood, London	James Martin	Rebecca (?)		Norwood, London	scholar
22695	Martin	Samuel	1848	Bethnal Green, London	Adam Martin	Mary Ann (?)		Whitechapel, London	
9296	Martin	Samuel	1850	Bethnal Green, London	Judah Martin	Rebecca Carcas		Bethnal Green, London	
28632	Martin	Sarah	1801	Whitechapel, London	(?)		(?) Martin	Spitalfields, London	hawker of sweetmeats
18155	Martin	Sarah	1811	Spitalfields, London	(?) Martin			Mile End, London	inmate of Portuguese Jews Hospital
28543	Martin	Sarah	1819	Bethnal Green, London	(?) Martin			Aldgate, London	slipper maker
18032	Martin	Soloman	1838	Chatham, Kent	Jacob Martin	(?)		Chatham, Kent	scholar
16361	Martin	Solomon	1840	City, London				Aldgate, London	boarding school pupil
18157	Martin	Welcome	1765	Middlesex, London	(?)		(?) Martin	Mile End, London	inmate of Portuguese Jews Hospital
3774	Martin (Martines Vaz)	Joseph	1831	Aldgate, London	David de Jona Vaz Martin	Deborah de Jacob Myers	Matilda Shannon	Spitalfields, London	cigar maker
6948	Martin (Martines)	Aaron Nunes	1812	Spitalfields, London	Israel de Joseph Nunes Martines	Sarah de David Fernandes	Rosa (Rosetta) Solomons	Whitechapel, London	fur dyer
332	Martin (Martines)	Abigail Nunes	1805	Clerkenwell, London	Moses (Moss) Nunes Martin (Martines)	Sarah (?)		Spitalfields, London	confectioner's daughter
11530	Martin (Martines)	Abraham	1842	Whitechapel, London	Solomon de Abraham Nunes Martines	Catharine (Kitty, Keturah, Yitla) de Sebi Hirsch		Spitalfields, London	scholar

ID	surname	given names	born	birthplace	father	mother	spouse 1	1851 residence	1851 occupation
313	Martin (Martines)	Abraham Nunes	1825	Whitechapel, London	Moses (Moss) Nunes Martin (Martines)	Sarah (?)	Marian (Miriam) Da Silva	Spitalfields, London	confectioner
21651	Martin (Martines)	Abraham Nunes	1851	Spitalfields, London	Moses Nunes Martin (Martines)	Rosetta (Rizka) de Abraham		Spitalfields, London	
19729	Martin (Martines)	Adelaide Nunes	1831	Middlesex, London	Abraham Nunes Martin (Martines)	Deborah Moravia		Whitechapel, London	
29435	Martin (Martines)	Agnes Nunes	1838	Mile End, London	Joseph Nunes Martin (Martines)	Catherine (Keturah) de Joseph Salamon		Spitalfields, London	assistant at home
29439	Martin (Martines)	Alice Nunes	1850	Mile End, London	Joseph Nunes Martin (Martines)	Catherine (Keturah) de Joseph Salamon		Spitalfields, London	
16183	Martin (Martines)	Amelia (Miriam) Nunes	1845	Spitalfields, London	Aaron de Israel Nunes Martin (Martines)	Rosa (Rosetta) Solomons		Whitechapel, London	
29436	Martin (Martines)	Amelia Nunes	1841	Mile End, London	Joseph Nunes Martin (Martines)	Catherine (Keturah) de Joseph Salamon	Isaac Lee	Spitalfields, London	scholar
22684	Martin (Martines)	Amelia Nunes	1845	Whitechapel, London	David de Israel Nunes Martines	Esther de Naphtali		Whitechapel, London	scholar
6785	Martin (Martines)	Anna (Hannah) Nunes	1845	Spitalfields, London	Moses Nunes Martin (Martines)	Rosetta (Rizka) de Abraham		Spitalfields, London	scholar
28008	Martin (Martines)	Barnett (Baruch) Nunes	1831	Bethnal Green, London	Joseph de Isaac Nunes Martines	Hannah de Benjamin Joseph	Sarah Levy	Spitalfields, London	general dealer
26904	Martin (Martines)	Barnett Nunes	1850	?, London	David Nunes Martin (Martines)	Betsey (Elizabeth) Lewis		Aldgate, London	
28009	Martin (Martines)	Benjamin	1832	Bethnal Green, London	Joseph de Isaac Nunes Martines	Hannah de Benjamin Joseph	Catherine Nelson	Spitalfields, London	general dealer
3888	Martin (Martines)	Benjamin Nunes	1808	?, London	Joseph de Moses Nunes Martinez	Dinah de Elimaleh Mudahi	Rebecca De Eliezer	Spitalfields, London	dealer in wearing apparel
6786	Martin (Martines)	Benjamin Nunes	1847	Spitalfields, London	Moses Nunes Martin (Martines)	Rosetta (Rizka) de Abraham		Spitalfields, London	scholar
26903	Martin (Martines)	Betsey (Elizabeth)	1833	?, London	Burnet Lewis		David Nunes Martin (Martines)	Aldgate, London	
16178	Martin (Martines)	Catharine (Keturah) Nunes	1838	Spitalfields, London	Aaron de Israel Nunes Martin (Martines)	Rosa (Rosetta) Solomons		Whitechapel, London	
11526	Martin (Martines)	Catharine (Kitty, Keturah, Yitla)	1809	Southwark, London	Sebi Hirsch		Solomon de Abraham Martin (Nunes Martines)	Spitalfields, London	
29432	Martin (Martines)	Catherine (Keturah)	1804	Whitechapel, London	Joseph Salamon		Joseph Nunes Martin (Martines)	Spitalfields, London	
11531	Martin (Martines)	Clara	1844	Whitechapel, London	Solomon de Abraham Nunes Martines	Catharine (Kitty, Keturah, Yitla) de Sebi Hirsch	Joseph Toledano	Spitalfields, London	scholar
11533	Martin (Martines)	Daniel	1833	?Bethnal Green, London	Jacob Nunes Martines	Esther de Judah Albujer	Esther Nunes Martin (Martines)	Spitalfields, London	general dealer
22677	Martin (Martines)	David Nunes	1805	Spitalfields, London	Israel de Joseph Nunes Martines	Sarah de David Fernandes	Esther de Naphtali	Whitechapel, London	fur cap maker
12323	Martin (Martines)	David Nunes	1815	?, London	Joseph de David Nunes Martin (Martines)	Lucky (Masaltob) de Abraham Levy	Frances (Fanny) de Benjamin Gomes Da Costa	Spitalfields, London	confectioner
20182	Martin (Martines)	David Nunes	1819	Mile End, London	Isaac Nunes Martin (Martines)		Rosetta Levy	Spitalfields, London	general dealer
26902	Martin (Martines)	David Nunes	1828	?, London	Joseph de Israel Nunes Martin (Martines)	Keturah de Joseph Salamon	Betsey (Elizabeth) Lewis	Aldgate, London	general dealer
16182	Martin (Martines)	David Nunes	1843	Spitalfields, London	Aaron de Israel Nunes Martin (Martines)	Rosa (Rosetta) Solomons		Whitechapel, London	
19727	Martin (Martines)	Deborah Nunes	1800	Bethnal Green, London	(?) Moravia		Abraham Nunes Martin (Martines)	Whitechapel, London	annuitant
3890	Martin (Martines)	Dinah Nunes	1832	Aldgate, London	Benjamin Nunes Martin (Martines)	Rebecca De Eliezer		Spitalfields, London	
17459	Martin (Martines)	Dinah Nunes	1841	Middlesex, London	Moses Nunes Martin (Martines)	Rosetta (Rizka) de Abraham	Aaron Mendoza	Spitalfields, London	scholar

ID	surname	given names	born	birthplace	father	mother	spouse 1	1851 residence	1851 occupation
3893	Martin (Martines)	Elias Nunes	1842	Aldgate, London	Benjamin Nunes Martin (Martines)	Rebecca De Eliezer	Harriet Symons	Spitalfields, London	scholar
16360	Martin (Martines)	Elias Nunes	1842	City, London	Jacob de Isaac Nunes Martines	Esther Mordecai	Rosa Belilo	Aldgate, London	boarding school pupil
29438	Martin (Martines)	Elias Nunes	1849	Mile End, London	Joseph Nunes Martin (Martines)	Catherine (Keturah) de Joseph Salamon		Spitalfields, London	
26533	Martin (Martines)	Elias Nunes	1851	Stepney, London	Israel Nunes Martin (Martines)	Sarah Abendana	Julia Nathan	Stepney, London	
19728	Martin (Martines)	Emma Nunes	1828	Bethnal Green, London	Abraham Martin (Martines Nunes)	Deborah Moravia		Whitechapel, London	annuitant
11528	Martin (Martines)	Esther	1832	Whitechapel, London	Solomon de Abraham Nunes Martines	Catharine (Kitty, Keturah, Yitla) de Sebi Hirsch	Daniel Nunes Martin (Martines)	Spitalfields, London	weaveress
28010	Martin (Martines)	Esther	1844	Bethnal Green, London	Joseph de Isaac Nunes Martines	Hannah de Benjamin Joseph	Benjamin Mendez	Spitalfields, London	
14687	Martin (Martines)	Esther Nunes	1791	Spitalfields, London	David de Moseh Nunes Martin (Martines)	Sarah de Elisah Arobas	Abraham de Abraham Silva	Spitalfields, London	confectioner's wife
22678	Martin (Martines)	Esther Nunes	1805	Southwark, London	Naphtali		David de Israel Nunes Martin (Martines)	Whitechapel, London	
16180	Martin (Martines)	Esther Nunes	1841	Spitalfields, London	Aaron de Israel Nunes Martin (Martines)	Rosa (Rosetta) Solomons		Whitechapel, London	
6784	Martin (Martines)	Esther Nunes	1843	Spitalfields, London	Moses Nunes Martin (Martines)	Rosetta (Rizka) de Abraham	Joshua Israel	Spitalfields, London	scholar
28006	Martin (Martines)	Hannah	1809	Whitechapel, London	Benjamin Joseph	Sarah de Solomon Mendoza	Joseph de Isaac Nunes Martin (Martines)	Spitalfields, London	
11532	Martin (Martines)	Hannah	1840	Spitalfields, London	Solomon de Abraham Nunes Martines	Catharine (Kitty, Keturah, Yitla) de Sebi Hirsch		Spitalfields, London	
3891	Martin (Martines)	Hannah Nunes	1835	Aldgate, London	Benjamin Nunes Martin (Martines)	Rebecca De Eliezer		Spitalfields, London	tailoress
16186	Martin (Martines)	Hannah Nunes	1850	Spitalfields, London	Aaron de Israel Nunes Martin (Martines)	Rosa (Rosetta) Solomons		Whitechapel, London	
3892	Martin (Martines)	Harriet Nunes	1840	Aldgate, London	Benjamin Nunes Martin (Martines)	Rebecca De Eliezer		Spitalfields, London	scholar
11534	Martin (Martines)	Henry (Haim)	1834	?Bethnal Green, London	Jacob Nunes Martines	Esther de Judah Albujer	Rebecca Nunes Martin (Martines)	Spitalfields, London	general dealer
22681	Martin (Martines)	Henry (Naphtali) Nunes	1837	Whitechapel, London	David de Israel Nunes Martines	Esther de Naphtali		Whitechapel, London	scholar
11539	Martin (Martines)	Hester (Esther) Nunes	1818	Spitalfields, London	Jacob de Joseph Nunes Martines	Esther de Judah Albujer	Nathaniel Isaacs	Spitalfields, London	
11538	Martin (Martines)	Isaac Nunes	1816	Spitalfields, London	Jacob de Joseph Nunes Martines	Esther de Judah Albujer		Spitalfields, London	confectioner
20184	Martin (Martines)	Isaac Nunes	1845	Whitechapel, London	David Nunes Martin (Martines)	Rosetta Levy	Elizabeth Harris	Spitalfields, London	scholar
16185	Martin (Martines)	Isaac Nunes	1849	Spitalfields, London	Aaron de Israel Nunes Martin (Martines)	Rosa (Rosetta) Solomons		Whitechapel, London	
20186	Martin (Martines)	Isabella (Bilha) Nunes	1849	Whitechapel, London	David Nunes Martin (Martines)	Rosetta Levy		Spitalfields, London	scholar
16181	Martin (Martines)	Israel (Isaac) Nunes	1842	Spitalfields, London	Aaron de Israel Nunes Martin (Martines)	Rosa (Rosetta) Solomons		Whitechapel, London	
26531	Martin (Martines)	Israel Nunes	1826	?, London	Joseph de Israel Nunes Martin (Martines)	Catherine (Keturah) de Joseph Salamon	Sarah Abendana	Stepney, London	
11536	Martin (Martines)	Jacob Nunes	1775	Spitalfields, London	Joseph Nunes Martines	Agar de Aron Mendosa	Esther de Judah Albujer	Spitalfields, London	confectioner
6783	Martin (Martines)	Jacob Nunes	1839	Whitechapel, London	Moses Nunes Martin (Martines)	Rosetta (Rizka) de Abraham		Spitalfields, London	scholar
11541	Martin (Martines)	Jacob Nunes	1840	Spitalfields, London	(?) Nunes Martin (Martines)	?		Spitalfields, London	
29437	Martin (Martines)	Jane Nunes	1845	Mile End, London	Joseph Nunes Martin (Martines)	Catherine (Keturah) de Joseph Salamon	Harris Bernstein	Spitalfields, London	scholar

ID	surname	given names	born	birthplace	father	mother	spouse 1	1851 residence	1851 occupation
11529	Martin (Martines)	Joel (Jacob)	1840	Whitechapel, London	Solomon de Abraham Nunes Martines	Catharine (Kitty, Keturah, Yitla) de Sebi Hirsch		Spitalfields, London	scholar
19730	Martin (Martines)	John (Jacob) Nunes	1832	Middlesex, London	Abraham Nunes Martin (Martines)	Deborah Moravia		Whitechapel, London	
28005	Martin (Martines)	Joseph Nunes	1798	Bethnal Green, London	Isaac de Joseph Nunes Martines	Sarah de Solomon Mendoza	Hannah de Benjamin Joseph	Spitalfields, London	confectioner
29431	Martin (Martines)	Joseph Nunes	1801	Spitalfields, London	Israel de Joseph Nunes Martines	Sarah de David Fernandes	Catherine (Keturah) de Joseph Salamon	Spitalfields, London	professor of music
22683	Martin (Martines)	Joseph Nunes	1842	Whitechapel, London	David de Israel Nunes Martines	Esther de Naphtali		Whitechapel, London	scholar
16184	Martin (Martines)	Joseph Nunes	1848	Spitalfields, London	Aaron de Israel Nunes Martin (Martines)	Rosa (Rosetta) Solomons	Deborah Levy	Whitechapel, London	
6787	Martin (Martines)	Joseph Nunes	1849	Spitalfields, London	Moses Nunes Martin (Martines)	Rosetta (Rizka) de Abraham		Spitalfields, London	
9294	Martin (Martines)	Judah Nunes	1813	Bethnal Green, London	Jacob de Joseph Nunes Martines	Esther de Judah Albujer	Rebecca Carcas	Bethnal Green, London	confectioner
22685	Martin (Martines)	Julia (Judith) Nunes	1846	Whitechapel, London	David de Israel Nunes Martines	Esther de Naphtali		Whitechapel, London	scholar
3894	Martin (Martines)	Julia Nunes	1844	Spitalfields, London	Benjamin Nunes Martin (Martines)	Rebecca De Eliezer		Spitalfields, London	scholar
3895	Martin (Martines)	Lambeth (Elhazar) Nunes	1846	Spitalfields, London	Benjamin Nunes Martin (Martines)	Rebecca De Eliezer		Spitalfields, London	scholar
11607	Martin (Martines)	Leah Nunes	1809	Spitalfields, London	Joseph Rodrigues	Abigail de Daniel Jerman	Mordecai Nunes Martin (Martines)	Aldgate, London	
16117	Martin (Martines)	Maria Nunes	1843	?, London	Abraham de Joseph Nunes Martin (Martines)	Martha (Miriam) de Asher Levy	Michael Israel	Aldgate, London	scholar
3896	Martin (Martines)	Mary (Malca) Nunes	1849	Spitalfields, London	Benjamin Nunes Martin (Martines)	Rebecca De Eliezer		Spitalfields, London	
11606	Martin (Martines)	Mordecai Nunes	1796	Whitechapel, London	David de Joseph de Moses Nunes Martines	Sarah de Mordecai Vitta	Leah de Joseph Rodrigues	Aldgate, London	confectioner
11608	Martin (Martines)	Mordecai Nunes	1841	Whitechapel, London	Mordecai de David Nunes Martines	Leah de Joseph Rodrigues		Aldgate, London	scholar
11535	Martin (Martines)	Moses	1822	?Bethnal Green, London	Jacob Nunes Martines	Esther de Judah Albujer	Rachel Lyons	Spitalfields, London	seaman
312	Martin (Martines)	Moses (Moss) Nunes	1786	Whitechapel, London	Isaac Martin (Nunes Martines)	Abigail (?)	Sarah (?)	Spitalfields, London	confectioner
22686	Martin (Martines)	Moses (Norris) Nunes	1850	Whitechapel, London	David de Israel Nunes Martines	Esther de Naphtali		Whitechapel, London	
6780	Martin (Martines)	Moses Nunes	1809	Shoreditch, London	Joseph Nunes Martine (Martines)		Rosetta (Rizka) de Abraham	Spitalfields, London	greengrocer
20185	Martin (Martines)	Moses Nunes	1847	Whitechapel, London	David Nunes Martin (Martines)	Rosetta Levy	Catherine (Keturah) Nunes Martin (Martines)	Spitalfields, London	scholar
16179	Martin (Martines)	Phoebe Nunes	1840	Spitalfields, London	Aaron de Israel Nunes Martin (Martines)	Rosa (Rosetta) Solomons		Whitechapel, London	
28007	Martin (Martines)	Raphael	1828	City, London	Joseph de Isaac Nunes Martines	Hannah de Benjamin Joseph	Hannah Nelson	Spitalfields, London	general dealer
3889	Martin (Martines)	Rebecca Nunes	1807	Aldgate, London	Eliezer		Benjamin de Joseph Nunes Martines	Spitalfields, London	
11527	Martin (Martines)	Rebecca Nunes	1829	Stepney, London	Solomon de Abraham Nunes Martines	Catharine (Kitty, Keturah, Yitla) de Sebi Hirsch		Spitalfields, London	milliner
22680	Martin (Martines)	Rebecca Nunes	1834	Whitechapel, London	David de Israel Nunes Martines	Esther de Naphtali		Whitechapel, London	

ID	surname	given names	born	birthplace	father	mother	spouse 1	1851 residence	1851 occupation
29434	Martin (Martines)	Rebecca Nunes	1836	Mile End, London	Joseph Nunes Martin (Martines)	Catherine (Keturah) de Joseph Salamon		Spitalfields, London	furrier
16176	Martin (Martines)	Rosa (Rosetta) Nunes	1812	Spitalfields, London	Isaac Solomons		Aaron de Israel Nunes Martin (Martines)	Whitechapel, London	
22682	Martin (Martines)	Rosa (Rosetta) Nunes	1839	Whitechapel, London	David de Israel Nunes Martines	Esther de Naphtali		Whitechapel, London	scholar
6781	Martin (Martines)	Rosetta (Rizka)	1812	Whitechapel, London	Abraham		Moses Nunes Martin (Martines)	Spitalfields, London	
20183	Martin (Martines)	Rosetta Nunes	1824	Southwark, London	Samuel Levy		David Nunes Martin (Martines)	Spitalfields, London	
11537	Martin (Martines)	Sarah Nunes	1806	Spitalfields, London	Jacob de Joseph Nunes Martines	Esther de Judah Albujer		Spitalfields, London	
14688	Martin (Martines)	Sarah Nunes	1815	Mile End, London	Moses Nunes Martin (Martines)	Sarah (?)		Spitalfields, London	confectioner's daughter
22679	Martin (Martines)	Sarah Nunes	1830	Whitechapel, London	David de Israel Nunes Martines	Esther de Naphtali		Whitechapel, London	fancy cloth cap maker
26532	Martin (Martines)	Sarah Nunes	1830	?, London	Elias Abendana	Nancy (Hannah, Ann, Yantla) de Jacob	Israel Nunes Martin (Martines)	Stepney, London	
29433	Martin (Martines)	Sarah Nunes	1834	Aldgate, London	Joseph Nunes Martin (Martines)	Catherine (Keturah) de Joseph Salamon	Abraham Solomons	Spitalfields, London	assistant at home
16177	Martin (Martines)	Sarah Nunes	1837	Spitalfields, London	Aaron de Israel Nunes Martin (Martines)	Rosa (Rosetta) Solomons	Benjamin Moss Goldhill	Whitechapel, London	
16116	Martin (Martines)	Sarah Nunes	1841	?, London	Abraham de Joseph Nunes Martin (Martines)	Martha (Miriam) de Asher Levy		Aldgate, London	scholar
16359	Martin (Martines)	Simon (Simeon) Nunes	1837	City, London	David Nunes Martin (Martines)		Miriam Hart	Aldgate, London	boarding school pupil
11525	Martin (Martines)	Solomon Nunes	1803	Shoreditch, London	Abraham de Joseph Nunes Martines	Hannah de Abraham Toledano	Catharine (Kitty, Keturah, Yitla) de Sebi Hirsch	Spitalfields, London	confectioner
6782	Martin (Martines)	Solomon Nunes	1836	Whitechapel, London	Moses Nunes Martin (Martines)	Rosetta (Rizka) de Abraham		Spitalfields, London	scholar
11540	Martin (Martines)	Sophia Nunes	1822	Spitalfields, London	Jacob de Joseph Nunes Martines	Esther de Judah Albujer	Baron Isaacs	Spitalfields, London	
16114	Martin (Martines) [Abrahams]	Martha (Miriam)	1811	?, London	Angel (Asher) Levy		Abraham de Joseph Nunes Martin (Martines)	Aldgate, London	general dealer
2745	Martines	Agnes (Hagar) Nunes	1851	Whitechapel, London	Aaron de Israel Nunes Martin (Martines)	Rosetta (Rose) Solomons	Baron Barnett	Whitechapel, London	
24323	Martinez	Isabella	1836	Bow, London	(?) Martinez	Rebecca (?)		Covent Garden, London	confectioner
24322	Martinez	Mariom	1834	Exeter, Devon	(?) Martinez	Rebecca (?)		Covent Garden, London	confectioner
24321	Martinez	Rebecca	1806	Liverpool			(?) Martinez	Covent Garden, London	confectioner
21635	Martins	Charlotte	1835	Islington, London	Elias Martins	Sarah (?)		Holloway, London	
21633	Martins	Elias	1816	Shoreditch, London			Sarah (?)	Holloway, London	weaver
21637	Martins	Eliza	1841	Islington, London	Elias Martins	Sarah (?)		Holloway, London	scholar
21636	Martins	Mary Ann	1837	Islington, London	Elias Martins	Sarah (?)		Holloway, London	servant
21634	Martins	Sarah	1816	St Pancras, London	(?)		Elias Martins	Holloway, London	laundress
7033	Marx	Karl Heinrich	1818	Trier, Germany [Trier, Prussia]	Heinrich Marx	Henriette Pressburg	Jenny (Johanna Bertha Julie) von Westphalen	Soho, London	doctor (philosophical and other)
28087	Maskell	Abraham	1825	?, Germany			Rosina (?)	Spitalfields, London	tailor
28088	Maskell	Rosina	1826	?, Germany	(?)		Abraham Maskell	Spitalfields, London	
21419	Mast	Israel	1832	Kutnow, Poland				Dewsbury, Yorkshire	traveller
13394	Mathews	Phebhe	1773	?, Holland	(?)		Abraham Mathews	Spitalfields, London	
23454	Matthews	Ellis	1831	?, Poland				Liverpool	upholsterer

490

ID	surname	given names	born	birthplace	father	mother	spouse 1	1851 residence	1851 occupation
2655	Matthews	Morris	1811	?, Poland				Glasgow, Scotland	clothier traveller
13851	Mayer	Adolphus	1851	Manchester	Saul Mayer	Emma (?Aronsberg)		Manchester	
14899	Mayer	Alfred James	1836	Bethnal Green, London				Bethnal Green, London	boarding school pupil
7813	Mayer	Alicia	1851	Manchester	Nathan Mayer	Caroline Franks	Isaac Brash	Manchester	
7810	Mayer	Amelia (Malka)	1801	?Sluzewiec, Poland [Sluzevi, Poland]	(?)		George Mayer	Hanley, Staffordshire	
18826	Mayer	Aubrey (Abraham)	1848	Manchester	Nathan Mayer	Caroline Franks		Manchester	
18825	Mayer	Caroline	1818	Manchester	(?Jacob) Franks		Nathan Mayer	Manchester	
14898	Mayer	Charles Henderson	1833	Bethnal Green, London				Bethnal Green, London	boarding school pupil
7730	Mayer	Emma	1827	Birmingham	(?) Samuel		Saul Mayer	Manchester	
7731	Mayer	Fanny	1847	Manchester	Saul Mayer	Emma (?Aronsberg)		Manchester	
7811	Mayer	George	1801	Warsaw, Poland			Amelia (Malka) (?)	Hanley, Staffordshire	jeweller
1912	Mayer	Joseph	1821	Gloucester, Gloucestershire			Phoebe (?)	Merthyr Tydfil, Wales	baker
7812	Mayer	Nathan	1816	?Sluzewiec, Poland [Sluzevi, Poland]	George Mayer	Amelia (Malka) (?)	Caroline Franks	Manchester	jeweller
1913	Mayer	Phoebe	1818	Mayfair, London				Merthyr Tydfil, Wales	
1914	Mayer	Sarah	1849	Merthyr Tydfil, Wales	Joseph Mayer	Phoebe (?)		Merthyr Tydfil, Wales	
7529	Mayer	Saul	1822	?, Poland [?, Prussia]	George Mayer	Amelia (Malka) (?)	Emma Samuel	Manchester	watchmaker + jeweller
14825	Mayers	?	1851	Finsbury, London	John Mayers	Louisa (?)		Finsbury, London	
14821	Mayers	Charles	1838	Finsbury, London	John Mayers	Louisa (?)		Finsbury, London	scholar
14822	Mayers	Frederick	1840	Finsbury, London	John Mayers	Louisa (?)		Finsbury, London	scholar
9771	Mayers	Henry	1840	Bristol				Kew, London	boarding school pupil
9992	Mayers	Isaac	1805	Great Yarmouth, Norfolk				Great Yarmouth, Norfolk	shopkeeper (fruit)
14823	Mayers	James	1842	Finsbury, London	John Mayers	Louisa (?)		Finsbury, London	scholar
14819	Mayers	John	1812	Finsbury, London			Louisa (?)	Finsbury, London	furrier --- master
14820	Mayers	Louisa	1820	Finsbury, London	(?)		John Mayers	Finsbury, London	straw bonnet maker
14824	Mayers	Louisa	1847	Finsbury, London	John Mayers	Louisa (?)		Finsbury, London	
7692	Mayers (Mayers)	Elizabeth	1818	Middlesex, London			Moses Myers (Mayers)	Marylebone, London	
18605	McCredie	Juliana	1827	Bradford, Yorkshire	(?) McCredie		Abraham Raphael	Ipswich, Suffolk	
14980	Mears	Elizabeth	1841	Hull, Yorkshire	(?) Mears			Bethnal Green, London	boarding school pupil
30237	Mears	Robert	1825	Shoreditch, London				Mile End, London	Hackney carriage driver
14904	Mears	Thomas	1839	Whitechapel, London				Bethnal Green, London	boarding school pupil
4753	Meckinheim	Louis R D	1823	?, France				Birmingham	pearl mfr
4754	Megers	Philip	1823	?, Poland [?, Prussia]				Birmingham	merchant's son
18041	Meider	Harris	1827	?, Latvia			Sarah (?)	Dudley, Worcestershire	painter + glazier
18042	Meider	Sarah	1818	?, Shropshire	(?)		Harris Meider	Dudley, Worcestershire	seamstress
9167	Meier	Abraham	1825	?Breznice, Czech Republic [Breschen, Prussia]				Whitechapel, London	tailor
9165	Meier	Mine	1831	Bock, Germany [Bock, Prussia]				Whitechapel, London	cap maker
30920	Meirkowsky	Harris	1786	?, Poland [?, Prussia]				Leeds, Yorkshire	commercial traveller
29022	Meldola	Abraham	1804	Middlesex, London	Raphael de Hezekiah Moses Meldola	Estelle (Estrella, Bella) (?)	Elizabeth (Sarah) (?)	Whitechapel, London	druggist
12021	Meldola	David	1801	?, Italy	Raphael de Hezekiah Moses Meldola	Estelle (Estrella, Bella) (?)	Esther (?)	Whitechapel, London	Jewish priest

ID	surname	given names	born	birthplace	father	mother	spouse 1	1851 residence	1851 occupation
12017	Meldola	Eleazer (Elhazar)	1810	Middlesex, London	Raphael de Hezekiah Moses Meldola	Estelle (Estrella, Bella) (?)	Marian (Miriam) Barend	Whitechapel, London	apothecary
29023	Meldola	Elizabeth (Sarah)	1808	?, Gloucestershire	(?)		Abraham Meldola	Whitechapel, London	
29025	Meldola	Estella	1836	Middlesex, London	Abraham de Raphael Meldola	Elizabeth (Sarah) (?)		Whitechapel, London	
12016	Meldola	Estelle (Estrella, Bella)	1781	?, Italy	(?)		Raphael de Hezekiah Moses Meldola	Whitechapel, London	annuitant
12022	Meldola	Esther	1791	Middlesex, London	(?)		David Meldola	Whitechapel, London	
12019	Meldola	Goodluck (Mazaltob)	1815	Middlesex, London	Raphael de Hezekiah Moses Meldola	Estelle (Estrella, Bella) (?)		Whitechapel, London	
12020	Meldola	Julia (Judith)	1815	Middlesex, London	Raphael de Hezekiah Moses Meldola	Estelle (Estrella, Bella) (?)		Whitechapel, London	
7271	Meldola	Matilda	1810	Frome, Somerset	Moses Abraham	Esther Emden	Samuel Meldola	Whitechapel, London	
29024	Meldola	Raphael	1832	Middlesex, London	Abraham de Raphael Meldola	Elizabeth (Sarah) (?)	Amelia Aria	Whitechapel, London	?apprentice from surgeon
7269	Meldola	Raphael	1849	Islington, London	Samuel Meldola	Matilda (?)	Ella Frederica Davis	Whitechapel, London	
7270	Meldola	Samuel	1813	Middlesex, London	Raphael de Hezekiah Moses Meldola	Estelle (Estrella, Bella) (?)	Matilda Abraham	Whitechapel, London	letter press printer
12018	Meldola	Sarah	1815	Middlesex, London	Raphael de Hezekiah Moses Meldola	Estelle (Estrella, Bella) (?)		Whitechapel, London	
23221	Melhado	Alfred	1844	Montego Bay, Jamaica, West Indies	(?)		(?) Melhado	Paddington, London	
23217	Melhado	Daniel	1830	Stoke Newington, London	Jacob Aaron Melhado	Rebecca Melhado		Paddington, London	
23218	Melhado	Emma	1834	Stoke Newington, London	Jacob Aaron Melhado	Rebecca Melhado		Paddington, London	
23222	Melhado	Gertrude	1849	Paddington, London	(?) Melhado	Sarah (?)		Paddington, London	
23216	Melhado	Harriett	1827	Kingston, Jamaica, West Indies	Jacob Aaron Melhado	Rebecca Melhado		Paddington, London	
23214	Melhado	Jacob Aaron	1800	Kingston, Jamaica, West Indies			Rebecca Melhado	Paddington, London	stock + share broker
23219	Melhado	Judith	1787	Spanish Town, Jamaica, West Indies	(?)		(?) Melhado	Paddington, London	
23215	Melhado	Rebecca	1807	Spanish Town, Jamaica, West Indies	(?) Melhado	Judith (?)	Jacob Aaron Melhado	Paddington, London	
23220	Melhado	Sarah	1814	Kingston, Jamaica, West Indies	(?) Melhado	Sarah (?)		Paddington, London	
14409	Mendel	Samuel	1814	Liverpool			Mary	Manchester	commercial merchant
6528	Mendelsohn	Meyer	1833	?, Poland [?, Prussia]	Saul Mendelsohn		Rebecca Silverstone	Newcastle Upon Tyne	Hebrew teacher
13448	Mendelson	Henry	1799	?, Germany			Leah (?)	Manchester	jeweller
13449	Mendelson	Leah	1809	Liverpool	(?)		Henry Mendelson	Manchester	jeweller
17554	Mendes	Abby	1848	Spitalfields, London	Joseph de Jacob Mendes	Hannah de Abraham Torres	Gilbert Barnet	Spitalfields, London	
17553	Mendes	Abraham	1843	Spitalfields, London	Joseph de Jacob Mendes	Hannah de Abraham Torres	Dinah Myers	Spitalfields, London	
18629	Mendes	Abraham Pereira	1828	Kingston, Jamaica, West Indies			Eliza (?)	Birmingham	Synagogue secretary
10598	Mendes	Charlotte	1791	Whitechapel, London	Joseph Habilho	Rebecca (?)	John (Jacob) de David Mendes	Spitalfields, London	
17550	Mendes	Charlotte	1837	Spitalfields, London	Joseph de Jacob Mendes	Hannah de Abraham Torres		Spitalfields, London	
10632	Mendes	Charlotte	1848	Spitalfields, London	George (Gershon) Mendes	Sarah Ben Sabat		Spitalfields, London	
18635	Mendes	Eliza Pereira	1830	Aldgate, London	David Aaron De Sola	Rebecca (Rica) Meldola	Abraham Pereira Mendes	Birmingham	

ID	surname	given names	born	birthplace	father	mother	spouse 1	1851 residence	1851 occupation
17551	Mendes	Esther	1843	Spitalfields, London	Joseph de Jacob Mendes	Hannah de Abraham Torres		Spitalfields, London	
10630	Mendes	George (Gershon)	1823	Southwark, London	John (Jacob) de David Mendes	Charlotte de Joseph Habilho	Sarah Ben Sabat	Spitalfields, London	general dealer
17549	Mendes	Hannah	1817	Spitalfields, London	Abraham Torres	Esther de Isaac Dias	Joseph de Jacob Mendes	Spitalfields, London	glass cutter
10597	Mendes	John (Jacob)	1787	City, London	David Mendes	Abigail Fernandez Da Silva	Charlotte de Joseph Habilho	Spitalfields, London	pickle merchant
17548	Mendes	Joseph	1814	Southwark, London	John (Jacob) de David Mendes	Charlotte de Joseph Habilho	Hannah de Abraham Torres	Spitalfields, London	glass cutter + paper + bound stionery dealer
10600	Mendes	Judah	1834	Whitechapel, London	John (Jacob) de David Mendes	Charlotte de Joseph Habilho	Sarah (?)	Spitalfields, London	cap peak maker
17555	Mendes	Maria	1850	Spitalfields, London	Joseph de Jacob Mendes	Hannah de Abraham Torres	Lewis Zusman	Spitalfields, London	
10599	Mendes	Maria (Miriam)	1830	Whitechapel, London	John (Jacob) de David Mendes	Charlotte de Joseph Habilho		Spitalfields, London	domestic assistant
10633	Mendes	Rachel	1850	Spitalfields, London	George (Gershon) Mendes	Sarah Ben Sabat		Spitalfields, London	
10634	Mendes	Reyna	1851	Spitalfields, London	George (Gershon) Mendes	Sarah Ben Sabat		Spitalfields, London	
10631	Mendes	Sarah	1825	Spitalfields, London	Jacob Ben Sabat	Rachel Rodrigues	George (Gershon) Mendes	Spitalfields, London	
17552	Mendes	Sarah	1845	Spitalfields, London	Joseph de Jacob Mendes	Hannah de Abraham Torres	Morris Freedman	Spitalfields, London	
18243	Mendes da Silva	Sarah	1785	Jamaica, West Indies	(?)		Solomon Mendes da Silva	Cheltenham, Gloucestershire	
5210	Mendes da Silva	Solomon	1781	Jamaica, West Indies			Sarah (?)	Cheltenham, Gloucestershire	landed proprietor
28637	Mendez	Abraham	1847	Brighton, Sussex	Joseph de Abraham Mendes	Sarah Esther Israel		Spitalfields, London	scholar
28638	Mendez	Benjamin	1849	?, Warwickshire	Joseph de Abraham Mendes	Sarah Esther Israel	Esther Nunes Martin (Martines)	Spitalfields, London	scholar
25996	Mendez	David	1818	Southwark, London	John (Jacob) de David Mendes	Charlotte de Joseph Habilho	Hannah Martin (Martines)	Aldgate, London	harness manufacturer empl 2
10447	Mendez	Esther	1799	Spitalfields, London	(?)		Joseph Rodrigues Mendez	Spitalfields, London	
25997	Mendez	Hannah	1805	Spitalfields, London	David de Joseph Martin (Martines)		David Mendez	Aldgate, London	
28634	Mendez	Joseph	1820	Middlesex, London	Abraham de David Mendes	Rebecca de Joseph Nunes Miranda	Sarah Esther Israel	Spitalfields, London	clothes renovator
10446	Mendez	Joseph Rodrigues	1799	Hamburg, Germany			Esther (?)	Spitalfields, London	general dealer
10450	Mendez	Joseph Rodrigues	1838	Sheffield, Yorkshire	Joseph Rodrigues Mendez	Esther (?)	Abigail Bitton (Bitto)	Spitalfields, London	cigar maker
10449	Mendez	Rebecca	1837	Sheffield, Yorkshire	Joseph Rodrigues Mendez	Esther (?)		Spitalfields, London	
28636	Mendez	Rebecca	1845	Brighton, Sussex	Joseph de Abraham Mendes	Sarah Esther Israel		Spitalfields, London	scholar
10448	Mendez	Sarah	1828	Manchester	Joseph Rodrigues Mendez	Esther (?)		Spitalfields, London	
28635	Mendez	Sarah Esther	1824	Middlesex, London	Solomon Cohen	Susan (?)	Joseph de Abraham Mendez	Spitalfields, London	
28639	Mendez	Solomon	1850	Spitalfields, London	Joseph de Abraham Mendes	Sarah Esther Israel		Spitalfields, London	
10905	Mendoza	Aaron	1818	Aldgate, London	David Mendoza	Hannah Jonas	Elizabeth (Brina, Betsey) Abrahams	Spitalfields, London	leather dealer
18914	Mendoza	Aaron	1834	Aldgate, London	Michael de David Mendoza	Esther de Aaron Gomes Da Costa	Rachel Raphael(?)	Aldgate, London	cigar maker apprentice
6612	Mendoza	Aaron	1836	Whitechapel, London	Israel Mendoza	Elizabeth (Betsey) Lesser	Caroline Solomons	Spitalfields, London	cigar maker apprentice
17457	Mendoza	Aaron	1838	Mile End, London	Daniel de Jacob Mendoza	Rosa de Abraham Levy	Dinah Martin (Nunes Martines)	Aldgate, London	cigar maker apprentice
12873	Mendoza	Abigail	1829	Mile End, London	Judah de Mordecai Mendoza	Rachel de Moses Dias	Angel Aarons	Aldgate, London	milliner

ID	surname	given names	born	birthplace	father	mother	spouse 1	1851 residence	1851 occupation
18916	Mendoza	Abigail (Bella)	1839	Aldgate, London	Michael de David Mendoza	Esther de Aaron Gomes Da Costa		Aldgate, London	
15708	Mendoza	Abraham	1825	?, London			Elizabeth De Sola	Aldgate, London	Minister of Jamaica Synagogue
6614	Mendoza	Abraham	1839	Whitechapel, London	Israel Mendoza	Elizabeth (Betsey) Lesser	Maria (Miriam) Defries	Spitalfields, London	scholar
16364	Mendoza	Abraham	1839	City, London				Aldgate, London	boarding school pupil
6618	Mendoza	Agnes (Hagar)	1848	Whitechapel, London	Israel Mendoza	Elizabeth (Betsey) Lesser	Baron A Barnett	Spitalfields, London	
12878	Mendoza	Amelia (Mazaltob)	1843	City, London	Judah de Mordecai Mendoza	Rachel de Moses Dias	Newman Franks	Aldgate, London	scholar
10908	Mendoza	Benjamin	1840	Spitalfields, London	Aaron de David Mendoza	Elizabeth (Brina, Betsey) Abrahams	Eliza (Leah) Lesser	Spitalfields, London	scholar
20541	Mendoza	Caroline (Jochabed)	1822	?, Holland	Moses Benjamin	(?)	Daniel Mendoza	Aldgate, London	fishmonger
9510	Mendoza	Catharine	1825	Spitalfields, London	Mordecai Nathan		Emanuel Mendoza	Aldgate, London	
9518	Mendoza	Catherine Sarah	1842	Spitalfields, London	Moses Mendoza	Hannah Hirsch		Spitalfields, London	
5665	Mendoza	Charlotte	1795	Birmingham	(?)		(?) Mendoza	Spitalfields, London	nurse
17452	Mendoza	Daniel	1797	Aldgate, London	Jacob Mendoza		Rosa de Abraham Levy	Aldgate, London	
20545	Mendoza	Daniel	1822	Aldgate, London	Israel Mendoza	Leah de Raphael Beracha (Bracho)	Caroline (Jochabed) Benjamin	Aldgate, London	dealer
18912	Mendoza	David	1829	Aldgate, London	Michael de David Mendoza	Esther de Aaron Gomes Da Costa	Miriam Joel	Aldgate, London	cigar maker journeyman
10907	Mendoza	David	1839	Spitalfields, London	Aaron de David Mendoza	Elizabeth (Brina, Betsey) Abrahams		Spitalfields, London	scholar
18166	Mendoza	Eleazer	1832	Middlesex, London				Mile End, London	patient in the Portuguese Jews Hospital
15707	Mendoza	Elizabeth	1830	City, London	Davis Aaron De Sola	Rebecca (Rica) Meldola	Abraham Mendoza	Aldgate, London	
17454	Mendoza	Elizabeth	1833	Aldgate, London	Daniel de Jacob Mendoza	Rosa de Abraham Levy		Aldgate, London	umbrella maker
18917	Mendoza	Elizabeth	1840	Aldgate, London	Michael de David Mendoza	Esther de Aaron Gomes Da Costa		Aldgate, London	scholar
6610	Mendoza	Elizabeth (Betsey)	1819	Sunderland, Co Durham	Abraham de Eliezer Lesser		Israel Mendoza	Spitalfields, London	
10906	Mendoza	Elizabeth (Brina, Betsey)	1820	Lambeth, London	Woolf (Zeev) Abrahams		Aron de David Mendoza	Spitalfields, London	domestic
9509	Mendoza	Emanuel	1824	Spitalfields, London	David Mendoza	Hannah Jonas	Catherine Nathan	Aldgate, London	cigar maker
10912	Mendoza	Emanuel	1849	Spitalfields, London	Aaron de David Mendoza	Elizabeth (Brina, Betsey) Abrahams		Spitalfields, London	
6619	Mendoza	Emanuel (Menahem)	1849	Whitechapel, London	Israel Mendoza	Elizabeth (Betsey) Lesser	Fanny Da Costa	Spitalfields, London	
18154	Mendoza	Esther	1769	Middlesex, London	(?)		(?) Mendoza	Mile End, London	inmate of Portuguese Jews Hospital
17578	Mendoza	Esther	1781	Middlesex, London	Micael Jonas		Eliezer (Elhazar) Mendoza	Spitalfields, London	
18910	Mendoza	Esther	1805	Aldgate, London	Aaron Gomes Da Costa	Fanny (Simha) (?)	Michael Mendoza	Aldgate, London	
17456	Mendoza	Esther	1837	Mile End, London	Daniel de Jacob Mendoza	Rosa de Abraham Levy		Aldgate, London	umbrella maker
9519	Mendoza	Esther	1844	Spitalfields, London	Moses Mendoza	Hannah Hirsch		Spitalfields, London	
10913	Mendoza	Esther	1850	Spitalfields, London	Aaron de David Mendoza	Elizabeth (Brina, Betsey) Abrahams	Henry Sternheim	Spitalfields, London	
12891	Mendoza	Eve	1825	?, London	Solomon de Jacob Mendoza	Hannah Mendes Quiros		Aldgate, London	dressmaker

ID	surname	given names	born	birthplace	father	mother	spouse 1	1851 residence	1851 occupation
18911	Mendoza	Fanny (Simha)	1828	Aldgate, London	Michael de David Mendoza	Esther de Aaron Gomes Da Costa	Moses Arrobus	Aldgate, London	household servant
7318	Mendoza	Frances (Fanny)	1817	Spitalfields, London	Jacob Levy		Jacob de Israel Mendoza	?Spitalfields, London	
15706	Mendoza	Frederick	1850	Jamaica, West Indies	Abraham Mendoza	Elizabeth De Sola		Aldgate, London	
9517	Mendoza	Gabriel	1839	Spitalfields, London	Moses Mendoza	Hannah Hirsch		Spitalfields, London	
26665	Mendoza	Haim	1820	?, London	Israel de Jacob Mendoza	Leah de Raphael Beracha	Rachel de Isaac Fernandez	Spitalfields, London	pedlar
9507	Mendoza	Hannah	1779	Aldgate, London	(?) Jonas		David de Moses Mendoza	Aldgate, London	general dealer
12898	Mendoza	Hannah	1799	Mile End, London	Abraham de Mordecai Levy		Samuel de Gabriel Costa	Spitalfields, London	
9513	Mendoza	Hannah	1801	Colchester, Essex	Gabriel Sebi Hirsch		Moses de David Mendoza	Spitalfields, London	tailor
7331	Mendoza	Hannah	1805	?, London	Moses Mendes Quiros	Eve de Mordecai Nathan	Solomon de Jacob Mendoza	Aldgate, London	
18913	Mendoza	Hannah	1832	Aldgate, London	Michael de David Mendoza	Esther de Aaron Gomes Da Costa		Aldgate, London	tailoress
9516	Mendoza	Isaac	1836	Spitalfields, London	Moses Mendoza	Hannah Hirsch	Rebecca Levy	Spitalfields, London	apprentice
12895	Mendoza	Isaac	1837	?, London	Solomon de Jacob Mendoza	Hannah Mendes Quiros	Maria (Miriam) Hart	Aldgate, London	general dealer
18920	Mendoza	Isaac	1846	Aldgate, London	Michael de David Mendoza	Esther de Aaron Gomes Da Costa	Annie Cohen	Aldgate, London	scholar
26666	Mendoza	Isaac	1846	Aldgate, London	Haim de Israel Mendoza	Rachel de Isaac Fernandez		Spitalfields, London	scholar
11622	Mendoza	Israel	1788	Aldgate, London	Jacob Mendoza	Polly (?)	Leah de Raphael Beracha (Bracho)	Aldgate, London	clothes dealer
6609	Mendoza	Israel	1811	Whitechapel, London	Mordecai Mendoza	Sipora Levy	Elizabeth (Betsey) Lesser	Spitalfields, London	general dealer
12892	Mendoza	Israel	1831	?, London	Solomon de Jacob Mendoza	Hannah Mendes Quiros	Mary Ann (?)	Aldgate, London	general dealer
20547	Mendoza	Israel	1850	?Aldgate, London	Daniel Mendoza	Caroline (Jochabed) Benjamin	Priscilla Jones	Aldgate, London	
21642	Mendoza	Jacob	1819	Whitechapel, London	Israel de Jacob Mendoza	Leah de Raphael Beracha	Sarah Levy	?Spitalfields, London	
9508	Mendoza	Jacob	1820	Aldgate, London	David Mendoza	Hannah Jonas	Amelia Samuel	Aldgate, London	general dealer
6606	Mendoza	Jacob	1832	Aldgate, London	Raphael de Solomon Mendoza	Charlotte de Hannah Solomons	Ellen (Luna) Rodrigues Brandon	Spitalfields, London	tailor's apprentice
17455	Mendoza	Jacob	1834	Spitalfields, London	Daniel de Jacob Mendoza	Rosa de Abraham Levy		Aldgate, London	cigar maker apprentice
12896	Mendoza	Jacob	1839	?, London	Solomon de Jacob Mendoza	Hannah Mendes Quiros		Aldgate, London	cigar maker
9522	Mendoza	Joseph	1829	Spitalfields, London	Moses Mendoza	Hannah Hirsch	Hannah Lazarus	Spitalfields, London	cigar maker
6617	Mendoza	Joseph	1846	Whitechapel, London	Israel Mendoza	Elizabeth (Betsey) Lesser	Alice (Elsie) Nathan	Spitalfields, London	scholar
5656	Mendoza	Judah	1800	Mile End, London	Mordecai Mendoza	Siporah Levy	Rachel de Moses Dias	Aldgate, London	sponge dealer
6615	Mendoza	Judah	1842	Whitechapel, London	Israel Mendoza	Elizabeth (Betsey) Lesser	Rebecca Davis	Spitalfields, London	scholar
10911	Mendoza	Judith	1847	Spitalfields, London	Aaron de David Mendoza	Elizabeth (Brina, Betsey) Abrahams		Spitalfields, London	
12876	Mendoza	Judith (Julia)	1838	City, London	Judah de Mordecai Mendoza	Rachel de Moses Dias	Angel Cohen	Aldgate, London	tailoress
12893	Mendoza	Julia	1834	?, London	Solomon de Jacob Mendoza	Hannah Mendes Quiros		Aldgate, London	cap maker
3341	Mendoza	Julia	1835	Aldgate, London	Michael Mendoza		Joel Harris	Aldgate, London	embroiderer apprentice
9511	Mendoza	Julia (Judith)	1847	Spitalfields, London	Emanuel Mendoza	Catherine Nathan		Aldgate, London	
9515	Mendoza	Keila	1835	Spitalfields, London	Moses Mendoza	Hannah Hirsch		Spitalfields, London	
6616	Mendoza	Lazarus (Elhazar)	1844	Whitechapel, London	Israel Mendoza	Elizabeth (Betsey) Lesser	Rebecca Keys (Israel)	Spitalfields, London	scholar
11623	Mendoza	Leah	1851	Aldgate, London	Daniel Mendoza	Caroline (Jochabed) Benjamin	Solomon Swaght	Aldgate, London	
26667	Mendoza	Leah (Sarah)	1848	Aldgate, London	Haim de Israel Mendoza	Rachel de Isaac Fernandez	Henry Cohen	Spitalfields, London	

ID	surname	given names	born	birthplace	father	mother	spouse 1	1851 residence	1851 occupation
13395	Mendoza	Maria (Miriam) Sarah	1796	City, London	Abraham Mathews	Phebhe (?)	Moses de Mordecai Mendez	Spitalfields, London	monthly nurse
18158	Mendoza	Mariah	1756	Middlesex, London	(?)		(?) Mendoza	Mile End, London	inmate of Portuguese Jews Hospital
12879	Mendoza	Martha	1844	City, London	Judah de Mordecai Mendoza	Rachel de Moses Dias	Solomon Cohen	Aldgate, London	scholar
18918	Mendoza	Mary (Miriam)	1842	Aldgate, London	Michael de David Mendoza	Esther de Aaron Gomes Da Costa		Aldgate, London	scholar
18909	Mendoza	Michael	1805	Aldgate, London	David Mendoza	Hannah Jonas	Esther de Aaron Gomes Da Costa	Aldgate, London	tailor working at home
9514	Mendoza	Michael	1827	Spitalfields, London	Moses Mendoza	Hannah Hirsch	Jane (Jael) Meyers	Spitalfields, London	general dealer
10910	Mendoza	Miriam	1845	Spitalfields, London	Aaron de David Mendoza	Elizabeth (Brina, Betsey) Abrahams		Spitalfields, London	scholar
9618	Mendoza	Mordecai	1774	Whitechapel, London	Moses Mendoza	Judith (?)	Sipora Levy	Spitalfields, London	infirm (formerly currier)
13396	Mendoza	Mordecai	1822	Whitechapel, London	Moses de Mordecai Mendoza	Maria (Miriam) Sarah Mathews	Rosetta (Rose) Lesser	Spitalfields, London	cigar maker
6611	Mendoza	Mordecai (Mark)	1835	Whitechapel, London	Israel Mendoza	Elizabeth (Betsey) Lesser	Frances Benjamin	Spitalfields, London	shoe maker apprentice
9512	Mendoza	Moses	1802	Whitechapel, London	David Mendoza	Hannah Jonas	Hannah de Gabriel Sebi Hirsch	Spitalfields, London	tailor
11621	Mendoza	Moses	1827	Aldgate, London	Israel Mendoza	Leah de Raphael Beracha (Bracho)	Elizabeth Fernandes	Aldgate, London	tailor empl ?2
6613	Mendoza	Moses Israel	1838	Whitechapel, London	Israel Mendoza	Elizabeth (Betsey) Lesser	Adelaide Benjamin	Spitalfields, London	scholar
20546	Mendoza	Moses M	1849	?Aldgate, London	Daniel Mendoza	Caroline (Jochabed) Benjamin		Aldgate, London	
18919	Mendoza	Nancy	1844	Aldgate, London	Michael de David Mendoza	Esther de Aaron Gomes Da Costa		Aldgate, London	scholar
26664	Mendoza	Rachael	1825	Aldgate, London	Isaac Fernandez	Sarah (?)	Haim de Israel Mendoza	Spitalfields, London	
5657	Mendoza	Rachel	1802	Mile End, London	Moses de Isaac Dias	Judith de Daniel Soares	Judah de Mordecai Mendoza	Aldgate, London	
10909	Mendoza	Rachel	1842	Spitalfields, London	Aaron de David Mendoza	Elizabeth (Brina, Betsey) Abrahams	Abraham Abrahams	Spitalfields, London	
17453	Mendoza	Rosa	1801	Aldgate, London	Abraham Levy		Daniel de Jacob Mendoza	Aldgate, London	waistcoat maker
12894	Mendoza	Rosa	1836	?, London	Solomon de Jacob Mendoza	Hannah Mendes Quiros	Simon Goldman	Aldgate, London	cap maker
12875	Mendoza	Sarah	1833	Mile End, London	Judah de Mordecai Mendoza	Rachel de Moses Dias	Angel Aarons	Aldgate, London	tailoress
6607	Mendoza	Sarah	1835	Spitalfields, London	(?) Mendoza	Charlotte (?)		Spitalfields, London	tailoress
6608	Mendoza	Selina	1837	Spitalfields, London	(?) Mendoza	Charlotte (?)		Spitalfields, London	cap maker
12897	Mendoza	Simon	1843	?, London	Solomon de Jacob Mendoza	Hannah Mendes Quiros		Aldgate, London	scholar
12890	Mendoza	Solomon	1799	?, London	Jacob Mendoza	Pyer (?)	Hannah de Moses Mendes Quiros	Aldgate, London	general dealer
12877	Mendoza	Sophia	1839	City, London	Judah de Mordecai Mendoza	Rachel de Moses Dias	Augustus Isaac	Aldgate, London	scholar
12874	Mendoza	Welcome	1831	Mile End, London	Judah de Mordecai Mendoza	Rachel de Moses Dias	Abraham Block	Aldgate, London	servant
29001	Mergen	Henry	1830	?, Poland				Whitechapel, London	tailor
26368	Merngstone	Alexander	1793	?, Poland			(?)	Aldgate, London	rabbi
26369	Merngstone	Moses	1838	?, Poland	Alexander Merngstone			Aldgate, London	
4220	Mesquita	Abraham Bueno de	1851	Whitechapel, London	David Mesquita (Bueno de Mesquita)	Jessy (Freha) Hadida	Frances Penina Cohen	Whitechapel, London	
4218	Mesquita	David Bueno de	1825	Utrecht, Holland	Abraham Bueno de Mesquita	Roza Fano	Jessy (Freha) Hadida	Finsbury, London	cigar maker

ID	surname	given names	born	birthplace	father	mother	spouse 1	1851 residence	1851 occupation
4219	Mesquita	Jessy (Freha) Bueno de	1831	?, London	Jacob Hadida	Simha (?)	David Bueno de Mesquita	Finsbury, London	
18440	Messeena	John Nathaniel	1796	?, Holland	Yehuda Leib		Rachel Gomes	Poplar, London	medical practitioner
18441	Messeena	Rachel	1794	Middlesex, London	Abraham Gomes		John Nathaniel Messeena	Poplar, London	
8727	Metz	Alexander	1851	Aldgate, London	John (Jacob) Metz	Harriet (Henrietta) Moss		Aldgate, London	
8726	Metz	Alice	1849	Aldgate, London	John (Jacob) Metz	Harriet (Henrietta) Moss		Aldgate, London	
8721	Metz	Charles	1825	Aldgate, London	Myer Joseph Metz	Phoebe Solomon		Aldgate, London	pianist
8722	Metz	Harriet (Henrietta)	1821	Whitechapel, London	Abraham Moss		John (Jacob) Metz	Aldgate, London	parasol maker
8720	Metz	John (Jacob)	1824	Aldgate, London	Myer Joseph Metz	Phoebe Solomon	Harriet (Henrietta) Moss	Aldgate, London	cigar maker
8724	Metz	Kate	1845	Aldgate, London	John (Jacob) Metz	Harriet (Henrietta) Moss		Aldgate, London	
8725	Metz	Mier	1847	Aldgate, London	John (Jacob) Metz	Harriet (Henrietta) Moss		Aldgate, London	
8718	Metz	Phoebe	1778	Aldgate, London	Jacob Solomon		Myer Joseph Metz	Aldgate, London	independent
8723	Metz	Phoebe	1843	Aldgate, London	John (Jacob) Metz	Harriet (Henrietta) Moss		Aldgate, London	
8719	Metz	Sarah	1816	Aldgate, London	Myer Joseph Metz	Phoebe Solomon		Aldgate, London	milliner
2656	Metzenberg	Barnet	1829	?, Ireland	Levy Metzenberg	Maria (?)		Glasgow, Scotland	furrier
2657	Metzenberg	Isaac	1845	?, Ireland	Levy Metzenberg	Maria (?)		Glasgow, Scotland	scholar
25624	Metzenberg	Levy	1805	Leszno, Poland [Lissa, Prussia]			Maria (?)	Dublin, Ireland	
2658	Metzenberg	Maria	1811	?, England	(?)		Levy Metzenberg	Glasgow, Scotland	
23698	Meyer	Adolph	1814	?, Germany				Liverpool	toy merchant's assistant
29171	Meyer	Albert	1846	City, London	Myer Henry Meyer	Hannah Meyers		Whitechapel, London	
29167	Meyer	Alfred	1837	City, London	Myer Henry Meyer	Hannah Meyers		Whitechapel, London	
29122	Meyer	Alfred	1848	?	Isaacs Meyer	Mary Ann (?)		Whitechapel, London	
22452	Meyer	Alfred Isaac	1845	Finsbury, London	Meyer Meyer	Sarah Moses		Finsbury, London	boarding school pupil
17012	Meyer	Barrington	1848	Middlesex, London	Meyer Meyer	Sarah Moses	Marion Emily Flora Montague-Marsden	Finsbury, London	
29169	Meyer	Bernard	1839	City, London	Myer Henry Meyer	Hannah Meyers		Whitechapel, London	
9032	Meyer	Caroline	1824	Wapping, London	Jacob Meyer	Hannah (?)	Abraham Brasch	Aldgate, London	
22656	Meyer	Charlotte	1817	Stepney, London	(?)		John Meyer	Whitechapel, London	
21077	Meyer	Edward	1839	?, London				Dover, Kent	boarding school pupil
5870	Meyer	Emily Sarah	1849	Finsbury, London	Meyer Meyer	Sarah Moses	Joseph Lyon Jacobs	Finsbury, London	
9029	Meyer	Esther	1829	Aldgate, London	Jacob Meyer	Hannah (?)	Samuel Zachariah	Aldgate, London	
29170	Meyer	Evelyn	1841	City, London	Myer Henry Meyer	Hannah Meyers		Whitechapel, London	
29166	Meyer	Frances	1836	City, London	Myer Henry Meyer	Hannah Meyers		Whitechapel, London	
9031	Meyer	Hannah	1790	Covent Garden, London	(?)		Jacob Meyer	Aldgate, London	
29165	Meyer	Hannah	1817	Middlesex, London	Kaufman Meyers	Eve Harris	Myer Henry Meyer	Whitechapel, London	
29123	Meyer	Hannah	1850	Aldgate, London	Isaacs Meyer	Mary Ann (?)		Whitechapel, London	
22657	Meyer	Harriet	1834	Bethnal Green, London	John Meyer	Charlotte (?)		Whitechapel, London	milliner
29168	Meyer	Henry	1838	City, London	Myer Henry Meyer	Hannah Meyers		Whitechapel, London	
13540	Meyer	Isaac	1823	?, Germany				Manchester	traveller, watches &c
29120	Meyer	Isaacs	1821	?, Russia			Mary Ann (?)	Whitechapel, London	dealer &c
9030	Meyer	Jacob	1780	abroad			Hannah (?)	Aldgate, London	draper + trimming seller
26194	Meyer	Jacob	1829	?, Germany				Aldgate, London	glazier
22655	Meyer	John	1802	?, Germany [Rassaufuldz, ?]			Charlotte (?)	Whitechapel, London	chemical porter
22658	Meyer	John	1837	Hackney, London	John Meyer	Charlotte (?)		Whitechapel, London	sawyer

ID	surname	given names	born	birthplace	father	mother	spouse 1	1851 residence	1851 occupation
22451	Meyer	Julius	1843	Southwark, London	Meyer Meyer	Sarah Moses		Finsbury, London	boarding school pupil
9033	Meyer	Louisa	1827	Aldgate, London	Jacob Meyer	Hannah (?)		Aldgate, London	
29121	Meyer	Mary Ann	1822	?, Germany	(?)		Isaacs Meyer	Whitechapel, London	
3565	Meyer	Meyer	1815	?, London	Solomon Myres		Sarah Moses	Finsbury, London	fur merchant
17013	Meyer	Montague	1847	Finsbury, London	Meyer Meyer	Sarah Moses		Finsbury, London	
29164	Meyer	Myer Henry	1807	Hamburg, Germany	Tsevi Hirsh HaCohen		Hannah Meyers	Whitechapel, London	[?wine and spirit] merchant
22659	Meyer	Rebecca	1839	Spitalfields, London	John Meyer	Charlotte (?)		Whitechapel, London	scholar
3564	Meyer	Sarah	1821	Bristol	Elias Moses [Marsden]	Judith Jacobs	Meyer Meyer	Finsbury, London	
22660	Meyer	Sarah	1850	Spitalfields, London	John Meyer	Charlotte (?)		Whitechapel, London	
29172	Meyer	Selina	1849	City, London	Myer Henry Meyer	Hannah Meyers	Simon Landsberger	Whitechapel, London	
22450	Meyer	Walter Solomon	1851	Finsbury, London	Meyer Meyer	Sarah Moses		Finsbury, London	
14018	Meyerheim	Adolph	1824	Dessau, Germany				Manchester	accountant
15362	Meyers	Ann	1804	Southwark, London	(?)		(?) Meyers	Waterloo, London	nurse
20393	Meyers	Augusta De Torre	1847	Hammersmith, London	Henry Meyers	Rachael (?)		Chelsea, London	
25475	Meyers	Barnett	1814	?Aldgate, London			Isabella Solomons	Tower Hill, London	cane merchant
20392	Meyers	Ben Braham	1847	Hammersmith, London	Henry Meyers	Rachael (?)		Chelsea, London	
20390	Meyers	David	1844	Middlesex, London	Henry Meyers	Rachael (?)		Chelsea, London	
15363	Meyers	Elizabeth	1832	Southwark, London	(?) Myers	Ann (?)		Waterloo, London	
29174	Meyers	Eve	1787	Middlesex, London	Behr HaLevi Harris		Kaufman Meyers	Whitechapel, London	
20389	Meyers	Felix	1840	Middlesex, London	Henry Meyers	Rachael (?)		Chelsea, London	
15364	Meyers	Frederick	1837	Southwark, London	(?) Myers	Ann (?)		Waterloo, London	
20387	Meyers	Henry	1811	Middlesex, London			Rachael (?)	Chelsea, London	medical practitioner + licentiate of Apothecaries Hall
29175	Meyers	Henry	1830	Middlesex, London	Kaufman Meyers	Eve Harris	Julia Davis	Whitechapel, London	cigar manufacturer
15365	Meyers	Henry	1842	Southwark, London	(?) Myers	Ann (?)		Waterloo, London	
17850	Meyers	Henry Lucas	1833	Amsterdam, Holland				Aldgate, London	tailor
17849	Meyers	Henry Lucas	1850	Middlesex, London	Johan Wilhelm Meyers	Mary Ann (?)		Aldgate, London	
25476	Meyers	Isabella	1821	Whitechapel, London	(?) Solomons		Barnett Meyers	Tower Hill, London	
17847	Meyers	Johan Wilhelm	1828	Amsterdam, Holland			Mary Ann (?)	Aldgate, London	tailor
9864	Meyers	Kate	1840	?, London				Fulham, London	boarding school pupil
29173	Meyers	Kaufman	1784	?, Poland [Speshing, Prussia]	Meir		Eve Harris	Whitechapel, London	fund holder
18268	Meyers	Lewis	1823	Leeds, Yorkshire				Whitby, Yorkshire	bookseller
15366	Meyers	Lezer	1846	Southwark, London	(?) Myers	Ann (?)		Waterloo, London	
17848	Meyers	Mary Ann	1829	?, Ireland	(?)		Johan Wilhelm Meyers	Aldgate, London	
6983	Meyers	Rachael	1822	Great Yarmouth, Norfolk	(?)		Henry Meyers	Chelsea, London	
20391	Meyers	Rose	1842	Middlesex, London	Henry Meyers	Rachael (?)		Chelsea, London	
28559	Meyers	Solomon	1818	Spitalfields, London				Spitalfields, London	general dealer
20388	Meyers	Sophia	1839	Middlesex, London	Henry Meyers	Rachael (?)		Chelsea, London	
15367	Meyers	Thomas	1848	Southwark, London	(?) Myers	Ann (?)		Waterloo, London	
30923	Meyers (Myers)	Abigail	1819	Middlesex, London	Zachariah Solomon	Caroline Woolf	Harris Meyers (Myers)	York, Yorkshire	
21997	Meyers (Myers)	Abraham	1822	Middlesex, London	Michael Myers		Elizabeth Leigh	Whitechapel, London	cigar maker
30925	Meyers (Myers)	Alfred	1847	York, Yorkshire	Harris Meyers (Myers)	Abigail Solomon		York, Yorkshire	scholar
11988	Meyers (Myers)	Barnett	1844	Whitechapel, London	Michael Meyers (Myers)	Jessie Solomons		Whitechapel, London	

ID	surname	given names	born	birthplace	father	mother	spouse 1	1851 residence	1851 occupation
22003	Meyers (Myers)	Clara	1849	Middlesex, London	Abraham Meyers (Myers)	Elizabeth Leigh		Whitechapel, London	
21998	Meyers (Myers)	Elizabeth	1822	Middlesex, London	Joseph Leigh		Abraham Meyers (Myers)	Whitechapel, London	
21999	Meyers (Myers)	Ephraim	1843	Middlesex, London	Abraham Meyers (Myers)	Elizabeth Leigh		Whitechapel, London	
11989	Meyers (Myers)	Evelyn	1846	Whitechapel, London	Michael Meyers (Myers)	Jessie Solomons		Whitechapel, London	
30922	Meyers (Myers)	Harris	1809	?, Poland	Meir		(?)	York, Yorkshire	tailor + draper master empl 4
5605	Meyers (Myers)	Isabella	1848	Whitechapel, London	Michael Meyers (Myers)	Jessie Solomons	Samuel Lazarus	Whitechapel, London	
11987	Meyers (Myers)	Jessie	1824	Middlesex, London	Benjamin Solomons		Michael Meyers (Myers)	Whitechapel, London	
22001	Meyers (Myers)	Jonah	1844	Middlesex, London	Abraham Meyers (Myers)	Elizabeth Leigh		Whitechapel, London	
30924	Meyers (Myers)	Meyers	1843	York, Yorkshire	Harris Meyers (Myers)	Abigail Solomon		York, Yorkshire	scholar
22000	Meyers (Myers)	Meyers H	1840	Middlesex, London	Abraham Meyers (Myers)	Elizabeth Leigh		Whitechapel, London	
11986	Meyers (Myers)	Michael	1813	Middlesex, London	Kaufman Meyers	Eve Harris	Jessy Solomons	Whitechapel, London	umbrella + parasolmaker
11991	Meyers (Myers)	Michael	1850	Whitechapel, London	Michael Meyers (Myers)	Jessie Solomons		Whitechapel, London	
22002	Meyers (Myers)	Nathaniel	1846	Middlesex, London	Abraham Meyers (Myers)	Elizabeth Leigh		Whitechapel, London	
30927	Meyers (Myers)	Sarah	1851	York, Yorkshire	Harris Meyers (Myers)	Abigail Solomon		York, Yorkshire	
30926	Meyers (Myers)	Simeon	1849	York, Yorkshire	Harris Meyers (Myers)	Abigail Solomon		York, Yorkshire	
25241	Meyerstein	William	1825	Hanover, Germany				Clerkenwell, London	merchant in foreign goods
25277	Michael	Aaron	1814	Holborn, London	Michael Michael		Julia Sailman	Holborn, London	tailor
17150	Michael	Abraham	1828	?, Germany				Newcastle Upon Tyne	glazier
4756	Michael	Abraham	1839	Birmingham	Henry Michael	Charlotte (?)		Birmingham	scholar
16784	Michael	Abraham	1848	Bristol	Joseph Michael	Rebecca Levy		Bristol	
25409	Michael	Albert D	1837	Middlesex, London	Jacob Michael	Rose (Rosetta) Hart		Holborn, London	at home
4467	Michael	Alexander	1838	Birmingham	Henry Michael	Charlotte (?)		Birmingham	scholar
5637	Michael	Caroline	1846	Bristol	Joseph Michael	Rebecca Levy	Alfred Nathan	Bristol	
29038	Michael	David	1791	Middlesex, London	Reuben Renner Michael	Esther Russell	Sarah Cohen	Whitechapel, London	watch movement maker
28658	Michael	David	1816	Middlesex, London				Spitalfields, London	general dealer
25283	Michael	Edward	1849	Holborn, London	Aaron Michael	Julia Sailman		Holborn, London	
21656	Michael	Elizabeth	1840	City, London	Samuel Michael	Esther Emanuel	Zuesman (Zuice, Solomon) Joel	Islington, London	
30587	Michael	Ephraim	1851	Aldgate, London	Harris Michael	Rebecca Nathan		Aldgate, London	
21750	Michael	Esther	1821	Aldgate, London	Joseph Emanuel		Samuel Michael	Islington, London	
16794	Michael	Esther M	1849	Bristol	Maurice Michael	Miriam Meyer	Edward Gosschalk	Bristol	
23021	Michael	Harris	1811	?, Poland [?, Prussia]	Moses Michael		Rebecca Nathan	City, London	fur merchant
28774	Michael	Henry	1803	Sheerness, Kent	Jonas Michael	Rebecca Russell	Charlotte (?)	Birmingham	furrier
25282	Michael	Isaac	1846	Holborn, London	Aaron Michael	Julia Sailman		Holborn, London	scholar
25404	Michael	Jacob	1796	Swansea, Wales	Yehuda Leib		Rose (Rosetta) Hart	Holborn, London	solicitor
16791	Michael	James	1844	Bristol	Maurice Michael	Miriam Meyer	Selina Levy	Bristol	
12376	Michael	John	1785	?, Poland				North Shields, Tyne & Wear	
22453	Michael	Jonas	1846	?				Gravesend, Kent	boarding school pupil
7611	Michael	Joseph	1813	Liverpool	Joseph Michael		Rebecca Levy	Bristol	pawnbroker
21748	Michael	Joseph	1839	Spitalfields, London	Samuel Michael	Esther Emanuel		Islington, London	
16790	Michael	Joseph	1841	Bristol	Maurice Michael	Miriam Meyer		Bristol	
25281	Michael	Joseph	1844	Holborn, London	Aaron Michael	Julia Sailman		Holborn, London	scholar

ID	surname	given names	born	birthplace	father	mother	spouse 1	1851 residence	1851 occupation
25278	Michael	Julia	1813	Portsmouth, Hampshire	Moses Sailman		Aaron Michael	Holborn, London	dressmaker
7816	Michael	Julia	1849	Bristol	Joseph Michael	Rebecca Levy	Charles Levy	Bristol	
25406	Michael	Lemon Hart	1825	Bloomsbury, London	Jacob Michael	Rose (Rosetta) Hart		Holborn, London	architect
25407	Michael	Louisa C	1829	?, London	Jacob Michael	Rose (Rosetta) Hart		Holborn, London	
28777	Michael	Maria	1812	Bow, London	(?) Phillips		Reuben Michael	Dover, Kent	
22454	Michael	Marion	1842	?	(?) Michael			Gravesend, Kent	boarding school pupil
28778	Michael	Mark	1841	Aldgate, London	Reuben Michael	Maria Phillips		Dover, Kent	
22455	Michael	Matilda	1843	?	(?) Michael			Gravesend, Kent	boarding school pupil
16788	Michael	Maurice	1810	Liverpool	Joseph Michael	Rachel Myers	Miriam Meyer	Bristol	pawnbroker + silversmith
21747	Michael	Michael	1838	Holborn, London	Samuel Michael	Esther Emanuel		Islington, London	
16789	Michael	Miriam	1819	Middlesex, London	Shlomeh Meyer		Maurice Michael	Bristol	
25279	Michael	Moses	1840	Holborn, London	Aaron Michael	Julia Sailman		Holborn, London	scholar
4757	Michael	Philip	1843	Birmingham	Henry Michael	Charlotte (?)		Birmingham	scholar
23023	Michael	Priscilla	1848	Aldgate, London	Harris Michael	Rebecca Nathan		City, London	
13148	Michael	Rachael	1834	Birmingham	Henry Michael	Charlotte (?)	Jonas Nathan	Aldgate, London	general servant
28775	Michael	Rebecca	1767	Middlesex, London	Michael Russell		Jonas Michael	Whitechapel, London	
23022	Michael	Rebecca	1821	?, Poland [?, Prussia]	Moses Nathan		Harris Michael	City, London	
16782	Michael	Rebecca	1822	Plymouth, Devon	Abraham Levy	Zipporah Benjamin	Joseph Michael	Bristol	
13149	Michael	Rebecca	1835	Birmingham	Henry Michael	Charlotte (?)		Aldgate, London	general servant
28776	Michael	Reuben	1813	Sheerness, Kent	Jonas Michael	Rebecca Russell	Maria Phillips	Dover, Kent	retired merchant
28779	Michael	Reuben	1846	Aldgate, London	Reuben Michael	Maria Phillips		Dover, Kent	
25405	Michael	Rosa (Rosetta)	1793	Penzance, Cornwall	Asher Lemel Hart		Jacob Michael	Holborn, London	
16786	Michael	Rosetta	1851	Bristol	Joseph Michael	Rebecca Levy		Bristol	
19184	Michael	Rosetta	1851	Bristol	Maurice Michael	Miriam (?)		Bristol	
21749	Michael	Samuel	1786	?, Poland	Yechiel Michael		Esther Emanuel	Islington, London	dealer in cloathe [sic]
28772	Michael	Samuel	1795	Middlesex, London	Jonas Michael	Rebecca Russell		Piccadilly, London	coffee house and brothel keeper
29039	Michael	Sarah	1788	Middlesex, London	Hirsh Cohen Organman		David Michael	Whitechapel, London	
21746	Michael	Sarah	1845	Spitalfields, London	Samuel Michael	Esther Emanuel	Solomon Joel	Islington, London	
16793	Michael	Selim	1847	Bristol	Maurice Michael	Miriam (?)		Bristol	
16792	Michael	Selina	1845	Bristol	Maurice Michael	Miriam (?)		Bristol	
25280	Michael	Simeon	1842	Holborn, London	Aaron Michael	Julia Sailman		Holborn, London	scholar
17130	Michael	Solomon	1829	?, Poland [?, Prussia]				Darlington, Co Durham	jeweller
25408	Michael	Walter A	1832	Middlesex, London	Jacob Michael	Rose (Rosetta) Hart		Holborn, London	clerk to underwriter
13468	Michaelis	Emma J	1850	Manchester	Michael Michaelis	Mary Ann (?)		Manchester	
13466	Michaelis	Mary Ann	1827	Manchester	(?)		Michael Michaelis	Manchester	
13465	Michaelis	Michael	1811	?, Poland [Lugde, Prussia]			Mary Ann (?)	Manchester	clerk in a shipping house
25159	Michaelis	R---	1812	?, Germany	(?)		S--- L--- Michaelis	Finsbury, London	
13467	Michaelis	Reuben	1849	Manchester	Michael Michaelis	Mary Ann (?)		Manchester	
25158	Michaelis	S--- L---	1813	?, Germany			R--- (?)	Finsbury, London	cap maker
28112	Michaels	Aaron	1826	City, London			Sarah Hart	Spitalfields, London	cigar maker
13810	Michaels	Abraham	1823	?, Poland [?, Prussia]				Manchester	traveller in hardware
27029	Michaels	Abraham	1827	?, London	(?) Michaels	Betsey (?)		Aldgate, London	cigar maker
19803	Michaels	Alexander	1829	?, Germany	Michael Michael		Sarah Drudinger	Spitalfields, London	tailor
20936	Michaels	Alice	1849	Aldgate, London	Michael Michaels	Esther (?)		Aldgate, London	

ID	surname	given names	born	birthplace	father	mother	spouse 1	1851 residence	1851 occupation
11011	Michaels	Anna	1793	Aldgate, London	(?)		Simon Michaels	Aldgate, London	tailor + renovator
28115	Michaels	Barnett	1848	Middlesex, London	Aaron Michaels	Sarah Hart		Spitalfields, London	
27028	Michaels	Betsey	1805	?, London	(?)		(?) Michaels	Aldgate, London	general dealer
27661	Michaels	Betsy?	1837	Whitechapel, London	(?) Michaels	Rebecca (?)		Aldgate, London	
20933	Michaels	Catherine (Kate)	1842	Whitechapel, London	Michael Michaels	Esther (?)		Aldgate, London	scholar
19805	Michaels	Cecilia	1847	Whitechapel, London	Alezxander Michaels	Sarah Drudinger		Spitalfields, London	scholar
20937	Michaels	Clara	1850	Aldgate, London	Michael Michaels	Esther (?)		Aldgate, London	scholar
11016	Michaels	David	1832	Aldgate, London	Simon Michaels	Anna (?)		Aldgate, London	tailor
11018	Michaels	Deborah	1836	Aldgate, London	Simon Michaels	Anna (?)		Aldgate, London	
20934	Michaels	Elizabeth (Betsy)	1844	Aldgate, London	Michael Michaels	Esther (?)	(?) Lipman	Aldgate, London	scholar
20930	Michaels	Esther	1819	Norwich, Norfolk	(?)		Michael Michaels	Aldgate, London	
20931	Michaels	Hannah	1838	Whitechapel, London	Michael Michaels	Esther (?)		Aldgate, London	
11012	Michaels	Henry	1818	Aldgate, London	Simon Michaels	Anna (?)		Aldgate, London	tailor + renovator
28116	Michaels	Henry	1850	?Spitalfields, London	Aaron Michaels	Sarah Hart		Spitalfields, London	
26282	Michaels	Herman	1831	Poznan, Poland [Exin, Posen, Prussia]				Aldgate, London	shoe maker
10739	Michaels	Isaac	1820	Aldgate, London				Spitalfields, London	general dealer
11013	Michaels	Isaac	1827	Aldgate, London	Simon Michaels	Anna (?)	Elizabeth Nathan	Aldgate, London	tailor + renovator
11014	Michaels	John	1829	Aldgate, London	Simon Michaels	Anna (?)		Aldgate, London	tailor + renovator
27030	Michaels	Joseph	1830	?, London	(?) Michaels	Betsey (?)		Aldgate, London	general dealer
28114	Michaels	Joseph	1846	Middlesex, London	Aaron Michaels	Sarah Hart		Spitalfields, London	scholar
11015	Michaels	Julia	1831	Aldgate, London	Simon Michaels	Anna (?)		Aldgate, London	tailoress
27660	Michaels	Leah?	1832	Whitechapel, London	(?) Michaels	Rebecca (?)		Aldgate, London	?dress maker
27662	Michaels	Lewis	1835	Whitechapel, London	(?) Michaels	Rebecca (?)		Aldgate, London	cigar maker's apprentice
13811	Michaels	Maurice	1820	?, Poland [?, Prussia]				Manchester	traveller in hardware
9562	Michaels	Michael	1811	Aldgate, London				Spitalfields, London	general dealer
20929	Michaels	Michael	1813	Whitechapel, London			Esther (?)	Aldgate, London	tailor + ?scourer
11017	Michaels	Moses	1834	Aldgate, London	Simon Michaels	Anna (?)		Aldgate, London	general dealer
20932	Michaels	Moss	1840	Whitechapel, London	Michael Michaels	Esther (?)		Aldgate, London	scholar
19806	Michaels	Myer	1849	Whitechapel, London	Alezxander Michaels	Sarah Drudinger		Spitalfields, London	
10398	Michaels	Priscilla	1832	Spitalfields, London	(?) Michaels			Spitalfields, London	servant
27659	Michaels	Rebecca	1803	Whitechapel, London	(?)		(?) Michaels	Aldgate, London	general dealer
19807	Michaels	Rebecca	1850	Whitechapel, London	Alezxander Michaels	Sarah Drudinger		Spitalfields, London	
28113	Michaels	Sarah	1825	Whitechapel, London	(?) Hart		Aaron Michaels	Spitalfields, London	
19804	Michaels	Sarah	1829	Stepney, London	Myer Drudinger		Alexander Michaels	Spitalfields, London	tailoress
11010	Michaels	Simon	1787	Aldgate, London			Anna (?)	Aldgate, London	tailor + renovator
20935	Michaels	Simon	1847	Aldgate, London	Michael Michaels	Esther (?)		Aldgate, London	scholar
30462	Michaelson	Absolom	1829	?Riga, Latvia [?Riga, Russia]				Newcastle-under-Lyme, Staffordshire	glazier
31016	Michaelson	David	1821	?, Poland				Halifax, Yorkshire	dealer in jewellery
13102	Michaelson	Fanny	1845	Manchester	David Michaelson		Daniel Barnard	Manchester	
13539	Michail	Bunna	1851	Manchester	Moritz Michail	Getty (?)		Manchester	
13536	Michail	Getty	1829	?, Poland [?, Prussia]	(?)		Moritz Michail	Manchester	
13535	Michail	Moritz	1820	?, Poland [?, Prussia]			Getty (?)	Manchester	master shoe maker empl 4

ID	surname	given names	born	birthplace	father	mother	spouse 1	1851 residence	1851 occupation
13537	Michail	Nathan	1845	?, Poland [?, Prussia]	Moritz Michail	Getty (?)		Manchester	
13538	Michail	Rebecca	1850	Manchester	Moritz Michail	Getty (?)		Manchester	
18319	Michal	Philip	1829	?, Poland [?, Prussia]				Sheffield, Yorkshire	tailor
12643	Michalowski	Catherine	1810	?, Ireland	(?)		Joseph Michalowski	Birmingham	
12642	Michalowski	Joseph	1799	?, Poland			Catherine (?)	Birmingham	slipper maker
14091	Michalsky	Julius	1821	?, Poland				Manchester	cap maker
20286	Michel	David	1829	?, Poland [?, Prussia]				Spitalfields, London	licensed hawker
21611	Michel	Elizabeth	1791	?, London	(?)		(?) Michel	Brighton, Sussex	lodging house keeper
7035	Micholls	Emmeline	1843	Manchester	Henry Micholls	Fredericka Behrens	Arthur Cohen	Manchester	
14411	Micholls	Frederica	1820	Manchester	Solomon Levi Behrens		Henry Micholls	Manchester	
14410	Micholls	Henry	1815	Whitechapel, London	Edward Emanuel Micholls	Rosetta (?)	Frederica Behrens	Manchester	merchant
7864	Micholls	Horatio Lucas	1825	Shoreditch, London	Edward Emanuel Micholls	Rosetta (?)	Rebecca Montefiore	Manchester	merchant
22555	Micholls	Rebecca	1825	Middlesex, London	Horatio Joseph Montefiore	Sarah de Daniel Mocatta	Horatio Lucas Micholls	Manchester	
23909	Micholls	Rosetta	1787	Kingston, Jamaica, West Indies	(?) Lucas		(?) Micholls	Marylebone, London	gentlewoman
22557	Micholls	Rosetta Horatia	1850	Manchester	Horatio Lucas Micholls	Rebecca Montefiore		Manchester	
3590	Micholls	Sallie (Sarah)	1851	Manchester	Horatio Lucas Micholls	Rebecca Montefiore	David Lionel [Moses] Beddington	Manchester	
18043	Mieder	Abraham	1829	?, Poland				Dudley, Worcestershire	travelling jeweller
6117	Mier	Caroline	1820	Southwark, London	Aaron Cohen		Morris Mier	Elephant & Castle, London	
4657	Mier	Joseph M	1810	Swansea, Wales			(?)	Birmingham	merchant
4659	Mier	Lavinia	1824	Haverfordwest, Wales				Swansea, Wales	
4658	Mier	Marcus (Marquis) Leon	1832	Oxford, Oxfordshire	Joseph M Mier	(?)	Sarah Ann Moses	Birmingham	
6119	Mier	Maria Miriam	1849	Elephant & Castle, London	Morris Mier	Caroline Cohen		Elephant & Castle, London	
6116	Mier	Morris	1811	Haverfordwest, Wales	Moshe Mier		Caroline Cohen	Elephant & Castle, London	
6118	Mier	Ray	1847	Elephant & Castle, London	Morris Mier	Caroline Cohen		Elephant & Castle, London	
26872	Miers	Abraham	1816	?, Poland [?, Prussia]			Mariah? (?)	Aldgate, London	tailor
3389	Miers	Ailsie (Alice)	1845	Whitechapel, London	Simeon (Sim) Lazarus Miers	Emma Burdett	Maurice Hart	Aldgate, London	scholar
25434	Miers	Benjamin Leon	1836	Whitechapel, London	Leon Meyer	Jane Woolf	Frances Roberts	Mile End, London	
24669	Miers	Diana	1825	?, Lincolnshire	(?)		Henry Miers	Kennington, London	
26876	Miers	Dinah	1840	?, London	Abraham Miers	Mariah? (?)		Aldgate, London	scholar
26879	Miers	Elisha	1850	?, London	Abraham Miers	Mariah? (?)		Aldgate, London	
18829	Miers	Emma	1819	Peterborough, Cambridgeshire	Peter Burdett		Simeon (Sim) Lazarus Miers	Aldgate, London	
24668	Miers	Henry	1823	Whitechapel, London			Diana (?)	Kennington, London	chair + sofa maker
24670	Miers	Henry	1849	Gateshead, Tyne & Wear	Henry Miers	Diana (?)		Kennington, London	
14216	Miers	Isaac	1825	?, Germany			Rosery (?)	Manchester	cloth cap maker
26878	Miers	Isaac	1848	?, London	Abraham Miers	Mariah? (?)		Aldgate, London	
3384	Miers	Isaac Levi	1801	Finsbury, London	Hananiah Lipman		?	Aldgate, London	warehouseman
3392	Miers	Isaac Lipman	1848	Whitechapel, London	Simeon (Sim) Lazarus Miers	Emma Burdett		Aldgate, London	

ID	surname	given names	born	birthplace	father	mother	spouse 1	1851 residence	1851 occupation
3391	Miers	Jacob	1847	Stepney, London	Simeon (Sim) Lazarus Miers	Emma Burdett		Aldgate, London	
20303	Miers	Jacob Levy	1830	Finsbury, London	Isaac Levi Miers	Elze (Ailsie, Alice) Lazarus nee Jacobs	Catherine Harris	Aldgate, London	warehouseman
21451	Miers	Joseph	1843	Bethnal Green, London				Gravesend, Kent	boarding school pupil
18830	Miers	Joseph Lazarus	1843	Whitechapel, London	Simeon (Sim) Lazarus Miers	Emma Burdett	Sarah Cecilia (Celia) Levy	Aldgate, London	
3394	Miers	Joshua	1851	Aldgate, London	Simeon (Sim) Lazarus Miers	Emma Burdett		Aldgate, London	
26875	Miers	Leah	1836	?, London	Abraham Miers	Mariah? (?)		Aldgate, London	scholar
26828	Miers	Lipman	1802	?, London			Rebecca (?)	Aldgate, London	general dealer
26874	Miers	Louisa	1835	?, London	Abraham Miers	Mariah? (?)		Aldgate, London	dressmaker
26873	Miers	Mariah?	1816	?, London	(?)		Abraham Miers	Aldgate, London	
26830	Miers	Mark	1830	Aldgate, London	Lipman Miers	Rebecca (?)		Aldgate, London	dealer
26831	Miers	Moses	1834	Aldgate, London	Lipman Miers	Rebecca (?)		Aldgate, London	dealer
26829	Miers	Rebecca	1802	?, London	(?)		Lipman Miers	Aldgate, London	
14217	Miers	Rosery	1826	?, Germany	(?)		Isaac Miers	Manchester	
26877	Miers	Rosina	1843	?, London	Abraham Miers	Mariah? (?)		Aldgate, London	scholar
3393	Miers	Samuel Frederick	1850	Stepney, London	Simeon (Sim) Lazarus Miers	Emma Burdett	?	Aldgate, London	
10850	Miers	Sarah	1796	?, Essex				Spitalfields, London	laundress at home
18828	Miers	Simeon (Sim) Lazarus	1819	Aldgate, London	Lazarus Miers		Emma Burdett	Aldgate, London	stay + shoe maker + hosier
27233	Migueres	Abraham	1842	?, London	Mordecai de Israel Migueres	Sarah de Abraham Dias Santillana		Aldgate, London	
27231	Migueres	Mordecai	1806	Tangier, Morocco	Israel Migueres		Sarah de Abraham Dias Santillana	Aldgate, London	confectioner
27232	Migueres	Sarah	1805	?, London	Abraham Dias Santillana	Judith de David Nunes Martines	Mordecai de Israel Migueres	Aldgate, London	confectioner
28913	Milhardo (Melhado)	Aaron	1830	Aldgate, London	Jonas Milhardo (Melhado)	Betsy (Elizabeth) Lipman	Sarah Moses	Spitalfields, London	general dealer
28916	Milhardo (Melhado)	Betsey	1849	Whitechapel, London	Aaron Milhardo (Melhado)	Sarah Moses		Spitalfields, London	
28918	Milhardo (Melhado)	Betsy (Elizabeth)	1805	Aldgate, London	Lipman		Jonas Milhardo (Melhado)	Spitalfields, London	
28919	Milhardo (Melhado)	Esther	1833	Aldgate, London	Jonas Milhardo (Melhado)	Betsy (Elizabeth) Lipman		Spitalfields, London	umbrella maker
28915	Milhardo (Melhado)	Hannah	1847	Whitechapel, London	Aaron Milhardo (Melhado)	Sarah Moses		Spitalfields, London	
28917	Milhardo (Melhado)	Jonas	1804	Amsterdam, Holland	Judah Milhardo (Melhado)		Betsy (Elizabeth) Lipman	Spitalfields, London	general dealer
10795	Milhardo (Melhado)	Levy (Louis)	1832	Spitalfields, London	Jonas Milhardo (Melhado)	Betsy (Elizabeth) Lipman	Rachel (?)	Spitalfields, London	
28922	Milhardo (Melhado)	Michael	1845	Aldgate, London	Jonas Milhardo (Melhado)	Betsy (Elizabeth) Lipman		Spitalfields, London	
10796	Milhardo (Melhado)	Rachel	1830	Gibraltar	(?)		Levy (Louis) Milhardo (Melhado)	Spitalfields, London	
28921	Milhardo (Melhado)	Rebecca	1841	Aldgate, London	Jonas Milhardo (Melhado)	Betsy (Elizabeth) Lipman		Spitalfields, London	

ID	surname	given names	born	birthplace	father	mother	spouse 1	1851 residence	1851 occupation
28920	Milhardo (Melhado)	Rosa	1835	Aldgate, London	Jonas Milhardo (Melhado)	Betsy (Elizabeth) Lipman	Uder (Judah?) Davis	Spitalfields, London	umbrella maker
28914	Milhardo (Melhado)	Sarah	1821	Aldgate, London	Samuel Moses		Aaron Milhardo (Melhado)	Spitalfields, London	general dealer
10797	Milhardo (Melhado)	Sarah	1851	Spitalfields, London	Levy (Louis) Milhardo (Melhado)	Rachel (?)		Spitalfields, London	
11980	Miller	David	1826	?, Poland				Whitechapel, London	tailor
14161	Miller	Joseph	1818	Hamburg, Germany				Manchester	merchant shipper
7236	Millingen	Abraham	1793	?, London	Zanvil Melingham		Nancy (Alsy) Solomons	Whitechapel, London	retired jeweller
19087	Millingen	Albert	1846	Spitalfields, London	Charles Millingen Joseph Millingen	Sarah Barnet		Spitalfields, London	
12346	Millingen	Betsey	1823	Aldgate, London	Abraham Millingen	Nancy (Alsy) Solomons		Whitechapel, London	stay maker
7733	Millingen	Charles	1816	Aldgate, London	Joseph Millingen		Sarah Barnet	Spitalfields, London	umbrella + parasol mfr empl 12
7449	Millingen	Charlotte	1787	Dover, Kent	(?) Moses		Michael Millingen	Whitechapel, London	housekeeper
7670	Millingen	Elizabeth	1827	Middlesex, London	Joseph Millingen			Fulham, London	school proprietor
19088	Millingen	Elizabeth	1847	Spitalfields, London	Charles Millingen Joseph Millingen	Sarah Barnet		Spitalfields, London	
9858	Millingen	Fanny	1842	?, London	(?) Millingen			Fulham, London	boarding school pupil
12344	Millingen	Frances	1821	Whitechapel, London	Abraham Millingen	Nancy (Alsy) Solomons		Whitechapel, London	stay maker
12349	Millingen	Henry	1834	Aldgate, London	Abraham Millingen	Nancy (Alsy) Solomons		Whitechapel, London	butcher
9856	Millingen	Hester	1832	?, London	Joseph Millingen			Fulham, London	assistant school proprietor
18952	Millingen	Isabella	1818	?, London	Michael Millingen	Charlotte Moses		Whitechapel, London	dressmaker
19086	Millingen	Joseph	1845	Spitalfields, London	Charles Millingen Joseph Millingen	Sarah Barnet		Spitalfields, London	
9855	Millingen	Joseph N	1789	Islington, London			?	Fulham, London	dealer in diamonds + ?
9857	Millingen	Kate	1840	?, London	(?) Millingen			Fulham, London	boarding school pupil
12350	Millingen	Louisa	1835	Aldgate, London	Abraham Millingen	Nancy (Alsy) Solomons		Whitechapel, London	stay maker
7669	Millingen	Maria	1831	?, London	Joseph Millingen			Fulham, London	assistant school proprietor
12347	Millingen	Matilda	1826	Aldgate, London	Abraham Millingen	Nancy (Alsy) Solomons		Whitechapel, London	stay maker
19090	Millingen	Matilda	1849	Spitalfields, London	Charles Millingen Joseph Millingen	Sarah Barnet	Charles Wells	Spitalfields, London	
18953	Millingen	Mich	1829	?, London	Michael Millingen	Charlotte Moses		Whitechapel, London	tailor
12351	Millingen	Michael	1845	Aldgate, London	Abraham Millingen	Nancy (Alsy) Solomons		Whitechapel, London	scholar
19089	Millingen	Morris	1848	Spitalfields, London	Charles Millingen Joseph Millingen	Sarah Barnet	Blanche Samuel	Spitalfields, London	
12343	Millingen	Nancy (Alsey)	1803	?, London	(?) Solomons		Abraham Millingen	Whitechapel, London	
22615	Millingen	Phineas	1793	Bethnal Green, London			Sarah (?)	Stepney, London	ostrich feather manufacturer
12345	Millingen	Samuel	1823	Aldgate, London	Abraham Millingen	Nancy (Alsy) Solomons		Whitechapel, London	butcher
22616	Millingen	Sarah	1796	Bethnal Green, London	(?)		Phineas Millingen	Stepney, London	ostrich feather manufacturer
19085	Millingen	Sarah	1816	at sea? [Bay of Biscay]	Moshe Barnet Joseph Millingen		Sarah Barnet	Spitalfields, London	

ID	surname	given names	born	birthplace	father	mother	spouse 1	1851 residence	1851 occupation
12348	Millingen	Sarah	1830	Aldgate, London	Abraham Millingen	Nancy (Alsy) Solomons		Whitechapel, London	feather maker
24333	Minden	Deborah	1820	Shoreditch, London	Emanuel (Menachem) Minden	Sarah Davis	Phillip Phillips	Covent Garden, London	
9436	Minden	Emanuel	1847	Whitechapel, London	Lewis Minden	Leah Lyons		Spitalfields, London	
24331	Minden	Emanuel (Menachem)	1791	Whitechapel, London	Eliezer Lezer Minden		Sarah Davis	Covent Garden, London	licensed victualler
30092	Minden	Eveline	1850	Spitalfields, London	Nathan Minden	Hannah Hart		Spitalfields, London	
30091	Minden	Hannah	1826	Paddington, London	Michael Hart		Nathan Minden	Spitalfields, London	
17322	Minden	John	1827	Whitechapel, London	Abraham Minden	(?Sarah Nathan)	Rebecca Kisch	Wapping, London	cigar maker
9433	Minden	Joseph	1825	?, London	Abraham Minden	Sarah Nathan		Wapping, London	cigar maker
30588	Minden	Joseph	1851	Spitalfields, London	Lewis Minden	Leah Lyons		Spitalfields, London	
9435	Minden	Leah	1824	Aldgate, London	(?) Lyons		Lewis Minden	Spitalfields, London	
9432	Minden	Lewis	1819	?, London	Abraham Minden	Sarah Nathan		Wapping, London	cigar maker
5988	Minden	Lewis	1823	Whitechapel, London	Emanuel (Menachem) Minden	Sarah Davis	Leah Lyons	Spitalfields, London	cigar maker
30090	Minden	Nathan	1827	Whitechapel, London	Emanuel (Menachem) Minden	Sarah Davis	Hannah Hart	Spitalfields, London	
24335	Minden	Rachel	1817	Spitalfields, London	(?) Minden			Covent Garden, London	
9437	Minden	Rachel	1849	Whitechapel, London	Lewis Minden	Leah Lyons		Spitalfields, London	
17323	Minden	Rebecca	1827	Whitechapel, London	Abraham Kisch		John Minden	Wapping, London	
9431	Minden	Sarah	1786	?, London	Moshe Nathan		Abraham Minden	Wapping, London	
24332	Minden	Sarah	1792	Spitalfields, London	Joseph Davis		(?)	Covent Garden, London	
24334	Minden	Sophia	1829	Whitechapel, London	Emanuel (Menachem) Minden	Sarah Davis		Covent Garden, London	
14953	Minson	Susan	1836	Middlesex, London	(?) Minson			Bethnal Green, London	boarding school pupil
9305	Miranda	Esther	1770	Whitechapel, London	Samuel Dina	Judith	Joseph de Jacob Nunes Miranda	Aldgate, London	poor
27285	Miranda	Moses	1830	?, Holland	Abraham Miranda		Sarah Ramos	Aldgate, London	cigar maker
18610	Miranda	Rachael	1827	?, Holland	Abraham Miranda		Hyman De Yonge	Aldgate, London	cigar maker
27283	Miranda	Sarah	1831	Brighton, Sussex	David de Isaac Ramos	Sarah de Jacob Hart	Moses Miranda	Aldgate, London	
13458	Mirlo	Aaron	1839	Manchester	Joseph Mirlo	Harriet (?)		Manchester	scholar
13463	Mirlo	Evelyn	1851	Manchester	Joseph Mirlo	Harriet (?)		Manchester	
13462	Mirlo	Frederick	1849	Manchester	Joseph Mirlo	Harriet (?)		Manchester	
6515	Mirlo	Harriet	1817	Liverpool	(?)		Joseph Mirlo	Manchester	
6514	Mirlo	Joseph	1800	?, Poland [?, Prussia]			Harriet (?)	Manchester	furrier + marine store dealer
13459	Mirlo	Rosina	1842	Manchester	Joseph Mirlo	Harriet (?)		Manchester	scholar
13460	Mirlo	Solomon	1844	Manchester	Joseph Mirlo	Harriet (?)		Manchester	scholar
13461	Mirlo	Victoria	1846	Manchester	Joseph Mirlo	Harriet (?)		Manchester	scholar
13505	Misell	Amelia	1850	Manchester	David Misell	Caroline Isaacs	Edward Henry Fox	Manchester	
13503	Misell	Asher	1845	Manchester	David Misell	Caroline Isaacs	Catherine (Kate) Fisher	Manchester	
13500	Misell	Caroline	1823	Manchester	Nathahn Isaacs		David Misell	Manchester	
13499	Misell	David	1809	Ipswich, Suffolk	Isaac Misell		Caroline Isaacs	Manchester	tobacconist
14121	Misell	David	1849	Liverpool	Moses Misell	Esther Jacobs		Manchester	
14118	Misell	Esther	1826	Birmingham	(?) Jacobs		Moses Misell	Manchester	
14120	Misell	Henry	1847	Salford, Lancashire	Moses Misell	Esther Jacobs		Manchester	scholar
13501	Misell	Hyman	1843	Manchester	David Misell	Caroline Isaacs	Della Rowas	Manchester	
13502	Misell	Isaac	1844	Manchester	David Misell	Caroline Isaacs	Mary Nolan	Manchester	

ID	surname	given names	born	birthplace	father	mother	spouse 1	1851 residence	1851 occupation
14122	Misell	Lewis (Louis)	1850	Manchester	Moses Misell	Esther Jacobs	Elizabeth (Bilha) Rogers (Rodrigues)	Manchester	
14119	Misell	Montague	1845	Manchester	Moses Misell	Esther Jacobs	Rachel Misell	Manchester	scholar
14117	Misell	Moses	1812	Ipswich, Suffolk			Esther Jacobs	Manchester	picture dealer
13504	Misell	Rachel	1848	Manchester	David Misell	Caroline Isaacs	Montague Misell	Manchester	
12617	Misncott	Hyman	1823	?, Poland [?, Prussia]				Birmingham	tailor
9926	Mitchell	Abraham	1835	Great Yarmouth, Norfolk	Michael Mitchell	Elizabeth Davis		Great Yarmouth, Norfolk	southwester maker
15638	Mitchell	Abraham	1841	Plymouth, Devon	Barnet Mitchell	Maria (?)		Plymouth, Devon	scholar
11557	Mitchell	Abraham	1848	Whitechapel, London	Hyam Mitchell	Eve Lipman		Spitalfields, London	scholar
5447	Mitchell	Barnet	1798	?, Russia			Maria (?)	Plymouth, Devon	
10001	Mitchell	Daniel	1838	Great Yarmouth, Norfolk	Michael Mitchell	Elizabeth Davis	Sophia Jacobs	Great Yarmouth, Norfolk	
11558	Mitchell	Dinah	1849	Spitalfields, London	Hyam Mitchell	Eve Lipman	Mordecai Mendoza	Spitalfields, London	scholar
8301	Mitchell	Elizabeth	1805	King's Lynn, Norfolk	(?Simon) Davis	(?Sarah) (?)	Michael Mitchell	Great Yarmouth, Norfolk	
6480	Mitchell	Emma	1842	Plymouth, Devon	Barnet Mitchell	Maria (?)	Anson Perels	Plymouth, Devon	scholar
11554	Mitchell	Ephrens	1841	Whitechapel, London	Hyam Mitchell	Eve Lipman		Spitalfields, London	scholar
26247	Mitchell	Esther	1834	?, London	(?) Mitchell			Aldgate, London	pastrycook
11551	Mitchell	Eve	1815	Whitechapel, London	Meir Lipman		Hyam Mitchell	Spitalfields, London	
5449	Mitchell	Fanny	1839	Plymouth, Devon	Barnett Mitchell	Maria (?)	Albert Louis	Plymouth, Devon	scholar
9925	Mitchell	George	1829	King's Lynn, Norfolk	Michael Mitchell	Elizabeth Davis	Esther E Jacobs	Great Yarmouth, Norfolk	southwester maker
11550	Mitchell	Hyam	1813	Whitechapel, London	Michael		Eve Lipman	Spitalfields, London	general dealer
29521	Mitchell	Isaac	1806	Aldgate, London	Abraham Mitchell		Rose (Rosa) Saunders	Spitalfields, London	pastry cook empl 7
15637	Mitchell	James	1824	Plymouth, Devon	Barnet Mitchell	Maria (?)		Plymouth, Devon	warehouseman
20326	Mitchell	Jane	1793	Aldgate, London	Jacob Cantor		Isaac Hart	Aldgate, London	
7012	Mitchell	Joseph	1800	City, London	David Mitchell	Mary Emanuel	Hannah Friedberg	Aldgate, London	accountant + editor, Jewish Chronicle
26250	Mitchell	Joseph	1810	?, London				Aldgate, London	
26248	Mitchell	Julia	1839	?, London	(?) Mitchell			Aldgate, London	pastrycook
9924	Mitchell	Julia Ann	1840	Great Yarmouth, Norfolk	Michael Mitchell	Elizabeth Davis		Great Yarmouth, Norfolk	scholar
9927	Mitchell	Kate	1843	Great Yarmouth, Norfolk	Michael Mitchell	Elizabeth Davis	Israel Jacobs	Great Yarmouth, Norfolk	
6483	Mitchell	Louisa	1837	Plymouth, Devon	Barnett Mitchell	Maria (?)	Michael Russell	Plymouth, Devon	
5448	Mitchell	Maria	1804	Middlesex, London			Barnett Mitchell	Plymouth, Devon	umbrella + parasol maker
7543	Mitchell	Mary	1775	?	Abraham Emanuel		David Mitchell	Aldgate, London	
7818	Mitchell	Mathew	1833	Great Yarmouth, Norfolk	Michael Mitchell	Elizabeth Davis	Elizabeth Jacobs	Hoxton, London	shoe packer
6482	Mitchell	Maud M	1849	Plymouth, Devon	Barnett Mitchell	Maria (?)		Plymouth, Devon	
7587	Mitchell	Michael	1802	Wymondham, Norfolk	Henry or Colman Mitchell		Elizabeth Davis	Great Yarmouth, Norfolk	
11555	Mitchell	Michael	1843	Whitechapel, London	Hyam Mitchell	Eve Lipman		Spitalfields, London	scholar
11553	Mitchell	Moses	1836	Whitechapel, London	Hyam Mitchell	Eve Lipman	Rose (Rosetta) Moss	Spitalfields, London	cigar maker
11556	Mitchell	Rachael	1846	Whitechapel, London	Hyam Mitchell	Eve Lipman	Barnett Alvares	Spitalfields, London	scholar
6481	Mitchell	Rachel	1847	Plymouth, Devon	Barnet Mitchell	Maria (?)		Plymouth, Devon	
26249	Mitchell	Rosa	1842	?, London	(?) Mitchell			Aldgate, London	pastrycook
29522	Mitchell	Rose (Rosa)	1809	?, France	Chapman Saunders		Rose (Rosa) Saunders	Spitalfields, London	
27137	Mitchell	Sarah	1821	?, London	(?)		(?) Mitchell	Aldgate, London	
26246	Mitchell	Sarah	1832	?, London	(?) Mitchell			Aldgate, London	pastrycook
11552	Mitchell	Sarah	1834	Whitechapel, London	Hyam Mitchell	Eve Lipman	Michael Nathan	Spitalfields, London	cap maker
26461	Mocatta	Abigail	1827	?, London	Abraham Mocatta	Grace Mendez Da Costa	Isaac Lindo Mocatta	Bloomsbury, London	

ID	surname	given names	born	birthplace	father	mother	spouse 1	1851 residence	1851 occupation
6183	Mocatta	Abraham	1797	Aldgate, London	Jacob Mocatta	Rebecca Baruh Lousada	Miriam Brandon	Bloomsbury, London	bullion broker
21553	Mocatta	Abraham Lindo	1796	Finsbury, London	Moses De Mattos Mocatta	Abigail Lindo		Bloomsbury, London	fundholder
7281	Mocatta	Ann	1815	Clapham, London	Alexander Susskind		David Alfred Mocatta	Hyde Park, London	
25519	Mocatta	Anna Maria	1844	Liverpool	Elias de Moses Mattos Mocatta	Julia de Leon	Francis John Stearns	Birkenhead, Cheshire	
9159	Mocatta	Benjamin	1784	?, London			Iphigenia (?)	Whitechapel, London	accountant
16353	Mocatta	Benjamin	1802	Vauxhall, London	Moses de Mattos Mocatta	Abigail Lindo	Miriam Montefiore	Hyde Park, London	gentleman
16357	Mocatta	Benjamin Elkin	1850	St Pancras, London	Jacob Mocatta	Juliana (?)	Marian Lucas	Bloomsbury, London	
25634	Mocatta	Charles John	1851	Wallasey, Cheshire	Maurice Mocatta	Elizabeth Woodburn		Wallasey, Cheshire	
15960	Mocatta	Constance Augusta	1838	?, London	Elias Mocatta	Eve Levy	Alfred Goldsmid	Paddington, London	scholar at home
7280	Mocatta	David Alfred	1806	Vauxhall, London	Moses de Mattos Mocatta	Abigail Lindo	Ann Susskind	Hyde Park, London	architect
25512	Mocatta	Elias	1798	?, London	Moses de Mattos Mocatta	Abigail Lindo	Julia de Leon	Birkenhead, Cheshire	merchant
6190	Mocatta	Elias	1804	Middlesex, London	Daniel Mocatta	Nancy (Canandala) de Guerson Goldsmid	Eve de Isaac Levy	Paddington, London	indigo broker
25631	Mocatta	Elizabeth	1819	Ulverston, Lancashire	John Woodburn	Margaret Laury	Maurice Mocatta	Wallasey, Cheshire	
24267	Mocatta	Emanuel	1804	Aldgate, London	Jacob de Abraham Mocatta	Rebecca de Daniel Baruch Lousada		Bloomsbury, London	Stock Exchange
25796	Mocatta	Esther	1796	Aldgate, London	Jacob de Abraham Mocatta	Rebecca de Daniel Baruch Lousada		Bloomsbury, London	
21554	Mocatta	Esther	1801	Vauxhall, London	Moses De Mattos Mocatta	Abigail Lindo		Bloomsbury, London	annuitant
6188	Mocatta	Frederick David	1828	Camberwell, London	Abraham Mocatta	Miriam Brandon	Mary Ada Goldsmid	Bloomsbury, London	banker
25518	Mocatta	Henry Robert Ker Porter	1842	Liverpool	Elias de Moses Mattos Mocatta	Julia de Leon	Penelope Rosamond Sneyd	Birkenhead, Cheshire	
9160	Mocatta	Iphigenia	1785	?, Hertfordshire	(?)		Benjamin Mocatta	Whitechapel, London	
16354	Mocatta	Isaac	1803	Walworth, London			Mary A (?)	King's Cross, London	fund holder
7283	Mocatta	Isaac Lindo	1818	?, London	Moses de Mattos Mocatta	Abigail Lindo	Abigail Mocatta	Brighton, Sussex	
6181	Mocatta	Jacob	1821	St Pancras, London	Abraham Mocatta	Miriam (?)	Juliana Elkin	Bloomsbury, London	East India broker
21555	Mocatta	Jessie	1811	St Pancras, London	Moses De Mattos Mocatta	Abigail Lindo	Thomas Robert Dobson	Bloomsbury, London	
25513	Mocatta	Julia	1805	Santa Cruz, Jamaica, West Indies	(?) De Leon		Elias de Moses Mattos Mocatta	Birkenhead, Cheshire	
6182	Mocatta	Juliana	1829	?, West Indies	Benjamin Elkin		Jacob Mocatta	Bloomsbury, London	
25517	Mocatta	Louisa	1836	?, London	Elias de Moses Mattos Mocatta	Julia de Leon	Frederick Charles Danvers	Birkenhead, Cheshire	
25632	Mocatta	Margaret	1845	Wallasey, Cheshire	Maurice Mocatta	Elizabeth Woodburn	Arthur Edmund Stearns	Wallasey, Cheshire	
16355	Mocatta	Mary A	1822	Rochester, Kent	(?)		Isaac Mocatta	King's Cross, London	
25514	Mocatta	Maurice	1821	St Thomas, Virgin Islands, West Indies	Elias de Moses Mattos Mocatta	Julia de Leon	Elizabeth Woodburn	Wallasey, Cheshire	stockbroker
25633	Mocatta	Maurice Sherbotoff	1848	Wallasey, Cheshire	Maurice Mocatta	Elizabeth Woodburn	Jessie Elizabeth West	Wallasey, Cheshire	
6184	Mocatta	Miriam	1796	Whitechapel, London	Gabriel Israel Brandon		Abraham Mocatta	Bloomsbury, London	
6186	Mocatta	Miriam	1823	St Pancras, London	Abraham Mocatta	Miriam Brandon	Samuel Mocatta	Bloomsbury, London	
6192	Mocatta	Miriam (Mary A)	1844	Islington, London	Isaac Mocatta	Mary A (?)	Barnard Lee	King's Cross, London	scholar
7282	Mocatta	Moses de Mattos	1768	Whitechapel, London	Abraham de Mattos Mocatta	Esther Lamego	Abigail Lindo	Brighton, Sussex	fundholder
6191	Mocatta	Rachel	1822	Clapham, London	Alexander Goldsmid		Elias Mocatta	Paddington, London	
19250	Mocatta	Rebecca	1811	Altona, Germany	(?) Mocatta			Paddington, London	governess
6185	Mocatta	Rebecca	1823	?, London	Abraham de Jacob Mocatta	Miriam Brandon	Sigismund Schloss	Liverpool	

ID	surname	given names	born	birthplace	father	mother	spouse 1	1851 residence	1851 occupation
6187	Mocatta	Samuel	1808	?, London	Moses Mocatta	Abigail Lindo	Miriam Mocatta	Brighton, Sussex	member of Stock Exchange
25516	Mocatta	William	1830	Caracas, Venezuela	Elias de Moses Mattos Mocatta	Julia de Leon	Mary Anne Menzies	Birkenhead, Cheshire	undergraduate at Trinity College, Dublin
12724	Mohr	Benjamin	1849	Birmingham	Isador Mohr	Susan (?)		Coventry, Warwickshire	
12722	Mohr	Isador	1821	Birmingham			Susan (?)	Coventry, Warwickshire	jeweller
12723	Mohr	Susan	1827	Birmingham	(?)		Isador Mohr	Coventry, Warwickshire	
11841	Molena	Hamed	1809	Tetouan, Morocco [Tetuan, Africa]				Whitechapel, London	cotton merchant
9457	Mombach	Israel (Julius) Lazarus	1813	Darmstadt, Germany	Eliezer Mombach		Katherine Hyams	Aldgate, London	professor of music
9458	Mombach	Katherine	1803	Hull, Yorkshire	Shlomeh Zalman Hyams		Israel (Julius) Lazarus Mombach	Aldgate, London	
9460	Mombach	Sarah	1833	Pfungstadt, Germany	Eliezer Mombach			Aldgate, London	
131	Montague	David	1820	Woolwich, London	(?Henry) Montague		Rachel (?)	Woolwich, London	fishmonger
134	Montague	David	1851	Woolwich, London	David Montague	Rachel (?)	Emma (?)	Woolwich, London	
12211	Montague	Henry	1829	Kensington, London			Louisa (?)	Whitechapel, London	watch maker
90	Montague	Jacob	1832	Woolwich, London	Robert Montague	Mary (?)		Woolwich, London	
12212	Montague	Louisa	1826	Manchester	(?)		Henry Montague	Whitechapel, London	dress maker
88	Montague	Mary	1798	Bexley, Kent			Robert Montague	Woolwich, London	
132	Montague	Rachel	1820	Woolwich, London			David Montague	Woolwich, London	
89	Montague	Rebecca	1825	Bermondsey, London	Robert Montague	Mary (?)		Woolwich, London	
133	Montague	Rebecca	1849	Woolwich, London	David Montague	Rachel (?)		Woolwich, London	
87	Montague	Robert	1797	Woolwich, London			Mary (?)	Woolwich, London	coal dealer
91	Montague	Sarah	1842	Crayford, Kent	Robert Montague	Mary (?)		Woolwich, London	
5937	Montefiore	Ada Rachel	1842	Middlesex, London	Jacob Eliezer Montefiore	Justina Lydia Gompertz	Joseph Lindo Alexander	Belgravia, London	
24212	Montefiore	Alexander Israel	1818	Middlesex, London	Judah Israel Montefiore	Judith (?)	Alice Abraham	Haggerston, London	clerk, marine insurance
24213	Montefiore	Alice Israel	1830	Middlesex, London	Israel Abraham		Alexander Israel Montefiore	Haggerston, London	
24214	Montefiore	Alice Israel	1848	Dalston, London	Alexander Israel Montefiore	Alice Abraham	Philip (Eliezer) Leon	Haggerston, London	
7102	Montefiore	Alice Julia	1851	Paddington, London	Nathaniel Montefiore	Emma Goldsmid	Henry Lucas	Hyde Park, London	
7868	Montefiore	Anne Horatia	1840	Hyde Park, London	Horatio Joseph Montefiore	Sarah de Daniel Mocatta	Leopold Schloss	Bayswater, London	
7819	Montefiore	Benjamin	1835	?, London	Horatio Joseph Montefiore	Sarah de Daniel Mocatta		Bayswater, London	
24218	Montefiore	Caroline Israel	1813	Woolwich, London	Judah Israel Montefiore	Judith (?)		Haggerston, London	
16327	Montefiore	Charlotte	1818	Stamford Hill, London	Abraham Montefiore	Henrietta Rothschild	Horatio Joseph Montefiore	Bayswater, London	
18125	Montefiore	David	1827	Plymouth, Devon	Abraham de Samuel Montefiore	Stella de Isaac Hatchwell		Mile End, London	
6691	Montefiore	Eliezor (Leslie) Jacob	1827	?London	Jacob Eliezor Montefiore	Justina Lydia Gompertz	Evelina (Eve, Adelaide) Montefiore	Belgravia, London	merchant
16331	Montefiore	Emanuel	1842	?, France	Horatio Joseph Montefiore	Sarah de Daniel Mocatta	Josephine Henriques	Bayswater, London	
7100	Montefiore	Emma	1819	Wandsworth, London	Isaac Lyon Goldsmid	Isobel Goldsmid	Nathaniel Montefiore	Hyde Park, London	
884	Montefiore	Emma Abigail	1832	?, England	Jacob Eliezer Montefiore	Justina Lydia Gompertz	Philip Salomons	Mayfair, London	
18128	Montefiore	Evelina	1839	Mile End, London	Abraham de Samuel Montefiore	Stella de Isaac Hatchwell		Mile End, London	
16329	Montefiore	Evelina (Eve, Adelaide)	1829	Bloomsbury, London	Horatio Joseph Montefiore	Sarah de Daniel Mocatta	Eliezor (Leslie) Jacob Montefiore	Bayswater, London	
18126	Montefiore	Flora	1835	Mile End, London	Abraham de Samuel Montefiore	Stella de Isaac Hatchwell	Moses Hartog Zwart	Mile End, London	

ID	surname	given names	born	birthplace	father	mother	spouse 1	1851 residence	1851 occupation
24215	Montefiore	Flora Israel	1851	Haggerston, London	Alexander Israel Montefiore	Alice Abraham	(?)	Haggerston, London	
16332	Montefiore	Helen	1849	Brighton, Sussex	Horatio Joseph Montefiore	Charlotte (?)		Bayswater, London	
18129	Montefiore	Helen (Hanah) E	1841	Mile End, London	Abraham de Samuel Montefiore	Stella de Isaac Hatchwell		Mile End, London	
5585	Montefiore	Henrietta	1791	?, Germany	(?) Rothschild		Abraham Montefiore	Mayfair, London	fundholder
7471	Montefiore	Horatio Joseph	1798	Middlesex, London	Joseph Elias Montefiore	Rachel de Abraham Mattos Mocatta	Sarah de Daniel Mocatta	Bayswater, London	stockbroker
876	Montefiore	Jacob Eliezor	1801	Barbados, West Indies	Eliezer Montefiore		Justina Lydia Gompertz	Belgravia, London	merchant
24556	Montefiore	John	1820	Barbados, West Indies			Julia Norman	Kennington, London	West Indies merchant
6690	Montefiore	Joseph Gompertz	1850	Belgravia, London	Jacob Eliezer Montefiore	Justina Lydia Gompertz	Eugenie Rose Emma de Wilton (Wilkins)	Belgravia, London	
7472	Montefiore	Joseph Mayer	1816	?, London	Abraham Montefiore	Henrietta Rothschild	Henrietta Francesca Sichel	Mayfair, London	fundholder
7256	Montefiore	Judith	1784	?, London	Levi Barent Cohen		Moses Haim Montefiore	Ramsgate, Kent	
16330	Montefiore	Judith	1837	Streatham, London	Horatio Joseph Montefiore	Sarah de Daniel Mocatta	Ernest Jacoby	Bayswater, London	
24217	Montefiore	Julia Israel	1812	Woolwich, London	Judah Israel Montefiore	Judith (?)		Haggerston, London	
875	Montefiore	Justina Lydia	1811	Kennington, London	Benjamin Gompertz	Abigail Joseph Montefiore	Jacob Eliezor Montefiore	Belgravia, London	
6694	Montefiore	Laura Judith	1838	?London	Jacob Eliezor Montefiore	Justina Lydia Gompertz	Jacob Wilkins (de Wilton)	Belgravia, London	
6689	Montefiore	Louis Phillip	1846	Brighton, Sussex	Jacob Eliezer Montefiore	Justina Lydia Gompertz		Belgravia, London	
6687	Montefiore	Louisa	1835	Middlesex, London	Jacob Eliezer Montefiore	Justina Lydia Gompertz		Belgravia, London	
16328	Montefiore	Moses	1832	Plymouth, Devon	Horatio Joseph Montefiore	Sarah de Daniel Mocatta		Bayswater, London	clerk to stockbroker
7255	Montefiore	Moses Haim	1784	Livorno, Italy	Joseph Elias Montefiore	Rachel Mocatta	Judith Barent Cohen	Ramsgate, Kent	baronet
7101	Montefiore	Nathaniel	1819	Brighton, Sussex	Abraham Joseph Elias Montefiore		Emma Goldsmid	Hyde Park, London	surgeon MRCS not practising
18127	Montefiore	Rachel	1838	Mile End, London	Abraham de Samuel Montefiore	Stella de Isaac Hatchwell	Benjamin Cohen	Mile End, London	
24216	Montefiore	Sarah Israel	1805	?, Jamaica, West Indies	Judah Israel Montefiore	Judith (?)		Haggerston, London	
6688	Montefiore	Sidney	1837	Middlesex, London	Jacob Eliezer Montefiore	Justina Lydia Gompertz	Madeline (?)	Belgravia, London	
18124	Montefiore	Stella	1804	Kingston, Jamaica, West Indies	Isaac de Moses Hatchwell		Abraham de Samuel Montefiore	Mile End, London	annuitant
16062	Moonshine	John	1826	?, Germany				Aldgate, London	boot maker
3933	Moore	Abraham (Alfred)	1850	Aldgate, London	Moss Godfrey Moore	Sarah Moss	Phoebe Marks	Whitechapel, London	
4760	Moore	Amelia	1834	Leeds, Yorkshire	Benjamin P Moore	Matilda (?)		Birmingham	
4758	Moore	Benjamin P	1807	?, Poland [?, Prussia]			Matilda (?)	Birmingham	china merchant
4766	Moore	Edward	1846	Birmingham	Benjamin P Moore	Matilda (?)		Birmingham	
4761	Moore	Eliza	1835	Birmingham	Benjamin P Moore	Matilda (?)		Birmingham	
3930	Moore	George	1839	Whitechapel, London	Moss Godfrey Moore	Sarah Moss	Sarah Levy	Whitechapel, London	
4767	Moore	Jane (Jeannie)	1851	Birmingham	Benjamin P Moore	Matilda (?)	Henry Barnett	Birmingham	
4768	Moore	Joseph	1821	Leszno, Poland [Lissa, Prussia]				Birmingham	merchant
4765	Moore	Lewis	1845	Birmingham	Benjamin P Moore	Matilda (?)		Birmingham	
3931	Moore	Lewis (Levy) Henry	1843	Whitechapel, London	Moss Godfrey Moore	Sarah Moss	Lucy Hadida	Whitechapel, London	
4759	Moore	Matilda	1811	Birmingham	(?)		Benjamin P Moore	Birmingham	
4762	Moore	Maurice	1840	Birmingham	Benjamin P Moore	Matilda (?)		Birmingham	
3927	Moore	Moss Godfrey	1818	Aldgate, London	Godfrey Moore	Harriet Nathan	Sarah Moss	Whitechapel, London	dealer of the meat to the Jewish congregation [kosher butcher]

ID	surname	given names	born	birthplace	father	mother	spouse 1	1851 residence	1851 occupation
3932	Moore	Phillip	1848	Whitechapel, London	Moss Godfrey Moore	Sarah Moss	Sarah Marks	Whitechapel, London	
4764	Moore	Rebecca	1844	Birmingham	Benjamin P Moore	Matilda (?)	Henry Bonas	Birmingham	
6374	Moore	Rosie	1842	Birmingham	Benjamin P Moore	Matilda (?)	Henry Harris	Birmingham	
3928	Moore	Sarah	1820	Aldgate, London	Joseph Moss	Julia (?)	Moss Godfrey Moore	Whitechapel, London	
19731	Moravia	Sarah	1784	Middlesex, London	(?) Moravia			Whitechapel, London	
18822	Morcoso	Edward M	1849	Birmingham	James Morcoso	Rebecca (?)	Hannah Samuels	Birmingham	
8539	Morcoso	Hannah	1846	Birmingham	James Morcoso	Rebecca (?)	Solomon Woolf (Wolf)	Birmingham	
4769	Morcoso	James	1793	Nakło nad Notecią, Poland [Nakel, Prussia Germany]			Rebecca Myers	Birmingham	general factor
4771	Morcoso	Phoebe	1844	Birmingham	James Morcoso	Rebecca Myers		Birmingham	scholar
4770	Morcoso	Rebecca	1821	?, Germany	(?) Myers		James Morcoso	Birmingham	
4773	Morcoso	Saul	1848	Birmingham	James Morcoso	Rebecca Myers		Birmingham	
4775	Morcoso	Teresa	1850	Birmingham	James Morcoso	Rebecca Myers		Birmingham	
6628	Mordecai	Abraham	1837	Spitalfields, London	Lazarus (Eleazer) Mordecai	Esther (?)		Spitalfields, London	cigar maker
9980	Mordecai	Ann	1798	Great Yarmouth, Norfolk	(?) Mayers		Isaac Mordecai	Great Yarmouth, Norfolk	shopkeeper's wife
26314	Mordecai	Barnett	1780	?Poland			Deborah (?)	Whitechapel, London	
6087	Mordecai	Benjamin	1823	Spitalfields, London	Eliezer Mordecai		Elizabeth Simmons	Aldgate, London	general dealer
24024	Mordecai	Benjamin	1846	Marylebone, London	Edward Mordecai	Rachael Abrahams		Marylebone, London	
13268	Mordecai	Catherine (Kate)	1823	Whitechapel, London	(?)		Joseph Mordecai	Spitalfields, London	umbrella maker
26313	Mordecai	Deborah	1781	?, Poland	(?)		Barnett Mordecai	Aldgate, London	
24017	Mordecai	Edward	1809	Marylebone, London	Eliahu Mordecai	(?Ryna Jacobs)	Rachael Abrahams	Marylebone, London	fruiterer
24019	Mordecai	Elias	1834	Marylebone, London	Edward Mordecai	Rachael Abrahams		Marylebone, London	fruiterer
14781	Mordecai	Elizabeth	1843	Aldgate, London	Moses Mordecai		Moss Woolf	Finsbury, London	scholar
18375	Mordecai	Ellen	1835	Paddington, London	(?) Mordecai			Maida Vale, London	servant
25462	Mordecai	Emanuel	1762	Aldgate, London				Aldgate, London	pensioner
11326	Mordecai	Emmanuel	1791	Aldgate, London				Aldgate, London	general dealer
6626	Mordecai	Esther	1791	Spitalfields, London	(?)		Lazarus (Eleazer) Mordecai	Spitalfields, London	clothes dealer
24025	Mordecai	Frances	1849	Marylebone, London	Edward Mordecai	Rachael Abrahams		Marylebone, London	
357	Mordecai	Henry	1834	Aldgate, London	Moses Mordecai	Kitty Isaacs	Eliza Matilda (Rebecca) Kingsman	Aldgate, London	fruiterer
24022	Mordecai	Henry	1842	Marylebone, London	Edward Mordecai	Rachael Abrahams		Marylebone, London	
9986	Mordecai	Isaac	1778	Great Yarmouth, Norfolk	Henry Mordecai		Ann Mayers	Great Yarmouth, Norfolk	shopkeeper (fruit)
13267	Mordecai	Joseph	1822	Whitechapel, London			Catherine (Kate) (?)	Spitalfields, London	clothes dealer
8835	Mordecai	Kitty (Kate)	1813	Aldgate, London	Shmuel Isaacs		Moses Mordecai	Aldgate, London	
16870	Mordecai	Lavina	1826	Ware, Hertfordshire			Mordecai Mordecai	Cambridge	
16871	Mordecai	Lavina Elizabeth	1850	Cambridge	Mordecai Mordecai	Lavina (?)		Cambridge	
13269	Mordecai	Lazarus	1848	Whitechapel, London	Joseph Mordecai	Catherine (Kate) (?)	Alice Hart	Spitalfields, London	scholar
6625	Mordecai	Lazarus (Eleazer)	1793	Spitalfields, London			Esther (?)	Spitalfields, London	clothes dealer
6084	Mordecai	Mark	1835	Spitalfields, London	Lazarus (Eleazer) Mordecai	Esther (?)	Hannah (?)	Spitalfields, London	cigar maker
9985	Mordecai	Martha	1831	Great Yarmouth, Norfolk	Isaac Mordecai	Ann Mayers	Henry (Harry) Jacobs	Great Yarmouth, Norfolk	shopkeeper's daughter
24023	Mordecai	Mary	1844	Marylebone, London	Edward Mordecai	Rachael Abrahams		Marylebone, London	
24021	Mordecai	Matilda	1840	Marylebone, London	Edward Mordecai	Rachael Abrahams		Marylebone, London	fruiterer
16869	Mordecai	Mordecai	1826	Cambridge			Lavina (?)	Cambridge	printer's compositor
360	Mordecai	Moses	1811	Aldgate, London	Tsebi Halevi		Kitty (Kate) Isaacs	Aldgate, London	cigar maker
24018	Mordecai	Rachael	1814	Marylebone, London	Naphtali Hirts Abrahams		Edward Mordecai	Marylebone, London	fruiterer

ID	surname	given names	born	birthplace	father	mother	spouse 1	1851 residence	1851 occupation
8839	Mordecai	Rachael	1846	Aldgate, London	Moses Mordecai	Kitty (Kate) Isaacs	Edward Jacobs	Aldgate, London	scholar
6627	Mordecai	Rebecca	1831	Spitalfields, London	Lazarus (Eleazer) Mordecai	Esther (?)	Isaac Hyams	Spitalfields, London	domestic at home
8836	Mordecai	Rebecca	1836	Aldgate, London	Moses Mordecai	Kitty (Kate) Isaacs		Aldgate, London	scholar
2036	Mordecai	Sarah	1829	Spitalfields, London	Lazarus (Eleazer) Mordecai	Esther (?)	Sydney Davis	Spitalfields, London	tailoress
8837	Mordecai	Sarah	1841	Aldgate, London	Moses Mordecai	Kitty (Kate) Isaacs	Simon Jacobs	Aldgate, London	scholar
13270	Mordecai	Sarah	1850	Whitechapel, London	Joseph Mordecai	Catherine (Kate) (?)		Spitalfields, London	
24020	Mordecai	Sophia	1838	Marylebone, London	Edward Mordecai	Rachael Abrahams		Marylebone, London	fruiterer
8838	Mordecai	Zelig	1844	Aldgate, London	Moses Mordecai	Kitty (Kate) Isaacs		Aldgate, London	scholar
22092	Mordicai	Elizabeth	1801	City, London	(?)			Aldgate, London	annuitant
11901	Morell	David	1842	?, Holland	Jacob Moses Morell	Gertrude (?)		Whitechapel, London	
11903	Morell	Fanny	1850	?, London	Jacob Moses Morell	Gertrude (?)		Whitechapel, London	
11899	Morell	Gertrude	1820	?, Holland	(?)		Jacob Moses Morell	Whitechapel, London	
11900	Morell	Hanah	1840	?, Holland	Jacob Moses Morell	Gertrude (?)		Whitechapel, London	
11898	Morell	Jacob Moses	1814	?, Holland	Moses Morell		Gertrude (?)	Whitechapel, London	cattle dealer
11902	Morell	Mary	1846	?, Holland	Jacob Moses Morell	Gertrude (?)		Whitechapel, London	
11904	Morell	Solchin	1830	?, Holland	(?) Morell			Whitechapel, London	
13683	Morgan	Edward	1831	?, Poland [?, Prussia]				Manchester	cap maker
13684	Morgan	Lewis	1834	?, Poland [?, Prussia]				Manchester	cap maker
28773	Morgan	Sara	1830	Middlesex, London	Henry Nathan	Catherine Michael	William Morgan	Glasgow, Scotland	
26380	Morisson	Lewis	1823	?, Germany				Aldgate, London	cigar maker
13553	Morris	Abraham	1815	?, Germany			Marley (?)	Manchester	master glazier
26850	Morris	Abraham	1831	Edinburgh, Scotland				Aldgate, London	student
18050	Morris	Albert	1846	Dudley, Worcestershire	Samuel Morris	Mary (?)		Dudley, Worcestershire	scholar
10830	Morris	Alexander	1824	Zurbmain, Poland	Moshe		Leah Lazarus	Spitalfields, London	jeweller
12052	Morris	Alfred	1837	Whitechapel, London	Samuel Morris	Celia Dyea		Whitechapel, London	
30839	Morris	Alfred	1849	Windsor, Berkshire	Lyons Morris	Mary Ann Meredew		Windsor, Berkshire	
12054	Morris	Amelia	1842	Whitechapel, London	Samuel Morris	Celia Dyea		Whitechapel, London	scholar
13552	Morris	Amelia	1843	?, Germany	Abraham Morris	Marley (?)		Manchester	
10832	Morris	Amelia	1851	Spitalfields, London	Alexander Morris	Leah Lazarus		Spitalfields, London	
26954	Morris	Anne (Hannah)	1849	Aldgate, London	Morris (Mordecai) Morris	Elizabeth Lawrence		Aldgate, London	
29185	Morris	Barnard	1793	?, Germany			Betty (?)	Whitechapel, London	cigar + snuff manufacturer empl 120
14835	Morris	Benjamin	1829	Bethnal Green, London			Esther (?)	Bethnal Green, London	cabinet maker
29186	Morris	Betty	1801	?, Germany	(?)		Barnard Morris	Whitechapel, London	
1166	Morris	Brina (Sabrina)	1811	Exeter, Devon			William (Henry) Morris	Plymouth, Devon	jeweller
26955	Morris	Caroline	1851	Aldgate, London	Morris (Mordecai) Morris	Elizabeth Lawrence		Aldgate, London	
11364	Morris	Catharine	1821	Aldgate, London	Isaac HaCohen Israel		Moses Morris	Aldgate, London	
12049	Morris	Celia	1812	Amsterdam, Holland	(?) Dyea	Victoa (?)	Samuel Morris	Whitechapel, London	
23091	Morris	Celig	1832	Hamburg, Germany				Aldgate, London	box maker
1167	Morris	Cordelia	1834	Plymouth, Devon	William (Henry) Morris	Brina (Sabrina) (?)		Plymouth, Devon	
1169	Morris	Deborah	1837	Plymouth, Devon	William (Henry) Morris	Brina (Sabrina) (?)	Wofe (William) Ullmann	Plymouth, Devon	scholar
13551	Morris	Dorothea	1849	?, Germany	Simon Morris	Rosa (?)		Manchester	
12050	Morris	Edward Samuel	1832	Whitechapel, London	Samuel Morris	Celia Dyea		Whitechapel, London	
6761	Morris	Edwin (Edward) Jacob	1850	Windsor, Berkshire	Lyons Morris	Mary Ann Meredew	Catherine Nathan	Windsor, Berkshire	

511

ID	surname	given names	born	birthplace	father	mother	spouse 1	1851 residence	1851 occupation
26952	Morris	Elizabeth	1823	Whitechapel, London	Abraham Lawrence		Morris (Mordecai) Morris	Aldgate, London	
2304	Morris	Esther	1827	?, Poland				Leeds, Yorkshire	
14836	Morris	Esther	1829	Bethnal Green, London	(?)		Benjamin Morris	Bethnal Green, London	fancy trimming weaver
26550	Morris	Esther	1830	Whitechapel, London	(?) Morris	Isabella (?)		Spitalfields, London	tailoress
29682	Morris	Fanny	1825	Whitechapel, London	Jacob Jonas		Hyam (Hyman) Morris	Whitechapel, London	
12051	Morris	Flora	1834	Whitechapel, London	Samuel Morris	Celia Dyea		Whitechapel, London	
12053	Morris	Frederick	1839	Whitechapel, London	Samuel Morris	Celia Dyea		Whitechapel, London	scholar
1168	Morris	George	1836	Plymouth, Devon	William (Henry) Morris	Brina (Sabrina) (?)		Plymouth, Devon	apprentice watchmaker
26549	Morris	Hanah	1826	Whitechapel, London	(?) Morris	Isabella (?)		Spitalfields, London	tailoress
1442	Morris	Hannah E	1844	Plymouth, Devon	Thomas Joel Morris	Mary Anne (?)		Plymouth, Devon	scholar
30977	Morris	Harris	1802	?, Poland			(?)	Walsall, Staffordshire	watchmaker
30980	Morris	Henrietta	1841	Walsall, Staffordshire	Harris Morris	(?)		Walsall, Staffordshire	scholar
31019	Morris	Henry	1831	?, Poland				Halifax, Yorkshire	tailor
30838	Morris	Henry	1848	Eton, Berkshire	Lyons Morris	Mary Ann Meredew		Windsor, Berkshire	
1440	Morris	Herbert O	1839	Plymouth, Devon	Thomas Joel Morris	Mary Anne (?)		Plymouth, Devon	scholar
29681	Morris	Hyam (Hyman)	1813	Poznan, Poland [Posen, Prussia]	M--- Morris		Fanny Jonas	Whitechapel, London	furrier
11365	Morris	Isaac	1850	Aldgate, London	Moses Morris	Catharine Israel		Aldgate, London	
13552	Morris	Isaac	1851	Manchester	Simon Morris	Rosa (?)		Manchester	
26548	Morris	Isabella	1796	Whitechapel, London	(?)		(?) Morris	Spitalfields, London	clothes dealer
239	Morris	Isidore	1830	Gdansk, Poland [Danzig, Poland]	Wolf Meyer Morris	Amalie Davidsohn	Clara Simons	Glasgow, Scotland	merchant (timber + esparto grass) + professor of music
12701	Morris	Israel	1832	Wolverhampton, Staffordshire				Birmingham	draper's apprentice
25818	Morris	Jacob	1815	Aldgate, London			Rebecca (?)	Aldgate, London	clothes dealer
1171	Morris	Jacob	1847	Plymouth, Devon	William (Henry) Morris	Brina (Sabrina) (?)		Plymouth, Devon	scholar
30981	Morris	Joel	1843	Walsall, Staffordshire	Harris Morris	(?)		Walsall, Staffordshire	scholar
29190	Morris	Johanna	1833	?, Germany	(?)		William Morris	Whitechapel, London	
14235	Morris	John	1827	?, Poland [?, Prussia]				Manchester	traveller (jeweller)
18047	Morris	John	1840	Birmingham	Samuel Morris	Mary (?)		Dudley, Worcestershire	errand boy
12055	Morris	John	1844	Whitechapel, London	Samuel Morris	Celia Dyea		Whitechapel, London	scholar
26551	Morris	Josepene	1833	Aldgate, London	(?) Morris	Isabella (?)		Spitalfields, London	tailoress
11896	Morris	Joseph	1826	?, Poland [?, Prussia]				Whitechapel, London	tailor
30979	Morris	Joseph	1839	Birmingham	Harris Morris	(?)		Walsall, Staffordshire	scholar
11362	Morris	Joseph	1848	Aldgate, London	Moses Morris	Catharine Israel		Aldgate, London	
1172	Morris	Judah	1849	Plymouth, Devon	William (Henry) Morris	Brina (Sabrina) (?)		Plymouth, Devon	
28485	Morris	Julia	1831	Margonin, Poland [Prussia]	(?)			Spitalfields, London	
25821	Morris	Julia	1838	Aldgate, London	Jacob Morris	Rebecca (?)		Aldgate, London	scholar
25822	Morris	Julia	1838	Mile End, London	Jacob Morris	Rebecca (?)		Aldgate, London	scholar
1170	Morris	Kate	1843	Plymouth, Devon	William (Henry) Morris	Brina (Sabrina) (?)	Joseph I Jacobs	Plymouth, Devon	scholar
2535	Morris	Koplik	1822	?, Poland			Ann (?)	Hull, Yorkshire	dealer in watches
10831	Morris	Leah	1827	Spitalfields, London	Eli Lazarus		Alexander Morris	Spitalfields, London	general dealer
25820	Morris	Leah	1837	Aldgate, London	Jacob Morris	Rebecca (?)		Aldgate, London	dressmaker apprentice
29189	Morris	Leopold	1839	Middlesex, London	Barnard Morris	Betty (?)	Sarah Boss	Whitechapel, London	scholar
25807	Morris	Levy	1821	Amsterdam, Holland				Aldgate, London	furrier journeyman

ID	surname	given names	born	birthplace	father	mother	spouse 1	1851 residence	1851 occupation
23827	Morris	Lewis	1829	?, Poland [?, Prussia]				Liverpool	hawker
237	Morris	Louis	1819	Gdansk, Poland [Danzig, Poland]	Wolf Meyer Morris	Amalie Davidsohn	Matilda Morris	Glasgow, Scotland	merchant
13556	Morris	Louisa	1848	?, Germany	Abraham Morris	Marley (?)		Manchester	
30840	Morris	Lyons	1821	Margonin, Poland [Margonin, Prussia]			Mary Ann Meredew	Windsor, Berkshire	tailor
2536	Morris	Marcus Carviel	1823	Kempen, Germany				Hull, Yorkshire	cap manufacturer
1441	Morris	Margaret J	1841	Plymouth, Devon	Thomas Joel Morris	Mary Anne (?)		Plymouth, Devon	scholar
13554	Morris	Marley	1813	?, Germany	(?)		Abraham Morris	Manchester	
18046	Morris	Mary	1817	Birmingham	(?)		Samuel Morris	Dudley, Worcestershire	
18048	Morris	Mary Ann	1842	Birmingham	Samuel Morris	Mary (?)		Dudley, Worcestershire	scholar
1439	Morris	Mary Anne	1802	Plymouth, Devon			Thomas Joel Morris	Plymouth, Devon	book binder
30841	Morris	Mary Anne	1822	Windsor, Berkshire	(?) Meredew		Lyons Morris	Windsor, Berkshire	tailor's wife
7444	Morris	Matilda	1819	?, London	Lewis Myer (Yehuda) Morris	Allice Marks	Louis Morris	Glasgow, Scotland	
13550	Morris	Maurice	1846	?, Germany	Simon Morris	Rosa (?)		Manchester	
16724	Morris	Michael	1829	Middlesex, London	Joseph Morris		Mary Barnett	Spitalfields, London	general dealer
26951	Morris	Morris (Mordecai)	1821	Aldgate, London	Joseph Morris		Elizabeth Lawrence	Aldgate, London	general clothes dealer
11363	Morris	Moses	1822	Aldgate, London	Joseph Morris		Catharine Israel	Aldgate, London	general dealer
17631	Morris	Moses	1825	?, Poland			Sarah (?)	Aldgate, London	jeweller
23822	Morris	Moses	1832	?, Russia				Liverpool	commercial traveller (pedlar)
11894	Morris	Nathan	1819	?, Poland [?, Prussia]				Whitechapel, London	tailor
29683	Morris	Pauline	1828	Poznan, Poland [Posen, Prussia]	(?)			Whitechapel, London	dressmaker
29188	Morris	Philip	1836	Middlesex, London	Barnard Morris	Betty (?)	Margaret (?)	Whitechapel, London	clerk, foreign manufacturer
30978	Morris	Rachael	1837	Birmingham	Harris Morris	(?)		Walsall, Staffordshire	scholar
16972	Morris	Rachel	1841	Dublin, Ireland	(?) Morris			Hammersmith, London	boarding school pupil
25819	Morris	Rebecca	1811	Mile End, London	(?)		Jacob Morris	Aldgate, London	char woman
2305	Morris	Rebecca	1848	Leeds, Yorkshire	Samuel Morris	Esther (?)		Leeds, Yorkshire	
13549	Morris	Rosa	1826	?, Germany	(?)		Simon Morris	Manchester	
12048	Morris	Samuel	1795	?, Germany			Celia Dyea	Whitechapel, London	tobacconist + cigar manufacturer
18045	Morris	Samuel	1807	Birmingham			Mary (?)	Dudley, Worcestershire	?horsley
238	Morris	Samuel	1823	Gdansk, Poland [Danzig, Poland]	Wolf Meyer Morris	Amalie Davidsohn	Augusta Morris	Glasgow, Scotland	merchant (timber + esparto grass)
2303	Morris	Samuel	1824	?, Poland			Esther (?)	Leeds, Yorkshire	shopkeeper
1432	Morris	Samuel	1826	?, Poland [?, Prussia]				Plymouth, Devon	pedlar
18049	Morris	Samuel	1843	Birmingham	Samuel Morris	Mary (?)		Dudley, Worcestershire	scholar
14837	Morris	Samuel	1850	Bethnal Green, London	Benjamin Morris	Esther (?)		Bethnal Green, London	
26376	Morris	Sarah	1751	?, Germany	(?)		(?) Morris	Aldgate, London	pensioner
17632	Morris	Sarah	1829	?, Poland	(?)		Moses Morris	Aldgate, London	cap maker
13548	Morris	Simon	1821	?, Germany			Rosa (?)	Manchester	master tailor
26552	Morris	Solomon	1834	Aldgate, London	(?) Morris	Isabella (?)		Spitalfields, London	fruiterer
26953	Morris	Sophia	1848	Aldgate, London	Morris (Mordecai) Morris	Elizabeth Lawrence		Aldgate, London	

ID	surname	given names	born	birthplace	father	mother	spouse 1	1851 residence	1851 occupation
18051	Morris	Thomas	1850	Dudley, Worcestershire	Samuel Morris	Mary (?)		Dudley, Worcestershire	
1438	Morris	Thomas Joel	1813	?, London			Mary Anne (?)	Plymouth, Devon	boot- + shoemaker
29187	Morris	William	1823	?, Germany	Barnard Morris	Betty (?)	Johanna (?)	Whitechapel, London	cigar + snuff manufacturer
1165	Morris	William (Henry)	1807	?, Poland [?, Prussia]			Brina (Sabrina) (?)	Plymouth, Devon	jeweller
18316	Morriss	Anne	1815	?, Russia	(?)		Harris Morriss	Sheffield, Yorkshire	
15161	Morriss	Elizabeth	1808	?Margate, Kent	(?)		Joseph Morriss	Haggerston, London	
18315	Morriss	Harris	1811	?, Russia			Anne (?)	Sheffield, Yorkshire	tailor
15160	Morriss	Joseph	1816	?, Poland			Elizabeth (?)	Haggerston, London	working jeweller travelling with ---
11366	Morriss	Julia	1830	Aldgate, London	(?) Morriss			Aldgate, London	furrier
18317	Morriss	Mena	1847	Sheffield, Yorkshire	Harris Morriss	Anne (?)		Sheffield, Yorkshire	
18318	Morriss	Mun	1849	Sheffield, Yorkshire	Harris Morriss	Anne (?)		Sheffield, Yorkshire	
15162	Morriss	Sarah Ann	1839	Shoreditch, London	Joseph Morriss	Elizabeth (?)		Haggerston, London	scholar
27814	Morse (Moses)	Sarah	1767	Holborn, London	(?)		(?) Morse (Moses)	Chelsea, London	
18600	Moryoseph	Abraham	1841	City, London	Judah Joseph de Shemaya Moryoseph	Luna de Raphael Meldola	Rebecca Josephs	Aldgate, London	
18599	Moryoseph	Deborah	1839	City, London	Judah Joseph de Shemaya Moryoseph	Luna de Raphael Meldola	Joseph Lang	Aldgate, London	
18595	Moryoseph	Judah Joseph	1787	Essaouira, Morocco [Mogador, Africa]	Shemaya Mor Joseph		Luna de Raphael Meldola	Aldgate, London	grocer
18596	Moryoseph	Luna	1811	Tuscany, Italy	Raphael Meldola		Judah Joseph de Shemaya Moryoseph	Aldgate, London	
18601	Moryoseph	Phineas	1846	City, London	Judah Joseph de Shemaya Moryoseph	Luna de Raphael Meldola	Yacota Emcurz	Aldgate, London	
18598	Moryoseph	Raphael (Reuben)	1834	City, London	Judah Joseph de Shemaya Moryoseph	Luna de Raphael Meldola		Aldgate, London	
18597	Moryoseph	Selina (Semanya)	1829	City, London	Judah Joseph de Shemaya Moryoseph	Luna de Raphael Meldola	Alfred Abrahams	Aldgate, London	
1049	Moschzisky	Blanche	1848	?, Devon		Laura (?Moschzisky)		Exeter, Devon	
1048	Moschzisky (Moschzisker)	Laura	1823	Oxford, Oxfordshire				Exeter, Devon	
1050	Moschzisky (Moschzisker)	Mathilda	1850	Pimlico, London		Laura (?Moschziski)		Exeter, Devon	
11773	Moseley	Alfred	1850	Aldgate, London	Ephraim Moseley	Rosetta Davis		Aldgate, London	
30589	Moseley	Benjamin	1851	Aldgate, London	Ephraim Moseley	Rosetta Davis		Aldgate, London	
11768	Moseley	David	1841	Aldgate, London	Ephraim Moseley	Rosetta Davis		Aldgate, London	
23684	Moseley	Dinah	1834	Limehouse, London	Moss Moseley	Hannah Lazarus	Morris Levy	Whitechapel, London	furrier
23682	Moseley	Edward	1831	Aldgate, London	Moss Moseley	Hannah Lazarus		Whitechapel, London	furrier
11766	Moseley	Ephraim	1810	Aldgate, London	Moses Moseley	Rosetta Samuel	Rosetta Davis	Aldgate, London	tobacconist + oilman
23680	Moseley	Esther	1828	Whitechapel, London	Moss Moseley	Hannah Lazarus		Whitechapel, London	parasol maker
11770	Moseley	Fanny	1846	Aldgate, London	Ephraim Moseley	Rosetta Davis	Louis Barnett Abrahams	Aldgate, London	
23683	Moseley	George	1835	Limehouse, London	Moss Moseley	Hannah Lazarus		Whitechapel, London	in the employ of Moses & Son
16599	Moseley	George	1850	Liverpool	Nathan Moseley	Louisa (?)		Liverpool	
23677	Moseley	George	1851	Finsbury, London	Lewis Moseley	Hannah Cohen		Finsbury, London	

ID	surname	given names	born	birthplace	father	mother	spouse 1	1851 residence	1851 occupation
23679	Moseley	Hannah	1796	Portsmouth, Hampshire	Jacob Eliezer Lazarus		Moss Moseley	Whitechapel, London	
23676	Moseley	Hannah	1830	Spitalfields, London	David Cohen		Lewis Moseley	Finsbury, London	
16595	Moseley	Jane	1845	Liverpool	Nathan Moseley	Louisa (?)		Liverpool	
11772	Moseley	Jessie	1849	Aldgate, London	Ephraim Moseley	Rosetta Davis		Aldgate, London	
197	Moseley	John Jacob	1824	Whitechapel, London	Moss Moseley	Hannah Lazarus	Priscilla Lialter	Whitechapel, London	sponge merchant
11779	Moseley	Judah Samuel	1819	Aldgate, London	Moses Moseley	Rosetta Samuel		Aldgate, London	trimming maker
11769	Moseley	Julius	1842	Aldgate, London	Ephraim Moseley	Rosetta Davis		Aldgate, London	
23675	Moseley	Lewis	1818	Southwark, London	Moos Moseley	Hannah Lazarus	Hannah Cohen	Finsbury, London	cigar maker
29018	Moseley	Lewis	1823	Bow, London			Selina (?)	Whitechapel, London	cigar maker
16593	Moseley	Louisa	1822	?, London	(?)		Nathan Moseley	Liverpool	
23678	Moseley	Moss	1791	Whitechapel, London	Jacob Moseley		Hannah Lazarus	Whitechapel, London	stationer &c
11771	Moseley	Moss	1847	Aldgate, London	Ephraim Moseley	Rosetta Davis		Aldgate, London	
16592	Moseley	Nathan	1817	Liverpool			Louisa (?)	Liverpool	watch manufacturer
16596	Moseley	Phillip	1846	Liverpool	Nathan Moseley	Louisa (?)		Liverpool	
23681	Moseley	Priscilla	1830	Limehouse, London	Moss Moseley	Hannah Lazarus		Whitechapel, London	parasol maker
11763	Moseley	Rosetta	1785	Holborn, London	Yehuda Konigsberg Samuel		Moses Moseley	Shoreditch, London	fundholder + watch + clockmaker + jeweller
11767	Moseley	Rosetta	1815	City, London	David Davis		Ephraim Moseley	Aldgate, London	
16594	Moseley	Rosina	1844	Liverpool	Nathan Moseley	Louisa (?)		Liverpool	
29019	Moseley	Selina	1823	York	(?)		Lewis Moseley	Whitechapel, London	
16598	Moseley	Victor	1849	Liverpool	Nathan Moseley	Louisa (?)		Liverpool	
16597	Moseley	Victoria	1847	Liverpool	Nathan Moseley	Louisa (?)		Liverpool	
8392	Mosely	Abigail	1850	Southampton, Hampshire	Henry Philip Mosely	Maria (?)		Southampton, Hampshire	
6402	Mosely	Abraham	1818	Birmingham			Ellen Ezekiel	Bristol	surgeon dentist
26614	Mosely	Abraham (Braham) P	1821	Swansea, Wales	Jacob Mosely	Abigail (?)	Hinda Levison	Southwark, London	jeweller
9770	Mosely	Alexander	1837	Middlesex, London	Ephraim Mosely	Julia (?)	Leah Keyser	Kew, London	boarding school pupil
9773	Mosely	Alfred	1842	Middlesex, London				Kew, London	boarding school pupil
2538	Mosely	Alice	1848	Middlesex, London	Simeon Mosely	Jessie Walkinshawe		Hull, Yorkshire	
17878	Mosely	Amelia Elizabeth	1833	Cheltenham, Gloucestershire	Lewin Charles Mosely	Lydia Alex		Fitzrovia, London	
26613	Mosely	Anna Catherine	1822	Swansea, Wales	Jacob Mosely	Abigail (?)	Michael Samuel	Maida Vale, London	
9774	Mosely	Benjamin	1837	Cheltenham, Gloucestershire				Kew, London	boarding school pupil
9598	Mosely	Deborah	1816	Whitechapel, London	Moshe Mosely			Spitalfields, London	furrier
6403	Mosely	Ellen	1818	Exeter, Devon	(?) Ezekiel	Betty (?)	Abraham Mosely	Bristol	
26612	Mosely	Emma	1813	Swansea, Wales	Jacob Mosely	Abigail (?)		Maida Vale, London	annuitant
17879	Mosely	Ferdinand Herman	1841	Fitzrovia, London	Lewin Charles Mosely	Lydia Alex		Fitzrovia, London	
6406	Mosely	Gerard	1851	Bristol	Abraham Mosely	Ellen Ezekiel	Louisa Blanckensee	Bristol	
2539	Mosely	Gertrude	1849	Middlesex, London	Simeon Mosely	Jessie Walkinshawe		Hull, Yorkshire	
26608	Mosely	Helen	1815	Swansea, Wales	Jacob Mosely	Abigail (?)		Brighton, Sussex	annuitant
26573	Mosely	Helena	1810	Swansea, Wales	Jacob Mosely			Brighton, Sussex	annuitant
8390	Mosely	Henry Philip	1811	Swansea, Wales	Jacob Mosely	Abigail (?)	(?)	Southampton, Hampshire	watchmaker + jeweller
2537	Mosely	Jessie	1827	Trinidad, West Indies	(?) Walkinshawe		Simeon Mosely	Hull, Yorkshire	
17881	Mosely	Leah	1846	Fitzrovia, London	Lewin Charles Mosely	Lydia Alex	John Phillips	Fitzrovia, London	
17876	Mosely	Lewin Charles	1808	Middlesex, London	Benjamin Mosely	Rose Levy	Lydia Alex	Fitzrovia, London	dentist
31151	Mosely	Louis J (Berla)	1849	Bristol	Abraham Mosely	Ellen Ezekiel		Bristol	

515

ID	surname	given names	born	birthplace	father	mother	spouse 1	1851 residence	1851 occupation
17877	Mosely	Lydia	1807	Middlesex, London	Pinchas Zelig HaCohen Alex		Lewin Charles Mosely	Fitzrovia, London	
6405	Mosely	Lydia (Lillie)	1847	Bristol	Abraham Mosely	Ellen Ezekiel	Samuel Hyman	Bristol	
8391	Mosely	Maria	1818	?, London	(?)		Henry Philip Mosely	Southampton, Hampshire	
16966	Mosely	Maria	1838	Middlesex, London	Ephraim Mosely		Eugene Cohen	Hammersmith, London	boarding school pupil
17882	Mosely	Maria	1848	Fitzrovia, London	Lewin Charles Mosely	Lydia Alex		Fitzrovia, London	
26572	Mosely	Maurice	1803	Swansea, Wales	Jacob Mosely	Abigail (?)		Brighton, Sussex	watchmaker + jeweller
6404	Mosely	Maurice Sinclair	1844	Bristol	Abraham Mosely	Ellen Ezekiel		Bristol	
2540	Mosely	Mira	1850	Hull, Yorkshire	Simeon Mosely	Jessie Walkinshawe		Hull, Yorkshire	
7942	Mosely	Rachel	1835	Cheltenham, Gloucestershire	Lewin Mosely	Lydia Alex	Albert Phillips	Fitzrovia, London	
10473	Mosely	Ralph	1799	Middlesex, London	Mosely Solomon			Mile End, London	dealer in sponges
16976	Mosely	Rosa	1843	Middlesex, London	Ephraim Mosely		Manuel Hirsch Javal	Hammersmith, London	boarding school pupil
17880	Mosely	Rosa Maria	1844	Fitzrovia, London	Lewin Charles Mosely	Lydia Alex		Fitzrovia, London	
2150	Mosely	Simeon	1817	Middlesex, London			Jessie Walkinshawe	Hull, Yorkshire	surgeon dentist
9772	Mosely	Simeon	1839	Middlesex, London			Malvina Oppenheim nee Harris	Kew, London	boarding school pupil
26610	Mosely	Zaleg Phillip	1807	Swansea, Wales	Jacob Mosely	Abigail (?)	Hinda Levison	Maida Vale, London	fundholder
15716	Moses	Aaron	1837	Bethnal Green, London	Moses Moses	Deborah Phillips		Spitalfields, London	egg seller
23336	Moses	Aaron	1838	Birmingham				Westminster, London	convict
308	Moses	Aaron	1841	Aldgate, London				Aldgate, London	
22771	Moses	Aaron	1845	Shoreditch, London	Joseph Moses	(?)		Whitechapel, London	scholar
3166	Moses	Abigail	1790	Aldgate, London	Shlomo Kany	?	David Moses	Stockwell, London	
456	Moses	Abigail	1826	Aldgate, London	David Moses	Hannah (?)	(?) Jacobs	Aldgate, London	dress maker
29923	Moses	Abraham	1777	Wurtemberg, Germany	Moshe		Clara Moses	Whitechapel, London	confectioner
10688	Moses	Abraham	1781	Spitalfields, London	Tsevi Hirsh		Rebecca Davis	Spitalfields, London	general dealer
10269	Moses	Abraham	1801	Amsterdam, Holland			Catharine Harris	Spitalfields, London	general dealer
6605	Moses	Abraham	1811	?				Spitalfields, London	tailor
25063	Moses	Abraham	1851	Spitalfields, London	Moses Moses	Rosetta Harris		Spitalfields, London	
25691	Moses	Abraham	1851	Aldgate, London	Moss Moses	Amelia (?)		Spitalfields, London	
10147	Moses	Abraham Keiley	1827	Whitechapel, London	Joseph Moses		Julia Davis	Whitechapel, London	cigar maker
3628	Moses	Abraham Lyon	1775	City, London	Henry Moses	?Fanny (?)	Abigail Lazarus	Shoreditch, London	gentleman
16742	Moses	Ada	1850	Bristol	Joseph Moses	Jane (?)		Bristol	
1916	Moses	Adelaide Matilda	1832	Swansea, Wales	John Moses Moses	Esther Davis	Samuel Levy Marks	Swansea, Wales	
1236	Moses	Agnes	1808	Plymouth, Devon				Plymouth, Devon	haberdasher
20653	Moses	Alexander	1807	?, Poland				Spitalfields, London	brazier
21965	Moses	Alexander	1822	Ipswich, Suffolk	Emanuel Moses	Ann (?)	Catherine Jacobs	Whitechapel, London	watch manufacturer
4013	Moses	Alexander	1823	Portsmouth, Hampshire	Isaac Moses	Esther Simmonds	Rosetta (Rosa) Hyams	Portsmouth, Hampshire	clerk
25687	Moses	Alfred	1836	Aldgate, London	Moss Moses	Amelia (?)		Spitalfields, London	asssistant to wholesale clothier
23143	Moses	Alfred	1846	City, London	Moses Moses	Elizabeth Levy		City, London	
30591	Moses	Alfred Henry	1835	Wapping, London	Henry Moses	Esther Nathan	Isabel Lindo Alexander	Shoreditch, London	
1919	Moses	Alfred Israel	1837	Swansea, Wales	John Moses Moses	Esther Davis	Rebecca Leah Lazarus	Swansea, Wales	scholar
2722	Moses	Alice	1823	Aldgate, London	Moses Moses	Elizabeth Jones	Jacob (John) Cohen	Aldgate, London	tailoress
12926	Moses	Alice	1834	City, London	Henry Moses	Esther Nathan	David Hyam	Shoreditch, London	
28037	Moses	Amelia	1790	?, London	(?) Moses			Spitalfields, London	fruit seller
25683	Moses	Amelia	1809	?, Canada	(?)		Moss Moses	Spitalfields, London	

ID	surname	given names	born	birthplace	father	mother	spouse 1	1851 residence	1851 occupation
24630	Moses	Amelia	1829	?, London	Phillip Marks		Joseph Moses	Waterloo, London	
7218	Moses	Amelia	1835	Shoreditch, London	Joseph Moses	Caroline Koenigswarter	George Jessel	Marylebone, London	
3570	Moses	Angelina Florence	1849	Hyde Park, London	Isaac Moses [Marsden]	Esther Gomes Silva		Hyde Park, London	
21964	Moses	Ann	1789	Bury St Edmunds, Suffolk	(?)		Emanuel Moses	Whitechapel, London	
22741	Moses	Ann	1793	Whitechapel, London	Jacob Coppel Reichenberg		Lazarus Moses	Whitechapel, London	
20837	Moses	Ann	1813	Covent Garden, London	(?)		Isaac Moses	Bloomsbury, London	
29621	Moses	Ann	1821	Whitechapel, London	David Davis		Maurice Lewis Moses	Aldgate, London	
28724	Moses	Ann	1841	?, London	Elias Moses	Maria Levy		Spitalfields, London	
30255	Moses	Ann	1841	?Finsbury, London	Ellis Moses	Mary b. Judah		?Finsbury, London	
22766	Moses	Ann	1826	Aldgate, London	Abner Jacobs		Joseph Moses	Whitechapel, London	
2543	Moses	Anna	1851	Hull, Yorkshire	Moses Moses	Diana (?)		Hull, Yorkshire	
5087	Moses	Anna (Hannah)	1785	Portsmouth, Hampshire	Jacob Levi	Elizabeth Jones	Aaron Moses	Portsmouth, Hampshire	
843	Moses	Anne (Hannah)	1821	Bristol	Levy Levy	Elizabeth Simon	Jacob Moses	Gloucester, Gloucestershire	
23200	Moses	Annie	1848	City, London	Solomon Moses	Frances Levi		City, London	
18831	Moses	Arthur Abraham	1845	Cheltenham, Gloucestershire	Israel Moses	Maria Abraham	Ada Myer	Worcester, Worcestershire	
16587	Moses	Asher	1828	?, London				Liverpool	assistant to surgeon dentist
3633	Moses	Assur Henry	1830	Whitechapel, London	Henry (Jacob) Moses	Marianna (Marianne Rebecca) Keyser	Henrietta Cohen	Wapping, London	?slopseller + merchant
23428	Moses	Behini	1772	?, London	(?)		(?) Moses	Aldgate, London	egg dealer
14507	Moses	Benjamin	1796	?, London			Rosetta (?)	Fitzrovia, London	silversmith, jeweller + dealer in antique china
16909	Moses	Benjamin	1814	Birmingham			Mary (?)	Sheffield, Yorkshire	Britannia metal smith
21703	Moses	Benjamin	1839	Bethnal Green, London	Michael Moses	Julia (?)		Islington, London	scholar
30256	Moses	Benjamin	1841	Clerkenwell, London	Ellis Moses	Mary b. Judah	Harriet Benjamin Cohen	?Finsbury, London	
16736	Moses	Bessie	1820	Frome, Somerset	Abraham Moses		George (Gershon) Delgado	Bristol	
463	Moses	Betsy	1839	?, London	Elias Moses	Catherine Abrahams		Spitalfields, London	tailoress
307	Moses	Betsy (Elizabeth)	1824	Aldgate, London	Samuel Moses		Barney (Barnett) Barnett	Aldgate, London	
1930	Moses	Braham	1851	Swansea, Wales	Emanuel Frederick Moses	Esther (?)		Swansea, Wales	
7220	Moses	Caroline	1812	Frankfurt, Germany	(?) Koenigswarter		Joseph Moses	Marylebone, London	
30048	Moses	Caroline	1831	Harrow, Middlesex	(?) Moses	Catherine (?)		Aldgate, London	carpet bag maker
10432	Moses	Catharine	1787	Aldgate, London	(?Naftali Mordecai)		Joseph Moses	Spitalfields, London	general dealer
10270	Moses	Catharine	1798	Amsterdam, Holland	(?) Harris		Abraham Moses	Spitalfields, London	
15714	Moses	Catharine	1832	Bethnal Green, London	Moses Moses	Deborah Phillips		Spitalfields, London	general dealer
3677	Moses	Catharine	1843	Spitalfields, London	Lewis Moses	Hannah (?)	Nathan Benjamin	Spitalfields, London	waistcoat maker
5086	Moses	Catherine	1775	Portsmouth, Hampshire	Isaac Elkin	Elizabeth (?)	Joseph Moses	Portsmouth, Hampshire	lady
22912	Moses	Catherine	1792	Aldgate, London	(?)		(?) Moses	Wapping, London	dairy keeper
30042	Moses	Catherine	1795	Whitechapel, London	(?)		(?) Moses	Aldgate, London	
461	Moses	Catherine	1813	Covent Garden, London	Joseph Abrahams	Rachel (?)	Elias Moses	Spitalfields, London	
27104	Moses	Catherine	1813	?, Germany	(?)		Samuel Moses	Aldgate, London	cap maker
23196	Moses	Catherine	1823	Sheerness, Kent	(?) Moses	Sarah (?)		City, London	fruiterer
16410	Moses	Catherine	1829	?, London	(?)		Solomon Moses	Aldgate, London	general dealer
25689	Moses	Catherine	1840	Aldgate, London	Moss Moses	Amelia (?)		Spitalfields, London	
29624	Moses	Catherine	1845	Southwark, London	Maurice Lewis Moses	Ann Davis		Aldgate, London	

ID	surname	given names	born	birthplace	father	mother	spouse 1	1851 residence	1851 occupation
30253	Moses	Catherine (Kate)	1835	Middlesex, London	Ellis Moses	Mary b. Judah		?Finsbury, London	
19955	Moses	Celia (Cecilia)	1845	Finsbury, London	Maurice Moses	Sarah Salomons		Whitechapel, London	
3668	Moses	Charles	1815	Harrow, Middlesex	Lewis Moses	Kate (?)	Elizabeth Alexander	Marylebone, London	dealer in wearing apparel
21978	Moses	Charles	1832	?, Germany	Simon Moses	Sophia (?)		Swansea, Wales	
8379	Moses	Charles M	1813	Sheerness, Kent	David Moses		Deborah Goldsmid	Southampton, Hampshire	fruiterer
12256	Moses	Charlotte	1837	Aldgate, London	Michael Moses	Julia Davis		Finsbury, London	
29924	Moses	Clara	1787	Aldgate, London	Shlomo Dov		Abraham Moses	Whitechapel, London	confectioner
20840	Moses	Clara	1840	St Pancras, London	Isaac Moses	Ann (?)		Bloomsbury, London	scholar
16730	Moses	Coleman	1845	Marylebone, London	Elias Moses	Catherine Abrahams		Spitalfields, London	scholar
3678	Moses	Cosman	1846	Spitalfields, London	Lewis Moses	Hannah (?)		Spitalfields, London	at home
19667	Moses	David	1782	abroad			Hannah (?)	Aldgate, London	clothes dealer
3165	Moses	David	1787	Aldgate, London	Eliezer (?Worms) Moses	?	Abigail Solomons	Stockwell, London	merchant
11198	Moses	David	1839	Aldgate, London				Aldgate, London	
8381	Moses	David	1840	?, London	Charles M Moses	Deborah Goldsmid	Rebecca Solomon	Southampton, Hampshire	
29623	Moses	David	1843	Southwark, London	Maurice Lewis Moses	Ann Davis		Aldgate, London	
462	Moses	David (Daniel)	1847	Marylebone, London	Elias Moses	Catherine Abrahams	Rebecca Valentine	Spitalfields, London	scholar
1921	Moses	David Gwynne	1840	Swansea, Wales	John Moses Moses	Esther Davis		Swansea, Wales	scholar
19957	Moses	David Maurice	1850	?, London	Maurice Moses	Sarah Salomons	Rosetta Lee	Whitechapel, London	
27505	Moses	Deborah	1806	Middlesex, London	Moshe Cohen		Coleman Moses	Aldgate, London	general dealer
8380	Moses	Deborah	1821	Kennington, London	Lamert Goldsmid	Esther Isaacs	Charles M Moses	Southampton, Hampshire	fruiterer
21700	Moses	Deborah	1825	Mile End, London	Michael Moses	Julia (?)		Islington, London	
5029	Moses	Deborah	1846	Paddington, London	Charles Moses	Elizabeth Alexander	Leopold Yates	Marylebone, London	
2542	Moses	Diana	1832	?, Germany			Moses Moses	Hull, Yorkshire	
10148	Moses	Dinah	1846	Southwark, London	Abraham Keiley Moses	Julia Davis		Whitechapel, London	scholar
22456	Moses	Dinah	1846	City, London	Michael Moses	Sarah Phillips		Gravesend, Kent	boarding school pupil
3571	Moses	Edith Josephine	1850	Hyde Park, London	Isaac Moses [Marsden]	Esther Gomes Silva	Henri Ettinghausen	Hyde Park, London	
20349	Moses	Eleazer	1832	?, Holland				Wapping, London	merchant
18330	Moses	Eleazer	1833	Wapping, London	Henry (Jacob) Moses	Marianna (Marianne Rebecca) Keyser		Cheltenham, Gloucestershire	clerk in woollen &c trade
460	Moses	Elias	1811	Spitalfields, London	Nathaniel Moses		Catherine Abrahams	Spitalfields, London	general dealer
28722	Moses	Elias	1816	Middlesex, London	Shmuel		Maria Levy	Spitalfields, London	general dealer
11205	Moses	Eliazer	1841	Aldgate, London	Michael Moses	Rachael (?)		Aldgate, London	
1240	Moses	Eliezer (Eleazar)	1838	Plymouth, Devon		Agnes (?)		Plymouth, Devon	scholar
13366	Moses	Elizabeth	1781	?, Holland	(?)		(?) Moses	Spitalfields, London	
15948	Moses	Elizabeth	1796	?, London	Judah Levy		Joseph Abrahams	Marylebone, London	independent
19188	Moscs	Elizabeth	1808	Covent Garden, London	(?) Moses			Covent Garden, London	glass + china warehouse
1411	Moses	Elizabeth	1818	Plymouth, Devon	(?)		(?) Moses	Plymouth, Devon	
23142	Moses	Elizabeth	1823	Whitechapel, London	Barnet Levy		Moses Moses	City, London	
19563	Moses	Elizabeth	1827	?Spitalfields, London	Ezekiel Moss	Elizabeth Moses	Hyam Moses	Spitalfields, London	
27117	Moses	Elizabeth	1836	Aldgate, London	Moses Moses	Sophia Solomons		Aldgate, London	tailoress
1100	Moses	Elizabeth	1844	Falmouth, Cornwall	Henry Moses	Joannah Richards		Falmouth, Cornwall	scholar
3667	Moses	Elizabeth (Betsy)	1826	Whitechapel, London	Isaac Alexander	Susan Levy	Charles Moses	Marylebone, London	
5830	Moses	Ellis	1802	Liverpool	Naphtali		Mary b. Judah	?Finsbury, London	
21963	Moses	Emanuel	1781	Biggleswade, Bedfordshire	David Moses		Ann (?)	Whitechapel, London	watch manufacturer
22770	Moses	Emanuel	1840	Strand, London	Joseph Moses	(?)		Whitechapel, London	scholar

ID	surname	given names	born	birthplace	father	mother	spouse 1	1851 residence	1851 occupation
1928	Moses	Emanuel Frederick	1825	Swansea, Wales	John Moses Moses	(?)	Esther (?)	Swansea, Wales	travelling jeweller
1926	Moses	Emily Amelia	1846	Swansea, Wales	John Moses Moses	Esther Davis	Louis Hyams	Swansea, Wales	scholar
13114	Moses	Emma	1825	Aldgate, London	Henry Moses	Rosa Hart	Edward Adolphus	Whitechapel, London	
12257	Moses	Emma	1839	Aldgate, London	Michael Moses	Julia Davis		Finsbury, London	
22204	Moses	Ephraim	1832	Whitechapel, London	Simon Moses	Phoebe (?)		Whitechapel, London	cigar maker
28726	Moses	Ester	1849	?, London	Elias Moses	Maria Levy		Spitalfields, London	
5090	Moses	Esther	1793	?, London	Jacob Simmonds	Leah Zachariah	Isaac Moses	Portsmouth, Hampshire	
3589	Moses	Esther	1796	City, London	Hyam (Chaim) Nathan		Henry Moses	Shoreditch, London	
23194	Moses	Esther	1809	Sheerness, Kent	(?) Moses	Sarah (?)		City, London	
1929	Moses	Esther	1827	Westminster, London	(?)		Emanuel Frederick Moses	Swansea, Wales	
10691	Moses	Esther	1827	Spitalfields, London	Abraham Moses	Rebecca Davis	(?) Defries	Spitalfields, London	dealer
1934	Moses	Esther	1828	Swansea, Wales	Moses Moses	(?)	Louis Cohen	Swansea, Wales	
1237	Moses	Esther	1829	Yealmpton, Devon		Agnes (?)		Plymouth, Devon	milliner
3635	Moses	Esther	1832	Wapping, London	Henry (Jacob) Moses	Marianna (Marianne Rebecca) Keyser	Lionel Lewis Cohen	Wapping, London	
22747	Moses	Esther	1835	Whitechapel, London	Lazarus Moses	Ann Jacobs		Whitechapel, London	lamp cotton cutter
13120	Moses	Esther	1839	?Aldgate, London	Henry Moses	Rosa Hart	Barnard (Barney, Barnet) Barnett	Whitechapel, London	
22457	Moses	Esther	1843	City, London	Michael Moses	Sarah Phillips		Gravesend, Kent	boarding school pupil
8384	Moses	Esther	1845	?, London	Charles M Moses	Deborah Goldsmid		Southampton, Hampshire	
20841	Moses	Esther	1846	Bloomsbury, London	Isaac Moses	Ann (?)		Bloomsbury, London	scholar
10500	Moses	Esther	1847	City, London	Moses Moses	Elizabeth Levy	Morris Walter	City, London	
24631	Moses	Esther	1851	Waterloo, London	Joseph Moses	Amelia Marks		Waterloo, London	
3187	Moses	Esther (Eugenie)	1850	Stockwell, London	Samuel Moses [Mostyn]	Elizabeth (Betsy) Davis	Wolf Myers	Stockwell, London	
1924	Moses	Esther Davies	1844	Swansea, Wales	John Moses Moses	Esther Davis		Swansea, Wales	scholar
22502	Moses	Fanny	1811	?, London	(?)		George Moses	Whitechapel, London	
12251	Moses	Fanny	1825	Southwark, London	Michael Moses	Julia Davis	Louis Berge	Finsbury, London	
12393	Moses	Fanny	1827	?, Russia	(?)		Mark (Marcus) Moses	North Shields, Tyne & Wear	
10434	Moses	Fanny	1828	Spitalfields, London	Joseph Moses	Catharine (?Mordecai)		Spitalfields, London	parasol maker
20636	Moses	Fanny	1834	?, Poland	Joseph Moses	Hannah (?)	Abraham Solomon	Spitalfields, London	tailoress
19954	Moses	Fanny (Frances)	1843	Finsbury, London	Maurice Moses	Sarah Salomons	Siegmund Jacoby	Whitechapel, London	
3637	Moses	Floretta	1835	Wapping, London	Henry (Jacob) Moses	Marianna (Marianne Rebeca) Keyser	Elias de Pass	Wapping, London	scholar at home
23199	Moses	Frances	1829	Birmingham	(?) Levi		Solomon Moses	City, London	
21968	Moses	Frances	1830	?, London	Emanuel Moses	Ann (?)		Whitechapel, London	
22746	Moses	Frances	1833	Whitechapel, London	Lazarus Moses	Ann Jacobs		Whitechapel, London	lamp cotton cutter
10694	Moses	Frances	1834	Spitalfields, London	Abraham Moses	Rebecca Davis		Spitalfields, London	
24225	Moses	Frances	1834	Whitechapel, London	(?) Moses			Hackney, London	general servant
23146	Moses	Frances	1836	Whitechapel, London	(?) Moses			City, London	
21702	Moses	Frances	1837	Bethnal Green, London	Michael Moses	Julia (?)		Islington, London	scholar
23145	Moses	Frances	1851	City, London	Moses Moses	Elizabeth Levy		City, London	
28727	Moses	Frances	1851	?Spitalfields, London	Elias Moses	Maria Levy		Spitalfields, London	
16739	Moses	Frederick	1844	Bristol	Joseph Moses	Jane (?)		Bristol	scholar
1917	Moses	Frederick Isaac	1834	Swansea, Wales	John Moses Moses	Esther Davis	Ellen Rachel Simmons	Swansea, Wales	

ID	surname	given names	born	birthplace	father	mother	spouse 1	1851 residence	1851 occupation
22501	Moses	George	1806	Liverpool			Fanny (?)	Whitechapel, London	inspector of meat for Jews
17934	Moses	George	1849	Paddington, London	Charles Moses	Elizabeth Alexander		Marylebone, London	
3572	Moses	Georgiana Hester	1851	Paddington, London	Isaac Moses [Marsden]	Esther Gomes Silva	Charles Lang	Hyde Park, London	
3202	Moses	Gertrude	1843	Hobart, Tasmania, Australia	Samuel Jacob Moses	Rosetta Blanche Moses	Frederick Elias Davis	Shoreditch, London	
9532	Moses	Hanah	1826	Spitalfields, London	(?Eliezer) Moses	Maria (?)		Spitalfields, London	clothes dealer
1295	Moses	Hannah	1780	Exeter, Devon			Philip Moses	Plymouth, Devon	
27121	Moses	Hannah	1780	Aldgate, London	Hyam Emanuel		Samuel Moses	Aldgate, London	
3675	Moses	Hannah	1816	Spitalfields, London			Lewis Moses	Spitalfields, London	tailoress
20635	Moses	Hannah	1821	?, Poland [?, Prussia]	(?)		Joseph Moses	Spitalfields, London	
6805	Moses	Hannah	1825	City, London	(?) Moses			Spitalfields, London	servant
22743	Moses	Hannah	1825	Spitalfields, London	Lazarus Moses	Ann Jacobs		Whitechapel, London	parasol maker
4015	Moses	Hannah	1829	Portsmouth, Hampshire	Isaac Moses	Esther Simmonds	Abraham Joseph Cohen	Portsmouth, Hampshire	housekeeper
20838	Moses	Hannah	1836	St Pancras, London	Isaac Moses	Ann (?)	Lewis Goldschmidt	Bloomsbury, London	scholar
27118	Moses	Hannah	1841	Aldgate, London	Moses Moses	Matilda Myers	Solomon Marks	Aldgate, London	
11206	Moses	Hannah	1843	Aldgate, London	Michael Moses	Rachael (?)		Aldgate, London	
1931	Moses	Harriet	1829	Swansea, Wales	Moses Moses	(?)	Manasseh Cohen	Swansea, Wales	milliner + dressmaker
1238	Moses	Harriet	1834	Plymouth, Devon		Agnes (?)		Plymouth, Devon	dressmaker
1925	Moses	Harriet (Henrietta) Rachel	1844	Swansea, Wales	John Moses Moses	Esther Davis	Isaac Levy	Swansea, Wales	scholar
13742	Moses	Harris	1825	?, Germany				Manchester	tailor
19956	Moses	Henrietta	1849	?, London	Maurice Moses	Sarah Salomons	Adolph Wiener	Whitechapel, London	
25460	Moses	Henry	1765	?, Czech Republic [?, Bohemia]				Aldgate, London	pensioner
3588	Moses	Henry	1791	Wapping, London	Samuel Eliezer Wintzenheimer [Moses]	Rachel Abrahams	Esther Nathan	Shoreditch, London	merchant (colonial)
13111	Moses	Henry	1794	Middlesex, London	Moses Moses		Rosa Hart	Whitechapel, London	slop seller
1097	Moses	Henry	1804	Falmouth, Cornwall	Philip Moses		Joannah Bristo nee Richards	Falmouth, Cornwall	hawker
25686	Moses	Henry	1834	Aldgate, London	Moss Moses	Amelia (?)		Spitalfields, London	asssistant to wholesale clothier
3629	Moses	Henry (Jacob)	1805	Aldgate, London	Abraham Lyon Moses	Abigail Lazarus	Marianna (Marianne Rebecca) Keyser	Wapping, London	merchant
16741	Moses	Hester	1848	Bristol	Joseph Moses	Jane (?)		Bristol	
20782	Moses	Hyam	1805	Middlesex, London	Nathaniel Moses		Rose (Rosetta) Lazarus	Spitalfields, London	clothier
10271	Moses	Hyam	1828	Spitalfields, London	Abraham Moses	Catharine Harris	Elizabeth Moss	Spitalfields, London	cigar maker
1942	Moses	Hyman	1849	Swansea, Wales	Simon Moses	Sophia (?)	Rose Joseph	Swansea, Wales	
5089	Moses	Isaac	1788	Portsmouth, Hampshire	Henry Moses	Jane (?)	Esther Simmonds	Portsmouth, Hampshire	general dealer
25348	Moses	Isaac	1790	Shoreditch, London				Finsbury, London	furniture dealer
20836	Moses	Isaac	1801	Covent Garden, London			Ann (?)	Bloomsbury, London	dealer in plate, watches, jewellery + plated goods + miscellaneous property
23721	Moses	Isaac	1806	?, Germany				Liverpool	pedlar
13359	Moses	Isaac	1811	Whitechapel, London	(?) Moses	Elizabeth (?)	Rosa (?)	Spitalfields, London	clothes dealer
22016	Moses	Isaac	1813	Boston, Lincolnshire	Emanuel Moses	Ann (?)		Whitechapel, London	jeweller

ID	surname	given names	born	birthplace	father	mother	spouse 1	1851 residence	1851 occupation
25861	Moses	Isaac	1821	?, Poland [?, Prussia]				Aldgate, London	bead maker journeyman
457	Moses	Isaac	1822	Aldgate, London	David Moses	Hannah (?)	Eve Zingerman	Aldgate, London	general dealer
10693	Moses	Isaac	1831	Spitalfields, London	Abraham Moses	Rebecca Davis		Spitalfields, London	hawker
22767	Moses	Isaac	1833	St Giles, London	Joseph Moses	(?)		Whitechapel, London	cigar maker
1241	Moses	Isaac	1841	Plymouth, Devon		Agnes (?)		Plymouth, Devon	scholar
16731	Moses	Isaac	1849	?, London	Elias Moses	Catherine Abrahams		Spitalfields, London	
8383	Moses	Isaac A	1844	?, London	Charles M Moses	Deborah Goldsmid		Southampton, Hampshire	
25811	Moses	Isaac Israel	1811	Amsterdam, Holland				Aldgate, London	painter journeyman
14332	Moses	Isaiah	1831	?, Poland				Manchester	glazier
836	Moses	Israel	1807	Gloucester, Gloucestershire	Moses Moses	Jane (?)	Maria Abraham	Worcester, Worcestershire	general outfitter
13675	Moses	Israel	1827	?, Germany			Sarah (?)	Manchester	hawker (rhubarb)
135	Moses	Israel	1834	Middlesex, London				Woolwich, London	
24895	Moses	Israel	1834	Middlesex, London				Plumstead, London	
30835	Moses	Israel	1850	Gloucester, Gloucestershire	Jacob Moses	Anne (Hannah) Levy		Gloucester, Gloucestershire	
842	Moses	Jacob	1812	Gloucester, Gloucestershire	Moses Moses	Jane (?)	Anne (Hannah) Levy	Gloucester, Gloucestershire	silversmith + pawnbroker
5088	Moses	Jacob	1816	New York, USA	Aaron Moses	Anna Levi		Portsmouth, Hampshire	
14272	Moses	Jacob	1830	?, Germany				Manchester	cloth cap maker
27107	Moses	Jacob	1850	?Aldgate, London	Samuel Moses	Catherine (?)		Aldgate, London	
8386	Moses	Jacob (John G)	1850	?, London	Charles M Moses	Deborah Goldsmid	Sophie Bennett	Southampton, Hampshire	
853	Moses	Jacob Richard	1843	Cheltenham, Gloucestershire	Israel Moses	Maria Abraham	Rosa Sternberg	Worcester, Worcestershire	scholar
25082	Moses	Jane	1806	Wapping, London	Joshua Jonas	Sophia Solomons	Samuel Moses	City, London	
16738	Moses	Jane	1817	Middlesex, London	(?)		Joseph Moses	Bristol	
10274	Moses	Jane	1834	Spitalfields, London	Abraham Moses	Catharine Harris		Spitalfields, London	milliner
15715	Moses	Jane	1835	Bethnal Green, London	Moses Moses	Deborah Phillips	Solomon Green	Spitalfields, London	tailoress
27506	Moses	Jane	1841	Middlesex, London	Coleman Moses	Deborah Cohen		Aldgate, London	scholar
30831	Moses	Jane	1843	Gloucester, Gloucestershire	Jacob Moses	Anne (Hannah) Levy		Gloucester, Gloucestershire	
839	Moses	Jane (Jennie)	1848	Cheltenham, Gloucestershire	Israel Moses	Maria Abraham		Worcester, Worcestershire	
8412	Moses	Jane (Jenny)	1849	Ryde, Isle of Wight	Samuel Moses	Kate Aaron		Ryde, Isle of Wight	
1920	Moses	Jane Davies	1839	Swansea, Wales	John Moses Moses	Esther Davis	Morris De Saxe	Swansea, Wales	scholar
20282	Moses	Jette Todorno	1806	?, Russia	(?) Todorno		Solomon Moses	Spitalfields, London	cap maker
1098	Moses	Joannah	1812	Hayle, Cornwall	John Richards		(?) Bristo	Falmouth, Cornwall	
22745	Moses	Joel	1831	Spitalfields, London	Lazarus Moses	Ann Jacobs	Matilda Lawton	Whitechapel, London	general dealer
4012	Moses	John	1814	Portsmouth, Hampshire	Isaac Moses	Esther Simmonds		Portsmouth, Hampshire	navy agent + dealer
22742	Moses	John	1821	Spitalfields, London	Lazarus Moses	Ann Jacobs		Whitechapel, London	labourer at cowkeeper
30047	Moses	John	1826	Harrow, Middlesex	(?) Moses	Catherine (?)		Aldgate, London	general dealer
1101	Moses	John	1846	Falmouth, Cornwall	Henry Moses	Joannah Richards		Falmouth, Cornwall	scholar
8413	Moses	John Jacob	1850	Ryde, Isle of Wight	Samuel Moses	Kate Aaron		Ryde, Isle of Wight	
1915	Moses	John Moses	1802	Bedford, Bedfordshire			Esther Davis	Swansea, Wales	pawnbroker
5085	Moses	Joseph	1762	Portsmouth, Hampshire	Isaac Moses	Hannah (?)	Judith (?)	Portsmouth, Hampshire	gentleman
10431	Moses	Joseph	1784	Whitechapel, London	(?Pinchas) Moses		Catharine (?Mordecai)	Spitalfields, London	general dealer
22765	Moses	Joseph	1809	Aldgate, London	Emanuel Moses		(?)	Whitechapel, London	general dealer
20634	Moses	Joseph	1811	?, Poland			Hannah (?)	Spitalfields, London	tailor

ID	surname	given names	born	birthplace	father	mother	spouse 1	1851 residence	1851 occupation
16737	Moses	Joseph	1815	Frome, Somerset	Abraham Moses		Jane (?)	Bristol	wine + spirit merchant
24047	Moses	Joseph	1819	Whitechapel, London	Lewis Moses		Rebecca Alice Van Goor	Marylebone, London	tailor empl 3
24629	Moses	Joseph	1829	?, London	Michael Moses		Amelia Marks	Waterloo, London	china dealer
27413	Moses	Joseph	1831	?, Poland [?, Prussia]				Whitechapel, London	tailor
26798	Moses	Joseph	1832	Aldgate, London				Aldgate, London	
12255	Moses	Joseph	1836	Aldgate, London	Michael Moses	Julia Davis		Finsbury, London	
16729	Moses	Joseph	1837	?, London	Elias Moses	Catherine Abrahams		Spitalfields, London	cigar maker
22769	Moses	Joseph	1838	Surrey, London	Joseph Moses	(?)		Whitechapel, London	scholar
13365	Moses	Joseph	1846	Aldgate, London	Isaac Moses	Rosa (?)		Spitalfields, London	
1103	Moses	Joseph	1850	Falmouth, Cornwall	Henry Moses	Joannah Richards		Falmouth, Cornwall	
10149	Moses	Joseph	1850	Whitechapel, London	Abraham Keiley Moses	Julia Davis		Whitechapel, London	
7219	Moses	Joseph Benjamin	1810	Whitechapel, London	Abraham Lyon Moses	Abigail Lazarus	Caroline Koenigswarter	Marylebone, London	bristle, ivory, tortoiseshell + mother of pearl shell merchant
25083	Moses	Joshua	1840	Wapping, London	Samuel Moses	Jane Jonas		City, London	
1239	Moses	Judah	1836	Plymouth, Devon		Agnes (?)		Plymouth, Devon	errand boy
25688	Moses	Judah	1838	Aldgate, London	Moss Moses	Amelia (?)		Spitalfields, London	asssistant to wholesale clothier
24780	Moses	Julia	1781	Aldgate, London	Shlomeh Cohen		Moss Moses	Elephant & Castle, London	
12250	Moses	Julia	1798	City, London	Moshe Davis		Michael Moses	Finsbury, London	
21699	Moses	Julia	1805	Holborn, London	(?)		Michael Moses	Islington, London	
22744	Moses	Julia	1829	Spitalfields, London	Lazarus Moses	Ann Jacobs		Whitechapel, London	parasol maker
10146	Moses	Julia	1830	Spitalfields, London	Joseph Davis	Dinah Jacobs	Abraham Keiley Moses	Whitechapel, London	dressmaker
30833	Moses	Julia	1847	Gloucester, Gloucestershire	Jacob Moses	Anne (Hannah) Levy		Gloucester, Gloucestershire	
1923	Moses	Julia Sarah	1843	Swansea, Wales	John Moses Moses	Esther Davis		Swansea, Wales	scholar
8411	Moses	Kate	1828	Brighton, Sussex	Solomon (?Saul Charles) Aaron		Samuel Moses	Ryde, Isle of Wight	
30832	Moses	Kate	1845	Gloucester, Gloucestershire	Jacob Moses	Anne (Hannah) Levy		Gloucester, Gloucestershire	
28259	Moses	Katherine	1822	Whitechapel, London	(?) Moses	Elizabeth (?)		Spitalfields, London	clothes hawker
838	Moses	Katherine	1841	Cheltenham, Gloucestershire	Israel Moses	Maria Abraham		Worcester, Worcestershire	scholar
13364	Moses	Katherine	1843	Aldgate, London	Isaac Moses	Rosa (?)		Spitalfields, London	
20637	Moses	Kitty	1840	?, Poland	Joseph Moses	Hannah (?)		Spitalfields, London	tailoress
1939	Moses	Lazarus	1841	Swansea, Wales	Simon Moses	Sophia (?)		Swansea, Wales	scholar
18200	Moses	Leah	1773	Middlesex, London	(?) Moses			Mile End, London	
6301	Moses	Lewis	1808	Covent Garden, London			Rosa (?)	Covent Garden, London	tailor
3674	Moses	Lewis	1815	Spitalfields, London	Nathan Moses	Rebecca (?)	Hannah (?)	Spitalfields, London	general dealer
29622	Moses	Lewis	1841	Spitalfields, London	Maurice Lewis Moses	Ann Davis		Aldgate, London	
24049	Moses	Lewis	1844	Marylebone, London	Joseph Moses	Rebecca Alice Van Goor		Marylebone, London	scholar
10690	Moses	Lipman (Lehman)	1825	Spitalfields, London	Abraham Moses	Rebecca Davis		Spitalfields, London	hawker
4014	Moses	Louis	1837	Portsmouth, Hampshire	Isaac Moses	Esther Simmonds		Portsmouth, Hampshire	shop boy
17933	Moses	Louis	1845	Paddington, London	Charles Moses	Elizabeth Alexander		Marylebone, London	
30834	Moses	Louis	1848	Gloucester, Gloucestershire	Jacob Moses	Anne (Hannah) Levy		Gloucester, Gloucestershire	

ID	surname	given names	born	birthplace	father	mother	spouse 1	1851 residence	1851 occupation
4777	Moses	Louisa	1821	Birmingham				Birmingham	
1918	Moses	Louisa Victoria	1835	Swansea, Wales	John Moses Moses	Esther Davis	Henry Barnett	Swansea, Wales	
22203	Moses	Lydia	1761	Aldgate, London	(?)		(?) Moses	Whitechapel, London	
20640	Moses	Marcus	1850	Whitechapel, London	Joseph Moses	Hannah (?)		Spitalfields, London	
9531	Moses	Maria	1781	?, Holland	(?)		(?Eliezer) Moses	Spitalfields, London	
837	Moses	Maria	1807	Bath	Jacob Abrahams		Israel Moses	Worcester, Worcestershire	
28723	Moses	Maria	1818	?, London	(?) Levy		Elias Moses	Spitalfields, London	
21966	Moses	Maria	1825	Ipswich, Suffolk	Emanuel Moses	Ann (?)		Whitechapel, London	
21234	Moses	Maria	1829	Whitechapel, London	(?) Moses			Spitalfields, London	
1936	Moses	Maria	1837	Swansea, Wales	Moses Moses	(?)	Isaac Seline	Swansea, Wales	
13363	Moses	Maria	1841	Aldgate, London	Isaac Moses	Rosa (?)		Spitalfields, London	
19953	Moses	Marian	1842	Finsbury, London	Maurice Moses	Sarah Salomons		Whitechapel, London	
3630	Moses	Marianna (Marianne Rebecca)	1805	?, London	Assur (Asher Anshel) Keyser		Henry (Jacob) Moses	Wapping, London	
21296	Moses	Mark	1839	Marylebone, London				Edmonton, London	boarding school pupil
12392	Moses	Mark (Marcus)	1823	?, Russia			Fanny (?)	North Shields, Tyne & Wear	glazier
26502	Moses	Martha	1798	Dover, Kent	(?) Moses			Dover, Kent	
19189	Moses	Martha	1806	Covent Garden, London	(?) Moses			Covent Garden, London	glass + china warehouse
16912	Moses	Martha	1850	Sheffield, Yorkshire	Benjamin Moses	Mary (?)		Sheffield, Yorkshire	
5831	Moses	Mary	1804	New---, Essex	Judah		Ellis Moses	?Finsbury, London	
16910	Moses	Mary	1810	Sheffield, Yorkshire	(?)		Benjamin Moses	Sheffield, Yorkshire	
5091	Moses	Mary	1827	Portsmouth, Hampshire	Isaac Moses	Esther Simmonds		Portsmouth, Hampshire	
27105	Moses	Mary	1845	?, Germany	Samuel Moses	Catherine (?)		Aldgate, London	scholar
1413	Moses	Mary	1847	Plymouth, Devon	(?) Moses	Elizabeth (?)		Plymouth, Devon	
16911	Moses	Mary H	1845	Sheffield, Yorkshire	Benjamin Moses	Mary (?)		Sheffield, Yorkshire	
27116	Moses	Matilda	1821	?, London	Woolf Myers		Moses Moses	Aldgate, London	
13115	Moses	Matilda	1827	Aldgate, London	Henry Moses	Rosa Hart	Saul Scott	Whitechapel, London	
1940	Moses	Matilda	1843	Swansea, Wales	Simon Moses	Sophia (?)		Swansea, Wales	
16740	Moses	Matilda	1846	Bristol	Joseph Moses	Jane (?)		Bristol	scholar
19951	Moses	Maurice	1811	?, Lincolnshire	Emanuel Moses		Sarah Salomons	Whitechapel, London	glass dealer
29620	Moses	Maurice Lewis	1818	Watford, Hertfordshire	Lewis Moses		Ann Davis	Aldgate, London	dealer general
21698	Moses	Michael	1796	Wapping, London			Julia (?)	Islington, London	furrier
12249	Moses	Michael	1799	Poznan, Poland [Posen, Prussia]	Aharon Moses		Julia Davis	Finsbury, London	gentleman funded property
23195	Moses	Michael	1811	Sheerness, Kent	(?) Moses	Sarah (?)		City, London	
28526	Moses	Michael	1811	Whitechapel, London				Spitalfields, London	glass cutter
11203	Moses	Michael	1817	Aldgate, London	Elias Moses	Elizabeth (?)	Rachael (?)	Aldgate, London	general dealer
26634	Moses	Michael	1823	Aldgate, London	Moses Moses	Elizabeth Jones	Sarah Isaacs	Aldgate, London	fruit dealer
12253	Moses	Michael	1827	Southwark, London	Michael Moses	Julia Davis		Finsbury, London	jeweller
14906	Moses	Michael	1839	Aldgate, London				Bethnal Green, London	boarding school pupil
8385	Moses	Michael A	1848	Lambeth, London	Charles M Moses	Deborah Goldsmid	Helena Rose Mosely	Southampton, Hampshire	
25214	Moses	Michael L	1824	?, Wales				Clerkenwell, London	importer of foreign goods
22205	Moses	Michall	1836	Whitechapel, London	Simon Moses	Phoebe (?)		Whitechapel, London	cigar maker

ID	surname	given names	born	birthplace	father	mother	spouse 1	1851 residence	1851 occupation
29782	Moses	Minna Alexander	1814	?, Poland	(?) (?Alexander)		(?) Moses	Whitechapel, London	wife of tin plate worker
13119	Moses	Montague Henry	1835	?Aldgate, London	Henry Moses	Rosa Hart	Caroline Woolf	Whitechapel, London	
10272	Moses	Morris	1832	Spitalfields, London	Abraham Moses	Catharine Harris		Spitalfields, London	cigar maker
13362	Moses	Morris	1839	Aldgate, London	Isaac Moses	Rosa (?)	Frances Isaacs	Spitalfields, London	cigar maker
25690	Moses	Morris	1844	Aldgate, London	Moss Moses	Amelia (?)		Spitalfields, London	
834	Moses	Moses	1768	?, London			Jane (?)	Cheltenham, Gloucestershire	retired pawnbroker
30982	Moses	Moses	1788	Dover, Kent				Dover, Kent	general dealer
26632	Moses	Moses	1795	Aldgate, London	Ralph (Raphael) Moses		Elizabeth Jones	Aldgate, London	clothes dealer
1932	Moses	Moses	1798	Leszno, Poland [Lissa, Prussia], Poland [Lissa, Prussia]	Moses Moses		(?)	Swansea, Wales	outfitter
27115	Moses	Moses	1811	?, London	Samuel Moses	Hannah Emanuel	Sophia Solomons	Aldgate, London	general dealer
23141	Moses	Moses	1814	Whitechapel, London	Aaron Moses		Elizabeth Levy	City, London	fur manufacturer
29925	Moses	Moses	1821	Whitechapel, London	Abraham Moses	Clara Moses		Whitechapel, London	general dealer
2541	Moses	Moses	1826	?, Germany			Diana (?)	Hull, Yorkshire	tailor
14237	Moses	Moses	1827	Middlesex, London				Manchester	cigar merchant
6199	Moses	Moses	1828	Aldgate, London	Joseph Moses	Elizabeth	Rosetta Harris	Spitalfields, London	cigar maker
10435	Moses	Moses	1831	Spitalfields, London	Joseph Moses	Catharine (?Mordecai)		Spitalfields, London	general dealer
22768	Moses	Moses	1836	Strand, London	Joseph Moses	(?)		Whitechapel, London	
28258	Moses	Moses	1847	Aldgate, London	Isaac Moses	Rosa (?)		Spitalfields, London	
16411	Moses	Moses	1848	?, London	Solomon Moses	Catherine (?)		Aldgate, London	
12394	Moses	Moses	1850	North Shields, Tyne & Wear	Mark (Marcus) Moses	Fanny (?)		North Shields, Tyne & Wear	
20205	Moses	Moses	1851	Spitalfields, London	Lewis Moses	Hannah (?)		Spitalfields, London	
26501	Moses	Moses Henry	1785	Dover, Kent				Dover, Kent	general dealer
3639	Moses	Moses Henry	1838	Wapping, London	Henry (Jacob) Moses	Marianna (Marianne Rebecca) Keyser	Rosetta Levy	Wapping, London	scholar at home
1927	Moses	Moses John	1848	Swansea, Wales	John Moses Moses	Esther Davis	Jessie Abrahams	Swansea, Wales	
20639	Moses	Moses Joseph	1844	?, Poland	Joseph Moses	Hannah (?)		Spitalfields, London	
24779	Moses	Moss	1779	Aldgate, London	Michael Moses		Julia Jacobs	Elephant & Castle, London	annuitant
25682	Moses	Moss	1801	Whitechapel, London			Amelia (?)	Spitalfields, London	wholesale clothier
20112	Moses	Moss	1806	?, Poland				Spitalfields, London	jeweller
24159	Moses	Moss	1825	?, Poland [?, Prussia]				Euston, London	journeyman(tailor?)
14905	Moses	Moss	1835	Spitalfields, London				Bethnal Green, London	boarding school pupil
20952	Moses	Moss	1836	Spitalfields, London				Aldgate, London	cigar maker assistant
11207	Moses	Moss	1850	Aldgate, London	Michael Moses	Rachael (?)		Aldgate, London	
27120	Moses	Myer	1846	Aldgate, London	Moses Moses	Matilda Myers		Aldgate, London	
27106	Moses	Nancy	1848	Spitalfields, London	Samuel Moses	Catherine (?)		Aldgate, London	scholar
12539	Moses	Nathan	1772	?, Germany				Norwich, Norfolk	fund holder
3672	Moses	Nathan	1792	Spitalfields, London			Rebecca (?)	Spitalfields, London	formerly fruit salesman
20951	Moses	Nathan	1831	Whitechapel, London				Aldgate, London	cigar maker
22711	Moses	Nathan	1831	Spitalfields, London				Whitechapel, London	costermonger fruit
16727	Moses	Nathan	1834	?, London	Elias Moses	Catherine Abrahams		Spitalfields, London	

ID	surname	given names	born	birthplace	father	mother	spouse 1	1851 residence	1851 occupation
3676	Moses	Nathan	1841	Spitalfields, London	Lewis Moses	Hannah (?)		Spitalfields, London	scholar
19186	Moses	Nathan	1850	Covent Garden, London	Lewis Moses	Rosa(?)		Covent Garden, London	
22458	Moses	Philip	1844	City, London	Michael Moses	Sarah Phillips		Gravesend, Kent	boarding school pupil
30050	Moses	Phillip	1823	Whitechapel, London	(?) Moses	Catherine (?)		Aldgate, London	general dealer
1099	Moses	Phillip Henry	1842	Falmouth, Cornwall	Henry Moses	Joannah Richards	Jane (?)	Falmouth, Cornwall	scholar
22202	Moses	Phoebe	1796	Whitechapel, London	(?)		Simon Moses	Whitechapel, London	
20784	Moses	Phoebe	1833	?, London	Hyam Moses	Rose (Rosetta) Lazarus		Spitalfields, London	
4510	Moses	Polly	1773	Bristol			(?) Moses	Birmingham	
3631	Moses	Priscilla	1829	Whitechapel, London	Henry (Jacob) Moses	Marianna (Marianne Rebecca) Keyset	Henry Behrend	Wapping, London	
13116	Moses	Priscilla	1829	Aldgate, London	Henry Moses	Rosa Hart	Abraham Hyams	Whitechapel, London	
11204	Moses	Rachael	1819	Aldgate, London	(?)		Michael Moses	Aldgate, London	slipper maker
1933	Moses	Rachel	1808	?, London	Solomon Isaacs		Moses Moses	Swansea, Wales	waistcoat maker
21967	Moses	Rachel	1827	Ipswich, Suffolk	Emanuel Moses	Ann (?)		Whitechapel, London	
12925	Moses	Rachel	1832	City, London	Henry Moses	Esther Nathan		Shoreditch, London	
1935	Moses	Rachel	1833	Swansea, Wales	Moses Moses	(?)	Samuel Fonseca	Swansea, Wales	
29785	Moses	Rachel	1833	?, Poland	(?) Moses			Whitechapel, London	cloth cap maker
464	Moses	Rachel	1843	Marylebone, London	Elias Moses	Catherine Abrahams	Benjamin Jacobs	Spitalfields, London	scholar
1941	Moses	Rachel	1845	Swansea, Wales	Simon Moses	Sophia (?)		Swansea, Wales	
3174	Moses	Rachel Frances	1840	Wapping, London	Samuel Moses [Mostyn]	Elizabeth (Betsy) Davis	Max Zossenheim	Stockwell, London	
19187	Moses	Ralph	1811	Covent Garden, London				Covent Garden, London	shopman
10273	Moses	Ralph	1835	Spitalfields, London	Abraham Moses	Catharine Harris	Maria Levett	Spitalfields, London	cigar maker
23197	Moses	Rebbeca	1826	Sheerness, Kent	(?) Moses	Sarah (?)		City, London	
3673	Moses	Rebecca	1793	Spitalfields, London			Nathan Moses	Spitalfields, London	domestic duties
26633	Moses	Rebecca	1801	Aldgate, London	Simon Solomons		Moses Moses	Aldgate, London	
29927	Moses	Rebecca	1825	Whitechapel, London	Abraham Moses	Clara Moses		Whitechapel, London	brush drawer
20638	Moses	Rebecca	1842	?, Poland	Joseph Moses	Hannah (?)		Spitalfields, London	
10689	Moses	Rebecca	1791	Spitalfields, London	Joseph Davis		Abraham Moses	Spitalfields, London	
3576	Moses	Rebecca (Kate)	1831	Middlesex, London	Isaac Moses [Marsden]	Rachel Hyam	John Asher Gomes da Silva [Templeton]	Paddington, London	
24048	Moses	Rebecca Alice	1823	Marylebone, London	Ezekiel Van Goor		Joseph Moses	Marylebone, London	
13118	Moses	Rhoda	1833	?Aldgate, London	Henry Moses	Rosa Hart	Emanuel Eberson	Whitechapel, London	
13112	Moses	Rosa	1795	Wapping, London	Benjamin Hart		Henry Moses	Whitechapel, London	slopseller
13360	Moses	Rosa	1812	Whitechapel, London	(?)		Isaac Moses	Spitalfields, London	clothes dealer
6302	Moses	Rosa	1826	Leigh, Essex	(?)		Lewis Moses	Covent Garden, London	
12254	Moses	Rosa	1829	Southwark, London	Michael Moses	Julia Davis		Finsbury, London	
20839	Moses	Rosa	1838	St Pancras, London	Isaac Moses	Ann (?)		Bloomsbury, London	scholar
5092	Moses	Rose	1834	Portsmouth, Hampshire	Isaac Moses	Esther Simmonds		Portsmouth, Hampshire	
20783	Moses	Rose (Rosetta)	1810	Middlesex, London	Nathan Lazarus		Hyam Moses	Spitalfields, London	
3172	Moses	Rose (Rosetta)	1839	Wapping, London	Samuel Moses [Mostyn]	Elizabeth (Betsy) Davis	Phineas (Ben) Cowan	Stockwell, London	
14508	Moses	Rosetta	1799	?, London	(?)		Benjamin Moses	Fitzrovia, London	
21701	Moses	Rosetta	1825	Holborn, London	Michael Moses	Julia (?)		Islington, London	
6200	Moses	Rosetta	1831	Aldgate, London	Abraham Harris		Moses Moses	Spitalfields, London	cigar maker
1922	Moses	Rosetta Frances	1842	Swansea, Wales	John Moses Moses	Esther Davis	Philip Hart	Swansea, Wales	scholar
306	Moses	Samuel	1787	Aldgate, London			(?)	Aldgate, London	shoe maker

ID	surname	given names	born	birthplace	father	mother	spouse 1	1851 residence	1851 occupation
25081	Moses	Samuel	1805	Wapping, London	Moses Moses		Jane Jonas	City, London	clothier
27103	Moses	Samuel	1813	?, Germany	Moshe		Catherine (?)	Aldgate, London	cap maker
8410	Moses	Samuel	1818	Poole, Dorset	Isaac Moses	Esther Simmonds	Kate Aarons	Ryde, Isle of Wight	clothier + outfitter
11694	Moses	Samuel	1831	Poznan, Poland [Posen, Prussia]				Aldgate, London	servant
25685	Moses	Samuel	1832	Aldgate, London	Moss Moses	Amelia (?)		Spitalfields, London	asssistant to wholesale clothier
22748	Moses	Samuel	1837	Whitechapel, London	Lazarus Moses	Ann Jacobs		Whitechapel, London	slipper maker
1412	Moses	Samuel	1841	Exeter, Devon	(?) Moses	Elizabeth (?)		Plymouth, Devon	scholar
8382	Moses	Samuel	1842	?, London	Charles M Moses	Deborah Goldsmid		Southampton, Hampshire	
27119	Moses	Samuel	1844	Aldgate, London	Moses Moses	Matilda Myers		Aldgate, London	
24050	Moses	Samuel	1845	Marylebone, London	Joseph Moses	Rebecca Alice Van Goor		Marylebone, London	scholar
12924	Moses	Samuel Henry	1829	City, London	Henry Moses	Esther Nathan	Zillah Simon	Shoreditch, London	merchant (colonial)
3176	Moses	Sara Kate	1841	Aldgate, London	Samuel Moses [Mostyn]	Elizabeth (Betsy) Davis	John Isaac Solomon	Stockwell, London	
23193	Moses	Sarah	1785	Middlesex, London	(?)		(?) Moses	City, London	
16735	Moses	Sarah	1803	Frome, Somerset	Abraham Moses			Bristol	
19952	Moses	Sarah	1814	?, London	L--- Salomons		Maurice Moses	Whitechapel, London	
3167	Moses	Sarah	1818	Boston, Lincolnshire	Emanuel Moses	Ann (?)	John Moses Moses	Whitechapel, London	
13113	Moses	Sarah	1823	Aldgate, London	Henry Moses	Rosa Hart		Whitechapel, London	
29926	Moses	Sarah	1823	Whitechapel, London	Abraham Moses	Clara Moses		Whitechapel, London	brush drawer
23354	Moses	Sarah	1824	Aldgate, London	(?) Moses			Strand, London	servant
13676	Moses	Sarah	1827	?, Germany	(?)		Israel Moses	Manchester	hawker (rhubarb)
10692	Moses	Sarah	1829	Spitalfields, London	Abraham Moses	Rebecca Davis	Angel Isaacs	Spitalfields, London	domestic assistant
16728	Moses	Sarah	1835	?, London	Elias Moses	Catherine Abrahams	Isaac Fromberg	Spitalfields, London	
28725	Moses	Sarah	1847	?, London	Elias Moses	Maria Levy		Spitalfields, London	
22772	Moses	Sarah	1849	Whitechapel, London	Joseph Moses	Ann Jacobs		Whitechapel, London	
25062	Moses	Sarah	1849	Aldgate, London	Moses Moses	Rosetta Harris		Spitalfields, London	
23201	Moses	Sarah	1850	City, London	Solomon Moses	Frances Levi		City, London	
7943	Moses	Sarah Ann	1841	Gloucester, Gloucestershire	Jacob Moses	Anne (Hannah) Levy	Marcus (Marquis) Leon Mier	Gloucester, Gloucestershire	
22116	Moses	Simeon	1829	?, Poland [?, Prussia]				Whitechapel, London	tailor
22201	Moses	Simon	1791	Spitalfields, London	(?) Moses	Lydia (?)	Phoebe (?)	Whitechapel, London	milkman
1937	Moses	Simon	1801	Warsaw, Poland			Sophia (?)	Swansea, Wales	traveller
12383	Moses	Simon	1832	?, Poland				North Shields, Tyne & Wear	glazier
1943	Moses	Simon	1850	Swansea, Wales	Simon Moses	Sophia (?)		Swansea, Wales	
20281	Moses	Solomon	1806	?, Russia			Jette Todorno	Spitalfields, London	cap maker
1944	Moses	Solomon	1818	Moldavia, Rumania				Swansea, Wales	glazier
16409	Moses	Solomon	1819	?, London			Catherine (?)	Aldgate, London	general dealer
10433	Moses	Solomon	1821	Spitalfields, London	Joseph Moses	Catharine (?Mordecai)	Catherine Lyons	Spitalfields, London	general dealer
23198	Moses	Solomon	1825	Sheerness, Kent	(?) Moses	Sarah (?)	Frances Levi	City, London	fruiterer
25684	Moses	Solomon	1830	Aldgate, London	Moss Moses	Amelia (?)		Spitalfields, London	asssistant to wholesale clothier
13361	Moses	Solomon	1837	Aldgate, London	Isaac Moses	Rosa (?)		Spitalfields, London	cigar maker
27507	Moses	Solomon	1843	Middlesex, London	Coleman Moses	Deborah Cohen		Aldgate, London	scholar

ID	surname	given names	born	birthplace	father	mother	spouse 1	1851 residence	1851 occupation
24051	Moses	Solomon	1850	Marylebone, London	Joseph Moses	Rebecca Alice Van Goor		Marylebone, London	
22773	Moses	Solomon	1851	Whitechapel, London	Joseph Moses	Ann Jacobs		Whitechapel, London	
30592	Moses	Solomon	1851	Spitalfields, London	Elias Moses	Catherine Abrahams		Spitalfields, London	
1938	Moses	Sophia	1812	Hanover, Germany			Simon Moses	Swansea, Wales	
12252	Moses	Sophia	1826	Southwark, London	Michael Moses	Julia Davis		Finsbury, London	
30049	Moses	Sophia	1835	Paddington, London	(?) Moses	Catherine (?)		Aldgate, London	general dealer
840	Moses	Sophia	1839	Cheltenham, Gloucestershire	Israel Moses	Maria Abraham	Sidney Myer	Worcester, Worcestershire	scholar
5829	Moses	Sophia	1839	Clerkenwell, London	Ellis Moses	Mary b. Judah	Michael Raphael	?Finsbury, London	
25084	Moses	Sophia	1844	Wapping, London	Samuel Moses	Jane Jonas		City, London	
29625	Moses	Sophia	1850	Finsbury, London	Maurice Lewis Moses	Ann Davis		Aldgate, London	
26526	Moses	Sophia	1851	Marylebone, London	Charles Moses	Elizabeth Alexander		Marylebone, London	
30254	Moses	Susan	1837	Middlesex, London	Ellis Moses	Mary b. Judah		?Finsbury, London	
22503	Moses	Susannah	1832	Westminster, London	George Moses	Fanny (?)		Whitechapel, London	dressmaker
13117	Moses	Sylvester	1832	Aldgate, London	Henry Moses	Rosa Hart	Rachel Isaacs	Whitechapel, London	clothier + dealer in silk handkerchiefs
13835	Moses	Theresa	1822	?, Poland [?, Prussia]				Manchester	dressmaker
12395	Moses	Theresa	1851	North Shields, Tyne & Wear	Mark (Marcus) Moses	Fanny (?)		North Shields, Tyne & Wear	
1102	Moses	Thomas	1848	Falmouth, Cornwall	Henry Moses	Joannah Richards		Falmouth, Cornwall	scholar
1242	Moses	Wolf	1845	Plymouth, Devon		Agnes (?)		Plymouth, Devon	scholar
25924	Moses	Woolf	1753	?, Germany			(?)	Aldgate, London	
10963	Moses (Moss)	Aaron	1836	Whitechapel, London	Elias Moses (Moss)	Elizabeth Levy		Aldgate, London	general dealer
6746	Moses (Moss)	Amelia	1837	Ipswich, Suffolk	Moses Moses (Moss)	Catherine Alexander	Herman Levy	Whitechapel, London	dressmaker
6332	Moses (Moss)	Amelia	1842	Aldgate, London	Elias Moses (Moss)	Elizabeth Levy	Isaac Defries	Aldgate, London	
10966	Moses (Moss)	Barnett	1840	Aldgate, London	Elias Moses (Moss)	Elizabeth Levy	Rose Myers	Aldgate, London	
6744	Moses (Moss)	Catherine	1792	Colchester, Essex	(?) Alexander		Moses Moses (Moss)	Whitechapel, London	dress maker
6747	Moses (Moss)	Clara	1825	Colchester, Essex	Moses Moses (Moss)	Catherine Alexander	(?) Levy	Whitechapel, London	dressmaker
10958	Moses (Moss)	Elias	1803	Spitalfields, London	Tsevi Hirsh HaLevi		Elizabeth Levy	Aldgate, London	general dealer
10959	Moses (Moss)	Elizabeth	1803	Spitalfields, London	Yissachar Baer		Elias Moses (Moss)	Aldgate, London	general dealer
14509	Moses (Moss)	Emanuel [Albert M]	1827	Fitzrovia, London	Benjamin Moses	Rosetta (?)	Amelia Isaacs	Fitzrovia, London	engraver + printer + watchmaker, jeweller + silvrsmith
10962	Moses (Moss)	Esther	1834	Spitalfields, London	Elias Moses (Moss)	Elizabeth Levy		Aldgate, London	general dealer
6745	Moses (Moss)	Harry (Henry)	1836	Ipswich, Suffolk	Moses Moses (Moss)	Catherine Alexander		Whitechapel, London	apprentice carver + gilder
10960	Moses (Moss)	Henry	1830	Spitalfields, London	Elias Moses (Moss)	Elizabeth Levy		Aldgate, London	general dealer
10965	Moses (Moss)	Isaac	1838	Whitechapel, London	Elias Moses (Moss)	Elizabeth Levy		Aldgate, London	general dealer
10968	Moses (Moss)	Lewis	1847	Aldgate, London	Elias Moses (Moss)	Elizabeth Levy		Aldgate, London	
10961	Moses (Moss)	Samuel	1832	Spitalfields, London	Elias Moses (Moss)	Elizabeth Levy		Aldgate, London	general dealer
3574	Moses [Beddington]	Edward Henry	1819	Wapping, London	Henry Moses	Esther Nathan	Julia Moses	Wapping, London	merchant colonial
3584	Moses [Beddington]	Esther Hannah	1850	Wapping, London	Maurice (Morris) Moses [Beddington]	Hannah Maria Neustadt	Henry Sylvester Samuel	Wapping, London	
3583	Moses [Beddington]	Hannah Maria	1829	Birmingham	(?) Neustadt		Maurice (Morris) Moses [Beddington]	Wapping, London	

ID	surname	given names	born	birthplace	father	mother	spouse 1	1851 residence	1851 occupation
3575	Moses [Beddington]	Henry Edward	1850	Wapping, London	Edward Henry Moses [Beddington]	Julia Moses	Floretta Marianna Cohen	Wapping, London	
5933	Moses [Beddington]	Jacob (John) Henry	1839	Wapping, London	Henry Moses	Esther Nathan	Jemima Alexander	Shoreditch, London	
3573	Moses [Beddington]	Julia	1829	Bristol	Isaac Moses [Marsden]	Rachel Hyam	Edward Henry Moses [Beddington]	Wapping, London	
3582	Moses [Beddington]	Maurice (Morris)	1821	Wapping, London	Henry Moses	Esther Nathan	Hannah Maria Neustadt	Wapping, London	merchant
3579	Moses [Beddington]	Rachel	1851	Wapping, London	Edward Henry Moses [Beddington]	Julia Moses	Hyman Moses [Montagu]	Wapping, London	
3168	Moses [Davis]	Israel Samuel (Isidore)	1833	Wapping, London	Samuel Moses [Mostyn]	Elizabeth (Betsy) Davis	Kate (Catherine) Stockley	Stockwell, London	
26064	Moses [Marsden]	Algernon	1847	Regent's Park, London	Isaac Moses [Marsden]	Esther Gomes Silva	Louise Frances Hyam	Hyde Park, London	
3556	Moses [Marsden]	Elias	1783	Bungay, Suffolk	Isaac Moses		Judith Jacobs	Stockwell, London	clothing retailer + manufacturer
3555	Moses [Marsden]	Esther	1827	Jamaica, West Indies	Moses Gomez Silva		Isaac Moses [Marsden]	Hyde Park, London	
3569	Moses [Marsden]	Herbert Phillip	1848	Hyde Park, London	Isaac Moses [Marsden]	Esther Gomes Silva	Henrietta Elizabeth de Jong	Hyde Park, London	
3554	Moses [Marsden]	Isaac	1809	?, London	Elias Moses [Marsden]	Judith Jacobs	Rachel Hyam	Hyde Park, London	clothing manufacturer + retailer
3566	Moses [Marsden]	Madeleine	1846	Paddington, London	Isaac Moses [Marsden]	Esther Gomes Silva	Salomon Fallek	Hyde Park, London	
12767	Moses [Marsden]	Martha Sarah	1812	Aldgate, London	Elias Moses [Marsden]	Judith Jacobs		Stockwell, London	
20343	Moses [Merton]	Ada	1844	?, London	Joseph Moses [Merton]	Caroline Koenigswarter		Marylebone, London	
3642	Moses [Merton]	Adeline (Adelina)	1811	?, Holland	Eleazer Jacob Symons	Hester (Esther) (?)	Eleazar Moses [Merton]	Manchester	
14003	Moses [Merton]	Alfred I	1841	Manchester	Eleazar Moses [Merton]	Adeline (Adelina) Symons		Manchester	scholar at home
14000	Moses [Merton]	Alice	1835	Whitechapel, London	Eleazar Moses [Merton]	Adeline (Adelina) Symons		Manchester	scholar at home
7040	Moses [Merton]	Benjamin M	1813	Whitechapel, London	Abraham Lyon Moses	Abigail Lazarus	Hannah Cohen	Marylebone, London	merchant
3641	Moses [Merton]	Eleazar (Lizer)	1808	Whitechapel, London	Abraham Lyon Moses	Abigail Lazarus	Adeline (Adelina) Symons	Manchester	fustian mfr
14005	Moses [Merton]	Eliza	1844	Manchester	Eleazar Moses [Merton]	Adeline (Adelina) Symons		Manchester	scholar at home
14001	Moses [Merton]	Emily P	1837	Manchester	Eleazar Moses [Merton]	Adeline (Adelina) Symons		Manchester	scholar at home
14002	Moses [Merton]	Frances	1839	Manchester	Eleazar Moses [Merton]	Adeline (Adelina) Symons		Manchester	scholar at home
7041	Moses [Merton]	Hannah	1816	Aldgate, London	Solomon Cohen	Hannah Samuel	Benjamin Moses [Merton]	Marylebone, London	
13998	Moses [Merton]	Henry	1832	Whitechapel, London	Eleazar Moses [Merton]	Adeline (Adelina) Symons	Emily Rachel Wagg	Manchester	apprentice to fustian mfr
18520	Moses [Merton]	Henry Merton	1848	Marylebone, London	Benjamin Moses [Merton]	Hannah Cohen		Marylebone, London	
20342	Moses [Merton]	James	1842	?, London	Joseph Moses [Merton]	Caroline Koenigswarter		Marylebone, London	
13999	Moses [Merton]	Jeanette	1834	Whitechapel, London	Eleazar Moses [Merton]	Adeline (Adelina) Symons		Manchester	scholar at home
3646	Moses [Merton]	Louis	1841	?, London	Joseph Moses [Merton]	Caroline Koenigswarter	(?) Pfeiffer	Marylebone, London	
7039	Moses [Merton]	Louisa Emily	1850	Middlesex, London	Benjamin Merton	Hannah Cohen		Marylebone, London	
14004	Moses [Merton]	Rebecca	1842	Manchester	Eleazar Moses [Merton]	Adeline (Adelina) Symons		Manchester	scholar at home
20341	Moses [Merton]	Victoria (Victorine)	1841	?, London	Joseph Moses [Merton]	Caroline Koenigswarter	Angelo Uzielly	Marylebone, London	
3181	Moses [Montagu]	Abigail Ellen (Nellie)	1845	Aldgate, London	Samuel Moses [Mostyn]	Elizabeth (Betsy) Davis	John Sefton Sewill	Stockwell, London	
3183	Moses [Montagu]	Albert Maurice	1846	Aldgate, London	Samuel Moses [Mostyn]	Elizabeth (Betsy) Davis		Stockwell, London	
3169	Moses [Montagu]	Charles	1835	Wapping, London	Samuel Moses [Mostyn]	Elizabeth (Betsy) Davis	Amy Maria Moses [Moss]	Stockwell, London	

ID	surname	given names	born	birthplace	father	mother	spouse 1	1851 residence	1851 occupation
869	Moses [Montagu]	Charlotte (Lettie) Victoria	1847	Aldgate, London	Samuel Moses [Mostyn]	Elizabeth (Betsy) Davis	Israel Hart	Stockwell, London	
3178	Moses [Montagu]	David Somers	1842	Aldgate, London	Samuel Moses [Mostyn]	Elizabeth (Betsy) Davis	Mary Gifford	Stockwell, London	
3186	Moses [Montagu]	Henry Havelock	1849	Aldgate, London	Samuel Moses [Mostyn]	Elizabeth (Betsy) Davis	Hannah Sophia Cowan	Stockwell, London	
3179	Moses [Montagu]	Hyman	1844	Aldgate, London	Samuel Moses [Mostyn]	Elizabeth (Betsy) Davis	Rachel Moses [Beddington]	Stockwell, London	
3171	Moses [Montagu]	Lawrence Elias	1837	Wapping, London	Samuel Moses [Mostyn]	Elizabeth (Betsy) Davis		Stockwell, London	scholar
12759	Moses [Montagu]	Rachel	1841	Aldgate, London	Samuel Moses [Mostyn]	Elizabeth (Betsy) Davis		Stockwell, London	
12758	Moses [Montagu]	Rosetta	1839	Wapping, London	Samuel Moses [Mostyn]	Elizabeth (Betsy) Davis		Stockwell, London	
12760	Moses [Montagu]	Sarah	1842	Aldgate, London	Samuel Moses [Mostyn]	Elizabeth (Betsy) Davis		Stockwell, London	
860	Moses [Montague]	Israel (Montague)	1849	Gloucester, Gloucestershire	Jacob Moses	Anne (Hannah) Levy	Ada Isaacs	Gloucester, Gloucestershire	
858	Moses [Montague]	Montague (Moses)	1841	Gloucester, Gloucestershire	Jacob Moses	Anne (Hannah) Levy	Hannah (Anne) Davis	Gloucester, Gloucestershire	boarding school pupil
3577	Moses [Montagu-Marsden]	Maurice Isaac	1832	?, London	Isaac Moses [Marsden]	Rachel Hyam	Amelia Fallek	Hyde Park, London	
3578	Moses [Montagu-Marsden]	Montagu	1833	Aldgate, London	Isaac Moses [Marsden]	Rachel Hyam	Flora Levyson	Hyde Park, London	
3537	Moses [Moses Jones]	Jane	1806	Wapping, London	Joshua Jones	Sophia (?)	Samuel Moses [Moses Jones]	Finsbury, London	
3538	Moses [Moses Jones]	Joshua	1840	Wapping, London	Samuel Moses	Jane Jones	Catherine (Kate) Jones	Finsbury, London	
3536	Moses [Moses Jones]	Samuel	1805	Wapping, London	Moses Moses	Elizabeth Levy	Jane Jones	Finsbury, London	clothier
3540	Moses [Moses Jones]	Sophia	1843	Wapping, London	Samuel Moses	Jane Jones		Finsbury, London	
5030	Moses [Moss Alexander]	George	1849	Paddington, London	Charles Moses	Elizabeth Alexander	Sybiel Kemp	Marylebone, London	
5028	Moses [Moss Alexander]	Lewis (Louis)	1845	Paddington, London	Charles Moses	Elizabeth Alexander	Catherine (Kate) Moss	Marylebone, London	
857	Moses [Mostyn]	Arthur Abraham	1845	Cheltenham, Gloucestershire	Israel Moses	Maria Abraham	Josephine Ada Myer	Worcester, Worcestershire	
66	Moses [Mostyn]	Elizabeth	1812	Woolwich, London	Israel Davis	Rosetta Levy	Samuel Moses [Mostyn]	Stockwell, London	
68	Moses [Mostyn]	Samuel	1810	Whitechapel, London	David Moses	Abigail Solomons	Elizabeth (Betsy) Davis	Stockwell, London	merchant
30784	Mosley	Charles	1806	?, London	(?Benjamin) Mosely	(?Rose Levy)		Preston, Lancashire	dentist
11839	Moss	Abigail	1827	?Aldgate, London	Aryeh Pais Moss	Rosa (Rosy) (?)		Whitechapel, London	annuitant
8113	Moss	Abraham	1778	Whitechapel, London			(?)	Poplar, London	dealer in shells, curiosities + hardwareman
30643	Moss	Adelaide	1835	Kingston, Jamaica, West Indies	Saul Moss	(?)		Bloomsbury, London	scholar
14267	Moss	Adeline S	1850	Manchester	Joel A Moss	Frances (?)		Manchester	
2879	Moss	Alexander Moses	1816	Poplar, London	Moses Moses (Moss)		Frances Sloman	Whitechapel, London	naturalist
5095	Moss	Alice Theresa	1827	Portsmouth, Hampshire	Joseph Moss	Amelia (?)	Levi Marks	Portsmouth, Hampshire	
5094	Moss	Amelia	1793	Portsmouth, Hampshire			Joseph Moss	Portsmouth, Hampshire	
22490	Moss	Amelia	1821	Whitechapel, London	(?)		Angel Moss	Whitechapel, London	
29679	Moss	Amelia	1823	?Soho, London	(?) Moss			Whitechapel, London	cook
30642	Moss	Amelia	1834	Kingston, Jamaica, West Indies	Saul Moss	(?)		Bloomsbury, London	scholar

ID	surname	given names	born	birthplace	father	mother	spouse 1	1851 residence	1851 occupation
27090	Moss	Amelia	1845	?, London	(?) Moss	Rachael (?)		Aldgate, London	scholar
22489	Moss	Angel	1816	Whitechapel, London			Amelia (?)	Whitechapel, London	cigar maker
21486	Moss	Ann	1819	Middlesex, London	Joseph Moss	Julia (?)		Whitechapel, London	parasol maker
5096	Moss	Ann	1829	Portsmouth, Hampshire	Joseph Moss	Amelia (?)	Isaac Ballin	Portsmouth, Hampshire	
17488	Moss	Ann	1834	Middlesex, London	Samuel Moss	Esther Norden		Spitalfields, London	
8441	Moss	Ann	1845	Portsmouth, Hampshire	Benjamin Woolf Moss	Catherine Levi		Portsmouth, Hampshire	
4781	Moss	Ann	1850	Birmingham	Joel Moss	Sarah Davis	Morris Harris	Birmingham	
22460	Moss	Barnet	1846	?				Gravesend, Kent	boarding school pupil
12057	Moss	Barnett	1809	Deptford, London	Moshe		Rachael (?)	Whitechapel, London	cabinet maker, carver, gilder + plate glass manufacturer + dealer in prints
16543	Moss	Barrow	1823	Plymouth, Devon	(?) Moss	Rachael (?)		Liverpool	licensed victualler
17211	Moss	Benjamin	1798	?, London			Sarah (?)	Spitalfields, London	general dealer
8436	Moss	Benjamin Wolf	1811	Portsmouth, Hampshire	Samuel Moses	Esther (?)	Catherine Levi	Portsmouth, Hampshire	navy agent + outfitter
17712	Moss	Betsy	1830	Whitechapel, London	Michael Moss	Clara (?)		Spitalfields, London	fur sewer
23520	Moss	Caroline	1826	Liverpool	(?) Sewill		Elias Moss	Liverpool	furniture dealer
2888	Moss	Catharine (Kate)	1849	Whitechapel, London	Alexander Moses Moss	Frances Sloman	Emanuel Victor Harris	Whitechapel, London	
8437	Moss	Catherine	1812	Portsmouth, Hampshire	Isaac Levi	Esther (?)	Benjamin W Moss	Portsmouth, Hampshire	outfitter
12059	Moss	Catherine	1831	Whitechapel, London	Barnett Moss	Rachael (?)	(Samuel Isaac Barnett? Or Isaac Michaels?)	Whitechapel, London	
16545	Moss	Charles	1825	Plymouth, Devon	(?) Moss	Rachael (?)		Liverpool	victualler
17711	Moss	Clara	1801	Amsterdam, Holland	(?)		Michael Moss	Spitalfields, London	
18767	Moss	Daniel D	1795	?, London			Rachel (?)	Hornsey, London	merchant general
21134	Moss	David	1851	Aldgate, London	David Moss	Rachael Isaacs		Aldgate, London	
22492	Moss	Dinah	1845	Whitechapel, London	Angel Moss	Amelia (?)		Whitechapel, London	scholar
22459	Moss	Edward	1847	?				Gravesend, Kent	boarding school pupil
23519	Moss	Elias	1813	?, London	Simon Moses		Caroline Sewill	Liverpool	furniture dealer
7397	Moss	Eliza	1820	Whitchurch, Shropshire	(?) Lazarus		Joseph Slazenger Mosss	Manchester	
9038	Moss	Eliza	1825	?, Cambridgeshire	(?) Moss			Aldgate, London	servant
8961	Moss	Elizabeth	1788	Aldgate, London	(?)		Jacob Moss	Aldgate, London	seamstress
6810	Moss	Elizabeth	1802	Spitalfields, London	Nathan Moses		Ezekiel Moss	Spitalfields, London	
30640	Moss	Elizabeth	1817	Middlesex, London	(?) Phillips		Saul Moss	Bloomsbury, London	
12210	Moss	Elizabeth	1827	Deptford, London	Samuel Moss		Isaac Israel	Whitechapel, London	
14143	Moss	Elizabeth	1827	Birmingham	(?)		(?) Moss	Manchester	commercial traveller's wife
19683	Moss	Elizabeth	1832	Spitalfields, London	Samuel Moss			Spitalfields, London	servant
27088	Moss	Elizabeth	1840	?, London	(?) Moss	Rachael (?)		Aldgate, London	cap maker
14766	Moss	Elizabeth	1847	Finsbury, London	Benjamin Moss	Frances Abraham		Finsbury, London	
14144	Moss	Ellen	1849	Manchester	(?) Moss	Elizabeth (?)		Manchester	
5756	Moss	Emanuel	1802	Middlesex, London	Jacob Moses			Piccadilly, London	jeweller, dealer in curios, antique furniture, china, stationery, clocks, bronzes, articles of vertu

ID	surname	given names	born	birthplace	father	mother	spouse 1	1851 residence	1851 occupation
5759	Moss	Emanuel	1817	Deptford, London			Rosetta (Rose) (?)	Aldgate, London	wholesale glass factor empl 14
17487	Moss	Esther	1800	Middlesex, London	Mordecai Norden		(?) Lyons	Spitalfields, London	
16607	Moss	Esther	1819	Liverpool	(?)		Saul Moss	Liverpool	
8438	Moss	Esther	1840	Portsmouth, Hampshire	Benjamin Woolf Moss	Catherine Levi		Portsmouth, Hampshire	
22491	Moss	Esther	1843	Whitechapel, London	Angel Moss	Amelia (?)		Whitechapel, London	scholar
6815	Moss	Ezekiel	1848	Spitalfields, London	Ezekiel Moss	Elizabeth Moses	Rebecca Harris	Spitalfields, London	
11229	Moss	Ezekiel	1848	Whitechapel, London	Mordecai Moss	Rebecca Samuel		Aldgate, London	scholar
18178	Moss	Fanny	1830	Plaistow, London	(?) Moss	(?) Saul		Mile End, London	
6814	Moss	Fanny (Frances)	1842	Spitalfields, London	Ezekiel Moss	Elizabeth Moses		Spitalfields, London	scholar
12836	Moss	Frances	1798	Whitechapel, London	(?)		Moses Moss	Whitechapel, London	dressmaker
14261	Moss	Frances	1816	Manchester	(?)		Joel A Moss	Manchester	
2880	Moss	Frances	1818	Whitechapel, London	Barnett Sloman		Alexander Moses Moss	Whitechapel, London	
14764	Moss	Frances	1818	Portsmouth, Hampshire	Abraham Braham (Abraham)		Benjamin Moss	Finsbury, London	
30648	Moss	Frances	1847	Bloomsbury, London	Saul Moss	Elizabeth Phillips		Bloomsbury, London	scholar
7398	Moss	Frances Annie Slazenger	1849	?, Lancashire	Joseph Slazenger Moss	Eliza Lazarus	Isidor Frankenburg	Manchester	
14767	Moss	Frank	1849	Finsbury, London	Benjamin Moss	Frances Abraham		Finsbury, London	
13691	Moss	Frederick	1810	Halle Wirtemberg, Germany			Ellen Foley	Manchester	
30649	Moss	George	1849	Bloomsbury, London	Saul Moss	Elizabeth Phillips		Bloomsbury, London	scholar
13144	Moss	George	1850	Middlesex, London	Emanuel Moss	Rosetta (Rose) (?)		Aldgate, London	
8488	Moss	George Isaac	1832	Portsmouth, Hampshire	Joseph Moss	Amelia (?)	Rebecca (Rose) Levy	Manchester	salesman
12838	Moss	Hannah	1836	Spitalfields, London	Moses Moss	Frances (?)		Whitechapel, London	
19681	Moss	Henry	1825	Spitalfields, London	Samuel Moss			Spitalfields, London	servant
15811	Moss	Henry	1831	?, London				Aldgate, London	tailor
2885	Moss	Henry	1845	Whitechapel, London	Alexander Moses Moss	Frances Sloman		Whitechapel, London	scholar
2545	Moss	Henry	1850	Hull, Yorkshire	Moses Moss	Rebecca Abrahams		Hull, Yorkshire	
16540	Moss	Henry E	1815	Plymouth, Devon	(?) Moss	Rachael (?)		Liverpool	coal merchant
20353	Moss	Henry Isaac	1839	Stepney, London	Isaac Moss	Sarah Ellen (?)		Whitechapel, London	scholar
16614	Moss	Henry L	1849	Liverpool	Saul Moss	Esther (?)		Liverpool	
5755	Moss	Isaac	1796	Whitechapel, London			Sarah Ellen (?)	Whitechapel, London	stay maker
5137	Moss	Isaac	1805	Arodna, Poland			Rosetta Jacobs	Sheffield, Yorkshire	watchmaker
8114	Moss	Isaac	1813	Shoreditch, London	Abraham Moss			Poplar, London	dealer in shells + curiosities
16544	Moss	Isaac	1821	Plymouth, Devon	(?) Moss	Rachael (?)		Liverpool	watch finisher
8439	Moss	Isaac	1841	Portsmouth, Hampshire	Benjamin Woolf Moss	Catherine Levi		Portsmouth, Hampshire	
7129	Moss	Isabella	1834	Portsmouth, Hampshire	Joseph Moss	Amelia (?)	Louis Leo	Whitechapel, London	governess
8440	Moss	Jane	1842	Portsmouth, Hampshire	Benjamin Woolf Moss	Catherine Levi	Isaac Levy	Portsmouth, Hampshire	
14765	Moss	Jane	1844	Shoreditch, London	Benjamin Moss	Frances Abraham		Finsbury, London	
16610	Moss	Jane	1844	Liverpool	Saul Moss	Esther (?)		Liverpool	
2886	Moss	Jane	1847	Whitechapel, London	Alexander Moses Moss	Frances Sloman	Oscar Youngman	Whitechapel, London	
13143	Moss	Jane (Jeannie)	1848	Middlesex, London	Emanuel Moss	Rosetta (?)	Henry Beyfus	Aldgate, London	
20356	Moss	Jane Sarah	1847	Stepney, London	Isaac Moss	Sarah Ellen (?)		Whitechapel, London	scholar
4778	Moss	Joel	1810	?, London	Solomon Moss		Sarah Davis	Birmingham	general dealer
2180	Moss	Joel	1819	?, Austria				Oxford, Oxfordshire	Hebrew scribe

ID	surname	given names	born	birthplace	father	mother	spouse 1	1851 residence	1851 occupation
2881	Moss	Joel	1837	Peckham, London	Alexander Moses Moss	Frances Sloman	Rosetta Solomon	Whitechapel, London	apprentice cigar maker
14260	Moss	Joel A	1811	Middlesex, London			Frances (?)	Manchester	pawnbroker
21485	Moss	John	1819	Middlesex, London	Joseph Moss	Julia (?)		Whitechapel, London	cigar maker
12837	Moss	John	1834	Spitalfields, London	Moses Moss	Frances (?)		Whitechapel, London	printer compositor
30646	Moss	John	1845	Clapton, London	Saul Moss	Elizabeth Phillips		Bloomsbury, London	scholar
2887	Moss	John	1848	Whitechapel, London	Alexander Moses Moss	Frances Sloman		Whitechapel, London	scholar
21483	Moss	Joseph	1781	Portsmouth, Hampshire			Julia (?)	Whitechapel, London	general dealer
5093	Moss	Joseph	1787	?, London			Amelia (?)	Portsmouth, Hampshire	gas fitter
8491	Moss	Joseph	1812	Poole, Dorset				Portsmouth, Hampshire	coal meter
16608	Moss	Joseph	1839	Liverpool	Saul Moss	Esther (?)		Liverpool	
17491	Moss	Joseph	1843	Middlesex, London	Samuel Moss	Esther Norden		Spitalfields, London	
11230	Moss	Joseph	1848	Whitechapel, London	Mordecai Moss	Rebecca Samuel		Aldgate, London	scholar
14264	Moss	Joseph A	1843	Preston, Lancashire	Joel A Moss	Frances (?)		Manchester	scholar
7396	Moss	Joseph Slazenger	1809	Manchester			Eliza Lazarus	Manchester	tailor + draper empl 16
3929	Moss	Julia	1795	Aldgate, London			Joseph Moss	Whitechapel, London	
16542	Moss	Julia	1831	Liverpool	(?) Moss	Rachael (?)		Liverpool	
18698	Moss	Julia	1837	Whitechapel, London	Barnett Moss	Rachael (?)	Henry Enthoven	Whitechapel, London	
22461	Moss	Julia	1839	?	(?) Moss			Gravesend, Kent	boarding school pupil
17190	Moss	Kate	1816	Middlesex, London				Fitzrovia, London	servant
17713	Moss	Katherine	1835	Whitechapel, London	Michael Moss	Clara (?)		Spitalfields, London	waistcoat maker
17714	Moss	Lazarus	1834	Whitechapel, London	Michael Moss	Clara (?)		Spitalfields, London	cigar maker journeyman
17492	Moss	Lear	1846	Middlesex, London	Samuel Moss	Esther Norden		Spitalfields, London	
19260	Moss	Lewis	1850	Whitechapel, London	Mark (Mordecai) Moss	Rosetta Simmons (Symons, Simons)		Whitechapel, London	
20355	Moss	Louisa Sarah	1843	Stepney, London	Isaac Moss	Sarah Ellen (?)		Whitechapel, London	scholar
16611	Moss	Marcus (Maurice)	1846	Liverpool	Saul Moss	Esther (?)	Frances Jane Moss	Liverpool	
14263	Moss	Marcus A	1841	Preston, Lancashire	Joel A Moss	Frances (?)		Manchester	scholar
7399	Moss	Marcus Slazenger	1846	?, Lancashire	Joseph Slazenger Moss	Eliza Lazarus	Kate Druiff	Manchester	
12060	Moss	Marion (Mary Ann)	1835	Whitechapel, London	Barnett Moss	Rachael (?)	Henry Calisher	Whitechapel, London	
3669	Moss	Mark Mordecai	1827	Harrow, Middlesex	Lewis Moses	Kate (?)	Rosetta Simmons (Symons, Simons)	Whitechapel, London	commercial traveller + money lender + merchant
26267	Moss	Mary	1796	?, London	Solomon Levy		(?) Moss	Aldgate, London	general dealer
19682	Moss	Mary	1825	Whitechapel, London	Samuel Moss			Spitalfields, London	servant
23521	Moss	Mary	1846	Liverpool	Elias Moss	Caroline Sewill		Liverpool	scholar at home
20352	Moss	Mary Ann	1830	Stepney, London	Isaac Moss	Sarah Ellen (?)		Whitechapel, London	hat trimmer
2889	Moss	Matilda	1851	Whitechapel, London	Alexander Moses Moss	Frances Sloman	Charles Hains	Whitechapel, London	
14265	Moss	Matilda R	1846	Preston, Lancashire	Joel A Moss	Frances (?)		Manchester	scholar
17710	Moss	Michael	1802	Spitalfields, London			Clara (?)	Spitalfields, London	commercial traveller
30644	Moss	Michael	1838	Kingston, Jamaica, West Indies	Saul Moss	(?)		Bloomsbury, London	scholar
11227	Moss	Mordecai	1824	Whitechapel, London	Ezekiel Moss	Elizabeth Moses	Rebecca Samuel	Aldgate, London	general dealer
19680	Moss	Morris	1823	Whitechapel, London	Samuel Moss			Spitalfields, London	cab proprietor
17696	Moss	Morris	1824	Soho, London				Holborn, London	coach builder
12839	Moss	Morris	1838	Spitalfields, London	Moses Moss	Frances (?)		Whitechapel, London	fruiterer

ID	surname	given names	born	birthplace	father	mother	spouse 1	1851 residence	1851 occupation
27174	Moss	Morris	1841	Whitechapel, London	Alexander Moses Moss	Frances Sloman		Whitechapel, London	
27089	Moss	Morris	1842	?, London	(?) Moss	Rachael (?)		Aldgate, London	scholar
20968	Moss	Morris	1850	Spitalfields, London	Michael Moss	Clara (?)		Spitalfields, London	
12835	Moss	Moses	1806	Aldgate, London			Frances (?)	Whitechapel, London	fruiterer
2151	Moss	Moses	1814	Exeter, Devon			Rebecca Abrahams	Hull, Yorkshire	picture dealer
6811	Moss	Moses	1832	Spitalfields, London	Ezekiel Moss	Elizabeth Moses	Sophia Levy	Spitalfields, London	cigar maker
17489	Moss	Moses	1836	Middlesex, London	Samuel Moss	Esther Norden		Spitalfields, London	
22493	Moss	Moses	1847	Whitechapel, London	Angel Moss	Amelia (?)		Whitechapel, London	
11232	Moss	Moses (Moss)	1851	Aldgate, London	Mordecai Moss	Rebecca Samuel		Aldgate, London	
17490	Moss	Nancy	1840	Middlesex, London	Samuel Moss	Esther Norden		Spitalfields, London	
5814	Moss	Nathan	1842	Liverpool	Saul Moss	Esther (?)	Esther Israel	Liverpool	
30645	Moss	Patrick	1843	Euston, London	Saul Moss	Elizabeth Phillips		Bloomsbury, London	scholar
27091	Moss	Philip	1847	?, London	(?) Moss	Rachael (?)		Aldgate, London	scholar
2884	Moss	Phoebe	1843	Whitechapel, London	Alexander Moses Moss	Frances Sloman	Bernhard Eberson	Whitechapel, London	
16539	Moss	Rachael	1790	Rochester, Kent	(?)		(?) Moss	Liverpool	retired pawnbroker
12058	Moss	Rachael	1813	Middlesex, London	(?)		Barnett Moss	Whitechapel, London	looking glass manufacturer
27087	Moss	Rachael	1813	?, London	(?)		(?) Moss	Aldgate, London	general dealer
21133	Moss	Rachael	1826	Finsbury, London	Samuel Isaacs	Leah Simmons	David Moss	Aldgate, London	tobacconist
18768	Moss	Rachel	1797	King's Lynn, Norfolk	(?)		Daniel D Moss	Hornsey, London	
17214	Moss	Rachel	1834	?, London	Benjamin Moss	Sarah (?)	Lewis (Lipman) Woolf	Spitalfields, London	tailoress
19684	Moss	Rachel	1837	Spitalfields, London	Samuel Moss			Spitalfields, London	servant
2882	Moss	Ralph	1839	Polar, London	Alexander Moses Moss	Frances Sloman	Louisa Ellen Downing	Whitechapel, London	scholar
14262	Moss	Ralph A	1840	Preston, Lancashire	Joel A Moss	Frances (?)		Manchester	scholar
7395	Moss	Ralph Slazenger	1845	Warrington, Cheshire	Joseph Slazenger Moss	Eliza Lazarus	Jane Stokes	Manchester	scholar
16613	Moss	Raphael (Ralph)	1848	Liverpool	Saul Moss	Esther (?)	Julia Cohen	Liverpool	
2544	Moss	Rebecca	1813	Newbury, Berkshire	(?) Abrahams		Moses Moss	Hull, Yorkshire	
11228	Moss	Rebecca	1824	Aldgate, London	Moshe Samuel		Mordecai Moss	Aldgate, London	dress maker
26269	Moss	Rebecca	1833	?, London	(?) Moss	Mary Levy		Aldgate, London	general dealer
20354	Moss	Reuben Isaac	1841	Stepney, London	Isaac Moss	Sarah Ellen (?)		Whitechapel, London	scholar
30647	Moss	Robert	1846	Bloomsbury, London	Saul Moss	Elizabeth Phillips		Bloomsbury, London	scholar
6813	Moss	Rosa	1839	Spitalfields, London	Ezekiel Moss	Elizabeth Moses	Moses Mitchell	Spitalfields, London	
11838	Moss	Rosa (Rosy)	1795	Middlesex, London	(?)		Aryeh Pais Moss	Whitechapel, London	annuitant
3670	Moss	Rosetta	1828	Whitechapel, London	Israel (Azriel) Simmons (Simonds, Simons)		Mark (Mordecai) Moss	Whitechapel, London	
27092	Moss	Rosetta	1850	?Aldgate, London	(?) Moss	Rachael (?)		Aldgate, London	
5138	Moss	Rosetta (Rosa)	1814	Middlesex, London	Samuel Jacobs	Eve (Eva) (?)	Isaac Moss	Sheffield, Yorkshire	
5760	Moss	Rosetta (Rose)	1827	Marylebone, London	(?)		Emanuel Moss	Aldgate, London	
19679	Moss	Samuel	1796	Covent Garden, London			(?)	Spitalfields, London	broker
17486	Moss	Samuel	1806	Middlesex, London	Nachmeh (?Nehemiah) Moss		Esther Norden	Spitalfields, London	general dealer
19102	Moss	Samuel	1824	Southampton, Hampshire				Fitzrovia, London	servant
26268	Moss	Samuel	1827	?, London	(?) Moss	Mary Levy		Aldgate, London	general dealer
15812	Moss	Samuel	1829	?, London				Aldgate, London	tailor
8489	Moss	Samuel Elias	1818	Portsmouth, Hampshire	Joseph Moss	Amelia (?)	Jeannette (Sheina) Vanderlyn	Whitechapel, London	commission agent

ID	surname	given names	born	birthplace	father	mother	spouse 1	1851 residence	1851 occupation
17212	Moss	Sarah	1801	?, London	(?)		Benjamin Moss	Spitalfields, London	
13096	Moss	Sarah	1806	Spitalfields, London				Whitechapel, London	pauper + maid of all work
16210	Moss	Sarah	1821	Aldgate, London	(?) Moss			Whitechapel, London	servant
4779	Moss	Sarah	1823	?, London	Mordecai Davis		Joel Moss	Birmingham	
30641	Moss	Sarah	1833	Kingston, Jamaica, West Indies	Saul Moss	(?)		Bloomsbury, London	scholar
6812	Moss	Sarah	1834	Spitalfields, London	Ezekiel Moss	Elizabeth Moses		Spitalfields, London	
16612	Moss	Sarah	1847	Liverpool	Saul Moss	Esther (?)	Henry Poland	Liverpool	
13876	Moss	Sarah	1848	?, Lancashire	Joseph Slazenger Moss	Eliza Lazarus		Manchester	
11231	Moss	Sarah	1849	Whitechapel, London	Mordecai Moss	Rebecca Samuel		Aldgate, London	
20351	Moss	Sarah Ellen	1816	St Pancras, London	(?)		Isaac Moss	Whitechapel, London	stay maker
30639	Moss	Saul	1805	Middlesex, London	Moshe		(?)	Bloomsbury, London	West India merchant
16606	Moss	Saul	1811	?, Kent			Esther (?)	Liverpool	looking glass manufacturer
12840	Moss	Simeon	1840	Spitalfields, London	Moses Moss	Frances (?)	Adelaide Cohen	Whitechapel, London	scholar
17213	Moss	Solomon	1832	?, London	Benjamin Moss	Sarah (?)		Spitalfields, London	cigar maker
14266	Moss	Theodore	1848	Preston, Lancashire	Joel A Moss	Frances (?)		Manchester	scholar
21045	Moss	Thomas	1842	?, London				Dover, Kent	boarding school pupil
15296	Moss (Moses)	Benjamin	1809	Southwark, London	Aharon		Hannah Levy	Shoreditch, London	general dealer
15299	Moss (Moses)	Fanny	1836	Spitalfields, London	Benjamin Moss (Moses)	Hannah Levy		Shoreditch, London	at home
15297	Moss (Moses)	Hannah	1806	Spitalfields, London	Isaiah HaLevi		Benjamin Moss (Moses)	Shoreditch, London	
15303	Moss (Moses)	Henry	1850	City, London	Zachariah Moss (Moses)	Rachel Judah		Shoreditch, London	
15300	Moss (Moses)	Isiac	1839	Spitalfields, London	Benjamin Moss (Moses)	Hannah Levy		Shoreditch, London	scholar
30590	Moss (Moses)	Joseph	1851	Shoreditch, London	Zachariah Moss (Moses)	Rachel Judah		Shoreditch, London	
15298	Moss (Moses)	Lewis	1831	Spitalfields, London	Benjamin Moss (Moses)	Hannah Levy		Shoreditch, London	general dealer
15302	Moss (Moses)	Rachel	1830	City, London	Moses Judah	Fanny (Frances) Solomon	Zachariah Moss (Moses)	Shoreditch, London	
4780	Moss (Moses)	Solomon	1848	Birmingham	Joel Moss	Sarah Davis	Rachael Cohen	Birmingham	
15301	Moss (Moses)	Zachariah	1828	Spitalfields, London	Benjamin Moss	Hannah (?)	Rachel Judah	Shoreditch, London	general dealer
7327	Moyel (Moyal)	Sarah	1799	City, London	Abraham Henriques Cardozo	Rebecca (?)	Solomon de Mordecai Moyel (Moyal)	?Aldgate, London	
16572	Mozley	Albert Charles	1842	Liverpool	Charles Mozley	Emma Brandon		Liverpool	scholar
23835	Mozley	Alfred J	1848	Liverpool	Elias Joseph Mozley	Rebecca (?)		Liverpool	
16573	Mozley	Amelia B	1844	Liverpool	Charles Mozley	Emma Brandon	Lionel Herbert Helbert	Liverpool	
16844	Mozley	Brandon L	1840	Liverpool	(?Charles Mozley			Brighton, Sussex	scholar
16571	Mozley	Charles	1801	Liverpool	Moshe HaLevi		Emma Brandon	Liverpool	banker
16669	Mozley	Charles	1837	Liverpool	Lewin Mozley	Fanny Joseph		Liverpool	scholar
16672	Mozley	Charlotte	1842	Liverpool	Lewin Mozley	Fanny Joseph		Liverpool	scholar at home
16674	Mozley	Edith	1848	Liverpool	Lewin Mozley	Fanny Joseph		Liverpool	scholar at home
7497	Mozley	Elias Joseph	1796	?			Rebecca (?)	Liverpool	banker
23836	Mozley	Eliza B	1850	Liverpool	Elias Joseph Mozley	Rebecca (?)		Liverpool	
16668	Mozley	Elizabeth	1836	Liverpool	Lewin Mozley	Fanny Joseph		Liverpool	scholar at home
18445	Mozley	Emma	1815	?, London	Joseph de Gabriel Israel Brandon	Rachel de Emanuel Piza	Charles Mozley	Liverpool	
16671	Mozley	Emma	1840	Liverpool	Lewin Mozley	Fanny Joseph		Liverpool	scholar at home
16676	Mozley	Fanny	1807	?Liverpool	(?) Joseph		Lewin Mozley	Liverpool	

ID	surname	given names	born	birthplace	father	mother	spouse 1	1851 residence	1851 occupation
7734	Mozley	Fanny	1842	Liverpool	Elias Joseph Mozley			Liverpool	
16843	Mozley	Frederick Barned	1840	Liverpool	(?Charles) Mozley	(?Emma Brandon)		Brighton, Sussex	scholar
23834	Mozley	Henry J	1844	Liverpool	Elias Joseph Mozley	Rebecca (?)		Liverpool	
16675	Mozley	Lewin	1793	?			Fanny Joseph	Liverpool	
16667	Mozley	Lewin Barned	1831	Liverpool	Lewin Mozley	Fanny Joseph	Rosetta Micholls	Liverpool	banker's apprentice
16575	Mozley	Lionel Barned (Bernard)	1847	Liverpool	Charles Mozley	Emma Brandon		Liverpool	
16670	Mozley	Miriam	1839	Liverpool	Lewin Mozley	Fanny Joseph	James Henry Enthoven	Liverpool	scholar at home
23832	Mozley	Rebecca	1809	Liverpool	(?)		Elias Joseph Mozley	Liverpool	gentlewoman
16673	Mozley	Sarah	1845	Liverpool	Lewin Mozley	Fanny Joseph		Liverpool	scholar at home
23833	Mozley	Sophia A	1834	Liverpool	Elias Joseph Mozley	Rebecca (?)		Liverpool	gentlewoman
16574	Mozley	William Elias	1846	Liverpool	Charles Mozley	Emma Brandon	Ethel Rebecca Lucas	Liverpool	
14318	Muller	Egmont	1826	?, Germany				Manchester	merchant
27793	Muller	Henry	1842	Aldgate, London	Nathan Muller	Sarah (?)		Spitalfields, London	scholar
27794	Muller	Louis	1845	Whitechapel, London	Nathan Muller	Sarah (?)		Spitalfields, London	scholar
27796	Muller	Moses (Morris)	1849	Whitechapel, London	Nathan Muller	Sarah (?)		Spitalfields, London	
27791	Muller	Nathan	1800	?, Germany	Menahem		Sarah (?)	Spitalfields, London	dealer in general
27792	Muller	Sarah	1813	?, Germany	(?)		Nathan Muller	Spitalfields, London	
27795	Muller	Solomon	1847	Whitechapel, London	Nathan Muller	Sarah (?)		Spitalfields, London	scholar
27797	Muller	Wolf	1851	Whitechapel, London	Nathan Muller	Sarah (?)		Spitalfields, London	
4783	Murcott	Hyman	1823	?, Poland [?, Prussia]				Birmingham	tailor
30223	Murray	Abraham James	1835	Middlesex, London	Joseph Murray	Leah (Leonora) (?)	Isabella (Bella) Joseph	Bayswater, London	articled clerk
30220	Murray	Joseph	1807	Southwark, London			Leah (Leonora) (?)	Bayswater, London	land proprietor
30221	Murray	Leah (Leonora) (?)	1809	Middlesex, London	(?)		Joseph Murray	Bayswater, London	
30222	Murray	Rose	1833	Marylebone, London	Joseph Murray	Leah (Leonora) (?)		Bayswater, London	
8268	Myer	?Londons	1806	?, Poland				Birmingham	
5193	Myer	Abraham Alfred	1796	Bornheim, Germany	Simeon (?Meyer)		Selina Davies	Hereford, Herefordshire	city councillor
10306	Myer	Elizabeth	1837	Spitalfields, London	Henry Myer			Spitalfields, London	scholar
5215	Myer	Grenville David	1848	Hereford, Herefordshire	Abraham Alfred Myer	Hannah Jones	Rachel (Ree) Maud Simmons	Hereford, Herefordshire	
5192	Myer	Hannah	1815	Great Yarmouth, Norfolk	David Jones	Leah Micholls	Abraham Alfred Myer	Hereford, Herefordshire	
10304	Myer	Henry	1803	Aldgate, London			(?)	Spitalfields, London	box maker
5216	Myer	Horatio	1850	Hereford, Herefordshire	Abraham Alfred Myer	Hannah Jones	Esther (Ettie) Joseph	Hereford, Herefordshire	
5214	Myer	Leah	1846	Hereford, Herefordshire	Abraham Alfred Myer	Hannah Jones	Alexander Jacob	Hereford, Herefordshire	
10305	Myer	Moses	1835	Spitalfields, London	Henry Myer			Spitalfields, London	apprentice to box maker
841	Myer	Sidney	1834	?, Russia	Baseman Myer		Sophia Moses	Hereford, Herefordshire	corn + hop merchant
5194	Myer	Sidney	1841	Hereford, Herefordshire	Abraham Alfred Myer	Selina Davies	Sophia Rose Alex	Hereford, Herefordshire	
29029	Myers	A---	1831	Woolwich, London	Abraham Myers	E--- (?)		Whitechapel, London	
28507	Myers	Aaron	1831	Aldgate, London	(?)	Catharine Myers		Spitalfields, London	labourer
10685	Myers	Aaron	1842	Spitalfields, London	Israel Myers	Julia (?)		Spitalfields, London	scholar
28513	Myers	Aaron	1851	Spitalfields, London	Samuel Myers	Eleanor (?)		Spitalfields, London	
27206	Myers	Abigail	1802	Aldgate, London	(?)		George Myers	Limehouse, London	
28602	Myers	Abraham	1761	?, Germany			(?)	Spitalfields, London	umbrella maker
29027	Myers	Abraham	1795	?, Poland [?, Russia Poland]			E--- (?)	Whitechapel, London	watch manufacturer
11109	Myers	Abraham	1803	Middlesex, London	Shlomeh Myers		Mary Simmons	Aldgate, London	picture dealer

ID	surname	given names	born	birthplace	father	mother	spouse 1	1851 residence	1851 occupation
12027	Myers	Abraham	1815	?, Poland [?, Prussia]	Meir		Sarah (?)	Whitechapel, London	tailor
11309	Myers	Abraham	1821	Aldgate, London	Isaac Myers	Rosetta (?)		Aldgate, London	general dealer
12616	Myers	Abraham	1833	?, Poland [?, Prussia]				Birmingham	jeweller + silversmith's assistant
4605	Myers	Abraham	1837	?, Poland				Birmingham	pawnbroker's assistant
26078	Myers	Abraham	1837	Middlesex, London	Benjamin Myers	Maria Israel		Aldgate, London	
28510	Myers	Abraham	1841	Aldgate, London	(?)	Catharine Myers		Spitalfields, London	
11400	Myers	Abraham	1844	Aldgate, London	Joseph Myers	Julia Davis	Phoebe Cohen	Aldgate, London	scholar
30593	Myers	Abraham	1851	Aldgate, London	Isaac Michael Myers	Caroline Aarons		Aldgate, London	
19668	Myers	Abraham Nathan	1804	Middlesex, London	Naftali Hirsch		Marian (Emma) Selig	Aldgate, London	toy + import merchant
26742	Myers	Abraham Saqui	1845	Aldgate, London	George Myers	Rachael Saqui		Aldgate, London	scholar
15648	Myers	Abram	1796	Whitechapel, London				Holborn, London	general dealer
4392	Myers	Adelaide	1845	Birmingham	Lewis Myers		Elias Lawrence Lee	Birmingham	scholar
21927	Myers	Adelaide (Betsey, Edella)	1823	?, London	Michael Myers	Hannah Israel	Hyman (Hyam) Benjamin	Aldgate, London	
20385	Myers	Albert	1844	Fitzrovia, London	Benjamin Joel Myers	Isabella (?)		Fitzrovia, London	
15025	Myers	Alfred	1825	Stepney, London				Bethnal Green, London	engraver
83	Myers	Alfred	1844	?, Poland				Woolwich, London	scholar at home
4798	Myers	Alfred Jacob	1840	Lymington, Hampshire	Jacob Myers	Juliana Aaron	Rosamond Joesbury	Birmingham	
12123	Myers	Amelia	1842	Whitechapel, London	Michael Myers	Esther (?)	Benjamin Israel	Spitalfields, London	scholar
31111	Myers	Amelia	1844	St Giles, London	Henry Myers	Lydia (?)		Bristol	scholar
30594	Myers	Amelia	1851	Whitechapel, London	Henry Myers	Elizabeth Barnett		Whitechapel, London	
15093	Myers	Andrew	1805	Westminster, London			(?)	Euston, London	boot maker
17244	Myers	Angelo	1824	Aldgate, London	Isaac Myers	Leah Miranda	Esther Davis	Aldgate, London	cigar maker journeyman
17337	Myers	Ann	1823	Wigan, Lancashire	(?) Myers			Spitalfields, London	house servant
14619	Myers	Ann	1828	Whitechapel, London	Michael Myers	Rosetta (Rosy) Solomons		Hoxton, London	milliner
26079	Myers	Ann	1838	Middlesex, London	Benjamin Myers	Maria Israel		Aldgate, London	
8971	Myers	Anne (Annie)	1846	Aldgate, London	Henry Myers	Sarah Barnard	(?) Gutmann	Aldgate, London	
24849	Myers	Annie	1838	?, London	(?) Myers	(?) Solomon		Elephant & Castle, London	
25183	Myers	Asher	1823	?, London			Kate Jacobs	Finsbury, London	cigar maker
2737	Myers	Asher Isaac	1848	Aldgate, London	Isaac Michael Myers	Caroline Aarons	Alice Cohen	Aldgate, London	
4787	Myers	Barnard (Bernard)	1834	Birmingham	Gedaliah Myers	Elizabeth (?)		Birmingham	
25474	Myers	Barnett	1814	?Aldgate, London			Isabella Solomons	Tower Hill, London	cane merchant
21186	Myers	Barnett	1850	Aldgate, London	Isaac Myers	Rebecca (?)		Aldgate, London	
22294	Myers	Baron	1836	Birmingham	(?) Myers	Maria (?)		Whitechapel, London	tailor
11037	Myers	Bella (Isabella)	1846	Aldgate, London	Moses (Morris) Myers	Phoebe Simmons	Henry Jones	Aldgate, London	scholar
8716	Myers	Benjamin	1813	abroad				Aldgate, London	silk mercer
6970	Myers	Benjamin	1837	Manchester	Isaac Myers	Elizabeth (?)	Rachel Levy	Whitechapel, London	cigar maker
3661	Myers	Benjamin Joel	1801	Maldon, Essex	Joel Myers		Isabella (?)	Fitzrovia, London	retired woollen draper
1232	Myers	Bessey	1832	Plymouth, Devon	Israel Myers	Zibiah Hyman	Hyman Harris	Plymouth, Devon	
11313	Myers	Betsey	1837	Aldgate, London	Isaac Myers	Rosetta (?)		Aldgate, London	cap maker
12122	Myers	Betsey (Elizabeth)	1840	Whitechapel, London	Michael Myers	Esther (?)	Jacob Danzig	Spitalfields, London	scholar
8949	Myers	Betsy	1791	?, Holland	(?)		John Myers	Aldgate, London	
4807	Myers	Betsy	1831	Sheffield, Yorkshire	(?) Myers	Leah (?)		Birmingham	patent collar sticker

ID	surname	given names	born	birthplace	father	mother	spouse 1	1851 residence	1851 occupation
22712	Myers	Burnett	1793	City, London			Wellcome (?)	Whitechapel, London	watch finisher
2732	Myers	Caroline	1820	St James, London	Shlomo Zvi Aarons	Mary (?)	Isaac Michael Myers	Aldgate, London	
6821	Myers	Caroline	1831	Amsterdam, Holland	(?)		Isaac Myers	Spitalfields, London	
7993	Myers	Caroline	1831	Spitalfields, London	Eleazer Levi	Catherine Moses	Joseph Myers	Spitalfields, London	
9839	Myers	Caroline	1841	?, London	Myer Myers	Rebecca Jacobs		Whitechapel, London	scholar
2309	Myers	Caroline	1842	Leeds, Yorkshire	Peter (Philip) Myers	Charlotte (?)	Myer Scherenski	Leeds, Yorkshire	
28506	Myers	Catharine	1804	?, Holland	(?) Myers	Sarah (?)	(?)	Spitalfields, London	dealer in fruit
26188	Myers	Catherine	1821	?, London	(?) Myers			Aldgate, London	governess
16262	Myers	Catherine	1831	Southwark, London	Yechutiel Abrahams		Lewis Myers	Southwark, London	
24653	Myers	Catherine	1831	Aldgate, London	Henry Myers			Kennington, London	
19373	Myers	Catherine	1833	Southwark, London	Raphael (Ralph) Myers	Elizabeth (Beila) Benjamin	Morris Harris	Bermondsey, London	
13257	Myers	Catherine	1839	Soho, London	Moses Myers	Sarah (?)		Spitalfields, London	scholar
8972	Myers	Catherine	1848	Aldgate, London	Henry Myers	Sarah Barnard		Aldgate, London	
30595	Myers	Catherine Rachel	1832	Covent Garden, London	Moses Henry Myers	Sarah Abraham		Aldgate, London	
24654	Myers	Charles	1832	Aldgate, London	Henry Myers			Kennington, London	cigar maker
14716	Myers	Charles	1838	Bethnal Green, London	Henry Myers	Elizabeth Levy	Ellen Samuel	Aldgate, London	
23468	Myers	Charles	1844	Liverpool	Daniel Myers	Julia Isaacs		Liverpool	scholar
24851	Myers	Charles	1848	Islington, London	(?) Myers	(?) Solomon		Elephant & Castle, London	
2307	Myers	Charlotte	1821	?, London			Peter (Philip) Myers	Leeds, Yorkshire	
20395	Myers	Charlotte	1823	Middlesex, London	(?)		Emanuel Myers	Walworth, London	
29030	Myers	Charlotte?	1835	Greenwich, London	Abraham Myers	E--- (?)		Whitechapel, London	
21945	Myers	Clara	1829	Whitechapel, London	(?) Myers	Rachel (?)	Henry Hart	Marylebone, London	
6842	Myers	Clara	1840	Amsterdam, Holland	(?) Myers	Sarah (?)		Spitalfields, London	tailoress
4803	Myers	Clara	1849	Portsmouth, Hampshire	Jacob Myers	Juliana Aaron		Birmingham	
23470	Myers	Claude	1845	Liverpool	Daniel Myers	Julia Isaacs		Liverpool	
6981	Myers	Daniel	1810	Maldon, Essex	Joel Myers		Julia Isaacs	Liverpool	draper + tailor
13249	Myers	David	1782	Aldgate, London			Harriet (?)	Spitalfields, London	clothes dealer
6203	Myers	David	1803	Wapping, London	Michael Myers	Hannah Israel	Leah Joshua	Aldgate, London	butcher
25566	Myers	David	1815	?, London	Levy Myers	Sarah Solomon	Rebecca Da Costa Noah	Aldgate, London	glass cutter dealer
23626	Myers	David	1828	?, London				Liverpool	professor of music
4799	Myers	David Joshua	1843	Lymington, Hampshire	Jacob Myers	Juliana Aaron	Elizabeth Jones	Birmingham	
12126	Myers	Deborah	1851	Whitechapel, London	Michael Myers	Esther (?)		Spitalfields, London	
8747	Myers	Diana	1832	Aldgate, London	Solomon Myers	Sarah (?)		Aldgate, London	tailoress
13258	Myers	Dinah	1840	Covent Garden, London	Moses Myers	Sarah (?)		Spitalfields, London	tailoress
30599	Myers	Dinah	1845	Aldgate, London	Moses Henry Myers	Sarah Abraham		Aldgate, London	
18185	Myers	Dinah	1846	Stepney, London	Lewis Myers	Sarah (?)		Mile End, London	
9838	Myers	Dinah	1847	?, London	Myer Myers	Rebecca Jacobs		Whitechapel, London	scholar
29028	Myers	E---	1795	Whitechapel, London	(?)		Abraham Myers	Whitechapel, London	
29032	Myers	E---	1834	Woolwich, London	Abraham Myers	E--- (?)		Whitechapel, London	
11848	Myers	Edward	1806	Amsterdam, Holland			Elizabeth (?)	Whitechapel, London	marine stores dealer
20386	Myers	Edward	1846	Fitzrovia, London	Benjamin Joel Myers	Isabella (?)		Fitzrovia, London	
28512	Myers	Eleanor	1830	Aldgate, London	(?)		Samuel Myers	Spitalfields, London	
5208	Myers	Elias	1785	Poznan, Poland [Posen, Prussia]				Cheltenham, Gloucestershire	retired pawnbroker

ID	surname	given names	born	birthplace	father	mother	spouse 1	1851 residence	1851 occupation
13260	Myers	Eliza	1847	Whitechapel, London	Moses Myers	Sarah (?)		Spitalfields, London	
27271	Myers	Elizabeth	1775	?, London	(?)		(?) Myers	Aldgate, London	clothes dealer
4784	Myers	Elizabeth	1790	Birmingham			Gedaliah Myers	Birmingham	pawnbroker
16193	Myers	Elizabeth	1791	?	(?)		Isaac Myers	Whitechapel, London	
12475	Myers	Elizabeth	1799	Aldgate, London	Myer Woolf		Lazarus Myers	Spitalfields, London	
20710	Myers	Elizabeth	1800	Wapping, London	(?) Hains		Andrew Myers	Whitechapel, London	
14714	Myers	Elizabeth	1805	Bethnal Green, London	Yehuda Leib Levy		Henry Myers	Aldgate, London	
28494	Myers	Elizabeth	1805	Spitalfields, London	(?)		(?) Myers	Spitalfields, London	fish dealer
11849	Myers	Elizabeth	1810	Amsterdam, Holland			Edward Myers	Whitechapel, London	
16266	Myers	Elizabeth	1813	Whitechapel, London	(?) Barnett		Henry Myers	Whitechapel, London	
11123	Myers	Elizabeth	1824	Aldgate, London	Emanuel Myers	Mary (?)		Aldgate, London	furrier
13251	Myers	Elizabeth	1825	Whitechapel, London	David Myers	Harriet (?)		Spitalfields, London	furrier
10684	Myers	Elizabeth	1840	Spitalfields, London	Israel Myers	Julia (?)	Moses Jacobs	Spitalfields, London	scholar
24850	Myers	Elizabeth	1840	City, London	(?) Myers	(?) Solomon		Elephant & Castle, London	scholar
11038	Myers	Elizabeth	1849	Aldgate, London	Moses (Morris) Myers	Phoebe Simmons	(?) Jacobs	Aldgate, London	scholar
19376	Myers	Elizabeth (Beila)	1798	Whitechapel, London	Michael Benjamin (Menachem Menke)	Beulah bat Naftali Hirsh	Raphael (Ralph) Myers	Bermondsey, London	
10458	Myers	Elizabeth (Betsey)	1846	Aldgate, London	Michael Myers	Jane Isaacs	Isaac Moses [Moss]	Aldgate, London	
29987	Myers	Elizabeth (Betsy)	1809	Middlesex, London	Yekutiel (Catriel) Jacobs		Michael Myers	Whitechapel, London	clothes dealer
15243	Myers	Ellen	1809	Whitechapel, London	(?)		Meir Myers	Shoreditch, London	nurse
11121	Myers	Emanuel	1783	Aldgate, London			Mary (?)	Aldgate, London	general dealer
20394	Myers	Emanuel	1819	Middlesex, London			Charlotte (?)	Walworth, London	professor of music + dealer in musical instruments
11035	Myers	Emanuel	1841	Middlesex, London	Moses (Morris) Myers	Phoebe Simmons	Emily Allen	Aldgate, London	scholar
19670	Myers	Emma	1833	Aldgate, London	Abraham Nathan Myers	Marian (Emma) Selig	Henry Eliezer Symons	Aldgate, London	
2313	Myers	Emmanuel	1850	Leeds, Yorkshire	Peter (Philip) Myers	Charlotte (?)		Leeds, Yorkshire	
27579	Myers	Ester	1828	Whitechapel, London	(?)		Lazarus Myers	Spitalfields, London	
23420	Myers	Esther	1791	?, London	Yehuda Leib Nathan		Naphtali Myers	Aldgate, London	
24796	Myers	Esther	1795	Middlesex, London	Samuel (Shmuel Zenvil) Nathan	(Hannah Mendes?)	Mendlewitz Myers	Elephant & Castle, London	
12119	Myers	Esther	1812	Whitechapel, London	(?)		Michael Myers	Spitalfields, London	
15543	Myers	Esther	1821	Covent Garden, London	(?Chanoch Enoch) Myers			Covent Garden, London	
14618	Myers	Esther	1825	Whitechapel, London	Michael Myers	Rosetta (Rosy) Solomons		Hoxton, London	milliner
20796	Myers	Esther	1828	Westminster, London	Mark Sloman	Sarah Nathan	Jacob Myers	Mayfair, London	trunk maker
30892	Myers	Esther	1833	Chelmsford, Essex	Wolf Myers	Hannah Samuel		Chelmsford, Essex	scholar at home
6955	Myers	Esther	1835	Aldgate, London	Jacob Myers	Rosetta (?)	Henry Levy	Spitalfields, London	
21182	Myers	Esther	1841	Aldgate, London	Isaac Myers	Rebecca (?)		Aldgate, London	
11217	Myers	Esther	1847	Middlesex, London	Levy Myers	Hannah (?)		Aldgate, London	
6637	Myers	Esther	1848	Spitalfields, London	Isaac Myers	Hannah Benjamin		Spitalfields, London	scholar
10686	Myers	Esther	1848	Spitalfields, London	Israel Myers	Julia (?)		Spitalfields, London	
16263	Myers	Esther	1848	Southwark, London	Lewis Myers	Catherine Abrahams		Southwark, London	
6822	Myers	Esther	1851	Spitalfields, London	Isaac Myers	Caroline (?)		Spitalfields, London	
6977	Myers	Esther	1851	?Aldgate, London	Morris Myers	Rachel Barnett		Spitalfields, London	

ID	surname	given names	born	birthplace	father	mother	spouse 1	1851 residence	1851 occupation
29177	Myers	Eva	1793	Amsterdam, Holland	(?)		Moss Myers	Whitechapel, London	boarding and lodging house
19278	Myers	Eve	1829	Whitechapel, London	David Myers	Leah Joshua		Aldgate, London	
26741	Myers	Eve	1843	Aldgate, London	George Myers	Rachael Saqui		Aldgate, London	scholar
8257	Myers	Ezra	1815	?			Rebecca Simon	Newark, Lincolnshire	
30702	Myers	Fanny	1785	Middlesex, London				Bloomsbury, London	cook
28108	Myers	Fanny	1788	?, Holland	(?)		(?) Myers	Spitalfields, London	capmaker
11124	Myers	Fanny	1826	Aldgate, London	Emanuel Myers	Mary (?)		Aldgate, London	tailoress
11311	Myers	Fanny	1828	Aldgate, London	Isaac Myers	Rosetta (?)		Aldgate, London	parasol maker
30894	Myers	Fanny	1838	Chelmsford, Essex	Wolf Myers	Hannah Samuel		Chelmsford, Essex	scholar at home
15899	Myers	Fanny	1840	Middlesex, London	(?) Myers			Hackney, London	boarding school pupil
12032	Myers	Fischell	1850	Whitechapel, London	Abraham Myers	Sarah (?)		Whitechapel, London	
29674	Myers	Flora	1825	Middlesex, London	(?) Meyers			Wapping, London	cook
24843	Myers	Flora	1831	Shoreditch, London	(?) Myers			Elephant & Castle, London	cook
22905	Myers	Frances	1784	Portsmouth, Hampshire	(?)		(?) Myers	Wapping, London	clothes dealer
24834	Myers	Frances	1795	Amsterdam, Holland	(?)		Herman Myers	Elephant & Castle, London	
21181	Myers	Frances	1838	Aldgate, London	Isaac Myers	Rebecca (?)		Aldgate, London	
5804	Myers	Frances (Fanny)	1848	Southwark, London	Solomon Myers	Rachel Lyons	Edward Wenkheim	Southwark, London	
23469	Myers	Frank	1845	Liverpool	Daniel Myers	Julia Isaacs		Liverpool	
10922	Myers	Frederick	1831	Spitalfields, London				Spitalfields, London	furrier
4788	Myers	Gabriel	1803	?, Germany			Maria (?)	Birmingham	cigar mfr (empl 14 men)
27205	Myers	George	1790	Spitalfields, London	Avraham		Abigail (?)	Limehouse, London	general dealer
26737	Myers	George	1811	Whitechapel, London	Michael Myers		Rachael Saqui	Aldgate, London	builder empl 2
20567	Myers	George	1835	Spitalfields, London	Lazarus Myers	(?)		Spitalfields, London	tailor
30896	Myers	George	1841	Chelmsford, Essex	Wolf Myers	Hannah Samuel		Chelmsford, Essex	scholar at home
23467	Myers	George	1843	Liverpool	Daniel Myers	Julia Isaacs		Liverpool	scholar
30602	Myers	Hagar	1851	Aldgate, London	David Myers	Rebecca Da Costa Noah		Aldgate, London	
8785	Myers	Hannah	1775	Aldgate, London			Levy Myers	Aldgate, London	
20021	Myers	Hannah	1775	Aldgate, London	Tsevi Hirsh Halevi		Angel (Abraham Asher Anshel) Myers	Aldgate, London	marine iron dealer
22948	Myers	Hannah	1777	Whitechapel, London	(?)		Morris Myers	Wapping, London	
25675	Myers	Hannah	1778	Aldgate, London	(?)		(?) Myers	Spitalfields, London	marine store dealer
6630	Myers	Hannah	1802	Southwark, London	Joseph Benjamin		Isaac Myers	Spitalfields, London	
11394	Myers	Hannah	1805	Amsterdam, Holland	Shmuel HaLevi			Aldgate, London	needlewoman
3551	Myers	Hannah	1811	Whitechapel, London	(?) Samuel		Wolf Myers	Chelmsford, Essex	cabinet maker + upholsterer mistress empl 2
11215	Myers	Hannah	1812	Middlesex, London	(?)		Levy Myers	Aldgate, London	
28703	Myers	Hannah	1815	Middlesex, London	Joseph		Joseph Myers	Spitalfields, London	
22010	Myers	Hannah	1821	Shoreditch, London	Barnet Hart	Elizabeth (?)	Israel Myers	Whitechapel, London	
4806	Myers	Hannah	1829	Nottingham, Nottinghamshire	(?) Myers	Leah (?)		Birmingham	cap maker
28268	Myers	Hannah	1830	Aldgate, London	(?) Myers			Aldgate, London	house servant
29989	Myers	Hannah	1832	Whitechapel, London	Michael Myers	Elizabeth (Betsy) Jacobs	Henry Marks	Whitechapel, London	furrier

ID	surname	given names	born	birthplace	father	mother	spouse 1	1851 residence	1851 occupation
6634	Myers	Hannah	1834	Shoreditch, London	Isaac Myers	Hannah Benjamin		Spitalfields, London	
6841	Myers	Hannah	1835	Amsterdam, Holland	(?) Myers	Sarah (?)		Spitalfields, London	cap maker
8262	Myers	Hannah	1839	Hull, Yorkshire	Ezra Myers	Rebecca (?)	Moses Feldman	Newark, Lincolnshire	
11243	Myers	Hannah	1840	Aldgate, London	(?) Myers	Susan (?)		Aldgate, London	
16971	Myers	Hannah	1840	Middlesex, London	(?) Myers			Hammersmith, London	boarding school pupil
30895	Myers	Hannah	1840	Chelmsford, Essex	Wolf Myers	Hannah Samuel		Chelmsford, Essex	scholar at home
26740	Myers	Hannah	1842	Aldgate, London	George Myers	Rachael Saqui		Aldgate, London	scholar
11036	Myers	Hannah	1844	Aldgate, London	Moses (Morris) Myers	Phoebe Simmons	Alexander Joseph (Josephs)	Aldgate, London	scholar
8790	Myers	Hannah	1845	Aldgate, London	John (Jacob) Myers	Harriet Levy	Abraham Hyams	Aldgate, London	
2738	Myers	Hannah (Annie)	1850	Aldgate, London	Isaac Michael Myers	Caroline Aarons		Aldgate, London	
13250	Myers	Harriet	1798	Aldgate, London	(?)		David Myers	Spitalfields, London	
8787	Myers	Harriet	1822	Aldgate, London	Solomon Levy		John (Jacob) Myers	Aldgate, London	
22983	Myers	Harriot	1803	?, Kent	(?)		Joel Myers	Poplar, London	
23471	Myers	Harvey	1849	Liverpool	Daniel Myers	Julia Isaacs		Liverpool	
24149	Myers	Helen	1845	?Strand, London	Andrew Myers	Rosa Samuel		Euston, London	
31113	Myers	Helen	1849	Bristol	Henry Myers	Lydia (?)		Bristol	
4819	Myers	Henrietta	1830	Birmingham	Myer Myers	Rebecca (?)	Leopold Cohen	Birmingham	
4790	Myers	Henrietta	1848	Birmingham	Gabriel Myers	Maria (?)	Alexander Jones	Birmingham	
19671	Myers	Henrietta	1848	Aldgate, London	Abraham Nathan Myers	Marian (Emma) Selig		Aldgate, London	
6942	Myers	Henry	1796	Whitechapel, London			(?)	Kennington, London	tailor
16265	Myers	Henry	1802	Spitalfields, London	Moses Myers	Hannah Marks	Elizabeth Barnett	Whitechapel, London	broker
4795	Myers	Henry	1803	?, London				Birmingham	broker
14713	Myers	Henry	1807	?, Holland	Angel (Abraham Asher Anshel) Myers	Hannah (Anna) (?)	Elizabeth Levy	Aldgate, London	general dealer
31108	Myers	Henry	1811	?, Poland [?, Prussia]			Lydia (?)	Bristol	wine + tea merchant
23113	Myers	Henry	1818	Aldgate, London			Hester (?)	Aldgate, London	cigar maker empl 5 apprentices
8969	Myers	Henry	1821	Aldgate, London	Levy Myers		Sarah Barnard	Aldgate, London	cook + confectioner
30226	Myers	Henry	1825	?London	Isaac Myers		Sophia Symons	Whitechapel, London	
21948	Myers	Henry	1827	Whitechapel, London	(?) Myers	Rachel (?)		Marylebone, London	clothier + outfitter
13252	Myers	Henry	1829	Mayfair, London	David Myers	Harriet (?)		Spitalfields, London	cigar maker
20381	Myers	Henry	1830	Southwark, London	Benjamin Joel Myers	Isabella (?)		Fitzrovia, London	
8671	Myers	Henry	1832	Clerkenwell, London	Lawrence Myers	(?)		Bloomsbury, London	clerk
13298	Myers	Henry	1832	Whitechapel, London	(?) Myers			Spitalfields, London	cigar maker
13724	Myers	Henry	1832	Birmingham	Isaac Myers	Rachael (?)	Caroline Salmon	Twickenham, London	no occupation
12121	Myers	Henry	1835	Whitechapel, London	Michael Myers	Esther (?)		Spitalfields, London	butcher's assistant
28508	Myers	Henry	1835	Aldgate, London	(?)	Catharine Myers		Spitalfields, London	labourer
31112	Myers	Henry	1846	St Giles, London	Henry Myers	Lydia (?)		Bristol	scholar
5416	Myers	Henry	1850	Gateshead, Tyne & Wear	(?) Myers			Gateshead, Tyne & Wear	
19378	Myers	Henry	1850	Southwark, London	Michael Henry Myers	Maria Samson		Camberwell, London	
24833	Myers	Herman	1791	?, Germany			Frances (?)	Elephant & Castle, London	?dealer in sponges + cigars
18186	Myers	Herman	1848	Stepney, London	Lewis Myers	Sarah (?)		Mile End, London	
23114	Myers	Hester	1831	Whitechapel, London	(?)		Henry Myers	Aldgate, London	
24148	Myers	Hester	1843	Clerkenwell, London	Andrew Myers	Rosa Samuel		Euston, London	

ID	surname	given names	born	birthplace	father	mother	spouse 1	1851 residence	1851 occupation
19379	Myers	Hester (Esther)	1849	Walworth, London	Michael Henry Myers	Maria Samson		Camberwell, London	
9837	Myers	Hirsch	1836	?, London	Myer Myers	Rebecca Jacobs		Whitechapel, London	clerk
3679	Myers	Hyam	1828	Aldgate, London	Lipman Myers (Miers)	Rebecca Mordecai	Maria Harris	Spitalfields, London	dealer in wearing apparel
21489	Myers	Hyam (Hyman)	1808	?London	Yehuda Leib		Sarah Emanuel	Clerkenwell, London	clothier
16192	Myers	Isaac	1784	Hanover, Germany			Elizabeth (?)	Whitechapel, London	general dealer
17241	Myers	Isaac	1793	Aldgate, London	Asher Enzley Myers		Leah Miranda	Aldgate, London	butcher empl 1
6629	Myers	Isaac	1795	Aldgate, London	Michael from Lenz		Hannah Benjamin	Spitalfields, London	watch maker
11307	Myers	Isaac	1798	Aldgate, London			Rosetta (?)	Aldgate, London	general dealer
21179	Myers	Isaac	1813	?, Poland	Meir		Rebecca (?)	Aldgate, London	general dealer
24939	Myers	Isaac	1813	Warsaw, Poland			Mary (?)	Bethnal Green, London	interpreter
6820	Myers	Isaac	1829	Amsterdam, Holland			Caroline (?)	Spitalfields, London	slipper maker
1461	Myers	Isaac	1837	Kalisz, Poland	Moses Myers	Reisele Zelda Michelsohn	Julia (?)	Manchester	cap mfr
30598	Myers	Isaac	1842	Aldgate, London	Moses Henry Myers	Sarah Abraham		Aldgate, London	
2310	Myers	Isaac	1845	Leeds, Yorkshire	Peter (Philip) Myers	Charlotte	Mary A (?Kidson)	Leeds, Yorkshire	
10457	Myers	Isaac	1845	Aldgate, London	Michael Myers	Jane Isaacs	Hannah Benjamin	Aldgate, London	
2731	Myers	Isaac Michael	1815	Amsterdam, Holland	Moses Myers		Caroline Aarons	Aldgate, London	school master + Hebrew teacher
20380	Myers	Isabella	1804	Middlesex, London	(?)		Benjamin Joel Myers	Fitzrovia, London	
12120	Myers	Isabella	1833	Whitechapel, London	Michael Myers	Esther (?)		Spitalfields, London	dress maker
1234	Myers	Isaiah (Frank)	1838	Plymouth, Devon	Israel Myers	Zibiah Hyman	Julia Lyons	Plymouth, Devon	scholar
10874	Myers	Israel	1774	Amsterdam, Holland	Meir		Rebecca Levy	Spitalfields, London	general dealer
1230	Myers	Israel	1791	Bavaria, Germany	Meir		Zibiah Hyman	Plymouth, Devon	general dealer
10682	Myers	Israel	1809	Whitechapel, London			Julia (?)	Spitalfields, London	general dealer
22009	Myers	Israel	1817	City, London	Meir		Hannah Hart	Whitechapel, London	cigar maker
17245	Myers	Israel	1826	Aldgate, London	Isaac Myers	Leah Miranda		Aldgate, London	butcher journeyman
29988	Myers	Israel	1831	Whitechapel, London	Michael Myers	Elizabeth (Betsy) Jacobs		Whitechapel, London	?pattern maker
28401	Myers	Israel	1845	Spitalfields, London	Joseph Myers	Phoebe Levy		Spitalfields, London	scholar
21069	Myers	J---	1836	?, London				Dover, Kent	boarding school pupil
11457	Myers	Jacob	1776	Bialystok, Poland [Balistock, Russia]				Aldgate, London	general dealer
4804	Myers	Jacob	1810	Strasburg, Germany [Strasburgh, Prussia]	Myer Myers		Juliana Aaron	Birmingham	pawnbroker
28109	Myers	Jacob	1810	?, Holland	(?) Myers	Fanny (?)		Spitalfields, London	jeweller
20795	Myers	Jacob	1825	Whitechapel, London	Michael Myers	Elizabeth Jacobs	Esther Sloman	Mayfair, London	trunk maker
4809	Myers	Jacob	1835	Nottingham, Nottinghamshire	(?) Myers	Leah (?)		Birmingham	shopman
28704	Myers	Jacob	1835	Middlesex, London	Joseph Myers	Hannah Joseph	Rosa (Rosetta) Harris	Spitalfields, London	
22295	Myers	Jacob	1838	Aldgate, London	(?) Myers	Maria (?)		Whitechapel, London	cigar maker
1235	Myers	Jacob	1845	Plymouth, Devon	Israel Myers	Zibiah Hyman		Plymouth, Devon	scholar
21185	Myers	Jacob	1848	Aldgate, London	Isaac Myers	Rebecca (?)		Aldgate, London	
13087	Myers	James	1822	Aldgate, London				Brixton, London	prisoner + tailor (journeyman)
13098	Myers	Jane	1793	Whitechapel, London	(?) Myers			Whitechapel, London	pauper + laundress
11211	Myers	Jane	1795	Aldgate, London	(?)		(?) Myers	Aldgate, London	general dealer
10455	Myers	Jane	1816	Aldgate, London	Henry Isaacs	Elizabeth (?)	Michael Myers	Aldgate, London	
19372	Myers	Jane	1837	Southwark, London	Raphael (Ralph) Myers	Elizabeth (Beila) Benjamin		Bermondsey, London	

ID	surname	given names	born	birthplace	father	mother	spouse 1	1851 residence	1851 occupation
21184	Myers	Jane	1842	Aldgate, London	Isaac Myers	Rebecca (?)		Aldgate, London	
12031	Myers	Jesse	1848	Woolwich, London	Abraham Myers	Sarah (?)		Whitechapel, London	
5805	Myers	Jessie	1849	Southwark, London	Solomon Myers	Rachel Lyons	Louis Ash Israel	Southwark, London	
22982	Myers	Joel	1802	?, Romania [?, Moldavia]			Harriot (?)	Poplar, London	interpreter
8948	Myers	John	1781	?, Holland			Betsy (?)	Aldgate, London	tailor
30891	Myers	John	1832	Chelmsford, Essex	Wolf Myers	Hannah Samuel		Chelmsford, Essex	cabinet maker apprentice
6968	Myers	John	1839	Whitechapel, London	Benjamin Myers	Maria Israel	Rachel (?)	Aldgate, London	
9776	Myers	John	1839	Middlesex, London				Kew, London	boarding school pupil
26739	Myers	John	1841	Aldgate, London	George Myers	Rachael Saqui		Aldgate, London	scholar
8951	Myers	John	1849	?, Holland	(?) Myers			Aldgate, London	
8786	Myers	John (Jacob)	1817	Aldgate, London	Levy Myers	Hannah (?)	Harriet Levy	Aldgate, London	cook + confectioner
2546	Myers	John D	1807	?, Germany				Hull, Yorkshire	
19280	Myers	John David	1832	Whitechapel, London	David Myers	Leah Joshua	Fanny Elizabeth Angel [Moses}	Aldgate, London	cigar maker
26284	Myers	Joseph	1791	?, Poland				Aldgate, London	cap maker
11392	Myers	Joseph	1794	Amsterdam, Holland	Shmuel HaLevi		Rebecca Cohen	Aldgate, London	boot + shoe maker
28702	Myers	Joseph	1811	Middlesex, London	Abraham		Hannah Joseph	Spitalfields, London	diamond merchant
17243	Myers	Joseph	1821	Aldgate, London	Isaac Myers	Leah Miranda	Sarah Nathan	Aldgate, London	umbrella maker journeyman
28397	Myers	Joseph	1822	Spitalfields, London	Morris Myers		Phoebe Levy	Spitalfields, London	rag merchant
7994	Myers	Joseph	1824	Whitechapel, London	Michael Myers		Caroline Levi	Spitalfields, London	master grocer
6632	Myers	Joseph	1829	Aldgate, London	Isaac Myers	Hannah Benjamin	Deborah Nathan	Spitalfields, London	cigar maker
14621	Myers	Joseph	1834	Whitechapel, London	Michael Myers	Rosetta (Rosy) Solomons		Hoxton, London	cooper
2308	Myers	Joseph	1840	?, London	Peter (Philip) Myers	Charlotte (?)	Catherine White	Leeds, Yorkshire	
4802	Myers	Joseph	1846	Portsmouth, Hampshire	Jacob Myers	Juliana Aaron	Sara Leonora Cowen	Birmingham	
13262	Myers	Joseph	1850	Spitalfields, London	Moses Myers	Sarah (?)		Spitalfields, London	
16269	Myers	Joshua	1838	Whitechapel, London	Henry Myers	Elizabeth Barnett		Whitechapel, London	
13259	Myers	Judah	1844	Aldgate, London	Moses Myers	Sarah (?)		Spitalfields, London	scholar
17743	Myers	Judah	1849	City, London	Woolf Myers	Leah Phillips		Aldgate, London	
11393	Myers	Julia	1803	Bethnal Green, London	Isaac Yitzhak		(?)	Aldgate, London	boot + shoe maker
10683	Myers	Julia	1811	Whitechapel, London	(?)		Israel Myers	Spitalfields, London	general dealer
6982	Myers	Julia	1814	Middlesex, London	Israel Isaacs	Rachel Andrade Da Costa	Daniel Myers	Liverpool	
23423	Myers	Julia	1827	?, London	Naphtali Myers	Esther Nathan		Aldgate, London	general dealer
11111	Myers	Julia	1830	Middlesex, London	Abraham Myers	Mary Simmons	Abraham Hart	Aldgate, London	waistcoat maker
13297	Myers	Julia	1830	Whitechapel, London	(?) Myers			Spitalfields, London	tailoress
28509	Myers	Julia	1837	Aldgate, London	(?)	Catharine Myers		Spitalfields, London	
16264	Myers	Julia	1850	Southwark, London	Lewis Myers	Catherine Abrahams		Southwark, London	
5801	Myers	Julia	1851	Southwark, London	Solomon Myers	Rachel Lyons	Flavian Ernst Lezard	Southwark, London	
23466	Myers	Julian	1840	Maldon, Essex	Daniel Myers	Julia Isaacs	Cecilia (Lielchen) Kulb	Liverpool	scholar
4797	Myers	Juliana	1822	Birmingham	David Aaron	Maria Myers	Jacob Myers	Birmingham	pawnbroker
6158	Myers	Lawrence	1803	Maldon, Essex	Joel Myers		(?)	Bloomsbury, London	merchant
12474	Myers	Lazarus	1803	?, London	M--- Myers		(?)	Spitalfields, London	tailor
27578	Myers	Lazarus	1828	Middlesex, London			Ester (?)	Spitalfields, London	general dealer
17242	Myers	Leah	1798	Aldgate, London	Joseph Rodrigues Miranda		Isaac Myers	Aldgate, London	
4805	Myers	Leah	1799	Portsmouth, Hampshire			(?) Myers	Birmingham	

ID	surname	given names	born	birthplace	father	mother	spouse 1	1851 residence	1851 occupation
19277	Myers	Leah	1803	Whitechapel, London	Abraham Cohen Joshua		David Myers	Aldgate, London	
17738	Myers	Leah	1825	?, Poland [?, Prussia]	(?) Phillips		Woolf Myers	Aldgate, London	
25247	Myers	Leah	1825	?Aldgate, London	(?)		(?) Myers	Holborn, London	artificial flower maker
30603	Myers	Leah	1849	Aldgate, London	John (Jacob) Myers	Harriet Levy		Aldgate, London	
8784	Myers	Levy	1778	Brighton, Sussex			Hannah (?)	Aldgate, London	cook + confectioner
11175	Myers	Levy	1789	Canterbury, Kent	Michael Land(au?)		Sarah Solomon	Aldgate, London	glass cutter
11214	Myers	Levy	1801	Middlesex, London			Hannah (?)	Aldgate, London	cap maker
8792	Myers	Levy (Lewis)	1850	Aldgate, London	John (Jacob) Myers	Harriet Levy		Aldgate, London	
18183	Myers	Lewis	1811	Middlesex, London			Sarah (?)	Mile End, London	House steward + tutor in school
14521	Myers	Lewis	1816	Middlesex, London				King's Lynn, Norfolk	traveller
16261	Myers	Lewis	1827	Southwark, London	Michael (Meir, Mendelwitz)		Catherine Abrahams	Southwark, London	general dealer
9836	Myers	Lewis	1829	Aldgate, London	Myer Myers	Rebecca Jacobs		Whitechapel, London	clerk
6978	Myers	Lewis	1831	Middlesex, London	Isaac Myers		Rachel Isaacs	Spitalfields, London	
14717	Myers	Lewis	1844	Spitalfields, London	Henry Myers	Elizabeth Levy		Aldgate, London	
16273	Myers	Lewis	1849	Whitechapel, London	Henry Myers	Elizabeth Barnett		Whitechapel, London	
10456	Myers	Lewis (Louis) Michael	1840	Aldgate, London	Michael Myers	Jane Isaacs	Elizabeth Harris	Aldgate, London	scholar
29990	Myers	Lewis Michael	1840	Whitechapel, London	Michael Myers	Elizabeth (Betsy) Jacobs	Elizabeth Harris	Whitechapel, London	
11216	Myers	Loue A	1843	Middlesex, London	Levy Myers	Hannah (?)		Aldgate, London	scholar
31114	Myers	Louis	1820	?, Poland [?, Prussia]				Bristol	wine + tea merchant
12124	Myers	Louis	1844	Whitechapel, London	Michael Myers	Esther (?)		Spitalfields, London	scholar
10875	Myers	Louisa	1801	Spitalfields, London	Israel Myers	(?Rebecca Levy)		Spitalfields, London	house keeper
10161	Myers	Louisa	1835	?London	Abraham Myers		Barnet (Baruh) Costa	Aldgate, London	dressmaker
8789	Myers	Louisa	1844	Aldgate, London	John (Jacob) Myers	Harriet Levy		Aldgate, London	
22012	Myers	Louisa	1847	Aldgate, London	Israel Myers	Hannah Hart		Whitechapel, London	scholar
4815	Myers	Louisa	1849	Birmingham	(?) Myers	Rebecca (?)		Birmingham	
31109	Myers	Lydia	1819	Preston, Lancashire	(?)		Henry Myers	Bristol	
4792	Myers	Mala (Matilda)	1849	Birmingham	Gabriel Myers	Maria (?)	Jacob Reuben Grant	Birmingham	
8717	Myers	Marcus	1833	?, London				Aldgate, London	silk mercer
22292	Myers	Maria	1812	Birmingham	(?)		(?) Myers	Whitechapel, London	carpet bag maker
4789	Myers	Maria	1817	?, London			Gabriel Myers	Birmingham	
3680	Myers	Maria	1823	Aldgate, London	Mordecai Harris	Sarah Lyon (Lyons)	Hyam Myers	Spitalfields, London	
19377	Myers	Maria	1827	Whitechapel, London	Lazarus Samson		Michael Henry Myers	Camberwell, London	
13253	Myers	Maria	1834	Whitechapel, London	David Myers	Harriet (?)		Spitalfields, London	tailoress
19669	Myers	Marian (Emma)	1815	Middlesex, London	Avi Ezrie Selig		Abraham Nathan Myers	Aldgate, London	
19492	Myers	Mark	1801	?, London				Covent Garden, London	violin maker
6086	Myers	Mark (Mordecai)	1849	Spitalfields, London	Hyam Myers	Maria Harris	Hannah Jacobs	Spitalfields, London	
3141	Myers	Marks	1805	?, Poland [?, Prussia]			Wilhelmina (?)	Sunderland, Co Durham	jeweller
15779	Myers	Martha	1836	Spitalfields, London	(?) Myers			Aldgate, London	apprentice servant
28907	Myers	Mary	1781	Aldgate, London	(?)		(?) Myers	Spitalfields, London	formerly nurse
11122	Myers	Mary	1791	Spitalfields, London	(?)		Emanuel Myers	Aldgate, London	
26187	Myers	Mary	1829	?, London	(?)		Michael Myers	Aldgate, London	cook
14968	Myers	Mary	1838	Middlesex, London	(?) Myers			Bethnal Green, London	boarding school pupil
12029	Myers	Mary	1842	?, Poland [?, Prussia]	Abraham Myers	Sarah (?)		Whitechapel, London	

ID	surname	given names	born	birthplace	father	mother	spouse 1	1851 residence	1851 occupation
2735	Myers	Mary	1844	Aldgate, London	Isaac Michael Myers	Caroline Aarons		Aldgate, London	
16272	Myers	Mary	1846	Whitechapel, London	Henry Myers	Elizabeth Barnett		Whitechapel, London	
19380	Myers	Mary	1848	Aldgate, London	Michael Henry Myers	Maria Samson	David Saul Levy	Camberwell, London	
28403	Myers	Mary	1850	Spitalfields, London	Joseph Myers	Phoebe Levy		Spitalfields, London	
11110	Myers	Mary	1809	Middlesex, London	Aharon Simmons		Abraham Myers	Aldgate, London	
8670	Myers	Mary Ann	1831	Aldgate, London	Lawrence Myers	(?)		Bloomsbury, London	at home
8672	Myers	Matilda	1833	Clerkenwell, London	Lawrence Myers	(?)	(?)	Bloomsbury, London	at home
20382	Myers	Matilda	1833	Southwark, London	Benjamin Joel Myers	Isabella (?)	Henry Simon Ansell	Fitzrovia, London	
30597	Myers	Matilda	1842	Aldgate, London	Moses Henry Myers	Sarah Abraham		Aldgate, London	
12030	Myers	Matilda	1846	?, Poland [?, Prussia]	Abraham Myers	Sarah (?)		Whitechapel, London	
4818	Myers	Maurice	1827	Birmingham	Myer Myers	Rebecca (?)	Matilda (?)	Birmingham	steel pen maker
6157	Myers	Maurice	1834	Aldgate, London	Lawrence Myers		Miriam van Noorden	Aldgate, London	clerk
20384	Myers	Maurie	1841	Fitzrovia, London	Benjamin Joel Myers	Isabella (?)		Fitzrovia, London	
4810	Myers	Maxe	1824	?, Poland				Birmingham	glazier
24795	Myers	Mendlewitz	1787	?, Poland [?, Prussia]	Aharon		Abigail Nathan	Elephant & Castle, London	general dealer
27245	Myers	Michael	1775	?, London	Asher Anshel (Enzly) Katsov		Hannah Israel	Aldgate, London	gentleman
18190	Myers	Michael	1781	Middlesex, London			(?)	Mile End, London	glass cutter
12118	Myers	Michael	1812	Whitechapel, London	Aharon Halevi		Esther (?)	Spitalfields, London	general dealer
10454	Myers	Michael	1816	Aldgate, London	Yehuda		Jane Isaacs	Aldgate, London	clothier
23422	Myers	Michael	1821	?, London	Naphtali Myers	Esther Nathan		Aldgate, London	general dealer
26186	Myers	Michael	1823	?, London			Mary (?)	Aldgate, London	licensed hawker
6631	Myers	Michael	1826	Aldgate, London	Isaac Myers	Hannah Benjamin		Spitalfields, London	shoe maker
28495	Myers	Michael	1831	Spitalfields, London	(?) Myers	Elizabeth (?)		Spitalfields, London	jobber
11312	Myers	Michael	1834	Aldgate, London	Isaac Myers	Rosetta (?)		Aldgate, London	cigar maker
19374	Myers	Michael Henry	1823	Southwark, London	Raphael (Ralph) Myers	Elizabeth (Beila) Benjamin	Maria Samson	Camberwell, London	auctioneer
13261	Myers	Micheal	1848	Spitalfields, London	Moses Myers	Sarah (?)		Spitalfields, London	scholar
4785	Myers	Miriam	1827	Birmingham	Gedaliah Myers	Elizabeth (?)		Birmingham	professor of music
8256	Myers	Miriam	1841	Grimsby, Lincolnshire	Ezra Myers	Rebecca (?)	Henry Davis Marks	Newark, Lincolnshire	
31110	Myers	Miriam	1842	St Giles, London	Henry Myers	Lydia (?)		Bristol	scholar
7738	Myers	Miriam Deborah	1840	Aldgate, London	Moses Henry Myers	Sarah Abraham		Aldgate, London	
22947	Myers	Morris	1779	Aldgate, London			Hannah (?)	Wapping, London	clothes shop keeper
9466	Myers	Morris	1801	Aldgate, London	Simon Myers		Sarah Fuller	Aldgate, London	rag merchant + Government contractor
25628	Myers	Morris	1810	?			(?)	Dublin, Ireland	
11310	Myers	Morris	1825	Aldgate, London	Isaac Myers	Rosetta (?)		Aldgate, London	general dealer
16271	Myers	Morris	1843	Whitechapel, London	Henry Myers	Elizabeth Barnett		Whitechapel, London	
4786	Myers	Moseley	1830	Birmingham	Gedaliah Myers	Elizabeth (?)	Rebecca Deborah Brasch	Birmingham	cigar manufacturer
13255	Myers	Moses	1815	Aldgate, London	Yehuda		Sarah (?)	Spitalfields, London	clothes dealer
6843	Myers	Moses	1842	Amsterdam, Holland	(?) Myers	Sarah (?)		Spitalfields, London	scholar
8950	Myers	Moses	1847	?, Holland	(?) Myers			Aldgate, London	
8748	Myers	Moses (Morris Moss)	1838	Bermondsey, London	Solomon Myers	Sarah (?)	Leah Raphael	Aldgate, London	
11033	Myers	Moses (Morris)	1814	Middlesex, London	Michael Myers		Phoebe Simmons	Aldgate, London	general dealer
7736	Myers	Moses Henry	1803	?, London	Chanov		Sarah Abraham	Aldgate, London	professor of Hebrew

ID	surname	given names	born	birthplace	father	mother	spouse 1	1851 residence	1851 occupation
29176	Myers	Moss	1811	Amsterdam, Holland			Eva (?)	Whitechapel, London	boarding and lodging house
4820	Myers	Myer	1798	?, Germany			Rebecca (?)	Birmingham	jeweller + silversmith
9835	Myers	Myer	1802	?, London			Rebecca Jacobs	Whitechapel, London	commission agent
28110	Myers	Myer	1817	?, Holland	(?) Myers	Fanny (?)		Spitalfields, London	jeweller
11401	Myers	Myer	1828	Amsterdam, Holland				Aldgate, London	cigar maker
6633	Myers	Myer	1831	Shoreditch, London	Isaac Myers	Hannah Benjamin	Esther Lyons	Spitalfields, London	watch maker
1233	Myers	Myer	1836	Plymouth, Devon	Israel Myers	Zibiah Hyman		Plymouth, Devon	scholar
21183	Myers	Myer	1841	Aldgate, London	Isaac Myers	Rebecca (?)		Aldgate, London	
22011	Myers	Myer	1844	Whitechapel, London	Israel Myers	Hannah Hart		Whitechapel, London	scholar
30601	Myers	Myer H	1836	Aldgate, London	Moses Henry Myers	Sarah Abraham	Rachel D'Oliveyra	Aldgate, London	
28939	Myers	Nancy (Priscilla)	1845	Whitechapel, London	Henry Myers	Sophia Symons	Moss Corper	Whitechapel, London	scholar
23419	Myers	Naphtali	1778	Amsterdam, Holland	Meir Englisher from Amsterdam		Esther Nathan	Aldgate, London	general dealer
23421	Myers	Nathan	1819	?, London	Naphtali Myers	Esther Nathan		Aldgate, London	general dealer
14895	Myers	Nathaniel	1840	Haggerston, London				Bethnal Green, London	boarding school pupil
29031	Myers	P---	1836	Greenwich, London	Abraham Myers	E--- (?)		Whitechapel, London	
2306	Myers	Peter (Philip)	1817	?, Poland			Charlotte (?)	Leeds, Yorkshire	shoemaker
13296	Myers	Pheobe	1825	Whitechapel, London	(?) Myers			Spitalfields, London	house keeper
6089	Myers	Philip	1840	Bermondsey, London	Solomon Myers	Sarah (?)	Rebecca Israel	Aldgate, London	scholar
11034	Myers	Phoebe	1814	Aldgate, London	Aaron Simmons		Samson Levy	Aldgate, London	
28398	Myers	Phoebe	1824	Whitechapel, London	Angel Levy	Maria (Miriam) Isaacs	Joseph Myers	Spitalfields, London	general dealer
30596	Myers	Phoebe	1839	Aldgate, London	Moses Henry Myers	Sarah Abraham	Moses Morris	Aldgate, London	
5973	Myers	Phoebe	1841	Spitalfields, London	Isaac Myers	Hannah Benjamin	Michael Lyons	Spitalfields, London	scholar
8788	Myers	Phoebe	1842	Aldgate, London	John (Jacob) Myers	Harriet Levy	Herman Haberer	Aldgate, London	
15766	Myers	Phoebe	1842	Soho, London	Moss Myers	(?) Abraham	Moses Morris	Soho, London	scholar
2736	Myers	Phoebe	1846	Aldgate, London	Isaac Michael Myers	Caroline Aarons	Henry van Ryn	Aldgate, London	
20383	Myers	Presilla	1836	Southwark, London	Benjamin Joel Myers	Isabella (?)		Fitzrovia, London	
4796	Myers	Rachael	1811	?, London	(?Asher Benjamin?)		Henry Myers	Birmingham	
26738	Myers	Rachael	1812	Bethnal Green, London	Abraham de Isaac Saqui	Hannah de Joseph Abendana	George Myers	Aldgate, London	
11397	Myers	Rachael	1827	Spitalfields, London	Joseph Myers	Sarah Solomons		Aldgate, London	tailoress
28125	Myers	Rachael	1827	?, London	(?)		(?) Myers	Spitalfields, London	
14715	Myers	Rachael	1831	Bethnal Green, London	Henry Myers	Elizabeth Levy		Aldgate, London	
6840	Myers	Rachael	1832	Amsterdam, Holland	(?) Myers	Sarah (?)		Spitalfields, London	tailoress
24147	Myers	Rachael	1833	Islington, London	Andrew Myers	(?)		Euston, London	
13254	Myers	Racheal	1842	Whitechapel, London	David Myers	Harriet (?)		Spitalfields, London	scholar
21947	Myers	Rachel	1795	Whitechapel, London	(?)		(?) Myers	Marylebone, London	retired clothier
6976	Myers	Rachel	1822	Aldgate, London	Isaac Barnett		Morris Myers	Aldgate, London	
5803	Myers	Rachel	1823	Newmarket, Suffolk	Joseph (Reuben) Lyon (Lyons)	Abigail Hyams	Solomon Myers	Southwark, London	
5615	Myers	Rachel	1829	Clerkenwell, London	Napthali Myers	Esther Nathan	Simeon Silverstone	Aldgate, London	tailoress
19279	Myers	Rachel	1831	Whitechapel, London	David Myers	Leah Joshua	Jacob White	Aldgate, London	
6979	Myers	Rachel	1832	Middlesex, London	Morris Isaacs		Lewis Myers	Spitalfields, London	
4814	Myers	Rachel	1848	Birmingham	(?) Myers	Rebecca (?)		Birmingham	
11218	Myers	Rachel	1851	Middlesex, London	Levy Myers	Hannah (?)		Aldgate, London	
6980	Myers	Rachel D	1838	Maldon, Essex	Daniel Myers	Julia Isaacs		Liverpool	scholar

ID	surname	given names	born	birthplace	father	mother	spouse 1	1851 residence	1851 occupation
19375	Myers	Raphael (Ralph)	1798	Southwark, London	Henry [Naftali] Myers		Elizabeth (Beila) Benjamin	Bermondsey, London	auctioneer, upholsterer + furniture dealer
22714	Myers	Rayner	1821	Spitalfields, London	Burnett Myers	Wellcome (?)		Whitechapel, London	
27581	Myers	Rebeca	1849	Middlesex, London	Lazarus Myers	Ester (?)		Spitalfields, London	
4415	Myers	Rebecca	1799	Birmingham			(?) Myers	Birmingham	
4817	Myers	Rebecca	1801	Birmingham			Myer Myers	Birmingham	jeweller + silversmith
12998	Myers	Rebecca	1802	City, London	Ephraim Samson	Hannah Myers	Reuben Myers	Bethnal Green, London	
21180	Myers	Rebecca	1817	Plymouth, Devon	(?)		Isaac Myers	Aldgate, London	
8258	Myers	Rebecca	1818	?	(?) Simon		Ezra Myers	Newark, Lincolnshire	
25567	Myers	Rebecca	1821	?, London	Benjamin Da Costa Noah	Agar de Joseph Abendanha	David Myers	Aldgate, London	
4813	Myers	Rebecca	1827	Birmingham			(?) Myers	Birmingham	clothes dealer
17246	Myers	Rebecca	1831	Aldgate, London	Isaac Myers	Leah Miranda		Aldgate, London	
16268	Myers	Rebecca	1835	Whitechapel, London	Henry Myers	Elizabeth Barnett		Whitechapel, London	
1243	Myers	Rebecca	1843	Plymouth, Devon	Israel Myers	Zibiah Hyman	Samuel Silver	Plymouth, Devon	scholar
2312	Myers	Rebecca	1848	Leeds, Yorkshire	Peter (Philip) Myers	Charlotte (?)		Leeds, Yorkshire	
4801	Myers	Rebecca Elizabeth	1844	Portsmouth, Hampshire	Jacob Myers	Juliana Aaron	Moritz Lotheim	Birmingham	
5279	Myers	Reuben	1791	City, London	Moses Myers	Rachel Levy	Rebecca Samson	Bethnal Green, London	keeper of the Jews' Burial Ground
14896	Myers	Reuben	1841	Warsaw, Poland				Bethnal Green, London	boarding school pupil
15094	Myers	Rosa	1811	Covent Garden, London	(?) Samuel		Andrew Myers	Euston, London	chorister
27580	Myers	Rose	1850	City, London	Lazarus Myers	Ester (?)		Spitalfields, London	
3772	Myers	Rosetta	1783	Aldgate, London	(?)		Jacob Myers	Spitalfields, London	nurse
11308	Myers	Rosetta	1798	Aldgate, London	(?)		Isaac Myers	Aldgate, London	
11395	Myers	Rosetta	1822	Middlesex, London	Joseph Myers	Rebecca Cohen		Aldgate, London	tailoress
24652	Myers	Rosetta	1830	Whitechapel, London	Henry Myers			Kennington, London	tailoress
12125	Myers	Rosetta	1846	Whitechapel, London	Michael Myers	Esther (?)		Spitalfields, London	scholar
2311	Myers	Rosetta	1847	Leeds, Yorkshire	Peter (Philip) Myers	Charlotte (?)		Leeds, Yorkshire	
14617	Myers	Rosetta (Rosy)	1803	Whitechapel, London	Joseph Solomons		Michael Myers	Hoxton, London	milliner
10451	Myers	Rosina	1827	Aldgate, London	(?) Myers			Aldgate, London	servant
18217	Myers	Rossetta	1838	Middlesex, London	(?) Myers			Mile End, London	scholar
27273	Myers	Samuel	1811	?, London	(?) Myers	Elizabeth (?)		Aldgate, London	clothes dealer
6551	Myers	Samuel	1814	Plymouth, Devon				Plymouth, Devon	army + navy trimming manufacturer
28511	Myers	Samuel	1826	Spitalfields, London			Eleanor (?)	Spitalfields, London	Hackney carriage driver
13912	Myers	Samuel	1829	Whitechapel, London				Manchester	salesman to tailor + draper
11396	Myers	Samuel	1832	Middlesex, London	Joseph Myers	Sarah Solomons	Leah Lyons	Aldgate, London	boot + shoe maker
28404	Myers	Samuel	1834	Spitalfields, London				Spitalfields, London	rag merchant
14622	Myers	Samuel	1835	Whitechapel, London	Michael Myers	Rosetta (Rosy) Solomons		Hoxton, London	pearl worker
28402	Myers	Samuel	1846	Spitalfields, London	Joseph Myers	Phoebe Levy		Spitalfields, London	scholar
8973	Myers	Samuel	1850	Aldgate, London	Henry Myers	Sarah Barnard		Aldgate, London	
28505	Myers	Sarah	1771	?, Holland	(?)		(?) Myers	Spitalfields, London	
11176	Myers	Sarah	1787	Middlesex, London	Meir Solomon		Levy Myers	Aldgate, London	
6839	Myers	Sarah	1804	Amsterdam, Holland	(?)		(?) Myers	Spitalfields, London	nurse
6974	Myers	Sarah	1805	Whitechapel, London	Moshe Emanuel		Hyam (Hyman) Myers	Holborn, London	

ID	surname	given names	born	birthplace	father	mother	spouse 1	1851 residence	1851 occupation
8746	Myers	Sarah	1808	Aldgate, London	(?)		Solomon Myers	Aldgate, London	
7737	Myers	Sarah	1809	Westminster, London	Victor Abraham	Rebecca Levy	Moses Henry Myers	Aldgate, London	
18184	Myers	Sarah	1811	Middlesex, London	(?)		Lewis Myers	Mile End, London	matron to house
12028	Myers	Sarah	1819	?, Poland [?, Prussia]	(?)		Abraham Myers	Whitechapel, London	
13256	Myers	Sarah	1824	Whitechapel, London	(?)		Moses Myers	Spitalfields, London	
8970	Myers	Sarah	1826	Chatham, Kent	Samuel Barnard	Louisa Benjamin	Henry Myers	Aldgate, London	parasol maker
5097	Myers	Sarah	1828	Gosport, Hampshire				Portsmouth, Hampshire	servant
20566	Myers	Sarah	1831	Spitalfields, London	Lazarus Myers	(?)		Spitalfields, London	tailoress
14620	Myers	Sarah	1832	Whitechapel, London	Michael Myers	Rosetta (Rosy) Solomons		Hoxton, London	milliner
4808	Myers	Sarah	1833	Nottingham, Nottinghamshire	(?) Myers	Leah (?)		Birmingham	cap maker
19371	Myers	Sarah	1840	Southwark, London	Raphael (Ralph) Myers	Elizabeth (Beila) Benjamin	Moss Cohen	Bermondsey, London	
16270	Myers	Sarah	1841	Whitechapel, London	Henry Myers	Elizabeth Barnett	Simon Pearl (Perle)	Whitechapel, London	
24797	Myers	Sarah	1842	Southwark, London	Mendlewitz Myers	Esther Nathan		Elephant & Castle, London	
28400	Myers	Sarah	1843	Spitalfields, London	Joseph Myers	Phoebe Levy		Spitalfields, London	scholar
6636	Myers	Sarah	1844	Spitalfields, London	Isaac Myers	Hannah Benjamin		Spitalfields, London	scholar
14718	Myers	Sarah	1846	Spitalfields, London	Henry Myers	Elizabeth Levy		Aldgate, London	
4241	Myers	Sarah	1848	Portsmouth, Hampshire	Jacob Myers	Juliana Aaron		Birmingham	
4816	Myers	Sarah	1850	Birmingham	(?) Myers	Rebecca (?)		Birmingham	
3681	Myers	Sarah	1851	Spitalfields, London	Hyam Myers	Maria Harris	Nathan Isaacs	Spitalfields, London	
22293	Myers	Saul	1834	Birmingham	(?) Myers	Maria (?)		Whitechapel, London	carpet bag maker
21284	Myers	Saul	1838	Chelmsford, Essex				Edmonton, London	boarding school pupil
22013	Myers	Simeon	1851	Whitechapel, London	Israel Myers	Hannah Hart		Whitechapel, London	
4822	Myers	Simon	1829	?, Poland				Birmingham	glazier
11399	Myers	Simon Simeon	1841	Middlesex, London	Joseph Myers	Julia Davis		Aldgate, London	scholar
8745	Myers	Solomon	1803	Aldgate, London			Sarah (?)	Aldgate, London	general dealer
8023	Myers	Solomon	1819	?, Poland [?, Prussia]	Myer Myers		Rachel Lyons	Southwark, London	watchmaker + jeweller
28111	Myers	Solomon	1821	?, Holland	(?) Myers	Fanny (?)		Spitalfields, London	musician
30148	Myers	Solomon	1824	City, London	Meir			Bloomsbury, London	surgeon dentist
16267	Myers	Solomon	1833	Whitechapel, London	Henry Myers	Elizabeth Barnett	Ann Benjamin	Whitechapel, London	
24655	Myers	Solomon	1834	Aldgate, London	Henry Myers			Kennington, London	printer
11398	Myers	Solomon	1843	Middlesex, London	Joseph Myers	Julia Davis		Aldgate, London	scholar
29991	Myers	Solomon	1843	Whitechapel, London	Michael Myers	Elizabeth (Betsy) Jacobs		Whitechapel, London	
8791	Myers	Solomon	1847	Aldgate, London	John (Jacob) Myers	Harriet Levy		Aldgate, London	
2733	Myers	Solomon Henry	1842	Aldgate, London	Isaac Michael Myers	Caroline Aarons	Mary Aarons	Aldgate, London	
28603	Myers	Sophia	1796	?, Germany	Abraham Myers			Spitalfields, London	umbrella maker
28938	Myers	Sophia	1826	Aldgate, London	Abraham Symons		Henry Myers	Whitechapel, London	
27272	Myers	Susan	1809	?, London	(?) Myers	Elizabeth (?)		Aldgate, London	clothes dealer
11242	Myers	Susan	1815	Strand, London	(?)		(?) Myers	Aldgate, London	furrier
30893	Myers	Susan	1835	Chelmsford, Essex	Wolf Myers	Hannah Samuel		Chelmsford, Essex	scholar at home
30600	Myers	Victor M	1849	Aldgate, London	Moses Henry Myers	Sarah Abraham	Rose Marks	Aldgate, London	
30890	Myers	Walter	1829	Chelmsford, Essex	Wolf Myers	Hannah Samuel		Chelmsford, Essex	woollen draper masterempl 2
22713	Myers	Wellcome	1792	Aldgate, London	(?)		Burnett Myers	Whitechapel, London	
14894	Myers	William	1811	Darlington, Co Durham			Susannah (?)	Bethnal Green, London	schoolmaster

ID	surname	given names	born	birthplace	father	mother	spouse 1	1851 residence	1851 occupation
17149	Myers	Wolf	1763	?, Poland [?, Prussia]			(?)	Newcastle Upon Tyne	jeweller + optician (pauper)
3188	Myers	Wolf	1842	Chelmsford, Essex	Wolf Myers	Hannah Samuel	Esther (Eugenie) Moses	Chelmsford, Essex	scholar at home
27229	Myers	Woolf	1791	?, Germany			(?)	Aldgate, London	tailor
17737	Myers	Woolf	1824	?, Poland [?, Prussia]			Leah Phillips	Aldgate, London	cap maker
1231	Myers	Zibiah	1807	Falmouth, Cornwall	Moses Hyman	Sarah (Sally) Levy (Levi)	Israel Myers	Plymouth, Devon	
12900	Myers (Mayers)	Henry	1837	Middlesex, London	Moses Myers (Mayers)	Elizabeth (?)		Marylebone, London	cigar maker
12901	Myers (Mayers)	Joseph	1842	Middlesex, London	Moses Myers (Mayers)	Elizabeth (?)		Marylebone, London	scholar
7735	Myers (Mayers)	Moses	1813	Middlesex, London			Elizabeth (?)	Marylebone, London	jeweller + curiosity dealer
12899	Myers (Mayers)	Ralph	1835	Middlesex, London	Moses Myers (Mayers)	Elizabeth (?)		Marylebone, London	cigar maker
11406	Myers (Mayers)	Rosa	1829	Middlesex, London	Raphael Myers			Aldgate, London	tailoress
11628	Myers (Miers)	Barnett	1839	Spitalfields, London	Michael Myers (Miers)	Sarah (?)		Aldgate, London	cigar boy
11626	Myers (Miers)	Hyman	1829	Spitalfields, London	Michael Myers (Miers)	Sarah (?)		Aldgate, London	cigar maker
11627	Myers (Miers)	Jane	1831	Spitalfields, London	Michael Myers (Miers)	Sarah (?)	Michael Mendoza	Aldgate, London	general dealer
11631	Myers (Miers)	Lewis	1849	Aldgate, London	Michael Myers (Miers)	Sarah (?)		Aldgate, London	
6082	Myers (Miers)	Lipman	1801	?, London	Mordecai Myers		Rebecca Mordecai	City, London	general dealer
21488	Myers (Miers)	Mark (Mordecai)	1830	Aldgate, London	Lipman Myers (Miers)	Rebecca Mordecai		Aldgate, London	dealer
11624	Myers (Miers)	Michael	1806	Aldgate, London			Sarah (?)	Aldgate, London	general dealer
6083	Myers (Miers)	Moses	1834	Aldgate, London	Lipman Myers (Miers)	Rebecca Mordecai	?	City, London	dealer
21487	Myers (Miers)	Rebecca	1800	Aldgate, London	(?) Mordecai		Lipman Myers (Miers)	Aldgate, London	
11630	Myers (Miers)	Samuel	1843	Spitalfields, London	Michael Myers (Miers)	Sarah (?)		Aldgate, London	scholar
11625	Myers (Miers)	Sarah	1807	Newcastle Upon Tyne	(?)		Michael Myers (Miers)	Aldgate, London	general dealer
8073	Myers (Miers)	Woolf	1841	Spitalfields, London	Michael Myers (Miers)	Sarah (?)	Esther Duran	Aldgate, London	cigar boy
14897	Myerson	Edward John	1837	Holborn, London				Bethnal Green, London	boarding school pupil
20661	Naeman	Davis	1833	?, Poland [?, Prussia]				Spitalfields, London	shoemaker
11377	Naphtali	Catharine	1845	Aldgate, London	Morris Naphtali	Maria Levy		Aldgate, London	scholar
11379	Naphtali	Elizabeth	1850	Aldgate, London	Morris Naphtali	Maria Levy		Aldgate, London	
28935	Naphtali	Fanny	1824	Soho, London	(?)		Solomon Naphtali	Whitechapel, London	commission dealer in jewellery
11376	Naphtali	Hannah	1843	Aldgate, London	Morris Naphtali	Maria Levy		Aldgate, London	scholar
13464	Naphtali	Israel	1800	?, Latvia [?, Courland]			Grace (?)	Manchester	Jewish missionary
28937	Naphtali	Joseph	1849	Aldgate, London	Solomon Napthali	Fanny (?)		Whitechapel, London	
28936	Naphtali	Julia	1847	Aldgate, London	Solomon Napthali	Fanny (?)		Whitechapel, London	
11375	Naphtali	Maria	1809	Aldgate, London	(?) Levy		Morris Naphtali	Aldgate, London	
11374	Naphtali	Morris	1806	Whitechapel, London			Maria Levy	Aldgate, London	professor of singing
11378	Naphtali	Sarah	1847	Aldgate, London	Morris Naphtali	Maria Levy		Aldgate, London	scholar
28934	Naphtali	Solomon	1815	Whitechapel, London	Joseph Napthali	Leah (?)	Fanny (?)	Whitechapel, London	commission dealer in jewellery
25900	Naphthali	Leah	1781	Aldgate, London	(?)		Joseph Naphthali	Aldgate, London	
5885	Natali	Alfred (Elias) J	1850	City, London	David Natali	Caroline Levy		Aldgate, London	
5886	Natali	Andrew Isaac	1848	City, London	David Natali	Caroline Levy	Rosetta Phillips	Aldgate, London	
5881	Natali	Caroline	1813	Stratford, London	Hyman (Haim) Levy		David Natali	Aldgate, London	
5889	Natali	Clara Frances	1845	City, London	David Natali	Caroline Levy		Aldgate, London	
5880	Natali	David	1812	Middlesex, London	Phineas Natali	Sarah Coshman	Caroline Levy	Aldgate, London	importer + dealer in foreign beads

ID	surname	given names	born	birthplace	father	mother	spouse 1	1851 residence	1851 occupation
16475	Natali	Elizabeth	1795	Whitechapel, London	Jacob Friedberg		Jacob Natali	Mile End, London	
5879	Natali	Elizabeth	1846	Aldgate, London	David Natali	Caroline levy	Emanuel Magnus	Aldgate, London	
10194	Natali	Elkanah	1839	City, London	David Natali	Caroline Levy		Aldgate, London	
5884	Natali	Hyman Henry	1843	City, London	David Natali	Caroline Levy		Aldgate, London	
10195	Natali	Isaac	1804	Middlesex, London	Phineas Natali	Sarah Coshman		Aldgate, London	
16474	Natali	Jacob	1782	Whitechapel, London	Isaac de Nathan Abraham Natali	Rachel Israel	Elizabeth Friedberg	Mile End, London	commission agent
5888	Natali	Julia	1841	City, London	David Natali	Caroline Levy	David Bernstein	Aldgate, London	
5882	Natali	Nathan Phineas	1838	City, London	David Natali	Caroline Levy		Aldgate, London	
5883	Natali	Rose	1849	City, London	David Natali	Caroline Levy		Aldgate, London	
5890	Natali	Sarah	1837	City, London	David Natali	Caroline Levy	Joseph Magnus	Aldgate, London	
22273	Nathan	?	1825	?			Mary (?)	Whitechapel, London	
29562	Nathan	A---	1826	Whitechapel, London	Samuel Nathan	R--- (?)		Whitechapel, London	general dealer
1371	Nathan	Aaron	1789	Plymouth, Devon	Yechiel Nathan		Mary (Maria) Mosely	Plymouth, Devon	police superintendent
1376	Nathan	Abigail	1817	Plymouth, Devon	Aaron Nathan	Mary (?)		Plymouth, Devon	boot + shoe binder
16097	Nathan	Abigail	1825	Holborn, London	(?) Nathan			Whitechapel, London	
5244	Nathan	Abigail	1848	Aldgate, London	Solomon Nathan	Hannah Abrahams	Abraham Lewis Jacobs	Aldgate, London	
20279	Nathan	Abigail	1849	Whitechapel, London	Lewis Nathan	Regina (Rachael) Kisch		Wapping, London	
18927	Nathan	Abraham	1813	Aldgate, London	(?) Nathan	Amelia (?)		Aldgate, London	furniture broker
28475	Nathan	Abraham	1818	Aldgate, London	L--- Nathan		Frances (Fanny) Abrahams	Spitalfields, London	general dealer
15372	Nathan	Abraham	1820	Lambeth, London			Mary (?)	Waterloo, London	labourer + dustman
19882	Nathan	Abraham	1820	?, Holland	David Nathan		Rose Cohen	Hartlepool, Co Durham	general dealer
16680	Nathan	Abraham	1825	Aldgate, London	David Nathan	Deborah Saltiel		Stepney, London	cigar maker
23347	Nathan	Abraham	1832	Lambeth, London	Henry Nathan	Catherine Michael	Annie (?)	Piccadilly, London	
22540	Nathan	Abraham	1833	Aldgate, London	(?) Nathan	Mary Ann (?)		Whitechapel, London	cigar maker
22776	Nathan	Abraham	1842	Shoreditch, London	Nathaniel Nathan	Eve Barnett		Whitechapel, London	scholar
6922	Nathan	Abraham	1843	Spitalfields, London	Henry Nathan	Sarah Costa	Katherine Lyons	Spitalfields, London	scholar
20031	Nathan	Abraham	1844	Spitalfields, London	Joseph Nathan	Marianne (?)		Aldgate, London	
28479	Nathan	Abraham	1849	Spitalfields, London	Abraham Nathan	Frances (Fanny) Abrahams		Spitalfields, London	
12785	Nathan	Abraham	1850	Spitalfields, London	Gewilder Nathan	Esther (?)		Spitalfields, London	cigar maker
17258	Nathan	Adelaide	1838	Aldgate, London	John Nathan	Rebecca (?Lyon)		Aldgate, London	scholar
20495	Nathan	Adelaide	1845	Nottingham, Nottinghamshire	Nathan (Nathaniel) Nathan	Louisa Jacobs	Lewis Jacobs	Strand, London	
12907	Nathan	Adolphus	1843	Clerkenwell, London	Mayer Moses Nathan	Sarina Levi		Clerkenwell, London	scholar at home
5635	Nathan	Alexander	1847	Whitechapel, London	Henry Nathan	Amelia Ellis		Whitechapel, London	scholar at home
5636	Nathan	Alfred	1838	?Whitechapel, London	Henry Nathan	Amelia Ellis	Caroline Michael	Whitechapel, London	
16019	Nathan	Alfred	1848	Middlesex, London	(?) Nathan	(?) Jacobs		Kensington, London	scholar at home
20049	Nathan	Alfred	1849	Covent Garden, London	Isaac John Nathan	Anna (?)		Covent Garden, London	
15749	Nathan	Ame	1839	Middlesex, London	Lewis (Louis) Nathan	Sophia Isaacs		Aldgate, London	scholar
18926	Nathan	Amelia	1794	Aldgate, London	(?)		(?) Nathan	Aldgate, London	clothes dealer
13902	Nathan	Amelia	1815	Manchester	Jacob Nathan	Jane (?)		Manchester	
5632	Nathan	Amelia	1821	Wapping, London	Alexander Ellis	Frances (?)	Henry Nathan	Whitechapel, London	
4824	Nathan	Ann	1815	Birmingham			Nathan Nathan	Birmingham	
21789	Nathan	Ann	1819	Aldgate, London	(?)		Hyam Nathan	Aldgate, London	
16096	Nathan	Ann	1824	Holborn, London	(?) Nathan			Whitechapel, London	
27713	Nathan	Ann	1845	Birmingham	Michael Nathan	Elizabeth Benjamin		Spitalfields, London	scholar
20041	Nathan	Anna	1815	Middlesex, London	(?)		Isaac John Nathan	Covent Garden, London	wife of fancy dress maker

ID	surname	given names	born	birthplace	father	mother	spouse 1	1851 residence	1851 occupation
25006	Nathan	Anne Elizabeth	1828	Bath	(?) Nathan			Holborn, London	coffee + chop house
14334	Nathan	Asher	1814	Manchester				Manchester	watch maker
22778	Nathan	Barnard	1846	Whitechapel, London	Nathaniel Nathan	Eve Barnett		Whitechapel, London	
12308	Nathan	Barnet	1784	?, London			Julia (?)	Dover, Kent	glass, china + earthenware dealer
28889	Nathan	Barnet Davis	1810	Emden, Hanover, Germany	Natan		Matilda (?)	Spitalfields, London	chiropodist
13915	Nathan	Barnett	1834	Dover, Kent				Manchester	clerk to tailor + draper
20563	Nathan	Benjamin	1827	Aldgate, London	Simon Nathan	Sarah Elias		Aldgate, London	cigar dealer
12915	Nathan	Benjamin	1841	Aldgate, London	Samuel Nathan	Rebecca Cohen		Spitalfields, London	scholar
27714	Nathan	Benjamin	1846	Birmingham	Michael Nathan	Elizabeth Benjamin		Spitalfields, London	scholar
4019	Nathan	Benjamin	1848	Portsmouth, Hampshire	Benjamin Nathan	Kate Hart		Portsmouth, Hampshire	
29700	Nathan	Benjamin	1850	?Aldgate, London	Michael Nathan	Elizabeth (?)		Aldgate, London	
20498	Nathan	Betsy (Elizabeth)	1850	Strand, London	Nathan (Nathaniel) Nathan	Louisa Jacobs		Strand, London	
24095	Nathan	Caroline	1822	City, London	Solomon Solomon		Solomon Nathan	Bloomsbury, London	upholsterer
6897	Nathan	Caroline	1828	Paddington, London	(?)		Emanuel Nathan	Spitalfields, London	
27715	Nathan	Casper Charles	1847	Birmingham	Michael Nathan	Elizabeth Benjamin		Spitalfields, London	scholar
10301	Nathan	Catharine	1843	Spitalfields, London	Lewis (Louis) Nathan	Hannah Cohen		Spitalfields, London	waistcoat maker
23901	Nathan	Catherina	1797	Plymouth, Devon	(?)		David Nathan	Westminster, London	
29701	Nathan	Catherine	1791	Middlesex, London	(?)		(?) Nathan	Aldgate, London	upholsteress
23346	Nathan	Catherine	1801	Sheerness, Kent	Jonas Michael	Rebecca Russell	Henry Nathan	Piccadilly, London	
13306	Nathan	Catherine	1833	Southwark, London	(?) Nathan			Spitalfields, London	servant
17256	Nathan	Catherine	1834	Aldgate, London	John Nathan	Rebecca (?Lyon)		Aldgate, London	
12916	Nathan	Catherine	1842	Spitalfields, London	Samuel Nathan	Rebecca Cohen		Spitalfields, London	scholar
5245	Nathan	Catherine	1850	Aldgate, London	Solomon Nathan	Hannah Abrahams	Edward Jacob Morris	Aldgate, London	
12843	Nathan	Charles	1828	Stepney, London	Henry Nathan	Sarah (?)		Whitechapel, London	draper assistant
24912	Nathan	Charles	1850	Bethnal Green, London	Israel Nathan	Isabella (Beila) Levi		Bethnal Green, London	
20444	Nathan	Charles Ellis	1832	Whitechapel, London	Phineas Nathan	Rachel (?)		Bloomsbury, London	assisting in wholesale jewellery + watch manufacturing business
13903	Nathan	Charlotte	1819	Manchester	Jacob Nathan	Jane (?)		Manchester	
24813	Nathan	Charlotte	1845	Southwark, London	David Nathan	Louisa East	William Van Dantzig	Elephant & Castle, London	
11483	Nathan	Clara	1817	Whitechapel, London	Isaac Lazarus		Nathan Nathan	Aldgate, London	
20497	Nathan	Clara	1847	Strand, London	Nathan (Nathaniel) Nathan	Louisa Jacobs	Isaac Kauffman	Strand, London	
30257	Nathan	Clara	1851	Covent Garden, London	Isaac John Nathan	Anna (?)		Covent Garden, London	
6997	Nathan	Clare Walter	1816	Finsbury, London	Walter (Falk) Nathan	Sophia Friedberg	Samuel Lindo	Bloomsbury, London	
10302	Nathan	Cosman	1846	Spitalfields, London	Lewis (Louis) Nathan	Hannah Cohen		Spitalfields, London	at home
23900	Nathan	David	1797	Plymouth, Devon			Catherina (?)	Westminster, London	general dealer
16615	Nathan	David	1801	Coventry, Warwickshire			Esther Levi	Liverpool	traveller + general dealer
16678	Nathan	David	1803	Aldgate, London	Abraham Nathan		Deborah Saltiel	Stepney, London	collector
30875	Nathan	David	1803	?, Poland			Mary (?)	Canterbury, Kent	furniture broker
24808	Nathan	David	1811	Southwark, London			Louisa East	Elephant & Castle, London	broker
12904	Nathan	David	1839	Aldgate, London	Mayer Moses Nathan	Sarina Levi		Clerkenwell, London	scholar
17380	Nathan	David	1843	Whitechapel, London	Samuel Nathan	Maria (?)		Whitechapel, London	scholar

ID	surname	given names	born	birthplace	father	mother	spouse 1	1851 residence	1851 occupation
27216	Nathan	David Moses	1839	Wapping, London	Moses Nathan	Mary Solomons	Ann Hart	Wapping, London	
16679	Nathan	Deborah	1805	Aldgate, London	Isaac Saltiel	Hannah de Abraham Moses	David Nathan	Stepney, London	
21767	Nathan	Deborah	1835	Whitechapel, London	Joseph Nathan	Elizabeth (?)	Joseph Myers	Aldgate, London	waistcoat maker
28891	Nathan	Deborah	1836	Spitalfields, London	Barnet Davis Nathan	Matilda (?)		Spitalfields, London	tailoress
11820	Nathan	Dinah	1785	Wapping, London	Eliezer Moses		Nathaniel Nathan	Whitechapel, London	retired clothes dealer
12313	Nathan	Dinah	1835	Dover, Kent	Barnet Nathan	Julia (?)	Nathaniel Hart	Dover, Kent	
5241	Nathan	Dinah	1842	Aldgate, London	Solomon Nathan	Hannah Abrahams	Bennet Cassel (Casril)	Aldgate, London	
29572	Nathan	E---	1828	?Whitechapel, London	(?)		Nathan Nathan	Whitechapel, London	dressmaker
10049	Nathan	Edward	1802	Lambeth, London			Esther Barnard	Southwark, London	dealer in ironmongery, tinware, boots + shoes
4782	Nathan	Edward	1823	Stepney, London			Jane (?)	Whitechapel, London	cigar maker
23488	Nathan	Edward	1832	Liverpool	Philip Nathan	Rosina Solomon Nathan		Liverpool	watchmaker
20396	Nathan	Edward Ezekiel	1802	Piccadilly, London	Jacob Hyam Nathan	Polly Isaacs	Rachel Davis	Spitalfields, London	slopseller
14065	Nathan	Elias	1810	Manchester			Mary (?)	Manchester	optician + jeweller empl 1
1389	Nathan	Elias	1819	Plymouth, Devon	Aaron Nathan	Mary (?)	(?)	Plymouth, Devon	cordwainer
24090	Nathan	Eliza	1821	Whitechapel, London	Nathaniel Nathan			Bloomsbury, London	
20484	Nathan	Eliza	1822	?Lambeth, London	(?)		Lewis Jacob Nathan	Soho, London	
13904	Nathan	Eliza	1823	Manchester	Jacob Nathan	Jane (?)		Manchester	
17201	Nathan	Eliza	1833	Whitechapel, London	Philip Joseph Nathan	Esther Lear		Whitechapel, London	
15073	Nathan	Eliza	1847	Whitechapel, London	James Nathan	Mary (?)		Bethnal Green, London	scholar
22915	Nathan	Elizabeth	1781	Whitechapel, London	Wolf Haltsman		Joseph Nathan	Wapping, London	dealer in clothes
14254	Nathan	Elizabeth	1791	?, Ireland	(?)		Lewis Nathan	Manchester	
21764	Nathan	Elizabeth	1791	Whitechapel, London	(?)		Joseph Nathan	Aldgate, London	greengrocer
29223	Nathan	Elizabeth	1795	City, London	(?)		Soesman Nathan	Whitechapel, London	
22847	Nathan	Elizabeth	1812	Ipswich, Suffolk	(?)		Morris Nathan	Whitechapel, London	governess of a dame school
27711	Nathan	Elizabeth	1815	Aldgate, London	(?) Benjamin		Michael Nathan	Spitalfields, London	tailoress
29698	Nathan	Elizabeth	1825	Middlesex, London	(?)		Michael Nathan	Aldgate, London	
29225	Nathan	Elizabeth	1828	Covent Garden, London	Soesman Nathan	Elizabeth (?)		Whitechapel, London	cap maker
24905	Nathan	Elizabeth	1830	Whitechapel, London	Israel Nathan	Isabella (Beila) Levi		Bethnal Green, London	
17200	Nathan	Elizabeth	1835	Spitalfields, London	Philip Joseph Nathan	Esther Lear		Whitechapel, London	
11484	Nathan	Elizabeth	1838	Whitechapel, London	Nathan Nathan	Clara Lazarus		Aldgate, London	
20400	Nathan	Elizabeth	1838	Spitalfields, London	Edward Ezekiel Nathan	Rachel Davis		Spitalfields, London	scholar
28477	Nathan	Elizabeth	1842	Spitalfields, London	Abraham Nathan	Frances (Fanny) Abrahams		Spitalfields, London	
20048	Nathan	Elizabeth	1846	Covent Garden, London	Isaac John Nathan	Anna (?)		Covent Garden, London	daughter of fancy dress maker
20415	Nathan	Elizabeth	1846	Strand, London	Lawrence Isaac Nathan	Julia Abraham (Abrahams)		Strand, London	scholar
17366	Nathan	Elizabeth	1848	Spitalfields, London	Emanuel Nathan	Julia (?)		Spitalfields, London	
22779	Nathan	Elizabeth	1848	Whitechapel, London	Nathaniel Nathan	Eve Barnett		Whitechapel, London	
15074	Nathan	Elizabeth	1849	Whitechapel, London	James Nathan	Mary (?)		Bethnal Green, London	scholar
22872	Nathan	Elizabeth	1850	Whitechapel, London	Henry Nathan	Jane (?)		Whitechapel, London	
16281	Nathan	Elizabeth (Betsy)	1771	Amsterdam, Holland	Jacob Isaacs		Isaac Barber	Spitalfields, London	dealer
20420	Nathan	Elizabeth (Lizzie)	1837	Middlesex, London	Morris Nathan	Louisa (Leah) Collins	Lewis Saunders	Marylebone, London	
17259	Nathan	Elizabeth (Lizzie)	1841	Aldgate, London	John Nathan	Rebecca (?Lyon)	Philip Druiff	Aldgate, London	scholar

ID	surname	given names	born	birthplace	father	mother	spouse 1	1851 residence	1851 occupation
30282	Nathan	Elizabeth Sarah	1835	Marylebone, London	Louis Nathan	Rosetta (?)		Soho, London	
23899	Nathan	Ellen	1837	Westminster, London	Isaac Nathan	(?)	Samuel Levy	Westminster, London	
6550	Nathan	Ellen	1847	Plymouth, Devon				?Plymouth, Devon	
3780	Nathan	Ellenor (Eleanor)	1801	Spitalfields, London	Meir Davis		Mark (Mordecai) Nathan	Spitalfields, London	
23115	Nathan	Emanuel	1778	?, London				City, London	black lead pencil maker
17362	Nathan	Emanuel	1815	Aldgate, London			Julia (?)	Spitalfields, London	engraver
28771	Nathan	Emanuel	1818	Middlesex, London	Henry Nathan	Catherine Michael	Ada Levenu	Piccadilly, London	coffee house and brothel keeper
6896	Nathan	Emanuel	1826	Spitalfields, London	Mordecai		Caroline (?)	Spitalfields, London	general dealer
20441	Nathan	Emma	1824	Whitechapel, London	Phineas Nathan	Rachel (?)	Henry Heap	Bloomsbury, London	
18612	Nathan	Emma Eliza	1850	Whitechapel, London	Edward Nathan	Jane (?)		Whitechapel, London	
12908	Nathan	Ernest	1845	Clerkenwell, London	Mayer Moses Nathan	Sarina Levi		Clerkenwell, London	scholar at home
20564	Nathan	Ester	1811	Lambeth, London	(?)		Samuel Nathan	Aldgate, London	general dealer
338	Nathan	Esther	1795	Aldgate, London			Israel Nathan	Aldgate, London	
16616	Nathan	Esther	1800	Birmingham	(?) Levi		David Nathan	Liverpool	traveller + general dealer
17198	Nathan	Esther	1800	Spitalfields, London	Isaac Lear	(?Ann Magnus)	Philip Joseph Nahan	Whitechapel, London	
11412	Nathan	Esther	1804	Rotherhithe, London	(?) Nathan		John (Jacob) Nathan	Aldgate, London	
28237	Nathan	Esther	1817	Middlesex, London	(?)		(?) Nathan	Spitalfields, London	
1377	Nathan	Esther	1821	Plymouth, Devon	Aaron Nathan	Mary (?)		Plymouth, Devon	lace maker
12784	Nathan	Esther	1827	Amsterdam, Holland	(?)		Gewilder Nathan	Spitalfields, London	
23350	Nathan	Esther	1838	Middlesex, London	Henry Nathan	Catherine Michael		Piccadilly, London	
24908	Nathan	Esther	1840	Waterloo, London	Israel Nathan	Isabella (Beila) Levi		Bethnal Green, London	
11486	Nathan	Esther	1842	Aldgate, London	Nathan Nathan	Clara Lazarus		Aldgate, London	
16685	Nathan	Esther	1842	Aldgate, London	David Nathan	Deborah Saltiel		Stepney, London	scholar
5243	Nathan	Esther	1846	Aldgate, London	Solomon Nathan	Hannah Abrahams	Charles Morris	Aldgate, London	
28896	Nathan	Esther	1849	Spitalfields, London	Barnet Davis Nathan	Matilda (?)		Spitalfields, London	
22775	Nathan	Eve	1821	Westminster, London	Abraham Barnett	Sophia (?)	Nathaniel Nathan	Whitechapel, London	
29226	Nathan	Eve	1830	Covent Garden, London	Soesman Nathan	Elizabeth (?)		Whitechapel, London	artificial flower maker
13305	Nathan	Eve	1851	Whitechapel, London	(?) Nathan	Rosa (?)		Spitalfields, London	
16617	Nathan	Ezekeal	1827	Birmingham	David Nathan	Esther Levi		Liverpool	watchmaker jobber
6548	Nathan	Ezra	1819	Plymouth, Devon				?Plymouth, Devon	
24964	Nathan	F---	1839	Aldgate, London	N--- Nathan	R--- (?)		Haggerston, London	
27456	Nathan	F---	1849	Aldgate, London	Nathaniel Levy Nathan	M--- (?)		Aldgate, London	
13073	Nathan	Fanny	1793	Poole, Dorset	Joshua Solomon		Jacob Hyam Nathan	Soho, London	
20413	Nathan	Fanny	1832	Southwark, London	Samuel Nathan	Hannah (?)	Benjamin Solomon	Elephant & Castle, London	crochet worker
26965	Nathan	Fanny	1832	Aldgate, London	(?) Nathan			Aldgate, London	tailoress
30878	Nathan	Fanny	1839	Canterbury, Kent	David Nathan	Mary (?)		Canterbury, Kent	
11416	Nathan	Fanny (Frances)	1839	Whitechapel, London	John (Jacob) Nathan	Esther Nathan	Morris Levene	Aldgate, London	scholar
20442	Nathan	Flora	1826	Whitechapel, London	Phineas Nathan	Rachel (?)		Bloomsbury, London	
6549	Nathan	Frances	1821	Plymouth, Devon	(?) Nathan			?Plymouth, Devon	
16095	Nathan	Frances	1822	Holborn, London	(?) Nathan			Whitechapel, London	
20046	Nathan	Frances	1840	Covent Garden, London	Isaac John Nathan	Anna (?)		Covent Garden, London	daughter of fancy dress maker
28476	Nathan	Frances (Fanny)	1816	Spitalfields, London	Abraham Abrahams		Abraham Nathan	Spitalfields, London	

ID	surname	given names	born	birthplace	father	mother	spouse 1	1851 residence	1851 occupation
3782	Nathan	Francis	1843	Whitechapel, London	(?) Nathan	(?)		Spitalfields, London	scholar
30604	Nathan	Frederick Magnus Henry	1851	Soho, London	Henry Nathan	Jane Magnus		Soho, London	
3663	Nathan	George	1805	Plymouth, Devon	Michael Nathan	Sarah (?)	Susan Alexander nee Levy	Whitechapel, London	picture dealer
17376	Nathan	George	1824	Stepney, London	Samuel Nathan	Maria (?)		Whitechapel, London	cigar maker
12834	Nathan	George	1830	Whitechapel, London	Henry Nathan	Sarah (?)		Whitechapel, London	draper's assistant
23497	Nathan	George	1850	Liverpool	Mosely Nathan	Louisa Abraham		Liverpool	
12783	Nathan	Gewilder	1821	Amsterdam, Holland			Esther (?)	Spitalfields, London	cigar maker
15786	Nathan	Grace	1806	Whitechapel, London	Walter (Falk) Nathan	Sophia Friedberg		Bloomsbury, London	
24089	Nathan	Grace	1813	Whitechapel, London	Nathaniel Nathan	Rachel (?)		Bloomsbury, London	
12664	Nathan	Hannah	1793	Coventry, Warwickshire				Birmingham	
20409	Nathan	Hannah	1796	Aldgate, London	(?)		Samuel Nathan	Elephant & Castle, London	dealer in pictures, china + furniture
21136	Nathan	Hannah	1797	?, Russia	(?)		Moses Nathan	Aldgate, London	general dealer
5240	Nathan	Hannah	1812	Aldgate, London	Abraham HaLevi Abrahams		Solomon Nathan	Aldgate, London	
10299	Nathan	Hannah	1816	Spitalfields, London	Moses Cohen		Lewis (Louis) Nathan	Spitalfields, London	tailoress
12310	Nathan	Hannah	1822	Dover, Kent	Barnet Nathan	Julia (?)	Judah Hart	Dover, Kent	
13751	Nathan	Hannah	1822	?, Poland [?, Prussia]	(?) Schoenthal		Louis Nathan	Manchester	housewife
20412	Nathan	Hannah	1830	Southwark, London	Samuel Nathan	Hannah (?)	Benjamin Lyons	Elephant & Castle, London	brace + garter maker
6293	Nathan	Hannah	1831	Wapping, London	John (Jacob) Nathan	Esther Nathan	Isaac Davis	Aldgate, London	artificial flower maker
21791	Nathan	Hannah	1831	Finsbury, London	(?) Nathan			Aldgate, London	waistcoat maker
15748	Nathan	Hannah	1837	Middlesex, London	Lewis (Louis)Nathan	Sophia Isaacs		Aldgate, London	domestic at home
22543	Nathan	Hannah	1839	Aldgate, London	(?) Nathan	Mary Ann (?)		Whitechapel, London	errand boy
27217	Nathan	Hannah	1840	Wapping, London	Moses Nathan	Mary Solomons		Wapping, London	
22777	Nathan	Hannah	1842	Spitalfields, London	Nathaniel Nathan	Eve Barnett		Whitechapel, London	
28894	Nathan	Hannah	1843	Spitalfields, London	Barnet Davis Nathan	Matilda (?)		Spitalfields, London	scholar
24805	Nathan	Hannah	1847	Southwark, London	John Nathan	Sarah Green		Elephant & Castle, London	
1379	Nathan	Hannah (Hanana, Ann)	1828	Plymouth, Devon	Aaron Nathan	Mary (?)		Plymouth, Devon	bonnet maker
3586	Nathan	Hariet (Hariette)	1819	Wapping, London	Henry Moses	Esther Nathan	Louis Nathan	Shoreditch, London	
12909	Nathan	Hariette	1847	Clerkenwell, London	Mayer Moses Nathan	Sarina Levi		Clerkenwell, London	
1256	Nathan	Harriet	1773	Plymouth, Devon	(?) Nathan			Plymouth, Devon	
2547	Nathan	Harriet	1805	Hull, Yorkshire				Hull, Yorkshire	
11821	Nathan	Harriet	1807	Wapping, London	Nathaniel Nathan	Dinah Moses	Edward Ezekiel Nathan	Whitechapel, London	retired clothes dealer
15787	Nathan	Harriet	1807	Whitechapel, London	Walter (Falk) Nathan	Sophia Friedberg		Bloomsbury, London	
29680	Nathan	Harriet	1825	Portsmouth, Hampshire	(?) Nathan			Tower Hill, London	
1373	Nathan	Henrietta (Haranitha, Hanata)	1830	Plymouth, Devon	Aaron Nathan	Mary (?)	Lewis Brock	Plymouth, Devon	dressmaker
12905	Nathan	Henriks	1841	Aldgate, London	Mayer Moses Nathan	Sarina Levi		Clerkenwell, London	scholar at home
12832	Nathan	Henry	1789	Aldgate, London			Sarah (?)	Whitechapel, London	draper empl 7
1409	Nathan	Henry	1793	Plymouth, Devon				Plymouth, Devon	proprietor of houses
23345	Nathan	Henry	1796	Whitechapel, London	Mier Nathan		Catherine Michael	Piccadilly, London	eating house keeper

ID	surname	given names	born	birthplace	father	mother	spouse 1	1851 residence	1851 occupation
27601	Nathan	Henry	1800	?	Isaac Nathan		Mary (Maria) Hyams	Spitalfields, London	
9392	Nathan	Henry	1806	Portsmouth, Hampshire	Jacob Nathan		Rosa Lee	Aldgate, London	tailor
5633	Nathan	Henry	1810	?	Jacob Nathan		Amelia Ellis	Whitechapel, London	merchant
13922	Nathan	Henry	1812	?, Poland	Michael Nathan		Matilda Jacobs	Manchester	brush factor
8434	Nathan	Henry	1821	Portsmouth, Hampshire	Joseph (Judah) Nathan		Ann Davis	Portsmouth, Hampshire	clothier
22868	Nathan	Henry	1823	Warsaw, Poland			Jane (?)	Whitechapel, London	master slipper-maker empl 1
18929	Nathan	Henry	1827	Aldgate, London	(?) Nathan	Amelia (?)		Aldgate, London	furniture broker
17378	Nathan	Henry	1831	Whitechapel, London	Samuel Nathan	Maria (?)		Whitechapel, London	cigar maker
5620	Nathan	Henry	1835	Southwark, London	Samuel Nathan	Hannah (?)	Emma (?)	Elephant & Castle, London	assistance in picture dealer's shop
30877	Nathan	Henry	1835	Canterbury, Kent	David Nathan	Mary (?)		Canterbury, Kent	
23352	Nathan	Henry	1842	Mayfair, London	Henry Nathan	Catherine Michael	Catherine Elmes	Piccadilly, London	
5622	Nathan	Henry	1843	Spitalfields, London	Lewis (Louis) Nathan	Sophia Isaacs	Ann Levy	Spitalfields, London	scholar
5634	Nathan	Henry	1843	Whitechapel, London	Henry Nathan	Amelia Ellis		Whitechapel, London	scholar at home
21453	Nathan	Henry	1843	Whitechapel, London				Gravesend, Kent	boarding school pupil
5625	Nathan	Henry	1844	Strand, London	Lawrence Isaac Nathan	Julia Abraham (Abrahams)	Clara Solomon	Strand, London	scholar
27606	Nathan	Henry	1845	?, France				Spitalfields, London	
28478	Nathan	Henry	1846	Spitalfields, London	Abraham Nathan	Frances (Fanny) Abrahams		Spitalfields, London	
18923	Nathan	Henry	1848	Aldgate, London	Joel Nathan	Rachael (?)		Aldgate, London	
22871	Nathan	Henry	1849	Whitechapel, London	Henry Nathan	Jane (?)		Whitechapel, London	
24911	Nathan	Henry	1849	Bethnal Green, London	Israel Nathan	Isabella (Beila) Levi		Bethnal Green, London	
30100	Nathan	Henry	1851	Bethnal Green, London	Nathaniel Nathan	Rebecca (?)		Bethnal Green, London	
5852	Nathan	Henry Jacob	1820	Middlesex, London	Yaakov		Jane Magnus	Soho, London	costumier
30309	Nathan	Henry John	1843	Aldgate, London	John Nathan	Esther Nathan		Aldgate, London	
21788	Nathan	Hyam	1816	Finsbury, London			Ann (?)	Aldgate, London	clothes dealer
20047	Nathan	Hyam	1843	Covent Garden, London	Isaac John Nathan	Anna (?)		Covent Garden, London	son of fancy dress maker
27244	Nathan	Hyman	1817	?, London				Aldgate, London	general dealer
21051	Nathan	Hyman	1839	?, London				Dover, Kent	boarding school pupil
23897	Nathan	Isaac	1807	Liverpool	Edward Nathan		?	Westminster, London	dealer in wearing apparel
6921	Nathan	Isaac	1844	Spitalfields, London	Henry Nathan	Sarah Costa		Spitalfields, London	scholar
20040	Nathan	Isaac John	1803	Middlesex, London			Anna (?)	Covent Garden, London	masquerade warehouse
11485	Nathan	Isaacs	1840	Spitalfields, London	Nathan Nathan	Clara Lazarus		Aldgate, London	
24904	Nathan	Isabella (Beila)	1814	Spitalfields, London	(?) Levi		Israel Nathan	Bethnal Green, London	
20042	Nathan	Isidore	1835	Middlesex, London	Isaac John Nathan	Anna (?)		Covent Garden, London	son of fancy dress maker
311	Nathan	Israel	1794	Aldgate, London	Simon Nathan		Esther (?)	Aldgate, London	butcher
24903	Nathan	Israel	1804	Aldgate, London			Isabella (Beila) Levi	Bethnal Green, London	draper
24962	Nathan	J---	1833	Middlesex, London	N--- Nathan	R--- (?)		Haggerston, London	
13899	Nathan	Jacob	1766	Bavaria, Germany			Jane (?)	Manchester	retired silversmith
1407	Nathan	Jacob	1784	Plymouth, Devon				Plymouth, Devon	pawnbroker
21137	Nathan	Jacob	1833	Aldgate, London	Moses Nathan	Hannah (?)	Caroline Sarah Lewis	Aldgate, London	cap maker
5248	Nathan	Jacob (John)	1850	Whitechapel, London	Lewis Nathan	Regina (Rachael) Kisch		Wapping, London	
13064	Nathan	Jacob Hyam	1780	Whitechapel, London	Hyam Nathan		Polly Isaacs	Soho, London	independent
15071	Nathan	James	1823	Whitechapel, London			Mary (?)	Bethnal Green, London	labourer
13900	Nathan	Jane	1779	Middlesex, London	(?)		Jacob Nathan	Manchester	

ID	surname	given names	born	birthplace	father	mother	spouse 1	1851 residence	1851 occupation
31047	Nathan	Jane	1813	Plymouth, Devon			Lazarus Elias Nathan	Plymouth, Devon	
23653	Nathan	Jane	1815	?, London	(?)		Lewis Nathan	Liverpool	
1378	Nathan	Jane	1824	Plymouth, Devon	Aaron Nathan	Mary (?)		Plymouth, Devon	boot + shoe binder
18611	Nathan	Jane	1824	Southwark, London	(?)		Edward Nathan	Whitechapel, London	
17199	Nathan	Jane	1826	Whitechapel, London	Philip Joseph Nathan	Esther Lear		Whitechapel, London	
5853	Nathan	Jane	1827	Chatham, Kent	Simon Magnus	Sarah Wolff	Henry Jacob Nathan	Soho, London	
22869	Nathan	Jane	1828	?, Wales [Upper ---isford, Wales]	(?)		Henry Nathan	Whitechapel, London	boot binder
16683	Nathan	Jane	1837	Aldgate, London	David Nathan	Deborah Saltiel		Stepney, London	scholar
23493	Nathan	Jane	1845	Liverpool	Mosely Nathan	Louisa Abraham		Liverpool	scholar at home
12906	Nathan	Janette	1842	Aldgate, London	Mayer Moses Nathan	Sarina Levi		Clerkenwell, London	scholar at home
28892	Nathan	Jesse	1837	Spitalfields, London	Barnet Davis Nathan	Matilda (?)		Spitalfields, London	cap maker
18921	Nathan	Joel	1821	Aldgate, London			Rachael (?)	Aldgate, London	furniture broker
20493	Nathan	Joel (Joseph)	1840	Waterloo, London	Nathan (Nathaniel) Nathan	Louisa Jacobs		Strand, London	
30131	Nathan	John	1794	?			Frances Samuel	Dublin, Ireland	watchmaker + jeweller
17254	Nathan	John	1808	Aldgate, London	Joseph HaLevi Nathan		Rebecca Lyon	Aldgate, London	clothier
12841	Nathan	John	1814	Strand, London	Henry Nathan	Sarah (?)		Whitechapel, London	draper assistant
24803	Nathan	John	1819	Southwark, London	Samuel (Shmuel Zenvil?) Nathan	(Hannah Mendes?)	Sarah Green	Elephant & Castle, London	broker
27632	Nathan	John	1823	Spitalfields, London			Julia (?)	Aldgate, London	cab man
27604	Nathan	John	1832	Whitechapel, London	Henry Nathan	Mary (Maria) Hyams		Spitalfields, London	
17282	Nathan	John	1833	Aldgate, London	Israel Nathan	Esther (?)		Aldgate, London	cigar maker apprentice
20408	Nathan	John	1838	Whitechapel, London				Southwark, London	
11411	Nathan	John (Jacob)	1801	Aldgate, London	Simon Katsov		Esther Nathan	Aldgate, London	butcher
24087	Nathan	Jonah	1810	Whitechapel, London	Nathaniel Nathan	Rachel (?)	Olivia Josephs	Bloomsbury, London	wholesale stationer
23349	Nathan	Jonas	1836	Middlesex, London	Henry Nathan	Catherine Michael	Rachael Michael	Piccadilly, London	
28740	Nathan	Jonas	1839	Middlesex, London	Lewis Nathan			Spitalfields, London	
5098	Nathan	Joseph	1776	Portsmouth, Hampshire	Gabriel Nathan		Sophia (?)	Portsmouth, Hampshire	clothes salesman
22914	Nathan	Joseph	1779	Spitalfields, London	Nathan Veilberg		Elizabeth Jacobs	Wapping, London	dealer in clothes
20029	Nathan	Joseph	1818	Spitalfields, London			Marianne (?)	Aldgate, London	general dealer
17135	Nathan	Joseph	1819	?, Germany				Bradford, Yorkshire	worsted stuff merchant
15078	Nathan	Joseph	1825	Whitechapel, London	Samuel Nathan	Sophia (?)		Bethnal Green, London	general dealer
6201	Nathan	Joseph	1830	Shoreditch, London	Philip Joseph Nathan	Esther Lear	Sarah Cohen	Whitechapel, London	
6206	Nathan	Joseph	1831	Aldgate, London	David Nathan	Deborah Saltiel	Mary Newsome	Stepney, London	
12312	Nathan	Joseph	1831	Canterbury, Kent	Barnet Nathan	Julia (?)		Dover, Kent	
6144	Nathan	Joseph	1837	Aldgate, London	Samuel Nathan	Rebecca (?)	Elizabeth Collins	Aldgate, London	cigar maker apprentice
22542	Nathan	Joseph	1837	Aldgate, London	(?) Nathan	Mary Ann (?)		Whitechapel, London	errand boy
22849	Nathan	Joseph	1841	Whitechapel, London	Morris Nathan	Elizabeth (?)		Whitechapel, London	scholar
12910	Nathan	Joseph	1848	Islington, London	Mayer Moses Nathan	Sarina Levi		Clerkenwell, London	
13068	Nathan	Joseph Edward	1835	Spitalfields, London	Edward Ezekiel Nathan	Rachel Davis	Dinah Marks	Spitalfields, London	out of situation
17365	Nathan	Joshau	1847	Spitalfields, London	Emanuel Nathan	Julia (?)		Spitalfields, London	
21790	Nathan	Joshua	1821	Finsbury, London				Aldgate, London	clothes dealer
12309	Nathan	Julia	1786	Middlesex, London	(?)		Barnet Nathan	Dover, Kent	
5627	Nathan	Julia	1814	Aldgate, London	Moses Abraham	(Fanny Jacob?)	Lawrence Isaac Nathan	Strand, London	
17363	Nathan	Julia	1818	Whitechapel, London	(?)		Emanuel Nathan	Spitalfields, London	

ID	surname	given names	born	birthplace	father	mother	spouse 1	1851 residence	1851 occupation
27633	Nathan	Julia	1824	Shoreditch, London	(?)		John Nathan	Aldgate, London	
17281	Nathan	Julia	1832	Aldgate, London	Israel Nathan	Esther (?)		Aldgate, London	
12914	Nathan	Julia	1836	Aldgate, London	Samuel Nathan	Rebecca Cohen	Michael Abrahams	Spitalfields, London	tailoress
16620	Nathan	Julia	1836	Liverpool	David Nathan	Esther Levi		Liverpool	scholar
20494	Nathan	Julia	1844	Nottingham, Nottinghamshire	Nathan (Nathaniel) Nathan	Louisa Jacobs	Richard Thompson Proctor	Strand, London	
27634	Nathan	Julia	1848	Shoreditch, London	John Nathan	Julia (?)		Aldgate, London	
4017	Nathan	Kate	1824	Tottenham, London	Eleazer Hart	Sarah Levy	Benjamin Nathan	Portsmouth, Hampshire	dealer in china, glass, hardware + stationery
20398	Nathan	Kate	1825	Marylebone, London	Edward Ezekiel Nathan	Rachel Davis		Spitalfields, London	furrier's finisher
9193	Nathan	Kate	1841	Boulogne, France	Solomon Nathan	Elizabeth Isaacs		Whitechapel, London	scholar
23654	Nathan	Kate	1850	Liverpool	Lewis Nathan	Jane (?)		Liverpool	
29563	Nathan	L---	1828	Whitechapel, London	Samuel Nathan	R--- (?)		Whitechapel, London	cigar maker
24812	Nathan	Lavinia	1843	Southwark, London	David Nathan	Louisa East		Elephant & Castle, London	
5626	Nathan	Lawrence Isaac	1804	Whitechapel	Isaac Nathan	(Catherine Solomon?)	Julia Abraham (Abrahams)	Strand, London	officer to Sheriff of Middlesex
26964	Nathan	Lazarus	1827	Whitechapel, London				Aldgate, London	boot maker
6491	Nathan	Lazarus Elias	1813	Plymouth, Devon			Jane (?)	Plymouth, Devon	tinman
21765	Nathan	Leah	1829	Whitechapel, London	Joseph Nathan	Elizabeth (?)	Asher Selig Harris	Aldgate, London	waistcoat maker
24907	Nathan	Leah	1836	Mile End, London	Israel Nathan	Isabella (Beila) Levi		Bethnal Green, London	
5630	Nathan	Leah	1851	Middlesex, London	Lawrence Isaac Nathan	Julia Abraham (Abrahams)	Angelo Jacobs	Strand, London	
13752	Nathan	Leei	1847	Manchester	Louis Nathan	Hannah Schoenthal		Manchester	
14253	Nathan	Lewis	1779	Manchester			Elizabeth (?)	Manchester	shoe maker
5100	Nathan	Lewis	1814	Portsmouth, Hampshire	Jacob Nathan	Hannah (?)	Maria Raphael	Portsmouth, Hampshire	clothier
23652	Nathan	Lewis	1820	Liverpool	(?) Nathan	Mary (?)	Jane (?)	Liverpool	shirt manufacturer [---]
18928	Nathan	Lewis	1824	Aldgate, London	(?) Nathan	Amelia (?)		Aldgate, London	fish dealer
12842	Nathan	Lewis	1826	Stepney, London	Henry Nathan	Sarah (?)		Whitechapel, London	draper assistant
5246	Nathan	Lewis	1829	Aldgate, London	Simon Nathan	Catherine Barnet	Regina (Rachael) Kisch	Wapping, London	cigar maker
17257	Nathan	Lewis	1836	Aldgate, London	John Nathan	Rebecca (?Lyon)		Aldgate, London	scholar at home
20044	Nathan	Lewis	1838	Covent Garden, London	Isaac John Nathan	Anna (?)		Covent Garden, London	son of fancy dress maker
20401	Nathan	Lewis	1839	Spitalfields, London	Edward Ezekiel Nathan	Rachel Davis		Spitalfields, London	scholar
28895	Nathan	Lewis	1847	Spitalfields, London	Barnet Davis Nathan	Matilda (?)		Spitalfields, London	scholar
15745	Nathan	Lewis (Louis)	1809	Middlesex, London	Abraham Nathan		Sophia Isaacs	Aldgate, London	furniture broker
10298	Nathan	Lewis (Louis)	1815	Spitalfields, London	Moses Nathan	Rebecca (?)	Hannah Cohen	Spitalfields, London	dealer in wearing apparel
13901	Nathan	Lewis H	1799	Manchester	Jacob Nathan	Jane (?)		Manchester	general practitioner (MRCS + LSA Lond)
20483	Nathan	Lewis Jacob	1812	Westminster, London			Eliza (?)	Soho, London	fancy costume tailor
7290	Nathan	Lipman	1833	?, Holland	Hyam Lipman	Ann (?)	Phoebe (Fanny) Silver	Aldgate, London	
30279	Nathan	Louis	1802	Covent Garden, London			Rosetta (?)	Soho, London	appraiser
3587	Nathan	Louis	1811	City, London	Nathan Lion Nathan	Sarah (?)	Hariet (Hariette) Moses	Shoreditch, London	ship owner + Australia merchant
13750	Nathan	Louis	1823	?, Poland [?, Prussia]			Hannah Schoenthal	Manchester	French polisher
16618	Nathan	Louis	1829	Birmingham	David Nathan	Esther Levi		Liverpool	watchmaker finisher
24091	Nathan	Louisa	1812	Whitechapel, London	(?) Nathan			Bloomsbury, London	

ID	surname	given names	born	birthplace	father	mother	spouse 1	1851 residence	1851 occupation
16094	Nathan	Louisa	1816	?, London	(?) Nathan			Whitechapel, London	
24809	Nathan	Louisa	1816	Bury St Edmunds, Suffolk	(?) East		David Nathan	Elephant & Castle, London	
20492	Nathan	Louisa	1818	Finsbury, London	Israel Jacobs		Nathan (Nathaniel) Nathan	Strand, London	
15788	Nathan	Louisa	1820	Finsbury, London	Walter (Falk) Nathan	Sophia Friedberg		Bloomsbury, London	
23491	Nathan	Louisa	1822	?, London	(?) Abraham		Mosely Nathan	Liverpool	
14007	Nathan	Louisa	1826	Middlesex, London				Manchester	lady's maid
20445	Nathan	Louisa	1828	Whitechapel, London	Phineas Nathan	Rachel (?)		Bloomsbury, London	
28238	Nathan	Louisa	1836	Whitechapel, London	(?) Nathan	Esther (?)		Spitalfields, London	dressmaker
24810	Nathan	Louisa	1839	Southwark, London	David Nathan	Louisa East		Elephant & Castle, London	
24910	Nathan	Louisa	1845	Finsbury, London	Israel Nathan	Isabella (Beila) Levi		Bethnal Green, London	
20496	Nathan	Louisa	1846	Strand, London	Nathan (Nathaniel) Nathan	Louisa Jacobs		Strand, London	
20419	Nathan	Louisa (Leah)	1813	Middlesex, London	Hayim HaLevi Collins	Mary (?)	Morris Nathan	Marylebone, London	
27455	Nathan	M---	1829	Aldgate, London	(?)		Nathaniel Levy Nathan	Aldgate, London	
29564	Nathan	M---	1829	Whitechapel, London	Samuel Nathan	R--- (?)		Whitechapel, London	cigar maker
17375	Nathan	Maria	1797	Southend, Essex	(?)		Samuel Nathan	Whitechapel, London	
21341	Nathan	Maria	1821	Southwark, London	(?)		Morris Nathan	Glasgow, Scotland	
5101	Nathan	Maria	1824	?, London	Ralph Raphael	Leah Hart	Lewis Nathan	Portsmouth, Hampshire	
18211	Nathan	Maria	1837	Middlesex, London	(?) Nathan			Mile End, London	scholar
20045	Nathan	Maria	1839	Covent Garden, London	Isaac John Nathan	Anna (?)		Covent Garden, London	daughter of fancy dress maker
20485	Nathan	Maria	1849	Westminster, London	Lewis Jacob Nathan	Eliza (?)		Soho, London	
20030	Nathan	Marianne	1823	Spitalfields, London	(?)		Joseph Nathan	Aldgate, London	
23487	Nathan	Marie	1828	Liverpool	Philip Nathan	Rosina Solomon Nathan		Liverpool	shopkeeper's assistant
5851	Nathan	Marion	1849	Piccadilly, London	Henry Jacob Nathan	Jane Magnus	Henry Rossner	Soho, London	
20039	Nathan	Mark	1796	Spitalfields, London			(?)	Aldgate, London	carman
11488	Nathan	Mark	1849	Aldgate, London	Nathan Nathan	Clara Lazarus		Aldgate, London	
3779	Nathan	Mark (Mordecai)	1797	Whitechapel, London			Ellenor (Eleanor) Davis	Spitalfields, London	glass cutter
15747	Nathan	Martha	1836	Middlesex, London	Lewis (Louis) Nathan	Sophia Isaacs	David Jacobs	Aldgate, London	domestic at home
28739	Nathan	Martha	1838	Middlesex, London	(?) Nathan			Spitalfields, London	tailoress
23651	Nathan	Mary	1789	?, London	(?)		(?) Nathan	Liverpool	
30876	Nathan	Mary	1805	Canterbury, Kent	(?)		David Nathan	Canterbury, Kent	
27213	Nathan	Mary	1806	Aldgate, London	Isaac Solomon		Moses Nathan	Wapping, London	
14066	Nathan	Mary	1815	Manchester	(?)		Elias Nathan	Manchester	
15373	Nathan	Mary	1825	Marylebone, London	(?)		Abraham Nathan	Waterloo, London	
15072	Nathan	Mary	1827	Aldgate, London	(?)		James Nathan	Bethnal Green, London	
22272	Nathan	Mary	1827	Surrey, London	(?)		(?) Nathan	Whitechapel, London	seamstress
15374	Nathan	Mary	1845	Lambeth, London	Abraham Nathan	Mary (?)		Waterloo, London	
11487	Nathan	Mary	1846	Aldgate, London	Nathan Nathan	Clara Lazarus		Aldgate, London	
1372	Nathan	Mary (Maria)	1797	Middlesex, London	Moshe Gykerleva Mosely		Aaron Nathan	Plymouth, Devon	
27600	Nathan	Mary (Maria)	1803	Middlesex, London	Menachem Hyam Manly Hyams		Henry Nathan	Spitalfields, London	hawker
5628	Nathan	Mary (Miriam, Marie)	1843	Strand, London	Lawrence Isaac Nathan	Julia Abraham (Abrahams)	Joseph Goodman	Strand, London	scholar
30283	Nathan	Mary A	1839	Marylebone, London	Louis Nathan	Rosetta (?)		Soho, London	

ID	surname	given names	born	birthplace	father	mother	spouse 1	1851 residence	1851 occupation
22538	Nathan	Mary Ann	1797	Aldgate, London	(?)		(?) Nathan	Whitechapel, London	fishmonger
30132	Nathan	Mary Ann	1825	?Liverpool	John Nathan	Frances Samuel	Adam Harpur	Dublin, Ireland	
28890	Nathan	Matilda	1815	Amsterdam, Holland	(?)		Barnet Davis Nathan	Spitalfields, London	
13923	Nathan	Matilda	1819	Nottingham, Nottinghamshire	Joseph Jacobs		Henry Nathan	Manchester	
9983	Nathan	Matilda	1827	Liverpool	John Nathan	Frances Samuel	Myer Jacobs	Dublin, Ireland	
21138	Nathan	Matilda	1841	Aldgate, London	Moses Nathan	Hannah (?)	Maximilian Berger	Aldgate, London	scholar
12902	Nathan	Mayer Moses	1800	Frankfurt, Germany	David		Sarina Levi	Clerkenwell, London	stock agent
27710	Nathan	Michael	1816	?, Poland [?, Prussia]			Elizabeth Benjamin	Spitalfields, London	tailor
29697	Nathan	Michael	1817	Middlesex, London	(?) Nathan	Catherine (?)	Elizabeth (?)	Aldgate, London	journeyman butcher
23116	Nathan	Michael	1822	City, London	Emanuel Nathan			City, London	black lead pencil maker
6924	Nathan	Michael	1823	Whitechapel, London	Simon Nathan		Sarah Green	Aldgate, London	journeyman cigar maker
12853	Nathan	Michael	1832	Plymouth, Devon				Spitalfields, London	cigar maker
12913	Nathan	Michael	1833	Aldgate, London	Samuel Nathan	Rebecca Cohen	Sarah Mitchell	Spitalfields, London	cigar maker apprentice
21290	Nathan	Michael	1839	Aldgate, London				Edmonton, London	boarding school pupil
22850	Nathan	Michael	1845	Whitechapel, London	Morris Nathan	Elizabeth (?)		Whitechapel, London	scholar
7550	Nathan	Miriam	1826	Liverpool	Philip Nathan	Rosina Solomon Nathan	Godfrey Levi	Liverpool	
23117	Nathan	Mitchel	1825	City, London	Emanuel Nathan			City, London	cigar maker
4016	Nathan	Mordecai (Mark)	1845	Portsmouth, Hampshire	Benjamin Nathan	Kate Hart	Gertude Joseph	Portsmouth, Hampshire	
22846	Nathan	Morris	1801	?, Holland			Elizabeth (?)	Whitechapel, London	clothier's shopman
13842	Nathan	Morris	1805	?, Poland				Manchester	hawker
20417	Nathan	Morris	1811	?, Poland			Maria (?)	Glasgow, Scotland	boot + shoe manufacturer empl 1
20418	Nathan	Morris	1814	Middlesex, London	Nathan		Louisa (Leah) Collins	Marylebone, London	auctioneer
30281	Nathan	Morris	1833	Marylebone, London	Louis Nathan	Rosetta (?)		Soho, London	
20416	Nathan	Morris	1848	Strand, London	Lawrence Isaac Nathan	Julia Abraham (Abrahams)		Strand, London	scholar
23490	Nathan	Mosely	1817	Liverpool	Philip Nathan	Rosina Solomon Nathan	Louisa Abraham	Liverpool	watch manufacturer
14247	Nathan	Moses	1773	Middlesex, London			(?)	Manchester	clothes dealer
10296	Nathan	Moses	1792	Spitalfields, London			Rebecca (?)	Spitalfields, London	formerly fruit salesman
27212	Nathan	Moses	1801	Wapping, London	Nathan		Mary Solomons	Wapping, London	slop seller
12694	Nathan	Moses	1802	Hanover, Germany				Coventry, Warwickshire	traveller (jewellery)
8530	Nathan	Moses	1822	Spitalfields, London			(?)	Westminster, London	convict (glass engraver)
6844	Nathan	Moses	1832	Amsterdam, Holland				Spitalfields, London	cigar maker
16684	Nathan	Moses	1838	Aldgate, London	David Nathan	Deborah Saltiel		Stepney, London	scholar
13470	Nathan	Myer A	1803	?, Germany				Manchester	merchant
24959	Nathan	N---	1800	Shoreditch, London			R--- (?)	Haggerston, London	butcher
1375	Nathan	Nancy	1816	Plymouth, Devon	Aaron Nathan	Mary (?)		Plymouth, Devon	mantle maker
11482	Nathan	Nathan	1811	Middlesex, London	Simcha HaLevi Nathan		Clara Lazarus	Aldgate, London	general dealer
4823	Nathan	Nathan	1813	Whitechapel, London			Ann (?)	Birmingham	papermaker
20994	Nathan	Nathan	1819	?, Poland [?, Prussia]				Aldgate, London	
29571	Nathan	Nathan	1825	Whitechapel, London			E--- (?)	Whitechapel, London	traveller
27603	Nathan	Nathan	1830	Whitechapel, London	Henry Nathan	Mary (Maria) Hyams	Julia Joseph	Spitalfields, London	
22848	Nathan	Nathan	1837	Whitechapel, London	Morris Nathan	Elizabeth (?)		Whitechapel, London	slipper maker apprentice
21452	Nathan	Nathan	1839	Bethnal Green, London				Gravesend, Kent	boarding school pupil
6070	Nathan	Nathan	1840	Spitalfields, London	Lewis (Louis) Nathan	Hannah Cohen	Sarah Isaacs	Spitalfields, London	scholar
17364	Nathan	Nathan	1843	Spitalfields, London	Emanuel Nathan	Julia (?)		Spitalfields, London	

ID	surname	given names	born	birthplace	father	mother	spouse 1	1851 residence	1851 occupation
15751	Nathan	Nathan	1848	Middlesex, London	Lewis (Louis) Nathan	Sophia Isaacs	Mary Levy	Aldgate, London	scholar
28897	Nathan	Nathan	1851	Spitalfields, London	Barnet Davis Nathan	Matilda (?)		Spitalfields, London	
20491	Nathan	Nathan (Nathaniel)	1809	Spitalfields, London	Joseph Nathan		Louisa Jacobs	Strand, London	fruit salesman
1408	Nathan	Nathaniel	1778	Plymouth, Devon				Plymouth, Devon	proprietor of houses
27453	Nathan	Nathaniel	1790	Aldgate, London			(?)	Aldgate, London	carcass butcher empl 3
22774	Nathan	Nathaniel	1819	Stepney, London	Israel Nathan		Eve Barnett	Whitechapel, London	umbrella maker
15101	Nathan	Nathaniel	1823	Stepney, London			Rebecca (?)	Bethnal Green, London	draper's assistant
27712	Nathan	Nathaniel	1843	Birmingham	Michael Nathan	Elizabeth Benjamin	Sarah Jacobs	Spitalfields, London	
24088	Nathan	Nathaniel	1844	Finsbury, London	Jonah Nathan	Olivia Josephs		Bloomsbury, London	
22274	Nathan	Nathaniel	1849	Middlesex, London	(?) Nathan	Mary (?)		Whitechapel, London	
11418	Nathan	Nathaniel J	1848	Aldgate, London	John (Jacob) Nathan	Esther Nathan		Aldgate, London	scholar
27454	Nathan	Nathaniel Levy	1822	Aldgate, London			M--- (?)	Aldgate, London	carcass butcher empl 6
27457	Nathan	Nathaniel Levy	1850	Waterloo, London	Nathaniel Levy Nathan	M--- (?)		Aldgate, London	
13304	Nathan	Ned	1849	Whitechapel, London	(?) Nathan	Rosa (?)		Spitalfields, London	
24963	Nathan	P---	1835	Whitechapel, London	N--- Nathan	R--- (?)		Haggerston, London	
13753	Nathan	Pelone (?Selina)	1850	Manchester	Louis Nathan	Hannah Schoenthal		Manchester	
28893	Nathan	Phebe	1841	Spitalfields, London	Barnet Davis Nathan	Matilda (?)		Spitalfields, London	scholar
16621	Nathan	Pheobe	1843	Liverpool	David Nathan	Esther Levi		Liverpool	scholar
16619	Nathan	Philip	1833	Liverpool	David Nathan	Esther Levi		Liverpool	watchmaker apprentice
27635	Nathan	Philip J	1850	Shoreditch, London	John Nathan	Julia (?)		Aldgate, London	
17197	Nathan	Philip Joseph	1786	Amsterdam, Holland	Joseph Nathan		Esther Lear	Whitechapel, London	
12911	Nathan	Philippe S	1850	Clerkenwell, London	Mayer Moses Nathan	Sarina Levi		Clerkenwell, London	
23494	Nathan	Phillip	1846	Liverpool	Mosely Nathan	Louisa Abraham	Louise Lyons	Liverpool	
20439	Nathan	Phineas	1792	Middlesex, London	Yitzhak Isaac		Rachel (?)	Bloomsbury, London	wholesale jewellery + watch manufacturer
12311	Nathan	Phoebe	1828	Dover, Kent	Barnet Nathan	Julia (?)	Abraham Joseph Vanderlyn	Dover, Kent	
18566	Nathan	Pierre John	1831	Whitechapel, London	John Nathan	Esther (?)	Julia Levene	Aldgate, London	
14188	Nathan	Pincus	1801	?, Poland			Rebecca Parkes nee (?)	Manchester	cap manufacturer
29573	Nathan	Polly	1850	Margate, Kent	Nathan Nathan	E--- (?)		Whitechapel, London	
29561	Nathan	R---	1799	?, Germany	(?)		samuel Nathan	Whitechapel, London	hawker
24960	Nathan	R---	1810	Portsmouth, Hampshire	(?)		N--- Nathan	Haggerston, London	
11413	Nathan	Rachael	1825	Whitechapel, London	John Nathan	Esther Nathan		Aldgate, London	book binder
18922	Nathan	Rachael	1827	Aldgate, London	(?)		Joel Nathan	Aldgate, London	
18930	Nathan	Rachael	1831	Aldgate, London	(?) Nathan	Amelia (?)		Aldgate, London	umbrella maker
23118	Nathan	Rachael	1831	City, London	Emanuel Nathan			City, London	
29699	Nathan	Rachael	1848	Middlesex, London	Michael Nathan	Elizabeth (?)		Aldgate, London	
18925	Nathan	Rachael	1850	Aldgate, London	Joel Nathan	Rachael (?)		Aldgate, London	
20440	Nathan	Rachel	1791	Liverpool	(?)		Phineas Nathan	Bloomsbury, London	
8707	Nathan	Rachel	1798	Aldgate, London	(?)		Samuel Nathan	Aldgate, London	
20397	Nathan	Rachel	1803	Westminster, London	(?) Davis		Edward Ezekiel Nathan	Spitalfields, London	
23485	Nathan	Rachel	1807	Coventry, Warwickshire	(?) Nathan			Liverpool	shopkeeper's assistant
16282	Nathan	Rachel	1813	Spitalfields, London	Symon Nathan	Elizabeth (Betsy) Isaacs		Spitalfields, London	dealer
18160	Nathan	Rachel	1815	Middlesex, London	(?) Nathan			Mile End, London	patient in the Portuguese Jews Hospital

ID	surname	given names	born	birthplace	father	mother	spouse 1	1851 residence	1851 occupation
20407	Nathan	Rachel	1823	Westminster, London	(?) Nathan			Southwark, London	assistant in the shops
13939	Nathan	Rachel	1824	Liverpool	Philip Nathan	Rose (?)		Manchester	
20562	Nathan	Rachel	1824	Spitalfields, London	Simon Nathan	Sarah Elias		Aldgate, London	cap maker
20411	Nathan	Rachel	1828	Southwark, London	Samuel Nathan	Hannah (?)		Elephant & Castle, London	dress maker
30936	Nathan	Rachel	1830	?, Poland	(?)		Solomon Nathan	Sheffield, Yorkshire	jeweller's wife
17377	Nathan	Rachel	1833	Whitechapel, London	Samuel Nathan	Maria (?)		Whitechapel, London	
6322	Nathan	Rachel	1839	Middlesex, London	John Nathan	Rebecca (?Lyon)	David Davis	Aldgate, London	
23351	Nathan	Rachel	1840	Middlesex, London	Henry Nathan	Catherine Michael		Piccadilly, London	
24806	Nathan	Rachel	1849	Southwark, London	John Nathan	Sarah Green		Elephant & Castle, London	
24815	Nathan	Rachel	1849	Southwark, London	David Nathan	Louisa East		Elephant & Castle, London	
27605	Nathan	Raphael	1839	Whitechapel, London	Henry Nathan	Mary (Maria) Hyams		Spitalfields, London	
10297	Nathan	Rebecca	1793	Spitalfields, London	(?)		Moses Nathan	Spitalfields, London	domestic duties
12912	Nathan	Rebecca	1799	Aldgate, London	Joseph Benjamin Zeev Wof HaCohen		Samuel Nathan	Spitalfields, London	
14189	Nathan	Rebecca	1809	?, Poland	(?)		(?) Parkes	Manchester	
17255	Nathan	Rebecca	1809	Aldgate, London	Moshe Lyon		John Nathan	Aldgate, London	
1380	Nathan	Rebecca	1827	Plymouth, Devon	Aaron Nathan	Mary (?)		Plymouth, Devon	lace worker
15102	Nathan	Rebecca	1831	Totnes, Devon	(?)		Nathaniel Nathan	Bethnal Green, London	
21766	Nathan	Rebecca	1832	Whitechapel, London	Joseph Nathan	Elizabeth (?)		Aldgate, London	waistcoat maker
23348	Nathan	Rebecca	1834	Vauxhall, London	Henry Nathan	Catherine Michael		Piccadilly, London	
5247	Nathan	Regina (Rachel)	1824	Whitechapel, London	Abraham Kisch		Lewis Nathan	Wapping, London	
15375	Nathan	Richard	1846	Lambeth, London	Abraham Nathan	Mary (?)		Waterloo, London	
9393	Nathan	Rosa	1803	?, London	Lazar b Gabriel Lee		Henry Nathan	Aldgate, London	
13303	Nathan	Rosa	1823	Whitechapel, London	(?)		(?) Nathan	Spitalfields, London	clothes dealer
27602	Nathan	Rosa	1826	Whitechapel, London	Henry Nathan	Mary (Maria) Hyams	Lewis Benjamin	Spitalfields, London	
30874	Nathan	Rosa	1837	Canterbury, Kent	David Nathan	Mary (?)	Henry A Hart	Canterbury, Kent	
14191	Nathan	Rosa	1840	Birmingham	Pincus Nathan	Rebecca Parkes nee (?)		Manchester	
24811	Nathan	Rosabella	1840	Southwark, London	David Nathan	Louisa East		Elephant & Castle, London	
19883	Nathan	Rose	1822	?, Holland	Benjamin Cohen		Abraham Nathan	Hartlepool, Co Durham	
29619	Nathan	Rosetta	1771	?, Germany				Aldgate, London	
30280	Nathan	Rosetta	1801	Aldgate, London	(?)		Louis Nathan	Soho, London	
20033	Nathan	Rosetta	1848	Spitalfields, London	Joseph Nathan	Marianne (?)		Aldgate, London	
22870	Nathan	Rosetta	1848	Whitechapel, London	Henry Nathan	Jane (?)		Whitechapel, London	
18924	Nathan	Rosetta	1849	Aldgate, London	Joel Nathan	Rachael (?)		Aldgate, London	
20486	Nathan	Rosetta	1850	Westminster, London	Lewis Jacob Nathan	Eliza (?)		Soho, London	
23898	Nathan	Rosey	1819	Spitalfields, London	Levy Simmons		Isaac Nathan	Westminster, London	
23492	Nathan	Rosina	1844	Liverpool	Mosely Nathan	Louisa Abraham		Liverpool	scholar
20043	Nathan	Rosina (Rosetta, Rachalla)	1837	Covent Garden, London	Isaac John Nathan	Anna (?)	Albert Blackmore Fullager	Covent Garden, London	daughter of fancy dress maker
23484	Nathan	Rosina Solomon	1797	Birmingham	(?) Nathan		Philip Nathan	Liverpool	shopkeeper
24961	Nathan	S---	1832	Middlesex, London	N--- Nathan	R--- (?)		Haggerston, London	

ID	surname	given names	born	birthplace	father	mother	spouse 1	1851 residence	1851 occupation
28738	Nathan	Sall (Saul?)	1825	Middlesex, London				Spitalfields, London	lamp glass dealer
24909	Nathan	Salomon	1842	Finsbury, London	Israel Nathan	Isabella (Beila) Levi		Bethnal Green, London	
22544	Nathan	Sampson	1842	Aldgate, London	(?) Nathan	Mary Ann (?)		Whitechapel, London	cricket ball maker
17374	Nathan	Samuel	1787	Coventry, Warwickshire			Maria (?)	Whitechapel, London	watch finisher
15076	Nathan	Samuel	1796	Aldgate, London			Sophia (?)	Bethnal Green, London	butcher journeyman
29560	Nathan	Samuel	1800	Spitalfields, London			R--- (?)	Whitechapel, London	general dealer
6145	Nathan	Samuel	1801	Plymouth, Devon	Yechiel (?Michael) Nathan		Rebecca Cohen	Aldgate, London	picture dealer
8706	Nathan	Samuel	1803	Portsmouth, Hampshire	Yaakov		Rachel (?)	Aldgate, London	clerk to a Society
11822	Nathan	Samuel	1808	Aldgate, London	Nathaniel Nathan	Dinah Moses		Whitechapel, London	general dealer
20565	Nathan	Samuel	1813	Middlesex, London	Simon Nathan	Sarah Elias	Ester Nathan	Aldgate, London	general dealer
4826	Nathan	Samuel	1818	Stepney, London	Nathan Nathan	Julia Solomon		Birmingham	commercial traveller in watch materials
14255	Nathan	Samuel	1827	?, London	Lewis Nathan	Elizabeth (?)		Manchester	warehouseman
20443	Nathan	Samuel	1830	Whitechapel, London	Phineas Nathan	Rachel (?)		Bloomsbury, London	assisting in wholesale jewellery + watch manufacturing business
11415	Nathan	Samuel	1835	Wapping, London	John (Jacob) Nathan	Esther Nathan		Aldgate, London	cigar maker apprentice
27215	Nathan	Samuel	1835	Wapping, London	Moses Nathan	Mary Solomons		Wapping, London	
4825	Nathan	Samuel	1839	Birmingham	Nathan Nathan	Ann (?)		Birmingham	
30879	Nathan	Samuel	1843	Canterbury, Kent	David Nathan	Mary (?)		Canterbury, Kent	
20032	Nathan	Samuel	1846	Spitalfields, London	Joseph Nathan	Marianne (?)		Aldgate, London	
14192	Nathan	Samuel	1847	Manchester	Pincus Nathan	Rebecca Parkes nee (?)		Manchester	
24807	Nathan	Samuel	1850	Southwark, London	John Nathan	Sarah Green	Rose Waterman	Elephant & Castle, London	
15790	Nathan	Samuel Walter	1817	Whitechapel, London	Walter (Falk) Nathan	Sophia Friedberg		Bloomsbury, London	custom house agent
19281	Nathan	Sarah	1755	Aldgate, London	(?)		Michael Nathan	Whitechapel, London	
20561	Nathan	Sarah	1788	Aldgate, London	Yosef Elias		Simon Nathan	Aldgate, London	general dealer
12833	Nathan	Sarah	1790	Aldgate, London	(?)		Henry Nathan	Whitechapel, London	draper's wife
15789	Nathan	Sarah	1815	Whitechapel, London	Walter (Falk) Nathan	Sophia Friedberg		Bloomsbury, London	
18173	Nathan	Sarah	1816	?	(?) Nathan			Mile End, London	lady's maid
20410	Nathan	Sarah	1817	Southwark, London	Samuel Nathan	Hannah (?)	Joseph Myers	Elephant & Castle, London	brace + garter maker
6925	Nathan	Sarah	1818	Spitalfields, London	Levy Ephraim Green	Amelia Hyams	Michael Nathan	Aldgate, London	
6920	Nathan	Sarah	1820	Aldgate, London	Moses Costa	Matilda de Zeheb Arye	Henry Nathan	Spitalfields, London	
12831	Nathan	Sarah	1820	?Whitechapel, London	Henry Nathan	Sarah (?)		Mile End, London	lady's maid
3781	Nathan	Sarah	1823	Spitalfields, London	Mark (Mordecai) Nathan	Ellenor (Eleanor) Davis		Spitalfields, London	cap maker
29224	Nathan	Sarah	1823	Covent Garden, London	Soesman Nathan	Elizabeth (?)		Whitechapel, London	waistcoat maker
24804	Nathan	Sarah	1827	Aldgate, London	Abraham Green	Rachael (?)	John Nathan	Elephant & Castle, London	
24906	Nathan	Sarah	1832	Whitechapel, London	Israel Nathan	Isabella (Beila) Levi		Bethnal Green, London	
27214	Nathan	Sarah	1832	Wapping, London	Moses Nathan	Mary Solomons		Wapping, London	
1374	Nathan	Sarah	1833	Plymouth, Devon	Aaron Nathan	Mary (?)		Plymouth, Devon	milliner
16681	Nathan	Sarah	1833	Aldgate, London	David Nathan	Deborah Saltiel		Stepney, London	
17379	Nathan	Sarah	1835	Whitechapel, London	Samuel Nathan	Maria (?)		Whitechapel, London	
17202	Nathan	Sarah	1837	Whitechapel, London	Philip Joseph Nathan	Esther Lear		Whitechapel, London	

ID	surname	given names	born	birthplace	father	mother	spouse 1	1851 residence	1851 occupation
14190	Nathan	Sarah	1839	Birmingham	Pincus Nathan	Rebecca Parkes nee (?)		Manchester	
11417	Nathan	Sarah	1841	Aldgate, London	John (Jacob) Nathan	Esther Nathan	Henry Silver	Aldgate, London	scholar
4018	Nathan	Sarah	1846	Portsmouth, Hampshire	Benjamin Nathan	Kate Hart	Asher Michaelson	Portsmouth, Hampshire	china dealer
24814	Nathan	Sarah	1848	Southwark, London	David Nathan	Louisa East		Elephant & Castle, London	
13924	Nathan	Sarah	1849	Whitechapel, London	Henry Nathan	Matilda Jacobs		Manchester	
20034	Nathan	Sarah	1850	Spitalfields, London	Joseph Nathan	Marianne (?)		Aldgate, London	
22275	Nathan	Sarah	1850	Middlesex, London	(?) Nathan	Mary (?)		Whitechapel, London	
6898	Nathan	Sarah	1851	Spitalfields, London	Emanuel Nathan	Caroline (?)	Isaac Baumin (Bowman)	Spitalfields, London	
12903	Nathan	Sarina	1819	Pesaro, Italy	Angelo Levi	Ricca Roselli	Mayer Moses Nathan	Clerkenwell, London	radical activist
2548	Nathan	Seby	1785	Whitechapel, London				Hull, Yorkshire	
29227	Nathan	Simon	1833	Bristol	Soesman Nathan	Elizabeth (?)		Whitechapel, London	cigar maker apprentice
6926	Nathan	Simon	1848	Aldgate, London	Michael Nathan	Sarah Green		Aldgate, London	
22780	Nathan	Simon	1850	Whitechapel, London	Nathaniel Nathan	Eve Barnett		Whitechapel, London	
5242	Nathan	Simon (Samuel)	1844	Aldgate, London	Solomon Nathan	Hannah Abrahams		Aldgate, London	
29222	Nathan	Soesman	1793	Aldgate, London			Elizabeth (?)	Whitechapel, London	furniture broker
2152	Nathan	Solomon	1795	?, Germany			(?)	Hull, Yorkshire	
5239	Nathan	Solomon	1817	Aldgate, London	Simon Nathan	Catherine Barnet	Hannah Abrahams	Aldgate, London	grocer + fruiterer
24094	Nathan	Solomon	1818	Marylebone, London	Nathaniel Nathan		Caroline Solomon	Bloomsbury, London	upholsterer
30935	Nathan	Solomon	1829	?, Poland			Rachel (?)	Sheffield, Yorkshire	jeweller
16682	Nathan	Solomon	1835	Aldgate, London	David Nathan	Deborah Saltiel		Stepney, London	chair + sofa maker
22541	Nathan	Solomon	1835	Aldgate, London	(?) Nathan	Mary Ann (?)		Whitechapel, London	cigar maker
15750	Nathan	Solomon	1840	Spitalfields, London	Lewis (Louis) Nathan	Sophia Isaacs		Aldgate, London	scholar
5099	Nathan	Sophia	1779	Portsmouth, Hampshire			Joseph Nathan	Portsmouth, Hampshire	
5746	Nathan	Sophia	1786	Whitechapel, London	Shmuel Friedberg		Walter (Falk) Nathan	King's Cross, London	
15077	Nathan	Sophia	1793	Strand, London	(?)		Samuel Nathan	Bethnal Green, London	
15746	Nathan	Sophia	1807	Spitalfields, London	Tsevi Hirsh Isaacs		Lewis (Louis) Nathan	Aldgate, London	
22539	Nathan	Sophia	1831	Aldgate, London	(?) Nathan	Mary Ann (?)		Whitechapel, London	bookbinder
3662	Nathan	Susan (Zeska)	1796	Whitechapel, London	Moses (Moshe Frenshman) Levy	Deborah (?)	Isaac Alexander (Yitzhak Isaac ben Meir)	Whitechapel, London	picture dealer
16280	Nathan	Symon	1764	Amsterdam, Holland	Nathan		Elizabeth (Betsy) Isaacs	Spitalfields, London	dealer
23489	Nathan	Theresa	1837	Liverpool	Philip Nathan	Rosina Solomon Nathan	Lewin Berrick	Liverpool	scholar
23496	Nathan	Victor	1849	Liverpool	Mosely Nathan	Louisa Abraham		Liverpool	
23495	Nathan	Victoria	1847	Liverpool	Mosely Nathan	Louisa Abraham		Liverpool	
15785	Nathan	Walter (Falk)	1767	City, London	Meir Nathan		Sophia Friedberg	Bloomsbury, London	coal merchant
23024	Natowski	Louis	1802	?, Poland				City, London	stationer
1945	Nayton (Nathan)	Levi	1798	?, Russia			Maria (?)	Merthyr Tydfil, Wales	pawnbroker
1946	Nayton (Nathan)	Maria	1798	Portsmouth, Hampshire			Levi Nayton (Nathan)	Merthyr Tydfil, Wales	
15226	Nehemias	Moses	1823	Gibraltar				Shoreditch, London	general merchant
366	Nelson	Abraham	1829	?, London				Aldgate, London	servant
14727	Nelson	Alace	1838	Bethnal Green, London	Moses Nelson	Hannah Abrahams		Spitalfields, London	scholar
5102	Nelson	Alexander	1824	?, Russia			Frances Isaacs	Portsmouth, Hampshire	watchmaker
16579	Nelson	Ann	1806	East Dereham, Norfolk	David Jones	Leah Micholls	Nathaniel Nelson	Liverpool	
16535	Nelson	Barnet	1841	Liverpool	Joseph Nathaniel Nelson	Elizabeth (Bruintje, Betty) Drielsma		Liverpool	

ID	surname	given names	born	birthplace	father	mother	spouse 1	1851 residence	1851 occupation
373	Nelson	Barnet	1843	?Aldgate, London	Isaac Nelson	Janetta (Jane) Moses		Aldgate, London	scholar
16546	Nelson	Bernard	1805	Dobrzyn, Poland [Dubrizin, Poland]			Frances (Fanny) Israel	Liverpool	watchmaker
14720	Nelson	Caroline	1838	?, London	Isaac Nathan	Janetta (Jane) Moses		Aldgate, London	scholar
17585	Nelson	Catherine	1813	Spitalfields, London	Isaac Davis	Rachael	Lewis Nelson	Spitalfields, London	
17586	Nelson	Catherine	1840	Whitechapel, London	Lewis Nelson	Catherine Davis		Spitalfields, London	scholar
17582	Nelson	Catherine	1844	Aldgate, London	Samuel Nelson	Elizabeth Levy		Aldgate, London	
279	Nelson	Elizabeth	1820	Aldgate, London	Nachum Levi		Samuel Nelson	Aldgate, London	
16533	Nelson	Elizabeth (Bruintje, Betty)	1816	Groningen, Holland	Isaac Jonas Drielsma	Theresa (Mietje) Meyer (Moses) Loewenstein	Joseph Nathaniel Nelson	Liverpool	
16548	Nelson	Emanuel	1840	Liverpool	Bernard Nelson	Frances (Fanny) Israel	Hannah Rebecca Berrick	Liverpool	
14728	Nelson	Emanuel	1841	Spitalfields, London	Moses Nelson	Hannah Abrahams		Spitalfields, London	scholar
16537	Nelson	Emma	1848	Liverpool	Joseph Nathaniel Nelson	Elizabeth (Bruintje, Betty) Drielsma	Abraham Levy	Liverpool	
26865	Nelson	Enleiss	1806	?, Poland	(?)		Samuel Nelson	Aldgate, London	
14725	Nelson	Frances	1833	Spitalfields, London	Moses Nelson	Hannah Abrahams		Spitalfields, London	button maker
17587	Nelson	Frances	1842	Whitechapel, London	Lewis Nelson	Catherine Davis		Spitalfields, London	scholar
16547	Nelson	Frances (Fanny)	1800	Dobrzyn, Poland [Dubrizin, Poland]	(?) Israel		Bernard Nelson	Liverpool	
17292	Nelson	George	1827	?, Russia				Spitalfields, London	jeweller
14723	Nelson	Hannah	1803	Spitalfields, London	Abraham		Moses Nelson	Spitalfields, London	
14722	Nelson	Hannah	1849	?Aldgate, London	Isaac Nathan	Janetta (Jane) Moses	Raphael Nunes Martin (Martines)	Aldgate, London	
17590	Nelson	Hannah	1851	Whitechapel, London	Lewis Nelson	Catherine Davis		Spitalfields, London	
26866	Nelson	Hershel	1835	?, Poland	Samuel Nelson	Enleiss (?)		Aldgate, London	tailor
277	Nelson	Isaac	1816	Amsterdam, Holland	Nathan		Janetta (Jane) Moses	Aldgate, London	general dealer
400	Nelson	Jane	1838	Spitalfields, London	Samuel Nelson		John Harris	Spitalfields, London	
30605	Nelson	Jane	1851	Aldgate, London	Samuel Nelson	Elizabeth Levy		Aldgate, London	
26869	Nelson	Janet	1844	?, Poland	Samuel Nelson	Enleiss (?)		Aldgate, London	
14719	Nelson	Janetta (Jane)	1818	?, London	Dov Behr Moses		Isaac Nelson	Spitalfields, London	
14729	Nelson	John	1845	Spitalfields, London	Moses Nelson	Hannah Abrahams	Sophia Abrahams	Spitalfields, London	scholar
5103	Nelson	John (Selig)	1832	Liepaja, Lithuania [Libau, Russia]			Esther Isaacs	Portsmouth, Hampshire	watchmaker
16532	Nelson	Joseph Nathaniel	1810	?, Poland			Elizabeth (Bruintje, Betty) Drielsma	Liverpool	grocer
26870	Nelson	Kate	1845	?, Poland	Samuel Nelson	Enleiss (?)		Aldgate, London	
286	Nelson	Lewis	1814	Spitalfields, London	Nathan Nelson		Catherine Davis	Spitalfields, London	general dealer
27501	Nelson	Lewis	1831	Middlesex, London				Aldgate, London	hawker
451	Nelson	Lewis	1835	Spitalfields, London	Samuel Nelson			Spitalfields, London	tassel maker?
14726	Nelson	Lewis	1835	Bethnal Green, London	Moses Nelson	Hannah Abrahams	Sarah Nelson	Spitalfields, London	errand boy
16534	Nelson	Louise	1840	Liverpool	Joseph Nathaniel Nelson	Elizabeth (Bruintje, Betty) Drielsma		Liverpool	
17589	Nelson	Martha	1848	Spitalfields, London	Lewis Nelson	Catherine Davis		Spitalfields, London	scholar
16536	Nelson	Morris	1844	Liverpool	Joseph Nathaniel Nelson	Elizabeth (Bruintje, Betty) Drielsma		Liverpool	

ID	surname	given names	born	birthplace	father	mother	spouse 1	1851 residence	1851 occupation
275	Nelson	Moses	1799	Aldgate, London	Nathan Nelson		Hannah Abrahams	Spitalfields, London	tailor
14724	Nelson	Nathan	1828	Bethnal Green, London	Moses Nelson	Hannah Abrahams	Dinah Jacobs	Spitalfields, London	general dealer
17588	Nelson	Nathan	1845	Whitechapel, London	Lewis Nelson	Catherine Davis		Spitalfields, London	scholar
16578	Nelson	Nathaniel	1801	Liverpool			Ann Jones	Liverpool	dentist
14721	Nelson	Nathaniel	1841	?, London	Isaac Nathan	Janetta (Jane) Moses		Aldgate, London	scholar
17583	Nelson	Rachael	1848	Aldgate, London	Samuel Nelson	Elizabeth Levy		Aldgate, London	
16538	Nelson	Rachael	1850	Liverpool	Joseph Nathaniel Nelson	Elizabeth (Bruintje, Betty) Drielsma	Samuel Moses Silverman	Liverpool	
26867	Nelson	Reuben	1838	?, Poland	Samuel Nelson	Enleiss (?)		Aldgate, London	
7440	Nelson	Rose	1842	Aldgate, London	Samuel Nelson	Elizabeth Levy	Lewis Allen	Aldgate, London	
16580	Nelson	Rose	1844	Liverpool	Nathaniel Nelson	Ann Jones		Liverpool	
399	Nelson	Samuel	1798	Spitalfields, London				Spitalfields, London	tailor
26864	Nelson	Samuel	1804	?, Poland			Enleiss (?)	Aldgate, London	tailor
278	Nelson	Samuel	1818	Aldgate, London	Isaac Nelson		Elizabeth Levy	Aldgate, London	orange dealer
26868	Nelson	Sarah	1842	?, Poland	Samuel Nelson	Enleiss (?)		Aldgate, London	
17584	Nelson	Sarah	1849	Aldgate, London	Samuel Nelson	Elizabeth Levy		Aldgate, London	
2549	Nelsons	Elia	1821	?, Poland			(?)	Hull, Yorkshire	
2551	Nelsons	Flossie	1846	?, Poland	Elia Nelsons	(?)		Hull, Yorkshire	
2553	Nelsons	Helen	1850	Hull, Yorkshire	Elia Nelsons	(?)		Hull, Yorkshire	
2550	Nelsons	Herman	1843	?, Poland	Elia Nelsons	(?)		Hull, Yorkshire	
2552	Nelsons	Rebecca	1849	Hull, Yorkshire	Elia Nelsons	(?)		Hull, Yorkshire	
14640	Neman	Charlotte	1845	St Pancras, London	Henry Neman	Elizabeth (?)		Hoxton, London	
14639	Neman	Elizabeth	1818	Sonning, Berkshire [Berks Sunning]	(?)		Henry Neman	Hoxton, London	dressmaker
14638	Neman	Henry	1812	Amsterdam, Holland			Elizabeth (?)	Hoxton, London	tailor
14641	Neman	Jacob	1847	St Pancras, London	Henry Neman	Elizabeth (?)		Hoxton, London	
14642	Neman	John	1849	St Pancras, London	Henry Neman	Elizabeth (?)		Hoxton, London	
4828	Nerwich	Abraham	1795	Poznan, Poland [Posen, Prussia]			Clara Aaron	Birmingham	retail tradesman
4829	Nerwich	Clara	1807	Birmingham	David Aaron	Maria Myers	Abraham Nerwich	Birmingham	
4832	Nerwich	Elizabeth	1836	Birmingham	Abraham Nerwich	Clara Aaron		Birmingham	
18778	Nerwich	Harriette Matilda	1850	Dublin, Ireland	Henry Nerwich	Jane Elizabeth Jacobs	Philip D Jacobs	Dublin, Ireland	
18779	Nerwich	Henry	1804	Poznan, Poland [Posen, Prussia]	Myer (Michael) Nerwich	Theresa (?)	Jane Elizabeth Jacobs	Dublin, Ireland	wholesale jewellery warehouse
18780	Nerwich	Jane Elizabeth	1819	?Finsbury, London	Henry Jacobs	Elizabeth (?)	Henry Nerwich	Dublin, Ireland	
18781	Nerwich	Louis Henry	1847	Dublin, Ireland	Henry Nerwich	Jane Elizabeth Jacobs	Bertha Bridgford	Dublin, Ireland	
18782	Nerwich	Louise Sophia	1849	Dublin, Ireland	Henry Nerwich	Jane Elizabeth Jacobs	B--- B--- Lyons	Dublin, Ireland	
4831	Nerwich	Matilda	1833	Birmingham	Abraham Nerwich	Clara Aaron		Birmingham	
25531	Nerwich	Myer	1780	Poznan, Poland [Posen, Prussia]			Theresa (?)	Dublin, Ireland	
4833	Nerwich	Selina	1838	Birmingham	Abraham Nerwich	Clara Aaron		Birmingham	
25532	Nerwich	Theresa	1783	?Poland [?Prussia]			Myer Nerwich	Dublin, Ireland	
14975	Netto	Rachel	1839	Middlesex, London	(?) Netto			Bethnal Green, London	boarding school pupil
14950	Netto	Sarah	1836	Middlesex, London	(?) Netto			Bethnal Green, London	boarding school pupil

ID	surname	given names	born	birthplace	father	mother	spouse 1	1851 residence	1851 occupation
23824	Neubour	Samuel	1832	?, Russia				Liverpool	commercial traveller (pedlar)
11949	Neugass	Esther	1824	Gibraltar	(?)		Henry Neugass	Whitechapel, London	
11948	Neugass	Henry	1819	?, Germany			Esther (?)	Whitechapel, London	boot maker
11950	Neugass	Solomon	1850	Aldgate, London	Henry Neugass	Esther (?)		Whitechapel, London	
12352	Neugass (Nugas, Neugan)	Samuel	1821	?, Germany	Solomon Neigass		Lina (Lucia) Marcus	Whitechapel, London	boot maker
1948	Neugent	Gershon	1833	Baden Gutenbach, Germany				Swansea, Wales	watchmaker
26384	Neumegen	Catherine	1805	?, Germany	(?)		Martin Neumegen	Aldgate, London	
26385	Neumegen	Deborah	1833	?, Germany	Martin Neumegen	Catherine (?)		Aldgate, London	carpet bag maker
26386	Neumegen	Lewis	1838	?, London	Martin Neumegen	Catherine (?)		Aldgate, London	tinker
26383	Neumegen	Martin	1792	?, Germany			Catherine (?)	Aldgate, London	carpet bag maker
26387	Neumegen	Matilda	1842	?, London	Martin Neumegen	Catherine (?)	Mark Abrahams	Aldgate, London	scholar
9752	Neumegen (Newmeyer)	Albert	1841	Highgate, London	Leopold Neumegen (Newmeyer)	Belinda (?)	Leonora Polak	Kew, London	
9749	Neumegen (Newmeyer)	Belinda	1809	Great Yarmouth, Norfolk			Belinda (?)	Kew, London	
9751	Neumegen (Newmeyer)	Edward	1839	Highgate, London	Leopold Neumegen (Newmeyer)	Belinda (?)		Kew, London	
9750	Neumegen (Newmeyer)	Hurwitz	1844	Kew, London	Leopold Neumegen (Newmeyer)	Belinda (?)		Kew, London	
9748	Neumegen (Newmeyer)	Leopold	1787	Poznan, Poland [Posen, Prussia]			Belinda (?)	Kew, London	school proprietor
4284	Neustadt	Maria	1798	Liverpool	Nathan Lyon	Phoebe Zipporah Aaron	Samuel Neustadt	Birmingham	(merchant) partner's wife
13557	Newbaur	David	1831	?, Poland [?, Prussia]				Manchester	cloth cap maker
26388	Newman	Abraham	1818	?, Poland			Hannah (?)	Aldgate, London	tailor
4834	Newman	Abraham	1823	?, Poland			Paulina (?)	Birmingham	glazier
30191	Newman	Abraham Benjamin	1851	Dudley, Worcestershire	Levy Newman	M--- V--- (?)		Dudley, Worcestershire	
28817	Newman	Adolphus	1804	abroad	Shlomeh		Rebecca Goulston	Spitalfields, London	printer + stationer
28821	Newman	Andrew	1835	Whitechapel, London	Adolphus Newman	Rebecca Goulston		Spitalfields, London	teacher
30183	Newman	Ann	1837	?, Poland	Joseph Newman	Sarah (?)		Dudley, Worcestershire	
5111	Newman	Barnett	1850	Portsmouth, Hampshire	Selig Newman	Eliza Nathan		Portsmouth, Hampshire	
30185	Newman	Bynne	1850	Dudley, Worcestershire	Joseph Newman	Sarah (?)		Dudley, Worcestershire	
28823	Newman	Catharine	1840	Spitalfields, London	Adolphus Newman	Rebecca Goulston		Spitalfields, London	scholar
17031	Newman	Debi	1814	?, Poland	(?)		(?) Newman	Edinburgh, Scotland	
5105	Newman	Eliza	1806	Portsmouth, Hampshire	Jacob Nathan	Hannah (?)	Selig Newman	Portsmouth, Hampshire	
5109	Newman	Elizabeth	1844	Portsmouth, Hampshire	Selig Newman	Eliza Nathan		Portsmouth, Hampshire	
5106	Newman	Emanuel	1837	Portsmouth, Hampshire	Selig Newman	Eliza Nathan		Portsmouth, Hampshire	
5110	Newman	Frances	1846	Portsmouth, Hampshire	Selig Newman	Eliza Nathan		Portsmouth, Hampshire	
30463	Newman	Frederick	1813	Wejherowo, Poland [Neustadt, Russia Poland]				Newcastle-under-Lyme, Staffordshire	glazier
26389	Newman	Hannah	1825	?, Poland	(?)		Abraham Newman	Aldgate, London	
5107	Newman	Hannah	1840	Portsmouth, Hampshire	Selig Newman	Eliza Nathan		Portsmouth, Hampshire	
4838	Newman	Harris	1849	Dudley, Worcestershire	Abraham Newman	Paulina (?)		Birmingham	

ID	surname	given names	born	birthplace	father	mother	spouse 1	1851 residence	1851 occupation
5108	Newman	Henrietta	1841	Portsmouth, Hampshire	Selig Newman	Eliza Nathan	Douglas Davis Samuel	Portsmouth, Hampshire	
17034	Newman	Isral	1843	?, Poland	(?) Newman	Debi (?)		Edinburgh, Scotland	scholar
30181	Newman	Joseph	1811	?, Poland			Sarah (?)	Dudley, Worcestershire	glazier
28819	Newman	Julia	1832	Southwark, London	Adolphus Newman	Rebecca Goulston		Spitalfields, London	
4843	Newman	Leah	1843	Leamington, Warwickshire	William Newman	Priscilla Davis	Isaac Lotinga	Birmingham	
30189	Newman	Levy	1825	?, Poland	(?)	Leane Benjamin	M--- V--- (?)	Dudley, Worcestershire	furniture dealer
30190	Newman	M--- V---	1823	?, Poland	(?)		Levy Newman	Dudley, Worcestershire	
30184	Newman	Minnie	1839	?, Poland	Joseph Newman	Sarah (?)		Dudley, Worcestershire	
4837	Newman	Morris	1847	Dudley, Worcestershire	Abraham Newman	Paulina (?)		Birmingham	scholar
28822	Newman	Nancy	1838	Finsbury, London	Adolphus Newman	Rebecca Goulston	Henry Hart Jacobs	Spitalfields, London	scholar
4835	Newman	Paulina	1827	?, Poland			Abraham Newman	Birmingham	
4842	Newman	Philip	1841	Leamington, Warwickshire	William Newman	Priscilla Davis		Birmingham	scholar
28824	Newman	Phoebe	1846	Spitalfields, London	Adolphus Newman	Rebecca Goulston		Spitalfields, London	scholar
4841	Newman	Priscilla	1823	?, Poland	(?) Davis	Hannah (?)	William Newman	Birmingham	
17032	Newman	Rebacia	1838	?, Poland	(?) Newman	Debi (?)		Edinburgh, Scotland	scholar
28818	Newman	Rebecca	1805	?, London	Mensha Goulston		Adolphus Newman	Spitalfields, London	
4839	Newman	Rebecca	1850	Dudley, Worcestershire	Abraham Newman	Paulina (?)		Birmingham	
4020	Newman	Rosa	1851	Portsmouth, Hampshire	Selig Newman	Eliza Nathan		Portsmouth, Hampshire	
4844	Newman	Samuel	1848	Birmingham	William Newman	Priscilla Davis		Birmingham	
30182	Newman	Sarah	1815	?, Poland	(?)		Joseph Newman	Dudley, Worcestershire	
17033	Newman	Sarah	1840	?, Poland	(?) Newman	Debi (?)		Edinburgh, Scotland	scholar
4836	Newman	Sarah	1846	Dudley, Worcestershire	Abraham Newman	Paulina (?)		Birmingham	scholar
5104	Newman	Selig	1804	?, Poland			Eliza Nathan	Portsmouth, Hampshire	clothes + general dealer
28820	Newman	Sophia	1834	Whitechapel, London	Adolphus Newman	Rebecca Goulston		Spitalfields, London	dressmaker
4840	Newman	William	1815	?, Poland [?, Prussia]	Phillip Newman		Priscilla Davis	Birmingham	watches + jewellery
17035	Newman	Zemul	1849	Edinburgh, Scotland	(?) Newman	Debi (?)		Edinburgh, Scotland	
25949	Newnberg (Newnberger)	Herman Louis	1823	Hanover, Germany			Mary Canty	Aldgate, London	hairdresser empl 1
6207	Newsome	Mary	1834	Spaldington, Yorkshire	Th--- Newsome		Joseph Nathan	St Pancras, London	
4285	Newstadt	Amelia	1823	Birmingham	(?) Newstadt	Maria Lyon		Birmingham	merchant's daughter
4286	Newstadt	Norton	1837	Birmingham	(?) Newstadt	Maria Lyon		Birmingham	scholar at home
15480	Newton	Abigail	1847	Surrey, London	Maurice (Moses) Newton	Catherine Cantor	Moss Levy	Whitechapel, London	
3447	Newton	Catherine	1826	City, London	Lewis Cantor	Agnes Woolf	Maurice (Moses) Newton	Whitechapel, London	
15482	Newton	Eadie Louisa	1850	Stepney, London	Maurice (Moses) Newton	Catherine Cantor		Whitechapel, London	
15479	Newton	Jacob	1845	Finsbury, London	Maurice (Moses) Newton	Catherine Cantor		Whitechapel, London	
15481	Newton	Lewis Abraham	1849	Stepney, London	Maurice (Moses) Newton	Catherine Cantor		Whitechapel, London	
15478	Newton	Maurice (Moses)	1820	City, London	Isaac Newton	Hannah Dias	Catherine Cantor	Whitechapel, London	cigar maker foreman
29350	Nicab (Necobb)	Esther	1828	Plymouth, Devon	Abraham Montefiore		Moses Nicab (Necobb)	Whitechapel, London	
29349	Nicab (Necobb)	Moses	1815	Algiers, Algeria	Samuel Necobb		Esther Montefiore	Whitechapel, London	traveller
7303	Nieto	Abraham Haim	1838	City, London	Jacob Nieto	Miriam (?)	Hannah Belasco	Aldgate, London	boarding school pupil
16358	Nieto	David	1842	City, London	Jacob Nieto	Miriam (?)	Esther Belasco	Aldgate, London	boarding school pupil
27739	Nisonthall	Aaron	1821	?, Russia				Spitalfields, London	jeweller
22857	Noah	Abraham	1840	Whitechapel, London	Joseph Noah	Mary (?)		Whitechapel, London	scholar
25952	Noah	Catherine	1808	Amsterdam, Holland	Aaron Simons		Joseph Abraham Noah	Aldgate, London	(tailor's?) shop worker
22859	Noah	Catherine	1844	Whitechapel, London	Joseph Noah	Mary (?)		Whitechapel, London	scholar

ID	surname	given names	born	birthplace	father	mother	spouse 1	1851 residence	1851 occupation
4846	Noah	Enoch	1823	Golin, Poland	Noah Noah		Sarah Robert	Birmingham	boot + shoe mfr
25955	Noah	Esther	1838	Whitechapel, London	Joseph Abraham Noah	Catherine Simons		Aldgate, London	cap maker
25956	Noah	Isaac	1842	Whitechapel, London	Joseph Abraham Noah	Catherine Simons		Aldgate, London	scholar
22852	Noah	Joseph	1806	Whitechapel, London			Mary (?)	Whitechapel, London	clothes dealer
25953	Noah	Joseph	1829	Amsterdam, Holland	Joseph Abraham Noah	Catherine Simons		Aldgate, London	hawker
25951	Noah	Joseph Abraham	1803	Amsterdam, Holland	Noah		Catherine Simons	Aldgate, London	tailor
25957	Noah	Levy	1844	Rotterdam, Holland	Joseph Abraham Noah	Catherine Simons		Aldgate, London	scholar
22853	Noah	Mary	1807	Oxford, Oxfordshire	(?)		Joseph Noah	Whitechapel, London	
25958	Noah	Mary	1847	Whitechapel, London	Joseph Abraham Noah	Catherine Simons		Aldgate, London	scholar
22854	Noah	Rachael	1833	Whitechapel, London	Joseph Noah	Mary (?)		Whitechapel, London	umbrella coverer
22858	Noah	Samuel	1842	Whitechapel, London	Joseph Noah	Mary (?)		Whitechapel, London	scholar
4847	Noah	Sarah	1831	Poznan, Poland [Posen, Prussia]	Jacob Robert	Elizabeth (?)	Enoch Noah	Birmingham	
22856	Noah	Sarah	1837	Whitechapel, London	Joseph Noah	Mary (?)		Whitechapel, London	umbrella coverer
25959	Noah	Simon	1850	Whitechapel, London	Joseph Abraham Noah	Catherine Simons		Aldgate, London	
22855	Noah	Sophia	1834	Whitechapel, London	Joseph Noah	Mary (?)		Whitechapel, London	umbrella coverer
11093	Noah (Da Costa Noah)	Abigail	1808	Middlesex, London	Moses Rodrigues Brandon	Luna (?)	Solomon Noah (Da Costa Noah)	Aldgate, London	confectioner
23079	Noah (Da Costa Noah)	Amelia (Miryam)	1824	City, London	Samuel Noah (Da Costa Noah)	Dinah Levy		Aldgate, London	bonnet maker
23080	Noah (Da Costa Noah)	Benjamin	1830	Middlesex, London	Samuel Noah (Da Costa Noah)	Dinah Levy	Emma Amelia Lyons [Pesman]	Aldgate, London	boot maker
11095	Noah (Da Costa Noah)	Benjamin	1839	Middlesex, London	Solomon Noah (Da Costa Noah)	Abigail de Moses Rodrigues Brandon		Aldgate, London	
11101	Noah (Da Costa Noah)	Deborah	1850	?Aldgate, London	Solomon Noah (Da Costa Noah)	Abigail de Moses Rodrigues Brandon		Aldgate, London	
23076	Noah (Da Costa Noah)	Dinah	1790	City, London	Samuel Levy		Samuel de Jacob Noah (Da Costa Noah)	Aldgate, London	traveller's wife
11096	Noah (Da Costa Noah)	Ellen (Luna)	1840	Middlesex, London	Solomon Noah (Da Costa Noah)	Abigail de Moses Rodrigues Brandon		Aldgate, London	
9324	Noah (Da Costa Noah)	Esther	1771	Whitechapel, London	Joseph Cohen		Jacob de Isaac Noah Da Costa	Aldgate, London	poor
11097	Noah (Da Costa Noah)	Esther	1843	?, London	Solomon Noah (Da Costa Noah)	Abigail de Moses Rodrigues Brandon		Aldgate, London	
23078	Noah (Da Costa Noah)	Fanny	1822	City, London	Samuel Noah (Da Costa Noah)	Dinah Levy		Aldgate, London	silk cleaner
11094	Noah (Da Costa Noah)	Hagar (Agatha)	1838	Middlesex, London	Solomon Noah (Da Costa Noah)	Abigail de Moses Rodrigues Brandon		Aldgate, London	confectioner
23081	Noah (Da Costa Noah)	Jacob (John)	1832	Middlesex, London	Samuel Noah (Da Costa Noah)	Dinah Levy	Esther Ventura	Aldgate, London	boot maker
11099	Noah (Da Costa Noah)	Jane (Jael)	1845	?, London	Solomon Noah (Da Costa Noah)	Abigail de Moses Rodrigues Brandon	Isaac Harris	Aldgate, London	
11100	Noah (Da Costa Noah)	Julia (Judith)	1847	?, London	Solomon Noah (Da Costa Noah)	Abigail de Moses Rodrigues Brandon		Aldgate, London	
11098	Noah (Da Costa Noah)	Moses	1843	?, London	Solomon Noah (Da Costa Noah)	Abigail de Moses Rodrigues Brandon		Aldgate, London	

ID	surname	given names	born	birthplace	father	mother	spouse 1	1851 residence	1851 occupation
23077	Noah (Da Costa Noah)	Samuel	1799	?, London	Jacob de Isaac Noah (Da Costa Noah)	Esther de Joseph Cohen	Dinah Levy	Aldgate, London	traveller
11092	Noah (Da Costa Noah)	Solomon	1817	Middlesex, London	Benjamin Da Costa Noah	Agar de Joseph Abendanha	Abigail de Moses Rodrigues Brandon	Aldgate, London	confectioner
25954	Noah [Joseph]	Aaron	1832	Spitalfields, London	Joseph Abraham Noah	Catherine Simons	Sarah Hermans	Aldgate, London	tailor
13712	Noiman	Adolph	1829	?Budapest, Hungary [Pesth]				Bloomsbury, London	journeyman tailor
30693	Norden	Charlotte	1821	Strand, London	Jacob Moses Norden	Catherine (Keila) Jacobs		Chelsea, London	dressmaker
20505	Norden	David	1836	Middlesex, London	Mark Jacob Norden	Jane Arrobus	Fanny Simons	Vauxhall, London	apprentice cigar maker
14689	Norden	Elizabeth	1845	Clerkenwell, London	Manasseh Norden	Isabella Barnett		Clerkenwell, London	
21442	Norden	Elizabeth	1850	Bury, Lancashire	Louis Norden	Esther Solomon		Bury, Lancashire	
14691	Norden	Emanuel Menahem	1849	Clerkenwell, London	Manasseh Norden	Isabella Barnett	Agnes Jessurun	Clerkenwell, London	
21441	Norden	Esther	1825	Nottingham, Nottinghamshire	(?) Solomon	Lydia (?)	Louis Norden	Bury, Lancashire	
20503	Norden	Esther	1833	Middlesex, London	Mark Jacob Norden	Jane Arrobus	Solomon Jacobs	Vauxhall, London	
20502	Norden	George	1832	Middlesex, London	Mark Jacob Norden	Jane Arrobus	Mary (Miriam) Phillips	Vauxhall, London	apprentice cigar maker
6205	Norden	Isabella	1820	Bloomsbury, London	(?) Barnett		Manasseh Norden	Clerkenwell, London	furrier
30691	Norden	Jane	1799	Westminster, London	Jacob Moses Norden	Catherine (Keila) Jacobs		Chelsea, London	
20500	Norden	Jane	1800	Clerkenwell, London	(?) Arrobus		Mark Norden	Vauxhall, London	
20504	Norden	Joseph	1834	Middlesex, London	Mark Jacob Norden	Jane Arrobus	Rachel Levi	Vauxhall, London	apprentice cigar maker
21807	Norden	Judah	1810	Strand, London	Jacob Moses Norden	Catherine (Keila) Jacobs	Sarah Lazarus	Chelsea, London	china dealer
30692	Norden	Leah	1815	Strand, London	Jacob Moses Norden	Catherine (Keila) Jacobs		Chelsea, London	dressmaker
14690	Norden	Lewis	1846	Clerkenwell, London	Manasseh Norden	Isabella Barnett	Sarah Jacobs	Clerkenwell, London	
21440	Norden	Louis	1823	Middlesex, London	Joseph Norden	Elizabeth (Beila) (?)	Esther Solomon	Bury, Lancashire	tailor + draper empl 6
22303	Norden	Louisa	1828	Holborn, London	Joseph Norden	Elizabeth (Beila) (?)	Henry Hyman	Hampstead, London	cook
6204	Norden	Manasseh	1819	Covent Garden, London	Joseph Norden	Elizabeth (Beila) (?)	Isabella Barnett	Clerkenwell, London	glass lustre manufacturer + fancy glass cutter (master)
20499	Norden	Mark Jacob	1799	Marylebone, London	Jacob Moses Norden	Catherine (Keila) Jacobs	Jane Arrobus	Vauxhall, London	accountant + fancy shop
20501	Norden	Rachel	1828	Middlesex, London	Mark Jacob Norden	Jane Arrobus	Harris Raphael	Vauxhall, London	artificial florist
26576	Norman	Harris	1830	?, Poland [?, Russian Poland]				Cambridge	hawker - a Jew
30312	Norton	Elizabeth	1798	Aldgate, London	(?)		Joseph Levy	City, London	
30314	Norton	Fitzroy	1836	City, London	Louis Norton	(?)		City, London	occasional assistant to solicitor + attorney
30315	Norton	Frederick	1837	City, London	Louis Norton	(?)		City, London	occasional assistant to solicitor + attorney
30313	Norton	Louis	1798	Whitechapel, London	Aharon		Maria (?)	City, London	solicitor + attorney
13558	Novetzka	David	1829	?, Germany				Manchester	cloth cap maker
23852	Novra	Benjamin	1834	?, London	George Novra	Rebecca Abrahams		Soho, London	
23848	Novra	George	1802	?, Poland [?, Prussia]	Tsevi Hirsch		Rebecca Abrahams	Soho, London	importer of foreign goods
23850	Novra	Henry	1832	?, London	George Novra	Rebecca Abrahams		Soho, London	clerk in foreign house
23853	Novra	Lewis	1838	?, London	George Novra	Rebecca Abrahams		Soho, London	
23851	Novra	Maria	1833	?, London	George Novra	Rebecca Abrahams		Soho, London	
23849	Novra	Rebecca	1802	?, London	Benjamin Abrahams		George Novra	Soho, London	
26947	Nowalzki	Bar	1833	?, Poland				Aldgate, London	tailor
13442	Nowitsky	Simon	1825	?, Poland				Manchester	clth cap mkr

ID	surname	given names	born	birthplace	father	mother	spouse 1	1851 residence	1851 occupation
13477	Nowitsky	Simon	1825	?, Poland [?, Poland Prussia]				Manchester	cloth cap maker
1947	Nuchamm	Abraham	1817	?, Russia				Swansea, Wales	servant
13543	Nun---	Lewis	1821	?, Germany				Manchester	clerk
24185	Nunes Nunes Israel)	Lydia	1786	Hackney, London	Abraham de Isaac Nunes Israel	Sarah de Abraham Del Valle		Hackney, London	house proprietor
24186	Nunes Nunes Israel)	Raffael (frederick)	1798	Hackney, London	Abraham de Isaac Nunes Israel	Sarah de Abraham Del Valle		Hackney, London	stockbroker
22282	Nunez	Hannah	1815	?, London	Moses Nunez	Sarah (?)		Whitechapel, London	
22283	Nunez	Judith	1838	?, London	Moses Nunez	Sarah (?)		Whitechapel, London	
10865	Nunez	Louisa (Leah)	1810	Spitalfields, London	Aaron Cohen De Azevedo	Judith (?)	Phineas Nunez	Spitalfields, London	
10864	Nunez	Phineas	1812	Spitalfields, London	Moses Nunez	Sarah (?)	Louisa (Leah) de Aaron Cohen De Azevedo	Spitalfields, London	cabinet maker empl 5
22281	Nunez	Sarah	1806	?, London	Moses Nunez	Sarah (?)		Whitechapel, London	
18637	Nuremberg	Jeanette	1845	Brighton, Sussex	Michael Simon Nuremberg	Miriam (?)	Abraham Morris	Brighton, Sussex	
18630	Nuremberg	Michael Simon	1813	?, Germany			Miriam Nathan	Brighton, Sussex	Synagogue secretary
18636	Nuremberg	Miriam	1823	?, Poland [?, Prussia]	(?) Nathan		Michael Simon Nuremberg	Brighton, Sussex	
18638	Nuremberg	Sarah	1847	Brighton, Sussex	Michael Simon Nuremberg	Miriam Nathan	Philip Isaacs	Brighton, Sussex	
2314	Nussbaum	Joseph	1828	?, Poland				Leeds, Yorkshire	hawker
30946	Nussbaum	Morris	1805	?, Germany				Hull, Yorkshire	dealer in stationery
28942	Nykerk	Morris	1825	Amsterdam, Holland	(?) Solomon			Whitechapel, London	cigar maker journeyman
30906	Obranski	Alfred	1845	Liverpool	Henry Obranski	Eliza (?)		Liverpool	
30904	Obranski	Eliza	1821	Middlesex, London	(?)		Henry Obranski	Liverpool	
30903	Obranski	Henry	1816	?, Poland			Eliza (?)	Liverpool	bookbinder
30905	Obranski	Mira	1843	?, America	Henry Obranski	Eliza (?)		Liverpool	
28053	Octofal	Michael	1831	Bydgoszcz, Poland [Bromberg, Prussia]				Spitalfields, London	traveller
23767	Oldenburg	Harriet	1821	Hamburg, Germany	(?) Kisch		Michael Oldenburg	Liverpool	
23766	Oldenburg	Michael	1813	Berlin, Germany [Berlin, Prussia]			Harriet Kisch	Liverpool	tailor master empl 6
23770	Oldenburg	Samuel	1851	Liverpool	Michael Oldenburg	Harriet Kisch		Liverpool	
23769	Oldenburg	Sarah	1849	Liverpool	Michael Oldenburg	Harriet Kisch		Liverpool	
23768	Oldenburg	Selina	1847	Liverpool	Michael Oldenburg	Harriet Kisch		Liverpool	
4063	Ollendorf	Mary	1842	Maidstone, Kent	(?) Ollendorf		Leon Emanuel	?Maidstone, Kent	
4361	Olsher	Julia	1834	?, London				Birmingham	shop assistant
27352	Onger	William	1820	Wrzesnia, Poland [Wreschen, Germany]				Aldgate, London	wholesale jeweller
10051	Onions	Mary Ann (Sarah)	1837	Bilston, Staffordshire	(?) Onions	Mary (?)	Alfred Barnard	Wolverhampton, Staffordshire	
26747	Openheim	Benjamin	1778	?, Germany				Aldgate, London	general dealer
17772	Oppenham	Adelade	1823	Hamburg, Germany	Myer Oppenham	M--- (?)	M---	Spitalfields, London	cap maker
17771	Oppenham	M---	1786	Hamburg, Germany			Myer Oppenham	Spitalfields, London	independent
17770	Oppenham	Myer	1766	Hamburg, Germany			M--- (?)	Spitalfields, London	independent
18140	Oppenheim	Abraham	1763	Whitechapel, London			(?)	Mile End, London	optician
11943	Oppenheim	Abraham Samuel	1816	?, Holland			Gertrude (?)	Whitechapel, London	cigar maker
14653	Oppenheim	Amelia	1815	Middlesex, London	Michael Oppenheim		Hirsch Fink	Hoxton, London	cabinet maker

ID	surname	given names	born	birthplace	father	mother	spouse 1	1851 residence	1851 occupation
13813	Oppenheim	Ann	1820	?, Poland [?, Prussia]	(?) Joel		S--- B--- Oppenheim	Manchester	
7740	Oppenheim	Augustus	1838	Shoreditch, London	Simeon Oppenheim	Maria Levy		Shoreditch, London	scholar at home
13814	Oppenheim	Benjamin	1841	?, Poland [?, Prussia]	S--- B--- Oppenheim	Ann Joel		Manchester	scholar
13815	Oppenheim	David	1843	?, Poland [?, Prussia]	S--- B--- Oppenheim	Ann Joel		Manchester	scholar
14928	Oppenheim	Edward John	1839	Hackney, London				Bethnal Green, London	boarding school pupil
7821	Oppenheim	Elizabeth (Betsy)	1798	Truro, Cornwall	Israel Levy	Hannah Moses	Samuel Oppenheim	Penzance, Cornwall	
18142	Oppenheim	Emanuel	1811	?, Belgium	Abraham Oppenheim	(?)	Goldje Sekkel	Mile End, London	jeweller
24192	Oppenheim	Emanuel	1812	Wroclaw, Poland [Breslau, Prussia]	Abraham Oppenheim		Golda Sekkel	De Beauvoir, London	merchant
14309	Oppenheim	Emma	1815	Hamburg, Germany	(?)		James Oppenheim	Manchester	
14311	Oppenheim	Emma	1845	Manchester	James Oppenheim	Emma (?)		Manchester	
23119	Oppenheim	Ernest (Baruch)	1823	?, France	Joseph Meyer Oppenheim		Clara Harris	City, London	foreign merchant
7832	Oppenheim	Evelina	1837	Shoreditch, London	Simeon Oppenheim	Maria Joseph		Shoreditch, London	
18143	Oppenheim	Fanny	1825	Stepney, London	Abraham Oppenheim	(?)		Mile End, London	
13818	Oppenheim	Fanny	1849	Manchester	S--- B--- Oppenheim	Ann Joel		Manchester	
14310	Oppenheim	George	1842	Hamburg, Germany	James Oppenheim	Emma (?)		Manchester	scholar
11942	Oppenheim	Gertrude	1821	?, Holland	(?)		Abraham Samuel Oppenheim	Whitechapel, London	cigar maker's wife
7827	Oppenheim	Hannah	1835	City, London	Simeon Oppenheim	Maria Joseph		Shoreditch, London	scholar at home
14962	Oppenheim	Henrietta	1838	Middlesex, London	(?) Oppenheim			Bethnal Green, London	boarding school pupil
24965	Oppenheim	Henry	1819	?, Holland			Cicely Catherine Obree	Haggerston, London	foreign agent
5374	Oppenheim	Israel	1843	Penzance, Cornwall	Samuel Oppenheim	Elizabeth (Betsy) Levy	Matilda Joseph	Penzance, Cornwall	
13817	Oppenheim	Jacob	1847	North Shields, Tyne & Wear	S--- B--- Oppenheim	Ann Joel		Manchester	
11945	Oppenheim	Jacob	1848	Whitechapel, London	Abraham Samuel Oppenheim	Gertrude (?)	Leah Phillips	Whitechapel, London	
14308	Oppenheim	James	1813	Middlesex, London			Emma (?)	Manchester	commission agent
14312	Oppenheim	James	1847	Manchester	James Oppenheim	Emma (?)		Manchester	
23186	Oppenheim	John M	1802	Hamburg, Germany				City, London	fur + skin merchant
18141	Oppenheim	Joseph	1799	?, Belgium	Abraham Oppenheim	(?)		Mile End, London	optician + tobacconist
9184	Oppenheim	Joseph	1805	?, Germany				Whitechapel, London	merchant
7826	Oppenheim	Lewis	1832	Whitechapel, London	Simeon Oppenheim	Maria Joseph		Shoreditch, London	
7739	Oppenheim	Maria	1803	Whitechapel, London	S--- Joseph		Simeon Oppenheim	Shoreditch, London	
23759	Oppenheim	Martha	1798	Middlesex, London	Isaiah Israel		Michael Solomon Oppenheim	Liverpool	
23758	Oppenheim	Michael Solomon	1795	?, Poland [?, Prussia]	Joseph Oppenheim		(?)	Liverpool	Minister of the Hebrew Congregation
18763	Oppenheim	Minna	1820	?, Germany				Euston, London	cook
14652	Oppenheim	Morris Michael	1820	?Middlesex, London	Michael Oppenheim		Sarah Mosely	Hoxton, London	dealer in sponge, walking sticks, umbrellas &c + timber merchant
7824	Oppenheim	Morris Simeon	1824	City, London	Simeon Oppenheim	Maria Joseph		Shoreditch, London	secretary of school institution
13816	Oppenheim	Mynna	1845	North Shields, Tyne & Wear	S--- B--- Oppenheim	Ann Joel		Manchester	
23120	Oppenheim	Palmir	1824	?, France	Joseph Meyer Oppenheim			City, London	
7828	Oppenheim	Priscilla	1843	Shoreditch, London	Simeon Oppenheim	Maria Joseph	Montague Louis Jonas	Shoreditch, London	scholar at home
7830	Oppenheim	Rebecca	1840	Shoreditch, London	Simeon Oppenheim	Maria Joseph	George Leon Abrahams	Shoreditch, London	scholar at home

ID	surname	given names	born	birthplace	father	mother	spouse 1	1851 residence	1851 occupation
23760	Oppenheim	Rosetta	1834	Liverpool	Michael Solomon Oppenheim	(?)		Liverpool	
11944	Oppenheim	Rosetta	1847	Whitechapel, London	Abraham Samuel Oppenheim	Gertrude (?)		Whitechapel, London	
13812	Oppenheim	S--- B---	1812	?, Poland [?, Prussia]			Ann Joel	Manchester	cap mfr
166	Oppenheim	Samuel	1794	?, Germany	Nathan Oppenheim		Elizabeth (Betsy) Levy	Penzance, Cornwall	clothier
7825	Oppenheim	Samuel	1827	City, London	Simeon Oppenheim	Maria Joseph		Shoreditch, London	
11946	Oppenheim	Samuel	1849	Whitechapel, London	Abraham Samuel Oppenheim	Gertrude (?)		Whitechapel, London	
14651	Oppenheim	Sarah	1825	Glasgow, Scotland	Moss Mosely		Morris Michael Oppenheim	Hoxton, London	cabinet maker's wife
7833	Oppenheim	Sarah	1830	City, London	Simeon Oppenheim	Maria Joseph	Joseph de Castro	Finsbury, London	
7475	Oppenheim	Simeon	1797	City, London	Yehiel		Maria Joseph	Shoreditch, London	gentleman + secretary of the Synagogue
4856	Oppenheimer	Leopold	1834	Hamburg, Germany				Birmingham	merchant
2554	Oppenhoim	Samson	1829	Hamburg, Germany				Hull, Yorkshire	
9304	Orobio	Betsy (Bathsheba) Mendoza	1778	?	Seby alias Barnet		Moses Mendoza Orobio	Aldgate, London	poor
12807	Osborn	Esther	1849	Chatteris, Cambridgeshire	John Osborn	Susan (?)	Jacob Da Silva	Chatteris, Cambridgeshire	
30945	Ossofiks	Herman	1830	?, Germany				Hull, Yorkshire	journeyman tailor
26216	Osterman	Lipman	1834	Amsterdam, Holland				Aldgate, London	cigar maker
17777	Ottolangui (Otolango)	Abraham	1846	Spitalfields, London	Henry Abrahams	Sarah Ottolangui		Spitalfields, London	
17773	Ottolangui (Otolango)	Alexander (Elisha)	1804	Mile End, London			Elizabeth De Beer	Spitalfields, London	general dealer
17774	Ottolangui (Otolango)	Elizabeth	1805	Spitalfields, London	Leb de Beer		Alexander Ottolangui (Otolango)	Spitalfields, London	
17775	Ottolangui (Otolango)	John	1842	Spitalfields, London				Spitalfields, London	scholar
17776	Ottolangui (Otolango) [Langley]	Alexander	1844	Spitalfields, London	Henry Abrahams	Sarah Ottolangui		Spitalfields, London	scholar
13277	Ottolengui	Aaron	1810	Aldgate, London	Israel Ottolangui	Miriam de Abraham Alevy	Regina (Reyna) de Jacob Bensabat	Spitalfields, London	chandler shop keeper
28868	Ottolengui	Abraham	1795	Whitechapel, London	Israel Ottolangui	Simha (?)	Sarah de Moses Toledano	Spitalfields, London	
13282	Ottolengui	Abraham (Richard)	1843	Spitalfields, London	Aaron Ottolengui	Regina (Reyna) de Jacob Bensabat	Katherine Dale	Spitalfields, London	scholar
13284	Ottolengui	Amelia (Miriam)	1847	Spitalfields, London	Aaron Ottolengui	Regina (Reyna) de Jacob Bensabat	David Romain (Romano)	Spitalfields, London	
28869	Ottolengui	Deborah	1788	Whitechapel, London	Isaac Martin		(?) Cohen	Spitalfields, London	
13285	Ottolengui	Eleazer	1849	Spitalfields, London	Aaron Ottolengui	Regina (Reyna) de Jacob Bensabat		Spitalfields, London	
13283	Ottolengui	Mordecai (Montague)	1845	Spitalfields, London	Aaron Ottolengui	Regina (Reyna) de Jacob Bensabat	Harriet Best	Spitalfields, London	
13279	Ottolengui	Rachel	1833	Middlesex, London	Aaron Ottolengui	Regina (Reyna) de Jacob Bensabat	Henry Simmons	Spitalfields, London	
13278	Ottolengui	Regina (Reyna)	1814	Aldgate, London	Jacob Bensabat	Rachel de David Rodrigues	Aaron Ottolengui	Spitalfields, London	
13289	Ottolengui [Langley]	Amelia	1832	Spitalfields, London	Moses (Moss) Ottolengui [Langley]	Emma de Jacob Bensabat	George (Gershon) Mendes	Spitalfields, London	

ID	surname	given names	born	birthplace	father	mother	spouse 1	1851 residence	1851 occupation
13293	Ottolengui [Langley]	David	1846	Spitalfields, London	Moses (Moss) Ottolengui [Langley]	Emma de Jacob Bensabat	Agnes Dossett	Spitalfields, London	scholar
29903	Ottolengui [Langley]	Elizabeth (Betsey, Brina)	1808	Portsmouth, Hampshire	Jacob Levy		Samuel Ottolengui [Langley]	Wapping, London	
13287	Ottolengui [Langley]	Emma	1820	Aldgate, London	Jacob Bensabat	Rachel de David Rodrigues	Moses (Moss) Ottolengui [Langley]	Spitalfields, London	
13280	Ottolengui [Langley]	Israel	1835	Middlesex, London	Aaron Ottolengui	Regina (Reyna) de Jacob Bensabat	Ellen Dewhurst	Spitalfields, London	cigar maker
13291	Ottolengui [Langley]	Israel [Alfred]	1841	Spitalfields, London	Moses (Moss) Ottolengui [Langley]	Emma de Jacob Bensabat	Mary Hannah (Ann) Selt [Jones, Cooper, Twomey]	Spitalfields, London	scholar
13288	Ottolengui [Langley]	Jacob (John)	1834	Spitalfields, London	Moses (Moss) Ottolengui [Langley]	Emma de Jacob Bensabat	Fanny Simmons	Spitalfields, London	general dealer
13281	Ottolengui [Langley]	Jacob (John)	1841	Spitalfields, London	Aaron Ottolengui	Regina (Reyna) de Jacob Bensabat	Clara Frances Burgess	Spitalfields, London	scholar
13294	Ottolengui [Langley]	Joshua (Josiah)	1848	Spitalfields, London	Moses (Moss) Ottolengui [Langley]	Emma de Jacob Bensabat	Sarah Ottolengui	Spitalfields, London	scholar
13286	Ottolengui [Langley]	Moses (Moss)	1808	Wapping, London	Israel Ottolangui	Miriam de Abraham Halevy	Emma de Jacob Bensabat	Spitalfields, London	general dealer
13290	Ottolengui [Langley]	Rachel	1837	Spitalfields, London	Moses (Moss) Ottolengui [Langley]	Emma de Jacob Bensabat	Lewis Solomon	Spitalfields, London	scholar
13292	Ottolengui [Langley]	Reyna	1845	Spitalfields, London	Moses (Moss) Ottolengui [Langley]	Emma de Jacob Bensabat	Abraham Joachim	Spitalfields, London	scholar
29902	Ottolengui [Langley]	Samuel	1805	Middlesex, London	Israel Ottolangui	Miriam de Abraham Alevy	Elizabeth (Betsey, Brina) Levy	Wapping, London	cab proprietor
11818	Oudkeek	Samuel	1803	Amsterdam, Holland				Whitechapel, London	porter (nk)
16447	Overweg	Augusta	1822	Hamburg, Germany				Shoreditch, London	governess
16446	Overweg	Wilhelmina	1821	Hamburg, Germany				Shoreditch, London	governess
21436	Owhsi	Jacob	1816	Cracow, Poland				Nottingham, Nottinghamshire	hawker of jewellery
10197	Pacifico	Clara	1806	Gibraltar	(?)		David (Chevaler Don) Pacifico	Aldgate, London	
10196	Pacifico	David (Chevalier Don)	1786	Gibraltar	Asher de Isaac Pacifico	Bella de Moseh Rietti	Clara (?)	Aldgate, London	annuitant
24096	Pacifico	Emanuel	1768	?, London	Asher de Isaac Pacifico	Bella de Moseh Rietti	Sarah de Jacob Israel Brandon	Bloomsbury, London	retired medical
10198	Pacifico	Esther	1836	Gibraltar	David (Chevalier Don) Pacifico	Clara (?)	Abraham de Moses Hassan	Aldgate, London	
24097	Pacifico	Sarah	1777	?, London	Jacob Israel Brandon	Sarah (?)	Emanuel Pacifico	Bloomsbury, London	
29054	Packman	Jacob	1828	Poznan, Poland [Duchy of Posen, Prussia]				Whitechapel, London	tailor
14062	Padr	Joshua	1832	Istanbul, Turkey [Constantinople]				Manchester	assistant (foreign ho)
30727	Paiba	Aaron	1839	Bethnal Green, London	Isaac de Aaron Paiba	Priscilla Phillips		Bethnal Green, London	scholar
30731	Paiba	Benjamin Frederick	1846	Bethnal Green, London	Isaac de Aaron Paiba	Priscilla Phillips		Bethnal Green, London	scholar
21337	Paiba	Edward	1793	Whitechapel, London			Pamela (?)	Walworth, London	harness maker

ID	surname	given names	born	birthplace	father	mother	spouse 1	1851 residence	1851 occupation
13063	Paiba	Harriet (Hannah)	1834	Covent Garden, London	Isaac de Aaron Paiba	Priscilla (Sprinza) de Moses Phillips	Morris Salinger	Bethnal Green, London	governess
24283	Paiba	Harriett	1834	?, London	(?) Paiba			Bloomsbury, London	
30728	Paiba	Henry	1839	Bethnal Green, London	Isaac de Aaron Paiba	Priscilla Phillips		Bethnal Green, London	scholar
13082	Paiba	Isaac	1796	Aldgate, London	Aaron Paiba	Sarah de Abraham Vanano	Priscilla (Sprinza) de Moses Phillips	Bethnal Green, London	leather seller
30730	Paiba	Kate	1845	Bethnal Green, London	Isaac de Aaron Paiba	Priscilla Phillips		Bethnal Green, London	scholar
30725	Paiba	Matilda	1829	Aldgate, London	Isaac de Aaron Paiba	Priscilla Phillips		Bethnal Green, London	dressmaker?
13084	Paiba	Phineas	1823	?London	Isaac de Aaron Paiba	Priscilla Phillips	Jeanette Lion Leman	Bethnal Green, London	merchant
13083	Paiba	Priscilla	1803	Aldgate, London	Moses Phillips		Isaac Paiba	Bethnal Green, London	leather seller
30729	Paiba	Rachael?	1844	Bethnal Green, London	Isaac de Aaron Paiba	Priscilla Phillips		Bethnal Green, London	scholar
30732	Paiba	Ronah Adelaide	1842	Bethnal Green, London	Isaac de Aaron Paiba	Priscilla Phillips	A--- Harris	Bethnal Green, London	
30726	Paiba	Samuel	1836	Aldgate, London	Isaac de Aaron Paiba	Priscilla Phillips	Ernesta Davis	Bethnal Green, London	clerk?
23417	Palache?	Abraham	1836	?, London				Aldgate, London	shop boy
9623	Palachy	Amelia	1848	Mile End, London	Mordecai Palachy	Hannah Henriques Julian		Aldgate, London	
9631	Palachy	Clara	1801	?Germany	(?)		Samuel Palachy	Spitalfields, London	
9622	Palachy	Esther	1847	Stepney, London	Mordecai Palachy	Hannah Henriques Julian		Aldgate, London	
9620	Palachy	Hannah	1821	?Barbados, West Indies	Moses Henriques Julian	Esther de Pass	Mordecai Palachy	Aldgate, London	cap maker
9630	Palachy	Mary (Mary Ann, Miriam)	1826	Aldgate, London	Harry Aaron		Moses Palachy	Spitalfields, London	
9621	Palachy	Mordecai	1818	?, Germany	Samuel Palachy	Clara (?)	Hannah Henriques Julian	Aldgate, London	cap maker
9626	Palachy	Moses	1826	Aldgate, London	Samuel Palachy	Clara (?)	Mary (Mary Ann, Miriam) Aaron	Spitalfields, London	general dealer
9625	Palachy	Samuel	1765	Hamburg, Germany			Clara (?)	Spitalfields, London	tailor
9624	Palachy	Samuel	1849	Stepney, London	Mordecai Palachy	Hannah Henriques Julian		Aldgate, London	
9777	Palak	James	1838	Monmouth, Wales				Kew, London	boarding school pupil
7291	Palgrave (Cohen)	Francis	1788	Kentish Town, London	Meyer Cohen	Rachel Levien	Elizabeth Turner	Hampstead, London	Knight + Deputy Keeper Public Records
14206	Pallor	Jetta	1828	?, Poland [?, Prussia]	(?)		(?) Pallor	Manchester	tailoress
14709	Paniel	Jacob	1815	?, Holland				Aldgate, London	boot maker
24523	Paravaynu	Joseph L	1805	Genova, Italy			Rose (?)	Stockwell, London	coral merchant
24524	Paravaynu	Rose	1811	Genova, Italy	(?)		Joseph L Paravaynu	Stockwell, London	
16363	Parety	Aaron	1838	City, London				Aldgate, London	boarding school pupil
14061	Pariente	Isaac	1822	?, Morocco [?, Barbary]	Jacob Pariente		Rachel Judith (Dita) Lazarus	Manchester	merchant (general)
7619	Pariente	Jacob	1798	?Morocco	Moses Pariente			Shoreditch, London	merchant
5919	Paris	Angelo	1811	Bridgetown, Barbados, West Indies	Isaac Paris	Esther Levi		Aldgate, London	
25710	Paris	David	1801	?, Poland [Yalnover, Galicia]			(?)	Spitalfields, London	dealer in general
22495	Paris	Dinah	1806	Whitechapel, London	(?)		Samuel Paris	Whitechapel, London	
22496	Paris	Elizabeth	1833	Whitechapel, London	Samuel Paris	Dinah (?)		Whitechapel, London	
5918	Paris	Esther	1788	Portsmouth, Hampshire	(?) Levi		Isaac Paris	Aldgate, London	keeper of Bath House
13741	Paris	Lewis	1826	?, Germany				Manchester	tailor
22494	Paris	Samuel	1808	Canterbury, Kent			Dinah (?)	Whitechapel, London	cigar maker
5917	Paris	Sarah	1813	Portsmouth, Hampshire	Isaac Paris	Esther Levi		Aldgate, London	

ID	surname	given names	born	birthplace	father	mother	spouse 1	1851 residence	1851 occupation
25711	Paris	Simeh (Simah)	1835	?, Poland [Yalnover, Galicia]	David Paris	(?)	David Eckstein	Spitalfields, London	
5915	Paris (Peres)	Amelia	1836	Middlesex, London	Abraham Paris (Peres)	Rachel (?)	Abraham Benabo	Whitechapel, London	parasol maker
29559	Paris (Peres)	Israel	1830	Canterbury, Kent	Abraham Paris (Peres)	Rachel (?)		Whitechapel, London	cigar maker
29557	Paris (Peres)	Rachel	1803	Sandwich, Kent	(?)		Abraham Paris (Peres)	Whitechapel, London	
29558	Paris (Peres)	Sarah	1828	Canterbury, Kent	Abraham Paris (Peres)	Rachel (?)		Whitechapel, London	cap maker
30650	Park	Blume (?)	1805	?, Holland	(?)		Eliezer Lezer Park	Spitalfields, London	general dealer
11791	Park	Lydia (Leah)	1838	Middlesex, London	Eliezer Lezer Park	Blume (?)	Louis Van Gelder	Shoreditch, London	
30652	Park	Rebecca	1835	Tower Hill, London	Eliezer Lezer Park	Blume (?)		Spitalfields, London	tailoress
30651	Park	Sarah	1833	?, London	Eliezer Lezer Park	Blume (?)		Spitalfields, London	tailoress
18757	Park	Simon	1830	?, Holland	Eliezer Lezer Park	Blume (?)	Julia Pereira	Spitalfields, London	servant
14194	Parkes	Amelia	1834	Nottingham, Nottinghamshire	(?) Parkes	Rebecca (?)		Manchester	
14193	Parkes	Ann	1833	Nottingham, Nottinghamshire	(?) Parkes	Rebecca (?)		Manchester	
14196	Parkes	Louisa	1837	Nottingham, Nottinghamshire	(?) Parkes	Rebecca (?)		Manchester	
14195	Parkes	Morris	1836	Nottingham, Nottinghamshire	(?) Parkes	Rebecca (?)		Manchester	
18148	Pass	Isaac	1786	Middlesex, London				Mile End, London	inmate of Portuguese Jews Hospital
18573	Pass	Leah	1826	New York, USA	(?) Pass			Shoreditch, London	annuitant
18574	Pass	Matilda	1840	Middlesex, London	(?) Pass			Shoreditch, London	
21527	Pass	Rebecca	1802	City, London	(?) Pass			City, London	housekeeper
18726	Pass (Paz de Leon)	Abigail	1845	Stepney, London	John (Jacob) Pass (Paz de Leon)	Sarah Leah Francis	George Davis	Whitechapel, London	
18729	Pass (Paz de Leon)	David	1847	Stepney, London	John (Jacob) Pass (Paz de Leon)	Sarah Leah Francis	Margaret Jordan	Whitechapel, London	
25649	Pass (Paz de Leon)	David	1847	Aldgate, London	Naphtali Pass (Paz de Leon)	Maria Solomon		Aldgate, London	
18731	Pass (Paz de Leon)	John (Jacob)	1817	Aldgate, London	David Pass (Paz de Leon)	Rebecca de Jacob Selomoh Solomons	Sarah Leah Francis	Whitechapel, London	gas fitter
25650	Pass (Paz de Leon)	John (Jacob)	1850	Aldgate, London	Naphtali Pass (Paz de Leon)	Maria Solomon		Aldgate, London	
18730	Pass (Paz de Leon)	Joseph	1850	Stepney, London	John (Jacob) Pass (Paz de Leon)	Sarah Leah Francis		Whitechapel, London	
25654	Pass (Paz de Leon)	Lewis (Judah)	1848	Aldgate, London	Naphtali Pass (Paz de Leon)	Maria Solomon	Rosetta (Posie) Hendriks	Aldgate, London	
18727	Pass (Paz de Leon)	Louisa	1839	Whitechapel, London	John (Jacob) Pass (Paz de Leon)	Sarah Leah Francis		Whitechapel, London	scholar
25648	Pass (Paz de Leon)	Maria	1825	Chatham, Kent	Lewis Solomon	Ann (?)	Naphtali Pass (Paz de Leon)	Aldgate, London	
18728	Pass (Paz de Leon)	Matilda	1841	Whitechapel, London	John (Jacob) Pass (Paz de Leon)	Sarah Leah Francis		Whitechapel, London	
25647	Pass (Paz de Leon)	Naphtali	1812	Aldgate, London	David Pass (Paz de Leon)	Rebecca de Jacob Selomoh Solomons	Maria Solomon	Aldgate, London	master butcher
25652	Pass (Paz de Leon)	Rebecca	1786	Aldgate, London	Jacob Selomoh Solomons		David Pass (Paz de Leon)	Aldgate, London	retired butcher
25651	Pass (Paz de Leon)	Rebecca	1851	Aldgate, London	Naphtali Pass (Paz de Leon)	Maria Solomon	Samuel Samuels	Aldgate, London	
18732	Pass (Paz de Leon)	Sarah Leah	1818	?, Essex	Joseph Francis		John (Jacob) Pass (Paz de Leon)	Whitechapel, London	
16437	Pass?	Emily	1839	Lambeth, London	(?) Pass?			Barnsbury, London	
14670	Patzochke	Julius	1814	?, Germany [?, Prussia, Germany]				Hoxton, London	(?bronze powder) manufacturer empl 4
30479	Peartree	Benjamin	1818	?, Poland [?, Prussia]	Haim Bournbaum		Caroline Lion	Whitechapel, London	commercial traveller
30480	Peartree	Caroline	1824	?Metz, France	Alexander Lion	Fanny (Frances) Lambert	Benjamin Peartree	Whitechapel, London	
27833	Peiro	Abraham	1813	?, Holland			Betsy (?)	Spitalfields, London	cigar maker
27834	Peiro	Betsy	1817	?, Holland	(?)		Abraham Peiro	Spitalfields, London	
27841	Peiro	Cyphus	1833	?, Holland				Spitalfields, London	traveller

ID	surname	given names	born	birthplace	father	mother	spouse 1	1851 residence	1851 occupation
27836	Peiro	Esther	1839	?, Holland	Abraham Peiro	Betsy (?)		Spitalfields, London	
27835	Peiro	Jacob	1837	?, Holland	Abraham Peiro	Betsy (?)		Spitalfields, London	cigar maker
27839	Peiro	Julia	1850	?, Holland	Abraham Peiro	Betsy (?)		Spitalfields, London	
27840	Peiro	Moses	1831	?, Holland				Spitalfields, London	traveller
27838	Peiro	Moses	1844	?, Holland	Abraham Peiro	Betsy (?)		Spitalfields, London	scholar
27837	Peiro	Rachel	1842	?, Holland	Abraham Peiro	Betsy (?)		Spitalfields, London	scholar
22477	Peiser	Adelaide	1839	Strand, London	Wolf Peiser	Rachel Barnard	Joseph Levy	Covent Garden, London	
14289	Peiser	Ellen	1803	Manchester	(?)		John Peiser	Manchester	
22479	Peiser	Esther	1841	Soho, London	Wolf Peiser	Rachel Barnard		Covent Garden, London	
14291	Peiser	Fanny	1832	Manchester	John Peiser	Ellen (?)		Manchester	
14288	Peiser	John	1803	?, Poland [?, Prussia]			Ellen (?)	Manchester	manufacturer - coach lace
14290	Peiser	Mary	1830	Manchester	John Peiser	Ellen (?)		Manchester	
22478	Peiser	Philip	1845	Soho, London	Wolf Peiser	Rachel Barnard		Covent Garden, London	
22475	Peiser	Rachel	1810	Portsmouth, Hampshire	Philip Barnard	Mary (?)	Wolf Peiser	Covent Garden, London	
22480	Peiser	Serena (Celina)	1850	Covent Garden, London	Wolf Peiser	Rachel Barnard	Louis Groedel	Covent Garden, London	
22476	Peiser	Wolf	1791	Copenhagen, Denmark			Rachel Barnard	Covent Garden, London	Reader of the Synagogue
29536	Peizer	Alexander	1823	abroad				Spitalfields, London	
16436	Pereira	Anna	1791	Holborn, London	(?) Pereira			Barnsbury, London	
28392	Pereira	David	1848	Spitalfields, London	Judah Pereira	Esther (?)		Spitalfields, London	
15264	Pereira	David L	1767	?, London			Rachel (?)	Shoreditch, London	retired from business
16435	Pereira	Eliza	1816	Holborn, London	(?) Pereira			Barnsbury, London	dress maker
12288	Pereira	Emily	1838	?, London	(?) Pereira			Finsbury, London	
29409	Pereira	Esther	1781	Amsterdam, Holland	(?)		Jacob Pereira	Spitalfields, London	nurse
28391	Pereira	Esther	1824	Amsterdam, Holland	(?)		Judah Pereira	Spitalfields, London	dressmaker
29408	Pereira	Jacob	1771	Amsterdam, Holland	Moses Pereira		Esther (?)	Spitalfields, London	outdoor relief, formerly cigar maker
29404	Pereira	Jacob	1842	Amsterdam, Holland	Moses Pereira	Sarah (?)	Rosa Phillips	Spitalfields, London	scholar
12286	Pereira	Jonathan	1805	?, London			Louisa Ann (?)	Finsbury, London	fellow of College of Physicians London practising
28390	Pereira	Judah	1821	Amsterdam, Holland			Esther (?)	Spitalfields, London	cigar maker
29406	Pereira	Julia	1850	Spitalfields, London	Moses Pereira	Sarah (?)		Spitalfields, London	
12289	Pereira	Louisa	1840	Acton, London	Moses Haim Picciotto	Laura (Louisa) (?)		Finsbury, London	
12287	Pereira	Louisa Ann	1810	Winchester, Hampshire	(?)		Jonathan Pereira	Finsbury, London	
29402	Pereira	Moses	1824	?, London	Jacob Pereira	Esther (?)	Sarah (?)	Spitalfields, London	cigar maker
29405	Pereira	Moses	1845	Amsterdam, Holland	Moses Pereira	Sarah (?)		Spitalfields, London	scholar
23075	Pereira	Rachel	1823	?, Holland	(?) Pereira			Aldgate, London	dressmaker
15265	Pereira	Rachel M	1765	?, London	(?) Pereira		(?) Pereira	Shoreditch, London	
29407	Pereira	Rebecca	1831	Amsterdam, Holland	(?) Pereira			Spitalfields, London	servant
7317	Pereira	Sarah	1812	Holborn, London	(?) Pereira			Barnsbury, London	dress maker
29403	Pereira	Sarah	1823	Amsterdam, Holland	(?)		Moses Pereira	Spitalfields, London	
28769	Perera	Rachel	1827	?, Holland	(?) Perera			Spitalfields, London	dressmaker
11829	Peres	Abraham	1844	Whitechapel, London	Peres Joseph Peres	Julia (?)		Whitechapel, London	scholar
11827	Peres	Julia	1814	Haarlem, Holland	(?)		Peres Joseph Peres	Whitechapel, London	
11826	Peres	Peres Joseph	1816	Haarlem, Holland			Julia (?)	Whitechapel, London	master tailor

ID	surname	given names	born	birthplace	father	mother	spouse 1	1851 residence	1851 occupation
11830	Peres	Priscilla	1850	Whitechapel, London	Peres Joseph Peres	Julia (?)		Whitechapel, London	
11828	Peres	Sare	1835	Haarlem, Holland	Peres Joseph Peres	Julia (?)		Whitechapel, London	
10614	Perez	Aaron	1843	Aldgate, London	Isaac Perez	Sarah Cohen De Azevedo		Spitalfields, London	scholar
10608	Perez	Clara	1825	Mile End, London	Isaac Perez	Sarah Cohen De Azevedo		Spitalfields, London	feather maker
10613	Perez	Esther	1841	Aldgate, London	Isaac Perez	Sarah Cohen De Azevedo	Moses Calo	Spitalfields, London	scholar
10606	Perez	Isaac	1802	Spitalfields, London	Moses Perez	Judith Torres	Sarah de Aaron Cohen De Azevedo	Spitalfields, London	painter + glazier
10611	Perez	Julia	1831	Aldgate, London	Isaac Perez	Sarah Cohen De Azevedo		Spitalfields, London	domestic assistant
10612	Perez	Leah	1838	Aldgate, London	Isaac Perez	Sarah Cohen De Azevedo		Spitalfields, London	scholar
17941	Perez	Maria	1836	Middlesex, London	Isaac de Moses Perez	Sarah de Aaron Cohen De Azevedo		Spitalfields, London	apprentice
10609	Perez	Moses	1827	Mile End, London	Isaac Perez	Sarah Cohen De Azevedo	Sophia (Sheba) Hart	Spitalfields, London	cigar maker
10607	Perez	Sarah	1800	Spitalfields, London	Aaron Cohen De Azevedo	Judith (?)	Isaac de Moses Perez	Spitalfields, London	painter + glazier
10610	Perez	Sarah	1829	Aldgate, London	Isaac Perez	Sarah Cohen De Azevedo		Spitalfields, London	domestic assistant
12638	Pergbylski	Ciprin	1802	?, Poland			Margret (?)	Birmingham	slipper maker
12639	Pergbylski	Margret	1830	Whitechapel, London	(?)		Cyprin Pergbylski	Birmingham	
12640	Pergbylski	Mary	1848	Whitechapel, London	Cyprin Pergbylski	Margret (?)		Birmingham	
12641	Pergbylski	Sarah Ann	1850	Birmingham	Cyprin Pergbylski	Margret (?)		Birmingham	
26995	Perir	Esther	1817	Aldgate, London			Morris Perir	Aldgate, London	tailoress
26997	Perir	Jacob	1845	Aldgate, London	Morris Perir	Esther (?)		Aldgate, London	
26994	Perir	Morris	1813	Hamburg, Germany [Hambro]			Esther (?)	Aldgate, London	tailor
26996	Perir	Sarah	1843	Aldgate, London	Morris Perir	Esther (?)		Aldgate, London	
13580	Pertuges	Harris	1791	?, Poland			Pepi (?)	Manchester	cap maker
13582	Pertuges	Mary	1832	?, Poland	Harris Pertuges	Pepi (?)		Manchester	
13581	Pertuges	Pepi	1806	?, Poland	(?)		Harris Pertuges	Manchester	
23238	Pesman	Ann	1805	Middlesex, London	(?)		Lewis Pesman	Hammersmith, London	
22958	Pesman	Catherine (Kate)	1824	Whitechapel, London	Alexander Lyons		Emanuel Pesman	Wapping, London	
22957	Pesman	Emanuel	1815	Whitechapel, London	John Pesman	Esther Capua	Catherine (Kate) Lyons	Wapping, London	slopseller
23237	Pesman	Lewis	1785	Middlesex, London			Ann (?)	Hammersmith, London	proprietor of houses
9166	Philip	Meier	1828	?Breznice, Czech Republic [Breschen, Prussia]				Whitechapel, London	glazier
14459	Philipp	Adolph	1808	Hamburg, Germany			Catherine Hogart nee (?)	Manchester	merchant
14460	Philipp	Catherine	1801	Sheffield, Yorkshire	(?)		(?) Hogart	Manchester	
17125	Philips	Jacob	1836	Aldgate, London				Sheerness, Kent	errand boy
6298	Philips	Mary (Miriam)	1801	Shoreditch, London	Issachar Benjamin		Philip Phillips	Shoreditch, London	
9865	Philips	Sarah	1840	?, London				Fulham, London	boarding school pupil
17601	Phillip	Betsy	1841	Finsbury, London	Solomon Phillip	Sarah? (?)		Aldgate, London	
17600	Phillip	Jessey	1841	Finsbury, London	Solomon Phillip	Sarah? (?)		Aldgate, London	
17599	Phillip	Lewis	1840	Finsbury, London	Solomon Phillip	Sarah? (?)		Aldgate, London	scholar
17603	Phillip	Moss	1850	Whitechapel, London	Solomon Phillip	Sarah? (?)		Aldgate, London	
17602	Phillip	Rachel	1849	Whitechapel, London	Solomon Phillip	Sarah? (?)		Aldgate, London	
17598	Phillip	Sarah?	1803	?Aldgate, London			Solomon Phillip	Aldgate, London	
315	Phillip	Solomon	1805	Whitechapel, London			Sarah? (?)	Aldgate, London	? maker
30956	Phillipp	Adolphus	1807	Hamburg, Germany			Catherine (?)	Bradford, Yorkshire	merchant
30952	Phillipp	Adolphus	1845	Bradford, Yorkshire	Jacob Phillipp	Jenny (?)		Bradford, Yorkshire	scholar

ID	surname	given names	born	birthplace	father	mother	spouse 1	1851 residence	1851 occupation
30957	Phillipp	Catherine	1803	?Germany	(?)		Adolphus Phillipp	Bradford, Yorkshire	
30950	Phillipp	Jacob	1818	Hamburg, Germany			Jenny (?)	Bradford, Yorkshire	stuff merchant
30951	Phillipp	Jenny	1820	Holstein, Germany	(?)		Jacob Phillipp	Bradford, Yorkshire	
30954	Phillipp	Morris	1848	Bradford, Yorkshire	Jacob Phillipp	Jenny (?)		Bradford, Yorkshire	
30953	Phillipp	Rebecca	1846	Bradford, Yorkshire	Jacob Phillipp	Jenny (?)		Bradford, Yorkshire	scholar
30955	Phillipp	William	1850	Bradford, Yorkshire	Jacob Phillipp	Jenny (?)		Bradford, Yorkshire	
20575	Phillips	Aaron	1784	Liverpool			Rosetta (?)	Spitalfields, London	general dealer
23598	Phillips	Aaron	1787	?, Poland			Esther (?)	Liverpool	hawker of sponges
20667	Phillips	Aaron	1834	Whitechapel, London0	Abraham Phillips	Rachael De Souza		Spitalfields, London	servant
25673	Phillips	Aaron	1847	Aldgate, London	Hyam Phillips	Hannah Lipman		Spitalfields, London	
30606	Phillips	Aaron	1851	Aldgate, London	Lazarus (Eleazer) Phillips	Bloomer (?)		Aldgate, London	
30609	Phillips	Aaron Samuel	1851	Aldgate, London	Woolf Benjamin Phillips	Dinah Levy		Aldgate, London	
9906	Phillips	Abigail	1789	Whitechapel, London	Simon Solomons		Henry Phillips	Elephant & Castle, London	
19441	Phillips	Abigail	1809	King's Lynn. Norfolk	(?)		Naftali Phillips	Wapping, London	slop seller
15783	Phillips	Abigail	1823	Aldgate, London	Michael Phillips	Frances Israel		Aldgate, London	general dealer
15352	Phillips	Abigal	1846	Southwark, London	John Phillips	Elizabeth Lewis		Waterloo, London	
23416	Phillips	Abraham	1774	?, Germany				Aldgate, London	shoe dealer
20662	Phillips	Abraham	1788	?, Holland	Tsevi Hirsch		Rachael De Souza	Spitalfields, London	fishmonger
24922	Phillips	Abraham	1793	Shoreditch, London			Jane (?)	Bethnal Green, London	silk weaver
3848	Phillips	Abraham	1799	Aldgate, London			Hana (Anna) (?Myers)	Spitalfields, London	general dealer
3244	Phillips	Abraham	1801	Aldgate, London	Alexander Saunders Phillips	Hannah Solomon		Aldgate, London	pen cutter
13643	Phillips	Abraham	1802	Warsaw, Poland			Sarah (?)	Manchester	tailor
27202	Phillips	Abraham	1817	?, London				Aldgate, London	tailor
11057	Phillips	Abraham	1821	Amsterdam, Holland				Aldgate, London	cigar maker
27179	Phillips	Abraham	1821	?, London				Aldgate, London	traveller
18181	Phillips	Abraham	1827	Aldgate, London	(?Moss) Phillips			Stepney, London	
24924	Phillips	Abraham	1828	Bethnal Green, London	Abraham Phillips	Jane (?)		Bethnal Green, London	silk weaver
6055	Phillips	Abraham	1843	Spitalfields, London	Lazarus Phillips	Louisa (Leah) Rogers (Rodrigues)	Jessie Isaacs	Spitalfields, London	scholar
11612	Phillips	Abraham	1847	Aldgate, London	Isaac Phillips	Esther Isaacs		Aldgate, London	
9465	Phillips	Abraham	1849	Aldgate, London	Barnett Phillips	Rachel Levy		Aldgate, London	
9911	Phillips	Abraham (Abram)	1833	Elephant & Castle, London	Henry Phillips	Abigail Solomons		Elephant & Castle, London	cigar maker
18848	Phillips	Ada Rose	1848	Regent's Park, London	Robert Abraham Phillips	Helen Levy		Regent's Park, London	
22863	Phillips	Adelaide	1798	Wapping, London	Isaac Cohen Barnett		Samuel Phillips	Whitechapel, London	
13533	Phillips	Adelaide	1847	Manchester	Henry Phillips	Emma (?)		Manchester	
4875	Phillips	Albert	1841	Birmingham	Philip Henry Phillips	Frances Armstrong	Rachel Mosley	Birmingham	scholar
25288	Phillips	Alexander	1785	City, London			(?)	Holborn, London	clothes salesman
18847	Phillips	Alfred	1845	Regent's Park, London	Robert Abraham Phillips	Helen Levy		Regent's Park, London	
18843	Phillips	Alfred	1846	City, London	Philip Saunders Phillips	Jane Lazarus		City, London	
18844	Phillips	Alice	1848	City, London	Philip Saunders Phillips	Jane Lazarus	Victor Haim Penso	City, London	
3281	Phillips	Alice Phoebe	1849	Regent's Park, London	Barnet Samuel Phillips	Helen Maria Samuel		Walton-on-Thames, Surrey	
30657	Phillips	Amelia	1799	?, Poland [?, Prussia]	(?)		Jacob Phillips	Spitalfields, London	tailor

ID	surname	given names	born	birthplace	father	mother	spouse 1	1851 residence	1851 occupation
16148	Phillips	Amelia	1801	Hamburg, Germany	(?)		Mark Phillips	Whitechapel, London	cutter
4872	Phillips	Amelia	1833	Birmingham	Philip Henry Phillips	Frances Armstrong		Birmingham	
26084	Phillips	Amelia	1846	Aldgate, London	Joseph Phillips	Dinah Joel		Aldgate, London	
15205	Phillips	Ann	1846	Shoreditch, London	Solomon Phillips	Mary (?)		Shoreditch, London	
12091	Phillips	Ann (Nancy)	1800	Whitechapel, London	Tsadok Woolf		Zelig (Solomon) Phillips	Spitalfields, London	
3220	Phillips	Annie	1840	Bloomsbury, London	Israel Phillips	Maria Samson	Adolphus Louis	Bloomsbury, London	
21160	Phillips	Asher	1843	Aldgate, London	(?) Phillips	Rachael (?)		Aldgate, London	
3261	Phillips	Augusta	1835	Strand, London	Lawrence (Eliezer) Phillips	Sarah Worms	Michael Simeon	Strand, London	
3251	Phillips	Barnet Lawrence	1818	Aldgate, London	Lawrence Phillips	Esther Spyer		Regent's Park, London	merchant
3279	Phillips	Barnet Samuel	1824	Aldgate, London	Samuel Phillips	Maria Samuel	Philippa Samuel	Walton-on-Thames, Surrey	general merchant
3246	Phillips	Barnett	1808	Aldgate, London	Alexander Saunders Phillips	Hannah Solomon	Rachel Levy	Aldgate, London	jeweller
12093	Phillips	Baruch	1834	Whitechapel, London	Zelig (Solomon) Phillips	Ann (Nancy) Woolf		Spitalfields, London	cap maker
20533	Phillips	Benjamin	1841	Marylebone, London	Lewis Phillips	Sarah Jonas	Elizabeth Hart	Marylebone, London	
24329	Phillips	Benjamin	1842	St Giles, London	Joseph Phillips	Esther (?)		Covent Garden, London	scholar
25252	Phillips	Benjamin	1850	Holborn, London	Michael Phillips	Hannah Davis		Holborn, London	
19179	Phillips	Benjamin	1851	Aldgate, London	Barnett Phillips	Rachel Levy		Aldgate, London	
24589	Phillips	Benjamin Lyon	1799	Tower Hill, London	Lyon Phillips		Hannah Aron Joseph	Lambeth, London	general merchant
3272	Phillips	Benjamin Samuel	1810	Whitechapel, London	Samuel Phillips	Hannah Jonas	Rachel Faudel	Streatham, London	spectacle maker
25250	Phillips	Betsey	1846	Holborn, London	Michael Phillips	Hannah Davis		Holborn, London	scholar
15599	Phillips	Betsy	1800	?, France	(?)		Samuel Phillips	Covent Garden, London	
10556	Phillips	Betsy	1840	Lambeth, London	Phillip Phillips	Maria (?)		Elephant & Castle, London	
9825	Phillips	Betsy (Elizabeth)	1847	Finsbury, London	Zaley (Zaleck, Solomon) Phillips	Sarah Cohen	Solomon Benjamin	Aldgate, London	
3216	Phillips	Bloom	1831	Holborn, London	Israel Phillips	Maria Samson	Abraham Salaman	Bloomsbury, London	
23437	Phillips	Bloom	1845	Liverpool	Charles Phillips	Esther (?)		Liverpool	scholar
12982	Phillips	Bloomer	1817	?, London	(?)		Lazarus (Eleazer) Phillips	Aldgate, London	
15784	Phillips	Bloomer	1825	Aldgate, London	Michael Phillips	Frances Israel		Aldgate, London	tailoress
12127	Phillips	Catherine	1801	Whitechapel, London	(?)		(?) Phillips	Spitalfields, London	general dealer
21147	Phillips	Catherine	1807	Aldgate, London	(?)		Phineas Phillips	Aldgate, London	
9912	Phillips	Catherine	1836	Elephant & Castle, London	Henry Phillips	Abigail Solomons		Elephant & Castle, London	
23438	Phillips	Catherine	1847	Liverpool	Charles Phillips	Esther (?)		Liverpool	scholar
21117	Phillips	Catherine	1849	Aldgate, London	Godfrey Phillips	Elizabeth Phillips		Aldgate, London	
18840	Phillips	Catherine (Kate)	1838	City, London	Philip Saunders Phillips	Jane Lazarus		City, London	
23433	Phillips	Charles	1809	?, London			Esther (?)	Liverpool	oyster dealer + tobacconist
4869	Phillips	Charles	1850	Birmingham	Joseph Phillips	Sarah (?)		Birmingham	
18839	Phillips	Charles Saul Aaron	1795	?			Maria (?)	Portsmouth, Hampshire	
15838	Phillips	Charlotte	1810	Swansea, Wales	Jacob b. Eleazer Mozely		Joseph Phillips	Hoxton, London	
31228	Phillips	Charlotte	1838	Hobart, Tasmania, Australia	Michael Phillips	Frances (?)		St Helier, Jersey, Channel Islands	annuitant
15841	Phillips	Charlotte H	1843	Haggerston, London	Joseph Phillips	Charlotte Mozely		Hoxton, London	
15203	Phillips	Clara	1834	Shoreditch, London	Solomon Phillips	Mary (?)		Shoreditch, London	
3267	Phillips	Clara	1843	Strand, London	Lawrence (Eliezer) Phillips	Sarah Worms		Strand, London	

ID	surname	given names	born	birthplace	father	mother	spouse 1	1851 residence	1851 occupation
3224	Phillips	Clara	1847	Holborn, London	Israel Phillips	Maria Samson	Carl Alberts	Holborn, London	
26680	Phillips	Clara	1848	Spitalfields, London	Philip Phillips	Elizabeth Israel		Spitalfields, London	scholar
26920	Phillips	Clara	1848	?, London	Moses Phillips	Miriam Franks		Aldgate, London	scholar
25003	Phillips	Clara	1851	Holborn, London	Henry Phillips	Leah Simons		Holborn, London	
3238	Phillips	Claude	1846	Middlesex, London	Robert Abraham Phillips	Helen Levy		Regent's Park, London	
11147	Phillips	Coleman	1820	Aldgate, London	Simon Phillips		Jane Harris	Aldgate, London	general dealer
25926	Phillips	Dadora	1830	Southwark, London	(?) Phillips	Rosata Moses		Aldgate, London	dressmaker
11695	Phillips	David	1811	Aldgate, London				Aldgate, London	servant
27322	Phillips	David	1813	Aldgate, London	Philip Phillips		Frances (?)	Aldgate, London	silversmith worker
2200	Phillips	David	1815	?, London				Oxford, Oxfordshire	jewellery dealer
26905	Phillips	David	1816	?, Poland			Sarah (?)	Aldgate, London	general dealer
1951	Phillips	David	1821	?, Poland	Wolf Phillips		Phoebe (?)	Cardiff, Wales	hawker
23435	Phillips	David	1843	Liverpool	Charles Phillips	Esther (?)		Liverpool	scholar
11224	Phillips	David	1846	Aldgate, London	Tobias Phillips	Hannah Harris	Sarah Woolf	Aldgate, London	scholar
8869	Phillips	David	1847	Aldgate, London	Joseph Phillips	Hannah Barnett		Aldgate, London	
13534	Phillips	David	1849	Manchester	Henry Phillips	Emma (?)		Manchester	
2555	Phillips	Davis	1817	?, Poland [?, Prussia]				Hull, Yorkshire	
10337	Phillips	Deborah	1824	Middlesex, London	(?) Cohen		Michael Phillips	Spitalfields, London	
24326	Phillips	Deborah	1832	Piccadilly, London	Joseph Phillips	Esther (?)		Covent Garden, London	
10339	Phillips	Deborah	1846	Middlesex, London	Michael Phillips	Deborah Cohen		Spitalfields, London	
5930	Phillips	Dinah	1828	Euston, London	Samuel Levy		Woolf Benjamin Phillips	Aldgate, London	
20530	Phillips	Dinah	1836	Marylebone, London	Lewis Phillips	Sarah Jonas		Marylebone, London	
27328	Phillips	Dinah	1845	Finsbury, London	David Phillips	Frances (?)		Aldgate, London	
6340	Phillips	Dinah	1846	City, London	Joel Phillips	Hannah (?)	Eskell (Ezekiel) Sutton	Aldgate, London	
11823	Phillips	Edward	1813	?, Poland [?, Prussia]				Whitechapel, London	bootmaker (clicker)/journeyman
29262	Phillips	Edward	1817	Whitechapel, London	Samuel Phillips	Hannah (?)		Whitechapel, London	
10972	Phillips	Edward Joseph	1844	?Southwark, London	Henry Phillips	Maria (?)		Aldgate, London	scholar
24252	Phillips	Edwin	1839	Bloomsbury, London	Emanuel Phillips	Sarah (?)		Bloomsbury, London	
13885	Phillips	Eleanor	1828	Poznan, Poland [Posen, Prussia]	(?) Phillips			Manchester	house servant
8461	Phillips	Eliza	1831	Brighton, Sussex	Charles Saul Aaron Phillips)	Maria (?)		Portsmouth, Hampshire	
24927	Phillips	Eliza	1839	Bethnal Green, London	Abraham Phillips	Jane (?)		Bethnal Green, London	scholar
18845	Phillips	Eliza	1850	City, London	Philip Saunders Phillips	Jane Lazarus		City, London	
28218	Phillips	Elizabeth	1776	?, Germany	(?)		(?) Phillips	Spitalfields, London	
22888	Phillips	Elizabeth	1784	Aldgate, London	Abraham Solomon		(?) Crabb	Wapping, London	
12271	Phillips	Elizabeth	1802	Whitechapel, London	Meir Nathan		Benjamin Phillips	Holborn, London	umbrella maker
28448	Phillips	Elizabeth	1813	City, London	(?) Isaacs		Lewis Phillips	Spitalfields, London	tailor (journeyman)
26674	Phillips	Elizabeth	1816	Spitalfields, London	Simon Israel		Philip Phillips	Spitalfields, London	watch finisher
15348	Phillips	Elizabeth	1817	Whitechapel, London	Chaim Lewis		John Phillips	Waterloo, London	
26744	Phillips	Elizabeth	1823	Aldgate, London	(?) Phillips			Aldgate, London	dressmaker
21114	Phillips	Elizabeth	1826	Greenwich, London	Phineas Phillips	Catherine (?)	Godfrey Phillips	Aldgate, London	
12274	Phillips	Elizabeth	1832	Clerkenwell, London	Benjamin Phillips	Elizabeth Nathan		Holborn, London	artificial flower maker
22866	Phillips	Elizabeth	1834	Whitechapel, London	Samuel Phillips	Adelaide Barnett	Abraham Fox	Whitechapel, London	umbrella maker
24926	Phillips	Elizabeth	1836	Bethnal Green, London	Abraham Phillips	Jane (?)		Bethnal Green, London	silk weaver

ID	surname	given names	born	birthplace	father	mother	spouse 1	1851 residence	1851 occupation
3853	Phillips	Elizabeth	1837	Aldgate, London	Abraham Phillips	Hana (Anna) (?Myers)	Isaac Cohen	Spitalfields, London	-
20532	Phillips	Elizabeth	1839	Marylebone, London	Lewis Phillips	Sarah Jonas		Marylebone, London	
23439	Phillips	Elizabeth	1848	Liverpool	Charles Phillips	Esther (?)		Liverpool	
30239	Phillips	Elizabeth (Pessa) Sarah	1789	City, London	Abraham		Joseph Phillips	Covent Garden, London	no trade
24648	Phillips	Ellen	1821	Aldgate, London	Hyam Phillips	Fanny Marks		Waterloo, London	shopwoman
21152	Phillips	Ellen	1845	Aldgate, London	Phineas Phillips	Catherine (?)		Aldgate, London	scholar
27329	Phillips	Ellen	1847	Finsbury, London	David Phillips	Frances (?)		Aldgate, London	
20534	Phillips	Ellen (Eleanor)	1843	Marylebone, London	Lewis Phillips	Sarah Jonas	Ellis Hart	Marylebone, London	
3223	Phillips	Ellis	1846	Holborn, London	Israel Phillips	Maria Samson		Holborn, London	
24250	Phillips	Emanuel	1812	Middlesex, London			Sarah (?)	Bloomsbury, London	rag + bottle dealer
12129	Phillips	Emanuel	1827	Whitechapel, London	(?) Phillips	Catherine (?)		Spitalfields, London	general dealer
24254	Phillips	Emanuel	1848	Bloomsbury, London	Emanuel Phillips	Sarah (?)		Bloomsbury, London	
27327	Phillips	Emila	1843	Finsbury, London	David Phillips	Frances (?)		Aldgate, London	
31227	Phillips	Emily	1835	Sydney, Australia	Michael Phillips	Frances (?)		St Helier, Jersey, Channel Islands	annuitant
15206	Phillips	Emily	1848	Shoreditch, London	Solomon Phillips	Mary (?)		Shoreditch, London	
29261	Phillips	Emma	1818	Whitechapel, London	Samuel Phillips	Hannah (?)		Whitechapel, London	
4859	Phillips	Emma	1821	Birmingham			John Phillips	Birmingham	
13531	Phillips	Emma	1825	Birmingham	(?)		Henry Phillips	Manchester	
21862	Phillips	Emma	1845	Clerkenwell, London	(?) Phillips			Clerkenwell, London	scholar
4861	Phillips	Emma	1848	Birmingham	John Phillips	Emma (?)	David Leon Lang	Birmingham	
2153	Phillips	Ephraim	1811	Czarnkow, Poland				Hull, Yorkshire	watchmaker + jeweller
30660	Phillips	Ester	1834	?, Poland [?, Prussia]	Jacob Phillips	Amelia (?)		Spitalfields, London	waistcoat maker
3911	Phillips	Esther	1791	?, London			Moses Phillips	Aldgate, London	
3248	Phillips	Esther	1792	Surrey, London	Pinchas Zelig Spyer		Lawrence Phillips	Marylebone, London	
3235	Phillips	Esther	1801	?, London	David Phillips	Bloomer Jonas		Mayfair, London	
23599	Phillips	Esther	1801	?, Poland	(?)		Aaron Phillips	Liverpool	
24325	Phillips	Esther	1808	Piccadilly, London	(?)		Joseph Phillips	Covent Garden, London	general dealer
11610	Phillips	Esther	1809	Spitalfields, London	Joseph Isaacs		Isaac Phillips	Aldgate, London	
25019	Phillips	Esther	1810	?, London	(?) Moses		Philip Phillips	Finsbury, London	
23434	Phillips	Esther	1815	Barnsley, Yorkshire	(?)		Chaerles Phillips	Liverpool	
29538	Phillips	Esther	1820	Spitalfields, London	Henry Beck	Sarah (?)	(?Godfrey/Louis) Phillips	Spitalfields, London	
19445	Phillips	Esther	1828	Wapping, London	Naftali Phillips	Abigail (?)		Wapping, London	
20527	Phillips	Esther	1830	Middlesex, London	Lewis Phillips	Sarah Jonas	?	Marylebone, London	
2943	Phillips	Esther	1833	Spitalfields, London	Phillip Phillips		Henry Davis	Whitechapel, London	
6059	Phillips	Esther	1834	Aldgate, London	Lazarus Phillips	Louisa (Leah) Rogers (Rodrigues)	Charles (Chebalis) Cohen Solal	Spitalfields, London	feather maker
12094	Phillips	Esther	1836	Whitechapel, London	Zelig (Solomon) Phillips	Ann (Nancy) Woolf	Henry Harris	Spitalfields, London	scholar
8225	Phillips	Esther	1841	Spitalfields, London	Isaac Phillips	Julia Hyman		Spitalfields, London	scholar
24999	Phillips	Esther	1842	Birmingham	Henry Phillips	Leah Simons		Holborn, London	
31173	Phillips	Esther	1843	Rochester, Kent	Jehiel (Jekiel) Phillips	Rosa (?)		Rochester, Kent	scholar
1954	Phillips	Esther	1844	?, Poland	Isaac Phillips	Fanny (?)		Cardiff, Wales	
25251	Phillips	Esther	1847	Holborn, London	Michael Phillips	Hannah Davis		Holborn, London	scholar
29074	Phillips	Eveline	1815	Holborn, London	Abraham Solomons		Solomon Phillips	Holborn, London	

ID	surname	given names	born	birthplace	father	mother	spouse 1	1851 residence	1851 occupation
25289	Phillips	Fanny	1820	Holborn, London	Alexander Phillips	(?)	Henry Alexander	Holborn, London	
10340	Phillips	Fanny	1848	Middlesex, London	Michael Phillips	Deborah Cohen		Spitalfields, London	
25674	Phillips	Fanny	1850	Aldgate, London	Hyam Phillips	Hannah Lipman		Spitalfields, London	
15782	Phillips	Frances	1781	Tower Hill, London	Aharon Israel		Michael Phillips	Aldgate, London	general dealer
4871	Phillips	Frances	1798	Gloucester, Gloucestershire	(?) Armstrong		Philip Henry Phillips	Birmingham	
20446	Phillips	Frances	1801	?, London	(?)		Michael Phillips	St Helier, Jersey, Channel Islands	annuitant
15849	Phillips	Frances	1808	Middlesex, London	Joseph Joseph		Coleman Lyon Phillips	Bloomsbury, London	
27323	Phillips	Frances	1810	Aldgate, London	(?)		David Phillips	Aldgate, London	silversmith worker
3249	Phillips	Frances	1814	City, London	Lawrence Phillips	Esther Spyer		Marylebone, London	
13532	Phillips	Frances	1840	Manchester	Henry Phillips	Emma (?)	Isaac Zagury	Manchester	
6268	Phillips	Francis	1839	?, Poland	Moses Phillips	Martha (?)	Amelia (?)	Portsmouth, Hampshire	
5928	Phillips	Frederick Abraham	1840	Bethnal Green, London	Joseph Phillips	Charlotte (?)	Eva Solomon	Hoxton, London	scholar
3270	Phillips	Frederick Samuel David	1833	Bloomsbury, London	Israel Phillips	Maria Samson	Rachel Joseph	Bloomsbury, London	tailor
20670	Phillips	Gabriel	1843	Whitechapel, London0	Abraham Phillips	Rachael De Souza		Spitalfields, London	scholar
10973	Phillips	George	1826	?, Dorset			Rachael (?)	Aldgate, London	baker
19234	Phillips	George Faudel	1841	Streatham, London	Benjamin Samuel Phillips	Rachel Faudel	Helen (?)	Finsbury, London	scholar
21113	Phillips	Godfrey	1826	Whitechapel, London	Eliayajum Getshlik		Elizabeth Phillips	Aldgate, London	cigar maker empl 30
19442	Phillips	Godfrey	1834	Wapping, London	Naftali Phillips	Abigail (?)		Wapping, London	cigar maker
3849	Phillips	Hana (Anna)	1803	Aldgate, London	(?Benjamin Myers)		Abraham Phillips	Spitalfields, London	
3240	Phillips	Hannah	1780	?	Aaron Solomon		Alexander Saunders Phillips	Aldgate, London	
26922	Phillips	Hannah	1790	?, London	(?)		Lewis Phillips	Aldgate, London	cap maker
24590	Phillips	Hannah	1812	Aldgate, London	Aron Joseph		Benjamin Lyon Phillips	Lambeth, London	
6338	Phillips	Hannah	1815	Whitechapel, London	Solomon Aarons	Rachael (?)	Joel Phillips	Aldgate, London	
20450	Phillips	Hannah	1819	Middlesex, London	Mark Mordecai		Marks Phillips	Weymouth, Dorset	clothier + outfitter
8867	Phillips	Hannah	1822	Whitechapel, London	David Barnett		Joseph Phillips	Aldgate, London	
11222	Phillips	Hannah	1824	Aldgate, London	Reuben Harris		Tobias Phillips	Aldgate, London	slipper binder
25249	Phillips	Hannah	1826	Holborn, London	John (Joseph) Davis	Leah Barnett	Michael Phillips	Holborn, London	
31137	Phillips	Hannah	1829	Aldgate, London	(?) Phillips	Sarah (?)		Margate, Kent	assistant in clothier's shop
16119	Phillips	Hannah	1832	?, London	Samuel Levy		Samuel Phillips	Aldgate, London	furrier
13832	Phillips	Hannah	1834	Manchester	Solomon Phillips	Sarah (?)		Manchester	
3913	Phillips	Hannah	1835	?, London	Moses Phillips	Esther (?)		Aldgate, London	
21860	Phillips	Hannah	1835	Clerkenwell, London	(?) Phillips			Clerkenwell, London	
20669	Phillips	Hannah	1839	Whitechapel, London	Abraham Phillips	Rachael De Souza		Spitalfields, London	scholar
11873	Phillips	Hannah	1840	Middlesex, London	(?) Phillips	(?)		Whitechapel, London	inmate of orphan school
15350	Phillips	Hannah	1841	Surrey, London	John Phillips	Elizabeth Lewis		Waterloo, London	
12983	Phillips	Hannah	1842	?, London	Lazarus (Eleazer) Phillips	Bloomer (?)		Aldgate, London	scholar
8227	Phillips	Hannah	1844	Spitalfields, London	Isaac Phillips	Julia Hyman		Spitalfields, London	scholar
26908	Phillips	Hannah	1848	?, London	David Phillips	Sarah (?)		Aldgate, London	
10945	Phillips	Hannah	1850	Spitalfields, London	Lazarus Phillips	Louisa (Leah) Rogers (Rodrigues)		Spitalfields, London	
25672	Phillips	Hannah	1822	Aldgate, London	Lewis Lipman	Mary (?)	Hyam Phillips	Spitalfields, London	

ID	surname	given names	born	birthplace	father	mother	spouse 1	1851 residence	1851 occupation
30241	Phillips	Hannah	1830	Tottenham, London	Aaron Hart		Samuel Phillips	Covent Garden, London	
30659	Phillips	Harriet	1824	?, Poland [?, Prussia]	Jacob Phillips	Amelia (?)		Spitalfields, London	waistcoat maker
21148	Phillips	Harriett	1837	Aldgate, London	Phineas Phillips	Catherine (?)		Aldgate, London	tailoress
6265	Phillips	Harriett	1842	?, Poland	Moses Phillips	Martha (?)	Woolf H Cohen	Portsmouth, Hampshire	
4863	Phillips	Harry P	1851	Birmingham	John Phillips	Emma (?)		Birmingham	
15713	Phillips	Hart	1767	?, Germany			(?)	Spitalfields, London	general dealer
3237	Phillips	Helen	1822	Middlesex, London	Moses Lyon Levy		Robert Abraham Phillips	Regent's Park, London	
9905	Phillips	Henry	1784	Whitechapel, London	Leib		Abigail Solomons	Elephant & Castle, London	general dealer
24994	Phillips	Henry	1804	?, London			Leah Simons	Holborn, London	clerk
10969	Phillips	Henry	1814	?, Dorset			Maria (?)	Aldgate, London	baker
18283	Phillips	Henry	1818	?, Poland [?, Polish Russia]				Salisbury, Wiltshire	traveller in jewellery
28527	Phillips	Henry	1818	Aldgate, London			Amelia Cardozo	Spitalfields, London	pickle merchant
13530	Phillips	Henry	1823	Manchester			Emma (?)	Manchester	steel pen agent
23530	Phillips	Henry	1832	?, Poland			Matilda (?)	Liverpool	merchant
20668	Phillips	Henry	1836	Whitechapel, London	Abraham Phillips	Rachael De Souza		Spitalfields, London	servant
15349	Phillips	Henry	1839	Whitechapel, London	John Phillips	Elizabeth Lewis		Waterloo, London	
25258	Phillips	Henry	1839	Holborn, London	Benjamin Phillips	Elizabeth Nathan	Mary Ann Davis	Holborn, London	
28449	Phillips	Henry	1840	City, London	Lewis Phillips	Elizabeth Isaacs		Spitalfields, London	tailor (journeyman)
1956	Phillips	Henry	1846	?, Poland	Isaac Phillips	Fanny (?)		Cardiff, Wales	scholar
26679	Phillips	Henry	1847	Spitalfields, London	Philip Phillips	Elizabeth Israel		Spitalfields, London	scholar
30614	Phillips	Henry	1851	Aldgate, London	Coleman Phillips	Jane Harris		Aldgate, London	
10971	Phillips	Henry John	1841	Lambeth, London	Henry Phillips	Maria (?)		Aldgate, London	scholar
3265	Phillips	Henry Joseph	1842	Strand, London	Lawrence Phillips	Sarah Worms	Leah Rachel Alex	Strand, London	
3282	Phillips	Herbert Samuel	1848	Regent's Park, London	Barnet Samuel Phillips	Philippa Samuel		Walton-on-Thames, Surrey	
15894	Phillips	Hester	1837	Bristol	Coleman Lyon Phillips	Frances (?)		Bloomsbury, London	boarding school pupil
1955	Phillips	Himan	1844	?, Poland	Isaac Phillips	Fanny (?)		Cardiff, Wales	scholar
25671	Phillips	Hyam	1813	Whitechapel, London	Michael Phillips	Frances Israel	Hannah Lipman	Spitalfields, London	clothes dealer
14872	Phillips	Hyam	1820	Stepney, London			Julia (?)	Finsbury, London	cigar manufacturer
21151	Phillips	Hyam	1843	Aldgate, London	Phineas Phillips	Catherine (?)		Aldgate, London	scholar
15353	Phillips	Hyman	1848	Southwark, London	John Phillips	Elizabeth Lewis		Waterloo, London	
24747	Phillips	Isaac	1761	?, Bavaria, Germany				Southwark, London	dealer in clothes
11609	Phillips	Isaac	1811	Whitechapel, London	Aaron Phillips		Esther Isaacs	Aldgate, London	general dealer
8224	Phillips	Isaac	1816	Whitechapel, London	Phillip Phillips	Sarah (?)	Julia Hyman	Spitalfields, London	pastry cook
1950	Phillips	Isaac	1818	?, Poland	Wolf Phillips		Phoebe (?)	Cardiff, Wales	hawker
11285	Phillips	Isaac	1825	Aldgate, London	Simon Phillips			Aldgate, London	general dealer
21504	Phillips	Isaac	1828	Middlesex, London	Michael Phillips	Leah (?)	Hannah Levy	Aldgate, London	looking glass frame maker
23867	Phillips	Isaac	1834	?, London	Samuel Phillips	(?)		Soho, London	
22867	Phillips	Isaac	1837	Whitechapel, London	Samuel Phillips	Adelaide Barnett		Whitechapel, London	clothes shop man
3855	Phillips	Isaac	1841	Aldgate, London	Abraham Phillips	Hana (Anna) (?Myers)	Maria Jane Warrington	Spitalfields, London	scholar
27326	Phillips	Isaac	1841	Finsbury, London	David Phillips	Frances (?)		Aldgate, London	
10943	Phillips	Isaac	1845	Spitalfields, London	Lazarus Phillips	Louisa (Leah) Rogers (Rodrigues)	Esther (Essie) Edwards	Spitalfields, London	scholar
20529	Phillips	Isaac (Alfred)	1833	Middlesex, London	Lewis Phillips	Sarah Jonas		Marylebone, London	cigar maker

ID	surname	given names	born	birthplace	father	mother	spouse 1	1851 residence	1851 occupation
24748	Phillips	Isaac I	1795	Aldgate, London	Isaac Phillips			Southwark, London	clerk + collector to the Southwark Synagogue
19444	Phillips	Isabella	1839	Wapping, London	Naftali Phillips	Abigail (?)		Wapping, London	scholar
226	Phillips	Israel	1803	?London	David Phillips	Bloomer Jonas	Maria Samson	Bloomsbury, London	tailor
30997	Phillips	Israel	1816	Warsaw, Poland				Bridgend, Glamorgan, Wales	travelling Jew
30656	Phillips	Jacob	1799	?, Poland [?, Prussia]			Amelia (?)	Spitalfields, London	tailor
11058	Phillips	Jacob	1819	Amsterdam, Holland				Aldgate, London	cigar maker
10940	Phillips	Jacob	1839	Spitalfields, London	Lazarus Phillips	Louisa (Leah) Rogers (Rodrigues)		Spitalfields, London	scholar
26917	Phillips	Jacob	1840	?, London	Moses Phillips	Miriam Franks		Aldgate, London	scholar
26776	Phillips	Jacob	1843	Aldgate, London				Aldgate, London	
8585	Phillips	James	1822	Lambeth, London	Henry Phillips	Abigail Solomons	Sarah Cohen	Southwark, London	fishmonger
24925	Phillips	James	1831	Bethnal Green, London	Abraham Phillips	Jane (?)		Bethnal Green, London	silk weaver
3254	Phillips	James Lawrence	1828	Aldgate, London	Lawrence Phillips	Esther Spyer		Marylebone, London	merchant
24923	Phillips	Jane	1801	Bethnal Green, London	(?)		Abraham Phillips	Bethnal Green, London	silk weaver
27359	Phillips	Jane	1801	Strand, London	(?)		(?) Phillips	Aldgate, London	no occupation
3242	Phillips	Jane	1819	Leigh, Essex	Laurence Lazarus	Catharine Phillips	Philip Saunders Phillips	City, London	
11146	Phillips	Jane	1822	Whitechapel, London	Solomon Harris	Frances Myers	Coleman Phillips	Aldgate, London	umbrella maker
4866	Phillips	Jane	1840	Birmingham	Joseph Phillips	Sarah (?)		Birmingham	
6299	Phillips	Jane	1841	Shoreditch, London	Philip Phillips	Mary (Miriam) Benjamin	Elias Cohen	Shoreditch, London	
24928	Phillips	Jane	1843	Bethnal Green, London	Abraham Phillips	Jane (?)		Bethnal Green, London	scholar
26919	Phillips	Jane	1845	?, London	Moses Phillips	Miriam Franks		Aldgate, London	scholar
25022	Phillips	Jane	1848	?, London	Philip Phillips	Esther Moses		Finsbury, London	
18567	Phillips	Jeannette	1838	Bloomsbury, London	Israel Phillips	Maria Samson	David L Jacobs	Bloomsbury, London	
18632	Phillips	Jehiel (Jekiel)	1802	?, Poland			Rosa (?)	Rochester, Kent	Rabbi to the Jewish congregation
31174	Phillips	Jesse	1846	Rochester, Kent	Jehiel (Jekiel) Phillips	Rosa (?)		Rochester, Kent	scholar at home
9824	Phillips	Jessy	1842	Finsbury, London	Zaley (Zaleck, Solomon) Phillips	Sarah Cohen		Aldgate, London	
6337	Phillips	Joel	1817	Aldgate, London	Philip Phillips		Hannah Aarons	Aldgate, London	watchmaker
12096	Phillips	Joel	1844	Spitalfields, London	Zelig (Solomon) Phillips	Ann (Nancy) Woolf		Spitalfields, London	
12985	Phillips	Joel	1850	?, London	Lazarus (Eleazer) Phillips	Bloomer (?)	Rebecca Levy	Aldgate, London	
26921	Phillips	Joel	1850	?Aldgate, London	Moses Phillips	Miriam Franks		Aldgate, London	
15347	Phillips	John	1810	Whitechapel, London	Henry Phillips	Abigail Solomons	Elizabeth Lewis	Waterloo, London	clothes salesman
4858	Phillips	John	1813	Birmingham			Emma (?)	Birmingham	gilt tray maker
12128	Phillips	John	1820	Whitechapel, London	(?) Phillips	Catherine (?)		Spitalfields, London	general dealer
27463	Phillips	John	1834	Brighton, Sussex				Whitechapel, London	clothier's clerk
4874	Phillips	John	1837	Birmingham	Philip Henry Phillips	Frances Armstrong	Leah Mosley	Birmingham	scholar
19443	Phillips	John	1837	Wapping, London	Naftali Phillips	Abigail (?)		Wapping, London	cigar maker
9464	Phillips	John	1847	Aldgate, London	Barnett Phillips	Rachel Levy		Aldgate, London	
12984	Phillips	John	1848	?, London	Lazarus (Eleazer) Phillips	Bloomer (?)		Aldgate, London	at home
4860	Phillips	John B	1846	Birmingham	John Phillips	Emma (?)		Birmingham	
10557	Phillips	Joseph	1764	Canterbury, Kent				Elephant & Castle, London	

ID	surname	given names	born	birthplace	father	mother	spouse 1	1851 residence	1851 occupation
30238	Phillips	Joseph	1786	City, London	Juda (Yehuda)		Elizabeth (Pessa) Sarah bat Abraham	Covent Garden, London	no trade
26081	Phillips	Joseph	1803	?, London	Avraham		Dinah Joel	Aldgate, London	shoe maker
15842	Phillips	Joseph	1805	?	Moshe Reuben Segal/Levy		Charlotte Mozely	Hoxton, London	
24324	Phillips	Joseph	1806	Middlesex, London			Esther (?)	Covent Garden, London	general dealer
15688	Phillips	Joseph	1815	Wapping, London	Saunders (Alexander) Phillips	Hannah Solomon		Aldgate, London	jeweller
4864	Phillips	Joseph	1816	Birmingham	Yehuda		Sarah (?)	Birmingham	pencil case maker
4857	Phillips	Joseph	1817	?, Poland [?, Prussia]				Birmingham	travelling hawker
18284	Phillips	Joseph	1820	?, Poland [?, Polish Russia]				Salisbury, Wiltshire	traveller in jewellery
8866	Phillips	Joseph	1821	Whitechapel, London	Mordecai Phillips		Hannah Barnett	Aldgate, London	orange dealer
26745	Phillips	Joseph	1826	Aldgate, London				Aldgate, London	cigar dealer
10342	Phillips	Joseph	1827	Middlesex, London				Spitalfields, London	general dealer
22865	Phillips	Joseph	1829	Whitechapel, London	Samuel Phillips	Adelaide Barnett		Whitechapel, London	clothes shop man
15839	Phillips	Joseph	1835	Middlesex, London	Joseph Phillips	Charlotte Mozely		Hoxton, London	scholar
27324	Phillips	Joseph	1838	Finsbury, London	David Phillips	Frances (?)		Aldgate, London	
15204	Phillips	Joseph	1840	Shoreditch, London	Solomon Phillips	Mary (?)		Shoreditch, London	
25020	Phillips	Joseph	1840	?, London	Philip Phillips	Esther Moses		Finsbury, London	
9462	Phillips	Joseph	1843	Aldgate, London	Barnett Phillips	Rachel Levy		Aldgate, London	
25000	Phillips	Joseph	1843	Birmingham	Henry Phillips	Leah Simons		Holborn, London	
26678	Phillips	Joseph	1845	Spitalfields, London	Philip Phillips	Elizabeth Israel		Spitalfields, London	scholar
21115	Phillips	Joseph	1846	Greenwich, London	Godfrey Phillips	Elizabeth Phillips		Aldgate, London	
21863	Phillips	Joseph	1846	Clerkenwell, London				Clerkenwell, London	
11226	Phillips	Joseph	1850	Aldgate, London	Tobias Phillips	Hannah Harris		Aldgate, London	
30308	Phillips	Joseph Henry	1851	Covent Garden, London	Samuel Phillips	Hannah Hart	Rachel Prince	Covent Garden, London	
8223	Phillips	Julia	1814	Falmouth, Cornwall	Moses Hyman	Sarah (Sally) Levy (Levi)	Isaac Phillips	Spitalfields, London	
14873	Phillips	Julia	1821	Stepney, London	(?)		Hyam Phillips	Finsbury, London	
19869	Phillips	Julia	1826	Whitechapel, London	Samuel Hart		Simon Phillips	Spitalfields, London	umbrella maker
3912	Phillips	Julia	1833	Aldgate, London	Moses Phillips	Esther (?)	Simon Goldman	Aldgate, London	
11897	Phillips	Julia	1840	?, Poland [?, Prussia]				Whitechapel, London	scholar
26676	Phillips	Julia	1841	Spitalfields, London	Philip Phillips	Elizabeth Israel		Spitalfields, London	scholar
20536	Phillips	Julia	1849	Marylebone, London	Lewis Phillips	Sarah Jonas	Alfred Isaac Hart	Marylebone, London	
8455	Phillips	Julia	1850	Portsmouth, Hampshire	Moses Phillips	Tybald (Martha) (?)	Israel Myer Wolfson	Portsmouth, Hampshire	
15851	Phillips	Julianna	1838	Streatham, London	Coleman Lyon Phillips	Frances Joseph		Bloomsbury, London	
23866	Phillips	Katherine	1833	?, London	Samuel Phillips	(?)		Soho, London	
12095	Phillips	Kitty (Catherine)	1841	Spitalfields, London	Zelig (Solomon) Phillips	Ann (Nancy) Woolf	Solomon (Saul) Davis [Solomons]	Spitalfields, London	scholar
3247	Phillips	Lawrence	1785	Aldgate, London	Barnet Phillips	Madeline (?)	Esther Spyer	Marylebone, London	merchant
3219	Phillips	Lawrence	1837	Bloomsbury, London	Israel Phillips	Maria Samson		Bloomsbury, London	tailor
21161	Phillips	Lawrence	1844	Aldgate, London	(?) Phillips	Rachael (?)		Aldgate, London	
23436	Phillips	Lawrence	1844	Liverpool	Charles Phillips	Esther (?)		Liverpool	scholar
234	Phillips	Lawrence (Eliezer)	1798	?, London	David Phillips	Bloomer Jonas	Sophia (Zippor) Rees	Strand, London	military tailor
8181	Phillips	Lawrence Barnett	1842	Aldgate, London	Barnett Phillips	Rachel (?)	Judith Cohen	Aldgate, London	
3255	Phillips	Lawrence David	1836	Strand, London	Lawrence Phillips	Sarah Worms		Strand, London	scholar
10936	Phillips	Lazarus	1806	?, Holland	Aryeh Pais Phillips		Esther Rodrigues	Spitalfields, London	miscellaneous dealer
12981	Phillips	Lazarus (Eleazer)	1815	?, London	Moshe HaLevi		Bloomer (?)	Aldgate, London	tailor

ID	surname	given names	born	birthplace	father	mother	spouse 1	1851 residence	1851 occupation
21503	Phillips	Leah	1797	?, Suffolk	(?)		Michael Phillips	Aldgate, London	
24995	Phillips	Leah	1815	?, London	(?) Simons	Elizabeth (?)	Henry Phillips	Holborn, London	
12272	Phillips	Leah	1823	Rochford, Essex	Benjamin Phillips	Elizabeth Nathan		Holborn, London	umbrella maker
20665	Phillips	Leah	1829	Whitechapel, London0	Abraham Phillips	Rachael De Souza	Jacob Rosenbloom	Spitalfields, London	furrier
28688	Phillips	Leah	1834	Middlesex, London	Ezekiel Abrahams		Phillip Phillips	Spitalfields, London	
11611	Phillips	Leah	1844	Spitalfields, London	Isaac Phillips	Esther Isaacs		Aldgate, London	
29076	Phillips	Leah	1847	Holborn, London	Solomon Phillips	Eveline Solomons	Adam Sampson	Holborn, London	
8870	Phillips	Leah	1849	Aldgate, London	Joseph Phillips	Hannah Barnett	Samuel Jacobs	Aldgate, London	
26681	Phillips	Leon	1850	Spitalfields, London	Philip Phillips	Elizabeth Israel		Spitalfields, London	
1466	Phillips	Leon (Lewis)	1850	?, London	Lewis Phillips	Sarah Solomons	Henrietta Bendix	Aldgate, London	
29539	Phillips	Levy	1847	Spitalfields, London	(?Godfrey/Louis) Phillips	Esther Beck		Spitalfields, London	
20524	Phillips	Lewis	1811	on the North Sea	Aryeh Pais Phillips		Sarah Jonas	Marylebone, London	clothier
20448	Phillips	Lewis	1813	?, Poland	?Hyman Cohen Phillips		(?)	Weymouth, Dorset	clothier + outfitter
28447	Phillips	Lewis	1813	Portsmouth, Hampshire			Elizabeth Isaacs	Spitalfields, London	tailor (journeyman)
1462	Phillips	Lewis	1814	Aldgate, London	Lewis (Judah) Phillips	Rose Cohen	Sarah Solomons	Aldgate, London	butcher
21858	Phillips	Lewis	1828	Clerkenwell, London				Clerkenwell, London	master tailor
17739	Phillips	Lewis	1833	?, Poland [?, Prussia]				Aldgate, London	cap maker
9913	Phillips	Lewis	1838	Elephant & Castle, London	Henry Phillips	Abigail Solomons		Southwark, London	fishmönger
26916	Phillips	Lewis	1838	?, London	Moses Phillips	Miriam Franks		Aldgate, London	scholar
26675	Phillips	Lewis	1839	Spitalfields, London	Philip Phillips	Elizabeth Israel		Spitalfields, London	
3263	Phillips	Lewis	1840	Strand, London	Lawrence (Eliezer) Phillips	Sarah Worms	Clara Moss	Strand, London	
9823	Phillips	Lewis	1840	Finsbury, London	Zaley (Zaleck, Solomon) Phillips	Sarah Cohen		Aldgate, London	scholar
12276	Phillips	Lewis	1841	Clerkenwell, London	Benjamin Phillips	Elizabeth (?)		Holborn, London	scholar
20473	Phillips	Lewis	1841	Middlesex, London				Covent Garden, London	
26909	Phillips	Lewis	1850	?, London	David Phillips	Sarah (?)		Aldgate, London	
31175	Phillips	Lewis	1850	Rochester, Kent	Jehiel (Jekiel) Phillips	Rosa (?)		Rochester, Kent	
18841	Phillips	Lionel (Lawrence)	1839	City, London	Philip Saunders Phillips	Jane Lazarus		City, London	
15850	Phillips	Lionel C	1836	Streatham, London	Coleman Lyon Phillips	Frances Joseph		Bloomsbury, London	clerk to a ship agent
25927	Phillips	Louis	1833	Middlesex, London	(?) Phillips	Rosata Moses		Aldgate, London	hat maker
3222	Phillips	Louis	1844	Holborn, London	Israel Phillips	Maria Samson		Holborn, London	
25021	Phillips	Louisa	1846	?, London	Philip Phillips	Esther Moses		Finsbury, London	
4862	Phillips	Louisa	1850	Birmingham	John Phillips	Emma (?)		Birmingham	
15207	Phillips	Louisa	1850	Shoreditch, London	Solomon Phillips	Mary (?)		Shoreditch, London	
10937	Phillips	Louisa (Leah)	1811	Aldgate, London	Abraham Rodrigues		Lazarus Phillips	Spitalfields, London	feather maker
20537	Phillips	Louisa (Lucy)	1851	Marylebone, London	Lewis Phillips	Sarah (?)	Moss (Moses) Hart	Marylebone, London	
18180	Phillips	Lydia	1817	Aldgate, London			Moss Phillips	Stepney, London	
19491	Phillips	Maria	1791	?, London	(?)		Samuel Phillips	Covent Garden, London	
8459	Phillips	Maria	1796	Portsmouth, Hampshire	(?)		Charles Saul Aaron Phillips)	Portsmouth, Hampshire	independent
10555	Phillips	Maria	1807	Middlesex, London	(?)		Phillip Phillips	Elephant & Castle, London	
3215	Phillips	Maria	1811	Bloomsbury, London	(?) Samson		Israel Phillips	Bloomsbury, London	tailoress
10970	Phillips	Maria	1820	Plymouth, Devon	(?)		Henry Phillips	Aldgate, London	baker
26827	Phillips	Maria	1824	Stepney, London	(?) Phillips			Aldgate, London	needlewoman
16147	Phillips	Mark	1796	?, Poland			Amelia (?)	Whitechapel, London	cutter

ID	surname	given names	born	birthplace	father	mother	spouse 1	1851 residence	1851 occupation
20449	Phillips	Marks	1817	?, Poland [?, Prussia]	Hyman Cohen Phillips		Hannah Mordecai	Weymouth, Dorset	clothier + outfitter
20535	Phillips	Martha	1846	Marylebone, London	Lewis Phillips	Sarah Jonas		Marylebone, London	
15201	Phillips	Mary	1804	Shoreditch, London	(?)		Solomon Phillips	Shoreditch, London	
21859	Phillips	Mary	1829	Clerkenwell, London	(?) Phillips			Clerkenwell, London	
26082	Phillips	Mary (Miriam)	1836	Aldgate, London	Joseph Phillips	Dinah Joel	George Norden	Aldgate, London	
23531	Phillips	Matilda	1832	?, Poland	(?)		Henry Phillips	Liverpool	
24997	Phillips	Matilda	1838	Birmingham	Henry Phillips	Leah Simons		Holborn, London	
21150	Phillips	Matilda	1841	Aldgate, London	Phineas Phillips	Catherine (?)		Aldgate, London	tailoress
18850	Phillips	Maximilian	1833	Brixton, London	Lawrence Phillips	Esther Spyer		Marylebone, London	clerk
31226	Phillips	Michael	1790	?, London			Frances (?)	St Helier, Jersey, Channel Islands	annuitant
6941	Phillips	Michael	1797	Middlesex, London			Leah (?)	Aldgate, London	pencil maker
10336	Phillips	Michael	1820	Middlesex, London			Deborah Cohen	Spitalfields, London	general dealer
25248	Phillips	Michael	1825	Holborn, London	Benjamin Phillips	Elizabeth Nathan	Hannah Davis	Holborn, London	fishmonger
30477	Phillips	Michael	1851	Spitalfields, London	Hyam Phillips	Hannah Lipman	Frances Phillips	Spitalfields, London	
26915	Phillips	Miriam	1813	?, London	Jacob Franks	Rachel Marks	Moses Phillips	Aldgate, London	cap maker
5229	Phillips	Miriam (Mary Ann)	1851	Spitalfields, London	Isaac Phillips	Julia Hyman	Joshua Barnett	Spitalfields, London	
4873	Phillips	Montague	1836	Birmingham	Philip Henry Phillips	Frances Armstrong		Birmingham	cigar maker
27475	Phillips	Morris	1834	Middlesex, London				Whitechapel, London	cap manufacturer
21116	Phillips	Morris	1848	Greenwich, London	Godfrey Phillips	Elizabeth Phillips		Aldgate, London	
15351	Phillips	Morriss	1843	Southwark, London	John Phillips	Elizabeth Lewis		Waterloo, London	
7235	Phillips	Moses	1775	?, Poland			(?)	Whitechapel, London	gentleman
3910	Phillips	Moses	1786	?, London	Nathan Sopher Phillips		Esther (?)	Aldgate, London	Hebrew writer
26914	Phillips	Moses	1815	?, London	Lewis Phillips	Hannah (?)	Miriam Franks	Aldgate, London	watchmaker
6266	Phillips	Moses	1818	?, Poland			Tybalt (Martha) (?)	Portsmouth, Hampshire	clothier + general dealer
11225	Phillips	Moses	1848	Aldgate, London	Tobias Phillips	Hannah Harris		Aldgate, London	scholar
10341	Phillips	Moses	1850	Middlesex, London	Michael Phillips	Deborah Cohen		Spitalfields, London	
11613	Phillips	Moses	1850	Aldgate, London	Isaac Phillips	Esther Isaacs		Aldgate, London	
8230	Phillips	Moses Hyman	1849	Spitalfields, London	Isaac Phillips	Julia Hyman	Julia Defries	Spitalfields, London	
18179	Phillips	Moss	1811	Stepney, London			Lydia (?)	Stepney, London	licensed victualler
31172	Phillips	Moss	1841	Rochester, Kent	Jehiel (Jekiel) Phillips	Rosa (?)		Rochester, Kent	scholar
9827	Phillips	Moss	1851	Whitechapel, London	Zaley (Zaleck, Solomon) Phillips	Sarah Cohen	Jane Jones	Aldgate, London	
12273	Phillips	Nathan	1830	Clerkenwell, London	Benjamin Phillips	Elizabeth Nathan		Holborn, London	cigar maker
12092	Phillips	Nathan	1831	Whitechapel, London	Zelig (Solomon) Phillips	Ann (Nancy) Woolf	Esther Rodrigues	Spitalfields, London	watch maker
1957	Phillips	Nathan	1835	Chatham, Kent				Cardiff, Wales	pawnbroker's clerk
11223	Phillips	Nathan	1843	Aldgate, London	Tobias Phillips	Hannah Harris	Eve Woolf	Aldgate, London	scholar
21861	Phillips	Nathaniel	1837	Clerkenwell, London				Clerkenwell, London	
3252	Phillips	Octavius	1827	Aldgate, London	Lawrence Phillips	Esther Spyer	Rebecca Hester Spyer	Bayswater, London	colonial banker
18849	Phillips	Palmyra Sarah	1850	Regent's Park, London	Robert Abraham Phillips	Helen Levy		Regent's Park, London	
18846	Phillips	Philip	1778	City, London				City, London	stockbroker
6297	Phillips	Philip	1800	Whitechapel, London			Mary (Miriam) Benjamin	Shoreditch, London	cane dealer
25018	Phillips	Philip	1809	?, London			Esther Moses	Finsbury, London	clothier
26673	Phillips	Philip	1813	Spitalfields, London	Lewis Phillips		Elizabeth Israel	Spitalfields, London	watch finisher
6057	Phillips	Philip	1828	Middlesex, London	Lazarus Phillips	Esther Rodrigues	Amelia (?)	Spitalfields, London	

ID	surname	given names	born	birthplace	father	mother	spouse 1	1851 residence	1851 occupation
9914	Phillips	Philip	1830	Elephant & Castle, London	Henry Phillips	Abigail Solomons		Elephant & Castle, London	fishmonger
15840	Phillips	Philip	1836	Finsbury, London	Joseph Phillips	Charlotte Mozely		Hoxton, London	scholar
18201	Phillips	Philip	1838	Middlesex, London				Mile End, London	scholar
5629	Phillips	Philip	1844	Weymouth, Dorset	Marks Phillips	Hannah Mordecai	Marie Nathan	Weymouth, Dorset	
25001	Phillips	Philip	1845	Birmingham	Henry Phillips	Leah Simons		Holborn, London	
6063	Phillips	Philip Gabriel	1851	Aldgate, London	Joel Phillips	Hannah (?)	Palmyre (Pauline) Lion	Aldgate, London	
4870	Phillips	Philip Henry	1794	Birmingham			Frances Armstrong	Birmingham	general factor
3241	Phillips	Philip Saunders	1801	Middlesex, London	Alexander Saunders Phillips	Hannah Solomon	Jane Lazarus	City, London	sponges merchant
13833	Phillips	Philip Solomon	1836	Manchester	Solomon Phillips	Sarah (?)	Julia Moses	Manchester	
3243	Phillips	Philip Zalig	1837	?City, London	Philip Saunders Phillips	Jane Lazarus		City, London	
3280	Phillips	Philippa	1827	Middlesex, London	Philip Samuel		Barnet Samuel Phillips	Walton-on-Thames, Surrey	
26988	Phillips	Phillip	1796	Amsterdam, Holland			Rebecca (?)	Aldgate, London	watch maker
10554	Phillips	Phillip	1799	Middlesex, London	(?Joseph) Phillips		Maria (?)	Elephant & Castle, London	hatter + cigar dealer
29741	Phillips	Phillip	1803	Whitechapel, London	Tsebi		Sophia Isaacs	Aldgate, London	fruit merchant
28221	Phillips	Phillip	1821	Aldgate, London	(?) Phillips	Elizabeth (?)		Spitalfields, London	butcher
28687	Phillips	Phillip	1823	?, Holland	Moses Phillips		Leah Abrahams	Spitalfields, London	confectioner
28260	Phillips	Phillip	1828	Middlesex, London				Spitalfields, London	fish salesman
20528	Phillips	Phillip	1831	Middlesex, London	Lewis Phillips	Sarah Jonas		Marylebone, London	clothier's shopman
12275	Phillips	Phillip	1835	Clerkenwell, London	Benjamin Phillips	Elizabeth Nathan	Fanny Davis	Holborn, London	apprentice to a carver
21159	Phillips	Phillip	1841	Aldgate, London	(?) Phillips	Rachael (?)		Aldgate, London	
24330	Phillips	Phillip	1845	St Giles, London	Joseph Phillips	Esther (?)		Covent Garden, London	scholar
19870	Phillips	Phillip	1849	Whitechapel, London	Simon Phillips	Julia Hart	Sipporah Rees	Spitalfields, London	
27330	Phillips	Phillip	1849	Finsbury, London	David Phillips	Frances (?)		Aldgate, London	
21118	Phillips	Phillip	1850	Aldgate, London	Godfrey Phillips	Elizabeth Phillips	Nena Elkan	Aldgate, London	
20664	Phillips	Phillips	1827	Whitechapel, London0	Abraham Phillips	Rachael De Souza		Spitalfields, London	fishmonger
21146	Phillips	Phineas	1803	?, Poland [?, Prussia]	Elikom		Catherine (?)	Aldgate, London	tailor
1952	Phillips	Phoebe	1823	?, Poland			Isaac Phillips	Cardiff, Wales	
1953	Phillips	Phoebe	1825	?, Poland			David Phillips	Cardiff, Wales	
20526	Phillips	Phoebe (Fanny)	1829	Whitechapel, London	Lewis Phillips	Sarah Jonas		Marylebone, London	waistcoat maker
3854	Phillips	Priscilla	1839	Aldgate, London	Abraham Phillips	Hana (Anna) (?Myers)		Spitalfields, London	scholar
20663	Phillips	Rachael	1802	?, Holland	Gabriel De Souza		Abraham Phillips	Spitalfields, London	
21158	Phillips	Rachael	1806	Sheerness, Kent	(?)		(?) Phillips	Aldgate, London	cap maker
31136	Phillips	Rachael	1827	Aldgate, London	(?) Phillips	Sarah (?)		Margate, Kent	assistant in clothier's shop
10974	Phillips	Rachael	1831	?, Ireland	(?)		George Phillips	Aldgate, London	scholar
10338	Phillips	Rachael	1843	Middlesex, London	Michael Phillips	Deborah Cohen		Spitalfields, London	
24554	Phillips	Rachel	1801	Middlesex, London	Aryeh Shirga Pais Phillips			Brixton, London	
3273	Phillips	Rachel	1810	Strand, London	Samuel Faudel		Benjamin Samuel Phillips	Streatham, London	
23865	Phillips	Rachel	1811	?, London	Jacob Davis		Samuel Phillips	Soho, London	general dealer
10687	Phillips	Rachel	1813	Usk, Wales	(?) Phillips			Spitalfields, London	servant
9461	Phillips	Rachel	1821	Covent Garden, London	Samuel Levy		Barnett Phillips	Aldgate, London	
1464	Phillips	Rachel	1847	Aldgate, London	Lewis Phillips	Sarah Solomons	Charles Joseph	Aldgate, London	
9826	Phillips	Rachel	1849	Whitechapel, London	Zaley (Zaleck, Solomon) Phillips	Sarah Cohen		Aldgate, London	

ID	surname	given names	born	birthplace	father	mother	spouse 1	1851 residence	1851 occupation
24996	Phillips	Ralph	1836	Birmingham	Henry Phillips	Leah Simons		Holborn, London	apprentice
9572	Phillips	Rebecca	1791	Aldgate, London	(?)		(?) Phillips	Spitalfields, London	general dealer
26989	Phillips	Rebecca	1791	Bristol	(?)		Phillip Phillips	Aldgate, London	dressmaker
24377	Phillips	Rebecca	1796	Spitalfields, London	(?) Phillips			Soho, London	cook
14457	Phillips	Rebecca	1814	Middlesex, London	(?)		Samuel Phillips	Manchester	
8460	Phillips	Rebecca	1827	Brighton, Sussex	Charles Saul Aaron Phillips)	Maria (?)		Portsmouth, Hampshire	
26746	Phillips	Rebecca	1829	Aldgate, London	(?) Phillips			Aldgate, London	dressmaker
6060	Phillips	Rebecca	1836	Spitalfields, London	Lazarus Phillips	Louisa (Leah) Rogers (Rodrigues)	Isidor Bernsdorff	Spitalfields, London	scholar
26083	Phillips	Rebecca	1838	Aldgate, London	Joseph Phillips	Dinah Joel		Aldgate, London	
8226	Phillips	Rebecca	1842	Spitalfields, London	Isaac Phillips	Julia Hyman	Joseph Jacobs	Spitalfields, London	scholar
25002	Phillips	Rebecca	1847	Birmingham	Henry Phillips	Leah Simons		Holborn, London	
3236	Phillips	Robert Abraham	1815	Abergavenny, Wales	Abraham Phillips		Helen Levy	Regent's Park, London	goldsmith, jeweller
31171	Phillips	Rosa	1807	?, Poland	(?)		Jehiel (Jekiel) Phillips	Rochester, Kent	
26907	Phillips	Rosa	1846	?, Poland	David Phillips	Sarah (?)		Aldgate, London	
20531	Phillips	Rosa (Rosetta)	1837	Marylebone, London	Lewis Phillips	Sarah Jonas		Marylebone, London	
25925	Phillips	Rosata	1801	Whitechapel, London	Woolf Moses	(?)	(?) Phillips	Aldgate, London	blouse maker
21149	Phillips	Rose	1839	Aldgate, London	Phineas Phillips	Catherine (?)		Aldgate, London	tailoress
1465	Phillips	Rose	1848	Aldgate, London	Lewis Phillips	Sarah Solomons	Leopold Myers	Aldgate, London	
5495	Phillips	Rose (Rosa, Rosetta)	1796	Aldgate, London	(?) Cohen		Lewis Judah Phillips	Aldgate, London	nurse
3221	Phillips	Rose (Rosetta)	1840	Bloomsbury, London	Israel Phillips	Maria Samson		Holborn, London	scholar
20576	Phillips	Rosetta	1787	Whitechapel, London	(?)		Aaron Phillips	Spitalfields, London	general dealer
3852	Phillips	Rosetta	1835	Aldgate, London	Abraham Phillips	Hana (Anna) (?Myers)		Spitalfields, London	tailoress
5887	Phillips	Rosetta	1849	City, London	Joel Phillips	Hannah (?)	Andrew Isaac Natali	Aldgate, London	
20666	Phillips	Samson	1832	Whitechapel, London0	Abraham Phillips	Rachael De Souza		Spitalfields, London	servant
19490	Phillips	Samuel	1793	?, Poland [?, Prussia]			Maria (?)	Covent Garden, London	retired tailor
22862	Phillips	Samuel	1798	Whitechapel, London	Joseph Phillips		Adelaide Barnett	Whitechapel, London	journeyman pencutter
15598	Phillips	Samuel	1801	?, Poland			Betsy (?)	Covent Garden, London	dealer in fancy goods
23864	Phillips	Samuel	1803	?, London	Aaron Cohen Phillips		?	Soho, London	general dealer
14456	Phillips	Samuel	1812	Manchester			Rebecca (?)	Manchester	carpet manufacturer
26743	Phillips	Samuel	1812	Aldgate, London				Aldgate, London	tailor
7292	Phillips	Samuel	1814	?Piccadilly, London	Philip Phillips		Rebecca Lyons	Sydenham, London	journalist
30240	Phillips	Samuel	1823	City, London	Joseph Phillips	Elizabeth (Pessa) Sarah bat Abraham	Hannah Hart	Covent Garden, London	hatter
15202	Phillips	Samuel	1830	Shoreditch, London	Solomon Phillips	Mary (?)		Shoreditch, London	greengrocer
16118	Phillips	Samuel	1833	?, London	Philip Phillips		Hannah Levy	Aldgate, London	general dealer
23600	Phillips	Samuel	1836	?, Poland	Aaron Phillips	Esther (?)		Liverpool	hawker of sponges
4867	Phillips	Samuel	1843	Birmingham	Joseph Phillips	Sarah (?)		Birmingham	
9463	Phillips	Samuel	1845	Aldgate, London	Barnett Phillips	Rachel Levy		Aldgate, London	
21153	Phillips	Samuel	1847	Aldgate, London	Phineas Phillips	Catherine (?)		Aldgate, London	scholar
23440	Phillips	Samuel	1850	Liverpool	Charles Phillips	Esther (?)		Liverpool	
27331	Phillips	Samuel	1850	Bethnal Green, London	David Phillips	Frances (?)		Aldgate, London	
30615	Phillips	Samuel	1851	Spitalfields, London	Simon Phillips	Julia Hart		Spitalfields, London	
3268	Phillips	Samuel Aaron	1844	Strand, London	Lawrence (Eliezer) Phillips	Sarah Worms	Amelia Solomon	Strand, London	

ID	surname	given names	born	birthplace	father	mother	spouse 1	1851 residence	1851 occupation
3276	Phillips	Samuel Henry Faudel	1838	City, London	Benjamin Samuel Phillips	Rachel Faudel	Sarah Georgina White	Streatham, London	scholar
20432	Phillips	Sarah	1777	Amsterdam, Holland	(?)		(?) Phillips	Aldgate, London	
13831	Phillips	Sarah	1792	?, Poland [?, Prussia]	(?)		Solomon Phillips	Manchester	
20447	Phillips	Sarah	1800	Aldgate, London	(?)		(?) Phillips	Margate, Kent	clothier
3256	Phillips	Sarah	1801	Stepney, London	Aaron Worms		Lawrence (Eliezer) Phillips	Strand, London	
3806	Phillips	Sarah	1801	Aldgate, London			(?) Phillips	Spitalfields, London	
9822	Phillips	Sarah	1803	Whitechapel, London	Moses Cohen		Zaley (Zaleck, Solomon) Phillips	Aldgate, London	
20525	Phillips	Sarah	1809	Middlesex, London	Isaac Jonas		Lewis Phillips	Marylebone, London	
13644	Phillips	Sarah	1814	Manchester	(?)		Abraham Phillips	Manchester	
24251	Phillips	Sarah	1815	Middlesex, London	(?)		Emanuel Phillips	Bloomsbury, London	
4865	Phillips	Sarah	1817	Birmingham			Joseph Phillips	Birmingham	
1463	Phillips	Sarah	1821	Portsmouth, Hampshire	Barnett Solomons	Betsey Isaacs	Lewis Phillips	Aldgate, London	
22864	Phillips	Sarah	1824	Whitechapel, London	Samuel Phillips	Adelaide Barnett		Whitechapel, London	umbrella maker
26906	Phillips	Sarah	1824	?, Poland	(?)		David Phillips	Aldgate, London	
9910	Phillips	Sarah	1828	Elephant & Castle, London	Henry Phillips	Abigail Solomons		Elephant & Castle, London	
3851	Phillips	Sarah	1834	Spitalfields, London	Abraham Phillips	Hana (Anna) (?Myers)	Benjamin Myers	Spitalfields, London	tailoress
24327	Phillips	Sarah	1834	St Giles, London	Joseph Phillips	Esther (?)		Covent Garden, London	
3274	Phillips	Sarah	1835	Middlesex, London	Benjamin Samuel Phillips	Rachel Faudel	William Barnet	Streatham, London	
27325	Phillips	Sarah	1839	Finsbury, London	David Phillips	Frances (?)		Aldgate, London	
29075	Phillips	Sarah	1840	Holborn, London	Solomon Phillips	Eveline Solomons	Alfred A Solomon	Holborn, London	
24998	Phillips	Sarah	1841	Birmingham	Henry Phillips	Leah Simons		Holborn, London	
26918	Phillips	Sarah	1843	?, London	Moses Phillips	Miriam Franks		Aldgate, London	scholar
6339	Phillips	Sarah	1844	City, London	Joel Phillips	Hannah (?)	Julius S Kramer	Aldgate, London	
8868	Phillips	Sarah	1844	Aldgate, London	Joseph Phillips	Hannah Barnett		Aldgate, London	
15780	Phillips	Sarah	1844	Spitalfields, London	Hyam Phillips	Hannah Lipman		Aldgate, London	scholar
24253	Phillips	Sarah	1844	Bloomsbury, London	Emanuel Phillips	Sarah (?)		Bloomsbury, London	scholar
8229	Phillips	Sarah	1848	Spitalfields, London	Isaac Phillips	Julia Hyman	Godfrey Abraham	Spitalfields, London	
25253	Phillips	Sarah	1851	Holborn, London	Michael Phillips	Hannah Davis		Holborn, London	
30613	Phillips	Sarah	1851	Spitalfields, London	Phillip Phillips	Leah Abrahams		Spitalfields, London	
3259	Phillips	Sarah Bloom	1834	Strand, London	Lawrence (Eliezer) Phillips	Sarah Worms	Solomon Abraham	Bloomsbury, London	
3239	Phillips	Saunders (Alexander)	1771	Wapping, London			Hannah Solomon	Aldgate, London	retired merchant
6061	Phillips	Selina (Simelia, Serina)	1841	Spitalfields, London	Lazarus Phillips	Louisa (Leah) Rogers (Rodrigues)	Lewis Isaacs	Spitalfields, London	scholar
22887	Phillips	Simon	1784	Aldgate, London	Phillip Isaacs (Aryeh)		(?)	Wapping, London	clothier
19868	Phillips	Simon	1816	Whitechapel, London	Phillip Phillips		Julia Hart	Spitalfields, London	butcher
11857	Phillips	Simon	1840	Middlesex, London	(?) Phillips	(?)		Whitechapel, London	inmate of orphan school
26677	Phillips	Simon	1843	Spitalfields, London	Philip Phillips	Elizabeth Israel		Spitalfields, London	scholar
13830	Phillips	Solomon	1790	?, Poland [?, Prussia]			Sarah (?)	Manchester	overseer of synagogue
15200	Phillips	Solomon	1801	Shoreditch, London			Mary (?)	Shoreditch, London	greengrocer
27360	Phillips	Solomon	1804	Aldgate, London				Aldgate, London	no occupation

589

ID	surname	given names	born	birthplace	father	mother	spouse 1	1851 residence	1851 occupation
27371	Phillips	Solomon	1811	Poznan, Poland [Posen, Prussia]				Aldgate, London	tailor
18282	Phillips	Solomon	1817	?, Poland [?, Polish Russia]				Salisbury, Wiltshire	traveller in jewellery
29073	Phillips	Solomon	1818	St Giles, London	Alexander Phillips		Eveline Solomons	Holborn, London	cigar manufacturer
24328	Phillips	Solomon	1841	St Giles, London	Joseph Phillips	Esther (?)		Covent Garden, London	scholar
8454	Phillips	Solomon	1844	?, Poland	Moses Phillips	Tybald (Martha) (?)		Portsmouth, Hampshire	
10193	Phillips	Solomon J	1842	City, London	Joel Phillips	Hannah (?)	Martha Garcia	Aldgate, London	
29742	Phillips	Sophia	1812	Walworth, London	Aharon Isaacs		Phillip Phillips	Aldgate, London	
3250	Phillips	Sophia	1816	Aldgate, London	Lawrence Phillips	Esther Spyer		Regent's Park, London	
14943	Phillips	Sophia	1835	Wellington, Shropshire	(?) Phillips			Bethnal Green, London	boarding school pupil
11895	Phillips	Susannah	1834	?, Poland [?, Prussia]				Whitechapel, London	tailor
18842	Phillips	Sydney	1843	City, London	Philip Saunders Phillips	Jane Lazarus		City, London	
3283	Phillips	Sydney Philip	1851	Regent's Park, London	Barnet Samuel Phillips	Philippa Samuel		Regent's Park, London	
30607	Phillips	Sydney Philip	1851	Regent's Park, London	Barnet Samuel Phillips	Helen Maria Samuel		Regent's Park, London	
30658	Phillips	Thomas	1823	?, Poland [?, Prussia]	Jacob Phillips	Amelia (?)		Spitalfields, London	tailor
4868	Phillips	Thomas	1845	Birmingham	Joseph Phillips	Sarah (?)		Birmingham	
11221	Phillips	Tobias	1823	Aldgate, London	Moses Phillips	Esther (?)	Hannah Harris	Aldgate, London	slipper maker
6267	Phillips	Tybald (Martha)	1819	?, Poland			Moses Phillips	Portsmouth, Hampshire	
1949	Phillips	Wolf	1796	?, Poland				Cardiff, Wales	hawker
5645	Phillips	Wolfe	1851	Cardiff, Wales	Isaac Phillips	Phoebe (?)	Hynda (Hinda) Bloom	Cardiff, Wales	
3850	Phillips	Woolf	1826	Aldgate, London	Abraham Phillips	Hana (Anna) (?)	Julia Bentolelar	Spitalfields, London	cigar maker
6056	Phillips	Woolf (Walter) L	1850	Spitalfields, London	Lazarus Phillips	Louisa (Leah) Rogers (Rodrigues)	Elizabeth (Bessie) E Levy	Spitalfields, London	scholar
5929	Phillips	Woolf Benjamin	1825	Aldgate, London	Moses Phillips	Esther (?)	Dinah Levy	Aldgate, London	
2796	Phillips	Zaley (Zelig, Solomon)	1809	City, London	L--- Phillips		Sarah Cohen	Aldgate, London	fishmonger
12090	Phillips	Zelig (Solomon)	1798	Spitalfields, London	Menahem HaLevi Phillips		Ann (Nancy) Woolf	Spitalfields, London	porter in general
3277	Phillips (Faudel Phillips]	George Faudel	1840	Streatham, London	Benjamin Samuel Phillips	Rachel Faudel	Helen Levy	Streatham, London	
8228	Phillips [Van Colom]	Philip	1846	Spitalfields, London	Isaac Phillips	Julia Hyman	Pauline Braun	Spitalfields, London	
29034	Phillipson	Berend (Behren)	1793	?, Holland	Jacob Phillipson		Rachel Isaacs	Whitechapel, London	grocer + cheesemonger
24572	Phillipson	Frederick	1849	Adelaide, Australia	Jonas Moses Phillipson	Matilda Constance Goldsmid		Brixton, London	
24573	Phillipson	Gertrude	1849	Adelaide, Australia	Jonas Moses Phillipson	Matilda Constance Goldsmid		Brixton, London	
24570	Phillipson	Jonas Moses	1816	Middlesex, London			Matilda Constance Goldsmid	Brixton, London	none
29035	Phillipson	L---	1826	Brighton, Sussex	Berend (Behren) Phillipson	Rachel Isaacs		Whitechapel, London	shopwoman
24571	Phillipson	Matilda Constance	1817	Middlesex, London	(?) Goldsmid		Jonas Moses Phillipson	Brixton, London	
29037	Phillipson	P---	1834	Brighton, Sussex	Berend (Behren) Phillipson	Rachel Isaacs		Whitechapel, London	domestic work
29036	Phillipson	P---	1830	Brighton, Sussex	Berend (Behren) Phillipson	Rachel Isaacs		Whitechapel, London	jeweller
24574	Phillipson	Walter J	1850	Brixton, London	Jonas Moses Phillipson	Matilda Constance Goldsmid		Brixton, London	
21076	Picard	Alphonse	1838	Paris, France	(?Samuel) Picard			Dover, Kent	boarding school pupil

ID	surname	given names	born	birthplace	father	mother	spouse 1	1851 residence	1851 occupation
21072	Picard	Raphael	1835	Rome, Italy	(?Samuel) Picard			Dover, Kent	boarding school pupil
7293	Picciotto	James Jacob	1830	Aleppo, Syria	Moses Haim Picciotto	Laura (Louisa) (?)	Mary Miriam Benoliel	Shoreditch, London	clerk
7295	Picciotto	Laura (Louisa)	1807	Tuscany, Italy	(?)		Moses Haim Picciotto	Finsbury, London	
7294	Picciotto	Moses Haim	1807	Aleppo, Syria			Laura (Louisa) (?)	Finsbury, London	general merchant + community leader
7296	Picciotto	Rachel	1809	Aleppo, Syria	(?)		Raphael Picciotto	Finsbury, London	
12290	Picciotto	Samuel	1836	Aleppo, Syria	Moses Haim Picciotto	Laura (Louisa) (?)		Finsbury, London	scholar
24657	Piddian	John	1830	Paddington, London				Kennington, London	cigar maker + writer
24656	Piddian	Sarah	1828	Paddington, London	(?) Piddian			Kennington, London	artificial florist
27356	Pike	Abraham	1831	?, Germany [Demscock, Germany]				Aldgate, London	?confectioner
27357	Pike	Simon	1830	?, Germany [Demscock, Germany]				Aldgate, London	tailor
15112	Pilichowski	Augusta	1791	Ipswich, Suffolk	(?)		Jakub Pilichowski	Bethnal Green, London	
15111	Pilichowski	Jakub	1792	?, Poland			Augusta (?)	Bethnal Green, London	fruit salesman
30973	Pin	Barnet	1830	?, Germany				Sheffield, Yorkshire	traveller
4876	Pinchas	Simon	1828	?, Poland [?, Russia Poland]				Birmingham	traveller
17023	Pincus	Moritz	1820	Mecklenburg Schwerin, Germany				Edinburgh, Scotland	general merchant -
1458	Pinkus	Emanuel (Myer)(Myer)(Myer)	1812	?, Poland			Priscilla Harris	Spitalfields, London	tailor
8626	Pinkus	Godfrey	1835	Mile End, London	Samuel Pinkus (Pincus)	Shebe (?)	Ann Morris	Aldgate, London	cigar maker
1459	Pinkus	Hannah	1825	?, Poland			Emanuel (Myer) Pinkus	Spitalfields, London	
8627	Pinkus	Henry	1843	Spitalfields, London	Samuel Pinkus (Pincus)	Shebe (?)		Aldgate, London	scholar
8628	Pinkus	Morris	1845	Spitalfields, London	Samuel Pinkus (Pincus)	Shebe (?)		Aldgate, London	scholar
8625	Pinkus	Pinkus	1831	Bedford, Bedfordshire	Samuel Pinkus (Pincus)	Shebe (?)		Aldgate, London	cigar maker
1460	Pinkus	Rachel	1847	City, London	Emanuel (Myer) Pinkus	Priscilla Harris	Marks Prince	Spitalfields, London	
69	Pinkus (Pincus)	Joseph	1841	Aldgate, London	Samuel Pinkus	Sheba (?)	Theresa Baum	Aldgate, London	scholar
70	Pinkus (Pincus)	Maria	1831	Bedford, Bedfordshire	Samuel Pinkus	Sheba (?)	Aaron Haim Gomes da Costa	Aldgate, London	tailoress
71	Pinkus (Pincus)	Samuel	1803	?, Poland [?, Prussia]			Sheba (?)	Aldgate, London	general dealer
8624	Pinkus (Pincus)	Sheba	1804	Bedford, Bedfordshire	(?)		Samuel Pinkus (Pincus)	Aldgate, London	
5112	Pinner	Lewis	1822	Pinnow, Germany [Pinner, Prussia]	Newman (Nahum) Pinner		Leah (Amelia) Abraham (Abrahams, Stockman)	Portsmouth, Hampshire	jeweller
10175	Pinto	Esther	1787	?, London	Moses de Israel Brandon		Abraham de Meir Pinto	Shoreditch, London	
10180	Pinto	Esther	1821	Middlesex, London	Hyman Collins	Mary (Maria) Davis	Jacob Pinto	Marylebone, London	
5387	Pinto	Esther	1849	Shoreditch, London	Henry (Haim) Pinto	Rosetta De Sola		Shoreditch, London	
5386	Pinto	Henry (Haim)	1815	?London	Abraham de Mier Pinto	Esther de Moses Brandon	Rosetta De Sola	Shoreditch, London	cigar manufactory
10179	Pinto	Jacob	1825	?, London	Abraham de Mier Pinto	Esther de Moses Brandon	Esther Collins	Whitechapel, London	cigar manufacturer
10178	Pinto	Joseph	1821	?, London	Abraham de Mier Pinto	Esther de Moses Brandon		Shoreditch, London	tobacconist
10176	Pinto	Meier	1813	?, London	Abraham de Mier Pinto	Esther de Moses Brandon	Anne Myers nee Keesing	Shoreditch, London	tobacconist
10177	Pinto	Moses	1818	?, London	Abraham de Mier Pinto	Esther de Moses Brandon		Shoreditch, London	
10174	Pinto	Rebecca (Rica)	1851	Shoreditch, London	Henry (Haim) Pinto	Rosetta De Sola		Shoreditch, London	
5385	Pinto	Rosetta	1822	Middlesex, London	David Aaron De Sola	Rebecca (Rica) Meldola	Henry Pinto	Shoreditch, London	

ID	surname	given names	born	birthplace	father	mother	spouse 1	1851 residence	1851 occupation
26535	Pirani	Abigail	1821	Leeds, Yorkshire	Gabriel Davis	Ann Aaron	James Cohen Pirani	Birmingham	
26539	Pirani	Agnes Elizabeth	1839	Birmingham	Charles Pirani	Elizabeth (?)		Birmingham	
26537	Pirani	Charles	1821	?, London	(?)		Charles Pirani	Birmingham	commercial traveller, confectionery
26538	Pirani	Elizabeth	1820	Birmingham			Elizabeth	Birmingham	
26541	Pirani	Ellen Louisa	1847	Birmingham	Charles Pirani	Elizabeth (?)		Birmingham	
26536	Pirani	Frederick Joy	1850	Birmingham	James Cohen Pirani	Abigail Davis	Marian Rennick	Birmingham	
26534	Pirani	James Cohen	1817	?, London			Abigail Davis	Birmingham	manager to woollen drapery, clothing + outfitting business
26540	Pirani	John	1842	Birmingham	Charles Pirani	Elizabeth (?)		Birmingham	
4879	Pisor	Ann	1843	?, Poland [?, Prussia]	Mendele Pisor	Dorah (?)		Birmingham	
4878	Pisor	Dorah	1821	?, Poland [?, Prussia]			Mendele Pisor	Birmingham	
4882	Pisor	Jacob	1850	Birmingham	Menedele Pisor	Dorah (?)		Birmingham	
4877	Pisor	Mendele	1811	?, Poland [?, Prussia]			Dorah (?)	Birmingham	tailor
4880	Pisor	Sarah	1845	?, Poland [?, Prussia]	Mendele Pisor	Dorah (?)		Birmingham	
4881	Pisor	Selina	1849	Aldgate, London	Mendele Pisor	Dorah (?)		Birmingham	
8959	Piza	Abigail (Augusta, Gusta)	1811	Southwark, London	Jacob Moss	Elizabeth (?)	Israel Piza	Aldgate, London	
19124	Piza	David	1817	Aldgate, London	Judah de Elias Piza	Rachel (?)	Hannah Isaacs	Aldgate, London	Minister of Synagogue
16400	Piza	Esther	1817	Aldgate, London	(?) Piza			Spitalfields, London	
19125	Piza	Hannah	1824	Aldgate, London	(?) Isaacs	Rebecca (?)	David de Judah Pisa	Aldgate, London	
8958	Piza	Israel	1813	?, Poland	Shmuel Piza		Abigail (Augusta, Gusta) Moss	Aldgate, London	general dealer
8960	Piza	John (Jacob)	1850	Aldgate, London	Israel Piza	Abigail (Augusta, Gusta) Moss		Aldgate, London	
19128	Piza	Judah	1846	City, London	David de Judah Piza	Hannah Isaacs	Janette Phillips	Aldgate, London	scholar
19126	Piza	Rachael	1842	?, Canada	David de Judah Piza	Hannah Isaacs		Aldgate, London	scholar
19127	Piza	Rebecca	1844	?, Canada	David de Judah Piza	Hannah Isaacs	Moses Levy Yuly	Aldgate, London	scholar
23264	Pizara	Jeanette	1834	?, Italy	(?) Pizara			Notting Hill, London	boarding school pupil
4884	Pizer	Dianna	1804	?, London			Tobias Pizer	Birmingham	
4885	Pizer	Dianna	1832	Birmingham	(?) Pizer			Birmingham	
4883	Pizer	Tobias	1803	?, Poland	Yitzchak		Dianna (?)	Birmingham	pawnbroker
14412	Plax	David	1820	abroad				Manchester	tailor + draper
12636	Plesena	Wolf	1828	?, Poland				Plymouth, Devon	traveller (with jewellery box)
22934	Plied	Edward F	1831	?, Holland				Wapping, London	tailor's shopman
30824	Pocock	Anne	1814	Middlesex, London	Isaac Pocock	Louisa Hime		Maidenhead, Berkshire	
8366	Pocock	Louisa	1787	Liverpool	Humphrey Hime	Sarah Levy	Isaac Pocock	Maidenhead, Berkshire	landed proprietor
8070	Polack	Abigail	1800	Southwark, London	Isaac Joseph		Mark Polack	Soho, London	
29442	Polack	Adelaide	1850	Spitalfields, London	Levy Polack	Catherine (?)	Elias Isaacs	Spitalfields, London	
15002	Polack	Amelia	1831	Spitalfields, London	Moses Polack	Jane (?)		Spitalfields, London	cap maker
15004	Polack	Barnett	1834	Spitalfields, London	Moses Polack	Jane (?)		Spitalfields, London	apprentice
29441	Polack	Catherine	1831	Whitechapel, London	(?)		Levy Pollack	Spitalfields, London	
27695	Polack	Edward	1846	Aldgate, London	(?)	Mary Polack		Spitalfields, London	

ID	surname	given names	born	birthplace	father	mother	spouse 1	1851 residence	1851 occupation
21088	Polack	Eleazer	1818	Hamburg, Germany				Dover, Kent	teacher
27699	Polack	Frances	1795	Aldgate, London	(?)		(?) Polack	Spitalfields, London	clothes dealer
15003	Polack	Gabriel	1833	Spitalfields, London	Moses Polack	Jane (?)	Betsey (?)	Spitalfields, London	apprentice
3712	Polack	Henry	1829	Aldgate, London	Michael Polack		Rachel Harris	Aldgate, London	general dealer
26439	Polack	Isaac	1827	?, Holland			Mina (?)	Aldgate, London	cigar maker
15001	Polack	Jane	1805	Amsterdam, Holland	(?)		Moses Polack	Spitalfields, London	hawker
27696	Polack	John	1847	Aldgate, London	(?)	Mary Polack		Spitalfields, London	
29440	Polack	Levy	1824	?, Holland	Isaac Polack		Catherine (?)	Spitalfields, London	cigar maker
8069	Polack	Mark	1801	Whitechapel, London			Abigail Joseph	Soho, London	lace and wardrobe dealer
27694	Polack	Mary	1827	Aldgate, London	(?) Polack	Frances (?)		Spitalfields, London	needlewoman
26440	Polack	Mina	1820	?, Holland	(?)		Isaac Polack	Aldgate, London	
27697	Polack	Rachael	1849	Aldgate, London	(?)	Mary Polack		Spitalfields, London	
27698	Polack	Rebecca	1851	Whitechapel, London	(?)	Mary Polack		Spitalfields, London	
10323	Polack (Pollock)	Abigail (Adelaide)	1841	Whitechapel, London	David Polack (Pollock)	Isabella (Betsey) Hyams	Elias Isaacs	Spitalfields, London	scholar
10321	Polack (Pollock)	David	1819	Spitalfields, London	Michael Polack		Isabella (Betsey) Hyams	Spitalfields, London	dealer in wearing apparel
10328	Polack (Pollock)	Elias	1850	Spitalfields, London	David Polack (Pollock)	Isabella (Betsey) Hyams		Spitalfields, London	
10324	Polack (Pollock)	Hannah	1849	Spitalfields, London	David Polack (Pollock)	Isabella (Betsey) Hyams	David Weber	Spitalfields, London	
10322	Polack (Pollock)	Isabella (Betsey)	1821	Whitechapel, London	Moses Hyams		David Polack (Pollock)	Spitalfields, London	dealer in wearing apparel
10327	Polack (Pollock)	Judah	1847	Whitechapel, London	David Polack (Pollock)	Isabella (Betsey) Hyams		Spitalfields, London	scholar
10325	Polack (Pollock)	Michael	1843	Spitalfields, London	David Polack (Pollock)	Isabella (Betsey) Hyams		Spitalfields, London	scholar
10326	Polack (Pollock)	Solomon	1845	Whitechapel, London	David Polack (Pollock)	Isabella (Betsey) Hyams		Spitalfields, London	scholar
30684	Poland	Alfred	1838	Whitechapel, London	Joshua Poland	Esther Isaacs	Hannah Da Costa Andrade	Whitechapel, London	scholar
30683	Poland	C---	1836	Whitechapel, London	Joshua Poland	Esther Isaacs		Whitechapel, London	fishmonger's clerk
22462	Poland	Charles	1843	Whitechapel, London	Joshua Poland	Esther Isaacs		Whitechapel, London	boarding school pupil
30682	Poland	E---	1834	Aldgate, London	Joshua Poland	Esther Isaacs		Whitechapel, London	milliner
30680	Poland	Esther	1801	Aldgate, London	Abraham Isaacs		Joshua Poland	Whitechapel, London	
30679	Poland	Joshua	1793	Aldgate, London	Yaakov Ha Cohen		Esther Isaacs	Whitechapel, London	fishmonger
21448	Poland	Juliet	1832	Aldgate, London	Joshua Poland	Esther Isaacs		Whitechapel, London	milliner
30681	Poland	M---	1827	Aldgate, London	Joshua Poland	Esther Isaacs		Whitechapel, London	fishmonger
21447	Poland	Rosetta	1828	Aldgate, London	Joshua Poland	Esther Isaacs	Henry Berkowitz	Whitechapel, London	milliner
30686	Poland	S---	1806	Aldgate, London				Whitechapel, London	fishmonger's clerk
30685	Poland	Sidney	1840	Whitechapel, London	Joshua Poland	Esther Isaacs	Rebecca Hands	Whitechapel, London	scholar
17151	Pollack	Abraham J	1831	?, Denmark				Newcastle Upon Tyne	merchant clerk
24291	Pollack	Frederick	1848	?, Austria	(?) Pollack	(?) Wertheimer		Bloomsbury, London	
23552	Pollock	Myer	1803	Amsterdam, Holland				Liverpool	picture dealer
24597	Poniger	Arnold	1826	Amsterdam, Holland	(?) Poniger	Rosina (?)		Lambeth, London	engraver
24596	Poniger	Fanny	1825	Amsterdam, Holland	(?) Poniger	Rosina (?)		Lambeth, London	
24598	Poniger	Henry	1830	Amsterdam, Holland	(?) Poniger	Rosina (?)		Lambeth, London	engraver
24595	Poniger	Maurice Lewis	1823	Amsterdam, Holland	(?) Poniger	Rosina (?)		Lambeth, London	musician
24594	Poniger	Rosetta	1819	Amsterdam, Holland	(?) Poniger	Rosina (?)		Lambeth, London	
24592	Poniger	Rosina	1791	Amsterdam, Holland	(?)		(?) Poniger	Lambeth, London	
24593	Poniger	Sarah	1817	Amsterdam, Holland	(?) Poniger	Rosina (?)		Lambeth, London	
24599	Poniger	William	1832	?, London	(?) Poniger	Rosina (?)		Lambeth, London	engraver

ID	surname	given names	born	birthplace	father	mother	spouse 1	1851 residence	1851 occupation
10894	Ponitzer	Adelaide	1836	Leszno, Poland [Lissa, Prussia], Poland [Lissa, Prussia]	Elias Ponitzer	Rachel (Rosetta) (?)	Theodor Bessinger	Spitalfields, London	fancy cap maker
10892	Ponitzer	Charlotte	1834	Leszno, Poland [Lissa, Prussia]	Elias Ponitzer	Rachel (Rosetta) (?)		Spitalfields, London	working at fur
10889	Ponitzer	Elias	1791	Leszno, Poland [Lissa, Prussia], Poland [Lissa, Prussia]			Rachel (Rosetta) (?)	Spitalfields, London	dealer in jewellery
10895	Ponitzer	Phebe	1838	Leszno, Poland [Lissa, Prussia], Poland [Lissa, Prussia]	Elias Ponitzer	Rachel (Rosetta) (?)		Spitalfields, London	fancy cap maker
10893	Ponitzer	Polona (Phina)	1834	Leszno, Poland [Lissa, Prussia], Poland [Lissa, Prussia]	Elias Ponitzer	Rachel (Rosetta) (?)	Soloman Broatmen	Spitalfields, London	domestic assistant
10890	Ponitzer	Rachel (Rosetta)	1803	Leszno, Poland [Lissa, Prussia], Poland [Lissa, Prussia]				Spitalfields, London	
10891	Ponitzer	Rosetta	1824	Leszno, Poland [Lissa, Prussia], Poland [Lissa, Prussia]	Elias Ponitzer	Rachel (Rosetta) (?)		Spitalfields, London	tailoress
19218	Pool	Edward (Eleazer)	1850	Whitechapel, London	Samuel Pool	Marianne Van Cleef		Whitechapel, London	
28953	Pool	Helena (Leah)	1851	Whitechapel, London	Salomon (Solomon) Pool	Sarah de Sola	Moses H Blok	Whitechapel, London	
5339	Pool	Marcus	1823	Rotterdam, Holland	Eleazer Pool		Ellen Phillips	Whitechapel, London	general merchant
19217	Pool	Marianne	1832	Arnhem, Holland	(?) Van Cleef		Samuel Pool	Whitechapel, London	
5340	Pool	Salomon (Solomon)	1823	Rotterdam, Holland	Eleazer Pool		Sarah de Sola	Whitechapel, London	importer of cattle
19216	Pool	Samuel	1822	Rotterdam, Holland	Eleazer Pool		Marianne Van Cleef	Whitechapel, London	importer of cattle
5341	Pool	Sarah	1820	Middlesex, London	David Aaron de Sola	Rebecca (Rica) Meldola	Salomon (Solomon) Pool	Whitechapel, London	
8125	Poole	Rosetta	1792	Poole, Dorset	Abraham HaLevi Poole			Tower Hill, London	
17020	Popowitz	Eleonora	1844	Edinburgh, Scotland	George Popowitz	(?)		Edinburgh, Scotland	
17017	Popowitz	George	1801	?, Hungary			(?)	Edinburgh, Scotland	photographic artist master empl 1
17018	Popowitz	Leon	1844	Edinburgh, Scotland	George Popowitz	(?)		Edinburgh, Scotland	scholar
17019	Popowitz	Louis (James)	1846	Edinburgh, Scotland	George Popowitz	(?)		Edinburgh, Scotland	scholar
13146	Popper	Eliza	1824	Whitechapel, London	G (Gotze?) P (Eliakim HaLevi) Beyfus	Cippy (?)	(?) Popper	Aldgate, London	Berlin woolworker
7337	Porter	Sarah Ricardo	1790	City, London	Abraham Ricardo	Abigail Delvalle	George Richardson Porter	Wandsworth, London	
13591	Portuges	Aaron	1822	Warsaw, Poland			Risel	Manchester	hawker of jewellery
13594	Portuges	Jane	1846	?, Poland	Aaron Portuges	Risel (?)		Manchester	
13595	Portuges	Lise	1850	?, Poland	Aaron Portuges	Risel (?)		Manchester	
13592	Portuges	Risel	1829	?, Poland	(?)		Aaron Portuges	Manchester	
13593	Portuges	Sarah	1844	?, Poland	Aaron Portuges	Risel (?)		Manchester	
27417	Posnansky	A---	1831	?, Poland [?, Prussia]				Whitechapel, London	tailor
27893	Powsnyskey	Amelia	1826	Kobylin, Poland [Koblin, Prussia]	(?)		Israel Powsnyskey	Spitalfields, London	tailoress
27894	Powsnyskey	Elizabeth	1849	Whitechapel, London	Israel Powsnyskey	Amelia (?)		Spitalfields, London	

ID	surname	given names	born	birthplace	father	mother	spouse 1	1851 residence	1851 occupation
27892	Powsnyskey	Israel	1821	Plock, Poland			Amelia (?)	Spitalfields, London	tailor
24120	Poznanski	Baruch	1798	?, Poland				Bloomsbury, London	Polish refugee
2206	Praag	Simon	1799	Amsterdam, Holland				Oxford, Oxfordshire	stationery dealer
16259	Praeger (Prager, Preagor)	Lauriah	1850	Spitalfields, London	Woolf Praeger (Prager, Preagor)	Rose Saunders		Spitalfields, London	
16256	Praeger (Prager, Preagor)	Louis (Lewis)	1841	Spitalfields, London	Woolf Praeger (Prager, Preagor)	Rose Saunders	Jane Saunders	Spitalfields, London	
16258	Praeger (Prager, Preagor)	Phillip	1846	Spitalfields, London	Woolf Praeger (Prager, Preagor)	Rose Saunders		Spitalfields, London	
16255	Praeger (Prager, Preagor)	Rosa	1818	Middlesex, London	Aryeh Pais Saunders		Woolf Praeger (Prager, Preagor)	Spitalfields, London	
16257	Praeger (Prager, Preagor)	Sarah	1843	Spitalfields, London	Woolf Praeger (Prager, Preagor)	Rose Saunders	Philip Myers	Spitalfields, London	
16254	Praeger (Prager, Preagor)	Woolf	1801	?, Poland [?, Prussia]	Yehuda Levi		Sarah Cohen	Spitalfields, London	tailor + cap maker
13772	Prager	Jeremiah	1820	?, Germany				Manchester	joiner + cabinet maker
4629	Prenders	Harris	1818	?, Poland				Birmingham	traveller
4709	Press	John	1824	?, Poland				Birmingham	
14210	Prestach	Valerian	1828	Lublin, Poland				Manchester	architect
28039	Price	Lewis	1829	?, Russia	Joseph Price		Julia Harris	Spitalfields, London	cap maker
27108	Prince	Abraham	1793	?, Poland [?, Prussia]	Woolf Prince		Rebecca Barnett	Aldgate, London	tailor
8846	Prince	Abraham	1845	Exeter, Devon	Henry Prince	Esther (?)		Aldgate, London	scholar
8844	Prince	Albert Naphtali	1840	Aldgate, London	Henry Prince	Esther (?)		Aldgate, London	scholar
8843	Prince	Alfred	1839	Aldgate, London	Henry Prince	Esther (?)		Aldgate, London	scholar
29568	Prince	Amelia	1775	Zutphen, Holland	(?)		Asher Prince	Whitechapel, London	
23568	Prince	Dinah	1843	Manchester	(?) Prince			Liverpool	
30458	Prince	Emanuel	1821	?, Poland				Newcastle-under-Lyme, Staffordshire	hawker
8842	Prince	Esther	1814	Aldgate, London	(?)		Henry Prince	Aldgate, London	
30944	Prince	George	1821	?, Poland [?, Prussia]				Wolverhampton, Staffordshire	traveller
29569	Prince	H---	1805	?, Holland	(?) Prince	A--- (?)		Whitechapel, London	picture dealer
8841	Prince	Henry	1807	?, Holland			Esther (?)	Aldgate, London	furrier + orange dealer
4886	Prince	Henry	1813	Marienberg, Germany [Marienburg, Prussia]				Birmingham	jeweller
8845	Prince	Henry	1842	Exeter, Devon	Henry Prince	Esther (?)		Aldgate, London	scholar
8847	Prince	Isaac	1846	Exeter, Devon	Henry Prince	Esther (?)		Aldgate, London	scholar
18277	Prince	John	1823	Amsterdam, Holland				Salisbury, Wiltshire	traveller in spices
4887	Prince	Joseph	1815	?, Holland	Asher Prins	Amelia (?)	Sarah (?)	Birmingham	sponge merchant
8849	Prince	Joseph	1850	Aldgate, London	Henry Prince	Esther (?)		Aldgate, London	
26297	Prince	Michael Samuel	1824	?, Germany	Marcus Prince		Rebecca Marks	Aldgate, London	bootmaker
29570	Prince	R---	1811	?, Holland	(?) Prince	A--- (?)		Whitechapel, London	dressmaker
27109	Prince	Rebecca	1796	?, London	Joseph Barnett		Abraham Prince	Aldgate, London	tailor
26298	Prince	Rebecca	1816	?, London	Henry Marks		Isaac Isaacs	Aldgate, London	
8848	Prince	Sarah	1849	Exeter, Devon	Henry Prince	Esther (?)	J--- Solomon	Aldgate, London	

ID	surname	given names	born	birthplace	father	mother	spouse 1	1851 residence	1851 occupation
26301	Prince	Sarah	1849	Aldgate, London	Michael Samuel Prince	Rebecca Marks		Aldgate, London	scholar
27110	Prince	William	1833	?, London	Abraham Prince	Rebecca Barnett		Aldgate, London	hawker
16630	Prince?	Dinah	1843	Manchester	(?) Prince?	(?) Wolf		Liverpool	
29753	Prins	Adelaide	1837	Whitechapel, London	Lion (Lipe, Lewis) Prins	Esther (?)		Aldgate, London	cap maker
29754	Prins	Asher	1839	Whitechapel, London	Lion (Lipe, Lewis) Prins	Esther (?)		Aldgate, London	scholar
29750	Prins	Esther	1803	Strand, London	(?)		Lion (Lipe, Lewis) Prins	Aldgate, London	
29749	Prins	Lion (Lipe, Lewis)	1796	?, Holland			Esther (?)	Aldgate, London	traveller
29751	Prins	Nancy	1828	Whitechapel, London	Lion (Lipe, Lewis) Prins	Esther (?)		Aldgate, London	umbrella maker
29752	Prins	Rebecca	1834	Whitechapel, London	Lion (Lipe, Lewis) Prins	Esther (?)		Aldgate, London	dress maker
29755	Prins	Samuel	1843	Whitechapel, London	Lion (Lipe, Lewis) Prins	Esther (?)		Aldgate, London	scholar
30618	Prochowski	Alfred	1851	Whitechapel, London	Samuel Newman Prochowsky	Betsy Schiff		Whitechapel, London	
22933	Prochowski	Betsy	1832	Liverpool	(?) Schiff		Samuel Newman Prochowski	Wapping, London	
22932	Prochowski	Samuel Newman	1816	?, Poland			Betsy Schiff	Wapping, London	tailor
15671	Procter	Abraham	1826	?, Holland	(?) Procter	Mary (?)	Rachael (?)	Aldgate, London	cigar maker
15675	Procter	Mary	1788	?, Holland	(?)		(?) Procter	Aldgate, London	nurse
15674	Procter	Moses	1834	?, Holland	(?) Procter	Mary (?)	Rachael (?)	Aldgate, London	slipper maker
15672	Procter	Rachael	1827	?, Holland	(?)		Abraham Procter	Aldgate, London	
15673	Procter	Solomon	1829	?, Holland	(?) Procter	Mary (?)		Aldgate, London	cigar maker
23089	Promull	Rodolph	1816	?, Poland [?, Prussia]				Aldgate, London	glue merchant
22181	Proops	Benjamin	1845	Whitechapel, London	Goodman Proops	Elizabeth (?)		Whitechapel, London	
27963	Proops	Catharine	1828	?, London	Elias Proops	Mary Marks		Spitalfields, London	
17567	Proops	Deborah	1807	Middlesex, London	Eliezer Mendoza	Esther de Micael Jonas	Israel Proops	Spitalfields, London	
17575	Proops	Eleazar (Ezekar)	1843	Middlesex, London	Israel Proops	Deborah Mendoza	Elizabeth Franks	Spitalfields, London	
27960	Proops	Elias	1800	?, Holland	Shlomeh HaCohen		Mary Marks	Spitalfields, London	general dealer
22178	Proops	Elizabeth	1816	Whitechapel, London	(?)		Goodman Proops	Whitechapel, London	
17572	Proops	Elizabeth	1836	Middlesex, London	Israel Proops	Deborah Mendoza	Julius Holz	Spitalfields, London	
17577	Proops	Ester	1849	Middlesex, London	Israel Proops	Deborah Mendoza	Henry Israel	Spitalfields, London	
22177	Proops	Goodman	1814	?, Holland			Elizabeth (?)	Whitechapel, London	journeyman butcher
17573	Proops	Hagar	1839	Middlesex, London	Israel Proops	Deborah Mendoza		Spitalfields, London	
17571	Proops	Hannah	1834	Middlesex, London	Israel Proops	Deborah Mendoza		Spitalfields, London	
10820	Proops	Hannah	1836	?, London	Joseph Solomon Proops	Judith S (?Cooper)	Henry Hacker	Spitalfields, London	dress maker
27965	Proops	Hannah	1838	?, London	Elias Proops	Mary Marks		Spitalfields, London	tailoress
22182	Proops	Hannah	1848	Whitechapel, London	Goodman Proops	Elizabeth (?)		Whitechapel, London	
10821	Proops	Isaac	1840	?, London	Joseph Solomon Proops	Judith S (?Cooper)		Spitalfields, London	scholar
17566	Proops	Israel	1806	?, Holland	Shlomo HaCohen		Deborah Mendoza	Spitalfields, London	general dealer
17570	Proops	Jane	1832	Middlesex, London	Israel Proops	Deborah Mendoza	Joseph David Isaacs	Spitalfields, London	
27964	Proops	Jane	1832	?, London	Elias Proops	Mary Marks	Israel Levine	Spitalfields, London	
27962	Proops	Joseph	1824	?, London	Elias Proops	Mary Marks	Rayner Lazarus	Spitalfields, London	cigar maker
17569	Proops	Joseph	1830	Middlesex, London	Israel Proops	Deborah Mendoza	Julia (?)	Spitalfields, London	
22183	Proops	Joseph	1850	Whitechapel, London	Goodman Proops	Elizabeth (?)		Whitechapel, London	
10817	Proops	Joseph Solomon	1800	?, Holland	Solomon Proops		Judith S (?Cooper)	Spitalfields, London	general dealer
10818	Proops	Judith	1806	?, Holland	Samson HaLevi (?Cooper)		Joseph Solomon Proops	Spitalfields, London	
17568	Proops	Julia	1828	Aldgate, London	Israel Proops	Deborah Mendoza		Spitalfields, London	
10932	Proops	Lewis	1772	?, Holland				Spitalfields, London	

ID	surname	given names	born	birthplace	father	mother	spouse 1	1851 residence	1851 occupation
17576	Proops	Lewis	1845	Middlesex, London	Israel Proops	Deborah Mendoza	Julia (Emily) Frankfort	Spitalfields, London	
10819	Proops	Louis	1834	?, London	Joseph Solomon Proops	Judith S (?Cooper)		Spitalfields, London	pocket book manufacturer
27961	Proops	Mary	1806	?, London	Jacob Coppel Marks		Elias Proops	Spitalfields, London	
27969	Proops	Rebecca	1849	Spitalfields, London	Elias Proops	Mary Marks		Spitalfields, London	
27968	Proops	Samuel	1844	?, London	Elias Proops	Mary Marks		Spitalfields, London	scholar
22179	Proops	Sarah	1841	Whitechapel, London	Goodman Proops	Elizabeth (?)		Whitechapel, London	scholar
27967	Proops	Sarah (Celia)	1843	Aldgate, London	Elias Proops	Mary Marks		Spitalfields, London	scholar
27966	Proops	Solomon	1840	?, London	Elias Proops	Mary Marks		Spitalfields, London	scholar
17574	Proops	Solomon	1841	Middlesex, London	Israel Proops	Deborah Mendoza	Jessie Cohen	Spitalfields, London	
22180	Proops	William	1844	Whitechapel, London	Goodman Proops	Elizabeth (?)		Whitechapel, London	
15781	Props	Sarah	1830	Spitalfields, London	(?) Props			Aldgate, London	tailoress
17531	Prosper	Adelaide	1825	Spitalfields, London	(?)		David Prosper	Spitalfields, London	
17530	Prosper	David	1825	Aldgate, London			Adelaide (?)	Spitalfields, London	grocer
17532	Prosper	Esther	1844	Spitalfields, London	David Prosper	Adelaide (?)		Spitalfields, London	
17534	Prosper	Fanny	1850	Whitechapel, London	David Prosper	Adelaide (?)		Spitalfields, London	
17533	Prosper	Prosper	1847	Aldgate, London	David Prosper	Adelaide (?)		Spitalfields, London	
9348	Proups	Abraham	1846	Aldgate, London	(?)	Rebecca Proups		Whitechapel, London	
9349	Proups	Joseph	1850	Aldgate, London	(?)	Rebecca Proups		Whitechapel, London	
9347	Proups	Rebecca	1824	Aldgate, London	(?) Proups			Whitechapel, London	milliner + dress maker
8153	Przins	Maria	1833	?, London	(?) Przins			Aldgate, London	servant
23646	Puresansky	Leaman	1831	?, Germany				Liverpool	glazier
7390	Pyke	Alexander	1833	Aldgate, London	Samuel Pyke	Eliza Alexander	Rose (Rosetta) A Calisher	Whitechapel, London	
7392	Pyke	Amelia	1835	Middlesex, London	Samuel Pyke	Eliza Alexander	Alexander Isaacs	Whitechapel, London	fancy worker
13129	Pyke	Amelia	1835	Whitechapel, London	John Leon Pyke	Dinah (?)	David Davis	Whitechapel, London	
13128	Pyke	Charles	1832	Whitechapel, London	John Leon Pyke	Dinah (?)	Rebecca Jacob	Whitechapel, London	
7387	Pyke	Charlotte	1840	Kensington, London	Samuel Pyke	Eliza Alexander	Simeon Singer	Whitechapel, London	scholar at home
13125	Pyke	Clara	1828	Whitechapel, London	John Leon Pyke	Dinah (?)		Whitechapel, London	
12917	Pyke	Clara	1830	Middlesex, London	Samuel Pyke	Eliza Alexander	David Asher	Whitechapel, London	school mistress
13130	Pyke	David	1835	Whitechapel, London	John Leon Pyke	Dinah (?)		Whitechapel, London	
13124	Pyke	Dinah	1795	Whitechapel, London	(?)		John Leon Pyke	Whitechapel, London	
7389	Pyke	Eliza	1806	Portsmouth, Hampshire	Solomon Alexander	Amelia Hart	Samuel Pyke	Whitechapel, London	quill dealer's wife
13126	Pyke	Ellen	1829	Whitechapel, London	John Leon Pyke	Dinah (?)		Whitechapel, London	
12918	Pyke	Ellen	1834	Middlesex, London	Samuel Pyke	Eliza Alexander		Whitechapel, London	governess
12598	Pyke	Esther	1845	Brighton, Sussex	(?) Pyke	(?) Cohen		Great Yarmouth, Norfolk	scholar
30055	Pyke	Isaac W	1839	Whitechapel, London	John Leon Pyke	Dinah (?)		Whitechapel, London	
13123	Pyke	John Leon	1790	?London	Leon Pyke		Dinah (?)	Whitechapel, London	sponge merchant + stationer
5859	Pyke	Joseph	1824	City, London			Sara Magnus	Chatham, Kent	
13131	Pyke	Kate	1810	Whitechapel, London	Leon Pyke			Whitechapel, London	dealer in fancy goods
13127	Pyke	Leon	1831	Whitechapel, London	John Leon Pyke	Dinah (?)		Whitechapel, London	
7394	Pyke	Maria	1839	Middlesex, London	Samuel Pyke	Eliza Alexander	Judah Afriat	Whitechapel, London	scholar at home
7388	Pyke	Samuel	1802	Whitechapel, London	Leon Pyke		Eliza Alexander	Whitechapel, London	sponge merchant + stationer
21449	Pyke	Samuel	1830	Middlesex, London				Gravesend, Kent	scholar

ID	surname	given names	born	birthplace	father	mother	spouse 1	1851 residence	1851 occupation
5858	Pyke	Sarah	1829	Chatham, Kent	Simon Magnus	Sarah Wolff	Joseph Pyke	Chatham, Kent	
12919	Pyke	Selina	1837	Middlesex, London	Samuel Pyke	Eliza Alexander		Whitechapel, London	scholar at home
16509	Pyke	Solomon	1833	Whitechapel, London				Holborn, London	clerk
19964	Pyke [Albert]	Eleazer (Albert)	1820	Portsmouth, Hampshire	Samuel Eleazer Pyke	(?) Abrahams	Rebecca Miriam Levy	Whitechapel, London	dentist
14444	Raalter	Mordecai	1833	Rotterdam, Holland				Salford, Lancashire	merchant
13089	Racobonski	Joseph	1808	?, Poland				Clerkenwell, London	prisoner + schoolmaster
2556	Rael	Hannah	1811	?, Germany			John	Hull, Yorkshire	
2557	Rael	John	1801	?, Germany			Hannah (?)	Hull, Yorkshire	
2558	Rael	Mary	1844	Hull, Yorkshire	John Rael	Hannah (?)		Hull, Yorkshire	
2315	Raiman	Lazarus	1828	?, Poland				Leeds, Yorkshire	hawker
17219	Rains	Barnett	1827	Amsterdam, Holland	Eleazer Rains		Sarah Harris	Spitalfields, London	cigar maker
20974	Rains	Solomon	1823	Amsterdam, Holland	Eleazer Rains		Rosetta Cantor	Spitalfields, London	cap peak manufacturer empl 5
30987	Raisack	Abram	1819	?, Poland [?, Prussia]				Nottingham, Nottinghamshire	hawker of jewellery
1253	Ralph	Abraham	1816	Plymouth, Devon		Hannah Nathan		Plymouth, Devon	marine store dealer
1255	Ralph	Amelia	1812	Plymouth, Devon		Hannah Nathan		Plymouth, Devon	
16080	Ralph	Edwin	1829	Plymouth, Devon	George Ralph	Jane (?)		Plymouth, Devon	professor of music
6473	Ralph	George	1801	Plymouth, Devon			Jane (?)	Plymouth, Devon	professor of music
1254	Ralph	Hannah	1768	Plymouth, Devon	(?) Nathan		(?) Ralph	Plymouth, Devon	
6474	Ralph	Jane	1806	Totnes, Devon	(?)		George Ralph	Plymouth, Devon	
15421	Ralph	Lazarus Hart	1809	?, Cornwall			Sarah (?)	Covent Garden, London	general dealer in furniture
15422	Ralph	Sarah	1807	Aldgate, London	(?)		Lazarus Ralph	Covent Garden, London	general dealer in furniture
6475	Ralph	William H	1832	Plymouth, Devon	George Ralph	Jane (?)		Plymouth, Devon	carpenter
26371	Ramos	David	1771	Amsterdam, Holland	Isaac Ramos		Sarah de Jacob Hart	Aldgate, London	traveller
30034	Ramos	Elias	1812	Spitalfields, London	David de Isaac Ramos	Sarah de Jacob Hart	Sarah de Abraham Mendes	Spitalfields, London	general dealer
26375	Ramos	Esther	1839	?, London	David de Isaac Ramos	Esther De David Nunes Carvalho	Mark Abrahams	Aldgate, London	
26372	Ramos	Esther	1803	?, London	David Nunes Carvalho	Abigail (?)	Isaac Carvalho	Aldgate, London	
26373	Ramos	Rosetta	1824	?, London	David de Isaac Ramos	Esther De David Nunes Carvalho	Lazarus Levy	Aldgate, London	furrier
26374	Ramos	Samuel	1835	?, London	David de Isaac Ramos	Esther De David Nunes Carvalho		Aldgate, London	cigar maker
30035	Ramos	Sarah	1814	Aldgate, London	Abraham de David Mendes	Rebecca de Joseph Nunes Miranda	Elias de David Ramos	Spitalfields, London	
30036	Ramos	Sarah	1838	Shoreditch, London	Elias de David Ramos	Sarah de Abraham Mendes		Spitalfields, London	general dealer
29857	Ramus	Agnes	1850	Whitechapel, London	Isaac de Simon Ramus	Martha (?)		Whitechapel, London	
29856	Ramus	Benjamin	1848	Whitechapel, London	Isaac de Simon Ramus	Martha (?)	Rachel Solomons	Whitechapel, London	
29850	Ramus	Isaac	1808	Whitechapel, London	Simon Ramus	Hagar de Joseph Cohen	Martha (?)	Whitechapel, London	warehouseman
29853	Ramus	Jacob (John)	1837	Finsbury, London	Isaac de Simon Ramus	Martha (?)	Fanny (Penina) Solomons	Whitechapel, London	cigar maker
29855	Ramus	Joseph	1847	Whitechapel, London	Isaac de Simon Ramus	Martha (?)		Whitechapel, London	scholar
29851	Ramus	Martha	1818	Whitechapel, London	(?)		Isaac de Simon Ramus	Whitechapel, London	
29854	Ramus	Samuel	1841	Whitechapel, London	Isaac de Simon Ramus	Martha (?)	(?)	Whitechapel, London	scholar
29852	Ramus	Simon	1836	Brighton, Sussex	Isaac de Simon Ramus	Martha (?)	Caroline (Keturah) Harty	Whitechapel, London	scholar
26750	Ransen	Sampson	1799	?, Poland				Aldgate, London	librarian

ID	surname	given names	born	birthplace	father	mother	spouse 1	1851 residence	1851 occupation
5845	Raphael	Abigail	1850	Aldgate, London	Michael Raphael	Mary Moses		Aldgate, London	
7925	Raphael	Abraham	1805	Tower Hill, London			Juliana McCredie	Ipswich, Suffolk	hat + cap warehouse wholesaler + retailer
5840	Raphael	Abraham	1806	Portsmouth, Hampshire	Ralph Raphael	Leah Hart	Elizabeth Jewell (Joel) nee (?)	Whitechapel, London	general dealer
26381	Raphael	Abraham	1818	?, Germany				Aldgate, London	tailor
28816	Raphael	Adelaide	1851	Spitalfields, London	Samuel Raphael	Sarah Franks		Spitalfields, London	
16444	Raphael	Agnes	1843	City, London	John Raphael	(?)		Shoreditch, London	scholar at home
16443	Raphael	Albert	1842	City, London	John Raphael	(?)		Shoreditch, London	scholar at home
6752	Raphael	Albert (Abraham) Phillip	1850	City, London	Phillip Raphael	Elizabeth Harris	Simmie Abrahams	Aldgate, London	
23505	Raphael	Alfred	1849	Liverpool	Joseph Raphael	Elizabeth (?)		Liverpool	
30167	Raphael	Ann	1841	Middlesex, London	(?) Raphael	(?) Levy	Sabbato Giuseppe Besso	Lambeth, London	scholar
5782	Raphael	Ann (Annie)	1848	City, London	Philip Raphael	Elizabeth Harris	Daniel Abraham Britton	Aldgate, London	
5823	Raphael	Caroline	1811	Bloomsbury, London	Samuel (Samson) Raphael	Charlotte Levy		Bloomsbury, London	annuitant
29677	Raphael	Caroline	1814	Whitechapel, London	(?) Raphael	Julia (?)		Whitechapel, London	annuitant
20713	Raphael	Clara	1826	Covent Garden, London	Moses Raphael	Sarah Levy		Soho, London	dress maker
16440	Raphael	Edward	1828	Hamburg, Germany	John Raphael	(?)		Shoreditch, London	merchant's clerk
7342	Raphael	Edward Lewis	1830	Whitechapel, London	Lewis Raphael	Rachael Mocatta	Helene (?)	Bloomsbury, London	merchant banker
26457	Raphael	Eliza	1824	Surrey, London	Henry (Hyam) Raphael	Julia Hart	Lazarus (Lewis) Lazarus	Covent Garden, London	waistcoat maker
20699	Raphael	Elizabeth	1803	Aldgate, London	Moses de David Ventura	Hanah (Nanny) de Uri Pays	Abraham Jewell (Joel)	Whitechapel, London	general dealer
5780	Raphael	Elizabeth	1811	City, London	Eliezer Lezer Harris		Philip Raphael	Aldgate, London	
23499	Raphael	Elizabeth	1818	Liverpool	(?)		Joseph Raphael	Liverpool	jeweller
29678	Raphael	Elizabeth	1818	Whitechapel, London	(?) Raphael	Julia (?)		Whitechapel, London	annuitant
10636	Raphael	Elizabeth	1824	Amsterdam, Holland	(?)		Henry Raphael	Spitalfields, London	
27682	Raphael	Elizabeth	1827	Covent Garden, London	(?) Raphael			Aldgate, London	servant
20781	Raphael	Elizabeth	1850	Bristol	Henry Raphael	Kate (Catharine) Moses	Gustave Barnett	Bristol	
15826	Raphael	Ellen	1824	Whitechapel, London	(?) Levy		Michael Raphael	Holborn, London	
28813	Raphael	Ellen	1839	Spitalfields, London	Samuel Raphael	Sarah Franks		Spitalfields, London	scholar
24312	Raphael	Ellen M	1824	England	(?)		(?) Raphael	Holborn, London	
16445	Raphael	Emilius	1844	City, London	John Raphael	(?)		Shoreditch, London	scholar at home
16439	Raphael	Emily L	1835	Whitechapel, London	Lewis Raphael	Rachel Mocatta		Bloomsbury, London	
20714	Raphael	Esther	1829	Covent Garden, London	Moses Raphael	Sarah Levy		Soho, London	dress maker
9679	Raphael	Esther	1839	Spitalfields, London	Michael Raphael	Mary Moses	Aaron Harris	Aldgate, London	tailoress
26736	Raphael	Esther	1844	Covent Garden, London	Lewis Raphael	Eve Myers	Judah Davis Krakauer	Spitalfields, London	scholar
26733	Raphael	Eve	1816	Aldgate, London	(?) Myers		Lewis Raphael	Spitalfields, London	clothes dealer
16442	Raphael	George	1832	Hamburg, Germany	John Raphael	(?)		Shoreditch, London	merchant's clerk
16840	Raphael	George Charles (Goethe)	1837	Whitechapel, London	Lewis Raphael	Rachel Mocatta	Charlotte Hanne Melchior	Bloomsbury, London	scholar
23501	Raphael	Hannah	1840	Manchester	Joseph Raphael	Elizabeth (?)	Samuel Davis	Liverpool	scholar
9681	Raphael	Hannah	1848	Spitalfields, London	Michael Raphael	Mary Moses	John Harris	Aldgate, London	scholar
12739	Raphael	Hayman	1832	Poznan, Poland [Posen, Prussia]				Ipswich, Suffolk	watch dealer
5792	Raphael	Henry	1827	Aldgate, London	Ralph Raphael	Leah Hart	Kate (Catharine) Moses	Bristol	
10635	Raphael	Henry	1827	Amsterdam, Holland			Elizabeth (?)	Spitalfields, London	cigar maker

ID	surname	given names	born	birthplace	father	mother	spouse 1	1851 residence	1851 occupation
23503	Raphael	Henry	1845	Liverpool	Joseph Raphael	Elizabeth (?)		Liverpool	scholar
7338	Raphael	Henry Lewis	1832	Whitechapel, London	Lewis Raphael	Rachael Mocatta	Henrietta Raphael	Bloomsbury, London	mercantile clerk
12714	Raphael	Israel	1820	Berlin, Germany			Sarah (?)	Coventry, Warwickshire	watch tool manufacturer
8202	Raphael	Jeannette (Janet)	1829	?Whitechapel, London	Lewis Raphael	Rachel Mocatta	Solomon Schloss	Bloomsbury, London	
4892	Raphael	Jette	1844	?, Poland [?, Prussia]	Saul Raphael	Mine (?)		Birmingham	
7343	Raphael	John	1802	Whitechapel, London	Joseph Raphael		(?)	Shoreditch, London	general merchant
9678	Raphael	John	1837	Spitalfields, London	Michael Raphael	Mary Moses		Aldgate, London	cigar maker
10638	Raphael	John	1850	Amsterdam, Holland	Henry Raphael	Elizabeth (?)		Spitalfields, London	
5783	Raphael	John George	1837	City, London	Philip Raphael	Elizabeth Harris	Sarah Louis	City, London	
23498	Raphael	Joseph	1808	Portsmouth, Hampshire	Ralph Raphael	Leah Hart	Elizabeth (?)	Liverpool	jeweller
6751	Raphael	Joseph	1844	City, London	Phillip Raphael	Elizabeth Harris	Sarah Coleman	Aldgate, London	
29676	Raphael	Julia	1771	Aldgate, London	(?)		(?) Raphael	Whitechapel, London	annuitant
26458	Raphael	Julia	1788	Portsmouth, Hampshire	(?) Hart		Henry (Hyam) Raphael	Covent Garden, London	housekeeper
20779	Raphael	Kate (Catharine)	1830	Aldgate, London	Hyam Moses	Rosetta Lazarus	Henry Raphael	Bristol	
28814	Raphael	Kitty (Catherine)	1841	Spitalfields, London	Samuel Raphael	Sarah Franks	Aaron Abrahams	Spitalfields, London	scholar
6663	Raphael	Kitty (Kate, Catherine)	1842	Aldgate, London	Michael Raphael	Mary Moses	Aaron Abrahams	Aldgate, London	scholar
6749	Raphael	Lazarus	1832	City, London	Philip Raphael	Elizabeth Harris		Aldgate, London	cigar maker
20802	Raphael	Leah	1787	Portsmouth, Hampshire	Moses Hart	Rachel (?)	Ralph Raphael	Whitechapel, London	annuitant
23500	Raphael	Leah	1838	Manchester	Joseph Raphael	Elizabeth (?)	Samuel Stern	Liverpool	scholar
17247	Raphael	Leah	1841	Covent Garden, London	Abraham Raphael	(?) Myers	Moses (Morris Moss) Myers	Aldgate, London	scholar
5789	Raphael	Leah (Laura)	1839	Aldgate, London	Philip Raphael	Elizabeth Harris	Emanuel Braham	Aldgate, London	boarding school pupil
7340	Raphael	Lewis	1794	Aldgate, London	Joseph Raphael		Rachel Mocatta	Bloomsbury, London	general merchant
4893	Raphael	Lewis	1849	Birmingham	Saul Raphael	Mine Raphel		Birmingham	
5791	Raphael	Lewis Philip	1846	City, London	Philip Raphael	Elizabeth Harris	Sara Isaacs	Aldgate, London	scholar
27992	Raphael	Louis	1849	?, London	Philip Raphael	Mina (?)		Spitalfields, London	
5843	Raphael	Mary	1815	Spitalfields, London	David Moses	Hannah (?)	Michael Raphael	Aldgate, London	
5785	Raphael	Mary Ann (Marianne, Mary)	1835	City, London	Philip Lazarus	Elizabeth Harris	Zadea Lazarus	Aldgate, London	
16441	Raphael	Mathilda	1829	Hamburg, Germany	John Raphael	(?)		Shoreditch, London	
23506	Raphael	Maurice	1834	Middlesex, London				Liverpool	
5784	Raphael	Maurice (Moss)	1834	Middlesex, London	Philip Raphael	Elizabeth Harris		Aldgate, London	
5842	Raphael	Michael	1805	Aldgate, London	Moshe Raphael		Mary Moses	Aldgate, London	clothes dealer
5828	Raphael	Michael	1823	Covent Garden, London			Ellen Levy	Holborn, London	cigar mker
27991	Raphael	Mina	1821	?, Germany	(?)		Philip Raphael	Spitalfields, London	
4889	Raphael	Mine	1821	?, Poland [?, Prussia]			Saul Raphael	Birmingham	
20711	Raphael	Moses	1781	City, London	Michael Kopf		Sarah Levy	Soho, London	general dealer
20715	Raphael	Moses	1843	Covent Garden, London				Soho, London	scholar
5844	Raphael	Moses	1846	Spitalfields, London	Michael Raphael	Mary Moses		Aldgate, London	scholar
28815	Raphael	Myer	1845	Spitalfields, London	Samuel Raphael	Sarah Franks		Spitalfields, London	scholar
9680	Raphael	Nancy (Annie)	1845	Spitalfields, London	Michael Raphael	Mary Moses		Aldgate, London	scholar
4891	Raphael	Naome	1843	?, Poland [?, Prussia]	Saul Raphael	Mine (?)		Birmingham	
5779	Raphael	Philip	1807	Portsmouth, Hampshire	Ralph Raphael	Leah Hart	Elizabeth Harris	Aldgate, London	travelling salesman
27990	Raphael	Philip	1825	?, Germany	Meir		Minna (?)	Spitalfields, London	tailor

ID	surname	given names	born	birthplace	father	mother	spouse 1	1851 residence	1851 occupation
23504	Raphael	Phillip	1848	Liverpool	Joseph Raphael	Elizabeth (?)		Liverpool	
16090	Raphael	Phoebe	1821	Covent Garden, London	Moses Raphael	Sarah Levy		Covent Garden, London	nurse
7341	Raphael	Rachael	1798	Stratford, London	(?) Mocatta		Lewis Raphael	Bloomsbury, London	
9677	Raphael	Rachael	1835	Spitalfields, London	Michael Raphael	Mary Moses	Aaron Mendoza	Aldgate, London	furrier
20780	Raphael	Ralph	1848	Whitechapel, London	Henry Raphael	Kate (Catharine) Moses		Spitalfields, London	
6750	Raphael	Raphael (Ralph)	1830	City, London	Phillip Raphael	Elizabeth Harris		Aldgate, London	cigar maker
4890	Raphael	Raphel	1841	?, Poland [?, Prussia]	Saul Raphael	Mine (?)		Birmingham	
28812	Raphael	Rebecca	1834	Spitalfields, London	Samuel Raphael	Sarah Franks		Spitalfields, London	cap maker
26735	Raphael	Rebecca	1846	Covent Garden, London	Lewis Raphael	Eve Myers		Spitalfields, London	scholar
5788	Raphael	Rose (Ruth) J	1839	Middlesex, London	Philip Raphael	Elizabeth Harris	Henry Jacques [Parker]	Aldgate, London	boarding school pupil
26459	Raphael	Rosetta (Rose)	1826	Aldgate, London	Henry (Hyam) Raphael	Julia Hart	John Benjamin	Covent Garden, London	book sewer + folder
23502	Raphael	Rosina	1842	Manchester	Joseph Raphael	Elizabeth (?)	Henry Fisher	Liverpool	scholar
28810	Raphael	Samuel	1797	?, Germany	Meir HaLevi		Sarah Franks	Spitalfields, London	cap maker
13920	Raphael	Samuel	1821	Covent Garden, London			Sarah (?)	Manchester	collector to tailor + draper
20712	Raphael	Sarah	1789	Whitechapel, London	Leib Levy		Moses Raphael	Soho, London	
28811	Raphael	Sarah	1812	?, Germany	Solomon Franks		Samuel Raphael	Spitalfields, London	cap maker
12715	Raphael	Sarah	1827	Birmingham	(?)		Israel Raphael	Coventry, Warwickshire	
26734	Raphael	Sarah	1840	Covent Garden, London	Lewis Raphael	Eve Myers		Spitalfields, London	scholar
10637	Raphael	Sarah	1849	Amsterdam, Holland	Henry Raphael	Elizabeth (?)		Spitalfields, London	
4894	Raphael	Sarah	1851	Birmingham	Saul Raphael	Mine (?)		Birmingham	
27993	Raphael	Sarah	1851	?, London	Philip Raphael	Mina (?)		Spitalfields, London	
4888	Raphael	Saul	1811	?, Poland			Mine (?)	Birmingham	pedlar
18904	Raphael	Simon	1826	Marylebone, London				Marylebone, London	
5793	Raphael	Victoria	1848	Middlesex, London	Philip Raphael	Elizabeth Harris	Lawrence Lezard (Lazarus)	Aldgate, London	boarding school pupil
11869	Raphal	Michal	1845	Middlesex, London	(?) Raphal	(?)		Whitechapel, London	inmate of orphan school
9220	Raphel	Caroline	1834	Mile End, London	(?) Raphel	Leach (?)		Spitalfields, London	dress maker
9221	Raphel	Esther	1837	Spitalfields, London	(?) Raphel	Leach (?)		Spitalfields, London	dress maker
9224	Raphel	Godfry	1848	Spitalfields, London	(?) Raphel	Leach (?)		Spitalfields, London	
28988	Raphel	Isaac	1829	Poznan, Poland [Lumter, Posen, Prussia]				Whitechapel, London	tailor
28989	Raphel	Jette	1832	Poznan, Poland [Lumter, Posen, Prussia]	(?) Raphel			Whitechapel, London	tailor
9222	Raphel	Joseph	1840	Spitalfields, London	(?) Raphel	Leach (?)		Spitalfields, London	scholar
9219	Raphel	Leach	1810	Finsbury, London	(?)		(?) Raphel	Spitalfields, London	dress maker
9223	Raphel	Rosseta	1846	Spitalfields, London	(?) Raphel	Leach (?)		Spitalfields, London	scholar
4023	Rapheles	Elizabeth	1832	Portsmouth, Hampshire	Lazarus Rapheles	Sarah Lazarus		Portsmouth, Hampshire	
4021	Rapheles	Esther	1842	Portsmouth, Hampshire	Lazarus Rapheles	Sarah Lazarus	Samuel Simons	Portsmouth, Hampshire	
4022	Rapheles	Phoebe	1843	Portsmouth, Hampshire	Lazarus Rapheles	Sarah Lazarus	Pinkus Samuel	Portsmouth, Hampshire	
14995	Rappaport	Abraham	1831	?, Poland [?, Prussian Poland]				Bethnal Green, London	bookbinder
14930	Rasenbury	Alfred Joseph	1838	York, Yorkshire				Bethnal Green, London	boarding school pupil
14929	Rasenbury	Francis Childs	1838	Ludlow, Shropshire				Bethnal Green, London	boarding school pupil
14932	Rasenbury	Henry Robert Herbert Abraham	1841	Middlesex, London				Bethnal Green, London	boarding school pupil

ID	surname	given names	born	birthplace	father	mother	spouse 1	1851 residence	1851 occupation
14931	Rasenbury	Joseph Robert Abraham	1841	Middlesex, London				Bethnal Green, London	boarding school pupil
22137	Rashintric	Caiba	1821	?, Poland [?, Prussia]				Whitechapel, London	tailor
30917	Rass	Harris	1810	?, Bavaria, Germany				Sheffield, Yorkshire	dealer
17625	Ratsham	Joseph	1830	?, Poland				Aldgate, London	tin worker
22312	Rees	Abigail	1823	Middlesex, London	Joshua Jacobs	Dinah Cohen	Isaac Rees	Southwark, London	
19603	Rees	Amelia	1835	Spitalfields, London	Barnett Rees	Sarah Isaacs	Hyman Davis	Aldgate, London	
19601	Rees	Barnett	1799	?, Holland	Baruch Bendit HaLevi		Sarah Isaacs	Aldgate, London	general dealer
19605	Rees	Benjamin	1831	Spitalfields, London	Barnett Rees	Sarah Isaacs	Rebecca Bittan	Aldgate, London	marine dealer
30526	Rees	Hannah	1758	Middlesex, London	(?)		(?) Rees	St Giles, London	retired linen draper
19608	Rees	Henry	1847	Spitalfields, London	Barnett Ress	Sarah Isaacs	Deborah Levy	Aldgate, London	
19604	Rees	Isaac	1828	Middlesex, London	Barnett Ress	Sarah Isaacs	Abigail Jacobs	Southwark, London	rag + bottle dealer
19606	Rees	Lawrence	1840	Spitalfields, London	Barnett Ress	Sarah Isaacs	Matilda Hyams	Aldgate, London	
30527	Rees	Michael	1789	Whitechapel, London	(?) Rees	Hannah (?)		St Giles, London	retired linen draper
19607	Rees	Michael	1843	Spitalfields, London	Barnett Ress	Sarah Isaacs	Jane Birne	Aldgate, London	
24374	Rees	Priscilla	1795	Piccadilly, London	(?)		(?) Rees	Soho, London	retired jeweller
19602	Rees	Sarah	1803	?, Holland	Moses Isaacs		Barnett Rees	Aldgate, London	
19600	Rees	Sophia	1849	Spitalfields, London	Barnett Rees	Sarah Isaacs	John Hyams	Aldgate, London	
4545	Reich	Edward	1830	?, Poland [?, Prussia]				Birmingham	hawker
22995	Reichfeld	Joseph	1822	?, Hungary				Whitechapel, London	tailor
2846	Reinberg	Esther	1841	Whitechapel, London	Magnus Reinberg	Rebecca Gollin		Whitechapel, London	
2845	Reinberg	Magnus (Menachim)	1814	Leszno, Poland [Lissa, Prussia], Poland [Lissa, Prussia]	Mordecai (?Reinberg)			Whitechapel, London	
2847	Reinberg	Marcus Woolf	1844	Whitechapel, London	Magnus Reinberg	Rebecca Gollin		Whitechapel, London	
2844	Reinberg	Rebecca	1816	Spitalfields, London	Wolf Josephson Gollin	Marlah (Martha) (?)	Magnus Reinberg	Whitechapel, London	
26979	Reinstein	Abraham	1809	?, Germany			Catherine (?)	Aldgate, London	tailor
26983	Reinstein	Adelaide	1844	Aldgate, London	Abraham Reinstein	Catherine (?)		Aldgate, London	
26980	Reinstein	Catherine	1809	?, Germany	(?)		Abraham Reinstein	Aldgate, London	clothes dealer
26982	Reinstein	Elizabeth	1839	?, Germany	Abraham Reinstein	Catherine (?)		Aldgate, London	
26981	Reinstein	Phebe	1836	?, Germany	Abraham Reinstein	Catherine (?)		Aldgate, London	
26984	Reinstein	Simon	1849	Aldgate, London	Abraham Reinstein	Catherine (?)		Aldgate, London	
25851	Reishman	?	1826	?, Poland			Samuel Reishman	Aldgate, London	?
25853	Reishman	Esther	1849	?, Poland	Samuel Reishman	(?)		Aldgate, London	
25852	Reishman	Mary	1847	?, Poland	Samuel Reishman	(?)		Aldgate, London	scholar
25850	Reishman	Samuel	1824	?, Poland			(?)	Aldgate, London	?
14471	Reiss	Leopold	1826	?, Germany				Salford, Lancashire	merchant
16241	Replat	Benjamin A	1822	?, Holland	Emanuel Replat	Betsey (?)	Debra (?)	Spitalfields, London	tailor
16240	Replat	Betsey	1793	?, Holland	(?)		Emanuel Replat	Spitalfields, London	
16242	Replat	Debra	1819	?, Holland	(?)		Benjamin A Replat	Spitalfields, London	
16239	Replat	Emanuel	1789	?, Holland			Betsey (?)	Spitalfields, London	tailor
16243	Replat	Emanuel	1848	?, London	Benjamin A Replat	Debra (?)		Spitalfields, London	
13575	Rermvaper	Marcus	1795	Warsaw, Poland				Manchester	slipper maker
16431	Reuben	Benjamin	1833	?, Poland	(?) Reuben	Jane (?)		Aldgate, London	slipper maker
29585	Reuben	Caroline	1850	Great Yarmouth, Norfolk	Salomon Reuben	Henrietta Van Raalte		Whitechapel, London	

ID	surname	given names	born	birthplace	father	mother	spouse 1	1851 residence	1851 occupation
26516	Reuben	Fanny	1822	Dover, Kent	Jacob Reuben	Sarah (?)		Dover, Kent	clothier's assistant
29583	Reuben	Henrietta	1824	?, Holland	Jacob Van Raalte	Hannah (?)	Salomon Reuben	Whitechapel, London	
26514	Reuben	Jacob	1788	?, London			Sarah (?)	Dover, Kent	clothier
16430	Reuben	Jane	1794	?, Poland	(?)		(?) Reuben	Aldgate, London	slipper maker
26518	Reuben	Julia	1832	Dover, Kent	Jacob Reuben	Sarah (?)		Dover, Kent	
26513	Reuben	Kate	1827	Dover, Kent	Jacob Reuben	Sarah (?)	Samuel Aaron	Dover, Kent	wholesale jeweller
26517	Reuben	Rachael	1824	Dover, Kent	Jacob Reuben	Sarah (?)	Benjamin Cantor	Dover, Kent	
29586	Reuben	Reuben	1851	Stepney, London	Salomon Reuben	Henrietta Van Raalte		Whitechapel, London	
29584	Reuben	Salomon	1817	?, London			Henrietta Van Raalte	Whitechapel, London	traveller watch materials
26515	Reuben	Sarah	1787	?, London	(?)		Jacob Reuben	Dover, Kent	
14470	Reuss	Ernest	1801	?, Germany			Sophia (?)	Manchester	merchant
7344	Reuter (Josaphat)	Julius (Paul) de (Israel Beer)	1816	Kassel, Germany	Samuel Levi Josaphat	Bette Sanders	Ida Marie Elisabeth Clementina Magnus	Finsbury, London	proprietor, news service agency
10481	Rewbin	Fanny	1776	?, Holland				Mile End, London	formerly clothes dealer
29181	Ribaus	Fredrik	1784	Hamburg, Germany [Hambrugh, Holland]				Whitechapel, London	merchant
7345	Ricardo	John Lewis	1812	Walthamstow, London	Jacob Ricardo		Katherine Duff	South Kensington, London	MP + prorietor of various securities
23316	Ricardo (Ricardo Israel)	Emily	1816	Walthamstow, London	(?Benjamin) Ricardo (Ricardo Israel)	(?Miriam de Elisha Lindo?)		Belgravia, London	
23315	Ricardo (Ricardo Israel)	Samson (Simson)	1792	Bow, London	Abraham de Joseph Israel Ricardo	Abigail de Abraham Del Valle		Belgravia, London	retired dealer in public funds
14271	Richer	Jacob	1826	?, Germany				Manchester	tailor
14863	Riches	Ann	1797	Norwich, Norfolk	(?) Riches			Bethnal Green, London	independent
2316	Richman	Morris	1830	?, Poland				Leeds, Yorkshire	hawker
2317	Riess	Herman	1819	?, Poland [?, Prussia]			Julia (?)	Leeds, Yorkshire	jeweller
2318	Riess	Julia	1820	?, Poland [?, Prussia]			Herman Riess	Leeds, Yorkshire	
2319	Riess	Max	1845	?, Poland [?, Prussia]	Herman Riess	Julia (?)		Leeds, Yorkshire	
2320	Riess	Rose	1847	?, Poland [?, Prussia]	Herman Riess	Julia (?)		Leeds, Yorkshire	
26412	Rifel	Aaron	1850	?Aldgate, London	Morris Rifel	Phoebe (?)		Aldgate, London	
26410	Rifel	Dinah	1845	?, Poland [?, Prussia]	Morris Rifel	Phoebe (?)		Aldgate, London	
26411	Rifel	Jacob	1847	?, Poland [?, Prussia]	Morris Rifel	Phoebe (?)		Aldgate, London	
26408	Rifel	Morris	1816	?, Poland [?, Prussia]			Phoebe (?)	Aldgate, London	tailor
26409	Rifel	Phoebe	1823	?, Poland [?, Prussia]	(?)		Morris Rifel	Aldgate, London	
12770	Rintel	Benedict Joseph	1809	Hamburg, Germany	Benedict Jacob Rintel	Therese Kalman	Fanny Simmons	Aldgate, London	professor of Hebrew
5451	Rintel	Fanny	1814	Penzance, Cornwall	Barnet Asher Simmons	Flora Jacob	Benedict Joseph Rintel	Aldgate, London	
26969	Rintle	Flora	1826	Dunbar, Scotland	Myer Moses Rintle	Sarah (?)		Aldgate, London	tailoress
26970	Rintle	Hyam	1830	Dunbar, Scotland	Myer Moses Rintle	Sarah (?)		Aldgate, London	tailor
26967	Rintle	Myer Moses	1778	?, Poland [?, Prussia]			Sarah (?)	Aldgate, London	Hebrew teacher
26968	Rintle	Sarah	1787	?, Poland [?, Prussia]	(?)		Myer Moses Rintle	Aldgate, London	
28252	Ritch	Caskel	1831	?, Poland [?, Prussia]				Spitalfields, London	tailor
2321	Ritman	Philip	1831	?, Poland				Leeds, Yorkshire	hawker
13648	Rittinbach	Israel	1825	?, Poland				Manchester	shoe mfr's partner
28933	Robbins	Abrahams	1850	?Spitalfields, London	Israel Robbins	Hannah (?)		Spitalfields, London	
28932	Robbins	Hannah	1823	?, Holland	(?)		Israel Robbins	Spitalfields, London	

ID	surname	given names	born	birthplace	father	mother	spouse 1	1851 residence	1851 occupation
28931	Robbins	Israel	1825	?, Holland			Hannah (?)	Spitalfields, London	cigar maker
21345	Robert	Elias	1843	Stourbridge, Worcestershire	Jacob Robert	Elizabeth (?)		Stourbridge, Worcestershire	scholar
4850	Robert	Elizabeth	1806	Poznan, Poland [Posen, Prussia]			Jacob Robert	Stourbridge, Worcestershire	
4848	Robert	Gabriel	1840	Stourbridge, Worcestershire	Jacob Roberts	Elizabeth (?)		Birmingham	scholar
21344	Robert	Henry	1842	Stourbridge, Worcestershire	Jacob Robert	Elizabeth (?)		Stourbridge, Worcestershire	scholar
4849	Robert	Jacob	1797	Poznan, Poland [Posen, Prussia]			Elizabeth (?)	Stourbridge, Worcestershire	general dealer
4851	Robert	Louis	1839	Birmingham	Jacob Robert	Elizabeth (?)	Harriet Fox	Stourbridge, Worcestershire	
23737	Roberts	Elizabeth	1830	Liverpool	Moses Roberts	Sarah (?)		Liverpool	
23738	Roberts	Jane	1834	Liverpool	Moses Roberts	Sarah (?)		Liverpool	
23742	Roberts	John	1843	Liverpool	Moses Roberts	Sarah (?)		Liverpool	scholar
23743	Roberts	Lewis Philip	1844	Liverpool	Moses Roberts	Sarah (?)		Liverpool	scholar
23739	Roberts	Mary	1835	Liverpool	Moses Roberts	Sarah (?)		Liverpool	scholar
23745	Roberts	Miriam	1848	Liverpool	Moses Roberts	Sarah (?)		Liverpool	
23735	Roberts	Moses	1806	Liverpool			Sarah (?)	Liverpool	commercial traveller to ship chandler
23746	Roberts	Moses	1849	Liverpool	Moses Roberts	Sarah (?)		Liverpool	scholar
23741	Roberts	Richard	1841	Liverpool	Moses Roberts	Sarah (?)		Liverpool	scholar
23736	Roberts	Sarah	1810	Chatham, Kent	(?)		Moses Roberts	Liverpool	shopkeeper
23744	Roberts	Sarah	1846	Liverpool	Moses Roberts	Sarah (?)		Liverpool	scholar
23740	Roberts	William	1837	Liverpool	Moses Roberts	Sarah (?)		Liverpool	scholar
4997	Robinson	Ann	1825	Birmingham				Birmingham	servant
4895	Robinson	Philip	1833	Exeter, Devon				Birmingham	traveller
23812	Robinson	Sophia	1845	Middlesex, London	Ralph Robinson [Lazarus]	Emily Johnson		Liverpool	
23813	Robinson	Thomas	1850	Liverpool	Ralph Robinson [Lazarus]	Emily Johnson		Liverpool	
30506	Robinson [Lazarus]	Emily	1824	Middlesex, London	Phineas Johnson		Ralph Robinson [Lazarus]	Liverpool	
7798	Robinson [Lazarus]	Ralph	1821	Middlesex, London	Moses Lazarus	(?) Joseph	Emily Johnson	Liverpool	cigar maker
4896	Robinzon	Lazarus	1809	Savillje, Poland				Birmingham	pawnbroker
19566	Robinzon	Matilda	1830	?, Poland	Lazarus Robinzon		Mark Gumpel Lyons	Birmingham	
10358	Rodrigues	Abraham	1822	Whitechapel, London	Joseph Rodrigues	Abigail de Daniel Jeerman	Leah (Lydia) Bitton	Spitalfields, London	general dealer
10594	Rodrigues	Abraham	1848	Spitalfields, London	Mordecai Rodrigues	Isabella (Bella, Blanca) Joseph	Ann Jacobs	Aldgate, London	scholar
21641	Rodrigues	Abraham	1851	Spitalfields, London	Abraham Rodrigues	Leah (Lydia) Bitton	Rachel Rodrigues	Spitalfields, London	
5666	Rodrigues	Clara	1801	Spitalfields, London	Emanuel Henriques Valentine		Samuel de Saul Rodrigues	Spitalfields, London	tailoress
29675	Rodrigues	Clara	1819	?, London	(?) Rodrigues			Wapping, London	house servant
30661	Rodrigues	D---	1799	Amsterdam, Holland			(?)	Spitalfields, London	iron dealer
10590	Rodrigues	David	1836	Mile End, London	Mordecai Rodrigues	Isabella (Bella, Blanca) Joseph		Aldgate, London	scholar
30662	Rodrigues	Edward	1825	Paris, France	D--- Rodrigues			Spitalfields, London	no trade

ID	surname	given names	born	birthplace	father	mother	spouse 1	1851 residence	1851 occupation
21731	Rodrigues	Eliza	1823	?London	Isaac Rodrigues	P--- (?)		Islington, London	
21732	Rodrigues	Ellen	1830	?London	Isaac Rodrigues	P--- (?)		Islington, London	
15733	Rodrigues	Emanuel	1836	?, Yorkshire	Samuel de Saul Rodrigues	Clara de Emanuel Henriques Valentine		Spitalfields, London	bedstead maker
21730	Rodrigues	Emma	1813	?London	Isaac Rodrigues	P--- (?)		Islington, London	
21728	Rodrigues	Isaac	1784	?, London			P--- (?)	Islington, London	meat salesman
10593	Rodrigues	Isaac	1845	Spitalfields, London	Mordecai Rodrigues	Isabella (Bella, Blanca) Joseph	Phoebe Belasco	Aldgate, London	scholar
10361	Rodrigues	Isaac	1847	Whitechapel, London	Abraham Rodrigues	Leah (Lydia) Bitton		Spitalfields, London	scholar
10588	Rodrigues	Isabella (Bella, Blanca)	1814	Portsmouth, Hampshire	Joseph de Jehiel		Mordecia Rodrigues	Aldgate, London	
10591	Rodrigues	Joseph	1839	Mile End, London	Mordecai Rodrigues	Isabella (Bella, Blanca) Joseph		Aldgate, London	scholar
10362	Rodrigues	Leah	1849	Whitechapel, London	Abraham Rodrigues	Leah (Lydia) Bitton		Spitalfields, London	
10359	Rodrigues	Leah (Lydia)	1820	Whitechapel, London	Isaac Bitton	Elizabeth (Eve, Hava) de Getschlik Elyakim	Abraham Rodrigues	Spitalfields, London	general dealer
10587	Rodrigues	Mordecai	1798	Whitechapel, London	David Rodrigues		Isabella (Bella, Blanca) Joseph	Aldgate, London	butcher
21729	Rodrigues	P---	1790	?London	(?)		Isaac Rodrigues	Islington, London	
10592	Rodrigues	Rachael	1843	Spitalfields, London	Mordecai Rodrigues	Isabella (Bella, Blanca) Joseph	Solomon Isaacs	Aldgate, London	scholar
15734	Rodrigues	Rebecca	1837	?, Yorkshire	Samuel de Saul Rodrigues	Clara de Emanuel Henriques Valentine		Spitalfields, London	servant
30663	Rodrigues	Richard	1827	Spitalfields, London	D--- Rodrigues			Spitalfields, London	no trade
10360	Rodrigues	Rosetta	1843	Whitechapel, London	Abraham Rodrigues	Leah (Lydia) Bitton	Laurence (Eliezer) Keys (Israel)	Spitalfields, London	scholar
9332	Rodrigues	Sarah	1791	Aldgate, London	(?)		David de Solomon Rodrigues	Aldgate, London	poor
10589	Rodrigues	Sarah	1834	Spitalfields, London	Mordecai Rodrigues	Isabella (Bella, Blanca) Joseph	Zelic Cohen	Aldgate, London	cap maker
15735	Rodrigues	Saul	1845	Middlesex, London	Samuel de Saul Rodrigues	Clara de Emanuel Henriques Valentine		Spitalfields, London	
21733	Rodrigues	Sophia	1834	?London	Isaac Rodrigues	P--- (?)		Islington, London	
27989	Roesfield	Isaac	1826	?				Spitalfields, London	butcher
12109	Rogers	Abigail	1795	Whitechapel, London	(?)		Joseph Rogers	Spitalfields, London	general dealer
26912	Rogers	Abigail	1822	?, London	(?)		(?) Rogers	Aldgate, London	
26913	Rogers	David	1846	?, London	(?) Rogers	Abigail (?)		Aldgate, London	
12110	Rogers	Esther	1831	Mile End, London	Joseph Rogers	Abigail (?)		Spitalfields, London	general dealer
12108	Rogers	Joseph	1781	Aldgate, London			Abigail (?)	Spitalfields, London	cigar dealer
26927	Rogers (Rodrigues)	Abigail	1848	?, London	Isaac de Joseph Rogers (Rodrigues)	Rebecca de Abraham Mendes		Aldgate, London	scholar
26726	Rogers (Rodrigues)	Abraham	1835	Aldgate, London	Daniel Rogers (Rodrigues)	Julia (Judith) de Haim Samuels	(?)	Spitalfields, London	jeweller apprentice
26724	Rogers (Rodrigues)	Daniel	1802	Aldgate, London	Abraham Rodrigues	Simha (?)	Julia (Judith) de Haim Samuels	Spitalfields, London	Jewish meat inspector
16412	Rogers (Rodrigues)	Daniel	1818	Middlesex, London	Joseph Rodrigues	Abigail de Daniel Jerman	Esther Costa	Aldgate, London	pencil maker

ID	surname	given names	born	birthplace	father	mother	spouse 1	1851 residence	1851 occupation
16419	Rogers (Rodrigues)	Deborah	1847	?, London	Daniel Rogers (Rodrigues)	Esther Costa		Aldgate, London	
16413	Rogers (Rodrigues)	Esther	1823	Middlesex, London	Samuel de Gabriel Costa	Hannah Levy	Daniel Rogers (Rodrigues)	Aldgate, London	
26926	Rogers (Rodrigues)	Esther	1847	?, London	Isaac de Joseph Rogers (Rodrigues)	Rebecca de Abraham Mendes		Aldgate, London	scholar
16420	Rogers (Rodrigues)	Eve	1850	?, London	Daniel Rogers (Rodrigues)	Esther Costa	Isaac de Aaron Gomes Da Costa	Aldgate, London	
16418	Rogers (Rodrigues)	Gabriel	1845	?, London	Daniel Rogers (Rodrigues)	Esther Costa		Aldgate, London	scholar
16414	Rogers (Rodrigues)	Hannah	1842	?, London	Daniel Rogers (Rodrigues)	Esther Costa		Aldgate, London	scholar
26728	Rogers (Rodrigues)	Hyam	1843	Aldgate, London	Daniel Rogers (Rodrigues)	Julia (Judith) de Haim Samuels		Spitalfields, London	scholar
26923	Rogers (Rodrigues)	Isaac	1816	?, London	Joseph Rodrigues	Abigail de Daniel Jerman	Rebecca de Abraham Mendes	Aldgate, London	general dealer
26925	Rogers (Rodrigues)	Joseph	1838	?, London	Isaac de Joseph Rogers (Rodrigues)	Rebecca de Abraham Mendes		Aldgate, London	scholar
16415	Rogers (Rodrigues)	Joseph	1842	?, London	Daniel Rogers (Rodrigues)	Esther Costa		Aldgate, London	scholar
26725	Rogers (Rodrigues)	Julia (Judith)	1806	Aldgate, London	Haim Samuels		Daniel de Abraham Rogers (Rodrigues)	Spitalfields, London	
16417	Rogers (Rodrigues)	Mordecai (Morris)	1844	?, London	Daniel Rogers (Rodrigues)	Esther Costa	Kate (Catherine) Cohen	Aldgate, London	scholar
26924	Rogers (Rodrigues)	Rebecca	1818	?, London	Abraham de David Mendes	Rebecca de Joseph Nunes Miranda	Isaac de Joseph Rogers (Rodrigues)	Aldgate, London	
16416	Rogers (Rodrigues)	Samuel	1843	?, London	Daniel Rogers (Rodrigues)	Esther Costa		Aldgate, London	scholar
26727	Rogers (Rodrigues)	Sophia (Simha)	1837	Aldgate, London	Daniel Rogers (Rodrigues)	Julia (Judith) de Haim Samuels	Morris Lyon	Spitalfields, London	
17136	Rollowski	John Charles	1805	Gdansk, Poland [Danzig, Prussia]				Bradford, Yorkshire	book keeper
10733	Romain	David Anidjar	1835	Spitalfields, London	Moses Anidjar Romain	Hannah Wolf	Dinah Jacobs	Spitalfields, London	
5955	Romain	Elizabeth (Betsy, Bilha) Anidjar	1840	Spitalfields, London	Moses Anidjar Romain	Hannah Wolf	John Joseph	Spitalfields, London	
10732	Romain	Hannah Anidjar	1811	Aldgate, London	Zeheb Wolf		Moses de Abraham Anidjar Romain	Spitalfields, London	general dealer
17451	Romain	Jacob	1825	?, Holland				Aldgate, London	hawker of fruit
10737	Romain	Julia (Judith) Anidjar	1842	Spitalfields, London	Moses Anidjar Romain	Hannah Wolf		Spitalfields, London	
10734	Romain	Louisa (Mazaltob, Lucky) Anidjar	1836	Spitalfields, London	Moses Anidjar Romain	Hannah Wolf		Spitalfields, London	
10731	Romain	Moses Anidjar	1807	Aldgate, London	Abraham Anidjar Romano (Romain)	Mazaltov (Lucky) (?)	Hannah Wolf	Spitalfields, London	general dealer
10738	Romain	Samuel Anidjar	1844	Spitalfields, London	Moses Anidjar Romain	Hannah Wolf		Spitalfields, London	
10735	Romain	Sarah Anidjar	1839	Spitalfields, London	Moses Anidjar Romain	Hannah Wolf	Henry Asher Davis	Spitalfields, London	
28354	Romain (Romano)	Aaron	1834	Mile End, London	John (Jacob) Romaine (Romano)	Hanah de Aaron Barnett		Whitechapel, London	butcher (out of employ)
28353	Romain (Romano)	Abigail	1803	Mile End, London	Jacob de Leon (Lyon)	Rebecca de Joseph Abendana	Barnet Benjamin	Whitechapel, London	cab driver
13274	Romain (Romano)	Abigail	1813	Whitechapel, London	Isaac Lyons		Joseph Romain (Romano)	Spitalfields, London	
28368	Romain (Romano)	Abigail	1843	Whitechapel, London	Emanuel (Menahem) Romain (Romano)	Rachel de Aaron Barnett		Whitechapel, London	scholar

ID	surname	given names	born	birthplace	father	mother	spouse 1	1851 residence	1851 occupation
28364	Romain (Romano)	Betsey	1833	Spitalfields, London	Emanuel (Menahem) Romain (Romano)	Rachel de Aaron Barnett		Whitechapel, London	waistcoat maker
13275	Romain (Romano)	David	1846	Aldgate, London	Joseph Romain (Romano)	Abigail Lyons	Amelia Ottolangui	Spitalfields, London	
28355	Romain (Romano)	Emanuel	1841	Mile End, London	John (Jacob) Romaine (Romano)	Abigail de Leon (Lyon)	Elizabeth Abrahams	Whitechapel, London	scholar
28360	Romain (Romano)	Emanuel (Menahem)	1798	Mile End, London	David Romano	Lucky (?)	Rachel de Aaron Barnett	Whitechapel, London	waterman at lunch stand
28369	Romain (Romano)	Esther	1846	Whitechapel, London	Emanuel (Menahem) Romain (Romano)	Rachel de Aaron Barnett		Whitechapel, London	scholar
28363	Romain (Romano)	Hannah	1831	Spitalfields, London	Emanuel (Menahem) Romain (Romano)	Rachel de Aaron Barnett	David Jacobs	Whitechapel, London	waistcoat maker
28352	Romain (Romano)	John (Jacob)	1808	Finsbury, London	David Romano	Rebecca (?)	Hanah de Aaron Barnett	Whitechapel, London	cab driver
13273	Romain (Romano)	Joseph	1820	Finsbury, London	David Romano	Rebecca (?)	Abigail Lyons	Spitalfields, London	Hackney carriage driver
28365	Romain (Romano)	Julia	1835	Spitalfields, London	Emanuel (Menahem) Romain (Romano)	Rachel de Aaron Barnett		Whitechapel, London	scholar
28366	Romain (Romano)	Katharine	1838	Whitechapel, London	Emanuel (Menahem) Romain (Romano)	Rachel de Aaron Barnett		Whitechapel, London	scholar
28356	Romain (Romano)	Nathan	1842	Spitalfields, London	John (Jacob) Romaine (Romano)	Abigail de Leon (Lyon)	Sarah Isaacs	Whitechapel, London	scholar
28357	Romain (Romano)	Rachael	1850	Whitechapel, London	John (Jacob) Romaine (Romano)	Abigail de Leon (Lyon)		Whitechapel, London	
28361	Romain (Romano)	Rachel	1801	Aldgate, London	Aaron Barnett		Emanuel (Menahem) de David Romano	Whitechapel, London	
13276	Romain (Romano)	Rebecca	1771	Aldgate, London	(?)		David Romano	Spitalfields, London	
28362	Romain (Romano)	Rebecca	1827	Spitalfields, London	Emanuel (Menahem) Romain (Romano)	Rachel de Aaron Barnett		Whitechapel, London	
28367	Romain (Romano)	Samuel	1839	Whitechapel, London	Emanuel (Menahem) Romain (Romano)	Rachel de Aaron Barnett		Whitechapel, London	scholar
28370	Romain (Romano)	Sarah	1829	Whitechapel, London	Emanuel (Menahem) Romain (Romano)	Rachel de Aaron Barnett	Michael Cohen	Whitechapel, London	
16492	Romanel	Abraham	1795	Amsterdam, Holland	Phineas Romanel	Leah (?)	Eve de Abraham	Mile End, London	leaseholder
16493	Romanel	Elizabeth (Brina)	1792	Aldgate, London	Abraham Hazan		Abraham de Phineas Romanel	Mile End, London	
12184	Romanell	Betsey (Elizabeth)	1827	Marylebone, London	(?Abraham) Romanell			Whitechapel, London	
14865	Roots	Eliza	1837	Bethnal Green, London	(?) Roots	(?) Cohen		Bethnal Green, London	
14866	Roots	Sophia	1840	Bethnal Green, London	(?) Roots	(?) Cohen		Bethnal Green, London	scholar
22082	Ropaky	Lodwing	1830	?, Russia [Wiziene, Russia]				Whitechapel, London	tailor
23699	Rose	Ferdinand	1827	?, Germany				Liverpool	toy merchant's assistant
26496	Rose	Kate	1822	Chatham, Kent	Lewis Lion Aaron	Mary (?)	Salomon Samuel Rose	St Giles, London	
30360	Rose	Kate (Catherine)	1811	Spitalfields, London	Baruch Benedet Solomons		Michael Elias Rose	St Giles, London	housekeeper
30359	Rose	Michael Elias	1801	?, Poland	Isaac		Kate (Catherine) Solomons	St Giles, London	housekeeper
26495	Rose	Salomon Samuel	1819	Hesse, Germany			Kate Aaron	St Giles, London	papier mache manufacturer empl 5
26497	Rose	Samuel Alfred	1851	St Giles, London	Salomon Samuel Aaron	Kate Aaron		St Giles, London	
16632	Rosefield	Aaron	1825	?, Poland [?, Prussia]				Liverpool	watchmaker
14512	Roseinberge	Ruben	1827	?, Poland [Reich Pole Crossing]			Sarah (?)	Birmingham	shoe maker
14513	Roseinberge	Sarah	1826	?, Poland [Reich Pole Crossing]	(?)		Ruben Roseinberge	Birmingham	shoe maker's wife

ID	surname	given names	born	birthplace	father	mother	spouse 1	1851 residence	1851 occupation
25862	Rosen	Benjamin	1831	?, Poland				Aldgate, London	bead maker journeyman
26283	Rosenbanks	Samuel	1832	Cracow, Poland				Aldgate, London	goldsmith
5721	Rosenbaum	Annie	1844	Whitechapel, London	Abraham Rosenbaum	Harriet Isaacson	John Chapman	?Finsbury, London	
15576	Rosenbaum	David	1828	Warsaw, Poland			Jane (?)	Covent Garden, London	printer
21417	Rosenbaum	Isidor	1833	Kovno, Poland [Kempen, Germany]				Dewsbury, Yorkshire	traveller
15577	Rosenbaum	Jane	1832	Mile End, London	(?)		David Rosenbaum	Covent Garden, London	
1366	Rosenberg	Aaron	1843	Plymouth, Devon	Abraham Moses Rosenberg	Fanny Solomon		Plymouth, Devon	scholar
15121	Rosenberg	Abraham	1798	?, Germany			Caroline (?)	Haggerston, London	cigar merchant
27873	Rosenberg	Abraham	1810	?, Russia			Rachael (?)	Spitalfields, London	slipper maker
4900	Rosenberg	Abraham	1848	?, Poland	Asher Abraham Rosenberg	Dimma (?)		Birmingham	
1364	Rosenberg	Abraham Moses	1815	Moscow, Russia			Fanny Solomon	Plymouth, Devon	
27876	Rosenberg	Adolph	1842	?, Russia	Abraham Rosenberg	Rachael (?)		Spitalfields, London	scholar
24528	Rosenberg	Adolphus	1838	Lambeth, London	Frederick Rosenberg	Mary (?)		Kennington, London	
9112	Rosenberg	Alethea (Elsie)	1826	Aldgate, London	(?) Barnett	Sarah (?)	(?) Rosenberg	Covent Garden, London	independent
24531	Rosenberg	Alfred	1844	Lambeth, London	Frederick Rosenberg	Mary (?)		Kennington, London	
24529	Rosenberg	Ann	1840	Lambeth, London	Frederick Rosenberg	Mary (?)		Kennington, London	
4897	Rosenberg	Asher Abraham	1821	?, Poland			Dimma (?)	Birmingham	master glazier
15122	Rosenberg	Caroline	1821	Middlesex, London	(?)		Abraham Rosenberg	Haggerston, London	
2323	Rosenberg	Catherine	1827	?, London	(?) Rosenberg	Charlotte (?)		Leeds, Yorkshire	piano teacher
2322	Rosenberg	Charlotte	1787	?, London				Leeds, Yorkshire	piano teacher
24533	Rosenberg	Clara	1849	Lambeth, London	Frederick Rosenberg	Mary (?)		Kennington, London	
4898	Rosenberg	Dimma	1823	?, Poland			Asher Abraham Rosenberg	Birmingham	lodging house keeper
13659	Rosenberg	Edward	1829	?, Germany				Manchester	cigar maker
23313	Rosenberg	Eliza	1764	Bath	(?)		(?) Rosenberg	Chelsea, London	annuitant
1365	Rosenberg	Fanny	1825	Warsaw, Poland	(?) Solomon		Abraham Moses Rosenberg	Plymouth, Devon	general dealer
24525	Rosenberg	Frederick	1797	Middlesex, London			Mary (?)	Kennington, London	artist + print colourer
4899	Rosenberg	Hannah	1844	?, Poland	Asher Abraham Rosenberg	Dimma (?)		Birmingham	
1369	Rosenberg	Henry	1847	Plymouth, Devon	Abraham Moses Rosenberg	Fanny Solomon		Plymouth, Devon	scholar
8096	Rosenberg	Henry (Heineman) Hertz	1817	Westphalia, Germany	Naphtali Rosenberg		Matilda Salamon (Salomon, Solomons)	Manchester	tobacconist
1958	Rosenberg	Herman	1849	Merthyr Tydfil, Wales				Merthyr Tydfil, Wales	
24532	Rosenberg	Jessey	1846	Lambeth, London	Frederick Rosenberg	Mary (?)		Kennington, London	
1367	Rosenberg	Joseph	1843	Plymouth, Devon	Abraham Moses Rosenberg	Fanny Solomon		Plymouth, Devon	scholar
8387	Rosenberg	Leah	1832	Southampton, Hampshire	(?) Rosenberg			Southampton, Hampshire	servant
5140	Rosenberg	Louis	1815	Westphalia, Germany				Sheffield, Yorkshire	tobacconist
13658	Rosenberg	Louis	1821	?, Germany				Manchester	tobacconist
13091	Rosenberg	Louis	1830	?, Germany				Clerkenwell, London	prisoner + labourer
27877	Rosenberg	Marcus	1846	?, Russia	Abraham Rosenberg	Rachael (?)		Spitalfields, London	scholar
23314	Rosenberg	Maria	1795	Bath	(?) Rosenberg	Eliza (?)		Chelsea, London	annuitant
24530	Rosenberg	Maria	1842	Lambeth, London	Frederick Rosenberg	Mary (?)		Kennington, London	
23703	Rosenberg	Mark	1834	?, Germany				Liverpool	toy merchant's apprentice
24526	Rosenberg	Mary	1805	Elephant & Castle, London			Frederick Rosenberg	Kennington, London	
8095	Rosenberg	Matilda	1822	Middlesex, London	Moses Salamon (Salomon, Solomons)	Ann Israel	Henry (Heineman) Hertz Rosenberg	Manchester	

ID	surname	given names	born	birthplace	father	mother	spouse 1	1851 residence	1851 occupation
1368	Rosenberg	Moses	1845	Plymouth, Devon	Abraham Moses Rosenberg	Fanny Solomon	Esther (?)	Plymouth, Devon	scholar
27874	Rosenberg	Rachael	1810	?, Russia	(?)		Abraham Rosenberg	Spitalfields, London	
24527	Rosenberg	Rosina	1831	Lambeth, London	Frederick Rosenberg	Mary (?)		Kennington, London	
30173	Rosenberg	S--- A---	1821	?, Poland				Dudley, Worcestershire	hawker, jewellery
27875	Rosenberg	Sarah	1843	?, Russia	Abraham Rosenberg	Rachael (?)		Spitalfields, London	scholar
1964	Rosenberg	Solomon	1794	?, Poland				Cardiff, Wales	invalid
26871	Rosenbergh	Thomas	1806	?, Poland				Aldgate, London	
22088	Rosenblock	Alexander	1839	?, London	Moses Rosenblock	Maria (?)		Whitechapel, London	
22090	Rosenblock	Henry	1843	?, London	Moses Rosenblock	Maria (?)		Whitechapel, London	
22089	Rosenblock	John	1841	?, London	Moses Rosenblock	Maria (?)		Whitechapel, London	
22087	Rosenblock	Maria	1813	Berlin, Germany	(?)		Moses Rosenblock	Whitechapel, London	
22086	Rosenblock	Moses	1804	Berlin, Germany			Maria (?)	Whitechapel, London	hawker
27655	Rosenbloom	Harriet	1842	Aldgate, London	(?) Rosenbloom			Aldgate, London	scholar
11709	Rosenbloom	Jacob	1831	?, Poland [?, Prussia]	Naphtali Rosenbloom	Katherine (?)	Leah Phillips	Aldgate, London	tailor
27650	Rosenbloom	Joseph	1805	?, Ireland			Rachel (?)	Aldgate, London	shoe maker empl 20
11708	Rosenbloom	Katherine	1801	Plocz, Poland [Plotze, Poland]	(?)		Naphtali Rosenbloom	Aldgate, London	
1965	Rosenbloom	Michael	1826	?, Poland				Merthyr Tydfil, Wales	watchmaker
27651	Rosenbloom	Rachel	1803	?, Ireland	(?)		Joseph Rosenbloom	Aldgate, London	
31104	Rosenbohm	Anne	1807	Newcastle Upon Tyne	George Rosenbohm	Catherine (?)		Gateshead, Tyne & Wear	
31103	Rosenbohm	Catherine	1784	Newcastle Upon Tyne	(?)		George Rosenbohm	Gateshead, Tyne & Wear	
31102	Rosenbohm	George	1781	?, Germany			Catherine (?)	Gateshead, Tyne & Wear	pawnbroker
21422	Rosenbohm	Harmond	1821	?, Germany			Mary Ann (?)	Liverpool	sugar maker
21425	Rosenbohm	Margaret	1850	Whitechapel, London	Harmond Rosenbohm	Mary Ann (?)		Liverpool	
21423	Rosenbohm	Mary Ann	1824	?, Sussex	(?)		Harmond Rosenbohm	Liverpool	
21424	Rosenbohm	Mary Ann	1848	Whitechapel, London	Harmond Rosenbohm	Mary Ann (?)		Liverpool	
31105	Rosenbohm	Sarah	1818	Jarrow, Tyne & Wear	George Rosenbohm	Catherine (?)		Gateshead, Tyne & Wear	
8406	Rosenbulish	Abraham	1823	?, Russia [Rhinish Russia]				Southampton, Hampshire	butcher
15589	Rosenburg	Adolphus	1785	Elven, France			?	Covent Garden, London	general dealer
2559	Rosenburg	Anshel	1823	?, Poland				Hull, Yorkshire	travels with jewellery
15591	Rosenburg	Elianor	1825	Southwark, London	Adolphus Rosenburg	(?)		Covent Garden, London	
4905	Rosenburg	Elizabeth	1816	?, Poland			Harris Rosenburg	Birmingham	lodging house keeper
25902	Rosenburg	Esther	1813	?, Poland	(?)		Magnus Rosenberg	Aldgate, London	milliner
4906	Rosenburg	Esther	1836	?, Poland	Harris Rosenburg	Elizabeth (?)		Birmingham	bookbinder
4907	Rosenburg	Gusta	1840	?, Poland	Harris Rosenburg	Elizabeth (?)		Birmingham	
30481	Rosenburg	Hankel	1829	?, Poland [?, Prussia]	(?) Rosenburg			Whitechapel, London	house servant
4904	Rosenburg	Harris	1817	?, Poland			Elizabeth (?)	Birmingham	hawker
4909	Rosenburg	Lyon	1849	?, Poland	Harris Rosenburg	Elizabeth (?)		Birmingham	
25901	Rosenburg	Magnus	1811	?, Poland			Esther (?)	Aldgate, London	barber master
15592	Rosenburg	Maria Ann	1834	Walworth, London	Adolphus Rosenburg	Mary Ann (?)		Covent Garden, London	
15590	Rosenburg	Mary Ann	1815	Spitalfields, London	(?)		Adolphus Rosenburg	Covent Garden, London	
4908	Rosenburg	Rebecca	1843	?, Poland	Harris Rosenburg	Elizabeth (?)		Birmingham	
21426	Rosenburgh	Abraham	1815	?, Poland				Liskeard, Cornwall	hawker, drapery
25187	Rosenfeld	Amelia	1850	Finsbury, London	John Rosenfeld	Rebecca (?)		Finsbury, London	
22649	Rosenfeld	Jacobs	1828	?, Poland				Whitechapel, London	journeyman slipper maker

ID	surname	given names	born	birthplace	father	mother	spouse 1	1851 residence	1851 occupation
25185	Rosenfeld	John	1822	?, Poland [?, Prussia, Duchy of]			Rebecca (?)	Finsbury, London	college cap maker
22650	Rosenfeld	Joseph	1833	?, Germany				Whitechapel, London	journeyman slipper maker
25188	Rosenfeld	Julia	1851	Finsbury, London	John Rosenfeld	Rebecca (?)		Finsbury, London	
22648	Rosenfeld	Lions	1818	Cracow, Poland [Kraku, Poland]				Whitechapel, London	journeyman slipper maker
30176	Rosenfeld	Orgunski?	1827	Warsaw, Poland				Dudley, Worcestershire	
25186	Rosenfeld	Rebecca	1830	Holloway, London	(?)		John Rosenfeld	Finsbury, London	
26358	Rosengarten	Aaron	1841	?, Poland	Elias Rosengarten	Rebecca (?)		Aldgate, London	scholar
26355	Rosengarten	Elias	1818	?, Poland			Rebecca (?)	Aldgate, London	tinplate worker
26361	Rosengarten	Hannah	1850	?Aldgate, London	Elias Rosengarten	Rebecca (?)		Aldgate, London	
26360	Rosengarten	Harriet	1846	?, London	Elias Rosengarten	Rebecca (?)		Aldgate, London	scholar
26359	Rosengarten	Jacob	1844	?, Poland	Elias Rosengarten	Rebecca (?)		Aldgate, London	scholar
26356	Rosengarten	Rebecca	1818	?, Poland	(?)		Elias Rosengarten	Aldgate, London	
26357	Rosengarten	Sarah	1839	?, Poland	Elias Rosengarten	Rebecca (?)		Aldgate, London	scholar
27431	Rosenheim	Barnett	1804	?, Poland			(?)	Whitechapel, London	furrier
27432	Rosenheim	Barron	1835	City, London	Barnet Rosenheim	(?)	Julia (?)	Whitechapel, London	furrier
27434	Rosenheim	Louisa	1839	City, London	Barnet Rosenheim	(?)		Whitechapel, London	
29964	Rosenheim	Myer	1831	City, London	(?) Rosenheim	(?) Barnett	Sarah Goldsmid	Whitechapel, London	cigar maker journeyman
27433	Rosenheim	Rebecca	1836	City, London	Barnet Rosenheim	(?)		Whitechapel, London	
27435	Rosenheim	Sarah	1842	City, London	Barnet Rosenheim	(?)		Whitechapel, London	
26195	Rosenheim?	Augustus	1827	?, Germany				Aldgate, London	glazier
25592	Rosenstein	Elizabeth	1838	Dublin, Ireland	Simon Rosenstein	Phoebe (?)		Dublin, Ireland	
25591	Rosenstein	Louis	1837	Dublin, Ireland	Simon Rosenstein	Phoebe (?)		Dublin, Ireland	
25590	Rosenstein	Phoebe	1810	?	(?)		Simon Rosenstein	Dublin, Ireland	
25589	Rosenstein	Simon	1794	?, Germany			Phoebe (?)	Dublin, Ireland	dealer in perfumery, jewellery + fancy goods
16290	Rosenstern	F---	1820	?, Germany				Dundee, Scotland	
13805	Rosentall	Jacob	1822	?, Germany				Manchester	jeweller
25521	Rosenthal	?	1825	?			Henry Rosenthal	Dublin, Ireland	
16922	Rosenthal	Abraham	1804	?, Poland				Sheffield, Yorkshire	comb maker
23913	Rosenthal	Adolphus	1821	?, Germany	Solomon Rosenthal		Sophia Stephany	Marylebone, London	cigar maker
10020	Rosenthal	Alfred	1815	Shoreditch, London			Emma (?)	Brixton, London	silk manufacturer
24249	Rosenthal	Alphonse	1849	St Pancras, London	Samuel Rosenthal	Elizabeth (?)		Bloomsbury, London	
8595	Rosenthal	Anny	1811	?, Poland	(?)		Simon Rosenthal	Spitalfields, London	
12196	Rosenthal	Benjamin	1845	?, Poland [?, Prussia]	Michael Rosenthal	Jane (?)		Whitechapel, London	scholar
12193	Rosenthal	Bertha	1836	?, Poland [?, Prussia]	Michael Rosenthal	Jane (?)		Whitechapel, London	waistcoat maker
12195	Rosenthal	Cecilia	1844	?, Poland [?, Prussia]	Michael Rosenthal	Jane (?)		Whitechapel, London	scholar
15330	Rosenthal	Charles	1803	Jerusalem, Israel	(?) Jacobs	Hannah (?)		Southwark, London	gentleman
23915	Rosenthal	Charles	1850	Marylebone, London	Adolphus Rosenthal	Sophia Stephany		Marylebone, London	
139	Rosenthal	Charlotte	1813	Verdun, France	Simon Bamberger	Katherine (?)	Lewis Julius (Loewe Judah) Rosenthal	Soho, London	
12633	Rosenthal	David	1826	?, Poland [?, Germany Poland]				Norwich, Norfolk	dealer
24246	Rosenthal	Edward	1843	Paris, France	Samuel Rosenthal	Elizabeth (?)		Bloomsbury, London	
24245	Rosenthal	Elizabeth	1819	?, Germany	(?)		Samuel Rosenthal	Bloomsbury, London	

610

ID	surname	given names	born	birthplace	father	mother	spouse 1	1851 residence	1851 occupation
12191	Rosenthal	Emily	1833	?, Poland [?, Prussia]	Michael Rosenthal	Jane (?)		Whitechapel, London	tailoress
24247	Rosenthal	Ernestine	1845	Paris, France	Samuel Rosenthal	Elizabeth (?)		Bloomsbury, London	
18857	Rosenthal	Esther	1801	?	(?)		Henry Rosenthal	Dublin, Ireland	
18859	Rosenthal	George	1803	Hanover, Germany				Dublin, Ireland	
24248	Rosenthal	Gustave	1846	?, Holland	Samuel Rosenthal	Elizabeth (?)		Bloomsbury, London	
8596	Rosenthal	Hanah	1835	?, Poland	Simon Rosenthal	Anny (?)		Spitalfields, London	
8597	Rosenthal	Harris	1839	?, Poland	Simon Rosenthal	Anny (?)		Spitalfields, London	
18856	Rosenthal	Henry	1798	Hanover, Germany			Esther (?)	Dublin, Ireland	
25520	Rosenthal	Henry	1825	?Dublin, Ireland			(?)	Dublin, Ireland	
29684	Rosenthal	Herman	1823	?, Germany				Shoreditch, London	interpreter
15621	Rosenthal	Isaac	1806	?, Poland [?, Prussia]			(?)	Spitalfields, London	fancy box maker
12190	Rosenthal	Jane	1808	?, Poland [?, Prussia]	(?)		Michael Rosenthal	Whitechapel, London	
12197	Rosenthal	Jane	1850	?, London	Michael Rosenthal	Jane (?)		Whitechapel, London	scholar
18858	Rosenthal	John David	1833	Dublin, Ireland	Henry Rosenthal	Esther (?)	Minna Solomons	Dublin, Ireland	university law student (TCD)
141	Rosenthal	Judah (Julius) Loewe	1846	Piccadilly, London	Lewis Julius (Loewe Judah) Rosenthal	Charlotte Bamberger	Alice Benjamin	Soho, London	scholar
31013	Rosenthal	Julia	1830	?, Germany	(?) Rosenthal			Manchester	cook
5508	Rosenthal	Leon Lowe	1848	Mayfair, London	Lewis Julius (Loewe Judah) Rosenthal	Charlotte Bamberger		Soho, London	
138	Rosenthal	Lewis Julius (Loewe Judah)	1814	Emden, Hanover, Germany	Juda Rosenthal		Charlotte Bamberger	Soho, London	professor of languages
12189	Rosenthal	Michacl	1813	?, Poland [?, Prussia]			Janc (?)	Whitechapel, London	traveller jeweller
12192	Rosenthal	Phillip	1834	?, Poland [?, Prussia]	Michael Rosenthal	Jane (?)		Whitechapel, London	cigar maker
12593	Rosenthal	Phillip L	1818	?, Hungary				Birmingham	professor of German
15623	Rosenthal	Rose	1828	?, Poland [?, Prussia]	(?) Busky		William Rosenthal	Spitalfields, London	
24244	Rosenthal	Samuel	1813	?, Germany			Elizabeth (?)	Bloomsbury, London	lithographic artist empl 20
8594	Rosenthal	Simon	1806	?, Poland			Anny (?)	Spitalfields, London	glazier
12194	Rosenthal	Solomon	1838	?, Poland [?, Prussia]	Michael Rosenthal	Jane (?)		Whitechapel, London	cigar maker
23914	Rosenthal	Sophia	1821	?, Germany	Coleman Stephany		Sophia Stephany	Marylebone, London	
15622	Rosenthal	William	1826	?, Poland [?, Prussia]	Isaac Rosenthal	(?)	Rose Busky	Spitalfields, London	bookseller agent
27096	Rosenthall	Angel	1811	?, Poland			Miriam (?)	Aldgate, London	tailor
24407	Rosenthall	Barnett	1850	Derby, Derbyshire	Joseph Rosenthall	Sarah Moses		Soho, London	
7674	Rosenthall	Deborah	1787	Folkestone, Kent	(?)		Lewin Rosenthall	Aldgate, London	shoe trimming mfr
17815	Rosenthall	Dina	1819	City, London	Lewin Rosenthall	Deborah (?)		Aldgate, London	shoe trimmer
21068	Rosenthall	E---	1838	Dublin, Ireland				Dover, Kent	boarding school pupil
24405	Rosenthall	Elizabeth	1845	Burton-on-Trent, Staffordshire	Joseph Rosenthall	Sarah Moses		Soho, London	
24403	Rosenthall	Emanuel	1844	Birmingham	Morris Moses		Joseph Rosenthall	Soho, London	
1966	Rosenthall	Haines	1801	?, Poland				Swansea, Wales	jeweller
13611	Rosenthall	Henrich	1828	?, Poland [?, Prussia]			Jette (?)	Manchester	baker
13610	Rosenthall	Jacob	1831	?, Poland [?, Prussia]				Manchester	bookbinder
24406	Rosenthall	Jeanette	1843	Middlesex, London	Joseph Rosenthall	Sarah Moses		Soho, London	
13612	Rosenthall	Jette	1826	?, Poland [?, Prussia]	(?)		Henrich Rosenthall	Manchester	

ID	surname	given names	born	birthplace	father	mother	spouse 1	1851 residence	1851 occupation
24402	Rosenthall	Joseph	1820	Manchester	Joseph Rosenthall	Sarah Moses		Soho, London	traveller (stationery trade)
24404	Rosenthall	Joseph	1820	Manchester	Barnet Rosenthal		Sarah Moses	Soho, London	traveller (stationery trade)
7673	Rosenthall	Juliet	1817	City, London	Lewin Rosenthall	Deborah (?)	Daniel Soman	Aldgate, London	shoe trimmer
27097	Rosenthall	Miriam	1813	?, Poland	(?)		Angel Rosenthall	Aldgate, London	
27098	Rosenthall	Moses	1836	?, Poland	Angel Rosenthall	Miriam (?)		Aldgate, London	tailor
26390	Rosenthall	Myer	1811	?, Hungary				Aldgate, London	clothes dealer
21067	Rosenthall	Samuel	1836	Dublin, Ireland				Dover, Kent	boarding school pupil
27474	Rosund	Isaac	1829	?, Poland				Whitechapel, London	tailor
27473	Rosund	Levy	1829	?, Poland				Whitechapel, London	tailor
2560	Roth	Frederick	1831	?, Germany			Charlotte (?)	Hull, Yorkshire	
31125	Roth	Julius	1821	Venice, Italy				Dalston, London	spice merchant clerk
7346	Roth	Mathias	1818	?, Hungary [Kaschau, Austria-Hungary]	Matyas Roth	Anna Schwartz	Anna Maria Collins	Marylebone, London	homeopath
5579	Rothschild	Alfred Charles de	1842	Piccadilly, London	Lionel Nathan de Rothschild	Charlotte von Rothschild		Piccadilly, London	scholar at home
5582	Rothschild	Annie de	1844	Piccadilly, London	Anthony Nathan de Rothschild	Louisa Montefiore	Eliot Yorke	Belgravia, London	
5583	Rothschild	Anthony Nathan de	1810	City, London	Nathan Mayer Rothschild	Hannah Barent Cohen	Louisa Montefiore	Belgravia, London	merchant banker
15632	Rothschild	Benjamin Lewin Myer	1811	?, Denmark			Esther (Hester) Levyson	Finsbury, London	jewel agent
20717	Rothschild	Caroline	1820	Oldenburg, Germany	(?) Frank		Michael Frank Rothschild	Liverpool	cigar manufacturer
23839	Rothschild	Celese	1842	?, France	(?) Rothschild			Liverpool	scholar
932	Rothschild	Charlotte de	1819	Naples, Italy	Carl Mayer von Rothschild	Adelheid Herz	Lionel Nathan de Rothschild	Mayfair, London	charitable worker
5581	Rothschild	Constance de	1843	Piccadilly, London	Anthony Nathan de Rothschild	Louisa Montefiore	Cyril Flower (Lord Battersea)	Belgravia, London	
18852	Rothschild	David	1846	Whitechapel, London	Marx (Max, Maroc) Rothschild	Hannah Schiff		Whitechapel, London	scholar
15634	Rothschild	Emma Dinah	1848	?, London	Benjamin Lewin Myer Rothschild	Esther (Hester) Levyson	Louis Goldschmidt	Finsbury, London	
15633	Rothschild	Esther (Hester)	1821	Marylebone, London	(?) Levyson		Benjamin Lewin Myer Rothschild	Finsbury, London	
5578	Rothschild	Evelina de	1839	Mayfair, London	Lionel Nathan de Rothschild	Charlotte von Rothschild	Ferdinand de Rothschild	Piccadilly, London	scholar at home
18851	Rothschild	Hannah	1811	Frankfurt-am-Main, Germany	Lazarus Schiff		Marx (Max, Maroc) Rothschild	Whitechapel, London	
5588	Rothschild	Hannah de	1851	?, London	Mayer Amschel de Rothschild	Juliana Cohen	Archibald Philip Primrose, Earl of Rosebery	Piccadilly, London	
23837	Rothschild	Harriet	1848	Dublin, Ireland	Michael Frank Rothschild	Caroline Frank		Liverpool	
6520	Rothschild	Henry	1825	Middlesex, London	Naphtali		Rebecca (?)	Exeter, Devon	
18853	Rothschild	Jannet R	1848	Finsbury, London	Marx (Max, Maroc) Rothschild	Hannah Schiff		Whitechapel, London	
2870	Rothschild	Joseph	1808	Pinczow, Poland			Matilda Jacobs	Bristol	watchmaker + jeweller
25593	Rothschild	Joseph	1810	Altona, Germany	Dov		Pauline (?)	Dublin, Ireland	tobacco dealer
5587	Rothschild	Juliana de	1831	Middlesex, London	Isaac Cohen	Sarah Samuel	Mayer Amschel de Rothschild	Piccadilly, London	
21321	Rothschild	Julius	1821	Hamburg, Germany				Dundee, Scotland	clerk to linen merchant
929	Rothschild	Leonora de	1837	Mayfair, London	Lionel Nathan de Rothschild	Charlotte von Rothschild	Alphonse de Rothschild	Piccadilly, London	scholar at home
18854	Rothschild	Leopold	1850	Finsbury, London	Marx (Max, Maroc) Rothschild	Hannah Schiff		Whitechapel, London	
5580	Rothschild	Leopold de	1845	Piccadilly, London	Lionel Nathan de Rothschild	Charlotte von Rothschild	Marie Perugia	Piccadilly, London	scholar at home

ID	surname	given names	born	birthplace	father	mother	spouse 1	1851 residence	1851 occupation
931	Rothschild	Lionel Nathan de	1808	City, London	Nathan Meyer Rothschild	Hannah Barent Cohen	Charlotte von Rothschild	Piccadilly, London	MP for City of London + merchant
5584	Rothschild	Louisa de	1821	?, London	Abraham Montefiore	Henrietta Rothschild	Anthony Nathan de Rothschild	Belgravia, London	philanthropist + writer
7691	Rothschild	Marx (Max, Maroc)	1801	Frankfurt-am-Main, Germany	David Rothschild		Hannah Schiff	Whitechapel, London	dealer in jewellery + watches
2878	Rothschild	Matilda	1807	Poole, Dorset	Abraham Jacobs	Elizabeth (Belly, Beila) Moses	Joseph Rothschild	Bristol	
5586	Rothschild	Mayer Amschel de	1818	City, London	Nathan Meyer Rothschild	Hannah Cohen	Juliana Cohen	Piccadilly, London	merchant banker + MP
20716	Rothschild	Michael Frank	1805	Bremen, Germany			Caroline Frank	Liverpool	cigar manufacturer + dealer in tobacco + snuff
930	Rothschild	Nathaniel (Natty) Mayer de	1840	?, London	Lionel Nathan de Rothschild	Charlotte de Rothschild	Emma Louisa von Rothschild	Piccadilly, London	scholar at home
6521	Rothschild	Rebecca	1832	Middlesex, London	(?)		Henry Rothschild	Exeter, Devon	
23838	Rothschild	Salis	1849	Liverpool	Michael Frank Rothschild	Caroline Frank		Liverpool	
15635	Rothschild	Sarah	1850	Finsbury, London	Benjamin Lewin Myer Rothschild	Esther (Hester) Levyson		Finsbury, London	
19185	Rothschild	Selina (Lena)	1851	Bristol	Joseph Rothschild	Matilda Jacobs	Wolfe Phillips	Bristol	
26052	Rottsand	David	1849	Aldgate, London	(?) Rottsand	Mary Fromberg		Aldgate, London	
26053	Rottsand	Jacob	1850	Aldgate, London	(?) Rottsand	Mary Fromberg		Aldgate, London	
25843	Rottsand	Mary	1831	?, Poland	Barnet Fromberg	Hannah (?)	(?) Rottsand	Aldgate, London	furrier journeyman
15104	Rozenbaum	Abraham	1800	?	Moshe Isaac Rozenbaum		Harriet Isaacson	Bethnal Green, London	bazaar keeper
15107	Rozenbaum	Anne	1843	Whitechapel, London	Abraham Rozenbaum	Harriet Isaacson		Bethnal Green, London	scholar
15108	Rozenbaum	Fanny	1847	Finsbury, London	Abraham Rozenbaum	Harriet Isaacson		Bethnal Green, London	
15103	Rozenbaum	Harriet	1803	Hoxton, London	Isaac Isaacson		Abraham Rozenbaum	Bethnal Green, London	bazaar keeper
15105	Rozenbaum	Lionel	1841	Aldgate, London	Abraham Rozenbaum	Harriet Isaacson		Bethnal Green, London	scholar
15106	Rozenbaum	Phineas	1842	Whitechapel, London	Abraham Rozenbaum	Harriet Isaacson		Bethnal Green, London	scholar
23008	Rubens	Caroline (Golda)	1814	Groningen, Holland	Isaac Jonas Drielsma	Theresa (Mietje) Meyer (Moses) Loewenstein	Salomon Jacobs Rubens	Liverpool	hawker's wife
31000	Rubens	Louisa	1840	?, Ireland	Salomon Jacobs Rubens	Caroline (Golda) Drielsma		Liverpool	scholar
23009	Rubens	Ruben	1841	Liverpool	Salomon Jacobs Rubens	Caroline (Golda) Drielsma	Caroline Drielsma	Liverpool	scholar
23007	Rubens	Salomon Jacobs	1815	?Holland			Caroline (Golda) Drielsma	Liverpool	hawker
31001	Rubens	Theresa	1849	Liverpool	Salomon Jacobs Rubens	Caroline (Golda) Drielsma		Liverpool	
25596	Rubinstein	Caroline	1849	Dublin, Ireland	Samuel Joseph Rubinstein	Sophia Dyte	Leopold Brull	Dublin, Ireland	
25597	Rubinstein	David	1850	Dublin, Ireland	Samuel Joseph Rubinstein	Sophia Dyte		Dublin, Ireland	
15150	Rubinstein	Henry	1819	?, Poland				Hoxton, London	gold chain maker
25594	Rubinstein	Samuel Joseph	1817	Jelgava [Mittau, Courland]	Yosef		Sophia Dyte	Dublin, Ireland	silversmith + jeweller
25595	Rubinstein	Sophia	1817	Middlesex, London	David Moses Dyte	Hannah Lazarus	Samuel Joseph Rubinstein	Dublin, Ireland	
15096	Rudzienski	Ann	1812	Bury St Edmunds, Suffolk	(?)		Joseph Rudzienski	Bethnal Green, London	slipper maker
15095	Rudzienski	Joseph	1803	?, Poland			Ann (?)	Bethnal Green, London	slipper maker
21460	Russell	Ann	1843	Sheerness, Kent	Samuel Russell	Catherine (?)		Sheerness, Kent	
18069	Russell	Benjamin	1837	Hornsey, London	Jacob Russell	Hannah C (?)		Southwark, London	pawnbroker's assistant
21455	Russell	Catherine	1802	Sheerness, Kent			Samuel Russell	Sheerness, Kent	
15547	Russell	Charlotte	1837	?, London	Israel Russell	Elizabeth (?Alexander)		Covent Garden, London	
19411	Russell	David	1831	Sheerness, Kent	Samuel Russell	Catherine (?)	Priscilla Benjamin	Sheerness, Kent	
15545	Russell	Elizabeth	1801	?, London	Isaac Alexander	Esther Barnard	Israel Russell	Covent Garden, London	

613

ID	surname	given names	born	birthplace	father	mother	spouse 1	1851 residence	1851 occupation
18071	Russell	Elizabeth	1840	Southwark, London	Jacob Russell	Hannah C (?)		Southwark, London	scholar at home
21459	Russell	Elizabeth (Betsy)	1840	Sheerness, Kent	Samuel Russell	Catherine (?)		Sheerness, Kent	
18065	Russell	Hannah C	1802	Coggleshall, Essex	(?)		Jacob Russell	Southwark, London	
18067	Russell	Hannah C	1832	Middlesex, London	Jacob Russell	Hannah C (?)		Southwark, London	
5865	Russell	Henry	1776	Sheerness, Kent	Michael Russell			?London	
7347	Russell	Henry	1813	Sheerness, Kent	Moses Russell	Sarah Levin	Isabella Lloyd	?, London	song writer + entertainer
21456	Russell	Henry	1833	Sheerness, Kent	Samuel Russell	Catherine (?)	Esther Davis	Sheerness, Kent	
15544	Russell	Israel	1799	Sheerness, Kent	Moses Russell	Sarah Levin	Elizabeth Alexander	Covent Garden, London	dealer in articles of virtu + pictures
18064	Russell	Jacob	1786	Elephant & Castle, London			Hannah C (?)	Southwark, London	pawnbroker
21461	Russell	Jessie	1845	Sheerness, Kent	Samuel Russell	Catherine (?)		Sheerness, Kent	
18068	Russell	Joseph	1835	Hornsey, London	Jacob Russell	Hannah C (?)		Southwark, London	pawnbroker's assistant
7834	Russell	Lionel	1844	?Middlesex, London	Israel Russell	Elizabeth (?Alexander)		Covent Garden, London	
15546	Russell	Louisa	1833	?, London	Israel Russell	Elizabeth (?Alexander)	John Moss	Covent Garden, London	
21458	Russell	Louisa	1838	Sheerness, Kent	Samuel Russell	Catherine (?)		Sheerness, Kent	
21647	Russell	Maria	1837	?, London	Israel Russell	Elizabeth (?Alexander)	Frederick Manassah Brandon (Brandon Israel)	Covent Garden, London	
18073	Russell	Martha	1842	Southwark, London	Jacob Russell	Hannah C (?)		Southwark, London	scholar at home
18072	Russell	Mary	1842	Southwark, London	Jacob Russell	Hannah C (?)		Southwark, London	scholar at home
6484	Russell	Michael	1821	Sheerness, Kent	Samuel Russell	Catherine (?)	Louisa Mitchell	Sheerness, Kent	
7349	Russell	Moses	1763	Whitechapel, London	Michael Russell		Sarah Levin	Soho, London	annuitant
21457	Russell	Moses	1836	Sheerness, Kent	Samuel Russell	Catherine (?)		Sheerness, Kent	
18074	Russell	Rebecca	1846	Southwark, London	Jacob Russell	Hannah C (?)		Southwark, London	scholar at home
21454	Russell	Samuel	1798	Sheerness, Kent			Catherine (?)	Sheerness, Kent	general dealer
18070	Russell	Sarah	1838	Hornsey, London	Jacob Russell	Hannah C (?)		Southwark, London	scholar at home
15548	Russell	Sarah	1841	?, London	Israel Russell	Elizabeth (?Alexander)	Morris Davidson	Covent Garden, London	
18066	Russell	William	1829	Middlesex, London	Jacob Russell	Hannah C (?)		Southwark, London	pawnbroker's assistant
26704	Saber	Agnes	1828	Liverpool	(?) Sewill		Lewis (Louis) Saber	Liverpool	
26700	Saber	Caroline	1828	Middlesex, London	(?) Moss		Woolf Saber	Liverpool	watchmaker
26702	Saber	Emanuel	1851	Liverpool	Woolf Saber	Caroline Moss	Frances Levy	Liverpool	
26705	Saber	Joseph	1847	Liverpool	Lewis (Louis) Saber	Agnes Sewill	Lizzie Lyon	Liverpool	furniture broker
26706	Saber	Joshua (George)	1847	Liverpool	Lewis (Louis) Saber	Agnes Sewill	Ada Siemms	Liverpool	furniture broker
26703	Saber	Lewis (Louis)	1825	?, Poland [Preussy, Prussia]			Agnes Sewill	Liverpool	furniture broker
26701	Saber	Moss (Moses)	1850	Liverpool	Woolf Saber	Caroline Moss		Liverpool	
26707	Saber	Sarah	1851	Liverpool	Lewis (Louis) Saber	Agnes Sewill		Liverpool	furniture broker
26699	Saber	Woolf	1819	?, Poland [Walsum, Prussia]			Caroline Moss	Liverpool	watchmaker
1967	Sabony	Solomon	1803	?, Morocco				Merthyr Tydfil, Wales	traveller
12632	Sachaczowskie	Abram	1826	?, Poland				Crediton, Devon	hawker in jewellery
3163	Sacks (Sachs)	Rachel	1790	Birmingham			Joseph Michael	Birmingham	
3162	Sacks (Sachs)	Solomon	1779	Glogow, Poland [Glogau, Prussia]	Shalom		Rachel Myers	Birmingham	retired pawnbroker
15896	Safire	Marianne	1836	Livorno, Italy [Leghorn, Italy]	(?) Safire			Hackney, London	boarding school pupil
17010	Salaman	Alice Rebekah	1849	?, London	Charles Kensington Salaman	Frances Simon		Marylebone, London	
4193	Salaman	Annette (Annie) Alice	1826	Strand, London	Simeon Kensington Salaman	Alice Cowen		Marylebone, London	

ID	surname	given names	born	birthplace	father	mother	spouse 1	1851 residence	1851 occupation
9060	Salaman	Betsy	1824	City, London	Isaac Salaman	Jane Raphael	M C Feist	Bloomsbury, London	feather maker
4180	Salaman	Charles Kensington	1814	Strand, London	Simeon Kensington Salaman	Alice Cowen	Frances Simon	Marylebone, London	composer of music
25603	Salaman	Elise (Eliza)	1846	Dublin, Ireland	Morris (Maurice) Salaman	Esther Cohen		Dublin, Ireland	
25599	Salaman	Esther	1820	Dublin, Ireland	Joseph Wolfe Cohen	Rebecca Lazarus	Morris (Maurice) Salaman	Dublin, Ireland	
7289	Salaman	Fanny	1831	City, London	Isaac Salaman	Jane Raphael	Lewis Nathan	Bloomsbury, London	feather maker
4182	Salaman	Frances	1817	Kingston, Jamaica, West Indies	Isaac Simon		Henry Simon	Marylebone, London	
25607	Salaman	Henry	1851	Dublin, Ireland	Morris (Maurice) Salaman	Esther Cohen		Dublin, Ireland	
4183	Salaman	Herbert Windsor	1851	Marylebone, London	Charles Kensington Salaman	Frances Simon		Marylebone, London	
17011	Salaman	Horatio	1841	?, London	(?) Salaman			Marylebone, London	scholar
227	Salaman	Isaac	1790	City, London	Aaron Solomon	Elizabeth (Betsy) (?)	Jane Raphael	Bloomsbury, London	feather seller
3225	Salaman	Jane	1796	City, London	Samuel Raphael	Charlotte (Guldah) Levy	Isaac Salaman	Bloomsbury, London	
17008	Salaman	Joseph (John) Seymour	1829	?Strand, London	Simeon Kensington Salaman	Alice Cowen	Louisa Solomons	Marylebone, London	articled to a solicitor
25606	Salaman	Joseph Wolfe	1849	Dublin, Ireland	Morris (Maurice) Salaman	Esther Cohen	Annie Samuel	Dublin, Ireland	
25605	Salaman	Julia	1848	Dublin, Ireland	Morris (Maurice) Salaman	Esther Cohen		Dublin, Ireland	
4192	Salaman	Kate	1821	?Strand, London	Simeon Kensington Salaman	Alice Cowen		Marylebone, London	artist in watercolours
25598	Salaman	Morris (Maurice)	1809	Warsaw, Poland	Solomon Salaman		Esther Cohen	Dublin, Ireland	
4171	Salaman	Myer	1835	City, London	Isaac Salaman	Jane Raphael	Sarah Solomon	Bloomsbury, London	scholar
9061	Salaman	Nathan	1825	City, London	Isaac Salaman	Jane Raphael		Bloomsbury, London	stationer
9062	Salaman	Rachel	1829	City, London	Isaac Salaman	Jane Raphael	Abraham J Simmons	Bloomsbury, London	feather maker
25602	Salaman	Rebecca (Rebekah)	1844	Dublin, Ireland	Morris (Maurice) Salaman	Esther Cohen		Dublin, Ireland	
17007	Salaman	Rosa	1816	Strand, London	Simeon Kensington Salaman	Alice Cowen	Julius Collins	Marylebone, London	authoress
23275	Salaman	Rosa	1818	Heidelberg, Germany	(?)		Samuel Salaman	Notting Hill, London	
25604	Salaman	Rose	1847	Dublin, Ireland	Morris (Maurice) Salaman	Esther Cohen		Dublin, Ireland	
23274	Salaman	Samuel	1823	Middlesex, London			Rosa (?)	Notting Hill, London	merchant clothier
25601	Salaman	Selim M	1843	Dublin, Ireland	Morris (Maurice) Salaman	Esther Cohen		Dublin, Ireland	
235	Salaman	Simeon Kensington	1789	Kensington London	Samuel Solomon	Julia Pyke	Alice Cowen	Strand, London	gold + silversmith, dealer in gold + silver lace, tailor, sword cutler, hatter, glover + hosier
15359	Salame	Emily	1836	Southwark, London	(?) Salame			Elephant & Castle, London	hat trimmer
15358	Salame	Joseph	1821	Greenwich, London			Jane Menzies	Elephant & Castle, London	hatter
2945	Salamon	Ann	1779	Aldgate, London	Isaiah Israel	Jane (?)	(?) Benson (Lazarus)	Chelsea, London	
24940	Salamons	Julius	1831	Whitechapel, London				Bethnal Green, London	fancy trimming maker
13062	Salinger	James	1849	Haggerston, London	Morris Salinger	Sarah Paiba		Haggerston, London	
21339	Salinger	Julia	1851	Bethnal Green, London	Morris Salinger	Sarah Paiba		Bethnal Green, London	
21338	Salinger	Lewis	1850	Bethnal Green, London	Morris Salinger	Sarah Paiba		Bethnal Green, London	
13060	Salinger	Morris	1822	Gneizo, Poland	Pinchas Zelig	Lena (?)	Sarah Paiba	Haggerston, London	trimming manufacturer
13061	Salinger	Sarah	1822	Bloomsbury, London	Isaac de Aaron Paiba	Priscilla (Sprinza) de Moses Phillips	Morris Salinger	Haggerston, London	
12558	Salkind	David	1846	Norwich, Norfolk	Simon Salkind	Hannah (?)		Norwich, Norfolk	scholar

ID	surname	given names	born	birthplace	father	mother	spouse 1	1851 residence	1851 occupation
12555	Salkind	Esther	1841	North Walsham, Norfolk	Simon Salkind	Hannah (?)		Norwich, Norfolk	scholar
12552	Salkind	Hannah	1816	?, Poland	(?)		Simon Salkind	Norwich, Norfolk	
12553	Salkind	Harriet	1838	Norwich, Norfolk	Simon Salkind	Hannah (?)		Norwich, Norfolk	school teacher
12559	Salkind	Rebecca	1850	Norwich, Norfolk	Simon Salkind	Hannah (?)		Norwich, Norfolk	
12557	Salkind	Samuel	1845	North Walsham, Norfolk	Simon Salkind	Hannah (?)		Norwich, Norfolk	scholar
12556	Salkind	Saul	1843	North Walsham, Norfolk	Simon Salkind	Hannah (?)		Norwich, Norfolk	scholar
12551	Salkind	Simon	1802	Middlesex, London			Hannah (?)	Norwich, Norfolk	furniture broker + general dealer
12554	Salkind	Solomon	1839	North Walsham, Norfolk	Simon Salkind	Hannah (?)		Norwich, Norfolk	scholar
15384	Salkinson	Moses	1820	?, Russia				Waterloo, London	student
25042	Salmon	Abraham	1827	?, Germany				Clerkenwell, London	clerk to boot, shoe + slipper manufacturer
4917	Salmon	Alfred	1843	Birmingham	Charles Moss Salmon	Rebecca (?)	Martha Woolf	Birmingham	scholar
4915	Salmon	Caroline	1839	Birmingham	Charles Moss Salmon	Rebecca (?)	Henry Myers	Birmingham	scholar
30296	Salmon	Catherine	1792	Middlesex, London	(?)		John Salmon	Piccadilly, London	
4911	Salmon	Charles Moss	1801	Birmingham			Rebecca (?)	Birmingham	hardwareman
4913	Salmon	Emma	1833	Birmingham	Charles Moss Salmon	Rebecca (?)		Birmingham	
9439	Salmon	Emma Sophia	1823	?, France	(?) Picard		Samuel Salmon	Aldgate, London	
25043	Salmon	Esther	1829	?, Germany	(?) Salmon			Clerkenwell, London	housekeeper
19310	Salmon	Eve	1811	Cambridge	Isaac Kyezor	Hannah Levy (Levi)	Salmon Salmon	Marylebone, London	
30300	Salmon	Frank	1829	Middlesex, London	John Salmon	Catherine (?)		Piccadilly, London	fruit
30298	Salmon	Hannah	1827	Middlesex, London	John Salmon	Catherine (?)		Piccadilly, London	professor singing
19312	Salmon	Hannah	1838	Cambridge	Salmon Salmon	Eve Kyezor		Marylebone, London	
19308	Salmon	Henry	1833	Norwich, Norfolk	Salmon Salmon	Eve Kyezor	Sophia Kyezor (Keyzor, Keysor)	Bloomsbury, London	watchmaker
17852	Salmon	Isaac	1808	Birmingham				Aldgate, London	general dealer
25044	Salmon	Jacob	1831	?, Germany				Clerkenwell, London	clerk to boot, shoe + slipper manufacturer
30297	Salmon	Jessy	1815	Middlesex, London	John Salmon	Catherine (?)		Piccadilly, London	
30295	Salmon	John	1782	Middlesex, London			Catherine (?)	Piccadilly, London	fruit merchant
4914	Salmon	John	1836	Birmingham	Charles Moss Salmon	Rebecca (?)		Birmingham	
19311	Salmon	Julius	1835	Cambridge	Salmon Salmon	Eve Kyezor		Marylebone, London	engraver
30299	Salmon	Kate (Katherine) Victoria	1831	Middlesex, London	John Salmon	Catherine (?)	Edward Rogers Griffiths	Piccadilly, London	
9440	Salmon	Leopold	1850	?, London	Samuel Salmon	Emma Sophia Picard		Aldgate, London	
4918	Salmon	Rachel	1846	Birmingham	Charles Moss Salmon	Rebecca (?)		Birmingham	scholar
4912	Salmon	Rebecca	1809	Walton-on-Thames, London	(?) (?Jacobs)		Charles Moss Salmon	Birmingham	
4916	Salmon	Rose	1841	Birmingham	Charles Moss Salmon	Rebecca (?)	Henry Lyons	Birmingham	scholar
19309	Salmon	Salmon	1792	?, France			Eve Kyezor	Marylebone, London	watchmaker
9438	Salmon	Samuel	1817	?, Germany			Emma Sophia Picard	Aldgate, London	cap peak manufacturer
25041	Salmon	Vots	1815	?, Germany				Clerkenwell, London	boot, shoe + slipper manufacturer
14284	Salmonson	Augusta	1824	Liverpool	(?) Critchley		Bernard Salmonson	Manchester	
14283	Salmonson	Bernard	1826	?, Holland			Augusta Critchley	Manchester	calico merchant
14287	Salmonson	Francis Bernard	1850	Manchester	Bernard Salmonson	Augusta Critchley		Manchester	

ID	surname	given names	born	birthplace	father	mother	spouse 1	1851 residence	1851 occupation
14285	Salmonson	Godfrey	1847	Manchester	Bernard Salmonson	Augusta Critchley		Manchester	
14286	Salmonson	John Henry	1848	Manchester	Bernard Salmonson	Augusta Critchley		Manchester	
12175	Salomo	Phoebe	1828	Spitalfields, London	Benjamin Zeev Wolf HaLevi		Salomo Salomo	Whitechapel, London	
12174	Salomo	Salomo	1814	?, Holland	Shmuel		Phoebe Levy	Whitechapel, London	agent to importers of cattle
17040	Salomon	Adolphe	1831	Rouen, France				Edinburgh, Scotland	boot maker assistant
7835	Salomon	Ann	1796	City, London	(?)		Naphtali Henry Salomon	Piccadilly, London	
9492	Salomon	Ansel	1769	Altona, Germany				Aldgate, London	retired merchant
17039	Salomon	Antoinette	1851	Edinburgh, Scotland	Henry Salomon	Clara (?)		Edinburgh, Scotland	
16451	Salomon	Caroline	1811	Paris, France			Joseph Israel Salomon	Holborn, London	
9493	Salomon	Clara	1818	Spitalfields, London	Isaac Salomon	Ann (?)		Aldgate, London	fund holder
17037	Salomon	Clara	1823	Nancy, France	(?)		Henry Salomon	Edinburgh, Scotland	corset maker
17038	Salomon	Edward	1849	Edinburgh, Scotland	Henry Salomon	Clara (?)		Edinburgh, Scotland	
16452	Salomon	Elizabeth	1840	Paris, France	Joseph Israel Salomon	Caroline (?)		Holborn, London	
9494	Salomon	Emma	1819	Aldgate, London	Isaac Salomon	Ann (?)		Aldgate, London	fund holder
21354	Salomon	Esther	1786	City, London				Mile End, London	annuitant
17036	Salomon	Henry	1819	Rouen, France			Clara (?)	Edinburgh, Scotland	boot maker master + importer of boots + shoes
16453	Salomon	Isaac	1846	Paris, France	Joseph Israel Salomon	Caroline (?)		Holborn, London	
7375	Salomon	Joseph Israel	1804	Falmouth, Cornwall			Caroline (?)	Holborn, London	agent for the sale of French manufactures
14131	Salomon	Moritz	1824	?, Germany			Sarah Briggs	Manchester	merchant
20900	Salomon	Moritz	1835	Altona, Germany				Liverpool	servant
7503	Salomon	Naphtali Henry	1792	Covent Garden, London			Ann (?)	Piccadilly, London	jeweller
20749	Salomon	Samuel	1810	?				Bath	boot + shoe maker + dealer
14132	Salomon	Sarah	1826	Nottingham, Nottinghamshire	(?) Briggs	Sarah (?)	Moritz Salomon	Manchester	
16291	Salomon (Solomon)	Julius	1831	?, Germany			Adele (?)	Dundee, Scotland	
3284	Salomons	Aaron	1813	Spitalfields, London	Barent Salomons	Rosy (?)	Adelaide (?)	Paddington, London	general merchant
3285	Salomons	Adelaide	1815	Whitechapel, London			Aaron Salomons	Paddington, London	
13749	Salomons	Adelaide	1838	Birmingham	Emanuel Solomons	Sophia Levien	Adolphe Landstein	Manchester	scholar
3286	Salomons	Adelaide (Addie)	1837	Finsbury, London	Aaron Salomons	Adelaide (?)	Walter Abrahams	Paddington, London	
7365	Salomons	Adeline	1840	Manchester	Henry Moses Salomons	Priscilla Lucas		Manchester	
18621	Salomons	Albert Lioel H	1840	Bloomsbury, London	Reuben Salomons	Sarah (?)		Hyde Park, London	scholar
7364	Salomons	Alfred	1830	Middlesex, London	Henry Moses Salomons	Priscilla Lucas		Manchester	
3287	Salomons	Alfred Hyman	1846	Paddington, London	Aaron Salomons	Adelaide (?)		Paddington, London	
16449	Salomons	Amelia Judith	1843	Marylebone, London	Philip Joseph Salomons	Cecilia Samuel		Marylebone, London	
17667	Salomons	Ann (Nancy)	1780	Whitechapel, London	(?) Hart		Lyon Salomons	Spitalfields, London	
16448	Salomons	Bertha	1841	Marylebone, London	Philip Joseph Salomons	Cecilia Samuel	Lionel Benjamin Cohen	Marylebone, London	
7352	Salomons	Cecilia	1812	Marylebone, London	Samuel Moses Samuel	Esther (?)	Philip Joseph Salomons	Marylebone, London	
18625	Salomons	Constance	1848	Hyde Park, London	Reuben Salomons	Sarah (?)		Hyde Park, London	
7350	Salomons	David	1797	Aldgate, London	Levy Salomons	Matilda de Metz	Jeanette Cohen	Marylebone, London	Alderman of London + JP

ID	surname	given names	born	birthplace	father	mother	spouse 1	1851 residence	1851 occupation
6693	Salomons	David Lionel	1851	Brighton, Sussex	Philip Salomons	Emma Abigail Montefiore	Laura Julia de Stern	Mayfair, London	
7361	Salomons	Edward	1828	?, London	Henry Moses Salomons	Priscilla Lucas	Carlotta Marion Montgorry (Montgarry)	Manchester	architect
24125	Salomons	Eliza	1829	Whitechapel, London	Michael Moses Salomons	Rosetta Joel		Bloomsbury, London	
18622	Salomons	Emily	1843	Islington, London	Reuben Salomons	Sarah (?)		Hyde Park, London	scholar at home
7355	Salomons	Emma (Anna) Hendellah	1839	Marylebone, London	Philip Joseph Salomons	Cecilia Samuel	Simon Waley Waley	Marylebone, London	
18620	Salomons	Esther Rose	1839	Shoreditch, London	Reuben Salomons	Sarah (?)		Hyde Park, London	scholar at home
17665	Salomons	Eve	1820	Whitechapel, London	Michael Isaacs	Elizabeth Levy	Jacob Salomons	Aldgate, London	
18624	Salomons	Frederick Barrent	1844	Hyde Park, London	Reuben Salomons	Sarah (?)		Hyde Park, London	scholar at home
3288	Salomons	Gertrude	1848	Paddington, London	Aaron Salomons	Adelaide (?)		Paddington, London	
16450	Salomons	Henrietta Esther	1845	Marylebone, London	Philip Joseph Salomons	Cecilia Samuel	Arthur Denis Samuel De Vahl	Marylebone, London	
18623	Salomons	Henry Hyman	1844	Hyde Park, London	Reuben Salomons	Sarah (?)		Hyde Park, London	scholar at home
7362	Salomons	Henry Moses	1794	?, Germany			Priscilla Lucas	Manchester	cotton merchant
24127	Salomons	Herman	1835	Whitechapel, London	Michael Moses Salomons	Rosetta Joel		Bloomsbury, London	
406	Salomons	Jacob	1821	Whitechapel, London	Lyon Salomons	Ann (Nancy) Hart	Eve Isaacs	Aldgate, London	Secretary to Hambro Synagogue
7351	Salomons	Jeanette	1803	Aldgate, London	Solomon Cohen	Hannah Samuel	David Salomons	Marylebone, London	
7354	Salomons	Joseph Philip	1838	Marylebone, London	Philip Joseph Salomons	Cecilia Samuel		Marylebone, London	scholar
7741	Salomons	Julia	1842	Islington, London	Reuben Salomons	Sarah (?)	Lewis Emanuel	Hyde Park, London	
24128	Salomons	Julia R	1845	Middlesex, London	Michael Moses Salomons	Rosetta Joel		Bloomsbury, London	
7366	Salomons	Julian Emanuel	1835	Birmingham	Emanuel Salomons	Sophia Levien	Louisa Solomons	Manchester	apprentice
17666	Salomons	Lyon	1850	Aldgate, London	Jacob Salomons	Eve Isaacs	Gertrude Maude Rosenthall	Aldgate, London	
11056	Salomons	Maria	1789	Amsterdam, Holland	(?)		Moses Salomons	Aldgate, London	general dealer
21330	Salomons	Marion	1833	?, London	(?) Salomons			Tonbridge, Kent	
24126	Salomons	Mary Ann (Marion, Mariam)	1833	Whitechapel, London	Michael Moses Salomons	Rosetta Joel		Bloomsbury, London	
30468	Salomons	Michael Moses	1797	?, Holland			Rosetta Emanuel	Bloomsbury, London	
11055	Salomons	Moses	1769	Amsterdam, Holland			Maria (?)	Aldgate, London	general dealer
885	Salomons	Philip	1796	Aldgate, London	Levy Salomons	Matilda de Metz	Emma Abigail Montefiore	Mayfair, London	Gentleman at Arms to Her Majesty, Esquire
7353	Salomons	Philip Joseph	1797	Marylebone, London	Joseph Salomons		Cecilia Samuel	Marylebone, London	annuitant
7363	Salomons	Priscilla	1801	Middlesex, London	(?) Lucas			Manchester	
7562	Salomons	Reuben	1811	Spitalfields, London	Barent Salomons	Rosy (?)	Sarah (?)	Hyde Park, London	merchant + warehouseman
24124	Salomons	Rosetta	1805	Aldgate, London	Joel Emanuel	Julia (Juliet) Lazarus	Michael Moses Salomons	Bloomsbury, London	
18619	Salomons	Sarah	1808	Highgate, London	(?)		Reuben Salomons	Hyde Park, London	
13748	Salomons	Sophia	1816	Bedford, Bedfordshire	(?) Levien		Emanuel Salomons	Manchester	schoolmistress
27427	Salomonsen	Isabella	1842	Whitechapel, London	Lewis (Ludvig) Solomon Salomonsen	Rebecca de Lara Cohen		Whitechapel, London	
27430	Salomonsen	Jeanette	1850	Stepney, London	Lewis (Ludvig) Solomon Salomonsen	Rebecca de Lara Cohen		Whitechapel, London	
27425	Salomonsen	Lewis (Ludvig) Solomon	1808	Copenhagen, Denmark	Solomon Salomonsen		Rebecca Cohen de Lara	Whitechapel, London	commission agent + dealer in stationery

ID	surname	given names	born	birthplace	father	mother	spouse 1	1851 residence	1851 occupation
27428	Salomonsen	Rachel	1844	Stepney, London	Lewis (Ludvig) Solomon Salomonsen	Rebecca de Lara Cohen		Whitechapel, London	
27426	Salomonsen	Rebecca	1813	Amsterdam, Holland	David Cohen De Lara		Lewis (Ludvig) Solomon Salomonsen	Whitechapel, London	
27429	Salomonsen	Sarah	1847	Stepney, London	Lewis (Ludvig) Solomon Salomonsen	Rebecca de Lara Cohen		Whitechapel, London	
14305	Salomonson	Godfried David	1847	Manchester	Henry Salomonson	Henrietta (?)		Manchester	
14304	Salomonson	Henrietta	1828	Utrecht?, Holland	(?)		Henry Salomonson	Manchester	
14303	Salomonson	Henry	1823	Utrecht?, Holland			Henrietta (?)	Manchester	general merchant
14306	Salomonson	Henry Louis	1850	Manchester	Henry Salomonson	Henrietta (?)		Manchester	
14307	Salomonson	Maurice	1823	Middleburg, Zealand, Holland				Manchester	general merchant
24625	Salomonson	Simon George	1814	Lambeth, London	(?Shlomo Zalman HaLevi Solomonson)			Kennington, London	solicitor
23968	Salthouse	Jane	1828	Southwark, London	(?) Marks	Sarah (?)		Marylebone, London	
17900	Saltiel	Joseph (Yomtob)	1808	Mile End, London	Isaac de Yomtob Saltiel	Hanah de Abraham Moses	Sarah de Joshua Lopes	Waterloo, London	accoucheur
17901	Saltiel	Rebecca	1814	Deal, Kent	Abraham Blitz		Joseph (Yomtob) Saltiel	Waterloo, London	
16300	Sampson	?	1820	?, Germany				Dundee, Scotland	
481	Sampson	Abraham	1834	Spitalfields, London	Samuel Sampson	Elizabeth (?)		Spitalfields, London	boot maker apprentice
14173	Sampson	Adam	1838	Manchester	Levi Sampson	Sarah (?)	Leah Phillips	Manchester	
14970	Sampson	Amelia A	1839	Middlesex, London	(?) Sampson			Bethnal Green, London	boarding school pupil
13541	Sampson	Asher	1824	Manchester	Levi Sampson	Sarah (?)		Manchester	fent --- master
489	Sampson	Betsy	1843	Spitalfields, London	Isaac Sampson	Nancy (?)		Spitalfields, London	
12987	Sampson	Betsy (Elizabeth)	1832	?, London	Joseph Sampson	Dinah de Young	Levie Lek	Aldgate, London	pedlar
30284	Sampson	Caroline	1818	Soho, London	(?) Nathan		(?) Sampson	Soho, London	
3194	Sampson	Catherine (Kate)	1781	Brentwood, Essex	Hyman Mossbach [Davis]	Esther (?)	Simeon Sampson	Marylebone, London	
355	Sampson	David	1850	Spitalfields, London	Samuel Sampson	Elizabeth (?)	(?)	Spitalfields, London	
12986	Sampson	Dinah	1812	Amsterdam, Holland	Moshe HaLevi De Young		Joseph Sampson	Aldgate, London	pedlar
498	Sampson	Eliza	1846	Whitechapel, London	John Sampson	Elizabeth (?)		Spitalfields, London	
331	Sampson	Elizabeth	1806	Aldgate, London			Samuel Sampson	Spitalfields, London	
497	Sampson	Elizabeth	1825	Bethnal Green, London			John Sampson	Spitalfields, London	
14455	Sampson	Elizabeth	1830	Middlesex, London	(?)		Lewis Sampson	Manchester	
495	Sampson	Elizabeth	1834	Shoreditch, London	(?) Sampson			Spitalfields, London	servant
14171	Sampson	Elizabeth (Betsy)	1830	Manchester	Levi Sampson	Sarah (?)		Manchester	
11196	Sampson	Esther	1778	Aldgate, London	(?)		(?) Sampson	Aldgate, London	general dealer
483	Sampson	Esther	1841	Spitalfields, London	Samuel Sampson	Elizabeth (?)	Louis Hyman Woolf	Spitalfields, London	scholar
14179	Sampson	Esther	1848	Manchester	Sampson Sampson	Matilda Solomon		Manchester	
10185	Sampson	Frances	1832	Aldgate, London	Lazarus Sampson	Celia Barnett	Asser Jean Cohen	Aldgate, London	
259	Sampson	Gershon	1850	Aldgate, London	Joseph Sampson	Dinah de Young		Aldgate, London	
12993	Sampson	Hannah	1846	?, London	Joseph Sampson	Dinah de Young	Jacob Abrahams	Aldgate, London	scholar
14178	Sampson	Henry	1847	?, London	Sampson Sampson	Matilda Solomon		Manchester	
487	Sampson	Isaac	1815	?, Poland			Nancy (?)	Spitalfields, London	tailor
12992	Sampson	Jane	1844	?, London	Joseph Sampson	Dinah de Young		Aldgate, London	scholar
471	Sampson	John	1806	Spitalfields, London			Mary (?)	Spitalfields, London	weaver
496	Sampson	John	1824	Spitalfields, London			Elizabeth (?)	Spitalfields, London	shoe maker
493	Sampson	John	1849	Walworth, London	Isaac Sampson	Nancy (?)		Spitalfields, London	

ID	surname	given names	born	birthplace	father	mother	spouse 1	1851 residence	1851 occupation
500	Sampson	John	1850	Spitalfields, London	John Sampson	Elizabeth (?)		Spitalfields, London	
240	Sampson	Joseph	1802	Amsterdam, Holland	Samson		Dinah de Young	Aldgate, London	pedlar
491	Sampson	Joseph	1845	Spitalfields, London	Isaac Sampson	Nancy (?)		Spitalfields, London	
14177	Sampson	Joseph	1846	?, London	Sampson Sampson	Matilda Solomon	Annie Bessie Abraham	Manchester	
499	Sampson	Joseph	1849	Spitalfields, London	John Sampson	Elizabeth (?)		Spitalfields, London	
10186	Sampson	Julia	1833	Aldgate, London	Lazarus Sampson	Celia Barnett	Charles Cohen	Aldgate, London	
14169	Sampson	Levi	1783	?, Holland			Sarah (?)	Manchester	warehouseman (empl 2)
14454	Sampson	Lewis	1826	Manchester	Levi Sampson	Sarah (?)	Elizabeth (?)	Manchester	job warehouseman
490	Sampson	Lewis (Louis)	1844	Spitalfields, London	Isaac Sampson	Nancy (?)		Spitalfields, London	
10190	Sampson	Louis	1845	Aldgate, London	Lazarus Sampson	Celia Barnett		Aldgate, London	scholar
10187	Sampson	Louisa	1836	Aldgate, London	Lazarus Sampson	Celia Barnett	Siegmund Jacque Sussman	Aldgate, London	scholar
351	Sampson	Mary	1801	Birmingham	(?)		John Sampson	Spitalfields, London	
12989	Sampson	Mary	1838	?, London	Joseph Sampson	Dinah de Young	Lewis Emanuel	Aldgate, London	umbrella maker
14176	Sampson	Matilda	1822	?, London	Lyon (Yehuda) Solomon	Esther (?)	Sampson Sampson	Manchester	
10184	Sampson	Matilda	1830	Aldgate, London	Lazarus Sampson	Celia Barnett	Simeon Greenberg	Aldgate, London	
12988	Sampson	Moses	1834	Middlesex, London	Joseph Sampson	Dinah de Young	Hannah Jacobs	Aldgate, London	cigar maker
484	Sampson	Moses	1845	Spitalfields, London	Samuel Sampson	Elizabeth (?)		Spitalfields, London	scholar
488	Sampson	Nancy	1817	Whitechapel, London	(?)		Isaac Sampson	Spitalfields, London	
10191	Sampson	Phenias	1847	Aldgate, London	Lazarus Sampson	Celia Barnett		Aldgate, London	scholar
12991	Sampson	Rachael	1842	?, London	Joseph Sampson	Dinah de Young		Aldgate, London	scholar
14174	Sampson	Rachel	1841	?Southwark, London	Levi Sampson	Sarah (?)		Manchester	
12485	Sampson	Rachel	1848	Spitalfields, London	Samuel Sampson	Elizabeth (?)	Israel Benjamin	Spitalfields, London	
494	Sampson	Rebecca	1850	Walworth, London	Isaac Sampson	Nancy (?)		Spitalfields, London	
485	Sampson	Rosa	1847	Spitalfields, London	Samuel Sampson	Elizabeth (?)		Spitalfields, London	scholar
26460	Sampson	Rosetta	1821	Middlesex, London	Simeon Sampson	Catherine (Kate) Davis		Marylebone, London	
12990	Sampson	Rosey (Rose)	1840	Spitalfields, London	Joseph Sampson	Dinah de Young	Joseph Soesan	Aldgate, London	scholar
24378	Sampson	Sampson	1796	City, London				Soho, London	butcher
14175	Sampson	Sampson	1821	Manchester	Levi Sampson	Sarah (?)	Matilda Solomon	Manchester	job warehouseman
241	Sampson	Sampson	1848	?, London	Joseph Sampson	Dinah de Young		Aldgate, London	at home
480	Sampson	Samuel	1803	Aldgate, London			Elizabeth (?)	Spitalfields, London	general dealer
479	Sampson	Samuel	1831	Spitalfields, London	Samuel Sampson	Elizabeth (?)		Spitalfields, London	
782	Sampson	Samuel	1834	?, London				Soho, London	upholsterer
14170	Sampson	Sarah	1806	Liverpool	(?)		Levi Sampson	Manchester	
10188	Sampson	Sarah	1838	Aldgate, London	Lazarus Sampson	Celia Barnett	Julius Sterner	Aldgate, London	scholar
492	Sampson	Sarah	1847	Whitechapel, London	Isaac Sampson	Nancy (?)		Spitalfields, London	
3193	Sampson	Simeon	1790	?, Poland [?, Poland Prussia]	Simhah		Sara Solomon	Marylebone, London	annuitant
10189	Sampson	Simeon	1844	Aldgate, London	Lazarus Sampson	Celia Barnett		Aldgate, London	scholar
14080	Sampson	Simon (Simeon)	1831	Manchester	Levi Sampson	Sarah (?)	(?)	Manchester	merchant
482	Sampson	Solomon	1835	Spitalfields, London	Samuel Sampson	Elizabeth (?)		Spitalfields, London	hatter apprentice
14172	Sampson	Sophia	1835	Manchester	Levi Sampson	Sarah (?)		Manchester	
783	Sampson	Theodor	1836	?, London				Soho, London	clerk in railway office
9784	Sampson	Walter	1836	Middlesex, London				Kew, London	boarding school pupil
2052	Samson	Agnes	1822	Mile End, London	Isaac Solomon	Maria Solomons	Reuben Samson	Bethnal Green, London	
14803	Samson	Albert	1849	Finsbury, London	Henry Samson	Harriet (?)		Finsbury, London	
14804	Samson	Alfred	1851	Finsbury, London	Henry Samson	Harriet (?)		Finsbury, London	

ID	surname	given names	born	birthplace	father	mother	spouse 1	1851 residence	1851 occupation
31213	Samson	Amelia	1819	Bath	(?)		Philip Samson	Totteridge, London	
2028	Samson	Asher	1812	Hull, Yorkshire	Lyon Samson	Sarah (?)	Ann Nichol	Clerkenwell, London	cigar maker
24299	Samson	Augustus	1806	St Giles, London			Maria (?)	Bloomsbury, London	jeweller + boarding house
9778	Samson	Baron	1839	Aldgate, London	Lazarus Samson	Celia Barnett	Caroline Emily Taylor nee Brown	Aldgate, London	boarding school pupil
10192	Samson	Baron	1846	Aldgate, London	Hyman Lazarus Samson	Hannah Samson	Fanny (?)	Whitechapel, London	scholar
14417	Samson	Bertha	1832	?, Germany	Sam Isaac Samson	Dorette (?)		Manchester	
9846	Samson	Clara	1851	Manchester	Leopold Samson	Emilia (?)		Manchester	
14414	Samson	Dorette	1811	?, Germany	(?)		Sam Isaac Samson	Manchester	
9844	Samson	Edward	1842	Hanover, Germany	Leopold Samson	Emilia (?)		Manchester	
14800	Samson	Elizabeth	1842	Finsbury, London	Henry Samson	Harriet (?)		Finsbury, London	scholar
31214	Samson	Ellen	1843	Colchester, Essex	Philip Samson	Amelia (?)		Totteridge, London	scholar
14419	Samson	Emil	1816	?, Germany				Manchester	
9843	Samson	Emilia	1818	Hamburg, Germany	(?)		Leopold Samson	Manchester	
2053	Samson	Ephraim	1845	Bethnal Green, London	Reuben Samson	Agnes Solomon	Rachel Corper	Bethnal Green, London	
7410	Samson	Esther	1842	Aldgate, London	Hyman Lazarus Samson	Hannah Samson	Henry Solomon	Whitechapel, London	scholar
9192	Samson	Eve	1820	Dover, Kent	Barnet Nathan	Julia (?)	Samson Asher Samson	Whitechapel, London	
7413	Samson	Fanny	1850	Whitechapel, London	Hyman Lazarus Samson	Hannah Samson	Barnett Samuel Woolf	Whitechapel, London	
31216	Samson	Frederick	1850	Totteridge, London	Philip Samson	Amelia (?)		Totteridge, London	
7411	Samson	Hannah	1823	Kalisz, Poland [Carlish, Prussia]	Eliezer Lezer Samson		Hyman Lazarus Sampson	Whitechapel, London	
5280	Samson	Hannah	1851	Bethnal Green, London	Reuben Samson	Agnes Solomon	John Creasey Squire	Bethnal Green, London	
14799	Samson	Harriet	1821	Stowmarket, Suffolk	(?)		Henry Samson	Finsbury, London	
14798	Samson	Henry	1821	Walworth, London			Harriet (?)	Finsbury, London	Br--- ---ant
14802	Samson	Henry	1847	Finsbury, London	Henry Samson	Harriet (?)		Finsbury, London	scholar
8531	Samson	Henry Jacob	1847	?Hanover, Germany	Leopold Samson	Emilia (?)	Esther (Pet) Levi Jonas	Manchester	
14416	Samson	Herman	1830	?, Germany	Sam Isaac Samson	Dorette (?)		Manchester	
7412	Samson	Hyman Lazarus	1813	Brodnica, Poland [Strasburg, Prussia]	David Samson		Hannah Samson	Whitechapel, London	outfitter for tailors
2054	Samson	Isaac	1846	Bethnal Green, London	Reuben Samson	Agnes Solomon	Julia Melado	Bethnal Green, London	
14934	Samson	James Lion	1841	Finsbury, London				Bethnal Green, London	boarding school pupil
14415	Samson	John	1829	?, Germany	Sam Isaac Samson	Dorette (?)		Manchester	
9842	Samson	Leopold	1815	Hanover, Germany			Emilia (?)	Manchester	merchant
2027	Samson	Lewis	1826	Liverpool	Lyon Samson	Sarah (?)	Martha Temple	Liverpool	shoemaker
14418	Samson	Louisa	1833	?, Germany	Sam Isaac Samson	Dorette (?)		Manchester	
9652	Samson	Moses	1805	Spitalfields, London	Ephraim Samson	Hannah Myers		Stepney, London	butcher
20718	Samson	Philip	1818	Colchester, Essex			Amelia (?)	Totteridge, London	coach + omnibus proprietor
31215	Samson	Philip	1845	Colchester, Essex	Philip Samson	Amelia (?)		Totteridge, London	scholar
2050	Samson	Reuben	1819	Whitechapel, London	Ephraim Samson	Hannah Myers	Agnes Solomon	Bethnal Green, London	bottle merchant
14413	Samson	Sam Isaac	1801	?, Germany			Dorette (?)	Manchester	merchant
18669	Samson	Samson	1824	Liverpool	Lyon Samson	Sarah (?)		?Liverpool	
2055	Samson	Samson	1849	Bethnal Green, London	Reuben Samson	Agnes Solomon	Louisa Lyons	Bethnal Green, London	
9191	Samson	Samson Asher	1811	?, London	Asher Samson	Amelia (?)	Eve Nathan	Whitechapel, London	cigar manufacturer
12155	Samson	Sarah	1790	Norwich, Norfolk	(?)		Lyon Samson	Whitechapel, London	annuitant

ID	surname	given names	born	birthplace	father	mother	spouse 1	1851 residence	1851 occupation
231	Samson	Simon (Simeon)	1814	Whitechapel, London				Holborn, London	tailor
14801	Samson	William	1846	Finsbury, London	Henry Samson	Harriet (?)		Finsbury, London	scholar
10183	Samson (Sampson)	Celia	1805	?, Poland [?, Prussia]	(?) Barnett		Lazarus Samson (Sampson)	Aldgate, London	
10182	Samson (Sampson)	Lazarus	1800	?, Poland [?, Prussia]			Celia Barnett	Aldgate, London	wholesale jeweller
25226	Samuda	Abigail R	1810	Aldgate, London	Abraham de Jacob Samuda	Joy (Simha) de Hananel Lopes Pereira alias Aguilar		Clerkenwell, London	
25224	Samuda	Abraham	1781	Middlesex, London	Jacob de Abraham Samuda	Abigail de Isaac de Pina	Joy (Simha) de Hananel Lopes Pereira alias Aguilar	Clerkenwell, London	colonial produce broker
7370	Samuda	Ada B	1845	Southwark, London	Joseph D'Aguilar Samuda	Louisa (Leah) Ballin		St John's Wood, London	
24476	Samuda	Angelique Gabrielle	1818	Paris, France	(?)		Joseph Samuda	Peckham, London	
19262	Samuda	Augusta	1840	Southwark, London	Joseph D'Aguilar Samuda	Louisa (Leah) Ballin		St John's Wood, London	
19263	Samuda	Cecil A	1849	Southwark, London	Joseph D'Aguilar Samuda	Louisa (Leah) Ballin		St John's Wood, London	
24480	Samuda	Charles Joseph	1850	Peckham, London	Joseph Samuda	Angelique Gabrielle (?)	Agnes Elizabeth Craig	Peckham, London	
21673	Samuda	David	1789	City, London	Jacob de Abraham Samuda	Abigail de Isaac de Pina		Islington, London	sugar merchant
21672	Samuda	Esther	1782	City, London	Jacob de Abraham Samuda	Abigail de Isaac de Pina		Islington, London	fundholder and land
24478	Samuda	Gabrielle	1844	?, Algeria [Chaliproski, Algeria]	Joseph Samuda	Angelique Gabrielle (?)		Peckham, London	scholar
24477	Samuda	Henriette	1841	Algiers, Algeria	Joseph Samuda	Angelique Gabrielle (?)		Peckham, London	
24479	Samuda	Isabel	1848	Peckham, London	Joseph Samuda	Angelique Gabrielle (?)		Peckham, London	
30490	Samuda	Jonathan	1805	Tottenham, London	David Samuda	Hannah (?)	(?)	Stoke-on-Trent, Staffordshire	secretary, North Staffordshire Railway
24475	Samuda	Joseph	1807	Tottenham, London	David Samuda	Hannah (?)	Angelique Gabrielle (?)	Peckham, London	solicitor's managing clerk
7368	Samuda	Joseph D'Aguilar	1813	Finsbury, London	Abraham Samuda	Joy D'Aguilar	Louisa (Leah) Ballin	St John's Wood, London	civil engineer + patentee of the atmosheric railway
25225	Samuda	Joy (Simha)	1785	?, London	Hananel Lopes Pereira alias Aguilar	Rebecca de Joseph Treves	Abraham de Jacob Samuda	Clerkenwell, London	
7369	Samuda	Louisa (Leah)	1817	Holloway, London	Samuel Ballin		Joseph D'Aguilar Samuda	St John's Wood, London	
19261	Samuda	Maria	1838	Southwark, London	Joseph D'Aguilar Samuda	Louisa (Leah) Ballin		St John's Wood, London	
25227	Samuda	Rosa	1815	Aldgate, London	Abraham de Jacob Samuda	Joy (Simha) de Hananel Lopes Pereira alias Aguilar		Clerkenwell, London	
25228	Samuda	Sarah	1818	Aldgate, London	Abraham de Jacob Samuda	Joy (Simha) de Hananel Lopes Pereira alias Aguilar		Clerkenwell, London	
24557	Samuda	Theodor Walsh	1820	Clapham, London			Louisa Frewin	Brixton, London	general merchant
29096	Samuel	A--- M---	1823	Berlin, Germany				Whitechapel, London	
22586	Samuel	Aaron	1824	Whitechapel, London			Phoebe Gotteil	Stepney, London	cigar maker
1968	Samuel	Aaron	1840	Skewen, Wales				Swansea, Wales	scholar
20885	Samuel	Aaron	1840	Liverpool	Israel Samuel	Catherine (?)		Liverpool	scholar
9989	Samuel	Aaron A	1848	Norwich, Norfolk	Samuel Samuel	Elizabeth Mordecai		Great Yarmouth, Norfolk	
12177	Samuel	Abigail	1802	Aldgate, London	(?) Lea---	Sarah (?)	Moses Samuel	Whitechapel, London	
21578	Samuel	Abigail	1832	Whitechapel, London	Godfrey (Alexander) Samuel	Rachel Joseph		Spitalfields, London	tailoress
10048	Samuel	Abigail (Abby)	1848	Whitechapel, London	Marcus Samuel	Abigail Moss	Issachar (Berman) Barnard	City, London	
29093	Samuel	Abraham	1776	?, London	Enzlie Brighton Cohen		Phoebe Levy	Whitechapel, London	watchmaker
6530	Samuel	Abraham	1801	Warsaw, Poland	Levy Samuel		(?)	Bridgend, Glamorgan, Wales	travelling Jew

ID	surname	given names	born	birthplace	father	mother	spouse 1	1851 residence	1851 occupation
2076	Samuel	Abraham	1819	Louth, Lincolnshire	Samuel Samuel	Deborah Myers	Jane Young	Louth, Lincolnshire	watchmaker empl 1 man
10376	Samuel	Abraham	1826	Whitechapel, London	Tsvi		Rainer Jacobs	Spitalfields, London	general dealer
16022	Samuel	Abraham	1830	?Shalford, ?Essex	Henry Samuel	Rachel (?)		Whitechapel, London	cabinet maker
12180	Samuel	Abraham	1833	Whitechapel, London	Moses Samuel	Abigail Lea---	(?)	Whitechapel, London	cabinet maker
27845	Samuel	Abraham	1834	Chatham, Kent	Isaac Samuel	Rebecca (?)	Isabella Jacobs	Spitalfields, London	slipper maker
10678	Samuel	Abram	1826	Amsterdam, Holland	Solomon Samuel	Esther (?)		Spitalfields, London	cigar maker
9479	Samuel	Ada	1849	Aldgate, London	Samuel Moss	Eliza (?)		Aldgate, London	
28788	Samuel	Adelaide	1818	Whitechapel, London	Lewin Phillip Samuel	(?)	Lewis Abrahams	Whitechapel, London	tailoress
7086	Samuel	Adelaide	1831	Liverpool	Louis Samuel	Henrietta (?)	Ellis Abraham Franklin	St Giles, London	
15891	Samuel	Agnes	1842	Rio de Janeiro, Brazil	Ralph H Samuel			Liverpool	boarding school pupil
21844	Samuel	Albert	1842	?, France	Isaac Samuel	Fanny (?)		Clerkenwell, London	scholar
30211	Samuel	Albert Aaron	1851	Liverpool	Henry Israel Samuel	Rachel Wolf	Fanny Durch	Liverpool	
20867	Samuel	Albert H	1844	Liverpool	Lewis Henry Samuel	Caroline H (?)		Liverpool	scholar
23334	Samuel	Alexander	1841	Westminster, London	Moses Samuel	Rosa Myers		Westminster, London	
23613	Samuel	Alfred	1832	Liverpool	Moses Samuel	Harriet (?)	Emma Wolf	Liverpool	watchmaker apprentice
7246	Samuel	Alice	1848	Shoreditch, London	Sampson Samuel	Esther Lazarus	Nathan Solomon Joseph	Shoreditch, London	
19159	Samuel	Amelia	1826	Sunderland, Co Durham	Samuel Lyon Samuel	Hannah Moses		Aldgate, London	fur sewer
11643	Samuel	Amelia	1829	Spitalfields, London	(?) Samuel			Aldgate, London	servant
24706	Samuel	Amelia	1832	Walworth, London	Isaac Samuel	Deborah (?)		Walworth, London	
28695	Samuel	Amelia	1835	Middlesex, London	(?) Samuel	Rebecca (?)		Spitalfields, London	
6433	Samuel	Amelia	1837	Aldgate, London	Henry Samuel	Rachel (?)	Hyman Davis	Whitechapel, London	
18115	Samuel	Amelia	1841	?, London	(?) Samuel			Mile End, London	scholar
13080	Samuel	Amelia	1849	Bury St Edmunds, Suffolk	Henry (Hart) Samuel	Charlotte Zimmerman		Marylebone, London	
7258	Samuel	Amelia (Emelia)	1789	?, Poland [?, Prussia]	Lazar Emanuel of Ramjets		Mendel Menachem Samuel	Wapping, London	clothier
9480	Samuel	Anette	1850	Aldgate, London	Samuel Moss	Eliza (?)		Aldgate, London	
24130	Samuel	Ann	1789	Portsmouth, Hampshire	(?)		(?) Samuel	Bloomsbury, London	annuitant
14753	Samuel	Ann	1798	Whitechapel, London	(?)		(?) Samuel	Finsbury, London	annuitant + mortgagee
1970	Samuel	Ann	1836	Bristol	John Samuel	Priscilla (?)		Swansea, Wales	
26638	Samuel	Ann	1840	Whitechapel, London	Mark Samuel	Elizabeth Allen		Aldgate, London	tailoress apprentice
2074	Samuel	Ann Elizabeth	1817	Louth, Lincolnshire	Samuel Samuel	Deborah Myers		Louth, Lincolnshire	
15670	Samuel	Anna	1842	?, Poland	David Samuel	Hannah (?)		Aldgate, London	
11752	Samuel	Barnet	1844	Shoreditch, London	(?) Samuel	Esther (?)		Shoreditch, London	scholar
5144	Samuel	Barnett	1810	Sheffield, Yorkshire			Martha (?)	Sheffield, Yorkshire	cutlery + comb dealer
16024	Samuel	Barnett	1838	?, London	Henry Samuel	Rachel (?)		Whitechapel, London	apprentice boot maker
1984	Samuel	Benjamin	1793	?, Poland				Merthyr Tydfil, Wales	watchmaker
8160	Samuel	Benjamin	1816	Aldgate, London	Hyam Samuel	Catherine (?)		Aldgate, London	general dealer
21576	Samuel	Benjamin	1826	Spitalfields, London	Godfrey (Alexander) Samuel	Rachel Joseph	Julia Solomons	Spitalfields, London	fruit dealer
20883	Samuel	Benjamin	1838	Liverpool	Israel Samuel	Catherine (?)		Liverpool	scholar
18863	Samuel	Benjamin	1840	Colchester, Essex	Michael Samuel	Emma Jacobs	Rosetta (?)	Colchester, Essex	boarding school pupil
24230	Samuel	Benjamin	1841	Hoxton, London	(?) Samuel	Lydia (?)	Emma Eliza Pavie	Hackney, London	scholar
8151	Samuel	Benjamin	1847	?, London	Samuel Samuel	Rebecca Lyons	(?)	Aldgate, London	scholar
28829	Samuel	Betsey	1808	?, Holland			Betsey (?)	Spitalfields, London	
24703	Samuel	Betsey	1824	City, London	Isaac Samuel	Deborah (?)		Walworth, London	
28830	Samuel	Betsey	1833	?, Holland	Mathew Samuel	Betsey (?)		Spitalfields, London	tailoress
2075	Samuel	Betsy (Elizabeth)	1830	Louth, Lincolnshire	Samuel Samuel	Deborah Myers		Louth, Lincolnshire	housekeeper to brother

ID	surname	given names	born	birthplace	father	mother	spouse 1	1851 residence	1851 occupation
16570	Samuel	Blanche	1848	Rio de Janeiro, Brazil	Ralph H Samuel			Liverpool	
16562	Samuel	Caby I	1788	Middlesex, London	(?)		(?) Samuel	Liverpool	annuitant
11889	Samuel	Caroline	1845	?, Poland	Lewis Samuel	Esther (?)		Whitechapel, London	scholar
28077	Samuel	Caroline	1845	Aldgate, London	Michael Samuel	Elizabeth Solomons		Spitalfields, London	
20865	Samuel	Caroline H	1811	Liverpool	(?)		Lewis Henry Samuel	Liverpool	
1973	Samuel	Catharine	1842	Swansea, Wales	(?) Samuel	(?Mary?) (?)		Swansea, Wales	
8147	Samuel	Catherine	1778	Aldgate, London	(?)		Hyam Samuel	Aldgate, London	
20880	Samuel	Catherine	1805	?, Poland	(?)		Israel Samuel	Liverpool	wife of grocer + provision dealer
27485	Samuel	Catherine	1822	Middlesex, London	(?) Samuel	Lydia (?)		Aldgate, London	dealer in hosiery
31049	Samuel	Catherine	1826	Richmond, London	(?) Samuel	Mary (?)		Richmond, London	
16346	Samuel	Catherine (Kate)	1844	Shoreditch, London	Sampson Samuel	Esther Lazarus	Martin Jaffe	Shoreditch, London	scholar at home
7848	Samuel	Cecilia L	1830	Middlesex, London	Mark (Mordecai) Wolff		Sylvester Lewis Samuel	Liverpool	
13982	Samuel	Charlotte	1821	Ipswich, Suffolk	(?) Samuel			Manchester	cook
13077	Samuel	Charlotte	1828	Bury St Edmunds, Suffolk	Godfrey Zimmerman	Martha (?)	Henry (Hart) Samuel	Marylebone, London	
18864	Samuel	Charlotte (Carlotta)	1842	Colchester, Essex	Michael Samuel	Emma Jacobs	Louis Schlesinger	Colchester, Essex	
19106	Samuel	Clara	1831	Stepney, London	James Samuel	Elizabeth Davis		Whitechapel, London	
29826	Samuel	Clara	1832	Shoreditch, London	(?) Samuel	Rebecca (?)		Wapping, London	dressmaker
15666	Samuel	David	1811	?, Poland	Shmuel		Hannah (?)	Aldgate, London	cap maker
19104	Samuel	David	1822	Stepney, London	James Samuel	Elizabeth Davis	Catherine (Kate) Leo	Whitechapel, London	stonemason
20884	Samuel	David	1840	Liverpool	Israel Samuel	Catherine (?)		Liverpool	scholar
11751	Samuel	David	1841	Shoreditch, London	(?) Samuel	Esther (?)		Shoreditch, London	scholar
16347	Samuel	David	1846	Shoreditch, London	Sampson Samuel	Esther Lazarus		Shoreditch, London	scholar at home
22592	Samuel	David	1850	Stepney, London	Aaron Samuel	Phoebe Gottheil		Stepney, London	
5282	Samuel	Deborah	1795	?, London	Moses Myers	Rachel Levy	Samuel Samuel	Louth, Lincolnshire	
30851	Samuel	Dinah	1787	Walton, Essex	(?)		Solomon Samuel	Bath	fur manufacturer
17701	Samuel	Dinah	1827	Portsmouth, Hampshire	(?) Samuel			Spitalfields, London	seamstress
19160	Samuel	Douglas Davis	1827	Whitechapel, London	Samuel Lyon Samuel	Hannah Moses	Henrietta Newman	Aldgate, London	fruit dealer
16349	Samuel	Edward	1850	Shoreditch, London	Sampson Samuel	Esther Lazarus		Shoreditch, London	
1974	Samuel	Edward	1851	Swansea, Wales	(?) Samuel	(?Mary) (?)		Swansea, Wales	
12782	Samuel	Edward Lyon	1833	?, London	Lyon Samuel	Rachael Mosely	Eliza Jacob	Aldgate, London	oilman's assistant
19105	Samuel	Edward?	1824	Stepney, London	James Samuel	Elizabeth Davis		Whitechapel, London	stonemason
3600	Samuel	Edwin Louis	1825	Liverpool	Louis Samuel	Henrietta Israel	Clara Yates	Liverpool	bullion merchant + banker
23335	Samuel	Elena (eve)	1843	Westminster, London	Moses Samuel	Rosa Myers		Westminster, London	
2869	Samuel	Elias	1830	Birmingham	Abraham Samuel	Lydia (?)	Hannah (?)	Birmingham	clothier + shopman
4922	Samuel	Elias Saul	1848	Birmingham	Saul Samuel	Louisa Lazarus		Birmingham	
23523	Samuel	Eliza	1807	Birmingham	(?)		Saul Samuel	Liverpool	
24132	Samuel	Eliza	1817	Chichester, Sussex	(?) Samuel	Ann (?)		Bloomsbury, London	annuitant
9477	Samuel	Eliza	1828	Liverpool	(?)		Moss Samuel	Aldgate, London	
19843	Samuel	Elizabeth	1755	?, Germany	(?)		(?) Samuel	Spitalfields, London	
18114	Samuel	Elizabeth	1766	Middlesex, London	(?)		(?) Samuel	Mile End, London	
19103	Samuel	Elizabeth	1800	Aldgate, London	Joseph Yespe Davis		James Samuel	Whitechapel, London	
23936	Samuel	Elizabeth	1806	City, London	(?)		Sim Samuel	Marylebone, London	

ID	surname	given names	born	birthplace	father	mother	spouse 1	1851 residence	1851 occupation
26636	Samuel	Elizabeth	1815	Whitechapel, London	Aryeh Leib Allen	Betsy Levy	Mark Samuel	Aldgate, London	fruit dealer
18429	Samuel	Elizabeth	1816	Ipswich, Suffolk	(?) Samuel			Bloomsbury, London	cook
23966	Samuel	Elizabeth	1822	City, London	Simon Samuel	Esther Moses Samuel		Marylebone, London	
28076	Samuel	Elizabeth	1826	Whitechapel, London	Henry Solomons		Michael Samuel	Spitalfields, London	
28691	Samuel	Elizabeth	1830	Middlesex, London	(?) Samuel	Rebecca (?)		Spitalfields, London	
21580	Samuel	Elizabeth	1837	Whitechapel, London	Godfrey (Alexander) Samuel	Rachel Joseph		Spitalfields, London	cap maker appentice
3768	Samuel	Elizabeth	1843	Aldgate, London	(?) Samuel	Jane (?)		Spitalfields, London	
21905	Samuel	Elizabeth	1847	Middlesex, London	Joseph Samuel	Esther (?)		Clerkenwell, London	
10378	Samuel	Elizabeth	1850	Whitechapel, London	Abraham Samuel	Rainer Jacobs		Spitalfields, London	
18862	Samuel	Elizabeth (Lizzie)	1839	Colchester, Essex	Michael Samuel	Emma Jacobs	Charles Louis Klisser	Colchester, Essex	scholar
4923	Samuel	Elizabeth (Lizzie)	1850	Birmingham	Saul Samuel	Louisa Lazarus	Montagu Davis	Birmingham	
23817	Samuel	Elizabeth Samuel	1843	Liverpool	(?Louis) Samuel	(?Henrietta Israel)		Liverpool	
23596	Samuel	Ellen	1816	Liverpool	Lewis Samuel	Kate (?)		Liverpool	
1971	Samuel	Ellen	1841	Chepstow, Wales	John Samuel	Priscilla (?)		Swansea, Wales	
24705	Samuel	Ellis	1829	Walworth, London	Isaac Samuel	Deborah (?)		Walworth, London	
8983	Samuel	Emanuel	1825	Bath	Solomon Samuel	Dinah (?)	Frances (Fanny) Ballin	Bath	fur manufacturer
15889	Samuel	Emily	1835	?Rio de Janeiro, Brazil	Ralph H Samuel		Max Hesse	Liverpool	boarding school pupil
18861	Samuel	Emma	1817	Piccadilly, London	(?) Jacobs		Michael Samuel	Colchester, Essex	wife of pawnbroker
31050	Samuel	Emma	1830	Richmond, London	(?) Samuel	Mary (?)		Richmond, London	
12578	Samuel	Emma	1848	Colchester, Essex	Michael Samuel	Emma Jacobs	Alfred Isaac Haldinstein	Colchester, Essex	
10740	Samuel	Esslirani	1801	?, Poland [?, Prussia]			Julia (?)	Spitalfields, London	general dealer
1977	Samuel	Ester	1807	Swansea, Wales			(?) Samuel	Swansea, Wales	mariner's wife
16325	Samuel	Esther	1783	?, England	(?)		Samuel Moses Samuel	Marylebone, London	
11194	Samuel	Esther	1799	Whitechapel, London	(?) Samuel			Aldgate, London	general dealer
11749	Samuel	Esther	1807	Finsbury, London	(?)		(?) Samuel	Shoreditch, London	cane dealer
16345	Samuel	Esther	1823	Leigh, Essex	Laurence Lazarus	Catharine Phillips	Sampson Samuel	Shoreditch, London	
11888	Samuel	Esther	1825	?, Poland	(?)		Lewis Samuel	Whitechapel, London	
21903	Samuel	Esther	1827	?, Kent	(?)		Joseph Samuel	Clerkenwell, London	
26639	Samuel	Esther	1841	Whitechapel, London	Mark Samuel	Elizabeth Allen		Aldgate, London	scholar
3771	Samuel	Esther	1848	Spitalfields, London	(?) Samuel	Jane (?)		Spitalfields, London	scholar
7749	Samuel	Esther	1851	Liverpool	Lewis (Louis) Samuel	Jane (?)	B D Smaje	Liverpool	
10677	Samuel	Esther	1791	Amsterdam, Holland	(?)		Solomon Samuel	Spitalfields, London	
23965	Samuel	Esther Moses	1787	?, London	Moses Samuel		Simon Samuel	Marylebone, London	
9991	Samuel	Eva Ella	1850	Norwich, Norfolk	Samuel Samuel	Elizabeth Mordecai	George Jacobs	Great Yarmouth, Norfolk	
23524	Samuel	Evelina	1837	Birmingham	Saul Samuel	Eliza (?)		Liverpool	
16565	Samuel	Fanny	1814	Liverpool	(?) Samuel	Caby I (?)		Liverpool	annuitant
21843	Samuel	Fanny	1818	?Boulogne, France	(?)		Fanny (?)	Clerkenwell, London	
28696	Samuel	Fanny	1843	Middlesex, London	(?) Samuel	Rebecca (?)		Spitalfields, London	
23593	Samuel	Fanny Yates	1819	Liverpool	Joseph Hess	Sarah Yates	Henry Solomon Samuel	Liverpool	merchant
7642	Samuel	Flora	1782	?, London	(?)		(?) Samuel	Liverpool	gentlewoman
16564	Samuel	Flora S	1814	Liverpool	(?) Samuel	Caby I (?)		Liverpool	annuitant
7744	Samuel	Florence	1841	Liverpool	Samuel H Samuel		Edward Rensburg	Liverpool	scholar
18469	Samuel	Frances	1775	Whitechapel, London	(?)		(?) Samuel	Whitechapel, London	annuitant
27486	Samuel	Frances	1826	Middlesex, London	(?) Samuel	Lydia (?)		Aldgate, London	dealer in hosiery
21577	Samuel	Frances	1830	Whitechapel, London	Godfrey (Alexander) Samuel	Rachel Joseph		Spitalfields, London	dress maker

ID	surname	given names	born	birthplace	father	mother	spouse 1	1851 residence	1851 occupation
22591	Samuel	Frances	1848	Stepney, London	Aaron Samuel	Phoebe Gottheil		Stepney, London	
16845	Samuel	Francis Samuel	1840	Philadelphia, USA	Frederick Samuel		Beatrice Julia Henriques	Brighton, Sussex	scholar
16326	Samuel	George	1808	Richmond, Surrey	Samuel Moses Samuel	Esther (?)		Marylebone, London	
2077	Samuel	George	1839	Louth, Lincolnshire	Samuel Samuel	Deborah Myers		Louth, Lincolnshire	scholar
18868	Samuel	George Michael	1851	Colchester, Essex	Michael Samuel	Emma Jacobs		Colchester, Essex	
16566	Samuel	Georgina	1839	Rio de Janeiro, Brazil	Ralph H Samuel		Raphael J Moses	Liverpool	scholar at home
1978	Samuel	Gitel	1825	?, Poland	(?)		Moses Samuel	Swansea, Wales	
13079	Samuel	Godfrey Zimmerman	1848	Bury St Edmunds, Suffolk	Henry (Hart) Samuel	Charlotte Zimmerman	Alice Lazarus	Marylebone, London	
23792	Samuel	Hanna Luhosua	1849	Liverpool	Jacob Samuel	Milga (?)		Liverpool	
19719	Samuel	Hannah	1779	?, Holland	(?)		Natan Halevi Samuel	Whitechapel, London	
19158	Samuel	Hannah	1790	Biggleswade, Bedfordshire	David Moses		Samuel Lyon Samuel	Aldgate, London	
15667	Samuel	Hannah	1815	?, Poland	(?)		David Samuel	Aldgate, London	
3766	Samuel	Hannah	1819	Whitechapel, London			(?) Samuel	Spitalfields, London	general dealer
8155	Samuel	Hannah	1819	Aldgate, London	Eliezer Mendoza		Lewis Samuel	Spitalfields, London	
11172	Samuel	Hannah	1830	Spitalfields, London	Joel HaLevi Abrahams		Mark Samuel	Aldgate, London	
1975	Samuel	Hannah	1844	Swansea, Wales	(?) Samuel	(?Mary) (?)		Swansea, Wales	
20869	Samuel	Harold H	1839	Liverpool	Samuel Henry Samuel			Liverpool	scholar
23610	Samuel	Harriet	1823	Middlesex, London	(?) Samuel			Liverpool	haberdasher's assistant
1982	Samuel	Harriet	1833	Swansea, Wales				Swansea, Wales	dressmaker
9990	Samuel	Helen A	1849	Norwich, Norfolk	Samuel Samuel	Elizabeth Mordecai		Great Yarmouth, Norfolk	
21850	Samuel	Helene	1848	Clerkenwell, London	Lambert Samuel	Leopoldine (?)		Clerkenwell, London	
3599	Samuel	Henrietta	1797	City, London	Israel Israel	Rebecca Pearl Solomon	Louis Samuel	Bloomsbury, London	
30846	Samuel	Henrietta	1810	Bath	Solomon Samuel	Dinah (?)		Bath	fur manufacturer
23955	Samuel	Henrietta	1829	Portsmouth, Hampshire	Horatio Joseph Montefiore	Sarah de Daniel Mocatta	Horatio Simon Samuel	Marylebone, London	
16020	Samuel	Henry	1802	North Shields, Tyne & Wear			Rachel (?)	Whitechapel, London	MRCS general practitioner
2073	Samuel	Henry	1824	Louth, Lincolnshire	Samuel Samuel	Deborah Myers		Louth, Lincolnshire	ship merchant
10681	Samuel	Henry	1833	Amsterdam, Holland	Solomon Samuel	Esther (?)		Spitalfields, London	cigar maker
19107	Samuel	Henry	1833	Whitechapel, London	James Samuel	Elizabeth Davis	Sarah Deborah Levy	Whitechapel, London	cigar maker
17075	Samuel	Henry	1836	Middlesex, London	Samuel Samuel	Sophia (?)		Glasgow, Scotland	message boy
28831	Samuel	Henry	1836	?, Holland	Mathew Samuel	Betsey (?)		Spitalfields, London	
13175	Samuel	Henry	1840	Aldgate, London	(?) Samuel			Aldgate, London	scholar
23940	Samuel	Henry	1840	Marylebone, London	Sim Samuel	Elizabeth (?)		Marylebone, London	scholar
18867	Samuel	Henry	1841	Colchester, Essex	Michael Samuel	Emma Jacobs	Caroline Haldinstein	Colchester, Essex	
9779	Samuel	Henry	1842	Middlesex, London				Kew, London	boarding school pupil
16567	Samuel	Henry (Harry) Sylvester	1843	Rio de Janeiro, Brazil	Ralph Henry Samuel		Esther Hannah Moses [Beddington]	Liverpool	scholar
13078	Samuel	Henry (Hart)	1818	North Shields, Tyne & Wear			Charlotte Zimmerman	Marylebone, London	
6575	Samuel	Henry Israel	1824	Liverpool	Moses Samuel	Harriet (?)	Rachel Wolf	Liverpool	watch + clockmaker + jeweller
23592	Samuel	Henry Solomon	1817	Liverpool			Fanny Yates Hess	Liverpool	merchant
13626	Samuel	Herman	1833	?, Poland [?, Prussia]				Manchester	tailor journeyman
24131	Samuel	Hester	1812	Chichester, Sussex	(?) Samuel	Ann (?)		Bloomsbury, London	annuitant
1980	Samuel	Holman	1850	Swansea, Wales	Moses Samuel	Gitel (?)		Swansea, Wales	

ID	surname	given names	born	birthplace	father	mother	spouse 1	1851 residence	1851 occupation
23954	Samuel	Horatio Simon	1825	City, London	Simon Samuel	Esther Moses Samuel	Henrietta Montefiore	Marylebone, London	colonial broker
8156	Samuel	Hyam	1843	Aldgate, London	Lewis Samuel	Hannah Mendoza		Spitalfields, London	scholar
24702	Samuel	Isaac	1793	City, London			Deborah (?)	Walworth, London	clothier
21842	Samuel	Isaac	1809	?, France			Fanny (?)	Clerkenwell, London	flower manufacturer
2868	Samuel	Isaac	1828	Birmingham	Abraham Samuel	Lydia (?)	Esther Barnett	Birmingham	clothes dealer
10680	Samuel	Isaac	1830	Amsterdam, Holland	Solomon Samuel	Esther (?)		Spitalfields, London	cigar maker
26347	Samuel	Isaac	1833	?, London	Morris Samuel	Phoebe Chen	Louisa Friedeberg	Aldgate, London	cigar maker
23938	Samuel	Isaac	1834	Marylebone, London	Sim Samuel	Elizabeth (?)		Marylebone, London	
16026	Samuel	Isaac	1842	?, London	Henry Samuel	Rachel (?)	Rosa Baumann	Whitechapel, London	scholar
26641	Samuel	Isaac	1849	Aldgate, London	Mark Samuel	Elizabeth Allen		Aldgate, London	
18855	Samuel	Isabel	1843	?, London	Lyon Samuel	Rachael Mosely	Reuben Hyams	Aldgate, London	
16568	Samuel	Isabel	1844	Rio de Janeiro, Brazil	Ralph H Samuel		Assur Keyser	Liverpool	scholar at home
31048	Samuel	Isabella	1822	Richmond, London	(?) Samuel	Mary (?)		Richmond, London	
23565	Samuel	Isabella	1829	Manchester	Abraham Samuel	Sophia Aarons		Liverpool	hosier assistant
1972	Samuel	Isabella	1848	Crickhowell, Wales	John Samuel	Priscilla (?)		Swansea, Wales	
20879	Samuel	Israel	1805	?, Poland			Catherine (?)	Liverpool	grocer + provision dealer
27844	Samuel	Israel	1832	Chatham, Kent	Isaac Samuel	Rebecca (?)		Spitalfields, London	slipper maker
29095	Samuel	J---	1812	?, London	Abraham Samuel	Phoebe Levy		Whitechapel, London	
2324	Samuel	Jacob	1825	?, Poland				Leeds, Yorkshire	general dealer
23789	Samuel	Jacob	1825	?, Poland			Milga (?)	Liverpool	grocer &c
12179	Samuel	Jacob Henry	1832	Whitechapel, London	Moses Samuel	Abigail Lea---		Whitechapel, London	cigar maker
8184	Samuel	James	1797	Spitalfields, London	Shmuel		Elizabeth Davis	Whitechapel, London	statuary + mason
27340	Samuel	Jane	1797	Aldgate, London	(?)		(?) Samuel	Aldgate, London	general dealer
2603	Samuel	Jane	1823	Whitechapel, London	Lewin Phillip Samuel		Samuel Isaacs	Whitechapel, London	umrella maker
7699	Samuel	Jane	1823	Hanover, Germany			Lewis (Louis) Samuel	Liverpool	
24133	Samuel	Jane	1829	Chichester, Sussex	(?) Samuel	Ann (?)		Bloomsbury, London	annuitant
25746	Samuel	Jesse	1827	Aldgate, London	(?) Samuel			Spitalfields, London	
20868	Samuel	Jessie H	1848	Liverpool	Lewis Henry Samuel	Caroline H (?)		Liverpool	
20429	Samuel	John	1761	Hamburg, Germany				Aldgate, London	
1969	Samuel	John	1791	?, Scotland			Priscilla (?)	Swansea, Wales	artist
28832	Samuel	John	1838	?, Holland	Mathew Samuel	Betsey (?)		Spitalfields, London	scholar
17077	Samuel	John	1841	Middlesex, London	Samuel Samuel	Sophia (?)		Glasgow, Scotland	scholar
3767	Samuel	John	1842	Aldgate, London	(?) Samuel	Jane (?)		Spitalfields, London	
1976	Samuel	John	1844	Swansea, Wales	(?) Samuel	(?Mary) (?)		Swansea, Wales	
2693	Samuel	Jonah	1820	?, Germany	Samuel Samuel	Isabella (?)		Nottingham, Nottinghamshire	
2659	Samuel	Joseph	1812	?, Poland			Roseanna (?)	Glasgow, Scotland	jeweller
21902	Samuel	Joseph	1822	City, London			Esther (?)	Clerkenwell, London	
17081	Samuel	Joseph	1825	?, England				Glasgow, Scotland	furrier
1983	Samuel	Joseph	1830	?, Poland				Swansea, Wales	watchmaker
15815	Samuel	Joseph	1831	?, London				Aldgate, London	salesman
17074	Samuel	Joseph	1833	Middlesex, London	Samuel Samuel	Sophia (?)		Glasgow, Scotland	silk button manufacturer
9780	Samuel	Joseph	1845	Middlesex, London				Kew, London	boarding school pupil
14754	Samuel	Joseph L	1819	Soho, London	(?) Samuel	Ann (?)		Finsbury, London	jeweller
19109	Samuel	Joseph S	1837	Stepney, London	James Samuel	Elizabeth Davis	Elizabeth Lyon	Whitechapel, London	

ID	surname	given names	born	birthplace	father	mother	spouse 1	1851 residence	1851 occupation
9781	Samuel	Judah	1840	?Aldgate, London	Lyon Samuel	Rachael Mosely	Rachel Cohen	Aldgate, London	boarding school pupil
10741	Samuel	Julia	1806	?, Holland	(?)		Esslirani Samuel	Spitalfields, London	
23597	Samuel	Julia	1825	Liverpool	Lewis Samuel	Kate (?)		Liverpool	
7180	Samuel	Julia	1832	Richmond, London	(?) Samuel	Mary (?)	Charles Isaacs	Richmond, London	
26637	Samuel	Julia	1837	Whitechapel, London	Mark Samuel	Elizabeth Allen	Hyam Woolf	Aldgate, London	scholar
8157	Samuel	Julia	1846	Aldgate, London	Lewis Samuel	Hannah Mendoza		Spitalfields, London	scholar
17078	Samuel	Julia (Juliet)	1844	?Aldgate, London	Samuel Samuel	Sophia (?)		Glasgow, Scotland	scholar
27045	Samuel	Julius	1821	?, Poland				Aldgate, London	tinman
22464	Samuel	Jullia	1844	?	(?) Samuel			Gravesend, Kent	boarding school pupil
15636	Samuel	Kate	1776	Bavaria, Germany	(?)		(?) Samuel	Finsbury, London	independent
23595	Samuel	Kate	1786	?, London	(?)		Lewis Samuel	Liverpool	
16563	Samuel	Kate	1812	Liverpool	(?) Samuel	Caby I (?)		Liverpool	annuitant
30848	Samuel	Kate	1818	Bath	Solomon Samuel	Dinah (?)		Bath	straw hat manufacturer + ?finisher
23564	Samuel	Kate	1827	Manchester	Abraham Samuel	Sophia Aarons		Liverpool	housekeeper
23941	Samuel	Kate	1842	Marylebone, London	Sim Samuel	Elizabeth (?)		Marylebone, London	scholar
22588	Samuel	Kate	1844	Whitechapel, London	Aaron Samuel	Phoebe Gottheil		Stepney, London	scholar
8158	Samuel	Kitty (Kate)	1847	Aldgate, London	Lewis Samuel	Hannah Mendoza		Spitalfields, London	scholar
21848	Samuel	Lambert	1812	?, France			Leopoldine (?)	Clerkenwell, London	commercial traveller
22590	Samuel	Lawrence	1847	Whitechapel, London	Aaron Samuel	Phoebe Gottheil		Stepney, London	scholar
16348	Samuel	Lawrence	1849	Shoreditch, London	Sampson Samuel	Esther Lazarus		Shoreditch, London	
8159	Samuel	Lawrence	1851	Spitalfields, London	Lewis Samuel	Hannah Mendoza		Spitalfields, London	
12181	Samuel	Lawrence Moses	1839	Whitechapel, London	Moses Samuel	Abigail Lea---	Maria Isaacs	Whitechapel, London	scholar
20642	Samuel	Lazarus	1833	?, Poland				Spitalfields, London	journeyman tailor
23943	Samuel	Lazarus	1846	Marylebone, London	Sim Samuel	Elizabeth (?)		Marylebone, London	scholar
19197	Samuel	Leah	1777	City, London	(?)		Samuel Samuel	City, London	
21849	Samuel	Leopoldine	1824	Wurtemberg, Germany	(?)		Lambert Samuel	Holborn, London	artificial florist
28787	Samuel	Lewin Phillip	1795	Canterbury, Kent			(?)	Whitechapel, London	glass dealer
23594	Samuel	Lewis	1783	Liverpool			Kate (?)	Liverpool	retired watch manufacturer
8154	Samuel	Lewis	1812	Aldgate, London	Hyam Samuel	Catherine (?)	Hannah Mendoza	Spitalfields, London	clothes dealer
11887	Samuel	Lewis	1821	?, Poland			Esther (?)	Whitechapel, London	tailor
23342	Samuel	Lewis	1830	Ipswich, Suffolk	Michael Samuel			Piccadilly, London	shopman
21579	Samuel	Lewis	1834	Whitechapel, London	Godfrey (Alexander) Samuel	Rachel Joseph		Spitalfields, London	cigar maker apprentice
23939	Samuel	Lewis	1838	Marylebone, London	Sim Samuel	Elizabeth (?)		Marylebone, London	scholar
4921	Samuel	Lewis	1840	?Birmingham	Abraham Samuel	Lydia (?)		Birmingham	
12182	Samuel	Lewis	1843	Whitechapel, London	Moses Samuel	Abigail Lea---		Whitechapel, London	scholar
7588	Samuel	Lewis (Louis)	1819	Middlesex, London	Abraham Samuel	Sophia Aarons	Jane (?)	Liverpool	haberdasher
20864	Samuel	Lewis Henry	1812	Liverpool			Caroline H (?)	Liverpool	watch manufacturer
4920	Samuel	Lewis Henry	1847	Birmingham	Saul Samuel	Louisa Lazarus	Hannah Solomon	Birmingham	
3598	Samuel	Louis	1794	City, London	Emanuel Menachem Samuel	Hanna (Hinde) Israel	Henrietta Israel	Bloomsbury, London	retired silversmith
30306	Samuel	Louis	1846	Colchester, Essex	Michael Samuel	Emma Jacobs		Colchester, Essex	
1979	Samuel	Louis	1847	?, Poland	Moses Samuel	Gitel (?)		Swansea, Wales	scholar
28835	Samuel	Louis	1849	Spitalfields, London	Mathew Samuel	Betsey (?)		Spitalfields, London	
15890	Samuel	Louisa	1838	?Rio de Janeiro, Brazil	Ralph H Samuel			Liverpool	boarding school pupil

ID	surname	given names	born	birthplace	father	mother	spouse 1	1851 residence	1851 occupation
20886	Samuel	Louisa	1843	Liverpool	Israel Samuel	Catherine (?)		Liverpool	
3471	Samuel	Louisa Harvey	1826	Aldgate, London	Lewis Henry Lazarus	Elizabeth (Eliza) Aaron	Saul Samuel	Birmingham	
26843	Samuel	Lucy	1777	?, London	(?) Samuel			Aldgate, London	shirt maker
2865	Samuel	Lydia	1783	Birmingham			Abraham Samuel	Birmingham	clothier
25293	Samuel	Lydia	1786	?, London			(?) Samuel	Holborn, London	
12780	Samuel	Lyon	1803	Portsmouth, Hampshire	Shmuel		Rachael Mosely	Aldgate, London	traveller
16025	Samuel	Lyon	1840	?, London	Henry Samuel	Rachel (?)		Whitechapel, London	scholar
21846	Samuel	Lyon	1849	Clerkenwell, London	Isaac Samuel	Fanny (?)		Clerkenwell, London	
21851	Samuel	Lyon Victor	1849	Clerkenwell, London	Lambert Samuel	Leopoldine (?)		Clerkenwell, London	
23563	Samuel	Maria	1815	Liverpool	(?) Samuel	Flora (?)		Liverpool	gentlewoman
24228	Samuel	Maria	1818	Spitalfields, London	(?) Samuel			Hackney, London	lint maker
16960	Samuel	Maria	1835	Birmingham	(?) Samuel			Hammersmith, London	boarding school pupil
26635	Samuel	Mark	1806	Whitechapel, London	Samuel Samuel	Betsy Levy	Elizabeth Allen	Aldgate, London	fruit dealer
11171	Samuel	Mark	1826	Aldgate, London	Moshe Samuel		Hannah Abrahams	Aldgate, London	general dealer
20641	Samuel	Mark	1827	?, Poland				Spitalfields, London	journeyman tailor
15668	Samuel	Mark	1839	?, Poland	David Samuel	Hannah (?)		Aldgate, London	
20881	Samuel	Marks	1833	Liverpool	Israel Samuel	Catherine (?)		Liverpool	
16958	Samuel	Martha	1779	Middlesex, London	(?) Samuel			Hammersmith, London	housekeeper
14008	Samuel	Martha	1828	Norwich, Norfolk				Manchester	cook
17702	Samuel	Martha	1829	Portsmouth, Hampshire	(?) Samuel			Spitalfields, London	seamstress
31051	Samuel	Mary	1791	Ramsgate, Kent	(?)		(?) Samuel	Richmond, London	jeweller &c
5740	Samuel	Mary	1815	Llanelli, Wales			(?) Samuel	Swansea, Wales	
21904	Samuel	Mary	1846	?, Kent	Joseph Samuel	Esther (?)		Clerkenwell, London	
23262	Samuel	Mary A	1814	Whitechapel, London	(?) Samuel			Notting Hill, London	fundholder
28828	Samuel	Mathew	1810	?, Holland			Betsey (?)	Spitalfields, London	pencil seller
23340	Samuel	Michael	1792	Ipswich, Suffolk			Mary Catherine Parker	Piccadilly, London	merchant [---]
18860	Samuel	Michael	1801	Ipswich, Suffolk			Emma Jacobs	Colchester, Essex	pawnbroker empl 2
26615	Samuel	Michael	1816	Whitechapel, London	Abraham Samuel		Anna Catherine Mosely	City, London	tailor + draper
28075	Samuel	Michael	1827	Whitechapel, London	Eleazer Samuel		Elizabeth Solomons	Spitalfields, London	general dealer
8150	Samuel	Michael	1845	Aldgate, London	Samuel Samuel	Rebecca Lyons	Martha (?)	Aldgate, London	scholar
23790	Samuel	Milga	1825	?, Poland [Charmon, Prusha]	(?)		Jacob Samuel	Liverpool	
30849	Samuel	Miriam	1830	Cheltenham, Gloucestershire	Solomon Samuel	Dinah (?)		Bath	fur manufacturer
11890	Samuel	Mitch	1849	Aldgate, London	Lewis Samuel	Esther (?)		Whitechapel, London	
28690	Samuel	Mordica	1824	Middlesex, London	(?) Samuel	Rebecca (?)		Spitalfields, London	general dealer
19108	Samuel	Morris	1835	Stepney, London	James Samuel	Elizabeth Davis		Whitechapel, London	general dealer
22589	Samuel	Morris	1846	Whitechapel, London	Aaron Samuel	Phoebe Gottheil		Stepney, London	scholar
3597	Samuel	Moses	1795	Middlesex, London	Emanuel Menachem Samuel	Hanna (Hinde) Israel	Harriet Israel	Southport, Lancashire	watchmaker + Hebrew scholar + professor of languages
12176	Samuel	Moses	1797	Aldgate, London			Abigail Lea---	Whitechapel, London	linen draper, hosier &c
23332	Samuel	Moses	1811	?, Poland	Samuel Moses		Rosa Myers	Westminster, London	clothier
31229	Samuel	Moses	1820	?, Poland			Gitel (?)	Swansea, Wales	watchmaker
24704	Samuel	Moses	1826	City, London	Isaac Samuel	Deborah (?)		Walworth, London	clothier
28693	Samuel	Moses	1833	Middlesex, London	(?) Samuel	Rebecca (?)		Spitalfields, London	
10386	Samuel	Moses	1836	Aldgate, London				Spitalfields, London	apprentice

ID	surname	given names	born	birthplace	father	mother	spouse 1	1851 residence	1851 occupation
9988	Samuel	Moses	1847	Norwich, Norfolk	Samuel Samuel	Elizabeth Mordecai		Great Yarmouth, Norfolk	
19429	Samuel	Moses (Moss)	1825	Whitechapel, London	Isaac Samuel	Sarah Davis	Moses Samuel	Kennington, London	
9476	Samuel	Moss	1820	Birmingham			Eliza (?)	Aldgate, London	jeweller + cigar dealer
11750	Samuel	Moss	1836	Finsbury, London	(?) Samuel	Esther (?)		Shoreditch, London	cane dealer shopman
3769	Samuel	Nathan	1845	Spitalfields, London	(?) Samuel	Jane (?)		Spitalfields, London	scholar
20887	Samuel	Nathan	1847	Liverpool	Israel Samuel	Catherine (?)		Liverpool	
23791	Samuel	Nathan	1848	Liverpool	Jacob Samuel	Milga (?)		Liverpool	
24044	Samuel	Philip	1787	Middlesex, London	Moshe Samuel		Phoebe Israel	Marylebone, London	Stock Exchange
16023	Samuel	Phillip Henry	1834	?Shalford, ?Essex	Henry Samuel	Rachel (?)	Rebecca Andrade Da Costa	Whitechapel, London	apprentice upholsterer
29094	Samuel	Phoebe	1786	?, London	Meir Levy		Abraham Samuel	Whitechapel, London	watchmaker
24045	Samuel	Phoebe	1791	Middlesex, London	Shlomeh Israel		Philip Samuel	Marylebone, London	
26345	Samuel	Phoebe	1805	?, London	Isaac Cohen		Morris Samuel	Aldgate, London	confectioner
22587	Samuel	Phoebe	1823	Whitechapel, London	Bernherd (Yissachar) Gottheil		Aaron Samuel	Stepney, London	
1981	Samuel	Priscilla	1813	?, Cornwall			John Samuel	Swansea, Wales	
21906	Samuel	Priscilla	1850	Middlesex, London	Joseph Samuel	Esther (?)		Clerkenwell, London	
30563	Samuel	Priscilla	1851	Aldgate, London	Mark Samuel	Elizabeth Allen		Aldgate, London	
12781	Samuel	Rachael	1809	?, London	Pinchas Zeligman Mosely		Lyon Samuel	Aldgate, London	
15669	Samuel	Rachael	1842	?, Poland	David Samuel	Hannah (?)		Aldgate, London	
10505	Samuel	Rachel	1792	Aldgate, London	(?)		Solomon Samuel	Mile End, London	formerly milliner
21575	Samuel	Rachel	1795	Spitalfields, London	Yosef		Godfrey (Alexander) Samuel	Spitalfields, London	clothes dealer
16021	Samuel	Rachel	1807	Oxford, Oxfordshire	(?)		Henry Samuel	Whitechapel, London	
23611	Samuel	Rachel	1830	Great Yarmouth, Norfolk	Shreiner Wolf	Matilda (?)	Henry Israel Samuel	Liverpool	
28692	Samuel	Rachel	1832	Middlesex, London	(?) Samuel	Rebecca (?)		Spitalfields, London	
26504	Samuel	Rachel	1839	Middlesex, London	(?) Samuel			Dover, Kent	
23942	Samuel	Rachel	1844	Marylebone, London	Sim Samuel	Elizabeth (?)		Marylebone, London	scholar
10744	Samuel	Rachel	1847	?, London	Esslirani Samuel	Julia (?)		Spitalfields, London	scholar
28834	Samuel	Rachel	1847	?, Holland	Mathew Samuel	Betsey (?)		Spitalfields, London	scholar
17080	Samuel	Rachel	1848	Glasgow, Scotland	Samuel Samuel	Sophia (?)		Glasgow, Scotland	
10377	Samuel	Rainer	1829	Whitechapel, London	(?) Jacobs		Abraham Samuel	Spitalfields, London	general dealer
18568	Samuel	Ralph Henry	1810	Liverpool	(?) Samuel	Caby I--- (?)		Liverpool	
28689	Samuel	Rebecca	1791	?Middlesex, London	(?)		(?) Samuel	Spitalfields, London	
27842	Samuel	Rebecca	1796	?, Poland	(?)		Isaac Samuel	Spitalfields, London	dealer in old clothes
29825	Samuel	Rebecca	1800	Brighton, Sussex	(?)		(?) Samuel	Wapping, London	dressmaker
30847	Samuel	Rebecca	1815	Bath	Solomon Samuel	Dinah (?)		Bath	straw hat manufacturer
27843	Samuel	Rebecca	1818	?, Poland	Isaac Samuel	Rebecca (?)		Spitalfields, London	afflicted - does nothing
23311	Samuel	Rebecca	1821	Middlesex, London	Pinhas Samuel			Mayfair, London	fundholder
8149	Samuel	Rebecca	1826	?, London	M--- Lyons		Samuel Samuel	Aldgate, London	furrier
10679	Samuel	Rebecca	1826	Amsterdam, Holland	Solomon Samuel	Esther (?)		Spitalfields, London	
14755	Samuel	Rebecca	1833	Birmingham	(?) Samuel	Ann (?)		Finsbury, London	
14506	Samuel	Rebecca	1835	Philadelphia, USA	(?) Samuel	Rebecca (?)		Torquay, Devon	fund holder's daughter
26503	Samuel	Rebecca	1837	Middlesex, London	(?) Samuel			Dover, Kent	
17076	Samuel	Rebecca	1838	Middlesex, London	Samuel Samuel	Sophia (?)		Glasgow, Scotland	scholar
10742	Samuel	Rebecca	1841	?, London	Esslirani Samuel	Julia (?)		Spitalfields, London	scholar
27341	Samuel	Reuben	1836	Wapping, London	(?) Samuel	Jane		Aldgate, London	upholsterer

ID	surname	given names	born	birthplace	father	mother	spouse 1	1851 residence	1851 occupation
16569	Samuel	Robert	1847	Rio de Janeiro, Brazil	Ralph H Samuel			Liverpool	
21847	Samuel	Rodolph	1850	Clerkenwell, London	Isaac Samuel	Fanny (?)		Clerkenwell, London	
23333	Samuel	Rosa	1809	?, Germany	Alexander Myers		Moses Samuel	Westminster, London	domestic
3116	Samuel	Rosa	1831	Birmingham	Abraham Samuel	Lydia (?)	Lewis Wulfson	Birmingham	
11173	Samuel	Rosa	1849	Aldgate, London	Mark Samuel	Hannah Abrahams		Aldgate, London	
23562	Samuel	Rose	1802	Liverpool	(?) Samuel	Flora (?)		Liverpool	gentlewoman
15973	Samuel	Rose	1839	Aldgate, London	(?) Samuel			Covent Garden, London	
7698	Samuel	Rosetta	1848	Liverpool	Lewis (Louis) Samuel	Jane (?)	Abraham Ahlborn	Liverpool	
2707	Samuel	Rosianna	1818	?, England			Joseph Samuel	Glasgow, Scotland	
23944	Samuel	Sam	1848	Marylebone, London	Sim Samuel	Elizabeth (?)		Marylebone, London	
7247	Samuel	Sampson	1806	Whitechapel, London	Sampson Samuel	Rachel Davis	Esther Lazarus	Shoreditch, London	solicitor + attorney
19196	Samuel	Samuel	1763	City, London			Leah (?)	City, London	shell merchant
4937	Samuel	Samuel	1766	?, Poland [?, Prussia]			(?)	Birmingham	
12734	Samuel	Samuel	1787	Ipswich, Suffolk				Ipswich, Suffolk	retired merchant general
2071	Samuel	Samuel	1793	Hull, Yorkshire	Elhannon Anly (Henry)	Gitla Abraham	Deborah Myers	Louth, Lincolnshire	retired jeweller, proprietor of land + houses, shipowner
8148	Samuel	Samuel	1811	?Aldgate, London	Hyam Samuel	Catherine (?)	Rebecca Lyons	Aldgate, London	general dealer
17072	Samuel	Samuel	1811	Middlesex, London			Sophia (?)	Glasgow, Scotland	printer compositor
16351	Samuel	Samuel	1815	?Wapping, London	Emanuel (Mendel Menachem) Samuel	Amelia (Emelia) Emanuel		Wapping, London	furrier
21347	Samuel	Samuel	1817	Ipswich, Suffolk				Ipswich, Suffolk	general dealer
19157	Samuel	Samuel Lyon	1781	Sunderland, Co Durham			Hannah Moses	Aldgate, London	Hebrew teacher
5565	Samuel	Samuel Morris	1831	Middlesex, London	Morris Samuel	Phoebe Cohen	Esther Abrahams	Aldgate, London	watchmaker
16324	Samuel	Samuel Moses	1774	City, London			Esther (?)	Marylebone, London	merchant
26842	Samuel	Sarah	1797	?, London	(?) Samuel			Aldgate, London	shirt maker
14505	Samuel	Sarah	1806	Stoke Newington, London	(?)		(?) Samuel	Torquay, Devon	fund holder
23937	Samuel	Sarah	1832	Marylebone, London	Sim Samuel	Elizabeth (?)		Marylebone, London	
29827	Samuel	Sarah	1835	Spitalfields, London	(?) Samuel	Rebecca (?)		Wapping, London	furrier
22463	Samuel	Sarah	1842	?	(?) Michael			Gravesend, Kent	boarding school pupil
10743	Samuel	Sarah	1843	?, London	Esslirani Samuel	Julia (?)		Spitalfields, London	scholar
26640	Samuel	Sarah	1844	Aldgate, London	Mark Samuel	Elizabeth Allen		Aldgate, London	scholar
28833	Samuel	Sarah	1844	?, Holland	Mathew Samuel	Betsey (?)		Spitalfields, London	scholar
3770	Samuel	Sarah	1847	Spitalfields, London	(?) Samuel	Jane (?)		Spitalfields, London	scholar
11174	Samuel	Sarah	1850	Aldgate, London	Mark Samuel	Hannah Abrahams	Morris Levy	Aldgate, London	
23609	Samuel	Sarah	1850	Liverpool	Lewis (Louis) Samuel	Jane (?)		Liverpool	
6124	Samuel	Sarah	1851	Aldgate, London	Samuel Samuel	Rebecca Lyons	Abraham Emanuel	Aldgate, London	
5778	Samuel	Sarah Dora	1844	Liverpool	Israel Samuel	Catherine (?)	Aaron Joseph Jacobs	Liverpool	
23522	Samuel	Saul	1807	Liverpool			Eliza (?)	Liverpool	engraver
3472	Samuel	Saul	1811	Manchester	Abraham Samuel	Lydia (?)	Louisa Lazarus	Birmingham	pawnbroker
23935	Samuel	Sim	1809	Oxford			Elizabeth (?)	Marylebone, London	tailor + salesman
23964	Samuel	Simon	1785	?, London	David Samuel	Judith Levy	Esther Moses Samuel	Marylebone, London	merchant
6229	Samuel	Simon	1844	?, London	(?) Samuel	Alice (?)		Covent Garden, London	scholar
30850	Samuel	Solomon	1773	?, Germany			Dinah (?)	Bath	fur manufacturer
10504	Samuel	Solomon	1782	Whitechapel, London	Joseph Samuel		Rachel (?)	Mile End, London	formerly doctor

ID	surname	given names	born	birthplace	father	mother	spouse 1	1851 residence	1851 occupation
10676	Samuel	Solomon	1790	Amsterdam, Holland			Esther (?)	Spitalfields, London	merchant
11193	Samuel	Solomon	1797	Whitechapel, London				Aldgate, London	general dealer
8161	Samuel	Solomon	1823	Aldgate, London	Hyam Samuel	Catherine (?)	Catherine Hyam	Aldgate, London	general dealer
23566	Samuel	Solomon	1831	Manchester	Abraham Samuel	Sophia Aarons		Liverpool	hosier assistant
17079	Samuel	Solomon David	1846	?, England	Samuel Samuel	Sophia (?)		Glasgow, Scotland	
22911	Samuel	Sophia	1774	Amsterdam, Holland	(?)		(?) Samuel	Wapping, London	hatter
27263	Samuel	Sophia	1786	?, London	Joseph Davis		(?) Samuel	Aldgate, London	
23567	Samuel	Sophia	1793	?, Poland	(?) Aarons		Abraham Samuel	Liverpool	housekeeper
7652	Samuel	Sophia	1795	?	(?)		(?) Samuel	Aldgate, London	
17073	Samuel	Sophia	1812	Walworth, London	(?)		Samuel Samuel	Glasgow, Scotland	
28789	Samuel	Sophia	1825	Whitechapel, London	Lewin Phillip Samuel	(?)	Lazarus Kohn	Whitechapel, London	umbrella maker
12178	Samuel	Sophia	1830	Whitechapel, London	Moses Samuel	Abigail Lea---	(?)	Whitechapel, London	
10379	Samuel	Sophia	1836	Whitechapel, London	(?) Samuel			Spitalfields, London	general dealer
28694	Samuel	Susan	1835	Middlesex, London	(?) Samuel	Rebecca (?)		Spitalfields, London	
9478	Samuel	Sydney Montague	1848	Aldgate, London	Samuel Moss	Eliza (?)		Aldgate, London	
7576	Samuel	Sylvester Lewis	1823	Liverpool	Lewis (Yehuda) Samuel		Cecilia Wolff	Liverpool	watch mfr empl 104
21845	Samuel	Theodore	1845	Clerkenwell, London	Isaac Samuel	Fanny (?)		Clerkenwell, London	scholar
23612	Samuel	Walter	1830	Liverpool	Moses Samuel	Harriet (?)	Harriet Wolf	Liverpool	watchmaker
10506	Samuel	William	1832	Aldgate, London	Solomon Samuel	Rachel (?)		Mile End, London	journeyman furrier
31230	Samuel	William	1844	Swansea, Wales	John Samuel	Priscilla (?)		Swansea, Wales	
20866	Samuel	William H	1841	Liverpool	Lewis Henry Samuel	Caroline H (?)		Liverpool	scholar
12732	Samuel	Wolf	1815	Ipswich, Suffolk				Ipswich, Suffolk	furniture broker
4140	Samuel	Woolf	1825	Manchester	Abraham Samuel	Sophia Aarons	Amelia Alexander	Liverpool	smallware + hosier dealer
11192	Samuel	Zadic	1785	Whitechapel, London				Aldgate, London	general dealer
17888	Samuel (De Samuel)	Amelia	1814	Middlesex, London	Moses Samuel	Esther Cohen	Dennis Moses Samuel (De Samuel)	Regent's Park, London	
17889	Samuel (De Samuel)	Arthur	1837	Regent's Park, London	Dennis Moses Samuel (De Samuel)	Amelia Samuel		Regent's Park, London	scholar
17887	Samuel (De Samuel)	Dennis Moses	1783	Middlesex, London	Moses Samuel		Amelia Samuel	Regent's Park, London	merchant
17890	Samuel (De Samuel)	Frank	1843	Regent's Park, London	Dennis Moses Samuel (De Samuel)	Amelia Samuel		Regent's Park, London	scholar
6013	Samuel (De Samuel)	Louisa	1835	Regent's Park, London	Dennis Moses Samuel (De Samuel)	Amelia (?)	George de Worms	Regent's Park, London	scholar
11339	Samuel (Samuels)	David	1814	Aldgate, London	Moses Samuel (Samuels)	Sarah Davis	Martha Harris	Aldgate, London	general dealer
2764	Samuel (Samuels)	Elizabeth	1827	Aldgate, London	Moses Samuels	Sarah Davis	George Marks	Aldgate, London	
11341	Samuel (Samuels)	Rachael	1837	Aldgate, London	Moses Samuel (Samuels)	Sarah Davis	Benjamin Blasswerren	Aldgate, London	scholar
11338	Samuel (Samuels)	Sarah	1793	Aldgate, London	Shmuel Haf-Met Davis		Moses Samuel (Samuels)	Aldgate, London	greengrocer
18897	Samuel [Montagu]	Montagu [Samuel]	1832	Liverpool	Louis Samuel	Henrietta Israel	Ellen Cohen	City, London	clerk
8083	Samuels	Aaron	1835	Aldgate, London	Michael Samuels	Rebecca Levy		Aldgate, London	butcher journeyman
22358	Samuels	Adelaid	1842	Middlesex, London	(?) Samuels	Ann Lewis		Aldgate, London	
30619	Samuels	Adelaide	1851	Whitechapel, London	Samuel Samuels	Esther (?)		Whitechapel, London	
19820	Samuels	Amelia	1829	Portsmouth, Hampshire	Isaac Cohen	Phoebe Myer	Maurice (Morris) Samuels	Spitalfields, London	
22357	Samuels	Ann	1821	Middlesex, London	John Lewis	Rachal (?)	(?) Samuels	Aldgate, London	
2325	Samuels	Barnet	1824	?, Poland			Selia (?)	Leeds, Yorkshire	tailor

ID	surname	given names	born	birthplace	father	mother	spouse 1	1851 residence	1851 occupation
30808	Samuels	Benjamin	1825	Aldgate, London			Sarah Bailey	Covent Garden, London	cigar maker
18569	Samuels	Caroline	1822	Middlesex, London	(?)		David Samuels	Shoreditch, London	
2937	Samuels	Catherine	1841	Aldgate, London	Michael Samuels	Rebecca Levy	Moses Davis	Aldgate, London	scholar
28419	Samuels	Catherine	1851	Whitechapel, London	Joseph Samuels	Hester (?)		Spitalfields, London	
30745	Samuels	Daniel	1800	Aldgate, London			Elizabeth (?)	Aldgate, London	master baker empl 8
7476	Samuels	David	1820	Middlesex, London			Caroline (?)	Shoreditch, London	umbrella + parasol manufacturer
2331	Samuels	David	1823	?, Poland				Leeds, Yorkshire	hawker
30199	Samuels	David	1848	Dudley, Worcestershire	Levi Samuels	Mary Ann Jones		Dudley, Worcestershire	
18571	Samuels	David Leon	1849	Islington, London	David Samuels	Caroline (?)		Shoreditch, London	
30748	Samuels	Elias	1836	Whitechapel, London	Daniel Samuels	Elizabeth (?)		Aldgate, London	gra--er apprentice
4929	Samuels	Eliza	1808	?, London				Birmingham	
30746	Samuels	Elizabeth	1801	Spitalfields, London	(?)		Daniel Samuels	Aldgate, London	
9987	Samuels	Elizabeth	1824	Great Yarmouth, Norfolk	Isaac Mordecai	Ann Mayers	Samuel Samuel	Great Yarmouth, Norfolk	
19440	Samuels	Emanuel	1838	Wapping, London	Isaac Samuels	Sarah R (?)		Wapping, London	scholar
4928	Samuels	Emanuel Isaac	1851	Birmingham	Joseph Samuels	Sara (?)		Birmingham	
30753	Samuels	Emma	1830	Chelsea, London	(?) Samuels			Bloomsbury, London	cook
26818	Samuels	Esther	1820	Southwark, London			Samuel Samuels	Whitechapel, London	
13205	Samuels	Esther	1823	Middlesex, London	(?) Samuels			Whitechapel, London	
16859	Samuels	Esther	1842	Sunderland, Co Durham	Levy Samuels	Sophia (?)		Sunderland, Co Durham	
26819	Samuels	Esther	1844	Middlesex, London	Samuel Samuels	Esther (?)		Whitechapel, London	scholar
1294	Samuels	Fanny	1850	Plymouth, Devon	Samuel Samuels	Jenette (Janette, Jeanette) Moses		Plymouth, Devon	
26820	Samuels	George	1845	Spitalfields, London	Samuel Samuels	Esther (?)		Whitechapel, London	scholar
22470	Samuels	Hannah	1825	?, England	(?)		Saul Samuels	St Helier, Jersey, Channel Islands	
17948	Samuels	Hannah	1833	?, London	(?) Samuels			Whitechapel, London	
1293	Samuels	Hannah	1849	Plymouth, Devon	Samuel Samuels	Jenette (Janette, Jeanette) Moses	Edward M Marcoso	Plymouth, Devon	
2048	Samuels	Hannah	1849	Aldgate, London	Michael Samuels	Rebecca Levy		Aldgate, London	
28418	Samuels	Hannah	1849	Whitechapel, London	Joseph Samuels	Hester (?)		Spitalfields, London	
19437	Samuels	Henry	1827	Wapping, London	Isaac Samuels	Sarah R (?)		Wapping, London	leather cutter
8084	Samuels	Henry	1838	Aldgate, London	Michael Samuels	Rebecca Levy		Aldgate, London	butcher
21041	Samuels	Henry	1842	Colchester, Essex				Dover, Kent	boarding school pupil
16861	Samuels	Henry	1845	Spitalfields, London	Levy Samuels	Sophia (?)		Sunderland, Co Durham	
28417	Samuels	Hester	1822	New York, USA	(?)		Joseph Samuels	Spitalfields, London	
22468	Samuels	Hyam	1849	St Helier, Jersey, Channel Islands	Moses Samuels	Rachel (Rebecca) Hart		St Helier, Jersey, Channel Islands	
9210	Samuels	Hyman	1814	?, Poland	Samuel Samuels			Spitalfields, London	watch maker
8085	Samuels	Hyman	1841	Aldgate, London	Michael Samuels	Rebecca Levy		Aldgate, London	scholar
19435	Samuels	Isaac	1796	Warsaw, Poland			Sarah R (?)	Wapping, London	watchmaker
18037	Samuels	Isaac	1812	?, Russia				Dudley, Worcestershire	hawker of jewellery
19822	Samuels	Isaac	1850	?, London	Maurice (Morris) Samuels	Amelia (?)		Spitalfields, London	
29240	Samuels	Isaacs	1815	Middlesex, London	Ariel		Sarah Moss	Whitechapel, London	clothier
2328	Samuels	Jacob	1848	Leeds, Yorkshire	Barnet Samuels	Selia (?)		Leeds, Yorkshire	

ID	surname	given names	born	birthplace	father	mother	spouse 1	1851 residence	1851 occupation
1291	Samuels	Jenette (Janette, Jeanette)	1821	Exeter, Devon	(?) Moses	Hannah (?)	Samuel Samuels	Plymouth, Devon	
22471	Samuels	Joel	1845	St Helier, Jersey, Channel Islands	Saul Samuels	Hannah (?)		St Helier, Jersey, Channel Islands	
24860	Samuels	John	1801	?Aldgate, London			(?)	Bermondsey, London	furrier
4926	Samuels	Joseph	1821	Limehouse, London	Emanuel (Menachem) Samuel	Polly Mayers	Sara Harris	Birmingham	lapidary
28415	Samuels	Joseph	1824	Whitechapel, London			Hester (?)	Spitalfields, London	general dealer
28416	Samuels	Joseph	1824	Whitechapel, London			Elizabeth Phillips	Spitalfields, London	general dealer
21073	Samuels	Joseph	1838	?, London				Dover, Kent	boarding school pupil
16863	Samuels	Joseph	1850	Sunderland, Co Durham	Levy Samuels	Sophia (?)	Fanny Hyams	Sunderland, Co Durham	
18572	Samuels	Joseph Naphtali	1850	Shoreditch, London	David Samuels	Caroline (?)		Shoreditch, London	
22359	Samuels	Julia	1844	Middlesex, London	(?) Samuels	Ann Lewis		Aldgate, London	
2047	Samuels	Julia	1845	Whitechapel, London	Michael Samuels	Rebecca Levy		Whitechapel, London	scholar
24510	Samuels	Kate	1816	Chichester, Sussex	(?) Samuels			New Cross, London	
2046	Samuels	Leah	1843	Whitechapel, London	Michael Samuels	Rebecca Levy		Aldgate, London	scholar
30196	Samuels	Levi	1826	?, Poland [?, Prussia]			Mary Ann Jones	Dudley, Worcestershire	glazier + painter
16856	Samuels	Levy	1811	?, Poland			Sophia (?)	Sunderland, Co Durham	glazier
16858	Samuels	Marian (Miriam)	1840	Sunderland, Co Durham	Levy Samuels	Sophia (?)	Isaac Abrahams	Sunderland, Co Durham	
24862	Samuels	Mary	1842	Southwark, London	John Samuels	(?)		Bermondsey, London	
30664	Samuels	Mary	1851	Whitechapel, London	Isaacs Samuels	Sarah Moss		Whitechapel, London	
30197	Samuels	Mary Ann	1820	Dudley, Worcestershire	(?) Jones		Levi Samuels	Dudley, Worcestershire	
22467	Samuels	Mary Ann Margaret (Minnie)	1846	St Helier, Jersey, Channel Islands	Moses Samuels	Rachel (Rebecca) Hart	David Crawcour	St Helier, Jersey, Channel Islands	
19819	Samuels	Maurice (Morris)	1822	Poznan, Poland [Posen, Prussia]			Amelia Cohen	Spitalfields, London	glazier
2043	Samuels	Michael	1813	Whitechapel, London	Hyam Samuel	Catherine (?)	Rebecca Levy	Aldgate, London	clothes dealer
19438	Samuels	Miriam	1829	Wapping, London	Isaac Samuels	Sarah R (?)		Wapping, London	straw bonnet maker
29246	Samuels	Morris	1849	Middlesex, London	Isaacs Samuels	Sarah Moss		Whitechapel, London	scholar
22465	Samuels	Moses	1822	?, Poland			Rachel (Rebecca) Hart	St Helier, Jersey, Channel Islands	
2330	Samuels	Paulina	1851	?, London	Barnet Samuels	Selia (?)		Leeds, Yorkshire	
30357	Samuels	Philip	1830	Whitechapel, London				St Giles, London	tailor's clerk
29245	Samuels	Phillip	1846	Middlesex, London	Isaacs Samuels	Sarah Moss		Whitechapel, London	scholar
1292	Samuels	Phillip	1848	Plymouth, Devon	Samuel Samuels	Jenette (Janette, Jeanette) Moses		Plymouth, Devon	
29244	Samuels	Rachael	1844	Middlesex, London	Isaacs Samuels	Sarah Moss		Whitechapel, London	scholar
2327	Samuels	Rachael	1847	Leeds, Yorkshire	Barnet Samuels	Selia (?)		Leeds, Yorkshire	
22466	Samuels	Rachel (Rebecca)	1822	?, England	(?) Hart		Moses Samuels	St Helier, Jersey, Channel Islands	
2044	Samuels	Rebecca	1815	Whitechapel, London			Michael Samuels	Aldgate, London	
29242	Samuels	Rosa	1838	Middlesex, London	Isaacs Samuels	Sarah Moss		Whitechapel, London	
26822	Samuels	Rosa	1849	Spitalfields, London	Samuel Samuels	Esther (?)		Whitechapel, London	scholar
16860	Samuels	Rose (Rosalie)	1843	Newcastle Upon Tyne	Levy Samuels	Sophia (?)	Jacob Simons	Sunderland, Co Durham	
9209	Samuels	Samuel	1779	Boston, USA			(?)	Spitalfields, London	watch maker

ID	surname	given names	born	birthplace	father	mother	spouse 1	1851 residence	1851 occupation
26817	Samuels	Samuel	1818	Whitechapel, London			Esther (?)	Whitechapel, London	watchmaker + finisher empl 16
1290	Samuels	Samuel	1819	Warsaw, Poland			Jenette (Janette, Jeanette) Moses	Plymouth, Devon	general dealer
30747	Samuels	Samuel	1834	Whitechapel, London	Daniel Samuels	Elizabeth (?)		Aldgate, London	
24861	Samuels	Samuel	1835	Southwark, London	John Samuels	(?)		Bermondsey, London	furrier
19439	Samuels	Samuel	1836	Wapping, London	Isaac Samuels	Sarah R (?)		Wapping, London	slipper maker
29243	Samuels	Samuel	1842	Middlesex, London	Isaacs Samuels	Sarah Moss		Whitechapel, London	scholar
16862	Samuels	Samuel	1848	Sunderland, Co Durham	Levy Samuels	Sophia (?)		Sunderland, Co Durham	
18570	Samuels	Samuel Levy	1848	Whitechapel, London	David Samuels	Caroline (?)		Shoreditch, London	
4927	Samuels	Sara	1828	Whitechapel, London	Henry Harris	Elizabeth Samuels	Joseph Samuels	Birmingham	
29241	Samuels	Sarah	1819	Middlesex, London	(?) Moss		Isaacs Samuels	Whitechapel, London	
30809	Samuels	Sarah	1824	Whitechapel, London	(?) Bailey		Benjamin Samuels	Covent Garden, London	
23911	Samuels	Sarah	1838	Whitechapel, London	(?) Samuels			Marylebone, London	patient
19821	Samuels	Sarah	1847	?, London	Maurice (Morris) Samuels	Amelia (?)		Spitalfields, London	
2329	Samuels	Sarah	1850	Leeds, Yorkshire	Barnet Samuels	Selia (?)		Leeds, Yorkshire	
19436	Samuels	Sarah R	1798	Aldgate, London	(?)		Isaac Samuels	Wapping, London	
22469	Samuels	Saul	1820	?, Poland			Hannah (?)	St Helier, Jersey, Channel Islands	dealer in jewellery + hardware
2326	Samuels	Selia	1826	?, Poland [?, Prussia]			Barnet Samuels	Leeds, Yorkshire	
22473	Samuels	Selina	1850	St Helier, Jersey, Channel Islands	Saul Samuels	Hannah (?)		St Helier, Jersey, Channel Islands	
30200	Samuels	Seth	1849	Dudley, Worcestershire	Levi Samuels	Mary Ann Jones		Dudley, Worcestershire	gun lock filer
30198	Samuels	Simeon	1846	Dudley, Worcestershire	Levi Samuels	Mary Ann Jones		Dudley, Worcestershire	
19285	Samuels	Simon	1820	?				Birmingham	hawker
16857	Samuels	Sophia	1811	Spalding, Lincolnshire	(?)		Levy Samuels	Sunderland, Co Durham	
26821	Samuels	Sophia	1847	Spitalfields, London	Samuel Samuels	Esther (?)		Whitechapel, London	scholar
22472	Samuels	Tobias	1848	St Helier, Jersey, Channel Islands	Saul Samuels	Hannah (?)		St Helier, Jersey, Channel Islands	
9916	Samuels (Samuel)	Abigail (Haby, Ellen)	1822	Lambeth, London	Samuel Levy		Lewis Samuels (Samuel)	Waterloo, London	general dealer
9917	Samuels (Samuel)	Benjamin	1839	Lambeth, London	Lewis Samuels (Samuel)	Abigail (Haby, Ellen) Levy		Waterloo, London	
9918	Samuels (Samuel)	Charles	1841	Lambeth, London	Lewis Samuels (Samuel)	Abigail (Haby, Ellen) Levy		Waterloo, London	
9921	Samuels (Samuel)	David	1849	Lambeth, London	Lewis Samuels (Samuel)	Abigail (Haby, Ellen) Levy		Waterloo, London	
9922	Samuels (Samuel)	Debiah	1850	Lambeth, London	Lewis Samuels (Samuel)	Abigail (Haby, Ellen) Levy		Waterloo, London	
9915	Samuels (Samuel)	Lewis	1812	Aldgate, London	Isaac Samuel	Deborah (?)	Abigail (Haby, Ellen) Levy	Waterloo, London	general dealer
9920	Samuels (Samuel)	Lipman	1845	Lambeth, London	Lewis Samuels (Samuel)	Abigail (Haby, Ellen) Levy	Elizabeth (?)	Waterloo, London	
9919	Samuels (Samuel)	Samuel	1842	Lambeth, London	Lewis Samuels (Samuel)	Abigail (Haby, Ellen) Levy	Selina Cloud	Waterloo, London	
25610	Samuelson	Clara (Chava)	1846	Dublin, Ireland	Elias Samuelson	Sarah (?)	Marcus Bebro	Dublin, Ireland	
25608	Samuelson	Elias	1826	Wroclaw, Poland [Breslau, Prussia]			Sarah (?)	Dublin, Ireland	military + merchant tailor
2561	Samuelson	Martin	1825	Hamburg, Germany			Sarah Vines (?)	Hull, Yorkshire	
25612	Samuelson	Rachel	1850	Dublin, Ireland	Elias Samuelson	Sarah (?)		Dublin, Ireland	
25611	Samuelson	Rodolph	1848	Dublin, Ireland	Elias Samuelson	Sarah (?)		Dublin, Ireland	
25609	Samuelson	Sarah	1824	Middlesex, London	(?)		Elias Samuelson	Dublin, Ireland	

ID	surname	given names	born	birthplace	father	mother	spouse 1	1851 residence	1851 occupation
2562	Samuelson	Sarah Vines	1827	Middle Cheney (Northumberland?)			Martin Samuelson	Hull, Yorkshire	
30172	Sandenierski	Eli	1821	?, Poland				Dudley, Worcestershire	glazier
11795	Sanders	Adel	1821	?, France	(?)		Mark Sanders	Shoreditch, London	
29329	Sanders	Anna	1849	?, London	Marcus N Sanders	Isabella (?)		Whitechapel, London	
29327	Sanders	Caroline	1844	?, Poland	Marcus N Sanders	Isabella (?)		Whitechapel, London	
29326	Sanders	Isabella	1823	?, Poland	(?)		Marcus N Sanders	Whitechapel, London	
11796	Sanders	Jane	1842	?, France	Mark Sanders	Adel (?)		Shoreditch, London	
30355	Sanders	Lewis	1831	Strand, London				St Giles, London	tailor's clerk
29325	Sanders	Marcus N	1813	?, Poland			Isabella (?)	Whitechapel, London	tailor
29328	Sanders	Maria	1848	?, Poland	Marcus N Sanders	Isabella (?)		Whitechapel, London	
11794	Sanders	Mark	1813	?, Holland			Adel (?)	Shoreditch, London	merchant
29330	Sanders	Solomon	1834	?, Poland				Whitechapel, London	tailor
29410	Sanders (Saunders)	Aaron	1802	Warsaw, Poland	Alexander Saunders		(?)	Spitalfields, London	stay maker
29411	Sanders (Saunders)	Rosetta	1805	Brussels, Belgium	Simon Marinus		Aaron Sanders (Saunders)	Spitalfields, London	stay maker
29413	Sanders (Saunders)	Sander	1843	Spitalfields, London	Aaron Sanders (Saunders)	Rosetta Marinus		Spitalfields, London	scholar
29412	Sanders (Saunders)	Sarah	1841	Whitechapel, London	Aaron Sanders (Saunders)	Rosetta Marinus		Spitalfields, London	scholar
25619	Sandheim	Abraham	1851	Dublin, Ireland	Julius Sandheim	Miriam (Marian) Davidson		Dublin, Ireland	
25615	Sandheim	Bendix Julius	1844	Dublin, Ireland	Julius Sandheim	Miriam (Marian) Davidson		Dublin, Ireland	
25618	Sandheim	David	1849	Dublin, Ireland	Julius Sandheim	Miriam (Marian) Davidson		Dublin, Ireland	
25616	Sandheim	Isaac	1846	Dublin, Ireland	Julius Sandheim	Miriam (Marian) Davidson	Annie Woodburn	Dublin, Ireland	
25613	Sandheim	Julius	1813	?			Marian (Miriam) Davidson	Dublin, Ireland	reader, shochet + mohel
25614	Sandheim	Marian (Miriam)	1818	Dublin, Ireland	Isaac Davidson	Catherine Ansell	Julius Sandheim	Dublin, Ireland	reader, shochet + mohel
25617	Sandheim	Martha	1848	Dublin, Ireland	Julius Sandheim	Miriam (Marian) Davidson	Norman Berlin	Dublin, Ireland	
15791	Sanguinos	Leon	1830	Gibraltar				King's Cross, London	commission agent
7376	Saphir	Adolph	1831	Budapest, Hungary	Israel Saphir	Henrietta Bondij	Sara Owen	Glasgow, Scotland	theology student
26668	Saqui	Abraham	1782	Whitechapel, London	Isaac de Abraham Saqui	Rebecca de Jacob Julião	Hannah de Joseph Abendana	Spitalfields, London	accountant
7478	Saqui	Abraham Austin	1834	Aldgate, London	Isaac de Abraham Saqui	Maria (Miriam) de David	Julia (Judith) Rothschild	Spitalfields, London	professor of music apprentice
27017	Saqui	Benjamin	1835	Middlesex, London	Jacob de Isaac Saqui	Maria de Menahem Manis		Aldgate, London	cigar maker
26669	Saqui	Hannah	1831	Shoreditch, London	Isaac de Abraham Saqui	Maria (Miriam) de David	Robert Hart	Spitalfields, London	
27018	Saqui	Hannah	1838	Middlesex, London	Jacob de Isaac Saqui	Maria de Menahem Manis	Michael Bersnstein	Aldgate, London	cap maker
18877	Saqui	Isaac	1806	Stepney, London	Abraham de Isaac Saqui	Hannah de Joseph Abendana	Maria (Miriam) de David Moss	Spitalfields, London	professor of music
27372	Saqui	Isaac	1822	Mile End, London	Jacob de Isaac Saqui	Maria de Menahem Manis		Aldgate, London	grocer empl 1
18880	Saqui	Julia (Judith)	1843	Stepney, London	Isaac de Abraham Saqui	Maria (Miriam) de David	William Green	Spitalfields, London	scholar
27016	Saqui	Maria	1808	Aldgate, London	Menahem Manis		Jacob de Isaac Saqui	Aldgate, London	general dealer
18881	Saqui	Rachel	1847	Spitalfields, London	Isaac de Abraham Saqui	Maria (Miriam) de David	Samuel Charles Lyons	Spitalfields, London	
18879	Saqui	Rebecca	1840	Shoreditch, London	Isaac de Abraham Saqui	Maria (Miriam) de David	William Smith	Spitalfields, London	scholar
26670	Saqui	Sarah	1819	Bethnal Green, London	Abraham de Isaac Saqui	Hannah de Joseph Abendana		Spitalfields, London	
18878	Saqui	Sarah	1838	Aldgate, London	Isaac de Abraham Saqui	Maria (Miriam) de David	Charles Eugene Pratt	Spitalfields, London	
9297	Sarfaty	Grace	1771	Sydenham, London	Abraham Sarfaty	Sarah Cortissos		Aldgate, London	poor
10811	Sarfaty	Miriam (Amelia)	1851	Spitalfields, London	Joseph Baruch Sarfaty (Searphita)	Hannah Mentser		Spitalfields, London	

ID	surname	given names	born	birthplace	father	mother	spouse 1	1851 residence	1851 occupation
10810	Sarfaty (Searphita)	Barnett Joseph	1849	Spitalfields, London	Joseph Baruch Sarfaty (Searphita)	Hannah Mentser	Margaret (Maggie) (?)	Spitalfields, London	
10809	Sarfaty (Searphita)	Hannah	1828	Amsterdam, Holland	(?)		Joseph Baruch Sarfaty (Searphita)	Spitalfields, London	
10808	Sarfaty (Searphita)	Joseph Baruch	1828	Amsterdam, Holland	Baruch Sarfaty		Hannah Mentser	Spitalfields, London	cigar maker
4901	Saskulch	Maxe	1825	?, Poland [?, Prussia]				Birmingham	tailor
18177	Saul	Harriot	1824	Aldgate, London	Saul Saul	(?)		Mile End, London	
18175	Saul	Jane	1810	Whitechapel, London	Saul Saul	(?)		Mile End, London	
14958	Saul	Sarah	1837	?, Portugal	(?) Saul			Bethnal Green, London	boarding school pupil
18174	Saul	Saul	1782	Aldgate, London				Mile End, London	meat salesman
18176	Saul	Sophia	1817	Whitechapel, London	Saul Saul	(?)		Mile End, London	
28674	Saunders	Abraham	1813	?, Poland	Solomon Sanders		Martha Solomons	Spitalfields, London	cap maker
28871	Saunders	Anah	1839	Spitalfields, London	(?) Saunders	Julia		Spitalfields, London	scholar
22689	Saunders	Asher	1841	Aldgate, London	Philip Saunders	Juliet (Julia) Myers		Whitechapel, London	scholar
3821	Saunders	Catherine	1808	Hull, Yorkshire			Moses Saunders	Spitalfields, London	dealer in slippers
18992	Saunders	Elizabeth	1831	Whitechapel, London	(?) Saunders			Aldgate, London	blackborderer
20789	Saunders	Elizabeth	1841	Spitalfields, London	Samuel Baruch Saunders [Solomons]	Sophia Jacobs	Lewis Levine	Aldgate, London	
18991	Saunders	Ellen	1823	Whitechapel, London	(?) Saunders			Aldgate, London	blackborderer
6330	Saunders	Esther	1837	Spitalfields, London	(?) Saunders	Catherine (?)	Morris Defries	Spitalfields, London	tailoress
20793	Saunders	Eva Rebecca	1849	Spitalfields, London	Samuel Baruch Saunders [Solomons]	Sophia Jacobs	Isaac Zachariah	Aldgate, London	
11586	Saunders	Fanny	1851	Whitechapel, London	Goodman Saunders	Phoebe (?)		Aldgate, London	
11578	Saunders	Goodman	1805	?, France			(?)	Aldgate, London	general dealer
13040	Saunders	Hannah	1817	Whitechapel, London	Asher Saunders			Spitalfields, London	tailoress
30665	Saunders	Hannah	1851	Whitechapel, London	Philip Saunders	Juliet (Julia) Myers		Whitechapel, London	
10757	Saunders	Hanny	1838	Whitechapel, London	(?) Saunders			Spitalfields, London	employed out doors NK
3826	Saunders	Jane	1840	Spitalfields, London	Moses Saunders	Catherine (?)	Louis (Lewis) Preager (Prager)	Spitalfields, London	scholar
20794	Saunders	John (Jacob) Barnet	1851	Spitalfields, London	Samuel Baruch Saunders [Solomons]	Sophia Jacobs		Aldgate, London	
4931	Saunders	Joseph	1825	?, Poland [?, Prussia]				Birmingham	dealer in watch materials
3823	Saunders	Joseph	1834	Spitalfields, London	Moses Saunders	Catherine (?)		Spitalfields, London	general dealer
28870	Saunders	Julia	1813	Portsmouth, Hampshire	(?)		(?) Saunders	Spitalfields, London	nurse
22688	Saunders	Juliet (Julia)	1816	Aldgate, London	Moses Myers		Philip Saunders	Whitechapel, London	
11584	Saunders	Kate	1845	Whitechapel, London	Goodman Saunders	Phoebe (?)		Aldgate, London	
20788	Saunders	Lazarus	1839	Spitalfields, London	Samuel Baruch Saunders [Solomons]	Sophia Jacobs	Elizabeth Levy	Aldgate, London	
22972	Saunders	Leah	1827	Whitechapel, London	(?) Saunders	(?) Woolf		Aldgate, London	fruit seller
28676	Saunders	Leah	1842	?Spitalfields, London	Abraham Saunders	Martha Solomons		Spitalfields, London	
4930	Saunders	Louis	1828	?, Poland [?, Prussia]				Birmingham	jeweller
11585	Saunders	Louisa	1847	Whitechapel, London	Goodman Saunders	Phoebe (?)		Aldgate, London	
3822	Saunders	Mark	1828	Manchester	Moses Saunders	Catherine (?)	Blanco Belasco	Spitalfields, London	general dealer
28675	Saunders	Martha	1809	Middlesex, London	Levy Solomons		Abraham Saunders	Spitalfields, London	
3827	Saunders	Mary	1843	Spitalfields, London	Moses Saunders	Catherine (?)	Aaron Levy	Spitalfields, London	scholar
22690	Saunders	Mary	1845	Spitalfields, London	Philip Saunders	Juliet (Julia) Myers		Whitechapel, London	

ID	surname	given names	born	birthplace	father	mother	spouse 1	1851 residence	1851 occupation
20792	Saunders	Mordecai (Mark)	1846	Spitalfields, London	Samuel Baruch Saunders [Solomons]	Sophia Jacobs	Rebecca Hains	Aldgate, London	
20790	Saunders	Moses (Daniel)	1842	Spitalfields, London	Samuel Baruch Saunders [Solomons]	Sophia Jacobs	Deborah Davis	Aldgate, London	
22687	Saunders	Philip	1817	Aldgate, London	Asher Saunders		Juliet (Julia) Myers	Whitechapel, London	rag merchant
11579	Saunders	Phoebe	1815	Whitechapel, London	(?)		Goodman Saunders	Aldgate, London	general dealer
11582	Saunders	Rosa	1841	Whitechapel, London	Goodman Saunders	Phoebe (?)	John Jacobs	Aldgate, London	
10756	Saunders	Rosy	1777	Aldgate, London	(?)		(?) Saunders	Spitalfields, London	
6582	Saunders	Sarah	1843	Whitechapel, London	Goodman Saunders	Phoebe (?)	Solomon (Judah) Isaacs	Aldgate, London	
3824	Saunders	Saunders	1835	Spitalfields, London	Moses Saunders	Catherine (?)		Spitalfields, London	errand boy
20791	Saunders	Saunders (Alexander)	1844	Spitalfields, London	Samuel Baruch Saunders [Solomons]	Sophia Jacobs	Catherine (Kate) Hains	Aldgate, London	
20787	Saunders	Solomon	1838	Spitalfields, London	Samuel Baruch Saunders [Solomons]	Sophia Jacobs	Sarah Brandon	Aldgate, London	
20785	Saunders [Solomons]	Samuel Baruch	1816	Czestchowa, Poland	Shlomo		Sophia Jacobs	Aldgate, London	cap maker + trader
20786	Saunders [Solomons]	Sophia	1814	Brummen, Holland	Eliezer Jacobs		Samuel Baruch Saunders [Solomons]	Aldgate, London	
2563	Sax	Abraham	1819	?, Poland			Teresa (Dorah) (?)	Hull, Yorkshire	plumber + glazier
31231	Sax	David	1851	Hull, Yorkshire	Abraham Sax	Teresa (Dorah) (?)		Hull, Yorkshire	
2565	Sax	Levi (Lewis)	1845	?, Poland	Abraham Sax	Teresa (Dorah) (?)		Hull, Yorkshire	
2566	Sax	Simon	1849	Hull, Yorkshire	Abraham Sax	Teresa (Dorah) (?)		Hull, Yorkshire	
2564	Sax	Teresa (Dorah)	1823	?, Poland			Abraham Sax	Hull, Yorkshire	plumber + glazier's wife
29953	Schaper	Joseph	1824	?, Germany				Whitechapel, London	glazier
29100	Schauchenberg	Henry	1804	Hanover, Germany			J--- (?)	Whitechapel, London	tobacco cutter
29905	Schaurig	Franz	1822	?, Germany				Wapping, London	cigar maker
2567	Scheaman	Alexander	1814	?, Germany				Hull, Yorkshire	
18940	Scherwin	Caroline	1812	Bavaria, Germany	(?)		(?) Scherwin	Shoreditch, London	cook
26227	Scherzwin	Moses	1817	Cracow, Poland				Aldgate, London	traveller
4283	Scheutrab	Clement	1825	?, Poland [?, Prussia]				Birmingham	working jeweller
17133	Scheyer	Emanuel B	1831	?, Germany				Bradford, Yorkshire	clerk, worsted yarn trade
7516	Scheyer	Solomon	1797	?			(?)	Whitechapel, London	wholesale shoe mfr
30620	Schiff	Abraham	1851	Whitechapel, London	Saling Schiff	Katherine Moseley		Whitechapel, London	
26040	Schiff	Amelia	1834	Deptford, London	Abraham Schiff	Ernestina (?)	Joseph Saunders	Whitechapel, London	domestic
26039	Schiff	Emma	1826	?, Poland [?, Prussia]	Abraham Schiff	Ernestina (?)		Whitechapel, London	domestic
26041	Schiff	Ernestina	1795	?, Poland [?, Prussia]	(?)		Abraham Schiff	Whitechapel, London	domestic
26038	Schiff	Jenny	1815	?, Poland [?, Prussia]	(?)		Lewis (Louis) Schiff	Whitechapel, London	cigar manufacturer
11775	Schiff	Katherine	1824	Aldgate, London	Moses Moseley	Rosetta Samuel	Saling Schiff	Whitechapel, London	
26037	Schiff	Lewis (Louis)	1818	?, Poland [?, Prussia]	Abraham Schiff	Ernestina (?)	Jenny (?)	Whitechapel, London	cigar manufacturer
2202	Schiff	Meyer	1804	Nordhausen, Germany [Prussia]				Oxford, Oxfordshire	jewellery dealer
11778	Schiff	Moses	1849	Whitechapel, London	Saling Schiff	Katherine Moseley		Whitechapel, London	
11776	Schiff	Saling	1823	?, Poland [?, Prussia]	Abraham Schiff	Ernestina (?)	Katherine Moseley	Whitechapel, London	cigar manufacturer (master)
11777	Schiff	Theresa	1847	Southwark, London	Saling Schiff	Katherine Moseley		Whitechapel, London	

ID	surname	given names	born	birthplace	father	mother	spouse 1	1851 residence	1851 occupation
29960	Schiler	Ludwig	1823	Dublin, Ireland				Whitechapel, London	butcher
14137	Schiller-Szinessy	Solomon Marcus	1820	Budapest, Hungary			Georgiana Eleanor (Sarah) Herbert	Manchester	local Rabbi of the Hebrew tongue
13615	Schilman	Joseph	1827	?, Poland [?, Prussia]				Manchester	tailor
26749	Schilsky	Julius	1829	?, Poland [?, Prussia]				Aldgate, London	hardwareman
14949	Schleinger	Caroline	1836	Liverpool	(?) Schleinger			Bethnal Green, London	boarding school pupil
30069	Schlesinger	Adelaide	1832	?, London	Michael Samuel Schlesinger	Annie (Hindela) (?)	Walter Oxford Ewer	Bloomsbury, London	
24294	Schlesinger	Alice	1850	?, London	Max Schlesinger	Belinda (Bella) Wertheimer		Bloomsbury, London	
30067	Schlesinger	Annie	1805	?, London	Eliezer		Michael Samuel Schlesinger	Bloomsbury, London	
30072	Schlesinger	Augustus Arnold	1835	Middlesex, London	Michael Samuel Schlesinger	Anette (Hindela) (?)	Nora Kelly	Bloomsbury, London	
24292	Schlesinger	Belinda (Bella)	1827	Whitechapel, London	John Wertheimer	Anette (?)	Max Schlesinger	Bloomsbury, London	
943	Schlesinger	Caroline	1809	Hamburg, Germany	(?)		(?Morris) Schlesinger	Exeter, Devon	
30068	Schlesinger	Charles Frederick	1827	Surrey, London	Michael Samuel Schlesinger	Annie (Hindela) (?)	Emily Elizabeth Streatfield	Bloomsbury, London	commission agent
30071	Schlesinger	Edward	1834	?, London	Michael Samuel Schlesinger	Annie (Hindela) (?)	Emma Louisa Pugh	Bloomsbury, London	writing clerk
30073	Schlesinger	Fanny Matilda	1839	Greenwich, London	Michael Samuel Schlesinger	Annie (Hindela) (?)	Alfred Barton Pearson	Bloomsbury, London	
30070	Schlesinger	Georgiana	1833	?, London	Michael Samuel Schlesinger	Annie (Hindela) (?)	Henry Speechley	Bloomsbury, London	
944	Schlesinger	Joanna	1835	?, Germany	(?Morris) Schlesinger	Caroline		Exeter, Devon	
24558	Schlesinger	Joseph	1819	Frankfurt-am-Main, Germany			Sarah Ann Herbert	Brixton, London	merchant
14154	Schlesinger	Louis	1828	Frankfurt-am-Main, Germany			Charlotte (Carlotta) Samuel	Manchester	clerk in shipping house
24293	Schlesinger	Max	1821	?, Hungary			Belinda (Bella) Wertheimer	Bloomsbury, London	doctor of medicine
24298	Schlesinger	Michael Samuel	1791	?, Poland [?, Prussia]	Samuel Schlesinger		Annie (Hindela) (?)	Bloomsbury, London	commission agent
1443	Schlesinger	Morris	1800	?, Poland [?, Prussia]			Caroline (?)	Plymouth, Devon	tobacconist
30074	Schlesinger	William James	1843	Holborn, London	Michael Samuel Schlesinger	Annie (?)	Louisa Morton	Bloomsbury, London	
16293	Schlochauer	William	1820	?, Germany				Dundee, Scotland	
7377	Schloss	David Frederick	1850	Liverpool	Sigismund Schloss	Rebecca Mocatta	Rachel Sophia Waley	Liverpool	
7381	Schloss	Herbert	1851	Liverpool	Sigismund Schloss	Rebecca Mocatta		Liverpool	
7867	Schloss	Leopold	1824	Frankfurt-am-Main, Germany	David Feist Schloss	Malchen (Amalia) Stiebel	Anne Horatia Montefiore	?Manchester	
8203	Schloss	Rebecca	1820	?, London	Abraham Mocatta	Miriam Brandon	Sigismund Schloss	Liverpool	
7378	Schloss	Sigismund	1813	Frankfurt-am-Main, Germany	David Feist Schloss	Malchen (Amalia) Stiebel	Rebecca Mocatta	Liverpool	shipping merchant
2665	Schloss	Solomon David	1815	Frankfurt-am-Main, Germany	David Feist Schloss	Malchen (Amalia) Stiebel	Jeannette (Janet) Raphael	Liverpool	commission agent
2568	Schluf	Betsey	1815	?, Germany				Hull, Yorkshire	
13547	Schmidt	Francis	1816	?, Poland [?, Prussia]				Manchester	furrier
20291	Schmuel	Abahm	1842	?, Russia				Spitalfields, London	scholar
27777	Schneiders	Abraham	1848	Aldgate, London	Zadok Schneiders	Netty (Jenetta, Jetta) Segahous		Spitalfields, London	scholar
30621	Schneiders	Berend	1851	Spitalfields, London	Zadok Schneiders	Netty (Jenetta, Jetta) Segahous		Spitalfields, London	
27773	Schneiders	Fanny	1837	Amsterdam, Holland	Zadok Schneiders	Netty (Jenetta, Jetta) Segahous		Spitalfields, London	cap maker
27778	Schneiders	Gerson	1849	Aldgate, London	Zadok Schneiders	Netty (Jenetta, Jetta) Segahous		Spitalfields, London	
27772	Schneiders	Joseph	1835	Amsterdam, Holland	Zadok Schneiders	Netty (Jenetta, Jetta) Segahous		Spitalfields, London	cigar maker
27775	Schneiders	Kitty (Kate)	1841	Amsterdam, Holland	Zadok Schneiders	Netty (Jenetta, Jetta) Segahous	Simon Jacobson	Spitalfields, London	scholar

ID	surname	given names	born	birthplace	father	mother	spouse 1	1851 residence	1851 occupation
27776	Schneiders	Michael (Mike)	1844	Amsterdam, Holland	Zadok Schneiders	Netty (Jenetta, Jetta) Segahous	Rose Bromet	Spitalfields, London	scholar
27771	Schneiders	Netty (Jenetta, Jetta)	1816	?, Belgium	Micael Segahous		Zadok Schneiders	Spitalfields, London	
27774	Schneiders	Rara	1839	Amsterdam, Holland	Zadok Schneiders	Netty (Jenetta, Jetta) Segahous		Spitalfields, London	cap maker
27770	Schneiders	Zadok	1805	Amsterdam, Holland			Netty (Jenetta, Jetta) Segahous	Spitalfields, London	cap maker
13754	Schoenthal	Ester	1834	?, Poland [?, Prussia]	(?) Schoenthal			Manchester	cap maker
1450	Schram	Abraham	1851	Plymouth, Devon	Nathaniel Schram	Anne (Anna) (?)		Plymouth, Devon	
1447	Schram	Angelina	1843	Truro, Cornwall	Nathaniel Schram	Anne (Anna) (?)		Plymouth, Devon	scholar
1445	Schram	Anne (Anna)	1816	?, Cornwall			Nathaniel Schram	Plymouth, Devon	
6545	Schram	Henrietta	1845	Truro, Cornwall	Nathaniel Schram	Anne (Anna) (?)	Mark Jacobs	Plymouth, Devon	scholar
1446	Schram	Jacob	1842	Falmouth, Cornwall	Nathaniel Schram	Anne (Anna) (?)		Plymouth, Devon	scholar
1449	Schram	Marianna (Mary)	1849	Plymouth, Devon	Nathaniel Schram	Anne (Anna) (?)	(?) Axworthy	Plymouth, Devon	scholar
1444	Schram	Nathaniel	1804	The Hague, Holland			Anne (Anna) (?)	Plymouth, Devon	herbalist
26792	Schrymoski	Samuel	1831	?, Germany				Aldgate, London	tailor
995	Schultz	Lewis	1787	Warsaw, Poland			Louisa (?)	Exeter, Devon	jeweller
996	Schultz	Louisa	1796	Warsaw, Poland			Lewis Schultz	Exeter, Devon	
14466	Schuster	Samuel	1837	?, Germany				Manchester	appentice merchant
2662	Schwabe	Adele	1840	Hamburg, Germany	Ludolph Schwabe	Helen (?)		Glasgow, Scotland	scholar
31204	Schwabe	Adelheid	1838	Manchester	Stephen Samuel Schwabe	Eliza (?)		Manchester	scholar
31199	Schwabe	Alfred James	1845	Manchester	Herman Morris Schwabe	Charlotte (?)		Manchester	scholar
31012	Schwabe	Catherine Marianna	1850	Manchester	Salis Schwabe	Julia (Ricke Rosetta) Schwabe		Manchester	
31209	Schwabe	Charles	1849	Manchester	Stephen Samuel Schwabe	Eliza (?)		Manchester	
31198	Schwabe	Charles Henry	1843	Manchester	Herman Morris Schwabe	Charlotte (?)		Manchester	scholar
31197	Schwabe	Charlotte	1819	?, Germany			Gherman Morris Schwabe	Manchester	
2663	Schwabe	Clara Helena	1848	Glasgow, Scotland	Ludolph Schwabe	Helen (?)		Glasgow, Scotland	
31208	Schwabe	Edward	1847	Manchester	Stephen Samuel Schwabe	Eliza (?)		Manchester	
31008	Schwabe	Edward Salis	1841	Middleton, Lancashire	Salis Schwabe	Julia (Ricke Rosetta) Schwabe		Manchester	scholar
31201	Schwabe	Eliza	1818	Middlesex, London	(?)		Stephen Samuel Schwabe	Manchester	
31202	Schwabe	Frederica	1835	Manchester	Stephen Samuel Schwabe	Eliza (?)		Manchester	
31010	Schwabe	Frederick	1845	Middleton, Lancashire	Salis Schwabe	Julia (Ricke Rosetta) Schwabe		Manchester	scholar
31009	Schwabe	George S	1844	Middleton, Lancashire	Salis Schwabe	Julia (Ricke Rosetta) Schwabe		Manchester	scholar
31007	Schwabe	Harriet	1839	Middleton, Lancashire	Salis Schwabe	Julia (Ricke Rosetta) Schwabe		Manchester	
2661	Schwabe	Helen Leonore	1817	?, Germany	(?) Scheuer		Ludolph Schwabe	Glasgow, Scotland	
31210	Schwabe	Henry	1850	Manchester	Stephen Samuel Schwabe	Eliza (?)		Manchester	
14346	Schwabe	Herman Morris	1813	?, Germany			Charlotte (?)	Manchester	general merchant
2640	Schwabe	Ida	1845	?, Germany	Ludolph Schwabe	Helen Scheuer		Glasgow, Scotland	

ID	surname	given names	born	birthplace	father	mother	spouse 1	1851 residence	1851 occupation
31011	Schwabe	Julia Rosetta	1848	?, France	Salis Schwabe	Julia (Ricke Rosetta) Schwabe		Manchester	
31200	Schwabe	Juliet	1850	Manchester	Herman Morris Schwabe	Charlotte (?)		Manchester	
14345	Schwabe	Leopold	1802	?, Germany			Emma F (?)	Manchester	
2660	Schwabe	Ludolph	1809	Bremerlehe, Germany	Marcus Herz Schwabe		Helen Leonore Scheuer	Glasgow, Scotland	cotton merchant
31203	Schwabe	Maria	1837	Manchester	Stephen Samuel Schwabe	Eliza (?)		Manchester	scholar
31206	Schwabe	Robert	1842	Manchester	Stephen Samuel Schwabe	Eliza (?)		Manchester	scholar
7383	Schwabe	Salis	1800	Oldenburg, Germany	Elias Herz Schwabe		Julia (Ricke Rosetta) Schwabe	Manchester	calico printer
14344	Schwabe	Stephen Samuel	1803	?, Germany			Eliza (?)	Manchester	general merchant
2664	Schwabe	Theodor Herman	1831	?, Germany	Herman Levy Schwabe	Augusta Bandmann	Sully (?Tully) Rothschild	Glasgow, Scotland	commission agent
31205	Schwabe	Thomas	1840	Manchester	Stephen Samuel Schwabe	Eliza (?)		Manchester	scholar
31207	Schwabe	Walter	1844	Manchester	Stephen Samuel Schwabe	Eliza (?)		Manchester	scholar
7382	Schwabe (Salis-Schwabe)	Julia (Ricke Rosetta)	1818	Bremen, Germany	Gottschalk Herz Schwabe		Salis Schwabe	Manchester	philanthropist + educationist
2569	Schwanfield	Emiel	1812	?, Poland [?, Prussia]				Hull, Yorkshire	farrier's man
26824	Schwartz	Caroline	1826	Stepney, London	(?) Phillips		Morris Schwartz	Aldgate, London	
26825	Schwartz	Ellen	1847	Aldgate, London	Morris Schwartz	Caroline Phillips		Aldgate, London	
9183	Schwartz	Joseph	1807	?, Germany				Whitechapel, London	messenger
26826	Schwartz	Julia	1849	Stepney, London	Morris Schwartz	Caroline Phillips		Aldgate, London	
26941	Schwartz	Michael	1833	?, Poland				Aldgate, London	tailor
26823	Schwartz	Morris	1822	?, Austria			Caroline Phillips	Aldgate, London	tailor empl 21
22880	Schwartzschild	Abigail	1829	Poplar, London	John Nathaniel Messeena	Rachel Gomes	Anschel Schwartzschild	Limehouse, London	
22879	Schwartzschild	Anschel	1816	?, Germany	Jacob Schwartzschild		Abigail Messena	Limehouse, London	foreign merchant
24191	Schweder	Julius E	1822	Berlin, Germany [Berlin, Prussia]				De Beauvoir, London	merchant
16818	Schweisen	Louis	1825	?, Poland [?, Prussia]				Colchester, Essex	jeweller
30187	Schwersen	Isaac	1826	?, Poland				Dudley, Worcestershire	hawker
2104	Schwersensky	Elizabeth	1841	Canterbury, Kent	Isaac Schwersensky	Hannah Isaacs		Liverpool	
22314	Schwersensky	Fanny	1846	Liverpool	Isaac Schwersensky	Hannah Isaacs		Liverpool	
2101	Schwersensky	Hannah	1810	Middlesex, London	Isaac Isaacs	Elizabeth Solomons	Isaac Schwersensky	Liverpool	
2102	Schwersensky	Isaac	1800	?Poland [Sarna, Prussia]	Joshua Schwersensky		Hannah Isaacs	Liverpool	outfitter + clothier
22315	Schwersensky	Joshua	1850	Liverpool	Isaac Schwersensky	Hannah Isaacs		Liverpool	
22313	Schwersensky	Nathaniel	1843	Liverpool	Isaac Schwersensky	Hannah Isaacs		Liverpool	
2103	Schwersensky	Philip	1840	Canterbury, Kent	Isaac Schwersensky	Hannah Isaacs		Liverpool	
28089	Scierpser	David	1829	?, Poland [?, Prussia]				Spitalfields, London	sugar boiler
28090	Scierpser	Herman	1833	?, Poland [?, Prussia]				Spitalfields, London	capmaker + furrier
17621	Seaman	Joseph	1831	?, Poland				Aldgate, London	tailor
16477	Sebag	Hannah	1826	Middlesex, London	(?) Sebag	Jane (?)		Mile End, London	needlewoman
16476	Sebag	Jane	1801	Middlesex, London	(?)		(?) Sebag	Mile End, London	annuitant
7479	Sebag	Joseph Montefiore	1823	?, Holland	Solomon Sebag		Adelaide (Ada) Cohen	Shoreditch, London	merchant + stockbroker
7577	Sebag	Solomon	1828	Whitechapel, London	Isaac de Solomon Sebag	Jane (Jael) de Jacob Senior Coronel		Aldgate, London	teacher of school
13309	Sebag (Sebas)	Jacob	1842	Essaouira, Morocco [Moggador]	Solomon Sebag (Sebas)	Welcome (?)		Spitalfields, London	

ID	surname	given names	born	birthplace	father	mother	spouse 1	1851 residence	1851 occupation
13311	Sebag (Sebas)	Judah	1848	Spitalfields, London	Solomon Sebag (Sebas)	Welcome (?)		Spitalfields, London	
13310	Sebag (Sebas)	Rebecca	1846	Mile End, London	Solomon Sebag (Sebas)	Welcome (?)		Spitalfields, London	
13307	Sebag (Sebas)	Solomon	1819	Essaouira, Morocco [Moggador]			Welcome (?)	Spitalfields, London	traveller in drugs
13308	Sebag (Sebas)	Welcome	1816	Spitalfields, London	(?)		Solomon Sebag (Sebas)	Spitalfields, London	
13941	Seelig	Ellen	1817	Rhodes, Lancashire	(?)		Julius Seelig	Manchester	confectioner's wife
13942	Seelig	Eugenie	1832	Heilbronn, Germany [Heilbrunn, Wurtemberg, Germany]	(?) Seelig			Manchester	confectioner's assistant
13940	Seelig	Julius	1821	Heilbronn, Germany [Heilbrunn, Wurtemberg, Germany]			Ellen (?)	Manchester	confectioner
27779	Segahous	Micael	1788	Amsterdam, Holland			(?)	Spitalfields, London	
15884	Segre	Abigail	1832	Liverpool	(?) Segre			Hackney, London	English teacher
14141	Segre	Caterilla	1837	?, America	Matthew John Segre	Esther Theresa Aaron		Manchester	scholar
14139	Segre	Esther Theresa	1806	Portsmouth, Hampshire	Jacob Arron	Alice (?)	Matthew John Segre	Manchester	lodging house keeper
14433	Segre	Theresa	1837	Liverpool	Matthew John Segre	Esther Theresa Aaron		Salford, Lancashire	
7089	Segre	Victoria (Virtuosa)	1835	Manchester	Matthew John Segre	Esther Theresa Aaron	Henry Abraham Franklin	Manchester	scholar
25876	Seigenberg	Adelaide	1831	Whitechapel, London	Israel Lippschutz	Harriet (?)	Charles Seigenberg	Aldgate, London	
16107	Seigenberg	Ann	1850	Aldgate, London	John Seigenberg	Julia Abrahams		Soho, London	
25875	Seigenberg	Charles	1828	Aldgate, London	Jonas Seigenberg		Adelaide Lippschutz	Aldgate, London	pencil maker empl 2
16106	Seigenberg	Flora	1848	Aldgate, London	John Seigenberg	Julia Abrahams		Soho, London	
16103	Seigenberg	John	1823	Whitechapel, London	Jonas Seigenberg		Julia Abrahams	Soho, London	pencil maker
6638	Seigenberg	Jonas (John)	1846	Aldgate, London	John Seigenberg	Julia Abrahams	Julia Jacobs	Soho, London	
16104	Seigenberg	Julia	1825	Aldgate, London	Michael Abrahams		John Seigenberg	Soho, London	
16105	Seigenberg	Lewis	1844	Aldgate, London	John Seigenberg	Julia Abrahams		Soho, London	
1137	Selig	Aaron	1849	Penzance, Cornwall	Benjamin Aaron Selig	Catherine Jacobs		Penzance, Cornwall	
13970	Selig	Adolphus	1847	Manchester	Julius Selig	Fanny Henry	Rozina Lena Siemms	Manchester	scholar
29339	Selig	Barnard (Baruch)	1823	?, Germany			Fanny (?)	Whitechapel, London	capmaker
1135	Selig	Benjamin Aaron	1814	Penzance, Cornwall	Aaron Selig	Hannah (?)	Catherine Jacob	Penzance, Cornwall	watchmaker
1136	Selig	Catherine	1820	Penzance, Cornwall	Samuel Jacob	Sarah (Sally) Levy	Benjamin Aaron Selig	Penzance, Cornwall	
29630	Selig	Conrad	1816	?, Poland [?, Prussia]			H--- (?)	Aldgate, London	cap maker
13966	Selig	Edwin	1838	Manchester	Julius Selig	Fanny Henry	Ellen Stadthagen	Manchester	scholar
13969	Selig	Emily	1844	Manchester	Julius Selig	Fanny Henry	M--- Marcus	Manchester	scholar
13965	Selig	Fanny	1816	Liverpool	(?) Henry	Leah (?)	Julius Selig	Manchester	boarding house keeper
29340	Selig	Fanny	1824	?, London	(?)		Barnard (Baruch) Selig	Whitechapel, London	
29634	Selig	Frances	1850	Middlesex, London	Conrad Selig	H--- (?)		Aldgate, London	
29631	Selig	H---	1819	?, Poland [?, Prussia]	(?)		Conrad Selig	Aldgate, London	
20287	Selig	Hemen	1831	?, Poland [?, Prussia]				Spitalfields, London	traveller
29342	Selig	Henry B	1851	Whitechapel, London	Barnard (Baruch) Selig	Fanny (?)		Whitechapel, London	
13968	Selig	Herman	1842	Manchester	Julius Selig	Fanny Henry		Manchester	scholar
13967	Selig	Honoria	1840	Manchester	Julius Selig	Fanny Henry	Marco Adutt	Manchester	scholar
1138	Selig	Lemon	1850	Penzance, Cornwall	Benjamin Aaron Selig	Catherine Jacobs		Penzance, Cornwall	
29633	Selig	Lisa	1847	Middlesex, London	Conrad Selig	H--- (?)		Aldgate, London	
27019	Selig	Myer	1850	Penzance, Cornwall	Benjamin Aaron Selig	Catherine Jacobs		Penzance, Cornwall	

ID	surname	given names	born	birthplace	father	mother	spouse 1	1851 residence	1851 occupation
29632	Selig	Rachel	1844	?, Poland [?, Prussia]	Conrad Selig	H--- (?)		Aldgate, London	
29343	Selig	Simond	1830	?, Germany				Whitechapel, London	cigar maker
29341	Selig	Solomon D B	1849	Whitechapel, London	Barnard (Baruch) Selig	Fanny (?)		Whitechapel, London	
27471	Seligmann	William	1817	?, Bavaria, Germany			(?) Mandelbaum	Whitechapel, London	shop assistant to importer of fancy goods
18891	Selim	Adolphus	1847	Middlesex, London	Henry Selim	Esther (?)		Chelsea, London	
7840	Selim	Elizabeth (Lizzie)	1849	Middlesex, London	Henry Selim	Esther (?)	J Otto Schuler	Chelsea, London	
7837	Selim	Esther	1821	Greenwich, London	(?)		Henry Selim	Chelsea, London	
7836	Selim	Henry	1817	Middlesex, London	Napthali Henry Salomon	Ann (?)	Esther (?)	Chelsea, London	silversmith + jeweller + traveller
7838	Selim	Henry J	1846	Middlesex, London	Henry Selim	Esther (?)		Chelsea, London	
7839	Selim	Isaac	1826	Middlesex, London	Naphtali Henry Salomon	Ann (?)		Marylebone, London	surgeon + money changer
5739	Seline	Hannah	1807	Hanover, Germany			Moses Seline	Swansea, Wales	
5737	Seline	Isaac	1842	Swansea, Wales	Moses Seline	Hannah (?)	Maria Moses	Swansea, Wales	scholar
5738	Seline	Moses	1801	?, Bavaria, Germany			Hannah (?)	Swansea, Wales	jeweller
19044	Sequerra	Hannah Bathsheba	1833	Mile End, London	Solomon de Shem Tob Sequerra	Simha de Solomon Aloof	Abraham Bitton	Aldgate, London	
7625	Sequerra	Mesoda	1835	Mile End, London	Solomon Sequerra	Simha de Solomon Aloof	Abraham Aloof	Aldgate, London	
19042	Sequerra	Simha	1810	Gibraltar	Solomon de Menahem Aloof		Solomon de Yom Tob Sequerra	Aldgate, London	
7626	Sequerra	Solomon	1808	Gibraltar	Shem Tob de Solomon Sequerra		Simha de Solomon Aloof	Aldgate, London	annuitant
19045	Sequerra	Stella	1837	Mile End, London	Solomon de Shem Tob Sequerra	Simha de Solomon Aloof	Solomon de Moses Sequerra	Aldgate, London	
29839	Serfaty	Solomon	1786	Gibraltar				Stepney, London	general clothes dealer
19229	Seringer	Rosetta	1801	Falmouth, Cornwall	(?)		(?) Seringer	Aldgate, London	
12076	Sewell	Michael	1829	?, Poland [?, Prussia]				Spitalfields, London	baker
870	Sewill	Caroline	1847	Liverpool	Joseph Sewill	Phoebe (?)	Israel Hart	Liverpool	
16605	Sewill	Francis Elias	1849	Liverpool	Joseph Sewill	Phoebe (?)		Liverpool	
16602	Sewill	Henry	1843	Liverpool	Joseph Sewill	Phoebe (?)		Liverpool	
16601	Sewill	Jane	1839	Liverpool	Joseph Sewill	Phoebe (?)	Arnold Gabriel	Liverpool	
3182	Sewill	John Sefton	1841	Liverpool	Joseph Sewill	Phoebe (?)	Abigail Ellen (Nellie) Moses	Liverpool	
7594	Sewill	Joseph	1814	Liverpool			Phoebe (?)	Liverpool	nautical instrument, watch and chronometermaker empl 5
16603	Sewill	Marcus	1845	Liverpool	Joseph Sewill	Phoebe (?)		Liverpool	
16600	Sewill	Phoebe	1821	Middlesex, London	(?)		Joseph Sewill	Liverpool	
30210	Shannon	Alice	1851	Bloomsbury, London	Morris (Moses) Shannon	Belinda Falcke	Lewis (Louis) White	Bloomsbury, London	
15312	Shannon	Anna (Hanah)	1828	Shoreditch, London	Samuel de Masaod Shannon	Miriam de Uri Sheraga Pais		Shoreditch, London	domestic servant
24122	Shannon	Belinda	1827	Great Yarmouth, Norfolk	Jacob Falcke	Hannah (?)	Morris (Moses) Shannon	Bloomsbury, London	
23353	Shannon	Mary (Miriam)	1801	Aldgate, London	Asher Levy		Samuel de Masaod Shannon	Strand, London	coffee house keeper
24121	Shannon	Morris (Moses)	1805	Middlesex, London	Jacob Shannon	Sarah (?)	Rachel de Levin Lamort	Bloomsbury, London	Sherriff's Officer
13731	Sharman	Clara	1800	?, London	(?) Sharman			Bloomsbury, London	

ID	surname	given names	born	birthplace	father	mother	spouse 1	1851 residence	1851 occupation
11947	Shemaul	Asher	1825	?, Holland				Whitechapel, London	com cigar [---]
4932	Shepover	Albert	1805	?, Poland			Rebecca (?)	Birmingham	slipper maker
4933	Shepover	Rebecca	1812	Middlesex, London			Albert Shepover	Birmingham	
20329	Sheyer	Jacob	1801	?				Aldgate, London	bootmaker
14064	Shidour	Adolphus	1827	?, Germany				Manchester	carver - wood + stone
14218	Shienfeld	Abraham	1831	Warsaw, Poland				Manchester	cap maker
14475	Shinefeld	Isaac	1829	?, Poland	King Shinefeld	Sarah (?)		Manchester	journeyman shoemaker
14473	Shinefeld	King	1803	?, Poland			Sarah (?)	Manchester	master shoemaker empl 9
14474	Shinefeld	Sarah	1811	?, Poland	(?)		King Shinefeld	Manchester	
7536	Shire	Elizabeth	1778	?, Holland	(?)		(?) Shire	Spitalfields, London	
21280	Shisa	James	1837	Aldgate, London				Edmonton, London	boarding school pupil
7979	Shoeps	Abraham	1808	?, Germany			Betsey Wulfson	Manchester	agent
7980	Shoeps	Betsey	1817	?, Germany	Michael Isaac Wulfson	Frederica (?)	Abraham Shoeps	Manchester	
7981	Shoeps	Emma	1834	Nottingham, Nottinghamshire	Abraham Shoeps	Betsey Wulfson		Manchester	
7984	Shoeps	Jacob	1849	Manchester	Abraham Shoeps	Betsey Wulfson		Manchester	
7983	Shoeps	Joseph	1848	Nottingham, Nottinghamshire	Abraham Shoeps	Betsey Wulfson		Manchester	
7982	Shoeps	Margret	1844	Nottingham, Nottinghamshire	Abraham Shoeps	Betsey Wulfson		Manchester	
9137	Sholl	Joseph	1815	Whitechapel, London			Sarah (?)	Whitechapel, London	shoe maker
9140	Sholl	Joseph	1845	Stepney, London	Joseph Sholl	Sarah (?)		Whitechapel, London	scholar
9141	Sholl	Margaret	1848	Stepney, London	Joseph Sholl	Sarah (?)		Whitechapel, London	scholar
9138	Sholl	Sarah	1819	Whitechapel, London	(?)		Joseph Sholl	Whitechapel, London	
9139	Sholl	Sarah	1844	Stepney, London	Joseph Sholl	Sarah (?)		Whitechapel, London	scholar
30465	Shomsky	Charles	1817	?, Poland				Stoke-on-Trent, Staffordshire	teacher
16880	Shriner	Samuel	1829	?, Poland [?, Prussia]				Cambridge	traveller
12154	Shuter	Alfred	1850	City, London	Joseph Shuter	Sarah Ann (?)		Aldgate, London	
9645	Shuter	Amelia	1851	Spitalfields, London	Samuel Shuter	Hannah (Annala) Woolf	Henry Mark Charig	Spitalfields, London	
12153	Shuter	Edward	1838	City, London	Joseph Shuter	Sarah Ann (?)		Aldgate, London	scholar
10868	Shuter	Hannah	1827	Stepney, London	Isaac Lesser	Sophia Benjamin Hart	Isaac Shuter	Stepney, London	
5742	Shuter	Hannah (Annala)	1824	Whitechapel, London	Abraham Woolf	Elizabeth Samuel	Samuel Shuter	Spitalfields, London	
10869	Shuter	Isaac	1823	Leszno, Poland [Lissa, Prussia]	Michael (Yechiel) Shuter		Hannah Lesser	Stepney, London	working furrier
12152	Shuter	James	1836	City, London	Joseph Shuter	Sarah Ann (?)		Aldgate, London	scholar
12150	Shuter	John	1826	City, London	Joseph Shuter	Sarah Ann (?)		Aldgate, London	grocer's assistant
12148	Shuter	Joseph	1800	City, London			Sarah Ann (?)	Aldgate, London	fruiterer
10870	Shuter	Michael	1850	Whitechapel, London	Isaac Shuter	Hannah Lesser		Stepney, London	
5741	Shuter	Samuel	1826	Leszno, Poland [Lissa, Prussia]	Michael (Yechiel) Shuter		Hannah (Annala) Woolf	Spitalfields, London	hat + cap maker
12149	Shuter	Sarah Ann	1802	Hornsey, London	(?)		Joseph Shuter	Aldgate, London	
12151	Shuter	William	1834	City, London	Joseph Shuter	Sarah Ann (?)		Aldgate, London	light porter
14390	Sichel	Amelia	1803	?, Germany	(?)			Manchester	
14389	Sichel	Augustus	1799	?, Germany			Amelia (?)	Manchester	merchant
14394	Sichel	Edward	1829	?, Germany	Augustus Sichel	Amelia (?)		Manchester	
14391	Sichel	Emil	1824	?, Germany	Augustus Sichel	Amelia (?)		Manchester	
14393	Sichel	Frederick	1827	?, Germany	Augustus Sichel	Amelia (?)		Manchester	

ID	surname	given names	born	birthplace	father	mother	spouse 1	1851 residence	1851 occupation
14392	Sichel	Gustavus	1825	Frankfurt-am-Main, Germany	Augustus Sichel	Amelia (?)	Henriette (?)	Manchester	
27101	Sichel?	Hazar	1840	Essaouira, Morocco [Mogador, Africa]				Aldgate, London	scholar
27099	Sichel?	Lazar	1790	Essaouira, Morocco [Mogador, Africa]			Sarah (?)	Aldgate, London	dealer in rhubarb
27102	Sichel?	Mashod	1843	Essaouira, Morocco [Mogador, Africa]				Aldgate, London	scholar
27100	Sichel?	Sarah	1797	Essaouira, Morocco [Mogador, Africa]	(?)		Lazar Sichel?	Aldgate, London	
13630	Side	Bernard	1837	?, Poland [?, Prussia]	Hyman Side	Hannah (?)		Manchester	shoemaker
13632	Side	Bronaly	1842	?, Poland [?, Prussia]	Hyman Side	Hannah (?)		Manchester	scholar at home
13628	Side	Hannah	1810	?, Poland [?, Prussia]	(?)		Hyman Side	Manchester	
13627	Side	Hyman	1805	?, Poland [?, Prussia]			Hannah (?)	Manchester	glazier
13629	Side	Morris	1835	?, Poland [?, Prussia]	Hyman Side	Hannah (?)	Louisa Lesset	Manchester	tailor
13633	Side	Salivea	1844	?, Poland [?, Prussia]	Hyman Side	Hannah (?)		Manchester	scholar at home
13631	Side	Selanen (?Selina)	1840	?, Poland [?, Prussia]	Hyman Side	Hannah (?)		Manchester	scholar at home
13634	Side	Sumple (?Gumpel)	1846	?, Poland [?, Prussia]	Hyman Side	Hannah (?)		Manchester	
9782	Sidney	Herbert	1836	Middlesex, London				Kew, London	boarding school pupil
9783	Sidney	Theodore	1838	Middlesex, London				Kew, London	boarding school pupil
29362	Siegenberg	Abraham	1814	Whitechapel, London	Jonas Seigenberg		Maria (Mary) Levy	Wapping, London	slopseller
27588	Siegenberg	Benjamin	1848	Aldgate, London	Henry Siegenberg	Sarah Isaacson		Spitalfields, London	
29367	Siegenberg	Clara	1847	Whitechapel, London	Abraham Siegenberg	Maria (Mary) (?Levy, ?Solomons)		Wapping, London	
9368	Siegenberg	Elizabeth	1829	Whitechapel, London	Jonas Seigenberg			Spitalfields, London	carpet bag maker
27590	Siegenberg	Flora	1850	Aldgate, London	Henry Siegenberg	Sarah Isaacson		Spitalfields, London	
27589	Siegenberg	Hannah	1849	Aldgate, London	Henry Siegenberg	Sarah Isaacson	Samuel Phillips	Spitalfields, London	
27584	Siegenberg	Henry	1818	Aldgate, London	Jonas Seigenberg		Sarah Isaacson	Spitalfields, London	pencil maker
29368	Siegenberg	Jacob	1849	Whitechapel, London	Abraham Siegenberg	Maria (Mary) (?Levy, ?Solomons)		Wapping, London	
29364	Siegenberg	Jonas	1842	Whitechapel, London	Abraham Siegenberg	Maria (Mary) (?Levy, ?Solomons)		Wapping, London	scholar
27587	Siegenberg	Kate	1845	Aldgate, London	Henry Siegenberg	Sarah Isaacson		Spitalfields, London	scholar
29366	Siegenberg	Lewis (Louis) Adolphus	1843	Whitechapel, London	Abraham Siegenberg	Maria (Mary) (?Levy, ?Solomons)	Charlotte (Lottie) Leah Redshaw	Wapping, London	scholar
29363	Siegenberg	Maria (Mary)	1815	Whitechapel, London	S--- Levy		Abraham Siegenberg	Wapping, London	
27586	Siegenberg	Morris (Morits)	1843	Spitalfields, London	Henry Siegenberg	Sarah Isaacson		Spitalfields, London	scholar
10445	Siegenberg	Samuel	1843	Spitalfields, London	(?) Siegenberg	(?) Isaacs		Spitalfields, London	scholar
27585	Siegenberg	Sarah	1822	Whitechapel, London	M--- Isaacson		Henry Siegenberg	Spitalfields, London	
29365	Siegenberg	Solomon	1844	Whitechapel, London	Abraham Siegenberg	Maria (Mary) (?Levy, ?Solomons)	Maria Joseph	Wapping, London	scholar
2332	Sigman	Selig	1825	?, Poland				Leeds, Yorkshire	hawker
2333	Sigmund	James	1827	?, Poland [?, Prussia]				Leeds, Yorkshire	furrier
17170	Silber	Moses	1832	Margonin, Poland				Newcastle Upon Tyne	jeweller
24118	Silberberg	Adam Alfred	1834	?, Poland [?, Russian Poland]	Solomon W Leopold	Anna (?)		Bloomsbury, London	attorney's lad
24115	Silberberg	Anna	1804	?, Poland [?, Russian Poland]	(?)		Solomon W Silberberg	Bloomsbury, London	

ID	surname	given names	born	birthplace	father	mother	spouse 1	1851 residence	1851 occupation
24991	Silberberg	Emma	1849	?Soho, London	Louis Silberberg	Theresa Asher		Strand, London	
24119	Silberberg	Leah	1836	?, Poland [?, Russian Poland]	Solomon W Leopold	Anna (?)		Bloomsbury, London	artificial florist
24116	Silberberg	Leopold	1830	?, Poland [?, Russian Poland]	Solomon W Leopold	Anna (?)		Bloomsbury, London	musician
24988	Silberberg	Louis	1820	Gdansk, Poland [Dantzig, Prussia]			Theresa Asher	Strand, London	tobacconist
24117	Silberberg	Louisa	1832	?, Poland [?, Russian Poland]	Solomon W Leopold	Anna (?)		Bloomsbury, London	artificial florist
24992	Silberberg	Louisa	1851	Strand, London	Louis Silberberg	Theresa Asher		Strand, London	
24990	Silberberg	Maria	1846	Gdansk, Poland [Dantzig, Prussia]	Louis Silberberg	Theresa Asher		Strand, London	
24114	Silberberg	Solomon W	1799	?, Poland [?, Russian Poland]			Anna (?)	Bloomsbury, London	Polish Refugee
24989	Silberberg	Theresa	1822	Wapping, London	(?) Asher		Louis Silberberg	Strand, London	
12077	Silberman	Mark	1828	?, Poland [?, Prussia]				Spitalfields, London	clerk
21421	Silberman	Masriel	1834	Czarkow, Poland				Dewsbury, Yorkshire	traveller
23122	Silberman	Theodor	1824	?, France				City, London	French agent
13472	Siligman	Herman	1765	?, Germany				Manchester	warehouseman
14159	Silkenstadt	John G	1823	Bremen, Germany				Manchester	clerk to merchant
27344	Silkman (Harrar)	Elias	1835	Mile End, London	Eliezer de Jacob Silkman (Harrar)	Louisa (Dina, Reyna) de Jacob Noah Da Costa	Sarah Boam	Aldgate, London	cigar maker
27343	Silkman (Harrar)	John (Jacob)	1834	Mile End, London	Eliezer de Jacob Silkman (Harrar)	Louisa (Dina, Reyna) de Jacob Noah Da Costa		Aldgate, London	boot maker
27342	Silkman (Harrar)	Louisa (Dina, Reyna)	1809	Mile End, London	Jacob de Isaac Noah Da Costa	Esther de Joseph Cohen	Eliezer de Jacob Silkman (Harrar)	Aldgate, London	embroiderer
27345	Silkman (Harrar)	Lucy (Lucky)	1838	Mile End, London	Eliezer de Jacob Silkman (Harrar)	Louisa (Dina, Reyna) de Jacob Noah Da Costa		Aldgate, London	
14116	Sillmann	Elkam	1801	?, Poland [?, Prussia]				Manchester	book keeper
14467	Siltzer	David	1811	?, Germany				Manchester	calico printer
29429	Silver	Abraham	1850	Spitalfields, London	Myers (Meyer) Silver	Rachel (?)		Spitalfields, London	
27190	Silver	Catherine	1823	?, Poland	(?)		Israel Silver	Aldgate, London	
29427	Silver	Clara	1846	Spitalfields, London	Myers (Meyer) Silver	Rachel (?)		Spitalfields, London	scholar
18743	Silver	Clara	1849	Spitalfields, London	Samuel Meijer Silver (Zilver)	Priscilla Salomon Proops	John Harris	Spitalfields, London	
27193	Silver	Elizabeth	1801	?, Poland	(?)		(?) Israel	Aldgate, London	
18677	Silver	Hannah	1795	Amsterdam, Holland	(?)		Henry Silver	Spitalfields, London	
18749	Silver	Hannah	1842	Middlesex, London	Samuel Meijer Silver (Zilver)	Priscilla Salomon Proops	Samuel J Nathan	Spitalfields, London	scholar
29426	Silver	Hannah	1844	Spitalfields, London	Myers (Meyer) Silver	Rachel (?)		Spitalfields, London	scholar
18676	Silver	Henry	1792	Amsterdam, Holland			Hannah (?)	Spitalfields, London	dealer in spectacles
29424	Silver	Henry	1839	Spitalfields, London	Myers (Meyer) Silver	Rachel (?)		Spitalfields, London	scholar
18750	Silver	Henry	1840	Middlesex, London	Samuel Meijer Silver (Zilver)	Priscilla Salomon Proops	Sarah Nathan	Spitalfields, London	scholar
18752	Silver	Isaac	1845	Middlesex, London	Samuel Meijer Silver (Zilver)	Priscilla Salomon Proops	Leah Rogers	Spitalfields, London	scholar
27189	Silver	Israel	1816	?, Poland	(?) Silver	Elizabeth	Catherine (?)	Aldgate, London	traveller
27191	Silver	Jacob	1844	?, London	Israel Silver	Catherine (?)		Aldgate, London	
18747	Silver	Joseph	1837	Middlesex, London	Samuel Meijer Silver (Zilver)	Priscilla Salomon Proops	Rebecca Cousins	Spitalfields, London	
18753	Silver	Lazarus (Eleazer)	1848	Spitalfields, London	Samuel Meijer Silver (Zilver)	Priscilla Salomon Proops	Leah (?)	Spitalfields, London	scholar
18751	Silver	Lewis Samuel	1843	Middlesex, London	Samuel Meijer Silver (Zilver)	Priscilla Salomon Proops	Esther Harris	Spitalfields, London	scholar
29428	Silver	Martha	1849	Spitalfields, London	Myers (Meyer) Silver	Rachel (?)		Spitalfields, London	

ID	surname	given names	born	birthplace	father	mother	spouse 1	1851 residence	1851 occupation
18746	Silver	Mary	1835	Middlesex, London	Samuel Meijer Silver (Zilver)	Priscilla Salomon Proops		Spitalfields, London	
18744	Silver	Michael (Myer)	1829	Middlesex, London	Samuel Meijer Silver (Zilver)	Priscilla Salomon Proops	Catherine Harris	Spitalfields, London	sugar maker
11916	Silver	Moses	1834	Amsterdam, Holland				Whitechapel, London	cigar maker
29422	Silver	Myers (Meyer)	1814	Amsterdam, Holland			Rachel (?)	Spitalfields, London	dealer in musical instruments
29425	Silver	Phoebe (Fanny)	1842	Spitalfields, London	Myers (Meyer) Silver	Rachel (?)	Lipman Nathan	Spitalfields, London	scholar
29423	Silver	Rachel	1819	Amsterdam, Holland	(?)		Myers (Meyer) Silver	Spitalfields, London	
18745	Silver	Sarah	1831	Middlesex, London	Samuel Meijer Silver (Zilver)	Priscilla Salomon Proops	Lazarus (Eleazer) Levy	Spitalfields, London	
27192	Silver	Sarah	1849	?, London	Israel Silver	Catherine (?)		Aldgate, London	
18678	Silver	Solomon	1831	Amsterdam, Holland	Henry Silver	Hannah (?)	Simmy Abrahams	Spitalfields, London	cigar maker
18748	Silver	Solomon	1840	Middlesex, London	Samuel Meijer Silver (Zilver)	Priscilla Salomon Proops		Spitalfields, London	scholar
18754	Silver	Woolf [John, Samuel]	1850	Spitalfields, London	Samuel Meijer Silver (Zilver)	Priscilla Salomon Proops	Sarah Elizabeth [Rebecca] Thomas	Spitalfields, London	
18756	Silver (Zilver)	Priscilla	1812	Amsterdam, Holland	Salomon (Shlomo) HaCohen Proops	Sarah Lioni	Samuel Meijer Silver (Zilver)	Spitalfields, London	
18755	Silver (Zilver)	Samuel Meijer	1806	Amsterdam, Holland	Meier Hartog Hirtz Zilver Hammelberg Zilver	Marianne Merle Salomon Samuel swaab	Priscilla Salomon Proops	Spitalfields, London	cook + confectioner
2570	Silverman	Marcus	1831	?, Poland				Hull, Yorkshire	travels with jewellery
26986	Silverstein	Minna	1822	?, Germany	(?) Silverstein			Aldgate, London	milliner
17824	Silverston	Abigail	1831	Brighton, Sussex	Jacob Michael Silverston	Sarah Phillips		Aldgate, London	
17828	Silverston	Abraham	1844	City, London	Jacob Michael Silverston	Sarah Phillips	Elizabeth Alexander	Aldgate, London	
17827	Silverston	Amelia	1842	Brighton, Sussex	Jacob Michael Silverston	Sarah Phillips	Aaron Woolf	Aldgate, London	scholar
29756	Silverston	Barnard	1799	?, Poland				Aldgate, London	dealer
17821	Silverston	Charlotte	1827	Southwark, London	Jacob Michael Silverston	Sarah Phillips		Aldgate, London	
17826	Silverston	Esther	1837	Brighton, Sussex	Jacob Michael Silverston	Sarah Phillips	Louis Platnauer	Aldgate, London	
17818	Silverston	Jacob Michael	1797	Kornik, Poland	Michael Silverston		Sarah Phillips	Aldgate, London	annuitant
17822	Silverston	Julia	1828	Brighton, Sussex	Jacob Michael Silverston	Sarah Phillips	George Platnauer	Aldgate, London	
17820	Silverston	Mark	1823	?Brighton, Sussex	Jacob Michael Silverston	Sarah Phillips	Julia (?)	Aldgate, London	bullion merchant
17823	Silverston	Michael	1829	Brighton, Sussex	Jacob Michael Silverston	Sarah Phillips		Aldgate, London	
17819	Silverston	Sarah	1799	?Poznan, Poland [?Posen, Prussia]	Mordecai Phillips		Jacob Michael Silverston	Aldgate, London	
17825	Silverston	Sophia	1833	Brighton, Sussex	Jacob Michael Silverston	Sarah Phillips	Michael Joseph Platnauer	Aldgate, London	
21294	Silverston	Zalig (Zaley)	1837	Brighton, Sussex	(Jacob Michael?) Silverston	(Sarah Phillips?)	Emma Solomon	Edmonton, London	boarding school pupil
1008	Silverstone	Abraham (Abram)	1849	Exeter, Devon	Israel Silverstone	Pauline (?)		Exeter, Devon	
28277	Silverstone	Augusta	1840	?, Poland [?, Prussia]	Jacob Silverstone	Jane (?)		Aldgate, London	
1000	Silverstone	Bella	1833	Honiton, Devon	Israel Silverstone	Pauline (?)	Berthold Albu	Exeter, Devon	lace mfr
1004	Silverstone	Clara	1840	Exeter, Devon	Israel Silverstone	Pauline (?)	Joseph Heilbron	Exeter, Devon	scholar
28280	Silverstone	Eliza	1851	Hull, Yorkshire	Jacob Silverstone	Jane (?)		Aldgate, London	
4934	Silverstone	Fanny	1821	?, Poland [?, Prussia]	Samuel Samuel		Philip Silverstone	Birmingham	
1009	Silverstone	Fanny	1850	Exeter, Devon	Israel Silverstone	Pauline (?)	Lionel P Lipman	Exeter, Devon	
1248	Silverstone	Hannah	1799	Redruth, Cornwall	(?)		Isaac Joseph	Plymouth, Devon	dealer in shells
4938	Silverstone	Hannah	1826	?, Poland [?, Prussia]	(?) Silverstone			Birmingham	
30329	Silverstone	Harriet	1816	Southwark, London	Solomon Alex	Rachel Jones	Simeon John Silverstone	Bath	
1003	Silverstone	Isaac	1838	Exeter, Devon	Israel Silverstone	Pauline (?)	Henrietta Blanckensee	Exeter, Devon	scholar
997	Silverstone	Israel	1807	?, Poland			Pauline (?)	Exeter, Devon	shopkeeper + silversmith

ID	surname	given names	born	birthplace	father	mother	spouse 1	1851 residence	1851 occupation
282	Silverstone	Jacob	1811	?, Poland [?, Prussia]			Jane (?)	Aldgate, London	traveller
28275	Silverstone	Jane	1813	?, Poland [?, Prussia]	(?)		Jacob Silverstone	Aldgate, London	
1006	Silverstone	John	1845	Exeter, Devon	Israel Silverstone	Pauline (?)	Julia Blanckensee	Exeter, Devon	scholar
28278	Silverstone	Lewis	1844	?, Poland [?, Prussia]	Jacob Silverstone	Jane (?)		Aldgate, London	
30330	Silverstone	Lewis Cohen	1850	Bath	Simeon John Silverstone	Harriet Alex		Bath	
4935	Silverstone	Mark	1848	Birmingham	Philip Silverston	Fanny Samuel		Birmingham	
1005	Silverstone	Maurice	1843	Exeter, Devon	Israel Silverstone	Pauline (?)	Alice Michael	Exeter, Devon	scholar
28276	Silverstone	Morris	1838	?, Poland [?, Prussia]	Jacob Silverstone	Jane (?)		Aldgate, London	
998	Silverstone	Pauline	1813	?, Poland			Israel Silverstone	Exeter, Devon	
4936	Silverstone	Rachel	1850	Birmingham	Philip Silverston	Fanny Samuel		Birmingham	
1002	Silverstone	Rebecca	1836	Exeter, Devon	Israel Silverstone	Pauline (?)	Myer Mendelsohn	Exeter, Devon	scholar
28279	Silverstone	Rosa	1845	?, Poland [?, Prussia]	Jacob Silverstone	Jane (?)		Aldgate, London	
999	Silverstone	Rosina	1832	Honiton, Devon	Israel Silverstone	Pauline (?)	Solomon Elzner	Exeter, Devon	lace mfr
1001	Silverstone	Sarah	1835	Honiton, Devon	Israel Silverstone	Pauline (?)		Exeter, Devon	lace mfr
1007	Silverstone	Selina	1847	Exeter, Devon	Israel Silverstone	Pauline (?)	Maurice Diefenthal	Exeter, Devon	scholar
1084	Silverstone	Simeon	1826	Cracow, Poland			Rachel Myers	Falmouth, Cornwall	traveller, stationery
30328	Silverstone	Simeon John	1812	Aldgate, London			Harriet Alex	Bath	jeweller + shopkeeper
5824	Silvester	Louisa (Laura)	1829	Whitechapel, London	(?) Silvester			Bloomsbury, London	teacher
24160	Simeon	Rosina	1826	Moscow, Russia	(?) Simeon			Euston, London	dressmaker
21416	Simmerman	Lazarus	1822	Cracow, Poland				Dewsbury, Yorkshire	traveller
17305	Simmonds	Bella	1836	Whitechapel, London	(?) Simmonds			Spitalfields, London	school teacher
8701	Simmonds	Benjamin	1835	Aldgate, London	Isaac Simmonds	Clarissa (?)		Wapping, London	assistant in veterinary business
8698	Simmonds	Clarissa	1805	Aldgate, London			Isaac Simmonds	Wapping, London	
8700	Simmonds	Clarissa	1833	Aldgate, London	Isaac Simmonds	Clarissa (?)		Wapping, London	
8699	Simmonds	David	1829	Aldgate, London	Isaac Simmonds	Clarissa (?)		Wapping, London	assistant in veterinary business
17562	Simmonds	Ester	1818	?, London	(?Joseph Simmonds)			Spitalfields, London	
23270	Simmonds	Esther	1839	Whitechapel, London	(?) Simmonds			Notting Hill, London	boarding school pupil
8697	Simmonds	Isaac	1788	Portsmouth, Hampshire			Clarissa (?)	Wapping, London	veterinary surgeon
29906	Simmonds	Isaac	1822	Bow, London			Rebecca (?)	Whitechapel, London	general dealer
17560	Simmonds	Joseph	1793	?, London			(?)	Spitalfields, London	general dealer
17564	Simmonds	Joseph	1845	?, London	(?Moses) Simmonds			Spitalfields, London	
8705	Simmonds	Mander	1846	Benenden, Kent	Isaac Simmonds	Clarissa (?)		Wapping, London	scholar
8703	Simmonds	Mary	1841	Benenden, Kent	Isaac Simmonds	Clarissa (?)		Wapping, London	scholar
28492	Simmonds	Michael	1829	Spitalfields, London				Spitalfields, London	porter
17561	Simmonds	Moses	1815	?, London	Joseph Simmonds		(?)	Spitalfields, London	general dealer
8704	Simmonds	Rachael	1844	Benenden, Kent	Isaac Simmonds	Clarissa (?)		Wapping, London	scholar
17565	Simmonds	Rachel	1851	?Spitalfields, London	(?Moses) Simmonds			Spitalfields, London	
14667	Simmonds	Rebecah	1794	City, London	(?) Simmonds			Hoxton, London	house servant
29907	Simmonds	Rebecca	1815	Bethnal Green, London	(?)		Isaac Simmonds	Whitechapel, London	
17563	Simmonds	Rosey	1831	?, London	(?) Simmonds			Spitalfields, London	
29908	Simmonds	Samuel	1850	Whitechapel, London	Isaac Simmonds	Rebecca (?)		Whitechapel, London	
8702	Simmonds	Sarah Ann	1839	Aldgate, London	Isaac Simmonds	Clarissa (?)		Wapping, London	scholar

ID	surname	given names	born	birthplace	father	mother	spouse 1	1851 residence	1851 occupation
2204	Simmonds (Simmons)	Simon	1833	Poznan, Poland [Posen, Prussia]			Theresa (?)	Oxford, Oxfordshire	jewellery dealer
28657	Simmonds (Simmons)	Adelaide	1850	?Spitalfields, London	John Simmonds (Simmons)	Jane Hart		Spitalfields, London	
28653	Simmonds (Simmons)	Hannah	1835	?, London	John Simmonds (Simmons)	Jane Hart		Spitalfields, London	
28656	Simmonds (Simmons)	Israel	1847	?, London	John Simmonds (Simmons)	Jane Hart		Spitalfields, London	
28652	Simmonds (Simmons)	Jane	1815	Birmingham	Lewis Hart		John Simmonds (Simmons)	Spitalfields, London	
28651	Simmonds (Simmons)	John	1811	?, London	Israel Simmons		Jane Hart	Spitalfields, London	general dealer
28655	Simmonds (Simmons)	Pheoby	1844	?, London	John Simmonds (Simmons)	Jane Hart		Spitalfields, London	
28654	Simmonds (Simmons)	Sarah	1842	?, London	John Simmonds (Simmons)	Jane Hart		Spitalfields, London	
17408	Simmons	Aaron	1826	Aldgate, London	Joseph Simmons		Elizabeth Coleman	Wapping, London	cigar maker
12492	Simmons	Aaron (Harry)	1841	Middlesex, London	(?) Simmons	Sarah (?)		Spitalfields, London	
26769	Simmons	Abagail	1840	Spitalfields, London	(?) Simmons	Sarah (?)		Aldgate, London	
27303	Simmons	Abigail	1799	Aldgate, London	(?)		(?) Simmons	Aldgate, London	clothes dealer
24753	Simmons	Abraham	1813	Whitechapel, London	Aharon Simmons		Hannah Solomon	Southwark, London	publican out of business
12547	Simmons	Abraham	1833	Great Yarmouth, Norfolk	Philip Simmons	Elizabeth (?)		Great Yarmouth, Norfolk	coach painter ap
12490	Simmons	Abraham	1835	Middlesex, London	(?) Simmons	Sarah (?)		Spitalfields, London	cigar maker
16175	Simmons	Abraham	1846	Spitalfields, London	Samuel Simmons	Matilda Mendoza		Spitalfields, London	scholar
8537	Simmons	Abraham	1848	Penzance, Cornwall	Moses Barnett Simmons	Rosa (?)	Annie Hyams	Aldgate, London	
5458	Simmons	Abraham Barnett	1831	Penzance, Cornwall	Barnet Asher Simmons	Flora Jacob	Leah Alman	Aldgate, London	
9063	Simmons	Abraham J	1833	Strand, London	John Simmons	Sarah (?)	Rachel Salaman	Covent Garden, London	artist
14048	Simmons	Abram Chas Albert	1850	Manchester	Keppel Simmons	Emily (?)		Manchester	
14708	Simmons	Agnes	1847	Aldgate, London	Joshua Simmons	Sarah Collins		Aldgate, London	scholar
14935	Simmons	Alexander	1840	Liverpool				Bethnal Green, London	boarding school pupil
25235	Simmons	Alfred	1842	Mile End, London	Shire, 'New Synagogue Birth Records'	Ellen Alice (?)		Clerkenwell, London	scholar
18577	Simmons	Alfred	1843	?Sydney, Australia	Isaac Simmons	Matilda (?)		St John's Wood, London	
5456	Simmons	Amelia	1825	Penzance, Cornwall	Barnet Asher Simmons	Flora Jacob	Isaac Davidson	Aldgate, London	embroiderer
27306	Simmons	Amelia	1839	Brighton, Sussex	(?) Simmons	Abigail (?)		Aldgate, London	clothes dealer
21497	Simmons	Ana	1837	Aldgate, London	Samuel Simmons	Rebecca Samuel		Aldgate, London	
14047	Simmons	Anna Fortunator	1849	Manchester	Keppel Simmons	Emily (?)		Manchester	
22970	Simmons	Anney	1827	Covent Garden, London	(?) Simmons	Rachel (?)		Aldgate, London	general dealer
6771	Simmons	Asher	1848	Spitalfields, London	Joshua Simmons	Esther Lyons nee Levy	Catherine (Kate) Jacobs	Soho, London	
187	Simmons	Barnet Asher	1784	Middlesex, London	Asher Simmons	Sarah (?)	Flora Jacob	Penzance, Cornwall	Jew Minister
24628	Simmons	Barnett	1829	Spitalfields, London	Moses Simmons	Clara Zadock		Waterloo, London	tin plate worker
13374	Simmons	Barnett	1835	Sydney, Australia	Isaac Simmons	Matilda (?)		St John's Wood, London	
30397	Simmons	Barnett Joshua	1817	Westminster, London	Joshua Simmons	Ann Levy	Fanny Levy	Sheffield, Yorkshire	
14634	Simmons	Benjamin	1839	Shoreditch, London	(?) Simmons	Sarah (?)		Hoxton, London	scholar

ID	surname	given names	born	birthplace	father	mother	spouse 1	1851 residence	1851 occupation
8396	Simmons	Bernard	1815	?, London				Southampton, Hampshire	outfitter's assistant
18903	Simmons	Betsy	1840	Marylebone, London	Simon Simmons	Catherine Davis		Marylebone, London	
6875	Simmons	Caroline	1816	Spitalfields, London	(?)		Joshua Simmons	Aldgate, London	
14627	Simmons	Caroline	1826	Leigh, Essex	Laurence Lazarus	Catharine Phillips	Mark Simmons	Hoxton, London	
18899	Simmons	Caroline	1833	Marylebone, London	Simon Simmons	Catherine Davis	Henry Raphael	Marylebone, London	
23997	Simmons	Catherine	1805	?Woolwich, London	Israel Davis	Rosetta Levy	Simon Simmons	Marylebone, London	
14632	Simmons	Charles A	1836	Shoreditch, London	(?) Simmons	Sarah (?)		Hoxton, London	clerk - London Dock
21500	Simmons	Charlot	1847	Aldgate, London	Samuel Simmons	Rebecca Samuel		Aldgate, London	scholar
15083	Simmons	Clara	1838	Lambeth, London	Michael Simmons	Fanny (?)		Mile End, London	scholar
24626	Simmons	Coleman (Charles)	1822	Spitalfields, London	Moses Simmons	Clara Zadock	Jane Benjamin	Waterloo, London	tin plate worker
9404	Simmons	Colly	1777	Aldgate, London				Aldgate, London	glass dealer
15098	Simmons	Daniel	1825	Stepney, London	(?) Simmons	Mary (?)	Esther (?)	Bethnal Green, London	blacksmith
16173	Simmons	Daniel	1842	Whitechapel, London	Samuel Simmons	Matilda Mendoza		Spitalfields, London	scholar
15100	Simmons	Daniel	1848	Bethnal Green, London	Daniel Simmons	Esther (?)		Bethnal Green, London	
12546	Simmons	David	1828	Great Yarmouth, Norfolk	Philip Simmons	Elizabeth (?)		Great Yarmouth, Norfolk	coach builder
12457	Simmons	Deborah	1815	Aldgate, London				Aldgate, London	house servant
14704	Simmons	Deborah	1835	?, London	Joshua Simmons	Sarah Collins		Aldgate, London	tailoress
25237	Simmons	Edward	1846	Mile End, London	Shire, 'New Synagogue Birth Records'	Ellen Alice (?)		Clerkenwell, London	scholar
21512	Simmons	Elias	1849	Soho, London	Joshua Simmons	Elizabeth Lyon (Lyons) nee Levy		Soho, London	
12544	Simmons	Elizabeth	1796	Hadiscoe, Norfolk	(?)		Philip Simmons	Great Yarmouth, Norfolk	
9403	Simmons	Elizabeth	1801	Whitechapel, London	(?)		Samuel Simmons	Aldgate, London	
30041	Simmons	Elizabeth	1803	?, London	(?) Simmons	Lydia (?)		Wapping, London	tailoress
14701	Simmons	Elizabeth	1827	?, London	Joshua Simmons	Sarah Collins		Aldgate, London	tailoress
5548	Simmons	Elizabeth	1832	Middlesex, London	(?)		Henry Simmons	Bethnal Green, London	
17409	Simmons	Elizabeth	1832	Aldgate, London	Benjamin Coleman	Jane (?)	Aaron Simmons	Wapping, London	
25232	Simmons	Elizabeth	1836	Mile End, London	Shire, 'New Synagogue Birth Records'	Ellen Alice (?)		Clerkenwell, London	
25693	Simmons	Elizabeth	1838	Aldgate, London	(?) Simmons	Hannah (?)		Spitalfields, London	
6879	Simmons	Elizabeth	1841	Spitalfields, London	Joshua Simmons	Caroline (?)		Aldgate, London	scholar
18576	Simmons	Elizabeth	1841	?Sydney, Australia	Isaac Simmons	Matilda (?)		St John's Wood, London	
21513	Simmons	Elizabeth	1850	Soho, London	Joshua Simmons	Elizabeth Lyon (Lyons) nee Levy		Soho, London	
12542	Simmons	Ellen	1848	Norwich, Norfolk	(?) Simmons	Sophia (?)		Norwich, Norfolk	
25230	Simmons	Ellen Alice	1807	Whitechapel, London			George (Gabriel) Simmons	Clerkenwell, London	skin merchant
18902	Simmons	Ellen Rachel	1842	Marylebone, London	Simon Simmons	Catherine Davis	Frederick Isaac Moses	Marylebone, London	
15504	Simmons	Emanuel	1793	?	Jacob Simmons		Rachael Belasco	Covent Garden, London	clothes salesman
14045	Simmons	Emily	1827	Livorno, Italy [Leghorn, Tuscany]	(?)		Keppel Simmons	Manchester	
11244	Simmons	Esther	1782	Aldgate, London	(?)		(?) Simmons	Aldgate, London	general dealer
21509	Simmons	Esther	1814	Aldgate, London	Isaac Levy		Mordecai Lyon (Lyons)	Soho, London	
15099	Simmons	Esther	1831	Bethnal Green, London	(?)		Daniel Simmons	Bethnal Green, London	
16172	Simmons	Esther	1840	Whitechapel, London	Samuel Simmons	Matilda Mendoza		Spitalfields, London	scholar
15084	Simmons	Esther	1841	Lambeth, London	Michael Simmons	Fanny (?)		Mile End, London	scholar

ID	surname	given names	born	birthplace	father	mother	spouse 1	1851 residence	1851 occupation
10710	Simmons	Esther	1844	Middlesex, London	Israel Simmons	Leah (?)		Spitalfields, London	scholar
13908	Simmons	Esther	1845	Manchester	Isaac Simmons	Kate (Catherine, Kitty) Solomon	Frederick Abraham Jackson	Manchester	scholar
30622	Simmons	Esther	1851	Holborn, London	Simeon Simmons	Nancy (Ann) Moses		Holborn, London	
30624	Simmons	Esther	1851	Waterloo, London	Coleman (Charles) Simmons	Jane Benjamin		Waterloo, London	
14628	Simmons	Fanny	1832	Whitechapel, London	George (Gabriel) Simmons	Ellen Alice (?)		Hoxton, London	
13375	Simmons	Fanny	1837	Sydney, Australia	Isaac Simmons	Matilda (?)		St John's Wood, London	
14633	Simmons	Fanny	1838	Shoreditch, London	(?) Simmons	Sarah (?)		Hoxton, London	at home
21499	Simmons	Fanny	1844	Aldgate, London	Samuel Simmons	Rebecca Samuel		Aldgate, London	scholar
15080	Simmons	Fanny	1807	Lambeth, London	(?)		Michael Simmons	Mile End, London	
28123	Simmons	Fanny (Frances)	1802	?, London	Yosef Woolf		John (Jacob) Simmons	Spitalfields, London	
19508	Simmons	Fanny (Frances)	1817	Westminster, London	Joshua Simmons	Ann Levy		Strand, London	assistant to fancy costumer
5450	Simmons	Flora	1789	Redruth, Cornwall	Moses Jacob		Barnet Asher Simmons	Penzance, Cornwall	
14635	Simmons	Frederick J	1841	Shoreditch, London	(?) Simmons	Sarah (?)		Hoxton, London	scholar
9106	Simmons	Gabriel	1840	Strand, London	John Simmons	Sarah (?)		Covent Garden, London	
25229	Simmons	George (Gabriel)	1803	?, Poland [?, Prussia]			Ellen Alice (?)	Clerkenwell, London	skin merchant
24754	Simmons	Hannah	1807	Aldgate, London	Isaiah Solomon		Abraham Simmons	Southwark, London	
19507	Simmons	Hannah	1812	Westminster, London	Joshua Simmons	Ann Levy		Strand, London	assistant to fancy costumer
25692	Simmons	Hannah	1816	Aldgate, London	(?)		(?) Simmons	Spitalfields, London	coffee house keeper
27304	Simmons	Hannah	1826	Brighton, Sussex	(?) Simmons	Abigail (?)		Aldgate, London	clothes dealer
20581	Simmons	Hannah	1827	Whitechapel, London	Eliezer Simmons			Spitalfields, London	tailoress
10709	Simmons	Hannah	1842	Spitalfields, London	Israel Simmons	Leah Marks	Harris Jacobs	Spitalfields, London	scholar
6884	Simmons	Hannah	1850	Spitalfields, London	Joshua Simmons	Caroline (?)		Aldgate, London	
5547	Simmons	Henry	1828	Middlesex, London	(?) Simmons		Elizabeth (?)	Bethnal Green, London	
6878	Simmons	Henry	1840	Spitalfields, London	Joshua Simmons	Caroline (?)		Aldgate, London	scholar
15086	Simmons	Henry	1847	Lambeth, London	Michael Simmons	Fanny (?)		Mile End, London	
13380	Simmons	Henry	1850	Marylebone, London	Isaac Simmons	Matilda (?)		St John's Wood, London	
18534	Simmons	Henry	1851	Bethnal Green, London	Henry Simmons	Elizabeth (?)		Bethnal Green, London	
14631	Simmons	Henry C	1834	Shoreditch, London	(?) Simmons	Sarah (?)		Hoxton, London	clerk (?actuaries)
9104	Simmons	Henry John	1835	Strand, London	John Simmons	Sarah (?)	Fanny Hart	Covent Garden, London	tailor
28385	Simmons	Isaac	1787	?, Germany				Spitalfields, London	hawker
13371	Simmons	Isaac	1805	Marylebone, London	Nathan		Matilda (?)	St John's Wood, London	gold merchant
13906	Simmons	Isaac	1806	Liverpool	Israel Simmons		Kate (Catherine, Kitty) Solomon	Manchester	watchmaker
12488	Simmons	Isaac	1830	Middlesex, London	(?) Simmons	Sarah (?)		Spitalfields, London	fruiterer
6885	Simmons	Isaac	1837	Middlesex, London	Joshua Simmons	Sarah Collins	Rose (?)	Aldgate, London	cigar maker
6881	Simmons	Isaac	1845	Spitalfields, London	Joshua Simmons	Caroline (?)	Rosa (?)	Aldgate, London	scholar
10711	Simmons	Isaac	1845	Middlesex, London	Israel Simmons	Leah (?)		Spitalfields, London	scholar
10707	Simmons	Israel	1815	Middlesex, London	Isaac Simons		Leah Marks	Spitalfields, London	general dealer
24627	Simmons	Jane	1819	Finsbury, London	Solomon Benjamin		Coleman (Charles) Simmons	Waterloo, London	
14046	Simmons	Jas Angelo	1847	Manchester	Keppel Simmons	Emily (?)		Manchester	at home
9101	Simmons	John	1805	Strand, London	Joshua Simmons	Ann Levy	Sarah b. Judah	Covent Garden, London	fancy costumier

ID	surname	given names	born	birthplace	father	mother	spouse 1	1851 residence	1851 occupation
28105	Simmons	John	1822	Spitalfields, London				Spitalfields, London	general dealer
11112	Simmons	John	1830	Middlesex, London	Aharon Simmons			Aldgate, London	cigar maker
12489	Simmons	John	1830	Middlesex, London	(?) Simmons	Sarah (?)		Spitalfields, London	fruiterer
25233	Simmons	John	1838	Mile End, London	Shire, 'New Synagogue Birth Records'	Ellen Alice (?)		Clerkenwell, London	scholar
21064	Simmons	John	1840	Sydney, NSW, Australia				Dover, Kent	boarding school pupil
28122	Simmons	John (Jacob)	1797	?, Poland	Simha		Fanny (Frances) Woolf	Spitalfields, London	furrier
3107	Simmons	Joseph	1793	Aldgate, London				Spitalfields, London	general dealer
18278	Simmons	Joseph	1815	?, Poland [?, Russia Poland]				Salisbury, Wiltshire	jeweller
18900	Simmons	Joseph	1835	Marylebone, London	Simon Simmons	Catherine Davis		Marylebone, London	
11856	Simmons	Joseph	1836	Middlesex, London	(?) Simmons	(?)		Whitechapel, London	inmate of orphan school
21498	Simmons	Joseph	1840	Aldgate, London	Samuel Simmons	Rebecca Samuel		Aldgate, London	scholar
13377	Simmons	Joseph	1845	Sydney, Australia	Isaac Simmons	Matilda (?)		St John's Wood, London	
30623	Simmons	Joseph	1851	Whitechapel, London	Aaron Simmons	Elizabeth Coleman		Whitechapel, London	
336	Simmons	Joshua	1801	?, London	Asher Simmons		Sarah Collins	Aldgate, London	general dealer
21508	Simmons	Joshua	1812	?, London	Joseph Simmons		Phoebe Cohen	Soho, London	
6874	Simmons	Joshua	1815	Spitalfields, London			Caroline (?)	Aldgate, London	licensed hawker
9103	Simmons	Joshua	1837	Strand, London	John Simmons	Sarah (?)		Covent Garden, London	
26768	Simmons	Joshua	1837	Spitalfields, London	(?) Simmons	Sarah (?)		Aldgate, London	
18108	Simmons	Judah	1849	Holborn, London	Simeon Simmons	Nancy (Ann) Moses		Holborn, London	
19506	Simmons	Julia	1811	Westminster, London	Joshua Simmons	Ann Levy		Strand, London	assistant to fancy costumer
24755	Simmons	Julia	1835	Aldgate, London	Abraham Simmons	Hannah Solomon		Southwark, London	
6877	Simmons	Julia	1836	Spitalfields, London	Joshua Simmons	Caroline (?)		Aldgate, London	tailoress
13376	Simmons	Julia	1840	Sydney, Australia	Isaac Simmons	Matilda (?)		St John's Wood, London	
25236	Simmons	Julius	1844	Mile End, London	Shire, 'New Synagogue Birth Records'	Ellen Alice (?)		Clerkenwell, London	scholar
13907	Simmons	Kate (Catherine, Kitty)	1825	Middlesex, London	Lyon (Yehuda) Solomon	Esther (?)	Isaac Simmons	Manchester	
14044	Simmons	Keppel	1812	Limburg, Germany [Limburg, Prussia]			Emily (?)	Manchester	general merchant
15081	Simmons	Laura	1834	Brighton, Sussex	Michael Simmons	Fanny (?)		Mile End, London	
25238	Simmons	Laurence	1848	Mile End, London	Shire, 'New Synagogue Birth Records'	Ellen Alice (?)		Clerkenwell, London	
13381	Simmons	Laurence	1851	Marylebone, London	Isaac Simmons	Matilda (?)		St John's Wood, London	
19180	Simmons	Laurence Mark	1851	Hoxton, London	Mark George Simmons	Caroline Lazarus		Hoxton, London	
11245	Simmons	Leah	1811	Aldgate, London	(?) Simmons	Esther (?)		Aldgate, London	
10708	Simmons	Leah	1819	Middlesex, London	Jacob Marks		Israel Simmons	Spitalfields, London	general dealer
28518	Simmons	Leah	1825	Whitechapel, London	(?)		Solomon Simmons	Spitalfields, London	
6882	Simmons	Leah	1846	Spitalfields, London	Joshua Simmons	Caroline (?)	Abraham Goldstein	Aldgate, London	scholar
5455	Simmons	Levy Barnett	1828	Penzance, Cornwall	Barnet Asher Simmons	Flora Jacob	Phoebe Levi	Aldgate, London	carver + gilder
25694	Simmons	Lewis	1788	Aldgate, London				Spitalfields, London	assistant to coffee house keeper
18279	Simmons	Lewis	1826	?, Poland [?, Russia Poland]				Salisbury, Wiltshire	silversmith
14707	Simmons	Lewis	1845	?, London	Joshua Simmons	Sarah Collins		Aldgate, London	scholar

ID	surname	given names	born	birthplace	father	mother	spouse 1	1851 residence	1851 occupation
13909	Simmons	Louisa	1847	Manchester	Isaac Simmons	Kate (Catherine, Kitty) Solomon	Edwin M Davis	Manchester	
14630	Simmons	Louisa Ann	1829	Shoreditch, London	(?) Simmons	Sarah (?)		Hoxton, London	at home
30040	Simmons	Lydia	1780	Portsmouth, Hampshire	(?)		(?) Simmons	Wapping, London	
14957	Simmons	Maria	1837	Liverpool	(?) Simmons			Bethnal Green, London	boarding school pupil
14626	Simmons	Mark George	1824	Whitechapel, London	George (Gabriel) Simmons	Ellen Alice (?)	Caroline Lazarus	Hoxton, London	fur merchant
6880	Simmons	Martha	1843	Spitalfields, London	Joshua Simmons	Caroline (?)		Aldgate, London	scholar
15097	Simmons	Mary	1781	Shoreditch, London	(?)		(?) Simmons	Bethnal Green, London	dressmaker
13145	Simmons	Mary	1830	Middlesex, London	(?) Simmons			Aldgate, London	
18901	Simmons	Mary Ann	1838	Marylebone, London	Simon Simmons	Catherine Davis	Isaac Raphael	Marylebone, London	
18107	Simmons	Mary Ann (Miriam)	1848	Holborn, London	Simeon Simmons	Nancy (Ann) Moses		Holborn, London	
12548	Simmons	Maryann E	1850	Great Yarmouth, Norfolk	(?) Simmons			Great Yarmouth, Norfolk	
13372	Simmons	Matilda	1811	Finsbury, London	Baruch		Isaac Simmons	St John's Wood, London	
16170	Simmons	Matilda	1811	Whitechapel, London	Daniel Mendoza		Samuel Simmons	Spitalfields, London	dress maker
14050	Simmons	Maurice	1833	Essen, Germany [Essen, Prussia]				Manchester	apprentice to general merchant
25234	Simmons	Maurice	1840	Mile End, London	Shire, 'New Synagogue Birth Records'	Ellen Alice (?)		Clerkenwell, London	scholar
21047	Simmons	Maurice	1842	Sydney, NSW, Australia				Dover, Kent	boarding school pupil
15079	Simmons	Michael	1808	Middlesex, London			Fanny (?)	Mile End, London	bookseller + stationer
22969	Simmons	Michael	1823	Soho, London	(?) Simmons	Rachel (?)		Aldgate, London	general dealer
21501	Simmons	Michal	1849	Aldgate, London	Samuel Simmons	Rebecca Samuel		Aldgate, London	scholar
27499	Simmons	Moses	1829	Middlesex, London				Aldgate, London	porter
5453	Simmons	Moses Barnett	1817	Penzance, Cornwall	Barnet Asher Simmons	Flora Jacob	Rosa Aaron	Aldgate, London	carver + gilder empl 3
18106	Simmons	Nancy (Ann)	1816	Middlesex, London	Judah Moses		Simeon Simmons	Holborn, London	
13379	Simmons	Nathan	1848	Marylebone, London	Isaac Simmons	Matilda (?)		St John's Wood, London	
27305	Simmons	Pheobe	1830	Brighton, Sussex	(?) Simmons	Abigail (?)		Aldgate, London	clothes dealer
12543	Simmons	Philip	1802	Great Yarmouth, Norfolk			Elizabeth (?)	Great Yarmouth, Norfolk	turner
12545	Simmons	Philip	1824	Great Yarmouth, Norfolk	Philip Simmons	Elizabeth (?)		Great Yarmouth, Norfolk	turner
6876	Simmons	Phoebe	1834	Spitalfields, London	Joshua Simmons	Caroline (?)	Barnet Burnstine	Aldgate, London	tailoress
3105	Simmons	Priscilla Gabriel	1823	?, London	Eliezer Lipman Gabriel	(?Judith Barnet?)	Solomon Simmons	Spitalfields, London	
14703	Simmons	Rachael	1833	?, London	Joshua Simmons	Sarah Collins		Aldgate, London	tailoress
13492	Simmons	Rachal	1777	?, Yorkshire	(?)		(?) Simmons	Manchester	
22968	Simmons	Rachel	1781	Aldgate, London	(?)		(?) Simmons	Aldgate, London	
21511	Simmons	Rachel	1841	Spitalfields, London	Joshua Simmons	Phoebe Cohen		Soho, London	
3106	Simmons	Rachel	1851	Spitalfields, London	Solomon Simmons	Priscilla Gabriel Green		Spitalfields, London	
21496	Simmons	Rebecca	1822	Aldgate, London	Samuel Bensadon		Samuel Simmons	Aldgate, London	
14706	Simmons	Rebecca	1841	?, London	Joshua Simmons	Sarah Collins		Aldgate, London	scholar
6883	Simmons	Rebecca	1848	Spitalfields, London	Joshua Simmons	Caroline (?)		Aldgate, London	scholar
8536	Simmons	Rosa	1823	Whitechapel, London	Abraham Aaron		Moses Barnett Simmons	Aldgate, London	
15085	Simmons	Rosa	1845	Lambeth, London	Michael Simmons	Fanny (?)	Daviid Levien	Mile End, London	scholar
11246	Simmons	Rose	1829	Aldgate, London	(?) Simmons	Esther (?)		Aldgate, London	
16174	Simmons	Rose	1844	Spitalfields, London	Samuel Simmons	Matilda Mendoza		Spitalfields, London	scholar
14702	Simmons	Rosetta	1831	?, London	Joshua Simmons	Sarah Collins		Aldgate, London	tailoress

ID	surname	given names	born	birthplace	father	mother	spouse 1	1851 residence	1851 occupation
12541	Simmons	Rosina	1842	Norwich, Norfolk	(?) Simmons	Sophia (?)		Norwich, Norfolk	scholar
9402	Simmons	Samuel	1795	Aldgate, London			Elizabeth (?)	Aldgate, London	glass dealer
21495	Simmons	Samuel	1803	Aldgate, London	Benjamin Simmons		Rebecca Samuel	Aldgate, London	cab driver
6945	Simmons	Samuel	1809	Whitechapel, London	Michael Simmons		Matilda Mendoza	Spitalfields, London	clothes dealer
13378	Simmons	Samuel	1847	Sydney, Australia	Isaac Simmons	Matilda (?)		St John's Wood, London	
12484	Simmons	Sarah	1775	Aldgate, London	Israel Simmons		Isaac Simmons	Aldgate, London	
12487	Simmons	Sarah	1800	Spitalfields, London	(?)		(?) Simmons	Spitalfields, London	general dealer
9102	Simmons	Sarah	1801	Strand, London	Judah		John Simmons	Covent Garden, London	
14700	Simmons	Sarah	1807	?, London	Benjamin Collins		Joshua Simmons	Aldgate, London	tailoress
14629	Simmons	Sarah	1809	Spitalfields, London	(?)		(?) Simmons	Hoxton, London	tambourine manufacturer empl 16
1131	Simmons	Sarah	1823	Penzance, Cornwall	Barnet Asher Simmons	Flora Jacob		Penzance, Cornwall	domestic assistant
13373	Simmons	Sarah	1831	Marylebone, London	Isaac Simmons	Matilda (?)		St John's Wood, London	
15082	Simmons	Sarah	1836	Lambeth, London	Michael Simmons	Fanny (?)		Mile End, London	scholar
16171	Simmons	Sarah	1838	Whitechapel, London	Samuel Simmons	Matilda Mendoza		Spitalfields, London	scholar
8016	Simmons	Sarah	1848	Manchester	Isaac Simmons	Kate (Catherine, Kitty) Solomon	Albert S Lewis	Manchester	
19505	Simmons	Simeon	1805	Westminster, London	Joshua Simmons	Ann Levy		Strand, London	fancy costumer + army and navy outfitter + tailor + dealer in camp equipage
18105	Simmons	Simeon	1818	Middlesex, London	Moses Simmons		Nancy (Ann) Moses	Holborn, London	tin plate worker
28124	Simmons	Simeon	1831	?, London	John (Jacob) Simmons	Fanny (Frances) Woolf		Spitalfields, London	cigar maker
9107	Simmons	Simeon J	1831	?Strand, London	John Simmons	Sarah (?)	Sophia Davis	Covent Garden, London	army + navy outfitter
23996	Simmons	Simon	1803	?	Joseph Simmons		Catherine Davis	Marylebone, London	clothes salesman
21510	Simmons	Simon	1839	Spitalfields, London	Joshua Simmons	Phoebe Cohen		Soho, London	
1132	Simmons	Simon Barnett	1836	Penzance, Cornwall	Barnet Asher Simmons	Flora Jacob	Rachel Joseph	Penzance, Cornwall	shop assistant
1086	Simmons	Solomon	1778	Truro, Cornwall				Falmouth, Cornwall	pedlar
28517	Simmons	Solomon	1823	Whitechapel, London			Leah (?)	Spitalfields, London	general dealer
3104	Simmons	Solomon	1826	?, London	Joseph Simmons		Priscilla Gabriel (Gabel) Green	Spitalfields, London	tailor
12540	Simmons	Sophia	1813	Hackford, Norfolk	(?)		(?) Simmons	Norwich, Norfolk	seamstress
25231	Simmons	Theresa	1833	Whitechapel, London	George (Gabriel) Simmons	Ellen Alice (?)		Clerkenwell, London	
18575	Simmons	Theresa	1839	?Sydney, Australia	Isaac Simmons	Matilda (?)		St John's Wood, London	
14049	Simmons	William	1826	Essen, Germany [Essen, Prussia]				Manchester	agent [to general merchant]
2203	Simmons	Wolf	1809	Poznan, Poland [Posen, Prussia]				Oxford, Oxfordshire	jewellery dealer
12491	Simmons	Woolf	1837	Middlesex, London	(?) Simmons	Sarah (?)		Spitalfields, London	
21502	Simmons	Woolf	1851	Aldgate, London	Samuel Simmons	Rebecca Samuel		Aldgate, London	
11202	Simmons (Simons)	Esther	1850	Spitalfields, London	Simon Simons	Hannah Moses		Aldgate, London	
11200	Simmons (Simons)	Hannah	1825	Aldgate, London	Elias Moses	Elizabeth (?)	Simon Simmons (Simons)	Aldgate, London	
11201	Simmons (Simons)	Lewis (Louis)	1848	Aldgate, London	Simon Simons	Hannah Moses	Leah Wilks	Aldgate, London	
11199	Simmons (Simons)	Simon	1822	Spitalfields, London	Levy Simmons		Hannah Moses	Aldgate, London	general dealer

ID	surname	given names	born	birthplace	father	mother	spouse 1	1851 residence	1851 occupation
24976	Simmons (Symonds)	Aaron	1837	St Giles, London	Isaac Simmons (Symonds)	Rachael Goodman		Holborn, London	cigar manufacturer
24977	Simmons (Symonds)	Fanny	1838	Holborn, London	Isaac Simmons (Symonds)	Rachael Goodman		Holborn, London	
24975	Simmons (Symonds)	Henry	1831	St Giles, London	Isaac Simmons (Symonds)	Rachael Goodman		Holborn, London	cigar manufacturer
24972	Simmons (Symonds)	Isaac	1806	Spitalfields, London	Aaron Simmons		Rachael Goodman	Holborn, London	general dealer + haberdasher
24979	Simmons (Symonds)	Josua	1847	Holborn, London	Isaac Simmons (Symonds)	Rachael Goodman		Holborn, London	
24974	Simmons (Symonds)	Julia	1829	St Giles, London	Isaac Simmons (Symonds)	Rachael Goodman		Holborn, London	
24978	Simmons (Symonds)	Mary	1843	Holborn, London	Isaac Simmons (Symonds)	Rachael Goodman		Holborn, London	
24973	Simmons (Symonds)	Rachael	1806	Whitechapel, London	Perets Goodman		Isaac Simmons (Symonds)	Holborn, London	general dealer + haberdasher
21374	Simon	Amelia	1834	Mainz, Germany	(?) Simon			Lincoln, Lincolnshire	
2571	Simon	Barnhardt	1810	?, Germany			Hulda (?)	Hull, Yorkshire	master tailor
4196	Simon	Charles Moncrieffe	1846	Hammersmith, London	John [Serjeant] Simon	Rachel Salaman	Adela Louise Behrens	Liverpool	
26343	Simon	Flora	1829	?, London				Aldgate, London	dressmakeer
17009	Simon	Frederic	1835	Jamaica, West Indies	Henry Simon	Frances Simon		Marylebone, London	lithographer
17134	Simon	Frederique Anthelme	1822	?, France				Bradford, Yorkshire	designer, worsted manufacturer
26653	Simon	Hannah	1823	?, Germany	(?)		Samuel Simon	Aldgate, London	
2335	Simon	Henrietta	1824	Leeds, Yorkshire			Julius Simon	Leeds, Yorkshire	
2572	Simon	Hulda	1822	?, Germany			Barnhardt Simon	Hull, Yorkshire	milliner
2573	Simon	Isidor	1847	?, Germany	Barnhardt Simon	Hulda (?)		Hull, Yorkshire	
4197	Simon	James Dunn	1847	Hammersmith, London	John [Serjeant] Simon	Rachel Salaman		Liverpool	
26342	Simon	John	1811	?, London				Aldgate, London	clothes dealer
26344	Simon	John	1832	?, London				Aldgate, London	cigar maker
2337	Simon	John (Henry)	1851	Leeds, Yorkshire	Julius Simon	Henrietta		Leeds, Yorkshire	
4195	Simon	John [Serjeant]	1818	Montego Bay, Jamaica, West Indies	Isaac Simon		Rachel Salaman	Liverpool	barrister at law
22083	Simon	Joseph	1832	?, Russia [Slaskowe, Russia]				Whitechapel, London	tailor
7523	Simon	Joseph	1851	Liverpool	John [Serjeant] Simon	Rachel Salaman		Liverpool	
2334	Simon	Julius	1813	?, Germany			Henrietta (?)	Leeds, Yorkshire	cloth merchant
2574	Simon	Julius	1850	?, Germany	Barnhardt Simon	Hulda (?)		Hull, Yorkshire	
24891	Simon	Louis M	1783	Middlesex, London			Matilda (?)	Lewisham, London	stockbroker
2336	Simon	Mary	1850	Leeds, Yorkshire	Julius Simon	Henrietta (?)		Leeds, Yorkshire	
7524	Simon	Naomi	1850	Liverpool	John [Serjeant] Simon	Rachel Salaman		Liverpool	
5115	Simon	Rachel	1819	Portsmouth, Hampshire	Joseph Simon	Sarah (?)	Benjamin Levy	Portsmouth, Hampshire	
4194	Simon	Rachel	1826	Westminster, London	Simeon Kensington Salaman	Alice Cowen	John [Serjeant] Simon	Liverpool	writer
26341	Simon	Rebecca	1785	?, London	(?)		(?) Simon	Aldgate, London	
5114	Simon	Rebecca	1815	Portsmouth, Hampshire	Joseph Simon	Sarah (?)		Portsmouth, Hampshire	
26652	Simon	Samuel	1826	?, Germany			Hannah (?)	Aldgate, London	tailor jobbing

655

ID	surname	given names	born	birthplace	father	mother	spouse 1	1851 residence	1851 occupation
5113	Simon	Sarah	1786	?, London			Joseph Simon	Portsmouth, Hampshire	living private
15163	Simon	Sarah	1816	Chatham, Kent	(?)		(?) Simon	Haggerston, London	
23809	Simon	Zillah	1844	?, Jamaica, West Indies	John [Serjeant] Simon	Rachel Salaman	Samuel Henry Moses	Liverpool	
21871	Simonds	Louisa	1833	Marylebone, London	(?) Simonds			Clerkenwell, London	servant
9716	Simons	Abraham	1843	Cheltenham, Gloucestershire	(?) Simons	(?) Aaron		Birmingham	
21599	Simons	Abraham	1843	Middlesex, London	(?) Simons	(?) Isaacs		Strand, London	
28203	Simons	Abraham	1845	Whitechapel, London	Simon Simons	Rachael Hyams		Spitalfields, London	scholar
30763	Simons	Abraham	1847	Finsbury, London	George Simons	Sarah Nathan		Finsbury, London	
4184	Simons	Adelaide	1841	?, London	Benjamin Simons	Rebecca Jacobs		Whitechapel, London	
17105	Simons	Ann	1835	?, England	(?) Simons			St Helier, Jersey, Channel Islands	general servant
3870	Simons	Ann	1850	Spitalfields, London	Solomon Simons	Jane Levy		Spitalfields, London	
30764	Simons	Barnett	1849	Finsbury, London	George Simons	Sarah Nathan		Finsbury, London	
236	Simons	Benjamin	1817	?, London	Philip Simons	Elizabeth Benjamin	Rebecca Jacobs	Glasgow, Scotland	fruit merchant
20626	Simons	Betsey	1841	Spitalfields, London	Henry Simons	Reyna Uzieli		Spitalfields, London	scholar
28283	Simons	Betsy	1847	Whitechapel, London	(?) Simons			Aldgate, London	
28274	Simons	Bluma	1793	Whitechapel, London	(?)		Simon Israel	Aldgate, London	dressmaker
14981	Simons	Caroline	1842	Middlesex, London	(?) Simons			Bethnal Green, London	boarding school pupil
30762	Simons	Caroline	1845	Finsbury, London	George Simons	Sarah Nathan		Finsbury, London	scholar at home
4186	Simons	Clara	1844	?, London	Benjamin Simons	Rebecca Jacobs	Isidore Morris	Whitechapel, London	
20623	Simons	David	1825	Spitalfields, London	Henry Simons	Reyna Uzieli		Spitalfields, London	cordwainer
2154	Simons	David	1827	Hull, Yorkshire	Samuel Simons	Sarah T (?)		Hull, Yorkshire	watchmaker
25004	Simons	Elizabeth	1776	Birmingham	(?)		(?) Simons	Holborn, London	annuitant
15464	Simons	Elizabeth	1836	Strand, London	Samuel Simons	Frances (?)		Covent Garden, London	
30759	Simons	Elizabeth	1840	Finsbury, London	George Simons	Sarah Nathan		Finsbury, London	scholar at home
3869	Simons	Elizabeth	1848	Spitalfields, London	Solomon Simons	Jane Levy		Spitalfields, London	
11717	Simons	Ester	1841	Aldgate, London	(?) Simons			Aldgate, London	scholar
26500	Simons	Esther	1812	Upton?, Kent	Samuel Simons	Sarah Moses		Dover, Kent	lodging house keeper
30760	Simons	Esther	1843	Finsbury, London	George Simons	Sarah Nathan		Finsbury, London	scholar at home
15462	Simons	Frances	1809	Spitalfields, London			Frances (?)	Covent Garden, London	
10883	Simons	Gabriel	1815	Aldgate, London			Rachel Benjamin	Spitalfields, London	general dealer
5616	Simons	George	1809	?Stratton, Cornwall	Abraham Simons		Sarah Nathan	Finsbury, London	watch manufacturer
28281	Simons	Hannah	1784	?, Holland	(?)		(?) Simons	Aldgate, London	
20625	Simons	Hannah	1833	Spitalfields, London	Henry Simons	Reyna Uzieli		Spitalfields, London	tailoress
21687	Simons	Henrietta	1809	Bideford, Devon	Abraham Simons			Islington, London	annuitant
20621	Simons	Henry	1779	Aldgate, London	Leib Tscherra Naz		Reyna Uzieli	Spitalfields, London	
15465	Simons	Henry	1838	Strand, London	Samuel Simons	Frances (?)		Covent Garden, London	
9717	Simons	Henry	1845	Bristol	(?) Simons	(?) Aaron		Birmingham	
17300	Simons	Henry	1845	Whitechapel, London	Joseph Simons	Leah Jacobs		Spitalfields, London	
28204	Simons	Hyman	1845	Whitechapel, London	Simon Simons	Rachael Hyams		Spitalfields, London	scholar
20624	Simons	Isaac	1831	Spitalfields, London	Henry Simons	Reyna Uzieli		Spitalfields, London	baker
28205	Simons	Jacob	1849	Whitechapel, London	Simon Simons	Rachael Hyams		Spitalfields, London	scholar
3867	Simons	Jane	1825	Sheffield, Yorkshire	Michael Levy		Solomon Simons	Spitalfields, London	
9236	Simons	Jane	1832	Bethnal Green, London	(?) Simons			Spitalfields, London	domestic servant
17301	Simons	Jane	1847	Aldgate, London	Joseph Simons	Leah Jacobs		Spitalfields, London	

ID	surname	given names	born	birthplace	father	mother	spouse 1	1851 residence	1851 occupation
17298	Simons	Joseph	1819	Whitechapel, London	Henry Simons		Leah Jacobs	Spitalfields, London	baker
28202	Simons	Julia	1844	Whitechapel, London	Simon Simons	Rachael Hyams		Spitalfields, London	scholar
1114	Simons	Kitty	1772	Redruth, Cornwall				Penzance, Cornwall	annuitant
17299	Simons	Leah	1819	Aldgate, London	Moses Jacobs	Anne (Hannah) Solomon	Joseph Simons	Spitalfields, London	
29414	Simons	Levi	1821	Amsterdam, Holland			Rebecca (?)	Spitalfields, London	cigar maker
3868	Simons	Lewis	1846	Spitalfields, London	Solomon Simons	Jane Levy		Spitalfields, London	
4939	Simons	Lewis (Louis)	1811	?, Poland				Birmingham	cap maker
10268	Simons	Lizer	1781	Spitalfields, London				Spitalfields, London	watchmaker
21686	Simons	Louisa	1807	Bideford, Devon	Abraham Simons			Islington, London	annuitant
30761	Simons	Margaret	1844	Finsbury, London	George Simons	Sarah Nathan		Finsbury, London	scholar at home
2575	Simons	Maria	1829	Hull, Yorkshire	Samuel T Simons	Sarah (?)		Hull, Yorkshire	
17101	Simons	Mary	1829	?, England	(?) Simons			St Peter Port, Guernsey, Channel Islands	house servant
4170	Simons	Michael	1842	?, London	Benjamin Simons	Rebecca Jacobs	Alice (Charlotte Elsie Alice Carlotta) Moses	Glasgow, Scotland	fruiterer
12078	Simons	Morris	1823	?, Poland [?, Prussia]				Spitalfields, London	tailor
21685	Simons	Moses	1795	Bude, Cornwall	Abraham Simons			Islington, London	watch manufacturer
15467	Simons	Philip	1844	Covent Garden, London	Samuel Simons	Frances (?)		Covent Garden, London	
15468	Simons	Phoebe	1850	Covent Garden, London	Samuel Simons	Frances (?)		Covent Garden, London	
28282	Simons	Priscilla	1827	Aldgate, London	(?) Simons	Hannah (?)		Aldgate, London	dealer in clothes
28201	Simons	Rachael	1820	Soho, London	(?) Hyams		Simon Simons	Spitalfields, London	
10884	Simons	Rachel	1809	Whitechapel, London	(?) Benjamin	Hannah (?)	Gabriel Simons	Spitalfields, London	seamstress
29416	Simons	Rachel	1848	Amsterdam, Holland	Levi Simons	Rebecca (?)		Spitalfields, London	scholar
15466	Simons	Ralph	1842	Whitechapel, London	Samuel Simons	Frances (?)	Miriam Somers	Covent Garden, London	
29415	Simons	Rebecca	1821	Amsterdam, Holland	(?)		Levi Simons	Spitalfields, London	cap maker
15463	Simons	Rebecca	1831	Lambeth, London	Samuel Simons	Frances (?)		Covent Garden, London	
20622	Simons	Reyna	1792	Whitechapel, London	Joseph Uzieli	(?Rachel) (?)	Henry Simons	Spitalfields, London	
10885	Simons	Reyna	1838	Whitechapel, London	Gabriel Simons	Rachel (?)		Spitalfields, London	
26498	Simons	Samuel	1778	Chatham, Kent			Sarah Moses	Dover, Kent	lodging house keeper
2155	Simons	Samuel	1786	?, Poland [?, Prussia]			Sarah T (?)	Hull, Yorkshire	Hull Hebrew reader
15461	Simons	Samuel	1807	Strand, London			Frances (?)	Covent Garden, London	tailor
26499	Simons	Sarah	1780	Dover, Kent	(?) Moses		Samuel Simons	Dover, Kent	lodging house keeper's wife
30758	Simons	Sarah	1813	Holborn, London	Barnet Nathan		George Simons	Finsbury, London	watch manufacturer
2576	Simons	Sarah T	1793	Middlesex, London			Samuel Simons	Hull, Yorkshire	
9718	Simons	Selina	1849	Ludlow, Shropshire	(?) Simons	(?) Aaron		Birmingham	
28200	Simons	Simon	1814	Aldgate, London			Rachael Hyams	Spitalfields, London	clothes dealer
3866	Simons	Solomon	1824	Spitalfields, London	Levy Simmons		Jane Levy	Spitalfields, London	general dealer
10882	Simons (Symonds)	Hannah	1843	Whitechapel, London	Gabriel Simons	Rachel (?)	Joseph de Jacob Gomes Da Costa	Spitalfields, London	
25495	Simonsen	Caroline	1831	Hull, Yorkshire	Solomon Meyer		Michael Ludwig Simonsen	Tower Hill, London	
25496	Simonsen	Lionel	1849	City, London	Michael Ludwig Simonsen	Caroline Meyer		Tower Hill, London	
25494	Simonsen	Michael Ludwig	1816	Copenhagen, Denmark	Levy Simonsen		Caroline Meyer	Tower Hill, London	merchant + colonial agent
25497	Simonsen	Sidney	1850	City, London	Michael Ludwig Simonsen	Caroline Meyer		Tower Hill, London	

ID	surname	given names	born	birthplace	father	mother	spouse 1	1851 residence	1851 occupation
7746	Simonson	Clara	1851	Salford, Lancashire	Michael Hart Simonson	Isabella Goldstone		Salford, Lancashire	
7745	Simonson	Isabella	1829	Liverpool	Michael Goldstone	Hannah (?)	Michael Hart Simonson	Salford, Lancashire	
7521	Simonson	Michael Hart	1804	?, Poland			Isabella Goldstone	Salford, Lancashire	shochet of Hebrew congragation
24561	Simpson	Charles	1844	?, London	(?) Simpson	Clara (?)		Brixton, London	scholar
24560	Simpson	Clara	1814	Wroclaw, Poland [Bresslau, Prussia]	(?)		Henry Simpson	Brixton, London	merchant's wife
24562	Simpson	Eleanor	1847	Aldgate, London	(?) Simpson	Clara (?)		Brixton, London	
4025	Simpson	Fanny	1785	Portsmouth, Hampshire	Simon Abrahams	Elizabeth Emanuel	Samuel Simpson	Portsmouth, Hampshire	
24564	Simpson	Fradel	1782	Zlotow, Poland [Flatow, Prussia]	(?) Simpson			Brixton, London	
24563	Simpson	George	1850	Brixton, London	Henry Simpson	Clara (?)		Brixton, London	
30666	Simpson	Henry	1802	Hamburg, Germany	Joshua Simpson		Clara (?)	Brixton, London	merchant
4024	Simpson	Samuel	1782	Portsmouth, Hampshire	Henry Simpson		Fanny Abrahams	Portsmouth, Hampshire	rag merchant
13704	Singer	Aaron	1843	Aldgate, London	Julius Singer	Fredericka (Rika, Rachel) Woolf		Bloomsbury, London	scholar
13739	Singer	Anna	1842	Manchester	Nathan Singer	Sophia Levy nee (?)		Manchester	
22124	Singer	Edward	1821	Győr, Hungary [Raab, Hungary]			Rachel (?)	Whitechapel, London	tailor
7386	Singer	Fredericka (Rika, Rachel)	1810	Hamburg, Germany	Woolf Woolf		Julius Singer	Bloomsbury, London	
13705	Singer	Jacob	1845	Whitechapel, London	Julius Singer	Fredericka (Rika, Rachel) Woolf		Bloomsbury, London	scholar
7385	Singer	Julius	1811	Raab, Hungary	Baruk Singer		Frederica (Rika, Rachel) Woolf	Bloomsbury, London	journeyman tailor
13706	Singer	Miriam	1849	Covent Garden, London	Julius Singer	Fredericka (Rika, Rachel) Woolf		Bloomsbury, London	
13736	Singer	Nathan	1805	abroad			Sophia Levy nee (?)	Manchester	marine store dealer
22125	Singer	Rachel	1823	?, London	(?)		Edward Singer	Whitechapel, London	
13740	Singer	Reuben	1844	Manchester	Nathan Singer	Sophia Levy nee (?)		Manchester	
7384	Singer	Simeon (Simon)	1848	Covent Garden, London	Julius Singer	Frederica (Rika, Rachel) Woolf	Charlotte Pyke	Bloomsbury, London	scholar
13735	Singer	Sophia	1807	Poznan, Poland [Posen, Prussia]	(?)		(?) Levy	Manchester	marine store dealer
22126	Singer	Sophia	1850	?, London	Edward Singer	Rachel (?)		Whitechapel, London	
14063	Singleton	Heinreich	1815	?, Germany				Manchester	merchant
13989	Sington	Adolphus	1812	Silesia, Poland	Joel		Frances Symons	Manchester	merchant (cotton fabrics)
14015	Sington	Adolphus	1850	Manchester	Nathan Sington	Fanny Bergmann		Manchester	
14013	Sington	Fanny	1824	?, Poland [?, Prussia]	(?) Bergmann		Nathan Sington	Manchester	
13990	Sington	Frances	1820	?Whitechapel, London	Eleazer Jacob Symons	Hester (Esther) (?)	Adolphus Sington	Manchester	
13992	Sington	Joseph George	1850	Manchester	Adolphus Sington	Frances Symons	Mary Florence Straus	Manchester	
14157	Sington	Julius	1822	Wroclaw, Poland [Breslau]				Manchester	warehouseman
14012	Sington	Nathan	1817	?, Poland [?, Prussia]			Fanny Bergmann	Manchester	commercial agent (dry salter)
13991	Sington	Nathan A	1849	Manchester	Adolphus Sington	Frances Symons		Manchester	
14014	Sington	Theodore	1848	Manchester	Nathan Sington	Fanny Bergmann		Manchester	

ID	surname	given names	born	birthplace	father	mother	spouse 1	1851 residence	1851 occupation
22645	Sira	Isidor	1826	Cracow, Poland [Krakuz, Poland]				Whitechapel, London	journeyman slipper maker
22646	Sira	Ozen	1831	Warsaw, Poland				Whitechapel, London	journeyman slipper maker
2156	Sitman (Sitner)	Hill	1827	?, Poland [?, Prussia]				Hull, Yorkshire	
19147	Slagar	Adolph	1813	?, Poland [?, Prussia]			(?)	Aldgate, London	tailor
19148	Slagar	Elias	1840	?, Poland [?, Prussia]	Adolph Slagar			Aldgate, London	tailor
23538	Slater	Daniel	1833	Schiedan, Holland				Liverpool	pedlar
23537	Slater	James	1827	Schiedan, Holland				Liverpool	jeweller
23535	Slater	Mary Jane	1819	Schiedan, Holland	(?)		(?) Slater	Liverpool	dressmaker
23536	Slater	Richard	1825	Schiedan, Holland				Liverpool	jeweller
30983	Sloman	Abraham	1813	?, Poland [?, Prussia]			Jane (?)	Nottingham, Nottinghamshire	cap manufacturer
31053	Sloman	Charles	1791	Rochester, Kent				Rochester, Kent	pawnbroker
15593	Sloman	Charlton H	1807	Covent Garden, London			(?)	Covent Garden, London	plater + teacher of music
15596	Sloman	Emanuel H	1837	Brighton, Sussex	Charlton H Sloman	(?)		Covent Garden, London	pianist
9354	Sloman	Isabella	1846	Westminster, London	Mark Sloman	Sarah Nathan		St Giles, London	
30984	Sloman	Jane	1811	?, Poland [?, Prussia]	(?)		Abraham Sloman	Nottingham, Nottinghamshire	cap manufacturer
2577	Sloman	John	1819	?, Germany				Hull, Yorkshire	
20723	Sloman	Joseph	1780	Chatham, Kent				Rochester, Kent	proprietor of houses + fundholder
15595	Sloman	Julia	1835	Brighton, Sussex	Charlton H Sloman	(?)	M--- Wallach	Covent Garden, London	pianiste
9355	Sloman	Louis M	1848	Westminster, London	Mark Sloman	Sarah Nathan	Rena Wilson	St Giles, London	
9350	Sloman	Mark	1799	Middlesex, London	Samuel (Solomon) Sloman		Sarah Nathan	St Giles, London	clothes salesman
15597	Sloman	Matilda	1839	Brighton, Sussex	Charlton H Sloman	(?)		Covent Garden, London	scholar
15594	Sloman	Maurice A	1834	Brighton, Sussex	Charlton H Sloman	(?)		Covent Garden, London	articled to professor of music
31052	Sloman	Mira	1778	Chatham, Kent	(?) Sloman			Rochester, Kent	
9353	Sloman	Morris	1840	Westminster, London	Mark Sloman	Sarah Nathan		St Giles, London	scholar
10538	Sloman	Phillis	1832	Elephant & Castle, London	(?) Sloman			Covent Garden, London	needle woman
30985	Sloman	Rebecca	1838	?, Poland [?, Prussia]	Abraham Sloman	Jane (?)		Nottingham, Nottinghamshire	
29228	Sloman	Rosetta	1796	City, London	(?) Nathan		(?) Sloman	Whitechapel, London	feather maker
9351	Sloman	Sarah	1805	?Middlesex, London	Nathaniel Nathan	Elizabeth (?Levy)	Mark Sloman	St Giles, London	
9352	Sloman	Sarah	1836	Strand, London	Mark Sloman	Sarah Nathan	Solomon M Benjamin	St Giles, London	
20797	Sloman	Selim	1851	St Giles, Lindon	Mark Sloman	Sarah Nathan	Amelia Lempert	St Giles, London	
9785	Sloman	William	1836	Middlesex, London				Kew, London	boarding school pupil
9374	Sloshman (Schlossman)	Caroline	1847	Hull, Yorkshire	Solomon Sloshman (Schlossman)	Esther Harriette Gerson	John David Davis	Spitalfields, London	
9373	Sloshman (Schlossman)	Esther Harriette	1824	Poznan, Poland [Posen, Prussia]	Aaron Gerson	Hannah (?)	Solomon Sloshman (Schlossman)	Spitalfields, London	
9372	Sloshman (Schlossman)	Solomon	1826	Jaroslav, Poland [Yaraslov, Galicia, Austria]	Aaron Schlossman	Pearl (?)	Esther Harriette Gerson	Spitalfields, London	slipper maker
25423	Slowman	Abraham	1800	Middlesex, London	Dovid HaLevi		Sarah Levy	Holborn, London	Officer to the Sheriff
25428	Slowman	Edward	1833	Middlesex, London	Abraham Slowman	Sarah (?)		Holborn, London	clerk

ID	surname	given names	born	birthplace	father	mother	spouse 1	1851 residence	1851 occupation
25429	Slowman	Eliza	1835	Holborn, London	Abraham Slowman	Sarah (?)		Holborn, London	
22195	Slowman	Ester	1832	Whitechapel, London	Nathaniel Slowman	Rosetta (?)		Whitechapel, London	seamstress
22193	Slowman	Henry	1836	Whitechapel, London	Nathaniel Slowman	Rosetta (?)		Whitechapel, London	scholar
9787	Slowman	Henry	1838	Middlesex, London				Kew, London	boarding school pupil
22192	Slowman	Joseph	1831	Whitechapel, London	Nathaniel Slowman	Rosetta (?)		Whitechapel, London	house decorator
25427	Slowman	Lewis C	1827	Middlesex, London	Abraham Slowman	Sarah (?)		Holborn, London	clerk
22190	Slowman	Nathaniel	1798	Whitechapel, London			Rosetta (?)	Whitechapel, London	house decorator
22191	Slowman	Rosetta	1801	Whitechapel, London	(?)		Natnaniel Slowman	Whitechapel, London	
22194	Slowman	Samuel	1839	Whitechapel, London	Nathaniel Slowman	Rosetta (?)		Whitechapel, London	scholar
25426	Slowman	Sarah	1808	Middlesex, London	Yehuda Leib Levy		Abraham Slowman	Holborn, London	
25431	Slowman	Theodore	1849	Holborn, London	Abraham Slowman	Sarah (?)		Holborn, London	
25430	Slowman	Walter	1847	Holborn, London	Abraham Slowman	Sarah (?)		Holborn, London	
12231	Smalhalden	Clara	1841	Middlesex, London	Elias Smalhalden	Henrietta (?)		Whitechapel, London	
12228	Smalhalden	Elias	1796	Amsterdam, Holland			Henrietta (?)	Whitechapel, London	commission agent?
12229	Smalhalden	Henrietta	1803	Amsterdam, Holland	(?)		Elias Smalhalden	Whitechapel, London	
12230	Smalhalden	Herman	1839	?, Holland	Elias Smalhalden	Henrietta (?)		Whitechapel, London	
28976	Smith	Abraham	1826	?, Poland [Germany Rush-Poland]	Yissachar		Rebecca (?)	Whitechapel, London	tailor
28978	Smith	Jacob Barnett	1834	?, Poland [Germany Rush-Poland]	Yissachar		Hannah Jacobs	Whitechapel, London	tailor
28977	Smith	Rebecca	1829	?, Poland [Germany Rush-Poland]	(?)		Abraham Smith	Whitechapel, London	
9407	Soares	Alice	1806	Whitechapel, London	(?)		Lewis Soares	Aldgate, London	
8661	Soares	Clara	1847	Aldgate, London	Frank Daniel Soares	Sarah Joseph		Aldgate, London	scholar
25484	Soares	Daniel	1781	Hackney, London	Daniel Soares	Clara (?)	Esther de David Fernandes	Tower Hill, London	alms house recipient - formerly hatter
8673	Soares	Daniel	1850	Aldgate, London	Frank Daniel Soares	Sarah Joseph		Aldgate, London	
27133	Soares	David	1822	?, Scotland	Jacob de Daniel Soares	Reyna (Rachel) Arrobas	Phoebe Romaine (Romano)	Aldgate, London	cigar maker
9409	Soares	Eliza	1836	Liverpool	(?) Soares			Aldgate, London	
25485	Soares	Esther	1785	Bethnal Green, London	David Fernandes	Miriam de Natan Espinosa	Daniel De Daniel Soares	Tower Hill, London	
8658	Soares	Esther	1837	Aldgate, London	Frank Daniel Soares	Sarah Joseph		Aldgate, London	waistcoat maker
8656	Soares	Frank Daniel	1806	Aldgate, London	Daniel de Daniel Soares	Esther de David Fernandes	Sarah Joseph	Aldgate, London	grocer + oilman
27349	Soares	Isaac	1839	Spitalfields, London	Jacob de Daniel Soares	Reyna (Rachel) Soares		Aldgate, London	
8660	Soares	Isaac Daniel	1842	Aldgate, London	Frank Daniel Soares	Sarah Joseph	Selina Harris	Aldgate, London	scholar
18164	Soares	Jacob	1779	Middlesex, London			(?)	Mile End, London	patient in the Portuguese Jews Hospital
27347	Soares	Jacob	1795	?London	Daniel Soares	(Clara?) (?)	Reyna (Rachel) Arrobas	Aldgate, London	
29145	Soares	John	1803	Spitalfields, London			Ann (?)	Whitechapel, London	clerk
27348	Soares	Joseph	1836	Spitalfields, London	Jacob de Daniel Soares	Reyna (Rachel) Soares		Aldgate, London	
8659	Soares	Julia	1840	Aldgate, London	Frank Daniel Soares	Sarah Joseph		Aldgate, London	scholar
9408	Soares	Leon	1833	Liverpool	Lewis Soares	Alice (?)		Aldgate, London	articled to a solicitor
9406	Soares	Lewis	1807	Liverpool			Alice (?)	Aldgate, London	landed proprietor
27134	Soares	Phoebe	1824	?, London	Emanuel (Menahem) de David Romano	Rachel de Aaron Barnett	David Soares	Aldgate, London	

ID	surname	given names	born	birthplace	father	mother	spouse 1	1851 residence	1851 occupation
27346	Soares	Reyna (Rachel)	1797	Mile End, London	David Arrobas	Miryam de David Zamira	Jacob de Daniel Soares	Aldgate, London	charwoman
8657	Soares	Sarah	1815	Aldgate, London	Isaac Joseph	Julia (?)	Frank Daniel Soares	Aldgate, London	
26942	Socheschoski	Aaron	1830	?, Poland				Aldgate, London	cap maker
27491	Soeson	Esther	1826	?, Holland	(?) Soeson			Aldgate, London	cap maker
30453	Sokolowska	Dora	1827	?, Poland [?, Prussia]				Hanley, Staffordshire	
29021	Sokolowski	Amada	1829	Bow, London			Laurey? Sokolowski	Whitechapel, London	
29020	Sokolowski	Laurey?	1808	?, Poland			Amada (?)	Whitechapel, London	tailor
30464	Sokolowski	Moses	1810	?, Poland				Newcastle-under-Lyme, Staffordshire	
13914	Soloman	Abraham	1834	Strand, London				Manchester	cashier for tailor + draper
18332	Soloman	Grace	1821	Southwark, London	(?) Soloman			Cheltenham, Gloucestershire	servant
1691	Soloman	John	1821	Whitechapel, London			Sarah (?)	Spitalfields, London	
14496	Soloman	Joseph	1796	Frankfurt-am-Main, Germany			Jane (?)	Coventry, Warwickshire	general dealer
14497	Soloman	Joseph	1818	Gdansk, Poland [Danzig, Prussia]				Plymouth, Devon	glazier
30791	Soloman	Joseph	1820	Warsaw, Poland				Preston, Lancashire	hardware dealer
1693	Soloman	Judah	1842	Spitalfields, London	John Soloman	Sarah (?)		Spitalfields, London	
23869	Soloman	Julia	1801	City, London	(?)		Samuel Soloman	Soho, London	
30928	Soloman	Moses	1798	?, Poland			(?)	Hull, Yorkshire	hawker
1696	Soloman	Nestor	1848	Spitalfields, London	John Soloman	Sarah (?)		Spitalfields, London	
23868	Soloman	Samuel	1798	City, London			Julia (?)	Soho, London	glass factor
1692	Soloman	Sarah	1822	Spitalfields, London			John Soloman	Spitalfields, London	
1695	Soloman	Sarah	1846	?Spitalfields, London	John Soloman	Sarah (?)		Spitalfields, London	
1690	Soloman	Solomon	1851	Spitalfields, London	John Soloman	Sarah (?)		Spitalfields, London	
1694	Soloman	Sophia	1844	?Spitalfields, London	John Soloman	Sarah (?)		Spitalfields, London	
22709	Solomans	Abraham	1807	Aldgate, London			Rebecca (?)	Whitechapel, London	dealer in wearing apparel
22764	Solomans	Rachel	1833	Spitalfields, London	(?) Solomans			Whitechapel, London	parasol maker
22710	Solomans	Rebecca	1806	Spitalfields, London	(?)		Abraham Solomans	Whitechapel, London	
12367	Solome	Clara	1830	Lambeth, London	David Solome	Sarah (?)	James Sargood	Lambeth, London	
12362	Solome	David	1795	Covent Garden, London			Sarah (?)	Lambeth, London	refiner
12368	Solome	Emanuel	1833	Lambeth, London	David Solome	Sarah (?)	Hannah Killinback	Lambeth, London	
12369	Solome	Josiah (Joshua)	1836	Lambeth, London	David Solome	Sarah (?)		Lambeth, London	
12364	Solome	Julia	1821	Lambeth, London	David Solome	Sarah (?)		Lambeth, London	
12366	Solome	Lewis	1828	Lambeth, London	David Solome	Sarah (?)		Lambeth, London	dealer
12370	Solome	Rosetta	1841	Lambeth, London	David Solome	Sarah (?)	Isaac Millward	Lambeth, London	scholar
12365	Solome	Samuel	1824	Lambeth, London	David Solome	Sarah (?)	Emma Wisenden	Lambeth, London	dealer
12363	Solome	Sarah	1800	Dover, Kent	(?)		David Solome	Lambeth, London	
16008	Solomon	?	1822	Covent Garden, London	(?)		Lewis Solomon	Covent Garden, London	
1689	Solomon	?	1827	?, Holland				Spitalfields, London	cigar maker
20344	Solomon	Aaron	1792	City, London	Kalonymus		Ann Lazarus	Shoreditch, London	general merchant
27234	Solomon	Aaron	1806	?, London			Sarah (?)	Aldgate, London	baker
29331	Solomon	Aaron	1818	?, Poland				Whitechapel, London	blacksmith
21463	Solomon	Aaron	1822	Stamford Hill, London	Abraham Solomon	Ellen Levy		Wolverhampton, Staffordshire	tailor's assistant

ID	surname	given names	born	birthplace	father	mother	spouse 1	1851 residence	1851 occupation
14636	Solomon	Aaron	1823	Aldgate, London			Mary Miles	Hoxton, London	traveller
1719	Solomon	Aaron	1840	Spitalfields, London	Solomon Solomon	Lydia (Leah) Lazarus		Spitalfields, London	scholar
10828	Solomon	Aaron	1850	Spitalfields, London	Phillip Solomon	Abigail (?)		Spitalfields, London	
30886	Solomon	Abigail	1810	Lewes, Sussex	(?) Solomon			Lewes, Sussex	
10823	Solomon	Abigail	1815	Whitechapel, London	(?)		Phillip Solomon	Spitalfields, London	
24768	Solomon	Abigail	1818	Aldgate, London	David Pass (Paz de Leon)	Rebecca de Jacob Selomoh Solomons	Joseph Solomon	Southwark, London	
24847	Solomon	Abraham	1766	?, Poland			Sarah (?)	Elephant & Castle, London	retail tea merchant + fruiterer
28151	Solomon	Abraham	1801	?, Holland				Aldgate, London	general dealer
6247	Solomon	Abraham	1803	Middlesex, London	(?)		Rachael Gershon	Holborn, London	dealer in clothes
7407	Solomon	Abraham	1812	Middlesex, London	Lyon (Yehuda) Solomon	Esther (?)	Julia Isaacs	Covent Garden, London	furniture dealer
20729	Solomon	Abraham	1818	Whitechapel, London	Alexander Solomon	Esther Lyons		Whitechapel, London	shoe maker
27566	Solomon	Abraham	1821	City, London	Solomon Solomon	Julia (?)		Spitalfields, London	tailor
28078	Solomon	Abraham	1821	?, Poland [?, Prussia]			Frederica (?)	Spitalfields, London	tailor
7400	Solomon	Abraham	1823	Aldgate, London	Michael (Myer) Solomon	Catherine Levy	Ella Hart	Fitzrovia, London	artist
21792	Solomon	Abraham	1825	Whitechapel, London			Esther Moses	Aldgate, London	trimming seller
9361	Solomon	Abraham	1829	Brighton, Sussex				Mayfair, London	manager to a tailor
12416	Solomon	Abraham	1835	?Strand, London	Nathaniel Saul (Solomon) Solomons		Deborah Levi	Strand, London	
23991	Solomon	Abraham	1835	Marylebone, London	Saul Solomon	Leagh (?)		Marylebone, London	
23173	Solomon	Abraham	1841	Shoreditch, London	Nathan Solomon	Julia (?)		Hoxton, London	
21608	Solomon	Abraham	1848	Chatham, Kent	Jacob Solomon	Esther (?)		Chatham, Kent	
2338	Solomon	Abraham	1850	Leeds, Yorkshire	(Jacob?) Solomon			Leeds, Yorkshire	
9429	Solomon	Abraham (Alfred)	1848	?, London	Charles Solomon	Deborah Minden	Julia Levy	Wapping, London	
16001	Solomon	Adelaide	1831	Covent Garden, London	Samuel Solomon	Ann (?)		Covent Garden, London	
15901	Solomon	Adelaide	1838	Middlesex, London	(?) Solomon			Hackney, London	boarding school pupil
19239	Solomon	Adele	1822	?, Devon	(?) Emanuel		Judah Solomon	Waterloo, London	
20724	Solomon	Alexander	1773	Middlesex, London			(?)	Bath	cabinet maker + upholsterer + furniture broker
20727	Solomon	Alexander	1786	Whitechapel, London	Baruch Benedit Rachmannet		Esther Lyons	Whitechapel, London	shoe maker
20734	Solomon	Alexander	1809	Rochester, Kent			Frances Ellen (?)	Pimlico, London	shirtmaker + hosier
20726	Solomon	Alexander	1811	Aldgate, London				Strand, London	fishmonger
31061	Solomon	Alexander	1825	Portsmouth, Hampshire	Solomon Solomon	Rachel Abraham		Southampton, Hampshire	
4966	Solomon	Alexander	1844	Warwick, Warwickshire	Joseph Solomon	Esther (?)		Birmingham	
30625	Solomon	Alexander	1851	Whitechapel, London	Joseph Solomon	Rebecca Hart		Whitechapel, London	
14500	Solomon	Alfred	1833	Norwich, Norfolk	Joshua E Solomon	Mary A (?)		Norwich, Norfolk	apprentice to watchmaker
4950	Solomon	Alfred	1843	Birmingham	George Solomon	Ann (?)		Birmingham	
29276	Solomon	Alfred	1843	?, London	Isaac Solomon	Frances (?)		Wapping, London	
16011	Solomon	Alfred	1844	Covent Garden, London	Lewis Solomon	?	Virginia (?)	Covent Garden, London	scholar
9786	Solomon	Alfred A	1838	Finsbury, London	Abraham Solomon	Julia Isaacs	Sarah Phillips	Covent Garden, London	boarding school pupil
23994	Solomon	Alice	1845	Marylebone, London	Saul Solomon	Leagh (?)		Marylebone, London	
9244	Solomon	Alice	1846	Middlesex, London	Samuel Solomon	Sarah (?)		Spitalfields, London	
22814	Solomon	Alice	1846	Middlesex, London	Saul Solomon	Sarah (?)		Spitalfields, London	

ID	surname	given names	born	birthplace	father	mother	spouse 1	1851 residence	1851 occupation
16144	Solomon	Amelia	1794	Whitechapel, London	(?)		(?) Solomon	Whitechapel, London	
10231	Solomon	Amelia	1796	Portsmouth, Hampshire	(?) Solomon	Elizabeth (?)		Aldgate, London	nurse
6252	Solomon	Amelia	1814	Penzance, Cornwall	Lemon Woolf		Philip Solomon	Shoreditch, London	
15677	Solomon	Amelia	1827	?, London	(?) Solomon	Esther (?)		Aldgate, London	furrier
24603	Solomon	Amelia	1843	Lambeth, London	Benjamin Solomon	Catherine Henry	Nathan Levi	Lambeth, London	
21606	Solomon	Amelia	1844	Chatham, Kent	Jacob Solomon	Esther (?)		Chatham, Kent	
3269	Solomon	Amelia	1846	Aldgate, London	Josiah Solomon	Bella Hart	Samuel Aaron Phillips	Aldgate, London	
1662	Solomon	Amelia (Miriam)	1818	Whitechapel, London	Jacob Fernandez	Rebecca Abendana	Solomons Solomon	Spitalfields, London	
21607	Solomon	Angel	1846	Chatham, Kent	Jacob Solomon	Esther (?)		Chatham, Kent	
10829	Solomon	Ann	1776	Whitechapel, London	(?)		Meir Solomon	Spitalfields, London	
20345	Solomon	Ann	1794	Aldgate, London	Henry (Hirsh) Lazarus	Perla (?)	Aaron Solomon	Shoreditch, London	
16007	Solomon	Ann	1796	Ipswich, Suffolk	(?)		Samuel Solomon	Covent Garden, London	
10873	Solomon	Ann	1801	Aldgate, London	(?Pinchas Zelig HaCohen Hart?)		Jacob Solomon	Spitalfields, London	shoe binder
4946	Solomon	Ann	1813	Birmingham			George Solomon	Birmingham	
19236	Solomon	Ann	1831	Fulham, London	(?)		Judah Solomon	St Giles, London	
4957	Solomon	Ann	1840	Middlesex, London	Isaac Solomon	Mary (?)		Birmingham	
1988	Solomon	Ann	1846	Bristol	Israel Solomon	Harriet Demery		Swansea, Wales	
16780	Solomon	Ann	1847	Bristol	Joseph Solomon	Catherine Benjamin	Emanuel Ezekiel	Bristol	
24605	Solomon	Ann	1850	Lambeth, London	Benjamin Solomon	Catherine Henry		Lambeth, London	
15986	Solomon	Ann	1851	St Giles, London	Judah Solomon	Leah (Ann) Coomer		St Giles, London	
21529	Solomon	Anna	1811	Stratford, London	(?)		Joseph Solomon	Mayfair, London	
5966	Solomon	Anna	1836	Whitechapel, London	Moses Solomon	Isabela Nathan	Samuel Lyons	Whitechapel, London	
6227	Solomon	Anne	1817	Poole, Dorset	Mark (Mordecai) Davis		Jonas Solomon	Aldgate, London	
3612	Solomon	Anne (Hannah)	1799	Aldgate, London	Baruch Benedet Solomons		Lewis Solomon	Chatham, Kent	
29070	Solomon	Asher	1818	Whitechapel, London	Lyon (Yehuda) Solomon	Esther (?)	Anne Russell	Covent Garden, London	furniture broker
12417	Solomon	Asher	1836	?, England	Nathaniel Saul (Solomon) Solomons	Rachael (?)		Strand, London	
18352	Solomon	Asher	1838	Canterbury, Kent	Phineas Solomon	Phoebe (?)	Esther Maria Andrade	Canterbury, Kent	scholar
26061	Solomon	Asher	1849	Westminster, London	Leon Solomon	Rose Joseph		Mayfair, London	
1653	Solomon	Banet	1794	Alsace, France [Elsas, France]			Lipman Solomon	Spitalfields, London	slipper dealer
8427	Solomon	Barnard	1804	?, Poland			Hannah (?)	Portsmouth, Hampshire	Jew - general dealer
18112	Solomon	Barnet	1786	Middlesex, London			Martha (?)	Mile End, London	burial ground keeper
9800	Solomon	Barnet	1840	Middlesex, London	Solomon Jacob Solomon	Catherine (Kitty) Joseph	Rose Lewis Jacobs	Spitalfields, London	
23557	Solomon	Barnet	1842	Liverpool	(?) Solomon	Jessie (?)		Liverpool	scholar
5924	Solomon	Bella	1816	Whitechapel, London	Henry Hart	Phoebe Myers	Josiah Solomon	Aldgate, London	domestic duties
18256	Solomon	Bella	1829	?, London				Cheltenham, Gloucestershire	
31157	Solomon	Bella (Isabel)	1795	Canterbury, Kent	(?) Solomon	Hannah (?)		Canterbury, Kent	straw bonnet maker
24600	Solomon	Benjamin	1812	Aldgate, London			Catherine Henry	Lambeth, London	general dealer
24773	Solomon	Benjamin	1822	Southwark, London				Southwark, London	cigar manufacturer
14773	Solomon	Benjamin	1831	Middlesex, London	George Solomon	Mary (?)		Finsbury, London	cigar maker
15680	Solomon	Benjamin	1834	?, London	(?) Solomon	Esther (?)		Aldgate, London	cigar maker
6756	Solomon	Benjamin	1845	Whitechapel, London	Solomon Jacob Solomon	Catherine (Kitty) Joseph		Whitechapel, London	
31062	Solomon	Bernard	1830	Portsmouth, Hampshire	Solomon Solomon	Rachel Abraham		Southampton, Hampshire	
27859	Solomon	Betsy	1769	?, Devon				Spitalfields, London	

ID	surname	given names	born	birthplace	father	mother	spouse 1	1851 residence	1851 occupation
15470	Solomon	Betsy	1774	Aldgate, London	(?)		Moses Solomon	Covent Garden, London	
15488	Solomon	Betsy	1821	Whitechapel, London	(?) Solomon			Covent Garden, London	
16000	Solomon	Borrett (?Barnett)	1829	Covent Garden, London	Samuel Solomon	Ann (?)		Covent Garden, London	
21291	Solomon	C---	1838	Finsbury, London				Edmonton, London	boarding school pupil
9174	Solomon	Caroline	1811	Piccadilly, London	Moses Eleazer Solomon	Betsy Hart		Whitechapel, London	none
25401	Solomon	Caroline	1811	Paris, France	(?)		Joseph Solomon	Holborn, London	
1035	Solomon	Caroline	1813	Exeter, Devon	Isaac Solomon	Rosetta Solomon	David Kaufman	Exeter, Devon	
4976	Solomon	Caroline	1820	Birmingham	William Eagles	Mary (?)	Moses Solomon	Birmingham	
16013	Solomon	Caroline	1846	Covent Garden, London	Lewis Solomon	?		Covent Garden, London	
16775	Solomon	Catherine	1809	?, London	Joel Benjamin		Joseph Solomon	Bristol	clothier
24601	Solomon	Catherine	1810	Southwark, London	Nathan Henry	Mary (?)	Benjamin Solomon	Lambeth, London	
29071	Solomon	Catherine	1818	?, London	Isaac Isaacs	Mary (Miriam, Polly) Solomons	Asher Solomon	Covent Garden, London	
21464	Solomon	Catherine	1826	Stamford Hill, London	Abraham Solomon	Ellen Levy		Wolverhampton, Staffordshire	
1720	Solomon	Catherine	1844	Spitalfields, London	Solomon Solomon	Lydia (Leah) Lazarus		Spitalfields, London	scholar
7404	Solomon	Catherine (Kate)	1802	Whitechapel, London	(?) Levy		Michael (Myer) Solomon	Hoxton, London	amateur painter
6319	Solomon	Catherine (Kate)	1843	Covent Garden, London	Lewis Solomon	?		Covent Garden, London	scholar
27741	Solomon	Catherine (Katherine)	1774	Whitechapel, London	Zadok Woolf		Isaac Solomon	Spitalfields, London	
6759	Solomon	Catherine (Kitty)	1803	Whitechapel, London	(?)		Solomon Jacob Solomon	Spitalfields, London	
13858	Solomon	Cathrine	1798	?, Poland	(?)		Phillip Solomon	Manchester	
4977	Solomon	Cecily (Emily)	1841	Birmingham	Moses Solomon	Harriet Lazarus		Birmingham	
24372	Solomon	Charles	1797	Covent Garden, London				Soho, London	printer
9427	Solomon	Charles	1819	Brussels, Belgium	Yehuda Leib (?Aaron Solomon)	(?Ann) (?)	Deborah Minden	Wapping, London	optician
3617	Solomon	Charles	1822	Chatham, Kent	Israel Solomon	Mary Israel Isaacs		Chatham, Kent	furniture broker
12921	Solomon	Charles	1833	Holborn, London	Abraham Solomon	Rachael Gershon		Holborn, London	cigar maker
21278	Solomon	Charles	1840	Edmonton, London	Henry Naphtali Solomon	Fanny Phillips		Edmonton, London	
22941	Solomon	Charles	1844	Westminster, London	Lewis Solomon	Louisa (?)		Wapping, London	scholar
4951	Solomon	Charles	1845	Birmingham	George Solomon	Ann (?)		Birmingham	
14504	Solomon	Charles	1846	Norwich, Norfolk	Joshua E Solomon	Mary A (?)		Norwich, Norfolk	scholar
29278	Solomon	Charles	1847	?, London	Isaac Solomon	Frances (?)		Wapping, London	
21609	Solomon	Charles	1850	Chatham, Kent	Jacob Solomon	Esther (?)		Chatham, Kent	
9691	Solomon	Charlotte	1814	Spitalfields, London	(?)		Morris Solomon	Whitechapel, London	tailor
1655	Solomon	Charlotte	1830	?London	Lipman Solomon	Banet (?)		Spitalfields, London	tailoress
15824	Solomon	Charlotte	1841	Whitechapel, London	Maurice Solomon	Louisa Raphael		Bloomsbury, London	scholar at home
16014	Solomon	Clara	1849	Covent Garden, London	Lewis Solomon	?	Montague P Hart	Covent Garden, London	
21143	Solomon	Coleman	1835	?, Poland	Moses Solomon	Rachel (?)		Aldgate, London	wholesale jeweller
22200	Solomon	Daniel	1781	Middlesex, London				Whitechapel, London	fund holder
15305	Solomon	Daniel	1821	Saxmundham, Suffolk				Shoreditch, London	light porter
17173	Solomon	David	1785	?, London			Sarah (?)	Newcastle Upon Tyne	cabinet maker
31158	Solomon	David	1785	Canterbury, Kent			(?)	Canterbury, Kent	retired silk merchant
29909	Solomon	David	1788	Wapping, London			Eliza (?)	Whitechapel, London	general dealer
813	Solomon	David	1825	Paddington, London	Saunders Solomon	Rachel Davis		Kensington, London	clothier + outfitter's assistant

ID	surname	given names	born	birthplace	father	mother	spouse 1	1851 residence	1851 occupation
18960	Solomon	David	1828	Holborn, London	Saul Solomon	Esther (?)		Whitechapel, London	hawker
18354	Solomon	David	1842	Canterbury, Kent	Phineas Solomon	Phoebe (?)		Canterbury, Kent	scholar
21605	Solomon	David	1843	Chatham, Kent	Jacob Solomon	Esther (?)		Chatham, Kent	
21520	Solomon	David	1849	Whitechapel, London	Lewis Solomon	Frances (?)		Wapping, London	
26062	Solomon	David	1850	Westminster, London	Leon Solomon	Rose Joseph		Mayfair, London	
1323	Solomon	David	1851	Plymouth, Devon	Josiah Solomon	Rose (?)		Plymouth, Devon	
6449	Solomon	David	1851	Spitalfields, London	Morris Solomons	Dinah Moses	Esther Lyons	Whitechapel, London	
9428	Solomon	Deborah	1813	?, London	Abraham Minden	Sarah Nathan	Charles Solomon	Wapping, London	
1060	Solomon	Deborah	1829	Exeter, Devon	(?) Lazarus		Myers Solomon	Exeter, Devon	
14775	Solomon	Deborah	1835	Middlesex, London	George Solomon	Mary (?)		Finsbury, London	apprentice
30459	Solomon	Dennis	1832	?, Poland				Newcastle-under-Lyme, Staffordshire	hawker
1679	Solomon	Dina	1835	Spitalfields, London	(?) Solomon	Julia (?)		Spitalfields, London	
19536	Solomon	Dinah	1769	Whitechapel, London			(?) Solomon	Strand, London	
21315	Solomon	Dinah	1797	Aldgate, London	(?) Solomon		(?) Solomon	Eton, Berkshire	retailer of beer + vinegar
6213	Solomon	Dinah	1820	City, London	David Moses	Hannah (?)	Morris Solomon	Whitechapel, London	
21272	Solomon	Dinah	1826	Spitalfields, London	Henry Naphtali Solomon	Fanny Phillips		Edmonton, London	
1665	Solomon	Dinah	1840	Middlesex, London	Solomons Solomon	Amelia (Miriam) Fernandez	Michael Woolf	Spitalfields, London	
26937	Solomon	Dorothea	1823	?, Poland			Dorothea (?)	Aldgate, London	
24444	Solomon	Ebenezer	1809	Spitalfields, London			Sarah (?)	Strand, London	shoe manufacturer
24770	Solomon	Edward	1775	Margate, Kent			Rachael (?)	Southwark, London	retired law clerk
14502	Solomon	Edward	1837	Norwich, Norfolk	Joshua E Solomon	Mary A (?)		Norwich, Norfolk	errand boy
4978	Solomon	Edward	1842	Birmingham	Moses Solomon	Harriet Lazarus		Birmingham	
29279	Solomon	Edward	1849	?, London	Isaac Solomon	Frances (?)		Wapping, London	
4940	Solomon	Edward Moss	1815	Birmingham	Daniel Solomon	Judith (?Davis)	Rosa Sloman	Birmingham	tailor
15970	Solomon	Elijah	1840	?, London	Henry Solomon	Rachel (?)		Aldgate, London	
23560	Solomon	Elisha	1849	Liverpool	(?) Solomon	Jessie (?)		Liverpool	scholar
16009	Solomon	Elisha (Elijah)	1841	Covent Garden, London	Lewis Solomon	?	Elizabeth Simmons	Covent Garden, London	scholar
6254	Solomon	Eliza	1850	Shoreditch, London	Philip Solomon	Amelia (?)		Shoreditch, London	
6349	Solomon	Eliza	1851	Mayfair, London	Leon Solomon	Rose Joseph		Mayfair, London	
10230	Solomon	Elizabeth	1753	Amsterdam, Holland	(?)		(?) Solomon	Aldgate, London	general dealer
22221	Solomon	Elizabeth	1782	Aldgate, London			(?) Solomon	Whitechapel, London	hawker
1712	Solomon	Elizabeth	1784	?, Holland	(?)		Jonas Solomon	Spitalfields, London	general dealer
4970	Solomon	Elizabeth	1791	?, London			Samuel Solomon	Birmingham	
25175	Solomon	Elizabeth	1824	Whitechapel, London	(?)		Solomon Solomon	Finsbury, London	
17177	Solomon	Elizabeth	1830	?, London	David Solomon	Sarah (?)		Newcastle Upon Tyne	
23995	Solomon	Elizabeth	1840	Chelsea, London	(?) Solomon			Marylebone, London	
25402	Solomon	Elizabeth	1840	Paris, France	Joseph Solomon	Caroline (?)		Holborn, London	
24602	Solomon	Elizabeth	1841	?Spitalfields, London	Benjamin Solomon	Catherine Henry		Lambeth, London	
14854	Solomon	Elizabeth	1843	Clerkenwell, London	Silverston Solomon	Frances (?)		Bethnal Green, London	scholar
4961	Solomon	Elizabeth	1848	Birmingham	Isaac Solomon	Mary (?)		Birmingham	
23177	Solomon	Elizabeth	1849	Shoreditch, London	Nathan Solomon	Julia (?)		Hoxton, London	
9067	Solomon	Elizabeth (Betsy)	1821	Aldgate, London	Michael (Myer) Solomon	Catherine Levy		Hoxton, London	
1687	Solomon	Elizabeth (Betsy)	1833	Spitalfields, London	Israel Solomon	Mary (?)		Spitalfields, London	tailoress

ID	surname	given names	born	birthplace	father	mother	spouse 1	1851 residence	1851 occupation
6770	Solomon	Ellen	1800	Whitechapel, London	(?)		Abraham Solomon	Wolverhampton, Staffordshire	tailor master empl 3
9644	Solomon	Ellen	1826	Whitechapel, London	(?) Solomon			Spitalfields, London	cap maker
9069	Solomon	Ellen	1827	Aldgate, London	Michael (Myer) Solomon	Catherine Levy		Hoxton, London	
21466	Solomon	Ellen	1831	Liverpool			Isaac Solomon	Wolverhampton, Staffordshire	
16003	Solomon	Ellen	1833	Covent Garden, London	Samuel Solomon	Ann (?)	John Lazarus	Covent Garden, London	
17141	Solomon	Ellen	1850	Deal, Kent	Emanuel Solomon	Sarah (?)		Deal, Kent	
1321	Solomon	Ellen E	1847	Plymouth, Devon	Josiah Solomon	Rose (?)		Plymouth, Devon	
1667	Solomon	Ellice (Alice)	1847	Spitalfields, London	Solomons Solomon	Amelia (Miriam) Fernandez		Spitalfields, London	
17139	Solomon	Emanuel	1815	Deal, Kent			Sarah (?)	Deal, Kent	general dealer
890	Solomon	Emanuel	1818	Bristol	Simon Solomon	Rosetta (?)		Bristol	clothier
21534	Solomon	Emelia	1846	Paddington, London	Joseph Solomon	Anna (?)		Mayfair, London	scholar at home
9245	Solomon	Emelia	1848	Middlesex, London	Samuel Solomon	Sarah (?)		Spitalfields, London	
22815	Solomon	Emelia	1848	Middlesex, London	Saul Solomon	Sarah (?)		Spitalfields, London	
16002	Solomon	Emily	1832	Covent Garden, London	Samuel Solomon	Ann (?)		Covent Garden, London	
15822	Solomon	Emma	1834	Whitechapel, London	Maurice Solomon	Louisa Raphael		Bloomsbury, London	scholar at home
27136	Solomon	Esther	1781	?, London	(?)		(?) Solomon	Aldgate, London	
18959	Solomon	Esther	1788	Westminster, London	(?)		Saul Solomon	Whitechapel, London	
20728	Solomon	Esther	1794	Whitechapel, London	Isaac Lyons		Alexander Solomon	Whitechapel, London	
15676	Solomon	Esther	1795	?, London	(?)		(?) Solomon	Aldgate, London	general dealer
26730	Solomon	Esther	1804	Spitalfields, London	(?)		Mark Solomon	Spitalfields, London	
21734	Solomon	Esther	1811	Holborn, London	(?)		(?) Solomon	Islington, London	
21601	Solomon	Esther	1813	Dartmouth, Devon	(?)		Jacob Solomon	Chatham, Kent	
19973	Solomon	Esther	1820	Deal, Kent	(?) Solomon	Sarah (?)		Deal, Kent	
4965	Solomon	Esther	1821	?, London			Joseph Solomon	Birmingham	
1658	Solomon	Esther	1826	Middlesex, London	Henry Solomon	Julia (?)	Samuel Shuter	Spitalfields, London	cap maker
21793	Solomon	Esther	1826	Spitalfields, London	Abraham Moses	Catharine Harris	Abraham Solomon	Aldgate, London	
9275	Solomon	Esther	1828	?Whitechapel, London			Isaac Solomon	Aldgate, London	
27631	Solomon	Esther	1829	City, London	(?) Solomon			Aldgate, London	umbrella maker
1680	Solomon	Esther	1837	Spitalfields, London	(?) Solomon	Julia (?)		Spitalfields, London	
18351	Solomon	Esther	1838	Canterbury, Kent	Phineas Solomon	Phoebe (?)		Canterbury, Kent	scholar
4956	Solomon	Esther	1839	Middlesex, London	Isaac Solomon	Mary (?)	(?) Barnett	Birmingham	
17006	Solomon	Esther	1842	Kensington, London	Saunders Solomon	Rachel Davis	Elias David Altston	Kensington, London	
9869	Solomon	Esther	1844	?, London				Fulham, London	boarding school pupil
10826	Solomon	Esther	1844	Spitalfields, London	Phillip Solomon	Abigail (?)		Spitalfields, London	scholar
21145	Solomon	Esther	1845	?, Poland	Moses Solomon	Rachel (?)		Aldgate, London	scholar
19970	Solomon	Esther	1847	Deal, Kent	Samuel Solomon	Rosetta (Rosa, Rose) Hart	Bryan Joseph A Keating	Deal, Kent	
24449	Solomon	Esther	1849	Aldgate, London	Ebenezer Solomon	Sarah (?)		Strand, London	
23561	Solomon	Esther	1850	Liverpool	(?) Solomon	Jessie (?)		Liverpool	
1718	Solomon	Eve	1837	Spitalfields, London	Solomon Solomon	Lydia (Leah) Lazarus		Spitalfields, London	tailoress
14855	Solomon	Eve	1846	Clerkenwell, London	Silverston Solomon	Frances (?)		Bethnal Green, London	scholar
20745	Solomon	Evelina	1825	?, Jamaica, West Indies	(?)		Philip Solomon	Westminster, London	
5927	Solomon	Evelina (Eva)	1850	Aldgate, London	Josiah Solomon	Bella Hart	Frederick Abraham Phillips	Aldgate, London	
4952	Solomon	Eveline	1849	Birmingham	George Solomon	Ann (?)		Birmingham	

ID	surname	given names	born	birthplace	father	mother	spouse 1	1851 residence	1851 occupation
946	Solomon	Fanny	1774	?, Poland [?, Prussia]			Nathan Solomon	Exeter, Devon	
21271	Solomon	Fanny	1798	Strand, London	Nehemia Phillips		Henry Naphtali Solomon	Edmonton, London	schoolmaster's wife
30885	Solomon	Fanny	1806	Lewes, Sussex	(?) Solomon			Lewes, Sussex	dressmaker
21273	Solomon	Fanny	1831	Hammersmith, London	Henry Naphtali Solomon	Fanny Phillips		Edmonton, London	
20744	Solomon	Fanny	1833	?Aldgate, London	Jacob Solomon	Sarah Levy		Westminster, London	
3616	Solomon	Fanny	1838	Chatham, Kent	Israel Solomon	Mary Israel Isaacs		Chatham, Kent	housekeeper
7135	Solomon	Fanny	1849	Portsmouth, Hampshire	Samuel Ellis Solomon	Fanny Carter	Hyman Levetus	Portsmouth, Hampshire	
10113	Solomon	Fanny	1824	City, London	(?)		Phineas Solomon	York, Yorkshire	
15686	Solomon	Fanny (Frances)	1811	?, London	Aharon Jacob		Morris Solomon	Clerkenwell, London	
20736	Solomon	Florence	1848	?Pimlico, London	Alexander Solomon	Frances Ellen (?)		Pimlico, London	
4953	Solomon	Florence	1850	Birmingham	George Solomon	Ann (?)		Birmingham	
21602	Solomon	Florina	1837	?, Jersey, Channel Islands	Jacob Solomon	Esther (?)		Chatham, Kent	
5117	Solomon	Frances	1795	?, London	Moses Davis	Rosey (?)	Moses Solomon	Portsmouth, Hampshire	
29272	Solomon	Frances	1810	Hamburg, Germany	(?)		Isaac Solomon	Wapping, London	
22222	Solomon	Frances	1811	Bethnal Green, London	(?) Solomon	Elizabeth (?)		Whitechapel, London	
14849	Solomon	Frances	1815	Covent Garden, London	(?)		Silverston Solomon	Bethnal Green, London	
21518	Solomon	Frances	1828	Whitechapel, London	(?) Braham		Lewis Solomon	Wapping, London	
16778	Solomon	Frances	1842	Bristol	Joseph Solomon	Catherine Benjamin		Bristol	
24604	Solomon	Frances	1846	Lambeth, London	Benjamin Solomon	Catherine Henry		Lambeth, London	
29811	Solomon	Frances	1849	Whitechapel, London	Joseph Solomon	Rebecca Hart		Whitechapel, London	
4943	Solomon	Frances	1850	Birmingham	Edward M Solomon	Rosa (?)		Birmingham	
6248	Solomon	Frances (Fanny)	1837	Middlesex, London	Abraham Solomon			Holborn, London	scholar
20735	Solomon	Frances Ellen	1823	Camberwell, London	(?)		Alexander Solomon	Pimlico, London	hosier
28079	Solomon	Frederica	1826	?, Poland [?, Prussia]	(?)		Abraham Solomon	Spitalfields, London	
14770	Solomon	George	1791	City, London			Mary (?)	Finsbury, London	paper stainer
4945	Solomon	George	1807	Birmingham			Ann (?)	Birmingham	parer dealer
20844	Solomon	George	1821	?, London	Nathaniel Solomon	Rebecca (?)		Euston, London	wool + tallow merchant
14776	Solomon	George	1837	Middlesex, London	George Solomon	Mary (?)	Janetta Kalischer	Finsbury, London	paper stainer
21277	Solomon	George	1837	Bloomsbury, London	Henry Naphtali Solomon	Fanny Phillips		Edmonton, London	
29275	Solomon	George	1840	?, London	Isaac Solomon	Frances (?)		Wapping, London	
21142	Solomon	Golda	1832	?, Poland	Moses Solomon	Rachel (?(		Aldgate, London	cap maker
27415	Solomon	H---	1833	?, Poland [?, Prussia]				Whitechapel, London	cap maker
21612	Solomon	Hanah	1808	?, London	(?)		(?) Solomon	Brighton, Sussex	lodging house keeper's assistant
23705	Solomon	Hanna	1805	Hamburg, Germany	(?)		Susman Solomon	Liverpool	
12307	Solomon	Hannah	1761	Shoreditch, London	(?)		(?)	Canterbury, Kent	
1651	Solomon	Hannah	1763	Finsbury, London	(?)		(?) Solomon	Spitalfields, London	hat binder
3190	Solomon	Hannah	1799	?, London	Isaac Isaacs	Phoebe (?)	Samuel Solomon	Chatham, Kent	
8428	Solomon	Hannah	1809	Portsmouth, Hampshire	(?)		Barnard Solomon	Portsmouth, Hampshire	
31044	Solomon	Hannah	1821	Penzance, Cornwall	(?) Jacob	Sophia (?)	John Solomon	Liverpool	
15999	Solomon	Hannah	1823	Covent Garden, London	Samuel Solomon	Ann (?)		Covent Garden, London	
26732	Solomon	Hannah	1831	Whitechapel, London	Mark Solomon	Esther (?)	Samuel Symons	Spitalfields, London	waistcoat maker journeyman
28941	Solomon	Hannah	1839	Aldgate, London	(?) Solomon			Whitechapel, London	scholar
21604	Solomon	Hannah	1841	Middlesex, London	Jacob Solomon	Esther (?)		Chatham, Kent	

ID	surname	given names	born	birthplace	father	mother	spouse 1	1851 residence	1851 occupation
15963	Solomon	Hannah	1846	Spitalfields, London	Morris Solomon	Dinah Moses		Whitechapel, London	scholar
18355	Solomon	Hannah	1847	Canterbury, Kent	Phineas Solomon	Phoebe (?)		Canterbury, Kent	scholar
29810	Solomon	Hannah	1847	Whitechapel, London	Joseph Solomon	Rebecca Hart		Whitechapel, London	
21795	Solomon	Hannah	1850	Whitechapel, London	Abraham Solomon	Esther Moses		Aldgate, London	
23178	Solomon	Hannah	1850	Shoreditch, London	Nathan Solomon	Julia (?)		Hoxton, London	
13993	Solomon	Harriet	1826	?, London	(?) Solomon			Manchester	house servant
1986	Solomon	Harriet	1828	Bath	(?) Demery		Israel Solomon	Swansea, Wales	
20362	Solomon	Harriet	1831	Stepney, London	Joseph Solomon		Lewis Lavinburg	Aldgate, London	servant
4979	Solomon	Harriet	1848	Birmingham	Moses Solomons	Caroline Eagles		Birmingham	
18193	Solomon	Henry	1770	Amsterdam, Holland			(?)	Mile End, London	tailor
6219	Solomon	Henry	1803	City, London			Rachel (?)	Aldgate, London	
8050	Solomon	Henry	1809	Exeter, Devon	Jacob Solomon	Sarah (?)	Sarah Adler	Finsbury, London	Birmingham warehouseman
19693	Solomon	Henry	1809	Exeter, Devon			Sarah (?)	Shoreditch, London	merchant
21522	Solomon	Henry	1816	Whitechapel, London				Wapping, London	clothier's shopman
25620	Solomon	Henry	1820	?			(?)	Dublin, Ireland	clothier
15487	Solomon	Henry	1823	Strand, London				Covent Garden, London	fishmonger
15965	Solomon	Henry	1828	?, London	Henry Solomon	Rachel (?)		Aldgate, London	cigar maker
3619	Solomon	Henry	1829	Chatham, Kent	Israel Solomon	Mary Israel Isaacs	Amelia Gallewski nee Green	Whitechapel, London	furniture broker
15821	Solomon	Henry	1832	Whitechapel, London	Maurice Solomon	Louisa Raphael	Eleanor Collins	Bloomsbury, London	
12922	Solomon	Henry	1837	?, London	Abraham Solomon	Rachael (?)		Holborn, London	cigar maker
19532	Solomon	Henry	1838	Covent Garden, London	(?) Solomon	Sarah (?)		Strand, London	
10824	Solomon	Henry	1840	Spitalfields, London	Phillip Solomon	Abigail (?)		Spitalfields, London	scholar
23556	Solomon	Henry	1840	?, London	(?) Solomon	Jessie (?)		Liverpool	scholar
4949	Solomon	Henry	1841	Birmingham	George Solomon	Ann (?)		Birmingham	
7409	Solomon	Henry	1841	Middlesex, London	Abraham Solomon	Julia Isaacs	Esther Samson	Covent Garden, London	
5926	Solomon	Henry	1842	Middlesex, London	Josiah Solomon	Bella Hart	Frances Solomon	Aldgate, London	scholar
1319	Solomon	Henry	1844	Plymouth, Devon	Josiah Solomon	Rose (?)		Plymouth, Devon	scholar
9430	Solomon	Henry	1850	?, London	Charles Solomon	Deborah Minden		Wapping, London	
24450	Solomon	Henry	1850	Norwich, Norfolk	Ebenezer Solomon	Sarah (?)		Strand, London	
28138	Solomon	Henry	1850	Middlesex, London				Spitalfields, London	
21270	Solomon	Henry Naphtali	1797	Spitalfields, London	Moses Eliezer Solomon		Fanny Phillips	Edmonton, London	schoolmaster
27565	Solomon	Hyam	1810	City, London	Solomon Solomon	Julia (?)		Spitalfields, London	cutler
17172	Solomon	Hyman	1834	Margonin, Poland				Newcastle Upon Tyne	glazier
22574	Solomon	Isaac	1761	?, Holland				Whitechapel, London	tailor
11009	Solomon	Isaac	1766	Aldgate, London				Aldgate, London	general dealer
1033	Solomon	Isaac	1776	?, Poland [?, Prussia]			Rosetta (?)	Exeter, Devon	retired jeweller
27740	Solomon	Isaac	1785	Whitechapel, London	Zelig Schneider Solomon		Catherine (Katherine) Woolf	Spitalfields, London	trimming manufacturer
2340	Solomon	Isaac	1806	?, Poland [?, Prussia]				Leeds, Yorkshire	general dealer
29271	Solomon	Isaac	1815	?, London			Frances (?)	Wapping, London	shoemaker
4954	Solomon	Isaac	1817	Middlesex, London	Pinhas		Mary (?)	Birmingham	clothier
12069	Solomon	Isaac	1821	?, Poland [?, Prussia]			Yetta (?)	Spitalfields, London	tailor
24969	Solomon	Isaac	1821	Portsmouth, Hampshire				Holborn, London	general dealer

ID	surname	given names	born	birthplace	father	mother	spouse 1	1851 residence	1851 occupation
9068	Solomon	Isaac	1825	Aldgate, London	Michael (Myer) Solomon	Catherine Levy		Hoxton, London	
9274	Solomon	Isaac	1826	Whitechapel, London			Esther (?)	Aldgate, London	fruiterer
3620	Solomon	Isaac	1827	Chatham, Kent	Israel Solomon	Mary Israel Isaacs		Chatham, Kent	
29317	Solomon	Isaac	1827	?, London				Wapping, London	cigar maker
21465	Solomon	Isaac	1828	Stamford Hill, London	Abraham Solomon	Ellen Levy	Ellen (?)	Wolverhampton, Staffordshire	tailor's assistant
21376	Solomon	Isaac	1832	Spitalfields, London	Israel Solomon	Mary (?)		Spitalfields, London	cigar maker
9799	Solomon	Isaac	1833	Middlesex, London	Solomon Jacob Solomon	Catherine (Kitty) Joseph		Spitalfields, London	furrier
19530	Solomon	Isaac	1833	Stepney, London	(?) Solomon	Sarah (?)		Strand, London	salesman
17955	Solomon	Isaac	1841	Aldgate, London	(?) Solomon	(?) Isaacs		Aldgate, London	scholar
6222	Solomon	Isaac	1844	City, London	Henry Solomon	Rachel (?)		Aldgate, London	
24446	Solomon	Isaac	1844	Wapping, London	Ebenezer Solomon	Sarah (?)		Strand, London	
25403	Solomon	Isaac	1846	Paris, France	Joseph Solomon	Caroline (?)		Holborn, London	
3177	Solomon	Isaac John	1835	Chatham, Kent	Samuel Solomon	Hannah Isaacs	Sara Kate Moses	Chatham, Kent	scholar
17204	Solomon	Isabella	1792	Portsmouth, Hampshire	Philip Nathan		Moses Solomon	Whitechapel, London	
24763	Solomon	Isabella	1825	Southwark, London	Edward Solomon	Rachael Joseph	I--- L--- Simmons	Southwark, London	
1671	Solomon	Isabella	1834	?, London	Woolf Solomon	Leah Hyman	Nathan Noah Joseph	Spitalfields, London	
15819	Solomon	Isabella (Elizabeth)	1829	Whitechapel, London	Maurice Solomon	Louisa Raphael	Horatio Micholls Jones	Bloomsbury, London	
17741	Solomon	Isador	1830	?, Poland [?, Prussia]				Aldgate, London	glazier
1685	Solomon	Israel	1801	?, Holland			Mary (?)	Spitalfields, London	commission agent
1985	Solomon	Israel	1816	?, Poland [?, Prussia]			Harriet Demery	Swansea, Wales	cheese dealer
5502	Solomon	Israel	1826	Portsmouth, Hampshire	Solomon Solomon	Rachel Abrahams		Southampton, Hampshire	
6315	Solomon	Israel	1828	Covent Garden, London	Samuel Solomon	Ann (?)	Martha Levy	Covent Garden, London	
11861	Solomon	Israel	1840	Middlesex, London	(?) Solomon	(?)		Whitechapel, London	inmate of orphan school
20739	Solomon	Jacob	1783	?, Germany	Ze'ev Bernsley		Sarah Levy	Westminster, London	retired tradesman
27268	Solomon	Jacob	1790	?, London			Maria (?)	Aldgate, London	general dealer
21600	Solomon	Jacob	1807	?Cracow, Poland [Carow, Poland]			Esther (?)	Chatham, Kent	surgeon + general practitioner
4963	Solomon	Jacob	1825	?, Holland				Birmingham	cigar maker
2339	Solomon	Jacob	1826	Warsaw, Poland	Isaac Solomon?			Leeds, Yorkshire	spoon dealer
30888	Solomon	Jacob	1833	?, London				Gloucester, Gloucestershire	engraver
1664	Solomon	Jacob	1838	Spitalfields, London	Solomons Solomon	Amelia (Miriam) Fernandez	Sarah Park	Spitalfields, London	
9696	Solomon	Jacob	1845	Whitechapel, London	Morris Solomon	Charlotte (?)		Whitechapel, London	
20846	Solomon	James	1831	?, London	Nathaniel Solomon	Rebecca (?)		Euston, London	
4948	Solomon	James	1839	Birmingham	George Solomon	Ann (?)		Birmingham	
22943	Solomon	James	1849	Clerkenwell, London	Lewis Solomon	Louisa (?)		Wapping, London	scholar
6757	Solomon	Jane	1831	Whitechapel, London	Solomon Jacob Solomon	Catherine (Kitty) Joseph	David Edward Winkler	Whitechapel, London	
13860	Solomon	Jane	1832	Manchester	Phillip Solomon	Cathrine (?)		Manchester	
1681	Solomon	Jane	1842	Spitalfields, London	(?) Solomon	Julia (?)		Spitalfields, London	
1990	Solomon	Jane	1849	Swansea, Wales	Israel Solomon	Harriet Demery		Swansea, Wales	
1688	Solomon	Jane (Janette)	1838	Spitalfields, London	Israel Solomon	Mary (?)		Spitalfields, London	cap maker
25026	Solomon	Jane G	1838	Finsbury, London	Saul Solomon	Julia Jacob		Finsbury, London	
19181	Solomon	Jeanette	1851	Finsbury, London	Henry Solomon	Sarah Adler		Finsbury, London	
23553	Solomon	Jessie	1814	Maldon, Essex	(?)		(?) Solomon	Liverpool	cigar maker's wife

ID	surname	given names	born	birthplace	father	mother	spouse 1	1851 residence	1851 occupation
28940	Solomon	Jessie	1837	Aldgate, London	(?) Solomon			Whitechapel, London	scholar
896	Solomon	Joel	1823	Bristol	Simon Solomon	Rosetta (?)	Henrietta Blanckensee	Bristol	pawnbroker
16779	Solomon	Joel	1845	Bristol	Joseph Solomon	Catherine Benjamin		Bristol	
16997	Solomon	Joel Woolf	1806	Covent Garden, London	?Woolf Solomon		Matilda Hart	Strand, London	artist - portrait painter
21834	Solomon	John	1777	Aldgate, London			Julia (?)	Clerkenwell, London	retired clothier
5147	Solomon	John	1803	Aldgate, London	Isaac Solomon		Sarah Davis nee Zusman	Aldgate, London	general dealer
892	Solomon	John	1820	Bristol	Simon Solomon	Rosetta	Amelia Levy	Bristol	wholesale clothier
3621	Solomon	John	1820	Chatham, Kent	Israel Solomon	Mary Israel Isaacs		Chatham, Kent	furniture broker
27242	Solomon	John	1823	?, London	Barnet Solomon	Hannah (Ann) Hart		Aldgate, London	general dealer
31043	Solomon	John	1826	Middlesex, London			Hannah Jacob	Liverpool	ship owner + merchant
24765	Solomon	John	1829	Southwark, London	Edward Solomon	Rachael Joseph		Southwark, London	
9362	Solomon	John	1835	Brighton, Sussex				Mayfair, London	assistant to manager to a tailor
14852	Solomon	John	1839	Aldgate, London	Silverston Solomon	Frances (?)		Bethnal Green, London	scholar
23558	Solomon	John	1844	Liverpool	(?) Solomon	Jessie (?)		Liverpool	scholar
4962	Solomon	John	1850	Birmingham	Isaac Solomon	Mary (?)	Kate (?)	Birmingham	
25028	Solomon	John W	1846	?, London	Saul Solomon	Julia Jacob		Finsbury, London	
1713	Solomon	Jonas	1785	?, Holland			Elizabeth (?)	Spitalfields, London	general dealer
6226	Solomon	Jonas	1812	Whitechapel, London	Mark Solomon		Anne Davis	Aldgate, London	master butcher empl 2
1716	Solomon	Jonas	1833	Spitalfields, London	Solomon Solomon	Lydia (Leah) Lazarus		Spitalfields, London	apprentice to cigar maker
10502	Solomon	Joseph	1784	Aldgate, London			Rachel (?)	Mile End, London	furrier
21528	Solomon	Joseph	1803	Whitechapel, London			Anna (?)	Mayfair, London	general dealer in wearing apparel
25400	Solomon	Joseph	1803	Falmouth, Cornwall			Caroline (?)	Holborn, London	agent for the sale of French manufactures
24767	Solomon	Joseph	1813	Sheerness, Kent	Edward Solomon	Rachael (?)	Abigail Pass (Paz de Leon)	Southwark, London	solicitor
23988	Solomon	Joseph	1820	Finsbury, London				St John's Wood, London	scripture reader
29808	Solomon	Joseph	1820	Bethnal Green, London	Selig Solomons		Rebecca Hart	Whitechapel, London	porter
4964	Solomon	Joseph	1823	Middlesex, London			Esther (?)	Birmingham	clothier
9798	Solomon	Joseph	1824	Middlesex, London	Solomon Jacob Solomon	Catherine (Kitty) Joseph		Spitalfields, London	morocco leather finisher
15489	Solomon	Joseph	1824	Strand, London				Covent Garden, London	farrier
16773	Solomon	Joseph	1827	Bristol	Simon Solomon	Rosetta (?)		Bristol	
9410	Solomon	Joseph	1829	?, London				Aldgate, London	clerk
21523	Solomon	Joseph	1831	Whitechapel, London				Wapping, London	clothier's shopman
4947	Solomon	Joseph	1837	Birmingham	George Solomon	Ann (?)		Birmingham	
23555	Solomon	Joseph	1838	?, London	(?) Solomon	Jessie (?)		Liverpool	tobacco stripper
15825	Solomon	Joseph	1840	Whitechapel, London	Maurice Solomon	Louisa Raphael		Bloomsbury, London	scholar at home
6221	Solomon	Joseph	1842	City, London	Henry Solomon	Rachel (?)		Aldgate, London	
6347	Solomon	Joseph	1847	Westminster, London	Leon Solomon	Rose Joseph	Leah Davis	Mayfair, London	
1683	Solomon	Joseph	1848	Spitalfields, London	(?) Solomon	Julia (?)		Spitalfields, London	
10827	Solomon	Joseph	1849	Spitalfields, London	Phillip Solomon	Abigail (?)		Spitalfields, London	
19971	Solomon	Joseph M	1849	?Deal, Kent	Samuel Solomon	Rosetta (Rosa, Rose) Hart		Deal, Kent	
22223	Solomon	Joshua	1827	Bethnal Green, London	(?) Solomon	Elizabeth (?)		Whitechapel, London	porter
14498	Solomon	Joshua E	1805	Norwich, Norfolk			Mary A (?)	Norwich, Norfolk	cabinet maker journeyman

ID	surname	given names	born	birthplace	father	mother	spouse 1	1851 residence	1851 occupation
1314	Solomon	Josiah	1810	Exeter, Devon			Rose (?)	Plymouth, Devon	jeweller/hardwareman
5925	Solomon	Josiah	1812	Exeter, Devon	Jacob Solomon	Sarah (?)	Bella Hart	Aldgate, London	merchant
6239	Solomon	Judah	1817	Elephant & Castle, London	Myer Solomons		Leah (Ann) Coomer	St Giles, London	tailor
19238	Solomon	Judah	1818	?, Devon			Adele Emanuel	Waterloo, London	loan office proprietor
16987	Solomon	Judah	1835	Whitechapel, London				Wapping, London	shoemaker apprentice
20730	Solomon	Judah	1846	Stepney, London				Whitechapel, London	scholar
24448	Solomon	Judah	1848	Shoreditch, London	Ebenezer Solomon	Sarah (?)		Strand, London	
4944	Solomon	Judith	1793	?, London	(?Naphtali Hirsh Davis?)		(?Godfrey?) Solomon	Birmingham	
21835	Solomon	Julia	1781	Aldgate, London	(?)		John Solomon	Clerkenwell, London	retired clothier
27563	Solomon	Julia	1781	City, London	(?)		Solomon Solomon	Spitalfields, London	
1657	Solomon	Julia	1795	Middlesex, London			Henry Solomon	Spitalfields, London	
25025	Solomon	Julia	1807	Finsbury, London	Aharon Jacob		Saul Solomon	Finsbury, London	
1678	Solomon	Julia	1815	Worcester, Worcestershire				Spitalfields, London	general dealer
7408	Solomon	Julia	1815	Middlesex, London	Isaac Isaacs	Mary (Miriam, Polly) Solomons	Abraham Solomon	Covent Garden, London	
23170	Solomon	Julia	1818	Stepney, London	(?)		Nathan Solomon	Hoxton, London	
8987	Solomon	Julia	1830	Portsmouth, Hampshire	(?) Carter		Samuel Ellis Solomon	Portsmouth, Hampshire	
6220	Solomon	Julia	1831	City, London	Henry Solomon	Rachel (?)		Aldgate, London	
16962	Solomon	Julia	1836	Bristol	(?) Solomon			Hammersmith, London	boarding school pupil
1673	Solomon	Julia	1837	Middlesex, London	Woolf Solomon	Leah Hyman	Henry Cohen	Spitalfields, London	
15687	Solomon	Julia	1838	Clerkenwell, London	Morris (Maurice) Solomon	Fanny (Frances) Jacob		Clerkenwell, London	
14853	Solomon	Julia	1841	Clerkenwell, London	Silverston Solomon	Frances (?)		Bethnal Green, London	scholar
19533	Solomon	Julia	1841	Covent Garden, London	(?) Solomon	Sarah (?)		Strand, London	
1320	Solomon	Julia	1845	Plymouth, Devon	Josiah Solomon	Rose (?)		Plymouth, Devon	scholar
4960	Solomon	Julia	1846	Birmingham	Isaac Solomon	May (?)		Birmingham	
18606	Solomon	Julia	1847	Aldgate, London	Josiah Solomon	Bella Hart		Aldgate, London	
1668	Solomon	Julia	1849	Spitalfields, London	Solomons Solomon	Amelia (Miriam) Fernandez		Spitalfields, London	
1061	Solomon	Julia	1850	Exeter, Devon	Myers Solomon	Deborah (?)	Edmund A Rosenthal (Rosenthall)	Exeter, Devon	
26938	Solomon	Julius	1845	?, Poland	Moses Solomon	Dorothea (?)		Aldgate, London	
17954	Solomon	Kate	1837	Aldgate, London	(?) Solomon	(?) Isaacs		Aldgate, London	scholar
4128	Solomon	Kitty	1815	Finsbury, London	Solomon Solomon			Spitalfields, London	boot binder
23176	Solomon	Laura?	1848	Shoreditch, London	Nathan Solomon	Julia (?)		Hoxton, London	
9692	Solomon	Laurence	1834	Whitechapel, London	Morris Solomon	Charlotte (?)		Whitechapel, London	cigar maker
30898	Solomon	Lazarus	1814	Deal, Kent	(?) Solomon	Sarah (?)		Deal, Kent	fruiterer
19535	Solomon	Lazarus	1850	Strand, London	(?) Solomon	Sarah (?)		Strand, London	
17000	Solomon	Lazarus (Lionel) Benson	1849	Covent Garden, London	Solomon Solomon	Marinda Salamon	Marion (?)	Strand, London	
23990	Solomon	Leagh	1815	?Aldgate, London	(?)		Saul Solomon	Marylebone, London	
1669	Solomon	Leah	1811	Falmouth, Cornwall	Moses Hyman	Sarah (Sally) Levy (Levi)	Woolf Solomon	Spitalfields, London	dressmaker
9797	Solomon	Leah	1821	Middlesex, London	Solomon Jacob Solomon	Catherine (Kitty) Joseph		Spitalfields, London	
12071	Solomon	Leah	1840	?, Poland [?, Prussia]	Isaac Solomon	Yetta (?)		Spitalfields, London	
23559	Solomon	Leah	1846	Liverpool	(?) Solomon	Jessie (?)		Liverpool	scholar
19237	Solomon	Leah	1851	St Giles, London	Judah Solomon	Ann (?)		St Giles, London	
1654	Solomon	Lehman	1828	?London	Lipman Solomon	Banet (?)		Spitalfields, London	hawker

ID	surname	given names	born	birthplace	father	mother	spouse 1	1851 residence	1851 occupation
6348	Solomon	Leon	1811	Warsaw, Poland			Rose Joseph	Mayfair, London	merchant jeweller
1710	Solomon	Levi	1828	Amsterdam, Holland				Spitalfields, London	cigar maker
1711	Solomon	Levi	1841	Amsterdam, Holland				Spitalfields, London	
29273	Solomon	Levy	1838	?, London	Isaac Solomon	Frances (?)		Wapping, London	
29212	Solomon	Lewis	1771	?, Germany			(?)	Whitechapel, London	optician
3611	Solomon	Lewis	1791	Aldgate, London	Isaac (John Zekel) Solomon	Maria (Merle) Israel	Anne (Hannah) Solomons	Chatham, Kent	tailor + navy agent
6317	Solomon	Lewis	1816	Waterloo, London			(?)	Covent Garden, London	fruiterer salesman &c
22939	Solomon	Lewis	1823	Aldgate, London			Louisa (?)	Wapping, London	china warehouseman
21517	Solomon	Lewis	1825	Whitechapel, London			Frances Braham	Wapping, London	clothier
2190	Solomon	Lewis	1826	Cracow, Poland	Judah Kraenger		Mathilda Levi	Oxford, Oxfordshire	jeweller
17175	Solomon	Lewis	1828	?, London	David Solomon	Sarah (?)		Newcastle Upon Tyne	cabinet maker
20889	Solomon	Lewis	1830	?, Poland [?, Prussia]				Bedford, Bedfordshire	watchmaker
13859	Solomon	Lewis	1832	Manchester	Phillip Solomon	Cathrine (?)		Manchester	pawnbroker's assistant
16777	Solomon	Lewis	1838	Bristol	Joseph Solomon	Catherine Benjamin		Bristol	
23993	Solomon	Lewis	1842	Marylebone, London	Saul Solomon	Leagh (?)		Marylebone, London	
6250	Solomon	Lewis	1847	Middlesex, London	Abraham Solomon	Rachael (?)		Holborn, London	
7406	Solomon	Lewis	1848	Covent Garden, London	Abraham Solomon	Julia Isaacs	Caroline Abrahams	Covent Garden, London	scholar
6313	Solomon	Lewis	1850	Whitechapel, London	Morris Solomon	Charlotte (?)	Priscilla Cohen	Whitechapel, London	
29280	Solomon	Lewis	1850	?Wapping, London	Isaac Solomon	Frances (?)		Wapping, London	
4129	Solomon	Lewis (Luke)	1811	Finsbury, London	Solomon Solomon			Spitalfields, London	boot + shoe maker empl 12
6211	Solomon	Lidia	1830	City, London	(?) Solomon	Esther (?)	Simon Solomon	Aldgate, London	furrier
1652	Solomon	Lipman	1788	Alsace, France [Elsas, France]			Banet (?)	Spitalfields, London	umbrella maker
233	Solomon	Louisa	1803	Bloomsbury, London	Samuel (Samson) Raphael	Charlotte Levy	Maurice Solomon	Bloomsbury, London	merchant's wife
3615	Solomon	Louisa	1812	Aldgate, London	Israel Solomon	Mary Israel Isaacs		Whitechapel, London	s
22940	Solomon	Louisa	1825	Elephant & Castle, London	(?)		Lewis Solomon	Wapping, London	
21352	Solomon	Louisa	1831	Chatham, Kent	Lewis Solomon	Ann (Hannah) Solomons		Chatham, Kent	
21275	Solomon	Louisa	1834	Bloomsbury, London	Henry Naphtali Solomon	Fanny Phillips	Matthias Levy	Edmonton, London	
15823	Solomon	Louisa	1837	Aldgate, London	Maurice Solomon	Louisa Raphael	Julian Emanuel Salomons	Bloomsbury, London	scholar at home
16015	Solomon	Louisa	1848	Covent Garden, London	Lewis Solomon	?	Michael Falk	Covent Garden, London	
20737	Solomon	Lucy	1850	?Pimlico, London	Alexander Solomon	Frances Ellen (?)		Pimlico, London	
21443	Solomon	Lydia	1788	Middlesex, London	(?)		(?) Solomon	Bury, Lancashire	
4958	Solomon	Lydia	1842	Waterloo, London	Isaac Solomon	Mary (?)	Benjamin Nathan	Birmingham	
1714	Solomon	Lydia (Leah)	1805	City, London	Aaron Lazarus		Solomon Solomon	Spitalfields, London	
29101	Solomon	Lyon (Yehuda)	1787	Finsbury, London			Esther (?)	Southwark, London	Manchester warehouseman
17041	Solomon	Margaret	1806	Liverpool				Edinburgh, Scotland	house servant
27269	Solomon	Maria	1792	?, London	(?)		Jacob Solomon	Aldgate, London	
21316	Solomon	Maria	1814	Aldgate, London	(?) Solomon			Eton, Berkshire	
24761	Solomon	Maria	1819	Southwark, London	Edward Solomon	Rachael Joseph		Southwark, London	
3618	Solomon	Maria	1821	?, London	Israel Solomon	Mary Israel Isaacs		Whitechapel, London	seamstress
16774	Solomon	Maria	1829	Bristol	Simon Solomon	Rosetta (?)	Bernhardt Sternberg	Bristol	
16145	Solomon	Maria	1832	Whitechapel, London	(?) Solomon	Amelia (?)		Whitechapel, London	
21274	Solomon	Maria	1832	Hammersmith, London	Henry Naphtali Solomon	Fanny (?)		Edmonton, London	
21532	Solomon	Maria	1839	Bayswater, London	Joseph Solomon	Anna (?)		Mayfair, London	feather maker

ID	surname	given names	born	birthplace	father	mother	spouse 1	1851 residence	1851 occupation
3191	Solomon	Maria	1840	Chatham, Kent	Samuel Solomon	Hannah Isaacs		Chatham, Kent	
12923	Solomon	Maria	1843	?, London	Abraham Solomon	Rachael (?)		Holborn, London	scholar
15964	Solomon	Maria	1850	Whitechapel, London	Morris Solomon	Dinah (?)		Whitechapel, London	
9867	Solomon	Marianne?	1842	?, London				Fulham, London	boarding school pupil
16999	Solomon	Marinda	1817	Whitechapel, London	Moses Salamon	Ann Israel	Solomon Solomon	Strand, London	
26729	Solomon	Mark	1784	Spitalfields, London			Esther (?)	Spitalfields, London	watch finisher
21530	Solomon	Mark	1835	Knightsbridge, London	Joseph Solomon	Anna (?)		Mayfair, London	cigar maker
18113	Solomon	Martha	1785	Dover, Kent	(?)		Barnet Solomon	Mile End, London	domestic affairs
31087	Solomon	Martha	1802	Brighton, Sussex	(?)		(?) Solomon	Brighton, Sussex	annuitant
1717	Solomon	Martha	1835	Spitalfields, London	Solomon Solomon	Lydia (Leah) Lazarus		Spitalfields, London	dress maker
1684	Solomon	Mary	1799	?, Holland	(?)		Israel Solomon	Spitalfields, London	
14771	Solomon	Mary	1800	City, London	(?)		George Solomon	Finsbury, London	
3830	Solomon	Mary	1801	Pinczow, Poland [Pincha, Poland]			Simon Solomon	Spitalfields, London	
21516	Solomon	Mary	1810	Shoreditch, London	(?)		Solomon Solomon	Bethnal Green, London	shoe binder
4955	Solomon	Mary	1813	?, London			Isaac Solomon	Birmingham	
14637	Solomon	Mary	1824	Ramsgate, Kent	(?) Miles		Aaron Solomon	Hoxton, London	
19529	Solomon	Mary	1832	Stepney, London	(?) Solomon	Sarah (?)		Strand, London	purse maker
31145	Solomon	Mary	1835	Bristol	Alexander Solomon	(?)		Bath	
1663	Solomon	Mary	1836	Middlesex, London	Solomons Solomon	Amelia (Miriam) Fernandez	Alexander (Abraham) Bittan	Spitalfields, London	parasol maker
14777	Solomon	Mary	1840	Middlesex, London	George Solomon	Mary (?)		Finsbury, London	at home
14499	Solomon	Mary A	1801	Norwich, Norfolk	(?)		Joshua E Solomon	Norwich, Norfolk	
14501	Solomon	Mary A	1835	Norwich, Norfolk	Joshua E Solomon	Mary A (?)		Norwich, Norfolk	pupil teacher model school
16010	Solomon	Mary Ann	1842	Covent Garden, London	Lewis Solomon	?		Covent Garden, London	scholar
2191	Solomon	Mathilda (Malka)	1825	?, Poland	Harris Levi	Hannah (?)	Lewis Solomon	Oxford, Oxfordshire	
20346	Solomon	Matilda	1803	City, London	(?) Solomon			Shoreditch, London	annuitant
24373	Solomon	Matilda	1803	Piccadilly, London	(?) Solomon			Soho, London	
1284	Solomon	Matilda	1805	Plymouth, Devon	Joseph Joseph	Edal (?)	(?) Solomon	Plymouth, Devon	lady
16146	Solomon	Matilda	1835	Whitechapel, London	(?) Solomon	Amelia (?)		Whitechapel, London	Berlin wool worker
22816	Solomon	Matthew	1851	Middlesex, London	Saul Solomon	Sarah (?)		Spitalfields, London	
15818	Solomon	Maurice	1800	?Spitalfields, London	Moses Eliezer Solomon		Louisa Raphael	Bloomsbury, London	merchant
4126	Solomon	Michael	1818	Finsbury, London	Solomon Solomon		Deborah Levi	Spitalfields, London	boot + shoe maker empl 12
24712	Solomon	Michael	1819	City, London				Walworth, London	glass + china maufacturer + dealer
6769	Solomon	Michael	1834	Stamford Hill, London	Abraham Soloman	Ellen (?)	Fanny (?)	Wolverhampton, Staffordshire	
14851	Solomon	Michael	1837	City, London	Silverston Solomon	Frances (?)		Bethnal Green, London	errand boy
17306	Solomon	Michael	1837	Whitechapel, London	(?) Solomon	(?) Jacobs		Whitechapel, London	scholar
229	Solomon	Michael (Myer)	1789	Aldgate, London	Aaron Solomon	Elizabeth (Betsy) (?)	Catharine (Kate) Levy	Hoxton, London	tailor + clothier
10825	Solomon	Michel	1842	Spitalfields, London	Phillip Solomon	Abigail (?)		Spitalfields, London	scholar
20845	Solomon	Miriam	1830	?, London	Nathaniel Solomon	Rebecca (?)	John Zachariah Laurence (Lawrence)	Euston, London	

ID	surname	given names	born	birthplace	father	mother	spouse 1	1851 residence	1851 occupation
31060	Solomon	Miriam	1832	Portsmouth, Hampshire	Solomon Solomon	Rachel Abraham	Robert Phillips Noah	Southampton, Hampshire	
17001	Solomon	Montague Benson	1850	Covent Garden, London	Solomon Solomon	Marinda Salamon		Strand, London	
9690	Solomon	Morris	1810	Whitechapel, London			Charlotte (?)	Whitechapel, London	tailor
6212	Solomon	Morris	1822	Middlesex, London	Phineas Solomon		Dinah Moses	Whitechapel, London	fishmonger
4903	Solomon	Morris	1826	?, Poland				Birmingham	glazier
202	Solomon	Morris (Maurice)	1806	?, London	Jacob Solomon		Fanny (Frances) Jacob	Clerkenwell, London	tailor + draper
10472	Solomon	Mosely	1759	Middlesex, London				Mile End, London	annuitant
15469	Solomon	Moses	1765	Aldgate, London			Betsy (?Hart)	Covent Garden, London	general dealer
11759	Solomon	Moses	1782	Whitechapel, London				Shoreditch, London	hawker
5116	Solomon	Moses	1786	Portsmouth, Hampshire	Samuel Solomon	Sarah (?)	Frances Davis	Portsmouth, Hampshire	navy agent
17203	Solomon	Moses	1795	Aldgate, London	Jacob Solomon		Isabella Nathan	Whitechapel, London	fundholder
21140	Solomon	Moses	1803	?, Poland			Rachel (?)	Aldgate, London	clothes dealer
4975	Solomon	Moses	1815	Birmingham			Harriet Lazarus	Birmingham	cabinet maker
26936	Solomon	Moses	1822	?, Poland			Dorothea (?)	Aldgate, London	traveller
15967	Solomon	Moses	1833	?, London	Henry Solomon	Rachel (?)		Aldgate, London	tailor
11868	Solomon	Moses	1844	Middlesex, London	(?) Solomon	(?)		Whitechapel, London	inmate of orphan school
1672	Solomon	Moses (Moss)	1835	Spitalfields, London	Woolf Solomon	Leah Hyman	Martha Green	Spitalfields, London	confectioner
9173	Solomon	Moses Eleazer	1775	Spitalfields, London	Kalman Kesselflicker		Betsy Hart	Whitechapel, London	school master
3833	Solomon	Myer	1839	Pinczow, Poland [Pincha, Poland]	Simon Solomon	Mary (?)		Spitalfields, London	
1059	Solomon	Myers	1822	?, Poland [?, Prussia]			Deborah Lazarus	Exeter, Devon	optician
21444	Solomon	Nathan	1829	Nottingham, Nottinghamshire	(?) Solomon	Lydia (?)		Bury, Lancashire	tailor + draper
945	Solomon	Nathan	1776	?, Poland [?, Prussia]			Fanny (?)	Exeter, Devon	retired jeweller
23169	Solomon	Nathan	1817	Stepney, London	Abraham Solomon	Phoebe (?)	Julia (?)	Hoxton, London	pencil maker
2181	Solomon	Nathan	1824	?, Poland [?, Prussia]				Oxford, Oxfordshire	journeyman tailor
31088	Solomon	Nathan	1825	Brighton, Susex	(?) Solomon	Martha (?)		Brighton, Sussex	printer
12356	Solomon	Nathan	1833	Whitechapel, London	Moses Solomon		Ellen Joseph	City, London	clothier's cashier
21438	Solomon	Nathan	1833	?, Poland				Nottingham, Nottinghamshire	hawker of jewellery
15968	Solomon	Nathan	1835	?, London	Henry Solomon	Rachel (?)		Aldgate, London	tailor
15820	Solomon	Nathan M	1830	Whitechapel, London	Maurice Solomon	Louisa Raphael	Annie Jones Levason	Bloomsbury, London	foreign agent
20842	Solomon	Nathaniel	1800	?, London			Rebecca (?)	Euston, London	
25005	Solomon	Nathaniel	1812	Sheerness, Kent			Elizabeth West	Holborn, London	printer + ticket writer
19235	Solomon	Nathaniel	1833	City, London	Lewis Solomon	Anne (Hannah) Solomons		City, London	apprentice (?tailor)
4967	Solomon	Noah	1791	?, Poland				Birmingham	general factor
6251	Solomon	Philip	1813	Exeter, Devon	Isaac Solomon		Amelia Woolf	Shoreditch, London	carpet bag maker
20741	Solomon	Philip	1813	Exeter, Devon	Jacob Solomon	Sarah Levy	Evelina (?)	Westminster, London	accountant
27270	Solomon	Philip	1829	?, London	Jacob Solomon	Maria (?)		Aldgate, London	general dealer
13857	Solomon	Phillip	1798	?, Poland			Cathrine (?)	Manchester	pawnbroker
10822	Solomon	Phillip	1805	Whitechapel, London	Meir Solomon	Ann (?)	Abigail (?)	Spitalfields, London	general dealer
1633	Solomon	Phillip Jacob	1828	Aldgate, London	Moses Solomon		Catherine (Kate) Benjamin	Spitalfields, London	tailor's trimming seller
18348	Solomon	Phineas	1799	Canterbury, Kent			Phoebe (?)	Canterbury, Kent	stationer
10112	Solomon	Phineas	1814	City, London			Fanny (?)	York, Yorkshire	
17137	Solomon	Phineas	1816	Middlesex, London				Bradford, Yorkshire	clothier manager
24970	Solomon	Phineas	1823	Portsmouth, Hampshire				Holborn, London	general dealer

ID	surname	given names	born	birthplace	father	mother	spouse 1	1851 residence	1851 occupation
23554	Solomon	Phineas	1837	Liverpool	(?) Solomon	Jessie (?)		Liverpool	cigar maker
23171	Solomon	Phoebe	1779	Poplar, London	(?)		Abraham Solomon	Hoxton, London	
18349	Solomon	Phoebe	1807	Whitechapel, London	(?)		Phineas Solomon	Canterbury, Kent	
24764	Solomon	Phoebe	1826	Southwark, London	Edward Solomon	Rachael Joseph		Southwark, London	
17178	Solomon	Phoebe	1832	?, London	David Solomon	Sarah (?)		Newcastle Upon Tyne	
23172	Solomon	Phoebe	1839	Shoreditch, London	Nathan Solomon	Julia (?)		Hoxton, London	
4942	Solomon	Phoebe	1849	Birmingham	Edward M Solomon	Rosa (?)		Birmingham	
20743	Solomon	Pricilla	1823	Exeter, Devon	Jacob Solomon	Sarah Levy		Westminster, London	
17205	Solomon	R---	1827	Aldgate, London	Moses Solomon	Isabella Nathan		Whitechapel, London	
24771	Solomon	Rachael	1791	Aldgate, London	(?)		Edward Solomon	Southwark, London	
12920	Solomon	Rachael	1803	?, London	(?) Gershon		Abraham Solomon	Holborn, London	
19531	Solomon	Rachael	1836	Stepney, London	(?) Solomon	Sarah (?)		Strand, London	flower maker
29274	Solomon	Rachael	1838	?, London	Isaac Solomon	Frances (?)		Wapping, London	
23174	Solomon	Rachael	1844	Shoreditch, London	Nathan Solomon	Julia (?)		Hoxton, London	
24447	Solomon	Rachael	1846	Wapping, London	Ebenezer Solomon	Sarah (?)		Strand, London	
24769	Solomon	Rachael	1851	Southwark, London	Joseph Solomon	Abigail Pass (Paz de Leon)		Southwark, London	
21445	Solomon	Rachel	1784	Buckingham, Buckinghamshire				Newport Pagnell, Buckinghamshire	washerwoman
10503	Solomon	Rachel	1786	?Aldgate, London	(?)		Joseph Solomon	Mile End, London	
5494	Solomon	Rachel	1790	Arundel, Sussex	Israel Abrahams	Elizabeth Davids	Solomon Solomon	Southampton, Hampshire	
812	Solomon	Rachel	1803	Stratford, London	Mark Davis		Saunders Solomon	Kensington, London	
21141	Solomon	Rachel	1805	?, Poland	(?)		Moses Solomon	Aldgate, London	
6223	Solomon	Rachel	1806	?, London	(?)		Henry Soloman	Aldgate, London	
23928	Solomon	Rachel	1824	Holborn, London	(?) Solomon			Marylebone, London	
16776	Solomon	Rachel	1835	Bristol	Joseph Solomon	Catherine Benjamin		Bristol	
18350	Solomon	Rachel	1835	Canterbury, Kent	Phineas Solomon	Phoebe (?)		Canterbury, Kent	dressmaker
4959	Solomon	Rachel	1844	Birmingham	Isaac Solomon	Mary (?)		Birmingham	
16963	Solomon	Rahel	1836	Middlesex, London	(?) Solomon			Hammersmith, London	boarding school pupil
20725	Solomon	Ralph	1819	Middlesex, London	Alexander Solomon		Rosetta (?)	Bath	cabinet maker
21836	Solomon	Ralph	1822	Clerkenwell, London	John Solomon	Julia (?)		Clerkenwell, London	tailor
11280	Solomon	Rebecca	1801	Aldgate, London	(?) Solomon			Aldgate, London	
20843	Solomon	Rebecca	1801	?, London	(?)		Nathaniel Solomon	Euston, London	
29809	Solomon	Rebecca	1828	Whitechapel, London	Samuel Michael Hart	Frances Phillips	Joseph Solomon	Whitechapel, London	parasol maker
7403	Solomon	Rebecca	1832	Aldgate, London	Michael (Myer) Solomon	Catherine (Kate) Levy		Fitzrovia, London	artist
3832	Solomon	Rebecca	1833	Pinczow, Poland [Pincha, Poland]	Simon Solomon	Mary (?)		Spitalfields, London	
1666	Solomon	Rebecca	1843	Spitalfields, London	Solomons Solomon	Amelia (Miriam) Fernandez	Jacob Elboz	Spitalfields, London	
230	Solomon	Reuben	1784	Aldgate, London	Aaron Solomon	Elizabeth (Betsy) (?)	Grace Ann Wells	Bethnal Green, London	shoe maker
9246	Solomon	Richard	1850	Middlesex, London	Samuel Solomon	Sarah (?)		Spitalfields, London	
25027	Solomon	Richard A	1839	Finsbury, London	Saul Solomon	Julia Jacob		Finsbury, London	
22942	Solomon	Robert	1847	Westminster, London	Lewis Solomon	Louisa (?)		Wapping, London	scholar
4941	Solomon	Rosa	1829	Middlesex, London	Barnet Sloman		Edward M Solomon	Birmingham	
1315	Solomon	Rose	1811	Penzance, Cornwall			Josiah Solomon	Plymouth, Devon	
26060	Solomon	Rose	1829	Penzance, Cornwall	Abraham Joseph	Eliza Woolf	Leon Solomon	Mayfair, London	
6543	Solomon	Rose	1830	Exeter, Devon	Woolf Solomon	Harriet (?)	Abraham Burstein	Exeter, Devon	lace manufacturer

ID	surname	given names	born	birthplace	father	mother	spouse 1	1851 residence	1851 occupation
1682	Solomon	Rose	1845	Spitalfields, London	(?) Solomon	Julia (?)		Spitalfields, London	
24762	Solomon	Rose (Rosetta)	1818	Southwark, London	Edward Solomon	Rachael Joseph		Southwark, London	
1034	Solomon	Rosetta	1781	?, Kent			Isaac Solomon	Exeter, Devon	
17145	Solomon	Rosetta	1818	Middlesex, London	Israel Solomon	Mary Israel Isaacs	Daniel Barnard	Aldgate, London	
20347	Solomon	Rosetta	1819	City, London	(?) Solomon			Shoreditch, London	
31144	Solomon	Rosetta	1823	Middlesex, London	(?)		Ralph Solomon	Bath	
14850	Solomon	Rosetta	1834	City, London	Silverston Solomon	Frances (?)		Bethnal Green, London	
21519	Solomon	Rosetta	1847	Whitechapel, London	Lewis Solomon	Frances (?)		Wapping, London	
19967	Solomon	Rosetta (Rosa, Rose)	1821	Canterbury, Kent	Joseph Hart	Miriam (Marian, Mary) Abrahams	Samuel Solomon	Deal, Kent	
1987	Solomon	Ruben	1844	Bristol	Israel Solomon	Harriet Demery	Mary (?)	Swansea, Wales	
30887	Solomon	Sally	1828	Brighton, Sussex	(?) Solomon			Lewes, Sussex	
9695	Solomon	Samson	1842	Whitechapel, London	Morris Solomon	Charlotte (?)		Whitechapel, London	
3189	Solomon	Samuel	1784	Aldgate, London	Isaac (John Zekel) Solomon	Maria (Merle) Israel	Hannah Isaacs	Chatham, Kent	slopseller
4971	Solomon	Samuel	1785	Birmingham				Birmingham	shoemaker
4969	Solomon	Samuel	1788	?, London			Elizabeth (?)	Birmingham	general dealer
16006	Solomon	Samuel	1797	?, London			Ann (?)	Covent Garden, London	fruiterer
30884	Solomon	Samuel	1801	Lewes, Sussex				Lewes, Sussex	master watchmaker
19968	Solomon	Samuel	1809	Deal, Kent			Rosetta (Rosa, Rose) Hart	Deal, Kent	general dealer
9242	Solomon	Samuel	1819	Middlesex, London			Sarah (?)	Spitalfields, London	boot maker master
20742	Solomon	Samuel	1819	Exeter, Devon	Jacob Solomon	Sarah Levy		Westminster, London	accountant
24772	Solomon	Samuel	1820	Southwark, London				Southwark, London	cigar manufacturer
29316	Solomon	Samuel	1823	?, London			Louisa (?)	Wapping, London	cigar maker
26731	Solomon	Samuel	1827	Whitechapel, London	Mark Solomon	Esther (?)		Spitalfields, London	cigar maker journeyman
17740	Solomon	Samuel	1830	?, Poland [?, Prussia]				Aldgate, London	tailor
21293	Solomon	Samuel	1837	City, London				Edmonton, London	boarding school pupil
23992	Solomon	Samuel	1837	Marylebone, London	Saul Solomon	Leagh (?)		Marylebone, London	
21603	Solomon	Samuel	1839	?, Jersey, Channel Islands	Jacob Solomon	Esther (?)		Chatham, Kent	
18353	Solomon	Samuel	1840	Canterbury, Kent	Phineas Solomon	Phoebe (?)		Canterbury, Kent	scholar
6249	Solomon	Samuel	1841	Middlesex, London	Abraham Solomon			Holborn, London	scholar
21533	Solomon	Samuel	1843	Paddington, London	Joseph Solomon	Anna (?)		Mayfair, London	scholar at home
16012	Solomon	Samuel	1845	Covent Garden, London	Lewis Solomon	?		Covent Garden, London	
23175	Solomon	Samuel	1846	Shoreditch, London	Nathan Solomon	Julia (?)		Hoxton, London	
6253	Solomon	Samuel	1847	Aldgate, London	Philip Solomon	Amelia (?)		Shoreditch, London	
14857	Solomon	Samuel	1850	Bethnal Green, London	Silverston Solomon	Frances (?)		Bethnal Green, London	
21521	Solomon	Samuel	1850	Whitechapel, London	Lewis Solomon	Frances (?)		Wapping, London	
25176	Solomon	Samuel	1850	Shoreditch, London	Solomon Solomon	Elizabeth (?)		Finsbury, London	
1317	Solomon	Samuel (Samuell)	1840	Plymouth, Devon	Josiah Solomon	Rose (?)		Plymouth, Devon	scholar
8986	Solomon	Samuel Ellis	1815	Plymouth, Devon			Julia Carter	Portsmouth, Hampshire	general dealer + toyman
24848	Solomon	Sarah	1766	?, London	(?)		Abraham Solomon	Elephant & Castle, London	
30899	Solomon	Sarah	1780	Canterbury, Kent	(?) Solomon	Sarah (?)		Deal, Kent	fruiteress
20740	Solomon	Sarah	1781	?, London	Yehuda Leib Levy		Jacob Solomon	Westminster, London	
5148	Solomon	Sarah	1787	Aldgate, London	Eliezer Zusman		Joshua Davis	Aldgate, London	
17174	Solomon	Sarah	1790	?, London	(?)		David Solomon	Newcastle Upon Tyne	

ID	surname	given names	born	birthplace	father	mother	spouse 1	1851 residence	1851 occupation
27235	Solomon	Sarah	1795	?, London	(?)		Aaron Solomon	Aldgate, London	
27564	Solomon	Sarah	1808	City, London	Solomon Solomon	Julia (?)		Spitalfields, London	
19537	Solomon	Sarah	1811	Strand, London	(?) Solomon	Dinah (?)		Strand, London	sells fruit
19694	Solomon	Sarah	1815	Hanover, Germany	(?)		Henry Solomon	Shoreditch, London	
19528	Solomon	Sarah	1817	Stepney, London	(?)		(?) Solomon	Strand, London	purse maker
24445	Solomon	Sarah	1823	Shoreditch, London	(?)		Ebenezer Solomon	Strand, London	
17140	Solomon	Sarah	1824	Canterbury, Kent	(?)		Emanuel Solomon	Deal, Kent	
9243	Solomon	Sarah	1825	Middlesex, London			Samuel Solomon	Spitalfields, London	
22813	Solomon	Sarah	1825	Middlesex, London	(?)		Saul Solomon	Spitalfields, London	
27243	Solomon	Sarah	1826	?, London	Barnet Solomon	Hannah (Ann) Hart		Aldgate, London	general dealer
3831	Solomon	Sarah	1831	Pinczow, Poland [Pincha, Poland]	Simon Solomon	Mary (?)		Spitalfields, London	
8049	Solomon	Sarah	1831	Hanover, Germany	Nathan Marcus Adler	Henrietta Worms	Henry Solomon	Finsbury, London	
21735	Solomon	Sarah	1834	Holborn, London	(?) Solomon	Esther (?)		Islington, London	
28137	Solomon	Sarah	1840	Middlesex, London	(?) Solomon			Spitalfields, London	scholar
21144	Solomon	Sarah	1841	?, Poland	Moses Solomon	Rachel (?(		Aldgate, London	scholar
1318	Solomon	Sarah	1842	Plymouth, Devon	Josiah Solomon	Rose (?)		Plymouth, Devon	scholar
18607	Solomon	Sarah	1844	Aldgate, London	Josiah Solomon	Bella Hart	Myer Salaman	Aldgate, London	scholar at home
19969	Solomon	Sarah	1844	Deal, Kent	Samuel Solomon	Rosetta (Rosa, Rose) Hart		Deal, Kent	
29277	Solomon	Sarah	1845	?, London	Isaac Solomon	Frances (?)		Wapping, London	
9426	Solomon	Sarah	1846	?, London	Charles Solomon	Deborah Minden	David Hyman Dyte	Wapping, London	
15213	Solomon	Sarah	1849	?, London	Philip Solomon	Amelia (?)		Shoreditch, London	
18958	Solomon	Saul	1786	Whitechapel, London			Esther (?)	Whitechapel, London	coal merchant
23989	Solomon	Saul	1806	City, London			Leagh (?)	Marylebone, London	broker
25024	Solomon	Saul	1806	Finsbury, London	Jacob Solomon	(Sarah Lazarus?)	Julia Jacob	Finsbury, London	tailor
22812	Solomon	Saul	1819	Middlesex, London			Sarah (?)	Spitalfields, London	boot maker master
25621	Solomon	Saul	1820	?			Polly (?)	Dublin, Ireland	clothing warehousew
17176	Solomon	Saul	1829	?, London	David Solomon	Sarah (?)		Newcastle Upon Tyne	cabinet maker
21531	Solomon	Saul	1836	Knightsbridge, London	Joseph Solomon	Anna (?)		Mayfair, London	dyer + ?clean starcher
10471	Solomon	Saul	1846	?, London	(?) Solomon	(?) Emanuel		Mile End, London	
9697	Solomon	Saul	1847	Whitechapel, London	Morris Solomon	Charlotte (?)		Whitechapel, London	
24760	Solomon	Saul Reginald	1816	Sheerness, Kent	Edward Solomon	Rachael Joseph	Elizabeth Levy	Southwark, London	solicitor
811	Solomon	Saunders	1795	Whitechapel, London	Sampson Solomon	Eliza Isaacs	Rachel Davis	Kensington, London	clothier + outfitter
5525	Solomon	Saunders	1848	Marylebone, London	Joseph Solomon	Anna (?)	Eveline Levi	Mayfair, London	scholar at home
15212	Solomon	Selim Solomon	1843	Newcastle Upon Tyne, Tyne & Wear	Philip Solomon	Amelia Woolf	Sophie Nathan	Shoreditch, London	
15679	Solomon	Selina	1832	?, London	(?) Solomon	Esther (?)		Aldgate, London	furrier
20847	Solomon	Selina	1833	?, London	Nathaniel Solomon	Rebecca (?)		Euston, London	
201	Solomon	Selina Sarah	1836	Clerkenwell, London	Morris (Maurice) Solomon	Fanny (Frances) Jacob	Joseph Lialter	Clerkenwell, London	
28080	Solomon	Sigmund	1849	?, Poland [?, Prussia]	Abraham Solomon	Frederica (?)		Spitalfields, London	
14848	Solomon	Silverston	1811	Finsbury, London			Frances (?)	Bethnal Green, London	tailor master
7402	Solomon	Simeon	1840	Aldgate, London	Michael (Myer) Solomon	Catherine (Kate) Levy		Hoxton, London	
888	Solomon	Simon	1784	abroad	Solomon Solomon		Rosetta (?)	Bristol	woollen draper + tailor + outfitter

ID	surname	given names	born	birthplace	father	mother	spouse 1	1851 residence	1851 occupation
3829	Solomon	Simon	1801	Pinczow, Poland [Pincha, Poland]			Mary (?)	Spitalfields, London	cap maker
6210	Solomon	Simon	1830	City, London	Henry Solomon	Rachel (?)	Lidia Solomon	City, London	cigar maker
889	Solomon	Simon (Solomon)	1814	Bristol	Simon Solomon	Rosetta (?)		Malmesbury, Wiltshire	licensed hawker
1322	Solomon	Simon W	1849	Plymouth, Devon	Josiah Solomon	Rose (?)		Plymouth, Devon	
15962	Solomon	Soloman	1844	Spitalfields, London	Morris Solomon	Dinah (?)		Whitechapel, London	scholar
27562	Solomon	Solomon	1781	City, London			Julia (?)	Spitalfields, London	clothes dealer
5493	Solomon	Solomon	1784	?, London	Henry Samuel Solomon		Rachel Abrahams	Southampton, Hampshire	navy agent + fancy goods + hotel keeper
21515	Solomon	Solomon	1801	Shoreditch, London			Mary (?)	Bethnal Green, London	sponge merchant
16998	Solomon	Solomon	1804	Covent Garden, London	(?Woolf) Solomon		Marinda Salamon	Strand, London	tailor
1715	Solomon	Solomon	1807	?, Holland	Jonas Solomon	?Elizabeth (?)	Lydia (Leah) Lazarus	Spitalfields, London	furniture broker
2341	Solomon	Solomon	1807	?, Holland				Leeds, Yorkshire	watch maker
25174	Solomon	Solomon	1821	Spitalfields, London	Pinchas		Elizabeth (?)	Finsbury, London	watchmaker
14772	Solomon	Solomon	1830	City, London	George Solomon	Mary (?)	Ann Hart	Finsbury, London	tailor
1144	Solomon	Solomon	1833	Plymouth, Devon	(?) Solomon	Mathilda Joseph	Lillie (?)	Plymouth, Devon	silversmith
1316	Solomon	Solomon	1838	Plymouth, Devon	Josiah Solomon	Rose (?)		Plymouth, Devon	scholar
15969	Solomon	Solomon	1838	?, London	Henry Solomon	Rachel (?)		Aldgate, London	tailor
1674	Solomon	Solomon	1841	Spitalfields, London	Woolf Solomon	Leah Hyman	Rebecca Van Gelder	Spitalfields, London	
9801	Solomon	Solomon	1841	Whitechapel, London	Solomon Jacob Solomon	Catherine (Kitty) Joseph		Spitalfields, London	
21794	Solomon	Solomon	1849	Whitechapel, London	Abraham Solomon	Esther Moses		Aldgate, London	
9796	Solomon	Solomon Jacob	1793	?, Holland	Isaac Solomon		Catherine (Kitty) Joseph	Spitalfields, London	commission agent
1661	Solomon	Solomons	1813	Amsterdam, Holland	Moses Solomons		Amelia (Miriam) Fernandez	Spitalfields, London	hawker
14774	Solomon	Sophia	1833	Middlesex, London	George Solomon	Mary (?)		Finsbury, London	paper stainer
1675	Solomon	Sophia	1846	Spitalfields, London	Woolf Solomon	Leah Hyman	Samuel Solomons	Spitalfields, London	
9693	Solomon	Susannah	1836	Whitechapel, London	Morris Solomon	Charlotte (?)		Whitechapel, London	
14856	Solomon	Susannah	1850	Bethnal Green, London	Silverston Solomon	Frances (?)		Bethnal Green, London	
23704	Solomon	Susman	1800	Hamburg, Germany			Hanna (?)	Liverpool	cigar manufacturer
21276	Solomon	Sydney	1835	Bloomsbury, London	Henry Naphtali Solomon	Fanny Phillips		Edmonton, London	horticulturist apprentice
9070	Solomon	Sylvester	1828	Aldgate, London	Michael (Myer) Solomon	Catherine Levy	Eliza Lipman	Hoxton, London	
18892	Solomon	Thomas	1822	Chatham, Kent	Israel Solomon	Mary (?)	Louisa (?)	Chatham, Kent	
14503	Solomon	William	1840	Norwich, Norfolk	Joshua E Solomon	Mary A (?)		Norwich, Norfolk	scholar
1989	Solomon	William	1847	Bristol	Israel Solomon	Harriet Demery		Swansea, Wales	
19534	Solomon	William	1849	Covent Garden, London	(?) Solomon	Sarah (?)		Strand, London	
4972	Solomon	Wolf	1777	?, Poland				Birmingham	watchglass maker
1370	Solomon	Wolf	1821	?, Poland				Plymouth, Devon	pedlar
1670	Solomon	Woolf	1811	?, London	Joseph Solomon		Leah Hyman	Spitalfields, London	general dealer
12070	Solomon	Yetta	1820	?, Poland [?, Prussia]	(?)		Isaac Solomon	Spitalfields, London	
9694	Solomon	Zaruh	1841	Whitechapel, London	Morris Solomon	Charlotte (?)		Whitechapel, London	
30537	Solomon (Solome)	Sarah	1819	Strand, London	(?) Meyers		Solomon David Solomon (Solome)	Waterloo, London	
30536	Solomon (Solome)	Solomon David	1819	Lambeth, London	David Solome	Sarah (?)	Sarah Meyers	Waterloo, London	silversmith + jeweller
16458	Solomon (Solomons)	Adelaide	1841	Waterloo, London	Henry Solomon (Solomons)	Esther Leman		Lambeth, London	

ID	surname	given names	born	birthplace	father	mother	spouse 1	1851 residence	1851 occupation
29767	Solomon (Solomons)	Amelia	1850	Whitechapel, London	Henry Solomon (Solomons)	Catherine Davis		Spitalfields, London	
10293	Solomon (Solomons)	Ann	1799	Vauxhall, London	Jacob Harris		Samuel Solomons	Spitalfields, London	slop worker
16456	Solomon (Solomons)	Benjamin	1839	Lambeth, London	Henry Solomon (Solomons)	Esther Leman		Lambeth, London	
29084	Solomon (Solomons)	Caroline	1822	Chelsea, London	Lyon Kesner	Isabella [Matilda, Elizbeth] David	Joseph Solomon (Solomons)	Whitechapel, London	
10294	Solomon (Solomons)	Catharine (Kitty, Kate)	1831	Aldgate, London	Samuel Solomons	Ann Harris	Isaac Symons (Simon)	Spitalfields, London	tailoress
29761	Solomon (Solomons)	Catherine	1817	Whitechapel, London	Benjamin Davis		Henry Solomon (Solomons)	Spitalfields, London	
17414	Solomon (Solomons)	David	1836	City, London	John Solomon (Solomons)	Phoebe Gershon		Wapping, London	
19386	Solomon (Solomons)	Elizabeth	1850	Lambeth, London	Henry Solomon (Solomons)	Frances (Fanny) Myers		Stockwell, London	
9698	Solomon (Solomons)	Ellen (Helen)	1828	Whitechapel, London	Isaac Solomon (Solomons)		Joel Woolf	Whitechapel, London	servant
29085	Solomon (Solomons)	Emanuel	1850	Whitechapel, London	Joseph Solomon (Solomons)	Caroline Kesner		Whitechapel, London	
24551	Solomon (Solomons)	Emma	1837	Whitechapel, London	Samuel Solomon (Solomons)	Sarah Phillips	Zalig Silverston	Brixton, London	
8133	Solomon (Solomons)	Emma	1849	Spitalfields, London	Simon Solomon (Solomons)	Rachel Lyon	James Eleazar Lazarus (Kingsley)	Finsbury, London	scholar at home
16455	Solomon (Solomons)	Esther	1816	Whitechapel, London	Aryeh Leib Leman		Henry Solomon (Solomons)	Lambeth, London	
29763	Solomon (Solomons)	Esther	1841	Spitalfields, London	Henry Solomon (Solomons)	Catherine Davis		Spitalfields, London	scholar
19383	Solomon (Solomons)	Esther	1844	Holborn, London	Henry Solomon (Solomons)	Frances (Fanny) Myers		Stockwell, London	
19382	Solomon (Solomons)	Frances (Fanny)	1825	Southwark, London	Raphael (Ralph) Myers	Elizabeth (Beilah) Benjamin	Henry Solomon	Stockwell, London	
17415	Solomon (Solomons)	Hannah	1839	City, London	John Solomon (Solomons)	Phoebe Gershon		Wapping, London	
16454	Solomon (Solomons)	Henry	1806	Spitalfields, London	Baruch Bendit		Esther Leman	Lambeth, London	brewer
29760	Solomon (Solomons)	Henry	1809	Whitechapel, London	Moshe Isaac Solomons	(?Blumah) (?)	Catherine Davis	Spitalfields, London	dealer in pens
19381	Solomon (Solomons)	Henry	1815	Whitechapel, London	Lyon (Yehuda) Solomon	Esther (?)	Frances (Fanny) Myers	Stockwell, London	upholsterer + furniture dealer
24549	Solomon (Solomons)	Henry Solomon	1834	Whitechapel, London	Samuel Solomon (Solomons)	Sarah Phillips		Brixton, London	
30628	Solomon (Solomons)	Isabella	1851	Whitechapel, London	Joseph Solomon (Solomons)	Caroline Kesner		Whitechapel, London	
17416	Solomon (Solomons)	Jane	1841	Whitechapel, London	John Solomon (Solomons)	Phoebe Gershon	Henry Barnet	Wapping, London	

ID	surname	given names	born	birthplace	father	mother	spouse 1	1851 residence	1851 occupation
16460	Solomon (Solomons)	Jeannette	1846	Lambeth, London	Henry Solomon (Solomons)	Esther Leman		Lambeth, London	
17410	Solomon (Solomons)	John	1801	Whitechapel, London	Samson Solomon		Phoebe Gershon	Wapping, London	tailor + clothes dealer
16459	Solomon (Solomons)	John	1844	Lambeth, London	Henry Solomon (Solomons)	Esther Leman		Lambeth, London	
29083	Solomon (Solomons)	Joseph	1815	Aldgate, London	Emanuel Solomon		Caroline Kesner	Whitechapel, London	?stencil plate --- maker
19385	Solomon (Solomons)	Joseph	1848	Lambeth, London	Henry Solomon (Solomons)	Frances (Fanny) Myers		Stockwell, London	
21931	Solomon (Solomons)	Joseph	1850	Aldgate, London	Phineas Solomon (Solomons)	Julia (Judith, Amelia) Davis		Aldgate, London	
24550	Solomon (Solomons)	Julia	1836	Whitechapel, London	Samuel Solomon (Solomons)	Sarah Phillips	Myer Marks	Brixton, London	
21930	Solomon (Solomons)	Julia (Judith, Amelia)	1813	?, London	Joseph Davis		Woolf Isaacs	Aldgate, London	
16457	Solomon (Solomons)	Leonora	1840	Lambeth, London	Henry Solomon (Solomons)	Esther Leman		Lambeth, London	
10295	Solomon (Solomons)	Louisa	1835	Aldgate, London	Samuel Solomons	Ann Harris		Spitalfields, London	apprentice to tailoress
24552	Solomon (Solomons)	Manuel	1841	Whitechapel, London	Samuel Solomon (Solomons)	Sarah Phillips		Brixton, London	
16461	Solomon (Solomons)	Maria	1850	Lambeth, London	Henry Solomon (Solomons)	Esther Leman		Lambeth, London	
19384	Solomon (Solomons)	Mary	1845	Holborn, London	Henry Solomon (Solomons)	Frances (Fanny) Myers		Stockwell, London	
30626	Solomon (Solomons)	Matilda (Millie)	1851	Stockwell, London	Henry Solomon (Solomons)	Frances (Fanny) Myers		Stockwell, London	
30627	Solomon (Solomons)	Miriam (Marian)	1851	Finsbury, London	Simon Solomon (Solomons)	Rachel Lyon		Finsbury, London	
6776	Solomon (Solomons)	Moses	1818	Middlesex, London	Isaac Solomons		Sarah Josephs	Spitalfields, London	general dealer
21929	Solomon (Solomons)	Phineas	1814	?, London	Solomon Solomons		Julia (Judith, Amelia) Isaacs nee Davis	Aldgate, London	general dealer
17411	Solomon (Solomons)	Phoebe	1801	Whitechapel, London	Joseph Gershon		John Solomon (Solomons)	Wapping, London	
29766	Solomon (Solomons)	Rachael	1849	Spitalfields, London	Henry Solomon (Solomons)	Catherine Davis		Spitalfields, London	
153	Solomon (Solomons)	Rachel	1824	Whitechapel, London	Isaac Leo Lyon	Hannah (Anna) Levi	Simon Solomon (Solomons)	Finsbury, London	dressmaker
17412	Solomon (Solomons)	Rachel	1826	City, London	John Solomon (Solomons)	Phoebe Gershon	Samuel Cohen	Wapping, London	umbrella maker
24548	Solomon (Solomons)	Rebecca	1833	Whitechapel, London	Samuel Solomon (Solomons)	Sarah Phillips	Emanuel Lambert Lion	Brixton, London	
29765	Solomon (Solomons)	Rosa (Rosetta)	1847	Spitalfields, London	Henry Solomon (Solomons)	Catherine Davis		Spitalfields, London	scholar

ID	surname	given names	born	birthplace	father	mother	spouse 1	1851 residence	1851 occupation
7571	Solomon (Solomons)	Samuel	1804	Middlesex, London	Moshe Eleazer Solomon		Sarah Phillips	Brixton, London	bookseller
18893	Solomon (Solomons)	Sarah	1806	Middlesex, London	Aryeh Shirga Pais Phillips		Samuel Solomon (Solomons)	Brixton, London	
6777	Solomon (Solomons)	Sarah	1820	Middlesex, London	Joseph Josephs		Moses Solomon (Solomons)	Spitalfields, London	
17413	Solomon (Solomons)	Sarah	1834	City, London	John Solomon (Solomons)	Phoebe Gershon		Wapping, London	umbrella maker
24553	Solomon (Solomons)	Sarah	1842	Whitechapel, London	Samuel Solomon (Solomons)	Sarah Phillips		Brixton, London	
29764	Solomon (Solomons)	Sarah	1844	Aldgate, London	Henry Solomon (Solomons)	Catherine Davis		Spitalfields, London	scholar
2927	Solomon (Solomons)	Simon	1825	Clerkenwell, London	Samuel Solomon		Rachel Lyon	Finsbury, London	fancy paper maker
29762	Solomon (Solomons)	Solomon	1837	Spitalfields, London	Henry Solomon (Solomons)	Catherine Davis		Spitalfields, London	butcher's boy
23164	Solomons	Aaron	1792	Aldgate, London			Sarah (?)	Hoxton, London	dealer in clothes
6943	Solomons	Aaron	1798	Whitechapel, London				Aldgate, London	watch maker
25806	Solomons	Aaron	1811	Amsterdam, Holland				Aldgate, London	pastrycook
9850	Solomons	Aaron	1835	?, London	Zachariah Solomons	Caroline Woolf		Aldgate, London	dressmaker
22371	Solomons	Abel	1847	?, Lincolnshire	Solomon Solomons	Sarah (?)		Whitechapel, London	
1635	Solomons	Abigail	1801	Spitalfields, London	(?) Solomons			Spitalfields, London	servant
29696	Solomons	Abraham	1790	Canterbury, Kent			(?)	Aldgate, London	optician
24565	Solomons	Abraham	1796	City, London			Betty (?)	Brixton, London	gentleman
21410	Solomons	Abraham	1827	Aldgate, London	Solomon Solomons	Susan (Susannah) Seinberg	Rebecca Isaacs	Bushey, Hertfordshire	
26793	Solomons	Abraham	1827	?, Poland				Aldgate, London	cap maker
11345	Solomons	Abraham	1831	?, Poland	Eleazer Solomon		Fanny Moses	Aldgate, London	tailor
6422	Solomons	Abraham	1845	Aldgate, London	Moses Solomons	Hannah (?)	Jane Simmons	Spitalfields, London	scholar
13236	Solomons	Abraham	1846	Whitechapel, London	Jacob Solomons	Rosa (Rosetta) Barnet		Spitalfields, London	
6421	Solomons	Abraham	1847	Shoreditch, London	Nathan Solomons (Solomon)	Eliza (Leah) Abrahams	Jessie Solomon	Bethnal Green, London	scholar
25977	Solomons	Abraham	1848	?, Poland [?, Prussia]	Harris Solomons	Hannah (?)		Aldgate, London	
3329	Solomons	Abraham	1849	Aldgate, London	Henry Solomons	Clara (?)	Alice (Abigail) Levy	Aldgate, London	
23691	Solomons	Abraham (Albert, Mish)	1850	Whitechapel, London	Lewis Solomons	Charlotte Samuel		Whitechapel, London	
26104	Solomons	Agatha (Hagar)	1816	?, London	Eliezer Mendoza	Esther de Micael Jonas	David Solomons	Aldgate, London	dress maker
1708	Solomons	Agnes	1826	Middlesex, London	(?)		Lewis Solomons	Spitalfields, London	tailoress
3625	Solomons	Albert	1840	Middlesex, London	Elias Solomons	Sophia Solomon	Ruth L Howard	Mayfair, London	scholar
22950	Solomons	Alexander	1774	Whitechapel, London	Benjamin Solomons		(?)	Wapping, London	straw hat maker
25315	Solomons	Alexander	1813	Whitechapel, London			Esther Lindo	Holborn, London	fishmonger
20317	Solomons	Alexander	1843	City, London	Zadoc (Zodiac) Solomons	Phoebe Lyon		Aldgate, London	
12422	Solomons	Alice	1831	Strand, London	Nathaniel Saul (Solomon) Solomons	Rachael (?)		Strand, London	servant
11646	Solomons	Amelia	1831	Aldgate, London	Joel Solomons	Hannah (?)	Isaac Levy	Aldgate, London	tailoress
25800	Solomons	Amelia	1834	Amsterdam, Holland	Levy Solomons	Reiber (?)	Henry Solomons	Aldgate, London	seamstress
4973	Solomons	Ann	1773	Stafford, Staffordshire				Birmingham	

ID	surname	given names	born	birthplace	father	mother	spouse 1	1851 residence	1851 occupation
1741	Solomons	Ann	1801	Aldgate, London	(?)		(?) Solomons	Spitalfields, London	shoe binder
9847	Solomons	Ann	1829	?, London	Zachariah Solomons	Caroline Woolf		Aldgate, London	dressmaker
11213	Solomons	Ann	1820	Aldgate, London	Benjamin Woolf		Isaac Solomons	Aldgate, London	baker
26379	Solomons	Anna	1850	Aldgate, London	Samuel Solomons	Hannah Bebarfield (Bebarfald)		Aldgate, London	
9863	Solomons	Annette	1839	?, London				Fulham, London	boarding school pupil
20319	Solomons	Annie	1846	City, London	Zadoc (Zodiac) Solomons	Phoebe Lyon	Abraham Sloman	Aldgate, London	
23288	Solomons	Benjamin	1793	Hull, Yorkshire			Mary (?)	Mayfair, London	optician
29848	Solomons	Benjamin	1837	Whitechapel, London	Isaiah Solomons	(?)		Mile End, London	cigar maker apprentice
9284	Solomons	Bertha	1838	Whitechapel, London	Henry Solomons	Maria (?)		Aldgate, London	cap maker
13235	Solomons	Betsey	1841	Whitechapel, London	Jacob Solomons	Rosa (Rosetta) Barnet		Spitalfields, London	
24566	Solomons	Betty	1808	Hamburg, Germany	(?)		Abraham Solomons	Brixton, London	
20314	Solomons	Blumah	1831	Aldgate, London	Zadoc (Zodiac) Solomons	Phoebe Lyon		Aldgate, London	
3592	Solomons	Caroline	1796	?, London	Aaron Woolf		Zachariah Solomons	Aldgate, London	
1648	Solomons	Caroline	1832	City, London	Mark Solomons	Rachel (?Levy)		Spitalfields, London	cap maker
20320	Solomons	Caroline	1851	Aldgate, London	Zadoc (Zodiac) Solomons	Phoebe Lyon	Abraham Joseph	Aldgate, London	
9868	Solomons	Catharine	1843	?, London				Fulham, London	boarding school pupil
9715	Solomons	Catherine	1776	Aldgate, London	(?)		(?) Solomons	St Giles, London	domestic
26848	Solomons	Catherine	1781	?, Germany	(?)		(?) Solomons	Aldgate, London	black lead pencil dealer
1659	Solomons	Catherine	1823	?, London	Joseph Simmonds	Esther (?)	Aaron (Gershon, George) Solomons	Spitalfields, London	general dealer
26427	Solomons	Catherine	1827	?, London	David Solomons	Betsey (Elizabeth) Cohen		Aldgate, London	tailoress
9283	Solomons	Catherine	1835	Whitechapel, London	Henry Solomons	Maria (?)		Aldgate, London	
27391	Solomons	Catherine	1848	Aldgate, London	Jacob Solomons	Mary (?)		Aldgate, London	
1709	Solomons	Catherine	1851	Spitalfields, London	Lewis Solomons	Agnes (?)		Spitalfields, London	
9851	Solomons	Catherine (Kate)	1838	?, London	Zachariah Solomons	Caroline Woolf		Aldgate, London	
29149	Solomons	Charles	1837	Finsbury, London	Philip Solomons	Sarah (?)		Whitechapel, London	scholar
23686	Solomons	Charlotte	1819	Wapping, London	Emanuel (Mendel Menachem) Samuel	Amelia (Emelia) Emanuel	Lewis Solomons	Whitechapel, London	chair + cabinet maker
26845	Solomons	Coleman	1830	?, London			Sarah Symonds	Aldgate, London	tailor
28310	Solomons	David	1791	Aldgate, London			Rebecca (?Harris)	Aldgate, London	hatter
24432	Solomons	David	1819	?, Holland			Elizabeth (?)	Strand, London	glass merchant
26103	Solomons	David	1822	?, London	Henry Solomons		Agatha (Hagar) Mendoza	Aldgate, London	cigar maker
29847	Solomons	David	1824	Whitechapel, London	(?) Solomons	Hannah (?)		Mile End, London	fishmonger
25874	Solomons	David	1835	?				Aldgate, London	hawker
12360	Solomons	David	1838	Strand, London	Nathaniel Saul (Solomon) Solomons	Rachael (?)		Strand, London	scholar
11862	Solomons	David	1842	Middlesex, London	(?) Solomons	(?)		Whitechapel, London	inmate of orphan school
5267	Solomons	David	1849	Aldgate, London	Zachariah Solomons	Paisley (Priscilla) Simmons	Esther (?)	Aldgate, London	
1736	Solomons	Deborah	1805	Whitechapel, London	Zeev Wolf Hyams		Philip Solomons	Spitalfields, London	general dealer
6246	Solomons	Deborah	1832	Whitechapel, London	(?) Solomon	Hannah Nunes Martines	(?) Levy	Aldgate, London	tailoress
6682	Solomons	Dinah	1840	Whitechapel, London	Samuel Solomons	Rachel Abraham	Benjamin Abrahams	Whitechapel, London	
21526	Solomons	Edward	1827	Whitechapoel, London				City, London	clothier's assistant
26106	Solomons	Eleazer	1845	?Aldgate, London	David Solomons	Agatha (Hagar) Mendoza		Aldgate, London	scholar

ID	surname	given names	born	birthplace	father	mother	spouse 1	1851 residence	1851 occupation
3623	Solomons	Elias	1798	Middlesex, London	Moshe Menachem (Demetri 'Manes') Solomons		Sophia Solomons	Mayfair, London	
7233	Solomons	Elijah	1801	?, London	Shmuel HaLevi Solomons		Rebecca Phillips	Whitechapel, London	jeweller
23405	Solomons	Elijah	1840	?, London	Henry Solomons	Rachael (?)		Aldgate, London	tailor
1721	Solomons	Eliza	1809	Portsmouth, Hampshire	(?)		(?) Solomons	Spitalfields, London	dress maker
27848	Solomons	Eliza	1811	Whitechapel, London	(?) Hyams		(?) Solomons	Spitalfields, London	cap maker
25295	Solomons	Elizabeth	1827	?London	John Solomons (Solomon)		Samuel Hart	Holborn, London	
24433	Solomons	Elizabeth	1828	?, Holland	(?)		David Solomons	Strand, London	
5573	Solomons	Elizabeth	1831	Aldgate, London	Zachariah Solomons	Caroline Woolf	Phillip Solomons	Aldgate, London	dressmaker
16140	Solomons	Elizabeth	1831	?, America	(?)		Ezekiel Solomons	Whitechapel, London	
29148	Solomons	Elizabeth	1835	Finsbury, London	Philip Solomons	Sarah (?)		Whitechapel, London	scholar
5264	Solomons	Elizabeth	1843	Aldgate, London	Zachariah Solomons	Paisley (Priscilla) Simmons		Aldgate, London	
25804	Solomons	Elizabeth	1847	Spitalfields, London	Levy Solomons	Reiber (?)		Aldgate, London	
27392	Solomons	Elizabeth	1850	Whitechapel, London	Jacob Solomons	Mary (?)		Aldgate, London	
25805	Solomons	Ellen	1849	Aldgate, London	Levy Solomons	Reiber (?)	Samuel Lisser	Aldgate, London	
26648	Solomons	Emanuel	1824	Aldgate, London			Rachael Simons	Aldgate, London	bricklayer journeyman
27849	Solomons	Emanuel	1837	Whitechapel, London	(?) Solomons	Eliza (?)		Spitalfields, London	apprentice to a tailor
18210	Solomons	Emanuel	1838	Middlesex, London				Mile End, London	scholar
1725	Solomons	Emanuel	1842	Spitalfields, London	(?) Solomons	Eliza (?)		Spitalfields, London	scholar
17195	Solomons	Emanuel	1842	Whitechapel, London	Samuel Solomons	Rachel Abraham		Whitechapel, London	
23690	Solomons	Emanuel	1849	Whitechapel, London	Lewis Solomons	Charlotte Samuel	Evalina Marks	Whitechapel, London	
20316	Solomons	Emelia	1835	Aldgate, London	Zadoc (Zodiac) Solomons	Phoebe Lyon		Aldgate, London	
24569	Solomons	Emma	1845	Clerkenwell, London, London	Abraham Solomons	Betty (?)		Brixton, London	
27526	Solomons	Ester	1801	Spitalfields, London	(?)		(?) Solomons	Aldgate, London	tripe dresser
25316	Solomons	Esther	1821	Holborn, London	(?) Lindo		Alexander Solomons	Holborn, London	
13057	Solomons	Esther	1825	Mile End, London	(?) Fernandes		Israel Solomons	Spitalfields, London	
22807	Solomons	Esther	1829	Spitalfields, London	(?) Solomons	Mary Solomons	Lewis Levy	Whitechapel, London	carpet bag maker
6767	Solomons	Esther	1830	Middlesex, London	David Solomons	Betsey (Elizabeth) Cohen	Walter Harris	Aldgate, London	tailoress
1722	Solomons	Esther	1832	Whitechapel, London	(?) Solomons	Eliza (?)		Spitalfields, London	furrier
18223	Solomons	Esther	1838	Middlesex, London	(?) Solomons			Mile End, London	scholar
27850	Solomons	Esther	1840	Whitechapel, London	(?) Solomons	Eliza (?)		Spitalfields, London	scholar
5552	Solomons	Esther	1841	Shoreditch, London	Nathan Solomons	Eliza (Leah) Abrahams	Joel Joel	Bethnal Green, London	scholar
12361	Solomons	Esther	1842	Strand, London	Nathaniel Saul (Solomon) Solomons	Rachael (?)		Strand, London	scholar
25814	Solomons	Esther	1849	Aldgate, London	Samuel Solomons	Mary Solomons	Henry Lesse	Aldgate, London	
29155	Solomons	Esther	1849	Whitechapel, London	Philip Solomons	Sarah (?)		Whitechapel, London	scholar
1728	Solomons	Eva	1766	?, Holland	(?)		(?) Solomons	Spitalfields, London	general dealer
2742	Solomons	Eva	1830	Pinczow, Poland	David Yehuda Leib (Davis)		Joseph Solomons	Whitechapel, London	cap maker
16139	Solomons	Ezekiel	1830	Plymouth, Devon			Elizabeth (?)	Whitechapel, London	clothes dealer
27036	Solomons	Fanny	1787	?, London	(?)		(?) Solomons	Aldgate, London	
1643	Solomons	Fanny	1847	Aldgate, London	Moses Solomons	Hannah (?)		Spitalfields, London	scholar
21411	Solomons	Frances (Fanny)	1829	Bushey, Hertfordshire	Solomon Solomons	Susan (Susannah) Seinberg	Charles Cohen	Bushey, Hertfordshire	
18552	Solomons	Francis	1820	Aldgate, London				Spitalfields, London	librarian
24567	Solomons	Frederick	1836	City, London	Abraham Solomons	Betty (?)		Brixton, London	
24093	Solomons	Gabriel	1807	City, London	(?) Solomons	Mary (?)		Bloomsbury, London	dealer in clothes

ID	surname	given names	born	birthplace	father	mother	spouse 1	1851 residence	1851 occupation
25318	Solomons	George	1848	Holborn, London	Alexander Solomons	Esther Lindo		Holborn, London	
15318	Solomons	Godfrey	1841	Aldgate, London	Michael Solomons	Matilda (?)		Shoreditch, London	scholar
1634	Solomons	Hannah	1782	Spitalfields, London	(?) Solomons		(?) Solomons	Spitalfields, London	fruit dealer
29844	Solomons	Hannah	1789	Aldgate, London	(?)		(?) Solomons	Mile End, London	fishmonger
11645	Solomons	Hannah	1796	Aldgate, London	(?)		Joel Solomons	Aldgate, London	pauper
25976	Solomons	Hannah	1827	?, Poland [?, Prussia]	(?)		Harris Solomons	Aldgate, London	
26378	Solomons	Hannah	1828	Wriezen, Germany [Wreshin, Prussia]	Myer Bebarfield (Bebarfald)	Shifra (Jane) (?)	Samuel Solomons	Aldgate, London	tailor
10997	Solomons	Hannah	1830	Aldgate, London	Jacob Solomons	Sarah Lazarus		Aldgate, London	general dealer
11258	Solomons	Hannah	1845	Aldgate, London	Moses Solomons	Rebecca (?)		Aldgate, London	
23689	Solomons	Hannah	1846	Whitechapel, London	Lewis Solomons	Charlotte Samuel	Mendel Cohen	Whitechapel, London	
23000	Solomons	Hannah	1850	Aldgate, London	Henry Solomons	Jane (?)		Finsbury, London	
26847	Solomons	Hannah	1850	?, London	Coleman Solomons	Sarah Symonds		Aldgate, London	
1641	Solomons	Hannah	1811	Aldgate, London			Moses Solomons	Spitalfields, London	
25975	Solomons	Harris	1825	?, Poland [?, Prussia]			Hannah (?)	Aldgate, London	shoe maker?
30756	Solomons	Helen (Ellen)	1851	Whitechapel, London	Samuel Solomons	Leah Symmons		Whitechapel, London	
9281	Solomons	Henry	1796	Whitechapel, London			Maria (?Da Costa)	Aldgate, London	watch finisher
21112	Solomons	Henry	1797	?, Poland				Aldgate, London	hair? Dealer
23397	Solomons	Henry	1803	?, London			Rachael (?)	Aldgate, London	pen cutter
29812	Solomons	Henry	1811	Whitechapel, London			Mary Ann (?)	Whitechapel, London	cabman
19958	Solomons	Henry	1817	?, London				Whitechapel, London	watchmaker
22998	Solomons	Henry	1823	Whitechapel, London			Jane (?)	Finsbury, London	tobacconist
4693	Solomons	Henry	1829	Birmingham	Elias Lonsman (?Solomons)		Caroline Lazarus	Birmingham	commercial traveller
12418	Solomons	Henry	1836	Strand, London	Nathaniel Saul (Solomon) Solomons	Rachael (?)		Strand, London	tailor
23400	Solomons	Henry	1838	?, London	Henry Solomons	Rachael (?)		Aldgate, London	cigar maker
22370	Solomons	Henry	1841	Whitechapel, London	Solomon Solomons	Sarah (?)		Whitechapel, London	
11257	Solomons	Henry	1843	Aldgate, London	Moses Solomons	Rebecca (?)		Aldgate, London	
15319	Solomons	Henry	1843	Spitalfields, London	Michael Solomons	Matilda (?)		Shoreditch, London	scholar
26108	Solomons	Henry	1849	?Aldgate, London	David Solomons	Agatha (Hagar) Mendoza		Aldgate, London	
26651	Solomons	Henry	1851	Aldgate, London	Emanuel Solomons	Rachael Simons		Aldgate, London	
9862	Solomons	Hester	1839	?, London				Fulham, London	boarding school pupil
28573	Solomons	Hester	1848	Spitalfields, London	John Solomons	Sarah (?)		Spitalfields, London	scholar
27390	Solomons	Hyman	1846	Poznan, Poland [Posen, Poland]	Jacob Solomons	Mary (?)		Aldgate, London	
24226	Solomons	Isaac	1773	Aldgate, London			Rosetta (?)	Hackney, London	keeper of Jews' Burial Ground
2343	Solomons	Isaac	1806	?, Germany				Leeds, Yorkshire	wool merchant
10994	Solomons	Isaac	1809	Aldgate, London	Jacob Solomons	Sarah Lazarus		Aldgate, London	general dealer
11120	Solomons	Isaac	1811	Aldgate, London				Aldgate, London	general dealer
11212	Solomons	Isaac	1825	Aldgate, London	Dov Behr Solomons		Ann Woolf	Aldgate, London	dress maker
19504	Solomons	Isaac	1826	Westminster, London				Strand, London	shopman [clothes]
12359	Solomons	Isaac	1827	Strand, London	Nathaniel Saul (Solomon) Solomons	Rachael (?)	Elizabeth Levi	Strand, London	tailor
25809	Solomons	Isaac	1831	Amsterdam, Holland				Aldgate, London	cigar maker journeyman

ID	surname	given names	born	birthplace	father	mother	spouse 1	1851 residence	1851 occupation
24229	Solomons	Isaac	1833	Bethnal Green, London				Hackney, London	cigar maker
3627	Solomons	Isaac	1840	Middlsex, London	Elias Solomons	Sophia Solomon		Mayfair, London	
23407	Solomons	Isaac	1844	?, London	Henry Solomons	Rachael (?)		Aldgate, London	
27524	Solomons	Isaac	1847	Aldgate, London	Judah Solomons	Maria (Miriam) Jacobs		Aldgate, London	
13058	Solomons	Isaac	1849	Whitechapel, London	Israel Solomons	Esther Fernandes		Spitalfields, London	
29846	Solomons	Isaiah	1821	Whitechapel, London	(?) Solomons	Hannah (?)	(?)	Mile End, London	fishmonger
25979	Solomons	Isidore	1829	?, Poland [?, Prussia]				Aldgate, London	cap maker
13056	Solomons	Israel	1818	St Giles, London	Pinchas		Esther Fernandes	Spitalfields, London	clothes dealer
5574	Solomons	Jacob	1790	?, London	Isaac Solomons		Maria (Mary, Polly) (?)	Aldgate, London	dealer in Government stores, tools + gas fittings
13233	Solomons	Jacob	1816	Whitechapel, London	Benjamin Zeev Wolf Solomons		Rosa (Rosetta) Barnet	Spitalfields, London	embroiderer
27388	Solomons	Jacob	1821	Poznan, Poland [Posen, Poland]			Mary (?)	Aldgate, London	cap + hatter empl 7
14129	Solomons	Jacob	1837	Manchester				Manchester	pawnbroker's clerk
22999	Solomons	Jane	1826	Bermondsey, London	(?)		Henry Solomons	Finsbury, London	
29152	Solomons	Jane	1843	Finsbury, London	Philip Solomons	Sarah (?)		Whitechapel, London	scholar
27525	Solomons	Jane	1849	Aldgate, London	Judah Solomons	Maria (Miriam) Jacobs		Aldgate, London	
29527	Solomons	John	1801	?, London				Spitalfields, London	fruit salesman's shopman
28568	Solomons	John	1821	Whitechapel, London			Sarah (?)	Spitalfields, London	shoe maker
9285	Solomons	John	1844	Whitechapel, London	Henry Solomons	Maria (?)		Aldgate, London	scholar
1700	Solomons	John	1850	Spitalfields, London	Moris Solomons (Solomon)	Caroline Abrahams		Spitalfields, London	
2743	Solomons	Joseph	1829	Warsaw, Poland	Zvi Hirsch Halevi		Eva Davis	Whitechapel, London	tailor
23406	Solomons	Joseph	1843	?, London	Henry Solomons	Rachael (?)		Aldgate, London	
23688	Solomons	Joseph	1845	Spitalfields, London	Lewis Solomons	Charlotte Samuel		Whitechapel, London	
6471	Solomons	Joseph	1848	Whitechapel, London	Solomon Solomons	Sarah (?)	Esther (?)	Whitechapel, London	
25978	Solomons	Joseph	1850	Aldgate, London	Harris Solomons	Hannah (?)		Aldgate, London	
12147	Solomons	Judah	1825	Exeter, Devon	Samuel Solomons	Matilda (?)		Aldgate, London	optician (journeyman)
27522	Solomons	Judah	1826	Aldgate, London	(?) Solomons	Esther (?)	Maria (Miriam) Jacobs	Aldgate, London	butcher
1723	Solomons	Judah	1835	Whitechapel, London	(?) Solomons	Eliza (?)	Rachel Isaacs	Spitalfields, London	shoe maker
25802	Solomons	Judah	1840	Amsterdam, Holland	Levy Solomons	Reiber (?)	Julia Abrahams	Aldgate, London	cigar maker journeyman
12549	Solomons	Judith	1800	Norwich, Norfolk	(?)		Abraham Solomons	Great Yarmouth, Norfolk	wife of silversmith
28570	Solomons	Judith	1842	Spitalfields, London	John Solomons	Sarah (?)		Spitalfields, London	scholar
356	Solomons	Julia	1791	Aldgate, London	(?)		(?) Solomons	Spitalfields, London	
11594	Solomons	Julia	1791	Aldgate, London	(?)		(?) Solomons	Aldgate, London	dealer in old clothes
8840	Solomons	Julia	1797	Aldgate, London				Aldgate, London	
10977	Solomons	Julia	1807	Middlesex, London	(?)		(?) Solomons	Aldgate, London	general dealer
29845	Solomons	Julia	1810	Whitechapel, London	(?) Solomons	Hannah (?)		Mile End, London	fishmonger
23399	Solomons	Julia	1825	?, London	Henry Solomons	Rachael (?)		Aldgate, London	
10996	Solomons	Julia	1828	Aldgate, London	Jacob Solomons	Sarah Lazarus		Aldgate, London	general dealer
10980	Solomons	Julia	1837	Middlesex, London	(?) Solomons	Julia (?)		Aldgate, London	
29151	Solomons	Julia	1840	Finsbury, London	Philip Solomons	Sarah (?)		Whitechapel, London	scholar
26105	Solomons	Julia	1842	Aldgate, London	David Solomons	Agatha (Hagar) Mendoza		Aldgate, London	scholar
13159	Solomons	Kate	1815	Whitechapel, London	(?) Solomons			Spitalfields, London	out of business
11255	Solomons	Katharine	1841	Aldgate, London	Moses Solomons	Rebecca (?)		Aldgate, London	

685

ID	surname	given names	born	birthplace	father	mother	spouse 1	1851 residence	1851 occupation
24794	Solomons	Kitty	1831	Middlesex, London	(?) Solomons			Elephant & Castle, London	servant
10993	Solomons	Lazarus	1806	Aldgate, London	Jacob Solomons	Sarah Lazarus		Aldgate, London	general dealer
28314	Solomons	Lazarus?	1825	Aldgate, London	David Solomons	Rebecca (?Harris)		Aldgate, London	hatter
6244	Solomons	Leah	1825	Whitechapel, London	(?) Symmons		Samuel Solomons	Whitechapel, London	
13059	Solomons	Leah	1851	Whitechapel, London	Israel Solomons	Esther Fernandes		Spitalfields, London	
24568	Solomons	Leopold	1842	Clerkenwell, London, London	Abraham Solomons	Betty (?)		Brixton, London	
25797	Solomons	Levy	1803	Amsterdam, Holland			Reiber (?)	Aldgate, London	shoe clicker
23685	Solomons	Lewis	1809	Whitechapel, London	Simon Solomons	Hannah (?)	Charlotte Samuel	Whitechapel, London	chair + cabinet maker
1707	Solomons	Lewis	1820	Aldgate, London	Avraham		Agnes (?)	Spitalfields, London	fruiterer
23978	Solomons	Lewis	1839	Soho, London	Samuel Solomons	Sarah (?)		Marylebone, London	historical painter
20318	Solomons	Lewis	1845	City, London	Zadoc (Zodiac) Solomons	Phoebe Lyon		Aldgate, London	
11261	Solomons	Lewis	1851	Aldgate, London	Moses Solomons	Rebecca (?)		Aldgate, London	
17251	Solomons	Lewis Sydie	1832	Whitechapel, London	Sydie Solomons	Rachel (?)	Julia Cohen	Aldgate, London	cigar maker journeyman
22373	Solomons	Lipman	1851	Whitechapel, London	Solomon Solomons	Sarah (?)		Whitechapel, London	
2342	Solomons	Louis	1806	?, London				Leeds, Yorkshire	general dealer
15813	Solomons	Louis	1830	?, London				Aldgate, London	tailor
23291	Solomons	Louisa	1835	Whitechapel, London	Benjamin Solomons	Mary (?)		Mayfair, London	
23292	Solomons	Lucy	1841	Mayfair, London	Benjamin Solomons	Mary (?)		Mayfair, London	
21414	Solomons	Marcus	1844	Bushey, Hertfordshire	Solomon Solomons	Susan (Susannah) Seinberg		Bushey, Hertfordshire	scholar
12424	Solomons	Maria	1840	Strand, London	Nathaniel Saul (Solomon) Solomons	Rachael (?)		Strand, London	scholar
27851	Solomons	Maria	1842	Whitechapel, London	(?) Solomons	Eliza (?)		Spitalfields, London	scholar
1644	Solomons	Maria	1848	Aldgate, London	Moses Solomons	Hannah (?)		Spitalfields, London	scholar
9282	Solomons	Maria	1804	Whitechapel, London	(?)		Henry Solomons	Aldgate, London	
20515	Solomons	Maria (Mary, Polly)	1792	?, London			Jacob Solomons	Aldgate, London	
27523	Solomons	Maria (Miriam)	1827	Spitalfields, London	(?) Jacobs		Judah Solomons	Aldgate, London	
1646	Solomons	Mark	1804	Aldgate, London			Rachel (?Levy)	Spitalfields, London	general dealer
8935	Solomons	Martha	1761	Aldgate, London				Aldgate, London	
1650	Solomons	Martha	1838	Whitechapel, London	Mark Solomons	Rachel (?Levy)		Spitalfields, London	furrier
24092	Solomons	Mary	1785	?, Poland [?, Prussia]	(?)		(?) Solomons	Bloomsbury, London	
23289	Solomons	Mary	1795	Aldgate, London	(?)		Benjamin Solomons	Mayfair, London	
15032	Solomons	Mary	1810	Shoreditch, London	(?)		Solomon Solomons	Bethnal Green, London	shoe binder
27389	Solomons	Mary	1820	Poznan, Poland [Posen, Poland]	(?)		Jacob Solomons	Aldgate, London	
25813	Solomons	Mary	1829	Amsterdam, Holland	Levy Solomons	Reiber (?)	Samuel Solomons	Aldgate, London	
10979	Solomons	Mary	1835	Middlesex, London	(?) Solomons	Julia (?)		Aldgate, London	
29813	Solomons	Mary Ann	1828	Whitechapel, London	(?)		Henry Solomons	Whitechapel, London	
12146	Solomons	Matilda	1787	Exeter, Devon	(?)		Samuel Solomons	Aldgate, London	housekeeper
15317	Solomons	Matilda	1828	?, Suffolk	(?)		Michael Solomons	Shoreditch, London	
3624	Solomons	Maurice (Morris) E	1832	Stepney, London	Elias Solomons	Sophia Solomons	Rosa Bethel Jacobs	Mayfair, London	paper ---
15316	Solomons	Michael	1820	Aldgate, London			Matilda (?)	Shoreditch, London	clothes man
28313	Solomons	Michael	1823	Aldgate, London	David Solomons	Rebecca (?Harris)		Aldgate, London	hatter
22369	Solomons	Michael	1838	Whitechapel, London	Solomon Solomons	Sarah (?)		Whitechapel, London	
21413	Solomons	Michael	1841	Bushey, Hertfordshire	Solomon Solomons	Susan (Susannah) Seinberg		Bushey, Hertfordshire	scholar

ID	surname	given names	born	birthplace	father	mother	spouse 1	1851 residence	1851 occupation
11259	Solomons	Michael	1847	Aldgate, London	Moses Solomons	Rebecca (?)		Aldgate, London	
6768	Solomons	Michael (Moses)	1832	Middlesex, London	David Solomons	Betsey (Elizabeth) Cohen		Aldgate, London	slopman
23290	Solomons	Minna	1834	Whitechapel, London	Benjamin Solomons	Mary (?)	John David Rosenthal	Mayfair, London	
1660	Solomons	Mordecai	1850	Spitalfields, London	Aaron (Gershon, George) Solomons	Catherine Simmonds		Spitalfields, London	
25810	Solomons	Morris	1821	Utrecht, Holland				Aldgate, London	hawker
1738	Solomons	Morris	1829	Spitalfields, London	Philip Solomons	Abigail (?)	Bloomah Barnett	Spitalfields, London	cigar maker
24675	Solomons	Morris	1839	Elephant & Castle, London				Kennington, London	apprentice to chair + sofa maker
25317	Solomons	Morris	1846	Holborn, London	Alexander Solomons	Esther Lindo		Holborn, London	
1640	Solomons	Moses	1806	Aldgate, London			Hannah (?)	Spitalfields, London	general dealer
11252	Solomons	Moses	1813	Southwark, London			Rebecca (?)	Aldgate, London	tailor
23402	Solomons	Moses	1833	?, London	Henry Solomons	Rachael (?)		Aldgate, London	tailor
27852	Solomons	Moses	1844	Whitechapel, London	(?) Solomons	Eliza (?)		Spitalfields, London	scholar
23168	Solomons	Moses	1845	Aldgate, London	Aaron Solomons	Sarah (?)		Hoxton, London	scholar
5268	Solomons	Moses	1851	Aldgate, London	Zachariah Solomons	Paisley (Priscilla) Simmons		Aldgate, London	
17194	Solomons	Moss	1835	Whitechapel, London	Samuel Solomons	Rachel Abraham		Whitechapel, London	apprentice upholsterer
29150	Solomons	Moss	1839	Finsbury, London	Philip Solomons	Sarah (?)		Whitechapel, London	scholar
26109	Solomons	Moss (Moses)	1850	Aldgate, London	David Solomons	Agatha (Hagar) Mendoza		Aldgate, London	
23403	Solomons	Nathan	1835	?, London	Henry Solomons	Rachael (?)		Aldgate, London	tailor
12419	Solomons	Nathaniel Saul (Solomon)	1791	Aldgate, London			Rachael (?)	Strand, London	tailor + clothes salesman
5263	Solomons	Paisley (Priscilla)	1820	Aldgate, London	Simon Simmons	Rachel Solomon	Zachariah Solomons	Aldgate, London	
10509	Solomons	Philip	1746	?, Poland			(?)	Aldgate, London	cap maker
1737	Solomons	Philip	1805	Spitalfields, London	Samson Solomon		Deborah Hyams	Spitalfields, London	general dealer
29146	Solomons	Philip	1806	Spitalfields, London			Sarah (?)	Whitechapel, London	general merchant
26849	Solomons	Philip	1819	?, London	(?) Solomons	Catherine (?)		Aldgate, London	pencil dealer
5572	Solomons	Phillip	1829	Aldgate, London	Jacob Solomons	Maria (Mary, Polly) (?)	Elizabeth Solomons	Aldgate, London	general dealer
17196	Solomons	Phoebe	1773	Aldgate, London	(?)		Emanuel (Menachem Mendele) Solomons	Whitechapel, London	
20313	Solomons	Phoebe	1809	City, London	Alexander Lyon		Zadoc (Zodiac) Solomons	Aldgate, London	general dealer
10995	Solomons	Phoebe	1826	Aldgate, London	Jacob Solomons	Sarah Lazarus	Angel Isaacs	Aldgate, London	general dealer
27165	Solomons	Phoebe	1826	?, London	Abraham Kalonymus Solomons		Benjamin Bensusan	Aldgate, London	house servant
1649	Solomons	Phoebe	1834	Whitechapel, London	Mark Solomons	Rachel (?Levy)	David Abrahams	Spitalfields, London	tailoress
1645	Solomons	Phoebe	1850	Aldgate, London	Moses Solomons	Hannah (?)		Spitalfields, London	
12420	Solomons	Rachael	1801	Aldgate, London			Nathaniel Saul (Solomon) Solomons	Strand, London	tailoress
23398	Solomons	Rachael	1806	?, London	(?)		Henry Solomon	Aldgate, London	
26649	Solomons	Rachael	1830	Spitalfields, London	(?) Simons		Emanuel Solomons	Aldgate, London	
25799	Solomons	Rachael	1831	Amsterdam, Holland	Levy Solomons	Reiber (?)		Aldgate, London	seamstress
10981	Solomons	Rachael	1844	Middlesex, London	(?) Solomons	Julia (?)		Aldgate, London	
11260	Solomons	Rachael	1848	Aldgate, London	Moses Solomons	Rebecca (?)		Aldgate, London	
1647	Solomons	Rachel	1806	Spitalfields, London			Mark Solomons	Spitalfields, London	
17249	Solomons	Rachel	1810	Aldgate, London	(?)		Sydie Solomons	Aldgate, London	school mistress
17193	Solomons	Rachel	1817	Finsbury, London	(?) Abraham		Samuel Solomons	Whitechapel, London	engraver

ID	surname	given names	born	birthplace	father	mother	spouse 1	1851 residence	1851 occupation
5266	Solomons	Rachel	1847	Aldgate, London	Zachariah Solomons	Paisley (Priscilla) Simmons		Aldgate, London	
15320	Solomons	Raff	1845	Spitalfields, London	Michael Solomons	Matilda (?)		Shoreditch, London	scholar
28311	Solomons	Rebecca	1789	Aldgate, London	(?) (?Harris)		David Solomons	Aldgate, London	
7234	Solomons	Rebecca	1800	?, London	Moses Phillips		Elijah Solomons	Whitechapel, London	
11253	Solomons	Rebecca	1821	Aldgate, London	(?)		Moses Solomons	Aldgate, London	
12421	Solomons	Rebecca	1829	Strand, London	Nathaniel Saul (Solomon) Solomons	Rachael (?)		Strand, London	tailoress
23166	Solomons	Rebecca	1833	Wapping, London	Aaron Solomons	Sarah (?)		Hoxton, London	dealer in clothes
26650	Solomons	Rebecca	1849	Whitechapel, London	Emanuel Solomons	Rachael Simons		Aldgate, London	
25815	Solomons	Rebecca	1850	Aldgate, London	Samuel Solomons	Mary Solomons	Abraham Emanuel Abrahams	Aldgate, London	
25798	Solomons	Reiber	1807	Amsterdam, Holland	(?)		Levy Solomons	Aldgate, London	
13234	Solomons	Rosa (Rosetta)	1818	Whitechapel, London	Abraham Barnet		Jacob Solomons	Spitalfields, London	tailoress
11254	Solomons	Rose	1833	Southwark, London	Moses Solomons	Rebecca (?)		Aldgate, London	
24227	Solomons	Rosetta	1784	Finsbury, London	(?)		Isaac Solomons	Hackney, London	
28312	Solomons	Rosetta	1819	Whitechapel, London	David Solomons	Rebecca (?Harris)		Aldgate, London	
10978	Solomons	Rosetta	1831	Middlesex, London	(?) Solomons	Julia (?)		Aldgate, London	
25803	Solomons	Rosetta	1842	Amsterdam, Holland	Levy Solomons	Reiber (?)		Aldgate, London	scholar
1726	Solomons	Rosetta	1847	Spitalfields, London	(?) Solomons	Eliza (?)		Spitalfields, London	scholar
18224	Solomons	Rossetta	1838	Middlesex, London	(?) Solomons			Mile End, London	scholar
29154	Solomons	Salomo	1847	Finsbury, London	Philip Solomons	Sarah (?)		Whitechapel, London	scholar
12145	Solomons	Samuel	1791	Leszno, Poland [Lissa, Poland]			Matilda (?)	Aldgate, London	housekeeper
23976	Solomons	Samuel	1793	Aldgate, London			Sarah (?)	Marylebone, London	dealer in curiosities
17192	Solomons	Samuel	1810	Deal, Kent	Emanuel (Menachem Mendele) Solomons	Phoebe (?)	Rachel Abraham	Whitechapel, London	engraver
30755	Solomons	Samuel	1818	Middlesex, London	(?) Symmons		Leah Symmons	Whitechapel, London	
26377	Solomons	Samuel	1824	?, Germany	Solomon Solomons		Hannah Bebarfield (Bebarfald)	Aldgate, London	tailor
25812	Solomons	Samuel	1826	Amsterdam, Holland	Solomon Solomons		Mary Solomons	Aldgate, London	cigar maker
21412	Solomons	Samuel	1831	Bushey, Hertfordshire	Solomon Solomons	Susan (Susannah) Seinberg		Bushey, Hertfordshire	
1724	Solomons	Samuel	1838	Whitechapel, London	(?) Solomons	Eliza (?)		Spitalfields, London	furrier
1740	Solomons	Samuel	1839	Spitalfields, London	Philip Solomons	Deborah (?)		Spitalfields, London	scholar
29153	Solomons	Samuel	1846	Finsbury, London	Philip Solomons	Sarah (?)		Whitechapel, London	scholar
3626	Solomons	Sara Maria	1836	Middlesex, London	Elias Solomons	Sophia Solomon		Mayfair, London	scholar
12997	Solomons	Sarah	1782	?, Holland	(?)		(?) Solomons	Aldgate, London	supported by family
10992	Solomons	Sarah	1786	Aldgate, London	Aharon Frankfurt Lazarus		Jacob Solomons	Aldgate, London	general dealer
23977	Solomons	Sarah	1796	Plymouth, Devon	(?)		Samuel Solomons	Marylebone, London	
23165	Solomons	Sarah	1806	Whitechapel, London	(?)		Aaron Solomons	Hoxton, London	dealer in clothes
29147	Solomons	Sarah	1816	Whitechapel, London	(?)		Philip Solomons	Whitechapel, London	
22368	Solomons	Sarah	1817	Whitechapel, London	(?)		Solomon Solomons	Whitechapel, London	
28569	Solomons	Sarah	1822	Spitalfields, London	(?)		John Solomons	Spitalfields, London	
9051	Solomons	Sarah	1825	Middlesex, London	(?) Solomons			Aldgate, London	servant
26846	Solomons	Sarah	1832	?, London	(?) Symonds	Flora (?)	Coleman Solomons	Aldgate, London	tailor's wife
9849	Solomons	Sarah	1833	?, London	Zachariah Solomons	Caroline Woolf		Aldgate, London	dressmaker

ID	surname	given names	born	birthplace	father	mother	spouse 1	1851 residence	1851 occupation
12423	Solomons	Sarah	1837	Strand, London	Nathaniel Saul (Solomon) Solomons	Rachael (?)		Strand, London	tailoress
11256	Solomons	Sarah	1842	Aldgate, London	Moses Solomons	Rebecca (?)		Aldgate, London	
12550	Solomons	Sarah	1843	Great Yarmouth, Norfolk	Abraham Solomons	Judith (?)		Great Yarmouth, Norfolk	scholar
28572	Solomons	Sarah	1846	Spitalfields, London	John Solomons	Sarah (?)		Spitalfields, London	scholar
1639	Solomons	Sarah	1850	Spitalfields, London	(?) Solomons	(?) Israel		Spitalfields, London	
20315	Solomons	Saul (Solomon)	1832	Aldgate, London	Zadoc (Zodiac) Solomons	Phoebe Lyon		Aldgate, London	
29156	Solomons	Selina	1850	Whitechapel, London	Philip Solomons	Sarah (?)		Whitechapel, London	
23687	Solomons	Simeon	1843	Spitalfields, London	Lewis Solomons	Charlotte Samuel	Adelaide Jones	Whitechapel, London	
23401	Solomons	Simon	1830	?, London	Henry Solomons	Rachael (?)		Aldgate, London	cigar maker
5265	Solomons	Simon	1845	Aldgate, London	Zachariah Solomons	Paisley (Priscilla) Simmons	Rachael Jacobs	Aldgate, London	
15321	Solomons	Sol	1847	Spitalfields, London	Michael Solomons	Matilda (?)		Shoreditch, London	scholar
15031	Solomons	Solomon	1801	Shoreditch, London			Mary (?)	Bethnal Green, London	sponge merchant
21408	Solomons	Solomon	1801	Middlesex, London	Meir (Michael?)		Susan (Susannah) Seinberg	Bushey, Hertfordshire	cattle dealer empl 1
22367	Solomons	Solomon	1815	Aldgate, London			Sarah (?)	Whitechapel, London	optician
25801	Solomons	Solomon	1837	Amsterdam, Holland	Levy Solomons	Reiber (?)		Aldgate, London	cigar maker journeyman
27037	Solomons	Solomon	1837	?, London	(?) Solomons	Fanny		Aldgate, London	baker
23404	Solomons	Solomon	1838	?, London	Henry Solomons	Rachael (?)		Aldgate, London	tailor
28574	Solomons	Solomon	1851	Spitalfields, London	John Solomons	Sarah (?)		Spitalfields, London	
26426	Solomons	Solomon M	1830	Middlesex, London	David Solomons	Betsey (Elizabeth) Cohen		Aldgate, London	dealer in tailors' trimmings
28571	Solomons	Sopheah	1844	Spitalfields, London	John Solomons	Sarah (?)		Spitalfields, London	scholar
3622	Solomons	Sophia	1810	Middlesex, London	Isaac (John Zekel) Solomons	Maria (Merle) Israel	Elias Solomons	Mayfair, London	
23293	Solomons	Sophia	1818	Boston, Lincolnshire	(?)		(?) Solomons	Mayfair, London	
23167	Solomons	Sophia	1834	Shoreditch, London	Aaron Solomons	Sarah (?)		Hoxton, London	dealer in clothes
26107	Solomons	Sophia	1846	Spitalfields, London	David Solomons	Agatha (Hagar) Mendoza		Aldgate, London	scholar
21409	Solomons	Susan (Susannah)	1806	?, Germany	Shmuel Ze'ev Seinberg		Solomon Solomons	Bushey, Hertfordshire	
17250	Solomons	Susanah	1808	Whitechapel, London	Sydie Solomons	Rachel (?)	Asher Davis	Aldgate, London	milliner
17248	Solomons	Sydie	1808	Whitechapel, London		Rachel (?)		Aldgate, London	tailor
1656	Solomons	Thom	1800	?, London				Spitalfields, London	shopman
1739	Solomons	Walter	1834	Spitalfields, London	Philip Solomons	Deborah (?)		Spitalfields, London	cigar maker
3591	Solomons	Zachariah	1791	?, London	Shlomo Zalman (Kany)		Caroline Woolf	Aldgate, London	glass dealer
5262	Solomons	Zachariah (Zalig)	1823	Aldgate, London	David HaLevi Solomons	Betsey (Elizabeth) Cohen	Paisley (Priscilla) Simmons	Aldgate, London	general dealer
20312	Solomons	Zadok (Zodiac)	1811	City, London	Moshe Isaac Solomons	(?Blumah) (?)	Phoebe Lyon	Aldgate, London	dealer in pens + sealing wax
18016	Solomons (Solomon)	Aaron	1844	Aldgate, London	Henry (Hyam) Solomons (Solomon)	Clara Moses		Aldgate, London	scholar
15988	Solomons (Solomon)	Abigail	1831	Whitechapel, London	(?) Solomon	Hannah Nunes Martines		Aldgate, London	tailoress
5895	Solomons (Solomon)	Abraham	1849	Aldgate, London	Coleman Solomons (Solomon)	Sarah Levy		Aldgate, London	
1699	Solomons (Solomon)	Ann	1848	Spitalfields, London	Moris Solomons (Solomon)	Caroline Abrahams		Spitalfields, London	
1697	Solomons (Solomon)	Caroline	1821	Aldgate, London	Lewis Abrahams (Abrahams)		Morris Solomons (Solomon)	Spitalfields, London	

ID	surname	given names	born	birthplace	father	mother	spouse 1	1851 residence	1851 occupation
18012	Solomons (Solomon)	Clara	1820	Aldgate, London	(?) Moses		Henry (Hyam) Solomons	Aldgate, London	
5891	Solomons (Solomon)	Coleman	1815	City, London	Yitzhak		Sarah Levy	Aldgate, London	general dealer
18013	Solomons (Solomon)	Coleman	1839	Aldgate, London	Henry (Hyam) Solomons (Solomon)	Clara Moses		Aldgate, London	scholar
15056	Solomons (Solomon)	Eliza (Leah)	1815	Hackney, London	Yehuda Abrahams		Nathan Solomons (Solomon)	Bethnal Green, London	
21266	Solomons (Solomon)	Esther	1847	City, London	Lewis (Eleazer) Solomons (Solomon)	Rosetta Isaacs		Barnsbury, London	
13045	Solomons (Solomon)	Flora	1845	Jamaica, West Indies	Philip Solomons (Solomon)	Evelina (?)	Alfred Fridlander	Marylebone, London	
26086	Solomons (Solomon)	Frances Green	1851	Aldgate, London	Coleman Solomons (Solomon)	Sarah Levy		Aldgate, London	
15987	Solomons (Solomon)	Hannah	1801	Whitechapel, London	Aaron de Abraham Nunes Martines	Welcome (Bemvenida) de Joseph Nunes Martines	(?) Solomon	Aldgate, London	
11798	Solomons (Solomon)	Hannah	1843	Shoreditch, London	Samuel Moses Solomons (Solomon)	Maria Jacobs		Shoreditch, London	scholar
26085	Solomons (Solomon)	Hannah	1847	Aldgate, London	Coleman Solomons (Solomon)	Sarah Levy		Aldgate, London	
18011	Solomons (Solomon)	Henry (Hyam)	1812	Aldgate, London	Mark Solomons		Clara Moses	Aldgate, London	jobbing carpenter
847	Solomons (Solomon)	Isaac	1837	?, London	Phineas Solomons	Julia (Judith) Moses		Cheltenham, Gloucestershire	scholar
5894	Solomons (Solomon)	Isaac	1845	Aldgate, London	Coleman Solomons (Solomon)	Sarah Levy		Aldgate, London	scholar
11283	Solomons (Solomon)	Jacob	1849	Aldgate, London	Solomon Solomons (Solomon)	Priscilla (Pruda) Phillips		Aldgate, London	
15058	Solomons (Solomon)	Jane	1835	Bethnal Green, London	Nathan Solomons (Solomon)	Eliza (Leah) Abrahams		Bethnal Green, London	lint maker
25294	Solomons (Solomon)	John	1780	Spitalfields, London			(?)	Holborn, London	clothes dealer
27729	Solomons (Solomon)	John	1822	Middlesex, London	Isaac Solomon	Catherine (Katherine) Woolf	Elizabeth Magnus	Spitalfields, London	trimming manufacturer
848	Solomons (Solomon)	Jonah	1840	?, London	Phineas Solomons	Julia (Judith) Moses		Cheltenham, Gloucestershire	scholar
18014	Solomons (Solomon)	Joseph	1841	Aldgate, London	Henry (Hyam) Solomons (Solomon)	Clara Moses		Aldgate, London	scholar
18017	Solomons (Solomon)	Julia	1846	Aldgate, London	Henry (Hyam) Solomons (Solomon)	Clara Moses		Aldgate, London	scholar
844	Solomons (Solomon)	Julia (Judith)	1805	Gloucester, Gloucestershire	Moses Moses	Jane(?)	Phineas Solomons	Cheltenham, Gloucestershire	
11284	Solomons (Solomon)	Leah	1851	Aldgate, London	Solomon Solomons (Solomon)	Priscilla (Pruda) Phillips		Aldgate, London	
15063	Solomons (Solomon)	Lewis	1845	Shoreditch, London	Nathan Solomons (Solomon)	Eliza (Leah) Abrahams		Bethnal Green, London	scholar

ID	surname	given names	born	birthplace	father	mother	spouse 1	1851 residence	1851 occupation
21264	Solomons (Solomon)	Lewis (Eleazer)	1817	Middlesex, London	Lyon (Yehuda) Solomon	Esther (?)	Rosetta Isaacs	Barnsbury, London	furniture dealer
21267	Solomons (Solomon)	Louisa	1849	City, London	Lewis (Eleazer) Solomons (Solomon)	Rosetta Isaacs		Barnsbury, London	
846	Solomons (Solomon)	Maria	1832	?, London	Phineas Solomons	Julia (Judith) Moses		Cheltenham, Gloucestershire	pawnbroker
15062	Solomons (Solomon)	Maria	1843	Shoreditch, London	Nathan Solomons (Solomon)	Eliza (Leah) Abrahams		Bethnal Green, London	scholar
1698	Solomons (Solomon)	Morris	1822	Spitalfields, London	Woolf Solomons		Caroline Abrahams	Spitalfields, London	cigar maker
15057	Solomons (Solomon)	Moss	1831	Bethnal Green, London	Nathan Solomons (Solomon)	Eliza (Leah) Abrahams		Bethnal Green, London	butcher
15055	Solomons (Solomon)	Nathan	1812	Hackney, London	Isaac Solomons	Rosetta (?)	Eliza (Leah) Abrahams	Bethnal Green, London	beadle to the Hambro Synagogue
25779	Solomons (Solomon)	Philip	1800	Aldgate, London	Simon Solomon		Hannah Solomon nee Nunes Martines	Aldgate, London	clothes dealer
845	Solomons (Solomon)	Phineas	1800	?, London			Julia (Judith) Moses	Cheltenham, Gloucestershire	pawnbroker
11800	Solomons (Solomon)	Phoebe	1850	Shoreditch, London	Samuel Moses Solomons (Solomon)	Rosetta (?)		Shoreditch, London	
3594	Solomons (Solomon)	Priscilla (Pruda)	1819	Aldgate, London	Simon Phillips		Solomon Solomons	Aldgate, London	
15990	Solomons (Solomon)	Rachael	1835	Spitalfields, London	Philip Solomons (Solomon)	Hannah Nunes Martines		Aldgate, London	cap maker
21265	Solomons (Solomon)	Rachel	1821	Middlesex, London	Lewis Eleazer Pyke		Lewis (Eleazer) Solomons (Solomon)	Barnsbury, London	
15059	Solomons (Solomon)	Rebecca	1837	Shoreditch, London	Nathan Solomons (Solomon)	Eliza (Leah) Abrahams		Bethnal Green, London	tailor
18015	Solomons (Solomon)	Rebecca	1843	Aldgate, London	Henry (Hyam) Solomons (Solomon)	Clara Moses		Aldgate, London	scholar
15060	Solomons (Solomon)	Rose	1839	Shoreditch, London	Nathan Solomons (Solomon)	Eliza (Leah) Abrahams	Emanuel Gershon	Bethnal Green, London	scholar
6278	Solomons (Solomon)	Rosetta	1814	Whitechapel, London	(?)		Samuel Moses Solomons	Shoreditch, London	
6277	Solomons (Solomon)	Samuel Moses	1803	Aldgate, London	Shlomo Dov		Maria Jacobs	Shoreditch, London	cane merchant + manufacturer of umbrella ribs
27730	Solomons (Solomon)	Sarah	1822	Bethnal Green, London	Samuel Lee		John Solomons (Solomon)	Spitalfields, London	trimming manufacturer
5892	Solomons (Solomon)	Sarah	1824	?, London	Henry Levy	Jane (?)	Coleman Solomons (Solomon)	Aldgate, London	
15989	Solomons (Solomon)	Sarah	1834	Aldgate, London	(?) Solomon	Hannah Nunes Martines		Aldgate, London	cap maker
3593	Solomons (Solomon)	Solomon	1809	Aldgate, London	Jacob Solomons	Sarah Lazarus	Priscilla (Pruda) Phillips	Aldgate, London	general dealer
11799	Solomons (Solomon)	Solomon	1848	Shoreditch, London	Samuel Moses Solomons (Solomon)	Rosetta (?)		Shoreditch, London	scholar

ID	surname	given names	born	birthplace	father	mother	spouse 1	1851 residence	1851 occupation
15065	Solomons (Solomon)	Solomon	1851	Bethnal Green, London	Nathan Solomons (Solomon)	Eliza (Leah) Abrahams		Bethnal Green, London	
6279	Solomons (Solomon)	Theresa	1846	Shoreditch, London	Samuel Moses Solomons	Rosetta (?)		Shoreditch, London	scholar
15991	Solomons (Solomon)	Welcome	1838	Aldgate, London	Philip Solomons (Solomon)	Hannah Nunes Martines	Philip Nelson	Aldgate, London	
1701	Soman	Abraham	1823	Whitechapel, London			Esther (?)	Spitalfields, London	watch guard maker empll 5
12537	Soman	Adelaide	1836	Norwich, Norfolk	David Soman	Rosetta Solomon		Norwich, Norfolk	shoe binder
1703	Soman	Adelaide	1845	Spitalfields, London	Abraham Soman	Esther (?)		Spitalfields, London	scholar
7671	Soman	Daniel	1831	Norwich, Norfolk	David Soman		Juliet Rosenthal	Norwich, Norfolk	shoemaker (cutter)
7672	Soman	David	1795	Epigal, Vosges, France			Rosetta Solomon	Norwich, Norfolk	shoemaker empl 30
1705	Soman	Elizabeth	1848	Spitalfields, London	Abraham Soman	Esther (?)		Spitalfields, London	scholar
1702	Soman	Esther	1823	Aldgate, London			Abraham Soman	Spitalfields, London	
12538	Soman	Juliet	1846	Spitalfields, London	(?) Soman			Norwich, Norfolk	scholar
12535	Soman	Lewes	1826	Great Yarmouth, Norfolk				Norwich, Norfolk	shoe maker
1706	Soman	Lewis	1850	Spitalfields, London	Abraham Soman	Esther (?)		Spitalfields, London	
12536	Soman	Philip	1835	Norwich, Norfolk	David Soman	Rosetta Solomon		Norwich, Norfolk	printer (compositor)
7844	Soman	Rosetta	1797	Whitechapel, London	Daniel Solomon		David Soman	Norwich, Norfolk	
1704	Soman	Rosetta	1847	Spitalfields, London	Abraham Soman	Esther (?)		Spitalfields, London	scholar
14482	Somers	Abraham	1815	?, Germany				Manchester	cloth cap maker
18709	Somers	Ann	1811	Aldgate, London	(?)		Judah George Somers	Aldgate, London	
21042	Somers	Charles	1844	?, London				Dover, Kent	boarding school pupil
18713	Somers	Dinah	1849	Aldgate, London	Judah George Somers	Ann (?)		Aldgate, London	
18701	Somers	Esther	1845	Aldgate, London	Judah G Somers	Ann (?)	Albert Louis Alexander	Aldgate, London	
18708	Somers	Judah George	1810	Aldgate, London			Ann (?)	Aldgate, London	stationer+ account book maker + print seller
18711	Somers	Lawrence A	1840	Aldgate, London	Judah George Somers	Ann (?)	Phoebe Lyons	Aldgate, London	
18712	Somers	Lewis John	1847	Aldgate, London	Judah George Somers	Ann (?)	Harriet (?)	Aldgate, London	
18710	Somers	Rebecca	1839	Boulogne, France	Judah George Somers	Ann (?)		Aldgate, London	
18717	Somers	Samuel	1831	Aldgate, London				?Aldgate, London	
18714	Somers	Sarah	1850	Aldgate, London	Judah George Somers	Ann (?)		Aldgate, London	
12075	Sossner	Morris	1848	?, Poland [?, Prussia]	Solomon Sossner	Yetta (?)		Spitalfields, London	
12074	Sossner	Rosa	1843	?, Poland [?, Prussia]	Solomon Sossner	Yetta (?)		Spitalfields, London	
12072	Sossner	Solomon	1817	?, Poland [?, Prussia]			Yetta (?)	Spitalfields, London	glazier
12073	Sossner	Yetta	1823	?, Poland [?, Prussia]	(?)		Solomon Sossner	Spitalfields, London	
26690	Souchay	Adelaide	1810	Emmerich, Germany [Emirich, Prussia]	(?)		Charles Isaac Souchay	Manchester	
26692	Souchay	Charles	1837	Manchester	Charles Isaac Souchay	Adelaide (?)		Manchester	scholar
14349	Souchay	Charles Isaac	1819	abroad			Adelaide (?)	Manchester	merchant
26693	Souchay	Ida Theckla	1839	Manchester	Charles Isaac Souchay	Adelaide (?)	Siegmund Maria Joseph Robert Lucius	Manchester	scholar
26691	Souchay	Juliana (Juliet) Maria	1836	Manchester	Charles Isaac Souchay	Adelaide (?)	Siegmund Maria Joseph Robert Lucius	Manchester	scholar
29589	Souweine	Adolphe	1833	?, Holland	William Souweine		Susan Van Raalte	Whitechapel, London	professor of languages

ID	surname	given names	born	birthplace	father	mother	spouse 1	1851 residence	1851 occupation
29588	Souweine	Felix	1826	?, Belgium	William Souweine		Hanna Van Raalte	Whitechapel, London	upholsterer
29587	Souweine	Hanna	1826	?, Holland	Jacob Van Raalte	Hannah (?)	Felix Souweine	Whitechapel, London	
116	Spanier	Adolph	1824	Poznan, Poland [Posen, Prussia]			Sarah (?)	Woolwich, London	glass merchant
119	Spanier	Magnus	1844	Berlin, Germany	Rodolph Spanier	Tena (?)	Alice E (?Roberts)	Woolwich, London	
118	Spanier	Mayer	1841	Berlin, Germany	Rodolph Sphanier	Tena (?)		Woolwich, London	
121	Spanier	Morris	1850	Woolwich, London	Rodolph Spanier	Tena (?)		Woolwich, London	
114	Spanier	Rodolph	1820	Poznan, Poland [Posen, Prussia]			Tena (?)	Woolwich, London	glass merchant (employing 2 men)
117	Spanier	Sarah	1819	?, Poland			Adolph Spanier	Woolwich, London	
115	Spanier	Tena	1819	Berlin, Germany			Rodolph Spanier	Woolwich, London	
2578	Sperling	Adolph	1819	Berlin, Germany			Hannah (?)	Hull, Yorkshire	tailor
2580	Sperling	Francis	1844	Berlin, Germany				Hull, Yorkshire	
2579	Sperling	Hannah	1824	Berlin, Germany			Adolph Sperling	Hull, Yorkshire	
2581	Sperling	Marcks	1847	Berlin, Germany	Adolph Sperling	Hannah (?)		Hull, Yorkshire	
14250	Spero	Solomon	1830	?, Poland [?, Prussia]				Manchester	shop man
17269	Sphania	Caroline	1827	Poznan, Poland [Posen, Prussia]	(?)		(?) Sphania	Aldgate, London	tailoress
17270	Sphania	Moris	1845	Poznan, Poland [Posen, Prussia]	(?) Sphania	Caroline (?)		Aldgate, London	scholar
3603	Spielman	Adam	1813	Poznan, Poland [Schocken, Posen]	Yehuda Spielman		Marian Samuel	City, London	bullion merchant
18895	Spielman	Amelia	1848	City, London	Adam Spielman	Marian Samuel		City, London	
18896	Spielman	Dora	1851	City, London	Adam Spielman	Marian Samuel		City, London	
18894	Spielman	Lionel Adam	1846	City, London	Adam Spielman	Marian Samuel		City, London	
3602	Spielman	Marian	1823	Liverpool	Louis Samuel	Henrietta Israel	Adam Spielman	City, London	
14463	Spier	Ansell	1796	?, Germany			Maria (?)	Manchester	furrier
13987	Spier	Arthur	1849	Manchester	Joseph A Spier	Catherine (?)		Manchester	
13986	Spier	Catherine	1821	Colchester, Essex	(?)		Joseph A Spier	Manchester	
4059	Spier	Eleanor	1843	Manchester	Ansell Spier	Maria (?)	Michael Emanuel	Manchester	
7487	Spier	Joseph A	1825	Manchester			Catherine (?)	Manchester	master furrier
4061	Spier	Julia	1843	Manchester	Ansell Spier	Maria (?)	Henry Herschel Emanuel	Manchester	
14464	Spier	Maria	1806	Liverpool	(?)		Ansell Spier	Manchester	
13988	Spier	Montague Hyam	1851	Manchester	Joseph A Spier	Catherine (?)		Manchester	
27724	Spiers	Barnet (Bernard)	1795	Gosport, Hampshire	Phineas Moses Spiers	Mariam Moses (?)	Charlotte (?)	Spitalfields, London	schoolmaster
27725	Spiers	Charlotte	1807	Deal, Kent	Phineas Moses Spiers	Mariam Moses (?)	Charlotte (?)	Spitalfields, London	schoolmistress
4985	Spiers	David	1844	Birmingham	Nathan Cohen Spiers	Sophia Aarons		Birmingham	
4988	Spiers	Elizabeth (Lizzie)	1850	Birmingham	Nathan Cohen Spiers	Sophia Aarons		Birmingham	
4986	Spiers	Henry C	1846	Birmingham	Nathan Cohen Spiers	Sophia Aarons	Rebecca Greenberg	Birmingham	
4980	Spiers	John	1791	Birmingham			Lucy (?)	Birmingham	cap maker
4987	Spiers	Lionel	1848	Birmingham	Nathan Cohen Spiers	Sophia Aarons		Birmingham	
4981	Spiers	Lucy	1801	Birmingham			John Spiers	Birmingham	
27726	Spiers	Marian (Miriam)	1830	Dublin, Ireland	Barnet (Bernard) Spiers	Charlotte (?)		Spitalfields, London	teacher
4982	Spiers	Morris (Moses)	1806	?, Poland	Samuel Spiers			Birmingham	watchmaker
4983	Spiers	Nathan Cohen	1797	Lublin, Poland			Elizabeth Aaron	Birmingham	pawnbroker

ID	surname	given names	born	birthplace	father	mother	spouse 1	1851 residence	1851 occupation
27727	Spiers	Phineas	1833	Plymouth, Devon	Barnet (Bernard) Spiers	Charlotte (?)	Matilda Ornstein	Spitalfields, London	cigar maker
27728	Spiers	Phoebe	1835	Portsmouth, Hampshire	Barnet (Bernard) Spiers	Charlotte (?)	Matilda Ornstein	Spitalfields, London	
4989	Spiers	Saul (Solomon) Cohen	1829	Birmingham	Nathan Cohen Spiers	Elizabeth Aaron	Rachel Benjamin	Birmingham	watchmaker
4984	Spiers	Sophia	1810	Birmingham	David Aaron	Maria Myers	Nathan Cohen Spiers	Birmingham	
29816	Spires	Sarah	1791	?, Germany	(?)		(?) Spires	Whitechapel, London	pensioner
26276	Spiro	Moritz	1811	Gniezno, Poland [Gnesen, Prussia]				Aldgate, London	
29954	Sporr	Elizabeth	1773	?, Germany	(?)		(?) Sporr	Whitechapel, London	broom seller
13711	Spriner	Wolff	1825	?, Poland				Bloomsbury, London	journeyman tailor
20981	Springer	Edward	1849	Aldgate, London	Sichel (Seckel) Leo Springer	Louisa Myers		Aldgate, London	
20982	Springer	Helene	1817	Bavaria, Germany	(?) Springer			Aldgate, London	annuitant
20978	Springer	Louisa	1812	?, London	(?) Myers		Sichel (Seckel) Leo Springer	Aldgate, London	
20977	Springer	Sichel (Seckel) Leo	1810	Bavaria, Germany	Yitzhak		Louisa Myers	Aldgate, London	bark merchant
20980	Springer	Solomon	1846	Aldgate, London	Sichel (Seckel) Leo Springer	Louisa Myers		Aldgate, London	scholar
20979	Springer	Walter	1845	Aldgate, London	Sichel (Seckel) Leo Springer	Louisa Myers		Aldgate, London	scholar
30696	Spyer	Grace	1803	Middlesex, London	Michael Josephs		Jones Spyer	Bloomsbury, London	
30699	Spyer	Grace Jones	1842	Bloomsbury, London	Jones Spyer	Grace Josephs		Bloomsbury, London	
30697	Spyer	Henry	1833	Middlesex, London	Jones Spyer	Grace Josephs		Bloomsbury, London	
30701	Spyer	Jane	1791	Middlesex, London	Pinchas Zelig Spyer			Bloomsbury, London	
30610	Spyer	John	1799	Whitechapel, London	Pinchas Zelig Spyer		Marianne Nunes Ribeiro	Bloomsbury, London	merchant
30695	Spyer	Jones	1796	Middlesex, London	Pinchas Zelig Spyer		Grace Josephs	Bloomsbury, London	solicitor
30698	Spyer	Joseph	1836	Middlesex, London	Jones Spyer	Grace Josephs		Bloomsbury, London	
30611	Spyer	Marianne	1803	?, Jamaica, west Indies	David Nunes Ribeiro		John Spyer	Bloomsbury, London	
29178	Spyer	Myer	1828	Amsterdam, Holland				Whitechapel, London	general merchant
3253	Spyer	Rebecca Hester	1827	Whitechapel, London	John Spyer	Marianne Nunes Ribeiro	Octavius Phillips	Bloomsbury, London	
17307	Spyer	Rosea	1781	?, Holland	(?)		(?) Spyer	Whitechapel, London	
20100	Spyer	Solomon	1830	City, London	Jones Spyer	Grace Josephs	Frances Bright	Bloomsbury, London	
30700	Spyer	Walter Joseph	1844	Bloomsbury, London	Jones Spyer	Grace Josephs		Bloomsbury, London	
7118	St Losky	Florence	1849	Finsbury, London	Samuel St Losky	Hannah Samuel	Frederic Michael Hyam (Halford)	Islington, London	
7120	St Losky	Hannah	1824	Liverpool	Louis Samuel	Henrietta Israel	Samuel St Losky	Islington, London	
7119	St Losky	Samuel	1816	?	Tsevi Hirsch (St Losky?)		Hannah Samuel	Islington, London	merchant
1146	Stadthagen	Arabella	1802	?, Cornwall	Isaac Joseph		Myer Stadthagen	Plymouth, Devon	
1150	Stadthagen	Ellen (Eliza)	1844	Plymouth, Devon	Myer Stadthagen	Arabella (?)	Edwin Selig	Plymouth, Devon	scholar
1145	Stadthagen	Myer	1804	?, Poland [?, Prussia]			Arabella Joseph	Plymouth, Devon	rabbi
1148	Stadthagen	Pheobe (Pheba)	1837	Plymouth, Devon	Myer Stadthagen	Arabella (?)		Plymouth, Devon	scholar
1149	Stadthagen	Sarah	1841	Plymouth, Devon	Myer Stadthagen	Arabella (?)	Edwin Woolf (Wolf)	Plymouth, Devon	scholar
1147	Stadthagen	Selina (Salina)	1835	Plymouth, Devon	Myer Stadthagen	Arabella Joseph	Barnett Barnett	Plymouth, Devon	
1991	Stall	Abraham J	1811	Warsaw, Poland			Rosa (?)	Swansea, Wales	glazier
1993	Stall	Esther	1833	Warsaw, Poland	Abraham Stall	Rosa (?)		Swansea, Wales	
1994	Stall	Phoebe	1837	Warsaw, Poland	Abraham Stall	Rosa (?)		Swansea, Wales	
1992	Stall	Rosa	1811	Warsaw, Poland			Abraham Stall	Swansea, Wales	
1995	Stall	Sarah	1851	Swansea, Wales	Abraham Stall	Rosa (?)		Swansea, Wales	

ID	surname	given names	born	birthplace	father	mother	spouse 1	1851 residence	1851 occupation
29003	Stared	Asher	1829	?, Poland				Whitechapel, London	tailor
25627	Stavenhagen	Samuel	1809	?, Germany	Gershon (?)		(?)	Dublin, Ireland	
11052	Stein	Abraham	1816	Bremen, Germany			Rachel Phillips	Aldgate, London	plumber + glazier
30916	Stein	Emanuel	1826	?, Bavaria, Germany				Sheffield, Yorkshire	licensed hawker
11054	Stein	Harriet	1851	Aldgate, London	Abraham Stein	Rachel Phillips		Aldgate, London	
11053	Stein	Louis H	1848	Hull, Yorkshire	Abraham Stein	Rachel Phillips		Aldgate, London	
3115	Stein	Rachel	1823	Aldgate, London	Lewis (Judah) Phillips	Rose Cohen	Abraham Stein	Aldgate, London	
13446	Steinberg	Ernest J	1844	Hamburg, Germany	Julius Steinberg	Fanny (?)	Minna R H (?)	Salford, Lancashire	
13444	Steinberg	Fanny	1817	Wuppertal, Germany [Eberfeld, Prussia]	(?)		Julius Steinberg	Salford, Lancashire	
13447	Steinberg	Francis (Frank)	1846	Hamburg, Germany	Julius Steinberg	Fanny (?)		Salford, Lancashire	
13443	Steinberg	Julius	1804	Neuenkirchen, Germany [Nuinkirchen, Prussia]			Fanny (?)	Salford, Lancashire	German merchant
13445	Steinberg	Lewis (Louis)	1842	Hamburg, Germany	Julius Steinberg	Fanny (?)	Bertha (?)	Salford, Lancashire	
14933	Steine	William	1841	Liverpool				Bethnal Green, London	boarding school pupil
17620	Steinhorn	Samuel	1832	?, Poland				Aldgate, London	glazier
23702	Steinwiche	Sigmann	1836	?, Germany				Liverpool	toy merchant's apprentice
17024	Stempeld	Emanuel	1827	Berlin, Germany				Greenock, Scotland	photographic artist
19572	Stephany	Benjamin	1843	Southwark, London	Israel Stephany	Leah Levy	Harriet Hyman	Southwark, London	
19574	Stephany	Coleman	1848	Southwark, London	Israel Stephany	Leah Levy		Southwark, London	
19571	Stephany	Esther	1841	Southwark, London	Israel Stephany	Leah Levy	Jacob Hyman	Southwark, London	
19575	Stephany	Isabella (Bella) Rebecca	1850	Southwark, London	Israel Stephany	Leah Levy	Moss Mozes Lion Corper	Southwark, London	
19568	Stephany	Israel	1805	?, Germany	Coleman Stephany		Leah Levy	Southwark, London	furrier
19569	Stephany	Leah	1815	Southwark, London	Jacob Levy	Zepporah (?)	Israel Stephany	Southwark, London	
19570	Stephany	Sarah	1840	Southwark, London	Israel Stephany	Leah Levy	Joseph Tuchman	Southwark, London	
19573	Stephany	Sophia	1845	Southwark, London	Israel Stephany	Leah Levy	Hyman Harris	Southwark, London	
20983	Stermer	Edmund	1837	Bavaria, Germany				Aldgate, London	merchant's clerk
12932	Stern	Alfred	1850	Middlesex, London	Herman Stern	Julias Goldsmid		Marylebone, London	
7415	Stern	David	1807	Frankfurt, Germany	Jacob Samuel H Stern	Theresia (?)	Sophia Goldsmid	Marylebone, London	merchant
16584	Stern	David	1850	Liverpool	Samuel Stern	Mary (?)	Lizette Mendoza	Liverpool	
4996	Stern	Elizabeth	1833	Birmingham	(?John) Stern	(?) (?Robinson)		Birmingham	
12931	Stern	Emily	1847	Middlesex, London	Herman Stern	Julias Goldsmid		Marylebone, London	
7418	Stern	Helena Caroline	1847	Middlesex, London	David Stern	Sophia Goldsmid		Marylebone, London	
7422	Stern	Herbert	1851	Brighton, Sussex	Herman Stern	Julia Goldsmid	Aimee Geraldine Bradshaw	Brighton, Sussex	
7419	Stern	Herman	1815	Frankfurt, Germany	Jacob Samuel H Stern	Theresia (?)	Julia Goldsmid	Marylebone, London	general merchant
16660	Stern	Ida	1850	Liverpool	Mayer Stern	Leonie (?Wolff)		Liverpool	
4995	Stern	John	1832	Birmingham	(?John) Stern	(?) (?Robinson)		Birmingham	clothier + tailor's son
7420	Stern	Julia	1823	Shoreditch, London	Aaron Asher Goldsmid	Sophia Solomons	Herman Stern	Marylebone, London	
16659	Stern	Leonie	1829	?, France	(?Maurice Wolff)	(?Regina) (?)	Mayer Stern	Liverpool	
16941	Stern	Leopold	1830	?, Germany				Brighton, Sussex	musician
16582	Stern	Mary	1823	Rotterdam, Holland	(?)		Samuel Stern	Liverpool	
16658	Stern	Mayer	1815	?, Germany	Eleazer Stern		Leonie (?Wolff)	Liverpool	Professor of French, German, Hebrew
16581	Stern	Samuel	1822	?, Germany [?, Prussia]			Mary (?)	Liverpool	traveller, jeweller

ID	surname	given names	born	birthplace	father	mother	spouse 1	1851 residence	1851 occupation
14465	Stern	Sigismund James	1810	?, Germany				Manchester	merchant
7416	Stern	Sophia	1821	Shoreditch, London	Aaron Asher Goldsmid	Sophia Solomons	David Stern	Marylebone, London	
16583	Stern	Sophia	1848	Liverpool	Samuel Stern	Mary (?)	Isaac Cohen	Liverpool	
7417	Stern	Sydney Davis James	1844	Middlesex, London	David Stern	Sophia Goldsmid		Marylebone, London	
11881	Sternberg	Alexander	1821	?, Poland [?, Prussia]			Theresa (?)	Whitechapel, London	tailor
11883	Sternberg	Amelia	1846	?, Poland [?, Prussia]	Alexander Sternberg	Theresa (?)		Whitechapel, London	scholar
894	Sternberg	David	1818	Kepno, Poland [Kempen, Prussia]	Solomon Sternberg		Henrietta Solomon	Cheltenham, Gloucestershire	pawnbroker
11885	Sternberg	Ellis	1850	Aldgate, London	Alexander Sternberg	Theresa (?)		Whitechapel, London	
1960	Sternberg	Hadis	1792	?, Poland [?, Prussia]			Israel Sternberg	Merthyr Tydfil, Wales	
891	Sternberg	Henrietta	1822	Bristol	Simon Solomon	Rosetta (?)	David Sternberg	Cheltenham, Gloucestershire	
1961	Sternberg	Ictehe (Irene?)	1828	?, Poland [?, Prussia]	Israel Sternberg	Hadis (?)		Merthyr Tydfil, Wales	
1959	Sternberg	Israel	1790	?, Poland [?, Prussia]			Hadis (?)	Merthyr Tydfil, Wales	glazier
902	Sternberg	Matilda	1826	Manchester	John Marks	Kate (?)	Nathan Sternberg	Manchester	
1963	Sternberg	Morris	1834	?, Poland [?, Prussia]	Israel Sternberg	Hadis (?)		Merthyr Tydfil, Wales	glazier
901	Sternberg	Nathan	1822	Kepno, Poland [Kempen, Prussia]	Solomon Sternberg		Matilda Marks	Manchester	
1962	Sternberg	Roben	1830	?, Poland [?, Prussia]	Israel Sternberg	Hadis (?)		Merthyr Tydfil, Wales	glazier
18255	Sternberg	Rosa	1850	Cheltenham, Gloucestershire	David Sternberg	Henrietta Solomon	Richard Jacob Moses	Cheltenham, Gloucestershire	
898	Sternberg	Samuel	1814	?, Germany	Solomon Sternberg		Hester Yoell	Cheltenham, Gloucestershire	pawnbroker + salesman
11884	Sternberg	Samuel	1848	Hull, Yorkshire	Alexander Sternberg	Theresa (?)		Whitechapel, London	
11882	Sternberg	Theresa	1821	?, Poland [?, Prussia]	(?)		Alexander Sternberg	Whitechapel, London	
24758	Sternhauss	Paul Hyman	1821	?, Austria				Waterloo, London	Minister + Missionary, Church of England
18655	Stibbe	David	1808	Amsterdam, Holland	Abraham Stibbe		Jansje Abrahams	Spitalfields, London	licensed hawker
18656	Stibbe	Emanuel	1837	Amsterdam, Holland	David Stibbe	Jansje Abrahams		Spitalfields, London	cigar maker
18658	Stibbe	Esther	1843	Amsterdam, Holland	David Stibbe	Jansje Abrahams	Mark Marks	Spitalfields, London	scholar
18659	Stibbe	Hannah	1845	Lambeth, London	David Stibbe	Jansje Abrahams	Samuel Greenberg	Spitalfields, London	
18657	Stibbe	John	1839	Amsterdam, Holland	David Stibbe	Jansje Abrahams	Kate Romaine	Spitalfields, London	scholar
18661	Stibbe	Joseph	1813	?, Holland				Spitalfields, London	licensed hawker
18660	Stibbe	Rosetta	1850	Spitalfields, London	David Stibbe	Jansje Abrahams	Myer Harris	Spitalfields, London	
22114	Stichs	Isaac	1829	?, Poland [?, Prussia]				Whitechapel, London	tailor
22322	Stiebel	Adelaide	1826	?, London	Samuel Stiebel	Sheina [Halutzah] bat Joseph called Raphael		Torquay, Devon	
22326	Stiebel	Adelina	1837	Bloomsbury, London	Sigismund (Asher) Stiebel	Eliza Mocatta	Charles Cleve	Bloomsbury, London	
22324	Stiebel	Charles Dan	1834	Tower Hill, London	Samuel Stiebel	Sheina [Halutzah] bat Joseph called Raphael		Torquay, Devon	
22318	Stiebel	Daniel Charles	1839	Bloomsbury, London	Sigismund (Asher) Stiebel	Eliza Mocatta	Ada Juliana Lousada	Bloomsbury, London	scholar
22327	Stiebel	Edward	1839	Bloomsbury, London	Samuel Stiebel	Sheina [Halutzah] bat Joseph called Raphael		Torquay, Devon	

ID	surname	given names	born	birthplace	father	mother	spouse 1	1851 residence	1851 occupation
22317	Stiebel	Eliza	1811	Middlesex, London	Jacob Mocatta	Rebecca Baruh Lousada	Sigismund (Asher) Stiebel	Bloomsbury, London	West Indian and South American merchant
22325	Stiebel	Flora	1836	Tower Hill, London	Samuel Stiebel	Sheina [Halutzah] bat Joseph called Raphael		Torquay, Devon	
22319	Stiebel	Jacob	1840	Bloomsbury, London	Sigismund (Asher) Stiebel	Eliza Mocatta		Bloomsbury, London	scholar
22320	Stiebel	Rebecca	1843	Bloomsbury, London	Sigismund (Asher) Stiebel	Eliza Mocatta		Bloomsbury, London	
22321	Stiebel	Samuel	1798	Frankfurt, Germany	Izaak Daniel Stiebel	Vogel Heienemann	Sheina [Halutzah] bat Joseph called Raphael	Torquay, Devon	merchant
22316	Stiebel	Sigismund (Asher)	1792	Frankfurt, Germany	Izaak Daniel Stiebel	Vogel Heienemann	(?)	Bloomsbury, London	West Indian and South American merchant
22323	Stiebel	Sigismunda	1832	Tower Hill, London	Samuel Stiebel	Sheina [Halutzah] bat Joseph called Raphael		Torquay, Devon	
15608	Stokvis	Mary S	1818	Woolwich, London	(?)		William (Woolfe) M Stokvis	Woolwich, London	
15607	Stokvis	William (Woolfe) M	1827	Amsterdam, Holland			Mary S (?)	Woolwich, London	tailor
15609	Stokvis	Wolf	1850	Woolwich, London	William (Woolfe) M Stokvis	Mary S (?)		Woolwich, London	
29636	Stoly	Tobias	1834	?, Poland [?, Prussia]				Aldgate, London	journeyman capmaker
4992	Stone	Amelia	1849	Birmingham	Benjamin Stone	Pauline (?)		Birmingham	
4990	Stone	Benjamin	1821	?, Germany	Judah Stone		Pauline Lyons	Birmingham	slipper maker
4991	Stone	Pauline	1828	?, Germany	Levi Lyons		Benjamin Stone	Birmingham	
4993	Stone	Rosanna	1850	Birmingham	Benjamin Stone	Pauline (?)		Birmingham	
13471	Stostun	Adolph	1824	?, Germany				Manchester	warehouseman
13598	Stradman	Jacob	1821	?, Poland				Manchester	cap maker
13599	Stradman	Simon	1801	Hamburg, Germany				Manchester	hawker of jewellery
26620	Stralets	Abraham	1847	Aldgate, London	Mark Stralets	Sarah Abrahams		Aldgate, London	scholar
26618	Stralets	Mark	1821	?, Germany			Sarah Abrahams	Aldgate, London	tailor
26619	Stralets	Sarah	1819	?, Germany	(?) Abrahams		Mark Stralets	Aldgate, London	tailor
28762	Strasburg	Aaron	1844	Middlesex, London	Adolphus Strasburg	(?Rosetta) (?)		Spitalfields, London	
28758	Strasburg	Adolphus	1797	?, Germany			(?Rosetta) (?)	Spitalfields, London	slipper maker
28760	Strasburg	Daniel	1838	?, Germany	Adolphus Strasburg	(?Rosetta) (?)		Spitalfields, London	
28761	Strasburg	Israel	1840	Middlesex, London	Adolphus Strasburg	(?Rosetta) (?)		Spitalfields, London	
28764	Strasburg	Jacob	1848	Middlesex, London	Adolphus Strasburg	(?Rosetta) (?)		Spitalfields, London	
28763	Strasburg	Many (Emanuel?)	1846	Middlesex, London	Adolphus Strasburg	(?Rosetta) (?)		Spitalfields, London	
28759	Strasburg	Meyer	1836	?, Germany	Adolphus Strasburg	(?Rosetta) (?)		Spitalfields, London	
15000	Strassburger	Herman	1824	?, Poland [?, Silesia Prussia]				Bethnal Green, London	compositor
14490	Straus	?	1849	Manchester	Henry Sigismund Straus	Henriette (?)		Manchester	
14487	Straus	Henriette	1827	Frankfurt, Germany	(?)		Henry Sigismund Straus	Manchester	
14384	Straus	Henry Sigismund	1810	Frankfurt, Germany			Henriette (?)	Manchester	merchant
14489	Straus	Isabella	1847	Manchester	Henry Sigismund Straus	Henriette (?)	Arthur Quixano Henriques	Manchester	
14383	Straus	Ralph S	1819	Frankfurt-am-Main, Germany				Manchester	merchant
14488	Straus	Rose Emily	1845	Manchester	Henry Sigismund Straus	Henriette (?)	Edward Micholls Henriques	Manchester	

ID	surname	given names	born	birthplace	father	mother	spouse 1	1851 residence	1851 occupation
11912	Strein	Julius	1820	?, Poland [?, Prussia]	Lazarus Strein		Harriet Israel	Whitechapel, London	tailor + dealer in silks, satins, watches + jewellery
25515	Strettel Clarke	Sarah	1823	St Thomas, Virgin Islands, West Indies	Elias de Moses Mattos Mocatta	Julia de Leon	Benjamin Strettel Clarke	Southport, Lancashire	
26570	Sulzberger	Abigail	1805	Aldgate, London	Levy Abrahams		Wolf Sulzberger	Whitechapel, London	clothier
26569	Sulzberger	Wolf	1807	?, Bavaria. Germany	Lazarus Sulzberger		Abigail Abrahams	Whitechapel, London	teacher of languages
9468	Summer	Hannah	1811	?, London	(?) Marks	Mary (?)	Isaac Summer	Aldgate, London	
9467	Summer	Isaac	1813	?, London			Hannah (?)	Aldgate, London	jeweller
9469	Summer	Maria H	1849	?, London	Isaac Summer	Hannah Marks		Aldgate, London	
25055	Summerfield	Hannah (Henrietta, Handel)	1814	Chodzież, Poland [Chodzesen, Prussia]	(?) Jacobs		James Summerfield	Newcastle Upon Tyne	
25056	Summerfield	Henry	1838	?, Poland [?, Prussia]	James Summerfield	Hannah (Henrietta, Handel) Jacobs	Matilda Summerfield	Newcastle Upon Tyne	scholar
25075	Summerfield	Israel	1827	?, Poland [?, Prussia]			Esther Wolf	Newcastle Upon Tyne	pawnbroker
25059	Summerfield	Israel (Isidor)	1845	Lobzenica, Poland [Lobsens, Prussia]	James Summerfield	Hannah (Henrietta, Handel) Jacobs	Adelaide Marks	Newcastle Upon Tyne	
25058	Summerfield	Jacob	1843	?, Poland [?, Prussia]	James Summerfield	Hannah (Henrietta, Handel) Jacobs	Dorothy Falk	Newcastle Upon Tyne	scholar
25054	Summerfield	James	1814	?Murowana-Goslina, Poznan, Poland			Hannah (Henrietta, Handel) Jacobs	Newcastle Upon Tyne	pawnbroker + tailor
25057	Summerfield	Rose Amelia	1839	?, Poland [?, Prussia]	James Summerfield	Hannah (Henrietta, Handel) Jacobs	Joseph Hyman Bernstone	Newcastle Upon Tyne	scholar
23271	Susner	Rosa	1843	?, Austria	(?) Susner			Notting Hill, London	boarding school pupil
26362	Sussman	Woolf	1791	?, Poland				Aldgate, London	rabbi
18339	Sutia	Mordica	1833	Wenteslawka, Poland				Brighton, Sussex	
14448	Sykes	Caroline	1801	?, Poland [?, Prussia]			Morris Sykes	Manchester	
14450	Sykes	Henry	1842	?, Poland [?, Prussia]	Morris Sykes	Caroline (?)	Sarah (?)	Manchester	
14447	Sykes	Morris	1802	?, Poland [?, Prussia]			Caroline (?)	Manchester	tailor
14449	Sykes	Susan	1838	?, Poland [?, Prussia]	Morris Sykes	Caroline (?)		Manchester	
7423	Sylvester	James Joseph	1814	Middlesex, London	Abraham Joseph			Holborn, London	barrister, mathematician + actuary
26844	Symonds	Flora	1786	?, London	(?)		(?) Symonds	Aldgate, London	nurse
16635	Symonds	George	1811	?, London				Liverpool	commercial traveller lace
30429	Symonds	Hannah	1776	Amsterdam, Holland	(?)		Woolf Emden	Aldgate, London	
9379	Symonds	Kitty	1836	Whitechapel, London	(?Abraham) Symonds	Sarah Lipman		Spitalfields, London	waistcoat maker
9378	Symonds	Sarah	1794	Middlesex, London	Phillip Lipman		(?Abraham) Symonds	Spitalfields, London	furrier
2088	Symonds	Sarah	1819	Carmarthen, Wales	Jacob Lazarus	Elizabeth Lazarus	William Symonds	Swansea, Wales	wife of a clerk
12414	Symons	Abraham	1818	Spitalfields, London				Spitalfields, London	general dealer
28126	Symons	Abraham	1828	?, London				Spitalfields, London	traveller
3843	Symons	Abraham	1837	Spitalfields, London	Henry Symons	Martha (?)		Spitalfields, London	cigar maker
11298	Symons	Asher	1829	Middlesex, London	(?) Symons	Rachael (?)		Aldgate, London	cigar maker
3846	Symons	Barnett	1847	Spitalfields, London	Henry Symons	Martha (?)		Spitalfields, London	
12460	Symons	Barnett	1849	?, London	Lewis Symons	Julia (?)		Spitalfields, London	
11295	Symons	Catharine	1817	Middlesex, London	(?) Symons	Rachael (?)		Aldgate, London	cap maker

ID	surname	given names	born	birthplace	father	mother	spouse 1	1851 residence	1851 occupation
12411	Symons	Catherine	1841	Spitalfields, London	Moses Symons (Simons)	Sarah Joseph		Spitalfields, London	
11420	Symons	Charles	1829	Middlesex, London				Aldgate, London	butcher
21357	Symons	Charlotte	1838	Islington, London	Henry Samuel Symons	Mary (Charlotte) (?)		Harringay, London	
19676	Symons	David	1821	Aldgate, London	Isaac Symons		Sarah Harris	Spitalfields, London	general dealer
3842	Symons	Deborah	1827	Amsterdam, Holland	Henry Symons	Martha (?)	Jonas Solomon Whalefish	Spitalfields, London	
10526	Symons	E Frances	1850	Soho, London	Eli Symons	Eliza Symons		Covent Garden, London	
13994	Symons	Eleazer Jacob	1783	Amsterdam, Holland	Yitzhak Yaacov		Hester (Esther) (?)	Whitechapel, London	Livorno broker
10524	Symons	Eli	1828	Westminster, London			Eliza Symons	Covent Garden, London	commercial clerk
24546	Symons	Elias	1850	Lambeth, London	Moses Symons	Hannah Nathan	Kate Van Oestren	Brixton, London	
10525	Symons	Eliza	1826	Bromley, Kent	(?) Symons	Sarah (?)	Eli Symons	Covent Garden, London	shirt maker
11296	Symons	Elizabeth	1824	Middlesex, London	(?) Symons	Rachael (?)		Aldgate, London	tailoress
3845	Symons	Emanuel	1843	Spitalfields, London	Henry Symons	Martha (?)		Spitalfields, London	scholar
24545	Symons	Eve	1848	Elephant & Castle, London	Moses Symons	Hannah Nathan		Brixton, London	scholar
10528	Symons	Frances	1823	Tonbridge, Kent	(?) Symons	Sarah (?)		Covent Garden, London	shirt maker
2582	Symons	Frances	1825	Hull, Yorkshire	(?) Symons	Julia Levy		Hull, Yorkshire	
11337	Symons	Hanah	1830	?, Holland				Aldgate, London	tailoress
24541	Symons	Hannah	1817	Southwark, London	Noah Nathan	(?Phebe Emanuel)	Moses Symons	Brixton, London	marine store + general dealer
11300	Symons	Hannah	1833	Middlesex, London	(?) Symons	Rachael (?)		Aldgate, London	
12324	Symons	Hannah	1845	Spitalfields, London	Moses Symons	Sarah (?)	Jacob (John) de Isaac Gomes Da Costa	Spitalfields, London	
9860	Symons	Harriet	1838	Falmouth, Cornwall	Isaac Symons	Rosetta (?)	Elias N Martinez	Fulham, London	boarding school pupil
3840	Symons	Henry	1802	Amsterdam, Holland			Martha (?)	Spitalfields, London	general dealer
21358	Symons	Henry	1842	Stoke Newington, London	Henry Samuel Symons	Mary (Charlotte) (?)		Harringay, London	
13996	Symons	Henry (Hyman) Eliezer	1826	Whitechapel, London	Eleazer Jacob Symons	Hester (Esther) (?)	Emma Myers	Whitechapel, London	Livorno broker
20758	Symons	Henry Samuel	1803	City, London			Mary (Charlotte) (?)	Harringay, London	lace manufacturer
13995	Symons	Hester (Esther)	1788	Rotterdam, Holland			Eleazer Jacob Symons	Whitechapel, London	
9875	Symons	Isaac	1797	Truro, Cornwall			Rosetta (?)	Whitechapel, London	annuitant
27489	Symons	Isaac	1800	?, Holland			Phebe (?)	Aldgate, London	shoe maker
3683	Symons	Isaac	1810	?, Holland			Rebecca (?)	Spitalfields, London	master tailor + draper
11501	Symons	Jacob	1806	Aldgate, London				Aldgate, London	general dealer
2158	Symons	John	1824	Hull, Yorkshire	(?) Symons	Julia Levy	Rose Levy	Hull, Yorkshire	assistant goldsmith
12461	Symons	Joseph	1850	?, London	Lewis Symons	Julia (?)		Spitalfields, London	
2583	Symons	Julia	1800	Portsmouth, Hampshire	S--- Levy		(?) Symons	Hull, Yorkshire	jeweller
12459	Symons	Julia	1820	Bermondsey, London	Benjamin Abrahams		Lewis Symons	Spitalfields, London	general dealer
9877	Symons	Julia	1826	Falmouth, Cornwall	Isaac Symons	Rosetta (?)		Whitechapel, London	annuitant's daughter
11297	Symons	Julia	1826	Middlesex, London	(?) Symons	Rachael (?)		Aldgate, London	tailoress
3686	Symons	Julia	1837	Whitechapel, London	Isaac Symons	Rebecca (?)		Spitalfields, London	
19678	Symons	Julia	1848	Aldgate, London	David Symons	Sarah Harris		Spitalfields, London	scholar
3689	Symons	Lewis	1819	?, Holland				Spitalfields, London	tailor
12458	Symons	Lewis	1823	Amsterdam, Holland	Isaac Symons		Julia Abrahams	Spitalfields, London	general dealer
24542	Symons	Lewis	1841	Elephant & Castle, London	Moses Symons	Hannah Nathan	Julia Joseph	Brixton, London	scholar
3844	Symons	Lucas	1841	Spitalfields, London	Henry Symons	Martha (?)		Spitalfields, London	scholar
3841	Symons	Martha	1809	Amsterdam, Holland			Henry Symons	Spitalfields, London	

ID	surname	given names	born	birthplace	father	mother	spouse 1	1851 residence	1851 occupation
21356	Symons	Mary	1828	Islington, London	Henry Samuel Symons	Mary (Charlotte) (?)		Harringay, London	
21355	Symons	Mary (Charlotte)	1802	Walworth, London			Henry Samuel Symons	Harringay, London	
12410	Symons	Mordecai	1835	Spitalfields, London	Moses Symons (Simons)	Sarah Joseph		Spitalfields, London	general dealer
24540	Symons	Moses	1811	Lambeth, London	Lewis Symons		Hannah Nathan	Brixton, London	marine store + general dealer
29162	Symons	Moses	1816	Amsterdam, Holland	Eleazer Jacob Symons	Hester (Esther) (?)	Charlotte (?)	Whitechapel, London	partner to export merchant
3847	Symons	Moses	1851	Spitalfields, London	Henry Symons	Martha (?)		Spitalfields, London	
3687	Symons	Myer	1839	Whitechapel, London	Isaac Symons	Rebecca (?)		Spitalfields, London	scholar
24543	Symons	Noah	1843	Elephant & Castle, London	Moses Symons	Hannah Nathan		Brixton, London	scholar
11299	Symons	Pheabe	1831	Middlesex, London	(?) Symons	Rachael (?)		Aldgate, London	cap maker
27490	Symons	Phebe	1787	?, Holland	(?)		Isaac Symons	Aldgate, London	
11294	Symons	Rachael	1797	Middlesex, London	(?)		(?) Symons	Aldgate, London	general dealer
3688	Symons	Rachael	1841	Whitechapel, London	Isaac Symons	Rebecca (?)		Spitalfields, London	scholar
12413	Symons	Rachel	1849	Spitalfields, London	Moses Symons (Simons)	Sarah Joseph		Spitalfields, London	scholar
3684	Symons	Rebecca	1808	Mile End, London			Isaac Symons	Spitalfields, London	
30217	Symons	Rebecca	1826	Covent Garden, London	(?) Symons			Piccadilly, London	
9861	Symons	Rebecca	1840	Falmouth, Cornwall	Isaac Symons	Rosetta (?)		Fulham, London	boarding school pupil
9876	Symons	Rosetta	1798	Penzance, Cornwall	(?)		Isaac Symons	Whitechapel, London	annuitant's wife
11500	Symons	Samuel	1831	Aldgate, London	Barnet Symons	Sarah (?)	Hannah Solomon	Aldgate, London	cigar maker
10527	Symons	Sarah	1787	Chichester, Sussex	(?)		(?) Symons	Covent Garden, London	schoolmaster's wife
11499	Symons	Sarah	1802	Whitechapel, London	(?)		Barnet Symons	Aldgate, London	cook
19677	Symons	Sarah	1823	Aldgate, London	Solomon Harris	Susan Solomons	David Symons	Spitalfields, London	
9859	Symons	Sarah	1834	Falmouth, Cornwall	Isaac Symons	Rosetta (?)		Fulham, London	boarding school pupil
3685	Symons	Sarah	1835	Whitechapel, London	Isaac Symons	Rebecca (?)		Spitalfields, London	
12412	Symons	Sarah	1847	Spitalfields, London	Moses Symons (Simons)	Sarah Joseph		Spitalfields, London	scholar
28127	Symons	Simon	1825	?, London				Spitalfields, London	clothes dealer
24544	Symons	Sophia	1846	Elephant & Castle, London	Moses Symons	Hannah Nathan	Joseph Cohen	Brixton, London	scholar
12408	Symons (Simons)	Moses	1820	Spitalfields, London	Levy Simons		Sarah Joseph	Spitalfields, London	general dealer
12409	Symons (Simons)	Sarah	1818	Spitalfields, London	Emanuel Joseph		Moses Simons	Spitalfields, London	
26987	Szerweska	Eliza	1811	Inowroclaw, Poland [Inarachlaw, Prussia] [Prussia]	(?) Szerweska			Aldgate, London	house servant
3887	Taller	Isaac	1824	?, Holland				Spitalfields, London	ink manufacturer
31177	Tallerman	Jacob	1836	Middlesex, London				Rochester, Kent	shoe trade
31176	Tallerman	Lewis	1846	Middlesex, London				Rochester, Kent	scholar
2344	Tannenberg	Simon	1825	?, Poland			Rachel Fox	Leeds, Yorkshire	hawker, general dealer
18586	Tarohn	Dinah	1846	Spitalfields, London	Nathan Tarohn	(?)	Asher Woolf	Spitalfields, London	
30754	Tarohn	Elizabeth	1850	Spitalfields, London	Nathan Tarohn	Rachael Martin		Spitalfields, London	
30667	Tarohn	Nathan	1804	Gdansk, Poland [Dantzig, Prussia]	Isaac		(?)	Spitalfields, London	
30668	Tarohn	Rachael	1819	Whitechapel, London	(?) Martin		Nathan Tarohn	Spitalfields, London	tailoress
26392	Taubb	Rachael	1823	?, Holland	(?) Taubb			Aldgate, London	needlewoman
5002	Taylor	Benjamin	1847	Birmingham	Harris Taylor	Rebecca (?)		Birmingham	
5000	Taylor	Bessiah	1841	Birmingham	Harris Taylor	Rebecca (?)		Birmingham	

ID	surname	given names	born	birthplace	father	mother	spouse 1	1851 residence	1851 occupation
5001	Taylor	Betsah	1843	Birmingham	Harris Taylor	Rebecca (?)		Birmingham	
19565	Taylor	Ellen	1840	Poplar, London	Howard Taylor		(?)	?Poplar, London	
4998	Taylor	Harris	1811	?, Germany			Rebecca (?)	Birmingham	traveller
4999	Taylor	Rebecca	1818	?, England			Harris Taylor	Birmingham	
28178	Taytasack	Hannah	1795	Whitechapel, London	Gabriel de PhineasTaitasack	Sarah de Isaac Nunes Henriques		Spitalfields, London	needlewoman
28177	Taytasack	Rachel	1793	Whitechapel, London	Gabriel de PhineasTaitasack	Sarah de Isaac Nunes Henriques		Spitalfields, London	needlewoman
1117	Teacher	Anna (Annie)	1850	Penzance, Cornwall	Solomon Teacher	Maria (?)	Myer Solomon Levy	Penzance, Cornwall	
1116	Teacher	Maria	1816	Penzance, Cornwall	Aaron Selig	Hannah (?)	Solomon Teacher	Penzance, Cornwall	
1115	Teacher	Solomon	1812	Bavaria, Germany	Markus Teacher		Maria Selig	Penzance, Cornwall	jeweller
18161	Tedesky	Susan	1777	Middlesex, London	(?) Tedesky			Mile End, London	patient in the Portuguese Jews Hospital
5003	Tepler	Louis	1821	?, Poland [?, Prussia]	Jacob Tepler		Rose Prush	Birmingham	licensed hawker
5004	Tepler	Rose	1825	?, Poland [?, Prussia]	Joseph Prush		Louis Tepler	Birmingham	
23631	Themans	Elizabeth	1828	?, Holland	Levi Themans			Liverpool	
29887	Themans	Jacob	1787	?, Holland			(?)	Wapping, London	tobacconist
23630	Themans	Levi	1790	?, Holland			(?)	Liverpool	
23632	Themans	Solomon	1830	?, Holland	Levi Themans		Hannah Lescenheim	Liverpool	cigar dealing commercial traveller
13710	Theodore	Holberg	1823	?, Poland				Bloomsbury, London	journeyman tailor
7488	Theodores	Tobias	1808	Berlin, Germany			Sarah Horsfall	Manchester	
23645	Tholander	Joseph	1836	?, Poland				Liverpool	traveller
16552	Tobias	Adeline	1840	Liverpool	George W Tobias	Matilda (?)		Liverpool	scholar
16554	Tobias	Alexander	1844	Liverpool	George W Tobias	Matilda (?)		Liverpool	scholar
16555	Tobias	Alice Maud	1846	Liverpool	George W Tobias	Matilda (?)		Liverpool	scholar
22809	Tobias	Catherine	1842	Whitechapel, London	Jacob Tobias	Mary Solomons		Whitechapel, London	scholar
16556	Tobias	Charles	1849	Liverpool	George W Tobias	Matilda (?)		Liverpool	
14124	Tobias	Charlotte	1823	Newcastle-under-Lyme, Staffordshire	Abraham Francks	Mary (?)	Jacob Tobias	Manchester	
16549	Tobias	George W	1811	Liverpool			Matilda (?)	Liverpool	merchant
16551	Tobias	Hannah	1837	Liverpool	George W Tobias	Matilda (?)		Liverpool	scholar
28781	Tobias	Hannah M	1811	Sheerness, Kent	Jonas Michael	Rebecca Russell	Isaac Tobias	Birmingham	
5005	Tobias	Henry	1818	?, Germany				Birmingham	musician
5007	Tobias	Herman	1831	?, Poland [?, Prussia]				Birmingham	cigar maker
28780	Tobias	Isaac	1810	?, Poland [?, Prussia]			Hannah Michael	Birmingham	fruiterer
14123	Tobias	Jacob	1821	?, Germany			Charlotte Francks	Manchester	watch dealer
25911	Tobias	Jacob	1823	?, Poland				Aldgate, London	cap maker empl 3
22810	Tobias	Jane	1808	Aldgate, London	Levy Tobias	Jane Jacobs		Whitechapel, London	domestic servant
28784	Tobias	Jonas	1845	Birmingham	Isaac Tobias	Hannah Michael		Birmingham	
24737	Tobias	Joseph	1791	?, Poland			Sarah (?)	Southwark, London	cloth cap maker
14167	Tobias	Joseph	1819	Berlin, Germany				Manchester	merchant
26945	Tobias	Joseph	1821	?, Poland				Aldgate, London	cap maker
24800	Tobias	Julius	1848	Elephant & Castle, London	Levy Tobias	Katherine Myers (Mendelwitz)		Elephant & Castle, London	

ID	surname	given names	born	birthplace	father	mother	spouse 1	1851 residence	1851 occupation
24798	Tobias	Katherine	1821	Southwark, London	Mendlewitz Myers	(Abigail? Esther?) Nathan	Levy Tobias	Elephant & Castle, London	
24799	Tobias	Levy	1812	?, Poland [?, Prussia]	Tobias Tobias		Katherine Myers (Mendelwitz)	Elephant & Castle, London	general dealer
22808	Tobias	Lewis	1840	Whitechapel, London	Jacob Tobias	Mary Solomons		Whitechapel, London	scholar
22806	Tobias	Mary	1807	Whitechapel, London	Reuben Solomons		(?) Solomons	Whitechapel, London	dress maker
16550	Tobias	Matilda	1811	Middlesex, London	(?)		George W Tobias	Liverpool	
16553	Tobias	Meyer	1842	Liverpool	George W Tobias	Matilda (?)		Liverpool	scholar
7799	Tobias	Morris	1771	Middlesex, London				Whitechapel, London	chronometer, watch + clock maker
24801	Tobias	Myer	1850	Elephant & Castle, London	Levy Tobias	Katherine Myers (Mendelwitz)		Elephant & Castle, London	
28785	Tobias	Rachel	1847	Birmingham	Isaac Tobias	Hannah Michael	Benjamin Emanuel	Birmingham	
28782	Tobias	Reuben Michael	1839	Edinburgh, Scotland	Isaac Tobias	Hannah Michael	Sarah King	Birmingham	
5006	Tobias	Robert	1827	?, Germany				Birmingham	musician
24738	Tobias	Sarah	1801	City, London	(?)		Joseph Tobias	Southwark, London	
28783	Tobias	Sarah	1841	Birmingham	Isaac Tobias	Hannah Michael	Isidor Solomon	Birmingham	
14125	Tobias	Theodore	1850	Manchester	Jacob Tobias	Charlotte Francks		Manchester	
28786	Tobias	Tobias	1849	Birmingham	Isaac Tobias	Hannah Michael	Johanna Reid	Birmingham	
15511	Toledano	Esther	1841	?London	Daniel Toledano		John (Jacob) Belasco	Spitalfields, London	
9298	Toledano	Jamilla	1793	Gibraltar				Aldgate, London	poor
11523	Toledano	Joshua	1800	?London	Moses de Abraham Toledano	Abigail de Joseph Nunes Martines	Sarah (?)	?Spitalfields, London	
11524	Toledano	Sarah	1800	?London	(?)		Joshua De Moses Toledano	?Spitalfields, London	
11522	Toledano	Sarah	1839	?Stepney, London	Joshua de Moses Toledano	Sarah (?)	Aaron Alvares	?Spitalfields, London	
18153	Tolendaza?	Abranel	1762	Middlesex, London				Mile End, London	inmate of Portuguese Jews Hospital
9299	Torres	Esther	1787	Bethnal Green, London	Isaac de Abraham Dias	Abigail de Isaac Gomes Da Costa	Abraham de Moseh Torres	Aldgate, London	nurse
10459	Tourass	Rebecca	1829	Bethnal Green, London				Aldgate, London	servant
17851	Trefgens	Johan	1822	Holstein, Germany				Aldgate, London	tailor
27988	Triber	Oliff	1814	?				Spitalfields, London	bootmaker
30461	Tubenich	Hyman	1832	Warsaw, Poland				Burslem, Staffordshire	dealer in sponges
29259	Tucker	Abraham Ben	1849	Whitechapel, London	Stephen Cochrane Tucker	Angelina Pinto	Stella Pereira Mendes	Whitechapel, London	
29253	Tucker	Angelina	1813	?, London	Abraham de Mier Pinto	Esther de Moses Brandon	Stephen Cochrane Tucker	Whitechapel, London	
29255	Tucker	Esther	1842	?, London	Stephen Cochrane Tucker	Angelina Pinto	Napthalie Gans	Whitechapel, London	scholar
29258	Tucker	Jane	1848	?, London	Stephen Cochrane Tucker	Angelina Pinto		Whitechapel, London	
29254	Tucker	Joseph Edward	1840	?, London	Stephen Cochrane Tucker	Angelina Pinto	Helene Hart	Whitechapel, London	scholar
29257	Tucker	Phoebe	1846	?, London	Stephen Cochrane Tucker	Angelina Pinto		Whitechapel, London	scholar
29256	Tucker	Rebecca	1844	?, London	Stephen Cochrane Tucker	Angelina Pinto		Whitechapel, London	scholar
29252	Tucker	Stephen Cochrane	1811	Plymouth, Devon			Angelina Pinto	Whitechapel, London	clerk to paymaster's office
31211	Ullman	Solomon	1831	Wrzesnia, Poland [Riesen, Prussia]				Winchester, Hampshire	importer, sponges + leather
2584	Ullman	Wolfe (William) Jacob	1835	Drezdenko, Poland [Driesen, Prussia]			Deborah Morris	Hull, Yorkshire	hawker of sponges

ID	surname	given names	born	birthplace	father	mother	spouse 1	1851 residence	1851 occupation
3140	Ullmann	Samuel	1818	?			Hortense Vallet (Walley)	Manchester	artificial florist + pattern designer
3126	Ulman	Hortense	1827	Paris, France	Ancill (Ansell) Walley (Vallet)		Samuel Ullman	Manchester	artificial flower maker + milliner
27921	Unger	Augusta	1847	Żerków, Poland [Gircof, Prussia]	Solomon Unger	Paulina Cohen		Spitalfields, London	
27922	Unger	Isaac	1849	Żerków, Poland [Gircof, Prussia]	Solomon Unger	Paulina Cohen	Sarah Aronheim	Spitalfields, London	
29904	Unger	Julius	1829	?, Germany				Wapping, London	cigar maker
27920	Unger	Paulina	1822	Żerków, Poland [Gircof, Prussia]	(?) Cohen		Solomon Unger	Spitalfields, London	
27919	Unger	Solomon	1821	Żerków, Poland [Gircof, Prussia]			Paulina Cohen	Spitalfields, London	tailor
30998	Unna	Caroline Susannah	1843	Leeds, Yorkshire	Jacob Arnold Unna	Serina (?)		Bradford, Yorkshire	
7932	Unna	Charles Frederick	1847	Leeds, Yorkshire	Jacob Unna	Serina (?)	Mathilde Bernheim	Bradford, Yorkshire	
5009	Unna	Eliza	1829	Liverpool			Joseph Adolph Unna	Birmingham	
7933	Unna	Jacob Arnold	1801	Hamburg, Germany			Serina (?)	Bradford, Yorkshire	merchant
16301	Unna	Joseph	1834	?, Germany				Dundee, Scotland	
5008	Unna	Joseph Adolph	1815	Hamburg, Germany			Eliza (?)	Birmingham	hat + cap mfr
7935	Unna	Serina	1813	Copenhagen, Denmark	(?)		Jacob Unna	Bradford, Yorkshire	
7934	Unna	Violetta Anna	1840	Leeds, Yorkshire	Jacob Arnold Unna	Serina (?)	Leopold Lewis	Bradford, Yorkshire	scholar
13707	Urban	Caroline	1835	Finsbury, London	(?) Urban			Bloomsbury, London	
27353	Vahia?	Abraham	1829	Muschen, Germany [Musheen, Germany]				Aldgate, London	tailor
11238	Valanca	Betsey	1844	?, Holland	Samuel Valanca	Mary Ann (?)		Aldgate, London	
11241	Valanca	David	1850	Aldgate, London	Samuel Valanca	Mary Ann (?)		Aldgate, London	
11237	Valanca	Mary Ann	1822	?, Holland	(?)		Samuel Valanca	Aldgate, London	
11236	Valanca	Samuel	1818	?, Holland			Mary Ann (?)	Aldgate, London	painter + glazier
11239	Valanca	Samuel	1847	?, Holland	Samuel Valanca	Mary Ann (?)		Aldgate, London	
11240	Valanca	Sarah	1849	?, Holland	Samuel Valanca	Mary Ann (?)		Aldgate, London	
13100	Valentine	Abigail	1782	Cowes, Isle of Wight				Whitechapel, London	pauper + washerwoman
17389	Valentine	Abraham	1799	Whitechapel, London	Nathan Breslau Valentine		Maria Jacobs	Whitechapel, London	general dealer
8192	Valentine	Abraham Henriques	1842	Aldgate, London	Isaac Henriques Valentine	Julia Solomons	Elizabeth Hyams	Aldgate, London	scholar
23267	Valentine	Amelia Henriques	1843	Shoreditch, London	Jacob de Elias Henriques Valentine	Amelia (Malka, Miriam) de Meir de Uri	Adolf (Abraham) Nieman	Shoreditch, London	boarding school pupil
8198	Valentine	Benjamin	1816	Mile End, London	Emanuel Valentine		Esther Hartell	Aldgate, London	general dealer
9614	Valentine	Betsy (Elizabeth, Bathsheba)	1840	Whitechapel, London	Abraham de Emanuel Henriques Valentine	Julia (Judith) Mordecai	Isaac Alvares	Spitalfields, London	scholar
21693	Valentine	Catherine	1805	Finsbury, London	(?)		Emanuel Valentine	Islington, London	
19578	Valentine	Catherine (Kate) Henriques	1848	Aldgate, London	Isaac Henriques Valentine	Julia Solomons	Lewis Emanuel	Aldgate, London	scholar
16521	Valentine	Charles Thomas	1847	Covent Garden, London	Isaac Valentine	Louisa Jane (?)		Clerkenwell, London	
10798	Valentine	David Henriques	1803	Spitalfields, London	Emanuel Henriques Valentine		Sarah de Hanoj Cohen	Spitalfields, London	marble paper maker
15182	Valentine	David Henriques	1805	Shoreditch, London	Elias (Elis) Henriques Valentine	Rebecca de Aaron Alvares Da Costa	Isabella Mordecai nee Benjamin	Stamford Hill, London	dry salter agent

ID	surname	given names	born	birthplace	father	mother	spouse 1	1851 residence	1851 occupation
27163	Valentine	David Henriques	1850	Aldgate, London	Isaac Henriques Valentine	Julia Solomons		Aldgate, London	
17391	Valentine	Deborah	1832	Whitechapel, London	Abraham Valentine	Maria Jacobs		Whitechapel, London	shoe binder
16522	Valentine	Edmund Conty	1849	Marylebone, London	Isaac Valentine	Louisa Jane (?)		Clerkenwell, London	
29386	Valentine	Edward	1828	Aldgate, London				Wapping, London	clothier's shopman
15175	Valentine	Elias (Elis) Henriques	1771	Aldgate, London	Isaac Henriques Valentine		Rebecca de Aaron Alvares Da Costa	Shoreditch, London	dry salter
21692	Valentine	Emanuel	1799	Clerkenwell, London			Catherine (?)	Islington, London	paper stainer
25154	Valentine	Emanuel	1827	Shoreditch, London	(?) Valentine	Julia (?)		Finsbury, London	paper stainer
9611	Valentine	Emanuel	1832	Whitechapel, London	Abraham Henriques Valentine		Fanny Woolf	Spitalfields, London	cabinet maker
21697	Valentine	Emanuel	1836	Finsbury, London	Emanuel Valentine	Catherine (?)		Islington, London	apprenticed
12448	Valentine	Emanuel	1849	Aldgate, London	Benjamin Valentine	Esther Hartell		Aldgate, London	
8878	Valentine	Emanuel Henriques	1834	Whitechapel, London	Abraham Henriques Valentine	Julia (Judith) Mendoza	Rebecca Martin	Spitalfields, London	cabinet maker
27162	Valentine	Emanuel Henriques	1838	?, London	Isaac Henriques Valentine	Julia Solomons		Aldgate, London	general dealer
8199	Valentine	Esther	1828	Whitechapel, London	Joseph Hartell		Benjamin Valentine	Aldgate, London	
21695	Valentine	Esther	1832	Clerkenwell, London	Emanuel Valentine	Catherine (?)		Islington, London	
10799	Valentine	Hagar (Agar) Henriques	1812	Whitechapel, London	Enoch (Hanoj) Cohen	Judith de Joseph Bendan	David de Emanuel Henriques Valentine	Spitalfields, London	
8187	Valentine	Hannah	1811	St Pancras, London				Victoria, London	housekeeper
23266	Valentine	Hannah H	1837	Shoreditch, London	Jacob de Elias Henriques Valentine	Amelia (Malka, Miriam) de Meir de Uri	Solomon Isaacs	Shoreditch, London	boarding school pupil
15176	Valentine	Hannah Henriques	1800	Aldgate, London	Elias (Elis) Henriques Valentine	Rebecca de Aaron Alvares Da Costa		Shoreditch, London	
17393	Valentine	Henery	1836	Whitechapel, London	Abraham Valentine	Maria Jacobs		Whitechapel, London	cigar maker
8183	Valentine	Isaac	1822	Marylebone, London			Louisa Jane (?)	Clerkenwell, London	jeweller + fancy dealer
25153	Valentine	Isaac	1825	Whitechapel, London	(?) Valentine	Julia (?)		Finsbury, London	paper stainer
8190	Valentine	Isaac Henriques	1815	Aldgate, London	Emanuel Henriques Valentine	Leah de Saul Rodrigues	Julia Solomons	Aldgate, London	general dealer
15183	Valentine	Isabella Henriques	1799	Strand, London	Yehuda Leib Benjamin		Michael Mordecai	Stamford Hill, London	
15178	Valentine	Jacob Henriques	1810	Aldgate, London	Elias (Elis) Henriques Valentine	Rebecca de Aaron Alvares Da Costa	Amelia (Malka, Miriam) de Meir de Uri	Shoreditch, London	dry salter
21694	Valentine	James	1826	Holborn, London	Emanuel Valentine	Catherine (?)		Islington, London	paper stainer
18188	Valentine	Jane	1826	Middlesex, London	(?) Valentine			Mile End, London	cook to house
9616	Valentine	Judah Henriques	1846	Whitechapel, London	Abraham de Emanuel Henriques Valentine	Julia (Judith) Mordecai	Jeannette (Jane) Cohen	Spitalfields, London	scholar
25151	Valentine	Julia	1783	Whitechapel, London	(?)		(?) Valentine	Finsbury, London	paper stainer
8191	Valentine	Julia	1816	Aldgate, London	Isaac Solomons		Isaac Henriques Valentine	Aldgate, London	
25155	Valentine	Julia	1829	Finsbury, London	(?) Valentine	Julia (?)		Finsbury, London	house servant
9609	Valentine	Julia (Judith)	1810	Whitechapel, London	Mordecai Mendoza	Sipora Levy	Abraham de Emanuel Henriques Valentine	Spitalfields, London	general shopkeeper
25152	Valentine	Leah	1817	Whitechapel, London	(?) Valentine	Julia (?)		Finsbury, London	paper stainer
9610	Valentine	Leah	1831	Whitechapel, London	Abraham de Emanuel Henriques Valentine	Julia (Judith) Mordecai	Benjamin Fonseca	Spitalfields, London	domestic
10800	Valentine	Leah Henriques	1829	City, London	David Henriques Valentine	Sarah Cohen	Moses Lipman	Spitalfields, London	dress maker
19577	Valentine	Leah Henriques	1846	Aldgate, London	Isaac Henriques Valentine	Julia Solomons	Michael Mitchell	Aldgate, London	scholar

ID	surname	given names	born	birthplace	father	mother	spouse 1	1851 residence	1851 occupation
8186	Valentine	Louisa Jane	1823	Marylebone, London	(?)		Isaac Valentine	Clerkenwell, London	
16520	Valentine	Louisa Mary	1845	Covent Garden, London	Isaac Valentine	Louisa Jane (?)		Clerkenwell, London	
17390	Valentine	Maria	1803	Whitechapel, London	Yechiel Jacobs		Abraham Valentine	Whitechapel, London	
21696	Valentine	Mary	1835	Finsbury, London	Emanuel Valentine	Catherine (?)		Islington, London	
8875	Valentine	Mordecai Henriques	1835	Whitechapel, London	Abraham Henriques Valentine	Julia (Judith) Mendoza	Hannah Nunes Martin	Spitalfields, London	cigar maker
16365	Valentine	Moses (Moss) Henriques	1842	City, London	Abraham Henriques Valentine	Julia (Judith) Mendoza	Sarah Joseph	Spitalfields, London	boarding school pupil
8195	Valentine	Philip	1827	Aldgate, London	Isaac Valentine	Sarah Green	Sarah Fonseca	Aldgate, London	printer compositor
17394	Valentine	Philip	1839	Whitechapel, London	Abraham Valentine	Maria Jacobs		Whitechapel, London	cigar maker
8189	Valentine	Rebecca	1844	Aldgate, London	Isaac Valentine	Julia Solomons	David (Daniel) Moses	Aldgate, London	scholar
15181	Valentine	Rebecca Henriques	1821	Aldgate, London	(?) Henriques Valentine			Shoreditch, London	
15179	Valentine	Rebecca Henriques	1833	?, America	Jacob de Elias Henriques Valentine	Amelia (Malka, Miriam) de Meir de Uri		Shoreditch, London	dress maker
19576	Valentine	Rebecca Henriques	1844	Aldgate, London	Isaac Henriques Valentine	Julia Solomons	David Moses	Aldgate, London	
17392	Valentine	Samuel	1834	Whitechapel, London	Abraham Valentine	Maria Jacobs		Whitechapel, London	cigar maker
29653	Valentine	Sarah	1821	Middlesex, London	Solomon Rivers		Saul Henriques Valentine	Spitalfields, London	
8196	Valentine	Sarah	1827	Aldgate, London	(?) Fonseca		Philip Valentine	Aldgate, London	general shop keeper
23265	Valentine	Sarah Henriques	1835	Shoreditch, London	Jacob de Elias Henriques Valentine	Amelia (Malka, Miriam) de Meir de Uri		Shoreditch, London	boarding school pupil
29652	Valentine	Saul Henriques	1793	Middlesex, London	Emanuel Henriques Valentine		Sarah Rivers	Spitalfields, London	gold refiner empl 1
9615	Valentine	Solomon (Saul)	1844	Whitechapel, London	Abraham de Emanuel Henriques Valentine	Julia (Judith) Mordecai	Sarah Ornstein	Spitalfields, London	scholar
9613	Valentine	Sophia	1838	Whitechapel, London	Abraham de Emanuel Henriques Valentine	Julia (Judith) Mordecai	Samson Levy	Spitalfields, London	scholar
29654	Valentine	Susan Henriques	1842	?Spitalfields, London	Saul Henriques Valentine	Sarah Rivers		Spitalfields, London	
16523	Valentine	Valentine	1851	Clerkenwell, London	Isaac Valentine	Louisa Jane (?)		Clerkenwell, London	
9330	Valentine	Welcome	1790	Whitechapel, London	(?) Valentine			Aldgate, London	poor
15180	Valentine	Welcome	1838	Shoreditch, London	Jacob de Elias Henriques Valentine	Amelia (Malka, Miriam) de Meir de Uri		Shoreditch, London	scholar
15177	Valentine	Welcome Henriques	1802	Aldgate, London	Elias (Elis) Henriques Valentine	Rebecca de Aaron Alvares Da Costa		Shoreditch, London	
15184	Valentine	Welcome Henriques	1842	Strand, London	David Henriques Valentine	Isabella Mordecai		Stamford Hill, London	
9325	Valentine (Valentine Henriques)	Rachel	1777	Whitechapel, London	(?)		David de Joshua Valentine Henriques	Aldgate, London	poor
9326	Valentine (Valentine Henriques)	Rebecca	1801	Mile End, London	David de Joshua Valentine Henriques	Rachel (?)		Aldgate, London	tailoress
2923	Valery	Flora (Floretta)	1818	City, London	Abraham Henry	Emma Lyon	Julius Isaac Valery	City, London	
8128	Valery	Julius Isaac	1811	Surinam, South America	Abraham Valery		Flora (Floretta) Henry	City, London	foreign importer
5010	Vallentine	Benjamin	1806	?, London			Rosa Nathan	Birmingham	toy warehouseman empl 2 men
5012	Vallentine	Benjamin	1843	Aldgate, London	Benjamin Vallentine	Rosa Nathan		Birmingham	
11262	Vallentine	Isaac	1794	Middlesex, London	Nathan Breslau Valentine		Sarah Green	Aldgate, London	printer

ID	surname	given names	born	birthplace	father	mother	spouse 1	1851 residence	1851 occupation
5013	Vallentine	Isabel	1847	Birmingham	Benjamin Vallentine	Rosa Nathan		Birmingham	
19481	Vallentine	Jacob	1799	Aldgate, London	Nathan Breslau		Rachel Samuel	Strand, London	general dealer
19482	Vallentine	Rachel	1798	Whitechapel, London	Mordecai Samuel		Jacob Vallentine	Strand, London	general dealer
5011	Vallentine	Rosa	1821	Whitechapel, London	Nathan Nathan	Julia Solomon	Benjamin Vallentine	Birmingham	
19483	Vallentine	Samuel	1821	Soho, London	Jacob Vallentine	Rachel Samuel		Strand, London	general dealer
11263	Vallentine	Sarah	1801	Aldgate, London	Ephraim HaLevi Green		Isaac Vallentine	Aldgate, London	
4910	Valshack	Jacob	1829	?, Poland				Birmingham	barber
30655	Van Boolen	Eleazer	1849	Spitalfields, London	Marks (Marquis) Van Boolen	Esther Park		Spitalfields, London	
30653	Van Boolen	Esther	1820	?, London	Eliezer Lezer Park	Blume (?)	Marks (Marquis) Van Boolen	Spitalfields, London	hawker
30654	Van Boolen	Marks (Marquis)	1813	?, Holland	Levy Van Boolen		Esther Park	Spitalfields, London	
29314	Van Coppelen	Jacob	1808	?, Holland			Martha (?)	Wapping, London	rag merchant
29315	Van Coppelen	Martha	1809	?, Holland	(?)		Jacob Van Coppelen	Wapping, London	
22532	Van Dam	Emanuel	1822	Hamburg, Germany			Emily (Amelia) (?)	Whitechapel, London	cigar maker
22533	Van Dam	Emily (Amelia)	1820	Hamburg, Germany	(?)		Emanuel Van Dam	Whitechapel, London	dress maker
22537	Van Dam	George	1850	Stepney, London	Emanuel Van Dam	Emily (Amelia) (?)		Whitechapel, London	
22536	Van Dam	Henry	1848	Stepney, London	Emanuel Van Dam	Emily (Amelia) (?)		Whitechapel, London	
22535	Van Dam	Rachael	1848	City, London	Emanuel Van Dam	Emily (Amelia) (?)		Whitechapel, London	
22534	Van Dam	Raphael	1846	City, London	Emanuel Van Dam	Emily (Amelia) (?)		Whitechapel, London	
28842	Van Dantzig	Barnard (Barnett)	1850	Whitechapel, London	Lyon Van Dantzig	Rebecca (?)	Abigail Nathan	Spitalfields, London	
28836	Van Dantzig	Lyon	1815	Zutphen, Holland			Rebecca (?)	Spitalfields, London	general dealer
28840	Van Dantzig	Michael	1845	Amsterdam, Holland	Lyon Van Dantzig	Rebecca (?)		Spitalfields, London	
28839	Van Dantzig	Rebecca	1820	Amsterdam, Holland	(?)		Lyon Van Dantzig	Spitalfields, London	milliner + dressmaker
28841	Van Dantzig	William	1845	Amsterdam, Holland	Lyon Van Dantzig	Rebecca (?)	Charlotte Nathan	Spitalfields, London	
11815	Van Delden	Eleazer	1850	Whitechapel, London	Henry Van Delden	Elizabeth (?)		Whitechapel, London	
11812	Van Delden	Elizabeth	1824	Groningen, Holland	(?)		Henry Van Delden	Whitechapel, London	
11811	Van Delden	Henry	1815	Amsterdam, Holland			Elizabeth (?)	Whitechapel, London	cigar maker/journeyman
11813	Van Delden	Hester	1848	Aldgate, London	Henry Van Delden	Elizabeth (?)		Whitechapel, London	
11814	Van Delden	Julie	1849	Whitechapel, London	Henry Van Delden	Elizabeth (?)	H--- Oppenheimer	Whitechapel, London	
29183	Van der Rifel	Samuel	1801	Groningen, Holland				Whitechapel, London	merchant
23096	Van Goor	Caroline	1828	Whitechapel, London	Ezekiel Van Goor	(?)	Emanuel Vandervelde	Aldgate, London	cap maker
23095	Van Goor	Charles Coleman	1827	Whitechapel, London	Ezekiel Van Goor	(?)	Theresa Woolf	Aldgate, London	watch manufacturer
23097	Van Goor	Ellen (Helen)	1829	Whitechapel, London	Ezekiel Van Goor	(?)	Solomon Goren	Aldgate, London	cap maker
23093	Van Goor	Ezekiel	1795	?Groningen, Holland			(?)	Aldgate, London	steel pen manufacturer
23098	Van Goor	Louisa	1831	Whitechapel, London	Ezekiel Van Goor	(?)	Michael Jackson	Aldgate, London	embroideress
23094	Van Goor	Sophia	1826	Whitechapel, London	Ezekiel Van Goor	(?)		Aldgate, London	
26071	Van Leer	Amelia (Melly)	1822	?, Holland	(?) Cohen		Lewis (Louis) Van Leer	Aldgate, London	tailor
26070	Van Leer	Lewis (Louis)	1821	?, Holland	Moses Van Leer		Amelia (Melly) Cohen	Aldgate, London	tailor
26072	Van Leer	Marks	1826	?, Holland	Moses Van Leer		Sarah Manus	Aldgate, London	cigar maker
26073	Van Leer	William	1831	?, Holland	Moses Van Leer			Aldgate, London	cigar maker
6161	Van Noorden	Katherine	1793	?			Moses Ezekiel van Noorden	Bloomsbury, London	
6162	Van Noorden	Louisa	1845	Newcastle Upon Tyne	Philip Ezekiel van Noorden	Kate (?)	Maurice Dukas	Newcastle Upon Tyne	
6159	Van Noorden	Miriam	1833	Edinburgh, Scotland	Ezekiel Moses van Noorden	Kate (?)	Maurice Myers	Newcastle Upon Tyne	

ID	surname	given names	born	birthplace	father	mother	spouse 1	1851 residence	1851 occupation
6160	Van Noorden	Phineas Ezekiel	1826	Edinburgh, Scotland	Ezekiel Moses van Noorden	Katherine (?)	Sarah Benjamin	Bloomsbury, London	professor + publisher of music
4215	Van Oven	Barnard (Bernard)	1796	?, London	Joshua Van Oven	Elisabeth Goodman	Sarah Frances Cohen	Bloomsbury, London	physician in practice
16993	Van Oven	Georgina	1828	Tower Hill, London	Barnard Van Oven	Sarah Frances Cohen	Abraham Levy (Walter) Symons	Bloomsbury, London	
4217	Van Oven	Lionel	1829	Aldgate, London	Barnard Van Oven	Sarah Frances Cohen		Bloomsbury, London	merchant clerk
20985	Van Oven	Manus	1787	?, Holland			(?)	Aldgate, London	out of employment
20986	Van Oven	Marian	1798	?, Holland	(?) Van Oven			Aldgate, London	
4216	Van Oven	Sarah Frances	1799	Jamaica, West Indies	Yehuda HaCohen		Barnard Van Oven	Bloomsbury, London	
21476	Van Praagh	Aaron	1846	Spitalfields, London	Lewis Van Praagh	Elizabeth (?)	Marie Lackinbach	Spitalfields, London	scholar
4113	Van Praagh	Barnett	1847	Whitechapel, London	Moses (Morris) Van Praagh (Van Praagh)	Sarah Boam		Whitechapel, London	
21470	Van Praagh	Barnett (Barnom)	1841	City, London	Joseph Van Praagh	Maria (?)	Louisa Hart	Spitalfields, London	
4108	Van Praagh	Benjamin	1834	Whitechapel, London	Moses (Morris) Van Praagh (Van Praagh)	Sarah Boam	Annie Louisa Jordan	Whitechapel, London	
12241	Van Praagh	Benjamin	1834	Whitechapel, London	Laurents Van Praagh	Nancy? (?)		Whitechapel, London	walking stick maker
21468	Van Praagh	Benjamin	1835	City, London	Joseph Van Praagh	Maria (?)		Spitalfields, London	cigar maker
21475	Van Praagh	Benjamin	1842	Spitalfields, London	Lewis Van Praagh	Elizabeth (?)	Anna Green	Spitalfields, London	scholar
29319	Van Praagh	Catherine (Clartje)	1827	?, Holland	Coenraad Sammes		Louis (Leon) Van Praagh	Wapping, London	dressmaker
29321	Van Praagh	Conrad	1792	?, Holland			(?)	Wapping, London	general dealer
21474	Van Praagh	Elizabeth	1817	City, London	(?)		Lewis Van Praagh	Spitalfields, London	
12245	Van Praagh	Elizabeth	1841	Tower Hill, London	Laurents Van Praagh	Nancy? (?)		Whitechapel, London	
30099	Van Praagh	Elizabeth	1851	Spitalfields, London	Lewis Van Praagh	Elizabeth (?)		Spitalfields, London	
12242	Van Praagh	Emelia	1835	Whitechapel, London	Laurents Van Praagh	Nancy? (?)		Whitechapel, London	servant
21467	Van Praagh	Emelie	1832	City, London	Joseph Van Praagh	Maria (?)		Spitalfields, London	
7774	Van Praagh	Emily	1851	Whitechapel, London	Moses (Morris) Van Praagh (Van Praagh)	Sarah Boam	William Van Praagh	Whitechapel, London	
12240	Van Praagh	Esther	1831	?, Holland	Laurents Van Praagh	Nancy? (?)		Whitechapel, London	umbrella maker
29320	Van Praagh	Esther (Hester)	1850	Finsbury, London	Louis (Leon) Van Praag	Catherine (Clartje) Coenraad Sammes	David Abrahams	Wapping, London	
12248	Van Praagh	Frances	1849	Tower Hill, London	Laurents Van Praagh	Nancy? (?)		Whitechapel, London	
4109	Van Praagh	Hannah	1835	Whitechapel, London	Moses (Morris) Van Praagh (Van Praagh)	Sarah Boam	John Cashmore	Whitechapel, London	
21478	Van Praagh	Hannah?	1834	City, London	Joseph Van Praagh	Maria (?)		Spitalfields, London	
4110	Van Praagh	Jacob (Jacques)	1839	Whitechapel, London	Moses (Morris) Van Praagh (Van Praagh)	Sarah Boam	Rebecca Levy	Whitechapel, London	
21471	Van Praagh	Joseph	1806	?, Holland			Maria (?)	Spitalfields, London	general dealer
7773	Van Praagh	Joseph	1847	Whitechapel, London	Moses (Morris) Van Praagh (Van Praagh)	Sarah Boam	Matilda Levy	Whitechapel, London	
21477	Van Praagh	Joseph	1848	Spitalfields, London	Lewis Van Praagh	Elizabeth (?)		Spitalfields, London	scholar
12238	Van Praagh	Laurents	1803	?, Holland			Nancy? (?)	Whitechapel, London	shop keeper
4111	Van Praagh	Lawrence (Lazarus)	1842	Whitechapel, London	Moses (Morris) Van Praagh (Van Praagh)	Sarah Boam	Abigail Alexander	Whitechapel, London	
21473	Van Praagh	Lewis	1819	?, Holland			Elizabeth (?)	Spitalfields, London	ironmonger
4112	Van Praagh	Lewis	1844	Whitechapel, London	Moses (Morris) Van Praagh (Van Praagh)	Sarah Boam	Jane Katherine Jacobs	Whitechapel, London	

ID	surname	given names	born	birthplace	father	mother	spouse 1	1851 residence	1851 occupation
29318	Van Praagh	Louis (Leon)	1823	?, Holland	Conrad (Yekutiel) Van Praag		Catherine (Clartje) Coenraad Sammes	Wapping, London	grocer
21472	Van Praagh	Maria	1803	City, London	(?)		Joseph Van Praagh	Spitalfields, London	
12243	Van Praagh	Matilda	1837	Whitechapel, London	Laurents Van Praagh	Nancy? (?)		Whitechapel, London	
12246	Van Praagh	Minetta (Minnie)	1843	Tower Hill, London	Laurents Van Praagh	Nancy? (?)	Meyer Jacobs	Whitechapel, London	
21469	Van Praagh	Morris	1837	City, London	Joseph Van Praagh	Maria (?)		Spitalfields, London	cigar maker
4106	Van Praagh	Moses (Morris)	1811	Groningen, Holland	Abraham Moses Van Praagh		Sarah Boam	Whitechapel, London	diamond merchant
12239	Van Praagh	Nancy?	1810	?, Holland	(?)		Laurents Van Praagh	Whitechapel, London	shop keeper
18578	Van Praagh	Rebecca Sarah	1842	?, London	Moses (Morris) Van de Praagh (Van Praagh)	Sarah Boam		Whitechapel, London	
12247	Van Praagh	Rosetta	1845	Tower Hill, London	Laurents Van Praagh	Nancy? (?)	Jacques Whyman	Whitechapel, London	
4107	Van Praagh	Sarah	1807	?, Holland	Jacob Boam		Moses (Morris) Van Praagh	Whitechapel, London	
4105	Van Praagh	Solomon	1839	City, London	Joseph Van Praagh	Maria (?)		Spitalfields, London	cigar maker
12244	Van Praagh	Solomon?	1839	Whitechapel, London	Laurents Van Praagh	Nancy? (?)		Whitechapel, London	
10848	Van Praagh	Woolf	1828	Amsterdam, Holland	Abraham Van Praagh		Esther Abrahams (Vos)	Spitalfields, London	cigar maker
21071	Van Pragh	Joseph	1841	?, London				Dover, Kent	boarding school pupil
22150	Van Raalte	Abraham	1845	?, Holland	Solomon Van Raalte	Esther (?)		Whitechapel, London	scholar
22152	Van Raalte	Bernardus	1848	?, Holland	Solomon Van Raalte	Esther (?)	(?)	Whitechapel, London	
29581	Van Raalte	Betsey	1834	?, Holland	Jacob Van Raalte	Hannah (?)		Whitechapel, London	
22151	Van Raalte	Emanuel	1846	?, Holland	Solomon Van Raalte	Esther (?)		Whitechapel, London	scholar
22145	Van Raalte	Esther	1810	?, Holland			Esther (?)	Whitechapel, London	
29579	Van Raalte	Hannah	1799	?, Holland	(?)		Jacov Van Raalte	Whitechapel, London	
22149	Van Raalte	Herman	1842	?, Holland	Solomon Van Raalte	Esther (?)	Fanny (?)	Whitechapel, London	scholar
29578	Van Raalte	Jacob	1801	?, Holland			Hannah (?)	Whitechapel, London	general merchant
29580	Van Raalte	Joel	1832	?, Holland	Jacob Van Raalte	Hannah (?)	Fanny Abrahams	Whitechapel, London	cigar maker
22147	Van Raalte	Joost	1837	?, Holland	Solomon Van Raalte	Esther (?)		Whitechapel, London	apprentice to cigar maker
22146	Van Raalte	Lion	1836	?, Holland	Solomon Van Raalte	Esther (?)	(?)	Whitechapel, London	apprentice to cigar maker
22148	Van Raalte	Margaret	1839	?, Holland	Solomon Van Raalte	Esther (?)	Hartog Benedictus	Whitechapel, London	scholar
22153	Van Raalte	Matilda	1850	Whitechapel, London	Solomon Van Raalte	Esther (?)		Whitechapel, London	
22144	Van Raalte	Solomon	1804	?, Holland			Esther (?)	Whitechapel, London	commercial traveller in cigars
29582	Van Raalte	Susan	1836	?, Holland	Jacob Van Raalte	Hannah (?)	Adolphe Souweine	Whitechapel, London	
23240	Van Vliet	Caroline (Lena)	1828	Middlesex, London	(?) Nathan		Emanuel Van Vliet	Chelsea, London	
23239	Van Vliet	Emanuel	1819	abroad	Yehuda HaLevi		Caroline (Lena) Nathan	Chelsea, London	bootmaker
23242	Van Vliet	Rosetta	1850	Westminster, London	Emanuel Van Vliet	Caroline (Lena) Nathan	Jonas David Oesterman	Chelsea, London	
23241	Van Vliet	Sarah (Rosa)	1848	Westminster, London	Emanuel Van Vliet	Caroline (Lena) Nathan		Chelsea, London	
21989	Van Werden	Alexander Elias	1829	?, Holland	Elias Van Werden	Caroline (?)	Matilda Marcus	Whitechapel, London	
21984	Van Werden	Caroline	1795	?, Holland	(?)		Elias Van werden	Whitechapel, London	
21983	Van Werden	Elias	1793	?, Holland			Caroline (?)	Whitechapel, London	commission agent
21988	Van Werden	Elizabeth	1831	?, Holland	Elias Van Werden	Caroline (?)		Whitechapel, London	
21986	Van Werden	Henry Elias	1825	?, Holland	Elias Van Werden	Caroline (?)	Julia Marcus	Whitechapel, London	commission agent
21985	Van Werden	Julia	1824	?, Holland	Elias Van Werden	Caroline (?)		Whitechapel, London	
21987	Van Werden	Margaret	1827	?, Holland	Elias Van Werden	Caroline (?)	Jacob Brunn	Whitechapel, London	
10933	Vandenberg	Abraham	1822	Amsterdam, Holland	Isaac Van den Berg		Rachel Coronel	Spitalfields, London	cigar maker
17317	Vandenberg	Christina	1809	Rotterdam, Holland	(?)		Jacob Vandenberg	Wapping, London	

ID	surname	given names	born	birthplace	father	mother	spouse 1	1851 residence	1851 occupation
17320	Vandenberg	Elizabeth	1845	Whitechapel, London	Jacob Vandenberg	Christina (?)		Wapping, London	scholar
17318	Vandenberg	Hendrik	1842	Rotterdam, Holland	Jacob Vandenberg	Christina (?)		Wapping, London	scholar
17321	Vandenberg	Henry (Hartog)	1847	Wapping, London	Jacob Vandenberg	Christina (?)		Wapping, London	
10935	Vandenberg	Isaac	1850	Spitalfields, London	Abraham Vandenberg	Rachel (?)		Spitalfields, London	
17316	Vandenberg	Jacob	1813	Rotterdam, Holland	Yehuda		Christina (?)	Wapping, London	rag + metal dealer
17319	Vandenberg	Lyon	1844	Rotterdam, Holland	Jacob Vandenberg	Christina (?)		Wapping, London	scholar
10934	Vandenberg	Rachel	1824	?, Holland	David Coronel		Abraham Vandenberg	Spitalfields, London	
2586	Vanderberg	Elizabeth	1828	?, Germany			George Vanderberg	Hull, Yorkshire	
2585	Vanderberg	George	1815	?, Holland			Elizabeth (?)	Hull, Yorkshire	
7578	Vanderlyn	Abraham Joseph	1831	?Aldgate, London	Joseph Vanderlyn	Catherine Moses	Phoebe Nathan	Aldgate, London	dealer in china, glass + earthenware
10002	Vanderlyn	Barnet Joseph	1842	Aldgate, London	Joseph Vanderlyn	Catherine Moses	Ellah Jacobs	Aldgate, London	
16995	Vanderlyn	Catherine	1805	Amsterdam, Holland	Dov Behr Moses		Joseph Vanderlyn	Aldgate, London	
16996	Vanderlyn	Isabella	1836	City, London	Joseph Vanderlyn	Catherine Moses	Morris Hart	Aldgate, London	dressmaker
8490	Vanderlyn	Jeannetta	1838	Aldgate, London	Joseph Vanderlyn	Catherine Moses	Samuel Elias Moss	Aldgate, London	scholar
16994	Vanderlyn	Joseph	1799	Amsterdam, Holland	Abraham Vanderlyn		Catherine Moses	Aldgate, London	tailor
29478	Vandersluis	Abraham	1831	?, Holland				Spitalfields, London	cigar maker
23894	Vandersluis	Benjamin	1824	?, Holland	Solomon Vandersluis		Catherine (Killty) Kesner	Westminster, London	journeyman tailor
23895	Vandersluis	Catherine (Kitty)	1825	Chelsea, London	Isaac Kesner	Rebecca (?Abrahams)	Benjamin Vandersluis	Westminster, London	
23890	Vandersluis	Hannah	1827	Chelsea, London	Isaac Kesner	Rebecca (?Abrahams)	Samuel Vandersluis	Westminster, London	
23896	Vandersluis	Salomon	1850	Westminster, London	Benjamin Vandersluis	Catherine (Killty) Kesner	Elizabeth Mendelson	Westminster, London	
23889	Vandersluis	Samuel	1819	?, Holland	Solomon Vandersluis		Hannah Kesner	Westminster, London	shopkeeper
23294	Vandervorst	John B---	1815	?, Belgium			Kezia (?)	Mayfair, London	tailor master
23295	Vandervorst	Kezia	1816	Plymouth, Devon	(?)		John B--- Vandervorst	Mayfair, London	
23296	Vandervorst	Kezia Elizabeth	1845	Middlesex, London	John B--- Vandervorst	Kezia (?)		Mayfair, London	tailor master
28768	Vanliner	Isaac	1824	?, Holland				Spitalfields, London	cigar maker
30843	Vanloo	Esther	1826	Wapping, London	(?) Vanloo			Wapping, London	house servant
30844	Vanloo	Jane	1826	Wapping, London	(?) Vanloo			Wapping, London	house servant
30289	Varicas	Esther	1784	Whitechapel, London	Gabriel de Joseph Israel Brandon	Leah de Joshua Israel Brandon	Abraham de Judah Varicas	Bloomsbury, London	fundholder
30290	Varicas	Judah (John)	1828	Covent Garden, London	(?)	Esther de Gabriel Israel Brandon		Bloomsbury, London	
30291	Varicas	Lionel Emanuel	1841	Covent Garden, London	Abraham Robert Varicas	Louisa (Keturah) Sarah Salaman		Bloomsbury, London	scholar
21688	Varkevisser	Arie	1830	?, Holland				Islington, London	gentleman
11914	Vegevene	David	1798	Amsterdam, Holland			Esther (?)	Whitechapel, London	hawker
11915	Vegevene	Esther	1796	Amsterdam, Holland	(?)		David Vegevene	Whitechapel, London	
16398	Ventura	Deborah	1821	?, Italy	Abraham Belais (Belize)	Naomi (?)	Isaac de Joseph Ventura	Spitalfields, London	wife of a retired drug merchant
7305	Ventura	Eleazar	1844	Aldgate, London	Isaac Ventura	Deborah Belais (Belize)	Buena Belasco	Spitalfields, London	scholar
16396	Ventura	Elias	1843	Aldgate, London	Isaac de Joseph Ventura	Deborah Belais (Belize)		Spitalfields, London	scholar
16397	Ventura	Esther	1845	Aldgate, London	Isaac de Joseph Ventura	Deborah Belais (Belize)	Jacob (John) Noah (Da Costa Noah)	Spitalfields, London	scholar
16399	Ventura	Isaac Joseph	1811	abroad	Joseph Ventura		Deborah Belais (Belize)	Spitalfields, London	retired drug merchant
15211	Ventura	Paulina	1803	?, Germany	(?)		Chaim Ventura	Shoreditch, London	

ID	surname	given names	born	birthplace	father	mother	spouse 1	1851 residence	1851 occupation
11793	Vesterman	Michal	1825	?, Holland				Shoreditch, London	cigar manufacturer
18269	Veverz	John	1832	Leeds, Yorkshire				Whitby, Yorkshire	bookseller
25987	Vible?	Coleman	1833	?, Poland [?, Prussia]				Aldgate, London	carpenter
17297	Victorson	Anne (Hannah)	1851	Spitalfields, London	Victor Isaacson	Catherine (Jate, Esther) Cohn		Spitalfields, London	
17296	Victorson	Catherine (Jate, Esther)	1816	?, Poland	Moses Cohn		Isaac Victorson	Spitalfields, London	
17295	Victorson	Isaac	1825	?, Russia	Lipman Victorson		Catherine (Jate, Esther) Cohn	Spitalfields, London	cap maker master empl 1
29829	Vilberg	Frances	1805	Amsterdam, Holland	(?)		(?) Goldsmid	Wapping, London	
29828	Vilberg	Gabriel	1816	Amsterdam, Holland			Frances Goldsmid nee (?)	Wapping, London	general dealer
15335	Vile	Charles	1839	Bermondsey, London	George Vile	Charlotte (?)		Southwark, London	
15333	Vile	Charlotte	1798	Ramsgate, Kent	(?)		George Vile	Southwark, London	
15332	Vile	George	1802	Deal, Kent			Charlotte (?)	Southwark, London	hatter journeyman
14319	Vile	Heymann	1826	?, Germany				Manchester	merchant
15334	Vile	Sarah	1835	Finsbury, London	George Vile	Charlotte (?)		Southwark, London	
10705	Vince	Lazarus	1834	Amsterdam, Holland	Nathan Vince			Spitalfields, London	apprentice to cigar making
10703	Vince	Louis	1827	Amsterdam, Holland	Nathan Vince		Sarah Goldsmid	Spitalfields, London	journeyman cigar maker
30629	Vince	Samuel	1851	Spitalfields, London	Louis Vince	Sarah Goldsmid		Spitalfields, London	
10704	Vince	Sarah	1831	Amsterdam, Holland	Samuel Goldsmid	Fanny Rachel (?)	Louis Vince	Spitalfields, London	
23845	Viner	Joseph	1829	?, Germany				Soho, London	tailor
28251	Vitcoski	Michael	1829	?, Poland [?, Prussia]				Spitalfields, London	tailor
21359	Vogel	Frances	1833	Finsbury, London	Abraham (Albert) Levi (Leopold) Joel Vogel	Phoebe Isaac		New Cross, London	
7424	Vogel	Julius	1835	Finsbury, London	Abraham (Albert) Levi (Leopold) Joel Vogel	Phoebe Isaac	Mary Clayton	New Cross, London	clerk
7425	Vogel	Phoebe	1810	Finsbury, London	Alexander Isaac	Sophia Levy	Abraham (Albert) Levi (Leopold) Joel Vogel	New Cross, London	
13455	Voorsanger	Abraham (Albert Edward)	1849	Manchester	Edward (Elias Abraham) Voorsanger	Rebecca Abrahams	Caroline Wilkinson Stubbs	Manchester	
13453	Voorsanger	Edward (Elias Abraham)	1806	Amsterdam, Holland	Abraham Elias Voorsanger Klover	Sophia Tsipr Hartog Ries Levie-Weiner	Rebecca Abrahams	Manchester	steel pen mfr
13454	Voorsanger	Rebecca	1815	Abbots Bromley, Staffordshire	(?) Abrahams		Edward (Elias Abraham) Voorsanger	Manchester	
29890	Vos	Isabella	1848	Wapping, London	Solomon Vos	Leah Themans		Wapping, London	
29889	Vos	Leah	1821	?, Holland	Jacob Themans		Solomon Vos	Wapping, London	
29888	Vos	Solomon	1801	?, Holland	L--- Vos		Leah Themans	Wapping, London	tobacconist
14158	Voss	Rudolph	1822	Hanover, Germany				Manchester	merchant
19700	Wagg	Arthur	1842	Marylebone, London	John Wagg	Harriet Cohen	Matilda (?)	Marylebone, London	
14960	Wagg	Charlotte	1837	Middlesex, London	John Wagg	Harriet Cohen		Marylebone, London	boarding school pupil
19701	Wagg	Edward	1843	Marylebone, London	John Wagg	Harriet Cohen		Marylebone, London	
19699	Wagg	Emily Rachel	1841	Marylebone, London	John Wagg	Harriet Cohen	Henry Moses Merton	Marylebone, London	
19696	Wagg	Harriet	1804	Aldgate, London	Solomon Cohen	Hannah Samuel	John Wagg	Marylebone, London	
14941	Wagg	Henry	1840	Southwark, London	John Wagg	Harriet Cohen		Marylebone, London	boarding school pupil

ID	surname	given names	born	birthplace	father	mother	spouse 1	1851 residence	1851 occupation
19698	Wagg	Jeannett	1840	Marylebone, London	John Wagg	Harriet Cohen		Marylebone, London	
19695	Wagg	John	1793	Aldgate, London	Haim		Harriet Cohen	Marylebone, London	stockbroker
19697	Wagg	Marian	1837	Marylebone, London	John Wagg	Harriet Cohen		Marylebone, London	
16299	Wagner	?	1820	?, Germany				Dundee, Scotland	
22531	Wagner	Louis	1826	Hamburg, Germany	Michel Wagner		Matilda Wittmund	Whitechapel, London	cigar maker
14017	Wagner	M--- K---	1818	?, Germany				Manchester	commercial agent
26101	Wail	Solomon	1767	?, London			(?)	Aldgate, London	labourer
26321	Waingold	Moses	1822	?, Poland				Aldgate, London	necklace maker
7359	Waley	Arthur Joseph	1850	Marylebone, London	Jacob Waley	Matilda Montefiore		Marylebone, London	
7357	Waley	Jacob	1818	Finsbury, London	Solomon Jacob Waley	Rachel Hort	Matilda Salomons	Marylebone, London	barrister + Professor of Political Economy, UCL
7358	Waley	Matilda	1829	Aldgate, London	Joseph Salomons	Rebecca Montefiore	Jacob Waley	Marylebone, London	
7684	Waley	Rachel	1791	Middlesex, London	Nachum Kempe Hort		Solomon Jacob Waley (Levy)	Marylebone, London	
16462	Waley	Samuel Waley	1828	Marylebone, London	Solomon Jacob Waley (Levy)	Rachel Hort		Marylebone, London	stockbroker
7360	Waley	Simon Waley	1827	Stockwell, London	Solomon Jacob Waley	Rachel Hort	Emma (Anna) Hendelah Salomons	Marylebone, London	member of Stock Exchange + composer
7356	Waley (Levy)	Solomon Jacob	1791	Portsmouth, Hampshire	Jacob Levi		Rachel Hort	Marylebone, London	stockbroker
15802	Wallach	Henry	1791	Piccadilly, London				Piccadilly, London	
15803	Wallach	Julius	1818	Hull, Yorkshire	Henry Wallach			Piccadilly, London	
28994	Wallenstein	C---	1848	?, Poland [?, Prussia]	L--- Wallenstein	L--- (?)		Whitechapel, London	
28992	Wallenstein	H---	1846	?, Poland [?, Prussia]	L--- Wallenstein	L--- (?)		Whitechapel, London	
28990	Wallenstein	L---	1802	?, Poland [?, Prussia]			L--- (?)	Whitechapel, London	oculist
28991	Wallenstein	L---	1822	?, Poland [?, Prussia]	(?)		L--- Wallenstein	Whitechapel, London	
28993	Wallenstein	M---	1847	?, Poland [?, Prussia]	L--- Wallenstein	L--- (?)		Whitechapel, London	
28995	Wallenstein	P---	1850	?, Poland [?, Prussia]	L--- Wallenstein	L--- (?)		Whitechapel, London	
7426	Wallich	Nathaniel	1785	Copenhagen, Denmark	Koebmand Wulff Lazarus Wallich	Hanne Jacobsen	Juliane Marie (Mary Ann) Hals	Bloomsbury, London	botanist
20902	Walsrode	Lewis	1836	Hamburg, Germany				Liverpool	servant
24981	Walter	Amelia	1808	?, Holland [Zealand]	(?)		Michael Walter	Strand, London	
31160	Walter	David	1845	Cardiff, Wales	Leon David Walter	Hannah Michael		Cardiff, Wales	scholar
24984	Walter	Esther	1835	Liverpool	Michael Walter	Amelia (?)		Strand, London	
29602	Walter	Frances	1846	Stepney, London	Morris Walter	Hannah (?)		Whitechapel, London	
29598	Walter	Hannah	1811	Hamburg, Germany	(?)		Morris Walter	Whitechapel, London	
31159	Walter	Hannah	1811	Swansea, Wales	(?) Michael		Leon David Walter	Cardiff, Wales	
31161	Walter	Joseph	1846	Cardiff, Wales	Leon David Walter	Hannah Michael		Cardiff, Wales	scholar
24982	Walter	Leah	1832	Hull, Yorkshire	Michael Walter	Amelia (?)		Strand, London	working stationer
31162	Walter	Leah	1848	Cardiff, Wales	Leon David Walter	Hannah Michael		Cardiff, Wales	
18631	Walter	Leon David	1816	?, Germany			Hannah Michael	Cardiff, Wales	woollen draper
24980	Walter	Michael	1805	Hull, Yorkshire			Amelia (?)	Strand, London	stationer
29601	Walter	Michael	1844	Stepney, London	Morris Walter	Hannah (?)		Whitechapel, London	
29597	Walter	Morris	1801	Hull, Yorkshire			Hannah (?)	Whitechapel, London	master boot maker
24987	Walter	Myer	1843	?, London	Michael Walter	Amelia (?)		Strand, London	scholar
24986	Walter	Philip	1840	?, London	Michael Walter	Amelia (?)		Strand, London	scholar
29599	Walter	Philip	1840	Stepney, London	Morris Walter	Hannah (?)		Whitechapel, London	

ID	surname	given names	born	birthplace	father	mother	spouse 1	1851 residence	1851 occupation
24983	Walter	Sarah	1833	Hull, Yorkshire	Michael Walter	Amelia (?)		Strand, London	working stationer
29603	Walter	Sarah	1849	Stepney, London	Morris Walter	Hannah (?)		Whitechapel, London	
24985	Walter	Walter	1837	?, London	Michael Walter	Amelia (?)		Strand, London	stationer's assistant
29600	Walter	Walter	1842	Stepney, London	Morris Walter	Hannah (?)		Whitechapel, London	
10488	Walters	Amelia	1842	Spitalfields, London	Lazarus Walters	Hannah Aarons	Samuel Jonas	Mile End, London	scholar
10498	Walters	David	1842	Spitalfields, London	Philip Walters	Rachel Phillips		Spitalfields, London	
10492	Walters	Esther	1845	Spitalfields, London	Lazarus Walters	Hannah Aaron		Spitalfields, London	
10496	Walters	Jane	1844	Spitalfields, London	Philip Walters	Rachel Phillips	Joseph Davis	Spitalfields, London	
10489	Walters	Lazarus	1810	?, Germany	Naphtali Hirsh Lazarus		Hannah Aaron	Spitalfields, London	tailor
10497	Walters	Louis	1842	Spitalfields, London	Philip Walters	Rachel Phillips		Spitalfields, London	
10491	Walters	Louis	1844	Spitalfields, London	Lazarus Walters	Hannah Aaron		Spitalfields, London	
10490	Walters	Morris	1841	Spitalfields, London	Lazarus Walters	Hannah Aaron	Hester Moses	Spitalfields, London	
10494	Walters	Philip	1808	?, Germany	Naphtali Hirsh Lazarus		Rachel Phillips	Spitalfields, London	tailor
10493	Walters	Philip	1846	Spitalfields, London	Lazarus Walters	Hannah Aaron		Spitalfields, London	
10495	Walters	Rachel	1821	Shoreditch, London	David Phillips		Philip Walters	Spitalfields, London	
22647	Wanz	Eisik	1836	?, Poland [Krakuz, Poland]				Whitechapel, London	journeyman slipper maker
20764	Warburg	Eliza	1822	Middlesex, London	Lewis Morris		Simeon Warburg	Whitechapel, London	tobacconist's wife
20767	Warburg	Henry	1822	?, London	John (Jacob) Warburg	Sarah Barnet	Isabella Abraham	Bristol	tobacco manufacturer
21104	Warburg	Isabella	1821	Frome, Somerset	Moses Abraham	Esther Emden	Henry Warburg	Bristol	
20765	Warburg	John (Jacob)	1783	?, Germany	Simon Warburg		Sarah Barnet	Whitechapel, London	tobacconist + cigar manufacturer
21154	Warburg	Morris	1825	?, Poland				Aldgate, London	tailor
20766	Warburg	Sarah	1784	Stepney, London	Aharon Yissachar Behr Barnet		John (Jacob) Warburg	Whitechapel, London	
16743	Warburg	Simeon	1818	?, London	John (Jacob) Warburg	Sarah Barnet	Eliza Morris	Whitechapel, London	tobacconist
13716	Warchau	?	1827	?, Poland				Bloomsbury, London	journeyman tailor
29335	Warschauer	Bernard	1831	?, Poland [?, Prussia]				Whitechapel, London	tailor
29333	Warschauer	Lipman	1801	?, Poland [?, Prussia]				Whitechapel, London	tailor
4902	Warsham	Abraham	1825	?, Poland				Birmingham	tailor
85	Warshawsky	David	1825	?, Poland				Woolwich, London	dealer in jewellery
12717	Warthman	Ann	1799	Coventry, Warwickshire			Ann (?)	Coventry, Warwickshire	shoe binder
12716	Warthman	Isaac	1804	Coventry, Warwickshire			Ann (?)	Coventry, Warwickshire	boot + shoe maker
12720	Warthman	Isaac	1838	Coventry, Warwickshire	Isaac Warthman	Ann(?)		Coventry, Warwickshire	boot + shoe maker
12719	Warthman	Louisa	1831	Coventry, Warwickshire	Isaac Warthman	Ann(?)		Coventry, Warwickshire	ribbon weaver
12718	Warthman	Mary Ann	1827	Coventry, Warwickshire	Isaac Warthman	Ann(?)		Coventry, Warwickshire	silk winder
12721	Warthman	William	1841	Coventry, Warwickshire	Isaac Warthman	Ann(?)		Coventry, Warwickshire	errand boy
20125	Webber	Charlotte	1838	Soho, London	(?) Webber	(?) Lee		Soho, London	scholar
3226	Weil	Solomon	1821	Paris, France	Baruch Weil		Henrietta (Hannah) Joseph	City, London	merchant
17029	Weill	Georgiana	1845	?, England	Reuben Weill	Sarah (?)		Edinburgh, Scotland	scolar
17027	Weill	Reuben	1829	?, England			Sarah (?)	Edinburgh, Scotland	
17028	Weill	Sarah	1816	?, England	(?)		Reuben Weill	Edinburgh, Scotland	
30161	Weiller	Blumy	1799	Portsmouth, Hampshire	Yechiel Michael Hart		Henry Weiller	Hendon, London	monthly nurse
19722	Weiller	Sarah	1838	Middlesex, London	Joseph Weiller		Jacob Herman Cohen	Mile End, London	scholar
5025	Weinberg	Abraham	1822	?, Poland	Isaac Weinburg		Rebecca Alexander	Rickmansworth, Hertfordshire	scholar at Stepney College
16287	Weinberg	Isaac Julius	1833	?, Germany				Dundee, Scotland	

ID	surname	given names	born	birthplace	father	mother	spouse 1	1851 residence	1851 occupation
2694	Weinberg	Jacob	1830	?, Germany				Nottingham, Nottinghamshire	trader
27418	Weinberg	S---	1829	?, Poland [?, Prussia]				Whitechapel, London	tailor
25844	Weinstock	Samuel	1818	?, Poland [?, Prussia]				Aldgate, London	gas fitter
13570	Weiss	Joseph	1831	Poznan, Poland [Posen, Prussia]				Manchester	hawker + jewellery
17903	Welfare	Adelaide (Abigail)	1809	Southwark, London	Elias Abrahams		Henry welfare	Southwark, London	
17905	Welfare	Alfred (Abraham)	1837	Southwark, London	Henry Welfare	Adelaide (Abigail) Abraham		Southwark, London	scholar
17906	Welfare	Elizabeth	1841	Southwark, London	Henry Welfare	Adelaide (Abigail) Abraham	Gustav Samuel Frank	Southwark, London	scholar
17902	Welfare	Henry	1811	?, Poland [?, Prussia]	Eliezer		Adelaide (Abigail) Abraham	Southwark, London	cap manufacturer
17908	Welfare	John	1845	Southwark, London	Henry Welfare	Adelaide (Abigail) Abraham	Rebecca Collins	Southwark, London	scholar
17904	Welfare	Louis (Lewis)	1836	Southwark, London	Henry Welfare	Adelaide (Abigail) Abraham	Matilda Jane Warren	Southwark, London	cap manufacturer's assistant
17907	Welfare	Morris (Maurice)	1843	Southwark, London	Henry Welfare	Adelaide (Abigail) Abraham		Southwark, London	scholar
2345	Werner	Herman	1828	?, Germany				Leeds, Yorkshire	tailor
29650	Wertheimer	Adelaide	1850	Aldgate, London	Simon Wertheimer	Celia Myers		Aldgate, London	
24288	Wertheimer	Annette	1800	?, Austria	(?)		John Wertheimer	Bloomsbury, London	
5949	Wertheimer	Asher	1843	Soho, London	Samson Wertheimer	Helena (Henrietta) Cohen	Flora Joseph	Soho, London	
29649	Wertheimer	Caroline	1846	Middlesex, London	Simon Wertheimer	Celia Myers		Aldgate, London	
18579	Wertheimer	Caroline	1847	Soho, London	Samson Wertheimer	Helena Cohen		Soho, London	
29647	Wertheimer	Celia	1812	Middlesex, London	Israel Myers		Celia Myers	Aldgate, London	
16980	Wertheimer	Charles	1842	Soho, London	Samson Wertheimer	Helena (Henrietta) Cohen	Freda (Frederica) (?)	Soho, London	
16981	Wertheimer	Esther	1844	Soho, London	Samson Wertheimer	Helena (Henrietta) Cohen		Soho, London	
16979	Wertheimer	Helena (Henrietta)	1818	Fiert, Germany	Jacob Cohen		Samson Wertheimer	Soho, London	
24287	Wertheimer	John	1800	Aldgate, London			Annette (?)	Bloomsbury, London	master printer empl 50
24290	Wertheimer	Juliette	1840	City, London	John Wertheimer	Annette (?)		Bloomsbury, London	
24289	Wertheimer	Marianne	1837	Shoreditch, London	John Wertheimer	Annette (?)		Bloomsbury, London	
4827	Wertheimer	Miriam	1825	Whitechapel, London	Nathan Nathan	Julia Solomon	Meyer (Martin) Victor Wertheimer	Birmingham	dealer in watch materials
29648	Wertheimer	Rebecca	1844	Spitalfields, London	Simon Wertheimer	Celia Myers		Aldgate, London	
16978	Wertheimer	Samson	1811	Fiert, Bavaria, Germany	Michael (Yechiel) Wertheimer		Helena (Henrietta) Cohen	Soho, London	embosser empl 6
29646	Wertheimer	Simon	1815	?, Sweden	Isaac Wertheimer		Celia Myers	Aldgate, London	general dealer
21722	Wetzler	Sarah	1808	?, Jamaica, West Indies	(?) Wetzler			Highbury, London	house servant
17668	Weyl	Simon	1806	?, Poland [?, Prussia]				Spitalfields, London	dealer in fancy goods + agent
21298	Wezlar	Charles	1841	?, Jamaica, West Indies				Edmonton, London	boarding school pupil
14483	Whalberg	Joseph S	1819	?, Germany			Sarah (?)	Manchester	traveller in silk
14484	Whalberg	Sarah	1815	?, France	(?)		Joseph S Whalberg	Manchester	traveller in silk
7686	White	Abraham	1801	Spitalfields, London	Moses (Pinchas Zelig) White		Elizabeth Levy	Aldgate, London	butcher
30206	White	Anthony	1810	Lviv, Ukraine [Lemberg, Galicia]			Louise Isaacs	Great Yarmouth, Norfolk	clothier
30208	White	Baron (Beren, Benjamin)	1843	Great Yarmouth, Norfolk	Anthony White	Louise Isaacs	Eveline Samuel	Great Yarmouth, Norfolk	scholar
9506	White	Catherine (Kate)	1836	Spitalfields, London	Abraham White	Elizabeth Levy	David Levy	Aldgate, London	

713

ID	surname	given names	born	birthplace	father	mother	spouse 1	1851 residence	1851 occupation
9502	White	Ellen	1824	Spitalfields, London	Abraham White	Elizabeth Levy		Aldgate, London	domestic
30207	White	Isaac	1841	Great Yarmouth, Norfolk	Anthony White	Louise Isaacs	Ann (Annie) Wolf	Great Yarmouth, Norfolk	scholar
9504	White	Jacob	1832	Spitalfields, London	Abraham White	Elizabeth Levy	Rachel Myers	Aldgate, London	butcher at home
20022	White	Leah	1838	Whitechapel, London	Abraham White	Elizabeth Levy		Aldgate, London	
30205	White	Lena	1831	Berlin, Germany	(?) Goldberg		Anthony White	Great Yarmouth, Norfolk	
30209	White	Lewis (Louis)	1845	Great Yarmouth, Norfolk	Anthony White	Louise Isaacs	Alice Shannon	Great Yarmouth, Norfolk	scholar
9505	White	Lewis A	1834	Spitalfields, London	Abraham White	Elizabeth Levy	Elizabeth Bernal	Aldgate, London	butcher at home
9503	White	Sarah	1831	Spitalfields, London	Abraham White	Elizabeth Levy		Aldgate, London	domestic
28999	Wiener	Anstin	1829	?, Germany	(?)		Louis Wiener	Whitechapel, London	
29000	Wiener	Hannah	1849	Whitechapel, London	Louis Wiener	?Anstin (?)		Whitechapel, London	
28998	Wiener	Louis	1815	?, Germany			Anstin (?)	Whitechapel, London	shoe maker
2590	Wiener	Luis	1811	?, Germany			(?)	Hull, Yorkshire	
21420	Wierwode	Israel	1830	Kutnow, Poland				Dewsbury, Yorkshire	traveller
26241	Wildas	Asher	1827	?, Poland				Aldgate, London	tailor
27338	Wilkaski	Luis	1825	?, Poland [?, Prussia]				Aldgate, London	tailor
3504	Wilks	?	1851	Spitalfields, London	Lewis Wilks	Clara Davis		Spitalfields, London	
3494	Wilks	Ann Solomon	1831	Spitalfields, London	Abraham Solomon Wilks	Rosetta Abrahams		Spitalfields, London	waistcoat maker
3497	Wilks	Clara	1817	Spitalfields, London	Judah Davis		Lewis Wilks	Spitalfields, London	
3480	Wilks	Edward Simeon	1837	Manchester	Isaac (Israel) Solomon Wilks	Rosetta (?)	Julia Lazarus	Whitechapel, London	
3486	Wilks	Elizabeth Solomon	1822	Spitalfields, London	Abraham Solomon Wilks	Rosetta Abrahams		Spitalfields, London	dress maker
3484	Wilks	Esther Solomon	1820	Spitalfields, London	Abraham Solomon Wilks	Rosetta Abrahams		Spitalfields, London	
3493	Wilks	Esther Solomon	1850	Spitalfields, London	Israel Solomon Wilks	Nancy (Anne) Mendoza	Elias Woolf	Spitalfields, London	
3498	Wilks	Hannah	1842	Spitalfields, London	Lewis Wilks	Clara Davis		Spitalfields, London	scholar
3478	Wilks	Isaac (Israel) Solomon	1798	Spitalfields, London	Simon Solomon Wilks	Elizabeth (?)	Rosetta (?)	Whitechapel, London	general dealer
3487	Wilks	Israel Solomon	1825	Spitalfields, London	Abraham Solomon Wilks	Rosetta Abrahams	Nancy (Anne) Mendoza	Spitalfields, London	dressmaker + cigar maker
3499	Wilks	Judah	1846	Spitalfields, London	Lewis Wilks	Clara Davis	Rachel Aarons	Spitalfields, London	scholar
3501	Wilks	Leah (Elizabeth)	1848	Spitalfields, London	Lewis Wilks	Clara Davis	Lewis Simmons	Spitalfields, London	scholar
3496	Wilks	Lewis	1817	Spitalfields, London	Philip Solomon Wilks	Hannah Levy	Clara Davis	Spitalfields, London	fish dealer
3491	Wilks	Nancy (Anne)	1825	Aldgate, London	Eliezer Mendoza		Israel Solomon Wilks	Spitalfields, London	dress maker
3495	Wilks	Philip Solomon	1789	Spitalfields, London	Simon Solomon Wilks	Elizabeth (?)	Hannah Levy	Romford, Essex	broker
13328	Wilks	Rebecca	1844	Spitalfields, London	Lewis Wilks	Clara Davis		Spitalfields, London	
3479	Wilks	Rosetta	1814	Walton-on-Thames, Surrey	Joseph (?Jacobs)		Isaac (Israel) Solomon Wilks	Whitechapel, London	dressmaker
3492	Wilks	Rosetta Solomon	1849	Spitalfields, London	Israel Solomon Wilks	Nancy (Anne) Mendoza		Spitalfields, London	
3485	Wilks	Sarah Solomon	1819	Spitalfields, London	Abraham Solomon Wilks	Rosetta Abrahams		Spitalfields, London	
29799	Wilks	Saul Solomon	1811	Aldgate, London	Abraham Solomon Wilks	Rosetta Abrahams		Spitalfields, London	traveller
3503	Wilks	Simon	1850	Spitalfields, London	Lewis Wilks	Clara Davis		Spitalfields, London	
28516	Wilks	Simon	1850	Spitalfields, London	Lewis Wilkes	Clara Davis		Spitalfields, London	
2596	Williams	Betsy	1825	?, Poland			Morris Williams	Hull, Yorkshire	
2598	Williams	Mary	1850	Hull, Yorkshire	Morris Williams	Betsy (?)		Hull, Yorkshire	
2597	Williams	Morris	1826	?, Poland			Betsy (?)	Hull, Yorkshire	hawker
14021	Willing	Andries G	1849	Manchester	Gabriel A Willing	Maria (?)		Manchester	
14019	Willing	Gabriel A	1825	?, Holland			Maria (?)	Manchester	cotton merchant
14020	Willing	Maria	1830	?, Holland	(?)		Gabriel A Willing	Manchester	

ID	surname	given names	born	birthplace	father	mother	spouse 1	1851 residence	1851 occupation
26229	Willkops	Hersh	1791	?Germany [Herzogthum]				Aldgate, London	tailor
23224	Wineberg	Hannah	1829	?	(?) Van Meegen		Herman Wineberg	Hyde Park, London	
23223	Wineberg	Herman	1824	?, Poland			Hannah Van Meegen	Hyde Park, London	dentist
23226	Wineberg	Herman	1848	Paddington, London	Herman Wineberg	Hannah Van Meegen		Hyde Park, London	
23225	Wineberg	Herminie	1848	Marylebone, London	Herman Wineberg	Hannah Van Meegen		Hyde Park, London	
29952	Wineburg	Marian	1828	?, Germany	(?)		Philip Wineburg	Whitechapel, London	
29951	Wineburg	Philip	1828	?, Germany			Marian (?)	Whitechapel, London	skin dresser
6758	Winkler	David Edward	1823	Westphalia, germany			Jane Solomon	Wapping, London	commission agent
10570	Winters	Rebecca	1831	Hamburg, Germany	(?) Winters			Whitechapel, London	house servant
26370	Wise	Marcus	1815	?, Austria				Aldgate, London	merchant
86	Wise	Samuel	1826	?, Poland [?, Prussia]				Woolwich, London	boat maker
29783	Wise	Zachariah	1829	?, Poland				Whitechapel, London	cloth cap maker
12137	Witcofski	Celia	1825	?, Poland [?, Prussia]	(?)		Simon Witcofski	Spitalfields, London	tailor's wife
12138	Witcofski	Marcus	1843	?, Poland [?, Prussia]	Simon Witcofski	Celia (?)		Spitalfields, London	scholar
12140	Witcofski	Rachael	1850	?, Poland [?, Prussia]	Simon Witcofski	Celia (?)		Spitalfields, London	
12136	Witcofski	Simon	1822	?, Poland [?, Prussia]			Celia (?)	Spitalfields, London	tailor
12139	Witcofski	Simon	1848	?, Poland [?, Prussia]	Simon Witcofski	Celia (?)		Spitalfields, London	scholar
27416	Witkowsky	Solomon	1831	?, Poland [?, Prussia]				Whitechapel, London	tailor
19269	Witmond	Louis	1830	Amsterdam, Holland	Aaron Witmond		Elizabeth Drukker	Spitalfields, London	cigar maker
6696	Witmond	Morris (Moses) Aaron	1824	Amsterdam, Holland	Aaron Witmond		Betsy-Barend Gomperts	Spitalfields, London	cigar maker
2599	Wittenburgh	Henry	1823	?, Poland [?, Prussia]				Hull, Yorkshire	journeyman shoemaker
25242	Wittgenstein	Charles	1828	?, Poland [?, Prussia]				Clerkenwell, London	merchant in foreign goods
2591	Wittkosky	Maurice	1827	?, Poland				Hull, Yorkshire	shoemaker
2592	Wittkowskie (Witkoski)	Levin	1798	?, Poland [?, Prussia]			Rachel (?)	Hull, Yorkshire	dealer in hardware
2595	Wittkowskie (Witkoski)	Marcus (Marks)	1832	?, Poland [?, Prussia]	Levin Wittkowskie (Witkoski)	Rachel (?)	Janette Jacobs	Hull, Yorkshire	journeyman tailor
2593	Wittkowskie (Witkoski)	Rachel	1799	?, Poland [?, Prussia]			Levin Wittkowskie (Witkoski)	Hull, Yorkshire	
2594	Wittkowskie (Witkoski)	Sarah	1830	?, Poland [?, Prussia]	Levin Wittkowskie (Witkoski)	Rachel (?)		Hull, Yorkshire	dressmaker
26231	Wittles	Moses	1815	Warsaw, Poland				Aldgate, London	slipper maker
22135	Wizesinsky	Casper	1849	Dorking, Surrey	(?) Wizesinsky	Rebecca Miller		Whitechapel, London	
22134	Wizesinsky	Esther	1847	Reigate, Surrey	(?) Wizesinsky	Rebecca Miller		Whitechapel, London	
22136	Wizesinsky	Jeanette	1850	Whitechapel, London	(?) Wizesinsky	Rebecca Miller		Whitechapel, London	
22133	Wizesinsky	Poline	1846	Horley, Surrey	(?) Wizesinsky	Rebecca Miller		Whitechapel, London	scholar
22132	Wizesinsky	Rebecca	1825	Reigate, Surrey	(?) Miller		(?) Wizesinsky	Whitechapel, London	haberdasher
13578	Wodinsk	Marks	1829	?, Poland				Manchester	slipper maker
13577	Wodinsk	Solomon	1831	?, Poland				Manchester	slipper maker
22077	Wohl	Aryder	1806	?, Russia			Rebecca (?)	Whitechapel, London	dealer in trinkets
22080	Wohl	Line	1846	?, Russia [Decktin, Russia]	Aryder Wohl	Rebecca (?)		Whitechapel, London	
22078	Wohl	Rebecca	1813	?, Russia [Teshinofke, Russia]	(?)		Aryder Wohl	Whitechapel, London	
22079	Wohl	Shene	1832	?, Russia [Teshinofke, Russia]	Aryder Wohl	Rebecca (?)		Whitechapel, London	tailoress

ID	surname	given names	born	birthplace	father	mother	spouse 1	1851 residence	1851 occupation
7073	Wolf	Aaron	1834	Great Yarmouth, Norfolk	Shreiner Wolf	Mathilda (?)	Adelaide Falcke	Manchester	antiquarian
9272	Wolf	Amelia	1786	Whitechapel, London	(?)		David Wolf	Aldgate, London	
16093	Wolf	Ann	1848	Birmingham	Henery Wolf	Sarah (?)		Birmingham	
13959	Wolf	Ann (Annie)	1841	Great Yarmouth, Norfolk	Shreiner Wolf	Matilda (?)	Isaac White	Manchester	
1300	Wolf	Aron (Aaron)	1821	Plymouth, Devon	Marcus (Woolf) Woolf	Kitty (Kate) (?)	Phoebe Levi	Plymouth, Devon	jeweller
24872	Wolf	Charlotte	1803	?, Devon	(?)		John Wolf	Bermondsey, London	
9271	Wolf	David	1767	?, Poland			Amelia (?)	Aldgate, London	general dealer
14815	Wolf	Edward	1788	Bermondsey, London			Sarah (?)	Finsbury, London	general dealer
13958	Wolf	Emma	1839	Great Yarmouth, Norfolk	Shreiner Wolf	Matilda (?)	Alfred Samuel	Manchester	
17446	Wolf	Fanny	1826	Spitalfields, London	(?)		Moses Wolf	Aldgate, London	
17447	Wolf	Frances	1850	Whitechapel, London	Moses Wolf	Fanny (?)		Aldgate, London	
13961	Wolf	Frederick	1846	St Pancras, London	Shreiner Wolf	Matilda (?)		Manchester	
13957	Wolf	George Garcia	1837	Great Yarmouth, Norfolk	Shreiner Wolf	Matilda (?)	Bertha Hoffnung	Manchester	
13956	Wolf	Harriet	1835	Great Yarmouth, Norfolk	Shreiner Wolf	Matilda (?)	Walter Samuel	Manchester	
16091	Wolf	Henery	1816	?, Germany			Sarah (?)	Birmingham	railway porter
13960	Wolf	Isaac	1843	Great Yarmouth, Norfolk	Shreiner Wolf	Matilda (?)	Bloom Phillips	Manchester	
16627	Wolf	Isabella	1829	Manchester	(?) Wolf	Sophia (?)		Liverpool	hosier assistant
24874	Wolf	Isabella	1833	Whitechapel, London	John Wolf	Charlotte (?)		Bermondsey, London	
24871	Wolf	John	1803	Finsbury, London			Charlotte (?)	Bermondsey, London	seal skin dresser
23723	Wolf	John	1825	?, Germany				Liverpool	pedlar
16878	Wolf	Joseph	1814	Gdansk, Poland [Danzig, Prussia]			(?)	Cambridge	traveller
24873	Wolf	Julia	1832	Whitechapel, London	John Wolf	Charlotte (?)		Bermondsey, London	
84	Wolf	Julius	1829	?, Russia				Woolwich, London	cloth cap maker
16626	Wolf	Kate	1827	Manchester	(?) Wolf	Sophia (?)		Liverpool	housekeeper
30996	Wolf	Lazarus	1804	Warsaw, Poland				Bridgend, Glamorgan, Wales	travelling Jew
2601	Wolf	Mary	1791	Hull, Yorkshire			William Wolf	Hull, Yorkshire	
13954	Wolf	Matilda	1809	?, London	(?)		Shreiner Wolf	Manchester	
17445	Wolf	Moses	1823	Berlin, Germany			Fanny (?)	Aldgate, London	tailor
2900	Wolf	Phoebe	1824	Plymouth, Devon	John Levi	Elizabeth (?)	Aaron Wolf	Plymouth, Devon	
11235	Wolf	Rachael	1776	Whitechapel, London	(?)		(?) Wolf	Aldgate, London	waistcoat maker
9273	Wolf	Rebecca	1831	Manchester				Aldgate, London	
16625	Wolf	Samuel	1825	Manchester	(?) Wolf	Sophia (?)		Liverpool	smallware + hosier
14867	Wolf	Samuel C	1794	?, Poland [?, Prussia]			Sarah	Bethnal Green, London	furrier
14816	Wolf	Sarah	1794	Kingston-upon-Thames, London	(?)		Edward Wolf	Finsbury, London	general dealer
14868	Wolf	Sarah	1794	?, Poland [?, Prussia]			Sarah	Bethnal Green, London	
16092	Wolf	Sarah	1819	Birmingham	(?)		Henery Wolf	Birmingham	
13955	Wolf	Sarah	1829	Great Yarmouth, Norfolk	Shreiner Wolf	Matilda (?)	Jacob (John) Saqui	Manchester	
18957	Wolf	Saul	1847	?, Devon				Whitechapel, London	
13953	Wolf	Shreiner	1799	?, Germany			Matilda (?)	Manchester	curiosity dealer
16628	Wolf	Solomon	1831	Manchester	(?) Wolf	Sophia (?)		Liverpool	hosier assistant
16629	Wolf	Sophia	1793	?, Poland	(?)		(?) Wolf	Liverpool	

ID	surname	given names	born	birthplace	father	mother	spouse 1	1851 residence	1851 occupation
24875	Wolf	Theresa	1835	Bermondsey, London	John Wolf	Charlotte (?)	Charles Coleman Van Goor	Bermondsey, London	
2600	Wolf	William	1795	?, Poland			Mary (?)	Hull, Yorkshire	glazier
30986	Wolf	William	1828	?, Poland				Nottingham, Nottinghamshire	glazier
28546	Wolf (Woolf)	Caroline	1803	Amsterdam, Holland	Elikom Getschlik Jacobs		Moses Wolf (Woolf)	Aldgate, London	
28547	Wolf (Woolf)	David	1833	Spitalfields, London	Moses Wolf (Woolf)	Caroline Jacobs		Aldgate, London	jobber
28550	Wolf (Woolf)	Elizabeth	1838	Spitalfields, London	Moses Wolf (Woolf)	Caroline Jacobs		Aldgate, London	
28552	Wolf (Woolf)	Eve	1844	Spitalfields, London	Moses Wolf (Woolf)	Caroline Jacobs		Aldgate, London	
28548	Wolf (Woolf)	Lewis	1836	Spitalfields, London	Moses Wolf (Woolf)	Caroline Jacobs		Aldgate, London	
28554	Wolf (Woolf)	Michael	1850	Spitalfields, London	Moses Wolf (Woolf)	Caroline Jacobs		Aldgate, London	
28545	Wolf (Woolf)	Moses	1795	Amsterdam, Holland	Binyamin Wolff		Caroline Jacobs	Aldgate, London	hawker
28549	Wolf (Woolf)	Polly	1837	Spitalfields, London	Moses Wolf (Woolf)	Caroline Jacobs		Aldgate, London	
28551	Wolf (Woolf)	Rachael	1842	Spitalfields, London	Moses Wolf (Woolf)	Caroline Jacobs		Aldgate, London	
28553	Wolf (Woolf)	Sarah	1846	Spitalfields, London	Moses Wolf (Woolf)	Caroline Jacobs		Aldgate, London	
23773	Wolfe	Barnett	1835	Middlesex, London	Lawrence Wolfe	Rebecca (?)		Liverpool	furniture broker's assistant
27742	Wolfe	Elizabeth	1797	Whitechapel, London	Zadok Woolf			Spitalfields, London	servant
23774	Wolfe	Elizabeth	1837	Middlesex, London	Lawrence Wolfe	Rebecca (?)		Liverpool	
23777	Wolfe	Ester	1845	Liverpool	Lawrence Wolfe	Rebecca (?)		Liverpool	
23775	Wolfe	Frances	1839	Middlesex, London	Lawrence Wolfe	Rebecca (?)		Liverpool	
19583	Wolfe	Francis	1837	Bath	Solomon Wolfe	Phoebe Lyon		Bath	
1045	Wolfe	George	1817	Exeter, Devon			Rachel(?)	Exeter, Devon	traveller, stationery
30901	Wolfe	George	1817	Exeter, Devon			Rachael (?)	Exeter, Devon	traveller with stationery
23776	Wolfe	Hannah	1841	Liverpool	Lawrence Wolfe	Rebecca (?)		Liverpool	
19584	Wolfe	Hannah	1842	Bath	Solomon Wolfe	Phoebe Lyon	Harris Freedman	Bath	
21062	Wolfe	Henry	1841	?, London				Dover, Kent	boarding school pupil
171	Wolfe	Joseph	1830	?, Poland [Wisseck, Prussia]	(?) Wolfe	Faugel (?)	Rosina Harris	Sunderland, Co Durham	broker
23771	Wolfe	Lawrence	1812	Middlesex, London			Rebecca (?)	Liverpool	furniture broker
7575	Wolfe	Marcus	1812	Middlesex, London				Liverpool	Secretary of Hebrew congregation
19582	Wolfe	Phoebe	1804	Bideford, Devon	Francis Lyon	Sarah Woolfe	Solomon Wolfe	Bath	shopkeeper old clothes
30902	Wolfe	Rachael	1818	Barnstaple, Devon	(?)		George Wolfe	Exeter, Devon	traveller with stationery
1046	Wolfe	Rachel	1818	Barnstaple, Devon			George Wolfe	Exeter, Devon	traveller, stationery
23772	Wolfe	Rebecca	1813	Middlesex, London	(?)		Lawrence Wolfe	Liverpool	
23778	Wolfe	Richard	1848	Liverpool	Lawrence Wolfe	Rebecca (?)		Liverpool	
5118	Wolfe	Sarah	1796	Portsmouth, Hampshire				Portsmouth, Hampshire	dressmaker
18627	Wolfe	Solomon	1786	?, Poland [?, Prussia]			Phoebe Lyon	Bath	Synagogue secretary
1047	Wolfe (Woolf)	Henry	1819	Exeter, Devon				Exeter, Devon	traveller, jewellery
5015	Wolff	Aaron	1811	Hamburg, Germany				Birmingham	cigar maker
15185	Wolff	Abraham	1819	Middlesex, London	Mordecai (Mark) Wolff	(?Matilda Joseph?)	Miriam Joseph	Shoreditch, London	member of the Royal College of Surgeons
21305	Wolff	Edward	1839	Spitalfields, London				Edmonton, London	boarding school pupil
14990	Wolff	Esther	1844	Brighton, Sussex	(?) Wolff			Bethnal Green, London	boarding school pupil
5016	Wolff	Fanny	1846	Birmingham	(?) Wolff	Sophia (?)		Birmingham	scholar

ID	surname	given names	born	birthplace	father	mother	spouse 1	1851 residence	1851 occupation
7427	Wolff	Joseph	1795	Weilersbach, Franconia, Germany	David Levi	Sarah Lipchowitz	Georgiana Mary Walpole	Ilminster, Somerset	Anglican vicar
21285	Wolff	Lewis	1836	Spitalfields, London				Edmonton, London	boarding school pupil
17191	Wolff	Mark	1848	Middlesex, London				Fitzrovia, London	
16661	Wolff	Maurice	1797	?, France			Regina (?)	Liverpool	silk merchant
15186	Wolff	Miriam	1824	Whitechapel, London	Aaron Joseph	Matilda Phillips	Abraham Wolff	Shoreditch, London	
14952	Wolff	Rachel	1836	Brighton, Sussex	(?) Wolff			Bethnal Green, London	boarding school pupil
16662	Wolff	Regina	1809	?, France	(?) Wolff		Maurice Wolff	Liverpool	
5014	Wolff	Sophia	1815	Poznan, Poland [Posen, Prussia]			(?) Wolff	Birmingham	cigar mfr
23912	Wolfsohn	Magnus Leon	1816	Gnosen, Poland			Hannah Cook	Marylebone, London	general merchant, [---], silks &c
19149	Wolfsohn	Wolf	1829	?, Poland [?, Prussia]				Aldgate, London	cap maker
6641	Wolfson	Alexander	1837	British Isles	Jacob Wolfson	Rosetta (Hannah Casper?)		Shoreditch, London	
2938	Wolfson	Frances	1827	Aldgate, London	Jacob Wolfson (Woolfson)	Hannah Casper	Myer David Davis	Shoreditch, London	scholastic teacher
2940	Wolfson	Hannah	1800	?	Asher Ansel Casper	?	Jacob Wolfson (Woolfson)	Shoreditch, London	
6642	Wolfson	Martha	1838	British Isles	Jacob Wolfson	Rosetta (Hannah Casper?)		Shoreditch, London	scholar
31223	Wolfson	Meyer	1806	?, Poland			Elizabeth	Bristol	grocer
6640	Wolfson	Walter	1835	British Isles	Jacob Wolfson	Rosetta (Hannah Casper?)		Shoreditch, London	cigar --- apprentice
2939	Wolfson (Woolfson)	Jacob	1796	?Jersey, Channel Islands	Zeev Woolf		Rebecca Casper	Shoreditch, London	
23549	Wollff	Henry	1836	Liverpool	Israel Wollff	Sarah (?)		Liverpool	cashier to shop keeper
23550	Wollff	Isaac	1839	Liverpool	Israel Wollff	Sarah (?)		Liverpool	scholar
23546	Wollff	Israel	1803	Berlin, Germany [Berlin, Prussia]			Sarah (?)	Liverpool	cap maker
23548	Wollff	Nathan	1835	Liverpool	Israel Wollff	Sarah (?)		Liverpool	cigar maker
23547	Wollff	Sarah	1811	Berlin, Germany [Berlin, Prussia]	(?)		Israel Wollff	Liverpool	
3122	Wollman	Cecilia	1849	Sunderland, Co Durham	Marks (Mark) Wollman (Wolman, Woolman)	Frances Cohen	Mark Goldman	Sunderland, Co Durham	
3121	Wollman	Esther	1847	Newcastle upon Tyne	Marks (Mark) Wollman (Wolman, Woolman)	Frances Cohen	Isaac Kempner	Sunderland, Co Durham	
3120	Wollman	Frances	1823	Margonin, Poland [Prussia]	Michael Cohen	Adaline (?)	Marks (Mark) Wollman (Wolman, Woolman)	Sunderland, Co Durham	
30127	Wollman	Joseph	1851	Newcastle Upon Tyne	Marks Wollman	Frances Cohen	Bertha Kaminski	Newcastle Upon Tyne	
3119	Wollman (Wolman, Woolman)	Marks (Mark)	1823	Kepno, Poland [Kempen, Prussia]	Josef (Joseph) Wollmann (Wollman)	Sarah Kohn	Frances Cohen	Sunderland, Co Durham	general clothes dealer
13769	Wolstone	Bertha	1840	?, Germany	Isadore Wolstone	Mary (?Prager)		Manchester	
13770	Wolstone	Caroline	1844	?, Germany	Isadore Wolstone	Mary (?Prager)		Manchester	
13767	Wolstone	Isadore	1820	?, Germany			Mary (?Prager)	Manchester	tailor + draper
13768	Wolstone	Mary	1817	?, Germany	(?) (?Prager)		Isadore Wolstone	Manchester	
13771	Wolstone	Solomon	1847	?, Germany	Isadore Wolstone	Mary (?Prager)		Manchester	
20775	Wood	Minna (Marina)	1817	?, Germany	(?)		Woolf Israel	Covent Garden, London	brothel keeper
20873	Woodburn	Hannah	1823	Liverpool	Moses Samuel	Harriet Israel	Samuel Woodburn	Southport, Lancashire	
20878	Woodburn	Harriet	1850	Liverpool	Samuel Woodburn	Hannah Samuel		Southport, Lancashire	

ID	surname	given names	born	birthplace	father	mother	spouse 1	1851 residence	1851 occupation
20877	Woodburn	Henry	1849	Liverpool	Samuel Woodburn	Hannah Samuel		Southport, Lancashire	
20876	Woodburn	Samuel	1818	Liverpool			Hannah Samuel	Southport, Lancashire	watchmaker
17278	Woofshon	Herman	1829	?, Poland [?, Prussia]				Aldgate, London	tailor
14153	Woolberg	Solomon	1829	Hanover, Germany				Manchester	clerk
10761	Woolf	?	1844	Whitechapel, London	Abraham Woolf	Sarah (?)		Spitalfields, London	
8407	Woolf	?	1821	?				Southampton, Hampshire	traveller
22665	Woolf	Abigail	1818	?, London	(?) Solomon		Phineas Woolf	Whitechapel, London	
4200	Woolf	Abigail (Abagail)	1822	Spitalfields, London	Michael Abrahams		Henry Woolf	Spitalfields, London	dress maker
5743	Woolf	Abraham	1790	Spitalfields, London	Meshullam HaLevi		Elizabeth Samuel	Aldgate, London	ladies shoe maker
10758	Woolf	Abraham	1806	Whitechapel, London	Jacob Woolf		Sarah Debias	Spitalfields, London	dealer in hardware
15814	Woolf	Abraham	1825	Penzance, Cornwall				Aldgate, London	tailor
20060	Woolf	Abraham	1836	?Liverpool	Lewis Woolf	Frances Lyons		Liverpool	
21481	Woolf	Abraham	1844	?, Poland [?, Prussia]	Henry Woolf	Fanny Benjamin		Aldgate, London	scholar
28407	Woolf	Abraham	1844	Whitechapel, London	Benjamin Woolf	Rachael Hart		Spitalfields, London	
11671	Woolf	Abraham	1846	Aldgate, London	Juda Woolf	Catharine (?)		Aldgate, London	
20061	Woolf	Albert Lewis	1837	Liverpool	Lewis Woolf	Frances Lyons	Lucy Helen Jones	Liverpool	
971	Woolf	Alfred	1850	Barnstaple, Devon				Exeter, Devon	boarding school pupil
27481	Woolf	Alice	1834	St Giles, London	Zadock Woolf	(?)		Aldgate, London	flower maker
30676	Woolf	Alice (Eliza)	1851	Wapping, London	Moss Woolf	Priscilla Solomon		Wapping, London	
18085	Woolf	Ann	1846	Middlesex, London	Samuel Woolf	Sophia Levy		Southwark, London	scholar
7061	Woolf	Ann	1849	?, Poland [?, Prussia]	Henry Woolf	Fanny Benjamin	Lewis (Louis) Cohen	Aldgate, London	
13344	Woolf	Ann (Nancy)	1824	Whitechapel, London	Moses Symons		Woolf Woolf	Spitalfields, London	umbrella maker
29356	Woolf	Anne	1844	Wapping, London	Moss (Moses) Woolf	Priscilla Solomons		Wapping, London	scholar
30672	Woolf	Anne	1844	Wapping, London	Moss Woolf	Priscilla Solomon		Wapping, London	scholar
21482	Woolf	Asher	1846	?, Poland [?, Prussia]	Henry Woolf	Fanny Benjamin	Elizabeth Lewis	Aldgate, London	scholar
13038	Woolf	Asher	1849	Spitalfields, London	Woolf Woolf	Sarah Saunders	Dinah Tarohn	Spitalfields, London	
2012	Woolf	Barnett	1832	Spitalfields, London	Benjamin Woolf	Sarah Levy	Phoebe Levy	Spitalfields, London	
27480	Woolf	Barnett	1833	St Giles, London	Zadock Woolf	(?)		Aldgate, London	cigar maker
27503	Woolf	Barnett	1833	Middlesex, London				Aldgate, London	cigar maker
7414	Woolf	Barnett Samuel	1849	Southwark, London	Samuel Woolf	Sophia (?)	Caroline Neustadt	Southwark, London	
29361	Woolf	Benjamin	1786	Whitechapel, London				Wapping, London	no occupation
30677	Woolf	Benjamin	1786	Whitechapel, London	Tsadok			Wapping, London	no occupation
27864	Woolf	Benjamin	1796	Rotterdam, Holland			Rebecca (?)	Spitalfields, London	chiropodist
2008	Woolf	Benjamin	1805	Spitalfields, London			Sarah Levy	Spitalfields, London	furniture broker
3228	Woolf	Benjamin	1808	?Spitalfields, London			Isabella (Bloom) Phillips	Mayfair, London	tailor (empl 6)
28405	Woolf	Benjamin	1810	Whitechapel, London	Abraham Woolf		Rachael Hart	Spitalfields, London	clothes dealer
28382	Woolf	Benjamin	1819	Whitechapel, London	Eliezer		Hannah Pass	Whitechapel, London	china + glass dealer
14940	Woolf	Benjamin	1841	Brighton, Sussex				Bethnal Green, London	boarding school pupil
29355	Woolf	Benjamin	1842	Wapping, London	Moss (Moses) Woolf	Priscilla Solomons		Wapping, London	cigar manufacturer
30671	Woolf	Benjamin	1842	Wapping, London	Moss Woolf	Priscilla Solomon		Wapping, London	cigar manufacturer
29605	Woolf	Bertha	1831	Aldgate, London	Benjamin Woolf	Phoebe (?)		Stepney, London	theatrical actor
26399	Woolf	Betsey	1849	?, London	Reuben Woolf	Rachael (?)		Aldgate, London	
3233	Woolf	Bloom	1840	?, London	Benjamin Woolf	Isabella (Bloom) Phillips	Levi Cohen	Mayfair, London	
29357	Woolf	Caroline	1846	Wapping, London	Moss (Moses) Woolf	Priscilla Solomons		Wapping, London	scholar
30673	Woolf	Caroline	1846	Wapping, London	Moss Woolf	Priscilla Solomon		Wapping, London	scholar

ID	surname	given names	born	birthplace	father	mother	spouse 1	1851 residence	1851 occupation
11669	Woolf	Catharine	1828	Spitalfields, London	(?)		Juda Woolg	Aldgate, London	general dealer
2209	Woolf	Catherine	1798	?, Poland			Isaiah Woolf	Oxford, Oxfordshire	
28876	Woolf	Catherine	1824	Spitalfields, London	(?) Benjamin		Isaac Woolf	Spitalfields, London	
13264	Woolf	Catherine	1829	Whitechapel, London	Shmuel Zenvil Goldsmid		Daniel Woolf	Spitalfields, London	parasol maker
8000	Woolf	Catherine	1849	Spitalfields, London	Henry Woolf	Abigail (Abagail) Abrahams		Spitalfields, London	
20059	Woolf	Cecilia	1834	?Liverpool	Lewis Woolf	Frances Lyons	Simeon Cohen	Liverpool	
13037	Woolf	Cecilia	1846	Aldgate, London	Woolf Woolf	Sarah Saunders	Samuel Lesser	Spitalfields, London	
22971	Woolf	Charles	1768	Aldgate, London				Aldgate, London	clothes dealer
30507	Woolf	Charles	1819	?, Germany	Mordecai Woolf		Elizabeth (?)	Whitechapel, London	tailor
3234	Woolf	Clara	1845	?, London	Benjamin Woolf	Isabella (Bloom) Phillips	Benjamin De Jongh	Mayfair, London	
13263	Woolf	Daniel	1828	Liverpool	Jacob HaLevi Woolf		Catherine Goldsmid	Spitalfields, London	clothes dealer
10760	Woolf	Daniel	1842	Whitechapel, London	Abraham Woolf	Sarah (?)		Spitalfields, London	
5017	Woolf	David	1824	?, Poland	Ephraim (Edward) Woolf	Julia (?)		Birmingham	master shoemaker empl 10 men
27866	Woolf	David	1824	Whitechapel, London	Benjamin Woolf	Rebecca (?)		Spitalfields, London	general dealer
15769	Woolf	David	1831	Aldgate, London	Abraham Woolf	Elizabeth Samuel		Aldgate, London	journeyman cigar maker
3231	Woolf	David	1835	?, London	Benjamin Woolf	Isabella (Bloom) Phillips	Louisa Davis	Mayfair, London	
28384	Woolf	David	1845	Whitechapel, London	Benjamin Woolf	Hannah Levy		Whitechapel, London	
19273	Woolf	Edward	1839	Spitalfields, London	Zive (Zwe) Woolf	Rebecca Lyons		Spitalfields, London	
9442	Woolf	Elenor	1811	Brighton, Sussex	David Woolf	Rosetta (?)		Aldgate, London	
29360	Woolf	Eliza	1851	Wapping, London	Moss (Moses) Woolf	Priscilla Solomons		Wapping, London	
5744	Woolf	Elizabeth	1798	North Shields, Tyne & Wear	(Shmuel Aryeh Pais) Samuel		Abraham Woolf	Aldgate, London	
30508	Woolf	Elizabeth	1816	Whitechapel, London	(?)		Charles Woolf	Whitechapel, London	
2011	Woolf	Elizabeth	1829	Mile End, London	Benjamin Woolf	Sarah Levy	Henry Woolf	Sheerness, Kent	
18226	Woolf	Elizabeth	1839	Middlesex, London	(?) Woolf			Mile End, London	scholar
18543	Woolf	Elizabeth	1848	Hackney, London	Lewis Woolf	Esther Cohen	Barnett Barnett	Stoke Newington, London	scholar at home
28877	Woolf	Elizabeth	1849	Spitalfields, London	Isaac Woolf	Catherine Benjamin		Spitalfields, London	
28207	Woolf	Elsey (Allice)	1796	Euston, London	Avraham		Jacob Woolf	Spitalfields, London	
24913	Woolf	Emanuel	1812	Shoreditch, London				Bethnal Green, London	carver
8059	Woolf	Emilie	1845	Tottenham, London	Lewis Woolf	Esther Cohen	Louis Hobinstock	Stoke Newington, London	
7944	Woolf	Emily	1839	Liverpool	Lewis Woolf	Frances Lyons	Louis Ezekiel Eskell	Liverpool	
5019	Woolf	Ephraim (Edward)	1798	?, Poland			Julia (?)	Birmingham	shoemaker
29627	Woolf	Esther	1813	Middlesex, London	Moses Mosely		Lewis Woolf	Aldgate, London	
18539	Woolf	Esther	1817	Whitechapel, London	Henry Cohen	Sarah Barrow (Beracho)	Lewis Woolf	Stoke Newington, London	
20304	Woolf	Esther	1828	Chatham, Kent	(?) Woolf			Aldgate, London	general servant
5293	Woolf	Esther	1835	Middlesex, London	Levy (Lewis) Woolf	Hannah Moses	Hyam Lyons	Spitalfields, London	
30057	Woolf	Esther Solomon	1813	Spitalfields, London	Philip Solomon Wilks	Hannah Levy	Moss Woolf	Romford, Essex	upholsteress
21480	Woolf	Fanny	1813	?, Poland [?, Prussia]	(?) Benjamin	Anne (?)	Henry Woolf	Aldgate, London	
1289	Woolf	Fanny	1830	Middlesex, London				Plymouth, Devon	servant
15770	Woolf	Fanny	1835	Aldgate, London	Abraham Woolf	Elizabeth Samuel	Emanuel Henriques Valentine	Aldgate, London	
10954	Woolf	Fanny	1836	Spitalfields, London	Isaac Woolf	Jane Jacobs	Samuel Lesser	Spitalfields, London	tailoress
30058	Woolf	Fanny	1842	Spitalfields, London	Moss Woolf	Esther Solomon Wilks		Romford, Essex	
5022	Woolf	Fanny	1846	Whitechapel, London	?	?		Birmingham	
2211	Woolf	Fanny (Frances)	1822	Romford, Essex	Isaac Freedman	Jane (?)	Jonas Woolf	Covent Garden, London	

ID	surname	given names	born	birthplace	father	mother	spouse 1	1851 residence	1851 occupation
2014	Woolf	Fanny (Frances)	1830	Mile End, London	Benjamin Woolf	Sarah Levy	Simon Rosenberg	Spitalfields, London	
2218	Woolf	Flora	1828	Romford, Essex	Isaac Freedman		Hoorshall Woolf	Oxford, Oxfordshire	tobacconist's wife
19978	Woolf	Flora Norma	1848	?, London	Lewis Woolf	Esther Cohen	Isaac Harris	Stoke Newington, London	
10105	Woolf	Frances	1782	Aldgate, London	(?)		(?) Woolf	Spitalfields, London	dealer in ladies wardrobe
20058	Woolf	Frances	1816	Portsmouth, Hampshire	Charles Lyons	Phoebe Levy	Lewis Woolf	Liverpool	
27479	Woolf	Frances	1820	Sheerness, Kent	Nathan Levy		Zadock Woolf	Aldgate, London	
5285	Woolf	Frances	1841	Whitechapel, London	Israel (Isaac) Woolf	Rachel Samson	Simon Ferdinand Feldman	Aldgate, London	
18083	Woolf	Frances	1844	Middlesex, London	Samuel Woolf	Sophia Levy		Southwark, London	scholar
17479	Woolf	Frances (Fanny)	1844	Spitalfields, London	Zive (Zwe) Woolf (Wolff)	Rebecca Lyons	Angel Cohen	Spitalfields, London	scholar
10763	Woolf	Gershon (Gill)	1846	Whitechapel, London	Abraham Woolf	Sarah (?)		Spitalfields, London	
28383	Woolf	Hannah	1805	Whitechapel, London	David Pass	Esther (?)	Benjamin Woolf	Whitechapel, London	china + glass dealer's wife
29517	Woolf	Hannah	1809	Spitalfields, London	Zvi Hirsch HaLevi Moses		Levy (Lewis) Woolf	Spitalfields, London	
27411	Woolf	Hannah	1832	?, Poland [?, Prussia]	Joseph Woolf	N--- (?)		Whitechapel, London	tailoress
27412	Woolf	Heinrich	1843	?, Poland [?, Prussia]	Joseph Woolf	N--- (?)		Whitechapel, London	scholar
28193	Woolf	Henry	1807	Whitechapel, London	Hyam Wolf		Julia Levy	Spitalfields, London	shoe maker
6478	Woolf	Henry	1819	Exeter, Devon			Martha Hocking	Exeter, Devon	traveller with jewellery
21479	Woolf	Henry	1819	?, Poland [?, Prussia]			Fanny Benjamin	Aldgate, London	boot + shoe factor
4199	Woolf	Henry	1821	Spitalfields, London	Yehuda HaLevi		Abigail (Abagail) Abrahams	Spitalfields, London	cigar maker
10771	Woolf	Henry	1823	?, Germany [Calssathin, Germany]	Mark Woolf		Sarah Asher	Spitalfields, London	tailor empl 6
25100	Woolf	Henry	1823	Middlesex, London				Finsbury, London	umbrella + parasol maker
15768	Woolf	Henry	1828	Aldgate, London	Abraham Woolf	Elizabeth Samuel	Leah Woolf	Aldgate, London	journeyman tailor
2010	Woolf	Henry	1833	Ramsgate, Kent	Samuel Woolf	Rosetta Myers	Elizabeth Woolf	Sheerness, Kent	clothes dealer
9788	Woolf	Henry	1839	Middlesex, London				Kew, London	boarding school pupil
22668	Woolf	Henry	1849	?, London	Phineas Woolf	Abigail Solomon		Whitechapel, London	
2217	Woolf	Hoorshall (Harris, Herschell)	1826	Poznan, Poland [Pozan, Poland]	Isaiah Woolf	Catherine (?)	Flora Freedman	Oxford, Oxfordshire	tobacconist
29519	Woolf	Hyam	1840	Whitechapel, London	Levy (Lewis) Woolf	Hannah Moses	Julia Samuel	Spitalfields, London	
10950	Woolf	Isaac	1801	Amsterdam, Holland			Jane Jacobs	Spitalfields, London -	general dealer
28875	Woolf	Isaac	1826	Spitalfields, London	Yehuda HaLevi		Catherine Benjamin	Spitalfields, London	general dealer
15772	Woolf	Isaac	1839	Aldgate, London	Abraham Woolf	Elizabeth Samuel	Clara Cohen	Aldgate, London	scholar
13345	Woolf	Isaac	1843	Aldgate, London	Woolf Woolf	Ann (Nancy) Symons		Spitalfields, London	scholar
26056	Woolf	Isaac (Israel)	1824	?, Poland	Ephraim (Edward) Woolf	Julia (?)	Sarah Cohen	Birmingham	boot + shoe manufacturer
10106	Woolf	Isabella	1821	Spitalfields, London	(?) Woolf	Frances (?)		Spitalfields, London	
3229	Woolf	Isabella (Bloom)	1808	?, London	David Phillips	Bloomer Jonas	Benjamin Woolf	Mayfair, London	
2208	Woolf	Isaiah	1795	?, Poland			Catherine (?)	Oxford, Oxfordshire	general dealer
5283	Woolf	Israel	1818	Spitalfields, London	B--- Woolf	(?Frances) (?)	Rachel Samson	Aldgate, London	bath keeper + dealer in weraing apparel
28206	Woolf	Jacob	1796	Euston, London	Benjamin Woolf		Elsey (Allice) Abrahams	Spitalfields, London	coal dealer
14938	Woolf	Jacob	1836	?, Germany				Bethnal Green, London	boarding school pupil
22667	Woolf	Jacob	1848	Aldgate, London	Phineas Woolf	Abigail Solomon		Whitechapel, London	
2212	Woolf	Jacob	1850	?, London	Jonas Woolf	Fanny (Frances) Freedman (Friedman, Freeman)	Rebecca Jacobs	Covent Garden, London	
10951	Woolf	Jane	1801	Amsterdam, Holland	(?) Jacobs		Isaac Woolf	Spitalfields, London	general dealer

ID	surname	given names	born	birthplace	father	mother	spouse 1	1851 residence	1851 occupation
10772	Woolf	Jane	1819	Amsterdam, Holland	Henry Silver		Henry Woolf	Spitalfields, London	
13483	Woolf	Jette	1839	?, Poland [?, Prussia]	(?) Woolf	Rosalie Beaver		Manchester	
10952	Woolf	Joel	1828	Whitechapel, London	Isaac Woolf	Jane Jacobs	Helen (Ellen) Solomons	Spitalfields, London	baker
29611	Woolf	John	1811	Hanover, Germany			Harriet (?)	Aldgate, London	merchant
9789	Woolf	John	1838	Middlesex, London				Kew, London	boarding school pupil
2210	Woolf	Jonas	1821	?, Poland	Isaiah Woolf	Catherine (?)	Fanny (Frances) Freedman (Friedman, Freeman)	Covent Garden, London	working jeweller
11670	Woolf	Jonas	1845	Aldgate, London	Juda Woolf	Catharine (?)		Aldgate, London	
30675	Woolf	Jos	1849	Wapping, London	Moss Woolf	Priscilla Solomon		Wapping, London	
27409	Woolf	Joseph	1807	?, Poland [?, Prussia]			N--- (?)	Whitechapel, London	tailor
26364	Woolf	Joseph	1810	?, Poland				Aldgate, London	traveller
10762	Woolf	Joseph	1849	Whitechapel, London	Abraham Woolf	Sarah (?)		Spitalfields, London	
29359	Woolf	Joseph	1849	Wapping, London	Moss (Moses) Woolf	Priscilla Solomons		Wapping, London	
11668	Woolf	Juda	1821	Spitalfields, London			Catharine (?)	Aldgate, London	general dealer
5020	Woolf	Julia	1801	?, Poland			Ephraim (Edward) Woolf	Birmingham	
28194	Woolf	Julia	1815	Whitechapel, London	Mordecai Levy		Henry Woolf	Spitalfields, London	shoe binder
29520	Woolf	Julia	1843	Spitalfields, London	Levy (Lewis) Woolf	Hannah Moses		Spitalfields, London	scholar
4201	Woolf	Julia	1847	Spitalfields, London	Henry Woolf	Abigail (Abagail) Abrahams		Spitalfields, London	
22669	Woolf	Julia	1850	Whitechapel, London	Phineas Woolf	Abigail Solomon		Whitechapel, London	
29004	Woolf	Julius	1832	?, Poland				Whitechapel, London	tailor
29628	Woolf	Kish	1843	Spitalfields, London	Lewis Woolf	Esther Mosely		Aldgate, London	
13215	Woolf	Leah	1790	Bideford, Devon	(?)		(?) Woolf	Spitalfields, London	
2213	Woolf	Levi	1835	Middlesex, London	Isaiah Woolf	Catherine (?)	Catherine Leah Hobinstock	Oxford, Oxfordshire	general dealer
29516	Woolf	Levy (Lewis)	1795	Whitechapel, London	Myer Woolf	Judith Cohen	Hannah Moses	Spitalfields, London	general dealer
20057	Woolf	Lewis	1809	Middlesex, London			Frances Lyons	Liverpool	watch manufacturer
18538	Woolf	Lewis	1814	Whitechapel, London	Lazarus Woolf	Elizabeth (?)	Esther Cohen	Stoke Newington, London	potter
29626	Woolf	Lewis	1815	?, Russia	Kisch Woolf		Esther Mosely	Aldgate, London	furrier
27867	Woolf	Lewis	1825	Whitechapel, London	Benjamin Woolf	Rebecca (?)		Spitalfields, London	general dealer
26397	Woolf	Lewis	1841	?, Poland [?, Prussia]	Reuben Woolf	Rachael (?)		Aldgate, London	
22666	Woolf	Lewis	1847	?, London	Phineas Woolf	Abigail Solomon		Whitechapel, London	
28408	Woolf	Lewis	1850	Spitalfields, London	Benjamin Woolf	Rachael Hart		Spitalfields, London	
26059	Woolf	Lewis	1851	Birmingham	Isaac (Israel) Woolf	Sarah Cohen	Kate Ann Joseph	Birmingham	
16150	Woolf	Lewis (Lipman)	1831	?, Poland [?, Prussia]	Isaac Woolf		Rachel Moss	Whitechapel, London	tailor
18086	Woolf	Louisa	1847	Southwark, London	Samuel Woolf	Sophia Levy		Southwark, London	
1298	Woolf	Marcus	1781	?, Poland			Kitty (Kate) (?)	Plymouth, Devon	general dealer
9441	Woolf	Marcus	1807	Brighton, Sussex	David Woolf	Rosetta (?)		Aldgate, London	watch manufacturer
15227	Woolf	Mary Ann	1829	Stanbridge, Essex	(?) Woolf			Shoreditch, London	housemaid
14520	Woolf	Maurice	1823	Exeter, Devon				King's Lynn, Norfolk	traveller
8819	Woolf	Michael	1814	Whitechapel, London			Rachael (?)	Aldgate, London	fruit merchant + Passover cake baker
29518	Woolf	Michael	1836	Whitechapel, London	Levy (Lewis) Woolf	Hannah Moses		Spitalfields, London	
26396	Woolf	Michael	1839	Poznan, Poland [Posen, Prussia]	Reuben Woolf	Rachael (?)		Aldgate, London	
14939	Woolf	Michael	1840	Bethnal Green, London				Bethnal Green, London	boarding school pupil
15774	Woolf	Miriam	1843	Whitechapel, London	Abraham Woolf	Elizabeth Samuel	Isaac Hart	Aldgate, London	scholar

ID	surname	given names	born	birthplace	father	mother	spouse 1	1851 residence	1851 occupation
13039	Woolf	Miriam	1851	Spitalfields, London	Woolf Woolf	Sarah Saunders	John Jacob Mendes	Spitalfields, London	
30509	Woolf	Montague	1848	Whitechapel, London	Charles Woolf	Elizabeth (?)		Whitechapel, London	
10775	Woolf	Montague	1850	Spitalfields, London	Henry Woolf	Jane Silver		Spitalfields, London	
30632	Woolf	Morris	1851	Whitechapel, London	Charles Woolf	Elizabeth (?)		Whitechapel, London	
26058	Woolf	Morris (Moses)	1850	Stepney, London	Isaac (Israel) Woolf	Sarah Cohen	Lizzie (Eliza) Davis	Birmingham	
13346	Woolf	Moses	1846	Whitechapel, London	Woolf Woolf	Ann (Nancy) Symons		Spitalfields, London	scholar
29629	Woolf	Moses	1850	Aldgate, London	Lewis Woolf	Esther Mosely		Aldgate, London	
21941	Woolf	Moses	1851	Southwark, London	Samuel Woolf	Sophia Levy	Martha (?)	Southwark, London	
30633	Woolf	Moses	1851	Aldgate, London	Zadock Woolf	Frances Levy		Aldgate, London	
5018	Woolf	Moses (Morris)	1840	Whitechapel, London	Ephraim (Edward) Woolf	Julia (?)	Rosalie Pinski	Birmingham	scholar
30669	Woolf	Moss	1798	Whitechapel, London	Tsadok		(?)	Wapping, London	cigar manufacturer
29353	Woolf	Moss (Moses)	1798	Whitechapel, London	Z--- Woolf		(?)	Wapping, London	cigar manufacturer
2005	Woolf	Myer	1836	Chatham, Kent	Samuel Woolf	Rosetta Myers	Katherine Cohen	Sheerness, Kent	clothes dealer
30631	Woolf	Myer	1851	Spitalfields, London	Woolf Woolf	Ann (Nancy) Symons		Spitalfields, London	
27410	Woolf	N---	1811	?, Poland [?, Prussia]	(?)		Joseph woolf	Whitechapel, London	
8072	Woolf	Nancy (Annie)	1837	Aldgate, London	Benjamin Woolf	Sarah Levy	Jacob Moses	Spitalfields, London	
27868	Woolf	Nathan	1830	Whitechapel, London	Benjamin Woolf	Rebecca (?)		Spitalfields, London	general dealer
26398	Woolf	Philip	1843	?, Poland [?, Prussia]	Reuben Woolf	Rachael (?)		Aldgate, London	
15771	Woolf	Phillip	1837	Aldgate, London	Abraham Woolf	Elizabeth Samuel		Aldgate, London	
22664	Woolf	Phineas	1821	?, Poland [?, Prussia]	Ze'ev		Abigail Solomon	Whitechapel, London	leather dyer
29604	Woolf	Phoebe	1786	Aldgate, London	(?)		Benjamin Woolf	Stepney, London	shirtmaker
18084	Woolf	Phoebe	1845	Middlesex, London	Samuel Woolf	Sophia Levy	Montague Woolf	Southwark, London	scholar
13217	Woolf	Pricilla	1831	Exeter, Devon	(?) Woolf	Leah (?)		Spitalfields, London	
29354	Woolf	Priscilla	1820	Whitechapel, London	Abraham Solomons		Moss (Moses) Woolf	Wapping, London	
30670	Woolf	Priscilla	1820	Whitechapel, London	(?) Solomon		Moss Woolf	Wapping, London	
10774	Woolf	Priscilla	1849	Spitalfields, London	Henry Woolf	Jane Silver	Leonard Van Boolen	Spitalfields, London	
28406	Woolf	Rachael	1816	Whitechapel, London	Henry Hart		Benjamin Woolf	Spitalfields, London	clothes dealer
8820	Woolf	Rachael	1817	?, Holland	(?)		Michael Woolf	Aldgate, London	tailor
26395	Woolf	Rachael	1821	?, Poland [?, Prussia]	(?)		Reuben Woolf	Aldgate, London	
15773	Woolf	Rachael	1841	Whitechapel, London	Abraham Woolf	Elizabeth Samuel	Samuel Abraham Cohen	Aldgate, London	scholar
13348	Woolf	Racheal	1850	Whitechapel, London	Woolf Woolf	Ann (Nancy) Symons		Spitalfields, London	
5284	Woolf	Rachel	1815	Aldgate, London	Ephraim Samson	Hannah Myers	Israel Woolf	Aldgate, London	
13216	Woolf	Rachel	1829	Plymouth, Devon	(?) Woolf	Leah (?)		Spitalfields, London	straw bonnet maker
2007	Woolf	Rachel	1842	Whitechapel, London	Samuel Woolf	Rosetta Myers		Chatham, Kent	
6740	Woolf	Rayner	1847	Whitechapel, London	Goodman Woolf	Hannah Ascher	Charles Marks	Wapping, London	
1257	Woolf	Rebecca	1782	Redruth, Cornwall				Plymouth, Devon	annuitant
27865	Woolf	Rebecca	1795	Whitechapel, London	(?)		Benjamin Woolf	Spitalfields, London	
23140	Woolf	Rebecca	1798	?, Poland	(?)		(?) Woolf	City, London	nurse
24914	Woolf	Rebecca	1809	?Aldgate, London	(?)		Emanuel Woolf	Bethnal Green, London	cap peak stitcher
26394	Woolf	Reuben	1816	?, Poland [?, Prussia]			Rachael (?)	Aldgate, London	rag merchant
4198	Woolf	Rosa (Rose)	1851	Spitalfields, London	Henry Woolf	Abigail (Abagail) Abrahams	Solomon Lazarus	Spitalfields, London	
13482	Woolf	Rosalie	1814	?, Poland [?, Prussia]	(?) Beaver		(?) Woolf	Manchester	
18541	Woolf	Rosalie	1842	Wapping, London	Lewis Woolf	Esther Cohen	Isaac Harris	Stoke Newington, London	scholar at home
9443	Woolf	Rosetta	1782	Aldgate, London	(?)		David Woolf	Aldgate, London	
2003	Woolf	Rosetta	1801	Hamburg, Germany	Zvi Hirsh Myers		Samuel Woolf	Chatham, Kent	

ID	surname	given names	born	birthplace	father	mother	spouse 1	1851 residence	1851 occupation
2015	Woolf	Rosey	1835	Aldgate, London	Benjamin Woolf	Sarah Levy		Spitalfields, London	
2002	Woolf	Samuel	1799	Margate, Kent	Joseph Woolf		Rosetta Myers	Chatham, Kent	umbrella maker
18081	Woolf	Samuel	1817	Spitalfields, London	Baruch		Sophia Levy	Southwark, London	clothes salesman
3230	Woolf	Samuel	1834	?, London	Benjamin Woolf	Isabella (Bloom) Phillips	Sarah Davis	Mayfair, London	tailor (assistant)
13265	Woolf	Samuel	1850	Whitechapel, London	Daniel Woolf	Catherine Goldsmid		Spitalfields, London	
2009	Woolf	Sarah	1802	Spitalfields, London	Benjamin Levy	Elizabeth (?)	Benjamin Woolf	Spitalfields, London	
10759	Woolf	Sarah	1806	Whitechapel, London	Joseph Debias		Abraham Woolf	Spitalfields, London	
13036	Woolf	Sarah	1824	Whitechapel, London	Asher Saunders		Woolf Woolf	Spitalfields, London	
26057	Woolf	Sarah	1824	Southwark, London	Moses Cohen	Abigail (?)	Isaac (Israel) Woolf	Birmingham	boot + shoe manufacturer
5021	Woolf	Sarah	1832	?, Poland	Ephraim (Edward) Woolf	Julia (?)	Solomon Isaacs	Birmingham	
10953	Woolf	Sarah	1834	Spitalfields, London	Isaac Woolf	Jane Jacobs		Spitalfields, London	cap maker
28195	Woolf	Sarah	1839	Whitechapel, London	Henry Wolf	Julia Levy		Spitalfields, London	shoe maker
18542	Woolf	Sarah	1844	Wapping, London	Lewis Woolf	Esther Cohen	F--- J--- Sessel	Stoke Newington, London	scholar at home
10773	Woolf	Sarah	1847	Spitalfields, London	Henry Woolf	Sarah Asher	Oscar Alexander	Spitalfields, London	
27482	Woolf	Sarah	1847	Middlesex, London	Zadock Woolf	Frances Levy	Emanuel Abrahams	Aldgate, London	
18540	Woolf	Sidney	1837	Wapping, London	Lewis Woolf	Esther Cohen	Isabella (Welcome) Nunes Carvalho	Stoke Newington, London	scholar at home
5668	Woolf	Sidney (Solomon Rees)	1844	Westminster, London	Benjamin Woolf	Isabella (Bloom) Phillips	Marie Goldstucker nee de Jongh	Mayfair, London	
13347	Woolf	Simon	1848	Whitechapel, London	Woolf Woolf	Ann (Nancy) Symons		Spitalfields, London	scholar
12631	Woolf	Solomon	1828	?, Poland [?, Prussia]				Birmingham	fireman
18088	Woolf	Solomon	1850	Southwark, London	Samuel Woolf	Sophia Levy	Clara Levy	Southwark, London	
30630	Woolf	Solomon Nathan	1851	Aldgate, London	Lewis Woolf	Esther Mosely		Aldgate, London	
18082	Woolf	Sophia	1820	Whitechapel, London	(?) Levy		Samuel Woolf	Southwark, London	
3232	Woolf	Sophia	1841	?, London	Benjamin Woolf	Isabella (Bloom) Phillips	Baruch Castello	Mayfair, London	
29358	Woolf	Sophia	1848	Wapping, London	Moss (Moses) Woolf	Priscilla Solomons		Wapping, London	
30674	Woolf	Sophia	1848	Wapping, London	Moss Woolf	Priscilla Solomon		Wapping, London	
13035	Woolf	Woolf	1821	Whitechapel, London	Isaac Woolf		Sarah Saunders	Spitalfields, London	boot maker
13343	Woolf	Woolf	1826	Whitechapel, London	Jacob Woolf		Ann (Nancy) Symons	Spitalfields, London	dealer in jewellery, china, glass + hardware
13266	Woolf	Woolf	1849	Whitechapel, London	Daniel Woolf	Catherine Goldsmid		Spitalfields, London	
28878	Woolf	Woolf	1850	Spitalfields, London	Isaac Woolf	Catherine Benjamin		Spitalfields, London	
27478	Woolf	Zadock	1809	Spitalfields, London	Baruch Woolf		(?)	Aldgate, London	broker (furniture)
1393	Woolf (Wolf)	Ann (Agnes)	1818	Portsmouth, Hampshire	John Levi	Elizabeth (?)	William Woolf (Wolf)	Plymouth, Devon	
1394	Woolf (Wolf)	Edwin (Ervin)	1840	Plymouth, Devon	William Woolf (Wolf)	Ann (Agnes) Levi	Sarah Stadthagen	Plymouth, Devon	scholar
1299	Woolf (Wolf)	Kitty (Kate)	1790	Palonas, Russia			Marcus Woolf	Plymouth, Devon	
1395	Woolf (Wolf)	Solomon	1847	Plymouth, Devon	Wiliam Woolf (Wolf)	Ann (Agnes) Levi	Annie Marcoso	Plymouth, Devon	scholar
1392	Woolf (Wolf)	William	1810	Exeter, Devon	Isaac Wolf		Ann (Agnes) Levi	Plymouth, Devon	tradesman
22601	Woolf (Wolfe)	Ephraim	1813	?, Poland	Woolf Woolf		Hannah Barnett	Stepney, London	shoe maker
22602	Woolf (Wolfe)	Hannah	1815	?, Cambridgeshire	Abraham Barnett		Ephraim Woolf (Wolfe)	Stepney, London	
22605	Woolf (Wolfe)	Maurice	1850	Whitechapel, London	(?) Woolf (Wolfe)	Sarah (?)		Stepney, London	
22603	Woolf (Wolfe)	Rachel	1845	Whitechapel, London	Ephraim Woolf (Wolfe)	Hannah Barnett		Stepney, London	scholar
22604	Woolf (Wolfe)	Sarah	1816	Whitechapel, London	(?)		(?) Woolf (Wolfe)	Stepney, London	
17482	Woolf (Wolff)	Annie	1851	Spitalfields, London	Zive (Zwe) Woolf (Wolff)	Rebecca Lyons		Spitalfields, London	

ID	surname	given names	born	birthplace	father	mother	spouse 1	1851 residence	1851 occupation
17476	Woolf (Wolff)	Elias	1779	?, Poland [?, Prussia]	Shmuel Lissa		Ann Josephson	Spitalfields, London	pencil maker + artist's colourman
19274	Woolf (Wolff)	Lewis	1842	Spitalfields, London	Zive (Zwe) Woolf (Wolff)	Rebecca Lyons		Spitalfields, London	
17481	Woolf (Wolff)	Naphtali Henry	1847	Spitalfields, London	Zive (Zwe) Woolf (Wolff)	Rebecca Lyons		Spitalfields, London	
17478	Woolf (Wolff)	Rebecca	1817	Spitalfields, London	Aaron Lyons	Abigail Solomon	Zive (Zwe) Woolf (Wolff)	Spitalfields, London	
17480	Woolf (Wolff)	Samuel	1846	Spitalfields, London	Zive (Zwe) Woolf (Wolff)	Rebecca Lyons		Spitalfields, London	
17477	Woolf (Wolff)	Zive (Zwe)	1814	Aldgate, London	Elias Woolf	Ann Josephson	Rebecca Lyons	Spitalfields, London	pencil maker + artist's colourman
23714	Woolfe	Amelia	1840	Liverpool	Nathan Woolfe	Rachael (?)		Liverpool	scholar at home
21050	Woolfe	Elias	1841	?, London				Dover, Kent	boarding school pupil
13496	Woolfe	Elizabeth	1800	Manchester	(?)		(?) Woolfe	Manchester	home keeper
13498	Woolfe	George	1837	Manchester	(?) Woolfe	Elizabeth (?)		Manchester	cigar maker
21155	Woolfe	James	1831	?, Poland				Aldgate, London	tailor
13497	Woolfe	Joseph	1834	Manchester	(?) Woolfe	Elizabeth (?)		Manchester	hooker
23712	Woolfe	Mena	1836	Liverpool	Nathan Woolfe	Rachael (?)		Liverpool	scholar at home
23710	Woolfe	Nathan	1806	?, Poland			Rachael (?)	Liverpool	general dealer in watches
23713	Woolfe	Nathan	1837	Liverpool	Nathan Woolfe	Rachael (?)		Liverpool	watchmaker's apprentice
23711	Woolfe	Rachael	1807	?, Poland	(?)		Nathan Woolfe	Liverpool	
29129	Woolff	Abraham	1818	Poznan, Poland [Posen, Prussia]			Mary (?)	Whitechapel, London	tailor
22735	Woolff	Elizabeth	1797	City, London	(?)		(?) Woolff	Whitechapel, London	
29131	Woolff	Henry	1851	?Whitechapel, London	Abraham Woolff	Mary (?)		Whitechapel, London	
22738	Woolff	Isaac	1827	Spitalfields, London	(?) Woolff	Elizabeth (?)		Whitechapel, London	general dealer
22736	Woolff	Jones	1823	Spitalfields, London	(?) Woolff	Elizabeth (?)		Whitechapel, London	general dealer
29130	Woolff	Mary	1823	Gothenburg, Sweden	(?)		Abraham Woolf	Whitechapel, London	
22740	Woolff	Nancy	1844	Spitalfields, London	(?) Woolff	Elizabeth (?)		Whitechapel, London	scholar
22737	Woolff	Samuel	1825	Spitalfields, London	(?) Woolff	Elizabeth (?)		Whitechapel, London	general dealer
22739	Woolff	Sophia	1832	Spitalfields, London	(?) Woolff	Elizabeth (?)		Whitechapel, London	dress maker
14937	Woolfgang	Elias	1841	?, Hungary				Bethnal Green, London	boarding school pupil
14936	Woolfgang	Samuel	1839	?, Hungary				Bethnal Green, London	boarding school pupil
20995	Woolfson	Aaron	1811	?, Poland				Aldgate, London	
6000	Worms	Amelia	1842	Whitechapel, London	Henry Worms	Rebecca Nathan	Edgar Lindo	Chelsea, London	scholar
21917	Worms	Amelia	1847	Clerkenwell, London	Solomon Worms	Mary (?)		Clerkenwell, London	
6015	Worms	Anthony de	1831	Regent's Park, London	Solomon Benedict de Worms	Henrietta Samuel	Emma A (?)	Marylebone, London	
15913	Worms	Aron	1850	Chelsea, London	Henry Worms	Rebecca Nathan		Chelsea, London	
28378	Worms	Eliza	1834	Whitechapel, London	Lewis Worms	Hannah Joseph		Whitechapel, London	
6006	Worms	Elizabeth	1801	Marylebone, London	(?)		Lewis Worms	Holborn, London	
24315	Worms	Elizabeth	1816	Middlesex, London	(?)		Morris Worms	Covent Garden, London	
15916	Worms	Ellen	1836	Marylebone, London	Solomon Benedict Worms (De Worms)	Henrietta Samuel	Adolph Landauer	Marylebone, London	scholar at home
28377	Worms	Emily	1833	Whitechapel, London	Lewis Worms	Hannah Joseph		Whitechapel, London	
6009	Worms	Emily	1845	Clerkenwell, London	Lewis Worms	Elizabeth (?)		Holborn, London	
21914	Worms	Emma	1833	Holborn, London	Solomon Worms	Mary (?)		Clerkenwell, London	furrier + sewer
6002	Worms	Esther	1848	Chelsea, London	Henry Worms	Rebecca Nathan		Chelsea, London	scholar
15914	Worms	Fanny	1832	Clerkenwell, London	Lewis Worms	Elizabeth (?)		Holborn, London	seamstress

ID	surname	given names	born	birthplace	father	mother	spouse 1	1851 residence	1851 occupation
21915	Worms	George	1839	Clerkenwell, London	Solomon Worms	Mary (?)		Clerkenwell, London	scholar at home
6012	Worms	George de	1829	Regent's Park, London	Solomon Benedict de Worms	Henrietta Samuel	Louisa De Samuel	Marylebone, London	gentleman
28379	Worms	Hannah	1805	Whitechapel, London	Simon Joseph		Lewis Worms	Whitechapel, London	linen draper
6011	Worms	Hannah	1835	Holborn, London	Lewis Worms	Elizabeth (?)		Holborn, London	seamstress
28381	Worms	Hannah	1848	Clapton, London	Lewis Worms	Hannah Joseph		Whitechapel, London	scholar
21916	Worms	Hannet	1843	Holborn, London	Solomon Worms	Mary (?)		Clerkenwell, London	scholar at home
5996	Worms	Henry	1808	Whitechapel, London	Aaron Cohen Worms	Rachel Lamert	Rebecca Nathan	Chelsea, London	boot + shoe maker
5999	Worms	Henry	1841	Whitechapel, London	Henry Worms	Rebecca Nathan	Louise Danziger	Chelsea, London	scholar
24135	Worms	Isabella	1815	Abergavenny, Monmouthshire, Wales	Nathan Isaacs		Matthew Aaron Worms	Bloomsbury, London	
24316	Worms	Isabella	1840	Middlesex, London	Morris Worms	Elizabeth (?)		Covent Garden, London	scholar
24319	Worms	Isabella	1847	Middlesex, London	Morris Worms	Elizabeth (?)		Covent Garden, London	
24317	Worms	Jane	1842	St Giles, London	Morris Worms	Elizabeth (?)		Covent Garden, London	
5995	Worms	Joseph	1806	Whitechapel, London	Aaron Cohen Worms	Rachel Lamert		Chelsea, London	
24318	Worms	Joseph	1845	St Giles, London	Morris Worms	Elizabeth (?)		Covent Garden, London	
28380	Worms	Joseph Lewis	1842	Bow, London	Lewis Worms	Hannah Joseph		Whitechapel, London	scholar
24320	Worms	Julia	1850	St Giles, London	Morris Worms	Elizabeth (?)		Covent Garden, London	
6007	Worms	Laetitia	1827	Whitechapel, London	Lewis Worms	Hannah Joseph		Whitechapel, London	
30375	Worms	Lewis	1791	?, Germany				Cheadle, Staffordshire	traveller vagrant
30488	Worms	Lewis	1791	?, Germany				Cheadle, Cheshire	traveller vagrant
6005	Worms	Lewis	1799	Spitalfields, London			Elizabeth (?)	Holborn, London	appraiser broker
28376	Worms	Lewis	1805	Spitalfields, London	Aaron Worms		Hannah Joseph	Whitechapel, London	linen draper
9790	Worms	Lewis	1839	Middlesex, London				Kew, London	boarding school pupil
21913	Worms	Mary	1808	Whitechapel, London	(?)		Solomon Worms	Clerkenwell, London	
24134	Worms	Matthew Aaron	1810	Whitechapel, London	Aaron Worms		Isabella Isaacs	Bloomsbury, London	upholstery merchant
24314	Worms	Morris	1809	Middlesex, London			Elizabeth (?)	Covent Garden, London	furniture dealer
6001	Worms	Rachel	1847	Chelsea, London	Henry Worms	Rebecca Nathan		Chelsea, London	scholar
5997	Worms	Rebecca	1813	Mile End, London	Joseph Nathan	Esther Lamert	Henry Worms	Chelsea, London	
5994	Worms	Rebecca	1814	Whitechapel, London	Aaron Cohen Worms	Rachel Lamert		Chelsea, London	annuitant
6008	Worms	Rosetta	1831	Whitechapel, London	Lewis Worms	Hannah Joseph		Whitechapel, London	house assistant
5998	Worms	Sarah	1841	Whitechapel, London	Henry Worms	Rebecca Nathan		Chelsea, London	scholar
21918	Worms	Sarah	1850	Clerkenwell, London	Solomon Worms	Mary (?)		Clerkenwell, London	
21912	Worms	Solomon	1806	Wapping, London			Mary (?)	Clerkenwell, London	labourer
6014	Worms	Solomon Benedict de	1801	?, Germany	Baruch Benedet de Worms	Jeanette (?)	Henrietta Samuel	Marylebone, London	gentleman
15915	Worms	Sophia	1842	Clerkenwell, London	Lewis Worms	Elizabeth (?)		Holborn, London	
21303	Worms	Sydney	1837	Whitechapel, London				Edmonton, London	boarding school pupil
3275	Worms [Pirbright]	Henry de	1840	Marylebone, London	Solomon Benedict de Worms	Henrietta Samuel	Fanny von Todesco	Marylebone, London	scholar at home
15228	Wrengensky	Amelia	1828	?, Poland	(?) Wrengensky			Shoreditch, London	cook
16295	Wulf	Albert	1820	?, Germany				Dundee, Scotland	
7954	Wulfson	Frederica	1790	?Germany	(?)		Michael Isaac Wulfson	Manchester	
14214	Wulfson	Hannah	1834	?, Germany	Michael Isaac Wulfson	Frederica (?)		Manchester	
7955	Wulfson	Herman	1823	Gdansk, Poland	Michael Isaac Wulfson	Frederica (?)	Leah Hart	Manchester	watch maker
14211	Wulfson	Julia	1824	?, Germany	Michael Isaac Wulfson	Frederica (?)		Manchester	
7938	Wulfson	Lewis	1825	?, Germany	Michael Isaac Wulfson	Frederica (?)	Rose Samuel	Manchester	watch maker

ID	surname	given names	born	birthplace	father	mother	spouse 1	1851 residence	1851 occupation
7953	Wulfson	Michael Isaac	1792	?, Germany			Frederica (?)	Manchester	
14215	Wulfson	Paulina	1838	?, Germany	Michael Isaac Wulfson	Frederica (?)	Henry Jacobs	Manchester	
14213	Wulfson	Taube	1824	?, Germany	Michael Isaac Wulfson	Frederica (?)		Manchester	
14212	Wulfson	Wulf (William)	1831	?, Germany	Michael Isaac Wulfson	Frederica (?)		Manchester	traveller
14671	Wummerlich	Edmund	1821	Bavaria, Germany				Hoxton, London	colour broker
21032	Ximenes	Ann	1824	Wigan, Lancashire	(?)		Henry Ximenes	Camden Town, London	
19233	Ximenes	Eliza	1814	Middlesex, London			John (Isaac) Levy Ximenes	Bloomsbury, London	
21033	Ximenes	Eliza	1847	Sydney, NSW, Australia	Henry Ximenes	Ann (?)		Camden Town, London	
21031	Ximenes	Henry	1819	Bermuda, West Indies			Ann (?)	Camden Town, London	retired officer + fundholder
19167	Ximenes	John (Giovanni, Isaac) Levy (Luigi)	1812	?, Holland	Samuel Levy Ximenes		Eliza (?)	Bloomsbury, London	teacher of music
2905	Yager	Joseph	1851	Exeter, Devon	Sigmund (Sigman) Yager	Tryphena (Trefinia, Traphenia) Levi		Exeter, Devon	
2902	Yager	Symond (Sigmund, Sigman)	1819	Wiesbaden, Germany			Tryphena (Trephina, Traphenia) Levi	Exeter, Devon	traveller
2901	Yager	Traphenia (Tryphena, Trephina)	1826	Plymouth, Devon	John Levi	Elizabeth (?)	Symond (Sigmund, Sigman) Yager	Plymouth, Devon	
2904	Yager [Wolf]	Isabella (Isabelle, Bella)	1850	Exeter, Devon	Symond (Sigmund, Sigman) Yager	Tryphena (Trefinia, Traphenia) Levi	Edouard Eugene Seligman	Exeter, Devon	
17927	Yates	Alfred	1825	City, London	Saul Yates	Sarah (?)		Aldgate, London	solicitor
3601	Yates	Clara	1837	Liverpool	Elias Samuel Yates	Kate (?)	Edwin Louis Samuel	Liverpool	scholar
23816	Yates	Daniel E	1849	Liverpool	Elias Samuel Yates	Kate (?)		Liverpool	
23815	Yates	Edward	1840	Liverpool	Elias Samuel Yates	Kate (?)		Liverpool	
7988	Yates	Emily	1840	?, London	Saul Yates	Sarah Isaacs	Jacob Alexander	Aldgate, London	
6218	Yates	George Samuel	1834	Liverpool	Elias Samuel Yates	Kate (?)	Hannah Keyser	Liverpool	
26543	Yates	Henry	1823	Liverpool				Birmingham	commercial traveller to outfitting business
23814	Yates	Kate	1803	Liverpool	(?)		Elias Samuel Yates	Liverpool	gentlewoman
17924	Yates	Leopold	1837	City, London	Saul Yates	Sarah (?)	Deborah Moses	Aldgate, London	boot maker's clerk
17926	Yates	Sarah	1801	City, London	Elias Isaacs		Saul Yates	Aldgate, London	
17925	Yates	Saul	1791	Liverpool	Benjamin Yates		Sarah Isaacs	Aldgate, London	solicitor
17928	Yates	Theodore	1844	City, London	Saul Yates	Sarah (?)		Aldgate, London	scholar
30188	Yellowich	Elias	1821	?, Poland				Dudley, Worcestershire	glazier
30186	Yerutsosk	Lions	1821	?, Poland			(?)	Dudley, Worcestershire	hawker
8418	Yoel	Samuel	1794	Portsmouth, Hampshire	Yoell Yoell	Mary (?)		Cowes, Isle of Wight	watchmaker
4032	Yoell	Abraham	1783	?, London	Yoell Yoell	Mary (?)	Amelia Aaron	Portsmouth, Hampshire	silversmith
4033	Yoell	Amelia	1787	Portsmouth, Hampshire	Jacob Aaron	Alice (?)	Abraham Yoell	Portsmouth, Hampshire	
4031	Yoell	Amelia	1841	Portsmouth, Hampshire	Lewis Yoell	Isabella Cohen		Portsmouth, Hampshire	
5576	Yoell	Caroline	1819	Portsmouth, Hampshire	Abraham Yoell	Amelia (?)	Edward Lowe	Portsmouth, Hampshire	
4035	Yoell	Frances Sara	1817	Portsmouth, Hampshire	Abraham Yoell	Amelia Aaron		Portsmouth, Hampshire	
8989	Yoell	Frances Sarah	1827	Portsmouth, Hampshire	Abraham Yoell	Amelia Aaron		Portsmouth, Hampshire	shirt manufactor
900	Yoell	Helen Amelia	1822	Portsmouth, Hampshire	Abraham Yoell	Amelia Aaron		Portsmouth, Hampshire	shirt manufactor
899	Yoell	Hester A	1832	Portsmouth, Hampshire	Abraham Yoell	Amelia Aaron	Samuel Sternberg	Portsmouth, Hampshire	shirt manufactor

ID	surname	given names	born	birthplace	father	mother	spouse 1	1851 residence	1851 occupation
4027	Yoell	Isabella	1808	Portsmouth, Hampshire	Isaac Cohen	Phoebe Myer	Lewis Yoell	Portsmouth, Hampshire	
4028	Yoell	Joseph	1835	Portsmouth, Hampshire	Lewis Yoell	Isabella Cohen	Sarah Abraham	Portsmouth, Hampshire	
4026	Yoell	Lewis	1792	?, London	Yoell Yoell	Mary (?)	Isabella Cohen	Portsmouth, Hampshire	general dealer
4029	Yoell	Rachel	1838	Portsmouth, Hampshire	Lewis Yoell	Isabella Cohen		Portsmouth, Hampshire	
4030	Yoell	Samuel	1839	Portsmouth, Hampshire	Lewis Yoell	Isabella Cohen		Portsmouth, Hampshire	
13097	Youell	Ann	1785	Exeter, Devon	(?)		(?) Youell	Whitechapel, London	pauper + laundress
2602	Youndkin	Jacob	1782	Rotterdam, Holland			(?)	Hull, Yorkshire	lunatic
8430	Yuly	Elizabeth	1812	Portsmouth, Hampshire	David Lazarus		Samuel Levy Yuly	Portsmouth, Hampshire	clothier
8431	Yuly	Judah	1832	Gloucester, Gloucestershire	Samuel Levy Yuly	Elizabeth Lazarus		Portsmouth, Hampshire	clerk
8432	Yuly	Phoebe	1836	Cheltenham, Gloucestershire	Samuel Levy Yuly	Elizabeth Lazarus		Portsmouth, Hampshire	
8429	Yuly	Samuel Levy	1797	Essaouira, Morocco [Mogador, Morocco]	?Judah Levy Yuly		Elizabeth Lazarus	Portsmouth, Hampshire	clothier
8433	Yuly	Sarah (Zorah)	1840	?, London	Samuel Levy Yuly	Elizabeth Lazarus	Jacob Myers	Portsmouth, Hampshire	
4041	Zachariah	Aaron	1843	Portsmouth, Hampshire	Seriaskie Zachariah	Julia (Ann) Moses		Portsmouth, Hampshire	
4037	Zachariah	Celia	1846	Portsmouth, Hampshire	Seriaskie Zachariah	Julia (Ann) Moses		Portsmouth, Hampshire	
4043	Zachariah	Edward	1848	Portsmouth, Hampshire	Seriaskie Zachariah	Julia (Ann) Moses	Frances (?)	Portsmouth, Hampshire	
8055	Zachariah	Esther	1849	Portsmouth, Hampshire	Seriakie (Seraiski) Zachariah	Julia (Ann) Moses	William Wasserzug	Portsmouth, Hampshire	
8484	Zachariah	Henry	1816	?, Poland				Gosport, Hampshire	silversmith
15691	Zachariah	John	1770	City, London			Phoebe (?)	Hampstead, London	proprietor of houses
4039	Zachariah	Julia (Ann)	1813	Portsmouth, Hampshire	Aaron Moses	Anna (Hannah) Levi	Seriaskie Zachariah	Portsmouth, Hampshire	
19021	Zachariah	Leah	1801	Middlesex, London	(?)		(?) Zachariah	Whitechapel, London	house servant
4042	Zachariah	Lewis	1844	Portsmouth, Hampshire	Seriaskie Zachariah	Julia (Ann) Moses		Portsmouth, Hampshire	
8403	Zachariah	Louis	1826	Portsmouth, Hampshire				Southampton, Hampshire	jeweller
15692	Zachariah	Phoebe	1780	Holborn, London	(?)		John Zachariah	Hampstead, London	
4040	Zachariah	Rebecca	1841	Portsmouth, Hampshire	Seriaskie Zachariah	Julia (Ann) Moses	Solomon Wax	Portsmouth, Hampshire	
7583	Zachariah	Samuel	1816	?, Poland	Eleazar Zachariah		Esther Meyer	Southampton, Hampshire	watchmaker + jeweller
4038	Zachariah	Seriaskie	1807	?, Poland			Julia (Ann) Moses	Portsmouth, Hampshire	silversmith
2182	Zacharias	Abraham (Israel)	1818	Kaliningrad, Russia [Konigsberg, Prussia]	Joel Zacharias		Leah Harris	Oxford, Oxfordshire	jeweller
2183	Zacharias	Leah	1821	Walworth, London	Abraham (Israel) Zacharias	Rose (Rosa) Jessel	Abraham (Israel) Zacharias	Oxford, Oxfordshire	
2184	Zacharias	Rebecca	1848	Oxford, Oxfordshire	Abraham (Israel) Zacharias	Leah Harris		Oxford, Oxfordshire	
2185	Zacharias	Rose (Rosa)	1849	Oxford, Oxfordshire	Abraham (Israel) Zacharias	Leah Harris	Daniel Davidson	Oxford, Oxfordshire	
21727	Zaguary	Simmy	1831	?, Portugal	(?) Zaguary			Highbury, London	
23317	Zalinger	August	1809	?, Norfolk				Belgravia, London	cook
29688	Zallman	Aaron	1822	?, Poland			Hannah Leavy	Shoreditch, London	cloth waterproofer
29692	Zallman	Godfrey	1849	Aldgate, London	Aaron Zallman	Hannah Leavy		Shoreditch, London	
29689	Zallman	Hannah	1821	?, Poland	Philip? J Leavy		Aaron Zallman	Shoreditch, London	
29690	Zallman	Jeanette	1845	Aldgate, London	Aaron Zallman	Hannah Leavy		Shoreditch, London	
29691	Zallman	Leah	1847	Aldgate, London	Aaron Zallman	Hannah Leavy		Shoreditch, London	
29693	Zallman	Sarah	1850	Aldgate, London	Aaron Zallman	Hannah Leavy		Shoreditch, London	
2000	Zaman (Seeman)	Julia	1826	Poznan, Poland [Exin, Posen, Prussia], Germany	Philip Seeman		Jacob Bene (Benny)	Whitechapel, London	tailoress
977	Zamoiski	Esther	1848	Exeter, Devon	Solomon Rodolph Zamoiski	Priscilla Aaron	Jacob Lowenthal	Exeter, Devon	
976	Zamoiski	Julia	1846	Exeter, Devon	Solomon Rodolph Zamoiski	Priscilla Aaron		Exeter, Devon	